ENCYCLOPAEDIA JUDAICA

ENCYCLOPAEDIA JUDAICA

SECOND EDITION

VOLUME 7
FEY–GOR

FRED SKOLNIK, *Editor in Chief*
MICHAEL BERENBAUM, *Executive Editor*

MACMILLAN REFERENCE USA
An imprint of Thomson Gale, a part of The Thomson Corporation

IN ASSOCIATION WITH
KETER PUBLISHING HOUSE LTD., JERUSALEM

Detroit • New York • San Francisco • New Haven, Conn. • Waterville, Maine • London

ENCYCLOPAEDIA JUDAICA, Second Edition

Fred Skolnik, *Editor in Chief*
Michael Berenbaum, *Executive Editor*
Shlomo S. (Yosh) Gafni, *Editorial Project Manager*
Rachel Gilon, *Editorial Project Planning and Control*

Thomson Gale
Gordon Macomber, *President*
Frank Menchaca, *Senior Vice President and Publisher*
Jay Flynn, *Publisher*
Hélène Potter, *Publishing Director*

Keter Publishing House
Yiphtach Dekel, *Chief Executive Officer*
Peter Tomkins, *Executive Project Director*

Complete staff listings appear in Volume 1

For more information, contact
Macmillan Reference USA
An imprint of Thomson Gale
27500 Drake Rd.
Farmington Hills, MI 48331-3535
Or you can visit our internet site at
http://www.gale.com

LIBRARY OF CONGRESS CATALOGING-IN-PUBLICATION DATA

Encyclopaedia Judaica / Fred Skolnik, editor-in-chief ; Michael Berenbaum, executive editor. -- 2nd ed.
v. cm.
Includes bibliographical references and index.
Contents: v.1. Aa-Alp.
ISBN 0-02-865928-7 (set hardcover : alk. paper) -- ISBN 0-02-865929-5 (vol. 1 hardcover : alk. paper) -- ISBN 0-02-865930-9 (vol. 2 hardcover : alk. paper) -- ISBN 0-02-865931-7 (vol. 3 hardcover : alk. paper) -- ISBN 0-02-865932-5 (vol. 4 hardcover : alk. paper) -- ISBN 0-02-865933-3 (vol. 5 hardcover : alk. paper) -- ISBN 0-02-865934-1 (vol. 6 hardcover : alk. paper) -- ISBN 0-02-865935-X (vol. 7 hardcover : alk. paper) -- ISBN 0-02-865936-8 (vol. 8 hardcover : alk. paper) -- ISBN 0-02-865937-6 (vol. 9 hardcover : alk. paper) -- ISBN 0-02-865938-4 (vol. 10 hardcover : alk. paper) -- ISBN 0-02-865939-2 (vol. 11 hardcover : alk. paper) -- ISBN 0-02-865940-6 (vol. 12 hardcover : alk. paper) -- ISBN 0-02-865941-4 (vol. 13 hardcover : alk. paper) -- ISBN 0-02-865942-2 (vol. 14 hardcover : alk. paper) -- ISBN 0-02-865943-0 (vol. 15: alk. paper) -- ISBN 0-02-865944-9 (vol. 16: alk. paper) -- ISBN 0-02-865945-7 (vol. 17: alk. paper) -- ISBN 0-02-865946-5 (vol. 18: alk. paper) -- ISBN 0-02-865947-3 (vol. 19: alk. paper) -- ISBN 0-02-865948-1 (vol. 20: alk. paper) -- ISBN 0-02-865949-X (vol. 21: alk. paper) -- ISBN 0-02-865950-3 (vol. 22: alk. paper)
1. Jews -- Encyclopedias. I. Skolnik, Fred. II. Berenbaum, Michael, 1945-
DS102.8.E496 2007
909'.04924 -- dc22

2006020426

ISBN-13:

978-0-02-865928-2 (set)
978-0-02-865929-9 (vol. 1)
978-0-02-865930-5 (vol. 2)
978-0-02-865931-2 (vol. 3)
978-0-02-865932-9 (vol. 4)
978-0-02-865933-6 (vol. 5)
978-0-02-865934-3 (vol. 6)
978-0-02-865935-0 (vol. 7)
978-0-02-865936-7 (vol. 8)
978-0-02-865937-4 (vol. 9)
978-0-02-865938-1 (vol. 10)
978-0-02-865939-8 (vol. 11)
978-0-02-865940-4 (vol. 12)
978-0-02-865941-1 (vol. 13)
978-0-02-865942-8 (vol. 14)
978-0-02-865943-5 (vol. 15)
978-0-02-865944-2 (vol. 16)
978-0-02-865945-9 (vol. 17)
978-0-02-865946-6 (vol. 18)
978-0-02-865947-3 (vol. 19)
978-0-02-865948-0 (vol. 20)
978-0-02-865949-7 (vol. 21)
978-0-02-865950-3 (vol. 22)

This title is also available as an e-book
ISBN-10: 0-02-866097-8
ISBN-13: 978-0-02-866097-4
Contact your Thomson Gale representative for ordering information.
Printed in the United States of America

10 9 8 7 6 5 4 3 2 1

TABLE OF CONTENTS

Historiated initial letter "F" of the word Fratibus *at the beginning of II Maccabees in a 12th-century manuscript from France. It illustrates the sending of the letter from the Jews of Jerusalem to their brethren in Egypt calling on them to observe the feast of Ḥannukah. Bordeaux, Bibliothèque Municipale, Ms. 21, fol. 256v.*

FEY–FU

FEYGENBERG (Imri), RAKHEL (1885–1972), Yiddish and Hebrew author, translator, and journalist. Rakhel Feygenberg was born in Luban, Minsk Province, Belorussia. She wrote about Russian-Jewish life, notably in her books on the 1919 pogroms, *A Pinkes fun a Toyter Shtot* ("Record Book of a Dead Town," 1926); *Oyf di Bregn fun Dnyester* ("On the Shores of the Dniester," 1925).). Her Shomer-influenced *Di Kinder-Yohren* (*Dos Naye Leben*, 1905; Warsaw, 1910) is an impressive achievement for a 20-year old. Her novel *Tekhter* ("Daughters") was serialized in Warsaw's *Moment* in 1913. She went to Palestine in 1924 for the first time, left in 1926, returned and settled in 1933, and under the name of Rakhel Imri came to write exclusively in Hebrew. A resident of Tel Aviv, she translated most of her Yiddish works into Hebrew, notably her *magnum opus, Megilot Yehudey Rusya: 1905–1964* ("Scrolls of Russian Jewry: 1905–1964," 1965).

BIBLIOGRAPHY: Rejzen, Leksikon, 3 (1929), 49–56; LNYL, 7 (1968), 343–6; Kressel, Leksikon, 1 (1965), 125–6.

[Leonard Prager (2nd ed.)]

FEYNMAN, RICHARD PHILLIPS (1918–1988), U.S. theoretical physicist. Born in New York City, Feynman was the son of an immigrant garment salesman and frustrated scientist whose curiosity and understanding of natural phenomena was a lifelong inspiration to his son. Educated at Massachusetts Institute of Technology (B.S. 1939; he had originally preferred Columbia but was apparently kept out by the Jewish quota) and Princeton (Ph.D. 1942), Feynman worked on the Manhattan (atomic bomb) Project from 1942 to 1946 in Princeton and at Los Alamos, New Mexico, where he was a computational group leader. He taught physics at Cornell University from 1946 to 1950 and at the California Institute of Technology from 1951 until his death.

Feynman won the Nobel Prize for physics in 1965 (jointly, with Julian Schwinger and Shinichiro Tomonaga) for the fundamental theoretical work that led to the development of quantum electrodynamics (from the quantum mechanics of the 1920s and 1930s). In the course of this work he also developed "Feynman diagrams," a widely used visual analytical technique. He also did important work on superconductivity and, in collaboration with his Cal Tech colleague (and rival) Murray *Gell-Mann, on quarks and other subatomic particles.

Near the end of his life Feynman served on the commission investigating the *Challenger* space shuttle disaster in 1986, creating a public sensation when he conducted, at a public hearing, a simple experiment that revealed the cause of the explosion. He also exposed the institutional management deficiencies that had made the disaster possible.

Feynman was early recognized as one of the most brilliant physicists of his generation and was widely respected as a teacher as well. His published lectures on physics are regarded as classics. He also had a reputation as a "character" – he was famous for his bongo drumming, his womanizing, and his general unconventional demeanor – and for his extreme individualism (said Gell-Mann, "I found that he had difficulty thinking in terms of 'us'"). In addition to publications in journals, he was the author of several popular books. Among his published works, both professional (mainly transcribed and edited lectures) and popular, are *The Theory of Fundamental Processes* (1961), *Quantum Electrodynamics* (1961), *The Feynman Lectures on Physics* (3 vols., 1963–65, with Robert B. Leighton and Matthew Sands), *The Character of Physical Law* (1965), *Quantum Mechanics and Path Integrals* (1965, with A.R. Hibbs), *Photon-Hadron Interactions* (1972), *QED: The Strange Theory of Light and Matter* (1985), *"Surely You're Joking, Mr. Feynman!": Adventures of a Curious Character* (1985, with Ralph Leighton), *Elementary Particles and the Laws of Physics: the 1986 Dirac Memorial Lecture* (1987, with Steven *Weinberg), and *"What Do You Care What Other People Think?": Further Adventures of a Curious Character* (1988, with Ralph Leighton). A biography, *Genius: The Life and Science of Richard Feynman* (1992, by James Gleick); *Selected Papers of Richard Feynman, with Commentary* (2000, edited by Laurie M. Brown); and a collection of letters, *Perfectly Reasonable Deviations from the Beaten Track* (2005, edited by his daughter Michelle Feynman), have been published. Feynman's life has inspired countless memoirs, a film, and two plays.

[Drew Silver (2nd ed.)]

FEZ, city in *Morocco, one of the most important in the Islamic world; founded by Idrīs I in 789, it became the capital of the kingdom in 808 under Idrīs II. The first inhabitants of Fez were pagan Berber\s, but it also included Christians and Jews. Idrīs II then admitted a large number of Jews who paid him an annual tax of 30,000 dinars. He assigned them a quarter, the al-Funduk al-Yahūdī. This community rapidly became influential and respected. Thus, when the ruler Yaḥyā – as it is told – became infatuated with a Jewess and forced his way into the public baths where she was at the time, there was an uprising in the town (c. 860).

A center of civilization, Fez also became a commercial center of prime importance, largely the result of the presence of the Jews, who from there traveled widely. Its position also encouraged a considerable development of the intellectual and religious life of the community: its yeshivot attracted such scholars as Judah *Ibn Quraysh in the 9th century. During the 10th–11th centuries its rabbis maintained a regular correspondence with *Sura and *Pumbedita. To Palestine went scholars such as David b. Abraham *Alfasi, author of a dictionary, R. Solomon b. Judah (d. 1051), who became head of the Jerusalem Academy, and to Spain grammarians of the stature of *Dunash b. Labrat and Judah Hayyūj. R. Isaac *Alfasi's (c. 1015–1105) most extended period of teaching was in Fez, where he wrote his long summary of the Talmud and answered queries on *halakhah* addressed to him from all over the world. Only in his old age did he arrive in Spain. During this golden era, which lasted several centuries, three grave events occurred: a section of the community was deported to Ashir (*Algeria) in about 987; 6,000 Jews were massacred in May 1035 by a fanatic who conquered Fez; and the town was ruthlessly sacked in 1068 by the *Almoravides. In about 1127 a pseudo-messiah, Moses Dari, brought some afflictions upon the community. In 1165 the official recognition of a new *Almohad monarch resulted in severe changes which went as far as forced conversion. Refusing to submit to this, the *dayyan* R. Judah ha-Kohen ibn Shushan was burnt alive and *Maimonides and his family, who had been living in Fez as refugees from Spain for five years, permanently left the country for *Egypt. In 1244 the Merinides established themselves in Fez, which once more became the capital of the kingdom. In 1275, there was an insurrection against the Jews, who were particularly well treated by the new masters, and it was the Merinide sultan himself who saved the community. The community lived in freedom and prosperity; its commerce, especially with Aragon, was of considerable importance; learning and science flourished. However, with the decline of the Merinides and the revival of fanaticism, the Jews were compelled in 1438 to live in a special *Jewish quarter situated on the site known as *mellah in New Fez. It was the first Jewish quarter in Morocco. Still, in order to straighten out public finances, Sultan ʿAbd al-Ḥagg turned to the Jews of Fez and one of them, Hārūn, became his prime minister. Subsequently, the town rose in revolt, the sultan and his minister were assassinated, and most of the Jews were massacred (1465). The community did not recover from this catastrophe until after 1492 with the arrival of the Spanish refugees; their numbers included some eminent personalities, but several, such as Jacob *Berab, later left for *Palestine.

One of the first Hebrew presses was set up in Fez, by Samuel b. Isaac Nedivot and his son Isaac who had learned their Hebrew printing in Lisbon. From 1516 (?) to 1524 they printed 15 Hebrew books.

The community, which numbered about 10,000, consisted of "Spanish exiles" (*megorashim*) and "natives" (*toshavim*). The former, by issuing *takkanot* based on Judeo-Spanish custom, became entirely detached from the latter; serious friction broke out between these two elements, but the *megorashim* finally gained the upper hand. Their descendants instituted the *Purim de Los Christianos* to commemorate the defeat of the Portuguese at the battle of al-Qaṣr al-Kabīr in 1578; they held the office of *nagid*, established in Fez at the beginning of the 16th century, and their yeshivot were headed by scholars including Naḥman b. Sunbal (d. after 1556), Samuel Ḥagiz (d. after 1596), Judah Uzziel (d. 1603), and Saul Serrero (d. after 1622). Their high standard was maintained over a lengthy period due to such personalities as Samuel Sarfaty (d. 1713), Judah ibn *Atar, and Ḥayyim ibn *Atar of *Salé. Scholars of the mellah recorded accounts of the events which they had witnessed. These. are valuable for the study of Moroccan history, and provide an insight into the psychology of the Jewish masses of the town living in a closed society.

During the same period many scholarly works were written in the mellah. Rabbis of Fez went to teach in communities abroad and became their spiritual leaders; this was the case, for example, with Isaac b. Abraham Uzziel, Aaron *Ibn Ḥayyim, and Jacob *Ḥagiz. Certain families, such as the Ibn Danāns, were the leading *dayyanim* of Fez for several generations and their authority was recognized by the Jews of the whole country. The preeminence of Fez only ended after the death of Jacob *Ibn Zur in 1753. Rabbis of Fez found refuge, whenever their communities were struck by a calamity, in the small town of Sefrou, near Fez. During the 18th and 19th centuries, rabbis of the Hota, Abitbol, and Elbaz families attracted many disciples from other parts of Morocco. A short while after its conquest by the Saʿdī Sharīfs (in 1550), Fez lost its political and economic importance. As a result, the Jewish community was deserted by its wealthiest and most influential elements and gradually fell into poverty. To secure Fez, where he was enthroned (in 1665), Moulay Rashīd, the founder of the Alawīte dynasty, entered the town by way of the mellah, where the Jews enabled him to spend the night. Having destroyed the bastion of the power of his enemies, the Zāwiya of Dila, this sultan in 1668 transferred the rich Jewish community of Dila with all its belongings to Fez: these 1,300 families changed the composition of the mellah, which lost its Spanish character and became more prosperous. In the period of anarchy, between 1720 and 1750, a few of them barely managed to obtain monopolies, e.g., over tobacco or the minting of coins; many of them continued to practice such traditional crafts as goldsmithing, the manufacture of gold thread, lace making, embroidery, and tailoring. But the community mostly lived in a state of spiritual and intellectual seclusion. In 1790 Moulay Yazīd destroyed its synagogues, ordered the plunder of the mellah, and expelled its inhabitants. The return of the Jews was authorized in 1792 by Moulay Suleiman, but the mellah was reduced to a quarter of its former size. Moreover, the Udayas stationed in New Fez (Fez al-Jadīd) persecuted the Jews; however, when these soldiers rebelled the sharif did not hesitate to bombard New Fez and the defeated Udayas were dispersed (1832). In commemoration of this deliverance the community instituted the "*Purim del Kor*" ("of the cannonballs"), celebrated every year on Kislev 22. Life in the mellah improved and the interest in studies was reawakened by such remarkable men as Abner Sarfaty (d. 1884) and Isaac ibn Danān (d. 1900). The community possessed many schools, five yeshivot, and an important benevolent society. A French school, which received the financial support of the notables of the community, was founded in 1884 by the Alliance Israélite Universelle.

In 1912, two weeks after the establishment of the French Protectorate, a revolt broke out in Fez. The mellah with a population of 12,000 was completely ransacked and set on fire by the mob; about 45 were killed and 27 were wounded. Under the pretext of munitions smuggling, the French military authorities had previously confiscated all the weapons of the Jews, who were left defenseless. The Sharīf received them within the precincts of the palace and ordered the distribution of food and clothes among them. From 1925 many Jews established themselves in the new town of Fez, together with the Europeans; it was only the poor and some Orthodox families who remained in the mellah where in 1942 the Vichy laws sought to reintegrate all those who had left it. In 1947 there were 22,484 Jews living in Fez and its surroundings. These included several physicians, lawyers, industrialists, and owners of agricultural estates. The traditional occupations disappeared with modernization, and commerce came under Muslim domination, with the exception of the precious metals and cereals businesses in which the Jews retained the leading role.

[David Corcos]

Zionist Activity

The Zionist association Ḥibbat Zion was created before the establishment of the French protectorate, at the end of 1908. It was the only Zionist association which the famous Rabbi Shaul Ibn Danān headed. The reactions of Jews in Fez and other communities in the region to the Balfour Declaration and the end of the war was mass immigration to Ereẓ Israel, but most of the Jews returned to Fez. We do not know the reasons for the failure of the immigration; however, its impact was very clear: Jews did not emigrate again from the region until the end of World War II.

After World War I a new Zionist association was created, Kol Mevasser, and Josef Halevy was its head. From 1924 Zionist activity almost ceased because of French opposition and the influence of the *Alliance on Jewish youth. Unofficially, Jews from Fez participated in Zionist conferences which took place at Casablanca. Eight delegates represented Fez in 1936, four in 1937, five in 1938, two in 1939, and seven in 1946. After World War II all Zionist parties and ideologies were represented in Morocco, including Fez.

Fez was a center of book printing in Morocco. The first printing house was established before 1922, named Imprimerie Allard. Nine printing houses are known in Fez, most of which were active in the 1920s.

[Haim Saadoun (2nd ed.)]

Contemporary Period

The Jewish population in Fez was about 10,000 in 1912, 14,000 in 1951, and 12,194 in 1961, comprising 7.5% of the Jewish population of Morroco. Most families had no more than six children. Most Jews left Fez in 1961–68. Until the community was dissolved, the town had many Jewish educational institutions run by the Alliance lsraélite Universelle, by Oẓar ha-Torah (which had 700 pupils in 1961), and Em ha-Banim. In 1961 these and other Jewish schools had a total of 2,823 pupils. Before the emigration in the 1950s and 1960s, there were also general Jewish organizations, such as the Zionist Bnei Akiva, a Ḥovevei ha-Safah for the study of Hebrew, several social welfare organizations, branches of WIZO, and a branch of the World Jewish Congress. Most of the Jews who left Fez made their way to Israel; others went to France and Canada. In 1969 there were only about 1,000 Jews in Fez.

[Ḥayyim J. Cohen]

BIBLIOGRAPHY: R. Le Tourneau, *Fès avant le protectorat* (1949); G. Vajda, *Un recueil de textes historiques judéo-marocains* (1951); Hirschberg, Afrikah, index; A. Chouraqui, *Between East and West* (1968), index; D. Corcos, *Les Juifs de Maroc et leur Mellahs* (1970), passim; idem, in: JQR, 54 (1963/64), 271–87; 55 (1964/65), 53–81, 137–50; idem, in: *Sefunot*, 10 (1965), 43–111; Bentov, *ibid.*, 413–82. **ADD. BIBLIOGRAPHY:** A. Elboim, *Ha-Edah ha-Yehudit be-Fez* (1972) H. Bentov, "*Umanim u-Ba'alei Melakhah be-Fez*," in: *Sefunot*, 10 (1965), 413–82; idem, "*Kehal ha-Toshavim be-Fez min ha-Me'ah ha-Tet-Zain…*," in: *Mi-Mizraḥ u-mi-Ma'arav*, 5 (1986), 79–108; S. Bar-Asher, *Ha-Kehillah ha-Yehudit be-Maroco* (1981); idem, *Yehudei Sefarad u-Portugal be-Maroco (1492–1753)* (1991); A. Mamman, "*Fez, Ereẓ Ẓemiḥato shel Meḥkar ha-Lashon ha-Ivrit ba-Magreb*," in: *Brit*, 3 (1988), 14–16; D. Ovadya, *Fez va-Ḥakhameha*, 1–2 (1979); M. Amar, "*Takannot Fez ve-Takkanot Mo'eẓet ha-Rabbanim be-Maroco*," in: *Sefer ha-Takannot, ha-Mishpat ha-Ivri be-Kehillot Maroco* (1980), 9–55; D. Bensimon-Donath, *L'évolution de la femme israëilite à fes* (1962); L. Brunot and E. Malka, *Textes judéo-arabes de Fes*; (1939); idem, *Glossaire judéo-arabes de Fes* (1940); J. Gerber, *Jewish Society in Fez 1450–1700* (1980); E. Bashan, "*Yehudei Fez 1873–1900 al pi Te'udot Ḥadashot*," in: *Asufot*, 15 (1993), 1–168; J. Tedgui, *Ha-Sefer ve-ha-Defus ha-Ivri be-Fez* (1994).

FICHMAN, JACOB (**Ya'akov**; 1881–1958), Hebrew poet, critic and literary editor. Born in Belz, Bessarabia, Fichman left home at the age of 14 and subsequently resided in various cities of czarist Russia and Western Europe, among which were Warsaw, Vilna, and Berlin, finally settling in Ereẓ Israel (1912).

He revisited Europe several times to carry out various editorial assignments, After spending World War I in Odessa, he returned to Ereẓ Israel in 1919 and then left again in 1922 for Warsaw on the invitation of the Stybel publishing house. From there he made his way back to Bessarabia in 1924, returning to Tel Aviv the next year. His occupations included teaching, the producing of textbooks, and working for the Tushiah and Moriah publishing houses. He was on the staff of the Warsaw paper *Ha-Ẓofeh*. In Palestine he edited the journals *Moledet* and *Ma'abarot* and, in collaboration with Joseph *Klausner, *Ha-Shilo'aḥ*. From 1936 to 1942 he was editor of *Moznayim*, the organ of the Hebrew Writers Association.

His first book of poems, *Givolim*, was published in Warsaw in 1911, and his first collection of essays, *Bavu'ot*, in Odessa in 1911. Fichman, a younger member of what is usually described as Bialik's school, is generally dubbed impressionist, both for the manner in which he handles his natural themes and images, and for his highly subjective and delicately intuitive criticism, which lacks theoretical interests and varies its criteria to fit the particular work under discussion. Such labels, and the affinities they imply, should however be treated circumspectly, in view of the gap separating the renascent Hebrew literature from the full-blown European context, as well as the often indirect and fragmentary nature of the influences involved. Fichman's criticism itself is an unwitting example of the dangers of facile generalization, as when it lumps together writers, poets, and philosophers of different periods and cultures, and contrasting temperaments. Thus his "imaginary museum" includes Emerson, Carlyle, Taine, Renan, Pisarev and Lessing, Goethe and Hoelderlin, Pushkin, Fet, Baudelaire, and Stefan George. Such lists attest to Fichman's strong desire to bring Hebrew criticism closer to European ideas and individual works. They also reflect, however, the eclectic and impressionistic approach for which he found it necessary to apologize in his essay, *Al ha-Bikkoret ha-Yoẓeret*.

Here he defines his role as that of a friend-critic who writes out of gratitude toward the poet for the moments of joy and the insight he has granted him. The task of such criticism is not to find fault, nor even to discriminate according to merit. In contrast to the "hostile critic" who criticizes that which is not – the flaws and shortcomings of the work of art – his task is to present that which is: to discover the center of a writer's "world" and manifest its uniqueness. The creative critic is thus able to appreciate writers of different, and even opposing, characteristics. Fichman does not shrink from subjectivity. Echoing Anatole France, he maintains that "in talking about the artist I am talking also about myself." Objectivity, he claims, may be a mere obstacle, while the subjective interrelation of critic and artist, and a close attention to the effect of the work on the sensitive reader, reveal its true power.

His point of departure, particularly in his essays on his contemporaries, is the impression which a writer or a particular work have made on him, or on those close to him. Positing a collective "we," he identifies his own sensibility and responses with those of his generation. At least once, however, he asserted his independence by welcoming the militant modernism of Shlonsky and his followers, notwithstanding that it was mainly directed against his own circle. It was only natural that a criticism as tolerant and eclectic as his would have little to do with the more innovatory trends of 20th-century Hebrew literature. It also refrained from questioning established reputations or calling attention to forgotten writers. Nor was its influence always salutary. Fichman's main merits – the charm of his vignettes, his broad-mindedness, and his desire to establish a "creative community" between writer and critic – were often disregarded by his more militant successors. His florid, cliché-ridden style had a definitely adverse effect on later "impressionists," lacking the strength of his tastes.

Fichman's poetry includes prose poems, folk poems, idylls and sonnets, dramatic poems, and verse on national and biblical themes. Like other contemporaries of his, such as Ya'akov Kahan, Zalman Shneour, Ya'akov Steinberg, and David Shimoni, he too underwent Bialik's formidable influence. But he was equally susceptible to the influence of the new Palestinian poetry led by Shlonsky, particularly in his later *Pe'at Sadeh* (1944). To the latter he is indebted for the Sephardi prosody, the structuring of the rhyme, and a somewhat harder image. Fichman was among the first of the Bialikites to renounce the-at the time almost compulsory-"prophetic mask," and concentrate on the smaller forms of artistic-conscious craftsmanship.

His more impressive achievements are attained in his symbolic nature-sketches, and in a series of pensive little lyrical poems, all composed in a minor key. The landscape is represented with an eye to its natural coloring and the interplay of light and shade. The moods are often derived from the familiar romantic and sentimental repertoire. Here, too, as in his criticism, there is no genuine originality, no daring, and little inventiveness. There is however the same respect for good craftsmanship.

Even in these later poems, Fichman's penchant for elevated language often causes him to resort to archaisms, abstractions, hackneyed metaphors, and words or phrases used solely to meet structural and rhythmic needs. He inclines to prefer the often trite poeticism to the concrete rendering of a physical reality. There is hardly a hint in his work of the new, more colloquial idiom which was gaining entry into Hebrew poetry; nor of other qualities usually associated with modern poetry, such as poetic irony and ambiguity. Particularly in his longer poems, it becomes clear that the poet was not capable of sustaining a longer work.

After his immigration to Palestine, Fichman became increasingly absorbed with the Palestinian landscape. Here too he is a member of a transitional generation. His attitude toward the new landscape is basically secular; he does not view it through the biblical-Zionist romanticism of Shimoni and other contemporaries. In this, too, he is a forerunner of the changes in Hebrew poetry, some of which he witnessed in his own lifetime.

For translations of his works into English, see Goell, Bibliography.

BIBLIOGRAPHY: Kressel, Leksikon, 2 (1967), 602–8; Y. Keshet, *Be-Dor Oleh* (1950), 95–132; Rejzen, Leksikon, 3 (1928), 68–72; Waxman, Literature, 4 (1960²), 306–11; M. Ribalow, *The Flowering of Modern Hebrew Literature* (1959), 189–206; R. Wallenrod, *The Literature of Modern Israel* (1956), index; G. Schoffmann (Shofman) *Kol Kitvei*, 4 (1960), index; *Davar* (Dec. 14, 1951), list of musical compositions to his poems. **ADD. BIBLIOGRAPHY:** B.Y. Michali, *Fichman be-Shirah u-ve-Masah* (1952); N. Govrin, "*J. Fichman, Al Yeẓirato,*" (1971), bibliography; R. Kartun-Blum, in: *Moznayim*, 32 (1971), 320–29; N. Govrin, in: *Arugot* (1973), 13–24; A. Kinstler, *Merḥav u-Zeman be-Te'urei ha-Teva shel Fichman* (1973); Y. Zemorah, *Arugot: Kovez le-Zikhro shel Y. Fichman* (1973); N. Govrin, "*Idilyot Yam le-Y. Fichman,*" in: *Sefer ha-Yovel le-S. Halkin* (1975), 627–53; A. Regelson, in: *Bizaron*, 67 (1976), 112–20; A.B. Jaffe, in: *Moznayim*, 51, 6 (1981), 415–20; K.A. Bertini, in: *Al ha-Mishmar* (Oct. 28, 1983; Nov. 4, 1983); L. Kupferstein, in: *Davar* (Mar. 9, 1984); Y. Zilberschlag, in: *Ha-Do'ar*, 63:30 (1984), 484–85; Z. Luz, *Shirat Ya'akov Fichman* (1989).

[Natan Zach]

°**FICHTE, JOHANN GOTTLIEB** (1762–1814), German philosopher. Fichte was the founder of ethical idealism, a philosophy which may be described as idealism in that it denies the independent existence of the world, and as ethical in that the reality of the world is determined by man's moral purpose. In his courageous *Reden an die deutsche Nation* (Berlin, 1808; trans. into Eng. as *Addresses to the German Nation*, 1922), originally delivered in Berlin then occupied by the French, he demanded that the foundation of the German national state be based on moral convictions. To achieve this goal, all Germans must be made aware of their moral obligations. These addresses some years later engendered the enthusiasm for the fight against Napoleon, and influenced the European national movements of the 19th century, including Zionism. Fichte's attitude toward Jews and Judaism was complex. Manifesting a reverent attitude toward the Bible, Fichte, in his *Grundlage der gesamten Wissenschaftslehre* (Leipzig, 1794), calls the biblical story of creation "an ancient document, worthy of respect, which contains profound and exalted wisdom and reaches conclusions to which all of philosophy must finally return." By contrast he completely rejected the Jewish religion. The Talmud contains, as he states in his *Kritik aller Offenbarung* (Koenigsberg, 1792), "ludicrously childish conceptions of God." Fichte was against awarding the rights of citizenship to Jews as long as the Jews manifested a strong resistance to the general love of mankind, and as long as they (so he held) believed in two sets of moral laws, one for Jews and another for non-Jews. Distinguishing between human rights and rights of citizenship, he held that "human rights must be granted to them [Jews] even though they do not grant them to us, for they are human beings and their injustice does not give us the right to be like them; but they must be denied the rights of citizens as long as even one Jewish idea remains with them" (for full text see *Beitrag zur Berechtigung des Urteils ueber die franzoesische Revolution*, Berlin, 1793).

This negative attitude toward Jews in general must be distinguished from his attitude toward individual Jewish philosophers, particularly Solomon *Maimon. In his *Ueber den Begriff der Wissenschaftslehre* (Leipzig, 1794), Fichte acknowledges the influence which Maimon's writings had exercised on his own philosophy, describing Maimon as "one of the greatest thinkers of our period."

BIBLIOGRAPHY: S.H. Bergmann, *The Philosophy of Solomon Maimon* (1967), ch. 12. A new edition of Fichte's works, sponsored by the Bayerische Akademie der Wissenschaften, has been in progress since 1962. It has excellent indices. **ADD. BIBLIOGRAPHY:** A. Pfahl-Traughber, "Aufklaerung und Antisemitismus – Kants, Lessings und Fichtes Auffassung zu den Juden," in: *Tribuene*, 158 (2001), 168–81; P.R. Sweet, "Fichte and the Jews – A Case of Tension between Civil Rights and Human Rights," in: *German Studies Review*, 16:1 (1993), 37–48; M. Voigts, "Fichte as Jew-hater' and Prophet of the Zionists," in: LBIYB, 45 (2000), 81–91; E. Fuchs, "Fichtes Stellung zum Judentum," in: *Fichte-Studien* 2 (1990), 160–77; W. Grab, "Fichtes Judenfeindschaft," in: *Zeitschrift fuer Religions- und Geistesgeschichte*, 44:1 (1992), 70–75; M. Voigts, "J.G. Fichte und das Judentum," in: *Judaica*, 57:4 (2001), 284–92.

[Samuel Hugo Bergman]

FICTION, HEBREW.

The Story in Talmudic-Midrashic Literature

Narrative creative writing has been a constant in Hebrew literature and can be found in every period of Jewish culture. The earliest biblical texts include stories, and the telling and retelling of stories continued in every age of Hebrew literature. The long talmudic-midrashic period, however, from the first *tannaim* to the first *geonim* is different from previous or later periods in that the Hebrew story was not regarded as an independent form of expression, nor were stories written as separate works; they formed part of the midrashic literary form, and were subordinate to its didactic and moralistic purposes. No collections of stories as such were published in that epoch. The Hebrew narrative of this period, as it reached medieval Jewish culture, was an integral part of the vast talmudic-midrashic literature with no special or specific literary standing. A great part of the narratives preserved in the Midrash developed the biblical story to conform to the exegetical purposes of the talmudic scholars. Frequently, the stories are biographies of early sages to serve as exempla to expound some moral, ethical, or halakhic doctrine. Other stories were included because of nothing more than a vague association with the problem under discussion; this connection, however flimsy it might be, was the only justification for their inclusion.

The subordinate status of the story did not, however, prevent a wealth of narrative material from being included in the talmudic-midrashic literature. L. Ginzberg has shown that this literature contains a complete retelling (in more than one version) of the biblical narrative from the creation to Ezra and Nehemiah; detailed, though sporadic, biographies; stories connected with most of the more important *tannaim* and *amoraim*; stories based on historical facts and legends covering the period of the Second Temple to the *Bar Kokhba War and after; and hundreds of popular stories (usually written in Aramaic, the vernacular of the time). Thus, while the literary aspect of the narrative was insignificant during this period, the narrative creative impulse did not disappear – it only lacked intellectual status as a separate, independent vehicle of expression. The Hebrew story in the Middle Ages opens, therefore, with the slow process of the genre achieving these aims: a separate status and an independent literary form.

The Development of Separate Stories Based on Midrashic Motifs

In the early centuries of the Middle Ages, a large group of independent Hebrew stories based, to some extent, on motifs included in the earlier midrashic literature emerged. Their literary form and content, however, developed independently of that tradition. While talmudic literature merely described the death of some tannaitic martyrs at the hands of the Romans, the medieval narrative "*Aggadat Aseret Harugei Malkhut*" ("The Legend of the Ten Martyrs," also known as "Midrash Elleh Ezkerah" in A. Jellinek, *Beit ha-Midrash*, 1 (1938²), 64–72) used the talmudic stories about R. *Akiva's death and that of other martyrs, and developed a new type of story: the *exemplum for Jewish martyrs in the Middle Ages. Historical truth, evident to some extent in the talmudic stories, was absolutely disregarded here, and the death of the ten *tannaim*, who had lived and died in different periods, was described as taking place at the same time.

Talmudic eschatology nursed the idea of two Messiahs, one the son of Ephraim and the other, the final deliverer, a descendant of the House of David. Sefer *Zerubbavel (*ibid.*, 54–57), a medieval tale, developed this idea into an apocalyptic eschatology. It describes, in biblical language, the visions of the last ruler of the House of David who was shown by an angel what is going to happen at the end of time. The main characters in the narrative are the Messiah's mother Ḥefẓi-Bah and Satan, called *Armilus, described as the son of a beautiful stone statue. These are literary figures unknown to talmudic legends. The writing shows independence of form (it is a separate work dedicated to one visionary story) and of content (the addition of new figures and new heroes not mentioned in older tradition).

Another example of this process is found in the tales told by *Eldad ha-Dani (*ibid.*, 2 (1938²), 102–13; 3 (1938²), 6–11; 5 (1938²), 17–21), who, at the end of the ninth century, traveled through Babylonia, North Africa, and Spain, telling strange stories about his travels and adventures. He described his native land, supposedly the home of four of the Lost *Ten Tribes, and his travel to the land of the other six tribes. Out of a few scattered remarks found in talmudic literature, Eldad spun a coherent and organic picture of the life of these tribes: their number, purity, wisdom, and military power. His description of the pure and holy life of the sons of Moses (the Levites), who live beyond the river *Sambatyon, is drawn both from Jewish and Moslem sources. A minor midrashic motif was here turned into a detailed and well-developed story which has been preserved in 17 different versions, some of them old and authentic, others including many later additions. This is an instance of a Hebrew medieval story coming into its own, achieving a new form, and developing an old theme in a new way. Eldad's stories about the Lost Ten Tribes later became part of the messianic eschatology when the belief developed (for which Eldad was not directly responsible) that the tribes were going to come with the Messiah and serve as his armies in the apocalyptic wars at the End of Days.

Using talmudic motifs, the medieval writers also developed the arts of biography and hagiography. They took material from the Talmud about some of the great sages and wove around them new legends, independent in form from their original talmudic setting (see *Hagiography).

The Retelling of Bible Stories

Medieval storytellers continued in the tradition that every period in Jewish culture retells the biblical story according to its own beliefs, views, and literary convention. This was also done in the first centuries of the Middle Ages when many anonymous writers freed the biblical story from its close connection with the exegetical Midrash and developed an independent literary form. The process took two directions: the telling of a short biblical episode as a fully developed independent short story whose plot revolved about a biblical hero or a biblical event; and attempts to retell great portions of the Bible in a new medieval manner.

To the first category belong "*Ma'aseh Avraham Avinu*" (*ibid.*, 1 (1938²), 25–34), a legend about Abraham; "*Divrei ha-Yamin shel Moshe Rabbenu*" ("The Chronicles of Moses," *ibid.*, 2 (1938²), 1–11); "*Midrash Va-Yisse'u*" (*ibid.* 3 (1938²), 1–5), a story about the battles of the sons of Jacob. Each of these is a short story using most, or even all, of the pertinent material in the Bible and in the Midrash, but reshaping it into a coherent independent plot, and usually adding many details with no source other than the author's imagination. In "*Midrash Va-Yisse'u*," biblical and fictional wars fought by Jacob and his sons in the area of Shechem are depicted in terms of medieval war strategy and medieval military practices. The valor of the sons of Jacob is characterized by medieval chivalry and knighthood concepts.

Other authors attempted to retell the biblical story in wider scope. The author of *Josippon (tenth century, Italy) dedicated most of his work to the war against the Romans and the destruction of the Second Temple. The work, however, starts with a short recapitulation of Jewish history, told in a medieval, fictional style. The more ambitious author of *Sefer ha-Yashar* (probably 11th century, Spain) retells, at great length, the story from the creation to the time of the Judges, i.e., the whole story of the Pentateuch. It is the most complete example of this type of medieval writing using biblical motifs, aggadic material, and fictional innovations to weave a new and captivating story. The literary scope of the work was unequaled by any later medieval writing.

The authors of *Josippon* and *Sefer ha-Yashar* added another aspect to the medieval story about biblical times: they attempted, and frequently succeeded, to incorporate non-Jewish legends, history, and mythology (especially Greek and Roman) into the biblical story. The Jews of the Byzantine Empire, Italy, and Spain accepted the legends and history of the people among whom they lived as being part of the history of the world, and argued that as such they form part of the Bible which was believed to include all the important events in human history. These authors, and others, therefore, developed a system of synchronization and analogy to establish a connection between non-Jewish stories and biblical heroes and chronology. The medieval Hebrew narrative, therefore, broke away from its cultural isolation which had prevailed, to a large extent, in the midrashic story, and it became an open form which accepted and drew on the wealth of non-Jewish stories that had become available to the scattered Jewish communities in the East and in Europe.

The Reawakening of the Apocrypha and Pseudepigrapha

One of the most significant differences between talmudic-midrashic literature on the one hand, and Second Temple literature and medieval Hebrew literature on the other, is the attitude toward the literature of the Second Temple, which was not included in the biblical canon. This literature was preserved in Greek, Latin, and other languages, and only recently have some Hebrew originals been found. During the long centuries of the development of the talmudic-midrashic literature, this material was almost completely ignored. The themes, ideas, and stories in the Book of *Jubilees, in the different versions of the Book of *Enoch, in *Tobit, in *Judith, and even in the historical Books of the *Maccabees are hardly mentioned.

After seven centuries of neglect, these works were again incorporated into the framework of Jewish culture by the Hebrew medieval writers. The process began in the early seventh century with **Pirkei de-Rabbi Eliezer*, which includes subjects from the Apocrypha. The author also used the Satan motif from the books of Enoch and Jubilees; his adaptation of the Bible story is deeply influenced by this long-disregarded or suppressed literature.

Early medieval Hebrew writers created different versions of the stories of Judith and Tobit usually stylistically influenced by popular folktales, and of stories based on the Books of the Maccabees, especially the story of the mother and her seven sons who were martyred by Antiochus. The story of the fallen angels, vividly told in the Book of Enoch, became the story of Uzza and Azael in the Middle Ages; it was transformed into a folktale, and used as a theological motif by kabbalists.

It is very doubtful whether the Hebrew medieval authors of these works had before them the Hebrew originals of the Second Temple literature, though it is not impossible. It would seem, however, that they used the Christian versions of the

Septuagint and the Vulgate. It is also probable that some of the writers had no direct knowledge of the Greek and Latin versions either, but heard the stories from their non-Jewish friends, since there are some significant variations between the originals and the medieval versions. Whatever the origin from which medieval writers drew their material, an important source of Jewish narrative literature, closed during the talmudic-midrashic period, became a living part of Hebrew medieval writing.

The First Collections of Stories

In the early Middle Ages another new literary form emerged, unknown to Hebrew literature, and scarcely found in other literatures of the time: collected stories in book form. The phenomenon indicates that the Hebrew story had taken its rightful place in Jewish literature. Books, devoted entirely or mainly to stories, began to be written. Four major works of this type were written between the 8th and 12th centuries:

(1) *Midrash Aseret ha-Dibberot* (in A. Jellinek, op. cit., 1 (1938²), 62–90; "Midrash of the Ten Commandments"), which is not a Midrash at all but a collection of about 50 stories (in different redactions the number varies) loosely associated with the Ten Commandments. The stories are interspersed with some midrashic aphorisms, but, their importance is clearly secondary. The Hebrew story thus completely reversed the previous situation. The literary aspect of the story, secondary and unimportant in talmudic-midrashic literature, became the main purpose, while the midrashic elements became merely ornamental.

Some of the stories included in the collection were taken from talmudic literature; others are based on the Apocrypha; many of them are new and were written for the first time in Hebrew, though they might have been previously told as folktales. The narratives are meant to serve as exempla, but do so in a peculiar way. There is no intention of teaching man to fulfill the Ten Commandments; this is so elementary, that it is obviously not the purpose. The aim of the work is to demonstrate the extremes of obedience demanded by the commandments. The moral expounded is usually excessive, without any practical didactic value. This tendency shows the first influence of Moslem ethics in Hebrew literature.

(2) *"Alfa Beta of Ben Sira"* ed. by M. Steinschneider (1858), a pseudepigraphical work attributed to *Ben Sira, which is in fact a medieval (ninth century?) collection of stories and epigrams. The aim of the work is a protest against accepted norms of Judaism. The stories ridicule some of the biblical figures, like David and Jeremiah, and parody the rabbinic way of learning. Some of the stories carry a bitter note, protesting against the way God conducts the world. These lively humorous tales structurally attained the highest artistic form to be found in early medieval Hebrew storytelling.

(3) *Sefer ha-Maasiyyot* ("Book of Stories," also *Ḥibbur Yafeh me-ha-Yeshu'ah*, ed. by H.Z. Hirschberg, 1954) by *Nissim b. Jacob of Kairouan (11th century), was originally written in Arabic. The Arabic original was forgotten; however, early Hebrew translations made the collection a part of Hebrew medieval literature. R. Nissim used mainly talmudic-midrashic stories and episodes, but added many medieval folktales, some of which had their origin in Judaism, others in Moslem and Arabic sources. His declared purpose was to strengthen the faith in God of a friend who had suffered some misfortune. The body of the collection, however, is not devoted only to this aim. The stories fall into all of the main categories of medieval popular narratives, such as stories about good and bad women, about witches and evil powers, about lust and repentance. In later Hebrew medieval writings, R. Nissim's stories had a life of their own, independent of their thematic and plot value in the original collection. They were told separately, and were included individually in many later collections.

(4) *The Exempla of the Rabbis*, a collection of stories published from a manuscript by M. Gaster (1924; 1968²), by far the largest to be compiled in the Middle Ages. It includes more than 200 tales. Most of them are talmudic, but many, especially in the second half of the collection, are medieval Hebrew folktales told in a captivating manner, Gaster claims that the collection is extremely old, and even suggests – without basis – that it was a source for the Talmud. The collection was most probably compiled in the 11th or 12th century, and shows that some artistic effort had been made to turn it into an organic and unified literary work by arranging the stories into different sequences, each connected to the other through the ending of the preceding narrative.

These four early collections of Hebrew stories mark the beginning of the medieval Hebrew story as a separate literary form, independent of the Midrash, and claiming its own place in Jewish culture.

Stories Included in Hebrew Historiographical Works

Simultaneous with the emergence of the Hebrew story as an independent literary form, Hebrew historiography evolved separately and in the process helped to preserve many Hebrew stories. The dividing line between history and legend, not clearly defined by the medieval historiographer, led to the literary genre of "fictional history" which tried to describe the history of a period, but succeeded mainly in collecting the major stories of it. A classical example is Megillat *Aḥima'aẓ ("The Chronicle of Ahimaaz," ed. by B. Klar, 1945), which was written in rhymed verse in Italy and describes the history of the Jews in southern Italy from the 8th to the 11th centuries. Most of the work is devoted to stories, which might have some historical foundation, but the writer was mainly interested in telling fables of wonder and mystery connected with the period: Abu Aaron, an eastern mystic living then in Italy, is the hero of a collection of these stories in which such things as his supernatural powers are described.

In Abraham *Ibn Daud's *Sefer ha-Kabbalah*, a more serious attempt to distinguish between history and legend is made. Some legends and tales are, however, included: e.g., the story of the four captives from Babylonia who, after they had been rescued, spread Jewish culture in many communities;

and the legendary material interwoven in the descriptions of the beginnings of Jewish culture in Spain. The same situation is found in many other and later historiographical works. A later example of this kind of "fictional history" is to be found in Gedaliah b. Joseph *Ibn Yaḥya's *Shalshelet ha-Kabbalah* ("The Chain of Tradition"), written in and influenced by Renaissance Italy. It is mainly a collection of stories, hagiographies, and exempla about great medieval scholars, including many demonological and supernatural tales.

The same lack of distinction between fact and fiction is to be found in another literary genre which developed in the Middle Ages: the peregrinations of great travelers, who had returned home full of wonderful and strange tales about faraway countries. Though these travel writings have much important historical data, most of the writers found special pleasure in telling fabulous stories (e.g., those by *Benjamin of Tudela, *Pethahiah of Regensburg, and Ḥayyim Joseph David *Azulai). Historiography and itineraries, therefore, formed part of the development of the Hebrew story in the Middle Ages.

The Romance in Hebrew Literature

From the 12th century, Hebrew literature began to include many detailed, long, and well-developed romantic stories. Most of the romances do not have their origin in Hebrew culture, but belong to the general medieval stock of fiction. Some are direct translations from Latin, Arabic, or other languages, while others show special Jewish adaptation as they passed from the original language into Hebrew. Most of the romances have more than one Hebrew rendition, and the Jewish elements in them, therefore, vary from one version to another.

Among the direct translations, to which very few or no Jewish motifs were added, are the 13th-century Hebrew version of the romance of King Arthur (Artus) and the Round Table (see *Arthurian Legend), and the *Tales of Sendebar* (ed. by M. Epstein, 1967), the classic cycle of stories about the faithfulness and unfaithfulness of women and sons, known in the West as the romance of "The Seven Sages of Rome." Whereas only one Hebrew version of the Arthurian legends is known, the *Tales of Sendebar* is found in many manuscripts and in several versions of various length and number of legends included.

The classic romance, "*The Gests of Alexander of Macedonia*" (*The Book of the Gests of Alexander of Macedon*, ed. and translated into English, by I.J. Kazis, 1962), exists in Hebrew in no less than five versions; four of them are based on Latin and Arabic sources in which some Jewish elements were added, the fifth seems to be an almost totally original work, bearing little affinity to the original classic Greek. The Jewish elements fuse well into the legends mainly because in the Greek original there are already a few anecdotes which associate Alexander with the Jews, and in the talmudic-midrashic tradition there are nearly a dozen stories about Alexander. It is not surprising, therefore, that in the Jewish version of the romance, Alexander even encounters the Lost Ten Tribes, is circumcised, and comes to believe in the God of the Jews.

Another medieval cycle of fables, *Kalila and Dimna (ed. by J. Derenbourg, 1881), which probably originated in India and was transmitted into European literature via Persian and Arabic writings, has two medieval Hebrew versions, one translated by a certain R. Joel (probably in the 12th century) and the other by R. Jacob b. Eleazar, a little later. *Ma'aseh Yerushalmi* ("The Story of the Jerusalemite," ed. by J.L. Zlotnik (1946)), a romance about a man who through a miracle had come to the land of the demons and was there forced to marry *Asmodeus' daughter, is only known from the Jewish original, though the motif exists both in Arabic and Latin literatures. Six Hebrew versions written from the 13th to the 17th centuries are found in Eastern and Western Jewish literatures. The differences in the texts are substantial; many, however, can be explained as a result of the development of the legend within Jewish literature and thought, and not because of non-Jewish literary influences. This is an example of a romance, which was probably first written down in 12th-century Europe, and was preserved, as well as developed, within Jewish culture, becoming one of the standard stories in every Hebrew collection.

The Hebrew view of Jesus' life found full expression in a well-developed and detailed medieval Hebrew romance. The legend, which is the Jewish answer to Christian versions about the birth, life, and death of Jesus, is of an earlier date; in the Middle Ages, however, it had grown into an independent, detailed work, Sefer *Toledot Yeshu. Mary is not unfavorably portrayed, and the author also shows some understanding of Jesus' deeds. It seems that hate itself could not support the development of the story, and when it became a romance, some sympathy had to be shown toward the main characters. Other medieval romances, mainly those originating in the East, reflecting Indian, Persian, and Arabic influences, were incorporated into Hebrew literature as tales in verse, mainly in the *maqama form, which in Hebrew is usually regarded as a poetic rather than a prose genre. The full acceptance of the medieval romance into Hebrew literature, both in its various forms and independent development, signifies that from the 12th century onward Hebrew fictional prose writing became a part of general medieval fiction. It used the stock heroes and plots of medieval fiction, but infused them with special Jewish motifs.

The Story in Hebrew Ethical Literature

With the development of Jewish ethical literature in the 11th century, the story found another major outlet, as well as a wide field for its development. Writers of ethical works, trying to reach as wide a public as possible and educate it according to their own ethical ideology, used every literary form which would popularize their works. This desire for a wider public made the use of stories, fables, legends, exempla, hagiographies, anecdotes, epigrams, imperative within the framework of ethical literature. As a result, many ethical works became treasure houses of all sorts of Hebrew fictional writings as well as the different literary genres devoted to the story exclusively.

Jewish philosophy, the first movement to develop Hebrew ethical literature (written mainly in Arabic and later translated into Hebrew), contributed little to the development of the story. Its authors were hostile toward narrative literary forms, going so far as to voice contempt for the narratives in the Bible itself. *Baḥya b. Joseph ibn Paquda in the preface to his *Ḥovot ha-Levavot* ("Duties of the Heart"), one of the most famous and influential philosophical-ethical works, explains that the narratives in the Bible were included by God to distinguish between the wise who will disregard them and study the wisdom in the Bible, and the fools, who will follow the narratives and thus reveal themselves as fools. The attitude was widely held by many Jewish medieval intellectuals, and even the *Zohar used the same fable that Baḥya did to demonstrate his contempt of the biblical narratives and narrative literature in general.

Despite their hostile attitude, the medieval philosophers did use the story, mainly in the form of long and well-developed fables and short anecdotes; philosophical-ethical writings, therefore, became another means through which the body of Jewish literature was enriched with anecdotes, epigrams, and fables. Many of them were taken from Arab philosophical and moralistic writings whose origin, as often as not, was in Indian literature. Views, too radical to be plainly stated, were often couched in fables; the wide disparity between the fable and the author's explanation served as an indication of the real views of the radical thinker. Baḥya himself often used this method in his work.

While philosophical-ethical literature did not contribute a great deal to the development of the Hebrew story, the two other main schools of Jewish medieval thought, the Ḥasidei Ashkenaz and the kabbalists, in their theological and their ethical works, were the main outlet for the fictional narrative which was to become inherent in popular Jewish culture.

The Story in Ashkenazi-Ḥasidic Literature

The writings of R. *Judah b. Samuel he-Ḥasid (d. 1217) and his disciples, both theological and ethical, are one of the main sources of the Hebrew narrative in the Middle Ages. The reason for this is at least partially theological. The Ḥasidei Ashkenaz believed that God's will and presence were not to be found in common phenomena of the everyday world and in laws of nature, but in miraculous wonderful happenings, If a Ḥasid, therefore, wanted to learn God's ways and essence, he had to look for unusual phenomena and deduce God's power from them. This attitude, naturally, caused the Ḥasidei Ashkenaz to write down and preserve stories and anecdotes about the exceptional, which was to them theological truth.

Most of these stories have some demonological elements and many describe meetings between men and witches, werewolves, demons, spirits, and ghosts. These supernatural powers did not represent any evil to the Ḥasidim; they regarded them as a part, though a dangerous and mysterious one, of the world created by God. Their theology made the Ḥasidim look for "true" stories which they could believe had actually happened. This is the reason that the literary element was neglected and most of the stories are "eyewitness" anecdotes. Consequently also 12th- and 13th-century German demonology is depicted and not traditional Jewish demonology and superstition. Many of the stories, told by the Ḥasidim as short anecdotes in the 12th century, were collected and developed 700 years later by the Grimm brothers as main stories of German mythology and folklore.

The second motive for the use of the story in Ashkenazi-ḥasidic literature was the ethical fanaticism of the Ḥasidim, as it is reflected in *Sefer Ḥasidim*, the major ethical work of Ḥasidei Ashkenaz. The extreme demands made by the Ashkenazi Ḥasidim on their followers were demonstrated in hundreds of exempla in which stories are told about men who succeeded in achieving the nigh impossible ethical standards set by the ḥasidic teachers. The latter, in turn, became heroes of cycles of legends (see *Legend; *Hagiography), written in the 13th, 15th, and 16th centuries and translated into Yiddish, in which supernatural deeds are attributed to them. Some of the later hagiographical legends sprang from original Ashkenazi-ḥasidic stories in which the heroes were anonymous.

Ashkenazi-ḥasidic ethical literature was one of the main influences on later Jewish ethics whose exponents made extensive use of *Sefer Ḥasidim* and other Ashkenazi-ḥasidic writings. The narratives of the Ḥasidei Ashkenaz were thus preserved long after the movement had died out (late 13th century), and this body of stories became one of the standard sources of later Hebrew fictional writing.

The Narrative in the Kabbalah

The Kabbalah, which flourished in Provence and Spain in the 12th century (reaching its maturity at the end of the 13th century), developed the medieval Hebrew narrative in three different forms:

(1) The hagiography. The teachers of the Kabbalah were treated by their disciples and followers as men of God who possessed secret knowledge and supernatural powers. Contemporaries of these sages and the following generations created hagiographical cycles of stories about them. The kabbalistic sages themselves also wrote hagiographies, often attributing their works to tannaitic sources, and describing the *tannaim* hagiographically. Works like the *Zohar, Sefer ha-*Kanah, and others include countless stories about the early sages.

(2) The mythological story. By introducing mythological elements into Jewish theology, the kabbalists opened many new possibilities to the Hebrew story (see *Kabbalah). The idea that processes in the divine spheres and the war between the divine powers of good and evil could be told in a narrative manner led the kabbalistic imagination to endow the saintly being with power to intervene in the divine spheres. The literary genre of the mythological story came to the fore only in later centuries, e.g., the story of R. *Joseph Della Reina (first recorded in 1519, published in 1913), and the stories and legends about *Shabbetai Ẓevi, who was regarded as having divine power by his believers.

(3) The mystical story. Mystical elements in the Kabbalah led kabbalists to describe their divine revelations and visions, through which they acquired mystical knowledge, in narrative form (see *Visions). The characteristics of the narrative were influenced by the individual kabbalist author: how he viewed his experience and his attitude to the form, Kabbalistic mysticism thus developed the aspect of the individual visions in the story.

The Kabbalah, between the 12th and 15th centuries, did not try to reach a wide public, and its exponents usually kept their knowledge and revelations a secret. Only at the end of the 15th and in the 16th centuries did the Kabbalah begin to reach wider and wider circles in the various Jewish communities and, therefore, it is in the later Middle Ages that the influence of the Kabbalah on the Hebrew narrative became predominant. It is in 16th-century Jerusalem, Safed, and Italy, and 17th-century Eastern Europe that the kabbalistic story came into its own.

The Hebrew Story in the Italian Renaissance

The Hebrew story in 16th-century Italy was influenced not only by the spirit of Italian Renaissance art and literature, but also by the catastrophe of the expulsion of the Jews from Spain and Portugal at the end of the 15th century. The combination of these two influences is reflected, for instance, in the dialogues found in *Shevet Yehudah*, a fictional-historical work by Solomon *Ibn Verga. It is devoted mainly to historical descriptions of the various catastrophes which befell the Jewish people since the destruction of the Temple. The originality of the work lies in the fictional dialogues between Christian kings, bishops, and scholars, sometimes also involving Jewish scholars and ordinary persons. Ibn Verga's views as to the causes of the catastrophes are unusual for his time. He states that the Jews themselves are to blame for their misfortunes which occurred because of their arrogance, fanaticism, and intolerance. The shock of the expulsion is fused here with the spirit of tolerance of the Renaissance to produce a work whose views were not again to come to the fore before the 19th-century Reform movement in Judaism.

The shock of the disaster of Spanish Jewry gave birth to messianic literature; the most famous examples are the autobiography of David *Re'uveni who styled himself as an emissary of the Lost Ten Tribes to the Pope and kings of Europe, and the autobiographical sketches and kabbalistic visions of Solomon *Molcho who felt that it was his destiny to announce the coming of the Messiah. Many more messianic stories were written in that period.

One of the most important literary contributions of the period to the Hebrew story was the art of autobiography (see *Biography and Autobiography). *Ḥayyei Yehudah by* Leone *Modena is one of the most intimate and revealing autobiographies written in Hebrew during the Middle Ages. Abraham *Jagel (Caliko) in one of the stories in *Gei Ḥizzayon* ("The Valley of Vision") relates how the spirit of his dead father visited him in prison and took him to the heavenly spheres. On their way, father and son met many spirits, good and wicked, who told their stories, and Abraham also told what had happened to him after his father's death. This literary form bears the mark of the Italian novella of that age, and the stories themselves were only slightly Judaized.

This period is marked by two conflicting developments in the Hebrew narrative. On the one hand, there is a closer connection and mutual influence between Hebrew and Italian cultures which benefited the Hebrew story. On the other hand, the Jewish situation of the time caused the Hebrew story to reflect the growing messianic hopes, resulting in a tendency toward isolation from outer influences. The Hebrew story thus came to express the emotions and tensions of a people torn between catastrophe and messianic hope.

The Hebrew Story in Palestine in the 16th Century

Concurrent with the Hebrew renaissance in literature in Italy, there was a Jewish literary and mystic renaissance in Palestine, especially in Safed. Kabbalistic thought, which prevailed in Safed at the time, filled the hearts of almost all the Jewish scholars with messianic expectations. At the beginning of the 16th century, from Jerusalem, came the first version of the story of Joseph Della Reina who tried to bring about the redemption through magic and Kabbalah. Here attention was focused on *Nevu'at ha-Yeled* ("The Prophecy of the Child" in Jacob Ḥayyim Ẓemaḥ's *Nagid u-Meẓavveh*, Constantinople, 1726), a story about a wonder child who revealed in obscure Aramaic prophecies the time of the redemption.

In Safed, stories were told about various sages who had performed unusual deeds and undergone all kinds of torture, in order to repent for the sins of all Israel, and in this way hasten the coming of the Messiah. In Safed also appeared R. Isaac *Luria whose teachings revolutionized the Kabbalah and gave it messianic direction; there the first body of hagiographical stories, preserved in various versions (see *Hagiography, *Toledot ha-Ari), was created around Isaac Luria and his school; and there Luria's foremost pupil, R. Ḥayyim *Vital, wrote his *Sefer ha-Ḥezyonot* ("Book of Visions") in which he describes his dreams of glory, believing Luria to be the Messiah who was to be a descendant of Joseph, and himself, the Messiah who was to be a descendant of David.

Many other kabbalists and non-kabbalists contributed to the development of the Hebrew story in Palestine at this period, At the beginning of the 17th century, their works began to spread to Eastern Europe, where most of the Jews and most of the more important communities were then located. Unlike the Hebrew literature of the Italian Renaissance, the literature of Safed had an enormous influence in shaping the culture of the Jewish communities in Eastern Europe. Therefore, the further development of the Hebrew story in the 17th and 18th centuries was a direct continuation of the Safed revival and not of the new forms supplied by the Hebrew renaissance literature in Italy.

The Hebrew Story in the 17th and 18th Centuries

Two major processes paved the way for the development of the Hebrew narrative in this period. The first was the spreading of the Lurianic Kabbalah throughout the Jewish world; the hagiographical cycle of stories woven around Luria was repeated in many versions, in many works, with similar stories told about other sages, most of them kabbalists. The second was the Shabbatean movement, which, although it did not produce much narrative literature, did lay the foundations for a new kind of legend: the messianic legend about Shabbetai Ẓevi who had styled himself as the Messiah. Some legendary biographies of Shabbetai Ẓevi and his prophet, Nathan of Gaza, were preserved, but there was probably much more narrative material which was either lost or suppressed by the opponents of Shabbeteanism. This had some delayed influence on ḥasidic literature.

Another change marking the development of the Hebrew story in Eastern Europe in this period was the wider use of Yiddish which had become the spoken, and often the written, language of the Jews. While sacred works in the field of *halakhah* and Kabbalah were always written in Hebrew, popular works, like stories and ethical literature, were either written only in Yiddish, or in Hebrew with a Yiddish translation. From this period on, it is impossible to distinguish between the development of Hebrew and Yiddish stories. Many originally Hebrew stories were written down in Yiddish, and many popular stories, which were told in Yiddish, were written down in Hebrew.

The wide use of printing also affected the field of narrative literature, and old and new stories were collected and published in small booklets and sometimes in larger collections. Attempts to collect medieval stories have been made by scholars in the East and West. Ḥayyim Joseph David Azulai, an eastern rabbi, wrote down and compiled the stories he had heard throughout his long life and wide travels. Unfortunately, he usually gave only a short description of the story and seldom went into details. Other eastern rabbis in the 18th and early 19th centuries collected hundreds of medieval stories; these, however, have remained in manuscripts until this very day. In the West, collections of stories were published more often; the largest and most important of them being the *Oseh Pele* ("Wonder Worker"). Modern scholars have taken an interest in this rich mine of narrative literature, and the greatest modern collection, which includes also a full bibliography of earlier collections, is M.J. Berdyczewski's *Mi-Mekor Yisrael* (1966²).

The Ḥasidic Story

The Hebrew narrative in its medieval form continued to develop in the modern period. Haskalah literature did not serve as a substitute for continued creative effort in the old types and forms of Hebrew narrative writing; on the contrary – the Hebrew story, in its medieval form, reached its zenith with the emergence of Haskalah literature. This phenomenon is due to the modern ḥasidic movement, founded by *Israel Ba'al Shem Tov (late 18th century) from which the medieval narrative drew new life.

Though Ḥasidism began much earlier, ḥasidic narrative literature as a written art came to the fore only at the beginning of the 19th century when *Shivḥei ha-Besht and the stories of R. *Naḥman of Bratslav were published (Berdichev, 1815). Later, hundreds of ḥasidic tales were compiled and published. They very often included not only ḥasidic material but also stories about medieval sages. The sanctity accorded to the story in ḥasidic life and ideology helped to preserve not only the ḥasidic story itself, but countless medieval narratives which would have been lost had the authors of ḥasidic narrative anthologies not looked for them and saved them from oblivion. The ḥasidic narrative and the medieval stories that were drawn into the body of ḥasidic literature did not use the wide range of literary forms which came into being in the Middle Ages and have been described above. The modern form almost exclusively belongs to the field of hagiography, and the stories were sometimes used as exempla. The other literary forms ceased to be a vehicle of expression; their place and possible development in Hebrew literature form part of the history of modern Hebrew literature, and not ḥasidic literature. For later developments see *Hebrew Literature.

BIBLIOGRAPHY: M.J. Bin Gorion (Berdyczewski), *Die Sagen der Juden* (1962²); J. Dan, *Torat ha-Sod shel Ḥasidut Ashkenaz* (1968), 184–202, 265–7 (incl. bibl.); idem, in: *Molad*, 23 (1965), 490–6; idem, in: *Tarbiz*, 30 (1961/62), 273–89; idem, in: *Zion*, 26 (1961/62), 132–7; idem, in: PAAJR, 35 (1967), 99–111; G. Scholem, *On the Kabbalah and Its Symbolism* (1965), 158–204; Zinberg, Sifrut, vols. 1–3; I. Tishby, *Mishnat ha-Zohar*, 1 (1957²), 1–98; J. Even-Shemuel (Kaufmann), *Midreshei Ge'ullah* (1954); *Kitvei Rabbi Avraham Epstein*, 1 (1950), 1–209, 357–90; A.M. Habermann, in: *Tarbiz*, 27 (1957/58), 190–202; J.L. Zlotnik, in: *Sinai*, 18 (1946), 49–58; F. Baer, in: *Sefer Dinaburg* (1949), 178–205; D. Flusser, in: *Zion*, 18 (1952/53), 109–26; idem, in: *Tarbiz*, 26 (1956/57), 165–184; L. Ginzberg, *Al Halakhah ve-Aggadah* (1960), 205–62; M. Guedemann, *Ha-Torah ve-ha-Ḥayyim be-Ẓarefat u-ve-Ashkenaz* (1968²), 157–81; Y. Raphael, in: *Aresheth*, 2 (1960), 358–77; 3 (1961), 440f. (*Shivḥei ha-Besht*, incl. bibl.). **ADD. BIBLIOGRAPHY:** J. Dan, *Ha-Sippur ha-Ivri bi-Yemei ha-Beinayim: iyyunim be-Toldotav* (1974); idem, *Ha-Sippur ha-Ḥasidi* (1975); A. Alba, *Midrás de los Diez Mandamientos y Libro precioso de la Salvación* (1989); idem, *Cuentos de los rabinos* (1991).

[Joseph Dan]

FIEDLER, ARTHUR (1894–1979), conductor and violinist. Fiedler was born in Boston, where his father was a violinist with the Boston Symphony Orchestra. Violinists or "fiedlers" had been in the family for three generations. As a boy, he studied the violin, the piano, and conducting at the Hochschule fuer Musik, Berlin. He made his debut there at 17 as a violinist, but returned to the U.S. on the outbreak of World War I and joined the Boston Symphony Orchestra as a viola player. In 1924 he founded the Boston Sinfonietta, an orchestra of 22 players. From 1929 he organized the successful outdoor series of Esplanade Concerts at Boston. A year later (1930), he was appointed conductor of the Boston Pops Orchestra, which he directed until his death. Fiedler extended the orchestral repertory to include show-tune medleys and arrangements of popular songs in a variety of styles, which brought him a wide reputation at home and abroad. From 1957 he also made international appearances as a guest conductor.

BIBLIOGRAPHY: Grove online; R. Moore: *Fiedler, the Colorful Mr. Pops* (1968), incl. discography; H.E. Dickson: *Arthur Fiedler and the Boston Pops* (1981).

[Israela Stein (2nd ed.)]

FIEDLER, LESLIE AARON (1917–2003), U.S. author and critic. Born in Newark, New Jersey, Fiedler taught at the University of Montana (1941–64) and, from 1965, was professor of English at the State University of New York at Buffalo. He wrote books of short stories, such as *Pull Down Vanity* (1962), and novels, including *The Second Stone* (1963), *Back to China* (1965), and *The Last Jew in America* (1966). He is however, best known for his literary studies and critical essays, which include a contribution to *Leaves of Grass: 100 Years After* (ed. by M. Hindus, 1955), in honor of Walt Whitman; an edition of Simone *Weil's *Waiting for God* (1959); *The Art of the Essay* (1969); *Love and Death in the American Novel* (1960); a contribution to *The Continuing Debate* (1964); and various articles in *Encounter, Preuves*, and *Partisan Review.* Fiedler tended to regard a literary work as the expression of an author's psychosexual desires, minimizing the importance of its structure and linguistic texture. Though not at first prominent in his works, Jewish themes played an increasing part in Fiedler's writing, notably in his *Image of the Jew in American Fiction* (1959) and *The Jew in the American Novel* (1966²), where he saw the Jew as the eternal alien and dissenter. *Fiedler on the Roof: Essays on Literature and Jewish Identity* appeared in 1991. *Nude Croquet* (1969), a volume of collected stories, is a bleak, guilt-ridden anthology, including much of Jewish interest. Fiedler was active in American-Jewish life.

BIBLIOGRAPHY: Bellman, in: *Congress Bi-Weekly* (Dec. 21, 1964), 10–12; Goodheart, in: *Midstream*, 7 no. 2 (1961), 94–100; Kostelanetz, *ibid.*, 9 no. 3 (1963), 93–97; Chase, in: *Chicago Review*, 14 (Autumn–Winter 1960), 8–18; Whalen, in: *Northwest Review*, 9 (Spring 1968), 67–73. **ADD. BIBLIOGRAPHY:** S. Kellman and I. Malin (eds.) *Leslie Fiedler and American Culture* (1999).

[Milton Henry Hindus]

FIELDS, DOROTHY (1904–1974), U.S. lyricist and librettist. Born in Allenhurst, New Jersey, Fields was the youngest of four children of the famous comedian Lew Fields. She and her two brothers, Herbert and Joseph, became writers in the entertainment field. In the 1920s Fields began a songwriting partnership with composer Jimmy McHugh that lasted almost a decade. Their first songs were written for shows performed at the famous Harlem night spot, the Cotton Club. Their greatest stage hit was *Blackbirds of 1928*, one of the longest-running Broadway shows with an all-black cast. In 1929 Fields and McHugh moved to Hollywood. Their most popular songs included "I Can't Give You Anything But Love" and "On the Sunny Side of the Street," both written for Broadway revues, and "Don't Blame Me" and "I'm In the Mood for Love," written for Hollywood films. In Hollywood in the 1930s Fields began working with other composers including Oscar *Levant and Fritz *Kreisler. Her favorite collaborator, and close friend, was Jerome *Kern. Kern and Fields wrote the scores for *The Joy of Living*, *I Dream Too Much*, and her best movie musical, *Swingtime*, which included the song, "The Way You Look Tonight," for which Kern and Fields won an Academy Award in 1936. In the 1940s, in collaboration with her brother Henry, Fields produced the books for four Broadway hits, *Let's Face It*, *Something for the Boys*, and *Mexican Hayride*, which had songs by Cole Porter, and *Annie Get Your Gun*, which had songs by Irving Berlin. Other composers with whom she worked included Sigmund *Romberg, Arthur Schwartz, Morton *Gould, Albert Hague, Harold *Arlen, and Harry Warren. After the deaths of her husband and her brother Herbert in 1958, Fields stopped writing for more than five years. She bounced back with one of her most popular stage plays, *Sweet Charity*, written with Cy *Coleman in 1966. Her final work, also written with Coleman, was *Seesaw.*

Fields won the Antoinette Perry (Tony) Award in 1959 for her work on *Redhead* and was elected as an inaugural member of the Songwriters Hall of Fame in 1971. Unlike earlier female lyricists, who worked in the field of operetta and tended to write songs of elevated sentiments, Dorothy Fields showed from the start a gift for the vernacular and an ear for the most up-to-date speech and slang. She is admired for her meticulous craftsmanship and her ability to combine clear-eyed sentiment with humor.

BIBLIOGRAPHY: D.G. Winer, *On the Sunny Side of the Street: The Life and Lyrics of Dorothy Fields* (1997).

[Charlotte Greenspan (2nd ed.)]

FIELDS, JACKIE (Jacob (Yonkel) Finkelstein; 1908–1987), U.S. welterweight boxing champion 1929–30 and 1932–33, featherweight Olympic Gold Medal winner, member of the Boxing Hall of Fame. Fields was born and raised in a Jewish neighborhood in Chicago, "where you had to fight your way to the swimming pool because the Italians, the Polish, the Irish, the Lithuanians were there." He began fighting at 14 at the Henry Booth Settlement House under the tutelage of one-time featherweight fighter Marty Fields, whose name he eventually adopted. After Fields' father, Morris, a butcher, contracted tuberculosis, the family moved to Los Angeles. Fields won 51 of 54 amateur bouts, and captured the Olympic Featherweight Gold medal at the 1924 Olympic Games at age 16, the youngest man ever to win an Olympic boxing crown. His first pro fight was February 2, 1925, and seven fights later, on November 12, 1925, Hall of Famer Jimmy McLarnin knocked him out in the second round, the only time Fields was stopped by a KO.

Fields won the National Boxing Association (NBA) Welterweight Championship on March 25, 1929, with a decision over Young Jack Thompson. Four months later, on July 25, he captured the unified world championship against Joe Dundee. The defending champion was knocked down five times in the second round, and was then disqualified after crawling on his hands and knees across the ring and punching Fields full-force in the groin, knocking him out. Thus Fields became the only fighter to ever win a title while flat on his back.

Fields lost the world title to Thompson on May 9, 1930, but regained it a second time on January 28, 1932, with a decision over Lou Brouillard, who had taken the crown from Thompson. He lost the title to Young Corbett III on February 22, 1933, and retired after one more fight, having lost his vision in one eye in an automobile accident a year earlier. Widely regarded as scientific boxer with tremendous stamina and a solid punch, Fields' record was 72 (30 KO's)–9–2. In 1965, Fields coached the U.S. boxing team at the Maccabiah Games in Israel.

[Elli Wohlgelernter (2nd ed.)]

FIG (Heb. תְּאֵנָה, *te'enah*), one of the seven species with which Ereẓ Israel was blessed (Deut. 8:8). It is mentioned in the Bible 16 times together with the vine as the most important of the country's fruit. The saying "every man under his vine and under his fig tree" depicts an era of peace and security in the past and the vision of an ideal future (I Kings 5:5; Micah 4:4; cf. Joel 2:22). On the other hand the prophets repeatedly warn against the destruction of the vines and the fig trees (Jer. 5:17; 8:13; Hos. 2:12; Hab. 3:17). The fig is also mentioned as a curative. A fig compress (*develah*) was used by Isaiah in the cure of King Hezekiah (II Kings 20:7; Isa. 38:21).

The cultivation of the fig in Ereẓ Israel goes back to very early times. Excavations at Gezer have uncovered remains of dried figs from the Neolithic Age, while an ancient Egyptian inscription refers to the destruction of the country's fig trees by its conquerors (Jeremias, Alte Test, 139). The spread of the fig in Ereẓ Israel is attested by place-names associated with the word *te'enah* or *develah*. The fig served as a basic food, possessing a high nutritional value, largely by virtue of its honey. The expressions "honey out of the crag" (Deut. 32:13) and "honey out of the rock" (Ps. 81:17) apparently refer to the honey of figs, the trees of which grow in rocky places (cf. Yal., Va-Era, 184). Similarly, the sages identify "honey" in the passage "a land flowing with milk and honey" with the honey of figs (Ket. 111b).

The fig tree sheds its leaves in winter, at the end of which, even before the tree is covered with leaves, the *paggim* ("green figs," Song 2:13) begin to develop in the form of small fruits, which are really tiny flowers covered with a soft skin, and which continue to grow during the summer months. Hosea (9:10) compared the young nation of Israel in the heyday of its glory to *bakkurot* ("first-ripe figs"), which are delicious and eagerly sought after (Isa. 28:4; Jer, 24:2). Not all the *paggim* reach the ripened stage, some falling off or withering (Isa. 34:4). Figs that ripen at the end of summer have an inferior taste (Micah 7:1), as do those that burst when overripe (Jer. 29:17). Figs were dried in the sun and were either left whole or cut up and pressed (*develah*, I Sam., 25:18; I Chron. 12:40). The word *kayiẓ* (II Sam. 16:1–2; Jer., 40:10, 12), which may refer to summer fruits as a whole, signifies primarily dried figs (cf. Isa. 16:9; Tosef., Ned. 4:1–2).

The importance of the fig in mishnaic and talmudic times is evidenced by the fact that more than 70 expressions connected with the fig occur in the literature of the period. Various strains of fig are mentioned: white and black (Ter. 4:8); those that ripen early and those that ripen late (*ibid.*, 4:6; Shev, 9:4), The *paggim* of certain strains were pierced or smeared with oil to make them ripen early (*ibid.*, 2:5). Other strains required caprification: to ensure the pollination of the fruit, branches bearing the fruit of the wild fig (*Ficus carica caprificus*) were hung up on the trees. These were infested with insects, which alone can pollinate the fruit of the cultivated fig (*Ficus carica domestica;* cf. Tosef., *ibid.*, 1:9; TJ, *ibid.*, 4:4, 35b).

At present, fig trees are cultivated in Ereẓ Israel mainly by Arabs, their economic value being limited in modern Jewish agriculture in that their fruit, not ripening simultaneously, must be picked almost daily by many hands (Num. R. 12:9). The fig tree has many branches, large leaves, and widely spread boughs. Large, shady fig trees are to be found in Israel, especially on the banks of streams and near springs, and are among the most beautiful trees in the country. The fig figures prominently in the *aggadah*, the consensus, on the basis of Genesis 3:7, being that the Tree of the Knowledge of Good and Evil was a fig tree (Ber. 40a; Gen, R. 15:7).

BIBLIOGRAPHY: F. Goldmann, in: REJ, 62 (1911), 216–32; Loew, Flora, 1 (1928), 224ff.; J. Feliks, *Olam ha-Ẓome'aḥ ha-Mikra'i* (1957), 33–39. **ADD BIBLIOGRAPHY:** Feliks, *Ha-Ẓome'aḥ* 167.

[Jehuda Feliks]

FIGO (Picho), AZARIAH (1579–1647), Italian rabbi and preacher, born in Venice. In his youth he devoted himself largely to secular studies, but later, regretting the time he had spent "loving the handmaiden" and "neglecting the mistress," he applied himself wholly to rabbinic studies. At the age of 28, he was appointed rabbi of Pisa. There he wrote *Giddulei Terumah* (Venice, 1643), a casuistic commentary on the *Sefer ha-Terumot* of Samuel *Sardi. After the burning of the Talmud in 1553, copies were very scarce, and when Figo wrote his book he possessed only the tractates *Bava Kamma, Shevu'ot*, and *Nazir* and had to borrow the other tractates from the neighboring communities. He completed the book in Venice, where he returned in 1627, and became preacher to the Sephardi community. Figo leaned toward a strict interpretation of Jewish law. He opposed the establishment of a theater in the ghetto of Venice and criticized the members of his community for usury, flaunting their wealth, internecine wrangling, laxity in ritual observances, and sexual irregularities, Figo was active in redeeming Jewish captives, and defended the Marranos, declaring them to be Jews. His most important work is his *Binah le-Ittim* (Venice (?), 1648), a collection of sermons delivered in Venice. They are based on the festivals and fasts of the Jewish calendar, and also include sermons based on *Avot* on such topics as charity and education. Since its first publication it has been reprinted 50 times. Some of his responsa are found in the *Devar Shemu'el* (1702) of Samuel Aboab. Figo died in Rovigo.

On his homiletical works, see *Homiletics.

BIBLIOGRAPHY: A. Appelbaum, *Azariah Figo* (Heb., 1907); Bettan, in: HUCA, 7 (1930), 457–95; M. Szulwas, *Ḥayyei ha-Yehudi be-Italyah bi-Tekufat ha-Renaissance* (1955), index; H.R. Rabinowitz, *Deyokena'ot shel Darshanim* (1967), 150–8.

[Chayim Reuven Rabinowitz]

FILDERMAN, WILHELM (1882–1963), Romanian Jewish leader. Born in Bucharest, in 1909 Filderman became a doctor of law in Paris. He returned to Romania and after teaching for two years at the high school of the Jewish community of Bucharest, started his law practice in 1912. In 1913 he was elected to the central committee of the Union of Romanian Jews. Filderman was an officer in the Romanian army during World War I and after the war became the acting leader of the Union of Romanian Jews. At the Versailles Peace Conference he was a member of the *Comité des Délégations Juives. He demanded the total emancipation of the Jews as an inalienable right and the inclusion of this principle in the peace treaty with Romania.

In 1920 Filderman became the representative of the *American Jewish Joint Distribution Committee (JDC) in Romania and in 1923 was elected president of the Union of Romanian Jews. Between the two world wars, he fought antisemitism, and worked for the effective realization of full citizenship for the Jews. Filderman also published a number of books against antisemitism. He was opposed to a national Jewish policy and a separate Jewish party. In 1927 Filderman was elected a member of the Romanian parliament on the Liberal Party list. He was also the president of the Jewish community of Bucharest (1931–33), and in the same period he became president of the Federation of Jewish Communities. In 1937, during the period of King Carol II's dictatorial reign, when all political groups were dissolved, the Federation of Communities also took over the functions of the political representation of the Jews, When the enlarged *Jewish Agency was constituted (1929), he was elected by the Federation of Communities as a non-Zionist delegate to its founding congress in Zurich.

After September 1940, when Ion *Antonescu took over the leadership of the country, Filderman intervened with him as a representative of the Federation, several times obtaining the revocation of serious measures, such as the wearing of the yellow badge, the deportation of Romanian Jews to Nazi camps in Poland, etc. At the beginning of 1942 the Federation of Communities was dissolved. Although Filderman no longer had an official status, he continued to address personal memoranda to the Romanian authorities denouncing the racial measures. He was a member of the underground Jewish Council, formed of representatives of the principal Jewish trends, When he expressed his opposition to the special tax of four billion lei demanded of Romanian Jewry by the Antonescu regime, he was sent to *Transnistria (March 1943), returning after three months through the intervention of the papal nuncio and the Swiss and Swedish ambassadors. Back in Bucharest, he immediately reported to the Romanian government on the terrible situation of the deportees in Transnistria and asked for their return, which was obtained at the end of the same year.

After the war, he again became president of the Federation of Communities and of the Union of Romanian Jews and representative of the JDC, Soon afterward, however, he came into conflict with the Jewish Communists, who wanted the Jewish institutions to affiliate with their party's policy. As a result of their instigations, Filderman was arrested in 1945 and liberated only after a five-day hunger strike. Afterward he was kept under house arrest for three weeks. He was increasingly attacked in the Communist press. In 1948 he secretly left Romania, after being informed that he would once again be arrested (this time on charges of spying for Britain), and settled in Paris. According to his will, his archives were transferred to Yad Vashem.

Filderman wrote *Adevărul asupra problemei Evreești din România, în lumina textelor religioase și a stasticii* ("The Truth on the Jewish Problem in Romania, in the Light of Religious Texts and Statistics," 1925), *Le problème du travail national et la crise du barreau en Roumanie* (1937), and *Manuila Sabin; Regional Development of the Jewish Population in Rumania* (1957).

BIBLIOGRAPHY: *Curierul Israelit* (Oct. 30, 1932); T. Lavi, in: *Yad Vashem Studies*, 4 (1960), 261–316.

[Theodor Lavi]

FILENE, family of entrepreneurs, social reformers, and philanthropists in Boston. Progenitor of the family in America was WILLIAM FILENE (1830–?) who emigrated to the United States after the German revolution of 1848, and became owner of two stores in Lynn, Mass. In 1881 William Filene founded William Filene's Sons Company, a department store, in Boston. He turned over control of his stores to his sons in 1890, and together they built a multimillion-dollar merchandising empire. EDWARD ALBERT. (1860–1937) and A. LINCOLN FILENE (1865–1957) were innovators in merchandising techniques and employer-employee relations. They introduced the idea of the "bargain basement" where goods were sold at reduced prices. They pioneered in establishing minimum wage scales for female employees, employee welfare plans, paid winter vacations for employees, employee purchasing discounts, profit sharing, health clinics, insurance programs, and credit unions, Filene's was the first department store in Boston to establish a five-day, 40-hour week.

Edward Filene was born in Salem, Mass. Entering his father's dry goods business in 1880, he became president of Filene's department store in 1908. He was a leading member of the Boston Chamber of Commerce, which he helped organize; later he was a founder of the United States Chamber of Commerce and the International Chamber of Commerce. As chairman of Boston's Committee on Industrial Relations, Edward played a pivotal role in the passage of Massachusetts' first workmen's compensation law in 1911, the first form of institutionalized social insurance in the United States. Edward believed that cooperative private enterprise and higher wages were necessary to raise consumer purchasing power and thereby avert economic depressions. He favored paying workers a "buying" wage instead of a near-subsistence "living" wage, In 1909 he secured enactment of the first credit union law in America in Massachusetts. In 1934 he organized the Credit Union National Association and donated $1,000,000 for its work, He also gave $1,000,000 to the Consumers Distribution Corporation to organize a national chain of cooperative retail stores. Throughout his life Edward took an active part in the world peace movement. In 1915 he joined the League to Enforce the Peace. After World War I he backed the League of Nations. In 1919 he founded the Twentieth Century Fund, which conducts investigations of social and economic problems with an emphasis on finding solutions. He wrote *Speaking of Change* (1939).

A. Lincoln Filene was born in Boston. He became treasurer and chairman of the board of Filene's in 1941, and was long active in civic and communal affairs, Lincoln believed that mass purchasing by department stores, and research to improve their efficiency, would benefit the consumer by allowing lower prices. He himself was a leader in the development of scientific methods of retail store management. In 1937 he established the Lincoln and Therese Filene Foundation, which funded the first educational television station in Boston in 1955. Lincoln Filene wrote *Merchants' Horizon* (1924).

Both brothers were social reformers who believed that capitalism had to operate more efficiently to avert radical reforms and advance the welfare of the individual. Both Edward and Lincoln Filene actively backed President Franklin D. Roosevelt's New Deal. At a time when most American employers attacked Roosevelt for being too radical, the Filene brothers helped prevent a complete split between the president and the business community.

BIBLIOGRAPHY: G.W. Johnson, *Liberal's Progress* (1948); Filler, in: DAB, supplement, 2 (1958), 183–5.

[Robert Asher]

FILIPOWSKI, ẒEVI HIRSCH (Herschell Philip; 1816–1872), Hebraist, editor, actuary, and mathematician. Born in Virbalis, Lithuania, Filipowski was instructed secretly by a Polish schoolteacher in mathematics and languages. In 1839 he emigrated to London, where he taught at a Jewish school while continuing his studies. Filipowski's first work, *Mo'ed Mo'adim* (1846), deals with the various calendars of the Jews, Karaites, Christians, and Muslims. He was the editor of the Hebrew annual *Ha-Asif* (2 vols., London, Leipzig, 1847–49), to which he contributed essays on Hebrew literature and mathematics. Later Filipowski, while working as an actuary in Edinburgh, pursued his interest in mathematics, publishing *Anti-Logarithms* in 1849. In addition, he translated Napier's *Canon of Logarithms* from Latin into English (1857) and edited Baily's *Doctrine of Life Annuities and Assurance* (1864–66). In 1851 Filipowski founded a Jewish antiquarian society, "Me'orerei Yeshenim" (a forerunner of the *Mekiẓe Nirdamim), for the purpose of publishing medieval Hebrew texts. Among the important works which he edited and published for the society (in type designed by himself) are Solomon ibn Gabirol's *Mivḥar ha-Peninim*, Abraham b. Ḥiyya's *Sod ha-Ibbur* (1851), Azariah dei Rossi's *Maẓref la-Kesef* (from the author's own manuscript), Menahem ibn Saruq's *Maḥberet* (1854), Dunash b. Labrat's criticism of Saruq's work (1855), and Abraham Zacuto's *Sefer Yuḥasin ha-Shalem* (1857). This edition of the *Yuḥasin* is still the best available; it was reissued by A. Freimann with an introduction, indices, etc. (Frankfurt, 1924; Jerusalem, 1963). In 1862 Filipowski printed a pocket edition of the prayer book, including his own English translation, for which he designed a special Hebrew type in which the vocalization is attached to the letters. In 1867 he founded the *Hebrew National*, but the journal ceased publication after six months. His last work was a pamphlet called *Biblical Prophecies* (1870) discussing the Jewish view of prophecy and messianism.

BIBLIOGRAPHY: Goldberg, in: *Ha-Maggid*, 16 (1872), 530ff. (repr. in: *Beit Oẓar ha-Sifrut*, 1 (1887), *Oẓar ha-Ḥokhmah* section, 72–74); Fuerst, Bibliotheca, 3 (1863), 85; Zeitlin, Bibliotheca, 83–85.

FILLER, LOUIS (1911–1998), U.S. historian. Born in Cincinnati, Ohio, Filler served as a research historian for the American Council of Learned Societies (1942–44), and as a historian for the War Department (1944–46). He joined the faculty of Antioch College, where he was appointed professor of American civilization in 1946. He was a fellow of the Social Science Research Council and American Council of Learned Societies (1953–54).

Filler's major work was in the field of American reform movements and cultural developments. Among his works are *Crusaders for American Liberalism* (1939, 1964), *Randolph Bourne* (1943), *The Crusade against Slavery, 1830–1860* (1960), *A Dictionary of American Social Reform* (1963), *The Unknown Edwin Markham* (1967), *Appointment at Armageddon: Muckraking & Progressivism in American Life* (1976), *Vanguards & Followers: Youth in the American Tradition* (1978),*The Rise & Fall of Slavery in America* (1980), *A Dictionary of American Social Change* (1982), *Dictionary of American Conservatism* (1987), *Distinguished Shades: Americans Whose Lives Live On* (1992), *The Muckrakers* (1993), *American Anxieties: A Collective Portrait of the 1930s* (1993), *Muckraking and Progressivism in the American Tradition* (1996), and *Slavery in the United States* (1998). In 1961 he received the Ohioana Book Award in nonfiction for *Crusade against Slavery*.

[Ruth Beloff (2nd ed.)]

FIMA (Reuytenberg), **EFRAIM** (1916–), painter. Fima was born into a Russian Jewish family in Harbin, China. His father, Alexander, had left Russia in 1904 with his wife, Sofia

Fishman. In 1934 Fima moved to Shanghai, where he started to learn painting in IZO, a Russian Academy of Art. He also began to study Chinese calligraphy and became passionately interested in Chinese philosophy. Fima immigrated to Israel in 1949. The revelation of the other side of the world and the exposure to Israel induced a period of doubt. Fima destroyed most of the canvases he had created up to that point. As with immigrants, he experienced difficulties. His working conditions were poor and he painted during the night. He married twice and in both cases the marriage ended in divorce. In 1958, after some one-man exhibitions in Israel, he began to sign his name Fima, shortening his Russian first name Yafim. In 1961 Fima and his wife Rama settled in Paris, coming to visit in Israel from time to time. After Rama's death he married Kaarina Jokinen in 1967. He had many exhibitions in Israel and in the United States and he taught at Haifa University. He lived and worked in Jerusalem and Paris.

The typical style of Fima was Abstraction. His paintings recall Abstract Expressionism and the Geometric Abstract but a closer examination of his works reveals that Fima is not interested in intellectual analysis. His outlines are not sharply defined, but are rather soft, misty, hazy and fluid. It seems to have been influenced by Chinese Taoism (*Red Calligraphy*, 1962, Israel Museum, Jerusalem).

When Fima focused on an object, whether it was a portrait, a flower, or beards, he described it in a general way with a background of one color. Nonetheless, the objects are vivid and appear in characteristic attitudes (*Self Portrait*, 1980, private collection).

The international influence on Fima's painting overshadows his Israeli Identity. Fima pointed out that only when he traveled on the canvas did he feel at home.

BIBLIOGRAPHY: Haifa, Mané-Katz Museum, *Fima – Shanghai Jerusalem Paris Jerusalem Works on Paper 1930–1990* (1998); Tel Aviv, Bineth Gallery, *Fima* (1990).

[Ronit Steinberg (2nd ed.)]

FINALE EMILIA, town near Modena, north-central Italy. Jews settled there in 1541 or even earlier; at first they were moneylenders but later they engaged in commerce in brandy and feed or in small industry, one of them producing mercury chloride from 1678. A first synagogue already existed in 1600 and another one was erected in 1630 (restored in 1839), and in the 1620s there was already an active Gemilut Ḥasadim confraternity. It was only in 1736 that the Jews were confined in a ghetto, where 201 Jews lived in 1799. Although there were 162 Jews still living in Finale in 1854, the community as such gradually dissolved between the 19th and 20th centuries. In the 1880s the commercial importance of Finale diminished and many families left and moved to other cities. The community was revived as a private association in 1878, but by then numbered only 50 members and before long ceased to exist. In the 1920s eight families lived in Finale and the Jewish community was attached to the Jewish community of Modena. In 1932 the synagogue was closed. The community of Finale died out completely in the second half of 20th century. In the 1990s the ancient cemetery with the most ancient tombstone from 1584 was completely restored by the Municipality and the Jewish community of Modena.

BIBLIOGRAPHY: Milano, Italia, index; Roth, Italy, index; Cammeo, in: *Vessillo Israelitico*, 42 (1894), 223–6, 257–9, 291–3; Servi, in: *Corriere Israelitico*, 10 (1871/72), 46–49. **ADD. BIBLIOGRAPHY:** A. Masina, *La comunità ebraica a Finale nel Seicento* (1988); M.P. Balboni, *L'antico cimitero ebraico di Finale Emilia* (1996).

[Attilio Milano / Federica Francesconi (2nd ed.)]

FINAL SOLUTION (**of the Jewish question**; Ger. "**Endlösung der Judenfrage**"), the Nazi plan for the extermination of the Jews. Rooted in 19th-century antisemitic discourse on the "Jewish question," "Final Solution" as a Nazi cover term denotes the last stage in the evolution of the Third Reich's anti-Jewish policies from persecution to physical annihilation on a European scale. Currently, Final Solution is used interchangeably with other, broader terms that refer to German extermination policies during World War II (Holocaust, Shoah), as well as more specifically to describe German intent and the decision-making process leading up to the beginning of systematic mass murder.

While the Nazi Party program adopted in February 1920 did not contain direct or indirect reference to the term, Nazi propaganda presented a radical elimination of anything deemed Jewish from all aspects of German life as prerequisite for national recovery. After Hitler's rise to power, party activists and bureaucrats competed in transforming the broad-based consensus that something had to be done about the "Jewish question" into government policy aimed at varying degrees of segregation, expropriation, and physical removal. In the process, applying force became increasingly attractive; however, use of the term in German documents produced prior to 1941 should be understood less as an expression of a preconceived blueprint for genocide than as an expression of radical, as yet unspecified intent.

With the beginning of war and the organized murder of "undesirable" non-Jewish groups among the German population in the so-called *Euthanasia program, hazy declarations of intent and expectation from the top leadership – most prominently Hitler's Reichstag statement of January 30, 1939, that a new world war would bring about "the annihilation of the Jewish race in Europe" – provided legitimization and incentive for violent, on occasion already murderous measures adopted at the periphery that would in turn radicalize decision making in Berlin. Heydrich's *Schnellbrief* to the *Einsatzgruppen* commanders in Poland dated September 21, 1939, on the "Jewish question" refers to secret "planned total measures" (thus the final aim) ("*die geplanten Gesamtmaßnahmen* (*also das Endziel*")); nevertheless, most Holocaust historians today agree that at the time this solution was still perceived in terms of repression and removal, not annihilation. The more frequent use of the term Final Solution in German documents beginning in 1941 indicates gradual movement toward the idea of physical elimination in the context of shattered plans for large-scale population resettlement (including the "Madagascar plan") and megalomanic hopes of imperial aggrandizement in Eastern Europe. American scholar Christopher Browning notes that "a 'big bang' theory" fails to adequately describe German decision making; instead, the process was prolonged and incremental, driven by "a vague vision of implied genocide."

If there was a caesura towards the implementation of the Final Solution through mass murder, it is marked by the German "war of destruction" waged against the Soviet Union from June 22, 1941. Provided with instructions that called for the rapid pacification of conquered areas and that stressed the "sub-human" nature of broad strata of the population as well as the need for drastic measures to fight the deadly threat posed by "Judeo-Bolshevism" to the Nazi grand design, German soldiers, SS-men, and policemen murdered Jews from the first days of the campaign. Regionally different patterns of persecution unfolded until the end of 1941; its most prominent feature – the broadening scope of the killings from male Jews of military age (Heydrich's notorious letter to the higher SS- and Police heads in the occupied Soviet Union dated July 2, 1941, listed "Jews in party and state positions" and "other radical elements" among those to be executed) to women and children – underscores the absence of a central order and the preference of the Berlin authorities for controlled escalation.

The murderous events in the occupied Soviet Union had – as envisaged in a directive by Alfred Rosenberg's Reich Ministry for the Occupied Eastern Territories – provided the German leadership with experiences on how to arrive at a "solution to the overall problem" (*"für die Loesung des Gesamt-Problems richtungsweisend"*) that could be applied elsewhere. On July 31, 1941, Goering signed a document that charged Heydrich with "making all necessary preparations with regard to organizational, practical and material aspects for an overall solution (*"Gesamtloesung"*) of the Jewish question in the German sphere of influence in Europe" and to draw up a plan "for the implementation of the intended final solution (*"Endloesung"*) of the Jewish question." By the time of the *Wannsee Conference held on January 20, 1942, the term Final Solution had become a common phrase among German government and party officials. Now reduced in its actual meaning to mass murder, its geographical scope expanded beyond German-dominated Europe: the protocol of the conference listed 11 million Jews in different countries to be engulfed in the "Final Solution of the European Jewish question," including England and neutrals like Sweden and Switzerland. The culmination of the Final Solution in mass deportations from various parts of Europe to the killing centers and death camps in Eastern Europe resulted, like earlier stages of the process, not from one single top-level decision, but from a complex mix of factors, with the Berlin center reacting as much as it was actively shaping events.

Its historical significance makes the term Final Solution the most important example of the ability of Nazi language to integrate potentially different if not divergent approaches towards the so-called Jewish question into a conceptual frame of reference that helped facilitate systematic mass murder and to hide the Third Reich's genocidal policies behind technocratic abstractions, thus providing legitimization for perpetrators and enabling bystanders to claim not to know what was going on. Despite its inherent problems, most notably in evoking the illusion of coordinated planning and systematic implementation, the term Final Solution remains crucial for recognizing the process character of the Holocaust as a key element in a broader history of state-sponsored mass murder during the Nazi era.

BIBLIOGRAPHY: G. Aly, *"Final Solution": Nazi Population Policy and the Murder of the European Jews* (1999); C.R. Browning (with contributions by J. Matthäus), *The Origins of the Final Solution: The Evolution of Nazi Jewish Policy, September 1939 – March 1942* (2004); R. Hilberg, *The Destruction of the European Jews* (2003[3]); P. Longerich, *Politik der Vernichtung. Eine Gesamtdarstellung der nationalsozialistischen Judenverfolgung* (1998).

[Jürgen Matthäus (2nd ed.)]

FINALY CASE, a cause célèbre after World War II in the struggle for the return to Judaism of two Jewish children rescued by non-Jews. A young Viennese Jewish doctor, Fritz Finaly, had fled to France with his wife after the 1938 *Anschluss* and settled in Grenoble, where they had two sons, Robert and Gerald, born in 1941 and 1942, respectively. Their father circumcised the boys on their birth. When the deportation of French Jews commenced, the Finalys entrusted the children to the care of a municipal school in Grenoble, in order to hide them from the Nazis. In February 1944 the parents were deported to Eastern Europe; they did not return. Friends of the family handed the children over to Notre Dame de Sion, a Catholic institution, which in turn put them in the hands of Antoinette Brun, the director of a municipal children's home in Grenoble. After the war, she wanted to keep the orphaned Finaly boys in her custody.

Fritz Finaly was survived by three sisters who made attempts to ascertain the fate of their brother and his family. The eldest sister succeeded in tracing the children to Brun and on contacting her, she was informed that the children were well and were being raised as Jews. At the same time, Brun obtained from the French authorities formal custody of the children and arranged for their conversion to Catholicism. The sisters, who were not aware of this development, agreed among themselves that the children should be brought up by the youngest, Hedwig Rosner, a resident of Gederah in Israel. In 1948, having failed in their attempts to obtain the children from Brun, the sisters resorted to legal action. The case lasted for five years, during which the children were moved from place to place and from one Catholic institution to another. The trial aroused great interest in France and abroad, and the arousing of public opinion, especially among teachers and intellectuals, had a great influence on the eventual outcome. A minority of the Catholic public in France accused the Jews of ingratitude and argued that the children were French citizens so that their transfer to Israel would be tantamount to kidnapping. However, even Catholic opinion was divided. François Mauriac, the author, initially took an anti-Jewish stand on the issue, but subsequently reversed it. At the height of the controversy the boys were smuggled out of France and handed over to Basque monks, and for a while their whereabouts remained unknown. In June 1953 France's highest court rejected Brun's claim; in July, the children were brought back to France and delivered to their aunt, who took them to Israel to be raised in her home.

BIBLIOGRAPHY: A. Danan, in: *Jewish Frontier*, 20 (June, 1953), 7–12; N. Baudy, in: *Commentary*, 15 (1953), 547–57; M. Kellen, *L'Affaire Finaly...* (1960); Rabi (pseud.), *L'Affaire Finaly* (1953); *Cahiers Sioniens*, 7 no. 1 (1953), 77–105.

[Chaim Yahil]

FINANCES, AUTONOMOUS JEWISH.

Internal Taxation

The public finances of the autonomous Jewish *community in the Middle Ages and early modern times were conditioned by the need to support communal institutions as well as to meet sudden and often huge demands for money in order to defend communities or individuals against attacks and libels (see also *Blood Libel; Desecration of the *Host). The provision of *charity by the communal purse also became urgent following massacres and expulsions. The methods of internal taxation adopted were often influenced, for better or worse, by the fact that the community was held collectively responsible for the collection and apportionment of taxes levied on Jews by the state, this being one of the main features of Jewish communal *autonomy. They were also shaped to a large extent by the methods of taxation of the gentile town where the community was located.

Under the **geonim* and **negidim* in the eastern countries and in Muslim Spain, up to the end of the 11th century and even beyond, local tax levies and allocations were mostly directed by the central leadership through local appointees. The finances of the Babylonian academies and the court of the *exilarch were regulated and their expenditure was covered by the levy of fixed imposts on the Jewish population, as well as by voluntary donations and income from landed property owned by these institutions.

In countries and periods in which the leadership was less centralistic, various methods of financial management were developed. *Takkanot* ascribed to *Gershom b. Judah, but in reality drawn up around the 12th century, envisage a case where "if the *kahalhas* established an ordinance to help the poor... with the agreement of the majority, the minority may not refuse to obey it" (L. Finkelstein, *Jewish Self-Government in the Middle Ages* (1924), 132); this is the first overt indication of a local system of taxation for charity within the framework of the medieval community.

In *takkanot of* Jacob b. Meir *Tam of the 12th century the period of residence before having to contribute to the charity fund is laid down: "to come under the *ḥerem* to 'bring the tithe to the treasure house' [Mal. 3:10] one must be but one month in the city. Members of a community who cannot give charity may compel others who can afford to give" (op. cit., 185–6; see also 209–10). This concept of the tithe (*ma'aser*) as a contribution to charity-whether enforced or voluntary-was to be one of the financial pillars of Ashkenazi communities. Thus certain medieval forms of internal Jewish taxes were based on and defined by ancient terminology and ideology.

In Christian Spain the communities largely covered their needs by an indirect consumption tax mainly on wine and meat, but combining this with direct taxation in the *cisa* system, subject to changes and variations of time and place.

In Poland-Lithuania, the intensive internal taxation and spending (cf. the various *takkanot* and budgets in the *Pinkas Medinat Lita* and *Pinkas Va'ad Arba Araẓot;* and see *Councils of the Lands) were not sufficient to cover needs, in particular as the harsh and irregular exactions of state dignitaries and the despotic nobility mounted. Eventually the Councils of the Lands as well as individual communities had to rely increasingly on loans, As their debts increased, higher interest rates were charged by Christian noblemen and churchmen, as well as by Jews. In several Polish communities of the 18th century the cost of defrayment of debts amounted to 40% of their annual budgets. In some instances these loans were of 150 years' standing. Separate collections were often made for the salaries of rabbis and preachers. The financial problems and methods of expenditure of a large community with a relatively secure

Poznan Jewry Budget, 1637–38

	Zlotys	percent
Taxes, etc.	12,000	37.1
King	200	0.6
Palatin	2,000	6.2
Vice-Palatin	1,000	3.1
Vice-Palatin's Secretary	150	0.5
The General	1,000	3.1
The General's Secretary	150	0.5
Other officials	250	0.8
Bishop	200	0.6
Clergy and monks	785	2.4
Town taxes and expenses	523	1.6
Officials in Gnessen	200	0.6
Other expenses	3,800	11.8
Various expenses at the fairs	1,400	4.3
Relief	4,809	14.8
Education (Talmud Torah)	692.20	2.1
The Palestine	303.20	1.0
Poor brides	150	0.5
Others	500	1.5
Salaries for rabbis, physicians and others	1,892	5.8
Guards	258	0.8
Various	95	0.3
Total	32,357.40	100.0

B.D. Weinryb, in PAJJR, 19 (1950), 50.

and legal position are shown in the budget of Poznan Jewry for 1637–38. (See Table: Poznan Jewry Budget.)

The much more detailed original Hebrew text of the budget (*ibid.*, no. 138, Heb. pagin. 57–60) shows very interesting items of expenditure. The highest-paid official of the community was the *shtadlan* who received 300 zlotys a year, while the rabbi was paid only 130 zlotys in salary and an allowance of 100 zlotys for living expenses. The main preacher was paid 156 zlotys while a separate collection for this purpose would bring in "approximately 107 zlotys." Six Jewish guards received 150 zlotys among them, while three Christian guards were paid 108 zlotys for the winter period only. Expenses for water pipes amounted to 400 zlotys. The main Christian dignitaries and the various Christian religious orders not only received fixed amounts of money but also spices and carpets on credit. To its foreseen outlay the community had to expend within the period 1637–38 to 1641–42 two payments on "tumults" and "all this in addition to various expenses amounting to thousands of zlotys given to the wojewoda [provincial governor], the general, and other dignitaries."

From about the middle of the 17th century local communities of Poland-Lithuania developed the **korobka* (basket tax), a system of indirect consumption tax frequently collected in dues for *sheḥitah*. It was later broadened under Russian and Austrian rule mainly in the form of a *candle tax (on candles for Sabbath and the like). Synagogues also gained an income from pew-selling. Scholars and the very poor were exempt in principle from most taxation.

With the advance of emancipation, the power of tax enforcement was gradually removed from communal jurisdiction, and all internal needs had subsequently to be financed on a voluntary basis.

The gap between the medieval *kehillah* and the modern fund-raising agencies was filled by the **ḥevrah* which assumed the function of activating voluntary giving as well as operating the social welfare and other institutions of the community. The most viable among these associations was the **ḥevra kaddisha*, the burial society, which by its monopolistic and lucrative ownership of the community's cemetery plots was sufficiently solvent not only to operate many social welfare, cultural, and educational enterprises, but also to help other associations maintain their services, As late as the 20th century, the dues of Central and South American burial societies financed communal activities. Sometimes the *ḥevra kaddisha* there assumed the functions of a *kahal* (e.g., in *Buenos Aires), In the 20th century the stupendous needs created by two world wars, the Nazi Holocaust, and the restoration of Israel prompted Jewish communities in Western countries to develop highly efficient fund-raising techniques. Thus the medieval system of compulsory financing was effectively converted into voluntary giving in modern times.

Methods of Tax Collection for the State

When having to act as collectors or farmers of state tax, the individual communities, Councils of the Lands, *federations of communities, **Landesjudenschaften*, or government-appointed rabbis (see *Kazionny Ravin) each had to develop their own methods of tax collection and apportionment according to circumstances as well as to try diplomatic means at negotiating an equitable tax load as far as possible, State imposition was usually mechanical. Taxes were generally imposed *per capita*, or according to the estimated combined wealth of the Jews of the given unit, The communal or other appointees in the Jewish leadership usually tried to calculate a just and equitable distribution of this burden among its members. Thus to assess the means of members they appointed special officers (Heb. *shamma'im*), and committees whose composition gave rise to class tensions in the larger and socially variegated communities. The assessment of taxes also involved problems of social justice and definitions of services and duties. In Christian Spain and Poland-Lithuania especially, the methods employed and principles involved were frequently called in question. An instructive example of application of these principles in Christian Spain is summed up by Y.F. Baer: The tax statute of the aljama [Jewish community] Huesca of the year 1340 opens with a paragraph dealing with the poll tax and exemptions from it. Among the groups exempted were members of the community whose wealth amounted to less than 50 sueldos, scholars 'who study day and night, having no other occupation,' the poor supported by charity, and servants. The communal leaders were authorized to exempt certain needy members from payment of this tax, provided the total sum involved in these exemptions would not exceed a certain specified figure. Then there followed a complex system of taxes of varying rates, levied upon both property and business transactions. A tax of one-half of one percent (½%) was levied on the value of houses and gardens adjoining them: and another, of one percent (1%) on fields, vineyards, and gardens not adjoining the owner's house. There was a tax of one and one half percent (1½%) on the amounts of direct loans of money and of commercial credits (*commendae*) in kind-grain, oil, honey, textiles, etc.-extended to Christians and Muslims. The tax on loans to fellow Jews was much lower, only five-twelfths of one percent (5/12%), since these bore no interest. Loans extended to aljamas, servants, and students and the sums involved in betrothal and marriage contracts and in wills went untaxed. There were taxes on mortgaged real estate, on rented homes and stores, on the purchase and sale of land, textiles, grain, foodstuffs, gold and silver, furs and other merchandise, as well as on the purchase of clothes and various other necessities. Finally the daily earnings of an artisan, if they were above a certain amount, were taxed. Teachers and the readers and sextons of the synagogues were exempted (Baer, Spain, 1 (1966), 206–7).

BIBLIOGRAPHY: Baron, Social², index; Baron, Community, index s.v. *Financial administration;* Baer, Spain, index; H.H. Ben-Sasson, *Hagut ve-Hanhagah* (1959), 147, 158, 229–32, 239; Roth, England, index s.v. *Taxation;* Roth, Italy, index; Milano, Italia, 485–514.

[Isaac Levitats]

FINBERT, ÉLIAN-J. (1899–1977), Jaffa-born author. Originally a camel driver and Nile boatman, Finbert published an anti-military novel, *Sous le règne de la Licorne et du Lion* (1925), for which Herni Barbusse wrote a preface. *Un homme vient de l'orient* (1930), the prizewinning *Le fou de Dieu* (1933), and *Le destin difficile* (1937) are novels on Jewish problems. Finbert edited a volume of essays, *Aspects du génie d'Israël* (1950) and wrote *Israël* (1955), a travel guide, and *Pionniers d'Israël* (1956).

°FINCH, SIR HENRY (1558–1625), English philo-Semite and precursor of Zionism. Finch was a member of parliament and distinguished jurist whose legal writings were studied for two centuries after his death. He was also an accomplished Hebraist and profoundly interested in theology. His *Explanation of the Song of Songs* (London, 1615) discussed the New Jerusalem. In his anonymous *The World's Great Restauration, or Calling of the Jews* (London, 1621) – one of the classics of Christian pro-Zionist literature – he invited the Jews to reassert their claim to the Promised Land, and Christian monarchs to pay homage to them. Although this was to be accompanied by the conversion of the Jews to Christianity, his views aroused much criticism. James I resented the suggestion that he should pay fealty to the Jews and the work was suppressed as derogatory to royal dignity. The author and the publisher were imprisoned until they expressed contrition for this "unadvised" writing.

BIBLIOGRAPHY: Kobler, in: JHSET, 16 (1952), 101–20. **ADD. BIBLIOGRAPHY:** ODNB online; D.S. Katz, *Philo-Semitism and the Readmission of the Jews to England, 1603–1655* (1982), index; W. Prest, "The Art of Law and the Law of God: Sir Henry Finch (1558–1625)," in: D. Pennington and K. Thomas (eds.), *Puritans and Revolutionaries* (1978), 94–117.

[Cecil Roth]

FINCI, ELI (1911–1980). Yugoslav editor and author. Born in Sarajevo, Bosnia, Finci first wrote for the literary magazine *Knijźevnost.* He founded and published a review, *Brazda,* in 1935, and translated literary works from French into Serbian. Later, in Belgrade, he served as department head in the publishing house "Geca Kon" and as a director of the Yugoslav Dramatic Theater. His published books include *Dva lika* ("Two Profiles," 1950) and *Više I manje yivota* ("More and Less than Life," 1954), *Stvarnost i iluzije* ("Reality or illusions," 1957). He also translated from French and published a study on Diderot. He was also prominent as a theatre critic.

FINE, REUBEN (1914–1992), U.S. chess master and psychoanalyst. Fine was born in New York City, where he studied at City College. Growing up in the East Bronx in a poor Russian-Jewish family, he first learned to play chess from an uncle at the age of eight. After winning several American tournaments as a youth, he turned to international competition. His important victories took place at Zandvoort, Amsterdam (1936), where he won an equal first prize with Flohr; Stockholm (1937); Moscow and Leningrad (1937); and Margate (1937). In the two top tournaments in the U.S.S.R., he was the first foreigner ever to come in first. At Nottingham in 1936 he was a joint third behind Capablanca and *Botvinnik. In the Avro Tournament of 1938, Fine tied for first place with Keres, and came in ahead of Capablanca, Alekhine, Botvinnik, Euwe, *Reshevsky, and *Flohr. Considered the second greatest American chess player, second to former world champion Bobby *Fischer, Fine competed in several U.S. championships but never won. But such international chess greats as Capablanca, Flohr, and Botvinnik could not beat him. Fine's chess style was logical, precise, and energetic, and he was equally at ease both strategically and tactically. According to most players, Fine's only weakness was his volatile temperament.

Soon after World War II, unable to properly support his family as a chess professional, Fine abandoned tournament chess to study psychology at the University of Southern California. He served with the United States Veterans Administration from 1948 to 1950 and at the Post-Graduate Center for Psychotherapy. He was professor of psychology at City College of New York from 1953 to 1958. Despite his preoccupation with his professional work, Fine continued to excel in "lightning" chess and won prizes in the American championships.

He wrote in both his fields of interest. On psychology, he wrote the following: *The Psychology of the Asthmatic Child* (1948), *Freud, A Critical Re-evaluation of his Theories* (1962), *History of Psychoanalysis* (1979), *The Intimate Hour* (1979), *The Healing of the Mind* (1982), *The Meaning of Love in Human Experience* (1985), *Narcissism, the Self, and Society* (1986), *The Forgotten Man* (1987), *Psychoanalysis around the World* (1987), *Troubled Men* (1988), *Love and Work* (1990), and *Troubled Women* (1992).

On the game of chess, he wrote: *My Best Games of Chess* (2 vols., 1927–38), *Basic Chess Endings* (1941), *Chess, the Easy Way* (1942), *Ideas behind the Chess Openings* (1943), *The World's a Chessboard* (1948), *The World's Great Chess Games* (1951), *Lessons from My Games* (1958), *Great Moments in Modern Chess* (1965), *The Psychology of the Chess Player* (1967), *Practical Chess Openings* (1973), *Bobby Fischer's Conquest of the World's Chess Championship* (1973), *Fifty Chess Masterpieces, 1941–1944* (1977), and *Reuben Fine's Best Games* (2002).

BIBLIOGRAPHY: A. Woodger, *Reuben Fine: A Comprehensive Record of an American Chess Career, 1929–1951* (2004).

[Gerald Abrahams / Ruth Beloff (2nd ed.)]

FINE, SIDNEY (1920–), U.S. historian. After serving as a Japanese language officer in the Navy (1942–46), Fine received his Ph.D. from the University of Michigan in 1948. That year, the university offered him a teaching position; he was appointed professor of history in 1959. His fields of research were the intellectual regions of 20th-century American reform and the automobile industry. Fine was active in Jewish communal affairs.

He retired in 2001 as the Andrew Dickenson White Professor Emeritus, History, College of Literature, Science, & the Arts. Having taught for 53 years, Fine is credited with having the longest active teaching career at the university and for leaving a lasting impression on his students. Recognized as an outstanding educator and historian, Fine was awarded the highest faculty honor, the University of Michigan's Henry Russel Lectureship, as well as the Golden Apple Award. Students select the Golden Apple recipient for excellence in teaching; the faculty chooses the Russel winner for national distinction in research and publication. Fine is the first professor to have received both these awards. He also received three honorary degrees; was named Professor of the Year for the state of Michigan in 1986 by the Council for Advancement and Support of Education; was named an International Man of the Year for 2000–1 by the International Biographical Centre of Cambridge, England; and eight of his books have won awards.

Over the years, Fine's work has involved the study of labor law and organized labor, trade unions, race relations, racial discrimination, and political history in Michigan. His books include *Laissez-Faire and the General Welfare of the State 1865–1901* (1956), *The Automobile under the Blue Eagle* (1963), *Sit-Down: The General Motors Strike of 1936–1937* (1969), *Frank Murphy: The Detroit Years* (1975), *Frank Murphy: The New Deal Years* (1979), *Violence in the Model City: The Cavanagh Administration, Race Relations, and the Detroit Riot of 1967* (1989), *Frank Murphy: the New Deal Years* (1993), *Without Blare of Trumpets: Walter Drew, The National Erectors' Association, and the Open Shop Movement* (1995), and *Expanding the Frontiers of Civil Rights: Michigan, 1948–1968* (2000). In the latter book he documents the fact that Michigan, as a leader among the states in civil rights legislation, embraced not only African-Americans but also women, the elderly, Native Americans, migrant workers, and the physically handicapped.

[Ruth Beloff (2nd ed.)]

FINEBERG, SOLOMON ANDHIL (1896–1990), U.S. rabbi and communal leader. Born in Pittsburgh, Penn., Fineberg served in the U.S. Marine Corps during World War I and then entered the University of Cincinnati and the Hebrew Union College, where he was ordained in 1920 along with Joseph L. *Baron, Bernard *Heller, and Jacob Rader *Marcus, a distinguished graduating class. He received his Ph.D. from Columbia University and later was honored with a D.D. from Hebrew Union College.

His first career was as a rabbi, serving congregations in Niagara Falls, N.Y. (1920–24), and then returning to Pittsburgh (1924–26). He moved to White Plains, N.Y. (1926–29), and then to Temple Sinai in nearby Mt. Vernon (1929–37), and for half that time simultaneously served as national chaplain of the Jewish War Veterans before joining the American Jewish Committee as National Community Relations Consultant. There he became, in the words of a colleague Isaiah Terman, "the foremost theoretician, strategist, practitioner, and adviser to Jewish community and intergroup organizations and to government agencies in the United States and abroad."

He is the author of several books including *Biblical Myth and Legend in Jewish Education* (1932) and *Overcoming Antisemitism* (1943), written at a critical time in the American Jewish experience. He wrote *Punishment without Crime* (1949), which both explores the sources of prejudice and suggests preventative programs to strengthen human relations. He took issue with the then current efforts of the American Jewish community to answer the charges of antisemitism, suggesting that they spread the libel. Instead he proposed an affirmative portrayal of the Jews. An anticommunist, he published *The Rosenberg Case* (1953), which demonstrated their guilt and suggested that the Jewish community not defend them, positions deeply unpopular with rank and file Jews. His work *Religion behind the Iron Curtain* brought attention to the plight of Soviet Jewry.

After formal retirement from the American Jewish Committee, he became a consultant to the National Conference of Christians and Jews for more than a dozen years (1965–78), working assiduously on race relations in New York at a time of great tension.

BIBLIOGRAPHY: *American Jewish Year Book* (1992), 594; I. Terman, "S. Andhil Fineberg," in: *Proceedings of the Central Conference of American Rabbis* (1990), 188–90.

[Michael Berenbaum (2nd ed.)]

FINEMAN, HAYYIM (1886–1959), U.S. educator and Zionist worker. Fineman, who was born in Russia, was taken to the United States by his parents in 1890. He became head of the English department at Temple University in Philadelphia in 1911. Throughout his life Fineman was active in *Po'alei Zion. He was one of the founders of the American organization in 1904. In 1919–20 he was secretary of the Po'ale Zion Commission sent to investigate conditions in Palestine, and on his return he became president of the organization. In 1929 Fineman took up a teaching position in Palestine, resuming his professorship at Temple University in 1933. He helped to establish the *Jewish Frontier* (1934), of which he was an editor. At a time when the majority of the leaders and members of Po'ale Zion belonged to the Yiddish-speaking community, it was Fineman's special role to present its standpoint to English-speaking Jews, particularly in the academic world. His son DANIEL (1915–) settled in Israel in 1953 and after teaching in the English department at the Hebrew University, Jerusalem, was appointed head of the English department at Tel Aviv University (1964–69) and was dean of the Faculty of Arts from 1966–69.

FINEMAN, IRVING (1893–1976), U.S. novelist. Born in New York, Fineman served in the navy during World War I, and worked as an engineer until 1929, when he turned to writing. His first two novels, *This Pure Young Man* (1930) and *Lovers Must Learn* (1932), dealt with American themes. His third, *Hear, Ye Sons* (1933), recreated the past from which his ḥasidic parents had come; *Doctor Addams* (1939) dealt with the dilemma of a successful scientist who is completely ineffective in dealing with personal and social problems. Of his later novels, *Jacob* (1941) and *Ruth* (1949) had biblical subjects, His biography of Henrietta *Szold, *Woman of Valor* (1961), aroused controversy because of its frank portrayal of a revered figure.

BIBLIOGRAPHY: S. Liptzin, *Jew in American Literature* (1966), 209–10.

[Sol Liptzin]

FINER, HERMAN (1898–1969), U.S. political scientist. Born in Herṭa (Gersta) Bessarabia, Finer was taken to England as a child and graduated from the London School of Economics where he lectured on public administration from 1920 to 1942. He was actively involved in Labour Party politics and London local government work as a member of the London School of Economics group of academics centered around Sidney and Beatrice Webb and Harold *Laski. From 1946 to 1963 he was professor of political science at the University of Chicago. Finer was one of the first to introduce comparative politics and public administration as academic subjects in universities. His massive *Theory and Practice of Modern Government* (1932) was a model for textbooks on comparative politics and served as an introduction to a generation of political scientists. He acquired fame by his *Road to Reaction* (1945), a polemical answer to Hayek's *Road to Serfdom.* Written in Finer's characteristically pungent style, this book defended national planning and the welfare state as not inconsistent with democracy. His other works include *English Local Government* (1935), *The Presidency: Crisis and Regeneration* (1960), and *Dulles Over Suez* (1964).

[Edwin Emanuel Gutmann]

FINES (Heb. קְנָסוֹת, *kenasot*) are distinguishable from *damages in that they are not commensurate with the actual amount of damage suffered, whether such damage has been sustained by tortious act or by breach of contract or by an offense (see also *Obligation, Law of; *Torts). However, in cases where for a particular tort only half of the sustained damage is recoverable, or where the law prescribes more than the full damage to be paid (e.g., in case of theft: Ex. 21:37), such payment is classified as a fine (Maim. Yad, Nizkei Mamon 2:7–8). Of the four instances of fines prescribed in biblical law, three are liquidated amounts (30 shekels of silver: Ex. 21:32; 100 shekels of silver: Deut. 22:19; 50 shekels of silver: Deut. 22:29), and one is unliquidated ("silver in proportion to the bride price for virgins": Ex, 22:16), The Talmud asserts that while the payment of damages commensurate to the damage caused is rational by law (*min ha-din*) the imposition of fines was something novel (*ḥadash*) decreed by heaven (Ket, 38a, Rashi *ibid.*), so that fines are not to be regarded as law proper but rather as royal (divine) commands (*ibid.*). Not being the normal compensation for the actual damage suffered, fines have a quasi-penal character ("penalties"), and hence can only be recovered on the evidence of two witnesses, and not on the *admission or *confession of the defendant (Ket, 42b–43a; Shev. 38b; Yad, loc. cit. and Genevah 3:8). Another consequence of the quasi-penal character of the fine is that it is merged in any graver penalty prescribed for the same act since not more than one penalty can be inflicted for the same offense; where *capital punishment or *flogging are prescribed for any offense, these alone will be inflicted and no fine imposed (Mak, 4b; Ket. 32b, 37a; BK 83b), The only exception to this rule is the case of wounding, where the payment of a fine and damages is to be preferred to any other punishment (Yad, Ḥovel u-Mazzik 4:9).

In talmudic law, the sanction of fines was introduced for a multitude of causes: e.g., where the damage is not visible to the eye (as where A ritually defiled B's food) and is not liable according to the law of the Torah (Git. 53a; Yad, loc. cit. 7:1–3); where it is doubtful which of several claimants is entitled to stolen goods (Yev. 118b; Yad, Gezelah ve-Avedah 4:9); for the alienation of immovables which cannot be the subject of theft (TJ, BK 10:6,7c); for selling slaves or cattle to heathens (Git. 44a); for *slander (BK 9 la; Yad, Ḥovel u-Mazzik 3:5–7); where a tortfeasor is not liable in damages because of a supervening act of a third party (TJ, Kil. 7:3, 3 la; see *Gerama* and *Garme*); et al. In some cases, the amount of the fine is fixed by law (e.g., in certain cases of slander and assault: TJ, BK 8:8, 6c; BK 8:6; for rape: Deut. 22:29; Ket. 3:1); in most cases, however, it is left to the discretion of the court in the exercise of its expropriatory powers (see *confiscation; MK 16a; Yad, Sanhedrin, 24:6; ḤM 2:1 and *Rema* ad loc.). Even where the amount had been fixed by law, instances are recorded in which the courts imposed heavier fines, e.g., on recidivists (BK 96b). Fixed tariffs have the advantage of assuring equality before the law (Ket. 3:7); and even where the amount of the fine was to be assessed according to the dignity and standing of the person injured, a great jurist held that all persons were to be presumed to be of equal rank and status (BK 8:6).

Contractual fines (see *contract) which a person undertook to forfeit in the event of his default were enforceable unless tainted by **asmakhta* (BB 168a). While formal jurisdiction for the imposition of fines ceased with the destruction of the Temple (see **bet din*), it was in post-talmudic law that fines became the standard sanction for minor (i.e., most) criminal offenses. Opinions are divided as to whether the present jurisdiction extends only to fines not fixed in the Bible or in the Talmud (Hagra to ḤM ln. 1) or whether fines fixed in the Talmud are included in this jurisdiction (*Piskei ha-Rosh* to Git. 4:41; Rema to HM 1:5); but there is general consensus that in matters not covered by biblical and talmudic law, courts have an unfettered discretion to impose fines (cf. Resp. Rosh 101:1) – a talmudic authority being invoked to the effect that fines may be imposed not only by virtue of law but also by virtue of custom (TJ, Pes. 4:3,30d).

A few examples of the many newly created offenses for which fines were imposed are: resisting rabbinical authority (Resp. Rosh 21:8–9); accepting a bribe for changing one's testimony (ibid. 58:4); refusing to let others use one's books (*ibid.*

93:3); instituting proceedings in non-Jewish courts (Resp. Maharam of Rothenburg quoted in *Mordekhai*, BK 195); frequenting theaters and other places of public entertainment, as well as *gambling (S. Assaf, *Ha-Onshin Aḥarei Ḥatimat ha-Talmud*, 116 no. 126); taking a dog into a synagogue (ibid., 95, no. 12); and many similar contraventions. But fines were also imposed for receiving stolen goods (ibid., 137, no. 163), fraudulent business transactions (ibid., 133 no, 157), and unfair competition (*ibid.*, 127, no. 141). Fines were also the alternative punishment for floggings, where these could not be imposed or executed (Rema to ḤM 2:1; *Darkhei Moshe* ad loc., n. 5; resp. Ḥatam Sofer ḤM, 181), as, conversely, flogging was imposed where a fine could not be recovered – although the standard sanction for the nonpayment of fines was *imprisonment (*Zikhron Yehudah* 36).

The greatest reform in post-talmudic law in respect of fines however concerned the nature of the payee. While both in biblical and talmudic law it was the person injured (or, in the case of a minor girl, her father) who was entitled to the fine and no fines were payable into any public fund, later courts ordered fines to be paid to the injured person only where he insisted (*Yam shel Shelomo* BK 8:49), but normally would order fines to be paid to public charities, at times giving the injured person a choice of the particular charity to be benefited (Resp. Maharyu 147). More often than not, the charity was left undefined, and the fine was then recovered from the debtor by the community treasurers in charge of collecting for general charities (cf. YD 256:1). But there are also instances of fines being imposed for named charities, such as the study of the Torah (Resp. Rosh 13:4); the maintenance of Torah students (*haspakah; Takkanot Medinat Mehrin*, 46 (no. 139), 47 (no. 140)); the poor of Jerusalem or of the Holy Land (*ibid.* 39, no. 117). A frequent destination of part of all fines recovered was the governor or government of the city or country in which the Jewish court was sitting. In many such cities or countries, the privilege of internal jurisdiction was granted to Jewish courts only on condition that part of all fines recovered would be paid into the official treasury (*ibid.* 39, no. 117; Resp. Rosh, 21:8–9). Whatever the destination was, however, it was the strict rule that the courts or judges were not allowed to appropriate any fines to themselves (Assaf. loc. cit., p. 43); and there are detailed provisions for accounts to be kept and published of the disposition of all fines imposed, recovered, and distributed (*Takkanot Medinat Mehrin*, 24, no. 74). Whether or not the fine was paid to the injured person, the court always insisted that the defendant did everything in his power to pacify him-even to the extent of proclaiming a **ḥerem* on him until he did so (Rif, *Halakhot* BK 187; *Piskei ha-Rosh* BK 2; Yad, Sanhedrin 5:17; *Sha'arei Ẓedek* 4:1,19). This rule applied even where the fine was irrecoverable owing to lack of jurisdiction; and where a man had possessed himself of a fine he could not recover in the courts, he was held entitled to retain it (BK 15b).

See also *Extraordinary Remedies.

[Haim Hermann Cohn]

Middle Ages and Early Modern Times

The power to fine – an important feature of Jewish *autonomy – was exercised by the *Councils of the Lands and *synods, the local *community, the law court, or the **ḥevrah*. According to talmudic law (i.e., before the fifth century when *ordination ceased), only a court of fully ordained judges was empowered to impose the fines prescribed for bodily injury. However, the principle was gradually established that the Jewish community had the right to decide fines and confiscate property as a deterrent or punishment. The proceeds of these monetary penalties went variously to *charity, the *kahal* heads, the *court*, the association, the guild, or the injured party, several of these very often sharing the sum. Fines were frequently imposed with other sanctions, or as a consequence of them, for instance, as the corollary of a **ḥerem*.

To prevent self-seeking by judges, the Lithuanian Council (see *Council of the Lands) adopted a resolution in 1662 that "no rabbi shall share in any way in the revenue from amercements he will impose himself or jointly with the leaders of the community." In some countries a portion or all of the fines were set aside for the royal or seigniorial treasury, either by demand or in order to act as a powerful impetus to their enforcement. From the 10th or 11th century there is reference to fines imposed by a *guild; it is stated: "each and every one of us [the injured members] will be free to give this fine to any ruler or official of his choice" (*Judah b. Barzillai al-Bargeloni, *Sefer ha-Shetarot*, no. 57). In the 13th century a synod of the Rhine communities decided; "Whoever transgresses any of these **takkanot* shall be under the excommunication of all the communities, and if he remains obdurate for a month, his property may be denounced to the king" (Finkelstein, Middle Ages, 249). The minute books of the many organs of self-government abound in statutory and penal fines of all kinds, imposed for various reasons, serious or petty. In 1563 the Lithuanian Council threatened the heads of the communities with heavy fines for the benefit of the poor of Ereẓ Israel, since they had failed to make proper collections for this fund. The Moravian Council in 1650 set an amount to be paid into the regional treasury by anyone whose appointment to a community office was secured on the order of the feudal lord. Fines imposed by Sephardi communities in the West on members refusing to undertake communal duties led in early modern time to desertion from the community, as in the case of Isaac *D'Israeli. The *ḥevrot* were particularly prone to controlling their members through a system of statutory fines for violation of the rules – a Mishnah *ḥevrah* in a Russian township adopted an ordinance that "if a member is in town and does not report to a class, he is to be fined one Polish *grosz* per day, unless he has an adequate reason." Guilds were equally strict with their members and exacted money payments for charity for violation of rules.

[Isaac Levitats]

Fines during the Period When There Is No Ordained Bet Din (Semikhah)

The fines established as punishments for various offenses detailed above were imposed by virtue of the authority invested in the court (*bet din*) or in community leaders to impose monetary punishments, whether by expropriation of an individual's assets on behalf of the community or by requiring payment of a fine to the injured party. By contrast, as stated above, these courts were not authorized to impose the fines stipulated by the Torah or those established in talmudic or geonic times. This point requires further detail.

The rule cited in the Babylonian Talmud is that cases involving the imposition of fines may not be adjudicated by anyone other than judges who have been ordained as judges (*semikhah*) (see **Bet Din*). During the period of the Babylonian Talmud, there were still some remaining sages in the Land of Israel who had received *semikhah*, whereas in Babylonia they no longer received it. Thus, in cases involving the requirement to impose a fine to be paid for damages caused by one party to another person, such as cases of "half-damages" (see *torts*), the courts in Babylonia could not adjudicate or impose the appropriate fine. There were two solutions to this problem. One was for the injured party to bring suit against the tortfeasor in Ereẓ Israel and, if the defendant failed to appear in court, a ban would be imposed on him (see **ḥerem*). The second solution was for the injured party to seize some of the tortfeasor's assets, and the court would refrain from confiscating them from him (BK 15b). The significance of the seizure remedy is based on a dispute among decisors and commentators in the post-Geonic era. According to Rabbenu *Tam (Tos. to BK 15b), the injured party may only seize the particular asset of the tortfeasor used by him to inflict the injury, but if he were to seize any other of the tortfeasor's assets, the court should wrest it from him. Rabbenu *Asher, however, was of the opinion that the injured party could seize any of the tortfeasor's assets, and if the property seized was of greater value than his losses, the court, after adjudication, could require the injured party to forfeit the additional amount. The rationale for this is that the seizure itself is a rabbinic enactment; accordingly, judicial deliberation regarding the value of seized property vis-à-vis the value of the damage does not constitute adjudication of a fine, but adjudication of a seizure under the terms of a **takkanah*. The Rif goes even further. In his opinion, the court may adjudicate the original suit for damages and assess the value of the damage, without any requirement to wait until after the aggrieved party's seizure of the other's property.

In practice, during the post-talmudic period, when there were no judges with *semikhah* even in the Land of Israel, the *geonim* enacted that, even though fines could not be collected in Babylonia, a tortfeasor could be subjected to a ban (see **ḥerem*) until he settled accounts with his victim, whether by payment or by agreement, or until he repaid the value of the damage (Rif on BK 30b). The rationale is that "a sinner should not be rewarded, nor damage-doing rampant among Israel" (Piskei ha-Rosh, BK 8.3, in the name of Rav Natronai Gaon).

*Maimonides ruled that the imposition of a ban is not only in order to exert pressure to pay for damages, but also to encourage the tortfeasor to go with the injured party to Ereẓ Israel for adjudication, as specified in the above-cited talmudic passage (Yad, Sanhedrin 5.16). In Maimonides' day, unlike the talmudic period, there were no longer ordained judges. Consequently, there are those who explained Maimonides' statement to mean that because, in his opinion, the *semikhah* of judges could theoretically be reinstituted at any ordination time, this is sufficient to argue that a court is empowered to order the banning of the tortfeasor should he refuse to litigate the case in court, thereby pressuring him to indemnify the injured party (Bet Yosef, Tur, ḤM, 295). By contrast, Rabbi Eliezer Waldenberg, one of the outstanding decisors of our times, rules on the basis of Maimonides' statement that, even in our day, courts in the Land of Israel may adjudicate cases in which the punishment is a fine, despite *semikhah* having fallen into desuetude (*Resp.* Ẓiẓ Eliezer 15.69).

Rabbi Joseph *Caro, in Shulḥan Arukh ḤM. 420.41), provides a detailed list of standardized payments for bodily damages, all of which are fines. Further on, he cites the monetary values of those payments in the currency of his time. It may be inferred from this that, even though in his opinion one cannot adjudicate cases requiring the payment of fines in the absence of judges with *semikhah* in Ereẓ Israel, a court is not entitled to refrain from adjudicating cases in which questions of damage arise for which recourse is the imposition of a fine, but must instead impose a ban until the tortfeasor pays the injured party the appropriate amount, or allow the seizure of the former's property by the injured party (Sh. Ar, ḤM, 1.5).

[Menachem Elon (2nd ed.)]

Bibliography: M.W. Rapaport, *Der Talmud und sein Recht* (1912), 2–69 (third pagination); S. Assaf, *Ha-Onshin Aḥarei Ḥatimat ha-Talmud* (1922), index, s.v. *Kenasot Mamon:* Gulak, Yesodei, 2 (1922), 15–17; J.M. Ginzburg, *Mishpatim le-Yisrael* (1956), 378 (index), s.v. *Dinei Kenasot;* ET, 1 (1951^3), 168–72; 2 (1949), 168–74; 3 (1951), 49–50, 162; 7 (1956), 376–82; 10 (1961), 98, 106f.; 12 (1967), 733f., 740; Finkelstein, Middle Ages, index s.v. *Fines.* MEDIEVAL AND MODERN TIMES: S. Assaf, op. cit., 17ff.; Neuman, Spain, 1 (1942), 126–9; Baer, Spain, passim; Halpern, Pinkas, passim; idem, *Takkanot Medinat Mehrin* (1952), passim; Baron, Community, index; J. Marcus, *Communal Sick-Care in the German Ghetto* (1947), index; I. Levitats, *Jewish Community in Russia* (1943), index; M. Wischnitzer, *History of Jewish Crafts and Guilds* (1965), 215, 271. **ADD. BIBLIOGRAPHY:** M. Elon, *Ha-Mishpat ha-Ivri* (1988), 1:8, 10, 20, 26, 30, 65, 97, 132, 332, 338, 387, 423, 496, 498, 504, 523, 540, 548, 558, 566, 567, 570, 579, 581, 592f., 599, 608, 610f., 621ff., 637, 646, 648, 657, 659, 665f., 693ff., 702, 704, 720; 2:885; M. Elon, *Jewish Law* (1994), 1:8, 9, 21, 28, 33, 72f., 109, 148f., 398, 406, 469; 2:516, 533, 604, 607, 614, 637, 658, 667, 679, 688, 689, 700, 713, 714, 732, 741, 752, 754f., 768, 789, 800, 802, 813, 815, 822, 846, 856ff., 869, 888; 3:1079; M. Elon and B. Lifshitz, *Mafte'aḥ ha-She'elot ve-ha-Teshuvot shel Ḥakhmei Sefarad u-Ẓefon Afrikah* (1986), 2:334–35; B. Lifshitz and E. Shohetman, *Mafte'aḥ ha-She'elot ve-ha-Teshuvot shel Ḥakhmei Ashkenaz, Ẓarefat ve-Italyah*, 321; R. Erusi, "*Dinei Kenasot be-Vatei ha-Din le-Mamonot ba-Zeman ha-Zeh*," in: *Teḥumin* 25 (2005) 233.

FINESHRIBER, WILLIAM HOWARD (1878–1968), U.S. Reform rabbi. Fineshriber was born in St. Louis, Missouri.

After ordination from Hebrew Union College in 1900, he was rabbi in Davenport, Iowa, for 11 years, and then served in Memphis, Tennessee, for 13 years. In 1924 Fineshriber was called to Philadelphia as rabbi of Reform Congregation Keneseth Israel and became rabbi emeritus in 1949. Fineshriber served on various community and government committees and was active in the American Council for Judaism, among other organizations.

BIBLIOGRAPHY: J. Jacobson, *A Man Who Walked Humbly with God: 50 Years in the Rabbinate with W.H. Fineshriber* (1950).

[Abram Vossen Goodman]

FINESTEIN, ISRAEL (1921–), British judge, historian, and communal leader. Born in Hull, Finestein had a distinguished career at the bar, serving as a county court judge in 1972–78. He combined this with an extraordinary array of senior communal positions, serving as president of the Board of Deputies of British Jews from 1991 to 1994 and as vice president of the World Jewish Congress during the same years. Finestein is at least as well known as an historian of the Anglo-Jewish community, serving as president of the Jewish Historical Society of England in 1973–75 and 1993–94. His prolific output on the history of the Jews in Britain, especially in Victorian times, includes *Anglo-Jewry in Changing Times: Studies in Diversity, 1840–1914* (1999) and *Scenes and Personalities in Anglo-Jewish Life, 1800–2000* (2002).

[William D. Rubinstein (2nd ed.)]

FINESTONE, SHEILA (1927–), Canadian politician and Jewish community worker. Finestone was born in Montreal, Quebec, daughter to Minnie and Monroe Abbey, a lawyer and former president of the Canadian Jewish Congress. Finestone earned a bachelor of science degree from McGill University, but it was human need not the study of science that was her passion. She began a long career in public service by volunteering in the Montreal Jewish community. By the mid-1970s she was actively engaged by issues in the larger public forum. Among her many community positions, Firestone was a founding member of the Alliance Quebec and from 1977 to 1980 she served as first Anglophone president of the 130,000-member Fédération des Femmes du Quebec. Deeply concerned with issues of community development and women's and minority rights, she was a member of the Board of Trustees of the Allied Jewish Community Services of Montreal and was outspoken on a wide range of social fronts.

She first entered the political arena in 1979 when she joined the Yvette Movement, the women's movement dedicated to keeping Quebec in Canada. She was the only woman to serve on the "No" Committee during the Quebec sovereignty referendum of 1980. In 1984 Firestone was elected to the federal Parliament for the Liberal Party in Montreal's heavily Jewish riding of Mount Royal, Pierre Trudeau's former seat. She was re-elected in each of the next three federal elections. In 1993 Firestone was appointed to the federal Cabinet as secretary of state for multiculturalism and the status of women. In this capacity she led the Canadian delegation to the 1995 United Nations World Conference on Women in Beijing. Leaving electoral politics, she was appointed to the Canadian Senate in 1999 where, along with her support for Israel, she took a special interest in the campaign to eliminate the use of landmines. Sheila Finestone retired for the Senate when she turned 75, the Senate's mandatory retirement age.

[Richard Menkis (2nd ed.)]

FINGERMAN, GREGORIO (1890–1976), Argentinean psychologist. Born in Bogopol, Russia, and taken to Argentina as an infant, Fingerman trained in medicine and then turned to education and finally to psychology. He was head of the National Institute for Secondary Education in Buenos Aires, and in 1934 was appointed director of the Institute for Professional Orientation. He also served as professor of psychology at the Escuela Superior de Comercio de la Nación. Among his several books are *Lecciones de Lógica* and *Lecciones de Psicología*. He was drama critic for *La Nación* and was a frequent contributor to the Jewish press in Buenos Aires.

FININBERG, EZRA (1889–1946), Soviet Yiddish poet. Ukrainian-born Fininberg made his literary debut in 1920, when his first poems were published in a Kiev Yiddish daily. His first volume of poems, *Otem* ("Breath," 1922), attracted immediate attention, and his second, *Lider* ("Poems," 1925), strengthened his position as one of the most popular Soviet Yiddish poets. While his early poems expressed a great deal of Jewish feeling and an appreciation of Jewish values, he later closely adhered to the Communist Party line. In his play *Yungen* ("Youngsters"), produced in Kharkov in 1927, he dramatized a number of important events of the Russian revolutionary movement; in his book *Galop* ("Gallop," 1926) he described the civil war in the Ukraine. Jewish themes recurred in his World War II poems, which were also filled with patriotism. In 1926–27 Fininberg belonged to the *Boy* ("Construction") literary group, which was later accused of Trotskyism. At a conference of the Yiddish writers of the Ukraine held in Kharkov in April 1931, this group was denounced and Fininberg alleged his ignorance of its having been organized by Trotskyites. He died in Moscow of wounds received in World War II. Among the major literary works which Fininberg translated into Yiddish are Victor Hugo's *The Year '93* and Goethe's *Faust.* His own works include *Fun Shlakht-feld* ("From the Battlefield," 1943); *In Rizikn Fayer* ("In the Great Fire"); *Geklibene Lider* ("Selected Poems," 1948).

BIBLIOGRAPHY: Rejzen, Leksikon, 3 (1929), 75–78; E. Schulman, *The Fate of Soviet Jewry* (New York, 1959), 19ff. **ADD. BIBLIOGRAPHY:** A. Vergelis, in: *Sovetish Heymland*, 12 (1969), 6–12; N. Oislender, in: *Sovetish Heymland*, 2 (1981), 119–33.

[Elias Schulman]

FINK, JOSEPH LIONEL (1895–1964), U.S. Reform rabbi. Fink was born in Springfield, Ohio, and ordained at Hebrew Union College in 1919, which also awarded him an honorary D.D. in 1949. He earned his B.A. from the University of Cincinnati in 1915, his M.A. from the University of Chicago in 1918, and his Ph.D. from Niagara University in 1919. He served first as rabbi of United Hebrew Congregation in Terre Haute, Indiana (1919–24), where as a civic leader, he incurred the wrath of the Ku Klux Klan, which at one point abducted him; he made such an impression on his captors, however, that after they released him and donated $1,800 to the local Community Chest, of which Fink was chairman.

In 1924, Fink was en route to Germany to pursue graduate studies when he stopped over in Buffalo, N.Y., and was instead persuaded to remain as rabbi of Temple Beth Zion. Over the course of the subsequent 40 years (34 as rabbi and six as rabbi emeritus, until his death), Fink was to become known as the leading spokesman for that city's Jewish community, as well as a radio personality and community affairs activist. His weekly broadcast, "The Humanitarian Hour," was a popular show for more than a generation of listeners (1930–56). He initiated interfaith dialogue with Catholic and Protestant clergy, served as chaplain of the Buffalo police force and fire department, and was called in as a mediator of civil disputes. Fink founded the local Board of Jewish Education, was president of the Buffalo B'nai B'rith Lodge, and a board member of many civic bodies, including the Community Chest, the Board of Community Relations, and the University of Buffalo. He was appointed to state commissions by the governor of New York, and engaged in public debates with Eugene V. Debs and Clarence Darrow.

A strong proponent of the separation of church and state, Fink for many years chaired the CCAR's Committee on Church and State and wrote position papers on religion and state for the rabbinic organization. He served on no fewer than 12 CCAR committees, chairing four of them. After having served as corresponding secretary (1928), member of the Executive Board (1948–50), member of the Liberal Judaism Education Board (1950), and vice president (1950–52), Fink was elected president of the *Central Conference of American Rabbis (1952–54). During his tenure as president, he initiated the publication of the CCAR *Journal: A Reform Jewish Quarterly*, and strengthened the ties between the recently merged *Hebrew Union College – Jewish Institute of Religion. Immediately after his term of office, he was elected president of the *World Union for Progressive Judaism (1952). He identified as a Zionist and encouraged Arab-Jewish dialogue early on in the history of the State of Israel.

BIBLIOGRAPHY: K.M. Olitzky, L.J. Sussman, and M.H. Stern, *Reform Judaism in America: A Biographical Dictionary and Sourcebook* (1993).

[Bezalel Gordon (2nd ed.)]

FINK, THEODORE (1855–1942), Australian press magnate, lawyer, and politician. Fink was born at Guernsey in the Channel Islands and was brought up in Melbourne. He built up a large practice in company and mercantile law. From 1894 to 1904 he sat in the Legislative Assembly of Victoria, and in 1899 was minister without portfolio. In 1902 he acquired a controlling interest in Herald Newspapers, which under his direction became the largest publishing house in the southern hemisphere. Fink presided over commissions on university, technical, and public education and in 1904 was thanked by Parliament for his services. It was to Fink that Australia largely owed the development of her news communications with the West. In politics, Fink evolved from progressive liberalism to right-wing conservatism. In 1998 a comprehensive biography of Fink was published by Don Garden, *Theodore Fink: A Talent for Ubiquity.*

ADD. BIBLIOGRAPHY: *Australian Dictionary of Biography*; H.L. Rubinstein, Australia I, 389–90.

[William D. Rubinstein (2nd ed.)]

FINKEL, ELIEZER JUDAH (1879–1965), Lithuanian *rosh yeshivah*. Finkel received his early education from his father Nathan Ẓevi *Finkel, known as the "*Sabba* ["grand old man"] of Slobodka." He continued his studies at some of the famous Lithuanian yeshivot, including Slobodka, Radin, and Mir. He married the daughter of Elijah Baruch Kamai, head of Mir yeshivah, who appointed him his deputy, and in 1907 he succeeded him. He devoted himself completely to the dissemination of Torah in his own yeshivah and elsewhere, revealing a talent as teacher, spiritual guide, and administrator. His great abilities were particularly manifest when the yeshivah was destroyed by fire in 1911. Within a short time he succeeded in rebuilding and extending it. His preaching and influence reached people in all sections of society. On the outbreak of World War I, he had to leave Mir and wandered throughout Russia, everywhere gathering students around him. In 1922 he accepted an invitation from the heads of the Mir yeshivah to return as its chief spiritual director. Thousands of students flocked there, making it one of the greatest in the world. When World War II broke out, he again was obliged to move from place to place with his students, finally settling in Jerusalem. There he was active in "Mir" and "Hebron" yeshivot and was esteemed as the "*zekan rashei yeshivot*" (the senior *rosh yeshivah*). The leading rabbis of his generation, including the Ḥafeẓ Ḥayyim and Ḥayyim Ozer *Grodzinski, gave him every support and encouragement. His monumental work *Divrei Eli'ezer* (1963) on the Talmud made an impression in scholarly circles.

BIBLIOGRAPHY: O.Z. Rand, *Toledot Anshei Shem*, 1 (1950), 98–99.

[Mordechai Hacohen]

FINKEL, JOSHUA (1904–1983), U.S. Orientalist and scholar. Finkel was born in Warsaw, Poland, and was taken to the United States in 1913. He was ordained at the Jewish Theological Seminary. He studied the relationship of Islam to Judaism. Part of his research included Persian, Egyptian, and Arabic texts in manuscript. He spent the years 1924–26 in research in *Egypt, where he procured the manuscripts of the three Arabic epistles of al-Jāḥiẓ (c. 776–868), a celebrated Muslim polygraph, which he published in *Cairo in 1926. From 1937 he taught Semitic languages at Yeshiva University. His later interest in psychoanalysis produced some studies in which he applied psychoanalytic theories to Jewish cultural phenomena.

Among his published works are *Three Essays of … al-Jahiz* (1926); "Jewish, Christian, and Samaritan Influences on Arabia" (in *The Mac-Donald (Duncan Black) Presentation Volume* (1933), 145–66); "Maimonides' Treatise on Resurrection" (in PAAJR, 9 (1938/39), 57–105); "Old Israelitish Tradition in Koran" (*ibid.*, 2 (1931), 7–21); and "The Arabic Story of Abraham" (in HUCA, 12–13 (1938), 387–409).

ADD. BIBLIOGRAPHY: S. Hoenig Sidney (ed.), *Joshua Finkel Festschrift* (1974).

[Abraham Solomon Halkin]

FINKEL, NATHAN ẒEVI BEN MOSES (1849–1927), *rosh yeshivah* and one of the leaders of the *Musar movement. Born in Raseiniai, Lithuania, Finkel was orphaned at an early age and brought up in his uncle's home in Vilna. At the age of 15 he was already acknowledged as a rabbinic scholar. A chance meeting in 1871 with Simḥah Zissel b. Israel *Broida, known as the "*Sabba* [grandfather] of Kelme" and one of the outstanding disciples of Israel *Lipkin (Salanter), founder of the Musar movement, had a profound effect upon Finkel. He was so struck by the forcefulness of Simḥah Broida's personality that he became his most devoted follower, dedicating his life to the dissemination of the doctrine of *musar.* Finkel first assisted Broida in directing his well-known yeshivah, Bet Talmud, which had recently transferred from Kelme to Grobina and aimed at combining the traditional method of Talmud study with that of *musar.* Because of a difference in views, however, Finkel left the yeshivah and established a *kolel for young married men, the first of its kind in *Slobodka. He also exerted a spiritual influence over the *kolel *perushim* of Kovno, established in 1879 and directed by Isaac Elhanan *Spektor, rabbi of the city. In addition to these activities Finkel was the overseer of the yeshivah Or ha-Ḥayyim.

In 1882 Finkel established in Slobodka his own independent yeshivah, Keneset lsrael, where hundreds of rabbis and talmudic scholars were educated. Finkel himself refused to accept any salary from the yeshivah. Supported from the proceeds of a small store managed by his wife, he was able to live with his students. In 1897 Finkel set up a branch of his yeshivah in Slutsk and also assisted in the founding of yeshivot in Telz, Bransk, Stutsin, Shklov, Lodz, and Grodno, as well as many minor yeshivot. At the outbreak of World War I the yeshivah of Slobodka was moved to Minsk and in 1916 to Kremenchug in the Ukraine, where it remained until 1920. In 1921 Finkel reestablished a *kolel*, Bet Yisrael, with 20 young married students, in Slobodka, and entrusted its administration to his son-in-law, Eisik Scherr. When in 1924 it was decided to establish a branch of the yeshivah in Ereẓ Israel, in Hebron, Finkel followed in 1925 and played a prominent role in its spiritual leadership. As a mark of the deep admiration which his students felt for him they dubbed him the "*Sabba* from Slobodka" in the manner of the title previously given to his own teacher, and it was thus that Finkel was best known.

Finkel, an outstanding pedagogue and educator, based his ethical system upon the eminence of man. "A soldier," he said, "who does not aspire to the rank of general is not even a soldier." He stressed the need for perfection and love of truth and for spirituality in one's daily life to justify the fact that "everything created was created for the sake of man." In 1881 he anonymously published *Ez Peri*, containing essays by Israel Lipkin and Isaac Elhanan Spector, with an introduction by Israel Meir ha-Kohen, author of the *Ḥafeẓ Ḥayyim*. In his regular talks with his pupils he stressed the greatness of man and the profound compassion of God toward His creatures, which demands a similar compassion on their part. Man's purpose in the world is to attain such perfection that he imitates the characteristics and ways of God.

Finkel left no manuscripts. His discourses and way of life were summarized after his death in the *Or ha-Ẓafun* (1928, 1959–68[2]), arranged according to the weekly portions of the Book of Exodus. These discourses were compiled from copies of the "*musar* talks" he delivered in Slobodka and Hebron. In most cases those who noted them did so in the manner in which they were delivered. At times, however, the editors expanded the contents and put the ideas in a more acceptable literary form. A collection of his discourses, *Siḥot ha-Sabba mi-Slobodka*, was published by Z. Kaplan (1955). At present there exist numerous yeshivot founded by his disciples where his system is studied. Of his sons, Moses was principal of the Hebron yeshivah, Eliezer Judah of the Mir yeshivah, and Samuel one of the promoters of the Grodno yeshivah.

BIBLIOGRAPHY: D. Katz, *Tenu'at ha-Musar*, 3 (n.d.), 17–316; Zinowitz, in: *Shanah be-Shanah*, 1 (1961), 347–52; H.E. Zeitschik, *Ha-Me'orot ha-Gedolim* (1967[3]), 206–59; M. Gerz, in: L.S. Dawidowicz (ed.), *Golden Tradition* (1967), 179–85.

[Itzhak Alfassi]

FINKEL, SHIMON (1905–1999), actor. Finkel was born in Grodno, Belorussia. He appeared on the local stage as a boy and later joined a Yiddish theatrical group. In 1922 he proceeded to Berlin, where he was accepted in the Max Reinhardt School of Dramatic Art. In 1923 he joined a group of actors who came from Ereẓ Israel to complete their studies in Berlin, with the aim of establishing a Hebrew theater in Ereẓ Israel. His first appearance in Hebrew was as Daniel in Menahem Gnessin's production of *Belshazzar* in Berlin in 1924. Emigrating to Ereẓ Israel in that year, he appeared in various productions of the Israel theater founded at the end of the year, and in 1927 joined Habimah, his first appearance being as Menashe in *The Dybbuk.* He toured in many countries and represented the Israel theater at various congresses of the International Theatrical Institute (ITI). In 1961–62 and 1971–75 he was artistic director of Habimah. In all, he wrote 11 books about the theater. He was awarded the Israel Prize for arts in 1969.

FINKELSTEIN, ARTHUR (1945–), U.S. political consultant and campaign director. Born in Brookyn to East European immigrant parents, Finkelstein was a graduate of Queens College. He served as a demographic analyst in Richard Nixon's 1972 reelection campaign and worked as a political consultant exclusively for Republican candidates, ranging from Jesse Helms, who in 1978 won a brutal race where the religion of his Jewish opponent was at issue, to Alfonse *D'Amato.

Finkelstein worked in the 1980 presidential campaigns of Ronald Reagan and Senator Robert Dole. Finkelstein's campaigns have a style all their own. He avoids the limelight, never giving interviews or press conferences, seldom if ever being photographed. He tries to tag the political opponent as liberal. His own Jewish identity and pro-Israeli leanings do not restrain him from pointing out the non-Christian religious beliefs of political opponents. He helped orchestrate Alfonse D'Amato's successful primary victory over veteran liberal Republican Senator Jacob *Javits in New York, where he successfully exploited Javits ill health – he had a degenerative muscular disease – without alienating voters or creating sympathy for the hitherto popular senator. He then skillfully positioned D'Amato to win the Senate seat in a three-way contest against two Jews, Representative Liz Holtzman and Javits, who stayed in the race as the Liberal Party candidate. He was to repeat his giant-killing ability in 1994 when he advised George Pataki in his race against three-term incumbent Mario Cuomo for governor of New York.

With the Americanization of Israel in the 1990s, this style of campaigning was introduced into Israeli politics by both the left and right. Labor candidates imported Democratic pollsters and strategists such as James Carville and the Likud, most especially Binyamin *Netanyahu, called in Arthur Finkelstein. He helped orchestrate Netanyahu's come-from-behind victory over Shimon *Peres. His string of victories was broken in 1998 when Senator D'Amato lost his reelection bid to Charles *Schumer and Senator Launch Faircloth of North Carolina lost to John Edwards. In anticipation of the 2006 reelection bid of Senator Hillary Clinton, he was the mastermind behind a Stop Her Now Political Action Committee seeking to weaken an expected 2008 Presidential bid.

Deeply private, even reclusive, about his personal life, Finkelstein surprised many Conservative admirers by marrying his long-time male companion in Massachusetts, the only state where such unions are permitted. They have adopted two children.

[Michael Berenbaum (2nd ed.)]

FINKELSTEIN, CHAIM (1911–2000), educator and Zionist leader in Argentina. Born in Brest Litovsk (Brisk), Poland, he studied in a secular Jewish school of CYSHO and in a secondary Tarbut school. Member of the Borochov youth movement, at 17 he became its local secretary. Without pedagogical training he started to teach children and gave evening courses for young people. Failing to obtain a certificate of immigration to Palestine, he immigrated in 1930 to Argentina. In 1931 he started to work as a teacher in one of the Borochov schools in Buenos Aires.

When in 1932 the Federal Police closed the Borochov schools that were suspected of communism, Finkelstein was arrested together with other teachers and activists. After being released from jail he started to promote the establishing of an organization of modern Jewish secular, left and Zionist schools. In January 1934, TZVISHO – Tzentral Veltlech Yiddishe Shul Organizatzie was founded as a new central secular and Zionist school organization. TVISHO and the schools Sholem Aleichem that it established, identified with Left Po'alei Zion.

At the end of the 1930s Finkelstein convinced the school activists that a new and modern building was needed for the school. With the economic support of large Jewish sectors and of the Hevra Kadisha (the Ashkenazi Community), they built a new school that was inaugurated in 1942 – the first modern Jewish school in Buenos Aires with its own new building. Finkelstein opened a teacher-training course with officially accredited teachers and formed a team that elaborated a new study program in Yiddish. Finkelstein introduced the study of Hebrew in 1947 in the upper classes of the primary school, and it gradually expanded to all the grades. In the 1960s it became the main language for Jewish studies. Finkelstein and his colleagues established as part of TZVISHO a summer camp, Kinderland; student clubs; and other enrichment programs. In the 1960s they also established the first TZVISHO day school – Ramat Shalom.

Finkelstein was secretary general of the Aḥdut ha-Avodad – Po'alei Zion party in Argentina. From 1946 he participated in the Zionist Congresses and from 1950 he was member of its Va'ad Ha-Poel (General Council). Following his election as head of the Department of Education and Culture in the Diaspora and the Executive of the World Zionist Organization (1968–1978) he settled in Israel. He also headed the Beit ha-Tanakh Ha-Olami (World Bible House, 1978–1994) in Jerusalem and Beit Rishonei Po'alei Zion in Tel Aviv.

[Efraim Zadoff (2nd ed.)]

FINKELSTEIN, HEINRICH (1865–1942), German pediatrician. Finkelstein was born in Leipzig where he studied medicine. From 1894 to 1901 he was assistant at the children's clinic of the Charité Hospital in Berlin. In 1901 he took over the management of the Berlin City Orphanage and in 1918 became director of the Kaiser und Kaiserin Friedrich children's hospital. He held this position until the Hitler regime forced him to emigrate. He went to Chile, where he died. As head of the Berlin orphanage, Finkelstein made a detailed study of the causes of diarrhea in newborn babies and came to the conclusion that many infant alimentary disorders are due to metabolic disturbances rather than to bacteria. This led him on to research which resulted in the discovery that carbohydrate and salt in milk are the principal causes of diarrhea in babies. He introduced "albumin milk," and thereby succeeded in substantially reducing infant mortality at the orphanage. Finkelstein proceeded to make a new clinical classification of alimentary disorders based on metabolic disturbances, dyspepsia, and alimentary toxication. He made studies of several other children's diseases, particularly those connected with the skin. His *Lehrbuch der Saeuglingskrankheiten* (1905) covered his findings in this field. He also published *Hautkrankheiten und Syphilis im Saeuglings-und Kindesalter* (1924).

BIBLIOGRAPHY: S.R. Kagan, *Jewish Medicine* (1952), 363.

[Suessmann Muntner]

FINKELSTEIN, ISRAEL (1949–). Israeli archaeologist, specializing in the Bronze and Iron Ages. Born in Tel Aviv, Finkelstein received his high school education in Petaḥ Tikva, before serving in the army. He undertook his graduate studies at Tel Aviv University in Archaeology and Near Eastern Studies, and in Geography, completing his M.A. in 1978, and writing a Ph.D. on the Izbet Sartah excavations in 1983. Finkelstein began teaching in various institutions from the late 1970s, serving as an associate professor at Bar-Ilan University (1987–90) and at the University of Chicago (1987), before taking up a full-time position at Tel Aviv University in 1990 and as a full professor (from 1992), becoming the director of the Sonia and Marco Nadler Institute of Archaeology between 1996 and 2003 and the incumbent of the Jacob M. Alkow Chair in the Archaeology of Israel in the Bronze and Iron Ages from 2002. Finkelstein has been the mentor and guide for many of the younger generations of Israeli archaeologists.

Having participated from the early 1970s in major archaeological excavations at Tel Beer Sheva, Tel Aphek and in surveys in Sinai, Finkelstein became the field director of the Izbet Sartah excavations between 1976–78, and later the director of excavations at Shiloh (1981–84), the director of the Southern Samaria Survey (1980–87), and more recently a co-director (together with D. Ussishkin and B. Halpern) of the important excavations at Megiddo. Finkelstein is a prolific writer with more than 130 articles to his credit, and numerous books, notably *The Archaeology of the Israelite Settlement* (1988) and *Living on the Fringe: The Archaeology and History of the Negev, Sinai and Neighbouring Regions in the Bronze and Iron Ages* (1995). In a key article published in 1996 titled "The Archaeology of the United Monarchy: An Alternative View" (*Levant* 28: 177–87), Finkelstein suggested lowering the conventional dates for the Early Iron Age by 75–100 years, thereby sparking off an important debate amongst scholars on matters relating to the absolute chronology of the Iron Age. Finkelstein's controversial views were summed up in his book *The Bible Unearthed: Archaeology's New Vision of Ancient Israel and the Origin of its Sacred Texts* (2001; co-authored with N.A. Silberman).

In 2005 Finkelstein was made laureate of the prestigious Dan David Prize in the Past Dimension – Archaeology.

[Shimon Gibson (2nd ed.)]

FINKELSTEIN, JACOB JOEL (1922–1974), U.S. Assyriologist, specializing in cuneiform law. Born in New York to Orthodox Jewish parents his early education included yeshivah training, but Finkelstein himself later moved far away from Orthodoxy. Though he graduated with honors from high school, full-time college was not within his means and he went to work as a presser. In World War II he served in the U.S. Army Air Corps, and at the war's end resumed his studies at Brooklyn College (B.A., 1948), and then at the University of Pennsylvania (Ph.D. 1953) where he was strongly influenced by his teacher, E.A. Speiser. After graduating, he was a research assistant with A. Goetze in the Near Eastern Languages Dept. at Yale University from 1953 to 1955. From 1956 to 1965 he taught Assyriology at the University of California in Berkeley, and in 1965 was appointed professor of Assyriology and Babylonian Literature at Yale University.

Finkelstein was the author of studies in Mesopotamian history, historiography, and law, but his interest focused increasingly on the last. At the time of his premature death of heart failure, he was preparing a fuller exposition of the contrast between biblical and Mesopotamian law based on an analysis of the "goring-ox rules" (cf. p. 269, n. 308 of "The Goring Ox" in the *Temple Law Quarterly,* 46:2 (1973), 169f.), which is a programmatic fragment of the intended work. His lasting contribution, however, will likely be his numerous copies of cuneiform texts, mainly from the collections of the British Museum and Yale University, which testify to his skill as an interpreter of tablets.

Among his studies are "Cuneiform Texts from Tell Billa," *Journal of Cuneiform Studies*, 7 (1953), 111f.; "Mesopotamian Historiography," *Proceedings of the American Philosophical Society,* 107 (1963), 461f.; "The Genealogy of the Hammurapi Dynasty," *Journal of Cuneiform Studies*, 20 (1966), 95f.; "Sex Offenses in Sumerian Law," *Journal of the American Oriental Society,* 86 (1966), 355f.; *Old Babylonian Legal Documents* (1968); "The Laws of Ur Nammu," *Journal of Cuneiform Studies*, 22 (1968), 66f.; "An Old Babylonian Herding Contract and Genesis 31:38f.," *Journal of the American Oriental Society,* 88 (1968), 30; "*Ha-Mishpat ba-Mizraḥ ha-Kadmon*," *Enẓiklopediya Mikra'it*, 5 (1968), 588f.; translations in J. Pritchard (ed.), *Ancient Near Eastern Texts* (1969): "Collections of Laws from Mesopotamia and Asia Minor," 523f., "Documents from the Practice of Law," 542f., *Late Old Babylonian Documents and Letters* (1972).

BIBLIOGRAPHY: H. Hoffner, Jr., in: JAOS, 95 (1975), 589–91; M. DeJong Ellis, *Essays on the Ancient Near East in Memory of Jacob Joel Finkelstein* (1977); J. Finkelstein, *The Ox that Gored* (published posthumously by Ellis; 1981); T. Frymer-Kensky, in, BA 45 (1982), 189.

[Aaron Shaffer]

FINKELSTEIN, LOUIS (1895–1991), U.S. Conservative rabbi, scholar, and educator. Finkelstein was born in Cincinnati. His father, an Orthodox rabbi, supervised his early Jewish education. He graduated from the College of the City of New York

(1915) and took his Ph.D. at Columbia University (1918). Ordained at the *Jewish Theological Seminary in 1919, Finkelstein served for more than ten years as rabbi of Congregation Kehilath Israel in New York City, but his close association with the seminary continued. A year after his ordination he began teaching Talmud there, and in 1924 he began teaching theology; from 1931 he was professor of theology. He rose to prominence early. He was president of the *Rabbinical Assembly from 1928 to 1930 at the age of 33. He was groomed by Cyrus Adler as his successor. He also assumed more and more administrative responsibility, as assistant to the president (1934), provost (1937), president (1940), and chancellor (from 1951–1972).

Under his leadership the seminary attained national prominence in both Jewish and interfaith activities, expanding its academic scope by initiating the Institute for Religious and Social Studies, for example, and its public education work through the *Jewish Museum and the radio and television program *The Eternal Light*, among other innovations.

Finkelstein was generally acknowledged to be the leading personality in the Conservative wing of Judaism and put his stamp on the movement, in general vigorously supporting more traditionalist segments, often over the initial opposition of the Seminary's alumni. The only other leader of Conservative Judaism who ever wielded such power and influence was Solomon *Schecter, but then the movement was small and its resources meager. In the Finkelstein era, the Conservative movement was the largest religious movement in American Judaism and the Seminary was the home of great scholars such as Louis *Ginzberg and Saul *Lieberman in Talmud and H.L. *Ginzberg in Bible. He recruited Abraham Joshua *Heschel to the Seminary Faculty in 1945 after Hebrew Union College had saved him from the Holocaust by sponsoring his immigration to the United States in 1939. The Seminary was a place of diverse views and differing ideologies. Kaplan and Heschel, Lieberman and Finkelstein coexisted and struggled for the loyalty of the students. Talmudic knowledge was most revered of all. The professors were described as cardinals, secure in their learning and stature, at a distance from their students and from the rabbis they had ordained.

Finkelstein oversaw attempts to create a Conservative movement-trained leadership and not to rely on recruiting the sons of Orthodox Judaism who sought entry into a wider American world. Leadership Training Fellowship was begun in 1946; Camp Ramah was inaugurated in 1947 and provided the leadership of the Conservative Movement for the next two generations.

Finkelstein became one of the most famous Jewish leaders of his age, at home with presidents and prime ministers. President Roosevelt in 1940 appointed him presidential adviser for Judaism on steps toward world peace; Finkelstein pronounced the prayers at the inauguration of President Eisenhower; President Kennedy appointed him to the U.S. delegation to the coronation of Pope Paul VI in 1963; President Nixon invited him to preach at special religious services in the White House. He was on the cover of *Time Magazine*.

At his core, Finkelstein remained a working scholar. He rose early and studied daily. He wrote and edited many books and articles on general problems in religion, sociology, culture, and ethics. He edited the widely used *Jews: Their History, Culture, and Religion* (1949, 1960[3]) as well as many of the publications of the seminary's Conference on Science, Philosophy and Religion and the seminary's Institute of Religious and Social Studies. He not only stimulated and assisted the research of other scholars but continued his own primary research and publication. Despite his manifold administrative and communal obligations, Finkelstein's central preoccupation remained what it was in his student days: study and research in the history and literature of classical Judaism. He published more than a hundred critical investigations of fundamental documents of Judaism, exploring the historical and social conditions reflected in liturgical texts, for example in the prayers *Shema*, *Amidah*, *Birkat ha-Mazon*, *Hallel*, and proving their antiquity, dating some of them very early, possibly as biblical; exploring the composition of several of the tannaitic Midrashim; and investigating the principal teachings and doctrines of Pharisaism, His social and economic studies of the Pharisees, especially his *Pharisees* (2 vols., 1938, 1966[3]), roused controversy because of his assertions that economic and social conditions influenced the formation of Pharisaic ideology. These studies lifted the discussion of historical problems from the parochial or purely doctrinal to the broad plane of social history. Finkelstein's *Jewish Self-Government in the Middle Ages* (1924, 1964[2]) remained an important source for medievalists and students of post-talmudic *halakhah* and institutions. He also edited *Commentary of David Kimhi on Isaiah* (1926, repr. 1969) and wrote *Akiba – Scholar, Saint, Martyr* (1936, 1962); *Ha-Perushim ve-Anshei Keneset ha-Gedolah* ("Pharisees and the Great Synagogue," 1950), which carried on in depth the investigation of his *Pharisees;* and *New Light from the Prophets* (1969), in which he traced certain Pharisaic emphases and sayings in the early Midrashim to the time of the prophets. He was drawn to the early classical treatises, which gave him insight into some of the earliest halakhic trends in Jewish Palestine. He also published the *Assemani Codex Manuscript of the Sifra* (1956, reissued 1970); *Sifrei* (1939, repr. 1969); and *Mavo le-Massekhtot Avot ve-Avot de-Rabbi Natan* (1950), an introduction to these talmudic treatises.

In all his scholarly work Finkelstein exhibited a fastidious attention to detail, particularly to textual variants in manuscripts, early printed editions, and citations in geonic and post-geonic literary works, and an awareness of what is central in each period. In both his scholarly and his administrative activities, he made enormous contributions to the understanding and acceptance of the values and insights of talmudic-rabbinic Judaism.

BIBLIOGRAPHY: H. Parzen, *Architects of Conservative Judaism* (1964); M. Davis, *Emergence of Conservative Judaism* (1963); M.

Sklare, *Conservative Judaism* (1955); AJYB, 45 (1943/44), 63; Liebman, *ibid.*, 69 (1968), 3–112.

[Judah Goldin / Michael Berenbaum (2nd ed.)]

FINKELSTEIN, NOAH (1871–1946), Zionist leader and Yiddish newspaper publisher, born in Brest-Litovsk. An active Zionist from the time of the first Zionist Congresses, at first in Brest-Litovsk and later in Warsaw, Finkelstein was among the supporters of the *Uganda project, and later became a *Territorialist. He belonged to the *Benei Zion circle of Zionist intelligentsia connected with the Sha'arei Zion Synagogue in Warsaw, which became a center of the Territorialists. In 1906, with his brother Nehemiah and his friend Samuel Jacob Jackan, Finkelstein began publication of *Yidishes Tagblat*, a newspaper which gained readers from groups who until then had not been attracted to the Hebrew or Yiddish press. Two years later, in 1908, they founded the daily **Haynt*, which became the most popular Zionist newspaper in Poland. Although Finkelstein was responsible for administration, he considerably influenced editorial policy. In 1912, during the elections to the Fourth *Duma, he was one of the most energetic organizers of Jewish defense against the violent antisemitic propaganda and *boycott proclaimed by the Polish right wing against the Jews in Warsaw, whose vote for the socialist candidate had caused the defeat of the right-wing nominee, After the amalgamation of *Haynt* with the Zionist organ *Dos Yidishe Folk*, Finkelstein left for Paris. From 1926 to 1940, also with the same partners, he began to publish the newspaper *Der Parizer Haynt*, which had to contend against opposition from Bundist and Communist immigrants who had arrived in France from Eastern Europe.

BIBLIOGRAPHY: Y. Gruenbaum, *Penei ha-Dor*, 1 (1957), 273–7; E. Steinman (ed.), *Sefer Brisk* (= EG, vol. 2, 1954), index; AJYB, 49 (1947/48), 621. **ADD. BIBLIOGRAPHY:** Ch. Finkelstein, *Haynt, a Tsaitung bay Yiden 1908–1939* (1978), index.

[Moshe Landau]

FINKELSTEIN, SHIMON (1861–1947), U.S. rabbi and author. Born in Slobodka, Lithuania. Finkelstein was recognized as a child as a brilliant talmudist by some of the great scholars of his learned city. After his bar mitzvah, he studied at the Kovno Yeshivah. At the age of 17 he came under the influence of a *maskil*, who encouraged him to leave his rabbinic studies and travel. This led his father to insist that he study a bit more, and he moved to Rumsheshok, where he was exposed to the teachings of the *Musar movement. He studied with a major disciple of Rabbi Israel *Salanter, Rabbi Isaac Blazer, and was ordained in 1882 by Rabbi Judah Meshil ha-Kohen, and one year later by Rabbi Isaac Elchanan *Spector.

With Spector's approval he immigrated to the United States in 1887, serving for three years in Baltimore and then from 1890 to 1896 in Cincinnati, where he was rabbi to Congregation Beth Tephila. In Cincinnati he was exposed to Reform Judaism and apparently even offered a position at Hebrew Union College, which he declined. He did, however, recognize that Reform Judaism was keeping some Jews Jewish who were unmoved by Orthodoxy and might otherwise have left Judaism. The salaries of Orthodox rabbis were quite low and Finkelstein got into some legal trouble while officiating at a divorce and was sued in secular court. He also for a time tried to produce kosher food products in competition with Manischewitz, a company that became synonymous with kosher food products in the United States. In 1896 he moved to Syracuse, New York, and six years later to Congregation Ohev Shalom in Brownsville, Brooklyn, New York, which had a rapidly growing Jewish community. He remained there for some four decades.

Finkelstein was a scholar and an authority on Jewish law. Among his books are *Reshut Bikkuri* (1889), *Bikkurei Anavim* (1899), and *Bet Yiẓḥak* (1923). Among his eight children was Louis *Finkelstein, a rabbinic scholar who became chancellor of the Jewish Theological Seminary and who, like his father, was personally punctilious in his observance while being open to and indeed changing Judaism for a changing world.

BIBLIOGRAPHY: M.D. Sherman, *Orthodox Judaism in America: A Bibliographical Dictionary and Sourcebook* (1996).

[Michael Berenbaum (2nd ed.)]

FINKIELKRAUT, ALAIN (1949–), French author and thinker. After a short academic career in which he taught in France and the United States, Finkielkraut devoted himself to writing books, articles, and radio programs, many of which deal with issues of contemporary Jewry. His books delineated the problems of the Jew in the Diaspora from the cultural and social aspects as well as the problem of his link to Jewish history and to Israel as a central issue (*Le Juif imaginaire*, 1980; *The Imaginary Jew*, 1994). He has dealt with antisemitism, the revisionist historians who have distorted the history of World War II (*L'avenir d'une negation*; 1982; *The Future of a Negation: Reflections on the Question of Genocide*, 1998), and incitement against the State of Israel (*La réprobation d'Israël*; 1983), using a system close to that of the "New Philosophers" of France. His thought was also influenced by that of the Jewish philosopher Emmanuel *Levinas: *La sagesse de l'amour* (1984; *The Wisdom of Love*, 1997) gave a tangible dimension to Levinas' concept of the relationship to otherness as the constituent element of humanity.

In 1986 Finkielkraut became the youngest recipient of the prestigious prize of French Jewry, the Prix de la Fondation du Judaisme Français. In *La défaite de la pensée* (1987; *The Defeat of the Mind*, 1995), Finkielkraut sharply denounced the rise of relativism in Western liberal societies. The book had a great impact and got him labeled a "conservative" thinker. Two years later he published his reflections on the collective memory of the Jewish genocide and on the idea of crimes against humanity in the context of the Klaus Barbie trial (*La mémoire vaine, du crime contre l'humanité*, 1989; *Remembering in Vain: The Klaus Barbie Trial and Crimes against Humanity*, 1992). In 1992, after an intellectual portrait of early 20th century French author Charles Peguy (*Le mécontemporain: Charles Pe-*

guy, lecteur du monde moderne), he published a selection of his writings relating to the Yugoslavian fighting of the early 1990s, during which he had supported the Croatians (*Comment peut-on être croate?*, 1992; *Dispatches from the Balkan War and Other Writings*, 1999). In 2002, the Second Intifada in the Palestinian-Israeli conflict and the rise of new forms of antisemitism led him to broadcast a weekly program on a Jewish radio station. While supporting a two-state solution and criticizing some aspects of Israeli policy, Finkielkraut took a strong stand against the penchant of intellectuals to call into question the legitimacy of Zionism and of Israel as the state of the Jewish people. In his 2002 chronicles (*L'imparfait du présent*) and his 2003 essay *Au nom de l'autre, sur l'antisémitisme qui vient*, he described how current hatred of Jews has adopted the fashionable Western dogma of radical universalism. Jews, asserts Finkielkraut, are no longer criticized for their cosmopolitanism: they are conversely accused of having replaced their supposed universal fate with what these new progenitors of antisemitism perceive as anachronistic and harmful efforts to persist as a specific human group, either as communities or in the framework of a nation-state. Finkielkraut came to be considered the most significant of young French thinkers who deal with current issues of Jewish existence.

ADD. BIBLIOGRAPHY: R. Kimball, "The Treason of the Intellectuals and 'the Undoing of Thought,'" in: *The New Criterion*, vol. 11, no. 4 (Dec. 1992); N. Rachlin, "Alain Finkielkraut and the Politics of Cultural Identity," in: *Substance: A Review of Theory and Literary Criticism*, vol. 24, no. 1–2 (1995), 76–77.

[Gideon Kouts / Dror Franck Sullaper (2nd ed.)]

FINLAND (Finnish Suomi) republic in N. Europe. Until 1809 it was part of the kingdom of Sweden, where Jews had been prohibited from settling within its borders. When in 1809 Finland became a grand duchy in the Russian Empire, Czar Alexander I declared that he would not change any of the existing Swedish laws, and the prohibition on Jewish settlement in Finland therefore continued. The first Jews to settle in Finland were *Cantonists who served in the garrisons in Helsinki (in the Sveaborg fort) and in Vyborg for up to 25 years, and were permitted when discharged to remain in Finland. Every residence permit issued to them, however, was bitterly opposed by the local authorities. When the Finnish authorities failed to have the permits given by the Russians canceled, they instead endeavored to undermine the position of the Jews by a series of severe restrictions, limiting their places of residence, curtailing their freedom of movement in the province, and limiting the occupations open to them. Jews were subject to constant control by the Finnish police, who required them to renew their residence permits every three months. They were permitted to deal in second-hand clothes only and forbidden to leave their city of residence or attend the fairs. The slightest violation of any of these limitations served as a ground for expulsion from Finland. Children were allowed to live with their parents only until coming of age. Jews conscripted to the army and transferred to Russia were not allowed to return to

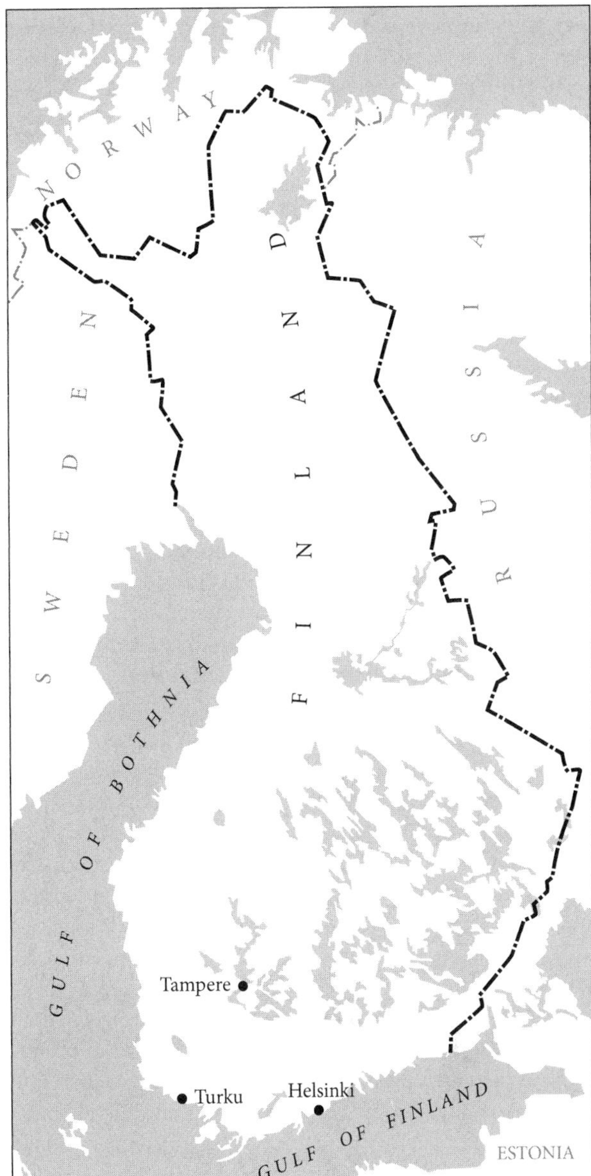

Major centers of Jewish population in Finland.

Finland after their discharge. For relief from these disabilities the Jews could only turn to the military governor in St. Petersburg who was responsible for the Jewish soldiers.

The struggle for equal rights for Jews continued for many decades and was taken up in the Finnish and Swedish press and in debates in the Finnish *diet* (*parliament*). Opposition came mainly from the clergy, while many landowners were sympathetic toward the Jewish problem. In 1872 two members of the *sejm*, Leo Mechelin and Antti Puhakka, called for the removal of some of these limitations on the Jews as the "people of the Book" but the *sejm* rejected the proposal. Toward the late 1870s Jews began to deal in new clothes which they produced or imported from factories in St. Petersburg. The debate on Jewish emancipation continued in the press during the 1880s. While the Swedish intelligentsia demanded reforms, the reactionary Finnish press obstinately opposed any change in the status of the Jews. The antisemites Meurman and Kihlman were opposed by Prof. Runeberg, son of the celebrated Finnish poet, by Bishop Alopaeus and by Barons Alfthan and Wrede. A law authorizing Jews to reside in the cities of Helsinki, Turku, and Vyborg was enacted in 1889. At that time there were 1,000 Jews resident in Finland.

At the beginning of the 20th century, mainly after the Russian revolution of 1905, signs of sympathy toward Jews were manifested by the nascent socialist movement in Finland. However in 1908 the restrictions still remained in force. The Danish-Jewish author Georg *Brandes, who went on a lecture tour in Finland that year, stated ironically in an interview with the Finnish press before he left: "I have committed three serious sins here. As a Jew, I was permitted to stay in your country for only three days, however I have stayed here for four consecutive days; as a Jew, I was permitted only to trade in rags, however here I lectured on world literature; and as a Jew, it is forbidden for me to marry here, but in spite of all this no one prohibited me from courting in your country...." In 1906 the third convention of Russian Zionists met in Helsinki and adopted the Helsingfors *Program. In 1909 the liberal elements in the Finnish parliament overcame the opposition of the extreme conservatives and by a majority of 112 to 48 a law was accepted abolishing the restrictions. However, the Russian government delayed its ratification and the Jews did not receive full civil rights until 1917 when Finland became independent.

Between the two world wars the Jewish population increased to 2,000 as a result of emigration from Russia during the early period of the revolution. Many of the Jewish youth studied in universities, and Jews entered the liberal professions as physicians, lawyers, and engineers. Others turned to industry and forestry, but the majority continued in the textile and clothing business. With a few isolated exceptions the Jews did not take part in internal party politics or join any political movement. The author and Mizrachi leader Simon *Federbusch officiated as chief rabbi of Finland from 1930 to 1940.

During the Finnish-Russian War of 1939–40, Jews fought alongside the Finns. When Viipuri (Vyborg) was annexed to the Soviet Union, the Jews (about 300 persons) evacuated the city along with the Finns. During World War II (1941–44) Finland fought on the German side against the Soviet Union, but, despite strong German pressure, the Finnish authorities, headed by Field Marshal Mannerheim refused to enforce anti-Jewish legislation. 160 Jews who did not possess Finnish nationality found refuge in neutral Sweden. At one stage the Finns yielded and allowed the Gestapo to deport 50 Jews from Finland who had arrived as refugees from Austria and the Baltic countries before the Nazi invasion. However, after the dispatch of the first transport of eight of the refugees, only one of whom survived, Mannerheim and the Finnish authorities refused to continue the operation. The peace treaty between the Allies and Finland prohibited racial discrimination and thereafter Jews again enjoyed full civil rights.

The Jewish community in Finland has always been deeply conscious of its Jewish traditions, and Yiddish is still used to some extent by the older generation. In 1968 the Jewish population numbered 1,750 (approximately 1,330 in Helsinki, 350 in Turku, and 50 in Tampere), dropping to around 1,100 at the turn of the century. The community was represented by a community council of 32 members. In Helsinki, a Jewish kindergarten (founded in 1953) and a comprehensive Jewish school (1918) with nearly 100 students were in operation, along with a full range of religious, cultural, and social services and active Zionist organizations. The rate of intermarriage was high. Twenty-nine Jewish youths from Finland fought in the Israel War of Independence, and over 100 Finnish Jews settled in the State of Israel, mostly in the agricultural sector. In 1979, Ben Zyskowicz became the first Finnish Jew to be elected to Parliament.

[Yehuda Gaulan]

Relations with Israel

In 1948 formal relations were established between Finland and Israel, first by reciprocal appointment of honorary consuls. In February 1951, Israel appointed Abraham Nissan, its minister in Sweden, as its nonresident minister in Helsinki. In 1953 a regular Israel legation was established in Helsinki, headed by a chargé d'affaires. In 1960 with the expansion of political and cultural ties between the two countries, a resident Israel minister was appointed in Finland and a Finnish minister in Israel. In 1962 both missions were elevated to the ambassadorial level. At that time Prime Minister David Ben-Gurion visited Finland on the invitation of its government, as part of his tour of Scandinavian countries, and was warmly received by the public and government officials. In May 1967 the prime minister of Finland, Raphael Paasio, reciprocated with an official visit to Israel. In 1968 Foreign Minister Abba Eban visited Helsinki on the invitation of the Finnish foreign minister.

The Six-Day War (1967) aroused great emotion in all sectors of the Finnish people. There were numerous expressions of support for and identification with Israel as a small nation fighting against great odds, reminiscent of the experience of the Finnish nation. Internationally its neutral status and proximity to the former U.S.S.R. dictated a cautious approach; its policy with regard to Israel has been neutral but sympathetic.

Cultural ties have developed between Finland and Israel. Many years ago a movement was established, mainly religiously based, called "Carmel," aimed at bringing to Israel annually a group of youngsters for a few months' training in the Hebrew language and acquaintance with Israeli life. Tourism from Finland to Israel increased, especially from 1968. In 1954 a League for Finnish-Israel friendship was established, with past Prime Minister K.A. Fagerholm as president. Finland's trade with Israel has increased steadily over the decades. The first trade agreement was signed in 1950, involving $7,000,000 in both directions. The major Israeli export to Finland was citrus and textiles, while Finnish exports to Israel comprised paper, cellulose, and paper products. In 1955 mutual trade reached $17,000,000. At the beginning the balance was in Israel's favor but later it shifted to Finland's favor. In 2003 bilateral trade between Finland and Israel amounted to €268 million. Whether for political-economic or other reasons, many Finnish products were shipped to Israel through a third country and therefore registered as trade with that country and thus unrecorded in the balance of trade between the two.

[Moshe Avidan]

BIBLIOGRAPHY: S. Federbusch, *World Jewry Today* (1959), 538–42; AJYB, 60 (1961), 223–7; A. Sarsowsky, *Gli ebrei in Finlandia* (1911 = *Settimana Israelitica*, 1910); P. Friedman, *They Were Their Brothers' Keepers* (1957), 143–8; J. Wolf, in: *Algemeyne Entsiklopedye Yidn*, 7 (1966), 292–9; N. Levin, *The Holocaust* (1968), 399–401. **WEBSITE:** www.jchelsinki.fi.

FINLAY-FREUNDLICH, ERWIN (1885–1964), astronomer. Born in Biebrich, Rhineland, Finlay-Freundlich became professor at the University of St. Andrews, Scotland. Prior to his activities as director of the St. Andrews University Observatory (1939–59), which he built up, he held the directorships of new institutes at Potsdam (1924–33), Istanbul (1933–36), and Prague (1936–39). Finlay-Freundlich was a versatile scientist and pursued research in celestial mechanics, stellar astronomy, theoretical physics, theory of relativity, solar research, and instrumental design. He equipped and directed several successful solar-eclipse expeditions, including two to Sumatra, in a determined effort to provide empirical tests of the theory of relativity through an exact verification of the minute effects of the gravitational light-deflection and the red-shift of spectral lines. He was one of the first pioneers in propagating the astronomical importance of Albert Einstein's concepts.

BIBLIOGRAPHY: Von Klueber, in: *Quarterly Journal of the Royal Astronomical Society*, 6 (1965), 82–84; *Astronomische Nachrichten*, 288 (1965), 281–6.

[Arthur Beer]

FINLEY, SIR MOSES (1912–1986), American-born British historian. Born Moses Finkelstein in New York, Sir Moses was educated at Syracuse and Columbia Universities and changed his name to "Finley" in 1936. In 1954, fearful of McCarthyism, he migrated to England, becoming a British subject in 1962. There, his distinguished academic career was spent at Cambridge, where he was professor of ancient history from 1970 to 1979. Finley was one of the most productive and highly regarded historians of the ancient world of his time, whose interests centered especially on the economy and society of ancient Greece. Among his best-known works are *The World of Odysses* (1956) and *The Ancient Economy* (1973). Finley received many academic honors and was knighted in 1979.

[William D. Rubinstein (2nd ed.)]

°**FINN, JAMES** (1806–1872), English philo-Semite, served as British consul in Jerusalem from 1845 to 1862. A pioneer for the resettlement of the Jews in Ereẓ Israel, Finn was a devoted friend of the Jews and often protected them from the Ottoman authorities. He was also active in promoting the idea of labor and agricultural development, and even invested funds in experiments to help organize his projects. After some time he went bankrupt. At the same time Finn engaged in missionary activities and tried to settle some Jewish converts to Christianity in the village of Artas (the biblical En-Etam) near Bethlehem, but this project was abandoned in 1864. When his appointment as consul ended, the leaders of the Jerusalem Jewish community and others addressed messages of appreciation and admiration to the British Government and to Finn himself for his services to the Jewish population. In assisting the Jews of Jerusalem, he had sometimes overlooked the instructions of his superiors and it has been suggested that this precipitated the end of his service in Ereẓ Israel.

After his death, his wife, Elizabeth Anne (née McCaul, 1825–1921), edited and published his book *Stirring Times* (1878), which contains detailed descriptions of the situation of the Jews in Ereẓ Israel at that time. Finn was also a pioneer in bringing to the knowledge of the Western world the Jews of *Kai Feng in his two works *Jews of China* (1849) and *The Orphan Colony of the Jews of China* (1872). Apart from this he wrote a superficial work on the *Sephardim* (1841). His wife assisted him in all his activities on behalf of the Jewish population of Ereẓ Israel. She wrote three books on Ereẓ Israel as well as memoirs on her life in Ereẓ Israel, under the title of *Reminiscences of Mrs. Finn* (1929), published posthumously.

BIBLIOGRAPHY: A.M. Hyamson, *British Consulate in Jerusalem ... 1838–1914*, 2 vols. (1939–47), index; I. Ben-Zvi, *She'ar Yashuv*, 1 (1966), 212, 520, 524; idem, *Meḥkarim u-Mekorot* (1966), 165; Ben-Zvi, Ereẓ Yisrael, 364, 409–10; A. Yaari, *Zikhronot Ereẓ Yisrael*, 1 (1947), 162–3, 175–8; M. Ish-Shalom, *Masei Noẓerim le-Ereẓ Yisrael* (1965), 44, 626–71. **ADD. BIBLIOGRAPHY:** ODNB online for Elizabeth Finn; H.L. and W.D. Rubinstein, *Philo-Semitism: Admiration and Support in the English-Speaking World for Jews, 1840–1939* (1999), 159–60; B.-Z. Abrahams, "James Finn: Her Britannic Majesty's Counsel at Jerusalem Between 1846 and 1860," in: JHSET, 27 (1978–80), 40–50.

[Abraham David]

FINNISTON, SIR HAROLD MONTAGUE (**Monty**; 1912–1991), British metallurgist and industrial administrator. Finniston was born in Glasgow (whose accent he retained), educated at Glasgow University, and became a lecturer at the Royal College of Science and Technology, Glasgow. He then became a metallurgist in industry and served in the Royal Naval Scientific Service during World War II. He was chief metallurgist at the United Kingdom Atomic Energy Authority, Harwell, from 1948 to 1958, and managing director of the International Research and Development Company from 1959 to 1967. He joined the board of the recently renationalized steel industry (British Steel Corporation) as deputy chairman (technical) in 1967, becoming chief executive in 1971 and chairman from 1973 to 1976. From 1976 he was active as chairman or director of industrial companies and from 1980 as a business consultant. Finniston was involved in many fields of research and in the Jewish community. He was chairman of the independent "think tank" of the Policies Institute from 1975 to 1984, chancellor of Stirling University, and pro-chancellor of the University of Surrey. He was knighted in 1975, had 15 honorary doctorates conferred upon him, and in 1969 was elected a Fellow of the Royal Society, of which he was later vice president in 1971–72. Sir Wally MacFarlane, the nationalized industry chairman portrayed in the popular British television comedy *Yes, Minister,* was based on Finniston.

ADD. BIBLIOGRAPHY: ODNB online.

[Vivian David Lipman]

FINZI, Italian family which can be traced back to the second half of the 13th century; the origin of the name is unknown, The first recorded members were loan bankers in Padua. Subsequently, the family spread to many other towns; some of them added the name of their city of origin to their family name (Finzi of Ancona, of Recanati, of Bologna, of Mantua, of Ferrara, of Reggio-Heb, ארי"ו – not Arezzo as usually transcribed). In Venice some of them became known as Tedesco-Finzi to emphasize their German origin. Other Finzis may be traced in the Balkans and in Jerusalem and later in England. Some of the most noteworthy members follow in chronological order.

MORDECAI (ANGELO) B. ABRAHAM (d. 1476), a versatile scientist, physician, and banker, who lived in Bologna and Mantua. He was known mainly for his mathematical and astronomical works, which included *Luḥot,* tables on the length of days (publ. Mantua, c. 1479, by Abraham Conat), and an astronomical work entitled *Netiv Ḥokhmah* (unpublished), He translated into Hebrew three important works by the Arab mathematician Abū Kāmil (850–930). He also translated into Hebrew various works on astronomy and geometry and wrote commentaries on some of them, described and explained recently invented astronomical instruments, and wrote treatises on grammar and mnemonics. SOLOMON B. ELIAKIM, rabbi in Forli (1536) and Bologna (1552). He wrote a methodological work, *Mafte'aḥ ha-Gemara* (Venice, 1622). It was reprinted in 1697 in Helmstedt with a Latin translation and notes by C.H. Ritmeier, and again reprinted in *Clavis Talmudica Maxima* (Hanau, 1714, 1740). GUR ARYEH HA-LEVI, rabbi in Mantua in 1665. He wrote a remarkable commentary on the Shulḥan Arukh, published (Mantua, 1721–23) by his great-nephew, Gur Aryeh b. Benjamin (d. 1754). SAMUEL (d. 1791), pupil of Isaac Lampronti, was a famous preacher and rabbi at Ferrara. His homilies are collected in *Imrei Emet* (1841^{2}). ISAAC RAPHAEL B. ELISHA (1728–1812), of Ferrara, was a widely esteemed preacher, some of whose sermons were published. He was a member of the French Sanhedrin in 1806 and was elected its vice president. JOSEPH (1815–1886), born in Mantua, was a patriot of the Italian Risorgimento. A confidant of Mazzini, Garibaldi, and Cavour, he took an active part in the risings against Austria from 1848 to 1853 and was entrusted with the funds for the Garibaldi's expedition to Sicily in 1860. From 1860 onward, he was a member of parliament for about twenty-five years and he was elected senator in 1886. The jurist MARIO (1913–1943) from Bologna was active in the Italian Resistance during World War II and he assisted Italian and German Jews from 1938; he was captured in 1943 during an attempt to help a Jew. GERALD (1901–1956), English musician and professor of composition at the Royal Academy of Music, wrote choral, orchestral, and chamber music.

BIBLIOGRAPHY: Roth, Italy, index; idem, *Jews in the Renaissance* (1959), index; Milano, Bibliotheca, index; Milano, Italia, 678; Ghirondi-Neppi, index; Mortara, Indice; A. Balletti, *Gli ebrei e gli Estensi* (1930^{2}), passim; V. Colorni, in: RMI, 9 (1934/35), 221–2; G. Bedarida, *Ebrei d'Italia* (1950), index; S. Simonsohn, *Ha-Yehudim be-Dukkasut Mantovah* (1956), index. **ADD. BIBLIOGRAPHY:** L. Carpi, *Il Risorgimento Italiano, Biografie Storico-Politiche d'Illustri Italiani Contemporanei,* 4 vols. (1888).

[Attilio Milano / Federica Francesconi (2nd ed.)]

FINZI, GIUSEPPE (1815–1886), Italian patriot and parliamentarian. Finzi studied in Padua from 1831 to 1835. In 1834 he joined the secret organization Giovane Italia. In 1844, he met with Giuseppe Mazzini in London, who entrusted him with the nationalist propaganda in both Switzerland and Lombardy. In 1848, Finzi fought behind the barricades in Milan. After serving for a time in the army of Charles Albert, he organized a regiment consisting of Mantuans. He first fought in Novara against Austria, and afterward in Rome against the papal troops. Having been taken prisoner, as a close friend of Mazzini, he was brought before an Austrian court-martial in Mantua. While many of his friends were condemned to the gallows, he was sentenced to 18 years imprisonment at Thereisenstadt and Josephstadt but an amnesty of 1856 set him free.

When Lombardy was freed from Austrian domination, Finzi was appointed royal commissary for the province of Mantua. He became the confidante of Giuseppe Garibaldi and was entrusted with the funds for the expedition to Sicily. The voluntary contributions not being sufficient, Finzi appealed to Count Camillo Benso di Cavour for more funding. Cavour supplied him with funds from the state treasury, under the strictest secrecy. Cavour urged Finzi to revolutionize Naples while Garibaldi was in Sicily. Accordingly, Finzi made his way there with others but had little success. He nevertheless paved the way for Garibaldi s entry later. Ill health compelled Finzi to resign the office of director general of public safety for the southern provinces, to which he had been appointed. He sometimes mediated between Garibaldi and Cavour, when their relations became strained. For about 25 years – from 1860 on – Finzi was a member of the Lower House, and highly esteemed by all parties. He was a man of unflagging energy but was not an orator. On June 7, 1886, he was made a senator, but died shortly thereafter.

FINZI-NORSA CONTROVERSY, Italian Jewish cause célèbre in the early part of the 16th century. Immanuel Norsa of Ferrara, reputed to be the second wealthiest Jew in Italy, was partner in a loan bank with Abraham Raphael Finzi of Bologna, who had suffered serious reverses in his other business interests. Although relations between the two men were strengthened by marriages between their children, it was still charged by Finzi's friends that directly or indirectly, Norsa had caused Finzi the loss of 5,000 gold florins. Since his partnership with Norsa was Finzi's only asset, he was compelled to dispose of it to satisfy his creditors. The wealthy Samuel da Pisa, Norsa's brother-in-law, agreed to buy out Finzi's share. However, due to Norsa's opposition, he reneged on the proposed transaction.

The creditors continued to press Finzi, who realized that Norsa would thwart any advantageous sale; Finzi was forced to accede to Norsa's conditions and let him have all the partnership rights at his own price. It is claimed that Norsa paid him only one-sixth the actual value. However, before Finzi went to Ravenna to conclude the sale, he made a *moda'ah* ("declaration") at Bologna before witnesses, on February 28, 1507, that he was only selling to Norsa under duress, and that all the statements he would make to Norsa to the effect that the sale was carried out with good will and without compulsion were in consequence null and void. He also retained all rights to sue his former partner in court at a more opportune time. About 12 years later, this document was submitted to a court of three rabbinical judges in Bologna. Finzi brought five witnesses to prove the power of Norsa in Ferrara and the impossibility of getting judgment against him in the latter's home town. The court granted him a change of venue and decided that the case should be tried before an impartial court outside Ferrara. Norsa refused to abide by this decision and insisted upon having the litigation in his city.

A vehement and vituperative controversy soon ensued solely on the validity of venue granted to Finzi. Norsa was supported by his local rabbis, particularly David Pizzighettone and by Abraham *Minz; Finzi was supported by almost all the Italian rabbinate, including Bendit Axelrod b. Eleazar, the head of the Venetian rabbinate, Israel b. Jehiel Isserlein of Rome, and Jehiel Trabotto b. Azriel of Pesaro. Above all, the famed Jacob *Pollak of Poland backed Finzi and finally excommunicated Abraham Minz for his role in aggravating the controversy. Finally, Norsa had to yield and appeared before an outside impartial court. No record of the decision reached on the monetary issue has been preserved.

BIBLIOGRAPHY: Marx, in: *Abhandlungen ... Hirsch Perez Chajes* (1933), 149–93 (Eng.).

[Aaron Rothkoff]

FIOGHI (Fiocchi), FABIANO (16th century), Roman Catholic theologian. Born a Jew in Monte Salvino, Fioghi was baptized in Rome, where he was active as teacher and catechist of the Jewish candidates for conversion at the House of *Catechumens, Fioghi published a missionary tract in Italian, entitled *Dialogo fra il Cathecumino et il Padre catechizante...* (Rome, 1582); a second edition, *Introduttione alla Fede fatta in forma di Dialogo*, appeared in Rome in 1628. Even 200 years later R. Joshua Benzion *Segre attacked the anti-Jewish introductory and concluding poems of this book. A Hebrew poem by Fioghi, addressed to Pope Gregory XIII, is to be found in the Vatican Library, together with a Latin translation.

BIBLIOGRAPHY: Wolf, Bibliotheca, 4 (1733), 948; M. Soave, in: *Vessillo Israelitico*, 29 (1881), 270; Vogelstein-Rieger, 2 (1896), 285; G. Sacerdote, in: REJ, 30 (1895), 267; M. Steinschneider, in: MGWJ, 43 (1899), 36; T. Weikart, in: ZHB, 5 (1901), 28 n. 4.

[Jefim (Hayyim) Schirmann]

FIORENTINO, SALOMONE (1743–1815), Italian poet. Fiorentino was born at Monte San Savino, a village in Tuscany where the Jewish presence went back at least to 1421. Son of a merchant, he studied traditional Jewish subjects in Siena, attending at the same time – as an external student – a Catholic school, where he distinguished himself. He had a shop selling cloth in Cortona and read Italian poetry and works of philosophy intensively. Starting to compose verse, he kept up a correspondence with outstanding Italian poets like Metastasio, Cesarotti, Monti, and Alfieri. The premature death of his beloved wife in 1789 was a turning point both in his private life and in his literary career; the three elegies he composed on this occasion won him a certain celebrity, so that Fiorentino was admitted to the important Accademia Fiorentina and named by the Grand Duke of Tuscany "poet laureate." In 1799, during the French occupation, the violence of the populace against the Jews (seen as Allies of the "heretic" French) forced Fiorentino, like many of his coreligionists, to leave his small villages and live in Siena, then in Florence; as a consequence of the riots, he lost all his property in Cortona and Monte San Savino. From 1800 to 1815, with the return of the French army, he could devote himself to literary activity and wrote moral poems, epithalamiums, poems in praise of the Habsburg emperors, as well as an Italian translation of the Sephardi prayer book of Livorno (Leghorn). His collected poems were printed several times. From 1801 to 1808, Fiorentino lived in Livorno, earning his living as a teacher of Italian in the local Jewish community; from 1808 to 1815, stricken by paralysis, he lived again in Florence, where he died. His poetry, though belonging to the Italian literary tradition, shows many Jewish elements: biblical references, a deep religiosity drawn from Jewish sources, even the centrality of family affection that had no poetical importance at the time. Fiorentino probably influenced the Italian poet Giacomo Leopardi, who inserted two of his elegies in his important anthology *Crestomazia italiana.*

BIBLIOGRAPHY: O. De Montel, *Sulla vita e sulle opere di Salomone Fiorentino* (1852); A.S. Toaff, in RMI, 15 (1949), 195–215; R.G. Salvadori, in: *Gli ebrei a Monte San Savino* (1994), 93–101; G. Milan, in: *Dizionario biografico degli italiani*, vol. 48 (1997), 160–62.

[Alessandro Guetta (2nd ed.)]

FIQH, the science of Islamic law. In the course of the eighth century, the term, which originally meant "knowledge" or "understanding," took on the meaning of Islamic jurisprudence on its two levels: certain knowledge, transmitted by the text of the Koran or a tradition relating to the Prophet (*sunna*); and legal conclusions derived by legal reasoning. The purpose of legal reasoning (*ra'y*), generally through analogy (*qiyās*), is to determine the *ratio legis* (motivation) for a legal rule. Consensus (*ijmā'*), the fourth source of Islamic law (after Koran, *sunna*, and *qiyās*), purports to ensure the truth of a rule or conclusion derived from textual sources. Those lawyers who deal with *fiqh* are known as *fuqahā*.

While *sharīca* is a general term for the totality of instructions and regulations in Islamic law, *fiqh* concentrates more on the legal aspect, though it too encompasses all areas of human behavior, religious as well as both private and public law. Accordingly, Islamic law recognizes five religious-ethical categories of human behavior (*al-ahakām al-khamsa*), ranging from obligatory (*farḍ*) to forbidden (*haarām*), with three intermediate categories: recommended (*mandūb*), reprehensible (*makrūh*), and indifferent (and permitted; *mubāha*). Parallel to this scale of religious-ethical qualifications is a scale of legal, rather than religious, validity of an action. While in theory the rules of *fiqh*, known as branches (*furūc*), are derived from the sources of Islamic law (*usūal-fiqh*) by the methodology prescribed in the *usūlal-fiqh* literature, some such rules actually stem from the customary law of pre-Islamic times (*jāhiliyya*) or the influence of other legal systems (Persian, Greek, Roman, Byzantine) or religions (Judaism, Christianity), whose full impact on Islamic law and its development have yet to be fully determined. Islamic law assimilated such influences in various ways, but not by way of custom (*curf, cāda*), which Islamic law in its initial phase did not recognize as an independent source of law; such recognition came at a later phase in the development of Islamic law.

One of the most salient characteristics of *fiqh* is its development by religious scholars (*fuqahā, culamā*) rather than judges. This at times led to divergences between theory and reality, with which the *fuqahā* had to deal by the application of, inter alia, legal devices and evasions (*ḥiyal*), as well as other legal principles, such as *istihsān* (discretionary decisions), or *istislāh* (consideration of the public interest). In some cases a special legal effort (*ijtihād*) was necessary to rule the law on the basis of the roots of the law, frequently by means of legal pronouncements (*fatāwā*, sing. *fatwa*) by high-ranking lawyers (*muftī*) – a phenomenon characteristic of the casuistic nature of Islamic law. In the mid-eighth century (758), ᶜAbdullah ibn al-Muqaffaᶜ proposed to the Caliph Al-Mansūr to draw up a codification of Islamic law, but his plan never came to fruition.

The legal oeuvre of the *fiqh* began to develop in the second half of the eighth century, beginning with the *fiqh* literature in all its variety, soon followed by the *usūl al-fiqh* literature. In addition to treatises devoted to detailed descriptions of specific areas of law, ranging from *cabādat* (ritual) to *mucāmalat* (pecuniary transactions), other literary genres of *fiqh* literature included works on differences between jurists and schools (*ikhtilāf*), which were a constant feature of Islamic law from its beginnings; legal formularies (*shurūt*); and works on legal devices (*ḥiyal*). The earliest work of *usūl al-fiqh* was the *Risāla* (that is, "epistle") of Idrīs Shāfiᶜī (820), generally considered the founder of Muslim legal theory, which defined its terms and set its limits against the background of a controversy that broke out in the early Middle Ages between two currents of opinion: supporters of legal tradition (*ahl al-ḥadīth*) and supporters of legal reasoning (*ahl al-ra'y*). The first work of *fiqh* was the *Muwaṭṭa'* ("paved path") of Mālik b. Anas. In parallel to the official system of Islamic law, a secondary system of criminal law, known as *al-naẓar fī'l-maẓālim* ("investigation of complaints") developed as an alternative to the rigid system of evidence and procedure of official Islamic law.

Islamic law recognizes the existence of different opinions, granting them equal status. Accordingly, several different legal schools emerged in the main centers of Islamic law: Medina, Kufa, and Syria. Through the second half of the ninth century and the early tenth century, these ultimately became the main legal schools (*madhhab*), each named for prominent early scholars of the law: The Ḥanafi school, after Abū Ḥānafa (767); the Mālikī school, after Mālik b. Anas (795); the Shāfiᶜī school, after Muḥammad ibn Idrīs al-Shāfiᶜī (820); and the Ḥanbalī school, after Aḥmad ibn Ḥanbal (855). A few other schools were formed but did not survive. Some of the differences between these schools reflect the legal traditions of a specific locality and time as well as prevailing social conditions (mainly the Malikī and Ḥanafi schools); others reflect a different attitude to the sources of law or to other legal principles. Each school created its own *fiqh* literature and summarized its legal outlook in a work known as *Mukhtaṣar* ("compendium"). Each school dominated a certain geographical region of the Muslim world. There may have been some connection between the formation of the schools and the anthologization of *ḥadīths* (the documentation of the *sunna*) and development of the science of *ḥadīth* criticism, since the two developments are related in subject matter and contiguous in time: The anthologies were drawn up during the ninth century, and soon after them came the consolidation of the schools. Probably also the transition from *ijtihād* (legal struggle or effort) to *taqlīd* is related to the appearance of the schools, since the *taqlīd* (reliance on legal tradition) expresses loyalty to the legal heritage of a particular school and its leader. The evolution of legal terminology may also have been influenced by the emergence of the schools, since it expressed a certain hierarchy of opinions and in a way functioned as a substitute for legal decision rules, which Islamic law lacks. Common to the schools was their acceptance of the legal theory of *usūl al-fiqh*, but this did not prevent the schisms of the seventh century, when the Shīᶜa split from the Sunna and the Khawārij seceded from mainstream Islam.

Muslim recognition of legal pluralism and the equal status accorded the legal schools created a degree of flexibility in Islamic law; thus, litigants were even permitted to shift from one school to another in a court composed of judges representing the four schools, and a judge could appeal to the ruling of a school other than his own. In modern times, Islam permits legislators to combine doctrines of more than one school in relation to specific clauses of the law (*takhayyur*), mainly in the context of protection of women's rights; this phenomenon blurs differences between the schools and promotes the unification of Islamic law.

Some characteristics of *fiqh* influenced Jewish law during and after the period of the *geonim*, in such areas as literary creativity, borrowing of legal terminology, and assimilation of legal principles and sometimes even of specific laws.

BIBLIOGRAPHY: "Fikh," in: EIS^2, 2 (1965), 886–91 (includes bibliography); I. Goldziher, *Introduction to Islamic Theology and Law* (1981), 31–66; W.B. Hallaq, *A History of Islamic Legal Theories* (1977); J. Schacht, *An Introduction to Islamic Law* (1964), 57–85.

[Gideon Libson (2nd ed.)]

FIRE (Heb. אֵשׁ).

In the Bible

Once humans discovered that fire could be maintained and exploited for their needs, it became one of their most important assets. Fire was used for light, warmth, cooking, roasting, baking, in waging war, and in various crafts, for sending messages, and for ritual purposes. Greek myth relates that fire was originally restricted to the gods before it was stolen by Prometheus and given to humans. Fire is one of the central elements of theophany. At the covenant with Abraham "a smoking oven and a flaming torch," representing the divine presence passed between the halves of the animals (Gen. 15:17). God appeared to Moses from the burning bush (Ex. 3:2); He went before Israel in a pillar of fire to guide them by night on their way out of Egypt (Ex. 13:21–22; 14:24; Num. 9:15–16 et al.); on the occasion of the giving of the Tablets of the Law, Mount Sinai is described as being covered in smoke, "for the Lord had come down upon it in fire" (Ex. 19:18). In Deuteronomy 9:3 Yahweh is described as "consuming fire." Yahweh breaths smoke, flames, and fire (II Sam. 22:9 [= Ps. 18:9]; Isa. 30:27, 33; 65:5). In cultic practice special importance was attributed to fire as a means of purification and cleansing: "any article that can withstand fire-these you shall pass through fire and they shall be clean" (Num. 31:23). Fire was used in several ways in worship: (1) a fire was lit daily in the temple (Ex. 27:20; Lev. 24:2; (2) a perpetual fire for burning sacrifices was maintained on the altar (Lev. 6:5, 6); (3) a fire was used for roasting sacrifices for human consumption; (4) a fire for burning incense was placed so that the smoke diffused throughout the shrine (Ex. 29:18; Lev. 16:13; et al.; see *Sacrifice). The power of fire both as a positive and destructive force is expressed in the poetic portions of the Bible: "and you call on the name of your god and I will call on the name of the Lord, and the God who answers by fire He is the God" (I Kings 18:24). God punishes the wicked by sending down fire from heaven: "the Lord rained upon Sodom and Gomorrah sulfurous fire from the Lord out of heaven" (Gen. 19:24). Fire is also an expression of great anger: "for a fire has flared in my wrath and burned to the bottom of Sheol, has consumed the earth and its increase, eaten down to the base of the hills" (Deut. 32:22).

[Ze'ev Yeivin / S. David Sperling (2nd ed.)]

In Talmudic Literature

Fire figures prominently both in the *halakhah* and the *aggadah*. In the former it occupies a central place in civil law as one of the four tortfeasors, the four principal categories of damage (see **Avot Nezikin*). It also occupies a special role with regard to the Sabbath; although kindling a fire is one of the main 39 categories of work forbidden on the Sabbath (Shab. 7:2), it is also specifically mentioned as a separate prohibition: "Ye shall kindle no fire throughout your habitations on the Sabbath day" (Ex. 35:3). There is a difference of opinion in the Talmud as to the reason for this distinctive mention. According to one opinion the reason is to make this particular prohibition a mere negative commandment, incurring the punishment of flogging, whereas violation of the others invokes *karet*. According to the other opinion it is specifically mentioned to establish the rule that a person is liable separately for each and every infringement of the prohibitions of the Sabbath (Shab. 70a). The rabbis, in contradistinction to the Sadducees (and later the Karaites) interpreted the verse to apply only to the actual kindling of a fire on the Sabbath but not to its existence. Therefore a fire lit before the Sabbath is permitted to continue to burn on that day (if no fuel is added during the day), permitting the distinctive feature of the home celebrations of Sabbath, the Sabbath lights on the table. This fire, according to some opinions, could be used to keep pre-cooked food warm on the Sabbath, and according to other opinions, it could also be used to allow partially cooked foods to continue cooking by themselves on the Sabbath itself. Among the forms of work forbidden on Sabbath and permitted on festivals, lighting a fire is one of only two such forms (along with carrying) which is permitted even if one does not use the fire to prepare food, in line with the principle that "once it was permitted for the need [of cooking] it was permitted when there is no such need" (Beẓah 12b).

Fire is extensively referred to in the *aggadah*. According to one account it was created on the second day of creation (PdRE 4) but according to another, it was created after the conclusion of the Sabbath, by Adam through the friction of two stones (Pes. 54a; TJ, Ber. 8:6, 12b). The fire of the altar came down from heaven (cf. Yoma 21b) and remained burning from the time of Moses until it was transferred to the Temple of Solomon (Zev. 61b), and it continued to burn until the reign of Manasseh (Yalkut, Kings 187). On the other hand the fire in the Second Temple was human fire (Yoma loc. cit.); nevertheless that fire was never extinguished by the rain. The "strange fire" which Nadab and Abihu, the sons of Aaron, offered up on the altar (Lev. 10:1) was "common" or human fire (Num. R. 2:23). Indeed, all that which is regarded as coming directly from God is said to have been given in fire. The Torah was given in a frame of white fire and the letters were engraved in black fire (TJ, Shek. 6:1, 48d). When God told Moses to institute the half-shekel, He showed him "a coin of fire" (*ibid.*, 1:6, 46b). Simultaneously with earthly fire was created the fire of Gehinnom, and earthly fire is one-sixtieth of that fire (Ber. 57b). Out of primordial fire was created light: "The fire became pregnant and gave birth to light" (Ex. R. 15:22).

Six kinds of fire are enumerated (Yoma 21b) and some such division is responsible for the formula of the blessing over light at the **Havdalah* ceremony. According to the school of Shammai the formula should be, "Who created the light of the fire." The school of Hillel, however, maintained that since there are many colors of fire, it was necessary to say, "Who created the lights of fire" in the plural (Ber. 52a) and the *halakhah* was established accordingly. The rabbis accepted the legend that the salamander was created out of fire (Ḥag. 27a; Tanh. *Va-Yeshev* 3, Ex. R. 15:28) and that its blood protected a person from the ill effects of fire. Fire beacons placed on the mountaintops were used to announce the arrival of the New Moon (RH 2:2–4).

[Louis Isaac Rabinowitz]

BIBLIOGRAPHY: S. Muehsam, *Das Feuer in Bibel und Talmud* (1869); E.B. Tylor, *Researches into the Early History of Mankind* (1878), index; Y. Yadin, *The Art of Warfare in Biblical Lands* (1963), passim. **ADD. BIBLIOGRAPHY:** W. Watson, in: DDD, 331–32.

FIRKOVICH, ABRAHAM (Even Reshef; 1787–1874), Karaite public figure in Eastern Europe. Firkovich was born in Luck (Lutsk), Poland. After his marriage in 1808 he worked as a miller. In 1813 he began to study Torah with the Karaite scholar Morekhai *Sultanski. In 1822 he moved from Lutsk to Evpatoria (Crimea) and was appointed *ḥazzan* of the local community. In 1825 he submitted a memorandum to the Russian government in which he suggested resettling Rabbanite Jews from the border areas in order to prevent them from smuggling and force them into agriculture.

In 1830 the Karaite *ḥakham* Simḥah *Babovich hired him as a tutor for his children and as his secretary to accompany him in his pilgrimage to the Land of Israel. During their visit to Jerusalem, Hebron, and Cairo Firkovich bought and copied many ancient books. In 1831–32 he moved to Istanbul, where he served as *ḥazzan*, *shoḥet,* and *melammed.* Following a conflict with the community there he returned to Evpatoria (Gozlow), where he organized a society for the publication of Karaite books. In 1834 he was appointed head of the Karaite publishing house there and published his biting anti-rabbinic book *Ḥotam Tokhnit*, accusing Rabbanites of crucifying Jesus and killing *Anan ben David.

In 1839 M. Vorontsov, the governor general of the Novorossya region and the Crimea, addressed a series of six questions to Babovich, who had become head of the Karaite Spiritual Council. These dealt with the origins of the Karaites and the time of their settlement in the Crimea, their character traits, occupations, important personalities, historical sources about their origins, time of their separation from the Rabbanites, and the differences between them. Babovich then recommended Firkovich investigate these questions and the latter initiated his archaeological and other expeditions in the Crimea and the Caucasus, uncovering ancient tombstones and manuscripts in order to produce an account of Karaite history. His main work, *Avnei Zikkaron* (1872) describes his travels and contains a collection of tombstone inscriptions with several pictures of these tombstones appended. In the course of his work Firkovich created a new concept of the origins of the Crimean Karaites, according to which they settled in the Crimea in 6 B.C.E.; therefore they could not share the responsibility for the crucifixion of Jesus. Firkovich wished to convince the authorities that the Karaites were a separate nation which differed historically, culturally, and anthropologically from the Rabbanites. He was the first Karaite author to apply a "scientific" research methodology to ameliorate the legal status of his congregation. To substantiate his claims Firkovich fabricated colophons and falsified some of the tombstone inscriptions. He changed the real dates on the tombs to earlier ones. He also "invented" some great figures of Karaite history, such as Isaac Sangari (identified in a late medieval source as the sage ("ḥaver") who in Judah *Halevi's account in the *Kuzari* converted the king of the *Khazars to Judaism). In Firkovich's version, Sangari converted the Khazars to the Karaite version of Judaism and died in Chufut-Qaleh.

Yet within a year of Firkovich's death, a controversy raged over the authenticity of the Firkovich material. Such prominent scholars as A. Harkavy, H. Strack, P.F. Frankl, and A. Kunik claimed that Firkovich's collections abounded in forgeries and fabrications. Even D. Chwolson, his most sympathetic critic, had to admit the general unreliability of Firkovich's manuscripts. Nevertheless, the manuscripts that he amassed were used or published by several well-known scholars in their studies about the Karaites. (S. Pinsker's *Likkutei Kadmoniyot* (1860) was based on Firkovich's materials; Fuerst and Graetz also unhesitatingly used this material.) Discussions of the authenticity of his materials stimulated the development of Jewish studies in Russia and Western Europe.

His manuscript collection is considered to be one of the most valuable collections of Hebrew manuscripts worldwide. Firkovich sold his first collection containing over a thousand Rabbanite, Karaite, and Samaritan manuscripts and Torah scrolls from the Crimea, Caucasus, and Middle East to the Imperial Library in St. Petersburg in 1862 and in 1870. His second collection, containing over 15,000 items, was sold after his death (1876). Most items originated in the Genizah of the Karaite synagogue in Cairo, which Firkovich visited in 1864. It is the largest collection of its kind in the world. These collections and his private archive, which are housed in the Russian National Library in St. Petersburg, were opened to researchers only after the breakup of the Soviet Union. Most of the material is available in microfilm at the Jewish National and University Library in Jerusalem.

Firkovich had six sons and five daughters. He died in Chufut-Qaleh and was buried in the cemetery in the Jehoshaphat valley.

BIBLIOGRAPHY: Z. Ankori, *Karaites in Byzantium* (1959), index; P. Frankl, *Aḥar Reshef* (1877); A. Harkavy, *Altjuedische Denkmaeler aus der Krim* (1876); Mann, Texts, 2 (1935), 695–7, and passim; D.H.L. Strack, *Abraham Firkowitsch und seine Entdeckungen* (1876); Z. Elkin – M. Ben-Sasson, in: *Pe'amim*, 90 (2002) 51–96; M. Polliack (ed.), *Karaite Judaism: A Guide to Its History and Literary Sources*, (2003), index. **ADD. BIBLIOGRAPHY:** E. Deinard, *Toledot Even-Reshef* (1875); R. Fahnn, *Sefer ha-Kera'im* (1929), 124ff.; A. Kahana, HUCA, 3 (192), 359–70; D. Shapira, *Firkowicz in Istanbul (1830–1832)* (2003); idem, in: *Pe'amim*, 98–99 (2004), 261–317.

[Haggai Ben-Shammai (2nd ed.)]

FIRSTBORN.

In the Bible

Primogeniture is a persistent and widespread institution whose legal, social, and religious features were reflected in the norms of ancient Israelite society. Biblical legislation gave the firstborn male a special status with respect to inheritance rights and certain cultic regulations, The latter, a part of a complex of cultic requirements, also applied to the first issue of the herds and the flocks, which, in the popular consciousness, were considered particularly desirable as sacrifices. Abel pleased God by offering Him firstlings of his flock (Gen. 4:4). The requirements of the cultic codes were based on the notion that the God of Israel had a claim on the first offspring of man and beast, which were to be devoted to Him in some manner. This notion also governed the prescriptions regarding the offering of the first fruits (see *First Fruits).

In biblical Hebrew usage the term *bekhor*, "firstborn [male]," and its derivatives, are somewhat ambiguous. The characterization of the human *bekhor* as *reshit on*, "the first fruit of vigor" (Gen. 49:3; Deut. 21:17; cf. Ps. 78:51; 105:36), stresses the relation to the father and adumbrates the firstborn's status of principal heir and successor of his father as head of the family. At the same time, the specification that the *bekhor* be "the first issue of the womb" (*peter reḥem*; Ex. 13:2, 12, 15, etc.; cf. Num. 8:16), which reflects the religious significance of the first products of the procreative process in human and animal life, stresses the biological link to the mother. Whereas it was usually possible to ascertain the paternity of human beings, this clearly did not hold true of animals, and there was never any attempt to base animal cultic regulations on considerations of specific paternity.

Two rather distinct conceptions can be made out: a socio-legal one, which assigned exceptional status to the first male in the paternal line; and a cultic one which assigned special status to the first male issue of the maternal line. The socio-legal conception was preserved in legislation governing inheritance. In cultic legislation, the *bekhor* of the legal tradition was required – in order for the cultic regulations to apply – to be also the first issue of his mother's womb.

According to Deuteronomy 21:15–17, a father was obliged to acknowledge his firstborn son as his principal heir, and to grant him a double portion of his estate as inheritance. (*Pi-shenayim* means "two-thirds" [see Zech. 13:8], but the intention of the text is that the firstborn shall get whatever fraction a double portion may come to; in the case posited in the text, where there are only two sons, it is two-thirds, but where there are three sons, it is one-half, and so on; cf. the correct inference drawn in BB 123a from I Chron. 5:1ff., which expressly terms Joseph's status as "firstborn" – Joseph received twice the portion of any of his brothers [Gen. 48:5, 22; ef. Rashbam to BB 123a].) This obligation was to apply irrespective of the status of the son's mother in a polygamous family. This inheritance right is termed *mishpat ha-bekhorah*, "the rule of the birthright" (Deut. 21:17), and the legal process by which the firstborn son was so designated is expressed by the verb *yakkir* "he shall acknowledge." Undoubtedly the acknowledgment involved certain formal, legal acts which are not indicated in biblical literature. In a different context, God acknowledged Israel as his firstborn (Ex. 4:22; ef. Jer. 31:8). A son, addressing his father, might also refer to his own status as firstborn son (Gen. 27:19, 32).

It is evident from the composition of biblical genealogies that the status of *bekhor* was a pervasive feature of Israelite life. In many such lists there is a formula which specifies the status of the first-listed son. For example, Numbers 1:20: "The sons of Reuben, the firstborn of Israel, were…" (cf. e.g., Gen. 35:23; 36:15; Ex. 6:14, and frequently in the genealogies of I Chron.). Even in genealogies which do not specifically indicate the status of the first son listed, it is clear that he is the firstborn. There are suggestions in the Bible that primogeniture carried certain duties and privileges in addition to the estate rights (see Gen. 27; 48:13; Judg. 8:20; I Chron. 26:10, etc.). The second in line was termed *ha-mishneh* (I Sam. 17:13; II Sam. 3:3; I Chron. 5:12).

The status of the firstborn in royal succession is not clearly defined. The Israelite kings were often polygamous, and the relative status of several royal wives figured in determining a succession, making the Deuteronomic law cited above appear more like an ideal than a reality so far as the king was concerned. A king might, for a variety of reasons, also be disposed to officially reject one of his sons, Accordingly, there were instances where the first in the royal line of succession did not, in fact, succeed his father. It is not known whether the firstborn in families of the high priests had a special status. From the exception noted in I Chronicles 26:10 it is inferable that the firstborn of a levitical clan was normally placed in charge of his brothers. There is some evidence that the firstborn daughter (*bekhirah*) was customarily married off before her younger sisters (Gen. 29:16ff.; I Sam. 18:17ff.).

In the Genesis narrative one sees how primogeniture was disregarded in the clan of Abraham. The son most suited to carry on the line of Abraham – with its attendant responsibility for transmitting the clan's unique religious belief – was acknowledged as the head of the family even if it meant passing by the firstborn; indeed even if it entailed banishing him from the household (Isaac was preferred to Ishmael, ch. 21: Jacob to Esau, ch. 27).

The terminology employed in Genesis, when compared

to that of Deuteronomy 21:17, is problematic, and allowance for a degree of inconsistency in technical usage must be made. In Genesis, Jacob contends with Esau over two matters: first, the *bekhorah*, which Jacob secured from Esau, who despised it, in exchange for a cooked meal (Gen. 25:29–34); and second, the *berakhah* ("blessing") which Jacob secured by deceiving his elderly father into thinking that he was blessing Esau (Gen. 27). Of the two terms, the *berakhah* counted for more, probably because pronouncing the blessing was considered to be the act formally acknowledging the firstborn as the principal heir. *Berakhah* connotes both the blessing which is to be pronounced and the effects of the blessing, i.e., the wealth transmitted as inheritance. In Deuteronomy 21:17 the term *bekhorah* refers specifically to the estate rights.

Owing to his favored status, the firstborn was considered the most desirable sacrifice to a deity where human sacrifice was practiced. On the verge of a defeat, Mesha, king of Moab, sacrificed his eldest son and acknowledged successor (II Kings 3:27). In a prophetic passage, the sacrifice of the firstborn is singled out as that offering which might be supposed the most efficacious for expiation (Micah 6:7). The importance of the *bekhor* is dramatized in the saga of the ten plagues God inflicted upon the Egyptians, the last of which struck down their firstborn (e.g., Ex. 11:5; 12:12). This serves as the etiology of the legal-cultic requirement that the male firstborn of man and beast in Israel were to be devoted to God. The Lord acquired title to Israel's firstborn, human and animal, by having spared them when he struck the firstborn of the Egyptians (Num. 3:13).

The priestly tradition goes on to explain that the Levites, as a group, were devoted to cultic service in substitution for all the firstborn Israelites (Num. 3:12). This would seem to be the historicization of a situation that in fact obtained independently of the particular events surrounding the Exodus. The laws governing the redemption of the firstborn (Ex. 13:15; 34:19, Deut, 15:19) presumably derived from a cultic matrix. At one time firstborn sons were actually devoted to cultic service as temple slaves, Nazirites, and the like; subsequently other arrangements were made for supplying cultic personnel while the erstwhile sanctity of the firstborn was lifted through redemption (cf. Lev. 27:1–8, and see below). This underlies the priestly traditions of the history of the levites and their selection for cultic service.

In the case of animals, male firstlings unfit for sacrificial use because they bore *blemishes or were of types considered impure could be redeemed by paying the assessed value of the animal, plus one-fifth (Lev, 27:26–27; cf. verses 9–13; Ex. 34:20; Deut. 15:19). The restriction of the requirement to male firstlings may reflect on economic consideration: very few males were needed for breeding purposes. This consideration may also figure in the predominance of male animals as sacrificial victims generally. Devoting firstlings to the cultic establishment served as a means of providing it with revenue (Num, 18:15–18; compare Deut. 15:19–23).

[Baruch A. Levine]

Redemption of the Firstborn

Rabbinic sources discuss at length methods of exchange and redemption (Mishnah, *Bekhorot* and *Temurah*). Neither kohanim nor levites need redeem their firstborn (Bek. 2:1). However, the firstborn son of a marriage between a kohen and a woman forbidden to him (e.g., a divorcee) does not have priestly rank and must be redeemed (Sh. Ar., YD 305:19), although the father may, in this case, keep the redemption money himself (R. Asher to Bek. 47b). In all cases the criterion is primogeniture from the mother's womb. A child is not regarded as a firstborn if his mother previously miscarried a fetus more than 40 days old (Sh. Ar., YD 305:23). Ordinary Jews whose wives are the daughters of kohanim or levites need not redeem their firstborn, but the son of a kohen's daughter and a non-Jew must be redeemed because his mother has forfeited her status. The firstborn son of a levite's daughter born under the same circumstances does not need to be redeemed (Bek. 47a). If there is a doubt regarding the primogeniture of a child, the child need not be redeemed (Sh. Ar., YD 305:22–25). The duty of redeeming the firstborn falls in the first instance upon the father. If he neglects to do so or if the child is an orphan, the son redeems himself when he reaches maturity (Kid. 29a). At one time a small medallion bearing the inscription *ben bekhor* was hung around the neck of such a child (Isserles to Sh. Ar., YD 305:15). It later became customary, however, for either the rabbinical court (*bet din*) or one of the child's male relatives to redeem him.

The Bible fixes the redemption fee at five silver shekels (Num. 18:16), and the father may choose any kohen to perform the ceremony by paying him this sum (in medieval times two Reichsthaler, today five U.S. dollars). It must be given in coins, but not money equivalents, such as securities, shares, etc. (Sh. Ar., YD 305:4). Special "redemption coins" are now minted in Israel for this purpose by the Bank of Israel and distributed by the Israel Government Coins and Medals Corporation. The kohen may return the money to the child's father (as did some rabbis in talmudic times, Bek. 51b), although the practice is condoned only when the father is very poor (Sh. Ar., TD, 305:8). On the other hand, the choice of a poor kohen (so as simultaneously to fulfill the *mitzvah* of charity) is approved.

The redemption ceremony (*pidyon ha-ben*) is held in the presence of the kohen and invited guests, and takes place on the 31st day after the birth. This is due to the fact that the child is not considered as fully viable until he survives the first 30 days of his life. Even if circumcision has not yet been performed (e.g., for health reasons), there should be no delay. Only if the 31st day is a Sabbath or festival is the ceremony postponed to the following weekday (*ibid.*, 305:11). During the ceremony, the father presents his son, often on a specially embellished tray, to the kohen who asks him, in an ancient Aramaic formula, whether he wishes to redeem the child or to leave him to the kohen. In some sources the formula is given in Hebrew. The father, in reply, expresses the desire to keep his son, hands the redemption money to the kohen, and recites one benediction for the fulfillment of the commandment of redemption, and another of thanksgiving (*She-Heḥeyanu*). The kohen, three times pronouncing "your son is redeemed," returns the child to the father, This dialogue is purely symbolic. A declaration by the father that he prefers the money to the child would have no legal validity. Finally, the kohen recites a benediction over a cup of wine, pronounces the priestly blessing on the child, and joins the invited guests at a festive banquet (*ibid.* 305:10 and Isserles ad loc.).

According to *halakhah* the biblical laws commanding the sacrifice of firstborn "clean" animals and the redemption of firstborn he-asses (Ex. 13:2,12–15; 34:19–20) should also be observed today. However, because of the suspension of the sacrificial system after the destruction of the Temple, the firstborn clean animals have to be given to a kohen after they have attained the age of 30 days (for sheep or goats) or 50 days (for large cattle). He keeps them, without deriving any benefit from them, either until they die a natural death – when the carcass may be used – or until they suffer a blemish which would have made them unfit as a sacrifice – when they may be eaten or used for any other purpose (Tur and Sh. Ar., YD 313:20). It is, however, forbidden to inflict a blemish deliberately (Sh. Ar., YD 313. 1). A firstborn he-ass should be redeemed from the kohen by giving him a sheep or its equivalent value in money (Tur and Sh. Ar., YD 321).

Fast of the Firstborn

Fast of the Firstborn (Heb. תַּעֲנִית בְּכוֹרִים, *ta'anit bekhorim*), fast observed by primogenital males on the 14th of Nisan i.e., the day before *Passover. This traditional custom seems to stem from the desire to express gratitude for the saving of the firstborn Israelites during the tenth plague in Egypt (Ex. 13:1ff.). According to talmudic sources (*Soferim*, ed. by M. Higger (1937), 21:1) the custom was already observed in mishnaic times. Another source mentions that R. Judah ha-Nasi fasted on this day; his fasting, however, is explained by some as a wish to stimulate his appetite for the *mazzah* (unleavened bread) at the *seder* meal (TJ, Pes. 10:1,37b and compare *Soferim*, loc. cit.). The fast became an accepted traditional custom obliging all males whether firstborn to their father or only to their mother, and in some opinions even firstborn women, to fast (Sh. Ar., OḤ 470:1). If a child is too young to fast (under the age of 13), his father fasts instead of him; if the father is firstborn, the child's mother fasts in lieu of the child (Isserles to OḤ 470:2). Should the first day of Passover be on a Sabbath, the fast is observed on the preceding Thursday; according to a more lenient ruling, it is suspended (*ibid.*). However, since one is permitted to break this fast in order to partake of a *se'udat mitzvah* (a meal accompanying a religious celebration, such as a circumcision) it was laid down that the celebration of the *hadran* constituted such a meal. The custom thus evolved to finish the study of a Talmud tractate on the morning before Passover, at which occasion a festive banquet is arranged in the synagogue, at which firstborns participate, and they need not therefore fast. Through this device, the Fast of the Firstborn is practically in desuetude (see *Fasting and Fastdays).

Legal Aspects Concerning the Firstborn

DEFINITION OF PRIMOGENITURE. The sole difference in the status of the firstborn son as compared with that of his brothers is his right to a greater share in their father's inheritance. This status is known as *bekhor le-naḥalah* (firstborn or primogeniture as to inheritance) and derives from the verse "he must acknowledge the firstborn the son of the unloved one, and allot to him a double portion of all he possesses; since he is the first fruit of his vigor, the birthright is his due" (Deut. 21:15–17). The firstborn in this context is the first son born to the father, even if not so to the mother, since it is written, "the first fruits of his vigor" (Bek. 8:1 and see commentators). Even if such a son is born of a prohibited union, e.g., the son of a priest and a divorced woman, or a *mamzer* born as first son to his father – he is included, on the strength of the words "he must acknowledge the firstborn, the son of the unloved one" (Deut., loc. cit.), the term a "loved" or an "unloved" wife being interpreted as relating only to the question whether the wife's marriage was "loved" or "unloved," i.e., permitted or prohibited (Yev. 23a and see Rashi and *Posekim* ad loc.). The prerogative of the firstborn never extends to a daughter, not even in a case where she has a right of inheritance (Sif. Deut. 215; see *Inheritance). A son born to a proselyte to Judaism, who had sons before he became a proselyte, does not enjoy the prerogative of a *bekhor le-naḥalah*, since he is not "the first fruits of his vigor" (Yev. 62a; Bek. 47a; *Posekim* ad loc.); on the other hand, if an Israelite had a son by a non-Jewish woman and thereafter has a son by a Jewish woman, the latter son does enjoy the prerogative, since the former is called her, and not his, son (Maim. Yad, Naḥalot 2:12). A first son who is born after his father's death, viz., if the mother gives birth to twins, is not considered a *bekhor le-naḥalah* since it is written "he must acknowledge" (Deut. 21:17) and the father is no longer alive to do so (BB 142b; Rashbam and *Posekim* ad loc.).

PROOF OF PRIMOGENITURE. In determining the fact of primogeniture reliance is placed upon the statements of three persons – the midwife, the mother, and the father. That the midwife is relied upon immediately after the son's birth (where twins are born) is derived from Genesis 38:28 (see TJ, Kid. 4:2,65d); the mother is relied on during the first seven days after childbirth, since the father has not yet succeeded in "accepting" or recognizing the child, as he does not pass out of his mother's hands until the circumcision; thereafter the father's determination is accepted at all times, since he "must acknowledge his son" – i.e., recognize the child as his firstborn son personally and before others. The father's determination is relied upon even if he thereby assails the status of his other sons, as may happen if he acknowledges as his firstborn the youngest of several sons borne by his wife after they married each other – thus characterizing the other sons as *mamzerim* (Yev. 47a; Kid. 74a and *Posekim* ad Lec.; see also *Mamzer*). However, the father is not believed in this last-mentioned case if the disqualified son already has children of his own, as the disqualification would also affect their status – for which purpose the law does not authorize reliance on his words (Yev. 47a and *Posekim; Ozar ha-Posekim*, EH, 1 (1955), 192, sec. 4:137).

4TH BIRTHRIGHT PREROGATIVE. The firstborn is entitled to a "double portion," that is, he takes twice the portion due to each of his brothers from their father's inheritance. Thus if the father has left a firstborn and two other sons, the former takes one-half and the latter one-quarter each of the estate (BB 122b–123a and *Posekim*). The prerogative does not extend to the mother's estate (BB 111b, 122b and Codes).

The firstborn takes a double portion only of the present and not of the contingent assets, i.e., only of the assets in the father's possession at the time of his death and not such as were due to come into his possession thereafter. Thus, if the father predeceased any of his own legators, the father's share in their estate passes through him to his own heirs, the firstborn taking only the share of an ordinary heir. This rule embraces debt still owing to the father at his death, even if under deed or bond, since the debt is considered an asset still to fall due and not yet in possession. If, however, the loan was secured by a pledge, or mortgage, the firstborn takes a double portion since in Jewish law the creditor acquires a right over the pledged property (Git. 37a) and a loan thus secured is therefore considered as an asset in possession (see generally Bek. 51b–52a; BB 125b; commentators and *Posekim* ad loc.). For the same reasons the firstborn does not take a double portion of improvements or increments from which the father's estate has benefited after his death, except with regard to natural increments – as for instance in the case of a sapling which has become full-grown (*ibid.*).

OBSERVANCE OF PREROGATIVE-PEREMPTORY ON THE FATHER. The above-mentioned underlying biblical injunction precludes the father from depriving the firstborn of his particular right of inheritance. Consequently, any form of testamentary disposition (see *Wills) by a father purporting to bequeath to the firstborn less than his prescribed double portion of the inheritance is null and void. This rule only applies, however, where the father has clearly adopted the language of a testator, since a father cannot change the laws of inheritance as such (Maim., Yad, Naḥalot 6:1). Consequently, if the father has expressed himself in terms of making a gift, his disposition will stand (although "the spirit of the sages takes no delight therein," BB 133b and see *Posekim*), since he may freely dispose of his assets by way of gift. Since the exercise of the birthright involves a corresponding greater liability for the debts of the estate, the firstborn may escape such additional liability by way of renouncing his prerogative before the division of the estate (BB 124a; Sh. Ar., ḤM 278:10).

STATE OF ISRAEL LAW. The Law of Inheritance 5725 – 1965 of the State of Israel does not include any prerogative of the firstborn.

[Ben-Zion (Benno) Schereschewsky]

BIBLIOGRAPHY: A.S. Hartom, in: EM, 2 (1954), 123–6 (incl. bibl.); I. Mendelsohn, in: BASOR, 156 (1959), 38–40; Redemption of the Firstborn: Eisenstein, Dinim, 43–4, 333–4; H. Schauss, *The Lifetime of a Jew* (1950), 18, 29, 48–50; N. Gottlieb, *A Jewish Child Is Born* (1960); Fast:, *Das mosaisch-talmudische Erbrecht* (1890), 12–14, nos. 16–20; R. Kirsch, *Der Erstgeborene nach mosaisch-talmudischem Recht*, 1 (1901); Gulak, Yesodei, 3 (1922), 10, 74–76, 78, 84f., 102, 131; Herzog, Instit, 1 (1936), 50; ET, 1 (1951^3), 4f.; 3 (1951), 276–83; 11 (1965), 37–39; B.-Z. Schereschewsky, *Dinei Mishpaḥah* (1967^2), 353–8. **ADD BIBLIOGRAPHY:** Elon, *Ha-Mishpat ha-Ivri* (1988), I, 110, 112, 279, 770, III, 1413; Idem., *Jewish Law* (1994), I, 124, 126, 329, II, 948, IV, 1683.

FIRST FRUITS, that portion of the fruits of each year's harvest that following the biblical injunction was to be taken to the Temple in Jerusalem.

In the Bible

The Hebrew term *bikkurim* and related terms for the "first fruits" derive from the same root as *bekhor*, "firstborn (see *Firstborn). On the same general principle that the firstborn of man and beast belonged to the God of Israel and were to be devoted to Him, the first fruits, including the first grains to ripen each season, were to be brought as an offering to God. Every Israelite who possessed the means of agricultural productivity was under this obligation (Ex. 23:19; 34:26, Num. 15:17–21; 18:12–13; Deut. 26:1–11). A frequent synonym for *bikkurim* is *reshit*, "the first [fruits]."

Deuteronomy 26:1–11 contains detailed procedures for the offering of the first fruits, including the text of a liturgical recitation incumbent upon any who offered their first fruits in the sanctuary. The manner of oblation prescribed in that passage represents a distinctive mode, whereby the substances involved were not burnt on the altar but were merely displayed, and later assigned to the priests as part of their cultic income (cf. Num. 18:12–13; Deut. 18:3–5). On the other hand, Leviticus 2:14 speaks of *minḥat bikkurim*, "a grain offering of first fruits," prescribing that part of it be burnt on the altar. It would seem, therefore, that at least some of the grain brought as first fruits was disposed of in that manner, although the prescription of Leviticus may reflect the tendency to accommodate older forms of sacrifice to the particularly Israelite practice of the burnt offering. It is difficult to identify this *minḥah* within the context of first fruit offerings. It has been identified with the "grain offering of fresh grain" (*minḥah ḥadashah*) of Leviticus 23:16; but that poses a problem, since the rule was that no leavened dough could be brought up on the altar, and the offering of fresh grain mentioned in that passage was to be baked from leavened dough. The offerings of first fruits were both an individual obligation and a part of public festival celebrations, particularly the celebration of *Shavuot, also called *Ḥag ha-Bikkurim*, "the first fruits festival" (Ex. 23:16; 34:22; Lev. 23:16–17; Num. 28:26).

A sheaf of the new barley harvest (*ʿomer*) was offered on the second day of the Passover festival (Lev. 23:10–11, 15–16). According to the Mishnah (Bik. 1:3, 6, 9), in Second Temple times the pilgrimage to the Temple for the purpose of offering the first fruits could be undertaken anytime between Shavuot, in the late spring, and *Sukkot, in the fall (but see below), but the festival of Shavuot was the first date for this offering. A rite notionally related to the offering of first fruits was the bringing of the fruit of trees during their fourth year of fruit bearing (Lev. 19:23–25). In both cases, an offering was required to release the fruit, as it were, for consumption by its owners. According to Leviticus 23:17, the offering of fresh grain was to be presented in the form of two loaves of baked, leavened bread.

There are no specifications as to the amounts or percentages of seasonal yield required for the offering of first fruits, but there does exist, on the other hand, a text for the recitation which was to accompany the offering, in Deuteronomy 26:5–10. A part of it has been incorporated in the Passover *Haggadah*. It consists of a review of Israel's early history, tracing Israelite origins to the pre-Egyptian period, and expressing gratitude to God for the redemption from Egypt. It culminates in an acknowledgment that as an Israelite, the one reciting the declaration is thankful for having been brought to the rich Promised Land, in recognition of which he is offering the first fruits of the land as a sacrifice. Only a few such recitations are preserved in the Torah, another being designated for the bringing of a type of tithe (Deut. 26:13–15).

Typologically, the offering of first fruits would seem to represent a very ancient practice, and yet it is not referred to in the historical books of the Bible, in descriptions of cultic activity, and most references are limited to the Pentateuch, post-Exilic literature and the Book of Ezekiel. The celebration mentioned in Judges 9:27, in connection with the grape harvest, may be related to the offering of first fruits, and a possible reference may be I Samuel 2:29. The Book of Proverbs (3:9) refers to the practice as a prerequisite to securing God's material blessings. As noted above, certain problems remain in reconciling the codes of Leviticus and Deuteronomy, and generally speaking, the biblical evidence leaves some gaps in understanding precisely how the rites connected with the first fruits operated.

[Baruch A. Levine]

In Halakhah

According to rabbinic interpretation the duty of bringing first fruits was confined to the seven distinct species growing in Ereẓ Israel, i.e., wheat, barley, grapes, figs, pomegranates, olive oil, and dates ("honey"). The fruits were given to the priests after the donor had recited the confession (Deut. 26; 1–11) acknowledging God as the one who redeemed the Israelites from the Egyptian bondage, and expressing gratitude to God who brought them to the Promised Land. The *bikkurim* were brought between Shavuot (hence its designation as *Ḥag ha-Bikkurim* – "the first fruits festival") and Sukkot. They could be brought as late as *Ḥanukkah, but after Sukkot no declaration was made.

If the fruits were stolen or became unclean or unfit for consumption, others had to be brought. A proselyte also had to offer the first fruits but he did not recite the confession as he could not say "which the Lord swore unto our fathers to give us" (Deut. 26:3). An Israelite (i.e., one who was not a priest or levite) was strictly forbidden to eat the first fruits; if he consumed them in error, a fifth of their worth in money had to be added as restitution (penalty). The Mishnah (Bik. 3:2–9) gives a vivid account of the first fruit offering ceremony in the period of the Second Temple. In the early morning hours, the people gathered in the open squares of the district towns and started their journey to Jerusalem, singing "Arise ye and let us go up to Zion, unto the Lord our God." The people walked in procession headed by an ox whose horns were wreathed with gold and silver, and his head with olive branches. The pilgrims were accompanied by musicians playing the flute. Rich people took the first fruits in baskets of silver and gold, while the poor carried them in wicker baskets made of peeled willow branches (which they gave to the priests together with the first fruits). The baskets contained the choicest fruits and had pigeons perched on top; these were sacrificed at the Temple. At the outskirts of Jerusalem, the procession was met by the Temple prefects and treasurers, and the pilgrims were escorted amid the cheers of the populace to the Temple Mount. There the choir of the levites welcomed them with the chanting of Psalm 30. Originally, everyone who could recite the confession did so by himself. However, in order not to shame those who did not know the text (and might, therefore, refrain from offering the first fruit) it was ordained that all people repeat the confession as it was read to them by the priest.

Those who lived close to Jerusalem brought fresh fruit and those who lived far, dried fruits. The minimum quantity of first fruits that could be offered was 1/60 of the harvest. The first fruit had to be brought only from the harvest of the soil of historic *Ereẓ Israel. According to rabbinic law, however, this included also sore parts of Transjordan and southern Syria.

The first-fruit offering was accompanied by other *shelamim* ("peace offerings") and the pilgrims were bound, out of respect for the Temple, to stay in Jerusalem overnight before returning to their villages (Deut. 16:7). Like all *terumah* ("heave offerings"), the first fruits were consumed by the priests. A priest in mourning for a relative was, however, forbidden to eat them. With the destruction of the Temple, the duty of first-fruit offerings was suspended. The description of the first-fruit offering in the Mishnah *Bikkurim* is corroborated by Philo (Spec. 2:215–222).

In modern Israel, the kibbutzim hold *bikkurim* celebrations on Shavuot which are evocative of the ancient Temple ritual. The children participate in a procession in which agricultural products are carried and donations are made to the Jewish National Fund for land reclamation.

BIBLIOGRAPHY: IN BIBLE: E.S. Hartom, in: EM, 2 (1954), 126–8, incl. bibl. IN HALAKHAH: Maim. Yad, Bikkurim 1–4; Eisenstein, Dinim, s.v. *Bikkurim;* S. Safrai, *Ha-Aliyyah la-Regel bi-Ymei ha-Bayit ha-Sheni* (1965), 224–8; H. Schauss, *The Jewish Festivals* (1938), 177–9. See also bibliography to *Shavuot.

FIRT (Fuerth), JULIUS (1897–1979), Czech journalist and publisher. Born in Sestrouň near Sedlčany (Bohemia), he became director of the Borový and Lidové Noviny publishing houses in 1936 and during the 1920s and 1930s attended the *Pátečníci* gatherings (see *Fischer, Otokar). He escaped from Czechoslovakia to England, where he worked for the Czechoslovak government-in-exile. Back home, from 1945 to 1948 he served as a deputy in Parliament and was in charge of the Melantrich publishing house. During his second exile, after 1948, he was director of Radio Free Europe in Munich.

Firt became well known for his book *Knihy a osudy* ("Books and Fates") published in exile and smuggled into Czechoslovakia, where it was published only in 1991. It presents a picture of the spiritual and cultural atmosphere of Masaryk's First Republic as well as a wealth of information about Czech writers, poets, and journalists such as Josef and Karel Čapek, Ferdinand Peroutka, Karel *Poláček, Ivan *Olbracht, Vítězslav Nezval, Karel Teige, Bedřich Fučík, the actor Hugo Haas, etc. Firt also contributed two articles about the role of Jews in the First Republic to *Die Burg* (1973–74; "The Castle"). His *Záznamy* (1985; "Notes") appeared posthumously describing Czechoslovakia's political situation in 1948 and his exile in London during World War II.

BIBLIOGRAPHY: A. Mikulášek et al., *Literatura s hvězdou Davidovou*, vol. 1 (1998); *Slovník českých spisovatelů* (1982).

[Milos Pojar (2nd ed.)]

FĪRŪZ, Karaite family, probably of Persian origin, prominent from the 12th to 19th centuries. Its members were authors, physicians, poets, envoys, copyists, and bibliophiles. Approximately 50 members of the family can be traced. They include: AL-SHAMS AL-KARĪM IBN, head of the Karaites in Cairo in 1465 and court banker; and MOSES BEN ISAIAH, Karaite scholar active in Damascus, 1630–45. An engraver by profession, Moses b. Isaiah is referred to as "Yerushalmi," indicating that he had made a pilgrimage to Jerusalem. Possibly he should be identified with Moses b. Isaiah Fīrūz, the *ḥazzan* in Damascus, a translator from Arabic into Hebrew, mentioned in the itinerary of the Karaite *Samuel b. David. His son DANIEL BEN MOSES, author and physician, active 1663–1700, wrote *Kitāb al-Murshid*, an Arabic compendium of the *Duties of the Heart* of *Baḥya b. Joseph ibn Paquda. Fīrūz included in this a Karaite chain of tradition. He is probably the author of an Arabic introduction to the Karaite prayer book according to the Damascus rite published by Margoliouth. Poznański listed Fīrūz' liturgical poetry and also published his polemical poems directed against *Shabbetai Ẓevi and *Nathan of Gaza.

BIBLIOGRAPHY: S. Pinsker, *Likkutei Kadmoniyyot* (1860), 61, 167–9 (second pagination); Steinschneider, Arab Lit, 158; G. Margoliouth, in: JQR, 18 (1905/06), 505–27; H. Hirschfeld, in: *Jews' College Jubilee Volume* (1906), 81–100; S. Poznański, in: MGWJ, 57 (1913), 44–58, 620; 60 (1916), 149–52; Mann, Texts, index.

[Isaak Dov Ber Markon]

FIRZOGERIN, Yiddish word for "foresayer" or "precentor"; also *zogerke*. It came to refer to the woman who led prayers in the women's section of the synagogue. Since women were separated from men during worship, sometimes in a separate room, they needed a leader to help them follow the proper order of the service. This leader, reciting vernacular translations, enabled less educated women, who did not know Hebrew and often were illiterate, to pray in their own language. The *firzogerin* was probably not an official position in the Jewish community until late in the 16th century, and it was not firmly established as an East European institution until the 18th century. However, there is evidence that women functioned in that capacity during medieval times, especially in Germany. According to a poetic eulogy written by her husband, *Eleazar ben Judah of Worms, in the late 12th century, *Dulcea of Worms was said to know "the order of the morning and evening prayers…. In all the cities she taught women, enabling their pleasant intoning of songs." The 13th-century Richenza of Nürenberg is described in a contemporaneous martyrology book as a leader in the women's synagogue, and the gravestone of Urania of Worms, a cantor's daughter, calls her a prayer leader who "officiated before the women to whom she sang the hymnal portions." In the 14th century, Guta bat Nathan was "… the important young woman who prayed for the women in her gentle prayers." Ashkenazi Jews migrating into Italy in the 15th century may have brought this custom with them. Sixteenth-century documents describe Anna d'Arpino leading women's prayers in the synagogue in Rome on Saturdays and holidays, a job for which she was paid (although this was not always the case). The poet Deborah *Ascarelli, a Sephardi woman living in Rome, may also have been a prayer leader. She knew Hebrew and translated many parts of the Sephardi service into Italian, especially for women.

As Jews moved into Eastern Europe, the female precentor became an accepted institution. Often, the *firzogerin* was the rabbi's wife or daughter; she was likely to be the most learned woman in the community and often had some knowledge of Hebrew. Some later *firzogerins* wrote their own Yiddish translations of the psalms and prayers, sometimes adding heartfelt appeals that related to women's lives. Beginning in the 17th century, many of these prayers had kabbalistic overtones and some revealed a high level of Jewish scholarship.

By the 18th century, a number of well-educated women were serving as *firzogerins*; some wrote petitionary prayers called *tkhines* for women to recite both in the synagogue and at home. The 18th-century pseudonymous Sarah *Bas-Tovim was a prolific writer of *tkhines*. After her death male writers appropriated her name to ensure the popularity of their own vernacular prayers. The figure of the *firzogerin* or *zogerke* continued into the 20th century; she is described in the anthropological study of the shtetl, *Life Is With People*, as a woman who "unlike most of them, is able to read and understand Hebrew. She reads the prayers and they repeat it after her, following each syllable and intonation…" A few of these women prayer leaders immigrated to the United States in the large migration of Jews that began in the 1880s, but by the second half of the 20th century, the *firzogerin* had disappeared in both Europe and the Americas, made obsolete by the Sho'ah and an almost universal standard of literacy for women.

BIBLIOGRAPHY: E. Taitz,, S. Henry and C. Tallan. *The JPS Guide to Jewish Women: 600 B.C.E.-1900 C.E.* (2003), 77–78, 101; C. Weissler, *Voices of the Matriarchs: Listening to the Prayers of Early Modern Jewish Women* (1998); M. Zborowski and E. Herzog, *Life Is with People: The Culture of the Shtetl* (1974), 54; I. Zinberg, *A History of Jewish Literature*, vol. 7, trans. and ed. Bernard Martin (1975), 23, 249–59.

[Emily Taitz (2nd ed.)]

FISCH, HAROLD (**Aharon Harel Fisch**; 1923–), author and critic. Fisch was born in Birmingham, England, where his father was rabbi. He studied at the University of Sheffield and at Oxford and in 1947 was appointed lecturer in English at Leeds University. In 1957, he immigrated to Israel, where he was appointed associate professor of English Literature and head of the English department at Bar-Ilan University. He became full professor in 1964 and served as rector of the university from 1968 to 1971. He served as the *Encyclopaedia Judaica* departmental editor for English literature. His publications include *The Dual Image: The Figure of the Jew in English and American Literature* (1959, 1971²), *Jerusalem and Albion: the Hebraic Factor in Seventeenth-Century Literature* (1964), *Hamlet and the Word: The Covenant Pattern in Shakespeare* (1971), *S.Y. Agnon* (1975), and *The Zionist Revolution* (1978).

He has also translated a number of works, including the Jerusalem Bible (1969). Fisch has been prominent in the Land of Israel Movement (*Ha-Tenu'ah le-Ma'an Ereẓ Israel ha-Shelemah). In 1971, he founded the Institute for Judaism and Contemporary Thought, of which he is chairman. This institute holds an international colloquium each year and conducts study groups on aspects of contemporary Jewish experience.

FISCHEL, ARNOLD (1830–1894), religious leader, historian, and advocate for the American Jewish chaplaincy. Born in Holland, Fischel began his career in 1849 as a speaker on Hebrew literature in Brighton and Portsmouth, England. He published essays on such themes as "The Cosmogony of Moses" and "The Laws of Israel as Represented by the Greeks and Romans," and translated Maimonides' *Moreh Nevukhim* (*Guide for the Perplexed*) from the Arabic original. In 1851, he was engaged as lecturer by the Old Hebrew Congregation of Liverpool.

In 1856, Fischel accepted the invitation of Shearith Israel of New York City, the oldest Jewish congregation in America, to become its first permanent lecturer. He was welcomed by both the Orthodox and Reform press, and was active in the Hebrew Benevolent Society, Chevra Bikur Cholim VeKadesh, and Touro Literary Institute, among others. His synagogue sermons stressed Orthodox beliefs and praised the United States as a haven for Jewish freedom. In his Thanksgiving Day sermon of 1860, he supported the Union in the Civil War as more sympathetic to the Jews than the individual states.

Fischel sought to give positive portrayals of Jewish history to Christian audiences, commencing with his address on the Holy Land to the American Geographical and Statistical Society in 1858. He established his reputation as a pioneering historian of American Jewry with his address on "the history of the Jews in America" at the New York Historical Society in 1859 and again in 1861. He correctly authenticated Medieval Spanish Jewish coins discovered in Ohio in his 1861 talk at the American Ethnographical Society.

In 1861, Congress had enacted a law requiring that all military chaplains be Christian ministers, and the first Jew to be elected a chaplain, Michael Allen, was forced to resign. As a challenge to the law, Fischel applied for a chaplaincy and was refused because of his religion. With the authorization of the (Orthodox) Board of Delegates of American Israelites, Fischel traveled to Washington, D.C., to lobby for a change in the law while serving as a civilian chaplain for Jewish soldiers in the region.

Fischel secured a meeting with President Lincoln on December 11, 1861, gained the president's support, and proceeded to lobby members of Congress. Christian views were divided between advocates of religious pluralism and Christian fundamentalists. After a broad public debate, the law was amended by Congress in July 1862 to accept chaplains of all religious denominations.

The Board of Delegates applied for a chaplaincy for Fischel, but the request was denied as unnecessary for the small number of Jewish soldiers in his region. Discouraged by this, and by a lack of support for other projects he envisioned on behalf of Jewish soldiers, Fischel returned permanently to Holland in 1864.

BIBLIOGRAPHY: J. Waxman, "Arnold Fischel 'Unsung Hero' in American Israel," in: *American Jewish Historical Quarterly*, 60:4 (June 1971), 325–43; B.W. Korn, *American Jewry and the Civil War* (1951); L.M. Berkowitz, "The Rabbi of the Potomac: Rev. Dr. Arnold Fischel ז"ל," in: *Torah Lives* (1995); H. Grinstein, *The Rise of the Jewish Community of New York* (1945); D. and T. de Sola Pool, *An Old Faith in the New World* (1955).

[Mark L. Smith (2nd ed.)]

FISCHEL, HARRY (1865–1948), U.S. businessman and philanthropist. Fischel was born in Meretz, Russia, and emigrated in 1885 to the United States, settling in New York City. There he entered the construction and real estate business and built up a sizable company employing largely Jewish builders, to whom he granted both Saturday and Sunday as paid days off at a time when the six-day week was universal in the trade. Fischel also soon became involved in Jewish communal affairs, concentrating on a number of institutions with which he remained associated in various capacities for the remainder of his life, particularly the Hebrew Immigrant Aid Society (after 1890), Beth Israel Hospital (after 1900), and the American Jewish Committee (after 1906). Shortly after the Balfour Declaration, he was active in the establishment of a number of development companies in Palestine. In 1932 he retired from business and devoted himself entirely to his philanthropic endeavors, which included the endowment of the Harry Fischel Foundation for Research in Talmud in Palestine (1933), and large donations to Yeshiva University during the depression of the 1930s. His attempts to get the New York Sabbath laws to recognize Saturday as the official Jewish day of rest are recorded in the biography of him by his son-in-law, Herbert Samuel *Goldstein, *Forty Years of Struggle for a Principle* (1928). Fischel died in Jerusalem, where he spent the final year of his life.

FISCHEL, WALTER JOSEPH (1902–1973), scholar of Oriental Jewry. Fischel was born in Frankfurt on the Main. From 1926 to 1945 he was a member of the faculty of Oriental studies in the Hebrew University of Jerusalem, taking part in several expeditions to all countries of the Near and Middle East and India. From 1945 he was professor of Semitic languages and literature at the University of California, Berkeley. After his retirement in 1970 he was appointed professor of Jewish studies and history at the Santa Cruz campus of the University of California. Fischel's publications centered around two major research areas: medieval Islamic civilization and Jewish civilization. In the former field, his major publications include *Ibn Khaldun and Tamerlane-Their Dramatic Meeting in Damascus in 1401* (1952), *Ibn Khaldun in Egypt* (1967), and *Jews in the Economic and Political Life of Medieval Islam* (1937; reissued with an essay as *The Court Jew in the Islamic World*, 1969). He wrote on economic aspects of medieval Islam. In his research on Jewish civilization, he stressed the history and literature of the Jewish Diaspora in the Orient, especially *Iraq, *Kurdistan, *Persia, *Afghanistan, *Bukhara, and *India. He discovered many significant documents in Dutch, Portuguese, and Indian archives. His works on Persia include *The Bible in Persian Translation*, *Israel in Iran–A Survey of the Judeo-Persian Literature*, and *History of the Jews in Persia and Central Asia and Their Literature*. On the Jews of India he wrote many monographs including a comprehensive work in Hebrew, *Ha-Yehudim be-Hodu* (1960). Fischel served as departmental editor of the *Encyclopaedia Judaica* for the history of the Jews in Persia, Afghanistan, Central Asia, and India.

FISCHELS, MEIR BEN EPHRAIM (also known as **Meir Fischels**; 1703–1769/70), rabbi and talmudist. He was born in Bunzlau, and was a descendant of Judah Leib b. Bezalel ("the Maharal") of Prague and a contemporary of Ezekiel Landau. His father is mentioned under the name Ephraim b. Meir Bums (Bimes) Margolioth of Bunzlau. Meir Fischels served for 40 years as head of the *bet din* and the yeshivah in Prague until his death. Of his work nothing has remained apart from a few responsa collected by his son and by his contemporary Eleazar Fleckeles, all his manuscripts having been burnt in the great fire that swept Prague in 1754, except for his novellae on *Bava Batra* and *Berakhot* that were still extant in 1905. He was a signatory of the ruling given in 1754 of the *Allufei ha-Kehillah* ("leaders of the community") with regard to the settlement of the disputes that arose in consequence of the conflagration. His name appears as Mayer Feischel Buntzl in the list of those who suffered loss through the fire. Ezekiel Landau refers to him as "enlightening me as well as halakhic scholars" (responsa *Noda bi-Yhudah*, YD, no, 82), makes appreciative reference to his erudition and capacity (no. 72), and mentions his halakhic decisions (nos.81, 83, 89).

BIBLIOGRAPHY: K. Lieben, *Gal-Ed* (1856), 55–56, no. 114 (German section); 60–61, no. 114 (Hebrew section); S.H. Lieben, in: JJLG, 2 (1904), 329–30; 18 (1927), 193; S. Seeligmann, *Catalog … hebraeischer und juedischer Buecher, Handschriften … Nachgelassen von N.H. Van Biema* (1904), xi–xiv; Ta-Shema, in: *Ha-Sefer*, 9 (1961), 47–49.

[Yehoshua Horowitz]

FISCHER, Czech family. MOSES (1759–1833), son of Meir *Fischels, was active in the *Haskalah movement in Prague. Fischer signed with Raphael *Joel a petition (1790) to allow Jews to serve in the army, stating that fulfillment of military service was more important than the meticulous observance of religious commandments. He corresponded with Moses *Mendelssohn on his commentary on the Pentateuch, among other subjects, and was a member of the *Gesellsehaft der jungen Hebraeer. Later he became Orthodox and from 1816 served as rabbi in Vienna and as *kashrut* supervisor. In 1829 he settled in Eisenstadt.

Moses' son MARCUS (Meir, Maier; 1788–1858) moved from Vienna to Prague around 1810 and became a clerk in the Bohemian Jewish tax administration. Influenced by Baruch and Ignaz *Jeiteles, Marcus began to write in both Hebrew and German on historical themes. In 1812 he published two parts of a history of Rome in Hebrew, *Korot Yemei Kedem* (the published parts covering the period until the fifth century B.C.E.), which he stated could teach devotion to duty, heroism, and patriotism. In 1817 Fischer published in Hebrew a history of Moroccan Jewry between the seventh and the ninth centuries based on historical material written in several languages.

Marcus falsified a manuscript, the so-called Ramshak or Wallerstein chronicle. He put German "translations" from the Aramaic and Yiddish sections that it allegedly contained at the disposal of Moses Wolf *Jeiteles who incorporated them in *Zikkaron le-Yom Aharon* (1828). These quotations show that there were good relations between Jews and gentiles during the *Hussite period, and attest to the existence of customs which the Prague *maskilim* were then intending to introduce. Fischer's falsification was apparently influenced by the nascent Czech national ideologies, which led the Czech patriot priest Wenceslas Hanka around the same time to falsify old manuscripts in order to demonstrate the antiquity of Czech literature. Fischer also published the *Historisches Taschenbuch fuer Israeliten und Israelitinnen* (1811), as well as a collection of poems, and several articles in *Sulamit*. His writings reflect his sympathies for republicanism, his appreciation of *Joseph II, and his opposition to the French Revolution.

BIBLIOGRAPHY: I. Gastfreund, *Die Wiener Rabbinen* (1879), 110–12; B. Wachstein, *Grabinschriften … Eisenstadt* (1922), 217–20, Heb. part, 153 no. 713; S.H. Lieben, in: JGGJČ, 1 (1929), 369–409; R. Kestenberg-Gladstein, *Neuere Geschichte der Juden in den boehmischen Laendern*, 1 (1969), index.

[Meir Lamed]

FISCHER, ANNIE (1914–1995), Hungarian pianist. Born in Budapest, Fisher studied in the Liszt Academy of Music with Arnold Szekely and Dohnani, and made her début in 1922, playing Beethoven's First Concerto. In 1922 she made her European début playing in Zurich. Fischer won the Franz Liszt international Competition in Budapest in 1933 with a mature and brilliant performance of Liszt's B minor sonata. She embarked on an international career, interrupted by the war years, which she spent mainly in Sweden. She made her American début in 1961 and appeared at the Salzburg festival in 1964. Although she toured throughout the world as concert pianist and recitalist, she remained essentially a European-based artist.

In 1949, 1955, and 1965 Fischer received the Kossuth prize, Hungary's highest cultural award. In 1965 she was made honorary professor at Budapest's Academy of Music and in 1974 received the Red Banner Order of Labor. Fischer established a reputation as a pianist of unique and visionary intensity. Her range of keyboard color was wide, from a tender crystal sound in Mozart, through a restrained and colorful Schumann, to a stormy and vigorous rendition of the Beethoven sonatas. As a profound pianist her interpretation was noble and intelligent, with a formidable command of structure. Fischer played music from Bach to Bartók. Mozart, Beethoven, and Schumann were central to her repertory, but she could equally master Chopin, Schubert, and Brahms. Inspirational and unpredictable, she made few recordings.

BIBLIOGRAPHY: Grove online; MGG²; A. Schiff and T. Vasary, *Annie Fischer* (2002); T. Vasary, "Memories of Annie Fischer," in: *The Hungarian Quarterly* (1995).

[Naama Ramot (2nd ed.)]

FISCHER, BERNARD (b. 1821), Austrian rabbi and author. Fischer was born in the village of Budikau, in Bohemia. He received his Ph.D. degree from the University of Prague in 1850. Fischer served as the rabbi of various small congregations in the district of Eger. He prepared new editions of Buxtorf's rabbinic lexicon (1873) and Wiener's Chaldaic grammar (1882). He also edited *Bikkurei Ha-Ittim*, an illustrated Hebrew monthly, in Leipzig in 1863.

°**FISCHER, CAROLUS** (**Karl**; 1755–1844), Christian Hebraist. Fischer was librarian of Prague University and served as government-appointed censor of Hebrew books and translator in Prague from 1788 (see *Censorship), the first layman to serve in this capacity. Fischer was on friendly terms with Eleazar *Fleckeles. His query about the validity of a Jew's oath to a gentile appears in Fleckeles' *Teshuvah me-Ahavah* (no. 26). He wrote notes to Moses *Landau's Aramaic-German dictionary and an introduction to Leopold *Dukes' German translation of Rashi's commentary on the Pentateuch. In 1813 he submitted to the authorities a memorandum concerning the use of the term *nokhri* in talmudic literature; he left a summary of his opinions on Jewish problems based on his experiences in censorship (dated 1814). Fischer's *Gutmeinung ueber den Talmud der Hebraeer* (completed in 1802) was published by Emanuel *Baumgarten in 1883 as a contribution to the *Bloch-*Rohling controversy over the Talmud. Two manuscript volumes mainly containing Fischer's Hebrew correspondence with Eleazar Fleckeles, Bezalel *Ranschburg, and other scholars, as well as paragraphs he had deleted from books, are in the Prague University library. Fischer was in personal contact with members of the *Gesellschaft der jungen Hebraeer, and permitted Israel *Landau and Meir (Marcus) *Fischer to use the university library, closed until then to Jews.

BIBLIOGRAPHY: G. Kisch, in: JGGJČ, 2 (1930), 469–70; F. Roubík, *ibid.*, 6 (1934), 292–5; 7 (1935), 305–16, 364–8; S.H. Lieben, in: MGWJ, 62 (1918), 49–56; R. Kestenberg-Gladstein, *Neuere Geschichte der Juden in den boehmischen Laendern* (1969), index; idem, in: *Judaica Bohemiae*, 4 (1968), 68–70.

FISCHER, EDMOND (1920–), U.S. biochemist. Fischer was born in Shanghai and from age seven was educated in Switzerland where he graduated in biology and chemistry from the University of Geneva and obtained his D.Sc. in chemistry under the direction of Kurt Meyer. After research appointments at the Rockefeller Institute, New York, and the California Institute of Technology, Pasadena, he joined the department of biochemistry of the University of Washington, Seattle (1953), where he was appointed professor (1961) and professor emeritus from 1990. Fischer's main research discoveries relate to protein phosphorylation, the process involved in vital metabolic activities such as providing energy from stored sugar in active muscles. He and his colleagues helped to elucidate the enzymes controlling phosphorylation and the regulation of these enzymes. He was awarded the Nobel Prize in Physiology or Medicine (1992) jointly with Edwin Krebs. Subsequently he made important contributions to elucidating the way in which protein phosphatases help to orchestrate the response of cells to external stimuli. His many honors include the Werner Medal of the Swiss Chemical Society, the Senior Passano Award, and election to the American Academy of Arts and Sciences (1972) and the U.S. National Academy of Sciences (1973). He is an accomplished pianist who contemplated a career in music before turning to chemistry.

[Michael Denman (2nd ed.)]

FISCHER, GYULA (**Julius**; 1861–1944), Hungarian scholar and rabbi, Born in Sárkeresztur, Fischer studied at the Budapest rabbinical seminary and was appointed rabbi of Györ (Raab) in 1887, Prague in 1898, and Budapest (1905) where he was chief rabbi (1921–43). In 1905 he became lecturer in rabbinic literature and Midrash at the rabbinical seminary, and for a time was acting director of the seminary. A man of wide Jewish and general erudition, Fischer wrote a monograph on Judah ibn Tibbon (1885) and translated into Hungarian Philo's *Life of Moses* (1925). He contributed many articles and essays in German and Hungarian to Jewish and general periodicals. Fischer was a gifted orator and one of the first Hungarian Neolog rabbis to support the rebuilding of Ereẓ Israel.

BIBLIOGRAPHY: I. Hahn, in; *Catalogue of the Jewish Theological Seminary of Hungary*, 67–69 (1946), 22–23 (Hg.).

[Baruch Yaron]

FISCHER, JEAN (1871–1929), Zionist leader in Belgium. Born in Cracow, Fischer emigrated to Belgium in his youth and became a prominent diamond merchant. He was an active supporter of Herzl's political Zionism. During World War I he initiated the transfer of the *Jewish National Fund office to the Hague and, together with Jaeobus *Kann, Nehemiah *de Lieme, and Julius *Simon, was a member of the committee established to run the activities of the Zionist Organization. Active in all spheres of Jewish public life in Belgium, Fischer headed the Zionist Federation for many years. In addition to many articles on Zionist matters, he published *Das heutige Palaestina* (1908), a book about his 1907 visit to Ereẓ Israel. The moshavah Kefar Yonah in the Plain of Sharon is named after him.

[Getzel Kressel]

His son MAURICE (1903–1965) was an Israeli diplomat. Born in Antwerp, he settled in Palestine in 1930 and was a founder of Kefar Yonah. In 1931 he founded the Mattaʾei ha-Sharon Agricultural Development Company. During World War II he served as an officer in the Free French Army and was twice decorated. In the crucial years of 1947–48 Fischer, then in France, served as official delegate of the Jewish Agency Political Department. Later he served in France as Israel's diplomatic representative, and eventually ambassador, until 1953. At the same time he headed the Israel delegation to UNESCO. In 1948 he was cosignatory of the Fischer-Chauvel Agreement, which defined the status of French institutions in the newly founded State of Israel. From 1953 to 1957 he was minister to Turkey, and from 1960 until his death ambassador to Italy.

[Netanel Lorch]

BIBLIOGRAPHY: Tidhar, 2 (1961), 3750–51; *Haolam* (1929), 1037; (1930), 15.

FISCHER, JOSEF (1871–1949), rabbi, historian of Danish Jewry. Born in Hungary, Fischer served as *dayyan* and librarian of the Copenhagen Jewish community from 1893, and was in charge of its welfare work from 1901 to 1932. He was a leading member of the Mizrachi movement in Denmark. Fischer wrote extensively on the genealogy of Jewish families in Denmark and the history of Danish Jewry in general; some of his studies were translated into English and German. He edited the *Tidsskrift for Jødisk Historie og Litteratur* ("Journal for Jewish History and Literature") in 1917–25 and contributed to the *Dansk Biografisk Leksikon.* His son LEO became president of the Copenhagen Jewish community in 1964.

[Bent Melchior]

FISCHER, LOUIS (1896–1970), U.S. author and journalist, authority on Soviet Russia. Fischer, who was born in Philadelphia, worked first as a teacher. In 1917 he enlisted in the Jewish Legion recruited by the British in World War I to fight in Palestine. The war was over by the time he arrived in Palestine, but he stayed on to familiarize himself with the country and to become acquainted with Jewish leaders. In 1922 he went to Russia where he remained for 14 years. No foreign journalist then or later came to know so many of the top leaders of the Revolution. *Oil Imperialism* (1926) was Fischer's first book on the Soviet Union. Permitted by the Foreign Commissariat to study their archives, he wrote the highly authoritative two-volume study, *The Soviets in World Affairs* (1930). With the Stalinist purges in the mid-thirties, when many of his close friends were sent to concentration camps or shot, Fischer left the Soviet Union and went to Spain. There he enlisted in the International Brigades and, after the collapse of the Republican regime, went on a tour round the world. He took a particular interest in India, where he became a close friend of Mahatma *Gandhi and Jawaharlal Nehru. Later Fischer became disillusioned with Communism and he participated in *The God that Failed* (1950), a symposium of noted writers who had abandoned their belief in Communism. His books include: *Why Recognize Russia?* (1933); *Soviet Journey* (1935); *The War in Spain* (1937); *Stalin and Hitler* (1940); an autobiography, *Men and Politics* (1941); *Dawn of Victory* (1942); *Gandhi and Stalin* (1947); *The Life of Mahatma Gandhi* (1950); *The Life and Death of Stalin* (1952); *Russia, America and the World* (1961); and *The Life of Lenin* (1964). In 1959 he became a member of the Institute of Advanced Study at Princeton University, and later a research associate and lecturer at the Woodrow Wilson School of the university.

[Maurice Gerschon Hindus]

FISCHER, MORITZ VON (1800–1900), Hungarian porcelain manufacturer. Fischer's porcelain company in Herend, Hungarian, rendered distinguished service to the country's industry and art. He was compelled to struggle against innumerable difficulties before he succeeded in developing his small factory in 1839. Because of the company s skills and talent, it became a veritable art institute, comparing favorably with the established porcelain establishments such as those in Berlin and Meissen. The company was represented at a large number of international exhibitions, and invariably was awarded first prizes. In recognition of his services, Fischer's grandson, Eugène von Fischer, was raised to the nobility by Emperor Francis Joseph I in 1869.

FISCHER, OTOKAR (1883–1938), Czech writer, poet, playwright, translator, and critic. Fischer, who was born into an assimilated Jewish family in Kolín, Bohemia, became professor of German literature at Prague's Czech university. He edited the literary reviews *Kritika* and *Jeviště*, contributed to other important Czech periodicals, and served as the director of the Prague National Theater. One of the outstanding exponents of Czech culture between the two world wars, Fischer was a prolific writer. His voluminous series of essays and monographs include two volumes on Heine, studies of Kleist and Nietzsche, and two collections of essays entitled *Duše a slovo* ("The Soul and the Word," 1929), and *Slovo a svět* ("The Word and the World," 1937). His works include more than a dozen volumes of poetry. In spite of his assimilated background, Fischer was always conscious of his Jewish spiritual roots and was tortured by a perpetual need for self-analysis. His second book of poems, *Ozářená okna* ("Lit Windows," 1916), proclaims his origin, and in the collection *Léto* ("The Summer," 1919), he again sees himself as a descendant of the *Wandering Jew. It was, however, only in the verse collection *Hlasy* ("Voices," 1923), which marks his maturity as a poet, that Fischer accepted the inescapability of his Jewish heritage. It was indeed no mere chance that Fischer's work on Heine (1922–24) was written at the same time as *Hlasy;* and in his translation of the *Poèmes juifs* of André *Spire, Fischer included a letter from Spire in which a parallel is drawn between the two poets. While both Heine and Fischer began writing not only in the language but also in the spirit of their environment, Spire notes, they could not in the end help returning to the Jewishness so deeply lodged in their souls. A number of Fischer's dramas – notably *Přemyslovci* ("The Přemysl Dynasty," 1918), *Herakles* (1919), and *Otroci* ("The Slaves," 1925) – were Czech stage successes. His outstanding translation from German literature is his version of Goethe's *Faust.* He also translated Heine, Kleist, Nietzsche, Schiller, Bruekner, Hofmannsthal, and Wedekind, as well as many other world-famous authors. He attended the informal *Pátečníci* gatherings ("Friday's visitors") which convened regularly every Friday on the initiative of the Czech writer Karel Čapek in the years 1924–1937, including President T.G. Masaryk and Foreign Minister E. Beneš. Fischer's younger brother JOSEF FISCHER (1891–1945), philosopher and sociologist, was executed by the Nazis.

BIBLIOGRAPHY: P. Váša and A. Gregor, *Katechismus dějin české literatury* (1925); B. Václavek, *Česká literatura XX. stoleti* (1935); Hostovský, in: *Jews of Czechoslovakia*, 1 (1968), 442–4. **ADD. BIBLIOGRAPHY:** *Lexikon české literatury* (1985); A. Mikulášek et al., *Literatura s hvězdou Davidovou*, vol. 1 (1998).

[Avigdor Dagan / Milos Pojar (2nd ed.)]

FISCHER, RUTH (née **Eisler**, also known as **Elfriede Golke** or **Friedlaender**; 1895–1961), Austrian Communist. Born in Leipzig, Ruth Fischer studied philosophy, politics, and economics at the University of Vienna where her father, Rudolph *Eisler, was a professor of philosophy. She was a sister of Gerhardt *Eisler and Hans *Eisler. She became co-founder of the Communist Party of Austria in November, 1918 and settled in Berlin during the following year. A leading figure in the German Communist Party, she was a member of the presidium of the Communist International and was elected to the Reichstag in 1924. In 1926 she was suspended from the party but continued to sit in the Reichstag until 1933, when she fled to Paris; she also remained a member of the Reichsrat from 1924 to 1928. In 1941 she immigrated to the United States, where she developed a more critical stance regarding Stalinism. After 1955 she returned to Paris, where she died in 1961. Ruth Fischer published several works on international Communism including: *Stalin and German Communism* (1948), *Von Lenin zu Mao; Kommunismus in der Bandung-Aera* (1956), and *Die Umformung der Sow etgesellschaft, Chronik der Reformen 1953–1958* (1958).

BIBLIOGRAPHY: *New York Times* (March 16, 1961). **ADD. BIBLIOGRAPHY:** R. Leviné-Meyer, *Inside German Communism: Memoirs of Party Life in the Weimar Republic* (1977).

FISCHER, SAMUEL (1859–1934), German publisher, Fischer, who was born in Liptószentmiklós, Slovakia, went to Berlin in 1881 and began trading there as a bookseller. In 1886 he founded the Fischer Verlag, specializing in the publication of foreign naturalist literature and of as yet little-known German authors. From 1898 onward, the character of the publishing house was largely determined by Moritz *Heimann, who was later succeeded as literary adviser by the poet Oskar Loerke. Fischer lent enthusiastic support to the "Freie Buehne," which sought to revitalize the German theater, and in 1889 began publishing its mouthpiece, the monthly *Die Neue Rundschau.* Until the Nazi seizure of power in 1933 the Fischer Verlag was Germany's leading literary publishing house. Fischer himself encouraged successive generations of aspiring young authors and secured the rights to publication of books by an impressive array of major writers, including Thomas *Mann, Arthur *Schnitzler, Jacob *Wassermann, Hugo von *Hofmannsthal, and Sigmund *Freud. Loerke, a staunch anti-Nazi, tried vainly to save the company under Hitler, and courageously delivered Fischer's funeral oration in 1934. Two years later, however, the publishing house was forced to move to Vienna and from there it was subsequently transferred to Stockholm (1938) and then to New York (1940). Gottfried Bermann-Fischer, the founder's son-in-law, assumed control of the firm in 1934 and maintained its activity abroad. In 1972 Gottfried Bermann-Fischer and his wife Brigitte, the daughter of Samuel Fischer, resigned from the Board of the Fischer Verlag and retired from all publishing activities.

In 1950 the Fischer Verlag resumed its publishing operations in Frankfurt. The well-known Fischer Buecherei, which specializes in paperback editions, was founded in 1952. *S. Fischer und sein Verlag* by Peter De Mendelssohn, giving a complete history of the publishing house, appeared in 1972.

BIBLIOGRAPHY: G. Berman-Fischer, *Der Fischer Verlag* (1967).

FISCHER, STANLEY (1943–), international economist and governor of the Bank of Israel. Born in Lusaka, Zambia, Fischer came to the United States in 1966 and was naturalized in 1976. He received both a bachelor and masters degree of science in economics from the London School of Economics and a Ph.D. in economics from MIT (Massachusetts Institute of Technology). He served as assistant professor of economics at the University of Chicago until 1973, after which he served as associate professor and finally professor at MIT's Department of Economics. During this time he was a visiting professor at the Hebrew University of Jerusalem and the Hoover Institution at Stanford. His ties to Israel are deep.

Fischer moved into international finance and economy in the business world in 1988 as vice president, development economics, and chief economist at the World Bank, then becoming the first deputy managing director of the International Monetary Fund from September 1994 through August 2001. Fischer then held several positions at Citigroup beginning in February 2002. In January 2005 Fischer agreed to become the next governor of the Bank of Israel after nomination by Prime Minister Ariel *Sharon and Finance Minister Binyamin *Netanyahu and a recommendation by the Israeli cabinet. He was appointed to the five-year term on May 1, 2005. While some criticized the appointment of a non-Israeli to the position, Finance Minister Netanyahu defended the decision, stating that Fischer is knowledgeable about Israeli economy and society. "The fact that a man like him is ready to finish his affairs at Citigroup, immigrate to Israel, and become the central bank governor here is a golden opportunity for the Israeli economy," Prime Minister Sharon said in a statement. Fischer's appointment meant a substantial pay cut, a long-distance move, and the necessity to become immersed in learning more of the Hebrew language, which he already spoke fairly well.

A Guggenheim Fellow, Fischer is also a Fellow of the Econometric Society and the American Academy of Arts and Sciences. His memberships include the Council on Foreign Relations, the G-30, the Trilateral Commission, and designation as research associate of the National Bureau of Economic Research. He served on boards for the Institute for International Economics, the International Crisis Group, Women's World Banking, and the International Advisory Board of the New Economic School in Moscow.

Fischer's lengthy list of published works includes extensive writings for scholarly and economic journals. He also held positions as associate editor, editor, and member of editorial advisor boards for a number of economic journals. Books authored or edited by Fischer include *Macroeconomics*, (co-author, 2004[9]); *IMF Essays from a Time of Crisis: The International Financial System, Stabilization, and Development* (2004); *The Economics of Middle East Peace* (co-editor, 1994).

[Lisa DeShantz-Cook (2nd ed.)]

FISCHHOFF, ADOLF (1816–1893), Austrian politician; one of the leaders of the 1848 revolution. As the first to suggest solutions to the problems of the Hapsburg monarchy by placing its various nationalities on an equal footing, he influenced the formulation of Jewish *Autonomism. Born in Budapest, Fischhoff went to Vienna in 1836 to study medicine. After the outbreak of the revolution, he became head of its highest governing body, the security council (*Sicherheitsausschuss*) and was active in various administrative capacities and in parliament. Fischhoff remained to face trial after the failure of the revolution. Acquitted in 1849, he was nonetheless deprived of political rights which were not restored to him until 1867. He practiced medicine in Vienna, but lost his assets in the stock-market crash of 1873. Subsequently he settled in Emmersdorf, Carinthia, where Austrian politicians came to consult the "sage of Emmersdorf." In collaboration with Joseph *Unger, he published anonymously Zur *Loesung der ungarischen Frage* (1861) outlining the compromise reached in 1867. In *Oesterreich und die Buergschaften seines Bestandes* (1869) he suggested the introduction of municipal autonomy, decentralization, and representative institutions, in conjunction with a conciliatory attitude toward the nationalities and their rights, a nationality law, and a court of national arbitration. In 1875 he published a pamphlet in favor of disarmament, *Zur Reduktion der kontinentalen Heere.* He was unsuccessful in an attempt in 1882 to found a Deutsche Volkspartei to rally liberals from all nationalities, the chief opposition coming from the Jewish leaders of the Vienna German liberals. Fischhoff's ideas were fundamental to the development of Jewish national policy in the Hapsburg domains. Joseph Samuel *Bloch tried to apply Fischhoff's ideas on relationships in the multi-national Austro-Hungarian Empire for the benefit of Galician Jewry. The *Juedische Volkspartei formulated its program along the lines of Fischhoff's Deutsche Volkspartei. Fischhoff was rarely active in Jewish affairs, but in 1851 he drew up, at the request of Leo *Herzberg-Fraenkel, a statute of association for Jewish agricultural colonization in Galicia. He signed the request to permit the founding of a *Kultusverein in Klagenfurt. He corresponded with some of his friends in Hebrew script. It was Fischhoff's express wish to be buried in the Jewish cemetery.

BIBLIOGRAPHY: J. Fischer, *Adolf Fischhof* (Heb., 1895); A. Frankl-Gruen, *Geschichte der Juden in Kremsier* (1896), 175–95 and passim; R. Charmatz, *Adolf Fischhof* (1910); W.J. Cahnman, in: YLBI, 4 (1958), 111–39; J.S. Bloch, *Reminiscences* (1923), 55–60; N.M. Gelber, *Aus zwei Jahrhunderten* (1924), 126–31; L. Goldhammer, in: *Juedisches Jahrbuch fuer Oesterreich* (1933), 126–30; M. Grunwald, *Vienna* (1936), index; R. Kann, *The Multinational Empire* (1950), index; R.J. Roth, *Viennese Revolution of 1848* (1957), index; P. Robertson, *Revolutions of 1848* (1960[2]), index; J. Guvrin, in: *Zeitschrift fuer die Geschichte der Juden* (1964), 83–98; Y. Toury, *Mehumah u-Mevukhah be-Mahpekhat 1848* (1968), index; J. Goldmark, *Pilgrims of '48* (1930). **ADD. BIBLIOGRAPHY:** W.J. Cahnmann, "Adolf Fischhof als Verfechter der Nationalität und seine Auswirkungen auf das jüdisch-politische Denken in Oesterreich," in: *Studia Judaica Austriaca*, 1 (1974), 78–91; W. Klimbacher, "Adolf Fischhof – Jude, revolutionärer Arzt und politischer Visionär," in: *Das jüdische Echo*, 45 (1996), 123–32; W.J. Cahnmann, "Adolf Fischhofs jüdische Persönlichkeit und Weltanschauung," in: *Kairos*, 14 (1972), 110–20.

[Meir Lamed]

FISCHHOFF, JOSEPH (1804–1857), Austrian pianist and composer. In 1813, Fischhoff began to study at the lyceum in

Brünn, at the same time receiving instruction in music from the pianist Jahelka and the bandmaster Rieger. After completing his studies at the lyceum, he went to the University of Vienna to study philosophy and medicine.

The sudden death of his father in 1827 changed Fischoff's career. He decided to devote himself from that time entirely to his art, and in 1833 became professor at the conservatory of music in Vienna. He was one of the most popular pianists in the Austrian capital, distinguishing himself particularly by his rendition of the compositions of Bach, Beethoven, Mendelssohn, and Chopin. He published a string quartet, many piano pieces, variations for the flute, and songs.

FISCHLER, STAN (1932–), U.S. author, sportscaster, leading authority on ice hockey. Born in Brooklyn, New York, and educated at Brooklyn College, Fischler covered hockey for over 50 years, beginning as a publicist for the New York Rangers. He wrote for the *Brooklyn Eagle*, the *New York Journal-American*, and the *Toronto Star* from 1955 through 1977, and then began his broadcasting career in Boston as an analyst for the New England Whalers of the WHA in 1973–74. Fischler joined SportsChannel New York (later FOX Sports Net) at its inception in 1975, for which he continued covering New York metropolitan area NHL teams. Known as "The Hockey Maven," Fischler with the help of his wife, Shirley, authored or co-authored more than 90 books on hockey, including *Fischler's Hockey Encyclopedia* (1975), *Great Book of Hockey: More Than 100 Years of Fires on Ice* (1991), and *Cracked Ice: An Insiders Look at the* NHL (1995). He wrote for various publications, including *The New York Times, The Sporting News, Sports Illustrated, Sport, Newsweek* and the *Hockey Digest*, and later became a columnist for *The Hockey News*. Fischler's other passions are subway systems and their history, and he has written a number of books on the subject, including *Uptown, Downtown: A Trip Through Time on New York's Subways* (1976), *Moving Millions: An Inside Look at Mass Transit* (1979), and *Next Stop Grand Central: A Trip Through Time on New York's Metropolitan Area Commuter Railroads* (1986). His writings have been included in *Best American Sports Writing of the Century* (1999).

[Elli Wohlgelernter (2nd ed.)]

FISCHMANN, NAḤMAN ISAAC (c. 1809–1878), Hebrew writer. A member of the young Haskalah group in Lemberg, Fischmann published his first book of poetry, *Eshkol Anavim*, in 1827. He was one of the group which published the *Ha-Ro'eh* pamphlets that sharply criticized the studies by Italian (Reggio and S.D. Luzzatto) and Galician (mainly S.J. Rapoport) scholars with the stated purpose of defending "Jewish traditions." Fischmann wrote two didactic biblical plays, *Sisera* (1841) and *Kesher Shevna* (1870), and published a second volume of poetry, *Ha-Et ve-ha-Meshorer*, in 1870. He left many unpublished poems and talmudic studies, some of which appeared later in various periodicals.

BIBLIOGRAPHY: J.L. Landau, *Short Lectures in Modern Hebrew Literature* (1938²), 262–70; S. Bernfeld, *Toledot ShIR* (1899), 98ff.

[Getzel Kressel]

FISCUS JUDAICUS, a fund of the Roman Empire into which was paid the money from the special tax levied on the Jews by *Vespasian after the destruction of the Temple (Jos., Wars 7:218; Dio Cassius 66:7,2). This imposition, a poll tax of two drachmae, was officially paid to Jupiter Capitolinus and took the place of the half-*shekel which the Jews throughout the world had contributed to the Temple while it stood. There is evidence to show that this tax was levied in Egypt from 71–72 C.E. onward. In these documents it is called "the Jewish tax" and a great deal is known about it, particularly from ostraca from Edfu. It is clear that in Egypt even women and children as young as three were liable, although they had been exempt from the half-shekel. The tax was probably paid in Egypt only until the age of 62. In Rome itself a special procurator called *procurator ad capitularia Judaeorum* was in charge of the fiscus (H. Dessau (ed.), *Inscriptiones Latinae Selectae*, 1 (1892), 330, no. 1519). In addition to the financial burden it imposed, the tax was humiliating for the Jews. During the reign of Domitian (81–96) the methods of collecting the tax were strengthened and apparently the Roman authorities became much more vigorous in determining who was liable for taxation. It was imposed on those who had been born Jews as well as those who concealed the fact that they were Jews, and on proselytes to Judaism. In various ways this opened the door to possibilities of calumny, causing suffering to many residents in Rome, and possibly beyond. Suetonius (*Vita Domitiani*, 12) relates that when he was young an old man of 90 was examined to see whether he was circumcised, which shows that during this period the tax was levied even on those above the age of 62. After the murder of Domitian in 96, the atmosphere changed for the better as is seen from the coins of Nerva which bear the inscription *fisci Judaici calumnia sublata*. However, the levy of the tax continued. The latest documentary evidence is a papyrus from the village of Karanis in Faiyum, upper Egypt (Tcherikover, Corpus, 3 (1964), 17–18, no. 460, line 7, dated 146 C.E. or 168 C.E.). Literary sources indicate that the tax was still in existence in the first half of the third century (Origen, *Ad Africanum*, 14). It is not known when the tax came to an end, but some attribute a decisive role in its abolition to *Julian the Apostate.

BIBLIOGRAPHY: Schuerer, Gesch, 2 (1907⁴), 315; 3 (1909⁴), 117f.; Juster, Juifs, 2 (1914), 282–6; M. Radin, *The Jews among the Greeks and Romans* (1915), 332–4, 362f.; J. Janssen, *C. Suetoni Tranquilli Vita Domitiani* (1919), 59; M.S. Ginsburg, in: JQR, 21 (1930/31), 281–91; Baron, Social², 2 (1952), 373–4n; Smallwood, in: *Classical Philology*, 51 (1956), 1–13; Tcherikover, Corpus, 2 (1960), 110–36; O. Hirschfeld, *Die kaiserlichen Verwaltungsbeamten* (1963³), 73; H.J. Leon, *Jews of Ancient Rome* (1960), 31, 33, 36, 252.

[Menahem Stern]

FISH, HAREL (**Harold**; 1923–), literary scholar specializing in general literature and the mutual relationship between

Jewish and non-Jewish culture in literature. Fish was born in Birmingham, served as an officer in the British army, and fought in World War II. He graduated in 1946 from Sheffield University, and in 1948 he received his B.Litt. from Oxford University, doing research on Bishop Josef Hall. From 1947 to 1957 he was a lecturer at Leeds University. In 1957 he immigrated to Israel and joined the faculty of Bar-Illan University, becoming a professor there in 1964. In 1968 he was named the rector of the university, a position he held until 1971. In 1971 he founded the David and Batya Kotler's Institute for Judaism and Contemporary Thought. From 1981 to 1987 he was chairman of the Lechter Institute for Literary Research. He published hundreds of articles and eight books, including (in Hebrew) *The Biblical Presence in Shakespeare, Milton and Blake* and *New-Old Stories: Biblical Patterns in the Novel from Fielding to Kafka*. In 2000 he was awarded the Israel Prize for literature.

[Shaked Gilboa (2nd ed.)]

FISH, STANLEY (1938–), U.S. literary theorist. Born in Providence, Rhode Island, Fish earned his doctoral degree in English literature from Yale University in 1962. He taught at the University of California, Berkeley, and at Johns Hopkins University, before becoming professor of English and of law at Duke University (1985–98). He also served as the executive director of the Duke University Press from 1993 to 1998. Fish was then dean of arts and sciences at the University of Illinois at Chicago from 1999 to 2004.

Considered a leading scholar on John Milton, Fish is a well-known and sometimes controversial literary theorist. His first published work, *John Skelton's Poetry*, appeared in 1965, but he rose to prominence with the publication of his second book, *Surprised by Sin: The Reader in "Paradise Lost"* (1967). Here Fish first presented his theory of "reader-response criticism," in which he argues that reading is a temporal phenomenon and that the meaning of a literary work is located within the reader's experience of the text. His *Self-consuming Artifacts* (1972) elaborated and developed the notion of reader response into a theory of interpretive communities, in which a reader's interpretation of a text depends on the reader's membership in one or more communities that share a set of assumptions. *Is There a Text in This Class? The Authority of Interpretive Communities* (1980), a collection of Fish's essays, established his position as one of the most influential literary theorists of his day.

In his later works, Fish extended literary theory into the arenas of politics and law, writing on the politics of the university, the nature of free speech, and connections between literary theory and legal theory. These works include *Doing What Comes Naturally: Change, Rhetoric, and the Practice of Theory in Literary and Legal Studies* (1989), *There's No Such Thing as Free Speech, and It's a Good Thing, Too* (1994), *Professional Correctness: Literary Studies and Political Change* (1995), and *The Trouble with Principle* (1999). *There's No Such Thing as Free Speech*, seen by some as a critique of liberalism, generated much debate. In *The Trouble with Principle*, Fish suggests that the application of principles impedes democracy, and he examines affirmative action as a case in point, again sparking wide-ranging critique. In 2005 Fish was named the Davidson-Kahn Distinguished University Professor of Humanities and Law at Florida International University, with a principal appointment in the College of Law and a role as lecturer in the College of Arts and Sciences.

[Dorothy Bauhoff (2nd ed.)]

FISH AND FISHING.

In the Bible and Talmud

The Bible says that humans are to exercise dominion over the fish as well as over all other subhuman life (Gen. 1:28). Fish are divided into clean and unclean by biblical dietary laws: "These you may eat, of all that are in the waters. Everything in the waters that has fins and scales … you may eat. But anything in the seas or the rivers that has not fins and scales … is an abomination to you" (Lev. 11:9–11). Water creatures lacking fins and scales are an abomination because they move like land animals, transgressing the boundaries of creation (Douglas in Bibliography). Similarly, certain fish were avoided because they looked like snakes (Firmage in Bibliography). When the Hebrews complain to Moses about their diet of manna, they recall the fish of Egypt, which they refer to as "meat" (Num. 11:4–5). Egypt was known for its abundance of fish, and as such they are mentioned as victims of the first plague (Ex. 7:18, 21). The likeness of any fish is included in the general prohibition of graven images in Deuteronomy 4:15–18. In the ancient period fishing served as a significant means of support and as an important economic factor both in Egypt and Babylonia, but probably less so in Israel. For most of the biblical period the southern Mediterranean coast was controlled by the Philistines and the north by Phoenicians. Natives of Israel would have fished in the Jordan and the Sea of Galilee (Firmage in Bibliography). Whereas *Hammurapi's laws 26–32 are devoted to fishermen in royal service (COS II, 338–39), no regulation of fishermen is found in biblical law. While Ashurnasirpal's banquet served 10,000 fishes (Wiseman in Bibliography), fish are absent from the delicacies of Solomon's table (I Kings 5:2–3). The Bible mentions "the Fish Gate" in Jerusalem (Zeph. 1:10; Neh. 3:3; II Chron. 33:14), which was named after the fish market nearby. Tyrian fish merchants selling their wares on the Sabbath in Jerusalem are mentioned in Nehemiah 13:16. The abundance of *halakhot* and *aggadot* about fishing and fishermen in both the Babylonian and Palestinian Talmuds and in various Midrashim indicates a considerable fishing industry in the periods of the Second Temple and the Talmud. This is also evident from the Gospels, as the first disciples of Jesus were fishermen on the Sea of Galilee. Josephus frequently refers to Jews engaged in that livelihood, as well as to a fleet of fishing vessels on the

Sea of Galilee. A Greek inscription from the second century C.E. about a family or band of Jewish fishermen has been found in Jaffa.

Although the Bible does not provide the name of any specific fish, it does mention many fishing implements: rod (Isa. 19:8), net (*ibid.*, and Hab. 1:15), trap (Eccles. 9:12), fishing net (Ezek. 26:5), spear (Job 40:31), and small fishing boats (Amos 4:2, according to the Targum). The word *reshet* ("net"), frequent in the Bible in other contexts, appears only once as a device to catch fish (Ezek. 32:3).

The Bible's most famous fish is the large one that swallowed Jonah and kept him in his belly for three days and nights (Jonah 2:1), and who, according to the New Testament, foreshadowed the underworld in which Jesus would spend three days and nights.

The Babylonian and Jerusalem Talmuds both mention the fishing rod and a variety of traps and nets (*akon*, from the Greek *o(n)gkīnos*, "hook," Kel. 23:5; *kefifa*, Tosef., Makhsh. 3:12; *pitos*, from the Greek *pithos*, TJ, Shab. 13:5, 14a; *leḥi, kokarei ve-oharei* in Shab. 18a, Git. 60b–61a, MK 11a; *ḥarmei*, the net-fishers of Tiberias, TJ Pes. 4:1, 30d). From the different fishing devices (such as snares in Kel. 23:5), it is possible to learn about other methods of fishing at that time (see Kid. 72a and BM 12b). The Midrash makes a reference to fishermen repairing their nets (Tanḥ., Va-Yelekh 2). According to the Testament of the Twelve Patriarchs, Zebulun "who shall dwell at the shore of the sea" (Gen. 49:13) was the first fisherman, and a detailed description of fishing is put into his mouth (Test. Patr., Zeb. 5:5–6, 8).

Fishing in the Halakhah

According to the Talmud the granting of fishing rights to all of the tribes around the Sea of Galilee was included in the "Ten *takkanot* of Joshua, the son of Nun," enacted by Joshua on the conquest of the land, even though that body of water was completely within the boundary of the tribe of Naphtali. "It is permitted to fish with an angle in the Sea of Galilee provided that no sail is spread, as this would detain boats" (BK 81a–b). Fish in the sea are considered ownerless property and whoever catches them has the right to keep them. It is stated that according to biblical law, this applies even to those fish already netted as long as the net has not been drawn from the water. "In the interests of peace," however, the rabbis ruled that the fish belong to the owner of the net (Git. 5:8). Details are given with regard to the prohibition of fishing on Sabbaths and festivals including the spreading of nets and the regulations concerning fishing on the intermediate days of festivals (Bezah 3:1–2; TJ, Pes. 4:1, 30d; Shab. 17b; Yoma 84b; MK 11a).

Fish in the Halakhah

In Jewish tradition only fish that have scales and fins are permitted for consumption (see *Dietary Laws). They need not be slaughtered ritually (*shehitah) and their blood is not prohibited. According to a belief held in talmudic times, the eating of fish together with meat was considered harmful and predisposed the body to leprosy. In accordance with the rule that considerations of health are as important as ritual prohibitions, the rabbis consequently forbade the cooking or eating of fish together with meat (Pes. 76b). No interval before eating meat, however, is necessary (Sh. Ar., YD 116:2–3); it is enough to rinse the mouth or to chew something after eating fish. Fish are *parve* (considered to be neither meat nor milk). It may be consumed or cooked with milk. Fish, as a favorite dish for Shabbat, is mentioned in the Talmud (Shab. 118b) and by the Roman poet Persius Flaccus (*Satires*, 5, 180ff.). The abundance of fish in the Babylonian rivers and canals, making it a food available to the poor, may be one possible reason. A more homiletical reason is found in the words "and God blessed them" which occur in the biblical account of the creation of fish on the fifth day (Gen. 1:22), as well as in the subsequent account of the sixth day (Gen. 1:28) and the Sabbath (Gen. 2:3). Fish, man, and the Sabbath are thus connected in a threefold blessing. Moreover, the Sabbath is said to be an anticipation of the messianic era which will be inaugurated by the eating of the legendary fish *Leviathan. Fishing from a river or pond is forbidden on Sabbath and on holidays; however, fish kept in a storage pond may be taken out (Bezah 3:1–2). Fish were thought to bring good luck because they are the zodiac signs of Adar, the month of Purim. Representations of fish are widespread in the Orient as amulets, and in Eastern Europe some boys were called Fishl as a good omen against the evil eye (see Ber. 20a; cf. Jacob's blessing of his grandchildren, Gen. 48:16). Fish was a favorite Sabbath food for Eastern European Jews living in poor economic conditions. This was presumably due to the abundance and cheapness of fish and to the special tax on kosher meat Jews had to pay to the government in the 18th century. Cooked, smoked, or salted fish was served as the main dish at the Third Meal (*Se'udah Shelishit) on Saturday afternoon, at the farewell meal (*Melavveh Malkah) on Saturday night at the end of the Sabbath and at communal dinners (see *Se'udah and *Siyyum). (See also *Food.)

BIBLIOGRAPHY: M. Shuvah, in: *Sefer ha-Yovel ...S. Krauss* (1937), 80–86; J. Newman, *Agricultural Life of the Jews in Babylonia* (1932), 136–40; Dalman, Arbeit, 6 (1939), 343–70; ET, 7 (1956), 202–26; Eisenstein, Dinim, 81f.; Goodenough, Symbols, 5 (1956), 3–61. **ADD. BIBLIOGRAPHY:** D. Wiseman, in: *Iraq*, 14 (1952), 24–44; M. Douglas, in: C. Meyers (ed.), *Identity and Ideology ...* (1996), 131–32; D. Sahrhage, *Fischfang und Fischkult in Aegypten* (1992); idem, *Fischfang und Fischkult im alten Mesopotamien* (1999); D. Sahrhage and J. Lundbeck, *A History of Fishing* (1992); E. Firmage, in: ABD, 6:1146–47.

FISHBANE, MICHAEL (1943–), U.S. scholar of Bible and Midrash. Born in Cambridge, Massachusetts, after early studies in philosophy and Jewish thought in America and Israel he became a student of Nahum M. *Sarna and Nahum N. *Glatzer and earned his M.A. and Ph.D. degrees from Brandeis University (1967 and 1971). He held a number of academic appointments in the Department of Near Eastern and Judaic

Studies at Brandeis University (1969–90). He served as the Nathan Cummings Professor of Jewish Studies in the Divinity School, the Committee on Jewish Studies, and the College of the University of Chicago (from 1990), where he was also a lecturer in the Law School.

Fishbane's initial work deals with literary and intertextual themes from the Hebrew Bible. In *Text and Texture: Studies in Biblical Literature* (1979), he demonstrates how biblical authors and redactors utilize stylistic and compositional devices in narratives and narrative units in speeches and prayers and in themes and motifs in order to convey the historical, cultural, and theological message of the Bible. In *Biblical Interpretation in Ancient Israel* (1985) Fishbane explores the existence and function of diverse forms of exegesis and interpretation in the Bible itself (scribal, legal, theological, prophetic-oracular). He thereby shows that not only is Hebrew Scripture the primary document for the exegetical tradition of Judaism and Christianity, but that it is an exegetical work in its own right. His *Biblical Myth and Rabbinic Mythmaking* (2003) is a study of myth in the Hebrew Bible and mythmaking in classical rabbinic literature and medieval Jewish mysticism. He demonstrates that certain types of myth are endemic in Jewish theology and are not contradictory to aspects of monotheism, diametrically opposing the contention that there was no myth in the rabbinic age (Ephraim E. Urbach), and that it is a late and foreign implant in medieval Spanish Kabbalah (Gershom *Scholem).

Fishbane's point that textual interpretation explicates the plain-sense of primary sources in their original cultural, historical, and social settings, while also generating new values and explications in subsequent eras, is found in his *The Garments of Torah: Essays in Biblical Hermeneutics* (1989). This interpretative process informing Jewish religious thought also illuminates his *The Exegetical Imagination: On Jewish Thought and Theology* (1998), a series of essays dealing with the role Scriptural exegesis plays in Jewish speculative theology as well as ritual practice. His *The Kiss of God: Mythical and Spiritual Death in Judaism* (1994), awarded the National Jewish Book Award for Jewish Thought, explores selected rabbinic, philosophic, and mystical texts on the passion for religious perfection expressed as the love of God unto death itself, including acts of martyrdom and ritual replacements for actual death. Fishbane is also the author of the first full-length commentary on the Sabbath and festival *Haftarot* (2002).

Fishbane's published articles and reviews in scholarly books and journals range from ancient biblical thought to the existential theology of Martin *Buber and Franz *Rosenzweig; and show how Jewish culture is permeated and regenerated by exegetical creativity. He served as editor-in-chief of the Jewish Publication Society Bible Commentary (for Prophets and Writings). Fishbane's life's work in tilling sacred texts and tracing subsurface traditions has led him to new explorations in the history of exegesis and theology and to projects involving cultural pedagogy and interreligious dialogue.

[Zev Garber (2nd ed.)]

FISHBEIN, MORRIS (1889–1976), U.S. physician, editor, and author. Fishbein, who was born in St. Louis, Mo., received his M.D. from Rush Medical College in 1912. He edited the *Journal of the American Medical Association* from 1924 to 1949, and was editor and coeditor of numerous other journals. Fishbein built the *Journal* into the world's largest medical periodical. He was considered the official mouthpiece of U.S. medicine. Fishbein also edited numerous reports, pamphlets, and books and wrote daily health columns for various American newspapers. Fishbein, in the course of his career, was also a vigorous opponent of chiropractors and medical quacks and faddists. His books include *Frontiers of Medicine* (1933); *Modern Home Medical Adviser* (1935); *Popular Medical Encyclopaedia* (1946); *History of the American Medical Association* (1947); *Medical Writing: The Technic and the Art* (1938); *New Advances in Medicine* (1956); *Modern Home Remedies and How to Use Them* (1966). From 1960 Fishbein was editor of *Medical World News*, and also medical editor of Britannica Book of the Year. He wrote an autobiography, *Morris Fishbein, M.D.* (1969).

BIBLIOGRAPHY: S.R. Kagan, *Jewish Contributions to Medicine in America* (1939), 106–8.

[Fred Rosner]

FISHBERG, MAURICE (1872–1934), U.S. physician and physical anthropologist. Born in Russia, Fishberg emigrated to the U.S. in 1889. He became clinical professor of medicine at the New York University and Bellevue Hospital Medical College. He served as chief physician and director of the tuberculosis service of the Montefiore Hospital and other institutions, and as medical examiner of the United Hebrew Charities of New York City. Fishberg became a recognized authority on pulmonary tuberculosis, and wrote a standard textbook on this subject, *Pulmonary Tuberculosis* (1916; 2 vols., 1932[4]). He was a pioneer in the use of pneumothorax treatment for this disease, and helped to stimulate a campaign for the prevention of the malady by his demonstration of its high incidence among New York City schoolchildren. The other focus of his intellectual concern was the scientific study of the anthropology and pathology of Jews, in which field he made extensive investigations not only in the United States but also in Europe and North Africa. His various investigations culminated in the summary volume *The Jews; A Study of Race and Environment* (1911), in which he maintained the heterogeneity in racial composition of modern Jews. As anthropological consultant to the Bureau of Immigration and on behalf of a U.S. Congressional Committee, he visited Europe in 1905 and 1907 to study aspects of the immigration problem. His report was published by the U.S. government at the direction of President Theodore Roosevelt. He also served as chairman of the anthropology and psychology section of New York Academy of Science and as vice president of the Academy (1909–11).

[Ephraim Fischoff]

FISHEL (Fischel), wealthy family prominent in Jewish society in *Cracow-Kazimierz, Poland, at the close of the 15th and first half of the 16th century; named after EPHRAIM FISHEL with whom the family arrived in Cracow from Bohemia. He and his four sons had commercial dealings with the Polish nobility. After initial friction with earlier-established Cracow Jews, the Fishel family took a leading place in the community, and two of its members were among the signatories of an agreement between the community leaders and the municipal council in Cracow in 1485. By 1475 Ephraim Fishel senior had died and his extensive business had been taken over by his sons. Of them MOSES (d. c. 1504), a banker and one of the community leaders, mentioned first in 1477, was principally engaged in the lease of customs duties and other royal revenues. In 1499 he was accused of extortion in collecting the poll tax from the Jews of the region of *Gniezno. In 1503, with his brother Jacob, Moses leased the royal customs revenues in the provinces of Great Poland and Masovia for an annual payment of 2,500 Hungarian florins, 24 kg. of saffron and 120 kg. of black pepper. His wife RACHEL (Raszka Moyżeszowa) engaged independently in moneylending from 1483. She was in contact with the courts of kings Casimir IV, John Albert, and Alexander. As creditor of Polish kings, she received compensation in an interesting way from King Alexander. In 1504 he annulled the crown debts due to her and her late husband and ordered the mint to mint coins from her silver bars; the coins were worth 1600 florins more than the bars, being 1000 as repayment of principal and 600 for interest. Of their daughters, Esther married Jacob *Pollak, Hendel married the kabbalist Asher Lemel, rabbi of Kazimierz, and Sarah married David Zehner of Buda, at the age of 12. Another son of Ephraim, STEPHAN (d. after 1532), a banker, converted to Christianity with his sons Jan and Stanislaw (their adopted Christian names), probably after the expulsion of the Jews from Cracow in 1494. His Jewish wife and their other children did not become baptized. Stephan continued to engage in finance and in 1503 leased the rights of collection of the Jewish poll taxes of Great Poland for a period of four years. In 1507 he and his two sons were adopted by the vice chancellor Jan Laski, into whose family he married, and he was ennobled, taking the name Powidzki. His descendants, still known as Powidzki, owned large landed estates in the 18th century. The relations between Stephan Powidzki and his Jewish kinsmen were strained, and on several occasions resulted in lawsuits. In about 1510, he befriended the notorious apostate Johannes *Pfefferkorn.

Moses' son, EPHRAIM FISHEL (late 15th and early 16th century), known as Franczek, a banker, tax and customs farmer, and communal leader, also engaged in many financial transactions with the Polish aristocracy. He was the first agent of Elizabeth (wife of Frederiek, prince of Silesia), the sister of King Sigismund I (1506–1548). In about 1512, he was appointed by the king, with *Abraham Judaeus Bohemus, as chief collector (*exactor*) of Jewish taxes throughout the kingdom, and was directly active in Little Poland and the province of "Russia," an appointment that gave him a central role in Jewish communal life there. His exceptional status was strongly opposed by the leaders of the communities and he had serious difficulties in collecting the taxes. In 1515 his failure to perform these offices became evident and he left Poland for a while. After a number of years, he returned to Cracow, and in 1524, with his wife Chwałka (Falka), he was appointed *servus regis* to Sigismund I and Queen Bona.

The son of Ephraim (Franczek) and Chwałka, MOSES died as a martyr in 1542. He was a pupil of Jacob *Pollak and studied medicine at Padua. After his return to Cracow, he practiced medicine as his sole occupation, achieving fame and becoming physician to state dignitaries. In consideration of his competence and achievements, the king exempted him from the payment of Jewish taxes in 1520. That year he signed the *ḥerem* ("ban") issued by Jacob Pollak against Abraham *Mintz. In 1532, on the death of Asher Lemel, Moses was appointed rabbi of the Polish community of Cracow (to be distinguished from that of the Bohemian Jews). At the end of 1541, in accordance with the Jewish policy of King Sigismund I, Moses was appointed, with *Shalom Shakhna b. Joseph of Lublin, as leader of the Jews (*senior generalis*) for Little Poland with authority extending over one quarter of the territory. The Jews, however, regarded this as an infringement of their autonomy and opposed the appointment. In 1541 Moses became involved in a false charge and appeared in a harsh trial concerning proselytes to Judaism. He was imprisoned and died soon afterward.

BIBLIOGRAPHY: *Russko-yevreyskiy arkhiv*, 3 (Rus. and Lat., 1903), nos. 26, 27, 44, 63, 64, 72, 81, 82, 83, 104, 108, 135, 147; I. Schipper, *Studya nad stosunkami gospodarczymi Żydów w Polsce podczas średniowiecza* (1911), index s.v. *Fiszel, Mojżesz* et al.; M. Bałaban, *Historja Żydow Krakowie i na Kazimierzu*, 1 (1931), 112–8.

[Arthur Cygielman]

FISHELS, ROIZL OF CRACOW (16th century), printer/publisher. In 1586 Fishels printed a book of Psalms translated from Hebrew into Yiddish by R. Moshe Standl; this volume also included her own autobiographical Yiddish poem, which was printed at the front of the book. In this poem, the principle source of information about her life, she indicates the date of the printing and relates part of her genealogy as the granddaughter of Yuda Levy, who ran a yeshivah in Ludomir for 50 years. She modestly describes her father, Yosef Halevi, as having "not a bad reputation among the *levi'im*," but her husband, whom she calls simply R. Fishels, is only named twice, without any description of his activities or accomplishments. All the male relatives she mentions were already deceased in 1586. At the end of the book Fishels again gave the date of completion and signed her name as "Roizl the Widow, daughter of R. Yosef Halevi."

Fishels offers no further personal details in her poem, but she does write that she "taught [the psalms] to all who wanted to know / Until they began to come, one and all, to me." This suggests that Roizl Fishels was a teacher, most likely of girls and women. Another line of the poem, "Here in the holy city of Hanover I donated [the psalms]" implies that she funded the printing of this Yiddish book so that it would be available "in our own mother tongue." Based on the frequency of Hebrew words in her writing, and her allusions to biblical characters, it is clear that she had at least some knowledge of Hebrew and was educated in Bible.

BIBLIOGRAPHY: A.B. Habermann, *Nashim Ivriyyot be-Tor Madpisot, Mesadrot, Motzi'ot le-Or ve-Tomekhot be-Meḥabrim* (1932–33), 8–10; M. Spiegel and D. Kremsdorf, *Women Speak to God: The Prayers and Poems of Jewish Women* (1987), 17; E. Taitz, S. Henry, and C. Tallan. *The JPS Guide to Jewish Women: 600 B.C.E.–1900 C.E.* (2003), 136.

[Emily Taitz (2nd ed.)]

FISHER, CARRIE FRANCES (1956–), U.S. actress and author. Born in Beverly Hills, Calif., to singer Eddie *Fisher and actress Debbie Reynolds and raised by her mother and shoe retailer Harry Karl following her parents' highly publicized divorce, Fischer attended the Professional Children's School in Los Angeles. She dropped out of Hollywood High School to join the Broadway musical *Irene* (1972) and made her film debut in *Shampoo* (1975), opposite Warren Beatty. She went on to study at the Central School of Speech and Drama in London for 18 months. After an audition with George *Lucas, Fisher landed the leading role of Princess Leia in the blockbuster film *Star Wars* (1977) as well as the next two films in the series, *The Empire Strikes Back* (1980) and *Return of the Jedi* (1983). Her connection to the original cast of the comedy TV show *Saturday Night Live* led her to take a small part as the jilted girlfriend of John Belushi's character in *The Blues Brothers* (1980) and a role as Chevy Chase's love interest in *Under the Rainbow* (1981). She appeared in smaller roles in such films as *The Man with One Red Shoe* (1985), *Hannah and Her Sisters* (1986), and *When Harry Met Sally* (1989). Fisher married singer Paul *Simon in 1983 after a seven-year relationship, but the couple divorced 11 months later in 1984. In 1985, Fisher nearly overdosed after wrestling with a Percodan addiction. At that time she entered a detox clinic and has remained drug-free since. The experience would later turn up in her 1987 bestselling novel *Postcards from the Edge*, which won the Los Angeles Pen Award and was adapted as a feature film in 1990 by director Mike *Nichols and starred Meryl Streep and Shirley MacLaine. *Postcards* was followed by the novels *Surrender the Pink* (1990), *Delusions of Grandma* (1994), and *The Best Awful There Is* (2004). Fisher continued to work in Hollywood as a script doctor and took on small parts in such films as *Austin Powers: International Man of Mystery* (1997), *Scream 3* (2000), and *Charlie's Angels: Full Throttle* (2003). In 2004, Fisher launched *Conversations with Carrie Fisher*, a cable TV talk show on the Oxygen network.

[Adam Wills (2nd ed.)]

FISHER, DONALD (1928–), U.S. entrepreneur, merchant. Fisher, a native Californian, was a real estate developer until he was 41. Then, frustrated at not finding a pair of jeans that fit properly, he and his wife, Doris, decided to open their own clothing store in San Francisco. That was the beginning of Gap Inc., a company that grew into the biggest specialty store chain in the U.S., with thousands of units in North America, Europe, and Japan. After earning a B.S. from the University of California in 1950, Fisher went into real estate development. He found his true calling in 1969 when, dissatisfied with the jeans he purchased, he launched his own business. The then popular phrase "generation gap" inspired the company name. At first, Gap sold only Levi's jeans as well as discounted record albums and tapes to lure younger customers. By the mid-1970s, Gap – which then had about 200 outlets – began adding private label merchandise, as did many other retailers. The company continued to open more stores, but it was apparent to Fisher that he needed someone with a merchant's eye to make the stores more compelling. In 1983, he hired Millard S. *Drexler as his deputy and Gap's fortunes began to soar. The same year, Fisher acquired Banana Republic, a chain of clothing stores specializing in safari looks. When that concept fell out of fashion, Banana Republic was restructured. In 1994, Gap launched another division, Old Navy, a discount chain that became an instant hit. The following year, Fisher stepped down as Gap's chief executive officer and gave the post to Drexler, whose merchandising acumen had propelled the company to unprecedented heights. A soft economy and increased competition hurt Gap's performance in the late 1990s and at the beginning of the new millennium, but a turnaround started in 2002. Fisher remained chairman until December 2003, relinquishing the title to his son Robert, a former Gap executive. At the time, Gap was a 3,070-unit retailing giant with annual sales of some $15 billion, and the Fishers' initial investment of $63,000 in 1969 had made them billionaires several times over. Fisher was named to the California Board of Education in 2001.

BIBLIOGRAPHY: *Fortune* (Aug. 1998).

[Mort Sheinman (2nd ed)]

FISHER, DUDU (1951–), Israeli singer and cantor. Fisher was born in Petaḥ Tikvah. He displayed his singing prowess at a very early age when he would entertain his fellow yeshivah high school students at parties with hits from abroad with the original English language lyrics replaced by a text of a far more religion-friendly nature. He spent his military tour of duty as a soloist in the choir of the IDF Chief Rabbinate and, after his release, began to work as a cantor in the Great Synagogue in Ramat Gan and Tel Aviv. He subsequently took his cantorial talents to South Africa and began to perform regularly for Jewish communities around the world. Alongside his cantorial duties, Fisher began to perform a wide range of material in Yiddish. The venture proved highly popular and he recorded his first album of Yiddish songs, *Goldener Lieder – Die Beste Yiddische Lieder* (Golden Songs – The Best Yiddish Songs) in 1986. The following year he competed unsuccessfully for the right to represent Israel in the Eurovision Song Contest. Fisher's contribution to Yiddish, ḥasidic, and cantorial music – both his recordings, such as *Mammamanyo*, and his numerous concerts around the world – were recognized by his award of the Shalom Aleichem Prize.

In 1987 Fisher auditioned for the Cameri Theater's Hebrew version of the musical *Les Miserables*. Despite the fact that the theater managers preferred a big name for the lead part of Jean Valjean, both the director and the producer of the show opted for Fisher, who was yet to become a star. The gamble proved successful and the show was a hit. Meanwhile, Fisher's recording work continued unabated and, in September 1988, he released two albums of ḥasidic and Yiddish songs. Fisher's international career really took off in 1993 when he starred in the English-language version of the Broadway production of *Les Miserables*, later playing the lead role when the production went to London's West End, where he performed in the presence of the Queen of England.

In 1989 Fisher performed in a show called *Over the Rainbow*, which included favorites from well-known musicals such as *Porgy and Bess, The Wizard of Oz*, and *Cats*. He subsequently released an album with material taken from the show. Fisher followed this with a production called *Steps to Heaven* in which he sang original and Hebrew-language versions of romantic hits performed in the 1960s by the likes of Paul Anka and Elvis Presley. Around this time Fisher cemented his lofty international status when he recorded an album of hits from musicals with the London Symphony Orchestra.

As an observant Jew, Fisher managed to keep his lead role in *Les Miserables* despite not taking part in the Friday evening or Saturday performances. In 1999 Fisher solved that logistical problem his own way when he put on a successful one-man off-Broadway show, aptly entitled *Never on Friday*.

[Barry Davis (2nd ed.)]

FISHER, EDDIE (**Edwin Jack Fisher**; 1928–), U.S. singer. Born in Philadelphia, the son of Russian Jewish immigrants, Fisher learned to sing in a synagogue. On tour in the Catskill Mountains in 1949, the young Fisher caught the attention of singer *Eddie Cantor. Fisher got his first wide exposure as a frequent guest performer on Cantor's early-1950s TV broadcasts. Within a year, he was idolized throughout the country. He gave considerable assistance to Jewish charities.

In 1953 Fisher was given his own 15-minute TV show, *Coke Time*, sponsored by Coca-Cola (1953–57). The show was so popular that the soft-drink company offered him an unprecedented one-million-dollar contract to be their national spokesperson. By 1954 Fisher had become one of the most popular singers in America. During that period he was, along with Perry Como and Elvis Presley, RCA Victor's top-selling pop vocalist. His many hits include "Anytime"; "Oh, My Papa"; "Wish You Were Here"; "I Need You Now"; "Dungaree Doll"; "I'm Walking Behind You"; "Heart"; "Games That Lovers Play"; "Somebody Like You"; "Thinking of You"; "Turn Back the Hands of Time;" "Tell Me Why"; "I'm Yours"; "Lady of Spain"; "Count Your Blessings"; and "Cindy, Oh Cindy."

In 1955 Eddie Fisher married actress Debbie Reynolds, but he divorced her and married Elizabeth *Taylor in 1959 after a highly publicized affair that damaged his career. His third wife was singer-actress Connie Stevens.

In addition to his many TV guest appearances, Fisher performed in three movies. He had a small part in the classic film *All about Eve* (1950). In 1956 he co-starred with Debbie Reynolds in the romantic comedy *Bundle of Joy*; and in 1960 he appeared in the drama *Butterfield 8* with Liz Taylor, a film that won her an Academy Award.

In 1963 Fisher recorded the live album *Eddie Fisher at the Winter Garden* for his own label, Ramrod. He returned to RCA in the mid-1960s to record the albums *Games That Lovers Play; People Like You*; and *You Ain't Heard Nothin' Yet.* He did not record much during the rest of his career, but he continued to perform on concert stages and in nightclubs around America.

Married five times, Fisher has four children, all of whom are in show business: Carrie Fisher and Todd Fisher (with Debbie Reynolds); and Tricia Leigh Fisher and Joely Fisher (with Connie Stevens).

Fisher has written two autobiographies, namely *Eddie: My Life, My Loves* (1981), and *Been There, Done That* (1999).

BIBLIOGRAPHY: M. Greene, *The Eddie Fisher Story* (1978).

[Ruth Beloff (2nd ed.)]

FISHER, MAX M. (1908–2005), U.S. industrialist and community leader. Fisher was born to Russian immigrant parents in Pittsburgh, Pennsylvania, and was raised in Salem, Ohio. He attended Ohio State University on a football scholarship, but after an injury he worked his way through college and graduated in 1930 with a degree in business administration. He then moved to Detroit, where he entered the oil business. He was a pioneer in the development of Michigan's oil industry and in the successful introduction of new oil-refining processes in the 1930s and 1940s. Fisher helped found the Aurora Gasoline Company and was chairman of the board until 1957. He also dealt in finance and real estate and was a board member of various prominent corporations.

In 1954 he made his first visit to Israel. From then on, he spent much of his life raising money for the Jewish state. He was also credited with leading and reorganizing every major Jewish organization in the U.S. Fisher raised hundreds of millions of dollars for Israel as well as for many charities, the city of Detroit, and the Republican Party.

A leading figure in the Republican Party in Michigan, Fisher was also a member of the Republican National Committee. Long interested in urban affairs, he was chosen chairman of New Detroit, Inc., a commission drawn from the city's industrial and business leadership to cope with the problems exposed by the 1967 summer riots. Soon after President Nixon's election (1968), he was appointed special presidential advisor on urban and community affairs. Fisher was active in Jewish life, serving as president of Detroit's Jewish Welfare Federation and chairman of its Allied Jewish Campaign, as general chairman of the United Jewish Appeal (1965–67), and its president (1967–71). He was chairman of the national executive of the American Jewish Committee (1968–72). He also served as chairman of the board of governors of the Jewish Agency from 1971. During the era of the Six-Day and Yom Kippur wars in Israel in the late 1960s and early 1970s, he urged military support for Israel and discouraged imposed peace plans. Later, he lobbied on behalf of Russian Jews who wished to immigrate to Israel.

In 1993, Ohio State's business college was named the Max M. Fisher College of Business. Regarded as one of the premier management institutions in the country, the business college's campus was largely endowed by Fisher.

In 1999 the board of the L.A. Pincus Fund for Jewish Education in the Diaspora established the Max M. Fisher Prize for Jewish education in the Diaspora in honor of Fisher's 90th birthday and in recognition of his role in supporting the advancement of Jewish education around the world. Established in 1977, the Jerusalem-based Pincus Fund works to strengthen Jewish education in the Diaspora through support for new and innovative programs. Fisher served as the fund's chairman since its inception.

In 2004 the Detroit Symphony Orchestra opened the Max M. Fisher Music Center performing arts complex. Fisher donated $10 million to the building, which is nicknamed "The Max." At age 96, Fisher was listed by *Forbes* magazine in 2004 as the oldest member of the Forbes 400, the list of the 400 wealthiest people in America.

ADD. BIBLIOGRAPHY: P. Golden, *Quiet Diplomat: A Biography of Max M. Fisher* (1992).

[Hillel Halkin / Ruth Beloff (2nd ed.)]

FISHER, SAMUEL, BARON FISHER OF CAMDEN (1905–1979), English communal worker. Samuel Fisher was born in London and from his youth was active both in Jewish communal affairs and in local politics. In 1953 he was elected mayor of the Borough of Stoke Newington, the first Jew to hold the office, and in 1965 of the newly created borough of Camden. His many public offices included chairmanship of the Metropolitan Water Board and of the Association of Labor Mayors. In the Jewish community he was one of the leading figures of the Jewish Friendly Society Movement, and in 1973–79 served as president of the Board of Deputies of British Jews. He was created a life peer in 1974 as Baron Fisher of Camden.

Fisher was an outstanding example of the new generation of Jewish communal leaders, whose roots were in the East End of London and who rose to the pinnacle of Jewish communal leadership without the advantage of birth or wealth but by hard work and a genuine concern for their fellows.

[Michael Wallach]

FISHER, SIR WOOLF (1912–1975), New Zealand industrialist and philanthropist. Born in Paraparaumu, he founded with his brother-in-law, M. Paykel, the firm of Fishel and Paykel, which developed into one of the largest manufacturers of refrigerators and home appliances in New Zealand. Fisher became one of the Dominion's leading industrialists. In 1959 he was appointed by the government to lead the New Zealand trade mission to Australia. From 1960 he headed New Zealand Steel Ltd., a vast enterprise, manufacturing steel from iron sands. Fisher helped to found the New Zealand Outward Bound Movement for the physical and moral training of youth. Among his other philanthropic undertakings was the establishment of the Woolf Fisher Scholarship Trust enabling New Zealand teachers to travel overseas. He was also a bloodstock breeder and owner of some of New Zealand's finest racehorses. Fisher was knighted in 1964 for his contributions to business life and philanthropy.

ADD. BIBLIOGRAPHY: *Dictionary of New Zealand Biography* (2003), online edition.

[Alexander Astor]

FISHMAN, JACOB (1878–1946), Yiddish editor and U.S. Zionist leader. Fishman was born in Poland and emigrated to the United States where he became active in pre-Herzl Zionist societies and later helped found the Zionist Organization of America. He wrote for and coedited the New York Yiddish dailies *Tageblat* (1893–1914) and *Varhayt* (1914–16), and from 1916 made his impact on the American Jewish scene as columnist and managing editor of the *Jewish Morning Journal.*

BIBLIOGRAPHY: Rejzen Leksikon, 3 (1929), 108ff.; LNYL, 7 (1968), 394–5.

[Sol Liptzin]

FISHMAN, JOSHUA AARON (1926–), U.S. educator, social psychologist, and sociolinguist. Born in Philadelphia, Fishman received his Ph.D. in social psychology from Columbia University in 1953. He was professor of social sciences at Yeshiva University (New York) from 1966. Fishman served as dean of the Ferkauf Graduate School of Humanities from 1960 to 1966 and as Yeshiva University's vice president of academic affairs from 1973 to 1975. He then served as the distinguished university research professor emeritus of social sciences of Yeshiva University.

An international leader in his field, Foreman did pioneering research in sociolinguistics, which explores the social concomitants of language behavior and behavior toward language. Within this field, he specialized in national language planning and in determining the circumstances of language maintenance and shift, and established techniques for measuring and describing patterns of societal bilingualism. He was also an internationally recognized authority on language policy in developing countries. Fishman's book *Language Loyalty in the United States* (1966) is a monumental work on the language maintenance efforts of non-English-speaking immigrants. His *Yiddish in America* (1965) is a significant study describing the efforts of American Jews of Eastern European origin to maintain their vernacular. In 1973 Fishman founded and became the ongoing general editor of the *International Journal of the Sociology of Language.* He also served as the editor of *YIVO-Bleter* from 1975 to 1977. He was appointed a Fellow of the Institute for Advanced Study at Princeton in 1975.

Among other books published by Fishman, the following have some Jewish content: *Language and Nationalism* (1972); *Language in Sociocultural Change* (1972); *Bilingual Education* (1976); *Language Planning Processes* (1977); *Advances in the Study of Societal Multilingualism* (1978); and *Advances in the Creation and Revision of Writing Systems* (1979), while *Studies on Polish Jewry: 1919–1939* (1973) and *Never Say Die: A Thousand Years of Yiddish in Jewish Life and Letters* (of which he was editor, 1980) are entirely of Jewish content. Subsequent books by Fishman include *Ethnicity in Action* (with M. and R. Gertner, 1985), *Readings in the Sociology of Jewish Languages* (1985), *Ideology, Society & Language: The Odyssey of Nathan Birnbaum* (1987), *The Influence of Language on Culture and Thought* (1991), *In Praise of the Beloved Language* (1996), *Can Threatened Languages Be Saved?* (2001), and *Reversing Language Shift* (2001).

Fishman was active in Yiddish cultural efforts. As a founding member and first chairman of the Research Planning Committee of the *YIVO Institute for Jewish Research in New York, he helped to develop a program for training new scholars in the social sciences and humanities as they relate to the Jewish field.

BIBLIOGRAPHY: *Who's Who in America*, 34 (1966–67), 684; LNYL, 7 (1968), 393–4. **ADD. BIBLIOGRAPHY:** S. Herman, *The Study of Jewish Identity Issues and Approaches* (1971).

[Leybl Kahn / Ruth Beloff (2nd ed.)]

FISHMAN, WILLIAM (1921–), British historian. Born to Russian immigrant parents in London's East End, Fishman left school at 14 to become a clerk and was involved in the *"Battle of Cable Street" in 1936. After World War II he received a degree from the London School of Economics and became probably the first British professionally trained historian of immigrant background to study the Jewish East End. From 1972 Fishman was Barnett Shine Senior Research Fellow at Queen Mary College. His best-known work, *East End Jewish Radicals,* appeared in 1975, and he has also written several other pioneering studies of the East End working class. Fishman has been very influential in broadening the traditional "meliorist" focus of Anglo-Jewish history from its elites to the inclusion of post-1880 immigrants and of radical groups. A Festschrift for Fishman, *Outsiders and Outcasts: Essays in Honour of William Fishman*, edited by Geoffrey Alderman and Colin Holmes, appeared in 1993.

[William D. Rubinstein (2nd ed.)

FISHMAN, WILLIAM HAROLD (1914–2001), biochemist. Fishman was born in Winnipeg, Canada, and became a U.S. citizen c. 1942. He graduated from the University of Saskatchewan (1935) and got his Ph.D. in biochemistry from the University of Toronto (1939). After postdoctoral research at the University of Edinburgh (1940) and Cornell University Medical School (1941), he joined the Bowman-Gray School of Medicine in Winston-Salem, North Carolina, followed by the University of Chicago (1945) and Tufts University, Boston (1948–76), where he became professor of pathology and first director of the Tufts Cancer Research Center (1971). In 1976 he and his wife and colleague Lillian Fishman founded the La Jolla Cancer Research Foundation (now the Burnham Institute), where he worked for the rest of his life. Fishman's research concerned the relationship between normal cell development and cancer (oncodevelopmental biology), and identifying markers for diagnosing cancer. His honors included the annual award from the International Society for Oncodevelopmental Biology and Medicine (1994), which recognized his pioneering role in this field.

[Michael Denman (2nd ed.)]

FITCH (Feiczewicz), LOUIS (1889–1956), Canadian Zionist. Born in Suceava, Bukovina, Fitch was taken to Canada in 1891 by his parents, who settled in Quebec. He was associated with Samuel W. Jacobs, who became a member of the Canadian parliament in 1917, in the Ortenberg trial. In this trial Jewish citizens of Quebec laid charges of libel against antisemitic agitators who had stated that the Talmud permits Jews to harm Christians. In 1919 he was one of the founders of the Canadian Jewish Congress, of which he was the first secretary. In the early 1920s he was chairman of the schools committee of the Montreal Jewish Community Council, which was fighting for a separate Jewish school system in Quebec; the case reached the Privy Council in London. He later became president of the Canadian ORT. In 1938 he was elected to the Quebec Provincial legislature, representing the Union Nationale Party, but was defeated the following year. Fitch published a number of historical works. He traveled extensively in Spain, North Africa, Mexico and Central America to research various aspects of the history of the Jews in Spanish-speaking countries, and made a special study of the Golden Age of Hebrew Literature in Spain.

Fitch remained an active Zionist throughout his life. He was vice president of the Zionist Organization of Canada from 1921 to 1940.

FITELBERG, GRZEGORZ (**Gregor**; 1879–1953), conductor and composer. Born in Dvinsk, Latvia, Fitelberg became conductor of the Warsaw Philharmonic Orchestra (1906–11), the Vienna Opera (1912–13), and, between 1914 and 1920, the Petrograd Musikalnya Drama Orchestra, the Moscow Bolshoi, and Diaghilev Ballet orchestras. He then returned to the Warsaw Philharmonic and formed the Polish radio's symphony orchestra. He spent World War II mainly in the U.S., and returned to the same orchestra, which he conducted until his death. Fitelberg's compositions include two symphonies (1905 and 1907), two overtures (1905 and 1906), and two orchestral rhapsodies. His son, JERZY FITELBERG (1903–1951), also a composer, was born in Warsaw and died in New York. He wrote mainly chamber and orchestral music in a neoclassical style, sometimes using Polish folk idioms.

FITERMAN, CHARLES (1933–), French politician. Born in Saint Etienne, France, Fiterman, a qualified electrician by trade, made his way to the number two position in the French Communist party, the second largest communist party in the Western world. In the first Mitterrand administration (1981–1984) he was one of the four communist ministers and was in charge of transport. Fiterman is a cool, moderate politician who follows traditional party lines.

His unsuccessful challenge to the leadership of the Communist party by Georges Marchais led to his exclusion from central positions in the party and he became one of the leaders of the "reformers" wing demanding reform and modernization of the remaining traditional communist parties in the world.

[Gideon Kouts]

FIVE SPECIES, the varieties of seed to which the *halakhot* concerning the agricultural produce of Ereẓ Israel apply. The Mishnah lists the five species as *ḥittim, se'orim, kusmin, shibbolet shu'al*, and *shippon* (Ḥal. 1:1). They are known in literature by the generic names *tevu'ah* ("produce," "increase"; Ḥal. 1:2) and *dagan* ("corn," i.e. grain). In the Bible, however, both terms have a wider meaning; *tevu'ah* denotes the "increase" of the threshing floor and the winepress (Num. 18:30), the vineyard (Deut. 22:9), and the corn (II Chron. 32:28); and *dagan* (often juxtaposed to "wine" and "oil") denotes the blessings of the earth. The term *bar* occurs only in the Bible, and applies to corn from which the chaff has been winnowed (Jer. 23:28; et al.). The exact definition of the five species is problematical. Feliks maintains that three of the five are species of the genus *Triticum* ("*wheat*"), and identifies (1) *ḥittim* as hard and bread wheat (*Triticum durum* and *vulgare*); (2) *kusmin* as rice wheat (*Triticum dicoccum*); (3) *shippon* as spelt wheat (*Triticum spelta*); the last two are species of the genus *Horedeum* ("barley"); (4) se'orim is six- and four-rowed barley (*Hordeum sativum* and *vulgare*); and (5) *shibbolet shu'al* is two-rowed barley (*Hordeum distichum*). All five species grew in Ereẓ Israel in ancient times, as was not the case with oats (the usual translation of *shibbolet shu'al*) or rye (that of *shippon*).

According to the *halakhah* these five species are subject to the laws relating to the blessings said before and after meals (see *Grace after Meals), to *ḥallah* (the separation of a portion of dough to the priests; Ḥal, 1:1), to the laws concerning leavened and unleavened bread on Passover (Ḥal. 1:2), and to the prohibition against harvesting or eating produce until the *omer* has been offered (Ḥal, 1:1). With respect to the law of *kilayim* (the prohibition on mixing heterogeneous plants in a field), *kusmin* and *shippon* are regarded as one species, and *se'orim* and *shibbolet shu'al* as another (Kil. 1:1). As regards combining different doughs to form the minimum quantity liable to *ḥallah*, in which taste is the determining factor, *ḥittim* and *kusmin* are reckoned as one species (Pes. 35a).

The Talmud records an important dispute between Johanan b. Nuri and the sages. The former maintained that rice, too, was a species of grain and, like the five species mentioned above, was subject to the laws of Grace after Meals, *ḥallah*, and unleavened bread. He also included as liable to *ḥallah, karmit* (Pes, 35a), apparently a plant of the order *Gramineae* which grows in swamps – the *Glyceria fluitans*. Although Johanan b. Nuri's view was not accepted as *halakhah*, there were places in Babylonia where *ḥallah* was separated from dough made of rice, since it was their staple food (Pes. 50b–51a). However, since rice is usually sown after Passover and does not ripen until the end of summer, Johanan b. Nuri is not reported as claiming that the laws of *omer* apply to it, since this would mean that it could not be eaten until the following spring.

BIBLIOGRAPHY: ET, 4 (1956), 226–9; J. Feliks, *Olam ha-Ẓome'aḥ ha-Mikra'i* (1957), 139–53; idem, *Kilei Zera'im ve-Harkavah* (1967), 24–32; idem, in: *Sefer ha-Shanah … Bar Ilan*, 1 (1962/63), 177–89; Loew, Flora, 1 (1924), 707ff.

[Jehuda Feliks]

°FLACCUS, AVILLIUS AULUS, prefect of Egypt 32–38 C.E. Until the death in 37 of Tiberius, to whom he owed his appointment, Flaccus discharged his duties with devotion and ability. However, with the accession of Caligula and the consequent uncertainty of his position, his attitude toward the Jews of Alexandria changed for the worse. He withheld their expression of homage to Caligula on the latter's accession, permitted the mob to jeer at the Jewish king Agrippa when he visited Alexandria, allowed them to place idols in the local synagogues, and issued an edict declaring the Jews to be aliens. He arrested and maltreated members of the *gerousia* (the local community council) and ordered Jewish homes to be searched and any weapons found to be confiscated. When the Jews were attacked and many of them killed by the Alexandrians, Flaccus made no attempt to restrain the mob. Suddenly arrested, he was sent to Rome and there banished to Andros, and later executed. Philo, who describes the entire episode in his *In Flaccum*, saw in his fate the hand of Providence.

BIBLIOGRAPHY: Pauly-Wissowa, 4 (1896), 2392, no. 3 and Suppl. 1 (1903), 228f.; U. Wilcken, *Griechische Ostraka aus Aegypten und Nubien*, 2 (1899), no. 1372; E. Groag and A. Stein (eds.), *Prosopographia Imperii Romani*, 1 (1933^2), 290f., no. 1414; H. Box, *Philonis Alexandrini in Flaccum* (1939).

[Lea Roth]

°FLACCUS, VALERIUS, Latin writer of the Flavian period, author of the *Argonautica*, describing the voyage of Jason and his companions. Only in the proem to the *Argonautica* does he touch upon matters pertaining to the Jews. It consists of a laudatory address to the emperor Vespasian, in which he refers to Titus' claim to military glory, the conquest of Jerusalem. The conquest of Judea (which he calls Idumea) and the burning of the Temple he describes in the words, "Thy son (i.e., Domitian) shall tell of the overthrow of Idumea – for well he can – of his brotherhood with the dust of Solyma, as he hurls the brands and spreads havoc in every tower." It is noteworthy that unlike *Josephus, who states that the Temple was destroyed against the wishes of Titus, Valerius Flaccus extols its destruction (although he refers generally to Jerusalem and not specifically to the Temple); this suggests that Josephus' description is an attempt to minimize the initiative taken by Titus in the destruction of the Temple. There is no reason to assume that the proem was composed immediately after the destruction or even during the reign of Vespasian; the conquest of Jerusalem was well remembered for many years. Scholars differ as to the date of the proem, some placing it in the reign of Titus, and others in that of Domitian.

BIBLIOGRAPHY: J. Bernays, *Ueber die Chronik des Sulpicius Severus* (1861), 48ff.; Syme, in: *Classical Quarterly*, 23 (1929), 135–7; V. Ussani, *Studio su Valerio Flacco* (1955); Smallwood, in: *Mnemosyne*, 4th series, 15 (1962), 170–2; Pauly-Wissowa, 2nd series, 15 (1955), 10, no. 170.

[Menahem Stern]

FLAG. There are indications that banners or emblems were in use among the Israelites even in biblical times (see *Banner). The expression אֹתֹת לְבֵית אֲבֹתָם – "the banner (or ensign) or their patriarchal house" (Num. 2:2) – appears to denote the physical emblem of a tribe, a patriarchal house, or a family, and it was thus understood in the Midrash (Num. R, 2:7), which gives the following description of the flags of the 12 tribes, with proof verses where the reason is not immediately obvious:

> There were distinguishing signs for each prince; each had a flag (*mappah*) and a different color for every flag, corresponding to the precious stones on the breastplate (lit. "heart") of Aaron. It was from these that governments learned to provide themselves with flags of various colors. Each tribe had its own prince and its flag whose color corresponded to the color of its stone. Reuben's stone was ruby, the color of his flag was red, and embroidered thereon were mandrakes. Simeon's was topaz and his flag was green, with the town of Shechem embroidered thereon. Levi's was smaragd (= emerald) and the color of his flag was a third white, a third black, and a third red; embroidered thereon were the Urim and Thummim. Judah's was a carbuncle and the color of his flag resembled that of the heavens; embroidered on it was a lion. Issachar's was a sapphire and the color of his flag was black like stibium; embroidered thereon were the sun and moon. Zebulun's was an emerald and the color of his flag was white, with a ship embroidered thereon. Dan's was jacinth and the color of his flag was similar to sapphire; embroidered on it was a serpent. Gad's was an agate and the color of his flag was neither white not black but a blend of black and white; on it was embroidered a camp. Naphtali's was an amethyst and the color of his flag was like clarified wine of a not very deep red; on it was embroidered a hind. Asher's was a beryl and the color of his flag was like the precious stone with which women adorn themselves; embroidered thereon was an olive tree. Joseph's was an onyx and the color of his flag was jet black; the embroidered design thereon for both princes, Ephraim and Manasseh, was Egypt because they were born there. A bullock was embroidered on the flag of Ephraim. A wild ox was embroidered on the flag of the tribe of Manasseh. Benjamin's stone was a jasper and the color of his flag was a combination of all the twelve colors; embroidered thereon was a wolf.

The word *nes*, mentioned in the Prophets (Isa. 5:26; 62:10; Jer. 4:6; Ps. 60:6), is also close to the modern "flag," standing as it does for a signal which may flutter in the breeze raised on a high place. It is also used to denote a sail (Isa. 33:23, also in the Mishna, BB 5a). Murals depicting Jewish ships, as found in Bet She'arim tombs and "Jason's tomb" in the Reḥaviah quarter of Jerusalem, reveal that the ships bore emblems. From Targum Jonathan to Numbers 2:3 it becomes apparent (see Num. R. 2:7; *Midrash Aggadah* (Buber ed. 79) *Arugat ha-Bosem* (Urbach ed.) A, 287/8) that during the time of the Targum colored flags, made of silk, were already known.

The term *degel* used in the Bible, especially in the description of the order in which the people of Israel pitched their tents and their battle array (Num. 2:1–3, 10–18, 25), was thought to have its present-day meaning – "flag." In fact, the term as employed there denotes a division of the people's army. This is the sense of Akkadian *diglu* (from *dagālu*; "to see," "behold,"), Aramaic *degel* of the fifth century B.C.E. *Elephantine papyri, and this is also the sense in which the term is mentioned in the Midrash (e.g., Num. R. 2:7; Song R. 6, 10); the Arabic word *dajjala* also means a very large group of men. Rashi (to Num. 2:2) explains *degel* in accordance with the examples he saw among the military formations of his time – a colored symbol identifying a military unit.

In the Dead Sea Scrolls – e.g., the "War of the Sons of Light with the Sons of Darkness" – the term *degel* is used in its biblical sense: an organizational unit, a battalion (*ibid.*, ed. Yadin 1955, p. 274; for other attestations DCH II, 415). The same scroll, however, devotes two chapters (*ibid.*, pp. 274–282, 284), to a description of the *otot* סֶרֶךְ אוֹתוֹת כּוֹל הָעֵדָה ("the customary symbols of the entire community"), which appear to have been actual flags. These symbols were of considerable sizes, depending on the size of the unit which they served, and contained various inscriptions: עַם אֵל ("the People of God"); שֵׁם יִשְׂרָאֵל וְאַהֲרֹן וּשְׁמוֹת שְׁנֵים עָשָׂר שִׁבְטֵי יִשְׂרָאֵל כְּתוֹלְדוֹתָם ("the name of Israel and Aaron and the names of the twelve tribes of Israel in the order of their birth"); נֵס אֵל (the pennant of God); שֵׁם נְשִׂיא הַשֵּׁבֶט (the name of the prince of the tribe); etc. To those who went into battle an order was issued "to inscribe on their symbols, as they went forth to war" further inscriptions, and, "when they returned from war" as victors, to add appropriate inscriptions (see DCH II, 166). If the scroll is not a literary fiction but reflects reality, there is here a description of the important role, very similar to that of the modern flag, ascribed to physical symbols in the organization of the community.

In the Diaspora, where there was no Jewish army or panoply of state, there was no room for flags in Jewish public life. In the late Middle Ages instances are known of the award of flags to individual Jews of communities by the secular rulers. In 1254 the emperor Charles IV granted a flag to the Jews of Prague; it was red in color and displayed the six-pronged star, which later became known as Shield of David. In 1592 R. Mordechai Meisel, also of Prague, was given permission to display in his synagogue "the flag of King David, similar to the flag in the Great Synagogue." In 1648 the Jews of Prague were again awarded a flag – still to be found in the Prague synagogue, the Altneuschul – in recognition of their part in the defense of the city against the Swedes; the flag is red and in the middle there is a yellow Shield of David with a Swedish star in its center. When the Jews of Ofen (= Buda) in Hungary welcomed King Matthias Corvinus in 1460, they carried a red flag containing two Shields of David and two other stars.

Jewish flags as an expression of national awakening appeared in the campaign of David *Reubeni among the Jews and the Christian rulers. His deportment was that of a prince and he used flags extensively as an expression of Jewish sovereignty. His flags were white, with the Ten Commandments or verses and names (according to one version, the letters of the word "Maccabee") embroidered on them in gold. Reubeni carried a flag of this kind when he appeared with Solomon *Molcho before Charles v in Regensburg in 1532. Molcho also signed his letters and writings by drawing a flag above his name (see illustrations under *Autographs).

The Shield of David acquired its status as a recognized Jewish symbol only as late as the middle of the 17th century. Official use of it was first made by the heads of the Jewish communities of Prague and Vienna, spreading from these places all over the world. The aristocratic Jewish families of Rothschild and Montefiore incorporated it in their family arms. The early *Ḥibbat Zion societies used it as a national emblem (e.g., in their official seals), generally inscribing the word *Ẓiyyon* in it.

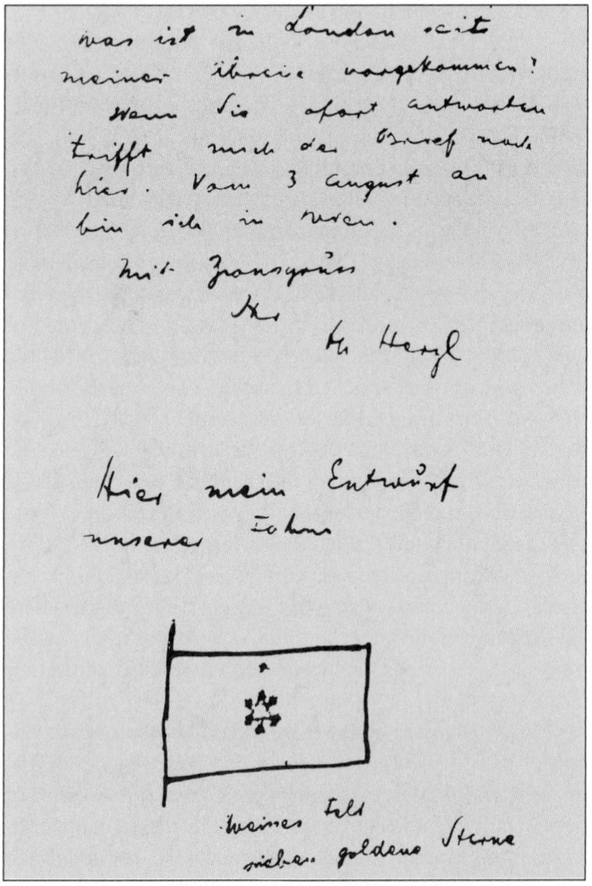

Theodor Herzl, who was not aware of the emblems used by the Ḥibbat Zion movement, made the following entry in his diary (June 12, 1895): "The flag that I am thinking of – perhaps a white flag with seven gold stars. The white background stands for our new and pure life; the seven stars are the seven working hours: we shall enter the Promised Land in the sign of work." This was also the flag that he proposed in *The Jewish State* (1896). Under the influence of the Zionist societies he accepted the shield of David as the emblem of the movement, but he insisted that the six stars should be placed on the six angles of the shield of David, and the seventh above it. In this form, with the inscription *"Aryeh Yehudah"* (the Lion of Judah) in the middle, the Shield of David became the first emblem of the Zionist Organization.

The combination blue and white as the colors of the Jewish flag is first mentioned in the latter part of the 19th century. In his poem *"Ẓivei Ereẓ Yehudah,"* written about 1860, the poet L.A. *Frankl declaims:

> All that is sacred will appear in these colors:
> White – as the radiance of great faith
> Blue – like the appearance of the firmament.

The Zionist flag in its present form – two blue stripes on white background with a Shield of David in the center – was first displayed in Rishon le-Zion in 1885. This, however, was not known to the delegates of the First Zionist Congress, and it was David Wolfsohn who created the flag of Zion on the model of the **tallit*, which, as he pointed out, was the traditional flag of the Jewish people, adding the Shield of David. In 1933, the 18th Zionist Congress decided that "by long tradition, the blue-and-white flag is the flag of the Zionist Organization and the Jewish people." This was also the flag which, by a special order issued by Winston Churchill, became the official flag of the Jewish Brigade Group in World War II.

Herzl's design for a Jewish flag, seven gold stars on a white field, sketched at the end of a letter to Jacob de Haas, probably 1896. The seven stars were intended to symbolize a seven-hour working day. From J. de Haas, Theodor Herzl, *1927.*

Flags of the State of Israel

As soon as the State of Israel was established, the question of its flags and emblems arose. Public opinion was unanimous in favor of proclaiming the flag of the Zionist movement as the state flag, but there was some apprehension lest this might cause problems to foreign members of the movement. The Provisional Council of State therefore decided only on flags of the navy and the merchant marine, and it was not until six months after the state had been proclaimed that the form of the national flag was officially determined; it was to be the flag of the Zionist movement, consisting of a white rectangle, with two blue stripes along its entire length and a Shield of David in the center made up of six stripes forming two equilateral triangles. In the original resolution, the color of the stripes and the Shield of David was described as "dark sky-blue," but this was later changed to "blue" for better visibility at sea.

The flag of the Israel navy is a dark blue rectangle, with a white isosceles triangle, with the vertex in the center of the rectangle and the base coinciding with its inner side, and a blue Shield of David inside the triangle. The flag of the Merchant Marine is a blue rectangle with a white oval with a blue Shield of David in its center.

The official emblem of the State, which was decided on in 1949, is the *menorah*, or candelabrum, the ancient symbol of the Jewish people, in the form seen in relief on the arch of Titus in Rome. The *menorah* is surrounded by olive branches, linked at the bottom by the inscription "Israel." The president's pennant is a square blue flag, with the state emblem in silver inside a silver frame. In the course of time more flags and pennants have been adopted: the flag of the Customs and Excise, a blue rectangle, with the national flag in its upper quarter and the inscription מֶכֶס וּבְלוֹ (Customs & Excise) inside a circle in the lower outer quarter.; the flag of the Israel Defense Forces, a blue rectangle with a thin gold stripe along three of its sides and in the lower outer quarter the badge of the IDF, consisting of a Shield of David in outline with a sword entwined with olive leaves inside it, and a strip bearing the inscription "צבא הגנה לישראל" (Israel Defense Army) at the bottom; the prime minister's pennant, a blue rectangle with the national flag in its upper inside quarter and the state emblem, superimposed on the IDF badge, in gold, in the lower outer quarter; the defense minister's pennant, similar to the prime minister's, but smaller by a quarter, and with the emblem in silver; the pennant of the chief of staff, the *allufim* (generals), the commander of the navy, the senior officer in a flotilla; the active service pennant, hoisted on naval vessels on active service; the flag of the air force; and the civil aviation pennant.

BIBLIOGRAPHY: M. Nimẓa-Bi, *Ha-Degel* (1948); State of Israel, *Iton Rishmi*, nos. 2, 32, 50 (1948–49); idem, *Sefer ha-Ḥukkim*, no. 8 (1949); idem, *Simlei Medinat Israel* (1953). **ADD. BIBLIOGRAPHY:** B. Levine, *Numbers 1–20* (1993), 146–48

[Michael Simon]

FLAM, HERB (1928–), U.S. tennis player. Born in Brooklyn, New York, and raised in California, Flam started playing at the age of 10 under the tutelage of his father and won his first tournament at 12. He first gained attention in 1943, when he won the U.S. Lawn Tennis Association (USLTA) Singles Championship as a 15 year old. As a Beverly Hills High School junior in 1945, he captured the USLTA Interscholastic titles in Singles and Doubles, with Hugh Stewart. The pair repeated their Doubles success in 1946. Flam earned national prominence in 1948, when as an undergraduate at UCLA, he entered the USLTA Singles Championships unseeded and reached the semifinals, earning him a No. 9 U.S. ranking. He won the USLTA Intercollegiate Singles and Doubles with Gene Garrett in 1950, and then reached the finals of the U.S. Singles championship, becoming the first Jewish tennis player ever to advance to those finals. Flam won the U.S. National Clay Court Singles that year, and teamed with Art Larsen to win the Clay Court Doubles crown as well. He reached the final eight of the Wimbledon Singles three times, and the semifinals in 1952. Flam also reached the quarterfinals of the U.S. Singles six times. After serving in the Navy in 1953–54, Flam won the 1955 U.S. Hard Court Championship, and in 1956 he won his second U.S. Clay Court title. He competed for the United States in Davis Cup matches starting in 1951, winning 12 of 14 matches through his final appearance in 1957. He was ranked No. 6 in the world in 1951, No. 10 in 1952, No. 7 in 1956, No. 5 in 1957 by World Tennis Magazine, and No. 4 in 1957 by the dean of British tennis writers, Lance Tingay. His U.S. rankings were as high as No. 2 in 1950, 1956, and 1957. Up until his time, Flam earned more world rankings than any other Jewish player.

[Elli Wohlgelernter (2nd ed.)]

FLANAGAN, BUD (1896–1968), British comedian. Born Chaim Reuben Weintrop, Flanagan teamed up with Chesney Allen after World War I. "Flanagan and Allen" toured the world and came to prominence in 1930 in George Black's "crazy" show at the London Pavilion. After World War II they were part of the "Crazy Gang," whose shows ran for many years at the Victoria Palace. Flanagan led the gang until it broke up in 1962. Most famous of Flanagan and Allen's song hits was "Underneath the Arches," a song of the depression of the 1930s. Flanagan sang the title song of the popular British television series *Dad's Army*. He wrote an autobiography, *My Crazy Life* (1962).

ADD. BIBLIOGRAPHY: ODNB online.

°**FLAVIUS, CLEMENS** (d. 95 C.E.), son of *Vespasian's elder brother, T. Flavius Sabinus. His sons were designated as successors to the childless emperor Domitian. In 95 C.E. he served as consul together with the emperor. Domitian, however, formally accused Clemens and his wife DOMITILLA, herself a granddaughter of Vespasian and a niece of *Titus and Domitian, of atheism (ἀθεοτης) which resulted in the execution of Clemens and the banishment of Domitilla. The earliest source, Dio Cassius (67:14, 1–2), expressly describes this heresy as a conversion to Judaism. Some scholars connect Flavius' conversion with the journey to Rome of R. *Gamaliel and his followers while others have depicted the couple as Christian martyrs.

BIBLIOGRAPHY: Schuerer, Gesch, 3 (1909), 168 n. 57; H. Vogelstein, *Rome* (1940), 70ff.; H.J. Leon, *Jews of Ancient Rome* (1960), 33–35, 252; E.M. Smallwood, in: *Classical Philology*, 51 (1956), 8; M. Stern, in: *Zion*, 29 (1964), 161–2; Alon, Toledot, 1 (1958), 74–75; G. Townend, in: *Journal of Roman Studies*, 51 (1961), 58; *New Catholic Encyclopedia*, 4 (1967), 994–5.

[Isaiah Gafni and Uriel Rappaport]

FLAX (Heb. פִּשְׁתָּה, *pishtah*, in the Bible; פִּשְׁתָּן, *pishtan*, in talmudic literature), plant cultivated in Ereẓ Israel. It is mentioned only once in the Bible. The "stalks of flax" mentioned in Joshua 2:6 are undressed flax fibers. Evidence of the cultivation of flax in Ereẓ Israel at the beginning of the period of the kingdom is to be found in the *Gezer Calendar, which mentions ירח עצד פשת, that is, "the month of the uprooting of flax," which is followed by "the month of the barley harvest." In the Bible there is frequent reference to flax products.

The cultivation of flax played an important role in ancient Egypt. The Bible states that during the plague of hail in Egypt, flax (which ripens early) was damaged (Ex. 9:31). Isaiah (19:5–9) describes the havoc caused to the Egyptian economy by the drying up of the Nile, the consequent withering of the flax, and the resulting ruin of the industries associated with it. Flax was, together with wool, one of the necessities of life (Hos. 2:7, 11), The Torah prohibited the wearing of a garment spun of both materials (Deut, 22:11; see *Shaatnez), a prohibition which the Midrash (PdRE 21) connects with the episode of Cain and Abel, the former having brought an offering of flax seeds, the latter of wool. Some contend that the prohibition reflects the antagonism between the farmer and the shepherd.

The Akkadian for flax is *kitannu*, from which are derived the biblical *ketonet* and the talmudic *kitna*. The sages differed on the interpretation of the phrase "garments (*kotnot*) of skins," with which Adam and Eve were clothed, one view being that it referred to flax "from which the [human] skin derives pleasure," another that it referred to wool, that "grows from skin" (Sot. 14a). Linen from c. 135 C.E. was discovered in Nahal Ḥever.

There are many references in talmudic literature to the growth and cultivation of flax. The quantity of flax produced was apparently subject to considerable fluctuations, there having been times when it was necessary to import hempen garments (Kil. 9:2), These, however, were no longer in demand in the amoraic period when flax was extensively grown (TJ, Kil. 9:5, 32d), Flax was attacked by plant diseases, and public prayers were offered up for their riddance (TJ, Ta'an 3:6, 66d), but after Hiyya and his sons came from Babylonia (to Ereẓ Israel), flax was free from disease (TJ, Ma'as. Sh. 5:8, 56d). Flax was regarded as a crop that impoverishes the soil and so was planted in the same field only once every three or seven years (BM 9:9; Tosef., BM 9:31). It bears beautiful blue flowers, which are followed after a few days by pods (Num. R. 7:4). Although grown mainly for its fiber, it was also cultivated for its seed, which was used as food and for medicinal purposes (BB 93a–b).

The Mishnah and the Talmud give many details about flaxen products and different kinds of cloth. A garment made of flax was usually a popular, strong, and very cheap form of clothing. When R. Judah ha-Nasi II, wearing a flaxen garment, came out to meet R. Johanan, he was told that it was more proper for a patriarch to wear clothes made of wool (TJ, Sanh. 2:8, 20c). There were, however, also fine, excellent clothes made of flax, a wealthy high priest having worn a flaxen garment which cost 20,000 zuzim (TJ, Yoma 3:6,40d). Although expensive flax material was imported (BM 29b), a high quality flaxen cloth was produced in Ereẓ Israel at Beth-Shean (Gen. R. 20:12); that made at Arbela was of a cheaper quality (*ibid.* 19:1 beginning). The flax in the Bible and in talmudic literature was the cultivated variety, *Linum usitatissimum*, of which there are many strains, some used in the manufacture of fiber, others for the extraction of oil from their seeds. Flax is hardly grown in Israel, but the wild flax of the species *Linum angustifolium*, which some regard as the original of the cultivated flax, grows extensively.

BIBLIOGRAPHY: Herschberg, in: *Ha-Kedem*, 3 (1909), 7–29 (Hebr. section); Loew, Flora, 2 (1924), 208–16; Krauss, Tal Arch, 1 (1910), 138–40; J. Feliks, *Olam ha-Ẓome'aḥ ha-Mikra'i* (1957), 279–84. **ADD. BIBLIOGRAPHY:** Feliks, Ha-Ẓome'aḥ, 130.

[Jehuda Feliks]

FLEA (Heb. פַּרְעֹשׁ, *parosh*). The flea symbolizes an insignificant, loathsome creature (I Sam. 24:15; 26:20). Nevertheless, the ancients did not refrain from calling themselves "parosh," and this was the name of a Judahite family that came with Ezra to Ereẓ Israel from Babylonia (Ezra 2:3), as well as of a Moabite prince (Neh. 10:15). The common flea, *Pulex irritans*, is a parasite living on human beings and other mammals. Another species is the *Chenopsylla cheopsis*, which attaches itself to rats. The flea is mentioned several times in talmudic literature where it is stated that contrary to several insects regarded as formed through spontaneous generation, its propagation is sexual (Shab. 107b). In modern times the flea has disappeared almost entirely from the inhabited regions of Israel.

BIBLIOGRAPHY: F.S. Bodenheimer, *Ha-Ḥai be-Arẓot ha-Mikra*, 2 (1956), 292ff.; Tristram, Nat Hist, 305.

[Jehuda Feliks]

FLECHTHEIM, ALFRED (1878–1937), German art collector, art dealer, and publisher. Flechtheim was born in Muenster/Westphalia into a prosperous family of grain dealers. After leaving school, he went to Geneva and Paris to complete his education. While working in the family business, he already engaged in collecting and participated in an art exhibition in Duesseldorf in 1906. Flechtheim was a co-founder of the Duesseldorf Sonderbund in 1909, which assisted young contemporary artists by offering them the possibility of exhibiting their works. Today, the fourth exhibition of the Sonderbund in Cologne in 1912, which had a direct impact on the New York Armory Show of 1913, is considered the most important presentation of European modern art prior to World War I. In the same year, Flechtheim opened his own gallery in Duesseldorf. Drafted into the army in 1914, Flechtheim had to dispose of his gallery and parts of his collection. However, he reopened it in 1919 and managed to open a second gallery in Berlin in 1921 and a third in Frankfurt-on-the-Main in 1922. Flechtheim sought out the works of contemporary French artists like Georges Braque, André Derain, Juan Gris, Pablo Picasso, and Maurice de Vlaminck but matched them with the works of contemporary German artists like Wilhelm Lehmbruck, Paul Klee, George Grosz, and Karl Hofer. As a dealer who introduced avant-garde art in Germany, he was in close contact with his colleague Daniel-Henry Kahnweiler in Paris, who was specialized mainly in the trade in Cubism, especially Picasso. In 1921, they joined forces and together became the most important art dealers and art patrons of the Weimar Republic. Many of his portraits, among them the famous one by Otto Dix (1926, Neue Nationalgalerie Berlin), offer vivid testimony of Flechtheim's leading position in the art world. Flechtheim was forced to close his galleries in 1933 and took refuge in London, where he continued to arrange exhibitions of modern art until his death in 1937.

BIBLIOGRAPHY: Kunstmuseum Duesseldorf, *Alfred Flechtheim. Sammler, Kunsthaendler, Verleger* (1987).

[Philipp Zschommler (2nd ed.)]

FLECK, BELA (1958–), U.S. banjo player, guitarist. The New York-born Fleck caught the banjo bug from hearing Homer and Jethro's theme for TV's *The Beverly Hillbillies* and acquired his first banjo at 15, although he was training as a French horn player at the High School of Music and Art. He spent his evenings playing with a bluegrass band, and it was in that musical genre that he first came to prominence as part of Newgrass Revival, a band that pioneered a fusion of bluegrass, jazz, rock, and country. In 1989 he joined with harmonica player/keyboardist Howard Levy, bassist Victor Lemonte Wooten, and "synth axe drumitar" player Roy "Futureman" Wooten to form the Flecktones, the band he continued to lead. The Flecktones, whose sound owes more to their leader's enthusiasm for Charlie Parker and John Coltrane than to Doc Watson and Bill Monroe, won numerous Grammy awards and made frequent national TV appearances.

BIBLIOGRAPHY: S. Hindin, "Bela Fleck," in *Down Beat Magazine* archives at: www.downbeat.com; N. Torkington, "Interview with Bela, April 21, 1996," at: http://prometheus.frii.com.

[George Robinson (2nd ed.)]

FLECKELES, ELEAZAR BEN DAVID (1754–1826), rabbi and author. Born in Prague, Fleckeles studied under Meir Fischeles (Bumsla), Moses Cohen-Rofe, and Ezekiel *Landau, In 1779 he was appointed rabbi of Kojetin in Moravia, but in 1783 returned to Prague, where he served as a member of the *bet din* of Ezekiel Landau and also headed a large yeshivah. After Landau's death, Fleckeles was appointed Oberjurist ("president") of the three-man rabbinate council which also included Samuel Landau, the son of Ezekiel. When the Frankists made their appearance in the city in 1800, Fleckeles headed the opposition to them. He was denounced by an informer and imprisoned, and on his release he wrote a pamphlet of thanksgiving entitled *Azkir Tehillot.* Fleckeles' fame rests on his volume of collected sermons, *Olat Hodesh* (4 parts, Prague, 1785–1800). It contains both halakhic and aggadic themes. Part II, *Olat Ẓibbur.* includes a sermon attacking Moses Mendelssohn's German translation of the Bible. In Part IV, *Ahavat David*, there are also included sermons against the Shabbateans and the Frankists. In these sermons, that reflect his outstanding ability as a preacher, Fleckeles expressed his vigorous opposition to various reforms resulting from the spread of the *Haskalah movement, warning on the one hand against excessive pursuit of secular studies and on the other concurring in the study of Kabbalah, but only on the basis of a sound knowledge of Talmud. Of his other books the following are noteworthy: *Teshuvah me-Ahavah*, a collection of 450 responsa (3 parts, Prague, 1809–21), in which he employed a new method of arranging the responsa according to the order of the Shulḥan Arukh, and at the same time adding his own comments on, and supplements to, other responsa; *Melekhet ha-Kodesh* (*ibid.*, 1812), a guide for scribes of *Sifrei Torah, tefillin*, and *mezuzot;* and *Hazon la-Mo'ed* (*ibid.*, 1824), 14 sermons for the month of Tishri. In the introductions to his works, he emphasizes the brotherhood of man and the duty of the Jews toward the Gentiles. In connection with the question put by the censor Karl Fischer, "whether there is any distinction between an Israelite swearing to his fellow Israelite and swearing to a Gentile," Fleckeles replied "that the force of an oath is great, and no distinction can be made between taking an oath to an Israelite and to a non-Jew" (*Teshuvah me-Ahavah*, pt. 1, no. 26). He was opposed to the hairsplitting methods of *pilpul* and to "labored solutions," and emphasized that he was not prone to stringency in his rulings (ibid., pt. 3, no. 325), He was careful to make allowance for traditional customs and gave information in his responsa about special customs that existed in various communities (*ibid.*, pt. 1, no. 90; pt. 2, no. 229).

BIBLIOGRAPHY: D. Kaufmann, in: MGWJ, 37 (1893), 378–92; G. Klemperer, in: HJ, 13 (1951), 76–80; S.H. Lieben, in: JJLG, 10 (1912), 1–33; Michael, Or, no. 485; J. Spitz, *Zikhron Eleazar* (1827); Zinberg, Sifrut, 5 (1959), 151, 156f., 356.

[Yehoshua Horowitz]

FLEG, EDMOND (originally Flegenheimer; 1874–1963), French poet, playwright, and essayist, whose outstanding works deal with Judaism and the Jewish people. Fleg's parents were prosperous and moderately observant Genevan Jews, but their religious compromises, together with his own secular studies, soon combined to weaken young Fleg's Jewish allegiances. He went to live in Paris, where he became a theater critic and a successful playwright. His plays included *Le Message* (1904), *La Bête* (1910), and *Le Trouble-fête* (1913), and French versions of Goethe's *Faust* (1937) and Shakespeare's *Julius Caesar* (1938). He also wrote the libretti for Ernest Bloch's *Macbeth* (1910) and Georges Enesco's *Oedipus* (1936). Fleg's dramatic return to Judaism, in the full sense, dates from the spiritual turmoil engendered by the *Dreyfus Affair (1894–1906), and the first three Zionist Congresses (1897–99), He was also impressed by the English author Israel *Zangwill, an early supporter of Zionism. Abandoning the path of easy success, he devoted himself to the study of Jewish history and thought, seeking reasons for the modern intellectual's remaining Jewish. His task was interrupted by World War I, in which he served in the French Foreign Legion. Thereafter, throughout 40 years of untiring activity, Fleg presented to the French reader the manifold aspects of Judaism in a style that shifts effortlessly from simple narrative to lyrical grandeur or brilliant psychological analysis. One of the most significant works was his *Anthologie juive des origines à nos jours* (1921, 1961; *The Jewish Anthology*, 1925). This discriminating and wide-ranging selection of Jewish writing down the ages constitutes a valuable introduction to Judaism.

Edmond Fleg's writing may be divided into three main categories: religious poetry, biographical works, and autobiographical and other essays on Jewish themes. He is perhaps best remembered for his verse cycle *Ecoute Israël*, a Jewish counterpart to Victor Hugo's *Légende des siècles*. The cycle comprises *Ecoute Israël* (1913–21), *L'Eternel est Notre Dieu* (1940), *L'Eternel est Un* (1945), and *Et Tu aimeras l'Eternel* (1948), the titles of which were taken from Deuteronomy 6:4. In 1954 the four parts were collected in one volume, starting with the creation and spanning the whole of Jewish history down to the era of the reborn Jewish State. Fleg's lyrical themes include the Jewish people's mission, messianic yearnings, and unswerving faith in humanity despite atrocities and persecution. From the Midrash, which he knew mainly from German translations, Fleg drew material for his legendary biographies *Moïse raconté par les Sages* (1928; *The Life of Moses*, 1928) and *Salomon* (1930; *The Life of Solomon*, 1929). Moved by ambivalent emotions of fascination and fear stemming from his childhood, Fleg also wrote *Jésus, raconté par le Juif Errant* (1933; *Jesus, Told by the Wandering Jew*, 1934), using quotations from the Hebrew Bible, talmudic literature, and the Gospels. Although Fleg presented a Jesus who was neither God nor Messiah, his sympathetic treatment of the Christian savior made a dubious impression on the Jewish reader. Of his essays, the most remarkable is probably *Pourquoi je suis Juif* (1928; *Why I am a Jew*, 1929), which was translated into English also by Victor Gollancz in 1943. A subtle and moving analysis of a young agnostic's spiritual progress and eventual return to Judaism, it also demonstrates Fleg's belief that the French genius owes much to the inspiration of Israel. The portrait of Fleg himself in *Pourquoi je suis Juif* may be regarded as a continuation of the one he painted in *L'Enfant prophète* (1926; *The Boy Prophet*, 1928). This romanticized account of a boy estranged from Judaism and rejected by Christian society tells how the child glimpses through the gloom of the Church a Jesus who is at once victim and persecutor, and how he at last seeks to revive his old faith through messianic expectation. Messianism also provided the theme of two early plays, *La Maison du Bon Dieu* (1920) and *Le Juif du Pape* (1925), the latter based on the encounter of Clement VII and Solomon Molcho. It continued to be a keynote of Fleg's writing over the years, as in *Ma Palestine* (1932; *The Land of Promise*, 1933) and *Nous de l'Esperance* (1949), which, together with *Pourquoi je suis Juif*, was collected in *Vers le Monde qui vient* (1960). In *La Terre que Dieu habite* (1953; *The Land in which God Dwells*, 1955) Fleg recorded the saga of the Zionist pioneers and his hopes for Israel's spiritual revival in the new Jewish State. His other works include translations of Shalom Aleichem and the Passover Haggadah (1925) and selections from Maimonides' *Guide* and from the Zohar. Fleg was an active member of the Alliance Israélite Universelle and of the French section of the World Jewish Congress. In Israel, a forest was dedicated in his honor in 1952.

BIBLIOGRAPHY: Laurencin, in: *Revue de la pensée juive*, 2 (Jan. 1950), 6–88; E. Fleg, *Pages choisies* (1954), introduction; Neher, in: *La Vie juive*, 45 (June 1958), 23–26.

[Jean Poliatchek]

FLEISCHER, CHARLES (1871–1942). U.S. rabbi. Fleischer, who began his career as a Reform rabbi articulating the ideal that American Jews could be both Americans and Jews, later developed a new American religion based upon the ideals of democracy. Born in Breslau, Germany, in 1871, Fleischer came to America at the age of nine. He moved to the Lower East Side, received his B.A. from the City College of New York in 1888, and advanced degrees from Hebrew Union College and the University of Cincinnati in 1893. He served as an assistant rabbi in Philadelphia until 1894, when he was named rabbi of Temple Israel in Boston. He remained at this post until 1911, and the following year founded the nonsectarian Sunday Commons, which he led from 1912 to 1918. Fleischer moved to New York in 1922, where he served as a newspaper editor, radio commentator, writer, and lecturer. During his tenure at Temple Israel, Fleischer introduced Sunday services (1906), and shared his pulpit with Unitarians, Trinitarians, and social reformers. He believed that ethics should be based on reason, rather than the fear of God, and that Judaism should strive to combat social problems. He often spoke to New England's Jewish and non-Jewish groups about Jewish-Gentile relations. Throughout his career, Fleischer struggled with his Jewish and American identities. Early on he possessed a pluralistic vision, believing that American Jews could be both Jews and Americans at the same time. But as early as 1902, Fleischer began to suggest that America should move beyond religious sectarianism, and that democracy itself was "potentially a universal spiritual principle, aye, a religion." In 1908 he advocated intermarriage, and when he left Temple Israel in 1911, he declared, "I am henceforth beyond… sectarianism."

True to his word, Fleischer founded the nonsectarian group Sunday Commons. He now argued that Jewish and Christian worship ran counter to universal values, and American religion should be based upon the values of heroes like Abraham Lincoln and texts such as the Declaration of Independence. Seventeen hundred people attended his services in their early years, where "aspirations" became a substitute for prayer.

BIBLIOGRAPHY: A. Mann, "Charles Fleischer's Religion of Democracy," in: *Commentary* 17, no. 6 (June 1954); "Dr. Chas. Fleischer, Editor and Lecturer," in: *New York Times* (July 3, 1942), 17.

[Michael Cohen (2nd ed.)]

FLEISCHER, JUDAH LOEB (Leopold, Lipot; 1886–1955), Hungarian scholar. Fleischer was born in Ersekujvar and founded a religious elementary school in Temesvar in 1918. He taught there and directed it until it was closed by the Communist regime in 1948. He wrote scholarly articles on Abraham Ibn Ezra, particularly the Bible commentaries, which appeared from 1912 onward in *Ha-Ẓofeh le-Ḥokhmat Yisrael, Sinai*, and other journals. Among his editions of Abraham Ibn Ezra are *Sefer ha-Ta'amim* (1951), *Sefer ha-Me'orot* (1933), *Sefer ha-Olam* (1937), and *Ibn Ezra le-Sefer Shemot* (1926). Some of his important works remain in manuscript.

His son Ezra FLEISCHER (1928–), Hebrew poet and scholar, was born in Temesvar (Timisoara), Transylvania. He was imprisoned after World War II by the Romanian authorities as a result of his activities on behalf of Bnei Akiva. In 1960 he immigrated to Israel, studied at the Hebrew University, became a lecturer on medieval Hebrew literature at Bar-Ilan University, and then at the Hebrew University. His poem, "*Massa Gog*" ("The Burden of Gog"), written during his imprisonment and published in the Israeli literary journal *Moznayim* (Nisan–Iyyar, 1959) under the pseudonym Y. Goleh, caused a literary sensation and won him the Israel Prize for 1959. He published poetry (under various pseudonyms) in the Hebrew press from 1956 and also two volumes, *Meshalim* (1957) and *Be-Heḥalek Laylah* (1961). Other important works include *Ha-Yoẓrot be-Hithavutam ve-Hitpatḥutam* (1984); a study of Hebrew poetry in the Middle Ages, *Shirat ha-Kodesh ha-Ivrit bi-Yemei ha-Beinayim* (1975); *Tefilah u-Minhagei Tefillah Ereẓ Yisraeliyim bi-Tekufat ha-Genizah* (1988).

BIBLIOGRAPHY: Ben-Menahem, in: KS, 33 (1958), 227–32 (bibliography of Fleischer's works); Breuer, in: S.K. Mirsky (ed.), *Ishim u-Demuyyot be-Hokhmat Yisrael* (1959), 404–14; A. Cohen, *Soferim Ivriyyim Benei Zemannenu* (1964), 209–10; M. Kushnir (Shnir), *Ha-Ne'imah ha-Aḥat* (1963), 228–30; CCAR *Journal*, 11 (1963), 48–49 (excerpt from "*Massa Gog*"). **ADD. BIBLIOGRAPHY:** R. Cohen, *Maẓa Matmonim: Bibliografyah shel Kitvei Ezra Fleischer* (2001)

[Getzel Kressel]

FLEISCHER, MAX (1883–1972), cartoonist and producer. Born in Vienna, Austria, Fleischer immigrated with his family to New York City at an early age, studying art at Cooper Union and the Art Students League. He worked as a commercial artist and cartoonist, but his interest in mechanics led him to animation. With his brothers Dave and Joe, he founded Fleischer Studios, one of the first animation studios. They turned out some of the most inventive films of the period.

Looking to find a method to produce animation more efficiently and economically, the brothers invented the rotoscope, a device used to trace movement from live-action film. With Dave working as his live model, Max Fleischer inaugurated his own cartoon series, officially titled "Out of the Inkwell" but more popularly known as "Koko the Clown." These short cartoons ingeniously combined animation with live action, usually in the form of an on-screen Fleischer drawing Ko-Ko before the viewers' eyes. Another innovation of Fleischer's was the sing-along cartoon. By "following the bouncing ball," theater audiences sang popular tunes together as they read the printed lyrics on the screen.

When the movie industry evolved from silent films to talking pictures, the Fleischer Studio was one of the few animation producers to survive the transition. When "the talkies" were permanently established in 1929, Fleischer began releasing his cartoons through Paramount Pictures, an association that continued for more than a decade.

At the end of the 1920s, the studio's top artist Grim Natwick came up with a new, seductive female character, Betty Boop. Fleischer also created Popeye the Sailorman and other popular cartoon characters. In 1941, Max and Dave launched the expensive Superman cartoon series. However, when the box office did not respond well, the two split up, and their animation staff was taken over by Paramount. Dave went to work at Columbia Pictures, while Max went into the industrial cartoon field.

During his career, Max Fleischer produced more than 600 cartoons and held 15 patents that were used in the motion picture industry. His feature cartoons include *Gulliver's Travels* (1939) and *Mr. Bug Goes to Town* (1941). Books by Fleischer are *Noah's Shoes* (1944), *Betty Boop* (1975), *Betty Boop's Hollywood Chronicles* (released in 1990), and *Betty Boop's Sunday Best: The Complete Color Comics, 1934–1936* (reprinted 1995).

His son is film director RICHARD FLEISCHER (1916–).

BIBLIOGRAPHY: L. Cabarga, *The Fleischer Story* (1976).

[Ruth Beloff (2nd ed.)]

FLEISCHER, MICHAEL (1908–1998), U.S. geochemist. Born in Bridgeport, Connecticut, to parents who emigrated from Germany, he received his B.S. in chemistry (1930) and Ph.D. (1933) from Yale University. From 1933 to 1936 he was a research associate, Department of Chemistry, Yale University, Fleischer joined the Geophysical Laboratory of the Carnegie Institute in Washington in 1936, and from 1939 to 1978 was with the United States Geological Survey. From 1978 to 1995, he was research associate, Department of Mineral Sciences, Smithsonian Institution. He was professorial lecturer (1957–65) at the George Washington University, assistant editor of *Chemical Abstracts* from 1940, and an associate editor of the *American Mineralogist*. He served as president of the Mineralogical Society of America, of the Geochemistry Commission of the International Union of Pure and Applied Chemistry, and as vice president of the Geological Society of America. In 1959 he was appointed president of the Commission on New Minerals and Mineral Names of the International Mineralogical Association.

Fleischer contributed many papers to scientific journals, dealing with chemical and analytical mineralogy, specific minerals (particularly of manganese), and the abundance of the individual elements in the earth's crust.

[Samuel Aaron Miller / Bracha Rager (2nd ed.)]

FLEISCHER, NATHANIEL STANLEY (**Nat**; 1887–1972), U.S. boxing historian, journalist, author, and member of the International Boxing Hall of Fame. Born on New York's Lower East Side, Fleischer first developed his love of boxing at age eight, when his father gave him photographs of boxers that were sold with cigarettes. He saw his first professional fight at age 11 on September 12, 1899, a bantamweight championship fight that saw Terrible Terry McGovern knock out Pedlar Palmer. It was the first time a championship bout ended in a first-round KO, and Fleischer was hooked on the sport. Standing only 5′ 2″ and weighing 122 pounds, Fleischer wanted to be a prizefighter himself, but he was knocked out in the first round of an amateur match when he was 15, and that ended his boxing ambitions.

Fleischer first wrote about sports for P.S. 15's monthly newspaper, and after graduating Townsend Harris High School, he was campus correspondent for two New York City newspapers while attending the City College of New York, where he organized with Dan *Daniel the school's first varsity basketball team in 1906. After graduating in 1908, Fleischer taught at P.S. 7, then took a commercial chemistry course at NYU and a forestry course at Yale, but soon realized that sports was his calling. He became sports editor at the *New York Press*, and continued when it merged with the *Morning Sun* in 1914. Fleischer proceeded to become sports editor at the *Morning Herald*, the *Mail-Telegram*, and the *Evening Telegraph*, but in 1929 he decided instead to devote himself entirely to a boxing magazine, *The Ring*, which he had co-founded with three associates in February 1922. It became the most influential publication in boxing history, earning Fleischer the moniker "Mr. Boxing." He refereed and judged more than 1,000 fights, established the Boxing Hall of Fame and Museum, initiated boxing's rating system, encouraged television coverage to maintain the public's interest, and helped establish boxing commissions around the world. Fleischer was the world's leading ring historian and the most prolific boxing writer of all time, publishing more than 60 books – an estimated 40 million words – including his autobiography, *Fifty Years at Ringside* (1958). His best-known work was the annual *Ring Record Book and Boxing Encyclopedia*, first published in 1941, which was considered the sports' authoritative source book. Fleischer was elected to the International Boxing Hall of Fame in 1990.

[Elli Wohlgelernter (2nd ed.)]

FLEISCHER, TSIPPI (**Tsipporah Dolgopolsky**; 1946–), Israeli composer and music education specialist, one of the Israeli women composers well known outside the country

Fleischer earned multiple bachelor's degrees (ranging from music theory to Arabic language, literature, and history), an M.A. in music education (NYU, 1975), and a Ph.D. in musicology (Bar-Ilan University, 1995). Initially interested in popular Israeli songs, especially the Hebrew canonic folk songs by composers such as Alexander *Argov, Moshe *Wilensky, and Naomi *Shemer, by the early 2000s, she had become an established composer of Western music (or, some would argue, composer of her unique version of World music) with a distinguished Middle-Eastern quality. She also revisited her research into the history of Israeli song in the past 120 years. From the late 1960s she taught at the Lewinsky Teachers College. Her book for music teachers, *Harmonization of Songs* (Hebrew), appeared in 2005.

From the 1980s she was committed to the ideology of Israeli style, first established by the founders of Israeli art music such as Paul *Ben-Haim and Mordecai *Seter. A perspective best conceptualized by Alexander *Boskovich, who held that an Israeli style can evolve only through the synthesis of ethnic local traits of Jewish and Arab music with techniques of Western classical music. In a 1986 interview she argued that her music is equally balanced between these traditions: not swaying toward the Western, with the Middle-Eastern source only an exotic flavor; nor toward the Eastern sources, when a work might not be fully artistic in Western terms.

Fleischer is a prolific composer. Her list of works includes her often-performed song-set *Girl-Butterfly-Girl* (1977, revised several times until the early 2000s); the cantata *Like Two Branches* (1989); the *Oratorio 1492–1992*; the collection *Ethnic Silhouettes* that includes four multimedia plays (1993–95, in Biblical Hebrew, Ugaritic, Old Babylonian, and Coptic); a collection of original miniatures; five short symphonies (1995–2004, illustrative symphonic poems and an ethnic collage); and two chamber operas, *Medea* (1995) and *Cain & Abel* (2002). Her music is inspired by the improvisatory quality of Arab oral traditions in music, and some of her melodies, both Arabic and Israeli, are compelling, as in her short toccata for strings, *Strings – Bow and Arrow* (1995).

Fleischer's works, especially of the 1980s and 1990s, synthesizing Arabic and Hebrew texts and musical modes with Western classical instrumentation, earned her a unique name as an established Middle-Eastern woman composer. Indeed, most of her earlier works reflected a local-regional, non-religious identity, smoothly mixing Mizrahi-Jewish and Arab elements, with a marked preference to the surrounding Arab character. She is perhaps the only Western woman composer in the Middle East whose music appeared on some sixteen commercial CDs, international Israeli.

In 2004, she wrote for the first time an explicitly Jewish work: the Fifth Symphony: *Israeli-Jewish Collage* for tape and accompanying orchestra, based on some of the most obvious Jewish identity markers – the *shofar* calls and the *Kol Nidrei* prayer.

BIBLIOGRAPHY: Robert Fleischer, *Twenty Israeli Composers*, Detroit: Wayne, 1997, p. 208–16.

[Ronit Seter]

FLEISCHMANN, GISI (1897–1944), Zionist women's leader in Bratislava who played a prominent part in rescue operations during the Holocaust. At the outbreak of World War II, she was in London and returned home to be with her family, which included a husband and two daughters as well as an ailing mother. She sent her two daughters to Palestine, but she herself remained in Bratislava, perhaps primarily for personal reasons and involved herself intensely in efforts to help the community. First she acted within the Ústredňa Židov (Jewish Council) as chief of the *Hicem department for emigration. In the summer of 1942 she became the guiding spirit of the "Working Group," a secret rescue organization for Jews that included herself and an ultra-Orthodox rabbi, Michael Weissmandel, who was related to her as a second cousin by marriage. It was rare, perhaps unprecedented, for an ultra-Orthodox rabbi and a woman Zionist to cooperate fully, and even more rare for the Zionist woman to assume the primarily leadership role. As a member of the Slovak Central Refugee Committee, she cooperated, albeit not without considerable tension, with Joseph Blum of the American Jewish Joint Distribution Committee, who later left for Hungary, and Fleischmann then became for all intents and purposes the Joint's person in Bratislava.

Fleischmann maintained a secret correspondence written in code with Jewish organizations in the free world, mainly with the He-Ḥalutz center at Geneva and with representatives of the *Jewish Agency in Istanbul. She reported on the condition of European Jewry under German occupation and she also traveled to Hungary to collect funds for rescue activities from the Hungarian Jewish communities. It was under her leadership though at Rabbi Weissmandel's initiative that a plan was devised to bribe Eichmann's representative in Slovakia, Dieter Wisliceny, to halt the deportation of the Jews. When an initial bribe and the promise of more funds to come seemed to work and the deportations of Slovakian Jewry were halted for a time, the working group devised a bold scheme, the *Europa Plan, to rescue the remaining Jews. Historians now know that is was not the bribe to Nazi officials but to Slovakian officials that halted the deportations and the chances of any success for the Europa plan were far-fetched. In 1943 she directed rescue operations of survivors of Polish ghettos, including groups of orphans, across the Polish-Slovak-Hungarian borders. In the spring of 1944 she conveyed the first eyewitness testimony on the death camps when the Auschwitz report was compiled by two men, Rudolf Vr'ba and Alfred Wetzler, who had escaped from Auschwitz on April 7, 1944, and reconfirmed by two later escapees, Arnost Rosin and Czeslaw Mordowicz, who reached Slovkia in June 1944. During the mass deportations in the autumn of 1944, she was arrested by the Germans and sent to Auschwitz with a special instruction, *RU-Rueckkehr unerwuenscht* ("return undesirable"), and on arrival in Auschwitz she was immediately killed. Fleishmann was described as a woman of organizational talent, intellectual ability, emotional involvement, and political savvy.

BIBLIOGRAPHY: L. Rothkirchen, *Ḥurban Yahadut Slovakyah* (1961), index, includes Eng. summary; O.J. Neumann, *Be-Ẓel ha-Mavet* (1958), passim; idem, *Gisi Fleischmann* (Eng., 1970); M.D. Weissmandel, *Min ha-Meẓar* (1960), passim; N. Levin, *The Holocaust* (1968), index. **ADD. BIBLIOGRAPHY:** J. Chapion, *In the Lion's Mouth: Gisi Fleishmann and the Jewish Fight for Survival*, (1987); Y. Bauer, *Rethinking the Holocaust* (2001), 1678–5; idem, *Jews for Sale* (1994).

[Livia Rothkirchen / Michael Berenbaum (2nd ed.)]

FLEISCHMANN, JULIUS (1872–1925), U.S. businessman and politician. Fleischmann was born in Cincinnati, Ohio, where his father, Charles Fleischmann, an immigrant from Hungary, had established a large concern for the manufacture of compressed yeast cakes. Fleischmann entered his father's business soon after leaving school.

Upon his father's death in 1897, he and his brother took over the business, which he ran by himself from 1905 on. Fleischmann's activity in local Republican politics led to his nomination for mayor in 1900. He was elected to the office and reelected in 1902. Though he declined to run for a third term, he served as Cincinnati's commissioner of parks during 1905–12, also attending several national Republican conventions as an Ohio delegate. An avid sportsman and breeder of horses, Fleischmann collapsed and died while playing in a polo game, leaving a large fortune. His financial speculations were so large that the stock market in Chicago suffered a sharp decline upon news of his sudden death.

FLEISHER, Philadelphia family originating in Memelsdorf, Germany. Members of this family and the related Liveright family arrived in the United States in the 1830s, and ultimately established prosperous yarn and clothing manufacturing businesses. Many descendants of BENJAMIN WOLF FLEISHER (1810–1845) and HANNAH TUCHNOR (1810–1903), who settled in Meadville, Pennsylvania, before moving on to Philadelphia, became leaders in Philadelphia Jewish and general affairs. Their sons SIMON B. (1840–1919) and MOYER (1842–1924) were partners in a yarn business in Philadelphia. They were both active in the Hebrew Education Society, and Moyer succeeded Moses A. Dropsie as its president in 1892. A son of Simon, BENJAMIN WILFRED (1870–1946), achieved distinction in Japan where he spent 40 years, becoming dean of American journalists there before the outbreak of World War II. SAMUEL STUART (1871–1944), brother of Benjamin Wilfred, was the founder and sole supporter, beginning in 1899, of the Graphic Sketch Club. Willed to the Philadelphia Museum of Art, the club nurtured the artistic talents of more than 40,000 young people. In 1923 Samuel became the first Jewish recipient of the prestigious Edward Bok Philadelphia Award. EDWIN ADLER (1877–1959), another brother, founded the Symphony Club of Philadelphia in 1909 and created a world-famed collection of music. The collection, eventually numbering over 11,000 pieces, was donated to the Free Library of Philadelphia, of which Edwin was a trustee. He had bought a large proportion of the scores on trips to Europe in which he scoured publishers' warehouses for long-neglected compositions. The Philadelphia Orchestra and the city's music academies have frequently used the collection. Samuel and Edwin, both members of Reform Congregation Knesseth Israel, were generous contributors to Jewish philanthropies, as was their cousin, ALFRED W. (1878–1928), prominent Philadelphia realtor. A partner in the firm of Mastbaum Brothers and Fleisher, Alfred was at least once the largest individual contributor to the Federation of Jewish Charities campaign. He was best known for his leadership in the field of progressive penology. For five years, beginning in 1923, he was president of the Board of Trustees of Eastern State Penitentiary and personally guided the construction of the prison at Gratersford. Edwin's nephew, STUART F. LOUCHHEIM, carried on the family tradition as president of the Academy of Music, which he rescued from potential bankruptcy and demolition. Louchheim was not a practicing Jew.

BIBLIOGRAPHY: H.S. Morais, *Jews of Philadelphia* (1894), 263–6; M. Stern, *Americans of Jewish Descent* (1960), 52–53; Bess, in: *Saturday Evening Post* (Feb. 6, 1943), 22ff.; Woolf, in: *New York Times Magazine* (April 4, 1937), 12ff.

[Bertram Wallace Korn]

FLEISHER, LARRY (1930–1989), head of the NBA players union from 1962 to 1988, member of NBA Hall of Fame. Born in the Bronx, New York, Fleisher graduated from DeWitt Clinton High School in 1946, New York University in 1950, and Harvard Law School in 1953, before serving in the U.S. Army from 1953 to 1955. His work as head of the NBA Players Association paved the way for pensions, minimum salaries, severance pay, and disability payments, among other benefits, and increased average yearly player's salary from $9,400 in 1967 to $600,000, without a strike. Fleisher was involved in the eventual merger of the ABA with the NBA, and was instrumental in developing the free agent system in 1976, known as the "Oscar Robertson Settlement" and allowing players to move more freely from team to team. In addition, he helped establish an Anti-Drug Agreement in 1983, the first such policy in pro sports, which provided for counseling and severe penalties for players involved in the use of hard drugs. Fleisher also negotiated the agreement that established the NBA salary cap system.

[Elli Wohlgelernter (2nd ed.)]

FLEISHER, LEON (1928–), U.S. pianist and conductor. Fleisher was born in San Francisco to Russian parents. He gave his first public recital at the age of six. From 1938 until 1948 he studied with Arthur *Schnabel in Italy and in New York. He made his New York debut at the age of 16, with Monteux, who also taught him conducting. Fleisher was the first American to win a major piano competition – the Queen Elisabeth International in Brussels (1952); he made several European tours and played highly successful recitals in South America. He gave the first performance of Leon Kirchner's Second Piano Concerto (1963), performed many modern works, and made numerous recordings. At his peak his playing combined intellectual power, warmth of feeling, grace, taste, and sensuous beauty.

In 1964 Fleisher began to suffer from cramps in the right hand, as a result of which he became incapable of regular playing. He began to conduct and to play the piano repertory for the left hand. Fleisher became conductor of the Annapolis Symphony Orchestra (1970), was associate conductor of the Baltimore Symphony Orchestra (1973–77), and made guest conducting appearances with major U.S. orchestras. In 1982, after surgery and many treatments, Fleisher returned gradually to the standard piano literature. He was appointed artistic director of the Tanglewood Music Center (1985–97), where in 1994 he gave the première of *Foss's Piano Concerto for left hand. From 1959 he was professor of piano at the Peabody Conservatory, Baltimore, where he later held the Andrew W. Mellon Chair in piano; he was also a visiting professor at the Rubin Academy of Music in Jerusalem.

BIBLIOGRAPHY: *Grove online*; MGG²; *Baker's Biographical Dictionary* (1997); D. Robert, in: *Clavier*, 38/8 (1999), 20–27.

[Max Loppert / Naama Ramot (2nd ed.)

FLESCH, family widely distributed throughout Central Europe. It originated in Frankfurt where a house named "Zur Flasche" ("The Flask") was built by Jacob of Prague in 1530. His son, AKIVA BEN JACOB FRANKFURTER (d. 1597), was a liturgical poet, and rabbi and preacher of the Frankfurt community. Another son, ABRAHAM VON SCHLESINGEN, with his sons, continued to live in the "Zur Flasche" house. Later descendants were merchants, *ḥazzanim*, and teachers in Frankfurt; they were also named Birnbaum and Flesch-Birnbaum.

A grandson of Akiva, the scholar ABRAHAM FLESCH (c. 1560–1640), was the first to bear the name in Austria, settling in Vienna in 1620. His descendants were scattered after the 1670 expulsion from Vienna.

MORDECAI (GUMPEL) FLESCH settled in Neu Raussnitz (Rousinov), Moravia, after 1670. One of his descendants, PHILIP (SOLOMON) FLESCH (1780–1852), founded a tannery in Brno (Bruenn). The descendants of Philip's 16 children were active in commerce and the professions; some settled in Brno. One of them, ADOLPH (1813–1879), continued the leather business and made it highly successful. Mordecai's great-grandson, ABRAHAM (1755–1828), was rabbi in Raussnitz, Moravia, and studied under Ezekiel *Landau. Abraham's son, JOSEPH (1781–1841), a merchant in Neu Raussnitz, was a pupil of Baruch Jeiteles, and among those who spread Haskalah into Moravia. He translated several of Philo's works into Hebrew and published exegetical and philological notes to Scripture (in *Bikkurei ha-Ittim*, 7, 9, and 11). He also provided the edition of the Bible published by M. *Landau with a list of Jewish exegetes and philologists, including modern scholars. Another member of the family was HEINRICH FLESCH (1875–1942), historian of Moravian Jewry. A native of Mattersdorf (now Mattersburg, in Burgenland, Austria), he was rabbi of Dolni Kounice, Moravia, from 1894 until his death. After World War I he was in charge also of the communities of Ivancice and Moravsky Krumlov. He published many articles on Moravian Jewry both in the local Jewish press and in learned journals, also editing the *takkanot* and records of several communities. He was a coeditor of Hugo *Gold's books on the communities of Moravia (1929), of Bratislava (1932), and Bohemia (1934). His archives are preserved in the Jewish State Museum in Prague. He also wrote a family history *Die Familie Flesch* (1914). His son JOSEPH had a Jewish bookstore and publishing house in Prague (the only one opened after 1918). Joseph perished in Auschwitz.

BIBLIOGRAPHY: L. Loew, *Gesammelte Schriften*, 2 (1890), 219–52.

FLESCH, CARL (1873–1944), violinist and teacher. Born in Moson, Hungary, Flesch studied in Vienna and Paris and made his debut in Vienna in 1895. After teaching at the conservatories of Bucharest (1897–1902) and Amsterdam (1903–08), he settled in Berlin, where his renown as a violin pedagogue came to equal his status as a virtuoso. From 1924 to 1928 he taught at the Curtis Institute in Philadelphia, and in 1933 left Germany, ultimately settling in Lucerne, Switzerland. He wrote the pedagogical works *Urstudien* (1910) and *Die Kunst des Violinspiels* (2 vols., 1923, 1928; Eng. trans. 1930 as well as translations into many other languages), and edited Kreutzer's and Paganini's études, the major violin concertos, and Mozart's violin sonatas (with Arthur *Schnabel). His memoirs were published posthumously by his son Carl Flesch, Jr. (Eng., 1957; Ger., 1960).

FLESH (Heb. בָּשָׂר, *basar*), a word used both in the Bible and Talmud for mortal man and for the flesh of animals (for the latter aspect, see *Meat). Eve is called by Adam "bone of my bones and flesh of my flesh" (Gen. 2:23), i.e., "my close relative" (cf. Gen. 29:4). In Genesis 6:3: The *basar* of humans is contrasted with *ru'aḥ* of God, which animates them. "My breath shall not abide (?) in the human forever, for that he is also flesh; therefore shall his days be a hundred and twenty years." Whereas God's breath is eternal, flesh is mortal. At death the flesh returns to the dust whence it came while the eternal breath returns to God (Gen 2:7; Eccl.. 12:7.) In Psalms 84:3 – "my heart and my flesh sing for joy unto the living God" – it designates the whole physical part of man. In Isaiah 66:16 "all flesh" is used as a synonym for mankind as a whole, while in the *Alenu* prayer "the sons of flesh" is used with the same connotation. In Talmud and Midrash the more comprehensive phrase *basar va-dam* ("flesh and blood") is used, largely to indicate the mortality of man as against the eternity of God, particularly in the contrast between the frailty and ephemerality of a mortal king compared with the "supreme King of kings, the Holy One blessed be He."

The corruptibility of flesh in the grave is constantly referred to. "The more flesh, the more worms" (Avot 2:7); "Know ... whither thou art going, to a place of dust, worms and maggot" (*ibid.* 3:1); and the word *basar* is regarded as an acronym of *bushah* ("shame"), *seruḥah* ("putrefaction") or *she'ol* ("the grave"), and *rimmah* ("worm"; Sot. 5a). At the same time, it is regarded metaphorically as the symbol of softness and pliancy in contrast with the hardness of bone (*ibid.*).

[Louis Isaac Rabinowitz / S. David Sperling (2nd ed.)]

FLEXNER, U.S. family. SIMON FLEXNER (1863–1946), U.S. physician and medical scientist, was born in Louisville, Ken., son of Morris Flexner, a Bohemian immigrant. He was the author of more than 350 scientific papers and monographs and joint author with his son, James Thomas Flexner, of the biography *William Henry Welch and the Heroic Age of American Medicine* (1941).

BERNARD FLEXNER (1865–1945) U.S. lawyer and Zionist leader, was born in Louisville, Ken., brother of Simon. After receiving a law degree from the University of Louisville (1898) and doing postgraduate work at the University of Virginia, he practiced law in Kentucky, later moving to Chicago (1911) and then to New York (1919). Throughout his career Flexner was much concerned with social welfare and labor problems. He was chairman of the Juvenile Court Board in Louisville and helped establish the first juvenile court in Chicago. Active in the National Probation Association, he served as president (1912–13) and as a committee member until his death. As a member of an American Red Cross mission to Romania in 1917, Flexner became convinced that Zionism was the solution to the problems of European Jewry. He entered actively into the U.S. Zionist movement and was counsel to the Zionist delegation at the Paris Peace Conference in 1919. When the *Palestine Economic Corporation was organized in 1925, Flexner became its first president, later serving as chairman of the board until 1944. He was also associated with many institutions, banks, and companies fostering the growth of the Jewish economy in Palestine. Among his other activities were membership on the executive committees of the American Jewish Joint Distribution Committee and the Jewish Agency for Palestine. Flexner was joint author of *Juvenile Courts and Probation* (1914) and *Legal Aspects of the Juvenile Court* (1922).

ABRAHAM *FLEXNER, U.S. educator, was a brother of Simon and Bernard. WASHINGTON FLEXNER (1896–1942), U.S. printer, was born in Louisville, Ken., brother of Simon, Bernard, and Abraham. In 1915 Washington Flexner organized the Lincoln Printing Company in Chicago, which became the largest financial printing company in the United States. JENNIE MAAS FLEXNER (1882–1944), U.S. librarian, was born in Louisville, Ken., daughter of Jacob Flexner. One of the pioneers of modern American librarianship, Jennie Flexner served as reader's adviser at the New York Public Library, and was author of *Circulation Work in Public Libraries* (1927) and *Making Books Work, a Guide to the Use of Libraries* (1943). JAMES THOMAS FLEXNER (1908–2003), U.S. author, son of Simon Flexner. James Thomas Flexner was the author of approximately 30 popular works on American art and civilization, including: *Doctors on Horseback: Pioneers of American Medicine* (1937), *America's Old Masters* (1939), *Short History of American Painting* (1950), and *American Painting: The Light of the Distant Skies* (1954). He also wrote a highly acclaimed four-volume biography of George Washington. (1965–72). His autobiography, *Maverick's Progress*, appeared in 1996.

BIBLIOGRAPHY: SIMON FLEXNER: *New York Times* (May 3, 1946); S.R. Kagan, *Jewish Contributions to Medicine in America* (1934), 294–7; Rous, in: *Science*, 107 (1948), 611–3; idem, in: Royal Society of London, *Obituary Notices of Fellows*, 18 (1949), 409–45. BERNARD FLEXNER: *New York Times* (May 4 and 7, 1945); *National Cyclopedia* *of American Biography*, 34 (1948), 517–8; JAMES THOMAS FLEXNER: *Who's Who in America* (1968–69), 746. WASHINGTON FLEXNER: *National Cyclopedia of American Biography*, 34 (1948), 265–66. JENNIE MAAS FLEXNER: *New York Times* (Nov. 18, 1944).

[Morton Rosenstock]

FLEXNER, ABRAHAM (1866–1959), U.S. scholar, and one of America's most creative educators. Flexner, who was born in Louisville, Kentucky, studied classics at Johns Hopkins University, and graduated in 1886. After teaching Latin and Greek at the Louisville High School (1886–90), he founded a unique college preparatory school which dispensed with rules, examinations, records, and reports. In 1905 he turned from the successful operation of his school to continue his studies at Harvard in psychology, philosophy, and science, with special reference to their bearing upon educational problems. During 1905–06, he studied the anatomy of the brain at the Rockefeller Institute for Medical Research, New York. He spent 1906–07 studying psychology and philosophy at the University of Berlin, where he came under the influence of Friedrich Paulsen, philosopher, pedagogue, and historian of German higher education. His review of higher education, *The American College*, published in 1908, attracted the attention of President Henry S. Pritchett of the Carnegie Foundation for the Advancement of Teaching, who commissioned Flexner to survey medical schools in the United States. The subsequent report, published in 1910 as *Medical Education in the United States and Canada*, was a critical analysis of 154 medical schools, seven of them Canadian. Although not a physician, Flexner was able to bring about a fundamental reform in all aspects of medical education in the United States. This was followed by an analysis of European medical schools during 1910–11 and the publication of *Medical Education in Europe* (1912). Another important study was *Prostitution in Europe* (1914). As a staff member and secretary of the General Education Board, 1912–28, Flexner undertook various educational inquiries and published, with F.P. Bachman as collaborator, *Public Education in Maryland* (1916) and *The Gary Schools* (1918). His *A Modern College* (1923) contained influential educational ideas and suggestions for the reform of secondary and higher education. His *Universities: American, English, German* (1930) was a severe criticism of functionalism in American higher institutions. His last major achievement was the founding, organization, and direction (1930–39) of the Institute for Advanced Study, Princeton. His other writings include: *Do Americans Really Value Education?* (1927); *Henry S. Pritchett: A Biography* (1943); *Daniel Coit Gilman, Creator of the American Type of University* (1946); and *Funds and Foundations* (1952). His autobiography, *I Remember* (1940), was revised, updated, and posthumously published as *Abraham Flexner: An Autobiography* (1960).

BIBLIOGRAPHY: F. Parker, in: *Journal of Medical Education*, 36 (1961), 709–14; idem, in: *History of Education Quarterly*, 2 (1962), 199–209; Strauss, in: *Journal of the American Medical Association*, 173 (1960), 1413–16; *New York Times*, Sept. 22, 1959.

[William W. Brickman]

FLOGGING, punishment by beating or whipping. This at all times has been the instinctive way to inflict disciplinary *punishment: a parent "disciplines" his son by beating him (cf. Deut. 8:5; 21:18; Prov. 19:18; 23:13–14; 29:17) as does a master his slave (Ex. 21:20,26). More than any other punishment, flogging is a means of correction rather than retribution, and, being a substitute for the capital punishment which, in the rabbinic view, every violator of God's word properly deserves, it reflects God's infinite mercy (cf. Sanh. 10a, Rashi *ibid.*).

In Biblical Law

It appears that, where no other punishment was expressly prescribed, flogging was in biblical law the standard punishment for all offenses (Deut. 25:2). The exegetical difficulties which arose in view of the preceding verse (25:1) gave rise to such restrictive interpretations as that the law of flogging applied only in limited cases of assault (Ibn Ezra, *ibid.*) or perjury (cf. Mak. 2b); but there need not necessarily be any connection between the two verses – the former being construed as a self-contained exhortation to do justice in civil cases as well as in cases of mutual criminal accusations (cf. Mid. Tan. to 25:1). It is noteworthy that flogging is the only punishment mentioned in the Bible as a general rule, and not in relation to any particular offense (but cf. Deut. 21:22 regarding postmortem hangings; see also *Capital Punishment), the only exception being the flogging prescribed, in addition to a *fine, for the slanderer of a virgin (Deut. 22:18).

The maximum number of strokes to be administered in any one case is 40 (Deut. 25:3), "lest being flogged further, to excess, your brother is degraded before your eyes" (*ibid.*). While this number was later understood as the standard, fixed number of strokes to be administered in each case (less one), there is no valid reason to assume that it was not in fact intended and regarded as a maximum limit – the preceding words, "as his guilt warrants" (25:2) indicating that the number of strokes was to be determined in each individual case according to the gravity of the offense, provided only they did not exceed the prescribed maximum. The scriptural intention to prevent any "degradation" of the human person is served by the fact that no discretion was allowed to the judges, who may tend to harshness or cruelty (Ibn Ezra, *ibid.*). There is no record of the manner in which floggings were administered in biblical times. Various instruments of beating are mentioned in the Bible (Judg. 8:7, 16; Prov. 10:13; 26:3; I Kings 12:11, 14; et al.), but any conclusion that they (or any of them) were the instruments used in judicial floggings is unwarranted.

In Talmudic Law

Talmudic law not only made detailed provision for the manner in which floggings were to be carried out, but also altered the concept of the biblical punishment; the maximum of 40 lashes was reduced to 39 (Mak. 22a), so as to avoid the danger of exceeding 40 even by mistake; and the offenses which carried the punishment of flogging were exactly defined, depriving it of its character as a residuary and omnibus punishment. The number of 39 lashes became the standard rather than the maximum number; but in order to prevent death by flogging – which would amount to a violation of the biblical injunction of "not more" than flogging – the person to be flogged was first physically examined in order to determine the number of lashes that could safely be administered to him (Mak. 3:11). Where, as a result of such examination, less than 39 lashes were administered, and it then turned out that the offender could well bear more, the previous estimate would be allowed to stand and the offender discharged (Maim. Yad, Sanhedrin 17:2). But the offender would also be discharged where physical symptoms manifested themselves during the course of the flogging, so that he would not be able to stand any more lashes, even though on previous examination he had been found fit to stand more (*ibid.* 17:5). It also happened that as a result of such examination, floggings were postponed for another day or later, until the offender was fit to undergo them (*ibid.* 17:3).

Offenses Punishable by this Method

The offenses carrying the punishment of flogging are, firstly, all those for which the *divine punishment of *karet* is prescribed; secondly, all violations by overt act of negative biblical injunctions (*ibid.* 18:1). However speech is not, as such, considered an overt act: thus, a person insulting the deaf or going about as a talebearer among the people in violation of express negative injunctions (Lev. 19:14–16) would not be liable to be flogged (Yad, loc. cit.). It is only when speech is tantamount to an act, as in vows substituting another animal for a sacred animal (Lev. 27:10), that flogging is inflicted (Tem. 3b); as it is also for swearing falsely by, or taking in vain, the name of God – "for the Lord will not clear one who swears falsely by His name" (Ex. 20:7; Deut. 5:11), but the court will, by flogging him (Tem. 3a). Flogging is also prescribed for cursing, i.e., wickedly using the name of God – because failure "to revere this honored and awesome Name" is expressly given as the cause of the infliction of *makkot*, a term meaning lashes as well as plagues (Deut. 28:58–59). Even though the offense is committed not just by speech but also by an overt act, it does not always result in a flogging: thus, where reparation must be made by money, as for the crime of stealing (Ex. 20:13; Deut. 5:17), the payment of *damages and fines is preferred to flogging; and as two punishments may not be inflicted for the same offense, the rule is that he who pays is not flogged (Mak. 1:2; 4b; Ket, 32a). For the same reason, no flogging can be inflicted where the offense carries capital (as distinguished from divine) punishment (Tosef., Mak. 5:17). Where the negative injunction is coupled with a positive one, as for instance: "thou shalt not take the dam with the young, thou shalt let the dam go, but the young thou mayest take" (Deut. 22:6–7), liability to be flogged only ensues if the negative injunction is violated and the positive disobeyed as well (Mak. 3:4; Ḥul. 12:4).

Floggings were administered with a whip made of calfskin on the bare upper body of the offender – one third of the lashes being given on the breast and the other two thirds on the back. The offender stood in a bowed position with the one administering the beating on a stone above him and the blows were accompanied by the recital of admonitory and consolatory verses from Scripture (Mak. 3:12–14; Yad, loc. cit. 16:8–11). If death ensued, even though the flogging was administered according to law, the executioner was not liable; but if the law had not been faithfully observed by him, he would be obliged to resort to a city of *refuge as in the case of any other accidental homicide (Yad, loc. cit. 16:12).

Disciplinary Floggings

There are reports in the Talmud of several extralegal floggings being prescribed (see *Extraordinary Remedies), for example, for having marital intercourse in public (Yev. 90b). In many cases, the flogging appears to have been sanctioned as a legal punishment, even though not falling within the categories set out above; for example, where a man and a woman seclude themselves (Kid. 81a), or for taking unreasonable vows (TJ, Suk. 5:2, 55b), or for falling asleep during watch duty in the Temple (Mid. 1:2); but these cases may also be regarded as instances of disciplinary rather than punitive measures, Disciplinary flogging (*makkat mardut*) was an innovation of the talmudic jurists. While the violation of a negative injunction calls for punishment, the act of violation being a matter of the past, the failure to obey a positive command calls for coercive measures calculated to enforce such obedience. Accordingly, while punitive floggings may (indeed, must) be restricted to a maximum number of blows, disciplinary floggings must be unrestricted – to be continued until the offender performs his duty. The maximum number of 40 lashes applies only where there has been a violation of a negative injunction, but in the case of positive commands, "as when they say to him: build a *sukkah* – and he refuses, or: take a *lulav* – and he refuses – he is flogged until his soul departs" (Ket. 86a–b). In the case of payment of a civil debt, which is also a positive command imposed by law, the question arose whether such payment could be enforced by a disciplinary flogging (*ibid.*); the better opinion appears to be that it could not, at any rate for so long as the debtor had any property attachable in execution proceedings or if he claimed to have no property only when he was attempting to avoid payment (*Piskei ha-Rosh*, Ket. 9, 13).

Disciplinary floggings were also resorted to where an offender was not liable to punishment for formal reasons, for example for lack of previous warning (Yad, loc. cit., 18:5). It was this innovation of the idea of a disciplinary flogging that enabled the courts, in post-talmudic times, to make use of the penalty of flogging for the maintenance of law and order and for the observance of religion. It is found to have been applied in an unlimited variety of cases and in different modes of execution. The flogging was mostly carried out in public, so as to have a deterrent effect: sometimes in the courthouse (Hai Gaon, comm. to Kel. 22, s.v. *safsal*), sometimes in the synagogue (*Yam shel Shelomoh*, BK 8:48, and Resp. Maharshal 28; Resp. Maharam of Lublin 46), and sometimes in the square outside the synagogue or in other public thoroughfares (Resp.

Ribash 351). Although because of jurisdictional doubts (see *Bet Din*), the application of a disciplinary, as opposed to that of punitive, flogging was preferred, the courts did not normally adopt the rule that disciplinary floggings ought not to be restricted, but ordered floggings to be limited to a certain amount of lashes – some holding that the biblical maximum applied *a fortiori* (*Yam shel Shelomo, ibid.*), some leaving the extent of the flogging in each individual case to the discretion of the court (*Sha'arei Ẓedek* 4:7, 39; *Halakhot Pesukot min ha-Geonim* 89; *Sha'arei Teshuvah* 181). The argument that such discretionary floggings constituted a much severer punishment for many much lighter offenses than the biblical flogging was countered with the assertion that the execution of the flogging should be so humane as to counterbalance the increased measure of strokes (Resp. Ribash 90). Indeed, it appears that the lashes were not normally inflicted on the bare body, nor with a leather whip, nor on the breast or back, but rather on less vulnerable parts. Following a talmudic dictum that a flogging is to be administered where an offense is reported but not proved (*malkin al lo tovah ha-shemu'ah:* Kid. 81a), post-talmudic courts introduced the punishment of flogging where an offense was threatened or commenced but not completed (Resp. Maharam of Rothenburg, ed. Prague 383; and cf. *Darkhei Moshe*, ḤM 421:35 n. 7); but mere suspicion alone was held insufficient to warrant flogging (*Halakhot Pesukot min ha-Ge'onim* 94), unless substantiated by at least one witness or by common repute (*Sha'arei Ẓedek* 3:6, 38). In many places, notables were exempt from floggings, and people were normally allowed to pay a fine instead (cf. *Yam shel Shelomo*, BK 8:49). Corporal punishment was abolished in Israel by the Punishment of Whipping (Abolition) Law 5710 – 1950. See entry *Punishment.

BIBLIOGRAPHY: S. Mendelsohn, *Criminal Jurisprudence of the Ancient Hebrews* (1891), 39f. (no. 21), 171f. (nos. 138, 139); S. Assaf, *Ha-Onshin Aḥarei Ḥatimat ha-Talmud* (1922), 146 (index), s.v. *Makkat Mardut* and *Malkot;* Jacob, in: MGWJ, 68 (1924), 276–81; Aptowitzer, in: *Ha-Mishpat ha-Ivri*, 5 (1935/36), 33–104; S. Katz, *Die Strafe im Talmudischen Recht* (1936), 63f.; ET, 1 (19513), 136; J.M. Ginzburg, *Mishpatim le-Yisrael* (1956), 381 (index), s.v. *Makkat, Malkot;* EM, 4 (1962), l 160f., s.v. *Malkot;* M. Elon, *Ḥerut ha-Perat be-Darkhei Geviyyat Ḥov ha-Mishpat ha-Ivri* (1964), 22–26, 207f. **ADD BIBLIOGRAPHY:** M. Elon, *Ha-Mishpat ha-Ivri* (1988), I, 180, 422f., 437f., 496, 499, 504, 558, 567, 579, 649, 692, 705, 720, II, 841; idem, *Jewish Law* (1994), I, 202, II, 515f., 534, 604, 608, 614, 679, 689f., 713, 803, 854, 870, 888, III, 1029; idem, *Jewish Law (Cases and Materials)* (1999), 398–404; M. Elon and B. Lifshitz, *Mafte'aḥ ha-She'elot ve-ha-Teshuvot shel Ḥakhmei Sefard u-Ẓefon Afrikah* (legal digest) (1986) (2), 332–334; B. Lifshitz and E. Shochetman, *Mafte'aḥ ha-She'elot ve-ha-Teshuvot shel Ḥakhmei Ashkenaz, Ẓarefat ve-Italiyah* (legal digest) (1997), 230–231.

[Haim Hermann Cohn]

FLOHR, SALO (Solomon Mikhailovitch; 1908–1983), Russian chess prodigy. Flohr, who was born in the Ukraine, escaped from a pogrom at an early age and found refuge in Czechoslovakia, which he represented in chess matches. He won several masters' tournaments between 1929 and 1939, went to Moscow during World War II, and became one of the leading Soviet grand masters and a chess writer of distinction. As he developed his game he changed his style from a brilliant incisive to a cautious one, and became a "drawing-master." Regarded at one time as the likely successor to Alekhine, Flohr was eventually displaced, notably by Botvinnik.

[Gerald Abrahams]

FLOOD, THE, deluge (Heb. *mabbul*) described in the Book of Genesis and brought by God to destroy humankind because of its sinfulness. Outside of the Noah tales in Genesis *mabbul* occurs only in Psalm 29:10. In Isaiah 54:9 the great flood is called "waters of Noah."

The Biblical Narrative (Gen. 6:5–9:17)

As punishment for the corruption and injustice rife on earth, God decided to bring a universal inundation to wipe out civilization. Alone of humankind, a blameless and righteous man named *Noah, together with his family, was to be saved. God informed him of His decision and gave him detailed instructions for the building of an ark and its provisioning (see *Ark of Noah). Noah was to take aboard the members of his family, together with male and female representatives of the animals, birds, and creeping things. When all the preparations were completed, the flood waters inundated the earth, blotting out all earthly existence, and lifting the ark above the highest mountain peaks. Then the rains ceased, the waters subsided and the ark came to rest on the mountains of *Ararat. Noah waited forty days and then sent out a raven, which, however, returned to the ark. Seven days later he released a dove, which came back bearing an olive leaf. After a further delay of seven days, he again dispatched the dove which did not return, and Noah knew it was safe to disembark. This he did on receiving instructions from God, and he thereupon offered sacrifices to Him. God, in turn, promised to restore the rhythm of the times and seasons and undertook never again to destroy humankind, setting his (war)bow in the sky as an everlasting symbol of this promise. He blessed Noah, his offspring, and everything on earth.

Extra-Biblical Accounts

Legends of a great inundation submerging much or all of the earth's surface are found in the traditions of a number of peoples. They are especially common among the Indians of the Western Hemisphere, the Aborigines of Australia, and the islanders of the Central and Southern Pacific, and also abound in the southern regions of Asia. Chinese and Japanese versions exist, but with the deluge circumscribed in extent. A few legends are found in Europe; that of Iceland depicts a flood of catastrophic proportions produced by blood gushing from the wounds of a giant. However, the accounts closest to that of the Bible are those emanating from southern Mesopotamia. The ancient Greek flood stories also may have been influenced by the earlier Mesopotamian diluvial traditions. There are no grounds for assuming that all or most of the widespread legends are related. It is apparent that many of them are rooted ultimately in man's fear, based on terrifying experiences, of being annihilated by violently surging water. Most of them developed quite naturally from memories of unusually disastrous floods. The alluvial plain of southern Mesopotamia was vulnerable to widespread flooding. In the Old Babylonian period in particular, catastrophic flooding was frequent, so that the myth of the ancient flood (*abūbu*) had special significance (Cole and Gash apud George, 509). Ancient memory blended with contemporary experience to produce tales of universal inundation. None of the flood accounts has received wider distribution than the biblical story. At the time it was incorporated into Jewish traditions, however, it was already countless centuries old. The earliest extant version of this tradition is known from a Sumerian clay tablet discovered at Nippur, the holy city of ancient Sumer. Unfortunately, only the lower third of the tablet has survived. Since the publication of the text by Arno Poebel in 1914, no additional fragments of the Sumerian flood story have come to light. Although the Sumerian text is badly broken, enough remains to give inklings of the content of the missing portions. The text, now known as "The Eridu Genesis" (COS I, 513–15) as a whole seems to provide a general history of humankind, in which the main episode is the deluge. Among the subjects touched are the creation of humans, the rise of kingship, and the establishment of cities. One of the deities declares his intentions of saving humankind from a destruction decreed by the gods. The coming of the flood is made known to King Ziusudra, who was noted for his receptiveness to divine revelations: "A flood will sweep over the temples. The decision, the declaration of the assembly of the gods, is to destroy the seed of humankind." The next section of the composition is missing but most likely contained instructions for Ziusudra to build an immense ship by which he might rescue himself from a watery grave. The lacuna is followed by a description of the inundation and the eventual reappearance of Utu the sun god, to whom Ziusudra offers sacrifices: "All the tempests attacked as one, very powerful. Simultaneously the deluge sweeps over the temples, After the flood had swept over the land for seven days and seven nights and the huge boat had been tossed about by the windstorms on the expansive waters, Utu the sun god who illumines heaven and earth came out. Ziusudra opened a window of the ship and heroic Utu shone into the great vessel. Before Utu, King Ziusudra prostrated himself; the king kills a steer and slaughters a sheep." Again there is a gap in the text, after which it is told that the king was granted eternal life and given a place of abode in a land called Dilmun, where the sun god rises. There the hero was to share immortality with his gods. The hero's name survived as Xisuthros in the flood story as retold in Greek by the Babylonian priest Berossus in the third century B.C.E.

The Sumerian account inspired a similar history of humankind written in the Old Babylonian dialect of Akkadian on three clay tablets, dated to around 1700 B.C.E., with fragments of two other versions inscribed about a thousand years later. The composition is now called the Epic of Atrahasis (COS I, 450–53) after its hero, whose name means "Exceeding Wise."

The first tablet begins in primordial times when the lesser gods were so burdened with toil that they engaged in the first-ever documented work-stoppage, and demonstrated against the great god Enlil. The dispute was resolved when it was decided that the midwife of the gods, Mami (also known as Nintu, Belet-ili, and Aruru), would create humans to work in place of the gods. One of the lesser gods was sacrificed and from an admixture of earth with his blood and flesh, humankind was brought into being. The second tablet relates that the world's population had increased so substantially that humans had become a nuisance to the head of the pantheon, Enlil. Provoked by the disruption of celestial serenity, Enlil announced before a divine convocation his intention to retaliate against human beings with a series of plagues, including a drought and famine. Obviously not satisfied with the results of these measures, the chief god then decided to destroy humanity by means of a flood. Humankind had a friend, however, in the wise god Enki (= Ea), who was permitted to be in charge of the inundation. The third tablet relates how Enki warned King Atrahasis. He spoke to the wall of the monarch's residence, rather than directly to the ruler, perhaps to avoid the appearance of revealing the gods' secrets to a human. Atrahasis was told to destroy his house and build a ship by which he would be able to save his life. Although much of the tablet is broken, the building of the ship, the loading of the animals, and the flood itself are documented. The gods ultimately decide that a more effective method of population control than a great flood is to create categories of women who cannot bear, and demonic baby-snatchers.

Parallels between the Epic of Atrahasis and the biblical Flood narrative may be cited, but even greater similarities to the Genesis account are present in another Babylonian epic whose hero bears the name Gilgamesh. (Thanks to the biblical similarities, the publication of this work in the late 19th century created a great stir in religious circles.) This epic skillfully and creatively blends several borrowed Sumerian literary motifs into what has come to be regarded as one of the masterpieces of world literature. It most likely came into existence around the beginning of the second millennium. Important sections written in classical (or Old) Babylonian are extant today, as are later rescensions extending over a millennium.

The Epic of Gilgamesh is divided into eleven tablets to which a twelfth, consisting of a literal translation from a Sumerian source, has been added. The fragments so far pieced together leave relatively few gaps in the epic. Tablet XI, in which the immortalized hero of the flood, usually called Utanapishtim ("He-Found-Life"), though occasionally also Atrahasis, relates the story of the flood to his mortal descendant Gilgamesh, is virtually intact, thus providing the most complete version of the deluge story in cuneiform script, The flood narrative in the Gilgamesh Epic is not part of a history of the world, as is the case in the epics of Ziusudra and Atrahasis. It is introduced rather as a story told to a hero obsessed with his quest for immortality.

Much of the epic is devoted to the heroic expeditions of Gilgamesh and his companion Enkidu. These episodes lead ultimately to the central theme, *viz.*, the inevitability of death. Enkidu's demise by divine decree, after the two adventurers had insulted the gods, brings Gilgamesh face to face with the one factor before which every person must yield. He then devotes himself completely to seeking a way to escape the destiny of all flesh. It is this confrontation with death that impels Gilgamesh to make his way to the person who was the Babylonian counterpart of the biblical Noah, a man named Utanapishtim, who, with his wife, had been blessed by the gods with immortality after surviving the diluvial catastrophe. From him Gilgamesh hopes to gain the secret of eternal life. After an arduous and perilous journey, Gilgamesh reaches the distant Utanapishtim and asks how he had obtained life without end. In reply, the ancient man recounts in detail the story of the deluge.

Utanapishtim relates to Gilgamesh how he was residing in Shuruppak, an urban center on the bank of the Euphrates, when he was warned of an impending disaster. For no stated reason, the gods, under the leadership of the warlike Enlil, felt compelled to bring a deluge of proportions sufficient to wipe out the human race. However, the god Ea, counterpart of the Sumerian Enki, made known the supernal counsel by speaking to the wall of the reed house in which Utanapishtim lived. Utanapishtim was told to tear down his house and build a ship, into which he must bring representatives of all living creatures, The boat was to be equal in width and length, with a covering over the top. At once, Utanapishtim confessed his desire to comply with the god's wishes, but also asked how he should explain his actions to the people of his community. Ea advised him to say that he has learned that he was to be the object of Enlil's hatred and, lest his presence in their midst bring disaster upon them, he must go into exile, journeying to Ea's dwelling-place in the marshlands near the Persian Gulf. (Cf. the explanation given by Jonah to his shipmates (Jonah 1:10) that his sea voyage is in flight from YHWH.) It was by this ruse that Utanapishtim obtained the assistance of the people of Shuruppak in constructing the ship. The finished vessel, a perfect cube of 120 cubits, had seven levels, each divided into nine compartments. Supplies were loaded onto it, including whatever silver and gold Utanapishtim had in his possession. His family and relatives came aboard and animals, craftsmen, and a boatman joined the company. When all was ready, the onset of the tempest was heralded by an evening of rain, Utanapishtim studied the storm apprehensively, then entered the ship and closed the door. At daybreak on the following morning, a black cloud rose from the horizon and subsequently darkness enveloped the landscape. The storm raged so fiercely that even the gods cowered in fear. For six days and nights the tempest assailed the earth, but on the seventh day it ceased and the tossing sea grew calm. Utanapishtim opened a window, and upon seeing the scene of death, wept. After the storm, the ship approached a peak called Mount Nimush (or Nisir) as it emerged from the subsiding water. The ship ran aground and could not free itself from its resting place. Six days elapsed and on the seventh day, Utanapishtim tested the situation by releasing a dove, It flew away and then returned without finding a place to land. A swallow was next let loose, but with the same result. Subsequently, a raven was released and did not return, for the water had abated. Utanapishtim interpreted this as a sign that the flood was over, He prepared a sacrificial offering "on top of the mountain", and burned incense to the gods, who, attracted by the sweet odor, "gathered like flies." Enlil arrived later than the others and was filled with rage when he saw that mortals had survived, but Ea soothed his wrath, explaining that it was through a dream that Utanapishtim had learned the secret plan of the gods, Thereupon Enlil boarded the ship, took the man and his wife on board, and, touching their foreheads as they knelt on either side of him, formally conferred immortality on them.

The Biblical-Mesopotamian Parallels

No parallels between the biblical and extra-canonical accounts are more remarkable and impressive than those between Utanapishtim's story and that of Genesis. At the same time, there are important and basic differences between the two sources.

In the Genesis story the flood marks a turning point in history. While this does not figure in the Gilgamesh Epic, the concept is apparent in other Mesopotamian sources, which divide epochs into "before the flood" and "after the flood" (cf. Ps. 29:10; see Cohen and Hallo in Bibliography.). In both accounts the flood is a result of divine decision and one individual, a deity's favorite, is chosen to be saved by constructing a large vessel, whose dimensions, together with building instructions, are divinely communicated. In each case the vessel is calked inside and out with a tar-like substance to render it seaworthy. Animals and birds are taken aboard in both narratives. Both traditions describe the utter devastation of the flood, and both have the ship coming to rest on a mountain peak, with the hero shortly thereafter sending forth birds to determine if the earth was again hospitable. Finally, in both narratives the hero offers sacrifices on emerging from his vessel, and receives a divine blessing.

In spite of these unmistakable and striking parallels, many details are not shared by the two accounts. Some of the dissimilarities are obviously due to the fundamental difference in religious orientation. The Book of Genesis is essentially monotheistic, while the Gilgamesh Epic and its predecessors are consistently polytheistic in outlook. Utanapishtim is elevated to the status of a god, while Noah remains human. In further contrast, the God of the Bible establishes a covenant with all humankind after the deluge, a concept alien to Mesopotamia.

While Noah is not identified with a particular city, Utanapishtim is said to be a citizen of Shuruppak. The former is told explicitly and directly that the flood will come, while Utanapishtim must deduce the course of events from a carefully worded warning obliquely delivered to the wall of a reed hut. Furthermore, Ea's warning is given without the knowledge of Enlil, who had insisted on destroying all humankind without exception. In the monotheistic framework of the Bible, however, the author of the Flood intentionally provides for a surviving remnant, though unlike the Babylonian version in which a considerable number of people were spared (Utanapishtim's relatives and a crew), in the Genesis story only Noah and his wife, sons, and daughters-in-law enter the ark. The ships in which Noah and his Babylonian counterpart ride out the storm differ considerably in size and shape, the craft of Utanapishtim having a displacement about five times that of Noah's vessel. It is highly significant that the Mesopotamian hero needed a boatman to navigate his ship, while that of Noah needed neither rudder nor sail nor any other navigational aid. The building of an ark, rather than a ship, is intended to attribute Noah's deliverance solely to the will of God, and not to any human skill.

In the Gilgamesh Epic there is no indication of when the deluge began and ended, but in one of the sections of the biblical account precise dates are given. As for the duration of the storm, the accounts are widely divergent: six days in the Gilgamesh Epic as against forty according to one of the figures in Genesis, and no fewer than 150 according to another. The site at which the biblical ark came to rest after the Flood is identified as Ararat, a range northeast of Lake Van near the 40th parallel. Utanapishtim's ship, however, grounded far to the south on Mount Nimush/Nisir, near the 35th parallel. From the latter vessel a dove, a swallow, and a raven, in that order, were released, whereas Noah first turned a raven loose and then twice sent out a dove.

In Genesis there is no doubt that the reason for the Flood is divine punishment for human injustice, lawlessness, and social unrighteousness, and that the salvation of Noah is solely conditioned by his moral worthiness. The same notion is not fully articulated in the Gilgamesh epic, but is, nonetheless, implicit in the god Ea's criticism of the god Enlil. Ea insists that only sinners should suffer for their crimes, whereas the flood caused by Enlil had punished the innocent as well. (Gilg XI, 181–95). The situation in the Mesopotamian narratives, however, is not at all clear in respect to the choice of the hero, whose deliverance involved the deception of one god by another.

Sacrifice is significant in both stories to the point of striking verbal similarity. According to Genesis 8:21, YHWH smelled the pleasing odor of the sacrifice, while Gilgamesh XI, 161 reads: "The gods smelled the savor, the gods smelled the sweet savor." The writer continues with "the gods gathered likes flies around the sacrificer," a formulation that the biblical writer could hardly have tolerated." Nor could he have described the biblical god in terms of a swarm of hungry flies. At the same time, the biblical story goes so far as to credit sacrifice with maintaining what would later be called the world (*olam*) a view still held, if attenuated in the Mishnah (Avot 1:2).

While it is clear that the biblical account is dependent on the much earlier Mesopotamian material, the numerous differences between the two versions may be due either to Israelite reworking of earlier sources or to an intermediary recension. The text was widely known even outside Mesopotamia, including Akkadian fragments from *Emar in upper Syria, *Megiddo in Israel and Hattušaš, the Hittite capital in Turkey. Hattušaš has also yielded Hittite and Hurrian adaptations.

When the deluge story became part of the Hebrew repertory, it was developed in more than a single tradition. Subsequently the products were carefully interwoven, but without eliminating some contradictions and duplications. The biblical narrative emerges, nonetheless, as a consistent moral indictment of the human race, designed to reveal the character of Israel's God and His ethical demands. It is this aspect of the Genesis diluvial presentation which makes it significantly different from its Mesopotamian analogues.

[Dwight Young / S. David Sperling (2nd ed.)]

In the *Aggadah*

God mourned for seven days for the world that He had created before He sent the Flood (Gen. R. 32:7). One view is expressed that the Flood did not cover the Land of Israel (Zeb. 113a). On the other hand, it is stated that the olive tree from which the dove took the leaf that provided evidence that the Flood had subsided was from a tree on the Mount of Olives (Har ha-Mishḥa); it is also stated that when the Canaanites heard of the exodus of the Children of Israel, they adopted a "scorched earth" policy and cut down all the trees (Ex. R. 20:16) which were, however, ancient and gnarled, since they had been planted after the Flood (Eccles. R. 3:11. no. 2.). The gigantic *Og, king of Bashan, survived the Flood (Nid. 61a).

[Louis Isaac Rabinowitz]

BIBLIOGRAPHY: Aa. Heidel, *The Gilgamesh Epic and Old Testament Parallels* (1946); E.A. Speiser, in: *Journal of World History*, 1 (1953), 311–27; idem, *Genesis* (1964); E. Sollberger, *The Babylonian Legend of the Flood* (1966^{2}); N.M. Sarna, *Understanding Genesis* (1966), 37–62; W.G. Lambert and A.R. Millard, ATRA-HASĪS, *The Babylonian Story of the Flood* (1969); J. Bright, in: *Biblical Archaeologist Reader* (1961), 32–40. **ADD. BIBLIOGRAPHY:** A. Kilmer, in: *Orientalia* 41 (1972), 160–77; idem, in: F. Rochberg-Halton (ed.), *Language, Literature, and History … Studies E. Reiner* (1987), 175–80; J.P. Lewis, ABD II, 798–803; J. Sasson, ibid., 1024–27; N. Sarna, in: *Genesis* (JPS; 1989), 46–60; C. Cohen, in: JANES, 19 (1989), 18–19; W. Hallo, in: MAARAV, 7 (1991), 173–81; A.R. George, *The Babylonian Gilgamesh Epic*, 2 vols. (2003).

FLORENCE (It. Firenze) city in Tuscany, central Italy. There is no evidence of a Jewish community in the Roman City of Florentia. Early medieval documents preserved in the Florence Archives mention names that can be Jewish. The first evidence of a Jewish presence is dated to the 13th century. However, only in 1396 did the Commune of Florence allowed Jews to practice banking in the city and therefore to settle there.

Representatives of the Jewish communities in Italy, assembled in Florence in 1428, obtained a letter of protection from Pope Martin v. In 1430 the municipal authorities invited Jewish bankers to set up shop, as they believed that they would be easier to control than their Christian counterparts. The first loan license was granted in 1437. Soon various Jewish families, such as the Da Pisas, Da Rietis, and Da Tivolis settled in Florence. Generally, the Jews met with hostility from the populace, while the aristocracy, especially the Medici family, protected them. The obligation to wear the Jewish *badge was frequently enforced and then suspended. Jews lived mainly on the other side of the Arno. A Via dei Giudei still exists in the area. There, until World War II, was possible to see the remains of a synagogue. The Jewish cemetery, within the city walls, was situated on the present Lungarno della Zecca. There were anti-Jewish demonstrations in 1458 and 1471. Further threats of violence were restrained with difficulty when Bernardino da *Feltre preached in Florence in 1488, and he was escorted from the city. However, the Medici often protected the Jews. In 1477 Lorenzo the Magnificent successfully stopped an attempt to expel the Jews from the city. On Lorenzo's death in 1492, the Jews of Florence faced new difficult times under the Republic. After the triumph of Savonarola a Monte di *Pietà was established, the Jewish bankers were compelled to transfer there their loan-bank licences. Later the Jews were expelled. In 1493 a Jew, falsely accused of having damaged the face of Giovanni Tedesco's statue of the Virgin in Orsanmichele Church, was brutally executed.

The Medici returned to Florence in 1512, and in 1514 Jewish moneylenders were recalled. In 1527 the Medici were again banished, and the Jews received orders to leave, their expulsion being delayed. On the accession of Alessandro de Medici as duke (1531), the anti-Jewish enactments were abolished. However, only with Cosimo I (1537–74) and his wife Eleonora of Toledo, who were on friendly terms with the *Abrabanel family of Naples (afterward of Ferrara), did the Jews of Florence enjoy a long period of peace. It was on Jacob Abrabanel's advice that the duke authorized an appeal, directed primarily to Jews, promising wide privileges to merchants willing to settle in Florence. In 1551 Cosimo made an official proclamation which granted various concessions to Levantine Jews. However, years later Cosimo consented to the burning of the Talmud in the cities within the duchy (1553). On the other hand, he offered refuge to many Jews who left the papal states as a result of Pope Paul *IV's repressive measures, which he refused to implement in Florence. Cosimo modified his attitude when seeking to obtain the pope's agreement to his assumption of the title of grand duke. Under Pius *V, he introduced the badge (1567) and established a ghetto (1571), both in Florence and Siena, the only two cities where Jews were authorized to live. The ghetto of Florence was planned by no less a personage than Bernardo Buontalenti, the Grand Duke's architect. It occupied a square area bounded to the east by Via dei Succhiellinai (Via Roma), to the south by Piazza del Mercato Vecchio, to the west by Via dei Rigattieri (Via Brunelleschi). In the central square stood two synagogues, serving the Spanish-Levantine and the Italian communities, respectively.

So far the development of Jewish intellectual life corresponded to the rich attainments of Florentine culture. Jewish men of letters were highly esteemed at the court of Lorenzo de' Medici (1449–92) by contemporary scholars and writers. Elijah *Delmedigo, Johanan *Alemanno, and Abraham *Farissol were closely connected with these circles of scholars and humanists. The banker Jehiel b. Isaac of *Pisa has been termed the "Lorenzo the Magnificent" of the Jewish community, and eminent scholars assembled at his home. Christians such as Giannozzo *Manetti, Marsilio *Ficino, Girolamo Benivieni, and Pico della *Mirandola were thus introduced to Hebrew language, literature, and philosophy. The 15th and 16th centuries were a fruitful period for Jewish literature and poetry, and other branches of Jewish learning, even though the community did not number much more than 100 families. The establishment of the ghetto terminated this renaissance. The number of Jews in Florence substantially increased, however, as they were forced to leave the provincial towns of the duchy and reside in the capital.

The legislation of 1571 restricted Jewish trade to second-hand goods and strictly enforced the ghetto system. Ferdinand I, the successor of Cosimo I, who became Grand Duke in 1587, granted a series of privileges to Levantine Jews and they were allowed to live outside the ghetto. Italian Jews, however, were not only confined to the borders of the ghetto but were also excluded from the city's guilds. In 1670 a fire destroyed the northern area of the ghetto. The damaged Italian synagogue was partly rebuilt. Under the rule of Cosimo III, the ghetto was extended to accommodate a growing population. In general the position of the Jews was more favorable than their legal status warranted.

In 1737 the Habsburg-Lorraine inherited the Grand Duchy of Tuscany from the defunct dynasty of the Medici. The situation of the Jews soon changed for better. Thus in 1750 the community was allowed to purchase the two buildings housing the synagogues. Certain civic rights were conferred on the Jews by the Grand Duke Leopold I (1765–90), one of the champions of the Enlightment in Europe, including the right to vote for the municipal council (1778). The first solely Hebrew printing press in Florence operated from 1734 to 1736, when Francesco Mouecke published a number of liturgical items. Isaac b. Moses di Pas printed there from 1744 to 1755. G. Campiagi printed a number of Hebrew books between 1778 and 1838, as did Rabbi G.V.A. Coën around 1828. When widespread popular disturbances broke out in 1790 against the reforms introduced by the ruler, the ghetto was attacked.

The Jews of Florence received their complete emancipation with the entry of the French Revolutionary army (March 25, 1799), which was subsequently forced to depart. In 1800 the French returned and the Jews regained their freedom. Florence, as well as Tuscany was annexed to Napoleonic France. Thus in 1808 a decree established consistories to govern the life of the Jewish communities in Tuscany, as in neighboring France.

After the restoration of the grand dukes (1814), Jews continued to enjoy wide toleration, albeit with some discrimination. Jews were permitted to own real estate and to work as physicians and pharmacists, but were barred from the legal profession and were excluded from military service. In this period various Jews, mainly from the Pontifical States, immigrated to the more tolerant Florence. Florence Jews as well as the Jews of the rest of Tuscany attained equality in 1848 under the constitution granted by Grand Duke Leopold II. Finally, in 1859, when Tuscany was incorporated in the Kingdom of Sardinia (from 1861 the Kingdom of Italy), the Jews were recognized as equal citizens of the new kingdom. In 1859 two Jews, the D'*Ancona brothers, held prominent positions in the provisional government of Farini before Tuscany was annexed to the Kingdom of Italy.

In 1864 Florence became the capital of Italy (until 1870). This probably influenced the community's decision to build a new synagogue. The building was erected in 1872, in the new district of the Mattonaia, in Via Farini 4. It was a building in the Moorish style, crowned by a huge dome. The original planner was the architect Marco Treves, later joined by Mariano Falcini and Vincenzo Micheli. The synagogue was twice visited by royalty: by Umberto I in 1887 and by Vittorio Emanuele III in 1911. Not all of Florence's Jews lived in the area. Thus in 1882 two small synagogues were opened in Via delle Oche 4. In 1899 the Collegio Rabbinico Italiano was transferred from Rome to Florence and placed under the guidance of Samuel Hirsch *Margulies. Through him and his pupils the community became the center of Hebrew culture in Italy. In 1931, 2,730 Jews lived in the community.

Hebrew Printing

The first solely Hebrew printing press in Florence operated from 1734 to 1736, when Francesco Mouecke published a number of liturgical items. Isaac b. Moses di Pas printed there from 1744 to 1755. G. Campiagi printed a number of Hebrew books between 1778 and 1838, as did Rabbi G.V.A. Coën around 1828. Publications appearing in Florence included *Rivista Israelitica* (1904–15), and *Settimana Israelitica* (1910–15), and the newspapers *Israel* (from 1916) and *Rassegna Mensile di Israel* (from 1925); both later appeared in Rome.

[Umberto (Moses David) Cassuto / Josef Levi (2nd ed.)]

Holocaust Period

The German occupation of Florence occurred on September 11, 1943. The perilous situation of the Jews immediately caused Rabbi Nathan Cassuto, son of the famous scholar Umberto *Cassuto, to seek assistance from the local clergy, and especially from the archbishop of Florence, Cardinal Elia Dalla Costa. Cassuto was concerned not only for the Florentine Jews but also for those refugees, mostly of East European origin, who after the announcement of the armistice between the Italians and the Allies on September 8, had followed the Italian Fourth Army occupying southeastern France on its retreat back into Italy. Many of the refugees were women and children. The Jewish-Christian relief committee that was born following the contacts between Cassuto and Dalla Costa became operative at the end of September 1943. This relief committee consisted of Cassuto himself; Father Cipriano Ricotti, prior of the Monastery of San Marco; Don Leto Casini, priest of Varlungo; Matilde Cassin (Rabbi Cassuto's young assistant, who attended to the contacts with the Florence monasteries and convents where the Jewish refugees were lodged); Eugenio Artom, a lawyer; Giuseppe Castiglioni, a lawyer; Guido De Angelis; Prof. Aldo Neppi Modona; and Giuliano Treves. Vital support to the relief committee was provided by Raffaele *Cantoni, who was in Florence following the dismissal of Mussolini as prime minister on July 25, 1943. Cantoni provided the committee with money, food, and clothing that were later distributed among the Jewish refugees lodged in the monasteries and convents. Giorgio La Pira, mayor of Florence after World War II, helped greatly in the search for monasteries and convents willing to take in the Jewish refugees.

The refugee committee was active for two months, from the second half of September to the second half of November 1943. The German raids against Jews in Tuscany began early in November 1943. On November 5 they took place in Siena and Montecatini. On November 6 the SS broke into the synagogue in Florence, seizing the custodian and a few refugees just arrived from France. They were deported to Auschwitz on November 9. On the evening of November 26, the SS invaded the premises of the Azione Cattolica, an Italian Catholic organization situated in Via dei Pucci, where a meeting of the Jewish-Christian relief committee was taking place, seizing Nathan Cassuto and other committee members. That same night, an SS unit with the active cooperation of a squad of Fascist soldiers invaded three monasteries in Florence: the convent of the Franciscan Missionary Sisters of Maria in the Piazza Carmine, where they seized 30 women and many children; the monastery of the Ricreatorio di San Giuseppe in Via Domenico Cirillo, where they arrested about 20 men; and the convent of the Sisters dell'Apparizione in via Gioberti, where they seized additional women and children. On the evening of November 29, as a result of betrayal, the Nazis apprehended, in the Piazza della Signoria, Anna Cassuto, the rabbi's wife; Saul Campagnano, Cassuto's brother-in-law; and Raffaele Cantoni. Most of the Jews arrested during the raids of late November 1943 were taken to the San Vittore prison in Milan, from where, on January 30, 1944, they were deported to Auschwitz. Cantoni managed to escape from the train, but the others arrived on February 6, 1944.

The relief activities of the Jewish-Christian committee continued clandestinely, but on a reduced scale, until the liberation of Florence in August 1944. About 243 Jews were deported from Florence, of whom only 13 returned. Eight Jews were murdered in circumstances related to their arrest, and four died while fighting with the partisans.

[Massimo Longo Adorno (2nd ed.)]

Contemporary Period

At the end of the war, 1,600 Jews were left in Florence. This number was reduced by 1965 to 1,276 out of a total of 455,000 inhabitants as a result of the constant excess of deaths over births. In 1962 the two oratories in Via delle Oche were sold. In 1970 there were approximately 1,250 Jews in Florence, including some in the surrounding area. By the turn of the century the number had dropped to around 1,000. In the floods of 1966, the muddy waters of the Arno River inundated the beautiful synagogue, causing great damage to the sacred objects and library. Today the synagogue is of the Sephardi rite, but there is also an Ashkenazi prayer house. The community had a kindergarten, an elementary school, and a high school as well as a rest home for elderly people, and a kosher restaurant. A review, *Ebrei d'Europa*, is published irregularly.

BIBLIOGRAPHY: Milano, Bibliotheca, index s.v. *Firenze*; Roth, Italy, index; U. Cassuto, *Ebrei a Firenze nell' eta' del Rinascimento* (1918); Roth, in: *Israel* (Apr. 17, and May 1, 1924); H.D. Friedberg, *Toledot ha-Defus be-Italya…* (1956), 88. **ADD. BIBLIOGRAPHY:** M., Bini, "Edificazione e demolizione del Ghetto di Firenze: prime ricostruzioni grafiche," in: *Architettura judaica in Italia: ebraismo, sito, memoria dei luoghi* (1994), 285–301; A. Boralevi, "Prime notizie sull' istituzione del Ghetto nella Firenze medicea," in: *Potere e lo Spazio: riflessioni di merito e contributi* (1980); U., Caffaz, "La cultura ebraica, Firenze nella cultura europea del Novecento," in: *Atti de Viesseux* (1993), 231–41; G. Carocci, *Il Ghetto di Firenze ed i suoi ricordi* (1886); M., Cassandro, "Per la storia delle comunita' ebraiche in Toscana nei secoli' XV–XVII," in: *Economia e Storia*, 4 (1977), 425–49; U., Fortis, *Ebrei e sinagoghe; Venezia, Firenze, Roma, Livorno, Guida pratica* (1973); L. Frattarelli Fisher, "Urban Forms of Jewish Settlement in Tuscan Cities (Florence, Pisa, Leghorn) during the 17th Century," in: WCJS, 10 (1993), 48–60; D. Liscia Bemporad, "La Scuola Italiana e la Scuola Levantina nel ghetto di Firenze: prima ricostruzione," in: *Rivista d'Arte* 38:5, IV, II (1986), 3–49; idem, "Firenze, nascita e demolizione di un ghetto," in: M. Luzzatti (ed.), *Il Ghetto ebraico, Storia di un popolo rinchiuso* (1988); V. Meneghin, *Bernardino Da Feltre e i Monti di Pietaà e i banchi ebraici* (1974); P. Pandolfi, *Ebrei a Firenze nel 1943, persecuzione e deportazione* (1980); R.G. Salvadori, *Gli ebrei toscani nell'eta' della Restaurazione (1814–1848)* (1993); idem, *Breve storia degli ebrei toscani* (1995); *Memorie della persecuzione degli ebrei con particolare riguardo alla Toscana*, ANED-ANFIM (1989); E. Salmon, *Diario di un ebreo fiorentino, 1943–1944* (2002); M. Longo Adorno, *Gli ebrei fiorentini dall'emancipazione alla Shoah* (2003); S. Minerbi, *Un ebreo fra D'Annunzio e il sionismo: Raffaele Cantoni* (1992).

FLORENTIN, MEVORAH (1895–1963), Venezuelan pioneer in the education of the blind. Florentin was born in Salonika, Greece. He lost the sight of one eye at the age of seven and his sight gradually deteriorated. In 1923, he settled in Caracas, Venezuela, and devoted himself to the study of Spanish until 1934 when, convinced that he would soon go completely blind, he turned to the study of Braille and the welfare of the blind. In 1936, he founded the Society for the Friends of the Blind, and after passing examinations in Braille and in typhlology (the scientific study of blindness) in Paris, he established a printing press for the publication of scholarly texts in Braille. In 1959, he founded the Eye Bank of the Venezuelan Institute for the Blind and the first School of Telephonists for the blind. In recognition of his services he was decorated four times by the Venezuelan Government, including the Order of Francisco de Miranda. After Florentin's death, the street in which the institute for the blind is located was named in his memory, and different educational institutions for the blind carry his name.

FLORETA CA NOGA, 14th-century Spanish physician. A document from 1381 indicating that Na Floreta Ca Noga of St. Coloma de Queralt was paid fifteen gold florins for her successful treatment of Sibila, Queen of Aragon, is among several records of royal payments for her services. She is one of a number of known female physicians of the medieval period, many of whom specialized in diseases of the eyes.

BIBLIOGRAPHY: A. Cardoner Planas, "Seis mujeres hebreas practicando la medicina en el reino de Aragon," in: *Sefarad*, 9:2 (1949), 443; A. López de Meneses. "Documentos culturales de Pedro el ceremonioso," in: *Estudios de Edad Media de la Corona de Aragón*, 5 (1953), #84, 736–37; E. Taitz, S. Henry, and C. Tallan. *The JPS Guide to Jewish Women* (2003).

[Judith R. Baskin (2nd ed.)]

FLORIDA, most southeasterly U.S. state, with a warm climate and long coastlines on the Atlantic Ocean and Gulf of Mexico. This combination creates a desirable quality of life that has attracted large numbers of people of all ages, among them many Jews. Florida (in 2005) boasted more than 17 million residents and had diversified its economy to become an important center of tourism, beef cattle, citrus, and space technology. Much of the growth in the Sunshine State since the end of World War II has been in its southern portions and South Florida had the third largest concentration of Jews in the U.S. after the New York and Los Angeles metropolitan areas.

Florida was discovered by Ponce de Leon for Spain in 1513 (21 years after the Spanish Inquisition) and some *Conversos may have come with him, as they did with Columbus. America's first permanent settlement was in St. Augustine in 1565. There are Sephardi names among those who lived there and evidence suggests that Pedro Menendez Marques, the third Spanish governor of Florida (1577–89) may have been a Converso. The perception that Jews were late arrivals in Florida parallels the belief that ascribes the founding of the U.S. to the pilgrims of Plymouth Rock. Current documentation shows that Jews have been *allowed* to live in Florida for nearly 250 years.

Until the mid-18th century Florida was for Catholics only. The Treaty of Paris (1762), which concluded the French and Indian War, gave Florida to the British and Louisiana to the Spanish. Jews living in Louisiana had to move. In 1763 three Sephardi Jews came from New Orleans to Pensacola: Samuel Israel, Joseph de Palacios, and Alexander Salomon. (Alexander Salomon may have been related to Haym *Salomon, who helped finance the American Revolution.)

Although Florida was returned to Spain following the American Revolution (1783), the Spanish needed settlers in the territory, so they tolerated a tiny Jewish presence. From the mid-18th century until Florida achieved statehood in 1845, Jews continued to trickle into northern Florida. The "Architect of Statehood" was a Jew, David Levy *Yulee, a son of pioneer Moses *Levy.

Eighty-one years before the First Zionist Congress in Basel, Switzerland (1897), Sephardi Jew Moses Elias Levy embarked on his own "Zion" plan to resettle oppressed European Jews in Florida. Born in Morocco in 1782, Moses Levy was descended from one of the many Jewish families who, having been expelled from the Iberian Peninsula at the end of the 15th century, found refuge in northern Africa. Raised in Gibraltar, Levy made his way to St. Thomas, V.I., in 1800. There he worked in the lumber business, accumulating a considerable fortune. He became interested in Florida and, in 1819, purchased 92,000 acres in the north central region.

Envisioning a haven for persecuted Jews, Levy called his settlement in Micanopy "Pilgrimage Plantation." He hired Frederick *Warburg, a member of the noted German Jewish banking family, to help him recruit Jewish settlers. Young Warburg, along with at least five other German Jewish families, lived on the Plantation. Included among them was Levy's son David, who became Florida's first U.S. senator. Moses Levy built a plantation house and houses for the settlers' families, as well as a blacksmith shop, stable, sugar mill, sawmill, and corn house. He brought in sugar cane, fruit trees, and seeds. In an effort to create a utopian Jewish settlement, Levy included among his projects a plan for the abolition of slavery, public schools, and a Jewish school.

The 1,000-acre plantation lasted from 1822 to 1835, when it was burned down by the Seminoles at the outbreak of the Second Seminole Indian War. Sustaining the plantation had been a challenge; in early 19th century Florida, it was virtually in the middle of nowhere. And the urban backgrounds of most of the Jewish settlers made adaptation to a rural outback difficult. As Levy said, "It is not easy to transform old clothes men into practical farmers."

Moses Levy left Florida a lasting legacy. Divorced, he had brought with him to Florida two of his four children, Elias and David. Elias was sent to Harvard; David boarded with the Moses Meyer family in Norfolk to get his Jewish education and then came to Florida by 1827 to manage some of his father's properties. He pursued law and was admitted to the Florida bar in 1832. David Levy became extremely active in politics. He helped draft Florida's constitution and eventually was sent to the U.S. Congress as the representative of the Territory of Florida (1841), where he argued for statehood. Being the first Jew to serve in the U.S. Congress, Levy faced discrimination when John Quincy Adams referred to him as the "alien Jew delegate."

With less than one hundred Jews in the state, David Levy was elected to the U.S. Senate when Florida became a state in 1845. He officially added the name of his father's Sephardi ancestry, Yulee. Yulee operated a 5,000-acre sugar plantation on the Homosassa River and another in Alachua County. He established a residence in Fernandina, where, in the 1850s, he organized and planned Florida's first railroad linking the Atlantic and Gulf coasts. On March 1, 1861, the first cross-state train of the Atlantic & Gulf Railroad left Fernandina at 7:15 A.M. and reached the outskirts of Cedar Key at 4 P.M., with eight stops in between.

Yulee resigned from the Senate when Florida seceded from the Union in early 1861. During the Civil War he served in the Confederate Congress. The war took a heavy personal toll. Union forces burned Yulee's plantation in Homosassa, his railroad lay in ruins, and, after the war, he was briefly imprisoned by the Union. Following his release, Yulee rebuilt his railroad, its operation continuing until the 1930s. Yulee moved to Washington, D.C., in 1880. He died six years later and is buried in Washington. Scholars contend there is no evidence that David Levy Yulee converted from Judaism, even though he married a Christian. Florida's Levy County and the town of Yulee (Nassau County) are among the places in Florida named for him.

Until 1822, Jews who lived in Florida came from somewhere else. The earliest known Jewish births are a girl (Virginia Myers) in Pensacola in 1822 and a boy (George Dzialynski) in Jacksonville in 1857. In that same year (1857), also in Jacksonville, Jews built the first Jewish cemetery in Florida. And in 1874 B'nai B'rith had a chapter in Pensacola.

Florida's first synagogue was constructed in Pensacola in 1876. By the end of the 19th century, there were six Jewish congregations and five Jewish cemeteries in Florida. Floridian Jews served on both sides of the Civil War. Following the Civil War, Jews began migrating south, settling in Tampa, *Orlando, Ocala, and even Key West. The west coast city of *Ft. Myers, founded in 1886, was named for a Jew – Abraham C. Myers, a West Point graduate and a descendant of the first rabbi of Charleston, South Carolina. Myers had served as quartermaster during the Second Seminole Indian War.

In 1879 German Jew Henry Brash was elected mayor of Marianna in north Florida, the first known of more than 150 Jews to serve their communities in this capacity. David Sholtz, a Russian Jew, became Florida's governor in 1933. Miami's Richard *Stone became the state's second Jewish U.S. senator in 1974 after serving as Florida's secretary of state. Scores of Jews have served in the state legislature and in the U.S. Congress. In 2005 Florida was represented in Washington by Debbie Wasserman Schultz and Robert *Wexler. More than 250 Jews have served as judges in Florida.

In 1915 Jacksonville Jew Ben Chepenik wrote his relatives in Massachusetts, "Sell everything; come quickly to Florida, the land of milk and honey; you can walk down the streets and pick citrus." And many did come. For Jews, Florida offered a variety of occupational opportunities. Some transferred their traditional dry goods businesses to Florida; others used the state's resources to develop or expand new ideas. In Florida, Jews became ranchers, farmers, cigar makers, architects, developers, hoteliers, artists, writers, scientists, retailers, educators, doctors, lawyers, civic leaders, and more.

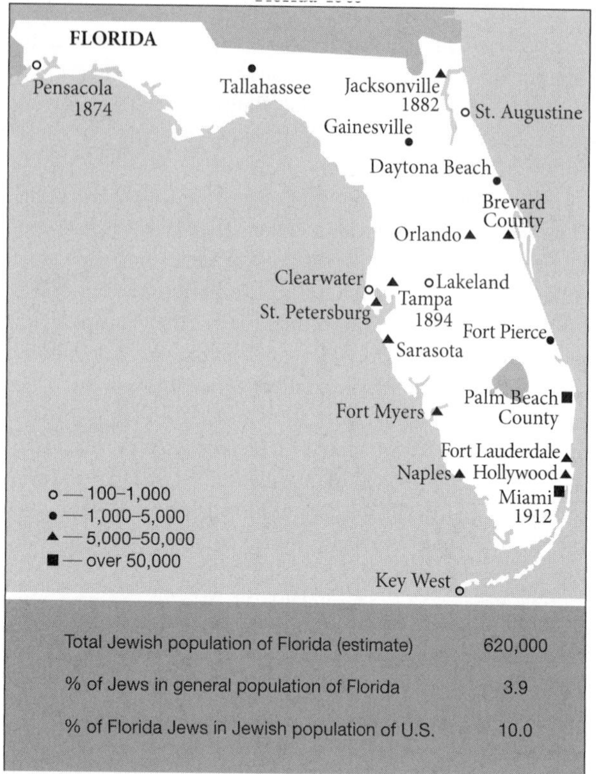

Total Jewish population of Florida (estimate)	620,000
% of Jews in general population of Florida	3.9
% of Florida Jews in Jewish population of U.S.	10.0

Jewish communities in Florida, with earliest dates of establishment. Population figures for 2001.

Jews owned the largest shade tobacco-packing factory in Quincy, near Tallahassee. Saul Snyder, a Russian Jew who immigrated to St. Augustine in 1904, founded the Florida Cattlemen's Association at a time when cattle was the state's major industry. The first Miss Florida was Jewish (1885). Much more recently, Marshall *Nirenberg of Orlando was awarded the Nobel Prize in medicine and physiology for breaking the genetic code (1968) and Isaac *Bashevis Singer – routinely associated with New York City but a Florida resident as well – received the Nobel Prize in literature in 1978. Four Jews have served on the Supreme Court of Florida, including as chief justice: Ray Ehrlich, Arthur England, Gerald Kogan, and Barbara Pariente.

Prior to the 20th century, most Jewish settlement in Florida was in the north or Key West (Key West was a port of entry for some European immigrants). But the development of railroads made accessible southern regions, and Jews headed south. Jewish migration throughout the state increased, but numbers increased exponentially after World War II, especially in Miami-Dade County. Air conditioning made Florida comfortable for year-round life.

The first South Florida community to host Jews was probably West Palm Beach, where Jews settled in 1892 when the railroad arrived there. Growth was slow at first; as late as 1940, the Jewish population in *Palm Beach County was only 1,000. In 2005 the Jewish population in Palm Beach County was the second largest in the state at about 220,000; the Boca Raton metropolitan area was more than 50% Jewish.

Many of the Jews who first settled in West Palm Beach were among the earliest settlers of *Miami. Miami, founded in 1896, was difficult to reach until Henry Flagler extended his railroad southward. But by the mid-1890s, the railroad rendered Miami and sites south accessible and Jews migrated accordingly. Other Jews migrated from Key West to Miami in the 1890s when a peddler's tax was imposed there. Some stayed after serving in the Spanish-American War. The first Jews settled on Miami Beach in 1913. After reaching its Jewish population zenith in 1975 (250,000), Miami-Dade County declined to about 113,000 in 2005 as elderly Jewish residents died and more recent retirees moved north, partly due to "white flight." At present, *Broward County, not Miami-Dade, has the largest number of Jews. Just as the center of the Jewish population moved south from *Jacksonville in the 1930s, it is now moving north.

Jews came to escape persecution in Europe, for economic opportunity, to join family members, to enjoy the climate, for their health, and to retire. In the 21st century, South Florida was an area stretching from Palm Beach to Miami where 15% of the population was Jewish. Most Jews came from other places in the United States, with considerable subsequent migration from Latin America as Jews were impacted by politics and economics. Jews have contributed in multiple ways to the development of the state, striving to maintain Jewish culture and institutions even as they've adjusted to the special nature of the place.

Sixteen percent of the American Jewish community lived in Florida in 2005. In the 1890s the Florida Jewish population was about 2,500; by the 1950s, the population had grown to 70,000; in 2005 it was nearly 850,000, about 5% of the general population, and still growing. Outside of South Florida, communities with noteworthy Jewish populations include Orlando, 35,000; Tampa, 25,000; St. Petersburg-Clearwater, 20,000; Sarasota, 17,000; Jacksonville, 13,000; Ft. Myers, 8,000; Naples, 6,000; Cocoa, Rockledge, Titusville, 6,000; Daytona, Ormond and environs, 5,500; Tallahassee, 4,400; Pensacola, 900 and Key West, 550. (See separate entries on other Jewish communities.)

In 2005 there were more than 350 congregations, 14 Federations that raised $82 million annually, 15 Jewish community centers, six university Judaic Studies programs, five Jewish homes for the aged, and eight Jewish newspapers. In Miami Beach were the Jewish Museum of Florida, a nationally recognized Jewish hospital (Mt. Sinai), and a major Holocaust Memorial. There was Florida Holocaust Museum in St. Petersburg as well as other Holocaust memorials and documentation and education centers around the state. The March of the Living and the Alexander Muss High School in Israel, two programs with international implications, began and are based in South Florida. There were nearly 100 kosher restaurants. And there was the full array of Jewish organizations, from the American Jewish Committee to the Zionist Organization of America. Few would deny that this was a significant American Jewish community.

[Marcia Jo Zerivitz (2nd ed.)]

°**FLORUS OF LYONS** (c. 860), successively secretary to the bishops *Agobard and *Amulo. Florus supplied no more than the literary material for the two bishops' anti-Jewish writings, which have often been wrongly attributed to him. However, he alone was responsible for two anti-Jewish compilations. The first, *De coertione Iudaeorum* ("On Forcing the Jews," c. 820), was in defense of Agobard, who was accused of using force in bringing Jewish children to baptism. The second, *De fugiendis contagiis Iuaeorum* ("On the Avoidance of Jewish Pollution," before 826), was included in a memorandum addressed to the emperor by Agobard and some of his colleagues.

BIBLIOGRAPHY: Blumenkranz, in: *Revue historique de droit français et étranger*, 33 (1955), 227ff., 560ff.; idem, *Les auteurs chrétiens latins…* (1963), 170–1.

[Bernhard Blumenkranz]

FLOSS, village in Bavaria, Germany. In 1685 a group of Jewish cloth merchants received a charter to settle and build on an unoccupied hill. Four houses were built in 1687 and the Jewish "colony" (juedische Kolonie), as it was called then, had 12 houses by 1712. In 1721 a synagogue was built. The community (referred to as "Judenberg" by contemporaries) retained its rights of self-government and jurisdiction well into the 19th century. When the government in 1819 ordered the incorporation of the Jewish community within the village according to the 1813 Bavarian edict (see *Bavaria), the Christian villagers protested, and in 1824 the Jewish community was again separated. It was totally incorporated in the village in 1869. There were 200 Jews living in Floss in 1799, 391 in 1840, 205 in 1871, and 19 in 1933. Floss served as a religious center for the Jews of the neighboring villages. On *Kristallnacht* (November 1938) the synagogue (consecrated in 1817) was burned down and the rabbi's house and communal center were ransacked. No Jews returned after the war. Yehoseph *Schwarz, pioneer Jewish geographer of Ereẓ Israel, was born in Floss.

BIBLIOGRAPHY: M. Weinberg, *Geschichte der Juden im Herzogtum Sulzbach* (1927); AWJD (Nov. 2, 1951), 9; S. Schwarz, *Die Juden in Bayern* (1963), 87, passim; PK Bavaryah.

FLOWERS. Almost all the very rich and variegated flora of Ereẓ Israel are flowering plants (*Phanerogamae*), and most of them have an attractively colored corolla. In Israel flowers bloom all year, in the cold and rainy season as well as in the burning heat of summer, but mainly during the spring. In this respect Israel differs from those countries where plants almost entirely cease blooming in winter and burst forth in spring in a blaze of flowers and greenery. The biblical "month of *Abib*" ("spring"; Ex. 13:4; et al.) refers to the time when the grains of corn in the ear are still tender. In point of fact, there are two seasons of the year in Israel: "Cold and heat, summer and winter" (Gen. 8:22); "Thou hast made summer and winter" (Ps. 74:17). The winter season begins after the early rains have fallen (October–November). Shortly afterward the ground is covered with a blanket of green grass. Appearing soon after the early rains, the first flowers bloom, mainly those of bulbous plants such as species of colchicum with their pinkish-white flowers and the crocus and saffron with their white ones. Masses of yellow dandelions and calendula appear a few weeks later. Once more the color of the fields changes, this time to the bright pink of the thousands of silene. In January the fields are covered with the blood-red flowers of the anemone, other colors of it – white, pink, and violet – growing in Galilee and on the Carmel. Their red is replaced shortly after by the fiery red flowers of the ranunculus, and here and there are to be seen the beautiful red blooms of the tulip, which in the 1930s and 1940s dominated the landscape of the Sharon and the mountains but have been greatly diminished as a result of ruthless picking. The red species of poppy, however, which bring the season of abundant flowering to a close, have not been affected in this way.

Such is the main cycle of the landscape's changing hues in Israel's Mediterranean areas until the arrival of summer. In addition to these there are hundreds of species of other flowers, some of them the most beautiful in the country, as well as several endemic species that are among the prettiest in the world, such as the cyclamen, conspicuous by its delicate flowers and picturesque leaves, which appears among the rocks as early as December. The fragrant narcissus is found in the valleys and prominent in March–May are many species of terrestrial orchids, not inferior in beauty despite their small flowers to their congener, the tropical epiphytic orchids. This period is rich in the blooming of floral species of the Iridaceae family, such as those of the gladiolus and iris, as well as flowers of the Liliaceae family, to which the *Lilium candidum* belong. Because of expanding agricultural settlement and the intensive picking of blooms, the areas of these beautiful flowers have been greatly reduced, but their number has been increasing year by year since the passing of the State of Israel's nature protection laws.

In the desert areas of Israel – the Negev and Aravah – flowering begins after the first rain and here also are many splendid flowers, particularly of the Liliaceae and Iridaceae families as well as species of the *Salvia* and crucifers. To the last belongs the desert *Mantur* which in winter covers the rocky hammada with a purple carpet of millions of flowers. The flowering period of the desert flora is short. Annuals have a brief existence, the entire life cycle of some – sprouting, growing, flowering, and seeding – lasting no more than ten weeks. In this way desert flora ensure their survival before the advent of the long, dry summer months. The Mediterranean single-season flora, too, have a brief span of life. Taking advantage of the rainy season, they grow rapidly, and flower for a few days, only to disappear suddenly with the coming of the first hot *sharav* ("sirocco") winds of spring. This phenomenon has found expression in many metaphors, such as those describing the end of man's life: "The grass withereth, the flower fadeth" (Isa. 40:7), and his short life: "In the morning it flourisheth, and groweth up; in the evening it is cut down, and withereth" (Ps. 90:6). The wicked, too, are likened to masses of single-season flowers that suddenly flourish in all their brilliance but with the coming of the hot *sharav* wind disappear without a trace (*ibid.* 92:8).

Besides wild annuals or bulbous and tuberous flora, there are many wild perennials – beautiful flowering shrubs and trees. Cyclical changes mirrored in the blossoms' hues on the dominant shrubs and trees can be distinguished in the color of the landscape. The first tree to bloom in Israel, when forest trees are still shedding their leaves is the *almond, covered with a white mantle of blossoms (some strains of the cultivated almond have pinkish flowers). Shortly after, in January, with the blossoming of the *Calycotome* shrub, the prevailing color of the woods changes to yellow. Next the rockrose (*Cistus*) shrubs bloom with their large pink and white flowers. The purple flowers of the Judas tree (*Cercis*) are conspicuous in the woods in March. Then yellow, the color of the spartium shrubs, once again becomes the predominant hue, to be replaced by the white of the flowers of the styrax and the hawthorn (*Crataegus*). The great majority of the country's shrubs and trees blossom in winter and spring, and only a few of them in the dry summer – the season when the eucalyptus flowers. Soon after the rains the various species of *citrus bloom, and the air is filled with the scent of their blossoms. The end of summer, with the approach of the rainy season, sees a revival in some species of flora known as "the harbingers of winter"; prominent among these is the *squill with its white flower, like an erect candle, which comes out of the bulb during the last months of summer. The *Pancriatum* – "lily of Sharon" – blooms in this season, its large, fragrant flowers visible from afar in the desolate landscape. Two species of the colchicum flourish at the end of summer. It is, at first sight, surprising that the Bible and talmudic literature seldom refer to the use of flowers for decorative purposes, but in ancient times the emphasis was laid on aromatic flora, and it is their fragrance which is emphasized. The picking of flowers is referred to in the Bible only once: "My beloved is gone down to his garden, to the beds of spices, to feed in the gardens, and to gather lilies" (Song 6:2). The Mishnah, too, speaks of the picking of lilies, but in a cemetery (Toh. 3:7). Mention is made of a "rose garden" which existed in Jerusalem since the days of the prophets (BK 82b). According to the Mishnah, figs grew there (Ma'as 2:5). But here, too, it is doubtful whether this garden was for decorative purposes or whether the fragrant roses were not used in the preparation of perfumes (see *Rose). The flowers mentioned in the Talmud, such as the saffron, jasmin, and narcissus, are chiefly mentioned as aromatic and medicinal flora.

The flower was a common motif in ancient Hebrew art: the ornamentation of the candlestick was in the form of "a calyx and petals" (Ex. 25:33). On the brim of the "sea" in the Temple were embellishments "like the brim of a cup, like the flower of a lily" (I Kings 7:26), while the boards of cedar in it were "carved with knops and open flowers" (*ibid.* 6:18). Josephus tells that the crown worn by the high priest was in the form of the calyx of the *Hyoscyamus* flower. Apparently the passage, "Woe to the crown of pride of the drunkards of Ephraim, and to the fading flower of his glorious beauty" (Isa. 28:1), alludes to floral wreaths. In apocalyptic literature it is stated that virgins wore floral chaplets, as did those celebrating Tabernacles and the victor in battle (II Bar. 10:13; Jub. 16:30; IV Macc. 17:15). The Talmud refers several times to chaplets of roses (Shab. 152a; BM 84a). It is also related that bridegrooms wore wreaths of roses and myrtle (Sot. 9:14; Tosef. 15:8) and that non-Jews garlanded the idols on their festivals with crowns of roses and corn (Av. Zar. 4:2; TJ, Av. Zar. 4:2, 43d).

Flowers of the Bible

Only three flowers are mentioned by name in the Bible, the *shoshan* or *shoshannah* ("lily" or "rose"), *shoshannat ha-amakim* (*shoshannah* "of the valleys"), and *ḥavaẓẓelet ha-Sharon* ("rose" or "lily" of the Sharon (Valley)). The complex question of the identification of the *shoshan* or *shoshannah* has provoked more studies than any other flora mentioned in the Bible, there being scarcely a beautiful flower found in Israel (and even beyond its borders) that has not been suggested. Symbolizing in the Bible beauty and fragrance, it is most probably to be identified with the *Lilium candidum* – the white (madonna) lily. Abraham Ibn Ezra (in his commentary on Song 2:1) had this flower in mind when he stated that *shoshan, shoshannah* is derived from *shesh* ("six"), "since it always has six white petals as well as a pistil and long stamens which likewise number six." On the basis of this identification and doubtless also because of its delightful smell, Ibn Ezra declared, contrary to the generally accepted view, that the expression "his lips are as lilies" (*ibid.* 5:13) refers "to scent and not to appearance," that is, not to the red color of the lips but to their sweet odor. The other descriptions of the word in the Bible fit in with "lily" (Song 6:2–3; 4:5; 5:13; 7:3). Previously doubt was cast on this identification on the grounds that it was not proved that in ancient times the lily grew wild in Ereẓ Israel, but this large, beautiful, and scented bloom is to be found in woods in the Carmel and Galilee areas. To see the lily's lovely fragrant flowers blooming at the beginning of summer among the various thorns that then dominate the landscape is an enchanting experience, and hence "as a lily among thorns, so is my love among the daughters" (Song 2:1–2). It is this passage that was responsible for the incorrect identification of *shoshannah* as a rose, having been explained as referring to a rose amid its thorny stems. The rose was not found in Ereẓ Israel in biblical times, however, and although two species of rose grow wild in the country, they are neither beautiful nor fragrant, nor do the name *shoshan* and its biblical description fit the rose. It must, however, be pointed out that its identification as a rose already appears in the Midrash which speaks of the "red *shoshannah*" and of "a *shoshannah* of a rose" (Lev. R. 23:3; Song R. 7:3, no. 2).

Although the identification of *shoshan/shoshannah* as a lily is almost certain, it is difficult to identify the *shoshannat ha-amakim* mentioned with it in the Song of Songs since the white lily does not grow specifically in valleys. Of the many suggestions put forward in identifying it, the most likely appears to be the narcissus (*Narcissus tazetta*), a fragrant flower with six enveloping petals that flourishes particularly in valleys with a heavy soil. *Ḥavaẓẓelet ha-Sharon* is mentioned in the same verse (Song 2:1) and also in the vision of the flowering of the desolate land which shall "blossom as the *ḥavaẓẓelet*" and to which "the excellency of Carmel and Sharon" shall be given (Isa. 35:1–2). The *ḥavaẓẓelet*, as also the *shoshannah*, is identified by the Septuagint as *κρίνον*, that is, a lily. The Targum on Song of Songs identifies it with a narcissus, while various exegetes have identified it with the country's beautiful flowers, such as the iris or rose (Ibn Ezra), the colchicum (Loew), the tulip, as well as other flowers of bulbous plants, since the word is very probably connected with *baẓal* ("bulb"). It is generally accepted that *ḥavazzelet ha-Sharon* is to be identified with the *Pancratium maritimum*, a bulbous plant with white, highly scented flowers which blooms at the end of summer in the coastal lowland; thus it appropriately symbolizes the flowering of the desolate land and its transformation into "the excellency of Carmel and Sharon."

[Jehuda Feliks]

Ceremonial Use

Man's awareness of the fragrance of flowers is an occasion for him to say the blessing, "Blessed art Thou, O Lord … who createst fragrant plants" (Ber. 43b). Yet flowers and plants were not generally used in synagogal or Jewish home ceremonies. On *Shavuot, however, it is customary to decorate the synagogue with fragrant grass, flowers, and branches. A threefold reason is given for this custom: the branches are a reminder that Shavuot is also the "Day of Judgment" for trees (RH 1:2); the fragrant grass is symbolic of the people of Israel assembled around Mount Sinai for the giving of the Torah (Ex. 34:3); and the flowers are a symbol for the betrothal of Israel to the Torah. The decorating of synagogues with flowers on Shavuot was opposed by some authorities on grounds of its similarity to the Christian practice (see *Ḥukkat ha-Goi). In modern times on Shavuot, synagogues are sometimes also adorned with sheaves of wheat, etc., symbolic of Shavuot as the festival of the wheat harvest and the offering of the *first fruits (*bikkurim*; see also Bik. 3:3). In the U.S. the custom has grown of having flowers at most family events, On Simḥat Torah in some congregations, a *ḥuppah* ("bridal canopy") made of plants and flowers is placed on the *bimah* ("platform"), and on Sukkot, the *sukkah* is embellished with fruits, flowers, and plants. Traditional Jewish mourning customs admit neither wreaths nor flowers at funerals or on tombstones (although in modern times, this custom is frequently disregarded). The planting of trees and shrubs around the synagogue building was the cause of heated debates a century and a half ago. Orthodox rabbinical authorities strongly objected to the landscaping of synagogue grounds, based on Deuteronomy 16:21 (see also Maim. Yad, Avodat Kokhavim 6:9). This objection, motivated by fear of innovation and reform, subsided in the course of time and yielded to the desire for an aesthetically appropriate setting for the synagogue.

BIBLIOGRAPHY: J. Feliks, *Olam ha-Ẓome'aḥ ha-Mikra'i* (1968[2]), 232–43; Loew, Flora, 2 (1924), 144ff; Z. Avidov and I. Harpaz, *Plants of Israel* (1968).

FLUSSER, DAVID (1917–2000), scholar of comparative religion; professor at the Hebrew University of Jerusalem beginning in 1962. Flusser's researches were devoted to Christianity, with a special interest in the New Testament; to Judaism of the Second Temple Period, and in particular to the *Dead Sea Scrolls; to the *Josippon Chronicle, and certain associated areas. Of great prominence were his researches into the Dead Sea Scrolls and the sect which produced them, especially as the Scrolls relate to the New Testament. His article "The Dead Sea Sect and Pre-Pauline Christianity" (*Scripta Hierosolymitana*, 1958) is central to any consideration of these problems. He has published over 1,000 articles in Hebrew, English, German, and other languages, distinguished by a great sensitivity to currents and types of religious thought as well as by their philological analysis. His published work also includes "Blessed are the Poor in Spirit," in: IEJ, 10 (1960), 1–12; *Die konsequente Philologie und die Worte Jesu* (1963); *De joodse oorsprong van het Christendom* (1964); *Yosippon: Kunteres le-Dugma* (1947); *Jesus in Selbstzeugnissen und Bilddokumenten* (1968) and *Jesus* (1969, 2001[3]); and translations into French and Dutch as well as "Jesus in the Context of History" (in: *The Crucible of Christianity* (1969), 225–34, ed. A. Toynbee). Later books include *Judaism and the Origins of Christianity* (1988) and *Judaism of the Second Temple Period* (2 vols., 2002). In 1980 he was awarded the Israel Prize for Jewish studies.

FLY (Heb. זְבוּב), which occurs in an analogous form in other Semitic languages, refers mainly to the housefly (*Musca domestica*) A dead fly turns foul anything it falls into (Eccles. 10:1). Among the visitations against which public prayer was offered up was a plague of flies (Ta'an. 14a). The Palestinian *amora*, Johanan, warned against flies as carriers of disease (Ket. 77b). One measure of a man's fastidiousness is how he reacts when a fly falls into his drink (Tosef., Sot. 5:9). One of the miracles that occurred in the Temple was that "no fly was seen in the slaughter house" (Avot 5:5). Rav reported from observation that "no fly is a year old"; in other words, that it does not live more than six months (cf. Deut, R. 5:2). Despite the repulsiveness of the fly, its existence was considered important in the balance of nature (TJ, Ber. 9:3, 13c). The people of Ekron worshipped an idol called Baal Zebub ("lord of the fly," see *Baal), perhaps regarded as a protector against the plague of flies (II Kings 1:2). Besides the housefly, there are to be found in Israel stinging, blood-sucking flies, as well as carrion and fruit flies. Carrion flies (*Lucillia*) lay their eggs in carcasses. From the eggs hatch maggots (referred to in biblical passages as *rimmah ve-tole'ah*), which cause the decomposition of the corpse (Isa. 14:11; et al.). The maggots of fruit flies (*Drosophila*) feed on fruit and sweet food (cf. Ex. 16:24); the olive fly (*Dacus olea*) causes the fruit to fall from the olive (Deut. 28:40).

BIBLIOGRAPHY: Tristram, Nat Hist, 327f.; J. Feliks, *Animal World of the Bible* (1962), 123f. **ADD. BIBLIOGRAPHY:** Feliks, Ha-Ẓome'aḥ, 224.

[Jehuda Feliks]

FOA (generally **Foà** in Italy), Italian family well-known from the 15th century; in the 18th century it became established also in Amsterdam, Constantinople, and France, where the forms Foi or Foy were adopted in due course. The origin of the name is unknown, but it may derive from Foix in southern France, where there was a Jewish community in the Middle Ages. A. Yaari (*Meḥkerei Sefer* (1958), 325–44) assembled the names of 100 distinguished members of the family. The family badge shows the Shield of David over a palm tree flanked by two lions. This was used as their distinctive *printers' mark by successive members of the Foa family from the middle of the 16th to the 19th century (see below).

ELIEZER NAHMAN (d. after 1641), rabbi and kabbalist, a disciple of Menahem Azariah da *Fano. He lived at Reggio Emilia where he became chief rabbi of the duchy of Modena. He was at the head of the pious association Ḥevrat ha-Aluvim which sponsored the printing of the commentary on the Passover *Haggadah, Midrash be-Ḥiddush* (Venice, 1641; complete ed. Leghorn, 1809). He also left a diffuse philosophic and kabbalistic commentary on the Pentateuch, *Goren Ornan* (Ms. in Mortara, Almanzi, and Ghirondi collections). MOSES BENJAMIN (1729–1822), bibliophile and bookseller of Reggio Emilia, supplied books to the ducal library at Modena and later became one of the most celebrated booksellers in Italy. He purchased the library of Israel Benjamin *Bassano, which he later presented to the Jewish community at Reggio. He wrote a Hebrew grammar and copied expertly several Hebrew manuscripts. ELIA EMANUEL (d. 1796) founded a Jewish school in Vercelli which attained a high standard and continued to flourish for over a century.

In more recent times, the following should be mentioned: CESARE (1833–1907), born at Sabbioneta and later rabbi in Soragna. He translated into Italian works by *Judah Halevi, Moses *Zacuto, and Jacob Daniel *Olmo. PIO (1848–1923), a pathologist, was born in Sabbioneta. He became a professor at the universities of Modena and Turin, and wrote a standard treatise on pathological anatomy. An ardent Italian patriot and in his youth a follower of Garibaldi, he was made a senator of the kingdom. His son CARLO (1878–n.a.), a physiologist, worked on the function of the glands of internal secretion, and was lecturer at various Italian universities. He was prize winner and later member of the Accademia dei Lincei. A member of another branch of this family was SALVATORE (1885–1962), born in Turin, who wrote several monographs on the history of the Jews in Piedmont. The French branch of the family produced well-known explorers, writers, and philanthropists. One of these, EDOUARD (1862–1901), explored the interior of Dahomey in 1886 and in 1894–97 crossed Africa from the mouth of the Zambesi on the Indian Ocean to Libreville in Gabon on the Atlantic Ocean, His books include *Le Dahomey* (1895) and *De l'Océan Indien à l'Océan Atlantique* (1900), and *Résultats scientifiques des voyages en Afrique d'Edouard Foa* (published posthumously, 1908).

[Giorgio Romano]

One section of the family devoted itself to Hebrew printing. TOBIAS BEN ELIEZER (16th century) set up a Hebrew printing press in his house in *Sabbioneta in 1551. In its last years, Tobias' sons ELIEZER and MORDECAI headed this enterprise, which had to close after difficulties with the censor, the last works on the press being finished in *Cremona and *Mantua. Tobias started the fashion of printing special copies, often on parchment, for wealthy patrons. NATHANEL BEN JEHIEL began his printing activity as a hobby in Amsterdam in 1702, prompted by his uncle and brother-in-law Joseph Ẓarefati. Most of the works he issued (12 up to 1715) were written by emissaries from Ereẓ Israel or were manuscripts which they had brought with them. ISAAC BEN GAD (b. c. 1700), physician and one of the leaders of the Venice Jewish community, ventured into Hebrew printing about the time of the birth of his son GAD (1730–1811) and produced mainly liturgical items until 1739. From 1741 Isaac was in the book trade proper. In 1742 he entered into partnership with his kinsman SAMUEL, who was also father of a son GAD, the two Gads later taking over the business. Gad b. Samuel appears as the sole printer between 1775 and 1778; he moved to *Pisa in 1796, producing 13 books at his own press or at that of David Cesna. His last major production, in association with Eliezer Saadun, was a handsome Hebrew Bible of 1803. Gad b. Isaac resumed printing in Venice in 1792 until 1809. Among the few major works produced by the Foas of Venice are the first four volumes of Isaac Lampronti's talmudic encyclopedia Paḥad *Yizḥak*.

BIBLIOGRAPHY: M. Mortara, *Indice alfabetico dei Rabbini e Scrittori Israeliti* (1886), s.v.; G. Pugleise, *Elia Emmanuel Foa ed il suo tempo* (1896); Ghirondi-Neppi, index; A. Balletti, *Gli Ebrei e gli Estensi* (1930²), 223–9; G. Bedarida, *Ebrei d'Italia* (1950), *indexes; A. Yaari, Meḥkerei Sefer* (1958), 324–419.

FOA, ESTHER EUGÉNIE REBECCA (1799–1853), French author. Born in Bordeaux, Esther Foa was the first Jewess to make her name as a French writer. Under various pen names, including Edmond de Fontanes, she wrote novels and stories on Jewish themes for juveniles. Among them are *Le Kiddouchim ou l'anneau nuptial des Hébreux* (4 vols., 1830), *La Juive, histoire du temps de la Régence* (1835), and *Le vieux Paris, contes historiques* (1840). She later abandoned Judaism.

FOA, RAIMONDO (1877–1940), Italian army officer. Born in Casale Monferrato, Foa was commissioned in 1899 and fought in the Italo-Turkish War (1911–12). He was an artillery commander in World War I and in 1919 worked in the technical service of the artillery. Foa became director of the Terni Ordnance Arms factory in 1927. He was promoted to the rank of lieutenant general in 1937.

ADD. BIBLIOGRAPHY: A. Rovighi, *I Militari di Origine Ebraica nel Primo Secolo di Vita dello Stato Italiano* (1999).

FOCSANI (Rom. **Focşani**) town in E. Romania founded in the 17th century. Jewish settlement there dates from the second half of the 17th century; there were 20 tax-paying families by 1820. The community numbered 736 in 1838, 1,855 in 1859 (19.2% of the total), and 5,954 in 1899 (25.2% of the total), 4,301 in 1930 (13.2 % of the total), and 4,935 in 1941 (10.5% of the total). Since this was a wine-growing area many of the Jews were vintners. Focsani was a center of anti-Jewish hostility. The oath "More Judaico" was introduced there for the first time in 1838. In 1859 there was a case of blood libel soon exposed as crime committed for gain. The antisemitic newspaper *Paznicul* was published in Focsani from 1900. The Romanians' Union, an association founded in 1910, proclaimed a boycott of the Jewish merchants. In March 1925 the trial was opened in Focsani of Corneliu Zelea Codreanu, head of the Iron Guard, accused of murdering the chief of the police in Jassy. Antisemitic gangs took the opportunity to pillage 300 Jewish houses, among them the school and the great synagogue. On the eve of World War II the community had eight synagogues, the oldest dating from the 18th century, two primary schools, a kindergarten, a medical dispensary, and three cemeteries. Focsani was a center of early Zionist activity, and the first conference of the Yishuv Erez Israel movement took place there on Jan. 11–12, 1882, with representatives from 32 localities. Rabbis of Focsani include the Hebrew author Jacob Nacht (1872–d. in Israel 1959), who officiated there from 1900 to 1919, and through whose influence Focsani became the center of Zionist cultural activity in Romania. The Hebrew writer Israel Teller, teacher at the Jewish school, also lived in Focsani. Solomon Zalman *Schechter, discoverer of the Cairo **Genizah*, was born in Focsani. Avram Moise Schwartz, known as *Cilibi Moïse, the first Jewish writer in the Romanian language, was also born in Focsani.

Holocaust Period

In 1941 there were 3,953 Jews living in Focsani out of a total population of approximately 37,000. At the beginning of the *Antonescu regime, the Jewish merchants were forced to hand over their shops to the Iron Guard; those who refused were sent to concentration camps at Târgo-Jiu and Caracal. Three of the synagogues were blown up by military engineers on the pretext that the earthquake of November 1940 had damaged their foundations, making them dangerous constructions.

When the war with the Soviet Union broke out (June 1941), all Jewish males aged between 16 and 60 were imprisoned. A few weeks later they were released, except for 65 hostages including the rabbi and community leaders. Three months later the number of hostages was reduced to ten; each was held for a while and then relieved by other Jews. The number of Jews in Focsani increased considerably with the arrival of Jews who had been driven out of the villages and towns in the district, as well as Jews from *Ploesti. They were cared for by the local community which also aided a group of 400 Jews from southern Transylvania who had been brought to the district as forced labor. A number of Jews from Focsani were also sent away on forced labor. In the spring of 1944, 210 Jewish orphans from *Transnistria were brought to Focsani and put under the care of the local community. On May 12, 1944, the local military commander mobilized all male and female Jews aged between 15 and 55, to dig anti-tank ditches for the defense of the town against the approaching Soviet forces.

In the postwar period the Jewish population, which numbered 6,080 in 1947, decreased to 3,500 by 1950 as a result of emigration. By 1970 continued emigration had reduced the number further to about 150 families. One synagogue remained open. In 1994, 80 Jews lived in Focsani, dropping to 70 in 2004.

BIBLIOGRAPHY: Joint Foreign Committee, *The Jewish Minority in Roumania* (1927), 6, 8, 14, 34; M. Schwarzfeld, in: *Analele Societăţii Istorice Iuliu Barasch*, 2 pt., 1 (1888), 41, 73; idem, *Momente din istoria evreilor in România* (1889), 7, 20, 23; M.A. Halevy, in: *Anuarul evreesc ilustrat pentru România* (1932), 126–8; *Almanahul Ziarului Tribuna Evreiască*, 1 (1937/8), 49–50; S. Cristian-Cris, *Patru ani de urgie* (1945), 122; M. Carp, *Cartea Neagră* 1 (1946), 156, 177; Y. Ariel, in *Voinţa* (Nov. 21, 1955), Th. Lavi, *Yahadut Romanyah be-Ma'avak al Hazzalatah* (1965), 147; idem, in *Viaţa Noastră* (Sept. 1, 1967). **ADD. BIBLIOGRAPHY:** Z. Ben Dov (Zilberman) *Focsani, Sippurah shel Kehillah* (2003); *Bună dimineaţa Israel* (July 19, 2004).

[Theodor Lavi / Lucian-Zeev Herscovici (2nd ed.)]

FODDER (Heb. מִסְפּוֹא, *mispo*, AV, JPS, "provender"), most often mentioned together with *teven* ("chaff," AV, JPS, "straw") as feed for camels and asses (Gen. 24:25; 43:24; Judg. 19:19). *Teven*, which was the most important food of domestic animals, was made from the bits of straw left after threshing. To it was usually added grain or pulse to produce *belil* (AV, JPS, "provender"), much loved by animals (Isa. 30:24; Job 6:5). The principal fodder, as also the customary ingredient of *belil*, was barley, which is suitable as feed for single-hoofed animals, horses, asses, and mules, and is mentioned as such for the horses and swift steeds in Solomon's stables (I Kings 5:8). Barley was unsuitable for ruminants, yet the Tosefta (BK 1:8) speaks of "an ass that ate barley and a cow that ate bitter vetch (*Vicia ervilia*)." The latter species is not mentioned in the Bible, but was clearly an ancient crop, seeds of it having been found in excavations at *Gezer dating from the beginning of the monarchy in Judah. The *carob, although similarly not mentioned in the Bible, was likewise used as fodder in ancient times, particularly for goats (Shab. 155a, et al.).

In addition to the fodder consisting mainly of grains or pulse, animals were given dry hay or green grass (*ḥaẓir*) that grows in winter in uncultivated fields (Ps. 147:8–9) and in summer alongside sources of water (I Kings 18:5; Isa. 44:4). In places where there is no water the grass dries up in spring (Isa. 37:27, et al.). In the rainy season animals graze in fields and eat natural grass. Sometimes the owner of a field cuts the green cereal and feeds it to his animals, and the cereal continues to grow "and does not diminish its grain" (Sif. Deut. 43, on the verse: "And I will give grass in thy fields for thy cattle"). Most often the grass was cut and dried as fodder (cf. 1 Kings 18:5), the usual talmudic term for green fodder being *shaḥat* (Pe'ah 2:1, et al.), and for dried *amir* ("a sheaf," in the Bible). For the latter, two species of legumes were specially sown, fenugreek (*Trigonella foenumgraecum;* see *Sifra, 7:1), and more particularly cowpea (*Vigna sinensis*) for its green pods and dry seeds, or for dry fodder (Shev. 2:8; et al.). To a limited extent vetch (*Vicia sativa*) was grown for fodder. In Babylonia, alfalfa (*Medicago*) was also sown.

BIBLIOGRAPHY: Loew, Flora, 1 (1928), 557, 571; 2 (1924), 92, 474, 476, 487ff.; Dalman, Arbeit, 2 (1932), 165ff., 268ff., 330; J. Feliks, *Ha-Ḥakla'ut be-Ereẓ Yisrael bi-Tekufat ha-Mishnah ve-ha-Talmud* (1963), 255f., 279–84; idem, *Olam ha-Ẓome'aḥ ha-Mikra'i* (1968²), 205ff.

[Jehuda Feliks]

FODOR, ANDOR (1884–1968), Israeli biochemist. Fodor was born in Budapest, Hungary, and in 1922 became professor of biochemistry at the University of Halle, Germany. In 1923, at the invitation of Chaim *Weizmann, he went to Palestine to establish a department of chemistry for the projected Hebrew University of Jerusalem. Before leaving Europe, he purchased the equipment and apparatus for this project, and himself supervised the actual building of the Institute of Chemistry on Mount Scopus. Fodor was the first professor appointed to the university, and held the chair of biochemistry and colloid chemistry for 28 years. Elected first dean of the faculty of science, he was responsible for training an entire generation of Israeli scientists. He did experimental research into protein structure and the action of enzymes, and was the author of *Dispersoidchemie* (1925) and *Das Fermentproblem* (1922, 1929).

[Samuel Aaron Miller]

FOERDER, YESHAYAHU (**Herbert**; 1901–1970), Israeli economist and banker. Foerder, born in Berlin, studied law and joined the Zionist student organization, *Kartell juedischer Verbindungen.* He was secretary of the German Zionist Organization from 1924 to 1926. Settling in Palestine in 1933, he was one of the founders of the Rassco Rural and Suburban Settlement Company (see *Israel, Housing), serving as its managing director until 1957. During the Mandate period Foerder represented Aliyah Ḥadashah, a party consisting mainly of German immigrants, in the Va'ad Leummi. In 1949 he was elected to the Knesset by the Progressive Party, which he represented until 1957. From 1957 he was chairman of the board of directors of Bank Leumi le-Israel and of the General Mortgage Bank. Foerder was the author of numerous publications on Zionism and on economic problems.

[Kurt Loewenstein]

FOGELBERG, DAN (1951–), U.S. composer and recording artist. Born in Peoria, Illinois, Fogelberg studied the piano from the age of 14, switched to guitar and played at local coffeehouses while majoring in art at the University of Illinois. Fogelberg's first album, *Home-free* (1972), attracted little attention. His second album, *Souvenirs* (1974), however, proved to be one of the finest collections of songs written in the 1970s. In 1975 Fogelberg was chosen as pop music's newcomer of the year and since then has recorded a number of best-selling albums including *Captured Angel* (1975), *Twin Sons of Different Mothers* (1979) with Tim Weisberg, *Phoenix* (1980), and *The Innocent Age* (1981). During the 1980s, none of his albums were platinum, but they continued to sell well among hardcore fans. During the 1990s he made several albums: *River of Souls* (1993), *No Resemblance Whatsoever*, a collaboration with Tim Weisberg (1995), *First Christmas Morning* (1999), and *Something Old New Borrowed and Some Blues* (2000).

[Jonathan Licht / Israela Stein (2nd ed.)]

FOIGHEL, ISI (1927–), German-born conservative politician. Foighel came to Denmark in 1932 and became a professor of law at Copenhagen University in 1964. From 1965 to 1971 he was president of the Danish Refugee Help organization and had considerable influence on refugee-related legislation. In 1972–73 he was president of the Jewish Community and subsequently head of the commission that prepared home rule for Greenland. In 1982–87 he was minister of taxation in the Danish government and in 1984–87 a member of Parliament. In 1988–98 Foighel was a judge at the European Court of Human Rights in Strasbourg, and in addition, in 1991–95, he was chairman of the board of Denmark's National Radio.

[Bent Lexner (2nd ed.)]

FOIX, formerly independent county, now part of Ariège department, southern France, with a capital town of the same name. During the Middle Ages there were Jews living in several localities of the county, notably in Foix itself, in Mazères, *Pamiers, and Troye-d'Ariège. In 1292, Roger-Bernard, count of Foix, obtained the agreement of Philip the Fair to exempt the Jews of the county from paying the royal poll tax. The count may also have protected the Jews in his domains from the French decree of expulsion of 1306. In 1321, several new Jewish communities are mentioned there which appear to have escaped the *Pastoureaux massacres. In 1394, the count refused to implement the decree of expulsion issued by Charles VI and at least succeeded in delaying its execution. At the end of the 14th century, four or five Jews figured among over 600 taxable inhabitants of the town of Foix.

BIBLIOGRAPHY: Gross, Gal Jud, 438; G. Saige, *Les Juifs du Languedoc* (1881), passim; A. de Dufau de Maluquer, *Rôle desfeux du comté de Foix* (1901), 21.

[Bernhard Blumenkranz]

FÖLDES, JOLÁN (1903–1963), Hungarian author. After leaving Hungary in the 1920s, Jolán Földes published the novel *Mária jól érett* (1932; *Prelude to Love*, c. 1938), but was forced to earn her living in menial occupations. She achieved fame with her prize-winning novel *A halászó macska utcája* ("The Street of the Fishing Cat," 1936), which portrayed the life of émigrés in Paris. She died in London.

°**FOLEY, FRANCIS** (1885–1958), British army officer and Righteous Among the Nations. British lieutenant Francis (commonly known as Frank) Foley arrived in Berlin in 1919 as an intelligence officer to check out the activities of Communist-led organizations. As a cover for his spy work, his official capacity was Chief Passport Control Officer in the British embassy, where he was given wide latitude to decide on the admission of foreigners into areas of the British Empire. With the Nazi rise to power in 1933, Foley's attention shifted to the rearmament of Germany, and he simultaneously began to be more preoccupied with helping Jews emigrate from Germany, a need which became urgent after the Nazi-staged pogrom of November 9–10, 1938, known as **Kristallnacht* ("Night of the Broken Glass"). Foley utilized legal means whenever possible, or exploited loopholes in British immigration laws. British regulations at the time forbade the issuance of entry visas to persons liable to compete with professional workers in England, as well as to the very old, the sick and handicapped, and persons associated with the Communist Party. As for entry to Palestine, £1,000 in hand was required to get a "capitalist" visa. This was a sizable sum at the time, and unavailable to many Jews whose bank and other assets had been frozen by the Nazi authorities. In the case of Elisheva Lernau (born Elsbeth Kahn), who could produce only £10, Foley decided that the balance of £990 would be available to her the minute she landed in Haifa, and on the strength of this issued her a visa for Palestine. Foley similarly bent the rules very liberally in the case of Wolfgang Meyer-Michael, accepting his cousin's guarantee in writing that the sum would be available once Wolfgang had crossed the border into the Netherlands. In this work, Foley was co-opted by Hubert Pollack, a Jewish community worker who brought to Foley's attention persons in desperate need of help to leave the country. In the case of Gunter Powitzer, jailed in Sachsenhausen for violation of the Nuremberg laws and having intimate relations with a non-Jewish girl, which produced a child, Foley personally went to Sachsenhausen to hand him an exit visa for Palestine, which included Gunter's semi-Jewish son, and both left Germany in February 1939. In the matter of a 20-year-old woman imprisoned because of her membership in the outlawed Community Party, Foley ruled that since she was 18 years old at the time of her arrest, her membership in the Party was to be viewed simply as "youthful fervor" and he granted her a visa. Others who gave accounts of being helped by Foley include Zeev Estrecher, Willi Preis, Heinz Romberg, Adele Wertheimer, and David Arian's aged mother. After the war, Pollack testified that "the number of Jews who were saved in Germany would have been ten thousand times – yes, ten thousand – less, if a 'competent official' had occupied that post instead of Captain Foley." Benno Cohn, head of the Zionist Federation in Germany, testified at the Eichmann trial in 1960 that immediately after *Kristallnacht*, he frantically called his superiors in Jerusalem to find ways to save the Jews of Germany, adding: "Nevertheless we succeeded in getting a sizable number of Jews to Palestine. That was thanks to a man who is to my mind to be counted among the Righteous Gentiles … Captain Foley [who] did all he could to enable Jews to immigrate to Palestine.… One may say that he saved thousands of Jews from death." Foley's wife, Katharine, also related that during the *Kristallnacht* pogrom period, Jews were temporarily hidden in their Berlin home. During World War II, Foley's intelligence work included the interrogation of Rudolf Hess, Hitler's close aide who landed in Scotland in May 1941 hoping to strike a deal between Germany and Britain. In 1999, Yad Vashem awarded the late Francis Foley the title of Righteous Among the Nations.

BIBLIOGRAPHY: Yad Vashem Archives M31–8378; M. Smith, *Foley: the Spy Who Saved 10,000 Jews* (1999); M. Paldiel, *Saving the Jews* (2000), 53–60.

[Mordecai Paldiel (2nd ed.)]

FOLIGNO, HANANEL (Da), apostate and anti-Jewish agitator in Rome in mid-16th century; his name after baptism was Alessandro Franceschi. Foligno was one of three apostates whose slandering of the Talmud to Pope *Julius III resulted in its burning in 1553. When in 1555 the Jews of Rome were accused of a ritual murder (*Blood libel), Foligno insisted on their guilt. After a public confrontation between him and representatives of the Jewish community, Pope Marcellus ordered the reconsideration of the charge. In due course, the true culprit was discovered and punished.

BIBLIOGRAPHY: Vogelstein-Rieger, 2 (1896), 146–51; Joseph ben Joshua ha-Kohen, *Emek ha-Bakha* (1895), 128, 133; REJ, 4 (1882), 95–96; F. Secret, *ibid.*, 122 (1963), 182–3; I. Sonne, *Mi Paulo ha-Revi'i ad Pius ha-Ḥamishi* (1954), 66, 103–5.

[Umberto (Moses David) Cassuto]

FOLKLORE.

This entry is arranged according to the following outline:

INTRODUCTION

Jewish folklore can be defined as the creative spiritual and cultural heritage of the Jewish people handed down, mainly by oral tradition, from generation to generation by the various Jewish communities. The process of oral transmission took place alongside the development of normative, written literature.

Jewish folklore may be classified according to the three main vehicles of transmission:

(1) Audio-oral, including the various branches of folk literature and folk music (discussed in the article on *Music);

(2) Visual, including arts, crafts, costumes, ornaments, and other material expression of folk culture;

(3) Cogitative, including popular beliefs, most of which find their expression in customs and practices.

The science of folklore ("folkloristics") is a discipline which studies the historic-geographic origin and diffusion of folklore institutions, their social backgrounds, functions, intercultural affinities, influences, changes, and acculturation processes and examines the meanings and interpretations of the institutions' individual components.

Folklore is not transmitted through a single medium. Most folklore combines the three categories, one of which, however, usually predominates. Thus, for example, the cogitative background of the commemoration of the Exodus from Egypt is expressed through rites, customs, and manners within the framework of the Passover festival. The main literal expression of the festival, however, the Passover *Haggadah*, is intertwined with audio-oral songs and legends and is recited at the *seder* which calls for special garb and ritual vessels, e.g., the cup of *Elijah. These constitute the visual elements of the Passover ritual which is comprised of many folk components.

The national cultural heritages of the gentile neighbors among whom the Jewish people has lived throughout its wanderings and dispersions have been assimilated into Jewish folklore. While mutual intercultural contacts are evident in many realms, Jewish folklore has certain specific features common to Eastern and Western Jews which are characteristic of the creative folk ego of the Jewish people. The Judaization and adaptation of universal traditions bear witness to the qualities, trends, and hopes of the Jewish transformers. Through a comparative study of neighboring cultures, normative Jewish religion, and folk evidence which is substantiated by the transmission of many generations and culture areas inhabited by Jews, the special character of Jewish folk tradition may be apprehended. This article is written from the viewpoint of comparative folklore, which frequently reaches conclusions and interpretations at variance with those traditionally held.

AUDIO-ORAL TRANSMISSION (FOLK LITERATURE)

Jewish oral literature (in Hebrew and in the various Jewish languages: Aramaic, Yiddish, Ladino, etc.) has been transmitted alongside the written literature, and both have exercised a mutual influence. Biblical literature (including the narrative tales in the Pentateuch, the legends interwoven into the fabric of the historical books, independent short stories such as the Books of Esther and Ruth, the gnomic (wisdom) literature, and the poetic literature) imbibed much from the oral heritage of the entire Near Eastern culture area. In sanctioning a written document (the Holy Scriptures), the sages differentiated between the holy writings and traditions which were regarded as *Oral Law. Exodus 34:27, "… for after the tenor of these words I have made a covenant with thee… ," was interpreted as (Git. 60b): "That which is by word of mouth, thou shalt not commit to writing." It was only with the failure of the Bar Kokhba revolt (135 C.E.), and the authoritative decision taken in the generation of Rabbi Akiva and his pupils, that the prohibition of committing to writing the oral traditions was revoked. The talmudic-midrashic literature of the *tannaim* and the *amoraim* is a mine of information of ancient Jewish folklore (mainly in Aramaic, which was then the spoken language of the people) handed down by word of mouth for hundreds of years before it was formulated. Rich folkloric material has also been preserved in postbiblical literature which was not transmitted in Hebrew: the Apocrypha and Pseudepigrapha, the works of Philo and Josephus, the New Testament, and the writings of the Church Fathers.

The various genres of Jewish folk literature are (1) folk narrative, including folktales, legends, jokes, and anecdotes transmitted mainly by word of mouth; (2) folk songs, usually performed or directed by a folk singer, whose music or musical interpretation has the approval and social sanction of the audience and whose text, music, and often gestures (handclapping) and folk dance movements constitute an integral whole between whose components it is hard to distinguish;

(3) proverbs and folk sayings which are part of gnomic (wisdom) literature and are perpetuated by a large section of the population, including the common people, in their daily speech; (4) riddles, usually woven into the fabric of a prose narrative (folktale), but constituting an independent literary genre; (5) folk dramas, performed on an improvised stage on specific (festive) occasions by either professional or amateur groups, and composed of several literary folk genres (listed above: stories, songs, etc.), but constituting a genre in themselves, evaluated according to folk transmission techniques.

Folk Narrative

The main kinds of universal folk narratives are also extant in the Jewish oral tradition, though the quantitative proportion between the various kinds differs in comparison with the respective proportion in the neighboring non-Jewish cultural areas. Thus the didactic story, and not the magic tale, is dominant in the Jewish folk narrative; similarly the legend in Jewish lore is a much more popular vehicle of expression than in general folklore.

Folk narrative research in recent decades has, by and large, solved the main classification problems through index systems subscribed to by folklorists. Those systems are general and ethnic (local): type indices and motif indices which are appended to the folktale (*Maerchen*), legend (*Sage*), myth, and humorous lore of various cultural areas. Thus the genres of Jewish folk narrative should be defined and described according to the accepted general division, mainly based on Aarne-Thompson's (AT) Type-Index and on Stith Thompson's Motif-Index:

MYTH ("A" MOTIFS). Myths constitute the imaginative answers to man's queries about the universe (cosmogony and cosmology), the creation and ordering of human and animal life, his own past, etc. They are basically etiological folktales which try to explain various life and nature phenomena and their plot is set in the remote past, at the beginning of creation. The main heroes are supernatural beings (gods, demigods, and cultural heroes) who perform supernatural deeds.

Most of the biblical narratives may, by this definition, be regarded as ancient Hebrew myths which, even after they became part of the "Written Law," continued to influence Jewish legendary lore, although most of the etiological elements were suppressed or omitted by normative monotheistic Judaism. The narrative elements in the Bible should be analyzed in the light of the rich repertoire of ancient Near Eastern mythological texts. Archaeological discoveries, text collections, and studies on the ancient cultures and religions of the Near East (T.H. Gaster, S.H. Hooke, E.O. James, S. N, Kramer, J.B. Pritchard, G. Widengren, and others) have shed fresh light not only on ancient Hebrew oral literature, its transmission through storytelling, and on the prebiblical dissemination of its narrative elements, but on ancient Hebrew folk religion, folk life, folk culture, and on the diffusion of their components.

C.H. Gordon's thesis that "Greek and Hebrew civilizations are parallel structures built upon the same Eastern Mediterranean foundation," stressing the Mediterranean diffusion by different oral vehicles, has not been accepted by biblical scholarship. The premise of general oral relationships between the Jewish and the Greco-Roman oral lore during the Hellenistic and talmudic periods serves as a basis for any comparative approach to the myths as preserved in the apocryphal, pseudepigraphic, and talmudic-midrashic literatures. Many etiological motifs in later Jewish folktales are remnants of ancient myths. In most cases they sanction newly invented or imported and Judaized customs, by stressing their antiquity and dating their origin and first observance to the creation, Noah's ark, the patriarchs, etc. Thus, for example, a midrashic etiological tale (PdRE 20) relates the custom of looking at the fingernails during the *Havdalah* ceremony (Sh. Ar., OḤ 298:3) to Adam, who, endowed with God-like wisdom, brought down fire and light from heaven. The resemblance between this legend and Greek (Prometheus) and cognate myths on the origin of fire (Motif A 1414) by means of theft – a culture hero steals it from its owner (Motif A 1415) – is evident (Ginzberg, Legends, vol. 5,113 n. 104). Similarly, most of the prevailing Jewish etiological stories explaining the origins of fascinating and strange phenomena and of established customs lacking authoritative, written explanations, are elaborated biblical narratives which are based on universal mythical concepts. The process is also manifest in European folklore. Thus the original midrashic story (Tanḥ, Noaḥ 13; Gen. R. 36:3–4; cf. Ginzberg, loc. cit., 190 n. 58) of Noah planting the vineyard with the help of Satan was transformed in European folklore into a typical etiological tale explaining the characteristics of wine (Motif A 2851). Its four qualities, as well as those of the drunken man, stem from the characteristic traits of the four animals sacrificed by Satan while planting the vineyard: the lamb, the lion, the monkey, and the pig. In Jewish and non-Jewish variants of the story some of the above animals are replaced by the peacock, the billy goat, etc. Unlike most of the non-Jewish variants, which are of an etiological character and not of a moralistic nature, the Jewish variants are didactic, severely condemning intoxication – the cause of all sins and the ruin of individuals.

ANIMAL TALE (AT 1–199). Many of the literary and oral Jewish fables were originally actual animal tales which reflected imaginative contemporaneous views on animal and plant life. (Animal tales which serve to illustrate daily life and to solve actual contemporary problems are transformed into moral fables by the added moral lesson.) The animal tale as an independent narrative genre is at present alive only among Jewish Oriental raconteurs, but even there it is based on the talmudic-midrashic fable and the beasts represent human traits. The main heroes are the lion and the serpent; usually human beings are also involved. The fox from whom the talmudic-midrashic name of the genre, "fox fables," is derived, does not play an important role.

ORDINARY TALE (AT 300–749). These stories are centered around supernatural beings who possess extraordinary knowledge and qualities enabling them to perform magic transformations and to rule the powers of nature, They are set neither in time nor in place, Folktales served as entertainment during all stages of Jewish history. Motifs characteristic of folktales (cf. Gunkel) are found in many of the biblical stories: Samson, David and Goliath, Jephthah's vow (Motif S 241), but especially in the aggadic lore of the Palestinian rabbis who adopted them from oral local (Greek) tradition.

Jewish raconteurs were both writers and disseminators of folktales:

Writers. Some of the best-known universal folktales are assumed to be of Jewish origin. Folktales were derived from Jewish written sources: thus the story of King Solomon's judgment (I Kings 3:16–28) influenced the cycle of folk stories about clever acts and words (AT 920–929) and the Tobias story influenced the "Grateful Dead" cycle (AT 505–508). In many cases the Jewish origin at first is not obvious and has been suggested only after penetrating analysis (Anderson, Goebel), for example (a) AT 331, "The Spirit in the Bottle": a man frees an evil spirit imprisoned in a bottle, but instead of receiving the promised reward he is endangered by the spirit whom he then tricks back into the bottle (cf. Grimm no. 99); (b) AT 332, "Godfather Death": Death endows a poor man, or his son, with the power to forecast how a sick person will fare according to the position of Death at the bedside, whether he is standing at the head or foot of the bed; Death is tricked, but avenges himself (cf. Grimm no. 44); (c) AT 922, "The King and the Abbot": a shepherd substitutes for the priest and answers the king's questions (cf. Grimm no. 152); and many other tales focusing on religious problems (see below, Religious Tale); on cleverness: wit ("outwitting the witty"), humor, answering riddles, performing great feats, and being put to severe tests; and on wise conduct.

Disseminators. The main Jewish contribution to the folktale was in the diffusion and dissemination of narratives from the East to the West. According to Thompson (cf. *The Folktale*, p. 17) the stories were brought by Jewish merchants from the East to Europe and became known first to the Jewish communities scattered throughout Europe.

Disciplina Clericalis (about 1110), a Latin work by Petrus Alphonsi, contains the earliest Eastern folktales in Western literature. Alphonsi, whose Hebrew name before his conversion to Christianity was Moshe Sefardi, was well versed in Eastern and Jewish traditional lore. The motifs in his work are found not only in medieval European folklore, but also in international narrative folklore (still extant today).

Medieval Jewish scholars translated **Kalila and Dimna* and *Sindbad* into European languages, the oral translations for narrating purposes preceding the literary written translations (see *Fiction). According to B.E. Perry the *Book of Sindbad* (*Sindabar) originated in Persia from which it passed to India and was assimilated into the rich Hindu folk literature. Leading folklorists of the 19th century (following Benfey) considered India to be the home of the European folktale. Modern scholarship however has shown that a direct chain of oral and written transmission links the Middle (including Persia) and Near East with Europe and that Jewish translators and storytellers were the main transmitters of Eastern (Islamic) culture to the Christian world. In modern scholarship there is full agreement between scholars of literature, both Jews (Epstein, Flusser, Peri, Schwarzbaum) and non-Jews (Holbek, Maeso, Quinn, Thompson), that Near Eastern folklore may have reached Europe directly through Jewish intermediaries and was not transmitted via India.

RELIGIOUS TALE (AT 750–849). Playing a most important role among Jewish folktales, the two main themes of the religious tale are theodicy ("God's justice vindicated") and reward and punishment. Several of the widespread universal religious folktales are of Jewish origin; among the best known are AT 759, "The Angel and the Hermit," which is representative of the theodician tale, and AT 757, "The King's Haughtiness Punished" or "The King in the Bath," which exemplifies the reward and punishment theme. In AT 759 an angel commits many seemingly unjust acts which arouse deep astonishment and strong words of protest from his companion the hermit; the hermit, however, upon learning the truth is convinced that each of the strange deeds was just. In many Jewish "legendarized" versions of AT 759 God, or the Prophet Elijah, plays the role of the angel, whereas the companion who learns his lesson ("The Rock, His work is perfect, for all His ways are justice," Deut. 32:4) is a hero in Jewish legend concerned with social justice: Moses (cf., Moses addressing God in Ex. 32:32 "Blot me, I pray Thee, out of Thy book"), *Joshua b. Levi, or Abraham *Ibn Ezra. Folktales starting with the hero's (a ḥasidic rabbi) enigmatic smile, whose significance is revealed as the plot unravels, also belong to this pattern of theodician tales.

In AT 757 a supernatural being (demon, angel, Elijah) takes the boasting king's place (or form) either by depriving him (in the bath) of his clothes or through other means. The wandering king (Solomon, Roderigo, Jovinian) is humiliated and rejected by all as a crazy liar; he is restored to the throne only when he repents of his haughtiness. According to Varnhagen this folktale is of Hindu origin, but the talmudic-midrashic Asmodeus-Solomon legend (Git. 68b; TJ, Sanh. 2:6, 20c; PdRK 169a) has influenced most of the Jewish oral versions.

The anonymous, often innocent, simpleton, around whom many religious tales originally centered, tends to be replaced by a historical, famous (talmudic, medieval, or local) sage, martyr, or scholar. The tales thus became part of the Jewish hagiographic lore. In their transitory stage many of the folktales are about one of the **Lamed-Vav Ẓaddikim*, the 36 anonymous and mysterious pious men, to whose humility, just deeds, and virtues the world owes its continued existence.

THE NOVELLA OR ROMANTIC FOLKTALE (AT 850–999). The novella in Jewish lore stresses the problem of fate. As marriages are decided in heaven (Gen. R. 68:3–4; Lev. R. 8:1), even before the bride and bridegroom were born, the question arises: Is this heavenly decision irrevocable or can it be changed? Thus the universal stories about heroes finding their way to each other, after overcoming often insurmountable obstacles, tend to become an integral part of Jewish matrimonial lore.

REALISTIC TALE (AT 1200–1999). Best known and the most widespread among the Jewish folklore genres, the realistic tale is mostly comprised of jokes and anecdotes depicting the comic aspects of life, especially as seen through Jewish eyes. The main heroes are fools, wits, misers, liars, beggars, tricksters, and representatives of various professions. The point of the Jewish joke, seemingly concluding it, is often followed by a "hyperpoint" – some clever and sophisticated addition to the humorous story, stressing a new, often specific Jewish aspect. Though the humorous motifs are universal, there is less of visual (situational) humor in Jewish jokes than in universal jests, and there is more of verbal humor, consisting of clever retorts, wordplay, "learned" interpretations of words and sentences, jests, and witty noodle stories. In most Jewish jokes the realistic background is typically Jewish, as are the heroes – well-known local wags (Hershele *Ostropoler, Motke Ḥabad, Froyim Greydinger, Jukha, etc.) whose fame has spread far beyond the border of their original place of activity. There are also "wise" places as, for example, *Chelm in Poland, Linsk (Lesko) in Galicia, etc., whose "wise" inhabitants (in fact, fools) perform the same deeds as their "wise" colleagues – the inhabitants of Abdera (Greece), Schildburg (Germany), Gotham (England), and other "cities of the wise."

Among the droll characters of the Jewish jokes, typical "Jewish" professions and types of socioeconomic failures are well represented: *schnorrers* ("beggars"), *shadḥanim* ("matchmakers"), cantors, preachers, but mostly *schlemiels* and *schlimazels.* Social misfits, their gawkishness, clumsy actions, and inability to cope with any situation in life make the listener enjoy his own superior cleverness (the feeling is often subconscious). A witty folk-saying distinguishes between the two characters: "A *schlemiel* is a man who spills a bowl of hot soup on a *schlimazel.*" Whereas the word *schlimazel* seems to be a combination of the German word *schlimm* ("bad") and the Hebrew word *mazal* ("luck"), the origin of *schlemiel* is obscure and has given rise to many German-Yiddish folk etymologies. It is first mentioned outside of Yiddish in Adalbert von Chamisso's famous German story *Peter Schlemihls wundersame Geschichte* (1813) whose hero sold his shadow to the devil. Many Jewish stories try to identify these types; stories are thus told about Moyshe Kapoyr ("Moses Upside-Down") – the hero of a comic strip in U.S. Yiddish newspapers in the early 1920s – and about similar heroes who are placed in a definite geographic-historical framework. Many of Shalom Aleichem's folk types, Tevye the Milkman and Menahem Mendel, have been given the traits of an irrepressible daydreaming *schlimazel*. Benyamin the Third, a character out of the world of Mendele Mokher Seforim, is similarly portrayed.

The undertone of sadness and frustration underlining many Jewish jokes is probably rooted in the ceaseless struggle for survival in an anti-Jewish society; the laughter is thus often through tears. While the jokes and anecdotes carry a note of satirical (sometimes even biting) self-criticism, they are a means of consolation as well, either through minimizing troubles and hoping for a happy end ("a Jew will find his way out"; "the troubles of many are half a consolation"), or by relating stories about rich, successful, and influential Jews (the Rothschilds, Baron Hirsch, and Jewish dignitaries "a (person) close to the (royal) court," etc.), with whom the poor Jewish listeners identify.

JEWISH LEGEND. Many Jewish folktales bear an exclusively Jewish national religious character, and their plot has no parallel in general folklore. They include stories about the Ten Lost Tribes living in their own Jewish independent kingdom on the other side of the miraculous river *Sambatyon, and about travelers who have been there (*Eldad Ha-Dani, David *Reuveni, etc.); stories of attempts to find the Ten Lost Tribes and to identify them in remote parts of the world, especially among strange Jewish communities (the *Bene Israel, *Beta Israel, *Khazars); tales of blood libels and other false anti-Jewish accusations; imaginative descriptions of the Messianic age and attempts to hasten the coming of the Redeemer (through kabbalistic means, by prompting Elijah the Prophet to herald the Messiah); stories about the eternal longing for and aspiration to get to the Promised Land (through a miraculous subterranean passage, by "the jump of the way," etc.); tales about proselytes and the extraordinary circumstances of their conversion to Judaism.

The legendary plot, which usually takes place in a definite period and in a specified place, dominates Jewish folk fiction. Besides an extension of the biblical and the talmudic midrashic story, mainly through translating it in terms of contemporaneous circumstances of the storytelling society (by means of many anachronisms), this type includes many local legends. Its heroes are universal-Jewish characters (biblical, talmudic, and medieval: Elijah the Prophet, King Solomon, Rabbi Akiva, Maimonides, and Rashi) and local figures (*Judah Loew b. Bezalel (the Maharal) of Prague, R. Ḥayyim Pinto of Morocco, Abdallah Somekh of Baghdad, R. Shalem Shabazi of Yemen, etc.). The dominant narrative motif is supernatural: the miraculous salvation of a Jewish community by the folk hero who is a sage not only versed in the Bible, Talmud, and Jewish law, but can also perform miracles and is learned in practical Kabbalah. Over the past few generations, some of the local heroes have become universal Jewish heroes, such as R. *Israel b. Eliezer Baal Shem Tov, the founder of the ḥasidic movement, who initially was legendary in Eastern Europe only; and R. Ḥayyim b, Attar (*"Or ha-Ḥayyim"*), whose legend originated in Morocco where he was born, and about whom legends were also woven in Jerusalem where he died. Certain heroes have become narrative stereotypes: King Solomon is the wise judge; Hershele Ostropoler, "the learned wag" who finds clever solutions for every problem and trial; Jukha, the innocent simpleton; and so forth. Many legends of the neighboring culture areas, revolving around non-Jewish figures (Harun al-Rashīd, Nāsir al-Dīn, Baron Muenchhausen, etc.) became a setting for Jewish heroes. Gentile characters in Jewish legends are mostly anonymous and referred to by title: king, vizier, etc. If named, they form a historical substantiation to the supernatural motifs. There are, however, non-Jewish heroes who play a dominant role in legends stressing the Jewish-gentile confrontation and conflict. One of them is Napoleon who recurs in about 150 Yiddish legends, folk songs, sayings, etc. (cf. Pipe).

The Jewish legendary folk hero is depicted as a pious and righteous man who "does justly and loves kindness" (cf. Micah 6:8) and his folk biography thus follows the international pattern (miraculous birth, dangerous exposure, growth in an alien environment, unintentional revelation of divine qualities, etc.). There are many common motifs between Jewish folk legends and tales revolving around biblical and aggadic exemplary heroes: Abraham, Joseph, Moses. The hero's good and "hearty" intention (*kavvanah*) are of utmost importance ("God requires the heart"), and he is therefore "holy" enough to perform (even willingly) miracles for the sake of the needy and oppressed. Many medieval legends which originated in Jewish oral tradition, as for example tales about a Jewish pope (Elhanan), or the *Golem of Prague, etc., have not survived in this medium, but since the end of the 19th century have been incorporated in chapbooks. On the other hand, many ḥasidic wonder tales which were first written found their way to raconteurs and became an integral part of Jewish oral literature.

Folk Song (Lyrics)

Songs whose lyrics are in Jewish languages and were transmitted orally from generation to generation are defined as Jewish folk songs. The classification may be according to (1) the folk language of the culture area in which the song was written (Yiddish of East Europe, Ladino of the Mediterranean area, etc.); (2) its musical style (Western, Oriental, etc.); (3) the text (contents). Most of the Jewish folk song collections and studies have adopted the last classification, yet the text of the folk song and its music are so intrinsically intertwined in Jewish folklore that no clear-cut division can be made.

RELIGIOUS FOLK SONGS AND FOLK MUSIC. The biblical books, especially the psalms and their "musical directions," influenced Jewish music, song, and dance and stressed their divine origin. The biblical names and actions associated with singing and playing music (Jubal, David playing before Saul, and his miraculous self-playing harp in the aggadah, Elisha feeling God's hand upon him while the minstrel played, the playing and singing prophets and levites, etc.) generally have a pleasant, positive connotation; thus the song (lyrics and melody) has always been part of the Jewish ritual. Throughout the ages this religious role has been extended from the limited realm of the synagogue (prayer melodies, biblical cantillation, etc.) to all aspects of Jewish religious and sociocultural life. The singing of the whole assembly strengthened the feeling of unity and of the values which were the common heritage of all Jews. Most songs of a religious nature stem from written Hebrew liturgical texts of the *siddur* or *maḥzor*. Many of them are, however, either bilingual (combining the Hebrew text and the Jewish vernacular) or sung in the vernacular only. Often the folk song expands or interprets the liturgical text. Thus, for example, the Hebrew verses of *Yismaḥ Moshe* are interspersed with Yiddish queries, and the song becomes a Hebrew-Yiddish dialogue whose lyrics are *Yismaḥ Moshe be-mattenat ḥelko. Vi hot men em gerufn? Ki eved ne'eman karata lo. Ven iz dos gevezn? Be-omedo lefaneikha al har Sinai*, etc. ("Let Moses rejoice over the gift of his portion. How did they call him – A faithful servant You called him. When did this happen? When he stood before You on Mount Sinai …"). The difference between the refrain (*Yismaḥ Moshe*), repeated by the audience, and the single strophes, sung by individuals, is emphasized by their melodic distinction. Many of the religious and devotional folk songs, sung as a part of the **zemirot* home ritual, became table songs for festive ritual meals at weddings, circumcisions, etc. They stress the close relationship between God, His Chosen People, the Torah and its precepts, and the Sabbath and festivals. As these were sung in the vernacular, all – the learned and the uneducated, young and old, women and children – could actively participate.

Although the melody of the religious folk song is strongly influenced by the artistic idiom of the **ḥazzan*, the folk singers and the audience that often joined them considered the lyrics the main feature of the song. On the other hand, many sophisticated groups (especially among the Ḥasidim) regarded the words (even when in Hebrew) a limitation of the divine nature of the song and stressed the value of the "pure" (without text) *niggun* (see *Ḥasidism, Musical Tradition). Many of the melodies, showing traces of local non-Jewish folk tunes, in their Jewish adaptation are characterized by a meditative mood. Traditional biblical cantillation motifs and later Oriental Jewish liturgies led to considerable changes in the adapted and "Judaized" folk tune, and this process was similar to that which had influenced the words.

SECULAR FOLK SONG. In spite of the negative attitude of normative rabbinic Judaism toward communal secular singing by both sexes, stemming from the talmudic saying *kol be-ishah ervah* ("a woman's voice is a sexual incitement"), the secular folk song was part of the life of the individual, the family, and the society on many occasions. The lyrics are very diverse and cover all aspects of Jewish life: the biblical past, the Messianic future, the year cycle, the lifespan ("from the cradle to the grave"), problems of livelihood, work and frustration, social protest, national hope, love, separation, luck, and misfortune.

Texts of the East European (Yiddish) folk song have been collected (An-Ski, Beregovski, Cahan, Ginzburg-Marek, Idelsohn, Prilutski, Rubin, Skuditski), popularized (Kipnis,

Rubin), studied, and analyzed (Cahan, Idelsohn, Mlotek, Weinreich) more than any other Jewish folklore genre. Recent annotated collections (Cahan, ed. Weinreich; Pipe, ed. Noy), as well as attempts at scholarly synthesis (see in bibl. Cahan's *Studies*; Rubin's *Voices*; Mlotek), see the Yiddish folk song as a well-defined artistic folk genre, both in its melodic (cf. Idelsohn, Sekuletz) and in its poetical form and contents. The lyrics are emotional, tender, and introspective, even if some of them, especially children's rhymes, are at times coarse, satirical, and comic. The melody is, almost always, in a minor key infusing the most joyous and even frivolous words with a touch of tenderness and sadness. According to Y.L. Cahan, the oldest among the Yiddish folk songs, going probably back to the European Renaissance period, are love and dance songs. Older Hebrew influences, stemming mainly from the Song of Songs and from remnants of love songs as preserved in talmudic literature (cf. Ta'an. 4:8–15th of Av song; Ket. 17a – a song "Before the Bride in the West," Palestine) are also evident.

Only a few collections and studies deal with the non-Yiddish, Oriental-Jewish folk song. Comparatively great attention has been paid to the folk song of the Yemenite Jews (Idelsohn, Ratzhabi, Spector) and to the romance and the *copla* (Spanish ballad or popular song) as sung in Ladino-speaking Sephardi communities dispersed all over the world: Tetuan, Spanish Morocco (Alvar, Armistead-Silverman, Palacin); Salonika, Greece (Attias); Atlanta, Georgia, U.S. (MacCurdy-Stanley); etc. (cf. also Avenary, Ben-Jacob, Gerson-Kiwi, Molho, Pelayo, Shiloah). The study of the Judeo-Spanish *romancero* ("a collection of ballads or romances"; Katz), is a very young branch of Jewish ethnomusicology (cf. *Ladino Literature).

Modern Palestinian and Israel folk songs are currently alive in Jewish folklore. The Holocaust put a tragic end to the Yiddish folk song which has become a subject for social-historical (Dvorkin), linguistic (Hrushovski), and folkloristic (Mlotek, Noy) studies, but no longer exists as a living tradition. The assimilation and emigration of Oriental Jewish communities, uprooted from their places of birth and traditional folkways, led to a similar process with regard to the Oriental-Jewish folk song transmitted in Ladino, Aramaic (by Kurdistan Jews; cf., Rivlin), and Judeo-Arabic dialects. Even if these non-Hebrew Jewish languages are still spoken by some young Jews, they are not their sole language of expression. Thus it would seem that only the Hebrew Jewish folk song, alive in a Hebrew-speaking society, is likely to survive.

The Palestinian folk song is characterized by two main traits: (1) the Hebrew lyrics; (2) the main theme, which is national. The central idea in the folk song focuses on the return of the Jewish people to their old-new homeland. The hope for the return is variously expressed and the trials and tribulations undergone are as diverse as the songs. Most of the songs were written by Palestinian authors and composers between the two world wars. Many others, dating back to the beginnings of the Jewish national revival and to the rise of the Zionist movement in 19th-century Russia, are strongly influenced by the songs of composers and bards like A. *Goldfaden and E. *Zunser. Some of the themes are: the yearning for Zion, the virtues of physical labor, self-defense, and pioneering in order to rebuild the land into a national home for the wandering Jew.

The Palestinian folk song celebrates the struggles of the young and ardent *ḥalutz* in his homeland: defense and standing guard (*haganah* and Trumpeldor songs); road building ("*Hakh Pattish*"); and agricultural work (*Sabba Panah Oref*) and love songs (*Saḥaki Saḥaki Al ha-Halomot*) were imbued with idealistic pathos alluding to national duties and hopes. Many of the Palestinian folk songs served as accompaniment (with or without words) to the various folk dances, The main musical influences on Palestinian folk songs (and folk dances) have been ḥasidic-Slavic, Oriental-Sephardi, Palestinian-Arabic, and Jewish-Yemenite (*Music in Ereẓ Israel.).

The destruction of the East European Jewish communities, the establishment of the State of Israel, the War of Independence, the 1967 Six-Day War, and other heroic deeds and achievements inspired many songs, but it is doubtful whether most of these will survive either orally or in folk memory during the coming generations. The songs (see Katsherginski in bibl.) written and sung in the ghettos and extermination camps during World War II were disseminated by oral transmission over wide areas, but their lifespan was limited. In the light of the above definition of a folk song, all songs composed and popular in Israel would be called *chansons* or folk-styled songs (*pizmonim*). On the other hand, many Yiddish, Ladino, and other Jewish folk songs, which were adapted for use in Ereẓ Israel (the text translated verbally or with modifications and the music also adapted), started a new folk lifespan in their Hebrew garb.

The establishment of musical research institutes by universities in Israel and the development of the study of liturgical poetry and music into scholarly disciplines, mainly in the training centers for cantors of the Jewish Theological Seminary, the Hebrew Union College, and the Israel Institute for Religious Music led to the study, analysis, and elaboration of many aspects of music and song in folk traditions. Data are collected and research is being continued in the field of East European Jewish musical folklore, stressing the role of folk musicians (*klezmerim*) and folk jesters (*badḥanim*). Other aspects emphasized are the social role of folk music, the interrelationship between sacred, liturgical, and ḥasidic music and religious folk songs (Geshuri, Vinaver), the music of the various Oriental-Jewish ethnic groups and the interrelationship of Jewish and non-Jewish folk music (Gerson-Kiwi; Idelsohn's *Thesaurus*; Tunisia-Lachman; Sephardi-Algazi; L. Levy). Many works on Jewish music and musicians (Avenary, Gradenwitz, Fater, Holde, Idelsohn, Rabinovitch, Werner) include studies on the lyrics of the folk song and on folk music.

The influence of Jewish folk songs on Jewish and non-Jewish modern composers is still to be investigated. Jews are among the most important composers of American jazz and the Jewish folk heritage might have had a considerable effect on their compositions. Many Yiddish folk songs entered the main popular musical stream of the U.S. and are sung by leading performers and millions of people (*Bei Mir Bist Du Schein*, *Joseph-Joseph*, etc.): through their penetration into a foreign setting, they have become alienated and disconnected from their original Jewish tradition (see also Music and Musical Life in Israel in *Music, and the various articles on the different ethnic communities).

Folk Proverb

A gnomic statement current in tradition, the folk proverb usually suggests a course of action or passes judgment on a situation. Originally, "the wit of one," it becomes in oral folklore "the wisdom of many" and thus is part of the didactic oral folk heritage. The folk saying is genetically related to proverbial lore. Most of the Jewish proverbs have been handed down (since the Book of Proverbs and other Hebrew wisdom literature) in written collections, and in many cases the oral character of the transmitted verse is doubtful. There are however more than one hundred talmudic-midrashic proverbs (cf. Sever) which begin with the statement: *haynu deamerei inshei* ("this is what people say"), indicating that the saying had prevailed in oral tradition. Proverbial lore was also deeply rooted in ancient Israel and the ancient Near East and there are many parallels of single biblical proverbs found in cuneiform proverbial texts (cf. Gordon, pp. 552f.); in the Egyptian gnomic literature attributed to Amen-em-Opet; in the story (teachings) of *Ahikar; and in others which testify to the wide diffusion and the oral transmission of many biblical proverbs.

Most of the Jewish proverb collections are compilations of single statements, aphorisms, and dicta, excerpted from the talmudic-midrashic and medieval literatures, or from specific post-biblical gnomic treatises, which have been transmitted in writing. The tannaitic *Avot*, for example, inspired many similar compilations. The classification and arrangement of the material is mostly in alphabetic order following the first word or the "catch word" rather than the subject matter. Only in recent decades have genuine collections of folk proverbs, committed to writing from the living oral tradition of the various Jewish communities, been published. The most comprehensive among them is I. Bernstein's collection of Yiddish proverbs, followed later by paroemiological collections and studies of Ayalti, Beem (Jewish-Dutch), Einhorn, Hurwitz, Kaplan (World War II death camps and ghettos), Landau, Mark, Rivkind, Stutshkov, and Yoffie. Other culture areas and ethnic groups represented in the various proverb collections and studies are: Judeo-Arabic (Yahuda); Judeo-Spanish (Besso, Kayserling, Luna, Saporta y Beja (Salonika) Uziel, Yahuda); Bukharan (Pinhasi); Neo-Aramaic from Iraqi Kurdistan (Rivlin, Segal); North African (Attal); Samaritan (Gaster); Yemenite (Goitein, Nahum, Ratzhabi, Shealtiel); Palestinian-Hebrew as current in the new kibbutzim and villages (Halter).

Jewish paroemiology has mainly been concerned with the written proverb, especially the Jewish and Arabic sources of the medieval collections and compositions of gnomic folklore as, for example, the 14th-century rhymed *Proverbios Morales* compiled by R. Shem Tov b. Isaac (*Santob de Carrion de los Condes) for King Pedro the Cruel of Castile (1350–1369); Solomon ibn *Gabirol's *Mivḥar ha-Peninim* ("Choice of Pearls"), and *Samuel Ha-Nagid's *Ben Mishlei* (cf. the studies of Ashkenazi, Braun, Davidson, Habermann, Ratzhabi). Only a few monographic studies have been devoted to particular proverbs, folk sayings, definite (Jewish) themes (Attal, Avida, Galante, Jellinek, Ratzhabi), and to proverbial lore in the writings of famous authors as, for example, in the work of Agnon and Shalom Aleichem (Toder). Any collection of Jewish proverbs and sayings in oral tradition shows strong biblical and talmudic-midrashic influences. Thus many Hebrew and even Aramaic literary proverbs and sayings penetrated the oral lore of the Yiddish and Ladino-speaking Jew. In many proverbs, extant in the vernacular, the Jewish allusions and references are so dominant that the proverb cannot be understood by a gentile without adequate explanation. Universal proverbs in their Hebrew form often acquired an original "Jewish touch." The Hebraization of the maxim "in vino veritas" (*nikhnas yayin yaẓa sod*, "wine entered, secret left") is based on the numerical value (*gematria*) of the words "secret" and "wine" (*yayin*, יין = (*sod*) 70 = סוד). Several recent Hebrew proverb compilations have used a comparative approach in their study of Jewish and foreign proverbs on the same theme (Blankstein, Cohen, Sharfstein).

Riddle

In ancient Jewish literature the riddle formed part of the narrative plot, as Samson's riddle in Judges 14:14 (Noy, Tur-Sinai, Wuensche), as well as the midrashic riddles through which the Queen of Sheba "came to test Solomon" (I Kings 10:1ff.; cf. Ginzberg, Legends, 4 (1913), 145ff.; Schechter). In medieval Hebrew literature the riddle is however an independent genre and the riddles of Abraham Ibn Ezra, *Judah Halevi, and Judah *Al-Ḥarizi are sophisticated aphorisms which were never part of the living oral tradition. Side by side with the tradition of literary riddles which were often rhymed and multistrophed, there were short and simple oral folk riddles. In the folk riddle proper the story in the question was always paralleled by the same or another relevant tale in the answer (solution), and the two parts could have existed independently. "Catch" questions and witty queries cannot be regarded by the folklorist as folk riddles, although informants and collectors often tend to term them as such.

There are only a few collections of Jewish riddles stemming from oral tradition in East Europe (An-Ski, Bastomski, Einhorn) and Yemen (Ratzhabi), as the genre was never popular with Jewish adults in those culture areas. Many of the riddles refer to biblical events and demand a knowledge of Hebrew and Jewish law and lore of the solver.

Folk Drama

Before World War II Jewish folk players put on folk dramas in many East European towns and villages, especially on Purim, or during the whole month of Adar. In most places, including yeshivot and *klaus*, the taboo on playing, decorations, and masks (cf., second commandment) was lifted during the Purim period to allow for merrymaking through stage performances. Playing in the open before a general and unselected audience was however often opposed by the local religious authorities who prohibited the performing of feminine roles by men. The *Purim-Shpil were therefore acted by youngsters of the lower social classes: tailor apprentices and workers.

There are many manuscripts, and printed copies, and descriptions in different works of various Purim *shpils*. Only one fourth of them dramatize the story of the Book of Esther. Most of them adapted such Pentateuchal stories as the sacrifice of Isaac (see **Akedah*) and the sale of Joseph in the light of the midrashic elaborations and interpretations of the original biblical narrative and according to folk fantasy.

Several folk plays depict postbiblical and even contemporary plots, among them the personal tragedy of Rabbenu Gershom b. Judah (Cahan, pp. 246–257), explaining why he imposed the ban on polygamy, and confrontations between Jews (merchant, innocent girl) and non-Jews (robber; cf. Lahad nos, 23–24).

VISUAL FOLKLORE

Folk arts and folk crafts comprise the realm of Jewish visual folklore, most of it belonging to ceremonial art. Though the second commandment ("Thou shalt not make unto thee a graven image …," Ex. 20:4; Deut. 5:8) imposed a taboo on plastic arts, associated in the ancient Near East mainly with idols and idol worship, it did not influence the aesthetic view of normative Judaism (see *Art). Throughout the ages Jews, in their homeland and in the Diaspora, have created beautiful vessels, dresses, and other artifacts for the performance of the Torah commandments.

Folk art objects are closely connected with (1) the ceremonial life cycle (from the cradle to the grave); (2) the ceremonial Jewish year cycle (Sabbath and the festivals); (3) *varia*, including the synagogue, the Jewish home, and other non-ceremonial artifacts.

Ceremonial Life Cycle

Of the four main festive occasions in the life cycle of a Jew, the wedding is the most picturesque: the marriage contract (**ketubbah*) which is frequently a parchment, the bridal canopy (*ḥuppah*), the "good-luck" wedding goblets ("cups of blessing"), the special wedding clothes and jewelry (amulets, rings, etc.) were richly wrought with Jewish and universal love and fertility symbols, traditional images, and biblical verses. The other three life cycle ceremonies are also represented in Jewish folk art:

(1) birth, by childbirth amulets, circumcision plates, and richly ornamented circumcision objects, particularly the handle of the knife, *Elijah's chair, embroidered cushions;

(2) *bar mitzvah, through frequently engraved and decorated cases (*battim*) for the phylacteries and the embroidered bag for the *tallit*;

(3) death, through traditional attire and various special objects of the **ḥevra kaddisha* including wine cups for the society's traditional annual festive meal (Seventh of Adar).

Ceremonial Jewish Year Cycle

Most of Jewish ceremonial art centers around the occasions of the *Sabbath and the festivals.

SABBATH. The kindling of the Sabbath lights inaugurates the Sabbath in the Jewish home. In Western Europe star-shaped hanging oil lamps were used; these became so typical for the Jewish home that they were called *Judenstern* ("Jewish star"), Since the 18th century, the suspended oil lamps have been replaced by candles and candlesticks and candelabra which have become precious family heirlooms.

The holiness of the Sabbath is proclaimed by the ancient *Kiddush* benediction (dating back to the Second Temple period) which is made over a cup of wine. The cup thus became a symbol of holiness, solemnity, and happiness in family life and is frequently made of silver, though it may be of other metals and even of glass. Usually in the form of an inverted dome, preferably with a stem and base, it became customary to inscribe the *Kiddush* cup with biblical quotations referring to the Sabbath, the festivals, light (Isa. 24:15; Prov. 6:23; 20:27), and the wine blessing. Special tablecloths, plates, and embroidered covers for the two Sabbath loaves are used. The *Havdalah* ceremony which concludes the Sabath and each festival includes wine, spices (*besamim*), and a twisted candle. The spice container, *hadas*, one of the most popular ceremonial artifacts ("no other ritual object shows as many variations," Kayser, p. 89), has many forms. The most common, the tower, originated among West European Jewish communities. It is reminiscent of the city hall tower where, in medieval times, spices and aromatic plants, which were then very precious, were stored. Other forms are: pear-shaped containers, turrets, boxes, fruits, windmills (Holland), fish (North Africa).

PASSOVER SEDER. The most important domestic event among all the Jewish festivals is the Passover *seder.* The table is festively set following certain prescriptive requirements: symbolic food (**mazzot, *maror*, etc., recalling the fate of the people of Israel in Egypt and their meal on the eve of their liberation) which are served on special plates and dishes; a cloth-covered tray, or a three-tiered plate for the three *matzah* symbolizing the priests, levites, and common Jews; the wine cups of glass or silver used for the drinking of the obligatory four cups during the Passover meal; and a special cup, usually the most precious, the cup of Elijah. The plates and other vessels are richly wrought with floral patterns, formulistic ornaments, and biblical scenes.

The *Haggadah*, the ceremonial text of the *seder* night, since it is only used in the home and not in the synagogue, was not subject to normative scrutiny and therefore has become the most illuminated of all Hebrew ceremonial prayer books. Most of the illustrations are traditional, transmitted from generation to generation by folk artists, copyists, and printers. Other Passover ceremonial items include an inscriptively embroidered cover for the *mazzot* and decorated **omer* scrolls used in the synagogue for counting the 49 days (seven weeks) between the second day of Passover and Shavuot (cf. Lev. 23:15–16).

SHAVUOT. The paper cuts used for window decorations are the folk art characteristics of Shavuot. As most of them have designs of roses, symbolizing Israel (cf. Song 2:2,16, and the exegetical Midrashim thereto), they are called by the Yiddish folk term *reyzele* ("little rose").

HIGH HOLIDAYS. The main ceremonial object of the High Holidays, the **shofar* has many interpretations in Jewish ritual, the most common being its role as a reminder of the sacrifice of Isaac. It also calls man to repentance and spiritual regeneration. As the horn of any animal of the sheep or goat family may be used for the *shofar,* it has various shapes depending upon the local fauna. While it is forbidden to embellish the *shofar,* either through painting, or by covering its mouthpiece with metal, it may be carved and on several old specimens inscriptions (biblical sentences referring to the *shofar,* Ps. 81:4, 5; 98:6, etc,) were found.

The traditional garb for the High Holidays is the *kitel,* a loose garment of white linen, reminiscent of the shroud and reminding the congregation of death and the last judgment. It is held together at the waist with a belt whose silver buckle is inscribed with a biblical verse relevant to the occasion or a quotation from the *Day of Atonement service.

SUKKOT. The only significant ritualistic object used during the *Sukkot festival is the box in which the *etrog* is kept. Generally assuming the shape of the fruit, there are also other forms. Another kind of folk art, especially folk painting, concentrates on the decoration of the *sukkah.* Besides fruits, vegetables, and the seven "kinds" the Holy Land has been blessed with, the *sukkah* is also embellished with pictures, verses and proverbs, trimmings, cutouts, and other ornaments.

ḤANUKKAH. The main ritual characteristic of the eight-day Ḥanukkah festival is the kindling of lights. The Ḥanukkah lamp, containing eight oil burners or candlesticks (the *shammash* – the auxiliary candle – is not counted), developed in the West from a simple Roman oil lamp into very elaborate forms. Two definite types can be distinguished: (1) "the bench type," which is usually small, has a back wall, and is often richly and symbolically ornamented; (2) the standing form (candelabrum) which developed during the Middle Ages and is reminiscent of the *menorah* in the Temple, with the main difference that instead of seven branches, the Ḥanukkah lamp has eight (with the *shammash* making up the ninth). In the synagogue, the Ḥanukkah *menorah* is placed to the right of the ark, corresponding to the location of the golden *menorah* in the Temple. The smaller Ḥanukkah *menorah* for the Jewish home was developed from the seven-branch standing candelabrum in the synagogue, since the 18th century also adapted for the use of candles.

Many of the motifs of the richly wrought Ḥanukkah lamp are associated with the miracle of the festival: the victory of Judah the Maccabee over the Syrians ("Greeks") in 165 B.C.E, and the burning of the sacred oil in the Temple seven days longer than its actual measure, which was sufficient for one day only. The ornaments are mostly lions (symbol of Judah), the figure of Judith holding the sword and the head of the slain Holofernes, Judah the Maccabee, cherubim, and eagles. The most common inscriptions are biblical, such as Exodus 25:37 and Proverbs 6:23, associated with the Ḥanukkah benedictions and prayers, and verses from the hymn *Ma'oz Ẓur* ("Mighty Rock of my Salvation").

The long nights of Ḥanukkah were ideal for games and play which, prohibited during the year (the main reason: they were a waste of time which should be devoted to the study of the Torah), were allowed on this occasion. The most popular game, especially with children, was *trendl* (*dreidl*, a top; in modern Hebrew *sevivon*) whose four sides were inscribed with the Hebrew letters נ, ג, ה, ש, standing for the words: נס גדול היה שם (*nes gadol hayah sham*, "a great miracle occurred there"; in Israel the ש is replaced by פ, the initial of פה (poh, "here")). The *dreidl* is an example of how foreign material was ingeniously Judaized: the original medieval dice used in Germany by gamblers was inscribed with the four letters: *N, G, H,* and *S,* which are the initials of *nichts* ("nothing"), *ganz* ("all"), *halb* ("half"), and *stellein* ("put in"). The four Hebrew parallel letters of the dice which became sanctified have the same numerical value as that of the word "Messiah" (מָשִׁיחַ = נגהש = 358) and appropriate conclusions were consequently reached. Cards were also Judaized and special "Jewish" card sets, inscribed with Hebrew letters and illustrated with "Jewish" pictures, were used.

PURIM. The Book of Esther is read in the synagogue from a parchment scroll (*megillah*) in a traditional chant. It has one roller, as distinct from the Torah scroll, which has two. Since the word for God does not appear in the Book of Esther artists felt free to illustrate it and it is thus the only biblical book in Judaism whose text, while in the form of a scroll, is traditionally illuminated. The cylindrical containers for the manuscript scroll, frequently of silver, are also richly ornamented. The main themes in the Scroll of Esther illustrations are scenes from the story: Haman leading Mordecai while Haman's wife (Zeresh) looks on; Haman and his ten sons on the gallows, etc.; all of them express the wishful thinking of the Jewish minority, oppressed and humiliated by many Hamans throughout the ages.

As Purim is dedicated to remembering the poor, charity, and "sending portions" (Esth. 9:19) and gifts to friends (*mishlo'ah manot* or Yid., *shalakh munes*), special plates, often made of pewter, are used for these purposes. Usually quotations from the Book of Esther are inscribed on the plates as well as scenes from the narrative. Here too the triumph of Mordecai is the most popular motif.

Varia: Synagogal and Home Ceremonial and Non-Ceremonial Objects.

Many ceremonial objects, whose origin (secular or religious) is often very vague, center around the synagogue and the Jewish home. The *mezuzah* (doorpost, cf, Deut. 6:9; 11:20), for example, is undoubtedly a Jewish home ceremonial object. A parchment scroll on which are sacred Pentateuchal portions, it is placed in a special metal or wood container and fixed on the upper part of the right doorpost of the house or occupied room (cf. Landsberger). The *mezuzah* has however many of the characteristics of the *amulet intended for protection. Most of the Jewish sages and rabbinic authorities did not approve of amulets being worn for purposes of protection against sickness, the "evil eye," and misfortune, and condemned the "magic" texts placed inside the amulet as non-Jewish superstition. The amulet could however be worn as an ornament, and it was particularly common among the Jewish population of the Mediterranean countries and of the Islamic culture areas. The ornaments on these amulets were often of a purely religious nature (priestly crowns, the tablets of the law, seven-branched candlestick) which did not hint at the protective qualities of the ornament.

PRAYER BOOK. The prayer book links the Jewish home, where it is usually kept as a family treasure, and the synagogue, where it is mainly used. The covers and bindings, often made of silver, gilded, or engraved, and inscribed with a biblical quotation and the owner's name or initials, are the prayer book's main adornments.

DECORATIONS IN THE SYNAGOGUE. The main synagogal ornaments and ritual objects are often part of the synagogue's architecture, Thus, for example, the laver (particularly used by the kohanim before the ceremony of blessing the congregation), often decorated, is built into the wall of the synagogue at the entrance, while the *shivviti* (the first word in Ps, 16:8: "I have set the Lord always before me") and *mizraḥ* ("East," designating the direction of prayer) are movable objects (plates or paper cutouts) hung on the wall facing Jerusalem or put on the cantor's stand which also serves as a sounding board.

The religious-ceremonial center of the synagogue is the holy *ark containing the Torah scrolls. Since the synagogue is compared to "… a little sanctuary in the countries" (Ezek. 11:16), the holy ark is reminiscent of the Holy of Holies (*Kodesh ha-Kodashim*) in the Temple. All objects associated with the Temple and the Torah were particularly cherished: the ark is ornamented with the two tablets of the Law, often wrought with inscriptions, rampant lions, and priestly (blessing) hands, etc.; the ark's curtain is made of costly brocade, velvet, or silk, frequently inscriptively embroidered (silver and gold) with the names of the donors; the wooden or metal (silver) case in which the Torah is kept among Eastern Jews, and the Torah mantle among Western Jews, are adorned with biblical and liturgical quotations surrounded by formulistic, traditional designs (floral or the seven "kinds" the Land of Israel is blessed with).

The *Torah ornaments consist of a crown (silver, often partly gilded and set with precious stones) wrought with biblical scenes and inscribed with donors' dedications; two finials (*"rimmonim*," pomegranates) to which small bells are attached; the silver pointer used in the Torah reading so that the parchment is not touched by hand; a richly decorated and inscribed *breastplate denoting the occasion of the usage of the Torah for congregational reading (Sabbath, a specific festival). The two columns of the sacred portal of the ark (*Jachin and Boaz) are the main symbol that associates the ark with the ancient Temple (cf., Goldman).

FOLK DRESS AND COSTUME. The Jewish folk dress and costume are part of the secular folk culture, if it is assumed that the origin of dress has its roots in man's desire to adorn himself. According to the Midrash (Tanḥ. B., Lev. 76) "God's glory is man and man's glory (ornament) is his clothes" (cf. Shab. 113a, 145b; Ex. R. 18; 5; A. Jellinek, *Bet ha-Midrash*, vol. 4, p. 86); thus all Jewish ethnic groups have concentrated on a particular type of dress. Most data about Jewish costumes of the past were gleaned from illustrated *minhagim* books or illuminated *Haggadot*, anti-Jewish Christian pamphlets, and travelers' accounts. Ethnographical fieldwork on extant folk dresses of Jewish communities is a very young discipline in the realm of Jewish ethnography and folkloristics (see *Dress).

Until the establishment of the State of Israel and the "ingathering of the exiles" from the various culture areas, the main interest of Jewish art "scholars" centered around ceremonial art and European specimens. Thus the first Jewish museums established in Germany (end of the 19th century) contained less than one percent of non-European material. With the growth of Jewish ethnography, the intensive study of folklore, sociology, and acculturation of the "tribes of Israel," and the establishment of specific ethnographic and folklore museums in Haifa and Tel Aviv there has been a rapid increase of interest in secular Jewish folk art in general, and in that of the non-European Jewish communities in particular. While pre-World War II folk art scholarship was mainly interested in historical roots (influence of Temple objects and symbols on the *Dura Europos synagogue and on later synagogue art; relation between traditional literary sources and ceremonial art, etc.), modern ethnographers are more interested in material culture in general (including secular folk art) and in ethnocultural and geographical comparisons. The folk museum collections and their various inventory and exhibition catalogs are still the most important source of knowledge of Jewish folk art in the past. These are often verified and substantiated by the testimonies of eyewitnesses or recollections of those who can delve into their own past or have memories of what they were told.

COGITATIVE FOLKLORE

Folk beliefs and customs constitute one creative complex. Belief, stemming from subconscious fears and desires and from a longing for psychological security, generates the wish to fight the causes of those fears which are man's hidden enemies. The strategies and tactics of man's warfare against his own fears which proved their "efficiency" and were transmitted (usually approved by social convention) from one generation to the next became folk customs. The customs continued to exist even after the beliefs that served as their basis had long been forgotten. Sometimes beliefs which have become detached from the customs that grew out of them, or from the phenomena which they explain, are regarded by the "progressive" society as "superstitions," due to changes in the society's view of the world and to a new interpretation of the phenomena in question. The novel explanation is in tune with the technological era whose society is fighting the old "superstitions" and "etiological folktales" lacking empirical proof.

Any period of transition, whether renewal and change of status in the cycle of the year (the summer and winter solstices, the vernal and autumnal equinoxes, etc.) or in the human life cycle (passage from embryo to child, from life to death, the first menstrual period, etc.) is always fraught with sociopsychological "crises" around which fears, anxieties, and inhibitions concentrate. These crises give rise to customs and rites which evolve in order to overcome the evil forces hostile to mankind that these crises seemed to set into motion. Thus ritual complexes, ceremonies, and festivals develop.

According to this interpretation the Jewish rites of passage in the life and year cycles manifest an interaction between universal beliefs, stemming from the realm of nature, and Jewish religious and national beliefs originating in the sphere of Jewish thinking and culture. The customs revolving around these rites would thus be rooted mainly in sympathetic magic which gradually adopted its Jewish character, mainly from the historical traditions related to the period of the nation's consolidation. Folkloristic research into Jewish customs and the folk beliefs underlying them therefore involves a study of their universal "prehistory" and their "Judaized" history. In universal practice the pouring of water on a stone, a sympathetic magic device to ensure rain and with it the fertility of the earth, animals, and mankind, is paralleled by a ritual performance of the sexual act. Judaized, the water libation rite as found in the Jewish normative books of laws and customs is a sacred ritual which was an integral part of the Sukkot celebrations (Simḥat Beit ha-Sho'evah, Feast of Water Drawing) in the Temple.

Most of the folk beliefs and customs concentrate on the life and year cycles and are usually considered according to these two groupings. Another category includes beliefs and customs not associated directly with one of the cycles – folk medicine, social beliefs, and social customs. The beliefs and customs which center around the Jew's life cycle, constituting the Jewish rites of passage, and around the general year cycle, comprising the Sabbath and the festivals, have throughout the ages undergone the same process of adoption and adaptation as other aspects of Jewish folklore. Thus the life-cycle "crises" in Judaism have universal-biological (*birth, coming of age, *marriage, menopause, death) and corresponding Jewish ritualistic (*circumcision, *bar mitzvah, *wedding, *burial) implications, as have the Jewish festivals and commemorative days.

The customs and their underlying folk beliefs discussed below are considered mostly from the point of view of their origin and function. The classification is according to their primary nature and to their similarity to the practices of hostile confrontation extant in prehistoric societies and in primitive intertribal warfare. Hostile confrontation may thus be divided into three main types: (1) direct (face-to-face) combat; (2) compromise (agreement and treaty); (3) deceptive stratagem.

Common to the three types of warfare is the belief that a person endowed with occult powers can, at propitious moments, compel and overcome supernatural, hostile, and harmful powers (*demons, *mazzikim*) and force their submission. Jewish literature never associates (*ta'amei minhagim*) Jewish folk customs and normative customs with their primitive and universal origin which gave rise to the magical elements inherent in them. Only customs of other peoples, usually pagan – neighboring culture or those rejected and fought against – are called magical and superstitions (*darkhei Emori*, "the Ways of the Amorites"). However, despite the legitimation of Jewish practices through association with biblical verses, hermeneutically explained or Judaized by other means, the belief in evil spirits (see *Demons) has remained basic to Judaism, and in many folk customs their magic nature is still clearly evident. As the existence of demons was presupposed, even in Jewish normative legislation (cf. *ru'aḥ* in Shab. 2:5; Er. 4:1, etc.), belief in them was not limited to the uneducated classes. This holds especially true in culture areas where the belief in evil spirits, which are hostile to mankind, was deeply rooted among the non-Jewish neighbors.

Direct (Face-to-Face) Combat

Some of the means with which spirits may be combated are specific colors (white, red) light, sound, and objects (iron, salt).

Demons usually dwell in dark places, ruined buildings (Ber. 3a, b), at the bottom of wells (Lev, R. 24:3), caves, dark and shadowy recesses (cf., the word צַלְמָוֶת *zalmavet*, originally meaning "darkness," as for example in Jer, 13:16; or in Job 12:22, interpreted as צֵל מָוֶת *zel mavet* "shadow of death"). They shun the light and therefore act at night. The Talmud (cf. Ber. 43b) commands that a person should not walk unaccompanied in the dark, but by the light of a torch or by moonlight. Similarly, the wedding, as well as other festive processions, was accompanied with torches and candles because of envying and hostile spirits. The Jewish traditional explanation (cf., A.I. Sperling, *Ta'amei ha-Minhagim* (1957), p. 407, no. 959) gives it an exclusively Jewish character: the *gematria* value of the two candles carried by the two best men is 500 (double *n[e]r* נֵר + נֵר), which is equal to the numerical value of God's first blessing to Adam and Eve פְּרוּ וּרְבוּ (*peru u-revu*, "be fruitful and multiply" = 500), Another explanation (*ibid.* no. 960) associates the wedding candles and torches with "the thunderings and the lightnings" at the revelation at Mount Sinai (Ex. 20:18), comparing the earthly ties of the human pair with the eternal bond of God and the Torah. A national modification of this wedding custom may be seen in the Jewish-Italian custom recorded at Pesaro and Modena (cf. D. Kaufmann, in REJ, 24 (1892), 289; Gaster, *The Holy and the Profane*, 110) where the bridegroom used to be accompanied by a man carrying a torch to which were attached six more lights, three on each side of the main flame. The allusion is to the seven-branched *menorah* in the Tabernacle and Temple, giving the wedding a Jewish-national character.

Spirits may be confronted with a white object since the color white frightens them away. This notion gave rise to many customs; for example, the white garments of the bride and bridegroom. The Jewish explanatory tradition, which regards the white nuptial attire as a symbol of innocence and penitence (cf. Isa. 1:18), since the espoused are on the threshold of a new "chapter in life," is a relatively late and sophisticated explanation (cf. Sperling, no. 957) of the universal white, as the statutory color of festive attire (cf. Cicero, *De Legibus*, 2:18–45: "White is the color most acceptable to gods"). The Roman custom harks back to the more ancient folk belief. The Jewish explanation associating the wedding day, a day of joy, with that of death, when the deceased is buried in white shrouds, is also a late interpretation (*Kolbo* no. 75). The custom of dressing the dead in white was common in ancient Greece (cf. Pausanias 4:1341), but there the white was to guard the dead against the powers of darkness and not a means of purification and a sign of penitence. The universality of the usage (Gaster, op, cit., 11–12), however, indicates that only powers who live under the cover of darkness may be subdued by light.

Spirits may be frightened away by sound. Their abodes cloaked in eternal silence (cf. Ps. 115:17, where the dead are paralleled with "those who go down into silence"), the demons themselves are mute creatures who are scared by such an alien element as noise. Much of the ritual and secular music performed at the various "crises" in a man's life cycle and in the natural year cycle stem from the belief that sound is a magic means to ward off demons (cf. also the common expression *le-arbev ha-Satan* ("to confuse Satan") associated with the blowing of the *shofar* on the High Holidays; RH 9b). Even some of the nonsense words in Jewish children's rhymes (cf., An-Ski, Pipe, ed. by Noy) and folk songs (as, for example, "lu-lu" in the refrains of cradle songs) may go back to the ancient, non-Jewish magic incantations, pointing to the functional character of this kind of folk poetry.

Another universal weapon directed against demons is iron. Spirits were thought to live in caves, mountains, and under stones, which "are cut by iron" (cf. BB 10a). Pieces of iron (sometimes even a real weapon – a sword, a dagger, or a simple knife) are thus placed in the bed or under the pillow of a woman in confinement and later in the child's cradle. In P.C. Kirchner's childbed scenes in *Juedisches Ceremoniel* (1734), a sword is prominently displayed beside the bed.

The circumcision knife especially is regarded as an effective weapon against demons. According to folk belief the night before the circumcision is the most critical for a mother and child, and a vigil, a "night of watching" (Yiddish: *vakhnakht*), is usually observed. Children of the *ḥeder*, accompanied by their *rebbe*, keep watch at the bedchamber and chorally chant prayers, mainly *Keri'at* **Shema* and Jacob's blessing to Ephraim and Manasseh (Gen. 48:16). The circumcision knife is often kept under the mother's pillow throughout the night.

The common usage of the sword as a real weapon against invisible demons (Gaster, op. cit., 3–11) led to many compendia of spells and magical formulae being entitled "the Sword" plus the name of a famous hero and wizard. *Ḥarba de-Moshe* ("The Sword of Moses," ed. M. Gaster, 1896) is one of the most famous and oldest Jewish collections of inscriptions of charms. In the folktales of Kurdistan Jews and in other Central Asian Jewish legends, the heroes go on quests to find the sword of Moses with which the redemption may be hastened (cf. D. Noy, *Sippurim mi-Pi Yehudei Kurdistan* (1968), 44–47, 59–60 and the aggadic details on the magic sword of Methuselah, in Ginzberg, Legends, 5 (1947), 165f.). In Afghanistan the iron sword is replaced by a cane called "Elijah's staff," (cf. *Yeda-Am*, 25 (1962), 64) not only because the Jews were forbidden to use swords but also to give a Jewish character to universal magic objects.

Iron is also used as a direct weapon to combat demons during the *tekufah* (the solstice or the equinox) when, according to folk belief, the waters may be poisoned by a drop of blood spilt by evil spirits from above (cf. Trachtenberg, *Jewish Magic and Superstition* (1961), 313, no. 12). Pieces of iron are placed on all vessels containing water and kept in the house to avert this danger. In Jewish lore the use of iron (Sperling, loc. cit., no. 900) is associated with the **notarikon* of the Hebrew word for iron בַּרְזֶל (BaRZeL), standing for the four mothers of the 12 tribes: Bilhah, Rachel, Zilpah, and Leah, who (and not the iron) avert all danger. Another explanation (*Yesod Emunah*, p. 384) changes the original text of Deuteronomy 8:9 from אֶרֶץ אֲשֶׁר אֲבָנֶיהָ בַרְזֶל to אֶרֶץ שֶׁבַּרְזֶל אֲבָנֶיהָ, thus adding to the *notarikon* the letter ש to include the two other matriarchs, Sarah and Rebekah (the ר standing both for Rachel and Rebekah).

Salt, a symbol of mortality, is also an effective "weapon with which demons may be repulsed" (cf. Ezek. 16:4; Shab. 129b). Other means to ward off demons and evil spirits are such symbols of life, health, and regeneration as herbs, honey, and oil. These usually play an important role as magic objects in folktales (cf. Thompson *Motif Index*, vol. 6, s.v.) and as helpful remedies in folk medicine.

Some of the demons are identified by name. Thus the child-snatching witch in Jewish folklore, *Lilith (often regarded as Satan's wife), seizes newborn babies and kills or injures their mothers. She also represents the "dream girl" who consorts with men in their sleep; because she is not impregnated through the sexual dream, the embittered and frustrated spirit takes her revenge upon the lawful wife and mother. In Jewish legend she was the first wife of Adam but after a quarrel deserted him. She was, however, overpowered by three angels (Sinoi, Sinsinoi, Samengelof) sent by God to bring her back, and she never enters a house in which their names are written. This story, with its emphasis on the three names, is found in most of the written or printed Hebrew amulets (known in Western countries as the *kimpettsetl* (corruption of the German *Kindbettzettel*, "childbed-charm")) which were hung in the lying-in chamber. Another kind of *kimpettsetl* is called *Shir ha-Ma'alot* ("Song of Ascents"), because it contains Psalm 121 (including verse 6, "The sun shall not smite thee by day, neither the moon by night"), which is one of the verses of the *Shir ha-Ma'alot* of the Book of Psalms (chs. 120–134).

Compromise (Agreement and Treaty)

Many Jewish customs go back to the notion that the vital and essential can be preserved by giving up the marginal and less important. In many cases the original offering (sacrifice), intended to appease demons, became highly institutionalized religious customs and rites in which God's or his representatives' holiness and superiority is acclaimed and exalted (cf. *circumcision, which is a direct "sign treaty" between God and man; tributes to the priests, **terumot*, and to the levites, *ma'aserot*; etc.).

Similarly, the custom of shaving a bride's head may also be explained as a sacrifice of a part in order to keep and to protect the whole. In many cultures, hair is regarded as a life index (Thompson, *Motif Index*, D 991, E 174, 12) which possesses an independent soul and is the seat of the vital spirit (cf. the Samson story). The belief in the magic power of hair as the seat of man's "life force" may have given rise to the taboos on cutting hair during the first year (or three years) of an infant's life, and the shearing of *pe'ot* (sidecurls). According to ritual ("*ḥalaqa*") the hair is cut after a year or three and is burned; in Jewish folklore the ritual takes place usually on *Lag ba-Omer, at the grave of Rabbi Simeon bar Yoḥai in Meron.

Deceptive Stratagem

Many customs stem from the notion that a wise and learned man can deceive the demons, who are stronger but more stupid than mankind, and thus gain the upper hand in a struggle with them. Various customs are therefore aimed at effecting an artificial change in a man's identity so that he may not be recognized by evil spirits or their representatives and messengers (the *Angel of Death). While in most customs the change is merely that of the name, this may exercise a profound influence on the person's ego, personality, character, and destiny. Meaningful changes of name often foreshadow the course of human destiny and reflect cosmic changes, evidence of which is already found in the Bible (Abraham and Sarah, Gen. 17:5; Jacob, Gen. 32:29; Joshua, Num. 13:16). In a talmudic story (Yoma 83b) Rabbi Meir refused to pass the night in an inn because the innkeeper's name, Kidor, was homonymic to a "negative" verse in the Bible (Deut. 32:20: כִּי דוֹר תַּהְפֻּכֹת הֵמָּה, *ki dor tahpukhot hemmah* – for they are a very forward generation, children in whom is no faith) and thus forebode trouble. A divine decree may be altered by changing a person's name. The well-attested custom of changing a sick person's name in order to bring about his speedy recovery (cf. *Sefer Ḥasidim* (1957), 245) is still a common practice among all Jewish ethnic groups. The evil forces may also be deceived by "selling" sick children to others so that they assume the buyer's name (see MGJV, 5 (1900), 18). The naming of the newborn child after a strong beast, a lion (*aryeh*) or a bear (*dov*), or a harmful animal, the bee (*devorah*), is also in many ways meant to deceive the evil spirit who is thus frightened away. Many of the naming practices (bestowing theophoric names or the name of a relative who passed away, so that the original name bearer may protect the newborn) stem both from the deceptive and from the compromising concepts. The compromise basis to the custom denotes homage to the supernatural forces as an inducement for their protection and to pacify and appease them through tributes.

Customs relating to sympathetic magic and contagious magic stem from a combination of the compromise and the deceptive trends. Thus by imitating the deeds of a supernatural power man admits its superiority and through his imitation pays tribute to the spirit. At the same time man incites the evil forces to act in his favor by challenging their power of action. The foolish spirits in trying to prove themselves play into man's hands.

Compromise and deceptive elements are also basic to the use of magic objects through which attempts are made to cause transformations in nature or in man. Man in using an object (part of an animal, plant, etc.) which the spirits have endowed with magic power imitates the evil powers and thereby shows his humility and submissiveness. On the other hand, he often uses his newly acquired power to combat the spirits from whom his own power now emanates. Many devices have thus been invented to overcome sterility and barrenness presumably imposed on man by malevolent supernatural forces who are strong enough to prevent sexual intercourse from resulting in conception. Plants or animals which were thought to have fertilizing properties were commonly used as aids to conception. Among the plants eaten were mandrakes and apples; the most popular animals were cocks and fish. Remedies such as touching a woman already with child, swallowing the foreskin of a newly circumcised infant, drinking the water with which a corpse has been washed (thereby transferring to the womb some of the life which has departed from the dead), and crawling under a gestating mare are based on contagious magic. They presuppose man's admission of the superiority of the object which originates from supernatural forces. These cures for barrenness (collected from Jewish informants, cf. Patai, "Jewish Folk-cures for Barrenness" in *Folklore*, vol. 4, p. 248; idem, "Birth in Popular Custom," in *Talpioth*, 9 (1965), 238–260; Gaster, op. cit., p. 4), which are not attested in normative Jewish *halakhah*, but are strongly opposed by it, still reflect general usage. In general folk culture and beliefs, the mandrake, for example, is regarded as a peculiarly potent aphrodisiac and, as such, it is referred to in the Bible (Gen. 30:14ff.; Song 7:14), probably because its root strikingly resembles the human form. Similarly the meat of fish was thought to induce fertility because of its pronounced philoprogenitive tendencies (cf. Gen. 48:16). Crawling under a mare was a means through which a woman could absorb some of the fertility of the mare which gestates for ten months.

Besides Judaized explanations and interpretations, there are many magic objects which are peculiarly Jewish. The sight of the ritual circumcision knife or a bowl of water placed under Elijah's chair at the circumcision ceremony drives spirits away. In folk medicine water in which the *kohanim* washed their hands before blessing the congregation, especially on the Day of Atonement, is a powerful cure for barrenness and other misfortunes. A uniquely Jewish practice or its explanation may sometimes have linguistic origins. Thus, for example, willow leaves which form part of the Hoshana Rabba rite induce conception not only because of their sympathetic magic qualities, paralleling the fertility of nature (prayer for rain) with human fertility, but because the willow (עֲרָבָה – *aravah*) and the word seed (זֶרַע – *zera*) have the same numerical value (277).

Many general practices are Judaized merely by the use of Hebrew (usually biblical verses), the holy tongue, which is believed to be the language of the Creator and the heavenly hosts and as such is a potent weapon against demons. It is often used by Christians and Arabs in their incantations.

A Jewish folk ceremony usually combines with many local non-Jewish magic practices and objects. Thus, for example, among German-speaking Jews a child is given a secular name on the fourth Sabbath after birth at the *Hollekreisch* ceremony. The invited guests, men in the case of a male birth and women in that of a female, range themselves in a circle (German *Kreis*) around the cradle. The baby is lifted thrice into the air while the guests call out each time *Holle! Kreisch!* and while appropriate biblical verses are recited. The magic circle wards off Frau Holle, a succubus in German mythology who attacks children. (Jewish folk etymology associates the word *Kreis* either with קרא, "call" or קרע, "tear.") The lifting is a survival of the concept that newborn babies must also be delivered from the womb of Mother Earth who gave birth to Adam, the first man (Gen. 2:7) and from which, according to folk legends, children emerge (cf. Midrashim and Rashi to Job 5:23 and Ginzberg Legends, vol. 5, page 50 note 148). It is also reminiscent of the concept that infants are symbolically sacrificed to the heavenly powers. On the other hand the biblical verses from Ecclesiastes 5:14 ("As he came forth of his mother's womb, naked shall he go back as he came") and Job 1:21 ("Naked came I out of my mother's womb and naked shall I return thither") endow the lifting custom with symbolic and ethical meaning through its counterpart practice, to deposit the dead in the ground soon after death.

A Jewish adaptation of a universal custom often also comprehends the national character of the Jewish people, stressing the everlasting bond between the nation and the Land of Israel. To plant a tree at the birth of a child (a cedar for a boy and a pine for a girl) is a Jewish birth custom which fell into desuetude, perhaps because the people became alienated from the soil and the Land of Israel. The two trees were cut down at marriage and used in the construction of the *ḥuppah* or bridal bower (cf. Git. 57a). The original universal custom stems from the general concept of the "external soul" (Thompson, Motif E. 710) which associates the life of man with some far-away object. This is a deceptive means whereby the hostility of the spirits may be diverted from their real targets. The Jewish interpretation stresses the Jew's roots in the Holy Land.

The specific Jewish character is also evident in the practice of placing a sachet of earth from the Land of Israel into the coffin of a Jew. The sachet serves as a substitute for actual burial in the Holy Land and ensures the earlier awakening of the dead on the Day of Resurrection. Since the resurrection will start in Zion, the buried need not roll to Zion before being resurrected. The dead are nevertheless buried with their feet toward the East so that they may be immediately on their way to the Land of Israel after resurrection. (This custom is also rooted in the basic concept of deception in which a part sanctifies the whole – *pars pro toto.*)

Judaizing tendencies exist especially with regard to customs and folk beliefs which are fundamentally contradictory to Jewish ethical teaching and thus threaten the Jewish ethnic ego. The pronounced Jewish character of betrothal and wedding ceremonies resulted from their refinement of the purely sexual relationships between man and woman. Nevertheless the Jewish rites of marriage have throughout the ages in all the culture areas where Jews have lived been accompanied by popular general practices aiming to ward off the evil spirits who envy man and want to abort his propagation (see *Lilith). The customs were, however, not adopted mechanically, but imbued with distinctive Jewish characteristics by incorporating Scriptures into the audio-oral prayers accompanying the rite, and in the Judaized explanation of the origin of the customs. Thus, for example, the bride and bridegroom must wear special wedding dresses and ornaments which originally were intended to protect them against evil spirits who abhor specific colors (white) and specific objects (iron). These have however acquired symbolic and aesthetic values. The clothes worn at the wedding are usually new and appropriate to the new phase of life; the bride's veil is not meant to hide her but is reminiscent of Rebekah who "took a veil and covered herself with it" (Gen. 24:65) when she first met Isaac, and is a sign of modesty. The customs of shaving the bride's head before going to the *ḥuppah* (and wearing a *sheitl* (wig)), and of her limping like an animal so as to seem blemished were originally intended to deceive the jealous spirits by showing them an ugly person not worth fighting for. Explanatory literature, however, invested these practices with deep ethical meaning:

man should not pay attention to outer form but inner value. Similarly, the customs of strewing ashes on the bridegroom's head and the breaking the glass at the wedding ceremony, which also have origins in general folklore, were interpreted as "reminder(s) of the destruction of the Temple." They were also meant to remind man of his vanity (*memento mori*).

In Israel, modern social life, especially in the secular sector and in kibbutz society, has stimulated the formation of new customs and the adaptation of religious ceremonies to a secular society which wants to keep the traditional, national folkways. This is evident, for example, in the bar mitzvah ceremony whose religious significance in a secular society is reduced but not eliminated. Since non-observant Jews do not "lay *tefillin*," which is the most outward sign of the bar mitzvah ceremony and the Jewish initiation rite, regarding them as a remnant of an ancient religious object (a kind of amulet containing scriptural verses), attempts have been made to revitalize the rite with other external symbols and the concept of *tefillin* has been completely eliminated. Under the initial impetus of the Reform movement, the individual ceremony has been substituted by a collective "confirmation" ceremony similar to that of the Christian rite. This takes place at the *Shavuot festival, chosen because it is the traditional date of the giving of the law on Mount Sinai, and consequently the proper season for adolescent boys and girls to celebrate their initiation into full Jewish adulthood. As the Shavuot festival coincides with the end of the school year, the ceremony, at times, bears the character of a graduation. In Israel the collective bar mitzvah has been introduced in nonreligious kibbutzim. The ceremony takes place after the children have performed some task, usually socioeducational, imposed upon each individual child (or pair) by the community, school, or youth movement (e.g., a week's stay in a new settlement with a newcomer's family in order to help them; or in a religious yeshivah in order to learn Jewish ways strange to them). The bar mitzvah child then has to write a composition on his experiences. He further relates his adventures during the performance of the task at the "confirmation" and the lessons derived therefrom are discussed by the whole assembly. These attempts, as well as the endeavors to introduce new agricultural festivals of a secular nature: Ḥag ha-Gez ("the Feast of Sheepshearing"), Ḥag ha-Keramim ("the Feast of the Vineyard," a "renewal" of the ancient Tu be-Av festival) have not been functioning long enough to become an integral and crystallized part of renewed or newly invented Jewish socio-cultural folkways, even in a limited segment of Jewish society. The artificial character of the new folk customs, as well as that of modern Israeli dances and folk music, is still evident.

Varia: Beliefs and Customs not Related to Cycles

A small proportion of Jewish customs and their underlying folk beliefs are not directly connected with the annual life cycle or with the crises of passage in man's life. Among these the Jewish customs pertaining to diet, nutrition, and food (including the biblical distinction between kosher and non-kosher food; the taboos of eating meat and milk together) and folk medicine practices are the two most important clusters of customs. Attempts have been made to relate them, to regard the dietary laws as part of ancient hygiene prescription, and to consider folk medicine and food customs as means of overcoming anxieties and fears.

FOLK MEDICINE. Folk beliefs and practices (remedies) for the prevention and cure of diseases have been transmitted by Jewish communities from generation to generation, even where there were normative medicine and physicians. The Bible recommends the use of the mandrake to produce fertility (Gen. 30:14). No decisive differentiation existed between the various ways of ensuring health and fertility and of combating disease and death: asking the doctor's advice, praying, and using folk remedies were all curative means emanating from God, the only healer (cf. Ex. 15:26). In Tobit (6:78) smoked liver, heart, and the gall of a fish are recommended as a cure for casting out a demon or evil spirit. Similar practices still prevail among Kurdish and Persian Jews and are indicative of the antiquity of many of the accepted folk cures.

Evidence of the widespread use of folk medicine in Palestine and Babylonia during the early centuries C.E. can be found in talmudic-midrashic literature. Magic practices and amulets received a Jewish "touch" through the use of biblical verses and by stressing the efficacy of relevant psalms. The tertian fever, for example, was to be cured with an amulet consisting of seven sets of seven articles hung around the neck (Shab. 67a). Amulets were also used against epilepsy (Shab. 61a); these were later sanctified and Judaized through biblical inscriptions. The concept that a cure may be effected by transferring the disease to animals, found so frequently in general folk medicine, is also present in Jewish folk medicine. According to talmudic sources the patient was recommended to go to a crossroad, pick up the first ant with a burden that he saw, and place it in a copper tube which was to be covered with lead and sealed. The tube should then be shaken and an incantation chanted: "What thou carriest on me, that I carry on thee" (Shab. 66b). Although practices of this kind were disapproved of by rabbinic authorities who regarded them as "Amorite rites" (folk practices alien to the spirit of Judaism), they persisted; most of them are based on principles of sympathetic magic. In the Middle Ages there is evidence of a more widespread use of folk medicine among Jews. There are many folk prescriptions in the *Sefer Ḥasidim* (13th century), most of them derived from the contiguous Christian culture. The remedy against premature birth was for a wife to wear a piece of her husband's stockings or waistband (a practice of contagious magic found in German folk medicine).

There are many folk medicine manuscripts extant from the late Middle Ages (16th–18th centuries) which contain prescriptions against fever and epilepsy. The mysterious nature of these diseases seems to have attracted the special attention of folk doctors in various culture areas. Some prescriptions deal with the improvement of family life, inducing love and fertility. Blood, a frequent element in general folk medicine, is rarely, if ever, used among Jews except in the case of nose-bleeding where the actual blood lost is sometimes baked into a cake and, following the principle prevailing in sympathetic magic, is given to a pig (*Sefer Refu'ot*, 14b).

Besides folk medicine, only a few customs are unrelated to any of the two main cycles of the Jewish year and life. Most of them have a distinctive Jewish character and have been based on Jewish legends and traditions. Thus, for example, feeding the birds in Eastern Europe on the winter Sabbath when the section on manna is read (Ex. 16) is associated with the legend that birds helped Moses defeat his opponents who wanted to prove that the Lawgiver had told a lie about manna. The same legend (cf. Ginzberg, Legends, 3 (1953), 46–47) also gave rise to the custom in Eastern Europe to feed birds on *Shabbat Shirah* when the section containing the Song of Moses (Ex. 15) was read in the synagogue.

Another social custom prevalent among Jews is to say "God bless you" (the exclamation *asuta* meaning "health") to anyone who sneezes. This custom is associated with the legend that in antiquity sneezing was a sign which forebode the sneezer's forthcoming death, but which no longer prevailed after the time of Jacob (cf. Ginzberg, Legends, vol. 5, 364, note 357). The origin of the custom, however, is not confined to Jews (Trachtenberg (1939), 306).

Jewish folklore and Jewish religion have always influenced each other. Often adapted from foreign sources, Jewish folklore was profoundly imbued with the Jewish religious spirit but in turn left its mark on Jewish religion. The religious practices extant in the various Jewish communities long ago freed themselves from their underlying superstitious beliefs and bear the character of monotheistic Judaism. However, in Jewish communities removed from the centers of learning and from religious leaders well versed in *halakhah* there still exist, side by side with the normative religion, complexes of popular beliefs and superstitions. Contrary to the explicit command of the Torah (Lev. 19:26; Deut. 18:9–14), beliefs in divination, the prognostic arts, interpretations of dreams, and astrology are still rooted in Jewish communities (cf. the still popular reprints of folk books like *Goralot Aḥitofel* ("Lots of Ahitophel," Jerusalem, 1965); *Sefer Ḥokhmat ha-Yad ha-Shalem* ("The Wisdom of Chiromancy," Jerusalem, 1966); *Sefer Ḥokhmatha-Parẓuf* ("Divination According to Features," Jerusalem, 1967) which are widely read and used by ethnic groups). Rabbinic authorities have tried to suppress customs which they regard not of Jewish origin, but in many cases they have not succeeded. Thus, for example, the customs of *kapparot* (propitiatory rite performed on the eve of the Day of *Atonement) and *tashlikh* (symbolic casting off of sins during *Rosh Ha-Shanah) are entirely foreign and considered by many Jewish authorities as pagan practices diametrically opposed to Judaism (cf. Rappoport, *The Folklore of the Jews*, p. 112–117); however, they are still commonly practiced in Jewish communities.

BIBLIOGRAPHY: FOLK NARRATIVE: W. Anderson, *Kaiser und Abt* (1923); A. Aarne, *The Types of Folktale* (1961 = AT in text); T. Benfey, *Pantschatantra* (1962); M. Epstein, *Tales of Sendebar* (1967); D. Flusser, in: *Tarbiz*, 26 (1956/57), 165–84; T.H. Gaster, *The Oldest Stories in the World* (1952); idem, *Thespis* (1966); Ginzberg, Legends; F.M. Goebel, *Juedische Motive im maerchenhaften Erzaehlungsgut* (1932); C.H. Gordon, in: HUCA, 26 (1955), 43–108; idem, *The Common Background of Greek and Hebrew Civilizations* (1962); H. Gunkel, *Das Maerchen im Alten Testament* (1917); B. Holbek, Notes to Chr. Pederson's Danish Aesop, *A esops levned og fabler* (1962); S.H. Hooke (ed.), *Myth, Ritual and Kingship* (1958); E.O. James, *The Ancient Gods …* (1960); S.N. Kramer (ed.), *Mythologies of the Ancient World* (1961); Pritchard, Texts; D.G. Maeso, in: *Miscelanea de Estúdios árabes y Hebráicos*, 5 (1956), 225–48; S. Thompson, *Motif Index of Folk-Literature*, 6 vols. (1955–58) (= Motif in text); H. Peri (Pflaum), *Der Religionsdisput der Balaam-Legende …* (1959); D. Noy, in: *Maḥanayim*, 115 (1967), 80–99; S.Z. Pipe, in: *Yivo Annual of Jewish Social Studies*, 1 (1946), 294–304; E.C. Quinn, *The Quest of Seth for the Oil of Life* (1962); Ch. Schwarzbaum, in: *Sefarad*, 21 (1961), 267–99; 22 (1962), 17–59; 321–44; 23 (1963), 54–73; S. Thompson, *The Folktale* (1951); H. Varnhagen, *Ein indisches Maerchen auf seiner Wanderung* (1882); G. Widengren, in: S.H. Hooke (ed.), *Myth, Ritual and Kingship* (1958), 149–203; idem, in: *Acta Orientalia*, 23 (1959), 201–62. RIDDLE: S. An-Ski, *Gezamlte Shriftn*, 15 (1925), 225–9; S. Bastomski, *Yidishe Folksreteishn* (1917); S. Einhorn, in: *Edoth*, 2 (1947), 278–81; 3 (1948), 95–98; Ginzberg, Legends; D. Noy, in: *Mahanayim*, 83 (1963), 64–71; Y. Ratzhabi, in: *Sinai*, 22 (1948), 36–44; idem, in: *Yeda-Am*, vol. 2 (1954), 36–41; S. Schechter, in: Folk-Lore, 1 (1890), 349–58; N.H. Tur-Sinai, *Ha-Lashon veha-Sefer*, 2 (1951), 58–93; A. Wuensche, *Die Raetselweisheit bei den Hebraeern, mit Hinblick auf andere Voelker* (1883). FOLK DRAMA: Y.L. Cahan (ed.), *Yidisher Folklor* (1938), 219–24, 310–18; E. Lahad, *Yiddish Folkplays* (1920), bibliography. FOLK SONG: L. Algazi, *Chants Sephardies* (1958); M. Alvar, in: *Boletín de la Universidad de Granada*, 23 (1951), 127–44; idem, *Endechas judeo-españoles* (1955); S. An-Ski, *Folklor un Etnografye* (1925), 171–91, 195–214; S.G. Armistead and J.H. Silvermann, in: *Sefarad*, 28 (1968), 395–98; M. Attias, *Romancero Sefaradi* (1956); idem, *La Romanza Sefaradi* (1958); idem, in: *Sefunot*, 2 (1958), 331–76; H. Avenary, in: *Sefarad*, 20 (1960), 377–94; S. Bastomski, *Baym Kval* (1923); B. Bayer, in: M. Zmona (ed.), *Yesodot Mizraḥiyyim u-Ma'arviyyim ba-Musikah be-Yisrael* (1968), 74–78; M.I. Bergovski, *Yidisher Muzik-Folklor* (1934); idem, *Yevreyskiye narodnye pesny* (1962); idem and I. Feffer, *Yidishe Folks-Lider* (1938); Y.L. Cahan, *Shtudyes vegn Yidisher Folksshafung*, ed. by M. Weinreich (1952); idem, *Yidishe Folkslider mit Melodyes* (1957); 1. Dobrushin and A. Yuditski, *Yidishe Folkslider* (1940); Y. Dworkin, in: *Studies in Biblical and Jewish Folklore* (1960), 201–21; I. Edel, *Ha-Shir ha-Ereẓ Yisre'eli* (1946); idem et al., *Zemer Am* (1946); I. Fater, *Yidishe Muzik in Poyln* (1970); E. Gerson-Kiwi, in: *Edoth*, 1 (1946), 227–33; 3 (1948), 73–78; idem, in: *Studies in Biblical and Jewish Folklore* (1960), 225–32; M.S. Geshuri, *Ha-Niggun ve-ha-Rikkud ba-Ḥasidut*, 3 vols. (1957–59); idem, in: *Yedi'ot ha-Makhon ha-Yisre'eli le-Musikah Datit*, 4 (1963), 141–6; S.M. Ginzburg and P.S. Marek, *Yevreyskiya narodniya pesnya v Rossii* (1901); Y. Goldberg, in: *Tsaytshrift* (Minsk), 1 (1926), 105–16; 2–3 (1927–28), 589–606; A.L. Holde, *Jews in Music* (1959); B. Hrushovski, in: *The Field of Yiddish*, 1 (1954), 224–32; E. Hurvitz, *Min ha-Meẓar* (1949); Idelsohn, Melodien; idem, *The Jewish Song Book* (1961); S. Katsherginski, *Lider fun di Getos un Lagern* (1948); F.M. Kaufmann, *Das juedische Volkslied* (1919); S.J. Katz, in: *Western Folklore*, 21 (1962), 83–91; M. Kipnis, *Hundert Folkslider* (1949); R. Lachman, *Jewish Cantillation and Song in the Isle of Djerba* (1940); S. Lehman, *A rbayt un Frayhayt* (1921), idem, *Ganovim Lider* (1928); I. Levy, *Chants judéo-espagnols* (1959); L. Levy, in: *Yeda*

Am, 3 (1955), 58–65, 5 (1958), 96f.; R.R. Mac-Curdy and D.P. Stanley, in: *Southern Folklore Quarterly*, 15 (1951), 221–38; E.G. Mlotek, in: *The Field of Yiddish* 1 (1954), 179–95; 2 (1965), 232–52; idem, in: *For Max Weinreich* (1964), 209–28; M. Molho, *Literatura Sefardita de Oriente* (1960); D. Noy, in: *Haifa Yorbukh*, 5 (1969), 177–224; A. de Larrea Palacin, *Cancionero judío del Norte de Marruecos*, 3 vols. (1952–54); M. Pelayo, in: *Antología de poetas líricas castellanos*, 9 (1945), 349–88; S.Z. Pipe, *Yidishe Folkslider fun Galitsye, ed.* by D. and M. Noy (1971); M. Prager, *Min ha-Meẓar Karati* (1956), N. Prilutski, *Yidishe Folkslider,* 2 vols. (1911–13); I. Rabinovitch, *Of Jewish Music ...* (1952); Y. Ratzaby, in: *Yeda-Am*, vol. 5 (1958), 85–89; Y.Y. Rivlin, *Shirat Yehudei ha-Targum* (1959); A. Rozentsvayg, *Sotsyale Diferentsyatsye inem Yidishen Folklorlid* (1934); R. Rubin, *A Treasury of Jewish Folksong* (1950); idem, *Voices of People* (1963); idem, *Jewish Folksongs in Yiddish and English* (1965); idem, in: *Tatzlil*, 8 (1968), 39–48; D. Sadan, in: *Yeda-Am*, vol. 1 no. 2 (1948), 33–35; no. 3–4 (1949), 30–32; no. 5–6 (1950), *Studies in Jewish and World Folklore* (1968), 409–17; E. Seculets, *Yidishe Folkslider* (1959); Sendrey, Music; A. Shiloah, in: *Folklore Research Center Studies*, 1 (1970), 349–68; K.Y. Silman, *Lekhu Nerannenah* (1928); A.I. Simon, *The Songs of the Jews of Cochin* (1947); Z. Skuditski, *Folklor-Lider,* ed. by M. Viner, 2 vols. (1933–36); J. Spector, in: *Reconstructionist*, 24 (1958), 11–16; idem, in: *Studies in Biblical and Jewish Folklore* (1960), 225–84; idem, in: *Yeda-Am*, vol. 3 (1955), 101–3; vol. 4 (1956), 24–28; Y. Stutshevski, *Folklor Muzikali shel Yehudei Mizraḥ Eiropah* (1958); idem, *Ha-Kleizmerim, Toledoteihem, Oraḥ Ḥayyeihem vi-Yziroteihem* (1959); B. Uziel, in: *Yeda-Am*, vol. 2 (1954), 75f., 172–7; ider, in: *Le Judaïsme Sephardi*, 18 (1959), 769–99; Ch. Vinaver, in: *Commentary*, 2 (1951), 85–87; U. Weinreich, in: *Yivo Bleter,* 34 (1950), 282–8; U. and B. Weinreich, *Yiddish Language and Folklore* (1959), nos. 294–347 (bibl.); E. Werner, in: HJS, 6 (1944), 175–88; idem, in: L. Finkelstein (ed.), *The Jews*, 2 (1949), 950–83; idem, *The Sacred Bridge* (1959); L. Wiener, in: *Germanica*, 2 (1898), 1–26, 33–59; A. Yaari, in: KS, 35 (1960), 109–26; 36 (1961), 264–72 (bibl. on *Badḥanim*). VISUAL FOLKLORE: Mayer, Art; D. Davidovitch, *Battei Keneset be-Polin ve-Ḥurbanam* (1960); B. Goldman, *The Sacred Portal, A Primary Symbol in Ancient Jewish Art* (1966); M. Golnitzki, *Be-Maḥazor ha-Yamim* (1963); Goodenough, Symbols; J. Gutmann, *Juedische Zeremonialkunst* (1963); S.S. Kayser, *Jewish Ceremonial Art* (1959); F. Landsberger, *A History of Jewish Art* (1946); idem, in: HUCA, 31 (1960), 149–66; G.K.L. Loukomski, *Jewish Art in European Synagogues* (1947); M. Narkiss, in: M. Davis (ed.), *Israel, Its Role in Civilization* (1956), 194ff.; J. Pinkerfeld, *Bi-Shevilei Ommanut Yehudit* (1957); Roth, Art; A. Rubens, *A Jewish Iconography* (1954); idem, *A History of Jewish Custom* (1967); Ch. Schwarzbaum, *Studies in Jewish and World Folklore* (1968), 435–40, 484f.; H. Volavková, *The Synagogue Treasures of Bohemia and Moravia* (1949); idem, *The Pinkas Synagogue in Prague* (1955); R. Wischnitzer, *Symbole und Gestalten der juedischen Kunst* (1935); idem, in: L. Finkelstein (ed.), *The Jews* (1949), 984–10 l o; idem, *The Architecture of the European Synagogue* (1964). COGNITIVE FOLKLORE: I. Abrahams, *Jewish Customs and Ceremonies* (1954); I. Abrahams, *Jewish Life in the Middle Ages* (1960); J. Bazak, *Le-Ma'lah min ha-Ḥushim* (1968); Y. Bergman, in: *Edoth*, 3 (1947/48), 58–66; L. Blau, *Das altjuedische Zauberwesen* (1898); R. Brasch, *The Star of David* (1955); Y.L. Cahan, *Shtudyes vegn Yidisher Folksshafung* (1952), 275–8; S. Daiches, *Babylonian Oil Magic in the Talmud and in Later Jewish Literature* (1913); A. Daron, in: *Transactions of the 11th International Congress of Orientalists* (1897), 259–70; Eisenstein, Dinim; L. Finkelstein (ed.), *The Jews*, 2 (1949), 1327–89; A.S. Freidus,, *Studies in Jewish Bibliography and Related Subjects in Memory of Abraham Solomon Freidus* (1929), lxxviiiff.; T.H. Gaster, *The Holy and the Profane: Evolution of Jewish Folkways* (1955); J. Jacobs, *Customs and Traditions of Israel* (1955); E, Tov, *Sefer ha-Toda'ah* (1960); E, Langton, *Essentials of Demonology: A Study of Jewish and Christian Doctrine* (1949); S.M. Lehrran, *Jewish Customs and Folklore* (1949); R. Lilienthal, in; *Yidishe Filologye*, 1 (1924), 245–71; A. Marmorstein, in: *Edoth*, 1 (1945/46), 76–89; J. Nacht, *Simlei Ishah* (1959); D. Noy, in: *Onot ha-Shanah*, 1 (1959); R. Patai, *Adam va-Adamah*, 2 vols. (1942–43); idem, *Man and Temple in Ancient Jewish Myth and Ritual* (1947), 4f.; S. Raskin, *Aron-hakodesh.. Jewish Life and Lore* (1955); I. Rivkind, *Yidishe Gelt* (1959); J. Soetendorp, *Symbolik der juedischen Religion; Sitte und Brauchtum im juedischen Leben* (1963); I. Sperling, *Sefer Ta'amei ha-Minhagim u-Mekorei ha-Dinim* (1957); J. Trachtenberg, *Jewish Magic and Superstition* (1939, repr. 1961); idem, *The Devil and the Jews* (1961^2). YEAR CYCLE BELIEFS AND CUSTOMS: A. Ben Ezra, *Minhagei Ḥagim* (1963); T.H. Gaster, *Festivals of the Jewish Year: A Modern Interpretation and Guide* (1956); P. Goodman, *Rejoice in Thy Festival* (1956); S. Goren, *Torat ha-Mo'adim* (1964); H. Leshem, *Shabbat u-Mo'adei Yisrael* (1965); Y.T. Lewinski (ed.), *Sefer ha-Mo'adim*, 3 (1953); J. Morgenstern, in: JQR, 8 (1917/ 18), 34–37; N. Wahrman, *Ḥagei Yisrael u-Mo'adav* (1961); M. Zobel, *Das Jahr des Juden in Brauch und Liturgie* (1936); H. Schauss, *The Jewish Festivals* (1938); idem, *Guide to Jewish Holy Days* (1962); M. Rabinovitch, *Ḥol u-Mo'ed* (1965). LIFE-CYCLE BELIEFS AND CUSTOMS: L.M. Epstein, *Sex Laws and Customs in Judaism* (1948); E. Ki-Tov, *Ish u-Veito* (1963); R. Patai, *Sex and Family in the Bible and the Middle East* (1959); H. Schauss, *The Lifetime of a Jew throughout the Ages of Jewish History* (1950); Ch. Schwarzbaum, *Studies in Jewish and World Folklore* (1968), 428ff. BIRTH AND CIRCUMCISION: E. Brauer, in: *Edoth*, 1 (1945/46), 129–138 (Kurdistan); W.F. Feldman, *The Jewish Child* (1917); M. Gaster, in: *Folk-Lore*, 11 (1900), 129–62; T.H. Gaster, *The Holy and the Profane* (1955), 3–41; A. Landau, in: *Zeitschrift des Vereins fuer Volkskunde*, 9 (1899), 72–77; J.Z. Lauterbach, in: CCARY, 42 (1932), 316–60; R. Lilienthal, in: MGJV, 25–26 (1908), 1–24, 41–53; M. Molho, in: *Edoth*, 2 (1946/47), 255–69 (Saloniki); R. Patai, in: *Folklore*, 54 (1943), 117–24; 56 (1945), 208–18; A.M. Posner, in: *Yeda-Am*, vol. 4 (1956), 41–44; A. Pritzker, *ibid.*, vol. 1 no. 1 (1948–53), 87–90; vol. 2 (1954), 22–23, 215–8; H. Schauss, in: *Yivo Bleter,* 17 (1941), 47–63; M. Zobel, in: *Almanach des Schocken Verlags* (1939), 98ff.; I. Zoller, in; *Filologishe Shriftn*, 3 (1929), 121–42. BAR MITZVAH: A. Ben-Gurion (ed.), *Yalkut Bar-Mitzvah* (1967); T.H. Gaster, *The Holy and the Profane* (1955), 66–77; J, Nacht, in: *Yeda-Am*, vol. 3 (1955), 106–11; 1. Rivkind, *Le-Ot u-le-Zikkaron* (1942). MARRIAGE: L.M. Epstein, *The Jewish Marriage Contract* (1927), incl. bib I.; I.Z. Lauterbach, in: HUCA, 2 (1925), 35 1ff.; Y.T. Lewinski, in: *Yeda-A m*, vol. 3 (1955), 91–97; *Maḥanayim*, 83 (1963). DEATH: S. An-Ski, in: *Filologishe Shriftn*, 3 (1929), 89–100; J. Avida, in: *Edoth*, 2 (1946/47), 217–25; A.P. Bender, in: JQR, 6 (1934/35), 317–47, 667–71; T.H. Gaster, *The Holy and the Profane* (1955), 137–95; Ch. Chajes, in: *Filologishe Shriftn*, 2 (1928), 281–328; A. Pritsker, in: *Yeda-Am*, vol. 3 (1955), 20f., 115–17; 4 (1956), 38–40; 5 (1957), 26–28; Ch. Schwarzbaum, in: *Yeda-Am*, vol. 6 (1960), 14–18. FOLK MEDICINE: Y. Bergman, *Ha-Folklor ha-Yehudi* (1953), 178–94; M. Bernstein, in: *Studies in Biblical and Jewish Folklore* (1960), 289–305; M.M. Firestone, in: *Journal of American Folklore*, 75 (1962), 301–10; M. Grunwald, in: *Jirbuch fuer juedische Volkskunde*, 1 (1923), 222–6; M. Kosover, *Yidishe Ma'akholim* (1958); R. Patai, in: *Folklore*, 54 (1943), 117–24; 56 (1945), 208–18; H.J. Zimmels, *Magicians, Theologians and Doctors* (1952). **ADD. BIBLIOGRAPHY:** D. Ben Amos, "Jewish Studies and Jewish Folklore," in: *Proceedings of the Tenth World Congress of Jewish Studies,* Division D (Art, Folklore, and Music), II (1990), 1–20); G. Hasan-Rokem, "Jewish Folklore and Ethnography," in: M. Goodman (ed.), *Oxford Handbook of Jewish Studies* (2002), 956–74, incl. bibl. The Israeli Folktale Archive at Haifa University in Israel (founded by Dov Noy) houses 25,000 narrative texts. An archive for proverbs at the Hebrew University of Jerusalem (founded by Galit Hasan-Rokem) houses 7,500 sayings. The Institute for Jewish Studies at the Hebrew University publishes the journal *Jerusalem Studies in Folklore.*

[Dov Noy]

FOLKMAN, JUDAH (1933–), U.S. medical scientist. Folkman was born in Cleveland, Ohio, and graduated with a B.A. from Ohio State University (1953) and an M.D. from Harvard Medical School (1957). His interest in research began while he was still an undergraduate with the development of a novel pacemaker. After training in surgery at Massachusetts General Hospital (1957–65), including service with the U.S. Navy (1960–62), he joined the staff of Harvard Medical School, where his subsequent senior appointments included professor of surgery (1967), pediatric surgery (1979), and cell biology (1994), and chief surgeon at Boston Children's Hospital. Folkman initiated research on the importance of new blood vessels (angiogenesis) to the growth and spread of cancers. This research showed that angiogenesis is stimulated by factors produced chiefly by the specialized cells (endothelial cells) lining the interior of the blood vessels of normal individuals and by cancer cells. It also promotes inflammation in many other diseases. Angiogenesis is inhibited by naturally occurring factors and by drugs such as endostatin and angiostatin designed as the result of this basic research. He has postulated that natural anti-angiogenesis factors are an important anti-cancer defense mechanism. Anti-angiogenesis drugs have proved effective in controlling experimental cancers but their relevance to clinical medicine awaits the outcome of the many clinical trials founded on this research. His achievements have been recognized by many honors, including election to the U.S. National Academy of Sciences (1990), the Gairdner Award (1991), the Wolf Prize (1992), and the Benjamin Franklin Award (2001). In 1999 he became a member of the International Scientific Board of the Israel Cancer Association.

[Michael Denman (2nd ed.)]

FOLKSPARTEI (Poland), "Yidishe Folkspartei in Polyn" (popularly known as **Folkist Party**), Jewish populist party in Poland organized during World War I and active in the interwar period; followed the ideology of the Russian *Folkspartei. The Folkist Party achieved its first successes among broad sectors of the Jewish electorate during the elections to the Warsaw municipal council of 1916. An agreement on the distribution of seats had then been signed between the united Jewish bloc – which comprised the Zionists, the Orthodox, and the assimilationists – and the Polish parties in order to break the tension existing between Poles and Jews since the proclamation of the anti-Jewish boycott in 1912. In opposition to this agreement a "People's Committee" (Folks Komitet) was formed on the initiative of a group of Yiddish authors and journalists led by the lawyer Noah *Prylucki. This presented a separate list calling for independent Jewish politics, cultural autonomy, and full political equality. As a result of the dissatisfaction among the small tradesmen and artisan class, the list won four seats.

The founding convention of the Folkspartei was held in November 1918. It drew up a program in general similar to that of the Russian Folkspartei but with the exclusive emphasis on Yiddish as the traditional language. In social outlook, the party was Democrat-Radical oriented, opposing the class struggle and aiming at productivization. Culture and education were to be of a secular character. The Folkspartei was headed by intellectuals and communal leaders who had left the Zionist and labor ranks (especially the Bund) like its principal leader, Noah Prylucki, the folklorist and Yiddish philologist, Samuel *Hirschhorn, Hillel *Zeitlin, H.D. *Nomberg, Lazar Cohen (Kahan), S. Stupnicki, and Ẓemaḥ *Shabad. The main centers of the movement were Warsaw, Lodz, and Vilna. Its organizational and ideological framework was not overly rigid, and its leaders achieved popularity through the Yiddish press and their efforts on behalf of individual causes.

In the elections to the Sejm (parliament) of 1919, the Folkists returned two members (Prylucki and Hirschhorn), but in the elections of 1922 were unsuccessful in the campaign against the minorities bloc, which attracted the decisive majority of the Jewish vote. Prylucki, who was elected as the party's sole representative to the Sejm, did not join the circle of other Jewish deputies. After this decline in the party's popularity, a split occurred in 1926 with the separation of the Vilna section, which proclaimed itself an independent faction ("Populist-Democrat") under the leadership of Shabad. In 1928, within the framework of the new political regime established in Poland after Pilsudski's coup, the supporters of Prylucki, in conjunction with Agudat Israel and the Merchants' Organization, joined forces with the list supported by the government against the second minorities bloc led by Yiẓhak *Gruenbaum. This affiliation with the Polish government camp did not enhance the status of the Folkist Party among the Jewish public. In 1929, an attempt was made to reunite the Folkspartei, and a national convention was held in 1931. During 1932–33 it published a monthly, *Folkistishe Heftn*, in order to explain the party ideology. All these efforts, however, were unable to compete with the growing Zionist and radical movements, especially the Bund, with which the Folkist Party collaborated in the fields of culture and Yiddish education.

BIBLIOGRAPHY: I. Schipper et al. (eds.), Żydzi *w Polsce odrodzonej*,, 2 (1933), 268–9; A. Levinson, *Toledot Yehudei Varshah* (1953), 270–1; R. Ben-Shem, in: EG, 6 (1959), 279–83.

[Moshe Landau]

FOLKSPARTEI (Russia), populist party; Jewish political party influential in most of Eastern Europe and active from 1906 to 1939. Its founder and mentor was Simon *Dubnow, who formulated with associates the party program on the basis of his ideology of *autonomism. According to this, the Jewish communal organization would serve as the secular cell of Jewish national existence and autonomy, to be administered on democratic lines. It was to establish Jewish schools whose language of instruction would be determined according to circumstances and the parents – Hebrew, Yiddish, or the language of the country – but the spirit and aims of this education should be Jewish. The local communities were to band together in a council on the lines of the *Councils of the Lands to represent the Jews vis-à-vis the authorities, whereby the state would grant it the right to collect taxes for internal Jewish requirements. The council would establish central institutions (rabbinical seminaries, teachers' training colleges, etc.), supervise the Jewish schools, and deal with economic and social matters (cooperatives, emigration, and welfare). On a higher plane, Dubnow visualized a world Jewish congress that would deal with problems concerning the whole of the nation in the Diaspora, such as the struggle for *emancipation in countries where it had not yet been achieved, and care for emigration and settlement in Ereẓ Israel and other countries. In 1911 a group of Autonomists-Socialists joined the Folkspartei. The party was led, in addition to S. Dubnow, by M. *Kreinin, I. *Yefroykin, S. *An-Ski, J.W. *Latzky-Bertholdi, Nahum *Shtif, and Joseph Tschernikhov.

After the Russian Revolution of February 1917, the party organized openly. It played a role in the political struggle among Jews during this period but made no headway against the Jewish socialist parties, the Zionists, and the Orthodox groups: in the elections to the Ukrainian Jewish Council of 1918, only four of its delegates were returned out of 125. Latzky-Bertholdi served as minister for Jewish affairs in the Ukrainian government for a short while in 1918. When the Soviets gained control of Ukraine and Belorussia, the activities of the party in these areas were brought to a halt. With the granting of *minority rights in international treaties, the Folkspartei considered that its program had been given international sanction.

In Poland the founding congress of the Folkspartei met in November 1918. The program adopted resembled the Russian one, differing in that it proclaimed Yiddish the sole language for the cooperative movement and for secular education and culture. Among the leaders of the party were: N. Prylucki, S. *Hirschhorn, J. *Zeitlin, H.D. *Nomberg, and others. In the elections to the Polish parlament (Sejm) two were elected: Prylucki and Hirschhorn; in the 1922 only Prylucki, but he did not join the Jewish Circle and the minorities bloc. In 1928 he joined forces with Agudat Israel and the government and not the second minorities bloc headed by Yiẓḥak *Gruenbaum. During the 1920s and 1930s, the party continued its activities in Poland and the Baltic countries. Its members took part in community affairs, and in conjunction with the Jewish leftist parties promoted secular Jewish schools with instruction in Yiddish (CYSHO [Central Yiddish School Organization]), and supported the Jewish cooperative movement and relief institutions (*ORT, *OSE). The party drew most of its adherents from the intelligentsia, small tradesmen, and artisans. While operating only in limited circles, it had some influence in communal life (see *Folkspartei, Poland). In the Baltic countries, the Folkspartei continued to exist until the rise of the dictatorial regimes and the abolition of Jewish autonomy. With the growing antisemitism and nationalism in the late 1930s, the party gradually disintegrated. Many of its members and leaders abandoned it, some joining the Zionists (such as Latzky-Bertholdi), and others the Territorialists (Tschernikhov).

BIBLIOGRAPHY: S. Dubnow, in: K. Pinson (ed.), *Nationalism and History* (1958); N. Kastelyanski, *Formy natsionalnogo dvizheniya* (1910).

[Yehuda Slutsky]

FOMIN, YEFIM MOISEYEVICH (d. 1941), Soviet soldier. In 1941 Fomin was a captain and commissar of a regiment during the Brest-Litovsk campaign. When the Germans broke through the Russian lines, Fomin conducted the defense of the Brest-Litovsk fortress for weeks after the rest of the front had retreated. Severely wounded, he was captured with the fall of the fortress and because he was a Jew, he was executed. He was posthumously made a Hero of the Soviet Union and a factory and a street in Brest-Litovsk were named after him.

FONDANE (Fundoianu), BENJAMIN (Barbu; 1898–1944), French and Romanian poet. Born in Jassy, Romania, Fondane studied law, then turned to literature, publishing some Romanian verse collections under his original name, Barbu Fondoianu. In 1923 he settled in France, where in common with other Romanian Jewish immigrants, such as Tristan *Tzara and Ilarie *Voronca, he made his name as a French writer. Unlike them, however, Fondane always remained a Jewish author, deeply conscious of his identity and painfully aware of the Jew's condition as an exile. Although he wrote philosophical essays which betray the influence of Kierkegaard, Fondane is primarily remembered as a visionary poet. In the vast lyrical frescos of *Ulysse* (1933) and *Titanic* (1937) he developed the theme of the *Wandering Jew, with pathetic descriptions of the wanderer's existence or of weary yet hopeful emigrants on the way to their Promised Land. Fondane's poetic testament, *L'Exode; superflumina Babylonis* (1965; written 1934–42), is more restrained and taut in tone. In this semiautobiographical work the author resigns himself to the inevitable, and in bitter words prophesies the ultimate catastrophe. Even as the darkness of Nazism descended on Jewry, Fondane continued to believe in the ultimate triumph of freedom. He was deported to the concentration camp at Birkenau (Auschwitz), where he was murdered.

[Wladimir Rabi]

FONDILLER, WILLIAM (1885–1975), U.S. electrical engineer. Born in Russia, Fondiller was taken to the U.S. He made his career with Western Electric Company (1909–25) and Bell Telephone Laboratories, of which he became vice president and treasurer. He was a research associate at Columbia University school of engineering from 1935 to 1950, and took out patents for loading coils, transformers, cables, etc. Fondiller was active in Jewish and Zionist affairs and was honorary president of the American Technion Society (1950).

FONSECA, ALVARO DA (c. 1657–1742), English merchant. Da Fonseca, known in synagogue as Jacob Jessurun Alvarez, arrived with his family in England in about 1670 from Nevis in the West Indies, became a successful merchant, and was active in synagogue affairs. About 1682 he left for India. In 1683 he and two other Portuguese-Jewish merchants, Bartholomew Rodriguez and Domingo do Porto, were authorized, though they were originally interlopers, to settle in Fort St. George (Madras). During the 17 years that he was in India (1683–1700) Da Fonseca served the English East India Company in a variety of functions. In 1690 he was appointed alderman of the Madras Corporation, representing the Jewish merchant group of Fort St. George. He built a vast commercial empire in collaboration with other Jewish merchants and opened up new markets in Asia for the English trade. He invested great sums in commercial transactions to China, Burma, and Bengal. The major commodities in which he dealt were diamonds and precious stones, textiles, and timber, frequently transported on his own ships. In March 1700 he returned with a large fortune to London, where he acted on behalf of the Madras governor Thomas Pitt in the appraisal and sale of the famous Pitt diamond.

BIBLIOGRAPHY: Diamond, in: JHSET, 19 (1960), 180–9; Fischel, in: *Journal of the Economic and Social History of the Orient*, 3 (1960), 78–107, 175–95. **ADD. BIBLIOGRAPHY:** ODNB online; E. Samuel, *At the Ends of the Earth: Essays on the History of the Jews in England and Portugal* (2004), 248–49; G. Yogav, *Diamonds and Coral: Anglo-Jews and Eighteenth Century Trade* (1978).

[Walter Joseph Fischel]

FONSECA, DANIEL DE (1672–c. 1740), Marrano physician and diplomat from Oporto (Porto), Portugal. His grandfather had been burned at the stake by the Inquisition; his father had escaped the same fate only by flight. Left behind in Portugal, his son was brought up as a priest. This did not prevent him from adhering to Judaism in secret. The secret reached the ears of the Inquisition and like his father he had to flee for his life, crossing the border into France. He studied medicine in Bordeaux, resided for a time in Paris, and then made his way to Constantinople, where he arrived in 1702. Once there, he openly embraced Judaism. Through his medical skill, De Fonseca soon became known in the Turkish capital, obtaining the confidence of many high officials. He showed himself an accomplished diplomat, consistently espousing the cause of France and thereby earning the dislike of the Court of Austria. He was appointed a physician to the French embassy, in which he occupied the position of confidential adviser. Subsequently, he became medical attendant to Prince Mavrocordato at Bucharest. On his return to Constantinople, he became physician to the sultan, continuing to occupy this office till 1730; and he was of great assistance to Charles XII of Sweden in his intrigues at the Sublime Porte against Russia and Poland. Finally he settled in Paris, where he mingled with the highest society of his age and earned the respect of Voltaire, who regarded him as "the only philosopher of his people."

BIBLIOGRAPHY: Rosanes, Togarmah, 4 (1935), 188f.; E. Carmoly, *Histoire des médecins Juifs* (1844), 198f.; Roth, Marranos, 310–11; A. da Silva Carvalho, *Daniel da Fonseca* (Fr., 1939); Marquis d'Argens, *Memoires* (1735), 114–5.

[Abraham Haim]

FONTAINEBLEAU, town in the Seine-et-Marne department, approximately 37 mi. (about 60 km.) S. of Paris, France. The Jewish community in Fontainebleau dates from 1799. During the 19th century, two important porcelain factories there were owned by Jews: Jacob Petit and Baruch Weil. At the time of the 1941 census, there were 58 Jews in Fontainebleau.

Holocaust and Postwar Periods

During the German occupation of World War II, Fontainebleau's synagogue, dating from 1857, was looted and destroyed; its eight-branch candelabrum, made of blue Sèvres porcelain and donated by Napoleon III to the Jewish community, was also smashed. After the war, a new Jewish community, composed mostly of North African Jews, settled there, numbering about 400 persons in 1969. The synagogue was rebuilt in 1965 and a new candelabrum was contributed by Allied (SHAPE) officers stationed in the town.

BIBLIOGRAPHY: Z. Szajkowski, *Analytical Franco-Jewish Gazetteer* (1966), 267.

[Bernhard Blumenkranz]

FOOD.

The Biblical Period

Diet in Ereẓ Israel during the biblical period was dependent mostly on the food supply of the closed agricultural economy. Most agricultural produce came from permanent settlements, and some wild plants were gathered, while meat was mainly supplied by cattle and sheep-raising nomads. Grain constituted the bulk of agricultural produce consumed and most meat was mutton. The Bible, in speaking of the produce of Ereẓ Israel, mentions three types of food: *dagan, tirosh*, and *yiẓhar* (Deut. 7:13; II Kings 18:32). *Dagan* ("corn" or "grain") represents the various agricultural crops, *tirosh* ("new wine")-wine, and *yiẓhar-oil.*

Food was made fit for eating by baking, boiling, frying, or roasting (see *Fire), or by a combination of these. Grain was prepared in two ways: roasting the kernels in order to break down their starches and soften them (Heb. *kali, qali*; "parched corn"; I Sam. 25:18; II Sam. 17:28; Ruth 2:14), or grinding and baking the item (see also *Bread). Cooked food was a mixture of meat and vegetables which were combined while heating (Heb. *marak*; "broth"; Judg. 6:19, 20; Isa. 65:4). Stew (Heb. *nazid*; Gen. 25:29; II Kings 4:38; et al.) was apparently a food cooked for a long time in water, most of which was boiled off. Fried foods, especially meat, were cooked in large quantities of boiling oil. Meat was also roasted over an open flame, which seared and softened it.

FORBIDDEN FOODS. The usual diet consisted of foods prepared from grain, wild and cultivated plants, and the meat of sheep, cattle, fowl, fish, and even certain insects. The Torah limited the meat a Jew could eat, both in terms of the animals permissible for eating, and the manner of their preparation (see also *Dietary Laws). Meat taken from a still living animal or from one found dead, and the drinking of blood were prohibited (see *Blood). Only animals specifically slaughtered for food or for use in the sacrificial service could be eaten. These animals had to have two characteristics: they chewed the cud and had cloven hoofs. An animal possessing neither or only one of these characteristics was forbidden. Some types of birds were permitted and the exceptions were specifically named (Lev. 11:13–19). The consumption of fish was limited to those possessing scales and fins. As to insects, only locusts (Heb. *ʾarbeh*) could be eaten.

THE FORM OF THE MEAL. The Bible uses several terms to describe meals. *ʾAruḥah* (from the root *ʾrḥ*, "to lodge") appears to refer to the usual daily meal, as in "a regular allowance [*ʾaruḥah*] was given him …" (II Kings 25:30; Jer. 52:34). It may also indicate a more modest meal, as in "Better is a dinner of herbs where love is, than a fatted ox and hatred with it" (Prov. 15:17). *Zevaḥ* (from the root *zbḥ*, "to sacrifice") generally indicates a meat meal connected with the religious worship, or with some other festive occasion (I Sam. 20:29). *Kerah* was a festive meal with many participants (II Kings 6:23). The verb *sʿd* ("to support") is frequently used to indicate eating: "Come home with me, and refresh thyself" (I Kings 13:7). *Leḥem* ("*bread") frequently refers to food or to a meal in general. Meat meals were not usual: the *kerah* or *zevaḥ*, as noted above, was part of some festive occasion such as a general holiday or special tribal or family occasion. Many people participated in a meat meal, of which nothing would be left over in order to prevent spoilage. Such meat meals were consecrated in order to enlist God's aid in human ventures, as a sign of thanks, or as a propitiatory offering (see also *Sacrifice). The everyday meal was eaten by the family either in the house or in the field. It was generally prepared by the woman, while the *zevaḥ* and *kerah* were prepared by both men and women, thus emphasizing the importance of these social events. A meal was an occasion for pleasure and enjoyment. It was eaten while seated and the established customs and manners were observed before and after the meal. The upper classes might sing and propose riddles during the mealtimes.

VEGETABLES. Cereals, such as wheat (Heb. *ḥiṭṭah*) and barley (Heb. *seʿorah*), *were cultivated* crops. Stew made of lentils (Heb. *ʿadashim*) or beans (Heb. *polim*) was common and was eaten after being softened by cooking. Other vegetable dishes were uncommon, most vegetables being picked wild as needed and then cooked for the daily meal. Wild melons (Heb. *ʾavaṭṭiʾaḥ*) and cucumbers (Heb. קשוא, *qeshu*) were among the wild vegetables eaten in Ereẓ Israel. In Egypt there were plots for the cultivation of melons and cucumbers. Sesame seeds (Heb. *shumshum*), also gathered wild, were used in the preparation of oil, or were eaten raw, in stews or in some other fashion. Garlic (Heb. *shum*) and onions (Heb. *bazal*) grew wild in Ereẓ Israel and served as food, while in Egypt they were cultivated. They were cultivated in Ereẓ Israel only in the post-biblical period.

FRUITS. The seven types of produce mentioned in Deuteronomy 8:8 include most of the fruit eaten in Ereẓ Israel. The vine (Heb. *gefen*) is mentioned after wheat and barley. Grapes (Heb. *ʿanavim*) were used mainly in the production of wine, although they were also eaten fresh. Grapes were dried in the sun to produce raisins (Heb. *ẓimmukim, ẓimmuqim*), which were preserved for substantial periods of time. Grapes were also used to produce a thick liquid like honey, called the grape honey (Heb. *devash ʿanavim*). Even today, grape honey (Ar. *dibes*) is produced in parts of Israel. Grape honey was made by treading in special vats: the liquid produced was not left to ferment, but was boiled in order to evaporate the water content, leaving behind a thick liquid resembling honey. Figs (Heb. *teʾenah*) were also common and were eaten either fresh when ripe, or dried, the dried figs (Heb. *develah*) being strung into a chain or made into a hard cake. This cake was made of figs stuck together and dried as a block. After sufficient drying, the fig block was sliced and eaten like bread. Pomegranates (Heb. *rimmonim*) were usually eaten fresh, although occasionally they were used in the preparation of wine for medicinal uses. Dates (Heb. *temarim*), too, were eaten fresh or were sun-dried. Like grapes, dates were made into a sweet, thick drink called date honey (Heb. *devash temarim*). This was prepared by soaking the fruit in water for some time during which it would disintegrate. The liquid was cooked down until thick and sweet. Olives (Heb. *zeitim*) were usually used to make oil (see below), although some were eaten after being preserved in tasty and fragrant spices, which removed their natural bitter flavor. The Bible also mentions nuts (Heb. *ʾegozim*), apples (Heb. *tappuḥim*), pistachios (Heb. *botnim*), and almonds (Heb. *shekedim, sheqedim*). Nuts were common in Ereẓ Israel, particularly in the post-biblical period. Apples, pistachios, and almonds were not cultivated, but grew wild. They were picked for occasional home use when they were available, although most were imported as a delicacy.

SPICES. The most common spice was salt (Heb. *melaḥ;* Job 6:6), there being hardly any food which was not seasoned with it. Salt served the additional function of symbolizing the making of a covenant (II Chron. 13:5), or the destruction of a city (Judg. 9:45). It was obtained in two ways: the most common method was mining, as at Sodom, although it was also produced by evaporating sea water and removing the salts from the sediment. The raw salt was rinsed in fresh water, purified, and then crushed until fine, in which form it was used for seasoning food and for other purposes. The flavor of food was also enhanced by spices derived from plants. Garlic and onions, as well as being eaten as vegetables, were used to season cooked foods. Other spices mentioned in the Bible are coriander (Heb. *gad*), cumin (Heb. *kammon*), and black cumin

(Heb. *keẓah*, *qeẓaḥ*). More delicate spices for special feasts were imported from Arabia and India, and were considered merchandise of the highest value. Among such spices were various types of pepper (Heb. *pilpel*), and ginger.

FOODS PRODUCED BY ANIMALS. During the biblical period, wild bee honey and eggs, especially birds' eggs, were eaten.

DAIRY FOODS. Most dairy items were produced from sheep or goat milk, since cattle were scarce in the country. The use of cow's milk is attested by Mesopotamian and Egyptian sources, such as the "Banner of Ur" and various Egyptian steles, as early as the fourth millennium B.C.E. In Ur, cows were milked from behind and in Egypt from in front of the udder, with their rear legs tied together. Milk, connected as it was with the miracle of reproduction, was used in pagan cults, in which a kid would be cooked in its mother's milk. This practice was forbidden for the Israelites (Ex. 23:19; et al.).

Milk was one the characteristic products of Ereẓ Israel (Ex. 3:8; 33:3; Joel 4:18). A nourishing food, it was frequently drunk cold or was cooked with other foods, as well as serving in other forms for medicinal purposes and ointments. Due to its importance, milk and its by-products served as offerings to gods and kings. The Bible mentions butter and various cheeses as milk-derived products. Butter was made by churning milk in vessels made especially for this purpose. Examples of these churns (Heb. *mahbeẓah*) have been found at Beersheba and elsewhere. The butterfat was separated as a result of the churning, and the excess liquid was evaporated in order to produce butter. In this concentrated form, it was used principally for cooking and frying. Cheese was made from soured milk. Milk was poured into special moulds in which it soured into hard lumps. These cheese lumps were dried in the sun or evaporated by cooking, producing curds (Job 10:10). A softer cheese was made in cloth bags filled with soured milk. The thin liquid filtered through the cloth while the soft cheese remained in the bag. The Hittites used cheese as an offering in their cult.

WINE. Most wine was produced from grapes. The vintage was brought to a winepress which was usually rock-cut. The grapes were spread on the broad upper surface of the press and tread upon by foot, in order to squeeze the liquid from them. This liquid (Heb. *tirosh*, "new wine") flowed down through a drainage channel into a vat in which the precipitates settled. From there it flowed to a second vat where it was collected. The drainage system was constructed so that the liquid flowed into the collecting vat only when the precipitation vat was filled. Thus, the heavier sediments such as waste matter, seeds, and skins had time to settle at the bottom of the vat, while the juice flowed into the collecting vat. The new wine was then transferred to vessels which were sealed and placed in a cool place to stand until the juice fermented by the action of the yeast in the fruit, becoming wine. There were several types of wine, some of which are mentioned in the Bible: a sparkling or foaming wine (Ps. 75:9); the wine of Helbon (Ezek. 27:18); spiced wine (Song 8:2); the wine of Lebanon (Hos. 14:8). The type of wine was determined by the grapes from which it was pressed, the time allowed for fermentation, and the age of the wine. Spices were added to improve the aroma and taste. The color was improved by steeping crushed grape skins in it. Sometimes wine was given an aroma by rubbing the winepress with wood resin. Wine was also made from raisins, dates, figs, and pomegranates.

Wine was considered the choicest of drinks. It was used in libations before gods, as payment of taxes to kings, and was highly regarded as an item of trade. It was measured by liquid measure: the *bat* (II Chron. 2:9) and the *hin* (Ex. 29:40; Samaria ostraca). Wine was hoarded in vessels of uniform size in the treasuries of the royal and the wealthy. Ereẓ Israel was known for its fine wines and advanced methods of production. Some indication of this may be gained from the widespread occurrence of presses in archaeological excavations throughout the country. A good example of a rock-cut winepress from the biblical period found at Gibeon has a broad surface for treading the grapes and several collecting vats. Wine was an intoxicant with a stimulating effect upon the human disposition. One who had taken Nazirite vows was therefore not permitted to drink it or to make any use of vine-derived products. The Bible mentions houses which were visited for the purpose of drinking and becoming intoxicated (Song 2:4). Another vine product was vinegar, which was produced by extra fermentation of new wine. It was used for seasoning foods, pickling vegetables, and medicinal purposes.

OIL. Oil was produced mainly from olives in olive presses designed for this purpose. There were three stages in its production. First, the hard olives were crushed into a soft paste. This was then squeezed, the crude oil flowing out as a result of the pressure. Finally, the crude oil was stored in vessels or vats for some time, in which the sediments and water from the olives settled and the pure oil rose to the surface. The oil was then collected in vessels for storage or use. Archaeological excavations have revealed numerous olive presses dating to the Hellenistic period. The earliest press excavated in the country was found at Tirat Yehudah near Lydda. This press has been reconstructed and transferred to the garden of the Israel Museum.

Oil was used as a condiment for various dishes, to fry foods, especially meats, and as a component in certain dishes. Specially purified oils mixed with spices were used as ointments or for medicinal purposes. Sesame oil, produced in a similar way, was particularly fine. Like wine, oil was used as an offering to the gods and for payment of taxes to kings. Oil production was advanced in Ereẓ Israel, as is attested by much documentary evidence, and the discovery of many olive presses in various locations.

[Ze'ev Yeivin]

Post-Biblical Period

CHARACTERISTICS OF JEWISH COOKERY. In their dispersion throughout the world Jews have adopted many dishes of the countries in which they found themselves, adapting them to conform to the requirements of the dietary laws. Economic factors have also played their part in the culinary sphere. Sometimes glamorous dishes have been created by enhancing poverty foods, influenced by local flavors and products.

The laws regarding use of animal food and its preparation require that all meat and poultry, having been killed in accordance with the laws of *sheḥitah, must be entirely drained of *blood. Observance of the dietary laws precludes the mixing or cooking of meat with milk; the Jewish cook is therefore debarred from using dairy products – butter, milk, or cream, etc. – in pastries, desserts, or other dishes which are to be eaten in conjunction with meat. *Parveh* (neutral) foods made with neither milk nor meat may be eaten with both. These include eggs, fish, vegetables, fruit, and liquors. A *parveh* substitute for milk or cream has been introduced into the modern kitchen.

The two main categories of Jewish cooking may be characterized as Oriental (broadly referred to as Sephardi) and Occidental (broadly referred to as Ashkenazi). While Sephardi cookery makes much use of spices, olive oil, rice, pulses, and lamb, Ashkenazi favors beef and bland vegetables, whose flavors are brought out by fats, sugar, and onions. Both feature many similar fowl and pastry dishes, and dishes having similar historical and religious significance. Because of this latter significance there has developed in modern times a sort of "culinary Judaism," by which many people identify with the Jewish religion mainly through this preference for traditional Jewish dishes. Indeed, assimilated Jewry in the orbit of the Hapsburg Empire from as early as the second half of the 19th century knew the conception of "*Fressfroemmigkeit*" for somebody whose devoutness finds its expression mainly or entirely in his eating the proper customary dishes on each holiday.

SEPHARDI AND ASHKENAZI TRADITION. Most of the foods of the Bible maintained their hold in the homes of the communities of the Mediterranean and Middle East where the same products are still grown. Grapes, dates, olives, melons, figs, mulberries, pomegranates, nuts, carobs, citrons, apricots, are still basically used in and around the Holy Land, not only as fresh fruits but as preserves such as dried apricot sheets, carob syrup (*dibbs*), and citron confiture. Pulses and cereals such as beans, lentils, cracked wheat (*burghul*), and spelt (rye) are used for Sephardi dishes as much as potatoes are in the West. The vegetables recorded in the Bible such as leeks, squash (also cucumbers of this family), and onions permeate Middle East cookery both for flavoring and as main dishes stuffed with meat. Cucumbers are preserved with dill, a herb that grows wild in Ereẓ Israel. Mint is used for flavoring many dishes, particularly vegetable salads. Frequently used spices and herbs include garlic in meat, saffron and cumin in cakes, coriander in coffee, and cinnamon not only in desserts but in meat and poultry dishes. Lamb fat and olive oil, so popular in the Bible, continue as the main fats used in Oriental Jewish cooking. The meat of goats and sheep is still eaten in the Middle East rather than beef and poultry. Pastries – usually deep fried – are dipped in honey or syrup among Eastern communities. Some Oriental groups – such as the Yemenites – even bake the bread (called *lakhoʾakh* or *ḥubs*) as in biblical days on the wall of a primitive earthen oven heated with embers, the fire being put out before baking, or bake it like a griddle cake on a rounded iron over embers. Bread is customarily put on the table for every meal, and also salt, symbolizing the covenant (see above).

In Eastern Europe among Ashkenazi communities milk foods and vegetables were the main fare during weekdays owing to impoverished circumstances and the shortage of *kasher* meat. Animals were generally slaughtered for food only for Sabbaths or festivals, or for celebrations. Figuring largely in the diet were *lokshen* (noodles) or other farinaceous food, potatoes, barley, peas, and beans. From time to time these were supplemented by fish. For celebrations of a circumcision or a wedding it was customary to provide fish and meat meals, and to bake festival bread and buns from cake dough, as well as sponge cake, sandwich cake, *fluden* (*fladen*), *strudel*, and egg cookies. In honor of the bride and bridegroom *gilderne yoikh* ("golden broth" of chicken soup) was served. During the summer in Eastern Europe, jams and confections would be prepared from the local fruits, which were added to tea, offered to guests, or served for the Sabbath or on festivals. The juice of raspberries, cherries, and other berries was also preserved. Preserves were made from plums and mushrooms, cucumbers were pickled, and sufficient sauerkraut was prepared for the whole year. In present-day Israel, Jewish cooking has been altered and adapted by each entry of new immigrants in the melting pot process of integration between East and West. This and the introduction of new products, such as avocado, formerly rarely known, has resulted in new trends in Jewish cooking.

Festival Cookery

SABBATH DISHES. For Sabbath and other holidays all sorts and shapes of *ḥallah* breads (called also *barkhes* or *tatsheres*) are baked. In most countries the Sabbath loaves are braided. The loaves are frequently sprinkled with (poppy or sesame) seeds to represent manna. Two loaves represent the double portion of manna gathered in the wilderness before the Sabbath. One of the two *ḥallot* on the tables of Ḥasidim is made of 12 rolls representing the 12 tribes, the loaf being referred to as *yud-bet* (= the number 12; Lev. 24:5–6). Fish is a standard food for Sabbath. The Talmud advises: "When may those who possess less than 50 shekels have the dish of vegetables and fish? Every Friday night of the Sabbath." In Eastern Europe, where fish was costly, the Jewish housewife made *gefilte* (filled) *fish* a popular dish. For *gefilte fish* the flesh is ground up, and bread, egg, onion, sugar, and pepper are added: after the fish is refilled it is stewed in onions. Carp and/or other types of fish may be used. Bukharan Jews eat fried fish dipped in garlic sauce with garlic bread.

A typical Sabbath dish popular in every community because it can be prepared beforehand and cooked overnight is *cholent* (Ashkenazi) – Oriental *ḥamin* – generally made with beans, fat meat, and potatoes. It is placed in a well-heated oven on Friday afternoon and allowed to cook slowly or simmer overnight until ready for the Sabbath meal. Ashkenazim may accompany the *cholent* with *kugel* (boiled pudding), stuffed *helzl* (neck skin), or *kishke* (stuffed derma), or a *lokshen* (noodle) pudding, sometimes made of leaf pastry, or a rice and raisin pudding. Bukharan Jews serve a rice cholent called *baḥsh*, layered with meat, liver, and vegetables, with rice and spices cooked in a bag in water: the liquid is not used. It was customary for gentiles to wait near the synagogue before prayers with kettles of boiling water; they would be given the *baḥsh* bag for cooking and return it after prayers. Bukharan Jews also bake *mamossa* (meat or fruit pie) for Sabbath, and eat cold meat (*yachni*) or *kabab-pieces* of meat and onion, dipped in salt and roasted on a spit before Sabbath. *Kishke* (Ashkenazi stuffed derma) is often eaten as a main dish for Sabbath, its Oriental equivalent being *nakahoris*. Ashkenazim use an onion and flour filling, and eastern communities fill the derma with ground meat, pine nuts, cinnamon, and sharp pepper. Persian Jews eat rice foods (*pilaw*) and a sort of meat pudding called *gipa* (stomach filled with rice). Often served as an appetizer on Sabbath is *pitcha* (also called *cholodny, pilsa, fisnoga, drelyes;* Heb. *regel* kerushah) – jellied calf's foot or jellied chicken with garlic and spices. In Yemen it is called *kur'i*. Other appetizers are chopped (*gehakte*) herring, chopped egg and onion, or chopped liver (Ashkenazi). A traditional accompaniment to the Sabbath meal in Ashkenazi homes is poultry soup – usually served with deep-fried pastas called *mandeln* ("almonds") to symbolize the manna of the Bible. Side dishes include *tsimes* (Ashkenazi), a stew made usually of carrots, parsnips, or plums with potatoes. The Lithuanian *rutabaga* is turnip *tsimes*. Compotes of dried fruits, such as flohmen *kompot* made with the addition of blanched almonds and honey, are a traditional East European Sabbath dessert. *Torten*-sponge cakes, *mandelbrot* – almond cookies – and *strudels*-filled rolled pastries, are of Central European origin. Yemenite Jews serve a traditional Sabbath pastry, similar to *kugel*, cooked overnight, sometimes with cottage cheese, called *ghininūn*, or an overnight baked yeast cake, *kubaneh*. *Pestelas* (sesame-seed-topped pastry filled with pine nuts, meat, onion, and delicately flavored) also called *burekas*, are often served in Sephardi homes after the Sabbath service. So as to be able to pronounce the blessings: *bore peri ha-eẓ*; *ha-gefen*; *ha-adamah*; *mezonot*, before the Sabbath repast and after, Yemenite Jews eat ga'le-roast peanuts, raisins, almonds, fruit, and candy. For *melavveh malkah* on Saturday night Ḥasidim eat a specially cooked barley soup with meat. Wine is drunk at the Sabbath meals, and brandy. Eastern Jews drink arak.

PASSOVER. Passover foods vary in Sephardi and Ashkenazi communities. Ashkenazim exclude rice, while it is served by Sephardim. Most Ashkenazim avoid the use of pepper because it is sometimes mixed with flour and crumbs by traders. Ḥasidim do not eat soaked matzah on Passover except on the last day (in the Diaspora).

The several varieties of *matzah* include *matzah shemurah*, egg *matzah*, and sugar *matzah*. The exclusion of leaven from the home has resulted in a rich menu of *matzah* meal and potato foods for Passover, such as dumplings and pancakes. Popular are the dumplings known as *kneydl* (Ashkenazi) of various types made from either *matzah* meal or broken up *matzah*. Some are filled with meat or liver or fruits, used for soups or side dishes or desserts. Potato flour is largely used in cakes along with finely ground *matzah* meal and nuts. Popular Ashkenazi dishes are *matzah brie* (fried crumbled *matzah* with grated onion), *matzah latkes* (pancakes) and *khremzlakh* (also called *crimsel* or *gres elies; matzah* meal fritters). Wined *matzah kugels* (puddings) have been introduced into modern Jewish cooking. For thickening soups and sauces at Passover fine *matzah* meal or potato flour is used instead of flour: for frying fish or cutlets, a coating of *matzah* meal and egg, and for stuffings, potatoes instead of soaked bread. "Noodles" may be made by making pancakes with beaten eggs and *matzah* meal which, when cooked, are rolled up and cut into strips. They may be dropped into soup before serving. *Matzah kleys* – dumplings – are small balls made from suet mixed with chopped fried onions, chopped parsley, beaten egg, and seasonings, dropped into soup and cooked. In Oriental countries and in old Jerusalem sheep-tail fat was prepared for Passover. Oriental Passover dishes are *fahthūt* (Yemenite) – a soup stew made with *matzah* meal – and Turkish *minas* and *mahmuras* – layers of *matzah* with fillings of cheese, vegetables, or meats. In Sephardi homes *ḥaroset* is served as a treat and not just as a taste. The *khreyn* – horseradish relish – originating as an Ashkenazi Passover dish – is popular all the year round. The radish *eyngemakhts*, still retained as a confiture among Ashkenazim, may have had its culinary beginnings in talmudic days when the radish was referred to as an elixir of life. A Passover beverage is mead, instead of beer, which includes leaven. Raisin wine is also used for the Four Cups at the *Seder*. A *kasher* liquor from potatoes was brewed in Eastern Europe.

SHAVUOT. Serving of dairy dishes on Shavuot is customary among Jews everywhere. In celebration of the giving of the Law from Sinai, Mount-Sinai-shaped sweets and cakes are served in many Eastern and Western communities. Ashkenazi Jews bake saffron bread, butter cookies with cheese, cheese twist or cheese *ḥallah* (in Germany called *kauletsch*, specially for those who have observed the sefirah-counting of the Omer). Popular Shavuot dishes are *blintses* (pancakes) filled with meat or cheese and sour cream, *kreplakh* (dough filled with cheese, meat, groats or fruit, shaped into triangles or hearts and boiled), *strudels* (Germany), cheese cakes (Poland), cheese pies (United States), and *knishes* (yeast dough filled with meat and/or potatoes, cheese or fruit and baked (Lithuania). A dairy beet *borsht* with sour cream, or a cold *chlodnik* (cucumber soup) or *shtshav* (cold sorrel soup) is also served on Shavuot. Some Sephardim bake a Seven Heavens cake to symbolize the "seven heavens" which God rent at the giving of the Torah. Sephardi Jews use ewe's salted cheese and make savory dairy dishes like *shpongous* (a cheese-spinach bake), Cottage cheese, popular everywhere, is associated with legends such as the Israelites' late return to the camp after receiving the Commandments from Mount Sinai when the milk had already soured.

AV. During the Nine Days between the First and Ninth of Av, no wine or meat is eaten (except on the Sabbath) as a sign of mourning for the destruction of the Temple. Both Ashkenazim and Sephardim eat farinaceous and other pastry food baked or boiled, and accompanied with cheese. The fast of the Ninth of Av is observed after a milk meal which includes a *bagel* – a crusty doughnut-shaped bun – or an egg dipped in ashes.

ROSH HA-SHANAH. On Rosh Ha-Shanah the *ḥallah* loaf is baked round or coin-shaped to signify blessings all the year round. All communities eat sweet fruits to evoke a sweet year, and honey for sweetness is added to many dishes. Until after Sukkot, bread is dipped in honey for the benediction instead of the usual salt in order to symbolize a sweet year. On the second night of New Year apples are eaten dipped in honey, also white grapes and watermelons. The *leykaḥ* honey cake is traditional among Ashkenazim, since *lekaḥ* means "portion" and the cake signifies the prayer "Give them a goodly portion."

Sweetened fish dishes with raisins and honey *lebkukhen, leibkuchen*, are primarily eaten in Western homes (originating in Switzerland). A head of a fish served without a tail (or the head of a lamb in Oriental homes) symbolizes, according to the Shulḥan Arukh, "being at the head and not the tail." In many Sephardi homes it is served to the father of the family.

All sorts of fruits and vegetables are selected for eating on Rosh Ha-Shanah because of their symbolic associations and endless possibilities of word play. Sephardim place on the table a *traskal* – a covered basket of fruit and vegetables – and as the father of the family takes out some fruit, those present repeat a suitable verse, as for the pomegranate, "May our merits multiply like pomegranate seeds." Carrot *tsimes* symbolizes prosperity because the slices are coin-shaped and golden in color and is also linked with an involved play of words in German. Ḥasidim use beetroots or beet leaves (*selek*) in the blessings *she-yistalleku oyeveinu* "to get rid of our enemies"; *bkeila*, a dish of this green leaf and beans, is popular among Tunisian Jewry. The Yemenite *hilbeh* (fenugreek sauce) is called *rubiya* in Hebrew and therefore eaten to signify *sheh-yirbu* ("to multiply").

EVE OF AND END OF DAY OF ATONEMENT. On the eve of the Day of Atonement Ashkenazim eat ladder-or bird-trimmed bread so that prayers should rise quicker to Heaven. In the morning many communities would distribute the loaves free at the entrance to the graveyard where people visited the graves of their forefathers, and honey cakes with a glass of wine. Before the fast, atonement (*kapparah*) meat is generally eaten. Ashkenazi homes usually serve *kreplakh* in the soup of the boiled *kapparah chicken* (though in many families the chicken is given to the poor). The white-feathered bird, symbolic of purity, assumes the role of the scapegoat slaughtered as a sin offering.

The fast is broken in Central European communities by eating *barkes*, or *shneken* – buns with cinnamon and nuts and/or raisins. To restock the body with salt, herring dishes such as chopped herring, pickled herring, or *zise-zoyre* (sweet and sour) pickled jellied fish are taken. Many Sephardi communities break the fast with spiced coffee-cinnamon (Dutch), cardamon (Syrian and Egyptian), and ginger with these spices (Yemen). Some Middle Eastern communities – Turkish, Greek, Iraqi – break the fast with a snow-white almond or other seed drink called *mizzo* or *soubiya* or *soumada*, the white color symbolizing purity. lraqi Jews eat *chadjoobadah* cardamon cakes. Italians serve *dolce Rebecca* (spiced mocha cake), and many Oriental groups eat sesame (*sumsum*) cakelets. *Bamya* (okra) in tomato sauce is an Iraqi end of Day of Atonement dish.

SUKKOT. Dishes traditional to Sukkot are adopted from the lands of the Diaspora, mostly because they proved convenient for serving in the *sukkah*. These include cabbage-meat *borsht* (Russian origin), Hungarian *goulash* – meat stew with paprika and onions: *kibbeh* – a Middle Eastern *burghul*-coated deep-fried meat dish served with various fillings; *kasher* Greek *moussaka* – eggplant meat casserole; *holeptses* also called *praakes, galuptzes* – rice and ground meat rolled in cabbage leaves – and *sarmis* – vine leaves filled with rice, pine nuts, and chopped meat filling. Still popular is the *fluden* (also known as *fladen*) – a layered dessert of dough and fruits symbolic of the harvested crops referred to in Judeo-German cooking records of the 12th century. For Hoshana Rabba, the seventh day of Sukkot, the *ḥallah* loaf is sometimes marked with a hand, symbolic of reaching for blessings, or key-shaped, that the door of heaven may be opened to admit prayers.

SIMḤAT TORAH AND SABBATH BERESHIT. For Simḥat Torah a round carrot sandwich (or slices) with honey symbolizes gold coins and the worth of the Torah. Sabbath *Bereshit* was formerly known in Vilna as the "honey Sabbath." The wives of religious functionaries baked honey cake with the honey their husbands received as a gift from the synagogue wardens for the festivals, and sold them. The proceeds enabled them to stock up with food and timber for the winter months.

HANUKKAH. For Ḥanukkah, Jews of all communities eat pastry and potato preparations fried in oil as a reminder of the miracle of the cruse of oil at the rededication of the Temple. Ashkenazim called them *latkes*, or *fasputshes*, or *pontshkes*. They are called *zalaviyye* (Yemen), *dushpire* (Bukhara), *ata-if* (Iraq), *spanzes* (Tripoli), and by Sephardim in general *birmenailes*. Hence the Israel *sufganiyyot* – doughnuts – of Ḥanukkah and the *levivot* (*latkes* – potato cakes) have a long tradition. A popular East European salad of this festival is the *retekh salat* of radish, turnip, olives, and onions fried in goose fat with *gribenes* or *grivn* (cracklings), all the ingredients being popular in the Maccabean era. As fat for Ḥanukkah is rendered from the goose used for Passover, this poultry (and related game like the Dutch *ganzebord*) is a popular Ḥanukkah dish, and *grivn* are often served with the latkes. In Czechoslovakia a shortbread cookie is made of goose cracklings (*grameln*) for this holiday. Yemen Jews eat *laḥis gizar* on Ḥanukkah, a sort of carrot stew, carrots being the vegetable in season.

TU BI-SHEVAT. As Sabbath Be-Shalaḥ falls only a few days before Tu bi-Shevat (the Fifteenth of Shevat) many foods for this day are linked to the New Year of Trees. Dutch Jews make *Be-Shallaḥ* calling it *kugel met waatz* to symbolize the manna and sauce for the Red Sea where the Egyptians were drowned pursuing the Israelites. Swiss French and some groups from Germany serve a wheat garnish in broth for this reason. Italians make a dish called *ruota di faraone* (Pharaoh's wheel). *Pomerantsen* – candied citrus fruits – are popular on this day.

Fresh and dried fruits are served to symbolize the harvests of the trees planted on Tu bi-Shevat in the Holy Land. The *bokser* – carob fruit (St. John's bread) – has found its way around the world for this festival. In Switzerland and other places 15 fruits to coincide with *Tu* (= 15) are eaten. Rich dried fruit *strudels* are often served on Tu bi-Shevat as harvest symbols.

In many Sephardi communities a home service is held at the table where blessings are pronounced over wheat, barley, grapes, figs, pomegranates, olives, and honey. Sephardim would distribute *ma'ot perot* ("fruit money"). At "white-red wine" parties each child is presented with a *bolsa de frutas* ("bag of fruit"). Ḥasidic groups arrange large fruit parties for which in the Diaspora they try to obtain fruit from Ereẓ Israel.

PURIM. The Purim festival has a long culinary history. Recorded in the humorous tractate *Massekhet Purim* written by Kalonymus b. Kalonymus is the Purim menu listing 27 different meat dishes. All communities make pastries representing Haman's hats, Haman's pockets, or Haman's ears, They are known by different names but similarly filled with poppyseed (Ger. *mohn* – a sound resembling "Haman"). Some Ashkenazi groups also fill them with *povidl* – plum jam – to commemorate the rescue of Jews in Bohemia about 250 years ago when a plum merchant was saved from persecution. In Italy *ciambella di Purim* is a popular pastry, as are *Hamantashen* in Eastern Europe and *mohn plaetzen* – poppyseed cookies – in Western Europe. Haman's ears (Heb. *oznei haman*) – a fried pastry sprinkled with sugar are called *Hamansoren* (Holland), *Hamman-Muetzen* (Germany), *Schunzuchen* (Switzerland and French-Lorraine), *Heizenblauzen* (Austria), *diples* (Greece), *shamleya* (Turkey), and *orecchie de Aman* (Italy). According to folk tradition the custom originates from the punishment of criminals whose ears were cut off before hanging. *Hamantashen* are symbolic of Haman's pockets stuffed with bribe money. The Purim *ḥallah* loaf (given the Russian name *keylitsh*) is giant-sized and braided, representing the long ropes used to hang Haman. Sephardim fill similar pastries with meat, vegetables, or fruit. For *mishlo'aḥ-manot* ("sending of presents") on Purim, women in Eastern communities make sugar-starch fingers in various colors, and non-Jews in Eastern lands call Purim *ʾīd al-sukar*, the sugar festival. It was customary in Persia to distribute, after the reading of the Book of Esther, *ha'alva kashka*, a pleasantly spiced dessert. All Sephardi and Eastern communities bake sweet cakes filled with almonds or other nuts, all sorts of marzipan, special *puralis* cake containing a whole egg, and various sorts of pancakes called in Iraq *zingula*. In Salonika and Istanbul, women baked *kulimas, barikas*, or *sambusach-khavsh* – dough filled with meat.

See also *Cookbooks.

[Molly Lyons Bar-David and Yom-Tov Lewinski]

BIBLIOGRAPHY: Dalman, Arbeit, 4 (1935), 260ff.; R.J. Forbes, *Studies in Ancient Technology*, 3 (1955), 50–105; C. Singer, et al. (eds.), *A History of Technology*, 1 (1954), 270–85; 2 (1956), 103ff.; N. de Garis Davies, *The Tomb of Nakht at Thebes* (1917), pl. 22; U. Cassuto, *A Commentary on the Book of Genesis*. 2 vols. (1961), passim; idem, *A Commentary on the Book of Exodus* (1967), passim; J.B. Pritchard, *Winery, Defenses and Soundings at Gibeon* (1964), 25–27, figs. 54–55; Z. Yeivin, in: *Attiqot* (English Series), 3 (1966), 52–62; S. Krauss, *Kadmoniyyot ha-Talmud*, 2 (1929), 93–276; A. Wiener, *Die juedischen Speisegesetze* (1895); J. Elzet (Zlotnik), *Yidishe Maakholim* (1920); M. Kosover, in: *Yuda A. Yofe-Bukh* (1958), 1–145; B. Safran, *Di Yidishe Kikh in Ale Lender* (1930); Y. Kafah, *Halikhot Teiman* (1962), chs. 1, 3–5; L. Cornfeld, *Ha-Bishul ha-Tov* (1967); idem, *Israeli Cookery* (1962); M.L. Bar-David, *Jewish Cooking for Pleasure* (1965); idem, *Sefer Bishul Folklori* (1964).

FORCALQUIERS, village in the Basses-Alpes department, S.E. France, approximately 50 mi. (about 80 km.) east of Avignon. The medieval Jewish community, which existed at least from 1275, occupied a separate quarter and owned a synagogue. The ledger of a single merchant of Forcalquiers records 20 Jews as his customers between 1330 and 1332. In 1351, possibly still in the aftermath of the *Black Death, anti-Jewish disorders broke out in Forcalquiers in which the population of the surrounding villages also took part. It is reported that in 1424 several inhabitants of Forcalquiers and Manosque formed a plot to kill all the Jews in the town. In 1472, a citizen of Forcalquiers was appointed guardian (*conservateur*) of all the Jews of Provence. The community in Forcalquiers was among the first to feel the effects of the definitive decrees of expulsion of 1486. Toward the end of the 18th century, some Jewish merchants, originating from the *Comtat Venaissin, attempted to settle in Forcalquiers but were expelled in 1775. In 1940 there were 72 Jews in the labor camp which had been set up in the district. About 14 Jewish families, mostly assisted by refugees' organization, were registered in Forcalquiers in 1942.

BIBLIOGRAPHY: Levi, in: REJ, 37 (1898), 259–65; 41 (1900), 274–5; C. Bernard, *Essai historique sur ... Forcalquiers* (1905), 90–91, 99, 122, 130, 153; Z. Szajkowski, *Franco-Judaica* (1962), nos. 14, 337; idem, *Analytical Franco-Jewish Gazetteer* (1966), 154.

[Bernhard Blumenkranz]

FORCED (Slave) LABOR. The term forced labor (*Zwangsarbeit*) is not well defined. Forced labor is commonly understood as an employment relationship of a member of a persecuted political or a specific ideological (*weltanschauliche*) grouping, or an ethnic group, or a people, a relationship arisen by force, and indissoluble, that did not consider the abilities, age, or sex of the forced laborer, that meant defenselessness concerning legal rights and a high rate of mortality due to bad living and working conditions as well as National Socialistic persecution. In Anglo-Saxon usage the term forced labor is distinguished from slave labor that ghetto and concentration camp prisoners and Jews in specific Forced Labor Camps (FLC) had to perform. Among other things slave labor is characterized by a considerably higher rate of mortality. In German-speaking usage the term slave labor has not become common, because slaves were without rights and they were exploited, but unlike SS and other NS organizations, the slaveholder ordinarily was interested in keeping the slave alive.

In the German Reich after January 30, 1933, at first prisoners of the early concentration camps were recruited to forced labor, for instance, politically persecuted Social Democrats or Communists. It was then already that murder was involved. From the end of 1938 on, German Jews were next and forced labor became an element of their persecution by the NS state. It was not until the outbreak of World War II, and the occupation of Poland, that forced laborers were recruited in vast numbers, when hundreds of thousands of Polish people were deported to the Reich. Also in the occupied Polish territory itself many forced laborers were deployed. From October 1939, the Jewish residents there became liable to work, later having a general duty of forced labor. Within the Reich forced laborers worked in agriculture, mining, and industry, as well as to enlarge military infrastructure.

The significant importance of forced labor for the Reich and its warfare becomes obvious regarding German agriculture. Without approximately 2 million foreign laborers, by the end of 1940, sufficient production of food to supply all the inhabitants would have become impossible. From autumn 1941 on the German wartime economy depended without other options on foreign labor. Since not enough foreigners came voluntarily, more and more forced recruitment was utilized, especially from spring 1942 on by Fritz Sauckel, general plenipotentiary for the employment of labor (*Generalbevollmaechtigter fuer den Arbeitseinsatz*). The largest number of foreign laborers in the area of the Reich was registered in August 1944 at 7,615,970. Among these were about 1.9 million prisoners of war and 5.7 million civilians. Of the 7.6 million, 2.8 million were from the Soviet Union, 1.7 million from Poland, and 1.3 million from France. Altogether, during World War II, up to 13.5 million men, women, and children were brought to the Reich and forced to labor.

With the expansion of the war and the successive occupation of a wider territory in Europe, forced laborers were displaced from those areas into the Reich, from 1942 onwards mainly inhabitants of the occupied Soviet Union. In addition, more and more forced labor was deployed within the occupied territories themselves. Likewise, in countries allied to the Reich, specific ethnic groups and other groupings were forced to labor. For example, in Bulgaria from 1941 onwards, there were Jewish labor battalions as well as Turkish and Greek ones. All of them worked particularly for the expansion of an infrastructure essential for the war. In Hungary, in addition to the Jews, also Serbs and Romanians were recruited for labor battalions. The importance of the Jewish labor battalions for Hungary becomes apparent, when it is observed that in October 1943 more than 112,000 Jews had to labor for the Hungarian army, and in October 1944 approximately 180,000. In Vichy-France as well, where from October 1940 there had been a special labor service for foreigners, among them many Jews who had fled from Germany and Austria and who, in the Groupements des Travailleurs Étrangers (GTE), were forced to carry out many kinds of labor. Also in Fascist Italy, in Croatia, Romania, and Slovakia, to a variable extent, people were obliged to do forced labor, among them, many Jews.

In the Reich there were considerable differences concerning the treatment of forced laborers. Subject to the most brutal conditions were the prisoners of concentration camps, including their subcamps (*Aussenlager*). The actual living conditions of the other forced laborers depended on the following factors:

1) Their ranking according to National Socialist race doctrine: Norwegians and Dutch were regarded as "Aryan" and "Germanic" and put on top of the hierarchy. Therefore they had to cope with less discrimination. People from the Soviet Union (but not people from the still independent Baltic States until 1940) were regarded as members of an inferior race and therefore were treated most brutally.

2) Country of origin: While people from the disintegrated states like Poland and Yugoslavia (insofar as Serbs and Slovenians were concerned) had no protection from their governments, French, Croatians, and Norwegians could at least hope for intervention by their governments, even though they were dependent on the Reich. People from allied countries, such as Bulgaria and Hungary, had conditions most similar to German workers. However, even these could not return home freely, at the earliest from 1943 onwards, and were exposed to discrimination in their German domiciles and their workplaces.

3) The work location: There were great differences depending on whether a forced laborer was deployed in rural areas or in the cities. In the country, surveillance and persecution by the NS authorities were less comprehensive and basic food was easier to come by. In the cities not only resources essential for survival like foodstuffs and clothing were hard to

get, also the oppression machinery was better developed and the threat of air raids was much more serious.

4) The firm: The larger the company and the more impersonal the contact between Germans and foreigners became, the more probable were brutal living and labor conditions. In big companies, where Germans and foreigners hardly interacted at all, bad living and labor conditions were more than likely.

There were roughly three phases of forced labor:

The first phase was the prewar period. Between 1933 and 1939 forced labor was of marginal importance. It was mainly used as a way to oppress political dissidents, and, from 1938 onwards, for the persecution of German Jews.

Phase Two began with the German aggression against Poland and ended with the turn of the year 1942. At that time, forced labor became a mass phenomenon. With the occupation of a wider territory many people came under the sway of the NS leaders. Therefore, even in Libya and Tunisia, Jews had to work for the German forces (*Wehrmacht*). At the same time, against the European Jews, forced labor was used as an element of mass murder. A similar attitude can also be observed in countries allied to the German Reich.

With the territorial changes, the Hungarians obtained control over parts of Slovakia, Romania, and Yugoslavia, including non-Hungarian parts of the population. In addition, forced labor tasks for Hungarian Jews were gradually increased and intensified. After the occupation of Yugoslavian and Greek territories, Bulgaria acted on a similar basis. Here, besides the Jews and Turks, forced labor was directed mainly against Greeks, not the Macedonian population, as the parts of Macedonia occupied in April 1941 (Vardar-Macedonia) were seen as an integral part of the state by the Bulgarian leaders, the core, of medieval Bulgaria.

The third and last phase began in 1943 and ended with the surrender of the Reich in May 1945. With the change of the war situation also the character of forced labor changed distinctly. On the one hand, discrimination against East Europeans with regard to labor laws and social rights were de jure gradually toned down. On the other hand, the threat to existence, from the security forces of the NS state, became more and more grave. In particular the change in jurisdiction concerning offenses by forced laborers from the judiciary to the *Reichssicherheitshauptamt* (RSHA) resulted in considerably more brutal persecution for even the slightest infraction. The RSHA sent many Poles and Soviet citizens (*Ostarbeiter*) to concentration camps, where most of them were murdered. During the last months of the war, arbitrary measures increased and grew to real mass murder; mainly East Europeans were the victims.

Jews and Forced Labor

The situation of Jewish forced laborers under German rule was different from all other cases. For them, in the occupied territories, there was special jurisdiction. At the latest from summer 1941 onwards, the National Socialist leaders had only one aim: the murder of all Jews. Accordingly, the phases of forced labor that involved Jews differ from the general kind of forced labor. For example, judicial reforms, especially for the East Europeans, did not concern Jews. Furthermore, certain factors did not affect their living conditions: within the Reich Jews were not designated to work in agriculture. Some of the allied countries, like Bulgaria and Croatia, were not interested in saving their Jewish citizens who were living in the German sphere of influence, and therefore they exposed them to death.

The German and Austrian Jews were the first to be systematically used for forced labor. From December 1938, all unemployed Jews and those on welfare were subjected to "locked-up labor" (*geschlossener Arbeitseinsatz*), organized by the employment offices. Their employees were instructed to put them in separate platoons or camps. All Jews, regardless of their educational background, were employed and remunerated as unskilled workers. In July 1939, already 20,000 Jews were in labor service working in road construction and underground engineering, in the construction of canals, and in dam projects, as well as on waste deposit sites.

After the war had begun, also more and more Jewish women were seized for forced labor. From autumn 1940 onwards, all Jewish men and women fit for work were conscripted and forced to work at various jobs, mostly in industry. In summer 1941, over 51,000 people were working as forced laborers, which represented about 30 per cent of the approximately 167,000 Jews still living in the territory of the Reich. These had to wear a special armband for identification. By January 1943, because of the deportation of many to the exterminations camps, their number was reduced to around 20,000. After the end of the so-called *Fabrikaktion*, in February 1943, another 12,000 were deported, and the remaining Jews (mostly "protected" by their intermarriage status) were forced to work until the end of the war. In autumn 1944, also so-called half-Jews (*Mischlinge*) had to work in "locked-up labor" for the Organisation Todt (OT), and were deployed in the Reich or in France.

In occupied Poland, the so-called *Generalgouvernement*, from October 1939 on, male Jews were on labor duty between the age 14 and 60, and later also women. This labor duty, however, did not yet lead to universal confinement of Jews in labor camps. There were numerous free de facto working relationships. Unlike the situation in the Reich, ghettos for the Jewish population were installed in many Polish cities. Some of the Jews detained there had to work outside, others were deployed in ghetto workshops. They worked for municipal institutions, for the ghetto administration, and for private firms based in and around the ghettos.

Besides the ghettos, a system of FLCs was developed. In summer 1942 up to 1.5 million Jews were in detention, and about half of them were in forced labor. The FLC were expanded especially from July 1942 on, after Heinrich *Himmler ordered the annihilation of all Polish Jews by the end of the year. Only those who performed forced labor in the arms industry were to be kept alive. These FLCs were run by the SS, and therefore the living and internment conditions were comparable to those in concentration camps. But even Jews from the FLCs and from the ghettos performing essential war labor were deported to the exterminations camps and murdered, or brought to concentration camps and forced to work there. The conditions were so bad that many Jews died of exhaustion after only a few weeks or months, if not selected out as "unfit for work" (*arbeitsunfaehig*) and murdered.

In the occupied territories of the Soviet Union, after the mass shootings in 1941, similar conditions existed. The Jews there were put into labor platoons and facilities, forced to work, e.g., for the *Wehrmacht*, and they, as well, were detained in ghettos and FLCs. Also the majority of these Jews, even if engaged in essential war work, were murdered, and only a few were deported to concentration camps to further exploit their productive capacity.

The conditions of the Jews doing forced labor in countries allied to the Reich varied greatly. The Hungarian Jewish labor battalions, especially the ones deployed on the eastern front or at mines in Bor, Serbia, as well as the Romanian labor battalions doing road and railway construction work and the Bulgarian labor battalions that were used for the expansion of the infrastructure, some of them also working for the OT, had to suffer from horrendous living and internment conditions similar to those in the concentrations camps of the SS. However, the circumstances of Italian Jews, in forced labor from 1942 on, were better. In Italy; probably none of the Jews died there, whereas in the Hungarian labor battalions tens of thousands were killed.

In spring 1944 the Nazis again changed their policy toward the Jewish forced laborers. Even though, until then, there was no provision made for the deployment of Jewish KZ prisoners in the Reich outside the concentration camp complex of Auschwitz, now, because of lack of workers, up to 100,000 Hungarian Jews were selected in Auschwitz for labor service in the territory of the Reich. Those Jews had to labor almost exclusively in the arms industry and for the construction of production facilities underground. Due to the disastrous conditions there and the very hard labor, the death rate was enormous.

After the end of World War II forced labor was not taken into account by the compensation laws decreed by the Federal Republic of Germany between 1953 and 1965. Only the imprisonment in ghettos, FLCs, and concentration camps was compensated, but only for a select circle of survivors. Most of the surviving forced laborers originated from Eastern Europe and returned to their home countries after the war. They did not receive any compensation because West Germany refused to made payments into Eastern Bloc countries.

The German Democratic Republic refused, on principle, to pay former East European forced laborers any benefits for the crimes of the National Socialists. The New York-based *Conference on Jewish Material Claims Against the German Nation, between the 1950s and the 1960s, succeeded in getting payments for former forced laborers in a handful of West German firms, such as I.G. Farbenindustrie, AEG/Telefunken, and Siemens. However, the majority of the forced laborers could not receive any compensation payments until the creation of the "Remembrance, Responsibility and Future" Foundation in 2000. From the year 2001 on approximately 1.6 million people received up to DM15,000 from the Foundation.

BIBLIOGRAPHY: HISTORY: E.L. Homze, *Foreign Labor in Nazi Germany* (1967); U. Herbert (ed.), *Europa und der "Reichseinsatz." Auslaendische Zivilarbeiter, Kriegsgefangene und KZ-Haeftlinge in Deutschland 1938–1945* (1991); H. Mommsen and M. Krieger, *Das Volkswagenwerk und seine Arbeiter im Dritten Reich* (1996); W. Gruner, *Der geschlossene Arbeitseinsatz deutscher Juden. Zur Zwangsarbeit als Element der Verfolgung 1938–1943* (1997); U. Herbert, *Fremdarbeiter. Politik und Praxis des "Auslaender-Einsatzes" in der Kriegswirtschaft des Dritten Reiches* (1999); A. Schaefer, *Zwangsarbeiter und NS-Rassenpolitik. Russische und polnische Arbeitskraefte in Wuerttemberg 1939–1945* (2000); W. Gruner, *Zwangsarbeit und Verfolgung. Oesterreichische Juden im NS-Staat 1938–45* (2000); M Spoerer, *Zwangsarbeit unter dem Hakenkreuz. Auslaendische Zivilarbeiter, Kriegsgefangene und Haeftlinge im Deutschen Reich und im besetzten Europa 1939–1945* (2001); M. Spoerer and J. Fleischhacker, "Forced Laborers in Nazi Germany: Categories, Numbers and Survivors," in: *Journal of Interdisciplinary History* 33 (2002), 169–204. BELGIUM: F. Selleslagh, *L'emploi de la main d'oeuvre belge sous l'occupation* (1972). BULGARIA: J. Hoppe, "Zwangsarbeit von Juden in Bulgarien waehrend des Zweiten Weltkriegs. Die juedischen Arbeitsbataillone 1941–1944," in: *Suedost-Forschungen* 64 (2006). FRANCE: J. Evrard, *La déportation des travailleurs français dans le IIIe Reich* (1972). HUNGARY: R. Braham, *The Wartime System of Labor Service in Hungary. Varieties of Experiences* (1995). NETHERLANDS: B.A. Sijes, *De Arbeidsinzet. De gedwongen arbeid van Nederlanders in Duitsland, 1940–1945* (1990). ROMANIA: R. Ioanid, *The Holocaust in Romania. The Destruction of Jews and Gypsies under the Antonescu Regime, 1940–1944* (2000). INDEMNIFICATION: B.B. Ferencz, *Less Than Slaves: Jewish Forced labor and the Quest for Compensation* (1979); C. Pross, *Wiedergutmachung. Der Kleinkrieg gegen die Opfer* (1988); C. Goschler, *Wiedergutmachung. Westdeutschland und die Verfolgten des Nationalsozialismus, 1945–1954* (1992); P. Zumbansen (ed.), *NS-Forced labor: Remembrance and Responsibility. Legal and Historical Observations* (2002); S.E. Eizenstat, *Imperfect Justice. Looted Assets, Slave Labor, and the Unfinished Business of World War II* (2003); S.S. Spiliotis, *Verantwortung und Rechtsfrieden. Die Stiftungsinitiative der deutschen Wirtschaft* (2003); H.G. Hockerts (ed.), *Nach der Verfolgung. Wiedergutmachung nationalsozialistischen Unrechts in Deutschland?* (2003).

[Jens Hoppe (2nd ed.)]

FORD, ALEXANDER (1908–1984), Polish film producer. Born in Lodz, Ford worked in Palestine in 1933 with a Polish unit making a story-documentary, *Sabra*. His *Droga Młodych* ("Road of the Young," 1936), banned in Poland, was exhibited in Paris. He became the director of Film Polski in 1945. He gained recognition for *Ulica Graniczna* ("Border Street," Venice gold medal, 1948), which dealt with the Warsaw ghetto. *Młodość Chopina* ("Youth of Chopin," 1952), *Piaétka z Ulicy Barskiej* ("Five Boys of Barski Street," Cannes Festival Prize, 1954); and *Krzyzacy* ("Crusader," 1960). Prevented from making a film on Janusz *Korczak, Ford left Poland in 1968 and settled in Israel in 1970.

FORD, HARRISON, (1942–), U.S. actor. Born in Chicago, Illinois, the son of a Russian Jewish mother and an Irish father, Ford's first career was as a professional carpenter. Dabbling as a film actor, he was noticed in a small role in George Lucas' *American Graffiti* (1973). Four years later, Lucas picked Ford for the lead role of Han Solo in his mega-blockbuster *Star Wars*, and Ford became an "instant" star. Steven Spielberg subsequently chose Ford for the leading role in his Indiana Jones cinematic trilogy.

Ford's other films include *The Conversation* (1974), *Heroes* (1977), *Force 10 from Navarone* (1978), *Hanover Street* (1979), *Apocalypse Now* (1979), *The Frisco Kid* (1979), *Star Wars: The Empire Strikes Back* (1980), *Blade Runner* (1982), *Star Wars: Return of the Jedi* (1983), *Witness* (1985), *The Mosquito Coast* (1986), *Working Girl* (1988), *Frantic* (1988), *Presumed Innocent* (1990), *Regarding Henry* (1991), *Patriot Games* (1992), *The Fugitive* (1993), *Clear and Present Danger* (1994), *Sabrina* (1995), *The Devil's Own* (1997), *Air Force One* (1997), *Six Days Seven Nights* (1998), *Random Hearts* (1999), *What Lies Beneath* (2000), *K-19: The Widowmaker* (2002), and *Hollywood Homicide* (2003).

In 1986 he was nominated for an Academy Award for Best Actor in the dramatic film *Witness*. In 1996 the U.S. Academy of Science Fiction, Fantasy, and Horror Films awarded him a Lifetime Achievement Award. In 1998, 1999, and 2000 he won the People's Choice Award for Favorite Movie Actor. And in 2002, Ford was presented with the Golden Globe's Cecil B. DeMille Award, which honors a performer's outstanding contribution to the entertainment field. In 1997 he was chosen by *People Magazine* as one of the 50 Most Beautiful People in the World, and in 1998 the magazine dubbed him "The Sexiest Man Alive." Ford is credited with having the highest worldwide box-office grosses of any actor in history.

ADD. BIBLIOGRAPHY: G. Jenkins, *Harrison Ford: Imperfect Hero* (1998); B. Duke, *Harrison Ford* (2004).

[Jonathan Licht / Ruth Beloff (2nd ed.)]

°FOREIRO (Forerius, Forerio), FRANCISCO (1510–1581), Portuguese Dominican and Hebrew scholar. Foreiro evinced a marked linguistic ability at an early age and was sent to Paris to study Greek and Hebrew. He represented King Sebastian of Portugal at the Council of Trent, where he was jointly responsible for preparing the *Index librorum prohibitorum* (Rome, 1564). His Latin translation of Isaiah from the Hebrew, *Isaiae prophetae vetus et nova ex hebraico versio, cum commentario*, was published in Venice in 1563, and he prepared a Hebrew lexicon as well as commentaries to the Prophets, Job, Psalms, and the biblical books ascribed to Solomon; all these remained unprinted.

BIBLIOGRAPHY: J. Quétif and J. Echard, *Scriptores Ordinis Praedicatorum*, 2 (Paris, 1721), 261f.; *Nouvelle Biographie Universelle*, 18 (1858), 170.

[Raphael Loewe]

FOREMAN, CARL (1914–1984), U.S. writer, producer, and director. Born in Chicago, Foreman saw army service during World War II, after which he began movie scriptwriting and prepared the scenarios for films such as *So This Is New York* (1948), *Champion* (1949), *Home of the Brave* (1949), *The Clay Pigeon* (1949), *Young Man with a Horn* (1950), *The Men* (1950), *Cyrano de Bergerac* (1950), *High Noon* (1952), *The Sleeping Tiger* (1954), *A Hatful of Rain* (1957), and *Bridge on the River Kwai* (1957). Called before a congressional committee during the McCarthy era, he declined to testify on whether he was a member of the Communist Party on the grounds of the Fifth Amendment; in 1956 he himself chose to testify before Congress, and was given what he described as "a clean bill of political health."

From the early 1950s he lived and worked in London, and headed his own production company there. He wrote and produced *Guns of Navarone* (1961); wrote, produced, and directed *Victors* (1963); produced *Born Free* (1965), *MacKenna's Gold* (1969), *The Virgin Soldiers* (1969), *Living Free* (1972); wrote and produced *Young Winston* (1972). He served as president of the Writer's Guild in England (1968), board member of the British Film Institute, and honorary president of the Screen Writers Guild of Israel (where he conducted a course in screenwriting).

Foreman returned to the U.S. in 1975, where he wrote such films as *Force 10 from Navarone* (1978); *EB* (1980); and *When Time Rain Out* (1980). In 1958 he was a winner of the Academy Award for Best Screenplay Based on Material from Another Medium for *Bridge on the River Kwai*. However, as he had been blacklisted at the time and received no screen credit, the Oscar was awarded to him posthumously in 1984. In his lifetime, Foreman earned five other screenwriting Oscar nominations and a Golden Globe nomination. As a producer, he was nominated six times for a Laurel Award.

[Ruth Beloff (2nd ed.)]

FOREMAN, MILTON J. (1862–1935), U.S. public official and army officer. Foreman was born in Chicago and was admitted to the bar in 1899. For the next 12 years he served on the Chicago City Council and held a number of other municipal positions. His interests, however, centered increasingly on his career in the Illinois National Guard, in which he first enlisted in 1895. Foreman served as a captain in the Spanish-American War, saw action along the Mexican border in 1916, and was a colonel with the field artillery in Europe during World War I. After the war he continued to rise in rank, retiring as lieutenant general in 1931. A prominent figure in the founding of the American Legion in 1919, Foreman was chairman of its first executive committee and later served as its national commander.

FORGERIES. Since the essential characteristic of a forgery is its intent to deceive, the pseudo-epigraphical literature, which consists of religious admonitions and prophecies ascribed to the biblical patriarchs in order to give them greater spiritual force (and similar writings found among the *Dead Sea Scrolls of the same period), are not in this category. There has been much controversy over the midrashic christological excerpts included by Raymond *Martini (13th century) in his *Pugio Fidei*: S. *Lieberman maintains that they derive from originals now lost; Y. *Baer, that they are fabrications. In the course of the scholarly discussions that followed the archaeological discoveries of the 19th and 20th centuries, many of them, e.g., the *Moabite Stone and the Dead Sea Scrolls, were denounced by some skeptics as forgeries. In 1883 M.W. Shapira attempted to sell to the British Museum for a fabulous sum certain Hebrew manuscript fragments of the Bible, purportedly from an ancient scroll of the book of Deuteronomy of the 9th or 10th century B.C.E. He was denounced at the time as a forger, but since the discovery of the Dead Sea Scrolls, some scholars have maintained that they may not have been forgeries. However, much material that passed through Shapira's hands as a dealer was certainly fabricated or altered. The Karaite scholar Abraham *Firkovich (1785–1874), in his attempts to prove the antiquity of the Karaites and, in particular, their settlement in the Crimea, published a number of obviously forged tombstone inscriptions and manuscript colophons. In addition, in view of his sectarian enthusiasm, a certain suspicion may be entertained about the details in any of the codices that passed through his hands (as also in the case of Shapira). At the first rumblings of the Reform movement in Judaism, Saul *Berlin (1740–1794), the brilliant son of Hirschel *Levin and rabbi of Berlin, produced a collection, *Besamim Rosh* (1793), purporting to be responsa by the medieval scholar R. Asher of Toledo, which ostensibly favored the new tendencies; when this was discovered, Berlin was driven into retirement (see R. Margoliot, in: *Aresheth*, 1 (1959), 424–5, no. 1737). In 1907–1909 S.J. *Friedlander published a substantial part of the fifth order of the Jerusalem Talmud from a Spanish manuscript dated 1212, which he claimed to have discovered in Turkey. It was, however, no more than a mosaic of passages from other parts of the Talmud, and after some initial excitement the work was dismissed as a fabrication.

Eliakim *Carmoly (1802–1875), rabbi of Brussels, published in profusion documents which he claimed to have in his rich library, but since some of them were obvious fabrications and some "improved," he undermined all confidence in what might have been genuine. B.H. *Auerbach's (1808–1872) edition of the *Sefer ha-Eshkol* (1868–69) by Abraham of Narbonne was also subjected to attack as a forgery. L. *Goldschmidt (1871–1950) admitted that in his youth he forged the book *Baraita de-Ma'aseh Bereshit* (cf. E.S. Rimalt, in: *Aresheth*, 1 (1959), 484–5). On the other hand, Goldschmidt leveled accusations of forgery against collectors of Hebrew printed books who made them appear as if they were incunabula (cf. L. Goldschmidt, *Hebrew Incunables* (1948)). H. Lieberman (b. 1892), the bibliographer, also deals with forged title pages (KS, 31 (1955/56) 397–8). G. *Scholem and his students discovered a number of forgeries in kabbalistic literature. In recent years with the increase in collectors of Jewish ritual art, very large numbers of forgeries in this sphere have been placed on the market, many of them very ingenious. Among the favorite methods are the appending of purportedly old inscriptions to modern objects, or the skillful adaptation of secular bric-à-brac to ostensibly Jewish purposes. Forged shekels (some of them bearing modern Hebrew lettering!) have been in circulation since the Renaissance period, having a special sentimental appeal to both Jews and Christians.

BIBLIOGRAPHY: C. Roth, in: *Commentary*, 43 (1967), 84–86.

[Cecil Roth]

FORGERY. Forgery of documents is not, either in biblical or in talmudic law, a criminal offense: it may be an instrument for the perpetration of *fraud and come within the general prohibition of fraudulent acts (Lev. 19:35; Deut. 25:13–16) or fraudulent words (Lev. 25:14). Nevertheless, it is a recognized evil which the law is called upon to prevent, and there are detailed provisions in the Talmud for the making of legally binding documents in such a manner that they cannot be forged: thus, documents must be written on and with material that cannot be effaced (Git. 19a et al.) and is enduring (Git. 22b, 23a); precautions must be taken that no space be left between the text of the document and the signatures, so that nothing could be inserted after signing (BB 162–7). The rule evolved that a document (**Shetar*) was valid only if executed in the manner of unforgeable bills (*Ke-Tikkun Shitrei Yisrael she-Einan Yekholin le-Hizdayyef*) to which nothing could be added and from which nothing could be erased (Maim. Yad, Malveh ve-Loveh 27:1).

Where a document appeared on the face of it to have been tampered with or added to, so that a suspicion of forgery arose in the eyes of the court, recourse was had to compulsory measures in order to induce the plaintiff to confess that he was suing on a false document (BB 167a). It is not clear what these compulsory measures were: literally translated, the reports say that the plaintiff was "bound, and then admitted the document to be false" (the word used for "binding" is the same as that used for the binding of a person to be flogged (cf. Mak. 3:12), as distinguished from and preliminary to the *flogging itself (Mak. 3:13); or for the functions of non-judicial officers attached to the courts, who "bind and flog people on orders of the court"; Rashi to Deut. 1:15). The binding (*koftin*) was later interpreted to mean compelling (*kofin*; Meir ha-Levi Abulafia, quoted in *Beit Yosef*, ḤM 42 n. 3–5), and the compulsion was authorized to be carried out by floggings (Tur and Sh. Ar., ḤM 42:3). It is, however, to be noted that these floggings – or any other compulsory measures – were not sanctions or punishments imposed for forging the documents, but only means to extort confessions of forgery: when a forgery was admitted or proved, the only sanction was that the claim based upon any such forged document was dismissed. It was only in much later times that forgers were punished by the courts, or more often – presumably because of the private law character of forgery in Jewish law – delivered for trial and punishment to the gentile courts (Assaf in bibliography, nos. 16, 112, 144). Even the notion that forgers of documents could be disqualified on that account from testifying or taking an oath was dismissed as unwarranted (*Ḥatam Sofer*, ḤM 39; *Pitḥei Teshuvah*, ḤM 34:7, n. 17).

In order to have a claim based on a document dismissed, it was not always necessary to prove that it was false – in certain circumstances it sufficed that it was reputed to be false (Ket. 36b; Maim. Yad, Edut 22:5). On the other hand, even the admitted forgery of a document would not necessarily vitiate a claim, as where a true document had been in existence and lost (BB 32b; Yad, To'en ve-Nitan 15:9). A man ought not to lend out his seal, so as not to tempt others to use it without his authority (BM 27b; Yev. 120b); his seal appearing (e.g., on a barrel of wine), it is presumed not to have been tampered with (Av. Zar. 69b). In the State of Israel, the Criminal Law Amendment (Offenses of Fraud, Extraction and Exploitation) Law 5723 – 1963 replaced the Criminal Code Ordinance 1936 mitigating the previous penalties for forgery (other than forgery of bank notes).

[Haim Hermann Cohn]

The offence of forgery was included in the Penal Code, 5737-1977. Sections 421-418 impose punishments of imprisonment for the forgery of documents or intentional use of a forged document. The law allows the imposition of severe punishments on a public servant who forges a document related to the area of his public responsibility for the purposes of obtaining a benefit; the offence of forgery includes the forgery of coins, deeds and stamps, and the forgery of documents for the purposes of stealing a car.

[Menachem Elon (2nd ed.)]

BIBLIOGRAPHY: M. Bloch, *Das mosaisch-talmudische Polizeirecht* (1879), 39, no. 20; Gulak, Yesodei, 2 (1922), 134–6; 4 (1922), 165–7; S. Assaf, *Ha-Onshin Aḥarei Ḥatimat ha-Talmud* (1922), passim; A. Gulak, *Urkundenwesen im Talmud* (1935), passim. **ADD BIBLIOGRAPHY:** Elon, *Ha-Mishpat ha-Ivri* (1988), 1, 642; Idem, *Jewish Law* (1994), II, 795.

FORGIVENESS, the act of absolving or pardoning; the state of being pardoned.

In the Bible

The biblical concept of forgiveness presumes, in its oldest strata, that sin is a malefic force that adheres to the sinner and that forgiveness is the divine means for removing it. This is demonstrated by the vocabulary of forgiveness which, in the main, stems from the cultic terminology of cleansing, e.g., *tiher* ("purify"; Jer. 33:8); *maḥah* ("wipe"; lsa. 43:25); *kibbes, raḥaẓ* ("wash"; Isa. 1:16; Ps. 51:4, 9); *kipper* ("purge"; Ezek. 16:63; Ps. 78:38). Even the most common verb for forgiveness, *salaḥ*, probably derives from the Mesopotamian cult where it connotes sprinkling in purification rites. More significantly, the most prominent epithet of God in His role of forgiver is *nose' 'avon/ ḥeṭ/ pesha'* (lit. he who "lifts off sin"; e.g., Ex. 34:7; Num. 14:18; Hos. 14:3; Micah 7:18; Ps. 32:5).

In the religion of ancient Israel, in contrast to that of its neighbors, rituals are not inherently efficacious. This point is underscored by the sacrificial formula of forgiveness. Whereas the required ritual is carried out by the priest, its desired end, forgiveness, is granted solely by God, e.g., "the priest shall make atonement for him for his sin and he shall be forgiven," i.e., by God (Lev. 4:26, and passim). Another limitation placed upon sacrificial means of obtaining forgiveness is that it can only apply to inadvertent errors (Num. 15:22–29). Blatant contempt of God cannot be expiated by sacrifice (Num. 15:30–31; I Sam. 3:14) or any other means (Ex. 23:21; Josh. 24:19). Moreover, contrition and compassion are indispensable coefficients of all rituals of forgiveness, whether they be expiatory sacrifices (Lev. 5:5–6; 16:21; Num. 5:6–7) or litanies for fasting (Joel 2:12–14; I Sam. 7:5–6).

Indeed, man's involvement both in conscience and deed is a *sine qua non* for securing divine forgiveness. It is not enough to hope and pray for pardon: man must humble himself, acknowledge his wrong, and resolve to depart from sin (e.g., David, II Sam. 12:13ff.; Ahab, I Kings 21:27–29). The psalms provide ample evidence that penitence and confession are integral components of all prayers for forgiveness (Ps. 32:5; 38:19; 41:5; Lam. 3:40ff.). The many synonyms for contrition testify to its primacy in the human effort to restore the desired relationship with God, e.g., seek the Lord (II Sam. 12:16; 21:1), search for Him (Amos 5:4), humble oneself before Him (Lev. 26:41), direct the heart to Him (I Sam. 7:3), and lay to heart (II Kings 22:19). The rituals of penitence, such as weeping, fasting, rending clothes, and donning sackcloth and ashes (II Sam. 12:16; Joel 1:13; Ezra 9:3ff.; 10:1, 6), are unqualifiedly condemned by the prophets if they do not correspond with, and give expression to the involvement of the heart (lsa, 1:10ff.; 29:13; Hos. 7:14; Joel 2:13).

At the same time, inner contrition must be followed by outward acts; remorse must be translated into deeds. Two substages are involved in this process: first, the negative one of ceasing to do evil (Isa. 33:15; Ps. 15; 24:4) and then, the positive step of doing good (Isa. 1:17; 58:5ff.; Jer. 7:3; 26:13; Amos 5:14–15; Ps. 34:15–16; 37:27). Again, the richness of the biblical language used to describe man's active role in the process testifies to its centrality, e.g., incline the heart to the Lord (Josh. 24:23), make oneself a new heart (Ezek. 18:31), circumcise the heart (Jer. 4:4), wash the heart (Jer. 4:14), and break one's fallow ground (Hos. 10:) However, all these expressions are subsumed and summarized by one verb which dominates the penitential literature of the Bible, שוב (*shuv, shwv;* "to turn; to return") which develops ultimately into the rabbinic doctrine of *teshuvah* ("repentance"). This doctrine implies that man has been endowed by God with the power of "turning." He can turn from evil to the good, and the very act of turning will activate God's concern and lead to forgiveness.

What is the source of the biblical optimism that man's turning will generate divine movement to pardon him? This confidence resides in a number of assumptions concerning the nature of God, as presumed by the unique relationship between God and Israel, the bond of the *covenant. Covenant implies mutuality of obligation, that Israel's fidelity to God's demands will be matched by God's response to Israel's needs, particularly in his attitude of forgiveness (e.g., II Sam. 24:14,

17; cf. Ps. 25:10–11; 80; 103:17–18; 106:45). That is why in the wilderness traditions, Moses can continue to plead with God despite the lapses of his people, because of his certainty that God's forgiveness is a constant of his nature (Num. 14:18–20; Ex. 32:11ff.; 34:6ff,). Again, the profusion of idioms expressing divine forgiveness (in addition to the cultic expressions, mentioned above), e.g., overlook sin (Micah 7:18), not reckon it (Ps. 32:2), not remember it (Ps. 25:7), hide his face from it (Ps. 51:11), suppress it, remove it (Ps. 103:12), throw it behind his back (Isa. 38:17) or into the sea (Micah 7:19), points to the centrality of this concept.

Another covenant image which invokes God's attitude of forgiveness is his role of Father and Shepherd. A father's love for his children (Ex. 4:22; Num. 11:12; Deut. 32:6, 19; lsa. 64:7) can lead them to hope that their sins will be forgiven (Jer. 3:19; 31:19; Hos. 11:1ff.). Furthermore, this parental relationship shows that Israel's suffering is not inflicted as retribution for their sins but as corrective discipline – "afflictions of love" so that Israel may correct its way (Deut. 8:5; Prov. 3:12).

Another component of the covenant is that God will accept the mediation of an intercessor. He is not bound to comply – in contradistinction to the coercive claims of the pagan magician – for God will reject even the mediation of the most righteous when Israel's sins have exceeded the limit of His forbearance (Jer. 15:1; Ezek. 14:13–20). Intercession is, first and foremost, the function of Israel's prophets. Indeed, the only time Abraham is called a prophet is at the precise moment when his intercessory powers are invoked (Gen. 20:7). Moses' main concern, to judge by the narratives of the Exodus and the wandering in the wilderness, is to intervene on behalf of others (e.g., Ex. 9:27ff.; 10:16ff.; 34:8–9; Num. 12:11ff.; 21:7ff.; Deut. 9:16–10:10; Jer. 15:1). The psalmist singles this out in his eulogy of Moses: "He (God) said He would have destroyed them, had not Moses, the chosen one, stood in the breach before Him" (Ps. 106:23). To "stand in the breach" is for Ezekiel the main function of the prophet (Ezek. 13:5; 22:30).

An equally significant concomitant of God's covenant is His promise to the forefathers that the people of Israel) will exist forever and that they will be in eternal possession of Ereẓ Israel. This aspect of the covenant is constantly invoked in pleas for forgiveness (Ex. 2:24; 3:6; 15–16; 4:5; 6:3–5; Lev. 26:42; Deut. 4:31, 37; 7:8, 12; 8:18; 9:5, 27; 13:18; 29:12; Josh. 18:3; 21:44; I Kings 18:36ff.; II Kings 13:23; Isa. 41:8; 51:2; Micah 7:20; Ps. 105:9; Neh. 9:7; II Chron. 30:6).

This promise to the forefathers bears a final corollary. Because of the covenant, God's honor is at stake in the world. Israel's woes will not be comprehended by the nations as divine punishment for its covenant violations but as God's inability to fulfill His covenant obligations. This argument features prominently in Moses' intercession (Ex. 32:12; Num. 14:13–16) and is mentioned repeatedly in subsequent prayers for Israel's pardon (Josh. 7:9; Ps. 74:10, 18; 83:3, 19; 92:9–10; 109:27; 143:11–12). Conversely, the argument continues, it is important for God to redeem Israel for the glorification and sanctification of His name throughout the world (Ps. 79:6; 102:16; 115:1; 138:3–5) even if Israel itself is undeserving of forgiveness (Isa. 48:9–11; Ezek. 36:22ff.).

See also *Repentance.

[Jacob Milgrom]

In Talmud and Jewish Thought

DIVINE FORGIVENESS. The theme of God's forgiveness for man's sins is recurrent in talmudic and midrashic literature and reappears in later rabbinic writings and the synagogue liturgy. Its main theological purport is to counterbalance, and indeed outweigh, the strongly entrenched rabbinic belief in the inevitable punishment of sin. The rabbinic outlook on the subject may be most simply expressed as "God is just"; He rewards the righteous and punishes the wicked (Principle number 11 of Maimonides' 13 principles of the Jewish faith). Only the unrepentant sinner incurs His wrath; the sinner who repents is always forgiven. Thus the Talmud states, "He who sins and regrets his act is at once forgiven" (Ḥag. 5a; Ber. 12b) and the Midrash states, "Says the Holy One, even if they [your sins] should reach to Heaven, if you repent I will forgive" (Pes. Rab. 44:185a; see Yal. Ps. 835). The Tosefta even gives a statistical figure to the matter, basing itself on Exodus 34:6–7, and says that God's quality of forgiveness is five hundred fold that of His wrath (Tosef., Sot 4:1).

The idea is more picturesquely expressed in the talmudic image of God praying to Himself that His mercy should prevail over His anger and that He should deal with His children *"li-fenim mi-shurat ha-din,"* i.e., that He should forgive them even though strict justice would demand their punishment (Ber. 7a). The whole of Jewish thought on the subject stems from the forgiving character of God depicted in the 13 Divine attributes as revealed to Moses (Ex. 34:6–7). The rabbinic mind embroiders the fundamental biblical idea in a homiletic way, thus giving encouragement and hope to the sinner who would turn to God but is troubled by the burden of his past deeds. The liturgy of the *Day of Atonement, and indeed its very role, bear eminent testimony to the central role that the idea of God's forgiveness plays within Jewish religious practice.

Maimonides formulates the breadth of the Jewish attitude on Divine forgiveness thus: "Even if a man has sinned his whole life and repents on the day of his death, all his sins are forgiven him" (Yad, Teshuvah 2:1). Though this forgiveness is always ultimately forthcoming, for various categories of sin it only comes into effect when the Day of Atonement, or the sinner's death, or both have finalized the atonement (Yoma 85bff.; Yad, loc. cit., 1:4).

In later rabbinic literature, ideas about God's forgiveness are variations on the original theme outlined above, though now and again, the emphasis is changed. In ḥasidic writings, for example, where the dominant notion of God is that of a merciful father, there is a tendency to overstress His quality of forgiveness at the expense of His quality of justice. Naḥman of Bratslav, one of the early ḥasidic leaders, writes: "There is no sin that will not be forgiven by sincere repentance. Every saying to the contrary in the Talmud and the Zohar is not to be understood literally" (*Likkutei Eẓot ha-Shalem* (1913), 119). R. Naḥman is adverting here to certain categories of sinners who, it is claimed, will never be forgiven because of the nature of their crimes, however genuine their repentance. Among those said to be excluded from God's grace are those whose sins involved a desecration of God's name or caused an evil repute to fall on their fellow, or even those who indulged in evil language in general (TJ, BK 8:10, 6c; ARN[1] 39, 116; Zohar, Num. 16la). But R. Naḥman's interpretation is according to the tradition that no sinner was ever absolutely excluded from the sphere of God's forgiveness (see Yad, Teshuvah, 1:4; RH 18a; S. Schechter, *Some Aspects of Rabbinic Theology,* ch. 18 and references cited). The intention of those texts that do seem to exclude certain classes of sinner can be interpreted as a way of emphasizing the gravity of the sins involved.

There are two further general points. Rabbinic literature is on the whole concerned with God's forgiveness for the individual sinner, rather than for Israel as a nation (the latter is more characteristic of the prophetic ethos than the rabbinic, for during most of the creative period of rabbinic thought, Israel had ceased to exist as a cohesive national entity). Forgiveness is always and only consequent on repentance (the idea of an arbitrary grace is almost totally absent; but see Ber. 7a on Ex. 33:19). Similarly the doctrine of the merit of the fathers, *zekhut avot*, was given an ethical interpretation (Sanh. 27b.).

The place of a forgiving God within the Jewish *Weltanschauung* has been of interest in modern times and is discussed by both Jewish and Christian scholars. The immediate causes of this interest were partly a desire to uncover the rabbinic roots of New Testament theology and partly an attempt to rectify the widespread but distorted image of the Jewish conception of God, according to which the Jewish God was seen as a legalistic and strict overlord who rewards and punishes according to man's deeds, and the Jew was thus thought to inhabit a somber religious world devoid of Divine compassion. A more thorough acquaintance with the sources shows how wrong such a picture was.

HUMAN FORGIVENESS. God's forgiveness, however extensive, only encompasses those sins which man commits directly against Him, *"bein adam la-Makom"*; those in which an injury is caused to one's fellow man, *"bein adam le-ḥavero"* are not forgiven until the injured party has himself forgiven the perpetrator. Hence the custom of seeking forgiveness from those one may have wronged on the eve of the Day of Atonement, without which proper atonement cannot be made (Yoma 8:9, basing itself on Lev. 16:30 "… all your sins before the Lord," i.e., and not to man; Yad, loc. cit., 2:9; Sh. Ar., OḤ, 605:1; see also RH 17b; Sifra, Aḥarei Mot, *Perek* 8).

The law regarding physical injury, for example, is explicit in that even after the various compensatory payments have been made, the inflicter of the damage must seek the forgiveness of the injured party for the suffering caused (BK 92a; Yad, Ḥovel u-Mazzik 5:9; Sh. Ar., ḤM, 422). Not only must he who sins against his fellow seek forgiveness from him, but the one sinned against is duty bound to forgive. "Man should be pliant as a reed, not hard like the cedar" in granting forgiveness (Ta'an. 20a). As the Talmud puts it: "All who act mercifully (i.e., forgivingly) toward their fellow creatures will be treated mercifully by Heaven, and all who do not act mercifully toward their fellow creatures will not be treated mercifully by Heaven" (Shab. 151b; see also RH, 17a; Meg. 28a). If the injured party refuses to forgive even when the sinner has come before him three times in the presence of others and asked for forgiveness, then he is in turn deemed to have sinned (see Tanh. Hukkat 19). He is called *akhzari* ("cruel"). The unforgiving man is not of the seed of Abraham (Beẓ. 32b), since one of the distinguishing marks of all of Abraham's descendants is that they are forgiving. The quality of forgiveness was one of the gifts God bestowed on Abraham and his seed (Yer. 79a; Num. R. 8:4; Yad, Teshuvah 2:10).

The rabbis go even further in the ethical demands made upon the injured party, for not only must he be ready to forgive his injurer, he should also pray that God forgive the sinner before he has come to beg forgiveness (Yad, loc. cit.; Tosef., BK 9:29; *Sefer Ḥasidim* ed. by R. Margalioth 1957, 267 no. 360). This demand is based on the example of Abraham, who prayed to God to forgive Abimelech (Gen. 20:17). The reasons the injured party should be ready to forgive the injurer are mixed. On the one hand is the self-regarding consideration, already mentioned, that forgiveness to one's fellow wins forgiveness from Heaven. As Philo states: "If you ask pardon for your sins, do you also forgive those who have trespassed against you? For remission is granted for remission" (ed. by Mangey, 2 (1742), 670; see also Yoma 23a). On the other hand there is the purer motive of *imitatio dei.* Just as it is in the nature of God to be merciful to His creatures, so man in attempting to imitate the ways of God should be forgiving toward those who have injured him (Shab. 133b; see Lev. 19:2). R. Naḥman combines both motives when he says: "Imitate God by being compassionate and forgiving. He will in turn have compassion on you, and pardon your offenses" (op. cit. 81–91).

[Alan Unterman]

BIBLIOGRAPHY: IN THE BIBLE: C.R. Smith, *The Biblical Doctrine of Sin* (1953); E.F. Sutcliffe, *Providence and Suffering in the Old and New Testaments* (1955); W.L. Holladay, *The Root šûbh in the Old Testament* (1958); W. Eichrodt, *Theology of the Old Testament*, 2 (1967), 380–495; J. Milgrom, in: JQR, 58 (1967), 115–25. IN TALMUD AND JEWISH THOUGHT: J. Abrahams, *Studies in Pharisaism and the Gospels*, 1 (1917), 139–67; G.F. Moore, *Judaism*, 1 (1927), 535–45; 2 (1927), 153–5; S. Schechter, *Some Aspects of Rabbinic Theology* (1909), 293ff.; R.T. Herford, *Talmud and Apocrypha* (1933), 157–61; E.E. Urbach, *Ḥazal. Pirkei Emunot ve-De 'ot* (1969), 396ff.; K. Kohler; *Jewish Theology* (1918), 112–7, 246–55; C.G. Montefiore and R. Loewe (eds.), *A Rabbinic Anthology* (1938), 460–469.

FORLÌ, city in N. central Italy. The philosopher *Hillel b. Samuel of Verona wrote his *Tagmulei ha-Nefesh* there about 1280. By the 14th century a number of Jewish loan bankers were established in the city and in 1373 Bonaventura Consiglio and a partner lent 8,000 ducats to Amadeo, count of Savoy, on the security of his crown and other valuables. Representatives of the communities of central and northern Italy met in Forlì in 1418 to discuss the raising of a fund for self-defense; they also passed a series of sumptuary regulations to limit shows of luxury and extravagance. Their action was probably decisive in obtaining the protection of Pope *Martin V, which he extended in the bull of Jan. 31, 1419. From the late 14th and through the 15th century several Jewish physicians lived in Forlì and a number of Hebrew manuscripts were copied there. In 1488 anti-Jewish disorders broke out: the Jewish loan banks were sacked and the loan bankers were forced to leave the city. Subsequently, however, their activities were resumed. At the beginning of the 16th century the papal government assumed the administration of the city, and in 1569 the community in Forlì ceased to exist with the expulsion of the Jews from the towns of the Papal States, though some craftsmen also lived there during the 16th and 17th centuries. A Jewish presence in the area of Romagna, and also in Forlì, is documented from the Napoleonic era. In 1938, 15 families in Forlì and 98 people in the entire province were considered Jewish. During the Nazi occupation, from 1943 until the liberation of November 13, 1944, a concentration camp operated in Forlì, where the majority of prisoners were Jews from the area or from Rome. In September 1944 the Nazis massacred 33 people at the airport of Forlì, including 19 Jews.

BIBLIOGRAPHY: Garzanti, in: *Romagna*, 5 (1908), 266–79; Roth, Italy, index; Milano, Italia, index; Milano, Bibliotheca, index; Finkelstein, Middle Ages, 281ff. **ADD. BIBLIOGRAPHY:** G. Caravita, *Ebrei in Romagna: 1938–1945: dalle leggi razziali allo sterminio* (1991); L. Picciotto, *Il libro della memoria: gli ebrei deportati dall'Italia, 1943–1945* (2001).

[Attilio Milano / Federica Francesconi (2nd ed.)]

FORMAN, MILOS (1932–), Czech-American film director. Forman's early years were spent in a town near Prague, where his father was a teacher. Both his parents, including his non-Jewish mother, were murdered in Auschwitz. In 1963 he made *Black Peter,* in 1964, *Loves of a Blonde*, a film distributed and internationally acclaimed. *The Fireman's Ball* (1968), a wry treatment of Czech bureaucracy, effected its own irony when it caused 40,000 fireman to quit after Novotny released the film. All were appeased when Forman offered his own critical interpretation (a parody in itself) of the film as broad allegory. Forman moved to Hollywood in 1970 and subsequently directed such films as *Taking Off* (1971), *One Flew over the Cuckoo's Nest* (1975), which was only the second film in cinema history to win all five major Academy Awards, *Hair* (1979), *Ragtime* (1981), *Amadeus* (1984), which again won Forman Oscars for Best Picture and Best Director, and *Valmont* (1989). Later films include *The People vs. Larry Flynt* (1996) and *Man on the Moon* (1999).

[Jonathan Licht]

FORMAN, PHILLIP (1895–1978), U.S. judge. Born in New York City, Forman was admitted to the bar in 1917. He attended the Temple University School of Law, where he received his LL.B. in 1919. During World War I he served in the United States Navy (1917–19). He had a private law practice in Trenton, New Jersey. In 1923 he was appointed assistant U.S. attorney for the southern district of New Jersey, and in 1928 district attorney. Forman became a district court judge in 1932, and in 1951 chief judge. Subsequently, in 1959, he was elevated to the U.S. Court of Appeals for the Third Circuit. He assumed senior status in 1961 and served in that capacity until his death.

Active in Jewish affairs, Forman was a founder of the Jewish Federation of Trenton, New Jersey, and a prominent figure in the *American Jewish Joint Distribution Committee, the *Jewish Welfare Board, and the *American Jewish Committee. He was also a member of the American Judicature Society and the American Legion. In 1940 Forman had the distinction of presenting Albert Einstein with his certificate of American citizenship.

[Morris M. Schnitzer / Ruth Beloff (2nd ed.)]

FORM AND MATTER (Heb. צוּרָה, *ẓurah*, and חֹמֶר, *ḥomer*), according to Aristotle, the two constituents of every physical substance, form being that which makes the substance what it is, and matter being the substratum underlying the form. In substantial change the form is that which is changed, while the matter remains constant throughout the change. Matter is defined by Aristotle as "that which in itself is not a this," form, as "that which is precisely in virtue of which a thing is called a this" (*De Anima* 2:1). Insofar as form makes the object what it is, it is equated with actuality, while matter is equated with potentiality. Insofar as form determines the nature of a substance it is likened to the species, while matter is likened to the genus.

*Plotinus, the first of the neoplatonists, accepting the Aristotelian notion of form as species and matter as genus, maintained that immaterial substances, since they can be defined in terms of genus and species, are also composed of matter and form. There exists, he maintained, a spiritual matter out of which incorporeal substances are formed. Only God is not composed of matter and form.

Among Jewish philosophers those who tended toward Aristotelianism generally followed the Aristotelian notion of form and matter, while those who tended towards neoplatonism, followed the Plotinian notion.

Solomon ibn *Gabirol devoted his major work, *Mekor Ḥayyim* (*Fons Vitae*), to a discussion of form and matter. He accepted the view that form and matter are constituent elements of corporeal and incorporeal beings alike. However, while Plotinus believed that there exist two types of matter, spiritual and corporeal, Gabirol held that matter is in itself incorporeal, and is common to corporeal and incorporeal substances. Gabirol, regarding form and matter as more than just the component parts of individual substances, saw them as cosmic forces – the two primary elements, which constitute intelligence, the highest of the emanated substances. Ibn

Gabirol is not clear concerning the origin of matter and form. At times he holds that matter emanates from God, and form, from an intermediary being, known as the divine will, while at other times he holds that both form and matter emanate from the divine will.

Joseph ibn *Ẓaddik, while he generally follows Aristotle in his natural philosophy, differs from Aristotle in his definition of matter and form. Matter, since it bears the form, is, for Ibn Ẓaddik, the one real substance, while form, insofar as it inheres in something else, has the same status as accidents (*Olam Katan* 1:2). For Aristotle, matter is that "which in itself is not a this."

Abraham *ibn Daud, the first of the Jewish Aristotelians, in his discussion of the concepts of form and matter, presents the example of a golden scepter, which is changed into a golden coin, then into a ring, and finally into a nose ring. He points out that gold is the matter underlying all these objects, while the scepter, the coin, the ring, and the nose ring are different forms that are imposed on the same matter. He deduces the existence of first matter and form from the reciprocal transmutation of the four basic elements. Having shown how the various elements are changed into one another he writes: "We thus know by observation that these elements are changed into one another... But it is inconceivable that the form, after passing away, should become the recipient... Hence we infer that they have a common underlying matter, which matter we call first matter" (*Emunah Ramah* 1:2). First matter is not in itself the matter out of which the four elements are formed, but rather first matter conjoined with the corporeal form. Maimonides, following Aristotle, maintains that "every physical body is necessarily composed of two things,... form and matter..." (*Guide* 2, intr., prop. 22). He maintains, further, that all privation and destruction of physical objects results from matter and not from form: "All bodies subject to generation and corruption are attained by corruption only because of their matter" (3:8; see also, 1:17). In the case of man, body is the matter and soul, form. It is the body, therefore, which is subject to destruction, and only the soul, which can attain immortality.

BIBLIOGRAPHY: Husik, Philosophy, index, s.v. matter; Guttmann, Philosophies, index; H.A. Wolfson, *Crescas' Critique of Aristotle* (1929), index; idem, in: JQR, 38 (1947/48), 47–61; idem, in: *Proceedings of the Sixth International Congress of Philosophy* (1926), 602–7; A. Altmann and S. Stern, *Isaac Israeli* (1958), 159–64.

[Alfred L. Ivry]

FORMIGGINI, ANGELO FORTUNATO (1878–1938), Italian publisher, editor, and writer. He was born in Modena, where his family had been court jewelers for generations and maintained their private synagogue. He was a publisher first in Modena (1908–11) and then in Genoa (1911–15) and Bologna; in 1916 he moved to Rome, where he won prominence for his innovations in publishing and the quality of his books.

Among his noteworthy publications the most important are *Classici del ridere*, a series of 106 volumes published from 1913 to 1938, including the best works of humorists from all countries (i.e., Giovanni Boccaccio, François Rabelais, Voltaire, Honoré de Balzac, Jonathan Swift, William Thackeray, Shalom Aleichem), and *Profili*, a series of 129 numbers, published from 1909 to 1937, which included brief essays on contemporary authors. Besides editing *Chi è, dizionario degli Italiani d'oggi*, the Italian *Who's Who* (first edition 1929–30), a dictionary of contemporary Italians, Formiggini served as managing editor of *L'Italia che scrive*, a monthly review of Italian literary and artistic activities, bibliography, and intellectual debate. In 1923 he published in the *Classici del Ridere* his *La ficozza filosofica sul Fascismo e la Marcia sulla Leonardo*, an ironic study of contemporary society and a defense of himself against the intellectual luminary Giovanni Gentile.

Between 1919 and 1921 he founded the Italian Institute for Cultural Propaganda Abroad and in 1929 he planned and organized the World Congress of Libraries and Bibliography. When the antisemitic laws of 1938 were promulgated, he committed suicide by jumping off the tower of Ghirlandina in Modena as an act of extreme protest and rebellion. His spiritual testament *Parole in libertà* was published posthumously (1945).

ADD. BIBLIOGRAPHY: L. Balsamo and R. Cremante, *A.F. Formiggini un editore del Novecento* (1981).

[Irving Rosenthal / Federica Francesconi (2nd ed.)]

FORMSTECHER, SOLOMON (1808–1889), German philosopher and rabbi. Formstecher was born in Offenbach. He studied philosophy, philology and theology at the University of Giesen, and served as the rabbi of the Offenbach community from 1842 until his death. He took an active part in the Reform movement and edited the periodicals *Der Freitagabend* and *Die Israelitische Wochenschrift*.

In his systematic work *Die Religion des Geistes – Wissenschaftliche Darstellung des Judentums nach seinem Charakter, Enwicklungsgaeng und Berufe in der Welt* (Frankfurt, 1841) Formstecher attempted to present a theoretical basis for the aims of the emancipation and Reform. Judaism is presented primarily as an idea, anchored in historical revelation and the full value of which is revealed through the gradual, progressive development of humanity. Formstecher used the philosophical categories of the German idealists Schelling and, to a lesser extent, Hegel in developing this concept.

The three central concepts of Formstecher's system are revelation, spirit, and nature. By revelation, which is the source of the ethical monotheism of Judaism, he means the divine communication concerning the true nature of good and evil. It is not the knowledge of God's existence that represents the true ideal, but the identification of God as a pure moral being. The God of Israel is not a supreme concept reached through philosophic understanding, but a supreme being transcending both spiritual and earthly nature. Therefore, Judaism as an idea is not a philosophic religion, but the manifestation of the true absolute revelation. The classical representatives of this idea were the prophets of Israel. They understood the truth of the original revelation – based on God's covenants with Noah and his *chosen people, symbolized by the Sinai covenant – through knowledge of the objective source of the absolute values, which was revealed to them by an immediate feeling.

Like Hegel, Formstecher meant by "spirit" the concretization of the absolute in the historic-conscious level of mankind. If, as he believed, religion in general is man's aspiration for a universe of values, then the religion of the spirit is the aspiration for the embodiment of an absolute moral idea, the source of which is divine revelation. Judaism as a phenomenon, i.e., historical Judaism, although subject to historical circumstances, clings to the aspiration of embodying the moral idea on earth.

This aspiration distinguished Judaism from all other religions, which are fundamentally religions of nature, or physical monotheism. Following Schelling, Formstecher defined the religion of nature (paganism) as the aspiration for universal life, in which the spirit is manifested as the "soul of the world". The philosophic pantheistic concepts, as well as speculative metaphysical thought, are therefore, the refined form of the pagan view of life. In proposing his argument Formstecher foreshadowed some of the anti-metaphysical trends in modern Jewish theology, represented by Rosenzweig and Buber, for example.

Judaism and paganism are polar phenomena, which by their very nature cannot coexist. Therefore, Formstecher rejected the concept of the mission of the Jews as the fundamental and direct heritage of Judaism. Within the framework of the dominant paganism, the isolation of Judaism among the nations is a direct result of its metaphysical nature. Nevertheless, Judaism does fulfill its mission among the nations, although not directly: it fulfills its mission through Christianity and Islam. These historical religions, in which pagan and spiritual elements are mingled, fulfill the requirement that paganism be overcome by the embodiment of the absolute moral value of the divine spirit. As the growth of the spirit and culture in modern times seemed to indicate, insofar as the human consciousness is aware of the moral source of all being, the universal human spirit will develop, and it will of itself bring about the removal of the barriers between the nations. Formstecher sincerely believed that the Emancipation was the social-political manifestation of this internal, spiritual process in the history of humanity.

BIBLIOGRAPHY: N. Rotenstreich, *Jewish Philosophy in Modern Times* (1968), 106–20 and index; Guttmann, *Philosophies* 308–13; **ADD. BIBLIOGRAPHY:** B. Ritter-Kratz, *Salomon Formstecher – Ein deutcher Reformrabbiner* (biography incl. full bibliography) (1991) (Wissenschaftliche Abhandlungen des Salomon Ludwig Steinheim-Instituts fuer deutsch juedische Geschichte, E. Heid (ed.), vol. 1); T., "Solomon Formstechers Religion des Geistes – Versuch einer Neulekture," in: *Aschkenas*, 13:2 (2003), 441–460; N.M. Samuelson, *An Introduction to Modern Jewish Philosophy* (1989), 150–53; M.A. Meyer, *Response to Modernity* (1988), 70–72, index.

[Moshe Schwarcz / Yehoyada Amir (2nd ed.)]

°**FORSTER (Foester, Vorster, Forsthemius), JOHANN** (1495–1556), German theologian and Hebraist. Forster studied under Reuchlin at Ingolstadt and later with Luther in Wittenberg. In 1539 he became professor of Hebrew at Tübingen and, ten years later, at the University of Wittenberg. He published a pioneering Hebrew-Latin lexicon, *Dictionarium hebraicum novum* (Basle, 1557; 1564²), which revealed the animosity of its author, a diligent Hebraist, toward the Jews. The lexicon's subtitle stressed that it was "not based on the commentaries of the rabbis or on those of our own scholars, with a foolish imitation … but derived from the treasures of the Bible." He was quite critical of Christian interpreters of the Kabbalah as well. Forster also published *Meditationes hebraicae in artem grammaticam* (Cologne, 1558). He attempted to derive the word *sibyl* ("oracle," "prophetess") from "kabula" (i.e., Kabbalah).

BIBLIOGRAPHY: Steinschneider, Handbuch, 48 no. 621; M. Adam, *Vitae Germanorum Medicorum* (1620), 302; F. Secret, *Les kabbalistes chrétiens de la Renaissance* (1964), 275–76. **ADD. BIBLIOGRAPHY:** L. Geiger, *Das Studium der hebraeischen Sprache in Deutschland* (1870), 97–102, 136–137; J. Friedman, in: *Bibliothèque d'Humanisme et Renaissance* 42 (1980), 61.

[Giulio Busi (2nd ed.)]

FORTAS, ABE (1910–1982), U.S. lawyer and Supreme Court justice. Fortas was born in Memphis, Tennessee, son of a cabinetmaker. A brilliant student, he graduated from Southwestern College (1930) and Yale Law School (1933), where he was *Law Journal* editor. Upon graduation, he was appointed to the Yale law faculty. Fortas married Carolyn Agger, who also became a distinguished lawyer. In 1937 he entered full-time government service with the Securities Exchange Commission and was general counsel for the Public Works Administration. From 1942 to 1946 he served as undersecretary of the interior and also was an adviser in 1945 to the American delegation at the San Francisco Conference which founded the United Nations. During this period Fortas became friendly with Lyndon B. Johnson, the future president.

In 1946 Fortas entered private legal practice. His firm, Arnold, Fortas & Porter, became one of the most prominent and wealthy in Washington, representing many important corporations. As counsel for Lyndon Johnson, Fortas successfully countered the challenge to the validity of Johnson's election to the U.S. Senate in 1948. In the 1950s Fortas and his firm became involved in civil liberties cases. He successfully defended Owen Lattimore, a victim of the McCarthy era communist charges. Some of his criminal cases became legal landmarks. In the Durham case, he persuaded the Federal District Court to adopt a new standard for criminal insanity, determining that an accused is not criminally responsible if his unlawful act was a product of mental disease or defect. In yet another, Fortas successfully argued that states should be required to provide free legal counsel for indigent defendants charged with major crimes. When President Johnson assumed office in 1963, Fortas became a key presidential aide and adviser. He worked out a complicated trust agreement for the

Johnson family, handled two sensitive administration scandals, aided the president in the Dominican crisis, and advised him on issues ranging from racial problems to the Vietnam War. In July 1965 Johnson appointed Fortas to the Supreme Court. As an associate justice, Fortas was known for his penetrating mind, skillful legal writing, and concern for individual rights. He generally joined the Court's libertarian, activist majority. One of the most significant of his opinions was in the Galt case, which extended the constitutional rights to due process of law to juveniles being tried in special juvenile courts. Fortas firmly believed in the protection of personal privacy, and opposed the widespread use of civil disobedience to attain political ends. His pamphlet *Concerning Dissent and Civil Disobedience* (1968) presented a rational yet passionate plea for the rejection of political violence and for respect for law and the democratic process.

In the summer of 1968 Johnson nominated Fortas to succeed retiring Chief Justice Warren. Opponents of the nomination succeeded in blocking Fortas' confirmation; they charged that he was too liberal and too close an adviser to President Johnson, and that the new appointment should be deferred until after the approaching presidential election. Moreover, while on the Court Fortas had accepted a fee for serving as lifetime consultant to the charitable Wolfson Family Foundation. When its founder, Louis E. Wolfson, was indicted for stock manipulation, Fortas returned the fee and severed his connection with the Foundation; but the disclosure of the association now aroused bitter public controversy. Fortas maintained that he had done no wrong; nevertheless, in May 1969 he resigned from the Court under heavy pressure and returned to private practice.

BIBLIOGRAPHY: Rodell, in: *New York Times Magazine* (July 28, 1968), 12–13, 63–68; Graham, *ibid.* (June 4, 1967), 26, 86–96; United States 90th Congress, 2nd Session, Senate; *Executive Report No. 8* (1968); 89th Congress, 1st Session, Senate Committee on the Judiciary, *Hearings* (Aug. 5, 1965).

[Barton G. Lee]

FORTES, MEYER (1906–1983), British social anthropologist. Born in South Africa, he settled in England. From 1934 to 1938 he was a research fellow of the International African Institute, London; he lectured at the London School of Economics, and at Oxford University (1939–41); was head of the department of sociology, West African Institute, Accra, Gold Coast (Ghana), from 1944 to 1946; and from 1950 until 1973 was professor of social anthropology at Cambridge University. Fortes conducted field research in Central and West Africa and initiated modern ethnographical research in Ghana. He studied ancestor worship, the development of a generalized theory of primitive social structure, and the demographical method in preliterate societies. With Evans-Pritchard he developed the modern theory of primitive political systems, and conducted research on the theory of kinship and social organizations in primitive societies. On the basis of his expertise in this realm, he analyzed structuralist theory and methodology. Among his books were *Dynamics of Clanship among the Tallensi* (1945) and *Oedipus and Job in West African Religion* (1959); he edited *African Political Systems* (1940, 1950[2]). Later he wrote *Kinship and the Social Order* (1969) and *Time and Social Structure* (1970).

ADD. BIBLIOGRAPHY: ODNB online: D.E. Hunter and P. Whitten (eds.), *Encyclopedia of Anthropology* (1976).

[Ephraim Fischoff]

FORTI, BARUCH UZZIEL BEN BARUCH (d. 1571), also called **Hazketto** (a Hebraized form of his name: *ḥazak* (*forte*, פורטי, "strong") and *-etto*, a diminutive ending), Italian rabbi. Forti was ordained rabbi in 1564 in Mantua, and later served as head of a yeshivah in Ferrara. In 1554 he took part in the conference of Italian Jewish communities in Ferrara. He intervened in the affair of the Venturozzo-Tamari divorce (see Moses b. Abraham *Provencale), taking the side of Tamari. He edited Isaac *Abrabanel's *Ma'yenei ha-Yeshu'ah* (Ferrara, 1551), and included his biography of Abrabanel. In this he expresses his thanks to Joseph and Samuel, Abrabanel's sons, then resident in Ferrara, for providing him with the necessary information. He also edited Moses *Alashkar's *Hassagot* on Shem Tov b. Shem Tov's *Sefer ha-Emunot* (*ibid.*, 1556) with an introduction. A responsum by Forti of 1565 is included in the responsa of Moses Isserles (Resp. Rema 36), while others are extant in the Mortara collection (at present in the Kaufmann Library of Budapest; M. Weisz, *Katalog … D. Kaufmann* (1906), nos. 152,157,160) and in a manuscript in the collection of Zadok Kahn (Paris). An alphabetical index of Maimonides' *Mishneh Torah* from a manuscript in Forti's possession was appended to the Venice 1574/76 edition.

BIBLIOGRAPHY: Ghirondi-Neppi, 53, 63; Carmoly, in: *Oẓar Neḥmad*, 2 (1857), 62; A. Pesaro, *Memorie Storiche sulla Comunitá Israelitica Ferrarese* (1878), 22; Michael, Or, no. 634; Finkelstein, Middle Ages, 302f.; Bernstein, in: HHY, 14 (1930), 58–60; S. Simonsohn, *Toledot ha-Yehudim be-Dukkasut Mantovah*, 1 (1962), 303; 2 (1964), 365, 369, 425; idem, in: *Tarbiz.* 28 (1958/59), 378, 383–6; Kupfer, *ibid.*, 38 (1968/69), 54–60.

[Umberto (Moses David) Cassuto]

FORTI (Heb. **Hazak**), **JACOB RAPHAEL HEZEKIAH BEN ABRAHAM ISRAEL** (1689–1782), Italian kabbalist. Forti studied under Mordecai *Bassani in Verona and later under Moses Ḥayyim *Luzzatto in Padua. He became chief rabbi of Padua, and Shabbetai Medini and Ariel Alatino were among his pupils. His glosses to the four *Turim* of *Jacob b. Asher and commentary to the Shulḥan Arukh as well as a methodology of the Talmud and the *posekim* and a collection of sermons survived in manuscript form. Some of his many responsa were published in the works of others. The records of his halakhic dispute with the rabbis of Venice regarding the business methods of its merchants are brought together in the *Mishpat Shalom* (in manuscript) of Isaac b. Asher Pacifico. Forti died in Padua.

BIBLIOGRAPHY: Ghirondi-Neppi, 148, 150.

[Samuel Abba Horodezky]

FORTIS (Heb. **Hazak**), **ABRAHAM ISAAC** (d. c. 1731), physician and communal leader in Poland. He is recorded in Poland around 1690, having come from Italy as a young man (*baḥur*). Moses *Zacuto, in the same year in Mantua, praised his wide knowledge in "Torah learning," in addition to his distinction in medicine. A clergyman who later became acquainted with him in Poland was amazed at his erudition in Christian theological literature. Fortis settled in the province of "Russia," living in Lvov, Jaroslaw, and Rzeszów (from 1706), and served as physician to Prince Lubomirski in Rzeszów, and to Count Potocki in Lezajsk, who tried to convert him. In 1710 he and another Jewish physician, who had also completed his studies in Italy, were summoned in connection with their qualifications before the crown tribunal of Lublin. Fortis also concerned himself with Jewish affairs. For many years he took part in the leadership of the Jews of the province (*galil*), and between 1726 and 1730 served as *parnas* of the *Council of Four Lands. He had several sons who became rabbis or physicians.

BIBLIOGRAPHY: Halpern, Pinkas, index, s.v. *Izḥak ben Shemu'el Ẓeynvil Rofe Ḥazak Fortis.*

[Israel Halpern]

FORTUNOFF VIDEO ARCHIVE FOR HOLOCAUST TESTIMONY. The archive began in New Haven, Connecticut, in 1979 when Laurel Vlock, a television journalist, and Dr. Dori Laub, a Holocaust survivor and psychiatrist met and recorded Dr. Laub's testimony. This initial effort led to the Holocaust Survivors' Film Project, Inc, a grassroots organization, created to videotape local Holocaust survivors and witnesses. The project was based on the belief that every survivor has a unique story to tell, that there was a diminishing window of opportunity to record their testimonies, and that video would be an effective vehicle for capturing Holocaust survivors' experiences. This initial effort recorded nearly 200 testimonies. These tapes were donated to Yale University in 1981, and in 1982 the Video Archive was established at the university's Sterling Memorial Library. Sterling Professor Geoffrey Hartmann, who had written extensively about Holocaust memory and testimony, became the faculty advisor and project director and a driving force in its development.

The archival collection has grown to over 4,300 items. These testimonies reflect the diversity of the witnesses and include accounts by Holocaust survivors, liberators, resisters, and bystanders. The tapes are catalogued and cross-referenced and are available to educators, researchers, and the public.

The Archive is an ongoing effort to preserve Holocaust memory. It works with affiliated video-testimony projects around the United States, Europe, Israel, and South America and has undertaken joint projects with the U.S. Holocaust Memorial Museums. Interviewers in affiliated projects are trained in its methodology and both the Archive and the affiliate receive a copy of the recorded testimony for their collections.

When the Video Archive was established it's interviewing philosophy was a departure from other oral history projects because it stressed the role of the witness rather than the interviewer in leading the interview. The interview is deliberately unstructured and open-ended; its content and direction determined by the witness rather than the interviewer. The latter asks questions primarily for clarification of time and place or for elaboration on a subject that the witness has already raised.

The Video Archive has an intensive training program. It is designed to prepare its interviewers both in methodology and in the background to the witnesses' experiences. The participants read and attend lectures on history, observe taped interviews, and discuss the Archive's interviewing techniques. The Archive has lent its expertise to other Holocaust organizations as well as international groups concerned preserving the memory of other genocides in the 20th century.

Education is a key to the goals of the Archive. In order to further the use of witness accounts in the classroom, it has created a library of edited video testimonies that are available to teachers and community groups. The Archive has also collaborated with educational organizations that have developed study guides using testimony. In addition, it sponsors academic conferences on Holocaust education and research.

The Fortunoff Archive for Holocaust Testimonies encourages use of its collection to the widest audience possible through its website: www.library.yale.edu. It has produced a television documentary of its own and spurred educational films.

[Beth Cohen (2nd ed.)]

FOSS (Fuchs), LUKAS (1922–), U.S. composer, pianist, and conductor. Born in Berlin, he immigrated to the U.S. in 1937. He was pianist with the Boston Symphony Orchestra from 1944 to 1950. He was the youngest composer to receive a Guggenheim Fellowship (1945), appeared as soloist in his own piano concertos with a number of orchestras in the U.S. and Europe, and conducted his first symphony in Pittsburgh in 1945. He taught composition at the Berkshire Music Center and at the University of California, Los Angeles. In 1963 he was appointed conductor and music director of the Buffalo Philharmonic Orchestra where he remained until 1970, when he became a freelance conductor and was visiting professor at Harvard University. He was chief conductor and advisor of the Israel Broadcasting Authority's Jerusalem Symphony Orchestra from 1972 until 1975. A precocious talent, he had some pieces published at the age of 15. His early works are neo-romantic in nature. Among them the most important are the cantata *The Prairie* (1942), the cantata *Song of Songs* (1947), an opera after Mark Twain *The Jumping Frog of Calaveras County* (1950), the cantata *A Parable of Death* (1953), the television opera *Griffelkin* (1955), and *Time Cycle* for soprano and orchestra (1960). Then Foss turned to ultramodernism using the extreme procedures of the avant-garde, including aleatory devices of "controlled improvisation." To this period belong his *Echoi* for instruments (1963) and *Elytres* for chamber orchestra (1964). His *Phorion* for strings, electronic organ, and amplified harpsichord and harp (1967) is a metamorphosis of a Bach prelude. In his later works Foss strove to combine his earlier, sometimes more conservative and sometimes specifically American, style with experiments of his modernist period (*American Cantata,* 1976; *Renaissance Concerto for Flute and Orchestra,* 1985). As a conductor, Foss always sought to popularize new music; in 1973 in Brooklyn he began "Meet the Moderns," a series of new music concerts as well as discussions with composers.

ADD. BIBLIOGRAPHY: NG²; MGG²; K.J. Perone, *Lukas Foss: A Bio-Bibliography* (1991).

[Nicolas Slonimsky / Yulia Kreinin (2nd ed.)]

FOSSANO, town in N.W. Italy. Fossano was one of the three communities, with Asti and Moncalvo, which preserved the special liturgy of French origin known as the *Apam rite. Jewish bankers in Fossano are first mentioned in the 1670s. A ghetto was established in 1724. There were then approximately 100 Jews living in Fossano. The "miraculous" escape of the Jews from a riot on the fourth night of Passover during the French revolutionary wars (1796) was long commemorated by a local Purim. The community ceased to exist before World War II.

BIBLIOGRAPHY: Roth, in: RMI, 5 (1930/31), 36–39; idem, in; HUCA, 10 (1935), 457–60; Colombo and Tedesco, in: RMI, 29 (1963), 129–41; Milano, Bibliotheca, index. **ADD. BIBLIOGRAPHY:** M. Acanfora Torrefranca, "Il rito APAM; una diversa tradizione musicale?," in: *Scritti sull'ebraismo in memoria di Emanuele Menachem Artom* (1996), 322–28.

[Daniel Carpi]

FOSSOLI, internment camp for British prisoners of war in the village of Fossoli, on the outskirts of the town of Carpi, in the province of Modena (Emilia), created by the Italian army in 1942. Opening in July, the camp consisted primarily of tents housing 1,800 British internees and 350 Italian guards under the command of Col. Giuseppe Ferraresi. In September a second section was opened and work began to substitute the tents with barracks. Living conditions for the prisoners were in accordance with international law, and representatives of the Red Cross visited regularly. By the summer of 1943, the two sections of the camp held about 4,000 prisoners.

After the Italian armistice with the Allies announced on September 8, 1943, the Germans began their long-planned occupation of Italy. Fossoli was under German control by the 9th. All Allied prisoners were deported to German camps, primarily Bergen-Belsen, during the second half of September.

At the end of November 1943, police order number 5 of the Ministry of the Interior of the Italian Social Republic announced that all properties of Jews were to be confiscated and that the Jews themselves should be arrested and detained. On December 5, the second section of the Fossoli camp was designated for Jewish prisoners and placed under the authority of the prefect of Modena, Bruno Calzolari. Within a few weeks, almost 1,000 Jews were detained in the camp. On March 15, the Germans officially took over the second section, which they had unofficially occupied since February, and placed it under the authority of the *Befehlshaber der Sipo-SD*, Wilhelm Harster, who resided in Verona. The second section then became a *Polizei- und Durchgangslager* controlled directly by the German SS and used as a base for the deportation of Jews and political prisoners to the East. The Italians continued to control the other section of the camp, where prisoners not destined for deportation were held. SS Untersturmfuehrer Karl Titho, aided by SS Hauptscharfueher Hans Haage, were awarded the direct command of the German section of Fossoli. Under them was a small group of SS, some Ukrainian volunteers, and some Italians from the Social Republic. Italians arrested for political or racial reasons, mainly in the northwestern region of the country, were sent to Fossoli. Deportations began on February 19, 1944, and ended on August 1 of that year, when the advancing Allies forced the Germans to retreat farther north. At that point, the Germans established their camp for political and racial prisoners at Bolzano-Gries. Altogether, about 5,000 prisoners were deported from Fossoli, of whom 2,461 were Jews.

Between autumn 1945 and the second half of the 1960s, Fossoli hosted various kinds of refugees: foreigners residing temporarily in Italy in the first postwar years as well as, after 1952, Italians fleeing from Dalmatia, controlled by Tito. The camp was then abandoned for several years. In 1973, the mayor of Carpi asked the Italian government for authority to turn Fossoli into a site of special remembrance. This was done in 1984. In 1996, a cultural foundation at the former camp was created for the purpose of educating new generations and nurturing the memory of the suffering that had occurred there. A study center dedicated to the memory of Primo *Levi, the great Italian Jewish writer who was deported to Auschwitz from the camp on February 22, 1944, was also created there.

BIBLIOGRAPHY: M. Sarfatti, *Gli Ebrei nell Italia fascista: Vicende, identità, persecuzione* (2001); C.S. Capogreco, *I Campi del Duce.* (2004).

[Guri Schwarz (2nd ed.)]

FOULD, family of French bankers and politicians. The Fould-Oppenheim banking house was founded by BER LEON FOULD (1767–1855) and expanded by his eldest son BENOÎT (Benedict; 1792–1858), who succeeded his father as manager. In 1827 he was made a judge of the commercial court and from 1834 to 1842 sat in the Chamber of Deputies as conservative member for St. Quentin. An expert on financial matters, Fould was active in Jewish communal affairs and spoke in parliament in connection with the *Damascus Affair, protesting against the fact that the French consul had permitted the use of torture. ACHILLE (1800–1867), second son of Ber Leon, shared the management of the bank with his brother Benoît, before entering public life as a member of the General Council of the Hautes Pyrénées. In 1842 he was elected to the Chamber of Deputies where he supported the conservative financial policies of the chief minister, Francois Guizot. When Guizot went into exile following the outbreak of the 1848 revolution, Fould withdrew from politics and wrote three pamphlets attacking the new government's financial policies. In the following year, he retired from the banking house to devote himself to politics and was made minister of finance by Louis Napoleon. He was responsible for the reform of the postal service, the abolition of income tax, and the initiation of old-age pensions. Fould was twice dismissed and twice recalled to the government; in 1852 he was made a minister of state, and was the first Jew to be appointed a senator. In 1861 Fould was appointed minister of finance for the third time to check the rising national deficit and in 1863 he reduced the floating debt by negotiating a loan of 300,000,000 francs. He retired in 1867. Though he remained a Jew, Fould married into a Protestant family and his children were brought up as Christians. Two sons ERNEST ADOLPHE (1824–1875) and EDOUARD MATHURIN (1834–1881) both sat in the Chamber of Deputies, as did his grandson ACHILLE CHARLES (1861–?). His third son GUSTAVE EUGÈNE (1836–1884) was a successful playwright and producer.

BIBLIOGRAPHY: P. Emden, *Money Powers of Europe* (1938), index, includes bibliography.

FOUNDATIONS. The earliest period for which there are records of Jews having established foundations is the Middle Ages. In particular, Joseph Ephraim ha-Levi of Ecija, Castile, is known to have endowed the school of the Jewish community in 1332. In the modern period Jonas *Fraenkel (1773–1846) bequeathed the greater part of his fortune to establish a seminary, which eventually opened in Breslau. In 1866 Moses *Montefiore set up an endowment to maintain a synagogue and college near his home at Ramsgate. On his death, control passed to the elders of the London Congregation of Spanish and Portuguese Jews. The philanthropy of Maurice de *Hirsch, apart from the Jewish Colonization Association, included substantial gifts of a permanent character, e.g., 12 million gold francs for the education of Jews in Austria (1888) and the Baron de Hirsch Fund, New York (1891).

[Dan S. Rosenberg and Sefton D. Temkin]

The evolution of much of Jewish philanthropy from a communal base to an entrepreneurial market-driven base is one of the important subtexts of late 20th century Jewish America. To understand contemporary American Jewry, one must explore the growth of Jewish foundations, their impact on communal structures, various models of foundation partnership and collaboration, and some projections for future development.

In the 1830s Alexis de Tocqueville described one of the unique attributes of American life: voluntarism. Whether due to mistrust of government or an emergence of a richer civic society, Americans strongly identified with the creation of voluntary associations aimed at improving quality of life along with fulfilling various affinity needs of the population. By the late 19th century this emerged into a serious third sector: a nongovernmental, not-for-profit sector whose existence was to improve the common good and as the 20th century tax structure developed this sector grew exponentially in recognition of the unique societal role this sector was playing.

At about the same time, led by figures such as Andrew Carnegie, John D. Rockefeller, and Henry Ford the creation of charitable foundations (many of which were to exist in perpetuity) to enhance the public good in the name of and as part of the legacy of entrepreneurs also became a component of the American scene. Philanthropy became serious business and even with increased regulations brought about by the 1969 Tax Reform Act, became a business of enormous growth. By the end of the 20th century more than 80,000 grantmakers, of which 60,000 were in the form of foundations, making over 500,000 grants, existed within the United States with assets in excess of a quarter of a trillion dollars. It is estimated that 10,000 of these are Jewish family foundations, an overrepresentation by more than eight times the Jewish representation in the population.

There are serious definitional problems in creating a taxonomy for Jewish foundations resulting in a paucity of reliable data as to both numbers, dollar values, and impact of these foundations. Among these issues are those that have to do with the definition of a Jewish foundation. Is it a foundation whose principal is/was Jewish? Whose board is primarily Jewish? Is it a foundation whose historic giving patterns were primarily to the Jewish community? Exclusively? Somewhat? Must its charter specify a Jewish purpose? Is a foundation Jewish if founded by a Jewish principal whose distributions throughout the first generation were for the benefit of Jewish causes but today is governed by the heirs who are no longer Jewish and who no longer support Jewish causes? What if that foundation gives exclusively to Israel causes? What if those Israel causes are to support the 18% of the Israeli population that is Arab?

Further, organizational definition problems also create a barrier to full understanding. Should we consider as Jewish foundations those donor-advised funds that sit either at Federations, Federation-supported community foundations, or general community foundations? These donor-advised funds are no longer the assets of an entity controlled by the donor. They are the assets of the community foundation. However, the foundation has indicated that it will generally follow the advisory role given to the donor (or his/her designees). With Federation-related foundation assets approaching $4 billion, the relevance of these questions becomes clear as one wants to understand the depth and breadth of the field.

The first two-thirds of the 20th century saw the development of the North American Federation system as the New World's replication of the European *kehillah*. While vastly different from the European model and far more voluntarily driven, the Federation became the community's address for collective responsibility of Jews one to another. Its fundraising prowess grew dramatically through the first half of the century and culminated in unprecedented support of the *United Jewish Appeal, the central overseas arm of this movement, in 1948. On an inflation-adjusted basis, this was the most powerful fundraising year in mature communities either before or since. For the birth of the State of Israel was the ultimate Jewish act of collective responsibility and even those who did not physically participate were prepared to fiscally contribute. The UJA/Federation campaigns were especially relevant at the most critical moments of Israel's life. The years 1956, 1967, 1973, 1982, and 1990 were significant blips on a long term donation curve showing the powerful relationship between *amkha* and an Israel in trouble (or in the case of 1990 with the coming Soviet *aliyah* of one million people in a moment of extraordinary opportunity). Non-donors became donors and lapsed donors gave again. Yet on an inflation-adjusted basis, the decline in the UJA/Federation annual campaign revenues is clear and evident with both a real dollar decline of almost one-third every decade and a market share decline of an equally significant proportion. Outside of times of crisis, federations engaged in serious planning processes aimed at determining how best to serve the need of Jews locally and around the world as community-driven, consensus-sensitive organizations. The processes required to govern called for serious and extensive involvement. Immediate and rapid decisions could not be made. Rarely, could an individual feel like (s)he as an individual, was determining the course of the future.

In many ways this corporate culture was antithetical to the successful entrepreneurs who built their businesses by making decisions and unilaterally determining the future. While the major Jewish philanthropists continued to financially support the UJA/Federation movement as well as many of the other Jewish organizational entities which emerged in North American life, many decided that they wanted more personal hands on involvement in their philanthropy and, often, shaping the Jewish world. At the same time their legal and tax advisors were encouraging them to set aside funds to meet their philanthropic obligations so as to take advantage of generous American (and less so, Canadian) tax policies in which they could forgo substantial taxes and only be required to annually spend five percent of the funds set aside in these tax exempt private foundations. By the 1990s, many of these foundations (Abraham, Bronfman, Crown, Goldman,Haas, Marcus, Schusterman, Spielberg, Steinhardt, Weinberg, Wexner) became household names in the organized Jewish world. They were the supporters of many initiatives of Jewish life.

An interesting dynamic began to occur at this time. The first was a planned initiative that was created so as to have many of these "mega" philanthropists in the Jewish community get to know one another. Following the very successful launch of Operation Exodus, the campaign to support the *aliyah* of Soviet Jews to Israel accompanying the opening of the Soviet Union, at which $54 million was raised at a breakfast of just a few major donors, the then-CEO of United Jewish Appeal recognized that these generous individuals did not know one another. He organized a Study Group of major foundation principals from North America and elsewhere, which came together twice a year to study together issues of contemporary Jewish life. Much of the time of the Study Group was devoted to its various members getting to know one another and to learn of each other's interests. Not surprisingly, a number of initiatives emerged in which members of the group partnered to change Jewish life. First among these was the rescue and resuscitation of Hillel, the American Jewish entity responsible for Jewish life on university and college campuses. Other initiatives which emerged came from the energy and vision of the various Group members. The Partnership for Excellence in Jewish Education (PEJE) developed as a partnership of a number of philanthropists (and one federation) initiated by a half dozen of the Study Group members. Within a year after two of its members launched Birthright Israel, eight Group members became founders with initial donations of $5 million each, unprecedented in the scope of non capital project related startups. This effort attracted both the government of Israel and the communities of the world through the Federations, Keren Hayesod, and the Jewish Agency for Israel as partners, resulting in more than 70,000 young adults from 36 countries having their first living and learning experience in Israel.

This emerging trend did not come without concerns with entrepreneurial unilateral decision-making becoming more prevalent. Would federations be expected to pick up the pieces after foundations became fatigued while funding a program (even if worthwhile) for several years? Have we created new ethical dilemmas replacing a democratic, open Federation model with an autocratic, closed one? In smaller communities what role would emerge from local foundations whose assets and annual revenues greatly exceeded that of the community's structures? While there was a century worth of experience in the general world of foundations, the world of Jewish foundations tends to be significantly younger, especially those with assets in excess of $100 million.

Further, the general infrastructure of Jewish family foundations is yet underdeveloped. The Jewish Funders Network, founded in 1991, became a membership organization that was designed to respond to the needs of individual Jewish funders and foundations. Its annual meeting which attracts close to three hundred has subjects ranging from a fifth generation Rockefeller's guidance on philanthropy to the Israeli-Palestinian situation with major speakers in a variety of areas and includes donors of as little as $25,000 a year to those who are responsible for distributing as much as $50 million a year. In recent years federation endowment funds and affiliated foundations are among those who have participated in Jewish Funders Network meetings and there has been serious engagement on the many ethical and planning issues with regard to the relationship between the funders, the independent funders, and their communal organizational brethren. As the Jewish Funders Network becomes a more sophisticated setting, it is developing affinity groups with interest in areas such as Jewish education, the needy in Israel, etc.

As with American foundations in general, the overwhelming majority of Jewish family foundations have no staff and are managed by the principals, with assistance from families and or businesses. Nevertheless, 24% give away more than $250,000 a year and, increasingly, professional assistance is being sought to facilitate the management thereof. As with all American foundations, increasing attention is being paid to philanthropic impact including the evaluation of programs and projects supported by these foundations and in some cases the external evaluation of the foundation's own performance. In the late 1990s a group was established in London which brought together European, Israeli, and North American foundations who operated multinationally. These tended to be larger foundations and the objective of the group was to create a setting where principals and/or chief professionals in the Jewish funding arena could engage in exchanges that better met the needs of these larger multinational foundations.

The federation communal structure, in recognition of these trends, began a number of initiatives aimed at providing donors with collaborative models for giving, distinct from the historical annual campaign in which the distribution of all available funds was determined by a volunteer-driven planning and allocations process. Beginning in Washington, and then moving on to Toronto, New York, and Los Angeles Jewish venture philanthropy funds were established to engage younger donors in collaborative funding. While many of these funds did not meet the technical terms of "venture philanthropy" they became important experiments in creating funding collaboratives within the Federation structure yet outside of the formal allocations process. Similarly, several federations created Jewish women's foundations, which brought together a different affinity group with some of the same attributes. It is highly likely that the next phase of Jewish philanthropic development will find various permutations of individual entrepreneurial and communal philanthropy as communities and donors learn from these experiences.

In addition to the challenge of maintaining the collective strength, which so highlighted the effectiveness of Jewish philanthropy, Jewish life is challenged in maintaining the interest of the most generous donors. In a study of American gifts of more than $10 million between 1995 and 2000, Jewish donors represented 18% of these "mega" gifts and 23% of the total giving in this category while being only 2% of the total population. Only 6% of this support went to Jewish causes.

In the early 21st century, Jewish American foundations will see the greatest transfer of wealth in history as those who earned great fortunes in the mid- to late-20th century bequeath their fortunes, thus creating a new generation of young philanthropists. This occurs at the same time there is a decentralization of Jewish philanthropy, moving away from the federation "central address" in favor of donor-driven programming. Simultaneously, philanthropy is becoming more hands-on with donor involvement beyond writing out checks. Donors are holding their own foundations and the community to higher standards of accountability. They seek not only greater involvement in decision-making as to the use of their support but also want to monitor the impact and effectiveness of its use. These dynamics will continue to create conflicts between systems of collective responsibility and the emerging entrepreneurial foundation generation. The evaluation of Jewish family foundations is early in its development, but already has radically altered the Jewish philanthropic scene.

See also *Philanthropy.

[Jeffrey R. Solomon (2nd ed.)]

ADD. BIBLIOGRAPHY: R. Greenberg, "Is It Good for the Jews?" in: *B'nai B'rith* (Winter 2003–4); G.A. Tobin, *Jewish Family Foundations Study* (1996); G.A. Tobin, J.R. Solomon, and A.C. Karp. *Mega-Gifts in American Jewish Philanthropy* (2003); U.S. Census Bureau, *Statistical Abstract of the United States 2004–2005*.

FOUR CAPTIVES, THE, story circulated in Spain in the Middle Ages on the subject of four rabbis who were taken captive. According to this story, which is preserved in Abraham *Ibn Daud's *Sefer ha-Kabbalah* (*The Book of Tradition*, ed. by G.D. Cohen (1967), 46–49, 63–67), a Muslim sea raider from Cordoba, Spain (probably Ibn Rumaḥis, 974) captured a ship which had set sail from Bari in southern Italy. On it were four rabbis who were on a mission (it is conjectured on behalf of the Babylonian academy) to raise funds for the dowries of poor brides. These rabbis were redeemed by Jewish communities: R. *Shemariah b. Elhanan in Alexandria, Egypt; R. *Ḥushi'el was sold in "Africa" (i.e., Tunisia) and became the leader of the Kairouan rabbis; R. *Moses b. Ḥanokh and his son *Hanokh were redeemed in Cordoba. The identity of the fourth captive and the place where he was redeemed was not stated.

There are various opinions among researchers as to the authenticity of this story. The principal argument against its veracity is to be found in a letter written by R. Ḥushi'el to R. Shemariah b. Elhanan and his son Elhanan, from which it is evident that he left his country (perhaps Italy) voluntarily in order to travel to Egypt, but remained in Kairouan to await the arrival of his son Elhanan. It also appears that R. Shemariah b. Elhanan was already in Egypt, as his father was the leader of Egyptian Jewry. Another objection is chronological. On the one hand, Ibn Daud writes (*ibid.*, 66/48) that the appointment of R. Moses b. Ḥanokh occurred during the lifetime of R. *Sherira Gaon in about 990, while on the other hand, it appears from his account that his appointment, as well as that of his son Ḥanokh several years later, occurred during the lifetime of *Ḥisdai ibn Shaprut, who died in about 990 (*ibid.*, 67). The story of Ibn Daud reflects the popular tradition which was current among the Jews of Andalusia during the generation after R. Moses Ḥanokh's arrival in Spain. A proof for the relative antiquity of the tradition is the fact that David *Conforte, in his *Kore ha-Dorot* (1846, 5a), recounts it on the authority of *Samuel ha-Nagid (993–1056). By this story Ibn Daud presumably wanted to demonstrate the historical fact of the disintegration of the spiritual center in Babylonia, its gradual removal to Spain from the beginning of the tenth century, and the end of the dependence of the Spanish rabbis on Babylonia. From the time of the arrival of R. Moses b. Ḥanokh in Spain the Spanish scholars became independent. Indeed, the story of R. Moses B. Ḥanokh's appointment to the position of chief *dayyan* in Cordoba in the place of the *dayyan R.* Nathan, who surrendered his position to R. Moses b. Ḥanokh when he became aware of the latter's erudition, is an ancient motif which already existed in talmudic literature (in the story of *Hillel and the *Benei Bathyra, Pes. 66a). It appears that Abraham Ibn Daud and the author of *Midrash Tanḥuma*, who brings a similar motif (Tanh. Ex. 277), drew this idea from an ancient source.

BIBLIOGRAPHY: S. Eppenstein, in: MGWJ, 55 (1911), 324–9, 464–77, 614–28; 56 (1912), 80–98; J. Mann, in: JQR, 9 (1918/19), 165–79; S. Schechter, in: JQR, 11 (1899), 643–50; G.D. Cohen, in: PAAJR, 29 (1961), 55–131; Auerbach, in: *Jahresbericht des Rabbiner-Seminars zu Berlin fuer 1925, 1926, 1927* (1928), 1–39; L. Blau, in: *Festschrift … David Simonsen* (1923), 129–33 (Ger.); Z. Javetz, *Toledot Yisrael*, 10 (1932), 238–43; Abramson, Merkazim, 159–61; Ashtor, Korot, 1 (1966[2]), 289–90; Hirschberg, Afrikah, 1 (1965), 24 lf., 382; M. Margalioth, *Hilkhot ha-Nagid* (1962), 6f.

[Abraham David]

°**FOURIER, FRANÇOIS MARIE CHARLES** (1772–1837), French philosopher and social reformer who inspired the Fourierist or Phalansterian school. Somewhat like Rousseau, Fourier pursued his aim – cure for social evils – with passionate dogmatism and intolerance. His dream of a better world went hand in hand with a phobia against foreigners, and above all Jews. For him commerce was "the source of all evil" and Jews were "the incarnation of commerce." In his earlier writings, Fourier leveled every accusation possible against the Jews. He believed that their economic activities were parasitic and rapacious and declared that there had never been "a nation more despicable than the Hebrews" (*Théorie des quatre mouvements et des destinées générales* (1808), 61, 253), the emancipation of slaves and Jews having been effected too suddenly. Yet, either because he saw the Jews as a nation or because he wanted them out of France, Fourier became a kind of Zionist. In his last book, *La fausse industrie* (1836), he no longer gave vent to antisemitic remarks and advocated the reconstitution of the Hebrew nation in Palestine around a model Jewish "*phalanstère*" – Fourier's own idea, a form of social organization in which goods and services were held in common – financed by Rothschild. However, Fourier's "Zionist" project remained unknown while his antisemitism was taken up by several of his followers, particularly A. *Toussenel. At the time of the Dreyfus case, the Fourierist newspaper edited by Adolphe Alhaïza was virulently antisemitic.

BIBLIOGRAPHY: E. Silberner, *Sozialisten zur Judenfrage* (1962), index; idem, in: JSOS, 8 (1946), 245–66; IESS, 5 (1968), 547–8; L. Poliakov, *Histoire de l'Anti-sémitisme, 3* (1968), 380–4; M. Bourgin, *Etude sur les sources de Fourier* (1905).

FOUR SPECIES (Heb. אַרְבָּעָה מִינִים, *arba'ah minim*), the four different plants which form an obligatory part of the rite of Sukkot according to the biblical commandment "And ye shall take you on the first day [of Sukkot] the fruit of goodly trees, branches of palm trees, and boughs of thick trees, and willows of the brook, and ye shall rejoice before the Lord your God seven days" (Lev. 23:40). "Ye shall dwell in booths for seven days" (Lev. 23:42) is also enjoined. Despite the fact that it would appear that in the time of Nehemiah, the plants in the first verse were regarded as referring to the materials from which the *sukkah* (see: *Sukkot), mentioned in the second verse, was to be constructed (Neh. 8:15), the traditional interpretation sees it as a commandment separate and distinct from the injunction of the *sukkah*.

Two of the species are given explicitly: the "branches of palm trees" are the *lulav*, and the "willows of the brook," the *aravot*. Tradition has universally identified the "fruits of goodly trees" with the *etrog* and the "boughs of thick trees" with *hadassim* ("myrtle"; Suk. 32b–33 but see the remarkable passage in Lev. R. 30:15). The four species are made up of three sprigs of myrtle and two of willow, which are bound to the *lulav* with strips of palm, the former on the right and the latter on the left of the *lulav*. They are held in the right hand and the *etrog* is held separately in the left (Suk. 37b).

During the Temple period the main ceremonial of the four species took place in the Temple. They were taken and waved during the seven days of Sukkot whereas elsewhere, the rite was confined to the first day only (Suk. 3:12). They were waved in a prescribed manner: toward the east, south, west, north, upward, and downward, in acknowledgment of the divine rule over nature (Suk. 37b). This took place during the recitation of Psalms 118:1–2 and 25 in the *Hallel*. After the Musaf sacrifice of the day had been offered, the four species were again taken, this time in procession around the altar while Psalms 118:25, or the words *ani va-hu hoshi'ah na, a* popular version of that verse, were chanted. On the first six days, only one circuit of the altar was made; on the seventh day, seven circuits. After the destruction of the Temple, R. *Johanan b. Zakkai ordained the Temple ceremonial as universal practice "in remembrance of the Temple" (Suk. 3:12); all the features of the Temple rite were included in the synagogue service (see: Sukkot, *Hoshana Rabba).

The popularity of the ceremony during the period of the Second Temple is reflected in the fact that *Ḥanukkah was celebrated by the Maccabees as a second Feast of Tabernacles, as well as in the incident in which the vast throng of worshipers in the Temple pelted King Alexander *Yannai with their *etrogim* during the festival, in protest against his disregard of the Feast of Water Drawing (see *Sukkot) (Jos., Ant., 13:372; cf. Suk. 4:9). The remarkable hold which the four species had on the sentiments of the people during the Second Temple period, and immediately afterward, is evidenced by the fact that even during the rigors of war, Bar Kokhba took special care to see that his warriors were supplied with them (see Yadin, in BJPES, 25 (1961), 60–62).

In the Bible no attempt is made to explain the symbolism of the four species. They probably symbolized the fertility of the land as evidenced in the harvest just concluded, and as desired for the coming season, especially with a view to the fact that the rains are due immediately after Sukkot. The Midrash gives a number of moral and homiletic interpretations (see Lev. R. 30:9–12); the most popular (*ibid.*, 30:12) is based on the qualities of the four trees. The *etrog* has both "taste and odor," the date (palm) only taste, the myrtle only odor, the willow none. "taste and odor" symbolize "Torah and good works"; respectively the four species represent four categories of Jews insofar as they possess both, one, or none of these virtues. But Israel is regarded as a whole, and the failings of one are compensated for by the virtues of the others.

Another interpretation depends upon the shape of the species. The *lulav* resembles the spine, the *etrog* the heart, the myrtle leaves the eye, and the willow leaves the mouth. Therefore one should submit these organs, and all the others, to the service of God, in accordance with Psalms 35:10, "All my bones shall say, Lord, who is like unto Thee" (Lev. R. 30:14). It has also been suggested that the four species represent the four agricultural areas of Israel: the *lulav*, the lowland; the *aravot*, the river; the *hadassim*, the mountains; and the *etrog*, the irrigated areas. Kabbalistic symbolism interprets the four species in terms of the doctrine of the *Sefirot.*

[Louis Isaac Rabinowitz]

FOX (Heb. שׁוּעָל), the *Vulpes vulpes.* The biblical name is *shu'al*, as in the passage: "Take us the foxes, the little foxes that spoil the vineyards" (Song 2:15). The comparison in Ezekiel 13:4 of the false prophets to foxes may be a reference to their craftiness or to their habit of frequenting ruins. Parables about the fox's cunning are contained in the folklore of various nations; R. Meir is said to have compiled 300 fox fables (Sanh. 38b). The word *shu'al* however is also used for the jackal, and the other biblical passages in which it occurs, e.g., the one in which Samson is said to have caught 300 *shu'alim* (Judg. 15:4), probably refer to it. The place-name Shaalbim (Judg. 1:35) or Shaalabbin (Josh. 19:42) is probably the etymon (in the plural) of the Arabic and Akkadian words for "fox," – *thaʿlab* and *sēlibu*, respectively.

BIBLIOGRAPHY: S. Bodenheimer, *Ha-Ḥai be-Ereẓ Yisrael* (1953), 244; Tristram, Nat Hist, 85–87. **ADD. BIBLIOGRAPHY:** Feliks, *Ha-Ẓome'aḥ*, 279.

[Jehuda Feliks]

FOX, BERNARD JOSHUA (1885–1978), Northern Irish judge. Born in Belfast, Fox was admitted to the Irish bar in 1914 and was legal adviser to the government of Northern Ireland from 1939 to 1944 when he was given a judgeship as Recorder of Belfast. He was chairman of several government committees including the wartime Price Regulation Committee for Northern Ireland. He retired in 1960.

FOX, CHAIM-LEIB (Fuks/Fuchs; 1897–1984), Yiddish author and journalist. Born in Lodz, Fox was at the center of its Yiddish literary life, which he described in a number of essays (e.g., "Dos Yidishe Literarishe Lodzh" ("Yiddish Literary Lodz"), in: *Fun Noentn Over,* 3 (1957), 189–284) and in his monograph *Lodzh shel Mayle* ("Heavenly Lodz," 1972). During World War I Fox was a labor conscript in Germany. After a brief period in the *Bund, he joined the Labor Zionist movement and, in Palestine (1936–38), the Haganah. During World War II he was in the Soviet Union (1940–46) and thereafter lived in Lodz, Paris (1948–53), and New York. He wrote for many periodicals and contributed over 3,000 articles to the *Leksikon fun der Nayer Yidisher Literatur.* A poet of intense religious and national feeling, he published seven volumes of poetry (1926–82) and wrote the historical novel *Gyoras Letster Veg* ("Giora's Final Road," 1939) and *100 Yor Yidishe un Hebreishe Prese in Kanade* ("100 Years of Yiddish and Hebrew Press in Canada," 1980).

BIBLIOGRAPHY: Rejzen, Leksikon, 4 (1929), 32–3; LNYL, 7 (1968), 322–5. **ADD. BIBLIOGRAPHY:** Kagan, Leksikon (1986), 439; I. Yanasowicz, *Penemer un Nemen* (1971), 262–72.

[Leonard Prager / Tamar Lewinsky (2nd ed.)]

FOX, CHARLES (1876–1964), British psychologist. Born in London, Fox lectured at the Westminster Hospital Medical School and at the Cambridge University Training College for Schoolmasters. In 1919 he was appointed principal of the Training College and director of training at Cambridge University, serving through 1939. A specialist in the field of educational psychology, his important books are *Practical Psychology* (1928), *Educational Psychology* (1925, 1950[4]), and *The Mind and Its Body* (1931). His basic approach was to extract the practical features from each of the conflicting theoretical schools – such as the Freudian and the Gestalt – and to coordinate them so that they could be incorporated into an expanding science of learning.

FOX, EMANUEL PHILIPS (1864–1915), Australian artist, generally known as E. Philips Fox. Born in Melbourne, Fox studied in Paris from 1886 to 1892, but returned to his birthplace, where he spent most of the rest of his life. His paintings, which include many commissioned portraits, are highly regarded and well-represented in Australia's galleries. Fox is probably the best-known Australian Jewish artist.

BIBLIOGRAPHY: Australian Dictionary of Biography; H.L. Rubinstein, Australia I, 446–47.

[William D. Rubinstein (2nd ed.)]

FOX, EYTAN (1964–), Israeli film director whose films often focus on homosexuals in Israel. His film *Yossi & Jagger* (2002) broke taboos in its depiction of a romance between two male IDF soldiers and won a Best Actor Award at the Tribeca Film Festival in New York for leading man Ohad Knoller. Fox followed it up with *Walk on Water* (2004), the story of a Mossad agent assigned to spy on the homosexual grandson of a notorious Nazi. *Walk on Water* was the first Israeli film ever selected to open the Panorama section of the Berlin Film Festival. Born in New York, Fox moved to Israel as a child and made his name directing *Florentine*, a popular television show in the 1990s about young people in Tel Aviv. His other directing credits include the films *Gotta Have Heart* (1997) and *Song of the Siren* (1994).

[Hannah Brown (2nd ed.)]

FOX (Fuchs), JACOB SAMUEL (1868–1938), journalist and educator. Born in Bialystok, Russia, he obtained his rabbinical diploma at the Berlin Rabbinical Seminary and pursued his secular studies at Berlin and Berne. Turning to journalism, he edited *Ha-Maggid he-Ḥadash* (1891–98) and (together with A. Guenzig) *Ha-Eshkol* (1898–1912). A research trip prompted his final move to England in 1902, after which Fox decided to foster Jewish education in Liverpool by founding a Hebrew higher grade school. He supported the establishment of the British Mizrachi and became principal of Aria College in Brighton. He was author of a monograph on Judah *Ibn Bal'am. His son, ISAAC SOLOMON FOX (1896–1971), practiced as a physician, was mayor of Chester (1932–33) and chairman of the British Zionist Federation (1955–56).

FOX, SIR JOHN JACOB (1874–1944), British chemist. Fox, who was born in London, studied at the Royal College of Science and entered government service in 1896. He was appointed government chemist in 1936 and retained this post until his death. In organic chemistry Fox obtained noteworthy results with hydroxyazo compounds. Later he turned to the application of physical methods to the solution of chemical problems and to analysis. He applied ultraviolet and infrared spectroscopy to the study of elements, and his work on diamonds was monumental. Fox was adept at improving both the procedures and the apparatus for analytical work, a major concern of the government's laboratory during both world wars. He was president of the Institute of Chemistry from 1940 to 1942 and in 1943 was elected a fellow of the Royal Society.

[Samuel Aaron Miller]

FOX, MARVIN (1922–1996), American Jewish educator. Born in Chicago, Fox received his B.A. in philosophy from Northwestern University in 1942, and his M.A. in the same field in 1946, obtained his doctorate from the University of Chicago in 1950, and completed his rabbinic studies at the Hebrew Theological College in that city. He served as a Jewish chaplain in the U.S. Army Air Force during World War II (1942–46). He taught at Ohio State University from 1948 through 1974, rising from instructor to professor of philosophy. He was appointed acting chairman of the department of philosophy from 1963 to 1964. He was a visiting professor of philosophy at the Hebrew University and Bar-Ilan University (1970–71).

In 1974 he was appointed director of the Lown School of Near Eastern and Judaic Studies at Brandeis University, chairman of the department, and in 1976 became the Philip W. Lown Professor of Jewish Philosophy. He was a founder and member of the executive committee of the Institute for Judaism and Contemporary Thought in Israel, a member of the Academic Board of the Melton Research Center of the Jewish Theological Seminary, and a member of the board of directors of the Library of Living Philosophers.

For many years Fox was active in the Hebrew Day School movement in the United States under the aegis of Torah Umesorah.

He received numerous academic awards, lectured widely at universities and at national and international academic conferences, and served as member of the National Endowment for the Humanities National Board of Consultants for new programs at colleges and universities.

A prolific writer, he was a consulting editor of the *Journal of the History of Philosophy* and was the author of more than 100 articles, which have appeared in scholarly journals, as well as in such general publications as *Commentary, Tradition*, and *Judaism*. Among Fox's important works are *Kant's Fundamental Principles of the Metaphysics of Morals* (1975), *Modern Jewish Ethics and Practice* (1975), *From Ancient Israel to Modern Judaism: Intellect in Quest of Understanding, Volume I* (1989), *Interpreting Maimonides: Studies in Methodology, Metaphysics, and Moral Philosophy* (1994), *Collected Essays on Philosophy and on Judaism, Volume One: Greek Philosophy, Maimonides* (ed. J. Neusner, published in 2003), *Collected Essays on Philosophy and on Judaism, Volume Two: Some Philosophers* (2003), and *Collected Essays on Philosophy and on Judaism, Volume Three: Ethics, Reflections* (2003).

In 1996, Dr. June Fox donated her late husband's book collections to the library of the University of Chicago. The Marvin Fox Memorial Book Collection of Philosophy and Judaica is an invaluable resource on Judaism, secularism, and textual interpretation.

[Ruth Beloff (2nd ed.)]

FOX (Fuchs), WILLIAM (1879–1952), U.S. film producer. Born in Tulchva, Hungary, Fox worked in his youth in New York's garment center. In 1904 he bought his first nickelodeon, installed a motion picture machine, opened a chain of movie theaters in the U.S. and abroad, and started a career that led him in 1915 to the presidency of Fox Film and Fox Theater Corporations. Dissatisfied with the quality of films distributed, he began to make his own films in a rented barn. In 1917 he built studios in Hollywood. By the 1920s he had created a multimillion-dollar empire that controlled a large portion of the exhibition, distribution, and production of film facilities during the era of silent film. Fox introduced organ accompaniment to the silent films shown in his theaters and was a pioneer in designing movie theaters for the comfort of its patrons. Through a well-orchestrated use of publicity, he developed Theda Bara into the first screen vamp and the first film star. Even during the Great Depression, Fox had the foresight and the wherewithal to outfit more than a thousand theaters with equipment to make possible the advent of talking pictures. In 1927 he developed the first commercially successful sound film, the news series *Movietone News*.

The stock market crash of 1929 and the entry of Wall Street into the film industry involved him in years of litigation and eventual loss of money and power. Charges of stock manipulation were filed against him in 1932, and he told a Senate subcommittee he was the target of a "bankers' conspiracy." He declared bankruptcy in 1936, and in 1942 served five months in prison on charges of obstructing justice in his bankruptcy claim. The Fox Film Corporation was the antecedent of Twentieth Century Fox.

BIBLIOGRAPHY: *Americana Annual 1953*. (1953), 259; J. Laurie, *Vaudeville* (1953), 410–1.

[Linda Gutstein / Ruth Beloff (2nd ed.)]

FOXMAN, ABRAHAM (1940–), Anti-Defamation League (ADL) executive. Born in Poland in 1940, Foxman survived the Holocaust when his parents entrusted him to their Catholic nursemaid, who baptized him and raised him as her own son. After the war, which Foxman's parents, Helen and Joseph, miraculously survived, they returned to claim him but faced several custody battles, which they ultimately won. Following their safe passage to a Displaced Person's Camp in the American Zone in Austria, the family eventually moved to the United States in January 1950.

Three imperatives that have shaped his life are the legacy of the Holocaust, particularly his experience as a hidden child, and his belief in the necessity of working to insure the security of the State of Israel and the safety of Jews to live freely as Jews everywhere, especially the United States.

Foxman's first assignment at the ADL was as assistant director of the Law Department, where he worked under the guidance of the legendary Arnold Forster and the leadership of the late national director Benjamin R. Epstein. His ascension through ADL's professional staff ranks mirrored the growth of the organization itself. As the first director of national leadership, Foxman created the annual Washington Leadership Conference. He founded and directed ADL's International Affairs Division, launching an Israel missions program that, at one point, had brought nearly one-third of all members of Congress on their first visit. When Nathan Perlmutter succumbed to cancer in July 1987, Foxman was appointed national director.

Foxman elevated the profile of ADL through a combination of passion, intuition, and intellect. Two seminal and defining events would propel him to a mantle of moral authority: the first was ADL's response to the virulently antisemitic, anti-Catholic, and anti-white diatribe delivered in November 1993 at New Jersey's Kean College by the Nation of Islam Lieutenant Khalid Abdul Mohammed. Among other rants, Mohammed wondered what was under the Pope's skirt, mocking the aging John Paul II and infuriating American Catholics. ADL's public rebuke of the NOI leader in a full-page *New York Times* ad triggered a hailstorm of condemnation, from the halls of Congress to pulpits across the country. By meeting such hate head-on, Foxman placed ADL on a stage that transcended the perceived boundaries of the organization's public advocacy.

Shortly thereafter, ADL released its benchmark survey on the growing influence of the Christian right. Titled *The Religious Right: the Assault on Tolerance and Pluralism in America*, this book-length report, intended to be a factual and critical assessment of some of the individuals and groups within the movement and their efforts to chip away at the wall of separation between church and state, was met with near universal hostility from those whom it addressed. Nonetheless, the resulting public hue and cry, and the "summit meetings" that would follow, established Foxman as the linchpin in a major national debate, which continued into the first decade of the 21st century, of the role of religion in American national life.

In 2000, Foxman rebuked Democratic vice presidential candidate Senator Joseph *Lieberman, who spoke of the need for religious values in American life, for injecting religion into the public square. Foxman did not repeat this call during the 2004 election, when religion again entered the public square, for he was still regaining his balance after a nearly year-long controversy over Mel Gibson's controversial film *The Passion of the Christ*. Foxman's initial private and respectful inquiries to Gibson went unanswered. Instead of following the customary American protocol and meeting with Jewish leaders in the hope of finding common ground, Gibson and his followers turned the tables and accused their accusers of being anti-Christian, a charge reiterated so often on cable television shows, in conservative newspapers, and among web "bloggers" that it became the dominant story. Some in the Jewish community would come to accuse Foxman of generating more interest in the film than it might have otherwise garnered.

[Richard S. Hirschhaut (2nd ed.)]

FRAENCKEL, LIEPMANN (1774–1857), miniature painter. Born in Germany, Fraenckel settled in Copenhagen in 1792. During a stay in Sweden from 1802 to 1805 he painted several members of the Swedish nobility. From 1814 he worked for the Danish court painting King Frederick VI and members of his family. Two hundred miniatures were made before 1830. In 1826 he founded a wallpaper factory, which still exists.

FRAENKEL (also **Frankel, Fraenckel, Frankl**, etc.), family widely scattered throughout Central and Eastern Europe. The name first appears in non-Jewish records as a designation for those who had immigrated to Vienna from "Frankenland," in the West. The family is traced back to two scholars in the Swabian town of Wallerstein in the 16th century, Moses ha-Levi Heller and Aaron Heller. Moses was the ancestor of Koppel Fraenkel ha-Levi "the rich" of Vienna (see below). Members of the family married into the patrician Teomim (called Munk in non-Jewish sources), Mirels, and Spiro families of Vienna and Prague. The name begins in Jewish use in the late 17th century, and after the expulsion of the Jews from Vienna (1670) is found throughout Central and Eastern Europe. KOPPEL FRAENKEL HA-LEVI (d. 1670), born in Baiersdorf, settled in Vienna around 1635 and became the richest man in the community. His sons DAVID ISAAC (Seckel), ISRAEL, and ENOCH (Hoenig) wound up the affairs of the Vienna community after the expulsion of 1670, giving 20,000 florins and the crown jewels of the principality of Moldavia (pawned to Koppel in 1665) as a security for the outstanding Jewish debts. They paid the city 4,000 florins for maintenance of the Jewish cemetery. With good conduct certificates, signed by Leopold I, they moved to Fuerth, where David Isaac became head of the community. Israel subsequently officiated as rabbi in Holesov, Uhersky Brod, Pinsk, and Wuerzburg. Enoch taught Hebrew to Johann Christoph *Wagenseil, and in 1683 sent him a letter stressing the importance of tolerance. Sons of Enoch were the ill-fated Ansbach Court Jews Elkan *Fraenkel and his brother Ẓevi Hirsch. GABRIEL and ZACHARIAS FRAENKEL, wealthy Court Jews to various south German principalities, resided in Fuerth but were not directly related to the Austrian levite branch. A son of David Isaac, ISSACHAR BERMAN (d. 1708), became chief rabbi of Schnaittach, Bavaria, **Landesrabbiner* of Ansbach, and rabbi of Brandenburg. Two of his sons, JUDAH LOEB and AARON LEVI, who published a collection of *seliḥot*, settled in Worms, where they and their descendants were prominent in communal life. The most noted of his numerous descendants was the founder of the Breslau seminary, Zacharias *Frankel. ISAAC SECKEL *FRAENKEL, the exponent of extreme Reform Judaism, was probably a descendant, as was L.A. *Frankl, the Austrian writer. Members of the family were among the Jews originally expelled from Vienna who settled in Berlin and Brandenburg, one of whom was appointed leader (*Obervorsteher*) of all the newly arrived Jews. BAERMANN FRAENKEL, another prominent communal leader, was fined 20 talers in 1705 for conducting a too-raucous Purim festival. The most famous of the Berlin Fraenkels was David ben Naphtali Hirsch *Fraenkel, teacher of Moses *Mendelssohn and rabbi of Berlin. His grandson JONAS FRAENCKEL (1773–1846), a wealthy Breslau merchant and philanthropist, donated the funds for the Breslau seminary. David Fraenkel's brothers, ABRAHAM and MOSES, were partners of V.H. *Ephraim in supplying precious metals to the mint. DAVID BEN MOSES FRAENKEL (d. 1865), director of the Dessau Franzschule and editor of **Sulamith*, was a grandnephew of David Fraenkel; the wife of Leopold *Zunz was his grandniece. The Fraenkel family belonged to the upper stratum of Jewish society and through intermarriage was connected with numerous scholars and community leaders including Avigdor *Kara, Yom Tov Lippmann *Heller, Jacob *Emden, and Baruch *Fraenkel Teomim. All Jews currently named Fraenkel may be descendants of the original Vienna family, though the exact relationship is no longer traceable.

BIBLIOGRAPHY: L. Bato, in: AJR *Information* (July 1964), 12; M.M. Fraenkel-Teomim, *Der goldene Tiegel der Familie Fraenkel* (1928); Ger., Heb.); A.F. Pribram, *Urkunden und Akten zur Geschichte der Juden in Wien*, 1 (1918), index; D. Kaufmann, *Die letzte Vertreibung der Juden aus Wien* (1889), 144–8; Fraenkel, in: ZGGJT, 2 (1931/32), 67–80; E.K. Frenkel, *Family Tree of R. Moshe Witzenhausen* (1969); H. Schnee, *Die Hoffinanz und der moderne Staat*, 3 (1955), index; 4 (1963), index; S. Stern, *Der preussische Staat und die Juden* (1962), index.

FRAENKEL, ABRAHAM ADOLF (1891–1965), Israeli mathematician. Born in Munich, Fraenkel received a thorough education in talmudic and Jewish studies in addition to mathematics. He held chairs of mathematics at Marburg (from 1922) and Kiel (1928). From 1929 to 1931 he was visiting professor at the Hebrew University, Jerusalem, and accepted a permanent chair there in 1933. Fraenkel made important contributions to set theory. His publications are listed in *Essays on the Foundations of Mathematics Dedicated to A.A. Fraenkel on His Seventieth Birthday*, ed. by Y. Bar Hillel (1966).

FRAENKEL, DAVID BEN NAPHTALI HIRSCH (1707–1762), German rabbi and commentator on the Jerusalem Talmud. Fraenkel was born in Berlin. He was descended from the Mirels family that originated in Vienna and was also known as David Mirels. He studied under his father who was a *dayyan* in Berlin and under Jacob b. Benjamin ha-Kohen *Poppers, author of *Shav Ya'akov*. After living for a time in Hamburg, in 1737 he was appointed rabbi of Dessau, where Moses *Mendelssohn was one of his pupils. In 1739–42 his father Naphtali and his brother Solomon undertook the printing of Maimonides' *Mishneh Torah* on his initiative. In 1743 he was appointed chief rabbi of Berlin. Mendelssohn followed him to Berlin and continued to study under him (particularly Maimonides' *Guide of the Perplexed*) and also provided for his material needs. In Fraenkel's letter of appointment it was expressly stipulated that he was not to act as judge or give rulings in cases where members of his family, of whom there was a great number in Berlin, were involved. Fraenkel's jurisdiction extended to the districts of Brandenburg and Pomerania.

Fraenkel's main achievement is his commentary to the Jerusalem Talmud which constitutes his life work. It is divided into two parts: the first part, *Korban ha-Edah*, following Rashi's commentary to the Babylonian Talmud, is a running commentary aimed at elucidating the plain meaning of the text; the second part, *Shirei Korban*, in the manner of the *tosafot*, gives novellae and various notes to reconcile contradictions in the *Gemara* and correct the errors and inaccuracies that had accumulated in the text. At times his explanations in this commentary differ from those in *Korban ha-Edah*. The commentary appeared in parts: part one (Dessau, 1743) on *Mo'ed*, part two (Berlin, 1757) on *Nashim*, and part three (*ibid.*, 1760–62) on *Nezikin*. He commenced with *Mo'ed* because for *Zera'im* there already existed the commentary of Elijah b. Judah Leib of Fulda published in 1710. His commentary has become one of the two standard commentaries to the Jerusalem Talmud. He wrote Hebrew poems following various events in Prussia – the end of the Silesian wars (1745) and the victory of Prussia in the Seven Years' War (1757) – and published sermons that were translated, in part by Mendelssohn, into German.

BIBLIOGRAPHY: E.L. Landshuth, *Toledot Anshei ha-Shem u-Fe'ullatam be-Adat Berlin* (1884), 35–60; M. Kayserling, *Moses Mendelssohn* (1862), 8ff.; M. Freudenthal, *Aus der Heimat Mendelssohns* (1900), 214ff., 229ff.; Z. Horowitz, in: *Oẓar ha-Ḥayyim*, 6 (1930), 188; Waxman, Literature, 3 (1960²) 708ff.; E. Wolbe, *Geschichte der Juden in Berlin* (1937), 177, 188, 191; L. Ginzberg, *Perushim ve-Ḥiddushim ba-Yerushalmi*, 1 (1941), 55f. (Eng. introd.); J. Meisl, in: *Arim ve-Immahot be-Yisrael*, 1 (1946), 103; idem (ed.), *Pinkas Kehillat Berlin* (1962), index.

[Yehoshua Horowitz]

FRAENKEL, ELKAN (c. 1655–1720), *Court Jew in Ansbach. His father became rabbi in Fuerth and Bamberg after the expulsion of the Jews from Vienna in 1670. However Elkan antagonized the Fuerth community by advocating the interests of the margrave of Ansbach against the prelate of Bamberg, the traditional guardian of Fuerth Jewry. In 1703, Fraenkel became Court Jew of the margrave displacing the *Model family in this post, who thus became his bitter enemies. In 1704, he became an elder (*parnas*) of Fuerth and Ansbach Jewry. Although he could exercise magnanimity, reducing a fine of 30,000 florins imposed on the community for usurious practices to 20,000 florins, he was in general despotic and aroused much opposition. In 1712 he was denounced by Essaja (Jesse) Fraenkel, the spendthrift son of a Fuerth printer and a convert to Christianity, and falsely accused of 16 charges including witchcraft, lèse-majesté, debauchery, possession of blasphemous books, and hindering the confiscation of Hebrew books in Fuerth in 1702. He was sentenced to a public whipping and life imprisonment. His possessions were confiscated and his wife and daughter expelled. His brother ẒEVI HIRSCH (d. 1723), appointed *Landesrabbiner* in 1709, was accused of witchcraft and use of kabbalistic devices to further Elkan's career. He received the same sentence and died in prison.

BIBLIOGRAPHY: S. Stern, *The Court Jew* (1950), 193–4, 237–8, 244, 256–7; H. Schnee, *Die Hoffinanz und der Moderne Staat*, 4 (1963), 26–28; Ziemlich, in: MGWJ, 46 (1902), 88–93; idem, in: *Gedenkbuch D. Kaufmann* (1901), 457–86; Weinberg, in: MGWJ, 50 (1906), 94–99; S. Haenle, *Geschichte der Juden im ehemaligen Fuerstenthum Ansbach* (1867), 72–86; D.Y. Cohen, *Irgunei "Benei ha-Medinah" be-Ashkenaz...*, 1 (1968), 141ff.; 2 (1968), 135–7 (mimeographed dissertation; English summary).

FRAENKEL, FAIWEL (Bar Tuviah; 1875?–1933), Hebrew author and publicist. He was born in Vasilkov, in the district of Kiev. In 1893 he published his first article on Polish Jewish history in *Ha-Meliẓ*. He moved to Kiev, and in 1899 published a Hebrew translation of Pinsker's *Autoemancipation*, and a Hebrew translation and adaptation of Edward Bellamy's *Looking Backward* titled *Be-Od Me'ah Shanah* ("One Hundred Years Hence"). An active socialist, he was forced to leave Russia in 1901. He went to Switzerland, studied at the University of Berne, and received his doctorate in 1906 for his dissertation *Buckle und seine Geschichtsphilosophie* (Berner Studien, 1906). He lived in Geneva (1906–12), San Remo (1912–17), and Nice. Bar-Tuviah published many articles in Hebrew literary-scholarly periodicals, including *Ha-Dor, Ha-Me'orer, Ha-Olam, He-Atid, Ha-Tekufah, Miklat*, and *Hadoar*. They deal primarily with social science, Jewish studies, and socialist theory. He was the first Hebrew writer to discuss social sciences in depth. In the field of Jewish studies he investigated the economic background of the formation of sects and parties in ancient Israel. His noteworthy contribution to this subject is his unfinished *Sefer ha-Nezirim*, a two-part history of asceticism among the Jews (1910). His more popular articles took up, in the main, questions of socialism and nationalism, and called for the negation of the Diaspora. His selected writings were published in 1964 by G. Elkoshi, accompanied by an evaluative biographical essay (9–40) and an annotated bibliography (729–808).

BIBLIOGRAPHY: Waxman, Literature, 4 (1960), 419ff.

[Gedalyah Elkoshi]

FRAENKEL, ISAAC SECKEL (1765–1835), Hebrew translator and banker. Fraenkel, who was born in Parchim, Germany, was self-educated. He acquired extensive knowledge of religious and secular subjects and of ancient and modern languages. In 1798 he moved to Hamburg where he engaged in banking and became one of the community leaders, particularly in its Reform congregation. Together with M.I. *Bresselau, Fraenkel edited a prayer book for the Hamburg Reform Temple (1818), which he defended in a German tract (*Schutzschrift des zu Hamburg erschienenen Israelitischen Gebetbuches*, 1819) when strong opposition against the new liturgy emerged among the traditionalists. Fraenkel's main literary project was the translation of the Apocrypha from Greek into Hebrew, entitled *Ketuvim Aḥaronim*. This work has frequently been reprinted since its first appearance in Leipzig (1830), its most recent edition appearing in Jerusalem in 1966. A bibliophile edition of the Books of the Maccabees, *Sefer ha-Ḥashmona'im*, appeared in Fraenkel's translation in 1964.

BIBLIOGRAPHY: *Kitvei Menahem Mibashan ha-Ḥadashim* (1937), 145–58; S. Bernfeld, *Toledot ha-Reformaẓyon ha-Datit be-Yisrael* (1923), 72–73 and appendix B (excerpts from the prayer book). **ADD. BIBLIOGRAPHY:** M.A. Meyer, *Response to Modernity* (1988), 54–60.

[Getzel Kressel]

FRAENKEL, JONAS (1879–1965), Swiss literary historian. Fraenkel was born in Cracow, Poland, studied at the Universities of Vienna and Berne, and became a lecturer at the latter in 1908 (professor extraordinary, 1921). He devoted himself to the investigation of German-Swiss literature and was the editor of the works of Gottfried Keller (17 vols., 1926–39). Other Swiss authors who engaged Fraenkel's attention were C.F. Meyer and his friend Carl Spitteler, whose unpublished works were bequeathed to Fraenkel for publication (*Spitteler – Huldigungen und Begegnungen*, 1945). In German literature Goethe and Heine were among his chief interests, and he published a new edition of Heine's poems (3 vols., 1911–13). Several of his essays were collected in *Dichtung und Wissenschaft* (1954).

ADD. BIBLIOGRAPHY: J. Schütt, *Germanistikm und Politik – Schweizer Literaturwissenschaft in der Zeit des Nationalsozialismus* (1996).

[Ludwig W. Kahn]

FRAENKEL, LEVI BEN SAUL (Schaulsohn; 1761–1815), apostate member of the rabbinical *Fraenkel family. In 1806 he was nominated by the authorities assistant of the *Breslau *bet din* and *Oberlandesrabbiner* for Silesia (excluding Breslau), despite local objections. A year later he left the city, addressing an open letter to the community in which he acclaimed the French *Sanhedrin, advocated the unification of all religions, and expressed messianic hopes centered around *Napoleon. His letter caused consternation. In the same year in Paris he embraced Catholicism and thereafter wandered throughout Europe, until his death in extreme poverty and neglect in a Jewish hospital in Frankfurt. He wrote a few mystical works.

BIBLIOGRAPHY: M. Brann, in: *Jubelschrift ... H. Graetz* (1887), 266–76; A. Freimann, in: ZHB, 4 (1900), 159. **ADD. BIBLIOGRAPHY:** *Biographisches Handbuch der Rabbiner*, 1 (2004), 323.

FRAENKEL, LOUIS (1851–1911), Swedish financier. Born in Germany, Fraenkel moved to Stockholm in 1874, where in 1880 he established a successful banking firm. In 1893 he became executive manager of the Stockholm Handelsbank (now Svenska Handelsbanken), which he developed into one of the largest financial institutions in the country. Fraenkel's activity was characterized by the personal manner in which he controlled his bank at a time when bureaucratic methods were becoming increasingly prevalent.

BIBLIOGRAPHY: *Svenska män och kvinnor*, 2 (1944).

[Hugo Mauritz Valentin]

FRAENKEL, OSMOND K. (1888–1983), U.S. constitutional lawyer. Fraenkel was the general counsel to the American Civil Liberties Union from 1955. He argued cases before the U.S. Supreme Court, seeking protection for political and religious groups, aliens, individuals holding dissident opinions, or persons convicted on the basis of improperly obtained confessions. He assisted in the Scottsboro case in the Alabama and Supreme Court hearings. In 1931 he wrote *The Sacco-Vanzetti Case*, arguing the innocence of the accused and the unfairness of the legal proceedings. He was the author of books on civil liberties, including *The Supreme Court and Civil Liberties* (1941, 1960^6); *Our Civil Liberties* (1944); *The Rights We Have* (1971); and *Georgetown Law Journal: Media and the First Amendment in a Free Society* (1973).

FRAENKEL-TEOMIM, BARUCH BEN JOSHUA EZEKIEL FEIWEL (1760–1828), rabbi in Poland and Moravia. Frankel-Teomim studied under Liber Korngold of Cracow, known as "Liber Ḥarif," and *David Tevele of Lissa. On the death in 1778 of Naphtali Herz Margolies, the *av bet din* of Wisznice, he was appointed his successor and served in this office until 1802. In that year he was appointed rabbi of Leipnik (Moravia), remaining there until his death. In Leipnik he founded a yeshivah which became renowned. Among his pupils were Ezekiel Panet, author of the *Mareh Yeḥezkel*, and Ḥayyim *Halberstamm, later his son-in-law (resp. *Ateret Ḥakhamim*, EH no. 9). During Fraenkel-Teomim's younger years *Ḥasidism began to spread in Poland and Galicia; at first he belonged to the circle of its opponents but later his opposition gradually diminished. Among the outstanding scholars with whom he was in contact may be mentioned Moses *Sofer (*ibid.*, ḤM nos. 12–15), with whom he was on intimate terms, David *Deutsch (*ibid.*, OḤ nos. 2,3), Ephraim Zalman *Margolioth (*ibid.*, EH no. 21), and Mordecai *Banet of Nikolsburg.

Fraenkel-Teomim saw his main task in the strengthening of his yeshivah and the education of many pupils. He did not devote himself to the same extent to the writing of books, for fear of dissipating his time. Only individual pamphlets by him are extant. These were written by his pupils, who noted down his novellae and homilies. Among the first to collect his teachings and publish them were his son Joshua Hoeschel and Ḥayyim Halberstamm. They published his *Barukh Ta'am* (1841), a selection of his novellae to which Halberstamm added glosses. Fraenkel is often referred to by the name of this book. Among his other works may be mentioned: (1) *Ateret Ḥakhamim* (1866) in two parts: pt. 1, responsa on the four sections of the *Shulḥan Arukh*; pt. 2, novellae and *pilpulim on talmudic themes; (2) *Margenita de-Rav* (1883; 2nd ed. with additions, 1957), a work on *aggadah* arranged in the order of the weekly scriptural readings, published by Menahem Eliezer Mahler from a manuscript in the possession of the author's grandchildren; (3) *Barukh she-Amar* (1905, 1966^2), novellae on many tractates and talmudic themes.

Fraenkel-Teomim left glosses written in the margin of his books of the *rishonim* and *aḥaronim*, and there is a list of 53 such works. His numerous glosses on the Shulḥan Arukh (OḤ, 1836; ḤM, 1860; YD, 1865; EH, 1904) under the title *Imrei Barukh* are highly regarded. His glosses to the Babylonian Talmud were published first in the Lemberg edition of the Talmud of 1862 and thereafter in all later editions; to the Jerusalem Talmud in Vilna in 1922; and to the Mishnah under the name *Mishnot Rav* in Lemberg in 1862. His *Derushei Barukh Ta'am* (edited by B.S. Schneersohn and E. Heilprin, 1963) contains homilies for the festivals, and eulogies. Other works remain in manuscript.

His responsa and *pilpulim* on talmudic themes are based on the *rishonim*, and penetrating deeply into their meaning he arrives at the *halakhah*. Although he indulged in *pilpul*, a simple answer was more important to him than casuistic exercises. Even though he showed himself in his responsa to be a great authority he mentions in various places that he "fears to give directives" (*Ateret Ḥakhamim*, EH 18, 22). In certain cases he did not wish to rely on his own opinion and sought the consent of other outstanding scholars for his view, stressing: "I am afraid to give expression to new ideas" (*ibid.*, YD 2:24).

BIBLIOGRAPHY: S.M. Chones, *Toledot ha-Posekim* (1910), 123; J.A. Kammelhar, *Dor De'ah* (1935), 143–9; J. Eibeschuetz, *Ohel Barukh* (1933); J.L. Maimon, in: *Sinai*, 44 (1959), 117–26, 204–12, 408–19; 45 (1959), 16–22, 97–106, 275–83; idem, *Middei Ḥodesh be-Ḥodsho*, 5 (1959), 49–57; Z. Horowitz, *Le-Korot ha-Kehillot be-Polanyah* (1969), 216f.; B. Fraenkel-Teomim, *Barukh she-Amar* (1966^2), introd. 13–28 (biography).

[Josef Horovitz]

FRAGA, city in Aragon, N.E. Spain; information concerning Jews there dates to the 13th century. The privileges which the Jews enjoyed, later confirmed by Alfonso IV of Aragon (1327–36), include the usual definition of civil rights. The maximum annual tax payable by the community was specified. The Jews were given the right to elect their representatives, who were granted a limited jurisdiction and the right to impose levies for communal purposes. They were permitted to maintain a synagogue, cemetery, and slaughterhouse, and were given the right of defending themselves against attacks. The Jews were promised that their quarter would be protected and its autonomy respected. In the 1380s there were 40 Jewish families living in Fraga. During the 1391 persecutions the synagogue was destroyed; many Jews left the town and others became converted to Christianity. In 1398 Queen Maria ordered 36 former members of the community to return to Fraga within a month, since they had undertaken not to leave without paying their share of the communal taxes. The most prominent member of the Fraga community, the physician and poet Astruc Rimoch, embraced Christianity in 1414 as Franciscus de Sant Jordi. In September 1414 Ferdinand I ordered a number of converts to pay the tax they owed before their conversion. By 1415 the Jewish community of Fraga had disappeared following the conversion of all its members. In 1436 John II permitted Jews to establish a new settlement in Fraga and Alfonso V promised privileges to Jews who would settle in Fraga. We have some information on the Jews in Fraga in 1451 and 1457 which suggests that the community apparently continued to exist until the expulsion in 1492.

The Jewish quarter was in the Collada, comprising one big street and several small byways leading to it.

BIBLIOGRAPHY: Baer, Urkunden, index; Baer, Spain, index; Salarrullana, in: *Revista de archivos, bibliotecas, museos*, 40 (1919), 69, 183, 431; Romano, in: *Sefarad*, 13 (1953), 75, 78. **ADD. BIBLIOGRAPHY:** J. Goñi Gaztambide, in: *Hispania Sacra*, 25 (1960), 205–6.

FRAM, DAVID (1903–1988), South African Yiddish poet. Born in Panevezys, Lithuania, he was a refugee with his parents in Russia during World War I, and returned to Lithuania in 1921. From 1923 he published poems in the Kaunas Yiddish press and in 1927 immigrated to South Africa, where he issued *Lider un Poemes* ("Songs and Poems," Vilna, 1931), nostalgic idylls of Jewish life in Lithuania, as well as South African poems. His later poetry dealt with South African themes, but remained rooted in Lithuanian Jewish tradition: "All the major actors on the South African stage step boldly forward in Fram's verse" (Sherman). His writings are marked by a deep compassion for the underdog and a sensitive lyrical quality. Outstanding examples are two long 1947 poems, "*Efsher*" ("Perhaps"), largely autobiographical, and "*Dos Letste Kapitl*" ("The Last Chapter"), an elegy on his destroyed Lithuanian homeland. Between the wars, Fram was active in Yiddish cultural circles in Johannesburg, a contributor to all Yiddish publications in South Africa, and wrote the libretti for two Yiddish operettas staged in Johannesburg. His later verse is anthologized in *A Shvalb oyfn Dakh* ("A Swallow on the Roof," 1984).

BIBLIOGRAPHY: LNYL, 7 (1968), 439. **ADD. BIBLIOGRAPHY:** J. Sherman, in: *The Mendele Review* (Jan. 14, 2004).

[Gustav Saron and Louis Hotz / Leonard Prager (2nd ed.)]

FRANCE (Heb. פְּרַאנְצִיָּה and צָרְפַת), country in Western Europe. This entry is arranged according to the following outline:

This article deals with the history of the Jews living within the territory corresponding to present-day France; the territories beyond the present frontiers (more particularly those of the north and southwest) which were subjected to the authority of the kings of France for short periods are not considered here. The provinces neighboring on the kingdom of France or enclosed within it before their incorporation within the kingdom (in particular *Brittany, Normandy, *Anjou, *Champagne, *Lorraine, *Alsace, *Franche-Comté, *Burgundy, *Savoy, *Dauphiné, the county of *Nice, *Provence, *Comtat Venaissin, *Languedoc, *Auvergne, Guienne, *Poitou) are dealt with. Those areas which formed part of these provinces, but which are today beyond the borders of France, are not included.

From the First Settlements until the Revolution

THE ROMAN AND MEROVINGIAN PERIODS. The earliest evidence of a Jewish presence in France concerns an isolated individual, perhaps accompanied by a few servants; he was *Archelaus, the ethnarch of Judea, who was banished by Augustus in the year 6 C.E. to *Vienne (in the present department of Isère), where he died in 16 C.E. Similarly, his younger brother Herod *Antipas, tetrarch of Galilee and Perea, was exiled to *Lyons (if not to a place also called Lugdunum on the French side of the Pyrenees) by Caligula in 39. A story taken as legend (intended to explain the origin of the prayer *Ve-Hu Raḥum*) states that after the conquest of Jerusalem, the Romans filled three ships with Jewish captives, which arrived in *Bordeaux, *Arles, and Lyons. Recent archaeological findings tend to find a basis for this legend. Objects identified as Jewish because of the *menorah* portrayed on them have been discovered around Arles (first, fourth, and early fifth centuries), and in Bordeaux and the neighboring region (third and early fourth centuries). Written sources, previously treated with some reserve, affirm that during the Roman period Jews had been present in *Metz (mid-fourth century), *Poitiers (late fourth century), *Avignon (late fourth century), and Arles (mid-fifth century).

Evidence is abundant from 465 onward. There were then Jews in Vannes (Brittany), a few years later in *Clermont-Ferrand and *Narbonne, in *Agde in 506, in *Valence in 524, and in *Orléans in 533. After Clovis I (481–511), founder of the Merovingian dynasty, became converted to Catholicism (496), the Christian population increasingly adopted Catholic doctrine. From 574 there were attempts to compel the Jews to accept the prevailing faith. In 576 Bishop *Avitus of Clermont-Ferrand offered the Jews of his town (who numbered over 500) the alternative of baptism or expulsion. His example was followed in 582 by Chilperic I, king of Neustria (the western part of the Frankish kingdom). In *Marseilles, where Jews from both these areas found refuge, there was also an attempt at forced conversion. Little information is available on a similar attempt made by Dagobert I between 631 and 639; had this been successful, the Jews would have been excluded from almost the whole of present-day France. However, this seems to have been far from the case; though documents make no mention of Jews for some time, there is a similar lack of information about other social and ethnic groups. Little is known of the Jews of Septimania (in southwest Gaul, then a Spanish province). The Jews there were spared the forced conversions and subsequent violent persecutions which befell their coreligionists in Visigothic *Spain.

During this period the number of Jews in France increased rapidly, initially through immigration, first from Italy and the eastern part of the Roman Empire and then from Spain, especially after Sisebut's persecutions, which began in 612. However, the increase in numbers was also due to Jewish proselytism, which found adherents mostly among the poorest classes and in particular among slaves.

At that time the Jews were mainly engaged in commerce, but there were already physicians and even sailors. In the absence of written Jewish sources, archaeological evidence once more provides information on the France of this early period. On a seal from Avignon (fourth century) the *menorah* is reproduced, although only with five branches. The same motif appears on the inscription of Narbonne (687/8), which also points to a scanty knowledge of Hebrew at the time; the whole text is in Latin with the exception of three words, *Shalom al Yisrael*, which are incorrectly spelled. Nothing at all is known of the internal organization of these Jewish groups, except for the presence of synagogues (*Paris 582; Orléans before 585), but it is known that there were contacts between them. The Marseilles community maintained relations with those of Clermont-Ferrand and Paris and even, beyond the borders, with that of Rome.

In spite of the attempts at forced conversion, relations between the Jewish and Christian populations seem to have been free, a state of affairs demonstrated by the repeated efforts of the church authorities to prohibit these relations. The main prohibition, frequently repeated, was on Jews and Christians taking meals together (Vannes, 465; Agde, 506; Épone, 517; etc.); another, aimed at separating the population further, forbade the Jews to go out-of-doors during the Easter holidays (Orléans, 538; Mâcon, 583; etc.); and finally – a measure designed to prevent Jewish proselytism – possession of not only Christian but also pagan slaves by the Jews was restricted or forbidden (Orléans, 541: Clichy, 626 or 627; etc.). Further, though at first sight negative, proof of good relations between Christians and Jews is provided by the frequent religious *disputations, discussions which were characterized by the great freedom in argument accorded to the Jews (particularly between King Chilperic I (561–84) and his Jewish purveyor *Priscus, 581). Another positive testimony – though this may be largely a pious invention – is to be found in the participation of the Jews in the obsequies of church dignitaries (Arles, 459 and 543; Clermont-Ferrand, 554).

FROM THE CAROLINGIANS UNTIL THE EVE OF THE FIRST CRUSADE. The reign of the Carolingians was the most favorable period for the Jews in the kingdom of France. *Agobard's attempted forced conversion of Jewish children in Lyons and

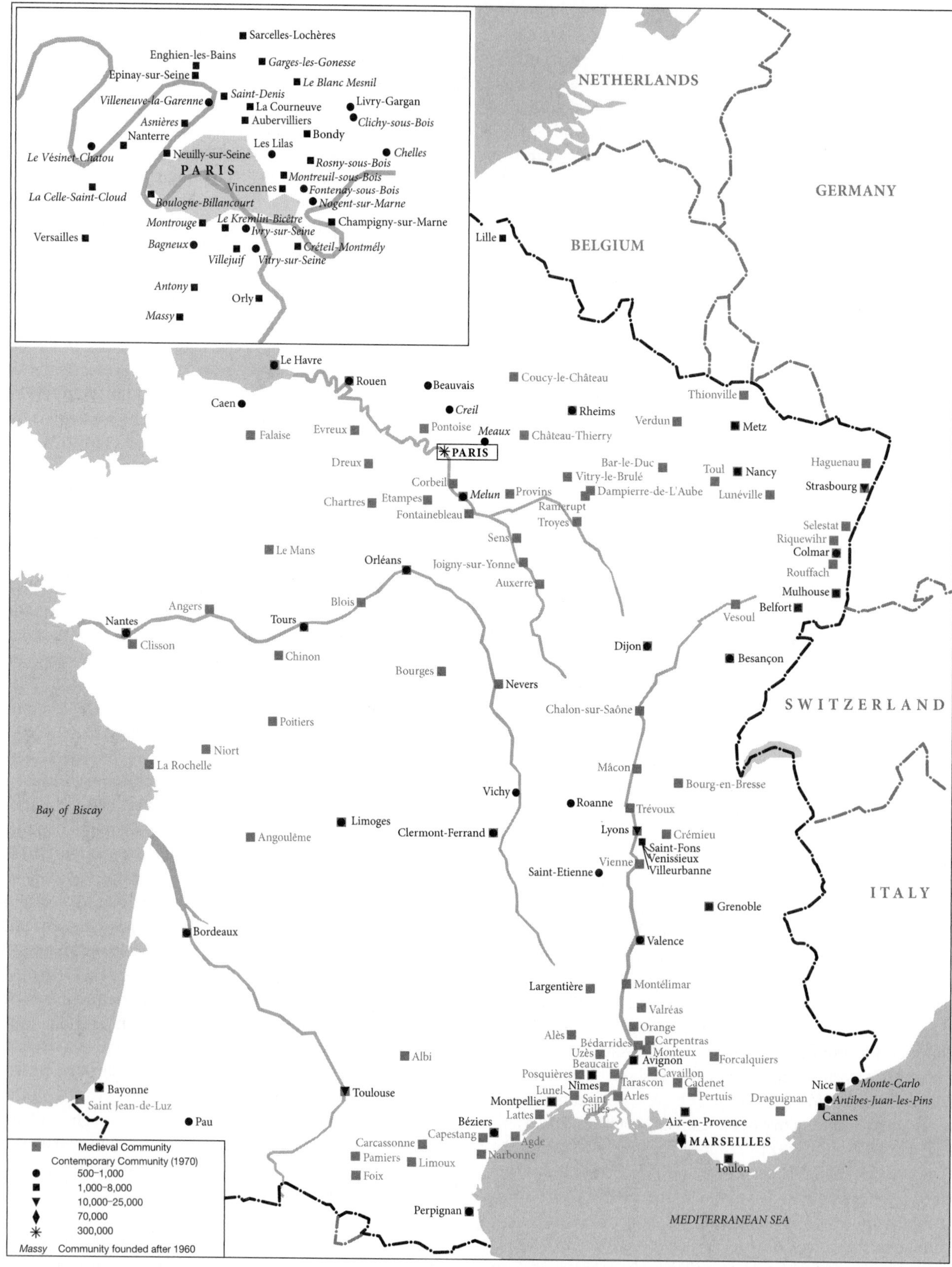

Main Jewish communities in France in the Middle Ages and in the latter 20th century. Insert shows detail of region surrounding Paris.

the district around 820 brought the bishop into disfavor with Louis the Pious (814–840).

The important Jewish settlement in the Rhone Valley, which had been in existence during the Roman and Merovingian periods, increased and expanded through the Saône Valley. Continued immigration from Italy and Spain was a source of demographic growth, as was proselytism affecting also the higher social classes; the best-known example is *Bodo, deacon of Louis the Pious, who converted to Judaism in Muslim Spain. From the second half of the tenth century and, at the latest, from the second half of the 11th century, there was also a trend toward migration to England.

The most intensive economic activity of the Jews of France, especially in the commercial field, belongs to this period. Some were accredited purveyors to the imperial court and others administered the affairs of Catholic religious institutions. Privileges granted to the Jews by the Carolingian emperors became the model for those coveted by other merchants. Their great concentration in agriculture and especially viticulture enabled them practically to monopolize the market; even the wine for Mass was bought from Jews. The few cases of moneylending known from this period were in fact connected with this agricultural activity; they were related to deferred purchases of agricultural estates intended to round off existing Jewish estates. In view of the wealth of general information available on the Jews of this period, the paucity of evidence concerning physicians suggests that there was a great decrease of interest in this profession. In the public services, Jews were employed both in the subordinate position of tax collector and in the most respected office of imperial ambassador (*Isaac for *Charlemagne; Judah for Charles the Bald).

The personal privileges and ordinances granted by the Carolingians assured the Jews complete judicial equality. Moreover, any attempt to entice away their pagan slaves by converting them to Catholicism was penalized; their right to employ salaried Christian personnel was explicitly guaranteed; any offense against their persons or property was punishable by enormous fines. Even more, the Jews enjoyed a preferential status, because they were not subjected to the ordeals ("judgments of God") which normally formed part of the judicial process. An imperial official, the *magister Judaeorum*, who ranked among the *missi dominici*, supervised the meticulous enforcement of all these privileges.

The activities of the church councils had little effect during this period. The Councils of Meaux and Paris (845–6) sought to legislate on the subject of the Jews, and a series of hostile canons concerning them were drawn up; these were in fact a kind of canonical collection and the work of *Amulo, Agobard's successor to the see of Lyons, and the deacon *Florus of Lyons, faithful secretary of both bishops. However, Charles the Bald (840–77) refused to ratify these canons. Another center of intensive Jewish settlement and powerful anti-Jewish reaction was *Chartres, where at the beginning of the 11th century, Bishop *Fulbert delivered a series of sermons to refute the Jewish assertion that, since there might yet be Jewish kings in distant lands, the Messiah had not yet come. Toward the close of the same century, *Ivo of Chartres inserted a series of violently anti-Jewish texts in his canonical collection. All of these, however, precisely by their concern to combat Jewish influences on the Christian faithful, emphasize the cordiality of the relations prevailing between Jews and Christians.

The so-called "Carolingian Renaissance" in the intellectual sphere had no counterpart on the Jewish scene, but strangely enough, subsequent tradition also attributes the impetus of Jewish learning in the West to Charlemagne (768–814). Just as he actually brought scholarly Irish monks to France, he is said to have brought the Jewish scholar Machir from Babylon. What is known of Hebrew works circulating in France derives from the testimony of Agobard, but, being a polemist, he mentions only those works he criticizes: a very ancient version of *Toledot Yeshu*, a parody of the Gospels, and *Shi'ur Komah*, a mystic work. The real upsurge of Jewish learning in France began during the 11th century. In the middle of the century, Joseph b. Samuel *Bonfils (Tov Elem) was active in Limoges, Moses ha-Darshan in Narbonne, and, a little later, *Rashi in Troyes. From the outset, the scholars' works comprised the principal fields of Jewish learning: liturgic poetry, biblical and talmudic commentaries, rabbinic decisions, grammar, and philology. The glory of Limoges and central France in general was shortlived, but Narbonne and Troyes heralded the great schools of Jewish scholars in both the extreme south and the extreme north of the country. The radical change in the situation resulted from the general upheaval which swept across the Christian West from the beginning of the 11th century and paved the way for the Crusades. Two local persecutions, in *Limoges at the end of the tenth and in the early 11th century, may be connected with the general persecution which raged through France from 1007 for at least five years. Launched by the clergy, it was rapidly supported by King Robert II the Pious (996–1031), then propagated by the general Christian population. The pretext for the riots was the accusation that the Jews of Orléans had joined in a plot against Christians with Sultan al-Ḥākim, who had indeed destroyed the Church of the Holy Sepulcher in Jerusalem. Thus the object of universal hatred, the Jews of France were then, if the sources are correct, either expelled from the towns, put to the sword, drowned in the rivers, or put to death in some other fashion, the only exceptions being those who accepted baptism. When one of the Jewish notables of France, Jacob b. Jekuthiel, intervened with Pope John XVIII (1004–09), the latter sent a legate to France to put a stop to the persecutions. Those Jews who had been forced to accept baptism immediately returned to Judaism. A similar situation arose in 1063: the "Spanish crusaders," who had set out to fight the Muslims, began by persecuting the Jews of southern France. On this occasion, however, they met with the opposition of the princes and the bishops, who were congratulated by Pope *Alexander II for their stand.

FROM THE FIRST CRUSADE UNTIL THE GENERAL EXPULSION FROM PROVENCE (1096–1501). The First Crusade (1096–99) had little immediate effect on the situation of the Jews, but it was in France that the first murderous persecutions occurred, accompanied by forced conversions in *Rouen and Metz (but not in southern France, as some scholars have asserted recently). Although the brunt of the brutalities was borne by the Jews of Germany, it was in Rouen that the crusaders justified their persecutions of the Jews: "If it is our desire [so they said] to attack the enemies of God after having covered lengthy distances toward the Orient while before our eyes we have the Jews, a nation whose enmity to God is unequaled, we will then follow a path which leads us backward." The first written legal act of a king of France which is extant is *Louis VII's decree of 1144 in which he banished from his kingdom those Jews who had been converted to Christianity and later returned to Judaism, that is those who – from the Christian point of view – had "relapsed into heresy." The Second Crusade (1147–49) gave rise to a controversy between *Bernard of Clairvaux and *Peter of Cluny on the question of the Jews; although they were spared the confiscation of all their belongings, as the abbot of Cluny had recommended in order to finance this expedition, they were nevertheless compelled to make a considerable financial contribution.

France's first *blood libel occurred in *Blois in 1171, when 31 Jews – men, women, and children – were burned at the stake after a parody of a trial, and in spite of the fact that not even a body was produced as proof of the murder. A series of similar accusations followed in Loches, *Pontoise, Joinville, and Épernay. Although Louis VII declared to the leaders of the Jewish community of Paris when they appealed to him that he regarded the ritual murder accusation as pure invention and promised to prevent the renewed outbreaks of similar persecutions, popular rumors continued to indict the Jews. According to his biographer, King *Philip Augustus (1180–1223), when only six years old, learned from his playmates that the Jews were in the habit of killing Christian children. The hatred thus nurtured prevailed, and he acted upon it soon after his accession to the throne. In 1181 he had all the wealthy Jews of Paris thrown into prison and freed them only in return for a huge ransom. In the following year (1182) he decreed their expulsion from the kingdom and the confiscation of their real estate. If the number of Jews affected by this measure was comparatively small, this was the result of the small size of the actual kingdom of France and the lack of royal authority over the nobles of the neighboring provinces, where the exiles found immediate refuge. Such a haven, however, was not always safe from the tenacious hatred of the king of France. Thus, in 1190, he pursued the Jews in Champagne (in *Bray-sur-Seine or in Brie-Comte-Robert) and exterminated a whole community which had the temerity to condemn one of his subjects to death for assassinating a Jew.

Driven by financial considerations, Philip Augustus authorized the return of the Jews to his kingdom in 1198, extorting from them what profit he could. Possibly another concern was also involved: from 1182 Philip Augustus had considerably expanded his territory. In all the lands incorporated within the kingdom, he found Jews living among a population which raised no objection to their presence, and he might have seriously angered the populace by expelling the Jews. Since he tolerated the Jews in the newly acquired parts of his kingdom, their banishment from its heart was no longer justified. Two months after their readmission, the king reached an agreement with Thibaut II, count of Champagne, on the division of their respective rights over the Jews living in their territories.

The Third Crusade (1189–92), which had such grave consequences for the Jews of England, did not affect those of France, but the crusade against the *Albigenses in southern France also spelled ruin to the Jewish communities. That of *Béziers, in particular, mourned many victims when the town was taken in 1209; the survivors crossed the Pyrenees and reestablished their community in *Gerona.

During the reign of *Louis IX (1226–70), severe anti-Jewish persecutions took place in 1236 in the western provinces, in Brittany, Anjou, and Poitou, which were not subject to the direct authority of the monarch. In 1240 Duke Jean le Roux expelled the Jews from Brittany. During the same year the famous disputation on the Talmud took place in Paris. Properly speaking, it was a trial of the Talmud inspired by a bull issued by *Gregory IX in 1239. The verdict had already been given in advance: the Talmud was to be destroyed by fire, a sentence which was carried out in 1242. In Dauphiné, which was still independent of the kingdom, ten Jews were burned at the stake in *Valréas in 1247 following a blood libel. Anti-Jewish agitation which resulted in the imprisonment of Jews and the confiscation of their belongings spread to several places in Dauphiné. There is no reason to believe that Louis IX had intended to expel the Jews or that he had even issued an order to this effect. Yet his brother, *Alphonse of Poitiers, to whom the king had ceded the government of several provinces, ordered the expulsion of the Jews from Poitou in July 1249. However, the order was not rigorously applied or it took effect for a brief period only. Nevertheless, the territory governed by Alphonse was the scene of the first local expulsion: from Moissac in 1271. Louis IX and Alphonse of Poitiers rivaled one another in their brutal methods of extorting money from the Jews. The king, ostentatiously scrupulous of benefiting from money earned through the sin of usury, dedicated it to the financing of the Crusade. With the same pious motive Alphonse of Poitiers incarcerated all the Jews of his provinces so that he could lay his hands on their possessions with greater ease. *Philip III the Bold, who reigned from 1270, was responsible for a widespread migration of the Jews when he forbade them, in 1283, to live in the small rural localities. The accession of *Philip IV the Fair (1285) was ushered in by the massacre of *Troyes, once more following on a blood libel; several notables of the community were condemned and burned at the stake in 1288. In 1289, first *Gascony (which was an English possession) and then Anjou (governed by the brother of the king of France) expelled the Jews. In 1291, Philip the Fair hastily published an ordinance prohibiting the Jews expelled from Gascony and England from settling in France.

Although Philip the Fair denied the clergy in general (1288) and the inquisitors in particular (1302) any judicial rights over the Jews, this was not the better to protect them but merely because he objected to sharing his authority in any way. It was therefore probably royal judges who tried the first *host desecration cases brought against several Jews of Paris in 1290. In order to guarantee the greatest financial gain from the expulsion order of 1306, Philip the Fair issued oral instructions only. After the imprisonment of all the Jews (July 22, 1306) and the seizure of their belongings, numerous written ordinances were issued by the royal chancellery in order to secure for the king, if possible, the sum total of the spoils. Over this very question of the Jews, the resurgent royal authority was revealed; indeed, the expulsion order won the successive support of an ever-growing number of lords until its provisions even spread to the territories of those lords who had not been consulted. As well as in the provinces which still evaded royal authority – Lorraine, Alsace, Franche-Comté, Savoy, Dauphiné, Provence with the principality of *Orange and Comtat Venaissin, the counties of *Roussillon and Cerdagne (Cerdaña) – the Jews banished from France found asylum in the present territories of Belgium, Germany, Italy, and Spain. Philip the Fair granted safe-conducts to a number of Jews to enable them to stay in his kingdom or return to it; they were to assist him in collecting the debts which had been seized. In 1311 they too were "permanently" expelled. Although the expulsion itself encountered scarcely any objections on the part of the lords, this was far from the case when the king tried to seize all the booty for himself: bitter disagreements often followed, as in Montpellier.

The recovery of all the spoils was still far from complete when *Louis x the Quarreler (1314–16), son and successor of Philip the Fair, considered allowing the Jews to return (May 17, 1315), which actually came into effect before July 28, 1315. A decree of that date, repudiating the "evil advisers" who had incited his father to expel the Jews and justifying Louis' decision to recall them because of the "general clamor of the people," defined the conditions of Jewish residence for a 12-year period. Under Philip v the Tall (1316–22) anti-Jewish massacres were perpetrated by the *Pastoureaux in 1320, and the Jews of *Toulouse and areas to the west of the town suffered heavily. There the king, his officers, and the church authorities combined in efforts to suppress the movement, principally because it was a serious threat to the social order. Popular mania against lepers spread to the Jews in several places in 1321, particularly in *Tours, *Chinon, and Bourges (or elsewhere in Berry). Without even a legal pretext, Jews were put to death in all these places, 160 in Chinon alone. As well as the confiscation of the belongings of the Jews thus "brought to justice," an immense fine was imposed on the whole of French Jewry. The expulsion – no text of the decree ordaining it remains – took place between April 7 and Aug. 27, 1322.

In 1338 and 1347 over 25 Jewish communities of Alsace were the victims of persecutions which were limited to the eastern regions. On the other hand, the massacres connected with the *Black Death (1348 and 1349), struck Jewish communities throughout the eastern and southeastern regions, notably in Provence, Savoy, Dauphiné, Franche-Comté, and Alsace. It was only due to the intervention of the pope that the Jews of Avignon and Comtat Venaissin were spared a similar fate. In Franche-Comté, after they had been accused of spreading the plague, the Jews were imprisoned for long periods and their possessions confiscated; they were expelled in 1349, although they reappeared there at the latest in 1355. In that same year Dauphiné was practically incorporated within the kingdom of France, yet the Jews of this province continued to enjoy their former freedoms and immunities.

The crown never revealed the financial motive behind the readmission of the Jews so blatantly as in 1359. *Charles v (1364–80), regent for his father John ii the Good who was held prisoner in England, then authorized their return for a period of 20 years simply in order to use the taxes to enable him to pay his father's ransom. Following the example of Louis the Quarreler, he allowed the Jews to reside in France for limited periods only, although in his case the residence periods which had been granted were more faithfully abided by. In 1360 John the Good (1350–64) ratified the authorization granted by his son.

When Charles v succeeded to the throne, he confirmed, in May 1364, the 20 years which were initially granted and prolonged the period by six years, then by a further ten years in October 1374. When *Charles vi (1380–1422) took over the government himself, in February 1388 and March 1389, he ratified the prolongations granted by Charles v; he did not ratify either the five or the six years accorded by Louis of Anjou, acting as regent for him (1380–88). Thus, after the decree of Sept. 17, 1394, stipulating that thenceforward the Jews would no longer be tolerated in the kingdom of France, the departure of the Jews became effective in 1395 (between January 15 and March 18), 36 years after the first concession for a new residence period granted by Charles v. Properly speaking, this was not actually an expulsion but rather a refusal to renew the right of residence. However, obviously it resulted in the departure of the Jews from the kingdom of France.

From 1380 the Jews were the victims of bloody persecutions, which followed in the wake of popular risings in several towns of the kingdom, especially in Paris and Nantes. There was a similar occurrence in 1382. Although the king exempted the Jews from returning the pawns which had been stolen from them on this occasion, he also granted a hasty pardon to the rioters. In 1389 the king allowed the town of Eyrieu the right of deciding for itself whether it would admit the Jews or not; although such a prerogative was subsequently granted to the towns of Alsace in general, this was at that time an exception within the kingdom. There was, however, no reason to regard this as a harbinger of the forthcoming generalized departure of the Jews. On the contrary, as late as July 15, 1394, the king issued a reasonably favorable decree to the Jews of Languedoc. When Charles VI terminated the residence of the Jews in his kingdom on September 17, he claimed that there had been "several grave complaints and outcries" concerning "the excesses and misdemeanors which the said Jews had committed and they continued to act in this manner every day against the Christians." He added that investigations had confirmed that the Jews had "committed and perpetrated several crimes, excesses, and offenses," particularly against the Christian faith, but such a justification for his action does not seem plausible. However, on this occasion there was no financial motive behind the expulsion, for it was not accompanied by confiscations. The move therefore remains inexplicable. This time the Jews of Franche-Comté shared the fate of their brothers in the kingdom, although the province did not then belong to the king of France.

From the second half of the 14th century, the voluntary movement of Jews from Dauphiné assumed ever greater proportions. The dauphin attempted to coax them back by offering fiscal advantages, but without success. By the early 16th century no more Jews lived in Dauphiné. In Savoy the situation of the Jews deteriorated throughout the 15th century: Jewish books were seized in 1417; there was a local expulsion from Châtillon-les-Dombes in 1429, a bloody persecution in 1466, and a general expulsion decree in 1492. In Provence, the greater part of the 15th century, especially during the reign of René I the Good (1431–80), was a favorable period for the Jews, aside from a few local incidents, for example in *Aix-en-Provence in 1430. Conditions changed from 1475 on when, for the first time since the Black Death, there were anti-Jewish outbreaks in several places. Between 1484 and 1486 attacks against the Jews occurred in numerous localities (notably in Aix, Marseilles, and Arles). After Provence was incorporated in France (1481), town after town demanded the expulsion of the Jews until the last remaining Jews were hit by a general expulsion order in 1498 which was completely enforced by 1501. There were therefore practically no Jews left within the present borders of France, with the exception of Alsace and Lorraine, Avignon, Comtat Venaissin, and the county of Nice.

THE COMMUNITIES IN MEDIEVAL FRANCE. Benjamin of Tudela records valuable details on the southern communities of the third quarter of the 12th century. According to his figures – confirmed for Narbonne by other contemporary sources – in six communities there were 1,240 heads of families, that is more than 6,000 souls. Another document of the same period, the list of the martyrs of *Blois, notes there were about 30 families or about 150 souls in this community, which would have been totally unknown if it had not been for the tragedy which befell it. The greatest number and widest dispersion of Jews in France was attained during the third quarter of the 13th century. There were about 150 localities inhabited by Jews in Île-de-France and Champagne, about 50 in the duchy of Burgundy, about 30 in Barrois – in spite of its small area – and many others. From 1283, as a result of the prohibition on residing in small places, the communities in the towns grew larger. The total number of Jews continued to increase, and some have estimated that about 100,000 Jews were affected by the expulsion of 1306. Migration resulting from this banishment and the losses during the Black Death – both by the plague itself and in the persecutions which it sparked off – considerably reduced the Jewish population until the middle of the 14th century. There was a slight increase from then on, especially after the authorization to return in 1359. However, after the 1394/95 expulsion from the kingdom of France and the subsequent expulsions from the other provinces or voluntary departures due to hostile pressure combined with ever greater fiscal extortions, only about 25,000 Jews at the most remained during the 15th century. By 1501 they numbered a few thousand only. If Catholic missionary activity did achieve some tangible results – due mostly to coercion if not outright violence – this was the least factor in the demographic decline of the Jewish community.

From the 12th century onward, moneylending became increasingly prominent as a Jewish occupation. It was particularly pronounced – to the point of being sometimes their sole activity – in the places where the Jews settled at a later date or after the readmissions to the kingdom of France. In the main, these were private loans, with a multitude of creditors and a small turnover. In the east and southeast the Jews were principally traders in agricultural produce and livestock. Throughout the south, particularly in Provence, there were a relatively large number of physicians who, in addition to practicing among Jews, were sometimes also appointed by the towns to take care of the Christian population. The agriculture, and especially viticulture, subsisting mainly outside the kingdom, supplied the needs of the Jewish population and only exceptionally the general market. Petty public officials, watchmen, toll-gatherers, etc., were found especially in the south, but rarely after the 13th century (one of the few exceptions was the principality of Orange). Halfway between commerce and public office was the activity of broker, often found in Provence.

The regulations of the Fourth *Lateran Council (1215), interpreted as the compulsory wearing of the Jewish *badge, were at first imposed in Languedoc, Normandy, and Provence (by councils held in 1227, 1231, and 1234); a royal decree enforcing this in the kingdom of France was not promulgated until 1269. However, compulsory residence in a Jewish quarter dates from 1294 in the kingdom of France, although only from the end of the first half of the 14th century in Provence. Although the French crown often sought to protect the Jews from Church jurisdiction – especially that of the inquisitors – it imposed the legal disabilities or measures of social segregation which had been first advocated by the church itself. Following the example of the *magister Judaeorum* of the Carolingian period, "guardians" of the Jews were often appointed; in the kingdom of France there was one for the Languedoc and another for the Langue d'Oïl which included approximately the regions situated to the north of the River Loire. Their authority extended to all legal suits in which Jews were one of the parties. Jewish internal jurisdiction was increasingly limited; thus in Provence even simple administrative matters in the synagogue were brought before the public tribunal. A special form of oath (see *Oath, more judaico) was laid down for Jews who were witnesses or parties to a trial.

In the 13th century Christian polemical writings increased considerably: in practice Judeo-Christian disputations were relatively free and still quite frequent. After early warnings, followed by the explicit church prohibition on the participation of laymen in such discussions, they became increasingly rare. The Jews lost none of their sharpness in these confrontations: the most outstanding examples are the *Sefer ha-Mekanne* and the polemic treatise which goaded *Nicholas of Lyra into a reply.

The Jewish communities organized themselves with increasing efficiency. Although the earliest confirmation of internal statutes dates from 1413 (Avignon), these were certainly current practice long before then. As well as these statutes – which regulated internal administration through elected officials (actual power lay in the hands of the wealthiest), financial contributions toward communal expenses, and religious obligations – sumptuary regulations were often laid down, intended to limit the ostentatious display of riches. The first synods (gatherings of communal representatives) are known from the middle of the 12th century. At the synod of Troyes in 1150, the representatives of the French communities were joined by officials from German communities. The 1160 synod, also held in Troyes, convened only representatives from the kingdom of France, Normandy, and Poitou. Therefore it is evident that this was not a firmly established institution convened at regular intervals. If, as seems apparent, these synods normally involved the attendance only of communities directly concerned, it is astonishing that the synod of *Saint-Gilles (1215) convened the representatives of the communities between Narbonne and Marseilles only to discuss a problem of the greatest importance for the whole of Jewry living in Christian countries: how to prevent the promulgation of the projected anti-Jewish canons by the Fourth Lateran Council. With the proliferation and increase of Jewish taxes, the civil authorities rapidly realized that a Jewish inter-communal organization covering the area under their authority served their interests; it became the task of this organization to assess and to collect all the taxes levied on the Jews. Although some communities tried to make use of this arrangement to reach a direct, and more advantageous, agreement with the authorities, when misfortune struck an isolated community, others often spontaneously revealed their active solidarity. Thus, at the time of the tragedy of Blois, the communities of Orléans and Paris brought relief to the persecuted.

SCHOLARSHIP IN THE MIDDLE AGES. The leading centers of Jewish scholarship were found in Île-de-France (principally Paris, then *Dreux, *Melun, Pontoise, *Corbeil, Coucy-le-Château, and Chartres) and in Champagne (led by Troyes, then *Dampierre-sur-Aube, *Vitry-le-Brulé, *Joigny-sur-Yonne, Joinville, *Château-Thierry, and *Ramerupt); there was also a concentration of centers of learning in the Loire Valley (Orléans, Tours, and Chinon). As well as this, there were a number of schools in Languedoc (headed by Narbonne, then Argentière, *Beaucaire, *Béziers, Lattes, *Lunel, *Montpellier, *Nîmes, *Posquières, *Capestang, and *Carcassonne) and in Provence (with Arles, Trinquetaille, and Marseilles, then Salon and Aix-en-Provence). A few other provinces were also active, though on a much more modest scale; in the wake of Ile-de-France came Normandy (with *Evreux and *Falaise and possibly also Rouen) and Brittany (Clisson); in the wake of Champagne, Burgundy (with *Dijon); following Provence, Comtat Venaissin (with Monteux and *Carpentras), as well as Orange and Avignon; and after Languedoc, Roussillon (with *Perpignan). Lorraine (with *Verdun, *Toul, and Metz) and Alsace (with *Strasbourg and *Sélestat) assured a link between northern France and the Rhineland. By contrast, Dauphiné (with only Vienne), and especially Franche-Comté and Savoy, hardly played any part in this intellectual ferment.

The north was principally the home of talmudic and biblical commentaries, anti-Christian polemics, and liturgical poetry. In the south scholarly activities extended to grammatical, linguistic, philosophical, and scientific studies, and innumerable translations (mostly from Arabic, but also from Latin). Of particular importance were the mystic circles which gave an impetus to the kabbalist movement. Both north and south produced decorated and even richly illuminated manuscripts.

FROM THE EXPULSION FROM PROVENCE TO THE EVE OF THE REVOLUTION. As soon as the Jews had left the southeast or been converted to Christianity and thus become permanently absorbed within the general population, the southwest witnessed the arrival of secret Jews, the *Conversos. From 1550, these "Portuguese merchants" or "New Christians" were granted letters patent by Henry II, who authorized them to live in France "wherever they desired." They settled mainly in Bordeaux and in Saint-Esprit, near *Bayonne. They were subsequently to be found in small places nearby: *Peyrehorade, *Bidache, and Labastide-Clairence, and toward the north in La *Rochelle, Nantes, and Rouen. However, of all the Marranos who arrived in France from the beginning of the 16th century, only a tiny minority remained faithful to Judaism. Since they sought to evade detection by externally practicing Catholicism while maintaining their Iberian language and customs, they were suspected in Bordeaux in 1596 of attempting to deliver the town into the hands of the Spaniards, and in 1625 their possessions were confiscated as a reprisal for the confiscation of French belongings by the king of Spain. They were also subjected to particularly severe taxes, which rose to 100,000 livres in 1723 in exchange for new letters patent; for the first time these recognized them as Jews, although they did not grant them the right to practice their religion openly. The Jews of Comtat Venaissin had taken in some Spanish refugees on a temporary basis only, as was the case with the parents of *Joseph ha-Kohen, the author of *Emek ha-Bakha*, who was born in Avignon but lived there only during his early years. The communities of Comtat Venaissin were themselves threatened with expulsion on several occasions. These decrees were not finally enforced, but the Jews were nevertheless compelled to leave all towns in the Comtat with the exception of Avignon, Carpentras, *Cavaillon, and *L'Isle-sur-la-Sorgue. Even there, the quarters assigned to them were constantly reduced in area so as to limit the Jewish population.

Jews seem to have lived in Lorraine without interruption although in small numbers only. After the French crown had occupied the region, progressively greater facilities were offered to the Jews to induce them to settle there. From three families in Metz in 1565, their number increased to 96 families in 1657. In the meantime, as a result of the Treaty of Westphalia (1648), the three towns and bishoprics of Metz, Toul, and Verdun were formally ceded to France. Although theoretically the expulsion order against the Jews of the kingdom still remained in force – and it was even reiterated in 1615 – the Jews in those parts of Lorraine which had become French were allowed to remain.

This was the first time since 1394 that Jews found themselves legally living in the kingdom of France. However, they were still confined to the town, or at best to the province, in which they lived. Considerable areas of Alsace were also incorporated within the kingdom of France by the Treaty of Westphalia. There also a firmly established Jewish population was not put in jeopardy by the new French administration; on the contrary, it was more effectively protected than in the past. In 1651, Jews from Holland settled in *Charleville, which belonged to the Gonzaga dukes (they had already admitted Dutch Jews for the first time from 1609 to 1633). Jews fleeing from the *Chmielnicki massacres in the Ukraine and Poland in 1648 arrived in Alsace and Lorraine. The general demographic decline which was a result of the Thirty Years' War (1618–48) explains the tolerance they encountered. Jews also arrived in the extreme southeast of France, where the duke of Savoy, to whom the county of Nice belonged, issued in 1648 an edict making Nice and *Villefranche de-Conflent free ports. Once more this was an indirect result of the Thirty Years' War, a search for an effective method of filling the economic vacuum it had created. Jews from Italy and North Africa immediately profited from the settlement facilities offered by this edict, strengthening the old Jewish community which had existed without interruption from the Middle Ages. However, Italian Jews who hoped to benefit from the apparently similar facilities offered in Marseilles by the edict of *Louis XIV in 1669 were disappointed; they were compelled to leave after a few years.

From the 17th century, the Jews of Avignon and Comtat Venaissin extended their commercial activity: besides frequenting the fairs and markets, mainly in Languedoc and Provence, they also attempted to remain in those towns and even to settle there. Following complaints from local merchants, the stewards of the king intervened on every occasion to remove them and restrict their presence at the fairs and markets as much as possible. With greater success, some Jews of Avignon and Comtat Venaissin – soon followed by Jews of Alsace – exploited the facilities granted to the "Portuguese" Jews, and from the beginning of the 18th century settled in Bordeaux. There they traded in the town or its environs, principally in textiles and to a lesser degree in livestock and old clothes.

From the beginning of the 18th century, some Jews began to settle in Paris, arriving not only from Alsace, Metz, and Lorraine, from Bordeaux, and from Avignon and Comtat Venaissin, but also from beyond the borders of France, mainly Germany and Holland. They were tolerated in Paris but no more. Even though they had benefited from most civil rights in their provinces of origin, they enjoyed no such privileges in the capital. In theory, if a Jew died in Paris his estate was confiscated in favor of the king and his burial had to be quasi-clandestine. In order to protect their rights and, initially, to obtain their own cemeteries, the Jews organized themselves into two distinct groups: southern Jews from Bordeaux, Avignon, and Comtat Venaissin, and Ashkenazim from Alsace, Lorraine, and a few other places. This was an early manifestation of the split which was later evident during the struggle for emancipation and afterward.

Just before the whole of Lorraine became part of France (1766), the request of some Jews of Lorraine to be admitted to the guilds gave rise to a lawsuit in which the advocate of Nancy, Pierre Louis de Lacretelle (1756–1824), called for their recognition as Frenchmen with rights equal to those of other citizens (1775). Although this suit was lost, nevertheless it left a powerful impression on the public who, from the beginning of the century, had become aware of the Jewish problem through the pronouncements of the great thinkers of the century, beginning with *Montesquieu. In 1781, Herz *Cerfberr, the representative of the Jews of Alsace, had the work of Christian Wilhelm von *Dohm (1751–1820), *Ueber die buergerliche Verbesserung der Juden* ("On the Civic Amelioration of the Jews"), translated into French. The first concrete result was Louis XVI's edict, drawn up in 1783 and published in January 1784, abolishing the humiliating "body tax" which for centuries had likened the Jews to cattle. In 1785 a competition by the Metz Société Royale des Arts et Sciences on the subject "Is there any way of rendering the Jews more useful and happier in France?" reflected this new trend of opinion, while strengthening it even further. The competition was initiated by P.L. *Roederer, a member of the *parlement* of Metz, and the best answers were submitted by the royal librarian Zalkind *Hourwitz (who defined himself as a "Polish Jew"), the advocate Thierry, and Abbé *Grégoire. Finally, in 1788, the minister *Malesherbes, who had successfully headed the commission charged with arranging civic rights for Protestants, was entrusted by Louis XVI with a similar mission with regard to the Jews.

[Bernhard Blumenkranz]

The Modern Period

THE REVOLUTION. On the eve of the French Revolution some 40,000 Jews were living in France. Those of the "German nation" were mainly concentrated in Alsace-Lorraine or Paris, while the "Spanish, Portuguese, or Avignonese" Jews were chiefly concentrated in the south. The former who, excepting residents of Nancy, almost exclusively spoke or wrote in Yiddish, formed the vast majority (84%) of French Jewry while the latter were closer to French language and culture, less observant in religious practice, and more nearly integrated within local society. These various groups would no doubt have been fairly satisfied to obtain civic rights provided that they were consonant with the continuation of their internal communal autonomy. After much petitioning and long-drawn-out parliamentary and public discussion, the Jews of France finally became French citizens, the Portuguese Jews on Jan. 28, 1790, and the Ashkenazim on Sept. 27, 1791. The law of 1791, however, although conferring civic rights on Jews as individuals, was coupled with the abolition of their group privileges, i.e., their religious-legal autonomy.

Later the communities in France suffered from the Reign of Terror (1793–94) in company with the other religious denominations. Synagogues were closed down and the communal organization abolished as a consequence of the general tendency to suppress all religious institutions. When the synagogues reopened their doors, the character of the former communities had already greatly changed. The opening up of the ghettos and the abolition of restrictions on residence encouraged many Jews to leave their former areas of residence and to reject, either entirely or partly, the discipline imposed by their erstwhile community.

MEASURES OF NAPOLEON. This anarchy, which led to complaints by former creditors of the dissolved Jewish communities, strengthened *Napoleon Bonaparte's determination to provide the Jews of France with a central organization supervised by the state and loyal to it, following the example of the arrangements he had already introduced for the other religions. Napoleon wished to create a Jewish "church organization" and at the same time to "reform" the Jewish way of life and Judaism, toward which he had an attitude of barely controlled hostility. Napoleon considered that the Jews were a "nation within a nation," and their emancipation had not produced the anticipated results. The Jews would therefore have to be corrected and regenerated; in particular a solution had to be found to solve the problem of usury, still a major Jewish occupation, especially in Alsace. With this in view, therefore, in 1806 he convened an assembly to serve as the "States General of French Judaism" (the *Assembly of Jewish Notables). Its first session was held on July 26. The Assembly had to reply to 12 questions put to it by the commissioners appointed by the government who were instructed to verify whether Jewish religious law held any principle contrary to the civil law. Having been informed of the deliberations of the Assembly and the answers it delivered, Napoleon determined on having them formulated into a type of religious code. He decided to convoke a Grand *Sanhedrin – a gesture which was also within the framework of his European ambitions – whose religious authority could not be called in question. The Sanhedrin, composed of 45 rabbis and 26 laymen, met on Feb. 9, 1807, and dispersed two months later on March 9, having fulfilled its role by codifying "religious" decisions in the spirit of the answers to the 12 questions delivered by the Assembly of Notables. The Sanhedrin then gave way to the Notables, who continued their task with the intention of proposing the establishment of an organization of the Jewish religion and measures to control Jewish economic activities.

THE CONSISTORIAL SYSTEM. The proposed regulation was amended by the Conseil d'Etat and promulgated by imperial edict in 1808, inaugurating what is usually called the consistorial system. This provided that a *consistory should be established for each department of France having a Jewish population of at least 2,000. Each consistory was constituted of a council composed of a *grand rabbin*, another rabbi, and three laymen elected by a small number of "notables." A central consistory composed of three *grand rabbins* and two laymen was to have its seat in Paris. Contrary to the provisions governing the organizations for the other recognized religions, expenses for religious purposes were still to be met by Jews. Thus, the new Jewish bodies were obliged, *ipso facto*, as inheritors, to repay the debts contracted by the former Jewish communities, whereas the other religions had been relieved of this burden. The consistorial system partially re-created the Jewish communities, and provided them with a means of action. It also constituted the recognition of Judaism as a religion, centralizing its organization, and placing it under strict government control. While the consistory was empowered to exercise absolute and exclusive authority in Jewish affairs, it mainly concerned itself with the strictly religious aspects. The consistory was supported by the rabbinate, which according to law was responsible for teaching the Jewish religion and the decisions of the Sanhedrin, promoting obedience to the civil laws, preaching in synagogue, and offering prayers for the imperial family. Although the authority of the rabbis was limited entirely to the religious sphere, it was nevertheless channeled into the service of the state.

These administrative measures were accompanied by complementary economic regulations. A decree abrogating a postponement previously granted on May 30, 1806, to persons owing money to Jews was issued, but it also laid down a mass of restrictive regulations. All debts contracted with Jews were to be annulled or liable to be annulled, reduced, or postponed by legal means (1808). As a result, a large section of the Jewish population of France, already in difficult circumstances, was brought to the verge of ruin. Any Jew who wished to engage in trade or commerce had to obtain a license to be renewed annually by the prefect of the department in which he resided. Further measures were issued in an attempt to compel the

Jews of France to assimilate into French society by regulating their place of residence. Thus a Jew who had not previously been resident in Alsace was prohibited from settling there. A Jew might settle in other departments only if he exercised a profession regarded as useful. In order to preserve the educational value in performing military service in company with their non-Jewish compatriots, Jews drafted for the army were prohibited from procuring substitutes. Another decree which, however, confirmed an existing situation, made it obligatory for Jews to adopt surnames in the presence of an official of the registry. The central consistory was set up on July 17, 1808. Its three *grand rabbins* were the president and two vice-presidents of the Sanhedrin, David *Sinzheim, Joshua Benzion Segré, who died shortly afterward and was replaced by Emanuel *Deutz, rabbi of Coblenz, and Abraham Vita *Cologna, rabbi of Mantua. After the death of Sinzheim in 1812 and the resignation of Cologna in 1826, Deutz remained the only *grand rabbin* in the central consistory until his death in 1842. Subsequently only one *grand rabbin* served for the whole of French Jewry.

OFFICIAL RECOGNITION. The Restoration was not received with hostility by the Jews of France. The Napoleonic regulations, while having the merit of organizing communal affairs, had nevertheless represented a step backward in revolutionary ideals. Without major difficulties they were able to ensure that the Napoleonic decree determining their activities and means of livelihood, commonly referred to by Jews as the *décret infâme*, was not renewed after the expiry of its ten-year time limit (1818). Soon the need for new rabbis became a matter for concern. Until the Revolution rabbis for the Ashkenazi communities had been trained in the yeshivah in Metz, in the small local yeshivot of Alsace, or otherwise drawn from abroad. The Sephardi communities in the south generally recognized the authority of the Dutch or Italian Sephardi rabbinates. The closing of the Metz yeshivah under the Revolution had greatly curtailed the recruitment of rabbis. Thus, from 1820 numerous attempts were made to obtain permission for the opening of a rabbinical school in Metz to supply the needs of all sectors of French Jewry. In 1829 the Ministry of Religions authorized the opening of a central rabbinical seminary in Metz. It was transferred to Paris in 1859, where it continues to function. Judaism was placed on the same footing as the other recognized religions when the chamber of peers passed a law making the Treasury responsible for paying the salaries of ministers of the Jewish religion (from Jan. 1, 1831). Thus almost the last sign of anti-Jewish discriminatory legislation in France disappeared.

ASSIMILATION. These political successes did not conceal the profound crisis through which French Jewry was passing. Many Jews born after the grant of emancipation were unprepared for the new world they were now facing. A wave of conversions followed, in which members of the most firmly established families left Judaism. Deutz's own son, notorious for his role in the arrest of the duchess of Berry, and his son-in-law David *Drach, who had pursued rabbinical studies and directed the Jewish school in Paris, both embraced Christianity, the latter even taking orders. The eldest son of the president of the Bas-Rhin Consistory, Marie-Theodore *Ratisbonne, became converted in 1826. He subsequently took orders and in celebration of the conversion of his youngest brother founded the order of Notre Dame de Sion to be devoted to missionary work among the Jews. The brother, who was an active member of the order, later built a monastery in Jerusalem. Although the lower ranks of the Jewish population were hardly affected by these conversions, such cases were numerous among their leaders.

The disappearance of the generation which had known the Revolution and taken part in the work of the Sanhedrin, coupled with the new spirit of liberal democracy, and the pressure in the new communities by arrivals from the rural areas of Alsace and Lorraine now necessitated a reform of the consistorial system. By an order in council of May 25, 1844, French Jewry continued to be directed by the central consistory, which was henceforth composed of the *grand rabbin* and a lay member from each departmental consistory. The electoral college was enlarged in 1844 and 1848, when every Jewish male aged over 25 obtained the right to take part in the elections of the departmental consistories. The Paris consistory finally obtained an increase in the number of its representatives on the central consistory because it had a large population under its jurisdiction. This system continued, apart from some minor modifications, until 1905, with the separation of church and state (see below).

ABOLITION OF THE "JEWISH OATH". The final obstacle to complete equality for Jewish citizens was removed with the abolition of the humiliating oath *more judaico*. The various courts that had been called upon to decide whether it was necessary for Jews to take the oath in that form had rendered conflicting decisions. It was only on the advice given to the rabbis by Adolphe *Crémieux, who became a member of the central consistory in 1831, to refuse to take the oath in this form that some progress was made. The Supreme Court of Appeal decided on its abolition in 1846. In the same period the debts of the former Jewish communities were finally settled by partial repayments effected by the successor communities.

WELFARE AND EDUCATION. While French Jewry was concerned with defense of its rights and its religious organization, it also promoted charitable and educational activities. The local charitable committees were generally offshoots of the traditional Jewish mutual aid societies or of the *ḥevrot* (see **ḥevrah*), which did not surrender their independence without hesitation or declared hostility. In the educational sphere, the first real development took place under the Restoration with the opening of Jewish primary schools. From 1818 schools were opened in Metz, Strasbourg, and Colmar. A boys' school had been functioning in Bordeaux from 1817 and a girls' school from 1831. In Paris the first Jewish boys' school was established in 1819 and the first girls' school in 1821. Parallel to these primary schools, the community also opened technical schools, at first in order to prepare their pupils for apprenticeship and later providing direct specialized training. The first Jewish trades school (Ecole de Travail) opened its doors in Strasbourg in 1825, and was followed by that of Mulhouse in 1842, and of Paris in 1865. This network grew in importance until the law making primary education compulsory was passed in 1882, and the church and state were separated in 1905, thus depriving it of state financial support.

PROTECTION OF JEWISH RIGHTS. The Jewish community in France was shocked into action to protect Jewish rights by the *Damascus Affair in 1840 and subsequently by the outbreak of anti-Jewish disorders in 1848. The hostile attitude shown by the French government and also by French public opinion when Jews in Damascus were accused of ritual murder, as well as the complicity of the French consul there, deeply stirred French Jewry. Crémieux therefore joined Sir Moses *Montefiore from England in a mission to Alexandria to intercede with *Muhammad Ali on behalf of the Damascus Jews. In February 1848, the peasants in Sundgau in Alsace took advantage of the general unrest to attack the Jews, some of whom managed to escape to Switzerland. The incidents spread northward, Jewish houses were pillaged, and the army was called out to restore order. Both this and the Damascus Affair strengthened the feeling among Jews in France that in certain situations they could rely only on self-defense. The formation of the provisional government, which included two Jews, Michel *Goudchaux and Crémieux, dispelled some of these anxieties, but Jewish concern was again heightened with the election of Prince Louis Napoleon to the presidency of the republic, and later his accession to the imperial title, since many feared that he would restore the discriminatory measures introduced by his uncle.

SOCIAL AND ECONOMIC ADVANCES. These fears proved unfounded. The Second Empire was a calm period for the Jews of France. Instances of anti-Jewish discrimination were the result of the influence of the Catholic circles surrounding the empress rather than of a determined will to start an antisemitic campaign. Jews, like other "nonbelievers," were often excluded from the universities. The social rise of the French Jews which had begun under the Restoration also continued under the Second Empire. In 1834 Achille *Fould became the first Jew to sit in the Chamber of Deputies, soon to be followed by Crémieux. The greatest and most rapid achievements were often through the civil service, candidates for which generally had to pass tests and competitive examinations. In 1836 Jacques *Halévy was elected a member of the Academy of Fine Arts. *Rachel, one of the greatest actresses of her time, never concealed her Jewish origin. In the commercial sphere, it was a period of success for the *Rothschild family and its head, Baron James, as well as for the *Pereire brothers to whom the Rothschilds were later violently opposed. Practically every career, including the army, was open to Jews.

NEW TRENDS IN JUDAISM. Events did not proceed without provoking the same unrest within the French community as had gripped German Jewry. The problem arose of maintaining Judaism in an open, modern society, and the influence of the *Reform movements from across the Rhine soon made itself felt. The French rabbinate was of a generally conservative frame of mind. Its members, who almost entirely hailed from the small towns of Alsace and Lorraine, were scarcely enthusiastic over the new ideas and the rabbinate found itself in retreat before the layman. A meeting of *grand rabbins* was held in Paris from May 13–21, 1856, to establish a common policy with which to confront the growing trend away from Judaism. The camps were clearly divided well before the meeting: the Alsatian communities, which were the most numerous, opposed the introduction of substantive reforms, for which they felt no necessity. However, since each consistory was represented by only one delegate, the majority of the representatives tended to opt for modifications. To prevent a breach, it was resolved that decisions would be taken according to a simple majority, but that the question of their application would be held in abeyance. The assembly decided to limit the number of *piyyutim*, to organize synagogue services for the blessing of newborn infants, to conduct the funeral service with more ceremonial, and to instruct rabbis and officiating ministers to wear a garb resembling that worn by the Catholic clergy. It was also resolved to make greater use of the sermon in synagogue, to reduce the length of services which were to be conducted in a more dignified manner, and to introduce the ceremony of religious initiation, particularly for girls, whose religious instruction was to be inspected and approved. The assembly also called for the transfer of the rabbinical seminary to Paris. Regarding the controversy which had arisen over the use of the organ in synagogue, it was decided that its use on Sabbath and festivals was lawful provided that it was played by a non-Jew. Its introduction would be subject to the authorization of the *grand rabbin* of the department concerned, at the request of the local rabbi. A breach in the community was therefore avoided at the price of compromises and half-measures. The different elements in French Jewry continued on good terms since the doctrinal independence of the local rabbi remained intact. Subsequently more ambitious attempts at reform were cut short by the Franco-German war of 1870–71. The French defeat cast an odium, a priori, on anything that smacked of German importation. As a result, French Jewry found itself in a state of arrested reform. Although moving away from Orthodoxy it remained firmly attached to the idea of an integrated community. To this day French consistorial Judaism has maintained great religious diversity, a situation which has always curbed the few attempts to establish dissident, Reform or Orthodox, communities. This flexibility later enabled the integration of immigrants from North Africa. The leading role still played in French communal affairs by the

Rothschild family also helped to give the community a large measure of stability.

ALLIANCE ISRAÉLITE UNIVERSELLE. The *Mortara case in 1858 once again brought up the question of freedom of conscience and reminded French Jewry of the Damascus Affair and the troubles of 1848. It again demonstrated the importance of organizing Jewish self-defense, this time on an international scale. The French Jews, who had been convinced that they had succeeded in assimilation by reconciling fidelity to Judaism with the gains achieved by democracy, felt compelled to react. However, it was typical of the existing situation that action was taken outside the framework of the central consistory which had by then withdrawn into a religious and representational role. In 1860, a group of young Jewish liberals founded the *Alliance Israélite Universelle with a central committee permanently based in Paris. The activities of this body were mainly directed to helping communities outside France and it had the great merit of again demonstrating that Jewish solidarity extended beyond modern nationalism.

ALSACE-LORRAINE AND ALGERIA. The 1870 war not only revived Franco-German hostility and put an end to many of the hopes for greater unity, but cut off from French Jewry its vital sources in Alsace and Lorraine. There was also the problem of integrating the Alsatian Jews who had opted to stay in France. This immigration considerably increased the importance of the communities in Paris and that part of Lorraine which had remained French. It also led to the creation of new consistories in Vesoul, Lille, and Besancon. The effects of the war also speeded up the naturalization of the Jews of *Algeria, where at the time of the French conquest there were a number of old-established communities. The French authorities took their existing arrangements into account but limited the powers of the "head of the Jewish nation" by attaching to him a "Hebrew council." The powers of the rabbinical courts were also restricted. However the Jews of Algeria officially remained part of the indigenous population with a personal status which was variously interpreted. In 1870, on the eve of the war with Prussia, and following numerous petitions by the Jews in Algeria, the imperial government was on the point of declaring the collective naturalization of Algerian Jewry.

The Government of National Defense sitting at Tours, at the pressing insistence of Crémieux, then minister of justice, proclaimed this naturalization by a decree issued on Oct. 24, 1870. Having become French citizens, the Jews of Algeria gave up their personal status and were on the same footing as the Jews of France. The consistorial system, which had been introduced in Algeria in 1845, was modified to permit a more active participation of the members of the Algerian community in the consistorial elections. The appointment of rabbis and *grand rabbins* was made by the central consistory.

ANTISEMITISM. Withdrawn into itself but enriched by the Algerian accession, the Jewish community of France soon had to face a formidable test. The advent of the Third Republic was not received by Jews with unmixed enthusiasm. Concerned at the progress of secularism and of movements demanding reform, royalist and clerical circles in France attempted to create an anti-Jewish diversion. Antisemitic newspapers began to appear. In 1883 the Assumptionists established the daily *La *Croix* which, with other publications, set out to prove that the Revolution had been the work of the Jews allied with the Freemasons. This trend was strengthened by the socialist antisemitism of the followers of *Fourier and *Proudhon. The various shades of antisemitism converged in Edouard *Drumont's *La France Juive* (1886), which became a bestseller. After the collapse of the Union Générale, a leading Catholic bank, the Jews in France provided a convenient scapegoat. In 1889 Drumont's ideas culminated in the formation of the French National Antisemitic League (see *Antisemitism: Antisemitic Political Parties and Organizations). In 1891, 32 deputies demanded that the Jews be expelled from France. In 1892 Drumont was able, with Jesuit support, to found his daily *La Libre Parole* which immediately launched a defamation campaign against Jewish officers who were accused of having plotted treason and of trafficking in secrets of the national defense. It also blamed Jews for the crash of the Panama Canal Company, creating a scandal which greatly increased its circulation. It was in this climate that Captain Alfred *Dreyfus was arrested on Oct. 15, 1894, on the charge of having spied in the interests of Germany. Many aspects of the affair are still unclear, although Dreyfus' innocence has been fully recognized. In any event, the affair went beyond the individual case of the unfortunate captain to rock the whole of France and Jews throughout the world.

In France the matter at stake was not the survival of the Jewish community: even its most virulent adversaries did not desire its physical disappearance, although cries of "death to the Jews" were uttered time and again by Paris crowds. On its part, the Catholic and right-wing press, and especially Drumont's *La Libre Parole*, frequently published "facts" about the machinations of a "World Jewish Syndicate" aimed at world domination. The Dreyfus case hastened the crystallization of the ideas of Theodor *Herzl, then press correspondent in Paris and a bewildered witness of the unleashing of antisemitism in a country reputed to be the most enlightened in Europe. The affair, by opposing the general trends of public opinion in France, led to a crisis of conscience rarely equaled in intensity. Its repercussions caused an upheaval in French political life with similar consequences for Jewish life.

SEPARATION OF CHURCH AND STATE. The disproportion between the origin of the affair and its consequences does not fail to astonish. In 1905, as a result of the victory of Dreyfus' supporters, a law was passed separating church and state. With the other recognized religions, the Jewish religion lost its official status, and state financial support was withdrawn with the abolition of state participation in religious expenses. Like the Protestants, but in contradistinction to the Catholics, the Jews accepted this resolution with goodwill. It would also have been difficult for them to oppose those who had supported

Dreyfus. At the same time *Grand Rabbin* Zadoc *Kahn died. His strong personality had dominated Jewish life since his election to the chief rabbinate of Paris in 1869 and a few years later to the chief rabbinate of France. His astonishing activity had revived French Judaism after the truncation of Alsatian Jewry, and he had interested Baron Edmond de *Rothschild in the colonization of Ereẓ Israel. The central consistory, disorientated after the passing of the 1905 act, thus had to transform itself while preserving its former framework as far as possible. Synagogues built with public subsidies were nationalized, but were immediately placed at the disposal of the successor religious associations. The central consistory became the Union des Associations Cultuelles de France et d'Algérie ("Union of the Religious Associations of France and Algeria"), and its office adopted the name Central Consistory. The regional consistories disappeared, but the large communities were changed into consistorial or religious associations. Practically all the departmental consistories remained in existence when the offices of the successor associations adopted the name consistory. The internal hierarchy, sanctioned by a century of tradition, continued. The perpetuation of the system, however, did not alter the fact that the organization of the Jewish community of France rested purely on a voluntary basis and on the recognition of a central authority freely accepted. In fact the French Jewish community became a federation of local communities which maintained a few joint central services, such as the chief rabbinate of France and the rabbinical seminary. Although this system increased the possibilities of fragmentation and disruption, the force of tradition maintained the moral authority of the various consistories, which became the principal, but not the exclusive, representation of a community undergoing a fundamental demographic transformation.

DEMOGRAPHIC CHANGES. During the 19th century, the relative importance of the Avignon communities had greatly decreased. The four Comtat communities had dispersed, their members moving to Marseilles and the large towns in southern France. The Bordeaux and Bayonne elements had never been very numerous. The extension of the French borders toward the north and east had opened up the country to a large Jewish immigration from Holland and the Rhineland. The Jewish population of Paris in 1789 numbered 500, out of the total French Jewish population of 40,000 to 50,000. There were 30,000 Jews living in Paris in 1869, out of a total of 80,000 for the whole of France. In 1880, following the loss of Alsace and Lorraine, 40,000 out of a total of 60,000 French Jews were living in Paris. This proportion has remained substantially unchanged. The pogroms in Russia of 1881 gave rise to a wave of Jewish emigration to the free countries and marked the beginning of the Russian, Polish, and Romanian immigration into France. A second wave of immigration took place after the abortive 1905 Russian revolution. From 1881 to 1914 over 25,000 Jewish immigrants arrived in France. The Russian element was in the minority. From 1908 a large Jewish influx also began from the Ottoman countries, chiefly from Salonika, Constantinople, and Smyrna. However, for a large number of immigrants, France served as a country of transit and not of refuge.

WORLD WAR I. The advent of World War I halted this immigration. In uniting all the forces of the nation, the war also put a stop to the antisemitic campaigns. The necessity for maintaining a common front (*union sacrée*) brought all the religions together. For some Jewish soldiers the war was to be a means of rejoining their families after the reconquest of Alsace and Lorraine. The victory restored to French Jewry these most vital communities. They had preserved their former consistorial organization since they had been in German territory in 1905 when the law separating church and state was passed. The French government, following a policy of pacification and taking into consideration the strong religious attachment of the population, did not apply the law to the regained territories. Thus religious life there continued to be organized on the old system.

INTER-WAR YEARS. After the war, Jewish immigration from the former Ottoman countries was resumed with greater intensity. The Jews from Turkey and Greece settled chiefly in Paris and in the large cities of the south. However, the largest immigration came from Eastern Europe in the wake of the Ukrainian and Polish pogroms. Romania also provided a significant number of Jews. Once again the Russian and Lithuanian elements were not numerous. This trend increased after 1924 following the prohibition of free immigration into the United States. From 1933 many Jewish refugees from Nazi Germany passed through France en route for America or Palestine. The number remaining in France was relatively insignificant. It is estimated that there were 180,000 Jews resident in Paris in 1939, one-third of them belonging to the old French Jewish community. By then the use of Yiddish had become widespread and the "Ashkenazation" of the community had increased. The freedom of religious organization, which the law separating church and state had ratified by abolishing the official organization of religion, had enabled the different groups of immigrants to organize an appropriate framework for their religious and social life. Thus in 1923 the Fédération des Sociétés Juives de France (FSJF), a body which united the majority of Landsmanschaften, was created. However, these organizations did not impair the prestige of the old-established French Jewish communal bodies. The new bodies lost much of their meaningfulness as their members assimilated into French life, and with the progress of social security which deprived them of much of their usefulness. Many of their members subsequently joined the ranks of the established community.

ECONOMIC, CULTURAL, AND SOCIAL POSITION. In the economic sphere, the position of French Jewry continued to improve. After 1850, the number of Jews engaged in crafts increased considerably, and many Jews entered the technical professions. Few were attracted to agriculture. In the period before World War I Jewish painters and sculptors had made the Paris school famous (see *Paris School of Art). Among a brilliant galaxy, the names of *Pissaro, *Soutine, *Pascin, *Kisling, *Chagall, and *Modigliani are well known. Sarah *Bernhardt, who was eventually baptized, brought luster to the French theater. Outstanding in literature and philosophy were Adolphe *Franck, Salomon *Munk, Henri *Bergson, Emile *Durkheim, Lucien *Lévy-Bruhl, Marcel *Proust, and André *Maurois.

Purely Jewish studies were not abandoned. From 1880 the *Société des Etudes Juives regularly published a learned periodical, *Revue des Etudes Juives*, and was responsible for the publication of the classic works of Heinrich *Gross (*Gallia Judaica*, 1897) and T. *Reinach (*Textes d'auteurs Grecs et Romains relatifs au Judaïsme*, 1895), and a modern translation of the works of Josephus. The French rabbinate published a magnificent translation of the Bible. On the other hand, talmudic studies in France ceased. The process of social assimilation continued, and in 1936 Léon *Blum became the first Jewish premier of France.

[Simon R. Schwarzfuchs]

Holocaust Period

On May 10, 1940, the Germans invaded France. *Paris fell on June 14. The armistice, which was signed two weeks later, divided France into an Unoccupied Zone in the South, and an Occupied Zone (subdivided into "general" and "forbidden" zones and several restricted areas) in the northern half of the country. The departments of Nord and Pas-de-Calais were attached to German military administration based in Brussels, while Alsace-Lorraine was annexed to the Reich. A new regime, based in Vichy, under the leadership of the World War I hero Marshal Philippe Pétain, took over the reigns of government. No official figures exist on the number of Jews living in France at the beginning of the war, since Jews were not singled out in the census and the documents on official and illegal entry or departure of refugees are unreliable. It is estimated that there were about 300,000 Jews in France prior to the invasion. During World War II, the Jews in France suffered from the combined impact of the Nazi "*Final Solution" and from traditional French antisemitism. By and large, French antisemitism did not tend toward physical extermination, but its existence unquestionably helped the Nazis in carrying out their scheme. A small coterie of French racist ideologues, largely in the Occupied Zone, expounded radical anti-Jewish sentiments. Most importantly, indifference to the fate of the Jews on the part of both Vichy government officials and French citizens led to callousness and disregard for the Jewish plight.

ANTI-JEWISH MEASURES AND ADMINISTRATION. Recent scholarship has demonstrated that the Vichy regime initiated many of its anti-Jewish policies and laws without any direct orders from and often in opposition to the German occupying powers. Much of the groundwork had been laid by laws passed by the Third Republic in its last years of existence restricting and controlling foreigners. With the defeat of France in June 1940, the Vichy government took the initiative to deal with the "Jewish question." In August 1940, it repealed the Marchandeau law, originally passed in April 1939, which had effectively outlawed antisemitic attacks in the press. The *Statut des juifs*, first enacted in October 1940 and then revised in June 1941, closed off top governmental positions to Jews. Its definition of Jews proved to be even more restrictive than those imposed by Nazis in Germany. Additional laws soon followed that effectively eliminated Jews from the liberal professions, commerce, the crafts, and industry. The Vichy regime also instituted a census in the Unoccupied Zone, and empowered the State to place all Jewish property in the hands of non-Jewish trustees. By late 1940, it is estimated that some 40,000 people were interned in camps, the vast majority of whom were foreign-born Jews. At the same time, German officials introduced various anti-Jewish measures in the Occupied Zone. The first *Verordnung* (ordinance) of Sept. 27, 1940, ordered a census of the Jews. Other ordinances soon followed, which placed Jewish property in the hands of so-called provisional administrators; extended the discriminatory category of "Jew" to individuals of Jewish origin who were not of the Jewish faith, and prohibited a number of economic activities. A proclamation issued by the German military authorities in December 1941 announced inter alia a fine of one million francs to be paid by the Jewish population, the execution of 53 Jewish members of the Resistance, and the deportation of 1,000 Jews (in fact, 1,100 Jews were actually deported on March 27, 1942, as a result of the proclamation). In 1942, German authorities established a curfew for Jews between 8 P.M. and 6 A.M., prohibited them from changing residence, and enlarged still further the scope of the definition of "the Jews." An ordinance of May 29, 1942, ordered all Jews to wear a yellow *badge. It was soon followed by a prohibition against Jews using public places, squares, gardens, and sports grounds Jews in the Occupied Zone were also restricted to one hour a day to make their purchases in shops and food markets.

The German *Verordnungen* were valid only in the Occupied Zone. Even after the Germans took control of all of France in November 1942, they were not extended to the newly occupied areas. Thus, for instance, the yellow badge never became compulsory in southern France. The statutes, laws, and ordinances of the Vichy government, on the other hand, were valid throughout the country, as was the rubber stamp *Juif* ("Jew") on identity cards. Whereas German measures were directed without exception against all Jews, the Vichy measures mainly affected Jews who were either foreign nationals or stateless, and later Jewish immigrants who had recently become French nationals. French Jews of long standing were generally spared, sometimes by means of the exceptions made in favor of ex-servicemen and individuals of outstanding merit. At the same time, the various discriminatory laws strongly suggest that the Vichy regime wished to consign all Jews to a subservient role and to subject them to severe restrictions.

With an eye to coordinating policies in the two Zones, the Gestapo and specifically the Paris branch of *Eichmann's IV B under the leadership of SS-Hauptsturmfuehrer Theodor Dannecker set about to create both a French government agency for anti-Jewish affairs and a *Judenrat, which would act as the French counterparts of the German IV B branch and the *Reichsvereinigung der Juden in Deutschland. With only minimal prompting and without prior submission to the German military administration, in March 1941 the Vichy government set up the Commissariat Général aux Questions Juives (CGQJ), headed by Xavier *Vallat, an extreme-right member of parliament. Vallat was a French politician and an antisemite in the French tradition, who believed that Jews were responsible for the very existence of democracy and the Third Republic, which had undermined France. After serving a year, he was dismissed after German authorities decided that he was too lax in carrying out anti-Jewish measures. Vallat was succeeded by the rabid antisemite Darquier de *Pellepoix. Under Darquier, the CGQJ accelerated the pace of "aryanization" of Jewish property and and forged stronger links with the German authorities. The Vichy government also created an official body called the *Union Générale des Israélites de France (UGIF) in November 1941 to represent French Jewry during the German occupation. It had two divisions – one in the Occupied Zone and one in the free one. The role of the UGIF continues to be the subject of much controversy. While helping to save many children and providing material aid to Jews in French internment camps, it generally proved unwilling to actively confront either German or Vichy authorities. Until at least 1942, leaders of the UGIF were convinced that government authorities would never betray the basic principles that allegedly underlie French society.

DEPORTATIONS AND FORCED LABOR. As the Germans accelerated their anti-Jewish activities in France after the *Wannsee Conference, held in January 1942, they recognized that though Vichy authorities were prepared to enforce the regulations to persecute "foreign" Jews, they were often reluctant to act against French Jews. For that reason, it was decided that any action taken against native Jews would be carried out by the Gestapo itself, whereas the French police would be responsible for the roundups of immigrant and foreign Jews. In June 1942, the Third Reich decided that France would supply 100,000 Jews, to be taken from both zones, for extermination. A series of roundups (*"rafles"* in French, *"Aktionen"* in German) soon followed. The most notorious roundup took place on July 16–17, 1942, in Paris and its suburbs, Carried out by French policemen and sanctioned by Premier Pierre Laval, it led to the arrest of 12,884 men, women, and children, most of whom were interned in the Velodrome d'Hiver, a large indoor sports arena in the south of Paris. Many more *"rafles"* took place both before and after the so-called "Grand Rafle" of the "Vel d'Hiv," as it became known. A major roundup of foreign Jews in the Unoccupied Zone took place between August 26 and 28. The great majority of the victims had settled in the southern part of France, where they had joined several thousand French Jews who had also fled from the Germans. The cities of Toulouse, Marseilles, Lyons, and Nice thus had large concentrations of Jews. Smaller towns, such as Limoges and Périgueux, also sheltered hundreds of Jews.

With the exception of a small number of wealthy individuals, the refugees from abroad were interned either in detention camps, such as Saint-Cyprien, Gurs, Vernet, Argelès-sur-Mer, Barcarès, Agde, Nexon, Fort-Barraux, and Les Milles, or in smaller so-called *Détachements de prestataires de travail*, i.e., forced labor detachments. Thousands of foreign Jews who had volunteered in 1939–40 for the French army were not demobilized after the armistice, but kept for a time in similar forced labor battalions, both in France and in North Africa (Djerada, Djelfa, and on the Mediterranean-Niger railway project). Their living and work conditions were similar to those of criminals sentenced to hard labor.

Jews generally were sent from internment camps to concentration camps in preparation for their deportations east. There were two main concentration camps for foreign Jews, Pithiviers and Beaune-la-Rolande near Paris, and a few smaller ones. *Drancy, a northern suburb, was the main transit camp to *Auschwitz. Some Jews were also deported from the Compiègne camp and a few deportation trains left from Pithiviers, Beaune-la-Rolande, and such towns as Angers, Lyons, and Toulouse. Deportation came in several waves, beginning on March 27, 1942, and was largely handled by the military administration. The second deportation during the summer and fall of 1942 followed the main roundup throughout the country. A third wave during the spring of 1943 came after the clearance and destruction of the Vieux-Port quarter of Marseilles. After the Germans occupied the former Italian zone in southeast France in the fall of 1943, many Jews who had found sanctuary there after German authorities took control of all of France in November 1942 were arrested. In Nice alone, about 6,000 Jews (out of 25,000) were deported. The first deportations of foreign Jews to Auschwitz occurred in March 1942. A convoy of French Jews soon followed them. Beginning in June 1942, the deportations were accelerated, and they continued almost without interruption throughout 1943. The unification of the two zones meant that the implementation of the Final Solution could now proceed without interruption and without differentiation between foreign-born and French Jews. The last convoy departed France in August 1944. An estimated 85,000–90,000 Jews, two-thirds of whom were immigrant and non-citizens, were deported in 100 convoys, largely to Auschwitz. Barely 3,000 of these survived. In addition, a few thousand Jews were deported or executed for political and resistance activities.

RESCUE AND RESISTANCE. Jewish institutions, such as *HICEM, helped a few of the foreign Jews to emigrate overseas. The fact that that the Vichy regime never officially prohibited emigration even after the occupation of the south meant there were opportunities for Jews to escape across the

Pyrenees and the Swiss border. Traditional religious and philanthropic Jewish organizations such as the largely native Consistoire israélite de France and the immigrant Fédération des sociétés juives de France continued their activities, mainly in southern France. The French rabbinate also arranged for religious and social assistance, which carried out in part by rabbis active in the resistance movement, such as René Kappel. Other institutions cared for the social and physical well-being of the internees. As persecution became more severe and as the pace of deportations increased, mutual-aid organizations such as the Fédération des sociétés juives increasingly combined their material aid with resistance activities, such as the falsification of identity and ration cards, and of addresses; and aid to those who had escaped deportation.

The Jews of France played an important role in the resistance to Nazism, both in French movements across the political spectrum – from Gaullist to Communist and Trotskyist groups – and in specifically Jewish groups, such as those organized by the Zionists and the Communists. The active role of the Zionists and the Communists in resistance gained them entry into the established Jewish community. The Zionist youth movements established a united Mouvement de la Jeunesse sioniste and later the Armée juive. Initially, the French-Jewish scout movement, the Eclaireurs israélites de France (EIF), was attracted to the ideology of the Vichy regime and particularly to the myth of Marshal Pétain. With the onset of deportations in 1942, however, the Scouts increasingly turned to active resistance, first aiding in the hiding of hundreds of children, and then engaging in armed struggle. Together with the Armée Juive, they established the OJC (Organisation Juive de Combat) Robert Gamzon (Castor), the national director of the Jewish Boy Scouts of France, largely contributed to this evolution. Other groups that were active in aiding Jews, especially children, were the Oeuvre de secours aux enfants (*OSE), and the Women's International Zionist Organization's (*WIZO) office in the Paris area. Jewish Communist groups, such as the Mouvement National contre le Racisme (MNCR), created in 1942, which benefited from the support of the French Communist Party, also played an active role in resistance. In contrast to other groups, which emphasized Jewish self-defense, they tended to view Jewish resistance to Nazism as part of the general struggle against Fascism.

During the course of the war, the attitude and behavior of the majority of French citizens toward Jews gradually shifted from open hostility or apathy to sympathy and support. At first, most Frenchmen approved of the discriminatory laws, especially against foreign-born Jews, as part of their general approval of Marshal Pétain's program of national revival. In time, however, the increasing brutality of the Vichy and Nazi policies beginning in 1942, which included the deportations of native-born Jews including women and children, and the fact that roundups were no longer limited to German-occupied areas, led to growing opposition to and resentment against the regime's anti-Jewish policies. Many individual Frenchmen hid children and adults, often at the risk of their own lives. For the first time, there were statements of opposition from established leaders. Before 1942, the French Catholic Church had remained silent in the face of Vichy's anti-Jewish pronouncements and policies. Alerted by Jewish religious authorities, a number of Catholic prelates, such as Monsignors Jules-Gérard Saliège and Pierre-Marie Théas, now strongly condemned the deportations of the Jews from their pulpits. In local areas, convents and monasteries offered shelter to Jews, particularly to children. For the most part, the Church hierarchy did not attempt to proselytize the Jewish children under their care, though some families did convert those whom they had taken in. The Protestant churches, numerically very small in France, were even more actively opposed to the persecution of Jews. Pastor Marc Boegner, president of the National Protestant Federation, denounced the Statut des juifs and the expropriation of Jewish-owned property in the Unoccupied Zone. The largely Protestant areas of the Haute-Loire, Hautes-Alpes, and the Tarnin in Central France became centers for active rescue of Jews. Of special note was the village of Le Chambon-sur-Lignon, whose efforts to hide Jews have been chronicled in numerous film documentaries and films.

[Lucien Steinberg / David Weinberg (2nd ed.)]

Early Postwar Period

NATIVE POPULATION AND WAVES OF IMMIGRATION. France was the only country in Europe to which Jews immigrated in significant numbers after World War II. In 1945, there were some 180 000 Jews in France. The community was composed of established Jewish families and immigrants from Central and Eastern Europe and Mediterranean countries. In 25 years the Jewish population tripled. Between 1945 and 1951 many Displaced Persons passed through France, and some settled there. In 1951 there were 250 000 Jews in the country. Between 1954 and 1961, approximately 100,000 Jews moved to France from Tunisia, Morocco, Egypt (1956), and Algeria. After the Bizerta incidents (in Tunisia) and the independence of Algeria (1962), immigration increased. By 1963, almost the entire Jewish community of Algeria (110,000 persons, all French citizens) had moved to France. Moroccan and Tunisian Jews continued to arrive in the late 1960s with a last peak following the Six-Day War (from the summer of 1967 to the summer of 1968, 16,000 Jews from Tunisia and Morocco sought sanctuary in France). French-speaking Jewry had undergone a new geographical distribution, diversification in occupations and social status, a change in community structure, and a fundamental reorientation in religious, ideological, and cultural trends.

Approximately 50% of the Jews who left North Africa settled in France, so that by 1968 the Sephardim were in the majority in the French Jewish community.

GEOGRAPHICAL DISTRIBUTION. In 1939 the Jewish population was concentrated in Paris and the surrounding region, Alsace-Lorraine, and several large towns. In 1968 about 60% of the Jewish population lived in Paris and its surroundings, about 25% in the Midi, and the rest were scattered throughout

France. Five provincial towns supported important communities: Marseilles (65,000), Lyons (20,000), Toulouse (18,000), Nice (16,000), and Strasbourg (12,000). Between 1957 and 1966 the number of localities in which Jews lived rose from 128 to 293. The dispersal of the immigrants from North Africa, which answered the need to absorb them into the economy, resulted in the establishment of Jewish communities throughout the country. In 1968, 76 rather isolated communities contained fewer than 100 Jews, and 174 communities numbered less than 1,000 (such communities were particularly numerous in the Paris district).

ECONOMIC AND SOCIAL STATUS. French Jewry succeeded in normalizing its economic status during the first two or three years following the liberation. Each successive wave of immigration, however, included a large group of impoverished persons who were forced to make recourse to social services run by the community or the state. Among both Ashkenazim and Sephardim, rapid and important changes in social status took place. Artisans from Eastern Europe or North Africa abandoned their traditional occupations in the second, if not in the first, generation in order to find jobs in modern industry, where the need for technical skills was great and through which a rapid rise on the social scale was possible. This trend was encouraged by the education offered in the seven *ORT schools, whose pupils were mainly from immigrant families. About 80% of North African Jews continued in the same occupation they had pursued in their countries of origin, and their influx into France slightly modified the distribution of occupations and social status of French Jewry. An estimated 15% of Algerian Jews were clerks employed at all levels of public administration; these were absorbed into urban administrations. Despite the resettlement loans granted by the government to repatriated citizens, some small businessmen and artisans had to abandon their previous status as self-employed persons and become salaried employees. Social advancement was rapid among North African Jews who were French nationals, as racial barriers that had seriously handicapped their advancement under colonial rule did not exist in France. Their settlement there opened new prospects for them, and many made their way in the liberal professions, commerce, and industry. The economic absorption of Moroccan or Tunisian Jews was more difficult. Nevertheless, they also chose France as their new country of residence as a result of their varying degrees of assimilation into French culture in their native countries. The social status and occupational distribution of French Jewry resembled the principal traits of the Diaspora in the West, i.e., a preponderance of members of the liberal professions, white-collar workers, businessmen, and artisans.

COMMUNITY ORGANIZATION. The period from 1945 to the end of the 1960s was a one of reconstruction of the community organization. The Consistoire Central Israélite de France et d'Algérie, the major religious organization, had to face numerous demands. Orthodox in orientation, it was the official representative of French Judaism, responsible for the training, nomination, and appointment of rabbis, religious instruction for young people, the supervision of *kashrut*, and the application of religious law in matters of personal status. In order to answer the new needs related to the sharp increase in the Jewish population, the Consistoire set up a program of new synagogue building projects (les Chantiers du Consistoire) and had to accompany the development of a more intense religious life (organizing the network of *sheḥita* and *hashgaḥah*, supplying more rabbis and *talmud torah* to teachers…). While in the 1950s the consistory synagogues generally practiced Ashkenazi rites (and a few the Portuguese or North African rituals), by the end of the 1960s a majority of the consistory synagogues had switched to North African rites. North African Jews often formed their own communal organizations, but were represented in all the consistorial organizations. After 1945, most of the pupils of the Ecole Rabbinique and the rabbinical seminary, the Séminaire Israélite de France, were of Egyptian and North African origin. The Union Libérale Israélite, affiliated to the World Union for Progressive Judaism, was no less active. It had greater influence in more assimilated circles of established and North African families and trained its ministers at the Institut International d'Etudes Hébraïques. Lastly, there were the independent religious bodies, including Sephardi and North African communities practicing their various local rites, Poles, and ḥasidim and kabbalists. Despite the amount of effort expended, only a small minority of French Jewry practiced their religion. There were, however, hundreds of associations and institutions of a cultural, social, or philanthropic nature. From 1945 efforts made to coordinate and channel the rather anarchic development of such organizations met with a measure of success. On a political level, the Conseil Représentatif des Juifs de France (CRIF), founded in 1944, was an example of such an effort. Created clandestinely during the war, it meant to illustrate the unity of the French Jewish community through its various trends, religious and non-religious, old established natives and newer immigrants, etc. In 1968, it was composed of 27 important organizations of diverse trends, including religious, Zionist, Bundist, and even Communist bodies. According to its statutes, the Council's aim was "to protect the rights of the Jewish community in France"; it also played an active role in fighting antisemitism. On the social and cultural level, the Fonds Social Juif Unifié (FSJU), founded in 1949 to centralize the various efforts of the community, rapidly became the central organizational body of French Jewry. It coordinated, supervised, and planned the community's major social, cultural, and educational enterprises, which it financed through its unified fund-raising campaign and the contributions of the *Joint Distribution Committee. Its community services played an important role in the integration of Jewish immigrants, and its numerous community centers aimed at involving peripheral elements without religious affiliations in community life. After the Six-Day War, the FSJU and the Appel Unifié pour Israël (United Israel Appeal) coordinated their activities and formed the Appel Unifié Juif de France, a joint fund-raising venture. Varied ideological and political orientations, from the assimilationists to the Zionists and from the left wing to the right, were freely expressed in the French Jewish community. Although the Landsmanschaften of Eastern European immigrants gradually died out, associations of immigrants from North African countries multiplied.

CULTURAL LIFE. The diverse cultural trends of French Jewry were expressed by its 40 or so weekly and monthly publications. In 1968, there were ten daily, weekly, or monthly publications in Yiddish. After 1945, due to the activities of the *Conference on Jewish Material Claims, many books on Jewish and Israeli subjects were published annually by large French publishing houses; there was also a weekly Jewish radio broadcast and a regular television program. Most French Jews preferred to provide their children with a secular state education. Less than 5% of Jewish schoolchildren studied in the Jewish day schools at all levels, but the numerous youth movements and organizations tried to attract as many young people as possible. Under an agreement between the French and Israel governments, Hebrew could be taught as a foreign language in the *lycées* (state high schools). Ten universities included Hebrew in their curriculum, the universities of Paris and Strasbourg taught Jewish history, literature, and sociology. All the major Zionist youth movements were represented in France. The French Zionist Federation included various Zionist parties; however, it was decimated by internal feuds and its influence was weak. Nevertheless, more and more French Jews expressed their solidarity with Israel.

Despite a certain latent but rarely virulent antisemitism (research conducted by the Institut Français de l'Opinion Publique in December 1966 showed that about 20% of the French public held seriously antisemitic opinions), Jews felt well integrated into French society. The efforts of numerous Jewish organizations did not retard the rate of assimilation. After the Six-Day War (1967), the explicit anti-Israel stance of de Gaulle and his government (see below), came as a shock to French Jewry. The feeling of uneasiness increased when the anti-Israel utterances of de Gaulle, his officials and commentators assumed a half-disguised, sophisticated antisemitic quality, particularly through hints at the Jews' "double loyalty." It reached its peak when de Gaulle, at a press conference (Nov. 27, 1967), defined the Jews as "*un peuple d'élite*, sûr de lui-même et dominateur" ("an elite people, self-assured and domineering"), thus giving a great impetus to overt expressions of latent antisemitism. This dictum aroused a wide public controversy in France and abroad. The chief rabbi, Jacob Kaplan, voiced his protest, reaffirming Jewish attachment to Israel and stressing that it did not contradict in any way the fact that the Jews of France are loyal Frenchmen. De Gaulle later told the chief rabbi that his words were not meant to be disparaging. At the same time, from the other extreme of the political scene, came the violently aggressive anti-Israel propaganda of the *New Left and of the "students' revolution" of May 1968, who supported Arab-Palestinian terrorism against Israel, though many of the movement's leaders were themselves young Jews (Daniel Cohn-Bendit, Marc Kravetz, Alain Krivine, and others). This agitation was the cause of embarrassment to most French Jews, not only because of its enmity toward Israel but also because of its extremist ideology of violence (Trotskyism, Maoism, anarchism, etc.), which could have easily aroused an antisemitic reaction in the mainly conservative French middle class, to whom most Jews belong. Physical clashes between Jews and Arabs in certain quarters of Paris, mostly provoked by pro-Palestinian North Africans, added to the malaise. As a result, migration from France to Israel, by both French and Algerian Jews, considerably increased in the late 1960s.

[Doris Bensimon-Donath]

Later Developments

DEMOGRAPHY. The Jews of France maintained a stable population variously estimated at 500,000–550,000 from the late 1960s to the early years of the 21st century (the former figure being the 2002 estimate based on a study by the Israeli sociologist Erik Cohen). Another 75,000 non-Jews were estimated in 2002 to be living in Jewish households. Following the decolonization of the former French possessions in North Africa, the Jewish population of France doubled between 1955 and 1965. Afterwards immigration was numerically insignificant. However, French Jewry changed from having an Ashkenazi majority to a Sephardi one (70 percent in 2002). France has taken in only a limited number of Jews who, since 1989, have left the former Soviet Union.

By the early 1990s the second as well as the third generation was French-born and educated. They were, of course, French, but maintained a conscious Jewish identity. The demographic trends among the Jewish population of France are similar to those of most other Diaspora countries: aging, low birth rates along with significant changes of the family units. Mixed marriages are an accepted fact and there are also increased numbers of couples living together and of divorces.

Some 50 percent of French Jews lived in Paris and its suburbs. Among the provincial communities the largest were those of Marseilles, Nice, Toulouse, and Montpellier in the south, Lyons and Grenoble in the southeast, and Strasbourg in Alsace. Jews also lived scattered throughout the country while having a tendency to congregate in middle-sized cities owing to the attraction of a better organized community life. In all, 72 percent of French Jews lived in just nine of its 30 départements

French Jewry constitutes the largest Jewish community in Europe. After the breakup of the Soviet Union and the mass emigration of Jews from there, France, in 1995, became the second largest Diaspora community (after the United States). Representing about 1 percent of the total French population, the Jews are only the third largest religious group: their number is greatly exceeded by the approximately 5 million Muslims, some stemming from the former French colonies, others French citizens. "Feujs" (young second and third generation Jews) and "Beurs" (young second and third generation Muslims) live in certain sections of the large cities and their suburbs, where at times they clash and at times live amicably.

EDUCATION AND CULTURE. During the 1970s there were significant developments in the sphere of all-day Jewish education. Both in Paris and in the provinces numerous primary and secondary schools, as well as kindergartens were opened. Parallel to the network controlled by the FSJU there were schools operating in accordance with the most Orthodox currents, such as the Otzar Hathora. In 1976 the FSJU and the Jewish Agency created the Fonds d'Investissement pour l'Education (FIPE), which, with the support and participation of a number of religious organizations, led to a significant expansion of the network of Jewish day schools. By 1979, approximately 10,000 children attended all-day Jewish schools, the most important of them having concluded agreements with the government whereby it covered the fees of the teachers who give general education.

According to a study made by Erik Cohen in 1986/88 (see bibliography), the number of full-time Jewish educational institutions – from nursery school to high schools – doubled from 44 in 1976 to 88 in 1986/87, at which time, 16,000 children and teenagers attended full-time Jewish schools. This trend has continued: by 1992, 20–25 percent of school-age Jews attended full-time Jewish schools. If one adds the *talmud Torahs* (preparatory courses for bar mitzvah and bat mitzvah), the youth movements, and other Jewish recreational organizations, 75 percent of Jewish youth have some more or less long term formal Jewish education.

Non-practicing Jewish families had, in the 1980s, a more favorable attitude than in the past to full-time Jewish education, but, more than the others, the religious circles have the maximum commitment to Jewish education. According to Cohen's study, in 1986/87, about one-third of the Jewish day schools were affiliated with organizations such as Lubavitch, Otzar Ha-Torah, or Or Yossef. In 1994, the FSJU opened the André Neher Institute intended to train educators who wish to work in the Jewish educational networks. This new institute stressed the recruitment of teachers of Jewish subjects who receive at the same time training in the university and pedagogical system charged with training teachers in France.

The majority of Jewish youth, however, study in public schools whose underlying principle is secularism, having as its objective the education of children and young people of every religion and every origin, with mutual tolerance. For over a century, the free, secular school has played an essential role in the integration of children born to every wave of immigration in French society. Still, the evolution of the French society by the end of the 20th century also echoed in the realm of the state schools. From the end of the 1980s, a broad public debate took place on the question of "conspicuous" religious signs worn by a few schoolchildren (mainly the Islamic veil for girls). The majority of those Jews who expressed themselves on the question strongly supported traditional French secularism as a protection for all minorities against certain over-assertive groups; nevertheless, some Jews – and among them the Consistoire Central, although for a very short period – were tempted by the idea of getting some exemptions made official, such as the exemption from school for observant Jewish children on Saturday. However, in 2004 a law finally banned all religious symbols from schools.

In the public school system, Hebrew was taught at a number of high schools as a foreign language which fulfills the matriculation requirement. In the universities, the study of Hebrew, Jewish languages, and Jewish civilization is now well represented.

The year 1992 was for the Jews of France the 50th anniversary of the beginning of the mass deportations: the Holocaust is at the heart of Jewish memory. During this decade, there was a significant increase in research studies into the responsibility of the Vichy government for the persecution of the Jews. President Mitterrand was called upon to admit officially France's responsibility for this persecution.

The year 1994 was the 600th anniversary of the expulsion of the Jews from France by Charles VI. A scientific colloquium presented information on this tragic period of the Jewish people.

The years 1994 and 1995 were marked above all by the celebrations of the 50th anniversary first of the Liberation of France and then of the extermination camps and finally of the victory of the Allies over Nazi Germany. While President Mitterrand had kept in 1992 the date of July 16th (the day of the big roundup of Jews in Paris in July 1942) as the official anniversary of the persecution of the Jews in France, President Chirac pronounced in 1995 a memorable speech acknowledging the responsibility of the French state in the tragic fate of the Jews. Jews and Jewish organizations were obviously associated with these national and international celebrations. Remembrance of the Holocaust is broadly presented and disseminated by the media. The Jews stress not only the persecution, but also the Resistance. There are increasing numbers of works dealing with what transpired and, more specifically, survivor accounts. The *Centre de Documentation Juive Contemporaine (CDJC) participates in an international project launched by Steven Spielberg, director of *Schindler's List*, for collecting Holocaust survivors' videotaped testimony.

The intellectual and cultural vitality of French Jewry is attested by artistic, literary, and scientific output. Each year, 200 to 300 works on Jewish themes are published in France. They cover the gamut of the field of Jewish studies, from the translation and interpretation of traditional texts of Jewish thought to the study of contemporary Jewish issues. At the same time, novels with Jewish themes are published and plays, movies, and works in the plastic arts are produced. The interest in Judaism and its culture is shared by the Jewish and non-Jewish public.

COMMUNITY. The Six-Day War was to a large extent a turning point for the French Jewish community. After 1967, the role played by Israel in the Jewish self-identification became even more central in France whereas Jewish institutions became increasingly involved in Jewish world politics. From 1970, the Conseil Representatif des Juifs de France (CRIF, which changed its name to the more precise one of Conseil Représentatif des Institutions Juives de France), expanded its range of activities. In the wake of the 1967 and 1973 wars in Israel, it took a new impulse under the dynamic leadership of Professor Ady *Steg. It played an important part in the struggle against antisemitism and was active in support of Soviet Jewry. While by 1970 the number of affiliated organizations reached34, the CRIF became more and more active in the public life, representing the Jews as a sort of sociological – and not purely religious – group. The impulse of the 1970s was confirmed in the three following decades, with the development of a regular dialogue with the authorities, symbolized since the 1980s by the yearly dinner at which the CRIF receives the French Premier. The last third of the century was also a period of enhanced development for the Fonds Social Juif Unifié, (FSJU), the main community organization in France, which collects and distributes funds for Jewish welfare and cultural activities. After the intense effort of the post-war reconstruction and the integration of a heavy immigration in the 1960s and 1970s, the FSJU had to adjust to the end of the support it had been granted by American Jewish Joint Distribution Committee while investing heavily in the development of formal education through Jewish schools and going on playing a major part in the organization and planning of the community social services in times which were not of full economic prosperity. At the same time, the FSJU statutes underwent a reform in favor of more democratic representation. In the religious sphere the most important event of the 1980s was the retirement of the chief rabbi, Jacob Kaplan, and the election for a seven-year period of Rabbi René Samuel *Sirat as his successor in June 1980. Born in Bone (Algeria), Sirat was a Sephardi and a university graduate; he placed the main stress on Jewish education and the spiritual renewal of French Jewry. This renewal took different forms. Whereas for some it consisted of a return to religious practice, in the case of others it meant the search for Jewish identity and a renewal of Sephardi and Yiddish culture. Together they embraced a significant number of individuals and an intense renewed literary activity is manifest.

In the 1980s organized community life was characterized by the rise of ever-increasing numbers of Sephardi Jews to positions of leadership and by a certain return to religion in strong opposition to humanistic and secular initiatives. The organization of the Jewish community of France continued to reflect the ideological heterogeneity of its members.

The consistories, which are in charge of the organization of Jewish religious worship and observances, tended to extend their spheres of activities.

In 1988, Joseph Sitruk, born in Tunisia, was elected chief rabbi after René Samuel Sirat and continued in that position into the 21st century. Jean-Paul Elkann was president of the Central Consistory in the 1980s. In June 1992, Jean-Pierre Bansard was elected. Born in 1940 in Oran, Algeria, and president of a financial company, Bansard represented a new Jewish leadership. In 1995 Jean *Kahn took over.

A most significant change, however, took place in the 1990s in the Board of the Association Cultuelle Israélite de Paris (ACIP), which is the most important regional consistory in France. A new team of a stricter Orthodoxy than its predecessor, headed by Benny Cohen, was elected, calling vigorously for a return to religious practice. This new tendency is strongly opposed by some of their coreligionists who affirm their Jewish identity only in a cultural mode. There are also more Orthodox Jews: in Paris, as in other cities, ultra-Orthodox groups and notably the Lubavitch Ḥasidim took root during the 1980s. They have established their neighborhoods and made their Judaism "visible" through billboard campaigns at Jewish holiday times and through lighting Ḥanukkah candles in large public places in Paris.

At the end of 1992, the new team of the ACIP changed some of the rules governing their association. As voted on December 20, 1992, the ACIP, which became the "consistory of Paris and the Ile de France," sought to reinforce its position as the heart of the central consistory organization and increase its powers with an eye on stricter observance of the *halakhah*. This transformation met with lively opposition on the part of representatives of more liberal tendencies within the consistory spheres themselves. Between 1992 and mid-1994 the debate was harsh between the more or less orthodox trends and finally a new president, Moïse Cohen, was elected who attempted to refocus the ACIP around its religious mission in a spirit open to the different trends in Judaism.

By the end of the 20th century, the CRIF had confirmed the trends that had affected it since the 1970s. It encompassed some 60 Jewish organizations, among them the most important in the country. After Alain de Rothschild, its presidents were Théo *Klein, Jean *Kahn, Henri Hajdenberg, and Roger Cukierman (from 2001). CRIF not only fought against antisemitism but also expanded its activities in the sphere of defense of human rights. In 2002 it organized a massive rally in Paris under the banner "Against Antisemitism. For Israel." Moreover, since 1986, first Theo Klein and then Jean Kahn served as president of the European Jewish Congress (CJE) created at the initiative of the World Jewish Congress. Since 1989 CJE has developed activities involving French Jewry, directly or indirectly, on behalf of Jewish communities in the ex-communist bloc. In 1992, Jean Kahn, within the framework of his functions, took part in humanitarian actions in the territory of former Yugoslavia.

The Fonds Social Juif Unifié (FSJU) celebrated in 2001 its 50th anniversary. This is the most important organization supporting and coordinating French Jewry's social, educational, and cultural activities. From 1982 David de Rothschild was its president.

Among the large Jewish organizations in France the Alliance Israélite Universelle (AIU), founded in 1860, plays an important role in the cultural domain. Prof. Ady Steg became its president in 1985. In September 1989 the AIU inaugurated a new library which is now the largest Jewish library in Europe. It also has a College of Jewish Studies focusing its activities on in-depth study of Jewish thought in its various expressions. The year 2000 brought a major development in the picture of institutions in France with the creation of the Fondation pour la Mémoire de la Shoah (the Endowment for the Memory of the Shoah, FMS). Although one cannot strictly consider the FMS as a Jewish community institution, it has started to play a major role in most important fields of the Jewish life. The FMS has been granted an inalienable endowment of some 393 million euros, a sum that corresponds to the wealth left in banks, insurance companies, etc. by the Jewish families who did not survive the Shoah in France. Only the product of the endowment is to be spent. In the first years of its existence, the FMS, whose president is Simone *Veil, started an impressive program which encompasses the transformation of the Jewish Shoah Memorial in Paris into an international museum, archive and research center on the Holocaust, social programs for survivors, support to cultural initiatives such as the House of Yiddish in Paris, training programs on Judaism for teachers in state schools, and more.

This overview of the large organizations gives only a partial picture of actual Jewish life in France. There are several hundred Jewish organizations in France, some with thousands of members, others with only a few dozen. Moreover, despite the impressive number of organizations, only 30–40 percent of the Jews have relations with the so-called organized community.

Since the end of the 1980s on, some Jewish secular and humanist movements have been organized, at least among the Ashkenazi Jews, and more recently, also among Sephardim.

It may be asked if one may speak of "a Jewish community" in the case of France. Heterogeneous in origins and orientations, embedded in a social, cultural, and political environment which offer aspirations different from those presented by Judaism, the French Diaspora does not constitute a community, in the strict sense. To be sure, at the local level or as voluntary societies based on origin or ideological sector, communities can come into being; they provide a firm foundation on which to affirm one's quest for Jewish identity. But this search exhibits different facets, even though, in France today, Jewish life is essentially crystallized around three poles: religion; culture; and the attitude to the State of Israel.

ANTISEMITISM. From 1978 the extreme right increased its racist and antisemitic attacks, including the desecration of monuments and Jewish cemeteries, hostile antisemitic inscriptions, and generally xenophobia in the context of economic crisis. Those responsible were extremely small groups who openly proclaim fascist doctrines. On Friday October 3, 1980, a bomb which exploded outside the synagogue on Rue Copernic, just before the conclusion of the services, killed three persons. Although this outrage was attributed at first to the French extreme right, it became clear after a while that the source was to be found in the Middle East. The reaction was immediate. Both in Paris and in the provinces public protest meetings took place in which Frenchmen of all the political trends and opinions participated. Middle Eastern terrorism struck again two years later, in August 1982, at the popular Jewish restaurant Goldenberg. Apart from the terrorist alarms coming from the Middle East, the 1980–1990 period was also marked by different events and trends that raised the issue of a possible renewal of antisemitism in France. Apart from the well-known antisemitism of the far-right, the development of the differencialist racialism of the Nouvelle Droite drew quite a lot of attention. The 1982 war in Lebanon favored some far-leftist, "anti-zionist" discourse that was on the verge of antisemitism. In the same period a wave of so-called revisionist works and publications questioning the Holocaust, produced by the far-right, the far-left, and pro-Palestinian circles, aroused very strong emotion. Despite the strength of the legal anti-racist apparatus in France, it was brought to further completion in 1990 by the Gayssot law which repressed the questioning of the existence of crimes against humanity and the publication and distribution of racist anti Semitic and revisionist writings. Some revisionist university workers were found guilty of questioning the Holocaust, but the suppression of antisemitic writings was insufficient.

Terrorism and antisemitic incidents marked the 1980s. At the beginning of the 1980s, a wave of terrorism raged with the bloodiest attack against Jews carried out in August 1982 against the Jo Goldenberg restaurant. At the end of the 1980s and in the early 1990s, desecrations of synagogues and, above all, cemeteries were prevalent. The most serious incident took place in Carpentras in 1990. At the end of 1992, the desecrations increased, particularly in Alsace where German Neo-Nazism and the French extreme-right cooperate. Only rarely have those guilty of these attacks been apprehended.

Other incidents were connected to the Holocaust past. In 1987 the trial against Klaus Barbie had widespread publicity. Sentenced to life imprisonment, Barbie died in prison on September 25, 1991. (See *Barbie Trial.)

Barbie was German, but the case of French Paul Touvier is more complicated. Touvier, head of the Lyon militia and Gestapo collaborator, was arrested in May 1989. On July 11, 1991, the Paris court (Chambre d'accusation) decided to release him. On April 13, 1992, this same court gave Touvier a general acquittal. This decision was accompanied by an interpretation of the Vichy role in the persecution of the Jews, considering it as totally subordinate to German authority. This decision unleashed fierce emotion in France and was repealed, at least in part, on November 27, 1992, by the Paris High Court of Appeal. The trial against Touvier, for the murder of seven Jews in June 1944 proceeded and in 1994 he was convicted and condemned to life imprisonment.

In November 1991 the media announced that the card file of the census of the Jews made in 1940 by the Vichy police had been found by the lawyer Serge Klarsfeld in the Ministry of Veteran Affairs. For 50 years historians have searched for this card file which had been said to have been destroyed. The file was transferred to the National Archives where it was studied by a commission of historians. On December 31, 1992, the Ministry of Culture made public the results of its study: this card file deals only with those Jews arrested and/or deported. The census made under the Vichy government seems to have been in fact destroyed in 1948 or 1949.

There was a decrease in terms of major antisemitic events in the 1990s, although the phenomenon of the profaning of graves continued (but not only in Jewish graveyards). But by the end of the 1990s one became aware of a new disturbing situation in schools among very young people. Against the French tradition of assimilation, there seems to have developed a "community attitude" in some schools in certain areas, with an increase of violence – first verbal and a strong trend to antisemitism. With the second Intifada in Israel, an ethnic type of anti-Jewish violence seemed to be on its way, carried out by people who perceived themselves as the "true" victims, both of history (colonization, slavery) and the present (poverty, racism).

ECONOMIC AND POLITICAL SITUATION. French Jews continued actively to support Israel.

The results of the Israeli elections of May 1977, which returned Menaḥem Begin, caused considerable dismay. Begin was considered the classical representative of the ultra-nationalism of the extreme right, so extreme and uncompromising that his coming to power was likely to bring about a new conflict in the Middle East. Daniel Mayer, a former Socialist minister and ex-president of the League of Human Rights, ceased to write his regular column in the Zionist periodical *La Terre Retrouvée*, which he had contributed for many years, on the grounds that from now on his socialist convictions would make it impossible for him to defend the Israeli cause under the new regime.

The visit of President Sadat to Jerusalem, however, and the Camp David agreement improved the image of Begin. Many French Jews, while expressing their sympathy with the State and concern for its survival, nevertheless criticize both the internal and foreign policies of the Israel government.

The French economy went through great changes from the 1980s to the 1990s. It became information oriented and automated, with a considerable increase in its production capacity. The battle against inflation succeeded and the currency was stabilized. The economy played an important and influential role in the creation of the European Economic Community whose borders opened on January 1, 1993, to free movement of goods among the 12 member-countries. European political union is more difficult to put into effect: in France, the September 20, 1992, referendum on the treaty of the European Union, called the Maastricht treaty, barely received a majority (51 percent); voting in favor was supported by several Jewish personalities.

This modernization of the economy had a corollary in increased unemployment. At the end of 1992, the threshold of three million unemployed was reached. Jews, too, were affected by this calamity, and social cases and problems reappeared. Poverty was also found among the Jews; in December 1992, Jewish social services launched an appeal called Tsedaka to collect funds to bring relief to 25,000 needy Jews.

From 1981 to 1995 France's president was François Mitterrand and its various governments had a socialist majority (except for the period of "cohabitation" from 1986 to 1988 during which the right-wing government was led by Jacques Chirac). From 1995 Jacques Chirac was president. Elections at different levels of political life are held frequently in France, and Jewish voters are regularly solicited by the political parties. Following an old tradition, the main Jewish organizations do not give any directions on how to vote. Nevertheless, some of them warn against voting for the FN. Jews constitute about 1 percent of the French electorate. Their votes can only play an important role in specific localities such as Paris and Marseilles. On the basis of analyses of voting behavior, it is known that the Jewish vote is spread among all parties, while within the machinery of every party Jews are active.

With the Mitterrand era coming to an end, his final "confessions" greatly troubled Jewish society which, first and foremost, appreciated his friendly relations with the Jews and the State of Israel. In fall of 1994, the book by Piere Péan, *Une Jeunesse française. François Mitterrand 1924–1947*, confirms rumors about relations between Mitterrand and the Vichy regime after his rejoining the Resistance and especially about certain meetings up to 1986 with René Bousquet, secretary general of the police in the Vichy government, who played an important role in the deportation of French Jews in 1942. Initially condemned by the High Court of Justice in 1949, Bousquet was immediately exempted from the sentences imposed on him by this same judicial body; he reintegrated into his political and financial milieu. Accused of crimes against humanity in 1991, René Bousquet was assassinated in June 1993. The ongoing relations between Mitterrand and Bousquet became an "affair" disseminated largely by the media. Yet, President Mitterrand expressed no regrets over his meetings with Bousquet, despite the exertion of pressure on him by several well-known individuals such as Elie Wiesel. Some Jews were embittered by this "affair." They were well disposed towards the new president, Jacques Chirac, who when mayor of Paris was known for his good relations with Jews, but they also recalled his former friendship with Saddam Hussein.

[Doris Bensimon-Donath / Nelly Hannson (2nd ed.)]

Relations with Israel

France played a major role on the Middle Eastern scene especially from World War I (see *Zionism; *Sykes-Picot; *Lebanon; *Syria; *Israel, State of: Historical Survey) until 1948. However, between the two world wars, France played a relatively minor role in Zionist policy, since the Zionist movement naturally directed its major political efforts toward London and Washington. Closer ties were established between the *yishuv* and Gaullist "Free France" during World War II, against the background of the Nazi conquests and on the basis of contact between the *yishuv* and the Free French in the Middle East. After the war, these ties were reinforced by their joint opposition to British policy. During the early post-war period, various French leaders provided moral and material support for the legal and "illegal" immigration of Jewish refugees to Palestine. France supported the UN partition resolution of Nov. 29, 1947, and played a decisive role in the internationalization of Jerusalem and its surroundings (mainly in order to protect the Holy sites and Christian religious institutions). France recognized the State of Israel de facto in January 1949 and de jure in May of the same year when Israel became a member of the UN. In the mid-1950s, developments paved the way for a closer cooperation between Israel and France. The tireless efforts of Shimon Peres, then director general of the Ministry of Defense, led to the conclusion in 1954 of arms agreements (tanks, artillery, aircraft) which were both beneficial for Israel's defense needs and for France's arm industries. The uprising against French colonial rule in Algeria (November 1954) gave a new impulse to the cooperation between both countries. It reached its climax with the Sinai Campaign (1956) when France, in partnership with Great Britain, coordinated their attack against Nasserite Egypt. Both countries shared a common interest in trying to weaken Egypt, because Nasser supported both the Algerian fellaghas and the Palestinian fedayins. Although the Suez campaign was a political failure, Franco-Israel friendship blossomed. France became Israel's major supplier of arms during that period, and remained so until the Six-Day War (1967). In 1957, France began to help Israel build the nuclear reactor in Dimona (Negev). A whole range of technical and scientific cooperation agreements were signed which enhanced cultural relations between the two countries. They included the establishment of chairs in French language and literature at Israeli universities and in Hebrew language and literature at a score of French universities; the teaching of French as a third language in Israeli secondary schools; exchanges of scientists, students and artists, and joint scientific projects. The advent to power of the General de Gaulle (1958) did not mark an abrupt break with previous policy. Only the close cooperation in nuclear matters and between the general staffs was phased out. French arms continued to be sold to Israel which was seen by de Gaulle as a strategic asset against Soviet expansion in the Middle East. Economic links were strong. In 1966, French exports to Israel amounted to $35,000,000 (imports did not exceed $19,000,000). Tourism from France to Israel reached the figure of 40,000. The reconsideration of French policy began slowly. On the occasion of Ben-Gurion's visits to France in 1960 and 1961, de Gaulle, who called Ben-Gurion "the greatest statesman of this century," hailed Israel as "our friend and ally." However, he firmly rejected a formal military alliance which Ben-Gurion wanted to conclude in 1963. At that time, de Gaulle has already begun a rapprochement with the Arab countries. After Algeria gained independence, the French president thought it was high time to resume diplomatic relations with Arab countries. Although there was a gradual shift in foreign policy, nothing foretold the about-face position taken by de Gaulle during the crisis which ended up with the Six-Day War (June 1967). In mid-May 1967 after the withdrawal of the UN truce observers at the request of Egypt and the closing of the Straits of Tiran to all shipping to Eilat, de Gaulle stated clearly to Abba Eban, minister of foreign affairs, that the situation was not a casus belli and that Israel should not take the initiative to go to war. To prevent the outbreak of a war, France announced an embargo on arms deliveries to "all Middle Eastern states," a decision which in practice hurt only Israel. This unilateral cancellation of French commitment towards Israel was seen in the Jewish state as a betrayal. De Gaulle justified his stand by arguing that Israel was militarily stronger and that the war would have long term destabilizing effects. He deeply resented the fact that Israel did not heed his advice on the eve of the 1967 war and went so far as to describe Israel in a famous press conference in November 1967 as a "warrior State determined to become larger." The Six-Day war was a breaking point in Israeli-French relations and put an end to a close cooperation which lasted almost 15 years. This abrupt change was misunderstood by many French people in the press, among politicians (even some Gaullists), among public opinion and, of course, in the Jewish community. It even aroused certain uneasiness when de Gaulle called the Jews "an elite people, self-assured and domineering…." After 1967, French-Israeli relations steadily deteriorated. De Gaulle's resignation in 1969 did not change much. Under Georges Pompidou's presidency (1969–1974), France drew nearer to the Arab world. The growing dependence on Arab oil and the attempts to penetrate the Arab markets economically (including through arm sales) moved France further way from Israel. Pompidou stated that Israel had the right to live in peace within secure and recognized borders but was also one of the first Western leaders to speak of the "rights of the Palestinian people" and used the nascent European political cooperation to promote the French position in the EEC. Valery Giscard d'Estaing made some positive gestures towards Israel: lifting of the arms embargo, official visit of the French foreign minister to Israel…. However, these moves cannot conceal the fact that France had clear pro-Arab leanings. A PLO office was opened in Paris (1975), and France was instrumental in the adoption by the Europeans of the Venice declaration (1980) which spoke of the Palestinian right to self-determination and called for PLO participation in the peace negotiations. At the same time, France had deep reservations regarding the Camp David accords because they were seen as leading towards a separate peace between Egypt and Israel, not to a global settlement of the Arab-Israeli conflict. These political stands strained relations with Israel. The election of Francois Mitterrand as president of France in May 1981 brought with it the hope that there might be a change favorable to Israel in French Middle East policy, because Mitterrand had a liking for the Jewish people and spoke in positive terms of Israel. The official visit he undertook in Israel in March 1982 – the first ever of a French president – was highly symbolic of his attachment to "Israel's unshakeable right to live" as he said during his speech at the Knesset. He welcomed also the Israeli president Haim Herzog for an official visit in 1988. However, this more cordial attitude towards the Jewish state went hand in hand with a deepening of French defense of the right of self-determination of the Palestinian people which had the right to have its own state, alongside Israel. President Mitterrand invited Yasser Arafat, in May 1989, for an official visit in Paris which aroused the opposition of the French Jewish institutions. He became more explicitly critical of Israel after the start of the first Intifada (1987) but returned a second time in Israel in November 1992. After the signing of the Oslo accords (1993), political relations improved notably. Paris became even a meeting point between Israelis and Palestinians. The economic part of the Israeli-Palestinian Interim Agreement was signed in Paris in April 1994. However, the lull was only temporary. Relations once again became strained after the advent to power of Binyamin Netanyahu in 1996 and, later on, with the start of the second Intifada in 2000. On the one hand, France denounced the re-occupation of Palestinian territories by the Israeli army and the confinement of Yasser Arafat; on the other hand, Israel denounced the alleged passivity of French authorities towards antisemitic actions undertaken, at least partially, under the false pretext of "solidarity with the Palestinians." The uneasy situation of the French Jewish community, French foreign policy and Israeli policies in the West Bank and Gaza intermingled dangerously. The new French government (right wing), set up in 2002, tried to improve relations with Israel, with such actions as the creation of a high council for research and scientific cooperation (2003) and official visits to France by Moshe Katzav and Ariel Sharon. These measures have bettered the general atmosphere between both countries which, on the economic level, have sustained relations (economic exchanges went up from €1.2 billion in 1992 to €1.8 billion in 2003).

[Alain Dieckhoff (2nd ed.)]

BIBLIOGRAPHY: UNTIL 1789: B. Blumenkranz, *Bibliographie des Juifs en France* (1961); idem, *Juifs et chrétiens* (1960); idem, in: *Fourth World Congress of Jewish Studies*, 2 (1968), 45–50; idem, in: *Annales de l'Est*, 19 (1967), 199–215; Aronius, Regesten; A. Neubauer and E. Renan, in: *Histoire littéraire de la France*, 27 (1877), 431–764; 31 (1893), 1–469; M. Schwab, *Inscriptions hébraïques en France…* (1899); L. Berman, *Histoire des Juifs en France* (1937); M. Catane, *Des croisades à nos jours* (1957); I.A. Agus, *Heroic Age of Franco-German Jewry* (1970); A. Hertzberg, *French Enlightenment and the Jews* (1968); L. Rabinowitz, *Social Life of the Jews of Northern France…* (1938); S. Schwarzfuchs, *Kahal: Communauté Juive de l'Europe Medievale* (1986); Z. Szajkowski, *Franco-Judaica* (1962); G. Nahon, in: REJ, 121 (1962), 59–80; R. Chazan, *ibid.*, 128 (1969), 41–65; G.I. Langmuir, in: *Traditio*, 16 (1960), 203–39; Gross, Gal Jud; E.E. Urbach, *Ba'alei ha-Tosafot* (1956); *Archives Juives* (1965 to date). MODERN PERIOD: P.C. Albert, *The Modernization of French Jewry: Consistory and Community in the Nineteenth Century*, (1977); L. Kahn, *Histoire des écoles communales et consistoriales israélites de Paris* (1884); idem, *Les professions manuelles et les institutions de patronage* (1885); idem, *Le Comité de Bienfaisance* (1886); idem, *Les Juifs à Paris depuis le VIe siècle* (1889); A.E. Halphen, *Recueil des lois, décrets… concernant les Israélites depuis la révolution de 1789* (1851); I. Uhry, *Recueil des lois, décrets… concernant les Israélites 1850–1903* (19033); R. Anchel, *Napoléon et les Juifs* (1928); idem, *Les Juifs de France* (1946); E. Tcherikower, *Yidn in Frankraykh*, 2 vols. (1942); Elbogen, Century, passim; Z. Szajkowski, *Jews and the French Revolution of 1789, 1830 and 1848* (1970); idem, *Poverty and Social Welfare among French Jews (1800–1880)* (1954); M. Roblin, *Les Juifs de Paris* (1952), S. Schwarzfuchs, *Brève histoire des Juifs de France* (1957); P. Lévy, *Les noms des Israélites en France* (1960). HOLOCAUST PERIOD: L. Poliakov, *Harvest of Hate* (1954); G. Reitlinger, *Final Solution* (1968^2), 327–51 and passim; R. Hilberg, *Destruction of European Jews* (1961), index; IMT, *Trial of the Major War Criminals*, 23 (1949), index; Z. Szajkowski, *Analytical Franco-Jewish Gazetteer 1939–1945* (1966); idem, in: *Yad Vashem Studies*, 2 (1958), 133–57; 3 (1959), 187–202; Ariel, *ibid.*, 6 (1967), 221–50; L. Steinberg, *Les autorités allemandes en France occupée* (1966); idem, *La révolte des justes – Les Juifs contre Hitler* (1970), 139–233. **ADD. BIBLIOGRAPHY:** J. Adler, *The Jews of Paris and the Final Solution* (1987), 198–201; M. Marrus and R. Paxton, *Vichy France and the Jews* (1982), passim; L. Poliakov, *Harvest of Hate* (1954); R. Poznanski, *Jews in Paris During World War II* (2001), passim; D. Weinberg, "France," in: *The World Reacts to the Holocaust* (1996), 3–44. CONTEMPORARY PERIOD: Bibliothèque du Centre de Documentation Juive Contemporaine, Catalogue no. 1, *La France de l'Affaire Dreyfus à nos jours* (1964); idem, Catalogue no. 2, *La France – le Troisième Reich – Israël* (1968); P., *From Dreyfus to Vichy: the Remaking of French Jewry, 1906–1939* (1979); Rabi (pseud.), *Anatomie du judaïsme francais* (1962); AJYB, 28 (1946/47–); *Annuaire du judaisme* (1950–52): Fonds Social Juif Unifié, *Communautés juives de France* (1966); R. Berg et al., *Guide juif de France* (1968); G. Levitte, in: JJSO, 2 (1960), 172–84; M. Catane, *Les Juifs dans le monde* (1962), 26–41; Donath, in: WLB, 21 no. 2 (1967), 24–26; Institut Français de l'Opinion Publique, *Sondages*, 2 (1967); E. Touati, in: *D'Auschwitz à Israël* (1968); L'Arche (1957–); *Information Juive* (1925–); *Community – Communauté* (French and English, 1958–); *Le Monde Juif* (1946–); *Les Nouveaux Cahiers* (1965–); D. Bensimon, *Les Juifs de France et leurs relations avec Israel 1945–1988* (1989); B. Berg, *Histoire du rabbinat francais: XVIe–XXe* (1992); P. Birnbaum, *Histoire politique des Juifs de France* (1990); E. Cohen, *L' eutude et l'education juive en France* (1991); R. Remond, *Paul Touvier et l'Eglise* (1992); S. Trigano, *La societé juive a travers l'histoire* (4 vol.; 1992/93); J.-D. Bredin, *L'Affaire* (1993); E. Conan, H. Rousso, *Vichy, un passe qui ne passe pas* (1994); F. Mitterrand, E. Wiesel, *Memoires à deux voix* (1995); P. Pean, *Une jeunesse Française. François Mitterrand. 1934–1947* (1994); Poznanski, R., *Etre Juif en France pendant la seconde guerre mondiale* (1994); David H. Weinberg, *The Jews in Paris in the 1930s: a Community on Trial* (1977). **ADD. BIBLIOGRAPHY:** E. Cohen, "Géographie des Juifs de France," données tirées du raport présenté au Conseil National du FSJU (2002); AJYB 2003. ISRAEL-FRANCE RELATIONS: M. Bar-Zohar, *Suez, Ultrasecret* (1964); Y. Tzur, *Yoman Paris 1953–1956* (1968); J. Bourdeillette, *Pour Israël* (1968); R. Aron, *De Gaulle, Israel and the Jews* (1969). **ADD. BIBLIOGRAPHY:** D. Lazar, *L'opinion française et la naissance de l'Etat d'Israël, 1945–1949* (1972); S Cohen, *De Gaulle, Les gaullistes et Israël* (1974); E. Barnavi & L. Rosenzweig, *La France et Israël. Une affaire passionnelle* (2002).

FRANCES, IMMANUEL BEN DAVID (1618–c. 1710), Hebrew poet. Born in Leghorn, he was educated by his father David, his brother Jacob *Frances, and especially by R. Joseph Fermo. Immanuel's life was filled with difficulties; not only was he forced to wander from one town to another to earn a living, but a succession of misfortunes befell him. His beloved father died in 1640, and his wife and two children in 1654. In

1657, he married Miriam, the daughter of R. Mordecai Visino, but both she and the son she bore him died in 1667. The same year saw the death of his brother, Jacob, to whom Immanuel was deeply attached, and together with whom he had fought against the supporters of Kabbalah. In his solitude, he devoted himself entirely to his literary work and to his activities as rabbi in Florence. In these he found his sole consolation for the remainder of his life.

His poetic work may be divided into three periods. The first extends from 1643 to 1660, when he was under the influence of two of Italy's most popular poets, Tasso and Guarini. At this time he wrote his love poems and his debates on women (*Vikku'aḥ Itti'el ve-Ukhal*), and rabbis (*Vikku'aḥ Rekhav u-Va'anah*), to which he appended satirical epigrams. The dramatic form he employed suited the literary style he had adopted to attack the corruption in contemporary Jewish society. From a traditional point of view he censured poets like Immanuel of Rome who introduced in their works frivolities and "prurient poems." During the second period, from 1664 to 1667, Immanuel, together with his brother Jacob, waged a literary war against Shabbetai Ẓevi, Nathan of Gaza, and their messianic movement, in which he saw a threat to the Jewish people: mysticism was in their opinion taking the place of the Halakhah. His book of satirical poems, *Ẓevi Muddaḥ* ("The Banished Gazelle [*Ẓevi*]"), belongs to this period and is the choicest of his literary work. The poems were published by M. Mortara (in *Kobez al jad*, 1 (1885), 99–131). A few poems have been translated into English: see Simonsohn (1977), 609–10, and Carmi (1981), 500–4. In the final period, from 1670 until after 1685, the poet adapted his religious poetry for use in synagogue services, giving it a dramatic and recitative character. He even wrote some poems in Latin that have not been preserved. While the poet preferred to use the Spanish-Arabic meter, he also introduced into his Hebrew poetry the *terza rima* and the *ottava rima* of Italian prosody. His poetic works were edited by S. Bernstein in 1932 under the title *Divan le-R. Immanu'el b. David Frances*. His work *Metek Sefatayim*, written in 1667 during a period of residence in Algiers, deals with various aspects of poetry and rhetoric. It was published in 1892 by H. Brody and deserves a new critical edition including all the new material that is known today; most of it has been translated into Spanish (del Valle, 1988).

BIBLIOGRAPHY: M. Hartmann, *Die hebraeische Verskunst nach dem Metek Sefatajim des Immanuel Fransis und anderen Werken juedischer Metriker* (Berlin, 1894); Davidson, Oẓar, 4 (1933), 459; s.v. *Immanuel Frances (ben David)*; Waxman, Literature, 2 (1960), 83–88. **ADD. BIBLIOGRAPHY:** M. Schulvass, *The Jews in the World of the Renaissance* (1973), 217; S. Simonsohn, *History of the Jews in the Duchy of Mantua* (1977), 617, 632, 710; T. Carmi (ed.), *The Penguin Book of Hebrew Verse* (1981), 500–4; A. Rathaus, in: *Annuario di Studi Ebraici*, 11 (1988), 159–73; Del Valle, *El divan poético de Dunash ben Labrat* (1988), 428–59.

[Yonah David]

FRANCES, ISAAC (18th century), preacher and the author of a collection of sermons, *Penei Yizḥak* (Salonika, 1753). No details are known of his life or where he lived. The sermons are based on the weekly portions of the Pentateuch, but there is usually more than one sermon for each portion, indicative of the author's long preaching career. Although Frances was influenced by the Kabbalah, often quoting and discussing kabbalistic sources in his sermons, he was not exclusively a kabbalist. He used both contemporary and ancient rabbinic sources extensively and even made some use of medieval philosophical writings, demonstrating the eclectic attitude common among 18th-century preachers. Frances's sermons are didactic, sometimes tending toward theological discourses, but more usually they are designed to foster the ethical improvement of his community, laying great emphasis on decent social behavior.

[Joseph Dan]

FRANCES, JACOB BEN DAVID (1615–1667), poet; elder brother of Immanuel *Frances. Born in Mantua, Jacob, a highly educated man, mastered not only Hebrew and Aramaic, but Latin, Italian, and Portuguese as well. The two brothers collaborated in their literary work, and in his book of poetics *Metek Sefatayim* Immanuel shows great esteem for his elder brother's talent, quoting his verses and calling him by the surname *Ha-harif*, "the sharp one." After Jacob's death, Immanuel corrected and completed some of his poems, to which he occasionally even attached additions of his own. Copyists inserted these additions into the poems without always noting that they were composed by Immanuel. At times they also attributed Immanuel's poems to Jacob, and vice-versa, because of the similarity in style, form, and content. There is still no definitive means of determining the true authorship of some of the poems; 54 sonnets, however, can almost certainly be ascribed to Jacob. In the manner of his contemporary poets, Jacob wrote on all subjects, including friendship, polemics, ethics, love, and marriage. As was customary in poetry at that time, some of his poems have a flavor of eroticism. Jacob quarreled fiercely with members of his community, chiefly attacking the sect of Shabbetai *Ẓevi that arose during his time, as well as the kabbalists who were closely associated with it. He and his brother regarded them as detrimental to Judaism and considered themselves duty-bound to stop them. In this struggle he aroused the opposition of Mantua's rabbis, who condemned a poem he published in 1660 or 1661 against the vulgarization of kabbalistic studies and destroyed almost all the copies of it (the poem was reprinted in 1704 by Samson Morpurgo at the end of his book *Eẓ ha-Da'at*, and again provoked the opposition of kabbalists like Solomon Aviad Basilea, who many years later condemned Morpurgo for having published it). Unlike his brother, Jacob held no communal post but engaged in business. He died in Florence, after having left Mantua because of his quarrel with the kabbalists. Only isolated poems were published during his lifetime. A collection of all his poems from manuscripts and printed works was published by Peninah Naveh (see bibliography). This publication has considerably changed the critical evaluation of his work, and Jacob is now considered by many scholars as one of the very outstanding Hebrew poets of his time, if not the greatest of them. D. *Pagis wrote that he is one of the most interesting poets in the entire Hebrew-Italian school of poetry, and that his work is rich in forms, genres, and psychological moods, and fascinating by virtue of its rhythmical flexibility and stylistic innovations; T. *Carmi defined him "the last major poet before the modern period" and translated some poems into English. Jacob's poetry clearly reveals his mastery of both the Hebrew language and Hebrew literary tradition, as well as his acquaintance with contemporary European literature. As some scholars have remarked, his poems (especially the love poems) are sometimes influenced by the style, the imagery, and the themes of Baroque poetry, and in a long poem written in ottava rima he anticipates the pastoral theme that later became very popular in both Italian and Hebrew literature of the 18th century.

BIBLIOGRAPHY: P. Naveh (ed.), *Kol Shirei Ya'akov Frances* (1969), incl. bibl.; A.M. Habermann, in: *Moznayim*, 29 (1969), 66–69; Davidson, Oẓar, 4 (1933), 415; Scholem, Shabbetai Ẓevi, 2 (1957), 425–8; E. Fleischer, in: KS, 45 (1969/70), 177–87. **ADD. BIBLIOGRAPHY:** A. Rathaus, "Ahavah le-Diokan," in: *Italia* 2, 1-2 (1980), 30-47; T. Carmi, *The Penguin Book of Hebrew Verse* (1981), 129-30, 493-500; M. Falk, "Jacob Frances, Two Love Sonnets," in: *Prooftexts* 1, 2 (1981), 153–57; D. Pagis, *Hebrew Poetry of the Middle Ages and the Renaissance* (1991), 60-61; D. Bregman, *A Bundle of Gold* (1997), 305-62 (Heb.).

[Abraham Meir Habermann /Ariel Rathaus (2nd ed.)]

FRANCHE-COMTÉ, region and former province in E. France, comprising the present departments of Haute-Saône, Doubs, and Jura. Since a document of 1220 mentions a Jewish quarter (*vicus Judaeorum*) in *Lons-le-Saunier, the Jews must first have come to Franche-Comté at a much earlier date, probably after the expulsion from the kingdom of France in 1182. From the middle of the 13th century, there is increased evidence of the presence of the Jews and the 40 or more places they had settled, including Baume-les-Dames, *Besançon, Lons-le-Saunier, and *Vesoul. Because they were a valuable source of income, the Jews were eagerly welcomed by various local lords, who granted them advantageous privileges, but they were not admitted to the Church domains. From a detailed list of the fiscal contributions of the Jews drawn up in 1296, it is apparent that by then several localities no longer permitted Jewish residence; those remaining paid an annual tax of 975 livres. Though Franche-Comté was temporarily under the control of the French kingdom at the time, the Jews were not affected by the expulsion order of 1306; however, they were included in that of 1322, though possibly it was not rigorously enforced. From 1332–33 at the latest, new immigrants joined those who had been able to remain in their homes; in a census of 86 Jewish families, 32 are described as recent arrivals. As during the 13th century, their principal occupation was moneylending.

During the *Black Death persecutions in 1348, the count appointed two commissioners, who promptly arrested the Jews and seized their belongings. They were imprisoned for many months (those of Vesoul for nearly ten months), some of them in Gray and the others in Vesoul. In spite of confessions extracted under torture, none was condemned to death but all were banished, and the regent, Jeanne de Boulogne, promised that Jews would no longer be tolerated in Franche-Comté. However, from 1355, there were Jews in the province once more, especially in Bracon and Salins-les-Bains, where a Christian loan bank was set up in 1363 so that there need be no recourse to Jewish moneylenders; the Jews were subsequently expelled from the town in 1374. In 1384, shortly after Franche-Comté was reunited with Burgundy, the duke authorized many Jewish families to settle there, but they did not escape the general expulsion from Burgundy ten years later. Many of them found refuge in Besançon, from where one Jew returned to settle in Champlitte. Driven out in 1409, he was the last Jew to live in Franche-Comté before the French Revolution.

BIBLIOGRAPHY: J. Morey, in: REJ, 7 (1883), 1–36; L. Gauthier, in: *Mémoires de la Société pour l'Emulation du Jura* (1914), 90ff.; J. Fohlen, in: *Archives Juives*, 5 (1968–69), 12–13.

[Bernhard Blumenkranz]

FRANCHETTI, RAIMONDO (1890–1935), Italian explorer. In 1910 Franchetti traveled alone through Indo-China and Malaysia. After World War I he explored the Sudan, East Africa, and Ethiopia. In *Nella Dancàlia Etiopica* (1935) he described the Danakil region of northeastern Ethiopia. His sympathetic understanding encouraged many of the Ethiopian tribal chiefs to join an alliance with Italy before hostilities began in 1934. Franchetti was killed in a plane explosion near Cairo airport.

FRANCIA, FRANCIS (b. 1675), English conspirator. He was the grandson of Domingo Rodrigues Isaac Francia, an ex-Marrano of Vila Real (Portugal) who arrived in London from Bordeaux in 1655 and became a leading member of the London community. Francis himself was born in Bordeaux and dealt in wine. He subsequently went to London where in 1717 he was tried on a charge of treasonable correspondence with adherents of the exiled Old Pretender James. Despite the weighty evidence against him, he was acquitted. He then apparently became a government agent and betrayed his former associates.

BIBLIOGRAPHY: Lipton, in: JHSET, 11 (1928), 190–205; L. Wolf, *Jews in the Canary Islands* (1926), 198–213; Roth, Mag Bibl, 248f. **ADD. BIBLIOGRAPHY:** Katz, England, 215–17.

[Cecil Roth]

°**FRANCIS I**, Austrian emperor 1792–1835, last Holy Roman Emperor (as Francis II) until 1806. In 1792 Francis ordered the *Judenamt* (office for Jewish affairs) to enforce the numerous restrictions on Jewish settlement in *Vienna and raised the *Bolleten* (tax paid by a Jew each time he entered the city). The preamble to his 1797 patent granted to Bohemian Jewry (see *Bohemia), proclaiming equality as its ultimate aim, raised expectations which remained unfulfilled. Most of the petitions for improvement of the status of the Jews addressed to him by representatives of the Jews in the empire were unanswered, though in 1798 Francis authorized the existence of 52 communities in *Moravia. He agreed to the official use of "Mr." instead of "Jew" in reference to Jewish citizens. During the Congress of *Vienna a petition requesting partial equality presented by B. *Eskeles, N.A. *Arnstein, and L. *Herz met with no success (see also *Metternich). In Francis' Italian provinces, however, *emancipation measures were not revoked. In Galicia, Francis supported Naphtali Herz *Homberg; knowledge of his catechism *Benei Zion* was made compulsory in 1810 for all Jewish couples registering their marriages. While regularly making use of Jewish finance and financial advice, Francis unhesitatingly blamed Jewish financiers for all the economic ills of the empire.

BIBLIOGRAPHY: A.F. Pribram, *Urkunden und Akten zur Geschichte der Juden in Wien*, 1–2 (1918), index; M. Grunwald, *Vienna* (1936), 168–71; Kisch, in: HJ, 8 (1946), 24; S. Baron, *Die Judenfrage an dem Wiener Kongress* (1920), 20–23, 118, 183; Dubnow, Weltgesch, 8 (1920–23), 280–93; R. Kestenberg-Gladstein, *Neuere Geschichte der Juden in den boehmischen Laendern*, 1 (1969), index.

FRANCISCANS, Roman Catholic Order. The presence in the Middle East of the Franciscan Friars, the Order founded by Francis of Assisi (Italy), officially approved by the Pope in 1221, started in the same year. The province of Terrae Sanctae (the Holy Land), or Siriae or the Promised Land, was founded in the year 1217. The first provincial or superior was Brother Elia from Assisi. In the year 1219 the founder himself visited the region in order to preach the Gospel to the Muslims, seen as brothers and not enemies. The mission resulted in a meeting with the sultan of Egypt, Malik al-Kamil, who was surprised by his unusual behavior. The Franciscan Province of the East extended to Cyprus, Syria, Lebanon, and the Holy Land. Before the taking over of Acre (on May 18, 1291), Franciscan friaries were present at Acre, Sidon, Antioch, Tripoli, Jaffa, and Jerusalem.

From Cyprus, where they took refuge at the end of the Latin Kingdom, the Franciscans started planning a return to Jerusalem, given the good political relations between the Christian governments and the Mamluk sultans of Egypt. Around the year 1333 the French friar Roger Guerin succeeded in buying the Cenacle on Mount Zion and some land to build a monastery nearby for the friars, using funds provided by the king and queen of Naples. With two papal bullae, *Gratias Agimus* and *Nuper Carissimae*, dated in Avignon, November 21, 1342, Pope Clement VI approved and created the new entity which would be known as the Franciscan Custody of the Holy Land (Custodia Terrae Sanctae).

The friars, coming from any of the Order's provinces, under the jurisdiction of the father guardian (superior) of the monastery on Mount Zion, were present in Jerusalem, in the Cenacle, in the church of the Holy Sepulcher, and in the Basilica of the Nativity at Bethlehem. Their principal activity was to ensure liturgical life in these Christian sanctuaries and to give spiritual assistance to the pilgrims coming from the West, to European merchants resident or passing through the main cities of Egypt, Syria, and Lebanon, and to have a direct and authorized relation with the Christian Oriental communities.

The monastery on Mount Zion was used by Brother Alberto da Sarteano for his papal mission for the union of the Oriental Christians (Greeks, Copts, and Ethiopians) with Rome during the Council of Florence (1440). For the same reason the party guided by Brother Giovanni di Calabria halted in Jerusalem on his way to meet the Christian Negus of Ethiopia (1482).

In 1551 the Friars were expelled by the Turkish Muslim Authority from the Cenacle and from their adjoining monastery. However, they were granted permission to purchase a Georgian monastery of nuns in the northwest quarter of the city, which became the new center of the Custody in Jerusalem and developed into the Latin Convent of Saint Savior (known as Dayr al-Latin).

In 1620 the Franciscans received in Galilee, from Fakhr ed-Din, the Druze amir of Sidon, Mount Tabor and the venerated Grotto of the Annunciation in Nazareth. In the following year they could partly rebuild the church of St. John the Baptist at *Ein Kerem on the mountain of Judea, where they opened a new friary.

New churches and monasteries were built in various, already venerated sites in the 19th century above the ruins of an older church: the Chapel of the Flagellation along the Via Dolorosa in Jerusalem in 1838; a chapel at Emmaus-Qubeibah in 1872; the church at Cana (Kefer Kanna) in 1880, and a chapel in the village of Naim; a chapel at Bethfage in 1883, and a chapel at the "Dominus Flevit" in 1891, both on the Mount of Olives.

New basilicas were built at Emmaus-Qubeibah in 1901 and at Nazareth – the so-called Church of Nutrition – in 1914; the Basilica of the Agony at Gethsemane in 1919–24; the Basilica of the Transfiguration on Mount Tabor in 1921–24, followed by the Chapel of the Good Shepherd in Jericho in 1924; the chapel on the west bank of the Jordan River in 1934; the Chapel of Primacy at Tabgha on the shore of the Sea of Galilee; the Church of the Visitation at Ein Keren in 1938–40; a new church at Bethany in 1952–54; a chapel in the Shepherds Field outside the village of Beit Sahur-Bethlehem; and a new chapel at "Dominus Flevit" in 1955. The new great Basilica of the Annunciation in Nazareth started in 1955 was consecrated in 1969. The Memorial of Saint Peter at Capernaum was completed in 1990. In Transjordan, the Memorial of Moses on Mount Nebo is managed by the Franciscans.

Historically, the Franciscan presence in the Holy Land resulted in a continuity with the keeping and recording of local Christian traditions. Over the centuries, in fact, the Franciscans published several important books in different languages supplying, revising, and updating a wealth of information useful for the guidance of pilgrims, as a result of first-hand experiences.

During the long period which officially started in the year 1342, they functioned as custodians of the Christian shrines on behalf of the Catholic Church, guides of the Christian pilgrims to the Holy Land, and consequently as authors of many publications about Palestinian subjects written with the intention of improving the knowledge of the Holy Land among the Christians of Europe.

Works such as *Il Libro d'Oltramare* ("A Voyage beyond the Seas") by Fra Niccolò da Poggibonsi, published in 1346; *Trattato di Terra Santa* ("Treatise on the Holy Land") by Fr. Francesco Suriano, written in 1485; *Piante dei Sacri Edifici* ("Plans of the Sacred Edifices of the Holy Land) by Fr. Bernardino Amico, which came out in 1609; and the work in two volumes of Fr. Francesco Quaresmi, *Elucidatio Terrae Sanctae* ("The Illustration of the Holy Land"), which appeared in 1626, bear witness to this activity.

The restoration and the rebuilding of the sanctuaries owned by the Custody of the Holy Land during the last century resulted in the archaeological exploration of the sites and their occupational history. The scientific work was entrusted to the archaeologists of the Studium Biblicum Franciscanum (SBF), an institute founded in Jerusalem in 1923.

As a scientific institution, the Studium Biblicum Franciscanum is closely related to the history of the Franciscan presence in the Holy Land. It was officially founded as a continuation of the work done by the Franciscan Fathers during the previous centuries. The Studium Biblicum Franciscanum is today a Roman Catholic faculty of biblical and archaeological studies in the Holy Land sponsored by the Franciscan Custody of Terrasanta. It is located in the Old City of Jerusalem, in the Flagellation monastery at the Second Station of the Via Dolorosa.

As a research center, the SBF specializes in the rediscovery and exploration of New Testament sites, as well as in the study of the local early Christian Church in the Holy Land, by means of both literary sources and excavations.

Reports on excavations are published annually in the review *Liber Annuus* and in the series *Collectio Maior* and *Collectio Minor*. Exegetical studies on the Bible are published in the series *Analecta*. The archaeological collections of the SBF are illustrated in the series *Museum*.

As a learning center, the SBF is presently authorized to confer pontifical academic degrees of Baccalaureate, Licentiate, and Doctorate in Biblical Sciences and Archaeology.

Added to the SBF is an archaeological museum opened in 1902 in the monastery of Saint Saviour. This original nucleus of the museum was transferred to the Monastery of the Flagellation in 1931. Findings from the SBF excavations, along with liturgical Latin codices of the 14th–15th centuries, a treasure trove of liturgical medieval objects from the Basilica of the Nativity in Bethlehem, and the 18th century pots of the pharmacy of the Franciscan monastery of Saint Saviour are displayed in the museum. The collection includes a numismatic section specializing in the city-coins of Palestine, Decapolis, and Provincia Arabia.

As a center of archaeological research, therefore, the Studium Biblicum specializes in the study of the Christian presence in the Holy Land in the sanctuaries of the Late Roman, Byzantine, and Crusader periods. Historically important for the geography of the Gospel are the discoveries of the localities of Nazareth, Capharnaum, Magdala, and Bethany.

The excavations in Nazareth, started by Fr. Prosper Viaud at the beginning of the 20th century, were resumed by Fr. Bellarmino Bagatti in 1954. Along with the discovery of the ancient village, he found the first signs of the Christian presence as evidenced by the Christian graffiti scratched on plaster found under the Crusader and Byzantine Basilica of the Annunciation.

At Capharnaum, the excavations started by Fr. Gaudenzio Orfali in the synagogue in 1921 were taken up again in 1968 and have been continued into the 21st century by Frs. Virgilio Corbo and Stanislao Loffreda. They have discovered among the ruins of the houses of the ancient village the *insula sacra* (the sacred insula) with the *domus-ecclesia* (house-church) of St. Peter under the Byzantine octagonal basilica. At the same time, they have unearthed under the Jewish synagogue, structures dating to the Late Roman period.

For the first century, which is the setting of the New Testament, one may mention the excavations of the Herodion palace near Bethlehem. This work was carried out by Fr. V. Corbo during the years 1962–67. The same archaeologist directed the excavations of the Herodian fortress of Machaerous in Jordan, in which, according to Josephus Flavius, *John the Baptist was jailed and murdered.

One of the main excavation and restoration projects undertaken by the Institute is the one at Mount Nebo in Jordan. The project started in 1933 under the direction of Fr. Sylvester Saller. The work was focused mainly on the Memorial Church of Moses, Prophet and Man of God. This memorial was built by the Christians of the region in the fourth century on the western peak of Siyagha. Around it a monastery developed in the Byzantine period.

Excavations were expanded to the nearby ruins of Khirbet el-Mukhayyat on the southern peak of Mount Nebo, where the Iron Age fortress and the Roman-Byzantine village identified with Nebo are located. Since 1984, the Studium has been excavating two Byzantine churches in the 'Uyoun Mousa valley, north of the mountain. At the same time, the Studium is cooperating with the Jordanian Department of Antiquities in excavating several monuments of the city of Madaba, such as the Church of the Virgin, the Hippolythus Hall, the Cathedral, and the Burnt Palace.

In the summer of 1986 work started at Umm er-Rasas, important ruins located in the steppe 20 miles (30 km.) southeast of Madaba, with the rediscovery of the ancient name of the ruins, Kastron Mefaa, in the inscriptions in the rich mosaic floor of the Church of St. Stephen built in the Umayyad period, with the biblical implications of this discovery. Moreover, a city plan of Kastron Mefaa was found along with these inscriptions. In the summer of 1989 a second plan of the city of Kastron Mefaa depicted in the mosaic floor of the church of the Lions was unearthed.

At Umm er-Rasas, as at Mount Nebo, Madaba, and other sites of the Holy Land, archaeological and historical research in the Roman-Byzantine and Arab periods (the main field of the scientific interest of the Studium) has proven to have deep historical implications with regard to the biblical world of both the Old and the New Testament, based on the continuity of life in the same land by the same populations, Jews, Christians, and Muslims.

BIBLIOGRAPHY: G. Golubovich, *Biblioteca Bio-Bibliografica della Terra Santa e dell'Oriente Francescano*, vol. 1–14 (1906–33); A.V.V., *The Custody of the Holy Land* (1979); M. Piccirillo (ed.), *La Custodia di Terra Santa e l'Europa* (1983); B. Bagatti (ed.), *Studium Biblicum Franciscanum. Nel 50° della fondazione (1923–1973)* (1973); B. Bagatti, *Il Museo della Flagellazione in Gerusalemme* (1939); M. Piccirillo, *Studium Biblicum Franciscanum Museum* (1983). The principal scientific publication produced by the Franciscan Printing Press, *Liber Annuus*, was founded in 1950. In regard to books, the *Collectio Maior* has now reached 34 titles; the *Collectio Minor* 34 titles; see also the series *Analecta* with 29 titles and *Museum* with 8 titles.

[Michele Piccirillo (2nd ed.)]

°FRANCIS JOSEPH I OF HAPSBURG (1830–1916), emperor of Austria 1848–1916. During his long reign he won popularity among all strata of Jewry in his empire and abroad. When he died the executive of the Austrian Zionists credited him with the betterment of the lot of the Jews in the empire, describing him as the "donor of civil rights and equality before the law, and their ever benevolent protector" (*Blochs Wochenschrift*, 33 (1916), 784). Antisemites nicknamed him "Judenkaiser." The Jewish masses referred to him as הקיר"ה (*ha-keisar, yarum hodo*: "the emperor, may his Majesty be exalted"), and many folklorist tales were told of him, among them that the prophet Elijah had promised him a long life. The synagogues were always full for the services held on his birthday, which were also attended by gentile dignitaries. Francis Joseph appreciated the role of the Jews as a sector of the population both devoted to and dependent on the monarchy at a time of growing internal national tensions. On the question of Jewish emancipation he assented to the liberal attitude of the 1848 Revolution (see also *Austria). In 1849 he granted the long-withheld recognition to the Vienna community simply by addressing its delegation as its representative (A.F. Pribram (ed.), *Urkunden und Akten...*, 2 (1918), 549). He intervened on behalf of the Jewish side in the *Mortara case. Francis Joseph signed the decree canceling restrictions on Jewish occupations and ownership of real estate (1860), and the Fundamental Law, which made Jews full citizens of the state (1867). In 1869 he met Jewish representatives in Jerusalem and gave a contribution to enable completion of the Nisan Bak Synagogue (Tiferet Yisrael). When visiting synagogues and other Jewish institutions he would assure Jews of his favor and praise their virtues, such as their devotion to family life and charity. He several times expressed his dislike of antisemitism, and in the Lower Austrian Diet called attacks on Jewish physicians a "scandal and disgrace in the eyes of the world" (1892). He twice refused to confirm the antisemite Karl *Lueger as mayor of Vienna, and on the day he finally did so conferred an order on Moritz *Guedemann, the chief rabbi of Vienna. He ennobled 20 Jews during his reign. After World War I many Jews of the former Hapsburg dominions looked back nostalgically to the reign of Francis Joseph as a golden age.

BIBLIOGRAPHY: G Deutsch, *Scrolls*, 2 (1917), 321–40; F. Coglievini, *Il viaggio in Oriente di S.M. Francesco Giuseppe I* (1869), 172–5; O. Gruen, *Franz Josef I in seinem Verhaeltniss zu den Juden* (1916); P.G.J. Pulzer, *The Rise of Political Anti-semitism in Germany and in Austria* (1964), index; J. Fraenkel (ed.), *The Jews of Austria* (1967), index; F. Heer, *Gottes erste Liebe* (1967), 320–1; J. Roth, *Werke*, 3 (1956), 40f.; D. Bronsen, in: *Tribüne*, 9 (1970), 3556–64.

FRANCK, ADOLPHE (**Jacob**; 1809–1893), French philosopher and writer. Franck, who was born at Liocourt, studied Talmud under Marchand Ennery, and later studied medicine and philosophy. He taught philosophy at several *lycées* (from 1840 in Paris) and lectured at the Sorbonne. In 1844 he was elected to the French Académie des Sciences Morales et Politiques, later being appointed to the Collège de France as extraordinary professor of ancient philosophy (1849–52) and professor of natural and international law (1854–86). In 1850 he represented the Jewish faith on the Conseil Supérieur de l'Instruction Publique. He was vice president of the Consistoire Israélite and later president of the Alliance Israélite Universelle. Franck took part in the activities of the French society for the translation of the Bible and the Societé des Etudes Juives (whose chairman he became in 1888). In 1870 he interceded in Bucharest with Prince Carol in favor of the Romanian Jews. Franck, who defended Judaism in several works, conceived of it as an idealistic expression of monotheism and vigorously opposed pantheism, atheism, materialism, and communism. He established and managed the journal of the anti-atheistic league, *La Paix Sociale*, and was coeditor of the *Journal des Savants*, and contributor to the *Journal des Débats* and the *Archives Israélites*. His works on general philosophy and the history of philosophy include *Esquisse d'une histoire de la logique* (1838); *Le communisme jugé par l'histoire* (1848); *Philosophie de droit pénal* (1864), in which Franck and others advanced the case against capital punishment; *Philosophie du droit ecclésiastique* (1864); *La philosophie mystique en France à la fin du XVIIIe siècle* (1866); *Philosophie et religion* (1857); and *Philosophes modernes* (1879); he also edited the *Dictionnaire des sciences philosophiques* (6 vols., 1844–52; 1885[3]).

Franck's chief work is in the field of Jewish studies: *La Kabbale ou philosophie religieuse des hébreux* (Paris, 1843; 1892[3]; *The Kabbalah; or the Religious Philosophy of the Hebrews*, 1926). This is the first attempt at a comprehensive, scientific description of the beginnings and contents of the Kabbalah in popular form. In the last (third) part Franck examines the religious and philosophic doctrines with which the Kabbalah has some traits in common (Platonism, the Alexandrinian school, the teachings of Philo, Christianity, the religions of the Chaldeans and the Persians). Two discussions on the Ḥasidim and the Frankists are appended. Franck's premises and hypotheses (early date for the beginnings of the Kabbalah; authenticity of Sefer *Yeẓirah; Persian influence) were strongly opposed (by Steinschneider, Jellinek, Jost, and Joel, among others). Other works of his of Jewish scholarly content are *Sur les sectes juives avant le christianisme* (1853); *La religion et la science dans le judaisme* (1882); and *Le panthéisme oriental et le monothéisme hébreu* (1889). His articles on Jewish subjects (all of which appeared in *Archives Israélites*) include: *"De la Création"* (1845); *"Le rôle des juives dans la civilisation"* (1855); and *"Le péché original et la femme"* (1885).

BIBLIOGRAPHY: H. Derenbourg, in: REJ, 4 (1882), 3–11; A. Kohut, *Beruehmte israelitische Maenner und Frauen* (1901); D.H. Joel, *Die Religionsphilosophie des Zohar* (1923); Jost, in: *Literaturblatt des Orients*, 6 (1845), 811; M. Steinschneider, *Jewish Literature from the Eighth to the Eighteenth Century* (1965), 299, 301; Pivacet, in: *Revue internationale de l'enseignement*, 40 (1920).

[Joseph Elijah Heller]

FRANCK, HENRI (1888–1912), French poet. A great-grandson of Arnaud Aron (1807–1890), chief rabbi of Strasbourg, Franck was born into a well-to-do Parisian family. He studied under Henri Bergson and became one of the circle of young French intellectuals who, in the aftermath of the *Dreyfus affair, opposed the rising tide of nationalism and sought a new national and metaphysical ideal that would save France from fanatical individualism. Endowed with a consuming ardor for life and learning, Franck refused to spare himself and died of tuberculosis at the age of 24. His works include philosophical essays and literary criticism, but his major achievement was a magnificent 2,000-verse poem, *La Danse devant l'Arche* (1912), which secured his reputation as one of the most gifted French poets of his generation. Encouraged by his close friend André *Spire, Franck sought to harmonize biblical inspiration with the French Cartesian tradition and saw himself as a new David dancing before the Ark of the Covenant. His poem concludes on a note of disillusion because of the refusal of his fellow Jews, so proud of their attenuated Judaism and atheistic French culture, to join him. Franck's spiritual conflict inspired his old friend and classmate, Jacques de *Lacretelle, to use him as a model for the tragic hero of his novel *Silbermann*.

BIBLIOGRAPHY: J. Durel, *La sagesse d'Henri Franck, poète juif* (1931); C. Jean, in: *Revue littéraire juive*, 2 (1928), 675–99, 797–823; A. Spire, *Quelques juifs et demi-juifs*, 2 (1928), 107–69; H. Clouard, *Histoire de la littérature française du symbolisme à nos jours*, 1 (1947), 404–5.

[M.J. Gottfarstein]

FRANCK, JAMES (1882–1964), physicist and Nobel prize winner. Franck, who was born in Hamburg, studied chemistry at Heidelberg and Berlin. He then devoted himself mainly to physics. In 1920 he became a professor of experimental physics, directing the second Physical Institute at Goettingen. In 1925 he and Gustav *Hertz jointly received a Nobel prize for their discovery of the laws governing the impact of an electron on an atom, corroborating Bohr's "obstacle" theory of spectra, according to which atoms cannot absorb any energy below a certain level. In 1933, after the Nazi regime was established, Franck moved to the United States. He became a faculty member of Johns Hopkins University and the University of Chicago and made further investigations into the structure of matter, especially the kinetics of electrons. He also developed brilliant optical methods for determining the dissociation temperatures of chemical combinations from molecular spectra, and confirmed the assumptions on which modern atomic theory rests. In addition, he carried out important investigations in photochemistry.

BIBLIOGRAPHY: Mc-Callum and Taylor, *Nobel Prize Winners* (Zurich, 1938); *American Men of Science* (1965).

[J. Edwin Holmstrom]

FRANCO, English family. In the 18th century, JACOB DE MOSES FRANCO (d. 1777) settled in London and amassed a large fortune in the coral trade in conjunction with his brothers RAPHAEL in Leghorn and SOLOMON (see below) in Fort St. George, Madras. He played a prominent part in the affairs of the London Sephardi community and was a member of the original Board of Deputies of British Jews in 1760. In that year, the College of Heralds accepted as evidence for his coat of arms the family badge which figured in the Leghorn synagogue. His brother SOLOMON (d. 1763) arrived in Bombay about 1743 under an agreement with the English East India Company as a "free merchant," moving to Madras in 1749. Described in his epitaph as "an eminent Hebrew merchant of Madras," he had huge interests in the coral and diamond trade. RALPH FRANCO (1788–1854), the great-grandson of Jacob, adopted the name of *Lopes, and was the ancestor of the barons Roborough.

BIBLIOGRAPHY: A. Rubens, *Anglo-Jewish Portraits* (1935), 33; J. Picciotto, *Sketches of Anglo-Jewish History* (1956²), index; A.M. Hyamson, *Sephardim of England* (1951), index; Wolf, in: JHSET, 2 (1894–95), 159–68. **ADD. BIBLIOGRAPHY:** Katz, England, 176–77; T. Endelman, *The Jews of Georgian England* (1999), 250.

[Cecil Roth]

FRANCO, AVRAHAM (1894–1993), Sephardi leader. Franco was born and raised in Hebron where his father was a religious leader. He had a traditional religious education and succeeded his father as *shoḥet* of the Sephardi community. In Hebron he taught Arabic at the New Talmud Torah but went on to study pharmacy, becoming the pharmacist of the Hebron municipality.

In World War I he served in the Turkish army, and after the war was a pharmacist at the Rothschild Hospital (which became the Hadassah Hospital) in Jerusalem. He then entered government service as a translator and became secretary of the Jerusalem municipality. As secretary of the Sephardi Federation, he introduced organizational changes in Jerusalem's Sephardi Public Council.

After the 1929 Hebron riots, he was active on behalf of the Hebron refugees, in aid of whom he went to London where he raised money, enabling some of the families to return to Hebron.

In 1947, Franco, as a Jewish employee of the Jerusalem municipality, was a target for assassination by Arabs. Sometime after escaping a bombing attempt aimed against the Jewish employees, two Arabs saved him from being stabbed by a potential assassin who entered the municipality specifically to kill him.

As secretary of the municipal council, he served as a bridge between Jews and Arabs. His experiences growing up in Hebron and living with Arabs helped him considerably in making friendships and initiating Jewish-Arab cooperation.

[Yitzhak Kerem]

FRANCO, GAD (1881–1954), Turkish lawyer. Franco was born in Milas, the son of Dardanelles Jewish community's chief rabbi and cousin of the journalist David *Fresco. He taught Turkish and French in 1901–02 at the Milas Jewish school. He started to publish his articles in the *Izmir newspapers *Ahenk* and *Hizmet.* In 1902 he moved from Milas to Izmir and started publishing the newspaper *El Nouvellista* with his cousin Hizkia Franco. Gad Franco was a fervent admirer of the Committee of Union and Progress and believed in the Ottomanization of the Jews. He graduated in 1909 from the Law School of Istanbul University and then went to Paris, where he graduated as a doctor of law from the Paris Faculty of Law. He returned to *Istanbul in 1923 and opened a law office together with two other Jewish lawyers, Henri Geron and Salamon Adato. Franco was a member of the Secular Council of Turkey's Chief Rabbinate and enjoyed very close relations with the Turkish Republic's leadership. In 1942, during the enforcement of the harsh capital tax law, he was unable to pay it and was sent to the labor camp of Aşkale. His works are *Muallimlere İrfan ve Terbiye Bahisleri* (1910), *Yunan-ı Kadimde Terbiye Nazariyeleri* (1910), *Conférence Faite par Maître Gad Franco au Local de l'Ecole de l'Alliance à Smyrne* (1910), *Tetebbüat* (1911), *Jan Jak Ruso'nun Terbiye Nazariyeleri* (1913), and *Développements Constitutionnels en Turquie* (1925).

BIBLIOGRAPHY: R.N. Bali, *Devlet'in Yahudileri ve "Öteki" Yahudi* (2004), 109–160.

[Rifat Bali (2nd ed.)]

FRANCO, MOSES (1837–1918), chief rabbi of Rhodes and later Rishon le-Zion, chief Sephardi rabbi of Ereẓ Israel from 1913 to 1916. He was born in Rhodes and brought back at the age of 45 from Milas, where he was working as a clerk, to become chief rabbi of Rhodes, which at the time was divided into factions over issues of finances and honor. In 1906, it was decided that he would serve as chief rabbi permanently. He occupied the post until 1911, when he decided to move to Ereẓ Israel. After the death of Rabbi Naḥman Batito, he was appointed acting-chief abbi (*ḥakham bashi*) of Jerusalem. Shortly afterwards, in 1913, the Ottoman authorities recognized his appointment. He endured the famine and misery of the period in Ereẓ Israel when Ottoman Turkey was at war with England in World War I. When the Ottoman Empire closed the borders to Ereẓ Israel and the inhabitants were restricted in their movements, and he himself was at an advanced age and unable to function in his position, he resigned, remaining in Jerusalem until he died.

His first cousin was RAHAMIM FRANCO, the "Harif," chief rabbi of Livorno, *av bet din* in Jerusalem, and chief rabbi of Hebron. His children included HIZKIYA, journalist and president of the Jewish community of Rhodes in the 1930s, and Elise Amateau of Izmir, father of Albert Jean *Amateau.

BIBLIOGRAPHY: M.D. Gaon, *Yehudei ha-Mizraḥ be-Ereẓ Yisrael*, Part 2 (1938), 567–68.

[Yitzchak Kerem (2nd ed.)]

FRANCO-MENDES, DAVID (Hofshi-Mendes; 1713–1792), Hebrew poet of the early Haskalah period. Born into an esteemed and affluent Portuguese family in Amsterdam, he received an excellent education and had a command of six languages besides Hebrew. In honor of his marriage to Rachel da Fonseca in 1750, his friend Benjamin Raphael Dias Brandon composed *"Keter Torah,"* an epithalamium. Franco-Mendes was considered an outstanding talmudic scholar and often handed down halakhic decisions. He was a leading Hebrew poet of his time and was greatly influenced by M.Ḥ. *Luzzatto during his stay in Amsterdam (from 1735). A central figure among a group of Dutch Hebrew poets even prior to the appearance of **Ha-Me'assef* in 1784, he became a member of Amadores das Musas, a Jewish literary society in 1769, and conducted an extensive correspondence with many Jewish literary personalities abroad. In the same year, he was also appointed honorary secretary of the Sephardi community of Amsterdam. A businessman, he was reduced to poverty in 1778, and compelled from then on to earn his living copying manuscripts. Franco-Mendes was one of the most zealous collaborators in the publication of *Ha-Me'assef*; *"Ahavat David"* (*Ha-Me'assef* (1785), 48), an article detailing a project for an encyclopedia in Hebrew, is one of his most noteworthy contributions to the periodical.

Franco-Mendes was a prolific writer. Among his dramas, most of them written in poetic form, his best-known work, *Gemul Atalyah* (Amsterdam, 1770), is reminiscent of Racine's tragedy *Athalie*. Many of his biographies of famous Sephardi Jews were published in *Ha-Me'assef* (1785ff.), and posthumously in *Ha-Maggid* (1860–66); some of his poems were also published in *Ha-Me'assef*, but the bulk survives in manuscript form. *Nir-le-David*, responsa from the years 1735 to 1792, was partly published in *She'elot u-Teshuvot* of the yeshivah Ets Ḥayyim. *Sefer Tikkunim* is a critical work on some of the writings of Maimonides. His works on the Portuguese and Spanish Jews of Amsterdam (still in manuscript) are of historical value.

BIBLIOGRAPHY: Klausner, Sifrut, 1 (1952), 200–3; J. Melkman, *David Franco-Mendes* (Eng., 1951), incl. bibl.; Schirmann, in: *Beḥinot*, 6 (1954), 44–52; Waxman, Literature, 3 (1960), 132–4; M. Gorali, in: *Tazlil*, 6 (1966), 32–46. **ADD. BIBLIOGRAPHY:** A.Z. Ben Yishai, *David Hofshi v-eha-Parodiya Haftara*, in: *Yed'a Am* 15 (1971, 37–38; 74–76; L. Fuks, in: *Studia Rosenthaliana* 7 (1973), 8–39; R. Fuks-Mansfield, "David Franco Mendes as a Historian," in: *Studia Rosenthaliana* 14, 1 (1980), 29–43; Y. Michman, *"Al Gemul Atalya,"* in: *Mikhmanei Yosef* (1994), 465–81; I.E. Zwiep, "An Echo of Lofty Mountains: David Franco Mendes, a European Intellectual," in: *Studia Rosenthaliana* 35, 2 (2001), 285–96.

FRANCOS (pl. of **Franco**, the Ladino equivalent of Arabic **Franji**, **Ifranji**), term used in Muslim countries of the Eastern Mediterranean to designate all Europeans. *Benjamin of Tudela (12th century) used the term in the same sense (*Massa'ot*, ed. by M.N. Adler (1907), 19, 23). Since the time of the *capitulations treaties between France and the Ottoman Empire (1535), the term has been generally used for the protected (Christian) merchants who came from European countries. In later times Jewish merchants from Europe were also protected under the capitulations treaties. Consequently, one finds the name Franco in Sephardi rabbinic literature from the 16th century onward as a term for European Jews. In Eastern Europe it first came to mean a Jew who was a Turkish subject, and then a Sephardi, Ladino-speaking Jew. In modern Hebrew slang the term *Franji* is used with the same meaning.

BIBLIOGRAPHY: Neubauer, Chronicles, 1 (1887), 157; E.W. Lane, *An Arabic-English Lexicon*, 6 (1877), 2389; R. Brunschvig (ed.), *Deux récits de voyage inédits en Afrique du Nord* (1936), 55, 121, 67, 135–6, 158, 192, and n. 3; Lutski, in: *Zion*, 6 (1940/41), 46–79; Baron, Community, 3 (1942), 101–2.

[Haïm Z'ew Hirschberg]

FRANK, ALBERT RUDOLPH (1872–1965), German chemical engineer and industrial chemist. Born in Stassfurt, the son of Adolph Frank, he joined his father's company, the Cyanidgesellschaft, in 1899, and was its president from 1901 to 1908. In 1905 he also joined Stickstoffwerke A.G., succeeding his father as head of this company in 1916. With his father, Nikodem *Caro, and Linde, Frank worked on the production of sulfites and of hydrogen, and particularly on calcium carbide. Frank tried to make cyanides (then wanted for a process for extracting gold) from calcium carbide and atmospheric nitrogen, but instead he got calcium cyanamide, which he deduced could be used as a fertilizer. In 1914, when Germany was cut off from supplies of Chile saltpeter, calcium cyanamide became of vital importance to the country's agriculture, and it remains of some importance to this day. Frank also investigated the use of calcium cyanamide as a chemical intermediate, and later found a way of converting it into cyanides. Frank also worked on other uses for calcium carbide (such as making acetylene black for dry batteries). He held many patents and made numerous contributions to scientific literature. The advent of the Nazis compelled him to leave Germany in 1938. He immigrated to the U.S., working for over 20 years with the American Cyanamide Company.

BIBLIOGRAPHY: *Chemie-Ingenieur-Technik*, 24 (1952), 609; *New York Times* (March 19, 1965).

[Samuel Aaron Miller]

FRANK, ANNE (1929–1945), teenage Holocaust victim who won fame following the posthumous publication of her now famous diary. Through the pages of this book, which she composed during more than two years of hiding from her Nazi persecutors, she has emerged as the preeminent symbol of the innocent but cruelly victimized Jewish child.

Anneliese Marie Frank was born in Frankfurt-am-Main. In the summer of 1933, following Hitler's accession to power, she left her native city with her parents and elder sister, Margot. After a stay of some months in Aachen, they settled in Amsterdam, where her father, Otto, had a business. Her early years in Amsterdam were relatively normal, but after Germany's invasion of the Netherlands on May 10, 1940, and especially after a series of harsh anti-Jewish decrees introduced in the following months, the situation of the Jews in the country worsened considerably. The Frank family sought safety by concealing themselves in several rooms in Otto Frank's office building. With four other Jews, they lived in this "Secret Annex" from July 6, 1942, until August 4, 1944, when they were betrayed and arrested. Sent first to Westerbork, a transit camp in Drente, in the north of Holland, they were deported a few weeks later to Auschwitz, the major Nazi death camp in Poland. After a little less than two months in this camp, Anne and Margot were then sent to Bergen-Belsen, in northern Germany, where, disease-ridden and emaciated, they died sometime in the early spring of 1945. Of the eight Jews in hiding in the "Secret Annex," only Otto Frank survived.

Anne's diary, parts of which were discovered and preserved by loyal co-workers of Otto Frank, was first published in Dutch in 1947. French and German translations appeared in 1950, and an English translation followed in 1952. Since then, the diary has been translated into some 60 languages and circulated in perhaps as many as 25 million copies. A highly popular stage version, written by Frances Goodrich and Albert Hackett, appeared in 1955, and a much acclaimed film version by famed director George Stevens followed in 1959. In subsequent years, Anne Frank's story has also been the focus of a number of other films and television programs, ballets, operas, other musical productions, paintings, drawings, works of sculpture, scholarly and popular books, postage stamps, commemorative coins, videotapes, CD-ROMS, and more. In addition to her presence in virtually all of the media of popular culture, Anne Frank's image has been enshrined in Otto Frank's former office building on the Prinsengracht, in central Amsterdam, which for years now has been one of Europe's most frequently visited memory sites, drawing very large crowds annually. As a result, Anne Frank's story has become familiar to millions of people throughout the world, so much so that she may be the best-known child of the 20th century.

On one level, the diary chronicles the trials and adventures, yearnings and frustrations, of its precociously bright and gifted author. Yet, while it has been prized chiefly as the personal confessions of an idealistic teenager doing her best to maintain her spirits and a measure of independence in confined and severely trying circumstances, the diary is also an important historical document. For it presents, often in vivid detail, the daily reflections of a highly intelligent and keenly observant young Jew struggling against the encroaching threats of the Nazi menace. Thus, the book has both universalistic and particularistic elements, and it can be and has been read in various ways.

The Goodrich and Hackett stage version of the diary elevated what Otto Frank himself energetically promoted as his daughter's "universal message" of goodness and hope and subordinated its darker and more specifically Jewish dimensions. Like the Hollywood film that followed it, the play features an Anne Frank who is basically cheerful, high-spirited, and ever optimistic. Its overarching "message" is summed up in words that have been broadly taken to constitute Anne Frank's signature line: "In spite of everything, I still believe that people are really good at heart."

The writer Meyer *Levin, who wrote an early adaptation of the diary for the theater, strongly objected to this interpretation of Anne Frank's story and fought for years to correct what he saw as an ideological distortion and political manipulation of the diary. He was largely unsuccessful, and his stage version has rarely been performed. More recently, however, the playwright Wendy Kesselman has adapted the Goodrich and Hackett stage play and given greater emphasis to the Jewish features of Anne Frank's story. Her version is in broader circulation today than Levin's ever was, and it may, over time, alter popular perceptions of her heroine's fate. In addition, new biographical, bibliographical, historical, and literary studies of Anne Frank's life and writings have appeared over the past two decades, and these have shown both the diary and its youthful author to be even more complex, interesting, and compelling than was earlier believed. At their best, these works have helped to demythologize the image of Anne Frank and to connect her more closely to the historical contexts in which she lived, wrote, and died. The meanings of Anne Frank's book no doubt will continue to be contested for years to come, including by those on the far-right revisionist fringe who have long denounced it as a "Jewish fabrication" and a "Zionist hoax," but the diary's place in the canon of 20th century literature is by now assured.

BIBLIOGRAPHY: D. Barnouw and G. van der Stroom (eds.), *The Diary of Anne Frank: The Critical Edition.* Prepared by the Netherlands State Institute for War Documentation (1989); *Anne Frank's Tales from the Secret Annex*, tr. R. Manheim and M. Mok (1984); *The Diary of Anne Frank,* dramatized by F. Goodrich and A. Hackett (1956);.*The Diary of Anne Frank*, by F. Goodrich and A. Hackett, newly adapted by W. Kesselman (2000); M. Gies, *Anne Frank Remembered: The Story of the Woman Who Helped to Hide the Frank Family* (1987); L. Graver, *An Obsession with Anne Frank: Meyer Levin and the Diary* (1995); R. Melnick, *The Stolen Legacy of Anne Frank: Meyer Levin, Lillian Hellman, and the Staging of the Diary* (1997); C.A. Lee, *The Hidden Life of Otto Frank* (2002); W. Lindwer, *The Last Seven Months of Anne Frank*, tr. A. Meersschaert (1991); M. Mueller, *Anne Frank: The Biography,* tr. R. and R. Kimber (1998); A.H. Rosenfeld, "Popularization and Memory: The Case of Anne Frank," in: P. Hayes (ed.), *Lessons and Legacies: The Meaning of the Holocaust in a Changing World* (1991), 243–78; idem, *Anne Frank and the Future of Holocaust Memory.* The Tenth Joseph and Rebecca Meyerhoff Annual Lecture, Washington, D.C., The United States Holocaust Memorial Museum (2005); H.A. Enzer and S. Solotaroff-Enzer, *Anne Frank: Reflections on Her Life and Legacy* (2000).

[Alvin H. Rosenfeld (2nd ed.)]

FRANK, BARNEY (1940–), U.S. congressman. Frank was born in Bayonne, N.J., to a politically active family. His sister, Anne Lewis, was a long-term Democratic Party activist, serving both in the Carter and the Clinton White House. Frank received his undergraduate and graduate education at Harvard and his political initiation from Allard Lowenstein. He worked as coordinator at Harvard for the Mississippi Freedom Summer of 1964, a cornerstone of the Civil Rights Movement, recruiting college black and white students – the whites overwhelmingly Jewish – to go down South. He was the chief assistant to Boston Mayor Kevin White (1967–71) and later on the staff of Michael Harrington, a liberal Boston congressman. Frank then sought office on his own, serving in the Massachusetts House of Representatives from 1973 to 1981. He excelled in the House and was an important early liberal voice on women's and homosexual rights.

He first ran for Congress in 1981 in an open district and won a narrow victory. In Congress, Frank was known for his liberal views. He was widely admired by the Asian community for his services as chair of the subcommittee that oversaw the bill granting compensation to Japanese-American for their internment during World War II. In the mid-1980s, the frumpish, overweight Frank gradually changed his appearance, losing 75 pounds and suddenly dressing stylishly. He came out of the closet after another congressman died of AIDS. He was thus the first openly gay congressman in the United States. He rose to the defense of others when they were attacked for their purported sexual practices. He often warded off attacks by threatening to "out" those who were hypocritical, attacking gay rights while secretly pursuing their homosexual lives. He would not attack those who chose to keep their behavior private as long as they did not engage in gay bashing.

Scandal struck when Frank was accused of employing a former male prostitute and fixing parking tickets on his behest. Local newspapers and even national columnists called for his resignation. Frank admitted that he had been suckered and asked the House Ethics Committee to investigate. Some urged expulsion or censure. In the end Frank apologized and was reprimanded. He was reelected in 1990 by a two to one margin.

Frank advised President Clinton on the issue of gays in the military; suggesting a middle way, commonly known as "Don't ask and don't tell." His compromise satisfied neither side. He was a staunch defender of President Clinton during the impeachment hearings where his wit often diffused tension. Political professionals rated him an outstanding legislator.

[Michael Berenbaum (2nd ed.)]

FRANK, BRUNO (1887–1945), German novelist and playwright. Born in Stuttgart, Frank studied philosophy and law at several German universities and then became a free-lance writer in Munich. After living for several years in Switzerland, he immigrated to the United States when the Nazis came to power. Frank began by writing lyric poetry, but his first published success was the novel *Die Fuerstin* (1915), a faithful portrait of contemporary society. He was at his best in recreating real or historical figures, as in *Tage des Koenigs* (1925), *Trenck* (1926), and *Politische Novelle* (1928), and in the plays *Die Schwestern und der Fremde* (1918) and *Zwoelftausend* (1927). In his last novel, *Die Tochter* (1943), one of the leading characters was a thinly veiled portrait of his mother-in-law, Fritzi Massary, the light-opera soubrette. It was in his novels rather than his plays that Frank's artistry and vivid imagination showed to their best advantage, but between the two world wars he was one of the most successful German dramatists.

BIBLIOGRAPHY: F. Lennartz, *Deutsche Dichter und Schriftsteller unserer Zeit* (1959[8]), 208–10.

[Rudolf Kayser]

FRANK, ELI (1874–1959), U.S. jurist. Frank was born in Baltimore. He taught law at the University of Maryland from 1900 on. In 1922, after serving on several state commissions, he was appointed judge on the Baltimore Supreme Bench. He held both positions until his retirement from public life in 1944. An authority on real estate law and the author of several books on the subject, Frank was highly active in Baltimore civic life and also in local Jewish activities. He served as president of the Hebrew Hospital and the Baltimore Federated Jewish Charities, was chairman of the American Jewish Relief Fund, and was a member of the executive committee of the American Jewish Committee. In 1929 he was appointed as one of the 44 non-Zionist American delegates to the Council of the Jewish Agency for Palestine.

FRANK, EVA (1754–1816), daughter of the charismatic Shabbatean leader Jacob *Frank (1726–1791) and Hannah Kohen, his wife. Eva was born in Nikopol, Bulgaria, then part of the *Ottoman Empire, into the Jewish-Muslim community of the *Doenmeh. Jacob Frank was a proponent of an antinomian anarchist approach that rejected all the prohibitions and restrictions of Jewish law, including the laws of incest. This annulment was inspired by medieval mystical traditions that the foremost expression of the messianic future would be the establishment of a new code, "the era of mercy," replacing the halakhah and the "era of harsh judgment." Frank, who brought his family to Poland in December 1755, was charged by the Jewish community of Brody, Galicia, with instigating illicit practices. He was tried, imprisoned, and excommunicated along with his followers in June 1756. Originally named Rachel, after Jacob Frank's mother, Rachel Herschel of Reischa, Eva is referred to in Frankist writings as the Lady, the Virgin, or *Matronita*, the Aramaic name of the mystical female entity *Shekhinah*. She became known as Eva following the conversion of her family to Christianity c. 1760. This conversion protected the Shabbatean group, which was being persecuted by Jewish communities in Galicia and Podolia for heretical views and unacceptable sexual behavior, and enabled the members to preserve their secret rituals based on messianism and anarchy in all aspects of life. The historian Peter *Beer knew Eva Frank and discussed the evolution of her names and her family's conversion in his work on Jewish sects (1823).

Jacob Frank's autobiographical writings, preserved in Frankist circles, included a Polish text entitled "The Sayings of the Master." This document set forth a mystical-mythical new reality in which Frank portrayed himself as a messianic figure, related to the biblical patriarch Jacob and associated with the kabbalistic entity of the divine male, *Tiferet* (divine glory). In this formulation, Frank's consort is portrayed as the biblical matriarch Rachel and is also associated with the mystical entity of the divine female, *Shekhinah*. Frank's wife Hannah, who was forced by her husband to play the public role of his mystical partner, the *Matronita*, died in great dismay at the beginning of 1770 when their daughter Eva was 16 years old. Frank did not allow his daughter to leave him or to marry, a prohibition he enforced on all his followers; they constituted a messianic community based on a communal sexual life with no incest restrictions or respect for marriage vows. He also demanded that Eva remain with him in prison when he was incarcerated between 1760 and 1772. Until his death in 1791, Eva played the roles of Rachel, the beloved of Jacob, and the *Shekhinah-Matronita*, the spouse of *Tiferet-*Ya'akov. Her father referred to his daughter with a citation from the *Zohar* describing the agonized *Shekhinah* who responds to her lover as "a beautiful maiden who has no eyes" (*Zohar*, Mishpatim).

Jacob Frank saw himself as the eternal messiah and told his followers that Eva-Rachel should be recognized as the mystical royal figure of the *Shekhinah* who would lead them as a messianic redeemer while he was temporarily absent. Ultimately, Frank claimed, he would be reborn and united with his daughter in "the unity of Messiah and *Shekhinah*." In the last decade of his life, Frank lived in Brno (Bruenn, then Austria) and in Offenbach in Germany with his daughter; he discussed Eva's messianic nature in inner Frankist circles while spreading the rumor in public that she was an illegitimate child of the Russian Empress Catherine of the house of Romanov. In 1777 Frank took Eva to Vienna where both were received at the royal palace. In that year he had portraits of his daughter sent to Frankist communities in Hamburg and Altona together with pronouncements of her messianic nature. After Jacob Frank's death in 1791, understood by his followers as a temporary disappearance, Eva led the Frankist court in Offenbach with her two younger brothers.

In 1800 Eva sent letters to hundreds of Jewish communities encouraging conversion to Christianity and enlistment in the Frankist movement (see Brawer, *Galicia*, pp. 270–75). Her request for financial help was supported by quotations from her father's teachings and promises of approaching messianic redemption. In 1803 the Offenbach court dismantled and the Frankists returned to Poland, where Eva conducted herself as a Romanov princess and lived as the Shabbatean-Frankist leader until her death in 1816. The anarchic aspect of the Frankist community, liberated from all restrictions imposed by tradition and taboo, did not survive her death. However, many Frankist families continued to keep a miniature of Eva Frank and honored her as a saintly woman who was falsely reviled.

BIBLIOGRAPHY: A. Kraushaar, *Frank i Frankisci polscy* I–II (1895); G. Scholem, "Jacob Frank," in: *Encyclopaedia Judaica* (1st ed., 1971); "Doenmeh," in: *ibid*; idem, *Mehkarim u-Mekorot le-Toledot ha-Shabbeta'ut ve-Gilguleiha* (1974): A. Brawer, *Galicia ve-Yehudeiha* (1965) 197–275; R. Elior, *"Sefer Divrei ha-Adon le-Ya'akov Frank,"* in: *Ha-Ḥalom ve-Shivero: The Sabbatean Movement and its Aftermath: Messianism Sabbatianism and Frankism* (ed. R. Elior), vol. 2 (2001) (Jerusalem Studies in Jewish Thought, vol. XVII, 471–548); H. Levin (ed.), *Ha-Kronikah, On Jacob Frank and the Frankist Movement* (1984); A. Rapoport-Albert, "On the Position of Women in Sabbatianism," in: *Ha-Ḥalom ve-Shivero: The Sabbatean Movement and its Aftermath: Messianism Sabbatianism and Frankism* (ed. Rachel Elior), vol. 1 (2001 (Jerusalem Studies in Jewish Thought, vol. 16, 168–69, 268–9. 279–94.

[Rachel Elior (2nd ed.)]

°**FRANK, HANS MICHAEL** (1900–1946), Nazi politician and lawyer responsible for the mass murder of Polish Jewry. A member of the Nazi Party from its inception, Frank participated in the Munich putsch of 1923. He fled to Austria for a time and then returned to Germany to finish his doctorate at the University of Kiel (1924). He left the Nazi Party for a time to protest Hitler's moderation, namely his willingness to renounce German claims over South Tyrol. During the last years of the Weimar republic, Frank was the Nazis' leading lawyer, defending hundreds of party members accused of political crimes and Hitler in his many libel cases. He also handled some other difficult assignments for Hitler, including researching his possible Jewish roots. With Hitler's accession to power, Frank proved less useful and was given seemingly important titles but little independent power. He was appointed head of the association of lawyers who were members of the Nazi party, and charged with the unification of the judiciary system of the Third Reich. His stature was reflective of two conflicting realities: his veteran status in the Nazi Party and Hitler's general aversion to law and to any limitations on his power. After the German conquest of Poland in the autumn of 1939, Frank was named governor general of the German-occupied Polish territories under the General Government. He was primarily responsible for the persecution of the population of Poland, the plundering of the country, and the murder of its Jews. Frank exhorted the Nazi leadership first of all to exterminate the Jews living in Poland. He was thus responsible for greatly hastening the program of the death camps in the East. Frank succeeded in depriving the Jews of the benefits and protection of the laws, beginning with his promulgation of a law on Oct. 27, 1939, ordering forced labor by the Jewish population and culminating in a law on Oct. 15, 1941, by which Jews were forbidden to leave their special districts under penalty of death. He confiscated their goods, forced them to wear a special insignia (the yellow badge), and concentrated them into ghettos, where they starved. His quest for power put him in conflict with the military occupation and with Hermann Goering regarding the economic use of Poles and Jews, as well as the SS. He never exercised control over the SS but did reach an accommodation with Goering and the military. His approach to the Poles general-government alternated between pragmatic stability and harsh brutality. He was stripped of his control of racial and police matters in March 1942 – prior to the deportation of the Jews from the ghettos – which were controlled by Himmler and Friedrich Wilhelm Kruger. Thus, as the major deportations began, Frank was a figurehead, deprived of all power. Hitler kept him that way, refusing all letters of resignation.

During his rule over Poland, until January 1945, Frank kept a diary in which he noted every speech and official engagement. He never concealed his plans for the "Final Solution" for Polish Jewry. Condemned to death by the International Military Tribunal at Nuremberg, after admitting his own guilt and that of Nazi Germany as a whole, Frank was hanged on Oct. 16, 1946.

BIBLIOGRAPHY: E. Davidson, *Trial of the Germans* (1966), 427–45; IMT, *Trial of the Major War Criminals*, 24 (1949), index; G.M. Gilbert, *Nuremberg Diary* (1947), 276–90; S. Piotrowski (ed.), *Hans Frank's Diary* (1961).

[Yehuda Reshef / Michael Berenbaum (2nd ed.)]

FRANK, ILYA MIKHAILOVICH (1908–1990), Russian Nobel laureate in physics. Frank, whose father was Jewish, was born in St. Petersburg (formerly Leningrad), graduated from Moscow State University in 1930, and received his doctorate in physico-mathematical sciences in 1935. He worked in the State Optical Institute in St. Petersburg (1931–34), followed by the P.N. Lebedev Institute of the U.S.S.R. Academy of Sciences. From 1941 he was in charge of the Atomic Nucleus Laboratory, becoming professor in 1944, and in 1957 he also became director of the Neutron Laboratory of the Joint Institute of Nuclear Investigations. He was a specialist in physical optics and his early interests concerned photoluminescence and photochemistry. He was awarded the Nobel Prize in 1958 (jointly with Pavel Alekseyevich Cherenkov and Igor Yevgenyevich Tamm) for his work on the Vavilov-Cherenkov effect, which concerns light emission by radioactive compounds. Solving the physical basis for this "glow" has had important applications in plasma physics, astrophysics, and radio wave generation. His later work concerned neutron physics.

[Michael Denman (2nd ed.)]

FRANK, JACOB, AND THE FRANKISTS. Jacob Frank (1726–1791) was the founder of a Jewish sect named after him which comprised the last stage in the development of the Shabbatean movement. He was born Jacob b. Judah Leib in Korolowka (Korolevo), a small town in Podolia. His family was middle class, and his father was a contractor and merchant, apparently well respected. His grandfather lived for a time in Kalisz, and his mother came from Rzesow. Although Frank's claim before the Inquisition that his father used to serve as a rabbi appears to have no foundation there is reason to believe that he did conduct services in Czernowitz, where he moved in the early 1730s. His father is depicted as a scrupulously observant Jew. At the same time, it is very likely that he already had certain connections with the Shabbatean sect, which had taken root in many communities in Podolia, Bukovina, and Walachia. Frank was educated in Czernowitz and Sniatyn, and lived for several years in Bucharest. Although he went to *ḥeder*, he gained no knowledge of Talmud, and in later years boasted of this ignorance and of the qualities he possessed as a *prostak* ("simple man"). His self-characterization as an ignoramus (*am ha-areẓ*) must be seen in the context of the contemporary usage of the word to mean a man who knows Bible and the *aggadah*, but who is not skilled in *Gemara*. In his memoirs he makes much of the pranks and bold adventures of his childhood and adolescence. In Bucharest he began to earn his living as a dealer in cloth, precious stones, and whatever came to hand. Between 1745 and 1755 his trade took him through the Balkans and as far as Smyrna.

Early Associations with the Shabbateans

Frank's accounts of his earliest associations with the Sabbateans are full of contradictions, but there is no doubt that these contacts go back to his youth. Apparently his teacher in Czernowitz belonged to the sect and had promised that Frank would be initiated into their faith after marriage, as was often customary among Shabbateans. He began to study the Zohar, making a name in Shabbatean circles as a man possessed of special powers and inspiration. When in 1752 he married Hannah, the daughter of a respected Ashkenazi merchant in Nikopol (Bulgaria), two Shabbatean emissaries from Podolia were at the wedding. Shabbatean scholars like these, some of whom Frank mentions in his stories, accompanied him on his travels, and initiated him into the mysteries of "the faith." There is no doubt that these men were representatives of the extremist wing formed by the disciples of Barukhyah Russo (d. 1720), one of the leaders of the *Doenmeh in Salonika. It was in the company of these teachers, themselves Ashkenazim, that Frank visited Salonika for the first time in 1753, and became involved with the Barukhyah group of the Doenmeh, but he followed the practice of the Polish disciples and did not convert to Islam. After his marriage it seems that trading became secondary to his role as a Shabbatean "prophet," and as part of his mission he journeyed to the grave of *Nathan of Gaza, Adrianople, and Smyrna, and again spent a good deal of time in Salonika in 1755. Through their letters, his Shabbatean teachers and companions from Poland spread the news of the emergence of a new leader in Podolia, and finally persuaded him to return to his early home. Frank, who was a man of unbridled ambition, domineering to the point of despotism, had a low opinion of the contemporary Barukhyah sect in Salonika, calling it "an empty house"; whereas, as the leader of the Shabbateans in Poland, he envisaged a great future for himself. Although in the circle of his close friends he was given the Sephardi appellation *Ḥakham Ya'akov*, at the same time he was considered to be a new transmigration or a reincarnation of the divine soul which had previously resided in *Shabbetai Ẓevi and Barukhyah, to whom Frank used to refer as the "First" and the "Second." At the end of the 18th century, the story that Frank had gone to Poland on an explicit mission from the Barukhyah sect was still circulating in Doenmeh sects in Salonika. In the first years of his activity he did in fact follow the basic principles of this sect, both its teaching and its customs.

Frank in Podolia

On Dec. 3, 1755, Frank, accompanied by R. Mordecai and R. Naḥman, crossed the Dniester River and spent some time with his relatives in Korolewka. After this he passed in solemn state through the communities in Podolia which contained Shabbatean cells. He was enthusiastically received by "the believers," and in the general Jewish community the news spread of the appearance of a suspected *frenk*, which was the usual Yiddish term for a Sephardi. Frank, who had spent about 25 years in the Balkans and was thought to be a Turkish subject, actually conducted himself like a Sephardi and spoke Ladino when he appeared in public. Subsequently he assumed the appellation "Frank" as his family name. His appearance in Lanskroun (Landskron) at the end of January 1756 led to a great scandal, when he was discovered conducting a Shabbatean ritual with his followers in a locked house. The opponents of the Shabbateans claimed that they surprised the sectarians in the midst of a heretical religious orgy, similar to rites which were actually practiced by members of the Barukhyah sect, especially in Podolia. Later Frank claimed that he had deliberately opened the windows of the house in order to compel the "believers" to show themselves publicly instead of concealing their actions as they had done for decades. Frank's followers were imprisoned but he himself went scot-free because the local authorities believed him to be a Turkish citizen. At the request of the rabbis an enquiry was instituted at the *bet din* in Satanow, the seat of the Podolia district rabbinate, which examined the practices and principles of the Shabbateans. Frank crossed the Turkish frontier; returning once more to his followers, he was arrested in March 1756 in Kopyczynce (Kopichintsy) but was again allowed to go free. After this he remained for at least three years in Turkey, first in Khotin on the Dniester, and afterward mainly in Giorgievo on the Danube. There, early in 1757, he became officially a convert to Islam, and was greatly honored for this by the Turkish authorities. In June and August 1757 he made secret visits to Rogatyn, in Podolia, in order to confer with his followers. During this period, he went to Salonika a number of times, and also paid one visit to Constantinople.

When Frank appeared in Poland he became the central figure for the vast majority of the Shabbateans, particularly those in Galicia, the Ukraine, and Hungary. It would appear that most of the Moravian Shabbateans also acknowledged his leadership. An inquiry of the *bet din* in Satanow had to a large extent uncovered the Shabbatean network of Barukhyah's followers, which had existed underground in Podolia. A considerable portion of the Satanow findings was published by Jacob *Emden. From this it is clear that the suspicions concerning the antinomian character of the sect were justified, and that "the believers," who conformed outwardly to Jewish legal precepts, did in fact transgress them, including the sexual prohibitions of the Torah, with the stated intention of upholding the higher form of the Torah, which they called *Torah de-aẓilut* ("the Torah of emanation"), meaning the spiritual Torah in contradistinction to the actual Torah of the *halakhah*, which was called the *Torah de-beri'ah* ("the Torah of creation"). The results of the inquiry were laid before a rabbinical assembly at Brody in June 1756, and confirmed at a session of the Council of the Four Lands held in Konstantynow in September. In Brody a *ḥerem* ("excommunication") was proclaimed against the members of the sect, which laid them open to persecution and also sought to restrict study of the Zohar and Kabbalah before a certain age (40 years in the case of Isaac *Luria's writings).

When printed and dispatched throughout the communities, the *ḥerem* provoked a wave of persecution against the members of the sect, particularly in Podolia. The Polish rabbis turned to Jacob Emden, well-known as a fierce antagonist of the Shabbateans, who advised them to seek help from the Catholic ecclesiastical authorities based on the argument that the Shabbatean faith, being a mixture of the principles of all the other religions, constituted a new religion, and as such was forbidden by canon law. However, the results of his advice were the opposite of what had been intended, as Frank's followers, who had been severely harassed, adopted the strategy of putting themselves under the protection of Bishop Dembowski of Kamieniec-Podolski, in whose diocese many of the Shabbatean communities were concentrated. If before they had acted in a two-faced manner with regard to Judaism, appearing to be outwardly Orthodox while being secretly heretical, they now decided, apparently on Frank's advice, to emphasize and even to exaggerate what beliefs they held in common with the basic principles of Christianity, in order to curry favor with the Catholic priesthood, although in fact their secret Shabbatean faith had not changed at all. Proclaiming themselves "contra-talmudists," they sought the protection of the Church from their persecutors, who, they claimed, had been angered precisely because of the sympathy shown by "the believers" toward some of the important tenets of Christianity. This extremely successful maneuver enabled them to find refuge with the ecclesiastical authorities, who saw in them potential candidates for mass conversion from Judaism to Christianity. In the meantime, however, members of the sect were constantly being impelled against their will by their protectors to assist in the preparation of anti-Jewish propaganda, and to formulate declarations which were intended to wreak destruction upon Polish Jewry. These developments strengthened mutual hostility and had dire consequences. Throughout these events Frank took great care not to draw attention to himself, except to appear as a spiritual guide showing his followers the way, as it were, to draw nearer to Christianity. It should be noted that the name "Frankists" was not used at this time, becoming current only in the 19th century. As far as the mass of Jews and rabbis were concerned there was no difference at all between the earlier Shabbateans and the Shabbateans in this new guise, and they continued to call them "the sect of Shabbetai Ẓevi." Even Frank's followers, when talking to one another, continued, to refer to themselves by the usual term *ma'aminim* ("believers").

Disputations

In the events that followed, it is difficult to differentiate precisely between the steps taken by Frank's adherents and those that were initiated by the Church and resulted from ecclesiastical coercion, although there is no doubt that M. Balaban (see bibliography) is right in laying greater stress on the latter. Shortly after the *ḥerem* at Brody the Frankists asked Bishop Dembowski to hold a new enquiry into the Lanskroun affair, and they petitioned for a public disputation between themselves and the rabbis. On Aug. 2, 1756 they presented nine principles of their faith for debate. Formulated in a most ambiguous fashion, their declaration of faith asserted in brief: (1) belief in the Torah of Moses; (2) that the Torah and the Prophets were obscure books, which had to be interpreted with the aid of God's light from above, and not simply by the light of human intelligence; (3) that the interpretation of the Torah to be found in the Talmud contained nonsense and falsehood, hostile to the Torah of the Lord; (4) belief that God is one and that all the worlds were created by Him; (5) belief in the trinity of the three equal "faces" within the one God, without there being any division within Him; (6) that God manifested Himself in corporeal form, like other human beings, but without sin; (7) that Jerusalem would not be rebuilt until the end of time; (8) that Jews waited in vain for the Messiah to come and raise them above the whole world; and (9) that, instead, God would Himself be clothed in human form and atone for all the sins for which the world had been cursed, and that at His coming the world would be pardoned and cleansed of all iniquity. These principles reflect the belief of the antinomian followers of Barukhyah, but they were formulated in such a way that they seemed to refer to Jesus of Nazareth instead of to Shabbetai Ẓevi and Barukhyah. They constitute a blatant plan to deceive the Church which the priests did not understand, and which, quite naturally, they were not interested in understanding.

The rabbis managed to avoid accepting the invitation to the disputation for nearly a year. However, after great pressure from the bishop, the disputation finally took place at Kamieniec, from June 20 to 28, 1757. Nineteen opponents of the Talmud (then called Zoharites) took part, together with a handful of rabbis from communities in the area. The spokesmen for the Shabbateans were also learned men, some of them being officiating rabbis who had secret Shabbatean tendencies. The arguments in the accusations and the defense of the rabbis were presented in writing, and were later published in a Latin protocol in Lvov in 1758. On Oct. 17, 1757, Bishop Dembowski issued his decision in favor of the Frankists, imposing a number of penalties upon the rabbis, chief of which was a condemnation of the Talmud as worthless and corrupt, with an order that it be burned in the city square. All Jewish homes were to be searched for copies of the Talmud. According to some contemporary accounts many cartloads of editions of the Talmud were in fact burned in Kamieniec, Lvov, Brody, Zolkiew, and other places. The "burning of the Torah" had a crushing effect on the Jewish community and the rabbis declared a fast in memory of the event. Jews who had influence with the authorities tried to stop the burnings, which took place mainly in November 1757.

A sudden reversal of fortune, in favor of the "talmudists" and to the detriment of the sectarians, resulted from the sudden death of Bishop Dembowski on November 9, at the very time of the burnings. News of the event, in which Jews saw the finger of God, spread like wildfire. Persecutions of the sect were renewed with even greater vehemence, and many of them fled across the Dniester to Turkey. There several converted to Islam, and one group even joined the Doenmeh in Salonika, where they were known as "the Poles." Meanwhile the spokesmen for the "contra-talmudists" turned to the political and ecclesiastical authorities and sought the implementation of the privilege which had been promised them by Dembowski, who allowed them to follow their own faith. They also sought the return of their looted property and permission for the refugees to come back to their homes. After some internal disagreements among the Polish authorities, King Augustus III issued a privilege on June 16, 1758, which accorded the sectarians royal protection as men "who were near to the [Christian] acknowledgment of God." Most of the refugees returned to Podolia at the end of September, and gathered mainly in and around the small town of Iwanie (near Khotin). In December, or the beginning of January 1759, Frank himself also left Turkey and arrived in Iwanie. Many of "the believers" scattered throughout eastern Galicia were summoned there.

Iwanie

In fact, the Frankists constituted themselves as a special sect with a distinctive character only during those months when "the believers" lived in Iwanie, an episode which became engraved on their memory as a quasi-revelatory event. Here it was that Frank finally revealed himself as the living embodiment of God's power who had come to complete the mission of Shabbetai Ẓevi and Barukhyah, and as "the true Jacob," comparing himself to the patriarch Jacob who had completed the work of his predecessors Abraham and Isaac. It was here that he unfolded his teaching before his followers in short statements and parables, and introduced a specific order into the ritual of the sect. There is no doubt that it was here that he prepared them to face the necessity of adopting Christianity outwardly, in order to keep their true faith in secret, just as the Doenmeh had done with regard to Islam. He declared that all religions were only stages through which "the believers" had to pass – like a man putting on different suits of clothes – and then to discard as of no worth compared with the true hidden faith. Frank's originality at this time consisted in his brazen rejection of the Shabbatean theology which was well-known to "the believers" from the writings of Nathan of Gaza and from the writings which were based on the extreme Shabbatean Kabbalah in Barukhyah's version. He asked them to forget all this, proposing in its place a kind of mythology freed from all traces of kabbalistic terminology, although in fact it was no more than a popular and homiletical reworking of kabbalistic teaching. In place of the customary Shabbatean trinity of the "three knots of faith," i.e., *Attika Kaddisha, Malka Kaddisha*, and the *Shekhinah*, which are all united in the Divinity (see *Shabbetai Ẓevi), Frank went so far as to say that the true and good God was hidden and divested of any link with creation, and particularly with this insignificant world. It is He who conceals Himself behind "the King of Kings," whom Frank also calls "the Great Brother" or "He who stands before God." He is the God of true faith whom one must strive to approach and, in doing so, break the domination of the three "leaders of the world," who rule the earth at this moment, imposing upon it an unfitting system of law. The position of "the Great Brother" is connected in some way with the *Shekhinah*, which becomes in Frank's terminology the "maiden" (*almah*) or "virgin" (*betulah*). It is obvious that he tried consciously to make this concept conform as closely as possible to the Christian concept of the virgin. Just as the extreme Shabbateans from the sect of Barukhyah saw in Shabbetai Ẓevi and Barukhyah an incarnation of *Malka Kaddisha*, who is the "God of Israel," so frank referred to himself as the messenger of "the Great Brother." According to him, all the great religious leaders, from the patriarchs to Shabbetai Ẓevi and Barukhyah, had endeavored to find the way to his God, but had not succeeded.

In order that God and the virgin be revealed, it would be necessary to embark upon a completely new road, untrodden as yet by the people of Israel: this road Frank called "the way to Esau." In this context, Esau or Edom symbolizes the unbridled flow of life which liberates man because its force and power are not subject to any law. The patriarch Jacob promised (Gen. 33:14) to visit his brother Esau in Seir, but Scripture does not mention that he fulfilled his promise, because the way was too difficult for him. Now the time had come to set out on this way, which leads to the "true life," a central idea which in Frank's system carries with it the specific connotation of freedom and licentiousness. This path was the road to consistent religious anarchy: "The place to which we are going is not subject to any law, because all that is on the side of death; but we are going to life." In order to achieve this goal it was necessary to abolish and destroy the laws, teachings, and practices which constrict the power of life, but this must be done in secret; in order to accomplish it, it was essential outwardly to assume the garb of the corporeal Edom, i.e., Christianity. The "believers," or at least their vanguard, had already passed through Judaism and Islam, and they now had to complete their journey by assuming the Christian faith, using it and its ideas in order to conceal the real core of their belief in Frank as the true Messiah and the living God for whom their Christian protestations were really intended.

The motto which Frank adopted here was *massa dumah* (from Isa. 21:11), taken to mean "the burden of silence"; that is, it was necessary to bear the heavy burden of the hidden faith in the abolition of all law in utter silence, and it was forbidden to reveal anything to those outside the fold. Jesus of Nazareth was no more than the husk preceding and concealing the fruit, who was Frank himself. Although it was necessary to ensure an outward demonstration of Christian allegiance, it was forbidden to mix with Christians or to intermarry with them, for in the final analysis Frank's vision was of a Jewish future, albeit in a rebellious and revolutionary form, presented here as a messianic dream.

The concepts employed by Frank were popular and anecdotal, and the rejection of the traditional kabbalistic symbolic terminology, which was beyond the comprehension of simple people, called into play the imaginative faculty. Frank therefore prepared his followers in Iwanie to accept baptism as the final step which would open before them, in a real physical sense, the way to Esau, to the world of the gentiles. Even in the organization of this sect Frank imitated the evangelical tradition: he appointed in Iwanie twelve emissaries (apostles) or "brothers," who were considered his chief disciples. But at the same time he appointed twelve "sisters," whose main distinction was to serve as Frank's concubines. Continuing the tradition of Barukhyah's sect, Frank also instituted licentious sexual practices among the "believers," at least among his more intimate "brothers" and "sisters." His followers who had been used to acting in this way did not see anything blameworthy in it, but they did not take kindly to this request that they eradicate from their midst all kabbalistic books, which had been superseded by Frank's teaching, and many of them continued to use ideas from Shabbatean Kabbalah, mixing them up in their writings with Frank's new symbols.

The group remained in Iwanie for several months until the spring of 1759. Frank established there a common fund, apparently in emulation of the New Testament account of the early Christian community. During this time, when they came into close contact with Frank, people were overcome and dominated by his powerful personality, which was compounded of limitless ambition and cunning, together with a facility of expression and marked imaginative faculty which even had a tinge of poetry. Perhaps it can be said of Frank that he was a mixture of despotic ruler, popular prophet, and cunning impostor.

The Disputation in Lvov

As events unfolded, an intermingling of two tendencies became manifest. On the one hand, it became clear to Frank and his disciples that they could not remain halfway between Judaism and Christianity. If they wished to restore their position after the severe persecutions they had suffered, baptism was the only course left open to them. They were even prepared to make a public demonstration of their conversion to Christianity, as the priests required as the price for their protection. On the other hand, there were quite different interests among important sections of the Church in Poland who from the very beginning did not associate themselves with the Frankist cause.

At this time there were several instances of the *blood libel in Poland, which were supported by some influential bishops and leading clergy. The Council of the Four Lands, Polish Jewry's supreme organized authority, was trying to act indirectly through different mediators with the ecclesiastical authorities in Rome, laying grave charges of deceit and insolence against those responsible for the promulgation of the blood libel. Their words did not go unheeded in Rome. It would appear that some priests in the bishoprics of Kamieniec and Lvov saw a good chance of strengthening their position with regard to the question of the blood libel, if Jews who represented a whole group could be found to come forward and verify this unfounded accusation. At the end of February 1759, when their position at Iwanie was at its peak, Frank's disciples requested Archbishop Lubieński in Lvov to receive them into the Church, claiming to speak in the name of "the Jews of Poland, Hungary, Turkey, Moldavia, Italy, etc." They asked to be given a second opportunity to dispute publicly with the rabbinic Jews, devotees of the Talmud, and promised to demonstrate the truth not only of the tenets of Christianity but also of the blood libel. Without doubt, the text of this request was composed after consultation with priestly circles and was formulated by the Polish nobleman Moliwda (Ignacy Kossakowski, who had once been head of the Philippovan sect), who was Frank's adviser in all these negotiations, right up to the actual baptism. Lubieński himself was not able to deal with the affair, since he was appointed archbishop of Gniezno and primate of the Polish Church. He handed over the conduct of the case to his administrator in Lvov, Mikulski, a priest who became extremely active in the preparation of the great disputation in Lvov, which was planned to end in mass baptism and verification of the blood libel.

In the months that followed, the Frankists continued to send various petitions to the king of Poland and to the ecclesiastical authorities in order to clarify their intentions, and to ask for specific favors even after their conversion. They claimed that 5,000 of their adherents were prepared to accept baptism, but at the same time requested that they be allowed to lead a separate existence as Christians of Jewish identity: they should not be compelled to shave their "sideburns" (*pe'ot*); they should be allowed to wear traditional Jewish garb even after conversion, and to call themselves by Jewish names in addition to their new Christian names; they should not be forced to eat pork; they should be allowed to rest on Saturday as well as on Sunday; and they should be permitted to retain the books of the Zohar and other kabbalistic writings. In addition to all this, they should be allowed to marry only among themselves and not with anyone else. In return for being allowed to constitute this quasi-Jewish unit, they expressed their willingness to submit to the other demands of the Church. In other petitions they added the request that they should be assigned a special area of settlement in Eastern Galicia, including the cities of Busk and Glinyany, most of whose Jewish inhabitants were members of the sect. In this territory they promised to maintain the life of their own community, and to establish their own communal life, setting up a "productivization" in contrast to the economic structure of the usual Jewish community. Some of these petitions, printed by the priests in Lvov in 1795, circulated very widely and were translated from Polish into French, Spanish, Latin, and Portuguese; they were also reprinted in Spain and Mexico and went through several editions there. The very presentation of these requests proves that Frank's followers had no thought of assimilating or of mixing with true Christians, but sought to gain for themselves a special recognized position, like that of the Doenmeh in Salonika, under the protection of both Church and State. It is obvious that they looked upon themselves as a new type of Jew and had no intention of renouncing their national Jewish identity. These petitions also show that the more extreme pronouncements of Frank within the closed circle of his followers had not wholly taken root in their hearts and they were not prepared to follow him in every detail. The prohibition against intermarriage with gentiles reiterates Frank's own words in Iwanie, yet on other matters there was apparently lively dispute between Frank and his followers. However, these isolated requests constituted only a transitional stage in the struggle which preceded the disputation in Lvov; and the spokesmen of the sect received a negative reply. The requirement of the Church was baptism without any precondition, although at this time the priests were convinced that the Frankists' intention was sincere, since they paid no heed to Jewish representatives who warned them continually about the secret Shabbatean beliefs of those who were offering themselves for baptism. The enormous publicity given to these events after the disputation at Kamieniec stimulated missionary activity on the part of some Protestant groups. Count Zinzendorf, head of "the Fellowship of the Brethren" (later the Moravian Church) in Germany, sent the convert David Kirchhof in 1758 on a special mission to "the believers" in Podolia in order to preach to them his version of "pure Christianity" (*Judaica*, 19 (1963), 240). Among the mass of Jews, the idea spread that Frank was in reality a great sorcerer with far-reaching demonic powers, prompting the growth of various legends, which had wide repercussions, concerning his magic deeds and his success.

The Frankists tried to postpone the disputation until January 1760, when many of the nobility and merchants would gather for religious ceremonies and for the great fair at Lvov. Apparently they hoped for considerable financial help because their economic situation had suffered as a result of persecution. The authorities in Rome and Warsaw did not regard the proposed disputation favorably and, for reasons of their own, sided with the Jewish arguments against a disputation, especially one which was likely to provoke disturbances and unrest as a result of the section on the blood libel. The raising of this subject, with all the inherent risk of organized and unbridled incitement against rabbinic Judaism, was equally sure to plunge the Polish Jewish authorities into profound anxiety. In this conflict of interests between the higher authorities, who wanted the straightforward conversion of Frank's followers without any disputation, and those groups who were concerned mainly with the success of the blood libel, Mikulski acted according to his own views and sided with the latter. He therefore fixed an early date for the disputation, July 16, 1759, to be held in Lvov Cathedral, and he obliged the rabbis of his diocese to attend.

The disputation opened on July 17, attended by crowds of Poles, and was conducted intermittently at several sessions until September 10. The arguments of both sides, the theses of the "contra-talmudists" and the answers of the rabbis, were presented in writing, but in addition vehement oral disputes took place. About 30 men appeared for the rabbis, and 10–20 for the sectarians. However, the number of the actual participants was smaller. The chief spokesman, and the man who bore the main responsibility on the Jewish side, was R. Ḥayyim Kohen Rapoport, the leading rabbi of Lvov, a highly respected man of great spiritual stature. Supporting him were the rabbis of Bohorodczany and Stanislawow. The tradition which sprang up in popular accounts circulating years later that *Israel b. Eliezer Ba'al Shem Tov, the founder of Ḥasidism, was also a participant, has no historical foundation. Frank himself took part only in the last session of the disputation when the blood libel question was debated. The sect's spokesmen were three scholars who had previously been active in Podolia among the followers of Barukhyah: Leib b. Nathan Krisa from Nodwarna, R. Naḥman from Krzywicze, and Solomon b. Elisha Shor from Rohatyn. After each session, consultations took place between the rabbis and the *parnasim*, who drafted written replies. They were joined by a wine merchant from Lvov, Baer *Birkenthal of Bolechov, who, unlike the rabbis, spoke fluent Polish, and he prepared the Polish text of their replies. His memoirs of the disputation in *Sefer Divrei Binah* fill in the background of the official protocol which was drawn up in Polish by the priest Gaudenty Pikulsi, and printed in Lvov in 1760 with the title *Złość Żydowska* ("The Jewish Evil"). In Lvov the Frankists' arguments were presented in a form accommodated as far as possible to the tenets of Christianity, to an even greater extent than at the earlier disputation. However, even then, they avoided any explicit reference to Jesus of Nazareth, and there is no doubt that this silence served the express purpose of harmonizing their secret faith in Frank as God and Messiah in a corporeal form with their official support of Christianity. Indeed, according to Frank himself, Christianity was no more than a screen (*pargod*) behind which lay hidden the true faith, which he proclaimed to be "the sacred religion of Edom."

Seven main propositions were disputed: (1) all the biblical prophecies concerning the coming of the Messiah have already been fulfilled; (2) the Messiah is the true God who became incarnate in human form in order to suffer for the sake of our redemption; (3) since the advent of the true Messiah, the sacrifices and the ceremonial laws of the Torah have been abolished; (4) everyone must follow the religion of the Messiah and his teaching, for within it lies the salvation of the soul; (5) the cross is the sign of the divine trinity and the seal of the Messiah; (6) only through baptism can a man arrive at true faith in the Messiah; and (7) the Talmud teaches that the Jews need Christian blood, and whoever believes in the Talmud is bound to use it.

The rabbis refused to reply to some of these theses for fear of being offensive to the Christian faith in their answers. The disputation began at the behest of the Frankists with a statement by their protector Moliwda Kossadowski. The rabbis replied only to the first and second of the theological arguments. It was obvious from the outset that the main attention would be centered on the seventh proposition, whose effects were potentially highly dangerous for the whole of Jewry. This particular argument came up for discussion on August 27. In the preceding weeks Frank had left Iwanie and passed through the cities of Galicia, visiting his followers. He then waited a long time in Busk, near Lvov, where he was joined by his wife and children. The Frankist arguments in support of the blood libel are a mixture of quotations from books by earlier Polish apostates, and absurd arguments and nonsensical discussions based on statements in rabbinic literature containing only the slightest mention of "blood" or "red." According to Baer Birkenthal the rabbis too did not refrain from using literary stratagems in order to strengthen the impression that their replies would have on the Catholic priests, and in the oral debates they all rejected all Polish translations from talmudic and rabbinic literature without exception, which resulted in some violent verbal exchanges. Behind the scenes of the disputation, contacts continued between the rabbinic representatives and Mikulski, who began to waver, both because of the opposition of the higher church authorities to the blood libel and also as a result of rabbinic arguments concerning Frankist duplicity. The debate on this point was continued in the last session on September 10, when Rabbi Rapoport made a stringent attack on the blood libel. As the disputation came to an end, one of the Frankists approached the rabbi and said: "You have declared our blood permitted – this is your 'blood for blood.'" The confused ratiocinations of the Frankists did not achieve the desired effect, and, in the end, Mikulski resolved to ask the rabbis for a detailed written answer in Polish to the Frankists' charges. However, the time for their reply was postponed until after the end of the disputation. In the meantime nothing concrete emerged from all the upheaval about the blood libel.

On the other hand, the conversion of many of the Frankists did actually take place. Frank himself was received with extraordinary honor in Lvov, and he dispatched his flock to the baptismal font. He himself was the first to be baptized on Sept. 17, 1759. There is some disagreement about the number of sectarians who were converted. In Lvov alone more than 500 Frankists (including women and children) had been baptized by the end of 1760, nearly all of them from Podolia but some from Hungary and the European provinces of Turkey. The exact numbers of converts in other places are not known, but there are details of a considerable number of baptisms in Warsaw, where Frank and his wife were baptized a second time, under the patronage of the king of Poland, in a royal ceremony, on Nov. 18, 1759; from then on he is named Josef Frank in documents. According to oral tradition in Frankist families in Poland, the number of converts was far greater than that attested by known documents, and it speaks of several thousands. On the other hand, it is known that most of the sectarians in Podolia, and in other countries, did not follow Frank all the way, but remained in the Jewish fold, although they still recognized his leadership. It would appear that all his followers in Bohemia and Moravia, and most of those in Hungary and Romania, remained Jews and continued to lead a double life, outwardly Jews and secretly "believers." Even in Galicia there remained many cells of "believers" in an appreciable number of communities, from Podhajce (Podgaytsy) in the east to Cracow in the west.

The Social Structure of the Sect

Contradictory evidence exists concerning the social and spiritual makeup of the sectarians, both of the apostates and of those who remained within the Jewish fold, but perhaps the two types of evidence are really complementary. Many sources, particularly from the Jewish side, show that a sizeable proportion of them were knowledgeable and literate, and even rabbis of small communities. Frank's closest associates among the apostates were doubtless in this category. As far as their social status was concerned, some were wealthy and owners of property, merchants and, craftsmen such as silver- and goldsmiths; some were the children of community leaders. On the other hand, a considerable number of them were distillers and innkeepers, simple people and members of the poorer classes. In Moravia and Bohemia they included a number of wealthy and aristocratic families, important merchants and state monopoly leaseholders, while in the responsa of contemporary rabbis (and also in the ḥasidic *Shivḥei ha-Besht*) incidents are related concerning scribes and *shoḥatim* who were also members of the sect. In Sziget, Hungary, a "judge of the Jews" (*Judenrichter*) is numbered among them, as well as several important members of the community.

The uncovering of the sect, which had hitherto practiced in secret, and the mass apostasy which had taken place in several of the Polish communities, received wide publicity and had various repercussions. The attitude of the Jewish spiritual leaders was not uniform, many rabbis taking the view that their separation from the Jewish community and their defection to Christianity were in fact desirable for the good of the Jewish people as a whole (A. Yaari in *Sinai*, 35 (1954), 170–82). They hoped that all the members of the sect would leave the Jewish fold, but their hopes were not realized. A different view was expressed by Israel Ba'al Shem Tov after the disputation at Lvov, namely, that "the *Shekhinah* bewails the sect of the apostates, for while the limb is joined to the body there is hope of a cure, but once the limb is amputated, there can be no possible remedy, for every Jew is a limb of the *Shekhinah*." Naḥman of Bratslav, a great-grandson of the Ba'al Shem Tov, said that his great-grandfather died of the grief inflicted by the sect and their apostasy. In many Polish communities traditions were preserved concerning Frankist families who had not apostasized, while those who were particular about family honor took care not to marry into these families because of the suspicion of illegitimacy (see **mamzer*) which attached to them through their transgression of the sexual prohibitions.

Frank's Arrest

Frank's journey to Warsaw in great pomp in October 1759 provoked a number of scandalous incidents, particularly in Lublin. Even after their apostasy Frank's followers were continually watched by the priests who had doubts about their reliability and the sincerity of their conversion. Records vary of the evidence given to the ecclesiastical authorities of their real faith, and it is possible that these did in fact emanate from different sources. It was G. Pikulski in particular who in December 1759 obtained separate confessions from six of the "brethren" who had remained in Lvov, and it became apparent from these that the real object of their devotion was Frank, as the living incarnation of God. When this information reached Warsaw, Frank was arrested, on Feb. 6, 1760, and for three weeks he was subjected to a detailed investigation by the ecclesiastical court, which also confronted with many of the "believers" who had accompanied him to Warsaw. Frank's testimony before the inquiry was a mixture of lies and half-truths. The court's decision was to exile him for an unlimited period to the fortress of Czestochowa which was under the highest jurisdiction of the Church, "in order to prevent him having any possible influence on the views of his followers." These latter were set free and ordered to adopt Christianity in true faith, and to forsake their leader – a result which was not achieved. Nevertheless, the "treachery" of his followers in revealing their true beliefs rankled bitterly with Frank until the end of his days. The court also issued a printed proclamation on the results of the inquiry. At the end of February Frank was exiled and remained in "honorable" captivity for 13 years. At first he was utterly deserted, but he quickly found ways of re-establishing contact between himself and his "camp." At this time the apostates were scattered in several small towns and on estates owned by the nobility. They suffered a good deal until they finally settled down, mainly in Warsaw, with the remainder in other Polish towns like Cracow and Krasnystaw, and organized themselves into a secret sectarian society, whose members were careful to observe outwardly all the tenets of the Catholic faith. They also took advantage of the unstable political situation in Poland at the end of its independence, and several of the more important families demanded noble status for themselves, with some degree of success, on the basis of old statutes which accorded such privileges to Jewish converts.

Frank in Czestochowa

From the end of 1760 emissaries from the "believers" began to visit Frank and transmit his instructions. Following these, they became once more involved in a blood libel case in the town of Wojsłwiec in 1761, as the result of which many Jews were slaughtered. Their reappearance as accusers of the Jewish people aroused great bitterness among the Jews of Poland, who saw in it a new act of vengeance. The conditions of Frank's imprisonment were gradually relaxed and from 1762 his wife was allowed to join him, while a whole group of his chief followers, both men and women, were allowed to settle near the fortress, and even to practice secret religious rites of a typical sexual orgiastic nature inside the fortress. When talking to this circle Frank added a specifically Christian interpretation to his view of the virgin as the *Shekhinah*, under the influence of the worship of the virgin which, in Poland, was actually centered on Czestochowa.

In 1765, when it was apparent that the country was about to break up, Frank planned to forge links with the Russian Orthodox Church and with the Russian government through a Russian ambassador in Poland, Prince Repnin. A Frankist delegation went to Smolensk and Moscow at the end of the year and promised to instigate some pro-Russian activity among the Jews, but the details are not known. It is possible that clandestine links between the Frankist camp and the Russian authorities date from this time. These plans became known to the Jews of Warsaw, and in 1767 a counterdelegation was sent to St. Petersburg in order to inform the Russians of the Frankists' true character. From then on, Frankist propaganda spread once more through the communities of Galicia, Hungary, Moravia, and Bohemia, by means of letters and emissaries from among the learned members of the sect. Links were also formed with secret Shabbateans in Germany. One of these emissaries, Aaron Isaac Te'omim from Horodenka, appeared in Altona in 1764. In 1768–69 there were two Frankist agents in Prague and Possnitz, the Shabbatean center in Moravia, and there they were even allowed to preach in the synagogue. At the beginning of 1770 Frank's wife died, and thenceforth the worship of "the lady" (*gevirah*), which was accorded her during her lifetime, was transferred to Frank's daughter Eva (previously Rachel), who stayed with him even when practically all of his "believers" had left the fortress and gone to Warsaw. When Czestochowa was captured by the Russians in August 1772, after the first partition of Poland, Frank was freed by the commander in chief and left the town early in 1773, going with his daughter to Warsaw. From there, in March 1773, he journeyed with 18 of his associates disguised as the servants of a wealthy merchant to Bruenn (Brno) in Moravia, to the home of his cousin Schoendel *Dobruschka, the wife of a rich and influential Jew.

Frank in Bruenn and Offenbach

Frank remained in Bruenn until 1786, obtaining the protection of the authorities, both as a respected man of means with many connections and also as a man pledged to work for the propagation of Christianity among his numerous associates in the communities of Moravia. He established a semi-military regime in his retinue, where the men wore military uniform and went through a set training. Frank's court attracted many Shabbateans in Moravia, whose families preserved for generations the swords that they wore while serving at his court. Frank went with his daughter to Vienna in March 1775 and was received in audience by the empress and her son, later Joseph II. Some maintain that Frank promised the empress the assistance of his followers in a campaign to conquer parts of Turkey, and in fact over a period of time several Frankist emissaries were sent to Turkey, working hand in glove with the Doenmeh, and perhaps as political agents or spies in the service of the Austrian government. During this period Frank spoke a great deal about a general revolution which would overthrow kingdoms, and the Catholic Church in particular, and he also dreamed of the conquest of some territory in the wars at the end of time which would be the Frankist dominion. For this, military training would be a deliberate preparation. Where Frank obtained the money for the upkeep of his court was a constant source of wonder and speculation and the matter was never resolved; doubtless some system of taxation was organized among the members of the sect. Stories circulated about the arrival of barrels of gold sent, some say, by his followers, but according to others, by his foreign political "employers." At one particular period there were in Bruenn several hundred sectarians who followed no profession or trade, and whose sole and absolute master was Frank, who ruled with a rod of iron. In 1784 his financial resources failed temporarily and he found himself in great straits, but his situation subsequently improved. During his stay in Bruenn the greater part of his teachings, his recollections, and his tales were taken down by his chief associates. In 1786 or 1787 he left Bruenn, and, after bargaining with the prince of Ysenburg, established himself in Offenbach, near Frankfurt.

In Bruenn and Offenbach, Frank and his three children played a part, which was unusually successful for a long time, in order to throw dust in the eyes of both the inhabitants and the authorities. While pretending to follow the practices of the Catholic Church, at the same time they put on a show of strange practices, deliberately "Eastern" in nature, in order to emphasize their exotic character. In his last years Frank began to spread even among his close associates the notion that his daughter Eva was in reality the illegitimate daughter of the empress Catherine of the house of Romanov, and that he was no more than her guardian. Outwardly, the Frankists shrank from social contact with Jews, so much so that many of those who had business or other dealings with the latter refused absolutely to believe Jewish charges concerning the true nature of the community as a secret Jewish sect. Even in the printed proclamations issued in Offenbach, Frank's children based their authority on their strong ties with the Russian royal house. There is some reliable evidence to show that even the prince of Ysenburg's administration believed that Eva should be regarded as a Romanov princess.

The last center of the sect was set up in Offenbach, where members sent their sons and daughters to serve at the court, following the pattern that had been established in Bruenn. Frank had several apoplectic fits, dying on Dec. 10, 1791. His funeral was organized as a glorious demonstration by hundreds of his "believers." Frank had preserved to the end his double way of life and sustained the legendary Oriental atmosphere with which his life was imbued in the sight of both Jews and Christians.

In the period between Frank's apostasy and his death the converts strengthened their economic position, particularly in Warsaw where many of them built factories and were also active in masonic organizations. A group of about 50 Frankist families, led by Anton Czerniewski, one of Frank's chief disciples, settled in Bukovina after his death and were known there as the sect of Abrahamites; their descendants were still living a separate life there about 125 years later. Several families in Moravia and Bohemia, who had remained within the Jewish fold, also improved their social status, had close connections with the *Haskalah movement, and began to combine revolutionary mystical kabbalistic ideas with the rationalistic view of the Enlightenment. Some of those who had converted in these countries under Frank's influence were accepted in the higher administration and the Austrian aristocracy, but they preserved a few Frankist traditions and customs, so that a stratum was created in which the boundaries between Judaism and Christianity became blurred, irrespective of whether the members had converted or retained their links with Judaism.

Only rarely did whole groups of Frankists convert to Christianity, as in Prossnitz in 1773, but a considerable proportion of the younger members who were sent to Offenbach were baptized there. Enlightening examples of family histories from the intermediate stratum mentioned above are those of the Hoenig (see *Hoenigsberg) and Dobruschka families in Austria. Some of the Hoenig family remained Frankist Jews even after their elevation to the nobility, and some of them were connected with the upper bourgeoisie and the higher Austrian administration (the families of Von Hoenigsberg, Von Hoenigstein, Von Bienefeld), while members of the Dobruschka family converted practically en bloc and several of them served as officers in the army. Moses, the son of Schoendel Dobruschka, Frank's cousin, who was known in many circles as his nephew, was the outstanding figure in the last generation of the Frankists, being known also as Franz Thomas von Schoenfeld (a German writer and organizer of a mystical order of a Jewish Christian kabbalistic character) and later as Junius Frey (a Jacobin revolutionary in France).

Apparently he was offered the leadership of the sect after Frank's death, and, when he refused, Eva, together with her two younger brothers, Josef and Rochus, assumed responsibility for the direction of the court. Many people continued to go up to Offenbach, to "*Gottes Haus*" as the "believers" called it. However, Frank's daughter and her brothers had neither the stature nor the strength of personality required, and their fortunes quickly declined. The only independent activity that emerged from Offenbach was the dispatch of the "Red Letters" to hundreds of Jewish communities in Europe in 1799 relating to the beginning of the 19th century. In these letters the Jews were requested for the last time to enter "The holy religion of Edom." By 1803 Offenbach was almost completely deserted by the camp of the "believers," hundreds of whom had returned to Poland, while Frank's children were reduced to poverty. Josef and Rochus died in 1807 and 1813 respectively, without heirs, and Eva Frank died in 1816, leaving enormous debts. In Eva's last years a few members of the most respected families in the sect, who were supported from Warsaw, remained with her. In the last 15 years of her life she acted as if she were a royal princess of the house of Romanov, and several circles tended to believe the stories circulating in support of this.

The sect's exclusive organization continued to survive in this period through agents who went from place to place, through secret gatherings and separate religious rites, and through the dissemination of a specifically Frankist literature. The "believers" endeavored to marry only among themselves, and a wide network of inter-family relationships was created among the Frankists, even among those who had remained within the Jewish fold. Later Frankism was to a large extent the religion of families who had given their children the appropriate education. The Frankists of Germany, Bohemia, and Moravia usually held secret gatherings in Carlsbad in summer round about the Ninth of Av.

Frankist Literature

The literary activity of the sect began at the end of Frank's life, and was centered at first at Offenbach in the hands of three learned "elders," who were among his chief disciples: the two brothers Franciszek and Michael Wołowski (from the well-known rabbinic family, Shor) and Andreas Dembowski (Yeruḥam Lippmann from Czernowitz). At the end of the 18th century they compiled a collection of Frank's teachings and reminiscences, containing nearly 2,300 sayings and stories, gathered together in the book *Slowa Pańskie* ("The words of the Master"; Heb. *Divrei ha-Adon*), which was sent to circles of believers. The book was apparently written originally in Hebrew since it was quoted in this language by the Frankists of Prague. In order to meet the needs of the converts in Poland, whose children no longer learned Hebrew, it was translated, apparently in Offenbach, into very poor Polish which needed later revisions to give it a more polished style. This comprehensive book illuminates Frank's true spiritual world, as well as his relationship with Judaism, Christianity, and the members of his sect. A few complete manuscripts were preserved in a number of families in Poland, and some were acquired by public libraries and consulted by the historians Kraushar and Balaban. These manuscripts were destroyed or lost during the Holocaust, and now only two imperfect manuscripts in Cracow University Library are known, comprising about two-thirds of the complete text. Also in Offenbach, a detailed chronicle was compiled of events in the life of Frank, which gave far more reliable information than all other documents, in which Frank did not refrain from telling lies. It also contained a detailed and undisguised description of the sexual rites practiced by Frank. This manuscript was lent to Kraushar by a Frankist family, but since then it has vanished without trace. The work of an anonymous Frankist, written in Polish about 1800 and called "The Prophecy of Isaiah," which puts the metaphors of the biblical book to Frankist use, gives a reliable record of the revolutionary and utopian expectations of the members of the sect. This manuscript, parts of which were published in Kraushar's book, was in the library of the Warsaw Jewish community until the Holocaust. A book was recorded in Offenbach which listed the dreams and revelations of which Eva Frank and her brothers boasted, but when two younger members of the Porges family in Prague, who had been sent to the court and been disillusioned with what they saw, fled from Offenbach, they took the book with them and handed it over to the rabbinical court in Fuerth, who apparently destroyed it.

The Frankists in Prague

Another center of intensive literary activity emerged in Prague, where an important Frankist group had established itself. At its head were several members of the distinguished Wehle and *Bondi families, whose forebears had belonged to the secret Shabbatean movement for some generations. They had strong connections with "the believers" in other communities in Bohemia and Moravia. Their spiritual leader, Jonas Wehle (1752–1823), was aided by his brothers, who were fervent Frankists, and his son-in-law Loew von Hoenigsberg (d. 1811), who committed to writing many of the teachings of the circle. This group acted with great prudence for a long time, particularly during the lifetime of R. Ezekiel *Landau, and its members denied in his presence that they belonged to the sect. However, after his death they became more conspicuous. In 1799 R. Eleazar *Fleckeles, Landau's successor, preached some fiercely polemical sermons against them, causing riotous disturbances in the Prague synagogue, and leading to the publication of libelous attacks on the group, as well as to both denunciations and defense of its members before the civil authorities. A great deal of evidence, extracted from "penitent" members of the sect in Kolin and other places, remains from this period. The important file on the Frankists in the Prague community archives was removed by the president of the community at the end of the 19th century, out of respect for the families implicated in it. The disturbances connected with the appearance of the "Red Letters" (written in red ink, as a symbol of the religion of Edom) helped to maintain a small, distinct Frankist group in Prague for years, and some of its members, or their children, were later among the founders of the first Reform temple in Prague (c. 1832). A similar distinct group existed for a long time in Prossnitz. Some of the literature of the Prague circle survived, namely, a commentary on the *aggadot* of *Ein Ya'akov* and a large collection of letters on details of the faith, as well as commentaries on various biblical passages written in German mixed with Yiddish and Hebrew by Loew Hoenigsberg in the early 19th century. Aaron Jellinek possessed various Frankist writings in German, but they disappeared after his death.

On Eva Frank's death the organization weakened, although in 1823 Elias Kaplinski, a member of Frank's wife's family, still tried to summon a conference of the sectarians, which took place in Carlsbad. After this the sect broke up, and messengers were sent to collect together the various writings from the scattered families. This deliberate concealment of Frankist literature is one of the main reasons for the ignorance concerning its internal history, allied to the decided reluctance of most of the sectarians' descendants to promote any investigation into their affairs. The only one of "the believers" who left any memoirs of his early days was Moses Porges (later Von Portheim). These he had recorded in his old age. A whole group of Frankist families from Bohemia and Moravia migrated to the United States in 1848–49. In his last will and testament, Gottlieb Wehle of New York, 1867, a nephew of Jonas Wehle, expresses a deep feeling of identity with his Frankist forebears, who appeared to him to be the first fighters for progress in the ghetto, a view held by many of the descendants of "the believers." The connection between the Frankists' heretical Kabbalah and the ideas of the new Enlightenment is evident both in surviving manuscripts from Prague, and in the traditions of some of these families in Bohemia and Moravia (where there were adherents of the sect, outside Prague, in Kolin, Horschitz (Horice), Holleschau (Holesov), and Kojetin).

There continued to be strong ties between the neophyte families in Poland, who had risen considerably in the social scale in the 19th century, and there may have been some kind of organization among them. In the first three generations after the apostasy of 1759-60 most of them married only among themselves, preserving their Jewish character in several ways, and only a very few intermarried with true Catholics. Copies of "the Words of the Master" were still being produced in the 1820s, and apparently it had its readers. The Frankists were active as fervent Polish patriots and took part in the rebellions of 1793, 1830, and 1863. Nevertheless the whole time they were under suspicion of Jewish sectarian separatism. In Warsaw in the 1830s most of the lawyers were descendants of the Frankists, many of whom were also businessmen, writers, and musicians. It was only in the middle of the 19th century that mixed marriages increased between them and the Poles, and most of them moved from the liberal wing of Polish society to the nationalist conservative wing. However, there still remained a number of families who continued to marry only among themselves. For a long time this circle maintained secret contacts with the Doenmeh in Salonika. An unresolved controversy still exists concerning the Frankist affiliation of Adam *Mickiewicz, the greatest Polish poet. There is clear evidence of this from the poet himself (on his mother's side), but in Poland this evidence is resolutely misinterpreted. Mickiewicz's Frankist origins were well-known to the Warsaw Jewish community as early as 1838 (according to evidence in the azdj of that year, p. 362). The parents of the poet's wife also came from Frankist families.

The crystallization of the Frankist sect is one of the most marked indications of the crisis which struck the Jewish society in the mid-18th century. Frank's personality reveals clear signs of the adventurer, motivated by a blend of religious impulses and a lust for power. By contrast, his "believers" were on the whole men of deep faith and moral integrity as far as this did not conflict with the vicious demands made on them by Frank. In all that remains of their original literature whether in German, Polish or Hebrew, there is absolutely no reference to those matters, like the blood libel, which so aroused the Jewish community against them. They were fascinated by the words of their leader and his vision of a unique fusion between Judaism and Christianity, but they easily combined this with more modest hopes which led them to become protagonists of liberal-bourgeois ideals. Their nihilist Shabbatean faith served as a transition to a new world beyond the ghetto. They quickly forgot their licentious practices and acquired a reputation of being men of the highest moral conduct. Many Frankist families kept a miniature of Eva Frank which used to be sent to the most prominent households, and to this day some families honor her as a saintly woman who was falsely reviled.

BIBLIOGRAPHY: J. Emden, *Sefer Shimmush* (Altona, 1762); idem, *Megillat Sefer* (1896); E. Fleckeles, *Ahavat David* (Prague, 1800); M. Balaban, *Le-Toledot ha-Tenu'ah ha-Frankit* (1934); idem, in: *Livre d'hommage à… S. Poznański* (1927), 25–75; N.M. Gelber, in: *Yivo Historishe Shriftn*, 1 (1929); idem, in: *Zion*, 2 (1937), 326–32; G. Scholem, *ibid.*, 35 (1920/21); idem, in: *Keneset*, 2 (1937), 347–92; idem, in: *Sefer Yovel le-Yitzḥak Baer* (1960), 409–30; idem, in: rhr, 144 (1953–54), 42–77; idem, *The Messianic Idea in Judaism, and Other Essays* (1971); idem, in: *Zeugnisse T.W. Adorno zum Geburtstag* (1963), 20–32; idem, in: *Max Brod Gedenkbuch* (1969), 77–92; idem, in: *Commentary*, 51 (Jan. 1971), 41–70; A. Yaari, in: *Sinai*, 35 (1954), 120–82; 42 (1958), 294–306; A.J. Brawer, *Galizyah vi-Yhudeha* (1966), 197–275; P. Beer, *Geschichte der religioesen Sekten der Juden*, 2 (1923); H. Graetz, *Frank und die Frankisten* (1868); idem, in: mgwj, 22 (1873); S. Back, *ibid.*, 26 (1877); A.G. Schenk-Rink, *Die Polen in Offenbach* (1866–69); A. Kraushar, *Frank i frankiści polscy* (1895); T. Jeske-Choiński, *Neofici polscy* (1904), 46–107; M. Wishnitzer, in: *Mémoires de l'Académie… de St. Pétersbourg*, series 8, Hist.-Phil. Section, 12 no. 3 (1914); F. Mauthner, *Lebenserinnerungen* (1918), 295–307; C. Seligman, in: *Frankfurter Israelitisches Gemeindeblatt*, 10 (1932), 121–3, 150–2; V. Zacek, in: JGGJČ, 9 (1938), 343–410; O. Rabinowicz, in: *JQR 75th Anniversary Volume* (1967), 429–45; P. Arnsberg, *Von Podolien nach Offenbach* (1965);

R. Kestenberg-Gladstein, *Neuere Geschichte der Juden in den boehmischen Laendern*, 1 (1969), 123–91; A.G. Duker, in: JSOS, 25 (1963), 287–333; idem, in: *Joshua Starr Memorial Volume* (1963), 191–201.

[Gershom Scholem]

FRANK, JEROME NEW (1889–1957), U.S. jurist and legal philosopher. Frank, who was born in New York City, practiced law in Chicago and New York City before being appointed general counsel to the Agricultural Adjustment Administration by President Franklin D. Roosevelt in 1933. Subsequently, he was appointed to important executive positions with the Federal Surplus Relief Corporation, the Reconstruction Finance Commission, and the Public Works Administration. As one of the more imaginative and articulate administrators of the New Deal program of President Roosevelt, he was often embroiled in argument and litigation in its defense, especially in the use of public power. Retiring to private practice in 1937, he was recalled by President Roosevelt in 1939 as commissioner and then chairman of the Securities and Exchange Commission. There, he played an important role in reorganizing the New York Stock Exchange. He also instituted new programs for public-utility holding companies under the 1935 Act. President Roosevelt named him to the U.S. Court of Appeals for the 2nd Circuit in 1941. He remained on the bench, and lectured at Yale Law School as well, until his death.

Basically a "legal realist," Frank developed the juristic concept of fact-skepticism, or the continuous questioning of factual assumptions to expose the realities of the judicial process. Legal philosophers, he insisted, should not think only in terms of law to determine whether justice prevails in any given case, but rather to concentrate on the processes by which facts are found and judged. Fact-skepticism led him to infer that the jury was an inept institution and that it ought to be abolished. He also warned against relying on jury verdicts to inflict capital punishment. Frank sought through fact-skepticism to liberalize and reform the trial process. He developed his thoughts in challenging and provocative books entitled *Law and the Modern Mind* (1930) and *Courts on Trial* (1949), as well as in many law review articles. In 1945 he wrote *Fate and Freedom*, in which he attacked Freud's deterministic psychology, Marxism, and natural-law doctrines as endangering individual freedom and moral responsibility. In *If Men Were Angels* (1942), Frank replied to critics of the new administrative agencies of the New Deal. In *Not Guilty* (1957), written with his daughter, he commented on a number of cases in which innocent people were convicted of crimes.

[Julius J. Marcke]

FRANK, JOSEF (1885–?), Austrian architect. Born in Baden, Frank was a progressive architect working in Austria after World War I and was best known for the Karl Marx Hof (Vienna, 1930), an ambitious workers' housing scheme which he designed with Oskar Wlach. In 1932 be emigrated to Sweden. Frank also taught at the New School of Social Research, New York (1941–44). He wrote *Architektur als Symbol* (1930).

°FRANK, KARL HERMANN (1898–1946), Sudeten German Nazi politician, leader of the radical wing of the Sudeten German Party and close associate of *Himmler. An Austrian army veteran of World War I, he became a bookseller in his native Karlsbad. In 1933 he entered local politics as propaganda chief to Konrad Henelein and later a Sudenten German Parliamentary delegate. In March 1939 he was appointed secretary of state to *Reichsprotektor* Constantin von Neurath in the Protectorate of Bohemia-Moravia. After the assassination of *Heydrich in 1942, Frank unleashed a wave of repression against the population of the Protectorate of Bohemia-Moravia that culminated in the destruction of the town of Lidice. One hundred ninety-two men and boys and 71 women had been murdered. The surviving women were sent to concentration camps. The children were dispersed, some to concentration camps, although a few who were considered sufficiently Aryan were sent to Germany. The SS then razed the town and tried to eradicate its memory. The name of Lidice was expunged from all official records. With the appointment of Wilhelm Frick as *Reichsprotektor*, Frank was nominated minister of state (1943) and became the virtual dictator of the Protectorate (see *Czechoslovakia). As SS and police officer with the rank of lieutenant-general, he was one of the persons mainly responsible for the annihilation of the Protectorate's Jewish population. Frank was hanged after the war (1946) by the verdict of a Czechoslovak court.

BIBLIOGRAPHY: G. Wrighton, *Heydrich...* (1962), index; IMT, *Trial of the Major War Criminals*, 24 (1949), index; E. Davidson, *Trial of the Germans* (1967), index.

[Yehuda Reshef / Michael Berenbaum (2nd ed.)]

FRANK, LEO MAX (1884–1915), engineer and the only Jew ever to have been murdered by a lynch mob in the United States. Frank, who was born in Cuero, Texas, of an immigrant German family, was raised in Brooklyn, and studied mechanical engineering. In 1907 he moved to Atlanta, Georgia, where his uncle, Moses Frank, owner of the National Pencil Company, offered him a job as plant superintendent. Here he became president of the local chapter of B'nai B'rith. On April 27, 1913, a 14-year-old employee of Frank's, Mary Phagan, was found murdered in the factory basement. Frank was arrested the next day and charged with the crime. The chief witness for the prosecution at his trial, which lasted for nearly two months, was a black employee of the factory, James Conley, who was suspected by many observers both at the time and subsequently of having been the true culprit. Despite the flimsy nature of the evidence, the dubious character of many of the prosecution's witnesses and Frank's own eloquent testimony on Aug. 23, 1913, the jury returned a verdict of guilty.

The issue of Frank's Jewishness was first raised at his trial by his own lawyers, who claimed that he was a victim of prejudice, a charge that the prosecution vigorously denied. Whether or not this denial was sincere, it became clear as the trial progressed that the mobs in and out of the courtroom that continually called for Frank's blood were inspired by antisemitic passions, which undoubtedly influenced the decision of the jury. It was only when the case was already being appealed, however, that a vicious antisemitic campaign was launched around it by the ex-populist and racist politician Tom Watson, who in his weekly *Jeffersonian Magazine* repeatedly demanded the execution of "the filthy, perverted Jew of New York." Watson helped found the "Knights of Mary Phagan," an antisemitic society which sought to organize a boycott of Jewish stores and businesses throughout Georgia.

Frank's lawyers fought his case all the way to the United States Supreme Court on the grounds that he had not been given a fair trial, and it became a cause célébre which enlisted the support of prominent Jews and gentiles. On May 18, 1915, however, the Court turned down Frank's final appeal. On June 21, shortly before his scheduled execution, his sentence was commuted to a life term by Governor John Slaton, who was personally convinced of his innocence. Slaton's decision, which was to cost him his political career, inflamed emotions in Georgia and did not save Frank's life for long: he was dragged from jail by a mob on Aug. 16, 1915, and lynched. There can be little doubt that Frank was innocent or that he would never have been brought to trial in the first place, much less convicted, had he not been a Jew.

In March 1986 Leo Frank was pardoned by the governor of Georgia.

BIBLIOGRAPHY: H. Golden, *A Little Girl Is Dead* (1965, republished in England as *Lynching of Leo Frank* (1966)); L. Dinnerstein, *Leo Frank Case* (1968); idem, in: AJA, 20 (1968), 107–26. **ADD. BIBLIOGRAPHY:** S. Oney, *And the Dead Shall Rise: The Murder of Mary Phagan and the Lynching of Leo Frank* (2003)

[Harry Golden]

FRANK, MENAHEM MENDEL (late 15th–first half of 16th century), rabbi. He at first served as *av bet din* in Poznan, Poland, and from 1529 was rabbi of Brest-Litovsk, Lithuania. Frank was granted judicial authority by the king to assist Michael Ezofovich in tax collection but met with opposition in Brest-Litovsk. In 1531, when Frank complained of the matter, the Jews under his jurisdiction were ordered by King Sigismund I to obey him and submit to any *ḥerem* he imposed, being forbidden to appeal against his decisions to a non-Jewish tribunal. Encountering opposition by members of the nobility and state courts, possibly incited by Frank's Jewish opponents, in 1532 he sought the protection of Queen Bona. Upon her recommendation, the king prohibited royal officials and judges from intervening in the rabbi's affairs and declared that Frank could not be summoned to account before the throne. Decisions by Frank appertaining to divorce bills and contracts are mentioned by *Shalom Shakhna b. Joseph of Lublin. According to some records Frank ended his days in Jerusalem.

BIBLIOGRAPHY: S.A. Bershadski (ed.), *Russko-yevreyskiy arkhiv*, 1 (1882), nos. 139, 147; A.L. Feinstein, *Ir Tehillah* (1886), 21–22, 64–65, 164–5.

[Arthur Cygielman]

FRANK, PHILIPP (1884–1966), philosopher and physicist. Born in Vienna, he was appointed professor of theoretical physics at the German University of Prague at 28, replacing Einstein. In 1938, he moved to the United States and taught mathematics and physics at Harvard. He established his reputation in physics by publishing with Richard von Mises, *Die Differential-und Integralgleichungen der Mechanik und Physik* (1925). Frank's most famous work was on philosophy of science. Following Duhem, Poincaré, Mach, and Einstein, Frank tried to clarify the philosophical foundations of the natural sciences. Frank's view is close to the positivism of the "Vienna Circle." He opposed the compartmentalization of individual sciences, stressing the unity of science. He also pointed out the neglected spheres between the individual sciences. Frank was a personal friend of Einstein and in 1947 wrote *Einstein: His Life and Times*. Frank opposed Mach's limited form of logical positivism and emphasized instead, relying on Einstein, that the principles of physics are the product of free human imagination and that they are symbols. These symbols are not arbitrary, but "true" ones, i.e., one should derive from them, by logical consequences, conclusions which are confirmed by experiment. This means that despite the emphasis on the empirical factor there still remains room for the researcher's productive activity. In his later years, he was especially interested in the sociological, historical, cultural, and psychological aspects of the natural sciences. Frank was a brilliant teacher and a lucid writer. A volume of *Boston Studies in the Philosophy of Science* (1965) was dedicated to him on his 80th birthday.

Frank's writings are an important source for the history of logical positivism and empiricism in the 20th century. They include *Das Kausalgesetz und seine Grenzen* (1932), *Théorie de la connaissance et physique moderne* (1934), *Das Ende der mechanistischen Physik* (1935), *Interpretations and Misinterpretations of Modern Physics* (1938), *Between Physics and Philosophy* (1941), *Modern Science and Its Philosophy* (1949), *Relativity: A Richer Truth* (1950), and *Philosophy of Science: The Link Between Science and Philosophy* (1957).

[Samuel Hugo Bergman]

FRANK, RAY (1861–1948), U.S. journalist and religious leader, the first Jewish woman to preach from a North American pulpit. Born in San Francisco (according to some sources in 1864 or 1865) to Leah and Bernard Frank, and raised in a "deeply religious home," she graduated from Sacramento High School in 1879, taught in Nevada for six years, and subsequently rejoined her family in Oakland, California. To support herself, Frank gave private lessons, wrote for several periodicals, and taught at First Hebrew Congregation, becoming superintendent of its religious school.

During the 1890s, Frank traveled throughout the Pacific Northwest as a correspondent for several Oakland and San Francisco newspapers. Arriving in Spokane, Washington (then Spokane Falls), in September 1890, just before the Jewish New Year, she found a small Jewish community torn apart by religious dissension. When she discovered that there was neither a synagogue nor planned religious services, she offered to deliver the sermon if a *minyan* could be assembled. As reported in a special edition of the *Spokane Falls Gazette*, Frank preached at the Opera House that evening, with one thousand Jews and Christians in attendance. She also spoke the next morning and on Yom Kippur. Moved by her plea that her coreligionists unite to form a congregation, a "Christian gentleman" offered to donate land on which to build a synagogue. Frank's call for communal cooperation was so successful that she healed congregational squabbles and helped create Orthodox and Reform congregations throughout the western and northwestern United States.

Hailed as a "latter-day Deborah" and erroneously labeled a "Lady Rabbi," she came to the attention of Isaac Mayer *Wise, who encouraged her to study at *Hebrew Union College. Enrolling in January 1893, she left after one semester, later maintaining that her intention was to study philosophy, not to become a rabbi. Wise, however, had earlier written that Frank's avowed purpose was to enter the "Jewish ministry," and he applauded her zeal and moral courage in breaking down "the last remains of the barriers erected in the synagogue against women." In September 1893 Frank delivered the opening prayer and a formal address on "Woman in the Synagogue" at the first Jewish Women's Congress, held in conjunction with the Parliament of World Religions at the Chicago World's Fair. She later spoke at synagogues and churches throughout North America and officiated in 1895 at High Holy Day services in an Orthodox synagogue in Victoria, British Columbia. She declined a Chicago Reform congregation's offer to become its full-time spiritual leader.

Frank's public career ended after her 1901 marriage to economics professor, Simon Litman. She remained active in local Jewish organizations and institutions in Urbana, Illinois, led a study group, and occasionally lectured in the community and throughout the Midwest. Her papers are housed at the American Jewish Historical Society.

BIBLIOGRAPHY: R. Clar and W.M. Kramer, "The Girl Rabbi of the Golden West," in: *Western States Jewish History*, 18 (1986), 91–111, 223–36, 336–51; P. Nadell, *Women Who Would Be Rabbis* (1998); S. Litman, *Ray Frank Litman: A Memoir* (1957).

[Ellen M. Umansky (2nd ed.)]

FRANK, ROBERT (1924–), photographer. Born into a wealthy family in Zurich, Switzerland, Frank was 15 when war broke out across Europe. While his family was unharmed and sat out the war in neutral Switzerland, Frank later said that "being Jewish and living with the threat of Hitler must have been a very big part of my understanding of people that were put down or who were held back." Frank took up photography as a way of breaking away from his family and Switzerland. At 16 he apprenticed himself to the photographer Hermann Segesser, who lived in the same apartment building as the Franks. He moved to New York in 1947 and soon began traveling the world, taking pictures for publications like *Harper's Bazaar* and the *New York Times*. After several years, Frank felt constrained. Encouraged by Walker Evans, he won Guggenheim Fellowships in 1955 and 1956, which allowed him the freedom to travel throughout the United States. He set off in a car loaned to him by Peggy *Guggenheim with his wife, Mary, and their two sons to document a culture that was uniquely American. He returned a year later with 28,000 black-and-white images, 83 of which became the photographs in his monumental and now-famous book called *The Americans*, first published in 1958. His style was as uninhibited and innovative as Jack Kerouac's and Allen *Ginsberg's, and his images, to many, came to epitomize the Beat Generation. In the book, which had an introduction by Kerouac, Frank's pictures dwelt on the disenfranchised, the lonely, the disconnected, and the insecure. The images that propelled him to prominence were his signature achievement, and the photographs, taken with a small Leica, retained their impact many years later. The images rejected the assumptions of the Eisenhower era, and one critic (Michael Kimmelman in the *New York Times*) wrote, "Frank discovered for himself a vast nation of empty highways and empty symbols, a country whose most notable rift was not the picturesque Grand Canyon but the one that divided the races." The photographs are considered classics of iconoclasm. They have an irreverence and a dark humor, Kimmelman wrote, whether it was the mysterious gleaming mass of a shrouded car in California or the glow of a jukebox in New York City. At the time, critics condemned his work as dark and depressing, made worse by their grainy, out-of-focus effects. In reality, they redefined street photography for a generation of American photographers.

Frank switched from photography to films in the late 1950s. His first film, the 1959 Beat classic, *Pull My Daisy*, was made to look improvised, but it was carefully plotted and scripted by Kerouac. His 1985 autobiographical video, *Home Improvements*, was a melancholy work. He returned to photography in the 1970s, but in a different style, somewhat like sculpture. He made collages combining photographs and words scratched roughly into them. To some, this work shows his grappling with tragedies in his life: the death of his daughter in a plane crash and the mental illness of his son, who eventually committed suicide. In later years, he divided his time between Nova Scotia and New York, where he lived from 1971 with the artist June Leaf after parting from his wife two years earlier. In 1990, Frank donated his vast archive to the National Gallery in Washington; it was the first time the museum ever collected the work of a living photographer.

[Stewart Kampel (2nd ed.)]

FRANK, SEMYON LYUDVIGOVICH (1877–1950), Russian philosopher. Frank was born in Moscow. He became an enthusiastic Marxist in P.B. Struve's group, but later rejected Marx and in 1912 joined the Orthodox Church. He lectured at St. Petersburg from 1912 to 1917, was professor at Saratov (1917–21), and was then appointed to Moscow University working with Berdyaev. The Soviets banished him in 1922 and he went to Germany. In 1937 he had to flee, spending eight years in France, before moving to England. A leading philosophical theologian, he contended that the world must be conceived as a "total-unity." He tried to give Christianity cosmic significance and to develop a religious humanism, seeing the glory of God in human creativity. His chief work, *Predmet Znaniya* ("The Object of Knowledge," 1915), appeared in French in 1937 as *La connaissance et l'être*. Two later works, *Nepostizhimoye* (1939; *God With Us*, 1946) and *Realnost i chelovek* (1956; *Reality and Man*, 1965), have appeared in English.

BIBLIOGRAPHY: P. Edwards (ed.), *Encyclopedia of Philosophy*, 3 (1967), 219f.; N.O. Lossky, *History of Russian Philosophy* (1952), 266–92; V.V. Zenkousky, *History of Russian Philosophy* (1953), 852–72.

[Richard H. Popkin]

FRANK, WALDO DAVID (1889–1967), U.S. novelist, critic, and philosopher. Born in Long Branch, New Jersey, Frank was educated in Europe and at Yale. His early travels also took him to Latin America (where his books later enjoyed particular success). His father, an American-born son of German immigrants, was a wealthy and assimilated lawyer but Waldo Frank underwent a mystical reconversion to Judaism in 1920. His first published book was a novel, *The Unwelcome Man* (1917). He later made several outstanding experiments in poetic prose, such as *Rahab* (1922), *City Block* (1922), and *Holiday* (1923), the last a study of race relations in the South. A man of intellectual energy and literary skill, Frank wrote many books and essays evaluating American culture, notably *Our America* (1919), *The Re-Discovery of America* (1929), and *In the American Jungle* (1937). His books on other cultures include *Virgin Spain* (1926), *America Hispana* (1931), *Dawn in Russia* (1932), and *Cuba, Prophetic Island* (1961). As editor of the important, although short-lived, magazine *Seven Arts* (1916–17), which he founded with James Oppenheim, and of *The New Republic* (1925–40), Frank profoundly influenced American liberalism. His later writings were imbued with a prophetic and mystical philosophy that demanded the rejection of materialism and atheistic rationalism and the recognition of an immanent God. Frank also urged that private life should be guided by the ethical tenets of the Judeo-Christian tradition, enriched by the concepts of Marx and Freud. *The Bridegroom Cometh* (1938), a Marxist novel paradoxically inspired by Frank's religious beliefs, illustrates the author's conviction that the fundamental problem of the time was "how to transform the great traditional religious energies of Western civilization into modern social action." Two works by Frank on Jewish subjects are *The Jew in Our Day* (1944) and *Bridgehead: The Drama of Israel* (1957). The latter insisted on Messianism as the purpose of Jewish survival and on Jewry's mission of world redemption through the prophet Micah's principles of justice, mercy, and humility before God.

BIBLIOGRAPHY: G. Munson, *Waldo Frank* (1923); W.R. Bittner, *Novels of Waldo Frank* (1958); S. Liptzin, *Jew in American Literature* (1966), 223; R.L. Perry, *Shared Vision of Waldo Frank and Hart Crane* (1966); P.J. Carter, *Waldo Frank* (Eng., 1967).

[Brom Weber]

FRANK, ẒEVI PESAḤ (1873–1960), chief rabbi of Jerusalem and halakhic authority. Frank was born in Kovno, Lithuania. His father, Judah Leib, was one of the leaders of the "Ḥaderah" society in Kovno which founded the village of *Ḥaderah in Ereẓ Israel. Frank studied under Eliezer *Gordon at Telz and under Isaac Rabinowitz at Slobodka. He attended the **musar* discourses of Israel *Lipkin of Salant. In 1893 he proceeded to Jerusalem where he continued his studies at the yeshivot of Eẓ Ḥayyim and Torat Ḥayyim. He acquired an outstanding reputation, combining a profound knowledge of the Talmud with sound common sense. Despite his youth, he was encouraged by Samuel *Salant, the rabbi of Jerusalem, who consulted with him in his halakhic decisions. In 1895 he married Gitah-Malkah, granddaughter of Ḥayyim Jacob Spira, head of the Jerusalem *bet din*. Subsequently he taught at a number of Jerusalem yeshivot. In 1902 he moved to Jaffa in order to be able to devote himself entirely to study. Rabbi A.I. *Kook had already taken up his appointment there, and later he and Frank associated in the efforts to establish the rabbinate of Israel.

In 1907 Frank was appointed by Salant and the scholars of Jerusalem as a member of the *Bet Din Gadol* in the Ḥurvah synagogue. Although he was its youngest member, the burden of the *bet din*, and the religious affairs of the city fell mainly upon his shoulders. He conducted single-handedly the spiritual administration of the city in the difficult days of World War I. The Turks tried to send him into exile in Egypt, but he hid in an attic from where he directed the rabbinical affairs of the city until the entry of the British (December 1917). The rabbinate was in a perilous state and Frank made strenuous efforts to raise its status, both materially and spiritually. He understood the importance of founding a central rabbinical organization, and immediately after the British occupation, took steps to found "The Council of Rabbis of Jerusalem." This organization, however, was short lived. Later, however, he established the "Rabbinate Office," which became the nucleus of the chief rabbinate of Israel, and on his suggestion A.I. Kook was invited to become chief rabbi of Palestine in 1921. In the violent controversy which resulted, fomented by the extreme religious section which saw no halakhic precedent for such an appointment, Frank brought proof to bear. In 1936 he was elected chief rabbi of Jerusalem. In consequence of his preeminence as a halakhist, the appointment was accepted by all parties, including those who opposed him on political grounds.

Frank was a rare Torah personality. He was approached on all difficult halakhic problems in Israel or in the Jewish world, and unhesitatingly gave his ruling. He was especially concerned about *agunot* (see *Agunah*) and the laws pertaining to the Land of Israel. Immediately after the *Balfour Declaration (1917) he expressed the opinion: "we have been worthy to see approaching signs of the redemption"; he began to clarify the laws of the Temple and sacrifices, and also headed the Midrash Benei Zion, an institute established for the clarification of the laws of the Land of Israel. He devised no novel procedure in halakhic ruling, but followed in the tradition of the renowned **posekim* Isaac Elhanan *Spektor and Samuel Salant. He fought against the military conscription of women and yeshivah students, exclusively secular education, and the desecration of the Sabbath. His statements sometimes raised a storm, but they were always received with respect. Together with Rabbi Isaac *Herzog he entered into an agreement with Hadassah Hospital on the circumstances under which autopsies could be performed according to the *halakhah*. He left many manuscripts, in particular responsa, constituting some 20 large volumes from which *Har Ẓevi* (1964), on *Yoreh De'ah; Mikdash Melekh* (1968); and *Har Ẓevi* (1969) on *Oraḥ Ḥayyim* were published.

[Shabbetai Devir]

The second part of Rabbi Frank's responsa on *Oraḥ Ḥayyim, Har Ẓevi*, has now been published, edited by R. Shabbetai Ẓevi Rosenthal under the auspices of the Makhon ha-Rav Frank. The volume consists of 132 responsa. Some of the responsa reflect the author's attitude toward the State of Israel. For instance, he regards those areas acquired in the War of Liberation as Israeli territory in every respect, legally acquired by Israel, with the result that the laws of *terumah* and *ma'aser* apply to it and vessels captured from the enemy are liable to *tevilah*, since they are to be regarded as legally belonging to Jews.

BIBLIOGRAPHY: *Keter Torah ve-Seder Hakhtarat ha-Rabbanut… Ẓevi Pesaḥ Frank* (1936); *Ha-Ẓofeh* (Dec. 11, 1960).

FRANKAU, English literary family. JULIA FRANKAU (1859–1916), novelist and critic, was a sister of the playwright James Davis (Owen Hall). Born in Dublin, she used the pseudonym "Frank Danby" for her fiction, and her first novel, *Dr Phillips, a Maida Vale Idyl* (1887), was a story of London Jewish life. Julia Frankau was an uneven craftsman, with an exuberant style. This is best shown in *Pigs in Clover* (1903), which deals with South Africans, *Uitlanders*, and Jews, all portrayed in lurid detail. In later life she held afternoon literary salons attended by many luminaries, including Max Beerbohm and Somerset Maugham. Her son GILBERT (1884–1952) maintained no connection with Judaism. He introduced Jews into his novels, treating them mostly in theatrical style. *The Love Story of Aliette Brunton* (1922) is a plea for the liberalization of English divorce law. Gilbert Frankau wrote two topical novelettes in verse, *One of Them* (1918) and *One of Us* (1919). He believed that the best antidote to the common antisemitic depiction of the Jews was Jewish patriotism, and was himself a strong right-winger. Frankau was one of the most popular British novelists of the interwar period. He wrote an autobiographical novel, *Self-Portrait* (1940). His daughter PAMELA (1908–1967), who became a Catholic in 1942, was also a well-known novelist and magazine writer.

BIBLIOGRAPHY: M.P. Modder, *The Jew in the Literature of England* (1939), 325–6. **ADD. BIBLIOGRAPHY:** ODNB online for all three; J. Sutherland, *The Longman Companion to Victorian Fiction* (1998); T. Endelman, "The Frankaus of London," in: *Jewish History* (U.S.), Vol. 8, 1–2 (1994), 117–50.

[William D. Rubinstein (2nd ed.)]

FRANKEL, BENJAMIN (1906–1973), British composer. Born in London, the son of a synagogue beadle too poor to give him a musical education, Frankel left school to work as a watchmaker's apprentice. Although largely self-educated, he managed to gain six months of piano study with Victor Benham in Berlin and Cologne as part of the exchange program after World War I. At the age of 17, he returned to London to earn his living as a piano teacher, café pianist, and jazz violinist, studying during the day at the Guildhall School of Music and eventually winning a composition scholarship there; in 1946 he returned to the Guildhall School as a composition teacher. He was a theater conductor (in, for example, Noel Coward revues) and orchestrator until 1931, when he completed his first film score; thereafter he was to write more than 100 scores for documentaries and stories such as *The Man in the White Suit, The Importance of Being Earnest*, and *The Battle of the Bulge*. As if in reaction, his "serious" works were written in a very different style from his commercial music, often being uncompromising in idiom. He wrote a violin concerto (1951) for Max Rostal in memory of "the Six Million," eight symphonies (all in the last 14 years of his life), and four string quartets. In the *String Trio No. 2* (1958) he seemed to have found a convincing solution to the problems of serialism that had interested him; thereafter most of his works showed the use of the 12-note technique. Frankel's other works include sonatas for unaccompanied violin and cello; *Sonata ebraica*, for cello and harp; *Élégie juive*, for cello and piano; *The Aftermath*, for tenor, trumpet, and strings; *Passacaglia*, for two pianos; and many other piano pieces. He was at work on the opera *Marching Song* (commissioned by the Stuyvesant Foundation) at the time of his death.

[Max Loppert (2nd ed.)]

FRANKEL, HEINRICH WALTER (1879–1945), German metallurgist. Frankel worked at universities of Heidelberg, Goettingen, and Zurich before joining the Frankfurt Institute of Physical Chemistry (1913). In 1919 he became professor of metallurgy at University of Frankfurt. Nazi accession to power forced him to migrate in the early 1930s to the U.S, where he became a researcher for American Smelting and Refining Company, Barber, New Jersey. He was the author of *Metallurgie: physikalisch-chemische Grundlagen* (1922).

FRANKEL, HIRAM D. (1882–1931), U.S. lawyer and community leader. Frankel, who was born in Mayfield, Ohio, served in appointive local and state government posts and was a member of the Minnesota Board of Regents. Frankel was also involved in journalistic and theatrical enterprises. He served as president of Mount Zion Hebrew Congregation in St. Paul, Minnesota, and of the Jewish Home for the Aged of the Northwest. He was a district president of B'nai B'rith, later director of the Canadian district, distinguishing himself in helping to break down barriers within the organization with Jews of East European origin. Frankel's large and meticulously preserved personal correspondence covering Jewish life in Minnesota and throughout the U.S. in the World War I period is housed in the Minnesota Historical Society, St. Paul.

BIBLIOGRAPHY: W. Gunther Plaut, *Mount Zion, 1856–1956* (1956), 65, 89; idem, *The Jews in Minnesota* (1959), passim.

[W. Gunther Plaut]

FRANKEL, LEE KAUFER (1867–1931), social worker and insurance executive. Kaufer was born in Philadelphia, Pennsylvania, and during the 1890s taught chemistry at the University of Pennsylvania and also worked as a consulting chemist. Frankel's friendship with Rabbi Henry *Berkowitz helped arouse his interest in Jewish community affairs and social work. Frankel went to New York City in 1899 as manager of the United Hebrew Charities. A brilliant administrator, he helped introduce professional social work standards into Jewish philanthropy. He stressed the importance of adequate relief geared to rehabilitation, the development of a pension program for such dependents as widowed mothers, and a program of assisted migration to reduce the concentration of the Jewish population in New York City. He became interested in the potential contribution of social insurance to the prevention and relief of poverty. The Russell Sage Foundation appointed him a special investigator in 1908; this led in 1910 to the publication of *Workmen's Insurance in Europe* which he wrote in cooperation with Miles M. Dawson and Louis I. Dublin. In 1909 Frankel became manager of the industrial department of the Metropolitan Life Insurance Company; he eventually advanced to the position of second vice president. At Metropolitan, Frankel pioneered the development of social and health programs under private insurance auspices. These included the distribution of many pamphlets on communicable diseases and personal hygiene, the organization of public health nursing services, and community health demonstrations. Throughout his career Frankel retained an interest in Jewish affairs. He served on the board of the American Jewish Joint Distribution Committee, and in 1927 was chairman of the commission that surveyed Palestine for the Jewish Agency. Frankel published many articles on health and welfare issues and was the coauthor of several books, including *The Human Factor in Industry* (1920), *A Popular Encyclopedia of Health* (1926), and *Health of the Worker, How to Safeguard It* (1924).

BIBLIOGRAPHY: Lowenstein, in: AJYB, 34 (1933), 121–40.

[Roy Lubove]

FRANKEL, LEO (1844–1896), Hungarian socialist. Born in Ó-Buda (now part of Budapest), Frankel was a goldsmith by trade. After living for a short time in Austria and Germany, he settled in Paris in 1867, where he became an active socialist. He was imprisoned by the French Imperial government for his political activities but was released on the outbreak of revolution in 1870 and helped to organize the uprising in the Paris Commune. In March 1871 Frankel was made minister of labor of the Commune, and on its overthrow two months later fled to London, where he became a member of the council of the Socialist International. In 1875 Frankel left for Austria, where he participated in the workers' conference at Wiener-Neustadt. He was arrested by the Austrian authorities and extradited to Hungary. He was imprisoned from 1876 to 1878, when he went back to Paris as Engels' assistant in the Socialist International. In 1889 he represented the Hungarian Social Democrats at the inaugural conference of the Second Socialist International.

Frankel was in constant correspondence with Karl Marx, whom he much admired, but also became interested in Zionism as a result of meeting Theodor Herzl. After his death in Paris, French workers organized a campaign to raise funds for a memorial in his name. In 1951 his portrait was used on a Hungarian stamp and in 1968 his remains were transferred to Budapest for reburial in the Workers' Pantheon.

BIBLIOGRAPHY: M. Aranyossi, *Leo Frankel* (Ger., 1957); T. Herzl, *Complete Diaries*, ed. by R. Patai, 1 (1960), 191–2.

[Yehouda Marton]

FRANKEL, MARVIN EARL (1920–2002), U.S. jurist. Frankel was born in New York City. After service in World War II, he studied law at Columbia, graduating in 1949. He served as an assistant to the solicitor general of the United States (1949–56) and then joined the New York firm of Proskauer, Rose, Goetz, & Mendelsohn, remaining until 1962 when he joined the faculty of the Columbia Law School.

In 1965 President Lyndon B. Johnson nominated Frankel to serve on the U.S. District Court for the Southern District of New York. Frankel quickly developed a reputation for great skill in handling complex federal civil litigation. He also became a leader in analysis of the administration of criminal justice. In 1974 he published *Criminal Sentences: Law without Order*, a landmark study of disparities in criminal sentencing. In 1977 he published *Grand Jury: An Institution on Trial*, a critical analysis of the history of the grand jury and abuse of the system for political ends.

He resigned from the court in 1978 and returned to the Proskauer, Rose firm for five years. In 1983 he joined the firm of Kramer, Levin, Naftalis, & Frankel, where he was the litigation director until his death in 2002. He became a champion of international humanitarian law, serving as chairman of the board of the Lawyers Committee for Human Rights. He criticized the repression of Soviet Jews, the mistreatment of political prisoners by the State of Israel, apartheid in South

Africa, and kidnappings and murders by military regimes in Argentina and Zaire.

In the last decade of his life Frankel wrote and litigated about religious liberty in the United States, but this phase of his work was not as distinguished as his advocacy for human rights. In 1994 he published an extended essay on religious freedom, arguing persuasively that officially established or preferred religion is never neutral and always entails preferences for one religious belief over another. Just before he died in 2002, Frankel argued his last case in the Supreme Court, urging the Court to invalidate a program of educational vouchers that included religious schools in Cleveland. The Court sustained this program by a vote of 5–4.

[Edward McGlynn Gaffney, Jr. (2nd ed.)]

FRANKEL, MAX (1930–), U.S. journalist; one of the most influential journalists of the 20th century as editorial page editor and executive editor of *The New York Times*. Frankel was born in Gera, Germany, but he and his family were forced to leave Nazi Germany in 1938. They crossed into the Soviet Union, where Jacob Frankel, his father, was arrested on suspicion of being a German spy and was given the choice of Soviet citizenship or a sentence of hard labor in Siberia. Because the family's intention was to reach the United States, Jacob refused citizenship and was sent to Siberia. Mary Frankel and her son Max arrived in the United States in 1940 and settled in New York City, where Jacob joined them after the war. Max had decided on a journalism career by the time he entered Columbia College, where he became editor of *The Spectator,* the student newspaper, and campus correspondent for *The Times*. He graduated from Columbia as a member of Phi Beta Kappa, the honorary society, in 1952 and earned a master's degree in American government from Columbia the following year.

Although he was hired as a full-time reporter for *The New York Times* in 1952, he served in the United States Army from 1953 to 1955. Upon his return, he worked as a reporter and rewrite man. In 1956 he attracted notice with his quick and impressive article, capturing the desperation and drama of the sinking of the Italian ocean liner *Andrea Dorea* off Nantucket Lightship after a collision with the Swedish ship *Stockholm*. Later that year he was sent overseas to cover stories arising from the Polish and Hungarian uprisings against Communism. From 1957 to 1960 he was a correspondent based in Moscow, where he wrote memorably about the international piano competition won by Van Cliburn, an American. He also wrote a series of colorful articles on Siberia that were described in the Soviet government newspaper *Izvestia* as coming "quite close to objectivity." After returning to the Western Hemisphere, he covered the United Nations and the Caribbean area, including Cuba, for a year before moving to Washington in 1961 as diplomatic correspondent. He won the Overseas Press Club award for foreign reporting in 1965 and the following year became White House correspondent. From 1968 to 1973 Frankel was chief Washington correspondent and then bureau chief.

As chief of the Washington bureau, Frankel paid more attention to bureau management than his immediate predecessors, in addition to writing analyses of Washington and foreign affairs. He won the George Polk Memorial Award for "best daily newspaper interpretation" of foreign affairs in 1970, and in 1972 he accompanied President Richard M. *Nixon on his historic trip to China. He filed 24 stories and won the Pulitzer Prize in 1973 for international reporting.

In Washington, Frankel was close to many high government officials, including Secretary of State Henry A. *Kissinger, but he resisted Kissinger's attempt to persuade him to suppress coverage of the American bombing of North Vietnam. In 1972, when some of his superiors and their lawyers at *The Times* balked at publication of the Pentagon Papers, the purloined Defense Department documents of the secret history of United States involvement in Vietnam, Frankel wrote a memorandum that helped change their minds. In the *Times*'s successful defense of its publication of the papers before the United States Supreme Court, Frankel's memo was an important affidavit. But in contrast to its aggressive publication of the Pentagon Papers, the Washington bureau, under Frankel, lagged behind the *Washington Post* in its coverage of the Nixon administration's involvement in the Watergate scandal.

He moved to New York in 1976 to serve as Sunday editor when the newspaper's daily and Sunday staffs were merged. The Sunday edition then had a circulation of 1.4 million copies and accounted for half of the paper's annual advertising linage. As Sunday editor, he had control over the Book Review, the magazine, the Arts and Leisure and Travel sections. Frankel is credited with restyling and enlivening the Sunday edition.

He did similar restructuring when he became editorial page editor in 1977. He had a lighter and more pragmatic touch than his predecessor, John B. *Oakes, and was less doctrinaire. As editor, Frankel supervised 10 to 12 editorial writers and worked closely with the publisher, Arthur Ochs *Sulzberger, and then his son, Arthur Jr. In 1986, when A.M. *Rosenthal, nearing the mandatory retirement age of 65, stepped down as executive editor of *The Times*, the highest-ranking news position, Frankel succeeded him. Under Frankel's leadership, the *Times* retained its position in the top ranks of journalism, winning Pulitzer Prizes in each of his years at the helm. In 1994, when he was approaching 65, Frankel turned the reigns over the Joseph *Lelyveld, and became a columnist for the *Times* Sunday magazine, writing on communications and the media. After he relinquished the column, Frankel wrote several books, including a memoir, *The Times of My Life and My Life With The Times* in 1999, which was a bestseller, and *High Noon in the Cold War: Kennedy, Khrushchev and the Cuban Missile Crisis* in 2004.

[Stewart Kampel (2nd ed.)]

FRANKEL, NAOMI (1920–), Israeli novelist. Born in Berlin into a wealthy, assimilated German-Jewish family, she joined Ha-Shomer ha-Ẓa'ir at an early age and went to Palestine in 1933. She studied Jewish history and Kabbalah, served in the

Palmaḥ during Israel's War of Independence, and later became a member of kibbutz Bet Alfa. Her panoramic trilogy, *Sha'ul ve-Yohannah* ("Saul and Joanna," 1956–67), describes the fate of German Jewry up to Nazi times, as reflected in the life of three generations of an assimilated Jewish family, whose granddaughter finds her way to a Zionist youth movement, and revolts against family tradition. Along with books for children, Frankel is the author of the novels *Dodi ve-Re'i* (1976), *Ẓemaḥ Bar* ("Wild Flower," 1981), and *Barkai* (1998). In 2004 she published *Predah,* a novel about Jerusalem in the 1950s, focusing on the relationship between Malkiel, a survivor of the pogrom in Hebron, and Yoske, his commander in the Palmaḥ. An ardent supporter of a Greater Israel, she moved to *Kiryat Arba in 1982 and later to Hebron.

BIBLIOGRAPHY: R. Gurfein, *Mi-Karov u-me-Raḥok* (1964), 122–5; J. Lichtenbaum, *Bi-Teḥumah shel Sifrut* (1962), 145–7. **ADD. BIBLIOGRAPHY:** Y. Orian, in: *Yedioth Aharonoth* (July 24, 1981); Y. Golan, in: *Davar* (July 24, 1981); E. Ben Ezer, "A Wild Flower for N. Frankel," in: *Modern Hebrew Literature* 8:11(1982/83), 48–52; G. Shaked, *Ha-Sipporet ha-Ivrit,* 4 (1993); P. Shirav, in: *Alei Si'aḥ,* 34 (1994), 69–82; T. Wald, *Sha'ul ve-Yohannah le-Naomi Frankel ve-Tafkido be-Iẓuv ha-Teguvah la-Traumah shel Milḥemet ha-Olam ha-Sheniyah ve-ha-Sho'ah* (2001); Z. Kochavi-Rini, "*Al Me'afyenim Le-shoniyim ba-Roman Barkai le-Naomi Frankel,*" in: *Balshanut Ivrit,* 54 (2004), 23–36.

[Getzel Kressel]

FRANKEL, SALLY HERBERT (1903–1996), South African economist. He was born and educated in Johannesburg, where he was professor of economics at Witwatersrand University from 1931 to 1946. He did research in maize marketing and government railway policy in South Africa, compiled calculations of the national income for the South African treasury (1941–48), and was a member of the Treasury Advisory Council (1941–45). Frankel investigated the railway system (1942) and mining industry (1945) for the Rhodesian government. In 1946 he was appointed professor of the economics of underdeveloped countries at Oxford. From 1953 to 1955 he was a member of the East African Royal Commission, and from 1957 to 1958 adviser to South Rhodesia's Urban African Affairs Commission. Frankel's publications include *Africa in the Re-Making* (1932), *Capital Investment in Africa* (1938), *Concept of Colonization* (1949), *Economic Impact on Underdeveloped Societies* (1953), *Some Conceptual Aspects of International Economic Development of Underdeveloped Territories* (1952), and *Investment and the Return to Equity Capital in the South African Gold Mining Industry, 1887–1965* (1967).

FRANKEL, SAMUEL BENJAMIN (1905–1996), U.S. naval officer. Born in Cincinnati, Ohio, Frankel graduated from the U.S. Naval Academy in 1929. He served on various U.S. warships in Nicaragua and in the Asiatic fleet between 1929 and 1936 before being sent to Riga, Latvia, to study Russian. During World War II he was assistant naval attaché at the United States embassy in Moscow and later assistant naval attaché for air in Murmansk-Archangel until 1944. He was sent to Pearl Harbor in 1945 to serve on the staff of the commander-in-chief of the United States Pacific Fleet and as officer in charge of the Joint Intelligence Center, Pacific Ocean Areas. In 1946 he served in the Office of the Chief of Naval Operations (Intelligence Division), assigned to the Central Intelligence Agency in Washington until 1948. He then served as naval attaché in Nanking, China. He remained in his post for a year after the Communist revolution before returning to the United States in 1950 to become director of the naval intelligence school. From 1953 to 1956 he was assistant head of naval intelligence in the Pacific fleet and was later a senior intelligence officer in the Navy Department in Washington, and promoted to rear admiral. In May 1960 Frankel became deputy director of naval intelligence and in the following year was appointed chief of staff of the Defense Intelligence Agency, a post he retained until his retirement in 1964.

Frankel was awarded the Distinguished Service Medal for his "exceptionally meritorious service" as assistant naval attaché in the U.S.S.R., in 1941–42; directing the repair and salvaging of damaged U.S. vessels; and helping in the rescue and repatriation of survivors of sunken ships. For several years Frankel served on the board of the Tolstoy Foundation, a New York-based organization dedicated to assisting displaced persons of Russian origin. In 1972 he retired to California, where he lectured on China and Russia at San Diego State University's Continuing Education Center of Rancho Bernardo.

[Ruth Beloff (2nd ed.)]

FRANKEL, WILLIAM (1917–), editor of the weekly **Jewish Chronicle*, published in London. Born in London, Frankel began his professional life as secretary of the British Mizrachi Federation. He was subsequently called to the Bar as a Member of the Middle Temple and practiced in London and on the South Eastern Circuit. In 1955 he was appointed the general manager of the *Jewish Chronicle* and two years later became its editor, a post he held until 1977. After his retirement, he remained a member of the Board of Directors of the *Jewish Chronicle* and became chairman in 1991. In 1971 he was appointed by the queen a commander of the Order of the British Empire. He wrote *Israel Observed* (1980) and was the editor of the annual *Survey of Jewish Affairs* from 1982 through 1992. Frankel also edited *Friday Nights* (1973), an anthology of important news as reported in the *Jewish Chronicle* from 1841 until 1971.

FRANKEL, YA'AKOV (1943–), Israeli economist. Frankel was born in Tel Aviv. In 1966 he received his B.A. degree in economics and political science from the Hebrew University of Jerusalem. He then received his M.A. in 1969 and Ph.D. in 1970 from the University of Chicago, both in economics. In 1971 he joined Tel Aviv University as a lecturer and in 1991 he became full professor. From 1994 he held the Wisefield Cathedra for Peace Economy and International Relations. From 1987 to 1991 he was chief economist and research director of the International Exchange Fund. He dealt with the debt problem of the developing countries and assisted states making the transition from a centralized to a market economy. In 1988 he joined the G-30 and from 2000 served as their chairman. In 1991 he was named governor of the Bank of Israel, a position he held until 2000. As governor he steered Israel into the global economy, liberalizing local money markets. He helped Israel stop inflation and achieve price stability, again making the country an attractive venue for investors. In 1991 he also joined the council of the G-7 and in 1992 he became a member of Ben-Gurion University's board. During 1995–96 he was the chairman of the board of governors of the American Bank for Rehabilitation and Development, while in 1999 he became deputy chairman of the board of governors of the European Bank for Rehabilitation and Development. From 2000 he was president of Merril Lynch and served as a member in the boards of Bar-Ilan and the Hebrew University. Frankel published over 300 articles and 18 books, including *The Monetary Approach to the Balance of Payments* (ed. with H.G. Johnson, 1976); *Exchange Rates and International Macroeconomics* (ed., 1983); *Fiscal Policies and the World Economy* (with A. Razin, 1987); *International Aspects of Fiscal Policies* (ed., 1988); and *The International Monetary System: Key Analytical Issues* (ed. with M. Goldstein, 1996). In 2003 he received the Israel Prize for his contribution in the field of economics.

WEBSITE: http://www.education.gov.il/pras-israel.

[Shaked Gilboa (2nd ed.)]

FRANKEL, ZACHARIAS (1801–1875), rabbi and scholar. Frankel was born in Prague. After receiving a talmudic education under Bezalel *Ronsburg, he studied philosophy, natural sciences, and philology in Budapest (1825–30). In 1831 the Austrian government appointed him district rabbi (*Keiserrabbiner*) of Leitmeritz (Litomerice) and he settled in Teppliz (Teplice) where he was elected local rabbi. He was one of the first rabbis to preach in German and express by that his positive attitude towards modernity and social integration of Jews within general society and culture. In 1836 he was called by the Saxon government to *Dresden to act as chief rabbi. The publication of his study on the Jewish *oath (see below) led to its abolition in several German states. He declined a call to Berlin in 1843, mainly because the Prussian government would not meet his stipulations (complete legal recognition of the Jewish faith – until then merely "tolerated"; denial to support to missionary activities among Jews, etc.). In 1845 he attended the second conference of Liberal rabbis in Frankfurt and advocated there a much more moderate-conservative approach than most of the participants to the issue of required reform in Judaism. He withdrew from the conference and broke his ties with Liberal rabbis once his direction was rejected and the conference adopted the idea of promoting both prayers and sermons in German rather than in Hebrew. In 1854, after having actively advocated its establishment, Frankel became director of the newly founded Juedisch-Theologisches Seminar (Jewish Theological Seminary) at Breslau, where he remained until his death.

Religious Outlook

As a theologian Frankel aimed at a synthesis between the traditional notion of Judaism as linear continuity anchored in divine revelation and based on Jewish law (*halakhah*) on the one hand and response to contemporary fundamental changes in the Jewish life on the other hand. He viewed Judaism as a dynamic balance between the Divine will, as expressed in the Torah, and the human response of the Jewish people, as manifested in the history of the Jewish people. This balance was articulated in the title he gave to the new denomination he established within Jewish life, namely "positive-historical" Judaism. The positive pole of this formulation referred both to the revealed-legalistic nature of Judaism and to its objective eternal and unchangeable content. The historic pole expressed the role Frankel ascribed to the human, ever-changing, and contextually dependent response of the Jewish community to this Divine content. Only the combination of these two poles determines what Judaism is and what is truly a *mitzvah*. The duty of the rabbis, as he understood it, was to combine loyalty to *halakhah* with sensitivity to the voice of *kelal yisrael* (the entire community or people of Israel). Frankel's approach thus led him to a rejection of both Reform and Orthodox notions of Judaism. In the Reform movement, led by Abraham *Geiger he saw both a negation of loyalty to Jewish law and the lack of genuine dialogue with the Jewish masses. The Reform rabbis mistakenly believed that they had the authority to determine Jewish dogma by themselves without taking popular sentiment and their way of life seriously into consideration. The Orthodox rabbis, led by S.R. *Hirsch, were criticized by him for not taking in account the historic dynamics and evolution of Judaism, and the need to free Judaism from its frozen state and irrelevance to current Jewish life. Both Reform and Orthodox ignored the very life of the *Volk*, the real source of authority for the work of the rabbi. It should be noted, that though Frankel wished to place himself at the "center," his critique of the Reform wing was much sharper and aggressive than that of Orthodoxy. The former were accused of transgressing Judaism altogether; the latter only of not properly relating to the current needs and concerns of the Jews. This imbalance represents the fact that it was Orthodoxy that designed for him the criteria for Jewish life, while his Reform counterparts were perceived as representing a much less urgent and acute challenge. Frankel promoted these ideas in his professional life in the way he designed the program of the Breslau seminary as well as in the kind of tendencies he developed within academic Jewish research (Wissenschaft des Jusentums). The Breslau seminary was the first modern institute for rabbinical education, combining clear emphasis on rabbinical studies – mainly in a traditional manner – with the study of the wider range of Jewish studies in connection with the local university. The unique nature of the Breslau seminary was questioned by Samson Raphael *Hirsch, who challenged Frankel, upon the seminary's opening, to state the religious principles that would guide instruction there. At the same time, Abraham Geiger criticized the seminary's classic method of talmudic instruction.

As a scholar Frankel focused on the study of rabbinic literature, presenting it as a human activity, reflecting its historical context, and hence a dynamic and open process of hermeneutics and adaptation of the Torah. By that he presented the rabbinic discourse and authority as the center of Jewish history and essence, in contrary to the Reform theologians and scholars who emphasized the Bible and theological discourse. At the same time Frankel presented the rabbis as the creators of Jewish legal tradition, in contrary to the traditional and Orthodox understanding of them as the carriers of the Divine oral law, revealed at Sinai. The "positive-historical" ("Breslau") school influenced later the *Conservative movement in the United States and served as its theoretical basis. In the controversy over the Hamburg prayer book (1841) and in his subsequent reply to the circular of the Hamburg preacher, Gotthold *Salomon (*Litteratur des Orients*, 3 (1842), nos. 23–24), he declared that only changes that were not in conflict with the spirit of historical Judaism should be permitted in the traditional ritual. He believed that the messianic belief, which expressed the "pious wish for the independence of the Jewish people" was of importance for the survival and development of Judaism, and that it brought a new spirit and vigor into the life of German Jews, even though "they already had fatherland which they would not leave." This statement and others express Frankel's deep devotion to Jewish peoplehood and national existence, a devotion not shared by Hirsch's neo-Orthodoxy or by contemporary Reform, but which was, in some ways, a precursor of later national Jewish thought. Frankel's monthly review, *Zeitschrift fuer die religioesen Interessen des Judentums* (1844–46), was a platform for his opinions. Frankel's view aroused opposition in both Reform and Orthodox quarters.

Works

Frankel's first work, on the Jewish oath, *Die Eidesleistung bei den Juden* (1840), arose out of a practical political need and was at the same time a pioneering attempt at scientific analysis of halakhic problems using the method of comparative jurisprudence. He further examined the question in *Der gerichtette Beweis nach talmdischem Rechte* (1846), a study of legal evidence according to talmudic law, and again in a series of articles in various periodicals: MGWJ, 2 (1853), 289–304, 329–47; 9 (1860), 321–31, 365–80, 406–16, 445–54; 16 (1857), 24–26, 70–72; and *Jahresbericht des Juedisch-Theologischen Seminars* (1860). Several of his works deal with the history of the oral tradition: in his first studies on the Septuagint, *Vorstudien zu der Septuaginta* (1841), he tried to show that traces of the Palestinian *halakhah* could be found in the Greek translation of the Bible; on this he based a further work on the influence of Palestinian exegesis on Alexandrian hermeneutics, *Ueber den Einfluss der palestinischen Exegese auf die Alexandrische Hermeutik* (1851). He published his research into the methodology of the Mishnah and the Talmud in *Darkhei ha-Mishnah* (1859; with supplement and index, 1867; new ed. 1923), which exercised a decisive influence on further research on the Mishnah. On the publication of that book Hirsch attacked him in his periodical *Jeschurun* in a series of critical essays in which he demanded that Frankel give a precise exposition of his views on rabbinical tradition and the revelation at Mount Sinai, an attack that was supported by a long line of other Orthodox rabbis. Confining himself to a brief statement in his journal, *Monatschrift fuer Geschichte und Wissenschaft des Judentums* (vol. 10 (1861), 159–60), Frankel stressed that it was not his purpose to dispute the worth of rabbinical tradition or to deny its antiquity, adding that the question as to which of its halakhic elements were to be considered of Mosaic origin was not yet resolved. Further scholarly works of Frankel are his *Mevo ha-Yerushalmi* (1870), an introduction to the Jerusalem Talmud. He also wrote *Ahavat Ziyyon*, a commentary to several tractates of the Jerusalem Talmud (*Berakhot*, *Pe'ah* 1847; *Demai* 1875), and *Entwurf einer Geschichte des Literatur der nachtalmudschen Responsen* (1865), the outline for a history of post-talmudic responsa literature. In 1851 he founded the scholarly journal *Monatschrift fuer Geschichte und Wissenschaft des Judentums*, editing it for 17 years and publishing numerous articles on Jewish cultural history. In the Breslau seminary, Frankel set the standards for modern rabbinical training, and his curriculum of study and the qualifications he established for both students and lecturers were adopted by all similar institutions.

ADD. BIBLIOGRAPHY: M. Brann, Verzeichtnis der Schriften und Abhandlungen Zacharias Frankel, in: M. Brann (ed.), *Zacharias Frankel, Gedenblaetter zu seinem hundersten Geburtstag* (1901), 144–160; R. Horwitz, *Zecharia Frankel ve-Reshit ha-Yahadut ha-Positivit Historit* (Zacharias Frankel and the Beginnings of Positive-Historical Judaism; 1984); A. Braemer, *Rabbiner Zacharias Frankel – Wissenschaft des Judentums und konservative Reform im 19. Jahrhundert* (2000; Netiva – Wege deutsch-juedischer Geschichte und Kultur; Studien des Salomon Ludwig Steinheim-Instituts, ed. Michael Brocke, 3) [biography, incl. full bibliography of Frankel's published and unpublished writings]; idem, "The Dilemmas of Moderate Reform – Some Reflections on the Development of Conservative Judaism in Germany 1840–1880," in: *Jewish Studies Quarterly*, 10:1 (2003), 73–87; M. Meyer, *Response to Modernity* (1988), 84–89 and index; I. Schorsch, "Zacharias Frankel and the European Origins of Conservative Judaism", in: *From Text to Context – The Turn to History in Modern Judaism* (1994), 255–265; E. Schweid, *Toledot Filosofiyyat ha-Dat ha-Yehudit ba-Zeman he-Ḥadash*, vol. 2 (2002), 144–56.

[Joseph Elijah Heller / Yehoyada Amir (2nd ed.)]

FRANKEN, ROSE DOROTHY LEWIN (1895–1988), U.S. playwright, director, fiction writer, and screenwriter. Franken was born in Gainesville, Texas, but grew up in New York City. The 450 performances of her play, *Another Language*, set a record for a first play. Burns Mantle, editor of the authoritative *Best Plays* yearbook, selected *Another Language* as one of the ten best of the 1931–32 season. Three more of Franken's plays subsequently won that distinction: *Claudia* (1940–41), *Outrageous Fortune* (1943–44), and *Soldier's Wife* (1944–45).

Franken was best known for the *Claudia* stories. Launched in 1939 as a series in *Redbook Magazine,* Claudia became the subject of seven novels, a radio series, two films, and a play. Directed by the author, it had a run of 722 performances in 1941–43. Claudia is a naïve young woman who only after marriage begins to recognize her ability to cope with adult responsibilities and adversities. *Claudia*'s subtitle, "The Story of a Marriage," points to Franken's predominant concerns. Her work captures the rapidly shifting mores of American society in the World War II years, seen through the eyes of women looking anew at their capabilities and desire for independence.

Another Language is the story of a rebellious woman in a family dominated by an authoritarian mother who keeps her sons and all but one of her obedient daughters-in-law on a short leash. Although the ethnicity of the Hallam family is unspecified, their ethnocentricity, gender roles, male professions, women's pastimes, and the materfamilias' attitudes about eating strongly suggest that they are middle-class Jews. Franken is more specific in *Outrageous Fortune*. This work, daring for its time, protests antisemitism and homophobia and deals forthrightly with the discontent spawned within middle-class Jewish clannishness. In the aptly titled *Soldier's Wife,* the eponym quite unintentionally becomes a successful writer during her husband's absence. Upon his return from military service, she chooses to give up her new career in deference to the domestic lifestyle of a conventional marriage, while acknowledging that "there's going to be a lot of money and success and independence in women that there's never been before."

Franken's work reflects her personal struggle with traditional gender roles and her ambivalence about balancing domestic and career commitments. Although her heroine in *Doctors Disagree* (1943) overcomes both her male colleagues' anti-feminism and other women's anti-professionalism, Franken confided in her autobiography a preference for "a traditional physician of the masculine sex." She often denied harboring any interests more urgent or fulfilling than home, husband, and her three sons, and claimed she wrote only for something to do while the children napped and a cake baked. She relinquished an opportunity for a Barnard College education in 1913 to marry Dr. Sigmund Franken, a dentist, who actively encouraged her writing. After his death in 1932, she pursued her writing career in Hollywood. In 1947, she married William Brown Meloney, a writer who produced her plays and collaborated with her on several serialized stories in popular magazines.

Not all of Franken's nine plays were produced. In addition to her eight novels and film scripts for Twentieth Century Fox and Samuel Goldwyn, she wrote her autobiography, *When All Is Said and Done* (1963).

BIBLIOGRAPHY: *Notable Women in the American Theatre* (1989).

[Ellen Schiff (2nd ed.)]

FRANKENBURGER, WOLF (1827–1889), lawyer and politician in Germany. Born at Obbach in Bavaria and educated in Wuerzburg, where he took an active part in the 1848 agitation. He settled in Nuremberg in 1861 to practice law. Frankenburger was first elected to the Bavarian diet in 1869 and remained a member until the end of his life. From 1874 to 1878 he was also the representative for Nuremberg in the German Reichstag. The first motion he proposed in the assembly was for freedom of the press and freedom of sale of literature. Frankenburger managed to obtain the abolition of the Jewish taxes then still in force in Bavaria and also obtained a salary increase for the poorly endowed rabbinical posts. Frankenburger was an eloquent advocate of the union of Bavaria with the German Empire and received from the Bavarian king the Class 1 Michaelisorden for his activities.

BIBLIOGRAPHY: A. Eckstein, *Beitraege zur Geschichte der Juden in Bayern – Die bayerischen Parlamentarier juedischen Glaubens* (1902), 23–33; E. Hamburger, *Juden im oeffentlichen Leben Deutschlands* (1968). **ADD. BIBLIOGRAPHY:** P. Müller, *Liberalismus in Nürnberg 1800–1871 – Eine Fallstudie zur Ideen- und Sozialgeschichte des Liberalismus in Deutschland im 19. Jahrhundert* (1990).

[B. Mordechai Ansbacher / Bjoern Siegel (2nd ed.)]

FRANKENHEIMER, JOHN MICHAEL (1930–2002), U.S. director. Born in New York City of Catholic-Jewish parentage, Frankenheimer graduated from La Salle Military Academy (1947). He wanted to be an actor, but when he was accepted into the Motion Picture Squadron of the Air Force, he discovered that his real skill lay behind the camera. He was a director for CBS television (1953–60), producing, among other programs, *The Turn of the Screw* and *Days of Wine and Roses.* He directed a total of 152 live television shows between 1954 and 1960, including such series as *Climax!* and *Playhouse 90.* Frankenheimer, who thoroughly enjoyed directing live television, was one of the first TV directors to use multiple camera angles, a moving camera, quick editing, and close-ups.

Ultimately, however, he became a successful director of feature films on the big screen. Through his movies, he used the opportunity to express his views on significant social and philosophical issues. Frankenheimer's films include *The Young Stranger* (1957); *The Young Savages* (1961); *All Fall Down* (1962); *Birdman of Alcatraz* (1962); *The Manchurian Candidate* (1962); *The Train* (1964); *Seven Days in May* (1964); *Grand Prix* (1966); *The Fixer* (1968); *The Gypsy Moths* (1969); *The Horsemen* (1971); *The Iceman Cometh* (1973); *The French Connection II* (1975); *Black Sunday* (1977); *Year of the Gun* (1991); *The Island of Dr. Moreau* (1996); *Ronin* (1998); *Reindeer Games* (2000); and *The Hire: Ambush* (2001). At the same time he produced and directed such TV fare as *The Rainmaker* (1982); *The Burning Season* (1994); *Andersonville* (1996); *George Wallace* (1997); and *Paths to War* (2002). During his career, he won four Emmy awards and was nominated for nine others.

In 2002 he was inducted into the Television Hall of Fame.

ADD. BIBLIOGRAPHY: G. Pratley, *The Cinema of John Frankenheimer* (1969); G. Pratley, *The Films of Frankenheimer: Forty Years in Film* (1998).

[Jonathan Licht / Ruth Beloff (2nd ed.)]

FRANKENSTEIN, CARL (1905–1990), Israeli psychologist and educator. Born in Berlin, he founded the Aid Society for Jewish Scientists, Artists, and Writers in Germany in 1928. Settling in Palestine in 1935, Frankenstein worked as probation officer of the Mandatory government until 1946. From 1948 to 1953 he was director of the Henrietta Szold Institute for Child Welfare, where he also founded and edited the education quarterly, *Megammot*. In 1951 Frankenstein began to teach at the Hebrew University first as a lecturer and later as professor of special education. He served on many government, municipal, and other public committees dealing with problems of welfare and education. In 1968 he was awarded the Israel Prize for education. He wrote books and essays in Hebrew, English, and German on depth psychology, juvenile delinquency, poverty, and impaired intelligence, including *Azuvat ha-Noʿar* ("Neglected Youth," 1947), *Psychopathy* (1959), *Persoenlichkeitswandel durch Fuersorge, Erziehung und Therapie* (1964), *The Roots of the Ego* (1966), *Psychodynamics of Externalization* (1968), *Varieties of Juvenile Delinquency* (1970), *They Think Again: Restoring Cognitive Abilities through Teaching* (1981), and *Between Philosophy and Psychotherapy* (1987).

BIBLIOGRAPHY: *Megammot*, 14 (1966), nos. 1–3 (articles on the occasion of Frankenstein's 60th birthday; in Hebrew, with English summaries).

[Zvi Lamm]

FRANKENTHAL, KÄTE (1889–1976), German physician and socialist politician. Born in Kiel, Frankenthal attended university against her parents' wishes. After passing her Abitur examination at the age of 20, she matriculated at the University of Kiel, and then studied in Heidelberg, Erlangen, Munich, and Vienna, before completing her doctorate in medicine in Freiburg in 1914. After the war broke out, she accepted a residency at a large Berlin hospital, but soon decided to take a position as a rural doctor, replacing a man who had been drafted into the army. Frankenthal applied for a job as a military physician; since the German army accepted women only as nurses, she volunteered for the Austrian army instead and served in the Carpathian Mountains and then on the Balkan front, where she was the only woman in the barracks. Towards the end of the war, Frankenthal returned to Berlin, where she worked at the Charité Hospital as an unpaid research assistant at the Institute for Cancer Research and as a resident directing a women's ward and treating tuberculosis patients in a clinic. In 1924, when women physicians were dismissed from their positions at the Charité to make room for war veterans, Frankenthal continued to do research in the Pathological Institute and to work in the University Women's Clinic as well as run a private practice.

An active member of the Social Democratic Party, Frankenthal ran a first aid station helping the injured in the 1919 civil war, working with other medics under a Red Cross flag. She campaigned for sex reform legislation in Germany, advocating rescinding the laws against abortion and homosexuality and promoting the establishment of marital counseling bureaus to provide sex education and birth control advice. In 1928, she gave up her busy medical practice to become the municipal physician for the working-class district of Berlin-Neukoelln. Frankenthal played a prominent role in both the Federation of Women Physicians and the Association of Socialist Physicians in Germany. She served as a Social Democratic municipal deputy representing the Tiergarten district in the Berlin City Council from 1925 to 1931 and was elected to the Prussian Landtag in 1930. In 1931, she left the German Social Democratic Party and joined the more leftist Socialist Workers Party, briefly serving on its executive board. Dismissed from her job in March 1933, Frankenthal escaped arrest for her political activities by fleeing to Prague, and later to Switzerland and Paris, before immigrating to the United States in 1936. After requalifying as a physician and training as a psychoanalyst, she eventually set up a private psychoanalytic practice in New York, specializing in marriage counseling and family therapy. In 1974, the City of Berlin honored Käte Frankenthal on the occasion of her 85th birthday. Her autobiography, *Der dreifache Fluch: Juedin, Intellektuelle, Sozialistin*, was published in 1981.

BIBLIOGRAPHY: *Encyclopedia of Jewish Women* (CD-ROM, 2005); H. Pass Freidenreich, *Female, Jewish, and Educated: The Lives of Central European University Women* (2002).

[Harriet Pass Freidenreich (2nd ed.)]

FRANKENTHALER, GEORGE (1886–1968), U.S. lawyer and arbitrator, Frankenthaler practiced law with his brother ALFRED (1881–1940) and in 1944 served for one year as justice in the New York Supreme Court. From 1948 to 1956 he was surrogate of New York County, the first Jew to hold this office and the first and last Republican ever elected to that position. He achieved distinction as an arbitrator in a strike of New York elevator operators and became a permanent arbitrator for that industry.

FRANKENTHALER, HELEN (1928–), U.S. painter and printmaker. Known as one of the most important artists of the second generation of Abstract Expressionists, New York-born Helen Frankenthaler earned a B.A. from Bennington College (1946–49), after which she returned to New York City. For three weeks in the summer of 1950, she studied with the avant-garde painter and teacher Hans Hoffman in Provincetown, Massachusetts. She first won public recognition after the influential art critic Clement *Greenberg selected her for a New Talent Show at the Kootz Gallery in December 1950. She had a small solo exhibition at the Tibor de Nagy Gallery the following year.

Employing thinned-down oil paint on an unprimed canvas, *Mountains and Sea* (1952) found Frankenthaler's signature style when she was only 23 years old after several years of experimenting with Cubist- and Surrealist-inspired imagery. Influenced by Jackson Pollock, Frankenthaler eschewed the paintbrush and the easel, instead placing a canvas on the floor and pouring pigment from coffee cans on the canvas. Known as stain painting, this watercolor-like technique emphasized the flat canvas while suggesting moods that are often described as lyrical. The importance of *Mountain and Sea* transcends Frankenthaler's own development as the canvas is well known for influencing Morris *Louis and Kenneth Noland; after seeing the painting in 1953 both artists adopted a staining technique. Although her paintings are abstract, they often find inspiration from reality; she painted *Mountains and Sea*, for example, after seeing the cliffs of Nova Scotia on a trip with Greenberg.

Her first retrospective exhibition was held at the Jewish Museum in 1960. Among the paintings shown there was *Jacob's Ladder* (1957, Museum of Modern Art, New York), a 9½ by nearly 6-foot abstract canvas soaked with floating colors that won first prize at the First Biennale de Paris in 1959. Among other venues, retrospectives have been held at the Whitney Museum of American Art (1969) and New York's Museum of Modern Art (1989).

In addition to painting, Frankenthaler has illustrated books, welded steel sculpture and made prints. Indeed, printmaking plays a significant yet underrated role in Frankenthaler's oeuvre. As innovative a printmaker as a painter, Frankenthaler made lithographs, screenprints, etchings, and woodcuts. From her first published print in 1961, a lithograph appropriately titled *First Stone*, Frankenthaler integrated abstraction, mostly through fluid lines rather than the rigid marks typical of printmakers, with her vital use of color to create 235 prints between 1961 and 1995.

BIBLIOGRAPHY: B. Rose, *Frankenthaler* (1979); J. Elderfield, *Frankenthaler* (1989); P. Harrison, *Frankenthaler: A Catalogue Raisonné, Prints 1961–1994* (1996); H. Frankenthaler, *After Mountains and Sea: Frankenthaler 1956–1959* (1998).

[Samantha Baskind (2nd ed.)]

FRANKFORT, HENRI (1897–1954), excavator, teacher, and author in the field of Near Eastern archaeology. Frankfort, who was born in Amsterdam, was concerned with the archaeology, culture, and religion of the entire Middle East. His wide-ranging scholarship enabled him to comprehend the ancient Near Eastern cultures in their totality, with a special awareness of their common features as well as the peculiarities of each. After studying in England with the great archaeologist W.M. Flinders *Petrie, Frankfort returned to Holland and received his Ph.D. at Leiden. He seems to have flirted briefly with Zionism but was generally uninterested in Judaism. (His mother perished in the Holocaust.) Frankfort participated in excavations at el-Amarna, Abydos, and Armant in Egypt, and at Tell Asmar, Khafaje, and Khorsabad in Mesopotamia. From 1932 to 1938 he was also professor at the University of Amsterdam and from 1939 to 1949 he was professor at the Oriental Institute of the University of Chicago. In the last phase of his career, Frankfort produced "cultural syntheses," namely, *The Intellectual Adventure of Ancient Man, An Essay on Speculative Thought in the Ancient Near East* (with others, 1946; abridged by the elimination of the chapter on the Hebrews, republished as *Before Philosophy*, 1951). Frankfort's wife, Henriette Groenwegen Frankfort, collaborated with him in this project.; *Kingship and the Gods, A Study of Ancient Near Eastern Religion as the Integration of Society and Nature* (1948, 1955[2]); *The Birth of Civilisation in the Near East* (1951); and *The Art and Architecture of the Ancient Orient* (1954). During this phase he returned to Europe and became director of the Warburg Institute and professor of pre-classical antiquity at the University of London. Thus, Frankfort's development began with the treatment of excavated materials, progressed to classification and interpretation of Near Eastern archaeological remains (the *Cylinder Seals…*, 1939), and culminated in a cultural-historical-archaeological interpretation of these early civilizations.

BIBLIOGRAPHY: P. Delougaz and T. Jacobsen, in: *JNES*, 14 (1955), 1–4 (incl. bibl. and photograph). **ADD. BIBLIOGRAPHY:** A. Joffe, in: JNES, 57 (1998), 232–34; D. Wengrow, *American Journal of Archaeology* (1999), 597–613.

[Penuel P. Kahane / S. David Sperling (2nd ed.)]

FRANKFURTER, DAVID (1909–1982), student of medicine who shot a Nazi official in protest against the persecution of Jews under the Nazi regime. The son of a rabbi, Frankfurter was born in Daruvar, Croatia (Yugoslavia). While studying in Germany, he witnessed the Nazi advent to power and the initiation of anti-Jewish measures. He left Germany and continued his studies in Switzerland. On Feb. 4, 1936, he shot and killed Wilhelm Gustloff, the leader of the Swiss branch of the Nazi party. A local court sentenced him to 18 years imprisonment, of which he served nearly nine. He was pardoned after the Nazi defeat but was banished forever from Switzerland. He settled in Israel and published a book about his experience, *Nakam* ("Vengeance," 1948). In 1969 the banishment order was rescinded and Frankfurter visited Switzerland. In Israel he worked for the Ministry of Defense.

BIBLIOGRAPHY: E. Ludwig, *Davos Murder* (1937).

[Yehuda Reshef]

FRANKFURTER, FELIX (1882–1965), U.S. jurist. Frankfurter, who was born in Vienna, was taken to the United States at the age of 12. His parents settled on the Lower East Side of New York, where his father, scion of a long line of rabbis, was a modest tradesman.

Early Years

Frankfurter graduated with distinction from the College of the City of New York in 1902; his real education, however, as he liked to recount, was derived from the books and newspapers that he devoured at the Public Library, Cooper Union, and the coffee shops of the city. Throughout his life he had a compulsive passion for reading, and he regularly scanned the newspapers of several continents. These he absorbed in no merely passive spirit; he came to have a wide acquaintance among journalists and publishers, and frequently he would pepper them with notes of compliment or rebuke. At Harvard Law School, from which he received his degree in 1906, Frankfurter developed his deep, indeed reverent, attachment to the values of the Anglo-American system of government under law, and as the leading student in his class found new horizons of achievement opened to him. On the recommendation of Dean Ames of Harvard Law School, he was invited by Henry L. Stimson, then United States Attorney in New York, to become an assistant in that office. Henceforth his professional life was divided between public service and teaching. The association with Stimson was one of the most significant experiences in Frankfurter's life, constituting living proof for him that the effective enforcement of the criminal law need not compromise the scrupulous standards of procedural decency that are encompassed in the guarantee of due process of law. When Stimson was appointed secretary of war in the administration of President Taft, Frankfurter became his personal assistant, with special responsibility for the legal affairs of overseas territories of the United States and the conservation of water resources. At this time his friendship began with Justice Oliver Wendell Holmes of the Supreme Court, which became a deep intellectual discipleship despite their disparity in background and temperament. Frankfurter admired not merely the style of Holmes – learning worn with grace – but his fastidiousness of mind and disinterestedness of judgment; and they shared an ardent love of country, instilled in the one by arduous service in the Civil War, in the other by the experience of seeing the vistas of opportunity opened to a gifted immigrant boy.

Professor and Public Servant

In 1914 Frankfurter accepted an appointment to a professorship at Harvard Law School, which he held until his appointment to the Supreme Court 25 years later. As a teacher and scholar he concentrated on the procedural aspects of law – the administration of criminal justice, the jurisdiction of the federal courts, the process of administrative tribunals, and the ill-starred use of the injunction in labor disputes. He earned a reputation as a radical reformer, but his concern was for the integrity of the law's processes, upon which a reasoned approach to the maintenance of a just society depended. Misunderstanding of his concern – its mistaken identification with the particular causes that motivated the victims of injustice – led some observers to conclude that Frankfurter was a radical who became a conservative on the bench. During World War I Frankfurter was called to Washington as legal officer of the President's Mediation Commission, charged with investigating and resolving serious labor disturbances. In that capacity he inquired into the vigilante action against strikers in the Arizona copper mines, finding that the companies' refusal to accept unionism was the root cause of the troubles, and he investigated the conviction of Tom Mooney on a bombing charge in California, finding that the trial had been vitiated by improper tactics of the prosecution. These were a forerunner of Frankfurter's involvement in the Sacco-Vanzetti murder case in Boston, the most bitter experience in his life, in which he fought unsuccessfully to have the verdict set aside on grounds of prejudicial conduct by the trial judge and prosecuting attorney, and thereby provoked against himself the burning hostility of the entrenched interests in the community. He was one of the founders of the American Civil Liberties Union, a legal adviser to the National Association for the Advancement of Colored People, and counsel to the National Consumers' League.

Zionist

Frankfurter became closely associated with Louis D. *Brandeis, who practiced law in Boston until his appointment to the Supreme Court in 1916. This association brought Frankfurter deeply into the Zionist movement, and in 1919 he went to Paris with the Zionist delegation to the peace conference. Through T.E. Lawrence he met Emir Feisal, head of the Arab delegation, and in consequence of their talks he received from Feisal the historic letter of 1st March, 1919, stating that the Arab delegation regarded the Zionist proposal as "moderate and proper," that they "will wish the Jews a most hearty welcome home," and that the "two movements complete one another" and "neither can be a real success without the other." In 1921 Frankfurter withdrew from formal participation in the Zionist movement, when the Brandeis-Mack-Szold group seceded over issues of organization and fiscal autonomy for American Zionism. Thereafter, nevertheless, he maintained his active interest in the upbuilding of the Jewish national home in Palestine, and in 1931, disturbed by the tendency of Britain to shirk its responsibility as the mandatory power, he published a notable and much-cited critical article in *Foreign Affairs* (9 (1931), 409–34), entitled "The Palestine Situation Restated." Despite the break with the formal Zionist organization, his relations with Weizmann remained cordial.

In Politics

In politics Frankfurter was more concerned with men and policies than with party labels. He served under Stimson in a Republican administration, was an admirer of Theodore Roosevelt, and in 1924 supported Robert M. La-Follette, the Progressive third-party candidate, for the presidency. In 1928 he campaigned for Alfred E. Smith, to whom he had been an informal adviser on problems of public-utility regulation when Smith was governor of New York. In 1932, quite predictably, he warmly supported Franklin D. Roosevelt. Roosevelt, as assistant secretary of the Navy, served with Frankfurter on an interdepartmental board concerned with wartime labor relations. When Roosevelt became governor of New York, he called on Frankfurter for counsel, and upon his election as president, Roosevelt asked Frankfurter to become solicitor general, intimating that if he held this post it would be easier to appoint him in due course to the Supreme Court. Frankfurter declined, however, on the ground that he could be more useful to the President's program without an official place in the administration. He continued to teach at Harvard while advising Roosevelt on certain appointments and lending a hand in speech writing and in the drafting of legislation, notably in relation to the regulation of securities and the stock exchange. When, in 1938, Justice Benjamin N. *Cardozo died, there was widespread sentiment that by virtue of intellect and philosophy – not for reasons of religion – Frankfurter was the rightful successor to this chair, which had been occupied before Cardozo by Justice Holmes. Disregarding the advice of some timorous Jewish friends who pointed to the fact that Justice Brandeis was still on the Court, Roosevelt made the nomination, which was confirmed on January 17, 1939.

Supreme Court Justice

Upon assuming judicial office, Frankfurter's roving commission in law and public affairs was ended, but the gravity of the world situation made it impossible for him to become a judicial recluse. He had recognized the menace of Hitler before most of his compatriots, and when war came, his insight, experience, and judgment were drawn upon. Perhaps his most notable service in this regard was his recommendation of his old mentor, Henry L. Stimson, to be secretary of war. As a judge Frankfurter conceived his role to be more complex than that of a teacher or publicist, since a judge on the Supreme Court must subordinate his merely personal views when judging the validity of the acts of a coordinate branch of government. He rejected the claims of absolutism for even the most cherished liberties of speech, assembly, and religious belief, maintaining that they must be weighed against the legitimate concerns of society expressed through government. When those concerns were relatively tenuous or could be satisfied in a less intrusive way, the liberty of the individual must prevail. Thus when a state attorney general conducted an investigation into the teaching of a college lecturer, Frankfurter wrote a powerful opinion upholding the sanctity of the university classroom against the threat of domination by the state (*Sweezy* v. *New Hampshire*, 354 U.S. 234 (1957)). When a school board introduced released-time instruction in religion in the public schools, on a voluntary basis, Frankfurter joined in condemning the program as a breach of the "wall of separation" between church and state (*Mc-Collum v. Board of Education*, 333 U.S. 203 (1948)). But when a compulsory flag-salute exercise in the public schools was resisted by Jehovah's Witnesses as a profanation of their religious tenets, Frankfurter concluded that the government had not gone beyond permissible bounds in seeking to inculcate loyalty and national pride in schoolchildren (*West Virginia State Board of Education* v. *Barnette*, 319 U.S. 624 (1943)). His dissenting opinion begins with his most explicit and deeply felt statement of his judicial philosophy in the troubled area of individual freedom:

> One who belongs to the most vilified and persecuted minority in history is not likely to be insensible to the freedom guaranteed by our Constitution. Were my purely personal attitude relevant I should wholeheartedly associate myself with the general libertarian views in the Court's opinion, representing as they do the thought and action of a lifetime.

But as judges we are neither Jew nor gentile, neither Catholic nor agnostic. We owe equal attachment to the Constitution and are equally bound by our judicial obligations whether we derive our citizenship from the earliest or the latest immigrants to these shores. As a member of this Court I am not justified in writing my private notions of policy into the Constitution, no matter how deeply I may cherish them or how mischievous I may deem their disregard.... The only opinion of our own even looking in that direction that is material is our opinion whether legislators could in reason have enacted such a law.

He joined wholeheartedly in the decisions holding legally segregated public schools to be a denial of equal protection of the laws (*Cooper* v. *Aaron*, 358 U.S. 1 (1958)). But in another pathbreaking action of the Court, upsetting malapportionment in legislatures, he dissented vigorously, on the ground that the courts were entering a "political thicket" that would enmesh them in party politics (*Baker* v. *Carr*, 369 U.S. 186 (1962)).

Retrospect

In 1962 Frankfurter suffered a stroke, and resigned from the Court. Though invalided, he was able the following year to receive the Presidential Medal of Freedom, the highest civilian honor within the bestowal of the President. The citation read: "Jurist, scholar, counselor, conversationalist, he has brought to all his roles a zest and a wisdom which has made him teacher to his time." The citation suggested the many-sided liveliness of the man, but could not capture the full measure of what he liked to call the Blue Danube side of his nature: the bouncy step, the love of argumentation, the steely grip on his interlocutor's elbow, the roars of laughter, what Dean Acheson called affectionately the "general noisiness" of the man. Nor could the citation capture his astonishing range of friendships, which embraced statesmen, scholars, artists, former students, and writers around the world. His correspondence was prodigious. He was refreshed by uninhibited communication as others are refreshed by solitude. Although not an observing Jew ("a believing unbeliever," he called himself), he retained a familiarity with Jewish lore, and toward the end of his life he felt drawn closer to his heritage.

Writings

Frankfurter's own talk and writings of interest to the general reader include: *Felix Frankfurter Reminisces* (1960); *Law and Politics* (1939); *Of Law and Men* (1956); *Of Law and Life* (1965); *Roosevelt and Frankfurter; their Correspondence 1928–1945; Felix Frankfurter on the Supreme Court* (1970).

BIBLIOGRAPHY: H.S. Thomas, *Felix Frankfurter: Scholar on the Bench* (1960); L. Baker, *Felix Frankfurter* (1969); W. Mendelson (ed.), *Felix Frankfurter: A Tribute* (1964); idem, *Felix Frankfurter: The Judge* (1964); Jaffe, in: *Harvard Law Review*, 62 (1949), 357–412; P.A.

Freund, *On Law and Justice* (1968), 146–62; For further bibliography see R. Dahl and C. Bolden (eds.), *American Judge* (1968), nos. 4274–92 and 6366–437; P.B. Kurland, *Felix Frankfurter on the Supreme Court* (1970). **ADD. BIBLIOGRAPHY:** J.D. Hockett, R.E. Morgan, and G.J. Jacobsohn (eds.), *New Deal Justice: The Constitutional Jurisprudence of Hugo L. Black, Felix Frankfurter, and Robert H. Jackson* (1996); J.F. Simon, *Antagonists: Hugo Black, Felix Frankfurter and Civil Liberties in Modern America* (1989); N.L. Dawson, *Louis D. Brandeis, Felix Frankfurter and the New Deal* (1980; M.I. Urofsky, *Felix Frankfurter: Judicial Restraint and Individual Liberties* (1991).

[Paul A. Freund]

FRANKFURTER, MOSES (1672–1762), author, *dayyan*, and printer in Amsterdam. Moses, the son of Simeon, established a printing press in 1721 from which he issued books both in Hebrew and Yiddish. He later moved to Frankfurt where he died. Frankfurter wrote *Nefesh Yehudah* (1701), a commentary on Isaac Aboab's *Menorat ha-Ma'or* with a Yiddish translation of the text. This very popular tract was often reprinted, as was *Sheva Petilot* (1721), an abbreviated version of the same work. Frankfurter translated into Yiddish and published his father's *Sefer ha-Ḥayyim* (1712). From it he compiled *Sha'ar Shimon* (1714), prayers for the sick, in two parts, the second in Yiddish. He also wrote *Zeh Yenaḥamenu* (1712), a commentary on the *Mekhilta de-R. Ishmael*. When Frankfurter was in serious distress he sought comfort in dedicating himself to the laborious task of correcting the text and commenting upon it. He also wrote *Tov Lekhet*, notes to the law of mourning of the Shulḥan Arukh, *Yoreh De'ah* (1746); *Ba'er Heitev*, glosses to the Shulḥan Arukh; *Ḥoshen Mishpat* (1749), patterned after Judah b. Simeon Ashkenazi's *Ba'er Heitev* (1736–42) on the other three parts of the Shulḥan Arukh. Frankfurter edited several works, the most important being a new edition of the rabbinic Bible *Mikra'ot Gedolot* (4 vols., Amsterdam, 1724–27), adding 16 previously unpublished commentaries on the various books of the Bible including his own commentary under the title *Kehillat Moshe*; another group of this compilation interpreting the whole Bible is *Komeẓ Minḥah, Minḥah Ketannah, Minḥah Gedolah*, and *Minḥat Erev*.

BIBLIOGRAPHY: M. Horovitz, *Frankfurter Rabbinen*, 2 (1883), 74f.

[Jacob Hirsch Haberman]

FRANKFURTER, SOLOMON FRIEDRICH (1856–1941), Austrian librarian, pedagogue, and classical philologist. Frankfurter was born in Pressburg and moved with his family to Vienna in 1859. In 1881 he began working as a volunteer at the University of Vienna library, where from 1919 to 1923 he served as director. In 1909 he was been appointed the first Jewish consultant on Jewish community questions to the Austrian Ministry of Culture and Education. Frankfurter was president of the Society for the Collection and Investigation of Jewish Historic Monuments, president of the B'nai B'rith, and member or consultant of many boards responsible for Jewish education and religion. He served briefly as director of the Vienna Jewish Museum, but also acted as an advisor. From 1934 to 1938 he was the only Jewish member of the Austrian Bundes-Kulturrat (Federal Board for Cultural Questions). When the Nazis invaded Austria (1938), he was arrested, but was released shortly afterwards.

Frankfurter's publications deal with archaeology; education, particularly the important role of a classical gymnasium education; biographies; and Jewish subjects. His works include *Unrichtige Buechertitel mit einem Exkurs ueber hebraeische Buechertitel* (1906); *Das altjuedische Erziehungs-und Unterrichtswesen im Lichte moderner Bestrebungen* (1910); *Josef Unger 1828–1857* (1917), dealing with Unger's youth; and *Zwei neugefundene mittelalterliche hebraeische Grabsteine in Wien* (1918).

U.S. Supreme Court Justice Felix *Frankfurter was his nephew.

ADD. BIBLIOGRAPHY: N.H. Tur-Sinai, "Viennese Jewry," in: J. Fraenkel (ed.), *The Jews of Austria: Essays on their Life, History and Destruction* (1967), 315; L. Kolb, "The Vienna Jewish Museum," in: *ibid.*, 149.

FRANKFURT ON THE MAIN (Heb. פרנקפורט דמיין; abbr. פפד"מ), city in Germany with an ancient and important community.

Early History

Reports and legends about Jews residing in Frankfurt go back to the earliest period in the city's history. Frankfurt was an important trading center, and Jewish merchants probably visited its annual fall fairs. In 1074 Emperor Henry IV mentions Frankfurt among the towns where the Jews of *Worms were permitted to trade without having to pay customs dues. During the 12th century Frankfurt had an organized and flourishing community, though still numerically small. Financial transactions and tax payments by Frankfurt Jews at that time are frequently mentioned: *Eliezer b. Nathan of Mainz makes repeated reference to the presence of Jewish merchants in Frankfurt. In 1241 the Jewish houses were demolished by the populace and over three-quarters of the approximately 200 Jews of Frankfurt were massacred. Among the victims were three rabbis, including the *ḥazzan*; many of the survivors accepted baptism. A special prayer for the martyrs has been retained in the liturgy for the Ninth of Av of the West German congregations. Subsequently Frederick II appointed a commission of inquiry, since the outbreak was an infringement of his imperial prerogative and interests. It apparently originated in a dispute over the forced conversion of a Jew. The city of Frankfurt was ultimately granted a royal pardon. The safety of the Frankfurt Jews was guaranteed and heavy penalties were ordered against Jew-baiters.

By around 1270 Frankfurt had again become a busy center of Jewish life. Two Jewish tombstones dated 1284 were found under the altar of the cathedral in 1952. During the following decades all the customary Jewish institutions developed in Frankfurt. The medieval community had a central synagogue ("Altschul"), a cemetery, a bathhouse, hospitals for local Jews and migrants, a "dance house" for weddings and other social events, and educational and welfare institutions. During the first half of the 14th century the financial burden on the Frankfurt community, exploited by both the city and the crown, grew steadily greater, but the profit derived from the Jews protected them against the current waves of persecution. However, the surge of bloodthirsty hatred aroused by the *Black Death engulfed them along with almost all the other communities in Europe. In 1349, shortly after Emperor *Charles IV had transferred his "Jewish rights" to the city against a substantial consideration, the community was completely wiped out, many of its members setting fire to their own homes rather than meet death by the mob. In 1360 Frankfurt reopened its gates to Jews. Their economic function was still vital to the flourishing city of merchants and craftsmen. However, the terms of resettlement imposed drastic changes. Jews had to apply individually for the privilege of residence, which usually had to be renewed annually in return for payment of heavy taxes and other dues. A set of statutes (*Staettigkeit*) regulated relations between the city and the community. Rabbis and communal leaders of note in the 14th century included Suesskind Wimpfen, who redeemed the body of *Meir b. Baruch of Rothenburg for ritual burial; and *Alexander Susslin ha-Kohen.

15th to 17th Centuries

During the first half of the 15th century, the Jewish community consisted of no more than 12 tax-paying families on the average. The expulsion of the Jews, or their relocation to a remote part of the city, was considered by the city council from the 1430s. From the 1450s the Jews were forced to wear a distinctive badge, and Christians were forbidden to visit Jewish festivities. After repeated interventions on the part of the emperor, and despite their strong resistance, the Jews of Frankfurt were finally forced to settle in a specially constructed street (*Judengasse*) outside the old city ramparts in 1462. Although existence in this ghetto entailed severe physical and social hardship to the community, its inner life developed even more intensively. There were 110 registered inhabitants of the ghetto in 1463, 250 in 1520, 900 in 1569, 1,200 in 1580, 2,200 in 1600, and about 3,000 in 1610. Since the ghetto was never permitted to expand beyond its original area, the existing houses were subdivided, and back premises and additional storeys were erected. The communal organization became stronger and more diversified. Religious and lay leaders (*Hochmeister* and *Baumeister*) were elected by the Jewish taxpayers, and a continual flow of *takkanot* laid the basis for powerful and jealously guarded local traditions in all spheres of religious, social, and economic life. Outstanding among the rabbis of the 15th century was Nathan Epstein. Johannes *Pfefferkorn confiscated some 1,500 Hebrew books from Frankfurt Jews. The Peasants' War and religious wars of the 16th century repeatedly endangered the community, and the guilds made serious inroads into their economic activities. Nevertheless, conditions were favorable to commercial enterprise, and by means of heavy financial contributions and skillful diplomacy the Frankfurt Jews managed to safeguard their privileges. By the end of the 16th century the community reached a peak period of prosperity. It had become a center of Jewish learning, and students from far away flocked to the yeshivot of Eliezer Treves and Akiva b. Jacob Frankfurter. The Frankfurt rabbinate and rabbinical court had become one of the foremost religious authorities in Germany. Decisions were made by the presiding rabbi in conjunction with the "members of the yeshivah" (*dayyanim*). General *synods of rabbinic and lay leaders were held at Frankfurt in 1562, 1582, and 1603.

However, economic and social antagonisms had long been simmering between the wealthy patrician families of the city and the guild craftsmen and petty traders, many of whom were in debt to Jews. The struggle flared into open rebellion when in 1614 the rabble, led by Vincent *Fettmilch, stormed the ghetto and gave vent to their anger by plundering the Jewish houses. The Jews were all expelled from the city, but the emperor outlawed the rebels, and their leaders were arrested and put to death (1616). Subsequently the Jews were ceremoniously returned to the ghetto, an event annually commemorated on Adar 20th by the Frankfurt community as the "Purim Winz" ("Purim of Vincent"). Possibly a group of wealthy Frankfurt Jews, among them Simeon Wolf, father of the celebrated Court Jew Samuel *Oppenheimer, used their influence at the imperial court to bring about this result. Among those who did not return to Frankfurt after the Fettmilch rebellion was Isaiah *Horowitz, the celebrated author of *Shenei Luḥot ha-Berit*, who had occupied the rabbinate from 1606. Other leading rabbis of the period included his son Shabbetai *Horowitz, Ḥayyim Cohen, grandson of *Judah Loew (the Maharal) of Prague, and Meir b. Jacob ha-Kohen *Schiff, a native of Frankfurt. Joseph Yuspa *Hahn recorded the ritual customs of the Frankfurt community in his *Yosif Omeẓ*. These were a source of special pride to the Frankfurt Jews, known for their local patriotism. Joseph Solomon *Delmedigo was for some years employed as communal physician. Aaron Samuel *Koidonover and his son Ẓevi Hirsh *Koidonover were also members of the Frankfurt rabbinate. The community did not grow numerically during the 17th century owing to the unhealthy conditions of their overpopulated quarter and the excessive taxes imposed upon them during the Thirty Years' War. In addition, the terms of residence were designed to keep their number stationary, allowing a maximum of 500 families and 12 marriage licenses annually. At the end of the 17th century the community made successful efforts to prevent Johann *Eisenmenger from publishing his anti-Jewish book.

18th Century

In 1711 almost the entire Jewish quarter was destroyed by a fire which broke out in the house of the chief rabbi, Naphtali b. Isaac *Katz. The inhabitants found refuge in gentile homes, but had to return to the ghetto after it had been rebuilt. J.J. *Schudt gave a detailed account of Jewish life at Frankfurt in this period. The importance of the Frankfurt Jewish community of that era is indicated by the official recognition of its representatives ("*Residenten*") in Vienna from 1718. The penetration of Enlightenment found the community in a state of unrest and social strife. Communal life had long been dominated by a few ancient patrician families, some of whom were known by signs hanging outside their houses, like the *Rothschild ("Red Shield"), Schwarzschild, Kann, and Schiff families. The impoverished majority challenged the traditional privileges of the wealthy oligarchy, and the city council repeatedly acted as arbitrator between the rival parties. Controversies on religious and personal matters such as the *Eybeschuetz-*Emden dispute further weakened unity in the community. Nevertheless, there was no decline in intellectual activity, and the yeshivot of Samuel Schotten and Jacob Joshua b. Ẓevi Hirsch *Falk attracted many students. The movement for the reformation of Jewish education fostered by the circle of Moses *Mendelssohn in Berlin found many sympathizers in Frankfurt, especially among the well-to-do class who welcomed it as a step toward *emancipation. Forty-nine prominent members of the community subscribed for Mendelssohn's German translation of the Bible (1782), but the chief rabbi, Phinehas *Horowitz, attacked the book from the pulpit. When in 1797 a project was advocated for a school with an extensive program of secular studies, Horowitz pronounced a ban on it. He was supported by most of the communal leaders, though many had their children taught non-Jewish subjects privately. The ban had to be withdrawn by order of the magistrate. Some years previously, Horowitz had acted similarly against the kabbalist Nathan *Adler. Meanwhile the French revolutionary wars had made their first liberating impact on Frankfurt Jewry. In 1796 a bombardment destroyed the greater part of the ghetto walls, and in 1798 the prohibition on leaving the ghetto on Sundays and holidays was abolished.

19th and 20th Centuries

The incorporation of Frankfurt in Napoleon's Confederation of the Rhine (1806) and the constitution of the grand duchy of Frankfurt (1810) gradually changed the status of the Frankfurt Jews, bringing them nearer emancipation. In 1811 the ghetto was finally abolished, and a declaration of equal rights for all citizens expressly included the Jews, a capital payment of 440,000 florins having been made by the community. However, the reaction following Napoleon's downfall brought bitter disappointment. The senate of the newly constituted Free City tried to abolish Jewish emancipation and thwarted the efforts made by a community delegation to the Congress of *Vienna. After prolonged negotiations, marked by the "*Hep-Hep" anti-Jewish disorders in 1819, the senate finally promulgated an enactment granting equality to the Jews in all civil matters, although reinstating many of the old discriminatory laws (1824). The composition and activities of the community board remained subject to supervision and confirmation by the senate. Meanwhile the religious rift in the community had widened considerably. Phinehas Horowitz's son and successor, Ẓevi Hirsch *Horowitz, was powerless in face of the increasing pressure for social and educational reforms. He did in fact renew his father's approbation of Benjamin Wolf *Heidenheim's edition of the prayer book which included a German translation and a learned commentary. However, this first stirring of *Wissenschaft des Judentums could not satisfy those in the community desiring reform and assimilation. In 1804 they founded a school, the Philanthropin, with a markedly secular and assimilationist program. This institution became a major center for reform in Judaism. From 1807 it organized reformed Jewish services for the pupils and their parents. In the same year a Jewish lodge of *Freemasons was established, whose members actively furthered the causes of reform and secularization in the community. From 1817 to 1832 the board of the community was exclusively composed of members of the lodge. In 1819 the Orthodox *ḥeder* institutions were closed by the police, and the board prevented the establishment of a school for both religious and general studies. Attendance at the yeshivah, which in 1793 still had 60 students, dwindled. In 1842 the number of Orthodox families was estimated to account for less than 10% of the community. In that year, a Reform Association demanded the abolition of all "talmudic" laws, circumcision, and the messianic faith. The aged rabbi, Solomon Abraham Trier, who had been one of the two delegates from Frankfurt to the Paris *Sanhedrin in 1807, published a collection of responsa from contemporary rabbis and scholars in German on the fundamental significance of circumcision in Judaism (1844). A year later a conference of rabbis sympathizing with reform was held in Frankfurt. A leading member of this group was Abraham *Geiger, a native of Frankfurt, and communal rabbi from 1863 to 1870. The revolutionary movement of 1848 hastened the emancipation of the Frankfurt Jews, which was finally achieved in 1864. The autocratic regime of the community board weakened considerably. A small group of Orthodox members then seized the opportunity to form a religious association within the community, the "Israelitische Religionsgesellschaft," and elected Samson Raphael *Hirsch as their rabbi in 1851. The Rothschild family made a large donation toward the erection of a new Orthodox synagogue. When the community board persisted in turning a deaf ear to the demands of the Orthodox minority, the association seceded from the community and set up a separate congregation (1876). After some Orthodox members, supported by the Wuerzburg rabbi, Seligmann Baer *Bamberger, had refused to take this course, the community board made certain concessions, enabling them to remain within the community. A communal Orthodox rabbi, Marcus *Horovitz, was installed and a new Orthodox synagogue was erected with communal funds. From then on the Frankfurt Orthodox community, its pattern of life and educational institutions, became the paradigm of German Orthodoxy. The Jewish population of Frankfurt numbered 3,298 in 1817 (7.9% of the total), 10,009 in 1871 (11%), 21,974 in 1900 (7.5%), and 29,385 in 1925 (6.3%). During the 19th century many Jews from the rural districts were attracted to the city whose economic boom owed much to Jewish financial and commercial enterprise. The comparative wealth of the Frankfurt Jews is shown by the fact that, in 1900, 5,946 Jewish citizens paid 2,540,812 marks in taxes, while 34,900 non-Jews paid 3,611,815 marks. Many civic institutions, including hospitals, libraries and museums, were established by Jewish donations, especially from the Rothschild family. The Jew Leopold *Sonnemann was the founder of the liberal daily *Frankfurter Zeitung*, and the establishment of the Frankfurt university (1912) was also largely financed by Jews. Jewish communal institutions and organizations included two hospitals, three schools (the Philanthropin and the elementary and secondary schools founded by S.R. Hirsch), a yeshivah (founded by Hirsch's son-in-law and successor Solomon *Breuer), religious classes for pupils attending city schools, an orphanage, a home for the aged, many welfare institutions, and two cemeteries (the ancient cemetery was closed in 1828). Frankfurt Jews were active in voluntary societies devoted to universal Jewish causes, such as emigrant relief and financial support for the Jews in the Holy Land (donations from Western Europe to the Holy Land had been channeled through Frankfurt from the 16th century). The yearbook of the Juedisch-Literarische Gesellschaft was published in Frankfurt, and the Orthodox weekly *Der Israelit* (founded in 1860) was published in Frankfurt from 1906. The Jewish department of the municipal library, headed before World War II by the scholar A. Freimann, had a rare collection of Hebraica and Judaica. During the first decade of the 20th century additional synagogues were erected, among them a splendid one situated at Friedberger Anlage. In 1920 Franz *Rosenzweig set up an institute for Jewish studies, where Martin *Buber, then professor at the Frankfurt university, gave popular lectures. Two additional yeshivot were established, one by Jacob Hoffman, who in 1922 succeeded Nehemiah Anton *Nobel in the Orthodox rabbinate of the community. Others prominent in Frankfurt Jewish life include the writer Ludwig *Boerne; the historian I.M. *Jost; the artists Moritz *Oppenheim and Benno *Elkan; the biochemist Paul *Ehrlich; the economist and sociologist Franz *Oppenheimer; rabbis Jacob *Horowitz and Joseph *Horowitz (Orthodox); Leopold Stein, Nehemiah Bruell, Caesar *Seligmann (Reform); and the Orthodox leaders Jacob *Rosenheim and Isaac *Breuer.

[Mordechai Breuer / Stefan Rohrbacher (2nd ed.)

Holocaust Period

After a number of attacks on individual Jews and the occupation of the famous Institut fuer Sozialforschung on March 5, 1933, the official Nazi action against the Jews began on April 1, 1933, with a boycott of Jewish businesses and professionals, followed on April 7 by the dismissal of Jewish white-collar workers, university teachers, actors, and musicians. State and party pressure subsequently resulted in the closing or "aryanization" of almost all Jewish-owned firms, while local SA units and Nazi students terrorized Jewish citizens. Though originally prohibited, these arbitrary actions were in later years legalized by the Reich government which helped to organize and coordinate them. The Jewish community reacted by expanding existing services, establishing new agencies for economic aid, reemployment, occupational training, schooling, adult education, and emigration. All institutions were under strict surveillance by the Gestapo.

On Nov. 10–11, 1938, the big synagogues of the two Jewish communities, situated at Friedberger Anlage, Dominikanerplatz (formerly Boerneplatz), Grosser Wollgraben (formerly Boernestrasse), and Freiherr-vom-Stein-Strasse were burned down. Community buildings including the Jewish Museum (Museum juedischer Altertuemer), the Jewish homes, and stores were stormed and looted by the SA, the SS, and mobs they had incited. More than 2,600 Jewish men were arrested and sent to the *Buchenwald concentration camp and around 530 to the *Dachau concentration camp. Members of the Orthodox Religionsgesellschaft were compelled to combine with the general community to form a single community organization which the Nazis named Juedische Gemeinde. In 1939 this autonomous community was forcibly merged into the state-supervised Reichsvereinigung. Jewish leaders were compelled to enter into Judenvertraege, transferring communal property to municipal ownership. Welfare foundations taken over by the municipal authorities in December 1938 were placed under direct Gestapo control in May 1940. Gestapo Officer Ernst Holland, who was also a city official, supervised until 1943 Jewish welfare and emigration, later organizing labor recruitment and "orderly proceedings" before deportation.

The Frankfurt community decreased by emigration from 26,158 in 1933, to 10,803 in June 1941, although there was an influx of Jewish families from the countryside. Deportations to Lodz began on October 19, 1941, and were followed by deportations to *Minsk, *Majdanek, *Kovno (Kaunas), *Theresienstadt, and other camps. In September 1943, after large-scale deportations stopped, the Jewish population in Frankfurt totaled 602, including half-Jews. The last deportation to Theresienstadt took place on March 15, 1945, only two weeks before the U.S. army occupied the city and liberated around 150 Jews and so-called Mischlinge.

[Eleanor Sterling-Oppenheimer / Jens Hoppe (2nd ed.)

After World War II

After the war, a new community was organized, consisting of those who had outlived the war in Frankfurt, survivors from concentration camps, and displaced persons, totaling 1,104 in 1952. They were joined by a number of pensioners and Israelis, and the community increased to 2,566 by 1959 and 4,350 by 1970, to become the largest in West Germany (excepting that of Berlin); the average age of its members was 45.4, and two thirds were aged over 40. One of the large synagogues was rebuilt, and by 1970 five prayer rooms were also in use. The first postwar Jewish elementary school in Germany was opened there in 1965, and a communal periodical *Frankfurter juedisches Gemeindeblatt* commenced publication in March 1968. A 200-bed home for the aged was opened in 1968. Due mainly to the immigration of Jews from the former Soviet Union, the number of community members rose from 4,842 in 1989 to 7,063 in 2003. The community has four synagogues. The Philanthropin was reopened as an elementary school in 2004. A Jewish museum was inaugurated in 1988 in the former palatial residence of the Rothschild family, with a branch opened in 1992 on the site of the Judengasse. The Frankfurt municipal and university library holds one of the most important collections of Judaica books and manuscripts in Germany.

[Henry Wasserman]

Printing

The book fairs of Frankfurt were visited by Jewish printers and booksellers as early as 1535. Some Hebrew printing was carried on in Frankfurt as early as the 16th century; in 1512 the brothers Murner published "Grace after Meals." Hebrew printing seriously developed in Frankfurt in the 17th century. The earliest work, *Megillat Vinẓ* (Fettmilch), was published by Isaac Langenbuch after the Fettmilch riots (see above). From 1657 to 1707 Balthasar Christian Wust and later his son (?) Johann issued a great number of Hebrew books. For this part of their work they employed Jewish printers and other Jewish personnel, and found Jewish financial backing. (As Jews could not obtain printing licenses, they used Christian firms as a front.) They printed mainly liturgical items, but also a Pentateuch with a German glossary (1662), and bibles (1677, 1694); and Wallich's Yiddish *Kuhbuch* (1672). Several other Hebrew printers published books in the late 17th and early 18th centuries. An important publisher was Johann Koellner, who in 20 years of printing was responsible for about half of the books issued in Frankfurt. Among his more important publications were the *Arba'ah Turim* (5 vols., 1712–16), and an excellent Talmud edition (1770–23). Soon after the completion of the latter, the whole edition was confiscated and was only released 30 years later. In the first half of the 19th century the names of seven non-Jewish printing houses are known. Subsequently Jewish printers emerged for the first time. Among them were J.H. Golda (1881–1920), E. Slobotzki (from 1855), and the bookseller J. Kauffmann, who took over the *Roedelheim press of M. Lehrberger in 1899. Hebrew printers were active in places like *Homburg, *Offenbach, *Sulzbach, Roedelheim, and others in the neighborhood of Frankfurt, because Jewish printers were unable to establish themselves in Frankfurt.

Music

The liturgical music and **ḥazzanut* of the Frankfurt community represent the archetype of the western Ashkenazi tradition. It can be traced to the 15th-century codifier Jacob *Moellin (Maharil), and is marked by an adherence to tradition which made any deviation from the customary melodies (some of which were credited with divine origin, "**mi-Sinai*") a religious offense. Thus the principal qualification required of cantors was a precise acquaintance with the details of musical custom (*minhag*). Liturgical poems (*piyyutim*) had a place of prime importance, especially as some of them were linked with the history of the community, and little scope was given to the cantor's capacity for musical invention or improvization. When at the beginning of the 16th century, the Sabbath hymn *Lekhah Dodi* came into vogue in many communities, it caused sharp controversy among Frankfurt Jews, and though finally accepted, it had to be chanted for many years by an assistant cantor in order to stress its non-compulsory character. Every special event in the Jewish year was marked by a festive, solemn, or plaintive tune, as the occasion demanded. Every month and every festival had an appropriate melody of its own, which was intoned by the cantor at the Blessing of the New Moon. Thus the liturgical music served as a "musical calendar." When a festival or New Moon fell on a Sabbath, the cantor had to give each its musical share ("*me-inyono*"). This was achieved mainly by mingling variants of the Kaddish melodies, of which there existed more than 25. On Simḥat Torah the "Year's Kaddish" recapitulated the whole range of the "musical calendar." Great stress was laid on correct reading and cantillation of the Bible, and many verses of special importance were chanted to particularly solemn tunes. In spite of the strict traditionalism, many Frankfurt melodies show the influence of German folksong; the one employed for the *Priestly blessing on the High Holidays is derived from the popular Frankfurt "Fassbaenderlied" (Coopers' song). The melody sung in the synagogue on the annual celebration of Purim Winz (see above) was derived from the march tune of the military escort that led the Jews back to the Frankfurt ghetto after the riots of 1616. In the 19th century the Reform movement installed an organ in the main Frankfurt synagogue, whereupon the Orthodox congregation introduced a male choir in their own synagogue with I.M. *Japhet as musical director.

[Mordechai Breuer]

BIBLIOGRAPHY: HISTORY: I. Kracauer, *Geschichte der Juden in Frankfurt a.M.*, 2 vols. (1925–27); A. Freimann and F. Kracauer, *Frankfurt* (Eng., 1929); H. Schwab, *Memories of Frankfurt* (1955); M. Horovitz, *Frankfurter Rabbinen*, 4 vols. (1882–85); J. Rosenheim, *Zikhronot* (1955), 9–111; E. Mayer, *Frankfurter Juden* (1966); Germ Jud, index; D. Andernacht and E. Sterling (eds.), *Dokumente zur Geschichte der Frankfurter Juden* (1963); D. Andernacht (ed.), *Das Philanthropin zu Frankfurt am Main* (1964): HJ, 10 (1948), 99–146; J. Katz, *Freemasons and Jews* (1970), index; M. Eliav, *Ha-Ḥinnukh ha-Yehudi be-Germanyah bi-Ymei ha-Haskalah ve-ha-Emanẓipaẓyah* (1960). **ADD. BIBLIOGRAPHY:** S. Scheuermann, *Der Kampf der Frankfurter Juden um ihre Gleichberechtigung* (1933); P. Arnsberg, *Bilder aus dem juedischen Leben im alten Frankfurt* (1970); idem, *Geschichte der Frankfurter Juden seit der Franzoesischen Revolution*, 3 vols. (1983); R. Heuberger, *Hinaus aus dem Ghetto. Juden in Frankfurt 1800–1850* (1988); I. Schlotzhauer, *Das Philanthropin 1804–1942* (1990); D. Andernacht, *Regesten zur Geschichte der Juden in Frankfurt am Main 1401–1519*, 5 vols. (1996–2002); G. Heuberger (ed.), *Wer ein Haus baut, will bleiben* (1998); M. Kingreen, *Nach der Kristallnacht* (1999); H. Thiel, *Die Samson-Raphael-Hirsch-Schule* (2001); K. Meier-Ude, *Die juedischen Friedhoefe in Frankfurt* (2004). HOLOCAUST: PK Germanyah; P. Friedman (ed.), *Bibliografyah shel ha-Sefarim ha-Ivriyyim al ha-Sho'ah ve-al ha-Gevurah* (1960), index; N. Bentwich, in: AJR *Information*, 25 (Aug. 1970), 8. PRINTING: B. Friedberg, *Ha-Defus ha-Ivri be-Merkaz Eiropah…* (1935); 62ff. **ADD. BIBLIOGRAPHY:** Juedisches Museum Frankfurt am Main (ed.), *"Und keiner hat fuer uns Kaddisch gesag …,"* in: *Deportationen aus Frankfurt am Main 1941 bis 1945* (2004). MUSIC: I.M. Japhet, *Schirei Jeschurun* (1922[4]);

S.Z. Geiger, *Divrei Kehillot* (1862); S. Scheuermann, *Die gottesdienstlichen Gesaenge der Israeliten fuer das ganze Jahr* (1912); F. Ogutsch, *Der Frankfurter Kantor* (1930).

FRANKFURT ON THE ODER, city in Brandenburg, Germany. Jews were living in Frankfurt before 1294, when a dispute between Jews and the slaughterers' guild there was settled. The Jews were not permitted to own houses, and lived in rented dwellings, referred to as *Judenbuden*. They mainly engaged in small trading and moneylending. In 1399 the community relinquished its cemetery for a larger one. From the second half of the 15th century the local merchants made continual complaints about economic competition by the Jews and the rate of interest they charged. In 1506 the synagogue was demolished and the new university was erected on the site. The Jews of Frankfurt were expelled with the rest of *Brandenburg Jewry in 1510. They later returned, and in 1564 there were nine Jewish familes living in Frankfurt, and 11 in 1567. They were again expelled in 1573. When a number of Jews were admitted to Brandenburg in 1671, a new community grew up in Frankfurt. The university there was the first in Germany to admit Jews. The first two Jewish students registered at the faculty of medicine in 1678, and others followed from all over Europe and even Jerusalem. Between 1739 and 1810 about 130 Jews studied there, and between 1721 and 1794, 29 graduated in medicine. The community numbered 592 in 1801; 399 in 1817; around 800 in the 1840s; and 891 in 1880. Subsequently it declined to 747 around 1900; 669 in 1925; and 586 in 1933.

In the 18th century many Jews from Poland attended the fairs in Frankfurt. In 1763 a conference of Polish rabbis headed by Gershon of Frankfurt settled a dispute between the printing houses of Amsterdam and Sulzbach concerning the publication of the Talmud.

Following the spread of the *Reform movement in the first half of the 19th century, the Orthodox members in Frankfurt seceded from the liberals and opened a prayer hall of their own. Samuel *Holdheim served as rabbi in Frankfurt from 1836 to 1840. In 1861 the first society for the colonization of Ereẓ Israel was founded in Frankfurt by Ḥayyim *Lorje. The scholar Judah *Bergmann officiated as rabbi there at the beginning of the 20th century, and the leader of liberal Judaism in Germany, Ignaz *Maybaum, was rabbi of the community between 1928 and 1936. In 1933 the community had a synagogue, a cemetery, three charitable societies, local chapters of the "Reichsbund Juedischer Frontsoldaten" and a *B'nai B'rith lodge. The Orthodox members rejoined the main community in 1934.

Under the Nazis the Frankfurt Jews suffered the same fate as those in the rest of Germany. Rabbi Maybaum was arrested and confined to the notorious Colombia prison in Berlin; later the charges against him were suspended. In the November pogrom known as Kristallnacht the synagogue was burned, Jewish businesses were destroyed, and several Jewish men were sent to Sachsenhausen. By May 1939 there were 184 Jews and 122 Mischlinge in the city. Jews were deported before the outbreak of World War II and eventually transported to Lublin Reservation. Twenty-four Jews from Frankfurt were deported to *Theresienstadt on Aug. 27, 1942, and three on June 16, 1943. The Jewish community was reestablished after the war and numbered 200 in 1958 but declined thereafter until the arrival of Jews from the former Soviet Union, who refounded the community in 1998. It numbered 222 in 2005. A memorial site (inaugurated in 1988) commemorates the destroyed synagogue. As Frankfurt on the Oder was divided after 1945 the Jewish cemetery is located in Slubice, Poland.

Printing

The earliest Hebrew book printed in Frankfurt on the Oder was a Pentateuch printed by J. and F. Hartman in 1595. Eighty years later J.C. Beckman, professor of theology at the local university, obtained a license to extend the privilege to print in Hebrew, and a Pentateuch with *haftarot* and the Five Scrolls, as well as other books, were published in 1677.

The most important work published there was a new edition of the Talmud (1697–99). The Court Jew Berend *Lehmann of Halberstadt invested in it and presented a large number of the 2,000 sets printed to various communities, *battei midrash*, and yeshivot. Further editions were printed in 1715–22 and 1736–39. Michael Gottschalk succeeded Beckman as manager and before 1740 Professor Grillo bought Gottschalk's press. It continued in his family until the end of the century, and in the hands of his successor, C.F. Elsner, until 1813. Grillos' turnover in trade of Hebrew books reached 80,000 Reichsthaler annually – a measure of the importance of the press for Germany and Eastern Europe. The main midrashim, *Yalkut Shimoni*, the Zohar, and other important rabbinic works were printed in Frankfurt on the Oder. As the result of the Prussian legislation of 1812, it was possible in 1813 for Hirsch Baschwitz, a Jew, to acquire the Hebrew printing press from Elsner. In turn, he sold the business in 1826 to Trebitsch & Son of Berlin.

BIBLIOGRAPHY: Germ Jud, 2 (1968), 251–2; FJW (1932), 65; A. Ackermann, *Geschichte der Juden in Brandenburg* (1906), 66, 70, 79, 80; S.L. Zitron, in: *Der Jude*, 2 (1917–18), 347–53, 670–7; L. Davidsohn, *Beitraege zur Sozial-und Wirtschaftsgeschichte der Berliner Juden vor der Emanzipation* (1920), 19, 39, 45, 46, 48; L. Lewin, in: JJLG, 14 (1921), 43–85, 217–38; 15 (1923), 59–96; 16 (1924), 43–85; idem, *Die Landessynode der grosspolnischen Judenschaft* (1926), 12, 14, 43, 49, 64; G. Kisch, in: *Juedische Familienforschung*, 10 (1934), 566–74, 598–602; B. Brilling, in: MGWJ, 80 (1936), 262–76; idem, in: SBB, 1 (1953–54), 84–94, 145–56, 183–96; 2 (1955–56), 79–96, 102–6; 8 (1966), 25–37; idem, in: *Archiv fuer Geschichte des Buchwesens*, 1 (1956), 325–30; idem, in: *Boersenblatt fuer den deutschen Buchhandel*, 13 (1957), 1537–48; S. Stern, *Der Preussische Staat und die Juden*, 2 (1962), Akten no. 1, 27, 43, 44, 142, 145, 149; PK Germanyah. **ADD. BIBLIOGRAPHY:** *Frankfurter Jahrbuch 1999 des Vereins der Freunde und Foerderer des Museums Viadrina, Jacobsdorf*, 79–98, 128–48; B. Meier, "Frankfurt/Oder," in: I. Diekmann and J.H. Schoeps (eds.), *Wegweiser durch das juedische Brandenburg* (1995), 125–41.

[Chasia Turtel]

FRANKINCENSE (Heb. לְבוֹנָה), the chief ingredient of the Temple *incense. It is mentioned a number of times among the treasures of the Temple (Neh. 13:5; I Chron. 9:29). It was burnt with the sacrifice of meal offering (Lev. 2:1) and placed upon the rows of showbread (Lev. 24:7). The frankincense on the meal offering along with a handful of the rest of its ingredients were scooped up by the priest as the "token portion" (*azkarah*) of the offering which he deposited on the altar to go up in smoke as a "soothing odor" offered to the Lord (Lev. 6:8; cf. Isa. 66:3). Pure frankincense was one of the four ingredients of the incense of the Tabernacle (Ex. 30:34; and cf. Ecclus. 24:15). It was brought to Ereẓ Israel from Sheba (Jer. 6:20). The maiden in the Song of Songs (3:6) came from the wilderness perfumed with myrrh and frankincense; in the erotic imagery of the Song of Songs, the lover refers to the body of his mistress as "the mountain of myrrh" and "the hill of frankincense" (Song 4:6), while the beloved is compared to "an enclosed garden" in which grow exotic perfumes including "all trees of frankincense" (Song 4:14–15). Ben Sira emphasizes its aromatic scent (Ecclus. 39:14; 50:9). Frankincense is frequently mentioned in rabbinic literature in connection with the laws of meal offerings, where it was used in the form of globules or grains (Men. 1:2). A potion of wine and frankincense was prepared for those condemned to death, "that they should not suffer pain" (Sem. 2:9; cf. Sanh. 43a). The name *levonah* is common in Semitic languages. It has its origin in the white color of the fresh sap, "pure frankincense." From the Semitic the name passed also into the Greek *libanos*.

Frankincense was extracted from trees of the genus *Boswellia*, of which there are two species: *Boswellia sacra Flückiger* (also known as *Boswellia Carterii*) found on the Arabian Peninsula and in North Somalia, and *Boswellia frereana Birdwood* found in North Somalia. These trees are still the source for the frankincense used as incense in the Catholic Church. In ancient Egypt, as in other countries of the east, frankincense was very important, and it seems that efforts were made to plant it locally. The bringing of pots of frankincense for planting in Egypt is depicted in ancient Egyptian drawings.

BIBLIOGRAPHY: Loew, Flora, 1 (1928), 312–4; J. Feliks, *Olam ha-Ẓomeʾaḥ ha-Mikraʾi* (1968[2]), 260–2. **ADD. BIBLIOGRAPHY:** HALOT, 493; DISO, 564; W. Holladay, *Jeremiah* 1 (1986), 222; W. Mueller, in: ABD II, 854.

[Jehuda Feliks]

FRANKL, ADOLF (1859–1936), rabbi, banker, and communal leader in Hungary. Born in Debrecen, he studied in various yeshivot and received his rabbinical ordination at the yeshivah of Pressburg. From 1888 Frankl was *nasi* of the Hungarian *kolel* of Jerusalem. In 1905 he was elected president of the organization of Orthodox communities and honorary president of the Orthodox community of Budapest. After the death of Koppel *Reich, Frankl was elected chief rabbi of the Orthodox community in Budapest, and sat as the delegate of Orthodox Jewry in the Hungarian Upper House (1930). He won esteem in all circles of the Jewish population of Hungary.

BIBLIOGRAPHY: *Magyar Zsidó Lexikon* (1929), 292.

[Baruch Yaron]

FRANKL, LUDWIG AUGUST (1810–1894), Austrian poet, secretary of the Vienna Jewish community, and founder of the Laemel School in Jerusalem. Born in Chrast, Bohemia, Frankl was one of the first Jews to attend a Bohemian secondary school. He also received a sound Jewish education under his relative, Zacharias *Frankel. Although he studied medicine at Vienna and Padua, he devoted himself mainly to literature. The patriotic flavor of Frankl's first collection of ballads, *Das Habsburgerlied* (1832), brought him a reward from Emperor Francis I. It was followed by *Morgenlaendische Sagen* (1834), a volume of poems on Jewish themes, and by the epic *Christoforo Colombo* (1836), for which he was made an honorary citizen of Genoa, the explorer's birthplace. In 1838 Frankl was appointed secretary and archivist of the Vienna Jewish community. The post enabled him to publish various works of Jewish interest, including a history of the Jews in Vienna (1853), but he really made his name as editor, from 1842, of the *Sonntagsblaetter*, which brought him into the circle of Austria's literary elite. In later years he was to publish studies of such of his new acquaintances as the dramatist Franz Grillparzer and the poet Nikolaus Lenau, but he also encouraged new writers, notably Moritz *Hartmann and Leopold *Kompert. His use of the elegant *Sonntagsblaetter* in support of the 1848 Revolution led to the paper's eventual suppression. During the Revolution Frankl served as an officer in the students' legion and achieved fame with his revolutionary lyric *Die Universitaet*, the first uncensored Austrian publication, which was circulated in half-a-million copies and was set to music no less than 28 different times: Frankl later edited the works of the revolutionary writer Anastasius Gruen (1877), and their correspondence was published by Frankl's son, Lothar. As the representative of Elisa Herz, Frankl went to *Jerusalem in 1856 and, in memory of her father, founded the Laemel School, which offered Jewish children a secular, as well as a religious, education. This aroused violent opposition on the part of the ultra-Orthodox Ashkenazi community, whose rabbinate placed Frankl under the ban of excommunication. He described his experiences in Ereẓ Israel in *Nach Jerusalem* (2 vols., 1858–60), which gives a valuable picture of the Jewish inhabitants of Jerusalem in the mid-19th century. The book was translated into Hebrew and other languages, and appeared in English as *The Jews in the East* (1859). A third volume, *Nach Aegypten*, appeared in 1860. Other works of Jewish interest are Frankl's *Elegien* (1842), *Rachel* (1842), *Libanon* (1855), and *Ahnenbilder* (1864). In 1876 he founded the Vienna Jewish Institute for the Blind, his philanthropic endeavors being rewarded with ennoblement as Ritter von Frankl-Hochwart. His memoirs appeared posthumously in 1910. His son LOTHAR (1862–1914) became professor of neurology at the University of Vienna in 1897.

BIBLIOGRAPHY: *Oẓar ha-Sifrut*, 5 (1896), 129–34, contains bibl.; E. Wolbe, *Ludwig August Frankl, der Dichter und Menschenfreund* (1910); S. Dollar, *Sonntagsblaetter von Ludwig August Frankl* (1932); Y. Yaari-Poleskin, *Ḥolemim u-Magshimim* (1967), 48–56; Schlossar, in: ADB, 48 (1904), 706–12. **ADD. BIBLIOGRAPHY:** H.I. Schmelzer, "Briefe von Leopold Zunz und Moritz Steinschneider an

Ludwig August Frankl," in: *Occident und Orient* (1988), 319–29; C. Walker, "Two Jewish Poetry Anthologies – Ludwig August Frankl's *Libanon* and Sigmund Kaznelson's *Jüdisches Schicksal in deutschen Gedichten*," in: *Jews in German Literature since 1945 – German-Jewish Literature* (2000), 21–34; N. Vielmetti, "Der Wiener jüdische Publizist Ludwig August Frankl und die Begründung der Lämelschule in Jerusalem," in: JIDG 4 (1975), 167–204.

FRANKL, PINKUS (Pinhas) FRITZ (1848–1887), German rabbi and scholar. Born in Uhersky Brod, Moravia, Frankl succeeded Geiger as rabbi of the Berlin community in 1877 and became lecturer in religious philosophy, medieval Hebrew literature, and homiletics at the Hochschule (Lehranstalt) fuer die Wissenschaft des Judentums in 1882. With Graetz he was coeditor of the journal **Monatsschrift fuer Geschichte und Wissenschaft des Judentums* (MGWJ). His studies were mainly about the Karaites: *Karaeische Studien* (1876); *Beitraege zur Literaturgeschichte der Karaeer* (1887); and articles in the Etsch-Gruber encyclopedia, MGWJ, and others. Frankl edited some *piyyutim* by Eleazar Kallir (in *Jubelschrift… L. Zunz*, 1884). A collection of his sermons, *Fest-und Gelegenheits-Predigten 1877–87*, was published posthumously (1888). In 1884 Frankl was one of the initiators of a "General Assembly of German Rabbis."

BIBLIOGRAPHY: S. Maybaum, *Trauerrede gehalten am 26. August, 1887 an der Bahre des Rabbiners Dr. P.F. Frankl* (1887).

FRANKL, VIKTOR EMIL (1905–1997), Austrian psychiatrist and founder of the school of existential psychotherapy known as logotherapy (or the Third Viennese School). Already as a student, Frankl was in touch with Sigmund Freud. Later on he became an adherent of Alfred Adler's school of psychoanalysis; however, he soon became a dissident here as well. In the following years he worked as a specialist in neurology and psychiatry at the Viennese Am Steinhof Psychiatric Clinic and from 1940 to 1942 he was head of the Rothschild hospital. Then, Frankl was sent to Dachau and Auschwitz for three years. During this period he gained new insights into human nature, which he later developed into his philosophy and theory of logotherapy. In contradistinction to the Freudian theories that analyzed human behavior in terms of determinism, the sex drives, and the repressed experiences of the past, and contrary to the Adlerian school which based explanations on the human desire for power and self-assertion, Frankl's philosophy focused on the human need for purpose, self-fulfillment, and the need to attain a higher meaning in life. By observing the behavior of the Auschwitz inmates he came to the conclusion that, "The prisoner who had lost faith in the future – his future – was doomed. With his loss of belief in the future, he also lost his spiritual hold; he let himself decline and became subject to mental and physical decay." Having survived the Holocaust, Frankl returned to Vienna and was in charge of the neurologic Policlinic in Vienna from 1946 to 1970. Frankl's books include *Ein Psychologe erlebt das Konzentrationslager* (1946, 2005; *From Death Camp to Existentialism*, 1959; republished as *Man's Search for Meaning*, 1964), and *Aerztliche Seelsorge* (1946, 2005; *The Doctor and the Soul*, 1955, 1965).

BIBLIOGRAPHY: Grollman, in: *Judaism*, 14 (1965), 22–38. **ADD. BIBLIOGRAPHY:** R. Nurmela, in: *Nordisk Judaistik*, 21:1–2 (2000), 149–55; T.E. Pytell, in: *Psychoanalytic Review*, 88:2 (2001), 311–34; idem, in: *Holocaust and Genocide Studies*, 17:1 (2003), 89–113; O. Zsok, *Der Arztphilosoph Viktor E. Frankl* (2005).

[Marcus Pyka (2nd ed.)]

FRANKL-GRUEN, ADOLF ABRAHAM (1847–1916), rabbi and historian in Moravia. Born in Uhersky Brod, Moravia, he officiated as rabbi of Kromeriz (Kremsier) from 1877 to 1911. Frankl-Gruen published many articles on biblical exegesis (see Gesamtindex of MGWJ (1966), 18) and homiletics, and a polemic against the antisemite H.S. *Chamberlain (1901). In 1903 he completed *Juedische Zeitgeschichte und Zeitgenossen*, on the contemporary Jewish scene. His three-volume *Geschichte der Juden in Kremsier* (1896–1901) and *Geschichte der Juden in Ungarisch-Brod* (1905), based mainly on documents previously unpublished, remain essential texts for the student of Jewish history in Moravia. In 1889 he became involved in a *blood libel in Kromeriz when a rumor was spread before Passover that a box containing the body of a Christian girl had been sent to him by railway.

His son OSCAR BENJAMIN FRANKL (1881–1955) studied philology at Vienna University. In 1918 he founded in Prague the German Urania Institute for adult education which he headed until 1938. He was appointed chief of the German department of the Czechoslovakian government radio and became an international authority on broadcasting. In 1939 he managed to escape to the United States through France. There he served as a researcher for Columbia University (1942–55) and was appointed lecturer at the Rand School of Social Science. His *Der Jude in den deutschen Dichtungen des 15., 16., und 17. Jahrhunderts…*, on the image of the Jew in German literature of the 15th to 17th centuries, and *Friedrich Schiller in seinen Beziehungen zu den Juden und zum Judentum*, on Friedrich Schiller's relations to Jews and Judaism (both published in 1905), are noteworthy.

BIBLIOGRAPHY: H. Gold (ed.), *Die Juden und Judengemeinden Maehrens…* (1929), 297.

FRANKLIN, English family active in communal, public, and economic life. BENJAMIN WOLF FRANKLIN (1740–1785), a teacher of Hebrew, went to England from Breslau about 1763. His youngest son, ABRAHAM (1784–1854), after spending his early life in Portsmouth, settled in Manchester and traded with the West Indies. Of Abraham's 12 children, three gained prominence: BENJAMIN (1811–1888) was a merchant in Jamaica where he was active in public and communal life. JACOB (1809–1877), first an optician and then a West Indies merchant, was a mathematician, accountant, and writer on accountancy. A staunch advocate of religious Orthodoxy, he founded and edited the *Voice of Jacob* as a mouthpiece against Reform (it was later merged with the *Jewish Chronicle*, to which he contributed as "She'erit Ya'akov"). Active in many communal organizations, he left the bulk of his fortune for educational projects, including the publication of Jewish textbooks. ELLIS ABRAHAM (1822–1909) moved from Manchester to London in 1842 and joined a banking house. Friendship with Samuel *Montagu, whose sister he married in 1856, led to his joining the firm established by Montagu and his brother in 1852. A patriarchal figure, he took an active interest in many communal organizations.

Ellis' daughter BEATRICE married Herbert *Samuel. His son, SIR LEONARD (1862–1944), senior partner in the family banking firm A. Keyser and Company, was a Liberal member of parliament, and was also active in synagogal administration. Another of his sons, ARTHUR ELLIS (1857–1938), besides his banking interests, was chairman of the Routledge publishing firm, president of the Jewish Religious Education Board, vice president of the Board of Guardians, and vice principal of the Working Men's College. He assembled a memorable collection of Jewish ritual art, now in the Jewish Museum, London. His son ELLIS (1894–1964) was similarly active in Anglo-Jewish communal life. Ellis' daughter, Rosalind *Franklin (1920–1958) was a distinguished chemist, particularly noted for her work on deoxyribonucleic acid (DNA). She died tragically young, just as the importance of her research was being noted. Her life has attracted a great deal of attention in recent years as an eminent woman scientist cut off in her prime, and who was arguably denied her full credit through the sexism of the time. A commemorative plaque was placed on the building where she lived in Chelsea, London.

BIBLIOGRAPHY: A.E. Franklin, *Pedigrees of the Franklin Family* (1915); idem, *Records of the Franklin Family and Collaterals* (1935²); J. Picciotto, *Sketches of Anglo-Jewish History* (1956²), index; V.D. Lipman, *Century of Social Service 1859–1959* (1959), index. **ADD. BIBLIOGRAPHY:** Bermant, *The Cousinhood*, 281–86; ODNB online for Jacob Franklin, Rosalind Franklin; John D. Watson, *The Double Helix* (1968); A. Sayre, *Rosalind Franklin and DNA* (1978); J. Glyn, "Rosalind Franklin, 1920–1958," in: E. Shils and C. Blacker (eds.), *Cambridge Women: Twelve Portraits* (1996), 267–82.

[Vivian David Lipman]

FRANKLIN, LEO MORRIS (1870–1948), U.S. Reform rabbi. Franklin was born in Cambridge City, Indiana and spent his youth in Cincinnati. Upon ordination at Hebrew Union College (1892), he served in Omaha, Nebraska, for seven years, then became rabbi of Temple Beth El, Detroit, in 1899, where he was a skilled organizational leader. Franklin was a proponent of classical Reform Judaism. He was president of the Central Conference of American Rabbis (1919–21). He organized the United Jewish Charities (1899) and was a founder of the Jewish Welfare Federation (1926). He led the first fight in the United States for open seating in synagogues instead of assigned seating and also fought to have his congregation provide Jewish education to all children regardless of their parents' ability to pay, which took on added importance during the Depression era. He tackled some important local issues of antisemitism with national implications, including efforts to expose the antisemitism of Father Charles Coughlin, and he maintained relations cordial and not so cordial with Henry Ford, whose influence in Detroit was major and whose support of antisemitism was significant. Franklin held many civic positions and was active in interfaith activities in Detroit. He belonged to the anti-Zionist American Council for Judaism until 1948, when he resigned and endorsed the State of Israel. He was one of the first rabbis to reach out to campus students, working with the Jewish students association at the University of Michigan, a forerunner of Hillel. Despite the formal policies and prevalent practices of the CCAR, Franklin officiated at intermarriages. He helped found smaller congregations throughout Michigan and worked with a movement to spur Jewish farmers in Michigan. He wrote *Rabbi, the Man and His Message* (1938) and many articles.

BIBLIOGRAPHY: Leo M. Franklin Section, Michigan Historical Collections, University of Michigan, Ann Arbor, Michigan.

[Irving I. Katz]

FRANKLIN, ROSALIND ELSIE (1920–1958), British biophysicist. Franklin was born in London, England, into an upper middle class Jewish family whose ancestors had come to England from Breslau in 1763. Her uncle, Sir Herbert *Samuel, was the first British High Commissioner to Palestine. In 1938 she was accepted to Newnham College Cambridge where she completed her studies in chemistry and physics and received her Ph.D. from Cambridge in the physical chemistry of carbon and graphite micro-structures (1945). During the war years she focused her research efforts on the analysis of high-strength carbon fibers, working at the British Coal Utilization Research Association (BCURA), work that later found use in the construction of carbon rods in modern nuclear power plants. She moved to Paris and lived there from 1947 to 1951, joining the Central Government Laboratory for Chemistry. Working under Jacques Mering she became proficient in X-ray diffraction analysis of coal structure. During this time, in addition to her science she perfected her French and culinary arts, embraced French fashion, and generally enjoyed the freedom and respect as a scientist and colleague, devoid of the prejudice women had to endure in England. Nonetheless, as a foreigner in France, she understood that it would be hard for her to establish herself as an independent researcher and so she returned to England and joined Kings College in London under Sir John Randall. It was here that she produced the essential basic data that paved the way for James Watson and Francis Crick of Cambridge University to propose the double helix structure of DNA, the molecule that genes are made of. At Kings College she and Maurice Wilkins independently studied DNA structure. Franklin perfected the X-ray diffraction equipment and technology to produce highly focused X-ray beams to study the fine DNA fibers she was able to extract. She soon discovered that DNA could assume two forms, which she called A and B. Through painstaking work and extreme care and patience in sample preparation she produced photographs of both A and B forms that led her to conclude that DNA was a double helical molecule in which the phosphate atoms must be on the outside of the structure and the nitrogen bases facing inside. These conclusions and Franklin's X-ray photographs enabled Watson and Crick to propose their double helix model of DNA in which base pairing created the bonds necessary to hold the anti-parallel strands of DNA together. In 1953, she moved to Birkbeck College to establish a new laboratory dedicated to the study of nucleic-acid protein complexes (when she left Kings College Sir Randall demanded that she stop working on DNA!). Franklin turned to the study of Tobacco Mosaic Virus (TMV) and with a young investigator, Aaron *Klug, discovered that TMV was an extended tube in which its proteins were arranged in helical fashion with RNA (ribonucleic acid) embedded amongst the protein molecules.

She made pivotal contributions in three areas of science; the analysis of the structure of carbon and coal, the elucidation of the structure of DNA, and the new field of structural virology as a pioneer. In 1956 she was diagnosed with ovarian cancer. Despite three operations and experimental chemotherapy she courageously continued her work on TMV and polio virus until her dying day. Four years later, Francis Crick, James Watson, and Maurice Wilkins received the Nobel Prize in medicine and physiology for their discoveries concerning the structure of DNA. In 1982 Sir Aaron Klug was awarded the Nobel Prize in chemistry for his structural elucidation of biologically important nucleic acid-protein complexes. It is not by chance that such profound science was so intimately associated with Rosalind Franklin. At the age of 37 she died of ovarian cancer, with little recognition of her monumental contributions to modern biophysics.

BIBLIOGRAPHY: B. Maddox, *Rosalind Franklin: The Dark Lady of DNA* (2002); A. Piper, "Light on a Dark Lady," in: *Trends in Biochem. Sci.* 23 (1998), 151–54; J.D. Watson, *The Double Helix* (1968).

[Jonathan Gershoni (2nd ed.)]

FRANKLIN, SELIM (1814–1883), Canadian politician. Born in Liverpool, England, Franklin was the son of a banker and acquired considerable wealth as a financier. He went to California during the gold rush of 1849 and in 1858 he and his brother, LUMLEY (1812–1873), were among the first Jews to settle in British Columbia. As British citizens, they were able to open a real estate auctioneering business in Victoria, conducting several government land sales of historical importance. In 1860 Selim was elected to the second Vancouver Island legislative assembly, despite allegations of ballot manipulation. Further trouble arose over his eligibility to take his seat because of the oath "on the true faith of a Christian," but the debate was ended by a ruling citing the British legal precedents of Jews and other non-Christians swearing oaths. With the right to assume his position in government recognized, Selim was a member of the assembly from 1860 to 1863 and from 1864 to 1866, when he returned to San Francisco. In 1865 Lumley Franklin became the first Jewish mayor in British North America when he was elected mayor of Victoria, taking an enthusiastic stance in favor of a political union with the mainland of British Columbia. Together, the two brothers played a prominent part in the social and cultural life of both the general and the Jewish community of Victoria. Both were gifted musicians and officers of the local Philharmonic Society. A river running into the Alberni Canal on Vancouver Island and a street in Victoria were named after Selim Franklin.

[Ben G. Kayfetz / Barbara Schober (2nd ed.)]

FRANKLIN, SIDNEY (**Frumkin**; 1903–1976), U.S. bullfighter. Born in Brooklyn, New York, to Russian Jewish immigrants, Franklin was the fifth of nine children. He graduated from Commercial High School and then attended Columbia University, where he studied commercial art. He opened a silk-screen poster business, but one day, after an argument with his father, he decided to go to Mexico to study Mayan history, setting sail on June 8, 1922, for Veracruz. There he opened another poster business, but after seeing his first bullfight, he was drawn to the sport and found his life's calling. Franklin debuted on September 23, 1923, losing his balance twice but killing the bull. The American was not given much of a chance in the Latin sport, but he became an admired matador, first in Mexico and then in Spain, where he moved in 1929 to become he first American ever to fight in that country. He later befriended Ernest Hemingway, who wrote in *Death in the Afternoon*, "Franklin is brave with a cold, serene and intelligent valor but instead of being awkward and ignorant he is one of the most skillful, graceful and slow manipulators of a cape fighting today … He is a better, more scientific, more intelligent, and more finished matador than all but about six of the full matadors in Spain today [1932] and the bullfighters know it and have the utmost respect for him…. You will find no Spaniard who ever saw him fight who will deny his artistry with a cape."

In his autobiography, *Bullfighter from Brooklyn: An Autobiography of Sidney Franklin* (1952), he wrote: "I have often been asked how I came to be a bullfighter; what there was in my background that led me into such a unique profession. Frankly, when I try to review my early life I am puzzled to find an answer to that riddle. To me, at the time, the journey from Jackson Place in Brooklyn to the Plaza de Toros Monumental in Madrid was an entirely natural though exciting one. One thing followed another and, instead of selling insurance or filling someone's teeth, I fought bulls."

[Elli Wohlgelernter (2nd ed.)]

FRANKS, English family, with an important branch in America. BENJAMIN FRANKS (c. 1649–c. 1716), son of an Ashkenazi merchant from Bavaria, was born in London but moved to the West Indies in the last decade of the 17th century. His checkered career took him to New York and Bombay where he made a deposition which was used in the piracy trial of Captain Kidd. He returned to London in 1698 and seems to have stayed there until his death. ABRAHAM (NAPHTALI HART)

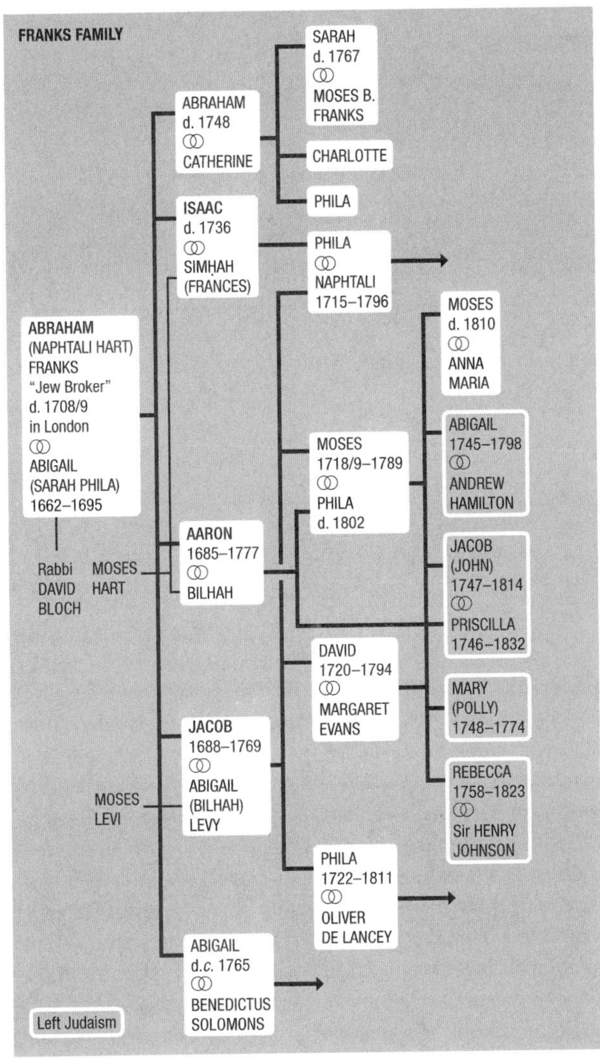

FRANKS (d. 1708–09) was a founder of the London Ashkenazi community admitted to the Royal Exchange in 1697. His son AARON (1685 or 1692–1777) attained great wealth as a jeweler, and was said to have distributed £5,000 yearly in charity without distinction of race or creed. At his country house in Isleworth near London he gave musical receptions and entertained members of the aristocracy. Like other members of the family, he was closely associated with the affairs of the Great Synagogue. He took the lead in 1745 in the attempt to secure the intervention of the English court on behalf of the Jews expelled from Prague. His brother JACOB *FRANKS (1688–1769) was head of the American branch of the family, some members of which in due course returned to England and played a part in communal and public life. (See the chart, "Franks Family.")

BIBLIOGRAPHY: C. Roth, *The Great Synagogue, 1690–1940* (1950), passim; Oppenheim, in: AJHSP, 31 (1928), 229–34; L. Hershkowitz and I.S. Meyer (eds.), *Letters of the Franks Family, 1733–48* (1968). **ADD. BIBLIOGRAPHY:** T. Endelman, *Jews in Georgian England*, index; Katz, England, 220–23, index.

[Cecil Roth]

FRANKS, BILHAH ABIGAIL LEVY (1696?–1756), Jewish letter writer. Franks was born in London; the sources are inconclusive about the exact date, just as they are unclear about when the Levy family migrated to New York City. Some documents demonstrate that her father, Moses Levy, a merchant, was there by 1703. At a young age, Franks shed the name Bilhah and signed herself Abigaill, which she always spelled with a double *l*. She is best known because of her surviving correspondence to her eldest son, Naphtali, who was sent to London in 1733 to learn the family business from his uncles. Abigail Franks' letters, among the earliest of any woman in the British colonies, are the oldest surviving communications by a Jewish woman in North America.

Little is known about Franks' youth. She had four brothers with whom she maintained close relations throughout their lives. Her mother died when she was 11 years old, and her father, as was customary, remarried a much younger woman, who in turn gave birth to eight more children. At the age of 16, Abigail married Jacob Franks, a young merchant who also had migrated from London and lived in the Levy household. Naphtali was born in 1715, followed by at least six other children.

Thirty-five letters survive, written between 1733 and 1748. Despite minimal spelling and punctuation skills, the letters reveal that she read broadly in literature and history. Naphtali sent her works of fiction and poetry, some classics, such as Alexander Pope, as well as popular literature. When she disapproved of a book, she chastised him for sending her "trash." She requested a two-volume history of Poland. Her letters demonstrate, as well, her interest in local government and serve as a source of information about early New York's fractious politics. She gossiped with her son about people known to them both, often with a tart tongue. Her observations about Judaism are sharp and critical, but she admonished her son to maintain the dietary laws as well as his daily devotions. While Franks fails to mention some important events in her life, including the deaths of two of her children, she reveals her own personality and much more. She never saw her son again, and none of his letters to her survive.

BIBLIOGRAPHY: E.B. Gelles (ed.), *The Letters of Abigaill Levy Franks (1733–1748)* (2004); L. Hershkowitz and I.S. Meyer, eds. *Letters of the Franks Family (1733–1748)* (1968); M.H. Stern. *First American Jewish Families: 600 Genealogies, 1654–1988* (1991).

[Edith B. Gelles (2nd ed.)]

FRANKS, DAVID (1720–1794), Colonial American merchant and Loyalist. Franks, who was born in New York, began his extensive mercantile career with his arrival in Philadelphia in 1738. In 1742 he entered a partnership with his uncle Nathan Levy. The following year he married a Christian and their children were baptized in Christ Church, Philadelphia. Franks, who had extensive holdings in Western lands, became an agent for the British Army in North America by 1754, along with his father. During the Revolution, Franks was deputy commissary of (British) prisoners for the Americas. However, because of dealings with his brother Moses and with England, he was relieved of his duties. In 1780, after several trials and a good deal of publicity, he was ordered out of Pennsylvania. Exiled to England, Franks vainly sought relief from the crown for his loyalty.

[Leo Hershkowitz]

FRANKS, DAVID SALISBURY (c. 1743–1793), U.S. merchant, a Revolutionary War officer, and patriot. Franks was born in Philadelphia. Three years after his registration in 1760 at the Philadelphia Academy (University of Pennsylvania), he went to Montreal as a merchant. He returned in 1776 after aiding the invading army of generals Richard Montgomery and Benedict Arnold in their unsuccessful attack on Quebec. He became an aide to Arnold, serving in the Pennsylvania line as a major. Exonerated of complicity in the Arnold treason in 1780, Franks was promoted to the rank of lieutenant colonel. In 1781 he was sent to bring government dispatches and advice to John Jay in Madrid and to Benjamin Franklin in Paris. He served as courier, consular official, and confidant to Thomas Jefferson, Robert R. Livingston, and John Adams at various times in Europe until 1787. In 1790 he was appointed assistant cashier to the Bank of the United States. Franks had served as *parnas* of the Congregation Shearith Israel in Montreal in 1775 and was a contributor to Mikveh Israel in Philadelphia.

BIBLIOGRAPHY: Rosenbloom, Biog Dict, 39.

[Leo Hershkowitz]

FRANKS, JACOB (1688–1769), New York City merchant and founder of a prominent mercantile family. Franks, born in London, arrived in New York in 1708 or 1709. He became a freeman of New York in 1711. A year later he married Abigail Bilhah Levy, daughter of Moses *Levy, one of New York's wealthiest Jews. The couple had nine children, three of whom – Moses, David, and Naphtali – became successful merchants in England and the provinces. A daughter, Phila, married Oliver De Lancey in 1742, thus linking the family with New York aristocracy. Franks' vast trade activities, engaged in part with Moses Levy and Nathan Simpson, as well as his sons, included dry goods, liquor, and slaves. Other partners in trade were members of the Van Cortlandt, Philipse, and Livingston families. Franks was elected constable of the Dock Ward in New York City in 1720, but declined to serve. He did serve in the militia during the French and Indian Wars. Franks contributed to the building of the steeple on Trinity Church in 1711. Much involved in the congregational affairs of Shearith Israel in New York, he served in a variety of offices, including that of president (1729). He was a founder of the congregation's Mill Street synagogue, and also helped to purchase the congregation burial ground off present-day Chatham Square. Frank's interest in religious affairs was not continued by his descendants, and the family disappeared as Jews by the end of the 18th century.

BIBLIOGRAPHY: L. Hershkowitz and I.S. Meyer (eds.), *Letters of the Franks Family (1733–1748)* (1968).

[Leo Hershkowitz]

FRANKS, JACOB (c. 1766–c. 1823), merchant and civic leader in Wisconsin and Michigan. Franks, who was born in England, was a nephew of David Salisbury *Franks. He immigrated to Montreal and in 1792 was sent to Green Bay, Wisconsin, as an agent for a Montreal firm. He soon purchased a large tract of land, opened his own trading post, and became one of the influential residents of the settlement, contributing much toward the development of the area. Franks moved to Mackinac, Michigan, in 1805 or earlier. During the War of 1812 Franks fought on the British side and aided in the capture of Mackinac. In 1815 he was listed as one of the "magistrates, merchants, traders and principal inhabitants of Michilimackinac and St. Josephs." When the British withdrew from Mackinac to Drummond Island, Michigan, in 1815, the Americans destroyed Franks' house at Mackinac. He returned to Montreal, where he became an army purveyor and was also a business associate of Henry Joseph, member of a leading Canadian Jewish family.

BIBLIOGRAPHY: I. Katz, *The Beth El Story* (1955), index; B. Sack, *History of the Jews in Canada* (1945), index; *Wisconsin Historial Collections*, 19 (1903–11), 292.

[Irving I. Katz]

FRANZBLAU, ABRAHAM NORMAN (1901–1982), U.S. educator and psychiatrist. Franzblau was born in New York. He began a long association with Hebrew Union College in 1923 as principal of its school for teachers in New York, serving until 1931, when he became professor of education and pastoral psychiatry at the College at Cincinnati. Franzblau received a Ph.D. in education from Columbia (1935), and then took up the study of medicine, receiving his M.D. in 1937. During World War II he was attached to the Surgeon General's Office as colonel. Franzblau returned to New York in 1946 as professor of pastoral psychology and dean of the Jewish Institute of Religion school of education. In 1948 he became associated with the psychiatric department of Mount Sinai Hospital and in 1958 retired from Hebrew Union College to devote himself entirely to psychiatry. A pioneer in the application of psychiatric knowledge to the work of the ministry, Franzblau lectured in this field at many seminaries. Besides texts, monographs, and research studies, he wrote *Religious Belief and Character Among Jewish Adolescents* (1934); *Road to Sexual Maturity* (1954); *Primer of Statistics for Non-Statisticians* (1958); and (with his wife Rose Franzblau) *Sane and Happy Life* (1963).

His wife ROSE NADLER FRANZBLAU (1905–1979) was a psychologist and columnist. She was born in Vienna and wrote human relations columns for the *New York Post* from 1947 and discussed psychological problems submitted by listeners to her daily radio program. She wrote *Race Differences in Mental and Physical Traits* (1935) and co-authored *Final Report, National Youth Administration* (1944) and *Tensions Affecting International Understanding* (1950). She also wrote *The Middle Generation* (1971).

ADD. BIBLIOGRAPHY: F. Fierman, "Abraham N. Franzblau: Revolutionary Jewish Educator," in: *El Paso Historical Review* (1988).

[Sefton D. Temkin / Ruth Beloff (2nd ed.)]

FRANZOS, KARL EMIL (1848–1904), Austrian novelist and journalist. Franzos' oeuvre reflects the identity crisis of emancipated European Jewry. His writings stage this crisis as a conflict between Western and Eastern Jews, between the Haskalah ideal of a transgressive "culture" and the inbred religious traditions of the shtetl. Born in the Galician town of Czortkow and raised in Czernowitz, he was brought up within a multi-ethnic and multi-religious society. After studying law in Vienna and Graz he returned to Galicia only a few years later – as a correspondent for the influential Viennese paper *Neue Freie Presse*. Defining his task as "to accompany the spirit of 'Bildung' and of progress in its war in the east as a humble, but honest correspondent," Franzos fleshed out various scenes of this "cultural war" in several tales and reports from the land of "darkness," which were published in two volumes under the title *Aus Halb-Asien* ("From Half-Asia") in 1876. His writings targeted Ḥasidism, considering it a harsh and brutal dictatorship of ignorance that prevented Eastern Jewry from leaving the halakhic paths and joining the process of Jewish acculturation and emancipation. On the other hand, it was Franzos' intention to produce a detailed impression of shtetl life and therefore his descriptions are also imbued with compassion and belie his fascination with the world whose structures are supposed to be struck down by the Enlightenment. Within these constellations, Franzos created his own particular kind of narrative within the genre of the so-called "ghetto novella," which he demonstrated first in his story collection *Die Juden von Barnow* (1877). The center of these novellas could be seen in the conflict between two laws (i.e., *torot*), between *halakhah* – as a law that has become insufficient to solve the daily problems of *galut* existence – and culture – as a new and superior law that is capable of making decisions that do not contradict ethical and moral values in order to find justice. The tragedy of this conflict is shaped in Franzos' novels *Moschko von Parm* (1880), *Judith Trachtenberg* (1889), and his famous *Der Pojaz* (published posthumously in 1905), which tells the story of the young Eastern Jew Sender Glatteis, who tries to get on the track of German culture in order to become an actor but who is finally not able to surmount the barriers of shtetl society with its restrictions.

For a long time the double-edged sense of Franzos' writings was overlooked, but in recent years it has become more and more clear that the crisis of Eastern Jewry diagnosed by his oeuvre mirrors the crisis of Western Jewry. The success of Franzos' writings at the end of the 19th century therefore points to the ambivalent status of German and Austrian Jewish society at the peak of the emancipation process: the enthusiastic reception of Franzos becomes a paradigm for the secular interpretation of Judaism as representing a longing for stabile cultural patterns of "Jewishness" as well.

Regarding his non-Jewish readers, Franzos saw himself always in the position of a mediator, whose mission was to explain the circumstances and conditions of East Jewish socialization, the effort it took for an Eastern Jew to bridge the gap between religious traditions and the sphere of the big humanist project which he identified with German culture. His ideal of a forthcoming German-Jewish symbiosis made him a sedulous fighter against any form of antisemitism. Franzos himself proved the value of Jewish participation in German cultural life – in 1879 he published the first edition of Georg Buechner's collected works.

BIBLIOGRAPHY: F. Sommer, *Halb-Asien. German Nationalism and the Eastern European works of Karl Emil Franzos* (1984); C. Steiner, *Karl Emil Franzos: 1848–1904. Emancipator and Assimilationist* (1990); P. Theisohn, *Eruv. Herkunft und Spiel an den Grenzen der Aufklärung in K.E. Franzos' "Der Pojaz,"* in: D. Bischoff et al. (eds.), *Herkuenfte* (2004), 171–90.

[Philipp Theisohn (2nd ed.)]

FRATERNAL SOCIETIES, organizations for mutual aid, fellowship, life insurance, relief of distress, and sick and death benefits, frequently modeled on the *Freemason pattern. Jewish fraternal societies originated in the 19th century. In England the Order Achei Brith and Shield of Abraham was organized in 1888, Ancient Maccabeans in 1891, Achei Ameth in 1897, Grand Order Sons of Jacob in 1900, followed by many others. In 1915 an Association of Jewish Friendly Societies was established there. In South and Central America these societies were organized as *Landsmannschaften, e.g., the Galician Farband or Bessarabian Landsleit Farein. The main society in the United States is the Independent Order *Bnai B'rith. Other bodies are the True Sisters (1846), the *Free Sons of Israel (1849), *Brith Abraham (1859), the Independent Order Brith Abraham (1887), and the defunct Order Kesher Shel Barzel (1860). Many others originated as *Landsmannschaften*. Many small-scale *Landsmannschaften* later enrolled in general orders, some of which were formed along political lines: the *Workmen's Circle (1900) stressed socialism; the Jewish National Workers' Alliance (1910) combined Zionism with socialism; the International Workers' Order (1930), later renamed Jewish People's Fraternal Order, was controlled by Communists. They established elementary and high schools with instruction in Yiddish and Hebrew and promoted adult education. With the growing popularity of commercial insurance, the commercialization of the mortuary business, and leisure time activities, the membership of fraternal orders rapidly declined.

BIBLIOGRAPHY: Baron, Community, index, s.v. *Landsmannschaften*; Weinryb, in: JSOS, 8 (1946), 219–44; AJYB, 39 (1938), 123–4; 50 (1949), 34–37; Levitats, in: *Essays on Jewish Life and Thought* (1959), 333–49.

[Isaac Levitats]

FRAUD, the prohibition against wronging another in selling or buying property (Lev. 25:14) is one of civil (see **Ona'ah*) rather than criminal law – although, since it is a negative injunction, its violation by any overt act may result in the punishment of *flogging (Tos. and *Penei Yehoshu'a* to BM 61a; cf. Maim. Yad, Sanhedrin 18:1). Where reparation can be made by the payment of money, no such punishment may be inflicted in addition (cf. Yad, loc. cit., 2 and Mekhirah 12:1; Ket.

32a; Mak. 4b, 16a). The express repetition, "And ye shall not wrong one another, but thou shalt fear thy God" (Lev. 25:17), was interpreted to prohibit the "wronging" of another not only in commercial transactions but also in noncommercial intercourse: the prohibition extends to "wronging by words" as distinguished from wronging by fraudulent deeds and devices; and wronging by words includes pestering people in vain as well as offending or ridiculing them (BM 4:10). It is said that wronging by words is even more reprehensible than wronging by fraudulent deeds, because while the latter is an offense against property only and can be redressed by the payment of money, the former is an offense against the person and his reputation, for which money will not normally be an adequate compensation (BM 58b; Yad, Mekhirah 14:12–18; see *Slander). However, though not constituting a cause of action for damages, wronging by words is not punishable by flogging either, because the mere utterance of words is not considered such an overt act of violation as may be punished in this way (cf. Yad, Sanhedrin 18:2). The admonition "but thou shalt fear thy God" (Lev. 25:17) is said to indicate that even though the offender may escape human punishment, divine retribution is certain to follow (Yad, Mekhirah 14:18; Ibn Ezra to Lev. 26:17).

The fact that fraud, even in the civil law meaning of the term, was in biblical times regarded as eminently criminal in character is well illustrated in Ezekiel's discourse on individual criminal responsibility: the same responsibility attaches for wronging the poor and needy, converting property, and not restoring pledges, as for murder, robbery, and adultery (Ezek. 18:10–13), and for all those misdeeds the same capital punishment is threatened (*ibid.*). Fraud and *oppression are usually found in the same context as *usury (Ex. 22:20, 24; Lev. 25:14, 17, 37; Deut. 23:17, 20; Ezek. 7–8; 12–13, 17). Fraud has also been held as tantamount to larceny (see *Theft and Robbery; Tur, ḤM 227). As fraud and oppression go hand in hand, their victims are often the weak and the underprivileged; hence there are particular prohibitions on fraud against strangers (Ex. 22:20), widows and orphans (Ex. 21), and slaves (Deut. 23:17). Wronging widows and orphans is so repulsive in the eyes of God that "if they cry at all unto Me… My wrath shall wax hot and I will kill you with the sword, and your wives shall be widows and your children fatherless" (Ex. 22:22–23). Wronging and vexing the poor and the stranger draws forth God's wrath (Ezek. 22:29–31 et al.) and is a cause of national disaster (Jer. 22:3–6).

In post-talmudic times, fraudulent business practices often resulted in the courts barring or suspending the offender from carrying on business. While isolated instances of fraud would be dealt with as civil matters, repeated and notorious fraudulent business practices might be punished by the sequestration of the offender's business, depriving him of his livelihood (S. Assaf, *Ha-Onshin Aḥarei Ḥatimat ha-Talmud* (1922), 43). On other aspects of fraud see also **Gerama*.

In the State of Israel, the criminal law on fraud and kindred offenses has been reformed and expanded by the Penal Law Amendment (Deceit, Blackmail and Extortion) Law, 5723–1963. Fraud is there defined as any representation of fact – past, present, or future – made in writing, by word of mouth, or by conduct, which the maker knew to be false or did not believe to be true. It is made a criminal offense not only to obtain anything by such fraud, but also to obtain anything by any trick not amounting to fraud or by the exploitation of another's mistake or ignorance. Particular instances of fraud mentioned in the Act are pretenses of sorcery or fortune-telling; forgeries and unauthorized alterations of documents and the use or uttering of the same; the fraudulent suppression or concealment of any document or chattel, and the fraudulent incitement of others to make, alter, or conceal documents; as well as the issue of a check where the drawer knew that the banker on whom it was drawn was not bound to honor it.

[Haim Hermann Cohn]

The Penal Code 5737–1977 included the contents of the legislated sections referred to above, pertaining to fraud in general. It also included sections establishing special offences for fraudulent acts in the context of corporations (sections 426–414 of the Law). Furthermore, section 576 of the Companies Ordinance [New Version] 5743–1983 deals with offenses committed by position holders in companies.

Regarding fraudulent betrothal (*kiddushin*), see *Marriage. Regarding a fraudulent judgment, see *Practice and Procedure

[Menachem Elon (2nd ed.)]

BIBLIOGRAPHY: ET, 1 (1951[3]), 160f.; 2 (1949), 18f.; EM, 1 (1950), 149f. **ADD. BIBLIOGRAPHY:** M. Elon, *Ha-Mishpat ha-Ivri* (1988), 1:536, 537, 576, 604, 622, 720; idem, *Jewish Law,* (1994) 2:652, 710, 748, 769, 888.

FRAUENSTAEDT, JULIUS (Christian Martin; 1813–1879), philosopher. Frauenstaedt, who was born in Bojanowo, Posen, became a Christian at 20. He studied theology and philosophy at Berlin. Originally a Hegelian, he met Schopenhauer in 1846 and became a student and follower of his. Frauenstaedt published the first complete edition of Schopenhauer's works in 6 volumes (1873–74) and was his literary executor, publishing his posthumous writings. He differed with Schopenhauer on various aspects of his philosophy, especially regarding his voluntarism and pessimism. Frauenstaedt wrote extensively on religion and ethics. His best-known works are *Aesthetische Fragen* (1853), *Der Materialismus* (1856), and *Blicke in die intellektuelle, physische und moralische Welt* (1869). He also wrote a *Schopenhauer-Lexikon* (1871), *Briefe ueber die Schopenhauer'sche Philosophie* (1854), and *Neue Briefe* (1876).

BIBLIOGRAPHY: H. Berger, *Julius Frauenstaedt, sein Leben, seine Schriften und seine Philosophie* (1911).

[Richard H. Popkin]

°**FREDERICK I** (1826–1907), grand duke of Baden, son-in-law of Kaiser William I, and uncle by marriage of Kaiser William II. Frederick ruled Baden from 1852 until his death and carried out many reforms in the school and voting system based on liberal ideas and was the first and almost the only influential political figure to help *Herzl wholeheartedly. When he learned of Herzl and *Der Judenstaat* from his sons' tutor, the Reverend William *Hechler, he followed Herzl's progress with deep sympathy. It was he who arranged the meeting between the German kaiser and Herzl when the former visited Ereẓ Israel in 1898, and he sent enthusiastic memoranda on political Zionism to the Russian czar. His efforts to arrange meetings between Herzl, the czar, and the king of England were unsuccessful, but the czar sent him a letter in support of political Zionism. Frederick received Herzl several times and they conducted an extremely friendly correspondence. The grand duke's picture, which he sent to Herzl, adorned the latter's study (and can be seen in the reconstruction of this room at the Herzl Museum, Jerusalem). After failures and disappointments in the diplomatic sphere, Herzl was greatly encouraged by his personal contacts with Frederick. The Zionist Organization sent a delegation (including David *Wolfsohn and Nahum *Sokolow) to Frederick's funeral in Karlsruhe.

The grand duke's correspondence with Herzl, the kaiser, the czar, and others in German, English, and French was found in 1959 by H. and B. Ellern, who published a facsimile edition in 1961. Later all the letters were published in the *Herzl Year Book*, 4 (1961–62), 207–70 by H. Zohn, together with an English translation of the letters in German and French.

ADD. BIBLIOGRAPHY: L. Schwarzmaier, "Grossherzog Friedrich I. und der Antisemitismus in Baden," in: F.-J. Ziwes, *Badische Synagogen aus der Zeit Friedrich I. in zeitgenössischen Photographien* (1997), 25–32; H.-G. Zier, "Theodor Herzl und Großherzog Friedrich I. von Baden – Zwei Streiter fuer den Judenstaat," in: *Juden in Baden 1809–1984* (1984), 109–30; W.P. Fuchs, *Grossherzog Friedrich I. von Baden und die Reichspolitik 1871–1907*, vol. 1–4 (1968–80); idem, *Studien zu friedirch I. von Baden* (1995).

[Getzel Kressel / Bjoern Siegel (2nd ed.)]

°**FREDERICK II** (**"the Great"**), king of Prussia 1740–86. Like his predecessors, Frederick II followed the policy of allowing into the kingdom only fixed numbers of **Schutzjuden* ("protected Jews"), and took pains to ensure that these remained within defined limits. In keeping with this policy, the General Regulation he issued in 1750 distinguished between "ordinary" and "extraordinary" protected Jews; hereditary residential rights – to which only one child could succeed – were granted to the former alone while the rights of the "extraordinary" Jews lapsed with their death. Prussia's severe tax burden weighed more heavily on the Jews than other citizens. Apart from fixed "protection" money and the taxes levied in lieu of military service, they were also made responsible for the export of the state's manufactured products, and had to purchase a specified quantity of porcelain – the so-called *Judenporzellan* – from the royal factory. The trades and occupations they could follow were restricted, and the oath *more Judaico* was reimposed in 1747. Although freethinking and a lover of art and literature, the king was prepared only after much persuasion to extend to Moses *Mendelssohn the privilege of *Schutzjude* – and an "extraordinary" one, at that.

BIBLIOGRAPHY: Stern-Taeubler, in: JSOS, 11 (1949), 129–52; S. Schwarz, in: YLBI, 11 (1966), 300–5.

[Reuven Michael]

°**FREDERICK II** (**"the Belligerent"**) **OF BABENBERG**, duke of Austria 1230–1246. In 1244 he granted to Jews the privilege known as the "Fridericianum," following the basic lines of the charters granted by Emperor *Frederick II of Hohenstaufen in Germany in 1236, and to the city of Vienna in 1238. The "Fridericianum," regarded by the historian J.E. Scherer as a "sparkling star in a dark night," served as the model for privileges granted to Jews in *Hungary in 1251, in *Bohemia in 1254, in *Poland in 1264, and in *Silesia in 1294. *Rudolf of Hapsburg confirmed it in 1278 in his capacity of Holy Roman Emperor. The charter remained valid in the territory of Austria proper, until the expulsion of the Jews in 1420 (see *Albert II; *Wiener Gesera). The "Fridericianum" granted the Jews autonomy and equality with Christians in civil law and equal rights for trading in wines, dyes, and medicaments. It prohibited forcible conversion and exempted Jews from having persons arbitrarily billeted in their houses. Jurisdiction over the Jews was transferred from the imperial to the ducal chamber. Security of their life and property was guaranteed including defense of their cemeteries and synagogues. Freedom of transit throughout Austria was permitted, including transportation of corpses for burial without paying tolls. In lawsuits between themselves Jews were entitled to judgment by their own *bet din*, while for settling disputes between Jews and gentiles the post of **Iudex Judaeorum* was created. If a gentile was suspected of murdering a Jew but the charge could not be substantiated, the duke was ready to supply a champion to fight him on behalf of the Jew. The transition of Jewish occupations from commerce to moneylending is reflected by the fact that 22 paragraphs out of 30 in the charter deal with matters connected with moneylending, fixing a weekly interest rate of eight pfennigs on one mark, i.e., 173.33% yearly. The "Fridericianum" took over the concept of accepting the statement of a Jew on oath that he had taken a pledge bona fide if it was proved to have been stolen or lost though not through his fault, thus continuing to give the moneylender protection against malicious claims.

BIBLIOGRAPHY: J.R. Marcus, *The Jew in the Medieval World* (1965), 28–33; J.E. Scherer, *Die Rechtsverhaeltnisse der Juden in den deutsch-oesterreichischen Laendern* (1901), 130–4; 173–315.

°**FREDERICK II OF HOHENSTAUFEN** (1194–1250), king of Sicily (with Apulia) from 1198; Holy Roman Emperor from 1215. He was in continuous and bitter conflict with the papacy, and was considered an arch-heretic by his opponents, who even termed him anti-Christ for his pamphlet *De tribus impostoribus* ("On the Three Impostors," i.e., Moses, Jesus, and Mohammed). However he had a lofty, if unusual, conception of the Christian religion, and of the royal duty to serve it. In his attitude toward the Jews and his reactions to them Frederick's complicated and powerful personality displayed an individual approach. In Sicily and in south Italy he confirmed the privileges accorded to the Jews by his Norman predecessors. He also had the dyeing and silk-weaving industries in south Italy, which were crown monopolies, administered by Jewish agents, as had the Norman rulers before him, who also employed Jewish artisans in the textile manufacture. In 1221, however, the Emperor decreed that Jews must be distinguished from Christians by their clothes and their appearance, thus conforming to the decisions of the Fourth Lateran Council (1215). The Jews of Sicily were ordered to wear blue coats over their clothes and grow beards, and the women to wear a blue stripe on their cloaks and head covering to distinguish them from the Christians; but there is no evidence that these strictures were actually enforced. Frederick finalized the legal definition governing the concept of Jewish servitude, which had evolved during the 12th century, describing the Jews in grants of privileges he issued in 1236 and 1237 as *"servi camerae *nostrae,"* which applied to all of his domains. In Sicily, the status of the Jews, formerly modeled by the Normans on the status of the **Dhimmis* in the lands of Islam, underwent a significant change as they became *servi camerae* and the monarch's property. Muslims living in Frederick's domains were accorded similar status.

Frederick invited Jewish translators and scholars to his court: Judah b. Solomon ha-Kohen (*Matkah), Samuel Ibn *Tibbon, and Jacob *Anatoli, who took part in its lively and variegated intellectual life, discussing philosophy and disputing diverse issues with Christian scholars. The emperor also took part in these discussions: in his introduction to *Malmad ha-Talmidim* ("A Goad to Scholars"), Jacob Anatoli referred to the emperor's own attempts at biblical interpretation.

The originality and force of Frederick's personality clearly emerged in the action he took in connection with the blood *libel. When the bodies of children alleged to have been murdered by the Jews in *Fulda (1236) were brought before him, he determined that he would finally settle the question. Frederick read about the problem himself and became convinced that the Jews were innocent of the charge. Being unable to obtain a clear-cut opinion or decision from the Church authorities or nobility, he had the original idea of convening a council of apostates, who as former Jews and devout Christians should be able to give a definitive answer. Frederick subsequently published their unequivocal refutation of the blood libel and prohibited the libel's circulation throughout his domains.

BIBLIOGRAPHY: Graetz, Hist, 3 (1949), 565–9; W. Cohn, in: MGWJ, 63 (1919), 315–32; A. Stern, in: ZGJD, 2 (1930), 68–77; J.P. Dolan, in: JSOS, 22 (1960), 165–74; G. Wolf, in: P. Wilpert (ed.), *Judentum im Mittelalter* (1966), 435–41; G. Kisch, *The Jews in Medieval Germany* (1949), index; L.I. Newman, *Jewish Influence on Christian Reform Movements* (1925), 291–9; *Der Adler: Mitteilungen der Heraldisch-Genealogischen Gesellschaft* (1931–34), 40–44; J. Cohn, *Die Judenpolitik der Hohenstaufen* (1934); S.W. Baron, in: *Sefer Yovel… Y. Baer* (1960), 102–24; R. Straus, *Die Juden im Koenigreich Sizilien unter Normannen und Staufen* (1910); Roth, Italy, index; S. Grayzel, *The Church and the Jews in the XIII*th *Century* (1966²), index. **ADD. BIBLIOGRAPHY:** G. Sermoneta, "Federico ii e il pensiero ebraico nell'Italia del suo tempo," in: A.M. Romanini (ed.), *Federico II e l'arte del duecento, Atti della settimana di studi* (1980), 183-97; D. Abulafia, *Frederick II. A Medieval Emperor* (1988); idem, "The Servitude of Jews and Muslims in the Medieval Mediterranean," in: *Mélanges de l'École française de Rome*, 112, 2 (2000), 687–714; C. Sirat, "La filosofia ebraica alla cortedi Federico II," in: P. Toubert and A. Paravicini Bagliani (eds.), *Federico II e le scienze* (1994); idem, "À la cour de Frédérick II Hohenstaufen: une controverse philosophique entre Juda Ha-Cohen et un sage Chrétien," in: *Italia*, 13–15 (2001), 53–78; Dietelkamp, "Der Vorwurf des Ritualmordes gegen Juden vor dern Hofgericht Kaiser Friedrichs II im Jahr 1236," in: *Religiose Devianz* (1990), 19–39.

[Reuven Michael /Nadia Zeldes (2nd ed.)]

°FREDERICK III OF HAPSBURG, duke of Austria (as Frederick V), and king of Germany (as Francis IV, 1440–86); Holy Roman Emperor 1452–93. Frederick III favored the Jews, whose enemies described him as "more a Jewish than a Holy Roman Emperor." The general charter he granted to Carinthia in 1444 contained provisions for the protection of the Jews there. He resettled the Jews in *Austria (though not in Vienna) after their expulsion in 1421, for which he obtained a *bull from Pope Nicholas V in 1451 permitting their return since this would provide for the "Jews' livelihood and the Christians' benefit." He confirmed this permission when emperor. Frederick resisted the frequent protests by the Estates against admitting Jews (1458–63). As emperor he intervened on behalf of Israel *Bruna who was accused in a *blood libel in 1474, although earlier he had him imprisoned as a hostage to extort payment of a coronation tax. Frederick also intervened on behalf of the Jews in the blood libel cases of *Endingen (1470), *Trent (1476), and *Regensburg (1478). He persuaded Pope Paul II to issue a bull in 1469 ordering priests not to deny religious sacraments to officials who upheld the rights of the Jews. Jacob b. Jehiel Loans was physician to Frederick III for many years, and according to tradition there was personal friendship between patient and physician. Frederick's attitude to the Jews was motivated both by the need to overcome his financial difficulties and to uphold the imperial authority including his jurisdictions over the Jews.

BIBLIOGRAPHY: J.E. Scherer, *Die Rechtsverhaeltnisse der Juden in den deutsch-oesterreichischen Laendern* (1901), 422–20; S. Babad, in: HJ, 7 (1945), 196–98; R. Strauss, *ibid.*, 12 (1950), 20.

°FREDERICK WILLIAM (Ger. **Friedrich Wilhelm**), name of several kings of Prussia.

FREDERICK WILLIAM III was king of Prussia from 1797 to 1840. The defeats in the Napoloenic Wars at Jena and Auerstädt and the peace treaty of Tilsit (1807) brought Prussia heavy territorial losses but opened the way to reform in the state system. The liberal-inspired 1812 edict (see *Prussia) concerning the civil status of the Jews was issued by Frederick William III, it had been forced on him by the statesmen *Hardenberg and *Humboldt. The king himself made determined efforts to exclude the Jews from participation in army service: when, after the Napoleonic wars, Jewish war veterans and invalids applied for pensions and posts, he denied even the rights of those who had received decorations. The king explicitly ordered that conversion to Christianity should be made a condition for employment in state posts, including those in universities. Frederick William gave official support to a Prussian society for propagating Christianity among the Jews, and declared conversion to Judaism illegal. He opposed the *Reform movement and had the private prayer rooms of I. *Jacobson closed down. It was with reluctance that he awarded regular advancements and decorations to Meno Burg, the first Jewish career officer in the Prussian army.

His son, FREDERICK WILLIAM IV, was king of Prussia from 1840 to 1861. Jewish hopes that he would follow a more liberal policy were soon disappointed. Imbued with a romantic-medieval concept of a Christian state, he proved even more reactionary than his father. He considered that Judaism was not a religion, but the remnant of a political constitution (see the ideas of Moses *Mendelssohn). Frederick William determined to reorganize the Jews as an independent corporation on medieval lines, alongside but not within the Prussian body. In December 1841, he ordered that the term "civil rights" should be replaced by "rights accorded by the 1812 edict," a preliminary for a new Jewish constitution under which the Jews were to have rights within their own community only. G. *Riesser, L. *Philippson, Johann *Jacoby, and Moritz *Veit led the struggle against the royal policy, supported by various Christian liberals as well as by the provincial estates, who were in favor of general and Jewish service in the army and full application of the 1812 edict. The king's most important supporters were F.J. *Stahl and *Bismarck. Despite vigorous opposition, he carried through his Jewish constitution in 1847 with only minor revisions. The king's "corporationist" plans were made obsolete by the 1848 revolution, but on the basis of the 1847 constitution the Prussian state recognized only individual Jewish communities. In 1849 he refused the offer of the parliament of Frankfurt to be emperor of Germany because he did not wish to have any connection with the revolution.

BIBLIOGRAPHY: H. Fischer, *Judentum, Steal und Heer in Preussen* (1968), index, s.v. *Friedrich Wilhelm*. **ADD. BIBLIOGRAPHY:** D.E. Barkley, *Frederick William IV. and the Prussian Monarchy 1840–1861* (1995); W. Busmann, *Zwischen Preußen und Deutschland – Friedrich Wilhelm IV. eine Biographie* (1992); D. Blasius, *Friedrich Wilhelm IV 1795–1861* (1992).

FREED, ALAN (1922–1965), U.S. disc jockey. Born in Salem, Ohio, Freed spent two years at Ohio State University, where he played the trombone and led the Sultans of Swing, a band named after a famous group in Harlem. After two years in the Army, Freed started a career in radio playing classical music. It was a far cry from his later years as the most important figure in the early years of rock 'n' roll, an outgrowth of rhythm and blues usually associated with "race" music and black audiences. In 1950, Leo Mintz, the owner of a Cleveland record store, lured Freed to be host of a program on a station geared to young white listeners after he discovered that many white suburban youths were going to his store to buy recordings by black artists. Freed played those records on the show and he and the music became sensations. He called himself Moondog and in 1952, at the Moondog Coronation Ball, considered the first rock concert, 20,000 fans crashed the 10,000-seat capacity Cleveland Arena. The dance was canceled.

Moving to New York in 1954, Freed's career took off, even as he tangled with radio stations, television networks, and the music business over playing the so-called black music. He brought rock 'n' roll into mainstream American society, a biographer wrote, "and he made a lot of enemies because of that. Here was this white guy bringing blacks and whites together to dance in the 1950s. It was unheard of." Freed's popularity over the air was matched on stage during school holidays, when he took over large movie palaces in Brooklyn and elsewhere and presented rock 'n' roll performers to mobs of youngsters. One such show, in Boston in 1958, resulted in Freed's arrest for anarchy and inciting to riot. The charges were later dropped. But Freed's "big beat" music was considerably less welcome afterward and a number of cities banned him altogether.

Freed's downfall came a few years later, when television quiz show scandals brought the subject of payola – the payment of fees by record producers to have their songs played on the air – into public view. Freed was charged with having taken bribes totaling $30,650 from six record companies for playing and promoting their releases on his program. In 1962 he pleaded guilty to part of the charge and received a six-month sentence, which was suspended, and a $300 fine. He then moved to the West Coast, where he lived quietly.

In 1986, at the inaugural ceremonies for the Rock and Roll Hall of Fame, Freed was inducted posthumously. It was not an accident that the hall was built in Cleveland.

[Stewart Kampel (2nd ed.)]

FREED (originally **Grossman**), **ARTHUR** (1894–1973), U.S. popular lyricist and producer of motion picture musicals. Freed was born in Charleston, S.C., and grew up in Seattle, Wash. He was a piano player for the music publishers Waterman, Berlin, and Snyder (see Irving *Berlin), toured the Chicago area with the *Marx brothers for several months, and later with Gus Edwards' vaudeville circuit for a year and a half. After army service in 1917–19, Freed wrote his first popular song hit, "I Cried for You, Now It's Your Turn to Cry over Me," with music by his partner, Nacio Herb Brown. He and Brown produced revues at the Orange Grove Theater using their own songs. Freed's work in motion pictures began when he and Brown wrote the songs for Metro-Goldwyn-Mayer's and Hollywood's first musical, *Broadway Melody of 1929*. In 1939 Freed produced, for MGM, *Babes in Arms*, the first of about 50 musicals, including *Strike Up the Band* (1940), *Cabin in the Sky* (1943), *Meet Me in St. Louis* (1944), *On the Town* (1949), *American in Paris* (1951), and *Singin' in the Rain* (1952), the title of the last being a Freed song originally performed in MGM's second musical, *Hollywood Revue*.

FREED, ISADORE (1900–1960), composer. Born in Brest-Litovsk, Russia, Freed was taken to the United States as an infant. He studied with Ernest *Bloch there and with Vincent d'Indy in Paris. Returning to the United States in 1934, he engaged in teaching, and was chairman of the music department of the Hart College of Music in Hartford, Connecticut, from 1944 until his death. He wrote two symphonies; violin and cello concertos; and an opera, *The Princess and the Vagabond* (1948); chamber music; and choral works. His works were of a moderately modernistic idiom, with some use of American folk themes, as in his *Appalachian Symphonic Sketches* (1946). His synagogal compositions include *Sabbath Morning Service* (1950), *Ḥasidic Service* (1954), Psalm settings, and a selection from Salamone de *Rossi's *Ha-shirim asher li-Shelomo* arranged as a service for cantor, chorus, and organ (1954).

FREED, JAMES INGO (1930–), U.S. architect. Born in Essen, Freed fled from Germany to France in 1938 and immigrated to the United States with his younger sister in 1939. He rose to become one America's most distinguished architects, winning a long list of awards such as the 1997 Award for Outstanding Achievement in Design for the Government of the United States. He received his bachelor's degree in architecture from the Illinois Institute of Architecture (1953), where he returned as dean of architecture two decades later. After serving with the U.S. Corps of Engineers and then working as an architect and planner in Chicago, Freed joined Mies Van der Rohe in New York in 1955. In 1956 he joined I.M. Pei and Partners, later known as Pei Cobb Freed and Partners. Freed taught architecture at every major architectural school in the United States. As an active participant in the public sphere, he was director of the Regional Plan Association of New York–New Jersey–Connecticut and from 1983 to 1991 served as architectural commissioner of the Arts Commission of New York City. In 1988 Freed was elected to the American Academy of Design. He was also a member of the American Academy of Arts and Letters and a fellow of the American Academy of Arts and Sciences. Among Freed's major building designs are the Jacob Javits Exposition and Convention Center in New York City (1986) and the U.S. Holocaust Memorial Museum in Washington, D.C. (completed in 1993). To prepare himself for the design of the Holocaust Museum, Freed visited the sites of the Nazi concentration camps in Europe and memorials in Israel. He studied films, tapes, and books, keeping a bound volume of photographs in his office of what he had seen. "It has been the most moving experience of my life," he said. "It couldn't be just another government building.... We want walls to speak, to impart a certain discomfort, a certain pressure, a certain evocation." Freed decided that his design would be outside current architectural dialogues and outside questions of style The main issue, Freed explained, was how people can be made to understand the Holocaust and keep it from happening again. Certain construction details in the building are evocative of the camps: the design of the lighting, the brick work, and cracked concrete walls. The museum is organized around a long, descending walk through the exhibits and ends in a Hall of Remembrance. In 1996 Freed designed the San Francisco Main Public Library. In 2001 he designed the reorganization of the Israel Museum complex, which includes buildings devoted to archaeology, art, sculpture, and the Shrine of the Book.

BIBLIOGRAPHY: A. Dannat, *United States Holocaust Memorial Museum: James Ingo Freed* (1995); J.I. Freed, "The United States Holocaust Memorial Museum," in: J.E. Young (ed.), *Art of Memory: Holocaust Memorials in History* (1994), 89–101.

[Betty R. Rubenstein (2nd ed.)]

FREEDMAN, BARNETT (1901–1958), British artist and book illustrator. Freedman, who was born in the East End of London, the son of a tailor, was bedridden from the age of 9 to 12 years. He then became a draftsman for monumental masons and attended evening classes in art. In 1922 he obtained a small annual grant and admittance to the Royal College of Art. In 1940 he was appointed an official war artist to the British Army, and later to the admiralty. His most important artistic achievement was as a book illustrator. In 1927 he illustrated Laurence Binyon's poem *The Wonder Night*, followed two years later by an edition of *Memoirs of an Infantry Officer* by Siegfried *Sassoon. In 1935 he designed the commemorative stamp for the Jubilee of King George V. He illustrated a series of classics published by Limited Editions Club and the Heritage Club of America. His paintings of street scenes and itinerant musicians were influenced by memories of his childhood in the Jewish working-class area.

BIBLIOGRAPHY: J. Mayne, *Barnett Freedman* (1948). **ADD. BIBLIOGRAPHY:** ODNB online.

[Charles Samuel Spencer]

FREEDMAN, HARRY (1922–), composer, English hornist. Born Henryk Frydmann in Lodz, Poland, Freedman was raised in Medicine Hat, Alberta, from 1925, and from 1931 in Winnipeg, where he studied painting and clarinet and became involved in big band jazz. After service in the Royal Canadian Air Force in World War II, he settled in Toronto, studying composition with John Weinzweig at the Royal Conservatory (1945–51) and with Olivier Messiaen and Aaron *Copland at Tanglewood (1949) and Ernst Krenek in Toronto (1953). From 1945 he studied oboe with Perry Bauman and played English horn in the Toronto Symphony in 1946–70. The Toronto Symphony's first composer-in-residence (1969–70), Freedman taught and was also composer-in-residence at the Courtenay Youth Music Centre, 1972–81. In 1989–91, he taught composition and orchestration at the University of Toronto – in 1990–91 as the Jean A. Chalmers Visiting Professor of Canadian Music.

Exceptional for his prolific output in a wide variety of musical idioms and genres, Freedman has written several works for film, theater, and ballet, including the electronic music for *The Shining People of Leonard Cohen* (1970). Also representative of his breadth are *Psalm 137: Al Naharot Bavel* (1974) for tenor and organ, *Celebration: Concerto for Gerry Mulligan* (1977), *And Now It Is Today Oh Yes* (1982), a musical entertainment for soprano and chamber players based on Gertrude Stein's *Everybody's Autobiography*, and *A Time Is Coming* (1982) for chorus based on Amos 9:13ff.

In 1970 he won an Etrog Award for best music in a Canadian feature film (*Act of the Heart* starring Donald Sutherland and Geneviève Bujold). The Canadian Music Council named Freedman Composer of the Year in 1980 and he was installed as an Officer of the Order of Canada in 1984. The recording of his 1989 *Touchings* by the Esprit Orchestra and the Nexus percussion ensemble won a Juno Award in 1996, and his *Borealis* for four choirs and orchestra was cited for "freshness of ideas and beauty of sound" at the 1998 International Rostrum of Composers in Paris. In 1998 he also received the Canada Council's Victor Martyn Lynch-Staunton Award.

BIBLIOGRAPHY: G. Dixon, *The Music of Harry Freedman* (2004).

[Jay Rahn (2nd ed.)]

FREEDMAN, JAMES O. (1935–), scholar of administrative law. Freedman was born in Manchester, New Hampshire. He received his bachelor of arts degree from Harvard in 1957 and graduated cum laude from Yale Law School in 1962. He served as a law clerk to Justice Thurgood Marshall, and then practiced law with a New York firm before joining the faculty of the University of Pennsylvania Law School in 1964. He became university provost in 1978 and dean of the law school in 1979. Freedman served as president of the University of Iowa from 1982 to 1987, then as president of Dartmouth College from 1987 to 1998, the second Jew to serve in that position. Dartmouth, which is the most rural and conservative of the Ivy League campuses, had their second Jewish president well before some of the other, more Jewish populated Ivy League colleges had their first.

A prominent scholar, Freedman published *Crisis and Legitimacy: The Administrative Process and American Government* in 1978. He wrote numerous articles and reviews for academic journals, including *Iowa Law Review*, *University of Pennsylvania Law Review*, *Administrative Law Review*, and others. In his writing, as well as in his role as university president, he was an outspoken supporter of liberal arts education and its role in moral leadership. His 1996 work *Idealism and Liberal Education* sets forth the importance of a liberal arts education in preparing students for leadership. Freedman cites Czech playwright Vaclav Havel as an example of an engaged intellectual involved with social and political concerns.

In "Ghosts of the Past: Anti-Semitism at Elite Colleges," an article written for *The Chronicle of Higher Education* in 2000, Freedman discusses his decision in 1997 to address the issue of antisemitism while presiding over the dedication of the Roth Center for Jewish Life at Dartmouth. His speech, which cited documents from the archives of Dartmouth and other institutions, chronicled the existence of a Jewish quota during the 1920s, 1930s, and 1940s. Freedman called for "a continuing vigilance about discrimination" against ethnic and religious groups. The speech generated widespread interest and praise.

Freedman was actively involved with the American Jewish Committee and served on the board of Brandeis University. In 2000 he was elected the forty-second president of the American Academy of Arts and Sciences. As president, he expressed a wish that the Academy address social concerns and inequality. In 2003 Freedman was named a member of Hebrew College's National Board.

[Dorothy Bauhoff (2nd ed.)]

FREEDMAN, SAMUEL (1908–1993), Canadian lawyer, community leader, chief justice of Manitoba. To a student who asked Samuel Freedman whether he should be addressed as "milord" or "Mr. Justice," Freedman replied: "Call me Sam." Sam Freedman was born in the Ukraine, the fifth of seven children. At age three he came to Canada with his family, settling in Winnipeg's immigrant North End. He graduated from the University of Manitoba with honors in classics in 1929 and went on to law school, where he became an accomplished debater. He graduated in 1933 and entered law practice, served four years as editor of the *Manitoba Bar News*, and was president of the Manitoba Bar Association in 1951–52. He was named to the Manitoba Court of Queens Bench in 1952; in 1954–55 he headed a commission investigating railroad labor problems; during 1959–68 he served as chancellor of the University of Manitoba. In 1960 Freedman was elevated to the Court of Appeal and in 1971 was appointed chief justice of Manitoba, a position he held until 1993. On his appointment as an Officer of the Order of Canada in 1984, the governor general of Canada cited his "discriminating mind and glowing humanity [as resulting] in brilliant legal judgements…."

Freedman was also much involved in the community. During his student years he was active in the Menorah Society and later in the YMHA and B'nai B'rith. A founder of the Winnipeg Chapter of the Canadian Friends of the Hebrew University, he served as a member of the organization's national board of governors. During 1955–58 he was division co-chair of the Canadian Council of Christians and Jews and in 1957–58 was campaign chairman for the Manitoba Heart Foundation. He was in great demand as a public speaker in Winnipeg and other centers in Canada and the United States.

His son Martin Freedman sat as a member of the Manitoba Court of Appeal in the seat once occupied by his father.

[Abraham Arnold (2nd ed.)]

FREEDOM. The concept of freedom in the Bible is found in the injunction that on the advent of the *Jubilee, "liberty was proclaimed throughout the land unto all the inhabitants thereof… and ye shall return every man unto his family" (Lev. 25:10). Thus the freedom envisaged encompassed not only the emancipation of slaves, but the return to one's ancestral lands which had been alienated by sale. This concept is extended in Jeremiah 34, in which the prophet denounces the people for later disregarding the order given by Zedekiah "that every man should let his man-servant and every man his maid-servant, being a Hebrew man or a Hebrew woman, go free; that none should make bondsmen of them, even of a Jew his brother" (34:9). Although the Talmud also uses the word freedom in antithesis to slavery (BK 15a), in general it employs the word in a wider sense as denoting absence of subservience, and the concept that it was morally and legally wrong under any circumstances for a Jew to be dependent upon or subservient to another Jew became one of the fundamental principles of the rabbis, but to the evil of the denial of freedom to Jew by his fellow Jew was added that of the subservience of the Jew to foreign rule.

The concept of that freedom was unique in the insistence on the freedom of the individual in order that he might be free to devote himself utterly and without restraint to the service of God and the fulfillment of His will. The locus classicus of this conception is the rabbinical interpretation given to the verse "For unto Me are the children of Israel servants," which is emphasized by the repetition "they are My servants" (Lev. 25:55), upon which the rabbis comment: "they are My servants, but not the servants of My servants." It is the basis of the reason given by Johanan b. Zakkai for the law that a Hebrew slave who chose to remain in slavery when the time came for his emancipation had to have his ear bored (Ex. 21:6), an interpretation which is called "a species of *ḥomer*" (probably "an important ethical principle") "Why the ear of all the organs of the body? God said: Because it was the ear which heard Me say upon Mount Sinai 'Unto Me are the children of Israel servants, but not servants to My servants,' yet its owner went and acquired a [human] master for himself, therefore let that ear be bored" (Kid. 22b; in the *Mekhilta* to Ex. 21:6 Simeon b. Judah ha-Nasi derives the same ethical lesson from the fact that the ear had to be placed against the doorpost).

It was in accordance with this principle of freedom from man in order to be free for the service of God that R. Joshua b. Levi stated, "No man is free but he who labors in the Torah" (Avot 6:2), which may be a protest against those who thought of freedom in purely physical or rational terms. This principle was enshrined to such an extent that the Talmud actually asks how, in view of this interpretation, it is permitted for a Jew even to be the employee of another Jew and replies that the right of the laborer to withdraw his labor at any time preserves his essential liberty (see *Labor). This conception of the right of the Jew to individual freedom was extended to include national freedom from foreign rule. R. Judah interprets the freedom which comes from the study of the Torah as "freedom from exile" (Ex. R. 32:1), and the theme that failure to exercise this freedom brings in its train political servitude was a favorite theme of the rabbis in the period immediately following the destruction of the Temple, when foreign rule became a grim fact. Thus Johanan b. Zakkai homiletically interprets Song of Songs 1:8, "You were unwilling to subject yourselves to heaven; as a result you are subjected to the nations of the world"; and his contemporary Neḥunya b. ha-Kanah states, "He who accepts the yoke of Torah will have the yoke of foreign rule removed from him, and he who casts off the yoke of Torah, upon him will be laid the yoke of foreign rule" (Avot 3:5). The striking statement of Samuel in the Talmud (Sanh. 91b et al.) that the only difference between the present world and the Messianic age is subjection to foreign rule is actually accepted as the *halakhah* by Maimonides in the last chapter of the *Mishneh Torah*, but he also emphasizes that the "sages and prophets did not long for the days of the Messiah that Israel might exercise dominion over the world, or rule over the heathens, or be exalted by the nations, or that it might eat, drink, and be merry. Their aspiration was that Israel be free to devote itself to the Torah and its wisdom, with none to oppress or disturb it" (Yad, Melakhim 12:4).

Most extreme in their passion for liberty were the members of the "Fourth Philosophy," the *Zealots or *Sicarii as the case may be. Josephus states of them that "this school agrees in all other respects with the opinions of the Pharisees, except that they have a passion for liberty that is almost unconquerable, since they are convinced that God alone is their leader and master. They think little of submitting to death, if only they may avoid calling any man master" (Ant. 18:23), a principle which they carried into practice with their mass suicide at *Masada rather than submit to the Romans. It has been suggested that the differences between them and the Pharisees with regard to the love of freedom was that whereas the Pharisees, while extolling the importance of liberty, did not include it among the cardinal principles for which one should suffer martyrdom rather than transgress, those members of the "Fourth Philosophy" did include it. The ideal of freedom was kept alive in the Jewish consciousness throughout the period of exile. The four cups of wine obligatory on the **seder* night of Passover, the festival of freedom (Pes. 108b), are the symbol of freedom, and in the daily liturgy in the evening prayer, the Exodus from Egypt is referred to as the emergence of the children of Israel to "everlasting freedom."

[Louis Isaac Rabinowitz]

Freedom of Thought

Because there never was a single body of official doctrine, Jewish tradition not only permitted, but even encouraged freedom of thought. Speculation about the fundamentals of faith was held to be a desirable and meritorious activity. *Baḥya ibn Paquda, the 11th century moralist and philosopher, states explicitly that, "On the question whether we are under an obligation to investigate the doctrine of God's unity or not, I assert that anyone capable of investigating this and similar philosophical themes by rational methods is bound to do so according to his powers and capacities… Anyone who neglects to institute such an inquiry is blameworthy and is accounted as belonging to the class of those who fall short in wisdom and conduct" (*Ḥovot ha-Levavot*, *"Sha'ar ha-Yiḥud,"* ch. 3). Maimonides echoes this view, as do many other major Jewish thinkers. The last major Jewish philosopher of the Middle Ages, Joseph *Albo, summarized this tradition of freedom of thought: "It is clear now that every intelligent person is permitted to investigate the fundamental principles of religion and to interpret the biblical texts in accordance with the truth as it seems to him" (*Sefer ha-Ikkarim*, pt. 1, ch. 2). This freedom is evident in the lack of any one official Jewish creed. Proposed creeds vary in content, principles, and number of articles. From antiquity to the present Judaism has found room for almost every conception of God known to civilized man so long as it is consistent with the principle of God's unity.

Alongside this tradition of freedom of thought there was also a restrictive drive which sought to limit what Jews might think and even what they might read. A Mishnah teaches that certain categories of Jews forfeit their share in the world to come, either because they hold erroneous beliefs or because they read forbidden books (Sanh. 10:1). This repressive aspect of the tradition receives its most extreme form in the codified rule that certain kinds of heretics may, or even must be put to death (Av. Zar. 26b; Sh. Ar., YD 158; 2). There is, however, little evidence that such a rule was ever put into practice. David *Hoffmann argued that this rule was codified at a time of extreme Christian religious zealotry, and was intended to show that Jews were also devoted to their faith. He denied that this rule was ever intended to be enforced, adding that in modern times such a rule is a profanation of God's name. Restrictions were also enacted against the study of certain subjects. The Mishnah records the decree that "no man should teach his son Greek" which is interpreted to mean the study of Greek philosophy (Sot. 9:14; 49b). The study of mystic traditions as well was restricted. The Talmud relates that only one of the four sages who "entered the Garden" (i.e., engaged in esoteric speculation) departed unhurt (Ḥag. 14b). In codifying these laws Moses Isserles stated, "It is only permitted to 'enter the Garden' after one has satiated himself with meat and wine," i.e., the study of mysticism is only allowed for he who is thoroughly grounded in the study of *halakhah* and the details of the commandments (Sh. Ar., YD 246:4). In the Middle Ages bans were also imposed on the premature study of philosophy and sciences. Solomon b. Abraham *Adret proclaimed in his ban of 1305 that physics and metaphysics could be studied from the age of 25, but laid no restriction on the study of astronomy and medicine (other communities in southern France banned the study of philosophy until the age of 30; see *Maimonidean Controversy).

Freedom of thought was also threatened by those who banned or burned books which they found offensive. An almost continuous line leads from the talmudic prohibitions against certain works to the 20th-century zealot who burned a nonorthodox prayer book in New York in 1944. Over the centuries there were bans on and burnings of the works of some *Karaites, Maimonides' *Guide*, the *Me'or Einayim* of Azariah de *Rossi, and even of some books of M.Ḥ. *Luzzatto. The rise of *Ḥasidism and of the *Haskalah generated such intense efforts to suppress their literatures that one writer asserts that "there was no period in Jewish history in which so large a number of books ... were banned or burned."

Such practical restrictions on freedom of thought came to an end in the 19th century. They can still be found only among some minor sects of the extreme orthodox right wing, but have no effect on the life and thought of the vast majority of Jews. In a peculiar way these restrictive elements in the Jewish tradition evoked a basic commitment to freedom of thought. Those who imposed bans on books could only enforce them locally, since there was no central authority. Such bans usually evoked counter-bans so that a book proscribed in one community found vigorous defenders in another. However great the stature of those who sought to prevent a book from being read, there were always men of equal stature who came to its defense and made it available. In this way, even when subjected to severe strains, freedom of thought was preserved and protected.

[Marvin Fox]

BIBLIOGRAPHY: In the Bible: L.I. Rabinowitz, in: *Sinai*, 55 (1964), 329–32; S. Goren, *Torat ha-Mo'adim* (1964), 334–45. In Jewish Philosophy: M. Carmilly-Weinberger, *Sefer ve-Sayif* (1966); R. Gordis, *The Root and the Branch* (1962), 31–53; D.J. Silver, *Maimonidean Criticism and the Maimonidean Controversy* (1965); E. Shmueli, *Bein Emunah li-Khefirah* (1962), 161–78.

FREEHOF, SOLOMON BENNETT (1892–1990), U.S. Reform rabbi, scholar, liturgist. Freehof, born in London, was taken to the United States in 1903 by his parents, who settled in Baltimore. The Freehof family name is derived from Freda, the daughter of Rabbi Shneur Zalman of Liady, the founder of Habad Hasidism. He graduated from the University of Cincinnati (1914) and a year later was ordained at Hebrew Union College, whose faculty he then joined. After serving as a chaplain with the American forces in Europe during World War I, Freehof became professor of liturgy at Hebrew Union College. In 1924 he became rabbi of Congregation Kehillath Anshe Maarav in Chicago, and in 1934 he was appointed rabbi of Congregation Rodef Shalom in Pittsburgh. He remained at Rodef Shalom until his retirement in 1966.

Freehof's scholarly endeavors were largely in two fields. The first was Jewish liturgy. In 1930 he was appointed chairman of the Reform Committee on Liturgy of the Central Conference of American Rabbis, whose work led to the publication of the two-volume *Union Prayer Book* (1940–45) and the *Union Home Prayer Book* (1951), both of which stressed relevance to modern life and the inclusion of contemporary material in the service. He served as President of the CCAR from 1943 to 1945. His second main interest was the development of Jewish law as displayed in the literature of the responsa and its bearing on modern Jewish practice. He was appointed head of the Responsa Committee of the Central Conference of American Rabbis in 1955. He wrote *Stormers of Heaven* (1931); *The Book of Psalms: A Commentary* (1938); *Modern Jewish Preaching* (1941); *The Small Sanctuary: Judaism in the Prayer Book* (1942); *In the House of the Lord* (1942); *Reform Jewish Practice and its Rabbinic Background* (1944); *Preface to Scripture* (1950); *The Responsa Literature* (1955); *The Book of Job: A Commentary* (1958); *Recent Reform Responsa* (1963); *A Treasury of Responsa* (1963); and *Current Reform Responsa* (1969). The last Responsa collection was *New Reform Responsa* published in 1980 at the age of 88.

BIBLIOGRAPHY: Rodef Shalom Congregation, *Essays in Honor of Solomon B. Freehof* (1964). **ADD. BIBLIOGRAPHY:** K. Weiss, "Reforming the Links: An Approach to the Authenticity of the Reform Rabbi in the Modern World" (DHL Dissertation, 1980).

[Hillel Halkin]

FREEMAN, JOSEPH (1897–1965), U.S. author, critic, and journalist. Freeman was taken to the U.S. from the Ukraine as a boy of seven. After his graduation in 1919, he joined the editorial staff of Harper's *Illustrated History of the World War*, but in the following year moved to Paris, where he worked for the *Chicago Tribune*, subsequently representing both the *Tribune* and the New York *Daily News* in London. In 1922 he returned to New York, where he used his journalistic talents in support of socialism, working first for *The Liberator* and later also for the *Partisan Review*. In 1926 he helped to found the monthly *New Masses*. He first represented the periodical in Moscow, and at various times during the 1930s was its editor. Freeman and Michael *Gold were the two outstanding American writers of the Left during the years preceding World War II. Freeman's works include *Dollar Diplomacy: A Study in American Imperialism* (1925), a radical assessment of U.S. foreign policy written in collaboration with S. Nearing; *Voices of October: Art and Literature in Soviet Russia* (1930), with J. Kunitz and L. Lozowick; and *The Soviet Worker* (1932). His autobiography, *An American Testament: A Narrative of Rebels and Romantics* (1936), is one of the most valuable source books on the radical literary politics of his time. Under the stress of the Nazi-Soviet pact of 1939 Freeman finally broke with the Communists. He later published two novels, *Never Call Retreat* (1943), which dealt with the frustrations of a political refugee, and *The Long Pursuit* (1947), set in postwar occupied Germany.

BIBLIOGRAPHY: D. Aaron, *Writers on the Left* (1961), 68–90, 119–48, 365–75; S.J. Kunitz, *Twentieth Century Authors*, first supplement (1955), s.v.; *New York Times* (Aug. 11, 1965), 35. **ADD. BIBLIOGRAPHY:** J. Bloom, *Left Letters: The Culture Wars of Mike Gold and Joseph Freeman* (1992).

[Milton Henry Hindus]

FREEMASONS, members of a secret society which developed out of craftmen's associations, originally consisting of masons proper. From the 17th century the society existed mainly as a social organization and cultivated a tradition of doctrines, passwords, and symbols, a ritual which is supposed to derive from the building of the First Temple in Jerusalem. The coat of arms of the English lodges is said to have been adapted from one painted by Jacob Judah Leon *Templo. Modern Freemasonry began in England around 1717; in 1723 the London Grand Lodge adopted a constitution formulated by the Reverend James Anderson, based on some older traditions. A printed constitution facilitated the foundation of new lodges on the basis of a recognized authority. During the next decades the lodges spread, in Britain, France, Holland, Germany, and many other countries. All the lodges regarded themselves as belonging to the same fraternity, and a Freemason appearing at any lodge with a certificate of membership was admitted to the work of the lodge and entitled to hospitality and help in case of need. The first paragraph of the constitution stated that anyone found to be true and honest, of whatever denomination or persuasion, was to be admitted. The constitution obliged the member only to hold "to that religion in which all men agree, leaving their particular opinions to themselves," a declaration of religious tolerance based on the current Deist trend, which postulated a Supreme Being who could be conceived of by any rational being. It is not known whether the possible aspiration of Jews to be accepted in the lodges influenced the wording of the constitution; yet it is formulated in a way that includes Jews as possible members. Thus, when a Jew asked for admission in 1732, one of the London lodges accepted him. The doors of the English lodges remained open to Jews in principle, although in practice there was some discrimination.

The Deistic declaration in the constitution did not remove some traces of Christian practice, including the New Testament, playing a part in the lodges. Nevertheless in the middle of the 18th century Jews joined the lodges, not only in England but also in Holland, France, and Germany. A Jewish lodge, the Lodge of Israel, was established in London in 1793.

Masonic tolerance weakened as a result of attacks made on it by the traditional sectors of all religions, who feared its all-embracing intentions. The Catholic Church banned – and still bans – Freemasonry in a bull promulgated by Pope Clement XII in 1738. The Deism of Freemasonry was clearly contrary to Church doctrines, and conservative Protestants and Jews also felt that its rituals were in conflict with their religious beliefs. To the objection of the Churches and other conservative elements in society, the Masons reacted by an apology which, in the main, tried to prove that Freemasonry was not an un-Christian institution, an argument supported by the fact that the Masonic fraternity consisted exclusively of Christians: Jews, Muslims, and pagans were not and should not be accepted. However, in England and Holland no objection in principle to Jewish applicants existed and in France the objections were swept away with the Revolution. Here Freemasonry became a kind of secular church in which Jews could participate freely. Adolphe *Crémieux was not only a Freemason from his early youth but in 1869 became the Grand Master of the Grand Lodge of the Scottish Rite in Paris.

In Germany objection to Jewish membership persisted, remaining a matter of controversy for generations. Until the 1780s only a few German Jews were admitted to Masonry. About this time Jewish applications for admission to the Masonic lodges became frequent. Though there were some attempts to open the lodges to Jews, no German Freemason of any standing at that time advocated Jewish admittance. Some German Jews became Freemasons when traveling abroad in England, Holland, and, particularly, in post-revolutionary France. In Germany itself French or French-initiated lodges were established during the Napoleonic occupation. A Jewish lodge, L'Aurore Naissante, was founded in Frankfurt, authorized in 1808 by the Grand Orient in Paris. These ventures, however, hardened the resistance of the indigenous lodges in Frankfurt and in other German towns, and some Masonic fraternities introduced amended constitutions specifically excluding Jews.

In the 1830s German intellectuals who were Freemasons protested against this exclusion, joined by Masons from Holland, England, France, and even by a lodge in New York, who resented the fact that their Jewish members were refused entrance to German lodges. By 1848 some lodges admitted Jews, if not as full members at least as visitors. The years of the 1848 Revolution swept away some of the paragraphs excluding Jews, and the Frankfurt Jewish lodges were now acknowledged by their Christian counterparts. The exceptions were the Prussian lodges, controlled by law from 1798 by the mother lodges from Berlin. In 1840 there were 164 Prussian lodges with a membership of 13,000. No Jew could ever be admitted to these, not even as a visitor, but many members, and sometimes entire lodges, wanted to reintroduce the original English constitution which excluded the attachment of Freemasonry to any specific religion. By the early 1870s most branches admitted Jews as visitors, sometimes even as permanent visitors, and in one of the branches of the Prussian lodges the restrictive paragraph was removed in 1872. A new wave of antisemitism, however, soon swept over the Bismarckian Reich, and by 1876 the lodges were already adopting an antisemitic tone. Those Jews who had been accepted by Prussian lodges left during the antisemitic outbreaks, followed by some liberal-minded Christians who were shocked by the behavior of a society ostensibly committed to the ideal of brotherhood.

Some Freemasons genuinely believed that confessing the Jewish faith was a disqualification for Freemasonry, which they regarded as a Christian institution, a view contested by those who adhered to the original English constitution and called themselves humanistic Freemasons. The struggle between the two trends continued during the 19th century.

In Germany in the 1860s Jews and Freemasons began to be identified as twin agencies responsible for undermining traditional society. This combined criticism of the two groups was transplanted to France, where a succession of books stressed *"le peril judéo-maçonnique."* The notion of a sinister alliance between the two played a conspicuous part in the *Dreyfus Affair and it became an antisemitic commonplace. The Protocols of the *Elders of Zion (first published in Russia in 1904) included the idea of a Jewish-Masonic plot to control the world. In Germany up to this time, Freemasonry was still thought of as a conservative and partly antisemitic association. When the *Protocols* were translated into German and English in the 1920s, Jews and Freemasons were identified as the sinister agents of the outbreak of World War I and of the German defeat. The slogan *Juden und Freimaurer* became a battle cry of the German right wing, and was utilized by Hitler in his rise to power. During World War II, Freemasons together with "Bolsheviks and Jews" were persecuted by the Nazis.

[*Encyclopaedia Hebraica*]

In the U.S.

Jewish names appear among the founders of Freemasonry in colonial America, and in fact it is probable that Jews were the first to introduce the movement into the country. Tradition connects Mordecai Campanall, of Newport, Rhode Island, with the supposed establishment of a lodge there in 1658. In Georgia four Jews appear to have been among the founders of the first lodge, organized in Savannah in 1734. Moses Michael Hays, identified with the introduction of the Scottish Rite into the United States, was appointed deputy inspector general of Masonry for North America in about 1768. In 1769 Hays organized the King David's Lodge in New York, moving it to Newport in 1780. He was Grand Master of the Grand Lodge of Massachusetts from 1788 to 1792. Moses *Seixas was prominent among those who established the Grand Lodge of Rhode Island, and was Grand Master from 1802 to 1809. A contemporary of Hays, Solomon *Bush, was deputy inspector general of Masonry for Pennsylvania, and in 1781 Jews were influential in the Sublime Lodge of Perfection in Philadelphia which played an important part in the early history of Freemasonry in America. Other early leaders of the movement included: Isaac da *Costa (d. 1783), whose name is found among the members of King Solomon's Lodge, Charleston, in 1753; Abraham Forst, of Philadelphia, deputy inspector general for Virginia in 1781; and Joseph Myers, who held the same office, first for Maryland, and later for South Carolina. In 1793 the cornerstone ceremony for the new synagogue in Charleston, South Carolina, was conducted according to the rites of Freemasonry.

The later history of Freemasonry in the United States shows a number of prominent Jewish names, but nothing corresponding to their influence in the earlier period. In 1843 the Grand Lodge in New York addressed a letter to the *Mutterloge* in Berlin complaining against the refusal of German lodges to accept registered Masons of the American Lodge because they were Jewish. Nonsectarianism in matters of religion has always characterized American Freemasonry, and regulations excluding Jews have not been part of their constitutions, though whether admissions policies have ever been restrictive would be difficult to establish. The apparatus of secrecy, ritual, and regalia which was a feature of *B'nai B'rith in its early years no doubt reflected the influence of Masonic practice as well as a desire to offer a substitute within the Jewish community.

[Sefton D. Temkin]

In Israel

In the Masonic world Jerusalem has always been regarded as the birthplace of Freemasonry; according to its tradition, there were Masonic lodges in the Holy Land at the time of the erection of King Solomon's Temple. Lodges are known there from the middle of the 19th century. During the Ottoman regime, six lodges were established in the country. The first regular one was founded in Jerusalem in May 1873, under the jurisdiction of the Grand Lodge of Canada. In 1891 another was established in Jaffa under the National Grand Lodge of Egypt. During the years 1910–11 the Grand Lodge of Scotland founded three lodges. During the British mandatory regime, Freemasonry flourished under several jurisdictions, in the main those of the Grand Lodges of Palestine and of Scotland. In 1932, four lodges in Jerusalem, holding under the National Grand Lodge of Egypt, constituted themselves into the National Grand Lodge of Palestine. Later, three of other jurisdictions joined it.

With the establishment of the State of Israel, a number of changes occurred: the lodges holding under the Grand Lodge of England and one holding under the Grand Lodge of Scotland moved out of the area. The remaining lodges of foreign origin and the five holding under the German Symbolic Grand Lodge in Exile joined the National Grand Lodge of Palestine. The five remaining lodges holding under the Grand Lodge of Scotland started to negotiate with their Grand Lodge to consecrate a Sovereign Grand Lodge of the State of Israel, which would encompass all the Masonic lodges in the country. The United Grand Lodge of the State of Israel was constituted in 1953 and since its consecration is the only sovereign grand lodge in Israel. In 1970 it consisted of 64 lodges, with some 3,500 active members drawn from all communities; Jews, Muslims, Christians, and Druze. The activities of the Grand Lodge and its several lodges included a mutual insurance fund; the Masonic old age home at Nahariyyah; Masonic temples all over the country; and a museum and library. By the early 21st century the number of lodges had increased to over 80.

[Abraham Fellman]

BIBLIOGRAPHY: J. Katz, *Jews and Freemasons* (1970); idem, in: JJSO, 9 (1967), 137–47; J.G. Findel, *Die Juden als Freimaurer* (1901); D. Wright, *The Jews and Freemasonry* (1930); S. Oppenheim, in: AJHSP, 19 (1910), 1–94; A.M. Friedenberg, *ibid.*, 95–100; H. Loewe, in: *Masonic News*, 1 (1928), 14–15.

FREE SONS OF ISRAEL, U.S. Jewish fraternal order. The organization was founded by nine men in New York City on January 18, 1849. Its purpose was to seek the deletion of clauses in the New York City charter that restricted the appropriation of land for burial purposes, in order to obtain ground for a Jewish cemetery. The order long consisted primarily of German Jews. By 1970 the Free Sons of Israel consisted of 46 self-governing lodges throughout the U.S., with approximately 10,000 men and women members. Each lodge provided membership benefits, which usually included burial, medical, and other benefits. The order consisted of an Insurance Fund and Fraternal Division and was headquartered in New York City. The order maintained a toy distribution program for handicapped children; a scholarship fund for the benefit of members and their families; a Federal Credit Union, which by September 1969, had disbursed $2,000,000 in loans; an insurance fund; travel service; blood bank; athletic association; and a newspaper, *The Free Sons of Israel Reporter.* Since that time it was the first organization of its kind to donate money to the Holocaust Museum in Washington., D.C., and has also contributed thousands of toys during the holidays to needy children in hospitals and care centers. On its 150th anniversary in 1999 it was commended by Rep. Carolyn McCarthy of New York in the House of Representatives.

FREE WILL, a philosophic and theological notion referring initially to the observation that man is able to choose between a number of possible courses of action, becoming, through his choice, the cause of the action which he selects. Among philosophers some accepted this observation as the true account of how men act, while others held that though man appears to be free to choose, his actions are, in fact, compelled, either by God or by laws of nature. While there were some Jewish philosophers who inclined toward a deterministic position, the majority affirmed that man, through choice, is the author of his own actions. Jewish philosophers generally considered a doctrine of free will as indispensable for accounting for man's moral responsibility for his own actions, and they considered it necessary for explaining God's justice in punishing evil-doers. Closely related to the notion of free will are those of divine *providence and divine omniscience.

In Jewish Philosophy

PHILO. The question of the freedom of man's will is discussed in a number of places in the writings of *Philo, but his position on this matter is not sufficiently defined. On the one hand, he clearly posits the freedom of man's will, i.e., the ability to choose between good and evil out of a knowledge of the difference between the two. On the other hand, he expresses the notion that man's choosing between good and evil is predetermined by the struggle between his inclinations and by the influence of external forces. Thus it cannot be said that Philo rejected determinism, since he did assume that all the occurrences in the world are a result of a necessary chain of causes and effects. Again, Philo in a number of places points to the similarity between man's free choice, which was granted to him by God, and the free will of God himself. It is evident that this refers to voluntary action, which is independent of the previously mentioned causal chain. Moreover, Philo's notion of man's free will contains a certain innovation in contrast to traditional Greek philosophy, since Aristotelians, for example, tended to view man's free choice as a defect and deficiency, contingent on his material being. On this point too, however, Philo is not consistent, for he also expresses the opinion that all the activities of created beings, including man, are actually caused by God. Philo's attempts to bridge this contradiction are artificial.

In some places in his writings Philo expresses the opinion that it is impossible to attribute to God's will those sins which are committed intentionally, while sins against fellowmen which are committed unintentionally sometimes result from natural order, and sometimes are instruments of divine punishment for the sins of the victim. In performing his good deeds, man needs God's help and divine grace, and he cannot ascribe his virtues to himself.

SAADIAH GAON. It appears that according to Philo, there is almost no connection between the notion of man's free will and the problem of divine justice. In contrast, *Saadiah, who was heavily influenced by Mu'tazilite philosophy (see *Kalām), maintains that the idea of God's justice necessarily implies the freedom of man's will. According to Saadiah, it is impossible to think that God could compel a man to do something for which he would later punish him. Furthermore, if man has no freedom of choice, both the righteous and the wicked should be rewarded equally since they would be equally fulfilling God's will. Saadiah brings another proof for free will: man feels that he can speak or be silent, that he can take something or leave it. Similarly, he feels that there is no one to deter him from doing as he wishes (*Book of Beliefs and Opinions*, ch. 4). Therefore, Saadiah states, in accordance with Mu'tazilite teachings, that every activity is preceded in time by the ability to carry it out or to refrain from doing so. This ability can be viewed as having a real existence, and its being prior to every action is what underlies free choice. Refraining from performing a certain action is also to be counted as an action in this respect.

Since the notion of man's free will as held by Saadiah results, wholly or in part, from his need to justify God's actions, it necessarily rests on the assumption that man's primary conceptions of good and evil are fundamentally identical with those of God. God, too, acts and is bound to act in accordance with these conceptions and, contrary to the Aristotelians, Saadiah maintains that it is one of the major functions of the human intellect to apprehend these conceptions directly (without any intermediary aid).

Thus it follows that the human intellect is permitted to question God's actions, especially with regard to sins which serve as punishment, such as Absalom's rebellion against David. On the one hand, Absalom sinned in rebelling against his father, and this sin originated in his free will. On the other hand, Absalom's attempted seizure of his father's throne served as punishment for David's sins.

In contrast to the more extreme Mu'tazilites, Saadiah does not see any contradiction between man's freedom of activity and God's prior knowledge of what man will choose to do. This foreknowledge, according to Saadiah, does not limit man's freedom, since it does not cause his actions.

BAHYA IBN PAQUDA. Baḥya ibn Paquda (*Ḥovot ha-Levavot*, ch. 3) briefly presents the ideas of those who believe that all of man's actions are predetermined by God, as well as opposing views, which maintain that man's will is free. He reaches the conclusion that whoever delves into this question must necessarily fall into error. Therefore, man must both conduct himself like one who believes that his actions are in his own hands (i.e., that he has freedom of choice), and at the same time trust in God like one who is certain that all his actions are predetermined. This view, which rejects a theoretical solution to the problem, stems from a desire to reconcile Saadiah's theodicy with total devotion to God (including the renunciation of one's freedom of action), which is characteristic of the Muslim *Sufis by whom Baḥya was influenced.

JUDAH HALEVI. Like Saadiah, *Judah Halevi accepts the notion of the freedom of man's will, which he supports by means of various proofs, some of which are similar to Saadiah's. One such proof is that a man feels that he can speak or be silent, act or refrain from acting. A proof of the existence of free will is found by Judah Halevi in the fact that only those actions which proceed from free choice are considered to be praiseworthy or culpable. Unlike Saadiah, however, he develops, in his discussion of free will, a classification of causes, in which he is strongly influenced by the Aristotelian school of thought.

The first cause of everything, according to Judah Halevi, is God, who produces the intermediary causes, according to which all actions and occurrences are either natural (i.e., resulting from natural order), accidental, or voluntary (resulting from human choice). Even the first two classes are not entirely brought about by necessity, but only free choice belongs completely to the realm of the possible; before the actual deed there is no necessity that it should be done.

Like Saadiah, Judah Halevi also maintains that there is no contradiction between the notion of free choice and the view that God knows in advance what will happen. Like Saadiah, he also maintains that God's foreknowledge cannot be regarded as a cause which brings about the event. Nevertheless, Judah Halevi states that his definition of free will as an intermediary cause, which is produced by the first cause, makes it necessary to see the voluntary acts as being under the influence of divine decree.

Man must conduct himself to the best of his ability. Exaggerated dependence on God may bring him into danger, thus, the warning; "Do not try the Lord." Sometimes, however, God acts without recourse to the intermediary causes, thereby bringing about miracles, such as Moses' being saved from starvation during the 40 days he was on Mount Sinai, or the defeat of Sennacherib.

ABRAHAM IBN DAUD. Abraham *Ibn Daud stated that he wrote his book *Ha-Emunah ha-Ramah* for the sole purpose of discussing the question of free will. Nonetheless, only a small section of the book (second treatise, 6:2, ed. by S. Weil, 93ff.) is devoted to this problem. Ibn Daud's position with regard to free will is similar to that of Judah Halevi. He classifies causes into divine, natural, accidental, and voluntary. There are some people, he says, in whom good or evil habits are so deeply ingrained that they are actually never required to exercise their free choice; but the majority of people are between these two extremes, and must therefore choose between good and evil. When they choose the good they become worthy of divine providence, while he who chooses evil is abandoned to his own resources. Ibn Daud is convinced that the existence of the possible in the world – and thus the non-existence of absolute determinism – is a defect. However, it should be pointed out, in this respect Ibn Daud departs from the teachings of his master, *Avicenna, whom he usually follows, since Avicenna believed that everything, including voluntary acts, is predetermined.

MAIMONIDES. In his *Guide of the Perplexed* *Maimonides deals with the question of free will in connection with providence (3:17). He distinguishes between five doctrines of providence, the last of which, that of the Torah, states that man can do everything according to his free choice. The question is whether Maimonides was convinced that man's choice and will are determined by prior causes, as was held by Muslim philosophers such as Avicenna, or whether he viewed the choice and voluntary activity of man as being uninfluenced by absolute determinism. There are various passages in the *Guide* which attest to his having followed the second opinion.

God's knowledge, which is only homonymous with human knowledge, controls each and every event, for God knows, "according to the view of our Torah," which of the possible outcomes will ultimately be actualized. This knowledge does not remove the things which are known, including human actions, from the realm of the possible. In his *Mishneh Torah*, which unlike the *Guide*, was intended for a popular audience, Maimonides takes a clearer position with regard to free will: every person may choose to be good or evil. God does not determine in advance whether a particular man will be righteous or wicked. A man can carry out any action, be it good or bad. If this were not so, the entire Torah would be purposeless; the wicked person could not be punished for his sins, nor the righteous be rewarded for his good deeds. In the same way that God instituted order in the universe, so it is His will that man be responsible for his own actions, by which he will be judged. Against the argument that God knows in advance whether a person will be righteous or wicked, Maimonides states that God's knowledge, being so unlike man's, cannot be apprehended by the human intellect. What is known beyond a shadow of a doubt is that man is responsible for his own deeds, and that God neither influences nor decrees that he should act in a certain manner. This is proven not only by religious tradition, but by clear arguments of reason (Yad, Teshuvah ch. 5).

Here, as in Saadiah, there is a clear connection between free will and the notion of God's justice. Unlike Saadiah and Judah Halevi, however, Maimonides does not avoid the difficulty involved in reconciling the idea of free will with the notion of God's omniscience. Contrary to some of his successors, he does not attempt to solve this difficulty, since he believes that its solution lies outside the scope of human understanding.

LEVI BEN GERSHOM. The post-Maimonidean Aristotelians placed great emphasis on the contradiction between God's all-inclusive foreknowledge and the idea of free will. *Levi b. Gershom accepts the notion of free will (*Milḥamot Adonai* 3:6), but offers his own solution to the difficulty by his interpretation of God's knowledge. According to him, God knows not only his own essence, but also (as does the active intellect) the general categories, i.e., the order of the universe, which is determined by the position of the stars. It is not necessary, however, that all events actually occurring in the world should correspond to his general order. By virtue of his free will man may act in contradiction to what has been predestined for him by the position of the stars. Thus, the knowledge of God and of the active intellect does not encompass those events which actually come into being, but they know only what should occur. Thus in his notion of free will Gersonides is following both the tradition of Jewish philosophy and Aristotelian Greek philosophy, which did not see absolute determinism as operating in the sublunar world.

HASDAI CRESCAS. A similar determinism underlies the idea of free will of Hasdai *Crescas (Or Adonai 2:5), which in some ways reverts to the Muslim philosophical tradition which held, following Avicenna, that man's choice is absolutely predetermined by a chain of prior causes: internal causes, based in man's character, and external causes, which are the factors influencing him. As Y. Baer has shown (in Tarbiz, 11 (1940), 188–206), Crescas was strongly influenced in this notion by *Abner of Burgos.

Crescas' notion, which is similar to that of Avicenna, is that voluntary actions are possible in themselves, but are necessary in terms of their causes. Crescas regards these actions as being necessary since they are known to God before their execution. He thinks, however, that this idea should not be made known to the masses who might use it as a justification for doing evil, since they will think that the punishment follows the sin in a causal chain of events. Despite this view, however, Crescas distinguishes between voluntary actions and acts carried out under compulsion. It is only proper, according to him, that only the former type should be subject to reward and punishment, and only in relation to this type of action can the commandments and prohibitions of the Torah act as a deterrent. Nevertheless, in this capacity, the commandments and prohibitions do not limit the activity of absolute determinism. On the other hand, man's beliefs and opinions do not depend on his own will and he should therefore not be rewarded or punished for them.

[Shlomo Pines]

In Talmud and Midrash

The doctrine of free will, expressed in the idea that man is free to choose between good and evil, was at the core of the Pharisaic outlook. Josephus indeed characterizes the differences between the Pharisees and their Sadducean and Essene opponents as between those who accepted both the freedom of man and divine providence (the Pharisees), those who ascribed everything to chance, denying providential guidance (the Sadducees), and those who denied human freedom, maintaining a doctrine of predestination (the Essenes; Wars 2:162ff; Ant. 13:171; 18:12f.). Though some doubt has been cast on Josephus' account because of his tendency to explain matters in terms of Greek philosophical schools (see G.F. Moore, *Judaism* vol. 3 p. 139), there seems no grounds for rejecting the main outlines of his characterization (Urbach, *Ḥazal: Pirkei Emunot ve-De'ot* (1969), 227).

Though both the doctrine of man's freedom and that of divine providence were adhered to by the rabbis as central to their faith, they do not seem to have been integrated in any systematic way in the talmudic texts which deal with the subject. On the one hand, one finds constant reference to the notion that nothing happens in this world which is not in some way determined from on high: "No man can touch that which has been prepared in advance for his friend" (Yoma 38b); "No man injures his finger here below unless it has been decreed for him on high" (Ḥul. 7b); "Never does a snake bite … or a lion tear [its prey] … or a government interfere in men's lives unless incited to do so from on high" (Eccles. R. 10:11); "Everything is in the hands [i.e., control] of heaven except cold and heat" (Ket. 30a); "Forty days before a child is formed a heavenly voice decrees so-and-so's daughter shall marry so-and-so" (Sot. 2a). On the other hand the whole rabbinic theological structure of reward and punishment turns on the idea that man is free to do evil or good (see Deut. 30:15–19; and Sif. Deut. 53–54). As Josephus mentions, the rabbis wished to maintain both doctrines despite the tension between them, though they were aware of this tension. Before conception the angel appointed over conception takes a seminal drop and asks God: "What is to become of this drop? Is it to develop into a person strong or weak, wise or foolish, rich or poor?" (Nid. 16b). But no mention is made of its becoming wicked or righteous, because "Everything is in the hands of heaven except the fear of heaven" (*ibid.*).

The combination of these two doctrines within rabbinic theology may be understood, not so much from the philosophical point of view, but rather from the practical point of view which underlies all rabbinic thinking. On the one hand it is necessary to think of the world as under the complete surveillance and control of heaven, a thought which adds to the confidence and trust of the Jew in God, and on the other the individual needs to make his choices and decisions on the assumption that evil and good are both within his grasp. The conceptual integration of these two ideas did not enter rabbinic thought forms. The philosophical problems surrounding God's foreknowledge and man's free will are dealt with in an equally cursory way in the texts. The most striking is the saying of Akiva, "Everything is foreseen, but freedom of choice is given" (Avot 3:15). This has been taken by some commentators – Maimonides, for example – to be a statement of the position that though God has foreknowledge of all our acts, still this does not limit our freedom (Maimonides, commentary to the Mishnah, Avot 3:15). Though such a doctrine – that God's foreknowledge is such as not to be philosophically irreconcilable with human freedom – may have been held in some inchoate form by the rabbis, the saying of Akiva has been interpreted as an assertion that God sees all man's acts, even those performed in the privacy of his room (see Rashi on Avot 3:15; Urbach, op. cit., 229–30).

In Modern Jewish Thought

For Hermann *Cohen, freedom of the will – in the sense of being unaffected by mechanical causes – does not exist. However, while he relates causation to the individual man, Cohen holds that freedom of the will does exist in the ethical realm when applied to the goal of mankind. We must assume an independent ethical realm of being in which man can make his own decisions in accord with the rules of that realm. The freedom of the individual depends on how far the individual acts in accord with the goal of mankind. Real freedom will exist only in the future – in the ideal society which is mankind's goal; as of now, freedom is not given but a task to be worked at (*Juedische Schriften*, 1 (1924), 28).

For Martin *Buber free will is given even though in the realm I–It, causality rules. But in the realm of relation, I–Thou – real decision can, indeed must, take place: "if there were a devil it would not be one who decided against God, but one who, in eternity, came to no decision" (*I and Thou* (1958), 52, cf. 51f.). For Buber the main problem is not whether there is choice (in the realm of I–Thou), but the quality of the choices made – for good or evil. Since man is free to choose evil he is also free to overcome evil. Modern man because of prevalent ideologies based on scientific materialism or its counterparts (e. g., dialectical materialism) is even more of a believer in blind fate than pagan man. However, according to Buber, man is really free in his depths, and his destiny is not decreed by fate but is his true fulfillment when met in free will: "… the free man has no purpose here and means there, which he fetches for his purpose: he has only the one thing, his repeated decision to approach his destiny" (*I and Thou*, 60). Free man is not without influences from outside himself, but only he can really respond to outside events and perceive the unique in each event. External events are preconditioned for his action, not determining factors in his character. The free man responds where others react. Man's freedom lies not in the absence of external limitations but in the ability, despite them, to enter into dialogue, i.e., I–Thou relation.

A.J. *Heschel makes a distinction in external happenings, dividing them into what he calls "process," a regular pattern, and "event," an extraordinary, or unique thing. The essence of man's freedom is his ability to surpass himself. To a certain extent man is enslaved by his environment, society, and character, but man can think, will, and take decisions beyond these limitations. If men are treated as "processes" freedom is destroyed. Man is free at rare moments; freedom is an "event." Everyone has the potentiality for freedom, but only rarely achieves it. Free will, the ability to choose between two alternatives, is not the same as freedom, for though the latter includes choice, its achievement lies in the fact that one goes beyond oneself, and disregards the self as its own end. Thus man must choose, although he can choose even to ignore freedom – which would be to choose evil (see *God in Search of Man* (1955), 409–13; *Man is not Alone* (1951), 142, 146).

Mordecai *Kaplan believes that the idea of free will as it was formulated in the past is out of step with the spirit of the present which looks for causality in everything. He therefore interprets the doctrine of free will as the expression of the idea that there can be no responsibility without freedom. The problem of freedom therefore becomes a spiritual one having to do with the significance of individuality and selfhood on the one hand, and liberation of personality from self-worship and desire for power, on the other (see *Meaning of God in Modern Jewish Religion* (1937), 270–296).

BIBLIOGRAPHY: H.A. Wolfson, *Philo*, 2 vols. (1947), index; idem, in: paajr, 11 (1941), 105–63; Husik, Philosophy, index, s.v. *Freedom of the Will*; Guttmann, Philosophies, index, s.v. *Will, freedom of the*; idem, in: *Jewish Studies in Memory of G.A. Kohut* (1935), 325–49; J. Guttmann, *Die Religionsphilosophie des Abraham Ibn Daud* (1879); idem, *Die Religionsphilosophie des Saadia* (1882); S. Schechter, *Some Aspects of Rabbinic Theology*, 285; J.B. Agus, *Modern Philosophers of Judaism* (1941), 73–74, 81–82; M. Friedman, *Martin Buber* (1960), 65–68, 198–9; F. Rothschild, *Between God and Man* (1959), 18–20, 26–30, 148–51.

FREHA BAT AVRAHAM, 18th century Hebrew writer. A member of the prominent Moroccan Bar Adiba family, Freha moved to *Tunis with her father and brother to escape anti-Jewish persecutions in *Morocco, probably some time in the 1730s. Unusually learned for a woman of her time and place, Freha was said to have been well versed in Torah and to have composed essays and poetry in Hebrew. Some of her poems survive and were first published in Tunis in the 1930s. Freha died in 1756 during the conquest of Tunis by Algerians. Her father built a synagogue in her memory and it became a place of pilgrimage for Tunisian Jewish women who revered Freha as a holy person (*kedoshah*) and invoked her name in times of distress. The synagogue stood until its destruction in 1936 when it was replaced by a new structure that also preserved Freha's name.

BIBLIOGRAPHY: J. Chetrit, "Freha bat Yosef: A Hebrew Poetess in Eighteenth-Century Morocco" (Heb.), in: *Peʿamim*, 4 (1980), 84–93; idem,"Freha bat Rabbi Abraham – More on a Hebrew Poetess in Morocco in the Eighteenth Century" (Heb.), in: *Peʿamim*, 15 (1993), 124–30; S. Kaufman, G. Hasan-Rokem, and T.S. Hess, *The Defiant Muse: Hebrew Feminist Poems from Antiquity to the Present* (1999), 74–77; E. Taitz, S. Henry, and C. Tallan, *The JPS Guide to Jewish Women* (2003), 171–72.

[Judith R. Baskin (2nd ed.)]

FREIBERG, U.S. family, prominent from the mid-1800s to the 1930s. JULIUS FREIBERG (1823–1905), who was born in Neu Leiningen, Germany, arrived in Cincinnati in 1847. In 1855 he established a distillery with Levi J. Workum. The business, which became quite successful, continued under family management until the passage of the Prohibition Amendment in 1918 forced it to close. Freiberg served as president of the Bene Israel (Orthodox) congregation for 25 years. Yet, when Isaac M. *Wise of Bene Jeshurun founded the Union of American Hebrew Congregations in 1873 and the Hebrew Union College two years later, Freiberg enthusiastically supported him. He served as vice president of the UAHC from 1873 to 1889, and as president from 1889 to 1903. Freiberg was a member of the Board of Governors of the HUC from 1875 to 1904, and a vice chairman for 26 years. He was a delegate to the Ohio Constitutional Convention of 1873 and held numerous other positions of public trust. In 1856 he had married Duffie Workum, the first Jewish female child born west of the Alleghenies. They helped found and support a number of Jewish charitable agencies.

His son JULIUS WALTER FREIBERG (1858–1921) also served as president of UAHC and served on the Cincinnati Charter Commission and several national Jewish organizations. His wife STELLA (née Heinsheimer; 1862–1962) was one of the nine founders in 1894 of the Cincinnati Symphony Orchestra. One of the founders of the National Federation of Temple Sisterhoods, she served as its president from 1923 to 1929. J. Walter's brother MAURICE J. FREIBERG (1861–1936), who was president of the family business from 1905 to 1918, was also known as a philanthropist and public servant. He donated the maternity wing of Cincinnati's Jewish Hospital in memory of his wife, served as vice president of the HUC Board of Governors, president of the Chamber of Commerce, and in many other Jewish and civic offices. ALBERT HENRY FREIBERG (1868–1940) and his son JOSEPH A. FREIBERG (b. 1898) were noted orthopedic surgeons and served as faculty members of the University of Cincinnati College of Medicine.

[Kenneth D. Roseman]

FREIBERGER, MIROSLAV/ ŠALOM (1903–1943), last rabbi of Zagreb, Yugoslavia, before the Holocaust. Born in Osijek (Croatia). During his youth he lived in Zagreb, actively participated in Zionist groups, and was a founding member of Aḥdut ha-Olim and the Federation of Jewish Youth Organizations. He studied at the Hochschule fuer Juedische Wissenschaften in Berlin, acquiring a Ph.D. in philosophy, and was ordained a rabbi.

On his return to Yugoslavia, he was appointed assistant rabbi in Osijek, then rabbi in Zagreb. He was the first locally born rabbi of the latter city. He published a new prayer book with Croatian translations and published various articles in the Jewish press, particularly in the Zionist weekly *Zidov*.

During the Holocaust, he refused to flee, not leaving his post as deportations and persecutions continued; he kept in touch with the Catholic archbishop, Stepinac (later cardinal), who promised to protect him. He was, however, deported on May 5, 1943, to Auschwitz, together with his wife and the last president of the community, Dr. Hugo Kon, all of them dying there. According to some testimonies, the archbishop tried to intervene, making telephone calls to the Croatian Ustashe police, but to no avail. In the reestablished Zagreb community the cultural association has been named after him.

BIBLIOGRAPHY: "Povijest Židova u Dubrovniku do izgona 1515," in: *Omanut* (Zagreb), no. 1 (1936/7), 30–37.

[Zvi Loker (2nd ed.)]

FREIBURG IM BREISGAU, city in Baden, Germany. Jews were imprisoned there in 1230 by the town's overlord, and released by King Henry VII. Rudolf I of *Hapsburg levied taxes from the Jews there in 1281. In 1300 the counts of Freiburg ratified the ancient rights of Freiburg Jewry. The rights to their taxes, which had been given for a short time to a Basle burgher, were restored in 1310 to the counts' authority, who granted the Jews a privilege in 1338. About this time the Jews owned 15 houses, near the synagogue and in other streets, shared by several families. The community, except pregnant women and children, was massacred by burning after one month's imprisonment, during the Black Death (January 1349). Emperor *Charles IV permitted the counts to resettle Jews in Freiburg in 1359. In 1373 a physician, master Gutleben, was admitted. In 1394 the Austrian overlord ordered that Jews should wear a special garb, with a coat and cap in dull shades; prohibited them from leaving their houses during Holy Week and from watching the religious procession; and set the weekly interest rate at 0.83%. In 1401 the Jews were expelled from the city although individual Jews were admitted from 1411 to 1423; the expulsion became final in 1424 but Jews continued to live in the nearby villages and towns. In 1453 they were prohibited from doing business in the city.

Some Hebrew works were printed in Freiburg in the 16th century as the result of difficulties with Hebrew printing in Basle. Israel *Ẓifroni printed a number of Hebrew books for Ambrosius Froben, among them Benjamin of Tudela's *Massa'ot* (1583), Jacob b. Samuel Koppelman's *Ohel Ya'akov*, and the first edition of Aaron of Pesaro's *Toledot Aharon* (1583–84). In 1503 and 1504, editions were issued of Gregorius Reisch's *Margarita Philosophica* including a page with the Hebrew alphabet in woodcut.

By the early 17th century Jews were able to enter Freiburg on business, accompanied by a constable. The first Jew received a medical degree from Freiburg University in 1791. There were 20 Jews living in Freiburg in 1846. Following the Baden emancipation law of 1862 a congregation was formed in Freiburg in 1863, and a synagogue was consecrated in 1885. It was burned down under the Nazis in 1938. The first rabbi, Adolf *Lewin, the historian of Baden Jewry, was succeeded by Max *Eschelbacher and Julius Zimmels. The legal historian Heinrich Rosen (1855–1927) was active in Jewish community life. Also of note at Freiburg University were the philosopher Edmund *Husserl, the economist Robert Liefmann, the jurist Otto Lenel, Fritz Pringsheim, the classical papyrologist, and the biochemist Siegfried Tannhauser. From 1933 to 1935, along with six other professors, they were dismissed (Pringsheim returned from England in 1945). The Jewish population numbered 1,013 in 1903; 1,320 in 1910 (1.58% of the total), 1,399 in 1925 (1.44%), and 1,138 in June 1933 (1.5%).

After the Nazi rise to power many Jews left the city. All 21 Jewish members of the faculty at the university were dismissed from their positions in 1933–35. Among those dismissed were Hans Adolf *Krebs, who later won the Nobel Prize for medicine in 1953. Jewish students were reduced in number from 183 to 54. Most Jewish businesses were Aryanized by November 1938. Polish Jews were expelled to the Polish border in October 1938 and on *Kristallnacht* the synagogue was destroyed and 100 Jewish men were sent to Dachau. In May 1939, 474 Jews remained. In 1940, 350 Jews were expelled from Germany and interned by the French in the *Gurs camp; another 30 were deported to Theresienstadt on August 23, 1942, as were almost all survivors from Gurs. After the war 15 survivors returned to Freiburg, and 78 displaced persons lived there in 1945. There were 58 Jews living in Freiburg in 1950, 111 in 1960, and 225 in 1968. A new prayer hall was consecrated in 1953. The university acquired the grounds where the synagogue once stood; it is commemorated by a memorial plaque. The *Freiburger Rundbrief*, a journal dedicated to Christian-Jewish understanding, was published in Freiburg. A new community center with a synagogue and a *mikveh* was inaugurated in 1987. A door from the old synagogue was integrated into the building, which was sponsored by the City of Freiburg and the Land (federal state) of Baden-Wuerttemberg. The community numbered 214 in 1989. Owing to the immigration of Jews from the former Soviet Union it increased to 700 in 2005. In 1998 the egalitarian Jewish Chawurah Gescher was founded in Freiburg. It was a member of the Union of Progressive Jews in Germany from 2004. Its membership numbered 30 in 2004.

BIBLIOGRAPHY: T. Oelsner, *The Economic and Social Conditions of the Jews in Southwestern Germany* (1931); Germ Jud, 1 (1963), 108; 2 (1968), 253–7; S.W. Baron, *Social and Religious History of the Jews*, 11 (1965); A. Lewin, *Juden in Freiburg i. B.* (1890); A. Marx, *Studies in Jewish History and Booklore* (1944), 318; G. Kisch, *Zasius und Reuchlin* (1961), 1–2, 59–60; B. Schwinekoeper and F. Laubenberger, *Geschichte und Schicksal der Freiburger Juden* (1963); A.G. von Olenhausen, in: *Vierteljahreshefte fuer Zeitgeschichte*, 14 (1966), 175–206; F. Taddey and G. Hundsknurscher, *Die juedischen Gemeinden in Baden* (1967); P. Sauer, *Dokumente ueber die Verfolgung der juedischen Buerger Baden-Wuerttembergs* 1933–1945 (1965). **ADD. BIBLIOGRAPHY:** R. Boehme, H. Haumann, *Das Schicksal der Freiburger Juden am Beispiel des Kaufmanns Max Mayer und die Ereignisse des 9.–10. November 1938*, Stadt und Geschichte, vol. 13 (1983); A. Maimon, M. Breuer, and Y. Guggenheim (eds.), *Germania Judaica*, vol. 3, 1350–1514 (1987), 395–8; F. Hundsnurscher, "Die juedische Gemiende Freiburg im Breisgau," in: J.B. Paulus (ed.), *Juden in Baden 1809–1984* (1984), 243–7.

[Toni Oelsner / Michael Berenbaum and Larissa Daemmig (2nd ed.)]

FREIDLINA, RAKHIL KHATSKELEVNA (1906–1986), Russian organic chemist. She graduated from Moscow University in 1930 and worked until 1934 at the Scientific Research Institute of Insectofungicides. In 1935–39 and 1941–45, she served at the Institute of Organic Chemistry of the U.S.S.R. Academy of Sciences; in the intervening period she was at the Moscow Institute of Fine Chemical Technology. In 1945 she was appointed chief of the laboratory of the Institute of Organometallic Compounds of the U.S.S.R. Academy of Sciences, and in 1958 became a corresponding member of the Academy. She contributed many papers to Soviet scientific journals. Some dealt with homolytic isomerization of organic compounds in solution, and her work on telomerization led to the development of the chemical precursors of some of the synthetic fibers now being made in Russia. Most of her work was with organometallic compounds. She was the author of *Sinteticheskiye metody v oblasti metalloorganicheskikh soyedineniy myshyaka* ("Synthetic methods ... Organoarsenic Compounds," 1945) and coauthor of *Khimiya kvazikompleksnykh metalloorganicheskikh soyedineniy iyavleniya tautomerii* ("Chemistry of Quasicomplex Organometallic Compounds ...," 1947).

[Samuel Aaron Miller]

FREIDUS, ABRAHAM SOLOMON (1867–1923), U.S. librarian and bibliographer. Freidus was born in Riga, Latvia. He lived in Paris, in the Palestinian agricultural settlement of Zikhron Ya'akov, and in London before going to New York in 1889. Freidus completed a course in librarianship at Pratt Institute in 1894 and began working as a cataloger. In 1897 he was appointed first chief of the Jewish Division of the New York Public Library, where he developed the classification scheme used for Judaica; it was adopted for many other large American Judaica collections as well. Because of his remarkable bibliographical knowledge, Freidus was an indispensable guide to scholars in locating materials. The editors of the 12-volume *Jewish Encyclopedia* (1901–06) were especially indebted to him.

BIBLIOGRAPHY: *Studies in Jewish Bibliography ... in Memory of Abraham Solomon Freidus* (1929), contains a list of writings by and about Freidus, xi–xvii; N. Ausubel, in: *Morning Freiheit* (Oct. 28, 1944), section 2, pp. 4, 6 (Eng.).

[Simcha Kruger]

FREIER (née **Schweitzer**), **RECHA** (1892–1984), founder of *Youth Aliyah. Recha Freier was born in Nordeney, Germany, and became a teacher and scholar of folklore. In 1932 she conceived the idea of Youth Aliyah and founded the first organization for the resettlement and agricultural training of young people in Palestine. After Hitler's rise to power, the idea was endorsed by the Zionist Congress of 1933, and the movement became a large-scale operation. After settling in Palestine in 1941, she founded the Agricultural Training Center for Israel Children for the education of underprivileged children in kibbutz boarding schools. She founded the Israel Composers' Fund in 1958 to foster original musical compositions, and, in 1966, established the Testimonium Scheme, a project aimed at recording major episodes in Jewish history in words and music based on authentic texts. In 1981 she was awarded the Israel Prize. She wrote the texts for two oratorios, *Massadah* and *Yerushalayim*. Her book *Let the Children Come: The Early History of Youth Aliyah* was published in 1961.

BIBLIOGRAPHY: Tidhar, 6 (1955), 2668–69.

[Arye Lipshitz]

FREIFELD, ABRAHAM (1921–), Chilean sculptor. Born in Romania, Freifeld immigrated to Chile in 1930 where he graduated in engineering and art. As a sculptor he preferred to work in metal, which he felt allowed him to express the inner tension he strove to achieve in each piece of sculpture. In 1960 he was appointed professor of sculpture at the Fine Art School of the University of Chile. In 1969 he was named director of the Institute for the Extension of Fine Arts at the University of Chile.

FREILICH, MAX MELECH (1893–1986), Australian manufacturer and communal leader. Born in Lesko, Poland, Freilich went to Australia in 1927. From 1932 he was managing director of the Safre Paper industry in Sydney. An active Zionist, he was president of the Australian Zionist Federation (1953–57) and of the Australian Keren Hayesod (1942–57). He was also vice president of the New South Wales Jewish Board of Deputies and chairman of the board of governors of the King David school. He published *Twenty-Five Years of Keren Hayesod* (1946).

ADD. BIBLIOGRAPHY: I. Porush, *The House of Israel* (1977), index; S. Rutland, *Edge of the Diaspora* (1988), index; H.L. Rubinstein, Australia 1, index.

FREIMAN, Canadian family. MOSES BILSKY (1831–1923) was a Canadian pioneer figure and an ancestor of the Freiman family by way of his daughter Lillian. He was born in Kovno and at the age of 14 went to Montreal with his father, moving to Ottawa in 1857. In the years 1861–67 he traveled throughout North and Central America, going to the Caribou gold fields in British Columbia overland by way of the isthmus of Panama, and enlisting in the Union forces in the U.S. Civil War. He returned to Ottawa and entered the jewelry business. There he founded the Adath Jeshurun synagogue in 1895, helped found the city's first Zionist Society in 1899, and led in community activity.

LILLIAN (1885–1940) was born in Mattawa, Ontario. In 1903 she married Archibald J. Freiman (see below) of Ottawa. She was identified closely with Zionist work in Canada all her life and attended the third Canadian Zionist convention in Montreal at the age of 17. From 1919 to her death she was president of Canadian Hadassah. She took the initiative in 1920–21 in bringing 150 Jewish pogrom orphans to Canada and touring her native country to raise funds and recruit foster parents. In 1918, at the time of the great influenza epidemic, the mayor of Ottawa placed her in charge of efforts to combat the disease. She played a prominent and stimulating role in a wide range of activities of a nonsectarian and Jewish nature, involving relief and succor to others, locally and overseas, Jew and gentile.

ARCHIBALD JACOB FREIMAN (1880–1944) was a Canadian merchant and Zionist leader. He was born in Wirballen, Lithuania, and went to Hamilton, Ontario with his parents in 1893. In 1902 he settled in Ottawa, where he established a department store. He was president of the Adath Jeshurun synagogue from 1903 to 1929 and from 1920 to his death was national president of the Zionist Organization of Canada.

Their son LAWRENCE FREIMAN (1909–1986), a merchant, was born in Ottawa. He served twice as president of the Zionist Organization of Canada, and was honorary president of the Federated Zionist Organization of Canada, and was a member of the board of governors of the Weizmann Institute of Science at Reḥovot. Freiman played a leading role in cultural activities in Canada, and was a director of the Ottawa Philharmonic Orchestra, the Canadian Festival of Arts, and the National Arts Center in Ottawa.

BIBLIOGRAPHY: H.M. Caiserman, *Two Canadian Personalities* (1948); C.E. Hart: *The Jew in Canada* (1926); Bernard Figler, *Lillian and Archie Freiman: Biographies* (1961).

[Ben G. Kayfetz]

FREIMANN, family of rabbis and scholars, ISAAC FREIMANN (d. 1886), who was born in Cracow, edited from a manuscript Abraham b. Ḥiyya's *Hegyon ha-Nefesh ha-Aẓuvah* (1860). His son ISRAEL MEIR FREIMANN (1830–1884) served as rabbi at Filehne (Wielen) and Ostrowo (Ostrow-Wielkopolski, both in Poznania), and declined an invitation to succeed Z. Frankel as head of the Breslau Jewish Theological Seminary. He prepared a critical edition of *Midrash Ve-Hizhir* (1875–80), and responsa of his were published in *Binyan Ẓiyyon* (1868), the responsa collection of his father-in-law Jacob Ettlinger, and elsewhere. His son was Aron *Freimann, his nephew and son-in-law was Jacob *Freimann, and Abraham (Alfred) *Freimann was his grandson.

FREIMANN, ABRAHAM ḤAYYIM (**Alfred**; 1889–1948), jurist and rabbinical scholar. Freimann, born in Holleschau (Holesov), Moravia, the son of Jacob *Freimann, studied rabbinics with his father and law in Frankfurt on the Main and Marburg. He served as a magistrate at Koenigsberg and county judge at nearby Braunsberg until the Nazis took power, when he immigrated to Palestine. There he at first worked for an insurance company, but in 1944 he began lecturing on Jewish law at the Hebrew University in Jerusalem. In 1947 Freimann was appointed head of an advisory committee for Jewish law concerning personal status in the proposed State of Israel. He was murdered by Arabs who attacked a convoy taking university staff to Mount Scopus.

Freimann's scholarly work was concerned with medieval rabbinics; later he devoted his efforts to the adaptation of Jewish law to modern conditions in a Jewish state. He was about twenty when he published two important studies on *Asher b. Jehiel and his descendants (in: JJLG, 12 (1918), 237–317; 13 (1920), 142–254). He edited a series of important responsa collections by Maimonides and members of his family: *Teshuvot ha-Rambam* (1934); *Teshuvot R. Maimon ha-Dayyan Avi ha-Rambam* (1935); *Teshuvot Rabbenu Avraham ben ha-Rambam* (1938); *Teshuvot ha-R. Yehoshu'a ha-Naggid mi-Benei Banav shel ha-Rambam* (1940); and *Teshuvot ha-Rambam le-R. Yosef ha-Ma'aravi Talmido* (1940); and one by Rashi, *Teshuvot Rashi* (1941). Freimann also prepared a second edition of Filipowski's edition of *Sefer Yuḥasin* by Abraham *Zacuto with an introduction and indexes (1925, repr. 1963). His major work *Seder Kiddushin ve-Nissu'in Aḥarei Ḥatimat ha-Talmud* (1945; repr. 1964), deals with changes in Jewish marriage laws after the talmudic period.

BIBLIOGRAPHY: E.E. Urbach, in: KS, 25 (1948/49), 105–8 (with full bibl.); idem, in: *Yavneh*, 3 (1949), 125–7, 225–36; P. Dickstein, in: *Ha-Peraklit*, 5 (1948), 67–70; M. Elon, in: ILR, 3 (1968), 443ff., 448ff.

FREIMANN, ARON (1871–1948), German scholar, historian, and bibliographer. Freimann was born in Filehne (Wielen), Poznan, the son of the local rabbi, Israel Meir Freimann. In 1898 he began working at the municipal library in Frankfurt, and under his direction the library in Frankfurt assembled one of the richest collections of Judaica and Hebraica in the world. He retired in 1933 when the Nazis came to power and immigrated to the United States in 1938. Between 1939 and 1945 he served as consultant in bibliography to the New York Public Library.

An industrious and erudite scholar, Freimann was the author or editor of scores of books and articles. In the field of bibliography one of his most important works is a systematic catalog of the Judaica collection of the Stadtbibliothek in Frankfurt on the Main, *Stadtbibliothek Frankfurt a. M. Katalog der Judaica und Hebraica* (vol. 1: Judaica, 1932); unfortunately, he was unable to complete the second part of the catalog, which was to have included the Hebraica collection. In *Thesaurus Typographiae Hebraicae Seculi XV* (1924–31), Freimann provided a complete collection of samples of facsimiles of all known Hebrew incunabula; this work also remained incomplete, missing the introduction and the discussion of the facsimiles. A most useful bibliographical reference tool is his *A Gazetteer of Hebrew Printing* (1946), in which he listed all the cities where Hebrew books were known to have been printed. For many years Freimann was working on a union catalog of all Hebrew manuscripts, but this work also remained incomplete. Freimann's handwritten cards, representing the material culled from all major and minor collections of Hebrew manuscripts, were photographically reproduced after his death as *Union Catalog of Hebrew Manuscripts and Their Location* (1964). Between 1900 and 1922 Freimann was the editor of the journal *Zeitschrift fuer Hebraische Bibliographie*, in which many of his bibliographical articles appeared.

Among Freimann's important historical works are *Geschichte der Israelitischen Gemeinde Ostrowo* (1896); a history of the Jews of Frankfurt in collaboration with I. Kracauer, *Frankfort* (Eng., 1929); an edition of Ḥ.J.D. Azulai's diary, *Ma'gal Tov ha-Shalem* (1921–34); and a collection of texts relating to Shabbetai Ẓevi, *Inyanei Shabbetai Ẓevi* (1912; index 1931). He was coeditor of *Germania Judaica*, a collection of monographs on medieval German Jewish communities (2 vols., 1917–34, 1963–68). From 1929 to the Nazi take-over he was also one of the editors of *Zeitschrift fuer die Geschichte der Juden in Deutschland*. Of his works in other fields his edition of L. Zunz's *Die synagogale Poesie der Juden* (1920) is particularly valuable. Freimann supplied many references and indexes to this classic work, making it much more useful than it had been previously. He also edited several Festschriften in honor of scholars, such as *Berliner Festschrift* (1903), *Brann-Festschrift* (1919), and *Simonsen-Festschrift* (1923).

In addition to his scholarly activities Freimann was active in Jewish communal life and in Jewish educational institutions. He was affiliated with the *Mekizei Nirdamim society from 1909 to his death, serving as president and board member. He owned a private collection of rare Hebraica and Judaica, part of which he sold to the library of Hebrew Union College in Cincinatti. On the occasion of his sixtieth birthday a Festschrift was edited in his honor by A. Marx and H. Meyer (publ. 1935), which included a short poem by Ḥ.N. Bialik and contained a complete bibliography of his writings to that time.

BIBLIOGRAPHY: A. Marx and B. Cohen, in: PAAJR, 17 (1947–48), xxiii–xxviii; S.D. Goitein, in: KS, 25 (1948/49), 109–12.

[Menahem Schmelzer]

FREIMANN, JACOB (1866–1937), German rabbi, scholar, and editor. Freimann studied under Simon Sofer (see *Sofer) and Akiva Kornitzer in his native Cracow, and under his uncle Israel Meir *Freimann at Ostrowo, as well as at Berlin and Tuebingen. He married Israel Meir Freimann's daughter. Jacob Freimann served as rabbi in Moravia at Kanitz (Dolni Kounice) and Holleschau from 1890 to 1913. In 1913 he succeeded Wolff Feilchenfeld as chief rabbi of Posen. In 1928 he joined the rabbinate of the Berlin Jewish community. Freimann was a member of the board of *Mekizei Nirdamim, editor of the department of rabbinics for the Eshkol encyclopaedias of Judaica in German and Hebrew, and lecturer on rabbinics and Jewish history at the Berlin Rabbinical Seminary. Freimann's scholarly interest was medieval rabbinical literature. Particularly important in this field are his editions of Joseph b. Moses' *Leket Yosher* (1903–04), Nathan b. Judah's *Sefer Maḥkim* (1909), *Ma'aseh ha-Ge'onim* (1909), and *Siddur Rashi* (1911) which was prepared by S. *Buber but completed by Freimann. He also contributed an introduction and indexes to the second edition of Wistinetzki's edition of *Sefer Ḥasidim* (1924).

BIBLIOGRAPHY: H. Levy (ed.), *Festschrift… Jacob Freimann* (1937), introd. 6–16 (includes bibliography); H. Gold. (ed.), *Juden und Judengemeinden Maehrens in Vergangenheit und Gegenwart* (1929), 233, 240, 270, 278; N. Lebovi, in: S. Federbush (ed.), *Ḥokhmat Yisrael be-Ma'arav Eiropah*, 2 (1959), 211–3.

[Hirsch Jacob Zimmels / Jacob Joshua Ross]

FRELENG, ISADORE "FRIZ" (also known as "**I.J.**"; 1905–1995), U.S. animator, cartoonist, director. Born in Kansas City, Missouri, Freleng began his career in animation in his hometown, working for fellow Kansas City native Walt Disney. When Disney moved to Hollywood, Freleng followed, teaming up with experienced cartoonists Hugh Harman and Rudy Ising. The three concocted the cartoon character Bosko, a Mickey Mouse-like hero, who became a star in Warner Brothers' new animated series *Looney Tunes*. When Harman and Ising left Warner Brothers in 1933, Freleng remained and was promoted to director. In the film *I Haven't Got a Hat* (1935), Freleng introduced Porky Pig to the world, one of the first cartoon characters to have a distinctive personality. Except for a brief stint at MGM in the late 1930s, Freleng remained with Warner Brothers for the next decades of his career. Best known perhaps for redesigning and introducing such immortal Warner Brothers' characters as Yosemite Sam and Speedy Gonzalez, Freleng also made the beloved short film *You Oughta Be in Pictures* (1940) in which Daffy Duck convinces Porky Pig to quit Warner Brothers and find work elsewhere. Freleng himself followed Daffy Duck's advice when Warner Brother's closed its doors in 1964 and Freleng and animator Dave DePatie opened their own operation in the San Fernando Valley, where they were commissioned to create the opening sequence of *The Pink Panther.* Freleng and DePatie came up with the iconic cool cat, whom they were able to transfer successfully to television in the years that followed.

[Casey Schwartz (2nd ed.)]

FRENCH LITERATURE.

Biblical and Hebraic Influences

The influence of the Hebrew Bible and other Jewish writings on early French literature is limited. With the exception of the 12th-century *Jeu d'Adam*, an Anglo-Norman verse-play, and the 15th-century *Mistère du Viel Testament*, only New Testament themes appear in medieval French plays, poetry, and stories. However, there was one interesting case of "infiltration": the *Midrash and **aggadah* became important sources for the French *fabliaux*. Fables, parables, and didactic tales were not rare in talmudic literature, and they remained part of the Jewish literary heritage throughout the Middle Ages. Indian tales and Aesop's fables mingled with talmudic "Fox Fables" (*Mishlei Shu'alim*), as is testified by compilations of Jewish writers such as *Berechiah b. Natronai ha-Nakdan and Isaac b. Joseph of *Corbeil. These compilations, translated into Latin by baptized Jews such as *Petrus Alfonsi and *John of Capua, thus passed into the French heritage in the form of the *fabliaux*. Literary transpositions also occurred, the medievalist Gustave Cohen being the first to note that the midrashic tale of the blind man and the lame (Sanh. 91a; Lev. R. 4:5) – which has a parallel in Aesop – had become the French story of St. Martin. The "Three Rings" tale was the source of the anonymous 13th-century *Dit du Vrai Aniel*, a Christian author transforming the old fable into propaganda for the Crusades. This tradition elsewhere influenced *Boccaccio and, later still, *Lessing.

In the Middle Ages biblical knowledge was primarily the preserve of the clergy, and it was through churchmen that Hebrew words, biblical expressions, idioms, and proverbs found their way into the French language from the 12th century right up to the 17th. As elsewhere in Europe, various Hebrew terms were absorbed by way of Greek and Latin. Certain French borrowings from Hebrew extend or modify the original meaning: *tohu-bohu* (chaos, disorder); *capharnaüm* (lumber room); *jérémiade* (lament); *moïse* (wicker cradle); *sabbat* (tumult, uproar); and *cabale* (conspiracy, intrigue). Hebrew idioms from the Bible found their way into French, as into other European languages: *trouver grâce* (find favor), *amis de Job* (Job's comforters), *bouc émissaire* (scapegoat). The inclusion of Hebraisms was given a new impetus with two versions of the Bible: the *Bible Complète* of the University of Paris (c. 1235) and the *Bible Historiale* of Guyart des Moulins (c. 1295) which was not a literal translation. Until the Reformation, these were the only full versions of the Scriptures in French.

THE RENAISSANCE. Apart from some stray references in the works of François Villon (c. 1431 – c. 1463), biblical subjects only make an appearance in French literature in the 16th century, under the combined impact of the Renaissance and the Reformation. At the same time there sprang up a widespread interest in the Hebrew language and the original biblical text. In 1530, Francis I established the Collège des Trois Langues (later renamed Collège de France) as a center of learning independent of the intolerant Sorbonne. Readers in mathematics and in Latin, Greek, and Hebrew were appointed in accordance with the humanistic principles of the Renaissance, and such was the liberalism of the era that the chair of Hebrew was first offered to a professing Jew, Elijah (Baḥur) *Levita, who declined the honor because of the exclusion of his fellow-Jews from the French realm. The post was not in fact given to a Jew until the late 19th century.

Humanism blazed a trail that was also followed by the new religious trends of the 16th century – early liberal Evangelism and Calvinism. The "return to the sources" inspired new Bible translations by Jacques Lefèvre d'Etaples (1523–30), Robert Olivétan (1535), a relative of John *Calvin and Sébastien Châteillon (1551). The Protestant poet Clément Marot composed beautiful metrical renderings of 50 of the Psalms (1545, and much reprinted), which John Calvin later accepted in his reformed hymnal, and which inspired many later imitations. François Rabelais placed considerable store on the study of the holy tongue and of the "thalmudistes et cabalistes," although he himself probably knew no Hebrew.

Later in the same century, Hebrew studies were pursued in a more systematic manner, by both Catholics and Protestants. Pontus de Tyard, a neoplatonist poet and later a bishop, published a French translation, *De l'Amour* (1551), of the *Dialoghi d'Amore* by Judah *Abrabanel (Leone Ebreo). Some leading French Christian Hebraists were Guillaume *Postel; Gilbert *Génébrard; Blaise de *Vignère; and Guy *Le Fèvre de la Boderie, a Bible scholar who wrote epic French verse full of kabbalistic references and Franco-Hebraic conceits. Two outstanding Protestant poets whose works owe much to biblical inspiration were Salluste *Du Bartas and Agrippa d'Aubigné, a militant Calvinist whose dramatic and satirical epic, *Les Tragiques* (1577–94), describes the sufferings of the French Protestants in a series of apocalyptic visions. Likening his coreligionists to the Children of Israel, d'Aubigné prophesies God's final vengeance on their persecutors.

Biblical drama also makes its appearance in the 16th century. *Saül le Furieux* (1572) by Jean de la Taille presents the theme of man's inability to understand the mysterious designs of Providence. Against God's command, Saul has spared the life of Agag, king of Amalek, and must be punished. This was a direct precursor of the classic French tragedy. In *Sédécie*, ou les Juives (1583), a drama in the Greek style by Robert Garnier, man's disobedience is again punished by God. Ignoring Jeremiah's injunction, Sédécie (Zedekiah) has sought an alliance with Egypt. The country and the Temple are destroyed, the king taken into captivity and blinded. Sédécie recognizes his sins and acknowledges God's justice. The chorus of Jewish women echoes the king's lament in strains reminiscent of Jeremiah. Minor biblical dramas of the period include: *Abraham Sacrifiant* (1576) by Théodore de Bèze; *Jephté* (1567) by Florent Chrestien, translated from the earlier Latin *Jephtes* (1554) by George Buchanan ("the Humanist"); and *Aman* and *David* (both 1601) by the talented Huguenot playwright and economist Antoine de Montchrestien.

THE CLASSICAL AGE. The 17th century manifests a dual character: classical and Christian. Naturally enough, biblical or post-biblical influences are felt primarily among writers of Christian inspiration; others return to the sources of classical antiquity. Among the great dramatists, Jean *Racine, deeply influenced by his Jansenist training and sympathies, was the only one for whom the Bible provided both subject matter and poetic inspiration. Racine's two biblical tragedies, *Esther* (1689) and *Athalie* (1691), rank among the great masterpieces of French drama. Two great French Christian writers of the century, Jacques-Bénigne Bossuet and Blaise *Pascal, were exceptionally aware of the importance of the biblical heritage. Bossuet, in his *Discours sur l'Histoire Universelle* (1681), presents a spiritual perspective of history in which the paths are traced by a mysterious but wise Providence. Here Israel is chosen for a particular mission to the world, and other nations of antiquity, however powerful and important they might appear in relation to the Jews, are but tools used by God to chastise or protect His chosen people. Israel is thus seen as the cornerstone of world history. Bossuet's biblical leanings are apparent in the lyrical and grandiose eloquence of his literary style; not only did biblical rhythm and imagery strongly influence all his works (including the sermons and the *Oraisons Funèbres*, 1663): he consciously transposed biblical passages and adapted them to contemporary circumstances. Pascal too, in his passionate search for God, saw in the Jews an exceptional and mysterious people, appointed by Providence to preside over human destiny. The Bible was to be read, studied, and interpreted symbolically, and Pascal drew heavily on the Midrash, which he considered a key to the understanding of the Scriptures. In his Platonic *Dialogues sur l'Éloquence* (1718), Fénelon regarded the Bible as a primary source of poetic inspiration and praised Judaism's religious purity.

In the 18th century, the "Age of Enlightenment," men like Denis *Diderot found it convenient to ridicule both the Bible and the Jewish people as an indirect method of attacking Christianity. Equally if not more virulent was *Voltaire, whose attitude was also more complex. Personally unfriendly toward the Jews, Voltaire, in his *Dictionnaire Philosophique* (1764), simultaneously attacked their alleged religious fanaticism and argued that Christians ought logically to practice Judaism, "because Jesus was born a Jew, lived a Jew, died a Jew, and said expressly that he was fulfilling the Jewish religion." Voltaire also condemned anti-Jewish persecution in his *Sermon du Rabin Akib* (1764). Another 18th-century writer, the atheistic Baron d'Holbach, strove in his *Esprit du Judaïsme* (1770) to prove that the Law of Moses was basically immoral, serving only to justify Jewish political ambitions. Although some other writers of the period, notably *Montesquieu and *Rousseau, made sympathetic references to Jews, they were not especially inspired by biblical or later Hebrew literature.

THE ROMANTIC AGE. The 19th-century Romantic movement brought with it a revival of interest in, and sympathy for, religion and Christian values. French poets displayed a noticeable reverence for the Bible and found inspiration in the Holy Land. Thus, François René de Chateaubriand praised the Bible's uniqueness and universality in his *Génie du Christianisme* (1802). In *Itinéraire de Paris à Jérusalem* (1811), he wrote a highly romanticized account of his journey to the Orient extolling the Jews' will to survive and their tenacious adherence to their heritage. Alphonse de Lamartine, a leading Romantic poet, acknowledged his debt to the Psalms and wrote a biblical drama, *Saül* (1818). After a grand tour which included Palestine, his *Souvenirs*, Impressions… Pendant un Voyage en Orient (1835) looked prophetically to the future: "Such a land, resettled by a new Jewish nation, tilled and watered by intelligent hands… would still be the Promised Land of our day, if only Providence were to give it back its people, and the tide of world events bring it peace and liberty."

Two other great French poets who were profoundly influenced by the Bible were Alfred de Vigny and Victor Hugo. Vigny, who knew the Bible by heart, based one-fifth of his poems on biblical themes and filled them with Hebrew images and expressions. They include "Moïse," "La fille de Jephté" (in *Poèmes Antiques et Modernes*, 1826) and "La colère de Samson" (in *Les Destinées*, 1864). Like all Vigny's heroes, the biblical figures are universal symbols – men of genius whose greatness condemns them to eternal solitude. Hugo was the preeminent biblical poet among the French Romantics. Despite his estrangement from Christian orthodoxy, Hugo constantly turns to biblical themes in such poems as "La Conscience," "Booz endormi," and "Salomon" (in *La Légende des Siècles*, 1859–83); "Le Glaive" (*Fin de Satan*, 1887); and "L'Aigle" (*Dieu*, 1891). He eulogized Isaiah and Ezekiel in *William Shakespeare* (1864); sought biblical support for his campaign against Napoleon III; and injected some basic knowledge of the Kabbalah (probably gained from his Jewish admirer, Alexandre *Weill) into *Les Contemplations* (1856).

Of the prominent 19th-century French novelists, Gustave Flaubert, another great traveler, recreated in his last work, *Hérodias* (the third of his *Trois Contes*, 1877), the Judea of the Roman era, the Dead Sea fortress of Machaerus, and the dramatic story of John the Baptist. Pierre Loti, a writer of Huguenot descent, wrote two travel books, *Jérusalem* (1895) and *La Galilée* (1896).

THE 20TH CENTURY. In more recent French literature, from the late 19th century onward, biblical and Christian inspiration again go hand in hand. Catholic writers such as Charles *Péguy, Léon *Bloy, and Paul *Claudel meditate on the Scriptures, and their poetic works (whether written in prose or verse) often take on a prophetic tone as they apply the biblical prophecies to contemporary events. Two biblically inspired dramas by Jean Giraudoux are his *Judith* (1932), a psychological tragedy; and *Sodome et Gomorrhe* (in *Théâtre complet*, vol. 10, 1947). In a class of his own stands the novelist and playwright André Gide, whose drama *Saül* (1898, publ. 1922) strips all heroism from its central character.

Some French Jewish poets of the early 20th century who rediscovered the Bible as a source of inspiration were Edmond *Fleg (*Ecoute Israël*, 1913, 1935), André *Spire (*Poèmes juifs*, 1919), Henri *Franck (*La danse devant l'Arche*, 1912), Albert *Cohen (*Paroles juives*, 1921), Gustave *Kahn (*Images bibliques*, 1929), and Benjamin *Fondane (*L'Exode*). Two important poets of the post-World War II era, both Catholic, both intoxicated with the Bible, were Pierre Emmanuel and Jean Grosjean. Emmanuel's mystical lyrics, reminiscent of Agrippa d'Aubigné and Victor Hugo, draw their images from the biblical text, and his vision (cf. *Babel*, 1951), like theirs, is prophetic, sometimes apocalyptic. Grosjean borrows almost all his themes from the Bible and the Kabbalah. The titles of his verse collections are eloquent: *Le livre du juste* (1952), *Fils de l'homme* (1953), and *Apocalypse* (1962). Other Jewish writers who sought inspiration in Jewish sources were Emmanuel *Eydoux, Arnold *Mandel, Armand *Lunel, Élie *Wiesel, and in Israel, three poets writing in French: Joseph *Milbauer, Jean *Loewenson, and Claude *Vigée.

The Image of the Jew

The appearance of Jewish characters in French literature is determined by the socio-historical role of the Jews in France, where they lived from Roman times until the expulsion of 1394. In medieval French literature, Jews generally appear in an unfavorable light. This attitude changes when they convert. Thus, in the 12th-century *Pèlerinage de Charlemagne a Jérusalem*, the Jew is presented like other "infidels" as a candidate for baptism. Confronted with the noble figure of the emperor, he readily accepts Jesus. In the 13th-century *Desputaison de la Synagogue et de la Saincte Eglise*, a play by Clopin which may reflect the Paris disputation of 1240, the representative of the Synagogue (i.e., the Jews) is a skillful woman debater who stubbornly refuses to acknowledge the superiority of the Church. A rare exception among medieval writers is Peter *Abelard (1079–1142), who composed a dialogue between a Jewish and a Christian philosopher which was quite favorable to Judaism.

The Jew's first appearance as a figure in French society in the 13th century is reflected in the literature of the period. The satirical poet Gautier de Coincy is particularly virulent against Jews, portraying them as not merely stubborn and blind, but also as rich oppressors of the poor. Two miracle plays, *Le Juif et le Chevalier* and *Le Miracle d'un Marchand et d'un Juif*, present a stereotyped Jew, crudely anticipating *Shakespeare's Shylock. In later mystery plays, the Pharisees represent the "hypocritical Jews," the "Christ-killers," filled with hatred and inspired by Satan. The performance of these plays in Paris was finally banned in 1548.

Throughout the 16th and 17th centuries the Jew is, by and large, absent from the French scene, and is virtually ignored by writers of that period. Even the liberal Michel de Montaigne (see below), a writer of partly Jewish descent who had personal contact with Jews in Italy, makes only a few random allusions to them in his *Essays*. Racine, however, defended the Jews in his drama *Esther*, where the heroine pleads their cause. The Jews, declares Racine, are peace loving, humble, and loyal to God and the king. Pascal also expresses his admiration for a Jewish people miraculously preserved through the ages and unique among nations for its unswerving loyalty to God, for its sincerity, and for its courageous devotion to the Law of Moses. Bossuet, too, marvels at Israel's miraculous survival. During his 17 years in Metz, whose Jewish community enjoyed royal protection, he met Jews and attempted to convert some of their youth. His unorthodox opponent in biblical controversies, the Hebraist Richard *Simon, was more enlightened. In 1690, he championed the Jews in the celebrated ritual murder trial of a Metz Jew, Raphaël Lévy, and in order to fight antisemitic prejudice, translated into French Leone *Modena's *Historia dei Riti Ebraici* (*Cérémonies et coustumes… parmi les Juifs*, Paris, 1674, 1681[2]).

THE 18TH-CENTURY PHILOSOPHERS. The few writers of the 18th century who were not blinded by anti-religious hatred expressed enlightened opinions about Jews and Judaism. Thus Montesquieu, who devotes no. 60 of his *Lettres Persanes* (1721) to the Jews, speaks of their passionate devotion to a religion which was the mother of Christianity and Islam. He then makes a plea for tolerance, repeated in the "Très humble remontrance aux Inquisiteurs d'Espagne et de Portugal" (*L'Esprit des Lois* (1748), 25:13), where the advocate of justice and humanity is a Portuguese Jew whose reasonableness makes a striking contrast to the violence of Christian fanatics. Among the many "Oriental" works inspired by the *Lettres Persanes* were the *Lettres Juives* (1736) of the Marquis d'Argens, which present an exceptionally favorable image of Jewish values and morality.

Voltaire and the Encyclopedists, on the other hand, presented a generally unsympathetic image of the Jews, whom they held to be as guilty of religious fanaticism as the Christians. Diderot, in his *Encyclopédie* article "Juifs," also reflects the prejudices of his time, but in his novel *Le Neveu de Rameau* (written c. 1774) he introduces a gullible and cowardly Jew who is, for once, neither vicious nor evil. In the fourth book of his *Emile* (1762), Rousseau, though scarcely better informed than his contemporaries, makes a remarkable plea for a more objective and sympathetic understanding of the Jews. "We shall never know the inner motives of the Jews," he says prophetically, "until the day they have their own free state, schools, and universities, where they can speak and argue without fear. Then, and only then, shall we know what they really have to say."

THE JEW IN FICTION. Throughout the 19th century the Jew's growing importance in French society found its reflection in literature, but the image of the Jew in plays and novels generally lacks nuance. George Sand, in her drama *Les Mississipiens* (1866; originally *Le Château des Désertes*, 1851), introduces a Jewish capitalist, Samuel Bourset, who is merely a Shylock in modern dress. Jews like Gobseck and Elie Magus in the giant (17 volumes) cycle, *La Comédie Humaine*, of Honoré de Balzac, are largely stereotypes: bankers and art collectors, generally crafty, rapacious, and miserly, who only partially redeem themselves by their devotion to their womenfolk. Only Balzac's "beau Juif," Naphtaly, is a figure of chivalrous virtue. In *Manette Salomon* (1867), a novel by the Gon-court brothers Edmond and Jules, the Jewish heroine is unsympathetically treated. She is the corrupting influence who forces the artist Caridis to abandon his ideals. *Les Rois en exil* (1879), by Alphonse Daudet, is a variation on the same theme.

In his dramas, Victor Hugo at first sacrificed truth to popular prejudice. The Great Protector's agent in *Cromwell* (1827) is a grotesque travesty of the historical *Manasseh Ben Israel, and another despicable Jewish usurer appears in *Marie Tudor* (prod. 1833; publ. 1834). Yet Hugo's last great play, *Torquemada* (1882), reveals the author's real sympathy for the Jewish victims of treachery and oppression – a sympathy he demonstrated publicly by presiding at a Paris rally on May 31, 1882, to protest against czarist persecution of Russian Jewry. Unpleasant Jewish types continued to make their appearance in the novels *Cosmopolis* (1893; Eng. tr. 1893) by Paul Bourget, *Mont-Oriol* (1887) by Guy de Maupassant, and *L'argent* (1891), part of the Rougon-Macquart novel cycle by Emile *Zola. Zola, however, by placing the Jewish Gundermann opposite a far more despicable Christian character, does succeed in restoring some sense of balance.

THE DREYFUS CASE. Some frankly antisemitic novels appeared at the turn of the century, reflecting the wave of ultranationalist feeling aroused by the *Dreyfus case. Such, for example, are *L'essence du soleil* (1890) by Paul Adam, Léon Cladel's *Juive-errante* (1897), and Léon *Daudet's *Le pays des* *parlementeurs* (1901) and *La lutte* (1907). In all these novels the Jew or Jewess is a rapacious intriguer, endangering the security of the nation and corrupting morals. A play in the same vein is *Le retour de Jérusalem* (1904) by Maurice Donnay. Bourget's *L'Etape* (1902) portraying an idealistic Jew, is a happy exception. Though often cast in the role of a prostitute, the Jewess in the short stories of Maupassant is treated sympathetically and proves herself more noble than her non-Jewish associates. Thus in *Mademoiselle Fifi* (1883), the Jewess Rachel alone resists the offensive Prussian officer, emerging as a symbol of French patriotism and courage. And in *La femme de Claude* (1873), a drama by Alexandre Dumas *fils*, it is the Jewess Rebecca who symbolizes feminine virtue and purity in a decadent and selfish society. The brothers J.-H. and S.-J. Rosny present a fierce and proud Jewess in *La Juive* (1907). The ambivalent Jewish characterization in the Erckmann-Chatrian novels of life in Alsace such as *L'ami Fritz* (1864; *Friend Fritz*, 1873), *Le blocus* (1867; *The Blockade*, 1869), and "Le Juif polonais" (in *Contes populaires*, 1866; *The Polish-Jew*, 1884) stems from their joint authorship: Emile Erckmann was a pro-Jewish Protestant, and Alexandre Chatrian a Catholic antisemite. Their best-known hero, Rabbi David Sichel (in *L'ami Fritz*), is a wholly admirable figure.

The Dreyfus case inspired not only a spate of nationalistic and antisemitic novels, but also some important works of an exactly opposite type by three great French writers. Zola's *Vérité* (1903) describes the "Affaire Simon," a romanticized Dreyfus case in which justice and secularism triumph over prejudice and clericalism. In *L'anneau d'améthyste* (1899), Anatole France presents a liberal who opposes bigotry, antisemitism, and racism, but it is in his charming *L'île des pingouins* (1908) that the *Affaire* is parodied with the most incisive wit. Society, eager to persecute the defenseless Jew Pyrot, is depicted in all its cowardice and greed. Anatole France also presents a likeable Jewish philologist, Schmoll, in *Le lys rouge* (1894). In *Jean Barois* (1913), Roger Martin Du Gard approaches the *Affaire* from a more philosophical standpoint. The central figure, a liberal journalist in search of truth and justice, speaks out on behalf of Dreyfus, under the influence of an admirable Jewish friend, Woldsmuth.

The *Affaire* also directed the attention of two great Catholic writers toward Jewry. Charles Péguy and Léon Bloy both devoted poems and meditations to the Jewish people, its destiny and mission. Paul Claudel did so too, in his drama *Le Père humilié* (1916), where the central figure is a blind Jewess, Pensée, who personifies the people of God. Two other writers of the period introduced Jewish figures. One was the poet Guillaume Apollinaire, who was fascinated by the figure of the *wandering Jew and used the Jew in his poems (particularly *Alcools*, 1913) and short stories as a symbol of exile and misfortune. The other was Marcel *Proust who, in the particular universe which he created, gave an important place to Jewish characters, including his own alter ego, the half-Jew Charles Swann.

WORLD WAR I AND AFTER. World War I marked a turning point in the treatment of Jewish characters in French literature, and they became increasingly numerous, varied, and interesting. Writers were preoccupied with the search for new social and moral values for a society shattered by war, and tended to give greater recognition to the Jew's specific identity. The Jew was no longer merely a persecuted human being to be defended for the sake of justice, but the bearer of a cultural and spiritual tradition worthy of a place in the broader French or European heritage. Such was the view of the former anti-Dreyfusard Maurice Barrès who, despite his ultranationalism and dislike of the Jew, assigned him in *Les diverses familles spirituelles de la France* (1917) a role akin to that of the Breton or Alsatian among the "families" constituting the French nation. With the brothers Jérôme and Jean *Tharaud, interest in the authentic Jew was transmuted into a search for the picturesque and the exotic in Jewish tradition. Even Zionism inspired a novel: *Le puits de Jacob* (1925) by Pierre Benoît, which deals with early pioneering in Ereẓ Israel. But it was Romain Rolland who, even before World War I, had given Jewish values a broad and universal meaning for modern civilization. Not only had the Jew his own traditions to contribute to the French heritage, he also had a special vocation in the western world, being the bearer of "Justice for all, of universal Right." The Jewish characters in Rolland's serial novel, *Jean Christophe*, are distinguished by their selfless devotion, their passion for improving the world, their boundless energy, and determination.

The first fully developed Jewish hero of 20th-century French literature was Silbermann, in the novel of that name by Jacques de *Lacretelle (1922). This deals with the friendship between two schoolboys, one a Christian and the other a Jew. The persecution of the brilliant and idealistic Silbermann by his antisemitic schoolmates forms the background to the story. The theme was taken up by André Gide in *Geneviève* (1936), which portrays a similar friendship between two girls. Henri de Montherlant, who otherwise dealt little with Jewish themes, wrote a "counterpart to Silbermann" in his autobiographical short story of World War I, "Un petit Juif à la guerre" (in *Mors et Vita*, 1932). The author, educated in a reactionary, antisemitic milieu, describes how he is attracted by a sensitive and intelligent young Jew whom he meets in the trenches. Georges Duhamel, in his serial novel *La chronique des Pasquier* (1933–41), presents a finely drawn Jew in Justin Weill, the loyal and idealistic friend of the storyteller-hero. Although the liberal Duhamel makes his Jewish hero an admirable figure, he is nevertheless presented as the perpetual stranger, alienated from both the French and the Jewish traditions. Throughout the *Chronicles* it is this fundamental alienation that accounts for the unsuccessful search for a Franco-Jewish synthesis. The same theme is given a slightly different interpretation by Paul Nizan in *La conspiration* (1938). Here the hero, Bernard Rosenthal, failing to involve the girl he loves in his own philosophical preoccupations, commits suicide. In all these works the Jewish hero has a central role, yet he is always analyzed in terms of the non-Jew's reactions.

To clarify the non-Jew's attitude toward the Jew, some French novelists have created minor, but striking, Jewish characters. Roger Martin Du Gard devotes *La belle saison* (1923), the third volume of his family cycle *Les Thibault*, to the story of Antoine Thibault, a young doctor, and Rachel, his Jewish mistress, who becomes intensely real although she is only seen through the eyes of her lover. Another interesting marginal character appears in *Thérèse Desqueyroux* (1927) by François Mauriac. It is a young Jew, Jean Azévédo, who brings a breath of fresh air into the stuffy atmosphere of a bigoted small town and precipitates Thérèse's revolt.

THE IMPACT OF NAZISM. The rise of racialism and Nazism between the two world wars led to the appearance of such antisemitic works as *Voyage au bout de la nuit* (1922; *Journey to the End of the Night*, 1959) by Louis-Ferdinand Céline and *Gilles* (1939) by Pierre Drieu La Rochelle – both writers who would compromise themselves in antisemitic politics under German occupation and Vichy government. On the other hand, in 1941, Antoine de Saint Exupéry wrote to his Jewish friend, Léon Werth, the *Lettre à un otage* (New York, 1943) which was a unique message of comfort and encouragement from a French Gentile to a Jew. Saint Exupéry's meditative *Citadelle* (1948) contains mystical thinking of Jewish interest.

World War II and Nazi persecution inspired few Jewish characters among French writers. Some exceptions were *La marche à l'étoile* (1943) by *Vercors; some minor characters in works like *La mort dans l'âme* (1949) by Jean-Paul Sartre; and *Le sang du ciel* (1961) by the Polish refugee Piotr Rawicz, a novel with a Jewish hero about the Nazi occupation of the Ukraine. The leading French writers of the postwar period did not introduce Jewish figures into their works, perhaps because of the irreparable mental shock caused by the war. Essays and theoretical writings on the Jewish question (by Sartre for example) were not rare, but Jewish characters and heroes became the exclusive concern of French Jewish writers.

The Jewish Contribution

Although Jews made no specific contribution to French literature before the 13th century, their links with French culture are more ancient. During the Middle Ages French Jews spoke Old French, which modified their pronunciation of Hebrew, and the somewhat Hebraized French dialect which they wrote in Hebrew characters is known as *Judeo-French. A parallel dialect in the south of France was *Judeo-Provençal. The *la'azim (glosses) which *Rashi and other Jewish commentators used to explain difficult Hebrew terms are an immensely valuable source for philologists and Romance specialists. Even Hebrew-Old French dictionaries have survived. In the 13th century, liturgical poems and a festival prayer book (the fragmentary Heidelberg *maḥzor*) were composed in Old French, using Hebrew orthography. The most important document of the period is another fragment, the *Complainte de Troyes*, commemorating the martyrs of the *Troyes massacre of 1288 (text in: E. Fleg, *Anthologie juive* (1951), 281). Its author was probably Jacob ben Judah de Lotra, who is known to have written a Hebrew *kinah* (elegy) on the same theme. Jews also began to write secular French verse: two 13th-century Provençal Jewish troubadours, Bonfils de Narbonne and Charlot le Juif, are mentioned and attacked in works by non-Jews; while some fragments have survived of poems by the convert Mathieu le Juif, a *trouvère* of Arras. With the expulsion of the Jews from France in 1394 this literary activity came to an end, although Alsace, and occasionally Provence, remained havens for Jewish refugees.

After a gap of nearly 200 years, writers of Jewish origin again made their appearance on the French literary scene. Outstanding among them were the celebrated astrologer and physician *Nostradamus (Michel de Nostre-Dame) and the great essayist Michel de Montaigne (1533–1592). The latter's mother, Antoinette de Louppes de Villeneuve, was a Christian descendant of Mayer Paçagon (Pazagón) of Calatayud who, after his forcible conversion at the beginning of the 15th century, took the baptismal name of Juan López de Villanueva. A skeptical humanist, more deistic than Christian, Montaigne in his *Essays* reveals a tolerant abhorrence of the Inquisition in Portugal, but only an outsider's interest in Jewish survival. In the revived Jewish community of Provence, *Purim plays had an honored place, a classic example being the dialect verse-drama *La Reine Esther*, written by Rabbi Mardochée Astruc and revised by Jacob de *Lunel, which was performed at Carpentras in 1774. But in French literature proper, Jews played no major literary role until the era of Louis Philippe (1830–48). Two early writers were the minor novelist Esther Foa and the prolific biographer, critic, and kabbalist Alexandre *Weill.

THE 19TH AND 20TH CENTURIES. Few of the many Jewish writers who rose to eminence in 19th-century France showed any real interest in Jewish themes. One rare exception was the poet and educator Eugène Manuel (1823–1901), author of *Pages intimes* (1866) and some very successful plays, who was a founder of the *Alliance Israélite Universelle. Other writers of this period were the poet and playwright Catulle *Mendès, the poet Ephraïm Mikhaël (1866–1890), the essayist and short-story writer Marcel *Schwob, and a host of playwrights and librettists – Adolphe Philippe d'Ennery (Dennery, 1811–1899); Hector Jonathan Crémieux (1828–1892) and his collaborator, Ludovic *Halévy; Georges de *Porto-Riche; Tristan *Bernard; and the stylish comedy writer Edmond Sée (1875–1959). By the beginning of the 20th century the number of Jewish playwrights had grown considerably. Notable among them were Fernand Nozière (pseud. of F. Weyl; 1874–1931) and Alfred Savoir (1883–1934), who collaborated in the writing of successful comedies and farces; André Pascal (Henri de Rothschild; 1872–1947), whose innovations at the Théâtre Pigalle included the revolving stage; the Belgians, Henry Hubert Kistemaeckers (1872–1938) and Francis de Croisset (1877–1937); Pierre Wolff

(1865–1944) and Romain Coolus (1868–1952), two writers of popular comedies; and Jean Jacques *Bernard, son of the more distinguished Tristan Bernard, who became a Catholic. Overshadowing most of these were the social dramatist Henry *Bernstein and the converted literary critic Gustave Cohen. Prominent writers in other literary spheres were the essayists André *Suarès, Julien *Benda, and Benjamin *Crémieux. Maurice *Sachs, a depraved but talented writer, was a World War II collaborator; and the eminent biographer André *Maurois at first supported Pétain. Outstanding poets of the early 20th century include the convert Max *Jacob, who died in a Nazi concentration camp; the half-Jew Oscar *Milosz, an esoteric writer detached from contemporary trends; and Yvan and Claire *Goll.

Almost all these authors, with the exception of Henry Bernstein, were Frenchmen who also happened to be Jews; but the Dreyfus case had a profound influence in reshaping the ideas of French Jewish writers. The publicists Victor *Basch and Bernard *Lazare were both roused to action by the affair. Even the half-Jew, Marcel *Proust, prevailed on Anatole France to intervene in Dreyfus' favor and, reassessing his own position in French society, gave a place of importance to Jewish characters in his great novel cycle *A la recherche du temps perdu.*

Two leading poets who rediscovered their Judaism were the symbolist Gustave *Kahn, who became an enthusiastic Zionist, and his even more militant contemporary, André *Spire, who inaugurated an entirely new Jewish and Zionist current in French literature. They were followed by Henri *Franck and Edmond *Fleg, the poet, playwright, and anthologist, whose rekindled devotion to Judaism led him to seek a symbiosis between the French and Jewish traditions.

In the 20th century the conflict of identity preoccupied several writers, including the novelists Jean-Richard *Bloch and Albert *Cohen. Their general approach was, however, very different. Bloch, a Communist, assigned to the Jew the role of "revolutionary ferment" in his adopted society; while Cohen, a Corfu-born poet and mystic, was strongly influenced by his Mediterranean background. The regional element is also important in the works of Armand *Lunel, who dealt primarily with Provençal culture, and Joseph *Kessel, who wrote some novels set in Israel. While Henri *Hertz, a leading French Zionist, devoted much of his attention to Jewish problems, other writers asserted their Jewishness mainly in their protests against antisemitism. Jean Finot (born Finkelstein, 1858–1922), a Warsaw-born lawyer, author of *Le préjugé des races* (1905; *Race Prejudice*, 1906), Emmanuel Berl (1892–1976), and Pierre Morhange (1901–1972) all belong to this category. So does Pierre Abraham (1892–1975), the brother of Jean-Richard Bloch, who directed the leftist monthly, *Europe*, and only recalled his Jewish identity in response to the Dreyfus case and, some 30 years later, to Hitler. A rare example of Jewish antisemitism was René Schwob (1895–1946), a convert to Catholicism, who wrote a series of unpleasant apologies, including *Moi*, juif (1928), *Ni grec ni juit* (1931), and *Itinéraire d'un juif vers l'église* (1940).

On the other hand, the themes of certain 20th-century writers, the problems they analyzed, the characters they depicted, the settings they chose were exclusively Jewish. Such were Myriam *Harry; Lily Jean-Javal (1882–1958), a novelist and poet; Michel Matvéev (b.1893), who evoked in novels such as *Ailleurs*, autrefois (1959) the tragic fate of the exiled and the persecuted; Pierre *Paraf; Josué Jéhouda; Pierre Neyrac; Joseph Schulsinger; Moïse Twersky, author of *L'épopée de Menasché Foïgel* (3 vols., 1927–28, with André Billy), the story of a Russian immigrant in France; and Irène Némirowsky (1903–1940), recently rediscovered – whose characters, however, seem to have been influenced by antisemitic stereotypes of the time. Two other figures of note who dealt with the religious implications of Judaism were Raïssa *Maritain, a Russian Jewess who became a Catholic, and Aimé *Pallière, a Catholic who became a liberal pro-Jewish propagandist.

A phenomenon worth consideration is the large number of Romanian-born Jews who either began or resumed their literary career in France. They include the novelist and playwright Adolphe Orna (1882–1925); Tristan *Tzara; the political poet Claude Sernet (1902–1968, born Ernst Spirt); Ilarie *Voronca; Eugène *Ionesco; and Isidore Isou. Another French poet of Romanian origin was the visionary Benjamin *Fondane (1898–1944), who came to France in the 1920s and then published *Ulysse* (1933), *Rimbaud le voyou* (1933), and *La conscience malheureuse* (1936) before being arrested and deported to Nazi camps.

Edmond *Jabès (1908–1991) has attracted considerable attention since the 1960s. His Le Livre des Questions has become the first of a series of works which consist of persistent questioning, sometimes in the form of narratives or dialogues, sometimes in the form of apocryphal talmudic discussions between imaginary rabbis or kabbalistic letter games. The condition of the Jew is for Jabès identified with that of the poet: both the creative writer and the Jew can exist only in the state of exile. The term is of course taken in a spiritual sense and has no political meaning. The title of the first volume is also the title of the whole series; the others are *Le Livre de Yukel* (1964), *Le Retour au Livre* (1965), *Yaël* (1967), *Elya* (1969), *Aely* (1972) and *El* (1973), which is the conclusion of a search for the unity of Judaism and literary creation, and at the same time a ceaseless questioning of the relevance of language His two-volume *Livre des Ressemblances* (1976–78) is in the same hermetic, broken poetic language as was his *Book of Questions*. In this new poetic work it is language itself which is being questioned. But the reader or the critic may query the deceptive dress of rabbinic discussion and kabbalistic tradition assumed by Jabès' writing. However, the glaringly inauthentic garment does not contradict the strikingly Jewish tone of this endless meditation, especially apparent in the author's philosophical essay: *L'ineffable*, L'inaperçu (1980). *Un étranger avec*, sous le bras, un livre de petit format (A Stranger Holding a Little Book under his Arm, 1989) seeks to characterize the stranger and to describe his role. The book is also a self-portrait. Jabès launches on a description of the central figure, stressing his Jewish specificity and his peculiar relation to the Book: "The Jew is a stranger because the Word in the Book, which adheres tightly to his Jewishness, is his." Yet this relationship of the Jew with the Word poses many questions. The Word is always imperfect since it cannot totally express our own inner self, even less our relationship to God. On the metaphysical level, the question remains unanswered. But the human quality of the Stranger and his function in our midst is more clearly defined. "The Stranger enables *you* to be yourself, when it turns you into a stranger." "You are the Stranger. And I? I am, for you, the Stranger. And *you*? The star always separated from the star. What brings them closer is only their will to shine together." The Stranger appears near-sighted, he is there and not there, present and absent, close and far away. "He lives in the margins of an inexhaustible book." Jabès concludes: "The writer is the Stranger *par excellence*," an eternal exile, like the Jew, who is "the hope and the wearing out of a book which he will never exhaust." In short, "in order to be himself, he must be alone." This is of course an old theme, on which Jabès had often touched, but it becomes the core of a very personal Jewish book and extends into the realm of the universal.

Jabès had, in a sense, prepared the way with an impressive collection of poems, *La mémoire et l'oubli* (To remember and to forget, 1987), a book which gathers a number of poetic texts composed between 1974 and 1980, some of which are directly or allusively tied to the Holocaust. *Le livre du partage* (The Book of Shares, 1990) appeared in English translation as the inaugural volume of a new series on religion and post-modernism at the University of Chicago Press. Whether this latest work indeed marks a new departure remains to be seen. The stricter conceptual essay form Jabès turns to is, at this juncture, dotted with apologies for the author's inadequacies and personal self-conscious remarks, such as: "Forgive my works. They have the excuse of despair."

THE MEMORY OF THE HOLOCAUST. A number of French Jewish authors wrote about the Hitler era and the Holocaust of European Jewry. Evoking the past was the main purpose of Roger *Ikor in *Les eau mêlées* (1955) as well as in *Pour une fois écoute mon enfant* (1975). Manes *Sperber with his trilogies *Ces temps* là (1976) and *Lele buisson devint cendre* (1948/1990) and other novels or essays such as *Etre juif* (1994) advocated for a "religion of memory." Anna *Langfus, in her semiautobiographical novels, described characters who, despite Nazi brutality ("I saw a man who stood up on another man who led on the earth"), succeeded in retaining their human dignity and moral values. One may quote *Le sel et le soufre* ("Salt and Sulfur," 1960) or *Les bagages de sable* ("Sandy Luggage," 1962). André *Schwarz-Bart, in the international bestseller, *Le dernier des justes* (1959; *The Last of the Just*, 1960), produced an epic on the age-old Jewish tragedy, while Elie *Wiesel, who was awarded the Nobel Prize in 1986, wrote a series of haunting novels on the Holocaust and its aftermath.

Wiesel, in *Entre deux soleils* (1970), unifies his vision of man through narrations, dialogues and legends, and emphasizes his role as witness. After two volumes of portraits and legends, *La Célébration hassidique* (1976) and *Célébration biblique* (1977) and a play, *Le procès de Shamgorod* (1979), very much in the tradition of the Yiddish theater, mixing irony and pathos, Elie Wiesel brought out a major novel, *Le Testament d'un poète juif assassiné* (1980), which bears witness to the agony and rebirth of Jewish consciousness among the young generation of Soviet writers. The book is couched in the form of a testament, written in a Soviet jail, by a Jewish poet accused of high treason and counterrevolutionary activities. Although the hero Paltiel Kossover is an imaginary figure, his itinerary closely resembles that of many a Jewish dissident. The son of a kind and pious father, he spent his youth in a Romanian shtetl. His messianic fervor took on the garb of revolutionary faith, claiming to bring salvation to mankind and Jews alike. The new Leninist religion, widely followed by young Russian Jews in the thirties, was to bring the hero to clandestine action in Nazi Germany and Palestine, and to fighting in the Spanish Civil War and the Red Army. But Paltiel, though a rebel against traditional Judaism, kept an obscure feeling of loyalty to his father, whose voice often calls out to him in the depth of night. Hardly knowing why, Paltiel carried his *tefillin* with him throughout. On the Russian front he meets Raïssa, seemingly a hardboiled communist. Though her role remains somewhat ambiguous, they will together uncover the sinister imposture of the Russian regime, and gradually Paltiel's poetry becomes the song of his people. Together they flee with their small son, Grisha, secretly circumcised by his father. The Soviet police submit the hero to its most refined physical and moral tortures, the chief result being to strengthen and elevate the spirit of the victim, who on the threshold of death writes a poignant spiritual autobiography as a legacy to his son. Grisha, the still unknowing child, instinctively feels the presence of a potential enemy: wanting to evade the questioning of a neighbor, a supposedly well-meaning doctor and father figure, he bites off his tongue and will remain mute. A strange witness of Paltiel's martyrdom and death is the clerk of the court, a Jew himself caught in the system, who carries the message to the mute son of the poet. Grisha will eventually reach Israel with a group of refuseniks, expecting his mother to follow. But will she ever come? The reader is carried into a dreamlike world of introspection, into the shadowy recesses of the psyche. Wiesel's book is an emotional and convincing statement of Jewish self-assertion.

The book *L'oublié* (1989) tells the story of a father and son and moves from Auschwitz to Israel. Its characters are convincing, while the search for a buried past is the motivation and the core of the book. The concluding message is clear: Israel, the land of the prophets, will be and must be the place where memory is kept intact, the land of truth and life, the land of Jewish hope. Elhanan Rosenbaum, born in a shetl of the Carpathian mountains, survives the Holocaust and discovers Palestine. In besieged Jerusalem he falls in love with Talia and a son, Malkiel, is born. In New York, where he settles with Malkiel, Elhanan preserves the memory of the terrible years. But Malkiel, already an American, although close to his father, has no link with Elhanan's past. One thing only is certain: his mother Talia died in bringing him into the world. Elhanan, who has been unable to reveal his treasured nightmare to his son, becomes ill and loses the ability to speak or to remember. Soon the past will be lost forever. Elhanan will have nothing to bequeath to his son who, in turn, will be unable to know the roots of his deepest convictions and to share them with his friend Tamar. The shipwreck of memory is averted in a dramatic manner: the father suddenly starts to tell the story of his tumultuous past, thus feeding his son's memory, while his own will finally be relieved of its intolerable burden. As the old man finally sinks into the night, forgetting all, his son, strengthened by the link regained, discovers the land of his ancestors. This marks his second birth and the revelation of his deeper self. He will conquer his truth with the help of his father's truth. Will Malkiel, in turn, be able to triumph over the indifference of a world devoid of memory? Will he remember his father's deepest hope? Elhanan's most fervent prayer had been never to forget. Indeed "to forget is to abandon, to betray." "Without memory, truth becomes a lie, a mere masking of the truth." A Jew must bear witness, both to joy and distress.

Wiesel also published his memoirs: *Tous les fleuves vont à la mer* (1994; All the Rivers Run to the Sea, 1995) and *Et la mer n'est pas remplie* (1996; *And the Sea Is Never Full*, 1999).

A writer whose reputation had continued to grow into the 21st century is Georges *Perec (1936–1982), whose stylistically dazzling masterpiece, *La Vie: mode d'emploi* (1978), was translated into English in 1987 as *Life: A User's Manual*. Called by Italo Calvino "the last great event in the history of the novel," it takes the reader into a Paris apartment house, examining the interlocking lives and possessions of its tenants as part of a shifting mosaic of signs and symbols. Until the end of his life he nurtured a profound memory of his parents, who died during World War II: "I am a writer because they left their indelible mark. Their tracks are writing, writing is the memory of their death and the assertion of my life." On these themes, Perec published *W ou le souvenir d'enfance* (1975), *Je me souviens* (1978) and *Récits d'Ellis Island* (1980), which he made into a film with Robert Bober.

In Quoi de neuf sur la guerre (1993), Robert *Bober evokes the post-war period and the survivors' painful personal process of rebuilding. *Berg & Beck* is the story of two young Jewish boys who one day have to put a yellow star on their coats while walking together to school. Beck is arrested and murdered in a Nazi camp. After the war, Berg regularly writes to him: "It's not because you never answer that History can do without you."

Two dramatists of outstanding talent, Liliane Atlan and Jean-Claude Grumberg merit attention. Liliane Atlan (1932–), born in Southern France to a Jewish family from Salonica, felt deeply the trauma of Nazi occupation. At the age of 17 she attended a Jewish communal school and after earning a diploma in philosophy, she started writing for the theater. Her early plays were Monsieur Fugue, staged in Paris in 1967 and in Israel in 1972 under the title Mar Slick; *Les Messies* (1969); *La Petite Voiture de Flammes et de Voix* (The Small Car of Flames and Voices), presented at the Avignon Festival in 1971. She also wrote three volumes of poetry in this period: *Les Mains Coupeuses de Mémoire* (Hands-Cutters of Memory, 1969), *Le Maître-Mur* (1964) and *Lapsus* (1971). The same themes recur both in her poems and in her plays. The first leitmotif is the difficulty in living, borne out by the awareness of the human condition: man, trapped by evil, contracts the incurable Earth-Sickness Le Mal de terre (the phrase serves as subtitle to the first two plays.) In Monsieur Fugue the author borrows elements from reality, yet the play is no documentary. Four Jewish children are being taken in a truck in the fog to Rotten Town, or the Valley of Dry Bones. Their guards are soldiers clad in green. One of them, Monsieur Fugue, decides to accompany the children, and during the journey he tells them stories and they enter the game. They live in imagination the life which they will never know in reality: adolescence, love, marriage, old age and natural death; at which point they are killed. But the imaginary has replaced the hideous reality. Dream here is no escape, but rather the only reality; and joy can thus spring forth out of despair. Joy is the recurrent countertheme. In *Les Messies*, Earth Sickness is no longer viewed from within, but from the outside or from higher up. All realistic elements have disappeared. A group of messiahs, set on an imaginary planet and representing all the ideals and hopes ever invented by mankind, await the moment to jump down and save the earth. But overtaken by dizziness caused by the Earth Sickness, they wait too long and fail. The myths of salvation are deceitful. Consolation lies not in the content of myths, as in *Monsieur Fugue*, but in the ability to invent them: after a dismal failure the messiahs will continue to pray and hope. *La petite voiture* represents a passage into subjective theater, set in a fantastic, apocalyptic universe. The two characters, Louise, an invalid in a wheel-chair pushed by Louli, are a projection of the author's split consciousness. How to live in an evil world is the agonizing question pursued in an obstinate, sometimes frenzied, dialogue-monologue. In the end Louli-Louise, facing an apocalyptic destruction, proclaims with all her meager might: joy will be for our descendants if not for us, an inner sun will shine and that's enough to smile for from tonight on. The Holocaust is still prevalent in Liliane Atlan's recent works, as may be seen in *Un opéra pour Terezin* (1997), which tells the true story of Jewish inmates in the Theresienstadt camp who decided to found an orchestra to play Verdi's Requiem; or in *Les Mers rouges* (1999), which collects survivors' testimonies, songs, and tales from the Salonika Jewish community mostly exterminated in gas chambers.

Jean-Claude Grumberg (1937–) was born in Paris, the grandson of a Yiddish-speaking immigrant from Cracow. Like Atlan, he felt the wound of Nazi oppression… For him too, the resulting anguish had to be exorcised in dramatic creations. But the tone is different: aggressiveness and humor are the dominant colors. Among his significant plays are *Amorphe d'Ottenburg* and *En revenant de l'Expo*, and above all *Dreyfus* (1974), unanimously hailed as a masterpiece. Grumberg seeks to reconcile History, and its seeming absurdity, with Man, trapped in his contradictions. History is invoked frequently, yet often treated with contempt. Man alone, in his human individual quality, really matters, with all his shortcomings. *Dreyfus* presents a potentially comical and pathetic situation. In a Vilna suburb in 1930, a group of townspeople rehearses a play about the Dreyfus Affair, written by Maurice, a young Jewish intellectual, who dreams of representing the Truth of History, of drawing a moral from past events and of creating genuine popular theater. But as the simple townspeople themselves see it, there is no historical truth; the only truth is what we see and recreate. If Maurice wants a moral, a lecture is preferable. As to popular theater, it has nothing to do with distant, foreign historical events. It must spring from experience and tradition. Michel, the cobbler, feels nothing in common with the French captain; he cannot play the role and remains wooden at rehearsals. Arnold, the barber, who plays the part of Zola, finds his text long and pompous; he would prefer a gay little Yiddish song. Motel, the tailor, sees no reason to make a blue uniform for Dreyfus, like in the pictures: he has a big reserve of red cloth. Zina, Arnold's wife, has to cross the stage, shouting Death to the Jews; she would rather be the captain's mother – a good *Yiddische mama*! – etc. In short, the townspeople, authentically alive, refuse the lifeless construction of the dreamy intellectual. The clash creates hilarious scenes. At times, emotion and even grandeur take over, as in the scene of the drunken Poles' attack, courageously repelled by the Jew, or the tale of the saintly ḥasidic rabbi who rose higher than God Himself. And finally in the last scene a taste of irony and tragic humor dominates: after the play's failure, Maurice goes to Warsaw and joins the Polish communist party. In a letter to his friends, one savors the bitter flavor of ideologies espoused by Jewish intellectuals whether communists of the 1930s or leftists of today. As a tragic echo comes a letter from Berlin, where two of the young actors have gone to seek their fortune: Germany is after all a civilized country, where one can build a future! Irony and humor, tempered by tenderness and sadness, contrive to make *Dreyfus* a great Jewish play and a masterpiece of comedy. His play, *L'Atelier* (1979) dwells, with typical tender Yiddish humor, on the sad life of the Holocaust survivors. After achieving great success, too, with *Zone libre* in 1990, he recalls the daily life of a Jewish immigrant family from Poland during the 1930s in *Conversations avec mon père* (2002) and in *Mon père*, inventaire (2003).

Among the writers of this generation, Emile Ajar (a pseudonym of Romain *Gary) has gained the greatest recognition with his two novels: *La vie devant soi* (1975) and *L'angoisse du roi Salomon* (1979). The first book, which created a sensation and won the much coveted Goncourt literary prize, presents a vivid picture of the Parisian Belleville slum, where Jews, Arabs, Blacks and other minorities live in close and generally friendly contact. The author chose to have his story narrated by a 14-year-old Arab boy, Momo, who, along with other semi-abandoned children of prostitutes, was raised by a Jewish mama, Madame Rosa, herself an ex-prostitute. Although the relationship between the kind and generous Madame Rosa and her precious and affectionate son appears to be an authentic and touching love story between mother and child, above and beyond racial and cultural barriers, the book has a very unreal quality. The numerous characters, perhaps with the exception of the old Jewish neighborhood doctor, seem to have walked out of a book of fables, including Momo, a cross between an innocent small boy and a knowledgeable social critic, and Madame Rosa herself, a victim of society and persecution on the one hand and a monumental monstrous delirious figure of terrorized womanhood on the other. Madame Rosa's Jewish cellar, which symbolically portrays an underground refuge in a hostile world, serves as the last retrenchment when death and madness overtake Madame Rosa's soul and body. In spite of the repeated Jewish references the central figure, Madame Rosa, could belong to any oppressed ethnic group: as the author himself admits, everyone is entitled to a secret hiding place. And if Momo, the little Arab, can grasp this, it is because Arab or Jew, where is the difference? *L'angoisse du roi Salomon* is also a kind of fable, where mythical representation and social realism are constantly intertwined. It is based on the story of an old noble-looking Jew, Mr. Salomon Rubinstein, former king of ready-to-wear fashion turned philanthropist devoted to helping lonely souls. The role of son and narrator is held by a young Paris taxi driver who, just as Momo did with Madame Rosa, finds in the old Jewish paternal figure the epitome of human compassion and kindness. King Salomon, who spent four years hidden in a cellar during the Nazi occupation, is scarred by pain and solitude. Like Madame Rosa he has sublimated the anguish by becoming a benevolent dispenser of kindness all around him. Ajar's style in both novels reproduces the language of the man in the street, savory, slangy, full of verve and irony, yet barely concealing a feeling of malaise and suffocation. In several books published under his own name, Gary tackles the memory of the Holocaust – for instance in *Education européenne* (1945), *La danse de Gengis Cohn* (1967), or *Chien blanc* (1970).

The post-war generation's need to find its Jewish roots has expressed itself in still other genres, spiritual or intellectual diaries, where remembrances either are mixed with religious, philosophical or political reflections or frankly give way to an essay commenting on insistent preoccupation with the Jewish condition in our age. In the category of essays one must mention the attempt by Alain Finkielkraut (1949–) to analyze the state of mind of his generation in *Le Juif imaginaire* (1980). Disappointed with leftist politics, tired of resisting his parents' recurrent "Jewish leitmotiv," he rediscovered for himself the significance of the Jewish message. Although he is well-read, his statement is based solely on his own intuitive subjective feeling. The impact felt by the works of a group of young philosophers appears to be a more lasting one. André Glucksmann (1937–) in *Les Maîtres penseurs* (1977) and Bernard-Henry *Lévy (1948–) in *La Barbarie à visage humain* (1977) and *Le Testament de Dieu* (1979) opened the way to a philosophical search of a Jewish view of man and God. They denounced not only fascism and marxism, but, in a rather sweeping manner, their Western masters (maîtres penseurs), guilty of politicizing all debates on life and history, basically because they were the heirs of platonic philosophy. What emerges here is the indictment of Athens in the name of Jerusalem. Bernard Chouraqui's (1943–) message in *Le Scandale juif ou la subversion de la mort* (1979) is more flamboyant and more mystical in its condemnation of Western rationalism. The latter is accused of having stifled the limitless freedom of man's spirit and more specifically the Jewish spirit. If permitted to fulfill its true vocation, Judaism can overcome death itself. The statement is often too grandiloquent to be totally convincing. Shmuel *Trigano (1948–) in *Le retour de la disparue* (1977) and *La nouvelle question juive* (1979) adopted a more restrained tone in dealing with the problem of Jewish identity. He too challenged the European humanism and rationalism, but in so doing he also condemned "Western oriented" Ashkenazi Judaism and Zionism itself. In the name of Kabbalistic tradition and Sephardi predominance he advocated a kind of revivalist Judaism, far from the Haskalah tradition. All these young thinkers, Glucksmann, Lévy, Chouraqui, Trigano, claim allegiance to the teachings of Emmanuel *Lévinas, the great Jewish philosopher.

Most of these prolific authors were disillusioned leftists. One of the most interesting was Pierre Goldman (1944–1979), a son of Polish immigrants who, after revolutionary activities, was accused of murder. He discovered his Jewishness in jail and started to study Judaism seriously. He wrote his first and best book in prison. After his release he was murdered under mysterious circumstances. In 1975 he composed *Souvenirs d'un Juif polonais né en France* ("Memories of a Polish Jew Born in Poland"), a rather remarkable testimony of the discovery of his Jewish consciousness. He proclaimed himself a Jewish revolutionary, who, in anguished self-concern, expressed his identification with his people through his revolutionary convictions. His Jewish self-identification remained divorced from either religious or Zionist feelings. A second book, *L'ordinaire mésaventure d'Archibald Rapoport* (1977) keeps up the same strident, ironic and desperate tone and attains the limit of poetic and metaphysical exasperation. The theme is couched in the form of a legend: the hero fulfills an angelic mission, that of exterminating all officialdom, because it represents a civilization responsible for Auschwitz.

A nostalgic feeling for the 1930s and the prewar period is also felt in Cyrille Fleischman's short tales, which always take place in the Pletzl, the Jewish quarter in Paris, from *Rendez-vous au métro Saint-Paul* (1992) to *Une rencontre près de l'Hôtel de ville* (2003).

Henri Raczymow's (1948–) *Contes d'exil et d'oubli* ("Tales of Exile and Oblivion," 1979) are an imaginary dialogue between a grandson in search of his Jewish self and a Polish grandfather transplanted to the Paris ghetto of Belleville. The tales contained in this short volume beautifully bring to life the charm and faith of the shtetl. *Un cri sans voix* (1985) tells the story of Esther who was totally obsessed with the memory of the Warsaw ghetto and committed suicide in the 1970s. Of note also is *Bloom & Bloch* (1993).

Raczymow also published an intriguing essay. He turned his attention, like others before him, to Swann, the half-Jewish Proustian hero. But the approach is new. The title of the book, *Le cygne de Proust* (1989), gives a clue of the direction chosen. Referring himself to one of the known models for Swann, namely Charles Haas, a dandy of the day (a German Jew), the essay pinpoints what links Swann to him and what separates Swann from his presumed model. The author's starting point is the translation from Haas to Swann. Haas (hare in German) was both too plebeian and too German for Proust's taste. Passing over to the English (more to the snobs' liking) he coined the new name Swann, only subtly reminiscent to the French reader of its translation (swan – and not Swann – evoking in English the noble and mythical bird: "le cygnet"). Such is the starting point for the essay. The author then answers the secret: how did the idea suggest itself? He observed in a painting representing a brilliant social circle, that Charles Haas was standing "near the door, facing the others, though on the side, as if he hesitated to mingle with them and penetrate inside the circle." Observing how Haas was "part of the circle, but remained on the periphery," the author told himself: "Haas was Jewish, had no title of nobility, no prestigious heredity, no tremendous fortune." From then on, that noble "cygne" (Swann) became less distant, almost a familiar, intimate person. One can see in this study a literary illustration of social marranism. Raczymow continued his study of Marcel Proust in *Le Paris retrouvé de Marcel Proust* (2005). On the other hand, he looks into his own boyhood in Avant *le déluge: Belleville années 50* (2005) and in *Reliques* (2005); in 2003, with *Le plus tard possible*, he evaluates his life, and "[his] experience of absolute loneliness."

Myriam Anissimov, born in 1943 in a refugee camp, wrote a Kafkaesque novel, *Rue de Nuit* (1977), the bizarre story of a couple accused of some unknown crime. In *La soie et les cendres* (Silk and ashes, 1989), Hannah, obsessed with the weight of her people's tragic past, deceives herself into believing that she has found the truth about herself and her link with the Holocaust. She has found an original "profession" for herself: she sells *shmattes* (old clothes) at the flea market. In so doing, she fantasizes that she is one with the pitiful remains (the "silk") of the victims at Auschwitz (the "ashes"). The book tells the sad and perverse nightmare of a Jewish girl, who eventually faces up to the essential duty of living creatively. She will find salvation through music, doubtless a finer memorial to the victims. Anissimov, who also published two successful biographies (on Primo Levi, 1998, and Romain Gary, 2004), wrote in *Dans la plus stricte intimité* (1992) about her childhood in a broken Jewish family after the war, from Lyon to Metz; and she also published a kind of autobiography, *Sa Majesté la Mort* (1999).

The difficult dialogue between a mother and her daughter is the original subject *L'immense fatigue des pierres* (1996) by of Régine Robin (1939–), but according to the author, the trauma of the Holocaust is at the root of linguistic hybridism and the plurality of identities. Robin had already devoted *Le deuil de l'origine* (1993) to the influence of their Jewish roots and the loss of their language (Yiddish or Ladino) on the works of several writers, such as Kafka, Celan, Freud, Canetti, and Perec. In her critical essay *La mémoire saturée* (2003) she questioned the function of the recent and widespread uses of commemoration of the past.

The memory of the Holocaust remains at the heart of some young writers' books. The first novel of Norbert Czarny deals with the problem of memory, or rather the ability to keep alive and convey the reality of the past. In *Les valises* (1989) the narrator's parents and grandparents, unlike the father in Wiesel's book, have been feeding the child endless stories of their past. But the child, threatened with suffocation, by the burden of those recollections, transforms, almost magically, a hard and somber tale into a legend full of poetic charm. Stephanie Janicot wrote her first novel, *Les Matriochkas* (1996), about the relationship between a young German and the Jewish family he lives with in Paris in the 1980s. Gila Lustiger (1963–), who grew up in Germany, published *L'inventaire* (1998) and *Nous sommes* (2005), telling the story of her family. In *Un amour sans résistance* (2004), Gilles Rozier (1963–) tells the story of a Gestapo translator in Paris who saves a young Jew, and more recently, in 2005, he published *La Promesse d'Oslo* centering on the will to life of an Orthodox Jerusalem woman whose son is murdered by a terrorist; after several months, she decides to have another child through artificial insemination, with her rabbi's consent. Cécile Wajsbrot (1954–) is increasingly obsessed with the Holocaust and its traumatic effects on succeeding generations, as evidenced by *Beaune-la-Rolande* (2004), *La trahison* (2005), and *Mémorial* (2005).

Although of Sephardi origin, Patrick *Modiano (1947–) is quite obsessed by the memory of the Holocaust. He is the author of successful novels – *La place de l'Étoile* (1968), *La ronde de nuit* (1969), *Les boulevards de ceinture* (1972), *Villa triste* (1975) and *Rue des boutiques obscures* (1978) – as well as an autobiography, *Livret de famille* (1977). The German occupation, which the author never experienced, is the recurrent and obsessive theme. A search for his true identity and for the meaning of his Jewish condition runs through the first novel, where the hero lives in fantasy through a thousand lives and identities. As a Jew, he sees himself sometimes as a king, sometimes a martyr. The same quest continues in the other books, down to the haunting search for the father in the last novel. The father is a pathetic, repulsive, ghost-like figure, victim and partner of a shady gang who lives it up under Nazi occupation. The ultimate question remains: is one ever free to choose or are we nothing but puppets in the hands of blind fate? The notion of Jewish identity has lost all moral or historic meaning. It has been reduced to an almost organic search for roots. The strained narratives are put forth in deliberately flat style, conveying tragic situations in a painfully grotesque manner. Modiano was awarded the Goncourt Prize in 1978. In the 1980s, Modiano deliberately turned to writing children's books. They included *Catherine Certitude* (1988), the charming story of a little girl who lives with her "papa" in a northern Parisian neighborhood close to Montmartre, part of a cosmopolitan world of little people who struggle as best they can, slightly out of the "real" French world. They find refuge in a world of dreams. Catherine will later realize that even the French sometimes have to escape a glittering, but cruel, reality. In fact, the "not quite French" depicted here are, in an implicit but clear fashion, Jewish immigrants, who always remain "out of it," even when they take on a new French name. The irony of Catherine's French surname resides in the fact that Catherine's father has been renamed by an employee of the city registrar, unable to read or spell the immigrant's foreign sounding name. "Certitude" had seemed to him clear and perfectly suitable! Catherine and her father eventually leave for New York, where Catherine's American mother now lives. Later Catherine, herself a mother, will realize that something in her parents' persistent estrangement from themselves and the world is part of their essential humanity. In this new vein of writing, Modiano, though still dealing with the hero's search to elucidate the darker of his parents' past, has found a lighter touch, devoid of bitterness and sarcasm. The mood is whimsical, sometimes ironic, but never cynical or nightmarish. The "happy ending" is suited to a delightful and moving children's book.

In *Dora Bruder* (1997) Modiano attempts to pick up the trail of a teenager who was deported from Paris in 1942, but "I will never know what she was doing all day long, where she was hiding, who she was with during Winter, then Spring …. It's her secret. Her poor and precious secret that torturers, camps, History could never rob her of…." In Un pedigree (2005) he gave the reader the biographical keys to his work.

THE SEPHARDI IDENTITY. Albert *Cohen (1895–1981) was still vigorously creative at 85, and after completing the saga of the Solals with a fourth novel, *Les Valeureux* (1969), a companion piece to *Mangeclous*, wrote what might be called his testament, a little book, which borrows its title from Villon's famous ballad: *O vous frères humains* ("O Ye, Human Brothers," 1972). Though the themes in Cohen's work – meditation on death, the universality and absurdity of human destiny, the tragic nobility of the Jewish condition – are not new, they reach to the heart of the Jewish writer's experience. A Jewish child encounters the implacable, stupid, cruel hatred of antisemitism and this banal and terrifying incident, prototype of all genocide, makes of him a Jew, an adult, and a poet. The bearer of this unified triple identity will have but one mission: to state the place of the Jew among the nations and send a cry of alarm to a mad world bent on hating, when love alone can save. In a poignant volume of diaries, *Carnets* (1978), the elderly writer returned to his timeless meditation. His style lost none of his brilliance, variety, sharpness, and opulence.

A group of writers, mostly Sephardi, has gradually emerged, characterized by books situated midway between the novel and the autobiography. Albert *Memmi's own search for identity takes on a radically different coloring. Cast in a sunny and intriguing decor, his two novels, *Le Scorpion* (1969) and *Le Désert* (1977), are full of old world wisdom and fancy, elegant pieces of French prose, a mixed genre between story-telling, autobiography and historical inquiry. Whereas, *Le Scorpion* is a sort of imaginary confession, depicting picturesque North African Jewish folk towards the end of the French protectorate, *Le Désert* presents a kind of Oriental tale, partly set in feudal Arab society, partly in desert Berber country (like many old Jewish Tunisian families. Memmi claims to have some Berber ancestry). Both books, no matter how remote from plain realism, have a remarkable, convincing ring of truth. In *La Statue de sel* (1953) Memmi confronted the question of his own Jewish identity.

To the same group belongs Jacques Zibi, who in *Ma* (1971) pays tribute to his mother. He tenderly and deftly evokes the mother's simple gestures, the intimacy of the Arab Jewish dialect of her native Tunisia, the purity and peace of the Jewish home. In a more humorous vein, Elie-Georges Berreby in *Le singe du Prophète* ("The Prophet's Monkey," 1972) takes up the Jonah theme. The modern reluctant prophet is forcibly pulled out of a quiet existence to denounce the sinful town, i.e., the nuclear city. Lucien Elia offers a painful experience of a real talent, presenting a degrading picture of his people.

In *Les ratés de la Diaspora*, where he depicts the ghettoes of Syria and Lebanon, the simple Oriental Jews are treated with caustic humor and contempt, though the villains are ostensibly the Arabs. In a second novel, *Fer blanc* (1973), he presents a downright antisemitic caricature of Israel. Jacques Sabbath, in *Le Bruit des autres* (1974), appears as a talented short-story writer.

Naim Kattan (born in Iraq in 1928) and Albert Bensoussan (born in Algeria in1935) similarly revive with great talent the land of their past. The first tells us of his youth in Baghdad, the second recalls Jewish life in Algiers. Kattan's *Adieu Babylone* (1975) portrays the life of a young Baghdad Jew in the modern age. Still part of an ancient Jewish tradition, he is exposed to Western modes when the arrival of British troops during the Second World War breaks into the unchanged quiet of the Oriental community. The hero is then caught between several alternatives: remaining within the bounds of traditional Jewish living, becoming an enlightened Westerner, identifying with the Arab nationalist struggle (in the guise of progressive politics) or with the Zionist pioneering ideal. Kattan is also the author of *La mémoire et la promesse* (1979) and *Le rivage* (1981). Bensoussan's two novels: *Frimaldjezar* (1976) and *Au nadir* (1978) do not deal so much with ideological choices as with the nostalgic feeling of a happy and sunny past, when an Algerian Jewish child could live in the cheerful fervent, popular milieu of a settled community. French colonial power then appeared as a permanent shield against all possible abuse on the part of the Arabs. The style, both lyrical and highly colorful, conveys the love of native surroundings where historical change was never to intrude. Around the turn of the century Bensoussan published several books, both prose and poetry, about the warm relationships between Jews, Arabs, and Christians in colonial Algeria, filling his books with colorful characters: *L'Oeil de la sultane* (1996), *Pour une poignée de dattes* (2001), and *L'Échelle algérienne. Voix juives* (2001).

In describing Jewish circles in Tunisia before independence or Jewish immigrants to Paris, Nine Moati (1937–) often focuses on women. In *Deux femmes à Paris* (1998), she describes the daily life of two neighbors in Paris, one is a young immigrant from Tunisia and the other a coquette whose lover is an extreme right-wing militant. In *Villa Week-end* (2003) she analyzes the evolutionary relationship between a young Jewish girl and her French friend in Tunisia in the 1930s, then under German occupation; and *L'Orientale* (2005) tells the story of Hannah, Duke Nessim's daughter from Leghorn, who becomes a "queen" in fashionable Paris before falling in love with an antisemitic French aristocrat.

The need to portray the life of now extinct Sephardi and Oriental communities also inspires a group of much younger writers, several of them women, who attempt to give a specific literary coloring to their childhood recollections. In the *Mémoire illettrée d'une fillette d'Afrique du nord à l'époque coloniale* (1979), Katia Rubinstein portrayed the life of a Tunis quarter where traditional Jews lived side by side with various other ethnic groups. The author chose an illiterate little girl as a narrator, gifting her with a colorful and truculent language, where French is interspersed with Jewish Arab, Jewish Italian and Jewish Spanish dialects.

Paula Jacques (born in Egypt in 1949) also focuses on women in her novels about Egyptian Jewry: *Lumière de l'œil* (1980) and *L'Héritage de tante Carlotta* (1987). *Les Femmes avec leur amour* (1997) describes the deep friendship between a young Jewish girl and her Muslim maid in Egypt, a few months before the Suez War in 1956; expelled by Nasser in 1957, like most of the Egyptian Jews, the heroine of *Gilda Stambouli souffre et se plaint* (Gilda 2001) sets up house in Paris, full of vigor, excesses, and insincerity, while at the same time her daughter tries to leave her kibbutz on the Syrian border.

In *Les herbes amères* (The Bitter Herbs, 1989), Chochana Boukhobza (1954–) has the heroine, Jane, who has made a clean break with her past, meditates on distant events and their true meaning. Marc, her beloved, is dead. Her mother, whom Jane always hated, committed suicide. Though she was a camp survivor, Jane never granted her even "a few minutes of loving grace." As for Marc, Jane knows that illness alone did not bring on his untimely end. Death has come into her world because a dark and tragic past could neither be spoken of nor allusively approached. Jane's inner self had created a deep gap with that past, which belonged to those closest to her. Memories must now be reconquered, if life is to go on. Still interested in women's approach, Boukhobza describes in *Un été à Jérusalem* (1999) the conflicting relationship of a young woman with Jewish tradition and with her father's rigorous authority.

The younger Karine Tuil (1967–) is not only interested in Jewish themes, but in her third novel, *Du sexe féminin* (2002), she describes tragi-comically the powerful influence of Jewish mothers on their children.

POEMS IN PROSE AND VERSE. Emmanuel Lévinas himself, though a philosopher in the strict traditional sense, has also written some interesting literary studies and poetic meditations. *Noms propres.* Sur M. Blanchot ("Surnames," 1976) is a series of short essays on writers as far apart as Agnon, Buber, Jabès, Proust and others. *Difficile liberté* ("Difficult Freedom," 1977) is a collection of fragments (meditations, exegesis, prose poems) dealing with Jewish existence, ethics and religion. The author rejects both mysticism and pathos, and always displays a sense of the profound nature of Jewish spiritual being.

Vigée's *Le soleil sous la mer* (The Sun under the Sea, 1972) consists of a collection of all his previous poetry, but it is preceded by an account of childhood recollections in Alsace – "the emergence… of a luminous beginning… the opening of life" – and followed by the poetic work, *L'acte du bélier* (The Act of the Ram). In his *Délivrance du souffle* (1977) the reader penetrates into the authentic realm of poetry, narration and reflection. Vigée deliberately mingles the three levels of writing, for he views poetic language as a fitting expression of his Jewish existential meditation and the narration of historic and personal experience as an indispensable adjunct to his reflection of life and Jewish destiny. The first part of this work is composed of poems which are not only inspired by Jewish themes and biblical subjects, but whose very poetic material (imagery, coloring, rhythms and sound) springs forth directly from an intimate knowledge and experience of the Hebrew language. Vigée has succeeded in creating his own poetic style, not by transposing biblical verse into typically French meter; but by speaking or rather breathing in accord with biblical poetry. In his "Diaspora Choral," the poet deplores the fact that the French language in its "subtle flavor" and sophisticated refinement inhibits the authentic "naked word" which in Hebrew "springs forth like fire between the teeth on the living tongue." The second part of *Délivrance du souffle* contains a moving diary of the Yom Kippur War. In sober and restrained tone in the midst of the peril threatening the nation, Vigée reflects on the meaning of Jewish destiny and of its presence in the Land. The third part of the book, "Motifs et variations," celebrates the beauty of Eretz Israel, an eerie beauty so penetrated with history and spiritual tradition as to wash it clean of all pagan seduction. Vigée's clear literary commitment to his Jewish heritage does not inhibit his rich contribution to Western culture, as his volume of critical essays, *L'Art et le Demonique* (1979), testifies.

The latest books of Arnold *Mandel and Claude Vigée should be noted, all representing a sum of their creation. Mandel's works display a decided leaning towards Kabbalah and ḥasidism. They deal, now as before, with the theme of Jewish vocation, destiny and character, whether it be in narrative form (*Le périple* ("The Journey"), 1972; *La Vierge au bandeau* ("The Virgin with a Blindfold"), 1974; *Tikoun*, 1980), in descriptive form (*La vie quotidienne des Juifs hassidiques* ("The Ḥasidims' Daily Life," 1977) or in essay form (*Nous autres juifs*, 1978). *Le périple*, a semi-autobiographical novel, shows a narrator through a long meandering journey, a sort of symbol of the Wandering Jew, who ends up in Israel. The end is a beginning. Israel is indeed the place of new beginnings, the only one where the Jew feels the West his very existence is questioned; for the Jews and non-Jews alike perceive that Jewishness is no contingent attribute, but an essential necessity of being. *La Vierge au bandeau* is a sequel in parable form to Mandel's earlier autobiographical novel *Le périple.* The author imagines the blindfolded figure of the Synagogue (the well-known gothic statue of the Strasbourg cathedral) having left her assigned place and becoming a modern Jewish girl named Myriam, who sets out to follow her lover Jacques Landau, hero of *Le Périple*, on his journey to Israel. But whereas Jacques will remain permanently in Jerusalem, Myriam will return to her traditional place in the Diaspora, where she still has a role to play. But is it a petrified one? *Nous autres Juifs* is a collection of essays dealing with the ambiguities of Jewish existence, its delights and trials. It is also an indictment of a sort of neutral Judaism, cut off from its religious and cultural tradition, or, worse still, the Jewish identification with revolutionary mythologies, in particular bolshevism. The chief title to fame of contemporary Jewry is, in the author's opinion, the rebirth of the Hebrew language and the creation of an original Hebrew culture in Israel. With *Tikoun*, an impressive novel bearing a Hebrew title, Mandel returns to his old favorite theme, i.e., the long circuitous journey of an exiled Jew in search of his true destination. But the setting has become broader, the tone one of gravity. The novel includes a large variety of imaginary characters, as well as historical figures, as far apart as Chaplin and Maimonides. This vast array of people and social situations is treated sometimes with biting satire, sometimes with kind humor. Postwar existentialism and the May 1968 abortive revolution are dealt with in the most ironic fashion. The story starts at the time of the Nazi occupation and culminates some 30 years later in Jerusalem, where the hero Ary Safran, a Hebrew teacher and writer, son of an angelic rabbi, finds comfort for his relative failures in life. The kabbalistic idea of *tikkun* is here applied to the hope that all quest for unity can some day somewhere be fulfilled.

Claude *Vigée, on the other hand, has persevered in the way he chose in recent years, namely the use of Judeo-Alsatian dialect to convey the true meaning of human existence. In *Le feu d'une nuit d'hiver* ("The Fire of a Winter Night," 1989), he went further. This poetic work is divided in two parts, the first of which is based on a volume written in dialect form in 1984. Composed in Jerusalem, it is a meditation on the somber past of our generation, which now faces new unknown perils. These perils are portrayed in an Alsatian epic, tender and ironic, burlesque and sinister, which unfolds in the guise of a country fair in the fall. The dual levels of expression in this dramatic tale bring forth our dual fate, revealing our earthly world which stands under the bright clarity of the eternal upper world. The poet says: "We have a good place elsewhere a trust well kept: in a welcoming 'elsewhere' the green vesperal light dies and flourishes anew in a muted spring."

This folk epic constitutes the prelude of the book, which in fact is more than half of the work: thirteen poems in all. Only a few bear titles, at once melancholy and whimsical: *La complainte du Tsigane Sékula*, *La foire d'arrière saison*, *Le chant d'après-minuit*. The last one, *L'amandier de Jérusalem*, marks a turning-point in locale, tone and spirit, serving as the transition for the "Jerusalem poems" of the second part. The very symbolic almond tree prepares the reader for the theme of renewed hope and youth. The poet addresses the beloved city: "Yes, though he threatens you, the Angel of Death, against him you stand in spite of all, in spite of all, you remain for me the summer bride my ever young, ever beautiful ever new Jerusalem."

Hebrew quotes from the liturgy abound in both parts of this volume.

The "10 Jerusalem poems," which constitute the second part, were composed between 1984 and 1988, with the exception of the first poem, "Chanson funèbre" (1982) where the poet echoes the "voice of the young soldiers" who died in the Lebanon War. The titles, as well as the content, bear the mark of the serious, sometimes solemn, but confident mood of the mature Jewish artist. Examples are "L'intime langue étrangère," "L'an futur," "Les trois portes de Jérusalem," "Passage du vivant," "La Bal des pénitents au Mont des Oliviers," and "La surface des choses." The title of the last poem, a final tribute to Jerusalem, is its first verse. "La demeure est le secret dont l'exil fut la quête." ("The dwelling is the secret. Exile was its quest," 1988).

In the mid-1990s and the early 21st century, Vigée described his family life in Alsace in his autobiography *Un panier de houblon*: *La Verte enfance du monde* (1994 and *L'Arrachement* (1995) and his refuge in the center of France during the 1940s in *La Lune d'hiver* (2002).

The poet Henny Kleiner, whose works had been little noticed, deserves mention. Born in Vienna, she lived in Israel during the war years, then settled in Paris in 1952 and thereafter wrote in French. Her most striking volumes of poems are *Mes cendres encore chair en terre* ("My ashes are still flesh down under the earth," 1979), followed by *Syllabaire de la gazelle*, and *Des ailleurs de toutes les couleurs* ("Elsewhere in many ways and colors," 1984). The recurrent themes of nature, tenderness, childhood, motherhood, mourning, beauty are characteristic of universal nostalgic lyricism. But the poet's gift for pictorial evocations and the musical quality of the verse make the poems special. The Jewish element is especially evident in *Mes cendres encore chair en terre*, and even more in its extension, *Syllabaire de la gazelle*. The poet often enters a biblical universe ("Moïse au Mont Nebo," "Jericho") or is in close contact with the Land of Israel ("Sel du désert," "Tiferet"). The poet also brings reminiscences of a grandmother on Sabbath Eve and moving allusions to the Holocaust.

One should also note an important translation into French of Paul Celan's *Pavot et mémoire* (1987). The great Jewish poet, born in 1920 in Bukovina, whose family was massacred by the Nazis, lived in Paris, but remained condemned to write in German, his only language. He lamented: how can I write in the language of my mother's murderers? Haunted by the tragic feeling of being a Jew without a people, without a country, without a home, he committed suicide in Paris in 1970. His poetry dwelt on many themes, but this particular volume is, in a way, a Jewish testament. In lyrical incantation Celan evokes the death of the Jews in the gas chambers, compelling the reader to the most serious meditation on the unspeakable evil of all evils. His poem "Fugue de mort" ("Todesfuge") is especially noteworthy.

There is a recurrent dispute about whether one can speak about a literary school of French-speaking Jewish writers, beyond their common language and – unequal – recognition by the Jewish community. Although it remains quite impossible to give an indisputable answer to this question, as can be seen above there are common themes that have concerned Jewish writers throughout the 20th century

Bibliography: J. Trénel, *L'Ancien Testament et la langue française du moyen âge* (1904); M. Debré, *Der Jude in der franzoesischen Literatur...* (1909; Eng.: *The Image of the Jew in French Literature from 1800–1908* (reprint, 1970)); A. Spire, *Souvenirs à bâtons rompus* (1962), 276–305; M. Lifschitz-Golden, *Les juifs dans la littérature française du moyen âge* (Thesis, Columbia University, 1935); E.S. Randall, *The Jewish Character in the French Novel, 1870–1914* (1941); R. Feigelson, *Ecrivains juifs de langue française* (1960), includes bibliography; F. Lehner, in: L. Finkelstein (ed.), *The Jews: Their History*, Culture, and Religion, 2 (19603), 1472–86, includes bibliography; E.J. Finbert (ed.), *Aspects du génie d'Israël* (1950); C. Lehrmann, *L'élément juif dans la littérature française*, 2 vols. (1960–61), includes bibliography; idem, *L'élément juif dans la pensée europèene* (1947), 177–202; P. Aubery, *Milieux juifs de la France contemporaine* (1962²), includes bibliography; D. Goitein, "Jewish Themes in Selected French Works" (Thesis, Columbia University, 1967); L. Berman, *Histoire des juifs de France* (1937), 323–37, 460–9; N.J.E. Rothschild, *Le Mistère du Viel Testament*, 6 vols. (1878–91), includes bibliographies. **ADD. BIBLIOGRAPHY:** M. Séguier, *Le Juif de l'écriture* (1985); G. Dugas, *La littérature judéo-maghrébine d'expression française* (1990); *Littérature et judéité dans les langues européennes*, special issue of *Pardès* (1995); M. Pariente, *Deux mille titres à thème juif parus en français entre 1989 et 1995* (1996); C. Lévy, *Ecritures de l'identité*. Les écrivains juifs après la Shoah (1998); C. Dana, *Fictions pour mémoire*. Camus, Perec et *l'écriture de la Shoah* (1998); E. Abecassis, *Le Livre des passeurs: de la Bible à Philip Roth*, trois mille ans de littérature *juive* (2006).

[Denise R. Goitein / Anne Grynberg (2nd ed.)]

FRENCH REVOLUTION.

Position of the Jews before the Revolution

The nature, status, and rights of the Jews became an issue of public consequence in *France in the last two decades before the outbreak of the Revolution in 1789. The Jewish population was then divided into some 3,500 Sephardim, concentrated mostly in southwestern France, and perhaps 30,000 Ashkenazim in eastern France. The Sephardim had arrived there after 1500 as *Marranos. By 1776, when the last *lettres patentes* in their favor had been issued by the crown, they had succeeded, step by step, in establishing their status as a merchant guild, avowedly Jewish, with at least the right to live anywhere within the authority of the *parlement* of *Bordeaux. The leading families of the Sephardim engaged in international trade. They were sufficiently assimilated to behave like bourgeois, and some were *Deists or nonbelievers before the Revolution. The Ashkenazim in eastern France were foreign and un-French in their total demeanor. This community spoke Yiddish and was almost totally obedient to the inherited ways of life. The power of the community over the individual was much larger among the Ashkenazim than among the Sephardim, for rabbinic courts were, in Metz and in Alsace, the court of first jurisdiction for all matters involving Jews. With the exception of a few rich army purveyors and bankers, Jews in eastern France made their living from petty trade, often in pursuits forbidden to them; by dealing in cattle; and from petty moneylending. More than any other, this last occupation embroiled the Jews in conflict with the poorest elements in the local population, the peasants.

Another economic quarrel involved the Jews in several places in France, and especially in Paris, with the traditional merchant guilds. In March 1767 a royal decree was issued creating new positions in the guilds and making these new posts freely accessible to purchase by foreigners. Jews managed to enter the guilds in a few places in eastern France, and to bid for entry in Bayonne. These efforts were fought in lawsuits everywhere. The new, Physiocratic insistence on productive labor had also helped sharpen the issue of "productivization" of the Jews in these years before the Revolution.

In the intellectual realm the Jews became a visible issue of some consequence in the 1770s and 1780s for a variety of reasons. The attack of the men of the Enlightenment on biblical religion inevitably involved these thinkers in negative discussion of the ancient Jews and, at least to some degree, of the modern ones. All of the newer spirits agreed that religious fanaticism, whether created by religion or directed against deviant faiths, needed to end. The Jews were thus an issue both as the inventors of "biblical fanaticism" and as the object of the hatred of the *Inquisition. Some of the great figures of the Enlightenment, with *Voltaire in the lead, argued that the Jews had an ineradicably different nature, which few, if any, could escape. The more prevalent, less ideological opinions were those of men such as the Marquis de *Mirabeau (the younger) and the Abbé *Grégoire, that the defects of the Jews had been created by their persecutors, who had excluded them from society and limited them to the most debasing of economic pursuits, leaving them entirely under the sway of their own leaders and their narrow tradition. With an increase in rights and better conditions, the Jews would improve.

Propaganda and pressure by Jewish leadership in eastern France, led by Herz *Cerfberr, the leading army purveyor in the region, had resulted in 1784 in the two last acts of the old order concerning Jews. In January 1784, Louis XVI, speaking in the accents of contemporary enlightened absolutism, forbade the humiliating body tax (see *Taxation) on Jews in all places subject to his jurisdiction, regardless of any local traditions to the contrary. In July of that year a much more general decree was published which attempted a comprehensive law for the Jews in Alsace. It was a retrograde act. A few increased opportunities were afforded the rich but no Jew could henceforth contract any marriage without royal permission and the traditional Jewish pursuits in Alsace, the trade in grain, cattle, and moneylending, were surrounded with new restrictions. The rich were given new scope for banking, large-scale commerce, and the creation of factories in textiles, iron, glass, and pottery. The Jewish leaders in Alsace fought against this decree, and especially against that part of it which ordered a census in preparation of the expulsion of all those who could not prove their legal right to be in the province. This census was indeed taken and its results were published in 1785. Nonetheless, Jews continued to stave off the decree of expulsion until this issue was overtaken by the events of the Revolution. These quarrels and the granting of public rights to Protestants in 1787 kept the question of the Jews before the central government in Paris. Under the leadership of Chrétien Guillaume de Lamoignon de *Malesherbes, the question was again discussed by the royal government in 1788. Delegations of both the Sephardi and the Ashkenazi communities were lobbying in Paris during these deliberations. The prime concern of the Sephardim was to see to it that no overall legislation for Jews resulted in which their rights would be diminished by making them part of a larger body which included the Ashkenazim. The representatives of the Jews from eastern France followed their traditional policy of asking for increased economic rights and of defending the authority of the autonomous Jewish community.

The Era of Revolution

In the era of the Revolution the Jews did not receive their equality automatically. The Declaration of the Rights of Man which was voted into law by the National Assembly on Aug. 27, 1789, was interpreted as not including the Jews in the new equality. The issue of Jewish rights was first debated in three sessions, Dec. 21–24, 1789, and even the Comte de *Mirabeau, one of their chief proponents, had to move to table the question, because he saw that there were not enough votes with which to pass a decree of emancipation. A month later, in a very difficult session on Jan. 28, 1790, the "Portuguese," "Spanish," and "Avignonese" Jews were given their equality. The main argument, made by Talleyrand, was that these Jews were culturally and socially already not alien. The issue of the Ashkenazim remained unresolved. It was debated repeatedly in the next two years but a direct vote could never be mustered for their emancipation. It was only in the closing days of the National Assembly, on Sept. 27, 1791, that a decree of complete emancipation was finally passed, on the ground that the Jews had to be given equality in order to complete the Revolution, for it was impossible to have a society in which all men of whatever condition were given equal rights and status, except a relative handful of Jews. Even so, the parliament on the very next day passed a decree of exception under which the debts owed the Jews in eastern France were to be put under special and governmental supervision. This was a sop to anti-Jewish opinion, which had kept complaining of the rapacity of the Jews. The Jews refused to comply with this act, for they said that it was contrary to the logic of a decree of equality. Opinion thus had remained divided even in the last days, when Jews were being given their liberty.

This division of opinion about the status of the Jews was, to some degree, based on traditional premises. Such defenders of the old order as Abbé Jean Sieffrein Maury and Anne Louis Henry de la Fare, the bishop of Nancy, remained in opposition, arguing that the Jews were made by their religion into an alien nation which could not possibly have any attachment to the land of France. The more modern of the two, Maury, went further, to quote Voltaire to help prove that the Jews were bad because of their innate character and that changes of even the most radical kind in their external situation would not completely eradicate what was inherent in their nature. De la Fare was from eastern France, and he was joined in the opposition to the increase of Jewish rights by almost all of the deputies from that region regardless of their party. That this would occur had already been apparent in the *cahiers* from eastern France which, with the exception of one writer under the influence of Abbé Grégoire, were almost uniformly anti-Jewish. The most notable of the left-wing figures from Alsace in the revolutionary parliament, Jean François Rewbell, remained an uncompromising opponent. He held that it was necessary to defend "a numerous, industrious, and honest class of my unfortunate compatriots who are oppressed and ground down by these cruel hordes of Africans who have infested my region." To give the Jews equality was tantamount to handing the poor of eastern France over to counterrevolutionary forces, for the peasant backbone of the Revolution in that region would see the new era as one of increased dangers for them. The only organized body in eastern France which was publicly in favor of increased rights for the Jews was the moderate, revolutionary Société des Amis de la Constitution in Strasbourg, with which the family of Cerfberr had close connections. This group argued that the peasants were being artificially whipped up and that their hatred of the Jews would eventually vanish. A policy of economic opportunity would allow the Jews to enter productive occupations and become an economic boon to the whole region. It was along this general line that the Jews, if they were regenerated to be less clannish and more French and if they were dispersed in manufacture and on the land, would be good citizens, that their friends argued for Jewish emancipation. In the first debate on the "Jewish Question" on Sept. 28, 1789, when the Jews of Metz asked for protection against the threat of mob outbreaks (there had been outbursts in Alsace that summer and some Jews had fled to Basle), Stanislas de *Clermont-Tonnerre, a liberal noble from Paris, had agreed that the existing Jews did merit the hatred against them but ascribed what was wrong with the Jews to the effects of oppression. The Jews themselves could not maintain any separatism, for "there cannot be a nation within a nation." The emancipation of the Jews in France eventually took place on the basis sketched out by him: "The Jews should be denied everything as a nation but granted everything as individuals …" Such views were argued in the revolutionary years by the Jacobins of Paris, who were pro-Jewish (almost all the others and especially those in eastern France were anti-Jewish) and by the main body of moderate revolutionaries, who ultimately made their feeling prevail, that emancipation was a moral necessity, its purpose being to improve the Jews so that they could be part of a regenerated society.

The final decree of Sept. 27, 1791, did not end the tensions in eastern France. The structure of the Jewish community remained, and in some places in eastern France local civil powers continued, at least briefly, to enforce the taxation imposed by the *parnasim* for the support of the Jewish community. It soon became apparent that the revolutionary government itself needed to keep some kind of Jewish organization in being. The decree of nationalization of the property of the Church and of the émigrés (Nov. 2, 1789) had contained a provision for the assumption of the debts of the churches by the government, but it refused to assume responsibility for the debts contracted by the Jewish communities. The one in Metz was heavily in debt, largely to Christian creditors, and the issue of the payment of these debts remained a source of irritation and of repeated legal acts well into the middle of the 19th century. Those who had lived in Metz before 1789 and their descendants who had moved far away, even those who had converted from the faith, were held to be liable.

Throughout the era of the Revolution there was recurring concern about the patriotism of the Jews (their *civisme*) and about the channeling of their young into "productive occupations" and making them into good soldiers of the Republic; that is, whether the Jews were indeed "transforming" themselves as their emancipators had envisaged. During the first decade of the Revolution some economic changes were taking place. Jews did participate in the buying of nationalized property, and in particular lent money to the peasants in Alsace, who thus acquired their own farms. This splitting of the estates of the Church and of the émigré nobility into small farms gave the peasantry a stake in the Revolution, but the contribution of Jewish creditors and speculators to this trade (it was significant though not dominant) earned them no gratitude. It remained a fixed opinion, especially among Jacobins, that the Jews were usurers and that they were using the new opportunities of the Revolution to become even more obnoxious. In general, the occupational structure of the Jews changed very little in the 1790s. They continued mostly to be middlemen or peddlers; very few were beginning to work in factories or even to own land, despite much propaganda and occasional pressure on them to take up agriculture. There were some difficulties about their joining the armies of the Revolution. In many places the

National Guard refused to accept Jews; sometimes it even attacked them and made minor pogroms, and it was regarded as a matter of unusual public importance that Max Cerfberr was accepted in Strasbourg in 1790. On the other hand, most Jews tried to avoid military service because of the problems of Sabbath and holiday observance which this created for them. A few of the sons of the richest families did become officers in the army as early as the 1790s, but the major military contribution of the Jews during the Republican period was in their traditional role as *contractors to the army. Jewish financiers were actually of minor importance, even here, but their visibility remained high and they were attacked with particular vehemence. Jews were involved in the military purchasing directory which was created in 1792, with Max Cerfberr as one of its directors. This body lasted just a few months, but it was at the center of much controversy during its existence, and thereafter. The Jews who were involved were subject to bitter criticism, but in this affair none was put to death for economic crimes or for treason.

The older Jewish leadership continued to dominate the Jewish community in the 1790s, but some newer forces were also arising. In southern France a group of Jewish Jacobins, whose club was named after Rousseau, became in 1793–94 the revolutionary government of Saint Esprit, the largely Jewish suburb of Bayonne. There were a few instances among both the Sephardim and the Ashkenazim of individual Jews who participated in the Religion of Reason. The overwhelming majority, however, both in the French Jewish communities and in those of the papal possessions, *Avignon and *Comtat Venaissin, which had been annexed to France in 1791, kept their religious traditions alive as best they could. No Jew was guillotined during the Terror (July 1793–July 1794) on the ground that his religious obduracy had made him an enemy of society, though such rhetoric was used by some of the Jacobins of eastern France in outraged reaction to the continuing practice of such traditions as Jewish burial. This was termed severely antisocial and a further expression of the supposed Jewish trait of hating the entire human race. During the Terror many synagogues and other Jewish properties were, indeed, nationalized and synagogue silver was either surrendered or hidden, as were books and Torah Scrolls. In some situations, such as in Carpentras in 1794, the Jews finally "willingly" gave their synagogue to the authorities. Nonetheless, religious services continued in hiding everywhere and after the Terror Jews were able not only to reopen many of their former synagogues but also to establish new conventicles in communities such as Strasbourg in which they had not had the right to live before the Revolution. As early as Aug. 4, 1794, within a few days after the fall of Robespierre, the Jews demanded the right to open a synagogue in Fontainebleau. There were a few cases of mixed marriage, though these remained very much the exception in the 1790s and did not become a trend of any significance until after the end of the century. The whole question of the status of Jewish acts in law remained confused, with many jurisdictions still continuing to restrict the personal freedom of Jews and the French courts still continuing to recognize Jewish law as determinant for Jews on matters of personal status, and especially marriage.

Anti-Jewish acts did not stop entirely with the end of the Terror. In November 1794, two Metz Jews were fined for carrying out Jewish burials and four years later five Jews were sentenced in Nice for building tabernacles for the Sukkot holiday. Thermidor was, however, regarded by Jews as a period in which religious persecution had ended. The problems of this period were mostly economic, for the civic tax rolls in various communities bore down heavily on Jews. From the very beginning of the Thermidor the central government ordered the protection of the Jews against agitation in eastern France. Occasional outbreaks continued and there were even some attacks on Jews for being in league, supposedly, with what remained of the Jacobins. Some angers that had been evoked by the emancipation of the Jews, and their involvement in the events of the first days of the Revolution, were evident during these days of reaction, but crucial was the fact that no change took place in the legal status of the Jews. Their emancipation was a fact and remained so; so was the economic conflict caused especially by their moneylending; so was the continued existence of their religious tradition and of their considerable communal apartness, even though the legal status of the community had been ended; so was the need of the central power to deal with the Jewish community in an organized way for many of its own purposes. All these questions, and an underlying concern about the "reform" of the Jewish religion and Jewish habits to accommodate the needs of the state, were deeded on to the next era, the period of *Napoleon.

Effects Outside France

The French Revolution brought legal equality to the Jews who dwelt in territories which were directly annexed by France. In addition to its operation in the papal possessions, Avignon and Comtat Venaissin, which were reunited with France in September 1791, just a few days before the final decree of emancipation for all of French Jewry, this legislation was applied to such border territories as Nice, which was conquered in 1792.

The German regions on the west bank of the Rhine were acquired by conquest in that same year, and the French conqueror, General A.P. de Custine, announced as his troops were entering the Rhineland that winter, that equality for Jews was one of his intentions. The formal enactments did not take place until 1797, when the supposedly independent Cisrhénane Republic was created. In the intervening years Jews who had begun by being suspicious of the new regime had become partisans of the Revolution.

In the *Netherlands there was a revolution in 1795, with help from the French army, and the Batavian Republic was proclaimed. A group of "enlightened" Jews had been among the prime organizers in Amsterdam of a body called *Felix Libertate. This association had as its purpose the furtherance of the ideas of "freedom and equality." There was substantial opposition in Holland even among some of the makers of the Revolution to the granting of full citizenship for Jews. The leaders of the official Jewish community were also opposed, for they fought bitterly against the disappearance of a Jewish separatist organization in a new regime of personal rights. There was a substantial debate, which culminated in eight days of discussion (Aug. 22–30, 1796), at the first session of the new revolutionary parliament. This debate was on a higher level than those held some years before in France; it resulted in the decision that Jews were to be given equal rights as individuals but that they had no rights as a people. The view of Clermont-Tonnerre in France in 1789 was thus upheld in Holland. In law this equality remained for the Jews in the Netherlands even after the fall of the Batavian Republic in 1806.

There were almost immediate echoes in *Italy of the French Revolution, but these stirrings were repressed in all of its various principalities. In the spring of 1790 the Jews were suspect of being partisans of the Revolution, and there were anti-Jewish outbreaks in both Leghorn and Florence; a comparable riot took place in Rome in 1793. There was almost no truth in all of these suspicions. A small handful of "enlightened" individuals were for the Revolution, but the organized Jewish communities looked forward only to some alleviations of their status by the existing regimes in Italy. Radical changes did take place toward the end of the decade, in 1796–98, when Napoleon Bonaparte conquered most of northern and central Italy, including the papal territories, in the course of two years of war. Everywhere the conquering French troops announced the end of the ghetto and equality for the Jews. In Italy the physical walls behind which Jews dwelt still existed in many places and the advent of the French armies gave the signal for the actual physical breaking down of these barriers by Jews and other partisans of the new order. Trees of liberty were planted in many places, especially in the Jewish quarters. Brief and even bloody revenge was taken on the Jews during Napoleon's absence in 1798–99 on his campaign in Egypt, as counterrevolutionary forces did battle against "Gauls, Jacobins, and Jews." In 1800 Napoleon, now as first consul, reconquered northern and central Italy and annexed it to France, ultimately to serve as the kernel of his future Kingdom of Italy. Jewish equality was secure in Italy until Napoleon's fall in 1815.

Elsewhere in Europe, the events of the French Revolution had enormous effects, but they did not lead to equality for the Jews. The French-inspired revolutionary Swiss regime of 1798 did not, even during its brief life, show any real desire to give the few Jews in Switzerland legal equality. In the Austrian Empire, the government was fearful of the Revolution and little was done in the 1790s that went beyond the several decrees of toleration that had been enacted in the spirit of enlightened absolutism by *Joseph II in 1781–82. The early years of the French Revolution coincided with the death agonies of independent Poland, leading to its partition and the end of Polish independence in 1795. Austria, Prussia, and Russia, among whom Poland was divided, were all either actively or passively arrayed against France throughout the 1790s. The influence of the French example, therefore, had no effect on their policy when these countries acquired among them the largest Jewish community, numbering some 800,000, in all of Europe. There was no change during the 1790s in the legal status of the Jews in any of the independent German principalities, not even those which sided with France in war. In the most important of the German states, *Prussia, despite notable and ongoing acculturation by members of the Jewish bourgeoisie in Berlin, the government refused to make any substantial changes in the regime of exclusion. A new decree that was issued at the beginning of 1790 spoke only of some future time, perhaps in three generations, when "regenerated Jews" might be admitted to civic equality. David *Friedlander answered on behalf of the leaders of Berlin Jewry that no changes at all were better than this "new imposition of chains"; what Jews wanted, he boldly added, was that such chains "be completely removed." To be sure, he and his circle were not insisting that equality be attained immediately by all Jews. Like the more successful Sephardim of France at that moment, the men whom David Friedlander led were interested almost entirely in their own rights. They proclaimed that the Jews in Berlin had already become culturally and intellectually the equal of the highest of German society, and they were, therefore, to be treated differently from their brethren in Bohemia or Poland, who were yet to wait until they had suitably prepared themselves by westernization for freedom.

The news from France was reported extensively and with exaltation in *Ha-Me'assef* for 1790, the Hebrew annual that was supported by this Berlin circle and by like-minded men on both sides of the Rhine and in Central Europe. These accents were soon suppressed in the name of patriotism, as Prussia went to war against France, but the example of equality in France, and of the United States Constitution of 1787, remained an ideal. For Jews everywhere in the next century after the French Revolution, the battle for emancipation became the central issue of their lives. Everywhere disabilities and exclusions were measured by the standards of France after 1791. In relation to the Jewish question Napoleon was the heir of the Revolution, and his victories after 1800 only extended the sphere of the emancipation. When he fell in 1815 the legal equality of Jews ended in much of his former empire, except in France and in Holland – and in Prussia, emancipation of 1812 had been a domestic decision, not forced upon Prussia by Napoleon. Nonetheless, the memory of the equality that Jews once held remained. Even in the many countries where nothing favorable to Jews had happened between 1789 and 1815, the example of the French Revolution was a dominant political force. Despite attempts at reaction in the 19th century the states of Europe had increasingly to contemplate full legal equality for all of their citizens, including Jews, as a central element of their entering modernity.

BIBLIOGRAPHY: Z. Szajkowski, *Jews and the French Revolutions of 1789, 1830, and 1848* (1970); A. Hertzberg, *French Enlightenment and the Jews* (1968); Milano, Italia, 339–51; Roth, Italy, 421–45; S.

Seeligman, *De Emancipatie der Joden in Nederland* (1913); Z.H. Ilfeld, *Divrei Negidim* (1799); I. Freund, *Emanzipation der Juden in Preussen* (1912); A. Kober, in: JSOS, 8 (1946), 291–322; M. Wiener, *Juedische Religion im Zeitalter der Emanzipation* (1933); R. Mahler, *Divrei Yemei Yisrael: Dorot Aḥaronim*, 1 (1952), 2 (1954), index.

[Arthur Hertzberg]

FRENK, BEER (Issachar Dov; 1770–1845), Hungarian rabbinic author and painter. His father emigrated from Turkey – hence the name Frenk, which was the appellation used for Ashkenazi Jews in Turkey – and went to Pressburg. Frenk studied under Moses *Sofer, who gave his approbation to a number of Frenk's works. He served as *shoḥet* and beadle of the Pressburg community for 41 years. He possessed literary talent and was a skilled painter, especially of miniatures. Among the portraits he painted was one of Moses Sofer, which was done without his knowledge, and Sofer rebuked him for it. His books, all written in German with Hebrew characters, were popular presentations of religious duties, such as the salting of meat, *niddah*, Sabbath lights, recitation of the *Shema*, etc.

BIBLIOGRAPHY: Ben-Menahem, in: *Sinai*, 64 (1968/69), 39–52; S. Schachnowitz, *Licht aus dem Westen* (1953^2), ch. 21.

[Naphtali Ben-Menahem]

FRENK, EZRIEL (or **Azriel**) **NATHAN** (1863–1924), Polish journalist and historian. Frenk was born in Wodzislaw to a ḥasidic family, but he was influenced by the Haskalah at an early age. In 1884 in Warsaw he began to write for the Jewish press, both in Hebrew and in Yiddish, and this remained his lifelong career. He published articles about current events, stories about ḥasidic life, and extensive studies on various subjects, mainly past and present problems of Poland's Jewry. Some of his historical writings, which had originally appeared in the daily press, were subsequently published in book form, notably, *Yehudei Polin bi-Ymei Milḥamot Napoleon* ("Jews of Poland in the Time of Napoleon," 1912), *Ha-Ironim ve-ha-Yehudim be-Polin* ("The Burghers and Jews in Poland," 1921), and *Meshumodim in Poyln in Nayntsn Yorhundert* ("Apostates in Poland in the 19th century," 2 vols., 1923–24). However, the bulk of his writing, including important studies of Polish Jewish life in the first half of the 19th century, remains scattered in various Hebrew and Yiddish newspapers and periodicals. Frenk also undertook translations, e.g., H. Sienkiewicz's *Ogniem i mieczem (Ba-Esh u-va-Ḥerev*, 4 vols., 1919–21).

BIBLIOGRAPHY: N.M. Gelber, in: S.K. Mirsky (ed.), *Ishim u-Demuyyot be-Ḥokhmat Yisrael be-Eiropah ha-Mizraḥit* (1959), 199–204; M. Balaban, *Yidn in Poyln* (1930), 314–9; idem, in: *Ha-Tekufah*, 21 (1924), 485–6; Kressel, Leksikon, 1 (1965), 682–3; Rejzen, Leksikon, 3 (1929), 228–37; LNYL, 7 (1938), 516–20.

[Israel Halpern]

FRENKEL (Frenel), ITZḤAK (1898–1981), Israeli painter. Frenkel was born in Ukraine, where he studied at the National Academy. He immigrated to Ereẓ Israel in 1919 but from 1920 to 1925 studied at the Académie des Beaux-Arts in Paris. In 1926 he became director of the Histadrut studio of painting in Tel Aviv. From 1929 to 1934 he was again in Paris, but returned to Ereẓ Israel and settled in Tel Aviv, where he devoted himself to painting stage settings. Frenkel was one of the formative forces of expressionism in painting in Israel. He painted the world surrounding him, especially Safed, but also Acre and Jerusalem – their landscapes and their synagogues, Jews at prayer, and typical people of the land. Rejecting unnecessary details and working with paint strokes, he created simple shapes bounded by heavy lines, and there is a spirit of mysticism in his canvases. A museum containing 100 of his works is located in Safed.

[Judith Spitzer]

FRENKEL, IZḤAK YEDIDIAH (1913–), Ashkenazi chief rabbi of Tel Aviv-Jaffa. Frenkel was born in Luntshits (Leczyca), Poland, and studied in Warsaw under Rabbi Menahem *Zemba, in whose home he stayed and whose works he prepared for publication. In 1935, he immigrated to Ereẓ Israel and was appointed rabbi of the poor Florentin area of Tel Aviv, mostly inhabited by Jews of Oriental origin. During the nearly 40 years that he held this position, he gained a reputation and endeared himself to the community as the "people's rabbi," entering into the lives of his community and exerting himself to the utmost in dealing with their many problems. His humble home was open to all. Frenkel was responsible for the institution of the Second Hakafot on the night after Simḥat Torah, which has become one of the major popular religious features of modern Israel. In 1973 he was elected unopposed as Ashkenazi chief rabbi of Tel Aviv in succession to Rabbi Shlomo *Goren.

FRENKEL, JACOB ILICH (1894–1952), Soviet physicist. Frenkel became an instructor at the University of the Crimea. From 1921 Frenkel lived in Leningrad. At first, he combined research work at the Physico-Technical Institute with lecturing at the Polytechnical Institute, where he headed the theoretical physics department for 30 years. He became a corresponding member of the Soviet Academy of Sciences in 1929. Frenkel's research was related to the physics of the atmosphere (particularly atmospheric electricity), terrestrial magnetism, biophysics, astrophysics, quantum theory, and the motion of electrons in metals. He laid foundations for the understanding of ferromagnetism and presented a theory of dielectric excitation, along with important ideas relating to defects in crystal lattices. He drew attention to certain similarities between liquid and solid structures, engaged in important research on the liquid state, and presented his conclusions in his book on the kinetic theory of liquids (1945). Soon after the first artificial splitting of the uranium atom, Frenkel advanced a theory to account for the phenomenon of fission, which provided a basis for practical applications of nuclear energy. He was a pioneer in the writing of original Russian handbooks on modern theoretical physics.

BIBLIOGRAPHY: *Bolshaya Sovetskaya Entsiklopediya*, 45 (1956^2); T. Kuhn, et al., *Sources for History of Quantum Physics* (1967), index.

[J. Edwin Holmstrom]

FRENKEL, VERA (1938–), Canadian multidisciplinary artist, video producer, poet, writer, educator. Frenkel was born in Bratislava, Czechoslovakia (now Slovakia). To escape the Nazis, her family fled to England and subsequently immigrated to Canada. Frenkel studied fine arts at McGill University and with Arthur Lismer at the Montreal Museum School of Fine Arts.

Already internationally recognized as a printmaker and sculptor, Frenkel began exploring video in 1974. At the forefront of contemporary Canadian art, Frenkel's interest in new media led her to produce video, web-based work and multimedia installations. Deeply concerned with human dilemmas, her art has examined the tyranny of received ideas, the mythological properties of popular culture, the impact of censorship, and the bureaucratization of experience. *...from the Transit Bar* (1992) explores the effects of cultural and geographic displacement. The *Body Missing Project* (1994 and ongoing), an interactive Internet site, originated with Frenkel's research on the cultural policy of the Third Reich and the proposed *Fuehrermuseum* in Linz, Austria. As in all of her work, *The Institute™: Or What We Do for Love* (2003 and ongoing) is an acerbic commentary on the institutionalization of contemporary society that plays documentary and fictional realities against each other.

Frenkel's work has been exhibited in major galleries throughout Canada, Europe, and Asia. She participated in the Venice Biennale (1972, 1997, and 1999), and represented Canada in *documenta IX* in Kassel, Germany (1992). Her work is internationally collected by, among others, the National Gallery of Canada, the Museum of Modern Art, New York, and the Ydessa Hendeles Art Foundation.

An innovative and inspiring teacher, Frenkel taught at the University of Toronto (1970–72) and at York University, Toronto (1972–95). Among many honors, she was awarded the Canada Council Molson Prize for the Arts (1989), the Toronto Arts Foundation's Visual Arts Award (1991), the Gershon Iskowitz Prize (1994), the Bell Canada Award (2001), and the CCCA Art Award (2004). Her writings have appeared in a range of Canadian and international journals and anthologies.

BIBLIOGRAPHY: E. Legge, "Of Loss and Leaving: Vera Frenkel's Body Missing Website," in *Canadian Art* (Winter 1996), 60–64; B. Grenville and L. Steele, *Vera Frenkel: Les Bandes Vidéo / The Videotapes* (Exh. cat. Ottawa, 1985); J. Gagnon et al., *... from the Transit Bar* (Exh. Cat. Ottawa, 1994); S. Schade, "Vera Frenkel: Body Missing," in: *Andere Koerper* (Exh. cat. Linz, 1994).

[Joyce Zemans (2nd ed.)]

FRENSDORFF, FERDINAND (1833–1931), German legal historian. Born in Hanover, Frensdorff was professor of law at the University of Goettingen and became known as an authority on medieval German law. His numerous writings include *Beitraege zur Geschichte und Erklaerung deutscher Rechtsbuecher* (1888–94), *Das statutarische Recht der deutschen Kaufleute in Novgorod* (1886), and *Das Wiedererstehen des deutschen Rechts* (1908).

ADD. BIBLIOGRAPHY: NDB, 3:625; 5:402.

FRENSDORFF, SOLOMON (1803–1880), German masoretic scholar. Frensdorff was born in Hamburg, the son of a rabbi. He studied with Isaac *Bernays and later at the University of Bonn, where he took up Semitic languages. A. *Geiger and S.R. *Hirsch were his contemporaries and friends. Between 1834 and 1837 he was assistant rabbi in Frankfurt; from 1837 he taught at the religious school in Hanover; and from 1848 he was head of the newly founded Teachers' Training College there. Frensdorff's major contribution to Jewish learning consists of a series of still valuable works on the masorah. He edited *Darkhei ha-Nikkud ve-ha-Neginot* (1847), ascribed to Moses ha-Nakdan, and the masoretic work *Okhlah ve-Okhlah* (1864, repr. 1969) from a Paris manuscript; the latter work had been published previously in a different version appended to rabbinic Bibles. Of a planned edition of *Die Massora Magna*, only the first part, an introduction, *Massoretisches Woerterbuch* (1876, repr. 1967), with a prolegomenon by G.E. Weil, appeared; the masorah notes are arranged alphabetically according to key words, giving the Bible passages where they occur. Part of Frensdorff's library is in the Jewish National and University Library in Jerusalem.

BIBLIOGRAPHY: Kressel, Leksikon, 2 (1967), 681; *Zum Andenken an unsern Vater... Sal. Frensdorff* (1903), contains sermons by S. Groneman and L. Knoller.

FRESCO, DAVID (1853–1936), Turkish journalist. Fresco started his journalistic activities in Yeheskal (Isaac) Gabay's *El Telegrafo*, where he worked for two years. He then moved to *El Tyempo* and became its last owner. *El Tyempo*, published in Ladino, soon became the most influential newspaper of its time, with a circulation of up to 10,000. After the Young Turk Revolt of 1908 it took a strong pro-Ottoman stance and reflected Fresco's anti-Zionist views. He closed the newspaper on March 27, 1930, and moved to Nice, where he spent his last years together with his sons. His books include *Le Sionisme* (1909) and *Lecture Edifiante de Morale Juive* (1929).

BIBLIOGRAPHY: "David Fresco, 55 années du journalisme juif," in: *Hamenora*, 8 (May 5 1930), 162–64; H.V. Sephiha, "David Fresco, 55 ans de journalisme judeo-espagnol," in: *La Terre Retrouvée*, 1 (Sept. 24 1981); M. Mizrahi, "David Fresco Direktor proprietario del jurnal El Tiempo," in: *Şalom*, 26 (Sept. 1956); A. Levy, "The Ladino *El Tyempo* of Istanbul during 1882–1883," in: *Gesher*, 13 (1993), 22–24; S. Abrevaya Stein, *Making Jews Modern – The Yiddish and Ladino Press in the Russian and Ottoman Empires* (2004).

[Rifat Bali (2nd ed.)]

FREUD, ANNA (1895–1982), psychoanalyst. Anna Freud was the youngest daughter of Sigmund *Freud, and was his companion on his vacation trips and his nurse during his prolonged illnesses. Her devotion to her father brought her into increasing contact with the developing thought and practice of psychoanalysis and she grew interested in child psychology. Between 1915 and 1920 she worked in her profession as a primary school teacher, deepened her knowledge in psychoanalysis, and started analysis as her father's patient. At the age of 28 she opened her own psychoanalytic practice, right across Sigmund Freud's treatment room in Berggasse 19. In 1927 she published a paper *Einfuehrung in die Technik der Kinderanalyse* (*Introduction to the Technique of Child Analysis*, 1928), in which she set out the analytical technique she had evolved. In 1936 she published *Das Ich und die Abwehrmechanismen* (*The Ego and the Mechanisms of Defence*, 1937) which described the ways by which painful ideas and emotions are warded off from consciousness and direct expression, e.g., by repression and replacement by the opposite idea. This book was a pioneer contribution to ego psychology and in understanding the adolescent.

She escaped from Austria with her father in 1938 and went with him to London, where Sigmund Freud died in 1939 and she continued to live until the end of her life. During World War II, together with her friend Dorothy Burlingham, she built up the Hampstead nurseries, where they took care of children separated from their families. In three books the two colleagues documented their experiences there, describing the treatment of children under conditions of war stress. They also described the development of children from narcissism to socialization, and set out the problems in the emotional life of institutional children despite their receiving advantages in physical care. These books were *Young Children in Wartime* (1942); *Infants without Families* (1943); and *War and Children* (1943).

The Hampstead nurseries closed in 1945. In 1947, with the help of Kate *Friedlander, Freud founded the Child Therapy Course. In 1951 she became director of the clinic which was opened in conjunction with the course. Freud's book *Normality and Pathology in Childhood* (1965) is a comprehensive summation of her thought. Freud's contribution to child analytic therapy and child psychology was fundamental. She was able to demonstrate the validity of the reconstructions made by Sigmund Freud of child development and pathology through his analysis of adults. Moreover she was able to add considerably to the information by her methods of direct observation of children. Of special interest was her employment of psychological understanding in the education of children and in preventive work with the child through its parents and educators. Her contribution to the knowledge of the reaction of young children separated from their parents and deprived of emotional relationships, particularly in institutions, has had a wide effect in social policy and direct child care. From 1968 her collected works appeared under the title *The Writings of Anna Freud.*

BIBLIOGRAPHY: E. Pumpian-Mindlin, in: F. Alexander, et al. (eds.), *Psychoanalytic Pioneers* (1966), 519–33; Sandler, in: J.G. Howells (ed.), *Modern Perspectives in Child Psychiatry* (1965), includes bibliography, 250f. **ADD. BIBLIOGRAPHY:** E. Young-Bruehl, *Anna Freud: a biography* (1989); U. Henrik Peters, "Anna Freud," in: H.J. Schultz (ed.), *Es ist ein Weinen in der Welt* (1990); R. Coles, *Anna Freud: The Dream of Psychoanalysis* (1992); W. Salber, *Sigmund und Anna* Freud (1999); R. Edgecumbe, *Anna Freud: a View of Development, Disturbance and Therapeutic Techniques* (2000); D.A. Rothe (ed.), "*… als käm ich heim zu Vater und Schwester*": *Lou Andreas-Salomé–Anna Freud Briefwechsel 1919–1937* (2004).

[Louis Miller / Mirjam Triendl (2nd ed.)]

FREUD, LUCIAN (1922–), English painter, grandson of Sigmund *Freud. Freud, who was born in Berlin, the son of an architect, was brought to London in 1933 with his parents. He was naturalized in 1939 and began to work full time as an artist after being discharged from the merchant navy in 1942. His *Interior at Paddington* won a prize at the Festival of Britain, putting him on the artistic map. In 1954 he represented Britain at the Venice Biennale. His work was often German in its influence and style, and closely resembled the later German expressionists in the Gothic intensity of his portraiture. His subject matter was largely portraits, nudes, and interiors. Freud is widely regarded as one of the greatest figurative artists of recent times, and is one of the best-known artists in contemporary Britain; his work was represented at most major galleries of modern art. He was made a Companion of Honour (CH) in 1993 and a member of the Order of Merit (OM) in 2002. He produced a book about his own work, *Lucian Freud,* in 1996.

ADD. BIBLIOGRAPHY: W. Feaver, *Lucian Freud* (1997); R. Hughes, *Lucian Freud* (2002).

FREUD, SIGMUND (1856–1939), Austrian psychiatrist and creator of psychoanalysis. Freud was born in the small town of Freiberg, Moravia (now part of the Czech Republic). When he was four his family moved to Vienna, where he graduated with distinction from gymnasium and then entered university as a medical student. As a Jewish student he encountered certain barriers, but he found a haven from the antisemitism of the university community in Ernst Bruecke's physiological laboratory. He worked productively in research with Bruecke from 1876 to 1882, and studied philosophy with Franz Brentano and biology with Carl Claus, a follower of Darwin.

In 1882 Freud became engaged to Martha Bernays. Though his interest was primarily in research, he decided to enter clinical practice as a resident at the Vienna General Hospital in order to establish himself sufficiently to be able to marry. While working as a clinician at the hospital, he continued to pursue his neurological research as an assistant to the brain anatomist T.H. Meynert.

The work with chronic nervous illnesses of the French neurologist Jean Charcot attracted Freud's interest, and he began to study the clinical manifestations of diseases of the nervous system. In 1885 he was awarded a traveling fellowship, which he spent studying with Charcot at the Salpetrière mental hospital in Paris. Charcot's demonstration that ideas could cause physical symptoms strengthened Freud's determination to investigate hysterical paralyses and anesthesias. In 1886 he married, resigned from the General Hospital, and set up a private practice in nervous diseases so that he could support his new wife.

Freud had already formed a friendship with the Viennese physician Josef *Breuer, who had stumbled upon an innovative treatment for hysteria. In 1880 Breuer had begun treating a young woman who suffered from severe hysterical symptoms – the patient made famous as Anna O. in Freud and Breuer's 1895 epoch-making collaboration *Studies in Hysteria*. Their work set out for the first time the theory that the unconscious damming up of emotions could produce symptoms of hysterical illness, and its corollary: that if, with the aid of hypnosis or some other method, patients could express this suppressed emotion and the fantasies that accompanied it, their symptoms would disappear.

Breuer was a well-established and respected general practitioner who had experimented with a new way of relieving neurotic symptoms with his patient Anna O. (what she called "the talking cure" or "chimney sweeping"). But as the treatment progressed, Breuer felt increasingly overwhelmed by the sexual nature of her behavior and symptoms; and he could not accept Freud's growing conviction that disturbances in sexual life were fundamental causal factors in neurosis and hysteria. A year after publishing *Studies in Hysteria*, Freud and Breuer parted company.

Now working on his own, Freud gave up hypnosis and the method of cathartic discharge for a new therapeutic technique. He asked his patients to relinquish self-censorship and to tell him whatever came into their minds. This process, which he called free association, is sometimes referred to as the fundamental rule of psychoanalysis. It allowed the patients to recall forgotten events and experiences, and so helped Freud uncover what he believed lay behind their symptoms. He soon concluded that an unacceptable impulse, feeling, or fantasy and the resistance that it engendered resulted in a special order of intra-psychic conflict. While the unacceptable impulse would (unconsciously) be repudiated and disavowed, less threatening methods of gratifying it in a disguised form would be pursued. The struggle to both thwart and pursue the impulse could manifest itself in mental or physical symptoms. The task of therapy was to uncover the repression and allow the repudiated impulse into consciousness, where it could be judged, and accepted or rejected; the result of this process was that the unconscious modes of regulation that had produced the symptom were no longer necessary and lost their force. Freud called this form of therapy psychoanalysis.

In 1896, almost immediately after his father's death, Freud began the difficult task of working through his own unconscious by analyzing his dreams. He came to the conclusion that a dream-thought is always related to a disavowed infantile (sexual) wish that emerges in the context of the dream only after passing through a mental censorship and distortion that camouflages the wish to such an extent that its expression can be tolerated. The dream thus serves as an exemplary model of the process whereby the repressed achieves expression in a disguised form. Freud articulated this theory in *The Interpretation of Dreams*, published in 1900, which he considered his most important work. He identified himself with the biblical character of Joseph, the dream-interpreter, and observed that "the interpretation of dreams is the royal road to a knowledge of the unconscious activities of the mind" (this sentence was added in 1909 to the second edition).

In 1904 Freud published *The Psychopathology of Everyday Life*, in which he showed that the numerous unconscious slips and mistakes that people make in everyday life are also the outcome of intra-psychic struggle; and that they are not merely accidental occurrences, but like dreams and neurotic symptoms have a meaning that can be discovered through psychoanalysis. In 1905 Freud's theories on the importance, from earliest infancy, of bodily experience, desire, and the Oedipus complex were elaborated and brought together in his *Three Essays on the Theory of Sex*. From this point on he continued to develop his notions of repression, symptom formation and sexuality.

Freud's sexual theories were no more acceptable to the medical profession at large than they had been to Breuer, and for almost a decade he was virtually ostracized by the establishment. But a small circle of colleagues interested in Freud's work slowly collected around him, and his professional isolation finally came to an end. He became concerned that attracting non-Jews to the psychoanalytic enterprise was necessary to avoid its becoming a "Jewish national affair" and encouraged non-Jews to take a prominent role in the newly formed International Psychoanalytic Association. In 1906 he heard that a group of psychiatrists in Zurich, one of whom was C.G. Jung (1875–1961), was interested in psychoanalysis. Freud and Jung met in the following year, and the Swiss psychiatrist became his foremost disciple.

Freud applied his psychological theories to primitive cultures, and to mythology and religion. In 1907 he suggested a relationship between obsessive acts and religious rituals. In 1913 in *Totem and Taboo* he concluded that the dread of incest was universal.

In 1909 Freud and Jung traveled together to the United States and gave a week of lectures at Clark University in Worcester, Mass. During that visit, Freud delivered his "Five Lectures on Psychoanalysis" (American Journal of Psychology, 21 (1910), 181–218). Their association lasted until 1912, when Jung went on to found his own school after advancing theories that Freud considered incompatible with psychoanalysis. Jung stressed the importance of universal archetypes in place of the infantile sexual wishes that were at the basis of Freud's view of the unconscious. In 1912 another prominent associate, the Austrian psychiatrist Alfred *Adler, also withdrew from psychoanalysis. Adler, like Jung, also repudiated infantile sexuality; but Adler thought it was the desire for power that was at the basis of character and neurosis.

Freud proposed that infancy is dominated by the pleasure principle, which later, during maturation, is modified and at least partially displaced by the reality principle. Under the regime of the pleasure principle immediate fulfillment and discharge of tension is demanded; while the reality principle operates in realistic terms, takes external conditions into account, includes delay and compromise, and allows the pursuit of gratification by pragmatic means. In 1911 he published "Formulations Regarding the Two Principles in Mental Functioning," which elaborated his view of these two basic principles. Meanwhile, between 1915 and 1917, he was attempting to construct a "metapsychology" by which he hoped to articulate and clarify the principal ideas of psychoanalysis. He explored these ideas in a series of influential papers that included "Instincts and their Vicissitudes" (1915), "The Unconscious" (1915), "Repression" (1915), and "Mourning and Melancholia" (1917).

After World War I Freud gave full scope to his speculative tendencies. In 1920 he published *Beyond the Pleasure Principle*; in 1921, *Group Psychology and the Analysis of the Ego*; and in 1923, *The Ego and the Id*. In *Beyond the Pleasure Principle* he brought the instincts for the preservation of the self and the species under the concept of Eros, a basic impulse toward life, love, and growth. He contrasted this with Thanatos, a death instinct. Many of his colleagues felt that the concept of a death instinct was purely speculative and not adequately grounded in empirical observation; it only found wide acceptance in the work of the later psychoanalyst Melanie Klein and her followers, who felt that the death instinct accounted for some of the self-destructiveness that seems to be part of human nature. In *The Ego and the Id*, Freud divided the mental apparatus into an ego, an id, and a superego: the ego supporting reason and reality, the id containing the passions, and the superego representing the internalized ethical standards of the parents.

Freud's work in understanding human psychology and mental disturbance is without parallel in history. He turned psychology's attention in a new direction. He made systematic contributions in three separate but related areas: human development (especially in childhood); the workings of the mind; and the treatment and cure of mental illness. A concern with biological and bodily processes, especially sexuality, underlay his developmental psychology. But Freud's perspective as a natural scientist was balanced by an emphasis on subjective experience and the formative relationships of childhood. Freud stressed the fundamental importance and dynamic nature of unconscious mental processes in everyday life and symptom formation: the centrality of the role of anxiety, the mechanisms of defense, and the functions of repression, sublimation, denial, and regression.

Freud's work has been faulted by many for its emphasis on sexuality and, in particular, for his belief in the universality of the Oedipal drama; on the other hand, there is no question that one of his major contributions was to open up the topic of sexuality for reexamination. Though Freud had a critical understanding of the role of culture and his psychology emphasized its importance in human development, his work has been extensively criticized for being limited by the assumptions of 19th-century science and of his Victorian social milieu. The development of psychoanalysis since Freud's death has involved the elaboration of many of his core ideas; his positions regarding the psychology of women and the contributions of the analyst to the psychoanalytic interaction are among those which have been challenged and significantly modified.

Freud's theories have had a wide and far reaching influence on our society. His contributions to other fields are almost as extensive as his contributions to clinical and theoretical psychoanalysis; and the nature of the wider impact his theories have had on our world has aroused as much interest and controversy as his psychology.

Freud and his daughter Anna *Freud, the child psychoanalyst, were hurried out of Vienna by his colleagues after the German-occupation in 1938. His other children and their families had already left; his sisters, who were old and infirm, refused to leave, and died in Auschwitz. Freud died the following year in London after a long and courageous battle with cancer.

Freud's complete psychological works in English were edited in 23 volumes by J. Strachey and others (1953–66), and his letters were published by E.L. Freud in 1961 (originally published in German 1960).

Freud's Jewish Identity

Sigmund Freud (born Sigismund Schlomo Freud) referred to himself as a "Godless Jew." He was a passionate atheist with a commitment to an ethical way of life and an aversion to religious ritual. At the same time, his Jewishness was a significant part of his identity, and throughout his life he felt a strong connection with the Jewish people. Both of his parents came from Orthodox homes in Galicia in the eastern part of the Austro-Hungarian empire. After Freud's birth, when the family moved to Vienna, they settled initially in the Jewish district of Leopoldstadt. It is likely that they celebrated the major Jewish holidays, and we know that Jakob Freud taught his son Bible stories; still, from the beginning, Sigmund Freud's life was also suffused with the liberal humanistic Jewish ideals of 19th century Vienna.

His gymnasium taught the classics-based curriculum of the German Enlightenment, although Jews in the school also studied the Bible and Jewish history and ethics. At a time when Austrian society allowed assimilated Jews to advance in society, Freud considered himself part of the wider German culture and, like many of his contemporaries, was ashamed of the "Ostjuden" (East European immigrants) who moved into his neighborhood in great numbers in the 1860s.

Although antisemitism was relatively quiescent in Vienna during his youth, a story his father told him of being humiliated as a young man by an antisemite left a lasting impression on the son. Freud recalled this story in his book *The Interpretation of Dreams*, along with his own disappointment in his father's passive response to the insult. The resurgence of antisemitism in Vienna, by the time Freud entered medical school, shattered his hopes of living a life of equality with non-Jews. When the option of assimilation was no longer available, Freud chose to express pride in his Jewishness, thus subtly defying those who sought to marginalize, and later to annihilate, him.

Freud chose to remain a Jew at a time when conversion was the only route to career advancement; as a result his promotion at the University of Vienna to full professor was delayed by more than 20 years. In 1897 he banded together with fellow Jews in the newly formed Jewish humanitarian organization *B'nai B'rith. He presented his developing ideas about psychoanalysis in that forum at a time when he felt excluded by the academic and medical community. At the 70th birthday party that his B'nai B'rith brothers prepared for him, he made that choice clear: "That you are Jews could only be welcome to me, for I was a Jew myself, and it had always seemed to me not only undignified, but quite nonsensical to deny it."

Freud never lost his emotional connection with Jewish culture. In private he used Jewish jokes and Yiddish folk tales and phrases to communicate with his friends and colleagues. In 1930 he accepted membership, along with Albert *Einstein and others, in the honorary praesidium of the *YIVO Institute (known in English as the Yiddish Scientific Institute) in Vilna, which was founded as a Jewish national academy in 1925 for the purpose of collecting, preserving, and studying Jewish culture and the Yiddish language.

Freud was sympathetic to the goals of Zionism, which his contemporary, Theodore *Herzl, was pursuing as a response to antisemitism. In 1930, in a letter to Einstein, he expressed pessimism over the possibility of a Jewish homeland in the Middle East. However, by 1935 he was to write a letter of support to the president of the *Keren Hayesod (the financial part of the World Zionist Organization) for his work "to establish a new home in the ancient land of our fathers." Freud approved when his sons joined Kadima, the Zionist student association at the University of Vienna, and at the age of 80 he asked to become an honorary member himself. He was particularly proud of the Hebrew University in Jerusalem, and served on its first Board of Governors, chaired by the university's founding father, Dr. Chaim *Weizmann.

Freud thought that religion was essentially a defensive fantasy: a primitive expression of infantile needs (*Future of an Illusion*, 1927) and unconscious guilt (*Totem and Taboo*, 1913). Although science and religion were often seen as battling for dominance in the late 19th century, Freud had contemporaries, such as the philosopher and psychologist William James, who held a much more nuanced understanding of religion. Interestingly, Freud married an Orthodox Jewish woman – Martha Bernays, the granddaughter of Rabbi Isaac *Bernays, who was the chief rabbi of Hamburg. Their marriage was a loving one, but Freud would not allow her to observe even the most basic Jewish ritual of lighting Sabbath candles.

In Freud's final years, he wrote *Moses and Monotheism* (1939), an exploration of issues that had long concerned him. Although he had often expressed pride in his Jewishness, he had always had difficulty defining what, in fact, connected him so strongly to the Jewish people, and what it meant to be a Jew. In *Moses and Monotheism*, he speculated on the nature and transmission of Jewish identity, and the origins of antisemitism. His account of the beginnings of the Jewish people breaks radically with tradition. In it, Moses was not a Jew but an Egyptian who taught an ancient Egyptian monotheistic religion to a semitic tribe. In the desert, the tribe rebelled against Moses and murdered him.

Freud had introduced the theme of the murdered father-figure in *Totem and Taboo*, hypothesizing that it was at the heart of all religion. In his account in *Moses and Monotheism*, the suppressed memory of this murder became so powerful that it served as the source of a tenacious religion, in this case, Judaism. The adoption of monotheism, Freud claimed, made the Jews a highly ethical and intellectual people, qualities that he identified as integral to Jewishness. He also associated the murder of Christ with the murder of Moses, and developed a case for this parallel being at the heart of antisemitism. This strange book, with its many complex twists of plot, offended Jews and Christians alike. Anthropologists, historians, and biblical scholars rejected its premises. With the passage of time, however, it has been interpreted more positively, with greater emphasis on what it reveals about its author. Upon dissolving the Vienna Psychoanalytic Society in 1938 and advising its members to flee the Nazi threat, Freud had invoked the memory of Rabbi *Johanan ben Zakkai, who was able to continue the Jewish tradition elsewhere after the destruction of the Temple in Jerusalem. Freud had tremendous respect for the power of knowledge, and although he was not interested in the continuation of ancient traditions, he may have hoped that publishing *Moses and Monotheism* from his new home in London, would ensure the survival of two crucial components of his life: psychoanalysis and the Jewish people.

BIBLIOGRAPHY: E. Jones, *Life and Work of Sigmund Freud*, 3 vols. (1953–57), includes bibliography; M. Robert, *From Oedipus to Moses* (1976); D. Klein, *Jewish Origins of the Psychoanalytic Movement* (1981); P. Gay, *A Godless Jew* (1987); idem, *Freud: A Life for Our Time* (1998); E. Rice, *Freud and Moses: the Long Journey Home* (1990); Y.H. Yerushalmi, *Freud's Moses: Judaism Terminable and Interminable* (1991); M. Gresser, *Dual Allegiance: Freud as a Modern Jew* (1994)

[Janice Halpern, Arnold Richards, and Sheldon Goodman (2nd ed.)]

FREUDEMANN, SIMḤAH (Ephraim ben Gershon ha-Kohen; c. 1622–1669), talmudist and author. Born in Belgrade, Freudemann studied under Judah Lerma II, the Sephardi rabbi of the Belgrade community, whom, despite his Ashkenazi descent, he succeeded as rabbi. In 1660 he was appointed rabbi of Ofen (Buda) in Hungary, but a dispute soon arose in the town on the grounds of his having relatives in the community, a disqualifying factor for the appointment of a rabbi under the terms of a ban included in the *takkanot* of the *dayyan* Aryeh Shraga Feivish of Vienna. In consequence, he left Ofen after a few months and returned to Belgrade where he remained until his death.

In 1647 he published Lerma's responsa, *Peletat Beit Yehudah* (Venice). Ten years later, there appeared in Venice his most important work, *Sefer Shemot* (referred to also as *Shemot ha-Gittin*), based on unpublished material of earlier Ashkenazi and Sephardi authorities, giving the correct Hebrew spelling of Jewish personal names of Hebrew, Latin, Spanish, and German origin, as well as the orthography of rivers and place-names for use in drawing up Jewish bills of divorce and other public documents in which accuracy was essential.

BIBLIOGRAPHY: S. Bechler, *A zsidók története Budapesten* (1901), 140–7; Conforte, Kore, 51b; J.J. (L.) Greenwald (Grunwald), *Pe'erei Ḥakhmei Medinatenu* (1910), 19; idem, *Ha-Yehudim be-Ungarya* (1913), 19f.; *Arim ve-Immahot be-Yisrael*, 2 (1948), 126; P.Z. Schwartz, *Shem ha-Gedolim me-Ereẓ Hagar*, 2 (1913), 42a, no. 94; Zipser, in: *Ben-Chananja*, 2 (1859), 172f.

[Samuel Rosenblatt]

FREUDENTHAL, ALFRED MARTIN (1906–1977), civil engineer. Born in Poland, his degrees in civil engineering were awarded in Prague (1929) and Lwow (1932). He worked as a structural designer in Prague and Warsaw before immigrating to Palestine and becoming resident engineer and then chief structural engineer of the Port of Tel Aviv (1935–45). For ten years he served on the faculty of Haifa Technion as professor of civil engineering. In 1947 he moved to the United States and in 1949 became professor of civil engineering at Columbia University. He later joined George Washington University's engineering department where he taught until his death. His specialties included metal fatigue and the theory of plasticity. He wrote *Verbundstuetzen fuer hohe Lasten* (1933) and *Inelastic Behavior of Engineering Materials and Structures* (1950). In honor of Freudenthal's exceptional contributions to research, in 1975 the American Society of Civil Engineers instituted the Alfred M. Freudenthal Medal, awarded to individuals in recognition of distinguished achievement in safety and reliability studies in civil engineering.

WEBSITE: www.asce.org/pressroom/honors.

[Ruth Rossing (2nd ed.)]

FREUDENTHAL, JACOB (1839–1907), German philosopher. His scholarly investigations were in the areas of Greek and Judeo-Hellenistic philosophy and the philosophy of Spinoza. Freudenthal was born in Hanover. In 1863 he taught at the Samson School in Wolfenbuettel and from 1864 lectured on classical languages and the history of religious philosophy at the Jewish Theological Seminary in Breslau. From 1875 he also taught at the Breslau University. He married a daughter of Michael *Sachs, the famous Berlin preacher and scholar.

Freudenthal was a foremost authority on Aristotle and published a series of works on his philosophy. In his studies of Xenophanes Freudenthal opposed the then prevalent opinion that Xenophanes was a consistent monotheist. His writings include *Hellenistische Studien* (1875–79); *Flavius Josephus beigelegte Schrift: Ueber die Herrschaft der Vernunft* (1869); *Zur Geschichte der Anschauungen ueber die juedisch-hellenistische Religionsphilosophie* (1869); "Spinoza und die Scholastik," in: E. Zeller, *Philosophische Aufsaetze* (1887), 85–138; *Die Lebensgeschichte Spinoza's in Quellenschriften…* (1899); *Spinoza, sein Leben und seine Lehre*, vol. 1 (1904), vol. 2 (1927).

BIBLIOGRAPHY: Baumgartner, in: *Chronik der Universitaet Breslau*, 22 (1907/8); Baumgartner and Wendland, in: *Jahresbericht ueber die Fortschritte der klassischen Altertumswissenschaft*; vol. 136, p. 152–63; M. Brann, *Geschichte des Juedisch-theologischen Seminars in Breslau* (1904), 129–30; B. Muenz, in: *Ost und West*, 7 (1907), 425–8; G. Kisch (ed.), *Das Breslauer Seminar* (1963), 322–3.

[Joseph Elijah Heller]

FREUDENTHAL, MAX (1868–1937), German liberal rabbi and writer. Freudenthal, who served as rabbi in Dessau, 1893–1900, Danzig, 1900–07, and Nuremberg, 1907–35, was one of the most resolute exponents of religious liberalism in Germany. His contributions to Jewish scholarship covered both philosophy and history. In philosophy he published *Die Erkenntnislehre Philos von Alexandrien* (1891): in history, *Aus der Heimat Moses Mendelssohns* (1900); *Die Familie Gomperz* (in collaboration with D. Kaufmann, 1907); *Die israelitische Kultusgemeinde Nuernberg*, 1874–1924 (1925), which includes his autobiography; and *Leipziger Messegaeste* (1928). Freudenthal contributed a wealth of basic material to the study of modern Jewish history in Germany. He wrote for various learned publications, and was coeditor of the *Zeitschrift fuer die Geschichte der Juden in Deutschland.*

BIBLIOGRAPHY: ZGJD, 7 (1937), 131–7.

FREUND, ERNST (1864–1932), U.S. jurist and legislative authority. Born in New York, Freund was educated in Germany and the United States. Freund practiced law in New York from 1886 to 1894, but was drawn to the teaching profession, concentrating on political and social sciences. As a professor at the University of Chicago from 1902, he made significant contributions to the field of public law, particularly in administrative law and legislation. Freund stressed the importance of social science in the legislative process. He served as a member of the National Conference of Commissioners on Uniform State Law from 1908 until his death and took part in the drafting of uniform state laws relating to marriage and divorce, the guardianship of children, child labor, narcotics, and the improvement of the legal position of illegitimate children. Two important books among his writings are *The Police Power, Public Policy and Constitutional Rights* (1904) and *Standards of American Legislation* (1917).

BIBLIOGRAPHY: *New York Times* (Oct. 21, 1932); *University Record* (January 1933); *Law Quarterly Review* (April 1933).

[Julius J. Marcke]

FREUND, GISÈLE (1908–2000), German photographer and reporter. Freund was born in Berlin and became acquainted with photography at an early age when her father presented her with a Leica after she finished school. She studied sociology in Freiburg and Frankfurt/Main under Theodor W. Adorno, Karl Mannheim, and Norbert Elias. After the National Socialist takeover in 1933 she fled to Paris, where she continued her studies at the Sorbonne. In her doctoral thesis she described the impact of photography on society in the 19th century. In Paris, she acquired French citizenship and started working as a professional photographer, portraying famous authors and artists. Freund used the newly developed 35-mm Technicolor film for her portraits of Walter Benjamin (1938), James Joyce (1939), Virginia Woolf (1939), and Jean-Paul Sartre (1939). In addition, she produced photojournalism for magazines like *Weekly Illustrated* and *Life*. After the German occupation she fled to Southern France in 1940 and two years later she settled in Argentina. She continued working as photographer and photojournalist and was active in the development of cultural relations between Argentina and France. After the war, Freund returned to France and went to work for the Magnum photo agency. She made several trips to America, reporting from there and lecturing on contemporary literature. After she did a piece on Evita Perón, she was banned for life from entering Argentina. The United States similarly refused her entry in 1954 on the grounds that she was a Communist sympathizer. In 1970 she published her autobiography, *Le monde et ma caméra*. In the 1980s she received several honors, such as the Chevalier de la Légion d'Honneur and the Officier du Mérite, both awarded by the French Republic. Late in life she received international recognition for her work, which was exhibited in such places as the Paris Musée d'art moderne (1968) and repeatedly in Germany, as in Bonn in 1977 (Rheinisches Landesmueum) and Berlin in 1988 (Werkbund-Archiv).

BIBLIOGRAPHY: G. Freund, *Gisèle Freund- itineraries* (1985); I. Neyer-Schoop and Th. Weski, *Gisèle Freund, Gesichter der Sprache* (Catalogue, Sprengel Museum Hannover, 1996); M. Braun-Ruiter (ed), *Gisèle Freund – Berlin Frankfurt, Paris, Fotografien 1929–1962* (1996);G. Freund: *Gisèle Freund – Die Poesie des Portraits* (1998).

[Philipp Zschommler (2nd ed.)]

FREUND, MARTIN (1863–1920), German organic chemist, born in Neisse. Freund became professor at Akademie fuer Sozial-und Handelswissenschaften (1905) and was rector there (1907–09). He was appointed head of the Chemical Institute of the newly founded Frankfurt University (1914). Some of his synthetic products became therapeutic pharmaceuticals.

FREUND, PAUL ABRAHAM (1908–1992), U.S. constitutional lawyer, educator, and author. Freund, who was born in St. Louis, Missouri, was appointed law clerk to Justice *Brandeis for the 1932–33 term of the U.S. Supreme Court, and served on the legal staffs of the Treasury Department and the Reconstruction Finance Corporation (1933–35), and was special assistant to the solicitor general (1934–39) and to the attorney general of the U.S. (1942–46). Freund lectured at the Harvard Law School from 1939 (named professor in 1940). He served as legal adviser to President Kennedy and to the State Department, and from 1957 as adviser to the American Law Institute on the drafting of the Restatement of the Conflict of Laws. A recognized authority on constitutional law, Freund believed that the U.S. Supreme Court in a federation has the responsibility of maintaining the supremacy of the Constitution and promoting the uniformity of law. He served as the president of the American Academy of Arts and Sciences in Cambridge, Massachusetts, from 1964 to 1967. His writings include *On Understanding the Supreme Court* (1949); *The Supreme Court of the U.S.* (1961); *On Law and Justice* (1968); *Experimentation with Human Subjects* (1970); and *Constitutional Law: Cases and Other Problems* (with A. Sutherland, 1977).

[Julius J. Marcke]

FREUND, SAMUEL BEN ISSACHAR BAER (1794–1881), rabbi and author of commentaries and glosses on the Mishnah and halakhic works. Born in Touskov, Bohemia, Freund was a pupil of Baruch Fraenkel-Teomim of Leipnik and Bezalel Ranschburg (Rosenbaum) of Prague. He served as rabbi in Lobositz, and afterward in Prague (1834–79), where he succeeded Samuel b. Ezekiel Landau as *dayyan*, or "Oberjurist." Freund initiated the founding of the "*Afike Jehuda" society for Jewish science in Prague (1869). He died in Prague.

Among his works are *Zera Kodesh* (pt. 1, 1827); novellae and expositions of the tractates *Berakhot, Pe'ah* and *Demai; Musar Av* (Vienna, 1839), a commentary on Proverbs; *Teshuvat Keren Shemu'el* (Prague, 1841), a responsum on the subject of eating legumes, rice, and millet during Passover, his conclusion being that they cannot be permitted; *Et le-Ḥannenah* (1850), glosses on the order *Mo'ed; Ir ha-Ẓedek* (1863), an abridgment of the *Sefer Mitzvot Gadol (Semag)* of Moses of Coucy, with glosses, novellae, and expositions; and *Amarot Tehorot* (1867), glosses to, and corrections of the works of commentators on the order *Tohorot*, together with his own *Ketem Paz* (1870), a commentary on *Avot*, and an appendix of glosses and novellae to *Berakhot*.

BIBLIOGRAPHY: *Der Israelit*, 22 (1881), 609, 636–8, 725; G. Klemperer, in: HJ, 13(1951), 80.

[Samuel Rosenblatt]

FREUND, VILMOS (1846–1920), Hungarian architect. He studied architecture in Zurich. Builder of three Jewish hospitals in Budapest, his works also include the New York Palace (1892) and the "Adria" building in Fiume (Rijeka, Yugoslavia). He favored historicizing neo-Baroque and neo-Renaissance styles.

[Eva Kondor]

FREUNDLICH, OTTO (1878–1943), German painter, sculptor, graphic artist, and teacher. Born into a Jewish family in Pomerania. Freundlich was educated by a foster mother in the Protestant tradition after the death of his mother. He studied history of art, then art; he traveled to Italy and Paris. From 1909, the year of his first exhibition, to 1914 he had a studio in Montmartre, where he worked with Picasso, Herbin, and Gris. Beside sculpture he was interested in the art of modern stained glass. He returned to Germany at the outbreak of World War I. Strongly sympathetic to the Left, Freundlich was a contributor to *Die Aktion*, a revolutionary anti-war publication in Berlin. Its September 1918 issue was dedicated to him and was illustrated with his drawings and woodcuts. After the war, he joined the short-lived *November Group*, which vainly endeavored to narrow the gap between the masses and the artists. Later he exerted a strong influence on the Dada movement. He returned to Paris in 1924 and took part in the exhibitions of the Abstraction-Creation group from 1932 to 1935. In 1936 he tried to establish a private academy but without success. In Nazi Germany, his works featured in the "Degenerate Art" show in 1937/38, and his near-abstract sculpture *Homme Nouveau* (1912) was singled out as an example of "Bolshevik-Jewish" art. When France was invaded in 1940, he fled to the Pyrenees but was caught by the Nazis and deported to Majdanek, where he perished. His works – sculpture, paintings, drawings, mosaics – were either close to pure abstraction or completely nonfigurative. The sculptures, often related to architecture, consist of rolling, cloud-like masses, joined together with great subtlety.

ADD. BIBLIOGRAPHY: J. Heusinger, *Otto Freundlich 1887–1943* (1978); G. Leistner, *Otto Freundlich. Ein Wegbereiter der abstrakten Kunst* (1994); J. Mettay, *Die verlorene Spur. Auf der Suche nach Otto Freundlich* (2005); O. Freundlich, *Kraefte der Farbe* (2001).

[Alfred Werner / Sonja Beyer (2nd ed.)]

FREUND-ROSENTHAL, MIRIAM KOTTLER (1907–1999), U.S. Hadassah leader. Born in New York City, she received her Ph.D. in American history from New York University, with a specialty in American Jewish history. She taught in the New York public high schools until 1944. From 1940, Freund-Rosenthal was a member of the National Board of Hadassah and held major positions in the organization. She was Youth Aliyah chairman (1953–56) and Hadassah national president from 1956 to 1960. She was instrumental in obtaining the services of Marc Chagall as creator of the twelve stained-glass windows in the synagogue at the Hadassah Medical Center.

Freund-Rosenthal edited the *Hadassah Magazine* from 1966 to 1971. She served as national education chairman, national vocational education chairman, national Youth Aliyah chairman, and national Zionist affairs chairman. Following her Hadassah presidency, she served as national Bond chairman, chairman for the Chagall exhibit, and chairman of the 1965 and 1977 national youth survey committee.

In appreciation for the work she did for Youth Aliyah to help North African Jewish children in Morocco, Youth Aliyah's Ohel Miriam in the synagogue in Ramat Hadassah Szold was named in her honor.

Freund-Rosenthal was also a founder of the Inter-Collegiate Zionist Youth Federation of America and a founding director of the Brandeis Youth Foundation. She was a national officer of the Jewish National Fund, as well as a national vice president of the Women's Division of Brandeis University. She also served as national associate chairman for the Women's Division of State of Israel Bonds. In 1991 she was elected an American regent of the International Center for University Teaching of Jewish Civilization. She also served as national chairman of library projects, as Hadassah's national historian, and as Hadassah's United Nations non-government representative

She wrote *Jewish Merchants in Colonial America* (1939), *Jewels for a Crown* (1963), and *In My Lifetime: Family, Community, Zion* (1989), as well as articles on Zionism and American history. She also compiled and edited the book *A Tapestry of Hadassah Memories* (1994). Later in life she settled in Jerusalem.

[Gladys Rosen / Ruth Beloff (2nd ed.)]

°**FREY, JEAN BAPTISTE** (1878–1939), French priest and archaeological scholar. In 1925 Frey was appointed secretary of the papal Bible commission and in 1933 rector-consultor of the Congregation "De propaganda fide" ("For Propagating the Faith"). His most important publication, though incomplete, is the two-volume *Corpus Inscriptionum Judaicarum* (entitled in French *Recueil des inscriptions juives du troisième siècle avant au septième siècle après J.C.*, vol. 1, *Europe*, 1936; vol. 2, *Asie-Afrique*, 1952). The second volume, despite its title, deals with *Egypt only. His other works include *La théologie juive aux temps de Jésus-Christ…* (1910), *Une ancienne synagogue de Galilée récemment découverte* (1933), and *Il delfino col tridente nella catacomba giudaica di Via Nomentana* (1931). Frey also contributed numerous articles to learned periodicals, chiefly on Judaism in the time of Jesus and on Semitic epigraphy.

FRIBOURG (Ger. **Freiburg**), capital of the Swiss canton of that name. Jews lived in the area before 1348 in Murten/Morat (1294/99). On the outbreak of the Black Death (1348–49), the Jews in the area, like those in the rest of Europe, were accused of causing the epidemic by spreading poison. After 1356 a number of Jews received permission to settle in the city of Fribourg as citizens and to engage in moneylending. As elsewhere in Switzerland, they lived in their own part of the town, although not confined to a ghetto. The decrees of expulsion of 1428 and 1463 were not permanent. Jews were subsequently granted the right to buy houses. Until at least 1481 Jews could live in the city. In that same year, Fribourg entered the Swiss Confederation. Eight Jewish doctors resided in Fribourg and others in the town of Murten, the most famous being Ackin de Vesoul.

The next mention of a Jewish presence in Fribourg dates from 1678, but Jews may have been present earlier. Jewish cattle dealers and peddlers were permitted to visit the city's open market, but the ban on Jewish commerce issued by nearby *Berne in 1787 also affected Fribourg until 1798. Restrictions against the settlement of Jews remained in force until 1864, though some privileged Jews received residence permits after 1843.

The present community was founded in 1895 by Alsatian Jews. In 2000, Jews in the canton of Fribourg numbered

138 persons; 66 were members of the community. The community built a synagogue in 1904 and acquired a cemetery. It was given official status in 1990/2001. The leading Nordmann family opened department stores. Jean Nordmann, president of the Jewish Community Association in 1973–80, was one of the first Jewish colonels in the Swiss army. Jewish subjects are taught at the local Catholic university.

BIBLIOGRAPHY: Kober, in: F. Boehm and W. Dirks (eds.), *Judentum, Schicksal, Wesen und Gegenwart*, 1 (1965), 162–3; A. Weldler-Steinberg, 2 vols. *Geschichte der Juden in der Schweiz* (1966/70), index s.v. *Freiburg*; **ADD. BIBLIOGRAPHY:** C. Agustoni, *Les Juifs de Fribourg* (1987). A, Kamis, *Vie Juive en Suisse* (1992), SIG (ed.), *Juedische Lebenswelt Schweiz. 100 Jahre Schweizerischer Israelitischer Gemeindebund* (2004).

[Uri Kaufmann (2nd ed.)]

FRIDMAN, GAL (1975–), Israeli windsurfer; first Israeli ever to win an Olympic gold medal and the first Israeli to win two Olympic medals. Born in the Israeli moshav of Karkur, near Haderah, Fridman – whose first name, Gal, means "wave" in Hebrew – began windsurfing when he was six years old and competing at age 11, under the coaching of his father, Uri. Young Fridman competed in international competitions in the youth categories in 1989 and 1991 while attending the ORT Ha-Shomron High School in Binyaminah. Fridman won the silver medal at the 1995 and 1996 World Championships and placed second in the European Championships both years. He then won a bronze medal at the Atlanta 1996 Summer Olympics, Israel's third medal-winner, and was named Israel's Sportsman of the Year. Fridman won a bronze in the European Championship in 1997; silver in the European Championship in 2002; gold at the Mistral World Championship in 2002; and a bronze at the World Championship in 2003. His winning the Olympic gold medal in Athens in 2004 was an historic moment in Israeli sports history. After crossing the finish line, Fridman pumped his fist, took a victory dip and then wrapped himself in an Israeli flag when he emerged from the water. "I am happy you all got to see the race live on television," he said to Israeli viewers in an interview. "I simply felt the entire country pushing me forward." It was the first time the national anthem Hatikvah was played at the Olympics. President Moshe Katzav, Prime Minister Ariel Sharon, and other senior Israeli officials and politicians called Fridman to congratulate him.

[Elli Wohlgelernter (2nd ed.)]

FRIED, AARON (1812–1891), Hungarian rabbi. Born in Hajduböszörmény, Fried studied under R. Moses Sofer in Pressburg from 1828 to 1831. In 1833 he married the daughter of Eleazar Loew (author of *Shemen Rokeʾaḥ*), the rabbi of Abaujszántó, and took up residence with him there until 1837. In the latter year, he was appointed rabbi of Mezöcsát where he remained until 1844. While there, all his possessions including his books and writings were lost in a fire. From 1844 to 1860 he was rabbi of Hajdusámson; he was then appointed to Hajduböszörmény. where he remained for the rest of his life. Fried took a prominent part in the establishment of the organization of the Hungarian Orthodox Jewish community, and in conducting their affairs. He is the author of: *Omer le-Ẓiyyon* (1872), talmudic novellae; *Ẓel ha-Kesef* (1878), 24 aggadic excursuses (no. 21 contains interesting references to the Hungarian Jewish congress held in 1868/69); *Responsa Maharaf*, including a long aggadic introduction with some interesting autobiographical data entitled *Todat Aharon*, as well as a commentary on the Mishnayot of the order *Zeraʿim* and tractate *Mikvaʾot*, entitled *Ḥallat Aharon* (1893); and *Zekan Aharon*, homilies (1904). The two latter books were published posthumously by Fried's son Eleazar (Lazar).

BIBLIOGRAPHY: A. Fried, *Sheʾelot u-Teshuvot Maharaf* (1893), 11a; P.Z. Schwartz, *Shem ha-Gedolim me-Ereẓ Hagar*, 1 (1913), no. 112; M. Stein, *Even ha-Meʾir*, pt. 1 (1907), 9b, no. 86; idem, *Magyar Rabbik*, 2 (1906), 72, no. 111.

[Abraham Schischa]

FRIED, ALFRED HERMANN (1864–1921), Austrian publicist and Nobel peace prize winner. Born in Vienna, Fried served as an Austrian diplomat for a short time but became discouraged and went to Berlin where he became a bookdealer and publisher. After 1891 he devoted himself to pacifist propaganda and founded and edited a number of journals for this purpose, among them *Die Waffen Nieder* which was owned by the famous Austrian pacifist-propagandist, Baroness von Suttner. Fried was the author of more than 70 books and pamphlets devoted to the advancement of peace and of nearly 2,000 newspaper articles. A member of the Berne Bureau and the International Institute for Peace, he was also European secretary of the Conciliation Internationale, secretary general of the Union Internationale de la Presse pour la Paix, and founder of the German and Austrian peace societies. Fried won the Nobel Prize for Peace in 1911. At the time of the Hague peace conferences (1899–1907) Fried was in constant touch with Ivan *Bliokh, the man who persuaded the czar to convene the conferences. His pacifist approach led to his being accused of treason; he left Austria on the outbreak of World War I and spent the war years in Switzerland. He was a prominent figure at the international workers meeting in Berne which fought to prepare a formula for a negotiated peace. After the war he advocated a European union of states similar to the Pan-American system. Fried's publications include *Handbuch der Friedensbewegung* (1905); *Die Grundlagen des revolutionaeren Pacifismus* (1908); *Der Kaiser und der Weltfrieden* (1910), a defense of Kaiser William II's policies; and *Der Weltprotest gegen den Versailler Frieden* (1920), an attack on the Versailles peace settlement.

BIBLIOGRAPHY: R. Goldscheid, *Alfred Fried* (Ger., 1922); H.F. Peterson, *Power and International Order; an Analytical Study of Four Schools of Thought and their Approaches to the War, the Peace and a Post-War System, 1914–1919* (1964). **ADD. BIBLIOGRAPHY:** E. Pistiner, "Der vergessene österreichisch-jüdische Friedens-Nobelpreistraeger Alfred Hermann Fried," in: ZGJ, 9 (1972), 17–32; A. Schou,

Histoire de l'imternationalisme III – Du Congrès de Vienna jusqu'a la Première Guerre Mondiale, 8 (1963), 365–68.

[Josef J. Lador-Lederer]

FRIED, ERICH (1921–1988), Austrian poet. Born in Vienna into an assimilated Jewish family, Fried was forced to flee to Great Britain after the annexation of Austria by Germany in 1938 and spent the remainder of his life in an English-speaking environment. In the late 1940s Fried worked intermittently for BBC radio until in 1952 he got full-time employment as a political commentator. Simultaneously he made various translations into German of English literature, including texts by John Donne, John Milton, Thomas Hardy, Rudyard Kipling, and T.S. Eliot, arousing the interest of German publishers and leading to the appearance of his own work. He published his first political poems in the collection called *Die Vertriebenen* (1941) and broached the subject of guilt in the poems of *Deutschland* (1944). The poems of *Oesterreich* (1945) followed in the formal footsteps of expressionistic antiwar verse. From the 1960s Fried also focused on European Jewry. He wrote poems about the Holocaust in *Anfechtungen* (1967) and *Warngedichte* (1964). These poems reflect the poet's attempts to come to terms with the Holocaust and his fear of another war. His only novel, *Ein Soldat und ein Maedchen* (1960), is a provocative love story involving an Allied soldier and a young female camp warden and reflects his harsh criticism of postwar Germany. In the following years Fried focused on contemporary social problems. *Vietnam und* (1966) contains shocking political poems using satirical elements and newspaper clippings to arouse the reader. In *Höre, Israel* (1967), a collection of anti-Zionist poems, Fried extended his political criticism to Israel and provoked heated discussion, as was the case with *So kam ich unter die Deutschen* (1977), which sought understanding for the motives of the German Red Army Faction terrorist group (Baader-Meinhof). Fried's collection of love poems, *Liebesgedichte* (1979), was very popular. Among his short prose works *Kinder und Narren* (1965) and *Das Unmass aller Dinge* (1982) are worthy of mention. Formal recognition came late in Fried's life. In 1973 he received the Austrian *Wuerdigungspreis fuer Literatur* and in 1980 the *Preis der Stadt Wien fuer Literatur.* Recognition from the Federal Republic of Germany came in the 1980s with the most prestigious West German literary award, the *Georg-Buechner-Preis* for his poetry and for his Shakespeare translations. Fried was a member of the German PEN Center and from 1986 on corresponding member of the *Deutsche Akademie fuer Sprache und Dichtung.*

BIBLIOGRAPHY: C. Jessen (ed.), *Erich Fried: eine Chronik; Leben und Werk; das biographische Lesebuch* (1998); G. Lampe, *"Ich will mich erinnern / an alles was man vergisst": Erich Fried, Biographie und Werk eines "deutschen Dichters"* (1998); N. Luer: *Form und Engagement: Untersuchungen zur Dichtung und Aesthetik Erich Frieds* (2004).

[Ann-Kristin Koch (2nd ed.)]

FRIED, LAZAR (1888–1944), Yiddish actor. Born in Minsk, Fried sang with Cantor *Sirota in Vilna and later appeared in German-Yiddish operettas in Vitebsk. In 1908 he joined *Hirschbein's company in Odessa. Boris *Thomashefsky took Fried to New York in 1913 and there he created the stage type *Moishe der Greener* ("Moishe the Greenhorn"). From 1919 he played serious parts, joined Schwartz's Jewish Art Theater in 1923, and played leading roles in New York and on tour.

FRIED (-Biss), MIRIAM (1946–), Israeli violinist. Born in Romania, Fried was brought to Israel at the age of two. She studied with Alice Fenives-Rosenberg at the Tel Aviv Rubin Academy, and pursued her training with Gingold at Indiana University (1966–67), and with Galamian at the Juilliard School (1967–69). Fried won the Paganini Geneval Competition in 1968 and the Queen Elisabeth of Belgium International Competition in Brussels in 1971. She is noted for her maturity of approach and vibrant expression, intelligent and perceptive musicianship as well as spirited brilliance of technique. She appeared as a soloist with many of the principle world orchestras, as a recitalist, and as a chamber music artist. She is a member of the Mendelssohn String Quartet and has collaborated with such distinguished artists as Isaac *Stern, Pinchas *Zukerman, Garrick Ohlsson, and her husband, violinist/violist Paul Biss. In 1986 she joined the faculty of Indiana University. From 1993 she served as artistic director of the Ravinia Institute, one of the leading summer programs for young musicians.

BIBLIOGRAPHY: Grove online; *Baker's Biographical Dictionary* (1997).

[Uri (Erich) Toeplitz and Yohanan Boehm / Naama Ramot (2nd ed.)]

FRIED, MORTON HERBERT (1923–1986), U.S. anthropologist. Born and educated in New York City, Fried received his B.S. from the City College of New York in 1942. He served in the U.S. Army (1943–46) and, under the Army Specialized Training Program, studied Chinese at Harvard, graduating in 1944. He did his graduate work at Columbia University, where he earned a Ph.D. in anthropology in 1951. He taught sociology and anthropology at New York City College (1949–50). He then became an instructor in the department of anthropology at Columbia University from 1950 to 1953; he was associate professor from 1957 to 1961 and then became a professor, teaching at Columbia for the next two and a half decades. He also served as chairman of the anthropology department (1966 –69).

Fried specialized in Asian studies and studied the Chinese in the Caribbean and Guianas (cf. his *Fabric of Chinese Society* (1953, 1968²), a study of the social life of a Chinese county seat). His other research interests included social kinship and social stratification in primitive society, especially China; evolution; and social and political organization, and evolution of the state. He was co-editor of *Readings in Anthropology* (2 vols., 1959, 1968²) and *Evolution of Political Society* (1967).

In 1981 he was invited by the People's Republic of China to act as a consultant to high government officials on implementing exchanges of scholars and students between the U.S. and China.

Fried's other books include *The Classification of Corporate Unilineal Descent Groups* (1957), *On the Evolution of Social Stratification and the State* (1957), *State: The Institution* (1968), *The Study of Anthropology* (1972), *Explorations in Anthropology: Readings in Culture, Man, and Nature* (1973), and *The Notion of Tribe* (1975).

[Ephraim Fischoff / Ruth Beloff (2nd ed.)]

FRIEDAN, BETTY (1921–2006), U.S. writer and feminist. Born Naomi Goldstein in Peoria, Illinois, she received her B.A. in psychology from Smith College in 1942. She then held a research fellowship in psychology at the University of California at Berkeley, assisted in early group dynamics at the University of Iowa, and worked as a clinical psychologist and in applied social research. She also turned to freelance writing, contributing to various magazines.

After her marriage in 1947, her main efforts were devoted to raising her three children. In 1963 she published *The Feminine Mystique*, which focused on the plight of women and their lack of equality with men. An immediate and controversial bestseller, it is now regarded as one of the most influential American books of the 20th century. This represented the start of the women's movement in the United States.

Friedan was the founder of the National Organization of Women (NOW) and served as its president from 1966 to 1970. The organization aimed at bringing women into full equal participation in American society, exercising all privileges and responsibilities. In 1970, she organized a march of 50,000 women through New York City. She was also a founder of the *National Women's Political Caucus* (1971) and the National Abortion Rights Action League (NARAL). In 1973 she became director of the First Women's Bank and Trust Company.

In 1978 Friedan chaired the Emergency Project for Equal Rights and the following year the National Assembly on the Future of the Family. Her second book, *The Second Stage* (1981), outlined new directions for the women's movement based on shared female experience. Friedan was seen in the 1980s as one of America's senior statespersons in the struggle for equal rights and was outspoken over what was perceived as backsliding on the issue of women's rights under the Reagan administration. During the span of her career she became more closely identified with Jewish issues and served on the board of *Present Tense – the Magazine of World Jewish Affairs.* She also denounced antisemitism and anti-Zionism at the UN.

Friedan traveled and lectured all over the world and wrote for such diverse publications as *McCall's*, *Harper's*, *The New York Times*, *The New Republic*, and *The New Yorker.* She was a Visiting Distinguished Professor at the University of Southern California, New York University, and George Mason University, an adjunct scholar at the Wilson International Center for Scholars at the Smithsonian, and Distinguished Professor of Social Evolution at Mount Vernon College.

In 1993 she was inducted into the National Women's Hall of Fame.

Other books by Friedan include *It Changed My Life: Writings on the Women's Movement* (1976); *The Fountain of Age* (1993), based on 10 years of research on changing sex roles and the aging process; *Beyond Gender: The New Politics of Work and Family* (1997); and *Life So Far: A Memoir* (2000).

BIBLIOGRAPHY: M. Meltzer, *Betty Friedan: A Voice for Women's Rights* (1985); S. Henry and E. Taitz, *Betty Friedan, Fighter for Women's Rights* (1990); S. Taylor-Boyd, *Betty Friedan: Voice for Women's Rights, Advocate of Human Rights* (1990); J. Blau, *Betty Friedan* (1990); J.A. Hennessee, *Betty Friedan: Her Life* (1999).

[Susan Strul / Ruth Beloff (2nd ed.)]

FRIEDBERG, town in Hesse, Germany. A community existed there by 1260 when a Gothic-style *mikveh* was constructed. About this time the community had a well-developed organization and tax system (Responsa of Meir b. Baruch of Rothenburg (1891), no. 187, pp. 204–6). In 1275 Rudolf I of Hapsburg granted a charter to the Friedberg community. The Jews there suffered persecution in 1338 and following the Black Death in 1349, the property of those who had been killed or fled was sold to the city by the imperial bailiff in 1350–54. Jews had been readmitted to Friedberg by 1360. The charter of 1275 was confirmed by successive German emperors. The right of the Jews in Friedberg to engage in the retail trade was upheld by the burgrave in 1623. In 1603 the Friedberg *bet din* was declared one of the five central Jewish courts. Between 1588 and 1640 the community was administered by six to ten *parnasim* and from 1652 the community elected an electoral committee of nine from which the *parnasim* and a taxation committee were elected. The Jews of Friedberg lived in an enclosed quarter near a square below the castle. In the late 18th century the gates were closed on Sundays. Jewish residence in Friedberg was subject to permission from both the burgrave and the community, and by around 1600 was restricted to persons owning 1,500 guilders. Exemptions were made during the Thirty Years' War, and after the expulsion of the Jews from the towns of Upper Hesse in 1662. In 1540 the Jewries of 14 villages and towns formed the community of the *Land* (*Kehillat* Friedberg). Its rabbinate had jurisdiction over Upper Hesse and the adjoining principalities as far as Westphalia, and over Hesse-Kassel from 1625 to 1656. *Ḥayyim b. Bezalel, the brother of *Judah b. Bezalel Loeb of Prague, was rabbi there in 1566. Elijah b. Moses *Loanz (d. 1636) also officiated there. A *ḥevrat gemilut ḥasadim* (charitable institution) was founded in 1687. There were about 16 Jewish families in 1536, 32 in 1550, 107 in 1609, 99 in 1617–24, 72 in 1729, 42 families in 1805, 506 persons in 1892, 491 in 1910 (5.17% of the total population), 380 in 1925 (3.44%), and 305 in 1933. The community had a very active cultural and orthodox religious life. The synagogue was burned in November 1938 and the Nazis initiated a pogrom. By summer 1939 only 58

Jews were living in Friedberg; those who did not subsequently emigrate were deported. In 1967 there were 21 Jews in Friedberg. The medieval bathhouse was restored by the municipality in 1957–58, as a historical monument, and various memorial plaques were put up in the town in subsequent years.

BIBLIOGRAPHY: A. Kober, in: PAAJR, 17 (1947/48), 19–60; Baron, Social², 13 (1969), 200f.; Wagner, in *Jeschurun*, 2 (1902), 437–9; Germ Jud, 1 (1963), 110–1; 2 (1968), 260–3 (incl. bibl.); W.H. Braun, in: *Wetterauer Geschichtsblaetter*, 11 (1962), 81–84; 16 (1967), 51–78; F.H. Herrmann, *ibid.*, 2 (1953), 106–10; H. Wilhelm, *ibid.*, 11 (1961), 67–85; B. Brilling, *ibid.*, 14 (1965), 97–103; FJW; PK; S. Goldmann, in: *Zeitschrift fuer die Geschichte der Juden*, 7 (1970), 89–93; E. Keyser (ed.), *Hessisches Staedtebuch* (1957), 163f., 166. **ADD. BIBLIOGRAPHY:** C. Kasper-Holtkotte, "Juedisches Leben in Friedberg (16.–18. Jahrhundert)" (*Kehilat Friedberg*, vol. 1; *Wettauer Geschichtsblaetter*, vol. 50) (2003); S. Litt (ed.), "Protokollbuch und Statuten der Juedischen Gemeinde Friedberg (16.–18. Jahrhundert)" (*Kehilat Friedberg*, vol. 2; *Wettauer Geschichtsblaetter*, vol. 51) (2003); H.-H. Hoos, "Kehillah Kedoscha – Spurensuche," in: *Zur Geschichte der juedischen Gemeinde in Friedberg und der Friedberger Juden von den Anfaengen bis 1942* (2002); idem, "Im Vordergrund steht immer das Sichtbare." Aspekte zur Rekonstruktion der Geschichte der juedischen Gemeinde und der Juden in Friedberg," in: *Wetterauer Geschichtsblaetter*, 38 (1989), 201–255; A. Maimon, M. Breuer, and Y. Guggenheim (eds.), *Germania Judaica* III 1350–1514 (1987), 407–413; F.H. Herrmann, "Die Friedberger Judengemeinde waehrend des Dreissigjaehrigen Krieges," in: *Wetterauer Geschichtsblaetter*, vol. 34 (1985), 53–77; H.H. Hoos, "Zur Geschichte der Friedberger Juden 1933–1942," in: M. Keller (ed.), *Von Schwarz-weiss-rot zum Hakenkreuz. Studien zu nationalsozialistischen Machtergreifung, zur Judenverfolgung und zum politisch-militaerischen Zusammenbruch in Friedberg* (*Wetterauer Geschichtsblaetter, Beihefte*, vol. 1) (1984).

[Toni Oelsner]

FRIEDBERG, ABRAHAM SHALOM (1838–1902), Hebrew author, editor, and translator. Born in Grodno, he received a traditional education and also studied watchmaking. After wandering from town to town in southern Russia, he returned to Grodno in 1858. His first book *Emek ha-Arazim* (adapted from *Vale of Cedars* by Grace Aguilar) was published in 1876 and enjoyed great popularity. After the pogroms of 1881 he joined the Ḥibbat Zion movement. In 1883 he went to St. Petersburg and became associate editor of **Ha-Meliẓ* and was influential in directing its editorial policy toward Zionism. He contributed numerous articles to the journal under the heading *Me-Inyanei de-Yoma* ("On Current Events"), which were signed H. Sh. for *Har Shalom*, the Hebrew translation of Friedberg. Failing to obtain a permit to remain in St. Petersburg, he left *Ha-Meliẓ* in 1886 and went to Warsaw, where he contributed to *Ha-Ẓefirah* and *Ha-Asif* and translated many books into Hebrew. He was an editor of the first Hebrew encyclopedia, *Ha-Eshkol* (1888), and was employed by the Aḥi'asaf publishing house. He wrote *Toledot ha-Yehudim bi-Sefarad* ("History of the Jews in Spain," 1893) based on Graetz, Kayserling, and others, translated into Hebrew M. Guedemann's *Geschichte des Erziehungswesens und der Kultur der abendlaendischen Juden*, 1880–88 (*Sefer ha-Torah ve-ha-Ḥayyim*, 1897–99), published *Sefer ha-Zikhronot* ("Book of Memoirs," 1899), a collection of literary articles and letters of well-known people, and edited the *Aḥi'asaf* yearbook (vols. 1–6). He also wrote for *Der Yid* and other Yiddish publications. His memoirs, which appeared in Sokolow's *Sefer ha-Shanah* (vols. 1 and 3) and in *Lu'aḥ Aḥi'asaf* (vol. 9), are important for the literary history of the period. His popular reputation was earned by his book *Zikhronot le-Veit David* ("Memoirs of the House of David," 1893–99), a series of stories embracing Jewish history from the destruction of the first Temple to the beginning of the Haskalah period in Germany. The first two volumes are an adaptation of *Geheimnisse der Juden* ("Secrets of the Jews") by H. Reckendorf, but the two remaining volumes were written by Friedberg himself. It was frequently republished and was translated into Arabic and Persian.

BIBLIOGRAPHY: Y. Rawnitzki, *Dor ve-Soferav* (1927), 170–4; Maimon (Fishman), in: *Ha-Toren*, 9, no. 3 (1922), 88–90; 9, no. 4 (1922), 91–95; Waxman, Literature, 4 (1960), 160, 434.

[Yehuda Slutsky]

FRIEDBERG, BERNARD (Bernhard, Ḥayyim Dov; 1876–1961), scholar and bibliographer. Friedberg was born in Cracow, and in 1900 moved to Frankfurt, where he worked for the publisher and bookseller Isaac *Kauffmann. In 1904 he set up his own firm and by 1906 had published two catalogs; in the same year he and J. Saenger founded the publishing house of Saenger and Friedberg. In 1910 the partnership broke up, and Friedberg entered the diamond trade, moving to Antwerp. When the Nazis occupied Belgium, he lost his valuable library and all his papers. In 1946 he settled in Tel Aviv, continuing to deal in diamonds but with his heart in books and his bibliographical and genealogical research.

Beginning in 1896, Friedberg published in Hebrew a number of biographies, e.g., on Joseph Caro (1896), Shabbetai Kohen (1898), and Nathan Spira (1899); family histories, e.g., Schor (1901), Landau (1905), and Horowitz (1911, 1928²); and a study on the old Jewish cemetery of Cracow, *Luḥot Zikkaron* (1897, 1904², 1969). Friedberg's first bibliographical effort was a history of Hebrew printing in Cracow, *Ha-Defus ha-Ivri be-Cracow* (1900), followed by a similar study on Lublin, *Le-Toledot ha-Defus ha-Ivri be-Lublin* (1901). In 1932 he began publishing a series of works on the history of Hebrew printing, *Toledot ha-Defus ha-Ivri*; the series included volumes on Poland (1932, 1950²); on Italy, Spain, Portugal, Turkey, and the Orient (1934, 1956²); on Central Europe (1935); and on Western Europe (1937). His greatest achievement was his bibliographical lexicon *Beit Eked Sefarim* (1 vol., 1928–31; 4 vols., 1951–56², the second edition listing Hebrew books published by 1950). Though Friedberg's works are not always accurate, they are indispensable bibliographical reference books.

BIBLIOGRAPHY: Tidhar, 5 (1952), 2268–69; Kressel, 2 (1967), 659.

[Naphtali Ben-Menahem]

FRIEDE, SHALOM (1783–1854), Dutch *ḥazzan*. Born in Amsterdam, he served as *ḥazzan* from 1809 until his death. His collection of about 200 melodies for various prayers, preserved in manuscript form at the Hebrew Union College, Cincinnati, added considerably to the knowledge of Polish cantoral and ḥasidic music. Of this collection, 15 melodies were published by A.Z. Idelsohn in *Oẓar Neginot Yisrael*. His preference for Polish and ḥasidic chants is reflected in his own compositions.

FRIEDELL, EGON, pseudonym of **Egon Friedmann** (1878–1938), Austrian playwright and cultural historian. Born in Vienna, Friedell studied there and at Heidelberg. A witty and versatile bohemian, he not only wrote plays but often acted in them, particularly at Max Reinhardt's theaters in Berlin and Vienna. Among the plays he wrote was *Die Judastragoedie* (1920). Beside his occupation as drama critic, theater director, and cabaret artist, he wrote essays and satires for popular dailies as well as Karl Kraus' *Fackel*, the *Schaubühne* and the *Neue Wiener Journal*. Friedell's magnum opus was the three-volume *Kulturgeschichte der Neuzeit* (1927; *A Cultural History of the Modern Age*, 1931–32). Ranging from the Reformation to World War I, this highly original work is no solemn historical study but a brilliant, aphoristic, and sometimes ironic survey of world history and culture. He also wrote *Kulturgeschichte des Altertums* (2 vols., 1936–49) and *Das Jesusproblem* (1921). Friedell, who converted to Protestantism at the age of 19, continuously displayed controversial attitudes toward Judaism until the Nazi rise to power in Germany. Refusing to emigrate, he stayed in Austria until 1938. On March 16 he committed suicide by jumping out of a window, when the SA came to arrest him a few days after the arrival of the German troops in Vienna.

BIBLIOGRAPHY: W. Schneider, *Friedell-Brevier* (1947); H. Zohn, *Wiener Juden in der deutschen Literatur* (1964), 61–64. **ADD. BIBLIOGRAPHY:** G. Patterson, "Race and Antisemitism in the Life and Work of Egon Friedell," in: *Jahrbuch des Instituts für Deutsche Geschichte*, 10 (1981), 3319–39; R. Innerhofer, *Kulturgeschichte zwischen den beiden Weltkriegen. Egon Friedell* (1990); W. Lorenz, *Egon Friedell: Momente im Leben eines Ungewöhnlichen* (1994); R. Reschke, "Ecce Poeta; Nachdenken über den Künstler in der Moderne; Egon Friedells eigenwillige Nähe zu Friedrich Nietzsche," in: Werner Stegmaier and Daniel Krochmalnik (eds.), *Jüdischer Nietzscheanismus* (1997).

[Harry Zohn / Mirjam Triendl (2nd ed.)]

FRIEDEMANN, ADOLF (1871–1932), one of Herzl's first supporters. Born in Berlin, Friedemann was a founder of the Juedische Humanitaetsgesellschaft in Berlin (1893), which later developed into the Jewish Student Zionist Organization in Germany (1895). When Herzl became active in Jewish affairs, Friedemann was his faithful companion, carrying out various missions on his behalf and accompanying him on his trip to Egypt in connection with the El-Arish Project (1902). He was a member of the Zionist General Council from 1903 to 1920, and after the Keren Hayesod was established, worked in its behalf in several countries. Friedemann published numerous articles and books on Zionism and Ereẓ Israel. His book *Das Leben Theodor Herzls* (1914) was the first biography of the founder of political Zionism to be published in book form. Other books are *Was will der Zionismus* (1903), *Reisebilder aus Palaestina* (1904, with illustrations by H. Struck), and a biography *David Wolffsohn* (1916). He was also the chief editor of the first lexicon of Zionism, *Zionistisches ABC Buch* (1908). He died in Amsterdam.

BIBLIOGRAPHY: T. Herzl, *Complete Diaries*, 5 vols. (1960), index; R. Lichtheim, *Die Geschichte des deutschen Zionismus* (1954). **ADD. BIBLIOGRAPHY:** Y. Eloni, *Zionismus in Deutschland* (1987); H. Lavsky, *Before Catastrophe – The Distinctive Path of German Zionism* (1996).

[Getzel Kressel]

FRIEDEMANN, ULRICH (1877–1949), German bacteriologist who made a significant contribution to the study of scarlet fever. Friedemann, who was born in Berlin, worked for two years as assistant to Paul Ehrlich, and then became professor of hygiene at Berlin University and head of the department of bacteriology at the Moabit city hospital in Berlin. He was also a member of the Robert Koch Institute. Friedemann left Germany soon after Hitler came to power in 1933 and, after three years as research worker at the National Institute for Medical Research in London, went to the United States. There he became chief of the division of bacteriology at the Jewish Hospital of Brooklyn, N.Y. In addition to his studies on scarlet fever, its causes and its effects, Friedemann did research on tetanus, virus diseases, latent infections and their significance to epidemiology, and the theory of anaphylactic shock.

BIBLIOGRAPHY: S.R. Kagan, *Jewish Medicine* (1952), 259; *Journal of the American Medical Association*, 142 (Jan. 1950), 43.

[Suessmann Muntner]

FRIEDENBERG, ALBERT MARX (1881–1942), U.S. lawyer and historian. Friedenberg was born in New York City. At the age of 19, he joined the *American Jewish Historical Society and became one of its leading members; he was largely responsible for the issuance of 17 volumes of the *Publications of the American Jewish Historical Society* (AJHSP, nos. 18–34). Friedenberg wrote numerous papers and articles on the early history of Jews in America, immigration, historical aspects of Zionism, Jews in Masonry, and the Jewish periodical press, and also on local German Jewish history, literature, and biography. He acted as the New York correspondent of the Baltimore *Jewish Comment* (1902–10) and the Chicago *Reform Advocate* (1905–31), and as contributing editor of the New York *Hebrew Standard* (1907–23).

BIBLIOGRAPHY: Coleman, in: AJHSP, 35 (1939), 115–37; Friedman, *ibid.*, 37 (1947), 461–2.

[Isidore S. Meyer]

FRIEDENBERG, SAMUEL (1886–1957), U.S. collector of medals. Brought to New York from Poland at the age of seven, Friedenberg later built up a fortune in the textile business and then in real estate, and became active in philanthropic and cultural work. Beginning with the purchase of a small collection of medals in 1935 from a German refugee, he established what became the most complete collection of Jewish medals in existence. He commissioned from artists such as I. Sors, Benno *Elkan, Paul Vincze, F. Kormis, a supplementary series of portrait medals, mainly of contemporaries. He left the collection to the New York Jewish Museum, where his son, Daniel M. Friedenberg, who wrote widely on the subject, became honorary curator of coins and medals.

BIBLIOGRAPHY: D.M. Friedenberg (ed.), *Great Jewish Portraits in Metal* (1963).

[Cecil Roth]

FRIEDENWALD, U.S. family of ophthalmologists and Jewish communal leaders.

JONAS FRIEDENWALD (1803–1893), a German immigrant who settled in Baltimore in 1831, was a businessman and one of the founders of the Hebrew Orphan Asylum and Chizuk Emunah Orthodox Congregation. His youngest son AARON FRIEDENWALD (1836–1902) was born in Baltimore and studied medicine at the University of Maryland. A distinguished ophthalmologist, he was the first president of the Medical and Chirurgical Faculty of Maryland and a prominent member of medical societies. In 1890 he organized the Association of American Medical Colleges. He was an active worker in local and national Jewish organizations, including the Baltimore Hebrew Orphan Asylum, Jewish Theological Seminary of America, Federation of American Zionists, and American Jewish Historical Society. He also published articles of Jewish and general medical interest.

HARRY FRIEDENWALD (1864–1950), eldest of Aaron's five sons, was born in Baltimore. He excelled in studies at Johns Hopkins University, and after two years at the Baltimore College of Physicians and Surgeons, spent two years traveling and studying ophthalmology in Berlin. He returned to Baltimore in 1891 and began his practice, teaching ophthalmology at the Baltimore College of Physicians and Surgeons (1894–1929). Harry Friedenwald was a member of Hevras Zion in Baltimore, probably the first American Zionist society, and was president of the Federation of American Zionists, 1904–18. In 1911 and 1914 he went to Palestine, where he served as a consultant for eye diseases in several Jerusalem hospitals. He was a member of the Provisional Committee of Zionist Affairs during World War I, and in 1919 he was chairman of the Zionist Commission to Palestine, where he spent the year.

Friedenwald wrote on medical history with special emphasis on medieval Jewish doctors and the use of the Hebrew language in medical literature; he also lectured frequently on Jews in medicine. In 1944 his collected and expanded historico-medical writings, *The Jews and Medicine* (2 vols.), were published. He wrote *Jewish Luminaries in Medical History* (1946). His son JONAS FRIEDENWALD (1897–1955) was also an ophthalmologist.

BIBLIOGRAPHY: L. Levin, *Vision: the Story of Dr. Harry Friedenwald of Baltimore* (1964); G. Rosen, in: H. Friedenwald, *Jews and Medicine* (1967).

[Gladys Rosen]

FRIEDER, ARMIN (1911–1946), Slovakian rabbi in the *status quo community at Zvolen and the *Neolog community of Nove Mesto had Vahom (from 1938), and an active Zionist. In 1942 he became a member of the underground "Working Group" (see *Slovakia, Holocaust) in Bratislava, set up to save the remaining Jews in Slovakia, and served as the underground's contact with Slovak government circles. Under his influence, the Ohel David Home for the Aged at Nove Mesto became a refuge before deportations. Following the suppression of the Slovak Uprising in the autumn of 1944, Frieder found refuge in a Catholic monastery. After the war he was chief rabbi of the Jewish communities of Slovakia.

[Livia Rothkirchen]

FRIEDERMAN, ZALMAN JACOB (c. 1865–1936), U.S. rabbi. Friederman was born in Meretch (Merkine), Lithuania, in 1865 or 1866. He studied at several yeshivot in Vilna and possibly in Kovno (Kaunas) and Eishishok (Eishishkes), but the most influential rabbinic figure in his formative years was Rabbi Judah Halevi Lifshitz of Meretch. In 1890 Friederman married Dora, daughter of Jacob Halevi Lifshitz, who was the secretary of Rabbi Isaac Elhanan *Spektor and Judah Lifshitz's brother. Shortly thereafter he was ordained as a rabbi, and during the same year, 1890, he relocated to Amsterdam to serve as a rabbi. His dissatisfaction with this job led him to immigrate to America in 1892, joining his sisters and their husbands who had immigrated earlier.

After spending a few months in New York as rabbi of congregation Kol Yisrael Anshe Polin, Friederman accepted an offer to serve as rabbi of congregation Anshe Vilkomir of Boston, to which he relocated in early 1893, notwithstanding the opposition of another local Orthodox rabbi, Moses S. *Margolies. In 1896 Margolies left Boston, and shortly thereafter Friederman was appointed as the rabbi the Union of Orthodox Congregations of Greater Boston. In addition, he was a member of the Union of Orthodox Rabbis of the United States and Canada, as well as Va'ad Harabanim of Massachusetts, founded a *talmud torah* in Boston, and over the years served as rabbi in several additional local congregations, such as Anshe Stonir, Anshe Zhitomir, and Sha'arei Zedek.

Friederman maintained close contacts with Rabbi Abraham I. *Kook and helped raise money for Jewish settlers in Palestine. In 1935 Friederman visited Palestine, where he died, being buried on the Mount of Olives, Jerusalem, close to Rabbi Kook.

Friederman wrote several polemic and homiletics books, all of which appeared during his lifetime: *Emet Ve-Emunah* (1895), *Minḥat Ya'akov* (1901), *Naḥalat Ya'akov* (1914), and *Shoshanat Ya'akov* (1927). In addition, he published many articles in East European and American Jewish newspapers, some of which relate to halakhic issues and others to contemporary aspects of American Jewry and Judaism, and contributed several entries to Judah *Eisenstein's encyclopedia, *Ozar Yisrael.*

BIBLIOGRAPHY: K. Caplan, *Ortodoksi'ah ba-Olam ha-Ḥadash: Rabbanim ve-Darshanut be-Amerikah (1881–1924)* (2002), 348–49; N.M. Kaganoff, *Organized Jewish Group Activity in 19th Century Massachusetts* (1979), 27, 29, 39, 232, 309, 311, 362; M.D. Sherman, *Orthodox Judaism in America: A Biographical Dictionary and Sourcebook* (1996), 70–72.

[Kimmy Caplan (2nd ed.)

FRIEDJUNG, HEINRICH (1851–1920), Austrian historian. Friedjung became professor of history in 1873 at Wiener Handelsakademie and participated in Georg von *Schoenerer's pan-German movement but parted with Schoenerer because of the latter's antisemitism. Dismissed from his post by the Education Ministry in 1881 for his radical political publicity, Friedjung entered upon a journalistic career. He founded and edited *Deutsche Wochenschrift* (1883–86) and became editor-in-chief of *Deutsche Zeitung*, the main publication of the Deutschnationale Partei. From 1891 to 1895, Friedjung was a member of the Vienna City Council. Because of growing antisemitism he had to leave the party and subsequently focused on scholarly works on the German Confederation, the Second German Empire, and the era of Francis Joseph. His *Der Kampf um die Vorherrschaft in Deutschland 1859–1869* (2 vols., 1907) went through 10 editions and spread his fame beyond the frontiers of Austria. His other works were *Benedeks Nachgelassene Papiere* (1904), *Oesterreich 1848–1860* (unfinished, 1907–12), and *Krimkrieg und die oesterreichische Politik* (1911²). His scholarly *Das Zeitalter des Imperialismus* (3 vols., 1919–22) was completed after his death by A.F. Pribram. Friedjung's Jewish origin barred him from a post at Vienna University, and, while he had little interest in Jewish affairs, he considered it undignified to buy a career through conversion.

ADD. BIBLIOGRAPHY: H. Bachmann, "Heinrich Friedjung 1851–1920,": in: *Die Juden in den Böhmischen Ländern* (1983), 201–08; R. Eder, *Heinrich Friedjung* (1991); A. Dechel, *Das "Linzer Programm" und seine Autoren – Seine Vorgeschichte unter besonderer Berücksichtigung der Rolle des Historikers Heinrich Friedjung* (1975).

[Herbert A. Strauss]

FRIEDKIN, WILLIAM (1935–), U.S. director. Born in Chicago, Illinois, Friedkin never went to college, instead going to work at WGN TV in Chicago just after finishing high school. There he directed hundreds of live television shows and documentaries. He then moved up to network television, but only after ten years did Friedkin have the opportunity to direct a feature film, *Good Times* (1967), with Sonny and Cher. He swiftly advanced to major motion pictures with *The Night They Raided Minsky's* (1968), and then directed a number of successful, critically acclaimed films, including *The Boys in the Band* (1970), a landmark film that introcuded gay life to a mainstream audience. He directed *The French Connection* (1971), which won five academy awards, including Best Picture and Best Director. Friedkin, then 32 years old, became the youngest person to win the Oscar for directing. Friedkin followed up this triumph with *The Exorcist* (1973), revolutionizing the horror genre. His other films include *Sorcerer* (1977), *The Brink's Job* (1978), *Cruising* (1980), *To Live and Die in L.A.* (1985), *The Guardian* (1990), *Blue Chips* (1994), *Jade* (1995), *Rules of Engagement* (2000), and *The Hunted* (2003). In 1998 he was nominated for an Emmy award for Outstanding Direction for the TV movie adaptation of *12 Angry Men*. Friedkin was married to actresses Jeanne Moreau, Lesley-Anne Down, and Kelly Lange. In 1991 he married actress/producer Sherry *Lansing.

ADD. BIBLIOGRAPHY: N. Segaloff, *Hurricane Billy: The Stormy Life and Films of William Friedkin* (1990); T. Clagett, *William Friedkin: Films of Aberration, Obsession, and Reality* (1990).

[Jonathan Licht / Casey Schwartz (2nd ed.)]

FRIEDLAENDER, DAVID (1750–1834), communal leader and author in Berlin, a pioneer of the practice and ideology of *assimilation and a forerunner of *Reform Judaism. Born in Koenigsberg, the son of a "protected Jew," Joachim Moses Friedlaender, a wholesale merchant, David settled in Berlin in 1770, and in 1776 established a silk factory there. As an expert in his field he was appointed counselor of the state commission of inquiry into the textile industry. In 1791 he forwarded a memorandum in the name of the manufacturers, advocating changes in the economic system against excessive government supervision over industry and the granting of protective tariffs to individual manufacturers. However, his interests ranged far beyond his business activities. Entering Moses *Mendelssohn's circle at the age of 21, Friedlaender absorbed Mendelssohn's ideas and became prominent among his followers. Through his marriage in 1772 with Blümchen Itzig, daughter of the banker Daniel *Itzig, he entered one of the wealthiest and most distinguished families of *Court Jews in Prussia.

In 1799 Friedlaender sent his famous *Sendschreiben* ("Open Letter") to Pastor Teller in which he expressed, "in the name of some Jewish householders," a deistic conception of religion. For this reason he rejected Christian dogma as well as the retention of Jewish ritual precepts. According to him the eternal truths around which enlightened Jews and Protestants should unite were synonymous with the pure teachings of Moses, i.e., with original Jewish monotheism. Throughout his life Friedlaender regarded Mosaic monotheism as an ideal to be followed; it was apparently the positive factor in his decision (in which he differed from many of his circle) against conversion to Christianity. "We are destined from time immemorial to guard and teach by example the pure doctrine of the unity and sanctity of God, previously unknown to any other people," Friedlaender wrote in 1815 in his *Reden der Erbauung* ("Edifying Speeches"). In his respect for biblical Judaism he was a faithful disciple of Mendelssohn, although Kant, who exercised an influence on Friedlaender, disparaged biblical Judaism. Friedlaender shared the educational ideals and belief in liturgical reform current among representatives of the Jewish enlightenment in Berlin after Mendelssohn, giving expression to these ideas in his writings.

After the issue of the 1812 edict in Prussia he published a paper on the reforms which he deemed necessary as a result of the new organization of the Jews in Prussia (reform of the divine service in the synagogues, of teaching institutions and subjects taught, and of their manner of education in general). Above all, he proposed substituting in the prayer in place of the expression of messianic hopes: "I stand here before God. I pray for blessing and prosperity for my compatriots, for myself and my family, not for the return to Jerusalem, not for the restoration of the Temple and the sacrifices. I do not harbor these wishes in my heart." He proposed that study of talmudic law should be replaced by study of the laws of the country. Friedlaender even wanted to enlist the help of the government in his endeavors for reform. In part as a result of his efforts, a "Jewish free school" was established in 1778; Friedlaender became the organizer and supervisor of the school, which he directed for almost 20 years, with his brother-in-law Isaac Daniel Itzig, along with the Hebrew press and bookshop associated with it. The institution aimed at putting into practice the ideals of enlightened education.

From 1783 to 1812 Friedlaender, as the representative of Prussian Jewry, fought assiduously for the implementation of its demands for equal rights. He headed the "general deputies" of the Jewish communities of Prussia who assembled in Berlin in order to submit their requests to the commission set up by Frederick William II in 1787. Under Friedlaender's leadership, the deputies rejected the unsatisfactory "Plan for Reform" proposed by the commission. In 1793 he published the documents pertaining to these negotiations under the title *Acktenstücke, die Reform der jüdischen. Kolonien in den preussischen Staaten betreffend.* In 1809 Friedlaender was the first Jew elected to sit in the municipal council. Continuing the struggle for emancipation, in 1810 he requested an audience with the Prussian chancellor, Carl August von *Hardenberg; as an argument in favor of granting emancipation he pointed to the "wave of baptisms" which indicated the degree of assimilation of Prussian Jewry. Friedlaender's efforts for the emancipation of Prussian Jews are especially important since in them are reflected the main dilemma of Jewish life in Prussia in the first generation after Mendelssohn: how to hold fast to a Jewish identity within a society based on universalist principles.

BIBLIOGRAPHY: M.A. Meyer, *The Origins of the Modern Jew* (1967); M. Eliav, Ha-Ḥinnukh ha-Yehudi be-Germanyah (1961); H. Fischer, *Judentum, Staat und Heer in Preussen* (1968). **ADD. BIBLIOGRAPHY:** H. Ritter, *David Friedlaender* (1861); S.M. Lowenstein, *The Jewishness of David Friedländer* … (1994); E. Friedländer, *Das Handelshaus Joachim Moses Friedlaender* … (1913).

[Michael J. Graetz]

FRIEDLAENDER, ISRAEL (1876–1920), scholar, Zionist, community activist. Friedlander was born In Kovel, Poland, and raised In Praga-Warsaw. After proving his ability at an early age to master biblical and rabbinic texts, he moved, like many promising scholars of his generation, to Berlin, where he enrolled in the Hildesheimer Rabbinical Seminary. Matriculating at the University of Berlin, he then transferred to the new German University of Strasbourg, where he earned a Ph.D. in Semitic languages under Theodor Noeldeke. In his dissertation, he argued for the purity of the Arabic language in Maimonides's *Guide to the Perplexed.*

Denied a German University post because of antisemitism, in 1903, Friedlaender welcomed an invitation by Solomon *Schechter to join the faculty of the reorganized Jewish Theological Seminary as a professor of Bible. Two years later, he married Lilian Ruth Bentwich, daughter of the prominent British Zionist Herbert *Bentwich.

Friedlaender's scholarly *oeuvre* was, in large part, devoted to drawing previously ignored connections between medieval Arabic and Jewish cultures, focusing upon their similarities in the areas of messianism, sectarian heterodoxy, and folklore. His writings include "The Heterodoxies of the Shiites in the Presentation of Ibn Hazm," in: *Journal of the American Oriental Society*, 27 and 29 (1907–8); "Shiitic Elements in Jewish Sectarianim," in: *Jewish Quarterly Review*, n.s. 1, 2, 3 (1910–1913); and *Die Chadirlegende und der Alexanderroman* (1913).

From Berlin the young Friedlaender had contacted the Jewish philosopher *Ahad Ha-Am and the historian Simon *Dubnow. He translated their writings throughout his career, and after 1905 transmitted their ideas in essays and public lectures delivered in many North American cities.

Friedlaender developed his social thought along lines laid out by Ahad Ha-Am. His view of the diaspora was influenced by Dubnow. While his Seminary colleagues remained ensconced in their ivory tower, Friedlaender also took part in communal activity. He and his friends Harry Friedenwald, Henrietta *Szold, and Judah *Magnes kept the FAZ (Federation of American Zionists) afloat in the lean years before World War I. His explications of Zionist history and ideology helped to convince Louis D. *Brandeis to seize the helm of the movement during the Great War.

Friedlaender aided Judah Magnes in founding the New York Kehillah and chaired its Bureau of Jewish Education. He founded together with Mordecai *Kaplan the first Young Israel synagogue where the sermon was given in English. Friedlaender was a trustee of the Educational Alliance, which helped Americanize immigrants. There he became a gadfly, advising the secularists who controlled the organization to schedule clubs, classes, and lectures with Jewish content.

The shock of war in 1914 turned Friedlaender's attention to Jewish suffering in Eastern Europe. In 1915, he published a short popular history of that community. His translation of Dubnow's *History of the Jews of Russia and Poland* appeared in three volumes between 1916 and 1920. Dubnow himself never published this work, so the English translation is the only available version. A collection of Friedlaender's essays entitled *Past and Present*, was published in 1919 and reprinted in part in 1961.

Two crises marked Friedlaender's final years. In 1918 he was appointed the Jewish representative on a Red Cross expedition to Palestine. As he was preparing to depart, New York newspapers published letters by prominent Zionists Stephen S. Wise and Richard Gottheil. Unfairly citing Friedlaender's previous ties to Germany, they recommended his removal from the commission on the grounds of disloyalty. In anger and sadness, Friedlaender resigned his place in the expedition.

To assuage the disappointment, the American Jewish Joint Distribution Committee (JDC) appointed Friedlaender to a commission formed to aid Jews in Ukraine, where postwar national frustrations and historic enmity had erupted into ferocious pogroms. In July 1920, Friedlaender and Rabbi Bernard *Cantor ventured into a battle-torn area near Kamenetz-Podolski. They were murdered on a lonely road and left naked in the mud. Despite careful investigation, neither the motive nor the identity of the killers was discovered. The Jewish community of Yarmolyntsi, the nearest town, buried the bodies and put up a crude monument.

Denied access to the cemetery from 1922 onward until Ukrainian independence, in 2001, at the request of Friedlaender's Jerusalem family, his body was exhumed and found its final resting place in the land of his dreams.

BIBLIOGRAPHY: B.R. Shargel, *Practical Dreamer: Israel Friedlaender and the Shaping of American Judaism* (1985); L. Friedlaender, J. Magnes, and A. Marx's tributes to Friedlaender, in: *Menorah Journal*, 6 (Dec., 1920); B. Cohen, *Israel Friedlaender: A Bibliography of his Writing with an Appreciation* (1936); M. Bentwich, *Lilian Ruth Friedlaender, A Biography* (1957).

[Baila Round Shargel (2nd ed.)]

FRIEDLAENDER, JOHNNY (1912–1992), French painter and printmaker. Friedlaender studied in Breslau, but after Hitler came to power, managed to immigrate to Czechoslovakia (1935) and from there to Paris (1937), where he fought with the Resistance. In 1945 Friedlaender returned to Paris and represented France in various international exhibitions. Friedlaender was particularly noted for his color etchings. His poetic and occasionally whimsical etchings are extremely decorative.

FRIEDLAENDER, MAX (1852–1934), musicologist. Born in Brieg, Silesia, Friedlaender became a noted bass singer, but after 1883 devoted himself to musicology. He accepted a teaching post at Berlin University in 1894 where he became professor. Friedlaender was an authority on German song. He discovered more than 100 lost songs by Schubert and published them in his complete edition of Schubert's songs. He also edited songs by Mozart, Beethoven, and Mendelssohn, and collections of German folk songs. His writings include the basic *Das deutsche Lied im 18. Jahrhundert* (3 vols., 1902) and *Franz Schubert: Skizze seines Lebens und Wirkens* (1928).

FRIEDLAENDER, MICHAEL (1833–1910), Orientalist, educator, and author. Born in Jutrosin (Posen province), Friedlaender served first as head of the *talmud torah* school in Berlin (from 1862), and from 1865 as principal of *Jews' College, London, Anglo-Jewry's rabbinical seminary, which under his leadership first became a fully developed rabbinical seminary. He remained in this position for 45 years, and exercised a great influence on generations of graduates. He published a German translation (with commentary) of the Song of Songs (*Das Hohelied*, 1867). His illustrated *Jewish Family Bible* (Hebrew and English, 1881, 1884, repr. 1953) became very popular, as did his standard work *Jewish Religion* (1891, 1913³) and its companion volume *Textbook of the Jewish Religion* (1891), which was also reprinted in many editions. Both represent a strictly traditionalist view.

He took an active part in the Society for the Diffusion of Jewish Literature under whose aegis he published his works on *Ibn Ezra and *Maimonides. The first was an edition of Abraham Ibn Ezra's commentary on Isaiah with an English translation together with the English translation of Isaiah, revised in accordance with Ibn Ezra's commentary, as well as a volume of essays on the latter's writings (4 vols., 1873–77; vols. 1 and 3 repr. 1964). His translation into English (with annotations) of Maimonides' *Guide of the Perplexed* (3 vols., 1881–85; repr. 1953) was an edition which owed much to S. Munk's Arabic text and translation (1856–66). A revised one-volume edition of the English translation (without the notes, 1904 and many reprints) was long the standard English version of the *Guide*. He took an active part in the communal and cultural life of Anglo-Jewry. His knowledge of mathematics and astronomy made him an expert on the Jewish calendar. Moses *Gaster was his son-in-law.

BIBLIOGRAPHY: JC (May 8, 1903 and Dec. 16, 1910); I. Cohen, in: L. Jung, ed., *Men of the Spirit* (1964), 467–76; *Jews College Jubilee Volume* (1906), xxxi–lxvi. **ADD. BIBLIOGRAPHY:** *Biographisches Handbuch der Rabbiner*, vol. 1 (2004), 345–46.

FRIEDLAENDER, MORITZ (1844–1919), writer, educator, and communal worker. Friedlaender, who was born in Hungary, studied for the rabbinate, but did not adopt it because of his liberal views. In 1875 he became secretary of the Israelitische Allianz, the Austro-Hungarian counterpart of the Alliance Israélite Universelle, and on behalf of both organizations visited Galicia to assist the immigration of Russian Jews to the United States. With the help of Baron Maurice de Hirsch and later of his widow, Friedlaender established and supervised more than 50 modern schools for boys, as well as vocational schools for girls in Galicia.

Friedlaender's scholarly interests lay in the direction of Hellenistic philosophy and the origins of Christianity. Among his published works are *Ueber den Einfluss der griechischen Philosophie auf das Judentum und Christentum* (1872); *Patristische und talmudische Studien* (1878); *Philo's Philantropie des juedischen Gesetzes*, translation and commentary (1889); *Apion, ein Kulturbild* (1882); *Zur Entstehungsgeschichte des Christentums* (1894); *Der vorchristliche juedische Gnostizismus* (1898); *Geschichte der juedischen Apologetik* (1903); *Die religio-*

ese Bewegung innerhalb des Judentums im Zeitalter Jesu (1906); *Der Kreuzestod Jesu* (1906). Friedlaender also wrote on his experiences in Galicia: *Fuenf Wochen in Brody* (1882) and *Reiseerinnerungen aus Galizien* (1900). He used the pseudonyms M. Freimann, Marek Firkowitsch, and Paul Frieda.

FRIEDLAENDER, OSKAR EWALD (1881–1940), Austrian philosopher. Friedlaender, who was born in Slovakia, taught in Vienna. Writing under the name "Ewald," he dealt with Kantianism, history of philosophy, and philosophy of religion. He opposed ethical relativism and empiricism. Friedlaender dealt with the relationship of romanticism to contemporary philosophy as well as offering an interpretation of Kant. In later writings, he sought to develop an undogmatic religion of humanity. His main works are *Richard Avenarius als Begruender des Empiriokritizismus* (1905), *Die Probleme der Romantik als Grundfragen der Gegenwart* (1904), *Kants kritischer Idealismus als Grundlage von Erkenntnistheorie und Ethik* (1908), *Die Religion des Lebens* (1925), and *Freidenkertum und Religion* (1927).

[Richard H. Popkin]

FRIEDLAENDER, SAUL (1932–), Israeli historian of the Third Reich and Holocaust. Born in Prague, Friedlaender fled with his family to France in 1939, where he was hidden in a Catholic boarding school following the German invasion of 1940. While in hiding, he developed a keen interest in Catholicism and even considered the priesthood. But when he was informed by one of his Catholic teachers about the Nazi genocide at the war's end, Friedlaender decided to reembrace his Jewish roots and moved to Israel in 1948, where he eventually embarked on a career as a historian.

Friedlaender long split his time as a historian between Europe, Israel, and the United States. From 1964 to 1987, he taught at the Institut des Hautes Etudes Internationales in Geneva, at first as a senior lecturer and after 1967 as professor. In that same year, he accepted a visiting professorship at the Hebrew University of Jerusalem and in 1969 was appointed professor of history and international relations. Friedlander remained in Jerusalem until 1975 at which point he moved to Tel Aviv University, where he was named Maxwell Cummings Chair of European History. In 1987 Friedlander was appointed to the 1939 Club Chair in Holocaust Studies at the University of California at Los Angeles, a position that he shared with his Tel Aviv post until retiring from the latter in 2000.

Friedlaender applied innovative methodologies to the study and writing of history. He began his academic career as a diplomatic historian, producing two incisive works in the mid-1960s: *Hitler et les Etats-Unis 1939–41* (1963; *Prelude to Downfall: Hitler and the United States*, 1967) and *Pie XII et le IIIe Reich* (1964; *Pius XII and the Third Reich*, 1966). The first study examined the diplomatic relations between Nazi Germany and the administration of Franklin D. *Roosevelt, while the second critically analyzed Pope *Pius XII's response to the Holocaust.

Friedlaender then turned towards psychology. His book *Kurt Gerstein, l'ambiguité du bien* (1967; *Kurt Gerstein; the Ambiguity of Good*, 1969), examined the complex motivations of a German SS officer who was involved in the Nazi Final Solution but later turned against it by attempting to inform neutral and Church figures of the gassing of Jews. His study *L'Histoire et psychoanalyse* (1975; *History and Psychoanalysis*, 1978) directly explored the virtues and limitations of psychoanalysis for historical inquiry.

Friedlaender's interest in psychology naturally led him to the study of historical memory. Friedlaender investigated the dynamics of remembrance at the individual level in his powerful autobiographical work, *Quand vient le souvenir* (1978; *When Memory Comes*, 1979), which focused on his own traumatic childhood in German-occupied France. Thereafter, he turned his attention to the study of cultural memory in *Reflets du nazisme* (1982; *Reflections of Nazism: A Study of Kitsch and Death*, 1984), which examined the lingering psychological appeal of Nazi imagery in works of contemporary European film and literature. Friedlaender expressed the concern that the memory of the Third Reich was becoming normalized within western consciousness and defined less by moral outrage than lurid fascination. By the late 1980s, he voiced these fears in a famous debate with the German historian, Martin Broszat over the "historicization" of the Nazi era. At a time in which conservative German historians were attempting to relativize the Nazis' crimes in an effort to create a normal sense of German national identity (the "Historians' Debate"), Friedlaender insisted that the singular nature of the Nazis' genocidal crimes against the Jews should prevent historians from viewing the 12 years of the Third Reich as they would any other era of German history.

In the 1990s, Friedlaender continued to explore theoretical issues while simultaneously returning to the empirically grounded and narrative-centered history of his early career. His 1992 volume *Probing the Limits of Representation* (based on a 1990 conference held at UCLA) explored the relevance of postmodern thought for the representation of the Final Solution. Sparked in part by American historian Hayden White's relativistic observations about the truth claims of all historical writing, Friedlander became deeply interested in the question of whether all methods of portraying the Holocaust were equally valid. His ensuing work of historical synthesis, published in 1997, *Nazi Germany and the Jews, Volume I: The Years of Persecution, 1933–1939*, examined the origins of the Final Solution from the interwoven perspective of the Nazi perpetrators as well as their Jewish victims, a pathbreaking approach that brought together narrative vantage points that had been kept apart by most previous historians. From the end of the 1990s, Friedlaender was busy completing the final volume of his two-volume study.

Friedlaender was involved in numerous other historical enterprises. Early in his career he worked closely with Nahum *Goldmann of the World Jewish Congress and with Shimon *Peres. He helped found the influential journal *His-*

tory & Memory in 1989. He served on the commission that examined the activities of the Bertelsmann publishing concern during the Third Reich and chaired the Independent Experts Commission that in 1999 issued a highly critical report on the policies of the Swiss government towards Jewish refugees during World War II. He was involved in Israeli-Palestinian dialogues and with leading Palestinian intellectuals such as Edward Said. For his outstanding scholarly achievements, Friedlaender was honored with the Israel Prize for history in 1983, the Geschwister-Scholl-Prize from the city of Munich in 1998, and a MacArthur Foundation "genius" Award in 1999.

[Gavriel Rosenfeld (2nd ed.)]

FRIEDLAENDER (Friedland), SOLOMON JUDAH (c. 1860–c. 1923), author and literary forger. Friedlaender gave contradictory biographical accounts of his life, claiming at various times to have been born in Hungary, Turkey, and Romania, but in all probability he was born in Beshenkovichi near Vitebsk, Belorussia. He supposedly studied at the yeshivah in Volozhin and afterward wandered throughout Europe. He was in Czernowitz (1880–1882), Mainz (1884), Frankfurt on the Main (1885), Mulhouse (c. 1888–c. 1895), Waitzen (1900–1902), Naszod (1902–1906), and finally in Szatmar, from 1906 onward. It seems that he died in Vienna. Friedlaender published a number of works of doubtful authenticity or pure forgeries. Among these were (1) *Ha-Tikkun*, published under the name of L. Friedland in Czernowitz in 1881. It pretends to be an authentic manual of ḥasidic customs, while in fact it is a crude and obscene parody of Ḥasidism in general and *Ḥabad Ḥasidism in particular; (2) *Tosefta, Seder Zera'im* and *Seder Nashim*, published in Pressburg in 1889 and 1890, with his commentary entitled *Ḥosak Shelomo*. He claimed to have edited a critical edition of the Tosefta text from an unpublished manuscript, but this was disputed by Adolf Schwarz and Rabbi Jacob Yanovsky of Kiev. Friedlaender responded to Schwarz's strictures in a pamphlet entitled *Kesher Bogedim* (Pressburg, 1891), replete with irrelevant matters and squalid abuse of his critics; (3) an edition of the tractate *Yevamot* of the Jerusalem Talmud, supposedly from a manuscript, along with a twofold commentary, *Ḥeshek Shelomo*, in Szinervaralja in 1905.

Friedlaender's most important forgery, however, was his pretended *Seder Kodashim* of the Jerusalem Talmud. Friedlaender proclaimed his fortunate discovery of an ancient Spanish manuscript, dated Barcelona 1212, which contained this long lost and most important talmudic text. He published *Zevaḥim* and *Arakhin* in 1907, and *Ḥullin* and *Bekhorot* in 1909, with his commentary *Ḥeshek Shelomo*. With these publications, he reached the summit of his audacity, claiming to be of pure Sephardi descent (*Sephardi tahor*) from the well-known Algazi family and a native of Smyrna. He asserted that he was assisted in the acquisition of the manuscript by his brother, Elijah Algazi, and a business associate of the latter, both citizens of Smyrna. Some of the leading scholars of this period, such as Solomon *Buber, Solomon *Shechter, and Shalom Mordecai *Schwadron of Brzezany accepted his story. However, the majority of scholars gave no credence to his tales, and B. Ritter of Rotterdam conclusively proved the fallaciousness of Friedlaender's claims. On the basis of internal evidence, Ritter showed that the text was an overt forgery. Ritter's conclusions were supported by many experts, including V. *Aptowitzer, W. *Bacher, D.B. Ratner and Meir Dan *Plotzki. The controversy continued for the next few years, and as late as 1913, Friedlaender still published booklets on this issue. He also edited a periodical entitled *Ha-Gan*, using the name of Judah Aryeh Friedland. It seems that only one issue appeared in Frankfurt in 1885. After his death, his son, M. Friedlaender, published his *Mavo la-Tosefta*, in Tirnovo, 1930. Friedlaender claimed at various times to have published, among others, a critical and annotated edition of the entire Tosefta, the *She'iltot* of Rav Aḥai Gaon, and the Sifra. No bibliographical evidence can be found to support these claims.

BIBLIOGRAPHY: B. Ritter, in: *Der Israelit*, 1907 and 1908; D.B. Ratner, in: *Haolam*, 1 (1907), 26ff.; *Tel-Talpioth*, 1907 and 1908.

[Abraham Schischa]

FRIEDLAND, East European family originating in Bohemia, presumably from the Bohemian town Friedland (Frydlant). During the 17th century NATHAN FRIEDLAND was known as the "head of the community and head of the province of Bohemia." During the 19th century, members of the family are found in Russia. MESHULLAM FEIVEL (1804–1854), a wealthy merchant of Slutsk, moved to Dvinsk in 1846 and was often among the delegates representing the communities of Lithuania before the authorities. His sons MEIR (d. 1902) and MOSES ARYEH LEIB (1826–1899) moved to St. Petersburg, where they ranked among the wealthiest Jews and philanthropists in the community. Moses for more than 30 years was general army contractor for the Russian government. He founded a Jewish orphanage with a school of handicrafts in St. Petersburg, and erected an old-age home in Jerusalem. In 1892 he presented his collection of about 13,000 Hebrew books (including 32 incunabula) and 300 manuscripts which he had assembled over many years to the Asiatic Museum in St. Petersburg (now the Leningrad Institute for Oriental Studies). The thousands of Hebrew books already in the museum were combined with his collection, given the name of Bibliotheca Friedlandiana. The bibliographer S. *Wiener catalogued these books (up to the letter *lamed*) in *Kohelet Moshe* (8 pts., 1893–1936). The genealogy and some of the history of the family is given by I.T. Eisenstadt and S. Wiener in *Da'at Kedoshim* (1897).

BIBLIOGRAPHY: S. Wiener, *Kohelet Moshe*, pt. 2 (1895), vii–xi.

[Yehuda Slutsky]

FRIEDLAND, ABRAHAM HYMAN (Ḥayyim Abraham; 1891–1939), poet, short-story writer, and educator. Friedland, who was born in Hordok, near Vilna, immigrated to America at the age of 15. In 1911 he founded the National Hebrew School in New York. In 1921 he assumed the post of superintendent of the Cleveland Hebrew Schools, and in 1924 was also appointed the first director of the Cleveland Bureau of Jewish Education. He was a leading member of the Jewish community in Cleveland and a champion of the community Jewish school which featured an intensive Hebraic curriculum and included a strong emphasis on the Zionist ideal. He wrote poems, short stories, and articles, edited educational texts, and published essays in Hebrew, English, and Yiddish on Hebrew literature. His poems and stories were collected in two volumes at the end of his life, *Sonettot* ("Sonnets," 1939), and *Sippurim* ("Stories," 1939), and in a posthumous volume of poems, *Shirim* ("Poems," 1940). His *Sippurim Yafim*, stories designed for children, were reissued in three volumes by the Cleveland Bureau of Jewish Education (1962). His narrative sonnets deal with the pathetic side of life, and his stories mainly portray American Jewish types.

BIBLIOGRAPHY: A. Epstein, *Soferim Ivrim be-Amerikah*, 2 (1952), 311–23; Waxman, Literature, 4 (1960), 1251–55; A. Ben-Or, *Toledot ha-Sifrut ha-Ivrit be-Dorenu*, 1 (1954), 139–41; *Sefer Zikhronot le-Ḥ.A. Friedland* (1940).

[Eisig Silberschlag]

FRIEDLAND, NATAN (1808–1883), rabbi, precursor of the *Ḥibbat Zion movement. Born in Taurage, Lithuania, Friedland studied in various Lithuanian yeshivot. The *Damascus Affair (1840) made a deep impression on him. He believed that the redemption of the Jewish people could be realized gradually, as a natural process, and periods of liberalism and progress should be used to achieve this. The miraculous redemption would ultimately occur with the arrival of the Messiah. Friedland was unaware that some of his contemporaries held similar views (e.g., Judah *Alkalai), and he spread his ideas verbally in Belorussia, Lithuania, and Germany, where he met Ẓevi *Kalischer. In 1859 he published two parts of his work *Kos Yeshu'ah u-Neḥamah* ("Cup of Salvation and Comfort"), in which he expounded his theories. Friedland met Adolphe *Crémieux and Albert *Cohen in Paris, and presented petitions from Kalischer and himself to Napoleon III, who granted him an audience. Sir Moses *Montefiore, whom he met in London, refused to cooperate with him. Friedland published a new edition of Kalischer's work *Derishat Ẓiyyon*, adding his own notes and essays. Friedland was an emissary of Ḥevrah le-Yishuv Ereẓ Israel ("Society for the Settlement of Ereẓ Israel"), established by Kalischer, and collected funds for it in Germany. During his visit to Holland, he handed the Dutch government a petition requesting their support for the restoration of Ereẓ Israel to the Jews. His greatest work, *Yosef Ḥen*, expounding his views, was published in a shortened version (1879). At the end of his life, he witnessed the beginnings of *aliyah* to Ereẓ Israel from Romania and Russia. In 1882 he went to Ereẓ Israel from London and died in Jerusalem.

BIBLIOGRAPHY: Klausner, in: *Ha-Ummah*, 18 (1967), 227–45.

[Israel Klausner]

FRIEDLANDER, ISAAC (1823–1878), U.S. businessman. Friedlander, born in Oldenburg, Germany, was taken to the U.S. as a child. After working in New York City and then in Savannah, Georgia, he went to San Francisco in 1849 to mine gold. Turning to business, Friedlander soon came to dominate the California flour market and in 1854 erected the Eureka Flour Mills, the largest in the state. He earned the title "Grain King" while speculating in the wheat market and by 1872 controlled nearly all California grain exported to foreign ports. A struggle by the California farmers' organization to circumvent him and export grain independently was unsuccessful. Friedlander also financed grain elevators and an irrigation project. He was one of the first regents of the University of California and was president of the San Francisco Chamber of Commerce.

BIBLIOGRAPHY: Paul, in: *Pacific Historical Review*, 27 (1958), 331–49; Anon, in: *California Mail Bag*, 9 (June 1876), 17–19; Reissner, in: YLBI, 10 (1965), 78.

FRIEDLANDER, KATE (1902–1949), criminologist and psychiatrist. After having completed her general medical studies in her native Innsbruck, she moved to Berlin where she specialized in mental and nervous diseases. She also trained as a psychoanalyst and worked as a specialist at the juvenile court in Berlin. In 1933 she migrated to London along with another prominent Jewish psychoanalyst, Paula Heimann (1899–1982), who later became a prominent child psychiatrist in London. Friedlander's main achievements were in the application of psychoanalysis to the theoretical and practical problems of dissocial character formation. Her book *The Psycho-Analytical Approach to Juvenile Delinquency* (1947, 1959[2]) is an important contribution to the understanding and treatment of juvenile delinquents. One of her principal interests, to which she devoted much of her life, was child guidance work for the elimination of unhappiness among children (in cooperation with Anna *Freud). She wrote many papers, most of which dealt with the emotional development of the child and were aimed at preventing juvenile delinquency and antisocial wayward behavior in general.

BIBLIOGRAPHY: Hoffer, in: *International Journal of Psycho-Analysis*, 30 (1949), 138–9; Jacobs, in: *New Era*, 30 (1949), 101–3.

[Zvi Hermon]

FRIEDLANDER, LEE (1934–), U.S. photographer. Born in Aberdeen, Wash., Friedlander took up photography at 14 and moved to California after graduation from high school. In 1956, he went to New York, where he became friendly with photographers like Robert *Frank, Walker Evans, Diane *Arbus, and Helen Levitt, and where he supported himself by taking pictures of jazz, blues, and gospel performers for various recording companies. He seems to have been greatly influenced by Frank, whose book *The Americans*, came out in 1958. Like Frank's photographs, Friedlander's were interpreted as a mirror of American society. His images were less emotional, however.

He got his first solo exhibition in the George Eastman House in Rochester, N.Y. in 1963. He always worked in series:

street images, flowers, trees, nudes, the industrial and postindustrial environment, portraits, and self-portraits. Among the important series he produced in the late 1970s and early 1980s was a reportage of forgotten memorials to events in American history, portraits of North American industrial areas threatened with unemployment, and photographs of computer operators. He thus gave shape to the banality of daily life and recorded the complexity of the American social landscape from a strong appreciation of the importance of formal values. His street scenes appear to be casual but are complicated compositions. The nudes reflect an almost obsessive attempt to capture the naked female body as it really is. He did not use models, but normal, reasonably well-shaped women marked by acne, bruises, fat, etc. He was also considered a master of the frame; his photographs nearly always include more details, telling or not, than the viewer expects. He used a viewfinder 35-millimeter camera and photographed in black and white. He received three Guggenheim fellowships, five grants from the National Endowment for the Arts and was awarded a MacArthur Foundation "genius" grant in 1990. More than a dozen books of his works have been published. He had one-man shows at the Museum of Modern Art in New York in 1972, 1974, and 1991. In 2001 MOMA acquired more than 1,000 of Friedlander's prints, spanning his entire career from the 1950s to work that had not yet been made public. It was the museum photography department's biggest purchase ever of works by a living artist.

[Stewart Kampel (2nd ed.)]

FRIEDLANDER, WALTER (1891–1984), U.S. social welfare expert and educator, born in Berlin. Friedlander was trained in law, began his career as a welfare worker among children, and later served as a juvenile court judge in Berlin. From 1931 to 1933 he was president of the German Child Welfare League. Moving to Paris in 1933, he served three years as the director of the Legal and Social Services for Refugees. Immigrating to the U.S., he lectured at the University of Chicago from 1936 to 1943 and then went to the University of California, Berkeley. Starting off at Berkeley as a lecturer in social welfare, he became an associate professor in 1948, then professor (1955) and professor emeritus (1959). After his retirement, he continued to teach as a visiting professor, first at Michigan State University (1959–60) and then at the University of Minnesota (1963–64).

Friedlander wrote a number of textbooks on social welfare, including *Youth in Distress* (1922) and *Introduction to Social Welfare* (1955). The latter has been republished in five editions, the last in 1980 (with Dr. Robert Apte as co-author). It has been translated into 10 languages and is considered to be the most widely used introductory text in undergraduate colleges and professional schools in the U.S. and abroad. Friedlander also wrote *Individualism and Social Welfare* (1962) and *International Social Welfare* (1975), and edited *Concepts and Methods of Social Work* (1958).

Friedlander was a founder of the International Conference of Social Welfare and was a member of the International Association of Schools of Social Work. He also served as chair of the Commission on International Social Work of the local chapter of the National Association of Social Workers.

Among his many honors, he received a Fullbright Teaching Fellowship at the Free University of West Berlin (1956); he won the Social Worker of the Year Award of the National Association of Social Workers, Golden Gate Chapter (1971); he was awarded the Great Cross of Merit, as well as the Marie Juchacz Medal (1976), from the German Federal Republic, for his contributions to the development of German social services; and he received the Outstanding Social Worker citation of the Oakland (California) City Council (1978). In 1984 Friedlander's friends and colleagues created the Walter Friedlander Fund to Promote Education in International Social Welfare.

[Joseph Neipris / Ruth Beloff (2nd ed.)]

FRIEDMAN, BENJAMIN (**Benny**; 1905–1982), U.S. football player. Friedman was born in Cleveland, Ohio, the fourth of six children to Russian immigrants Mimi (Atlevonik) and Lewis, a ladies furrier and tailor. In 1923, he graduated from Glenville High School ranked as its top student, president of his senior class, and was chosen to deliver the commencement address. He starred in football, baseball, and basketball, leading the school to the 1922 Cleveland city championship and to the mythical national high school championship over Chicago's Oak Park High School.

The 5′8″, 172-pound Friedman then starred at the University of Michigan his last two and a half years as the consummate triple threat man – runner, passer, and kicker – who led the team to an 18–3 record in the games he was the starting quarterback. In his junior year the 1925 team outscored its opponents 227–3. The Wolverines finished the season ranked No. 2 in the nation, and Friedman was named a consensus first team All-American. In his senior year Friedman was named team captain, the first Jew to be so honored, as well as Big Ten Most Valuable Player and an All-American.

Friedman began playing professional football upon graduation in 1927, and immediately established himself as the game's first great passer, one who would throw anytime, and anywhere, to anybody. His multiple talents had a singular impact on the evolution of the sport, changing football from a straightforward running contest to the modern pass-and-run game.

Friedman played his first season with the Cleveland Bulldogs, for whom he threw a league-record 11 touchdown passes as a rookie, and while with the Detroit Wolverines the following season, he led the league in scoring, extra points, and rushing – to this day the only player in NFL history ever to lead the league in passing and rushing in a single season. The New York Giants then purchased the entire Detroit franchise in order to acquire the contract of Friedman, paying him a $10,000 salary as the highest-paid player in the pro ranks of his day, when most players were getting $100 a game. Friedman's first season with New York in 1929 saw him throw a record 20 touchdown passes – the next highest total was six – considered one of the greatest feats in NFL history, considering the passing rules in effect at the time and the watermelon shape of the ball. Friedman led the league in passing yards and touchdowns (11, 9, 20, and 13) his first four seasons, he was named All-Pro all four years, and his 66 career TD passes were an NFL record until 1944. He moved from the Giants to the Brooklyn Dodgers in 1932, but only played part-time for two more seasons as he began college coaching, first at Yale, and then from 1934 through 1941 as head football coach at City College of New York, compiling a 27–31–4 record. After serving as a lieutenant commander in the U.S. Navy in WWII, Friedman served as athletic director at Brandeis University from 1949 to 1963, as well as head coach of the school's football team from 1951 through 1959, when they discontinued the sport. His record was 34–32–4.

Ill health late in life left him despondent, and in 1982 he was found in his New York apartment dead of a self-inflicted gunshot wound.

Friedman attributed his good fortune to his mother's faith in Judaism and her practice of putting 18 cents in her *pushke* (charity box) every Saturday on his behalf. Friedman was never injured throughout his high school, college, and pro career. "I never questioned whether it was my ability that kept me aloof from injury. I let it go that it was *chai* working for me."

Friedman was elected as a charter member of the College Football Hall of Fame in 1951, and was elected to the Pro Hall of Fame in 2005. He is the author of *The Passing Game* (1931).

[Elli Wohlgelernter (2nd ed.)]

FRIEDMAN, BRUCE JAY (1930–), U.S. novelist and playwright. Friedman was regarded as one of the leaders of the school of "black humor." He was a frequent contributor to *Esquire*, the *Saturday Evening Post*, and the *New York Times Book Review*. His fiction includes *Stern* (1962), *Far from the City of Class* (1963), *A Mother's Kisses* (1964), *Black Angels* (1966), and *A Father's Kisses* (1996). The last edition of *The Collected Short Fiction of Bruce Jay Friedman* was published in 2000. His first play, the notable comedy *Scuba Duba* (1967), had a long run in New York.

BIBLIOGRAPHY: M. Schulz, *Bruce Jay Friedman* (1974).

FRIEDMAN, DEBORAH LYNN (1951–), singer and songwriter of late 20th century American Jewish liturgical and popular music. Beginning in the early 1970s, Friedman, a native of Utica, N.Y., produced 19 recordings and seven song books of contemporary Hebrew and English music. Her compositions combined traditional Jewish texts and liturgy with newly written lyrics and melodies influenced by both American and Israeli popular music. By the beginning of the 21st century, her liturgical music had "crossed over" from its initial origins in Reform Judaism's youth movement to Conservative and modern Orthodox congregations as well as to educational and camp settings. Many Christian groups also adopted some of her English religious songs. Friedman, who moved to New York City in 1995, gave a concert at Carnegie Hall in 1996 to commemorate 25 years of singing and song writing. Despite a terrible blizzard, thousands turned out to see her performance. That year she also won the Covenant Foundation Award for her impact in Jewish education and the ASCAP Annual Popular Awards.

Friedman's recordings included *Ani Ma'amin* (1976), *If Not Now, When* (1980), *And the Youths Shall See Visions* (1981), *And You Shall Be a Blessing* (1989), *Live at the Dell* (1990), *The World of Your Dreams* (1993), *Renewal of Spirit (1995), Debbie Friedman at Carnegie Hall* (1996), *It's You* (1998), *The Water in the Well* (2001), and *Light These Lights* (2001). Her song *Misheberach*, which she called a "sermon in song," became an anthem of the Jewish healing movement. Friedman's close association with feminist circles involved her in creating songs and settings for traditional and new Passover texts for the *Ma'yan Haggadah*, written in collaboration with Tamar Cohen, for use at women's seders.

Friedman's music caused controversy in the Jewish community. Many standard bearers of *ḥazzanut* opposed the entry of her music into the synagogue, claiming that it, lacked *nusaḥ* or any Jewish rootedness. However, the greater American Jewish community widely recognized her achievements: the National Federation of Temple Youth made her a lifetime member, and she was awarded the Jewish Fund for Justice Woman of Valor Award (1997). She was honored by the Jewish Women's Archive; received the Jewish Cultural Achievement Award in Performing Arts from the National Foundation for Jewish Culture in 2002; and received the Lion of Judah Award in 2004, among many other accolades.

[Judith S. Pinnolis (2nd ed.)]

FRIEDMAN, DÉNES (1903–1944), Hungarian rabbi and scholar. In 1927 he succeeded L. *Venetianer as rabbi of Ujpest, and in 1935 joined the staff of the Budapest rabbinical seminary. While still a student he edited, with D.S. *Loewinger, a manuscript of the *Alphabet of Ben Sira* (in *Ve-Zot li-Yhudah*, 1926). He wrote *A zsidó irodalom főrányai* ("The Main Trends of Jewish Literature," 1928). He prepared *Bibliographie der Schriften Ludwig Blaus* (1926; enlargement of Hg. ed., 1926), and biobibliographies of graduates of the Budapest rabbinical seminary (in *Magyar Zsidó Szemle*, 44 (1927), 340–68). When the Nazis invaded Hungary in 1944, Friedman was deported to his death after witnessing the murder of his only son.

BIBLIOGRAPHY: J. Wassermann (ed.), *Dr. Friedman Dénes irodalmi munkássága* (1943); List of his works; I. Hahn, *Az Országos Rabbiképzö Intézet Évkönyve*... (1946), 23–24.

[Baruch Yaron]

FRIEDMAN, HERBERT A. (1918–), U.S. rabbi, executive chairman of the national United Jewish Appeal for over 20 years. Born in New Haven, Conn., to immigrant parents, Friedman graduated from Yale University (B.A.) in 1938, attended Columbia University Graduate School of Business Administration, and graduated from the Jewish Institute of Religion with a M.H.L. degree. He was ordained as a rabbi in 1944. He served as a chaplain with the Ninth Infantry Division in Germany and after World War II spearheaded efforts to help Jewish survivors of the Nazi death camps, including work with *Beriḥah, while ministering to the needs of American soldiers. Later he served as assistant advisor on Jewish affairs to General Lucius D. Clay, commander of U.S. Occupation Forces in Germany, working with Rabbi Philip *Bernstein. His efforts included a visit to Kielce immediately after the July 4, 1946, pogrom that resulted in the decision to open the American sector to Jews fleeing Poland. During that period, he was secretly recruited into the *Haganah and worked in the *illegal immigration operation called "Aliyah Bet." He was subsequently decorated by the State of Israel for that service.

While serving an anti-Zionist congregation in Denver, he was active in clandestinely securing desperately needed arms for Israel. He was one of the founders of the Israel Bond organization, invited by David Ben-Gurion to the formation meeting in Jerusalem in September 1950. In 1955, he became the executive vice chairman of the UJA national campaign and executive chairman in 1970.

Throughout three decades he was present at critical moments in the life of Jewish communities in many countries: pogroms in Morocco in 1955; flight of Hungarian and Egyptian refugees in 1956; exodus from Romania in 1957. He also studied conditions in Iran, Poland, and Tunisia. Just before the outbreak of the Six-Day War in 1967, he was in Israel for talks with Jewish Agency and government leaders, which resulted in the historic Israel Emergency Fund that raised millions of dollars for Israel in the fearful days preceding the war and the immediate post-war euphoria.

He created the UJA Young Leadership Cabinet, bringing together young men and women from all over the country and instilling within them a philosophy of Judaism and a sense of commitment. He also created a peer network among the most Jewishly philanthropic young Jews. He developed the UJA Overseas Mission concept, which has escorted scores of thousands of American Jews to Israel, and many thousands to the sites of the Nazi camps. He established the Israel Education Fund, which built high schools, libraries, and kindergartens throughout the country. Friedman and his family settled in Jerusalem in 1971.

Upon returning to the U.S. in 1978, Friedman assumed the position of president of the American Friends of Tel Aviv University. At an age when many would retire, he entered an even more creative phase. He was co-founder with Leslie Wexner in 1985 of the Wexner Heritage Foundation, dedicated to the education of leadership groups in Jewish communities throughout the United States, training cadres of young and promising affluent and highly positioned Jews in a two-year seminar in Jewish history and tradition so that they are prepared to assume leadership roles.

BIBLIOGRAPHY: H.A. Friedman, *Roots to the Future* (1999).

[Lori Baron (2nd ed.)]

FRIEDMAN, JACOB (1910–1972), Yiddish poet. Born in Mielnica, Galicia, Friedman lived after World War I in Czernowitz, except for the years 1929–32, which he spent in Warsaw. In 1941 the Romanian authorities deported him to the Bershad camp in Transnistria. Liberated in March 1944, he eventually came to Bucharest and was active in the revival of Jewish cultural life there until 1947. He tried to make his way to Palestine, but reached Israel only in February 1949 after spending a year interned in Cyprus. His poetry, which he began publishing in 1927, is often filled with religious fervor. It acquired new depth due to his experience during and after the Holocaust. His lyrical and dramatic poems, first published in various journals, were included in several collections, among them: *Pastekher in Yisroel* ("Shepherds in Israel," 1953), *Libshaft* ("Love," 1967) and the posthumous *Lider un Poemes* ("Poems," 3 vols., 1974); four volumes appeared in Hebrew translation (1970, 1972, 1977, 1983).

BIBLIOGRAPHY: S. Bickel, *Shrayber fun Mayn Dor* (1958), 175–81. **ADD. BIBLIOGRAPHY:** LNYL, 7 (1968), 478–80; E. Sela-Saldinger, *A Torn Chord Trembling in the Dark*, 2 vols. (1996); idem, *From Transnistria to Israel* (2003).

FRIEDMAN, JEROME ISAAC (1930–), physicist. Friedman studied at the University of Chicago from which he received his A.B. (1950), his M.A. (1953), and his Ph.D. (1956) in physics. After working as a research associate there and at Stanford University, he joined the faculty of MIT in 1960, becoming a professor in 1967 and an institute professor in 1991. At MIT he was also the director of the laboratory for nuclear science (1980–83) and head of the physics department (1983–88). In addition, he served as president of the American Physical Society in 1999. He was co-recipient of the 1990 Nobel Prize in physics with Richard Taylor and Henry Kendall for work they had done at the Stanford Linear Acceleration Center 1967–73, which showed that protons and neutrons were composed of quarks rather than being fundamental particles. In doing so, they also proved the existence of quarks which had been regarded until then as theoretical and highly implausible by most of the physics community. Their work also established the experimental foundations for the development of quantum chromodynamics, the theory of the so-called strong force, which is responsible for binding quarks together to form all hadronic matter.

FRIEDMAN, KINKY (**Richard F.**; 1944–), U.S. country singer, novelist, political activist. Friedman was born in Chicago to Minnie and Tom, who had flown 35 bombing missions over Germany during World War II. The family moved to Texas, where Friedman's father was a speech therapist and an educational psychology professor at the University of Texas. The Friedmans also ran their own summer camp for children in the Texas hill country, called Echo Hill Ranch. It was there that young Richard Friedman began life as an entertainer, originating ideas for comedy routines on camp skit nights, and writing the winning songs for bunk song night.

Friedman founded his first band while at the University of Texas, King Arthur & the Carrots, a group that poked fun at surf music and recorded one single, "Schwinn 24" / "Beach Party Boo Boo" in 1966. After graduation, Friedman served in the Peace Corps from 1966 to 1968 in the jungles of Borneo.

In 1971, Friedman founded his second band, Kinky Friedman & the Texas Jewboys, an irreverent group reflected in their name as well as in their songs, which included "The Ballad of Charles Whitman," about the Texas sniper; satirical responses to antisemitism called "We Reserve the Right To Refuse Service To You" and "They Ain't Making Jews Like Jesus Anymore"; "Ride 'Em Jewboy," the only country song written about the Holocaust; and the politically incorrect, "Get Your Biscuits in the Oven & Your Buns in the Bed." Many Jewish-owned chain stores thought the name of the band was antisemitic or self-hating, and refused to carry the group's first album, *Sold American*. The group also elicited bomb threats from the Jewish Defense League.

In 1976, Friedman and his band toured with Bob Dylan & the Rolling Thunder Revue. That same year he made his third album, *Lasso from El Paso*, featuring Dylan and Eric Clapton. Three years later the Texas Jewboys disbanded and Friedman moved to New York, where he often appeared solo at the Lone Star Café sporting a yellow Star of David on his guitar strap. He also began writing mystery thrillers, featuring a Jewish country singer turned Greenwich Village private eye named Kinky Friedman, who, like his creator, always wore a black Stetson and smoked Cuban cigars. To everyone's surprise, Friedman's fiction was well received and a new career was born, resulting in 17 books in the detective series and five million books sold – including *Greenwich Killing Time* (1986), *Elvis, Jesus and Coca-Cola* (1993), *God Bless John Wayne* (1995), and *The Mile High Club* (2000); a non-fiction work, *Kinky Friedman's Guide to Texas Etiquette: Or How to Get to Heaven or Hell Without Going Through Dallas-Fort Worth* (2001); and a novel, *Ten Little New Yorkers* (2005), which Friedman announced would be his final literary effort.

In 1999, singers Willie Nelson, Dwight Yoakam, Tom Waits, and Lyle Lovett covered Friedman's music on the tribute album, *Pearls in the Snow: The Songs of Kinky Friedman*. In 2002 a documentary was made about Friedman by Simone de Vries called *Proud to Be an Asshole from El Paso*.

In March 2005, Friedman announced his independent candidacy for governor of Texas in 2006, with slogans such as "How Hard Could It Be?" and "Why the Hell Not?" and a campaign promise: "If you elect me the first Jewish governor, I'll reduce the speed limit to 54.95."

[Elli Wohlgelernter (2nd ed.)]

FRIEDMAN, LEE MAX (1871–1957), U.S. lawyer, historian, and patron of learning. Friedman was born in Memphis, Tennessee, of German Jewish descent. He became a noted trial attorney in Boston and a teacher and scholar of law. He was vice president and professor of law at Portia Law School, Boston, contributing learned articles to law journals. Friedman was deeply interested in American Jewish history, and in 1903 he began his association with the American Jewish Historical Society, eventually serving as president (1948–53) and honorary president (1953–57). In 1905 he was chairman of the celebration in Boston of the 250th anniversary of Jewish settlement in the United States, and half a century later he was the main speaker at Symphony Hall, Boston, on the occasion of the tercentenary. As a historian, Friedman contributed many articles and notes to the *Publications of the American Jewish Historical Society*, covering a wide range of subjects that included Judah Monis, Cotton Mather, and Aaron Lopez. The volumes he published in the field of Jewish history included some of European Jewish interest: *Robert Grosseteste and the Jews* (1934), and *Zola and the Dreyfus Case: His Defense of Liberty and Its Enduring Significance* (1937); and others on American Jewish themes: *Early American Jews* (1934), *Rabbi Haim Isaac Carigal: His Newport Sermon and His Yale Portrait* (1940), *Jewish Pioneers and Patriots* (1942), and *Pilgrims in a New Land* (1948). He presented books and manuscripts to the American Jewish Historical Society, and a bequest in his will enabled the Society to establish its own headquarters adjoining Brandeis University.

Friedman's approach to cultural, philanthropic, civic, and communal endeavors was conservative. He served in leading positions with the Boston Art Museum, Harvard College Library, General Theological Library, and Boston Public Library. He was active in Boston Jewish life and was prominent in such national bodies as the Union of American Hebrew Congregations and the World Union for Progressive Judaism.

BIBLIOGRAPHY: Kozol, in: AJHSQ, 56 (1967), 261–7; Meyer, *ibid.*, 47 (1958), 211–5; Norden, *ibid.*, 51 (1961), 30–48 (bibl.).

[Isidore S. Meyer]

FRIEDMAN, MILTON (1912–), U.S. economist. Friedman, who was born in Rahway, New Jersey, received his B.A. from Rutgers University in 1932, his M.A. from the University of Chicago in 1933, and his Ph.D. from Columbia University in 1946. He began working for the U.S. government in 1935 and taught at several American universities before becoming professor of economics at the University of Chicago (1946–76). There, he acquired an international reputation and served as consultant to national and international institutions. He also acted as adviser to President Nixon. Friedman became the leader of the "Chicago school" of economic thought, opposed to those following the generally accepted theories of John Maynard Keynes. He argued that the U.S. government relied too much on changes in taxation and government spending instead of controlling the money supply, in order to regulate the economy. In addition, he maintained that the

U.S. Federal Reserve Board repeatedly erred in the rate at which it changed the money supply and, as a result, intensified the fluctuations in economic growth. Friedman favored a simplified taxation system, floating exchange rates, and the demonetization of gold. He also advocated the abolition of the social welfare system, which he considered paternalistic, ineffective, and inefficient. In its place he wanted a "negative income tax," which would provide ready cash for the poor to pay for their basic needs.

Friedman was awarded the Nobel Prize for economics in 1976 for "his achievements in the field of consumption analysis, monetary history and theory, and for his demonstration of the complexity of stabilization policy." By that time he had become one of the most influential and high-profile economic theorists of his day. His theory of monetarism – which related increases in the money supply to inflation – was adopted by the English Conservative party under Margaret Thatcher, which followed his prescriptions for reducing the money supply during the early years of the 1980s.

Friedman was a member of the research staff of the National Bureau of Economic Research (1937–81). He also served on the President's Economic Policy Advisory Board during President *Reagan's administration in the 1980s.

After retiring from the University of Chicago in 1977, Friedman became Paul Snowden Russell Distinguished Service Professor Emeritus of Economics at the University of Chicago and a senior research fellow at the Hoover Institution at Stanford University. In 2002 the Cato Institute in Washington established the Milton Friedman Prize for Advancing Liberty, a cash prize awarded every second year to a person who has made a significant contribution to the advancement of freedom.

A prolific writer, Friedman was the author of *A Monetary History of the United States* (1963; with Anna Schwarz), a major work on economic history in which he showed that declines in the supply of money have led to nearly every recession in the U.S. economy in the last hundred years. Among his other writings are *A Theory of Consumption Function* (1957), *A Program for Monetary Stability* (1960), *Price Theory* (1962), *Essays in Positive Economics* (1966), *Capitalism and Freedom* (1967), *A Theoretical Framework for Monetary Analysis* (1971), *There's No Such Thing as a Free Lunch* (1975), *Tax Limitation, Inflation and the Role of Government* (1978), *Bright Promises, Dismal Performance: An Economist's Protest* (1983), *The Essence of Friedman* (with K. Leube, ed., 1992), *Why Government Is the Problem* (1993), *Foreign Economic Aid: Means and Objectives* (1995), *A Choice for Our Children: Curing the Crisis in America's Schools* (with A. Bonsteel and S. Sugarman, 1997), and *Two Lucky People: Memoirs* (with Rose Friedman, 1998).

ADD. BIBLIOGRAPHY: R. Gordon (ed.), *Milton Friedman's Monetary Framework: A Debate with His Critics* (1975); D. Goldman and L. Lerouche, *The Ugly Truth about Milton Friedman* (1980); E. Butler, *Milton Friedman: A Guide to His Economic Thought* (1985); E. Rayack, *Not So Free to Choose: The Political Economy of Milton Friedman and Ronald Reagan* (1986); A. Hirsch, *Milton Friedman: Economics in Theory and Practice* (1990); J. Wood, *Milton Friedman: Critical Assessments* (1990); N. De Marchi and A. Hirsch, *Milton Friedman: Economics in Theory and Practice* (1991); W. Frazer, *The Legacy of Keynes and Friedman: Economic Analysis, Money, and Ideology* (1994); J. Hammond, *Theory and Measurement: Causality Issues in Milton Friedman's Monetary Economics* (1996); W. Frazer, *The Friedman System: Economic Analysis of Time Series* (1997); J. Hammond (ed.), *The Legacy of Milton Friedman as Teacher* (1999).

[Joachim O. Ronall and Rohan Saxena / Ruth Beloff (2nd ed.)]

FRIEDMAN, NAPHTALI (1863–1921), Jewish deputy to the Russian *Duma (parliament). Born in Shaulai (Shavli), Lithuania, after graduating in law at the University of St. Petersburg Friedman practiced in Ponevezh, Lithuania. In 1907 he was elected to the Third Duma for the district of Kovno. He joined the Kadets (Russian Constitutional Democratic Party), taking an active part in the committees of the Duma, and with the other Jewish delegate L. *Nisselovich several times defended the Jews from attacks by the antisemitic deputies. Many Jews and non-Jews were impressed by his defense of the Jewish victims of the pogroms at the end of the 1880s. Friedman was also elected to the Fourth Duma (1912) where he continued to represent the interests of Russian Jewry with the two other Jewish delegates, M. Bomash and E. Gurewich. After the outbreak of World War I, Friedman joined with the representatives of the other national minorities in declaring that the Jews were ready to fight alongside the rest of the Russian peoples for victory. Friedman combated the allegations of Jewish treason trumped up by military circles in an attempt to cover up their defeats at the front. After the February Revolution of 1917 he cooperated for a while with the provisional government, but after the October Revolution he returned to Lithuania and practiced law in Panevezys. He was elected to the founding Parliament of independent Lithuania. He died in a health resort in Germany.

BIBLIOGRAPHY: M. Sudarski et al. (eds.), *Lite* (Yid., 1951), 1411–18.

[Yehuda Slutsky / Shmuel Spector (2nd ed.)]

FRIEDMAN, PHILIP (1901–1960), Polish-Jewish historian. Friedman studied at the universities of Lvov and Vienna, and obtained his doctorate for a thesis on *Die Galizischen Juden im Kampfe um ihre Gleichberechtigung (1848–1868)*, 1929. In further research on the history of Polish Jewry, mainly in the 19th century, Friedman described changes in the economic structure and the growth of the great Jewish center at Lodz. He took part in editing periodicals in Hebrew, Yiddish, and Polish, and contributed to *Miesiecznik Żydowski* ("The Jewish Monthly"). Friedman published Hebrew textbooks for Jewish high schools, and taught Jewish history at the Jewish High School in Lodz and at the Institute of Jewish Studies in Warsaw. During World War II he went into hiding in Lvov. After the liberation, Friedman moved to Lublin, where he organized the Central Jewish Historical Commission, later the Jewish Historical Institute, in Warsaw, which undertook extensive documentation on the fate of Polish Jewry. In 1946 Friedman was appointed to organize an educational project for the Holocaust survivors in the American zone of occupation in Germany. In 1948, after the displaced persons camps were closed, Friedman immigrated to the United States, where he directed the Jewish Teachers' Institute in New York. He also lectured on Jewish history at Columbia University. Friedman was a member of the YIVO staff and director of the bibliographical series of the Joint Documentary Projects of YIVO and Yad Vashem. Almost all Friedman's postwar publications dealt with the Holocaust period, on which he became a leading expert. His writings up to 1955 are listed in *Writings of Philip Friedman. A Bibliography* (1955). His later works include *Martyrs and Fighters* (1954), a collection of sources on the Warsaw Ghetto uprising; and *Their Brothers' Keepers* (1957), about non-Jews who saved Jewish lives in occupied countries. The bibliographies of the Holocaust which he edited are *Guide to Jewish History under Nazi Impact* (coeditor J. Robinson, 1960), *Bibliography of Books in Hebrew on the Jewish Catastrophe and Heroism in Europe* (1960), and *Bibliography of Yiddish Books on the Catastrophe and Heroism* (coeditor J. Gar, 1962).

BIBLIOGRAPHY: S.W. Baron, in: PAAJR, 29 (1960/61), 1–7; JBA, 18 (1960/61), 76–80 (Yid.); *Yad Vashem Bulletin* 6/7 (1960), 3–7; YIVO, *Newsletter*, no. 74 (1960), 1, 7; B. Orenstein, *Das Leben un Shafen fun Ph. Friedman* (1962).

[Shaul Esh]

FRIEDMAN, SHAMMA (1937–), Talmud scholar. His publications over several decades constitute an important contribution to our understanding of the Babylonian Talmud and related literature. He was the first to provide clear and objective criteria for differentiating between different literary and historical strata within the text of the Babylonian Talmud, subsequently applying these criteria systematically in the form of a continuous commentary to an entire chapter of the Babylonian Talmud (Yevamot X, with a General Introduction to the Critical Study of the Talmudic Sugya (1978)). The insight that many of the difficulties which have baffled generations of interpreters of the Talmud are rooted in the tensions which exist between these different literary and historical levels led Friedman to a more fundamental and (for some) revolutionary conclusion: that these tensions and difficulties are not the result of errors in transmission, or confusion in the interpretation of earlier tradition, but rather the result of a conscious process of synthetic creative reinterpretation which inheres in every level of talmudic literature, from the earliest tannaitic sources, through the statements of the amoraim, and down to the latest commentaries and additions of the savoraim. While continuing to develop and refine the methodolgy for analyzing and interpreting the different redactional levels within the talmudic text, Friedman went on to apply the notions of "development" and "evolution" to two other scholarly issues: the origin and significance of variant readings (especially in the manuscript tradition of the Babylonian Talmud), and the so-called "synoptic problem," i.e., the existence of and relation among alternative versions of a given textual tradition preserved in different talmudic and midrashic works. The notion that later talmudic sages often self-consciously reinterpreted and reformulated earlier versions of a given tradition has proved to be a powerful tool in solving many formerly intractable problems in the history of talmudic halakhah and aggadah. In addition to the many scholarly articles in which these ideas and methods were developed – including numerous studies in the field of Hebrew and Aramaic linguistics – Friedman's major publications in recent years have included *Talmud Arukh, Bava Metzi'a vi: Critical Edition with Comprehensive Commentary* (1990 and 1996), published by JTS press, and *Tosefta Atikta, Synoptic Parallels of Mishna and Tosefta Analyzed, with a Methodological Introduction* (2002), published by Bar-Ilan University.

The comprehensive critical methodology which has emerged from Friedman's literary efforts has provided the foundation for a number of important scholarly projects in which he has played a leading role. In 1985, Friedman founded the Saul Lieberman Institute of Talmudic Research at the Jewish Theological Seminary of America, which encourages innovative Talmud scholarship and provides sophisticated tools for its implementation. The Institute today, under Friedman's direction, distributes a computerized database containing the text of almost all surviving Talmud manuscripts, first printed editions and fragments, as well as a computerized page-by-page bibliography of hundreds of books dealing with talmudic literature. The product of decades of work, these resources are aimed at opening new horizons in the field of Talmud Study. In the early 1990s, Friedman established the Society for the Interpretation of the Talmud, a collaborative venture in which a group of scholars has undertaken the preparation of an edition of the Babylonian Talmud with commentary based on scholarly standards and aimed to a wide reading audience. A preliminary volume containing representative analyses of selected talmudic sugyot (*Five Sugyot from the Babylonian Talmud*) was published in 2002, and the first three volumes covering entire chapters of the Talmud are currently in the press, with preparations for more extensive publications well under way. Friedman also directs an Internet site at Bar Ilan University (developed together with Prof. Leib Moscovitz) devoted to bringing together all the primary textual witnesses of Tannaitic literature, with Tosefta and halakhic midrashim currently represented.

Friedman is the Benjamin and Minna Reeves Professor of Talmud and Rabbinics at the Jewish Theological Seminary and teaches in the Talmud Department at Bar Ilan University. He was born in Philadelphia in 1937 and settled in Jerusalem in 1973. He has held a variety of positions at the Seminary, including acting librarian, and editor of Hebrew publications of the Schocken Institute. During the 1970s and 1980s, Friedman was the dean and director of JTS's Jerusalem campus, now known as the Schechter Institute of Jewish Studies, where he teaches. In addition to his professorship at JTS and Bar Ilan, Friedman has taught at several universities, including Harvard, the Hebrew University, and Tel Aviv University, and has sponsored more than 25 graduate students in advanced degrees. He was elected to the Israel Academy of the Hebrew Language and the American Academy of Jewish Research, is Talmud division editor of the *Encyclopaedia Judaica*, and is a member of the editorial board of *Jewish Studies*, an Internet journal.

[Stephen G. Wald (2nd ed)]

FRIEDMAN, THEODORE (1908–1992), U.S. Conservative rabbi and scholar. Friedman was born in Stamford, Conn. He was a graduate of the City College of New York (1929) and was ordained at the Jewish Theological Seminary (1931). He received his Ph.D. two decades later from Columbia University (1952). As was common in the rabbinate of his day, Friedman moved from congregation to congregation before finding his permanent prestigious pulpit. He served as rabbi of Beth El in North Bergen, N.J. (1931–42), Beth David in Bufflalo (1942–44), the Jewish Center of Jackson Heights, N.Y., during 1944–54, and from 1954 until his retirement in 1970 of Beth El of South Orange, N.J., then a growing suburb of Newark during the first great wave of suburbanization. He then moved to Jerusalem. A leader of the centrist group within Conservative Judaism, which advocates controlled change within Jewish law, Friedman served as chairman of the Law Committee, where he worked with the Jewish Theological Seminary on solving the problem of the **agunah*. The result was a joint Law Conference of the Seminary. He was co-chair of the Steering Committee and secretary of its *bet din* and of the Rabbinical Assembly for matters dealing with marriage and divorce and was president of the Rabbinical Assembly in 1962–64. During turbulent times he embraced the cause of civil rights and was an early participant in the effort to rescue Soviet Jewry. He co-authored with Morris *Adler and Jacob *Agus the responsum permitting the use of electricity on the Sabbath and allowing congregants to drive to synagogue on the Sabbath.

He was managing editor of *Judaism*, a journal of Jewish thought, during 1953–61. He was coeditor with Robert Gordis of *Jewish Life in America* (1955), and wrote *Letters to Jewish College Students* (1965), relating Jewish teachings to the concerns of contemporary college students, and of *Judgment and Destiny* (1956), sermons. From Jerusalem, he wrote a "Letter from Jerusalem" published in *Conservative Judaism*.

[Jack Reimer / Michael Berenbaum (2nd ed.)

FRIEDMAN, THOMAS L. (1953–), U.S. journalist. Born in Minneapolis, Minn., Friedman earned a bachelor's degree summa cum laude from Brandeis University with a specialty in Mediterranean studies, which helped prepare him for a career in writing and reporting on foreign affairs. He became known for advocating a compromise peace between Israel and the Palestinians, for modernization of the Arab world, and for globalization and laissez-faire capitalism.

During his undergraduate years, Friedman spent semesters abroad at the Hebrew University of Jerusalem and the American University in Cairo. He then attended St. Antony's College, Oxford University, on a Marshall scholarship and received a master's degree in modern Middle East studies. He joined the London bureau of United Press International and spent a year there as a general assignment reporter before being assigned to Beirut. He reported from Beirut from 1979 to 1981, and then was hired by the *New York Times*, which sent him to Beirut as bureau chief in 1982, six weeks before the Israeli invasion. Fluent in Arabic and Hebrew, he reported extensively on the war and won the Pulitzer Prize for international reporting, particularly for his articles on the Sabra and Shatilla massacres. In June 1984 Friedman became the *Times*'s bureau chief in Israel, the first Jew to serve in that position, and worked in Jerusalem until 1988. He won another Pulitzer Prize for his reporting of the first Palestinian Intifada. He chronicled his assignment in the Middle East in the book *From Beirut to Jerusalem*, published in 1989. It was on the *New York Times* bestseller list for nearly 12 months and won the National Book Award for nonfiction and the Overseas Press Club Award for Best Book on Foreign Policy. The book has been published in 10 languages, including Japanese and Chinese, and is used as a basic textbook on the Middle East in many high schools and universities. Friedman has been attacked by right-wing Jewish organzations and individuals for his reporting from Beirut and for his support of a two-state solution a decade before the Oslo agreements. Given his background and his manifest commitments to Judaism and to Israel, they had considerable difficulty portraying him as a self-hating Jew, however much they tried.

In January 1989 Friedman was posted to Washington as the *Times*'s chief diplomatic correspondent. For the next four years he traveled 500,000 miles, covering Secretary of State James A. Baker and the end of the Cold War. When Bill Clinton became president, he was named White House correspondent and in 1994 his assignment became the intersection of foreign policy and economics. In 1995 he became a foreign affairs columnist for *The Times*.

Initially, Friedman focused on the intersection of globalization and finance, and summarized his views in *The Lexus and the Olive Tree* (1999). It, too, became a bestseller. The two objects in the title symbolized the interaction between globalization and local tradition. The book also discussed the role of new technology in reshaping global politics and argued that nations must sacrifice a degree of economic sovereignty to institutions like the International Monetary Fund to achieve Western-style prosperity. After the attacks of September 11, 2001, Friedman's columns concentrated on the threat of terrorism, and he won the 2002 Pulitzer Prize for commentary. He supported the invasion of Iraq in 2003, although he had grave misgivings about the way the Bush administration waged it. Friedman also wrote *Longitudes and Attitudes* (2002) and *The World is Flat* (2005).

When the *Times* developed a television channel, it engaged Friedman to draw on his extensive contacts to report and write documentaries about the Middle East and other parts of the world. As such, he became a familiar figure in American homes. He also appeared frequently on television panels and spoke often at colleges and public forums. He was a member of the board of trustees of Brandeis and of the advisory board of the Marshall Scholarship Commission.

[Stewart Kampel (2nd ed.)]

FRIEDMANN, ABRAHAM (d. 1879), chief rabbi of Transylvania. Among the first rabbis there to introduce the preaching of sermons in the synagogue in Hungarian, he encountered strong opposition from Orthodox rabbis. When officiating in Simánd (province of Arad) in 1845 he preached in Hungarian on the occasion of the birthday of King Ferdinand I. The address, entitled *Egyházi beszéd*, was published the same year. Previously Friedmann published a pamphlet, also in Hungarian, in defense of Jewish rights entitled *Az izraelita nemzetnek védelmére* (1844). In 1845 the council of electors of the Jews of Transylvania, convened by the Catholic bishop of *Alba-Iulia, elected him chief rabbi of the grand principality. He subsequently settled in the capital, Alba-Iulia. During his period of office he also played a political role as representative of Transylvanian Jewry and became involved in bitter disputes and polemics. In 1872 his opponents obtained his removal from office. He was the last chief rabbi to hold office for the whole of Transylvania. One of his main opponents was Hillel *Lichtenstein.

BIBLIOGRAPHY: *Magyar Zsidó Lexikon* (1929), 295.

[Yehouda Marton]

FRIEDMANN, ARON (1855–1936), German *ḥazzan*. Born in Szaki, Lithuania, Friedmann studied in Berlin and in 1882 was appointed chief *ḥazzan* of the Old Synagogue of the Berlin community, a post he held until 1923. He received the title of Koeniglicher Musikdirektor, Royal Academy of Art, Berlin, 1907. In 1901, he published *Shir li-Shelomoh*, a collection of cantorial music in traditional style for the prayers of the year. He also wrote *Der synagogale Gesang* (1904) and *Lebensbilder beruehmter Kantoren* (3 vols., 1918–27), containing biographies of 19th-century *ḥazzanim.*

FRIEDMANN, DANIEL (1936–), Israeli professor of law. Born in Israel, Friedman studied law at the Hebrew University of Jerusalem prior to his army service. He is a professor of law at Tel Aviv University, where he was also dean of the Law Faculty, 1974–78. Friedmann was a member of the Commission of Inquiry (chaired by Justice M. Beiski) appointed by the president of the Supreme Court to investigate the price manipulation of bank shares. He as a member of a number of legislative advisory committees and the Advisory Committee for the Codification of Civil Law in Israel (chaired by Chief Justice A. *Barak) appointed by the minister of justice. He also served as an adviser to the Restatement (Third) of the Law of Restitution. Friedmann participated in the establishment of the Cegla Institute for Comparative and Private International Law at Tel Aviv University and was its first director. He also participated in establishing the Law School of the College of Management and was its first dean. He published numerous books on various spheres of law: insurance, contract, damages, and other topics. In 1991 he received the Israel Prize for social sciences.

FRIEDMANN, DAVID ARYEH (1889–1957), Hebrew critic and editor. After studying medicine at Moscow University, he emigrated in 1925 to Palestine, where he was a practicing ophthalmologist and active member of the medical association. Friedmann wrote many articles in the Hebrew press on medicine, literature, and the arts, most of which were published posthumously in two volumes: *Iyyunei Shirah* (1964), and *Iyyunei Prozah* (1966). He was an editor of Ayanot Publishing Co. as well as of *En Hakore* (1923); he also edited the Medical Association's journal, *Ha-Refu'ah,* from 1929.

BIBLIOGRAPHY: B. Shmueli, *Maḥberet ha-Ayinin* (bibliography of works by Dr. D.A. Friedmann, 1912–42, 280 items); idem, in: *Ha-Refu'ah*, 39 no. 1 (1950), 13 (summary as well as comprehensive appreciation by Y.L. Roke'aḥ); *Hadoar* (Sept. 20, 1957).

[Getzel Kressel]

FRIEDMANN, DAVID BEN SAMUEL (also called **"Dovidel" Karliner**; 1828–1917), Lithuanian rabbi and *posek*. Friedmann was born in Biala and lived for a time in Brest-Litovsk after 1836. On the advice of Leib Katzenellenbogen he moved to Kamenets-Litovsk where he studied under the supervision of his older brother Joseph until 1841. In that year he made the acquaintance of the philanthropist Shemariah Luria of Mohilev, who entrusted to him the education of his brother-in-law Zalman Rivlin of Shklov. Friedmann later married Luria's daughter. From 1846 to 1866 he devoted himself to concentrated study in the house of his father-in-law, where he compiled his *Piskei Halakhot*. After the death of his father-in-law in 1866 he accepted the rabbinate of Karlin near Pinsk (in 1868) where he remained until his death.

Friedmann's renown rests upon his *Piskei Halakhot* (pt. 1, 1898; pt. 2, 1901), an exposition and summary of matrimonial law, with a commentary entitled *Yad David*, an appendix entitled *She'ilat David* containing responsa on the laws of *mikva'ot ("ritual baths"). The text of the *Piskei Halakhot* follows that of Maimonides. In his comprehensive exposition, Friedmann endeavors to establish clear-cut decisions. His work is distinguished by the fact that he relies to an overwhelming extent on the Babylonian and Jerusalem Talmuds and on the *rishonim, disregarding the *aḥaronim. He eschewed casuistry and tried to penetrate to the essence of the *halakhah* by a logical approach. Among the rabbis who turned to him with their problems were Menahem Mendel *Schneersohn, the head of the Lubavitch (Chabad) dynasty, and David *Luria. When religious extremists in Jerusalem excommunicated the *bet midrash* of his brother-in-law, Jehiel Michael *Pines, because he supported the establishment in Jerusalem of an orphanage "where they would also learn a foreign language," Friedmann attacked them in his *Emek Berakhah* (1881). It consists of four essays in which he discusses the question of a ban and the regulations and conditions under which it should be imposed, emphasizing that a handful of rabbis of Jerusalem had no right to impose such a ban. Pines wrote a long introduction to the book. Even though he tended to view with favor secular knowledge and the study of languages, Friedmann was opposed to compromise with regard to Torah education and the character of the traditional *ḥeder and in 1913 vehemently opposed the plan of the society Mefiẓei Haskalah be-Rusyah ("Disseminators of Secular Education in Russia") to change the accepted curriculum of the *ḥeder.*

During a certain period of his life, Friedmann participated actively in the Ḥibbat Zion movement. From 1863 he published articles in the *Levanon* which reflect his favorable attitude towards this movement, and he thus influenced many observant Jews to join it. He debated with Ẓ.H. *Kalischer on the problems of the movement and, together with L. *Pinsker and Samuel *Mohilever, participated in the *Kattowitz conference of 1885 as a delegate of the Pinsk branch of the Ḥovevei Zion. In a letter to A.J. Slucki he stressed that the noble idea of the nationalist movement deserves to become dear to "our brethren who are anxious for the word of God," and he testifies of himself that "the fire of love for our holy land burns in my heart" (ed. by A.J. Slucki, *Shivat Ẓiyyon*, 1 (1891), 18–19. In the course of time, however, he changed his attitude and following the decision of Zionist parties to include national secular education among their activities became an opponent of the Zionist idea. His grandson SHMUEL ELIASHIV (Friedmann, 1899–1955), jurist and author, served as first ambassador of the State of Israel to the U.S.S.R.

BIBLIOGRAPHY: S.N. Gottlieb, *Oholei Shem* (1912), 172–4; Masliansky, in: *Hadoar*, 17 (1938), 455f.; *Toyzent yor Pinsk* (1941), 87, 93, 171, 269–71; Zinovitz, in: *Ba-Mishor*, 6 (1945), no. 255 p. 4f.; *Yahadut Lita*, 1 (1960), 250f., 344, 494, 513; 3 (1967), 79; S. Eliashiv, in: *Sefer Biala-Podlaska* (1961), 334–6.

[Yehoshua Horowitz]

FRIEDMANN, DESIDER (1880–1944), lawyer and Zionist leader. Born in Boskovice, Moravia, he was an active Zionist from 1898. When Vienna became the first great Jewish community in the West with a Zionist majority, Friedmann was elected vice president of its Israelitische Kultusgemeinde (Jewish community; 1920–24) and from January 1933 its president. In May 1934 Friedmann was appointed a member of the Austrian Council of State (*Staatsrat*). He was a courageous fighter for Jewish rights and enlarged the cultural, educational, and social activities of the Kultusgemeinde. The Austrian chancellor Schuschnigg dispatched him abroad in 1938, a few weeks before the annexation of Austria to Nazi Germany (the *Anschluss*), to negotiate support for Austrian currency. Immediately after the *Anschluss*, the Nazis arrested him, allegedly for his financial aid to the Schuschnigg government. On April 1, 1938, he was deported to the Dachau concentration camp with the so-called *Prominententransport* (transport of prominent people) and later to other concentration camps. In the autumn of 1944 he, his wife, and other Zionist leaders of Vienna were transferred from Theresienstadt to the gas chambers at Auschwitz.

BIBLIOGRAPHY: J. Fraenkel (ed.), *Jews of Austria* (1967), index; H. Gold (ed.), *Die Juden und Judengemeinden Maehrens…* (1929), 92. **ADD. BIBLIOGRAPHY:** L. Brenner, *Zionism in the Age of Dictators – A Reappraisal* (1983).

[Josef Fraenkel / Bjoern Siegel (2nd ed.)]

FRIEDMANN, GEORGES (1902–1977), French sociologist, born in Paris, educated at the Ecole Normale Supérieure and the University of Paris. During World War II he organized the resistance movement in the Toulouse region. Friedmann, an expert in vocational education and the sociology of work and industry, was appointed inspector general of technical education in France in 1945 and participated in the work of the commission for educational reform. Friedmann became professor for the history of labor at the Conservatoire des Arts et des Métiers in 1946 and director of studies at the Ecole Pratique des Hautes Etudes at the Sorbonne in 1948; he was administrator of the Centre d'Etudes Sociologiques, 1949–51. In 1956 he was president of the International Sociological Association. His position in industrial sociology is that the psycho-physiological problems of labor in industry must be considered not only within the individual enterprise, but also in the context of the larger social structure and cannot be solved without comprehensive changes in the social order. Among his major works are *Problémes du machinisme en U.R.S.S. et dans les pays capitalistes* (1934), *La crise du progrès: Esquisse d'histoire des idées (1895–1935)* (1936), *De la Sainte Russie à l'U.R.S.S.* (1938), *Leibniz et Spinoza* (1946), *Les problèmes humains du machinisme industriel* (1946), *Humanisme du travail et humanités* (1950), *Où va le travail humain?* (1951), and *Le travail en miettes; spécialisation et loisirs* (1956). Friedmann was editor and coeditor of *L'Homme et la machine and of Annales des Economies, Sociétés, Civilisations* and author of numerous articles on human and technological problems in industrial development. Several of his works were translated into English and German. In 1965, after an extended stay in Israel, Friedmann published *La Fin du peuple Juif?* (1965; *The End of the Jewish People?*, 1967). In this book he dealt with the present problems and future prospects of the State of Israel and the Jewish people. He held that the decline of religious orthodoxy, the growth of cultural assimilation in Israel and elsewhere, and the rise of a secular Israel nationalism will endanger the continued existence of the Jewish people in the Diaspora, as well as the Jewishness of Israelis.

[Werner J. Cahnman]

FRIEDMANN, JANE (1931–), Swedish actress. She appeared in Stockholm at Dramatiska Teatern, the national theater of Sweden, and at the Stockholm City Theater. Her first great success was in the title role of *The Diary of Anne Frank* (1956). She also acted in *L'Ecole des femmes* by Molière; *Three Knives from Wei*, a Chinese story by the Swedish poet, Harry Martinson; and the modern English polemical play *Oh, What a Lovely War!* (1963). She also has a number of contemporary Swedish roles to her credit, such as in *Between the Summers* (1995) and *The Prompter* (1999).

FRIEDMANN, MEIR (pen name **Ish-Shalom**; 1831–1908), rabbinic scholar. Friedmann was born in Horost, Slovakia. From 1843 to 1848 he studied in Ungvar at the yeshivah of his relative Meir Asch. Between 1848 and 1858 he underwent several crises and changes. Successively, he lived as an ascetic Ḥasid preparing for immigration to Ereẓ Israel, temporarily came under the influence of the Haskalah, returned to the study of the Talmud and was ordained, married, and became a farmer; his wife died, he was impoverished, and he became a *maggid*. In 1858 he settled in Vienna and attended the university as a non-matriculated student. From 1864 on he served as librarian, Bible teacher to adults, and Talmud teacher to the young at the *bet midrash* in Vienna. After 1894 he also taught at the rabbinical seminary there. Among his students were V. *Aptowitzer, Z.P. *Chajes, and S. *Schechter.

In his lifetime Friedmann was known for his studies of and lectures on *aggadah*, and even earned the title *mara de-aggadeta* ("master of *aggadah*"). His most important contributions are concerned with the halakhic Midrashim. He discovered lost sources, determined correct versions, and illuminated difficult passages; his writing is exceptionally erudite, profound, logical, and elegant of expression. His influence on Jewish scholarship was considerable. Many of the commentaries and interpretations of later talmudic scholars and researchers originated in his work. Friedmann maintained that "the Talmud is the foundation of Judaism and whoever abandons it is abandoning life"; this conviction affected all his creative work and activities. At the height of the Haskalah Friedmann was calling for traditional education, even drawing up plans for traditional Jewish secondary schools and universities. He was also active in the Zionist movement and founded the Association for the Dissemination of the Hebrew Language.

Friedmann edited midrashic texts with introductions and commentaries, the commentaries entitled *Me'ir Ayin*. The halakhic Midrashim include *Mekhilta* (1870), *Baraita de-Melekhet ha-Mishkan* (1908), and *Sifrei* (1864); a part of the *Sifra*, which he had begun editing, was published posthumously (1915). He published *Pesikta Rabbati* (1880) and *Tanna de-vei Eliyahu* (1902), aggadic texts; *Talmud Bavli: Massekhet Makkot* (1888) with a short interpretation as an example of a scientific edition of the Talmud; and a pamphlet about translating the Talmud, *Davar al Odot ha-Talmud* (1885). He published many works on the literature of *halakhah* and *aggadah*, its characteristics and principles, as well as books and articles on other Jewish subjects, including Bible, particularly commentaries on the Pentateuch, Judges, Samuel, Isaiah, Hosea, and Psalms; and the Targums of Onkelos and Aquila; the Holy Land; and Jewish prayer and poetry. He produced a number of sample textbooks on the Talmud and Mishnah for schools, and several of his lectures and sermons were published, although most of them can only be found incorporated into the works of his contemporaries. With I.H. Weiss Friedmann edited the periodical *Beit ha-Talmud* (1881–89). Most of his articles appeared in that and other publications under his pen name "Ish Shalom."

BIBLIOGRAPHY: B.Z. Benedikt, in: KS, 24 (1947/48), 263–75; idem, in: *Aresheth*, 2 (1960), 269–84; T. Preschel, *ibid.*, 3 (1961), 468; J. Friedmann (ed.), *Lector M. Friedmann zur 100 Wiederkehr seines Geburtstages…* (1931), a bibliography; Kressel, Leksikon, 1 (1965), 98; J. Bergman, in: *Sefer ha-Zikkaron le-Veit ha-Midrash le-Rabbanim be-Vina* (1946), 37–45; S. Schechter, *Seminary Addresses and Other Papers* (1915, repr. 1959), 135–43.

[Binyamin Zeev Benedikt]

FRIEDMANN, MORITZ (1823–1891), Hungarian *ḥazzan*. Born in Hraboc, Friedmann was a noted boy soprano. When he went to Budapest as a youth, the *ḥazzan* David Broder accepted him in his choir. Later he went to Oedenburg (Sopron) and obtained a post as assistant cantor and Hebrew teacher in a nearby congregation. In 1857 he was appointed chief *ḥazzan* in Budapest, where he conducted services in the *Sulzer style, with a large choir and set psalms and prayers to music for solo and choir. His collection of Jewish synagogue songs, *Izráelita vallásos énekek…* (1875), was used in the synagogues of most Hungarian communities. He also edited the paper *Ungarische Israelitische Kultusbeamtenzeitung* (1883–97), in which he published articles on cantorial music.

BIBLIOGRAPHY: *Friedmann Album*, 2 vols. (1877–85); Sendrey, Music, indexes; M. Rothmueller, *The Music of the Jews* (1967).

[Joshua Leib Ne'eman]

FRIEDMANN, PAUL (1840–?), philanthropist and author, initiator of a settlement scheme for Jews in Midian. A Protestant of Jewish descent, Friedmann was born in Koenigsberg, Prussia, but the place and year of his death are unknown. After accumulating a vast fortune, he traveled over Europe to gather material for his works, *Les Dépêches de G. Michiel, Ambassadeur de Venise en Angleterre pendant les années 1554 à 1557* (1896) and *Anne Boleyn – A Chapter of English History 1527–1535*, 2 vols. (1885^2). In 1891 he privately published *Das Land Madian* (Arabic for Midian), in which he described the possibilities of colonizing this land without mentioning Jews as the prospective settlers. Influenced by the Russian pogroms of the 1880s, he envisioned the unpopulated land of Midian as a haven for the victims of such persecution, and ultimately even as a Jewish state. With the assent of Sir Evelyn Baring (later Lord Cromer), Britain's representative in *Egypt, Friedmann opened negotiations with the British authorities. He simultaneously set out to enlist the first settlers and was finally able to persuade a group of 17 men, 6 women, and 4 children from Austrian Galicia to join his expedition. He acquired a yacht, which he called "*Israel*," that reached Suez on December 1, 1893, with a total of 46 persons. The Prussian officer in command exercised strictest discipline, which proved unbearable, and 18 persons left the group. After one of them was found dead in the Sinai desert, Friedmann was blamed for the "murder." Leaving the women and children in *Cairo, the group finally reached the Sinai Peninsula and prepared to cross the Red Sea to Midian. News reached them, however, that the Turks had occupied the Midianite city of Dhaba and that in accordance with Turkish law no non-

Muslim was permitted to settle in this area, which is part of the Hejaz.

A number of Friedmann's group deserted the camp and arrived in Cairo, spreading gruesome stories about the enterprise. As Friedmann's scheme had been favored by Baring, it was branded in the local press as a British attempt to occupy Midian, and bitter controversies arose between the British and Turkish authorities. Finally Friedmann was compelled to abandon his efforts. He was then a broken man, financially as well as spiritually, and although he brought successful court actions against a number of newspapers that attacked him, the litigation took many years and was, ultimately, of no avail.

BIBLIOGRAPHY: O.K. Rabinowicz, in: *In Time of Harvest: Essays in Honor of Abba Hillel Silver* (1963), 284–319; J. Fraenkel, in: *Herzl Year Book*, 4 (1961), 67–117; J.M. Landau, in: B. Dinur et al. (eds.), *Shivat Ẓiyyon* (1950), 169–78; N.M. Gelber, in: *ibid.*, 2–3 (1953), 351–74.

[Oskar K. Rabinowicz]

FRIEDRICHSFELD, DAVID (c. 1755–1810), German author. Friedrichsfeld was born in Berlin, where he was influenced by the Jewish Enlightenment movement. In 1781 he settled in Amsterdam, where he became one of the leaders in the fight for Jewish emancipation. After Amsterdam was occupied by the French revolutionary forces, he became one of the leaders of the *Felix Libertate society. A follower of Moses Mendelssohn, he expounded his views in works such as *Beleuchtung... in Betreff des Buergerrecht der Juden* (Amsterdam, 1795), *De Messias der Jooden...* (The Hague, 1796), *Appell an die Staende Hollands* (Amsterdam, 1797), and *Kol Mevasser* (Amsterdam, 1802). He also wrote a work on Hebrew phonetics, *Ma'aneh Rakh* (Amsterdam, 1808), and contributed short articles and poems to *Ha-Me'assef.*

BIBLIOGRAPHY: Graetz, Hist, 5 (1895), 400–1, 454; Klausner, Sifrut, 1 (1952^2), index. **ADD. BIBLIOGRAPHY:** H. Graetz, *Geschichte der Juden von den ältesten Zeiten bis auf die Gegenwart*, 2 (1900); M. Brenner, S. Jersch-Wenzel, and M.A. Meyer, *Deutsch-jüdische Geschichte in der Neuzeit,* vol. 2 (1996).

FRIEDSAM, MICHAEL (1858–1931), U.S. businessman, public servant, philanthropist, and art collector. Friedsam, who was born in New York, began working for the B. Altman & Company department store at the age of 17. He became a company partner in 1900 and a vice president in 1909. Upon the death of company president Benjamin Altman in 1913, Friedsam became president of the company and of the Altman Foundation, established to disburse the bulk of Altman's fortune for charitable and educational purposes. During World War I Friedsam, as a New York State representative of the Federal Food Administration, participated in government efforts to regulate consumption and check profiteering. He also held the rank of colonel in the New York State National Guard. In 1925 Friedsam chaired the committee appointed by Governor Al Smith that recommended increased New York State financial aid to public schools. Friedsam willed portions of his extensive fine arts collection to the New York Metropolitan Museum of Art and the Brooklyn Institute of Arts and Sciences. In 1932, under the terms of his will, the Friedsam Foundation was established, for assisting the young and aged and for educational purposes.

[Richard Skolnik]

FRIEND, CHARLOTTE (1921–1987), U.S. oncologist, microbiologist. Friend was born in New York City to parents who immigrated from Russia. She finished her undergraduate studies at Hunter College, New York, and upon graduating in 1943 she served in the U.S. Navy during World War II and was second in command of the hematology laboratory at the naval hospital in Shoemaker, California. In 1950, she received her Ph.D. from Yale University. After graduation she was hired by the director of the then new Sloan Kettering Institute and was an associate professor of microbiology until 1966 when she moved to Mount Sinai School of Medicine and was appointed professor of microbiology. She remained there until she died in 1987. Friend made many important contributions to cancer research. Her first discovery was that a leukemia could be induced experimentally by a virus now known as the Friend Leukemia Virus (FLV), which at the time was received with skepticism and hostility because until then there had been no known link between viruses and cancer. Friend paved the way for a great many avenues of research. Her demonstration of inducible differentiation of leukemic cells by DMSO has served as an inspiration for evaluating the potential of therapeutic effects of differentiation-inducing agents in human cancer. Friend was a woman of strong convictions and a fighter. She openly supported the blacklisted academics and dissidents even in the McCarthy and Nixon era. She believed in the State of Israel and was a fervent supporter of the women's movement. Charlotte Friend received many prizes and awards. In 1976 she was elected to the National Academy of Sciences.

BIBLIOGRAPHY: Leila Diamond, Biographical Memoirs.

[Bracha Rager (2nd ed.)]

FRIEND, HUGO MORRIS (1882–1966), U.S. lawyer and judge. Friend, who was born in Prague, was brought to the United States when he was two. In his youth he distinguished himself as an athlete and was a member of the U.S. team at the 1906 Olympic Games. In 1908 he was admitted to the Illinois bar and started to practice in Chicago. Friend was made a master in chancery for Cook County, and in 1920 was appointed to fill a vacancy in the circuit court. He was reelected to office until 1930, when he was appointed to the appellate court for the first district. Friend took some part in the charitable work of the Jewish community. In 1917–18 he was president of the Young Men's Jewish Charities; he was a vice president of the Jewish Home Finding Society, board member of Mount Sinai Hospital, president of the Jewish Children's Bureau (1945–48), and a director of the Jewish Charities of Chicago.

[Sefton D. Temkin]

FRIENDLY, FRED W. (**Fred Wachenheimer**; 1915–1998), U.S. television writer and director. Born in Providence, Rhode Island, Friendly began his career as a radio announcer in 1937. During World War II he was a correspondent for army publications, and in 1948 joined the National Broadcasting Company. He collaborated with veteran journalist Edward R. Murrow in the *Hear It Now* radio series. These were followed by several years of producing *CBS Reports* (1959–64) for the Columbia Broadcasting System. Friendly was president of CBS News from 1964 to 1966. He produced the innovative investigative TV news series *See It Now*, hosted by Murrow; it was the first TV program to be broadcast coast to coast across America (1951–57). He also produced the TV series *Back That Fact* (1953); the documentary film *Satchmo the Great* about legendary jazz musician Louis Armstrong (1958); and the CBS News documentary *Harvest of Shame* (1960), which dealt with the plight of migrant farmworkers in America.

In 1966 Friendly resigned from CBS when his decision to carry the live U.S. Senate hearings on Vietnam was overruled and the network chose to air reruns of *I Love Lucy* instead. Friendly then became a television adviser to the Ford Foundation, where he developed the Public Broadcast Laboratory, and was a professor of journalism at Columbia University.

Recognizing that animosity was growing between journalists and the judiciary in America, in 1974 Friendly collaborated with some of the country's leading lawyers, journalists, and politicians to create a series of debates centered on society and the media. Now known as the Fred Friendly Seminars, broadcasts of these programs became highly popular fare on the Public Broadcasting Service.

Among his many honors and accolades, Friendly garnered 35 major awards for *See It Now*; 40 major awards for *CBS Reports*; and 10 Peabody Awards for TV production. In 1994 he was inducted into the Academy of Television Arts and Sciences' Hall of Fame.

Books written by Friendly include *"I Can Hear It Now" 1933–45* (with E.R. Murrow, 1948); *Due to Circumstances Beyond Our Control* (1967); *The Good Guys, the Bad Guys, and the First Amendment: Free Speech vs. Fairness in Broadcasting* (1976); *Minnesota Rag: The Dramatic Story of the Landmark Supreme Court Case That Gave New Meaning to Freedom of the Press* (1981); and *The Constitution: That Delicate Balance* (1984).

ADD. BIBLIOGRAPHY: A. Sperber, *Murrow: His Life and Times* (1986); L. Paper, *Empire: William S. Paley and the Making of CBS* (1987); D. Schoenbrun, *On and Off the Air: An Informal History of CBS News* (1989).

[Barth Healey / Ruth Beloff (2nd ed.)]

FRIENDLY, HENRY JACOB (1903–1986), U.S. judge. Considered by lawyers, judges, and legal scholars as one of the ablest lawyers of his generation and the preeminent federal appellate judge of his time, Friendly made a legendary record as a student at Harvard Law School. He became law clerk to Justice Louis D. Brandeis. He turned down an offer to teach at Harvard Law School and joined the prestigious law firm of Root, Clark, Buckner, and Ballantine, of which he became a partner in 1937. In 1946 he formed his own law firm; he was vice president, director, and general counsel of Pan-American Airways System. Thus, for over 30 years he was in private law practice with no involvement in public activities. In 1959 he was appointed judge of the United States Court of Appeals for the Second Circuit, in which he served until his death in March 1986. In the estimation of the legal profession, Friendly deserved to be coupled with Learned Hand for judicial competence and eminence. Felix Frankfurter in 1963 considered him the best judge writing judicial opinions. Professor Paul Freund wrote that Friendly "combined massive documentation and sharply critical, often astringent, analysis with invariably constructive, or reconstructive, proposals." He was especially expert in administrative law, federal jurisdiction, criminal procedure, trademark, railroad, and commercial law. He was chief judge of his court for two years, and from 1974 to the time of his death he was also presiding judge of the special court set up by an act of Congress on railroad reorganization.

Judge Friendly served on the Council of the American Law Institute, on the board of overseers of Harvard University, and was the author of several books, including *Benchmarks* (1967) and *Federal Jurisdiction: a General View* (1973). In 1977 he was awarded the Presidential Medal of Freedom, and in the following year the Thomas Jefferson Memorial Award in Law.

BIBLIOGRAPHY: *Harvard Law Review* 99 (1986); K. Johnson, *N.Y. Times* (June 10, 1986).

[Milton Ridvas Konvitz]

FRIENDSHIP, a relationship between people arising from mutual respect and affection. The ideal of friendship in the Western world is largely derived from classical Greece. Not only do the myths and legends point to friendship as one of the great human achievements, but the philosophers make it one of the primary virtues of existence. The Romans continued this exaltation of friendship, as is evident in Cicero's essay on the topic, *De amicitia*. Biblical tradition seems to take friendship, as it does so many other general values, for granted and accords it respect; yet it never raises the close relationship between one person and a chosen companion to the status of a major ideal. There can be no question that the significance of true friendship is recognized in the Bible. A friend (*re'a*) is defined, almost accidentally, in Deuteronomy 13:7 as "one who is like your very self"; in Proverbs 18:24 a friend (*ohev*) is one "who sticks closer than a brother." There are few depictions of friendship in the Bible; the most notable examples are those of David and Jonathan (I Sam. 20), David and Barzillai (II Sam.17:27–29, 19:32–40), and Ruth and Naomi (Ruth 1:7–3:17). When Jephthah's daughter goes off to bewail her fate she asks permission to do so with her companions (Judg. 11:37). The Bible seems to emphasize proper concern for one's neighbor as a means for the creation of a sacred society, rather than intense person-to-person relationships. This may be a safeguard against homosexuality, which was so much a part of the Greek conception of friendship.

Typical of the Bible's ethical concern in human relations is the frequent reference to false friendship in the book of Proverbs. As the worthy friend is he who stands by you, so the bad friend is he who deserts you when you are in need. Thus the warning is issued that the rich, not the poor, have many friends (14:20); that friends flock to the gift giver (19:6); and that he who has many friends has reason to worry (18:24). The rabbinic tradition, like the biblical, shows appreciation of friendship. The friendship of David and Jonathan is held up as the supreme example of altruistic love (Avot 5:19). It does not consider it a major concern, however, though the good *ḥaver* (associate or colleague, *ibid.*, 1:6; 2:13) and the good neighbor (2:13) are mentioned as ideals to be sought. The *amora* Rav is reported to have praised the friends of Job for going to see him when they learned of his suffering, even though they lived at a great distance from him. In response to Rav, Rabbah quoted the popular saying "Either a friend like the friends of Job or death" (BB 16b). The Talmud reports that Rabbi Zera showed friendship even to some lawless men who lived near him. It chides some of the other sages who did not do so for their hardness of heart but praises them for their repentance (Sanh. 37a). Modern Jewish thought, responding to the ethical implications of the concept of friendship, has shown a renewed interest in this subject, exemplified in the writings of Martin *Buber (*I and Thou*, 1952^2, passim) and Hermann *Cohen (*Religion der Vernunft* (1929^2), 510).

[Eugene B. Borowitz]

FRIENDSHIP LEAGUES WITH ISRAEL. Societies established in various countries for the promotion of friendly and cultural relations between their countries and Israel. Listed below are the countries where such societies exist. They have a total membership of about 30,000. Although a number of them were formed immediately after the establishment of the State in 1948, the majority were formed after 1965.

The leading members of these societies include distinguished citizens from all walks of life. The societies organize lectures, seminars, Israeli art exhibitions and concerts, and receptions for Israeli personalities. Some of them also organize annual study tours to Israel for their members. They publish pamphlets, quarterlies, and books on life in Israel. In Latin America, these organizations take the form of "cultural institutes."

Though a few societies tend to be of a more political nature, the majority concentrate on cultural relations. They are composed mainly of non-Jews, but in some countries Jewish community leaders are also active as officers or members. In addition to the friendship leagues, there are a number of pro-Israel parliamentary groups e.g., in Great Britain, West Germany, and France. In Britain three such groups, Conservative Friends of Israel, Labour Friends of Israel, and Liberal Friends of Israel, are active mainly in political circles.

In Israel, corresponding societies promote friendship with 27 countries, while the Israel-Asia Friendship Council and the Israel-Africa Friendship Association are roof organizations to promote relations with the two continents as a whole, and the Central Cultural Institute in Jerusalem coordinates the work done for Spanish- and Portuguese-speaking countries.

The Council of Israel Friendship Leagues coordinates all these activities, which include the spreading of information of the respective countries and their cultures, contacts with sister societies abroad, entertaining visitors, and arranging concerts and exhibitions.

In their respective countries the friendship societies cooperate with the local Zionist federations and with other Jewish bodies, receiving support from the External Relations Department of the World Zionist Organization.

By the late 1970s the countries with Friendship Leagues and Cultural Institutes were as follows: Australia, Mauritius, New Zealand; in Europe – Austria, Belgium, Denmark, Finland, France, Greece, Holland, Ireland, Italy, Norway, Spain, Sweden, Switzerland, the United Kingdom, and Germany; in North America – Canada and the U.S.; in Asia – India, Japan, Nepal, Philippines, South Korea; Latin America (Cultural Institutes) Argentina, Bolivia, Brazil, Chile, Colombia, Costa Rica, Ecuador, El Salvador, Guatemala; Honduras, Mexico, Nicaragua, Panama, Peru, Uruguay, and Venezuela; Australia. Through its Youth Ambassador Student Exchange program for secondary school students, the America-Israel Friendship League, founded in 1971, has brought together over 5,000 students.

BIBLIOGRAPHY: Letter, published periodically by External Relations Department, Jewish Agency, Jerusalem (Jan. 1962–June 1965); *Record of Activities of the Friendship Leagues Abroad and in Israel* (November, 1965–); Benjamin Jaffe, *Twenty Years of Activities* (1977). **WEBSITE:** www.aifl.org.

[Benjamin Jaffe]

°FRIES, JAKOB FRIEDRICH (1773–1843), German antisemitic philosopher. He lectured in Jena and Heidelberg and published authoritative works on philosophy and psychology. On the one hand, Fries was an advocate of enlightenment, civil and constitutional rights and the equality of man. On the other hand he propagated a cultural, religious, and *voelkisch* conception of a homogeneous German nation excluding Jews as an ethnic and religious minority. In his pamphlet *Ueber die Gefaehrdung des Wohlstandes und Charakters der Deutschen durch die Juden* (Heidelberg, 1816), Fries accused the Jews of "physical separation" from the German people and demanded an enforced integration by the complete adoption of German culture and values and the destruction of Judaism and Jewish traditions: "We do not declare war on the Jews, our brothers, but on Jewry" (*Judenschaft*). Immediately after the Napoleonic wars, Fries took part in the nationalistic student agitation and was the only member of the professional staff present at the 1817 Wartburg demonstration. His popularity with the students contributed to the success of his anti-Jewish writings. Under his influence, the Burschenschaft (students' associations) decided not to accept Jews as members. Although Fries' antisemitic attitude was not principally racist, his rabid language and the frequent use of the words "destruction" and "annihilation" in particular paved the way for radical forms of racial antisemitism.

BIBLIOGRAPHY: J. Katz, *From Prejudice to Destruction. Anti-Semitism 1700–1933* (1980); G. Hubmann, "Voelkischer Nationalismus und Antisemitismus im fruehen 19. Jahrhundert. Die Schriften von Ruehs und Fries zur Judenfrage," in: R. Heuer and R.-R. Wuthenow (eds.), *Antisemitismus, Zionismus, Antizionismus 1850–1940* (1997), 10–34; G. Hubmann, "Menschenwürde und Antijudaismus. Zur politischen Philosophie von J.F. Fries," in: W. Hogrebe (ed.), J.F. Fries, *Philosoph, Naturwissenschaftler und Mathematiker* (1999), 141–63

[Leon Poliakov]

FRIGEIS, LAZARO DE (16th century), physician. Scholars disagree on whether he was a native of Hungary or Holland. When Andrea Vesalius (1514–1564), the great anatomist, came to Padua, Frigeis became a member of his close circle of friends. He furnished Vesalius with the Hebrew names for some of the anatomic structures described in Vesalius' epoch-making work *De Humani Corporis Fabrica* and possibly also those appearing in *Tabulae Anatomicae*. The Hebrew anatomical terms used are for the most part taken from the Hebrew translation of the *Canon* of Avicenna and in some cases directly from the Talmud.

BIBLIOGRAPHY: S.E. Franco, in: RMI, 15 (1949), 495–515, incl. bibl.; C. Singer and C. Rabin, *Prelude to Modern Science* (1946), xxvi, 24, 30.

[Suessmann Muntner]

FRISCH, DANIEL (1897–1950), U.S. Zionist leader. Frisch, who was born in Ereẓ Israel, was taken by his family to Romania when he was one year old. He immigrated to the U.S. in 1921, settled in Indianapolis, Indiana, and eventually became an investment broker and the head of a large salvage firm. In 1934 Frisch, a militant General Zionist from his youth, became a member of the Zionist Organization of America's (ZOA) Administrative Council. In the course of the next 25 years he held numerous other Zionist posts before being elected ZOA president in 1949. In that same year, largely through Frisch's efforts, the ZOA, the Jewish Agency, and the World Confederation of Zionists reached agreement for financing various projects in Israel. Frisch's approach to Zionism was reflected in his belief that Israel's growth and welfare were dependent upon the strength of the General Zionist movement and in the need for the development of a strong private sector in the Israeli economy. A collection of his essays, sketches, and letters was published as *On the Road to Zion* (1950).

FRISCH, EFRAIM (1873–1942), Austrian author and journalist. Born at Stry in the Ukraine, Frisch was a member of an Orthodox family. Following the success of his novel *Das Verloebnis* (1902), he worked at Max *Reinhardt's Deutsches Theater in Berlin as director of drama from 1904 to 1908. In 1902 his writing was also included in the first volume published by the Jüdischer Verlag, the *Jüdischer Almanach*, among contributions from Stefan Zweig and Max Liebermann. His views on the stage are contained in *Von der Kunst des Theaters* (1910). After some years with a Munich publishing house, Frisch co-edited with Wilhelm Hausenstein *Der Neue Merkur* (1914–1925), a literary and political monthly whose contributors included Gottfried Benn, Bertholt Brecht, Martin Buber, André Gide, Yvan Goll, Bernard Shaw, and Arnold Zweig. He also published translations from the French (Giraudoux, Cocteau), English (Priestley), Polish, and Yiddish (Mendele Mokher Seforim).

Zenobi (1927), a brilliantly written novel generally considered Frisch's masterpiece, shows how a gentle, impractical, and naïve fool becomes the touchstone for a depersonalized and corrupt world of materialism, militarism, and technology. Frisch's positive attitude toward Judaism is clear from the frequent and sympathetic presentation of the East-European Jewish milieu in his fiction. He once published a special Jewish issue of *Der Neue Merkur* and in 1935 delivered four public lectures on Judaism at Ascona, Switzerland, where he later died.

BIBLIOGRAPHY: Stern, in: LBIY, 6 (1961), 125–49. **ADD. BIBLIOGRAPHY:** G. Stern, *War, Weimar, and Literature: The Story of Der Neue Merkur* (1971); G. Mattenklott, "Literarische Kritik im Kontext deutscher Judaica (1895–1933)"; M. Heimann and E. Frisch, in: *Studi germanici. Rivista bimestrale dell'istituto italiano di studi germanici.* (1990), 303–20; idem, in: W. Barner (ed.), *Literaturkritik – Anspruch und Wirklichkeit* (1992), 87–97; idem, in: M. Ponzi (ed.), *Tradizione ebraica e cultura di lingua tedesca* (1995), 150–62; *Juedische Autoren Ostmitteleuropas im 20. Jahrhundert* (2000).

[Harry Zohn]

FRISCH, EPHRAIM (1880–1957), U.S. Reform rabbi. An outspoken rabbi who held pulpits in Arkansas, New York, and Texas, Frisch stirred controversy throughout his career by praising communism, denouncing the poll tax, criticizing Zionism as a "menace," and ridiculing legislators who banned evolution texts from the schools.

A native of Shubocz, Lithuania, Frisch was the son of Rabbi David and Hannah Baskowitz Frisch. He immigrated to the United States in 1888 through the Great Lakes port of Duluth, Minn. Religious scholarship and political liberalism were prevalent in his family tree. His maternal great-grandfather, Rabbi Alexander Sender, who was hailed as a *gaon*, wrote the talmudic commentary, *Hatarat Nedarim* (1880), discussing contracts and vows. Frisch's cousin, Leonard Frisch (1890–1984), was a national Zionist leader and the editor of *American Jewish World*, a Twin Cities weekly.

Frisch grew up in Minneapolis and was ordained in 1904 from Hebrew Union College, where he was founding editor of the college annual. At his first pulpit, Anshe Emeth (1904–1912) in Pine Bluff, Ark., he launched the state's first county tuberculosis association, supported an African American minister who hosted biracial gatherings, and criticized the governor for referring to Jesus in a Thanksgiving Day proclamation. In 1912, Frisch moved to Temple Israel in Far Rockaway, Queens. There he established a temple social service department that created Children's Haven of Far Rockaway for temporary care of indigent youngsters.

In the spring of 1915 Frisch founded the New Synagogue, a Manhattan congregation whose credo stressed humanitarian deeds, social action, flexible rituals, and liturgy augmented with secular readings. The following year, he married Ruth Cohen (1890–1934), a pianist and writer and the daughter of Galveston's Rabbi Henry Cohen (1863–1952). Her connections and congeniality drew people to the budding congregation. The *New York Evening Post* hailed Frisch and his congregation as "post/Darwin." By 1918, however, Frisch's opposition to the Balfour Declaration and his characterization of Zionism as a "menace" led to rebuffs from colleagues, disenchantment among congregants, and a line in the *American Hebrew* denigrating him as an "obscure rabbi."

In 1923 Frisch became rabbi of Temple Beth-El in San Antonio. In the conservative South, Frisch was a lightning rod for controversy. He criticized compulsory Bible reading in the schools, urged an American boycott of the Berlin Olympics, sympathized with the city's underpaid pecan shellers, and denounced the city's squalid slums. Jewish youth, inspired by Frisch's idealism, gravitated to the rabbi and his wife, who launched a young adult group that staged plays, dances, book reviews, and political debates. Older congregants were less enamored of the rabbi. During sermons favoring the New Deal and Filipino independence, some congregants walked out or spoke up in opposition. In June 1942, despite two years left on Frisch's contract, the congregation voted the rabbi into retirement. For a short time he directed the Social Justice Commission of the Central Conference of American Rabbis, then quit over administrative matters. Embittered and now a widower, he spent his remaining years living alone in New York.

BIBLIOGRAPHY: H.A. Weiner, *Jewish Stars in Texas: Rabbis and their Work* (1999), 156–81.

[Hollace Ava Weiner (2nd ed.)]

FRISCH, OTTO ROBERT (1904–1979) physicist, nephew of the physicist Lise *Meitner. Frisch was born in Vienna but was naturalized as a British citizen (1943). After gaining his D.Phil. in physics from the University of Vienna (1926) he worked at the national physics laboratory in Berlin (1927–30) and with the Nobel physics laureate Otto *Stern in Hamburg (1930–33). With the coming of the Nazis, he left Germany in 1933 to work in Patrick Blackett's laboratory in Birkbeck College, London, before joining Niels *Bohr's laboratory in Copenhagen (1934–38). With the threat of war and invasion, Frisch moved to Mark Oliphant's laboratory in Birmingham, England (1939–40) but joined James Chadwick's laboratory in Liverpool as this was more appropriate for his work. With the merging of U.K. and U.S. research on nuclear weapons he moved to Los Alamos (1943–46), returning to England in 1946 as head of the nuclear physics division at the Atomic Energy Establishment in Harwell. In 1947 he was appointed Jacksonian Professor of natural philosophy at Cambridge University and a fellow of Trinity College, working in the Cavendish Laboratory. He retired in 1972. His initial research in Germany concerned the physical properties of nuclear particles, including the discovery of the magnetic moment of protons. In Copenhagen he studied radioactive isotopes and the outcome of collisions between neutrons and nuclei. At the end of 1938 he and Lise Meitner calculated the enormous energy which could potentially be released by what they termed "fission," the process just described by Otto Hahn and Fritz Strassman whereby uranium nuclei are split by colliding neutrons. He rapidly identified the fission products experimentally in Bohr's laboratory. Frisch was early to recognize the practical implications of sustained fission and, in collaboration with Rudolf Peierls, he calculated that neutrons could induce a chain reaction in a small enough quantity of pure uranium 235 to make a bomb feasible. In Los Alamos he worked in considerable personal danger on the chain reactions in pure uranium 235 and plutonium underlying the first fission bombs. In Cambridge he developed devices for tracking particles, one of which was marketed successfully under his chairmanship. He was also deeply interested in science education and he wrote many well received books for general readers. He continued his commercial and literary interests in retirement. He was elected a fellow of the Royal Society in 1948.

[Michael Denman (2nd ed.)]

FRISCHMANN, DAVID (1859–1922), one of the first major writers in modern Hebrew literature. Versatile and prolific in his literary creativity, Frischmann was an innovator in style and in the treatment of his subject, especially in the Hebrew short story, the ballad, the essay, criticism, and the lyric-satiric feuilleton. He also distinguished himself as a translator of world literature, and as an editor. In introducing Western aestheticism into Hebrew literature, Frischmann was a major influence in the development of Hebrew literature according to the aesthetic concepts of the world.

Early Career

He was born in Zgierz, near Lodz, into a well-to-do mercantile family which, although traditional, approved of the Haskalah. His education included Hebrew religious studies as well as humanities. At a young age, Frischmann already showed signs of literary talent and was considered a prodigy. At 15, his first writings were published – the sonnet "*Yesh Tikvah,*" a translation of Heine's "Don Ramiro," and "*Tarnegol ve-Tarnegolet,*" an original short story (*Ha-Boker Or*, 1874). He published satirical writings in *Ha-Shaḥar, whose editor, *Smolenskin, hailed him as a "brilliant star that has risen in our literary spheres – Boerne and Heine in German and Frischmann in Hebrew."

Short Stories

Frischmann's early satirical narratives, with their inherent social criticism, influenced by the writings of J.L. *Gordon and

K.E. *Franzos, gave way to the short story whose purpose was mainly aesthetic. Jewish life was now portrayed more objectively. Frequently, the main characters were Jews who had come into direct conflict with the mores of the traditional society in which they lived and who, because of these conflicts, had either become estranged from it, or were rejected by it. In *"Yom ha-Kippurim"* (1881), a Jewish girl attracted to the world of music becomes a famous singer but abandons her people and traditions. At a recital in the church of her native town, on the Day of Atonement, she meets her death at the hand of her widowed mother who, out of shame and pain, has become demented. In *"Ha-Ish u-Miktarto,"* a famous rabbi is so addicted to smoking that he is forced to violate the Sabbath, first furtively, and later publicly; as a result, he is excommunicated. Frischmann empathizes with these protagonists who succumb to human weaknesses and describes them with compassion and understanding.

Ba-Midbar (1923), a series of fictional biblical tales, alluding to biblical motifs and written in a biblical style and language, are original both in their choice of subject and in form. Set in the desert, immediately after the exodus of the Israelites from Egypt, the characters are torn between the half-pagan primitive habits and lusts that they still cling to, and the new moral life preached by Moses as the word of God. Their leaders and priests, responsible for the observance and teaching of the new precepts, are themselves not always faithful to them. These stories, while evoking nostalgia for the ancient era, also reflect universal themes relevant to Frischmann and his time: the conflict between religion as an act of faith and as law, and instinct.

Literary Critic

Frischmann frequently was a scathing literary critic. Thus in an article, *"Mi-Misterei Sifrutenu"* (*Ha-Boker Or*, 1880), he violently admonished P. Smolenskin, the leading authority in Hebrew literature at that time, whom he accused of plagiarizing from M. *Hess's *Rome and Jerusalem*. In *Tohu va-Vohu* (1883), he mocks and scorns the Hebrew literary journalism of his day because of its inefficiency and provincialism. In due course, Frischmann became an authoritative arbiter of good taste and a champion of literary writing for art's sake. He defended J.L. Gordon against the attacks of M.L. *Lilienblum – who had accused Gordon of not being sufficiently nationalistic in his writings (in a critical article published in *Ha-Asif*, 1894). His admiration for Gordon did not, however, prevent him from criticizing Gordon on another matter. He claimed that Gordon, after joining the editorial board of *Ha-Meliẓ*, had abandoned those liberal views which he had expounded for 30 years previously.

An Iconoclast Poet

Frischmann's literary nonconformism, expressed in two of his earliest poems *"Lo Elekh Immam"* and *"Elilim,"* were to become the motto of his life and his literary credo. In *"Lo Elekh Immam,"* he voices his refusal to follow the old path and expresses his fearless criticism:

> I shall not go with them, I shall not go; their ways are not mine,
> I cannot bear their prattle, their expressions, their talk or their conversation.
> I cannot tolerate their ways, their manners, or their thoughts,
> Their prophets are not my prophets, their angels are not my angels.
> Thoughts repel me, thoughts without minds,
> I detest feelings, feelings without hearts.

"Elilim" points to Frischmann the iconoclast; the poem harks back to the patriarch Abraham whom he sees as the first iconoclast. The poet claims that Abraham in smashing the idols had not completed the act, since the largest of the idols still survived. He calls upon the patriarch to endow him with his ancient venerated spirit, so that he might smite surviving idols.

A non-observant Jew, Frischmann rejected as futile and impractical the attempts at religious reforms in the 19th century, whose purpose was the adaptation of Judaism to the spirit of the times. In *"Ani va-Avi Zekeni,"* Frischmann argues that the grandfathers who cling to Judaism would not assent to any reform of the *mitzvot* which, in their view, were all "given to Moses at Sinai," whereas the younger generation, with which the author identifies, does not need the sanction of tradition to act according to its conscience.

Frischmann and European Culture

Like many of his contemporaries, Frischmann's introduction to European culture was by way of German, a language he had studied in his youth. Two German-Jewish authors, *Heine and *Boerne, exercised a profound influence upon his writing. Frischmann visited Germany several times, and during his 1882 stay, became personally acquainted with a number of authors and scientists, among them B. Auerbach, a German-Jewish writer, and A. *Bernstein, whose large popular scientific work, *Knowledge of Nature*, Frischmann was to translate in part. Between 1890 and 1895, he studied philology, philosophy, and the history of art at the University of Breslau. He returned to Warsaw in 1895, and until 1910, translation became his regular occupation. The works he rendered from German, Russian, and English into Hebrew during that period include J. Lippert's *The History of the Perfection of Man* (1894–1908), George Eliot's *Daniel Deronda* (1893), legends and tales of Hans Christian Andersen (1896), selected poems of Alexander Pushkin (1899), Byron's *Cain* (1900), and Nietzsche's *Also sprach Zarathustra* (1900). Frischmann devoted his entire life to literature and avoided all public office or public involvements. His many opponents accused him of anti-Zionism. In actuality, it was his rejection of the use of art for ideological or propagandistic purposes that caused him to refrain from advocating social or political views.

Frischmann as a Hebrew Journalist

In the 19th century, the dividing line between belles lettres and journalism had not been clearly defined, and most authors engaged in both disciplines without differentiating between them. Frischmann published a series of short stories, *Otiyyot Poreḥot* (1893), a series of book reviews, and a series of feuilletons on practical subjects, called *"Ba-Kol-mi-Kol-Kol"* in *Ha-Asif.* His adversaries often dismissed him as "merely a feuilletonist." Frischmann, who did not accept the old forms, and left on all the genres he employed his mark as innovator – in style, structure, choice of content and its treatment – saw the feuilleton as a new form of poetry whose range extended far beyond that of any other type of poetry. In his eulogy of Theodor *Herzl, Frischmann wrote:

> I knew him as an artist in his field long before he became famous as the father of Zionism. My enthusiasm for Herzl, the feuilletonist, was so great, that for a time I almost hated Zionism because it had robbed me of his poetic powers and transformed a great poet into a man of public affairs concerned with petty politics. However immense his contribution to Zionism may have been, the loss to literature is immeasurable.

Frischmann had a special affinity for political leaders who had literary talents. He wrote with enthusiasm about the diary of Ferdinand *Lassalle, and about the private letters of Rosa *Luxemburg.

Editor and Publisher of Journals

Frischmann published several short stories in the German literary monthly *Salon* (Leipzig, in 1885), in *Ha-Meliẓ* (whose editor, J.L. Gordon, invited him to join its editorial board in 1896); and in *Ha-Yom*, the first Hebrew daily. Frischmann preferred *Ha-Yom* because it was an independent journal and its editor and principal contributors, among them J.L. *Kantor, and J.L. Katznelson, shared the same liberal outlook as he. Frischmann served as assistant editor and published his feuilletons almost daily; the series "Letters Concerning Literature" became one of the foundation stones of modern Hebrew criticism.

In 1901 Frischmann became editor of *Ha-Dor*, a literary weekly whose high literary standard attracted the most talented writers of the day. After one year it was forced to close down, due to its small circulation. Frischmann tried to revive it three years later, but failed after publishing 38 additional issues. Zalman *Shneour, describing the *Ha-Dor* period in his memoirs, says: "Frischmann was generally considered a quarrelsome man; his antagonists considered him a cynic. In truth, he was a mild, pleasant man who loved talented and promising young people."

In 1903 Frischmann became editor of the literary supplement of the Vilna daily newspaper *Ha-Zeman*, in 1909, in Warsaw, of the short-lived *Ha-Boker*; between 1908 and 1910 of the literary collections *Sifrut* (1909–10); and of *Reshafim* (1909–10; pocket-sized literary anthologies) in which he published, in serial form, his translation of *Also sprach Zarathustra*.

Frischmann in Yiddish

Hebrew was Frischmann's literary vehicle of expression, and he was faithful to biblical Hebrew, which he had mastered probably better than any contemporary author, rejecting the "synthetic" Hebrew developed by *Mendele Mokher Seforim and his school. Occasionally, however, he also wrote in Yiddish and in German. The few poems that he composed in Yiddish are lyrical in tone. He also wrote short stories and feuilletons in that language. His first Yiddish articles were published in *Shalom Aleichem's *Yudishe Folksbibliothek* (1888–89), but he also contributed Yiddish poems and articles to the literary annual *Hoys-Fraynd*, the weekly *Der Yud*, and the daily *Fraynd*. From 1908, he was a regular contributor of weekly feuilletons to the Warsaw Yiddish daily *Haynt*. His collected Yiddish stories were published in two volumes by the Lodz Pedagogue editions, and his Yiddish articles on drama and literature were published by the Warsaw Progress editions. These collected works are only a small part of Frischmann's Yiddish writings, most of which are still uncollected.

Frischmann's Visits to Palestine

Frischmann visited Palestine twice, in 1911 and 1912, each time with groups organized by *Haynt*, in which he published his travel impressions. These he also published in Hebrew in a small book entitled *Ba-Areẓ* (1913). Overwhelmed by his experiences, he wrote emotionally about the holy places he had visited, the landscape, his meetings with the pioneers, and the beginnings of the revival of Hebrew. His initial skepticism gave way to enthusiasm, and he candidly and openly retracted his reservations about the rebirth of Hebrew as a vernacular.

Frischmann in Russia During World War I and the Revolution

At the outbreak of World War I, Frischmann was on a visit in Berlin, where he was interned as an enemy alien. Eventually, he was set free and allowed to return to Poland. When the conquering German army neared Warsaw, he left for Odessa where he remained until the Russian Revolution. While in Odessa, he wrote some of his most beautiful lyrical poems, translated *The Conversations of the Grimm Brothers* for the Moriah editions of Bialik-Rawnitzki and the poetry of the Indian poet Rabindranath Tagore. Frischmann's translation of Tagore's poetry is a masterpiece. The translation, together with several original poems, and a series of literary obituaries, were published in *Keneset* (1917), edited by *Bialik. During his stay in Odessa, he also contributed weekly feuilletons to the Odessa Yiddish newspaper *Undzer Lebn*, until the Russian authorities closed down the paper.

After the revolution of February 1917, a Hebrew literary center was formed in Moscow, and Frischmann was invited to be the chairman of the editorial board of the A.J. Stybel publications. He was named editor of *Ha-Tekufah, the quarterly published by Stybel. There he published his translations of Goethe, Heine, Byron, Oscar Wilde, Anatole France, and Tagore. He also continued his biblical stories of the *Ba-Midbar* series. Stybel's generous support enabled him, as well as many other authors, to devote themselves entirely to writing. The publication program of the house was outlined by Frischmann in his address on "Belles Lettres" at the second Hebrew Language and Culture congress in Vienna (1913).

In 1919 the Stybel publishing house was closed down in Moscow, and reestablished in Warsaw, where Frischmann continued in his capacity of editor. There he also published a series of "New Letters Concerning Literature" in the monthly *Miklat* (another Stybel project, edited by Y.D. *Berkowitz in New York), and translated the "Legends" (*Aggadot*) of Max Nordau (1923[2]) and Shakespeare's *Coriolanus* (published in 1924). Grave illness compelled him to travel to Berlin to seek medical treatment; there he died and was buried.

Frischmann's Conversations and Letters

Besides his great literary prolificacy, perseverance in pursuing an idea or belief, and his immense contributions to the different branches of literature, Frischmann's talent also revealed itself in his letters to friends (few unfortunately survive), and in conversation. Some of his conversations were written down later, from memory, by his admirers: J. *Fichmann, E. *Steinman, and Z. *Shneour. His letters to his contemporaries, rarely personal, are a valuable source of information on Frischmann and on the history of the Hebrew literature of his period. Eleven of his letters, *Iggerot David Frischmann* ed. by E.R. Malachi, were collected and published in New York (1927); others were published in different periodicals.

Collected writings of Frischmann have been published in various editions: (1) *Ketavim Nivḥarim* (4 vols., Piotrokow-Warsaw, 1899–1905), a selection of his writings with an introduction by Y.L. Kantor; (2) *Ketavim Ḥadashim* (5 vols., Warsaw, 1909–12); (3) *Kol Kitvei David Frischmann u-Mivḥar Tirgumav* (16 vols., Warsaw, 1922[2]), his complete writings and a selection of his translations, as well as an additional volume (vol. 17) of his articles; (4) *Kol Kitvei Frischmann* (8 vols., Warsaw-New York, 1939), his complete writings; (5) *Kol Kitvei Frischmann* (8 vols. published until 1968), his complete works; (6) *Tirgumim* (1954), a collection of all his literary translations. Four books of Frischmann's collected Yiddish writings were published by the Pedagogue editions (1909) in Lodz, and the Progress editions (1911) in Warsaw. Many of Frischmann's writings in Hebrew, as well as in Yiddish and German, have not yet been collected in book form and are still scattered in different periodicals. For English translations, see Goell, Bibliography, 674–81, 2046–91, 2794–95.

BIBLIOGRAPHY: D. Frischmann, in: *Ha-Tekufah*, 16 (1923; autobiographical letter, written in 1893 to S.L. Zitron); E.R. Malachi (ed.), *Iggerot Frischmann* (1927); N. Sokolow, in: *Ha-Tekufah*, 16 (1923); J. Fichmann, *Ruḥot Menaggenot* (1952), 117–74: E. Steinman, *Mi-Dor el Dor: Seder Frischmann* (1951); Z. Shneour, *David Frischmann ve-Aḥerim* (1959); Y.D. Berkowitz, *Ha-Rishonim ki-Venei Adam, bein Shalom Aleikhem u-Frischmann* (1943); Y.H. Rawnitzki, *Dor ve-Soferav* (1927; in memory of D. Frischmann); Lachower, Sifrut, 3 pt. 1 (1963), 123–78; R. Brainin, *Ketavim Nivḥarim, Avot: David Frischmann* (1950); A.A. Ben-Yishai, in: *Sefer ha-Shanah shel ha-Ittona'im be-Yisrael* (1961); Rejzen, Leksikon, 204–28; Z. Fishman, in: *En Hakore* (1923); Waxman, Literature, index; N. Slouschz, *David Frischmann* (Fr., 1913). **ADD. BIBLIOGRAPHY:** Sh. Kremer, "*Hista'aruto shel Frischmann al Sifrut ha-Haskalah*," in: *Moznayim* 35 (1972), 230–35; M. Gilboa, *Bein Re'alizm le-Romantikah: Al Darko shel D. Frischmann ba-Bikkoret* (1975); G. Shaked, *Ha-Sipporet ha-Ivrit*, 1 (1977), 114–30; S. Kramer, *Frischmann ha-Mevaker: Monografyah* (1984); U. Shoham, in: *Te'udah* 5 (1986), 101–15; Z. Kagan, "*Ma'aseh ha-Sippur: Sippurei 'Ba-Midbar*,'" in: *Dapim le-Meḥkar ba-Sifrut* 7 (1990). 95–110; M. Gilboa (ed.), *David Frischmann: Mivḥar Ma'amrei Bikkoret al Yeẓirato* (1988), bibliography; E. Mats, "Tenses in Frischmann's *Ba-Midbar*," in: *Jewish Studies in a New Europe* (1998), 223–28; I. Parush, *Kanon Sifruti ve-Ideologyah Le'ummit: Bikkoret ha-Sifrut shel Frischmann be-Hashva'ah le-Bikoret ha-Sifrut shel Klozner u-Vrener* (1992); Y. Peleg, *Reinterpreting the East: Orientalism in Hebrew Literature 1890–1930* (2000); R. Scheneld, "*Mashber ba-Mishpaḥah*," in: *Mi-Vilnah li-Yerushalayim* (2002), 343–59.

[Aharon Zeev Ben-Yishai]

°**FRITSCH, THEODOR** (1852–1933), German antisemitic publicist and politician. One of the leading early racists, in 1886 he joined the Deutsche Anti-semitische Vereinigung (see *Antisemitism) which strove to repeal the emancipation law. In 1887 he published the *Antisemiten-Katechismus ...* (1887) as a catalog of "Jewish misdeeds." Later renamed *Handbuch der Judenfrage*, it went through 49 editions until 1944. In 1902 Fritsch established the periodical *Hammer* as a forum for antisemitic authors of the *voelkisch* movement in Germany. In the following years Fritsch played a leading role in the foundation of antisemitic and *voelkisch* organizations like the *Reichshammerbund* (founded in 1912), the *Deutschvölkische Schutz- und Trutzbund* (founded 1919), a mass organization with more than 200,000 members, and the *Deutschvölkische Freiheitspartei* (founded 1922, in 1924 Fritsch become one of its Reichstag members). The Nazis honored Fritsch as their *Altmeister*, and Hitler characterized the *Handbuch der Judenfrage* as important contribution that "paved the way for the National Socialist antisemitic movement."

ADD. BIBLIOGRAPHY: Michael Bönisch, "Die 'Hammer'-Bewegung," in: U. Puschner et al., *Handbuch zur "Völkischen Bewegung" 1871–1918*, (1996), 341–65; A. Volland, *Theodor Fritsch (1852–1933) und die Zeitschrift Hammer* (1994); S. Breuer, *Ordnungen der Ungleichheit. Die deutsche Rechte im Widerstreit ihrer Ideen 1871–1945* (2001); S. Tabary, "Theodor Fritsch (1852–1933). Le 'Vieux Maitre' de l'antisemitisme allemand at la diffusion de l'idée 'völkisch,'" (Diss., Strasbourg 1998).

FRITTA (**Friedrich Taussig**; 1909–1944), Czech painter and graphic artist. In 1942 he was deported to the concentration camp at *Theresienstadt. Here, together with fellow artists Leo *Haas, Otto Ungar, Friedrich Bloch (an Austrian painter), and later Karel Fleischmann, he formed a group of painters who assigned themselves the task of creating a pictorial record of the last days of men facing death. Fritta's contribution to this unique documentary was probably the largest. Their works were smuggled out of Theresienstadt over a two-year period. In July 1944 the Nazis discovered some of Fritta's works depicting shocking scenes of ghetto life. Fritta was imprisoned and deported to Auschwitz, where he died after undergoing torture. About 150 of his Theresienstadt drawings, buried in a tin case, were unearthed after the war, together with the works of other Theresienstadt artists. They are in the Jewish Museum in Prague.

BIBLIOGRAPHY: Frýd, in: *Terezin*, published by the Council of Jewish Communities in Czech Lands (1965), 206–18; Haas, *ibid.*, 156–62.

[Avigdor Dagan]

FRIULI-VENEZIA GIULIA, northeastern region of Italy. Jews were already settled in antiquity at Aquileia in Friuli. Between 1028 and 1420 the patriarch of Aquileia ruled over Friuli. Under his protection, Jewish merchants and moneylenders settled in *Cividale, Cormons (1340), Gemona (1395), Pordenone and Porcia (1399), San *Daniele, *Trieste (1348), Udine (1387), and Venzone (1333). Within a brief period, prosperous Jewish communities formed around them. When Friuli was annexed by the Republic of Venice in 1420, there was no essential change in the status of the Jews. However, at the end of the 15th and during the 16th centuries the preaching of friars and the Counter-Reformation movement led to deterioration in the situation of the Jews and the expulsion from Udine in 1556 and Cividale in 1572. The situation of the Jews living in Habsburg territory also deteriorated. However, in the middle of the 17th century Jews still lived at Gorizia and there was a new settlement at Gradisca. Jews were then segregated in ghettos, including Trieste in 1696.

In 1777, Jews were expelled from all the settlement in the territory of the Republic of Venice. However, for Jews living in Habsburg territory, the 18th century was a period of growth in both Gorizia and Trieste. With Joseph II's reforms, Habsburg Trieste became the center of attraction for Jews in Friuli. While in the course of the 19th century, all the other Jewish communities, with the exception of Gorizia, begun a steady decline, Trieste grew to become one of the most prosperous communities of the Habsburg Empire.

The end of World War I, and the passage of the whole region to Italy, as well as the deterioration of the economic situation, produced a decline in the Jewish population in Friuli. The Holocaust weighed heavily on Friuli's Jews, concentrated in Trieste. In the early 21st century, in all of Friuli, Jews lived only in Trieste.

BIBLIOGRAPHY: C. Roth, *Venice* (1930), 269, 349; F. Luzzatto, *Cronache storiche della Università degli ebrei di San Daniele del Friuli…* (1964); idem, in: RMI, 16 (1950), 140–6; Modona, in: *Vessillo Israelitico*, 47 (1899), 327–34, 366–8; Roth, Dark Ages, index. **ADD. BIBLIOGRAPHY:** S.G. Cusin, and P.C. Ioly Zorattini, *Friuli Venezia Giulia, Itinerari ebraici, I luoghi, la storia, l'arte* (1998), 9–19; M. Del Bianco Controzzi, *La comunita' ebraica di Gradisca d'Isonzo, Istituto di storia dell'Universita' di Udine*, Serie monografica di storia moderna e contemporanea (1983).

[Daniel Carpi / Samuele Rocca (2nd ed.)]

FRIZZI, BENEDETTO (Benzion Raphael Kohen; 1756–1844), Italian physician, engineer, and scholar from Ostiano near Mantova. He graduated from Pavia and practiced in Trieste. In 1790 he founded the first Italian medical journal and published six *Dissertazioni di polizia medica sul Pentateuco* (Pavia and Cremona, 1787–90) on precepts of the Law, presenting them in a modern scientific and apologetic manner. He also wrote *Difesa contro gli attacchi fatti alla nazione ebrea nel libro intitolato dell'influenza del ghetto nello Stato* (Pavia, 1784), an apologetic and polemical work, which intended to disprove the accusations by a contemporary Italian – Giovan Battista D'Arco from Mantua, author of *Dell'influenza del Ghetto nello Stato* (Venice, 1782) that Jews hated Christians and that their economic activities tended to impoverish the countries they lived in. He described Jewish theology, philosophy, and ethics and then analyzed in great detail and with many examples the economic role of Jews in Europe, particularly in Italy. He outlined the valuable functions they fulfilled historically and attributed their success as merchants to attention to details and quality, realistically low prices, avoidance of borrowing at interest, and trade in perennially useful products rather than luxury items for which demand varies. Frizzi enumerated markets and services opened and developed by Jews and described their business methods at length.

In *Dissertazione in cui si esaminano gli usi ed abusi degli ebrei nei luoghi ed effetti sacri e si propone la maniera di renderli utili in società* (Milan, 1789), he analyzed contemporary Judaism from a critical point of view, focusing in the first part on the inappropriate luxury of the synagogues and the tendency of rabbis to become preachers instead of scholars and doctors of theology; and in the second part on the prayers in general (Psalms, *Amidah*, etc.) and on the need to behave properly during the services. Finally, in the third part, he criticized bad sermons with their threatening manner and grammatical errors and also dealt with public and private charity.

He wrote his Hebrew work, *Petaḥ Enayyim*, in 3 vols. (Leghorn, 1815–25), to demonstrate that the rabbis' teachings were based on scientific knowledge, expounding the book *Ein Ya'akov Ein Yisrael* (Frankfurt am Main, 1723) of Ya'aov Kabyb, a masterpiece of the religious and normative culture of Italian Jewish communities. He hoped both to increase his contemporaries' respect for Torah and to attack traditionalists who saw Jewish law as untouchable and untouched by the modern spirit.

In addition, Frizzi published *Giornale medico e letterario di Trieste*, (4 vols., Trieste, 1790–91), *Opuscoli filosofici e medici* in (4 vols., Trieste, 1791–92), *Accademia letteraria sul metodo degli studi ebraici nella logica e altri filosofici rami* (Trieste, 1791), *Dissertazione sulla lebbra degli ebrei* (Trieste, 1795), and *Dissertazione di biografia musicale* (Trieste, 1803). A man of great learning and wide renown, Frizzi was considered one of the outstanding Jewish scholars of the Enlightenment in Western Europe.

BIBLIOGRAPHY: Nissim, in: RMI, 34 (1968), 279–91; Dinaburg, in: *Tarbiz*, 20 (1948/49), 241–64.

[David Niv / Federica Francesconi (2nd ed.)]

FROEHLICH, ALFRED (1871–1953), pharmacologist. He was born in Vienna and became professor of pharmacology and toxicology at the University of Vienna in 1912. In 1939 he settled in the U.S. and became associated with the Jewish

Hospital in Cincinnati. He was the first to describe in 1901 adiposo-genital dystrophy, a form of obesity which is associated with a tumor in the pituitary gland and deficient development of the sex organs. He collaborated with Otto *Loewi on the pharmacology of the autonomous nervous system, and as a result of their discoveries, the use of a combination of adrenalin and cocaine was established in medical practice. Together with the neurologist L.F. Hochward, Froehlich recommended the use of hypoglysin during delivery, a practice that became universally accepted. He and H.H. Mayer investigated the contracture of striated muscle fibers under influence of tetanus toxin. He carried out experimental research in increasing the effect of certain drugs and made extensive investigations into the effect of theophylline.

BIBLIOGRAPHY: S.A. Kagan, *Jewish Medicine* (1952), 209–12.

[Suessmann Muntner]

FROG (Heb. צְפַרְדֵּעַ; *ẓefarde'a*). One of the ten plagues visited upon Egypt was that of frogs (Ex. 7:29; Ps. 78:45; 105:30). They apparently made life intolerable for the Egyptians by their shrill croaking and by contaminating food with their moist bodies. The frog, *Rana esculenta*, is found in Israel near bodies of water. The word *ẓefarde'a* may also refer to the toad (*Bufo*). While the frog is, according to the laws of the Torah, prohibited as food, it is not included among the swarming things which, by contact, make man, vessels, and food unclean (cf. Lev. 11:29–30; Toh. 5:4).

BIBLIOGRAPHY: Tristram, Nat Hist, 280f.; J. Feliks, *Animal World of the Bible* (1962), 112. **ADD. BIBLIOGRAPHY:** Feliks, Ha-Ẓome'aḥ, 272.

[Jehuda Feliks]

FROHLICH, HERBERT (1905–1991), British physicist. Frohlich was born in Rexingen, Germany, in 1905. He earned his doctorate from the University of Munich at the age of 24 and lectured at Freiburg University before immigrating to England in 1933. There he was a research physicist, lecturer, and reader in theoretical physics at the University of Bristol (1935–1948), after which he became professor of theoretical physics at Liverpool. His varied research included electrical conductivity and he contributed to the microscopic theory of superconductivity. He held a number of visiting professorships, including one at Purdue University in the U.S.

In 1951 Frohlich was elected a fellow of the Royal Society. He was the recipient of numerous awards and honors, including the prestigious Max Planck Medal. His publications over a half century include two books and more than 140 original papers and review articles.

[Ruth Rossing (2nd ed.)]

FROHMAN, U.S. family of theatrical figures, born in Sandusky, Ohio. DANIEL (1851–1940), theater manager and producer, began his career as a journalist, but later turned to theater management. In 1880 he became business manager of the Madison Square Theater. Later he bought the Lyceum Theater (1885) and appointed David *Belasco as stage manager. He staged plays by Belasco, A.W. Pinero, V. Sardou, and H.A. Jones, and such stars as William Faversham, Henry Miller, and E.H. Sothern acted under his management. He also managed Daly's Theater (1899–1903) and, after the Lyceum closed, opened the New Lyceum (1903). Later he went into film production and became a director of the Paramount Company. In 1933 he returned to Broadway to produce an English version of the Yiddish drama *Yoshe Kalb* at the National Theater, but the play closed after four performances. Daniel was president of the Actors' Fund of America from 1903 until his death and remained a revered figure of the American stage. He recalled his career in *Memories of a Manager* (1911), *Daniel Frohman Presents* (1935), and *Encore* (1937).

His brother, GUSTAVE (1855–1930), a theater manager, interested Charles (see below) in the theater and persuaded Daniel to leave journalism.

A third brother, CHARLES (1860–1915), theater manager and producer, was for some years a booking agent with connections throughout the United States. Later he helped organize a theatrical syndicate which controlled U.S. theaters for several years. Frohman acquired the Empire Theater in New York and had controlling shares in others. He also had interests in five theaters in England. As a producer, he scored his first real success with *Shenandoah* (1889). He was the first U.S. producer to become famous outside the country and produced some 125 plays in London. Charles managed and developed many stars of the stage of his day, some of the best known being Maude Adams, Ethel Barrymore, John Drew, William Gillette, and Otis Skinner. He also introduced Oscar Wilde and Somerset Maugham to the American public. Frohman dominated the U.S. stage in his time and with his death, on the torpedoed *Lusitania*, an era ended.

[Jo Ranson]

FROHMAN, DOV (1939–), Israeli engineer. Born in Amsterdam, Frohman reached Israel with Youth Aliyah; his parents were murdered in the Holocaust. He received his B.Sc. from the Haifa Technion and his M.Sc. and Ph.D. degrees in electrical engineering and computer science from the University of California, Berkeley. Much of his work was devoted to the development of semi-conductor memories, and he developed the first EPROM products. Joining the staff of the Hebrew University in 1974, he headed the School for Applied Science and Technology there (1975–80), during which time he established a laboratory for the development of semi-conductor devices as a basis for applied research on memory devices. In 1981 he began to direct Intel activity in Israel, eventually becoming its general manager in Israel. In 1991 he received the Israel Prize for engineering and technology.

FROLKIS, VLADIMIR VENIAMINOVICH (1924–1999), Ukrainian physiologist and gerontologist. Frolkis was born in the Ukraine (Zhitomir). He was one of the founders of the Institute of Gerontology in Kiev, where he headed the Department of Biology of Aging and the Laboratory of Physiology. His research interests covered all major fields of experimental gerontology with particular emphasis on neurohormonal mechanisms of aging and longevity. He developed the adaptive-regulatory theory of aging. He was the author of more than 700 works, including 25 monographs and 15 handbooks. Among them is a fundamental work on *Life Span Prolongation* (1991). Frolkis was a full member of the National Academy of Sciences and vice president of the Academy of Medical Sciences of the Ukraine, a member of the International Parliament of Humanitarians, and a Merited Professor of the International Science Foundation. He received many awards, including a State Prize in Science and Technology, the A.A. Bogomolets Award and the I.I. Mechnikov Award from the National Academy of Sciences of Ukraine, and the Fritz Verzar Medal.

BIBLIOGRAPHY: V.V. Bezrukov, in: *Gerontology* (1999), 239–40.

[Vadim Fraifeld (2nd ed.)]

FROMAN, IAN (1937–), Israeli tennis developer. Born in Johannesburg, South Africa, Froman received his degree in dentistry in 1961 from the University of Witwatersrand. In 1964 he immigrated to Israel. A tennis player from his youth, he represented South Africa in the Wimbledon championship in 1961, participated in Maccabiahs as a South African and as an Israeli, was captain of the Israeli Davis Cup team and trainer of the national tennis team. He left dentistry in 1974 to devote himself full time to advancing a tennis center for Israeli youth which opened in 1976. There are now eight such tennis centers throughout Israel with thousands of young people participating in the sport. In 1989 he was awarded the Israel Prize for sport and physical culture. In 2004 he was chosen to be the chairmen of the Israeli tennis association, and was one of the torch carriers during the independence ceremony.

[Fern Lee Seckbach]

FROMM, ERICH (1900–1980), U.S. psychoanalyst, social philosopher, and author. Fromm, who was born in Frankfurt of rabbinic descent, studied at German universities and received his professional training at the Psychoanalytic Institute of Berlin. He worked at the Institute for Social Research in Frankfurt from 1929 to 1932, but immigrated to the U.S. when Hitler came to power in Germany. His first appointment in America was at the International Institute for Social Research in New York City (1934–39). He was on the faculty of Bennington College, Vermont, from 1941 to 1950. In 1951 he was appointed professor at the National University of Mexico. He was also professor at Michigan State University (1957–61) and New York University (1962). In 1974 he settled in Switzerland. A theoretician of the neo-Freudian school, he pursued an independent road in the application of psychoanalysis to the problems of culture and society. His psychological studies on the meaning of freedom for modern man have had a wide influence on western thought.

A student of the Bible and the Talmud, "brought up in a religious family where the Old Testament touched me and exhilarated me more than anything else I was exposed to," Fromm was a disciple of Ludwig Krause and Nehemia Nobel, and was greatly influenced by Hermann Cohen. Fromm believed that everyone has a religious need and that religion is "the formalized and elaborate answer to man's existence." He postulated two major kinds of religion: the authoritarian and the humanistic. He rejected the former, for here man is utterly powerless, and adopted the humanistic religion in which man experiences oneness with the All, achieving his greatest strength and self-realization, as in the Jewish prophets, where their doctrines have an underlying humanity and where freedom is the aim of life. He differed from Freud, and considered "the religious cult as vastly superior to neurosis, because man shares his feelings, his oneness, security, and stability with his fellow men, which the neurotic person lacks in his isolation."

Fromm claimed that Judaism is an "untheological religion, where the stress is on the underlying substratum of human experience." Making extensive use of Judaic texts and practices, he demonstrated their contemporary relevance to the human condition, showing, in a nontheological way, how the idea of God is a permanent challenge to all kinds of idolatry. In Fromm's view, alienation, which is identical to idolatry in the Bible, is the sum and substance of human misery in our society. To save Western man from "depersonalization," society must recognize the sovereignty of the individual. In contrast to Freudian orthodoxy, Fromm emphasized the need for a social and cultural orientation in psychoanalysis.

Fromm's belief in the need for a society which recognizes man as a responsible individual is expounded in *The Sane Society* (1955). This society he regarded as the best antidote to the totalitarianism that he denounces in *Escape from Freedom* (1941). His other studies deal with the interrelation of psychology and ethics, psychoanalysis and social history, myth and religion, and dream symbolism. These books include: *Man for Himself* (1947); *Psychoanalysis and Religion* (1950); *The Forgotten Language* (1952); *The Art of Loving* (1956); and *You Shall Be as Gods* (1967), a psychiatric commentary on the biblical view of God in which he declares that the "Old Testament is a revolutionary book because its theme is the liberation of man."

Fromm's first wife was Frieda *Fromm-Reichman, whom he married in 1926.

BIBLIOGRAPHY: J.S. Glen, *Erich Fromm: a Protestant Critique* (1966); Friedenberg, in: *Commentary*, 34 (1962), 305–13.

[Menachem M. Brayer]

FROMM, HERBERT (1905–1995), German-born American organist, conductor, and composer. Born in Kitzingen on the Main, Bavaria, Fromm studied at the Academy of Music in Munich with Paul Hindemith. He worked as a theater conductor in Bielefeld (1930) and Wuerzburg (1931–33). In 1937 the Nazis forced him out of Germany and he went to the United States. There he became organist and director of music at

Temple Beth Zion, Buffalo, and from 1941 until 1973 at Temple Israel in Boston. He composed many works for the synagogue, and also a number of secular works. His synagogue compositions include *Adath Israel*, a service for Friday evening (1952); *Song of Miriam*, for women's choir, organ, or piano (1945); *Six Madrigals* (1951), for Sabbath and festivals; *Avodat Shabbat* (1960); *Psalm Cantata*, for mixed voices, organ, trumpet, viola, flute, and timpani (1963); *Ḥemdat Yamin*, a service for Sabbath morning (1964); *Chamber Cantata* (text by Judah Halevi), for mixed voices and eight instruments (1966); *Ḥag ha-Matzot*, suite on Passover melodies for harpsichord, flute, and cello (1967); and numerous anthems and organ compositions. In addition to his articles and essays in various journals and newspapers, he wrote *The Key of See: Travel Journey of a Composer* (1967), *Seven Pockets* (1977), and *On Jewish Music: A Composer's View* (1979). Fromm received the Ernest Bloch Award in 1945).

ADD. BIBLIOGRAPHY: Baker's Biographical Dictionary (1997); N.M. Steinberger and E. Kahn, An Inventory of the Herbert Fromm Collection (1995).

FROMM-REICHMANN, FRIEDA (1889–1957), U.S. pioneer of psychoanalytic psychiatry and psychotherapeutic teaching and research. Born in Karlsruhe, Germany, Frieda Fromm-Reichmann studied medicine, practiced in several German cities, and founded the South West German Psychoanalytic Institute. She worked at the "Weisser Hirsch" Sanatorium in Dresden, which was a crossroads of psychoanalysis, social reform, Jewish orthodoxy, and existentialist philosophy. With the advent of Nazism she left Germany in 1933 and went to the U.S., where she joined the Washington Psychoanalytic Society in 1935, worked at the William Alanson White Institute in New York, and at Chestnut Lodge in Rockville, Maryland. She believed in the voluntary acceptance of life's commitments and in acquiring the strength to accept criticism. She was also fearlessly critical, for instance, of Freud's concept of narcissistic neurosis, a psychotic withdrawal which he held to be inaccessible to treatment. She stimulated the application of linguistic and communications research to psychoanalysis, when participating in 1955 and 1957 at the Center for Advanced Studies in the Behavioral Sciences, Stanford, California. She influenced a wide circle of pupils. The popular fictional work *I Never Promised You a Rose Garden* (1964), written by Joanne Greenberg, a former patient, presented her therapeutic technique.

Her major books include *Principles of Intensive Psychotherapy* (1950) and *Psychoanalysis and Psychotherapy* (1959, with full bibliography).

She was married to Erich *Fromm for four years from 1926.

BIBLIOGRAPHY: A. Grinstein, *Index of Psychoanalytic Writings*, 2 (1957), 701–3; 6 (1964), 3256–58; *Journal of the American Medical Association*, 164 (Aug. 3, 1957), 1601. **ADD. BIBLIOGRAPHY:** Gail A. Hornstein, *To Redeem One Person Is to Redeem the World: The Life of Frieda Fromm-Reichmann* (2000.)

[Janos A. Schossberger]

°**FRONTO, MARCUS CORNELIUS** (c. 100–175), Roman rhetorician. Addressing his former pupil, Marcus *Aurelius, he refers to numerous casualties (not recorded elsewhere) inflicted on Roman armies by the Jews during Hadrian's reign.

[Jacob Petroff]

FROST, MARTIN (1942–), U.S. congressman. Frost was born in California but raised in Fort Worth, Texas. As a youngster he was deeply involved in the National Federation of Temple Youth, the Reform Youth Movement where he was a regional and national officer. He went to the University of Missouri, where he received a bachelor of journalism degree. He then worked for a Delaware newspaper and later for the *Congressional Quarterly* while he trained to be a lawyer at Georgetown University Law Center. Upon graduation, he clerked for Judge Sarah T. Hughes until 1972. He was also a legal commentator on Dallas television.

He first ran for Congress in 1974 and was defeated in a primary against a very popular TV weatherman. He sat out the next campaign while he ran Jimmy Carter's presidential campaign in North Texas. His district was more than one-third African American and 15 percent Hispanic, not necessarily an ideal political base for a Jewish candidate. Yet, with perseverance and organization, two traits that were to characterize his political career, he ran again in 1978 in the Democratic primary against the same incumbent weatherman and in a very big upset, prevailed.

Upon entering Congress Frost allied himself with then-Majority Leader James Wright, a fellow Texan who rewarded the freshman with a seat on the powerful House Rules Committee. He was an ally to Wright and his fortunes rose when Wright became speaker of the House. They dipped after Wright was forced to resign, but he rose again to leadership as chairman of the Democratic Congressional Campaign Committee and then as chairman of the Democratic Caucus, the third most important position in the House.

Frost was a successful fundraiser and very savvy political strategist and organizer; he headed the Democratic Congressional Campaign Committee in both the 1996 and 1998 cycles. In the 106th Congress he became chair of the Democratic Caucus, the first Jew ever to hold that position. His wife, Kathryn George Frost, retired as a major general and former adjutant general of the United States Army. She was the highest-ranking female in the United States Army. Frost raised three daughters, one of whom became a rabbi and one a chef.

Entering Congress in 1978, Frost served for 13 terms until he was defeated in the 2004 election after the mid-decade reapportionment bill, orchestrated by fellow Texan, House Majority Leader Tom Delay, passed the Texas Legislature. His district, which was once primarily a minority district was transformed by absorbing Republican strongholds, and what had been a secure seat was lost to the Republicans. When he was retired, he was one of the most senior Democrats in the House, in the South, and of the Jewish delegation.

He remained in Washington but also taught at the Kennedy School of Government at Harvard and served as a commentator for Fox News.

[Marshall Brachman (2nd ed.)]

FRUG, SHIMON SHMUEL (1860–1916), Russian poet. Frug was born in a Jewish agricultural colony in Kherson province, Russia; he was self-educated. He began his poetic career writing in Russian, published three volumes of verse, and was the first poet to treat Jewish themes in Russian verse. His poem "The Goblet," written under the impact of the pogroms of 1881, was translated into Yiddish as "*Der Kos*" by I.L. Peretz and sung by Jews the world over. Soon Frug himself began to write in Yiddish, but his first collection of Yiddish songs and ballads did not appear until 1896. A complete edition in three volumes followed in 1904 and again, with additions, in 1910. His Yiddish national songs were keyed to the needs of his generation. In his popular song "*Zamd un Shtern*" ("Sand and Stars") he argues with God, asking why He had only fulfilled half His promise to Abraham, making Jews as numerous as sand: but "where are the stars?" The song "*Hot Rakhmones*" ("Have Pity"), composed after the Kishinev Pogrom of 1903, bore the refrain "Have pity, give shrouds for the dead and for the living – bread." It was recited and sung at mass meetings protesting against Czarist oppression of Jews. In his socialist and Zionist lyrics, he pleaded for a return of the Jews to productive labor on their ancestral soil. His songs inspired the early Zionist pioneers. He also composed ballads based on Jewish folklore, of which the best known is "*Dem Shames Tokhter*," "The Sexton's Daughter," a Jewish parallel to the Greek tale of Admetus and Alcestis. Frug, who suffered from poverty, misfortune, illness, and family troubles in his last years in Odessa, characterized himself as a poet who wept all his life.

BIBLIOGRAPHY: Rejzen, Leksikon, 3 (1929), 138–62; Feinberg, in: JBA, 17 (1959/60), 65–72; Singer, *ibid.*, 24 (1966/67), 87–90; S. Liptzin, *Flowering of Yiddish Literature* (1963), 65–72; E.H. Jeshurin, *S. Frug, Bibliografye* (1960); L. Wiener, *History of Yiddish Literature* (1899).

[Melech Ravitch]

FRUM, Canadian family. BARBARA ROSENBERG FRUM (1937–1992), radio and TV journalist, was born in Niagara Falls, New York, and educated at the University of Toronto. She wrote for numerous magazines and performed on TV and radio, but was best known for hosting CBC Radio's popular current affairs show *As It Happens*. From 1982 until her death she was a host of *The Journal*, CBC-TV's nightly current-affairs program. Barbara Frum received the Order of Canada in 1979 and the National Press Club of Canada Award for Outstanding Contribution to Canadian Journalism in 1975. Following her death from leukemia in 1992, she was awarded an honorary degree from the University of Toronto and the Academy of Canadian Cinema and Television John Drainie Award for Distinguished Contributions to Broadcasting.

Her husband, MURRAY FRUM (1931–), was a real estate developer and arts patron. He was born in Toronto, Ontario, and received his degree in dentistry from the University of Toronto in 1956. He began his career in property development soon after graduation and became chairman and CEO of the Frum Development Group. A long-time patron of the arts, Frum chaired the Ontario Arts Council Foundation and the Ontario Cultural Attractions Fund, and was a trustee of the Art Gallery of Ontario. The Frum Collection of Primitive Art and Sculpture has been exhibited at such prestigious institutions in Canada and the U.S. as the National Gallery in Ottawa, the Art Gallery of Ontario in Toronto, the Museum of Modern Art and the Guggenheim Museum in New York, the Smithsonian Institute and the National Gallery of Art in Washington, D.C., and the Baltimore Museum of Art. Frum was awarded the Order of Canada in 2001.

Their son DAVID FRUM (1960–), author, journalist, and political pundit, was born in Toronto, Ontario. He received simultaneous B.A. and M.A. degrees in history from Yale in 1982 and graduated cum laude from the Harvard Law School in 1987. Between 1994 and 2001, he was a senior fellow at the Manhattan Institute for Public Policy Research, and from January 2001 to February 2002, was economic speechwriter for President George W. Bush. He wrote for *The Wall Street Journal, Forbes, The Weekly Standard, The New York Times*, and Canada's *National Post*, and published five books. Frum was the Reader's Digest resident fellow at the American Enterprise Institute and a contributing editor for *National Review*, writing a daily column for National Review Online. He regularly appeared on National Public Radio and contributed to Britain's *Daily Telegraph*.

Barbara and Murray Frum's daughter LINDA FRUM (1963–), author and journalist, was also born in Toronto, Ontario. In 1984 she earned a B.A. in arts from McGill University. Her work appeared in many Canadian publications, particularly the *National Post*, and she published two books, including a memoir of her late mother, *Barbara Frum: A Daughter's Memoir* (1996). She was appointed chair of UJA Federation's Women's Campaign & Advocacy and was a member of the board of directors of the Canada-Israel Committee.

[Andrea Knight (2nd ed.)]

FRUMKIN, ALEKSANDR NAUMOVICH (1895–1976), Russian physical chemist. He graduated from the University of Odessa in 1915, where he taught 1920–22. In 1928–29 he was a lecturer on colloid chemistry at the University of Wisconsin, and from 1930 professor of electrochemistry at the University of Moscow. Frumkin was director of the Institute of Physical Chemistry of the U.S.S.R. Academy of Sciences 1939–49, and from 1958 of the Academy's Institute of Electrochemistry. He became an academician in 1932, and was awarded the Lenin Prize in 1931 and the Stalin Prize in 1941. He wrote on surface phenomena, the theory of electrochemical processes, the electric double layer, diffusion processes in solution under the influence of electric fields, and other topics. His work was applied in the U.S.S.R. to the generation of electricity by chemical means, the wetting of metals by electrolytes, flotation, and heterogenous catalysis. He was the author of *Elektrokapillyarnye yavleniya i elektrodnye potentsialy* ("Electrocapillary Effects and Electrode Potentials," 1919) and a coauthor of *Kinetika elektrodnykh protsessov* ("Kinetics of Electrode Processes," 1952).

[Samuel Aaron Miller]

FRUMKIN, ARYEH LEIB (1845–1916), rabbinical scholar and writer; pioneer of Jewish settlement in Ereẓ Israel. Frumkin studied rabbinics in his native Kelme, Lithuania, and at the Slobodka Yeshivah. He visited Ereẓ Israel in 1867, and after two years in Odessa, returned to Jerusalem in 1871. There he began research for a history of the rabbis and scholars of Jerusalem, *Toledot Ḥakhmei Yerushalayim* (Vilna, 1874; ed. by E. Rivlin, Jerusalem, 1928–30, repr. 1969, with biography and index). Frumkin's account of his first visit to Jerusalem, *Massa Even Shemu'el* (1871), gives important source material on conditions in Ereẓ Israel at the time. Returning to Lithuania, Frumkin was ordained a rabbi and took a rabbinical post at Ilukste, Latvia. After the 1881 pogroms, Frumkin participated, representing Ḥovevei Zion, in the consultations held in Germany to consider the plight of Russian Jewry. There he advocated settlement in Ereẓ Israel as a solution, opposing emigration to the United States. With the financial support of Emil Lachman, a wealthy Berlin Jew, he bought land in *Petaḥ Tikvah, built the first house there, and began a heroic ten-year period as a farmer-scholar, braving malaria and other dangers, establishing a *talmud torah* and a small yeshivah, and persuading more settlers to move there from *Yehud. Lachman eventually refused to continue endowing the enterprise and Frumkin was compelled to leave the settlement. In 1894 he went to London and was active in Jewish life in the East End. He established a wine business, using the income to return to Ereẓ Israel in 1911, where he lived first in Jerusalem and then returned to Petaḥ Tikvah.

Apart from *Toledot Ḥakhmei Yerushalayim*, Frumkin's main contribution to Jewish scholarship is his edition of *Seder Rav Amram* (of *Amram ben Sheshna) which he published as a large *siddur* (from an Oxford Ms.), with a commentary and notes (Jerusalem, 1910–12). He also published a biographical sketch of his uncle, Elias b. Jacob, called *Toledot Eliyahu* (1900), a Passover *Haggadah* (with *Gei Ḥizzayon* commentary, 1913), and an edition of the Book of Esther with two commentaries (1893).

BIBLIOGRAPHY: M. Harizman and J. Poleskin, *Sefer ha-Yovel le-Fetaḥ Tikvah* (1929), 321–51; E. Rivlin, in: A.L. Frumkin, *Toledot Ḥakhmei Yerushalayim*, 1 (1928), 11–56, first pagin.; A.I. Trywaks and E. Steinman, *Sefer Me'ah Shanah* (1938), 399–410.

FRUMKIN, BORIS MARKOVICH (1872–after 1939), pioneer of the *Bund and among its most prominent publicists; first historian of the Jewish labor movement in Russia. He graduated from Geneva University. From the middle 1890s, Frumkin ranked among the leading ideologists of the Jewish Social Democrat circles in Minsk. He was the editor of the *Arbayter Bletel* of Minsk (1897), the first periodical published by the Jewish Social Democrats in Russia. He helped to organize the Bund in Lodz, where he was imprisoned in 1898 for revolutionary activity. In 1906 he left Russia and became a member of the "Committee Abroad" of the Bund and secretary of the Organization of Workers' Societies and Relief Groups for the Bund Abroad. After his return to Russia, he was again active in Lodz and edited (1913–14) the principal legalized organ of the Bund in St. Petersburg, *Di Tsayt, Undzer Tsayt*. After the February 1917 Revolution, Frumkin wrote for the Bundist press. During the split in the Bund in 1920–21 he joined the Combund (the faction that later joined the Communist Party). He was seen in Moscow in the mid-1930s. Later, he disappeared from the literary and public scene. He appears to have been still alive on the eve of World War II, but there is no information available on his end.

Frumkin's historiographical writings include: "*Iz istorii revolyutsionnogo dvizheniya sredi yevreyev v 1870-kh godakh*" ("From the History of the Revolutionary Movement among the Jews in the 1870s"), in: *Yevreyskaya Starina*, 4 (1911), 221–48, 513–40; "*Ocherki iz istorii yevreyskogo rabochego dvizheniya v Rossii 1885–1897*" ("From the History of the Jewish Labor Movement in Russia 1885–1897"), *ibid.*, 6 (1913), 108–22, 245–63; and "*Zubatovshchina i yevreyskoye rabocheye dvizheniye*" ("The Zubatov Movement and the Jewish Labor Movement"), in: *Perezhitoye*, 3 (1911), 199–223. Over the signature of "B. Gorenberg" he wrote the Bund's report on the problem of emigration, *Zur Emigrationsfrage* (also Yid., *Emigratsye un Imigratsye*) for the Stuttgart congress of the Second International (1907). He was coauthor of "*Der 'Bund' in der Revolutsye fun 1905–06*" ("The 'Bund' in the Revolution of 1905–06," 1930), which also appeared in *Archiv fuer Sozialwissenschaft und Sozialpolitik*.

BIBLIOGRAPHY: F. Kursky, *Gesamlte Shriftn* (1952), index; *Di Geshikhte fun Bund*, 2 vols. (1960–62), indexes.

[Moshe Mishkinsky]

FRUMKIN, ISRAEL DOV (1850–1914), pioneer journalist in Ereẓ Israel. Frumkin was born in Dubrovno, Belorussia and was taken to Jerusalem when he was nine. In 1870 he started contributing to the weekly *Ḥavaẓẓelet* founded by his father-in-law, Israel *Bak. Frumkin soon became its publisher and editor, and turned it into a militant paper that attacked financial corruption in the Jerusalem community. His enemies caused the sporadic banning of his paper and even his imprisonment. In *Ḥavaẓẓelet* he advocated the consolidation of the separate communities in Jerusalem, higher standards in education, and the inclusion of secular studies and vocational training in the schools. His early support of agricultural settlement in Ereẓ Israel turned to adamant opposition as its secular character became apparent. Frumkin was especially hostile to Aḥad Ha-Am, the Ḥovevei Zion, and the Herzl brand of Zionsim in Ereẓ Israel. He also fiercely opposed missionary activities. *Ḥavaẓẓelet* declined after the turn of the century and ceased publication in 1910.

BIBLIOGRAPHY: I. Kressel, in: *Mivḥar Kitvei I.D. Frumkin* (1954), 13–114, 205–29; G. Frumkin, *Derekh Shofet bi-Yrushalayim* (1955), opening chapters; *Tidhar*, 1 (1947), 489–91.

[Yehuda Slutsky]

°**FRY, VARIAN** (1907–1967), U.S. journalist and Righteous Among the Nations. On hearing of the fall of France to the Germans, in June 1940, a group of intellectuals, headed by Frank Kingdon, met at the Commodore Hotel in New York and decided to create an Emergency Rescue Committee in order to spirit out of the country well-known artists and intellectuals as well as German and Austrian socialist leaders – mostly Jews – who because of their past activities and anti-Nazi stance stood in danger of being turned over to the Germans under clause 19 of the Franco-German armistice, which obliged France "to surrender on demand all persons under German jurisdiction named by the German government." The committee chose Varian Fry, a Harvard graduate and editor of several liberal journals, as its emissary to Vichy France. He was given $3,000, and instructed to explore rescue possibilities for the individuals on his list. He was to leave on August 4, 1940, and return within a month, with a possible extension of two more months. Arriving in Marseilles, he began writing letters from his hotel room to all those on his 200-name list whose addresses were known. The resultant stampede of people to his hotel room led him to open an office called the Centre Américain de Secours. He discovered that some intellectuals were afraid to disclose their whereabouts or, as in the case of Walter *Benjamin, had preferred to end their life. As the job was beyond the capacity of one man, he assembled a staff of trustworthy people to help him in what would become a vast rescue operation, including Albert Hirschman, Mary Jane Gold, former French police officer Daniel Bénédite, Miriam Davenport-Ebel, Willi Spira (a Viennese cartoonist who helped to falsify credentials), Marcel Verzeano, and Johannes (Hans) and Lisa Fittko. The aim now was to get as many people as possible out of the country, in whatever way possible. In Fry's words, "I had come to think of illegal emigration as the normal, if not the only way to go." The escape routes included Route A: from Marseilles to Lisbon through Spain, via the French border town of Banyuls; B: to Spain over the Pyrenees; C: with authentic-looking forged papers, from Pau (France) to Saragossa (Spain); D: Cuban visas on questionable passports; E: from Marseilles by boat to Oran (Algeria); F: an alternate crossing into Spain: G: from Marseilles to the French colony of Martinique. By May 1941, the office had handled more than 15,000 requests, of which 1,800 fell within the scope of Fry's direct work, representing some 4,000 people. Altogether 1,000 were sent out of the country, and support and allowances were distributed to 560 others. Many others were referred to separate welfare agencies. Persons helped to leave France included novelists Franz *Werfel and Lion *Feuchtwanger, painter Marc *Chagall, sculptor Jacques *Lipchitz, political scientist Hannah *Arendt, physiologist Otto *Meyerhof, and many others. The French lodged protests with the American consul in Marseilles over Fry's illegal emigration methods, and the police several times raided Fry's offices in search of incriminating documents. The French wanted him out of the country, as did U.S. diplomats in Vichy France (including the consul-general in Marseilles, Hugh S. Fullerton, and the U.S. ambassador, Admiral William Leahy), who felt that Fry's methods were hurting the good relations existing then between the U.S. and Vichy France. In Washington D.C., the U.S. State Department complained that Fry's "continued presence was an embarrassment to everybody." Fry was continuously followed by French secret agents, "part of a campaign to frighten me into leaving France of my own free will." In a June 1941 letter to his wife, Eileen, Fry wrote, "If I leave, I abandon those human beings, many of whom I have come to know and to like very much, and most of whom have come to depend on me." Finally, in August 1941, Fry was arrested and given an hour to pack, driven to the Spanish border, and told that his expulsion had been ordered by the Ministry of the Interior, "with the approval of the American embassy." Fry's office continued to function, headed by his French aide Bénédite, until the office was closed by the authorities on June 2, 1942. After his forced return to the U.S., Fry criticized the State Department's immigration policy. As a result, he was placed under FBI surveillance as a subversive agent on the orders of J. Edgar Hoover. In a piece called "The Massacre of the Jews," published in *The New Republic* in December 1942, Fry called upon the Allied governments to immediately set up tribunals to begin to collect evidence on the Nazi massacres of Jews, while at the same time open their doors to any refugees fleeing the Holocaust, and for the Pope to threaten with excommunication all Catholics who in any way participated in these frightful crimes.

In 1967, a few months before his death, France, which had expelled him in 1941, conferred upon him the Chevalier de Légion honor. In a ceremony at Yad Vashem, on February 2, 1996, U.S. Secretary of State Warren Christopher apologized on behalf of the State Department for its earlier abusive treatment of Fry and underlined the pride of the U.S. that a man of such high moral caliber was now honored as a great humanitarian under the Yad Vashem-sponsored "Righteous Among the Nations" program. Fry is the only American ever to receive the Righteous Among the Nations Award.

BIBLIOGRAPHY: Yad Vashem Archives M31–6150; V. Fry, *Surrender on Demand*, (1997); A. Marino, *American Pimpernel* (1999); M. Paldiel, *Saving the Jews* (2000), 61–73; idem, *Sheltering the Jews* (1996), 137–41.

[Mordecai Paldiel (2nd ed.)]

FRÝD, NORBERT (**Fried**, also **Nora F.**, 1913–1976), Czech writer and journalist. Born in České Budějovice (Bohemia) into a mixed Czech-German family, he studied law and modern literature at Charles University in Prague. He was active in left-wing culture and influenced by surrealism. His professional career as a scriptwriter, as well as his personal life, was interrupted by the Nazi occupation of Czechoslovakia. He was sent to the Theresienstadt, Auschwitz, and Dachau concentration camps and was the only member of his family to survive. He recorded his experiences from the Holocaust in his novel *Krabice živých* (1956; "A Box of Living People"). The Protectorate's atmosphere is depicted in the story *Kat nepočká* (1958; "The Hangman Will Not Wait"). After the war, Frýd entered the Czechoslovak Foreign Service and spent several years in Mexico. His stay there inspired him to write the journalistic pieces *Mexiko je v Americe* (1952; "Mexico Is in America") and *Usměvavá Guatemala* (1955; "Smiling Guatemala"), the novels *Studna supů* (1953; "The Well of Vultures"), *Prales* (1965; "The Primeval Forest"), and *Císařovna* (1972; "The Empress") and some other works of prose. Beginning in the late 1960s Frýd published a fictionalized trilogy chronicling the life of his family and its fate. The first volume, *Vzorek bez ceny a pan biskup* (1966; "Sample without Value and Mister Bishop"), and the second, *Hedvábné starosti* (1968; "Silken Worries") deal with the time of his grandparents and parents, i.e., Bohemian Jewry in the second half of the 19th and the beginning of the 20th century; the third volume *Lahvová pošta* (1971; "The Bottle Post"), is a testimony of the 1930s in Prague and of Frýd's stay at the Theresienstadt ghetto and other concentration camps.

BIBLIOGRAPHY: *Českožidovští spisovatelé v literatuře 20. století* (Czech-Jewish Writers in the Literature of the 20th Century), Praha, Židovské muzeum (2000); *Lexikon české literatury* 1 A–G (Dictionary of Czech Literature vol. 1 A–G), Praha, Publ. House Academia (1985); V. Menclová, *Norbert Frýd*, Praha, Čs. spisovatel (1981)

[Milos Pojar (2nd ed.)]

FRYMER-KENSKY, TIKVA, scholar of biblical studies. She received her bachelor's degree from City College of New York in 1965 and her doctorate from Yale University in 1977. She was a visiting associate professor at the University of Michigan and the Jewish Theological Seminary before becoming the director of biblical studies at Reconstructionist Rabbinical College in 1988. In 1995 she joined the faculty of the University of Chicago Divinity School as professor of Hebrew Bible and the history of Judaism.

Frymer-Kensky's areas of specialization include, in addition to Bible studies, Assyriology and Sumerology, Jewish studies, and women and religion. Her 1992 work, *In the Wake of the Goddesses: Women, Culture, and the Biblical Transformation of Pagan Myth*, attracted widespread attention and critical acclaim. The work traces the shift in the Middle East from polytheism, which included the worship of goddesses, to monotheism; it examines changes in the role of women and questions whether religious experience would be different for women were the deity defined as female.

Motherprayer: The Pregnant Woman's Spiritual Companion (1995) is a collection of biblical interpretations, prayers, ancient Sumerian incantations, and meditations that draw from more recent Jewish and Christian tradition. Intended as a spiritual guide for mothers-to-be, the work follows the stages of pregnancy through birth. Though rooted in Frymer-Kensky's scholarly research, it found a wide audience outside academia.

Frymer-Kensky received the Koret Jewish Book Award in 2002 and a National Jewish Book Award in 2003 for *Reading the Women of the Bible* (2002). Noting that a text from a patriarchal society would not be expected to contain so many stories about women, she examines four female groups: victors, victims, virgins, and "voice." She suggests that the stories of women as both victors and victims originate during an absence of central power, coming before the rise of the Israelite monarchy and after its fall, and she relates the understanding of these stories to an Israeli conception of their subjugation by other groups.

Frymer-Kensky was editor, with David Novak, Peter Ochs, David Fox Sandmel, and Michael A. Signer, of *Christianity in Jewish Terms* (2000). This collection of essays examines aspects of Christianity that renounce antisemitism and that view Judaism as a spiritual path compatible with that of Christianity. She also served as editor, with Victor H. Matthews and Bernard M. Levinson, of *Gender and Law in the Hebrew Bible and the Ancient Near East* (1998). Her later work involves a commentary on Ruth and further investigation of biblical theology. She is a fellow of the American Academy for Jewish Research.

[Dorothy Bauhoff (2nd ed.)]

FUBINI, GUIDO (1879–1943), Italian mathematician. Fubini was professor of mathematics at Catania in 1901, at Genoa in 1906, and at Turin from 1908 until the Fascist anti-Jewish laws resulted in his dismissal in 1938. He immigrated the following year to the United States and worked successively at the Institute of Advanced Studies, Princeton, and New York University. Fubini, who was a member of the Accademia Nazionale dei Lincei, made important contributions to projective differential geometry, theory of Lie groups and analysis. His collected works in three volumes entitled *Opere Scelte* (1957–62) were published in Rome. The first book of this edition contains a record of his publications together with a biographical introduction.

[Barry Spain]

FUBINI, MARIO (1900–1977), Italian literary historian and critic. Born in Turin, Fubini belonged to the group that gathered around the young liberal intellectual Piero Gobetti (killed by the Fascists in 1926). Fubini was first a schoolteacher and later a professor of Italian literature at the universities of Palermo (1937–39), from which he was removed owing to the antisemitic laws promulgated by the the Fascist regime, Trieste (1945–49), Milan (1949–67), and Pisa at the prestigious Scuola normale superiore (1967–77). He took an early interest in French literature, publishing two monographs, *Alfred de Vigny* (1922) and *Jean Racine e la critica delle sue tragedie* (1925), but subsequently concentrated on Italian literature, particularly that of the Renaissance and Romantic periods. He wrote a number of studies of fundamental importance including *Ugo Foscolo* (1928); *Studi sulla critica letteraria del Settecento* (1934); *Vittorio Alfieri: il pensiero – la tragedia* (1937, 1960³); *Dal Muratori al Baretti* (1946); *Foscolo Minore* (1949); *Ritratto dell' Alfieri e altri studi alfieriani* (1951, 1963²); *Romanticismo italiano* (1953); and *La cultura illuministica in Italia* (1957). Stressing the indissolubility of the connection between culture and literature, Fubini formulated various modifications of Croce's aesthetics, to which he basically adhered. The results of Fubini's research on linguistic problems are contained in *Stile e umanità di Giambattista Vico* (1946), *Studi sulla letteratura del Rinascimento* (1947), and *Metrica e poesia* (1962). An authority on Dante, Fubini also published a collection of essays, *Il peccato di Ulisse e altri studi danteschi* (1966). He was editor of the *Giornale Storico della Letteratura Italiana*, and he promoted and directed the publication of several classical Italian texts, to which he appended important introductions and notes.

ADD. BIBLIOGRAPHY: Ceserani-Giuntini-Roberti, "Bibliografia degli scritti di Mario Fabini, 1918–1970," in: *Critica e storia letteraria. Studi offerti a Mario Fabini* (1970) i, xvii–lxxxvii, G. Grana, *Letteratura italiana. I critici*, 5 (1973), 3503–532; Chiesa-Pozzi, "Bibliografia degli scritti 1977–1978," in: *Giornale storico della letteratura italiana*, 155 (1978), 91–99.

[Louisa Cuomo / Alessandro Guetta (2nd ed.)]

FUCHS, ABRAHAM MOSHE (**Fuks**; 1890–1974), Yiddish short story writer and journalist. Born in Ozerna, East Galicia (now Ukraine), Fuchs lived in Lemberg (Lvov), where he formed part of the literary group "Yung-Galitsye" before immigrating to New York in 1912. During World War I he lived in Vienna as a journalist. In 1938 he fled from the Nazis and went to London. In 1950 he settled in Israel. Fuchs began to publish short stories in 1911 and served as correspondent of the New York *Forverts* (1921–45). His books are *Eynzame* ("Loners," 1912), *Oyfn Bergl* ("On the Hill," 1924), *Unter der Brik* ("Under the Bridge," 1924), *Di Nakht un der Tog* ("Night and Day," 1961), and *Dertseylungen* ("Tales," 1976). Fuchs' protagonists are poor Galician Jewish villagers, whose natural surroundings he describes. His later tales are set in Israel. Some of his works have been translated into Hebrew, Polish, German, and English.

BIBLIOGRAPHY: Rejzen, Leksikon, 3 (1929), 26–32; M. Ravitch, *Mayn Leksikon*, 3 (1958), 334–8; S. Bickel, *Shrayber fun Mayn Dor*, 2 (1965), 361–6. **ADD. BIBLIOGRAPHY:** LNYL, 7 (1968), 319–22; M. Naygreshl, *Fun Noentn Over*, 1 (1955), 322–34.

[Jon Silkin / Tamar Lewinsky (2nd ed.)]

FUCHS, ALFRED (1892–1941), Czech journalist, publicist, translator and author. Born in Prague, Fuchs was a Zionist in his youth, but later he became an assimilationist and edited publications of the organized assimilationist movement of Czech Jews (see *Čechů Židů, Svaz). One of his first works was *O židovské otázce* ("On the Jewish Question," 1919). Above all he translated Heine's works. Ultimately he was baptized and became one of the leading Catholic publicists in Czechoslovakia. He learned Hebrew in order to read kabbalistic literature (together with his friend, the Hasidic poet Jiří Mordechai *Langer), but found greater affinity in the Catholic mystic philosophers. After a career with the Catholic press, he became chief of the press department of the prime minister's office. He was a leading expert on canon law and published a number of penetrating studies on Vatican policy. Fuchs described his road to Catholicism in an autobiographical novel *Oltář a rotačka* ("Altar and Printing Press," 1930). He never concealed his Jewish origin, and at the peak of the antisemitic wave under Hitler, he wrote that if he were forced to wear the yellow star of David, he would wear that and his Vatican decorations with equal pride. In 1941 he was taken by the Gestapo from a monastery where he had found refuge and was tortured to death in the Dachau concentration camp.

ADD. BIBLIOGRAPHY: O. Donath, *Židé a židovství v české literatuře 19. a 20. století* (1930); F. Langer, *Byli a bylo* (1963); E. Hostovský, in: *Jews of Czechoslovakia* 1 (1968), index; A. Mikulášek et al., *Literatura s hvězdou Davidovou*, vol. 1 (1998).

[Avigdor Dagan / Milos Pojar (2nd ed.)]

FUCHS, DANIEL (1909–1993), U.S. novelist and screenwriter. Raised in the Williamsburg section of Brooklyn, Fuchs wrote three naturalistic novels based upon his experiences there: *Summer in Williamsburg* (1934), *Homage to Blenholt* (1936), and *Low Company* (1937). These were later published as one volume in 1961. The stories he wrote for the *Saturday Evening Post* led him to Hollywood, where he wrote a number of successful scripts for motion pictures. *West of the Rockies* was published in 1971. *The Apathetic Bookie Joint* appeared in 1979; *The Golden West: Hollywood Stories* was published in 2005.

BIBLIOGRAPHY: M. Krafchick, *World Without Heroes: The Brooklyn Novels of Daniel Fuchs* (1988); G. Miller, *Daniel Fuchs* (1979).

FUCHS, LILLIAN (1901–1995), U.S. violist and one of the first women to perform as a permanent member of a string quartet in America. Her musical family included her father, Philip, an amateur violinist; and brothers JOSEPH (1899–1997), a well-known violinist, and HARRY (1908–1986), a cellist. After early study of the piano, Lillian switched to the violin, studying with Louis Svencenski (1862–1926). She enrolled in the Institute of Musical Art (now Juilliard) and studied violin with Franz Kneisel (1865–1926) and composition with Percy Goetschius (1853–1943). In 1924, she earned the silver medal for highest honors, the Morris Loeb Prize, and the Seligman Prize in composition. Fuchs married Ludwig Stein, a business man and amateur musician in 1930. They had twin daughters, Carol Stein (Amado), a violinist, and Barbara Stein (Mallow), a cellist, born in 1935.

Fuchs's debut concert as a violinist took place in 1926. That same year, invited by Marianne Kneisel to join an all-female string quartet, she switched to viola. In 1927, Lillian joined the Perolé String Quartet as violist. In addition to live concerts, the Perolé Quartet was featured on regular Sunday radio broadcasts over WOR in New York City. Fuchs performed with them for 15 years and went on to play with the Budapest String Quartet as a second violist, which gave her acceptance in the highest ranks of chamber music.

In 1940 she began to concertize with her brother Joseph Fuchs. Their highly acclaimed performances of the Mozart *Sinfonia Concertante*, helped bring this and other classic duos to new life. Fuchs also enjoyed a career as a soloist with major symphony orchestras. Fuchs championed contemporary music and several composers created works written especially for her, including Bohuslav Martinu, *Three Madrigals* (*Madrigaly*, 1947) and *Sonata for Viola and Piano* (1955); Quincy Porter, *Duo for Viola and Harp* (1957); and Jacques de Menasce, *Sonata for Viola and Piano* (1955). Fuchs adapted many works for viola, such as Bach's *Six Suites for Unaccompanied Cello*; she was the first violist to record all six Bach suites, which she did on Decca records. She composed some of her own music, including *Jota*, for violin and piano, and wrote a number of works devoted to the development of viola technique.

In her long career, Fuchs taught and coached other chamber music performers, including Isaac *Stern and Pinchas *Zukerman. In 1962, the Manhattan School of Music engaged her to coach chamber music. She accepted a post at Juilliard in 1971 and in 1989, she joined the faculty at Mannes College of Music, teaching at both institutions until 1993.

BIBLIOGRAPHY: A.D. Williams. *Lillian Fuchs, First Lady of the Viola* (1994).

[Judith S. Pinnolis (2nd ed.)]

FUCHS, MOSES ẒEVI (1843–1911), Hungarian rabbi. He was born in Lovasbereny, where his father, Benjamin Ze'ev Wolf, was rabbi, and Moses succeeded him in 1873. In 1882 he moved to Grosswardein (now Oradea), Romania, where he served until his death. His *Yad Ramah* (1940) includes important halakhic responsa, many of which reflect the problems facing European Jewry in his time.

Fuchs saw in Ḥasidism an antidote to Haskalah and assimilation, stating in one of his responsa: "The love of God and His Torah is the essence and source of Ḥasidism. When economic circumstances permit, one should occupy oneself in the study of Torah with deep deliberation and spiritual joy. It is also important to visit the *ẓaddik* from time to time, in order to learn from his ways. The wise man should learn from the *ẓaddikim* and their true disciples but pay no attention to the masses who go running after them."

BIBLIOGRAPHY: S.N. Gottlieb, *Oholei Shem* (1912), 226; Z. Schwartz, *Shem ha-Gedolim me-Ereẓ Hagar*, 2 (1914), 14b–15a; E. Goldmann, *Shalshelet Zahav* (1942), 9–46.

[Naphtali Ben-Menahem]

FUCHSBERG, JACOB D. (1913–1995), U.S. jurist. For many years, Fuchsberg was a leading trial lawyer. He argued many cases before the U.S. Supreme Court, hundreds of cases before the New York State Court of Appeals and other appellate courts, and thousands of trials covering almost every facet of litigation. Some of the precedent-setting or socially significant cases he participated in as trial and appellate counsel were *Oliver v. Postel*, keeping the courts open to the press and public under the Sixth Amendment to the U.S. Constitution; the *Knights of Pythias* case, attacking color discrimination in fraternal organizations; the *De Martino* "Baby Lenore" case, which led to reform of New York adoption statutes and raised important questions of full faith and credit under the U.S. Constitution and a number of tort cases setting precedents in the award of adequate damages.

Fuchsberg served as president of the Association of Trial Lawyers of America (1963–64). In 1974 he was elected judge in the highest appellate court of the State of New York – the New York State Court of Appeal. He retired from the Court of Appeals in 1983 and founded the Jacob D. Fuchsberg law firm.

Fuchsberg wrote *Examination of Witnesses* (with L. Harolds and J. Kelner, 1965) and compiled *Class Actions Primer* (1973). He edited and authored a number of books on the law of damages and trial advocacy and wrote many articles on a variety of legal subjects for professional periodicals. He founded and edited *Trial* Magazine.

Fuchsberg was active in many Jewish causes and served as vice president of the Zionist Organization of America. He represented the New York Conference on Soviet Jewry.

[Julius J. Marcke]

FUENN, SAMUEL JOSEPH (1818–1890), Hebrew writer of the more traditional wing of the Russian Haskalah and an early member of Ḥovevei Zion. Fuenn, who was born in Vilna, received a traditional Jewish education, and afterward joined the circle of Haskalah supporters there. He was a founder of the first Jewish school in the city (1841) where he taught Bible and Hebrew. Together with L. Hurwitz he published the literary magazine *Pirḥei Ẓafon* (1841–44), the first such Hebrew work to appear in Russia. When the government rabbinical school opened in Vilna in 1847 he joined it as a teacher of Bible and Hebrew language. In 1856 he was appointed inspector of the government Jewish schools in the Vilna District. In 1863 he opened a Hebrew printing press in Vilna. He edited and published *Ha-Karmel* (1860–81) which appeared first as a weekly and then as a monthly. Fuenn wrote extensively in Hebrew and Russian for this periodical, and his articles included studies of the history of Russian Jewry and literary criticism, as well as the first chapters of his autobiography, *Dor ve-Doreshav*. Because of his moderate views on the Haskalah, his traditional way of life, and his financial independence, Fuenn achieved a prominent role in the leadership of the Vilna Jewish community. He was also highly respected by the civilian authorities and was the recipient of government medals. When the Ḥibbat Zion movement began, he helped establish a society in Vilna and headed it, together with L. Levanda. He was later elected to the central committee in Russia. In his later years Fuenn devoted himself to two important works. The first was a biographical lexicon of notable Jews, *Keneset Yisrael* (1886–90). The second was an extensive Hebrew dictionary, *Ha-Oẓar*, which was the first in the history of Hebrew lexicography to cover the Bible, Mishnah, Talmud, the Hebrew poets, and medieval philosophers; the dictionary also included a translation of terms into Russian and German. Only the first volume, comprising the first seven letters *alef* to *zayin*, appeared in the author's lifetime; the remaining three volumes were completed from Fuenn's notes by S.P. *Rabbinowitz (1900–03). For the meaning of Hebrew words Fuenn relies upon the works of the medieval grammarians, especially Ibn Janaḥ and David Kimḥi, as well as modern lexicographers. His Hebrew dictionary is a summary of the knowledge available in his generation, which still lacks systematic etymological insight. Its strong point is the collection of references to the sources, the Mishnah, the Jerusalem Talmud, and liturgical and Aramaic texts. He died in Vilna. Fuenn's other works include a history of the Second Temple, *Divrei ha-Yamim li-Venei Yisrael* (Vilna, 1871–77), *Kiryah Ne'emanah* (Vilna, 1860), a monograph on the Vilna community, and a number of textbooks and translations of juvenile historical novels and short stories.

BIBLIOGRAPHY: Klausner, Sifrut, 4 (1953[2]), 115–20; Z. Vilnai, in: *Gilyonot*, 15 (1943), 236–43; G. Elkoshi, in: *Yahadut Vilna*, 1 (1959), 438–41.

[Yehuda Slutsky]

FUERST, JULIUS (pseudonym **Alsari**, 1805–1873), Polish Hebraist, bibliographer, and historian. Fuerst was born in Zerkow, Poland, the son of a *darshan* ("expounder" of the Bible). He studied at the University of Berlin, where Hegel was one of his teachers, and at the universities of Breslau and Halle, where he was the pupil of *Gesenius. He settled in Leipzig and taught Hebrew, Syriac, Aramaic grammar and literature, Bible exegesis, and other subjects at the university there (professor, 1864).

Fuerst owes his reputation to his monumental bibliographical work *Bibliotheca Judaica* (2 vols., 1849–51, 2 vols. in 3, 1863[2], reprint 1960). The work is based solely on his findings without taking into account the important research done in the field by his contemporary M. *Steinschneider. His history of the Karaites, *Geschichte des Karaeerthums* (3 vols., 1862–69), was superseded by later works, even by the time of its publication. Fuerst also wrote *Lehrgebaeude der aramaeischen Idiome* (1835), *Ḥaruzei Peninim* (1836), *Oẓar Leshon ha-Kodesh* (1837–40), a revision of *Buxtorf's Bible concordance in collaboration with Franz *Delitzsch, and *Hebraeisches und Chaldaeisches Handwoerterbuch ueber das Alte Testament* (2 vols., 1851–61), with the supplement *Zur Geschichte der Hebraeischen Lexicographie* (1867[3]; translated into English by S. Davidson, *A Hebrew and Chaldee Lexicon to the Old Testament*). He translated Saadiah Gaon's *Emunot ve-De'ot* into German (1845), and wrote a comprehensive history of Hebrew literature, *Geschichte der juedischen Literatur und des juedisch-hellenistischen Schrifttums* (2 vols., 1867–70); *Der Kanon des Alten Testaments nach den Ueberlieferungen in Talmud und Midrasch* (1868); and several Hebrew–Aramaic dictionaries and grammars. He collaborated with L. *Zunz and also worked on the publication of an edition of the Bible, *Illustrierte Prachtbibel* (1874), comprising 24 books with German translation and explanatory notes. He was a close friend of Franz Delitzsch, whom he assisted in writing his work on the history of Jewish poetry.

Fuerst founded and edited the weekly magazine *Orient* (1840–52), in whose scientific supplement *Literaturblatt des Orients* many of his scientific articles were published. Although most of Fuerst's works are by now obsolete, he is thought to be one of the forerunners of scientific research in all branches of Judaic studies. His library was bequeathed to the *Hochschule fuer die Wissenschaft des Judentums in Berlin.

BIBLIOGRAPHY: M. Steinschneider, in: HB, 13 (1873), 140; Fuenn, Keneset, 438–40; W. Schochow, *Deutsch-juedische Geschichtswissenschaft* (1969), 286–7.

FUERSTENBERG, CARL (1850–1933), German banker. Born in Danzig, Fuerstenberg worked for the Berlin banking house of S. *Bleichroeder from 1871 to 1883, when he left to join the Berliner Handels-Gesellschaft, another prominent issuing and investment bank. Under Fuerstenberg's guidance the Berliner Handels-Gesellschaft became one of the leading financial institutions of late Imperial Germany operating in global business. It developed especially close connections with German heavy and electrical industries, and introduced Russian and United States securities to the Berlin Stock Exchange. Fuerstenberg also established firm relations with the New York firm of *Hallgarten and Company which were useful after World War I, when Germany needed foreign credit. Fuerstenberg married a Jewish woman whose family came from Poland. His attitude towards his Jewishness was strongly influenced by the idea of acculturation. His son Hans was educated as a Protestant. Fuerstenberg was known for his caustic wit. He refused all offers of titles and decorations. His memoirs were published by his son Hans.

BIBLIOGRAPHY: R.E. Lueke, *Die Berliner Handels-Gesellschaft 1856–1956* (1956), H. Fuerstenberg, *Carl Fuerstenberg: Die Lebensgeschichte eines deutschen Bankiers* (1961, first printed 1931). **ADD. BIBLIOGRAPHY:** *Erinnerungen: Mein Weg als Bankier und Carl Fürstenbergs Altersjahre* (1965); Hans Fuerstenberg (ed.), *Carl Fuerstenberg – Anekdoten: Ein Unterschied muß sein* (1978).

[Joachim O. Ronall / Christian Schoelzel (2nd ed.)]

FUERTH (Heb. פיורדא, פירד), city in Bavaria, Germany. Jewish moneylenders are mentioned there in 1440. They were later expelled, but in 1528 Jews were allowed to resettle in the town. There were 200 Jewish residents in 1582. A rabbi is mentioned in 1607. The Jews were represented on the municipal council by two of their *parnasim*. The community dispersed during the Thirty Years' War (1618–48). In 1670 refugees from Vienna augmented the Jewish community, which was concentrated around the Geleitsgasse. The "old synagogue" (near Koenig-strasse) was built in 1617, a new one in 1697, and that of the *Fraenkel family in 1707. The first cemetery dates from 1607 and the hospital (*hekdesh*) from 1653.

In 1719 the status of the community (consisting of 400 households) was regulated by the bishop. In return for annual payments, the Jews were promised protection for their lives and property; they were allowed to build synagogues and to employ a cantor, beadle (*Schulklopfer*), and gravedigger; cases between Jews were to be tried by a Jewish court, while litigation between Jews and gentiles came under the jurisdiction of the cathedral court. The Fuerth community regulated its internal affairs by a series of *takkanot* in 1728. The first Jewish orphanage in Germany was established in Fuerth in 1763 and from the 17th century until 1824 there was an important yeshivah in the town. An Orthodox elementary school was established in 1862 and officially recognized as a secondary school in 1899. In 1811 Elkan *Henle of Fuerth published a pamphlet calling for emancipation of the Jews in Bavaria; Gruensfeld of Fuerth became the first Jewish lawyer in Bavaria (1843), David Morgenstern, the first Jewish deputy to the Landtag (1849), and Solomon Berolzheimer, the first Jewish judge (1863). Fuerth Jews contributed much to the economic, cultural, and political development of the city.

Hebrew printing was begun in Fuerth in 1691 by S.S. Schneur and his sons Joseph and Abraham and son-in-law Isaac Bing. From 1691 to 1698 they issued 35 works, including *Sifra with commentaries. Hirsch Frankfurter opened a press which issued nine books, between 1691 and 1701. Confiscations of Hebrew books from 1702 onward account for a pause in printing until it was resumed by the Schneur family from 1722 to 1730. Between 1737 and 1774, Ḥayyim b. Hirsch of Wilhermsdorf published 80 works and his press continued in the family until 1868; their non-Jewish successor issued a Pentateuch with *haftarot* as late as 1876. Between 1760 and 1792 Isaac b. Loeb Buchbinder (not Bamberg) printed 73 Hebrew books. Joseph Petschau and his son Mendel Beer printed 17 books between 1762 and 1769. S.B. Gusdorfer was active as a printer from 1852 to 1867.

The Jewish population numbered 1,500 in 1720; 2,434 in 1816 (19% of the total); 3,336 in 1880; and 2,000 (2.6% of the total) in 1933. In 1933–1941 1,400 Jews mangaged to leave Fuerth, mainly to the United States and Shanghai. Among those leaving was Henry Kissenger, the first Jewish secretary of state of the United States, who came to New York together with his brother and parents. Kissenger said: "By the time we left Germany it took no foresight, merely opportunity." On Nov. 10, 1938, the main synagogue was burned down; the other six synagogues and innumerable Jewish shops and homes were demolished. One hundred and fifty men were sent to Dachau. By May 17, 1939, only 785 Jews remained; the community was destroyed in three stages. On November 28, 1941, 83 Jews were deported to Riga. On March 24, 1942, 224 Jews, almost all Jews under the age of 65 were deported to Izbica, a way station to Belzec and on September 10, 1942, 153 Jews, mainly the elderly and children in an orphanage were deported to Theresienstadt. After the war some 40 Jews returned. The synagogue was restored and consecrated. There were 200 Jews living in Fuerth in 1970. In 1989 the community numbered 179. The membership increased to 587 in 2003. About 98% of them were immigrants from the former Soviet Union. Fuerth (together with Schnaittach) is one of the sites of the Jewish Museum of Franconia. The museum in Fuerth – which was founded in 1997 – is dedicated to the history and culture of the Jews in Fuerth and Franconia and to the present and future life of the Jewish community.

BIBLIOGRAPHY: F. Neubuerger, in: MGWJ, 45 (1901), 404–22, 510–39; M. Brann, in: Gedenkbuch D. Kaufmann (1900), 385–450; L. Loewenstein, *Zur Geschichte der Juden in Fuerth* (1913, 1967²) (=JJLG, 6 (1909), 153–233); S. Schwarz, *Juden in Bayern* (1963); PK; *Nachrichten fuer den juedischen Buerger Fuerths* (1961–to date); H. Barbeck, *Geschichte der Juden in Nuernberg und Fuerth* (1878). **ADD. BIBLIOGRAPHY:** M. Berthold-Hilpert, *Orte der Verfolgung und des Gedenkens in Fuerth. Einladung zu einem Rundgang* (2002) (Orte juedischer Kultur); M. Berthold-Hilpert, "Juedisches Leben in Franken am Beispiel der Gemeinde Fuerth," in: G. Och, H. Bobzin (eds.), *Juedisches Leben in Franken* (2002) (Biblioteca academica, Reihe Geschichte, vol. 1), 197–212; G. Blume (ed.), *Gedenke. Zum Gedenken an die von den Nazis ermordeten Fuerther Juden 1933 – 1945 = Remember* (1997); I. Schwierz, *Steinerne Zeugnisse juedischen Lebens in Bayern. Eine Dokumentation* (1992), 155–158; W.J. Heymann (ed.), *Kleeblatt und Davidstern. Aus 400 Jahren juedischer Vergangenheit in Fuerth* (1990).

[Ze'ev Wilhem Falk / Michael Berenbaum and Larissa Daemmig (2nd ed.)]

FUERTH, HENRIETTE (1861–1938), German social worker. Fuerth was born in Katzenstein, Germany. Herself the mother of 11 children, she was one of the founders of the Mother's Welfare Movement, an organization which concerned itself with family and health problems affecting mothers and their families. She established and directed the Organization for the Prevention of Venereal Diseases. Interested in politics as a means of achieving her welfare goals, she served for nine years as a socialist member of the Frankfurt City Council.

She wrote a great number of books and articles on social welfare, especially in relation to working women, sexual problems in society, and population policy. Among her works are *Staat und Sittlichkeit* (1912), *Die soziale Bedeutung der Kaeufersitten* (1917), *Kulturideale und Frauentum* (1906).

ADD. BIBLIOGRAPHY: H. Krohn, "'Du sollst dich niemals beugen' – Henriette Fuerth – Frau, Jueden, Sozialistin," in: P. Freimark (ed.), *Juden in Deutschland* (1991), 326–43; A. Epple, *Henriette Fuerth und die deutsche Frauenbewegung im deutschen Kaiserreich* (1996); I. Schroeder, *Grenzgängerinnen – Jüdische Sozialreformerinnen in der Frankfurter Frauenbewegung um 1900* (2001).

[Joseph Neipris]

FUKS, ALEXANDER (1917–1978), Israeli historian. Fuks was born in Wloclawiek, Poland, and joined the history faculty of the Hebrew University in 1949, being appointed professor of ancient history and classics in 1957. Fuks was the author of numerous scholarly articles, including studies of political life in classical Athens, and social revolution in Sparta in the Hellenistic period. His books include *The Ancestral Constitution: Four Studies in Athenian Party Politics at the End of the Fifth Century* B.C.E. (1971) and *Social Conflict in Ancient Greece* (1984). In the field of Jewish history, he wrote "Aspects of the Jewish Revolt in A.D. 115–117" (*Journal of Roman Studies*, 51 (1961), 98–104) and "The Jewish Revolt in Egypt (C.E. 115–117) in the Light of the Papyri" (*Aegyptus*, 33 (1953), 131–58). He collaborated with Victor *Tcherikover on the *Corpus Papyrorum Judaicorum* (3 vols., 1957–69), a collection of papyri written in Greek relating to Jews and Jewish affairs.

[Irwin L. Merker]

FUKS, LAJB (1908–1990), librarian and Yiddish scholar. Born in Poland, Fuks immigrated to Holland in 1934. In 1946 he became assistant librarian of the Bibliotheca Rosenthaliana, the Hebraica and Judaica Department of the Amsterdam University Library (see Jewish *Libraries), and was its librarian from 1949 until his retirement in 1973. He lectured in Modern Hebrew and Yiddish at the University of Amsterdam from 1964. His main scholarly interest was the history of Old Yiddish language and literature. He edited *The Oldest Known Literary Document of Yiddish Literature (c. 1382)*, 2 vols. (1957); and wrote *Die hebräischen und aramäischen Quellen des altjiddischen Epos Melokîm-Bûk* (1964). His other works deal with the history of Dutch Jewry, especially the history of Hebrew printing and bibliography in Holland. Together with R.G. Fuks-Mansfeld he edited *Hebrew and Judaic Manuscripts in Amsterdam Public Collections*, 2 vols. (1973–75), and *Hebrew Typography in the Northern Netherlands 1585–1815*, 2 vols. (1984–87). He was the editor of and frequent contributor to the *Studia Rosenthaliana* from its founding in 1967.

[Henriette Boas / Shlomo Z. Berger (2nd ed.)]

°FULBERT OF CHARTRES (d. 1028 or 1030), bishop of Chartres (France). In 1009, Fulbert delivered a series of three sermons based on Genesis 49:10: "The scepter shall not depart from Judah." They dealt with Jewish objections to the Christian argument that since royalty no longer existed among the Jews, the Messiah had already come and that he was Jesus. The Jews claimed that their present distress was only temporary, as had been their captivity in Babylon; moreover, there might be Jewish kings in other parts of the world and there were still wise and powerful Jews who enjoyed an almost royal power.

BIBLIOGRAPHY: J.-P. Migne (ed.), *Patrologia Latina*, 141 (1880), 305–18; B. Blumenkranz, *Juifs et Chrétiens…* (1960), index; idem, *Les auteurs chrétiens latins…* (1963), 237–43.

[Bernhard Blumenkranz]

FULD, AARON BEN MOSES (1790–1847), defender of Orthodoxy and communal worker in his native Frankfurt. Fuld in his early youth met R. Phinehas ha-Levy Horowitz, author of the *Hafla'ah*, and was close to the circle of his son, Ẓevi Hirsch Horowitz. He was also a pupil of Solomon Zalman Trier who headed the Frankfurt *bet din*, and to whom he used to refer as: "my esteemed teacher, the high priest." Fuld engaged in business and never held any rabbinical post. Although opposed to the Reform movement, he strove for the inclusion of secular subjects in the curriculum of Jewish schools. In a letter to Akiva *Eger, Fuld asked for the approval of a curriculum in which secular subjects were included, stressing that the rabbis of "every city and province should strive with all their might that there be no slackening of the study of these subjects, essential nowadays so as not to provide an opening for the criticism of those who have risen against us" (*Beit Aharon*, Introd., V–VI). In another letter, of 1843, written on behalf of the Frankfurt rabbinate, he protested strongly against the desecration of the Sabbath and the abolition of circumcision, attendant upon the strengthening of the Reform movement. On one occasion, when Fuld was rebuked by Moses *Sofer (Schreiber) for having, according to his informant Akiva b. Abraham Moses *Lehren, permitted shaving during the intermediate days of a festival, he wrote a letter of vindication, stating, "Those who said I permitted shaving during the intermediate days have spoken falsely about me, for such a thing never entered my mind" (*Beit Aharon*, introd., II). At the same time, Sofer mentions Fuld with respect in his responsa as "the sharp-witted, learned rabbi" (responsa *Ḥatam Sofer*, YD (1841), nos. 88, 224, 319, 323).

Fuld's work, *Beit Aharon*, comprises five sections: (1) *Meshivei Milḥamah Sha'rah*, 17 responsa written between 1823 and 1830; (2) glosses to the Talmud; (3) glosses to the Arukh (also published as an appendix to the 1959 edition of Arukh); (4) *Haggahot ha-Tishbi* to the *Sefer ha-Tishbi* (Isry, 1541) of Elijah b. Asher ha-Levi Baḥur; (5) *Haggahot ha-Meturgeman* to the *Sefer ha-Meturgeman (ibid.*, 1541) of Elijah b. Asher ha-Levi Baḥur. Fuld's notes to the *Shem ha-Gedolim* of Ḥ. J.D. Azulai were published at the end of volume two of the Frankfurt edition (1847).

BIBLIOGRAPHY: Ḥ.M. Horowitz, in: A. Fuld, *Beit Aharon* (1890), i–xiv (introd.); S.A. Trier, *Rabbinische Gutachten ueber die Beschneidung* (1844), xix.

[Yehoshua Horowitz]

FULD, STANLEY HOWELLS (1903–2003), U.S. attorney. Born in New York, Fuld received his LL.B. from Columbia University in 1926. After occupying a number of state legal offices in New York, Fuld was appointed to the New York Court of Appeals in 1946. In 1966 he was elected chief judge of the Court of Appeals in the State of New York, serving until 1973. Fuld defended personal rights against what he believed was infringement by the state, often dissenting in cases such as eavesdropping, public school prayers, and the Fifth Amendment. He was a member of the New York County Republican Committee and was active in communal and Jewish affairs. He was chairman of the law division of the Joint Defense Appeal (1945–46), the National Hillel Commission (1947–56), and the board of the Jewish Theological Seminary from 1966. He was a member of the American Bar Association, B'nai B'rith, and the Knights of Pythias. He also served for many years as a director of the Atlantic Legal Foundation. The State Bar Association's Section on Commercial and Federal Litigation has created the Stanley H. Fuld Award for Outstanding Contributions to Commercial Law and Litigation.

[Ruth Beloff (2nd ed.)]

FULDA, city in Hesse, Germany. Jews are first mentioned there in 1235, when 34 martyrs were burned to death following a blood *libel. Emperor Frederick *II, after inquiries, refuted the charge in his judgment of the case. The martyrs were commemorated by Pesaḥ ha-Kohen, a relative and friend of some of the victims, in three *seliḥot*. In 1301 King Albert I pledged the taxes of the Jews of the diocese to the abbot of Fulda. In 1310 Henry VII transferred full authority over them to the abbot. In 1349 they fell victim to the Black *Death persecutions. Jews had been readmitted to Fulda by 1399. By the 16th century Fulda became the seat of a rabbinate which extended its jurisdiction over the entire region, for some time as far as *Kassel. At the Frankfurt *synod of 1603 Fulda was made the seat of one of the five Jewish district courts in Germany. Aaron Samuel b. Moses Shalom of *Kremenets taught at the yeshivah from 1615 to 1620, and Meir b. Jacob ha-Kohen *Schiff (Maharam Schiff) from 1622 to 1640. Judah b. Samuel Mehler, who studied in Fulda and left the city in 1629 at the age of 20, wrote an informative autobiography. Jews of Fulda dealt in wine-retailing but were opposed by the burghers. Regulations restricting Jewish trade were issued in 1699, 1739, 1788, and 1792. There were 75 Jewish families living in Fulda in 1633 (compared with 292 Christian households). The whole community, apart from five families, was expelled in 1677. By 1708 their number had increased to 19 taxpayers. The community had a well, and owned houses, homesteads, and stables in the Jews' street (first mentioned in 1367); by 1740 some lived outside this area. The synagogue and bathhouse were located on the "Jews' Hill" near the community's hospital, and the cemetery in a suburb. A Jewish school was established in 1784. The community numbered 321 in 1860; 675 in 1905; 957 in 1913 (4.26% of the total population); 1,137 in 1925 (4.44%); and 1,058 in June 1933 (3.8%). Under its rabbi, Michael Cahn (1849–1919), Fulda was a center of Orthodoxy. Its yeshivah remained open until 1939. The synagogue was set on fire in November 1938, destroying its Memorbuch, which dated back to 1550, and reducing the synagogue to rubble. In 1940 the cemetery was destroyed. Four hundred and fifteen Jews remained in Fulda on May 17, 1939; 131 of those unable to leave were deported to Riga on December 12, 1941, 36 were sent to the Lublin district, and an additional 76 in September 1942 to *Theresienstadt and unknown destinations in the East. The few Jews who survived the Holocaust and returned to Fulda after the war turned their cemetery into a paved courtyard to protest against the frequent desecrations there. There were 17 Jews living in Fulda in 1967. The new Jewish community center and synagogue was inaugurated in 1987. As a result of the immigration of Jews from the former Soviet Union the number of Jews increased to 500 in 2005. Almost all activities of the community werre focused on the new immigrants. There are commemorative plaques at the former and new Jewish cemetery and near the site of the destroyed synagogue.

BIBLIOGRAPHY: Germ Jud, 1 (1963), 113–4, 2 (1968), 267–8; G. Kisch, *Jews in Medieval Germany…* (1949), index; Bloch, in: *Festschrift… Martin Philippson* (1916), 114–34; Baron, Community, 1, 341–43; Baron, Social², 9 (1967), 143f., 311f.; 10 (1967), 146f., 359; 13 (1969), 201f.; Salfeld, Martyrol; M. Stern, in: ZGJD, 2 (1888), 194–9; L. Loewenstein, in: ZHB, 19 (1917), 26–37; A. Schmidt, *Fuehrer durch Fulda* (1955³), 35; A. Jestadt, in: *Veroeffentlichungen des Fuldaer Geschichtsvereins*, 38 (1937), 55, 62–70; 40 (1950), 59; S.M. Auerbach, *The Auerbach Family: The Descendants of Abraham Auerbach* (1957), 78–80; FJW, 86, 200, 318; P.N. Emeking, *Das Hochstift Fulda unter seinem letzten Fuerstbischof* (1935), 119f.; E. Keyser (ed.), *Hessisches Staedtebuch* (1957), 174–76; PK. **ADD. BIBLIOGRAPHY:** M. Imhof, "Legalisierter Raub," in: *Fulda. Die Entrechtung und Ausraubung der Fuldaer Juden im Nationalsozialismus. Dokumentation* (2004); H.-J. Hoppe, *Das juedische Fulda. Ein historischer Stadtspaziergang* (1999); G. Renner, J. Schulz and R. Zibuschka (eds.), "*… werden in Kuerze anderweit untergebracht …". Das Schicksal der Fuldaer Juden im Nationalsozialismus. Eine Dokumentation* (1992²) (Regionalgeschichtliche Schriften der Geschichtswerkstatt, Hessisches Institut fuer Lehrerfortbildung, Aussenstelle Fulda); K. Krolopp (ed.), *Der juedische Friedhof in Fulda* (1987²) (Fulda imformiert. Reihe Dokumentationen zur Stadtgeschichte, vol. 2); P. Horn and N.H. Sonn, *The History of the Jews in Fulda. A Memorial Book* (1971).

[Toni Oelsner / Larissa Daemmig (2nd ed.)]

FULDA, LUDWIG (1862–1939), German playwright. Born in Frankfurt, Fulda's early interest was the German baroque poets; he received his Ph.D. in Heidelberg with a dissertation on Christian Weise (1883) and this was followed by an edition *Die Gegner der zweiten schlesischen Schule* in the series of Kürschners *National-Literatur* (1883). Fulda then came under the influence of Sudermann's Naturalism in Berlin, became an Ibsen enthusiast, and in 1889 helped to found the *Freie Buehne*. During this period he wrote plays of a sociological nature, such as *Das verlorene Paradies* (1892) and *Die Sklavin* (1892), remarkable for their clever stage effects and insight into social problems, but lacking in great depth or style. Fulda's greatest success came with his change to a neo-romantic mood in *Der Talisman* (1892). This comedy on the theme of the fairy tale "The Emperor's New Clothes," was awarded the Schiller Prize, but its performance was banned by the kaiser. *Die Zwillingsschwester* (1901) displayed his talent for writing graceful verse. Fulda published translations of Molière's *Meisterwerke* (1892), Beaumarchais' *Figaro* (1897), Rostand's *Cyrano de Bergerac* (1898), Shakespeare's *Sonnets* (1913), Ibsen's poems and *Peer Gynt* (1916), and the Spanish dramatists' *Meisterlustspiele der Spanier*, 2 vols. (1925). In 1928 he was elected president of the Prussian Academy. He was dismissed after Hitler's rise to power and lived in retirement until the Nazis stripped him of his most prized possessions. He then committed suicide.

BIBLIOGRAPHY: A. Klaar, *Ludwig Fulda* (1922). **ADD. BIBLIOGRAPHY:** B. Gajek, "Fulda, Ludwig," in: W. Killy (ed.), *Literatur Lexikon*, vol. 4 (1989), 64–65. H. Dauer, *Ludwig Fulda. Erfolgsschrift-*

steller. Eine mentalitätsgeschichtlich orientierte Interpretation populär-dramatischer Texte (1998).

[Samuel L. Sumberg]

FULLER, SAMUEL MICHAEL (1912–1997), U.S. film writer-director. Born in Worcester, Mass., to a Polish Jewish mother and Russian Jewish father, Fuller said that his father dropped the Rabinovitch family name and took Fuller from the *Mayflower* passenger registry. Samuel Fuller started out as a journalist, beginning his career at the age of 12 as a copyboy at the *New York Evening Journal*; by 17, he was the newspaper's crime reporter. He would go on to write for the *New York Evening Graphic* and the *San Diego Sun*, among other newspapers. From 1942 to 1945 he served in the U.S. Army's First Infantry Division in Europe and North Africa, earning the Silver Star and Bronze Star. Fuller toiled in Hollywood for 11 years before he directed his first film, the western *I Shot Jesse James* (1949). He drew upon his war experiences for the insightful films *The Steel Helmet* (1951) and *Fixed Bayonets* (1951), both of which were set in and released during the Korean War. He next wrote and directed *Park Row* (1952) and co-wrote *Scandal Sheet* (1952), based on his acclaimed 1944 novel *The Dark Page*. His 1963 film *Shock Corridor* features a journalist seeking a Pulitzer for solving a murder in an insane asylum. He followed this with the crime drama *The Naked Kiss* (1964). In the late 1970s, with financing from Lorimar Productions and United Artists, Fuller was able to direct the film he had wanted to make about his own experiences in World War II, *The Big Red One* (1980), which was partially shot in Israel. The film fell flat at the box office, and Fuller went to Europe to find backing for projects in the 1980s and 1990s.

[Adam Wills (2nd ed.)]

FULVIA (1st century C.E.), Roman proselyte. A lady of high rank, she was attracted to Judaism and entered the Jewish faith. She was then persuaded by a certain Jew, who had come from Ereẓ Israel, to send presents of purple and gold to the Temple in Jerusalem. The gifts, deposited with this Jew and his three confederates, were never delivered. Fulvia urged her husband to report the matter to Emperor Tiberius. The latter thereupon expelled all the Jews from Rome (19 C.E.). Four thousand young Jews were drafted into military service and sent to fight the brigands in the island of Sardinia. The expulsion is mentioned by the Roman historians, Suetonius, Tacitus, and Dio Cassius, all of whom connect the incident in some manner with proselytism.

BIBLIOGRAPHY: Jos., Ant., 18:81–84; Schuerer, Gesch, 3 (1909[4]), 168; Heidel, in: *American Journal of Philology*, 41 (1920), 38–47; Rogers, *ibid.*, 53 (1932), 252–6; Roth, Italy, 9f.; Vogelstein-Rieger, 1 (1896), 14f.

[Isaiah Gafni]

FUNES, town in Navarre, northern Spain. A charter granted to Funes and the neighboring town of Viguera at the beginning of the 12th century also regulated relations between Jews and Christians, including the mode of establishing evidence in litigation. Ordeal by battle between Jews and Christians was prohibited and a high blood price was fixed for the murder of a Jew. Jewish landowners were required to pay tithes to the church. In 1171 King Sancho VI extended the same privileges to the Jews of Funes as those he had granted to the Jews of *Tudela in 1170, based on the *fuero* ("municipal charter") of Nájera. The Jews were freed from other dues in return for undertaking maintenance of the citadel of Funes, and they were not to be held responsible for the death of a Christian killed by them during an attack on the citadel, where they were living. In 1328, following the death of Carlos IV, the Jews of Funes were attacked. Many Jews were killed. The Jewish community had its own executive official, the *bedinus*. Much may be learned of life in the community in the 13th century from the list of fines imposed on members who had transgressed the law. Little of importance is known of the Jews in Funes from the 14th century onward.

BIBLIOGRAPHY: M. Kayserling, *Die Juden in Navarra* (1861), index; Baer, Urkunden, 1 (1929), index.

FUNK, CASIMIR (1884–1967), U.S. biochemist, originator of the word "vitamin." He was born in Warsaw and obtained his doctorate at the University of Berne in 1904. In 1910 he went to the Lister Institute in London where he studied beriberi, a deficiency disease in rice eaters. He found a substance in rice shavings (and also in yeast and milk) which prevented the disease, and called it "vitamine." This was vitamin B, later known to be a complex of several vitamins. He worked as head of the department of chemistry at the Cancer Hospital Research Institute until he went to America in 1915. With the support of the Rockefeller Foundation, he went back to Warsaw as head of biochemistry at the School of Hygiene (1923–27). During 1928–39 he operated his own Casa Biochemica at Rueil-Malmaison, France, also serving as consultant from 1936 to the U.S. Vitamin Corporation. During World War II he returned to America, and from 1948 was president of the Funk Foundation for Medical Research. Funk contributed numerous papers to scientific periodicals on various matters of synthetic organic chemistry and on other biochemical topics such as internal secretions, diabetes, and cancer. He wrote the book *Die Vitamine* (1914; *The Vitamins*, 1922). Funk's hypotheses on the importance of vitamins A, B5, C, and D to normal growth and development stimulated other investigators in the field of nutrition and laid the foundation for rational child nutrition and modern dietetics in general.

BIBLIOGRAPHY: B. Harrow, *Casimir Funk, Pioneer in Vitamins and Hormones* (1955); S.R. Kagan, *Jewish Medicine* (1952), 192–3.

[Samuel Aaron Miller]

FUNK, SOLOMON (1867–1928), rabbi and scholar. Funk was born in Hungary and served as rabbi at Sarajevo, Bosnia, Boskovice, Czechoslovakia, and in Vienna. Among his published works are *Die haggadischen Elemente in den Homelien des persischen Weisen Aphraates* (1891); *Die Juden in Babylo-*

nien 200–500 (2 vols., 1902–08); *Grundprinzip des biblischen Strafrechts...* (1904), a comparative discussion of the Bible and the Hammurapi Code; *Entstehung des Talmuds* (1919^2); and *Talmudproben* (1921^2). The last two small but well-presented volumes, which appeared as volumes 479 and 583 in the popular Goeschen series, did much to convey a balanced view of the world of the Talmud to non-Jewish readers. Other publications of Funk were *Die Hygiene des Talmuds* (1912); "Bibel und Babel" (in *Monumenta Talmudica*, 1913); and a pro-Zionist tract, *Der Kampf um Zion...* (1921).

BIBLIOGRAPHY: S. Krauss, in: *Die Wahrheit* (Dec. 11, 1925), 7; *Wiener Morgen-Zeitung* (Dec. 12, 1925); JJLG, 20 (1929), 7; *Arim ve-Immahot be-Yisrael*, 1 (1946), 279.

[Naphtali Ben-Menahem]

FUNKENSTEIN, AMOS (1937–1995), scholar. Born in Tel Aviv, he was educated in Palestine and Berlin where he got his doctorate in 1965. While in Berlin, he was active in smuggling refugees from east to west Berlin. He was professor of history and philosophy of science at Tel Aviv University, the scientific revolution, and Bible commentary in medieval and modern times. Among his books was *Theology and the Scientific Imagination from the Middle Ages to the 17th Century*. He wrote on Maimonides and his views on messianism, on the connection between the thought of Maimonides and Thomas Aquinas, and on contemporary Jewish religious movements and their messianic ideology. In his writings he challenged the traditional view of the contradiction between science and religion and noted the contribution of Christian theology to the development of the new scientific outlook, from 1980. He also founded the departments for Jewish history at UCLA and at Stanford and Berkeley, California. In Berkeley he was professor of Jewish history and culture. He specialized in many fields of research including Jewish thought and culture, general intellectual history. In 1995 he was awarded the Israel Prize for historical research.

FUNT, ALLEN (1914–1999), U.S. radio and television personality. Born in Brooklyn, New York, Funt studied at Pratt Institute before earning a bachelor's degree in fine arts from Cornell University. While working at an advertising agency, he became an idea man who dreamed up gimmicks for radio programs. In World War II he used his radio experience in the Army Signal Corps, learning to handle a portable wire recorder, predecessor of the tape recorder, and began to experiment with concealment techniques. After the war, Funt created *Candid Microphone*, which had its premiere on the ABC radio network in 1947, using hidden microphones to snare the unwary. The format, though embarrassing to many of the prey, proved highly popular. The program moved to television in 1948 and was renamed *Candid Camera* a year later. As creator, producer, director, and editor of *Candid Camera*, Funt was part humorist, part psychologist, and part con artist, catching unsuspecting people in "the act of being themselves," as he put it. In a typical stunt, passers-by were startled by a talking mailbox or by a hand reaching out of a sewer grating, angling for a hat just out of reach. In New York, many people just handed the hat to the hand and walked on. Funt, who sometimes participated in disguise as a dentist or garage mechanic, ended the ploy by saying "Smile! You're on *Candid Camera*."

[Stewart Kampel (2nd ed.)]

FURAYDIS, AL-, Arab village in Israel at the foot of Mt. Carmel, near *Zikhron Ya'akov. The village of al-Furaydis and the nearby Jewish settlers developed close economic and social ties, which date back to the founding of Zikhron Ya'akov. During the *War of Independence (1948), the Arab village did not participate in the attacks on Jewish traffic in the vicinity. It was the only Arab village of the region which remained fully populated and unchanged after Israel's independence (1948). In 1952 it received municipal status. Al-Furaydis, with 2,810 inhabitants in 1969, engaged in intensive farming. By 2002 the population had increased to 9,350 inhabitants. Like the Hebrew word "Pardes," the village's name is assumed to be derived from the Greek "paradeisos" (the origin also of "paradise").

[Efraim Orni]

FURCHGOTT, ROBERT F. (1916–), U.S. pharmacologist and Nobel Laureate in medicine. Furchgott was born in Charleston, South Carolina, and received his B.S. in chemistry at the University of North Carolina, Chapel Hill (1937), and his Ph.D. in biochemistry at Northwestern University, Chicago (1940). His first postdoctoral appointment was at Cornell University Medical School (1940–49), where he studied mediators of shock. He was assistant professor in the pharmacology department of Washington University, St Louis (1949–56), where he developed his lifelong interest in drug-receptor interactions, particularly in the adrenergic system which regulates blood vessel flow and smooth muscle tone. His experimental methods were largely based on rabbit aorta preparations. He was chairman of the new department of pharmacology at the State University of New York (now called the SUNY Health Science Center at Brooklyn; 1956–82), where his research work centered on the anomalous response of rabbit aortic preparations to drug and other stimuli, which often produced relaxation of the vessel instead of the expected contraction. This was attributable to the unsuspected release of a factor from the cells lining the internal surface of the preparation (called endothelial cells), which later proved to be nitric oxide (NO). This discovery followed meticulous analysis of a serendipitous observation and led to the award of the Nobel Prize (1994, jointly with Louis J. Ignarro and Ferid Murad). Wider roles for NO have now been identified, including defense against infection and blood pressure regulation. After retirement in 1989 Furchgott maintained active contacts in teaching and research with his former department and the pharmacology department of the University of Miami School of Medicine. His honors include the Gairdner Award (1991) and the Lasker Award for basic medical research.

[Michael Denman (2nd ed.)]

FURIE, SIDNEY J. (1933–), Canadian film producer-director-writer. Toronto-born Furie traces his career inspiration back to *Captains Courageous*, which he saw in 1937 at the age of four. He went to Pittsburgh to train in directing and scriptwriting at the Carnegie Institute of Technology, and in 1954 joined the Canadian Broadcasting Corporation as a writer and director, creating the series *Hudson's Bay*. His first feature efforts, *A Dangerous Age* (1957) and *A Cool Sound from Hell* (1958), were teenage rebellion films. Furie immigrated to England in 1960 and first tried his hand at horror films, *Dr. Blood's Coffin* (1961) and *The Snake Woman* (1961). Furie experienced his first box-office hit with the teenage musical *The Young Ones* (1961), which helped launch Cliff Richard. His success led to the cult film *The Leather Boys* (1964). In 1965, Furie was hired to direct the Len Deighton spy thriller *The Ipcress File*, starring Michael Caine. He followed with the western *The Appaloosa* (1966), and *The Naked Runner* (1967), starring Frank Sinatra. Furie turned to Hollywood when Paramount Pictures offered the director a four-picture deal, which included *The Lawyer* (1970), *Little Fauss and Big Halsy* (1970), *Lady Sings the Blues* (1972), and *Hit* (1973). His next film was *Sheila Levine Is Dead and Living in New York* (1975), a romantic comedy of unrequited Jewish love. After the Vietnam-era love story *Purple Hearts* (1984) fell flat, Furie turned to directing action films, including *Superman IV* (1987), the *Iron Eagle* series (1986, 1988, 1995), and *The Taking of Beverly Hills* (1991). In 1994, Furie returned to Canada to direct the pilot episode of the *Lonesome Dove* series. He continued to shoot made-for-television films, as well as direct-to-video features.

[Adam Wills (2nd ed.)]

FURMAN, YISROEL (Israel Fuhrmann; 1890 or 1887–1967), Romanian-born Yiddish folklorist. Born in Sereth, Furman lived in Czernowicz from 1920 to 1939 and after World War II in Bakau, Transylvania. A doctor of jurisprudence (University of Vienna), he worked as an attorney and was also a Yiddish poet and a key supporter of Yiddish schools in Bukovina but is best known as a Yiddish folklorist. He settled in Jerusalem in 1965 and worked intensively on his magnum opus, *Yidishe Shprikhverter un Rednsartn: Gezamlt in Rumenye – Besarabye, Bukovine, Moldeve un Transilvanye* ("Yiddish Proverbs and Expressions: Collected in Romania – Bessarabia, Bukovina, Moldovia and Transylvania," Tel Aviv, 1968), based on expressions actually heard in, or from natives of, these regions; he also published a study of the terminology of bakers (*Yidishe Shprakh*, 33 (1974), 32–37). In his later years he turned to writing poems, which were published only on a website devoted to his poetry (http://home.interlog.com/~jfuhrman).

BIBLIOGRAPHY: B. Kagan, *Leksikon fun Yidishe Shraybers*, 439; Y. Paner, in: *Di Goldene Keyt*, 65 (1969), 260–62.

[Leonard Prager (2nd ed.)]

FURST (Fürst), MORITZ (1782–1840), early U.S. medalist. Furst was born near Pressburg, and after immigrating to the United States in 1807, he worked as an engraver for the United States Mint in Philadelphia from 1812 to 1839. He received quick recognition, and 33 of his patriotic commemoratives and portraits are still issued by this mint; his best-known work was struck commemorating the War of 1812. He also did the first recorded American Jewish medal, the homage paid to the patriot and religious leader Gershom Mendes Seixas on his death in 1816. Official portraits were struck by him for presidents James Monroe, John Quincy Adams, Andrew Jackson, and Martin Van Buren.

BIBLIOGRAPHY: *Magyar Zsidó Lexikon* (1929) 300; *Price List of Bronze Medals for Sale by the U.S. Mint*; D.M. Friedenberg, in: *The Numismatist* (July 1969), 904–5.

[Daniel M. Friedenberg]

FURSTENBERG, HILLEL (Harry) (1935–), Israeli mathematician. Furstenberg was born in Berlin but immigrated to the United States and studied at Yeshiva University, New York, obtaining both his B.A. and his M.Sc. in 1955, and his doctorate from Princeton in 1958. In the same year he was appointed instructor at Princeton and at MIT from 1959 to 1961; assistant professor at the University of Minnesota (1961–63); and full professor (1964–65). He relocated to Israel in 1965 on his appointment as professor of mathematics at the Hebrew University. Furstenberg works in the area of probability theory and dynamics and their applications to combinatorics and group theory. He was awarded the Rothschild Prize in 1978 and the Israel and Harvey Prizes in 1993. He is a member of the Israel Academy of Sciences and Humanities, the American Academy of Arts and Sciences, and the U.S. National Academy of Sciences.

FURTADO, ABRAHAM (1756–1817), politician and communal leader in France. His parents originally lived in Portugal as Marranos, but after his father's death in the Lisbon earthquake (1755), his mother moved to London, where Abraham was born, and returned to Judaism. In 1756 she settled in Bayonne. They later moved to Bordeaux, where Furtado was educated. His dealings in property eventually enabled him to devote himself to literature, philosophy, and history, and to enter politics. In 1788 he and David *Gradis were invited to sit on the *Malesherbes commission for considering proposals for the amelioration of the Jewish position, as representatives for southern France. Furtado became a municipal counselor in Bordeaux shortly before the French Revolution. A sympathizer with the federalist-minded Girondins, Furtado was proscribed with them in 1793. After the downfall of Robespierre, however, he was reinstated in civic office in Bordeaux. He was elected president of the *Assembly of Jewish Notables (1806–07) convened by Napoleon and acted as secretary of the Paris *Sanhedrin (1807). Furtado, who knew Napoleon personally, traveled to Tilsit in June 1807 to present a memorandum to the emperor in the hope of preventing restrictive measures against the Jewish community. His efforts were only partially successful. In 1808 he published in Paris his *Mémoire d'Abraham Furtado sur l'Etat des Juifs en France jusqu'* *à la Révolution*. After Napoleon's return from Elba, Furtado refused the appointment of vice-mayor of Bordeaux, but accepted it from Louis XVIII when the monarchy was restored for a second time.

BIBLIOGRAPHY: M. Berr, *Eloge de M. Abraham Furtado* (1817); AI, 2 (1841), 361–8 (biography); R. Anchel, *Napoléon et les Juifs* (1928), index.

FUR TRADE AND INDUSTRY. Jews arrived at the fur trade and industry through their commerce between the Mediterranean littoral and Continental Europe, in particular Eastern Europe. Their active participation in the central European fairs enabled them to play an important role in the development of the fur trade. During the ninth century the Jewish merchants known as Radanites were among the principal agents in the international fur trade. They may have purchased the furs at the northern end of their European itinerary, but more likely bought them in the land of the *Khazars, since pelts could be obtained there cheaply, and secured for the Khazar kingdom a central position in the international trade (taxes there were occasionally collected in furs). The report of Ibrahim ibn *Ya'qub in the tenth century shows that Jewish and Muslim merchants in Prague dealt in furs and hides of various kinds, among other goods. The fur trade must have remained an important part of the business of Jewish merchants visiting Russia (*holkhei Russia*) in the 11th and 12th centuries. Furs were among the wares of the 11th-century Mediterranean merchant Naharay b. Nissim. The extent to which the fur trade and payment in furs figured in Jewish life and imagination is shown in a 13th-century tale about "a Jew who went afar and saw in his dreams a Jew whom exalted ones were weighing in a balance, and his sins were found to weigh heavier; they said: as his sins are heavier he will have no part in the world to come. [Then] others came and said: you did not weigh fairly, and they put pelts and other furs on the man, and he was heavier; they said: he shall enter the world to come.... And they said: those furs they put on him were furs he paid in tax" (*Sefer Ḥasidim*, ed. R. Margalioth (1924), no. 654, p. 421).

In the 13th century Jewish merchants imported furs from Hungary into Little Poland. The Jews of Volhynia and Red Russia, especially at the close of the 14th and beginning of the 15th centuries, held a prominent place among the merchants who imported Oriental goods and traded at the fairs of Lvov and Kiev – these imported, among other articles, furs and horses. During the second half of the 15th century, and especially after 1454, following the extension of Polish rule to *Gdansk (Danzig), participation of Jews in the northern trade intensified; among the cargoes rafted down the rivers there were hides and furs. Furs held an important place among the goods supplied by Jews to the courts of the Polish kings. Sebastian *Miczyński (1618) tells that "there are two Israelite brothers who, upon arriving in Lvov where various goods arrive from Turkey... took into their possession almost all the furs ... and this is not all.... They [the Jews], despite existing laws and privileges, import from Bohemia, Moravia, and Germany finished goods and prepared furs, fox furs made from the hide of the belly." Throughout the 17th century, the Jewish merchants of Poland played a main role in the overland export of hides and furs. The regulations of the furriers' guild of Cracow of 1613 show that its members were, in fact, fur merchants. In Bohemia during the 15th to 16th centuries the Jews were prominent in the fur retail trade. In 1515, when the municipal councillors of Prague sought to reduce Jewish competition in trade, they prohibited them, among other things, from preparing or selling cloths and new furs. On the other hand, they were authorized to sell used clothes and furs at the fairs. During the 17th and 18th centuries the Jews of Amsterdam also engaged in the trade of furs, which they imported from Frankfurt. The city of *Leipzig was an important center of the fur trade. Here, the Jewish merchants of Austria, Germany, and Russia played a pioneering role through their participation in the fairs of the city from the beginning of the 16th century. In recognition of their contribution toward the import of raw materials for the hide and fur industries, the Jews of Poland and Russia were authorized in 1747 to settle in Leipzig without paying taxes. Jewish merchants from Brody, Lissa (Leszno), and Shklov were among the most active fur traders at the fairs of Leipzig. During this period, the other principal centers of the fur trade in Germany were Breslau and Gross-Glogau (for furs imported from Russia, from the region of Crimea), as well as Luebeck and Hamburg (for furs from Siberia and the Scandinavian countries).

In North America the Jews played an important role in the fur trade during the colonial period. George Croghan, a prominent fur trader in the second half of the 18th century, was assisted by many Jewish suppliers. In 1765 the brothers Barnard and Michael *Gratz established an extensive commercial partnership with non-Jewish merchants and their activities included trade in furs. Other important fur traders in the colonial period were Hayman *Levy, Joseph *Simon, Salomon Simson, and David *Franks. In Canada, the town of Trois Rivières became the center of the fur trade, in which Aaron *Hart and Samuel *Judah, who exported furs to England, played a considerable role. The sales of the American-Russian Fur Company were handled by the J.M. Oppenheim firm, London's largest fur house. Before the purchase of Alaska by the United States in 1867 the Russian firm began selling furs to independent fur traders of San Francisco, many of whom were Jews, eager to penetrate the lucrative seal islands of Alaska. Indeed the negotiations of Hutchinson, Kohn, and Co. for purchasing the Alaskan fur monopoly influenced the decision to purchase the territory. The Russian company's rights and assets were subsequently bought by this firm. Californian Jews were prominent in the "fur rush" to Alaska. The Alaska Commercial Company, headed by Lewis *Gerstle and Louis Sloss, continued to dominate the fur trade after Alaska was purchased by the United States. On the east coast a number of German-Jewish firms sprung up for the processing of fur products, the largest being A. Hollander and Sons of Newark, New Jersey.

The year 1815 was the start of a prosperous period for the fur trade of Leipzig as a result of which a local fur industry was established. The first Jewish company, founded by Marcus Harmelin in 1830, existed until 1939. With the unification of Germany in 1871, the Jewish fur industry of Leipzig received new momentum when Jewish fur merchants of Berlin, Breslau, Brody, Frankfurt, Fuerth, and Hamburg settled there or opened branches of their businesses. Even the new Jewish companies then beginning trade in New York, such as Ullmann and Boskovitz, opened branches there. The fur trade between Russia and Germany remained at a peak level until World War I, and the important Jewish furriers of Leipzig took part annually in the large fairs of Russia. According to the census of 1897, Jews formed 90% of the fur merchants in Congress Poland, and according to the census of 1900 in Galicia they formed 80% of the hide and fur merchants. Even though World War I brought a crisis to the fur trade, the principal companies in Germany recuperated immediately afterward, when trade relations with the United States intensified. In 1921 the trade was also renewed with the Soviet Union. It has been estimated that in 1929 there were about 1,228 fur industry enterprises in Leipzig of which at least 513 were owned by Jews. Of the 794 fur merchants then living there, 460 were Jews. Before Hitler's rise to power, the Leipzig fur industry saw a period of prosperity during which many Jewish companies began to open branches in other places. Subsequently the Jewish fur industry throughout Germany was brought to an end. The centers of the Jewish fur industry were then transferred to other places, with refugees who had succeeded in escaping Nazi Germany occasionally occupying leading positions.

Though the fur-working industry in the United States in the 19th century was largely in the hands of Germans, the large Jewish emigration from Eastern Europe from the 1880s on had brought a flood of Jewish workers into the profession, many of whom were forced to labor under sweatshop conditions. In 1912 an estimated 7,000 out of 10,000 fur workers in the United States were Jewish, the great majority concentrated in New York, Philadelphia, and Chicago. A Jewish Furriers Union was organized in 1906 but soon dissolved. In 1913 the International Fur Workers Union came into being, the leadership and rank and file of which were both heavily Jewish. Under the leadership of Benjamin *Gold, the Furriers International was for years among the most politically radical unions in America.

A study undertaken in 1937 indicated that approximately 80% of the employees in the fur industry in the United States, and over 90% of the employers, were Jewish. The largest of these Jewish fur firms was Eitington-Schild of New York City, whose president, Motty Eitington, was a leading figure for many years in the Associated Fur Manufacturers, as was another large Jewish fur dealer, Samuel N. Samuels. In Canada, Jews became prominent in this branch, notably in Montreal, Toronto, Winnipeg, and Vancouver. A census held in 1931 shows that 48.65% of the employers and directors and 31.82% of the workers in this industry were Jews. Most had acquired their professional knowledge in their countries of origin in Eastern Europe, and they contributed largely to promoting the industry in Canada.

In London Jewish companies were estimated in the 1960s to constitute about two-thirds of the city's fur enterprises. They contributed considerably toward the development and improvement of methods employed in the fur industry, such as the preparation and dyeing of furs. In Argentina in the same period about 80% of the fur enterprises were owned by Jews who organized a trade association, the Sociedad Mercantil de Peleteros. In Israel the fur trade and industry employed in 1969 about 500 workers in 70 firms specializing mainly in broadtail and karakul. Production, primarily aimed at export, earned approximately $1,000,000 in 1963 and over $3,500,000 in 1969. A small number of minks and chinchillas were reared on farms. In subsequent years Jewish participation in the trade declined with the general decline in the wearing of fur and the hostility of pro-animal protestors, not to mention the movement of Jews away from traditional trades. Israel joined nearly 100 other countries in banning the use of traps. In 2003 Israel exported just $1 million worth of leather products and dressed furskins.

BIBLIOGRAPHY: I. Schipper, *Di Virtshaftsgeshikhte fun di Yidn in Poiln be-Eysen Mitelalter* (1926), passim; F. Dublin, in: PAJHS, 35 (1939), 14–16; L. Rosenberg, *Canada's Jews* (1939), 178–9, 186; N. Barou, *Jews in Work and Trade* (1948³), index; L. Rabinowitz, *Jewish Merchant Adventurers* (1948), 82 ff., 164 ff.; P.S. Foner, *Fur and Leather Workers Union* (1950), 20–21, 24–26: R. Glanz, *Jews in American Alaska* (1953), 46; M.U. Schappes, *Jews in the United States* (1958), index; W. Harmelin, in: YLBI, 9 (1964), 239–66; J.R. Marcus, *Early American Jewry*, 2 vols. (1951–53), index; idem, *American Jewry Documents* (1959), index; H.A. Immis, *Fur Trade in Canada* (1956); M. Wischnitzer, *History of Jewish Crafts and Guilds* (1965), index.

FURTUNĂ, ENRIC (pseudonym of **Henry Peckelmann**) (1881–1965), Romanian poet. Born in Botoșani, Furtună practiced as a physician in Jassy. He spent much of his time writing poetry which he published both in Jewish periodicals, such as *Ha-Tikvah* and *Adam*, and in general Romanian journals. Two important verse collections were *De pe Stâncă* ("From the Rock," 1922) and *Poemele resemnării* ("Poems of Resignation," 1940). Many of Furtună's poems had Jewish themes and he showed particular concern for the tragic homelessness of the Jewish people, for which the only remedy he saw was a return to Zion. Some of his poems are on biblical themes, the last being *Abișag*, a dramatic work published in Tel Aviv in 1963 when Furtună was over 80. There are other poems which show a biblical influence. Furtună also wrote plays and translated Hebrew poetry, especially that of Ḥ.N. Bialik and David Shimoni, and Yiddish writers, notably Itzik Manger and Halper Leivick. Furtună emigrated to Ereẓ Israel in 1944 but he left after two years and returned to Romania. In 1958 he settled in Brazil where he died in São Paulo.

BIBLIOGRAPHY: E. Lovinescu, *Evolutia poeziei lirice* (1927), 161–3; S. Lazar, in: *Viața noastră* (July 20, 1965).

[Abraham Feller]

FUST (Fuerst), MILÁN (1888–1967), author and poet. A descendant of the court Jew Jacob Bassevi von *Treuenberg, Füst wrote verse remarkable for its ghostly atmosphere and preoccupation with death. He also wrote novels – notably *A feleségem története* ("The Story of My Wife," 1942) and *Látomás és indulat a müvészetben* ("Vision and Impulse in Art," 1948) – and various plays and short stories.

FUTORANSKY, LUISA (1939–), Argentinian writer, Futoransky was born in Buenos Aires. From 1971 she lived in Spain, Italy, Japan, and China, and settled in Paris in 1981, where she worked as a journalist. She conducted poetry workshops in U.S. universities and visited Israel frequently. In her poetry and prose, an uncommonly sharp and painful insight into feelings and circumstances is reinforced by an equally sharp humor, all of which is conveyed in a rich style that combines high language and everyday idiom. Love, voyage, exile, and womanhood are her basic themes in addition to explicit Jewish and Israeli motifs concerning Jewish identity and experience. An anthology published in 2002 (*Antología*, Buenos Aires) includes a selection of previous books such as *Partir, digo* (1982); *La sanguina* (1987); *La parca, enfrente* (1995); *Cortezas y fulgores* (1997); and *De dónde son las palabras* (1998). Her novels include *Son cuentos chinos* (1986); *De Pe a Pa* (1986); and *Urracas* (1992). Her essays appear in *Pelos* (1990) and *Lunas de miel* (1996). She has received awards in Argentina and Spain. Her works have been translated into several languages.

BIBLIOGRAPHY: L. Beard, "A is for Alphabet, K is for Kabbalah. Luisa Futoransky's Babelic Metatext," in: *Intertexts* (1997); D.B. Lockhart, *Jewish Writers of Latin America. A Dictionary* (1997); F. Masiello, *Bodies in Transit: Travel, Translation and Gender* (1997).

[Florinda Goldberg (2nd ed.)

Initial letter "G" of the word "Ge" ("I" in old French) at the opening of a paraphrase of and commentary on I Sam. 19:11 in Old French and Latin. The historiated initial in this 13th-century manuscript depicts Saul sending messengers after David. Munich, Bayerische Staatsbibliothek, Cod. gall. 16, fol. 36r.

GA–GOR

GAAL (Heb. גַּעַל), the son of Ebed, head of a band that fought *Abimelech son of Gideon (Judg. 9:26–41), who, with the help of mercenaries, had imposed his rule over Mt. Ephraim. Gaal's band is reminiscent of those that accompanied Jephthah (Judg. 11:10) and David (1 Sam. 22:2; 23:1–13). During Abimelech's absence from Shechem, Gaal incited the inhabitants to revolt and took advantage of the social, and possibly also of the racial, tension prevailing among the various sections of the town's population. It appears that Gaal conspired with the ancient nobility in the locality, which claimed descent from Hamor the father of Shechem (9:28) and which apparently belonged to the Canaanite population hostile to Abimelech. The immediate cause of the friction was the highway robbery conducted by the Shechemites (9:25). Apparently, the ruling families seized control of the roads and interfered with Israelite commerce. Informed by Zebul, the city prefect, Abimelech quickly returned and, by a clever stratagem, crushed the revolt. Gaal was driven from the city (9:30–41) and was not heard of again.

BIBLIOGRAPHY: A. Malamat, in: B. Mazar (ed.), *Ha-Historyah shel Am Yisrael* (1967), 226–8; idem, in: H.H. Ben-Sasson (ed.), *Toledot Am Yisrael bi-Ymei Kedem* (1969), 77. **ADD. BIBLIOGRAPHY:** Y. Amit, *Judges* (1999), 171–80.

GA'ATON (Heb. גַּעְתּוֹן), kibbutz in the hills of northern Israel, east of *Nahariyyah, affiliated with Kibbutz Arẓi Ha-Shomer ha-Ẓa'ir. It was founded in October 1948 while under fire from nearby Arab positions. The founding group of settlers hailed from Hungary; later, Israeli-born members and immigrants from Egypt and other countries formed the majority. Kibbutz factories manufacture cardboard and medical equipment. A boarding school for the performing arts, mainly dance, is located in the kibbutz. In 2002 the population was 422.

The name is historical, mentioned (Tosef., Shev. 4:11) as an enclave on the northern border of the area occupied by the returning exiles from Babylonia, having been preserved in the Arabic names of the nearby ruin Khirbat Ja'tūn and the Ga'aton brook, which runs down from there to its outlet in Nahariyyah.

[Efraim Orni]

GABBAI, family of Hebrew printers. ISAAC BEN SOLOMON (b. second half of 16th century) lived in Leghorn and was the author of the Mishnah commentary *Kaf Naḥat* (appended to Mishnah, ed. Venice, 1614). Early in the 17th century he worked as a typesetter for *Bragadini in Venice. His son JEDIDIAH acquired the Bragadini type and decorations and set up the first Hebrew press in *Leghorn, which was active there from 1650 to 1660, issuing a number of important works. With part of the equipment and staff of this press, Jedidiah's son ABRAHAM in 1657 established a printing house in Smyrna, which existed until 1675. Abraham himself moved to Constantinople in 1660, where he was a printer for a number of years. His corrector (proofreader) was SOLOMON BEN DAVID GABBAI – probably not of the same family – author of the kabbalistic work *Me'irat Einayim* (between 1660 and 1665) and a theological work *Ta'alumot Ḥokhmah* (Bodleian Library, Ms. Opp. 602).

GABBAI, family with many branches in *Baghdad and India. Noteworthy members include ISAAC BEN DAVID BEN YESHU'AH (d. 1773), known as Sheikh Isḥāq Pasha because he ruled with the firmness of a pasha from 1745 to 1773 as *nasi* of the Jewish community and as **ṣarrāf bāshī* ("chief banker") for the governor of Baghdad. On the other hand, his contemporaries praised his good deeds, especially his efforts to encourage R. Ẓedakah Ḥusin who was very active in propagating the study of the Torah among Iraqi Jewry. He died together with his three sons in the plague of 1773. EZEKIEL BEN JOSEPH NISSIM MENAHEM GABBAI (d. 1826), also known as Baghdadli, was a prominent banker in Baghdad. With his assistance, Talʿat Effendi succeeded, in 1811, in suppressing the rebellion of Suleiman Pasha, the governor of Baghdad. Gabbai was called to Istanbul, where he became a favorite of Khālid Effendi, the secretary to the Sultan. He was introduced to the court of the sultan and appointed *ṣarrāf bāshī*. In this position he revealed exceptional talents and wielded tremendous unofficial influence; many honors were bestowed upon him, and he succeeded in displacing the Armenian faction from the court. He exploited his position for the benefit of his coreligionists and family in the leadership of the Baghdad community. The *nasi* Sasson ibn Ṣāliḥ was replaced by his brother Ezra who held the position from 1817 until 1824. When the Armenian faction regained its influence, Ezekiel was exiled, and both brothers were later executed as a result of libels brought against them. EZEKIEL GABBAI (1825–1898), a grandson of Ezekiel b. Joseph, was the first Jew to hold office in the Ottoman Ministry of Education. He was also an active member of the Istanbul community. In 1860, he founded a Ladino newspaper, *El Zhurnal Izraelit*, in which he fought for reforms within the Jewish community. He also summarized the laws of the Ottoman State in regard to the Jews. His son ISAAC published until 1930 the newspaper *El Telegrafo*, which followed a similar policy to that of his father. EZEKIEL BEN JOSHUA GABBAI (1824–1896), the disciple and nephew of R. Abdallah *Somekh of Baghdad, traveled in 1842 to India, where he became wealthy. He was accustomed to set aside *ma'aser* ("a tenth") of his income for charities in India, Iraq, and Ereẓ Israel. He extended his business to China in 1843, becoming one of the first Baghdadis to trade there. In 1853, he married ʿAzīza (d. 1897), the daughter of Sir Albert (Abdallah) *Sassoon. The traveler Jacob *Saphir wrote of him in 1860 that he was a distinguished scholar, sharp-witted and shrewd, cultured and industrious. His five sons and five daughters included Flora (Farḥa), the wife of Sir Solomon *Sassoon, David, president of the Jewish community in Shanghai, and one son who became a judge in Bombay. EZEKIEL BEN ṢĀLĪḤ GABBAI (1812–1887) traveled in 1842 from Baghdad to India, where he was "*gabbai* ("treasurer") of the Four Lands" (Jerusalem, Hebron, Tiberias, and Safed) for 40 years. Under his direction, large sums were collected for Ereẓ Israel. In 1870, the traveler Solomon *Reinmann (*Masot Shelomo*, 182) stated that Ezekiel possessed a fortune amounting to several million francs. He later lost most of his wealth and became the manager for David Sassoon and Company in Calcutta.

AARON (d. 1888) and Elijah (d. 1892), sons of Shalom Gabbai, were born in Baghdad. In 1840, they journeyed to Calcutta and amassed a fortune in the opium trade between India and China. Outstanding philanthropists, they contributed generously to charitable causes in India, Iraq, and Ereẓ Israel. Elijah lived in China for a time and later returned to Calcutta, where he became a member of the municipal council and an agent for David Sassoon and Company. RAPHAEL BEN AARON GABBAI (d. 1923) was also born in Baghdad and later settled in Calcutta. Another noted philanthropist, he left a bequest of £100,000 to be distributed among charitable institutions in Ereẓ Israel, Baghdad, Calcutta, and London. SASSON BEN EZEKIEL MORDECAI GABBAI, "*gabbai* of the Four Lands" in Bombay during the 19th century, raised considerable funds for charities in Ereẓ Israel. JOSHUA BEN SIMEON GABBAI (1828–1898) settled in Calcutta in 1851, where he was a communal worker and *gabbai* of the Maghen David Synagogue.

[Abraham Ben-Yaacob]

SOLOMON SALIH GABBAI (1897–1961), poet and educator in Iraq. After having taught for many years in Baghdad, he became rabbi of Amara (1943–44) and later rabbi of the Iraqi community in Teheran. He wrote many poems in Hebrew and collected them in two booklets entitled *Shirei ha-Kerem* (Baghdad, 1925–26); some of these are poems on Zion. He also wrote an elegy on the massacre of the Jews in Baghdad during June 1941. He settled in Israel in 1951.

[Haim J. Cohen]

BIBLIOGRAPHY: A. Ben-Jacob, *Yehudei Bavel* (1965), index; D.S. Sassoon, Ohel Dawid, 1 (1932), 36,430–1; idem, *History of the Jews in Baghdad* (1949), index.

GABBAI (Heb. גַּבַּאי, גַּבַּי), lay communal official. Derived from the Hebrew *gavah* (גָּבָה – to exact payment), the word is actually part of the complete title *gabbai ẓedakah* (charity warden) and all the relevant regulations, such as that individuals could not act as a *gabbai*, but collectors had to work in pairs, refer to this charity collector. In the Middle Ages, however, the meaning of the word was extended to include other communal officials. The original meaning of collector of taxes or treasurer merged in the usage of the medieval community with the parallel ancient meanings of collector for charities or administrator of them, and also came to connote supervisor and executive leader. The executive officer of a *ḥevrah or *guild was named *gabbai*. He was an unpaid lay-elected officer who administered the affairs of the particular association, whether burial, sick care, or the host of other purposes served by these groups. Very large societies had as many as 12 *gabba'im*, each serving one month in the year, when he was *gabbai ḥodesh*. Smaller organizations elected only one or more executives. Where the work was plentiful, the *gabbai* had the services of a beadle and other paid employees. In the small association the *gabbai* usually did all the work himself. In the communal administration the *gabbai* was an officer in charge of a particular committee or activity. In the Cracow community there were officers termed exalted, *gabba'im gevohim*. Some served as *gabba'im* in the synagogue, managing its affairs and distributing honors, especially at the Reading of the Torah. There were also *gabba'ei Ereẓ Yisrael*. In 1749, for example, at the Jaroslaw session of the Polish *Council of Four Lands, such officers were appointed in local or regional communities to make collections for the maintenance of the poor in Ereẓ Israel. In modern times there were also *gabba'im* of the *kolelim* (see also *ḥalukkah). The manager and supervisor of the affairs of a ḥasidic rabbi was also named *gabbai*. Female heads of associational activities were called *gabbaites*. The elected heads of the synagogues, mainly among Ashkenazi Jewry, were titled *gabbai*. British Jews employed the term *parnas in a congregational context instead of *gabbai*, using the latter for the warden of the synagogue; the president is called *parnas* in Hebrew.

BIBLIOGRAPHY: Baron, Community, index s.v. *Gabba'im*, Elders; J. Marcus, *Communal Sick-Care* (1947); I. Levitats, *Jewish Community in Russia* (1943); Halpern, Pinkas, 329, 338; C. Roth, *Records of the Western Synagogue* (1932), 58.

[Isaac Levitats]

GABBAI, MEIR BEN EZEKIEL IBN (1480–after 1540), kabbalist of the generation of Spanish exiles. The details of his life are not known. Apparently he lived in Turkey and possibly died in Ereẓ Israel. He wrote three books dealing with the principal problems of Kabbalah. They are *Tola'at Ya'akov* (written in 1507 and first printed in Constantinople, 1560), on the prayers; *Derekh Emunah* (written in 1539 and first printed in Constantinople, 1560), an explanation of the doctrine of the *sefirot* in the form of questions and answers, based on *Sha'ar ha-Sho'el* by *Azriel of Gerona and incorporating views of the *Zohar; and *Avodat ha-Kodesh*, on the entire doctrine of the Kabbalah, in four parts – on the unity of God, the worship of God, the purpose of man in the universe, and an explanation of esoteric aspects of the Torah – an important work which he wrote from 1523 to 1531. The last is the most comprehensive and organized summary of the doctrine of the Kabbalah prior to the Safed period and was one of the most popular books on Kabbalah even with recent generations. It was first printed in 1566–68 under the name *Marot Elohim*. Gabbai was one of the leading proponents of the view that the *Sefirot* are the essence of divinity.

[Gershom Scholem]

Ibn Gabbai is also one of the most important exponents of the theurgical approach in Kabbalah, which found its elaborate and complex expressions in both *Tola'at Ya'akov* and *Avodat ha-Kodesh*.

[Moshe Idel (2nd ed.)]

BIBLIOGRAPHY: Yaari, in: KS, 9 (1933), 388–93; Zunz, Lit Poesie, 381; Blau, in: ZHB, 10 (1906), 52–58. **ADD. BIBLIOGRAPHY:** E.K. Ginsburg, *Sod ha-Shabbat, from the Tola'at Ya'aqov of R. Meir ibn Gabbai*, (1989); R. Goetschel, *R. Meir Ibn Gabbai; Le Discours de la Kabbale espagnole* (1981).

GABBAI, MOSES BEN SHEM-TOV (d. c. 1443), scholar of Spain and North Africa. He lived for a time in Calatayud and then moved to Teruel where he served as rabbi. He settled in Majorca (before 1387) but during the riots of 1391 escaped to North Africa and was appointed rabbi of Honein. Gabbai was closely connected with the royal Spanish court and King John I of Aragon granted him freedom of passage between Spain and Majorca to attend to his affairs in Majorca (from a document dated 1394). His sister was the wife of Simeon b. Ẓemaḥ *Duran; Gabbai corresponded with the latter and with *Isaac b. Sheshet Perfet, both of whom he greatly respected. The poet Solomon b. Meshullam *Da Piera praised him in several of his poems. The latest mention of his name is in a responsum of Duran (*Tashbeẓ*, 2:99) addressed to him at Honein. From its contents it is clear that it was written in 1443, and not in 1427, as has been erroneously stated by his biographers. His extant writings are a supercommentary (written in 1421) on the commentary of Rashi on the Pentateuch (in manuscript); and a *bakkashah* (petitional prayer) which is also in manuscript.

BIBLIOGRAPHY: I. Epstein, *The Responsa of Rabbi Simon ben Ẓemaḥ Duran* (1903), index; A. Hershman, *Rabbi Isaac bar Sheshet Perfet and His Times* (1943); Baer, Urkunden, 1 (1929), 720f.

[Israel Moses Ta-Shma]

GABBAI IZIDRO (Ysidro), ABRAHAM (d. 1755), Sephardi rabbi. A Spanish Marrano, his wife was tried by the Inquisition while he escaped to London and reentered Judaism. He studied later with David Israel *Attias in Amsterdam and published in 1724 a sermon containing some interesting autobiographical details. Thereafter he was rabbi in *Surinam and then *Barbados. In old age, he returned to London where he died. He left in manuscript a kabbalistic verse commentary, *Yad Avraham* on the *Azharot, which was published (Amsterdam, 1758) by his widow, who had settled in Bayonne.

BIBLIOGRAPHY: Kayserling, Bibl, 48; JHSAP, 29 (1925), 13.

[Cecil Roth]

GABEL, MAX (1877–1952), Yiddish actor and playwright. He is credited with having written 114 plays, mostly melodramas and adaptations of Broadway successes. His first play was *The Sea King*, 1895, performed in New York. Later he managed Gabel's Star Theater and other New York playhouses. He wrote and produced plays for his wife, actress/singer/writer/producer JENNIE GOLDSTEIN (1896–1960), whom he married when she was 16. These plays included *Girl with a Past* and *Everything for Love*. The couple starred together in his plays, and Gabel's productions enjoyed extended runs. He toured with his wife until they divorced in 1930 and he retired to California.

[Ruth Beloff (2nd ed.)]

GABÈS (Ar. **Qābis**; the ancient **Tacapae**), maritime town in *Tunisia, situated in a luxuriant palm forest. Gabès was an important commercial and industrial center. Under Arab rule the Jews were farmers and manufacturers, who wove silk and exported – mainly precious cloth; they gained considerable wealth as a result of their trade with Sicily, the Orient, and the interior of Africa. Some of them were merchants of worldwide importance. In Gabès many Jews devoted themselves to poetry and music, and their intellectual leaders, such as the Ibn Jamaʿ family, succeeded in converting their academy into a religious center whose importance was comparable to that of *Kairouan. These rabbinical scholars maintained contact with *Sura and *Pumbedita, where the *gaon* Abraham al-Qābisi (i.e., of Gabès) had already settled at the beginning of the ninth century. During the 12th century they frequently communicated with the Jews of *Spain; Abraham *Ibn Ezra stayed in Gabès. After incursions by the Normans of *Sicily (1117, 1147) the community was destroyed by the *Almohads in 1159. Once reconstituted, the community did not return to its former importance. During the following centuries, the Jews of Gabès generally lived in peace. Many of them were engaged in commerce. The weaving of cloth and the wood and jewelry trades were principally Jewish crafts. The community, which numbered about 3,200 before World War II, suffered extensively under the German occupation of 1942–43. From 1948 its members immigrated to France and Israel. Only about 200 families of wealthy Jewish landowners still lived in Gabès in 1970.

[David Corcos]

During the Hafisit period Gabès was an economic and administrative center of its region. We do not have any real information about Jewish life in Gabès before the middle of the 19th century. In 1858 Benjamin the Jewish traveler found out about 100 families in Gabès but this is the only information about the Jewish community. A French explorer of the Sahara and the Tuareg, Henri Duveyrier (1840–1892), visited Tunisia in 1860, and his observations on the Jewish community of Gabès were of great importance. Jews lived in both parts of the ancient town, Menzel and Jara. Some Jews came from Leghorn and integrated into the autochthonous community. Their economic life was based on the Trans-Sahara trade, maritime commerce, and agriculture. Some Jews enjoyed European citizenship.

During the French protectorate the Jewish community grew to 1,271 in 1909 and more than 3,300 in 1946. Thus the community became one of the largest in south Tunisia. Most Jews came from *Djerba and the south. The French developed the port, the industry, and the minerals in the region of Gabès. Jews took part in those new economic opportunities. The Jewish community of Gabès was based on Djerba rabbinical authority. The rabbis came from Djerba and were committed to *takkanot* from Djerba. Gabès became the northern frontier of the Djerba periphery. For example, owing to its French nature, the Alliance Israélite Universelle could not open a school in Gabès. The rabbis in Djerba strongly opposed the Alliance initiative. Moreover, Rabbi Haim Khuri, the most famous sage in the 20th century, was born in Djerba and immigrated to Gabès, where his influence on Jewish life in Gabès was of great importance. He was the author of the books *Bene Moshe*, *Derekh Haim*, and *Maẓa Hayyim*. He was buried in Beersheba, and his grave became a holy place at which his sons organize a *hillula* every year. In 1909 the French created the communal committee, La Caisse de Secours et de Bienfaisance, as in all other large towns in Tunisia. Simon Seror was the president of the committee between the two World Wars and Haouti Zana was president after World War II. Jews sent their children to *talmud torahs* and some of them even to French schools, which provided the only modern education.

The only Zionist activity in Gabès was the creation of the Zionist association Ḥerut Zion just after World War I but Jews contributed to the national funds. As far as we know, Jews lived in coexistence with the Muslims. For example, at the fish factory of the Journo family, Arabs and Jews worked together in friendly relations. The only exception was the riot of May 20, 1941, in which seven Jews were killed and about 20 were wounded. After World War II and as a result of the German occupation, Zionist activity was stronger than before the war. All political trends took part in Zionist activity: Betar, Ẓeʿirei Ẓion (a Marxist group), Torah va-Avodah, and others. Even a self-defense group was created but had little importance.

[Haim Saadoun (2nd ed.)]

BIBLIOGRAPHY: R. Brunschwig, *La Berbériè orientale sous les Hafṣides*, 2 vols. (1940–47), index; Hirschberg, Afrikah, index; S.D. Goitein, *A Mediterranean Society*, 1 (1967), index. **ADD. BIBLIOGRAPHY:** M. Ben-Sasson, "The Jewish Community of Gabès in the 11th Century, Economic and Residential Patterns," in: M. Abitbol (ed.), *Communautes juives des marges sahariennes du magrhreb* (1982), 265–84; D. Vitalis, *Juifs du Sud, note du voyages* (April 1950); "Gabès," in: I. Abramski-Bligh, *Pinkas ha-Kehillot* (1997), 306–18.

GABIN (Pol. **Gąbin**; Rus. **Gombin**), small town in Warszawa province, central Poland. Of the 352 houses there in 1564, seven were owned by Jews. The wooden synagogue was erected in 1710. The community numbered 365 in 1765, 2,539 in 1897, and 2,564 in 1921 (out of a total population of 5,777). R. Abraham Abele *Gombiner author of *Magen Avraham*, was born there. Yehuda Leib *Avida (Zlotnik) was rabbi of Gabin from 1911 to 1919. Between the wars the Jews suffered economic hardship but community life flourished. Following the Nazi occupation in September 1939, some were sent to forced labor camps; the rest were ghettoized in early 1940. In May 1942 the Jews were deported to Chelmno; around 180 survived the war, most of them subsequently immigrating to Israel.

BIBLIOGRAPHY: S. Pazyra, *Geneza i rozwój miast mazowieckich* (1959), index; *Miasta polskie w tysiącleciu* (1967), index; S. Huberband, *Kiddush ha-Shem* (1969), 278; D. Dąbrowska, in: BŻIH, no. 13–14 (1955), 122–84 and passim. **ADD. BIBLIOGRAPHY:** *Dos Leben un Umkum fun a yiddish shtetl in Poylen* (1969); Jewish Life, 1, 440, s.v. "Gombin."

°**GABINIUS, AULUS**, Roman governor of Syria from 57 to 55 B.C.E. He was granted extensive authority, and his system of rule was characteristic of Roman imperialistic methods toward the end of the period of the republic. He put into effect Pompey's decision to diminish the area of the territory of Judea, deprived Hyrcanus of the title ethnarch, divided the country into five districts, and rehabilitated the Greek cities which the Hasmoneans had destroyed. He defeated the efforts of Aristobulus II and his son Alexander to seize power in Judea.

BIBLIOGRAPHY: A. Schalit, *Ha-Mishtar ha-Roma'i be-Ereẓ Yisrael* (1937), 4–5, 32ff.; idem, *Hordos ha-Melekh* (1964), index; A.H.M. Jones, *The Herods of Judaea* (1938), 20, 24–26.

GABIROL, SOLOMON BEN JUDAH, IBN (c. 1021–c. 1057; Ar. Abu Ayyub Sulayman ibn Yahya ibn Gabirul; Lat. Avicebron), Spanish poet and philosopher.

His Life

The main source of information on Ibn Gabirol's life is his poems, although frequently they offer no more than hints. A number of details can be found in the works of *Ibn Saʿīd and in the *Kitab al-Muhadara wal-Mudhakara* by Moses *Ibn Ezra (published by A. Halkin (1975), 36b, 37a, etc.), and some information can be deduced from Ibn Gabirol's introduction to his ethical work, *Tikkun Middot ha-Nefesh* (Constantinople, 1550). His family left Córdoba in the unsafe years of the beginning of the 11th century, and he was very likely born in Malaga – or at any rate he lived there and regarded it as his native city, signing a number of his poems "Malaki," i.e., from Malaga – but as a child he was taken to Saragossa, where he acquired an extensive education. Orphaned at an early age, he wrote a number of elegies on the death of his father; on his mother's death in 1045, he mourned both his parents in "*Niḥar be-Kore'i*" (14). Ibn Gabirol complained in his poems of his weak physique, small stature, and ugliness, and if we understand his words literally, he was frequently ill from his childhood on, suffering particularly from a serious skin disease that he seems to describe in his strange and terrifying poem "*Ha-Lo Ezdak*." Being unusually mature for his age, he began to write poetry at a very young age, at the latest 16 when he wrote *Azharot* (Venice, 1572). Ibn Gabirol likened himself to a 16-year-old with the heart of an 80-year-old ("*Ani ha-Sar*," 8). According to his contemporaries, his character, at times verging on arrogance, brought him into frequent conflict with influential men of his day, whom he attacked virulently, and with society in general. Since he wanted to devote his life to philosophy and poetry, he was dependent on the support of wealthy patrons, a subservience against which he rebelled from time to time. In 1038 Ibn Gabirol wrote a number of elegies on the death of *Hai b. Sherira Gaon. One of his more important supporters was Jekuthiel b. Isaac ibn Ḥasan, whom he praised in a number of poems for his knowledge of the Talmud and the sciences, his interest in poetry, and his generosity ("*Ve-At Yonah*"). When Jekuthiel was killed in 1039 as a result of court intrigues, Ibn Gabirol wrote two elegies, one of which ("*Bi-Ymei Yekuti'el Asher Nigmaru*") is regarded as one of the greatest of Jewish medieval secular poems. With the loss of his patron, Ibn Gabirol's financial status and social standing were drastically lowered and his incessant squabbling with the town nobles caused him considerable suffering. At the age of 19, he completed his great didactic poem, "*Anak*." It is thought that he wrote *Tikkun Middot ha-Nefesh* ("The Improvement of the Moral Qualities") in 1045, and soon afterward he seems to have left Saragossa; from then on few details are available on his life and work. Some scholars believe that he lived for some time in Granada, where his patron was *Samuel ha-Nagid, with whom he later quarreled as a result of his criticisms of Samuel's poems. Ibn Gabirol appears to have spent the year 1048–49 under the patronage of *Nissim b. Jacob ibn Shahin, but it is doubtful if he ever was actually Nissim's student. He was on friendly terms with Isaac ibn Khalfun and Isaac ibn Kapron. According to Moshe Ibn Ezra, Ibn Gabirol died in Valencia at the age of 30, while Abraham Ibn Daud states that he died in 1070, when he was approximately 50. However, the most exact date seems to be that given by Ibn Saʿīd: 450 A.H. or 1057–58, when he was between 36 and 38. The many legends surrounding his life attest to the awe in which the man and his works were held after his death. One legend (found in the commentary to *Sefer Yeẓirah* (publ. Mantua, 1562), attributed to Saadiah Gaon) relates how Ibn Gabirol made a female *golem* out of wood; another (in *Shalshelet ha-Kabbalah* by Gedaliah ibn Yaḥyā, Venice, 1587) tells how he was murdered by an Arab.

Works

In one of his poems, Ibn Gabirol boasts of having written 20 books, but only two are extant that can certainly be attributed to him: *Mekor Ḥayyim* and *Tikkun Middot ha-Nefesh*. Both are written in Judeo-Arabic. *Sefer Al ha-Nefesh* (*Liber de Anima*), which has been preserved in Latin, and *Mivḥar Peninim* (Venice, 1546) are frequently attributed to Ibn Gabirol, but in both cases there is insufficient proof of his authorship. In their commentaries on the Bible, Abraham ibn Ezra and David Kimḥi quote some of his interpretations, mostly allegorical, but it is not known if he composed a complete commentary of his own. The difficult task of recovering and identifying Ibn Gabirol's poems, which were scattered in prayer books, anthologies, and single pages dispersed in many libraries, was first undertaken in the 19th century by J.L. Dukes, S.D. Luzzatto, S. Sachs, and H. Brody, who brought out the first collection of his verse. The discovery in the *Genizah* in the early part of the 20th century of an ancient index of poems by Ibn Gabirol, Ibn Ezra, and Judah Halevi proved that there had been a very early collection of Ibn Gabirol's poems, and later a complete *divan* was found in manuscript (Schocken 37). Bialik and Ravnitzky did not regard their seven-volume edition of Ibn Gabirol's collected works (1924–32) as complete. Brody and Schirmann published a scientific edition of his secular poems in 1974. D. Jarden collected and annotated the secular (1975) and liturgical (1976) poems in four volumes. Ibn Gabirol's poems have been translated into most Western languages (I. Goldberg, 1998). There is a good English translation of many of his poems by P. Cole (2001); a German translation by F. Bargebuhr (1976); E. Romero translated into Spanish a large selection of his secular poems (1978), and M.J. Cano translated his secular poetry (1987) and a significant part of his liturgical poems (1992).

Poetry

In his poetic works Ibn Gabirol displays his great knowledge of biblical Hebrew and his linguistic virtuosity, while avoiding the complexity of many of his predecessors, including Samuel ha-Nagid. Employing images and idioms from Arabic poetry, he fuses them into an original style, with brilliant intellectual metaphors. He can be a formalist in some conventional genres, but he also attains lyrical heights that are unusual in the Middle Ages, with deep reflections on his own life and his search for wisdom. While he wrote in biblical Hebrew, like all Andalusian poets, he was not a purist, and allowed himself some neologisms that provoked the censure of his most intransigent critics. In spiritual tone his poetry is shaped by Bible and talmudic literature as well as by early mystical Midrashim. In its mystical tendencies, his work is sometimes described as closely akin to Sufi poetry. Both his scientific knowledge, especially of astronomy, and his neoplatonic leanings are evident in his poems.

SECULAR POETRY. In accordance with contemporary tradition, most of Ibn Gabirol's secular poetry was composed in honor of patrons whom he describes in extravagant panegyric. As he employs the full range of the Hebreo-Arabic rhetoric of the time in poems of praise and poems of friendship, it is often difficult to differentiate between the two. In the tone of the Arabic poems of self-praise, he refers to himself as a "violin unto all singers and musicians" ("*Ani ha-Sar*") before whom are opened the "doors of wisdom" that are closed to the rest of his nation ("*Ha-Tilag le-Enosh*"). Following convention, especially that of the great Arab pessimistic poets, he emphasizes the contrast between himself and the society in which he lives, frequently voicing complaints against time, i.e., fate, and his inability to find his place among his fellows, involved as they are in mundane matters and temporal successes. Nonetheless, he was alive to the impulses of youth and while he composed few love poems those few are powerful lyrics. An erotic note is sounded in his description of his relation to poetry, which he portrays as a desirable young girl. In his most personal poetry, he expresses the internal tensions of his own search for knowledge, his solitude and his confrontation with destiny and with the men of his time, his bitterness and despair, mourning his inability to enjoy the pleasures of the world and of love, and finding refuge in wisdom and in God.

In his "wisdom poetry" he depicts himself as devoting his life to knowledge in order to prepare his soul to rejoin the "Source of Life" on its release from its bodily prison. Knowledge has two aspects consisting both of the effort of the intellect to scale the heights of the heavenly spheres and of the soul's introspection. At first pleading with God to let him live, the poet soon begins to deride the world and time, regarding them as valueless and insignificant obstacles on the way to eternity. From the height of his identification with the infinity of the Godhead and of eternity, he regards with disgust the trials of the world below, the illusions of the senses, and the weakness of the flesh.

In accordance with the rules of rhetoric, some of Ibn Gabirol's extensive nature poetry seems to have served as an introduction to his laudatory verse, for the patron's generosity was often likened to the ordained plenitude of nature. It is clear from his nature poetry that he was influenced by the Islamic culture prevalent in Spain at the time, but within this traditional framework, the fine descriptions are accurately observed. Some of his winter poems ("autumn" according to the poet) include a few of his finest creations, e.g., "*Avei Sheḥakim*," and "*Yeshallem ha-Setav Nidro*."

A part of Ibn Gabirol's poetry reflects his lack of social adaptation and his pessimistic view of the society of his time. His response is to complain in a harsh, satirical tone. If his contemporaries are not able to recognize his qualities, he pays them back with contempt, fustigating their ignorance and their wretchedness.

In another large section of Ibn Gabirol's work, his ethical poems, he addresses the reader directly, propounding an ethic based upon individual introspection. These poems deal with the transience of life and the worthlessness of bodily existence in all its aspects as opposed to the eternal values of spiritual life and the immortality of the soul. Ibn Gabirol's didactic tendency also finds expression in the many riddles he composed, which were possibly appended to letters, and it is also apparent in the dialogue form in which many of the longer poems were written. This style, developed in medieval Arabic poetry, was also used to introduce variety into the long poems which otherwise tended to be monotonous as a result of the identical rhyming of all the stanzas. The only secular verse he wrote in a strophic form is "*Ki-Khelot Yeini*" – a humorous poem that became a popular Purim song.

RELIGIOUS POETRY. Through his combination of pure Hebrew with the varied meters of Arabic poetry, Ibn Gabirol enhanced his poetic stature in the estimation of his contemporaries. Today, however, these qualities are dimmed by the great wealth of complex strophic forms he employed in his religious poetry. Stylistically, liturgical poets were always the elite of medieval Jewish poetry and Ibn Gabirol's works in this genre are the apogee of the tradition. Ibn Gabirol composed a substantial number of religious poems in the difficult style of the early school of liturgical poets, possibly because they were commissioned by various communities or synagogues. Despite this, the freshness and vivacity of his imagery is striking. Many of these liturgical poems have been preserved, not only in Sephardi and Ashkenazi prayer books but also in those of the Karaites. It is on the basis of these poems that Ibn Gabirol is regarded as the major religious poet of Spanish Jewry, and many of them, such as "*Reshut*" and "*Shaḥar Avakkeshkha*," are outstanding lyrical-religious creations even outside this particular context. In contrast to the long compositions of the classical *piyyut* Ibn Gabirol writes many short poems that reflect the feelings and predilections of the Andalusian believer in his relation with God. At the same time, he introduces many elements of secular poetry in the liturgical poems. Although his God is a personal deity, to whom he may turn in confession or supplication, Ibn Gabirol, unlike Judah Halevi, does not describe his great love for God as the relationship between the lover and the beloved. The poet, who in his secular verse is strong-willed and contemptuous of the base world about him, becomes humble in his religious poetry as he begins to understand himself and man in general. When addressing God, he realizes his insignificance and his inability either to combat desire or to understand the essential evil of the senses for which there is no succor except in the compassion of God (*"Adonai, Mah Adam," "Shokhenei Battei Ḥomer"*). At times, these expressions of longing and of profound love for God are akin to the emotions expressed in the love poems (*"Shaḥar Aleh Elai Dodi"*).

As it was customary to compose liturgical poems according to a system of acrostics, most of the religious poems begin with the letter *shin* (S). In his shorter poems, Ibn Gabirol set out his own name "Shelomo" in the first letters of each verse, whereas in the longer ones he duplicated this name a number of times, combining it with that of his father Judah ibn (or ben) Gabirol. Other poems were composed according to an alphabetical sequence, but even in these he wove his own name, at times beginning an alphabetically arranged poem with a verse containing his name. Although surpassed by Judah Halevi's poems in the same vein, Ibn Gabirol's national poetry overshadows the modest efforts of Samuel ha-Nagid and should be regarded as a link between the two. This poetry emerged from a combination of the traditional longing for deliverance and the particular fate of Spanish Jewry. Political events, the fate of Jekuthiel, and the murder of an anonymous Jewish statesman by Christians in the forests along the border (*"Asher Teshev Shekhulah"*; *"Lekhu Bo'u ve-Hikkaveẓu"*) must have reinforced Ibn Gabirol's awareness of the dangers of exile. In *"Ge'ullot"* and *"Ahavot"* the people of Israel speak to their God as a woman to her lover, telling of her sorrows, while her lover comforts her with promises of her deliverance. In these poems fear of the final destruction and of the end of the prophetic vision mingle with a fervent belief in the advent of the Messiah. *Rashuyyot*, a collection of limpid short poems, is marked by extreme yearning for the savior. According to Abraham ibn Ezra, Ibn Gabirol was among those who tried to predict the Day of Judgment and this tendency is apparent in his poetry. The concepts and visions in Ibn Gabirol's mystical poems are very difficult to reconcile with the philosophical concepts expressed in his other works. In these poems, knowledge of the Divinity can be apprehended only by the elect who have plumbed the mysteries of creation through which God manifests Himself. The very names of God are endowed with mystical significance, becoming potent symbols of the power of the Creator and the wonders of His creation. The account of the creation is similar to that which appears in *Sefer Yeẓirah*. Many midrashic elements, as well as God's reply out of the whirlwind in Job, join to form a dynamic, mystery-shrouded account of creation breaking forth from the turmoil of primordial chaos into reality and form. There are detailed descriptions of the upper spheres, the curtain of the heavens, and the abodes of the angels, written in the spirit of **heikhalot* literature and the *Pirkei de-Rabbi Eliezer*. The close relationship between imagery and content in some of these poems, e.g., *"Ha-Ra'ash ha-Gadol,"* and *"Shinanim Sha'ananim,"* suggests that they may have been written in moments of ecstasy. *Ha-Anak* is a didactic poem apparently intended to teach the basic rules of Hebrew. According to Abraham ibn Ezra (introduction to *Moznayim*, 1809), the poem contained 400 stanzas, of which only 88 are extant, and was based upon a series of acrostics. An introduction on the superiority of the Hebrew language is followed by an explanation of how the words in the language are related to 22 letters of the alphabet in the same way that form is related to matter. *"Ha-Anak,"* which Ibn Gabirol called *Iggeret* and *Maḥberet*, is written in plain, flowing language, and was apparently designed for study, perhaps for teachers. The book was greatly admired by Abraham ibn Ezra, who regarded it as an important contribution to the understanding of the Hebrew language. The peak of Ibn Gabirol's poetic achievement is *Keter Malkhut*, a long composition in rhymed prose dealing in high style with the essence of God, the work of the creation, with a description of the "spheres," and a confession of the low condition of man, prone to sin (see below). The many editions, manuscripts, translations, and imitations (most important by David ibn Zimra) of the work bear witness to the widespread and continuing admiration it has aroused.

Judah *Al-Ḥarizi has the highest praise for Ibn Gabirol's poetry: "All the poets of his age were worthless and false in comparison… He alone trod the highest reaches of poetry, and rhetoric gave birth to him in the lap of wisdom… all the poets before him were as nothing and after him none rose to equal him. All those who followed learned and received the use of poetry from him" (*Tahkemoni*, "Third Gate").

[*Encyclopaedia Hebraica* / Angel Sáenz-Badillos (2nd ed.)]

Philosophy

METAPHYSICS. Gabirol presents his philosophic views in his major work, *Mekor Ḥayyim* ("The Source of Life"). Written in Arabic, but no longer extant in that language, the full work has been preserved in a medieval Latin translation under the title *Fons Vitae*. A Hebrew translation of several extracts by Shem Tov ibn Falaquera (13th century), who claimed that it contained all of Gabirol's thought, is also extant under the title *Likkutim mi-Sefer Mekor Ḥayyim*. In studying *Mekor Ḥayyim*, however, the loss of the Arabic original makes it difficult to explain certain terms.

Mekor Ḥayyim is written in the form of a dialogue between master and pupil, a style also current in Arabic philosophic literature of that period. However, it is not a typical Platonic dialogue, in which the student discovers true opinions for himself through discussion with the master; instead, the student's questions serve to enable the master to expound his views. *Mekor Ḥayyim*, divided into five treatises, is devoted primarily to a discussion of the principles of matter and form. The first treatise is a preliminary clarification of the notions of universal matter and form, a discussion of matter and form as they exist in objects of sense perception, and a discussion of the corporeal matter underlying qualities. The second treatise contains a description of the spiritual matter that underlies corporeal form. The third is devoted to demonstrating the existence of simple substances. The fourth deals with the form and matter of simple substances, and the fifth, with universal form and matter as they exist in themselves. The doctrine of matter and form is, in Gabirol's view (*Mekor Ḥayyim*, 1:7), the first of the three branches of science, the other two being, in ascending order, the science of (God's) will and the science of the First Essence, God. Gabirol states (5:40) that he has written a special book devoted to God's will, but no further evidence of such a book is available.

Gabirol's cosmological system generally has a neoplatonic structure but with modifications of his own. The first principle is the First Essence, which can be identified with God. Next in order of being are the divine will, universal matter and form, then the simple substances – intellect, soul, and nature, and finally the corporeal world and its parts. Gabirol holds that all substances in the world, both spiritual and corporeal, are composed of two elements, form and matter. This duality produces the differences between various substances, but, according to some passages, it is specifically the forms that distinguish one substance from the other, while according to others, it is matter. Matter is the substratum underlying the forms; forms inhere in it. All distinctions between matter and form in the various substances stem from the distinction between universal matter and universal form, the most general kinds of matter and form, which, according to Gabirol's account of being, are the first created beings. However, Gabirol presents conflicting accounts of their creation. According to one account (5:42), universal matter comes from the essence of God, and form, from the divine will, but according to another (5:36–38), both of these principles were created by the divine will. In some passages Gabirol holds that universal matter exists by itself (2:8, 5:32), which deviates from the Aristotelian account of matter, but in other passages he states, in accord with Aristotle's view, that matter is akin to privation, and form to being, and that matter exists only in potentiality (5:36).

All forms, in addition to appearing in various levels of being, are also contained in universal form. Matter and form do not exist by themselves; their first compound is intellect, the first of the spiritual substances, from which the soul emanates, it, too, being composed of matter and form. Hence, as opposed to the Aristotelian views, spiritual matter exists, and it is found in all incorporeal substances. All spiritual, or simple, substances emanate forces that bestow existence upon substances below them in the order of being. Thus, soul is emanated from intellect. There are three kinds of soul, rational, animate, and vegetative, which, besides being cosmic principles, also exist in man. In contrast to the opinion of the Aristotelians, nature as a cosmic principle emanates from the vegetative soul. Nature is the last of the simple substances, and from it emanates corporeal substance, which is below nature in the order of being. Corporeal substance is the substratum underlying nine of the ten Aristotelian *categories. The tenth category, substance, is universal matter as it appears in the corporeal world, and the nine other categories are universal form as it appears in the corporeal world.

For soul to be joined to body a mediating principle is required. The mediating principle joining the universal soul to the corporeal world is the heavens; the mediating principle joining the rational soul of man to the body is the animal spirit. The relation of man's body to his soul is also said to be like the relation between form and matter (a parallel which is difficult to reconcile with Gabirol's account of these two principles). The soul comprehends the forms but not matter, since the latter principle is unintelligible. In order to comprehend sensible forms the soul must use the senses, because these forms do not exist in the soul as they are in the corporeal world. The forms which always exist in the soul are the intelligible forms. However, since the soul was deprived of its knowledge as a result of its union with the body, these forms exist in the soul only potentially, not actually. Therefore, God created the world and provided senses for the soul, by means of which it may conceive tangible forms and patterns. It is through this comprehension of the sensible forms and patterns that the soul also comprehends ideas, which in the soul emerge from potentiality to actuality (5:41).

All forms exist in intellect, also, but in a more subtle and simple manner than in soul. Furthermore, in intellect they do not have separate existence, but are conjoined with it in a spiritual union. "The form of the intellect includes all the forms, and they are contained in it" (4:14). Intellect, which is composed of universal form and matter, is below these two principles, and therefore can conceive them only with great difficulty.

Above the knowledge of form and matter there is a far more sublime knowledge: that of the divine will, which is identical with divine wisdom and divine logos. This will in itself, if considered apart from its activity, may be thought of as identical with the Divine Essence, but when considered with respect to its activity, it is separate from divine essence. Will according to its essence is infinite, but with respect to its action is finite. It is the intermediary between divine essence and matter and form, but it also penetrates all things. In its function as the efficient cause of everything, it unites form with matter. The will, which causes all movement, be it spiritual or corporeal, is in itself at rest. The will acts differently on different substances, this difference depending upon the particular matter, not upon the will (5:37). The First Essence, i.e., God, cannot be known because it is infinite and because it lacks any similarity to the soul. Nevertheless, its existence can be demonstrated.

The goal to which all men should aspire is defined in *Mekor Ḥayyim* (1:1, 2:1) as knowledge of the purpose for which they were created, i.e., knowledge of the divine world (5:43). There are two ways to achieve this goal: through knowledge of the will as it extends into all matter and form and through knowledge of the will as it exists in itself apart from matter and form. This knowledge brings release from death and attachment to "the source of life."

SOURCES. On a number of points, Gabirol's philosophy is close to the neoplatonic system current in medieval thought, for example, the concept of emanation that explains the derivation of simple substances and the concept of the parallel correspondence between different grades of being. Nevertheless, it differs on two very important points from the Muslim neoplatonism: the concept of form and matter (especially the latter) and the concept of will.

Gabirol's concept of matter is not internally coherent. On the one hand, it reflects distinct Aristotelian influence, but on the other, the occasional identification of matter with essence (*substantia*) suggests a Stoic influence, possibly the result of Gabirol's reading of the Greek physician Galen (second century). A concept that particularly characterizes Gabirol's system is spiritual matter. One possible source of this concept is the neoplatonist Plotinus (205?–270) in his *Enneads* (2:4), but there is no known Arabic translation of the latter's text (see *Neoplatonism). Theorem 72 of Proclus' *Elements of Theology*, which was translated into Arabic, sets forth a view of matter akin to Gabirol's. Like Gabirol, Plotinus and the Greek neoplatonist Proclus (c. 410?–485) regard matter as the basis of all unity in the spiritual world as well as in the physical. However, they do not maintain that universal form and matter are the first simple substances after God and His will. Pseudo-Empedoclean writings set forth the view that matter (Heb. *yesod*) and form are the first created beings and are prior to intellect. Ibn Falaquera states explicitly that Gabirol followed the views expressed by "Empedocles," that is, in the Pseudo-Empedoclean writings. It is even more likely that Gabirol's views on form and matter were influenced by certain texts of the tenth-century philosopher Isaac *Israeli or by a pseudo-Aristotelian text (see J. Schlanger, *La philosophie de Salomon Ibn Gabirol* (1968), 57–70) that appear to have influenced the latter as well as other authors.

In the identification of divine will and the logos and in the concept of the omnipresence of will, Gabirol's concept of will finds a parallel in *Saadiah Gaon's commentary to *Sefer Yeẓirah*. There is also a partial similarity of Gabirol's teachings to those of the Muslim Ismaili sect. In the text of *Mekor Ḥayyim* Plato is the only philosopher mentioned.

INFLUENCE OF MEKOR ḤAYYIM. *Mekor Ḥayyim* is unique in the body of Jewish philosophical-religious literature of the Middle Ages, because it expounds a complete philosophical-religious system wholly lacking in specifically Jewish content and terminology. The author does not mention biblical persons or events and does not quote the Bible, Talmud, or Midrash. To some extent this feature of the work determined its unusual destiny. Among Jewish philosophers *Mekor Ḥayyim* is quoted by Moses ibn Ezra in his *Arugat ha-Bosem*. Abraham ibn Ezra was apparently influenced by it, although he makes no direct reference to the work, and Joseph ibn Ẓaddik, the author of *Ha-Olam ha-Katan* ("The Microcosm"), also drew on it. There is also a clear similarity between the views of the Spanish philosopher and kabbalist Isaac ibn *Latif and those of *Mekor Ḥayyim*. Traces of Gabirol's ideas and terminology appear in the Kabbalah as well.

On the other hand, *Mekor Ḥayyim* was severely attacked by Abraham *Ibn Daud, an Aristotelian, in his book *Emunah Ramah*. Despite these influences, however, *Mekor Ḥayyim* was slowly forgotten among Jews. In its own time it was not translated into Hebrew, and the original Arabic text was lost.

In the 12th century *Mekor Ḥayyim* was translated into Latin by Johannes Hispalensus (Hispanus) and Dominicus Gundissalinus. Hispalensus, also known as Aven Dauth, may possibly have been the same Ibn Daud who criticized Gabirol. Gabirol's name was corrupted to Avicebron, and he was generally regarded a Muslim, although some Christians thought he was a Christian. Some Christian thinkers were greatly influenced by *Mekor Ḥayyim*. Aristotelians, such as Thomas *Aquinas, sharply criticized Gabirol's views, but the Franciscan philosophers, who favored Augustine, accepted some of them. The Jewish philosophers Isaac *Abrabanel and his son Judah *Abrabanel, better known as Leone Ebreo, seem to have been familiar with some of Gabirol's works. Leone Ebreo, who quotes him by the name Albenzubron, regards him as a Jew, and states his own belief in Gabirol's views. It was only in the 19th century, 350 years after the Abrabanels, that Solomon *Munk, the French scholar, rediscovered the Falaquera extracts and through them identified Avicebron as Solomon ibn Gabirol, a Jew. Among modern philosophers, Schopenhauer noted a certain similarity between his own system and that of Gabirol.

ETHICAL WORK. *Tikkun Middot ha-Nefesh.* ("The Improvement of the Moral Qualities"), Gabirol's book on ethics, was written around 1045 and has been preserved in the original Arabic as *Kitāb Iṣlāḥ al-Akhlāq* and in Hebrew by Judah ibn Tibbon's Hebrew translation (1167). In this work Gabirol discusses the parallel between the universe, the macrocosmos, and man, the microcosmos. There is no mention in the book of the four cardinal virtues of the soul, a Platonic doctrine which was popular in Arabic ethical writings. Gabirol developed an original theory, in which each of 20 personal traits is assigned to one of the five senses: pride, meekness, modesty, and impudence are related to the sense of sight; love, mercy, hate, and cruelty, to the sense of hearing; anger, goodwill, envy, and diligence, to the sense of smell; joy, anxiety, contentedness, and regret, to the sense of taste; and generosity, stinginess, courage, and cowardice, to the sense of touch. Gabirol also describes the relation between the virtues and the four qualities: heat, cold, moistness, and dryness, which are incorporated in pairs in each of the four elements of which the earth is composed: earth, air, water, and fire.

PHILOSOPHICAL POETRY. Gabirol gives poetic expression to the philosophical thought of *Mekor Ḥayyim* in the first part of his poem *Keter Malkhut* (*The Kingly Crown*, tr. by B. Lewis, 1961). Although the conceptual framework of *Keter Malkhut* is not identical in every detail to that of *Mekor Ḥayyim*, the differences are in many cases only of phrasing or emphasis.

The conceptual variations reflect the contradictions apparent in *Mekor Ḥayyim* itself. *Keter Malkhut* opens with praise for the Creator and an account of His attributes: His unity, existence, eternity, and life and His greatness, power, and divinity. God is also described as "Light," according to the neoplatonic image of the deity, "Thou art the supreme light and the eyes of the pure soul shall see thee" (tr. Lewis, 31). Nevertheless, Gabirol stresses that God and his attributes are not distinguishable: we refer to attributes only because of the limited means of human expression.

The next section speaks of divine "Wisdom" and the "predestined Will" (*ha-Ḥefeẓ ha-Mezumman*), which together parallel the single concept of will (*Raẓon*) in *Mekor Ḥayyim*. "Thou art wise, and from Thy wisdom Thou didst send forth a predestined will, and made it as an artisan and a craftsman, to draw the stream of being from the void..." (*ibid.*, 33). His description of the creative activity of the predestined will corresponds with the concept of will in *Mekor Ḥayyim*, but despite the close ties between them, wisdom and will are not as closely identified with each other in *Keter Malkhut* as in *Mekor Ḥayyim*. In *Mekor Ḥayyim* Wisdom is seated upon the Throne, which is the first matter; in *Keter Malkhut* the link between these two substances is not clearly stated: "Who can come to Thy dwelling place, when Thou didst raise up above the sphere of intelligence the throne of glory, in which is the abode of mystery and majesty, in which is the secret and the foundation to which the intelligence reaches..." (*ibid.*, 47). Apparently, in *Keter Malkhut* the foundation or element (*ha-Yesod*) is the first matter.

The will is the instrument and the means of creation; after the description of the will the poet goes on to describe the structure of the world according to Ptolemaic cosmology. The earth, "half water, half land," is surrounded by a "sphere of air," above which there is a "sphere of fire." The world of the four elements is circumscribed by the spheres of the moon, Mercury, Venus, the sun, Mars, Jupiter, Saturn, the zodiac, and the diurnal sphere, "which surrounds all other spheres." The distance of these spheres from the world, the length of their orbit, the magnitude of the heavenly bodies found within them, and, particularly, their forces and their influence upon nature, worldly events, and the fate of man are all described according to Ptolemaic and Muslim astronomy. However, beyond the nine spheres there is yet another, which is the result of philosophical abstraction: "... the sphere of the Intelligence, 'the temple before it,'" from whose luster emanates the "radiance of souls and lofty spirits ... messengers of Thy Will" (*ibid.*, 45). Above this sphere is "the throne of glory, in the abode of mystery and majesty," and beneath it is "the abode of the pure souls" (*ibid.*, 47). In this exalted sphere, also, the punishment of sinful souls will be meted out. This part of the poem ends with a description of the soul that descends from the upper spheres to reside temporarily in matter, the source of sin, from which the soul can escape only by "the power of knowledge which inheres" in it (*ibid.*, 50). The concluding section of the poem contains a confession of sins (*viddui*), and for that reason *Keter Malkhut* was included in the Day of Atonement prayer book of some Jewish rites.

Among the translations and editions of Gabirol's philosophical works are: the Hebrew text of Ibn Falaquera's *Likkutim mi-Sefer Mekor Ḥayyim*, with a French translation by S. Munk, in the latter's *Mélanges de philosophie juive et arabe* (1859, 1927^2); a German edition by C. Baemker of the Latin translation by Johannes Hispanus (Hispalensus) and Dominicus Gundissalinus (1895); *Fountain of Life*, a partial translation by H.E. Wedeck with an introduction by E. James (1962); *La Source de Vie, Livre III*, translated with introduction, notes, and bibliography by F. Brunner (1950); *Sefer Mekor Ḥayyim*, a modern Hebrew translation by J. Bluwstein (1926); *Fountain of Life* in an English tranlation by A.B. Jacob (1987); *Improvement of the Moral Qualities*, including the Hebrew text, translated with an introduction by S. Wise (1901); *Keter ha-Malkhut*, edited by I.A. Zeidman (1950).

[Shlomo Pines]

BIBLIOGRAPHY: POETRY: Moses ibn Ezra, *Shirat Yisrael*, ed. by B. Halper (1924), 69–72; M. Sachs, *Die religioese Poesie der Juden in Spanien* (1845), 213–48; Zunz, Lit Poesie, 187–94; S. Sachs, *Shelomo b. Gabirol u-Keẓat Benei Doro* (1866); A. Geiger, *Salomo Gabirol und seine Dichtungen* (1867); D. Kahana, in: *Ha-Shiloʾaḥ*, 1 (1897), 38–48, 224–35; J.N. Simhoni, in: *Ha-Tekufah*, 10 (1921), 143–223; 12 (1922), 149–88; 13 (1923), 248–94; Solomon b. Gabirol, *Selected Religious Poems* tr. by I. Zangwill, ed. by I. Davidson (1923), introd.; J. Klausner, introd. to *Mekor Ḥayyim* tr. by J. Bluwstein (1926); A. Marx, in: HUCA, 4 (1927), 433–48; D. Yellin, *Ketavim Nivḥarim*, 2 (1939), 274–318; A.M. Habermann, in: *Sinai*, 25 (1943), 53–63 (bibliography on *Mivḥar ha-Peninim*); A. Orinowski, *Toledot ha-Shirah ha-Ivrit bi-Ymei ha-Beinayim*, 1 (1945), 85–133; J. Millás-Vallicrosa, *Selomo ibn Gabirol como poeta y filósofo* (1945); H. Schirmann, in: *Keneset*, 10 (1947), 244–57; J. Schirmann, *Shirim Ḥadashim min ha-Genizah* (1966), 166–84 (166f. a bibliographical list of poems published since 1935); *Seis Conferencias en Torno a Ibn Gabirol* (Malaga, 1973); J. Schirmann, in: REJ, 131 (1972), 323–50; F.P. Bargebuhr, in: EB (1973), 9:145; H. Brody and J. Schirmann with the participation of J. Ben-David, *Solomon Ibn Gabirol, Secular Poems* (1974); F. Bargebuhr, *Salomo Ibn Gabirol. Ostwestliches Dichtertum* (1976). **ADD. BIBLIOGRAPHY:** D. Yarden (ed.), *The Secular Poetry of Rabbi Solomon Ibn Gabirol* (Heb., 1975); idem, *The Liturgical Poetry of Rabbi Solomon Ibn Gabirol* (Heb., 1976); D. Pagis, *Change and Tradition in the Secular Poetry of Spain and Italy* (Heb., 1976); P. Cole, *Selected Poems of Solomon Ibn Gabirol* (2001); E. Romero, *Poesía secular* (1978); M.J. Cano, *Ibn Gabirol: poemas seculares* (1987); idem, *Ibn Gabirol: poesía religiosa* (1992); I. Goldberg, *Solomon ibn Gabirol: a Bibliography of His Poems in Translation* (1998); I. Levin, *Mystical Trends in the Poetry of Solomon Ibn Gabirol* (Heb., 1986); Schirmann-Fleischer, *The History of Hebrew Poetry in Muslim Spain* (1995), 257–345 (Heb.); R. Loewe, *Ibn Gabirol* (1989); A. Sáenz-Badillos, *El alma lastimada: Ibn Gabirol* (1992); idem, in: MEAH 29:2 (1980), 5–29; A. Tanenbaum, *The Contemplative Soul* (2002). PHILOSOPHY: J. Schlanger, *La Philosophie de Salomon ibn Gabirol* (1968); Guttmann, Philosophies, index s.v. *Ibn Gabirol*; idem, *Die Philosophie des Salomon ibn Gabirol* (1889); F. Brunner, *Platonisme et aristotélisme: La Critique d'Ibn Gabirol par St. Thomas d'Aquin* (1965), incl. bibl.; idem, in: REJ, 128 (1970), 317–37; Heschel, in: *Festschrift J. Freimann* (1937), 68–77; idem, in: MGWJ, 82 (1938), 89–111; idem, in: HUCA, 14 (1939), 359–85; R. Palgen, *Dante und Avencebrol*, 1958; Pines, in: *Tarbiẓ*, 27 (1957/58), 218–33; 34 (1964/65), 372–8; Husik, Philosophy, index; G.

Scholem, in: *Me'assef Soferei Ereẓ Yisrael* (1960), 160–78. **ADD. BIBLIOGRAPHY:** J. Guttman, *Philosophie des Salomon Ibn Gabirol (Avicebron) Dargestellt und Erlautert* (1979); J. Lomba, *La corrección de los caracteres* (1990); F. Brunner, *Metaphysique d'Ibn Gabirol et de la Tradition Platonicienne* (1997).

GABLER, MILTON (1911–2001), U.S. jazz impresario. Born in Harlem in New York City, Gabler said he fell in love with jazz at his family's summer cottage in Throgs Neck, the Bronx. While a student in high school, he worked at his father's hardware store and then transferred to another shop his father owned nearby, the Commodore Radio Corporation, a popular supply store. Gabler hooked up a loudspeaker over the door and tuned in a local radio station. Customers kept asking if the store sold records. It didn't, but it soon did. By 1934, the renamed Commodore Music Shop became the country's most important source of records and a meeting ground for fans and musicians. The store later had three addresses on East 42nd Street and had a branch on 52nd Street, where the jazz clubs were clustered. Also in 1934, Gabler began buying boxes of out-of-print jazz recordings from major record companies that had no plans to re-release them. Gabler then became the first person to sell re-issued records and was the first to print the names of all participating musicians on jazz records. In 1939, Gabler recorded Billie Holiday's chilling and now-classic ballad about lynching, "Strange Fruit," after her record producer refused for fear of losing sales in the South. On Commodore Records, Holiday sang, "Southern trees bear a strange fruit. Blood on the leaves and blood at the root." Throughout the 1930s and 1940s, Commodore issued almost 90 recordings, using more than 150 musicians and singers. In 1941, Gabler was hired by Decca Records, although he continued to produce records for Commodore until 1950. He produced records for Peggy Lee, the Weavers, and the Ink Spots, among many others. He was the first to pair Louis Armstrong and Ella Fitzgerald on record and, as a lyricist, he wrote the words for "In a Mellow Tone" for Duke Ellington and "Love" for Nat King Cole. Gabler was one of the first to make recordings of Broadway shows and was a midwife at the birth of rock 'n' roll. In 1954, he signed Bill Haley and the Comets to Decca. They were scheduled to record two songs. The first, "13 Women," was considered more promising. The other was "Rock Around the Clock." The group rehearsed one quick verse to set sound levels and recorded the song live in one take. Sound engineers were said to be alarmed at the high sound levels, but the song soon energized the market for the new sound of rock 'n' roll. Gabler was the uncle of entertainer Billy *Crystal.

[Stewart Kampel (2nd ed.)]

GÁBOR (Greiner), ANDOR (1884–1953), Hungarian poet and journalist. Gábor first wrote for the Jewish press, publishing violent attacks on Hungarian antisemitism. He wrote a prize-winning translation of Frédéric Mistral's Provençal epic, *Mirélo*, and was a founder of and writer for Hungary's political cabaret. After the failure of Béla *Kun's Communist regime. Gábor was an exile in Vienna and Moscow, but returned to Budapest after World War II and edited a satirical paper.

GABOR, DENNIS (1900–1979), British physicist and electrical engineer of Hungarian birth. Gabor wrote on electrical transients, gas discharges, electron dynamics, communication theory, and physical optics. He was also greatly concerned with the impact of science and technology upon society. Gabor taught at the University of Berlin-Charlottenburg as an assistant for two years. From 1926 to 1933 he worked first for the German research association for high voltage equipment and then as a research engineer in an engineering company. Gabor settled in England in 1933. Gabor theorized about a process of photographic recording which he named holography (1947). In the 1960s with the invention of laser beams the theory was realized, permitting cameraless three-dimensional full color photographic images. He was elected a Fellow of the Royal Society of London in 1956 and became professor of applied electron physics at the Imperial College of Science and Technology, University of London, two years later. Gabor was awarded the Nobel Prize for physics in 1971.

[J. Edwin Holmstrom]

GÁBOR (originally **Lederer**), **IGNÁC** (1868–1944), Hungarian philologist. Born in Abaujkomlos, Gábor studied at the Budapest rabbinical seminary and at the universities of Budapest and Paris, where he specialized in Semitic and Indo-European philology. His research was confined mainly to the theory of rhythm, and he translated medieval Hebrew poetry and various Sanskrit, Norse, French, Italian, Dutch, and other works into Hungarian. He initiated the "Popular Jewish Library," and edited a French-language newspaper, *Le Progrès* (1896–99). His works include a translation into Hungarian of the 13th-century Icelandic *Poetic Edda* (1905); *Manoello élete és költészete* ("Poems and Life of Imanuel of Rome," 1922); *A magyar ritmus problémája* ("The Problem of Rhythm in Hungarian," 1925); and *Der hebraeische Urrhytmus* (1929). Gábor and most of his family died in the Holocaust at the end of 1944.

BIBLIOGRAPHY: *Magyar Zsidó Lexikon* (1929), 302; *Magyar Irodalmi Lexikon*, 1 (1963), 375.

[Baruch Yaron]

GABOR, JOLIE (1894–1997), **MAGDA** (1914–1997), **ZSA ZSA** (1917–), and **EVA** (1919–1995). The three Gabor sisters (Magda, Zsa Zsa, and Eva) and their mother, Jolie, were among the first celebrities in post-World War II America to be famous for being famous. Although renowned for their beauty, glamour, and quick wit, the Gabors were also notorious for their many marriages to wealthy men. In truth the Gabors were smart business women whose fortunes were all self-made and who, more often than not, suffered broken hearts. Matriarch Jolie was born Jansci Tilleman in Budapest, Hungary, and married Vilmos Gabor, father of her daughters Magda, Sári (Zsa Zsa), and Eva. Zsa Zsa, already a beauty in Budapest, married the Turkish consul at 16 (she is rumored to have had an affair with Kemal Attaturk). By 1939 Eva was already in Hollywood, launching her acting career. During the war Magda was active in resistance activities in Budapest. Her reported relationship with the Portuguese consul afforded her the protection to escape to the border and to also have her parents escape from Hungary. After the war, Zsa Zsa, by then Mrs. Conrad Hilton, was able to appeal to Secretary of State Cordell Hull to have her parents admitted to the United States. Zsa Zsa's career was launched in 1951 when she became a regular on the TV show *Bachelor's Haven*, displaying her razor-sharp wit. Movie roles followed in such films as *Moulin Rouge* (1952), *Lilli* (1953), and *Touch of Evil* (1958). She married eight times, and had one daughter, Constance Francesca Hilton. For many years Zsa Zsa made a considerable income from department store appearances and other endorsements. Zsa Zsa gained a new measure of infamy for a 1989 trial after she slapped a police officer in Beverly Hills. Eva, the most serious actress of the three sisters, appeared in such films as *A Royal Scandal* (1945), *The Last Time I Saw Paris* (1954), and *Don't Go Near the Water* (1957). She is best known for her role as the socialite wife of Eddie Albert in the 1960s CBS sitcom *Green Acres*. She is also known to countless generations of children as the voice of "Duchess" in the animated film *The Aristocats*. She married five times, all of which ended in divorce. For many years, Eva maintained a very successful wig business.

[Adam Wills (2nd ed.)]

GABRIEL, GILBERT W. (1890–1952), U.S. drama critic and author. Born in Brooklyn, New York, Gabriel graduated from Williams College in 1912. He worked at first as a reporter on the *New York Evening Sun*, then became literary editor (1915–17), music critic (1917–24), and drama critic (1925–29). He subsequently worked for *The New York American* (1929–37). He also wrote articles, drama criticism, and stories for such magazines as *Vanity Fair, The New Yorker, Town and Country, The Stage, Harper's Bazaar,* and *Collier's*. He lectured on drama and criticism at New York University and created the *New Yorker* "Profile" department. During World War II, Gabriel was second lieutenant in the Army and served two years in Alaska. In 1944 he went to London as deputy chief of publications. He left the service later that year with the rank of lieutenant colonel. Gabriel became drama critic for *Theatre Arts* magazine and in 1949 began to work for *Cue* magazine. Gabriel's books include *The Seven-Branched Candlestick* (1916), *Jiminy* (1922), *Brownstone Front* (1928), *Famous Pianists and Composers* (1928), *Great Fortune* (1933), *Love from London* (1946), and *I Thee Wed* (1948).

[Ruth Beloff (2nd ed.)]

GABRIELOVITCH, OSIP SOLOMONOVICH (1878–1936), pianist and conductor. Born in St. Petersburg, Gabrielovitch studied there with Anton *Rubinstein, Liadov, and Glazunov, and later with Leschetizky in Vienna. After 1896 he toured Europe and the United States as an internationally renowned concert pianist and conductor. In 1918 he was appointed conductor of the Detroit Symphony Orchestra. Ten years later he became, additionally, joint conductor of the Philadelphia Orchestra with Leopold Stokowski. He was also known for his series of historical concerts illustrating the development of keyboard music from Bach to his own day. He married the contralto Clara Clemens, the daughter of Mark Twain.

GAD (Heb. גָּד, "fortune"; cf. Gen. 30:11), a deity of fortune, equivalent in function and meaning to the Greek Tyché and Latin Fortuna. In Isaiah 65:11 Gad is mentioned together with Meni as the beneficiary of a food offering: "Who prepare a table for Gad, and who give Meni a full drink offering." Although the name appears here (according to the masoretic pointing) preceded by the definite article, it refers to the deity (and see below). The Septuagint translates "for Gad" as *tō daimoniō*, "for the demon"; while Vulgate renders both Gad and Meni by Fortuna. The rite described has elements in common with the Roman lectisternium in which food was spread on a table before an image of the deity. The Roman ceremony was meant to propitiate gods and repel pestilence and enemies. The rite condemned by the prophet may have served a similar function. This is the only unequivocal mention of the deity in the Bible. There are other references, however, which might be connected with the deity. Thus a place named Baal-Gad, "Lord of fortune," is mentioned as the extreme northern limit of Joshua's conquest (e.g., Josh. 11:17); Migdal-Gad, "Tower of Gad," appears as a place in the southwest lowlands of Judah (Josh. 15:37). The word *gad* also occurs in proper names, but probably as the appellative meaning "(good) fortune" rather than as the name of a god, e.g., Gaddi (Num. 13:11), Gaddiel (Num. 13:10), and Azgad (Ezra 2:12). This is almost certainly the case in the name Gaddiyo ("YHWH is my fortune"), which occurs on one of the Samaria ostraca. The character of the element *gad* in the names Gad Melekh and Gad-Marom, on seals from the fifth to fourth centuries B.C.E. and an earlier period respectively, found in Jerusalem, is uncertain.

Gad also appears in other Semitic religions as an element in names. Though the meaning cannot always be determined, in many cases it is possible to interpret the element *gad* as an appellative meaning "fortune." Thus in a number of Palmyrene inscriptions the word occurs in combinations where the second element is the name of Nabū, Bel, and other Babylonian deities. One Palmyrene inscription found at a sacred spring (Efka), reading "Gadda," clearly points to a deity to whom the spring was sacred. A bilingual inscription of the second century CE equates Palmyrene Gad with Greek Tyché. In Phoenicia the word is found as an element in personal names (e.g., גדי, גדעזיז). A Punic (overseas Phoenician) inscription of the 4th–3rd century B.C.E. from Sardinia reads: *lrbt ltnt pn bʿl wgd*, "for the Lady, for Tinit Face-of-Baal and Gad." An early second century B.C.E. Punic inscription from Spain (KAI 72) reads: *lrbt ltnt ʾdrt whgd*, "For the Lady, for mighty Tinit and the Gad" (cf. the definite article used with Gad in Isa. 65:11). It appears also as an element in Nabatean (e.g., גדטב), Aramaic (e.g., גדיא), and South Arabian (e.g., עמגד) names. As a heterogram, GDE survived into Middle Persian, where it is read as *xwarrah*, "fortune." Babylonian talmudic גדא refers to the god/genius of fortune and serves as well as the common noun "luck."

BIBLIOGRAPHY: R. Dussaud, *Notes de mythologie syrienne* (1905), 73ff.; idem, *La pénétration des Arabes en Syrie avant l'Islam* (1955), 91, 110ff., 144; J. Hastings (ed.), *Encyclopaedia of Religion and Ethics*, 1 (1908), 662; E. Littmann, *Thamūd und Ṣafā* (1940), 108; O. Eissfeld, in: *Der alte Orient*, 40 (1941), 94, 123; S. Bottéro, in: S. Moscati (ed.), *Le Antiche Divinità Semitiche* (1958), 56; H.B. Huffmon, *Amorite Personal Names in the Mari Texts* (1965), 179; M. Hoefner in: H.W. Haussig (ed.), *Woerterbuch der Mythologie*, 1 (1965), 438–9. **ADD. BIBLIOGRAPHY:** S. Ribichini, in: DDD, 339–41; idem, in: DBJA, 260; J. Linderski, *Oxford Classical Dictionary*, 837; J. Blenkinsopp, *Isaiah 56–66* (AB; 2003), 274–79.

[Yuval Kamrat / S. David Sperling (2nd ed.)]

GAD (Heb. גָּד), one of the 12 tribes of Israel, tracing its descent to Gad, a son of Jacob, borne to him by Zilpah, the maidservant of Leah (Gen. 30:10–11). The tribe was comprised of seven large families, the Zephonites, Haggites, Shunites, Oznites, Erites, Arodites, and Arelites, named after the seven sons of Gad (Num. 26:15–17; with slight differences in Gen. 46:16). During the period of the Conquest of Canaan, Gad's fighting men numbered 40,500 (Num. 26:18). According to Jacob's blessing, "Gad shall be raided by raiders; but he shall overcome at last" (Gen. 49:19). Moses declared: "Poised is he like a lion to tear off arm and scalp" (Deut. 33:20), showing that Gad was a tribe of fighting warriors. Indeed, in the era of the monarchy, the Gadites are described as "expert in war," as having faces "like the faces of lions," and as being "as swift as gazelles upon the mountains" (I Chron. 5:18; 12:9).

Its Territory

When Transjordan was conquered by Israel in the time of Moses, the Gadites (together with the Reubenites and half of Manasseh) requested permission to settle in the pasture lands east of the Jordan because of their abundant cattle. Moses acceded to their request, but stipulated that they first cross the Jordan and participate fully with all the tribes in the wars of conquest (Num. 32; Deut. 3:12–20; Josh. 1:12–18; 22:1ff.). Accordingly, the Gadites settled in Gilead, which was in the center of Transjordan, between the territory of Reuben in the south and that of the half tribe of Manasseh in the north. In the east their territory bordered that of the Ammonites and that of various nomadic desert tribes. On the west was the Jordan, from the Sea of Chinnereth to the Dead Sea; in the south, the vicinity of Heshbon and the northern tip of the Dead Sea; in the north the border passed by way of Mahanaim (Khirbet Mahna south of Nahal-Jabesh) and Lidbir (probably Lo-Debar (II Sam. 9:4), south of Naḥal-Arav) to the edge of the Sea of Chinnereth. The eastern border apparently receded westward to the region of Rabbath-Ammon, and then extended northeastward to the region of the upper Yarmuk whence it turned to Mahanaim. This description of the territory of Gad in ac-

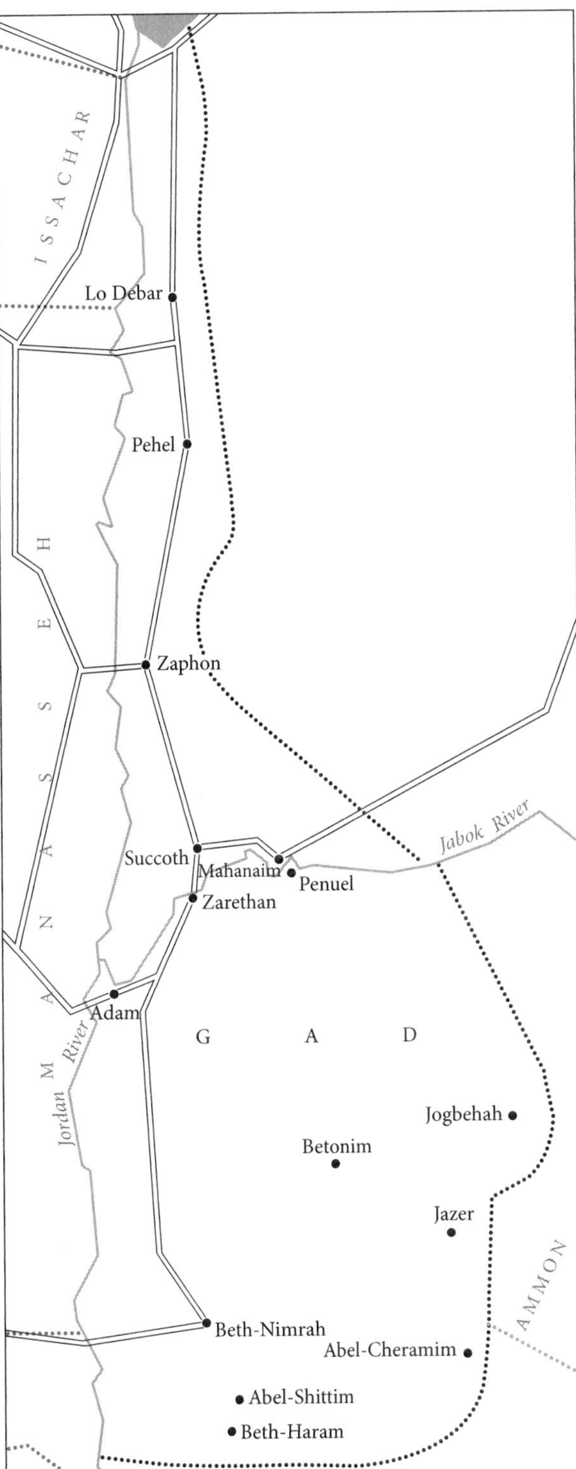

Territory of the tribe of Gad. After Y. Aharoni in Lexicon Biblicum, *Dvir, Tel Aviv, 1965.*

cordance with the Book of Joshua (13:24–28; 20:8; 21:36–37) certainly reflects the reality of a definite period; however, some hold it to be very early and, like most of the borders of the Book of Joshua, merely theoretical and ideal. Political developments subsequently caused changes in the region of the tribe's settlement, sometimes for the worse (e.g., I Kings 22:3; II Kings 10:33) and sometimes for the better (e.g., I Chron. 5:11).

Its History

The history of the tribe consists of a succession of wars with Ammon and Moab in the south, with the Kedemites, the Hagrites, and nomadic tribes in the east, and with Arameans in the north. During the era of the Judges, the submission of the people of Succoth and Penuel to the Midianites and the Kedemites led them into a fratricidal war with *Gideon (Judg. 8; cf. verse 5; Josh. 13:27). The Gileadites as a whole were saved from the Ammonites by Jephthah (Judg. 11). At this time the Gileadites (= Gad) and the Benjamites entered into marital ties and a fraternal alliance (Judg. 21). In addition, the reign of the Benjamite Saul was a period of relief and respite for the tribes of Transjordan (I Sam. 11; I Chron. 5). Hence, the notable act of loyalty of the Gileadites to the slain Saul (I Sam. 31:11–13) and to his family. The capital of Saul's son Ish-Bosheth was Mahanaim (II Sam. 2:8–9). Saul's grandson Mephibosheth took refuge in Lo-Debar (II Sam. 9:4–5), but this, in northern Gilead, was probably not Gadite but Manassite.

David's wars with Aram, Ammon, and Moab greatly strengthened the position of Israelite Transjordan. In consequence the Gileadites supported David, and Mahanaim became his base, in his war against Absalom (II Sam. 17:24–27; 19:33). Mahanaim later became the station of one of Solomon's 12 commissioners (I Kings 4:14). In the era of the divided kingdom, Gad belonged to the kingdom of Samaria. Elijah the prophet was a native of Gilead (I Kings 17:1). When King Mesha of Moab rebelled against Israel, he dealt harshly with the Gadites of Ataroth (*Mesha Stele*, 10–13, in: Pritchard, Texts, 320). The Gileadites suffered greatly from the Arameans and the Ammonites during Israel's weakness in the first half of the rule of the House of Jehu (see *Jehu, *Jehoahaz; cf. Amos 1:3, 13); but Gilead was reconquered by Jeroboam II (cf. Amos 6:13; Lo-Dabar and Karnaim = Lo-Debar and Ashteroth-Karnaim). The reign of Jeroboam son of Joash seems to have been a period of respite in their history (II Kings 14:28; cf. I Chron. 5:17). There are allusions to some sort of ties between Gilead and the kingdom of Judah during the reign of Jotham king of Judah, on the eve of the destruction of Gilead (I Chron. 5:17; II Chron. 27:5). In 732 B.C.E. the territory of Gad was laid waste by Tiglath Pileser III, and most of its inhabitants were exiled from their land (II Kings 15:29), which was then invaded by the Ammonites (Jer. 49:1). However, there are indications that a remnant of the Gadites remained in southern Gilead, and it is possible that the Tobiads known at the beginning of the Second Temple period derived from them. The Gadite remnant and the Judean refugees in Ammon (Jer. 41) formed the foundation of the Jewish community that developed in Transjordan in the days of the Second Temple.

[Yehuda Elitzur]

In the *Aggadah*

Gad was born on the tenth of Ḥeshvan and lived to the age of 125 (Yal. Ex. 162). He was born circumcised (Rashi to Gen. 30:11). His name "Gad" was a portent of the manna (which was "like coriander seed," Heb. *gad*, Ex. 16:31; Ex. R. 1:5). He was among the brothers whom Joseph did not present to Pharaoh, lest Pharaoh, when he saw their strength, would enlist them in his bodyguard (Gen. R. 95:4). Gad was ultimately buried in Ramia, in the portion of his tribe, on the east bank of the Jordan (*Sefer ha-Yashar*, end). According to some, Elijah was a descendant of Gad (Gen. R. 71:8).

BIBLIOGRAPHY: A. Bergman, *The Israelite Occupation of Eastern Palestine in the Light of Territorial History* (1934); A. Alt, in: PJB, 35 (1939), 19ff.; Abel, Geog, 2 (1938), 67, 77, 82, 103, 123, 138; N. Glueck, in: AASOR, 18–19 (1939), 150ff.; idem, in: D. Winton Thomas (ed.), *Archaeology and Old Testament Study* (1967), 429ff.; Albright, Arch Rel, 218; idem, in: *Miscellanea Biblica B. Ubach* (1954), 131–6; M. Noth, in: MNDPV, 58 (1953), 230ff.; idem, in: ZDPV, 75 (1959); S. Yeivin, in: EM, 2 (1954), 423–9; Y. Kaufmann, *The Biblical Account of the Conquest* (1954), 26–28, 46–52; Y. Aharoni, *Ereẓ Yisrael bi-Tekufat ha-Mikra* (1962), 178–9, 228, 304–5; B. Mazar (ed.), in: *Historyah shel Am-Yisrael, ha-Avot ve-ha-Shofetim* (1967), 191–2, 197; Y. Aharoni, *ibid.*, 214–5; Z. Kallai, *Naḥalot Shivtei Yisrael* (1967), 221–8.

GAD (Heb. גָּד), the seer (Heb. *ḥozeh*); one of the three prophets during the days of King *David. Gad joined David when the latter fled from Saul to Adullam and he persuaded him to return to Judah (I Sam. 22:5). He also instructed David to purchase the threshing floor of *Araunah the Jebusite and to build an altar there (II Sam. 24:18ff.); this later became the site of Solomon's Temple (I Chron. 22:1). It is known that he remained in the court of David when the latter reigned in Jerusalem (II Sam. 24:11–14; I Chron. 21:9–30). He was also one of the organizers of the levitical service in the Temple (II Chron. 29:25) and, according to Chronicles, one of the chroniclers of the history of David (I Chron. 29:29). An anonymous opinion in the Babylonian Talmud (BB 15a) credits Gad along with the prophet Nathan with completing the Book of Samuel following Samuel's death.

BIBLIOGRAPHY: M.Z. Segal, *Sifrei Shemu'el* (1961), 178; Yeivin, in: VT, 3 (1953), 149–65; O. Eissfeldt, *The Old Testament. An Introduction* (1965), 55, 533. **ADD. BIBLIOGRAPHY:** S. Japhet, *I & II Chronicles* (1993), 516–17.

[Josef Segal]

GAD, DEVORAH (1914–), architect and interior decorator. Gad was born in Bukovina and studied architecture and construction engineering in Vienna. Immigrating to Ereẓ Israel in 1936 she first worked with Professor Oskar Kaufmann but later opened her own office together with her husband Yeḥezkel Gad. Among other commissions the firm designed the first buildings of the Israel embassies abroad, the residence of the foreign minister, the offices of El Al and Zim in New York, London, and Paris, and together with Professor Alfred Mansfeld the interiors of nine passenger ships, including the *Shalom*. Together with her partner L. Noy she also designed the interior of the Knesset in Jerusalem. She was awarded the Israel Prize for arts in 1966.

GADARA, ancient city of Gilead. It is first mentioned as a Hellenistic settlement in the description of the conquest of Ereẓ Israel by *Antiochus III (Polybius, 5:71, 3). Although the name is of Semitic origin, the new settlers called it Gadara after a Macedonian city. It was among the cities captured by Alexander *Yannai, but *Pompey took it from the Jews and included it in the *Decapolis. It was part of *Herod's domain in the Roman period and later became autonomous with the right of minting coins. An important center of Hellenistic culture, it was the birthplace of the poets *Meleager and Menippus and the philosopher *Philodemus. Jews lived there both during and after the Jewish War (60–70/73). In the days of R. Gamaliel and R. Akiva there is a reference to "Shizpar, the head of Geder" (RH 22a); the philosopher Oenomaus of Gadara (called "ha-Gardi" in the Talmud) was a friend of R. Meir (Lam. R., Proem 2; cf. Ḥag. 15b). In the Byzantine period, bishops of Geder are mentioned up to the sixth century. Under Arab rule the city declined and is the present-day village of Muqays (Umm Qeis) situated at a height of 1,194 ft. (364 m.) with a splendid view of the Sea of Galilee, the Jordan Valley, Galilee, and Mt. Hermon. First identified by Seetzen in 1806, the site has been frequently explored and excavated, especially since 1974 with the work of the German Evangelical Institute for the Archaeology of the Holy Land. The site contains many traces of ancient habitation: paved colonnaded streets; two temples, a fortified acropolis, baths, two theaters, a stadium; ruins of houses; tombs with sarcophagi, inscriptions, and statues, etc. The Jewish presence at Gadara is represented by the discovery of two blocks carved with a wreath containing a *menorah* flanked by a *shofar* and a palm branch; these may have come from a synagogue. On the bank of the Yarmuk are hot springs known as *Ḥammat Gader. The city's area may have extended to the Sea of Galilee as indicated in the New Testament story of the "Gadarene swine" but variants of the text mention different cities, e.g., Gerasa (Matt. 8:28; Mark 5:1; Luke 8:26).

BIBLIOGRAPHY: S. Klein (ed.), *Sefer ha-Yishuv*, 1 (1939), s.v.; G. Schumacher, *Northern Aylun* (1890), 46ff.; Schuerer, Gesch, 2 (1907[3]), 157–61. **ADD. BIBLIOGRAPHY:** S.J. Saller, *Second Revised Catalogue of the Ancient Synagogues of the Holy Land* (1972), 84; S. Holm-Nielsen et al., "Umm Qeis (Gadara)," in: D.H. Fredericq and J.B. Hennessy (eds.), *Archaeology of Jordan*, vol. 2 (1989); T. Weber, *Umm Qeis, Gadara of the Decapolis* (1989).

[Michael Avi-Yonah / Shimon Gibson (2nd ed.)]

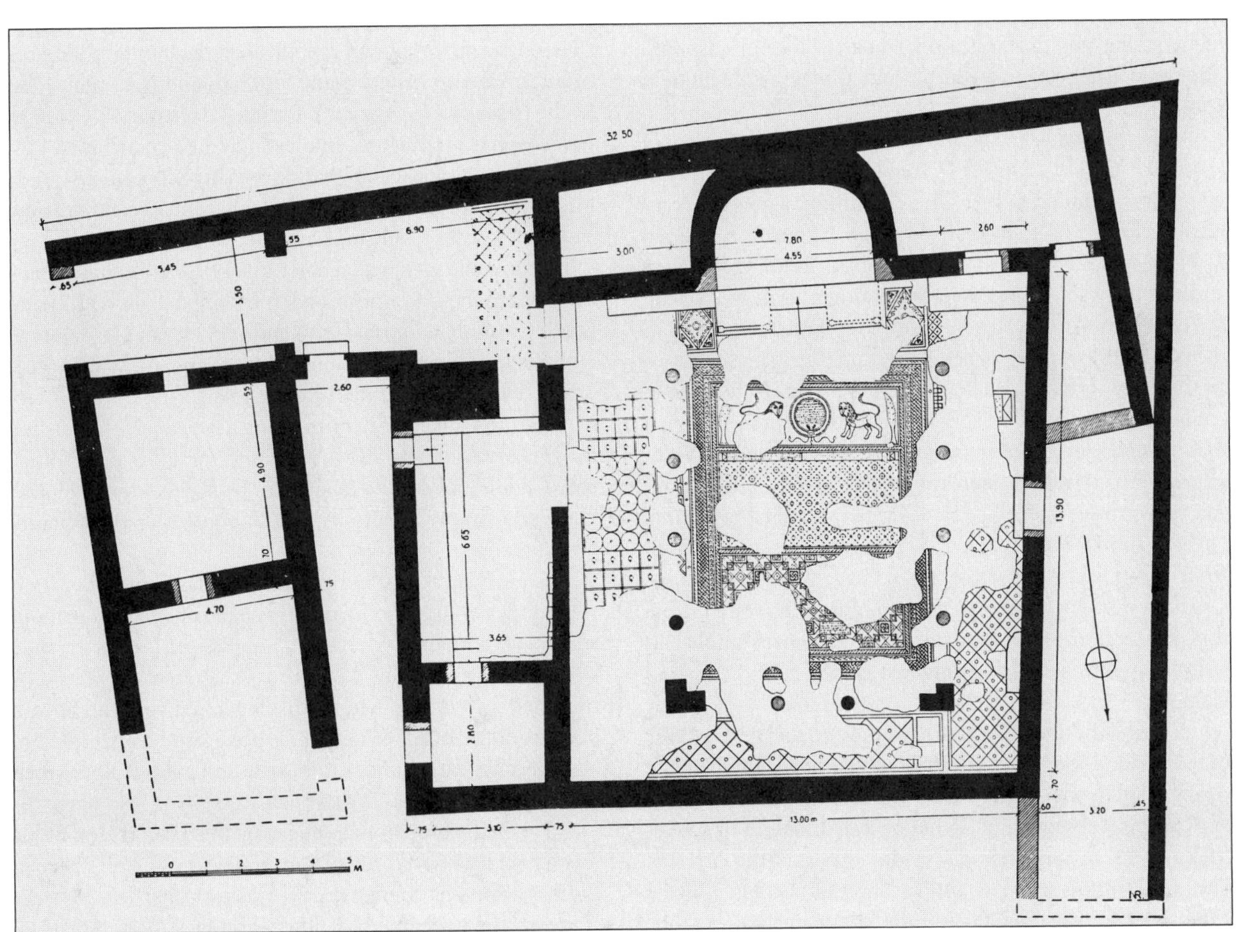

Ground plan of the synagogue of Ḥammat Geder (Gadara), fifth century C.E., *showing the excavated floor mosaics. From* Journal of the Palestine Oriental Sociey, *Vol.* XV, *1935.*

GADNA (Heb. גדנ"ע; abbr. for גְּדוּדֵי נֹעַר, *Gedudei No'ar*; "Youth Corps"), Israel government youth movement for training 13- to 18-year-olds in defense and national service. Gadna, whose membership is voluntary, functions in high schools and youth clubs. It trains its members in firsthand knowledge of Israel's geography and topography, physical fitness, marksmanship, scouting, field exercises, comradeship, teamwork, and mutual aid. It is administered by the Gadna Command which functions in the framework of the Israel Defense Forces and the Ministry of Defense and cooperates with the Ministry of Education and Culture. The corps may be activated in an emergency by special permission of the chief of staff.

In addition to regular training, Gadna organizes route marches for 16-year-olds, sharpshooting clubs with nationwide contests on Lag ba-Omer, and an international Bible contest for youth. In its air section (Gadna-Avir) youngsters construct model planes, study aviation, and practice gliding, under the direction of Air Force officers. In the naval section (Gadna-Yam) naval officers teach swimming, rowing, sailing, navigation, diving, and underwater fishing. There is a Gadna orchestra, which has played abroad. During vacations third-year high school students go to Gadna work and training camps in border settlements and immigrant villages, or participate in national service projects in landscape improvement, archaeological excavation, and assistance in hospitals. The corps also helps to reeducate and reintegrate delinquent youth.

Gadna, established in 1948, was the successor to Ḥagam (*Ḥinnukh Gufani Murḥav*; "Extended Physical Training"), which was founded in 1939, and Alummim, a general organization for the 14- to 18-year-old group. Its purpose, defined by Prime Minister Ben-Gurion in 1949, was "training for peace and not for war." In 1951 a Gadna training farm was set up at *Be'er Orah in the Negev, followed by others at Nurit in the Gilboa Hills, and at *Sedeh Boker and Keẓiot in the Negev. In the early 1950s Gadna youngsters went out to help newcomers in immigrant villages and introduce them to Israeli life through Hebrew lessons, Israel songs, and games. Gadna's work has been of interest to visitors from African and Asian countries, and a Gadna delegation traveled to Ghana, Nigeria, and Liberia in 1959. The first Gadna course for youth from Africa and Asia was organized in 1961, and Gadna instructors were later sent to various countries. In 1968 a Gadna unit was organized for *Druze youth. The corps published a monthly newspaper *Be-Maḥaneh Gadna* ("In the Gadna Camp").

During the Sinai Campaign of 1956 and the Six-Day War of 1967, Gadna youngsters effectively replaced personnel in the postal system, civil defense, schools, hospitals, industry, and agriculture. Subsequently Gadna operated mainly in school frameworks. In some schools, Gadna is part of the curriculum, while others send students for a week to Gadna military camps that prepare them for military service, including weapons training and discipline. Different military branches run their own Gadna groups, such as the Air Force and Navy.

BIBLIOGRAPHY: E. Shomroni, *Maggal va-Ḥerev* (1955²), 7–22, 159; *Israel Year Book* (1949–).

[David Coren]

GADOL, MOISE S. (1874–1941), U.S. founder and editor of *La America*. Gadol was born in Rostchuck, Bulgaria. At the age of 14 he was offered an opportunity to study in the Alliance School in Paris but felt compelled instead to assist his family who were of modest means. His early career was varied: a clerk in a law office, a salesman, and army service, among other jobs. He continued to study and organized the first Zionist society in Rostchuck.

He came to the United States for a visit and was drawn to the Sephardi community of New York whom he felt lacked any sense of self-identity and was ignored by the far more numerous Ashkenazim. His tool was the first Judeo-Spanish newspaper and he became a publisher, adding to the rich variety of local newspapers prevalent among the immigrant populations of New York. He entitled his publication *La America*. According to historian Marc *Angel, Gadol convinced the leaders of the Hebrew Immigrant Aid Society to establish an Oriental Bureau in order to help the "Oriental" Jews. Gadol himself served as the secretary of the Oriental Bureau, initially as a volunteer, and spent many hours helping newly arrived Sephardi immigrants get through the immigration procedures. He also helped many find jobs and keep their jobs. In the pages of *La America*, he printed a glossary in order to teach Sephardim English. Interestingly, he also included Yiddish definitions, believing that since many Sephardim worked for Yiddish-speaking employers, Sephardim needed to know Yiddish in order to advance in America.

The newspaper included news items about Sephardi communities in the U.S. and abroad. It included poetry and some literary work. Gadol was a forceful spokesman for Zionism, which caused resentment among some Sephardim of Turkish origin, who were cautious about endangering Turkish-Jewish relations. Like other immigrant newspapers, he pushed for the advancement of workers and for individual initiative. Gadol printed several articles by a person who signed her name simply as Miss A, which argued for the equality of women.

Gadol's successes, however, did not last. His publication went under in 1925 and he tried his hand at business without success, eventually serving as a supplier of leather to shoe stores. The death of his wife in 1933 shattered him and only the intervention of a fellow Rostchuck native brought him back from the brink of despair. Once again he attempted to start his publication and he did write and publish a pamphlet *Christopher Columbus Was a Spanish Jew.*

He died a broken man and only the intervention of his former mentor saved him from potter's field. Still, even in death he remains controversial. A historical article by Marc Angel led to a vehement denunciation by Albert *Amateau, who, at the age of 101, wrote an angry recollection of his dealings with Gadol.

BIBLIOGRAPHY: A.J. Amateau, "The Sephardic Immigrant from Bulgaria: A Personal Profile of Moise Gadol," in: *American Jewish Archives* (1989); M.D. Angel, *La America: The Sephardic Experience in the United States* (1982); J.M. Papo, *Sephardim in Twentieth Century America* (1987).

[Michael Berenbaum (2nd ed.)]

GADYACH, city in Poltava district, Ukraine. From the beginning of the 19th century, the city had a small Jewish community and was renowned as the burial place of the founder of Chabad Ḥasidism, R. *Shneur Zalman of Lyady. He died in 1813 while fleeing from the armies of Napoleon and was brought to Gadyach, where a monument was built over his tomb. The Jewish community numbered 883 in 1847, and by 1897 had increased to 1,853 (24% of the total population). With the outbreak of pogroms in October 1905, Jewish property was looted. Under the Soviet regime the Jewish population declined as many left for the larger towns. In 1926 Gadyach had 1,764 Jews (17.3% of the total), dropping to 633 (5,8%) in 1939. Gadyach was occupied by the Germans on September 27, 1941, and the remaining Jews there were soon murdered. The life of the Jews under German occupation is described in *Esh ha-Tamid* by A. Ẓefoni (Ẓvi Preigerzon) (1966). In 1970 the number of Jews in Gadyach was estimated at about 75 (15 families). From the 1990s hundreds of ḥasidim from all over the Ukraine gathered annually in the town to pray at Shneur Zalman's grave.

[Yehuda Slutsky / Shmuel Spector (2nd ed.)]

GAER, FELICE D. (1946–), international human rights activist. Born in Englewood, N.J., to Beatrice and Abraham Gaer and educated at Wellesley College and Columbia University (receiving a master's in political science, 1974), Gaer became a program officer of the International Division of the Ford Foundation in 1974, focusing on Soviet and East European programs, including advocating emigration rights and refugee assistance for Soviet Jewish refuseniks. From 1982 to 1991, she served as executive director of the International League for Human Rights, where she pressed for information about the whereabouts of Soviet dissident Andrei Sakharov. She also encouraged the Carter administration to ratify international human rights treaties and successfully lobbied the U.N. Sub-Commission on the Prevention of Discrimination and the Protection of Minorities to adopt the first U.N. resolution critical of China after the Tiananmen Square massacre in 1989. Beginning in 1993, Gaer directed the Jacob Blaustein Institute for the Advancement of Human Rights of the American Jewish Committee. From 1999, she served as the first American and first woman on the U.N. Committee Against Torture. In 2001, she was appointed by then House Minority Leader Richard Gephardt to the U.S. Commission on International Religious Freedom, serving as its chair (2002–03) and vice chair (from 2003); she was reappointed by House Minority Leader Nancy Pelosi in 2004.

Between 1993 and 1999, Gaer was appointed to nine U.S. delegations, six to the U.N. Commission on Human Rights and three to U.N.-sponsored world conferences, and she served on numerous boards. She was the chair of the Steering Committee of the National Coalition on the 50th Anniversary of the Universal Declaration of Human Rights (1997–99), a member of the board of directors of the Andrei Sakharov Foundation (from 1993), a member of the Steering Committee of Human Rights Watch/Europe and Asia (from 1996), vice president and a member of the board of governors of the International League for Human Rights (from 1991), and a member of the Council on Foreign Relations (from 1991).

Gaer advocated for repeal of the infamous U.N. "Zionism = Racism" resolution of Nov. 10, 1975, a goal which was achieved in 1991, and she played the key role in ensuring passage by consensus of the U.N. General Assembly's first-ever condemnation of antisemitism on Dec. 9, 1998, the 50th anniversary of the Universal Declaration of Human Rights. Later she worked with the Organization for Security and Cooperation in Europe on regional measures to combat antisemitism. In her address to the first U.N. conference on antisemitism on June 21, 2004, at U.N. headquarters in New York, she argued that antisemitic incidents are a form of human rights abuse and should be treated as such by U.N. bodies. Gaer was also the architect of many initiatives linking women's rights to human rights. After the Srebenica massacres in the Bosnia conflict, Gaer helped craft a joint statement of 27 NGOs arguing that rape and other gender-specific crimes must be prosecuted by international war crimes tribunals

[Michael Galchinsky (2nd ed.)]

GAETA, town N.W. of Naples. According to the Chronicle of *Ahimaaz (1054), *Aaron of Baghdad lived for a time in Gaeta in the ninth century, teaching his mystical and esoteric doctrines. The main occupation of the Jews of Gaeta in the 12th century was dyeing, on which they had to pay a special tax. From the 15th century Jewish loan-bankers and pawnbrokers were also active there. In 1468 the city requested the permission of King Ferrante I to expel a Jewish moneylender for usurious practices and to limit the sale of pawned goods. In 1471 the city again demanded that the Jews living in Gaeta should not be permitted to give loans at interest (with the exception of a certain Salomon), and that the sale of objects given in pawn should be regulated by the royal court. In 1492–93 a number of refugees from Sicily and Spain settled there. In 1495 the city resisted the invasion of Charles VIII of France and many of its inhabitants were killed, including a number of Jews. The expulsion of 1510–11 did not bring the Gaeta community to an end, and in 1521 there were still Jewish moneylenders living there as attested by the deliberations of the city council that once again demanded the regulation of such activities. The Jews were finally expelled from Gaeta in 1541 in the general expulsion from the kingdom of Naples. A few Jewish families came to Gaeta in the 18th century, probably attracted by the favorable policy of Charles III of Bourbon who in the edicts of 1728 and 1740 invited Jews to live and trade in the kingdom of the Two Sicilies, but these attempts encountered strong political opposition and in July 1747 the Jews were again expelled from the whole kingdom. Jews returned to Gaeta in the 19th century. After World War II ships carrying Jewish illegal immigrants to Ereẓ Israel passed through the port of Gaeta.

BIBLIOGRAPHY: Roth, Italy, index; Milano, Italia, index. **ADD. BIBLIOGRAPHY:** N. Ferorelli, *Ebrei nell' Italia meridionale…* (1990); V. Giura, *Gli ebrei e la ripresa economica del regno di Napoli, 1740–1747* (Naples, 1978); P. Capobianco, *Gli ebrei a Gaeta* (Gaeta 1981); A. Sereni, *I clandestini del mare: L'emigrazione ebraica in terra d'Israele dal 1945 al 1948* (1973; Hebrew, *Sefinot lelo deghel*, 1975).

[Ariel Toaff / Nadia Zeldes 2nd ed.]

°GAFFAREL, JACQUES (1601–1681), French Catholic theologian and Hebrew scholar. Gaffarel, who was particularly interested in kabbalistic literature, published a description of the manuscripts used by *Pico della Mirandola (Paris, 1651). Gaffarel's writings include: (1) *Les tristes pensées de la fille de Sion sur les rives de l'Euphrate (ibid.*, 1624); (2) *Abdita divinae cabalae mysteria contra sophistarum logomachiam defensa (ibid.*, 1625; translated into French by Samuel b. Ḥesed as *Les profonds mystères de la Cabale divine*, Paris, 1912); and *Jom JHWH, Dies Domini* (*ibid.*, 1629; according to *Steinschneider the fictitious author's name Elḥa b. David was invented by Gaffarel). He also published, with an introduction – without the author's consent – the *Historia de gli riti Hebraici* by Leon *Modena, whom he had met in Venice in 1633. His *Curiosités inouyés sur la sculpture talismanique des Persans; Horoscope des Patriarches et lecture des estoilles* (first published in 1632 or 1637) was published in a Latin translation with an extensive commentary by M.G. Michaelis (Hamburg, 1676).

BIBLIOGRAPHY: Wolf, Bibliotheca, 1 (1715), 223; 2 (1721), 1244; 3 (1727), no. 223; Steinschneider, Cat Bod, 919 no. 4526; G. Scholem, *Bibliographia Kabbalistica* (1933), 51 no. 396–400; S. Stern, *Der Kampf der Rabbiner gegen den Talmud im 17. Jahrhundert* (1902), 184; *Biographie Universelle*, 15 (1856), 347.

[Joseph Elijah Heller]

GAGIN, ḤAYYIM (b. circa 1450), Moroccan rabbi and poet, first known member of a family which produced many talmudic scholars. Gagin was born in Fez, but when still young, probably at the time of the massacre of the Jews of Fez in 1465, he left for Spain. There he studied under R. Isaac Aboab, the last *gaon* of Castile, and the talmudist R. Joseph Uzziel. Having acquired a vast and profound knowledge, he returned to Fez where he was appointed *av bet din* of the native-born community to which his family belonged. Disputes often broke out between this community and the newly constituted one of the Spanish and Portuguese refugees, both over economic questions and differences in customs. Gagin was a staunch defender of the customs of the native Jews and of their manner of interpreting the laws. His intransigence on the subject of the insufflation of the lungs of slaughtered animals was the origin of the lengthiest and most severe controversy in which his community came into conflict with that of the Spanish Jews who had settled in Fez. It was only in 1535, after 10 years of disputes in which the Muslim authorities were also involved, that this struggle, first of a purely religious character but which had degenerated into a social conflict, ended with the victory of the viewpoint of the Spanish Jews. The vicissitudes which resulted from this dispute were described by Gagin in *Eẓ Ḥayyim*, lengthy extracts of which were published by J.M. Toledano in his *Ner ha-Ma'arav* (1911). He also wrote numerous *kinot*, particularly on the Spanish expulsion. Nothing is known of his descendants until the 18th century, when they immigrated to Jerusalem, where the Gagin family produced a number of talmudic scholars, among whom was R. ḤAYYIM ABRAHAM *GAGIN, the first *ḥakham bashi* of Ereẓ Israel.

BIBLIOGRAPHY: J.M. Toledano, *Ner ha-Ma'arav* (1911), index; J. Benaim, *Malkhei Rabbanan* (1931), 36a; M.D. Gaon, *Yehudei ha-Mizraḥ be-Ereẓ Yisrael*, 2 (1938), 178–9.

[David Corcos]

GAGIN, ḤAYYIM ABRAHAM BEN MOSES (1787–1848), chief rabbi of Jerusalem. Gagin was born in Constantinople. He became *rishon le-Zion* (Sephardi chief rabbi) in 1842 and was the first to bear the official title of *ḥakham bashi*. Gagin was responsible for the taxes of the Jews to the government, and was granted authority to impose taxation within the community on meat ('gabela'), *maẓẓot*, wine, etc. He lived in the Old City of Jerusalem in the courtyard of his grandfather, Shalom *Sharabi, the kabbalist, and the government placed a guard of ten soldiers near his dwelling to protect the Jewish quarter. In his time a violent dispute broke out among the rabbis of Jerusalem with reference to the *Kolelim and the distribution of the funds for them which arrived from abroad. The following of his works were published: *Minḥah Tehorah* (Salonika, n. d. c. 1825–36), *Ḥukkei Ḥayyim* (1843); *Ḥayyim mi-Yrushalayim* (1882); and *Yeri'ot ha-Ohel* (2 pts., 1886–1904).

BIBLIOGRAPHY: Frumkin-Rivlin, 3 (1929), 276–8; M.D. Gaon, *Yehudei ha-Mizraḥ be-Ereẓ Yisrael*, 2 (1938), 179–82.

[Abraham Ben-Yaacob]

GAGIN, SHALOM MOSES BEN ḤAYYIM ABRAHAM (d. 1883), talmudist and emissary of Ereẓ Israel. He was the son of Ḥayyim Abraham *Gagin, from whom he inherited a large library, of which *Frumkin made use in his *Toledot Ḥakhmei Yerushalayim*. Shalom was a member of the kabbalist circle of scholars at the yeshivah "Bet El" in Jerusalem. From 1862–65, as an emissary of Jerusalem, he visited Tripoli and Algeria, as well as Tunis, where he influenced Caid Nissim Shamama to bequeath a large sum of money to Ereẓ Israel. In 1870, on a second mission, Shalom spent some time in Rome. He died in Jerusalem.

His works, most of whose titles include the word *Samaḥ* (from the initials of his name), include (1) *Yismaḥ Lev*, responsa, pt. 1 (1878), pt. 2 (1888); (2) *Yismaḥ Moshe* (1878), rulings relevant to the testament of Nissim Shamama; (3) *Samaḥ Libbi* (1884), homilies; (4) *Saviv ha-Ohel* pt. 1 (1886), pt. 2 (1904), on the tent of meeting, consisting of additions to *Yeri'ot ha-Ohel*, the commentary of Ḥayyim Abraham Gagin (Agan) on the *Ohel Mo'ed* of Samuel b. Meshullam *Gerondi; (5)

Samaḥ Nefesh (1903), on the laws of blessings. Shalom also arranged the publication of *Sha'ar ha-Pesukim* (1863) of Ḥayyim Vital, and *Ḥayyim mi-Yrushalayim* (1888), a collection of his father's sermons. Some of his poems were published in *Devar Adonai mi-Yrushalayim* (1873) of Aaron b. Isaac Pereira.

BIBLIOGRAPHY: M.D. Gaon, *Yehudei ha-Mizraḥ be-Ereẓ Yisrael*, 2 (1938), 188; Yaari, Sheluḥei, 738f.; Frumkin-Rivlin, 1 (1929), 60, 66 (introduction); 3 (1929), 121, 277, 312.

[Simon Marcus]

GAḤAL (acronym for Hebrew *Gush Ḥerut Liberalim* (Ḥerut-Liberal Bloc)). Israeli parliamentary group established towards the end of the term of the Fifth Knesset in 1965 by two opposition parties, the *Ḥerut Movement and the Israel Liberal Party. The two parties agreed that while maintaining separate political organizations, they would act as a single parliamentary group and run in a single list in the elections to the Sixth Knesset, with Menaḥem *Begin as its leader. The new alignment moved the Ḥerut Movement, which for 17 years had been Israel's most extreme right-wing party and had existed more or less in total political isolation, to the center of the political spectrum, providing it with legitimization in wider parts of the population. Not all the members of the Liberal Party joined Gaḥal, as its members who had previously belonged to the Progressive Party preferred to form a new parliamentary group and party under the name *Independent Liberal Party. Within Gaḥal, as within the *Likud later on, the Liberal Party component advanced the line of economic liberalism. At the end of the Fifth Knesset the Gaḥal parliamentary group had 27 seats. In the elections to the Sixth Knesset in 1965 it received 26 seats, losing four in the course of the Knesset's term. Upon the outbreak of the Six-Day War Gaḥal joined the coalition under Levi *Eshkol with two of its members, Menaḥem Begin and Yosef *Sapir, becoming ministers without portfolio. In the elections to the Seventh Knesset in 1969 Gaḥal received 26 seats, also increasing its strength in the municipal elections and in the elections to the *Histadrut conference. In the new government formed after the elections by Golda *Meir, Gaḥal was represented by six ministers, of whom two, Begin and Arie *Dulzin, were without portfolio. Gaḥal resigned from the coalition in August 1970 after the Meir government expressed willingness to accept the Rogers Plan, which was based on the principle of territories for peace. Prior to the elections to the Eighth Knesset the Ḥerut Movement and Liberal Party decided to establish a new list together with several other parties and groups, which was called the *Likud.

[Susan Hattis Rolef (2nd ed.)]

GAINES, WILLIAM M. (1922–1992), U.S. magazine publisher. Gaines, the publisher of the wildly satirical *Mad* magazine, was the son of Max Gaines, publisher of the All-American Comics division of DC Comics and also an influential figure in the history of comics, having tested the idea of selling comics on newsstands, inspiring the creation of the character Wonder Woman. A veteran of the U.S. Army, William attended New York University. Upon his father's death, he inherited a faltering comic-book empire in the late 1940s and turned it into a huge success with science fiction, fantasy, and realistic war comics. His horror comics were subtle satiric approaches to horror with genuine dilemmas and startling outcomes, often drawn from classic authors like Edgar Allan Poe and H.P. Lovecraft. His fantasy titles dealt with adult issues such as racism and the meaning of progress and had stories adapted from the work of Ray Bradbury and others. The books featured artists who came to be among the most prominent commercial illustrators of the 20th century, including Will *Elder.

The first issue of *Mad* reached the newsstands in 1952 and had sharp sendups of movies, advertising celebrities, and comic strips: Mickey Mouse became Mickey Rodent and Superman was Superduperman. To the delight of its largely teenage audience, it brought satire into the mainstream, along with up-to-the minute New York humor sprinkled with Yiddish, nonsense, and non sequiturs. The cover featured a goofy-faced, gap-toothed boy named Alfred E. Neuman with the caption "What? Me worry?" It was an image and slogan that proved iconic, and the character appeared on the cover of virtually every issue of *Mad* and was picked up and satirized in other national publications.

Gaines's comics may have appealed to adults, but the general public considered comic books to be aimed at children. With the publication of Dr. Fredric Wertham's *The Seduction of the Innocent*, which found damaging material in the comics, comic books in the Gaines style drew the attention of the U.S. Congress and other moralists. Under questioning by a Congressional committee, Gaines defended his magazine. "The truth is that delinquency is the product of the real environment in which the child lives," Gaines told the committee in voluntary testimony, "and not of the fiction he reads." But the Comics Code Authority, modeled on motion-picture production rules, banned bloodthirsty material and Gaines suspended publication of his horror comics. He reissued *Mad* as a magazine in 1955 to skirt the code.

[Stewart Kampel (2nd ed.)]

GAISIN (**Gaysin**), city in Vinnitsa district, Ukraine, formerly within Poland. There were 65 Jews living in the town in 1765. After it passed to Russia Gaisin became a district capital. The Jewish population numbered 2,018 in 1847, 4,321 (46% of the population) in 1897, and 5,190 (34%) in 1926. It dropped to 4,109 (27.7%) in 1939. Gaisin was occupied by the Germans on July 25, 1941. Some of the Jews were murdered in the first months of occupation. Others were put to work building Highway Number 4, from Lvov to Stalino (Donetsk). Because of the terrible conditions, many died or were killed, so in 1942 Jewish deportees from Bessrabia and Bukovina were brought in from Transnistria. Most of the new Jewish workers also died or were "liquidated" in "selections" and "*Aktionen.*" Only a few survived to the day of liberation on March 13, 1944.

BIBLIOGRAPHY: YE, 6 (c. 1910), 31; PK Romanyah, 1 (1970), 518–22.

[Yehuda Slutsky / Shmuel Spector (2nd ed.)]

GÁL, FEDOR (1945–), Slovak publicist, political scientist, sociologist, and publisher, born of Slovak parents in the Terezín concentration camp. He attained a master's degree in chemistry and doctorates in both sociology and economics and worked in the field of prognostics. In 1989 he was a founder and chairman of the political movement the Public against Violence, which won the elections in Slovakia in 1990. Due to internal disagreements in the movement and antisemitism aimed at him, he left Slovakia. From 1991 he lived in Prague. Gál is active in numerous civic non-governmental organizations; he issued an animated TV series for children; and co-produced a CD ROM, *Franz Kafka Lived in Prague* (in three languages).

He published the following works: a futurologist monograph *Možnosť a skutečnosť* ("Possibility and Reality," 1990); a reflection of events in Slovakia after 1989 *Z prvej ruky* ("From the First Hand," 1991); a study of the identity of Jews and Romas *O jinakosti* ("On Diversity," 1998); a series of essays *Vízie a ilúzie* ("Visions and Illusions," 2000); essays on the identity of the human being *Lidský úděl* ("The Human Fate," 2004); and *1 + 1* (2004).

[Milos Pojar (2nd ed.)]

°**GALACTION, GALA** (literary pen name of the priest Grigore Pişculescu; 1879–1961), Romanian novelist and writer. Galaction was one of Romania's outstanding literary figures, and his humanitarian outlook made him a great friend of the Jews. Jewish types abound in his novels and stories, and their high moral character is contrasted with their bitter struggle for survival. He attributed this survival to a divine miracle. In two novels, *Roxana* (1930) and *Papucii lui Mahmud* ("Muhammad's Slippers," 1932), he makes a plea for understanding between Christians, Muslims, and Jews. As a result of his friendship with Jewish intellectuals Galaction used to deliver lectures to Jewish organizations, and he also wrote articles on Jewish festivals and religious lore for Romanian-Jewish periodicals.

An admirer of Theodor Herzl, whom he considered a successor to the biblical prophets, Galaction wrote many pro-Zionist essays which were collected in *Sionismul la prieteni* ("Zionism among Friends," in *Herzl*, 1929). A visit to Palestine (1926) inspired a series of articles in *Adam* (1929) and the novel *Scrisori către Simforoza: In pămantul făgăduinţei* ("Letters to Simforoza: In the Promised Land," 1930). Galaction exerted a notable influence by his literary translation of the Bible (1938; in collaboration with Vasile Radu). His translations of the Song of Songs and the Book of Psalms are particularly remarkable. It is significant that, even at the height of World War II, Galaction courageously maintained his close ties with the Jewish community of Romania, and when the Jews were forced to clear the streets of snow, he insisted on joining them.

BIBLIOGRAPHY: G. Călinescu, *Istoria literaturii române…* (1941), 601–3; T. Vianu, *Arta prozatorilor români* (1941), 257–63; M. Sevastos, *Aminitiri de la "Viața Românească"* (1957), 117–20; F. Aderca, *Mărturia unei generații* (1967), 85–94; T. Vârgolici, *Gala Galaction* (1967). **ADD. BIBLIOGRAPHY:** G. Voicu, in: *Contribuția scriitorilor evrei la literatura română* (2001).

[Dora Litani-Littman]

GALAI, BINYAMIN (1921–), Hebrew writer and poet. Born in Vladivostok, Siberia, his family went to Palestine in 1926. He lived in Tel Aviv for many years, then moved to Haifa where he served as press adviser to the municipality. Among his volumes of poetry are *Im ha-Ru'aḥ* (1946); *Armonim* (1949); *Shivah Shelishit* (1953); his collected poems, *Al Ḥof ha-Raḥamim* (1958) and *Massa Ẓafonah* (1968); *Mi-Yam le-Yam* (1985); and *Shirim Aḥaronim* (1995). He also published volumes of plays, *Sedom Siti* ("Sodom City," 1952) and *Shotim u-Melakhim* ("Fools and Kings," 1971); a selection of sketches, *Al Kafeh Hafukh* ("Over White Coffee," 1960); radio plays, *Mayim Genuvim* (1964); and two volumes of children's stories. Galai wrote *Sippur ha-Aḥ ha-Niddaḥ, o Via Dolorozah* (1983) and a historical novel, *Ha-Mavet ha-Shaḥor o Divrei Yemei Gemini* (1976). A list of his works translated into English appears in Goell, Bibliography, 23f.

BIBLIOGRAPHY: Y. Zmora, *Sifrut al Parashat Derakhim*, 2 (1949), 288–93; M. Shamir, *Be-Kulmos Mahir* (1960), 117–26; Kressel, Leksikon, 1 (1967), 480. **ADD. BIBLIOGRAPHY:** Y. Zemora, in: *Moznayim* 43 (1976), 418–24; N.H. Toker, in: *Moznayim* 46 (1978), 141–43; M. Shamir, in: *Apiryon* 10–11 (1988), 22–25; G. Sagiv, in: *Moznayim* 74 (2000), 56–59.

[Getzel Kressel]

GALANT, ELIAHU (Ilya) VLADIMIROVICH (1868–after 1929), historian of Ukrainian Jewry. Galant, who was born in Nezhin, Ukraine, taught Jewish religion in high schools in Kiev. His studies of the persecution of Ukrainian Jewry from the 17th to the 19th centuries, particularly the blood-libels charged against them, appeared in *Yevreyskaya Starina* and other Russian-Jewish papers. In 1919 Galant was associated with the establishment of a Jewish Historical-Archeographical Commission, known as the "Galant Commission," founded under the auspices of the Ukrainian Academy of Sciences. The commission's task was to conduct research on the history of Ukrainian Jewry based on government archival material, which was not accessible under the czarist regime. The commission's work was interrupted by the ensuing civil war and it was not revived until 1924 with Galant as secretary. He edited the first two volumes of its proceedings, *Zbirnyk prats Zhydivskoy istorychno-arkheografichnoy komisiyi* (1928–29). Shortly afterward, Galant became suspect to the *Yevsektsia, which criticized his work, and was forced to discontinue his scholarly activities in 1929.

BIBLIOGRAPHY: A. Greenbaum, *Jewish Scholarship in Soviet Russia 1918–41* (1959), passim; B.A. Dinur, *Bi-Ymei Milḥamah u-Mahpekhah* (1960), 393–7.

[Yehuda Slutsky]

GALANTA, town in N.W. Slovakia. Until 1992 Czechoslovak Republic, since Slovak Republic. Jews started to settle in Galanta by the end of the 17th century. The earliest document is from 1729, when Count Ferdinand Eszterhazy granted the

Jewish community a room for prayer and ground for a cemetery. In 1830, 556 Jews lived in Galanta (31.2% of the total); in 1840 there were 430; and in 1850 there were 670 Jews in the town. In 1880 they numbered 714 (32.8%) and in 1900 there were 937. The second Czechoslovak census of 1930 reported 1,274 Jews.

The first rabbi was Wolf Duces (1757), during whose leadership the first synagogue was built. In 1760 the Jewish community of west Slovakia protested against Empress *Maria Teresa's Toleration Tax (*Toleranz Steuer*) that Jews were forced to pay. The community benefited from the legislation of Emperor Josef II (1780–90), which permitted Jews to engage in agriculture and a variety of commercial activities. At that time, the community had a *talmud torah*, a *mikveh*, and a cemetery. In the mid-1860s a yeshivah was established, which became renowned not only in Hungary but also abroad, and students flocked there from many European countries. It was recognized by the Czechoslovak authorities as an institute of higher education. In 1889 Samuel Neufeld opened a printing shop that produced rabbinical literature, including two printings of the Talmud. The shop existed under a variety of names until 1944. During the Spring of Nations, the Magyar national movement was supported by many local Jews. In 1918 Galanta, along with many other cities in Slovakia, was subjected to pogroms and looting of Jewish property.

After the Hungarian Jewish Congress of 1868, the Galanta Jewish community chose the Orthodox path. In 1891 a major dispute erupted over who should inherit the rabbinical seat. This led to a rift within the Jewish community and the establishment of two Orthodox congregations. The community split in 1893; the authorities made an uncharacteristic decision and recognized both congregations. Each chose its own rabbi, had a synagogue, a *talmud torah*, and other religious institutions. The dispute drew attention in Hungary and abroad, and received international press coverage. The Czechoslovak authorities also recognized both congregations. It was uncommon to have two Orthodox congregations in a single community.

Between the wars, Jewish communal life thrived in Galanta. Agudat Israel was the main political force there, but the Zionist movement existed as well. The Galanta Jewish community was renowned for the religious-folkloric celebration of the (alleged) birth and death of Moses, on the seventh of Adar. The ceremony is still observed today.

The Award of Vienna, October 2, 1938, assigned southern Slovakia to Hungary, including Galanta. The anti-Jewish legislation in Hungary was applied to the conquered territories. By the beginning of 1940, Jews – including those of Galanta – were recruited to special forced labor army units (*munkaszolgalat*), where many perished. On March 19, German troops occupied Hungary; shortly thereafter, they began to deport Jews to Auschwitz. In May 1944, the Jews of Galanta and its environs were assembled in the Kurzweil brick factory in *Nove Zamky. About 1,560 were deported on June 26, 1944; several survived.

In 1947 there were 272 Jews in Galanta. The Jewish community repaired one of the synagogues and the *mikveh*, and a kosher public kitchen provided meals until the survivors could adjust themselves. The *ḥevra kaddisha* was revived, and regular prayers resumed. In March 1985 the ancient small synagogue was torn down under the pretext that the space was needed for an apartment building. The congregation was given an apartment in which to hold its services. This, too, was replaced with another building in September 1983.

In 1947, upon their return from the concentration camps, members of the community founded a successful carpentry cooperative which, at its peak, had 250 workers. The communist regime, which followed the February 1948 coup d'état, nationalized the factory, and the Jews lost all their investment, including the money and the tools invested by the JDC. For years after the migration of 1948–49, Galanta served the Jews of southern Slovakia as a meeting point to celebrate the seventh of Adar as well as for bar-mitzvahs for youngsters from the entire region. The community was still active in 2005.

BIBLIOGRAPHY: R. Iltis (ed.), *Die aussaeen unter Traenen…* (1959), 142–5. **ADD. BIBLIOGRAPHY:** E. Bàrkàny and L. Dojč, *Židovské náboženské obce na Slovensku* (1991), 139–44.

[Sarlota Rachmuth-Gerstl / Yeshayahu Jelinek (2nd ed.)]

GALANTE, family of Spanish origin which produced a large number of scholars. An ancestor of the family was MORDECAI GALANTE, who was among the Spanish exiles of 1492 and lived in Rome during the first half of the 16th century, dying there after 1541. His original family name was Angello. Because of his handsome appearance and his dignified behavior he was nicknamed by the Roman nobility *galant' uomo*, from which was derived the surname Galante adopted by his descendants. Both of his sons, Moses *Galante and Abraham *Galante, migrated to Safed. The former had three sons: JONATHAN (d. 1678), who became a rabbi in Jerusalem, Jedidiah *Galante, the author of *Ḥiddushei Galante* (Willhermsdorf, 1716), and ABRAHAM, who served as *dayyan* in the *bet din* of Damascus. Moses *Galante II, the son of Jonathan, succeeded his father in Jerusalem. Around the year 1700 a certain JOSEPH GALANTE functioned as rabbi in Tyre. During the latter half of the 18th century another MORDECAI GALANTE (d. 1781), who was a scion of the same family, was rabbi and head of a yeshivah in Damascus. He corresponded about matters of Jewish law with the foremost Sephardi rabbinical authorities of his time. A number of his halakhic dissertations are contained in the responsa *Berekhot Mayim* by Mordecai *Meyuḥas (Salonika, 1789), Solomon *Laniado (Constantinople, 1775) and *Bigdei Yesha* of Isaiah *Attia (1853). A collection of his sermons was published in Leghorn under the heading of *Divrei Mordekhai*. To these were appended responsa by him entitled *Gedullat Mordekhai* as well as homilies by his son Moses under the title of *Kolo shel Moshe*. Mordecai Galante of Damascus was succeeded by his son MOSES (d. 1806). The latter also wrote responsa, which were published in Leghorn in 1809 under the name of *Berakh Moshe*. Attached to the volume was an appendix entitled *Zikkaron la-Rishonim*. It included also glosses on Joseph Caro's Shulḥan Arukh *Ḥoshen Mishpat* by Moses b. Mordecai (I) Galante, as well as notes by Ḥayyim *Modai on Shulḥan Arukh *Oraḥ Ḥayyim* and *Yoreh De'ah*, and on *Hezekiah da Silva's *Peri Hadash*, and Ḥayyim *Benveniste's *Keneset ha-Gedolah*. Moses Galante died in Damascus. Abraham *Galanté, the historian, also belonged to this family.

BIBLIOGRAPHY: Azulai, 1 (1852), 10 no. 36, 132 no. 111; Michael, Or, no. 176; S. Hazan, *Ha-Ma'alot li-Shelomo* (1894), 43a no. 20, 55b no. 1, 57a no. 14, 57b no. 15, 58b no. 23; Ghirondi-Neppi, 251 no. 41; Frumkin-Rivlin, 1 (1929), 56, 150; Rosanes, Togarmah, 3 (1938^2), 281–2; Fuenn, Keneset, 16; Vogelstein-Rieger, 2 (1896), 35, 86; J. Rivlin, in: *Reshumot*, 4 (1926), 114; A. Elmaleh, in: *Talpioth*, 9 (1964), 364–86.

[Samuel Rosenblatt]

GALANTÉ, ABRAHAM (1873–1961), Turkish politician, scholar, and historian born in Bodrum, Turkey. Galanté was a teacher and inspector in the Jewish and Turkish schools of Rhodes and Smyrna. He protested the misrule of Sultan Abdülhamid II and partly in consequence of this he left for Egypt, where from 1905 to 1908 he edited the Ladino newspaper *La Vara* and also contributed to Arabic, French, and Turkish newspapers and periodicals. He encouraged the acculturation of Turkish Jewry to its homeland, and conducted an active campaign for the adoption of the Turkish language by the Jews. At the same time he fought vigorously for Jewish rights. After the revolution of the Young Turks, Galanté returned to Istanbul, at whose university he was appointed professor of Semitic languages in 1914 and later professor of the history of the Ancient Orient. Galanté was a delegate to the first Turkish National Assembly after World War I and also a member of the Parliament which met in 1943. His principal field of scholarly activity was the study of Jewish history in Turkey, but he also wrote against the adoption of Latin characters for the Hebrew alphabet. His works (mainly in French) include *Don Joseph Nassi, Duc de Naxos* (1913), *Esther Kyra* (1926), *Documents officiels turcs concernant les Juifs de Turquie* (collections, 1931–54), *Nouveaux documents sur Sabbetai Sevi* (1935), *Histoire des Juifs d'Anatolie* (1937–39; appendix 1948), and *Histoire des Juifs d'Istanbul* (1941–42). In the 1990s his collected works were published by the Isis Press in Istanbul.

BIBLIOGRAPHY: A. Elmaleh, *Le Professeur Abraham Galanté* (1947); idem, *Ha-Profesor Abraham Galanté* (1954), incl. bibl.; Shunami, Bibl, index. **ADD. BIBLIOGRAPHY:** J.M. Landau, in: KS, 27 (1950–51), 212.

[Martin Meir Plessner / Jacob M. Landau (2nd ed.)]

GALANTE, ABRAHAM BEN MORDECAI (second half 16th century), kabbalist in Safed. He was the brother and a pupil of Moses b. Mordecai *Galante and a disciple of Moses *Cordovero. Galante, who was known as a distinguished and modest Ḥasid, received the title, "*Ha-Kadosh*" ("the saint"). He was the first to cite Joseph Caro's *Maggid Meisharim*. His works include (1) *Yare'aḥ Yakar*, a commentary on the *Zohar (extant in manuscripts, to Exodus-*Terumah* 140:2). The work was abridged by Abraham Azulai, entitled *Zohorei Ḥammah*, and published in Venice (1655, and later in Piotrkow, 1881); (2) *Kinat Setarim*, a kabbalistic commentary on Lamentations (publ. by R.I. Gershon in the work *Kol Bokhim*, Venice, 1589); (3) *Zekhut Avot*, a kabbalistic commentary on the tractate *Avot* (in the work *Beit Avot*, Bilgoraj, 1911); and (4) *Minhagei Ḥasidut*, published by S. Schechter (1908). Ḥ.J.D. *Azulai relates that Galante built the court of Meron where the graves of *Simeon b. Yoḥai and his son Eleazar are located.

BIBLIOGRAPHY: S. Schechter, *Studies in Judaism*, 2 (1908), 208–9, 273–5, 294–7; G. Scholem, *Kitvei Yad be-Kabbalah* (1930), 102–4; idem, *Bibliographia Kabbalistica* (Ger., 1933), 187–8; M. Benayahu, *Toledot ha-Ari* (1967), 111–5, index; D. Tamar, *Meḥkarim be-Toledot Yehudim be-Ereẓ Yisrael u-ve-Italyah* (1970), 101–6.

[David Tamar]

GALANTE, JEDIDIAH BEN MOSES (17th century), scholar and emissary. From 1607 to 1613 Galante visited the Italian communities as an emissary of Safed, possibly on behalf of its Italian community to which his family belonged. During his travels he wrote several halakhic responsa in reply to problems addressed to him and relayed the remarkable deeds attributed to Isaac *Luria (the Ari). In 1608 he published in Venice the responsa of his father, Moses *Galante. When some Italian Jews, who objected to one of Jedidiah's rulings on a subject that divided the rabbis of Italy, accused him of embezzling the donations for Ereẓ Israel, he took dramatic action. On a Sabbath in Elul 1609, after his sermon to a large Venetian congregation before which he had been invited to preach, he took a Scroll of the Law from the Ark and in the presence of the whole congregation swore to his complete innocence. The incident, which made a profound impression, was publicized by the lay leaders and rabbis of Venice in a specially printed notice circulated among the Italian communities.

BIBLIOGRAPHY: Sonne, in: *Koveẓ-al-Yad*, 5 (1950), 205–12; Yaari, Sheluḥei, 152, 247, 842–3.

[Avraham Yaari]

GALANTE, MOSES BEN JONATHAN (II) (1620–1689), Jerusalem rabbi. Galante was called "*Ha-Rav ha-Magen*" after his major work *Elef ha-Magen* which includes one thousand responsa and cases (unpublished). He was the grandson of Moses b. Mordecai *Galante (I). He studied in Safed and later moved to Jerusalem where he became a leading rabbi and headed the yeshiva Bet Ya'akov. His students included *Hezekiah b. David Da Silva, author of *Peri Hadash*, Israel Jacob Ḥagiz, his son-in-law (the father of Moses *Ḥagiz), and Abraham Yiẓḥaki, the rabbi of Jerusalem. He and other scholars instituted an ordinance (*takkanah*) that the scholars of Jerusalem would not use the title "rabbi" (in order that one scholar would not have authority over another). From 1667–68 he served as an emissary of Jerusalem to the cities of Turkey and Hungary. In 1673 he was again in Jerusalem. Galante was influenced by the Shabbatean movement for a time. In 1665 he and other rabbis from Jerusalem went to Gaza in order to seek purification of the soul from *Nathan of Gaza. At the end of 1665 or early in 1666 Galante was in Aleppo where he was among the leading Shabbatean "prophets." According to the testimony in a letter from Aleppo (in Ms. Epstein, Vienna, Jewish Community Library 141[8]), Galante was the "*ḥakham* Moses Galante" who accompanied Shabbetai Ẓevi to Smyrna at the end of 1665 and was appointed by him "King Yehoshaphat." He also accompanied Shabbetai Ẓevi to Constantinople. R. Abraham Yiẓḥaki testified that Galante said "Although I would not believe in Shabbetai Ẓevi, I would not deprecate him. But after I saw that in writing to one of his followers here, he signed himself 'I the Lord your God' [i.e., he wrote the Tetragrammaton in his own handwriting], I excommunicate him daily." His published works include *Zevaḥ ha-Shelamim*, commentaries on the Torah with the glosses of Galante's grandson Moses Ḥagiz (Amsterdam, 1708), and *Korban Ḥagigah*, sermons for the Three Festivals and novellae on the tractate *Ḥagigah* and on Maimonides' *Yad ha-Ḥazakah* (Venice, 1704, 1709).

BIBLIOGRAPHY: Frumkin-Rivlin, 2 (1928),56–60, 150; Habermann, in: *Kovez-al-Yad*, 13 (1940), 210; Yaari, Sheluḥei, 290–1; I. Tishby, *Ẓizat Novel Ẓevi le-Rabbi Ya'akov Sasportas* (1954), 74f.; Scholem, Shabbetai Ẓevi, name index.

[David Tamar]

GALANTE, MOSES BEN MORDECAI (I) (fl. 16th century), talmudist and kabbalist, one of the scholars ordained in Safed in the second half of the 16th century. Galante, who was born in Rome, was the brother of Abraham b. Mordecai *Galante. He was well acquainted with Ḥayyim *Vital's disciples. Galante was a disciple of Joseph *Caro who ordained him at the age of 22 (Responsa of Moses Galante, par. 124). His teacher in the field of Kabbalah was Moses *Cordovero. From 1580 he served as *av bet din* in Safed as the successor of Moses di Trani. He lived to be over 90 and apparently died after 1612. His works include: (1) responsa, only partly published (124 paragraphs) by his son Jedidiah, with the addition of his novellae (Venice, 1608); (2) *Mafte'aḥ ha-Zohar*, an index of the biblical passages interpreted in the Zohar (incomplete; Venice, 1566); and (3) *Kohelet Ya'akov*, a partly homiletic and partly kabbalistic commentary on Ecclesiastes (Safed, 1578).

Some of his sermons were published in the commentary on Ruth of Obadiah of Bertinoro (Venice, 1585).

BIBLIOGRAPHY: G. Scholem, *Bibliographia Kabbalistica* (Ger. 1927), 195; Benayahu, in: *Sinai*, 35 (1954), 60; Tamar, in: *Tarbiz*, 27 (1958), 111–6.

[David Tamar]

GALATI (Rom. **Galați**; Ger. **Galatz**), port on the River Danube, in Moldavia, eastern Romania, first mentioned in the 15th century. Jews first settled there at the end of the 16th century. A cemetery which has not been preserved, was probably established in 1629; another, recently restored, was established in 1774. In 1803, 72 Jews paid taxes. Until the beginning of the 19th century the *ḥevra kaddisha* was responsible for the communal administration. Following a *blood libel in 1796, outrages were perpetrated against the Jews. In 1821 Greek revolutionaries who entered the town set fire to several synagogues, and in 1842 there were renewed attacks on the community by local Greeks. In 1846 anti-Jewish outbreaks again occurred in which synagogues were looted and Jewish houses and shops were destroyed. In 1859, in a similar attack, many Jews were killed. In 1867 a number of Jews among those expelled from the country drowned in the Danube near Galati: the catastrophe provoked a storm of protest throughout Europe. The Jewish bakers were expelled from Galati for refusing to break the strike of their fellow workers and party members in 1893. The Jewish population numbered around 7,000 in 1841, 14,500 in 1894, 12,000 in 1910 (22% of the total), 19,912 in 1930 (20%), and 13,000 in 1942. Jewish artisans and merchants contributed considerably to the city's economic and commercial development. In 1895 a community association with legal recognition (1906) was founded. The Zionist Baruch Zosmer was elected deputy mayor in 1928. Among the rabbis who functioned between the two world wars and after World War II were Abraham Jacob Derbaremdigher, Jacob Margulies, and Isaac Schapira. Ḥasidic courts such as that of Rabbi Abraham Joshua Heschel Friedman also functioned in Galati. Before World War II the community had 22 synagogues, a secondary school, two elementary schools for boys and one for girls, a kindergarten, a trade school, a hospital, an orphanage, an old-age home, and two ritual bathhouses. In 1881–1919 Galati was the center of the Zionist movement in Romania. In 1926, the Zionist Revisionist Organization of Romania was founded in Galati. There was also a cultural-religious society, a Zionist society, a youth organization Ẓe'irei Zion, and a "culture" club. The Jews in Galati were subjected to constant persecution by the pro-Nazi authorities during World War II. The community was not destroyed during the Holocaust, but subsequently diminished through emigration. It numbered 13,000 in 1947, 9,000 in 1950, and 450 families in 1969, with two synagogues. In 2005, 252 Jews lived in Galati, with a synagogue, a kosher restaurant and a cemetery.

BIBLIOGRAPHY: *Monografia Comunității Israelite din Galați* (1906); *Almanahul Ziarului Tribuna Eyreească*, 1 (1937/38), 260–3; L. Preminger-Hecht, in: *Ostjuedische Zeitung*, 10 (1928), no. 1107; PK Romanyah, 90–99. **ADD. BIBLIOGRAPHY:** O. Lazar and S. Weinberg, in: SAHIR, 6 (2001), 11–27, idem, in: *Jaloane pentru o viitoare istorii* (1999), 227–31; FEDROM-*Comunitati evreiesti din Romania* (Internet, 2005).

[Haim Karl Blum / Lucian-Zeev Hersovici (2nd ed.)]

GALATIA, district in Asia Minor, which became a Roman province in 25 B.C.E. Evidence of the existence of Jews in Galatia is scanty, but it is likely that Jewish settlement began with the establishment of Jewish military colonies by Antiochus III in adjoining Phrygia and Lydia (Jos., Ant. 12:147ff.) toward the end of the third century B.C.E. Jews lived in the neighboring countries of *Pergamum, *Cappadocia (I Macc. 15:22), and *Bithynia (Philo, *Embassy to Gaius*, 281) in the second century B.C.E., and the first century C.E. Josephus tells of an edict of Augustus published in Ancyra, capital of Galatia, granting the Jews, among other privileges, the right to practice their ancestral traditions, and to transfer funds to Jerusalem (Ant. 16:162–5). However, "Ancyra" is a correction proposed by Scaliger from a faulty text which cannot be absolutely relied upon. Clearer evidence is available from accounts of the missionary activities of the apostle Paul among the various communities in the first century (I Cor. 16:1; Acts 16:6; 18:23), in particular his *Epistle to the Galatians*. Jewish names in inscriptions found in the precincts of Galatia include "Esther" and "Jacob," appearing on a tomb at Germa, southwest of Ancyra (Frey, Corpus, 2 (1952), 48, no. 796) and "Levi," inscribed elsewhere (Henderson, in *Journal of Hellenistic Studies*, 19 (1899), 285, no. 178). The word "Galia," recurring a number of times in talmudic literature, is in some instances considered to refer to Galatia, e.g., the journey of R. Akiva to "Galia" (RH 26a). It is similarly thought that Nahum or Menahem of "Galia" came from Galatia although others identify "Galia" with France or with a settlement in Judea. (Ket. 60a: Tosef., Er. 11:10; TJ, Ber. 4:4, 8b). In II Maccabees 8:20, it is specifically mentioned that Jews fought against the Galatians at the side of Seleucid kings in Babylonia, defeating them and taking much loot, but there is no available information as to which war is referred to, or its details.

BIBLIOGRAPHY: Schuerer, Gesch, 3 (1909[4]), 22–23; Juster, Juifs, 1 (1914), 193; W.M. Ramsay, *Cities and Bishoprics of Phrygia*, 2 (1897).

[Lea Roth]

°GALATINUS, PIETRO COLUMNA (1460–1540), Italian theologian and Christian kabbalist. A Franciscan friar who believed himself to be the "Angel Pope" first prophesied by followers of Joachim of Fiore in the 13th century, Galatinus wrote a monumental work of Christian mysticism, *De arcanis catholicae veritatis* (Ortona, 1518), first printed by Gershom *Soncino. Though anti-Jewish in tone, it was published in defense of the great German humanist Johann *Reuchlin and did much to promote Christian Hebraism. The book, which assembled a vast number of polemical texts, inspired many later Christian kabbalists, including the French visionary Guillaume *Postel. It was prefaced by laudatory Hebrew verses and laid great stress on numerology. The most popular work of its kind in the 16th century, the *Arcana* was praised by *Amatus Lusitanus. Galatinus anticipated Daniel *Bomberg by advocating the publication of the Talmud. He "explained" early Christianity's lack of explicit reference to the Kabbalah by citing a passage in the Babylonian Talmud (Ḥag. 11bff.), which forbids the indiscriminate transmission of the creation and chariot mysteries (see *Merkabah Mysticism), especially in writing.

BIBLIOGRAPHY: D.W. Amram, *Makers of Hebrew Books in Italy* (1909), 124–6; C. Roth, *Jews in the Renaissance* (1959), 182; F. Secret, *Les kabbalistes chrétiens de la Renaissance* (1964), 102–6; idem, in: *Studi francesi*, 3 (1957), 379ff.

[Godfrey Edmond Silverman]

GALBANUM (Heb. חֶלְבְּנָה, *ḥelbenah*), a gum resin mentioned among the ingredients of the incense in the Tabernacle (Ex. 30:34) and by Ben Sira as a spice (Gr. χαλβάνη). It was included in a *baraita* (Ker. 6a), dating from Second Temple times, among the constituents of the incense used in the Temple. The *Gemara* (Ker. 6b) states that it was an ingredient of incense despite its offensive smell, thus demonstrating that a malodorous substance, when mixed with fragrant spices, also contributes to the general pleasant odor, thereby symbolizing that sinners of Israel are an integral part of its society. Greek and Roman natural and medical writers, referring to the medicinal qualities of galbanum, praise the spices imported from Syria (Pliny, *Historia Naturalis*, 12:25; Dioscorides, *De Materia Medica*, 3:87). In Israel six species of galbanum grow wild, but their resin is not used for any known purpose. A substance called umbelliferone, employed as a remedy for convulsions, is extracted from two species of galbanum, from *Ferula galbaniflua* which grows in Syria and *Ferula schair* which grows in Turkestan. These plants are of the Umbelliferae family whose stems contain a milk-like resin congealing on contact with air. It is also used in the lacquer industry.

BIBLIOGRAPHY: Loew, Flora, 3 (1924), 455–7; J. Feliks, *Olam ha-Ẓome'aḥ ha-Mikra'i* (1968[2]), 276–7.

[Jehuda Feliks]

°GALEN (Galenus), CLAUDIUS (131–c. 201 C.E.), prominent physician in antiquity and author of important philosophical works. Galen was born in Pergamum (Asia Minor) and died in Rome. Medieval Hebrew authors and translators regarded Galen as "the greatest physician" (*gedol ha-rofe'im, rosh ha-rofe'im*). A popular legend among the Jews in the Middle Ages identified Galen with the patriarch Gamaliel II, who was said to have written a handbook of medicine for Titus after the destruction of Jerusalem. This did not, however, prevent *Maimonides and other Jewish authors from sharply criticizing Galen for his attacks on the law of Moses (see R. Waltzer, *Galen on Jews and Christians*, 1949) and denying his authority in any field other than medicine (*Pirkei Moshe* (1888), 25). *Jedaiah ha-Penini launched a sharp attack on Galen (*Iggeret Hitnaẓẓelut*, in *Iggerot ha-Rashba* (1881), 61), and *Immanuel of Rome relegated him to hell (*Maḥbarot*, vol. 2 (1967), no. 28, p. 515). A derogatory opinion on Galen as a philosopher is also found in a work by Shem-Tov ibn *Falaquera (*Ha-Mevakkesh*, 33). On the other hand, on the question of the eternity of the world, Maimonides sided with Galen against al-*Fārābī (*Guide of the Perplexed*, 2:15). As Galen was a physician and author of medical works, his reputation among Jews was beyond dispute. Maimonides wrote Arabic compendia of the 16 "canonical" books and of several other works by Galen, and his Arabic commentary on Hippocrates' *Aphorisms* is based primarily on Galen. Maimonides' own aphorisms (*Pirkei Moshe*) are also primarily a selection from Galen's works and the latter's commentary on Hippocrates (as stated by Maimonides in the introduction).

The following works by Galen appeared in Hebrew translation (generally based on the Arabic text of Ḥunayn ibn Isḥāq, but in some instances also on Latin versions) or as Hebrew adaptations: (1) *Ars Parva* (*Melakhah Ketannah*), translated by Samuel ibn *Tibbon in 1199 (manuscripts in Leiden and Paris) together with the Arabic commentary by the Egyptian physician Ali ibn Riḍwān. This commentary was translated again under the title of *Sefer ha-Tegni* (manuscript in Rome and extracts in Paris) by *Hillel b. Samuel, but this time from the Latin translation by Gerard of Cremona. (2) Four books dealing with various diseases, their causes, and symptoms were translated by Zeraḥiah b. Isaac *Gracian under the title of *Sefer ha-Ḥola'im ve-ha-Mikrim* (manuscript in Munich). (3) Three treatises on compound drugs were also translated by Gracian under the title of *Katagenē* (manuscript in Hamburg). (4) The "Book of Crises" was translated by Solomon Bonirac of Barcelona under the title *Sefer Baḥran*, based on the Arabic text by Ḥunayn. (5) The treatise on bloodletting exists in two Hebrew translations: one, based on the Arabic text, was made by Kalonymus b. Kalonymus in Arles (manuscript in Leiden); the other is an anonymous work based on the Latin translation and bears the title *Sefer ha-Hakkazah shel Gidim* (manuscript in Guenzburg collection). (6) *De clysteriis et colica*, translated by Kalonymus from the Arabic of Ḥunayn (manuscript in Leiden). (7) Treatise on the regimen to be followed by epileptic boys, anonymous translation under the title *Sefer be-Hanhagat ha-Na'ar ha-Nikhpeh*, based on Ḥunayn's Arabic text (manuscript in Munich). (8) *De malitia complexionis diversae*, translated by David b. Abraham Caslari in Narbonne under the title *Sefer Ro'a Mezeg Mitḥallef*, probably on the basis of the Latin text by Gerard of Cremona (Bodleian manuscript). (9) The Alexandrians' compendia of Galen's 16 "canonical" writings were translated from the Arabic version by Samson b. Solomon under the title *Sefer ha-Kibbuẓim la-Aleksandriyyim*. Several manuscripts are extant, all fairly complete.

Apart from the compendia translated by Samson b. Solomon, there existed several compendia of individual works by Galen. Two of these exist in anonymous Hebrew translations: *Kelalei Sefer Galenus ba-Marah ha-Sheḥorah* (on melancholy), based on the translation by Stephanus, as revised by Ḥunayn; and *Asifat Marot ha-Sheten*, on the colors of urine (three manuscripts). A second translation of the latter work bears the title *Kibbuẓei Sifrei Galenus be-Minei ha-Sheten* (manuscript in Leiden).

Galen's commentary on the Aphorisms by Hippocrates was translated from the Arabic by Nathan b. Eliezer ha-Me'ati in Rome, together with Hippocrates' own work (many manuscripts have been preserved). A second translation from the Arabic of both works was made by Jacob b. Joseph ibn Zabara (manuscript in New York), and a third, based on the Latin version of Constantinus Africanus, is probably the work of Hillel b. Samuel.

A large number of works attributed to Galen were also translated into Hebrew, including *Sefer ha-Em*, *Sefer Issur ha-Kevurah*, *Panim le-Fanim*, *Sefer ha-Nefesh*, and *Likkutei Segulot u-Refu'ot mi-Galeno*. Other works by Galen also influenced medieval Jewish literature, even though they were not translated into Hebrew. Thus, for example a work by Galen was quoted in *Saadiah Gaon's commentary on *Sefer Yeẓirah* (4:5), in *Baḥya ibn Paquda's *Ḥovot ha-Levavot* (2:5), in *Judah Halevi's *Kuzari* (5:8), and in a letter by Zerahiah b. Isaac Gracian addressed to Hillel b. Samuel (in *Oẓar Neḥmad*, 2 (1857), 141).

BIBLIOGRAPHY: D. Kaufmann, *Die Sinne* (1884), 6, 192, and passim; M. Steinschneider, *Alfarabi* (1869), 31, 34, 134, 142; Steinschneider, Uebersetzungen, index; Steinschneider, Arab Lit, 214ff., 217, 232; Steinschneider, Cat Bod, 2 (1931), 997; A. Marx, in: *Devir*, 2 (1924), 208–12.

[Moshe Nahum Zobel]

GALICH ALEXANDER ARKADYEVICH (Ginzburg; 1919–1977), Russian poet and dramatist. Galich was born in Dnepropetrovsk (Ukraine). He studied acting with Stanislavski theatrical studio and appeared with an army troupe at the front during WWII. From 1945 he was a drama teacher and wrote a number of plays, the most popular one being the comedy *Was vyzyvaiet Taimir* ("Taimir Is Calling You, 1948). He also wrote the screenplay *Vernyie Druzia* ("Faithful Friends," 1958). Another of his plays, *Matrosskaya Tishina* ("The Seaman's Silence"), was banned in the Soviet Union. From the beginning of the 1960s he wrote poems which he set to music, performed, and recorded. His poems were critical of Soviet thinking and the language of the press. Some had Jewish themes, such as the poem "Korchak" ("Kaddish") for the actor *Mikhoels and a cycle of poems on the emigration of Soviet Jews to Israel. In the 1960s he turned to Christianity. His poems were published outside the Soviet Union. He also fought for human rights. For all these reasons he was ejected in 1971 from the Union of Writers and Filmmakers. In 1974 he settled in Paris. He visited Israel twice, performing his songs in concerts.

[Shmuel Spector (2nd ed.)]

GALICIA (Pol. **Galicia**; Ger. **Galizien**; Rus. **Galitsiya**), geographical-political region of E. Europe, in S.E. Poland and N.W. Ukraine, extending northward from the Carpathians into the Vistula Valley to the San River.

After numerous changes in the Middle Ages, Galicia was incorporated within the kingdom of Poland. The major part passed to the Hapsburg monarchy during the first partition of Poland in 1772; with the third partition of Poland the area under Hapsburg rule was extended to the north and northwest of the region. From 1803 Galicia formed a separate administrative unit (province). With the dissolution of the monarchy after World War I Galicia again passed to Poland (1918–19). In 1939, after the outbreak of World War II, western Galicia was occupied by the Germans and eastern Galicia by the Soviet Union, which incorporated it in the Ukrainian S.S.R. Eastern Galicia was also occupied by the Germans in 1941 and the Jews there suffered the fate of the rest of the Jews of Poland and the Ukraine. After the war western Galicia returned to Poland, while eastern Galicia remained within the Ukrainian S.S.R.

During the period of Polish rule until 1772 Galicia was known as Little Poland (see *Lesser Poland), which within the Jewish organizational framework of the *Council of the Lands formed one of the four "lands" (provinces). For the history of the Jews in this period, see *Poland-Lithuania.

[Simha Katz]

After the 1772 Annexation to Austria

At the time of the region's annexation to Austria in 1772, its Jewish population numbered 224,980 (9.6% of the total). Jews were to be found in 187 cities, 93 small towns, and 5,467 villages and homesteads. By 1773 the number of Jews had declined to 171,851 (6.5%), and by 1776 to 144,200. In 1780 the Jewish population stood at 151,302; in 1782 at 172,424, and in 1785 at 212,002. In 1776 the area in the region of Cracow was extracted from Austria, but it was returned in 1795 and structured administratively as "western Galicia" (including the *Lublin district). Until 1809 the Zamosc district was also in Galicia, under Austria, and between 1786 and 1818 *Bukovina was included administratively in Galicia. In 1815–46 Cracow and its environs constituted an autonomous republic, while the Ternopol district came under Russian rule, during 1809–15.

The non-Jewish population of western Galicia was almost entirely Polish in 1776, Jews constituting 3.1% of the population. Eastern Galicia was mostly Ukrainian, and the Jews there were 8.7% of the total population. Six towns (*Brody, *Belz, *Rogatin, *Peremyshlyany, Delyatin, and *Sokal) were almost entirely Jewish, nine other towns had a Jewish majority, and in seven cities (including *Lvov) the Jews constituted one-third or more of the total population. Initially, the Jews of Galicia continued in the framework of the socioeconomic structure of old Poland-Lithuania. In the villages Jews were occupied in *arenda; in the towns and townlets the majority of Jews were retailers or craftsmen, especially in the household industry (textiles, sackcloth, and sail cloth) and the garment industry (as tailors, furriers, and hatters). The export and import trade of the region was mainly in the hands of Jews, as the transit between Turkey and Russia in the east and Germany in the west centered in *Brody.

The Austrian "Code of Regulations Concerning the Jews" (1776) allowed the autonomy of the Jewish community to stand. A 12-member supreme Jewish council was created, headed by the chief rabbi of the region. The following specific taxes were levied on the Jews: protection and toleration tax (4 guldens per family), property and employment tax (the same), marriage tax (according to the wealth of the family, from 4 to 300 ducats). All Jewish beggars were expelled from Galicia. Aryeh Leib *Bernstein became chief rabbi, Mordecai Ze'ev Orenstein vice chief rabbi.

Emperor *Joseph II included Galicia in his statutes (1785–89) directed at the improvement of the condition of the Jews (see *Emancipation) and their ultimate *assimilation. His 1789 *Toleranzpatent mentioned 141 organized Jewish communities, each administered by three *parnasim, except for Lvov and Brody, which had seven. The autonomy of the community, the rabbinical court, and the craftsmen's guilds were abolished. In 1786 the supreme council, established in 1776, was dissolved. The expulsion of the Jews from the villages began; various trade branches, peddling, and *arenda* were prohibited to them. At the same time they were actively encouraged to take up agricultural work. Close to one-third of the Jewish population was deprived of its means of livelihood as a result of these regulations. In 1789 Jews were included in the obligation to do military service (there was some active resistance to this by the Jews of Brody) and had to adopt German family names. Government-sponsored schools were established for the Jews, and attendance was made compulsory. A tax was levied on *kasher* meat (see *Korobka), and in 1797 on Sabbath and holiday candles as well (see *Candle Tax); this tax became the basis for the vote in the community. The average yearly income from the tax on *kasher* meat was 500,000–700,000 gulden, while that on candles brought in some 350,000 gulden annually.

In 1787 Naphtali Herz *Homberg was appointed chief inspector of the network of more than 104 government schools established for the education of the Jews. Both he and the teachers – who came mainly from Bohemia and Germany –were enthusiasts for total Jewish assimilation into German culture. Jews were bitterly opposed to this school system and as far as possible prevented their children's attendance. In 1806 all these Jewish schools in Galicia (attended by 3,550 pupils) were closed. The plan for settling 1,410 Jewish families on government-owned land, initiated in 1786, also failed, and by 1822 there were only 836 Jewish farmers in all of Galicia. On the other hand, Jewish physicians were granted equality with Christian ones and secondary schools and institutions of higher learning were opened to Jews. Nonetheless only 158 Jewish students attended such schools in 1827. Polish society in Galicia showed a relatively pro-Jewish attitude, its representatives including in their program for the region – presented to Emperor Leopold II – a demand for civil rights for Jews, though not the right to own estates or to hold elective office.

By 1827 there were about 115,000 Jewish males in Galicia, about 50,000 of whom were of working age. Of the latter, 28,524 (less than 60%) were gainfully employed, the majority in business, transportation, services, and the free professions. During the late 18th and early 19th centuries Jewish cultural and social life in Galicia was rich. The *Haskalah entered Galicia almost in its beginnings, Brody being its center. Mendel *Levin (Lefin), first at Brody and later in Ternopol, and J.L. Ben *Ze'ev were its pioneers there, followed by Dov Berish Ginsburg, Jacob Samuel *Bick, and Joseph *Perl. The years 1815 to 1850 represent the high point of the Haskalah in Galicia. In this period the following men were active in Galician social and literary life: Nachman *Krochmal, S.J. *Rapoport, Isaac *Erter, Meir *Letteris, Solomon *Rubin, Samson *Bloch, Joshua Heschel *Schorr (editor of *He-Ḥalutz*), his brother Naphtali Mendel *Schorr, Abraham *Krochmal, Samuel Leib *Goldenberg, Jacob *Bodek, Isaac Mieses, M. Silberstein, Abraham Menahem Mendel *Mohr, Joseph *Kohen-Ẓedek, and others. Their literary and educational activity made Galicia of the 19th century a major center of Jewish thought and creativity. Traditional Torah education and scholarship continued in full measure in Galicia throughout the 19th century. Some of the great Talmud scholars of this period there were Joseph Saul ha-Levi *Nathanson; Jacob Meshullam Orenstein, both of Lvov; Solomon b. Judah Aaron *Kluger of Brody; Aryeh Leib b. Joseph ha-Kohen (*Heller) of Stry, the author of *Keẓot ha-Ḥoshen*; Shalom Mordecai b. Moses *Shvadron of Berezhany; Joseph *Engel, and others. Social life in Galicia was imprinted first by the acrimonious strife between *mitnaggedim* and Ḥasidim, and then, later between Ḥasidim and the Haskalah.

*Ḥasidism spread steadily in Galicia during the 19th century, and despite the opposition of the leading rabbis, it succeeded in permeating all strata of the population. Local rabbis of the smaller communities, in particular, had to accept the influence of the ḥasidic *ẓaddik* whose followers were the strongest group in their community. The important figures of Galician Ḥasidism were the *Belz dynasty, founded by Shalom Rokeaḥ in 1816; Zanz, founded by Ḥayyim *Halberstam in 1830; and the dynasties of the sons of Israel *Ruzhin (Friedmann), in *Sadgora (c. 1855) and in *Chortkov (1860). All Orthodox elements united against the Haskalah, which fought the Orthodox majority not only through education and propaganda, but through alliance with the state authorities and sometimes through the denunciation to them of the Orthodox, in particular, and of the Ḥasidim (in this Joseph Perl excelled). In the 1870s the Ḥasidim of Belz began to intervene in political matters. The Haskalah was influential in the large cities, e.g., Brody, Lvov, Ternopol, and *Zholkava, where Joseph Perl and others instituted Jewish schools with German as the language of instruction, and Haskalah leaders founded "reform" synagogues of varying trends. In 1816 Jacob Meshullam Orenstein excommunicated the *maskilim* of Lvov but was compelled by the authorities to rescind his decree. During the 1830s and 1840s the number of *maskilim* and their influence continued to increase in the large cities. In 1838 the communal leadership of Lvov installed a Reform rabbi Abraham *Kohn, who was poisoned in 1848. The striving of the Haskalah in Galicia for assimilation into German culture changed in the 1860s and the 1870s to a preference for assimilation into Polish culture; the extreme Orthodox tended to support Polish political aims.

The 1848 revolutionary parliament, which included three Galician Jews, rescinded the special taxes on the Jews, and in the constitution of March 1849, Jews were granted equality of rights. At the end of 1851, however, the government revoked the constitution and restricted the civil rights of the Jews. In 1859–60 most of the restrictions on Jews were lifted. Jews were also granted the right to be elected to the Galician Sejm, and consequently there were four Jewish deputies in 1867–72. In 1867 the Sejm elected a Jewish deputy to the parliament in Vienna, as the Austrian constitution of 1867 granted Jews equal rights.

The economic life of the Jews of Galicia also improved at about that time. Rich Jews entered *banking, large-scale export and import, industry, and the oil trade and industry. From 1867 the number of Jewish estate owners grew markedly. Jews entered the civil service and the judiciary (in 1897 Jews constituted 58% of the civil servants and judges). The majority, however, only felt a slight improvement. They resented attempts to draw them to the village and agricultural life and as a result failed in these areas. In the early 20th century the number of Jewish estate owners or lessees again increased significantly, Jewish merchants and industrialists eagerly investing in these fields. There was a corresponding increase in the number of Jews in agricultural management, and in agricultural schools and experimental farms for Jews.

In 1874, 98 Jews sat on 71 regional councils. In the Galician Sejm, five of the 155 deputies were Jews. There were 261 Jews on various municipal councils in Galicia, and in 45 municipalities they were the majority. Ten cities had Jewish mayors. The leadership of the Haskalah movement, as well as of the assimilationists – German or Polish – gradually passed into the hands of a new, university-educated group of writers like Ludwig *Gumplowicz, Joseph Ettinger, Moritz Rapoport, Dr. Eliezer Englewicz, Meir Letteris, Marcus Landau, Joseph Kobak, Jacob *Goldenthal, Leo Herzberg-Fraenkel, K.E. Franzos, Marcus Dubs, and Meir Mintz. The number of Jewish students in the secondary schools (301 in 1856; 703 by 1867) and in the universities continued to grow. At the same time, a network of educational institutions was established under Jewish auspices.

From 1867 the assimilationist circles were split between those tending to Polish assimilation – organized in the Aggudat Aḥim (Fraternal Society) of Poles of Mosaic Faith – and those tending to German assimilation culture – organized in the *Shomer Israel (Guardians of Israel). In the elections of 1873, Shomer Israel of eastern Galicia allied itself with the Ukrainians against the Poles and succeeded in electing four Jewish deputies; the Jewish deputy from Cracow joined the Polish group in parliament. In 1878, on the initiative of Shomer Israel, a congress of Jewish communities was convened and resolved regulations for all communities, as well as the establishment of a rabbinical seminary. The Orthodox, led by the rabbi of Cracow, Simeon *Sofer, and the *ẓaddik* of Belz, Joshua Rokeaḥ, opposed the convention and encouraged a boycott of it. In 1882 the Orthodox convened a rabbinical conference (in Lvov) whose regulations for the communities were diametrically opposed to those of the congress of Jewish communities. Only those who lived according to the *Shulḥan Arukh and paid their communal dues would be entitled to a vote in the communities. The Austrian authorities refused to endorse this Orthodox regulation despite the support of the Polish group in parliament. In 1890 the Ministry of Religion and Culture formulated a regulation of its own, approved by parliament and enforced until 1918. A proposal to establish a rabbinical seminary, adopted in 1907 by the Galician Sejm, was frustrated by the opposition of the Orthodox, who organized themselves in the *Maḥzike Hadas ("Upholders of the Faith"), headed by the above-mentioned leaders. The Orthodox allied themselves with the Poles in the parliamentary elections of 1878 and elected Rabbi Sofer, who joined the Polish group in Parliament.

A number of monthly and weekly Hebrew periodicals circulated in 19th-century Galicia: *Yerushalayim* (1865–90); *Ha-Mevasser* (1860–70); *Nesher* ("Eagle"); *Meged Yeraḥim* (1855, 1859); *Oẓar Ḥokhmah* (1849–65); *He-Ḥalutz*, edited by Joseph Kobak; *Ha-Ivri*, edited by Baruch and Jacob Werber. In 1848–49 several Yiddish weeklies made their appearance: *Tsaytung* (1848–49); *Di Yidishe Post* (1849); *Yidishe Tsaytung* ("The Jewish Weekly"; 1865–67); *Naye Yidishe Prese* (1872), and *Israelit* (1875–76).

Between 1860 and 1880 anti-assimilationist works and new trends in Haskalah, mainly influenced by Peretz *Smolenskin, began to appear. In 1875 the first society in Galicia for the settlement of Palestine was established in *Przemysl. In the 1880s Ḥovevei Zion (see *Ḥibbat Zion) gained momentum in Galicia. Growing antisemitism among the Poles aided this development. In 1884 the organ of the Polish trend of assimilation, *Aguddat Aḥim*, ceased publication, confessing in its last issue that the Jews of Galicia could only "emigrate to Palestine or convert to Christianity." In Lvov and in the outlying towns, the first Zionist organizations were formed. The student Zionist organization of Lvov, Zion, published the first Zionist newspaper in the Polish laguage, *Przyszłość* ("Future," 1892); the periodical *Wschód* ("East") followed. Nonetheless, assimilationists continued to lead the communities, and, with the help of the Poles and brutal acts of terror, succeeded in electing their candidates to parliament until as late as 1907. These joined the Polish group and supported the demands of the Poles, even when they conflicted with Jewish interests.

In 1893 a Catholic convocation in Cracow proclaimed an economic boycott on Jews. From 1900 Poles and Ukrainians combined to exclude the Jews from the merchandising of agricultural produce through the establishment of a network of agricultural cooperatives and through propaganda among the peasants not to buy from or sell to Jews, and the various organizations of estate owners formed their own associations for buying and selling. In 1910 the Jews were forbidden to sell alcoholic beverages; 15,000 Jewish families lost their source of livelihood. This occurred at a time when the number of Jews had doubled in Galicia (between 1857 and 1910). As the table Jewish Population in Galicia, 1857–1910, shows, up to 1890 the percentage of Jews increased from 9.6% to 11.7%; from 1890 it was constantly declining and by 1910 became 10.9%.

The economic structure of Galician Jewry is reflected in the table Economic Structure of Galician Jewry, 1910.

The boycott and economic pressure impoverished the masses of Jews in Galicia. In 1908 there were 689 cooperative lending funds, most of which had been established with the help of Jews abroad. Between 1881 and 1910 a total of 236,000 Jews emigrated from Galicia. Impelled by circumstances, the Zionist movement entered local politics in 1906. In the general elections of 1907, three Zionist candidates – Adolf *Stand, Arthur *Mahler, and Heinrich Gavel – were successful. Together with the Zionist deputy from Bukovina, they formed the first "Jewish Club" in the Austrian parliament. In the general elections of 1911, all Zionist candidates failed, due to the terror exercised by the local authorities (mainly Poles) on behalf of assimilationist candidates (in Drogobych, for example, 20 Jews were murdered; see Nathan *Loewenstein). Despite the terror of 1911, Zionists continued the struggle against the assimilationists. The strife was further embittered when the Galician authorities canceled the licenses of 8,000 Jewish merchants of alcoholic beverages, who were consequently deprived of a livelihood (with their families, about 40,000 people were involved). The Zionists brought the merchants to Vienna to demonstrate, but the assimilationist Jewish deputies did nothing. Although the Austrian ministers promised their assistance, they failed to keep their word.

In the latter part of the 19th and the beginning of the 20th centuries, the Jewish labor movement of Galicia was organized. At first it was associated with the Polish *PPS, the Labor Zionist movement making its appearance later. The first convention of its various chapters took place in Cracow, in 1903. At the second convention, in 1904, the *Po'alei Zion party was founded. A number of Jewish organizations dissociated themselves from PPS and in 1906 established the *Jewish Social Democratic Party (ZPS). The PPS countered by establishing a "Jewish section," which existed until 1914. Some of its members then joined the ZPS.

At the outbreak of World War I tens of thousands of Jews fled to Hungary, Bohemia, and Vienna. During the Russian occupation of Galicia, the Jews who remained suffered greatly. Following the fall of the Hapsburg monarchy in November 1918, the Jews of Galicia were caught in the Polish-Ukrainian war. The central government of the Western Ukrainian Republic (Eastern Galicia, see *Ukraine) was prepared to grant the Jews full national autonomy, but its civil service and the military continued to oppress the Jews. On November 22 and 23, following the occupation of Lvov, the Poles conducted a series of pogroms in which 72 Jews were killed and 443 injured. By the summer of 1919 the armies of Poland had captured all of Galicia. The particular motifs which had developed among the Jews of Galicia continued to leave their mark on that community, even as it fused with the Jewry of Poland during the period between the two world wars. The major ideological currents – Ḥasidism, the Zionist movement, the many devotees of Polish and German culture, respectively, and those who had traditionally cooperated with the Poles – continued to be the forces which shaped the internal and external character of Polish Jewry from 1919 to 1939. The Zionist deputies from Galicia, headed by L. *Reich and O. *Thon, came to terms with the Polish government in a July 4, 1925, "compromise" agreement (see *Ugoda). S.Y. *Agnon, like many others, immortalized the cultural atmosphere of the Galician *shtetl in his works.

Jewish Population in Galicia, 1857–1910

Year	Total pop.	Catholics	Eastern Orthodox	Jews	Others
1857	4,632,864	2,072,633	2,077,112	448,971	34,148
1869	5,444,779	2,509,105	2,315,782	575,918	43,974
1880	6,018,907	2,706,977	2,578,408	686,596	46,926
1890	6,607,816	2,999,716	2,790,894	768,845	48,361
1900	7,315,939	3,345,780	3,108,972	811,183	50,004
1910	8,025,675	3,731,569	3,379,613	871,895	42,598

The Economic Structure of Galician Jewry, 1910

Occupation	Percentage	Number
Agriculture and forestry	10.7	93,471
Industry and crafts	24.6	214,184
Commerce, alcoholic beverages, and transportation	53.5	462,004
Liberal professions, civil service, and military	11.4	102,145

For the position of the Jews in eastern Galicia after World War II, see *Ukraine.

[Nathan Michael Gelber]

BIBLIOGRAPHY: M. Stoeger, *Darstellung der gesetzlichen Verfassung der galizischen Juden* (1833); J. Buzek, *Wpływ polityki rządu austryackiego w latach 1772–1778 na wzrost zaludnienia żydowskiego w Galicyi* (1903); F. Bujak, *Galicya*, 2 vols. (1908–10); S. Gruziński, *Materjañy do kwestji żdowskiej w Galicji* (1910); A.J. Brawer, *Galizien wie es an Oesterreich kam* (1910); idem, in: *Ha-Shilo'aḥ*, 23 (1910), 29–39, 147–54, 331–43, 427–34; idem, *Galiẓyah vi-Yhudeha* (1956); M. Balaban, *Dzieje Zydów Galicji i w Rzeczypospolitej Krakowskiej 1772–1868* (1910); idem, in: *Ha-Tekufah*, 14–15 (1923); M. Weissberg, in: MGWJ, 57 (1913), 513–26, 735–49; 71 (1927), 54–62, 100–9, 371–87; 72 (1928), 71–88, 184–201; I. Schiper, in: *Neue juedische Monatshefte*, 2 (1917/18), 223–33; J. Tenenbaum, *Żydowskie problemy gospodarcze w Galicji* (1918); idem, *Galitsye Mayn Alte Heym* (1952); N.M. Gelber, *Aus zwei Jahrhunderten* (1924); idem, *Szkice do historji Żydów Rzeczypospolitej Krakowskiej* (1924); idem, in: I. Halpern (ed.), *Beit Yisrael be-Polin*, 1 (1948); idem, in: EG, 4 (1956); F. Friedmann, *Die galizischen Juden im Kampfe um ihre Gleichbe rechtigung in den Jahren 1848–1868* (1929); G. Bader, *Medinah va-Ḥakhameha* (1934); idem, *Mayne Zikhroynes* (1953); S. An-Ski, *Ḥurban ha-Yehudim be-Polin, Galiẓyah u-Bukovinah*, 2 vols. (R. Mahler, *Der Kamf Tsvishn Haskole un Khasides in Galitsye…* (1942); idem, *Divrei Yemei Yisrael, Dorot Aḥaronim*, vol. 1, 2–4 (1954–56). **ADD. BIBLIOGRAPHY:** F. Bujak, *Rozwoj gospodarczy Galicji 1772–1914* (1917); H. Diamand, *Polozenie ekonomiczne Galicji przed wojna* (1915); F. Friedman, *Die Galizischen juden im kampfe um ihre Gleichberechtigung 1848–1868* (1929); I. Cohen and D. Sadan (eds.), *Pirkei Galiẓyah* (1957); S. Unger, *Poalei Zion be-Keisarut ha-Ostrit 1904–1914* (2001).

GALIL, UZIA (1925–), Israeli high-tech entrepreneur. Galil earned a B.Sc. from the Technion and an M.Sc.EE. degree from Purdue University. He began his high-tech career in R&D at Motorola in Chicago from 1953 to 1954 and in the Israeli Navy from 1954 until 1957. From 1957 to 1962 he served as the head of the electronics department at the Technion. From 1980 to 1990, Uzia Galil was chairman of the International Board of Governors of the Technion. In 1962 he founded Elron, a technology group specializing in defense electronics, communications, semiconductors, and medical imaging technologies, serving as its chairman and CEO until 1999. During this period he also acted as chairman and/or member of the board of directors of the publicly traded Elron affiliates – Elbit Ltd., a communications company, Elbit Systems Ltd., a defense electronics company, EMI Ltd. and Elscint Ltd., medical imaging companies, and the private companies in the Elron group. He continued to serve as a member of the boards of directors of Orbotech Ltd., Partner Communications Co. Ltd., and NetManage Inc., and as chairman of Zoran Corporation (all publicly traded). Subsequently he served as president and CEO of Uzia Initiatives and Management Ltd., a company he founded in 1999. In 2000 he founded the Galil center for telemedicine and medical information at the Technion, a joint venture with the Faculty of Medicine. Galil has been awarded an honorary doctorate in technical sciences by the Technion in recognition of his contribution to the development of science-based industries in Israel as well as honorary doctorates from the Weizmann Institute of Science, Ben-Gurion University, and Polytechnic University, New York. In 1997 he received the Israel Prize for his special contribution to Israeli society.

WEBSITE: www.uzia.co.il.

[Shaked Gilboa (2nd ed.)]

GALILEE (Heb. הַגָּלִיל, *Ha-Galil*), the northernmost region of Ereẓ Israel.

Name

The name Galilee is derived from the Hebrew *galil* which comes from the root גלל ("to roll"), and thus means a circle. It appears in the Bible in the combination *Gelil ha-Goyim* "Galilee of the nations" (Isa. 8:23), a formula repeated in I Maccabees 5:15. The town of Kedesh (see *Kadesh) is mentioned several times with the addition "in Galilee" (Josh. 20:7; 21:32; I Chron. 6:61); in I Kings 9:11 the 20 cities Solomon gave to *Hiram of Tyre (in the region of Cabul) are defined as being "in the land of Galilee." In the *Zeno papyri (259 B.C.E.) the name appears as Galila. The form Galilee as the name of the northernmost region of Ereẓ Israel west of the Jordan is firmly established in the writings of *Josephus, the New Testament, and talmudic literature.

History

In prehistoric times the eastern part of Galilee was settled by Neanderthal man in the Lower Paleolithic period: remains of human skeletons have been found in the *Arbel and 'Amūd valleys. With the establishment of urban civilization in the Early Canaanite period, cities were founded in the plains surrounding the Galilean mountain massif and in its northern plateau while the wooded core of the country was left unoccupied. Egyptian documents mention only the cities (apart from those in the Jordan Valley and the coastal plain) lying on the branch of the Via Maris (the road leading from Damascus to the sea) which crosses the southeastern corner of Lower Galilee: Shemesh-Adom, Adummim, Anaharath, Hannathon, and apparently cities in northern Galilee: Beth-Anath, Kanah, Meron, and probably Kedesh.

The armies of the Pharaohs and of the invading *Hyksos avoided the difficult mountain region as far as possible. Archaeological evidence indicates that the Israelite tribes exploited this situation by infiltrating into the forested hill country before attacking the Canaanite strongholds in the plains (see *Archaeology).

The victories of Joshua at the waters of Merom and of *Deborah at Mt. *Tabor ensured Israelite supremacy over the whole of Galilee. In biblical times Galilee was divided between four tribes: *Asher in the northwest, *Zebulun in the southwest, *Naphtali in most of the eastern half, and *Issachar in part of the southeast (see Twelve *Tribes: Book of *Joshua). By conquering the remaining Canaanite cities in the *Jezreel Valley, David annexed the whole of Galilee to his kingdom. Under *Solomon, Galilee was divided into three districts, each roughly corresponding to a tribal area: the ninth district included Zebulun and probably Asher, the eighth, Naphtali, and the tenth, Issachar. With the division of the monarchy Galilee became part of the northern kingdom of *Israel and was in the forefront of the struggle with Aram-Damascus (see *Aram-Damascus). In 732 B.C.E. *Tiglath-Pileser III, king of Assyria, conquered Galilee and turned it into the Assyrian province of Magiddu (*Megiddo). Some of the Israelite inhabitants were deported but the remaining remnant renewed its relations with Jerusalem in the time of Josiah who may have reunited Galilee with his kingdom (see *Ten Lost Tribes). Nothing is known of Galilee under the Babylonians and Persians; it was possibly administered from *Acre or Hazor since Megiddo had lost its importance by this time (see Israel; *History, Second Temple). In the Ptolemaic period some estates in Galilee were held by Greeks; it appears in the Zeno papyri as a supplier of wheat to Tyre. It was part of the eparchy of Samaria in Seleucid times (see *Seleucia); its administrative center was the royal fortress on Mt. Tabor (Itabyrion). According to I Maccabees 5:15 there were Jewish settlements in western Galilee in the confines of Acre-Ptolemais. These were evacuated by Simeon but others remained in eastern Galilee; *Bacchides, the Seleucid general, is reported to have attacked the Jews of Arbel on the Sea of Galilee. Galilee was incorporated into the Hasmonean kingdom by *Judah Aristobulus I (104 B.C.E.). It rapidly became completely Jewish, for only two years later at the beginning of the reign of Alexander *Yannai, its cities could be attacked on a Sabbath for an easy victory. After *Pompey's conquest (63 B.C.E.) Galilee was left to Judea; *Gabinius' attempt to cut it off from Jerusalem by establishing a separate council (*synedrion*) at *Sepphoris did not succeed. Galilee was then a province (*meris*), a division established by Alexander Yannai, containing the sub-districts of Sepphoris, Araba, Tarichaea, and Gischala in Upper Galilee. Under Hyrcanus II, *Herod was governor of Galilee for a time; when he became king, Galilee was one of the centers of opposition to his rule and it remained a *Zealot stronghold until the fall of Jerusalem. After Herod's death Galilee was inherited by Herod Antipas, who founded its second largest city – *Tiberias. From Herod *Antipas it passed to *Agrippa I and then to Roman *procurators. In the last years of Nero, Tiberias and its vicinity were granted to *Agrippa II. In 66 C.E. Galilee joined in the Jewish revolt against Rome; it was the home of *John of Giscala, one of the foremost Zealot leaders. The defense of the Galilee was in the hands of the historian Josephus who lost it to Vespasian in 67. The Romans took no measures against the Jews of Galilee, some of whom, especially those of Sepphoris and Tiberias, favored the Roman cause. Under Trajan Tiberias became an autonomous city; Hadrian turned Sepphoris into a Roman city called Diocaesarea but its population remained largely Jewish. Galilee did not take part in the *Bar Kokhba War (132–135; although historians dispute this point); what is certain is that after the expulsion of the Jews from Judea, Galilee was throughout the mishnaic and talmudic periods the stronghold of Judaism in Ereẓ Israel. The activities of *Jesus and the early Christian apostles had no effect on the Jewishness of Galilee. The national authority of the patriarchate was reconstituted there in the second century, and the *Sanhedrin continued to sit in various cities, settling later in Sepphoris and finally in Tiberias. The priestly families which had been dispersed from Judea settled in Galilee. The remains of a score of synagogues and of a central necropolis at *Bet She'arim are material evidence of the prosperity and vitality of Galilean Jewry from the second to the sixth centuries, and the completion of the Mishnah and the Palestinian Talmud, of its spiritual productivity. The establishment of Christianity as the official religion did not at first influence the Jewishness of Galilee even though the Church set up an ecclesiastical hierarchy there and built numerous churches in the sixth century. Galilee was the center of the Jewish revolts against Gallus Caesar (351) and the Byzantines (614). It fell to the Muslim Arabs in 635/6 and became part of the province of al-Urdunn (Jordan) with its capital in Tiberias. The Jewish villages continued diminishing but some existed until the time of the *Crusades. Under Crusader rule Galilee was formed into a principality held by the Norman Tancred. It was lost in 1187 after their disastrous defeat at the Horns of Hittin, but part of it was regained in 1198 and all of it in 1240 only to be lost again during the 1260s. Ruins of Crusader castles (at *Miʿilyā, Montfort, etc.) attest to their rule. Under the *Mamluks Galilee was part of the *mamlaka* ("province") of *Safed; under the Turks it was ruled by the semi-independent pashas of Acre. In the 16th century Safed became the center of Jewish kabbalism and Tiberias was resettled by Don Joseph *Nasi as the center of a proposed Jewish province.

[Michael Avi-Yonah]

In the second half of the 19th century, Galilee's population increased and, on the whole, progressed, thanks to an extended period of peace. The Jewish community, concentrated mainly in Safed, somewhat improved its standard of living, although it continued to be dependent on *ḥalukkah* (donations from the Diaspora). In 1856, Ludwig August *Frankl found 2,100 Jews in Safed, and 50 in *Peki'in, the only other Jewish community in Upper Galilee at that time. Until 1895, the number of Jews in Safed increased to 6,620, and in Peki'in to 96. Even before the arrival of settlers of the Ḥovevei Zion and Bilu movements, there were stirrings within the Safed community for a more productive way of life, and in 1878 a group formed to settle at Gei Oni, the forerunner of *Rosh Pinnah; later a second group which formed to settle in the Golan eventually established Benei Yehudah. Rosh Pinnah became the cornerstone of a Jewish settlement network in eastern Upper Galilee and on the rim of the *Ḥuleh Valley. In 1891, Russian Jews founded Ein Zeitim north of Safed. A second phase began in 1900 when the *Jewish Colonization Association (ICA) bought rather flat land with basalt soil in eastern Lower Galilee with the object of establishing "true" farming villages, i.e., based on grain crops, and *Ilaniyyah, *Kefar Tavor, *Jabneel, and other settlements were founded. More moshavot were added through private initiative, and a training farm was set up on *Jewish National Fund (JNF) land at *Kefar Ḥittim. The Galilean moshavot set the stage for the beginnings of the cooperative movement of Jewish laborers and of *Ha-Shomer ("Guardsmen's" Association). In the following decade, however, the Galilean moshavot and the Tiberias community stagnated, and those of Safed and Peki'in even decreased. As a result of World War I Safed's Jewish community was decimated, whereas Galilee's Arab rural society, based on a solid foundation of agriculture, emerged from the war unscathed and was even consolidated.

The Third, Fourth, and Fifth *aliyot*, which gave a powerful impulse to Jewish settlement in other regions, hardly touched Galilee, although all around it new Jewish areas were created, in the Jezreel Valley to the south in the 1920s, and in the Zebulun Valley to the southwest in the 1930s. The expansion of the *Stockade and Watchtower network during the 1936–39 Arab riots completed this outer ring, in the Acre Coastal Plain to the northwest, in the Bet Shean Valley to the southeast, and in the Ḥuleh Valley to the northeast. In Galilee proper, only the kibbutz Kefar ha-Ḥoresh was established in 1935 near Nazareth.

It was at the end of the decade that settlement spread into the hills near the Lebanese border in the northwest (*Ḥanitah, *Eilon, *Maẓẓuvah), while *PICA and the JNF, reacting to the British *White Paper of 1939, strengthened the "settlement bridge" in southeastern Lower Galilee connecting the *Jezreel and the *Kinnarot valleys (e.g., the settlements *Sharonah, *Ha-Zore'im, etc.). In the 1940s, several more outpost settlements were set up, some of them at particularly difficult and isolated sites (e.g., *Manara, *Yeḥi'am, *Misgav Am).

The largest part of Galilee, however, continued to be exclusively non-Jewish, causing the UN partition plan of 1947 to allocate to the proposed Arab state the bulk of the area, from the Lebanese border south to, and including, Nazareth and from the shore of the Acre Plain east to the vicinity of Safed; only a strip of eastern and southeastern Galilee was left to the Jewish state. In the War of Independence, the Jewish villages, many of them isolated, held their ground without exception. In battles before the State of Israel was proclaimed (May 14, 1948), new positions were gained and continuous fronts consolidated: the southeastern corner of Lower Galilee was cleared of enemy strongholds; Tiberias and Safed became unexpectedly all-Jewish towns when the Arabs left them; and when on May 12–13, 1948, the Acre Plain was occupied by Jewish forces, direct contact was renewed in western Upper Galilee with the Ḥanitah bloc and Yeḥi'am. In the ten days of fighting between the first and second truces ("Operation Dekel," July 9–18, 1948), western, southern, and more of southeastern Galilee were taken, Arab forces were dislodged from their positions, and *Sepphoris and Nazareth came into Israeli hands. The rest of Galilee, corresponding to the previous British Mandate borders, was brought under Israeli control in "Operation Ḥiram" (Oct. 29–31, 1948); this fact was endorsed in the 1949 Armistice Agreement with Lebanon, in which a strip of territory west of the Naphtali Ridge which Israel had occupied returned to Lebanon.

In contrast with the events in other parts of the country, the movement of Israeli forces in Galilee was followed by only a minor exodus of the Arab population; although a considerable part of the Muslims left, most of the Christians and almost all of the Druze remained. This caused a relative increase of the latter two communities in Galilee's total population, with the following pattern of ethnic distribution thus emerging: Druze inhabit villages in western Upper Galilee, between Acre and Mount Meron, and one village, al-Maghār, further southeast. Around Nazareth in southwestern and central Lower Galilee, there are mostly Greek Orthodox and Roman Catholic villages, but also a number of Muslim villages which remained intact. Two villages of the Greek Catholics, Miʿilyā and Fassūṭa, lie in western Upper Galilee, and one of the Maronite faith (Gush Ḥalav = Jish), near the Lebanese border further east. During and immediately after the War of Independence, 12 new kibbutzim were created, not only in the Acre Plain (Sa'ar, *Gesher ha-Ziv, *Kabri, etc.) but also in the hills near the Lebanese border (*Ga'aton, Yiftaḥ, *Sasa, Baram, etc.) and in Lower Galilee (*Lavi, *Ein-Dor, etc.). In the beginning of the 1950s, about 30 moshavim were added, many of them initially in the form of "work villages," the settlers earning their livelihood as hired workers in soil reclamation, afforestation, and other projects until a minimum of land became available for their own farms. This was intended to create more or less continuous chains of Jewish settlements across Galilee from west to east. In the same period many newcomers were absorbed in Tiberias and Safed, but the growth of both towns later slowed down. Two new urban centers were established in southern Galilee – *Migdal ha-Emek in 1952, and Upper Nazareth in 1957. In the northwest, *Ma'alot and *Shelomi were founded as nuclei of development towns, but their progress was far from satisfactory. The new moshavim in the hills also encountered difficulties, as their infrastructure of cultivable land and available water proved too narrow and the choice of farming branches was limited by local conditions.

The non-Jewish villages of Galilee, on the other hand, entered a phase of prosperity. Provided through government aid with access as well as internal roads, water installation, electricity, educational facilities, and municipal and social services, they modernized their farming methods and added new branches (e.g., deciduous fruit orchards) to the traditional ones (such as olives, tobacco, sheep, goats); many inhabitants worked in the cities as skilled or semi-skilled laborers, but kept their dwellings and holdings in the villages. Housing improved, and the built-up areas of the villages expanded, as most of them doubled or even tripled their population between 1948 and 1968. When surveys showed that Galilee's opportunities were still far from being fully used and that more settlers could be absorbed there, both urban and rural settlement was furthered. Upper Nazareth grew quickly in the 1960s, and the initial stagnation at Migdal ha-Emek was overcome by industrialization. In 1963 a Central Galilee development project was started by the Israeli government, the JNF, and the Jewish Agency settlement department. Within its framework, a new village bloc was established near the Lebanese border (Biranit, Shetulah, Netu'ah, Zarit) and development work was carried out in the Yodefat-Mount Ḥazon area. In 1964, the town of *Karmi'el was founded, which expanded mostly after 1967. In the 1980s a new plan to keep Galilee Jewish was launched, focusing on the establishment of small communities (Miẓpim, or Lookout Points) located on hills and mountains. Until 1982, 33 such Miẓpim were established. These new settlements are concentrated in two major areas – the Segev zone and Tefen zone. Inside the Tefen zone there is an industrial area founded by the industrialist Stef *Wertheimer. Many of the Galilee settlements earn their livelihoods from tourism, mainly renting out guest rooms.

The northern part of the Galilee area, mainly Kiryat Shmoneh and the rural settlements around it, suffered for years from bombardments by Palestinian organizations operating in Lebanon. These attacks led to Operation Peace for Galilee in 1982, a full-scale invasion of Lebanon culminating in the siege of Beirut and the expulsion of Arafat and the Palestinian terrorists under his command. The IDF fell back to a narrow buffer zone in 1986 and withdrew from Lebanon completely in 2000.

Northern Israel, comprising in addition to the Galilean hill regions areas in the Upper and Central Jordan Valley, in the Jezreel Valley, and in the Acre Plain, increased its population from 53,400 in the 1948 census to 1,111,500 in 2003 (with nearly half Arabs). In Galilee proper (i.e., the natural regions of eastern Upper and Lower Galilee, the Hazor Region, the Nazareth-Tir'an hills, and western Upper and Lower Galilee) the total population was around 400,000.

[Efraim Orni]

BIBLIOGRAPHY: Maisler, in: BJPES, 11 (1944), 39ff.; Alt, in: PJB, 33 (1937), 52ff.; idem, in: ZDPV, 52 (1929), 220ff.; S. Klein, *Ereẓ ha-Galil* (1946); Y. Aharoni, *Hitnaḥalut Shivtei Yisrael ba-Galil ha-Elyon* (1957); Avi-Yonah, Land, index; Abel, Geog, 2 (1938), passim; Aharoni, Land, passim; EM, 2 (1965), 506–7; R. Dafni, *Galilee* (1961).

GALILI (Berchenko), ISRAEL (1911–1986), Israeli politician and former *Haganah commander; member of the First and Third to Eighth Knessets. Born in Brailov, in the Ukraine, Galili was brought to Ereẓ Israel by his parents in 1914. He studied printing at an elementary school in Tel Aviv. In 1924 he was among the founders of the No'ar ha-Oved ve-ha-Lomed youth movement, and in 1930 one of the founders of kibbutz Na'an. Galili was active within the Youth Center in the *Histadrut, and in 1927 joined the *Haganah. In 1935 he became a member of its Central Command on behalf of the Histadrut. During World War II Galili played an active role in the preparation for a possible German invasion of Palestine. When the split took place in *Mapai in 1944, after Si'aḥ B broke away, he became one of the leaders of *Aḥdut ha-Avodah-Po'alei Zion. After the war Galili played an active role in the armed underground activities against the British Administration and was placed in charge of the Haganah's purchasing and arming department. On "Black Saturday" on June 29, 1946, he managed to evade arrest by the British. In the years 1946–48 he was chief of the Territorial Staff of the Haganah, in which capacity he participated in the preparation of the Israeli War of Independence. During the war one of his main tasks was arms acquisition. In the Provisional Government formed by Ben-Gurion in 1948 Galili was appointed deputy minister of defense, in which capacity he opposed the breakup of the *Palmaḥ as ordered by Ben-Gurion. In January 1948 Galili supported the union of Aḥdut ha-Avodah with *Mapam and was elected to the First Knesset in 1949 on the Mapam list. He was not elected to the Second Knesset, but in 1954 he supported the split of Aḥdut ha-Avodah-Po'alei Zion from Mapam, against the background of differences of opinion regarding the Soviet Union. He was reelected to the Third Knesset on the Aḥdut ha-Avodah-Po'alei Zion list. In the Third to Fifth Knessets he was a member of the Knesset Foreign Affairs and Defense Committee. In 1965 he supported the establishment of the first Alignment with Mapai, and in 1968 supported the establishment of the *Israel Labor Party. In the years 1966–77 he served in successive governments as minister without portfolio, except for a brief period after the Six-Day War when he served as minister of information. Galili was always a behind-the-scenes figure, acting as adviser to Prime Minister Golda Meir and Yitzhak *Rabin. Several months before the elections to the Eighth Knesset Galili prepared a policy proposal, known as the Galili Document, which outlined the Labor Party's policy in the occupied territories for the next four years. The document was considered relatively hawkish and was opposed by the Labor Party doves. The document advocated that Israel develop the economy, infrastructures, and social services for the Arab population in the West Bank and Gaza Strip, and economic ties between Israel and the territories; hold municipal elections in the territories (this was actually done in 1976); continue the open bridges policy initiated by Moshe *Dayan; enable the employment of Arabs from the territories in Israel while ensuring equal salary and employment conditions for them; build permanent housing for the refugees in the Gaza

Strip; acquire land for Jewish development and settlement in the territories; encourage Jewish settlement activities more or less within the parameters of the Allon Plan; and continue the development of Jewish Jerusalem. Galili was not chosen as a candidate on the Labor list in the elections to the Ninth Knesset, and gradually turned into one of the "party elders" and a mentor to former members of Aḥdut ha-Avodah. He encouraged Yigal *Allon to contend for the Labor Party leadership in 1980, and after Allon's death encouraged Yitzhak Rabin.

[Susan Hattis Rolef (2nd ed.)]

GALINSKI, HEINZ (1912–1992), leader of the Berlin Jewish community after World War II. Born in West Prussian Marienburg, Galinski worked in a textile retail store in Rathenow before he moved to Berlin on the eve of World War II. After being taken for forced labor, he was deported to Auschwitz in February 1943. His father had already been killed in Berlin before the deportation; his mother and his wife were murdered in Auschwitz. Galinski was liberated by British troops in Bergen-Belsen on April 15, 1945.

Galinski was involved in preparing the first restitution laws and in rebuilding the Berlin Jewish community. In 1947, he married again; a daughter was born two years later. In 1949, he was elected president of the Berlin Jewish community, an office he held until his death in 1992. Jewish life in Berlin was clearly shaped by his activities. In contrast to his predecessors and some other German-Jewish politicians, Galinski saw German-Jewish life after the Holocaust not as the closing chapter of a long German-Jewish history but rather as a period for reconstructing the future. During his 43 years in office, the Berlin Jewish community built a new community center (inaugurated in 1959) and an elementary school and opened its doors to Jewish immigrants, mainly from the Soviet Union. In 1971, he signed a treaty with the Berlin city government which defined the position of the Jews.

From 1988 until his death, Galinski served as president of the Zentralrat der Juden in Deutschland, an office he took over from Werner *Nachmann, who had died amidst allegations of fraud and embezzlement. It was Galinski's prime task to clear the name of German Jewry's central institution. Galinski had been Nachmann's political rival for decades. While Nachmann kept up close contacts with conservative politicians and represented a more lenient position toward dealing with the Nazi past, the memory of the Holocaust and the prosecution of Nazi crimes always played a central role in Galinski's activities. Among the many honors he received were an honorary doctorate from Bar-Ilan University (1983) and the title of honorary citizen of Berlin (1987).

BIBLIOGRAPHY: A. Nachama, "Der Mann in der Fasanenstrasse," in: A. Nachama and J.H. Schoeps (eds.), *Aufbau nach dem Untergang* (1992); K. Schuetz, *Heinz Galinski* (2004).

[Michael Brenner (2nd ed.)]

GALIPAPA, ELIJAH MEVORAKH (d. 1740), Turkish rabbi. Galipapa was born in Sofia and went to Jerusalem in 1702. He fled from there after being imprisoned for his inability to pay the heavy taxation imposed on him, and reached Rhodes where, in 1704, he became deputy to the chief rabbi, Elijah ha-Kohen ibn Ardut. Galipapa is the author of *Yedei Eliyahu* (Constantinople, 1728) in two parts: (1) the *takkanot* (ordinances) instituted by the prophets; (2) novellae. Many more of his novellae remain unpublished. His tombstone still stands in Rhodes.

BIBLIOGRAPHY: Azulai, 1 (1852), 21 no. 155; 2 (1852), 59 no. 7; Fuenn, Keneset, 104; Frumkin-Rivlin, 2 (1928), 158f.; Rosanes, Togarmah, 4 (1935), 240, 348–9.

[Simon Marcus]

GALIPAPA, ḤAYYIM BEN ABRAHAM (1310–1380), Spanish talmudist. Galipapa was born in Monzon, Aragon. He served as rabbi of Huesca and subsequently of Pamplona. The following works by him are known: *Emek Refa'im*, a commentary to the tractate *Semaḥot* which includes a description of the *Black Death and the persecutions of the Jews which came in its train in Catalonia and Provence during the years 1347–50 – extracts from it are given by *Joseph ha-Kohen in his *Emek ha-Bakha* and *Divrei ha-Yamim le-Malkhei Ẓarefat*; *Iggeret ha-Ge'ullah*, mentioned by Joseph Albo in his *Ikkarim* (4:42); a commentary on the *Seder Avodah* (for the Day of Atonement) of Joseph b. Isaac ibn Avitur, extracts from which are given in the *Kovez Ma'asei Yedei Ge'onim Kadmonim* (1856; pt. 2, 120–2). There is also extant a letter by *Isaac b. Sheshet (Resp. Ribash 394) to Galipapa from which the latter's views on *halakhah* can be seen. Galipapa's place in the Spanish Judaism of his time was determined by the great daring he displayed both in thought and in *halakhah*. According to Joseph Albo (loc. cit.), Galipapa maintained that all Isaiah's prophecies of deliverance had reference to the Second Temple and Daniel's vision in chapter 7 to the Hasmoneans. It is evident that in his work Galipapa intended to abolish belief in the coming of the Messiah or at least to deny that there was a basis for such belief in the Bible. Galipapa also showed an exceptional tendency toward leniency in *halakhah*. He maintained that there was no need to conceal permissive laws out of fear that the permission would cause the ignorant to fall into error with regard to things forbidden "for they are all wise and with understanding, knowing the Torah, expert in the minutiae of the precepts, and as full of precepts as is the pomegranate of seeds" (Isaac b. Sheshet, loc. cit.). In opposition to the opinions of all authorities before him he ruled that combing the hair on the Sabbath is not forbidden. To find a basis for this permissiveness Galipapa was compelled arbitrarily to amend the text of the Talmud, thus aggravating still more the opposition to him.

BIBLIOGRAPHY: Michael, Or, no. 866; Graetz-Rabbinowitz, 5 (1897), 309–11; Weiss, Dor, 5 (1904[4]), 147f.; I.F. Baer, *Toledot ha-Yehudim bi-Sefarad ha-Noẓerit* (1959[2]), 271.

[Jacob S. Levinger]

GALIPAPA, MAIMON (14th–15th century?), Spanish satirical poet. Galipapa, called "En" (= Don) Maimon Galipapa, was possibly identical with the Galipapa mentioned in a document of 1353 from Valencia. He is the author of *Ma'amarei ha-Rofe'im*, a parody on the *Aphorisms* of Hippocrates, a medical work highly popular in the Middle Ages, and *Neder Almanah*, a satire about a widow who quickly forgets her late husband. Presumably he also wrote the anonymous humorous pamphlet *Midyenei Ishah* ("Contentions of a Wife") which appeared together with *Ma'amarei ha-Rofe'im* in Ferrara in 1551.

BIBLIOGRAPHY: I. Davidson, *Shalosh Halaẓot… Meyuḥasot le-R. Yosef Zabara* (1904); J. Zabara, *Sefer Sha'ashu'im*, ed. by I. Davidson (1914²), xcix–ci, 73; Davidson, Oẓar, 4 (1933), 433; H. Friedenwald, *Jews and Medicine*, 1 (1944), 69–83; Schirmann, Sefarad, 2 (1956), 547–54.

[Jefim (Hayyim) Schirmann]

GALLEGO, JOSEPH SHALOM (d. 1624), Hebrew poet. Originating in Salonika, Gallego was for 14 years *ḥazzan* in Amsterdam. He later migrated to Ereẓ Israel. His "*Imrei No'am*" (Amsterdam, 1628) is a collection of devotional poems for the festivals, fast days, weddings, and circumcisions. The Spanish songs according to whose tune they were to be sung are generally indicated. Some of the poems are by Gallego; other poems of his are included in the collection *Kol Tefillah ve-Kol Zimrah* by David *Franco-Mendes (Ms.). He also translated into Spanish the ethical writings of *Jonah Gerondi (*Sendroe* [Sendero] *de Vidas*, Amsterdam, n.d. and 1640²).

BIBLIOGRAPHY: Dukes, in: *Litteraturblatt des Orients*, 5 (1844), 440–1; 6 (1845), 146; Steinschneider, Cat Bod, 485 no. 3216; I.S. da Silva Rosa, *Geschiedenis der portugeesche Joden te Amsterdam* (1925), 8, 26; Davidson, Oẓar, 4 (1933), 408, s.v. *Yosef Shalom Galliano.*

[Jefim (Hayyim) Schirmann]

GALLICO (or **Gallichi**), Italian family of French origin. The family first lived in Rome where it was known from the 14th century. In 1323, a "Gallichi" (which may however imply "French") synagogue is mentioned there. Later the Gallico family spread to other Italian towns. MALACHI (Angelo) GALLICO was physician and rabbi in Cori, a village of Rome, in 1565 when the community decided to accept the invitation of Joseph *Nasi and move en masse to Tiberias. SAMUEL GALLICO, rabbi and kabbalist, published a summary of Moses *Cordovero's *Pardes Rimmonim*, under the title of *Asis Rimmonim* (Venice, 1601). In the 16th, 17th, and 18th centuries several other rabbis and scholars belonging to this family are mentioned in Mantua, Modena, and Siena. Another member of the family was the Hebrew scholar and poet Abraham b. Hananiah dei Gallichi *Jagel.

BIBLIOGRAPHY: A. Milano, *Ghetto di Roma…* (1964), index; Mortara, Indice; C. Roth, *The House of Nasi: Duke of Naxos* (1948), 125–30; D. Kaufmann, in: JQR, 2 (1889/90), 291–7, 305–10.

[Attilio Milano]

GALLICO, ELISHA BEN GABRIEL (c. 1583), talmudic scholar and kabbalist in Safed. Gallico was a pupil of Joseph *Caro and a member of the latter's *bet din*. After the death of Caro, he was a member of Moses *Trani's *bet din*. Gallico was the teacher of Samuel *Uceda. Gallico's signature appears – once together with the other scholars of Safed – on several responsa (in Caro's *Avkat Rokhel*, etc.). After Caro's death, according to his instructions, Gallico banned Azariah dei *Rossi's *Me'or Einayim*. The collection of Gallico's responsa has been lost; however several of them are quoted both in the work *Keneset ha-Gedolah* and in the responsa *Ba'ei Ḥayyei* by Ḥayyim *Benvenisti. Gallico wrote homiletic and kabbalistic commentaries on all the five scrolls. The commentaries on Ecclesiastes (Venice 1578), Esther (Venice 1583), and the Song of Songs (Venice 1587) have been published. Toward the end of his life he headed a yeshivah in Safed.

BIBLIOGRAPHY: L. Zunz, in: *Kerem Ḥemed*, 5 (1841), 141; Michael, Or, no. 474; D. Tamar, in: *Sefunot*, 7 (1963), 173; idem, in: KS, 33 (1958), 378.

[David Tamar]

°GALLING, KURT (1900–1987), German Lutheran biblical scholar. He was professor at Halle from 1928 to 1945, at Mainz from 1946 to 1954, from 1955 at Goettingen, and from 1962 at Tuebingen. A student of Hugo Gressmann, Galling was a versatile and prolific scholar and a pioneer in bringing precision into biblical archaeology, especially through his *Biblisches Reallexikon*. Galling published works and articles on archaeology and biblical history, theology, and exegesis, including *Der Altar in den Kulturen des Alten Orients* (1925), *Die Erwaehlungstraditionen Israels* (1928), *Biblisches Reallexikon* (1937), *Der Prediger Salomo* (1940, 1964²), *Das Bild vom Menschen in biblischer Sicht* (1947), *Die Buecher der Chronik, Esra, Nehemia* (1954), and *Studien zur Geschichte Israels im persischen Zeitalter* (1964). From 1957 to 1962 Galling edited the third edition of *Die Religion in Geschichte und Gegenwart*, to which he contributed scores of articles in various fields.

BIBLIOGRAPHY: RGG³, Registerband (1965), 69–70; *Theologische Literaturzeitung*, 85 (1960), 153–8, incl. extensive bibl. **ADD. BIBLIOGRAPHY:** T. Thompson, in: DBI, 1:430.

GALLIPOLI, port in European Turkey, on the S. coast of the Gallipoli peninsula. Benjamin of Tudela, the 12th-century traveler, found 200 Jews in Gallipoli; they are also mentioned during the reign of Michael VIII Palaeologus in 1261. In the Byzantine period there were a few cases of conversion in the 13th century. In 1354 Gallipoli came under Ottoman rule. Mehmed the Second transferred, after 1453, many Jews from Gallipoli to Istanbul. They founded a separate congregation, one of the "Sürgün" congregations in Istanbul. But in the 16th century there were only three or four members in this congregation and at the beginning of the 17th century it ceased to exist. Jews are registered in the census of 1488/1489 of Gallipoli. Jews in Gallipoli served as *sarrafs* (bankers), and in the 15th century they paid for the privilege of a license to work as a group in this profession. There were also Jews in Gallipoli who owned real estate. It seems that a group of Romaniots returned to Gallipoli before 1492, but they remained with a status of "Sürgün" and paid their taxes in Istanbul. The number of Jews increased at the end of the 15th century, when the Romaniot Jews were joined by refugees from Spain and Portugal. In the census of the year 1519, 15 Jewish families and two bachelors were registered along with three merchant Jews from Istanbul who were staying in the city. In 1520–35, 23 Jewish families lived in the city, representing 0.3% of the general population. There were 5,001 Muslim and 3,901 Christian inhabitants. Between the years 1547 and 1557 a first firman for the Sephardim and Romaniots was enacted. It exempted the Romaniots from part of the Ottoman taxes and community taxes. The Sephardim were considered wealthy. At the same time new orders were issued which related to the economic rivalry between the Sephardim and Ashkenazim in the community. But in 1577 the Sephardim complained about economic hardship and their inability to pay the Ottoman taxes. New community regulations from the middle of the 16th century tried to prevent the transfer of Jewish real estate to the Gentiles and the entry of Gentiles into the Jewish quarter. In that century Rabbis Judah Ibn Sanghi and Ishai Morenu were active in the community. In 1600–01, 30 Jewish families lived in the city (1.72% of the population), all in the Jewish quarter. Local Jews were the tax farmers in the city during the 17th century, but in 1648 the "emin" of the city threw the Jews out of this position.

The emissaries Rabbi Moses ha-Levi and Joseph ha-Cohen visited the community between 1668 and 1684, and the emissary Ḥayyim Ya'akov visited it in 1670. The traveler Samuel ben David visited in 1641–42 and wrote that there were two synagogues in the city, but it seems that the community was united under the leadership of one rabbi. In 1656 the local Jews ransomed an Ashkenazi woman from Eastern Europe. In 1666 the pseudo-messiah *Shabbetai Ẓevi was confined to the fortress of Abydos (called by the Jews *Migdal Oz*, "Tower of Strength") in the vicinity of Gallipoli; his prison became a center of Shabbateanism. Abraham *Cardozo visited the community in 1682 and was boycotted by the local Jews..

The majority of Jews were peddlers and merchants, but there were also wine manufacturers who sent their products to Istanbul. Jews from Gallipoli traveled for their businesses especially to Egypt, Istanbul, Bursa, Edirne, Salonica, and Rhodes. Jews from Gallipoli founded the community of Çanakkale. The famous rabbi of the community was Meir di *Boton (born in Salonica, 1575), who wrote a book of responsa. He served the community many years and died in Gallipoli in 1649. The rabbis of the city during the 17th century were Simeon Ibn Haviv (died 1712), Ishai Almoli (served as the community rabbi c. 1665–90), and Raphael Ibn Haviv. Other rabbis and scholars in the 17th century were Eliezer ha-Cohen, Joseph Sasson (b. 1570), and Nathan Gota. The *av bet din* of the community in the middle of the 19th century before his departure to Istanbul was Raphael Jacob ha-Levi.

During the 19th century the Jewish community prospered. Among the Jews were merchants, artisans, and civil servants. The rabbi of the city was Raphael Ḥayyim Binyamin Peretz, who was earlier a *dayyan* in Istanbul and came to Gallipoli after 1878. He wrote that the community of Gallipoli was small and had to adopt the religious regulations of the Istanbul community in those special cases in which the wealthy leaders of Gallipoli did not know how to decide. Peretz wrote the well-known halakhic work *Zokhreno le-Ḥayyim* (3 vols, Salonica, 1867–72). Another rabbi of the community was Jacob Ibn Haviv (d. 1863). At the end of the 19th century Rabbi David Pardo (b. Istanbul, 1838) served there for seven years. The Jews of Gallipoli had many commercial and economic connections with the Gentiles. The majority spoke and wrote Ladino.

In 1912 there were 2,500 Jews in Gallipoli. The earthquake in the same year destroyed the Jewish quarter with the two synagogues which had been active from the 19th century onwards, but no Jews were killed. During the Balkan Wars (1912–13) refugees, including Jews, streamed into Gallipoli. The Va'ad ha-Hazzalah ("Rescue Committee"), founded then, aided the refugees, as well as Jewish soldiers from Syria and Iraq. In 1915 the Zion Mule Corps, as part of the British Army, fought the Turks on the Gallipoli peninsula (see *Jewish Legion). Until c. 1920 there lived in the city 600 Jewish families with three synagogues. From 1933 all religious and administrative affairs of the Gallipoli community were subordinated to the district rabbinate of *Çanakkale. As a result of emigration to Istanbul and the United States between the two world wars and subsequently to Israel, the number of Jews in Gallipoli decreased. Two of the three synagogues of the community were burned during World War II. In 1948 there were about 400 Jews in Gallipoli, and in 1951 about 200. By 1970 the few remaining families in Gallipoli were mainly engaged in commerce. In 1977 the Jews of the city numbered only 22 persons, of whom four were youngsters. Of the breadwinners six were merchants. In August 1977 no Jew remained in the city after the immigration of local Jews to Istanbul and Israel. The Jewish cemetery contains 835 tombstones, of which the oldest is from 1628 and the latest is from 1986.

BIBLIOGRAPHY: Angel, in: *Almanakh Izraelit* (1923), 109–11 (Ladino); Rosanes, Togarmah, 1 (1930²), 4; 3 (1938²), 127–8; Scholem, Shabbetai Ẓevi, index; Y.M. Toledano, *Sarid u-Palit*, 40–4; A. Ya'ari, *Masot Ereẓ Yisrael* (1976), 227; N. Todorov, *The Balkan City, 1400–1900* (1983), 52; J. Haker, in: *Zion*, 55 (1990), 71; M.A. Epstein, *The Ottoman Jewish Communities and their Role in the Fifteenth and Sixteenth Centuries* (1980), 78, 112–13; S. Tuval, in: *Pe'amim*, 12 (1982), 134–35; S. Bowman, *The Jews of Byzantium, 1204–1453* (1985), 61, 76 n., 116; A. Shmuelevitz, *The Jews of the Ottoman Empire in the Late Fifteenth and the Sixteenth Centuries* (1984), 133; L. Bornstein-Makovetsky, *Pinkas Bet ha-Din be-Kushta – Pinkas Bet Din Issur ve-Heter, 1710–1903* (1999), 42–43.

[Leah Bornstein-Makovetsky (2nd ed.)]

GALON (Heb. גָּלְאוֹן), kibbutz in southern Israel, northeast of *Kiryat Gat, affiliated with Kibbutz Arẓi ha-Shomer ha-Ẓa'ir. It was founded on the night of Oct. 6, 1946, as one of 11 settlements established simultaneously in the Negev. The founding members hailed from Poland, where a number of them lived in ghettos or were partisans fighting the Nazis. In the *War of Independence (1948), Galon served as a vantage point for Israeli columns in dislodging Arab forces from the Bet Guvrin and southern foothills area. In 1968 it had a population of 350 inhabitants, rising slightly to 385 in the mid-1990s and dropping to 287 in 2002. Its farming was based on field crops, flowers, avocado plantations, citrus groves, dairy cattle, poultry, and ostriches. The kibbutz owned a factory producing fans for industry and agriculture and motors for air-conditioners and ran a guesthouse and facilities for hosting seminars. Its name, meaning "Monument to Strength," commemorates fallen ghetto fighters.

WEBSITE: www.galon.org.il.

[Efraim Orni / Shaked Gilboa (2nd ed.)]

GALSKÝ, DESIDER (1921–1990), Slovak publicist and journalist, born in Michalovce, Slovakia, lived in Prague. Galský took part in the Slovak National Uprising against the Nazis and was imprisoned. After the war, he worked for two decades as an editor in publishing houses. He served as chairman of the Council of Jewish Religious Communities in Czechoslovakia (1981–86) and was dismissed by the Communist regime. He assumed the position again after the Velvet Revolution in 1989. He was killed in a car accident in 1990. A master of non-fiction, Galský wrote dozens of books on such topics as M. Bormann, F. Lesseps, and world discoveries, but not any Jewish-related subjects.

[Milos Pojar (2nd ed.)]

GALUT (Golah) (Heb. גָּלוּת, גּוֹלָה), exile.

The Concept

The Hebrew term *galut* expresses the Jewish conception of the condition and feelings of a nation uprooted from its homeland and subject to alien rule. The term is essentially applied to the history and the historical consciousness of the Jewish people from the destruction of the Second Temple to the creation of the State of Israel. The residence of a great number of members of a nation, even the majority, outside their homeland is not definable as *galut* so long as the homeland remains in that nation's possession.

Only the loss of a political-ethnic center and the feeling of uprootedness turns Diaspora (Dispersion) into *galut* (Exile). The feeling of exile does not always necessarily accompany the condition of exile. It is unique to the history of the Jewish people that this feeling has powerfully colored the emotions of the individual as well as the national consciousness. The sense of exile was expressed by the feeling of alienation in the countries of Diaspora, the yearning for the national and political past, and persistent questioning of the causes, meaning, and purpose of the exile. Jewish mystics perceived a defect in the Divine Order which they connected with alienation in this world – "the exile of the Divine Presence."

The Diaspora Pattern

The process of Jewish dispersion in various countries during different periods was due to the combination of national catastrophes, military defeats, destructions, persecutions, and expulsions, as well as to normal social and economic processes – migration to new places of settlement and transition to new means of livelihood. The expression "Egyptian Exile" for the period before the Exodus is merely a homiletic conception of later date; but there is no doubt that Jewish dispersion had already begun in a normal way a long time before the concept of exile developed. The conquests of the Arabs between 632 and 719 changed the pattern of the Diaspora by uniting large parts of the Jewry of the Roman Empire with that of the Persian Kingdom. The Muslim armies extirpated the Jews from the Arabian peninsula, with the exception of those in Yemen and Wadi al-Qara, but created favorable conditions of development for the exiles in the remainder of the lands of Islam. In the Christian world, this period is marked by the progress of the Jewish dispersion in Gaul and later in Germany and Britain. From the 11th century, the Jewry of the West (see *Germany) managed to maintain itself under increasingly difficult conditions and even spread to central Germany. The changes in the territorial supremacies of Christianity and Islam as a result of the Crusades and the Reconquest in Spain, as well as the *expulsions in the Christian countries, brought changes in the configuration of the Jewish Diaspora from one period to another.

By processes of both expulsion and attraction, the Jews penetrated the expanses of Poland-Lithuania during the 15th century. The migration eastward was halted by the total prohibition imposed on the admission of Jews by the grand duchy of Moscow (see *Russia). After 1497 there were no professing Jews (except for the underground of forced converts – **anusim*) left in all of the lands bordering the Atlantic, including England. During the 17th century, however, the Jews returned and penetrated to the Netherlands and England. The Jewish population in the Ottoman Empire had increased in numbers after the Spanish Expulsion. The largest Jewish concentrations during the 16th to 18th centuries were to be found in the Ottoman Empire and the kingdom of Poland-Lithuania. The persecutions of 1648–49 (see Bogdan *Chmielnicki) started off the migration of Jews in Eastern Europe toward the West, a process which continued and intensified throughout the modern era.

At the close of the 18th century, the partitions of Poland as well as the French Revolution led to a Jewish expansion toward the western provinces of Russia, the northeastern provinces of Austria, the Kingdom of Prussia, and the French territories. Economic, social, cultural, and political developments made Ashkenazi European Jewry the most important in the Diaspora, both numerically and in dynamism, throughout the 19th century and the first 30 years of the 20th. As formerly, liberalist or restrictive trends in this period also determined the pattern of Jewish dispersion in the world. It was only in 1917 that the revolution in Russia abolished the *Pale of Settlement and removed the last barriers to the settlement of Jews throughout the territory of the great Eurasian power.

In America individual Sephardi Jews had already begun to arrive during the 16th century. However, the emigration of considerable groups of Jews there was only to begin during the mid-19th century when many left Germany; the transfer of masses of Jews from Eastern Europe to the new world, especially the United States, only began during the last quarter of the 19th century. The flow of mass imigration to the United States and later also to Canada and the South American countries, coupled with the impetus of Zionism and trends of modern nationalism, have contributed to the shift to new centers of gravity. The catastrophe of the persecutions in Germany from 1933, the conquests of the Nazis until 1939, and the decimation of European Jewry in the Holocaust from 1939 until 1945, created a situation in the 1970s such that the numerical majority in the Jewish Diaspora was to be found on the American continent, while Ereẓ Israel had the third largest Jewish concentration in the world (Soviet Russia was the second). In the early 21st century, after the collapse of the Soviet Union and the exodus of over one million Jews, the largest Diaspora communities were the United States and France. In Ereẓ Israel, the independent Jewish politico-national center has been revived. As in the Second Temple era, through the State of Israel, the Jewish nation has regained the basic pattern of a Diaspora with a state as its center (see *Diaspora).

Second Temple and Mishnah Period

It can be assumed that the severe persecutions in the days of Antiochus Epiphanes and the success of the ensuing rebellion contributed to the Jews' feeling of being out of place in the Diaspora and their yearning for Judea. Despite this, the growth of the Diaspora was more pronounced in the hellenistic kingdoms and in the Roman Empire. Prophecies and poems of pietists gave expression to the tragedy of the *galut* combined with the feeling of the inevitability and continuity of the Diaspora. In the second half of the second century B.C.E. the sibyls explain to their nation, "it is thy fate to leave thine holy soil" (Or. Sibyll. 3:267), a fate described as encompassing the whole world and causing hatred toward those who are dispersed because of their way of life (*ibid.* 3:271–2). In the second half of the first century it was stated that, "among every nation are the dispersed of Israel according to the word of God" (Ps. of Sol. 9:2); the conquests of Pompey were also seen as a cause of the *galut* (*ibid.* 17:13–14, 18). Even prior to the destruction of the Temple were sensed the dangers which stemmed from the general dispersion, as foretold in the biblical warnings (Test. Patr., Ash. 7:2–7). On the other hand there were groups who expressed the feelings of the people in their own cultural terms and wrote favorably of the Diaspora and their neighbors, tending to regard the dispersion as a normal and even desirable situation (Philo, *De Legatione ad Gaium*, 281; Jos., Ant., 4:115–6).

After the destruction of the Temple the question of the *galut* as existence under foreign rule without a Temple and without a spiritual center was discussed. In the spirit and the style of the Bible, it was said that "behold we are yet this day in captivity, where Thou hast scattered us, for a reproach and a curse and a punishment" (I Bar. 3:8); but thought was directed mainly to the possibility of existing in a land of gentiles and under their rule (*ibid.* 1:12, 4:6). The question of the meaning and the justification of the exile begins to be asked in all earnestness: the evil nations dwell in prosperity and the chosen people suffer; the author of IV Ezra (3:32–34; 6:59) argues with his Creator, asking: "Have the deeds of Babylon been better than those of Zion? Has any other nation known Thee besides Zion?… If the world has indeed been created for our sakes, why do we not enter into possession of our world? – How long shall this endure?" He is bitter about the fact of "the reproach of the nations" and the profaning of God's name which occurs in the *galut* (*ibid.* 4:23–25), but he lays no stress on the physical suffering entailed. Accepting neither the cosmic explanation of the exile, nor the mysteriousness of the ways of the Lord, nor the world to come, which nullify the valuation of the events in this world (*ibid.* 4:9–10), he seeks to explain the exile as a road of suffering which must be traveled in order to reach the good (*ibid.* 7:3–16). He is comforted in the exile by the vision of the lion – the Messiah – who will destroy the eagle – Rome (*ibid.* ch. 12).

The author of II Baruch (10:9–16) almost despairs of all life, from the survival of the people to cultivating the land, a mood which is also found in the "ascetics who multiplied" (BB 60b) after the destruction of the Temple. The essence of the tragedy of the exile seems to him, too, to be a diminution of the honor of God in the eyes of the gentiles and the degradation of the Jewish people (II Bar. 67:2–8). The deep spiritual shock which followed in the wake of the dispersion is expressed in this book: there were Jews who despaired of the possibility of spiritual leadership of the people after the destruction of the Temple and the cessation of the sacrifices and the priesthood (*ibid.* 77:13–14). In the spirit of Jabneh and from the power of the Torah, which exists even in the *galut*, the author answers their despondency: "Shepherds and lamps and fountains come from the law…if therefore ye have respect to ponder on the law and are intent upon wisdom the spiritual leadership will not be lacking" (*ibid.* 77:15–16).

Thus the problems of the *galut*, its meaning, and its essence were considered in great depth and with considerable apprehension during the first two generations after the destruction of the Temple. It is true that the ideas voiced in the Apocrypha were not heard by the people in general and their influence was not noticeable, but they reflect a feeling and emotional state which are similar to those expressed in the Mishnah, the Talmud, and the Midrashim.

The thinking of the *tannaim* and *amoraim* on the *galut* and its meaning is extensive and varied, developing in the light of the changes which took place from the days of the Second Temple until about the fifth century C.E. In general the patterns of thought and the imagery of the Bible prevail, together with those of many apocryphal works. However, they express their feelings with greater and more penetrating detail, arising from the depths of their degradation and the suffering occasioned by the rise of Christianity, when they passed from subjugation to alien pagans to subjugation to the rule of a Jewish heresy.

Apprehension of the pain of the destruction was so severe that "the ascetics in Israel who refused to eat meat and to drink wine increased"; this recourse to complete abstinence, whose intention was self-annihilation of the nation ("it is fitting that we should decree upon ourselves not to marry nor beget children") was not accepted, and the moderate path of limited mourning and remembering the destruction of the Temple was followed instead (BB 60b). Yet from the beginning the *galut* was a phenomenon which demanded an explanation: even the gentiles asked: "And His people, what did they do to Him that He exiled them from their land?" (ARN[2] 1, 4). The sages could not be satisfied with a general answer about the sins of the people, and they gave their opinion about the specific causes of the destruction of the Second Temple. Unlike the first exile, which resulted from idol worship, incest, and the shedding of innocent blood, the second destruction was caused by baseless hatred and the love of money (Yoma 9b). Alongside these realistic types of explanation, there is a widespread tendency to connect the *galut* with the past and to find in it links for the future. Abraham had to decide whether to choose for his children either "Gehinnom or foreign kings," and some say that Abraham chose Gehinnom for himself and God chose the foreign kings for him (Gen. R. 44:21). Even the ram struggling among the thorns was a symbol for Abraham that "thy children will be trapped by iniquities and be entangled by troubles … and by foreign kings" (TJ, Ta'an. 2:4, 65d; Gen. R. 56:9; Mid. Ḥag. to Gen. 22:13). When the tribes in the desert "wept without cause," "from that hour it was determined that the Temple would be destroyed in order that Israel would be exiled among the nations" and there would then be a reason for their weeping (Num. R. 16:20; Ta'an. 29a). R. Abbahu, at the end of the third century, compares the expulsions of the people and their banishment as punishment for violating the covenant with the expulsion and banishment of Adam from the Garden of Eden after he had transgressed the commandment of the Lord (PdRK 119b). The exile from "country to country" was considered one of the ten decrees proclaimed against Adam (ARN[2] 42, 116). The sages give varied interpretations to the dispersion and its temporary nature, regarding as a specially severe decree the fact that the Jews were not concentrated in one place, but scattered among the nations "as a man scatters grain with a winnowing shovel and not one grain sticks to another" (Sifra 6:6). Everywhere the Jews are only "temporary" (i.e., wanderers) and the "dwellers" (the permanent population) are the children of Esau (Deut. R. 1, 22). The suffering of the exile is equal to all other suffering combined (Sif. Deut. 43); it is "like death and the abyss" (Mid. Ps. to 71:4). In the *galut* Israel is a mendicant (*ibid.* to 9:15), deprived of its pride, which has been given to the gentiles (Ḥag. 5b). There is no way for the exiled nation to defend itself since "Israel is among the 70 mighty nations; what can [Israel] do?" (PR 9:32a).

The very soul of the Jew is affected in the *galut*, which renders him "unclean with iniquities" (Song R. 8:14). Nor is the individual soul alone affected: the *galut* detracts from the completeness of the Kingdom of Heaven (Mid. Ps. to 97:1). The *Shekhinah* "moans like a dove" and the "Holy One blessed be He roars like a lion" over the destruction of the Temple and over the children of Israel … "Whom I have exiled among the nations" (Ber. 3a; cf. Ḥag. 5b). From the time of R. Akiva it became accepted belief that "in every place where Israel was exiled the *Shekhinah* was exiled with them" (Mekh., Pisḥa 14; Meg. 29a; TJ, Ta'an. 1:1, 64a; etc.). This idea connected the exile of Israel with the fate of the world as a whole and became a source of encouragement and faith.

Despite the feeling of suffering and the oppression of the exile, the rabbis at all times firmly believed that the *galut* would not mean total destruction. God had made the nations of the world swear that "they would not subjugate Israel overmuch"; the great sufferings in the *galut* constituted a violation of this oath, and this would hasten the advent of the Messiah (Ket. 111a; Song R. 2:7).

The rabbis saw a cause for satisfaction even in the negative aspects of the *galut*. The suffering emphasizes the faithfulness of Israel and gives it an opportunity to say to God "How many religious persecutions and harsh edicts have they decreed against us in order to nullify Thy sovereignty over us, but we have not done so" (Mid. Ps. to 5:6). The sages saw the dispersion as a prerequisite for the redemption: in the settlement of Jews throughout the whole Roman Empire ("if one of you is exiled to Barbary and another to Sarmatia") they saw (in the second half of the second century) a fulfillment of this condition (Song R. 2:8; PdRK 47a–48a; PR 15:71b). Nevertheless, according to the opinion of Rav: "When Israel merits it, the majority of them will be in the land of Israel and a minority in Babylonia, but when they are unworthy of it, the majority will be in Babylonia and the minority in Ereẓ Israel" (Gen. R. 98:9).

The increase in the number of converts in the Roman Empire gave added meaning to the dispersion. At the beginning of the third century the *amoraim* R. Johanan and R. Eleazar gave the interpretation that "the Lord did not exile Israel among the nations except in order that there should be added to them converts" (Pes. 87b). In the eyes of the homilists who expressed similar sentiments, the people of Israel was like a "flask of perfume," which emits its scent only when it is shaken, and to Abraham, who made converts, it was said, as a sign for his descendants, "Wander about in the world, and your name will become great in my world" (Song R. 1:4). This evaluation of the Diaspora is similar to that of Philo and Josephus, and it is possible that the *amoraim* are only repeating views which were widespread for a long time before them, when the conversion movement was at its height. With the adoption of Christianity by the Roman Empire and with the decrease in conversion, the dispersion took on an additional aspect of national security. When a Christian sectarian boasted, "We are better than you," for "when you were given permission to destroy Rome, you left none in it except a pregnant woman" and "you have been with us many years and we do not do anything to you," R. Oshaiah answered that it is not the mercy of the rulers which assured survival in exile, but the political situation. Their wide dispersion saves the Jewish people from total destruction and thus "the Lord did a righteous thing to Israel in scattering them among the nations" (Pes. 87b; cf. SER 11:54). As a favor to His exiled people the Lord sees to it that no one kingdom dominates the world: "He divided His world into two nations, into two kingdoms … in order to preserve Israel" (*ibid.* 20:11, 4). In the ancient promise to the patriarchs that their children would be "as the dust of the earth," the rabbis found a symbol of the *galut*; "As the dust of the earth is scattered from one end of the world to the other, thus your children will be scattered from one end of the world to the other, as the dust of the earth causes even metal vessels to wear out but exists forever, so Israel is eternal but the nations of the world will become nought … as the dust of the earth is threshed, so thy children will be threshed by the nations …" (Gen. R. 41:9).

Like Ezekiel, and in the same language and spirit, the sages deal with the problem of religious observance in the Diaspora. The absence of sacrifices and of the Temple was liable to undermine the foundations of the religion. Some maintained that from a religious point of view the Jewish people in exile could be compared to a slave who had been sold and the laws obtaining in his former master's house did not apply to him: "When we were in His city and in His house and in His Temple we served him; now that we have been exiled among the nations – let us act as they do" (SER 29:159; Sifra, Be-Ḥukkotai 8:4). An echo of the fear expressed by the author of I Baruch is heard in the saying of the sages that in the exile "knowledge has been taken from them … they will be lacking in the study of the Torah" (Mekh., Ba-Ḥodesh, 1). These were, however, the effects of the first shock. The people overcame them, finding solace in the teaching of the sages. The commandments assumed new value in the *galut* and the Torah was studied. When the national organism sought means of defense and survival for its separate life as a community in an alien environment, it was realized that in exile the nation had lost all signs of social-national unity; "for what has remained to them … all the boons which had been given to them have been taken from them; and were it not for the Torah which remained to them, they would be no different from the nations of the world" (Sifra, Be-Ḥukkotai 8:10). In the *galut* the Torah was both the anchor and the protective wall for survival, preserving unity; this had already been symbolized in the promise of the "dust of the earth": "As the dust of the earth is not blessed except with water, so Thy children are not blessed except by the virtue of the Torah" (Gen. R. 41:9). Even God wondered at the way they maintained their religious-national status in the long exile: "My child I am full of wonder, how did you wait for Me all these years? – and Israel answered … were it not for the *Sefer Torah* which Thou hast written for us the nations of the world would already have made us lost to Thee" (PdRK). The Torah is the marriage contract which was given to the faithful wife.

To the sages, the social and psychological battle of the people as a whole and of each individual to resist the blandishments of *assimilation in the exile gave meaning to the trouble and sufferings which resulted from it. From their knowledge of the conditions of life in the exile they understood that "had they found a refuge, they would not have returned" (Gen. R. 33:6). In interpreting the ideas expressed by Ezekiel, they saw the social disabilities and the physical suffering of the exile as a means of annulling the desire to abandon the Torah: "Without your consent, against your will, I imposed My sovereignty upon you … for they immediately humble their heart in repentance" (Sifra, Be-Ḥukkotai 8:4–5). It is stated even more emphatically, perhaps as a result of the increase in their troubles and persecutions: "When your bones are crushed and your eyes are put out and the blood of your mouths spill to the ground, you cause His kingdom to reign over you" (SER 29:159). The sufferings on their part add a special reward and meaning to the observance of the Torah and its study: "The later generations are better than the former; although there is subjugation to foreign kings, there is study of Torah" (Yoma 9b).

The spiritual struggle to explain and justify the exile became intensified from the time that Judaism was obliged, from the fourth century onward, to contend with Christianity, which saw in the exile of Israel a witness and a sign that the divine favor had been taken from Israel and given to the church and its adherents. This polemic tone is particularly noticeable in the words of the *paytanim* and in late Midrashim (see *Apologetics).

As the duration of the exile extended, fears grew: when they saw that oppression increased "with taxes… and with poll taxes … Jacob became afraid … would it last forever?" The people found their consolation in Messianic promises which were bound up with the liquidation of the *galut* and the ingathering of the exiles – "from Babylonia … from Gaul and from Spain" (PdRK 151a–b). When despair grew until they even went as far as to complain, "Is there any remedy for a servant whose master creates evils and troubles for him?" – the remedy for this weakness of spirit was found in the doctrine that the troubles themselves were a sign of the true election of Israel (Ḥag. 5a).

The concept of exile and the description of the feelings it inspired which occur in the Mishnah, Talmud, and Midrashim reveal a community battling against adverse conditions and finding a rationale for accepting its sufferings and looking forward to the end of the *galut*. Through this concept the essence of the phenomenon, the reason for the dispersion among the nations, the religious, social, and national qualities of the nation for whom there remained only the Torah were considered; and in it expression was also given to the struggle against the religion which sought to find in the condition of the exile itself support for its claim that Judaism had come to an end, and that it could claim to be its heir.

Ideology in the Medieval World

During the Middle Ages both the reality of *galut* and its image acquired new intensity. Changes were wrought by the power and violence of events, the strength and fervor of continuous religious *disputations with the surrounding nations, and the soul searchings among Jews on the implications of *galut*, which appeared as a central element of both faith and world destiny. Every change in the fate of the exiles of "Edom" (as Christendom was termed) or "Ishmael" (Islam), in their legal position, and in their spiritual confrontation with Christianity and Islam, required fresh adaptation of the concept of *galut* to the new challenges.

In fact the position of the Jews and their status differed with time, place, and the attitude adopted in principle and practice toward them by Christian and Muslim rulers and peoples (see *History; *Blood Libel; Jewish *Badge; Covenant of *Omar; *Dhimmi).

Despite these distinctions, however, a fundamental conception of *galut* remained. Basically, throughout the Middle Ages exile was for the Jews everywhere a political and social condition characterized by alienation, humiliation, and servitude, and regarded as such by both non-Jews and Jews. Danger to life and limb and the actuality of expulsion were its permanent accompaniments. It was this situation which gave rise to ideas and imagery concerning the exile and its meaning in the minds of the dispersed and downtrodden nation.

The challenge of exile induced in response a system of thought which viewed *galut* as a course of suffering which uplifted the spirit, a penance for sins in this world, and a preparation for redemption. As an outcome both of medieval thinking in general and of the Jewish spiritual legacy in particular, Jewish thinkers emerged who, while they viewed exile against all its horrors, showed the majesty of God's purpose, and the greatness of the Jewish heritage, and who reinforced the faith of fellow Jews and countered the arguments of gentiles. The attitude of the Jews to exile during the Middle Ages can be measured by the extent of the response made by different generations to the appearance of pseudo-messiahs and *messianic movements, which were a direct and spontaneous expression of the desire to abolish the exile. The condition of alienation in the Diaspora also found perpetual expression in tradition, customs of mourning for Jerusalem, and the symbols perpetuating the memory of the destruction of the Temple. The immediate preparedness of individuals or groups of Jews to return and settle in Ereẓ Israel, the support given by the Diaspora for the immigrants, and the calls for aid and immigration from those in the Holy Land and their emissaries continued in all periods. The stories current in Jewish tradition concerning the *Ten Lost Tribes criticize under the veil of utopian legend Israel's lack of kingship and sovereignty and express the desire for their restoration. In conjunction with these popular expressions of the condition of *galut*, in which ideas concerning the exile and redemption are interwoven, Jewish thinkers advanced their views on the meaning of the sufferings and purpose of *galut*, and developed the ideology a stage further.

During the seventh century, with the rise of Islam and its victories over Christianity, it appeared to the Jews that contemporary events constituted a retribution on Israel's enemies and that it was the intent of Providence to ease the yoke of the exile (see **Nistarot de-Rabbi Shimon bar Yoḥai*). During the eighth century, *Anan b. David confirmed the custom of preserving strict mourning for Zion, and prohibited the eating of meat and drinking of wine. During the tenth century, after a number of messianic movements had failed, rationalist and skeptical outlooks increased within the community and a kind of Judaism that did not anticipate redemption was conceived (Saadiah Gaon, *Beliefs and Opinions*, treatise 8). The ideas of the Karaite *Al-Kirkisānī testify that a similar attitude was emerging among certain Karaites (L. Nemoy, in HUCA, 7 (1930), 395; J. Mann, in JQR, 12 (1921/22), 283). However, the majority of the people did not agree with such extremes.

With time, the constant humiliation to which Jews in the Islamic Empire were subjected was felt more intensely, and in the period of unrest, when the Abbasid caliphate was in process of disintegration, the misfortunes of exile multiplied. Exile under Islam appeared a terrible fate to those living in it. Saadiah Gaon expressed the sentiments of those who remained among the faithful despite all adversities: "the servitude has been drawn out and the yoke of the [alien] kingdoms has been prolonged, behold every day we are increasingly impoverished and our numbers are reduced as time advances" (prayer for period of misfortune, to be found in *Siddur Rav Sa'adyah Ga'on* (1963), 77–78, see also 350–1).

Out of this conception of the harshness of the exile, systematic arguments were advanced to prove that the *galut* was only temporary, and explanations were given on the meaning of the sufferings it entailed and the methods to be followed to bring about its termination. The Karaite "Mourners of Zion" (*Avelei Zion) gathered in Jerusalem, where they mortified themselves and prayed for the end of the exile, proclaiming their emotions in words saturated with the feeling of the misery of exile and expressing in their poetry the pain for the condition "of our poor mother," "whom we lifted up our eyes to see and could not recognize as a result of her ill appearance" (*Koveẓ le-Divrei Sifrut*... (1941), 141–2). They considered that "Karaism is the path toward redemption, while the Rabbanite prolongs the exile" (J. Mann, in JQR, 12 (1921/22), 283).

Saadiah Gaon developed a theory of his own to explain the meaning of the exile: he considered that its imposition as a temporary punishment had substantial internal sense. Exile had befallen the nation "partly as punishment and partly as a test" (*Beliefs and Opinions*, treatise 8, 291), while this trial also had a purifying value: "to refine our dross ... and to terminate our impurities ... He has exiled us and scattered us among the nations, so that we have swum in the roaring waves of the kingdoms, and, as the smelting of silver in the furnace, in their fires ... we have been purified (*Siddur Rav Sa'adyah Ga'on* (1963), 78). Because of these principles "we patiently await" (*Beliefs and Opinions*, treatise 8, 292).

According to this conception, the endurance of the nation is a result of its historical experience and religious faith, and cannot be conceived by one "who has not experienced what we have experienced nor believed as we have believed" (*ibid.*, 293). Saadiah Gaon points to the certainty of the justice of God as perceived by the believer, and the strength which he has revealed in his struggle against the severity of the exile as manifested in the present time, to prove that there must be meaning and end to *galut*: it is inconceivable "that He is not aware of our situation or that He does not deal fairly with us or that He is not compassionate … nor … that he has forsaken us and cast us off" (*ibid.*, 294). In the exile "some of us are being subject to punishment and others to trials." This is the correct religious manner of explaining "every universal catastrophe … such as famine, war, and pestilence" (*ibid.*, 295). In this respect, *galut* is not to be distinguished from other natural and historical calamities which do not differentiate between the righteous and the wicked.

An explanation advanced by an anonymous profound thinker in some fragments extant from the tenth century gives the meaning of the exile as a mark of Israel's election, as a divine gift and the "blessing of Abraham" (HUCA, 12–13 (1937–38), 435ff). In his opinion, as far as can be discerned from the fragments, the purpose of the dispersion among the nations is that Israel should assume the function of the priest of the world, who atones for the sins of the nations and guides them by means of the yoke of the sufferings which he bears on his back and by the arguments which he constantly voices in their ears. The anonymous author is firmly convinced that "just as the dispersion has come about and materialized, so will the ingathering come about and be realized without delay" (*ibid.*).

From the beginning of the 11th century the academies of Babylonia were in a state of continuous decline, while Islam not only failed to disintegrate but also received additional strength by the accession of the Turks. The political situation with which Jews were faced was that of a hostile Islamic and Christian world composed of fragmented states. This situation called forth *Hai b. Sherira Gaon's description of the nation as "a threshold over which every passerby tramples" (Ḥ. Brody, *Mivḥar ha-Shirah ha-Ivrit*, ed. by A.M. Habermann (1946), 59). Protests emerged against God that the nation is "like Job … forgotten … in judgment and not remembered in mercy … the King has rejected me … He has seen me slaughtered and devoured and has not rebuked those who consumed me" (*ibid.* 59–60).

From the beginning of the tenth century, plentiful evidence is available concerning the feelings of exile among the Jews of Christian Europe. In Germany, Simeon b. Isaac (Simeon the Great) described the state and feeling of exile during the period. Next to the fact of material suffering, he places especial stress on the spiritual danger which faced Jews in the Christian arguments that the exile is a proof of the Jews' responsibility for the sin of the crucifixion and their punishment for it, so that the exile can only be ended by their conversion to Christianity (*Piyyutei R. Shimon ha-Gadol*, ed. by A.M. Habermann (1938), 40–41). *Gershom b. Judah also felt the pressure of missionary arguments based on *galut* during the 10th to 11th centuries: "the enemy urges … your yoke to remove … to accept a despised idol as a god" (Ḥ. Brody, op. cit., 69–71).

Conditions deteriorated after the massacres of the First Crusade (1096) and the numerous cases of martyrdom (see **Kiddush ha-Shem*) that accompanied it (see *Crusades). A thousand years had elapsed since the destruction of the Temple and the beginning of the exile, and pertinence was thus added to the claim of the Christians that an exile of over one thousand years was a proof that God had abandoned the nation. The Reconquest in Spain transferred many Jews under Islamic rule to Christian dominance. Rashi was a witness of this change for the worse. He explains the hatred of the Christians for Jews because Israel does not "pursue after their lie in order to accept their erroneous belief" (on Ps. 69:5). He felt strongly the degradation of Israel and the mocking that their mourning evoked (on Isa. 52:14; Ps. 69:11; 88:9). The root of the evil was that the nation "is exiled … from Ereẓ Israel" (on Isa. 53:8). With a vivid plasticity of expression his commentaries (particularly to Isa. 53) convey the feeling of calamity experienced by the generation which underwent the persecutions of 1096. The sufferings related of the "servant of God" by the prophet are understood by Rashi in terms of the tragedy which befell his nation in Germany. There is a special religious justification for the acceptance of these sufferings in the concept of sanctification of the Holy Name: "His soul [of the martyr] is given over and sacrificed for My holiness, to return it to me as a trespass offering for all that he has transgressed … this is an indemnity [Old French: *amende*] which a man gives to the one whom he has sinned against." Even so, Rashi is unable to reconcile himself to the flourishing state of the cruel nations, which weakens the hands of the God-fearing from His service as well as undermining their trust in Him (on Ps. 69:7; 88:11). On the subject of the sufferings of the righteous in the exile, Rashi follows the doctrine of Saadiah Gaon. In the climate of perpetual controversy with Christianity, Rashi conceives that the cause for the cruel persecution of the Jews originates in the jealousy of the nations of the Divine election of Israel, a fact which – despite everything – still applies (e.g., on Ps. 102:11). This explanation came to be generally accepted by Jews.

During the 12th century, *Eliezer of Beaugency, in France, advanced in his commentaries the idea that the perseverance of Jews in their faith in the Christian environment is the outcome of divine decree: "I will not put it in your heart to worship wood and stone, so that you become one nation with them and they do you no further evil; but I will harden your hearts against their faith … and they will hate you so that among them you will fall by the sword, by fire, by captivity, and by plunder" (on Ezek. 20:32–33). Jews long to die "in battle," but their endurance of the life of exile is also an exposure to mortal danger. Ezekiel's vision of the "valley of the dry bones" is interpreted by Eliezer as referring to the House of Israel which had died in exile, to be "a great comfort to all those who have died for the unity of His Name, and even if they have not been done to death, since all their lives they have endured disgrace and shame and have been smitten and struck because they do not believe in their idol – and with this they have also died" (on Ezek. 37:9–15; cf. *Sefer Ḥasidim*, no. 263).

Of the tosafists (see **Tosafot*) *Eliezer b. Samuel of Metz, the disciple of Jacob b. Meir *Tam, emphasizes the bane of the exile from its spiritual aspect and attributes it to lack of political independence: "… our intelligence is confused, because we are in captivity without a king or country, and people who are not settled have neither heart nor knowledge" (*Sefer Yere'im ha-Shalem*, ed. by A.A. Schiff (1892), 72, nos. 31–32). *Moses b. Jacob of Coucy ascribes to the exile an ecumenical significance and purpose for drawing proselytes by serving as an example of moral conduct: "now that the exile has been prolonged more than necessary, Israel must abstain from the vanities of the world and take up the seal of God, which is truth, so as not to lie either to Israel or to the nations and not to lead them into error in any matter, and [Israel] must sanctify themselves even in that which is permitted … and when God shall come to deliver them, the nations will say: He has done justly, because they are honest men and their Law is sincerely observed by them. But if they behave toward the Gentiles with deceit, they will say: see what the Lord has done, that He has chosen as His portion thieves and swindlers … God sows Israel in the lands so that proselytes may be added to them, and so long as they deal deceitfully, who will join them?…" (*Semag*, Assayin 74).

The conception of exile of the *Ḥasidei Ashkenaz is dominated by the phenomenon of *Kiddush ha-Shem*, which permeates all their thoughts on life. A description of the rigor of exile in 12th-century France was put into the mouth of the Jew in the disputation composed by Peter *Abelard (cf. Baer, in *Zion*, 6 (1934), 152–3). Spanish Jewry from the 11th century envisioned exile as an element in specific ideological-mystical configurations. In his *Megillat ha-Megalleh*, *Abraham b. Ḥiyya ha-Nasi considers that history was immanent in the Creation; thus even "this harsh exile in which we find ourselves today was decreed by the King in the six days of Creation"; the sins of the nation, which were its direct cause, were also foreseen in this primordial decree. Thus predestinational-astrological conception moves exile away from the notion of punishment, facilitating the discussion of the subject with Christians and especially with the mystics among them.

Powerful expression of the inner dilemma arising from the search for the reason for the exile is given by *Judah Halevi in his poetry and thought. His *Kuzari* was written "to defend the humiliated religion," and its dominant motif is the knowledge that the Christian and Muslim worlds "despise us for our degradation and poverty" (Judah Halevi, *The Kuzari*, tr. by H. Hirschfeld (1964), pt. 1 no. 113). To meet the arguments of the oppressors who claim that the degradation of the Jews in the exile shows that "their degree in the next world [will be] according to their station in this world" (*ibid.* no. 112), he advances his theory on the ethnic election of the Jewish people. Israel suffers for the sins of the nations which are by nature inferior to itself; "Israel among the nations is like the heart amid the organs of the body," and the diseases with which it is afflicted – its degradation – are a sign of its central position in human history and the nobility of its character (pt. 2 nos. 29–44). The Jewish nation is entitled to be proud of its affliction in the exile, as all monotheistic religions glory in martyrdom. However, only a minority of Jews willingly and lovingly accept the yoke of the exile, while for the remainder the affliction is enforced, a fact which explains the length of the exile. Every Jew who suffers in the exile nevertheless has great merit, whether he bears the yoke of exile by compulsion or out of free choice "for whoever wishes to do so can become the friend and equal of his oppressor by uttering one word, and without any difficulty" (pt. 1 nos. 112–5). Judah Halevi did not relinquish his optimistic faith in final victory. He enlarges upon the ancient simile that the nation in exile is to be compared to "the seed which falls into the ground": to the person who observes the external condition of the seed, its sowing signifies its destruction; but to the one who has real knowledge, the sowing "transforms earth and water into its own substance, carries it from one stage to another until it refines the elements and transfers them into something like itself" (pt. 4 no. 23). Judah Halevi admits that for some Jews the acceptance of the yoke of exile is no more than merely passive agreement (pt. 2 nos. 23–24). The survival of the sick and dispersed nation which resembles "a body without a head … scattered limbs …" in this lengthy exile is in itself a proof that "He who keeps us … in dispersion and exile" is "the living God" (*ibid.* nos. 29–32). The sorrows of exile continue: "we are burdened by them, whilst the whole world enjoys rest and prosperity. The trials which meet us are meant to prove our faith, to cleanse us completely, and to remove all taint from us" (no. 44). With realistic insight into the sensation of exile, Judah Halevi promises the one who accepts these consolations with sincerity the peace of mind required to lead a human existence in the exile, because "he who bears the exile unwillingly loses his first and his last rewards" (pt. 3 no. 12).

During the second half of the 12th century, despair also seized the exiles of the Islamic world. In about 1160, *Maimon b. Joseph addressed to his brothers in Arabic the *Iggeret ha-Neḥamah* ("Letter of Consolation"), when he himself had left his place of residence from fear of the Muslim *Almohads. He particularly stresses the constant terror and anguish of a life where security is absent. To fortify the souls which find themselves in this distress, Maimon formulated his meditation on exile in metaphor. The Torah is a lifeline which is thrown to one who is drowning in the sea of exile, "and whoever seizes it has some hope." The exile is only lengthy viewed in human dimensions. From the terrifying description of the storms of the sea and the weakness of the man caught up in them, he evokes a picture of consolation: "it so happens … that while the current overthrows walls and hurls up rocks, the frail thing remains standing. Thus with the exile … the Holy One, blessed be He, will save the frail nation…"

His son, *Maimonides, considered the exile of his time to be part of the continuous attempts through history to turn the Jewish people from its religion. Some have attempted this by force and others by persuasion; Christianity has merely introduced the innovation "that for its purpose it combined the two, that is coercion and arguments … because it realized that this was more effective for achieving the effacement of the nation and the Torah" (*Iggeret Teiman*). Islam learned this combined method from Christianity. However, the attitude of Islam is the hardest and most degrading: "there has never risen against Israel a worse nation" than Ishmael (*ibid.*). When Maimonides imputes responsibility for "the loss of our kingdom and the destruction of our Temple" to "our ancestors … who did not study the art of war and the conquest of lands" because they believed in the foolishness of astrology (from his responsa to the rabbis of Marseilles), this realist-political explanation is only considered by him a description of the natural punishment which had resulted from having sunk into one of many sins. Born into a generation which had been tried by forced *conversions, and having witnessed religious coercion and escaped from it, he conceived the exile as a furnace whose purpose is to purify and test "until religion is retained only … by the pious of the offspring of Jacob … who are pure and clean, who fear God" (*Iggeret Teiman*). The exile and the sufferings of the people "and all that will befall them is as a holocaust upon the altar" (*ibid.*); these words are accompanied by an enumeration of the sacrifices actually demanded of his contemporaries.

The feeling of exile as experienced in Spain during the Reconquest period, with the changes in political situations and conjunctions where the plight of the Jew remained unaffected, was expressed by David *Kimḥi in his simile of the animals which were ensnared within a circle in the forest and which, in turn, the lion encircled with his tail; "thus, we in the exile are as within the circle, we cannot leave it without falling into the hands of the carnivores: for if we can extract ourselves from the rule of the Ishmaelites, we fall under the dominion of the uncircumcised … we therefore withdraw our hands and feet for fear of them" (commentary to Ps. 22:17); Jewish adherence to faith in persecution and suffering is stressed (on Isa. 26:13; Ps. 44:21).

During the middle of the 13th century, a period bringing an upsurge of mystical thought and an intensification of rationalistic tendencies among Jews, Moses b. Naḥman (*Naḥmanides) attributed a most profound and penetrating religious significance to exile, and his thought was to exercise tremendous influence within Judaism in coming generations. Naḥmanides visualized exile as a crisis in Divinity itself. He explains the sayings of the rabbis on the special bond with which the inhabitants of Ereẓ Israel are linked to God as an allusion to the distinction between "the venerable God, blessed be He, the God of gods when abroad" and the "God of Ereẓ Israel, which is the possession of God" (on Lev. 18–25); there is "additional" power in God as lord of His own estate compared with the power which He has in the remainder of His world; exile is the disruption of the link with this special "emanation" of the Divinity. This divine crisis is followed by a religious crisis, "because the precepts are essentially intended for those living in the land of God" (*ibid.*). Ereẓ Israel, the earthly Temple, and the condition of exile in the lower world become symbols of the situation and the events in the celestial world (*ibid.*; also on Deut. 4:28; 11:18). It is not only the property of prophecy which is impaired as the result of the exile, but the nature of faith, world, and God. Another aspect of Naḥmanides' approach is his theory – based on the passage of *Sifra*, *Be-Hukkotai* 10:5, and Rashi (on Lev. 26:32) and his own historical experience – that the desolation of Ereẓ Israel is a sign that though the alliance between God and the Jews has been broken in some of its elements, the alliance of the "Owner of the estate" has not been established with any other nation. The estate will not be cultivated and the Owner will not be worshiped in this aspect of His Divinity until His children return to His land (on Lev. 26:16). Naḥmanides' profound recognition of the religious aspect of the tragedy of exile did not overshadow his realistic appraisal of the actual situation in the 13th century. He recognizes the potentials of the physical and spiritual existence of the remainder of the nation and the possibility of preservation to a certain degree of the link with God (on Deut. 4:27; and in other words in *Sefer ha-Ge'ullah*, 4). Naḥmanides minimizes the extent of the economic decadence in the exile, no doubt influenced by the flourishing condition of the Jews in Spain in his time (on Deut. 28:42). Like *Baḥya b. Joseph ibn Paquda (*Ḥovot ha-Levavot*, "*Sha'ar ha-Beḥinnah*," 5), who had preceded him during the prosperous days under Islamic rule, Naḥmanides concludes that "as a result of our exile in the lands of our enemies, our affairs have not fared for the worse… for in these lands we are as the other nations living there, or even better than them" (on Deut. 28:42). Menahem b. Solomon *Meiri, in the generation which followed Naḥmanides, criticized Christian persecution of the Jews since they pray for the peace of the monarchy, "and our prayer is pure and sincere, unlike their thoughts; if only our prayers for them would be fulfilled in our own persons" (on Ps. 35). This lends a new note to the feeling of exile – the bitterness over suffering even while the Jews demonstrate sincere loyalty to Christian rule.

The conception of Naḥmanides that the world and the Divinity had become impaired as a result of the exile assumed a more practical and concrete meaning for the generations which followed the expulsion from Spain, Portugal, and Sicily (1492, 1497). Exile presented itself from the viewpoint of Kabbalah as the misery arising from a cosmos fractured internally, as the terror of a world in which a struggle was taking place between light and darkness, purity and impurity; a world situation in which Israel, the nation of light, is delivered into the hands of the children of darkness, that is the children of Edom, who in this array of symbols are subjected to a double measure of hatred. A dynamic mystic-universal meaning was attributed to efforts to amend the world by deeds, knowledge, and example (a meaning taken up by the kabbalists of *Safed, and the *Shabbateans).

An explanation of the negative phenomena of the exile and the manifestations of continuing survival in it were given

15th-century realities and concepts by Isaac *Arama. Its torments and persecutions are attributed to being in close relation to gentiles by residence "in their towns and settlements." Yet in its state of semi-serfdom and semi-protection, and to a large measure thanks to this enslavement and protection by the crown, the nation has been able to survive exile. Isaac Arama also places the forced converts within his tableau of the exile: "even though they have become assimilated within the nations … their feet have not found complete rest; because they [the nations] constantly insult and despise them and contrive against them … libels … and they always consider them as reverting to Judaism" (*Akedat Yiẓḥak*, Deut., *sha'ar* 98). The underground life of the *anusim* is depicted as exile accompanied by even heightened terrors. To the question of the length of the exile, of the shining of the Divine countenance on the Christian world and its success, which had already been asked in former generations and disturbed the generation of the Expulsion with even greater urgency (*ibid.*, Lev., *she'arim* 70 and 60), Isaac Arama attempted to offer several answers. Jewish history until this exile "was merely to be considered as a betrothal …"; the marriage had not yet taken place. There is therefore no reason to speak of a divorce (*ibid.*, Ex., *sha'ar* 50). Moreover, even according to Christian thinking, the Law was only revealed thousands of years after the Creation, while Jesus came to redeem souls from the original sin long after this revelation. By comparison Israel's wait for redemption is not long, even if anguished (*ibid.*, Deut., *sha'ar* 88). Purification from sins and removal of the evil inclination from the heart are also advanced as reasons for the intensification of the sufferings and their prolongation (*ibid.*, Gen., *sha'ar* 14).

Isaac *Abrabanel vividly contrasts the kind fate accorded to the gentile nations and the evil which had befallen Israel in the exile (introduction to *Ma'yenei ha-Yeshu'ah*).

He distinguishes between the cause of the hatred by the Christians – the crucifixion of Jesus – and that of the hatred by the Ishmaelites – the rejection of the Koran (on *Hinneh Yaskil Avdi*). Exile is also characterized for him by the fact that "the exiles … will not become tillers of the land … but will engage to a limited extent in the commerce of goods …" (*Yeshu'ot Meshiḥo, iyyun* no. 2 ch. 1), but he considers this laudable, because the acquisition of land abroad would reduce the yearning for redemption (*ibid., iyyun* no. 1 ch. 1). The steadfastness of Israel as manifested in endurance of suffering, in holding fast to the faith in disputations and in maintaining purity of religion and worship, Abrabanel regards as a threefold gain from the *galut* (on *Hinneh Yaskil Avdi*). The steadfastness of the faithful stands out in contrast to the conduct of the *anusim*, who silenced their voices and hid their faith; he stresses the merit of those who gave up their homes and belongings and went into exile with pride in order to practice Judaism openly. Even during those evil days Abrabanel believed that by its spiritual strength the nation would yet succeed in its desire to "bring the Gentiles under the wings of the Divine Presence,… by its knowledge and wisdom … it would remove them from their false beliefs"; Israel will act kindly toward its tormentors and will instruct its torturers (*ibid.*).

The words of these scholars preserve the strength and originality of men who observed the condition of a physically stricken but spiritually intact and healthy nation, of thinkers who drew from the sources of tradition and who perceived the past in the light of the present and the present in the light of the past. However, the words of Solomon *Ibn Verga, written about 30 years after the Expulsion, reveal the mood of a man who has lost contact with the social framework against which he should direct the sharpness of his rebuke. His thought is abstract and presented in the form of analogies detached from concrete situations. The subsidiary reason for the exile advanced by Maimonides – that the Jews were defeated because they did not study the art of war and relied upon astrology – becomes a recurrent argument of Ibn Verga, that "at first, when the Jews found favor in the eyes of God, He fought their wars … they did therefore not study … war … and when they sinned … they were not familiar with the instruments of war, and God was not with them … and they fell as a flock without a shepherd" (*Shevet Yehudah*). The condition of exile caused the Jews to forfeit their wisdom: "our mind is in exile, being enslaved to the exile, to the search for means of livelihood, to the taxes and decrees of the state; how can it preoccupy itself with wisdom?" (*ibid.*). Analysis of the situation, accompanied by wishful inclination, leads Ibn Verga to conclude that it is the Christian masses who hate the Jews, while "the kings in general … the princes, the wise, and all the notables of the land loved them"; even the pope "loves the Jews" because he authorizes them to live in his country and trade there. Ibn Verga, however, realizes that the fury of mass passions is an overwhelming power "and if the king safeguard us and the populace rise against us, how can we be secure?" (*ibid.*).

Ibn Verga is preoccupied with searching for "the reason for the great hatred felt by the Christians against the Jews." This he finds in a combination of religious and natural factors: on the one hand, religious fanaticism which paves the way to belief in fantastic libels against the Jews, on the other, the desire for loot and the fact that every community "seeks to absorb its neighbor and to integrate it within itself"; the Gentiles therefore hate the Jews who refuse to assimilate into them. He also echoes the steadfast pride of the exile who declares to the "Master of the world: You go to great lengths that I should abandon my religion … despite the dwellers of heaven, I am a Jew … and will remain as such" (*ibid.*). This divine persecution is explained through the ancient and powerful answer of the prophet: "You only have I known of all the families of the earth; therefore, I will visit upon you all your iniquities" (Amos 3:2). But concomitantly, exile continues naturally because of religious hatred, "the jealousy of women, the envy of money," and the accusations brought against the totality of Jewry because of the sins of individuals "who have sought to dominate the nations."

The thought of *Judah Loew b. Bezalel (the Maharal of Prague) on the exile at the beginning of the 17th century bears the imprint of the situation which followed the Spanish Expulsion on the one hand and the relative prosperity in his country, Bohemia-Moravia, in his time; it is based upon both the fundamentals of Kabbalah and the rabbinical systems of *halakhah* and homiletics current during the 16th to 17th centuries. The mainstream of his thought is expressed in *Neẓaḥ Yisrael*, and marginally in *Gur Aryeh*, *Or Ḥadash*, and *Be'er ha-Golah*. The Maharal divides the "night of exile" into three "watches": the first is one of painful slavery, the second of massacres and forced conversions, while the third – that in which he is living and which appears to him the last before dawn – consists essentially of consecutive expulsions. Like Ibn Verga, he too preferred the order of the king's peace and protection according to God's will against the popular frenzy and violence which did not spare the weak. The Maharal analyzed the religious-spiritual-social nature of the exile in terms which anticipate the theories of organic nationalism of the 19th century: "Exile is a change and a departure from order: for God has situated every nation in the place which is appropriate to it … According to the natural order the suitable place for them [the Jews] is Ereẓ Israel where they are to live in independence.… As with every natural existing object, they are not to be divided into two … since the Jewish people is one nation, more indivisible and inseparable than all the other nations … dispersion is unnatural to them…; moreover, according to the natural order, it is improper that one nation be enslaved by another… because God has created every nation for itself.… It is therefore unbecoming that in the order of nature Israel should be under the dominion of others." In several aspects, exile is thus an anomaly in the eternal natural order, every deviation from which cannot be but casual and temporary.

This combination of natural factors is the guarantee for the redemption from the unnaturalness of exile. For "all things which are removed from their natural place are unable to survive in a place which is not natural to them … because if they subsisted … the unnatural would become natural and this is impossible … therefore, from the exile, we can perceive the redemption." In the meantime, however, the exile continues by the express will of God (because "that which … departs from the limits of reality requires excessive supervision and reinforcement in order to survive"), and it is by Him also that assimilation in the exile is prevented. So long as this anomaly is maintained, it has its own legitimacy and roots to feed on by the laws of nature: the rule of Edom over the world becomes the defective condition of this world. There is an essential spiritual contrast, even if the depths of its profundity cannot be perceived, between Edom and Jacob: as between "water and fire, although not endowed with intelligence or will, are opposed to each other by nature." The struggle between the two is for the totality of the creation, because "each desires the possession of all that exists, which is this world … and the world to come, and thus repels his opponent." In the present stage of this struggle "Esau has gained for himself out of the quarrel a world of shame and disgrace … to which he is related; Jacob is removed from it, because impurity is foreign to him and he was born the last"; it is impossible that Jacob and Esau should possess both worlds together, because, if so, there would be two extremes in one subject. With pride he sees the exile as an expansion into far-flung regions where the dispersed Jews await the era of perfection of the world, which they will rule.

In opposition to the physical dispersion of the material reality, there are spiritual factors which unite the nation. This is unity created and symbolically expressed both by consciousness of national solidarity and by Torah study and prayer. Engaged in the latter the nation is in a state resembling redemption. To the question: "If … the Divine Presence is indeed with Israel in exile … why does Israel spend most of its days in this world undergoing oppression and expulsions?" the Maharal replies that "this world is not the portion of Israel"; hence, it is to the advantage of the Jews to be removed from its benefits. The Maharal developed a theory against censorship of thought and literature and religious coercion which regarded these as the exercise of tyranny, and the struggle against them as the true and full expression of the free divine spirit in man.

The *galut* feeling in Poland-Lithuania, an exile which appeared relatively easy during the 16th to 17th centuries, is reflected in the commentaries of Samuel Eliezer b. Judah ha-Levi *Edels (the Maharsha) on the *aggadot* of the Talmud. He was grateful to the Turks for the refuge which the exiles had found in their country, and he considered the "Kings of Ishmael" "merciful kings" (*Ḥiddushei Aggadot*, on BB 74b), while "Esau and his offspring … have tormented us in every generation more than all the other nations …" (*ibid.* on Meg. 11a). With their persecutions, the Christians are intent on placing obstacles in the path of the Jewish people toward perfection (*ibid.* on Bek. 8a).

Edels accepted the viewpoint of the author of *Shevet Yehudah* concerning the difference of attitude toward the Jews on the part of the various classes: "It is obvious that by the king and the princes they will be not humiliated and despised also when in exile, but only by the populace and the masses of the nations" (on Ta'an. 20a). On the other hand, the hatred of the populace saves the Jews from being appointed officials in "most contemptible crafts" (*ibid.*). Of special interest is the discussion of Edels with the Christians on the subject of the destruction of the Temple, the cessation of its existence, the revelation of the Divine Presence within its walls, and the length of the exile as evidence of the departure of the Holy Spirit from Israel. The Jew insists that the Divine Presence is not really bound up fully with one location only; partially at least the Jews can carry on the divine task even in dispersion and exile (*ibid.* on Bek. 8a and Ar. 10b).

*Ephraim Solomon b. Aaron of Luntschitz (Leczyca) regarded the exile as a social problem, part of the problem of justice in the world. He arranges a kind of double confrontation, between the wealthy of Israel and the condition of their nation and between the nations of the world and the distribution of material bounty among them; as result of this comparison "the superiority of victory is always upon my lips to reply to the nations who adduce a proof for their religion from their success … to refute their opinion and to overthrow their towers: because in every generation … our eyes witness that God has handed over all the benefit of temporary success to those who are unworthy of it, and this forms part of His profound and wonderful counsel – in order that the axe should not become proud against him that hews therewith, and that the nations should not say our hand is powerful; because they [i.e., the Gentiles] also agree that there are among them wicked people that are unworthy of success and even so they see their houses filled with wealth, while according to their evil ways [i.e., the Christian faith] they do not deserve that God should bestow of his abundance on them." However, the goods of this world, which are putrid flesh and stale bread, are thrown to the dogs of this world (*Olelot Efrayim*, 1 (1883), 3 nos. 5–6). He warns the "blind in the camp of the Hebrews" not to rely on their prosperity and to remember the communities which have been destroyed.

Once Italian Jewry had established itself in a renewed structure in the towns and states of the post-Renaissance period, it became imperative to explain the exile to the urban dwellers whose minds were inclined toward rationalistic reasoning and commercial considerations. In 1638 Simone (Simḥah) *Luzzatto completed his *Discorso circa il stato de gl'hebrei…* ("Discourse on the State of the Hebrews …"), in which he attempted to shed light on the exile in a manner most acceptable to the rulers in Venice – by the exploitation of humanist trends of thought and mercantile considerations. This apologetic tractate, which was intended to convince despots governed by cold political considerations and commercial-utilitarian motivations of the usefulness of the Jews, also reflects the self-criticism resulting from feelings of inferiority induced by the contrast with gentile existence. Many ideas which had formerly been expressed within the Jewish framework of the concept of exile were now brought out to the non-Jewish world and illumined with the cold and harsh light of realistic calculation.

In the 17th century *Manasseh Ben Israel also addressed himself to Gentiles in order to overcome objections to the return of Jews to England by the members of the Protestant sects who were prejudiced by religious fervor in addition to their economic considerations. Manasseh Ben Israel expressed not only the desire for survival of the *galut* but also its tendency toward extension with the expansion of the known world and the discoveries of new territorial and social horizons. Much of his reasoning is drawn from the arguments of Luzzatto, but, voiced by Manasseh, they assume a more religious content and a less submissive tone. He is not deterred from declaring to the nations in their own language, in the manner of the early medieval debators, that the sufferings of the "Servant of God" had befallen the Nation of God, and that the nations in their various countries "have slaine them, not for wickednesses, which they did not commit, but for their riches which they had" (*The Hope of Israel*, sec. 29). Even the expulsions serve the process of the expansion of the exile, because when one ruler expels them, the second accepts them with affability and grants them a "thousand priviledges" (*ibid.*, sec. 33). Commerce enables the Jews to live in wealth and with the acquisition of properties, as a result of which they "not only become gracious to their Princes and Lords" but also causes "that they should be invited by others to come and dwell in their Lands," because "wheresoever they go to dwell, there presently the Traficq begins to florish" (*A Declaration to the Common-wealth of England*, fol. 1–2). The central theory of Manasseh on the continuation of the exile and its extension is that so long as the prophecy of Daniel remains unfulfilled and the exiles have not yet been scattered to the extremities of the world, the redemption will not come.

Ideology in Modern Times

The feeling that there was room for expansion and progress for the Jews in general society, the apologetic trend of appeal to the non-Jewish world, and the awareness of new attitudes intensified with the changes in society and opinions of 18th-century Europe. In the modern era the nature of the debate on the exile assumed a different character as a result of social experiments made by Jews and non-Jews to abolish the exile. From the 18th century, ideas on and explanations of the exile were channeled to new methods of expression, both through organized movements which attempted to remold the character of Judaism and through individual thinkers (see *Emancipation; *Reform; *Haskalah; *Assimilation; *Ḥasidism; *Ḥibbat Zion; *Zionism; *Agudat Israel; M. *Mendelssohn; S.R. *Hirsch; J.L. *Pinsker; *Aḥad Ha-Am; S. *Dubnow; M.J. *Berdyczewski (bin Gorion); J.Ḥ. *Brenner; J. *Klatzkin; A.D. *Gordon; A.I. *Kook; F. *Rosenzweig; S. *Rawidowicz). The conception of the exile of these movements and personalities cannot be separated from their essential standpoints and lines of thought and should be considered within their specific contexts. Even those whose thinking followed ancient paths ascribed their views to innovations brought about by these movements in the modern era. Until the second half of the 19th century, it appeared that supremacy was being achieved both in reality and in ideology by the trends which sought to abolish the exile through integration within the surrounding nations or through continuing a respected existence within their midst by finding a meaning in this situation either as a divine punishment or as part of a sublime religious purpose. However, from the second half of the 19th century, this reality deteriorated in the emergent world of nationalism. Jews increasingly viewed the exile in terms of anger and despair, which even though presented in modern idioms, resembled in content the ancient conception of the exile expressed by former generations. Numerous efforts were made toward finding a means of preserving the distinctiveness and historic continuity of the nation within new and changing circumstances.

By the second half of the 20th century and into the 21st, the two fundamental conceptions in Jewish ideology of the modern era on the subject of the exile have resumed their struggle with renewed intensity. One line of thinking points to the Holocaust in Europe, the brutality of its perpetrators, and the apathy manifested by the majority of the nations of the world during the years 1939–45. It was argued that hatred of the Jews has not disappeared even after the atrocities of Hitler, while the Jews are subject to powerful forces of assimilation in places where they have free social interchange. There is the reality of the establishment of the State of Israel in contrast to the difficulties of maintaining the unity of world Jewry and the ties between the nation in its country and the minorities abroad. All these phenomena are interpreted as signaling the degeneration of the Jewish position and the danger attached to the continuation of the exile, and are put forward as decisive proofs for the necessity of its liquidation.

Adherents of the other line of thinking point to the political freedom and equality of rights legally granted to individual Jews in all the countries of the world and the authorization accorded in most states to Jewish organizations to pursue their cultural and social activities. They stress the organizational, spiritual, literary, and philanthropic achievements of the Diaspora communities; the political and material strength which is added to the State of Israel by the support of Diaspora Jewry; and the role of the Diaspora as exemplified in the Second Temple era. The success that the Germans achieved in modern times in uniting their dispersed nation around their country is noted. These believe – in common with the Jews in the days of *Philo and *Josephus, the geonic period, and the 19th century – that the Diaspora has a reason, and a right of existence; that there is national utility in the maintenance of the Diaspora according to its potentialities in its diffusion throughout the world. In fact, many who approve the existence of the exile are inclined to consider the state as a more favorable form of Jewish survival and sympathize with the principle of the "ingathering of the exiles." On the other hand, the majority of those who condemn the exile recognize that there is no possibility in sight of terminating the Diaspora. The Six-Day War (1967) and its aftermath strengthened both the consciousness of identity and feelings of interdependence between Israel and the Diaspora for the majority of Jews. However, a radical and vocal minority expresses strong disapproval of this tie. The link with Israel has become a touchstone and testing furnace for the existence of Jews in present-day Communist-ruled countries.

Down through its history the feeling of *galut* has been one of the most permanent and prolific incentives in Jewish thought. It has expressed the desire for redemption and preservation as a nation even in the most difficult days. The discussion between Jews and adherents of other monotheistic religions on this subject, the spiritual pride and religious feeling it engendered, resulted in the formulation of new patterns of explanation of the exile from generation to generation which enabled the Jew to bear his suffering without losing his humanity or his faith in God and justice. The spirit of Jacob has been saved out of the tragedy of the exile because the feeling of exile has been one of the principal factors creating the particular sensitivity to questions of divine and social justice among most Jews. As the result of a specific situation, according to Judah Loew b. Bezalel, the Jewish nation has become different from the other nations of the world through its experience of suffering and humiliation and detachment from the rest of society for generation after generation, and through alert and proud reaction to this trial.

BIBLIOGRAPHY: S. Dubnow, *Mikhtavim al ha-Yahadut* (1937), 96–103; Aḥad Ha-Am, *Parting of the Ways…* (1905); EM, 2 (1965), 496–506; J.M. Guttmann, *Mafte'aḥ ha-Talmud*, 3 pt. 2 (1930), s.v. *Ereẓ Yisrael, Malkhuyyot*; G. Rosen, *Juden und Phoenizier* (1926²); A. Posnanski, *Schiloh* (Ger., 1904); Y. Kaufman, *Golah ve-Nekhar*, 2 vols. (1954–61); *Galut: Le-Verur Mashma'ut ha-Galut ba-Mikra u-ve-Sifrut ha-Dorot* (1959); J. Klatzkin, *Galut ve-Ereẓ* (1920); *Soẓyologyah shel Toledot ha-Golah ha-Yehudit le-Or ha-Marxism* (1951): S. Rawidowicz, *Bavel vi-Yrushalayim* (1957); M. Kamrat (ed.), *Mashma'utah shel Galut ba-Amerikah…* (1964); H.H. Ben-Sasson, *Ha-Yehudim mul ha-Reformaẓyah* (1969); N. Rotenstreich, *Jewish Philosophy in Modern Times* (1968); Y. Baer, *Galut* (Eng., 1947); idem, in: *Zion*, 5 (1933), 61–77; 6 (1934), 149–71; B. Dinur, *Israel and the Diaspora* (1969); L. Baeck, *This People Israel* (1965); J.B. Agus et al., in: *Midstream*, 9 (1963), 3–45; D. Polish, *Eternal Dissent* (1961), 147–61; Baron, Social², index; Scholem, Mysticism, index, s.v. *Exile, Tikkun*; idem, *Ra'yon ha-Ge'ullah ba-Kabbalah* (1946).

[Haim Hillel Ben-Sasson]

GALVESTON PLAN, a project to divert European Jews immigrating to the United States from the large eastern ports of the United States to the southwestern states. In 1907 Jacob H. *Schiff initiated and financed the plan, hoping to alleviate the concentration of immigrants in the big cities of the northeast and middle west. The Jewish Territorial Organization undertook to continue the task. A Jewish Immigrants' Information Bureau (JIIB), directed by Morris D. *Waldman, was established in 1907 in Galveston, Texas, to settle and sustain the immigrants, who began to arrive in July of that year. Rabbi Henry *Cohen of Galveston was instrumental in the entire effort. The Jewish Territorialist Organization (ITO) was established in 1901 by the United Hebrew Charities of New York, the B'nai B'rith, the Baron de Hirsch Fund, and other Jewish immigrant aid agencies. Its stated aim was to disperse Jewish immigrants to other communities and thus alleviate the plight of Jewish charities in New York. The ITO helped the Jewish emigrants get from Russia to Bremen, Germany, and from there, the Hilfsverein der Deutschen Juden cared for the Jewish emigrants and put them on ships for Galveston. Once the Jews got to Texas, the JIIB assumed responsibilities for them and helped them resettle in other communities.

However, several major Jewish immigration organizations refused to assist, and in 1910 the U.S. Department of Commerce and Labor deported a large number of immigrants who had arrived at the port of Galveston, alleging that the immigrants had violated labor laws or were liable to become public charges. Nevertheless, the Galveston plan managed to settle 10,000 immigrants before it ceased operations at the outbreak of World War I as relationships between the Jewish organizations had deteriorated and potential immigrants were less willing to go to Galveston.

For Galveston, see *Texas.

BIBLIOGRAPHY: M.D. Waldman, in: *Jewish Social Service Quarterly*, 4 (1926); Z. Szajkowski, in: JSOS, 29 (1967), 22–26, 81; L. Shpall, in: *Jewish Forum*, 28 (June-Aug. 1945), 119–20, 139–40, 156–8. **WEBSITE:** www.AJHS.org.

[Michael Berenbaum (2nd ed.)]

GAMA, GASPAR DA (c. 1440–1510), Jewish traveler; his original name is unknown. Born, according to one account, in Posen (Poland), he made his way to Jerusalem and then Alexandria, was taken prisoner and sold as a slave in India, where he obtained his freedom and entered the service of the ruler of Goa. When the Portuguese explorer Vasco da Gama arrived off Angediva in 1498, he was greeted in a friendly fashion by this long-bearded European on behalf of his master, but Vasco da Gama treacherously seized the Jew and compelled him to embrace Christianity under the baptismal name of Gaspar da Gama. He now had to pilot the fleet in Indian waters and was subsequently brought back to Portugal. In Lisbon, Gaspar was granted a pension by the king, who employed his linguistic ability in subsequent Portuguese naval expeditions. In 1500 he accompanied Cabral on his voyage in western waters and was with Nicolau Coelho when he first stepped ashore in Brazil. On the return voyage he met Amerigo Vespucci, the Tuscan explorer after whom America is named, at Cabo Verde and was consulted by him. Later he went to India once more with Vasco da Gama (1502–03) and again in 1505 with Francisco d'Almeida. He took part in the latter's expedition against Calicut in 1510, when he may have died.

BIBLIOGRAPHY: A. Wiznitzer, *Jews in Colonial Brazil* (1960), 3–5; Huemmerich, in: *Revista da Universidade de Coimbra* (1927); W.J. Fischel, *Ha-Yehudim be-Hodu* (1960), 15–30; M. Kayserling, *Christopher Columbus…* (Eng., 1928^2), 113–9.

[Walter Joseph Fischel]

GAMALA (Gamla), ancient city in lower Golan. It was called Gamala because it was situated on a hill shaped like a camel's hump (Heb. *gamal*, "camel"). According to the Mishnah it was fortified in the time of Joshua (Ar. 9:16). Alexander Yannai (Jannaeus) captured the city (83–80 B.C.E.) and it continued to be inhabited by Jews (Jos., Ant., 13:394); it belonged to the Herodian territory of Gaulanitis (Jos., Wars, 1:105). During the war against Rome it was fortified by Josephus and since the Jewish rebels could maintain contact with Babylonia by way of Gamala, the city underwent a prolonged siege in 67 C.E. Because of its nearly impregnable position and strong fortifications, it was captured only after very severe fighting; Vespasian killed many of its inhabitants while others committed suicide (Wars, 4:11–54, 62–83). First identified by Y. Gal at a rocky spur between the branches of Naḥal Daliyyot, close to the village of Deir Qeruh, the site was surveyed and subsequently excavated by S. Guttman for ten years from 1976. More recently new excavations have been conducted at the site by D. Syon, who is also in charge of the publication of the late Guttman's work. The earliest remains at the site date from the Early Bronze Age. The principal archaeological remains at the site are the remains of the town dating from the Late Hellenistic period to the destruction by the Romans in 67 C.E. The settlement was built on the slope of a spur with a fortification wall along the unprotected sides. The buildings were built inside the town on terraces. Residential and industrial buildings were found separated by alleyways. A large public columned building was uncovered with benches along the walls, and it was identified by the excavator as a synagogue. A large olive press was also excavated as well as a number of residential buildings. Large quantities of finds were uncovered, including pottery, chalk vessels, coins, arrowheads, and ballista balls.

BIBLIOGRAPHY: G. Schumacher, *Across the Jordan* (1886), 74–76, 84–85; Dalman, in: PJB, 7 (1911), 25–26; 8 (1912), 52ff. **ADD. BIBLIOGRAPHY:** S. Guttman, "The Synagogue at Gamla," in: L.I. Levine (ed.), *Ancient Synagogues Revealed* (1981), 30–34; idem, *Gamla – A City in Rebellion* (1994); D. Syon and Z. Yavor, "Gamla – Old and New," in: *Qadmoniot*, 34 (2001).

[Michael Avi-Yonah / Shimon Gibson (2nd ed.)]

GAMALIEL, RABBAN, the name and title of six sages, descendants of *Hillel, who filled the office of *nasi* in Ereẓ Israel.

RABBAN GAMALIEL HA-ZAKEN ("the elder"), a grandson of Hillel, lived in the first half of the first century. As president of the Sanhedrin he maintained close contact not only with the Jews of Ereẓ Israel, but also with those in the Diaspora. The Tosefta has preserved three letters, containing reminders about the times of separating tithes and information about the leap year, which Rabban Gamaliel dictated to the scribe Johanan, while seated in the company of sages upon the steps of the Temple Mount. In these letters he addresses "our brethren in Upper Galilee and in Lower Galilee," "our brethren of the Upper South and of the Lower South," and "our brethren of the exile of Babylon, the exile of Media, and the other exiles of Israel" (Tosef, Sanh. 2:6; TJ, Sanh. 1:2, 18 d; Sanh. 11b). Like his grandfather, Hillel, Gamaliel was responsible for many *takkanot*, many of them bearing the formula, "for the benefit of humanity" (Git. 4:2–3), particularly on behalf of women (*ibid.*). Of particular importance is his decision permitting a woman to remarry on the evidence of a single witness to the death of her husband (Yev. 16:7). Stories have been preserved testifying to his ties with the royal family, apparently that of *Agrippa I (Pes. 88b). Among his pupils were Simeon of Mizpeh, Joezer of Ha-Birah, and Nehemiah of Bet Dali (Pe'ah 2:6; Or. 2:12; Yev. 16:7). According to Acts Gamaliel was tolerant toward the first Christians, and Paul was one of his pupils (22:3). Of his children there are known Simeon, who succeeded him, and a daughter who married Simeon b. Nethanel ha-Kohen (Tosef., Av. Zar. 3:10). The sages' regard for Gamaliel was expressed in their saying: "When Rabban Gamaliel the elder died the glory of the Torah ceased, and purity and saintliness [lit. "separation"] perished" (Sot. 9:15).

RABBAN GAMALIEL II, also called Rabban Gamaliel of Jabneh, grandson of (1), succeeded *Johanan b. Zakkai as *nasi* c. 80 C.E. He saw his life's work as the strengthening of the new center at Jabneh and the concentration and consolidation of the people around the Torah, constituting an authority that would be capable of filling the place of the Temple and of the Sanhedrin which had met in the Chamber of Hewn Stones. To this end he worked energetically for the elevation of the dignity of the *nasi's* office, and for the unification of *halakhah*. The Talmud reports a heavenly voice "that was heard in Jabneh" establishing the *halakhah* in accordance with Bet Hillel (Er. 13b; TJ, Ber. 1:7, 3b), corresponding to the aims of much of Gamaliel's activity. It also describes his vigorous exertions as not directed to increasing his own honor or that of his household, but rather to preserving the unity of the nation and the Torah (BM 59b). In his private life and in his personal relationships he was modest and easygoing, showed love and respect toward his pupils and friends, and even to his slave, and was tolerant of gentiles (Tosef, BK 9:30; Ber. 2:7; Sanh. 104b; et al.; Sif. Deut. 38). In respect to laws and prohibitions he was at times lenient to others and strict with himself (Ber. 2:6; TJ, Ber. 1:2, 3a). In spite of this, his firmness as *nasi* and his endeavors to increase the power of the new center aroused the strong opposition of the elder scholars of his generation. According to later talmudic tradition this led to a severe struggle in which Gamaliel did not hesitate to excommunicate his own brother-in-law, *Eliezer b. Hyrcanus (BM 59b). Of greatest consequence was Gamaliel's dispute with *Joshua b. Hananiah on the fixing of the new moon (see *Calendar). Gamaliel regarded the affair as a test of the authority of his *bet din* and ordered R. Joshua to demonstrate publicly that he accepted the discipline of the *nasi*: "I charge you to appear before me with your staff and your money on the day which according to your reckoning should be the Day of Atonement." On the advice of his colleagues, Akiva and Dosa b. Harkinas, R. Joshua bowed to the command. When he came before Rabban Gamaliel, the *nasi* rose, kissed him on his head and said to him: "Come in peace my teacher and pupil – my teacher in wisdom and my pupil because you have accepted my decision" (RH 2:8–9). From this passage in the Mishnah it would seem that the tensions between Gamaliel and Joshua had been resolved. According to the Talmud, however, they did not cease with this affair. The firmness of Gamaliel was regarded by most of the scholars as an insult to the dignity of R. Joshua and led to a revolt against his authority which ended with his removal from the office of *nasi* and the appointment of *Eleazar b. Azariah in his place (Ber. 27b–28a). The nobility of Rabban Gamaliel's character was vindicated, however, by his not absenting himself from *bet ha-midrash* and by his participation in the establishment of the *halakhah* under the direction of the new *nasi*. In the end Gamaliel appeased Joshua, and the scholars, meeting him halfway "out of respect for his father's house," reinstated him as *nasi*. According to the Jerusalem Talmud (Ber. 4:1) he alone was *nasi*, Eleazar b. Azariah only serving as his deputy, *av bet din*, but according to the Babylonian Talmud (*ibid.*) Eleazar b. Azariah continued to share the post of *nasi* with him.

Rabban Gamaliel was recognized as one of the greatest scholars of his generation by his colleagues, by his many pupils, and even by his opponents. His halakhic pronouncements, among them traditions from his father and grandfather, are abundantly cited in the Mishnah and *beraitot*. His activity, together with that of his colleagues and pupils in Jabneh, laid the foundation of the Mishnah. Exceptionally important *takkanot* with respect to religion and worship are associated with the name of Rabban Gamaliel, their aim being to face up to the new reality created by the destruction of the Temple by the implementation of laws and customs designed to serve as a "reminder of the Temple." Rabban Gamaliel played a large part in formulating Passover eve ceremonial after the destruction of the Temple (Pes. 10:5), in determining the final version of the 18 benedictions (*Amidah*), in making it a duty for each individual to pray, and in deciding in favor of the custom of praying three times a day. It is clear that Rabban Gamaliel was close to the general culture and learning of his time, permitting among other things the study of Greek (Tosef., Sot. 15:8). His son Simeon's testimony that many youngsters studied Greek wisdom in his father's house (Sot. 49b) seemed incomprehensible to the scholars, who later explained the phenomenon in terms of the political activity of the *nasi* and in the light of the need to maintain good relations with the ruling powers. He did not refrain from bathing in the bathhouse of Aphrodite in Acre, regarding the image there as serving a decorative purpose only (Av. Zar. 3:4). Gamaliel's son, Ḥanina, testified that it was customary in his father's house to use seals which had figures in relief (TJ, Av. Zar. 3:1, 42c). He was apparently also acquainted with the principles of Greek science. He used astronomical diagrams to examine the witnesses of the new moon (RH 2:8), and he fashioned an instrument to measure distances (ER. 43b). Gamaliel was not only the chief religious authority but also the recognized national-political leader. It is probable that the Roman government also recognized him as the spokesman of the Jews. In any event he made journeys – either alone or in the company of other scholars – to the governor in Syria to receive "authority" (Eduy. 7:7; Sanh. 11a) and also to Rome in order to intercede for his people (TJ, Sanh. 7:19, 25d). In his contacts with non-Jews, he also appeared as the spokesman of Judaism in its battle against idolatry and heresy (Av. Zar. 3:4, 4:7, et al.). Associated with his name is the introduction of the *Birkat ha-Minim* in the *Amidah*, aimed at excluding the Christians from the Jewish fold (Ber. 28b; Meg. 17b).

The year of his death is not known, but in all probability he did not live to witness the revolt in the time of Trajan (c. 116 C.E.). The life and death of the great *nasi* are embellished in the *aggadah*. Tradition assigns to him the great *takkanah* – on behalf of the poor – of abrogating ornate and expensive funerals and introducing the practice of burying the dead in simple flaxen raiment.

GAMALIEL III or Rabban Gamaliel be-Rabbi, the son of *Judah ha-Nasi, lived in the first half of the third century. He was appointed *nasi* in accordance with the testament of his father who instructed him to conduct his office with firmness (Ket. 103b); his brother Simeon was appointed *ḥakham* in the same testament. In the Mishnah Gamaliel rejects the extremist desideratum of isolation from the affairs of the world, takes a positive view of occupation and labor, and exhorts those occupied with communal affairs to work for the sake of heaven and not for their own benefit and honor. He counsels (apparently on the basis of his own experience) caution and suspicion in one's dealings with the government (i.e., Roman authority), even when it appears friendly (Avot 2:2–3). It is reported of Rabban Gamaliel and his *bet din* that they voted to invalidate ritual slaughter performed by Samaritans (Ḥul. 5b and Rashi, *ibid.*). Not many of his halakhic sayings have been preserved, but the greatest *amoraim* of the first generation – Samuel, Hosea, Ḥanina, and Johanan – were his disciples and highly valued his teachings. Among the discoveries in the Bet *She'arim excavations of 1954 were two adjoining decorated sepulchers, bearing the inscriptions in Hebrew and Greek, "Rabbi Gamaliel" and "Rabbi Simeon" respectively, which are thought to be the graves of the *nasi* and his brother.

RABBAN GAMALIEL IV, the son of *Judah Nesiah, lived in the second half of the third century.

RABBAN GAMALIEL V, the son of Hillel II, lived in the second half of the fourth century; very little is known of either father or son.

Rabban Gamaliel VI, the last *nasi*. An order of the emperors Honorius and Theodosius II, dated 415, has been preserved, which deprived Gamaliel of the post of *nasi* and of the titles of honor given by the government to that office as a penalty for having built a synagogue without authorization and for having defended the Jews against the Christians. Gamaliel's death in 426 brought to an end the institution of the *nasi*. From an allusion in the works of the medical author Marcellus (fifth century) it would seem that this Gamaliel was also a physician.

BIBLIOGRAPHY: Graetz, Hist, index; Weiss, Dor, 1 (1924[4]), 234 (index), s.v.; 2 (1924[4]), 236 (index), s.v.; 3 (1924[4]), 38ff.; Halevy, Dorot, vol. 1, pt. 5 (1923), 41ff.; Hyman, Toledot, 304–21; Urbach, in: *Beḥinot*, 4 (1952/53), 66; Alon, Toledot, 1 (1958[3]), 114ff.; L. Finkelstein, 775–7 and index; idem, ed., *The Jews*, 1 (1949), 149–52; 2 (1949), 1790–91 and index; Baron, Social[2], index; G.F. Moore, *Judaism*, 2 (1946), index.

GAMALIEL BEN PEDAHZUR (fl. first half of 18th century), pseudonym of the author of *The Book of the Religion, Ceremonies, and Prayers of the Jews* (London, 1738). This is the earliest translation of the Jewish prayer book, published in English with a scurrilous introduction. It appears from a letter in *The Gentleman's Magazine* (28 (Oct. 1758), 468) that the author was an apostate named Abraham Mears. The work throws interesting light on the life and customs of London Jewry in the 18th century.

BIBLIOGRAPHY: Roth, in: JHSEM 2 (1935), 1–8; Singer, in: JHSET, 3 (1896–98), 51–53. **ADD. BIBLIOGRAPHY:** Katz, England, 231–32.

[Cecil Roth]

GAMARNIK, YAN BORISOVICH (1894–1937). Born in Zhitomir, Gamarnik joined the Communist Party in 1916, taking part in preparing the October Revolution of 1917 in Kiev and in 1918–19 heading the Communist organizations and revolutionary councils of Odessa, Kharkov, Crimea, and Kiev. In 1919–20 he served as a divisional commissar on the southern front. From 1929 until his death in 1937 he was head of the political administration of the Soviet army and a member of the Party Central Committees of the Ukraine, Belorussia, and ultimately the U.S.S.R. He also served from June 1930 as deputy people's commissar for defense and chief editor of the Red Army journal *Krasnaya Zvezda*. He was awarded the highest state distinctions. During the mass arrests he committed suicide. His wife was the sister of Ḥayyim Nahman *Bialik's wife.

GAMBLING. Gambling was known to the ancient world. Games of chance were an appreciated pastime, often turning into addiction, among the Greeks – Herodotus relates that the Lydians supposedly invented some games (*History* 1:94); among the Romans, who are known to have bet heavily on chariot races; and among the Teutons, of whose gambling habits Tacitus states that in their less sober moments they even gambled themselves into slavery (*Germany*, 24). While the Hebrews were also acquainted with gambling (Judg. 14), it was only from mishnaic days onward that the rabbis took a definitive attitude toward gambling.

Professional and Compulsive Gambling

Professional gambling in any shape or form, whether among Jews or non-Jews, was severely frowned upon. The professional gambler was considered a parasite who was engaged in a useless endeavor and contributed nothing to better the world. Some rabbis went so far as to declare the professional gambler a robber whom the Mishnah (Sanh. 3:3) disqualified from giving testimony; he was looked upon as a spineless wastrel who, instead of engaging in the study of Torah or in the pursuit of an honest livelihood (Maim., Comm. to Mishnah, Sanh. 3:3), frittered his time and efforts away on a demeaning occupation and unseemly conduct (*Rabban* (ed. 1920), 224d; *Mordekhai*, Sanh. nos. 690, 695).

The rabbis recognized the inability of the compulsive gambler to control his passion for the game (*Shiltei ha-Gibborim*, Sheb. 756), considered him a moral weakling, and consequently dealt with him severely. One medieval rabbi advised: "Do not show pity to the gambler who pleads 'pity me in order that I may not be shamed and disgraced by him who has won a gulden.' Better he be disgraced…" (Judah he-Ḥasid, *Sefer Ḥasidim*, ed. by R. Margaliot (1957), no. 1026; cf. no. 400). So vehement was his opposition to the gambler that if the latter were to lose his money and require assistance from charity, it was to be denied to him.

Public calamities that befell the Jewish community were often considered the consequence of, and the punishment for, excessive gambling. In 1576, in Cremona, three scholars proposed a ban on gambling after a pestilence had abated. They maintained that the popular passion to gamble was the main source of all calamities that had befallen the community. A similar view had been expressed earlier by Judah Katzenellenbogen (Isaac Lampronti, *Paḥad Yiẓḥak*, 3 (Venice, 1798), 54a).

Effects of Gambling

Community leaders, keenly aware of the painful and destructive effects of gambling upon an individual's character, meted out severe punishment. Gambling debts could not be collected through the Jewish courts (Resp. Rashba, vol. 7, no. 445). The gambler was often placed under ban, dismissed from the burial society (*ibid.*, nos. 244, 270; Resp. Rosh 13:12), at times prohibited from holding his wedding in the synagogue courtyard (Loewenstein, in JJLG, 8 (1910), 184f.), not called to the Torah (Finkelstein, Middle Ages, 282–95), etc. Family life was also disrupted by gambling habits, and there is much evidence readily available to show how difficult relationships were between gamblers and their wives (Resp. Rashba, vol. 2, nos. 35, 286; vol. 7, no. 501; Rosh, resp. 82:2, inter alia). Women refused to live with such husbands; wife-beating and drinking were common (*Zikhron Yehudah* no. 71; responsa Maharyu no. 135) and the education of children was jeopardized (Rosh, resp. 82:2). Repelled by the conditions under which they were forced to live, gamblers' wives often sought divorce. The gambler's desertion of his family was not an uncommon occurrence. One moralist even suggested that women should join their husbands in their acts of gambling in order to save their marriages (Moses of Jerusalem (Moses Henochs), *Brant-Shpigel*, ch. 10).

Gambling was denounced not only by Jewish law and by Jewish moralists, but its evils and terrible consequences were warned against by popular folk singers, in colloquial expressions, and in proverbs. "Gambling poems," describing the sorrow of a home where the man gambles, speak pitifully of the mental anguish of the gambler's "widow," the hidden tears, and the neglect of the children.

Curbs on Gambling

Jewish writings mention many gamblers who made conscious efforts to curb their passion and activities. A common practice among them was to take an oath not to indulge in games of chance, although this usually resulted in a double violation: gambling and breaking a vow. The vows varied: some gamblers set a time limit to their vows; others excluded specific days or special occasions; while still others only refrained from placing monetary stakes, but played, for example, for stakes of fruit (Resp. Rashba, vol. 3, no. 305; Maharshal, resp. no. 185). Rabbis discouraged hasty vows, realizing that these did not lessen the lure of games of chance.

Exemptions

Communal restrictions to suppress gambling were often enacted; the frequency of these enactments, however, shows how futile the prohibitions were and how popular the games. Taking into consideration the attraction of games and gambling, the enactments were flexible: on many festive occasions (e.g., Ḥanukkah, Purim, the intermediary days of Passover and Sukkot, and the New Moon) the restrictions were lifted (Israel Bruna, resp. no. 136). Special family occasions also received communal dispensation for gambling (Finkelstein, Middle Ages, 228–42, 284–91). In general, however, the prohibitions were enforced and accompanied by severe penalties: excommunication and flagellation were commonly meted out to transgressors (Resp. Rashba, vol. 7, nos. 244, 270); fines were imposed and honorary functions within the synagogue withheld.

Types of Games of Chance

The medieval gambler was enticed by all sorts of games. Dice were known from ancient times, and games such as "odds or evens" played with pebbles, knucklebones, and bowling were also quite old. Games with nuts, although often played by children, were also a pastime for the gambler (*Haggahot Mordekhai*, Sanh. nos. 722–3; Resp. Maharam of Rothenburg, ed. Prague, no. 94). Not until the 15th century did cards capture the fancy of the Jewish masses (I. Abrahams, *Jewish Life in the Middle Ages* (1932^2), 415ff.). Tennis, popular among the Jews of Italy during the 16th century, was, just as chess, not merely played as a pastime but enormous stakes were wagered upon the outcome of such matches (Henderson, in JQR, 26 (1935/36), 5; for cards and chess see *Games). By the 18th century, lotteries were very popular. The different types of gambling were not universal; each country had its own fads and favorite games.

Many authorities felt that it was permissible to indulge in games of chance on occasions (*Mordekhai*, Sanh. 690f.). Gambling, however, carried with it a stigma; but while public opinion looked down upon it, all the private and communal efforts to stem the tide of gambling did not stop Jews from indulging frequently. One scholar even urged the abolition of all decrees against gambling since men could not withstand such temptation (*Mordekhai*, Shev. 787).

Synagogue Gambling

Gaming in the synagogue was not uncommon; a sharp contrast was drawn, however, between the usual forms of gambling and cases where the primary motive was not personal gain. A multitude of responsa cite instances where the winnings at games of chance were not considered fruits of sin (e.g., Resp. Maharam of Rothenburg, ed. Prague, no. 493). One of the clearest statements was made by Benjamin *Slonik who differentiated between gambling for private gain and that in which the winnings, even if only in part, went to charity. He saw no violation in the latter case and demanded full payment of gambling debts to charity. There were many instances where the rabbis and communities joined in games of chance. One rabbi ruled that he who wins at a lottery should pronounce the blessing *She-Heḥeyanu*; should one win together with a partner, one must also add the blessing *ha-tov ve-ha-metiv* (B. Levin, *Shemen Sason* (1904), 53 no. 27; see *Benedictions). It seems hardly likely that any blessing should be required if the winnings were considered the rewards of sinful acts. It would thus appear that Jewish law proscribes the professional and compulsive act of gambling; frowns severely and condemns the occasional act of gambling when indulged in for personal gain; while occasional gambling, where all or part of the winnings go to charity, has never aroused condemnation and frequently even has had the approval of the Jewish communities.

These findings might have bearing on the modern controversy over congregationally sponsored bingo and card games organized to raise funds to meet the tremendous budgets of the synagogues. Jewish history and rabbinic literature shows that such methods are not new. Synagogues and communities have indulged in similar games in the past, and the revenues have been used to meet their financial obligations. Rabbis not only did not frown upon such acts but frequently encouraged them. The *United Synagogue of America at successive conventions has, however, ruled that bingo is a form of fund-raising not to be permitted by their congregations, the opinion being that it is not in keeping with the spirit of Judaism.

[Leo Landman]

In Jewish Law

It is said that people who play games of dice are the sinners "in whose hands is craftiness" (Ps. 26:10), calculating with their left hand and covering with their right, and defrauding and robbing each other (Mid. Ps. to 26:7). Dice are variously named in the Talmud as *kubbiyyah* (RH 1:8; Sanh. 3:3; et al.), *pesipas* (Sanh. 25b), or *tipas* (Tosef., Sanh. 5:2), apparently all words of Greek origin denoting small, wooden, mostly painted cubes. The player is sometimes called *kubiustos*, and it is said of him that he is afraid of daylight (Ḥul. 91b). Slaves are said to be notorious gamblers – which is the reason given for the rule that the sale of a slave could not be rescinded where it turned out that he was a *kubiustos* (BB 92b–93a and Rashbam *ibid.*).

However sinful and reprehensible gambling may be, it was not regarded as a criminal offense in talmudic law. A gambler who had no other trade but lived by gambling was disqualified as a judge and as a witness (RH 1:8; Sanh. 3:3), and in order to have his disqualification removed, had first to pay back (or to distribute to charities) all the money he had earned from his gambling (Sanh. 25b; *Piskei ha-Rosh*, Sanh. 3:10). For the purpose of such disqualification, moreover, the concept of gambling was expressly extended to include betting on animal races and the flights of pigeons and other birds (Sanh. 25a–b). Opinions differ as to the reason for such disqualification: some hold that taking money from another by way of game or sport, without giving valuable consideration in return, is like larceny; others hold that wasting time and money in gambling, instead of engaging in studies or in a trade or profession, amounts to ignoring the "general welfare of the world" (*yishuvo shel olam*); both schools conclude that gamblers cannot, therefore, be reliable (*ibid.*; and Yad, Gezelah Va-Avedah 6:10–11 and Edut 10:4). The rule did not apply to occasional gamblers who earned their livelihood by an honest trade (Sanh. 3:3; *Rema*, ḤM 370:3; *Mordekhai*, Sanh. 690; *Kesef Mishneh*, Edut 10:4; et al.). A vow not to earn money was understood to mean not to win money by gambling (TJ, Ned. 5, 4, 39b). As gambling easily grows into an irresistible obsession, vows and oaths to abstain from it in the future were frequently taken, and the question arose whether such vows were irrevocable: those who held that they were regarded gambling as offensive and prohibited anyway (cf., e.g., TJ, Ned. *ibid.* and *Korban Edah* and *Penei Moshe ibid.*; Resp. Rashba, vol. 1, no. 756; Resp. Radbaz 214; Resp. Maharashdam, YD 84; et al.); others also considered the psychological aspect and held such vows to be impossible to maintain (Resp. Ribash 281, 432; et al.). But so long as the vow had not been lawfully revoked, any gambling in contravention of it would be punished with *flogging and heavy *fines (Resp. Rosh 11:9).

In the Middle Ages, the playing of games of chance came to be recognized in many communities as a criminal offense: with the impoverishment of ghetto populations, the public danger of gambling and the necessity to suppress it called for drastic measures. The following is an example of a communal law (*takkanah*) on gambling: "Nobody may play at cards or dice or any other games whatsoever that the mouth could speak or the heart think, even on Rosh-Ḥodesh, Ḥanukkah, Purim, *ḥol ha-mo'ed*, and other days on which no *Taḥanun* is said, and even at the bed of a woman confined in childbirth or at a sickbed – and everybody whoever it may be, including boys and girls, manservants and maidservants, shall be punished if they should (God forbid) contravene and play; if the offender is well-to-do, he shall pay for every occasion two silver coins, one for the *talmud torah* and one for the poor of Jerusalem; and if he is poor so that he cannot be punished by fine, he shall be punished by *imprisonment and tortured by iron chains as befits such offenders – always according to his blameworthiness and the exigencies of the day; and in any case shall his shame be made public, by announcing that this man has contravened this law" (*Takkanot Medinat Mehrin*, ed. I. Halpern, 92f.).

The modern distinction between games of skill (which are lawful) and games of chance (which are prohibited) was already made in Jewish medieval sources: some scholars held that games of skill were allowed and games of chance prohibited on a Sabbath (*Shiltei ha-Gibborim*, Er. 35b); some doubted the validity of the distinction and held that all games, even chess, were prohibited on Sabbath (several responsa on the subject are printed in full in *Paḥad Yiẓḥak* (by Isaac Lampronti) s.v. *Shevu'ah she-Lo Lisḥok*). Games of skill, such as chess, were never made a criminal offense, though disapproved of as a waste of time which should properly be devoted to study; and domestic gambling, even for money, became customary during the night of Christmas.

The Israel Penal Law Amendment (Prohibited Games; Lottery and Betting) Law, 5724 – 1964, provides for the punishment, with imprisonment up to one year and a fine of up to 5,000 pounds, of professional gamblers (and much lighter punishment for occasional gamblers); the prohibition attaches to games in which money or other material benefits can be won, and the results of which depend more on chance than on understanding or skill, or – as in the case of bets – depend purely on guesswork.

[Haim Hermann Cohn]

The Validity of an Agreement Dependent on Casting Lots

AN AGREEMENT DEPENDENT SOLELY ON CASTING LOTS. Casting lots is mentioned in tannaitic literature as an acceptable way of dividing property amongst heirs (BB 106b). The *amoraim* discussed the nature of the legal mechanism of *acquisition (*kinyan*) after the results of the lots are obtained. The conclusion reached in the Babylonian Talmud is that the benefit derived by each of the siblings from the very fact of the mutual agreement to disband the partnership creates the wholehearted agreement required in order for the transaction to be valid (Rashbam, *ibid.*). Similarly, any agreement in which the sides undertake to make payment in accordance with the results of casting lots has binding force, albeit on condition that a formal *kinyan* was performed so long as there was no *kinyan* the sides can withdraw from the agreement (*Me'irat Einayim* on Sh. Ar., ḤM 207:33).

The conditions required to validate an agreement involving lots or gambling are that it be carried out fairly; and that each participant enjoy equal chances of winning. Rabbi Jair Hayyim Bacharach was asked about a case in which people had cast lots, the stakes being a golden goblet. In the particular case he adjudicated, the lots were cast in an unfair, unequal manner; hence, he ruled that the lottery was invalid. Had the lots been cast fairly, he ruled that they would carry binding validity for "we see from the Torah, the Prophets, and the Writings that lots were relied upon when they were cast without human thought or intervention… Most likely, if the lots are cast fairly, an element of divine intervention obtains" (Responsa *Havot Ya'ir* §61).

AGREEMENTS DEPENDENT ON BOTH LUCK AND SKILL OF PARTICIPANTS. In the case of games involving a combination of both skill and luck, we find a controversy regarding whether the agreement among the sides is valid or not. As stated earlier, the *amoraim* argued in the Talmud (Sanh. 24b) as to why dice-players are disqualified from serving as witnesses or judges. According to Rabbi Shesheth, it is because "they are not concerned with the general welfare." In his view, their disqualification is more societally oriented. Rami bar Hama, by contrast, argues that their disqualification stems from the invalidity of the agreement among them, which transforms the transfer of money among them into theft, thereby disqualifying them as witnesses or judges.

In this second view, games of dice "constitute an *asmakhta* [a transaction built upon a fallacious presumption], and an *asmakhta* is not binding" (BM 66b. See *Asmakhta*). Each participant presumes that he has the skill and ability to beat his opponent and to win the money; hence, when he initially agrees with the other parties to abide by the results of the game, his consent is not sincere. Hence, the required act of acquisition does not take place among the sides, and the money that ultimately goes to the winner is in a sense stolen (Rashi, *ibid.*).

The law was decided in favor of Rabbi Shesheth, who said that the reason that dice-players are disqualified from serving as judges or witnesses is their "lack of concern with the general welfare." Some explain this in the sense that dice-players, being unfamiliar with the normal workings of the world, are thereby unfit to serve as judges. This approach would seem to imply that, from a monetary standpoint, the agreement among dice-players is valid (Rashi, *ibid.*). Yet according to Maimonides (Yad, Gezelah 6:11), even the rationale of "lack of concern with the general welfare" includes the issue of theft. In his view, winning money in a dice game still involves a "trace of theft" to it, thus making it rabbinically prohibited. No full-fledge acquisition takes place between the sides; what occurs is instead a farce (*Me'irat Einayim* on Sh. Ar., ḤM, 34:40. In the view of Alfasi [*Teshuvot ha-Ge'onim* (ed. Harkabi, 5647, §84)], or that of the Talmudic text he had before him, it follows that Rabbi Shesheth does not disagree with the principle that dice-games constitute an *asmakhta*.).

When the dice game is played for money that is not literally lying on the table before the players, but only exists as a debt, such that each participant undertakes to pay in the future if he loses, the winner is unable to claim the money from the loser through the rabbinic court. The reason for this is that such a case constitutes an outright *asmakhta*, or because such an act is devoid of any act of acquisition (Tosafot, Er. 82a; Tur, ḤM 207:17).

GAMES OF SKILL. We find a controversy among the halakhic authorities regarding games in which winning depends on skill rather than luck. The Talmud (Er. 104a) mentions such a game between women employing nuts and apples, and the game is deemed prohibited on the Sabbath. *Or Zarua* (Pt. II, Hilkhot Yom Tov, §357) rules that even on weekdays that game is prohibited, because it is like dice games.

By contrast, *Shiltei ha-Gibborim* rules that this game is exclusively one of skill, and as such cannot be likened to dice games. In wake of this controversy, later authorities disagreed regarding chess: should chess be considered not an *asmakhta*, as it requires skill and only people of good character play it, or should we not distinguish between different types of games, and instead consider even games of skill an *asmakhta*? (see, for example, *Responsa Torat Emet* §180).

PURCHASING LOTTERY TICKETS. Contemporary halakhic authorities deliberated the issue as to whether one is permitted to purchase lottery tickets. Rabbi Ovadiah Yosef ruled that, owing to the problem of *asmakhta*, it is forbidden to purchase such tickets. By contrast, Rabbi Avraham Shapira, when he served as chief rabbi of Israel (see Bibliography: Shapira), ruled that the purchase of lottery tickets differs from playing games of dice, because the person purchasing the tickets knows full well that the money with which he purchased the ticket will not return to him. Rather, it will be transferred, via an agent, to the bank account of the lottery company. It is therefore clear that he is making an outright gift of the money to the company. His hopes of winning remain a separate issue, independent of his agreement to pay the cost of the ticket, much like any other person who invests in a business and hopes to earn a profit from his investment. Subsequent disappointment does not suffice to transform the investment to theft. In addition, he makes the point that "we need to be aware of a major principle, that we mustn't question a practice of the entire Jewish People. Heaven forfend that we say the entire Jewish people have fallen pray to a sin." Furthermore, many sources indicate that Jews customarily purchase lottery tickets, and the great rabbis of Israel, even if they viewed such purchases as indicating weak faith in God, did not suggest that the practice involved the least hint of theft.

The Law in the State of Israel

Articles 224–235 of the 1977 Penal Code deal with gambling. According to the law, a "forbidden game" is one in which "a person is supposed to win money, goods, or benefits based on the outcome of a game, and that outcome depends on luck more than on understanding or ability." The law imposes prison sentences on anyone participating in forbidden games, and larger punishments on those who organize such games. There is likewise a prohibition against operating or maintaining premises in which such games are played, and the police are authorized to close them down.

At the same time, when games are earmarked for a specific group of people, are not played in a place where forbidden games are played, and their purpose is entertainment alone and not profit, the law does not forbid them. The Finance Minister likewise has the authority to permit certain games, and the National Lottery is allowed to operate in accordance with a special license received from the minister.

The Supreme Court of the State of Israel relied on the stance of Jewish Law regarding games of chance in the "Ninety Balls Incident" (CA 4436/02 *Ninety Balls* v. *the Haifa Municipality*, PD 58 (3) 782), vis-à-vis the underlying reasoning for the negative approach to gambling. The Court (Justice Asher Grunis) quoted from R. Menahem Meiri (*Bet ha-Behirah, Sanhedrin*, ad loc.). Meiri explains that two reasons stand behind this negative relationship. The first involves the fact that, just as gamblers are accustomed to lying during their gambling, they will not consider lying a shameful act in their other activities. According to the second explanation, just as gamblers take a cavalier attitude to their own money where gambling is concerned, so are they liable to take a cavalier attitude to the money of others. Hence, they will not consider what it means for someone to lose money as a result of their own false testimony.

[Menachem Elon (2nd ed.)]

BIBLIOGRAPHY: L. Loew, *Die Lebensalter in der juedischen Literatur* (1875), 323–37; V. Kurrein, in: MGWJ, 66 (1922), 203–11; I. Rivkind, in: *Tarbiz*, 4 (1932/33), 366–76; idem, in: *Horeb*, 1 (1934), 82–91; idem, *Der Kamf kegen Azartshpilen bay Yidn* (1946); I. Jakobovits, *Jewish Law Faces Modern Problems* (1965), 109–12; L. Landman, in: JQR, 57 (1966/67), 298–318; 58 (1967/68), 34–62; idem, in: *Tradition*, 10:1 (1968/69), 75–86; I. Abrahams, *Jewish Life in the Middle Ages* (1932[2]), 397–422; ET, 2 (1949), 113; 5 (1953), 520–2; J. Bazak, in: *Ha-Peraklit*, 16 (1960), 47–60; idem, in: *Sinai*, 48 (1961), 111–27. **ADD. BIBLIOGRAPHY:** M. Elon, *Ha-Mishpat ha-Ivri* (1988), 1:193f, 576, 658, 665; idem, *Jewish Law* (1994), 1:218f.; 2:710, 814, 822; M. Elon and B. Lifshitz, *Mafte'aḥ ha-She'elot ve-ha-Teshuvot shel Ḥakhmei Sefarad u-Ẓefon Afrikah* (legal digest), 1 (1986), 15; B. Lifshitz and E. Shohetman, *Mafte'aḥ ha-She'elot ve-ha-Teshuvot shel Ḥakhmei Ashkenaz, Ẓarefat ve-Italyah* (legal digest) (1997), 13; Sh. Warhaftig, *Dinei Ḥozim be-Mishpat Ivri* (5735 – 1975), 212–31; idem, "The Contract Involved in Lotteries and Gambling According to Jewish Law," in: *Sinai*, 71 (5732 – 1972), 229–40; B. Lipschitz, *Asmakhta – Ḥiyyuv ve-Kinyan be-Mishpat ha-Ivri* (1988), 81–83; A.C. Shapira, "Purchasing Lottery Tickets," in: *Teḥumin*, 5 (1984), 301–2; Y. Cohen, "A Married Woman's Winning the Lottery," in: *Teḥumin*, 5 (1984), 303–14.

GAMES. Jews, like all other peoples, have played games from earliest times. There are ample references to games in the Bible. Guessing games were played in biblical days (Judg. 14: 12ff.; I Kings 10:1–3). Jews were also acquainted with sports and military games such as horseback riding, racing, and archery (I Sam. 20:20–21; Jer. 12:5; Ps. 19:6). Twelve young men from Benjamin waged a fencing contest with twelve of David's followers (II Sam. 2:14ff.). Children played at home and in the streets (Zech. 8:5). During the Second Temple period, games of Babylonian, Persian, Greek, and Roman origin were introduced into Israel. Jews rarely originated games, usually adopting them from their neighbors. There are many reports on the mass games held on the nights of Sukkot during the Feast of Water Drawing. The leaders of the people, such as Hillel the Elder and Simeon b. Gamaliel, took an active part in the proceedings. The levites played and danced on the steps, and platforms were erected from which the people could view the scene. Here men and women mixed together, although in later times they were separated at social functions. The national leaders set the tone by engaging in acrobatic exercises, in dancing and juggling with eight burning torches, knives, or eggs (Suk. 5:1–4; Tosef. Suk. 4:1–5). The custom of holding youth festivals in the vineyards was observed as late as the Second Temple period (Ta'an. 4:8). Traces of it are still found in the traditions observed by some communities, such as Caucasia and Yemen, on the conclusion of the Day of Atonement.

The paraphernalia of games in ancient times included nuts, fruits, eggs, balls, bones, and stones. The Jerusalem Talmud (Ta'an. 4:8, 69a) states "Tur-Shimon <?> was destroyed because its inhabitants played ball" (on the Sabbath, see *Korban ha-Edah*, ad loc.). Certain games with nuts and apples were played by women on the Sabbath (Er. 104a). Other games mentioned in the Talmud are akin to modern dominoes, checkers, and chess. There was betting (on pigeon races, called "*Mafriḥei Yonim*") and *gambling with dice. Persons who engaged in these pursuits were not regarded as trustworthy witnesses (San. 3:3). Weddings were another occasion for joyous play. To fulfill the commandment of helping the bridal pair to rejoice, the sages would leave their studies and perform juggling tricks, pour oil and wine, and dance with the bride on their shoulders (Ket. 17a). Holding live fowl in their hands, they would dance before the bride or clap their hands and stamp their feet (Git. 57a). The tradition of merrymaking in honor of the bride and groom developed further in the Middle Ages with the *Marshalek*, a professional comedian who would amuse the wedding party by telling jokes, extemporaneously composing songs, and putting on various acts. Weddings were a time for the abandonment of restraint, when public entertainment was permitted. A "guard" of men wearing extravagant uniforms, some of them mounted on horses, accompanied the bridal parade, dancing women beat cymbals, and children raced along with burning torches. Bearded old men danced and clapped their hands, or sang songs and prayers.

Under the new medieval environment in which the Jews found themselves, the form of entertainment likewise changed. The carnival made its way into the Jewish quarter, and on *Purim especially there would be masquerades, death dances, stage shows, and street parades. Purim was the only season of the year during which Jewish communities, in all times and places, observed unlimited rejoicing. The period of merrymaking began on the first of Adar, when wandering musicians appeared in the Jewish quarter. People donned Purim costumes and danced in the streets, and stage shows were performed with the story of Esther and Ahasuerus as their theme. Young men on horseback amused the public by trying to push one another off their mounts. Children made stuffed dolls and burnt Haman in effigy. Shots were fired, and the sound of the "*grager*" (noisemaker) filled the air. Jews in Italy held sports tournaments in which boys fought on foot throwing nuts, while their fathers rode on horses, and, amidst a background of horns and bugles blowing, attacked a model of Haman with wooden staves, later burning it on a mock funeral pyre. In some communities, such as Hebron, Yemen, and Baghdad, Ḥanukkah was observed in a similar manner, though on a smaller scale, as was Simḥat Torah and the second day of Shavuot. In the yeshivot, the great occasion for play was Purim. Preparations would start right after Ḥanukkah, and the usual theme for the play was "The Sale of Joseph" or "David and Goliath." Young artisans would also put on Purim plays, their favorite theme being the Esther story. In Sephardi communities, the play would be a parody based on the life of Esther, Haman's wedding to Zeresh, Haman's funeral, etc. In Iraq and other communities, a Haman figure would be put up on Purim to serve as a target for young and old alike. The games played at home were *cards, *chess, dominoes, and checkers. Card playing was sharply condemned, and the rabbis often excluded card players from religious functions and social life. Yet the habit persisted. The 14th century *Kalonymus b. Kalonymus in his *Even Boḥan* sharply criticized those card players who reduced their opponents to utter despair. Maimonides compared such persons who gamble to robbers (Yad, Gezelah ve-Avedah 6:7). A synod in Forli, Italy, enacted a ruling in 1416 that the Jewish community must refrain from playing dice, cards, and other games of chance, except on fast days and in time of illness, in order to relieve the distress. Similar measures were taken in Bologna and Hamburg. The numerical value of the letters making up *karten* (Yid. for cards) was found to be the same as that of "Satan," and hence a pious Jew should keep away from them. The 17th century *Ḥavvot Ya'ir* of Jair Ḥayyim *Bacharach permitted card playing without money on Ḥanukkah, Purim, and *ḥol ha-mo'ed (p. 126). On Christmas eve, playing for money was tolerated. Leone Modena was plagued by his obsessive love for card playing. The rabbis of Venice issued a ruling in 1628 ex-communicating any member of a congregation who played cards, and there were many instances of oaths taken by individuals who wanted to avoid all games of chance. In the course of time, Yiddish terms were introduced into the card games: a six became a "*vover*" (the letter "*vav*" having the numerical value of six), a seven a "*zayner*," a nine a "*teser*"; hearts became "*lev*" and trumps were "*yom tov*" (holiday). The card deck was called the small "*Shas*" (the Talmud) or the "*Tillim'l*" (the Book of Psalms), etc. Chess, on the other hand, was a respected pastime, although some rabbis disapproved of the game. There was a legend ascribing its invention to King Solomon. Rashi observed that chess drives boredom away and causes the player to contemplate (Ket. 61b). Poets and philosophers set down the rules of the game, and R. Abraham *Ibn Ezra composed a poem on it, as did Bonsenior ibn Yahia in the 15th century (both translated into Latin by Thomas Hyde in *De Ludis Orientalium*, Oxford, 1694). There were rabbis who excelled in the game of chess. One legend has it that R. Simeon, the chief rabbi of Mainz (11th century), played chess with the pope and recognized in him his long lost son. The *Magen Avraham* of Abraham Abele b. Ḥayyim ha-Levi *Gombiner (17th century) tells of people who had special silver chess sets for use on the Sabbath. Here, too, Yiddish and Hebrew terms were introduced into the game. Checkers was also a popular game. Yeshivah students would draw a checkerboard on the blank inside cover of the Talmud volume and make their own black and white pieces of wood. Rabbi Nahum of Stefanesti found in the game an allegory of life: you take one step in order to gain two. You must not take two steps at once. You may only go up; once you have reached the top, you may go wherever you like (A.Y. Sperling, *Ta'amei ha-Minhagim* (1957), 367).

The world of children in both Ashkenazi and Sephardi communities was a world of games. For every holiday the Jewish child prepared special toys, made from whatever material was available, with the assistance of the rabbi in the *ḥeder* or of older children. The Jewish child was said to be a jack-of-all-trades: on Passover he makes holes in the *maẓẓot*, on Shavuot he becomes a gardener, on Lag ba-Omer he is a soldier, on Sukkot a builder, on Ḥanukkah he pours lead, on Purim he is a gunsmith, and for Rosh Ha-Shanah he trains as a trumpeter (to blow the *shofar*). For Ḥanukkah the boys would prepare a "*dreydel*" (a four-sided top), either carving it out of wood or pouring lead into a form. This game is still popular and has also been adopted by Yemeni and Sephardi children. It came upon the Jewish scene in the early Middle Ages, and the four sides of the *dreydel* were marked with the Hebrew letters *Nun, Gimmel, He, Shin* (standing for Yiddish words *Nimm, Gib, Halb, Shtell* meaning take, give, half, and put). Soon, however, the letters were interpreted as standing for the Hebrew *Nes Gadol Hayah Sham* ("a great miracle happened there"). In modern Israel the last word was changed to *Po*, so as to read "a great miracle happened here." *Dreydel* spinning was one form of Ḥanukkah gambling. Older children made their own Yiddish cards known as *"Lamed-Alef-niks"* or *"Kvitlakh."* For Purim, noise-making toys, *"gragers"* or boxes, to drown the sound of Haman's name in the synagogue reading of the Book of Esther, masks, costumes, and Haman dolls were made by young folk. Passover games were played with walnuts. For Lag ba-Omer the equipment was bows and arrows, and the children spent the day in the woods, engaging in various warlike operations under the command of the "Lag ba-Omer general." On Shavuot girls decorated the windows with paper roses, and the boys brought field flowers and ivy from the forest and adorned the doors, windows, and lamps. There was also a custom of piercing eggs, emptying them of their contents, drawing a string through the empty shells, gluing feathers to them, and hanging them up in the open to swing in the wind like birds. On the eve of the Ninth of Av children armed themselves with wooden swords and played as soldiers fighting the Turks for possession of Ereẓ Israel. The "Rabbi" game in which boys mimicked their teachers was popular between the 17th of Tammuz and the Ninth of Av, when children were free from punishment. Even adults enjoyed this game on Purim. Throughout the year in their spare time children played war games (often based on biblical themes), cops and robbers, hide-and-go-seek, "Simple Simon," etc. More sedate games were played with buttons, pocketknives, heads or tails, paper cutouts, and drawing on walls.

Concerning adults, there are records of Jews dueling. In Spain, some enjoyed wearing arms, considering themselves knights, and using stately names. In Provence, Jews used trained falcons in hawking while riding horses. Occasionally, they joined Christian friends in hunting, although they could not eat the game killed that way because of the *dietary laws (see Cruelty to *Animals and *Hunting). All ages enjoyed a variety of word games, often based on biblical verses. A *"samekh-pe"* game, relating to finding open or closed lines in the Pentateuch, was popular. The "Moses" game was played by children who would turn to pages of the Bible and compete with each other to be the first to locate the Hebrew letters of Moses' name among the last letters on the page. Letter games with *Gematria, i.e., in which corresponding words and phrases were searched for with each having the same numerical value, were enjoyed, e.g., the identical numerical value of the Hebrew phrases for "blessed is Mordecai" and "cursed be Haman." Riddles were a form of amusement, and early examples were found in the series of moral riddles in the 13th chapter of Proverbs. *Eḥad mi Yode'a, a song from the Passover *seder*, is an illustration. Hebrew *acrostics were popular, combined with arithmetical puzzles. Abraham Ibn Ezra wrote several of these, some expressly for Ḥanukkah. Judah Halevi also composed poetic riddles. In the 13th century riddles about general folk legends like "Solomon and Marcom" were also known to Jews. Yet at this time the most common games involving words were table riddles, such as found abundantly in the Hebrew romances of Al-Ḥarizi and Joseph Zabara. The Talmud reported an example of such a riddle from Adda the fisherman: "Broil the fish with his brother (salt), plunge it into its father (water), eat it with its son (sauce), and drink after it its father (water)" (MK 11a). Jewish gatherings in later times were often enlivened by witty puzzles. *Kabbalah also had a part in such wordplay, as when children would direct some invocation to the angel *Sandalfon at the start of their games. There were formal occasions for performances by teenagers at the end of the school term or the conclusion of a tractate of the Talmud (see *Siyyum) on the 15th of Shevat, etc. In Ashkenazi communities, *Shabbat Naḥamu* (the Sabbath following the Ninth of Av) would be marked by a festive meal and children's show. Sephardi children in the old city of Jerusalem, Hebron, Baghdad, etc. would mark the last day of Ḥanukkah with a play, *"Miranda di Ḥanukkah."* In Tripoli, Tunis, and Salonika, on the sixth or seventh day of Ḥanukkah, a celebration would be held for girls who had reached the age of twelve. Also on Ḥanukkah, Sephardi children would play "Caricas di Sol" ("Face of Salt"), or act as soldiers fighting the Greeks. This was also the custom among the children of Yemen, who wore blue clothes for the occasion. Jewish children in Persia marked Ḥanukkah by playing various games of chance known as *"Kab," "Kemar,"* and *"Tachte-ner"* (a kind of checkers, known as *"Shesh-Besh"* in Arabic). Yemeni children played with fruit stones (now played in Israel with apricot stones). Their Ḥanukkah top (*"Duame"*) was made of nutshells; the Purim *"grager"* was called *"Khirye."* Other games were *"Umey"* (blindman's buff), *"Kez Almakez"* ("horses," or jumping over one another's bent backs), etc. In Tripoli the young men had the custom of holding donkey races on the Ninth of Av, for on that day the Messiah was expected to come, riding on a donkey. On Shavuot they would pour water on the passers-by (also customary in other eastern communities). The last day of Passover was the occasion for a *"Maimuna" carnival, when young and old would pelt one another with flowers and vegetable leaves. In all communities, girls had their own games, such as playing ball, dolls, "cat-and-mouse," "golden bridges," etc. They also played an elaborate form of "bride-and-groom," accompanied by songs. Rarely did boys and girls join in games together, although girls would also engage in games usually reserved for boys. After World War I, various forms of modern sports and gymnastics were introduced into the Jewish communities, taking the place of the traditional forms of entertainment. Some of the old games, however, still survive and are handed down by children from one generation to the next.

BIBLIOGRAPHY: J.J. Schudt, *Juedische Merckwuerdigkeiten*, 2 (1714), 312; 3 (1714), 202; A. Berliner, *Aus dem inneren Leben der deutschen Juden im Mittelalter* (1871); M. Steinschneider, *Schach bei den Juden* (1873); M. Guedemann, *Geschichte des Erziehungswesens und der Cultur der abendlaendischen Juden*, 3 vols. (1880–88); I. Abrahams, *Jewish Life* in the Middle Ages, ed. by C. Roth (1932), 397–422; I. Rivkind, *Der Kamf kegen Azartshpiln bay Yidn* (1946); Y. Stern, *Kheyder un Bes-Medresh* (1950); C. Roth, *Jews in the Renaissance* (1959), 28–30; M. Molho, *Literatura sefardita de Oriente* (1960), 177–82; Yahadut Luv (1960), 367–99; Y. Kafih, *Halikhot Teiman* (1961), passim; J. Yehoshua, *Yaldut bi-Yrushalayim ha-Yeshanah* (1965).

[Yom-Tov Lewinski]

GAMES, ABRAM (1914–1996), British graphic designer. Born in Whitechapel, London, to Moshe Joseph Gamse, a photographer from Dvinsk, Latvia, and Sarah Rosenberg from Semyatitz, Russo-Poland, Games achieved early recognition for his poster designs before being conscripted in 1940. Subsequently he was posted to the War Office and awarded the unique title "Official War Poster Artist," in which position he created some 100 posters until his demobilization in 1946, many of which became recognized classics.

Games was responsible for creating many iconic posters and numerous emblems, including those for the Festival of Britain and the Queen's Award to Industry. His stamp designs led to his appointment to the Advisory Committee of the Council of Industrial Design and his giving a course for designers of the Israel Philatelic Services. He did much work for Jewish organizations. In addition, Games was a lecturer at the Royal College of Art and was later made an honorary fellow, and was an active painter, product designer (including the famous Cona coffee maker), and inventor. He was awarded the Queen's OBE in 1957 and appointed Royal Designer for Industry in 1959. His book *Over My Shoulder* was published by Studio Books in 1960 and he later summarized his work through a traveling exhibition called "60 Years of Design." In 1968 the United Nations Industrial Development Organization appointed Games as consultant on Graphic Design at the Bezalel School of Art in Jerusalem. He was the designer of the original motif and cover for the first edition of the *Encyclopaedia Judaica*, an exceptional concept combining Hebrew and English calligraphy of text from the Book of Isaiah in the form of a menorah.

[Naomi Games (2nd ed.)]

GAMORAN, EMANUEL (1895–1962), U.S. educator. Born in Belz, Russia, he was taken to the U.S. in 1907. From 1917 to 1921 Gamoran was associated with the New York Bureau of Jewish Education, becoming in 1923 the educational director of the Commission of Jewish Education of the Union of American Hebrew Congregations, a post he held until his death. He was also president of the National Council for Jewish Education in 1927–28. Under Gamoran's direction, the Reform Commission on Jewish Education produced numerous textbooks and curricula for its affiliated schools, and pioneered the use of audiovisual aids in Jewish education. Gamoran wrote *Changing Conceptions in Jewish Education* (1924) as well as graded textbooks for Jewish schools and many articles on Jewish education.

BIBLIOGRAPHY: *Jewish Education*, 34 (1964), 67–86 (several articles in honor of Gamoran).

[Leon H. Spotts]

GAMORAN, MAMIE GOLDSMITH (1900–1984), U.S. writer. Born in Jersey City, N.J. to Nathan and Mamie Aronson Goldsmith, Gamoran was a prolific author of Jewish children's textbooks and fiction. Raised in a non-observant home, she received no formal Jewish education as a child. Her interest in Judaism was stimulated by her involvement in a Jewish girls club, the Bronx chapter of the Association of Jewish High School Girls (which later merged with a parallel boys club and became the League of Jewish Youth). The club was created by Dr. Samson *Benderly, director of the New York Bureau of Jewish Education and a revolutionary force in Jewish education in the early 20th century. Her exposure to Benderly's educational approach was intensified when she came to work at the Bureau as Benderly's personal secretary. There she also became acquainted with the so-called "Benderly Boys," the group Benderly was grooming for leadership positions in Jewish education. These included her future husband, Emanuel Gamoran. Mamie also studied at the Jewish Theological Seminary, and was a member of the first graduating class of the Israel Friedlaender extension school (1922).

After their marriage in 1922 the Gamarons moved to Cincinnati, Ohio, where Emanuel became education director of the Union of American Hebrew Congregations, the lay arm of the Reform movement. There, Mamie taught in area supplementary schools and served for two years as principal of the Conservative affiliated Adath Israel religious school. A central facet of her husband's work included commissioning and editing religious school textbooks. Always in need of writers, he encouraged Mamie's literary aspirations. Among her best-known books was *Hillel's Happy Holidays* (1939), one of the earliest Jewish holiday primers for young children, and a three-volume Jewish history series for junior high school students, *The New Jewish History* (1953–57).

Gamoran co-edited her husband's biography following his death, *Emanuel Gamoran: His Life and His Work* (1979), and wrote a memoir, *A Family History* (1985), published by her son, Rabbi Nathaniel Hillel Gamoran, after her death.

BIBLIOGRAPHY: M. Lehman, "Gamoran, Mamie," in: P.E. Hyman and D.D. Moore (eds.), *Jewish Women in America*, vol. 1 (1997), 495–96.

[Jonathan Krasner (2nd ed.)]

GAMUS GALLEGOS, PAULINA, Venezuelan lawyer and politician. Gamus Gallegos was born in Caracas and attended the Moral y Luces Herzl Bialik High School there. She obtained her law degree from the Universidad Central de Venezuela in 1959. After working as a lawyer for two years, she served in various capacities in public administration. In 1974 she became adjunct legal adviser to the president of the country and executive secretary of the Women's Advisory Commission of the president. She served as director of information of the Ministry of Education from 1975 to 1977 and in the latter year was vice minister of information and tourism.

In 1977 she was also chosen by presidential candidate Luis Pinerua Ordaz as his campaign public relations director. Gamus Gallegos was elected councilor representing the Democratic Action Party for the Federal District in 1977, becoming head of that faction in 1981. She chaired the Committee on Environment and was a member of the Permanent Committee for Culture and Town Planning. In December 1983 she was elected principal delegate of the Democratic Action Party in the Federal District and in January 1984 became the co-director of the parliamentary faction. She belonged to the Legislative Commission, to the bicameral commission for a new employment law, to the bicameral commission for the reform of municipal government, and was chairman of a number of special committees. In January 1986 she was appointed a minister in the government, Ministra de Estado-Presidenta del Consejo Nacional de la Cultura (CONAC).

Gamus Gallegos was a journalist from 1969 with a column in the daily newspaper *El Nacional* and from 1981 with a column in the daily newspaper of Caracas. She has also contributed to the magazines *Resumen* and *De Frente*. In addition, she has represented Venezuela at numerous international meetings.

GAMZON, ROBERT (1905–1961), French Jewish leader. In 1923 he helped to found the Eclaireurs Israélites de France (EIF), which was to become the most popular Jewish youth movement in France and in North Africa. Gamzon gave a broad interest to the EIF movement which attracted Jews from a wide range of backgrounds and ideologies.

During World War II Gamzon served as a communications officer in the Fourth French Army from 1939 to 1940. After the armistice of June 1940, he reestablished the EIF framework in the towns in southern France where Jewish refugees had gathered. In Algeria he worked to open homes for children, handicraft centers, and rural work camps in order to provide an educational framework for Jewish youth. In 1942 Gamzon created "La Sixième," a clandestine escape network manufacturing false identity papers and taking children and teenagers to safety in Spain or Switzerland by illegal means. In December 1943 he set up a Jewish underground movement in the Tarn area with youth from rural work camps and veteran members of EIF and played a major role in the unification of Jewish resistance groups in France. In June 1944 his group, now a full-fledged military unit, was incorporated in the Free French Army as the Marc Haguenau Company. As area commandant, Gamzon received and assisted Allied specialists in sabotage who parachuted into his zone and set up ambushes against German convoys. On August 19, 1944, the EIF company seized a whole armored convoy and two days later liberated the towns of Castres and Mazamet.

After the war, in 1947, he established a school for community workers in a Parisian suburb. In 1949, he immigrated to Israel at the head of a group of 50 EIF veterans. In Israel Gamzon, an electro-acoustical engineer by profession, worked as laboratory head at the Weizmann Institute where he invented an isophase loudspeaker used by manufacturers of high fidelity musical instruments. He met his death by accidental drowning.

Gamzon wrote an essay on Jewish thought, *Tivliout*, published in 1945 in Paris, and his wartime journal, *Les Eaux Claires, Journal 1940–1944* (1982).

[Lucien Lazare]

GAMZU, ḤAYYIM (1910–1982), Israel drama and art critic. Born in Chernigov, Russia, he went to Palestine with his parents in 1923, and later left to study art and philosophy at the Sorbonne and the University of Vienna. The director of the Tel Aviv Museum, from 1962 he taught at the Ramat Gan School of Drama, and wrote regularly on painting, sculpture, and the theater, mainly for the daily *Haaretz*. His criticism was erudite and often harsh and could make or break an exhibition or production. Insisting that Hebrew drama must maintain European standards, he often expressed dissatisfaction with its achievements. His books, consisting of reproductions of works of art and accompanying text, include *Ḥannah Orloff* (1949), *Ẓiyyur u-Fissul be-Yisrael ve-ha-Yeẓirah ha-Ommanutit be-Ereẓ Yisrael ba-Ḥamishim Shanah ha-Aḥaronot* ("Painting and Sculpture in Israel and Artistic Creation in the Land of Israel in the Past 50 Years," 1957); *Ze'ev Ben-Zvi* (1955); *Ommanut ha-Pissul be-Yisrael* ("The Art of Sculpture in Israel," 1957). The Tel Aviv Museum's prize for the advancement of the arts is named for him.

[Getzel Kressel]

GANCHOFF, MOSES (Maurice [Moshe] (1905–1997), *ḥazzan*. Ganchoff was born in Odessa but came to the United States as a child. During his formative years he studied with Simon Zemachson and later came under the influence of the creative talents of Mendel Shapiro and Aryeh Leib Rutman. Even at that tender age, he was already a skilled interpreter of the many recitatives of the most important composer of *ḥazzanut* of that generation, Jacob *Rappaport. After serving in a number of congregations, in 1958 he was appointed cantor to the synagogue in Grossinger's Resort in New Yok's Catskill Mountain Borscht Belt, remaining there until 1978. In 1963 he was invited by the Government of Israel to participate in the Israeli Music Festival. He was lecturer in *ḥazzanut* in the faculty of *ḥazzanut* of Hebrew Union College. Ganchoff was one of the last of the great classical East European *ḥazzanim* and the title of "Ḥazzan's Ḥazzan," by which Ganchoff is known, was apt and well deserved. A number of publications by the Cantors' Assembly and Tara Publications include Ganchoff's: *Mincha* and *Ma'ariv* for Weekdays, "*Tefillot Moshe*," and Favorite Recitatives, all skillfully transcribed and notated by Noah Schall. Barry Serota, record collector and publisher of "Musique Internationale," has issued an entire series of cassettes devoted to the cantorial art of Ganchoff. They are based on standard recordings, radio broadcasts, and live concerts and services that Ganchoff participated in through the course of his long active carreer as a performing *ḥazzan*.

[Akiva Zimmerman / Raymond Goldstein (2nd ed.)

GANDELSONAS, MARIO (1938–), architect. Gandelsonas was born in Buenos Aires and received his degree in architecture from the University of Buenos Aires. In 1977, he and his wife, Diana *Agrest, designed a group of apartment buildings in Buenos Aires. In 1980, they formed the firm of A&G Development Consultants, Inc. Subsequently, Gandelsonas taught at Yale, Harvard, the University of Illinois, and the University of Southern California, later becoming professor of architecture at Princeton University and director of international programs there. Under Gandelsonas' direction, a group of 20 students from Hong Kong University and Tongii University in Shanghai together with Princeton students worked to redesign Hangzou's Wulin Square, including plans for a new cultural center. The city was once the capital of the Southern Song dynasty and today is a tourist center for the 17 million people who come to visit the nearby West Lake. Gandelsonas believes that globalization is making a powerful impact on architecture and his work has inspired other international student projects. The students choose the projects and exchange cultural studies and visits to the sites. The Melrose Community Center (2000) in the Bronx is a good example of the work of A&G, Inc. Set amid high-rise apartment buildings, the center serves about 3,000 young people. With its curved exterior of silver and red, the building beckons young people to use, among other facilities, its basketball court, darkroom, restaurant-size kitchen, and computer lab. The interior is also decorated in silver and red. Gandelsonas received high praise for his Vision Plan (1990–92), a design for central Des Moines. Known for home and apartment design as well as urban planning, he is the author of *The Urban Text* (1991) and *X-Urbanism* (1999), both showing the influence of his studies in Paris with Roland Barthes and also the theories of Sigmund Freud.

BIBLIOGRAPHY: "Joint Study with Asian Universities Inspires Students," in: *Princeton Bulletin*, vol. 90, no. 12 (Dec.11, 2000); M. Gandelsonas (ed.), *Shanghai Reflections: Architecture and Urbanism, and the Search for an Alternative Modernity* (2002).

[Betty R. Rubenstein (2nd ed.)]

°GANDHI, MOHANDAS KARAMCHAND (1869–1948), Indian political leader. Gandhi had several Jewish friends resulting from his 21-year stay in South Africa (1893–1914). This was a period of formative influence in which he formulated and first put into practice his conception of *satyagraha* (nonviolent resistance) and crystallized most of the elements of his ethos and lifestyle. The most intimate of his non-Indian colleagues and confidants in South Africa were Jews, notably H.S.L. (Henry) Polak and Hermann *Kallenbach. However, while evincing sympathy for the Jews as the historic underdog of Western society, Gandhi was less sympathetic to the Jewish religion. Neither Polak nor Kallenbach could authentically interpret Judaism for him since they were both alienated from the Jewish religion and community. Gandhi's formative perception of Judaism derived less from his Hinduism than from the particular circumstances of his exposure, as a Hindu, to Christian influence. While he had reservations about Christianity, he at least understood it on its own terms, whereas Judaism was perceived by him through Christian-tinted glasses. Thus he regarded Jesus as "the finest flower of Judaism" and identified Judaism wholly with the Old Testament which he did not like much. This attitude was reinforced by his contact with the Calvinist Boers of South Africa in whom he saw the products of Old Testament influence.

Gandhi's distorted view of Judaism also prejudiced his perception of Zionism. Thus he insisted that Zion was not geographical but "lies in the heart." It therefore could be realized by Jews anywhere and ought not to mean "the reoccupation of Palestine." Moreover, his overriding striving for Muslim-Hindu amity in an undivided India influenced him to support the Muslim-Arab case against that of Zionism. In March 1921 he made a statement supporting the demand of the Indian Muslim Khilafat (Caliphate) movement that Muslim control be retained over Palestine. He argued on moral grounds but the partiality of his stand is evident in his dismissal of Jewish religious sentiment regarding Palestine, in contrast to his uncritical affirmation of Muslim religious sentiment. Concerned by the increasing hostility to Zionism in India, Moshe Shertok urged Kallenbach, who had meanwhile become a Zionist in South Africa, to visit India with a view to gaining Gandhi's sympathy for the Zionist cause. Kallenbach visited him in May 1937 and succeeded in making the Mahatma more sympathetic to Zionism. Gandhi permitted him to deliver a private statement to the Zionist leadership accepting, in principle, the validity of the Jewish aspiration to found a home in Palestine, but rejecting any reliance on British power, and insisting that fulfillment of Zionist goals be dependent on Arab approval. However, constrained by his solidarity with Muslim feelings in India, Gandhi never gave public expression to such private sentiments. At the same time, not wishing to harm either Jews or Arabs, Gandhi was reluctant to make public statements on the Arab-Jewish conflict. Yet, urged by Kallenbach and others to make his voice heard in the light of Nazi persecution of the Jews, he finally did so in November 1938. But in this statement he again averred that Palestine belonged to the Arabs and advised the Jews to cultivate a spiritual rather than a geographical Zion. He unreservedly condemned Hitler's wanton persecution of the Jews but recommended that the Jews of Germany observe organized *satyagraha* in response to Nazi atrocities and not leave Germany.

Martin Buber and Judah Magnes, both admirers of Gandhi, wrote open letters to him in response to this statement. But they remained unanswered. It is not clear whether Gandhi actually received them. However, he did publicly answer another open letter from Ḥayyim Greenberg, in which he reiterated his views and denied that they were motivated by the desire to win Muslim friendship. It would appear that the nature of Nazi treatment of the Jews lay utterly beyond his comprehension. He remained convinced that "the stoniest German heart will melt" if only the Jews would adopt "active non-violence."

After World War II, Gandhi again expressed some sympathy for the Zionist case in private conversations with the Anglo-Jewish M.P. Sidney Silverman and with his American Jewish biographer, Louis Fischer. But when publicity was given to these sentiments, he reiterated his reservations and condemned violence. His public statements thus remained consistently unsympathetic to Zionism.

As far as the Jews of India are concerned, it appears that they have had a positive view of Gandhi. According to their oral accounts, in 1931 Gandhi met with a number of *Bene Israel to discuss the possible participation of Indian Jews in the nationalist movement and suggested that they join hands with Indian nationalists in the event of their victory but not get involved in wider politics before that time, as they represented such a small minority that they should be concerned chiefly with their own safety.

ADD. BIBLIOGRAPHY: M. Buber, *The Letters of Martin Buber: A Life of Dialogue* (1991); M. Chatterjee, *Gandhi and His Jewish Friends* (1992); E.N. Musleah, *On the Banks of the Ganga: The Sojourn of Jews in Calcutta* (1975); J.G. Roland, *The Jewish Communities of India* (1999).

[Gi. Sh. / Yulia Egorova (2nd ed.)]

GANDZ, SOLOMON (1887–1954), Semitics scholar and historian of mathematics. Gandz was born in Austria. He studied mathematics, Semitics, and rabbinics in Vienna and taught at a Viennese high school from 1915 to 1923. He emigrated to the United States in 1924 and was librarian and instructor in medieval Hebrew and Arabic at the Rabbi Isaac Elchanan Theological Seminary until 1935. From 1942 until his death he taught the history of Semitic civilization at Dropsie College.

Gandz's particular field of study was ancient Oriental mathematics, astronomy, and science and Jewish study of these specialties in the Middle Ages. Among his works in this field is a translation of *Mishnat ha-Middot* (in *Quellen und Studien zur Geschichte der Mathematik, Astronomie und Physik*, Abteilung A, 2, 1932), a second-century Hebrew geometry and its ninth-century Arabic version. A selection of his many essays was collected in *Studies in Hebrew Astronomy and Mathematics* (1970). In Semitics, he contributed an annotated German translation of Imru' al-Qays' sixth-century poems, "Die Muʿallaqa des Imrulqais" (in *Sitzungsbericht der Kaiserlichen Akademie der Wissenschaften in Wien*, 170, Abhandlung 4, 1913). He was associate editor of the international periodical *Osiris*, devoted to the history of science, to which be contributed "The Dawn of Literature" (7 (1939), 261–522). He also contributed the section on public law to the second volume of *Monumenta Talmudica* (Ger., 1913). For the Yale Judaica Series English edition of Maimonides' Mishneh Torah, Gandz did the translation of Book 3, *Book of Seasons* (1961; with Hyman Klein) and of Book 3, Treatise 8, published separately as *Treatise on the Sanctification of the New Moon* (1956).

BIBLIOGRAPHY: J. Dienstag, in: *Hadoar*, 34 (May 14, 1954), 528–9; Levey, in: *Isis*, 46 (1955), 107–10, includes bibliography.

GAN ḤAYYIM (Heb. גַּן חַיִּים), moshav in central Israel in the southern Sharon near *Kefar Sava, affiliated with Tenu'at ha-Moshavim. It was founded in 1935 by veteran farm workers from Russia and other East European countries. The moshav expanded in 1949 when settlers from Romania joined it. Citriculture constituted a prominent farm branch. The population in 1968 was 220, rising to 350 in the mid-1990s and 607 in 2002 after expansion. The moshav is named after Chaim *Weizmann.

[Efraim Orni]

GANNEI TIKVAH (Heb. גַּנֵּי תִּקְוָה), town in central Israel. In 1949 a settlement called Shikkun ha-Yovel was set up by the Jewish Agency on the outskirts of *Petaḥ Tikvah. The new settlement absorbed immigrants from Romania, Poland, Yemen, and Morocco and was only connected to the water system in 1950 and to the electricity grid in 1952. In 1954 its name was changed to Gannei Tikvah and it received municipal status. In 2002 its population was 11,500, with a land area of 0.75 sq. mi. (1.9 sq. km.). The town has many green areas, where sculptures of well-known artists are on display, and in 2002 Merkaz ha-Bamah, a culture center, was opened. The center has a theater group which performs original plays as well as the standard repertoire.

WEBSITE: www.gantik.org.il.

[Shaked Gilboa (2nd ed.)]

GANNEI YEHUDAH (Heb. גַּנֵּי יְהוּדָה; "Gardens of Judea"), moshav with municipal council status in the Judean coastal plain of Israel near Petaḥ Tikvah, affiliated with Ha-Iḥud ha-Ḥakla'i, founded in 1950. The founding settlers were mainly immigrants from South Africa and engaged principally in citriculture. In 1968 Gannei Yehudah had 580 inhabitants, rising to 731 in 2002. In 2004 it was united with the nearby municipal council of Savyon.

[Efraim Orni / Shaked Gilboa (2nd ed.)]

GANS, BIRD STEIN (1868–1944), U.S. educator. Gans was born in Allegheny City, Pennsylvania. In 1896 she became director of the Society for the Study of Child Nature in New York, the first organization in the U.S. engaged in the field of parent education. With the growth of similar societies in other cities, the organization changed its name to the Federation for Child Study in 1898 and Bird Gans was elected its first president. In 1924 the organization became the Child Study Association of America. Gans organized similar groups in Japan (1924) and England (1929). By 1941 the association was conducting extensive experiments and research in child psychology and providing its results to approximately 100 groups throughout the country. Gans was president of the organization until 1933 and honorary president for the next six years. She served on the National Board of Review and the film censorship organization, and she was associated with several organizations devoted to the investigation and solution of youth welfare problems.

GANS, DAVID BEN SOLOMON (1541–1613), chronicler, astronomer, and mathematician. Born in Lippstadt, Westphalia, Gans studied rabbinics with Reuben Fulda in Bonn; Eliezer Treves in Frankfurt; Moses Isserles in Cracow; and Judah Loew (the *Maharal*) in Prague. Encouraged, so it is said, by Isserles, he devoted himself to the study of mathematics and astronomy. In the house of his first father-in-law Gans apparently found a Hebrew translation of Euclid by Moses ibn Tibbon; his second father-in-law was the physician Samuel Rofe who had become famous for his mercury cures of syphilis. Gans was one of the few German Jews of his time, when rabbinics ruled supreme, to undertake serious secular studies for which he found and quoted older Jewish authorities. In Prague he corresponded with the astronomer Johann Mueller (Regiomontanus) and was in friendly contact with Johann Kepler and Tycho Brahe, for whom he translated the Alfonsine Tables from Hebrew into German.

Gans's main astronomical (and also geographical) work was *Neḥmad ve-Na'im* ("Delightful and Pleasant," Jesnitz, 1743; shortened version *Magen David*, Prague, 1612) in which he rejects the new Copernican system in favor of Ptolemy's, the former going back (according to Gans) to the Pythagorean system. Astronomy (and mathematics) – he held – was first studied by Jews from whom the Egyptians had learned the science, passing it on to the Greeks. Ptolemy had studied with Alexandrian Jewish scholars. The study of astronomy was important not only for the Jewish calendar but as proof for the cultural achievements of the Jewish people. Other works by Gans on mathematics, the calendar, and the geography of Ereẓ Israel remained unpublished.

Gans wrote his chronicle *Ẓemaḥ David* ("Offspring of David," Prague, 1592) in two parts, one dealing with Jewish history to the date of publication, the other with general history. He had written it for "householders like myself and of my worth," while justifying the inclusion of general history by the fact that it contained ethical teachings of emperors, which ordinary people would accept coming from such illustrious mouths. The first part of the work summarizes that of his predecessors, such as Ibn *Daud and *Zacuto, but he dissociates himself from the untraditional approach of Azariah dei *Rossi. For the second part his sources are contemporary German chroniclers like Cyriak Spangenberg and Laurentius Faustus, though in his introduction he expresses doubts as to their reliability. Gans shows an interest in economics; his description of historical events and situations reflects the spirit and taste of the 16th-century Jewish "householder" in Bohemia and Poland. The *Ẓemaḥ David* remained a standard work up to the Haskalah period. The second edition by David b. Moses of Reindorf (Frankfurt, 1692) brings the chronicle up to the date of publication, also giving a long poetical description of the *Fettmilch riots of 1614. It was translated into Latin by W.H. Vorst (Leyden, 1692); into Yiddish by Solomon Zalman Hanau (Frankfurt, 1698); and parts of it into German by G. Klemperer (ed. Moritz Gruenwald, 1890). The Warsaw edition of 1849, also brought up to date, was reproduced in 1966 with introductions in Hebrew and English and an index.

BIBLIOGRAPHY: K. Lieben, *Gal-Ed* (1856), Hebrew section 4; German section 10–12; M. Steinschneider, *Geschichtsliteratur der Juden* (1905), para. 132; idem, *Copernikus nach dem Urteil des David Gans* (1871); M. Grunwald, in: D. Gans, *Ẓemaḥ David*, Ger. tr. by G. Klemperer (1890), introd.; S. Steinherz, in: JGGJČ, 9 (1938), 171–97; G. Alter, *Two Renaissance Astronomers* (1958).

GANS, EDUARD (1789–1839), jurist and historian in Berlin. From 1816 to 1819 he studied law and philosophy in the universities of Berlin and Heidelberg; at Heidelberg he was influenced by *Hegel and his system and became one of the philosopher's closest students. In 1820 Gans was appointed lecturer at the University of Berlin where he became celebrated for his inspiring lectures. In contrast with Hegel and Kant, Gans argued that Judaism should be seen as one of the major sources of Western culture and the origin of its notion of religion and morals. He considered Rabbinic Judaism to be a vital development of prophetic Biblical Judaism and a dynamic response to the surrounding cultures of the time. Nevertheless, throughout the centuries and owing to Christian anti-Jewish pressure traditional Judaism degenerated. Contemporary Judaism must adjust itself to the values and cultural level in order to regain its vitality and to overcome its isolationist tendency. As an expression of this notion he founded in 1819, in conjunction with Leopold *Zunz and Moses *Moser, the *Verein fuer Kultur und Wissenschaft der Juden (Society for Culture and Science of the Jews), the objective of which was to establish a scientific modern study of Judaism, to bring general education to Jewish youth by expanding their cultural horizons, and the reform of traditional Jewish thinking. The society, which proved to be the first step towards the development of Wissenschaft des Judentums, was dissolved in 1824. In this period not much was done in terms of actual research but major programmatic formulations – not the least by Gans himself – laid the ground for the further work done in the next generations. Gans' inclination to *assimilation, and the government's objection to the appointment of a Jew to a permanent academic position, led Gans to become an apostate to Christianity at the end of 1825. In 1826 he was appointed associate professor at Berlin University, and in 1829 a full professor. In his lectures on jurisprudence, which attracted an enormous audience, Gans developed the Hegelian philosophical system rejecting the historical system of Savigny. On history, he elaborated the concept of the Prussian state and its sovereignty, and the central role of the ruler as the incarnation of the concept of the state. He saw the French Revolution as a new and crucial factor in European history, and explained the historical concept of "Europe" as a synthesis of different peoples incorporating the best in the cultures of Israel, Greece, Roman, Christianity, and the West in its development; Gans was opposed to nationalism and the romantic glorification of the Middle Ages and its Christian culture.

His works include (on law) *Scholien zum Gaius* (1821); *System des roemischen Civilrechts im Grundrisse* (1827); *Ueber die Grundlage des Besitzes* (1839); *Beitraege zur Revision der preussischen Gesetzgebung* (1830–32); *Das Erbrecht in weltgeschichtlicher Entwicklung* (4 vol., 1824–35; repr.), a fundamental work on comparative law; and a historical work, *Vorlesungen ueber die Geschichte der letzten fuenfzig Jahre* (1833–34). He also edited Hegel's lectures on the philosophy of history (vols. 8 and 9 of G.W.F. Hegel's *Werke*, 1833–37). In 1827 he founded the *Jahrbuecher fuer wissenschaftliche Kritik*. An essay on the principles of the law of inheritance in the Pentateuch and Talmud, a chapter from his work *Das Erbrech in weltgeschichtlicher Entwicklung*, appeared in the *Zietschrift fuer die Wissenschaft des Judentums* (vol. 1 (1822–23), 419–71), which also published his study of the Roman legislation concerning the Jews ("Gesetzgebung ueber Juden in Rom"). The reports of the society, including several of his addresses, are preserved in manuscript in the Zunz archives in Jerusalem.

BIBLIOGRAPHY: B. Kurzweil, in: *Haaretz* (April 24, 1967); H.G. Reissner, *Eduard Gans: ein Leben in Vormaerz* (1965); idem, in: YLBI, 2 (1957), 179–86; 4 (1959), 92–110; M. Wiener, in: YIVOA, 5 (1950), 190–3. **ADD. BIBLIOGRAPHY:** Eduard Gans, *Rueckblicke auf Personen und Zustanede* (autobiography), ed. with introduction by N. Waszek (1995); N. Waszek, *Eduard Gans (1797–1839) – Hegelianer, Jude Europaeer – Texte und Dokumente* (1991); J. Braun, *Judentum, Jurisprudenz und Philosophie – Bilder aus dem Leben des Juristen Eduard Gans (1797–1839)* (1997); J.M. Harris, "Fitting in or sticking out – constructs of the relationships of Jewish and Roman law in the nineteenth century," in: H. Lapin and D.B. Martin (eds.), *Jews, Antiquity and the Nineteenth Century Imagination* (2003), 53–63.

[Nachum Glatzer / Yehoyada Amir (2nd ed.)]

GANS, MOZES ("Max") HEIMAN (1917–1987), Dutch author, journalist, and jeweler. Gans grew up in the building of the "Joodse Invalide." This was the institute for poor Jewish invalids, an outstanding example of modern Jewish charity of which the controversial Rebbe Meijer de Hond (1882–1943) was the spiritual father and Gans' own father, Isaac Gans, the founder and director.

In 1943 Max Gans managed to escape to Switzerland, where he founded the Joodse Coördinatie Commissie in Genève, which acted as much as possible on behalf of the Dutch Jews under Nazi occupation. Upon his return to Amsterdam he took over the jeweler's shop of his father-in-law (who had been deported to his death), Premsela & Hamburger, specializing in silverware. Later he would write a standard work on antique silver.

At the same time he was active in Jewish affairs, becoming the head of the Central Committee for Jewish Education of the Netherlands Ashkenazi Congregation (NIK) and in 1950 assistant editor and then, from 1956 to 1966, the editor of the Dutch Jewish Weekly *Nieuw Israelitisch Weekblad* (NIW). As the (assistant) editor of the NIW he criticized what he saw as the short Dutch national memory of the persecution of the Dutch Jews, the apologetical attitude towards the Jewish Council by the Jewish author and lawyer Abel Herzberg (1893–1989), and the opportunistic way in which the German *Widergutmachungs* money was handled by the Dutch authorities.

A private collector of Judaica, Gans published in 1971 his monumental *Memorbook, A Pictorial History of Dutch Jewry from the Middle Ages to 1940*, with some 1,100 illustrations, which in 1987 went into its sixth printing, with an English translation published in 1977. In addition, he published three smaller albums on the Amsterdam Jewish quarter before 1940 and after – all of which were also translated into English. In 1976–77 he held the appointment of professor extraordinary in Dutch Jewish history at the University of Leiden.

ADD. BIBLIOGRAPHY: S. Bloemgarten and P. Bregstein, *Herinnering aan Joods Amsterdam* (1978); M. Bossenbroek, *De Meelstreep. Terugkeer en opvang na de Tweede Wereldoorlog* (2001); J. Gans-Premsela, in: *Memorboek* (fifth printing, 1988), 840–45; idem, *Vluchtweg. Aan de bezetter ontsnapt* (1999); C. Kristel, *Geschiedschrijving als opdracht. Abel Herzberg, Jacques Presser en Loe de Jong over de jodenvervolging* (1998); I. Lipschits, *Honderd jaar NIW. Het Nieuw Israëlietisch Weekblad 1865–1965* (1966); S.R. de Melker, in: *Dutch Jewish History*, 2 (1989), 411–24.

[Henriette Boas / Evelien Gans (2nd ed.)]

GAN SHELOMO (Heb. גַּן שְׁלֹמֹה; previously known as Kevuzat Schiller), kibbutz near Reḥovot, affiliated with Iḥud ha-Kevuẓot ve-ha-Kibbutzim. It was founded in 1927 by a pioneer group of former students from Galicia. Affiliated with Ḥever ha-Kevuẓot (of *Mapai orientation), the settlers nevertheless preserved their political ties with Ha-Oved ha-Ẓiyyoni (Independent Liberals). Citriculture, field crops, orchards, poultry and dairy cattle constituted principal farm branches, and the kibbutz also had a textile factory. Gan Shelomo is named in memory of Solomon *Schiller. In 1968 its population was 265, rising to 413 in 2002.

[Efraim Orni]

GAN SHEMU'EL (Heb. גַּן שְׁמוּאֵל), kibbutz in central Israel near *Ḥaderah, affiliated with Kibbutz Arẓi ha-Shomer ha-Ẓa'ir. Members of Odessa's Ḥovevei Zion first settled there in 1884, laying out plantations of *etrogim* ("citrons"). They named the place "Samuel's Garden" after Samuel *Mohilever. In 1912 a laborers' group settled there temporarily, and in 1921 settlers from Eastern Europe took over. In 1968 Gan Shemu'el had 700 inhabitants, and in 2002 a total of 827. The kibbutz's economy has been based on intensive farming (fieldcrops, orchards, dairy cattle, fishery, turkeys, and ducks) and a food preserves factory.

WEBSITE: www.ganshmuel.org.il.

[Efraim Orni /Shaked Gilboa (2nd ed.)]

GAN SHOMRON (Heb. גַּן שׁוֹמְרוֹן), moshav in central Israel, northeast of *Ḥaderah, founded in 1934 by middle-class settlers from Germany and unaffiliated with any moshav association. It expanded after 1945, when World War II veterans and new immigrants settled there. Its economy was based on intensive farming (especially citriculture). The name Gan Shomron refers to the location of the village near the Samaria Hills. In 1969 its population was 322, rising to 599 in 2002.

[Efraim Orni]

GANSO, JOSEPH (17th century), rabbi, author, and *paytan*. He lived in Bursa, Turkey, and, in his old age, immigrated to Jerusalem, where he died. Famed as a leading hymnologist he composed a book of *piyyutim* of which only one incomplete copy is extant (in the library of the Jewish Theological Seminary in New York). The hymns, written in a lucid style, reveal the influence of R. Israel *Najara, but they are also original in a manner typical of his contemporaries and of his time. Several of the hymns are in Aramaic. The most important of Ganso's pupils was R. Solomon *Algazi.

BIBLIOGRAPHY: Conforte, Kore, 50a, 51a; Ghirondi-Neppi, 197; Rosanes, Togarmah, 3 (1914), 160; Davidson, Oẓar, 4 (1933), 493–4.

[Abraham Meir Habermann]

GANTMAN, JUDAH LEIB (Leo) (1888–1953), *ḥazzan*. Judah Leib Gantman was born in Berlin and, as a child, participated in the choir of his father, Cantor Benjamin Gantman, who composed melodies for many portions of the prayer service. He continued his studies in music and in 1908 moved to Odessa, where he studied at the Music Conservatory. He served in the Russian army as conductor of the military orchestra, both in the Czarist army and in the revolutionary army, until he was released in 1919. From 1920 to 1927 he conducted the Odessa Opera, after which he moved to Antwerp, where he conducted the synagogue choir of the "Machsiké Hadass" community. Gantman left hundreds of compositions for sections of the prayer service. He trained many cantors, some of whom are still serving in many parts of the world.

[Akiva Zimmerman (2nd ed.)]

GAN YAVNEH (Heb. גַּן יַבְנֶה), town in the coastal plain of Israel, southwest of *Yavneh. The municipal council area is 4 sq. mi. (10.5 sq. km.). It was founded as a moshavah in 1931 by a Zionist group, the Aḥuzah society in New York, most of whose members failed to arrive. The moshavah was considerably enlarged by new immigrants in 1949 and in 1950 received its municipal council status. The population of the settlement constantly grew, reaching 2,840 inhabitants in 1968, 4,790 in the mid-1990s, and 12,200 at the end of 2002. Its name refers to the historical site of Jabneh, which is 5½ mi. (9 km.) away.

[Efraim Orni / Shaked Gilboa (2nd ed.)]

GANZFRIED, SOLOMON BEN JOSEPH (1804–1886), rabbi and author. Ganzfried was born in Ungvar, Hungary, where he also died. Orphaned in his childhood, he was brought up in the house of the local rabbi Ẓevi Hirsch Heller, one of the outstanding scholars of his time. From 1830 to 1849 Ganzfried served as rabbi of Brezewicz and subsequently as head of the *bet din* of Ungvar. He was one of the chief speakers for orthodox Jewry at the Jewish congress which took place in Budapest in 1869. He also published a polemic against the Reform movement. His first published work, *Keset-ha-Sofer* (1835; 1871[2] with additions by the author), was on the laws of writing a *Sefer Torah*, and was highly recommended by Moses *Sofer as a necessary textbook for scribes of Torah scrolls, *tefillin*, and *mezuzot*. Ganzfried's fame, however, rests mainly upon his *Kiẓẓur Shulḥan Arukh* ("Abridged Shulḥan Arukh," 1864); it achieved great popularity and widespread circulation and was accepted as the main handbook for Ashkenazi Jewry. It encompassed all the laws relating to the mode of life of the ordinary Jew living outside Ereẓ Israel (including such subjects as etiquette, hygiene, etc.), but omitting such details as were common knowledge and practice at that time (see his introduction to ch. 80) or that were not essential knowledge for the ordinary man (see especially the laws of matrimony, ch. 145). The *Kiẓẓur Shulḥan Arukh* is based upon the Shulḥan Arukh of Joseph *Caro with the glosses of Moses *Isserles. It is written in simple, popular language, with a lively style, and interest is sustained by the ethical maxims with which it is interlaced. Unlike his predecessor Abraham *Danzig, author of the *Ḥayyei Adam*, Ganzfried does not detail and explain the different views but usually gives his decision without the reasoning. The book had already achieved 14 editions during its author's lifetime, and since then it has gone through scores of editions, displacing all previous abridgments of the Shulḥan Arukh. It also became a basic work to which many scholars added marginal notes and novellae.

The important editions of the work are Lublin, 1888, with the commentaries, "*Pe'at ha-Shulḥan*" by the author himself, *Ammudei ha-Shulḥan* by Benjamin Isaiah b. Jeroham Fishel ha-Kohen, and *Misgeret Zahav*, by Moses Israel; Leipzig, 1924, with source references (*Meẓudat Ẓiyyon*), supplements (*Meẓudat David*) and with illustrations, edited by D. Feldman; Jerusalem, 1940, a vocalized edition with the addition of the laws and customs applying in Ereẓ Israel at the present day, edited by J.M. Tykocinski, and one with the additions *Misgeret ha-Shulḥan* and *Leḥem ha-Panim* of Ḥayyim Isaiah ha-Kohen Halbersberg and a summary of those precepts connected with the land of Israel in accordance with the rulings of Abraham Isaiah *Karelitz, edited by K. Kahana (Jerusalem, 1954).

The book was also translated into many languages (English by H.E. Goldin (1928)). Ganzfried's other published works are a commentary on the prayer book with notes and supplements to the prayer-book commentary *Derekh ha-Ḥayyim* of Jacob Lorbeerbaum (first published in the prayer book printed in Vienna in 1839); *Penei Shelomo* (1845), novellae to Bava Batra; *Torat Zevaḥ* (1849), on the laws of *sheḥitah; Leḥem ve-Simlah* (1861), on the laws of menstruation and ritual immersion; *Appiryon* (1864; with the author's additions in 1876), homilies on the Pentateuch and on some *aggadot; Oholei Shem* (1878), on the laws of names in bills of divorce and on the writing of deeds; and *Shem Shelomo* (1908), on talmudic themes. There have remained in manuscript *Leshon ha-Zahav*, on Hebrew grammar; *Penei Adam*, notes to the *Ḥayyei Adam; Kelalim be-Ḥokhmat ha-Emet*, a commentary on the Zohar; and his responsa.

BIBLIOGRAPHY: Brody, in: *Oẓar ha-Sifrut*, 3 (1889/90), 55–61 (4th pagination); J. Banet, in: S. Ganzfried, *Shem Shelomo* (1908), introd.; J.L. Maimon, in: S. Ganzfried, *Kiẓẓur Shulḥan Arukh* (1950), introd.

[Jacob S. Levinger]

GAON (pl. **Geonim**), formal title of the heads of the academies of Sura and Pumbedita in Babylonia. The *geonim* were recognized by the Jews as the highest authority of instruction from the end of the sixth century or somewhat later to the middle of the 11th. In the 10th and 11th centuries this title was also used by the heads of academies in Ereẓ Israel. In the 12th and 13th centuries – after the geonic period in the exact sense of the term – the title *gaon* was also used by the heads of academies in Baghdad, Damascus, and Egypt. It eventually became an honorific title for any rabbi or anyone who had a great knowledge of Torah. Apparently, the term *gaon* was shortened from *rosh yeshivat ge'on Ya'akov* (cf. "the pride of Jacob," Ps. 47:4). Other explanations of the origin of the term offered by modern scholars are not acceptable.

The Geonim of Sura and Pumbedita

The exact time when the title of *gaon* came into use cannot be established. *Sherira and later rabbis automatically designated as *gaon* the heads of the two academies from the year 900 according to the Seleucid calendar (589 C.E.), when the academies renewed their normal activity. But Sherira also mentions a tradition that Ravai, of Pumbedita (c. 540–560), was already *gaon*. However, some hold that this title and the special privileges of the academies were not granted until after the Arab conquest of Babylonia (657 C.E.), Sura receiving them first and later Pumbedita. Together with the title *gaon* they also used the titles *resh metivta* or *rosh yeshivah* ("head of the academy") as was customary in the talmudic period, and the title *rosh yeshivah shel ha-golah* ("head of the academy of the exile"), which is not found in the Talmud. According to a tradition that originated in the Sura academy (Neubauer, Chronicles, 2 (1895), 78), only the heads at Sura were called *gaon* and not their counterparts in Pumbedita. This was accepted by some historians but is contradicted by R. Sherira's account and other sources. The existence of separate traditions, one in Sura that enumerates "the qualities in which Sura is superior to Pumbedita" (*ibid.*), and that of Pumbedita which emphasizes that "the rabbis of Pumbedita are the leaders of the Diaspora from the time of the Second Temple" (*Iggeret Rav Sherira Ga'on*, ed. B.M. Lewin (1921), 82), emphasizes the competition between the two. Hints of tension and even open quarrels are found in other sources. Nevertheless, Sura and Pumbedita dominated the intellectual landscape of the period to the extent that little or nothing is known about other scholars or academies.

In the talmudic period the heads of the academies were chosen by the scholars of the academies (BB 12b) while in the geonic period they were appointed by the exilarchs. *Geonim* usually (although not always) rose through the hierarchy of positions in the academies until they attained this highest office. Persons of average ability therefore also attained the gaonate, and in the entire period of 400 years only a few *geonim* were outstanding men who made a lasting impact on Judaism. These included *Yehudai, *Amram, *Saadiah, Sherira, *Samuel b. Hophni, and *Hai. At times the exilarchs misused their authority and appointed *geonim* whom they expected to be subservient to them and who were not outstanding scholars. For example, it is related that an exilarch rejected *Aḥa of Shabḥa, author of the *She'iltot*, and appointed his disciple Natronai Kahana to the gaonate in Pumbedita (Ibn Daud, *Sefer ha-Kabbalah*, 47–49). Thus, the academy in Sura was generally disturbed by the interference of the exilarchs. Sherira (*Iggeret Sherira Ga'on*, 105) argues that because of the interference of the exilarchs he could not exactly record the names of the *geonim* of Sura until the year 1000 of the Seleucid calendar (689 C.E.). After the authority of the exilarchs had weakened under *David b. Judah (*ibid.* 93) in the times of the caliph al-Ma'mun, from 825, the influence of the group of scholars on the appointment of the *gaon* increased, especially in Pumbedita. Traditionally, the *gaon* had multiple roles. First and foremost, the *gaon* was the head of the academy, teaching privately and publicly, especially during the *kallah* months (see below). In addition, he served as judge and the head of the equivalent of a supreme court. He also was empowered to administer the courts and appoint judges. The leading *geonim* also wrote numerous responsa, i.e., correspondence answering halakhic questions from near and from far. As an arbiter of Halakhah, the *gaon* was also responsible for legal innovation when the situation warranted it. Numerous *geonim* were authors of commentaries, legal codes, and works of theology (see *Geonic Literature). Finally, some of the *geonim* were involved in politics beyond the Jewish community. They represented the community to the local and state Muslim governments.

There were cases when the exilarch and the group of scholars could not agree on the appointment of the *gaon* and each side appointed its own candidate. If the two sides did not reach a compromise as a result of the pressure of public opinion, the quarrel might last until the death of one of the candidates. Generally, assistants to the heads of academies were appointed *gaon* and were called *dayyanei de-bava* or *av* (abbreviation of *av bet din*). Distinguished *geonim*, such as Sherira, Samuel b. Hophni, and Hai had first served as *av bet din*; a deviation from this practice was considered derogatory. Because only those who already possessed such honorific titles as *aluf and *resh kallah and who had formerly served as scribes or assistants to heads of *yeshivot*, were appointed to the gaonate, the choice often fell on old men who could fill the position for only a few years.

In this period the academies in Babylonia served as the cultural center for world Jewry, and not only Babylonian-Persian Jewry as was the case in talmudic times. Hence, the influence of the *geonim* was now all-important. The *geonim* viewed themselves as the heirs to the Babylonian talmudic tradition. They continued the work of the Babylonian **amoraim* as passed on by the **savoraim*. This in turn was the source of their supreme authority in matters of *halakhah*. During the geonic period the Babylonian Talmud existed as both oral law and as written texts. Indeed, the *geonim* always quoted the oral tradition before citing the written texts. Since their knowledge of the Talmud was the result of an unbroken tradition, the text had a certain fluidity. The *gaon* would often quote from differing oral versions of the Talmud, even without determining the "correct" version. The *geonim* had a three-fold responsibility regarding the Talmud: (a) They were part of the chain of tradition, transmitting the Talmud to the next generation. (b) They endeavored to provide the correct interpretation of the Talmud. (c) They actively facilitated the practice of Judaism according to the Talmud. Until the second half of the 10th century, very few of their interpretations were written down. They were simply taught in the academies. Since the *geonim* spoke an Aramaic dialect very similar to that of the Babylonian *amoraim*, they had an added advantage of correctly understanding the Talmud. They clearly were intimately aware of the spirit of talmudic discourse and enjoyed a sensitivity to its literary nature. This profoundly influenced their interpretations in general and greatly affected the practical application of the Talmud text. The *geonim* became skilled at utilizing the advanced communication and travel technologies developed by the Muslim Empire to get their message to far-flung Jewish communities in North Africa and in Spain.

The *geonim* made the academies a supreme court and source of instruction for all Jewry. Thousands of persons, occupied with their personal affairs for most of the year, would assemble in the academies in the *kallah months of Elul and Adar to hear lectures on *halakhah*. During those months, three types of study took place: (a) A specific tractate of Talmud was studied in depth; (b) individual students were tested to see if they were worthy of the stipend; and (c) the assembly would discuss questions in *halakhah*, many of which were sent from throughout the Diaspora. The floor was open to all scholars. However the *gaon* made the final decision. The academies were actually filled with students only during the *kallah* months. Throughout the rest of the year, only a small group of serious students remained. These students received stipends from the academies.

While the Talmud and Talmud study were the center of the geonic universe, the *geonim* engaged in other areas of Jewish study. One such area is biblical exegesis. The innovator was Saadiah Gaon. Other geonim followed Saadiah's lead in writing biblical commentary; the most important of them was Samuel ben Hophni. Saadiah was the first gaon to write monographs on specific topics, a number of which he devoted to biblical translation and commentary. Saadiah translated the entire Pentateuch, as well as the books of Isaiah, Proverbs, Psalms, Job, and Daniel. He wrote commentaries on all of these books, with the exception of the latter half of the Pentateuch. Samuel ben Hophni translated and wrote commentaries on three of the five books of the Pentateuch. Each monograph begins with a lengthy and elaborate introduction in which the *gaon* describes the biblical text and explains the methodology of his commentary. On the whole, the commentaries emphasize the linguistic components of the text, the conflict between the literal and metaphoric meaning of the text, and theological and polemical concerns. The *geonim* commented on the non-legal portions of the Bible, leaving the legal sections to be dealt with in their halakhic works. At the same time, their commentaries are more disciplined and far less imaginative than earlier rabbinic exegesis. Samuel ben Hophni's commentaries do include homilies but they are not based on a specific text. Rather, they derive from the overall thrust of the whole portion of the text.

There were two major courts in Sura and two in Pumbedita. In each academy there was the *gaon*'s court and that of the *av bet din*. In addition, the gaonate had jurisdiction over the organization of the courts in all the districts of Babylonia. However, the judges were appointed by the exilarch with the assent of the *geonim*. Only under Hai Gaon did the supreme court (*bet din ha-gadol*) of Pumbedita appoint the judges (Neubauer, Chronicles, 2 (1887), 85; *Teshuvot ha-Ge'onim*, ed. Harkavy, no. 180). The *geonim* were not satisfied with halakhic conclusions derived from the Talmud; they also made new regulations regarding contemporary needs. Their *takkanot* ("ordinances") had legal validity because the *geonim* considered themselves presidents of the Sanhedrin of their generation. The halakhic decisions of the geonim were not made without influence from the general, non-Jewish legal environment. It has been demonstrated that a number of geonic customs had their origins in Islamic practice. For example, the question arose as to how a widow who lost her **ketubbah* would receive payment. Ẓemaḥ Gaon suggested that the determination should be made by consulting the ketubbot of her relatives. Both Sherirah and Hai disagreed with this ruling because it had no basis in the Talmud. However, a similar practice existed in Islamic law. Interestingly, the custom was accepted by later authorities, including Solomon *Duran, Solomon *Aderet and *Asher ben Jeḥiel.

All these tasks required a large establishment; therefore, the academies employed scribes, directors of the *kallah* assemblies, and other officials. Their expenditure was covered by taxes levied on districts, which were directly subject to their authority. In addition, the communities which addressed their questions to the *geonim* sent them contributions. In isolated instances the *geonim* would turn to the communities in the Diaspora with a request for financial support and usually their request was answered. Real estate also served as a source of income for the academies. The requests for support of the academies increased, especially, toward the end of the geonic period. Thus, the candidates for the office of head of the academies had to be not only learned, but they also had to possess administrative talents. Descent was also a factor; six or seven families provided most of the *geonim* of Sura and Pumbedita. Three of these were priestly, while Sherira traced his ancestry to King David (*Iggeret Sherira Ga'on*, 92). His family produced several *geonim*, many assistant heads of academies, and other important officials in Pumbedita. In Sura positions were held for 200 years by three families. The *geonim* Jacob, Ivomai, Moses, and *Kohen Ẓedek (b. Ivomai) belonged to one priestly family; another such family produced the *geonim* *Hilai (788), *Natronai b. Hilai (853), Jacob, and Joseph (942), while a third priestly family produced the *geonim* Kohen Ẓedek of Pumbedita, his son *Nehemiah, Samuel b. Ḥophni grandson of Kohen Zedek, his son *Israel, and his grandson Azariah of Sura. The *geonim* Zadok, Kimoi, *Nahshon, *Zemah b. Ḥayyim, and Hai b. Nahshon were members of one family. However, the position of *gaon* was not hereditary. Although Hai attained the gaonate immediately after his father Sherira, Nahshon did not become *gaon* until 53 years after the death of his father Zadok, seven members of other families serving as *geonim* in the interim. The difference in time between the death of Hilai and the appointment of his son Natronai was similar. *Dosa did not attain the gaonate until 71 years after the death of his father Saadiah and when he was more than 80 years old.

On the appointment of a new *gaon* a festive ceremony was held, in which participated the scholars of the two academies and the dignitaries of all the communities in Babylonia, headed by the exilarch. According to *Nathan ben Isaac ha-Bavli (Neubauer, Chronicles 2 (1895), 86), the ceremony resembled the installation of the exilarch and the people honored the *geonim* royally. Following the method of talmudic references to heads of academies, Sherira throughout used the word "*malakh*" ("reigned") to designate the term of service of the *gaon*.

The *geonim* were considered the intellectual leaders of the entire Diaspora and their decisions and responsa had absolute legal validity in most Jewish communities. It cannot be assumed that they attained their influence without a struggle and conflict with other centers, especially Ereẓ Israel. Ben Baboi (see *Pirkoi Ben Baboi) the pupil of Yehudai Gaon, attested to the intervention of the *geonim* in the affairs of Ereẓ Israel, "and he wrote to Ereẓ Israel regarding… all the *mitzvot* which are not observed properly according to the *halakhah* but according to practice in times of persecution and they did not accept his intervention and they replied to him: 'a custom suspends a *halakhah*'" (Ginzberg, *Ginzei Schechter*, 2 (1929), 559). Baboi attacked practices of Ereẓ Israel (*Tarbiz*, 2 (1931), 396–7). He claimed that only the Babylonian customs and practices were valid. To follow the customs of Ereẓ Israel was a sin. Seventy years later, Amram polemized against those who followed the customs of the westerners who deviated from the right path. The aim of the Babylonian *geonim* was to impose the Babylonian Talmud and the doctrines of their academies also in Ereẓ Israel and in this way to lessen the attachment of the Diaspora to Ereẓ Israel.

The gaonate had a specific political, communal function at the side of the exilarch. The recognition of the gaonate as a political representation of the Jewish community is attested by the fact that on the death of the exilarch his income was given to the *gaon* of Sura until the appointment of a new exilarch. The *geonim* also attempted to influence the policy of the government toward the Jews via Baghdad Jewry, who had representatives in the court of the caliphs. However, the particular achievement of the *geonim* was their success in giving legal validity to the laws of the Talmud and spreading the knowledge of the Talmud among the thousands of people who came to Babylonia from all parts of the world. Their writings in the fields of commentary and *halakhah* made an impact on the entire period which is named after them. Their great importance to Jewry is attested by the paragraph in the **Kaddish* where the *geonim* are mentioned together with the exilarch (*Gedenkbuch… D. Kaufmann* (1900), Hebrew section, 52ff.; *Ginzei Kedem*, 2 (1923), 46; 3 (1925), 54). They and other high officials in the academies are also mentioned with the exilarch in the prayer *Yekum Purkan*. R. *Ẓemaḥ b. Ḥayyim, the *gaon* of Sura, expressed this feeling of authority in his responsa to the community in Kairouan: "And when Eldad said that they pray for the scholars of Babylonia and then for those in the Diaspora, they are right. For the major scholars and prophets were exiled to Babylonia, and they established the Torah and founded the academy on the Euphrates under Jehoiachin, king of Judah until this day, and they were the dynasty of wisdom and prophecy and the source of Torah for the entire people…" (*Eldad ha-Dani*, ed. by Abraham Epstein (1891), 8).

Even though the leading *geonim* were those of the later generations, the gaonate already had declined as the cultural, religious center of Judaism far before it had ceased to exist. This was as a result of a combination of internal and external causes. A sign of its public decline was that from the late ninth century most *geonim* no longer lived in the cities of the two academies. They lived in Baghdad, the center of the authorities and the residence of the exilarch. On the one hand, the decline of the academies in the eyes of the Diaspora was caused by the competition between Sura and Pumbedita and the quarrels in the academies regarding the appointment of the *gaon*. On the other hand, the essence of the fulfillment of the mission of the *geonim* – the spread of the Talmud – lessened its importance. With the emergence of new centers for talmudic studies and the appearance of great scholars throughout the Diaspora, its dependence on the two academies and on the *geonim* ceased and its attachment to them weakened. Independent-minded scholars stopped sending questions to the academies and their *geonim*, and even important *geonim* such as Sherira and Hai expressed their anger at the weakening of the links with North Africa and with Spain (Mann, Texts, 1 (1931), 109, 120–1). *Ḥanokh b. Moses of Cordoba did not even answer the letters of *Sherira. The scholars of Spain found encouragement from the authorities in their tendency to break their dependence on the *geonim* of Babylonia. The Umayyad caliphs in Cordoba did not approve the

Jewish attachment to the academies in Babylonia which were under the Abbasids (cf. Abraham ibn Daud's statement, "The king was delighted by the fact that the Jews in his domain no longer had need of the people of Babylon," Ibn Daud, *Sefer ha-Kabbalah*, 66).

The decline of the Baghdad caliphate, the impoverishment of Babylonian Jewry which caused the academies to depend completely on contributions from abroad, the greatness and the independent intellectual development of the Diaspora, and the persecutions by the Abbasid and Seljuk rulers put an end to the institution of the gaonate in about 1040.

List of the Geonim of Sura and Pumbedita

Because of the dearth of sources the exact chronology of the *geonim* cannot be established. The letter of R. Sherira serves as the basis for the list but it contains contradictions and many variant versions. (See Table: Chronological List of Geonim in Sura and Pumbedita.) The list of Abraham *Ibn Daud in the *Sefer ha-Kabbalah* does not clarify these contradictions. Nonetheless, the letter of Sherira remains the major source for the chronology of the Babylonian *geonim*. But there is much material on the history of their period, both in Babylonia and in other countries, in the collections of the responsa of the *geonim* (see bibliography).

Chronological List of the Geonim in Sura and Pumbedita (dates according to year of appointment)

Sura		Pumbedita
	589	Hanan of Iskiya
Mar bar Huna	591	(?) Mari b. Dimi (formerly of Firuz-Shapur and Nehardea)
Ḥanina	614	Ḥanina of Bei-Gihara (Firuz-Shapur)
		Ḥana (or Huna)
Huna	650	
Sheshna (called also Mesharsheya b. Taḥlifa)	...	
	651	Rabbah
	...	Bosai
Ḥanina of Nehar-Pekod	689	Huna Mari b. Joseph
	...	Ḥiyya of Meshan
	...	Ravya (or Mar Yanka)
Hilai ha-Levi of Naresh	694	
Jacob ha-Kohen of Nehar-Pekod	712	
	719	Natronai b. Nehemiah
	...	Judah
Samuel	730	
	739	Joseph
Mari Kohen of Nehar-Pekod	748	Samuel b. Mar
	752	(?) Natroi Kahana b. Mar Amunah
	...	Abraham Kahana
Aḥa	756	
Yehudai b. Naḥman	757	
Aḥunai Kahana b. Papa	761	Dodai b. Naḥman (brother of Yehudai the gaon of Sura)
	764	Hananiah b. Mesharsheya
Ḥaninai Kahana b. Huna	769	
	771	Malkha b. Aḥa
	773	Rabbah (Abba) b. Dodai
Mari ha-Levi b. Mesharsheya	774	
Bebai, (Bivoi, Bivi) ha-Levi b. Abba of Nehar-Pekod	777	
	781	Shinoi
	782	Ḥaninai Kahana b. Abraham
	785	Huna ha-Levi b. Isaac
Hilai b. Mari	788	Manasseh b. Mar Joseph
	796	Isaiah ha-Levi b. Mar Abba
Jacob ha-Kohen b. Mordecai	797	
	798	Joseph b. Shila
	804	Kahana b. Ḥaninai
	810	Ivomai (in both academies)
Ivomai, uncle of his predecessor	811	
	814	Joseph b. Abba
Zadok b. Jesse (or Ashi)	816	Abraham b. Sherira
Hilai b. Ḥanina	818	
Kimoi b. Ashi	822	
Moses (Mesharsheya)	825	
Kahana b. Jacob		
	828	Joseph b. Ḥiyya
	833	Isaac b. Hananiah
	836[1]	
Kohen Ẓedek b. Ivomai	838	
	839	Joseph b. Ravi
	842	Paltoi b. Abbaye
Sar Shalom b. Boaz	848	
Natronai b. Hilai	853	
	857	Aḥa Kahana b. Rav
Amram b. Sheshna[2]	858	Menahem b. Joseph b. Ḥiyya
	860	Mattathias b. Mar Ravi
	869	Abba (Rabbah) b. Ammi
Nahshon b. Zadok	871	
	872	Ẓemaḥ b. Paltoi
Ẓemah b. Ḥayyim	879	
Malkha	885	
Hai b. Nahshon	885	
	890[3]	Hai b. David
Hilai b. Natronai	896	
	898	Kimoi b. Ahai
Shalom b. Mishael	904	
	906	Judah b. Samuel (grandfather of Sherira)
Jacob b. Natronai	911	
	917–926	Mevasser Kahana b. Kimoi
Yom Tov Kahana b. Jacob	924	
	926–936	Kohen Ẓedek b. Joseph (appointed during the lifetime of his predecessor)

Sura		Pumbedita
Saadiah b. Joseph	928	
	936	Zemah b. Kafnai
	938	Hananiah b. Judah
Joseph b. Jacob	942–944	
	943	Aaron b. Joseph haKohen Sargado
	960	Nehemiah b. Kohen Ẓedek
	968	Sherira b. Hananiah
Ẓemaḥ b. Isaac (descendant of Paltoi)	988	
(?) Samuel b. Hophni ha-Kohen	997	
	998	Hai b. Sherira
Dosa b. Saadiah	1013	
Israel b. Samuel b. Hophni	1017	
Azariah ha-Kohen (son of Israel?)	1034	
(?) Isaac	1037	
	1038–(1058)	Hezekiah b. David (exilarch and head of the academy)

1. Until 838 position not filled in Sura.
2. Ruled with above 853–858.
3. The first of the geonim who lived in Baghdad (R. Isaac ibn Ghayyat, Sha'arei Simhah, pt. 1 no. 64).
4. The academy was closed for about 45 years. However, several teachers and pupils apparently remained.

[Simha Assaf and Jehoshua Brand]

Geonic Responsa

The collecting of scattered material in the anthologies of geonic responsa, both printed and in manuscript, and in their editing, according to the order of the tractates of the Babylonian Talmud, was begun by B.M. Lewin in *Oẓar ha-Ge'onim*, which he published in 12 volumes to *Bava Kamma* (1928–43). The 13th volume was published posthumously to part of *Bava Meẓia* and one volume of *Oẓar ha-Ge'onim* to *Sanhedrin* was published by H.Z. Taubes (Jerusalem, 1966).

The following are the editions of geonic responsa: *Halakhot Pesukot min ha-Ge'onim* (Constantinople, 1516, and again published by J. Mueller, 1893); *She'elot u-Teshuvot me-ha-Ge'onim* (Constantinople, 1575); *Sha'arei Ẓedek* (Salonika, 1792; Jerusalem, 1966); *Sha'arei Teshuvah* (in *Naharot Dammesek* of Solomon Kamondo, Salonika, 1802, and separately; Leipzig, 1858; Leghorn, 1869; New York, 1946); *Teshuvot Ge'onim Kadmonim* (Berlin, 1848); *Ḥemdah Genuzah* (Jerusalem, 1863); *Toratam shel Rishonim* (published by Ch. M. Horowitz, Frankfort, 1881); *Teshuvot Ge'onei Mizraḥ u-Ma'arav* (published by J. Mueller, Berlin, 1888); *Kohelet Shelomo* (published by S.A. Wertheimer, Jerusalem, 1899); *Ge'on ha-Ge'onim* (published by S.A. Wertheimer, Jerusalem, 1925); *Mi-Sifrut ha-Ge'onim* (published by S. Assaf, Jerusalem, 1933); *Teshuvot ha-Ge'onim* (standard title for different texts), published by J. Musafia (Lyck, 1864); by N.N. Coronel (Vienna, 1871); by A. Harkavy (Berlin, 1887); by S. Assaf (Jerusalem, 1927, 1928, 1942); by A. Marmorstein (Déva, 1928). Geonic responsa appeared also in several anthologies and periodicals such as *Ta'am Zekenim* (ed. by E. Askenazi, 1855); *Oẓar ha-Ḥayyim* (ed. by Ch. Ehrenreich, 1925–38); *Ginzei Kedem* (1922–44); in REJ, JQR, *Tarbiz*, KS, *Sinai* (see their index volumes), and in various Festschriften.

The Geonim of Baghdad after the Geonic Period

The heads of the Baghdad academy saw themselves as the successors of the *geonim* of Sura and Pumbedita because the last of them had lived in Baghdad after the tenth century. It may be assumed that many students and teachers from the older academies came to the academy that opened in the second half of the 11th century. The heads of the academies in Baghdad attempted to preserve, if at all possible, the continuity of their connection with the geonic period and called themselves, in the manner of their predecessors in Sura and Pumbedita, *rosh yeshivat ge'on Ya'akov* and *rosh yeshivah shel ha-golah*. The first known Baghdad *gaon* was Isaac b. Moses b. Sakri who came to the East from Spain in about 1070 after he failed to receive recognition in his native country. There is no information on the academy of Babylon, except for the period of 1140–50 when its head was Eli ha-Levi, the rabbi of David *Alroy. The names of the *geonim* who followed him are known from letters and responsa. The most famous was *Samuel b. Ali ha-Levi who opposed *Maimonides; he is praised by the travelers *Benjamin of Tudela and *Pethahiah of Regensburg. Judah *Al-Ḥarizi found that the liturgical poet *Isaac b. Israel ibn Shuwaykh was the head of the Baghdad academy. He was also known because of his connections with Abraham *Maimuni. In 1258 Baghdad Jewry was threatened by the attack of the Mongols and with the decline of Babylonian Jewry the position of gaonate declined as well. In 1288 the head of the Baghdad academy was Samuel b. Abi al-Rabīʿa ha-Kohen. This is known from his letter concerning the Maimonidean controversy (published by Halberstam in J. Kobak's *Jeschurun*, vol. 7, pp. 76–80). Henceforth, nothing is known about the fate of the Baghdad academy in the Middle Ages.

Chronological List of the Baghdad Geonim

1070	Isaac b. Moses
1140	Ali ha-Levi
1150	Solomon
1164	Samuel b. Ali ha-Levi
1194	Zechariah b. Barachel
1195	Eleazar b. Hillel
1209	Daniel b. Eleazar b. Ḥibbat Allah
1218	Isaac b. Israel ibn Shuwaykh
1240	Daniel b. Abi al-Rabīa ha-Kohen
1250	Eli II
1288	Samuel b. Daniel b. Abi al-Rabīa ha-Kohen.

The Gaonate in Ereẓ Israel

Little information on the beginnings of the gaonate in Ereẓ Israel is available. Sources increase only in the beginning of the 10th century as a result of the dispute between Saadiah Gaon and Aaron *Ben Meir and the bitter polemic between Rabbanites and Karaites. However, even here there is no reliable information on the gaonate in Ereẓ Israel, as was the case with the letter of R. Sherira regarding Babylonia, and was similarly true concerning the chronology of the *geonim* in Ereẓ Israel as given by Ben Meir. In any case it is clear that the title of *gaon* was not used in Ereẓ Israel until the academy of Tiberias moved to Jerusalem, which was several generations after its use in Babylonia. One may assume that the Babylonian *geonim* did not recognize the right of the heads of academies in Ereẓ Israel to use this title which they called *rosh ḥavurah* or *rosh yeshivah*. Since the Jerusalem academy was considered the successor to that of Tiberias, its leaders were sometimes called "*ge'on Teveryah*." The scholars in Ereẓ Israel could not compete in Talmud interpretation and *halakhah* with the scholars of Babylonia. A crucial turning point in the relationship between the gaonate in Babylonia and that of Ereẓ Israel was the dispute between Aaron Ben Meir and Saadiah Gaon. Ben Meir announced a new calendar computation that resulted in Passover beginning on a Sunday as opposed to the Babylonian calendar that determined the beginning of the holiday on a Tuesday. Six months later, by New Year 922 the debate was over, Saadiah had won and the Babylonian calendar was again used universally. The leadership of the academy of Ereẓ Israel was held by a group of seven scholars, often called "*Sanhedrin Gedolah*," and at its head was *ha-shelishi ba-ḥavurah* ("the third of the group of scholars"), the *gaon* and the *av bet din* or his substitute. The rest of the five members were called *ha-revi'i ba-ḥavurah* ("the fourth of the group of scholars"), etc., or briefly, *ha-shelishi*, etc. The appointment to positions was done according to a fixed hierarchy. After the death of the *gaon*, his position reverted generally to the *av bet din* and the rest of the leadership was promoted according to the hierarchy of positions. It is possible, however, that this order began only after the death of Ben Meir. Contrary to the Babylonian practice, the position of the *gaon* in Ereẓ Israel was hereditary. Sometimes the father would serve as *gaon*, one of his sons as *av bet din*, and the second son would be *shelishi* or *revi'i* in the *ḥavurah*; there is no doubt that this practice negatively influenced the matters of study in the academy of Ereẓ Israel.

The *geonim* of Ereẓ Israel in the 10th and 11th centuries were mainly from the family of Ben Meir, which claimed relation to *Judah ha-Nasi and thus to King David, and two families of kohanim, one of which was the family of *Abiathar and was related to *Eleazar b. Azariah. However, S. Abramson concludes that the family of kohanim that claimed relation to the House of David stemmed from the academy in Ereẓ Israel in one family. Abramson discovered in the *Genizah* fragments of an unknown document, which contained a list of the heads of academies for several generations. From this document it is apparent that one family of kohanim was merely a branch of the Ben Meir family. Thus, the gaonate of Ereẓ Israel was held by one family and its different branches for perhaps 200 years. *Solomon b. Judah, a native of Fez, next to Ben Meir the most famous of the *geonim* in Ereẓ Israel and whose family is not known, and his successor *Daniel b. Azariah, a descendant of one of the families of the exilarchate in Babylonia, were heads of academies and were not descendants of the *geonim* of Ereẓ Israel. Daniel was known as a strong leader, was esteemed by his contemporaries, and was a friend of Samuel ha-Nagid (Ibn Nagrela).

Besides managing the academy, the work of the *gaon* included all Jewish affairs in Ereẓ Israel. The designation of powers among the heads of academies and exilarchs, as was practiced in Babylonia, was not known in Ereẓ Israel. The *geonim* ordained the *ḥaverim*, appointed the *dayyanim* in Ereẓ Israel and Syria, and managed the economic affairs of the Jewish community in Ereẓ Israel. They were recognized by the foreign ruler as the representatives of the Jewish community in Ereẓ Israel. After Ereẓ Israel was politically allied with Baghdad and later with Egypt, the *geonim* corresponded with highly influential Jewish dignitaries in the two capitals. In these cases of emergency they were accustomed to travel there personally to negotiate in the court of the rulers. The halakhic and literary activity of the *geonim* is attested by some responsa. Hundreds of letters asking the *geonim* to aid the Jewish community and the academies were discovered in the Cairo *Genizah*. The *geonim* of Ereẓ Israel were not as learned as the *geonim* in Babylonia. Their major achievement was the maintenance of the continuity of the tradition of the academies in Ereẓ Israel under difficult political conditions.

Abrahamson assumes that Ẓemaḥ, who served as head of the academy from about 884–915, was a fourth-generation descendant of *Anan b. David, the founder of the Karaites, and he was a *nasi* and a *gaon*. Aaron Ben Meir succeeded in deposing Anan's family only after a bitter struggle in which he was assisted by the scholars and heads of the Baghdad community.

Chronological List of the Geonim of Ereẓ Israel

...	Moses (head of the academy?)
...	Meir I (head of the academy?)
884–915	Ẓemaḥ
915–932	Aaron b.Moses Ben Meir
932–934	Isaac (son of Aaron)
934–948	... Ben Meir (brother of Aaron)
948–955	Abraham b. Aaron
c. 955	Aaron
...	Joseph ha-Kohen b. Ezron (ruled two years)
...	...(ruled thirty years)
988-?	Samuel b. Joseph ha-Kohen
...	Yose b. Samuel
...	Shemaiah
1015	Josiah b. Aaron ('member of the Great Synagogue') b. Abraham (lived in Ramleh)
1020–1027	Solomon b. Joseph ha-Kohen
1027–1051	Solomon b. Judah
1051–1062	Daniel b. Azariah (*nassi* and *gaon*)
1062–1083	Elijah b. Solomon b. Joseph ha-Kohen
1084–1109	Abiathar b. Elijah

The Geonim of Erez Israel in Damascus, and the Geonim of Egypt

The occupation of Jerusalem by the Seljuks in 1071 completely destroyed the city's Jewish community. The *gaon* *Elijah b. Solomon moved the academy to Tyre, which was subject to Fatimid rule. Elijah's son Abiathar headed the Tyre academy until the conquest of the city by the crusaders. Afterward he moved to Tripoli, Syria, where he died before 1110. His brother Solomon, who served as an *av bet din*, fled in 1093 to Hadrak (near Damascus) because of the decrees of David b. Daniel b. Azariah, head of Egyptian Jewry. In Hadrak he assembled the survivors of the Erez Israel academy which apparently included his brother's son Elijah b. Abiathar. Later his position was given to his son Mazli'aḥ, who went to Egypt in 1127 where he received the title of *gaon*. The academy of Erez Israel was moved from Hadrak to Damascus and still existed during the 12th century when *Benjamin of Tudela reported that it was subject to the rule of the Babylonian gaonate (Baghdad). The names of two *geonim* who were descendants of the Abiathar family, Abraham b. Mazhir and his son Ezra, are known. The latter was ordained by Samuel b. Ali of Baghdad. In his time or shortly afterward the continuity of the *geonim* of Erez Israel was broken. It is possible that he was followed by Zadok, who was dismissed from his position (*Taḥkemoni*, ed. by A. Kaminka (1899), 354).

In Fostat, Egypt, the academy existed in the time of Elhanan, the father of Shemariah, who is known from the story of the "*Four Captives." His title "chief rabbi" and his position were inherited by his son and then his grandson Elhanan who called himself *rosh ha-seder* or "*rosh ha-seder* of all Israel." *Shemariah and Elhanan, both of whom had previously studied in the Pumbedita academy, corresponded with Sherira and Hai. Only after the decline of the Babylonian and Palestinian academies did the large communities in Egypt request the establishment of their own gaonate. David b. Daniel (1083–89) was the first who attempted to do this. Like his strict father, he hoped to become *nasi* and *gaon* and to exert his power even over the head of the Tyre academy and on the communities in the coastal cities of Erez Israel. However, the *nagid* Mevorakh, who supported him at first, later rejected him. In 1127 Mazliaḥ b. Solomon, the aged head of the Erez Israel academy, moved from Hadrak to Fostat and called himself *rosh yeshivat ge'on Ya'akov*. Several of his documents and letters are extant. After his death in 1138, his position was apparently given to Moses ha-Levi b. Nethanel; however, it is possible that Samuel b. Hananiah, who met Judah Halevi when he traveled from Egypt to Erez Israel, was given the position. After Moses, his son Nethanel was *gaon* (1160–70) and was followed on his death by his brother Sar Shalom who was appointed *gaon* at Fostat. Sar Shalom, who was perhaps of Palestinian geonic descent, sometimes called himself *rosh yeshivat Erez ha-Zevi*, as if his activities were a continuation of the academies of Erez Israel not only in Damascus but also in Fostat. With his death the gaonate in Egypt ceased to exist. Maimonides, who lived at that time in Egypt, did not possess the title of *gaon*.

The Title of Gaon in Other Countries

The title of *gaon* was also used by great scholars in other countries. Maimonides writes in his introduction to the *Mishneh Torah*, "the *geonim* of Spain and France." The *geonim* of Africa, Lotharingia (Lorraine), Mainz, and Narbonne are mentioned in the literature of the early *posekim*. Thus, the title was given to well-known individuals from the early rabbinic period, such as R. *Hananel, R. *Nissim, R. *Moses b. Ḥanokh and his son *Ḥanokh, R. *Joseph b. Abitur, R. Kalonymus of Lucca and his son R. Meshullam, and others.

[Simha Assaf / David Derovan (2nd ed.)]

BIBLIOGRAPHY: GENERAL: Assaf, Ge'onim; Abramson, Merkazim; Mann, Egypt; Mann, Texts. BABYLONIA: L. Ginzberg, *Geonica*, 2 vols. (1909, repr. 1968); idem, *Ginzei Schechter*, 2 (1929); J. Mueller, *Mafte'aḥ li-Teshuvot ha-Ge'onim* (1891); B.M. Lewin, *Meḥkarim Shonim bi-Tekufat ha-Ge'onim* (1926); V. Aptowitzer, *Meḥkarim be-Sifrut ha-Ge'onim* (1941); M. Ḥavazzelet, *Ha-Rambam ve-ha-Ge'onim* (1967); H. Tykocinski, *Die gaonaeischen Verordnungen* (1929); S.D. Goitein, *Sidrei Ḥinnukh* (1962); *Iggeret Rav Sherira Ga'on*, ed. by B.M. Lewin (1921); S. Abramson, in: *Sinai*, 54 (1963/64), 20–32; 56 (1964/65), 303–17; Epstein, in: *Festschrift... A. Harkavy* (1908), 164–74 (Heb. sect.); Y.L. Fishman (Maimon), in: *Sefer ha-Yovel... B.M. Lewin* (1940), 132–59; Krauss, in: HHY, 7 (1923), 229–77; J. Mann, in: JQR, 7 (1916/17), 457–90; 8 (1917/18), 339–66; 9 (1918/19), 139–79; 10 (1919/20), 121–51, 309–65; 11 (1920/21), 409–71; idem, in: *Hebrew Union College Jubilee*

GAON, MOSES DAVID (1889–1958), Israel educator, journalist, and writer. Gaon was born in Travnik, then under Austro-Hungarian administration (now in Yugoslavia), and studied in the University of Vienna. He emigrated to Erez Israel in 1909. He taught Hebrew and was principal of elementary schools in Jerusalem, Smyrna, and Buenos Aires. In his last years he was an official of the Jerusalem municipality and was active in the Committee of the Sephardi Community. He co-founded the Mizrachi Pioneers' Federation. For several decades Gaon contributed articles to the Hebrew press on Oriental Jewry and its relation to the Holy Land, which was also the subject of his book *Yehudei ha-Mizraḥ be-Erez Yisrael* (2 vols., 1928–37). He also wrote a study of a popular Ladino moralistic work, *Maskiyyot Levav* on *Me-Am Lo'ez (1933), *Ba-Mishol* (1936) on the history of the Hebrew press in Palestine up to 1914, etc. He edited the jubilee volume in honor of Jacob *Meir *Zikhron Me'ir* (1936) with M. Laniado; *Sefer ha-Zikhronot* (1938) by Ben-Zion Cuenca; and a volume on the Jerusalem family Azriel (1950). He compiled a bibliography of the Ladino press in *Ha-Itton
ut be-Ladino – Bibliografyah* (1965). The Gaon Center for Ladino Culture at Ben-Gurion University is named for him. His son Yehoram *Gaon, a popular Israeli entertainer, often included Sephardi music in his repertoire. He also appeared in several films and on the musical stage, notably in the Israeli musical *Kazablan*.

BIBLIOGRAPHY: Tidhar, 1 (1947), 500; 10 (1959), 3648.

[Getzel Kressel]

GAON, NESSIM DAVID (1922–), philanthropist and communal worker. Gaon's family originated in Turkey but moved to Egypt. His father was a political officer with the Sudanese government in Khartoum, where he was born. He graduated from the Comboni College in that city. During World War II he joined the British army in Cairo and was subsequently commissioned as a lieutenant, seeing active service in Syria, Iraq, Iran, Italy, and North Africa. After his discharge in 1946 with the rank of captain, he joined the family business in the Sudan. In 1957 Gaon moved to Geneva where he built up a world-wide business corporation in import-export, investment, and real estate, including one of Geneva's biggest hotels, the Noga Hilton.

Gaon is prominent in Jewish communal affairs. In Khartoum he served as secretary and vice president of the Jewish community and succeeded in uniting the Ashkenazi and Sephardi congregations in Geneva, becoming president of the United Community in 1966.

Gaon's main communal activity has been with regard to the Sephardi community and in the academic world, in addition to his munificent contributions to Israel. He has served as president of the *World Sephardi Federation since 1971; He was a vice president of the World Jewish Congress.

In 1971 he became a member of the Board of Governors of Bar-Ilan University and two years later of Ben-Gurion University in Beersheba of which he was appointed chairman of the Board of Governors.

GAON, SOLOMON (1912–1994), English Sephardi rabbi. Born in Travnik (Yugoslavia), Gaon studied for the rabbinate at Jews' College, London. After acting as senior *ḥazzan*, he was in 1949 appointed haham of the Spanish and Portuguese Jews' Congregations in the British Commonwealth. On retiring as haham of the Spanish and Portuguese congregation of London in 1977 Gaon was appointed haham of the Association of Sephardi Congregations with the object of converting that organization into the effective center of leadership and rabbinical administration of the increasingly diversified Sephardi component of Anglo-Jewry. In view of its failure to expedite the setting-up of a centralized *bet din* he resigned in 1980. He also acted for some time as visiting minister to the She'erit Israel Sephardi Congregation of New York. He published *Influence of Alfonso Tostado on the Pentateuch Commentary of Abravanel* (1943).

GAON, YEHORAM (1939–), Israeli pop singer, actor, television personality. Gaon is possibly the nearest thing the Israeli entertainment world has to a Mr. Consensus. Gaon was born in Jerusalem to a family steeped in Ladino traditions. As a high school student he considered an academic career in Eastern Studies but, on his recruitment to the IDF, tried out successfully for the Naḥal entertainment troupe. Initially, he was accepted for his acting talents, and it was not until 1959, two years after he joined the band, that he was given his first chance to demonstrate his vocal abilities. From then on there was nothing to stop him.

Shortly after he was demobilized, Gaon joined The Roosters which included promising young singers such as Ḥanan Goldblatt, Gavri Banai, Israel Poliakov (Banai and Poliakov later made up two-thirds of renowned comedy trio *Ha-Gashash ha-Ḥiver), and Lior Yeini. The Roosters were a smash hit and turned out several hit songs before disbanding in 1963. Gaon left the group in 1961 to further his acting career. He joined the Cameri Theater and appeared in productions such as *Kinneret Kinneret* (1961), *Torah* (1963), and *French Fries with Everything* (1964).

In 1964 Gaon's musical career took off when he formed the highly successful Yarkon Bridge Trio, along with Arik *Einstein and Benny Amdursky. However, he left the band after just one year to pursue a solo career, releasing his debut solo album, *Kol ha-Ir Merakhelet Aleinu* ("The Whole Town's Talking about Us"), in 1965. The record spawned several successful singles, such as *Eyfo Hen ha-Bakhurot ha-Hen* ("Where Are Those Girls") and *Az Areh La* ("Then I'll Show Her").

In 1966 Gaon left for the United States to study theater acting and television directing but, at the end of the year, returned to Israel to audition for the musical *Kazablan*. He got the lead role and the show was an enormous success, and only ended when Gaon decided he had had enough.

Gaon's superstar status was cemented when he won the first two places in the 1969 Israeli Song Festival and put out a string of hit singles and albums throughout the 1970s, including *Rosa* and *Mediterranean Love*. During this period he also maintained his theater and cinema interests, playing star roles in such movies as *Kol Mamzer Melekh* ("Every Bastard's A King") and *Mivẓa Yonatan* (*Entebbe: Operation Thunderbolt*). Later he starred in a popular TV series called "Neighbors. Neighbors."

His musical career tailed off in the 1990s but in 2003 he became a popular TV personality when he began to present a musical talk show called *Gaon on Friday*. In 2004 Gaon received the ultimate accolade when he was awarded the prestigious Israel Prize for his services to Israeli popular music.

[Barry Davis (2nd ed.)]

GAPONOV, BORIS (**Dov**; 1934–1972), translator from Georgian and Russian into Hebrew, lexicographer of Hebrew. Gaponov was born in Eupatoria, Crimea, but grew up in Kutaisi, Georgia, where his family moved during World War II. As a youth he acquired a basic knowledge of Hebrew from his grandfather, afterwards continuing to study the language on his own. For a short period of time he studied Persian at the Oriental Languages Institute of Moscow University but had to give it up because of financial difficulties. He also worked as a reporter for the newspaper of the Kutaisi automobile plant. In the 1960s he turned to literary translation, translating both Russian and Georgian prose and poetry into Hebrew.

In 1969 his translation of the greatest masterpiece of Georgian medieval literature, *The Man in the Panther's Skin*

(12th century) by Shot'ha Rust'haveli, was published in Israel. This monumental work, executed with brilliance and faithful to the form and spirit of the original, testified to Gaponov's great poetic talent and immediately became a classic among poetic translations into Hebrew. In 1970 Gaponov was awarded the Tchernichowsky Prize for this work.

In 1971 he came to Israel and in the same year published his translation of *A Hero of Our Time* by Lermontov, which was also highly praised by the critics. In 1972 he received the Shazar Prize for refugee repatriate writers, but died shortly after. A. *Shlonsky played a prominent role in the literary fate of Gaponov. Their correspondence began when Gaponov was still living in the U.S.S.R. and continued for many years. Among Gaponov's unpublished works are a dictionary of Hebrew phrases, a work of considerable merit on which he had been working for 15 years, as well as numerous translations of poems by Lermontov, articles on the Rust'haveli epic, and poems in Russian on Jewish themes.

[Michael Zand]

GARBUZ, YAIR (1945–), Israeli artist. Garbuz studied painting under Rafi Lavi between 1962 and 1967 as well as at the Avni Institute in Tel Aviv. He began to exhibit in 1967, participating in group and individual exhibitions in Israel and abroad. Garbuz also taught from 1973 at the Hamidrashah School of Art, serving as its director from 1997, at the Avni Institution, Tel Hai College, and the Bezalel Art Academy. In addition, he wrote and lectured widely on art, and was an editor of the satirical newspaper *Davar Aḥer*. He appeared as a media critic on the *Tik Tikshoret* TV talk show. In 2004 he was awarded the EMET Prize by the Ministry of Education and Culture.

In his art, Garbuz moved from abstraction to the use of collages incorporating photographs, texts, and various materials, all serving to produce personal and social/cultural narratives.

[Shaked Gilboa (2nd ed.)]

GARDEN OF EDEN (Heb. גַּן עֵדֶן), a garden planted by the Lord which was the first dwelling place of *Adam and Eve (Gen. 2–3). It is also referred to as the "garden in Eden" (Gen. 2:8, 10; 4:16), the "garden of YHWH" (Gen. 13:10; Isa. 51:3), and the "garden of God" (Ezek. 28:13; 31:8–9). It is referred to by Ben Sira 40:17 as "Eden of blessing." There existed in early times an Israelite tradition of a "garden of God" (i.e., a mythical garden in which God dwelt) that underlies the story of the Garden of Eden in Genesis 2–3. Ezekiel (28:11–19; 31:8–9, 16–18) in his description introduces new and variant details not present in the Genesis narrative of the Garden of Eden. Thus, in Genesis there is no trace of the "holy mountain" of Ezekiel 28:14 and no mention of the "stones of fire" of Ezekiel 28:14, 16. While Genesis speaks only in general terms about the trees in the garden (2:9), Ezekiel describes them in detail (31:8–9, 18). The term "garden of YHWH" occurs in literary figures in a number of other passages in the Bible (Gen. 13:10; note Isa. 51:3: "He will make her wilderness (*midbar*) like Eden and her desert (*arabah*) like the garden of YHWH," Joel 2:3). The name Eden has been connected with Akkadian *edinu*. But this word, extremely rare in Akkadian, is borrowed from the Sumerian *eden* and means "plain," "steppe," "desert." In fact, one Akkadian synonym list equates*edinu* with *ṣēru*, semantically equivalent to Hebrew *midbar*, "desert." More likely is the connection with the Hebrew root *ʿdn*, attested in such words as *maʿdanim*, "dainties," "luxury items" (Gen. 49:20; Lam. 4:5) *ʿednah*, "pleasure," (Gen. 18:12), *ʿadinah*, "pampered woman" (Isa. 47:8); and in Old Aramaic *mʿdn* "provider of abundance," which would be a transparent etymology for the name of a divine garden. The Septuagint apparently derived Eden from *ʿdn*, translating *gan ʿeden* (Gen. 3:23–4) by *ho paradeisos tēs truphēs*, "the park of luxuries," whence English "paradise." Akkadian provides a semantic parallel in *kiri nuhši*, "garden of plenty" (McCarter apud Stager). Several references (Gen. 2:8 ("in Eden"), 10 ("from Eden)," 4:16 ("east of Eden)," indicate that Eden was a geographical designation. According to 4:10 a single river flowed out of Eden, watered the garden and then diverged into four rivers whose courses are described and themselves named. This datum encouraged scholars ancient (see below) and modern to attempt to locate the site of the garden of Eden intended by the author.

[S. David Sperling (2nd ed.)]

In the Aggadah

The Garden of Eden appears in the *aggadah* in contradistinction to Gehinnom – "hell" (e.g., BT Sotah 22a). However, talmudic and midrashic sources know of two Gardens of Eden: the terrestrial, of abundant fertility and vegetation, and the celestial, which serves as the habitation of souls of the righteous. The location of the earthly Eden is traced by the boundaries delineated in Genesis 2:11–14. Resh Lakish declared, "If paradise is in the land of Israel, its gate is Beth-Shean; if it is in Arabia, its gate is Bet Gerem, and if it is between the rivers, its gate is Dumaskanin" (Er. 19a). In *Tamid* (32b) its location is given as the center of Africa. It is related that Alexander of Macedon finally located the door to the Garden, but he was not permitted to enter. The *Midrash ha-Gadol* (to Gen. 2:8) simply states that "Eden is a unique place on earth, but no creature is permitted to know its exact location. In the future, during the messianic period God will reveal to Israel the path to Eden." According to the Talmud, "Egypt is 400 parasangs by 400, and it is one-sixtieth of the size of Ethiopia; Ethiopia is one-sixtieth of the world, and the world is one-sixtieth of the Garden, and the Garden is one-sixtieth of Eden …" (Ta'an. 10a). The rabbis thus make a clear distinction between Eden and the Garden. Commenting upon the verse "Eye hath not seen, O God, beside Thee," R. Samuel b. Naḥamani states, "This is Eden, which has never been seen by the eye of any creature." Adam dwelt only in the Garden (Ber. 34b., cf., Isa. 64:3). The word *le-ovedah* ("to dress it"; Gen. 2:15) is taken to refer to spiritual, not physical, toil, and is interpreted to mean that Adam had to devote himself to the study of the Torah and the fulfillment of the commandments (Sif. Deut. 41). Although the eating of meat was forbidden him (Gen. 1:29), it is stated nevertheless that the angels brought him meat and wine and waited on him (Sanh. 59b; ARN 1, 5).

The boundary line between the earthly and heavenly Garden of Eden is barely discernible in rabbinic literature. In fact, "The Garden of Eden and heaven were created by one word [of God], and the chambers of the Garden of Eden are constructed as those of heaven. Just as heaven is lined with rows of stars so the Garden of Eden is lined with rows of the righteous who shine like the stars" (Ag. Song 13:55).

BIBLIOGRAPHY: IN THE BIBLE: M.D. Cassuto, in: *Studies in Memory of M. Schorr* (1944), 248–53; idem, in: EM, 2 (1954), 231–6; J.L. Mc-Kenzie, in: *Theological Studies*, 15 (1954), 541–72; E.A. Speiser, *Genesis* (1964), 14–20; idem, *Oriental and Biblical Studies*, ed. by J.J. Finkelstein and M. Greenberg (1967), 23–34; N.M. Sarna, *Understanding Genesis* (1966), 23–28. IN THE AGGADAH: Ginzberg, Legends, index. **ADD. BIBLIOGRAPHY:** A. Millard, in: VT, 34 (1984), 103–6; J. Rosenberg, *King and Kin: Political Allegory in the Hebrew Bible* (1986), 2–12; J. Kennedy, in: JSOT, 47 (1990), 3–14; H. Wallace, in: ABD, 2:281–83; S.D. Sperling, *The Orginal Torah* (1998), 37–9; L. Stager, *ErIsr*, 26 (Cross Volume;1999), *183–*94.

GARDOSH, KARIEL (Charles, "Dosh"; 1921–2000), Israel cartoonist. He created the figure of "Little Israel," a young boy who became the popular symbol of the State and its people. "Dosh," as he signed himself, was born in Budapest and educated there and in Paris. He immigrated to Israel in 1948 and five years later joined the staff of the afternoon paper *Ma'ariv* as editorial cartoonist. His drawings were marked by comic irony which won him a wide following. They were regularly reprinted in the *Jerusalem Post*, in the Tel Aviv Hungarian daily *Uj Kelet*, and in many newspapers abroad. Gardosh illustrated books, wrote short stories and one-act plays, and held exhibitions in Israel and other countries. He published several collections of cartoons, including *Seliḥah she-Niẓẓaḥnu!* (1967; *So Sorry We Won!*, 1967) and *Oi la-Menaẓẓeḥim* (1969; *Woe to the Victors*, 1969) with text by Ephraim *Kishon, dealing with the Six-Day War and after.

BIBLIOGRAPHY: Tidhar, 8 (1957), 3048.

GARFIELD, JOHN (Julius Garfinkle; 1913–1952), U.S. actor. Born in New York, Garfield, deeply disturbed by the death of his mother, was a chronic truant, but was persuaded by a child psychologist to study acting. He attended drama school and later joined the Group Theater Company, where he won acclaim for his role in *Awake and Sing*. He first played on Broadway in Elmer *Rice's *Counselor-at-Law* (1931) and then took the lead in Clifford *Odets' *Golden Boy* (1937) and in its revival in 1952. His other Broadway performances include *Johnny Johnson* (1936–37), *Having a Wonderful Time* (1937–38), *Heavenly Express* (1940), *Skipper Next to God* (1948), *The Big Knife* (1949), and *Peer Gynt* (1951).

Embittered over being passed over for the lead (the part went to William Holden) in the 1939 film version of *Golden Boy*, which was written for him, he signed a contract with Warner Brothers and won enormous praise for the role of the cynical Mickey Borden in the film *Four Daughters* (1938). Although he began his film career typed as a "tough," he played the lover in *Saturday's Children* (1940) and the role of Danny in John Steinbeck's *Tortilla Flat* (1942). In 1947 he had the opportunity to put on the boxing gloves once again when he starred as the prizefighter in *Body and Soul*. Other films of his include *They Made Me a Criminal* (1939), *Pride of the Marines* (1945), *The Postman Always Rings Twice* (1946), *Nobody Lives Forever* (1946), *Humoresque* (1946), *Gentleman's Agreement* (1947), *Force of Evil* (1948), *We Were Strangers* (1949), *Under My Skin* (1950), *The Breaking Point* (1950), and *He Ran All the Way* (1951).

Active in liberal political and social causes, he found himself caught up in the Communist scare of the late 1940s. Although he testified before Congress that he was never a Communist, his opportunities to secure acting roles decreased. When John Garfield died of a heart attack at age 39, his funeral was attended by thousands of fans, the largest turnout for an actor since the death of silent film idol Rudolph Valentino.

ADD. BIBLIOGRAPHY: L. Swindell, *Body and Soul: The Story of John Garfield* (1975); H. Gelman, *The Films of John Garfield* (1975); R. Nott, *He Ran All the Way: The Life of John Garfield* (2003).

[Ruth Beloff (2nd ed.)]

GARFUNKEL, ART (1941–), U.S. singer and actor. Born in Forest Hills, New York, Garfunkel met singer/songwriter Paul Simon while they were both in their early teens. Garfunkel received his B.A. in art history (1965) and his M.A. in mathematics from Columbia University (1967). He and Paul Simon formed the duo Simon & Garfunkel and began recording Simon's songs together in 1960 ("Hey, Schoolgirl"). In 1964, Simon and Garfunkel signed a one-album contract with Columbia Records and released *Wednesday Morning, 3 A.M.* It failed to generate interest, and Garfunkel left the music business to teach mathematics. The sudden and unexpected success of a single song culled from the album ("The Sounds of Silence") brought Garfunkel back with Simon, and together they recorded a long string of hit songs that include "Homeward Bound," "I Am a Rock," "A Hazy Shade of Winter," "The Dangling Conversation," "The 59th St. Bridge Song," "Mrs. Robinson," "The Boxer," "Fakin' It," and "Bridge over Troubled Water."

In 1973, Garfunkel began a solo career and recorded such albums as *Angel Clare* (1973), *Breakaway* (1975), *Watermark* (1978), *Fate for Breakfast (Double for Dessert)* (1979), *Art Garfunkel* (1979), and *Scissors Cut* (1981). Garfunkel is the recipient of Grammy Awards for "Mrs. Robinson" (1969) and "Bridge over Troubled Water" (1970). As an actor, Garfunkel appeared in such films as *Catch-22* (1970), *Carnal Knowledge* (1971), *Bad Timing* (1980), *Good to Go* (1986), *Boxing Helena* (1993), and *54* (1998).

In 1989, Garfunkel published a book of prose poems entitled *Still Water*. He was inducted into the Rock and Roll Hall of Fame (as a member of Simon & Garfunkel) in 1990. After the September 11, 2001, terrorist attacks on New York and Washington, Garfunkel contributed generously toward helping the survivors and the victims' families. He continued to give concert tours and in 2002 released the album *Everybody Wants to Be Noticed.* In 2003, he reunited with Paul Simon for the first time in 20 years on a nostalgia tour.

ADD. BIBLIOGRAPHY: J. Morella and P. Barey, *Simon and* Garfunkel: Old Friends (1991); V. Kingston, *Simon & Garfunkel: The Definitive Biography* (1996).

[Jonathan Licht / Ruth Beloff (2nd ed.)]

GARIH, ÜZEYIR (1929–2001), Turkish industrialist. Garih graduated in 1951 as a mechanical engineer from the Istanbul Technical University. In 1954 he established together with İshak *Alaton the Alarko Company. Alarko became a major holding company engaged in tourism and leisure-time activities as well as being a large-scale contractor for infrastructure projects like the construction of airports, dams, and roads, operating in both Turkey and the new Turkish republics of the former Soviet Union. Garih was a regular contributor to various Turkish newspapers on business and management and was particularly concerned with the education of youth. In 1984 he was granted the title of honorary doctor by the Istanbul Technical University. From 1990 he was the honorary consul of the Philippine Republic. He was murdered during a robbery.

[Rifat Bali (2nd ed.)]

GARLIC (Heb. שׁוּם, *shum*), plant mentioned once in the Bible among the vegetables which the Israelites ate in Egypt and for which they longed when wandering in the wilderness (Num 11:5). Garlic (*Allium sativum*) is a condiment which was extremely popular among the peoples of the East from very early times. Herodotus states that an inscription on the pyramid of the pharaoh Cheops refers to the large sum spent on garlic as food for the men who worked on the pyramids. The ancients attributed to garlic aphrodisiac qualities (Pliny, *Historia Naturalis*, 20:23), and an enactment ascribed to Ezra decrees that it is to be eaten on Friday evenings since "it promotes love and arouses desire" (TJ, Meg. 4:1, 75a). Because it was their custom to eat garlic, the Jews referred to themselves as "garlic eaters" (Ned. 3:10). The fastidious loathed the smell, and it is related of Judah ha-Nasi that he asked those who had eaten garlic to leave the *bet midrash* (Sanh. 11a). In this he may have been influenced by the Roman aristocracy's objections to garlic eating, the emperor Marcus Aurelius having criticized Jews for exuding its smell (Ammianus Marcellinus, *Res gestae*, 22:5). Garlic was regarded as a remedy for intestinal worms (BK 82a), a view also held by Dioscorides (*De Materia Medica*, 2:181). It belongs to the genus *Allium*, to which belong also the *onion and the *leek (*ḥaẓir*, to be distinguished from its usual sense of grass: *fodder), which are mentioned together with garlic in the Bible (Num. 11:5). Many species of the genus *Allium* grow wild in Israel, and are picked and eaten by the local population.

BIBLIOGRAPHY: Loew, Flora, 2 (1924), 139–49; J. Feliks, *Olam ha-Ẓome'aḥ ha-Mikra'i* (1968^2), 172f. **ADD BIBLIOGRAPHY:** Feliks, Ha-Ẓome'aḥ, 156.

[Jehuda Feliks]

GARLOCK, JOHN HENRY (1896–1965), U.S. surgeon. Born and educated in New York City, Garlock was assistant attending surgeon at the New York Hospital and instructor in surgery at the Cornell Medical College from 1924 to 1937. He was then appointed chief of surgery at New York's Mount Sinai Hospital and clinical professor of surgery at Columbia University. He was consultant in surgery to many hospitals and held membership in numerous professional societies. Among his many contributions to medical literature are several chapters in standard textbooks of surgery. His book, *Garlock's Surgery of the Alimentary Tract* (1967), was published posthumously by his colleagues. Garlock was chairman of the American Jewish Physicians Committee, which raised money to start the Hebrew University Faculty of Medicine.

[Fred Rosner]

GARMENT, LEONARD (1924–), U.S. lawyer and counsel to President Richard M. *Nixon. Garment was born to immigrant parents in Brooklyn, New York. After graduating from Brooklyn College and Brooklyn Law School, he was admitted to the bar of New York in 1949, and later to the bar of the District of Columbia (1967). Garment was a brilliant law student, graduating first in his class (summa cum laude). He financed part of his education by playing tenor saxophone and clarinet with a leading popular jazz band of the time in the company of such artists as Billie Holiday and Woody Herman.

He joined the prestigious law firm later known as Nixon, Mudge, Rose, Guthrie, and Alexander, becoming a partner in 1957 and head of its litigation department. In this capacity, he worked closely with Nixon, handling the trial work on his cases. Nixon admired his ability, and in 1969, as president, appointed him as his special consultant concentrating on civil and human rights, voluntary action, and the arts. In this role, he termed himself Nixon's "odds and ends man." As a result of the Watergate scandal, Nixon appointed him as his counsel, replacing John Dean, to represent the administration in matters relating to the congressional Watergate investigation.

Garment, a Democrat by political affiliation, was regarded as one of the "liberals" in the Nixon administration.

After Nixon's resignation, Garment continued to move in Washington legal and political circles. He served as assistant to President Ford in 1974. Ford named him U.S. representative to the United Nations Human Rights Commission, where he served until 1977. He was also counselor to the U.S. delegation to the United Nations (1975 –76).

Garment was a frequent contributor to the *New York Times'* op-ed page. He wrote his autobiography, *Crazy Rhythm: My Journey from Brooklyn, Jazz, and Wall Street to Nixon's White House, Watergate, and Beyond* (1997), and the highly controversial *In Search of Deep Throat: The Greatest Political Mystery of Our Time* (2000).

[Julius J. Marcke / Ruth Beloff (2nd ed.)]

GARMISON, SAMUEL (17th century), scholar and prolific author. Born in Salonika, Samuel immigrated to Jerusalem. In about 1647 he traveled as an emissary of Jerusalem apparently to Italy but was taken captive during the journey by Maltese pirates, from whom he was ransomed by a society for the redemption of captives centered in Venice. He was rabbi in Malta until c. 1660. Subsequently he seems to have officiated in Jerusalem. In 1666 he attacked Shabbetai Ẓevi in a sermon which is included in his *Imrei No'am*. Only one of his works has been published: *Mishpetei Ẓedek* (1945), responsa on the Shulḥan Arukh, *Arba'ah Turim* and *Beit Yosef*. Among others still in manuscript are *Kevod Ḥakhamim*, sermons on the Bible; *Imrei No'am*, sermons on the Pentateuch; *Imrei Tevunah ve-Imrei Kodesh*, on the Talmud and codes; a commentary on the Mishnah; novellae to the tractates *Ḥullin, Bekhorot, Zera'im, Tohorot*, and *Berakhot*; works on the tractates *Beẓah, Kiddushin*, and *Ḥullin*.

BIBLIOGRAPHY: Benayahu, in: *Scritti… S. Mayer* (1956), 25–31 (Heb. part); M.D. Gaon, *Yehudei ha-Mizraḥ be-Ereẓ Yisrael*, 2 (1938), 208; Scholem, Shabbetai Ẓevi, 1 (1957), 152, 156, 201, 290; Frumkin-Rivlin, 2 (1928), 53f.

[Simon Marcus]

°**GARSTANG, JOHN** (1876–1956), British archaeologist; professor of archaeology at the University of Liverpool from 1907 to 1941. From 1900 to 1908 he conducted excavations in Egypt, Nubia, Asia Minor, and northern Syria, and from 1909 to 1914 he worked at ancient Meroë in Sudan uncovering important remains of the Roman-Nubian culture. After the British conquest of Palestine, Garstang was director of the British School of Archaeology in Jerusalem (1919–26). At the same time he served in the British Mandatory government as the first director of its Department of Antiquities, organizing the department and excavating at Ashkelon. In 1930–36 he resumed work in Palestine at Jericho, his findings there attracting wide attention at the time, although some of his conclusions were not borne out by subsequent investigations. By dating Jericho's double wall to the Late Bronze Age ca. 1400 B.C.E., Garstang found confirmation of the fall of the city to Joshua (Joshua 6), which fit the then-popular 15th century date assigned to the exodus. Katheen Kenyon's subsequent excavations showed that the fallen walls dated to Early Bronze and that Late Bronze remains were few; there was no wall as depicted in Joshua. After resigning from the University of Liverpool, Garstang continued working in Asia Minor (at Mersin, etc.) on behalf of the British Institute of Archaeology at Ankara. His publications, all characterized by a conservative trend, include studies in Hittite history, historical topography of Palestine and the Bible, and numerous excavation reports. During the controversy aroused by the 1939 White Paper, Garstang adopted an anti-Zionist position and was active in British public affairs on behalf of the Arabs. He was the author of *Hittite Empire* (1929), *Joshua, Judges* (1931), and *Heritage of Solomon* (1934).

BIBLIOGRAPHY: J. Day, in: DBI, 1, 431.

[Michael Avi-Yonah]

GARTNER, LLOYD P. (1927–), American-Israeli historian. Educated in the United States, Gartner was a professor at the City University of New York and the Jewish Theological Seminary before becoming professor of history at Tel Aviv University. He is probably best-known for his work *The Jewish Immigrant in England, 1870–1914* (1960), a pioneering work on Anglo-Jewish history which was among the earliest to study the post-1881 "New Diaspora" in Great Britain. Gartner has also written or edited a number of works on American Jewish history, including *Jewish Education in the United States: A Documentary History* (1969) and co-authored histories of the Jewish community in Los Angeles, Milwaukee, and Cleveland. In 2000 Gartner produced a comprehensive *History of the Jews in Modern Times*.

[William D. Rubinstein (2nd ed.)]

GARY, "The Steel City," founded in 1906 by the United States Steel Corporation; situated on the southern tip of Lake Michigan; the second largest city in Indiana. Gary has a population of approximately 120,000, less than 1,000 of them Jewish. Jewish families made their way into Gary's sand dunes and swamps along with the earliest pioneers, and in September 1908 the first Orthodox Jewish house of worship was dedicated. Subsequent years brought a series of ever larger structures, and in 1955 the modern Temple Israel was completed. The Reform Congregation was incorporated in 1910, and services are now conducted in the large, fifty-year-old Temple Israel in the Miller Section of Gary.

Gary's Jewish community is active in government, business, civic, and philanthropic circles. During most of the time from 1964 to 1968 the mayor, city attorney, superintendent of schools, health commissioner, and municipal judge were Jewish. There was little overt antisemitism, but Jews were excluded from the all-white Gary Country Club and the University Club. The Gary Jewish community continues to be involved in social justice issues but with the change in demographics it is not as involved politically as it once was. The Gary Jewish Welfare Federation was formed in 1941. Enlarged in 1958–59 to include East Chicago and Hammond, the name was changed to the Northwest Indiana Jewish Welfare Federation. This Federation possesses archives which include historical material on the Jewish communities in the area.

[Ida Kay Sacks / Stanley Halpern (2nd ed.)]

GARY (originally **Kacew**), **ROMAIN** (1914–1980), French novelist. Gary, who was of mixed parentage, "part Cossack and Tartar, part Jew" to use his own phrase, was born in Vilna. When he was seven, his family moved to Poland and finally, in 1926, to Nice. He was a fighter pilot in the French Air Force at the outbreak of World War II, and then joined De Gaulle's Free French in England in 1940. After the liberation, he entered the French diplomatic service. His final appointment was that of consul-general in Los Angeles (1956–60).

Gary's first novel *Education européenne* (1945; *Forest of Anger*, 1944, reissued as *A European Education*, 1960) includes many elements of Jewish interest, notably the description of a clandestine Friday evening service held by Jewish underground fighters. His other novels include *Tulipe* (1946); *Le grand vestiaire* (1948; *The Company of Men*, 1950); *Les Racines du ciel* (1956; *The Roots of Heaven*, 1958), an adventure story about a group of idealists bent on saving a herd of elephants from hunters, which won the Prix Goncourt; *La Promesse de l'aube* (1960; *Promise at Dawn*, 1961), memories of the author's Jewish mother; and *Le Mangeur d'étoiles* (1966; *The Talent Scout*, 1961). Two works which first appeared in English are *Lady L* (1958), a social satire, and *The Ski Bum* (1965). Jewish characters constantly make an appearance in Gary's novels, but they were mostly viewed from the outside until the writer's traumatic experience in a Warsaw war museum savagely wakened him to reality. *La Danse de Gengis Cohn* (1967; *The Dance of Genghis Cohn*, 1969), the title of which sardonically reflects Gary's own ancestry and predicament, tells with cruel humor the story of a Jewish comedian shot by the Nazis, who relentlessly haunts his executioner. He also wrote *La Tête Coupable* (1968; *The Guilty Head*, 1969).

BIBLIOGRAPHY: C. Lehrmann, *L'Elément juif dans la littérature française*, 2 (1961), 198–205; *Livres de France*, 18 no. 3 (1967), special issue devoted to Gary. **ADD. BIBLIOGRAPHY:** D. Bona, *Romain Gary* (1987); J.-M. Catonné, *Romain Gary, Emile Ajar* (1990); P. Bayard, *Il était deux fois Romain Gary* (1990); N. Huston, *Tombeau de Romain Gary* (1995); F. Larat, *Romain Gary: un itinéraire européen: essai biographique* (1999); R.W. Schoolcraft, *Romain Gary: The Man Who Sold His Shadow* (2002); M. Anissimov, *Romain Gary, le caméléon* (2004).

[Moshe Catane]

GASCONY, a duchy under English rule from 1152 to 1453, and later (with Guyenne) a province of the kingdom of France. There have been Jews in Gascony from at least the fourth century, especially in *Bordeaux. From 1242 or earlier the English ruler appointed special judges over the Jews, who were particularly numerous in *Agen and its vicinity. A first expulsion order was issued in 1289, even before the expulsion from England itself. Debts owing to the Jews were confiscated and collected at half their value for the king's treasury. Royal agents were appointed to seize the Jews and their belongings. However, the expulsion order was not vigorously enforced or rapidly became obsolete, for in 1292 there were again Jews in Gascony; the king ordered their expulsion once more. In 1305 they returned and must this time have obtained official authorization since in 1308 a judge was again in charge of Jewish affairs. A further expulsion order followed in 1310, which was repeated in 1313 and 1316. However, there were Jews in Gascony in 1320, when they were massacred by the *Pastoureaux. Some Jews were still found in Bordeaux until at least 1362. Jews bearing the surname of Gascon may have originated from there. Marrano refugees from Spain took refuge in this region from the close of the 15th century. Through them the Bordeaux community later became important again.

BIBLIOGRAPHY: Gross, Gal Jud, 144–5; E. Gaullieur, in: REJ, 11 (1885), 78–100; I. Rosenthal, in: PAAJR, 26 (1957), 127–34; Ch. Bemond and Y. Renouard (eds.), *Rôles Gascons*, 2 (1900), nos. 1067, 1128, 1181, 1192; 3 (1906), nos. 2054, 4786; 4 (1962), nos. 246, 488, 489, 490, 1127, 1138, 1233, 1670; Ch. Samaran, *La Gascogne dans… Trésor des Chartes* (1966), nos. 43, 44, 428; H.G. Richardson, *English Jewry under Angevin Kings* (1960), 225–7, 232–3.

[Bernhard Blumenkranz]

GASKELL, SONJA (1904–1974), Dutch dancer, choreographer, and ballet director. Gaskell was born in Villkaviskis, Lithuania. She studied in Paris and danced there in Diaghilev's Ballets Russes. In 1939 she followed her Dutch husband to Amsterdam, where she taught ballet dancers Russian technique. After World War II she founded her own groups, Ballet Studio '45 (1945) and Ballet Recital (1949–51), became the artistic director of Het National Ballet of Amsterdam, and established the first Netherlands academy of ballet in the Hague, where she was director of the Het Nederlands Ballet. As a choreographer, she created several ballets. From 1968 she worked as a member of the board of the dance department of UNESCO before taking over the Amsterdam company in 1961. In 1966 Gaskell was named officer of the Orde van Oranje-Nassau.

[Marcia B. Siegel / Amnon Shiloah (2nd ed.)]

GASSER, HERBERT SPENCER (1888–1963), U.S. neurophysiologist and Nobel Prize winner. Gasser was born in Platteville, Wisconsin. He collaborated with Joseph *Erlanger in investigating the electrical properties of nerve fibers. Utilizing a cathode-ray oscilloscope and a sensitive amplification system they recorded the electrical impulses passing over isolated nerve fibers. The measurements of the potential cycles of different nerve fibers revealed three distinct patterns indicating that there were three major types of fibers. It was also shown that the rate of conduction varied directly with the thickness of the fiber. These studies were the foundation of the modern knowledge of action currents in nerves and were of great importance toward an understanding of the complexities of nerve impulse transmission. As a result of this work Gasser and Erlanger shared the 1944 Nobel Prize for medicine.. Working with Erlanger and others, Gasser also contributed much to the understanding of the differences between sensory and motor nerves. He also dealt with problems involving the perception of pain and the contraction of muscle as well as the coagulation of blood.

BIBLIOGRAPHY: L.G. Stevenson, *Nobel Prize Winners in Medicine and Physiology, 1901–1950* (1935), 223–8; *Biographical Memoirs of Fellows of the Royal Society*, 10 (1964), 75–82.

[Norman Levin]

GASSING, extermination of Jews and others during the *Holocaust in installations specially constructed for mass-killing by gas, mostly in specific *camps. The idea of systematic and organized extinction of inoffensive human beings emanated from the conception which abolished the basic belief in the sanctity of human life and substituted the postulated predominance of the Aryan race whose superior value and whose purity had to be secured. As Hitler said in *Mein Kampf*: "A corrective measure in favor of the better quality must intervene" (Eng. transl. (1939), 248.)

Racial-biological "eugenics" were at first not applied to the Jews but to the elements in the German people itself. The "Law for the Prevention of Progeny with Hereditary Disease" was proclaimed already on July 14, 1933. The problem was further dealt with at the Nazi Party convention on Sept. 1, 1933, where the director of the "Racial-Policy Office" called compassion for people suffering from hereditary disease "false humanity" and a "sin against the Creator's own laws of life."

The implementation of the "Euthanasia Program" was prepared as from July 1939, together with the war. It was a top secret program carried through and supervised by the staff of Hitler's private chancellery. The action included the concentration of the mental patients chosen for the "merciful death" and their transportation from there to the nearest euthanasia station, short "medical" investigation of each patient, mainly in order to decide on the most plausible fictitious "cause of death" and then gassing of 20–30 people at one time in hermetically shut chambers disguised as shower rooms, cremation in the crematorium-annex after gold teeth had been broken off and some of the brains secured for "medical research."

Between January 1940 and August 1941, 70,273 German people were killed in five euthanasia institutions by this *Sonderbehandlung* (special treatment). The carbon monoxide gas was provided compressed in steel containers and released through pipes into the gas chamber. People were dead after 6–7 minutes. The first experiment was done by Kriminal-Kommissar Christian Wirth; later a specially trained chemist, Dr. Kallmeyer, became responsible for the whole gassing process. In August 1941 Hitler called the program officially off following the evolving unrest in the population, legal complications, and mounting protests, especially by the Churches. In fact, the institutions continued to function until 1944 but death was administered partly by gas, partly by injections, and partly by gradual starvation. Also put to death were the chronically ill, gypsies, foreign forced laborers, Russian prisoners of war, children from mixed marriages, and others "unworthy of life."

When in October 1941 the mass-shooting of Jews by the *Einsatzgruppen* became problematic (see *Holocaust), the three experts of the killing operation came together and decided on the use of gas: Erhard Wetzel, director of the Racial-Policy Office of the Nazi Party and the consultant on Jewish affairs of the Reich Minister for the Occupied Eastern Territories Alfred *Rosenberg; Victor Brack, deputy director of the Chancellery of the Fuehrer, the man mainly responsible for the implementation of the euthanasia program; and Adolf *Eichmann (Source: NO-997). Since the euthanasia program had just been officially discontinued it must have seemed reasonable to use the experience for the new project. The two technical experts, Christian *Wirth and Dr. Kallmeyer, were sent to the East to make the necessary installations. Physicians who had conducted the euthanasia program were also transferred. In the meantime gas had been employed in the fight against partisans in Yugoslavia. Here vans were used into which the exhaust fumes of their diesel engines were channeled. This method was now applied to the first killing center at *Chelmno. Then *Globocnik seized the idea and used it for the installation at *Belzec and *Treblinka. *Gerstein met Wirth there as the chief operator. Wirth now used the exhaust fumes the way the carbon monoxide gas had been handled in the euthanasia operation installing the whole process with the shower-room camouflage and securing gold teeth and other valuables. *Hoess brought the system to perfection in *Auschwitz. He went back to the easier use of chemical gas but chose hydrogen cyanide, the so-called Zyklon B crystals, instead of the carbon monoxide, apparently because it could easily be provided in great quantities. He also developed the crematorium scheme which had been in use in the euthanasia installations. Following the semantics of the previous stages the working teams were now called *Sonderkommando.* Zyklon B was also used in minor scale in Majdanek and in the concentration camp Gross-Rosen which was used for the extermination of concentration camp inmates in Germany. The gas chambers in Dachau and Theresienstadt were never put into action.

BIBLIOGRAPHY: R. Hilberg, *Destruction of the European Jews* (1967), index; G. Reitlinger, *Final Solution* (1968[2]), 130–64 and index; M. Weinreich, *Hitler's Professors* (1946), passim; A. Mitscherlich and F. Mielke, *Doctors of Infamy* (1949); K. Binding and A. Hoche, *Die Freigabe der Vernichtung unwerten Lebens, ihr Mass und ihre Form* (1920, 1922[2]); *Trials of War Criminals…*, 1 (1949); *Anklageschrift des Generalstaatsanwalt Frankfurt a. M. gegen den frueheren Arzt Horst Schuman von 12. 12. 1969*, Yad Vashem, no. 0404/20–83; K. Doerner, in: *Viertelsjahrhefte fuer Zeitgeschichte*, 15 (1967), no. 2, 121–52.

[Leni Yahil]

GASSNER, JOHN (1903–1967), U.S. author, critic, and anthologist. He was playreader in the 1930s for Theater Guild, and in 1940 established the playwriting seminar of Erwin Piscator's Dramatic Workshop. Gassner also functioned as dramatic critic for various publications. He was professor of playwriting and dramatic literature at Yale from 1956. He was one of two members of the drama jury of the Pulitzer Prize who resigned in 1963 when the trustees rejected the verdict for Edward Albee's *Who's Afraid of Virginia Woolf?* and made no award. His writings include (with B. Mantle) *Treasury of the Theater* (3 vols., 1935), *Masters of the Drama* (1940), *The Theater in Our Times* (1954), *Heritage of World Literature* (1946, vol. 7 of *Literature*, ed. by E.A. Cross), and *Best American Plays 1918–1958* (1961).

GASTER, MOSES (1856–1939), rabbi, scholar, and Zionist leader. Gaster was born in Bucharest and studied at the University of Breslau and the Jewish Theological Seminary of Breslau, where he was ordained in 1881. He taught Romanian language and literature in the University of Bucharest, 1881–85, published a popular history of Romanian literature, *Literatura Populară Română* (1883), and began his great chrestomathy of Romanian literature *Chrestomatie Română* (2 vols., 1891). In 1885, because of his protests against the treatment of the Jews, he was expelled from Romania. He settled in England where he was appointed to teach Slavonic literature at Oxford University in 1886. In 1887 he was appointed haham of the English Sephardi community.

Gaster's abilities as a scholar and an orator gave him an outstanding position both in the Anglo-Jewish community and in those areas of intellectual life in which he became a recognized authority, e.g., folklore and Samaritan literature. However, Gaster had a stubborn and combative personality, and this led to an unwillingness to retreat from a position once taken, which did not enhance his reputation. When he was principal of Judith Montefiore College, Ramsgate (1891–96), he endeavored to make it an institution for training rabbis, but the attempt failed. In 1918, after disagreements with his congregation, Gaster retired from the office of haham.

Gaster was active in Ḥibbat Zion and later in the Zionist movement. He accompanied L. *Oliphant on his visits to Romania, Constantinople, and Ereẓ Israel, and also played a considerable part in the establishment of Zikhron Ya'akov and Rosh Pinnah in Palestine, the first colonies settled by Romanian Jews. He became one of Herzl's early supporters but opposed him on the *Uganda Scheme, and this also brought him into conflict with the leaders of the English Zionist Federation, of which he was president in 1907. Throughout these years Gaster was a prominent figure at Zionist Congresses, being elected a vice president at the first four. It was to Gaster that Herbert *Samuel, then in the British Cabinet, turned when he wished to establish contact with the Zionists. The conference held at Gaster's home in February 1917 between the Zionist leaders and Sir Mark Sykes of the British Foreign Office was an important stage in the events leading to the *Balfour Declaration. After World War I he returned to his dissociation from official Zionist policy; this was partly the result of his failure to satisfy his ambition of becoming the official leader of the organization.

Gaster's writings covered many branches of learning, including Romanian literature, comparative and Jewish folklore, Samaritan history and literature, rabbinic scholarship, liturgy, Anglo-Jewish history, and biblical studies. A selection of Gaster's scattered essays appeared under the title *Studies and Texts in Folklore, Magic, Medieval Romance, Hebrew Apocrypha*… (3 vols., 1925–28). Other publications are listed in the bibliographies below. Gaster assembled a magnificent library, including many manuscripts, most of which he sold to the British Museum in 1925, but he continued his literary work, despite almost total blindness.

His son, THEODOR HERZL GASTER (1906–1992), educator and scholar, was born in London, and taught comparative religion at Dropsie College, Philadelphia, and at several universities in the United States and elsewhere. His writings include *Passover; its History and Traditions* (1949), *Purim and Hanukkah in Custom and Tradition* (1950); *Thespis; Ritual, Myth and Drama in the Ancient Near East* (1950, 1961[2]), *Festivals of the Jewish Year* (1953), *Holy and the Profane* (1955), and *New Year; Its History, Customs and Superstitions* (1955). He edited J.G. Frazer, *The New Golden Bough* (1959), edited and translated *Oldest Stories in the World* (1952), and translated the *Dead Sea Scriptures* into English.

BIBLIOGRAPHY: B. Schindler (ed.), *Occident and Orient… Gaster Anniversary Volume* (1936), includes bibliography; idem, *Gaster Centenary Publication* (1958), contains revised bibliography; C. Roth, in: JHSET, 14 (1940), 247–52; DNB, supplements, 5 (1949), 309–10.

[Cecil Roth]

GASTON-MARIN (Grossman), GHEORGHE (1919–), Romanian Communist politician and engineer. Born in Padureni, (Arad county), Transylvania, Gaston-Marin completed secondary school at Petrosani (1937) and was active in Zionist circles in his youth. He went to Paris and studied mathematics and physics at the Sorbonne (1937–38), afterwards at the Polytechnical Institute of Grenoble (1934–40), where he qualified as an electrical engineer and was a member of the French Resistance during World War II. After the war he returned to Romania (1945), joined the Communist Party, and was made minister of electrical energy in 1949. In 1954 he became first vice chairman of the State Planning Commission and from 1962 to 1969 was head of the Romanian industrialization program with the rank of deputy-premier; from 1969 to 1982 he was president of the State Council for Prices; from 1952 to 1985 he was a member of Romanian Parliament and from 1964 to 1982 Romanian representative to international economic organizations.

BIBLIOGRAPHY: G. Gaston-Marin, *In serviciul Romaniei lui Gheorghiu-Dej* (2000).

[Lucian-Zeev Herscovici (2nd ed.)]

GAT (Heb. גַּת), kibbutz in southern Israel, N.E. of *Kiryat Gat, affiliated with Kibbutz Arẓi ha-Shomer ha-Ẓa'ir, founded by East European settlers in 1942, as one of the first outposts established in the framework of the program to extend the settlement network to the south and northern Negev. The kibbutz economy was based on highly intensive farming (field crops, citrus groves, poultry, and dairy cattle), recreation facilities, a juice factory in partnership with Kibbutz Bet Nir, and a factory for wood products. The kibbutz name was chosen due to its proximity to the tell, then identified with biblical *Gath. In 1968 there were 435 inhabitants. The population rose to 560 in the mid-1990s but then dropped to 392 in 2002.

WEBSITE: www.gat.org.il.

[Efraim Orni / Shaked Gilboa (2nd ed.)]

GATESHEAD ON TYNE, industrial town in N.E. England. The first known Jew to settle in Gateshead was Zachariah Bernstone in the 1890s, a Russian immigrant who rebelled and broke away from the lesser observant congregation of adjoining *Newcastle-upon-Tyne. With his protégé E. Adler and their families from Eastern Europe, he attempted to establish a community at the beginning of the 20th century. On the initiative of a group of scholars, including *shoḥet* David Dryan, David Baddiel, and Moshe David Freed (son-in-law of Z. Bernstone), a yeshivah, now world-famous with some 250 pupils, was opened in 1929 under the direction of Rabbi N. Landynski and his assistant, L. Kahan. It represented the realization of a dream of those scholars who had seen their own yeshivot in Europe destroyed in pogroms. The first students from the U.K. were joined in the 1930s by refugees fleeing Nazi Germany and later by students from all over the world. Rabbi N. Shakowitzky, formerly of Lithuania, became community leader in the 1930s, up to which time the community and its houses of learning were of a strictly Russian-Polish character.

When refugees from Nazi Germany came to England, only the strictly observant were attracted to Gateshead. A college for advanced talmudical students (*kolel*), the first of its kind in Britain, was founded by E.G. *Dessler. German Jews who came to Gateshead after the war established further institutions of learning – a teachers' training college for girls, founded by A. Kohn, and a boarding school founded by M.L. Bamberger, 1944. Other institutions include a Jewish primary school, a kindergarten, and a *ḥeder*. The first scientific *shaatnez bureau in Britain was established in Gateshead. In 1966 the Gateshead Foundation for Torah was established to further the publication of Jewish literature. The community numbered 350 in 1970. In the mid-1990s the Jewish population numbered approximately 430, and according to the 2001 British census, the Jewish population of Gateshead had risen to 1,564. It had a range of strictly Orthodox institutions unknown in Britain outside of London and Manchester and its yeshivah and kolel were internationally known.

BIBLIOGRAPHY: M. Donbrow, in: *Jewish Chronicle* (London, 1959). **ADD. BIBLIOGRAPHY:** M. Dansky, *Gateshead: Its Community, Its personalities, Its Institutions* (1992).

GATH (Heb. גַּת), name of several Canaanite cities often appearing with a toponymic addition to differentiate them (e.g., Gath-Hepher, Gath-Rimmon, Gath-Gittaim, etc.). Four cities called Gath are listed among the conquests of Thutmose III and several Gath (or Gintis) are mentioned in the *El-Amarna letters: Ginti, Ginti-Kirmel, and Giti-Padalla. The last, which also appears in the city list of Pharaoh Shishak, is identified with the Arab village of Jatt in the Sharon. Pliny mentions a Gitta north of Mt. Carmel (*Natural History* 5:75); it was the home town of the famous sorcerer Simon Magus (Justinus Martyr, *Apologia* 1:26, 5–6). Eusebius locates a Gath between Antipatris and Jamnia (Jabneh; Onom. 72:2) and it is similarly situated on the Madaba Map. This is probably Gath-Gittaim, which Jewish tradition identifies with Ramleh and for which B. Mazar proposes the site of Ras Abu Ḥumayd (or Ḥamīd), east of Ramleh.

The best known Gath is "Gath of the Philistines." It was originally inhabited by Anakim ("giants"; Josh. 11:22; I Chron. 20:6, 8; II Sam. 21:20, 22) and later by one of the five Philistine lords (Josh. 13:3; etc.). It was one of the cities to which the Ark was brought after its capture (I Sam. 5:8). The Philistines fled from Gath after the defeat of Goliath (*ibid.* 17:52). Persecuted by Saul, David escaped to take refuge with Achish king of Gath (*ibid.* 21:11) from whom he received Ziklag in the Negev, a fact which indicates the extent of the territory ruled by Gath in the south. When Israel again became strong and united under David, Gath is mentioned in connection with his victory over the Philistines (I Chron. 8:13); the parallel account in II Samuel 8:1, however, contains the enigmatic "Metheg-Ammah" instead of Gath. The people of Gath were subdued and Ittai the Gittite became one of the captains of David's guard and remained faithful to him when Absalom rebelled (II Sam. 15:19–22; 18:2). A descendant of Achish, however, continued to rule Gath at the beginning of Solomon's reign (I Kings 2:39ff.); thus the Gath fortified by Rehoboam cannot be Gath of the Philistines and is possibly Moresheth-Gath, as proposed by Y. Aharoni. In his campaign of c. 815–814 B.C.E., Hazael of Aram-Damascus advanced as far as Gath (II Kings 12:18); his destruction of the city may be that alluded to by Amos (6:2). Gath was conquered by Uzziah, king of Judah (II Chron. 26:6) and Sargon mentions the capture of Gath (Ginti) during his campaign against Ashdod in 711 B.C.E. It is doubtful, however, whether these two references are to Gath of the Philistines or to the more northern Gat-Gittaim. In later times Eusebius mentions a village called Gath, five Roman miles from Eleutheropolis on the road to Diospolis-Lydda (Onom. 68:4ff.); it is also mentioned by Jerome (*Epistulae* 108:14).

The identification of Gath is a much debated problem. Albright proposed to locate it at Tell al-ʿUrayna, west of Bet Guvrin (Eleutheropolis) but six seasons of excavations by S. Yeivin have shown that most of the site contained no Iron Age (Philistine) remains. Only on the upper mound were remains from that period found, but its small size (3–4 acres) precludes an identification with Gath. A subsequent proposal to identify Gath with Tell al-Najīla has also been disproved so far by excavations; in two seasons of excavations a large Middle Bronze Age city was found but almost no Iron Age remains. The current proposal returns to its old identification with Tell al-Ṣāfī (as suggested by Elliger, Galling, and later, Aharoni). This large mound, excavated in 1899/1900, has produced large quantities of Philistine pottery.

BIBLIOGRAPHY: EM, s.v.; F.J. Bliss and R.A.S. Macalister, *Excavations in Palestine* (1902), pl. 44; Albright, in: AASOR, 2–3 (1923), 7–17; Elliger, in: ZDPV, 57 (1934), 148–52; Bulow and Michell, in: IEJ, 11 (1961), 101–10; S. Yeivin, *First Preliminary Report on the Excavations at Tel Gat* (1961); Mazar, in: IEJ, 4 (1954), 227–35; Aharoni, Land, index.

[Michael Avi-Yonah]

GATH-HEPHER (Heb. גַּת חֵפֶר), a town on the border of the territory of *Zebulun, between *Japhia and Eth-Kazin (Josh. 19:13). It is referred to as the birthplace of the prophet *Jonah (II Kings 14:25). The biblical site has been identified with Khirbat al-Zurraʿ (now called Tel Gath Hepher), near the Arab village of Mashhad, 2½ mi. (4 km.) southeast of *Sepphoris. An examination of the tell has revealed Iron Age pottery on its surface. A tomb in the village traditionally that of Jonah (al-Nabī Yūnis) attests the existence of a local tradition which was already noted by Jerome in the preface to his Latin commentary on the Book of Jonah.

BIBLIOGRAPHY: Albright, in: BASOR, 35 (1929), 8; EM, S.V.

[Michael Avi-Yonah]

GATH-RIMMON (Heb. גַּת רִמּוֹן).

(1) Levitical city in the territory of Dan (Josh. 21:24; I Chron. 6:54). It is located in the vicinity of Jehud, Bene-Berak, and Me-Jarkon ("the waters of Yarkon") in Joshua 19:45 and it is possibly mentioned in the list of conquests of Thutmose III in c. 1469 B.C.E. (line 63) in the same general area, between Jaffa and Lydda. In the opinion of some scholars, the Giti-rimunima in the *El-Amarna letters (ed. by Knudtzon, 250) refers to this locality. Gath-Rimmon is commonly identified with Tell Jarīsha, which was excavated from 1934. The finds included remains of a Hyksos wall and glacis of the Middle Bronze II Age, a Late Bronze Age tomb, and evidence of a settlement up to the ninth century B.C.E.

(2) Levitical city of the tribe of Manasseh west of the Jordan (Josh. 21:25). Some scholars consider it identical with the Giti-rimunima of the el-Amarna letters mentioned above, and as evidence that a second Gath-Rimmon existed in the region, they cite the worship of Hadadrimmon in the Jezreel Valley (Zech. 12:11). In the parallel text of levitical cities in I Chronicles 6, however, Bileam (Ibleam) appears instead of Gath-Rimmon, and the mention of the latter twice in Joshua 21 may have been due to an error.

BIBLIOGRAPHY: EM, S.V. (includes bibliography); QDAP, 4 (1935), 208–9; 6 (1938), 225; 10 (1944), 55ff., 198–9, excavation reports of Gath Rimmon (1); Aharoni, Land, index.

[Michael Avi-Yonah]

GATIGNO, family of rabbis and scholars that first appeared in Spain and Portugal in the 14th century and settled in Turkey after the expulsion. Some consider the name to derive from the French province of Gatines. EN SOLOMON ASTRUC of Barcelona, called the "*kadosh*," is regarded as one of the first members of this family, but others cast doubt upon his connection with them. He was the author of the commentary on the Pentateuch called *Midreshei ha-Torah*, apparently composed after 1376. Some identify him with Ezra B. SOLOMON, while others maintain that Ezra was his son, who lived in the second half of the 14th century in Saragossa and Acrimonte. Ezra wrote a supercommentary (still in manuscript) on Abraham ibn Ezra's commentary to the Pentateuch, explaining his exegesis and his homiletical interpretations. ḤAYYIM BEN SAMUEL GATIGNO was among the exiles from Spain in 1492 who reached Italy. He worked in Rome as a copyist between the years 1542 and 1553 and then as a proofreader in Cremona.

From the beginning of the 18th century members of the family are found especially in Smyrna and Salonika. ELIAKIM BEN ISAAC GATIGNO served as rabbi of Smyrna, where he died in 1795. He was the author of: *To'afot Re'em* (Smyrna, 1762), an exposition of Elijah *Mizraḥi's supercommentary to Rashi; responsa, *Agurah be-Ohalekha* (Salonika, 1781), which include responsa taken from manuscripts by David b. Zimra (Radbaz), Isaac Escapa, and Abraham ha-Kohen of Safed, and appended to the volume are passages which he omitted from the *To'afot Re'em*; and *Yiẓḥak Yerannen* (*ibid.*, 1786), glosses to Maimonides' *Mishneh Torah*. Eliakim's son, ISAAC, was the author of: *Beit Yiẓḥak* (*ibid.*, 1792), also glosses to the *Mishneh Torah; Beit Mo'ed* (*ibid.*, 1839), novellae to the tractates *Mo'ed Katan* and *Makkot* with additions by his pupil Ḥayyim *Palache, who also wrote an introduction to the work; and *Mi-Yagon le-Simḥah* (*ibid.*, 1795), a commentary on the laws of mourning (nos. 1–32) of *Meir of Rothenburg. Among the rabbis of this family who served in Salonika during the 18th and 19th centuries are: ḤAYYIM ABRAHAM BEN BENVENISTE, kabbalist, a pupil of Solomon *Amarillo, and the author of *Tirat Kesef* (*ibid.*, 1736), sermons on the weekly scripture portions; and *Ẓeror ha-Kesef* (*ibid.*, 1756), responsa, glosses, and novellae on the Shulḥan Arukh, talmudic themes, and on the *Mishneh Torah*. These were published by BENVENISTE (Mercado), son of Ḥayyim Abraham, with an introduction and additions. Benveniste was the author of a halakhic work, *Terumat ha-Kesef*, which, together with a work by his son Abraham, *Elef Kesef*, was published with the comprehensive title *Maẓref le-Kesef* (1867). ABRAHAM BEN BENVENISTE GATIGNO was elected *ḥakham bashi* ("chief rabbi") of Salonika in 1875. He died in 1895. He was the author of the responsa *Ẓel ha-Kesef* (1872) to which are appended ten homilies. Abraham was the founder of the first modern Jewish school in the town. BENVENISTE BEN MOSES was the author of homilies on the Torah which were published together with additions by his son JUDAH under the title, *Meḥushakim Kesef* (1839). Judah's son SAMUEL (d. 1885) was a *dayyan* in Salonika.

BIBLIOGRAPHY: S. Eppenstein (ed.), *Midreshei ha-Torah* (1899), introd.; A. Freimann (ed.), *Inyanei Shabbetai Ẓevi* (1912), 147 nos. 142, 146; M. Steinschneider, *Gesammelte Schriften*, 1 (1925), 1–8; Baer, Urkunden, 1 (1929), 579f.; B. Wachstein, *Mafte'aḥ ha-Hespedim*, 1 (1922), 18, 24, 31, 54, 62; 2 (1927), 3, 25, 31, 41; 3 (1930), 4, 18, 50, 63, 84; 4 (1932), 33; I.S. Emmanuel, *Maẓẓevot Saloniki* (1963), no. 531; Molḥo and Amarijlio, in: *Sefunot*, 2 (1958), 55f.; *Saloniki Ir va-Em be-Yisrael* (1967), 15, 19, 77.

[Yehoshua Horowitz]

GAUNSE, JOACHIM (d. 1619), mining engineer; member of the Gans family of Prague. In 1581 he was in England, where he reorganized the copper mining at Keswick in Cumberland, and later at Neath, Wales. He was arrested in Bristol (1596) for indiscreet remarks during a theological dispute and declared himself a Jew. He was sent to London for trial before the Privy Council and presumably was expelled from England. He is probably identical to the Zalman b. Zeligman Gans whose tombstone in Prague (S. Hock, *Die Familien Prags*, 1892, no. 997) describes him as having endangered his life to wreak vengeance among the gentiles. Gaunse has one remarkable distinction: In 1584 he was recruited by Sir Walter Raleigh to join the first Virginia Company's expedition to the New World and served as supervisor of mining on the ill-fated Roanoke Expedition of 1595. Gaunse was thus the first known Jew to set foot in North America, at least in the area ruled by England.

BIBLIOGRAPHY: M.B. Donald, *Elizabethan Copper...* (1956), passim; Abrahams, in: JHSET, 4 (1903), 83–101.

[Cecil Roth / William D. Rubinstein (2nd ed.)]

GAVISON (or **Gavishon**), Spanish family. In the 14th century the Gavison family were among the most respected Jews of Seville, but they were forced to flee to Granada during the persecutions of 1391. There, in the 15th century, almost all the Gavisons were murdered; only JACOB and ABRAHAM, the sons of JOSEPH GAVISON, escaped in 1492 to Tlemcen, Algeria. JACOB BEN JOSEPH was a physician and the author of *Derekh ha-Sekhel*, a work directed against the opponents of Maimonides, no longer extant. Poems in praise of this work were written by Solomon al-Malaki, Jacob Berab, and Abraham (2?) Gavison. One of Joseph Gavison's descendants was ABRAHAM BEN JACOB (d. 1578) of Tlemcen, a physician, who lived for some time in Algiers, author of *Omer ha-Shikhḥah* (unfinished). His son JACOB edited the poetical portion of this work and added poems written by himself and his own son ABRAHAM (1586–1605), a gifted young man who died of the plague (see *Omer ha-Shikhḥah*, 127b–128a, and Abraham's poems, 120b). MOSES (d. 1696), a merchant of Algiers, belongs to the same branch of the family; he also died of the plague. The same fate overtook in 1745 the two sons of ABRAHAM (4), who in 1748 published his ancestor's *Omer ha-Shikhḥah* in Leghorn. MEIR and SOLOMON were contemporaries of R. Jacob de *Castro in Egypt in the second half of the 16th century. MEIR GAVISON, originally from Damascus, went to Egypt as a merchant and later joined the academy of the *dayyan* Ḥayyim Kaposi; his responsa were seen in manuscript by Ḥ.Y.D. *Azulai. SOLOMON GAVISON, also a halakhic authority (see responsa of Solomon ha-Kohen (Maharshak) III, Salonika, 1594), was sharply attacked by Castro (responsa *Oholei Ya'akov*, no. 33), because he delivered a halakhic opinion favorable to the Karaites. In the second half of the 19th century VIDAL served as a rabbi in Gibraltar.

BIBLIOGRAPHY: A. Gavison, *Omer ha-Shikhḥah* (1746), preface and supplement; A. Cahen, *Juifs dans l'Afrique septentrionale* (1867), 104ff.; M. Mendez-Bejarano, *Histoire de la Juiverie de Séville* (1922), 125; Rosanes, Togarmah, 3 (1938), 246, 247, 250ff.; Hirschberg, Afrikah, 2 (1965), 46–47.

[Jefim (Hayyim) Schirmann]

GAVISON, RUTH (1945–), Israeli jurist. Gavison was born in Jerusalem and spent her childhood years in Haifa. In 1969 she received her LL.B. with distinction and in 1970 she graduated in philosophy and economics, both degrees from the Hebrew University of Jerusalem. From 1969 she taught in the Faculty of Law of the Hebrew University. In 1970 she clerked under Justice B. Halevi of the Israel Supreme Court and in 1971 she was admitted to the Israeli bar. In the same year she finished her LL.M. with distinction at the Hebrew University and in 1975 she received her Ph.D. in legal philosophy from Oxford University. In 1984 she was named to the H. Cohn Chair for Human Rights at the Hebrew University and in 1990 she became full professor. In addition to her academic career, Gavison was active in the Association for Civil Rights in Israel, serving as its president from 1996 to 1999. In 1997 she joined the International Commission of Jurists and the Israel Democracy Institute. She also served as a member of several public committees, such as the Kahan Committee on Privacy in 1976, a public committee on Orthodox-secular relations in Israel from 1987 to 1990, and the Shamgar Committee on the Appointment of the Attorney-General and Related Issues in 1997–98. Gavison is a familiar public figure in Israel owing to her participation in numerous media debates on legal issues. She received the Zeltner Prize for Legal Research in 1997 and the EMET prize in 2003. Her fields of interest are philosophy of law and legal theories and processes. She published numerous books and articles, among them *Discretion in Law Enforcement: The Power of the Attorney General to Stay Criminal Proceedings* (1991); *Human Rights in Israel* (1995); *The Constitutional Revolution: A Reality or a Self-Fulfilling Prophecy?* (1998); *Israel: A Jewish and Democratic State* (1999); and *The Role of the Supreme Court in Israeli Society* (with M. Kremnitzer and Y. Dotan, 2000). In 2000 she published together with Rabbi Ya'akov Madan a document defining secular-religious relations in Israel. Gavison is identified with the right wing and has criticized Supreme Court decisions. She called for a curbing of the legal activism spearheaded by Supreme Court President Aharon *Barak. She believes that the Supreme Court cannot act as the highest moral authority of the state, but should respect the political system and its decisions and the Jewish character of the state. In 2005 her name came up as a candidate for the Supreme Court, which led to much heated debate.

BIBLIOGRAPHY: Y. Yoaz, "Ruthie's Agenda," in: *Haaretz* (Dec. 2, 2005).

[Shaked Gilboa (2nd ed.)]

°**GAWLER, GEORGE** (1796–1869), English Christian who propagated the idea of Jewish settlement of Ereẓ Israel. Gawler took part in the Battle of Waterloo as a senior commander and was the first governor of the newly established colony of South Australia (1838–41). On his return to England he took up the cause of the agricultural settlement of Ereẓ Israel by Jews and persisted in the propagation of this idea until the end of his life. He sought to provide a solution both to the permanent unrest in the Middle East and to the Jewish problem in Europe and proposed that his plan should be executed by the British. He first introduced his ideas in a pamphlet entitled *Tranquilization of Syria and the East: Observations and Practical Suggestions in Furtherance of the Establishment of Jewish Colonies in Palestine … the Most Sober and Sensible Remedy for the Miseries of Asiatic Turkey* (London, 1845), and followed this up with a series of pamphlets in which he discussed other plans, including *Emanicipation of the Jews Indispensable for the Maintenance of the Protestant Profession of the Empire; and Most Entitled to the Support of the British Nation* (1847). His experience in Australia led him to believe that it was possible to settle an uninhabited land within a few years. He accompanied Sir Moses *Montefiore on the latter's third trip to Ereẓ Israel (1849) and seems to have been the one who persuaded Montefiore to initiate agricultural settlement in the country, in spite of the opposition of large sections of the Jewish population to the idea. Over the course of the years, Gawler contributed numerous articles to the Jewish press in Britain (*Voice of Jacob, Jewish Chronicle)*; in one of these articles he stated: "I should be truly rejoiced to see in Palestine a strong guard of Jews established in flourishing agricultural settlements and ready to hold their own upon the mountains of Israel against all aggressors, I can wish for nothing more glorious in this life than to have my share in helping them do so" (JC, Aug. 10, 1860). The only result of his plans was Montefiore's acquisition of an orange grove near Jaffa on his fourth trip to the Holy Land (1855), where Jewish workers were employed (now known as the Montefiore Quarter in Tel Aviv).

His son, JOHN COX GAWLER, took up his father's cause and in 1874 published a detailed plan for the settlement of Ereẓ Israel by Jews on businesslike and technological principles. He also sought to gain Montefiore's interest in the plan. The plan aroused great interest in Jerusalem, and a Hebrew translation of it by I.D. *Frumkin was published in *Ḥavaẓẓelet*. By publishing the plan, Frumkin encouraged certain groups of the old *yishuv* to put the plan into practice, and, as a result, four years later *Petaḥ Tikvah was founded.

BIBLIOGRAPHY: M. Montefiore, *Diaries of Sir Moses and Lady Montefiore*, 2 (1890), 15; N. Sokolow, *History of Zionism*, 2 vols. (1919), index; G. Kressel (ed.), *Mivḥar Kitvei I.D. Frumkin* (1954), index; G. Yardeni, *Ha-Ittonut ha-Ivrit be-Ereẓ-Yisrael* (1969), index. **ADD. BIBLIOGRAPHY:** Australian Dictionary of Biography; ODNB online; H.L. Rubinstein and W. D Rubinstein, *Philosemitism*, 152–54.

[Getzel Kressel]

GAY (Froehlich), PETER JACK (Joachim; 1923–), U.S. historian. Gay, who was born in Berlin, Germany, immigrated to the United States in 1941 and began teaching at Columbia University in 1948. In 1969 he became professor of comparative European intellectual history at Yale. Later he was director of the Center for Scholars and Writers at the New York Public Library and Sterling Professor Emeritus of History at Yale University. Gay's chief interest was the Enlightenment, of which he presented a sympathetic view. His major publications in this field are *Voltaire's Politics* (1959), *Party of Humanity* (1964), and *The Enlightenment, an Interpretation: The Rise of Modern Paganism* (1966). He wrote many other books as well, including *The Dilemma of Democratic Socialism* (1952), *A Loss of Mastery* (1966), *Weimar Culture* (1968), *Style in History* (1976), *Art and Act: On Causes in History – Manet, Gropius, Mondrian* (1976), *Freud, Jews and Other Germans* (1978), *The Bourgeois Experience* (1983), *Education of the Senses* (1984), *The Tender Passion* (1986), *A Godless Jew* (1987), *The Cultivation of Hatred* (1993), *Pleasure Wars* (1998), *My German Question* (1998), *Schnitzler's Century* (2002), and *Savage Reprisals* (2002).

[Joseph I. Shulim / Ruth Beloff (2nd ed.)]

GAYLORD, MITCHELL (1961–), U.S. gymnast, winner of four medals at the 1984 Olympics. Born in Los Angeles, California, Gaylord was named the city's high school athlete of the year in 1979. He attended UCLA, and saw his first international competition at the 11th Maccabiah Games in 1981, winning six gold medals and one silver – coming in second to his brother, Chuck. The seven medals tie him for the most won by an individual athlete at a single Maccabiah Games. Gaylord earned a 10 on the high-bar at the 1982 U.S.A. Championships, resulting in a gold medal, won the all-around championship at the 1982 National Sports Festival, and was the No. 1-ranked gymnast in 1983 and 1984. Gaylord invented two skills now named internationally after him – the Gaylord Flip and the Gaylord Two, considered two of the most difficult feats in gymnastics. Gaylord won the U.S. national championship in 1983 and 1984, when his 117.85 set an American record, and the all-around title representing UCLA at the 1984 NCAA championship with a score of 116.95.

At the 1984 Olympic Games in Los Angeles, Gaylord won a gold medal in the team event, a silver in vaulting, and bronze medals in both rings and parallel bars. His score of 59.45 in the team competition is a U.S. record, and he was the first American gymnast in history to receive a perfect "10." President Ronald Reagan thereafter appointed him to the President's Council for Physical Fitness. Gaylord is co-author with his brother of *Working Out Without Weights* (1987).

[Elli Wohlgelernter (2nd ed.)]

GAZA (Heb. **עַזָּה, Azzah**), city on the southern coastal plain of Ereẓ Israel. From earliest times it served as the base of Egyptian operations in Canaan. Unlike the neighboring sites of Tell el-'Ajjul and Tell Ali Muntar, Gaza itself did not have much strategic and economic importance during the third and second millennia B.C.E. An important Middle Bronze II settlement, however, has been discovered at al-Moghraqa in the area of Wadi Gaza. Gaza was apparently held by Thutmose III (c. 1469 B.C.E.) and in his inscriptions it has the title of "that-which-the-ruler-seized" signifying its role as the chief Egyptian base in Canaan. In the reliefs of Seti I (c. 1300 B.C.E.) it is called "the [town of] Canaan." It is also mentioned in the Tell el-Amarna and Taanach tablets as an Egyptian administrative center. According to biblical tradition its original inhabitants were the Avvites (Deut. 2:23; Josh. 13:3). At the time of the Israelite conquest it was allotted to the tribe of Judah (Josh. 15:47; Judg. 1:18) but it remained in the possession of the Canaanites until the beginning of the 12th century B.C.E. when it was occupied by the Philistines – possibly at first as an Egyptian garrison. It became the southernmost city of the Philistine Pentapolis (Josh. 13:3; I Sam. 6:17; Jer. 25:20). At Gaza Samson performed some of his famous deeds and there too he perished in the temple of Dagon in the great slaughter of his enemies (Judg. 16). With the weakening of Egyptian support, the Philistines finally submitted to David (II Sam. 5:25). In 734 B.C.E. Tiglath-Pileser III of Assyria took Gaza but it remained a Philistine city and the short conquest of Hezekiah (II Kings 18:8) did not alter its status. Pharaoh Necho II occupied Gaza briefly in 609 B.C.E. Under the Persians (after a siege in 529 B.C.E. by Cambyses) Gaza became an important royal fortress called Kadytis by Herodotus (2:159). In 332 B.C.E. it was the only city in Ereẓ Israel to oppose Alexander, who besieged it and sold its people into slavery. In the Hellenistic period Gaza was the outpost of the Ptolemies until its capture by Antiochus III in 198 B.C.E. Its commercial importance increased in Persian and Hellenistic times when it served as the Mediterranean outlet of the Nabatean caravan trade and as the gateway for Greek penetration into southern Ereẓ Israel. The city was attacked by Jonathan the Hasmonean in 145 B.C.E. (I Macc. 11:61–62) but was taken only by Alexander Yannai in 96 B.C.E. after a long siege. It was restored by Pompey and rebuilt by Gabinius in 57 B.C.E. It was held by Herod for a short time. Gaza prospered under Roman rule and contained a famous school of rhetoric. It was fanatically devoted to its Cretan god Marnas, even under Christian rule; only in the fifth century was its temple destroyed and Christianity made the ruling religion. Although Jews were settled there in the talmudic period, the city was regarded as being outside the halakhic boundaries of the Holy Land. Gaza is shown as a large city on the Madaba Map – "splendid, delicious" are the words of the traveler Antoninus – with colonnaded streets crossing its center and a large basilica in the middle, probably the church erected on the temple of Marnas. A depiction of the city of Gaza also appears in a mosaic floor uncovered at Umm er-Rasas in Jordan. In antiquity Gaza controlled an extensive territory, including the areas of Anthedon and its harbor, Maiumas. The sources mention an "Old Gaza." This was probably at Beth-Eglaim – Tell al-Ajūl (the tell at the city proper however contains evidence of settlement from the Bronze Age onward). "Gaza the desert" in the New Testament (Acts 8:26), which is the city proper, was so called because of its devastation by Alexander Yannai. The "New City" (Neapolis) was the harbor; a synagogue was found there paved with mosaics and dated 508/9. In 1965 a mosaic floor was uncovered on the seashore of Gaza's harbor. Its figures include one of King David as Orpheus, dressed in Byzantine royal garments and playing the lyre. The name "David" in Hebrew letters appears above it. A Greek inscription at the center of the floor, which mentions the names of the two donors (Menahem and Jesse) of the mosaic to the "holy place," and the name "David," testify to the fact that a synagogue stood there. The synagogue was cleared by A. Ovadiah in 1967/68. Evidence of a considerable Jewish population during the talmudic period in Gaza is provided also by a relief of a *menorah*, a *shofar*, a *lulav*, and an *etrog*, which appear on a pillar of the Great Mosque of Gaza; and various Hebrew and Greek inscriptions. According to the Karaite Sahl b. Maẓli'aḥ, Gaza, Tiberias, and Zoar were the three centers of pilgrimages in Ereẓ Israel during the Byzantine period. Gaza was situated 3 mi. (5 km.) from the sea in a fertile plain rich in wheat, vineyards, and fruits. Its fair (*panegyris*) was one of the three main fairs in Roman Palestine.

In a great battle fought near Gaza in 635, the Arabs vanquished the Byzantines; the city itself fell soon afterward. It remained the seat of the governor of the Negev, as is known from the Nessana Papyri. The Jewish and Samaritan communities flourished under Arab rule; in the eighth century, R. Moses, one of the masoretes, lived there. In the 11th century R. Ephraim of Gaza was head of the community of Fostat (old Cairo). King Baldwin I of Jerusalem occupied the city which was known in Crusader times as Gadres; from the time of Baldwin III (1152) it was a Templar stronghold. In 1170 it fell to Saladin. Under Mamluk rule Gaza was the capital of a district (*mamlaka*) embracing the whole coastal plain up to Athlit. After the destruction of Gaza by the Crusaders the Jewish community ceased to exist. Nothing more was heard of it until the 14th century. Meshullam of Volterra in 1481 found 60 Jewish householders there and four Samaritans. All the wine of Gaza was produced by the Jews (A.M. Luncz, in *Yerushalayim*, 1918). Obadiah of Bertinoro records that when he was there in 1488, Gaza's rabbi was a certain Moses of Prague who had come from Jerusalem (*Zwei Briefe*, ed. by A. Neubauer (1863), 19). Gaza flourished under Ottoman rule; the Jewish community was very numerous in the 16th and 17th centuries. The Karaite Samuel b. David found a Rabbanite synagogue there in 1641 (*Ginzei Yisrael be-St. Petersburg*, ed. by J. Gurland (1865), 11). In the 16th century there were a *bet din* and a yeshivah in Gaza, and some of its rabbis wrote scholarly works. Farm-owners were obliged to observe the laws of *terumah* ("priestly tithe"), *ma'aserot* ("tithes"), and the sabbatical year. At the end of the 16th century the Najara family supplied some of its rabbis; Israel *Najara, son of the Damascus rabbi Moses Najara, author of the "*Zemirot Yisrael*," was chief rabbi of Gaza and president of the *bet din* in the mid-17th century. In 1665, on the occasion of Shabbetai Ẓevi's visit to Gaza, the city became a center of his messianic movement, and one of his principal disciples was *Nathan of Gaza. The city was occupied by Napoleon for a short time in 1799. In the 19th century, the city declined. The Jews concentrated there were mainly barley merchants; they bartered with the Bedouins for barley which they exported to the beer breweries in Europe. It was a Turkish stronghold in World War I; two British attacks made on Gaza in 1916–17 failed and it was finally taken by a flanking movement of *Allenby. Under Mandatory rule Gaza developed slowly; the last Jews left the town as a result of the anti-Jewish Arab disturbances in 1929.

[Michael Avi-Yonah / Shimon Gibson (2nd ed.)]

In 1946 Gaza's population was estimated at 19,500, all Muslim except for 720 Christians. In the Israel *War of Independence, the invading Egyptian army occupied Gaza (May 1948). The town, together with the newly formed *Gaza Strip, was put under Egyptian administration by the armistice agreement of 1949. The influx of Arab refugees from the areas which became part of Israel swelled the city's population at least fourfold. The 1967 census showed that 87,793 inhabitants lived in the city proper, while 30,479 lived in the refugee camp within municipal boundaries. Of these, 1,649 were Christian and the rest Muslim. In the *Sinai Campaign (1956), Gaza was occupied by the Israeli army (November 2, 1956) and evacuated in March 1957. The Egyptian army reinstalled itself in the Strip, but in the Six-Day War (1967), Israeli forces captured the town on June 6, and an Israeli military government was set up in the town. From 1969, there were frequent acts of terrorism and sabotage in the town, which remained the center of activity in the Gaza Strip. (For political developments see *Gaza Strip.)

It appears that in the historic past Gaza's built-up area alternately expanded and decreased in size, particularly in the area between the city core and the seashore about 2 mi. (3 km.) distant. This expanse of dunes lay waste in the 20th century, until the British Mandate authorities allocated land for a nominal fee to anyone promising to build his house there within five years of signing a contract. Gaza's principal east-west artery now runs through this area, up to the shore. From the 1940s the city also expanded eastward. In the northwest Gaza gradually links up with Jabalya and Nazala. Within the municipal area, there are orchards, fields, and kitchen gardens. Farming and sea fishing retain a place with small commerce and industries in the city economy, while pottery constitutes a prominent branch. After 1967, larger manufacturing plants (food, textiles, and other branches) were established there.

BIBLIOGRAPHY: M.A. Meyer, *History of the City of Gaza from the Earliest Times to the Present Day* (1907); G. Downey, *Gaza in the Early Sixth Century* (1963); Kena'ani, in: BJPES, 5 (1937), 33–41; Benayahu, *ibid.*, 20 (1955), 21–30; Avi-Yonah, *ibid.*, 30 (1966), 221–3; M. Ish-Shalom, *Masei Noẓerim le-Ereẓ Yisrael* (1965), index; Ben Zvi, Ereẓ Yisrael, index; J. Braslavski (Braslavi), *Le-Ḥeker Arẓenu – Avar u-Seridim* (1954), index; idem, *Me-Reẓu'at Azzah ad Yam Suf* (1957); S. Klein, *Toledot ha-Yishuv ha-Yehudi be-Ereẓ Yisrael* (1935), index; S. Assaf and L.A. Mayer (eds.), *Sefer ha-Yishuv*, 2 vols. (1939–44). **ADD. BIBLIOGRAPHY:** J. Garstang, "The Walls of Gaza," in: PEFQS (1920), 156–57; C.A.M. Glucker, *The City of Gaza in the Roman and Byzantine Periods* (1987); J. Clarke et al., "The Gaza Research Project: 1998 Field Season," in: *Journal of Palestinian Archaeology*, 2 (2001), 4–11; L. Steel et al., "Gaza Research Project. Report on the 1999 and 2000 Seasons at al-Moghraqa," in: *Levant*, 36 (2004), 37–88; "Ghazza," in: EIS[2], 2, 1056–57 (incl. bibl.).

GAZA STRIP (Heb. רְצוּעַת עַזָּה; Ar. قطاع غزة), an area located on the coastal plain between Israel and Egypt, cover-

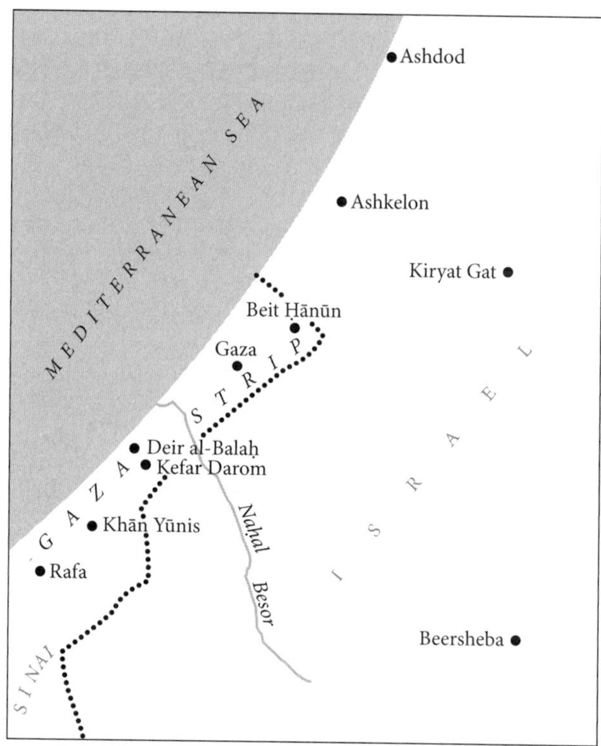

The Gaza Strip.

ing around 140 sq. miles (362 sq. km.), and between 3 and 4.5 miles (5–7 km.) wide and 28 miles (45 km.) long. The Gaza Strip is not a separate geographical unit, but rather a political one that emerged after the Arab-Israeli War of 1948, when the territory of Palestine, a British Mandate from 1920 to 1948, was divided into three major entities: the independent State of Israel, inhabited predominantly by Jews, and the two Palestinian Arab "territories" of the West Bank (ruled by Jordan at that time) and the Gaza Strip (ruled by Egypt).

Gaza Strip under Egyptian Rule

The Armistice Agreement of February 1949 between Israel and Egypt established the borders of the Gaza Strip according to the ceasefire boundaries, although the districts of Beit Ḥānūn and ʿAbasān were given to Egypt by Israel. This agreement proved to be fragile. From the early 1950s, Palestinian *Fidāʾiyyūn* (lit. those who are ready to sacrifice their lives for their cause) launched attacks from the Gaza Strip on Israeli military and civilian targets. Taking the view that Egypt had initiated these attacks, Israel carried out several raids in the Strip. In 1956, as part of the *Sinai Campaign, Israel occupied the Strip and held it between November 2, 1956, and March 8, 1957. The subsequent period of Egyptian control that followed was relatively quiet, until the outbreak of the Six-Day War in June 1967, when Egypt lost the Strip to Israel (and Jordan lost the West Bank to Israel).

Demographic change was much more radical in the Strip during the 1948 War than in the West Bank, and had significant economic and social consequences. Some estimates suggest that during the 1948 War the population of the Strip multiplied by 4.5 times (from 80,000 to 360,000) due to the influx of Palestinians from Arab villages in Israel pouring into the Strip in search of protection from the Egyptian army. Eight refugee camps were set up and administered by the newly created United Nations Relief and Works Agency (UNRWA) where their residents obtained food, basic housing, medical care, and schooling. Unemployment was high because there were not enough jobs in the local economy, largely based on agriculture and small businesses; employment outside the Strip was not permitted until 1952, when Egypt opened its border to allow workers to enter. Yet even then job opportunities were limited. At least half of the labor force remained unemployed, and those who found work earned very little.

In 1957, after regaining control of the Strip, Egypt took some measures to relieve the situation, which included improving the seaport of *Gaza and encouraging exports. Although this had a positive effect for some Palestinians, it did not bring about fundamental structural change, and "national output" from the Strip did not significantly increase; in the last full year of Egyptian control over the Strip, per capita GNP stood at only US$80 (about 1,500 NIS in 2005 prices).

From Direct Control to Disengagement: Israel and the Gaza Strip

At the end of the Six-Day War in June 1967, Israel seemed very determined to hold on to the Strip. Prime Minister Levi *Eshkol declared that "Israel intends to keep the former part of Jerusalem and the Gaza Strip" and his defense minister, Moshe *Dayan, declared that "the Gaza Strip is Israel's and steps will be taken to make it part of this country." Even so, a full annexation did not follow these declarations. Although small settlements of Israeli Jews were established in the Gaza Strip, it was only in stages that the notion of annexation was replaced by that of separation.

In the Camp David Accords between Israel and Egypt in 1978, Israel signed "a framework for peace in the Middle East" which called for the implementation of an autonomy plan for the West Bank and Gaza Strip, but left open the question of sovereignty over these territories. In 1994–95, in the Oslo Accords between Israel and the Palestine Liberation Organization (PLO), a timetable was drawn up for the withdrawal of Israeli forces from the Gaza Strip and the West Bank, and for the formation of a self-governing Palestinian entity, leading to the establishment of a Palestinian state. The so-called permanent status issues such as the fate of Palestinian refugees, the future of Israeli settlements in the West Bank and Gaza, and agreed borders between Israel and a Palestinian entity, were deliberately excluded from the Accords and left for future negotiations. Subsequently, the Palestinian Authority (PA) was established as the new governing regime in the Strip. Israel handed over some areas in which both civilian and security authority were transferred to the PA. However, violence and violations on both sides have held back progress in accordance with the Oslo Accords timetable. Nevertheless, the process of separation has been ongoing.

In September 2005, Israel withdrew its troops and all Jewish settlers from the Gaza Strip and relinquished control of certain areas of the northern West Bank, in accordance with its unilateral Disengagement Plan, and the PA took control of the Strip. Israel, however, was to continue to control the Strip's borders and gateways, although the southern border – the "Philadelphi Road" – was to be guarded by Egypt. While the Israeli government expressed its hope that existing economic relations with the PA would be maintained, the Hamas victory in the Palestinian parliamentary elections in January 2006 threw future relations into doubt.

[Amos Nadan (2nd ed.)]

Nationalism, Politics, and Violence

The history of Gaza since 1967 should be seen within the context of the reemergence of Palestinian nationalism, Islamic political revival in Palestinian politics that began in the 1970s, and attempts to settle the Israeli-Palestinian and Arab conflict, especially since the outbreak of the Intifada in 1987. Regarding the ebb and flow of politics and violence within Gaza itself, it was highly volatile in the first years of Israeli rule, quiescent and peaceful between 1972 and the early 1980s, and after the eruption of the Intifada in December 1987, became steeped in almost perpetual violent struggle against Israeli rule. Gaza also became the scene to the most extreme forms of internecine political contention and violence, mostly between Fatah, the largest nationalist faction within the PLO, and the Hamas, the major Islamic movement.

Why violent opposition to Israeli rule was greater in Gaza than in the West Bank during the first years of Israel's rule had to do with Egyptian policy before the Six-Day War. Unlike Hashemite Jordan, which went to great efforts to stifle Palestinian identity and curtail PLO political activity, Egypt, the former ruler, had been engaged since 1959 in actively promoting a Palestinian identity and institutions in Gaza as part of its political offensive against Israel. After 1964, this included the PLO and its military arm, the Palestinian Liberation Army; their performance against the Israel Defense Forces (IDF) in the Six-Day War won high marks from Israeli military analysts.

It was these former officers and soldiers in the PLA who served as the nucleus of violent opposition to Israeli rule that began in 1968 and reached its zenith in 1970–early 1971 when 17 Israelis were killed in Gaza as a result of terrorist activity emanating from there. Terrorist activity was virtually stamped out by Israeli forces under General Ariel Sharon, Head of Southern Command, who employed techniques such as specialized anti-terror units acting in disguise and the employment of armored military craft in urban warfare, which later became better known in subsequent more intense rounds of Israeli-Palestinian violence under increasing media scrutiny.

Yet Israel's response in itself was hardly sufficient to wipe out terrorism. Israel, after initial hesitation, opened its labor market during these years to a job-hungry population (see below) while an additional ten percent of the workforce was directly linked to providing transportation for these commuters. Employment in Israel was the major factor in the vast improvement in the standard of living. It also had its limitations – the Israeli market offered blue collar work only – a form of employment that became a growing source of frustration for an increasingly educated Palestinian workforce. Nevertheless, prosperity brought tranquility until the early 1980s.

Calm gave way to increasing tension as the PLO, principally Fatah and the Islamic Brotherhood, began forming "front" social and political institutions that not only provided social services but had the added advantage of employing the new augmented ranks of high school and university students. There was also political friction, focused mainly around Gaza University, established in 1978, between student blocs affiliated to Fatah, Islamic Jihad, formed in 1983, and the local Muslim Brotherhood, which in early 1988, after the outbreak of the Intifada, became known as the Hamas.

These organizations became recruiting grounds for the "military" wing of these political forces in Gaza with the result that even before the outbreak of the Intifada, Gaza became the stage of increasing acts of terror, the most dramatic of which was the clash in October 1987 between three al-Jihad al-Islami members who had escaped detention and Israel General Security agents, leading to the death of an Israeli agent. The incident had a dramatic effect; for the first time since 1971, "the resistance," as it was known in Palestinian society, had succeeded in killing a member of an elite security unit of almost mythic proportions.

The trend of increasing violence paled in comparison to the mass violence that broke out on December 8, 1987, in Jabaliyya Refugee Camp and elsewhere over rumors that an Israeli had deliberately crashed into a vehicle killing four Palestinians. Thousands took to the streets in massive daily confrontations against a small hard-pressed Israeli military presence in Gaza. If political forces were not responsible for the outbreak of Intifada, they were crucial in assuring its persistence; the Unified National Command of the West Bank and Gaza, consisting of members of the four major factions under the PLO umbrella, Fatah, the Popular Front for the Liberation of Palestine, the Democratic Front for the Liberation of Palestine, and the Palestinian Communist Party, organized activity directly and through a series of leaflets; the Hamas and Islamic Jihad did much the same through its own separate organizations and leaflets.

Soon mass activities and violence, characterized by stone throwing and use of incendiary bombs, gave way to increasing terrorist activity by a professional "salaried" hard core; the establishment of the ʿIzz al-Dīn al-Qassām Brigades in Gaza, Hamas' military wing in 1989, and its kidnapping and killing of an Israeli soldier in that year were, in retrospect, the most significant actions. This ushered in a series of killings culminating in the expulsion to Lebanon of nearly 413 Hamas and Jihad activists in December 1992. Their expulsion and even more so their subsequent repatriation, was an egregious mistake; in Lebanon they perfected their skills to use explosives, under the aegis of Hizbullah, leading to the introduction of suicide-bombing, a new and more lethal mode of terrorism. The first suicide bombing, by a member of the al-Jihad al-Islami, took place in April 1993 in the Jordan Valley. Nevertheless, Fatah was still the major political and military force, even in Gaza, when the Palestinian Authority as part of the Oslo peace process was created.

For a brief period in Palestinian politics between the establishment of the PA in July 1994 and the entry of the PA into the six major towns of the West Bank in January 1996, Gaza held the limelight as Yasser *Arafat set up headquarters in the city of Gaza. Even afterwards, Arafat, realizing the popularity of the two major Islamic organizations native to Gaza, spent much of his time, if not most, in Gaza to assure his control in the area. Most of the other formerly Tunis-based Palestinian politicians and organizations preferred, however, Ramallah and even though sessions of the Palestinian Legislative Council, elected in January 1996, took place in both, increasing government business was transacted in the latter.

Arafat's political instincts were correct. For the PA and Arafat, Gaza became a major source of opposition; in November 1994, PA security forces gunned down 12 mostly Hamas activists coming out of mosque in the city of Gaza to quell a continuation of mass protests against the PA for arresting and harassing its members; the three suicide bombings of late February–early March 1996 resulting in 57 deaths in Israel were all planned, organized, and carried out in Gaza by the Hamas. Israel reacted to suicide-bombing by curtailing work permits and targeting Hamas and Islamic Jihad terrorists.

Nevertheless, there was some room for hope and prosperity. An airport in Dahaniya in Gaza was opened, the Erez industrial park in the north rapidly expanded, and another industrial park was established in Karni, but none of these developments could make up for restricted and much reduced access to the Israeli labor market and led to a 40 percent decline in the average income level since the Oslo peace process in 1993.

Access to the Israeli labor market terminated almost completely with the outbreak of armed conflict between the PA and the Palestinian factions in September 2000; Gaza became the stage of mass armed demonstrations and protests and soon thereafter of recurring armed assaults and suicide attacks against the Israeli military and civilian presence there, including 18 settlements established since 1971. Unlike Judea and Samaria, where two massive IDF military offensives in 2002 and the partial reoccupation of its towns brought about a significant reduction of terrorism and armed attacks, in Gaza terrorism and guerrilla activity increased from 2002 to 2005 reaching levels of violence unparalleled in Judea and Samaria, which even the assassination of Ahmad Yasin, the founder and leader of Hamas in March 2004, and one month afterwards of his successor, ʿAbd al-ʿAzīz al-Rantīsī, only temporarily reduced.

[Hillel Frisch (2nd ed.)]

Socioeconomic Features under Israeli Rule

The Israeli occupation of the Gaza Strip in 1967 brought immediate economic relief to Gaza's residents, as Israel opened its labor market to Palestinians. In 1968, according to Israeli statistics, about 82.5% of the Strip's laborers were employed. In 1973 this figure reached 99.1%, with about one-third (32.7%) of these workers finding their main employment in Israel. The level of employment in Israel continued to increase. In 1979 it stood at 42.4% and in 1986 at almost half of the total (46.1%); in Israel, the Palestinian workers from Gaza were engaged in labor-intensive jobs, but their wages were far lower by 59% than those of the Israeli workforce. From 1968 to 1986 the average annual population growth in the Strip stood at 2.2%, with an annual growth of 2.5% in per capita GDP (from 3,508 NIS to 5,964 NIS in 2005 prices); yet this deteriorated between 1979 and 1985 (from 6,593 NIS to 5,346 NIS). These trends were significantly different from the more economically viable West Bank: in 1968 per capita GDP in the Gaza Strip was 18% less than in the West Bank, but by 1986 it was lower by 55%.

The Intifada ("uprising") of 1987 was the first Palestinian national revolt since the Israeli occupation 20 years earlier. The socioeconomic roots and consequences of this Intifada were significant. At its onset, the 1987 Intifada was a spontaneous disturbance, not directed by a recognized national leadership; it also started in the poorest region – the Gaza Strip – and spilled over into the West Bank. The group of rebels who initiated the revolt was essentially people who used to work in Israel, who felt poor and discriminated against, and hoped for change. To some extent, the Intifada of 1987 acted as a labor-separator between the Strip and Israel. By 1993, the level of Gazan workers employed in Israel and in Israeli settlements had dropped to 26.5%. Moreover, several suicide attacks by Palestinians in Israel in 1994 and 1995, and the border "closure policy" of the Israeli government, brought a further reduction of Gazans employed in Israel: in 1995 only 3.3% of Gazans who were employed had found work in Israel. However, this gradually changed, and by 1998 the number had risen to 16.2%.

The Intifada of 2000, the second revolt against Israeli occupation, was supported and sustained from the outset by the PA, as well as by the Islamic opposition groups in Gaza. While per capita GDP figures suggest that the economic crisis of the first Intifada was not particularly serious, the socioeconomic consequences of the 2000 Intifada were undoubtedly much more severe. There was an average annual decline of more than 14% in GNP in Gaza between 1999 and 2002, and the average level of Gazan employment in Israel fell to below 1% between October 2000 and mid-2004.

[Amos Nadan (2nd ed.)]

ADD. BIBLIOGRAPHY: O. Eran, "Arab-Israel Peacemaking," in: A. Sela (ed.), *The Continuum Political Encyclopedia of the Middle East* (2002), 127–47; A.M. Lesch and M. Tessler, *Israel, Egypt, and the Palestinians: From Camp David to Intifada* (1988); The Palestinian Authority, Palestinian Central Bureau of Statistics, *Labour Force Survey: Annual Report, 1998*; Z. Schiff and E. Ya'ari, *Intifada: The Palestinian Uprising – Israel's Third Front* (1990); State of Israel, Central Bureau of Statistics, *National Accounts of Judea, Samaria and the Gaza Area 1968–1993* (1996); United States, Department of State, *The Camp David Summit* (1978); World Bank, *Four Years – Intifada, Closures and Palestinian Economic Crisis: An Assessment* (2004); Regularly updated data about Gaza Strip and the West Bank are available on the Internet: http://www.pcbs.org; http://www.cia.gov/cia/publications/factbook/.

GAZELLE (Heb. צְבִי, *ẓevi*). The gazelle is included among the seven wild animals permitted as food (Deut. 14:5; 12:15), and is the only one among them that has survived in Israel. Though it was almost extinct in the early 1940s, there has been a considerable increase in the number since the passing of the Wild Life Protection Law by the State of Israel, which made hunting the gazelle an offense, and today hundreds of them are to be found in the Judean hills and in the Negev. There are two species of gazelle in Israel; the more common is the *Gazella gazella*, which is grayish-brown in color, 55 inches (140 cm.) in length, and up to 27½ inches (70 cm.) in height. The other species, *Gazella dorcas*, which is found in the Negev, is light-brown in color, has large ears and diverging horns, and stands only 23½ inches (60 cm.) high. The gazelle's delicate appearance, its slender legs, narrow body, and beautiful eyes, made it a symbol of grace and beauty (Song 2:9; 4:5; 7:4). It was hunted extensively for its delicious meat (Isa. 13:14; Prov. 6:5). Its light-footedness became a symbol of speed (II Sam. 2:18). In Song of Songs (2:7; 3:5) there twice occurs the adjuration "by the gazelles and by the hinds of the field," the reference being to the habit of the males and females of living apart during most of the year and meeting again at the mating season. Perhaps the maiden here intimates that her beloved will surely return to her. Because the gazelle is not found in Europe, the translators of the Bible there identified the *ẓevi* with the *deer (Heb. אַיָּל), which abounds there. Whereas, however, the horns of the deer are branched and solid ("antlers"), the Talmud clearly states that those of the *ẓevi* are unbranched (Ḥul. 59b) and hollow (TJ, Er. 1:17, 19b). "Gazelle" and not "deer" is also the meaning of the Aramaic and Arabic cognates of *ẓevi*. The *halakhah* refers to the prohibition of crossbreeding the gazelle with the goat, which it resembles (Kil. 1:6), the progeny of such crossbreeding being, according to some, the animal known as the *koi* (Ḥul. 132a).

BIBLIOGRAPHY: I. Aharoni, *Torat ha-Ḥai*, 1 (1923), 87; F.S. Bodenheimer, *Ha-Ḥai be-Ereẓ Yisrael* (1953), 246; Tristram, Nat Hist, 127–30; J. Feliks, *Animal World of the Bible* (1962), 11. **ADD BIBLIOGRAPHY:** Feliks, Ha-Ẓome'aḥ, 270.

[Jehuda Feliks]

GAZIT (Heb. גָּזִית; "hewn building stones," Isa. 9:9), kibbutz in eastern Lower Galilee, Israel, S.E. of Kefar Tavor, affiliated with Kibbutz Arẓi Ha-Shomer ha-Ẓa'ir, first founded in 1943 by a group known as "Irgun Borochov," and taken over by a Ha-Shomer ha-Ẓa'ir group in the summer of 1947. A year later, the present kibbutz was established, while the battles of the *War of Independence were in progress nearby. Its members were pioneers from Argentina, Romania, and other countries. The kibbutz economy was based on field crops, orchards, beef cattle, dairy cattle, and poultry along with plastics, rubber, and furniture factories. Its population was 415 in 1968 and 581 in 2002.

[Efraim Orni / Shaked Gilboa (2nd ed.)]

GDANSK (Ger. **Danzig**), major commercial port in Poland, situated at the estuary of the Vistula on the Baltic. In 1308 the city passed to the Teutonic Order, which prohibited Jewish settlement there. During the first half of the 15th century Jews from Poland and Lithuania frequently visited the town but this tolerance was limited in 1438. Around 1440 a "Judengasse" ("Jewish Lane") existed on the bank of the Motława. Toward the end of the 15th century, after the town had been incorporated in Poland, it became the wealthiest city of Poland, and the entrepôt for the large commerce in grain and goods between Western and Eastern Europe. This created many commercial possibilities for Jews. However, their activities were restricted by the autonomous status of Gdansk, which enabled the city to discriminate against them. In 1476 the Polish king recommended the city council to permit two Jews to enjoy equal rights with the other merchants.

A Jewish settlement grew up in Gdansk after 1454, but owing to the opposition of the merchants in 1520 the Jews had to move to the Schottland suburb which was not under municipal jurisdiction. Subsequently Jews also settled in other places outside the jurisdiction of the city. On the intervention of King Sigismund I in 1531, the council withdrew the regulation prohibiting Jews from trading at the fair, but a resolution of the *Sejmik* (small parliament) of Prussia prohibited the extension of further rights to the Jews. In retaliation, the Jews of Lithuania boycotted the Gdansk banking house in Kaunas (Kovno) which had to be liquidated, and ousted the merchants of Gdansk from the Lithuanian salt trade. In 1577 an agreement was concluded between King Stephen Báthory and Gdansk approving the existing restrictions. The citizens also demanded that Jewish residence and trade in the city should be entirely prohibited. Jews were not allowed to hold religious services there, and in 1595 the city council permitted them to stay in Gdansk during fair days only. In 1616 the Gdansk authorities had to pay large indemnities for their arbitrary exclusion of Jewish merchants coming from Polish cities; subsequently Jews were allowed to stay six days in Gdansk against payment of a high poll tax.

Around 1616 about 400 to 500 Jews were living in Gdansk in addition to those settled in lands owned by the gentry or clergy. In 1620 the king permitted Jewish residence in Gdansk. They were permitted to trade in grain and timber in the commercial sector and Langengarten which belonged to the port area, and after these quarters were incorporated into Gdansk in 1626 these rights were extended to the whole of the city. However, the Polish-Swedish wars of the 17th century interrupted the trading activities of the Gdansk Jews. In the middle of the 17th century about 50 Jews became apostates to Christianity. One of them, Johann Salama, a teacher in the seminary of Gdansk, carried on missionary activity among Jews. Cramer, the pastor of Gdansk, in a sermon published in 1664, *Der verstockte Jude*, describes the martyrdom of a Jew who refuses to accept Christianity. During the 18th century, the main opposition to the Jews in Gdansk came from the representatives of small trades and crafts. The third Northern War, strengthening the position of Catholicism in Gdansk, aggravated the hostility to the Jews, and they were moved away from some of their quarters. However, a *ḥevra kaddisha* and *bikkur ḥolim* were founded in the old Jewish quarter in Schottland (Stary Schottland) in 1724. The Jews who had been expelled returned in 1748, although according to a regulation endorsed by the king in 1750 they could only stay temporarily in Gdansk. There were about 1,098 Jews living in Gdansk in the areas outside the city jurisdiction in 1765, of whom 504 were living in Schottland and Hoppenbruch, 230 in Langfuhr, and 364 in Weinberg. In 1773, 50 families received the rights of citizenship in Gdansk and 160 Jews were permitted to reside there.

After Gdansk was incorporated into Prussia upon the second partition of Poland in 1793, the restrictions on the Jews remained in force. In 1813 Langfuhr and Schottland were destroyed, and the Jews there moved within the city. Between 1807 and 1814 Gdansk was a Free City, and after its renewed occupation by Prussia the Jews there obtained rights of citizenship by the Prussian liberation decree. There were anti-Jewish incidents during the *Hep! Hep! riots in September 1819 and again in August 1821. Thirty-three Jews were received into the merchants' guild, but by then the city's commercial importance had declined. Jews were permitted to engage in crafts, and in 1823 the Society for the Promotion of Crafts Among the Jewish Population was founded.

Some Hebrew printing was done there in the 16th century in connection with Phillip Wolff's *Spiegel der Juden*. In 1843 the printing house of Rathke and Schroth issued the Mishnah with the *Tiferet Yisrael* commentary by Israel *Lipschuetz, who was rabbi at Danzig. They also published some works of Ẓevi Hirsch *Edelmann from 1844 to 1845, including an edition of his Passover *Haggadah, Leil Shimmurim*. Abraham Stein, an adherent of Reform and later preacher in Prague, was rabbi of Schottland from 1850 to 1864. In 1888 the communities of Schottland, Langfuhr, Weinberg, Mattenbunden, and Breitegasse were amalgamated. The Jewish population numbered 3,798 in 1816, 2,736 in 1880 (2.4% of the total), 2,390 in 1910 (1.4%), and 4,678 in 1924.

In 1920 Gdansk was again declared a Free City, having a population of approximately 356,000. There were 7,292 Jews living in the territory of the Free City in 1923, and 9,230 in 1924, of whom 53.4% lived in Gdansk itself. A large number of Jewish emigrants passed through the port on their way to the United States and received assistance from the *American Jewish Joint Distribution Committee and *Hias. The community had four synagogues and various Jewish organizations. The "Jung-Juedischer Bund-Danzig" was founded in 1920. A communal organ, *Juedisches Wochenblatt*, was published from 1929 to 1938. The Jews in Gdansk engaged in commerce and the liberal professions; more than 150 Jews were employed in crafts. Adjoining Sopot was a popular summer and sea resort for many Polish Jews between the two world wars. It also attracted a number of Jewish émigrés from Soviet Russia. Despite large Nazi gains in the elections of 1933 and 1935, civil and economic order was upheld by Hermann Rauschning, president of the senate, until 1937, when the *minority rights provided for under the League of Nations lapsed. Albert Forster, the Nazi gauleiter, dismissed almost all Jews from practice in the liberal professions. In October 1937 a full-scale pogrom was initiated. Half of the Jews left Gdansk within a year, the Polish government offering them no protection. Between Nov. 12 and 14, 1938, two synagogues were burned down and two others were desecrated. Shops and homes were looted. The Jewish community decided to organize emigration and many left. By September 1939 barely 1,700 remained, mostly elderly persons, and by early 1941, just 600. The last group to leave sailed for Palestine on the ill-fated *Patria*, which was sunk by the British in Haifa port. Of those who remained, 395 were deported during February and March 1941 to Warsaw and 200 from the Jewish old age home were sent to Theresienstadt. Twenty-two Jewish partners of mixed marriages who remained in Gdansk survived the war. After the city reverted to Poland in 1945, a number of Jews settled there. Few remained by the end of the 1960s.

BIBLIOGRAPHY: P. Simson, *Geschichte der Stadt Danzig*, 4 vols. (1913–18); E. Keyser, *Danzig's Geschichte* (1923); A. Stein, *Die Geschichte der Juden zu Danzig* (1933[2]); *Gdańsk, przeszłość i teraźniejszość* (1928); M. Aschkewitz, *Zur Geschichte der Juden in Westpreussen* (1967); i C.J. Burckhardt, *Meine Danziger Mission 1936–1939* (1960); MGWJ, 6 (1857), 205–14, 241–50, 321–31, 401–11; K. Sander, in: *Unser Danzig*, 12 (1960), 21–24; *Zeitschrift fuer Demographie und Statistik der Juden*, 4 (1927), 126–7; E. Cieślak and C. Biernat, *Dzieje Gdańska* (1969); S. Echt, *Die Geschichte der Juden in Danzig* (1973) E. Soidekat, BLBI, 8 (1965), 107–49; T. Loevy, *ibid.*, 9 (1966), 190–2; AJYB, 32 (1930/31), 249–51; D. Weinryb, in: PAAJR, 19 (1950), 1–110 (Heb. sect.); Halpern, Pinkas, index. **ADD. BIBLIOGRAPHY:** A. Stern, *Koroteihem shel Yehudei Danzig me-az ha-Emanẓipaẓiyah ve-ad ha-Gerush bi-Mey ha-Shilton ha-Naẓi* (1978); M. Andrzejewski, "Terror w Wolnym Miescie Gdansku w 1937–1939," in: BŻIH, 141 (1962), 111–27; E. Lichtenstein, *Die Juden der Freien Stadt Danzig unter der Herrschaft des Nationalsozializmus* (1973); E. Stern, *Yehudei Danzig 1840–1943* (1983); Jewish Life, 1, 420.

[Jacob Goldberg]

GEBA (Heb. גֶּבַע; "hill"), common name of inhabited places in Ereẓ Israel from biblical times onward; its Arabic form (Jabaʿ) has survived in the names of several Arab villages. Important places bearing this name include:

(1) A city of *Benjamin, near the northern border of the tribe, the present-day Jabaʿ, a Muslim village some 5½ mi. (9 km.) north of *Jerusalem and 2 mi. (3 km.) east of al-Rāma, situated on an ancient tell containing Iron Age remains. Because of the similarity between the names Geba, Gibeah, and other places in the area, it is sometimes difficult to determine exactly which place the Bible refers to, especially since there are also interchanges and probable errors in the text (e.g., in Judg. 20:10 *Gibeah is meant and in II Sam. 25 Gibeon, according to the parallel verse in I Chron. 14:16). It is therefore not certain whether Geba of the Benjaminite cities (Josh. 18:24) is the one under discussion or a more northerly city known to Eusebius, 5 Roman miles north of *Gophnah (Onom. 74:2). Geba is one of the levitical cities (Josh. 21:17; I Chron. 6:45) and was apparently the seat of the family of Ehud, the son of Gera (Judg. 3:13; I Chron. 8:6, following the Septuagint reading Ehud (ʾΑωδ) instead of Eḥud). Strategically located south of Wadi Ṣuwaynīṭ, opposite *Michmas, it played a central role in Saul's wars with the Philistines. His son Jonathan seized control of the city after his victory over its Philistine garrison (I Sam. 13:3). From the continuation of the war between Geba and Michmas (*ibid.* 13:16; 14:5), it is clear that this Geba is meant. Moreover, the assumption that a Philistine garrison was stationed at Gibeah before Saul established his capital there has been refuted by excavations at this site. It thus also appears that the "hill of God" (Gibeath ha-Elohim), which was the site of the Philistine garrison (I Sam. 10:5), is identical with the Geba being discussed, and this indicates that a "high place" existed there during the time of Saul.

Asa fortified Geba with stones taken from nearby Ramah (I Kings 15:22; II Chron. 16:6); excavations at Geba have also established that this reference is not to Gibeah, as some scholars have claimed. Geba's strategic position on the eastern branch of the northern highroad is described by Isaiah (10:29) and it is logical that this is the same city which is mentioned on the border of the kingdom of Judah in the latter days of the First Temple (II Kings 23:8; Zech. 14:10; Neh. 11:31). From the statement that *Josiah brought the priests to Jerusalem "from Geba to Beer-Sheba" (II Kings 23:8) it seems likely that up to his time a sanctuary was located in the city (especially after the discovery of an Israelite temple of this period at *Arad on the southeastern border of the kingdom). Geba's destruction came about with the fall of the First Temple and it was rebuilt in the post-Exilic period; the exiles who returned to it are listed together with those from neighboring Ramah (Ezra 2:26; Neh. 7:30; and see Neh. 12:29).

[Yohanan Aharoni]

(2) Geba-Parashim (Gr. *Geba Hippeon*, "Geba of the Horsemen"), city in Lower Galilee near the Jezreel Valley founded by Herod who settled demobilized cavalrymen there (Jos., Ant., 15:294; Wars, 3:36). It served as a Herodian and Roman administrative center in the valley and enjoyed several urban privileges, including the right to mint city-coinage. During the Jewish War (66–70/73) fighting between the Romans and the Galilean rebels under the command of Josephus took place near Geba (Jos., Life, 115). The city was in existence until the fourth century C.E. and was the seat of a Christian bishop. Most scholars identify it with Khirbat Ḥarithiyya near a key road at the entrance of the Jezreel Plain. Another suggestion is that Hellenistic Geba corresponds to the Geba mentioned in the list of Thutmose III's conquests (No. 41, Geba-Shemen) which has been identified with Tell al-ʿAmr in the same neighborhood.

(3) Geba, a place mentioned in the Mishnah (Kelim 17:5) and Tosefta (Kelim; BM 6:10) as being inhabited by Kutim (Cutheans). This city has been identified with the Arab village of Jabaʿ, 3 3/4 mi. (6 km.) north of Samaria. It is also mentioned in the Samaria ostraca from the eighth century B.C.E.

[Michael Avi-Yonah]

BIBLIOGRAPHY: Abel, Geog, 2 (1938), 328–9; Aharoni, Land, index; EM, s.v.; IDB, s.v. *Gibeah*; Maisler (Mazar), in: BJPES, 11 (1945), 37ff.; Avi-Yonah, Geog, 145.

GEBIHA OF BE-KATIL (first half of the fifth century), Babylonian *amora*. Gebiha headed the academy of Pumbedita during the years 419–33 (*Iggeret Sherira Ga'on* (1921), 96) and lectured on *halakhah* at the *bet ha-midrash* adjoining the house of the *exilarch. His younger contemporaries *Amemar and *Ashi discussed the meaning of his pronouncements (Beẓah 23a). Gebiha, who spanned a number of generations of *amoraim*, mentions the rulings of Abbaye (Ḥul. 64b; Me'il. 10a), transmits cases that came before Rava (Av. Zar. 22a), and is also frequently found debating halakhic topics with Ashi (Ḥul. 26b; et al.).

BIBLIOGRAPHY: Hyman, Toledot, 300.

[Jacob Eliahu Ephrathi]

GEBINI (first century), Temple crier of the Second Temple (Shekalim 5:1). His role was to rouse those on duty to the performance of the Temple rites. According to the *baraita* his cry was, "Priests, bestir yourselves to your service, levites to your platform (for song), Israelites to your posts" (*Ma'amad*; Yoma 20b; TJ, Shek. 5:2, 48d). The Mishnah states that his voice could even be heard as far as Jericho (Tam. 3:8). His stentorian voice became legendary. The *baraita* adds that King Agrippa heard his voice at a distance of three (another version, eight) parasangs, and sent him a gift in admiration. It is believed that the name became an eponym for all subsequent Temple criers.

BIBLIOGRAPHY: Hyman, Toledot, 300.

[Jacob Eliahu Ephrathi]

GEBIRTIG, MORDECHAI (originally **Bertik**; 1877–1942), Yiddish poet and songwriter. Born in Cracow, he worked as a carpenter and for many years a used furniture restorer. Although untrained musically, he wrote songs of great popular appeal, many of which assumed folksong status. Amateur actor, devoted socialist, army nurse in World War I, he wrote and sang political songs and songs of compassion for the poor as well as entertaining cabaret songs that found their way into the Yiddish theater. His first collection, *Folkstimlekh* ("Folk-Like," 1920) included 20 poems but no melodies; a second collection published in Vilna in 1936 numbered over 50 songs with melodies (later reprinted with additions: New York 1942, 1948, and Paris 1949), including the famous "Undzer Shtetl Brent" ("Our Town is Burning"). The poet was murdered by the Nazis in June 1942, together with his wife and two daughters. His popularity has steadily grown; his songs are performed worldwide; and new collections of his work have continued to appear: e.g. *Mayn Fayfele: Umbakante Lider* ("My Little Pipe: Unknown Songs," 1997) prints 80 songs hitherto unknown (ed. N. Gross, with Y. Luden's Yiddish translation of Gross's Hebrew introduction).

BIBLIOGRAPHY: Rejzen, Leksikon, 1 (1926), 595–7; LNYL, 2 (1958), 286–90. **ADD. BIBLIOGRAPHY:** N. Gross, *Zydowski Bard: Gaweda o Zyciu i Tworczosci Mordechaja Gebirtiga* (2000); idem, in: *Polin*, 16 (2003), 107–17; G. Schneider (ed.), *Mordechai Gebirtig: His Poetic and Musical Legacy* (2000); B. Davis, in: S. Kerbel (ed.), *Jewish Writers of the Twentieth Century* (2003), 171–2.

[M. Rav. / Leonard Prager (2nd ed.)]

GECKO, reptile of the order Lacertilia. Six genera belonging to the Gekkonidae family are to be found in Israel. The most common is the house gecko, *Hemidactylus turcicus*, a nocturnal lizard up to about 4¾ inches (12 cm.) in length, with a soft speckled hide and prehensile feet which enable it to climb walls. Two animals referred to in the Bible are likely to be identical with the gecko. The *anakah* is included among the unclean swarming things (Lev. 11:30) and has, according to the Mishnah (Ḥul. 9:2), a soft hide. The word *anakah* means "groan", and the gecko does in fact emit a sound reminiscent of the groan of a sick person. The Book of Proverbs, in its enumeration of the "things which are little upon the earth, but… are exceeding wise" (30:24), mentions the *semamit*, which "taketh hold with her hands, and is in kings' palaces" (*ibid.*, 28). This description fits the ubiquitous gecko which climbs on walls with feet that resemble hands. Although many other identifications have been suggested for the *anakah* and the *semamit*, the gecko fits them best.

BIBLIOGRAPHY: I. Aharoni, *Torat ha-Ḥai*, 1, pt. 3 (1930), 62–66; Tristram, Nat Hist, 265f.; J. Feliks, *Animal World of the Bible* (1962), 97. **ADD BIBLIOGRAPHY:** Feliks, Ha-Ẓome'aḥ, 207.

[Jehuda Feliks]

GEDALGE, ANDRE (1856–1926), music theorist, teacher, and composer. Born in Paris, Gédalge studied composition with Guiraud at the Paris Conservatory, where he later became a professor of counterpoint and fugue (1905). In 1885 he won the second Prix de Rome (1885) for his cantata *La Vision de Saul*. He became famous as a teacher, and his *Traité de la fugue* (1901) is still considered one of the best books on the subject. He also wrote two volumes on ear training (1921–23). His experience, as an inspector of provincial conservatories (1906), led him to write his *L'enseignement de la musique par l'éducation méthodique de l'oreille* (Paris, 1920). Gédalge composed four symphonies; chamber music such as String Quartet (1892) and two violin sonatas (op. 12 in 1897; op. 19 in 1900); the ballet *Phoebé* (1900); pieces for piano such as *Préludes et fugues*, op. 2 and three préludes de concert, op. 23 (1903); an opéra-comique, *Pris au piège* (1895); a drame lyrique, *Hélène* (1893), which won the Prix Cerescent in 1895; and songs. He remained uninfluenced by the developments of impressionism and continued to follow the tradition of Saint-Saëns and

Lalo. However, his main contribution to French music was through his influence on composers such as Florent Schmitt, Ravel, *Milhaud, and Honegger, who were his pupils.

BIBLIOGRAPHY: Grove online; MGG[2]; G. Fauré, Silhouettes du Conservatoire: Charles-Marie Widor, André Gédalge, Max d'Ollone (1986).

[Israela Stein (2nd ed.)]

GEDALIAH (Heb. גְּדַלְיָה, גְּדַלְיָהוּ), son of Ahikam. Gedaliah was appointed by the Babylonians as governor of Judah after the capture of Jerusalem in 586 B.C.E.; members of his family had held important posts during the last decades of the kingdom of Judah. His grandfather *Shaphan and his father *Ahikam supported Josiah during the latter's reforms (II Kings 22:3ff., 12ff.). Ahikam held an important post during the reign of Jehoiakim and was able to save Jeremiah from the anger of the people after his speech at the Temple gate (Jer. 26:24). Evidently this family followed a line of moderation and submission to Babylon, which explains the choice of one of its members to govern the remnant in Judah (see also *Elasah, *Jaazaniah). Gedaliah may even have been a man of influence and status before this time (II Kings 25:22; Jer. 40:5). He has been identified with the official of the same name, who was "in charge of the house"; the identification was made by means of a seal impression reading *lgdlyhw ʾšr ʿl hbyt*, which was found at the town gate of *Lachish, a town burned and destroyed in the last days of the kingdom of Judah.

Gedaliah resided at *Mizpah in the territory of Benjamin. The remaining people of Judah who gathered around him included army officers who had escaped capture and deportation by the Babylonians. May and other critics claim that Gedaliah served as the representative of the exiled *Jehoiachin who was still considered king of Judah, but there is no real basis for this assumption. The center at Mizpah was not long lived and Gedaliah, together with the Judahites and Babylonians stationed at Mizpah, was murdered by *Ishmael b. Nethaniah, who was in contact with *Baalis, king of the Ammonites. The assassination was instigated apparently with the hope of overthrowing Babylonian rule. Those who were spared, including several army officers, fled to Egypt, taking Jeremiah with them, out of fear that the Babylonians might consider them responsible for the murder of Gedaliah (II Kings 25:25–26; Jer. 41:1ff.).

Several scholars have suggested that the Babylonian Exile from Judah in the 23rd year of Nebuchadnezzar's reign (Jer. 52:30) is connected with the murder of Gedaliah (cf. Jos., Ant. 10:181), but this assumption requires the dating of the murder in 582/1 B.C.E., whereas according to the biblical record, Gedaliah governed only for a short time, either until the seventh month of the year of destruction (587/6) or the seventh month of the following year (586/5). The day of Gedaliah's death was observed as a fast day, and is called "the fast of the seventh month" in the Bible (Zech. 7:5; 8:19) and, at a later date, the Fast of Gedaliah (see *Fasts and Fasting). According to tradition it is observed on the third of Tishri (RH 18b).

BIBLIOGRAPHY: Bright, Hist, index; Yeivin, in: *Tarbiz*, 12 (1940/41), 253, 255–8, 266–8; May, in: AJSLL, 56 (1939), 146–8; C.C. Mc-Cown et al., *Excavations at Tell en-Nasbeh*, 1 (1947), 30–34, 46–48; EM, 2 (1965), 440–2. **ADD. BIBLIOGRAPHY:** W. Holladay, *Jeremiah* 2 (1989), 293–303; R. Althann, in: ABD, 2:923–24; S. Ahituv, *Handbook of Ancient Hebrew Inscriptions* (1992), 125; O. Lipschits and J. Blenkinsopp (eds.), *Judah and the Judeans in the Neo-Babylonian Period* (2003).

[Jacob Liver]

GEDALIAH, (Don) JUDAH (d. c. 1526), Hebrew printer. Gedaliah, who was born in Lisbon, worked there at Eliezer *Toledano's Hebrew press (1489–95) until the expulsion from Portugal (1497). He settled in Salonika, establishing the first Hebrew printing press there using fine type fonts he had brought from Lisbon. Between 1515 and 1535 he, his daughter, and his sons (who continued the firm after his death) carefully edited and printed about 30 Hebrew books including the first edition of *Ein Ya'akov* of R. Jacob ibn Ḥabib (1516–22). The latter, in his introduction, highly praised Gedaliah for his efforts in spreading the knowledge of Torah among the other Iberian refugees in Salonika.

BIBLIOGRAPHY: A. Freimann, in: ZHB, 11 (1907), 52–53; J. Bloch, *Early Hebrew Printing in Spain and Portugal* (1938), 34–54; H.D. Friedberg, *Toledot ha-Defus ha-Ivri bi-Medinot Italyah…* (1956), 130ff.

[Jacob Hirsch Haberman]

GEDALIAH, JUDAH BEN MOSES (16th century), scholar in Salonika. Nothing is known of his life, but his important works remain. They are *Masoret Talmud Yerushalmi*, indexes of parallels to the Jerusalem Talmud (Constantinople, 1573); notes on the *Midrash Rabbah* and the Five Scrolls (Salonika, 1593/94). In this latter work Gedaliah reveals a sound critical aptitude and extensive philological knowledge. He explains most of the difficulties found in the Midrash, and is extensively quoted by later commentators. His notes on the *Zohar Ḥadash* (Salonika, 1596/97) also reveal his critical insight. In the Bodleian Library there are preserved a few volumes of the Bomberg edition of the Babylonian Talmud with his notes in manuscript.

BIBLIOGRAPHY: Michael, Or, no. 980; Fuenn, Keneset, 393; Steinschneider, Cat Bod, no. 1326.

[Itzhak Alfassi]

GEDALIAH HA-LEVI (d. after 1610), kabbalist and rabbi in Safed, Ereẓ Israel. Gedaliah, the brother-in-law of Ḥayyim *Vital, was one of the "initiates" of Isaac *Luria, i.e., one of his important and early disciples. His signature appears on the writ of association of Luria's disciples (1575). He edited and arranged according to Luria's instructions the *Derushei ha-Melakhim she-Metu*, which appeared in *Kol ba-Ramah* (Korets, 1785) and exists in several unsigned manuscripts. Solomon Shlomel Dresnitz, author of *Shivḥei ha-Ari*, heard tales about Luria directly from Gedaliah.

BIBLIOGRAPHY: A.Z. Aescoly (ed.), *Sefer ha-Ḥezyonot* (1954), 56, 221; G. Scholem, *Kitvei Yad be-Kabbalah* (1930), 138; idem in: *Zion*, 5 (1940), 146–7, 149; D. Tamar, *Meḥkarim be-Toledot ha-Yehudim be-Ereẓ Yisrael u-ve-Italyah* (1970), 171.

[David Tamar]

GEDALIAH OF SIEMIATYCZE (early 18th century), Jerusalem emissary. Gedaliah, followed by his brother R. Moses of Siemiatycze, arrived in Jerusalem on Oct. 14, 1700, in the group headed by R. *Judah Ḥasid. For most of the immigrants, including Gedaliah, the objective of this *aliyah* was to hasten the redemption by ethical conduct, repentance, prayer, fasting, and self-mortification. Gedaliah was sent later on, as the emissary of the Ashkenazi community of Jerusalem, to Western Europe where he published his work on the virtues of Ereẓ Israel, *Sha'alu Shelom Yerushalayim* ("Pray for the Peace of Jerusalem," Berlin, 1716). In it Gedaliah describes the *aliyah* of R. Judah Ḥasid and his group; the arrival of the group in Jerusalem and the death of their leader soon after; the arrangements of the "courtyard" which they acquired; the oppression of the authorities who extorted a great sum of money from them in the form of taxes and bribery; and the methods of collecting the poll tax. He also depicts Jerusalem life in general: the food, the fruits and vegetables, the methods of baking and cooking, the water supply, clothing, the means of travel, the houses, the bathhouses, and the markets, the holy places, and especially the prayers at the Western Wall. An account is also given of the decrees issued by the government and the unrest during the first years after the arrival of the group.

His brother, R. Moses of Siematycze, was accepted in 1702 as one of the teachers in the yeshivah founded by Abraham *Rovigo in Jerusalem; about 1711, he visited Metz as the emissary of the Ashkenazi community of Jerusalem. He died after 1716.

[Avraham Yaari]

°GEDDES, ALEXANDER (1737–1802), Catholic Bible scholar. Born in Scotland, he studied in Paris, learning Hebrew at the Sorbonne. After ordination he served as priest in various places in Scotland in the years 1764–80. In 1781 he was dismissed by his bishop for his liberal views. He moved to London, where under the patronage of a wealthy Catholic he was able to devote himself to biblical studies. A versatile scholar and prolific writer, Geddes published after many preparatory works *The Holy Bible … translated from the corrected Text of the Original; with various readings, explanatory notes, and critical remarks* (2 vols., 1792–97; embracing only the historical books). Already in conflict with the Church, Geddes was suspended from exercising his priestly functions on account of the critical attitude contained in his *Critical Remarks on the Hebrew Scriptures, Corresponding with a New Translation of the Bible; Containing Remarks on the Pentateuch* (1800). He disputed Moses' divine inspiration, explained the miracles in a natural way, and saw in the Pentateuch an assemblage of numerous and mostly post-Mosaic fragments. He thus established the "fragments" hypothesis, which was accepted and developed by J.S. Vater, and one of whose outstanding exponents was W.M.L. de *Wette.

BIBLIOGRAPHY: DNB, 7 (1889/90), incl. bibl. **ADD. BIBLIOGRAPHY:** R. Fuller, in: DBI, 1:434–35.

[Rudolf Smend]

GEDERAH (Heb. גְּדֵרָה), moshavah with municipal council status (since 1949), in the Coastal Plain of Israel, 8 mi. (13 km.) S.W. of Reḥovot. It was founded in 1884 by young members of the *Bilu movement from Russia. Gederah was for a long time the southernmost Jewish settlement in the country and also the only veteran moshavah independent of Baron Edmond de *Rothschild's aid and administration. Initially, grapes and grain constituted Gederah's principal farm branches; later citrus orchards, cotton, and other intensive field crops were added. In the 1930s a number of rest houses, among them sanatoriums for respiratory ailments, were established there. The moshavah had a few small industrial enterprises in food and other branches. Its municipal boundaries included Uri'el, a village for the blind who were employed in certain branches of agriculture and handicrafts, and Kannot, a *Youth Aliyah children's village. In 1970 its population was 5,200. By the mid-1990s the population had risen to approximately 9,650, and by the end of 2002 it was 11,700, occupying an area of 5.6 sq. mi. (14.5 sq. km.). The town served as an urban center for its rural neighbors. Residents earned their living in agriculture, industry, commerce, and services.

Gederah's name is derived from the neighboring Arab village Qaṭra – abandoned since 1948. Most scholars assume Qatira to be identical to the town of *Gederah belonging to the tribe of Judah (Josh. 15:36), and, with greater certainty, to the town Kedron mentioned in I Maccabees (15:39; 16:9) as the scene of one of Judah's victories over Syrian forces. The Greek form of the name has been preserved by moshav Kidron founded north of Gederah in 1949.

WEBSITE: www.allgedera.co.il.

[Efraim Orni / Shaked Gilboa (2nd ed.)]

GEDERAH, GEDEROTH (Heb. גְּדֵרָה, גְּדֵרוֹת), name of several localities in Ereẓ Israel formed from the root גדר ("to wall in").

(1) A place in the northern Shephelah of Judah mentioned in Joshua 15:36. It may be identical with the home of Jozabad, a "mighty man" of Dav id (I Chron. 12:5), and of Baal-Hanan, the overseer of David's olive and sycamore trees (the latter being especially plentiful in the Shephelah; I Chron. 27:28). The city has been tentatively identified with Khirbat Jadīra (Judayra), ½ mi. (1 km.) south of Beit Nattif.

(2) A Gederoth mentioned in Joshua 15:41 together with Beth-Dagon and Naamah is perhaps identical with the Gedrus of Eusebius (Onom. 68:22). The Kedron in I Maccabees 15:39, the tell of Qaṭra, has been suggested as its site.

(3) A locality appearing among the cities conquered

by the Philistines during the reign of Ahaz. Since it is mentioned together with Soco, Timnah, Gimzo, Beth-Shemesh, and Aijalon (II Chron. 28:18), *Albright has identified it with Khirbat el-Jadīra (Judayra), 1 mi. (2 km.) west of Latrun, in the Aijalon Valley.

(4) A place mentioned in I Chronicles 4:23 (JPS translation, "hedges"), probably identical with (1) or (2) above.

BIBLIOGRAPHY: EM, s.v. (includes bibliography).

[Michael Avi-Yonah]

GEDILIAH, ABRAHAM BEN SAMUEL (d. 1672), rabbi and author. Born in Jerusalem, Abraham journeyed to Italy in 1648 and resided in Leghorn and Verona. On his return journey in 1660, he stayed for a time in Egypt. In Italy he was friendly with Samuel *Aboab and Moses b. Mordecai *Zacuto. While in Leghorn, he worked as a proofreader in the printing works of Jedidiah Gabbai. In 1657–60 he published the *Yalkut Shimoni with his own commentary, *Berit Avraham*. In 1665 he sent a letter from Gaza to the rabbis of Italy, expressing his belief in the messianic claims of *Shabbetai Ẓevi and in the prophecy of *Nathan of Gaza. This letter, the first of its kind to be sent by a scholar of Ereẓ Israel, made a deep impression. Abraham died in Jerusalem. Some of his homilies are included in the *Mizbaḥ Eliyahu* of *Elijah ha-Kohen of Smyrna (Smyrna, 1867). Many members of the Gediliah family were rabbis in Hebron, and some in Tiberias and Safed. His grandson, Abraham Gediliah of Hebron, was an emissary of Ereẓ Israel.

BIBLIOGRAPHY: Frumkin-Rivlin, 2 (1928), 33f.; Yaari, Sheluḥei, 158, 272, 845; idem in: KS, 25 (1948/49), 113f.; Tishbi, *ibid.*, 230f.; Scholem, Shabbetai Ẓevi, 198, 289f., 478.

[Avraham Yaari]

GEDOR (Heb. גְּדוֹר).

(1) A city of Judah mentioned in the Bible together with *Halhul and *Beth-Zur (Josh. 15:58). It has been identified with Khirbat Jadūr, 2½ mi. (4 km.) north of Beth-Zur, where surface pottery from the Early Iron (Israelite) Age has been found.

(2) The city Gedor appears in I Chronicles 4:18. It is probably identical with *Gederah (1). Another Gedor – the home of two of David's "mighty men," Joelah and Zebadiah, sons of Jeroham (1 Chron. 12:8), may be identical with either (1) or (2).

(3) One of the cities of Simeon (I Chron. 4:39). It is called Geder in Joshua 12:13, Gerar in the Septuagint, and is not listed among Simeon's cities in Joshua 19:1–9.

(4) The capital of Perea in post-Exilic times (now al-Tell near ʿAyn Jadūr in the vicinity of al-Ṣalṭ in Transjordan (Jos., Wars 4:413)). In the Mishnah it is included among the cities fortified in the time of Joshua (Ar. 9:6).

BIBLIOGRAPHY: L. Haefeli, *Samaria und Peraea...* (1913), 107ff.; Dalman, in: PJB, 6 (1910), 22–23; Aharoni, Land, index.

[Michael Avi-Yonah]

GEDUD HA-AVODAH (Heb. "The [Yosef Trumpeldor] Labor Legion"), first countrywide commune of Jewish workers in Palestine. The Gedud was founded in the autumn of 1920 by 80 pioneers of the Third Aliyah, disciples of Yosef *Trumpeldor. In the winter of 1920 the Gedud contracted to build part of the Tiberias–Tabgha road in Galilee. The members decided to establish a permanent form of communal life at their camp near Migdal, with a common treasury. In the spring of 1921 some of the members were sent to Rosh ha-Ayin to lay the branch railroad to Petaḥ Tikvah and at the same time to serve as the nucleus of a second Gedud, which soon grew to 300 members. In early summer representatives of the groups met at Migdal and defined the Gedud's aim as "the building of the land by the creation of a general commune of the workers of the Land of Israel." The members were to be organized in disciplined groups, which would be at the disposition of the *Histadrut for labor and defense. In the course of time it was intended that the Gedud would encompass all workers and merge with the Histadrut. Among its leaders were M. Elkind and Y. Kopeliovitz (*Almog); Yiẓḥak *Sadeh was an active member. As road work diminished, "companies" of the Gedud went to the Jezreel Valley, where they founded *Ein Ḥarod (1921) and *Tel Yosef (1923), forming a single farming unit. A large group went to Jerusalem to work in building and quarrying and to strengthen the armed defenses of the *yishuv* there. Others worked in agriculture and building and provided services at British army camps. At its zenith the Gedud had some 700 members. In July 1923 the Tel Yosef-Ein Ḥarod group split over a minority demand for economic autonomy, about one-third of the members settling in Ein Ḥarod and the majority in Tel Yosef. A minority attempt to turn the Gedud into a political party, with syndicalist and pro-Communist tendencies, resulted in another split, in 1926, into right-wing and left-wing factions. The left wing soon disintegrated, as some of its members, including Elkind, went to the Soviet Union. They set up a communal farm in the Crimea, Via Nova, which was disbanded in 1931–32. The Gedud was seriously weakened, and in December 1929 the three surviving groups – Tel Yosef, Kefar Giladi, and Ramat Raḥel – joined *Ha-Kibbutz ha-Me'uḥad.

At its peak the Gedud played an important pioneering role in settlement, defense, and labor. Over 2,000 pioneers passed through its ranks, and its influence was out of proportion to its membership. It published a periodical, *Me-Ḥayyenu* and maintained a dramatic studio, *Massad* ("Foundation").

BIBLIOGRAPHY: Al Inyenei Ein Ḥarod (1923); *Koveẓ Ḥavrei Gedud ha-Avodah ba-Kibbutz ha-Me'uḥad* (1932); *Koveẓ ha-Kibbutz ha-Me'uḥad* (1932); I. Bar-Ḥayyim, *Mi-Naftulei Gedud ha-Avodah ba-Kur* (1941); Sh. Lavi, *Megillati be-Ein Ḥarod* (1947); D. Horowitz, *Ha-Etmol Shelli* (1970), 160–98.

GEFFEN, AVIV (1973–), Israeli rock singer, songwriter. Geffen is a unique phenomenon on the Israeli rock scene. He was the first artist to create a following among Israeli youth that bordered on hysteria. He was also one of the first to develop a highly successful career based on protest and uncompromising social comment. As a conscientious objector he controversially refused to serve in the Israeli army.

As the son of writer, lyricist, satirist Yehonatan Geffen, the young Geffen was exposed to the music and entertainment industry as a child. He recorded his first single, "*Ḥaver*" ("Friend"), when he was just 17. Although the song did not meet with success Geffen immediately set about recording his debut album, *Zeh Rak Or ha-Yare'aḥ* ("It's Only the Moonlight") with his band Ha-Ta'uyyot ("The Mistakes"). He began to tour the country intensively and gradually built up a faithful and enthusiastic following, particularly among teenagers. His lyrics largely addressed burning issues of the day, such as the Middle East conflict, violence, drug and alcohol abuse, and parent-child relationships.

Other artists began discovering Geffen's songwriting talents, and popular singers such as Nurit Galron and Dafna Armoni recorded his material. Geffen received the ultimate accolade for a young Israeli songwriter when iconic singer Arik *Einstein recorded his song "*Livkot Lekha*" ("Crying For You").

Geffen's second album, *Akhshav Me'unnan* ("It's Cloudy Now"), released in 1993, sold well and reflected Geffen's musical influences from the 1960s, including the likes of the Beatles and Pink Floyd. Geffen was now a superstar and played to a hysterical audience at that year's Arad Festival. His one-of-a-kind image was also enhanced by the use of heavy make-up on stage. In particular, Geffen's mid-song shout of the song title "*Anaḥenu Dor Mezuyan*," which translates "we're a screwed-up generation," got a wild response from the festival audience and aroused the ire of the country's educators.

In 1995 Geffen found himself drawn into mainstream Israeli culture when he was the last artist to perform at the peace rally at which Prime Minister Yitzhak *Rabin was assassinated. Eight days later, in the same place, he performed "*Livkot Lekha*," which became something of an anthem for Israeli youth. In subsequent years Geffen toned down his stage persona and devoted much of his time to developing an international career. In November 2003 he released a single entitled "Hello" together with British artist Steven Wilson and the duo's album, *Blackfield*, came out the following year.

[Barry Davis (2nd ed.)]

GEFFEN, DAVID (1944–), U.S. record producer. Born in New York, Geffen began his career in the mailroom of the William Morris Agency, moved up the ladder to a position as agent, and then founded his own agency with Elliot Roberts in 1968. Taking such stars as Joni Mitchell and Neil Young under his managerial wing, Geffen founded the now major recording label Asylum Records (1970). He picked up recording artists such as Jackson Browne and built his company up to the point where it merged with long-established Electra Records, with Geffen installed as president (1973–76). In 1975 he was made vice chairman of Warner Brothers Pictures and in 1977 became executive assistant to the chairman of Warner Communications. In 1980 Geffen founded a new record label under his own name and signed John Lennon and Yoko Ono, as well as Bob Dylan, Elton John, and Donna Summer. The Lennon-Ono *Double Fantasy* (1980) album was the first released on Geffen Records. Geffen's original signings continued to bring his company success through the 1980s and into the 1990s, when Guns N'Roses proved one of the most successful groups in rock history. His ability to recognize talent was instrumental in helping to launch or develop the careers of such entertainers as Crosby, Stills, Nash & Young, the Eagles, and Tom Cruise.

In 1981 he branched out into producing Broadway musicals and had success with *Dreamgirls* and *Cats*, which became the longest-running musical in Broadway history. Geffen's incursions into stage as well as film production (*Personal Best*; *Risky Business*; *Interview with the Vampire*) netted him millions of dollars. By 1996 he was a billionaire. He sold Geffen records to MCA, receiving stock valued at $545 million in exchange, and received a further $710 million when the Matsushita Corporation bought MCA a few months later. In 1994 he launched the DreamWorks film studio project in partnership with Steven *Spielberg and Jeffrey *Katzenberg.

Geffen taught at Yale and UCLA. In 2002 he donated $200 million to the UCLA medical school, the largest single donation to a U.S. medical school in history. The school is named the David Geffen School of Medicine. The campus already includes the Geffen Playhouse, which was named for him when he donated $5 million. Geffen has also contributed generously to the Democratic National Party; Los Angeles's AIDS Project; New York's Gay Men's Health Crisis; and AIDS Action in Washington, D.C.

ADD. BIBLIOGRAPHY: S. Singular, *The Rise and Rise of David Geffen* (1997); T. King, *The Operator: David Geffen Builds, Buys, and Sells the New Hollywood* (2000).

[Jonathan Licht / Rohan Saxena and Ruth Beloff (2nd ed.)]

GEFFEN, JOEL (1902–1988), U.S. Conservative rabbi. Born into a distinguished rabbinic family (his father was Tobias *Geffen) in Kovno, Lithuania, Geffen came to the United States when he was a year old, where he was raised in Atlanta. He graduated from Emory University in 1944 and was ordained by the Jewish Theological Seminary four years later. His first pulpit was in Harrisburg, Pennsylvania, where he organized the congregation of 200 families. In 1929 he moved to Temple Beth El in Troy, New York, where he again built the congregation and organized a community *talmud torah* along with adult education and youth groups. He joined the Jewish Theological Seminary in 1944 as director of the Department of Field Activities and Communities Education, a position that he served in for four decades until his retirement. He was involved in the establishment of Leadership Training Fellowship, an elite training program for Conservative youngsters, and also in the establishment of Camp Ramah in Wingdale, New York. For four decades he was the unpaid but exceedingly dedicated spiritual adviser of the National Federation of Jewish Men's Clubs during years of significant growth. For a dozen years he also directed the Metropolitan New York region of United Synagogue, the congregational arm of the Conservative movement and edited with, Milton Berger and M. David Hoffman, *Roads to Jewish Survival* (1967). He also contributed to the *American Jewish Historical Quarterly*.

BIBLIOGRAPHY: P.S. Nadell, *Conservative Judaism in America: A Biographical Dictionary and Sourcebook* (1988), 95–96.

[Michael Berenbaum (2nd ed.)]

GEFFEN, TOBIAS (1870–1970), Lithuanian-born U.S. rabbi, community leader, and activist. Born in Kovno, Lithuania, to Kuna Real Strauss and Yosef Geffe, Geffen studied privately in Kovno, Slobodka, and Grodno. After marrying Sara Hene Rabinowitz in August 1898, he entered the Kovno Kollel, and his wife operated a paper store to support them.

In 1903, a month after the Kishinev pogrom, Geffen left Kovno for the United States with his wife, two children, and his wife's siblings. A few weeks before they left he received *semikhah* from Rabbi Moshe Danishevsky of Slobodka and the Kovner Rav Shapiro.

After part-time work at a family sweatshop in New York City, Geffen became rabbi of the Beit Knesset Ahavat Tzedek Bnai Lebedove in 1904. Several months later Geffen attended the Agudat ha-Rabbonim convention where he first met his colleagues. In a major authentification initiative, the famous Ridbaz ordained rabbis at the convention. Geffen received his third *semikhah* from the Ridbaz in July 1904.

While soliciting funds for the Kovno Kollel, Geffen spent a Shabbat in Canton, Ohio. Invited to be the rabbi there, he moved his family, now four children, to Canton in 1907.

After a visit to the Shearith Israel Congregation in Atlanta, Geffen was chosen as rabbi. He served the congregation from 1910 until his death in 1970. As the rabbi of the smaller orthodox synagogue in the city, Geffen, nevertheless, took quick action by creating a religious school, which would try to eliminate all the "*melammedim*." Most important, he introduced a daily class in Talmud, which soon became occasions to present **hadranim* at conclusions of different treatises of the Talmud. The earliest ones delivered in Atlanta were published in the *Ha-Meassef* halakhic journal in Jerusalem. Later Geffen published his *hadranim*, his *derashot*, and a few responsa in the eight books, which he published from 1924 to 1962.

The public highlights of Geffen's career were varied. In 1913, he visited Leo Frank, who had been convicted unjustly of the murder of Mary Phagan, and instituted regular prayers for Frank for the two years of his incarceration. Upon Frank's lynching in 1915, Geffen urged his congregants to remain calm but vigilant and not to leave Atlanta. In the early 1920s Geffen led a campaign calling upon the U.S. Congress not to adopt the new immigration law because it was discriminatory against Jewish refugees. In 1933 he and his son, attorney Samuel Geffen, successfully lobbied the governor for the release of a "Yankee Jew" from a Georgia chain gang prison.

His most famous act involved the drink Coca-Cola, whose home is in Atlanta, Georgia. After rabbis throughout the northeast and midwest gave their *hekhsher* to Coca-Cola for use on Passover and the entire year without any knowledge of the ingredients, Geffen was requested by the Agudat ha-Rabbonim to see what he could ascertain. Permitted to have access to the highly secret formula, Geffen analyzed the soft drink with the assistance of his daughter Helen Geffen, a food chemist. In a responsum published in 1935, he showed that Coca-Cola was non-kosher and not kosher for Passover. However, since "so many people do drink this product," Geffen identified two substances which could be substituted for the problematic ones in the drink. In 1935 the change was made by the company, and that year for Passover (in Atlanta only), Geffen's *hekhsher* written by him in Hebrew appeared on the Coca-Cola bottle cap.

Geffen's papers are found in the archival collections of the American Jewish Historical Society.

[David Geffen (2nd ed.)]

GEHAZI (Heb. גֵּחֲזִי, גֵּיחֲזִי), servant of *Elisha. In the story of the wealthy Shunammite woman (II Kings 4:8–37), Gehazi is portrayed as Elisha's faithful messenger and loyal protector (4:27). In the story of Naaman (II Kings 5), he is portrayed as a greedy character who, contrary to the instructions of Elisha, cunningly solicited a reward from the Syrian general and then tried to practice deception on his master, the prophet Elisha. In punishment, Elisha cursed Gehazi and his descendants forever with the "leprosy" of Naaman (biblical *ṣaraʿat* is not true leprosy, i.e., Hansen's disease, but more likely psoriasis). In the Bible *ṣaraʿat* is punishment for disloyalty and challenge to authority (Zakovitch).The third time that Gehazi appears is in connection with the woman from Shunem and the king of Israel (II Kings 8:1–6). In this story Gehazi reported to the king on the great deeds which Elisha had performed. These three stories, so it would appear, did not occur in the chronological order in which they are now arranged in Kings, since it is unlikely that Gehazi would have stood before the king recounting Elisha's great deeds after he had been cursed with leprosy. It is reasonable to assume that they reflect two separate traditions. The first and third stories, which are related in content, constitute one tradition, while that of Naaman stems from a different circle.

[Isaac Avishur]

In the Aggadah

Gehazi is one who set his eyes upon that which was not proper with the result that he was not granted that which he sought, and lost whatever he possessed (Sot. 9b). Although learned, he was jealous of Elisha's learning, sensual (in his actions toward the Shunamite), and did not believe in the resurrection of the dead. Instead of obeying Elisha's order not to greet anyone on his way to the Shunamite's son (II Kings 4:29), he made sport of his mission and deliberately asked everyone he met whether they really believed that Elisha's staff, which he was carrying, could restore the dead to life (PdRE 37).

Gehazi was punished with "leprosy" because Elisha had been studying the law of the eight unclean creeping things when Naaman first consulted him. When Elisha accused Gehazi of taking eight things from Naaman (II Kings 5:26), he implied that he would be punished as would one who caught any of the eight creeping things – with "leprosy" (ARN 9). According to another tradition, Gehazi was thus punished because he showed disrespect by calling his master by name (cf. II Kings 8:5; Sanh. 100a). Gehazi never repented. Instead, he sinned further either by hanging a magnet over Jeroboam's idol and suspending it between heaven and earth in order to deceive people, or by engraving the name of God on it, so that it spoke the first two commandments (Sanh. 107b). When Elisha met him in Damascus and exhorted him to repent, he replied: "Thus have I learnt from thee. He who sins and causes the multitude to sin, is not afforded the means of repentance" (*ibid.*). Elisha, however, is criticized for "thrusting Gehazi away with both hands," instead of using only one for that purpose, and the other for drawing him toward himself (Sot. 47a). Gehazi is one of the four commoners who have no share in the world to come (Sanh. 10: 2). He was even undeserving of speaking the praises of God and His servant Elisha.

BIBLIOGRAPHY: Ginzberg, Legends, index; I. Ḥasida, *Ishei ha-Tanakh* (1964), 97–98. **ADD. BIBLIOGRAPHY:** Y. Zakovitch, *Every High Official* (1986), 142–45: D. Wright and R. Jones, in: ABD, 4:277–82; S.D. Sperling, in: HUCA, 70–71 (1999–2000), 48–9.

GEHINNOM (Heb. גֵּי בֶן־הִנֹּם, גֵּי בְנֵי הִנֹּם, גֵּיא בֶן־הִנֹּם, גֵּיא הִנֹּם; Gr. Γέεννα; "Valley of Ben-Hinnom, Valley of [the Son (s) of] Hinnom," Gehenna), a valley south of Jerusalem on one of the borders between the territories of Judah and Benjamin, between the Valley of *Rephaim and *En-Rogel (Josh. 15:8; 18:16). It is identified with Wadi er-Rababi.

During the time of the Monarchy, Gehinnom, at a place called Topheth, was the site of a cult which involved the burning of children (II Kings 23:10; Jer. 7:31; 32:35 et al.; see *Moloch). Jeremiah repeatedly condemned this cult and predicted that on its account Topheth and the Valley of the Son of Hinnom would be called the Valley of the "Slaughter" (Jer. 19:5–6).

In Judaism the name Gehinnom is generally used as an appellation of the place of torment reserved for the wicked after death. The New Testament used the Greek form Gehenna in the same sense.

ADD. BIBLIOGRAPHY: D. Watson, in: ABD, 2:926–28.

GEHRY, FRANK OWEN (**Ephraim Goldberg**; 1929–), U.S. architect. Gehry was responsible for some of the most creative architecture of the 20th century with 30 existing buildings, public and private, in America, Europe, and Asia. He was born in Toronto, Canada. After moving to the United States in 1947, he received his degree in architecture from the University of Southern California and then served in the U.S. military during the Korean War. After the war, he went to Harvard Graduate School to study city planning. In 1962, Gehry Partners was launched. From his earliest work, he was opposed to the straight line and flat surfaces of most modern and postmodern designs. His use of chain link fencing on his home in Santa Monica aroused the wrath of his neighbors and the bewilderment of professional architects. Gehry simply explained that he was using ordinary materials in a different way. At first, Gehry was skeptical of the computer, but his engineer, Jim Glymph, convinced him that the best way to transform his creative drawings into economically practical applications was through the computer. In addition, much research went into finding the particular materials Gehry wanted to use to accentuate the play of light and color on the surface of his buildings. The Guggenheim Museum in Bilbao, Spain, the Rock Music "Temple" (EMP) in Seattle, Washington, and the Los Angeles Walt Disney Concert Hall are handsome and startlingly different from the boxlike structures of his predecessors. Gehry's forms are fluid, organic, and colorful, growing out of his flowing sketches. In the case of the Guggenheim Museum, he finally found a special formula for titanium that would reflect the changing light of the sun, clouds, and sky. For the rock-'n'-roll building (known as the EMP – Experience Music Project) in Seattle, non-fading auto body paint in red, blue, even gold, silver, and purple mark different sections of this 140,000-square-foot building. The shapes and surfaces of Gehry's buildings develop out of deeply ingrained images in his consciousness. He recounts that he was fascinated by the forms of the live fish his grandmother used to bring home from the market. He used to play with them in the bathtub before they were cooked. His Fishdance Restaurant in Kobe, Japan (1987), is unmistakably the shape of a large fish. The scalelike surfaces of the Guggenheim Museum and the EMP exemplify the same influence. Gehry won an invited design competition in 1987 for the Walt Disney Concert Hall in Los Angeles. Begun before the Bilbao museum, 16 years went by before completion. Gehry received a long list of awards including the Pritzker Prize for architecture in 1989, the most prestigious award given to an architect, and more than 100 awards from the American Institute of Architects to honor outstanding architectural design. On March 2, 2005, representatives of the City of Las Vegas, Nevada, announced that Gehry would be the architect for the Alzheimer's Research Center, one of the projects that will make up the 61-acre downtown urban village. The mayor of Las Vegas said Gehry's building "will be a piece of artwork that will draw people from around the world who will marvel at its beauty."

[Betty R. Rubenstein (2nd ed.)]

GEIGER, ABRAHAM (1810–1874), pioneer of the *Wissenschaft des Judentums and founder of *Reform Judaism. Geiger was born in Frankfurt am Main to an Orthodox family and received a traditional religious education. Already in his childhood, he began studying classical history, which gave rise to doubts concerning biblical claims to divine authority. At the age of 17, Geiger began writing a study of the Mishnah, differentiating its legal style from biblical and talmudic law, and a dictionary of Mishnaic Hebrew.

With funding from friends, Geiger began university studies at the University of Heidelberg in April 1829, to the dismay of his family. He concentrated on philology, Syriac, Hebrew, and classics, but also attended lectures in Old Testament, philosophy, and archaeology. After one semester, he moved to the University of Bonn, where he joined a group of Jewish students, many of whom were preparing for careers in the rabbinate, that included Samson Raphael *Hirsch, Solomon *Munk, Joseph Derenbourg, and other future scholars of Judaism.

At Bonn, Geiger's studies focused on Oriental languages, philosophy, and theology, but he was offended by some of his professors' ignorance of Judaism and occasional antisemitic comments. He began an intense study of Arabic and the Koran under the distinguished Orientalist Georg Freytag, winning a prize for his essay "Was hat Mohammed aus dem Judenthume aufgenommen?" The essay, which earned Geiger a doctorate at the University of Marburg, demonstrated the influence of rabbinic literature on the text of the Koran. Published as a book in 1833, it won great acclaim as opening a new avenue for Islamic scholarship, and was the first step in Geiger's larger intellectual project, demonstrating Judaism's central influence on Christianity and Islam. Neither possessed religious originality, but simply carried the Jewish message of monotheism to the pagan world.

Since no university professorships were available in Germany to Jews, Geiger took a position as rabbi to the Jewish community of Wiesbaden from 1832 to 1837 and continued his academic publications primarily through the scholarly journals he founded and edited, *Wissenschaftliche Zeitschrift fuer juedische Theologie* (1835–39) and *Juedische Zeitschrift fuer Wissenschaft und Leben* (1862–75). His journals became an important vehicle in its day for publishing Jewish scholarship, and they included historical and theological studies as well as discussions of contemporary Jewish affairs.

While in Wiesbaden, Geiger introduced some synagogue reforms, abolishing the recitation of medieval Hebrew poems of lamentation for the destruction of the Second Temple, and other prayers he felt were theologically inappropriate. In 1837 Geiger convened a meeting of reform-minded rabbis in Wiesbaden, and he continued to be a driving force behind subsequent synods of liberal rabbis, held in Braunschweig in June 1844, Frankfurt in July 1845, and Breslau in 1846.

In 1838 Geiger became a finalist for a rabbinic post in Breslau, but divisions between conservative and liberal factions within the Jewish community led to heated opposition to his appointment. His religious commitments were under suspicion by conservative factions, who accused him of being a Karaite or Sadducee. Geiger replied that rabbinic Judaism meant "not to be slaves to the letter of the Bible." As a result of the opposition, he was not able to take up a position as assistant rabbi until 1840, and only with the death of Breslau's Orthodox rabbi Solomon Tiktin in 1843 did Geiger become chief rabbi. That appointment led to the secession of the Orthodox faction, under the rabbinic leadership of Gedaliah Tiktin. In Breslau Geiger established a school for religious studies and a group for the study of Hebrew philology. Geiger was one of the most active participants in the synods held by the Reform rabbis in Frankfurt am Main (1845) and Breslau (1846).

The tensions in Breslau continued throughout his tenure, and when the Juedisch-Theologisches Seminar was founded there in 1854, thanks in part to Geiger's efforts, he was not appointed to its faculty, though he had long been at the forefront of attempts to establish a faculty of Jewish theology. His exclusion from the Breslau seminary resulted from pressures by conservative Jews who considered his theological position too liberal. In 1863 Geiger left Breslau to serve as rabbi of the Reform congregation in his hometown of Frankfurt am Main, and in 1870 became rabbi in the Berlin community. Ultimately, in 1871, he was appointed to the faculty of the newly founded Reform rabbinical college in Berlin, Hochschule fuer die Wissenschaft des Judentums, where he spent his final years.

Geiger's rejection of Orthodox Judaism in favor of a more liberal approach developed, he tells us in his diaries, during his adolescence, and began to flourish in his university days. Judaism was distinguished for Geiger by its monotheism and ethics. Whereas the Greek genius had introduced philosophy to Western civilization, the Jews were possessed of a "religious genius," and it is the latter, according to Geiger, that gives morality a firm basis in society. However, Judaism's ethical imperative had been lost in the rigidity of talmudic legalism, developed over centuries of ghettoization inflicted by Christian intolerance. In the Middle Ages, Jews were better off in Islamic countries than under Christian rule, he argued; Geiger praised Islamic tolerance and the Jews in Islamic Spain as "heroes of Wissenschaft," producing poets and philosophers who contributed their work to the general culture by writing in Arabic, not Hebrew. Theirs was a pure Judaism, he argued: monotheistic, based on divine revelation, but without the constraints and narrowness of Jewish life within medieval Christendom.

While Reform Judaism initially developed as lay Jews simply lost interest in the strict observances required of Orthodoxy, with many seeking shorter services, more frequent sermons, and organ music, modeled after Protestant churches, Geiger sought a more coherent ideological framework to justify innovations in the liturgy and religious practice. In his view, Reform Judaism was not a rejection of earlier Judaism, but a recovery of the Pharisaic halakhic tradition. Geiger's magnum opus, *Urschrift und Uebersetzungen der Bibel* (1857), argued that the Pharisees and early rabbis of the Mishnah had sought a liberalization and democratization of Jewish law, in opposition to the conservative, aristocratic Sadducees, who controlled the priesthood and Temple as the central religious institutions of Jewish life. Drawing on methods developed by F.C. Baur and the Tuebingen School, Geiger uncovered the religious and political tendencies in Greek, Aramaic, and Syriac biblical translations, as well as apocryphal and pseudepigraphical literature, to formulate a picture of Second Temple Judaism in tension between progressive and reactionary proclivities: the Sadducees "were joined by everything which counted itself as part of the aristocracy… they had administration and judicial functions. The Pharisees consisted of the citizenry which had national and religious inclinations, and constituted the opposition to the aristocracy, whom they eventually overcame. The differences are based more on political and partisan viewpoints than on diverging religious principles; gradually they became different religious sects." The theological principle of Pharisaic tradition, according to Geiger, "is nothing other than the principle of continual further development in accord with the times, the principle of not being slaves to the letter of the Bible, but rather to witness over and over its spirit and its authentic faith-consciousness."

In his subsequent survey of Jewish history, *Das Judentum und seine Geschichte*, a series of lectures he delivered in Frankfurt and Berlin, Geiger depicted the eras of Jewish engagement with the surrounding culture as ideal. The Pharisees, who sought to liberalize and democratize Jewish practice and supplant the Temple priesthood with a priesthood of all believers, represented authentic Judaism. Jesus was a liberal Pharisee who "walked in the way of Hillel…. [and] did not utter a new thought." Christianity began when Paul carried Jesus' Jewish message to the Greco-Roman world and distorted Jewish monotheism with Hellenistic paganism. The Pharisaism of both Jesus and the early rabbis was lost in the Middle Ages, Geiger argued, when Christian persecution forced Judaism to retreat from the liberalizing tendencies of the Mishnah and turn the Talmud into a petrified system of legal restrictions. Jesus failed to gain many Jewish disciples in Judea because his teachings were not original, but the common beliefs of the Pharisees. Following the destruction of the Temple in 70 C.E., Geiger argued, the Sadducees joined the early Jesus movement and expressed their long-standing opposition to the Pharisees in various New Testament passages, such as Matthew 23.

Geiger's position within the Reform movement was moderate, mediating between the more radical efforts of Samuel *Holdheim and Kaufmann *Kohler, and the conservative, proto-nationalist factions represented by Zacharias *Frankel and Heinrich *Graetz. Geiger preferred German as the language of Jewish liturgy: "If Hebrew were to be represented as an essential element of Judaism, then Judaism would be pictured as a national religion." Similarly, Geiger felt that the dietary laws were "inane, thereby so very damaging to social life, and, indeed, the inward brotherhood among people nonetheless transcends the renewal of a separatist, bleached-out and very dubious religious feeling." At the same time, while he considered circumcision a "barbaric, bloody act," he opposed the call of the radical Frankfurt Reformverein to abolish it.

Geiger became a major liturgist of the Reform movement, editing prayer books in 1854 and 1870 that became influential models for Reform Jews worldwide. In accord with other liberal Jews of his day, he eliminated the hope for a return to Zion in the messianic era from the prayer book, and while retaining the Hebrew original, changed the German translation of certain phrases; for example, "reviver of the dead" became "source of eternal life." Geiger himself remained an observant Jew throughout his life, but permitted certain liberalizations of religious practice. He relaxed some Sabbath restrictions and allowed organ music in the synagogue, and shortened the prayer services, but he opposed the abolition of circumcision and shifting Sabbath observance to Sundays.

Although criticized sharply for his opposition to Jewish national identity, notably in his refusal to intervene on behalf of the Jews of Damascus accused of ritual murder in 1840, Geiger sought to instill a deep sense of pride in Jews. He argued that Jews deserve credit for giving birth to the three major monotheistic traditions of the West, and also for those principles of religious tolerance and freedom of belief that constitute the basis of modern society.

Writings

Geiger's most significant writings include his doctoral dissertation *Was hat Mohammed aus dem Judenthume aufgenommen* (1833) and *Urschrift und Uebersetzungen der Bibel in ihrer Abhaengigkeit von der innern Entwickelung des Judenthums* (Breslau: Julius Heinauer, 1857); the second edition was published with an introduction by Paul Kahle, a postcript by Nachum Czortkowski, and a Hebrew essay by Geiger, reprinted from *Oẓar Neḥmad*, 3 (1860), 1–15, 115–21, 125–28 (Frankfurt am Main: Verlag Madda, 1928); in Hebrew translation with an introduction by Joseph Klausner, *Ha-Mikra ve-Targumav* (Jerusalem: Bialik Foundation, 1949; reprinted 1972). See also Geiger's *Sadducäer und Pharisäer* (Breslau: Schlettersche Buchhandlung, 1863), reprinted from JZWL, 2:11–54. The two journals he edited contain numerous articles of scholarly and theological significance: *Wissenschaftliche Zeitschrift fuer juedische Theologie* (1835–39) and *Juedische Zeitschrift fuer Wissenschaft und Leben* (1862–75). *Das Judenthum und seine Geschichte* (3 vols., 1865–71) appeared in English as *Judaism and Its History* (1865, 1911). Also important are Geiger's *Lehr- und Lesebuch zur Sprache der Mischnah* (1845) and *Parschandatha; die nordfranzösische Exegetenschule* (1855). Other writings include a study of Maimonides (1850); an edition of the *Divan* of Judah Halevi (1851); a study of Ibn Gabirol (1867); translations of a number of their poems in German verse; a treatise on the Karaite Isaac b. Abraham Troki (1853); and a study on Leon Modena (1856). He published several valuable manuscripts (collected in *Melo Chofnajim*, 1840). Geiger contributed regularly to the *Zeitschrift der Deutschen Morgenländischen Gesellschaft*, the leading journal in the fields of Oriental studies, Semitics, philology, and Islamic studies.

Geiger's son, Ludwig Geiger, wrote the most comprehensive biography to date in the introduction to *Abraham Geiger: Leben und Lebenswerk* (Berlin: Georg Reimer, 1910), which also contains a superb collection of studies about Geiger's work by leading scholars. Ludwig Geiger also edited five volumes of Geiger's articles and correspondence, with biographical in-

The Jewish cemetery in Prague, where some of the headstones date from the 14th century. *Photo: Z. Radovan, Jerusalem.*

For a Jew the stages of life are accompanied by various rituals and ceremonies, from birth through education and bar/bat mitzvah to marriage and family to death. Items may relate to an individual, such as birth amulets, *tefillin* bags, and dowries, or to the community, such as the *ḥevra kaddisha* (burial society) appurtenances. The locale of each community influenced the materials and styles reflected in the various objects and events shown here.

LIFE CYCLE

A funeral in Prague. Lowering the body into the grave—from a series of oil paintings commissioned by the Prague *ḥevra kaddisha. Jewish Museum, Prague.*

(opposite page) TOP: Copy of reliefs on tombstones in the Jewish cemetery in Curaçao, Netherlands Antilles, 1980. Generally, the decoration related to the name of the person buried. For example, the decoration on the tombstone of Eliau Namias De Orasto, center, represents the name Elijah—a chariot of fire ascending to heaven. On the right, the motif of the felled tree indicates a man who died in his prime. The portrayal of ships shows that the man was a sailor or was engaged in commerce. *Photo: Micha Bar-Am, Israel. By courtesy of Beth Hatefutsoth Photo Archive, Tel Aviv and courtesy of Mordechai Arbell, Israel.*

(this page) ABOVE: Burial Society glass, Prague, Bohemia, 1713. Glass, enamel, and paint; 24.5 x 15.7cm. *Collection, The Israel Museum, Jerusalem. Photo © The Israel Museum, Jerusalem, by Yoram Lehmann.*

(this page): Gold filigree birth amulet set with rubies and diamonds, Italian or English, mid 19th century. *Jewish Museum, London.*

(opposite page): Abraham and the Three Angels (Fol.165), who came to inform Abraham of the pending birth of Isaac. From the *Rothschild Miscellany*, Northern Italy, c. 1450–1480. Vellum, pen and ink, tempera, and gold leaf. *Collection, The Israel Museum, Jerusalem. Photo © The Israel Museum, Jerusalem, by David Harris.*

Red velvet and bright flowers on a circumcision cushion; embroidered by Simcha Janiver-Diskin, Jerusalem, 1898. *© Dr. David Darom.*

Circumcision set, Holland, 1827 and 1866. Box: Silver filigree, cast and hammered; inlaid with semi-precious stones. Utensils: Silver filigree, cast and hammered; mother-of-pearl, carved. Box 9.5 x 7.375 x 4.125" (24.1 x 18.7 x 10.5 cm). *The Jewish Museum, New York. The H. Ephraim and Mordecai Benguiat Family Collection.*

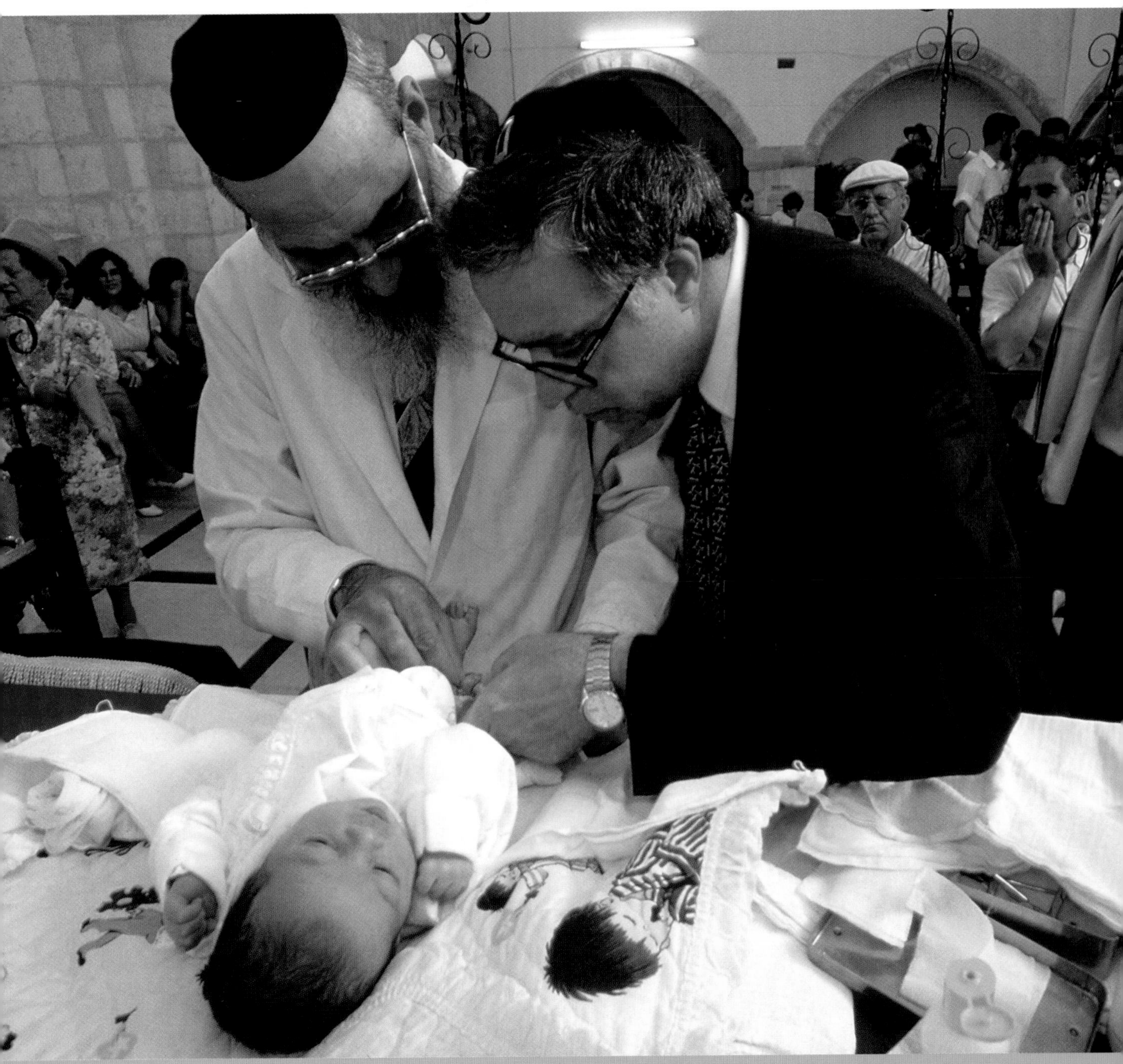

A mohel performs performs a *brit milah*, or circumcision, in a Jerusalem synagogue, 1994. © *Bojan Brecelj/Corbis.*

troductions: *Abraham Geigers Nachgelassene Schriften* (Berlin: Louis Geschel Verlagsbuchhandlung, 1875–78; reprinted New York: Arno Press, 1980). English translations of excerpts from Geiger's publications and private correspondence, with a biographical introduction, are found in Max Wiener, ed., *Abraham Geiger and Liberal Judaism: The Challenge of the Nineteenth Century*, tr.. E.J. Schlochauer (Philadelphia: Jewish Publication Society, 1962). Selections in Hebrew translation appear in M.A. Meyer (ed.), *Avraham Geiger: Mivḥar Ketavav al ha-Tikkunim ba-Dat*, tr. G. Eliashberg (Jerusalem: Merkaz Zalman Shazar u-Merkaz Dinur, 1949; reprinted 1979) and S.A. Poznanski (ed.), *Kevuẓat Ma'amarim* (Berlin: Louis Gerschel, 1877; reprinted Warsaw: Tushiyah, 1910; reprinted Haifa: Student Union of Haifa University, 1966).

BIBLIOGRAPHY: J.J. Petuchowski (ed,), *New Perspectives on Abraham Geiger: An HUC-JIR Symposium* (1975), incl. bibl., 55–58. S. Heschel *Abraham Geiger and the Jewish Jesus* (1998); M. Wiener, "Abraham Geiger and the Science of Judaism," in: *Judaism*, 2 (Jan. 1953), 41–48; idem, *Juedische Religion im Zeitalter der Emanzipation* (1933), passim; M.A. Meyer, "Christian Influence on Early German Reform Judaism," in: C. Berlin (ed.), *Studies in Jewish Bibliography, History and Literature in Honor of I. Edward Kiev* (1971), 289–303; idem, "Reform Jewish Thinkers and Their German Intellectual Context," in: J. Reinharz and W. Schatzberg (eds.), *The Jewish Response to German Culture*, (1985); J. Fleischmann, *Be'ayat ha-Naẓerut ba-Maḥshavah ha-Yehudit mi-Mendelson ad Rozentsvaig* (1964); I. Heinemann, *Ta'amei ha-Mitzvot be-Sifrut Yisrael*, 2 vols. (1966). For additional bibliography, see J. Auerbach, "Abraham Geiger," in: *Allgemeine deutsche Biographie*, 8 (1878; reprinted Berlin: Duncker & Humblot, 1968), 786–93.

[Susannah Heschel (2nd ed.)]

GEIGER, BERNHARD (1881–1964), Austrian philologist. Geiger, born in Bielitz (Bielsko), Upper Silesia, attended the universities of Vienna, Bonn, and Heidelberg. Originally his field of study was Hebrew, but one of his teachers in Vienna aroused his interest in Iranian and Sanskrit, and it was in those languages that he made his principal contributions to scholarship. From 1909 to 1938 he taught at the University of Vienna, being forced to leave that position by the Nazis. In 1938 he immigrated to the United States and from 1938 to 1951 was professor of Indo-Iranian philology at the Tibetan-Iranian Institute (later the Asia Institute), New York. In 1951–56 he taught Indo-Iranian at Columbia University. In 1949 the shah of Iran conferred upon him the Order of Humayoun.

Geiger's publications include *Die Aməša Spəntas* (1916); *Die Religion der Iranier* (1929); and *Middle Iranian Texts* (1956; repr. from *The Excavations at Dura-Europos, Final Report*, 7 pt. 1 (1936), 283–317). Geiger was one of the contributors to the volume of *Additamenta* to A. Kohut's *Aruch Completum* (1937), being mainly responsible for the detailed philological study of talmudic words of Iranian origin.

ADD. BIBLIOGRAPHY: S. Winninger (ed.), *Grosse Jüdische Nationalbiographie*, vol. 7 (1936), 568.

GEIGER, LAZARUS (Eliezer Solomon; 1829–1870), German philosopher and philologist. Geiger, who was born in Frankfurt, was a nephew of Abraham *Geiger. He studied classical philology at the Universities of Marburg, Heidelberg, and Bonn. Unlike his uncle, he belonged to the Orthodox religious group of German Jewry. From 1861 until his death he was a teacher at the Jewish educational institute Philanthropin in Frankfurt. He saw in language the source of human reason. Language, according to Geiger, was formed from meaningless expressions – the reactions of early man to his visual impressions. These expressions became fixed and stabilized into permanent concepts. Geiger's research won a certain amount of contemporary approval, but his conclusions were rejected by subsequent scholarship. His main works are *Ursprung und Entwicklung der menschlichen Sprache und Vernunft* (2 vols., 1868–72; the second volume was published after his death by his brother Alfred Geiger) and *Der Ursprung der Sprache* (1864).

BIBLIOGRAPHY: G. Peschier, *Lazarus Geiger, sein Leben und Denken* (1871); L.A. Rosenthal, *Lazarus Geiger* (Ger., 1883). **ADD. BIBLIOGRAPHY:** B. Mueller, *Ohr der Seele – Lazarus Geiger und die sprachphilsophischen Reflexionen der Kosmiker* (2000).

GEIGER, LUDWIG (1848–1919), German literary historian; a fervent adherent of the symbiosis of Judaism and Germanness. Son of Abraham *Geiger, he studied philology and history in Heidelberg, Goettingen, and Berlin and concluded his academic studies in 1873 with a dissertation, presented to Leopold von Ranke on the attitude of Greek and Roman authors to Judaism and Jews. In 1880 he was appointed extraordinary professor of the history of literature at Friedrich Wilhelm University, Berlin. Later he additionally became a lecturer at the Lehranstalt fuer die Wissenschaft des Judentums. Geiger was a versatile scholar, editor, and translator. His major contributions were to Renaissance, Humanism, and Reformation studies, German-Jewish history, and research on Goethe and other writers of the 19th century. Even when treating the first and last subjects he remained particularly conscious of the Jewish aspect. Appreciation of Geiger's work on the Rennaissance led the Swiss historian, Jacob Burckhardt – a notorious antisemite – to appoint him editor of all future editions of his *Die Cultur der Renaissance in Italien* ("Civilization of the Renaissance in Italy"). Geiger's major work in this subject was *Renaissance und Humanismus in Italien und Deutschland* (1882). He published the letters of Johann *Reuchlin (1875) and the latter's biography, *Johann Reuchlin, sein Leben und seine Werke* (1871). Founder and editor of *Zeitschrift fuer die Geschichte der Juden in Deutschland* (1887–92), he also wrote *Geschichte der Juden in Berlin* (2 vols., 1871), *Die deutsche Literatur und die Juden* (1910), and numerous articles on German Jewish history. The *Goethe Jahrbuch* was founded by him in 1880; he continued to edit it until 1913, when he had to leave in the aftermath of an acrimonious dispute. His major works on Goethe were *Goethe und die Seinen* (1908) and *Goethe, sein Leben und Schaffen dem deutschen Volke erzaehlt* (1910); he also wrote on Goethe's relationship to Jews and Judaism. Geiger edited his father's *Nachgelassene Schriften* (5 vols., 1875–78) and other works; he also wrote a biography of his father, *Abraham Geiger, Leben und Lebenswerk* (with others, 1910).

Geiger was a vigorous exponent of liberalism and Reform Judaism and an opponent of political Zionism and Orthodox Judaism. In 1911, in his birthday letter to the kaiser, he courageously protested against the social discrimination to which German Jews were subjected. From 1909 he edited the leading Jewish newspaper, *Allgemeine Zeitung des Judentums.* His unpublished works include a projected edition of the correspondence of Leopold *Zunz.

BIBLIOGRAPHY: G. Lauer, in: C. König (ed.), Internationales Germanistenlexikon 1800–1950 (2003), 547–549. **ADD. BIBLIOGRAPHY:** H. Hague, B. Machosky, and M. Rotter, "Waiting for Goethe. Goethe's Biographies from Ludwig Geiger to Friedrich Gundolf," in: *Goethe in German-Jewish Culture* (2001), 84–103; H.-D. Holzhausen, "Ludwig Geiger (1848–1919) – ein Beitrag ueber sein Leben und sein Werk unter dem Aspekt seiner Bibliothek und weiterer Archivalien," in: *Menora,* 2 (1991), 245–69; C. Koenig, "Cultural History as Enlightenment. Remarks on Ludwig Geiger's Experiences of Judaism, Philology and Goethe," in: *Goethe in German-Jewish Culture* (2001), 65–83.

[Rudolf Kayser / Sebastian Panwitz (2nd ed.)]

GEIGER, MORITZ (1860–1937), philosopher. Moritz Geiger, a nephew of Abraham *Geiger, was born in Frankfurt and became professor in Munich and Goettingen. After the rise of the Nazis in 1933 he moved to the U.S. and was professor at Vassar College. Geiger was first a disciple of Th. Lipps, then a fellow student of *Husserl, and the first to apply the objective "eidetical" method developed in Husserl's *Logische Untersuchungen* in aesthetics. Geiger did not accept the "transcendental-subjective" method that was already Husserl's main concern. Geiger saw the aesthetic values of the object as based, not on its real characteristics, but on its phenomenal ones. From this he concluded that a student of aesthetics is obliged to investigate its objects from the point of view of their phenomenal characteristics. In this way Geiger brought about a change toward the objectivity of aesthetics, which was adopted by many in the teaching of art and beauty, and became the basis for interpreting "aesthetic pleasure" in the school of phenomenalism. Other studies led Geiger to an analysis of the unconscious. He showed that the laws of psychological reality are not to be understood as laws of consciousness. Additional studies were devoted to philosophical problems of mathematics and physics, the theory of relativity and axiomatic geometry. His work on essential relations and essential meaning in aesthetics induced him to turn to metaphysics; the philosophy of ontology and the question of the division of the sciences caused him to reconsider the problem of "the ultimate existence, the unattached existing within itself," and "independent metaphysics." He wrote *Bemerkungen zur Psychologie der Gefuelselemente und Gefuelsverbindungen* (1904), *Die philosophische Bedenkung der Relativitaetstheorie* (1921), *Systematische Axiomatik der euklidischen Geometrie* (1924), *Aesthetik* (1921), and *Die Wirklichkeit der Wissenschaften und die Metaphysik* (1930).

BIBLIOGRAPHY: Zelker, in: *Zeitschrift fuer philosophische Forschung,* 14 (1960), 452–66.

GEIGER, SOLOMON ZALMAN (ben Abraham, d. 1775), community notable of Frankfurt on the Main. In 1738 he published a philosophic-kabbalistic homiletical commentary *Kerem Shelomo* which was at first well received. However, in 1742 the rabbis of Frankfurt withdrew his right to be chosen as *gabbai,* interdicted him from serving as precentor in the Great Synagogue for nine years, and apparently made a public declaration against his book, the official reason being that Geiger had not comported himself correctly in the community meetinghouse. Geiger compiled an anthology of writings of medieval Jewish philosophers (unpublished).

BIBLIOGRAPHY: M. Horovitz, *Frankfurter Rabbinen,* 2 (1883), 90; 3 (1884), 15, 19–21, 60; 4 (1885), 35.

[Jacob S. Levinger]

GEIRINGER, KARL (1899–1989), musicologist. Born in Vienna, Geiringer studied with Guido *Adler and Curt *Sachs, and earned his doctorate at the University of Vienna in 1922 for a dissertation on musical instruments in Renaissance painting. In 1929 he was appointed to the commission of the Denkmäler Tonkunst in Oesterreich and a year later became custodian of the museum and library of the Gesellschaft der Musikfreunde, Vienna. Following the Nazi invasion of Austria in 1938, he went to London, where he worked for the BBC, wrote articles for the fourth edition of the *Grove's Dictionary,* and taught at the Royal College of Music. In 1941 he was appointed professor of history and theory of music at Boston University, where he remained for 21 years. He was elected a fellow of the American Academy of Arts and Sciences in 1959 and was an honorary member of the American chapter of the Neue Bach-Gesellschaft and of the Oesterreichische Gesellschaft fuer Musikwissenschaft. In 1962 Geiringer was appointed professor of music at the University of California, Santa Barbara, where he retired in 1971. Geiringer's writings include *Musical Instruments: Their History in Western Culture,* (1943), *Haydn: a Creative Life in Music* (1946), *Brahms: His Life and Work* (1936), *The Bach Family* (1954), *A Thematic Catalog of Haydn's Settings of Folk Songs from the British Isles* (1953), *Johann Sebastian Bach: The Culmination of an Era* (1966). He edited *Antonio Caldara: Ein Madrigal und achtzehn Kanons,* Cw, XXV (1933), *Music of the Bach Family: An Anthology* (1955), *Joseph Haydn: 100 schottische Lieder* (Munich, 1961); and *J. Haydn: Symphony No. 103 in E-Flat Major* (New York, 1974).

BIBLIOGRAPHY: Grove online; MGG[2]; Karl Geiringer, *A Checklist of his Publications in Musicology* (1969); H.C.R. Landon and R.E. Chapman (eds.), *Studies in Eighteenth-Century Music: a Tribute to Karl Geiringer* (1970).

[Israela Stein (2nd ed.)]

GEKHT, SEMEN GRIGOREVICH (1903–1963), Russian writer. Gekht was born in Odessa and from the mid-1920s lived in Moscow where he worked on the newspaper *Gudok.* With his first prose work, the novella *Chelovek, kotoryj zabyl svoyu zhizn'* ("The Person Who Forgot His Life," 1927) Gekht appeared as a representative of Russian-Jewish literature. The basic theme of his books (including the novel *Pouchitel' naya istoriya* ("An Instructive Story," 1939); stories for children; *Syn sapozhnika* ("Son of the Cobbler," 1931); *Efim Kalyuzhny iz Smidovichey* ("Efim Kalyuzhny from Smidovichi," 1931), etc., is the transformation of Jewish life in the post-revolutionary period and the participation of Jewish youth from the shtetl in the struggle for the industrialization of the country. In his major novel *Parokhod idet v Yaffu i obratno* ("The Steamship Goes to Jaffa and Back," 1936), set in Palestine of the first third of the 20th century. Gekht describes positively the daily life of the *ḥalutzim,* accurately depicts the bloody attacks of the Arabs in Jerusalem and Jaffa, and reproduces at length passionate speeches of Zionists about assimilation and antisemitism. Some Soviet critics accused the novel of manifesting "camouflaged Zionism."

During World War II Gekht was military correspondent for the newspaper *Gudok.* At the end of the 1940s his works were suppressed but he was rehabilitated in 1956.

Gekht maintained his Jewish themes throughout his career (see *Budka solov'ya* ("Nightingale Booth," 1957), or *Dolgi serdtsa* ("Debts of the Heart," 1963)). His heroes are Jews whose lives are ruined by the war. Even his works in which the characters are non-Jews contain tragic motifs concerning the destruction of Ukrainian Jewry, with references to Babi Yar, the tractor factory in Kharkov (the site of another massacre of Ukrainian Jews), and so on. In 1960 Gekht wrote memoirs about E. Bagritsky, I. *Ilf, and others. He translated from Yiddish works by Sholem *Asch, Shalom *Aleichem, and M. *Daniel.

[Mark Kipnis / *The Shorter Jewish Encylopaedia in Russian*]

°GELASIUS I, pope, 492–6. A council convened in Rome by Gelasius in 494 established the Catholic canon of biblical texts. On a personal level, Gelasius was not hostile to the Jews; among his favorites was a Jew, Telesinus, who won the pope's trust to the extent that in 495 Gelasius recommended Telesinus' nephew, the Jew Antius or Antonius, to the bishop Quinigesius. In 496, when the pope was apprised that the slave of a Jew had claimed that, although he had been a Christian from childhood, his Jewish master had forced him to be circumcised, Gelasius ordered the investigators to act with scrupulous justice so that religious interests should not be wronged nor the slave unfairly removed from his master's authority.

BIBLIOGRAPHY: Vogelstein-Rieger, 127f.; B. Blumenkranz, *Auteurs chrétiens latins* (1963), 48f.

[Bernhard Blumenkranz]

GELB, ARTHUR (1924–), U.S. journalist and author. Born in New York, the son of immigrants from Ukraine, Gelb was educated at the City College of New York and at New York University. He was hired by *The New York Times* as a copyboy, the lowest newsroom job, in 1944 and made a mark by founding an in-house newsletter, *Timesweek*, which brought him to the attention of people who could promote him. He became a general assignment reporter and then gravitated to the drama department, where he became assistant drama critic in 1958, working under Brooks Atkinson, the paper's chief critic, and hoped to succeed him. Instead, he became chief cultural correspondent, serving from 1961 to 1963. In addition to reviewing Broadway and Off Broadway theater, Gelb wrote stories on little-known performers like Woody *Allen, Barbra *Streisand, and others. At the same time, Gelb began working with his wife, Barbara, the stepdaughter of the playwright S.N. *Behrman, on the first definitive biography of the American playwright Eugene O'Neill. The book, published in 1962, and called simply *O'Neill*, became a bestseller. It had taken the Gelbs six years to research and write the book.

When Gelb's close friend A.M.*Rosenthal was named metropolitan editor of *The Times*, Gelb was installed as his deputy. In 1967 he succeeded Rosenthal and then rose to assistant managing editor, deputy managing, and finally managing editor from 1986 as Rosenthal moved up to executive editor of *The Times.* Their professional closeness reached a crescendo with their coverage of the killing of Kitty Genovese, a young woman in Kew Garden, Queens, whose final screams were heard by 38 people who chose not to call the police. Gelb also helped expose a local member of the American Nazi Party, who was, in fact, Jewish. When his background was made known, the man, Daniel Burros, committed suicide.

During his tenure as metropolitan editor, Gelb was a fount of ideas, nurtured the careers of countless *Times* reporters and editors, and passionately presided over the coverage of dozens of important stories, from the New York City fiscal crisis of the mid-1970s through political campaigns, a major exposure of police corruption in New York, and disasters such as airplane crashes. Along the way Gelb and Rosenthal wrote and edited several travel books. After his tenure as managing editor, Gelb became president of The New York Times Foundation and dispensed thousands of dollars each year to cultural organizations, educational groups, and organizations dealing with disadvantaged youth. He also founded a *Times* scholarship program for high school students and headed it until he was past 80 years of age.

Thirty-five years after the O'Neill biography was published, the Gelbs decided to revisit O'Neill and write a new biography. The first of three volumes, *O'Neill: Life with Monte Cristo*, was published in 2000. The Gelbs were also working with the documentary filmmaker Ric Burns on an O'Neill series for public television. In 2003, *City Room*, a memoir, recalled Gelb's career and key decisions in the news room of *The Times*. In 2005, one of his two sons, Peter, was named general manager of the Metropolitan Opera in New York.

[Stewart Kampel (2nd ed.)]

GELB, IGNACE JAY (1907–1985), U.S. Assyriologist. Born in Tarnow, Poland, Gelb studied in Rome with the Sumerologist, Anton Deimel. In 1929 he went to the Oriental Institute at the University of Chicago, with which he remained associated. After serving in the armed forces in World War II, he returned to the Institute as professor of Assyriology in 1947 and began the reorganization and replanning of the monumental multi-volume dictionary of the Akkadian language entitled *Assyrian Dictionary of the Oriental Institute of the University of Chicago* (= CAD, 1956ff.; almost complete by 2005) a project which had been begun in 1921. He served as editor of the dictionary from 1947 to 1955. He was also the editor and chief contributor of the auxiliary project, *Materials for the Assyrian Dictionary* (from 1951). His contributions to the field of Assyriology are centered on the ethno-linguistic foundations of the Ancient Near East. Among his works on this subject are *Hurrians and Subarians* (1944); *Nuzi Personal Names* (with M. Puryes and A.A. MacRae, 1943); *La lingua degli Amoriti* (1958); "The Early History of the West Semitic Peoples" (in: *Journal of Cuneiform Studies*, 15 (1961), 27ff.). Of fundamental importance are his penetrating studies of the Old Akkadian dialect: *Sargonic Texts from the Diyala Region* (1952), *Old Akkadian Writing and Grammar* (1952, 1961[2]), *Glossary of Old Akkadian* (1957), and *A Sequential Reconstruction of the Proto-Akkadian* (1969). He published a popular scientific work, *A Study of Writing* (1952, 1965[2]). After Gelb's death his personal library and his papers and unfinished manuscripts became the basis of the Gelb Memorial Library of the University of California.

BIBLIOGRAPHY: Chicago University, Oriental Institute, *Assyrian Dictionary*, 1 (1956), introd. **ADD. BIBLIOGRAPHY:** J. Hayes, in: *Orientalia*, 42 (1973), 1–8 (bibliography of Gelb's publications).

[Evasio de Marcellis and Pinhas Artzi]

GELB, MAX (1907–1987), U.S. rabbi. Born in Austria, Gelb immigrated to New York City with his parents at the age of seven. He was educated at Yeshiva Rabbi Chaim Berlin and Yeshiva Yitzhak Elchanan, earned his B.A. from City College in 1929, and was ordained by the Jewish Theological Seminary in 1932. His first pulpit was in Harrisburg, PA (1933–39), a congregation that was undergoing financial difficulties as well as problems of morale in post-depression America. He strengthened the education and youth activities of his congregation, thereby gaining the support of their parents. He left that congregation in significantly better condition than when he had assumed the pulpit. He moved to White Plains, NY, where he was rabbi of Temple Israel, a suburban congregation before the onset of suburbanization. Within a decade membership had grown fourfold. He fought for strong Jewish programming within his congregation at a time when other rabbis were seeking to attract young people without regard to the content of what happened once they entered the building. He became a leader in Westchester Jewish communal life. An ardent Zionist, he was president of the White Plains Region of the Zionist Organization of America and president of the West Council of Rabbis. He helped establish with Orthodox colleagues the first day school in Westchester County and then broke with the school to establish in 1965 the Solomon Schechter School, more akin to his own brand of Conservative Judaism. Among his achievements was finding the compromise language by which the Conservative liturgy rewrote the morning blessing, recited by men praising God for not making them a woman and women praising God for making them according to His will. His solution was as elegant as it was simple. Both men and women praise God for creating them in the Divine image.

He edited *Understanding Conservative Judaism*, essays by Robert Gordis, which were part of a Rabbinical Assembly series on Conservative Jewish Thought. Upon his death, he was still working on the English translation of Abraham Joshua Heschel's *Torah Min Shamayim*, a project that was brought to conclusion by his successor at Temple Israel, Rabbi Gordon Tucker, and published as *Heavenly Torah: As Refracted by the Generations* (2005).

BIBLIOGRAPHY: P.S. Nadell, *Conservative Judaism in America: A Biographical Dictionary and Sourcebook* (1988); *Proceedings of the Rabbinical Assembly* (1989).

[Michael Berenbaum (2nd ed.)]

GELBER, Canadian family. MOSES GELBER (1876–1940), born in Brzezany, Galicia, settled in Toronto in 1892, where he established a wool importing business. He was a founder of Jewish education in Toronto, serving as first president of the Toronto Hebrew Free School (later the Associated Hebrew Schools). A vice president of the Zionist Organization of Canada, Gelber was among the first supporters of the project to reclaim the Sharon Valley in Palestine. His son EDWARD ELISHA (1903–1971) was born in Toronto. He studied at Columbia and the Jewish Theological Seminary, and was admitted to the Ontario bar (1934) and the Palestine bar (1937). Gelber played a leading role in Jewish education in Toronto; in the Canadian Jewish Congress; and in the Zionist Organization of Canada, of which he was national president in 1950–52. In 1954 he moved to Jerusalem where he served as chairman of the executive of the Hebrew University, and vice chairman of Yad Vashem.

LOUIS GELBER (1878–1968) brother of Moses, was born in Brzezany, Galicia, and in 1896 went to Canada where he was associated in business with his brother Moses. He was a founder of the Toronto Hebrew Free Loan Association. His son LIONEL MORRIS (1907–1989), born in Toronto, was a writer on international affairs. Lionel Gelber was a Rhodes scholar and studied at Oxford. He wrote *Rise of Anglo-American Friendship* (1938), *Peace by Power* (1942), *Reprieve from War* (1950), *American Anarchy* (1953), and *Alliance of Necessity* (1966). He served as special assistant to Canadian Prime Minister John Diefenbaker during 1960–61. Louis' daughter SYLVA (1910–2003) was born in Toronto. During 1934–37 she was a social worker in Jerusalem and became probation officer in the Magistrate's Court, appointed to the department of labor of the Palestine government in 1942. She joined the Department of National Health and Welfare in Ottawa in 1950, and in 1969 was appointed head of the women's bureau of the Canadian Department of Labour. Her brother MARVIN (1912–1990), also born in Toronto, was a student of economics and politics. He wrote for various journals and was a Liberal member of parliament for York South (1963–65). He was national president of the United Nations Association of Canada; head of the Canadian delegation to the U.N. Economic and Social Council (1967); and delegate to the U.N. General Assembly (1968). He was closely associated with Zionist and Jewish community activity. Another brother ARTHUR E. (1915–1998), born in Toronto, was a Jewish community leader. He was president of the United Jewish Welfare Fund of Toronto and active in the United Jewish Appeal, Canadian Jewish Congress, and United Jewish Refugee Agencies. He took a leading role in settling Jewish refugees in Canada in the post-World War II period. Prominent in cultural activities in Canada, he was president of the Canadian Conference of the Arts and the National Ballet. A fourth brother SHOLOME MICHAEL (1918–), born in Toronto, served in the RCAF during World War II. He then worked for the Joint Distribution Committee in postwar Europe. He served as dean of the Academy for Higher Jewish Religion in New York, and then in 1966 began teaching at New York University in the department of religion. He wrote *Failure of the American Rabbi* (1961).

BIBLIOGRAPHY: A.D. Hart (ed.), *Jew in Canada* (1926), 133, 319; *Who's Who in Canadian Jewry* (1965), 310, 387.

[Ben G. Kayfetz]

GELBER, JACK (1932–2003), U.S. playwright and director. Gelber achieved international success with *The Connection* (1959), which dealt with drug addiction. Its subject (drug addicts waiting for their "connection" to buy drugs), raw language, and a renovating realism (for example, actors cadging money from the audience) vitalized both theater-goers and a generation of writers. It also made the Living Theater, at whose center were Judith Malina and Julian Beck, a focus of attention. Among his plays are *The Apple* (1961), *Square in the Eye* (1964), *The Cuban Thing* (1968), *Sleep* (1972), and *Rehearsal*, first produced in 1976. In 1964, his novel *On Ice* was published.

[Lewis Fried (2nd ed.)]

GELBER, NATHAN MICHAEL (1891–1966), Austrian historian and Zionist leader. Gelber was born in Lvov, Galicia and studied at the universities of Vienna and Berlin. He served in World War I as an officer in the Austro-Hungarian army; thereafter he assumed the post of general secretary of the Eastern Galician delegation of the Va'ad Le'ummi in Vienna (1918–21) and, subsequently, became an active participant in the Austrian Pro-Palestine Committee and first secretary of the Austrian Zionist Organization (1921–30). In 1934 he immigrated to Palestine where, until his retirement in 1954, he worked in the Keren Hayesod head office in Jerusalem. His last years were devoted to Jewish scholarship, which he had pursued extensively, though not professionally, all his life.

Gelber was a prolific author who published close to 1,000 books and articles in Hebrew, German, Yiddish, and Polish on Jewish history and contemporary Jewish life, in addition to scores of articles on contemporary issues in daily newspapers. He was a major contributor to the *Juedisches Lexikon*, the *Encyclopaedia Judaica*, the *Encyclopaedia Hebraica*, and other encyclopedias. His most significant works deal with the history of Zionism and Galician Jewry. Among them are *Zur Vorgeschichte des Zionismus* (1927); *Haẓharat Balfour ve-Toledoteha* (1939); *Toledot ha-Tenu'ah ha-Ẓiyyonit be-Galiẓyah, 1875–1918* (2 vols., 1958); *Aktenstuecke zur Judenfrage am Wiener Kongress 1814–1815* (1920); *Die Juden und der polnische Aufstand* (1923); a volume on Brody (vol. 6 of *Arim ve-Immahot be-Yisrael*, 1955); and "*Toledot Yehudei Lvov*" (in EG, 4 (1956), 22–390). After his death his article "History of the Jews in Kalisch" (*Kalisch Book*, vol. 2) was published, in 1968.

BIBLIOGRAPHY: H. Gold, in: *Sefer ha-Yovel le-Nathan Michael Gelber* (1963), 235–64.

[Michael A. Meyer / Bjoern Siegel (2nd ed.)]

GELBHAUS, SIGMUND (**Joshua Samuel**; c. 1850–1928), East European rabbi and writer. Gelbhaus was born in Tysmienica (Galicia) and served as rabbi in Karlovac (Karlstadt, Croatia), Nordhausen (Germany), Prague, and Vienna. In Vienna he also lectured at the Israelitisch-Theologische Lehranstalt and at the Hebrew Paedagogium. A prolific writer, he published numerous articles, books, and translations into Hebrew. Among them are *Rabbi Jehuda Hanassi und die Redaktion der Mischna* (1876), *Die Mittelhochdeutsche Dichtung in ihrer Beziehung zur biblisch-rabbinischen Literatur* (3 vols., 1889–93), *Esra und seine reformatorischen Bestrebungen* (1903), *Religioese Stroemungen in Judaea waehrend und nach der Zeit des babylonischen Exils* (1912), and *Die Metaphysik der Ethik Spinozas im Quellenlichte der Kabbala* (1917).

BIBLIOGRAPHY: Wininger, Biog, 2 (1928), 399; 6 (1931), 614.

GELBRUN, ARTUR (1913–1985), composer and conductor. Born in Warsaw and educated in his native city and in Italy, Gelbrun settled in Israel in 1949 and became a teacher at the Rubin Academy of Music, Tel Aviv. He regularly conducted most of the orchestras in Israel as well as in Europe. His compositions include two symphonies, chamber music, ballets, orchestral suites, and songs with orchestra.

[Jehoash Hirshberg (2nd ed.)]

GELDERN, SIMON VON (1720–1788), German adventurer and traveler. Von Geldern, who was born in Duesseldorf into a family of Court Jews (see Van *Geldern), studied at yeshivot, and also acquired a secular education. He went wandering through many countries and eventually reached Palestine where he spent six months studying the Kabbalah in Safed. Armed with letters of recommendation from Safed scholars headed with the words *Kitvei Kodesh u-Meliẓot Ḥakhamei Yisrael* (printed in Amsterdam, c. 1759) and with contributions from public and private charity chests, he set off on another journey, calling himself "an emissary from the Holy Land." Von Geldern engaged in the book trade, mainly selling copies of the *Zohar. Assuming the title of "Chevalier von Geldern" and posing as an Oriental sage, he led a life of adventure, gambling, and the pursuit of amorous affairs in Christian society and among royalty. His grandnephew, Heinrich *Heine, speaks admiringly of his exploits in North Africa. Von Geldern was the first person to mention the Cairo *Genizah*. He made an English adaptation, entitled *The Israelites on Mount Horeb* (1773), of a French oratorio by the Abbé de Voisinon, which in its turn was based on the Italian original by a fellow adventurer, Giacomo Casanova. Von Geldern also published a Hebrew version of the Book of Judith. He spent the last ten years of his life in the service of the grand duke of Hesse-Darmstadt. He provided Abbé *Gregoire with the material for his *Essai sur la regénération physique, morale et politique des Juifs* (1789). Von Geldern's travel diaries (facsimile of Ms. (original probably lost) in Schocken Library, Jerusalem) and his personal papers, including a family tree, have survived.

BIBLIOGRAPHY: F. Heymann, *Der Chevalier von Geldern* (19632); Brilling, in: BLBI, 8 (1965), 315ff; D. Kaufmann, *Aus Heinrich Heines Ahnensaal* (1896); *Archiv fuer juedische Familienforschung*, 1 nos. 2–3 (1913), 18ff., nos. 4–6, 32ff; Loewenstein, in: MGWJ, 51 (1907), 205ff.; idem, in: JJLG, 10 (1912), 121; Yaari, Sheluḥei, 180, 446ff.

GELDERN, VAN, Duesseldorf family of *Court Jews. The prefix in the surname indicates the family's origin from the Dutch province or from the village near Duesseldorf where JOSEPH JACOB (Juspa) VAN GELDERN (1653–1727) established himself as supplier and banker to the elector of Hanover, who had made Duesseldorf his capital. Juspa maintained business connections with Leffmann *Behrends and his daughter married the son of Jost *Liebmann. He built a synagogue for the community, of which he was *Obervorgaenger* ("chief representative") for more than 30 years; he paid one tenth of the community's dues. His son, LAZARUS (d. 1769), inherited the office in the community and became Court Jew of *Juelich and *Berg, but lost most of the immense family fortune in lawsuits. Lazarus' son, GOTTSCHALK, was a prosperous physician whose daughter Betty married Samson Heine, descendant of the Schaumburg-*Lippe family of Court Jews. Their son Heinrich Heine, the poet, immortalized his great-uncle, the adventurer Simon van *Geldern, Lazarus' other son.

BIBLIOGRAPHY: D. Kaufmann, *Aus Heinrich Heine's Ahnensaal* (1896); G. Wilhelm (ed.), *Heine Bibliographie* (1960^2), 44f.; S. Stern, *The Court Jew* (1950), index; H. Bieber and M. Hadas, *Heinrich Heine, A Biographical Anthology* (1956), 38–40.

GELDMAN, MORDECHAI (1946–), Hebrew poet. Geldman was born in Germany and has lived in Tel Aviv since the age of three. He obtained a B.A. in literature and an M.A. in clinical psychology and worked as a psychotherapist. Geldman began publishing poetry in 1966 and his first poetry collection *Zeman ha-Yam u-Zeman Ha-Yabbashah* ("Sea Time, Land Time") appeared in 1970. This was followed by the collections: *Ẓippor* (1975), *Ḥalon* ("Window," 1980), *66–83* (1983), *Milano* (1988), *'Ayin* ("Eye," 1993), *Sefer Sheal* ("Book of Ask," 1997), *Shir ha-Lev* ("The Song of the Heart," 2004). Geldman's highly personal, often narcissist poetry, highlights the dialectics of the hidden and the overt, describes male-friendship and erotic attraction and reflects on dependence and loneliness. A Geldman poem accompanied by nine etchings by Moshe Gershuni appeared in 1997 under the title *Time*. Geldman also wrote two non-fiction books: "Dark Mirror" (1995) and *Sifrut u-Psikhologiyyah* ("Psychoanalytic Criticism," 1998). He published the collection *Shir ha-Lev* in 2004. Individual poems have been translated into a number of languages and information is available at the ITHL website, www.ithl.org.il.

BIBLIOGRAPHY: A. Barkai, "*Mas'a Toda'ati*," in: *Al ha-Mishmar* (December 19, 1980); Z. Shamir, in: *Maariv* (October 17, 1980); Sh. Levo, "*Shirat ha-Tavvas she-Avad ve-Nimẓa*, in: *Davar* (January 30, 1981); A. Feinberg, "M. Geldman's Poetry," in: *Modern Hebrew Literature*, 7 (1982); N. Calderon, "*Ḥamesh Reshimot*," in: *Siman Keriah*, 15 (1982), 20–37; G. Moked, "*Izzun al gabbei Ḥevel Matu'aḥ*," in: *Akhshav*, 47/48 (1983), 66–68; M. Knei-Paz, "*Le-Karev et ha-Raḥok*," in: *Yedioth Aharonoth* (July 13, 1984); Y. Ben David, "*Ha-Meshorer ke-Ẓoref Zahav*," in: *Ahavah mi-Mabbat Sheni* (1997), 199–205; U. Hollander, in: *Haaretz* (Feb. 18, 2004).

[Anat Feinberg (2nd ed.)]

GELFAND, IZRAIL MOISEVICH (1913–), Russian mathematician. Gelfand was born in Krasnye Okny (now Moldova) and obtained his Ph.D. at Moscow University (1938), where he was professor at the Academy of Sciences Institute of Mathematics from 1943. He worked mainly in Banach algebra, the representation theory of Lie groups related to quantum mechanics, and in solving the algebraic problems of mathematics applied to physics, subjects on which he published for over 60 years. His many honors include the Wolf Prize (1978) and election to the Russian National Academy of Sciences, the U.S National Academy of Sciences, and the Royal Society of London.

[Michael Denman (2nd ed.)]

GELFOND, ALEKSANDR OSIPOVICH (1906–1968), Soviet mathematician. Gelfond was appointed professor of mathematics at Moscow University in 1931. He made important contributions to number theory, complex analysis, and theory of transcendental numbers. Of his works, the following were translated into English: *The Solution of Equations in Integers* (1961) and *Transcendental and Algebraic Numbers* (1960).

GELFOND, ALEXANDER LAZAREVICH (pseud. **Parvus**; 1869–1924), activist in the Russian and German revolutionary movements. Gelfond was born in Berezino, Belorussia. He graduated from the Basel university in 1891 and lived in Germany, where he joined the left wing of the Social-Democratic movement, He wrote and edited periodicals for the movement and became known as a Marxist economist. In 1905 he returned to Russia, and became a member of the workers soviet in Peterburg. Together with Rosa *Luxemburg he developed the theory of the "permanent revolution," which was adopted by *Trotsky. In December 1905 he was arrested and exiled for three years to Siberia but fled to Germany. In 1910–17 he lived in Turkey and the Balkans, where he made a fortune in trade. During WWI he lived in Berlin and busied himself supplying the German army. He tried to get the German Foreign Office to support the Russian revolutionary parties and helped transfer German funds to them. He tried to return to Russia after the October 1917 Revolution, but was prevented from doing so by Lenin, who was afraid that Gelfond's financial transactions would be discovered. In 1918 he tried to settle in Switzerland, but was sent back to Germany and ceased his political activity. After his death he was accused by Lenin and Gorky of being "immoral, chauvinistic, and an adventurist in politics."

[Shmuel Spector (2nd ed.)]

GELIL YAM (Heb. גְּלִיל יָם), kibbutz in central Israel near Herzliyyah, affiliated with Ha-Kibbutz ha-Me'uḥad. It was founded in 1943 by a group which had maintained a transitory camp near Tel Aviv for over a decade, while working as hired laborers in the Tel Aviv port and on the railways. The founding settlers from Russia and Poland were later joined by immigrants from different countries. Its economy was based on a concrete plant and a factory producing household faucets. Its population was 310 in 1968 and 320 in 2002. The kibbutz stopped receiving new members due to privatization processes. It was located on one of the most highly valued tracts of land in Israel, with the city of Herzliyyah expanding around it over the years. Gelil Yam's name is based on the Arabic denomination of the site, Jalīl.

WEBSITE: www.glil-yam.org.il.

[Efraim Orni / Shaked Gilboa (2nd ed.)]

GELLÉRI, ANDOR ENDRE (1907–1945), Hungarian novelist. Gelléri, who was born in Budapest, worked as a dyer and as a locksmith. His literary talents were first discovered in a short-story competition run by the evening newspaper *Az Est*. His prize enabled him to complete his education in Germany. Gelléri's first novel, *Nagymosoda* ("The Laundry," 1931), combined reality with dreams and visions. His characters were wretched slum dwellers, some of them Jews. His other works include *Szomjas inasok* ("Thirsty Apprentices," 1933); a book of short stories, *Hold utca* ("Hold Street," 1934); *Kikötö* ("The Harbor," 1935); and *Villám és esti tüz* ("Lightning and Evening Fire," 1940). Following the Nazi occupation of Hungary he was sent to the Mauthausen concentration camp at the end of 1944 and died at the Wells camp in Germany, a victim of typhus, two days after the liberation in May 1945. Gelléri's autobiography, *Egy önérzet története* ("The Story of One Man's Self-Respect"), appeared posthumously in 1957.

BIBLIOGRAPHY: M. Szabolcsi (ed.), *A magyar irodalom története*, 6 (1964), 757–66; *Magyar Irodalmi Lexikon*, 1 (1963), 390–1.

[Baruch Yaron]

GELLÉRT, OSZKÁR (1882–1967), Hungarian poet and journalist. One of the editors of *Nyugat*, Gellért at first wrote biblical and religious verse but later turned to radical themes. His collections include *Ötven év verseiből* ("Selections from Fifty Years," 1952), *Emberség, Szerelem* ("Humanity, Love," 1957) and *Egy író élete* ("The Life of a Writer," 1958).

GELLMAN, LEON (1887–1973), U.S. Zionist journalist and leader. Gellman, who was born in Yampol, Russia, immigrated to the U.S. at the age of 23. He settled in St. Louis where he worked as a principal of various Hebrew schools (1911–17), and later as editor (1918–35) and publisher (1923–35) of the Yiddish *St. Louis Jewish Record*, in which he advocated the creation of a great religious Zionist movement. An organizer of the U.S. Mizrachi movement, he subsequently served as its executive secretary (1914–17), national vice president (1930–35), and president (1935–39). Moving to New York, he was editor of Mizrachi publications from 1935 to 1949, including *Der Mizrachi Weg* (1936–49) and (with Pinkhos Churgin) the *Mizrachi Jubilee Publication* (1936).

Gellman moved to Israel in 1949 and became chairman of the World Mizrachi Organization in that year, later becoming honorary chairman. From 1948 to 1953 he was a deputy member of the Executive of the Jewish Agency. He was a frequent contributor to *Ha-Ẓofeh*, the Israeli national religious daily, and to New York Yiddish newspapers. A prevalent theme in Gellman's writing is that the survival of Israel is contingent upon adherence to traditional Jewish faith and values. Among his numerous books, primarily collections of essays, are: *Eynem Kampf far der Yidishe Medine* (1948), *Ha-Yahadut be-Ma'avakah* (1956), *Neẓaḥ ha-Ummah* (1958), *Bi-Shevilei ha-Yahadut* (1967), and *Be-Darkhei No'am* (1969).

GELL-MANN, MURRAY (1929–), U.S. theoretical physicist. Born in New York City and educated at Yale, which he entered at the age of 15 (B.S. 1948), and Massachusetts Institute of Technology (Ph.D. 1951), Gell-Mann studied physics rather than the languages and archaeology he originally preferred, because his father, who ran a language school, warned him that he would never be able to make a living. Gell-Mann taught at the Institute for Nuclear Studies of the University of Chicago from 1952 to 1955, while studying under Enrico Fermi, and at California Institute of Technology from 1955 until his retirement as Robert Millikan Professor of Theoretical Physics, Emeritus, in 1993. He held numerous visiting professorships at American and European universities, was made a member of the National Academy of Sciences, a fellow of the American Physical Society and other academic institutions, and served on a number of official bodies including the President's Science Advisory Committee (1969–72), the Board of Regents of the Smithsonian Institution (1974–88), and the President's Committee of Advisors on Science and Technology (1994–2001). He was later a distinguished fellow at the Santa Fe Institute, a research foundation which he helped to found in 1982 in Santa Fe, New Mexico. He also taught part of the year at the University of New Mexico in Albuquerque.

Gell-Mann was awarded the Nobel Prize for physics in 1969 for his revolutionary work in particle physics, a field in which he was preeminent for over 20 years. The explanatory theory he formulated in 1963 accounted for the presence of the many particles discovered in atomic nuclei and posited that all such particles are composed of basic units that Gell-Mann named "quarks" (a word taken from one of his favorite books, James Joyce's *Finnegans Wake*), which his own and others' research indicated were one of three fundamental, irreducible building blocks of matter (the others are leptons and intermediate vector bosons). The existence of quarks, and the accuracy of Gell-Mann's theoretical prediction that there were likely six types, was confirmed by experimentation with particle accelerators in the 1980s and 1990s. Gell-Mann's work led to the development of the field theory of quantum chromodynamics, which describes the interactions of subatomic particles.

From the 1980s Gell-Mann, who had a well-deserved reputation as a polymath (he described his interests as including "natural history, historical linguistics, archaeology, history, depth psychology, and creative thinking, all subjects connected with biological evolution, cultural evolution, and learning and thinking"), tried to develop a theory of complex adaptive systems that would reflect his concerns about the environment: "restraint in population growth, sustainable economic development, and stability of the world political system." His 1994 book *The Quark and the Jaguar*, written for general readers rather than fellow scientists, had its origins in this concern. At the Santa Fe Institute he also headed the Evolution of Human Languages Program, which seeks to establish the historical relationships among human languages, on the assumption that all of them may belong to "superfamilies" derived from an original "proto-language" whose characteristics may be discovered.

Gell-Mann's publications include *Lectures on Weak Interactions of Strongly Interfacing Particles* (1961), *The Eightfold Way: A Review with a Collection of Reprints* (1964, with Yuval Ne'eman), *The Quark and the Jaguar* (1994), and two edited collections, *The Evolution of Human Languages* (1992, edited with John A. Hawkins) and *Understanding Complexity in the Prehistoric Southwest* (1994, edited with George J. Gumerman). In addition, a full-scale biography of Gell-Mann was published by George Johnson: *Strange Beauty: Murray Gell-Mann and the Revolution in 20th-Century Physics* (1999).

[Drew Silver (2nd ed.)]

GELLNER, FRANTIŠEK (1881–1914), Czech writer, poet, and cartoonist, and the outstanding satirist of his time. Born in Mladá Boleslav, Bohemia, into a poor family, Gellner studied painting first in Munich and then in Paris, where he published his early cartoons in *Rire, Cri de Paris*, and other French periodicals. He soon found, however, that he could express his anarchist creed better through the medium of verse, and his three books of poetry, modeled on the style of François Villon, contain some of the best satirical verse ever written in Czech. They are *Po nás at přijde potopa* (After us the Deluge, 1901), *Radosti života* (Pleasures of Life, 1903), and *Nové verše* (New Poems, 1919). In 1911 he joined the leading Czech newspaper *Lidové Noviny*, as a cartoonist and feature editor, and then began writing prose: his only novel, *Potulný národ* (Nation Errant, 1912), *Cesta do hor a jiné povídky* (Trip to the Mountains and Other Stories, 1914), and *Povídky a satiry* (Stories and Satires), which appeared in 1920 after his death. Because in many of his articles and short stories Gellner did not hesitate to subject Jewish weaknesses to the merciless lash of his satire, he has been criticized as an anti-Jewish writer. He disappeared while serving on the Russian front early in World War I. New editions of his works appeared in 1952, 1964, and in the 1990s.

BIBLIOGRAPHY: F. Gellner, *Spisy*, 3 (1928), postscript by M. Hýsek; P. Váša and A. Gregor, *Katechismus dějin české literatury* (1925); O. Donath, *Židé a Židovstvi v české literatuře 19. a 20. století*, 2 (1930), index. **ADD. BIBLIOGRAPHY:** F. Gellner, *Radosti života* (1974); A. Mikulášek et al., *Literatura s hvězdou Davidovou*, vol. 1 (1998); *Lexikon české literatury* 1 (1985).

[Avigdor Dagan / Milos Pojar (2nd ed.)]

GELMAN, JUAN (1930–), Argentinean poet. He was born in Buenos Aires into a family of immigrants from the Ukraine. His political involvement with the left since his youth went together with an active critical dissent, which made him break with the Communist Party in 1964 and with the Montonero Peronist Movement in 1979. In the 1960s he became a journalist in leading magazines and newspapers. He went into exile in Mexico in 1975. In 1976 his son and pregnant daughter-in-law were abducted and murdered by the military government; in 2000 he was able to locate his granddaughter in Montevideo. His poetry expresses his worldview and the tragedies of Argentina through a personal blend of social involvement and pure aesthetics. High poetic language intertwines with colloquial expressions, love poems alternate with protest texts, history and ideology with tiny events of daily life and common people. The poems of *dibaxu* ("Beneath," 1994) are written in Ladino, in which he saw a means of connecting his Spanish-speaking culture with Jewish identity. *Com/posiciones* ("Com/positions," 1984) includes his translations-rewritings of poems by Judah Halevi. Among his main books are *Violín y otras cuestiones* ("Violin and Other Matters," 1956); *Gotán* ("Tango," 1962); *Cólera buey* ("Ox-like Anger," 1963 and 1971); *Si dulcemente* ("If Sweetly," 1980); *Salarios del impío* ("Wages of the Godless," 1992); *Tantear la noche* ("Feeling Up the Night," 2000); *Incompletamente* ("Incompletely," 1997); and *Debí decir te amo* (*Antología personal*) ("I Should Have Said I Love You," personal anthology, 1997). Considered a leading poet of the Spanish-speaking world, among the many awards he received are the Argentine Nacional Poetry Prize (1997), the Mexican López Velarde Award (2004), the Iberoamerican Pablo Neruda Prize (2005), and the Queen Sofía Poetry Award in Spain (2005). His work has been translated into ten languages, including Hebrew.

BIBLIOGRAPHY: D.B. Lockhart, *Jewish Writers of Latin America. A Dictionary* (1997); M.C. Sillato, *Juan Gelman. Las estrategias de la otredad* (1996); R. Spiller, *Culturas del Río de la Plata (1973–1975):*

transgresión e intercambio (1995); S. Schreibman, *Selected Poems of Juan Gelman* (1990); L. Uribe, *La poesía de Juan Gelman* (1995).

[Florinda F. Goldberg (2nd ed.)]

GELMAN, MANUEL (1910–1993), Australian educator. Born in London, Gelman was taken to Australia as an infant. From 1946 to 1964 he was a lecturer in methods of modern languages at Melbourne University's Faculty of Education. From 1950 he headed the department of languages at the Secondary Teachers' College. From 1961 to 1964 Gelman was president of the Modern Languages Teachers' Associations of Victoria and founded the Australian Federation of Modern Language Teachers' Associations. His activities within the Jewish community included membership in the Board of Governors of Mount Scopus College, Melbourne (1959–61) and chairmanship of its Education Committee.

[Harry Freedman]

GELNHAUSEN, town in Germany. The Gelnhausen Jews paid their annual tax to the imperial treasury jointly with the Frankfurt community in 1241. In 1347 Emperor Louis IV offered the revenues from Gelnhausen Jewry as security on a loan. The community was annihilated during the *Black Death persecutions (1349) and the burghers were released from their debts to the Jews. By 1360 Jews had again settled in the town. In the late 17th century they were active as moneylenders, despite restrictions and threats of expulsion. A burial society was founded in 1711 and in 1734 the synagogue was rebuilt. The community then numbered 33 families. It remained approximately the same size in the 19th century (some 200 persons) and until the Nazi advent to power. The last Jew left Gelnhausen on Oct. 1, 1938. After World War II several Jews returned to the region but no organized community was formed. They numbered 27 in 1960.

BIBLIOGRAPHY: Roth, in: ZGJD, 5 (1892), 188; *Aus Alter und Neuer Zeit* (June 25, 1925); Germ Jud, 2 (1968), 273–5; FJW, 187; Yad Vashem Archives; PKG.

GELSENKIRCHEN, city in North Rhine-Westphalia, Germany. A community was established there in 1874 and a synagogue built in 1885. There were 120 Jews living in Gelsenkirchen in 1880, 1,171 in 1905, and 1,600 in 1933. The community maintained an elementary school which in 1906 had 121 pupils. Siegfried Galliner officiated as rabbi before World War II. In Gelsenkirchen, as in most Westphalian congregations, Reform Judaism was dominant but an Orthodox congregation was established with its own synagogue and institutions. For some time from 1922 the rabbi of the Association for the Safeguarding of Traditional Judaism in Westphalia (founded 1896) had his seat in Gelsenkirchen. Under the Nazi regime two-thirds of the Jews left. The synagogue was destroyed on *Kristallnacht*, Nov. 9, 1938. On January 27, 1942, 350 of the remaining 500 Jews were deported to the Riga ghetto. The last Jews were deported to Warsaw and Theresienstadt. By June 17, 1939, only 720 Jews remained. On Sept. 9, 1939, the men were deported to the *Sachsenhausen concentration camp. Their families followed in 1942. There were 69 Jews in Gelsenkirchen in 1946. In 1958, a synagogue and communal center was built for the newly established *Kultusgemeinde*. The community numbered 110 in 1967 – mostly new residents – and had its own cantor and teacher. In 2005 the Jewish population was around 450, with a new synagogue under construction.

BIBLIOGRAPHY: *Festschrift der Synagogen-Gemeinde Gelsenkirchen…* (1924); H.C. Meyer (ed.), *Aus Geschichte und Leben der Juden in Westfalen* (1962), 63–66, 162–3, 188, incl. bibl.; PKG. **ADD. BIBLIOGRAPHY:** S. Spector (ed.), *Jewish Life Before and During the Holocaust* (2001).

GEMARA (Aram. גְּמָרָא; lit. "completion" or "tradition"), a word popularly applied to the Talmud as a whole, or more particularly to the discussions and elaborations by the *amoraim* on the Mishnah. The word appears (abbreviated) in the printed editions of the Babylonian Talmud to indicate the beginning of that discussion and it has been adopted in the Vilna (Romm) edition of the Jerusalem Talmud. There is a *Gemara* to both the Babylonian and the Jerusalem Talmuds, though not to all or to the same tractates.

For a fuller discussion of the precise meaning of the word see *Talmud.

GEMARIAH (Heb. גְּמַרְיָהוּ, גְּמַרְיָה; "Yahu has accomplished"), two biblical figures.

(1) Gemariah son of Hilkiah was one of Zedekiah's emissaries to Nebuchadnezzar, who brought the letter written by Jeremiah to the elders in exile (Jer. 29:3). He is mentioned nowhere else. Although Jeremiah's father was also named Hilkiah that is probably coinicidental.

(2) Gemariah son of Shaphan was a high official in the time of Jehoiakim (Jer. 36:10). He was a member of one of the influential pro-Babylonian families in the last days of Judah (see *Shaphan), and was also one of the royal officers on friendly terms with Jeremiah. Baruch read Jeremiah's scroll in Gemariah's chamber (Jer. 36:10–12). The latter's son Micaiah reported this to Jehoiakim, who ordered the scroll destroyed after it was read to him. Gemariah was among the officials who tried to dissuade him. The mention of Gemariah's chamber in the Temple is interesting, yet the reason for his having one is not entirely clear. Such chambers were commonly intended for priests and levites (Neh. 10:38–39; 13:4–9; I Chron. 9:26, 33) and also for high officials of the king (II Kings 23:11; Jer. 35:4), but the purpose of these chambers is unknown (cf. I Sam. 9:22; Neh. 13:4–9). A bulla (stamp-seal impression) reading *lgmryhw [b]n špn*, "belonging to Gemariahu [so]n of Shaphan," was found in excavations in Jerusalem.

The name Gemariahu son of Hizziliahu occurs on the *Lachish Ostraca.

BIBLIOGRAPHY: Yeivin, in: *Tarbiz*, 12 (1940–41), 255, 257–8. **ADD. BIBLIOGRAPHY:** W. Holladay, *Jeremiah* 2 (1989), 140; S. Ahituv, *Handbook of Ancient Hebrew Inscriptions* (1992), 32–3, 128–29.

GEMATRIA (from Gr. γεωμετρία), one of the aggadic hermeneutical rules for interpreting the Torah (*Baraita of 32 Rules, no. 29). It consists of explaining a word or group of words according to the numerical value of the letters, or of substituting other letters of the alphabet for them in accordance with a set system. Whereas the word is normally employed in this sense of manipulating according to the numerical value, it is sometimes found with the meaning of "calculations" (Avot 3:18). Similarly where the reading in present editions of the Talmud is that Johanan b. Zakkai knew "the heavenly revolutions and *gematriot*," in a parallel source the reading is "the heavenly revolutions and calculations" (Suk. 28a; BB 134a; Ch. Albeck, *Shishah Sidrei Mishnah*, 4 (1959), 497).

The use of letters to signify numbers was known to the Babylonians and the Greeks. The first use of *gematria* occurs in an inscription of Sargon II (727–707 B.C.E.) which states that the king built the wall of Khorsabad 16,283 cubits long to correspond with the numerical value of his name. The use of *gematria* (τὸ ἰσόψηφον) was widespread in the literature of the Magi and among interpreters of dreams in the Hellenistic world. The *Gnostics equated the two holy names Abraxas (Ἀβράξας) and Mithras (Μίθρας) on the basis of the equivalent numerical value of their letters (365, corresponding to the days of the solar year). Its use was apparently introduced in Israel during the time of the Second Temple, even in the Temple itself, Greek letters being used to indicate numbers (Shek. 3:2).

In rabbinic literature numerical *gematria* first appears in statements by *tannaim* of the second century. It is used as supporting evidence and as a mnemonic by R. Nathan. He states that the phrase *Elleh ha-devarim* ("These are the words") occurring in Exodus 35:1 hints at the 39 categories of work forbidden on the Sabbath, since the plural *devarim* indicates two, the additional article a third, while the numerical equivalent of *elleh* is 36, making a total of 39 (Shab. 70a). R. Judah inferred from the verse, "From the fowl of the heavens until the beast are fled and gone" (Jer. 9:9), that for 52 years no traveler passed through Judea, since the numerical value of *behemah* ("beast") is 52. The Baraita of 32 Rules cites as an example of *gematria* the interpretation that the 318 men referred to in Genesis 14:14 were in fact only Eliezer the servant of Abraham, the numerical value of his name being 318. This interpretation, which occurs elsewhere (Ned. 32a; Gen. R. 43:2) in the name of *Bar Kappara, may also be a reply to the Christian interpretation in the Epistle of Barnabas that wishes to find in the Greek letters τιη, whose numerical value is 318, a reference to the cross and to the first two letters of Jesus' name, through which Abraham achieved his victory; the Jewish homilist used the same method to refute the Christian interpretation. These *gematriot* are based on the first of four methods of calculating the numeral value of the letters of the Hebrew alpha. Known as *Mispar Hekhreḥi*, absolute or normative value, each letter is given a specific numerical equivalent. *Alef* equals 1, *bet* equals 2, *gimmel* equals 3, and so on until *yod*, the tenth letter, which equals 10. The next letter, *kaf*, equals 20, then *lamed*, which equals 30, and so on until *kuf*, which equals 100. The last three letters, *resh, shin, taf*, equal 200, 300, and 400, respectively. The final forms of the letters, *kaf, mem, nun, pei*, and *ẓadi*, used when these letters appear at the very end of a word, are often given the same numerical equivalent as the standard form of the letter. Sometimes, they are given the values 500, 600, 700, 800, and 900, respectively. This brings the numerical equivalencies of the Hebrew alphabet to 1,000, for the *alef*, the first letter, can also symbolize 1,000. The word *alef* can also be read as *elef*, meaning 1,000.

The next two methods of *gematria* calculation are *Mispar Sidduri*, ordinal value, where each of the 22 letters of the Hebrew alphabet are given a number between 1 and 22, and *Mispar Katan*, reduced value, where every letter is equal to a single digit number. This is accomplished by removing the value of 10 or 100. Thus, the *alef* equals 1, but so do the *yod* and the *kuf*, which equal 10 and 100 in the absolute or normative value system. In these last two systems, the five letters that have final forms are usually given the same value as the standard form of the letter. At times, they are assigned special value.

The fourth method, *Mispar Katan Mispari*, integral reduced value, reduces the total value of the word to a single digit number. If the sum exceeds nine, then the integer values of the total are added together again and again until a single digit number is received. For example, the word, *ḥesed* (lovingkindness) has an absolute or normative value of 72. The *ḥet* equals 8, the *samakh* equals 60, and the *dalet* equals 4. The numbers of the sum of 72 are then added together (7 plus 2) to equal 9. It should be pointed out that the integral reduced value of the ordinal value and the reduced value of *ḥesed* also add up to 9.

In Kabbalah, an additional system of *gematria* is used. The absolute or normative value of a word is calculated by treating each letter as a word and then adding up all of the numerical equivalencies of these letter-words. This system is called *milu'i* or *milu'im*. Since some letters can be spelled differently as words, different numerical equivalencies can be achieved for a single word. Thus, the Tetragrammaton, *yod, hei, vav*, and *hei*, has the values of 72, 63, 45, or 52, each of which has vital significance in Kabbalah.

The form of *gematria* which consists of changing the letters of the alphabet according to *atbash*, i.e., the last letter ת is substituted for the first א, the penultimate ש for the second ב, etc., already occurs in Scripture: Sheshach (Jer. 25:26; 51:41) corresponding to Bavel ("Babylon"). The Baraita of 32 Rules draws attention to a second example: *lev kamai* (Jer. 51:1) being identical, according to this system, with *Kasdim. Another alphabet *gematria* is formed by the *atbaḥ* system, i.e., ט is substituted for א, ח for ב, etc., and is called "the alphabet of Ḥiyya" (Suk. 52b). Rav, the pupil of Ḥiyya, explained that Belshazzar and his men could not read the cryptic writing because it was written in *gematria*, i.e., according to *atbaḥ* (Sanh. 22a; cf. Shab. 104a).

Gematria has little significance in *halakhah*. Where it does occur, it is only as a hint or a mnemonic. The rule that when a man takes a nazirite vow for an unspecified period, it is regarded as being for 30 days, is derived from the word *yihyeh* ("he shall be") in Numbers 6:5, whose numerical value is 30 (Naz. 5a). Even in the *aggadah*, at least among the early *amoraim*, *gematria* is not used as a source of ideas and homilies but merely to express them in the most concise manner. The statements that Noah was delivered not for his own sake but for the sake of Moses (Gen. R. 26:6), that Rebekah was worthy to have given birth to 12 tribes (*ibid.* 63:6), and that Jacob's ladder symbolizes the revelation at Sinai (*ibid.* 68:12), do not depend on the *gematriot* given there. These homilies are derived from other considerations and it is certain that they preceded the *gematriot*.

Gematriot, however, do occupy an important place in those Midrashim whose chief purpose is the interpretation of letters, such as the *Midrash Ḥaserot vi-Yterot*, and also in the late aggadic Midrashim (particularly in those whose authors made use of the work of *Moses b. Isaac ha-Darshan), including *Numbers Rabbah* (in *Midrash Aggadah*, published by S. Buber, 1894) and *Bereshit Rabbati* (published by Ḥ. Albeck, 1940; see introduction, 11–20). Rashi also cites *gematriot* that "were established by Moses ha-Darshan" (Num. 7:18) and some of the *gematriot* given by him came from this source even if he does not explicitly mention it (Gen. 32:5, e.g., "I have sojourned with Laban" – the *gematria* value of "I have sojourned" is 613, i.e., "I sojourned with the wicked Laban but observed the 613 precepts," is the interpretation of Moses ha-Darshan, *Bereshit Rabbati*, 145). Joseph *Bekhor Shor, one of the great French exegetes of the Torah, made extensive use of *gematriot*, and nearly all the tosafists followed him in this respect in their Torah commentaries (S. Poznański, *Mavo al Ḥakhmei Ẓarefat Mefareshei ha-Mikra*, 73). A wealth of *gematriot* occur in *Pa'ne'aḥ Raza*, the commentary of Isaac b. Judah ha-Levi (end of 13th century), and in the *Ba'al ha-Turim*, the biblical commentary of *Jacob b. Asher. The Kabbalah of the *Ḥasidei Ashkenaz also caused *gematriot* to enter the *halakhah*. In his *Ha-Roke'aḥ*, *Eleazar of Worms uses *gematriot* to find many hints and supports for existing laws and customs; with him the *gematria* at times embraces whole sentences. Thus he establishes by *gematria* from Exodus 23:15 that work which can be deferred until after the festival may not be performed during the intermediate days (*Ha-Roke'aḥ*, no 307). *Gematriot* of the Ḥasidei Ashkenaz occupy a prominent place in their commentaries on the liturgy and on *piyyutim*. Abraham b. Azriel incorporated the teachings of Judah he-Ḥasid and Eleazar Roke'aḥ in his *Arugat ha-Bosem*, and followed their lead. These *gematriot*, which were part of the Kabbalah of the Ḥasidei Ashkenaz, established the definitive text of the prayers, which came to be regarded as sacrosanct. Some authorities forbade it to be changed even when the text did not conform with the rules of grammar. *Naḥmanides, on the other hand, tried to limit the arbitrary use of *gematriot* and laid down a rule that "no one may calculate a *gematria* in order to deduce from it something that occurs to him. Our rabbis, the holy sages of the Talmud, had a tradition that definite *gematriot* were transmitted to Moses to serve as a mnemonic for something that had been handed down orally with the rest of the Oral Law… just as was the case with the *gezerah shavah* [see *Hermeneutics] of which they said that no man may establish a *gezerah shavah* of his own accord" (*Sefer ha-Ge'ullah* ed. by J.M. Aronson (1959), *Sha'ar* 4; see his commentary to Deut. 4:25).

Despite *Naḥmanides' attempt to limit its use, *gematria* found its way into biblical commentary. The *Pane'aḥ Raza* by Isaac ben Judah ha-Levi (late 13th century) and *Ba'al ha-Turim* by Jacob ben Asher (c. 1270 to 1340) both make frequent use of *gematria*. Indeed, *gematria* became a staple element in kabbalastic literature. For example, the 17th-century work, *Megalleh Amukkot*, by Nathan Nata ben Solomon Spira, uses *gematria* extensively. The followers of *Shabbetai Zevi used *gematria* as proof of his messianism.

Gematria is still used to this very day. Indeed a search on the "Google" internet search engine reveals over 106,000 references to *gematria* on the World Wide Web, a great number of these sites deal with Christianity, witchcraft, and general (non-Jewish) mysticism. Numerous contemporary Jewish books have been published about *gematria* as well as assisting the reader to find his own *gematria* equivalencies. For instance, one such book, *Sefer Gematrikon* (Jerusalem, 1990) provides *gematria* equivalents for the numbers 1 to 1,000.

[*Encyclopaedia Hebraica* / David Derovan (2nd ed.)]

In Kabbalah

The use of *gematria* was developed especially by the Ḥasidei Ashkenaz and circles close to them in the 12th and 13th centuries. It is possible that traditions of *gematriot* of Holy Names and angels are from an earlier date, but they were collected and considerably elaborated only in the aforesaid period. Even among the mystics *gematria* is not generally a system for the discovery of new thoughts: almost always the idea precedes the inventing of the *gematria*, which serves as "an allusion *asmakhta." An exception is the *gematria* on the Holy Names, which are in themselves incomprehensible, or that on the names of angels whose meaning and special aspect the German Ḥasidim sought to determine via *gematria*. Often *gematria* served as a mnemonic device. The classic works of *gematria* in this circle are the writings of *Eleazar of Worms, whose *gematriot* are based – at any rate partially – on the tradition of his teachers. Eleazar discovered through *gematria* the mystical meditations on prayers which can be evoked during the actual repetition of the words. His commentaries on books of the Bible are based for the most part on this system, including some which connect the midrashic legends with words of the biblical verses via *gematria*, and some which reveal the mysteries of the world of the *Merkabah ("fiery chariot") and the angels, in this way. In this interpretation the *gematria* of entire biblical verses or parts of verses occupies a more outstanding place than the *gematria* based on a count of single words. For example, the numerical value of the sum of the letters of the entire verse "I have gone down into the nut garden" (Songs 6:11), in *gematria* is equivalent to the verse: "This is the depth of the chariot" (*merkavah*). Several extensive works of interpretation by means of *gematria* by the disciples of Eleazar of Worms are preserved in manuscript.

In the beginnings of Sephardi Kabbalah *gematria* occupied a very limited place. The disciples of *Abraham b. Isaac of Narbonne and the kabbalists of Gerona hardly used it and its impact was not considerable on the greater part of the Zohar and on the Hebrew writings of *Moses b. Shem Tov de Leon. Only those currents influenced by the tradition of the Ḥasidei Ashkenaz brought the *gematria* into the kabbalistic literature of the second half of the 13th century, mainly in the work of *Jacob b. Jacob ha-Kohen and Abraham *Abulafia and their disciples. The works of Abulafia are based on the extensive and extreme use of *gematria*. His books require deciphering before all the associations of the *gematriot* in them can be understood. He recommended the system of developing power of association in *gematria* to discover new truths, and these methods were developed by those who succeeded him. A summary of his system is found in *Sullam ha-Aliyyah* by Judah *Albotini, who lived a generation after the Spanish expulsion (*Kirjath Sefer*, 22 (1945–46), 161–71). A disciple of Abulafia, Joseph *Gikatilla, used *gematria* extensively as one of the foundations of the Kabbalah in *Ginnat Egoz* (Hanau, 1615; the letters *gimmel, nun, tav* of *Ginnat* are the initials of *gematria notarikon*, and *temurah* – the interchange of letters according to certain systematic rules). This work influenced considerably the later Zohar literature, *Ra'aya Meheimna* and *Tikkunei Zohar*.

Two schools emerged as the Kabbalah developed: one of those who favored *gematria*, and another of those who used it less frequently. In general, it may be stated that new ideas always developed outside the realm of *gematria*; however, there were always scholars who found proofs and wide-ranging connections through *gematria*, and undoubtedly attributed to their findings a positive value higher than that of a mere allusion. Moses *Cordovero presented his entire system without recourse to *gematria*, and explained matters of *gematria* only toward the end of his basic work on Kabbalah (*Pardes Rimmonim*). A revival of the use of *gematria* is found in the Lurianic Kabbalah, but it is more widespread in the kabbalistic works of Israel *Sarug and his disciples (mainly Menahem Azariah of *Fano and Naphtali *Bacharach, author of *Emek ha-Melekh*) than in the works of Isaac *Luria and Ḥayyim *Vital. The classic work using *gematria* as a means of thought and a development of commentative ideas in the Kabbalah in the 17th century is *Megalleh Amukkot* by Nathan Nata b. Solomon Spira, which served as the model for an entire literature, especially in Poland. At first only the part on Deut. 3:23ff. was published (Cracow, 1637) which explains these passages in 252 different ways. His commentary on the whole Torah (also called *Megalleh Amukkot*) was published in Lemberg in 1795. Apparently Nathan possessed a highly developed sense for numbers, which found its expression in complex structures of *gematria*. In later kabbalistic literature (in the 18th and 19th centuries) the importance of the methods of commentary via *gematria* is well-known and many works were written whose major content is *gematria*, e.g., *Tiferet Yisrael* by Israel Ḥarif of Satanov (Lemberg, 1865), *Berit Kehunnat Olam* by Isaac Eisik ha-Kohen (Lemberg, 1796; complete edition with commentary of *gematria*, 1950), and all the works of Abraham b. Jehiel Michal ha-Kohen of Lask (late 18th century).

In the Shabbatean movement, *gematriot* occupied a place of considerable prominence as proofs of the messianism of *Shabbetai Ẓevi. Abraham *Yakhini wrote a great work of Shabbatean *gematriot* on one single verse of the Torah (*Vavei ha-Ammudim*, Ms. Oxford), and the major work of the Shabbatean prophet Heshel *Zoref of Vilna and Cracow, *Sefer ha-Ẓoref*, is based entirely on an elaboration of *gematriot* surrounding the verse *Shema Yisrael* ("Hear O Israel"; Deut. 6:4). In ḥasidic literature *gematria* appeared at first only as a by-product, but later there were several ḥasidic rabbis, the bulk of whose works are *gematria*, e.g., *Igra de-Khallah* by Ẓevi Elimelekh Shapira of *Dynow (1868), *Magen Avraham* by Abraham the Maggid of Turisk (1886), and *Sefer Imrei No'am* by Meir Horowitz of Dzikow (1877).

The systems of *gematria* became complicated in the course of time. In addition to the numerical value of a word, different methods of *gematria* were used. In Ms. Oxford 1,822, one article lists 75 different forms of *gematriot*. Moses Cordovero (*Pardes Rimmonim*, part 30, ch. 8) lists nine different types of *gematriot*. The important ones are the following:

(1) The numerical value of one word (equaling the sum of the numerical value of all its letters) is equal to that of another word (e.g., גבורה (*gevurah*) = 216 = אריה (*aryeh*)).

(2) A small or round number which does not take into account tens or hundreds (4 = ת; 2 = כ).

(3) The squared number in which the letters of the word are calculated according to their numerical value squared. The Tetragrammaton, יהו"ה $= 10^2 + 5^2 + 6^2 + 5^2 = 186 =$ מקום ("Place"), another name for God.

(4) The adding up of the value of all of the preceding letters in an arithmetical series (ד (*dalet*) = 1 + 2 + 3 + 4 = 10). This type of calculation is important in complicated *gematria* that reaches into the thousands.

(5) The "filling" (Heb. *millui*); the numerical value of each letter itself is not calculated but the numerical values of all the letters that make up the names of the letter are calculated (בי"ת = 412; דל"ת = 434; יו"ד = 20). The letters ה and ו have different "fillings" – הו, הה, הא and וו, ואו, ויו; *millui de-alefin* (*alef* "filling"), *millui de-he'in* (*he* "filling"), or *millui de-yudin* (*yod* "filling"), respectively. These are important in Kabbalah with regard to the numerical value of the Name of God (יהו"ה), the Tetragrammaton, which varies according to the four different "fillings" יוד, הא, ואו, הא (= 45, in *gematria* אָדָם (Adam), symbolizing the 45-letter Name of God); יוד, הה, וו, הה (= 52, in *gematria* ב"ן, representing the Holy Name of 52 letters); יוד, הי, ואו, הי (= 63, in *gematria* ס"ג, the 63-letter Name);

יוד, הי, ויו, הי (= 72, in *gematria* ע"ב, representing the Holy Name of 72 letters).

Other calculations in *gematria* involve a "filling" of the "filling," or a second "filling." The *gematria* of the word itself is called *ikkar* or *shoresh*, while the rest of the word (the "fillings") is called the *ne'elam* ("hidden part"). The *ne'elam* of the letter י is וד = 10; the *ne'elam* of שד"י is ין, לת and וד = 500.

(6) There is also a "great number" that counts the final letters of the alphabet as a continuation of the alphabet (500 = ם; 600 = ן; 700 = ץ; 800 = ף; 900 = ך). However, there is a calculation according to the usual order of the alphabet whereby the numerical values of the final letters are as follows: ך = 500, ם = 600, ן = 700, etc.

(7) The addition of the number of letters in the word to the numerical value of the word itself, or the addition of the number "one" to the total numerical value of the word.

Criticism of the use of *gematria* as a justified means of commentary was first voiced by Abraham *Ibn Ezra (in his commentary on Gen. 14:14) and later by the opponents of the Kabbalah (in *Ari Nohem*, ch. 10). But even several kabbalists (e.g., *Naḥmanides) warned against exaggerated use of *gematria*. Joseph Solomon *Delmedigo speaks of false *gematriot* in order to abolish the value of that system. When the believers in Shabbetai Ẓevi began to widely apply *gematriot* to his name (*shaddai* (God) and its "filling" = 814), those who denied him used mock *gematriot* (*ru'aḥ sheker* = ("false spirit") = 814). In spite of this, the use of *gematria* was widespread in many circles and among preachers not only in Poland but also among the Sephardim. To this day the homiletical and allegorical literature according to the method of *Pardes (the four levels of meaning of a text), especially of the North African rabbis, is full of *gematria*.

[Gershom Scholem]

According to the findings of Stephen Lieberman, a variety of techniques similar to gematria are found already in Mesopotamia. Among the *Ḥasidei Ashkenaz books devoted to the *gematria'ot* found in the Bible are known, as is the case with R. *Judah he-Ḥasid, and his descendant R. *Eleazar ha-Darshan (Ms. Munchen 221). An interesting example of wide-ranging gematria in most of its varieties is found in the manuscript writings of a contemporary of Eleazar of Worms, R. Nehemiah ben Solomon the Prophet, which reflect the centrality of this technique outside the circle of Kalonymide esotericism in Worms. One of the most famous *gematriot*, *Elohim = teva* = 86, presumably had an influence on Spinoza's philosophy.

[Moshe Idel (2nd ed.)]

BIBLIOGRAPHY: W. Bacher, *Exegetische Terminologie…*, 1 (1899), 125–8; 2 (1905), 124; F. Dornseiff, *Das Alphabet in Mystik und Magie* (1925[2]), 91–118; A. Berliner, *Ketavim Nivḥarim*, 1 (1945), 34–37; S. Lieberman, *Hellenism in Jewish Palestine* (1950), 69–74; H. Waton, *Key to the Bible* (1952); T. Wechsler, *Ẓefunot be-Masoret Yisrael* (1968); Scholem, Mysticism, index; S.A. Horodetzky, in: EJ, 7 (1931), 170–9. **ADD. BIBLIOGRAPHY:** H. Gabai, *Judaism, Mathematics and the Hebrew Calendar* (2002); Y. Ginsburgh, *The Hebrew Letters: Channels of Creative Consciousness* (1990); *Sefer Gematrikon* (1990); M. Munk, *The Wisdom of the Hebrew Alphabet: The Sacred Letters as a Guide to Jewish Deed and Thought* (1983); M. Zuriel, *Or ha-Torah: Bi'ur le-Darkhei ha-Gematriot be-Toratenu* (1983); S. Sambursky, in: *Journal of Jewish Studies*, 29:1 (1978), 35–38; G. Locks, *The Spice of Torah – Gematria* (1985). KABBALAH: D. Abrams, "From Germany to Spain: Numerology as a Mystical Technique," in: JJS, vol. 47 (1996), 85–101; J. Dan, "The Ashkenazi Hasidic *Gates of Wisdom*," in: G. Nahon and Ch. Touati (eds,), *Hommages à Georges Vajda* (1980); I.R. Gruenwald, "Uses and Abuses of Gematria," in: M. Bar Asher (ed.), *Rabbi Mordechai Breuer Festschrift* 2 (1992), 823–32 (Heb.); M. Idel, *Absorbing Perfections: Kabbalah and Interpretation* (2002); idem, *Language, Torah and Hermeneutics in Abraham Abulafia* (1989); idem, "*Deus sive natura*" – the Metamorphosis of a Dictum from Maimonides to Spinoza, in: R. Cohen and H. Levinw (eds.), in: *Maimonides and the Sciences* (2000), 87–110; D. Abrams and I. Ta-Shma (eds.), *Sefer Gematriot of R. Yehudah the Pious* (1998); S. Lieberman, "A Mesopotamian Background for the So-Called Aggadic 'Measures' of Biblical Hermeneutics?," in: HUCA vol. 58 (1987), 157–225; D. Segal, *Sefer Sodei Razei Simmukhim* (2001); A. Wasserstein, in: *Tarbiz*, vol. 43 (1974), 53–55 (Heb.). **WEBSITES:** www.inner.org/gematria/gematria.htm; www.jhom.com/topics/envy/letters/gematria.html.

GEMEN, town in Westphalia, Germany. Jews are known to have lived there from the mid-16th century. After 1771 they came under the jurisdiction of the rabbi of *Muenster. The community numbered 28 persons in 1809; 49 in 1911; and 52 in 1933. The synagogue (erected in 1912) was destroyed in November 1938, and shortly afterward the congregation ceased to exist.

BIBLIOGRAPHY: E. Loewenstein, *Aus Vergangenheit und Gegenwart der israelitischen Gemeinde Gemen* (1912); PKG.

GEMILUT ḤASADIM (Heb. גְּמִילוּת חֲסָדִים; lit., "the bestowal of lovingkindness"), the most comprehensive and fundamental of all Jewish social virtues, which encompasses the whole range of the duties of sympathetic consideration toward one's fellow man. The earliest individual rabbinic statement in the Talmud, the maxim of *Simeon the Just, mentions it as one of the three pillars of Judaism ("Torah, the Temple service, and *gemilut ḥasadim*) upon which the [continued] existence of the world depends" (Avot 1:2).

The first Mishnah of *Pe'ah* enumerates it both among the things "which have no fixed measure" and among those that "man enjoys the fruits thereof in this world, while the stock remains for him in the world to come," i.e., its practice affords satisfaction in this world while it is accounted a virtue for him on the Day of Judgment. This, incidentally, is an exception to the general rule that pleasure in this world is at the expense of one's spiritual assets. With regard to the former, the Jerusalem Talmud (Pe'ah 1:1, 15b) differentiates between *gemilut ḥasadim* expressed in personal service ("with his body") and with one's material goods. It maintains that only the former is unlimited in its scope, whereas the latter is limited by the general rule that one should not "squander" more than a fifth of one's possessions on good works. With regard to the latter, the text of the Mishnah mentions only "honoring one's parents, *gemilut ḥasadim*, and bringing about peace between man and his fellow." The prayer book version adds, inter alia, "hospitality to wayfarers, visiting the sick, dowering the bride, attending the dead to the grave." These additions, culled from various *beraitot* and other passages, are actually redundant since they are merely aspects of the comprehensive virtue of *gemilut ḥasadim* which embraces them and many other expressions of human sympathy and kindness (cf. Maim., Yad, Evel 14:1).

Gemilut ḥasadim encompasses a wider range of human kindness than does *charity: "Charity can be given only with one's money; *gemilut ḥasadim*, both by personal service and with money. Charity can be given only to the poor; *gemilut ḥasadim*, both to rich and poor. Charity can be given only to the living; *gemilut ḥasadim*, both to the living and the dead" (Suk. 49b). Thus, helping a lame man over a stile is an act of *gemilut ḥasadim*, though not of charity; a gift given with a scowl to a poor man may be charity; the same amount given with a smile and a word of good cheer raises it to the level of *gemilut ḥasadim*. Almost humorously the rabbis point out that the only provable example of genuine altruistic *gemilut ḥasadim* is paying respect to the dead, for in it there is not the unspoken thought that the recipient may one day reciprocate (Tanḥ., Va-Yeḥi 3; cf. Rashi to Gen. 47:29).

Gemilut ḥasadim is regarded as one of the three outstanding, distinguishing characteristics of the Jew, to the extent that "whosoever denies the duty of *gemilut ḥasadim* denies the fundamental of Judaism" (Eccles. R. 7:1); he is even suspected of being of non-Jewish descent. Only he who practices it is fit to be a member of the Jewish people (Yev. 79a), for the Jews are not only practicers of *gemilut ḥasadim* but "the scions of those who practice it" (Ket. 8b). That *gemilut ḥasadim* is essentially a rabbinic ethical conception, is explicitly stated by Maimonides (loc. cit.).

During the Middle Ages the grand conception of *gemilut ḥasadim* as embracing every aspect of benevolence and consideration to one's fellow both in attitude and in deed became severely limited to the single aspect of giving loans without interest to those in need. It is not unlikely that this limitation was due to the fact that the main source of economic existence for the Jew was moneylending (to non-Jews), with the result that in lending money without interest he was depriving himself of his essential stock in trade. It is to this connotation of *gemilut ḥasadim* that the free-loan *gemilut ḥasadim* societies refer.

[Louis Isaac Rabinowitz]

Modern Period

Burial societies in the communities of Central and Eastern Europe in the 18th century were known as **ḥevra kaddisha* or *kabranim* with the added appellation *gemilut ḥasadim*. They were also called *gomelei ḥesed shel emet* (Gen. 47:29). This application came to signify the acts of lovingkindness connected with burial and consolation of the bereaved. The Prague community in 1792 had an association with triple functions: the provision of *gemilut ḥasadim*, of burial duties, and of *sandakim* at circumcisions. In Koenigsberg and many other communities the local *bikkur ḥolim* was also called *gemilut ḥasadim*. The Hambro Synagogue in London in 1795 had a ladies' auxiliary, *ḥevra kaddisha u-gemilut ḥasadim mi-nashim*. In the United States *ḥesed shel emet* societies have specialized in burial of the poor. Such an association, founded in 1888 in St. Louis, Missouri, amassed considerable wealth from its large cemetery holdings and was able to support local, national, and overseas charities from its considerable income.

[Isaac Levitats]

BIBLIOGRAPHY: ET, 6 (1954), 149–53; C.G. Montefiore and H. Loewe (eds.), *A Rabbinic Anthology* (1938), ch. 16; Rabinowitz, in: *Fourth World Congress of Jewish Studies*, Papers, 1 (1967), 145–8 (Heb. pt.); J. Marcus, *Communal Sick-Care in the German Ghetto* (1947); I. Levitats, *Jewish Community in Russia* (1943); idem, in: *Essays… in Honor of S.W. Baron* (1959), 337ff.

GENEALOGY.

In the Bible

Genealogical lists in the Bible are of two main types:

(1) those which are simply lists of historical, ethnographic, and even legendary traditions, and which constitute most of the lists in Genesis that are called "generations" or "books of generations" (Gen. 5:1; 6:9; 10:1; et al.);

(2) those which are tribal genealogies or lists reflecting clan traditions, the census lists in Numbers, and the genealogical accounts in Chronicles.

A third type consists of detailed lists giving the genealogical background of individual families, usually where that family played an important historical role, such as in the case of the house of David (I Chron. 2:10–15; 3:1–24), the house of Zadok (I Chron. 5:28–41; et al.), and the house of Saul (I Chron. 8:33ff.; et al.). Sometimes, less important families (I Chron. 2:31–41; 5:14; et al.), and also individuals (II Kings 22:3; Jer. 36:14), are represented in the same way as in the third type of list. The Bible does not distinguish these different types from each other, and the historico-ethnographic and tribal genealogies are all based on the view (common also among the Arabs) that nations, tribes, and clans all develop in the same way: every human grouping is descended from a single father. Nor is it always easy to classify a genealogy as belonging to one or another type.

It is not known when the tradition of recording genealogies became established in Israel, but it is undoubtedly an ancient one, as only by proving connection with some family or clan could an individual claim the privileges of citizen status. The important role of the genealogy is indicative of a society based on a tribal, patriarchal tradition. Consequently, certain family groups or individuals from among the local population or from closely related tribes, who joined the Israelites during the period of the Conquest or in the early monarchy, were included in the genealogical framework of the tribe as one way of truly incorporating them into the community. In like manner artisans, wise men, and poets, whose profession was customarily hereditary, were generally linked with some ancient ancestor (cf. I Chron. 2:55; 4:21, 23), and

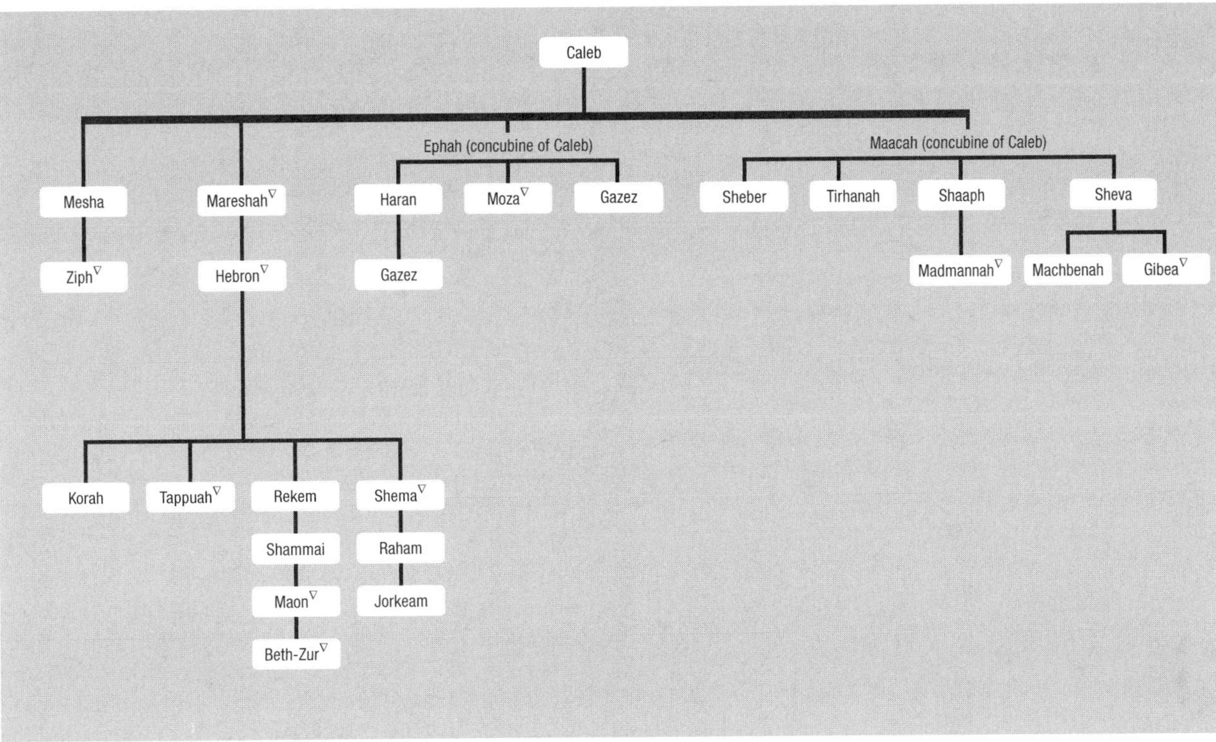

The line of Caleb (I Chron. 2:42–49). ∇ indicates names of towns in Judah.

whoever joined such a group was as a matter of course attached to it genealogically even though he did not actually stem from its line.

Such written lists were definitely family and clan genealogies and not those of individuals; in part they were composed for official purposes, such as for a national census, military service, or the levying of taxes. Genealogical lists in Israel are known from the time of the First Temple, from what is related in Ezra 2:62 of priestly families who on returning to Zion sought proof of their pedigree but could not find it. Nehemiah (7:5) also mentions the "book of the genealogy of those who came up at first." It seems that the institution of genealogical lists is the background of certain figurative expressions in the Bible (cf. Ex. 32:32; Ezek. 13:9; Ps. 139:16; et al.). Apparently genealogies of individual families were based on oral traditions passed down among the families concerned, or even on national traditions. Some think that the list of Aaron's priestly descendants (I Chron. 5–6) goes back to a text in which many generations were missing, and that the editors filled some of the gaps by repeating some of the names.

In the period of the return to Zion the question of genealogy acquired a special significance. Of primary importance was the lineage of the priests and the levites, for without proving their priestly descent they could not qualify for service in the Temple; but the other returning families were no less keen to prove their descent in order to claim family property. Consequently, a special interest developed in the ancient genealogical lists, some of which are reproduced in the opening chapters of Chronicles and presumably were written toward the end of the Persian period. Similarly, in the short historical stories of Esther, Judith, and Tobit, also written at the end of the Persian period, the lineage of the main hero of the story is given in detail, e.g., those of Mordecai (Esth. 2:5; cf. I Sam. 9:1), Tobit (1:1; cf. Gen. 46:24), and Judith (8:1; cf. Num. 1:6). It is hard to suppose that these are authentic genealogies, yet each of these books claims to relate an event that happened long before the time of composition.

In the genealogical lists, particularly those of I Chronicles, there are three main elements which are usually combined. One represents the relationship of clans through lines of descent from father to son; another sees it in the names of settlements (usually so-and-so, the "father" of the settlement); and a third, in the names of families (e.g., the Tirathites (I Chron. 2:55)). The line of Caleb's descendants (I Chron. 2:42–49) illustrates the mixture.

Various scholars have sought to find in the genealogical schemes of the Bible a conventional way of handing down ethnographic records and information concerning regional history and the pattern of settlement of local clans and families. These scholars have even attempted to establish rules to interpret the various genealogical schemes. Thus, the fusing of two ethnic groups or tribes can be expressed by an account of a marriage; and the integration of a newly settled tribe in the indigenous population can be indicated by the head of the tribe marrying one of the native women, or taking one as a concubine. Daughters generally represent settlements subject to a larger urban center, and sons naturally represent the strongest and oldest of these. Individuals from outside the "family" circle who appear in a genealogy usually symbolize weak families who joined a stronger tribe and so on.

Though such rules cannot provide the sole interpretation of the genealogical lists, they are an aid to the unraveling of the complicated process of Israelite settlement. One, of course, must bear in mind that several of the stories and traditions concerned derive from a combination of schematic descriptions, as regards the historic reality, together with legends and folktales.

It frequently happens that a given name – of a nation, tribe, or family – occurs in different genealogical contexts, or even in a compound list, once as father, once as son, uncle, or brother. For example, Aram is listed in Genesis 10:23 as the father of Uz, whereas in Genesis 22:20–21 Uz is a son of Nahor and an uncle of Aram. In Genesis 36:5, 14 Korah is a son of Esau, but in Genesis 36:16 the clan of Korah is descended from Esau's son Eliphaz. In I Chronicles 2:9 Ram is a son of Hezron and brother of Jerahmeel, yet in the same chapter, verse 27, Ram is the eldest son of Jerahmeel. Sometimes one name can be included in several genealogical lists in association with different ethnic or tribal units. For instance, Zerah, Korah, and Kenaz, who are included in the Edomite list in Genesis 36, are also found on the list of families in the tribe of Judah in I Chronicles 2 and 4; Beriah appears as one of the sons of Ephraim (I Chron. 7:23), and also as one of the sons of Asher (Gen. 46:17); and Hezron is listed as the son of Reuben (Gen. 46:9), and also as one of the sons of Perez son of Judah (Gen. 46:12). At times it may seem plausible that two entirely separate ethnic groups bore the same name, but generally such duplication is caused by uncertainty concerning genealogical attribution or the existence of parallel traditions. These may have had various causes; sometimes they reflect changes in historical circumstances – the power relations between tribes, families and clans; the migration of several tribes or clans from one region to another; or a mingling of various ethnic elements.

The editors of the genealogical lists in the Bible, particularly those of I Chronicles, were confronted with conflicting lists and traditions, often mutually contradictory. The combination of the various lists, without altering their different, individual character, was possible because the editors of the comprehensive lists regarded them as genealogies of individuals, the progenitors of families and tribes. Thus, the repeated recurrence of the same name provided no difficulty. They did not regard such recurrences as conflicting data concerning families and clans, but merely as showing that the same name kept recurring among individuals related to one another.

[Jacob Liver]

In the Second Temple Period

Purity of descent played an important role in the Second Temple period. It concerned mainly the kohanim ("priests") and those Israelite families who laid claim to the eligibility of their daughters to marry kohanim. Other families, who had no record of their descent but on the other hand were not suspected of impure lineage, were referred to as *issah* ("dough"). The kohanim, in order to preserve their pure status, were restricted to marital ties with families whose purity of descent was not in doubt, and were therefore required to know in detail their own genealogy and that of the families whose daughters they married. Families laying claim to purity of blood kept ancestral lists, which served as evidence of their seniority and legitimacy, for the very possession of such lists enhanced their standing. For the kohanim, a general genealogical list was maintained in the Temple, which recorded genealogical information on all priestly families; even the kohanim who lived in the Diaspora provided this genealogical center in Jerusalem with full details of their marriages (cf. Jos., Apion, 1:7).

A priestly tribunal, which convened in a special room in the Temple, was responsible for the upkeep of the genealogical lists and the verification of genealogical data. They functioned in accordance with established rules, and also based their findings on the evidence of witnesses and genealogical documents. One such rule followed in the Second Temple period was that families who traditionally performed certain functions were beyond suspicion and their purity of descent required no further examination: priestly families who served in the Temple "from the altar and upward" and "from the *dukhan* [the place from which the kohanim blessed the people] and upward," and members of the *Sanhedrin and other families who performed certain official functions (Kid. 4:4–5; Sanh. 4:2; Ar. 2:4). Other duties, such as participation in the priestly blessing or partaking in the *terumah* (the contribution made to kohanim), did not in themselves put the priestly family in question beyond the need for further proof. It should be pointed out that the various offices in the Temple service passed from father to son.

It is important to note that the sages did not owe their positions of leadership to their descent from prominent families. Some of the sages, it is true, were of noble lineage (such as *Judah ha-Nasi), but others came from families with no genealogical record and there were even a few who were the descendants of proselytes. In their society, the rabbi took the place of the father, and the tradition of the academies (the yeshivot) took precedence over the tradition of the family. Talmudic legends went so far as to "invent" a gentile origin for some sages, including some of the greatest (*Akiva, *Meir, and others); some sages were even said to have been descended from infamous and evil gentiles (Sisera, Sennacherib, Haman, Nero) who had repented of their ways and had become Jews. The evident purpose of such legends was to demonstrate that the acquisition of Torah learning and piety was not dependent upon noble descent.

Purity of blood did, however, play a role in the struggle for secular power among the prominent families, and even the royal houses had to resort to genealogical proofs in order to strengthen their position. Thus the *Hasmoneans, who had to defend themselves against the contention that only Davidic descendants could lay claim to kingship, in turn questioned the purity of David's blood, in view of his descent from Ruth the Moabite. *Herod, who also had to face a challenge to the legitimacy of his rule, forged for himself a pedigree going back to David, after first destroying the genealogical records maintained in the Temple (according to the third-century Christian historian Africanus). Later sources reflect the great danger inherent in any attempt to probe the purity of leading families, for the latter would not hesitate to use force against anyone casting doubt upon their pure descent (Kid. 71a). *Johanan b. Zakkai therefore decreed (apparently on the eve of the destruction of the Temple) that no rabbinical court would deal with matters concerning genealogy (Eduy. 8:3). A similar consideration led to an early rejection of *Sefer Yuḥasin*, which seems to have been a Midrash on Chronicles (Pes. 62b).

After the destruction of the Temple, when the kohanim lost their function, they prized even more their purity of descent, for it was the only symbol left to them of their exalted status. This emphasis on descent continued up to the end of the era of the *amoraim* (sixth century), in both Ereẓ Israel and Babylon. One result was that a man who wished to ensure the continued purity of his family would marry only his sister's daughter (Yev. 62b, et al.); many of the great sages followed this practice. The Damascus Sect (see Book of the Covenant of *Damascus) disapproved of it. It is doubtful whether the rabbis of the tannaitic and talmudic era had real knowledge of their own – and contemporary – genealogy. Numerous families are mentioned in the Mishnah and the *Gemara*, and some of these are described as being of traceable descent (Tosef., Pe'ah 4:11; Yev. 16b; Ta'an. 4:5, etc.). The list in the Mishnah Ta'anit 4:5 originates from the Persian period. Some of the genealogies ascribed to these families are undoubtedly of a legendary character, while the rest are disputed by scholars. A special problem is posed by the later genealogy of the house of David, a subject which also concerned the early Christians (Matt. 1:1–17, Luke 3:23–38).

The Mishnah (Kid. 4:1) lists ten social groups who returned from the Babylonian exile, in the order of their genealogical precedence. The first three – kohanim, levites, and Israelites – are of equal status, except that the kohanim are restricted in their choice of wives; the *ḥalalim* are the sons of the marriages of disqualified kohanim and are themselves disqualified from service in the Temple and marital ties with kohanim; next are *gerim* (converts to Judaism) who are equal to Israelites in most respects, except that they may enter certain marriages which are prohibited to an Israelite by descent; the sixth group are the *ḥarurim*, manumitted slaves; the seventh are the **mamzerim*, i.e., bastards, the children of one of the unions prohibited on pain of death or **karet*; next are the *nethinim*, the descendants of the Gibeonites who were circumcised at the time of Joshua and were not regarded as full Jews because their ancestors' conversion was incomplete; the ninth group are the *shetukim* ("the silent ones") who do not know the identity of their father; and the tenth, and lowest, group are the *asufim* ("foundlings") who know neither mother nor father. A chapter in the Talmud (Kid. 4) is devoted to the relationships between these groups, i.e., the rules applying to intermarriage between one group and another. Not included in the scale are gentiles and slaves; these have no genealogical status at all, and when they convert or are set free achieve their own "descent" and are legally free to marry even their closest relatives. This genealogical scale applied to marriage and honorific matters; it was not deemed relevant in respect of Torah learning and piety, and the Mishnah states clearly that "a learned bastard takes precedence over an uneducated high priest" (Hor. 3:8).

Babylonian Jewry considered that the purity of its descent was of a higher order than that of Ereẓ Israel, basing its claim on the tradition that all those whose purity was in doubt had returned to Ereẓ Israel with Ezra. In the course of time, however, Babylonian *amoraim* declared the population of entire areas as Jews who were not fit "to enter the assembly of God" (i.e., for marriage with other Jews; Kid. 70b). The rabbis of Ereẓ Israel made several attempts to change the existing rule which regarded Babylonian lineage as superior but failed in their attempt; this was a result of the general reluctance to take up genealogical questions prevailing in Ereẓ Israel, as well as the rising importance of Babylonian Jewry at this time (beginning of third century). Babylonian Jews continued to claim greater purity, and the Talmud (Kid. 71b) tells of an impostor who feigned a Babylonian accent to claim Babylonian descent.

This development testifies to the degeneration of the concept of genealogy which, with the destruction of the Temple ceased to have practical significance and merely became a symbol of social status. The Talmud makes frequent references to honorable families and individuals who quarreled with one another about their lineage, even stating: "When men quarrel among themselves, they quarrel over birth" (Kid. 76a). The *amoraim* tackled the problem from two angles: on the one hand they decided that "anyone with a family stigma stigmatizes others and never praises anyone" (according to the correct reading in DER 1), and Samuel added that "he stigmatizes with his own stigma" (Kid. 70b). It is also related in this same spirit of the people of Ereẓ Israel: "When two people quarrel they see which becomes silent first and say to him 'This one is of superior birth'" (*ibid.* 71b); on the other hand they included within their homilies abundant praise of birth, such as "When the Holy One causes His divine Presence to rest, it is only upon Israelite families of pure birth" (Kid. 70b); "The Holy One is reluctant to uproot a name from its place in a genealogical tree" (Gen. R. 82:11; cf. TJ, Suk. 5:8). The sages also protested against "anyone who takes a wife not fit (i.e., with a stigma) for him" (Kid. 70a) because he disregards the importance of birth. The sages included among their homilies sayings in the style of prophecies of comfort that God will purify Israel's genealogy in time to come. They stressed, however, that for the time being one can only act carefully and be guided by the rule that "a family once mixed up remains so" (Kid. 70b) – an important rule which they regarded as "a charity shown by God to Israel" since it is likely to abolish the obstacles of genealogical stigmas: one should not reveal the truth concerning families that have become mixed up and whose stigma has been forgotten (see also *Family).

The Talmud records the Davidic descent of the patriarchs of the Ereẓ Israel community in the talmudic era, and of the Babylonian *exilarchs. Similarly, in the post-talmudic era the exilarchs were regarded as descending from the house of David. The same claim was made about some of the *geonim* (such as *Hai Gaon). In the Middle Ages, Davidic lineage was claimed for some great scholars, e.g., *Rashi, and in consequence his grandsons Jacob b. Meir *Tam and *Samuel b. Meir were said to have descended from *Johanan ha-Sandlar, who in turn was regarded as being of Davidic descent.

In the Modern Period

From the 12th century onward, the term **yiḥus* (birth) assumed additionally a new and positive meaning among the Jews of Central and Eastern Europe. Dynastic connection not only ensured the family concerned against any suspicion of impure birth, but also provided it with family privileges (*zekhut avot*) applicable in many matters. These dynastic genealogies stemmed from superiority of their pious and scholarly forefathers, the founders of the family, and its main importance was in connection with arranging marriages. Many families possessed genealogical trees – whether of substance or otherwise – which they took great pains to preserve. Some of these lists were published in order to add further luster to the family name. Many rabbis strongly criticized this custom and stressed the value of a man creating his own good name. In *Ḥasidism, descent from the **zaddik* was endowed with special significance, rooted in the belief that the *ẓaddik* transmitted some of his sanctity to his descendants. With the development of dynasties of *ẓaddikim* the term *yiḥus* acquired also great formal institutional value. In 19th-century Germany the study of genealogy held an important place in Jewish public affairs, because of the aspiration to prove that the Jewish community was deeply rooted in the locality. Scientific journals dealing with this topic were founded and much scientific and archival material published.

[Israel Moses Ta-Shma]

Genealogical Research

INTRODUCTION. Jewish genealogy is a popular and even scholarly pursuit in many parts of the world today. Since Judaism is not only a community of faith but a people that claims descent from common ancestry, there has always been an interest in tracing and validating descent. To this day there are Jews who trace their descent from the ancient priests (*kohanim*) and levites (*leviim*) of the biblical period and who receive special recognition as such in the synagogue service. *Sephardim are particularly scrupulous in maintaining family genealogical records in order to demonstrate that they are indeed "pure" Sephardim (*sefardi tahor*).

RABBINIC GENEALOGY. Because of the importance attached to Torah learning in the Jewish tradition, genealogical records of rabbis and ḥasidic leaders (*rebbes*) are relatively abundant and carefully recorded. Genealogical research is facilitated by the frequency with which these families intermarried.

Rabbinic genealogical information may be found in biographical works, rabbinic manuscripts, scholarly works and responsa literature. *Yizkor* books on the *shtetls* of Eastern Europe contain stories about the town rabbis and their families. Because rabbis and scholars held positions of esteem in the Jewish world, their writings were preserved and their *yahrzeits* observed. Therefore it may be possible to trace farther back into time if one is of rabbinic descent even if the family did not maintain records.

Amongst the problems in creating a rabbinic family genealogy is the fact that despite large numbers of children born into rabbinic families, only those sons who were rabbis and daughters who married rabbis were usually recorded.

Research has been complicated by the changing of family names. A son-in-law might take the name of a scholarly father-in-law or that of a beloved mother-in-law in place of the patronym. Adding to the confusion is the usage of the Hebrew word *ḥatan*, which refers to both son-in-law, father-in-law, and husband. Encyclopedic works may record rabbis according to first names. Since words in rabbinic literature are used sparingly, rabbis were often known by *rashe tevot* (first letter abbreviations) or by the names of books they authored (see B. Friedberg, *Bet Eked Sefarim*). The use of the title "Reb" as sign of respect for a non-rabbi also leads to misunderstandings. Publication of a rabbi's writings often contained bibliographies of the author and *yahrzeit* dates for members of the family. Introductory *haskamot* (approbations) by rabbis who read the manuscript included their own biographical notes about the author and his family, recording the names of other scholars in the family. *She'elot* and *teshuvot* (rabbinic responsa) also may contain genealogical references.

WHAT IS GENEALOGY TODAY? In contrast to the traditional view of genealogy as simply a compilation of ancestors' names and dates in a chronological order from the past to the present, genealogy today differs both in direction and in scope. Starting with the present, the researcher works back into history, recording personal characteristics and history as well as names and dates. Since the search has a personal motivation, which is self-understanding, the term genealogy is being used interchangeably with family history or personal history. Genealogy previously had been primarily an activity of the elderly. The "new" genealogy has attracted a much younger constituency.

It is not unusual to hear that a genealogist has been researching his ancestry for 30 years. Starting with two parents, four grandparents, eight great-grandparents, continually increasing their number, we find that, within ten generations, if successful, a person will have 1,024 direct ancestors. The number grows proportionally as we add brothers, sisters and their spouses and children at each generational level.

Key elements in genealogy are names, dates, places, and relationships. These records have been recorded on many artistic charts and trees. Information can be collected and stored in albums or books, on tapes, maps, and slides. Today, with a computer, people with large genealogies produce computerized copies of their ancestry.

Starting with oneself, the genealogist poses the following questions. What were the personal, historic, economic, religious, and social reasons that brought my ancestors to uproot themselves and move from one country to another? How have my parents' and ancestors' decisions, beliefs, and needs affected my environment and my life? A family tree is only the framework for family history. Stories, legends, and events in the life of members of the family give drama and meaning to the genealogy. Often a family maintains that it is descended from the Ba'al Shem Tov, the Vilna Gaon, the Maharal of Prague, Rashi, and other famous personalities. These traditions add excitement and encouragement for the genealogist.

An explosion of interest in genealogy across the United States of America was sparked by the bicentennial celebration of American independence in 1976 and ignited by the television screening of Alex Haley's bestseller *Roots* in 1977. These events carried a strong message of encouragement to all Americans to take pride in their ethnic origins. Along with other ethnic groups Jews have joined the "Back to Roots" movement.

In 1977, Dan Rottenberg published *Finding Our Fathers: A Guidebook To Jewish Genealogy* which provided a major resource for Jewish genealogists. In 1979 there were three Jewish genealogical societies in North America and by 1984 there were 17, located in New York, Washington, Los Angeles, Chicago, Philadelphia, Cleveland, St. Louis, Pittsburgh, Tidewater (Virginia), Orange County, San Diego, San Francisco, Detroit, Boston, southern Florida, Cincinnati, and Montreal. These organizations function as a support system for the researcher and a forum for sharing discoveries, methods, and sources of research, and genealogical skills and techniques.

In 1977 the first American journal of Jewish genealogy, *Toledot: The Journal of Jewish Genealogy*, was published in New York, followed by *Roots Key* from Los Angeles, Philadelphia's *Newsletter, Mishpacha* from Washington, and *Search* from Chicago.

In 1981, the First National Summer Seminar on Jewish Genealogy took place in New York City. Subsequently, national seminars were held in Washington in 1982, Los Angeles in 1983, and Chicago in 1984. The First International Seminar, sponsored by the Jewish Genealogy Society of Greater Washington, was held in Jerusalem in 1984. These seminars provide participants with the opportunity to visit local archives, libraries, and cemeteries, to meet other genealogists from different cities and countries, and to attend educational workshops.

The shock of the Holocaust was a significant factor in stimulating Jewish genealogy. Jewish attention was turned back to Eastern Europe. Jews were tormented by questions of what and who had been lost. Questions about ancestral roots were reawakened. Grievous family losses created a hunger for the reuniting of families and a fierce desire to know who survived. In response agencies were created that are important resources for genealogists: the International Tracing Service (ITS) in Arolsen, West Germany, and the Search Bureau for Missing Relatives in Jerusalem.

The ITS, administered by the International Red Cross, maintains a master index on an alphabetic Soundex System. Among the holdings of the ITS are indexes and name lists of concentration camp victims, deportation lists of Jews, and lists of children separated from families. Postwar holdings include lists of inhabitants of the displaced person camps. The staff of the ITS can respond to queries in most languages.

In 1945 the Jewish Agency for Palestine established the Search Bureau for Missing Relatives. The office published *The Register of Jewish Survivors*, listing 58,000 persons. Now they have computerized their list of World War II survivors. Also, the Agency maintains a computerized family finder for Israeli residents indexed by surname, country, and town.

French Holocaust research can be done at The Memorial Library in Paris. The book by Serge Klarsfeld, *Le Memorial de la Déportation des Juifs de France*, contains vital statistics of some 80,000 Jews deported from France.

Post-Holocaust Archives. At this time also archives were established to gather, save, and preserve what remained of Jewish records from before the Holocaust and those concerning that period. *Yad Vashem was founded in Israel in 1945. The Leo Baeck Institute, an important archive for German Jewish records, was established in Israel in 1955; its New York Archive has valuable genealogical materials.

Yad Vashem became a major center for the collection of oral, photographed, and written testimonies of Holocaust survivors. It has a copy of the ITS holdings; however, it is not equipped to deal with queries or research. There is at Yad Vashem a plan to create a separate file on those who gave testimony and a computer series in Hebrew and English characters listing the victims and significant information about them.

Motivated by a need to remember and record life in their native villages and towns now destroyed by Nazis, the landsmannschaft organizations began to produce *yizkor bikher* ("memorial books"). These *yizkor bikher* now number over 500 and are an indispensable source of information on the destroyed Jewish communities of Eastern Europe. They include lists of local residents, photographs, stories about personalities who lived in the town, and history of the town itself. Many books have hand-drawn maps of the town which outline the main streets of the *shtetl*, cemeteries, synagogues, and details not normally found on a map. These books are written mostly in Yiddish and Hebrew, with some English. Most Jewish libraries carry some of the volumes. The most complete selection is at Yad Vashem in Jerusalem and YIVO in New York City. The most recent listing of these volumes can be found in *Appendix I* by Zachary M. Baker in *A Ruined Garden* (see Bibliography).

Yad Vashem also has put online names and information for more than three million victims of the Holocaust gathered over the past half century. The names of those murdered are a prominent feature of the new museum exhibition with the Hall of Names and are now accessible for all to search. In 2005, it signed an exchange agreement with the United States Holocaust Memorial Museum for the exchange of names of victims taken from lists of deportee and concentration camp records, which will join the affidavits of those murdered that Yad Vashem has painstakingly gathered. Yad Vashem will also have access to the Ben and Vladka Meed National Registry of Jewish Holocaust Survivors collected by the *American Gathering of Jewish Holocaust Survivors since 1981. The more than 50,000 pre-interview questionnaires of the Survivors of the Shoah Visual History Foundation, under the auspices of the University of Southern California, also contain an extensive list of Holocaust victims as well as survivors; the material was not yet accessible online in late 2005. In addition, the Jewish Historical Institute in Warsaw is the home of a genealogical search for records of Jews in Poland. Yale Reisner developed the project with major financial assistance from the Ronald S. Lauder Foundation.

GENERAL METHODOLOGY. (1) Interview family, starting with the oldest in each branch of the family. Record and tape everything carefully. The most valuable sources are the oldest living members of the family. Their memories of events and recollection of family experiences cannot be replaced. Fortunate is the researcher who has a relative from the immigrant generation, for this person may remember those who remained behind and were lost in the Holocaust.

(2) Locate all relatives; interview or contact by letter or phone. Record dates of all contacts.

(3) Search for diaries, biographies, family papers and letters, diplomas, journals and newspaper clippings, photographs, passports, vital records, *yahrzeit* records, and inscriptions in Bibles and prayer books.

(4) Try to discover through family and survivors of the Holocaust who of the family remained in Europe during World War II and what happened to them. Contact International Tracing Service, D-3548 Arolsen, Federal Republic of Germany.

(5) Contact or visit Yad Vashem to see if your relatives are recorded in the pages of testimony filed there. These pages list the name and address of the testifier who is often a family member.

(6) Search for death records at home, in cemeteries, at funeral parlors, and in synagogues, *ḥevra kaddisha* records, society and landsmannschaft records, vital statistics departments of the government, newspaper or journal obituaries and notices.

(7) Search for birth records at home, in maternity clinics, in government health record centers, and in physicians' files, circumcision records, and vital records in government and state archives.

(8) Obtain immigration and naturalization records. In the U.S. petitions for naturalization, "first papers," are particularly valuable since they may record the name of the ship, date, and port of arrival, and destination in the new country. They may have the immigrant's birthplace.

(9) Search for steamship passenger manifests. Write for steamship passenger arrival lists, to American and Canadian ports, using the original family names prior to immigration. Ship manifests are available in the National Archives and Record Service (NARS) in Washington D.C., at the archive of the Genealogy Society of Utah, at *YIVO Institute for Jewish Research in New York, and at HIAS (Hebrew Immigrant Aid Society; see 15: 1539) in New York. HIAS holds steamship ticket records for 1907–10, and passenger lists for 1884, 1886, 1887, 1891–95, 1898, 1901, 1912, 1913. The State Archive in Hamburg holds passenger lists from their heavily used port. Hamburg passenger lists from 1850–1914 may also be found at the Museum of Hamburg, Historic Emigration Office, Holstenwall 24, 2000 Hamburg 36 (there is a users' fee). Some of these archives also hold passenger arrival records from Dutch ports of Amsterdam and Rotterdam; Antwerp, Belgium from years 1854–1855; Trieste, Naples, and Le Havre. The Bremen passenger lists were lost in World War II.

(10) Search in old telephone and city directories in larger libraries for addresses of relatives. Census and military records are based on address and ward in large cities. An uncommon name can sometimes be used to find relatives. Old city directories may include occupation and wife's names. The N.Y. Public Library Annex has some pre-Holocaust books from cities in Austria, Poland, Yugoslavia, and Czechoslovakia, and post-Holocaust ones which help to locate family.

(11) For the U.S., obtain U.S. census records taken every ten years; currently available are those from 1790 through 1910. They may provide date of immigration and birth date and place. The National Archives of the United States houses the United States federal census records. The records are filed geographically and by Soundex. These records may be obtained on interlibrary loan or through a regional branch of the Federal Archives. Pamphlets on "How to Get Census and Other Records" are available from the United States Government Printing Office, Washington D.C. 20402. In other countries turn to state archives for census records.

(12) Examine court and probate records, pension and social security records, land and tax records, military and draft registration records, business employment records, adoption and divorce records.

(13) Visit the local branch of Mormon Genealogical Library. Use gazeteer to find the province where towns are located. Examine town records for Jewish holdings. Order birth, marriage, or death records, census records, and ships' passenger lists.

(14) Visit Jewish historical societies, Jewish libraries, large public libraries with genealogy departments, and Jewish archives.

(15) Request to see synagogue records and bulletins, old-age home records, landsmannschaft and other society records.

(16) Examine *yizkor* books of the towns from which the family came.

(17) For the U.S., obtain information from HIAS records concerning ships' passenger lists, steamship records, and passage order books. HIAS records can be obtained from YIVO in New York or from a branch of the Genealogical Society of Utah. Also, HIAS processes inquiries for missing persons through a Search and Location Department in New York City.

(18) For the U.S., write to the United States Government Printing Office, Washington, D.C. 20402, for pamphlets on "Where to Write For Birth, Death and Marriage."

(19) For Canada, write to the Public Archives of Canada (395 Wellington, Ottawa KIA ON3, Canada) for a booklet called "Tracing your Ancestors in Canada."

(20) In Holland, two organizations of assistance in research of Sephardi genealogies are the Netherlands Joods Familienarchif at Amsteldijk 67, Amsterdam and the Centraal Bureau voor Genealogie, POB 11755, 2502 AT, The Hague.

GENEALOGY IN ISRAEL. The first guide to the use of modern techniques of genealogical research in Israel is "Eretz Israel Jewish Genealogy, An Introduction to the Sources for the Late Ottoman and Mandate Periods" by Michael Plotkin, which appeared in *Toledot*, 3 (4), 1983.

Traditional research in Jewish genealogy relied almost exclusively on Jewish sources such as citations in rabbinic works, family records, *ḥevra kaddisha* records, cemetery registers, and oral traditions. Modern methods of genealogical research incorporate the technique of quantitative history, including census records, birth, marriage, and divorce registrations in the civil courts, steamship passenger lists, immigration and naturalization records, court records, name changes, wills, and estate and land records. Plotkin, a trained archivist at the Israel State Archives, has shown that these techniques can be used in research in Israel. He also shows how Jewish Agency and World Zionist Organization *aliyah* records, the *Pinkas Ha-Bogrim* of the *Yishuv* in Mandatory Palestine, and histories of local settlements can be utilized for genealogical research. Simultaneous with the publication of Plotkin's pioneering article, the first Jewish genealogical society was organized in Jerusalem.

In 1971 under the leadership of Dr. Isaac Halbrecht of Tel Aviv University, the World Zionist Organization established Moreshet Beit Saba (the "Society for Jewish Family Heritage"). The purpose of the society is "to spark a movement centered in Israel that would encourage interest in Jewish family heritage and roots." A questionnaire was formulated in several languages suited in part for computer processing with a genealogical component which is being distributed worldwide to Jewish organizations and educational institutions. In order to preserve the genealogical and ethnographic contents of the questionnaire and to facilitate the study of personal and family history, there is a plan to create an archive and a computer center in Israel which will be available to roots searchers. Moreshet Beit Saba is also supported by the Israel Ministry of Education to foster "a dialogue between the generations through oral history and the roots program in the public schools of Israel."

Moreshet Beit Saba is in some ways a response to the revolt against the Jewish tradition which marked some ideologies within the Zionist movement. These ideologies often resulted in feelings of disdain for the Yiddish language and the traditional East European Jewish style of life. The determination to create a new society, a new culture, a new Jew produced a mass movement to adopt new Hebraic names in place of the old, Yiddish, East European names. This movement was given impetus by the insistence that official representatives of the State of Israel abroad had to assume new Hebrew family names. Moreshet Beit Saba is designed to repair some of the disruptions and discontinuities which these Zionist ideologies of revolt produced.

MORMON GENEALOGICAL ARCHIVES. The Mormon Church of the Latter Day Saints (LDS), established in 1830, has the largest holdings of microfilmed genealogical data in the world. These are stored in six disaster-proof storage vaults in Granite Mountain in Salt Lake City, Utah. Daniel Schlyter is archivist of Jewish records and has provided valuable assistance for Jewish genealogical research. Over 400 branch libraries throughout the world maintain microfilm indices of their holdings which the public may view, and from which it may order specific films for a minimal fee. The LDS fund this program as a religious duty, since a believer who can document his ancestors can bring them posthumously into the Church. The records consist of annual records of births, marriage, and death documents written in archaic foreign script, mainly from 1826 to 1865. Jewish records (approx. 2,500 films) from Poland and Hungary and 220 rolls of film on Jewish records from Alsace-Lorraine have been purchased through the efforts of Dr. Isaac Halbrecht. They are not yet available to researchers. "A Translation Guide to 19th-Century Polish Language Civil-Registration Documents," written by Judith R. Frazin (published by the Jewish Genealogical Society of Illinois, 1984), was prepared specifically for these documents.

Most people assume that because of the destruction of life and property during the Holocaust, no Jewish records remain in Europe. Though Nazi Germany destroyed Jews they did not deliberately destroy Jewish records. In fact they maintained scrupulous records of the destruction itself.

Only recently, with the publicity about the Jewish records of the Genealogical Society of Utah (Mormons) we have become aware that much remains to research. To the surprise of many Jewish genealogists, despite the many losses of records due to fires, pogroms, frequent moves, lack of or careless record keeping, documents remain, even in Eastern Europe. It has recently become known that the governments maintained vital and census records in the countries where Jews settled and lived.

By 1826 in Poland and Hungary and by 1865 in Germany, there were uniform vital records of the Jewish communities in official archives. Archives of some small towns were included among those of the larger nearby towns, often mixed with Catholic or general records. Thus far, records have been released for microfilming from c. 1740 to c. 1870 enabling genealogists to examine 124 years of Jewish records.

Wherever and whenever possible, Jews avoided creating records. They had valid reasons to fear placing census and birth records in government hands, since these would be used to draft Jewish men and boys for the army or to collect taxes. Jewish congregations though they did not ordinarily record births and marriages often kept burial records, if they maintained a burial ground or cemetery.

In the late 1960s the Mormon Church filmed 100-year-old vital records in the towns and cities of West Germany, Poland, Hungary, Lithuania, and France. We find the following relevant birth, marriage, and death records among the Mormon microfilms:

(1) Hungarian records of cities and towns within the former borders of Hungary, which include areas now in the former Soviet Union, Romania, Austria, Yugoslavia, and Czechoslovakia from the early to middle 1800s to 1895, were filmed in the Budapest Archive. Also, there is a Jewish census from some old Hungarian counties in the year 1848. Hungarian Jewish Registers from 1840 are complete within modern borders. There were uniform vital Jewish records in Hungary from 1826.

(2) German records of the German empire, which is now Germany, the former Soviet Union, France, and Poland from 1800 to 1895. East German Jewish records are being withheld at this time.

(3) French civil records for Jews exist since 1792, many of which have not yet been filmed. Nineteenth-century Jewish records are in the Consistoire, and in the Alliance Israélite Universelle in France. Civil records for Jews are also in State Archives of Alsace and Lorraine.

(4) Polish records: Russian and German areas of Poland had separate civil registers for Jews from 1826. Polish records in the Austrian territory of Galicia, except for Cracow and Tarnow, have not yet been filmed at the Polish State Archives. In most cases, Polish records which have been filmed provide records up to 1870.

(5) Czechoslovakian Jewish records were centralized in Prague during World War II. Slovakian records were gathered in Bratislava. The records from Prague have been microfilmed and are also in the Archives of the History of the Jewish People in Jerusalem. The Czechoslovakian Embassy in Washington has a user's fee for genealogical research.

(6) Soviet records have not been microfilmed. Government records are not made available to the researcher. However, there exist Jewish census records in Russia from 1794, 1811, 1815, 1833, 1850, and 1887. Jewish records are held in the Central State Archives in Minsk; Warsaw and Vilna Archives in Poland hold some pre-1917 Russian census records which are costly to obtain but are available. Russian-Polish vital records from Suwalki have been filmed.

There are some pre-Holocaust Russian records in the Archives of the History of the Jewish People in Jerusalem, including birth, death, and marriage records in Hebrew and Russian from c. 1857 to 1878.

Russian Consular Records from 1860 to the 1920s, left behind in Washington, D.C. by the Czarist government, have been discovered recently in storage in the National Records Center in Suitland, Maryland. Many files exist on Canadian and American Jews of Russian origins. Efforts are being made to index, catalogue, and translate these records from Russian to English. The Canadian Public Archives in Ottowa hold the Vancouver and Montreal files. They contain valuable genealogical materials. These files may be useful to Polish, Galician, Ukrainian, and other nationals who lived within the borders of Imperial Russia.

The Mormon Church is now microfilming records from 1840 in Yugoslavia, which was under Austrian rule at that time.

The Polish, Hungarian, and German Jewish records of the Genealogical Society of Utah were first published in *Toledot: The Journal of Jewish Genealogy* in 1978–79. An update of these records can be found at the Mormon library or at the Archives of the History of the Jewish People in Jerusalem or in John Cherny, *The Source: A Guidebook of American Genealogy*, "Jewish American Research," ch. 21 (1984).

GENEALOGY AND EDUCATION. Currently, genealogy is being used in schools as a method of personalizing Jewish history. Examining one's own family history leads to a more significant understanding of the total Jewish experience. History teachers are assigning students the task of preparing a chart and a map of family migrations in order to lead them into a study of the world of their direct forebears. An awareness of genealogical connectedness helps a group to maintain its distinctiveness. Genealogy binds individuals to the family and to their history.

Genealogists write of their deepened interest in Jewish history, geography, and religion as a result of their genealogical research. They express a desire to study Yiddish and Hebrew in which so much Jewish family history is recorded.

It is rare that a Jewish genealogist does not find that the family suffered grievous losses during the Holocaust. Forty years after the Holocaust, Jewish genealogists, as a result of their research, are finding for the first time that members of their families were among the six million. This discovery leads to a search for names and information about the deceased. The genealogist adds these names to records and charts, ensuring that the victims are memorialized and remembered within the embrace of the family. This personalizing of the Holocaust is a major concern of Jewish educators today.

SURNAMES AND GENEALOGICAL RESEARCH. Name changes, both of a voluntary and involuntary nature, create problems for the genealogist. Most East and Central European Jews used patronymics (e.g., Moshe ben Amram). Surnames were rare, unless the family was in commerce, and traveling between cities. Around 1800, the governments in Central Europe began to demand surnames for the Jews. By 1844, Russia and Poland mandated that surnames be registered. However, even these names underwent a metamorphosis when they passed through the immigration gates of America. Hardly able to understand the heavily accented pronunciation of names, immigration officials wrote down phonetic sounds as they heard them. They would anglicize, change, or shorten names, as the mood struck them. Without a family record it is exceedingly difficult to trace families earlier than the 18th century. With marriage, women's maiden names were dispensed with and lost. Federal census records list the head of the household and occasionally the number of family members. Jewish tombstones usually refer to a person's father, and rarely the mother.

PROBLEMS IN GENEALOGICAL RESEARCH. (1) Because of war and change of borders, it is often hard to know in which country to do your research.

(2) Frequently, Jews were married in Europe by religious ceremony (*ḥuppah* and *kiddushin*) but not with a civil license. Anti-Jewish legislation often forbade Jewish marriages, so couples often married secretly. Children of these marriages were not recognized by civil authorities as legitimate. Therefore, children took their mothers' surnames. Only sons were not conscripted by the Russian army. Additional sons were placed with families without sons and took that family's name.

(3) Record keeping in Eastern Europe was careless. Control of fires was poor in small villages and records were irreparably lost.

(4) Children were born at home and not in hospitals. Parents remembered the time of year ("around" which holiday) at which they were born but not the exact date.

(5) Russian records since the end of World War I are not available to the public.

(6) The pronunciation of town names varies greatly from their conventional spelling. There can be as many as 50 towns with similar sounding names all located within the same country.

(7) Documents and genealogical material may be in Yiddish, Hebrew, Russian, Polish, or other official languages.

COMPUTER AND GENEALOGY. A major problem in genealogy is information storage. The ongoing growth of genealogical information requires a constant revision of charts. For this reason many genealogists with very large inclusive family histories, resort to holding material in notebook form with sections assigned to each branch of the family. The computer with its various programs designed especially for genealogical study has become a very important tool.

In 1982 the Jewish Genealogical Society, Inc. (New York) published the first computerized Family Finder. The purpose is to enable members of all Jewish genealogy societies to list names and towns being researched in one central location. This aims at reducing the duplication of research. Entered into the computer are the name and address of the researcher along with family surnames, and the names of towns, cities, and countries being researched. (The computer service for this project is Data Universal, Teaneck, New Jersey.) The printout is updated regularly, with the inclusion of new researchers' data, and sent to Jewish genealogy societies throughout the United States so that their members can utilize the information.

Two Jewish books have been published by the Computer Center for Genealogy by Dr. Neil Rosenstein (*The Margolis Family* and *Latter Day Leaders*). This appears to be the wave of the future.

Beth Hatefutsoth, the Museum of the Diaspora, in Tel Aviv has a computer department that holds information about Jewish names, cities, and towns and stores genealogical information. Famous published genealogies are being computerized.

[Sara Schafler]

In Latin America

The Asociación de Genealogía Judía de Argentina – AGJA (Association of Jewish Genealogy of Argentina) – was founded in 1996 and is affiliated to the *International Association of Jewish Genealogical Societies – IAJGS. AGJA undertook voluntary work in documentation and digitalization of vital records, creating the database of the Jewish cemeteries in Argentina (with more than 215,000 names), and promoted similar work in Chile, Uruguay, and Peru. It digitized lists of settlers in the agricultural colonies of the Jewish Colonization Association (ICA) and is working on the lists of weddings and bar mitzvahs celebrated in synagogues in Buenos Aires.

AGJA also promoted educational activities, conferences, and courses in Buenos Aires and in other communities for adults and students. It publishes the journal *Toldot* and has published the *Diccionario de apellidos judíos* ("Dictionary of Jewish Surnames," 2003) by Benjamin Edelstein.

[Efraim Zadoff (2nd ed.)]

For additional information see *International Association of Jewish Genealogical Societies.

BIBLIOGRAPHY: BIBLICAL: Klein, in: *Zion* (*Me'assef*), 2 (1927), 1–16; 3 (1929), 1–16; 4 (1930), 14–30; Maisler (Mazar), in: *Zion*, 11 (1946), 1–16; U. Cassuto, *A Commentary on the Book of Genesis*, 1 (1961), 249–89; 2 (1964), 141–224, 250–77; J. Liver, *Toledot Beit David* (1949); idem, in: *Sefer D. Ben-Gurion* (1964), 486–99; S. Yeivin, *Meḥkarim be-Toledot Yisrael ve-Arẓo* (1960), 131ff.; Luther, in: ZAW, 22 (1901), 33–76; E. Meyer, *Die Israeliten und ihre Nachbarstaemme* (1906); W. Robertson Smith, *Kinship and Marriage in Early Arabia* (1903³), 3–39; Freund, in: *Festschrift A. Schwarz* (1917), 265–311; M. Noth, *Das System der zwoelf Staemme Israels* (1930); W. Duffy, *The Tribal Historical Theory on the Origin of the Hebrew People* (1944); De Vaux, Anc Isr, 4–7; Malamat, in: JAOS, 88 (1968), 163–73. POST-BIBLICAL AND MODERN: A. Buechler, in: *Festschrift Adolf Schwarz*

(1917), 133–62; L. Freund, *ibid.*, 163–209; A.S. Hershberg, in: *Devir*, 2 (1923), 92–100; idem, in: *Ha-Tekufah*, 28 (1935), 348–62; V. Aptowitzer, *Parteipolitik der Hasmonaeerzeit im rabbinischen und pseudoepigraphischen Schrifttum* (1927); idem, in: *Sefer Zikkaron… A.A. Poznański* (1927), 145–69; S. Klein, in: *Zion*, 4 (1939), 30–50, 177–8; idem, in: *Sefer ha-Yovel… B.M. Lewin* (1939), 86–92; J. Katz, in: *Zion*, 10 (1945), 21–54; H.L. Poppers, in: JSOS, 20 (1958), 153–79; Shunami, Bibl, 466–9; E.E. Urbach, in: *Divrei ha-Akademyah ha-Le'ummit ha-Yisre'elit le-Madda'im*, 2 (1969), 31–54. RESEARCH, GENERAL: M.Z. Baker, "Eastern European Jewish Geography; Some Problems and Suggestions," in: *Toledot: The Journal of Jewish Genealogy*, 2 (1978–79); idem, "Landsmannschaften and the Jewish Genealogist," in: *Toledot: The Journal of Jewish Genealogy*, 4 (1983); idem, "Russian Consular Collection at the Public Archives of Canada; Genealogical Implications," in: *Toledot: The Journal of Jewish Genealogy*, 4 (1983); C.G. Cohen, *Shtetl Finder Gazeteer* (1980); J. Cherny, "Jewish American Research," in: *The Source: A Guidebook of American Genealogy*, (1984); J.W. Clasper and M.C. Dellenbach, *Guide to the Holdings of the American Jewish Archives in Cincinnati* (1979); S. David, "In Search of a Sephardic Tradition," in: *Toledot: The Journal of Jewish Genealogy*, 2 (1978–79); Israeli Archives Association, *Guide to Archives in Israel* (1973); S. Gorr, *Official Gazette 1921–1948, Extract of Public Announcement of Legal Changes of Names during British Mandate in Palestine* (4 volumes; 1983); P. Grayevsky, *Avnei Zikkaron* (1920); D. Kranzler, *My Jewish Roots, A Practical Guide to Tracing and Recording Your Genealogy and Family History* (1979); A. Kurzweil, *From Generation to Generation, How to Trace Your Jewish Genealogy and Personal History* (1980); B.C. Kaganoff, *A Dictionary of Jewish Names and their History* (1977); J. Kugelmass and J. Boyarin, *A Ruined Garden, The Memorial Books of Polish Jewry* (1983); A. Morton, *Directory of European Passenger Steamship Arrivals* (1931); S. Milton, "Genealogical Sources of the Leo Baeck Institute," in: *Toledot: The Journal of Jewish Genealogy* (1979); National Archives, *Guide to Genealogical Research in the National Archives* (1983); M. Plotkin, "Eretz-Israel and Jewish Genealogy, An Introduction to the Sources for the Ottoman and Mandate Periods," in: *Toledot: The Journal of Jewish Genealogy*, 3 (1983); A. Segall, *Guide to Jewish Archives* (1981); N. Rosenstein, *The Margolis Family* (1983); idem, *Polish Jewish Cemeteries* (1984); N. and E. Rosenstein, *Latter Day Leaders, Sages and Scholars Bibliographical Index* (1983); D. Rottenberg, *Finding Our Fathers, A Guide Book to Jewish Genealogy* (1977); M.H. Stern, *Jewish Genealogy: An Annotated Bibliography Leaflet* (1976); idem, *First American Jewish Families, 600 Genealogies from 1654–1977* (1977); *Who's Who in World Jewry* (1955, 1956, 1968, 1972, 1978, 1981); D.S. Zubatsky and I.M. Berent, *A Source Book of Family Histories and Genealogies* (1984). RABBINIC: C.J.D. Azulai, *Shem ha-Gedolim ha-Shalem* (1905); I. Alfasi, *Ha-Ḥassidut* (1974); D. Einsiedler, *Rabbinic Genealogy: A Research Guide*, an annotated bibliography, (1983); B. Friedberg, *Beit Eked Sefarim* (1956); N.Z. Friedman, *Oẓar Ha-Rabbanim* (1975); N.S. Gottlieb, *Ohalei Shem* (1912); J. Levenstein, *Dor Dor ve-Dorshav* (1949); H. Michael, *Or ha-Ḥayyim* (1965); N. Rosenstein, *The Unbroken Chain*, New York (1976); N. Rosenstein and E. Rosenstein, *Latter Day Leaders, Sages and Scholars Bibliographical Index*, Computer Center for Jewish Genealogy (1983); A. Stern, *Meliẓei Eish* (1974); A. Walden, *Shem Ha-Gedolim Ha-Ḥadash* (1879); M. Wunder, *Me'orei Galicia; Encyclopedia Le-Ḥahkmei Galicia*, vol. I–II (1978); Encyclopedia Judaica, Ḥasidic Dynasties. EXAMPLES OF SOME OUTSTANDING BIOGRAPHIC GENEALOGIES: S.M. Auerbach, *The Auerbach Family* (1957); S. Epstein, *Mishpahat Luria* (1910); *The Feuchtwanger Family*; L. Lauterbach, *Chronicles of the Lauterbach Family*; A. Siev, *Rabbeinu Moshe Isserles* (REMA) (1972); E.B. Weill, *Weil-De Veil, A Genealogy 1360–1956* (a Rabbinic family with Christian branches; 1957). SEPHARDI RESEARCH: A.L. Frumkin, *Sefer Toldot Ḥakhmei Yerushalayim* (1910); J. Gelis, *Encyclopedia le-Toledot Ḥakhamei Eretz Israel* (1973); C. Neppi and M. Ghirondi, *Toledot Gedolei Israel ve-Geonei Italia* (1853); M. Markowitz, *Shem ha-Gedolim ha-Shelishi* (1910); S. Rosanes, *Korot ha-Yehudim be-Turkiah ve-Ateret ha-Kedem* (1905, 1945); R. Halperin, *Atlas Eẓ Ḥayyim* (sections on Spain, Egypt, Israel, Italy, Turkey, and North Africa) (1978); A.M. Hyamson, *The Sephardim in England: A History of the Spanish and Portuguese Jewish Community 1492–1951*; A. Chouraqui, *Between East and West: A History of the Jews in North Africa* (1973); C. Roth, *World of Sephardim; A History of the Marranos* (1954); M. Angel, *La America* (1982); Keyserling, *Bibliotheca Espagnol-Portugesa-Judaica* (German; 1890); *Encyclopaedia Sephardica Neerlandica* (Dutch; 1949); R. Singerman, *The Jews in Spain and Portugal*, a bibliography (1975). RABBINIC FAMILY GENEALOGIES: *Avot Atarah le-Banim*, for the families Katzenellenbogen, Wahl, Lifschutz back to Rashi; *Mishpaḥat Luria*, for families Luria, Treves, Spira; *Shem mi-Shimon*, for families Schapira, including the Baal Shem Tov; *Mishpaḥot Atikot be-Yisrael*, on Schapira and others related to them; *Toledot Mishpaḥat Horowitz, ha-Dorot ha-Rishonim*, Horowitz Family; *Toledot Mishpaḥat ha-Rav mi-Liady*, for the Schneersons of the Lubavitch Dynasty; *Daat Kedoshim*, intertwined families; *The Auerbach Family; Chronicles of the Lauterbach Family; Sefer Ḥut ha-Meshullash*, on the Sofer-Schreiber and Eiger families; *Nitei Ne'emanah*, on the Rubinstein family; *Toledot Mishpaḥat Schor; Toledot Mishpaḥat Rosenthal, The families from Hungary; Reshimoth Aboth: Eine Ahnentafel von 27 Generationen bis zum Yahre 1290*, on the Rabbinic families, Seckbach, Auerbach, Hirsch, Marx, Bodenheimer. **ADD. BIBLIOGRAPHY:** A. Kurzweill and M. Weiner, *Encyclopedia of Jewish Genealogy* (1994). HOLOCAUST: M. Weiner, *Jewish Roots in Poland: Pages from the Past and Archival Inventories* (1997); idem, *Jewish Roots in Ukraine and Moldova: Pages from the Past and Archival Inventories* (2000).

°GÉNÉBRARD, GILBERT (1537–1597), French theologian and Hebraist. Born in Riom, Auvergne, Génébrard, a pupil of the Provençal convert Abraham de Lunel, who is said to have reverted to Judaism in his latter years, was a polymath, specializing in biblical exegesis, theology, patristics, liturgy, chronology, and rabbinics. Unlike many of his contemporaries, he was in general opposed to the Kabbalah. From 1569 Génébrard was professor of Hebrew and Bible at the Collège de France and from 1593 he was archbishop of Aix-en-Provence. His outspoken support for the Catholic League – which opposed Henry of Navarre, a Protestant – incurred official wrath after the latter's accession (as Henry IV). Génébrard died in disgrace. As a Hebraist, he was considered an expert on the correct pronunciation of the "holy tongue." He was a prolific writer, translator, and editor: Steinschneider lists about two dozen of his publications.

His works include *Commemoratio divorum et ritus nuptiarum, e libro Maḥzor* (published with *Symbolum fide); Eldad Danius … De Judaeis clausis* (Paris, 1563), a Latin version of the Travels of *Eldad ha-Dani; *De metris Hebraeorum ex libro R. David Jechiae…* (Paris, 1562–63), an edition of the *Sha'ar bi-Melekhet ha-Shir* of R. David b. Solomon *Ibn Yaḥya; ΕΙΣΑΓΩΓΗ *rabbinica ad legenda et intelligenda Hebraeorum Rabbinorum Commentaria sine punctis scripta…* (Paris, 1563); *Alphabetum Hebraicum* (Paris, 1564); and *Symbolum fidei Judaeorum … Precationes …* DCXIII *legis Praecepta e capitulis* *ultimis More Nebuchim* (Paris, 1569), based on *Maimonides. Génébrard also published *Chronologia Hebraeorum Major* (Paris, 1578), a Latin version of the *Seder Olam* of *Yose b. Ḥalafta, a shortened version of which, *Hebraeorum breve Chronicon usque ad 1112*, had appeared earlier (Paris, 1573); there are various later editions of this book. Two other works by Génébrard are *Jakob Salomonis cap. Chelek* (published with the *Chronicon*), a Latin edition of the commentary by Jacob b. Solomon Habib on a chapter of the tractate *Sanhedrin* (of the Babylonian Talmud) much studied by Renaissance Christian Hebraists and kabbalists; and an edition of the Song of Songs with three rabbinical commentaries (Paris, 1570). Gilbert Génébrard's pupils included the French diplomat and kabbalist, Blaise de *Vigenère.

BIBLIOGRAPHY: F. Secret, *Les Kabbalistes Chrétiens de la Renaissance* (1964), 201–3; idem, *Le Zôhar chez les Kabbalistes Chrétiens de la Renaissance* (1964^2), 88–91; Steinschneider, Cat Bod, nos. 1006–08; *Dictionnaire de théologie catholique*, 6 (1920), 1183–85.

[Godfrey Edmond Silverman]

GENERAL ZIONISTS, Zionist and Israeli party. The General Zionists were originally a loose political group within the Zionist movement, made up of those Zionists who were neither socialists nor religious and who at first did not draw up a program of their own. Their number at the Zionist Congresses kept dwindling from one Congress to the next. In Ereẓ Israel the General Zionists began to organize in 1922, the first meetings being attended by *Aḥad Ha-Am, Meir *Dizengoff, B. Mossinson, Ze'ev *Gluskin, and others.

The first world conference of the representatives of these "civilian circles," as they were called, occurred in 1929, in the course of the Zionist Congress that took place in Zurich. The moving force behind this organization was Isaac Ignacy *Schwarzbart. In 1931 the World Union of General Zionists held its founding conference, adopting the following principles: (1) Ereẓ Israel and the Jewish people take priority over class and sectarian interests; (2) labor and property should unite to serve the people; (3) in addition to the support afforded by the national funds for the activities of the pioneers, encouragement should be given to private enterprise and the settlement of individuals with limited means; (4) partisan control over all educational, health, and welfare institutions should be abolished. These principles remained the basis of the General Zionist program throughout the years.

Among the founders of the World Union were Leo *Motzkin, Stephen S. *Wise, Louis *Lipsky, Kurt *Blumenfeld, Menahem *Ussishkin, Benzion *Mossinson, Moshe *Gluecksohn, Yehoshua *Suprasky, Peretz *Bernstein, Emil Schmorak, and Schwarzbart. Though operating most of the time on his own, Chaim *Weizmann was also associated with the new movement.

The World Union did not survive as a unified organization for long, and the General Zionists formed numerous factions, the main ones being General Zionists A, headed by Weizmann, which was closer to the Labor movement, and General Zionists B, headed by Ussishkin. The reasons for the frequent splits varied, and combined elements of personal rivalry and ideological issues on the political, economic, and social levels.

As was common among the other Zionist parties and groupings, the General Zionists had their own youth movements from the 1920s, especially in Eastern Europe. These movements bore names such as Ha-No'ar ha-Ivri, Ha-Shomer ha-Tahor, Ha-No'ar ha-Ẓiyyoni, and Akiva. Some of them advocated pioneering and formed the General Zionist He-Ḥalutz.

The first group of General Zionist youth, made up of members of Ha-No'ar ha-Ivri in Galicia, settled in Ereẓ Israel in 1930 and established the first General Zionist kibbutz, near Petaḥ Tikvah. They were followed by others, from various countries, constituting the core group of a General Zionist labor movement. In the initial stage, they all joined the *Histadrut, though they objected to the Histadrut's socialist ideology, advocating a syndicalist approach. In 1934 an independent General Zionist workers organization was established by some of the General Zionist workers, though others remained in the Histadrut as the Oved ha-Ẓiyyoni faction. However, most of the General Zionists in Ereẓ Israel belonged to the middle class rather than the working class. In Ereẓ Israel, as in the Diaspora, splits also took place within the ranks of the General Zionists, especially over the question of whether to fight for their views from within the *Va'ad Le'ummi (and later the Government of Israel) or as an external opposition.

In the early 1940s the various factions reunited, under Moshe *Sneh. In 1946 the General Zionist workers' organization rejoined the Histadrut, and became a separate faction in it, side by side with Ha-Oved ha-Ẓiyyoni.

The reunion of the General Zionists did not survive, and prior to the establishment of the State in 1948, they entered the political scene as two separate parties, one by the name of the General Zionist Party and the other, which also included members of Aliyah Ḥadashah, which had been formed in 1942 by immigrants from Central Europe, by the name of the Progressive Party. Both parties participated in the Provisional Government, but while the Progressive Party also joined the first regular government formed by David *Ben-Gurion after the elections to the First Knesset, and joined most of the governments formed in subsequent years, the General Zionists remained in opposition, except for the years 1952–55. Both parties opposed the over-politicization of the labor-dominated system that controlled the employment agencies and public health system, and fought against the separate trends in education. Both also supported a liberal approach to economic policy.

The General Zionists ran independently in elections to the First to Fourth Knessets, receiving 7 seats in the First Knesset, 20 seats in the Second (which grew to 23 when the Sephardi and Yemenite parliamentary groups joined it), 13 seats in the Third, and 8 seats in the Fourth.

In 1961 the General Zionist Party and the Progressive Party united and established the Liberal Party. Four years later, in 1965, the general council of the Liberal Party voted in favor of the establishment of a joint bloc with the *Ḥerut movement for elections to the Sixth Knesset and the local authorities (see *Gaḥal). It was finally mostly the former General Zionists who joined the new bloc, while most of the former Progressives broke away to form the *Independent Liberal Party.

In the Zionist Organization, both parties belonged to the World Union of General Zionists and participated in its work, but by the late 1960s the Independent Liberals became an independent group on the Zionist scene as well.

BIBLIOGRAPHY: K. Sultanik (ed.), *General Zionist Movement* (1956); M. Kol, *Misholim* (1964); J. Klausner, *Mahutah u-She'ifoteha shel ha-Ẓiyyonut ha-Kelalit* (1943); M. Gluecksohn, *Im Ḥillufei Mishmarot*, 1 (1939), 98–105 and passim; M. Kleinman, *Ha-Ẓiyyonim ha-Kelaliim* (1945). **ADD. BIBLIOGRAPHY:** Y. Drori, *Bein Yamin le-Semol: ha-Ḥugim ha-Ezraḥiyyim bi-Shnot ha-Esrim* (1990); D. Sha'ari, *Mi-"Setam Ẓiyyonut" le-"Ẓiyyonut Kelalit": Iḥud u-Fillug be-Reshit Darka shel ha-Ẓiyyonut ka-Kelalit ha-Olamit 1929–1939* (1990); S. Zalman Abramov, *Al Miflagah She-Ne'elmah ve-al-Liberalizm* (1995); N. Shiloah, *Merkaz Holekh ve-Ne'alam: Ha-Ḥugim ha-Ezraḥiyyim be-Ereẓ Yisrael bi-Shnot ha-Sheloshim* (2003).

[Susan Hattis Rolef (2nd ed.)]

GENESIS, BOOK OF, the first book of the Pentateuch. The English title refers to the opening theme of the book and is derived, via the Latin transliteration, from the tradition of the Alexandrian Jews as reflected in the Septuagint Greek: *genesis*, "origin"). The book describes not only the origin of what would later be called the universe, but the origins of the people Israel and some of its specific practices including the Sabbath and circumcision. Genesis includes numerous etiologies for, among others, labor pains and fruitless labor. The Joseph story, which concludes the book, provides the background for Israel's descent into Egypt, and accordingly, for the enslavement, exodus, and arrival at the border of the promised land to which the next four books of the Pentateuch are devoted. The popular Hebrew name (Heb. בְּרֵאשִׁית) is based on the initial word (cf. TJ, Meg. 3:1, 74a; TJ, Sot. 1:10, 17c; Gen. R. 3:5; 64:8). Some medieval Hebrew manuscripts also use the titles "First Book" (*Sefer Ri'shon*) and the "Book of the Creation of the World" (*Sefer Beri'at ha-Olam*). Another title occasionally in use was the "Book of the Upright" (*Sefer ha-Yashar*), referring to the patriarchal narratives (cf. Av. Zar. 25a; TJ, Sot. 1:10, 17c).

The book is traditionally divided into 12 *parashiyyot*, "annual pericopes," and 43 (in some Mss. 45) *sedarim*, "triennial pericopes." There are 43 *petuḥot*, "open sections," and 48 *setumot*, "closed sections." Printed Hebrew Bibles, based upon the Vulgate system, divide the book into 50 chapters containing 1,534 verses in all.

The Contents

Genesis is a narrative account of the span of time from the creation of the world to the death of Joseph. (See Table: Book of Genesis- Contents.) It divides naturally into two main parts, the first dealing with the universal history of early humankind (chapters 1–11), the rest being devoted to the story of the patriarchs and their families (chapters 12–50). The time span purportedly covered by the book is 2,307 (or 2,309 cf. 11:10) years according to the accepted received Hebrew text. This may be calculated by combining the sum of the ages of the fathers of mankind at the birth of their respective successors (1,946 or 1,948 years; Table 1: The time span from Adam to Abraham's birth) with the years that elapsed between the birth of Abraham and the death of Joseph (361; Table 2: The time span from Abraham's birth to the death of Joseph). Great imbalance in the presentation of the material is evident, for the first 11 chapters deal with a time span of over 2,000 years while the other 39 are devoted to only one eighth of the period treated. Moreover, the only themes elaborated in detail in the universal history are Creation, the Flood, and the ethnic division of mankind. This disproportion may be taken as indicative of the aims and purposes of Scripture. It is less interested in recording history for its own sake than in the utilization of events as vehicles for the demonstration, objectification, and transmission of the verities of biblical faith.

Composition – The Critical View

Genesis itself contains no information about its authorship, nor can any biblical passage be cited in support of a tradition concerning it. Based on expansive readings of such passages as "Moses wrote this Torah" (Deut. 31:9) post-biblical Judaism, followed by classical Christianity, accepted the unitary origin of the entire *Pentateuch as the divinely inspired work of *Moses, so that Genesis in its present form is regarded as being a homogeneous composition, the product of Mosaic authorship. (For the traditional view see *Pentateuch; Traditional View.) Serious biblical study of the past few centuries has shown that there is no basis for the claim of Mosaic authorship. The presence of anachronisms, the use of different Hebrew names for God, diversity of style and vocabulary, and the existence of duplicate and sometimes varying and even contradictory accounts of the same event all serve as the criteria for literary analysis that leads to the conclusion that Genesis is really a composite work put together from different documents deriving from varying periods. For example, the sanctity of (Jeru)salem and its priesthood in the period of David and Solomon is justified by Abr(ah)am's actions in Gen. 14. Jacob's vow to build a temple at Beth-el (Gen. 28:22) would seem to be directed to a tenth-century audience as a justification for the construction of the Beth-el temple by Jeroboam (I Kings 12). The table of nations in Gen. 10 knows of the kingdoms of Babylonia and Assyria but not of Persia, an unlikelihood after the rise of that empire in the sixth century B.C.E. The flood story, although going back to third millennium tales, cannot have reached its present form before the early first millennium when *Ararat (Gen. 8:14) replaced the former name for what would later be called Armenia. Genesis 1, which emphasizes the goodness of the creation in direct opposition to Isa. 45: 7 (Weinfeld) is a Jewish adaptation of the Zoroastrian "good creation" by Ahuramazda (Sperling 1999).

Book of Genesis – Contents

1:1–11:32	**PART I: Universal History**
1:1–6:4	**Creation from Adam to Noah**
1:1–2:4a	The story of Creation; the Sabbath.
2:4b–3:24	Adam and Eve in the Garden of Eden.
4:1–16	Cain and Abel.
4:17–26	The genealogy of Cain; the rise of civilization.
5:1–32	The line of Adam to Noah.
6:1–4	The "sons of God" and the daughters of men.
6:5–11:32	**From Noah to Abraham**
6:5–8:32	The Flood.
9:1–17	The blessing and the covenant with man.
9:18–29	Noah's drunkenness.
10:1–32	The table of nations.
11:1–9	The Tower of Babel.
11:10–32	The line of Shem to Abraham.
12:1–50:26	**PART 2: Patriarchal History**
12:1–25:18	**Abraham**
12:1–9	The call of Abraham; the migration to Canaan.
12:10–20	Abraham and Sarah in Egypt.
13:1–18	Abraham and Lot.
14:1–24	The battle of the kings; Abraham blessed by Melchizedek.
15:1–21	The covenant with Abraham.
16:1–16	Abraham, Sarah and Hagar; Divine promises regarding Ishmael.
17:1–27	The covenant concerning circumcision.
18:1–33	Abraham and the three messengers; the intercession for Sodom.
19:1–29	The destruction of Sodom and Gomorrah.
19:30–38	Lot and his daughters; the birth of Moab and Ammon.
20:1–18	Abraham and Sarah at Gerar.
21:1–8	The birth of Isaac.
21:9–21	The expulsion of Hagar and Ishmael.
21:22–34	Abraham and Abimelech at Beer Sheba.
22:1–19	The binding of Isaac (Akedah).
22:20–24	The line of Nahor.
23:1–20	The purchase of Machpelah and the burial of Sarah.
24:1–67	The marriage of Isaac to Rebekah.
25:1–6	The line of Keturah.
25:7–18	The death and burial of Abraham; the line of Ishmael.
25:19–36:43	**Isaac and Jacob**
25:19–34	The birth of Jacob and Esau; the sale of the birthright.
26:1–33	Isaac,Rebekah and Abimelech at Gerar.
26:34–35	Esau's Hittite wives.
27:1–28:5	Jacob's deception of Isaac.
28:6–9	Esau's Ishmaelite wife.
28:10–22	Jacob at Bethel.
29:1–30:43	Jacob with Laban.
31:1–54	Jacob's flight from Laban.
32:1–32	Jacob at Mahanaim and Penuel; Jacob wrestles with the angel.
33:1–20	Jacob meets Esau; his purchase of land at Shechem.
34:1–31	The rape of Dinah.
35:1–15	Jacob revisits Bethel.
35:16–29	Family affairs in Canaan.
36:1–43	The lines of Esau and Seir the Horite; early kings of Edom.
37:1–50:26	**Joseph and his brothers**
37:1–36	Joseph and his brothers.
38:1–30	Judah and Tamar.
39:1–23	Joseph in Potiphar's house.
40:1–23	Joseph in prison.
41:1–57	Pharoah's dreams; Joseph's rise to power; the years of abundance and the start of the famine.
42:1–44:34	Joseph encounters his brothers.
45:1–28	Joseph discloses his identity.
46:1–47:10	The migration of the Israelites to Egypt.
47:11–27	Joseph's agrarian policy.
48:1–50:21	Jacob's farewell blessings; his death and burial.
50:22–26	The death of Joseph.

ANACHRONISMS. Abraham's native city is called "Ur of the Chaldeans" (11:28, 31; 15:7) although the people known by that name did not penetrate southern Mesopotamia before the end of the second millennium B.C.E., long after the period in which the patriarchal narratives are set. Genesis 12:6 relates that "the Canaanite was then in the land," while 13:7 states that "the Canaanites and Perizzites were then dwelling in the land," implying that neither people existed at the time of the writer, whereas both survived as late as Solomon's time (I Kings 9:16, 20; cf. Josh. 16:10; Judg. 1:27–33; II Sam. 24:7). The reference to Dan (Gen. 14:14; see Kimhi a.l.) is irreconcilable with later history (Josh. 19:47; Judg. 18:29). The mention of Philistines (Gen. 21:32, 34; 26:1, 8, 14, 15, 18; cf. 10:14) presents a similar problem since that particular ethnic group did not settle on the Canaanite coast before the end of the 12th century B.C.E. The city of Beersheba (Gen. 26:33) was not settled until the 11th century. A phrase like "committing an outrage in Israel" (34:7) is difficult as a direct quotation from Jacob's time (though not in the time of Moses) but seems rather to be of a proverbial nature (cf. Judg. 20:6, 10; Jer. 29:23) deriving from a period when "Israel" was already designated as an established ethnic or cultic community. The list of eight Edomite kings (Gen. 36:31–39) would cover about 150 years of history. Since the Edomites were not settled in Transjordan before the 11th century B.C.E. (LEVY). This conclusion is buttressed by the phrase "before any king reigned over the Israelites" (36:31) which would set the passage in the time of the Israelite monarchy, as was seen by Yizhaki apud Ibn Ezra.

DUPLICATIONS. There are two irreconcilable accounts of Creation. In the one (1:26–28), man and woman are created simultaneously as the climax of creation after the birds and animals; in the other (2:7, 18, 19, 22), the order is man, animals, birds, then woman. The Flood story presents similar contradictions. One passage demands a single pair of each species of beast, bird, and creeping things to be taken into the ark (6:19–20), while another has orders to Noah to take aboard seven pairs of clean animals and birds and one pair of unclean (7:2–3), and still a third passage reports that Noah took two of each species irrespective of their clean or unclean status (7:8–9). One account refers to 40 days of rain and a further 14 days until the waters had finally subsided (7:4, 12, 17; 8:6–11); another speaks of a duration of 150 days (7:11; 7:24–28:1; 8:3–4) and an entire year and ten days before Noah was able to emerge from the ark (7: 11; 8:13–14). Sarah was twice taken from her husband, once by Pharaoh (12:11–20) and once by Abimelech (20:1–18). A similar story is related about Rebekah and Abimelech (26:6–11). In all three accounts the wife is passed off by the spouse as his sister for his own protection. Hagar twice leaves her mistress in flight to the wilderness (16:6–14; 21:9–19). Both narratives have in common the presence of a well, an angelic visitation, and divine assurances of greatness for Ishmael. Two accounts of the origin of the name Beer-Sheba in the days of Abimelech are given, one concerning Abraham (21:22–32) and the other concerning Isaac (26:26–33). The story of Isaac's expectation of imminent death (27:1–2) does not seem to be compatible with his still being alive at least 20 years later (35:28). The names of Esau's wives given in 26:34 and 28:9 do not correspond with those recorded in 36:2–3. There are duplicate etiologies for the names Bethel (28:17–19; 35:14–15) and Israel (32:29; 35:10). Rachel's death (35:19) seems not to be in consonance with Jacob's reaction to Joseph's dream 17 years later (37:10), and the birth of Benjamin near Bethlehem (35:16–17) makes difficult his inclusion in the list of Jacob's sons born in Paddan-Aram (35:23–26). Finally there seem to be two separate traditions about the identity of those who bought and sold Joseph; they are variously called Midianites (37:28a, 36) and Ishmaelites (37:27, 28b; 39:1).

THE DIVINE NAMES. The foregoing material has to be supplemented by the variant use of divine names. Genesis employs YHWH about 150 times whether in direct quotation (cf. 4:1; 14:22; 15:2, 7, 8 and so about 30 times), or in the narrative (over 100 times). The patriarchs built altars to YHWH (12:7, 8; 13:18, cf. 8:20) and invoked His name (12:8; 13:4; 21:33; 26:25; cf. 4:3; 25:21, 22). According to 4:26 this practice began as early as the days of Enosh. It is clear, however, from Exodus 3:14 and 6:2–3 that another tradition existed which ascribed the initial revelation of the name YHWH to the time of Moses. Indeed, large sections of Genesis do not use that divine appellative at all, employing Elohim or some other name instead.

On the basis of all the phenomena just described, critical scholars have attempted to reconstruct the literary history of Genesis. The classical critical position is that there once existed a Judahite history which began with the creation of the world and which preserved the tradition of the early use of the name YHWH (J source). Later on, a parallel Ephraimite history appeared which commenced with Abraham and which, preserving the tradition of a later origin of YHWH, used ʾElohim (E source) exclusively in the patriarchal narratives. A redactor (R) fused the two accounts into a single narrative (JE). Still another source, this time of priestly origin (P), which had the same tradition about YHWH as did E, was interwoven with JE, so that the present Genesis is a composite of JEP with admixtures of R. Each source, it is claimed, betrays its own peculiarities of literary style and phraseology and displays its own distinctive religious and theological outlook.

The basic distribution of Genesis according to the classical three-source hypothesis of the Graf-Wellhausen school appears in the table: Book of Genesis – Analysis of the Book of Genesis.

It should be noted that chapter 14 cannot be fitted into any of the sources. In some instances such as chapters 31 and 45:1–28, the J and E sources have been so interwoven that disentanglement of the strands is precarious.

In the course of time the inadequacies of the original Graf-Wellhausen hypothesis have led to an expansion of the three sources through the continuous subdividing of each document and by the isolation of still other sources. Some time ago O. Eissfeldt claimed to identify an L (lay) document which, he claimed, is the oldest narrative strand. More recently, claims have also been made for a separate "Promises" writer. Recent scholarship questions the very existence of E as a separate source. Some scholars have effectively revived the fragmentary theory of the early 19th century arguing that there are no continuous sources in the Pentateuch but rather redactional notes. Others have revived the supplementary hypothesis according to which an original narrative has been supplemented by later authors (On these matters see Carr, Hendel, Houtman, Jenks in Bibliography, and *Pentateuch). Despite the diversity of contemporary critical opinion there is no returning to the pre-critical position of Mosaic authorship.

The Distinctiveness of Genesis within the Pentateuch

Despite the contradictions and duplications, and what seems sometimes like a collection of collages, the book has a character all its own, distinguished by numerous features not shared by the other four. It is almost entirely narrative, and in the number and variety of its stories it is unparalleled. Because of its setting in the pre-Israelite period, Genesis, unlike the rest of the Torah, contains the biographies of individuals, not an account of the fortunes of the nation.

The patriarchal sagas have preserved certain social institutions that are unknown elsewhere in the Bible, although they are now documented in extra-biblical sources of the second and first pre-Christian millennia. Among these are brother-sister marriage (Gen. 20:12); concubinage and surrogate motherhood as a remedy for childlessness (16:2; 30:2–3), (perhaps) the role of the household gods in inheritance (Gen. 31:19) and the transference of the birthright (see below).

The book is peculiar, too, in its onomasticon (namestock). Of the 38 personal names connected with the patriarchal family, 27 never recur in the Bible. Nowhere else is there mention of the place-name Paddan-Aram used here so frequently (25:20; 28:2, 5, 6, 7), or is Hebron referred to as Mamre (13:18; 14:13, 18:1; 23:17, 19; 25:9; 35:27; 49:30; 50:13).

Genesis is further differentiated by some stylistic characteristics. It employs the phrase "These are the generations of" ((ו) אֵלֶּה תּ(וֹ)לְד(וֹ)ת) ten times (2:4; 6:9; 10:1; 11:10, 27; 25:12, 19; 36:1, 9; 37:2; cf. 5:1; 10:32; 25:13), which occurs only once in the

ANALYSIS OF THE BOOK OF GENESIS

Sources	Chapters and verses
P	J 4b–25 J 29 1 E 2 J 3 4 E 5 P 1–4a P 1–28
J E P	1–8 1–5 7–10 12 16b 17b 6 7 30–32 9–22 6 11 13–16a 17a 18–21
J E P	22–23 2b–3a 6–12 13b 20–22 8 9 24 1–2a 3b–5 13a 14–19 1–17
J E P	18–27 8–19 21 24–30 1–9 10 11 28–29 1–7 20 22–23 31–32
J E P	28–30 1–4a 6–20 1–5 7–11a 12 13 10–27 31–32 4b–5 6 11b–12a
J E P	12b–18 1–2a 3b–4 6–12 17–21 (14?) 15 2b–3a(?) 5(?) 13–16(?)
J E P	1b–2 4–14 J 16 P 17 J 18 E 19 1a 3 15–16 P
J E P	1–28 30–38 J 1a 2a 33 E 20 E 21 6–32 34 29 P 1b 2b–5
J E P	20–24 J 1–6 22 1–19 P 23} J 24 E 25 P
J E P	11b 18 21–26a 27–34 1–33 1–45 26 27 7–11a 12–17 19–20 26b 34–35
J E P	10 13–16 19 21b 1–14 28 11–12 17–18 20–21a 22 29 46 1–9
J E P	31–35 3–5 7–16 20b 15–23 25–28 30 30 1–2 6 17–20a 21–23 24 28b–29
J E P	24–43 } 1–18a } 19–54 4–33 1–17 31 32 1–3 33 18b 18a
J E P	J 14 21–22a 18b–20 J 34 E 35 1–8 16–20 P 9–13 15 22b–29
P	J 2b–20 25–27 28b 36 E 37 21–24 28a 28c–36 J 38 P 1–2a
J	J 27–28 39 E 40 E 41 1–45 46b–57 42 1–26 P 46a
J E P	J J 1 29–38 J 43 44 E } 45 E 46 2–5 P 6–27
J E P	28–34 1–5a 6b 13–27a 29–31 47 48 1–2 5b–6a 7–12 27b–28 3–7
J E P	1b–28a 1–11 14 } 8–22 49 50 15–26 1a 28b–33 12–13

rest of the Torah (Num. 3:1; cf. Ruth 4:18). It has God speaking in the first person plural (Gen. 1:26; 3:22; 11:7; otherwise only Isa. 6:8) which is unusual, and combines the divine names YHWH-ʾElohim, "Lord God," nearly 22 times in two chapters (2–3), such a conjunction appearing otherwise only once in the Pentateuch (Ex. 9:30).

The patriarchal narratives contain much material at variance with the legislation of the Torah. Deuteronomy 21:15–17 explicitly interdicts the transference of the birthright in contrast to what takes place in the case of Jacob and Esau (Gen. 25:23, 30–34; 27:1–33), Reuben (49:3–4; cf. I Chron. 5:1–2) and Ephraim and Manasseh (Gen. 48:13–20). Abraham entered into marriage with his paternal half-sister (20:12), something repeatedly forbidden in the Torah code (Lev. 18:9, 11; 20:17; Deut. 27:22). Jacob was simultaneously married to two sisters (Gen. 29:23, 28, 30), a state of affairs to which Leviticus 18:18 is opposed. Judah had a relationship with his daughter-in-law (and the offspring was not thereby delegitimated; Gen. 38:16; cf. Ruth 4:18). This contrasts strongly with pentateuchal law (Lev. 18:15).

Turning to the area of the cult, the same anomalous situation is apparent. Abraham planted a sacred tree in connection with worship (Gen. 21:33; cf. 12:6–7; 13:18 and see Josh. 24:26), a practice abhorred in the legislation (Deut. 16:21; cf. Ex. 34:13; Deut. 12:3). Jacob set up sacred stone pillars at Bethel (Gen. 28:18, 22; 31:13; 35:14) and Gilead (31:44–53), cultic paraphernalia otherwise outlawed by the Torah (Deut. 16:22; cf. Ex. 23:24; 34:13; Lev. 26:1; Deut. 7:5; 12:3).

The religious situation is further distinguished by other extraordinary features. The war on idolatry is unknown and there is no religious tension between the patriarchs and their neighbors. The appellation "the God of my (your/his) father" (Gen. 26:24; 28:13; et al.) is peculiarly characteristic of the book as is also the employment of numerous Divine Names, several of them unique: *ʾEl ʿElyon* (14:18, 22), *ʾEl Roʾi* (16:13), *ʾEl ʿOlam* (21:33), *ʾEl Bet-ʾEl* (31:13; 35:7), *ʾEl ʾElohe Yisrael* (33:20), *ʾEl Shaddai* (17:1; 28:3; et al.), *Paḥad Yiẓḥaq* (31:42), *ʾAbbir Yaʿaqov* (49:24). Another peculiarity, though not unique to Genesis, is the frequent appearance of angels, which are encountered by Hagar (16:7ff.; 21:17), Abraham (18:1ff.; cf. 22:11,15; 24:7, 40), Lot (19:1, 15), and Jacob (28:12; 31:11; 32:2; cf. 48:16).

The Age of the Material

The Wellhausen School had maintained that Genesis contained no creditable records dating to the second pre-Christian millennium, and that therefore, we can only extract reliable information about the time in which individual narratives were composed. Thus, an eighth-century narrative about Abraham, for example, could be employed only to illuminate the circumstances of the eighth-century writer and his audience. Crucial to Wellhausen's conclusions was his assumption that writing was unknown in Syria-Palestine of the second millennium, rendering impossible the preservation of accurate ancient traditions. In a similar vein, Wellhausen asserted that the proper names of Israel's ancestors were simply retrojections of tribal names of the first millennium. Beginning in the 1920s, continuing archaeological discoveries in the Middle East brought the second millennium into the light of history. It became clear that Wellhausen's assertions about writing were unfounded and that such ancestral names as Benjamin, Israel, Ishmael, and Jacob were genuine second millennium names. Legal procedures and documents from the second millennium provided "parallels" that seemed to demonstrate that the traditions behind Genesis were ultimately of great antiquity. The "biblical archaeology" movement, particularly associated with the name of W.F. *Albright, which employed archaeological evidence to demonstrate the "general accuracy" of Genesis' portrayal of the patriarchal period, was especially influential among Christian and Jewish religious moderates in the United States and Israel for several decades. But the pendulum has swung back. Thanks to the refinement of archaeological technique, the critical re-evaluation of reading the Bible archaeologically, especially by Thompson, and van Seters (1975), and the opening of "biblical Israel" and the Sinai to Israeli excavation following the 1967 war, opinion began to shift in the mid-1970s, i.e., shortly after the present *Encyclopaedia Judaica* entry appeared in its original form. For example, a celebrated claim had been made by E.A. Speiser that the thrice-told wife-sister story (Gen. 12, 20, 26) was an attempt by Hebrew writers to account for an ancient form of marriage known in second millennium Mesopotamia but forgotten in the course of time. Ingeniously, Speiser argued that the multiple accounts demonstrated that the writers of Genesis preserved truly ancient traditions even when they no longer understood them. Subsequent studies showed that Speiser had completely misunderstood the Nuzi documents and, indeed, misrepresented them. In other cases, true parallels, such as surrogacy as a solution for childlessness, were shown not to be confined to the second millennium and therefore irrelevant for dating the narratives of Genesis. Equally irrelevant to dating is the argument from patriarchal deviance from laws from (allegedly) later legislation. The fact that the patriarchs entered into marriages prohibited elsewhere in the Torah (see above) does not demonstrate that the patriarchal traditions are old. Rather, the prohibitions demonstrate that such marriages were common enough to elicit prohibition. The same can be said for the prohibition against alienating a birthright. Rachel's theft of the household gods has been adduced as a distant mirror of the practice known from Nuzi (in eastern Iraq) of the second millennium in which a female heir might serve the household gods. On that basis Rachel would have stolen the gods to ensure her rights to Laban's property. But the service of the gods by Nuzi women does not itself mean that the gods are the property of the women. Nor is there evidence that receipt of the gods conveyed property rights (Paradise.) Similarly inconclusive is the evidence of female cultic service from Syrian Emar (Huehnergard). Strong evidence for a first millennium background, or at the earliest, a late second millennium background, is the Aramean connection of the patriarchs. Abraham (then Abram) left Aramean Haran, his homeland (Gen. 12:1; 24:7, 10) for Canaan (The tradition of migration from Ur of the Chaldees (11:28; 15:7) originated later among Babylonian Jews.) Abraham's slave came to Haran to find a wife for Isaac (Gen. 24:4ff.); Jacob fled to Haran from the wrath of Esau (Gen. 28:2, 10) and spent a good deal of his life there. All the tribes, with the exception of Benjamin, originated in this area. Jacob's uncle Laban utters the only Aramaic phrase in the Torah (Gen. 31:47). All of this is consistent with the stories in I and II Kings of the ninth-century Hebrew prophets Elijah and Elisha healing Arameans and prophesying to them; with the "wandering/fugitive Aramaean" ancestry attributed to Israelites in Deuteronomy 26:5; with the Jacob traditions known to Hosea (Hos. 12:5) in the eighth century; and if it is not anachronistic, with the David-Absalom connection to Aramaean Geshur (II Sam. 15:8). This conclusion receives independent support from the fact that the personal names of the patriarchal ancestry are often identical with place-names in the vicinity of Haran. This is true of Terah, Abraham's father (11:24–32), of Nahor, the name of his grandfather (11:22–25) and of his brother (11:26–27, 29), of Serug, Terah's grandfather (11:20–23) and of Peleg, the grandfather of Serug (10:25; 11:16–19). In addition to allusions to the period of David and Solomon and Jeroboam noted above, the absence of any reference to Baal would point to the composition of narratives in a period between that god's fall from grace in the pre-monarchic period (Judg. 6) and his restoration under Ahab in the ninth century. Some preservation of ancient memory is indicated by the contrast between the known historic realities of the post-settlement period and the traditions about Jacob's sons. Thus, Reuben is depicted as Jacob's firstborn son (29:32; 49:3), and his name always takes pride of place in the tribal lists (35:23; 46:8) even though he lost the birthright (49:3–4; cf. I Chron. 5:1–2). Nevertheless, Reuben enjoyed no tribal supremacy in the recorded post-patriarchal history of Israel (cf. Deut. 33:6; Judg. 5:15–16). The identical situation exists in respect of Manasseh, firstborn of Joseph (Gen. 41:51; 48:14, 18–19) who likewise lost the birthright (48:1–20). The tribe was wholly eclipsed by Ephraim in later times. The image of Levi in Genesis is of a warlike and ruthless adversary (34:1–31; 49:5–7). This is at variance with the priestly and cultic functions of the tribe which played no role in the wars of conquest. Simeon is depicted as the partner of Levi in its act of violence (34:1–31), but in Joshua's campaigns Simeon was allied with Judah (Josh. 19:9; Judg. 1:3). The organization of the tribes according to matriarchs does not correspond to the post-conquest reality. Maternally related tribes did not enjoy any special political associations and their tribal territories were not always contiguous. All this makes it likely that some Genesis narratives have preserved some authentic reminiscences of early tribal history.

Abraham and Isaac enter into pacts with various peoples (14:13; 21:22–32; 26:28–31); Jacob's sons Judah and Simeon intermarry with Canaanites (38:2; 46:10); the Arameans and the Patriarchs are portrayed as being consanguineous (22:21; 24:24, 38; 25:20).

The Major Themes and Teachings

The distinctive nature of Genesis within the pentateuchal complex does not mean that it can be understood apart from the other books. On the contrary, it is the indispensable prologue to the drama that unfolds in Exodus. It provides the ideological and historical background for the relationship between God and Israel as it found expression in the events connected with the national servitude and the liberation. Its unique concept of God, of humanity, of the nature of the world, and of their interrelationships is essential to the understanding of those events.

THE GOD OF CREATION. The external points of contact between the Genesis creation account and the ancient Near Eastern cosmologies are sufficiently numerous and detailed as to leave no doubt about the influence of the latter on the former. The Genesis creation narrative, like the Egyptian Memphite Theology (COS I:21–3), presupposes a single creator god Ptah, but in contrast to Elohim, Ptah himself creates other gods, who themselves are objects of worship. The Genesis creation stories contrast with other ancient Near Eastern myths that regularly depict creation as the aftermath of the creator god's victory over the forces of chaos, a motif found in poetic biblical texts as well (e.g. Isa. 27:1; Ps. 89:10–11; 93; Job 26:11–13). Creation by divine fiat (Gen. 1:3, 6, 9, 11, 14, 20, 24) emphasizes the concept of the omnipotent, transcendent God whose will is unchallengeable. In this connection, the external literary form in which the account of cosmogony has been cast is highly instructive (See Table 3: The process of Creation (Gen. 1:1–2:3).) The creative process is divided into two groups of three days each, the first of which represents the stage of preparation or creation of the elements, the second the stage of completion or creation of those who are to make use of them. Each three-day group embraces the same number of creative acts, and in each case the first day witnesses a single deed, the second a bipartite act, and the third two distinct creations. The products of the middle days in the two groups are chiastically arranged. The seventh day is climactic and pertains to God alone. (The human institution of the Sabbath is not mentioned.) This symmetrically arranged literary pattern serves to underscore the fundamental idea that the world came into being as the free, deliberate, and meaningful expression of divine will.

HUMANITY. Another basic teaching is that the creation of humans is the culmination of the cosmogonic process. (This situation contrasts strongly with the Babylonian myth of Atar-Hasis, which like Genesis moves from creation to the great flood (COS I:450–53]), in which humans are created to do all the work that the minor deities rebelled against doing.) Only here is the divine act preceded by an annunciation of intention (1:26). Only humans are created "in the image of God" (1:26, 27), and to them alone is the custody and exploitation of nature's resources entrusted (1:26, 28, 29). In the second account of the creation of humans, their unique position is emphasized by the fact that their appearance constitutes the sole exception to creation by divine fiat and requires, as it were, a special and personal effort by God, from whom they directly receive the breath of life (2:7). At the same time, the exceptional mention of the material out of which the human was formed (2:7) is suggestive of the limitation of humanity's God-like qualities.

EVIL. The sevenfold affirmation of the goodness of God's creative acts (1:4, 10, 12, 18, 21, 25, 31) is singular in the Bible and indicates the influence of Zoroastrian theology whereby the creator-god effected a good creation. The Jewish writers of Genesis 1 who lived in the post-exilic period adapted the Persian notion to the needs of Jewish monotheism.

THE MORAL LAW. The divine punishment of Cain for fratricide (4:3–16) and the visitations upon the generation of the Flood for its corruption (6:9–8:22) and upon Sodom and Gomorrah for their wickedness (chapters 18–19) all presuppose the existence of a divinely ordained order of universal application, for the infraction of which humans are ultimately and inevitably brought to account.

THE UNITY OF HUMANKIND. The idea of the derivation of all mankind from one common stock is manifested through the divine creation of a single pair of humans as ancestors to all humanity. It is reinforced by the genealogical lists that illustrate the process of development from generation to generation. This concept of the family of humanity and its essential unity receives its consummate expression in the "Table of Nations" (chapter 10), in which the totality of ethnic entities is schematized in the form of a family genealogical tree deriving from the three sons of Noah and their wives, the only human survivors of the Flood.

DIVINE ELECTION. The universal focus in Genesis is gradually narrowed through a process of divine selectivity. Noah is singled out for salvation from the rest of humankind (6:8). Of his sons, Shem is especially blessed (9:26), and his line receives outstanding attention (10:21–31; 11:10–32). His genealogy is continued to the birth of Abraham (11:26) who becomes the elect of God and founder of a new nation (cf. 18:19). Again, of Abraham's two sons, Ishmael is rejected and Isaac chosen (17:7–8, 19, 21; 21:14; 25:6; 26:3–4), and the selective process is repeated in respect of his offspring (35:9–12). The divine blessing of Jacob is the final stage, since at this point the patriarchal period ends and the national era begins. Nevertheless, the universal interest is not neglected entirely for the divine promises involve Israel in the international community (12:1–3; 18:18; 22:18; 26:14; 28:14).

THE COVENANT AND THE PROMISES. One of the most extraordinary features of Genesis is its conception of the relationship between God and humankind in terms of a covenant by which, as an act of grace, God commits Himself unconditionally to the welfare of humankind. This is first explicated in the case of Noah (6:18; 9:8–17; cf. 1:28–29). With the advent of Abraham, the covenant becomes the dominant theme of the entire book, to which all else is preparatory and which itself becomes prologue to the rest of the Bible. The oft-repeated promises to the Patriarchs consist basically of two parts – a future national existence and the possession of national territory. Abraham is to father a great people destined to inherit the land of Canaan (12:2–3; 13:14–17; 15:4–5, 18–21; 17:2, 4–8; 22:17–18). The same is reaffirmed to Isaac (26:3–4) and Jacob (28:13–14; 35:10–12; cf. 46:2–4; 48:3–4). In fact, most subsequent scriptural references to the three Patriarchs are in connection with these promises, and the measure of their paramount importance may be gauged both by the frequency of their repetition and by the fact that the book closes on this very theme (50:24).

The promissory covenant in Genesis lacks mutuality. It is a unilateral obligation freely assumed by God. The solemnity and immutable nature of the act of divine will is conveyed through a dramatic covenant ceremonial (chapter 15). Abraham's worthiness is indeed stressed (18:19; 22:12, 16; 26:5), and his offspring to come, throughout the ages, are to observe the rite of circumcision as the symbol of the covenant (17:9–14). It should be noted, though, that the idea of a national covenant on Sinai with all its implications for the religion of Israel is beyond the horizon of Genesis, which sees in the promises to the Patriarchs the guarantee of God's eternal grace to Israel and the assurance of eventual deliverance from Egypt (cf. 15:14; 50:24; Ex. 6:4–5).

GOD AND HISTORY. The concepts of God and the covenant in Genesis inevitably mean that the presence of God is to be felt on the human scene. History is thus endowed with meaning. A literary characteristic of the Genesis narratives is the employment of schematized chronology, the featuring of neatly balanced periods of time and the use of symbolic numbers to give prominence to this idea.

The ten generations from Adam to Noah are paralleled by a like number separating Noah from Abraham. The birth of each personality represents, from the biblical point of view, the arrival of an epochal stage in history. It is not accidental that the arts of civilization appear precisely in the seventh generation after Adam (Gen. 4:20–22), through the sons of Lamech who himself lived 777 years (5:31). See Table 1.

Turning to the period of the Patriarchs, it is significant that Abraham lived 75 years in the home of his father and the same number of years in the lifetime of his son Isaac, that he was 100 years of age when Isaac was born, and sojourned 100 years in Canaan (12:4; 21:5; 25:7). Jacob lived 17 years with Joseph in Canaan and 17 years with him in Egypt (37:2; 47:9, 28). See Table 2.

The Patriarchs resided a total of 250 years in Canaan (21:5; 25:26; 47:9), which is exactly half the duration of their descendants' stay in Egypt (Ex. 12:40; according to the Greek and Samaritan versions the correspondence is exact). The important events in their lives are recorded in terms of a combination of the decimal and sexagenary systems with the occasional addition of seven (See Table 4: Important events in the lives of the Patriarchs). The idea is clearly projected that what is happening is the stage by stage unfolding of the divine plan of history.

Table 1. The time span from Adam to Abraham's birth

Genesis	Personality	Age at birth of first-born
5:3	Adam	130
5:6	Seth	105
5:9	Enosh	90
5:12	Kenan	70
5:15	Mahalalel	65
5:18	Jared	162
5:21	Enoch	65
5:25	Methuselah	187
5:28	Lamech	182
5:32	Noah	500
11:10	Shem	100
11:12	Arpachschad	35
11:14	Shelah	30
11:16	Eber	34
11:18	Peleg	30
11:20	Reu	32
11:22	Serug	30
11:24	Nahor	29
11:26	Terah	70
		1946[1]

[1] or 1948 according to Gen. 11:10

Table 2. The time span from Abraham's birth to the death of Joseph

Genesis	Personality	Age
21:5	Abraham at the birth of Isaac	100
25:26	Isaac at the birth of Jacob	60
47:28	Life span of Jacob	147
41:46 45:6 47:28 50:26	From the death of Jacob to the death of Joseph	54
		361

Table 3. The process of Creation (Gen. 1:1–2:3)

Group I		Group ii	
Day	Element	User	Day
1	Light (1:3–5)	Luminaries (1:14–19)	4
2	Sky Terrestial Waters (1:6–8)	Marine life (fish) Sky life (fowl) (1:20–23)	5
3	Dry land Vegetation (1:9–13) (Lowest form of organic life)	Land animals Man (1:24–31) (Highest form of organic life)	6
7 *Divine cessation from creativity* (2: 1–3)			

Table 4. Important events in the lives of the Patriarchs

Personality	Event	Age	Source
			Genesis
Abraham	Migrated from Haran	75	12:4
	Married Hagar	85	16:3
	At birth of Isaac	100	21:5
	At death	175	25:7
Sarah	At birth of Isaac	90	17:17
	At death	127=2x60+7	23:1
Isaac	Married Rebekah	40	25:20
	At birth of twins	60	25:26
	At Esau's Marriage	100	26:34
	At death	180=3x60	35:28
Jacob	At migration to Egypt	130	47:9
	At death	147=2x70+7	47:28
Joseph	At sale to Egypt	17=10+7	37:2
	At rise to power	30	41:46
	At death	110	50:26

BIBLIOGRAPHY: COMMENTARIES: H.E. Ryle (Eng., 1921); B. Jacob (Ger., 1934); J. Skinner (Eng., 19302); S.R. Driver (Eng., 1948[15]); C.A. Simpson and W.R. Bowie (Eng., 1952); U. Cassuto (Eng., 2 vols. 1961–64); G. Von Rad (Eng., 1961). GENERAL STUDIES: A.T. Chapman, *An Introduction to the Pentateuch* (1911); Kaufmann Y., Toledot, 1 (1960), 207–11; idem, in: *Molad*, 17 (1959), 331–8; M.H. Segal, in: JQR, 46 (1955/56), 89–115; 52 (1961/62), 41–68; 53 (1962/63), 226–56; B. Gemser, in: OTS, 12 (1958), 1–21; J. Finegan, *In the Beginning* (1962); U. Cassuto, *The Documentary Hypothesis* (1965[4]); O. Eissfeldt, *The Old Testament…* (1965), 194–9; N.M. Sarna, *Understanding Genesis* (1966); B. Mazar, in: JNES, 28 (1969), 73–83. ON CHAPTERS 1–11: W.F. Albright and S. Mowinckel, in: JBL, 58 (1939), 87–103; U. Cassuto, in: *Knesseth*, 8 (1943), 121–42; S.N. Kramer, in: JAOS, 63 (1943), 191–4; 64 (1944), 7–23, 83; idem, in: *Studia Biblica et Orientalia*, 3 (1959), 185–204; R.A.F. Mackenzie, in: CBQ, 15 (1953), 131–40; K. Cramer, *Genesis 1–11* (1959); B.S. Childs, *Myth and Reality in the Old Testament* (1960); A. Heidel, *The Babylonian Genesis* (1963); idem, *The Gilgamesh Epic* (1963); G.C. Westerman, *The Genesis Accounts of Creation* (1964). On patriarchal period see bibliographies to *Abraham, *Isaac, *Jacob, *Joseph, *Patriarchs. **ADD. BIBLIOGRAPHY:** E.A. Speiser, in: J. Finkelstein and M. Greenberg (eds.), *Oriental and Biblical Studies… Writings of Speiser* (1967), 62–82; M. Weinfeld, in: *Tarbiz*, 37 (1968), 105–32; T. Thompson, *The Historicity of the Patriarchal Narratives* (1974); J. van Seters, *Abraham in History and Tradition* (1975); idem, IDB Sup, 645–48; idem, *The Pentateuch: A Social Science Commentary* (1999); J. Huehnergard, in: CBQ, 47 (1985), 428–34; J. Paradise, in: D. Owen and M. Morrison (eds.), *Nuzi and the Hurrians*, vol. 2 (1987), 203–13; C. Westermann, *Genesis*, 3 vols., tr. J. Scullion (1985–87); N. Sarna, *JPS Torah Commentary Genesis* (1989); G. Plaut, in: *DBI*, 1:436–42; C. Houtman, in: *DBI*, 2:257–62; A. Jenks, in: ABD, 2:478–82; R. Hendel, ibid., 933–41 (extensive bibliography); D. Carr, *Reading the Fractures of Genesis* (1996); S.D. Sperling, *The Original Torah* (1998), 75–102; idem, in: R. Chazan et al., *Ki Baruch Hu…Studies…Levine* (1999), 373–85; T. Levy et al., in: *Antiquity*, 78, no. 302 (2004), 865–79.

[Nahum M. Sarna / S. David Sperling (2nd ed.)]

GENESIS RABBAH (Heb. בְּרֵאשִׁית רַבָּה), aggadic Midrash on the Book of Genesis, the product of Palestinian *amoraim*.

Title

The earlier title of the Midrash was apparently *Bereshit de-Rabbi Oshaya Rabbah* (*Genesis of R. Oshaya Rabbah*) so named after its opening sentence, "R. Oshaya Rabbah took up the text…" (Gen. R. 1:1), this being later abbreviated to *Genesis Rabbah*. This explanation is superior to the suggestion that it was so called in order to distinguish it from the biblical Book of Genesis of which it is an expansion (*rabbah* means "great").

Structure

Genesis Rabbah is an exegetical Midrash which gives a consecutive exposition of the Book of Genesis, chapter by chapter, verse by verse, and often even word for word. It is a compilation of varying expositions, assembled by the editor of the Midrash. The work is divided into 101 sections (according to the superior Vatican 30 manuscript; other manuscripts and the printed versions have minor variations in the number of sections). Often the division into sections was fixed according to the open and closed paragraphs of the Torah (see *Masorah), and at times according to the triennial cycle of the weekly readings of the Torah in Ereẓ Israel which had been customary in earlier times. All of the sections, with seven exceptions, are introduced by one or several proems, one section having as many as nine. The total for the entire work is 246. The proems are of the classical type common to amoraic Midrashim, opening with an extraneous verse which is then connected with the verse expounded at the beginning of the section. Most (199) of the proems in *Genesis Rabbah* are based on verses from the Hagiographa (principally Psalms and Proverbs), only a small number being from the Prophets (37) and the Pentateuch (10). The proems are largely anonymous and in most instances commence without any of the conventional introductory formulae or *termini technici*. Those that are ascribed to authors are mostly amoraic, only two being tannaitic. Generally, the sections have no formal ending, but some conclude with the verse with which the following section begins, thus providing a transition. On rare occasions the ending carries a message of consolation. Characteristic of *Genesis Rabbah*, as of the other early amoraic Midrashim, tannaitic literature, and the two Talmuds, are its repetitions. An exposition or story is often transferred in the Midrash where an expression appears in more than one context.

Language

The language of *Genesis Rabbah* closely resembles that of the Jerusalem Talmud. It is mostly written in mishnaic Hebrew with some Galilean Aramaic. The latter is used especially for the stories and parables, in which many Greek terms and expressions are also interspersed.

The Redaction of the Midrash

In the early Middle Ages, some scholars ascribed the work to the author of the opening proem of the Midrash, Oshaya, of the first generation of Palestinian *amoraim*. The fact, however, that *Genesis Rabbah* mentions the last group of Palestinian *amoraim* who flourished in the second half of the fourth century C.E. (about 150 years after Oshaya) shows this ascription to be erroneous.

The editor used early Aramaic and Greek translations of the Bible (the translation of *Aquila is quoted three times in the Midrash), but was unacquainted with Targum *Onkelos on the Pentateuch, which was used in a Babylonian milieu. While he clearly used the *Mishnah, some scholars have assumed that he did not make use of our *Tosefta, or of the extant **Midreshei Halakhah* (Albeck, *Mavo*), though this issue needs further investigation. They also conclude that he made no use of **Avot de-Rabbi Nathan*, a relatively late aggadic compilation, or even of the much earlier *Seder Olam Rabbah*. Since there are many parallel passages in *Genesis Rabbah* and the Jerusalem *Talmud, scholars have understandably devoted considerable attention to the complex question of their relation to each other. Recently H. Becker devoted an entire study to a reexamination of this issue. In an extended review of this work, C. Milikowsky criticizes the author for not drawing a clear distinction between the question of literary dependence between individual passages found in these two works, and the larger question of literary dependence between these compositions as complete and fully redacted literary works. Milikowsky, however, falls prey to this very confusion when he writes (concerning Lev. R. and Pes. deRav Kahana) "if we succeed in reconstructing which text used the other, then we have the rare opportunity of seeing exactly what a rabbinic redactor does with the material he is revising" (528). Milikowsky rightly draws our attention here to what may be the only matter of substance in this entire scholarly debate. Nevertheless, the question of "exactly what a rabbinic redactor does with the material he is revising" can be determined *only* on the level of individual passages, and it is more than likely that in some cases the redactor of *Genesis Rabbah* reworked an earlier literary tradition which is preserved in a more original form in the Jerusalem Talmud, whereas in other cases the opposite may be the case. This can be explained by positing that some of the *aggadot* and *halakhot* which occur in both *Genesis Rabbah* and the Jerusalem Talmud were derived from earlier common sources (perhaps from oral traditions). Alternatively, both *Genesis Rabbah* and the Jerusalem Talmud may have undergone successive revisions (as did the Babylonian Talmud), even after they took on a fairly distinct and identifiable literary form as redactional wholes, such that either one of them could have drawn upon a version of the other which differs in some respects from the works which we possess today. Therefore the artificial linking of the important issue of the nature of rabbinic redactional revision of earlier literary sources to the broader (and far less significant) question of possible literary dependence of one or the other of these two finished and complete literary works on the other only leads to methodological and conceptual confusion.

On the basis of its language, of the names of sages mentioned in it (most of whom were Palestinian *amoraim*), and of various historical allusions, it is clear that the work was edited in Ereẓ Israel, probably in the beginning of the fifth century C.E. *Genesis Rabbah* is thus the earliest amoraic aggadic Midrash extant; it is also the largest and the most important. The other amoraic aggadic Midrashim, including *Leviticus Rabbah* and *Lamentations Rabbah*, already made use of it. The first explicit reference to the work, however, occurs in *Halakhot Gedolot*.

The editor drew upon both written and oral sources. *Ben Sira is mentioned four times in *Genesis Rabbah*, on one occasion being introduced by the phrase, "As it is written in the book of Ben Sira" (Gen. R. 91:4). *Genesis Rabbah* contains many *aggadot* which also occur in the other Apocrypha, the Pseudepigrapha, and in the works of *Philo and *Josephus. No conclusions, however, are to be drawn from this regarding any relation between *Genesis Rabbah* and these works, it being highly probable that they drew upon a common source or early oral traditions. In addition, *aggadot* and ideas from Jewish-Hellenistic literature often reached the sages through indirect channels. In addition to amoraic statements, *Genesis Rabbah* naturally contains much tannaitic aggadic material. Having assembled all of this material, the editor arranged it according to the order of the verses in the Book of Genesis, abbreviating, or modifying as he saw fit.

Later Additions

In *Genesis Rabbah* there are several parts (in 75, 84, 88, 91, 93, 95ff.) whose language, style, and exegetical character do not form an integral part of the original Midrash but are later additions. In most manuscripts the original expositions on the end of the pentateuchal portion of *Va-Yiggash* and the beginning of that of *Va-Yeḥi* are omitted and replaced by others of later origin and which belong to a type of **Tanḥuma Yelammedenu* Midrash.

Editions

Genesis Rabbah was first published in Constantinople in 1512 together with four other Midrashim on the other books of the Pentateuch, though these latter have nothing in common, as regards style and date of editing, with *Genesis Rabbah*. This edition and Midrashim on the five scrolls (which were previously published separately) were reprinted in Venice in 1545 and reissued several times.

Genesis Rabbah has appeared in a scholarly, critical edition based on manuscripts and containing variant textual readings and comprehensive commentary. This edition is one of the finest such works of modern rabbinic scholarship. It was begun by J. *Theodor in 1903 and completed in 1936 by Ḥ. *Albeck, who also wrote the introduction. From the numerous manuscripts at his disposal, Theodor chose the London manuscript, written about the middle of the 12th century. Careful examination of the manuscripts by Albeck, however, established the manuscript Vatican 30, copied in the 11th century, as superior. The London manuscript is probably a later formulation of the same tradition recorded in the Vatican manuscript. This conclusion has been subsequently confirmed by Y. *Kutscher's linguistic studies of the Vatican 30 manuscript which have shown it to represent an accurate archetype of Galilean Aramaic. A facsimile edition of the Vatican 30 manuscript was published in 1971 with an introduction by M. Sokoloff, and in the following year a facsimile edition of a previously unknown manuscript of *Genesis Rabbah* (Vatican 60), which was at first thought to be equal in importance or perhaps even superior to the Vatican 30 manuscript, but after a detailed analysis of this manuscript by M. Kahana, this has proven not to be the case. *Genesis Rabbah* was translated into English in the Soncino series by M. Friedman (1939) and again more recently by J. Neusner (1985).

BIBLIOGRAPHY: Frankel, Mevo, 51b–53a; M. Lerner, *Anlage und Quellen des Bereschit Rabba* (1882[2]); Weiss, Dor, 3 (1883), 252–61; Ḥ. Albeck, *Mavo le-Midrash Bereshit Rabbah* (1936); idem, *Midrash Bereshit Rabbati* (1940), 1–54 (introd.); J. Mann, *The Bible as Read and Preached in the Old Synagogue*, 1 (1940); Zunz-Albeck, Derashot, 76–78, 123–124. **ADD. BIBLIOGRAPHY:** L.M. Barth, *An Analysis of Vatican 30* (1973); M. Sokoloff, *The Geniza Fragments of Bereshit Rabba* (Hebrew) (1982); O. Meir, in: *Proceedings of the Tenth World Congress of Jewish Studies*, 3:1 (1990), 101–8; idem, in: *Te'uda*, 9 (Hebr.) (1996), 61–90; M. Kahana, in: *Te'uda*, 9 (1996), 17–60 (Hebr.); H. Becker, in: *The Synoptic Problem in Rabbinic Literature*, ed. S. Cohen (2000), 145–58; idem, *Die grossen rabbinischen Sammelwerke Palästinas: Zur literarishen Genese von Talmud Yerushalmi und Midrash Bereshit Rabba, Texte und Studien zum antiken Judentum 70* (1999); C. Milikowsky, in: JQR, 92:3–4 (2002), 521–67; A. Goldberg, in: *Meḥkarei Talmud*, 3:1 (2005), 130–52.

[Moshe David Herr / Stephen G. Wald (2nd ed.)]

GENESIS RABBATI (Heb. בְּרֵאשִׁית רַבָּתִי), a Midrash on the Book of Genesis usually ascribed to *Moses ha-Darshan of Narbonne (first half of 11th century). The Midrash was published from the only extant manuscript by Ḥ. Albeck (Jerusalem, 1940). However *Raymond Martini in his *Pugio Fidei* included many excerpts from "*Genesis Rabbah* of Moses ha-Darshan," which he termed "The large *Genesis Rabbah*," calling the well-known *Genesis Rabbah "The Minor [or short] *Genesis Rabbah*." The relationship between these extracts and *Genesis Rabbati* has been a subject of dispute among scholars. Zunz, whose sole knowledge of it was derived from S.J. Rapoport, assumed that the quotations found in Martini's work had been extended and given the name *Genesis Rabbati*. In this way he explained the differences between *Genesis Rabbati* and the fragments in the *Pugio Fidei*. S. Buber argued that *Genesis Rabbati* should not be ascribed to Moses ha-Darshan on the specious ground that he could not find in it certain quotations from Moses ha-Darshan cited by Rashi, the *tosafot*, and Abrabanel in his *Yeshu'ot Meshiḥo*. Epstein held that *Genesis Rabbati* is an abridged form of "the large *Genesis Rabbah*" mentioned in the *Pugio Fidei*, finding support for his view in the very fact that many of the quotations cited by Martini in the name of Moses ha-Darshan do not occur in *Genesis Rabbati*. He came to the conclusion that in fact "the large *Genesis Rabbah*" was not the work of Moses ha-Darshan, but of an anthologist who used some of Moses' work. Ḥ. Albeck accepted the view of Epstein concerning the relationship between *Genesis Rabbati* and "the large *Genesis Rabbah*." He reinforced his view by a comparison between the *Midrash Aggadah* published by Buber (which is based upon the Midrash of Moses ha-Darshan) and with *Numbers Rabbah* to the portions *Ba-Midbar* and *Naso* (chapters 1–15), which is also based, as he succeeded in proving, upon the Midrash of Moses ha-Darshan (an opinion already expressed by S.D. Luzzatto in his notes to *Numbers Rabbah*).

Genesis Rabbati is based upon the classical sources of the *halakhah*, viz., the two Talmuds, the *targumim, Sefer Yeẓirah*, and all the known Midrashim, but reveals an especially wide knowledge of variant readings in the Midrashim. In the main, however, it is based upon *Genesis Rabbah* (of which it also gives variant readings). The unique quality of *Genesis Rabbati* lies in its quotations from the Apocrypha and Pseudepigrapha, and particularly from the Testaments of the Twelve Patriarchs, quoting it either directly or from the *Midrash Tadshe*, which is to a considerable extent dependent upon these works. Epstein even maintains that *Midrash Tadshe* is the work of Moses ha-Darshan. Quotations from the latter are mostly cited in the name of *Phinehas b. Jair to whom the *Midrash Tadshe* is attributed because of its opening words. Similarly, in quoting from other Midrashim which were attributed to definite authors, Epstein attributes such statements to their presumed author. *Genesis Rabbati* does not quote its sources verbatim but adapts them (as is the case with the other Midrashim based upon the Midrash of Moses ha-Darshan). Moses was accustomed to combine sources, to change one source in order to equate it with another, to explain one by means of the other, etc. He also added his own explanations and made great use of **gematria*. His treatment of the sources and his additions, while having a precedent in the early Midrashim, clearly indicate his desire to create a new Midrash which would however reflect the biblical exegesis of the rabbis of the Midrash, and this aim is equally evident in the additions. The importance of this Midrash lies not only in its quoting of the sources but also in its biblical exegesis and in its exposition of the Ashkenazi **piyyut* which came into being at about this time. There are no clear proofs of the direct use of *Genesis Rabbati* by authors of this period, though certain references by authors to *Genesis Rabbah*, which do not occur there, may refer in fact to *Genesis Rabbati*.

BIBLIOGRAPHY: A. Epstein, *R. Moshe ha-Darshan mi-Narbona* (1891); Ḥ. Albeck, *Midrash Bereshit Rabbati* (1940), introduction. **ADD. BIBLIOGRAPHY:** Y. Ta-Shma, *Rabbi Moshe ha-Darshan ve-ha-Sifrut ha-Ḥitẓonit* (2001); S. Yahalom, in: *Peamim*, 94–95 (2003), 135–58.

[Jacob Elbaum]

GENETIC ANCESTRY, JEWISH.

Background

The human genome refers to approximately three billion chemical letters (nucleotides) comprising the sequence of deoxyribonucleic acid (DNA) in almost every cell of each human being. There are four different nucleotides (adenine, guanine, cytosine, thymidine), such that each of the approximately three billion sites of the human DNA sequence comprising the human genome is occupied by one of these four nucleotide chemical letters. Human genome analysis has revealed that on the face of the planet, on average, any two individuals differ from each other at fewer than merely 0.1% (1⁄10,000) of these sites. These differences among individuals arise from inaccuracies during the process wherein DNA is replicated and transmitted from generation to generation. Furthermore, the pattern of variable sites is not randomly scattered across the 3 billion-nucleotide genome. Rather, certain combinations of variable sites are often transmitted in blocks known as haplotypes.

DNA sequence variants are detected by genotyping or DNA sequencing methods. In the minority of cases, such variable sites may predispose to disease (disease-predisposing mutations), but for the most part they simply serve as "neutral DNA markers." In addition to medical and forensic applications, DNA sequence variation markers are convenient for tracing shared ancestries, family relations, genealogic networks, migratory patterns, and geographic origins of individuals, communities, and populations. This discipline is called DNA sequence based phylogenetics or phylogeography.

While analysis of the genome provides important insights with respect to population history, including Jewish origins and history – for both scientific and ethical reasons, such analysis does not provide an appropriate tool for establishing Jewish or any other religious or ethnic identity at an individual or community level. Scientifically, the variation in DNA sequence identity among Jews is too broad, and overlaps that of non-Jews sufficiently, so as to negate the concept of unique or characteristic genomic markers for Jews. Furthermore, Jewish identity is a concept based on tradition, law, culture, and custom, rather than on physical considerations, including DNA sequence. Attempts to use any biological markers to establish Jewish identity in individuals have been fraught with unwanted and tragic consequences in the past. Therefore, inferences regarding patterns of DNA sequence variation should be interpreted with great caution, with regard to both scientific and societal considerations.

DNA markers are distributed across all of the various distinct regions of the genome, which in humans consists of 22 pairs of autosomal chromosomes, the sex chromosomes (XX in females and XY in males), and mitochondrial DNA. Most of the genome is diploid, meaning that there is representation of each nucleotide site from both parents. However, the Y-chromosome of the genome in males, and mitochondrial DNA in both males and females are haploid, meaning that there is only representation from one parent (uniparental). In the case of the Y-chromosome, the DNA sequence including its variable site markers is transmitted only from fathers to their sons. In the case of mitochondrial DNA, the DNA sequence including its variable site markers is transmitted only from mothers to both their male and female offspring. Furthermore, at these uniparentally inherited haploid regions the genome is free of a process called recombination, which does occur at the diploid regions of the genome. Recombination shuffles markers between the two parental copies at corresponding genomic regions. For most of the length of the Y-chromosome (the nonrecombining or NRY region) and for the entire mitochondrial DNA, no recombination occurs. Thus, analysis of DNA markers on the NRY region of the Y-chromosome and mitochondrial DNA has emerged as a powerful tool in phylogenetics of male and female lineages respectively. Markers outside of these haploid regions have also been used in genome based phylogeographic analysis. However, the dual inheritance, with biparental presentation together with recombination, renders the interpretation of shared ancestry and phylogenetics more complex and often ambiguous. It should be noted, that when DNA sequence variants anywhere in the genome are disease-predisposing mutations, differences in their frequency among Jewish communities in comparison with non-Jews can contribute to certain health and disease epidemiologic patterns (see *Genetic Diseases in Jews). The current entry will be divided into a description of genomic analysis of Jewish populations along male and female lineages, followed by an integrated overview.

Application of Phylogenetics to Jewish Populations

The molecular principles described above have been usefully applied to the evolutionary studies of humankind as a whole, as well as to the phylogenetics of various populations of interest. These studies address questions related to geographic origins, ancestry, history, migration, and demography of populations. Likewise, it is possible to phrase similar questions with regard to the parental ancestry of contemporary Jews. To do so, it is necessary, first, to delineate accepted nomenclatures and classifications for Jewish communities and second, to clarify how the use of different classes of genetic markers enables distinct questions of interest to be addressed. To this end, contemporary Jews can be considered as descending from two large population groups which had somewhat separate demographic histories during the past approximately two millennia. These are the Ashkenazi and non-Ashkenazi groups, which in turn are comprised of numerous different communities. It is clear that this division oversimplifies the relations and hierarchy between the various Jewish communities. Thus the Ashkenazi population of Europe, which refers to Jews whose recent ancestry traces to Central and Eastern Europe, is, often regarded as one population subgroup, despite clearly being composed of multiple communities. This classification has emerged because of shared adherence to similar religious rituals, liturgical style, and the shared use of the Yiddish language, and geographic location in Central and Eastern Europe. Of relevance to phylogenetics was the practice of a high level of endogamy, wherein Ashkenazi Jews married within the population subgroup. The non-Ashkenazi population subgroup is a much more culturally and geographically diverse population. The majority of the non-Ashkenazi population is composed of communities that resided in the Near and Middle East, North Africa, and geographic locations to which the Jews fled following the Iberian expulsions, beginning in 1492 C.E. These communities share similar religious rituals, most probably due to their presumed common historical origin from a gradual movement of Babylonian Jews, and are sometimes collectively referred to as the "Sephardi (Spanish)" or "Mizraḥi (Eastern)" Jews. In the current entry, we shall adhere to this convention though, where appropriate, based on available information, the term "Spanish exile" will refer to members of Jewish communities descended from the Iberian expulsions, and shall use the term "non-Ashkenazi" when the detailed geographic origin does not permit a more precise description. Moreover, neither the term "Sephardi" nor "Mizraḥi" takes into account some additional Jewish communities such as some of the Italian, Georgian, Yemenite, and Indian communities.

Following the foregoing definitions, two complementary sets of questions arise. First, what is the overall pattern of the contemporary NRY and mitochondrial DNA sequence variation at the level of the entire Jewish population in comparison to non-Jews, and of individual population subgroups or communities? More specifically this set of questions relates to our overall ability to trace recent or contemporary Jewish communities to a particular geographic origin such as the Near East, and allows analysis of parameters such as admixture and gene flow with Diaspora host populations. Second, DNA marker analysis enables clarification of micro-evolutionary mechanisms and events that have shaped the population history of each of the Jewish communities. These include the actual number of founding ancestors, their rate of expansion, their most likely geographic origin, and the level of identity between the various Jewish founding ancestors in different Jewish communities. The answers to both sets of questions are addressed separately for paternal and maternal population history, using the NRY-region of the Y-chromosome and mitochondrial DNA respectively, and in some cases these are expected to yield different patterns.

To gain a clearer understanding of the way in which these questions can be addressed, it is important to clarify the different kinds of DNA sequence variation markers that are available for analysis, and the ways in which they can be combined to generate phylogenetic trees, with different levels of temporal resolution. Haplogroups are generally defined by a series of hierarchically arranged stable variations or polymorphisms in DNA sequence (usually at a single nucleotide site and hence termed single nucleotide polymorphisms or SNPs) that have usually occurred only once in the course of human evolution. These are binary or bi-allelic, since there are only two variants in the human population, rather than multiple different variants. Numerous such binary sites are located throughout the NRY, and when combined they define major haplogroups. Individuals belonging to the same NRY haplogroup share common paternal ancestry at a level of resolution and timeframe that is a function of the number and choice of such binary sites. In the case of mitochondrial DNA, these binary sites are usually located in the portion of the circular mitochondrial DNA genome that is termed the coding region, and these define maternal haplogroups. Haplogroups enable the most basic level of phylogenetic assignment of humans into populations on the basis of shared paternal or maternal ancestry and hence phylogeographic origin. Such haplogroup analysis has been used to trace African origins and subsequent major migration routes for all anatomically modern humans on the planet. In the case of paternal haplogroups, defined by binary markers on the NRY, these have been given designations of major haplogroups A through R, based on the use of a few dozen binary markers, and each such haplogroup can be further refined and subdivided into a hierarchical tree of subhaplogroups, using many additional binary markers. These subhaplogroups are given additional lower case letter and number designations. As an example, NRY haplogroups A and B are dominant in Africa and absent in the Americas. Of relevance to the origin of Jewish populations, the Near East as a whole is populated by a varied mix of major haplogroups among which the most frequent are E and J. Similarly the mitochondrial major haplogroups are designated by letters A through Z, and then again further subdivided using numbers and lower case letters, using additional coding region binary markers. In the case of mitochondrial DNA haplogroups, the major L haplogroup is dominant in Africa and absent in the Americas. Of relevance to Jewish population origins, and as is the case for the Y-chromosome, the Near East is populated with a long list of major mitochondrial haplogroups, among which H, J, T, U, and K are frequent. It is important to emphasize that the most common major haplogroups can be found across very large geographic expanses, and in turn comprise numerous lineages that usually coalesced many thousand years ago. Lineages refer to branches within a given haplogroup or subhaplogroup which can be related to each other by additional classes of DNA sequence variation markers. Many such additional classes of markers exist, and together they are distinguished from haplogroup-defining binary markers in several ways. First, there may be more than two variants – such as in the case of simple tandem repeat markers (STRs) on the NRY. Also, they represent DNA sequence mutation events which may occur at a much more rapid rate compared to haplogroup defining binary markers, and as such may also have occurred at a given site repeatedly many times in human history, as occurs in the D-loop or control region of mitochondrial DNA. Such repeat markers are often said to define haplotypes within haplogroups, or lineages. Thus a phylogenetically defined lineage represents a cluster of related evolving haplotypes within a haplogroup. As noted, a haplogroup at any level of binary marker resolution is composed of numerous such coalescing lineages, whose relatedness can be determined using analysis of haplotype-defining repeat markers. Thus, while documentation or comparison of haplogroup frequencies within or among populations of interest provides important information regarding large but specific geographic origins, this does not effectively allow determination of the real number of ancestral parental lineages that gave rise to the present-day diversity in a population. This can be likened to the hands on a clock, in which haplogroups are like the hour hand, and haplotypes are like the minute hand, and a lineage represents a given number of minutes within the interval defined by the hour hand. There is a slight difference in the way haplotypes are measured and determined for the NRY and for mitochondrial DNA, with a greater emphasis on the use of STRs in the case of the NRY, and use of D-loop sequence variants in the case of mitochondrial DNA. The advantage of using haplotype-defining repeat markers is invaluable in the study of the genomic structure of population groups, since they evolve quickly enough to trace recent historical events from DNA samples of extant living individuals. It is this genomic tool which has provided several important insights regarding Jewish populations, whose demographics and histories had previously been described on the basis of oral tradition, archival records, linguistic and liturgical analysis. Analysis of the genome has provided a complementary tool to these more classical approaches, and yielded additional insights.

Jewish Paternal Ancestry – View from the NRY Markers of the Y-Chromosome

The first recorded studies at the level of the genomic DNA sequence variation appeared in 1993, and compared Sephardi and Ashkenazi Jews in comparison to non-Jewish Czech males. These reported that the two Jewish population subgroups show a great similarity of NRY DNA marker frequencies, and appear to show very little evidence for admixture with host non-Jewish neighbors. Of interest, comparison with Lebanese non-Jews supported the notion of a shared Near East origin for both Ashkenazi and Sephardi Jewish population subgroups examined. Studies over the subsequent decade utilized progressively larger and more diverse sample sets, and a greater number of DNA sequence markers. Taken together this decade of work on the NRY markers strongly supports the hypothesis that the paternal gene pool of Jewish communities from Europe, North Africa, and the Middle East descended from a common Near Eastern ancestral population, and suggest that most Jewish communities have remained relatively isolated from neighboring non-Jewish communities during and after the Diaspora. The two most prevalent major NRY haplogroup affiliations shared among all Jewish communities are those denoted J and E. Further research based on haplogroup markers has shown that, with some notable rare exceptions, the NRY chromosome pool of both Ashkenazi Jews and non-Ashkenazi Jews originates as an integral part of the genetic landscape of the Near East. Further analysis at the haplotype level suggested that the pattern of haplotype differentiation within these shared haplogroups differs between the Jewish population and non-Jewish Near Eastern populations. This is entirely consistent with a shared remote Near East origin but subsequent separation of the ancestors of contemporary Jews from their non-Jewish Near East shared ancestral population. Such separation involved the establishment of a separate ethnic identity and restriction in marital admixture. The separation would have been accentuated by migration of the Jewish population from the Near East and into other parts of the world, during the Diasporas. In others words, the biological events leading to the emergence of the major haplogroups observed in Jews and non-Jews with whom they share common Near East ancestry are much older than the populations in which these haplogroups are found. While the similar and shared Near Eastern background at the haplogroup level predates the ethnogenesis in the region, the haplotype structure is more recent and has evolved after the establishment of the Jews as a population group. To date, the Ashkenazi subpopulation of the Jews has been studied in the greatest detail, though there is a steadily increasing accumulation of comparably detailed genomic information for non-Ashkenazi communities. In the most detailed paternal phylogenetic study of the Ashkenazi to date by Behar and Skorecki in collaboration with an international team of scientific colleagues, a detailed resolution of the haplogroup structure according to the Y Chromosome Consortium recommendations was obtained. Based on the genotyping results, the Ashkenazi haplogroups were divided into the following three categories: major founder haplogroups, minor founder haplogroups, and shared haplogroups. The first two categories included those haplogroups likely to be present in the founding Ashkenazi population (and that now occur at high and low frequency respectively). The latter category is comprised of haplogroups that either entered the Ashkenazi Jewish gene pool recently as the result of introgression from European host populations, and/or that were present in both European and Jewish populations before the dispersal of the ancestral Ashkenazi population through Europe.

Haplogroup E-M35 and haplogroup J-12f2a fit the criteria for major Ashkenazi Jewish founding subhaplogroups, because they are widespread both in Ashkenazi Jewish communities and in Near Eastern populations, and occur at much lower frequencies in European non-Jewish populations. Subhaplogroups G-M201 and Q-P36 show a similar pattern, but are found at lower frequency, and are therefore considered to have been part of the founding paternal Ashkenazi Y-chromosome pool. It has not yet been established if these minor subhaplogroups are shared with non-Ashkenazi Jews. The best candidates for subhaplogroups that entered the Ashkenazi Jewish population more recently via admixture from the neighboring European populations include I-P19, R-P25, and R-M17. Taken together these results confirmed that the majority of NRY haplogroups found among contemporary Ashkenazi Jews originated in the Near East, with an approximately 8% introgression from non-Jewish European populations. Two events of interest seem to have made very specific independent contributions to this minor degree of introgression, and these will be described in the subsequent section. However, overall genomic analysis provides definitive evidence refuting a major contribution to the Ashkenazi Y-chromosome pool of any large scale entry into the population from the Caucasus, the putative geographic location of the Khazarian Kingdom, or from any other European or Eurasian source population. While a study of this detail in non-Ashkenazi communities is still to be done, multiple lines of evidence from the genomic literature strongly support a common Near Eastern paternal origin for all Jewish communities, with low levels of introgression from neighboring non-Jews in the Diasporas. These findings also provided the backdrop for detailed analysis of lineages to clarify demographic patterns and microevolutionary forces that have shaped the detailed population structure of different Jewish communities and Jewish population subgroups. A number of illustrative examples are provided herein.

GENOMIC ANALYSIS OF THE JEWISH PRIEST AND LEVITE CASTES. Phylogenetic analysis is based upon relatedness of individuals within a group. Genetic analysis has confirmed that all of humankind is phylogenetically related as descendents of a common maternal and paternal ancestor. In some societies, extensive records are maintained which document relationships and establish pedigrees extending over many generations, and this information can be used to facilitate genomic studies. While such biparental pedigree information is not available extending back to the early history of the Jewish people, there exists an oral tradition which may provide information about shared paternal ancestry, which has proven to be of interest, and must be taken into account in phylogenetic studies of Jews. In particular, a long-established system of Jewish male tribal or caste affiliation categorizes Jewish men into three groups: Jewish *priests or kohanim, *levites, and Israelites. Within the Jewish community, membership in the male castes noted above, is determined by patrilineal descent. Kohanim are, in biblical tradition, the descendants of Aaron, who along with his brother Moses was a male descendant of Levi, the third son of biblical patriarch Jacob. According to the same tradition, Levites are considered to be those remaining male descendants of Levi who are not kohanim. These categories are recognized and affiliations of individual Jewish males to one of the three castes is widely known in virtually all Jewish communities, including Sephardi, Ashkenazi, and other.

More specifically, self-identification with the Jewish priestly caste reflects an oral tradition of transmission by inheritance from father to son with no halakhically sanctioned mechanism for introgression of males who are not descendents along the paternal line from the founder of this male dynasty. Accordingly, this tradition carries with it specific scientific predictions based on the molecular genomics of the Y-chromosome. Since, as noted, the Y-chromosome is also transmitted from fathers only to their male offspring, it is predicted that the Y-chromosome of historically and geographically dispersed priests should have a significantly greater similarity of DNA sequence markers compared to Y-chromosomes of other groups. Comprehensive clarification of the patterns of paternal relatedness, based on NRY marker analysis, requires combining haplogroup with haplotype analysis, to trace actual lineages. Indeed, several research studies beginning in 1997, and carried out over many years and across several continents, reveal a statistically significant greater degree of similarity of such NRY markers among contemporary Jewish priests compared to other groups tested. This similarity applied equally when tested across Ashkenazi and non-Ashkenazi communities. This finding has been durable and has withstood the test of a decade of verification. Utilization of NRY STR markers, whose rate of change occurs at a surmised rapid pace, enabled the tracing of lineages and also determination of lineage coalescence times, in order to bracket an approximate timeframe for the establishment of this patrilineal Jewish priestly dynasty. Thus for example, using a set of six STR markers (DYS19, DYS388, DYS390, DYS391, DYS392, and DYS393), a single haplotype, termed the Cohen Modal Haplotype, was found to be the most frequent, and to be shared among priests from both the non-Ashkenazi and Ashkenazi communities. The scores (corresponding to the number of repeats in each named STR marker respectively) for this six-STR haplotype are 14, 16, 23, 10, 11, and 12 and are now known to belong to NRY haplogroup J, which, as noted above, is the most frequent haplogroup in the Near East and among Jews in particular. In a 1998 study, the modal haplotype frequencies were found to be 0.449 and 0.561 for the Ashkenazi and Sephardi kohanim, respectively. The corresponding modal frequencies for the Ashkenazi and Sephardi Israelites in this same study were found to be 0.132 and 0.098, respectively. This lower frequency highlights the difference in criteria for overall Jewish affiliation compared to affiliation with the Jewish priesthood. Overall Jewish identity, since at least talmudic times (100 B.C.E.–500 C.E.) has traditionally been acquired either by descent from a Jewish woman, or alternatively by rabbinically authorized conversion, without the need to establish descent from a common male (or female) ancestor. In contrast as noted above, affiliation to the Jewish priesthood was restricted along patrilineal lines of descent. The use of one-step mutation haplotypes, termed the Cohen Modal Cluster, allowed the calculation of the coalescence to the most common recent ancestor by standard accepted mutation rates. This calculation gave an estimate of approximately 106 generations, which for a generation time of 25 years gives an estimated range which brackets a mean of 2,650 years before the present. These results establish the common origin of the Jewish priesthood caste in the Near East, coinciding with a timeframe beginning at approximately the biblically attributed date of the exodus from Egypt and extending to the Temple period. However, it should be noted that such dating estimates are based on numerous inherent assumptions and carry with them a wide error margin. The availability of more binary as well as STR markers for the NRY is now enabling further refinement at both the haplogroup and haplotype levels, and these numerical estimates may change based on future genome analysis. Furthermore, the discovery of a modal haplotype and cluster is based on statistical analysis, and does not permit specific validation of priestly status for a given individual. The latter depends upon cultural, religious, and social considerations which are not related to genome analysis for a given individual.

Of interest, the same studies in 1997 and 1998 found high frequencies of multiple haplogroups in the levites, indicating that no single recent origin could be inferred for the majority of this group, despite an oral tradition of a patrilineal descent similar to that of the kohanim (with some exceptions outlined in talmudic tractate *Bekhorot*). This led to a more detailed NRY analysis of the levites. In particular, given the importance of the paternally defined levite caste in Jewish history, together with multiple theories of the ethnogenesis of the Ashkenazi Jewish community, and a suggestion that Yiddish is a re-lexified Slavic tongue, Behar and Skorecki, together with an international team of scientific collaborators, reported in 2003 a detailed investigation of the paternal genetic history of Ashkenazi levites. They compared the results with matching data from neighboring populations among which the Ashkenazi community lived during its formation and subsequent demographic expansion. The finding clearly demonstrated among the Ashkenazi levites, a major tightly clustered lineage within NRY haplogroup R-M17, which comprises 74% of Ashkenazi levites within this haplogroup and 52% of Ashkenazi levites overall. The presence of the R-M17 haplogroup within Ashkenazi levites is striking for several reasons. Firstly, this haplogroup is found at high frequency in the Ashkenazi levites but not in Sephardi levites, nor any other geographically or religiously designated Jewish grouping examined to date. This means that a large and closely related subgroup of the Ashkenazi levites and the Sephardi levites differ in paternal ancestry. This is a very different pattern from that observed among the kohanim. Second, the STR marker-based haplotypes within this Ashkenazi levite haplogroup form an exceedingly tight phylogenetic cluster, indicative of a very recent origin from a single common ancestor. Coalescence calculation following the same principles used for the Cohen Modal Haplotype point to a founding event that occurred approximately 1,000 years before the present, with the same caveats regarding time estimates based on genomic analysis as were pointed out above. Third, the haplogroup is extremely rare in other Jewish groups and in non-Jewish groups of Near Eastern origin, but is found at high frequency in populations of East European origin. This contrasts with the Cohen Modal Haplotype, which belongs to a haplogroup that is abundant in the Near East. For the reasons stated above, it is likely that the event leading to a high frequency of R-M17 Y-chromosomes within the Ashkenazi levites involved very few, and possibly only one, founding paternal ancestor. The question then arises regarding the possible origins of the founder(s). Haplogroup R-M17 is found at very low frequency in other Jewish groups. It is possible, therefore, that this haplogroup was also present at very low frequency among the levites present within the Ashkenazi founding community, followed by exceeding reproductive success, rendering the descendents of one such Levite, with this rare haplogroup, more numerous. Likewise, the haplogroup is also found at very low frequency within some populations of Near Eastern origin. It is therefore also possible that a conversion event prior to the establishment of the Ashkenazi founding population led to the founding of this haplogroup and its subsequent emergence at high frequency within the Ashkenazi levites. While it is not possible to formally refute either of these two possible explanations, it would be a remarkable coincidence that the geographic origins and demographic expansion of the Ashkenazi levites are within northern and eastern Europe and that this haplogroup is found at very high frequency within neighboring non-Jewish populations of European origin, but not at high frequency elsewhere. An alternative explanation, therefore, would postulate a founder(s) of non-Jewish European ancestry, whose descendents were able to assume levite status. While neither the NRY haplogroup composition of the majority of Ashkenazi Jews nor the STR haplotype composition of the R-M17 haplogroup within Ashkenazi levites is consistent with a major Khazar or other European origin for the Ashkenazi community, as has been speculated by some scholars, one cannot rule out the important contribution of a single or a very few individual male founders from the Khazarian or another Eurasian population group among contemporary Ashkenazi levites. A similar study focusing on non-Ashkenazi levites is yet to be carried out, and will no doubt shed additional light on the detailed paternal lineages comprising contemporary levites.

DUTCH JEWS AND LEMBA. Two additional illustrative examples of geographic rather than caste designation can be given wherein genomic analysis of NRY marker variation has provided insights of relevance to Jewish population history. NRY analysis of Ashkenazi Dutch Jewish males has shown that approximately 25% of their NRY chromosomes belong to the most prevalent haplogroup in Western Europe and one that is rare in the Near East, R-P25. Therefore, when various indices of genetic distances are measured between this Ashkenazi community and the non-Jewish host population, greater similarities are observed, reflecting more substantial male-origin gene flow from the host population to the Ashkenazi Dutch community. This is consistent with greater religious tolerance which may have characterized Dutch society. Interestingly, the pattern of this possible introgression is different from that observed for the R-M17 haplogroup described for the levites. The genetic distances between the haplotypes comprising haplogroup R-P25 in contemporary Ashkenazi Dutch Jews coalesce prior to the migration of Jews to Europe and therefore are likely explained by repetitive introgression events (admixture) of European non-Jewish males into this community. Another group of interest has been the *Lemba tribes of Southern Africa. While not identified as Jews in religious or halakhic terms, these individuals relate an oral tradition of descending from a group of men who migrated via the Hadramout from the ancient kingdom of Judea in the Near East. Following their eventual settlement in their current villages, located in modern-day South Africa, Mozambique, and Zimbabwe, the Lemba founders are said to have intermarried with local Bantu-speaking women, and to have adopted the language and many cultural practices of their neighbors. However, they also maintained some traditions, reminiscent of a Near East and Jewish origin. Genomic analysis of NRY markers at the haplogroup and haplotype level indeed confirmed a pattern of admixture, with clear-cut evidence of Y-chromosomes of Near East origin in a substantial number of Lemba males, with frequencies approaching those found in some Ashkenazi and Sephardi Diaspora Jewish communities, with a strikingly high frequency of Lemba males with the Cohen Modal Haplotype. These are virtually absent among the non-Lemba neighboring populations. More detailed STR-based lineage and coalescence analysis with a large number of markers could provide additional insights of historical interest.

Additional studies have been done, and are continuing to focus on the mechanisms that shaped the population genomic structure of the remaining majority of Jewish groups and communities. Questions of special interest amenable to this type of analysis include these: how limited is the number of founders which gave rise to the contemporary global Jewish population? Do Ashkenazi and various non-Ashkenazi Jewish populations share overlapping or distinct founding lineages? Can geographic origins for each of the Jewish haplogroups be determined with greater accuracy? Studies carried out between 2002 and 2004 have provided some initial information in this regard. By focusing initially on the Ashkenazi population and investigating the STR marker variation within each of the founding haplogroups, Behar and Skorecki, together with an international group of scientific collaborators, confirmed previous findings that Ashkenazi Jews show high levels of haplogroup diversity compared with their non-Jewish counterparts. However, a vastly reduced number of haplotypes within Ashkenazi Jewish haplogroups, as well as reduced haplotype variance within haplogroups, was clearly observed. What do these contrasting patterns tell us about the possible role of a bottleneck in the Ashkenazi population? Despite the fact that Ashkenazi Jews represent a recently founded population in Europe, they appear to derive from a large and diverse ancestral source population in the Near East, a population that may have been larger than the source population from which European non-Jews derived. This is consistent with the finding that contemporary Ashkenazi Jews display higher levels of haplogroup diversity than European non-Jewish populations. The reduced haplotype diversity within Ashkenazi Jewish haplogroups compared to non-Jewish populations may be the signature of a founder event/population bottleneck in the Ashkenazi population history. Indeed, the extremely low STR-based haplotype diversity of some of the less frequent founding haplogroups (e.g., NRY haplogroups R-M17, Q-P36) suggest a single male lineage expansion comprising most or all of these and other haplogroups in Ashkenazi Jews. Comparable analyses have yet to be carried out for the many non-Ashkenazi communities. In addition, the study demonstrated that the many different Ashkenazi communities in Central and

Eastern Europe cannot be readily distinguished from each other either at the haplogroup or haplotype level, based on genetic markers at both the haplogroup and haplotype levels. This can be attributed to a common origin from a shared ancestral deme and due to continuous migration among the Ashkenazi communities, and is entirely consistent with nongenetic disciplines identifying all Ashkenazi communities as a relatively homogeneous population.

Jewish Maternal Ancestry: View from Mitochondrial DNA

The available data on the maternally inherited mitochondrial DNA in Jewish communities is still scant, but is being collected at a rapid rate as DNA sequencing and genotyping technology improves, and is also fueled by the interest of the public in genealogic questions. An initial study, which focused only on a region of the D-loop of mitochondrial DNA known as hypervariable sequence 1 (HVS-1), demonstrated greatly reduced mitochondrial DNA diversity in the Jewish populations in comparison with the host populations, together with a wide range of different modal haplotypes specific to each of the different communities. The results indicated specific founding events in the Jewish populations. A simple explanation for this exceptional pattern of mitochondrial variation across Jewish populations was that each of the different Jewish communities is composed of descendants of a small group of maternal founders. After the establishment of these communities, inward gene flow from the host populations must have been very limited. As the study focused on haplotype diversity and did not include deep haplogroup analysis, a putative origin of each of the founding lineages was not suggested. A subsequent study conducted by Behar and Skorecki, together with an international group of scientific collaborators, focused in greater detail on the Ashkenazi population using a large set of samples from descendents of numerous communities across Europe, and utilized markers which permitted deep phylogeographic analysis at the mitochondrial haplogroup and haplotype levels. The analysis of Ashkenazi mitochondrial sequence variation portrays a pattern of highly reduced diversity, with an unusually large proportion of haplotypes that are unique to the Ashkenazi gene pool, and a reduction in frequency of rare haplotypes and singleton sites compared with both European and Near Eastern populations. At the haplogroup level, the Ashkenazi mitochondrial DNA variation was found to have a number of peculiarities. For example, in two separate studies nearly ten years apart, haplogroup K appears as the most common haplogroup, with its frequency almost an order of magnitude greater than among European or Near Eastern non-Jewish populations. More detailed sequence analysis enabled the construction of mitochondrial DNA-based phylogenetic networks, which resolved the haplogroup K samples into three separate lineages, whose phylogeographic origins are thought to antedate by far the founding of the Ashkenazi population. Furthermore, mitochondrial DNA haplogroup N1b, rare in most European populations, was found to comprise nearly 10% of the Ashkenazi mitochondrial DNA pool, and strikingly, haplotype analysis of this N1b haplogroup in Ashkenazi Jews revealed only a single lineage. These Ashkenazi mitochondrial DNA lineages were virtually absent from surrounding non-Jewish populations, and therefore provide a genetic signature of the Ashkenazi maternal gene pool, and bear witness to the strong effects of genetic drift acting on this population. Similar to the observation for male ancestry based on Y-chromosome analysis in the Ashkenazi population, the mitochondrial DNA results also show that the various Ashkenazi communities throughout Central and Eastern Europe cannot be readily distinguished from each other, likely reflecting shared recent origins from a common small ancestral deme, followed by continuous migration among the Ashkenazi communities.

Micro-Evolutionary Mechanisms that Have Shaped Mitochondrial DNA Sequence Variation in Jewish Communities

Based on the foregoing, and with the development of advanced technological approaches to facilitate DNA sequence analysis, the highest possible level of maternal phylogeographic resolution can be obtained from compete sequencing of the entire approximately 16,500 nucleotides of mitochondrial DNA from samples of interest. Recent studies by Behar and Skorecki and their international scientific collaborators, as well as other research groups, are utilizing such an approach in an attempt to shed light on the absolute number of individual women who gave rise to the lineages among Ashkenazi Jews, to shed light on their putative origin. Based on the complete sequencing analysis in Ashkenazi Jews and existing complete sequences from non-Jews, the exact phylogenetic branches in which the Ashkenazi lineages could be traced were identified. The new information was used to screen a global set of haplogroup K samples to include or exclude them from these Ashkenazi lineages. The results showed that the Ashkenazi lineages were virtually absent in other populations, with the important exception of low frequencies among non-Ashkenazi Jews. These results indicate that the three Ashkenazi haplogroup K lineages are virtually restricted to this population, and are likely to be of Near Eastern rather than European origin. The same approach was followed for mitochondrial DNA haplogroup N1b, and concluded that for this haplogroup all samples belong to one expanding lineage. Taken together, these four lineages indicate that four individual women gave rise to fully 40% of contemporary Ashkenazi Jews, or approximately 3.5 million people. The coalescence times for the expansion of these four lineages coincide well with the historical timeframe of less than 2,000 years for Ashkenazi population expansion from a small founding deme, providing the most powerful and detailed information about the maternal Ashkenazi population founding event. Similar studies in non-Ashkenazi Jewish communities remain to be carried out, and should provide comparable information regarding absolute numbers of founding maternal lineages, as well as their approximate founding dates and possible ancestral locations.

Integration of the Paternal and Maternal Genetic History

Taken together, the data available from Y-chromosome and mitochondrial DNA phylogenetic analysis of Jewish populations has been very informative in uncovering patterns and mechanisms that complement information gleaned from more conventional historical, linguistic, archival, liturgical, and archeological approaches. Furthermore, NRY and mitochondrial DNA markers continue to be used to seek possible Near East origins for communities which claim shared remote ancestry with the majority of Jewish population groups (so-called "Lost Tribes"). At the population level it seems that the genetic histories of the maternal and paternal ancestors tell different stories about population genomic structure of the Jews. Y-chromosome genomic analysis strongly points to a common origin in the Near East while the genetic data from the mitochondrial DNA point to separate local events with a putative geographic origin that might or might not be in the Near East. Y-chromosome and mitochondrial DNA analyses are congruent in suggesting that a limited number of founding ancestors gave rise to the various Jewish communities, with remarkably low levels of introgression from the host populations. It is also clear that many questions remain unanswered and the scope of future studies is potentially very large. Data on the non-Ashkenazi population is needed to answer more accurately questions pertaining to the mechanisms that have shaped each of the communities and the possible connection among them and with the Ashkenazi and host populations. It is important to note that information gleaned from the study of the haploid regions of the genome provide information that is of relevance to population level genomic effects. Population level effects, such as founder and bottleneck events, influence overall patterns of DNA sequence variation across the genome as a whole. Thus a founder effect, followed by population expansion, may lead to the drift to high frequencies of specific disease-predisposing or phenotype-modifying sequence variants at other parts of the genome. However, they do not substitute for direct analysis at these diploid and autosomal regions of the genome in ascertaining mutations. Furthermore, recombination, which characterizes the pattern of inheritance at the diploid regions of the genome, accounts for the influence of even small degrees of admixture of Jews with their non-Jewish neighbors on diverse traits or phenotypes that are determined by DNA sequence variation throughout the genome. This partly explains some of the differences in physical features that may be noted among Jewish communities, despite common ancestral origins, and high levels of intra-community endogamy. Interestingly, recently it has been shown that in other parts of the genome as well, there may be regions of limited recombination, or regions in which DNA sequence variation markers are inherited in a block like pattern. This finding may open up the ability to utilize such diploid regions to enhance our understanding of population genomic history, especially with respect to disease predisposition. The potential implication of findings such as paucity of ancestors and their possible effect on other parts of the genome, especially those relevant for diseases prevalent among Jews, remains an important continuing frontier for study with respect to genomic analysis of Jewish populations. These questions are particularly important for the Ashkenazi community in which the reasons for the well-documented excess of rare recessive disorders have been repeatedly discussed without a definitive resolution. It is anticipated that future studies integrating analysis of the haploid genomic regions and other genomic regions such as the X-chromosome and the autosomes will be complementary and shed additional light of historical and population health importance. The future holds great promise in clarifying these important chapters in the history of the Jewish people.

BIBLIOGRAPHY: B. Bonné-Tami, M. Korostishevsky, J. Redd, Y. Pel-O, M.E. Kaplan, M.F. Hamme, "Maternal and Paternal Lineages of the Samaritan Isolate: Mutation Rates and Time to Most Recent Common Male Ancestor," in: *Ann. Hum. Genet.*, 67 (2002), 153; D.M. Behar, D. Garrigan, M.E. Kaplan, Z. Mobasher, D. Rosengarten, T.M. Karafet, L. Quintana-Murci, H. Ostrer, K. Skorecki, M.F. Hammer, "Contrasting Patterns of Y Chromosome Variation in Ashkenazi and Host Non-Jewish European Populations," in: *Hum. Genet.*, 114 (2004a), 354–65; D.M. Behar, M.G. Thomas, K. Skorecki, M.F. Hammer, E. Bulygina, D. Rosengarten, A.L. Jones, K. Held, V. Moses, D. Goldstein, N. Bradman, M.E. Weale, "Multiple Origins of Ashkenazi Levites: Y Chromosome Evidence for Both Near Eastern and European Ancestries," in: *American Journal of Human Genetics*, 73 (2003), 768–79; D.M. Behar, E. Metspalu, T. Kivisild, A. Achilli, Y. Hadid, S. Tzur, L. Pereira, A. Amorim, L. Quintana-Murci, K. Majamaa, H. Herrnstadt, N. Howell, D. Gurwitz, B. Bonné-Tamir, A. Torroni, R. Villems, K. Skorecki, "The Matrilineal Ancestry of Ashkenazi Jewry: Portrait of a Recent Founder Event," in: *Amer. J. Hum. Genet.*; S. DellaPergola, "Major Demographic Trends of World Jewry: The Last Hundred Years," in: B. Bonné-Tamir, A. Adam (eds.), *Genetic Diversity among Jews: Diseases and Markers at the DNA Level* (1992), 3–32; M.F. Hammer, A.J. Redd, E.T. Wood, M.R. Bonner, H. Jarjanazi, T. Karaget, S. Santachiara-Benerecetti, A. Oppenheim, M.A. Jobling, T. Jenkins, H. Ostrer, B. Bonné-Tamir, "Jewish and Middle Eastern Non-Jewish Populations Share a Common Pool of Y-Chromosomes Biallelic Haplotypes," in: *Proceedings of the National Academy of Sciences USA*, 97:6769–74; M.A. Jobling, C. Tyler-Smith, "The Human Y Chromosome: an Evolutionary Marker Comes of Age," in: *National Review of Genetics*, 4:598–612; M.C. King, A.G. Motulsky, "Human Genetics. Mapping Human History," in: *Science*, 298:2342–43; A. Nebel, D. Filon, B. Brinkmann, P.P. Majumder, M. Faerman, A. Oppenheim, "The Y Chromosome Pool of Jews as Part of the Genetic Landscape of the Middle East," in: *American Journal of Human Genetics*, 69 (2001), 1094–1112; A. Nebel, D. Filon, M. Faerman, H. Soodyall, A. Oppenheim, "Y Chromosome Evidence for a Founder Effect in Ashkenazi Jews," in: *European Journal of Human Genetics*, 13:388–91; A. Nebel, D. Filon, D.A. Weiss, M. Weale, M. Faerman, A. Oppenheim, M.G. Thomas, "High-Resolution Y Chromosome Haplotypes of Israeli and Palestinian Arabs Reveal Geographic Substructure and Substantial Overlap with Haplotypes of Jews," in: *Human Genetics*, 107:603–41; M.B. Richards, V.A. Macaulay, H.J. Bandelt, B.C. Sykes, "Phylogeography of Mitochondrial DNA in Western Europe," in: *Ann. Hum. Genetics*, 62, Pt. 3 (1998), 241–60; A.S. Santachiara-Benerecetti, O. Semino, G. Passarino, A. Torroni, R. Brdicka, M. Fellous, G. Modiano, "The Common Near-Eastern Origin of Ashkenazi and Sephardi Jews Supported by Y-Chromosome Similarity," in *Ann. Hum. Genetics*, 57, Pt. 1 (1993), 55–64; K. Skorecki, S. Selig, S. Blazer, R. Bradman, N.

Bradman, P.J. Warburton, M. Ismajlowicz, M.F. Hammer, "Y Chromosomes of Jewish Priests," in: *Nature*, 385 (1997), 32; M.G. Thomas, T. Parfitt, D.A. Weiss, K. Skorecki, J.F. Wilson, M. le Roux, N. Bradman, D.B. Goldstein, "Y Chromosomes Traveling South: the Cohen Modal Haplotype and the Origins of the Lemba – the 'Black Jews of Southern Africa'," in: *American Journal of Human Genetics*, 66 (2000), 674–86; M.G. Thomas, K. Skorecki, H. Ben-Ami, T. Parfitt, N. Bradman, D.B. Goldstein, "Origins of Old Testament Priests," in: *Nature*, 394 (1998), 138–40; M.G. Thomas, M.E. Weale, A.L Jones, M. Richards, A. Smith, N. Redhead, A. Torroni, R. Scozzari, F. Gratrix, A. Tarekegn, J.F. Wilson, C. Capelli, N. Bradman, D.B. Goldstein, "Founding Mothers of Jewish Communities: Geographically Separated Jewish Groups Were Independently Founded by Very Few Female Ancestors," in: *American Journal of Human Genetics*, 70 (2002), 1411–20.

[Doron Behar and Karl Skorecki (2nd ed.)]

GENETIC DISEASES IN JEWS. The abnormal genes and DNA sequences underlying most inherited genetic diseases in Jews have been identified. This progress has helped to understand the nature of these diseases, to increase the prospects for treatment, to facilitate genetic counseling, and to elucidate the population genetics underlying the segregation of these diseases in Jewish communities. Classically, genetic disorders are classified according to their mode of inheritance. Individuals inheriting one abnormal dominant gene or two abnormal recessive genes develop disease. In contrast, individuals who inherit one copy of a recessive gene do not develop disease but are carriers at risk of transmitting the disease. However, progress has revealed further complexities. Diseases formerly attributed to a single abnormal gene are often associated with different or multiple abnormal genes. There is also an imperfect correlation between inheriting an abnormal gene and the clinical features and severity of the resulting disease. Increased recognition of mild forms of classical disease has forced a re-evaluation of disease prevalence in Jewish as in other populations. Furthermore, although mutation in identifiable genes is responsible for most genetic diseases, interaction with other genes and with environmental factors often determines disease susceptibility and expression.

Genetic diseases with a high prevalence in Jews are mostly recessive. In general, over 1,000 recessive diseases have been discovered. Most are rare but the prevalence of some of these diseases is increased 100-fold or more in Jewish as in other isolated ethnic groups with predominant inbreeding. This increased prevalence is usually but not invariably confined to individual Jewish ethnic groups ("*edot* Israel") and not found in Jews in general. Most are severe and often lead to early death. In some diseases genetic analysis has identified the first appearance of an abnormal "founder" gene originating in a small number of individuals within a Jewish group. This creates a genetic bottleneck whereby the prevalence of a recessive genetic disease is maintained at a high level by subsequent inbreeding.

These principles and the practical issues are illustrated by examples of the most common genetic diseases. Ashkenazim are a relatively homogeneous group despite their settlement in different European countries for centuries. The high prevalence of some 20 "Ashkenazi diseases" in this group dates from founder effects and bottlenecks in the era after 75 C.E. and between 1100 and 1400 C.E. The most common of these diseases are the neurodegenerative Tay-Sachs disease and Gaucher type I disease, which has more widespread clinical features. These "lysosomal storage" diseases result from enzyme deficiencies. Familial dysautonomia affects peripheral nerves and predominantly affects certain Ashkenazi groups. The carrier rate in Ashkenazim in Israel of Polish descent is 1 in 18 compared with 1 in 99 in those of non-Polish descent.

Ashkenazi women with a family history of breast cancer are at increased risk of developing this disease, especially of early onset, due to the high (2.5%) prevalence of BRCA1 and BRCA2 gene mutations in this population. They also have a high incidence of ovarian cancer of which a large percentage, estimated at up to 41%, are attributable to "founder" mutations in these genes. Approximately 1 in 25 Ashkenazim are carriers for one of these disorders, resulting in the birth of one affected child in approximately every 3,000 Ashkenazi live births for each condition. Screening is essential at least in those with a family history. The gene mutations responsible for other less common diseases with a high prevalence in the Ashkenazi population have also been identified allowing accurate diagnosis in at risk families. Prevention programs have already reduced the number of affected children born to these families by over 90%.

In contrast, genetic analysis in cystic fibrosis is more problematical. This disorder has many clinical features in addition to the characteristic lung and pancreatic involvement. There is a high carrier rate (1 in 23) in Ashkenazi Jews but it is similar in the general northern European population. Over 900 genetic abnormalities have been associated with cystic fibrosis and there is a poor correlation between these abnormalities and disease features and severity.

Sephardi Jews are genetically much more heterogeneous than Ashkenazi Jews and genetic diseases in high prevalence in Sephardi communities reflect their country of origin such as Iraq, Yemen, and Morocco. Some genetic disorders characteristic of the Mediterranean region are relatively common in all Sephardi and in non-Jewish communities, marking constant migration. Genetic screening for the abnormal hemoglobin responsible for thalassemia is well established. Familial Mediterranean fever (FMF) is an intermittent febrile illness, often difficult to diagnose. Five variants of abnormal sequence have been detected in the defective gene associated with FMF which give important insights into disease severity and its occurrence in different communities. However, genetic analysis has not solved the diagnostic problems. See also *Sickness.

BIBLIOGRAPHY: Y. Kleiman, *DNA and Tradition* (2004); E. Abel, *Jewish Genetic Diseases* (2001).

[Gideon Bach (2nd ed.)]

GENEVA, capital of Geneva canton, Switzerland. Jews apparently first settled there after their expulsion from France by *Philip Augustus in 1182, receiving protection from the local bishop. The first mention of a Jew in an official document dates from the end of the 13th century. At first Jews were not authorized to settle in Geneva itself but only in the vicinity. They engaged in moneylending and moneychanging as well as in commerce on a partnership basis with Christian merchants. There were also some physicians among them. Jews having to pass through Geneva on business paid a poll tax of four denarii (pregnant women paid a double tax). In 1348, at the time of the *Black Death, the Jews were accused of having poisoned the wells and many were put to death. From the early 15th century, the merchants and the municipal council restricted the Jewish activities, and from 1428 Jewish residence was confined to a separate quarter (near the present Rue des Granges). The relations between the Jews and the Christian merchants were strained and the Jewish quarter was frequently attacked by the populace. The most serious attack occurred at Easter 1461. The duke's representatives admonished the city authorities but the situation of the Jews continued to deteriorate. In 1488, Jewish physicians were forbidden to practice there and in 1490 the Jews were expelled from the city. Subsequently no Jews lived in Geneva for 300 years. A proposal to allow a group from Germany to settle if they undertook to pay a high tax and perform military service obligations was rejected by the municipal council in 1582. In 1780 Jewish residence was permitted in the nearby town of Carouge, which was then under the jurisdiction of the dukes of Savoy. After the French Revolution, Geneva was annexed by France and remained under French rule until 1814. During this period, the Jews enjoyed equal rights of citizenship. However, in 1815 Geneva became a canton within the Swiss confederation, and subsequently their position deteriorated. The acquisition of real estate by Jews throughout the territory of the canton was now prohibited. The Jews in Geneva were not granted civic rights until 1841, and freedom of religious worship until 1843. The Jewish community was recognized as a private corporation in 1853 and a synagogue was inaugurated in 1859. The first rabbi of Geneva was Joseph Wertheimer (1859–1908), who also lectured at the University of Geneva. At the turn of the century, Geneva University attracted many Jewish students from Russia. Chaim *Weizmann lectured there in organic chemistry in 1900–04. As early as 1925 there existed a Sephardi fraternal group which in 1965 merged with the Communauté Israelite.

[Zvi Avneri]

Modern Period

As the seat of the *League of Nations, Geneva was also the seat of the Comité pour la Protection des Droits des Minorités Juives, headed by Leo *Motzkin, and of the Agence Permanente de l'Organisation Sioniste auprès de la Société des Nations, represented by Victor *Jacobson and, after his death, by Nahum *Goldmann. The *World Jewish Congress was founded in Geneva in 1936, and the last Zionist Congress before World War II took place there in August 1939. During World War II, the city served as an important center for information about the fate of Jews in Nazi-occupied Europe. After the war, although the headquarters of the United Nations were established in New York, Geneva preserved its international importance as seat of the European office of the United Nations and of many UN and other international agencies. Consequently, many Jewish organizations, including the *Jewish Agency, the World Jewish Congress, the *American Jewish Joint Distribution Committee, and *ORT, established their European headquarters there. The government of Israel maintains a permanent delegation to the European office of the United Nations, headed by an ambassador. The Jewish community of Geneva numbered 2,245 in 1945, and 3,000 in 2004; 4,356 persons declared themselves to be Jewish in 2000. After World War II a number of East European Jews settled in Geneva, and later Jews from North Africa and the Middle East also settled there. The community, which consists of separate Ashkenazi and Sephardi congregations, has two synagogues (the Sephardi Hekhal ha-Ness was built in 1972), a *mikveh*, and a community center (Bâtiment de la Communauté, opened in 1951) with a library. From 1948 Alexandre *Safran, former chief rabbi of Romania, served as chief rabbi of the Geneva Jewish community. After 1980 a Jewish day school was founded. In 1970 a liberal community came into being, "Groupe Israelite Liberal" (= GIL) which in 2005 has some 1,000 members. There is also a Chabad group and Machsike ha-Dass, a version of Hungarian Orthodoxy.

In Geneva there is a strict separation between religion and state following the French model of 1905. Even confessional cemeteries are forbidden, so that the Jewish community erected a new one on French soil, the mere entrance being on the territory of Geneva. The university has a small Centre des Ètudes Juives. There is a private lecturership for Jewish philosophy, first filled by A. Safran and then by his daughter, Esther Starobinsky-Safran.

[Chaim Yahil / Uri Kaufmann (2nd ed.)]

Hebrew Printing

From the 16th to the 19th centuries, non-Jewish printers issued a considerable number of Hebrew books in Geneva, mostly Bibles or individual books of the Bible with the Greek or Latin versions, or Hebrew grammars, primers, and dictionaries using Hebrew type. Thus Robert Estienne printed a Hebrew Bible with Latin translation in 1556, and a year later a Hebrew-Chaldee-Greek lexicon. Calvin's commentaries on Daniel (1561) and Psalms (1564) were printed in Geneva with the Hebrew text. J.H. Otho's *Lexicon rabbinico-philologicum* … of 1675 included the Mishnah tractate *Shekalim* in the original with a Latin translation. The 18-volume duodecimo edition of the Hebrew Bible (1617–20) is usually ascribed to Geneva, and so is the volume of Proverbs, with interlinear Latin translation of 1616 by the same printer (אילן כאפא). The possibility that the Hebrew transcription גנווא should be read as Genoa cannot be excluded.

BIBLIOGRAPHY: E. Ginsburger, in: REJ, 75 (1922), 119–39; 76 (1923), 7–36, 146–70; A. Nordmann, *Histoire des Juifs à Genève de*

1281 à 1780 (1925); J. Jéhouda, *L'histoire de la colonie juive de Genève, 1843–1943* (1944); A. Weldler-Steinberg, *Geschichte der Juden in der Schweiz* (1966), index, s.v. *Genf*; K.J. Luethi, *Hebraeisch in der Schweiz* (1926), 35ff; L. Mysysowicz, "Université et révolution. Les étudiants d'Europa Orientale à Genève en temps de Plékhanov et Lénine," in: *Schweizer Zeitschrift fuer Geschichte* (1975), 514–62; idem, "Les étudiants 'orientaux' en médecine à Genève," in: *Gesnerus*, 34 (1977), 207–12; D. Neumann, *Studentinnen aus dem Russischen Reich in der Schweiz (1867–1914)* (1987); L. Leitenberg, *La population juive de Carouge 1870–1843* (1992); idem, "Evolution et perspectives des communautés en Suisse romande," in: Schweiz. Isr. Gemeindebund (ed.), *Jüd. Lebenswelt Schweiz* (2004); *100 Jahre Schweiz. Isr. Gemeindebund*, 153–66, 464–66.

GENIZAH (Heb. גְּנִיזָה; literally "storing"), a place for storing books or ritual objects which have become unusable. The *genizah* was usually a room attached to the synagogue where books and ritual objects containing the name of God – which cannot be destroyed according to Jewish law – were buried when they wore out and could no longer be used in the normal ritual. As a result ancient synagogues can preserve books or sections thereof of great antiquity. The word is derived from the root גנז from the Persian *ginzakh* ("treasury"), the root meanings of which are to "conceal," "hide," or "preserve." Eventually it became a noun designating a place of concealment. In Scripture there occur *ginzei ha-melekh* ("the king's treasuries"; Esth. 3:9; 4:7) and *beit ginzayya* (Ezra 5:17; 6:1; 7:20) with the sense of a "treasury" or "archive." In talmudic and midrashic literature, however, it is used as a *nomen actionis* (Shab. 16:1; Lev. R. 21:12; Meg. 26b), as a place for the putting away of all kinds of sacred articles, such as sacred books no longer usable, as well as the books of Sadducees and heretics, and other writings of which the sages disapproved but which were not required to be burned (Mid. 1:6; Shab. 116a); whence the expression *sefarim genuzim* ("books to be hidden away"). The expression *beit genizah* ("storeroom," Pes. 118a) means a treasury "powerfully and strongly guarded" (Rashbam, ad loc.). There was an ancient custom of honoring a dead man by putting holy books next to his coffin (BK 17a; see also Meg. 26b; MGWJ, 74 (1930), 163). In times of war and forced conversion, Jews used to hide their books in caves or tombs in order to preserve them. The letter of *Ḥisdai ibn Shaprut to the king of the Khazars relates, in the name of the elders (*yeshishei ha-dor*), that during a period of forced conversion "the scrolls of the law and holy books" were hidden in a cave. In 1947 certain scriptural scrolls, books, and fragments were discovered in a cave at ʿAyn al-Fashkha in the Judean wilderness and later in other caves in that vicinity. It is probable that the sectarians who lived there hid the books when compelled to leave (see *Dead Sea Scrolls). There were also *genizah* sites between the stone courses of sacred buildings (Shab. 115a), under the foundation stones of synagogues (as in Mainz), and attics and special cupboards kept in synagogues. When the cupboards and attics could take no more, the tattered pages, which, because they contained the Divine Name, were known as *shemot* ("names," i.e., of God), were buried in the cemetery. The day on which the *shemot* were conveyed from the *genizah* for burial in "one of the caves on the slope of Mount Zion" was celebrated in a festive way in Jerusalem, even during the modern period. The participants in the ceremony would play musical instruments, sing, dance, and play games "facing one another with drawn swords in order to magnify the joyousness of the affair" (*Yerushalayim* (ed. Luncz), 1 (1882), 15–16). There is evidence that a similar custom prevailed in other areas.

Such *genizot* existed in a great number of both Eastern and Western communities. Although they usually contained only the worn-out remnants of books in daily use such as the Pentateuch and the prayer book, rare or historically important books and documents were sometimes hidden among them. In the majority of cases the material of the *genizot* was so damaged by dampness and mildew that the collections were of no value for the purposes of historical research.

For the Cairo *Genizah*, see following entry.

BIBLIOGRAPHY: Masseri, in: *Mizraḥ u-Maʿarav*, 1 (1920), 27–31 (English version in *Jewish Review*, 4 (1913), 208–16); Halper, in: *Ha-Tekufah*, 19 (1923), 261–76; 20 (1924), 261–84; A.M. Habermann, *Ha-Genizah* (1944); idem, *Edah ve-Edut* (1952), introd.; E.L. Sukenik, *Megillot Genuzot*, 1 (1948), introd.; 2 (1950), introd.; idem (ed.), *The Dead Sea Scrolls of the Hebrew University* (1955), introd.; Zulay, in: *Luʿaḥ Haaretz li-Shenat 5710* (1950), 110–26; Teicher, in: JJS, 1 (1948/49), 156–8; Golb, in: *Judaism*, 6 (1957), 3–16; P.E. Kahle, *The Cairo Genizah* (1960²); S.D. Goitein, *A Mediterranean Society*, 1 (1967), 1–28; idem, in: PAAJR, 23 (1954), 29–40; Allony, in: *Aresheth*, 3 (1961), 395–425.

[Abraham Meir Habermann]

GENIZAH, CAIRO.

Introduction

The term *genizah* is a word shortened from the rabbinical Hebrew phrase *bet genizah* (see also *Genizah). Its counterpart in late biblical Hebrew is *genez* (pl. *genazim, ginzei*) which in Esther evidently means a "treasury," as well as the term *ganzak* (1 Chron. 28:11, *ve-ganzakkav*). The term *ganzakkah* occurs a few times in rabbinical Hebrew, along with *bet genazim*, in the sense of "treasury." The verbal noun *genizah* signifies the act of storing something away, and is used a few times with *bet* in the phrase *bet genizah* to signify a "house of storing"; subsequently, in colloquial but not literary usage, the *bet* was dropped and *genizah* alone came to mean "the [place of] storing." There are other cases of verbal nouns used as nouns of place in Semitic languages.

The Jewish custom of storing away old books and manuscripts seems to have grown out of the rabbinical rule that worn-out Torah Scrolls should be buried, hence that all papers bearing the Tetragrammaton or other divine appellations should likewise be buried. Such manuscripts as a rule were only temporarily stored away in some chamber of the synagogue until such time as they were able to be given a permanent burial in the cellar or in the local cemetery; but in time the first process seems to have become as important as the second, and in some places, to take precedence over it. Such was the case with the *genizah*, or *bet genizah*, of the ancient synagogue of Fustat.

The term "*genizah*" (pl. *genizot*) should be used and understood as a generic term. There was more than one *genizah*. In Cairo alone there was apparently more than one such storage, or deposit place, for old, outworn writings, mostly, but not exclusively, in Hebrew script. An important *genizah* was at a Karaite synagogue, which was apparently the source of much of the material that came to be known as the Firkovitch Collection, housed in the National Russian Library in St. Petersburg. There were additional such institutions in other communities of the east as analyzed by Y. Khalfon-Stillman and M. Cohen.

Therefore, any *genizah* is not an organized comprehensive archive or deposit library. Furthermore, *genizot* are not representative of the daily or spiritual life of their users. Yet, they are more representative than any private archive or collection of books. In the absence of comprehensive archives and deposit libraries the importance of the *genizot* lies in their randomness. It is this randomness which makes the contents of *genizot* so varied and rich, and which kept for us organized family archives of such families who were not immortalized in "classical" sources together with haphazardly preserved documents, official documents relating to communities or persons or properties that were no longer extant and were of no interest to anybody. The same randomness also preserved for posterity complete or fragmentary literary works that at some point of time seem to have lost their attraction or importance for their owners in particular, or for the reading public at large, or for book collectors and dealers. The common denominator of almost all texts found in Cairo *genizot* is the Hebrew letter; not necessarily the language. The Hebrew letter was regarded holy since it was studied in the context of religious life; it was taught in order to participate in the public synagogue ceremonies and prayers, expecting children to present what they had learnt in class. The less the Hebrew language was understood the more it became holy since the sign became a symbol and reminder to the elementary studies of the language. Hence any remnants of it were regarded holy and kept in the most respectable way discards could be kept. No wonder therefore that the *genizot* contain all signs of documented life, even the most secular ones like bankers' accounts, merchants' lists, children's jottings, and even transliterations of other religious texts as the Koran or the New Testament or any scientific text.

A large section of the material relevant both to history, i.e., documents, and religious thought, as in fact many other areas of knowledge and learning, is in Judeo-Arabic. Hebrew translations to Arabic and Judeo-Arabic works, started mainly in the second half of the 12th century, are rather rare among the *genizot*.

During *Fatimid rule in Egypt (969–1171) the newly-founded city of Cairo mainly served as the political and administrative center of the country and the realm. The great metropolis of Egypt was Fustat, a few miles to the south, and the majority of the Jewish population lived there. This community had a tripartite religious complexion: aside from the sectarian Karaite Jews, there were two groups of Rabbanites – the one showing allegiance to the Jewish academies of Babylonia; and the other group, the "Palestinians," whose allegiance was to the Palestinian academy. These groups had many differing customs and legal regulations; they consequently possessed separate synagogues in each of which a different custom prevailed. The one which has survived until today and from which the Cairo *Genizah* fragments come, was not the one of the Karaites (as a number of writers formerly thought) but that of the Palestinian Rabbanite Jews. This synagogue is still standing in Old Cairo after its renovation by the World Jewish Congress in the 1980s, almost a century after the previous community renovations of the site that might have led to the discovery of the *Genizah*.

Many documents have been discovered during the years which throw light on the history of the synagogues of Fustat and Cairo and on the basis of them scholars traced with some exactness the important changes through which the communities passed, including the status of the *waqf*, or property holdings, of the several synagogues during the reign of al-Ḥākim. It seems most likely that due to this series of acts there is relatively little documentary material of the preceding age among the *Genizah* papers.

Collections of *Genizah* Documents

The largest and most usable collection of the Ben-Ezra synagogue's *Genizah* manuscripts is at University Library, Cambridge, where the individual fragments were set, at the beginning, either under glass or in bound volumes, or, in the case of some thousands, were placed loosely in large shelve-boxes. Holdings are dispersed: Cambridge University Library Taylor-Schechter *Genizah* Collection, containing some 135,000–150,000 "fragments." This *Genizah* collection accounts apparently for about 60% of all *Genizah* fragments known and available today; New York – The Library, Jewish Theological Seminary of America (JTSA), has about 30,000 *Genizah* "fragments." Other more modest collections are scattered all over the world.

WRITING MATERIALS OF THE GENIZAH TEXTS. University Library, Cambridge, possesses fragments of a papyrus scroll found in the *Genizah* and containing old liturgical poetry (T-S. 6). A few papyrus documents, perhaps emanating from the *Genizah*, are also located in the Erzherzog-Rainer Papyrus-Sammlung in Vienna and in Heidelberg. All other texts from the *Genizah*, however, are written either on vellum, parchment, or paper, with the preponderance of texts being written on paper. The vellum and parchment texts are either fragments of Scripture used for worship purposes (which by halakhic precept had to be written on skin) as well as for ceremonial purposes or, more importantly, old texts (10th–11th centuries) of either a literary or documentary nature. A few are written in a palimpsest way, namely, rewritten on deleted elder text. The few very old documents emanating from non-Islamic countries are written on these materials. Texts written on paper seem to have come largely into vogue during the 11th century. The paper of 11th–13th-century texts is of a heavy weight, and as a rule brown in color, whereas *Genizah* papers of later periods tend to be thinner and more lightly colored.

History of *Genizah* Discoveries

Knowledge of the existence of the Cairo *Genizah* spread slowly to the West. The first traveler who appears to have been there in modern times was Simon van *Geldern, a grand-uncle of Heinrich Heine, who in 1752 visited Egypt and recorded in his diary that he had been to the "synagogue of Elijah" and made a search through the *Genizah*, situated within it. Moshe Haim Capsutto met an Italian scholar and traveler who visited the synagogue and gave a generous description of the site and relying on this source some reconstruction of the site was suggested. Capsutto, however, did not refer to the chamber and its content. Abraham *Firkovich, the Russian Karaite who on his trips to the East collected great numbers of rare, valuable, and ancient manuscripts, visited Egypt in September/October 1864 (to wit, the second half of Elul 5624) during his second visit to the Middle East (1863–65). He gave explicit and detailed descriptions about his findings and whereabouts during his visit. His main and first interest in Egypt was the Karaite *genizot* of Cairo, and indeed he took back with him to Crimea a substantial amount of Mss that were sold to the Russian National Library in 1876, two years after his death. The Firkovitch Collection is by far the world's largest and most important collection of Judeo-Arabic manuscripts, containing over 10,000 Judeo-Arabic manuscripts ranging in size from a single page to 800 folios. And indeed, the way Firkovitch described his work in the *genizot* (before arriving to Egypt and in Egypt likewise) points to a very selective method – he would choose the best of manuscripts and leave the others in order to avoid un-needed investment both in time, money, and loads. While dedicating almost all of his time to the Karaite "*genizah*," Firkovitch visited Ben-Ezra synagogue, accompanied by the chief rabbi, R. Elijah Israel Shirizly, and claimed to be requested to take with him also the treasures of Ben-Ezra and of the Rabbanite synagogue of Alexandria. Firkovitch described in his letter to his son-in-law, Gabriel, in Russia that he saw the Ben-Ezra *Genizah* and planned to take care of it likewise. Shortage of money and length of his stay in the region may have accompanied his desire/haste to share his findings from this second visit with colleagues and scholars and brought him to leave the Middle East without emptying, or even taking, the Ben-Ezra hoard. According to his letters and tentative catalogues the material brought from Egypt (named by him *Gefen Mitzrayim* after the verse in Psalms 80:9 and also *pinkas kadmoniyot shel genizat Miẓrayim*) was from the Karaite *genizah* and Basatin cemetery, and indeed it consists of dominant Karaite material. Some important rabbinical works are testified to be owned by prominent Karaite scholars and affluent members of that community. A major question remains however whether some of the material sold to the Russian National Library came from the Ben-Ezra room, since in a few cases other parts of the same copies can be found in western libraries thought to brought from Ben-Ezra. At the same time it might as well be the case that fragments left by Firkovitch, that were originally part of the books he took with him, were brought by others to these libraries mistakenly referred to as Ben-Ezra. At this time of writing (October 2005) not all Firkovitch and other related archives have been searched and new data may clarify this point.

In the same summer of 1864 the traveler Jacob *Saphir attempted to see the manuscripts hidden in Ben-Ezra synagogue, but he was not as fortunate as Firkovich had been. The beadle was reluctant to allow him entrance into the chamber, which he claimed to be an abode of snakes and demons; once inside, he could not get to many of the manuscripts, for the entire collection had been buried under debris that had been deposited there by workmen some years previously. He had to content himself with a few worthless scraps, but later remarked in his travel diary, "Yet who knows what else is to be found underneath?"

Toward the end of the 19th century local dealers in antiquities began the clandestine task of removing certain fragments from their old hiding place. Cyrus *Adler visited Egypt in 1891 and was able to purchase a small collection of manuscripts, which he brought back with him to the United States and later bequeathed to *Dropsie College, now the Center of Advanced Jewish Studies of the University of Pennsylvania. Oxford's *Bodleian Library also acquired about 2,600 fragments in the same way, mainly through the periodic purchases of Greville Chester and A.H. Sayce. In 1896 Elkan N. *Adler made a trip to Egypt, and while in Cairo was permitted by the Jewish communal authorities to take a sack full of *Genizah* documents with him; using an old Torah-mantle which they gave him for that purpose, he stuffed in as many of the documents as he safely could and took them back with him to England. These manuscripts later found their way to the U.S. and became the nucleus of the collection of the *Jewish Theological Seminary of America. By this time the fame of the *Genizah*, induced partly by the reports of the above-mentioned travelers and partly by publications in the early 1890s of *Genizah* studies by Rabbi S.A. *Wertheimer (who also sold fragments to the Bodleian Library), had begun to spread. In May 1896 Mrs. A.S. Lewis and Mrs. M.D. Gibson of England brought manuscripts which they had purchased to Cambridge and showed them to Solomon *Schechter. He was able to identify one of the leaves as part of the original Hebrew text of *Ben Sira (Ecclesiasticus). Thereafter, Schechter sent word of his discovery to Adolph *Neubauer at Oxford, who soon announced that he had discovered nine leaves of this same long-forgotten text among the *Genizah* manuscripts of the Bodleian Library. Schechter at once proposed that a trip be made to Cairo to ascertain the possibilities of bringing the *Genizah* treasures to England. Money was secured for this purpose from Charles Taylor, the master of St. John's College; in December 1896 Schechter sailed for Egypt, and once there proceeded immediately with his task of securing the documents. The communal authorities consented to allow him to take practically that entire precious "hoard of Hebrew manuscripts" back to England.

With Schechter's return to Cambridge the first period of activity involved in making the new manuscript sources available to the world came to an end. The old Ben-Ezra synagogue of Fustat had been almost completely emptied of its contents, which were scattered throughout the length and breadth of Europe, and had also reached the U.S. During the years, many public and private libraries – in London, Cambridge, Oxford, Manchester, Paris, Strasburg, Breslau, Frankfurt, Vienna, Budapest, St. Petersburg (then Leningrad), Kiev, Moscow, New York, Washington, D.C., Philadelphia, Toronto, Tel Aviv, and Jerusalem University Library – managed to acquire *Genizah* fragments in smaller or larger quantities, with Cambridge in the foremost place. Soon after Schechter's return to Cambridge, the time came to explore the texts themselves. The discovery among the *Genizah* manuscripts of fragments of Ben Sira immediately set off a search for still further remnants of this old work, and for other ancient texts which were (rightly) assumed to be hidden either among the hundreds of thousands of leaves brought back by Firkovitch and by Schechter, or in the other collections. Due to past Soviet policy which prevented access of western scholars to the Firkovitch collections, these manuscripts have been largely unknown to scholars. The vast majority of the works contained in the manuscripts are not known from other sources. Study of these manuscripts and publication of their contents is expected to revolutionize the knowledge of Judeo-Arabic culture and to be a major contribution to the study of Jewish history overall. This collection was photographed due to an agreement between the Russian National Library and the Jewish National and University Library in Jerusalem. Scholars had access in the last decade of the 20th century to the treasures of the Firkovitch collection and a great deal of attention has been given to its deciphering and cataloguing.

Luckier were most other collections. A new period in the history of Jewish studies opens after the arrival of the fragments from Cairo to Western libraries. As scholars began their explorations ancient texts came to light – not only Hebrew sources, but Greek and Syriac ones as well. Among the Greek fragments brought to light were portions of the Jews translation made by Aquila. This translation, which differed from that of the Septuagint in being far more literal and meticulous, yet considerably less comprehensible, constituted one of the columns of the multi-versioned Jews, the Hexapla, edited by Origen in the first part of the third century. It was employed mainly by Jews in the synagogal service, but fell into disuse when Greek declined in reading and speaking by the people after the Islamic conquests. In the case of these fragments and of texts containing parts of the Palestinian Syriac version of the Jews and of the Hexapla, the original writing, while still legible, was partially effaced through long and constant use, and a later scribe had employed the parchments to copy down some Hebrew liturgical hymns which to the men of that age were undoubtedly of much greater worth than the incomprehensible words written beneath. Another fact of interest is related to a statement of Origen, to the effect that "in the more exact [biblical] versions, the Name [of God] is written in Hebrew characters – not the modern [Aramaic square] Hebrew, but the ancient [Canaanite] kind." Tallying exactly with the description given by Origen, the Greek fragments of Aquila were found to employ consistently the old Canaanite letters rather than the square characters or the Greek word for God [*Kyrios*] when mentioning the Tetragrammaton.

While these discoveries were in progress Schechter worked on important sectarian manuscripts. One of these turned out to be fragments of the Aramaic law book of *Anan ben David (eighth century); when added to the previously published parts of Anan's law book (edited by the Russian Jewish scholar Albert *Harkavy in 1897–98), it considerably increased understanding of the methods of this schismatic. Another short document created a sensation when finally published by Schechter in 1910. At about the turn of the century he uncovered fragments of a text containing laws and quasi-historical statements of an unknown Jewish sect; a study of the text brought him to the conclusion that the represented schismatic group was related to the "*saddukiyya*" especially mentioned by the Karaite writer al-*Kirkisānī as being a Jewish sect of pre-Exilic times. Since the views of this sect did not conform to those of the historical Sadducees, but in a few important respects did correspond to certain doctrines of al-Qirqisānī's "*saddukiyya*," Schechter judged the leaves to be fragments of a work written by "Zadokites," i.e., people belonging to the sect mentioned by al-Kirkisānī, or to a closely similar one; thus, while the text was copied down in medieval times, the document itself went back to Second Temple times. An extensive controversy over the age and importance of this text followed its publication. The discovery in 1947 and following years of the first *Dead Sea Scrolls – some of which proved to be closely related in phraseology and ideas to the Cambridge document – made it evident that Schechter had been correct in his intuition that this text had been conceived perhaps 21 centuries previously. It is not known how it came into the *Genizah* in fragments of two medieval copies.

Another of Schechter's early discoveries was the remains of an extensive literary epistle concerning the kingdom of the *Khazars. The ruler of this Caspian kingdom, and along with him many of his subjects, accepted Judaism before the ninth century. Some correspondence between the Khazar king Joseph and Ḥisdai ibn Shaprut had been published at the end of the 16th century and much later (in 1879) by Harkavy who used material brought from Cairo to Russia; the Cambridge document considerably increased the knowledge of the conversion and of subsequent Khazar history, and supplied many useful geographical details as well. In recent years still another Cambridge *Genizah* manuscript pertaining to the Khazars was discovered by N. Golb.

Information about the "*Four Captives" – Shemariah, Ḥushi'el, Moses, and Ḥanokh – who were thought to have come from Babylonia or Southern Italy in the tenth century, been captured by pirates, and subsequently sold out of captivity, and later to have founded the new seats of learning in Egypt, North Africa, and Spain, also came to light in the Cambridge documents. In this case some of the legendary stories surrounding these figures were seen as suspicious; as it could be shown from a letter of Ḥushi'el's (written by his son Hannan'el/Elhannan) that he had settled in Kairouan (now *Tunisia), after a trip there from some Christian country, probably Italy. Shemariah, on the other hand, turned out to be a native of Egypt. Thus, the whole story of the capture by pirates, as told, at least of these two sages was evidently a fabrication.

A personality which emerged most clearly from the *Genizah* was that of *Saadiah ben Joseph al-Fayyumi, the *gaon* of Sura. It became clear from *Genizah* texts that it was Saadiah who was chiefly responsible for conducting the struggle over the calendaric authority of the Babylonian academy which had been initiated by Aaron ben Meir, the head of the rival Palestinian school (922), and that he initiated a bitter quarrel with the exilarch, who had appointed him *gaon* (928), and with the latter's followers. Other polemics of his also came to light with the publication of treatises against the heretic Ḥiwi al-Balkhi, the masoretic scholar Aaron ben Asher, and Anan ben David and various later Karaites, many of whom fought Saadiah with equal vigor. Another side of the *gaon*'s personality was revealed in some of his letters which were discovered during the early years of the 20th century. Many fragments of his Arabic commentary on the Jews were found, especially by Hartwig Hirschfeld, and parts of his grammatical treatises – probably the first systematic works on Hebrew grammar to be composed – were edited years afterward by S.L. Skoss, although a beginning had been made by Harkavy. Fragments of his legal (by M. Ben-Sasson and R. Brody) and philosophical (by H. Ben-Shammai and S. Stroumsa) writings were also discovered, and one manuscript emanating from his children gave the exact date of his birth (882) and the approximate time of his emigration from Egypt to Palestine, Syria, and finally Babylonia. Indeed, if all the Saadiah fragments that were discovered in the *Genizah* had not been found, it is unlikely that H. Malter's richly documented study of the *gaon* would have been possible. Much important research on the Saadiah fragments, and on the polemic literature of that age, was carried out by Moshe Zucker, Yehuda Ratzaby, Eliezer Schlossberg, and Haggai Ben-Shammai, especially on Saadiah's biblical translations and commentaries. Saadiah's poetry was enriched and studied through the reconstruction of his *Siddur* (S. Assaf, I. Joel, I. Davidson, E. Fleischer, R. Brody, and J. Tobi).

The search for lost writings of the *gaon* of Sura also led to the discovery of numerous legal responsa of the other *geonim* of Babylonia; many of the Hebrew ones were first edited by A. Harkavy, S. Assaf, and L. Ginzberg and later also those in Judeo-Arabic by Sh. Abramson, R. Brody, and M.A. Friedman. These fragments were of value not only for the legal discussions they contained, but also for the inadvertent descriptions which the *geonim* gave of the way of life pursued by their countrymen. L. Ginzberg and J. Sussman found old leaves of the Jerusalem Talmud, which were of service in clearing up numerous obscurities in the printed texts of this work. Letters of the *geonim* were recovered by Schechter, J. Mann, and B.M Lewin, and new discoveries were made in the field of midrashic literature. A work of considerable interest was the Book of Precepts by Ḥefeẓ b. Maẓli'aḥ, a tenth-century dignitary of *Mosul, which was published by Benzion Halper in 1915. Much work has been done on the legal and halakhic texts by S. Abramson of Jerusalem, who published works on R. Nissim Gaon and on other subjects, based mainly on *Genizah* manuscripts.

Another area of *Genizah* studies was initiated with Paul Kahle's arrival in England from Germany. A considerable number of biblical manuscripts were being discovered in the collections which exhibited different systems of vocalization from the one commonly in use (i.e., the so-called Tiberian system, with most of the vowel signs written below the line). Such texts, which possessed supra-linear punctuation, and which later were discovered to be of three different kinds, had indeed been known before. Specimens of the two "Babylonian" systems were published during the last half of the 19th century, and the third system, "punctuation of the Land of Israel," was mentioned as far back as the 12th century in Simḥah b. Samuel's *Maḥzor Vitry*. The *Genizah* fragments greatly supplemented the then-known collections of Babylonian texts and gave the first examples of the Palestinian variety. Kahle was the first to realize the possibilities inherent in the new finds and to take full advantage of them. During his several trips to England, where he settled after the advent of Nazism, Kahle copied and photographed large quantities of material, and in the course of the years was able to publish extensive studies on the biblical traditions of the Babylonian and Palestinian Jews. This was of importance not only for determining what were the various systems of punctuation, their probable dates of inception, and spheres of influence but also for arriving at the pronunciation of Hebrew, before the time of the Tiberian punctuators, in the various countries of the Arabic world where Jews lived. Furthermore, it was possible to see in what ways the ninth-century biblical scholars of Tiberias had been influenced by other traditions in evolving their own "standard" pronunciation of Hebrew.

The "punctuation of the Land of Israel" could be discovered in only a few of the *Genizah* biblical fragments. Kahle, however, found other kinds of texts which preserved this system – fragments of the Palestinian Aramaic translation of the Torah and a few leaves of the Mishnah and of early liturgic poetry (*piyyut*). Almost without exception, each of these proved to have its own particular value for the history of Hebrew vocalization. Kahle and his students contributed much to the understanding of these texts. The various texts of the Aramaic translation of the Jews which came to light were highly instructive, for they supported the view of scholars such as Geiger and Zunz that there were earlier substrata in the official Aramaic translations (Targum Onkelos to the Torah and Targum Jonathan to the Prophets). To a large extent these were preserved in *Genizah* manuscripts of the so-called Palestinian Targum, the author(s) of which version not only interpreted some passages differently but also added homiletic remarks. The standard Targum Onkelos itself was then able to be subjected to renewed scrutiny, as collections in the *Genizah* collections of fragments of this Targum were found that had been written and vocalized in Babylonia many centuries previously. This field enjoyed two more generations of scholars focusing their works on it – E.J. Revel, Y. Yahalom, I. Yevin, and I. Eldar.

The *Genizah* also supplied specimens of the Mishnah text vocalized in the Babylonian manner. There is, of course, no traditional Tiberian vocalization of the Mishnah, the pronunciation having been handed down orally from generation to generation. This Babylonian tradition of the pronunciation of mishnaic Hebrew, which differs considerably from that employed by Jews of the West, is corroborated to a very high degree by the living Yemenite tradition of pronouncing post-biblical Hebrew – a fact demonstrated later by H. Yalon and S. Morag.

Thus, even during the first few decades of *Genizah* research, outstanding discoveries were made in many fields of Jewish learning. The job of sorting out the Leningrad Fragments has been at the core of the work of several scholars over the last century, among them Harkavy, Strack, Kahle, Fenton, Sklare, Beit Arie, Glazer, Almagor, Ben-Shammai, Stroumsa, and Ben-Sasson, but it is still far from being completed. A large part of the Cambridge fragments was studied by Schechter, E.J. Worman (a librarian at Cambridge), and Hartwig Hirschfeld who published a considerable number of manuscripts. Not only the Hebrew fragments but thousands of Arabic documents were placed in their respective places in boxes, bound volumes, or – in the case of exceptionally valuable and fragile pieces – under glass. In the last decades the management of the Cambridge *Genizah* Research Unit has been allocating substantial attention and resources with the goal of intensive cataloguing of its collection according to subjects and fields. In Oxford, Neubauer and A. Cowley issued a catalog of the fragments deposited there; the same was accomplished at the British Museum by Margoliouth, and was eventually also done for the Adler collection at Dropsie College and the Freer Collection of Detroit (later removed to Washington). The collection given by the Russian archimandrite of Jerusalem, Antonin Kapustin, was fully described by Harkavy, who was in charge of the Hebrew collections at the Russian Imperial Library in St. Petersburg and was later published by A.I. Katsh.

The publication of important fragments from the Cairo *Genizah*, covering many aspects of Judaism, has continued. Many manuscripts and fragments in the various libraries of the world, particularly in the Russian National Library of St. Petersburg [= Leningrad], the Schechter-Taylor collection in Cambridge and the Jewish Theological Seminary of New York (N. Danzig catalogue), have been catalogued and edited by different scholars. As a result of these, it has become possible to reconstruct the position of the Jews in Ereẓ Israel and the Middle East in the religious, cultural, and economic spheres from the 10th to the 13th centuries. On the other hand, a large number of texts and thousands of fragments remain un-catalogued, and it is estimated that there are no less than 250,000 *Genizah* items, of which about 50,000 deal with biblical exegesis, language, Jewish law, Talmud, and *piyyut*.

Liturgy and Poetry

The poetic literature of the *Genizah* was especially prominent and its discoveries enabled new understanding of the history of Jewish worship as well as of the diversity of Jewish literature in the late Byzantine and Muslim periods. A new field of research emerged which is credited to the discoveries of Cairo *genizot* – the study of the Ereẓ-Israeli [known also as Palestinian] rite of prayers and synagogue life. At an early date Kahle realized the value of the Palestinian liturgical fragments for the history of Hebrew vocalization, but the literary significance of these texts, in the minds of many scholars, was far greater. While it is quite frequently difficult to make sense of the hints and allusions of the early liturgists (*paytanim*), and to comprehend their poetic vocabulary, it is also true that what can be understood is often poetry of supreme beauty and fine religious feeling.

The first paytanic texts were published in facsimile at the end of the 19th century – but only for the Greek and Syriac writing which they contained underneath. Israel Davidson recognized in the later script five compositions of the early Palestinian poet Yannai, of whose writings only a single poem was known during the previous centuries. Davidson's publication (1919) marked the beginning of systematic investigations in the field of *paytanic* literature. Kahle's students took a considerable part in this work, as did Davidson himself. At the same time the most important step was taken with the founding, in 1930, of the Schocken Research Institute for Hebrew Poetry, which began its activities in Berlin and transferred to Jerusalem a short time after the rise of Nazism. In the first few years of its existence the Schocken Institute collected several thousand photographs of *Genizah* manuscripts, including many in Leningrad. Among them were scores of fragments containing the *piyyutim* of Yannai, on the basis of which Menahem Zulay published in 1938 a collection of over 800 compositions by this poet.

The scholars of the institute – H. Brody, J. Schirmann, A.M. Habermann, and Zulay – were chiefly responsible for knowledge of literary activities of the *paytanim*, and of the religious and secular poets of Spain. Brody discovered many religious poems and encomiums of Hai Gaon, Moses ibn Gikatilla, and Abraham Ibn Ezra among the *Genizah* fragments. A score of contemporary poems by Moses Ibn Ezra were described by Schirmann, whose success in this research was greatly aided by *Genizah* manuscripts. Schirmann was the first to systematically explore the poetic fragments in the libraries of England, and he catalogued these and had them photostatted for the institute. Zulay demonstrated that the paytanic literature was of a class seldom equaled in the poetic literature of the Jews. He not only discovered the writings of many of the unknown early Palestinian poets but also added immensely to the knowledge of those already known – Yannai, Kallir, and Solomon al-Sanjari. He also proved that the country which in the time of Zunz had been regarded as barren of all creative production during the early Middle Ages was in reality a center, if not the center, of paytanic activity that continued unabated until the Crusades. These poems, far from artificial, could not be considered as only a subterfuge by which the Jews sought to avoid the consequences of Justinian's decrees prohibiting the *deuterosis* (or study of the rabbinic exposition of Scripture). Zulay showed – on the basis of the *Genizah* texts – that the Jews of Palestine constantly had to add to the set prayers of the day, and inspire them with new vigor. Much important work on these texts was conducted by Ezra *Fleischer of Jerusalem through the second half of the 20th century. Fleischer represents the demand to publish broad scholarly works based on the *genizot* in contradiction to previous generations' work of publishing fragments and small pieces of information reflecting the excitement of the very early meeting with new material. His broad works consist of extensive reconstruction of complicated oeuvres of the time and their analysis in the broadest cultural and historical contexts. Among his works one may find an intensive analysis of the Palestinian rites based on earlier publications (J. Mann, N. Wieder, and N. Fried), correcting their partial pictures and drawing a fresh new representation of that forgotten rite; the profile of old-new poets like Sa'id Ben Babshad, Solomon the Babylonian, and even R. Judah Halevi. A group of students of Schirmann, Fleischer, and S. Spiegel of the JTS has continued the research and opened new venues: Y. Yahalom, Y. Tobi, R. Scheindlin, Sh. Elizur and T. Be'eri. In this discipline, as in any other of the *Genizah* research, typical publications of the fourth generation consist of two aspects – publication of extensive new material and the drawing up of a broad analysis of a substantial part of a scholarly field.

Historical Discoveries

In 1915 Jacob Mann began to search through the British collections. During 1915–20 he studied the fragmentary documents of the *Genizah*, gathering data for a history of the Egyptian and Palestinian Jews from the 10th to the 12th centuries. There were extant remnants of the copies of letters of the Jewish community of Cairo-Fustat, once one of the leading centers of Jewish population. On the basis of these fragments it was possible to reconstruct the personalities of the people and the significant events in their collective history.

The task that Mann first set out to accomplish was twofold: that of establishing a chronological sequence from the mass of data, and of describing the important religious and communal authorities of Egypt and Palestine during the period involved. These are the chief characteristics of his study, *The Jews in Egypt and in Palestine under the Fatimid Caliphs* (2 vols., 1920–22). Later, when professor of history at Hebrew Union College, he was able to supplement this material in two additional volumes entitled *Texts and Studies in Jewish History and Literature*. Such outstanding figures as Solomon b. Judah and Ephraim b. Shemariah, leading dignitaries of Egyptian Jewry, were first fully revealed by Mann. It became clear from his work in what towns of Palestine and Egypt the Jews had chiefly settled. There was much that he elucidated about the communal ban (*ḥerem*), the ransoming of captives, the functions of the head of the Jews [= the **nagid*], and the Palestinian custom of completing a Torah cycle only once every three years (to this latter subject he devoted his final book, *The Bible as Read and Preached in the Old Synagogue*, which is also based chiefly on *Genizah* material). Mann described the whole complicated story of the relations between the Rabbanites and Karaites – especially those in Jerusalem – and cast new light on the writings and activities of such Karaite notables as Daniel al-Qumisi, Sahl b. Maẓli'aḥ, and Salomon b. Jeroham. Ḥisdai ibn Shaprut was revealed as a statesman of the first rank, to whom appeals were sent from other lands, and who corresponded with Helena the empress of Byzantium. Mann also uncovered the story of the Norman proselyte to Judaism, Obadiah ha-Ger. His historical research in the *Genizah* treasures provided a scientific foundation which could be built upon and elaborated by later scholars.

The first scholars who explored the *Genizah* manuscripts pursued their own particular interests in studying the documents. They turned, in so doing, mainly to the documents written in Hebrew and Aramaic, languages which were prominent in the *Genizah* finds. Only a few researchers gave their attention to the mass of documents written in Arabic, which for hundreds of years had been the vernacular of the Jews of Egypt and the Near East. The score or more of Judeo-Arabic fragments which Hartwig Hirschfeld published were mainly of literary interest: remnants of the writings of Saadiah Gaon, some texts pertaining to the polemics between Karaites and Rabbanites, a few autograph fragments of *Maimonides, and some short documents pertaining to *Muhammad and the Jews of Khaybar. Samuel Poznański used some Judeo-Arabic fragments (some from the Russian *genizot* collections) for his own researches on the Karaites and leading rabbinic figures of the Middle Ages; and other scholars – I. *Goldziher, W. Baecher, and G. Margoliouth – also made contributions. This work, however, was sporadic in nature, and gave few clues to the value of the Judeo-Arabic fragments. Even Mann relied mainly on Hebrew documents in producing his works; however, his appreciation of the Arabic texts grew in time, and considerably more of them were used in his *Texts and Studies* than in his first work. All agreed that the fragments were important, but little was done to make their contents known.

In the early 1930s the *Genizah* papers became a subject of interest in Jerusalem, mainly as a result of Mann's investigations and the establishment of the Institutes of Jewish Studies and Oriental Studies at the Hebrew University, Jerusalem. There it was possible to study the way of life of numerous communities from Arabic-speaking lands and to become intimately acquainted with their language. Some of the scholars in Jerusalem thus developed a close familiarity with the cultures of the Middle East, and under these conditions it was possible to make considerable advances in *Genizah* research.

D.H. Baneth did the most important work in establishing Arabic *Genizah* research on a sound philological basis. Philological correctness and exactitude were essential to the proper understanding of these texts; sometimes scholars who preceded Baneth had been led into making blunders in understanding the vernacular used in the manuscripts (which quite often differed considerably from the literary language). In conjunction with S. Assaf, Baneth published a series of *Genizah* studies which rank as exemplary specimens of such writing. The historical information he elucidated from them was also of value; he discovered in one document that it had been a prevalent custom among the Egyptian Jews to determine, through witnesses, whether a couple who planned to marry were of the same social and economic status (Heb. *hagunim*).

Assaf was mainly interested in the *Genizah* papers for the information they contained about the legal, social, and cultural history of the Jews. He found numerous documents about the Jews in Palestine from the time of its conquest by Omar until the period of the Crusades, and afterward as well. It was learned from a tradition represented in one document which he discovered that when the Arabs conquered Jerusalem, Omar allowed them to build or occupy only 70 homes (although they had asked for 200); they chose the southern part of the city as their quarter, and the first Jews to resettle there were some families from Tiberias. Other texts which Assaf published and elaborated upon provided information about the slave trade, in which he thought to confirm that the Jews of that time engaged in it (although they could not take Muslims as slaves); new information was derived about Jewish trade in the Mediterranean, as well as the main centers of learning in Palestine and elsewhere. Other texts of importance pertaining to Palestine were published by Braslavski, among them a "tourist guide" to Jews who came in pilgrimage to the holy city, mentioning local sites of interest. E. Strauss (later Ashtor), the historian of Jewish life during the Mamluk period, published a letter in 1940 which was written in Aden and addressed by the sender to a business associate in Fustat; it mentions Jews traveling to India on their own ships, taking various goods with them to sell in Malabar. Other texts, when finally deciphered and interpreted, revealed the economic and social life of the Jews of Egypt and neighboring lands in great detail, and, incidentally, matters pertaining to general Islamic history and economic development. Ashtor's later publications, including his *History of the Jews of Muslim Spain*, numerous articles on economic and social life, and his book-length study of prices and salaries in the medieval Near East (*Histoire des prix et des salaires dans l'Orient médiéval*, 1969), rely heavily on *Genizah* manuscripts.

However, with all the real importance of Mann's works as pioneering ones, which guided generations of historians, and his awareness of the uniqueness of these materials in comparison to whatever sources of Jewish history that had been known previously, and with his enthusiasm to publish this wealth of materials, he saw this history mainly as a rather formal history of texts, and not of concrete human and social actualities and processes, the like of Ashtor's works based on these documents.

The most important accomplishment, or achievement, in the field of history is no doubt the monumental oeuvre of S.D. *Goitein. Goitein was initially educated within this unusual combination of deep rooted Jewish tradition and 19th-century German humanism. He was then trained as a philologist and developed it in the years he worked at the Hebrew University, Jerusalem, in the rigorous methods so typical of German universities. He later turned his attention to Islamic historical sources, and still later made another turn, to *Genizah* studies, mainly on the documentary material. In his works the extent to which the *Genizah* has shaped the picture of the medieval history of Jewish communities in the East came to its fullest manifestation. The uniqueness of his works is imaginable only as a result of the uniqueness of the material, namely the fact that here we have at our disposal direct sources that shed light not only on the actions and the views of the leaders of the communities, but also, and mainly, of many ordinary individuals that made up the rank and file of these communities. Already in his early *Genizah* studies Goitein paid special attention to the light shed on the social structure of the communities in the *Genizah* documents. He focused his attention on individuals whose personalities and activities could not have been known from the formal, literary sources. Such was his study of Ibn ʿAwkal, a noble North African Jewish merchant who settled in Cairo in the early 11th century, conducted from there his international commercial ventures, and became a prominent figure in the local community. Already in the early stages of Goitein's work on the *Genizah* documents he also encouraged his students to work on individual personalities from the *Genizah*. At that stage it already became clear that certain segments of the *Genizah* documents were not just randomly disposed off by their owners, but constituted entire family "archives," or at least parts of such archives, while others were parts of court archives, mainly from Fustat. This recognition led Goitein and his students to pursue the remains of such archives. The first such archive that served as a subject of a Ph.D. thesis by Murad Michael was that of Nahray b. Nissim, another North African Jewish merchant who settled in Cairo in the middle of the 11th century. From there he directed his merchant banker activities that stretched virtually over three continents, from Spain, through North Africa and Egypt, to the Fertile Crescent and further through Yemen as far as India. When Michael finished his work on the archive over 30 years ago, he was able to trace about 260 documents.

Since then over 100 additional documents from that archive have come to light through Goitein, Udovitch, and Gil, and enabled us to draw a fascinating picture of commercial and postal connections, banking practices of the High Middle Ages, transportation routes in the Mediterranean Basin, variations and prices of a very wide range of commodities, communal and family ties of the Cairene merchant banker and his agents who were stationed in many important ports and commercial centers, as well as in some important communal centers such as Jerusalem.

In the late 1940s S.D. Goitein began his researches in the field of *Genizah* manuscripts. He soon became convinced that they were of inestimable value for both general and Jewish history. He found eyewitness accounts of the crusaders' attack on Jerusalem: from one letter it was learned that the story of the massacre of the inhabitants, so widely accepted by students of the Crusades period, was really somewhat exaggerated – it had been a savage attack, but many lives were spared, evidently so that those taken prisoners could be ransomed for a handsome sum of money. Another letter made it evident that, contrary to the contention of many scholars, other nationalities than the French were represented among the crusaders, for in it mention was made of the "cursed ones who are called Ashkenazim." Other letters emanating from Palestine made it clear that the crusaders' attack on Beirut in February 1110 was a surprise attack, and that the Jews were driven out of Jerusalem during the second occupation by the crusaders, under the command of Frederick of Hohenstaufen. Goitein also found further fragments pertaining to Obadiah the Proselyte, from which it was learned that he was not a crusader, as had been contended by Mann and others, but a man of some learning who converted because his religious studies convinced him of the truth of Judaism and who was saved from Christian persecution by some fellow Jews who brought him to *Aleppo. One of the most unusual discoveries made by Goitein consisted of fragments from Cambridge and the Jewish Theological Seminary which turned out to be letters sent by Judah Halevi to his friend Ḥalfon b. Natanel al-Dimyati of Cairo, an affluent trader who engaged in large business with India. Three of the letters deal mainly with Judah Halevi's endeavors to raise the dinars necessary for the ransom of a Jewish woman kept in prison by the ruling authorities, while in a fourth he expresses the fond wish to travel to the East, as he indeed did some years later.

Goitein also gathered over 400 letters on the Mediterranean trade with India. This commerce, which went by way of Egypt, East Africa, and South Arabia, was the chief economic factor in the status quo of the countries of the Middle East. Not only did Goitein discover complete itineraries of the journey to India, descriptions of the dangerous voyage through the Indian Ocean, and the names and prices of numerous goods which made up that trade, but he also found eyewitness accounts of events barely known from the writings of the Arabic historians. One such account, in a letter from Aden to Egypt, gives a detailed description of the number of soldiers, the types of boats, and even the military tactics used by the rulers of the island of Kish (in the Persian Gulf) when they tried to extend their control over the sea route to India by conquering Aden.

Goitein collected all of the documents from the Cairo *genizot* that pertain to trade between India and the Mediterranean, and was preparing them for publication, translating the Judeo-Arabic documents and adding notes. Goitein did not finish preparing his work on Indian trade (referred to by him as the "India Book"), when he passed away. One of his leading students, M.A. Friedman, agreed to complete the work. The final book (scheduled for publication in 2006 by the Ben-Zvi Institute) will be the product of work by both scholars. The book, which contains more than 400 texts from the *genizot* in the original language, generally Judeo-Arabic and in Hebrew translation, is a remarkable source of information on the contacts – commercial, social, and cultural – between India and the Middle East in the Middle Ages. Because of the great interest in these matters in the scholarly world and among the educated public, the book will be published in both Hebrew and English versions.

Goitein published over 250 articles based on *Genizah* documents. This work was climaxed by his magisterial study, *A Mediterranean Society: The Jewish Communities of the Arab World as Portrayed in the Documents of the Cairo Genizah*, in five volumes enabling the description of a society and its daily life as well as its beliefs and views, based on their own writings – the documentary *genizot*.

Goitein's approach paved the way towards comprehensive historical studies that were focused on specific sections of the material, such as geographical ones (the most important one to date is by Moshe Gil on Palestine), or social ones (such as the studies of Menahem Ben-Sasson on the beginnings of communal organization in North Africa in the ninth century), or social and halakhic ones (the most important to date are M.A. Friedman's studies on marriage documents and practices). Such works resulted from a synthesis between the unique primary *Genizah* material and well-known literary materials from a wealth of Jewish and non-Jewish sources. On the solid basis of Goitein's approach and oeuvre, it is possible to conduct many and diversified cross sections, which can shed light on every imaginable aspect of Jewish life and culture in the Middle Ages, such as Joel Kraemer's projects on women's letters from the *Genizah*, the several projects dedicated to Maimonides and his descendants by P.B. Fenton, M.A. Friedman, and M. Ben-Sasson, and a new comprehensive collection of Maimonides' letters by J. Kraemer. In fact Goitein's first published book on the *Genizah* was a study on education. Goitein's final, concluding work in the field was the multi-volume *A Mediterranean Society* in five volumes. When Goitein started this work he had already been well into the studies of economic, social, and cultural history. This fact had a decisive impact on the structure and plan of this gigantic opus. It is basically planned along social lines – its five volumes corresponding to five social levels:

I: Economic Foundations; II: The Community; III: The Family; IV: Daily Life; V: The Individual (see below).

Goitein inspired many researchers, such as N.A. Stillman, Y. Khalfon-Stillman, M. Gil, M.A. Friedman, and M.R. Cohen.

The *Genizah* manuscripts also aided in the study of post-Inquisition Jewish history. Already S. Schechter, S. Assaf, and J. Mann published documents and other literary texts having to do with this period. A major contribution was made by Meir Benayahu who found on trips to England and the U.S. approximately 2,000 documents relating to the Jews of the Mediterranean after 1492. On the basis of photostats of these manuscripts in the possession of the Ben-Zvi Institute in Jerusalem, Benayahu made an extensive study of the Jewish communities during the 15th–18th centuries. He found that even at this late period the Jews were enterprising merchants, traveling to such places as India, North Africa, Spain, and Italy, carrying on an extensive trade in pepper and skins. During this period there was considerable migration to Palestine, and many talmudic academies were founded there; in some documents there are descriptions of the dormitories which the yeshivah students occupied, and in one dating from the 15th century there is an account of the rebellion staged by a group of students against their academy for having allowed poor living conditions to prevail in the dormitories. A most important document gives a detailed history of the Hebron community. Moreover, Judeo-German and Judeo-Spanish texts are included among these relatively late manuscripts, which have been studied by several scholars in recent decades. The work on the post-expulsion generations has been continued by I. Tishbi, J. Hacker, A. David, and E. Gutwirth (the latter extended the research to texts written in Judeo-Spanish).

There is rich information in the *Genizah* about many aspects of life, such as the role of women in society, loans and interest, the communal organization, the Jews as *ahl al-dhimma* (people of the covenant, or tolerated minority), their actual place in Muslim society, etc. Information on the following salient topics, inter alia, may be found in the *Genizah* texts: the Jews of Alexandria; Babylonian Jews; letters of Byzantine Jews; begging letters; book lists and letters about books; communal records and affairs; dated letters; diseases; Fustat and Cairo; geographical data; houses and housing; Jerusalem; Karaites; Maimonides; medicine – practice and theory; relations with Muslims and Christians; occupations; plagues; police; prisoners; letters of recommendation; seafaring and warfare; Sephardim, i.e., Spanish Jews; synagogues; Syria, including Ereẓ Israel; tenth-century documents.

Many additional topics are included, such as individual personalities of the time, place-names of Egyptian-Jewish settlements, artifacts, etc. On the other hand, a few topics deserve special treatment:

(1) *Documents of European Provenience, or Containing Information about European History.* The first to publish such fragments and documents were D.S. Schechter, L. Ginzberg, J. Mann, and S. Assaf – some enlightening events and phenomena back in the early ninth and tenth centuries. After a long pause in such publications it was N. Golb who drew attention to the *Genizah*'s importance for the reconstruction of the history of these communities. He published an article (*Sefunot*, 8 (1964), 87–104) based on the U.L. Cambridge manuscript 1080 J, no. 115, in which he shows that the document is a letter of recommendation sent from a certain Samuel b. Isaac the Spaniard in Jerusalem to Shemariah b. Elhanan in Fustat at the beginning of the 11th century (more precisely c. 1006), and that it concerns a Jewish proselyte from a prominent Christian family who fled his homeland, arrived in Damascus, thereafter made a pilgrimage to Jerusalem, and from there, because of persecution by the Christian community in Jerusalem, decided to go on to Egypt, where, we may assume, he finally settled. On the basis of internal evidence, it appears that the proselyte is probably the Slovenian cleric Wecelinus (cf. Alpertus Mettensis, *De diversitate temporum*, 1.7; II. 22, 23), who converted to Judaism in 1005 C.E. This proselyte, who fled to Egypt, is the earliest of the 11th century converts to Judaism described in the *Genizah* fragments, and the manuscript in question furnishes additional evidence pointing to the phenomenon – already brought to light in prior *Genizah* publications – of conversion to Judaism on the part of prominent European Christians in the 11th century, who subsequent to their conversion left their homelands to settle in non-Christian countries. Other such proselytes of the 11th century were Andreas, the archbishop of Bari, who converted about 1070; an anonymous proselyte of the last half of the 11th century; an anonymous proselyte from a wealthy family who first settled in France during the same period; and finally, Obadiah the Norman proselyte, who had been demonstrated by N. Golb and A. Scheiber to be the scribe of a musical manuscript (Adler 4096b). Documents of actual European provenience include a Cambridge manuscript (T.S. 16.100), evidently from the town of Monieux, Provence (Golb, in: *Proceedings of the American Philosophical Society*, 113 (1969), 67–94); and a British Museum manuscript (Or. 5544, Vol. 1), evidently written in Arles and concerning a wealthy Jew of Rouen.

(2) *Illuminated Genizah Fragments.* Still almost totally unutilized, and lying undisturbed among *Genizah* manuscripts of Cambridge, Oxford, and the British Museum, are approximately 60 illuminated fragments of the Fatimid and Ayyubid periods which, taken collectively, characterize both the quality and the content of the Judeo-Arabic culture during the period of its highest development. In addition, among the *Genizah* fragments one should count also around a dozen wood pieces engraved in the same period; fragments that testify to the history of the Ben-Ezra Synagogue and the Maimonidean circles (Ben-Sasson, *Synagogue and Fortress*). Artistic remains of any kind from the Fatimid period are rare; besides architectural subjects, all that have been previously known are illuminated Korans, some wood carvings, linens and decorated bowls, and a certain number of items of glass and metal. The addition to this material of a body of 60 illuminated fragments may therefore stimulate research not

only in the field of medieval Jewish art (students of which have heretofore had no knowledge whatsoever of these manuscripts) but also in the general area of Islamic art and culture. The illuminated fragments, mostly at Cambridge, may be classified as follows:

(A) Marriage contracts, approx. 20 items; (B) Children's readers and school books, approx. 10 items; (C) Bible leaves and prayer book leaves, approx. 20 items; (D) Miscellaneous fragments, as follows: (1) Architectural plan of Ezekiel's temple, 1 page; (2) Leaf from an early *materia medica*, 2 folios; (3) Illustrations from a book of magic, 2 folios; (4) Child's drawing of a boat, 1 page; (5) Two warriors engaged in combat, margin of 1 page; (6) Painting of two water birds, standing on either side of a tree (of life?) within a decorative border, 1 page. The richness of this material is all the more surprising in view of the previously held opinion that for the entire Fatimid period only a single illuminated fragment had survived, namely, the Bodleian *ketubbah* of the 11th century.

(3) *Historical Geography.* E. Ashtor and N. Golb have studied the work of the historical geography of the Jews in medieval Egypt. The main purpose of this research has been to clarify the problem of the continuity, or lack of continuity, of Jewish life in Egypt between the Hellenistic period and the Middle Ages. The salient result of their study of *Genizah* fragments bearing upon this problem (in: *Journal of Near Eastern Studies*, Summer 1965) is the conclusion that the Jewish community of medieval Egypt represents not a new phenomenon but the continuation of an ethnic and cultural pattern which stretched far back in time, and that in this respect it is very difficult to accept the view that the small number of Hebrew documents of the Byzantine period, "extending over 300 years, may serve as a good indication of the gradually declining importance of Egyptian Jewry in the Byzantine period" (*Corpus Papyrorum Judaicarum*, ed. V. Tcherikover et al., 3 (1964), 88). Just the contrary may be claimed – that there was a continuous, if necessarily irregular, line of development from ancient times through and despite cultural reorientation, political upheavals, and the assimilation of a fair proportion of the people. This is made especially manifest by the comparison of the known places of settlement of Egyptian Jews in antiquity with their more than one hundred communal settlements in the Middle Ages, which stretched from the very border of Egypt far up the river to Elephantine-Aswan.

It is thus apparent how valuable these preponderantly Arabic papers and the hundreds of others like them are for purposes of historical research. If studied together with the responsa and historiographic literature of that age, unparalleled source material can be found among them for this still obscure period in medieval life; and it may therefore be concluded that when all the material has been systematically edited and the texts brought into proper relationship with one another, there will be an integrative account of the Jewish community of medieval Egypt, and a reliable record of the general social and economic conditions prevailing at that time in Egypt and the Middle East.

Genizah Research, 1960s–1980s

The following survey reviews in more detail some of the specific work that has been done from the 1960s to the 1980s in fields of scholarship which rely extensively on **Genizah* sources. Only books and monographs have been taken into account, since the inclusion of periodical publications would have swelled the survey beyond permissible bounds. A complete list of publications relating to the *Genizah* can be found in *Published Material from the Cambridge Genizah Collections: A Bibliography*, produced by the Taylor-Schechter Genizah Research Unit under the direction of Dr. Stefan Reif, published by Cambridge University Press for the University Library's Genizah Series. It should also be noted that G. Khan of the Taylor-Schechter Genizah Research Unit is now preparing a more comprehensive description of publications relating to the *Genizah*, including both books and periodicals. Bibliographical details on the books discussed in the present survey can be found in the bibliography accompanying this article.

DOCUMENTS. The private and legal documents of the *Genizah* have provided the primary source material for several studies in the socio-economic history of the medieval Near East. S.D. Goitein in Volume I of *A Mediterranean Society* made a synthesis of information gleaned from hundreds of *Genizah* documents in order to build up a comprehensive portrait of the economic foundations of the Jewish communities in the Arab world during the High Middle Ages. The bulk of this study concentrates on commerce and finance with special attention to overseas trade. This latter area of economic activity is particularly well documented in the many commercial letters that have been preserved in the *Genizah*. Such correspondence indicates that trade was conducted for the most part on the basis of mutual trust and personal friendship rather than formal agreements. Goitein also published a collection of 80 letters of medieval Jewish traders which reflect this personal aspect of overseas commerce. These letters show how a man's piety and fear of God were invoked when he was urged to adhere to good business practices. Moreover, although distant trade involved interaction between people of different social classes, it seems that the long months spent together in foreign parts or on perilous voyages brought people close together. Two of Goitein's research students, M. Michael and N.A. Stillman, have made a specialized study of *Genizah* letters which relate to specific Jewish traders. Michael's dissertation deals with the correspondence of the medieval businessman and community leader Nahray ben Nissim and includes an edition of many of his letters together with those of his son Nathan. Stillman analyzes and edits documents relating to Joseph ibn ʿAwqal, who likewise was both a trader and a leader of the community. The business correspondence of both Nahray and ibn ʿAwqal reveals the great diversity of goods which were handled by the traders of their time and gives a detailed picture of the organization of medieval business houses.

Ashtor in his *Histoire des Prix et des Salaires dans l'Orient Médiéval* made extensive use of *Genizah* documents as a basis for a detailed analysis of the standard of living in medieval (mainly Fatimid and Ayyubid) Egypt. The documentary portion of the *Genizah* furnishes a unique source for such a study, for it contains many specific references to contemporary prices. By contrast most Muslim sources for the period are literary texts that are often tendentious and prone to adapting figures that suit their purpose. The *Genizah* papers also give firsthand evidence of changes in currency. They demonstrate, for instance, that there was a shift from gold to silver during the Ayyubid period. The Egyptian scholar Hassanein Rabie has used *Genizah* sources for a large portion of his work on the financial system of Egypt between 1164 and 1341. He relied for the most part on Cambridge University Library's Taylor-Schechter documents which are written in Arabic script (viz. T-S Ar. 38–42) as opposed to those in Hebrew script. Rabie has shown that the *Genizah* gives us valuable information on the poll tax (*jawālī*) and the *mawārīth ḥaṣriyya*, i.e., the law determining that property without heirs was to be confiscated by the state.

Volume II of Goitein's monumental *Genizah* synthesis, *A Mediterranean Society*, deals with the social and communal life of the Jewish minority in Egypt between the 11th and 14th centuries, with the most abundant information being provided for the earlier part of this period. The topics discussed include the communal authorities at the national, regional, and local levels. He not only brings a great deal of new material to bear on the nature of these institutions, their historical development, and their relations with the politically dominant Muslim authorities but, in the case of the *nagid*, has totally and conclusively revised the accepted view of the origin of this office. The description of the organization and operation of the local communities is particularly valuable, since the unmediated character of the *Genizah* documents makes them a unique source for information about everyday life and ordinary people. Goitein portrays the medieval Egyptian Jewish community as a "religious democracy" in which there was a balance between authority and communal sanction. The loosely structured and highly mobile Islamic society in which the community was situated also influenced its structure. There is, for instance, no reference in the *Genizah* to enactments restricting the entry of strangers into the community analogous to the *ḥerem ha-yishuv* of the communities in medieval Christian Europe.

M.R. Cohen in his book *Jewish Self-Government in Medieval Egypt* develops Goitein's thesis with regard to the origin of the office of the Egyptian *nagid*. Goitein first showed by means of a wide selection of *Genizah* documents, that, contrary to the opinion of earlier scholars, the nagidate was not instituted by decree of the Fatimid caliph. Rather it evolved within the Jewish community in the second half of the 11th century. Cohen emphasized that the nagidate evolved in response to the political and spiritual vacuum created by the decline of the Palestinian yeshivah, to which a large portion of Egyptian Jewry had given allegiance.

A number of Goitein's research students have worked on *Genizah* documents relating to the communal life of the Egyptian Jewish community. The general format of these doctoral dissertations is similar to those of Michael and Stillman, in that considerable space is devoted to editing the documents which constituted their source material. G. Weiss has edited 255 legal documents written by the court scribe Ḥalfon ben Manasseh during the period 1100 to 1138. A large proportion of the legal documents which are preserved in the *Genizah* were written by this scribe. Apart from providing ample material for research on legal formularies, the study demonstrates the value of working on a corpus of documents written by the same hand. For instance, undated fragments can be more easily dated and a greater accuracy of reading achieved. A.L. Motzkin has made a study of Judge Elijah ben Zechariah (first half of 13th century) and his family on the basis of their correspondence which has been found in the *Genizah*. *Genizah* documents have been employed by M. Gil as a source for a detailed examination of the medieval Jewish institution of the *kodesh* or "pious foundation" which was essentially equivalent to the Moslem *waqf*. Although these Jewish foundations flourished during the Fatimid period there is no evidence of their existence under the Ayyubid dynasty. The chief motivation for the Jews to dedicate property to a pious cause was apparently religious, charity being one of the most important precepts of Jewish law. The institution was, however, also exploited to circumvent Islamic legislation, especially the *mawārīthaṣriyya* (see above).

Volume III of Goitein's *A Mediterranean Society* is concerned with the family. The body of the book deals with the nuclear family and marriage, the main source for which are the many medieval *ketubbot* (see **Ketubbah*) which have been preserved in the *Genizah*. From an examination of over 600 of these Goitein has illuminated the manifold economic and social aspects of marriage. He shows that divorce was common and that 45% of brides whose marriages are recorded were marrying for the second time. From the itemization of the dowry in the *ketubbot* of the High Middle Ages Goitein concludes that prices were remarkably stable during this period. The mobility of the population often disrupted family life; this especially applied to the long business trips which were undertaken by many members of the community. In general, the *Genizah* portrays a male-oriented society. Private letters and genealogical lists usually mention only sons. Nevertheless many women played an active role in economic life. They owned properties, took charge of them, and also made or took loans.

Since the Middle Ages the marriage contracts of all known Jewish communities have followed the basic model of the Babylonian *geonim*. Scholars assumed that the *ketubbah* formulary had remained uniform since early Talmudic times. M. Friedman, however, has discovered in the *Genizah* a substantial number of fragments of medieval marriage contracts, mostly emanating from Palestine, which reveal traditions of formulating the *ketubbah* distinct from that of the Babylonian *geonim*. He has made a thoroughgoing study of these Palestinian-style *ketubbot* in his book *Jewish Marriage in Pales-*

tine. They contain many distinctive features. For instance, the woman is granted the right to initiate divorce proceedings and the husband is obliged to bury his wife, should she predecease him, or to care for her if she becomes insane. Friedman also shows that the Palestinian formulary influenced the marriage contracts of several Jewish communities along the northern shores of the Mediterranean and North Africa.

Y. Stillman, in her doctoral thesis, examines the female attire of medieval Egypt as portrayed in the trousseau lists of the *Genizah ketubbot*. These lists contain the names and details of many previously unknown garments and fabrics. Moreover, on the basis of the prices which are given for each item Stillman has been able to establish a relative scale of quality between many varieties of textiles. J. Sadan, in a similar manner, has made extensive use of *Genizah* trousseau lists in order to study household furniture in the medieval Near East. These two aspects of material culture, viz. clothing and furniture, are dealt with in Vol. IV of Goitein's *A Mediterranean Society*.

Several scholars have used *Genizah* documents as a basis for studies in the socio-economic history of medieval Palestine. Gil has studied many aspects of life in Palestine during this period on which the *Genizah* has shed considerable light. These include the institution of the Palestinian yeshivah together with the personalities who headed it and its relations with Jewish communities in Egypt, Syria, and the Byzantine Empire; the relationship between Karaites and Rabbanites; Jewish life in Jerusalem and in many other localities in Palestine; problems of taxation; pilgrimage and immigration, etc. Goitein has published a collection of studies on *Genizah* texts pertaining to the history of Palestine, in particular its Jewish population, in the century preceding the Crusades and during the Crusader period itself. The documents show that life in Palestine returned to normal relatively quickly after the Crusader conquest. Several documents refer to the activities of Moses Maimonides in the ransoming of prisoners captured by the Franks when King Amalric I took Bilbays, Lower Egypt, in November 1168. Goitein suggests that Maimonides' meteoric rise to the leadership of Egyptian Jewry, only a few years after his arrival in the Nile country, is partly to be attributed to his initiative in the ransoming of these captives.

In connection with the history of Palestine we should mention two works under the editorship of J. Prawer: *The History of Eretz-Israel under Moslem and Christian Rule* (634–1291), some of whose contributions employ *Genizah* documents as source material, and *Sefer Ha-Yishuv*. The latter work presents a wide variety of source material, much of it from the *Genizah*, relating to the Jewish community in Palestine during the period from the Crusader domination until the Ottoman conquest at the beginning of the 16th century.

In the course of Gil's research on the history of Palestine he published a short study on the Tustarī family which had considerable influence on Palestinian Jewry. The information about this family is pieced together largely from *Genizah* documents. Its two most illustrious members were the two sons of Sahl, Abū Naṣr Faḍl (Ḥesed) and Abū Saʿd Ibrāhīm (Abraham). They engaged in trade and banking and involved themselves in the political affairs of both the Fatimid court and the Jewish community. Gil attributes the Tustarīs' influence on Palestinian Jewry to the fact that Ḥesed was secretary to a Fatimid general much involved in Palestinian affairs. He also argues that the Tustarīs belonged to a distinct Karaite sect known as Tuṣtarians or Dastarians.

The documentary portion of the *Genizah* has also furnished sources for the history of Jewish communities outside the Mediterranean area. Goitein has published a collection of articles about the Jews of Yemen, several of which had previously appeared in a variety of periodicals. The section on medieval Yemenite Jewry is based almost entirely on *Genizah* sources. These documents show that the Yemenite Jews enjoyed considerable prosperity in the High Middle Ages, since they formed the link between the Mediterranean and the India trade, and that they remained in close contact with the Jewish academies of Iraq and Palestine.

N. Golb and O. Pritsak have made a contribution to the history of the Jewish *Khazars in their book *Khazarian Hebrew Documents of the Tenth Century*. This work contains an edition and detailed analysis of a recently discovered *Genizah* document relating to the Khazars together with a re-edition and reassessment of the *Genizah* letter from a Khazarian Jew to the Spanish dignitary Ḥisdai ibn Shaprut which was published by Schechter in 1912. All the sources which refer to the conversion of the Khazars to Judaism are reexamined with special attention to the extent to which they reflect the historical and geographical background of Khazaria in the Crimea. The newly discovered document (T-S 12.122) is the autograph of a letter of recommendation written by Khazarian Jews residing in Kiev in the first half of the tenth century. It is signed by Jews with Khazarian names and contains a remark in the Khazarian language written in runic Turkic script. This document proves conclusively that the judaization of the Khazars is a fact and not a forgery or romance, a view which has been canvassed by many scholars. Golb and Pritsak also show that the text which was edited by Schechter could have been written only by a Jew of Khazaria who had firsthand acquaintance with the historical and geographical circumstances of his country during the first half of the tenth century.

We must also include Volume III of Ashtor's *History of the Jews in Egypt and Syria under the Rule of the Mamluks*, published in 1970 (the first volume appeared in 1944). This final volume contains the texts of the *Genizah* documents referred to in the preceding volumes. Finally, the sources for Ashtor's *A Social and Economic History of the Near East in the Middle Ages* and Stillman's *The Jews of Arab Lands* include *Genizah* documents, principally in sections which deal with the socio-economic realities of the Southern Mediterranean in the High Middle Ages.

The focus of M. Ben-Sasson's research has been the social and intellectual history of medieval Jewry in Muslim lands from the 7th to the 14th centuries; based on work integrating legal, historical, and literary *Genizah* fragments. In examining social structures of Jewish public life from the perspectives of both the central leadership and the local community, each in its special locations and each with its special expression, institutional form, intellectual achievements, and self-consciousness, he pointed to the shift of power from the Eastern centers to the Maghreb, the building of the local Jewish community through a reconstruction of the *Genizah* corpus related to the community of Kairouan. He also found that the Maghebri-Jewish immigrants became involved in the central Jewish leadership in the East starting in the second half of the tenth century. Their involvement signified the beginning of a process of building a regional and local functional leadership. In this venue he published sources on the history of the Jews of Sicily. The analysis of the Babylonian-Iraqi center was done by means of research on the activities and personality of Saadiah Gaon. With Prof. R. Brody (Dept. of Talmud, The Hebrew University) he prepared a critical edition of the first halakhic book written in Judeo-Arabic. It is the "lost" Book of Deeds and Decrees of Saadiah Gaon, compiled in the year 926. They reconstructed the book almost *in toto*, on the basis of more then 100 *Genizah* pieces scattered over 25 libraries in the East and in the West. This book was written according to the order and with the terminology of Islamic legal works. Like many of Saadiah's books, this had great influence on most of the Jewish legal monographs and on the practical life of world medieval Jewry in its formative years.

Then Ben-Sasson turned to a *Genizah* study of the Maimonidean dynasty that headed the Jewish communities of the East from the 12th to the early 15th centuries.

BIBLICAL COMMENTARY. The commentary of Isaac ibn Ghayyat to the Book of Ecclesiastes was published from fragments in Cambridge and New York and the commentary of Samuel ben Ḥophni Gaon to the Pentateuch was published by Aaron Greenberg in Jerusalem (1979).

COMMENTARIES AND NOVELLAE ON MISHNAH AND TALMUD. 1. Abraham I. Katsh has published *Ginze Talmud Babli* (Vol. 1, 1976; Vol. 2, 1979). The first volume includes 178 pages of the Babylonian Talmud from nine tractates from the Antonin Collection in the National Library of Leningrad, and the second, 90 pages from 11 other tractates. A comparison between these fragments and the printed edition, as well as the Munich manuscript, reveals important variations. 2. Tractate *Bikkurim* with a list of the *variae lectiones*, which indicates the extent to which the readings differ from those in the printed texts. 3. Fragments of the Mishnah with Palestinian vocalization. 4. Mishnah fragment of *Berakhot* 1:1–3:1; *Peah* 4:3–6:3, written in the tenth century. 5. Tractate *Shevi'it*. 6. Fragments of the TJ *Berakhot*, Chap. 3; *Shabbat*, Chap. 12; *Kiddushin*, Chap. 3, written in the early style of the Jerusalem Talmud. 7. A fragment of TJ *Shabbat*, Chap. 10. 8. Fragments from tractates *Bava Meẓia*, *Bava Batra*, and *Sanhedrin*, revealing considerable variants from the standard texts.

Texts from the Talmud provide readings that approximate more closely those of Rashi and Alfasi than the printed version. Scores of *ketubbot* include an undertaking by the bridegroom not to take a second wife, even though legally he was permitted to do so. When an additional wife was taken, a detailed agreement was made binding the husband to treat all his wives equally.

An example of the wealth of new material in this sphere is seen in the recent publication of tractates *Ketubbot* and *Sotah* by the Institute for the Complete Israel Talmud (see *Talmud, Recent Research). Altogether 150 pages or fragments of the tractate *Ketubbot* from the *Genizah* were collated (pp. 75–91) for this purpose. *Genizah Fragments of Rabbinical Literature; Mishnah, Talmud and Midrash* (1973), edited by N. Aloni, contains no less than 219 facsimile pages of 60 *Genizah* manuscripts in the various libraries. This collection is of special importance in that it includes rabbinical texts with the Palestinian system of vocalization. *Genizah Bible Fragments with Babylonian Masorah and Vocalization* (5 vols., 1973), edited by Y. Yeivin, provides the scholar with all the ancient sources with the Babylonian vocalization.

MIDRASH. Of particular interest is *Ginze Midrash* by Z.M. Rabinowitz (1977). The author deals with the early form and style of the Midrash as revealed in the texts, which are written in the early Palestinian script and belong to the 11th and 12th centuries. The copyists later changed the text – both the Hebrew and Aramaic – to conform with the Babylonian usage. Although the majority of the fragments are from well-known Midrashim, they also include a few hitherto unknown ones.

THE GEONIC PERIOD. S. Abramson's *Inyanot be-Sifrut ha-Geonim* (1973) includes an appendix (pp. 319–89) on the text of the *She'iltot* of *Aḥa of Shabḥa and deals with the *variae lectiones* therein. The *Genizah* fragments have vastly increased the knowledge of the development of the *halakhah* in Ereẓ Israel after the completion of the Jerusalem Talmud. The publication of *Hilkhot Ereẓ Israel min ha-Genizah* by M. Margaliot, set up for publication by I. Ta-Shema (1973), disproves the theory that the gaonate in Ereẓ Israel was reestablished in the 10th and 11th centuries in order to fight against Karaism. There was an unbroken chain of authority and heads of yeshivot until the end of the geonic period, and it seems that there was a separate halakhic tradition in Ereẓ Israel, deriving from the Jerusalem Talmud and differing from the Babylonian tradition. Various fragments of this tradition have now been published (cf. *Sefer ha-Ma'asim li-Benei Ereẓ Israel)*. The *Hilkhot Ereẓ Israel* includes an appendix on another Ereẓ Israel work, *Perek Zera'im*, edited by J. Feliks, which is the most complete work on agricultural products and nature found in ancient Jewish literature. M.A. Friedman was the latest to publish additional fragments of *Sefer ha-Ma'asim*.

Other items on the geonic period, also published by M.A. Friedman, are (1) Additional material on Pirkoi Ben *Baboi. (2) Fragments of a large collection of geonic responsa which include the following: the intervention of the authorities in Kairouan in the case of the divorce of a betrothed woman; the concluding portion of a responsum dealing with the complaint of a woman whose marriage settlement had been sold by her husband, or lost. It provides data on the custom of Kairouan with regard to a *moredet* (a wife who "rebels" against her husband), and on the community and the relationship between the civil authorities and the Jewish leader. There have also been found fragments from the *Siddur* of R. *Amram Gaon, providing details of the compilation of the work. 3. Fragments of geonic commentaries to tractate *Shabbat* which are ascribed to Sherira Gaon and Hai Gaon.

MAIMONIDES. 1. Fragments of the *Mishneh Torah* written by Maimonides himself. It has been shown that these fragments are from a first text of the *Mishneh Torah*, whereas all later editions were based on a second edition which he wrote. The differences between this holograph and the printed are considerable, including the order of the books and the chapters, and sometimes even the order of the individual laws in the chapter, and there are also differences in language. 2. A commentary by Maimonides on the *Laws of Tefillin* from the *Sefer ha-Menuḥah* of Manoah of *Narbonne. M.A. Friedman and Sh. Abramson added new findings from the *genizot* reflecting students' shorthand writings in Maimonides' school as well as the school's traditions.

RISHONIM. 1. Fragments from the novellae of Yom Tov b. Abraham Ishbili (the *Ritba) to tractate *Beẓah*. 2. New fragments from the commentary of Ḥananel b. Ḥushiel on Bible and Talmud. They consist of many pages, partly fragments of complete works and partly fragments of commentaries on individual chapters. They include commentaries on tractates *Berakhot, Kiddushin, Sotah, Bava Kamma, Bava Batra*, and *Sanhedrin*, as well as portions of his commentary to tractate *Zevaḥim*. 3. A complement to a commentary of a pupil of Naḥmanides to tractate *Pesaḥim*.

LITURGY. Following the publication of "An Unknown Blessing on the Reading of the Chapter *Bameh Madlikin* (Shabbat 2) from the *Genizah*," N. Wieder has come to the conclusion that the inclusion of this chapter in the liturgy was the result of the controversy between the Rabbanites and the Karaites. This blessing, which has been completely forgotten, was in the nature of a public declaration of faith in the authority of the rabbis and the continuation of tradition, and of the authority for kindling lights for the Sabbath which was forbidden by the Karaites. N. Wieder deals with the formula of the *'Amidah* in early Babylonian usage and shows that the words "Possessor of heaven and earth" were included in the formula of both Israel and Babylon.

POETRY. The last two decades have seen the publication of many critical editions of early *piyyutim* and of medieval religious and secular poetry, the majority of which draw to a greater or lesser extent on *Genizah* sources. The *Genizah* has preserved not only many previously unknown poems of the famous poets but also a substantial number of the works of forgotten or little-known poets.

J. Schirmann published an anthology of Hebrew poems discovered in the *Genizah*. This collection includes secular and religious poetry from the Jewish communities of the East and from Spain, North Africa, Italy, and Byzantium. Especially worthy of note are the oldest example of a Hebrew poem in praise of a beautiful youth; the full text of a *muwaššaḥ* (*muwashshaḥ*, see 13: 684) of Samuel ha-Nagid, of which previously only a few lines were known; three secular poems of Judah Halevi which are not known from other sources; several *muwaššaḥat* of Abraham Ibn Ezra including one which describes his flight from Spain; and Hebrew *maqāmāt* (see *Maqāma*) including a section of *maqāmat Yamīma*, an allegorical love story, of which Israel Davidson published some fragments in the 1920s. This new fragment enabled Schirmann to identify the author of this work as Joseph bar Judah ben Simeon, the famous pupil of Maimonides. Also noteworthy are a number of rhymed proverbs, many of which show that their authors must have been familiar with the Hebrew version of Ben Sira.

Several scholars have collected the works of various *paytanim* which have been preserved in the *Genizah*. A. Mirsky used *Genizah* sources extensively in his edition of the *piyyutim* of the early *paytan* Yose ben Yose. These *piyyutim* show that Yose ben Yose was one of the first Hebrew poets to make the oral law a basis of his works. Wallenstein published and analyzed a number of *Yoẓerot* by Samuel ha-Shelishi (10th–11th century), discovered in the *Genizah*, to which Ezra Fleischer and Yoseph Yahalom dedicated substantial scholarly work. E. Fleischer has critically edited 580 short liturgical compositions from the *Genizah* which were all written by the same anonymous author (called "Anonymous" by Zulay). These poems (called *pizmonim* by the copyist of the *Genizah* manuscript) were composed in the late tenth century and were intended to serve as choral additions to several pieces of a cycle of *kedushtaot* written by R. Simeon ha-Kohen b. R. Megas, an early Palestinian *paytan* who was active in the seventh century. They reflect the increase in the participation of the choir in synagogue worship towards the end of the first millennium C.E. Fleischer has also used *Genizah* sources in his edition of the *piyyutim* of the tenth-century Italian *paytan* Solomon ha-Bavli, who was one of the first Hebrew poets to write in Europe. His works molded the Italian Ashkenazi school of *paytanim*. The *Genizah* has also preserved many of the poems of his pupil Elya bar Shemaya, which have been edited by Y. David.

Owing to the ties between the Andalusian and Egyptian Jewish communities, manuscripts of religious and secular poems written in Spain found their way into the *Genizah*. Consequently scholars who have collected the works of the Spanish medieval Hebrew poets have found abundant source material among the *Genizah* papers. This applies to the following collections: the liturgical poems of Solomon ibn Gabirol, the religious poems of Judah Halevi and the *Diwan* of Samuel ha-Nagid by Jarden; the collections of the secular poems of Ibn Gabirol by Allony and Jarden and by Brody and Schirmann; the religious poems of Abraham Ibn Ezra by Levin; the poems of Isaac ben Abraham Ibn Ezra by Schmelzer; the poems of Levi Ibn al-Tabban by Pagis, and the poems of Joseph Bensuli by David. Mirsky has published a collection of poems by Isaac Ibn Khalfun (10th–11th century), almost all of which were recovered from the *Genizah*. These poems show that Ibn Khalfun played an innovative role in the development of Hebrew verse in that he was one of the first to compose secular poems and introduce elements of personal experience into his poetry. D. Jarden published an anthology of medieval Hebrew verse *Ẓefunei Shirah*. This includes several poems of little-known or anonymous authors which have been discovered in the *Genizah*: 1. A list of secular poems by Solomon ibn Gabirol hitherto unknown from any other source. 2. A *kerovah* of the liturgical poet *Yannai to the portion *Ha'azinu* (Deut. 32). 3. *Piyyutim* to the *Avodah* on the Day of Atonement. They include a "bibliographical" *piyyut* giving a detailed list of the titles of ten such orders of service. 4. Early Yemenite *piyyutim* and *Seliḥot* for the Day of Atonement.

HISTORICAL. S.D. Goitein devoted himself particularly to the economic life of the Jews as revealed in the *Genizah* documents and fragments. He points out that as a result of the economic changes which took place in the Middle East as a whole, in which trade superseded agriculture as the basis of the economy, Jews tended to abandon agriculture and engage in skilled occupations and trade. In one text a Jewish girl writes to her widowed mother urging her to see that her brother, in addition to studying Torah, also learn a trade, adding "if he will have a trade, he will be a man."

Other published material includes (1) Documents appertaining to the life of the Jewish community of Egypt. (2) M. Gil's *Documents of the Jewish Pious Foundations from the Cairo Genizah* (1976) gives the religious and sociological motivation behind them, the halakhic aspect, income and expenditure, etc. (3) Horoscopes from the *Genizah* (1977). (4) A letter from the community of al-Mahdiya in Tunis to Fustat in Egypt in the 11th century reflects the commercial movements between the ports on the Mediterranean Sea in which Jews played a prominent role. The letter was addressed to Nahray b. Nissim, originally of Kairouan, who later settled in Egypt, and reflects the golden period of the Fatimids in the first half of the 11th century. (5) There has been discovered the earliest document emanating from *Salonika, a letter from an Egyptian scholar who immigrated there, dated approximately 1090. (6) Three documents from the beginning of the Crusades, consisting of letters from Tyre and Tripoli in Lebanon and Arqa in northern Syria which reflect the need of the Jews for mutual assistance in the difficult circumstances which prevailed at the end of the 11th century, and lastly, evidence of the connection between the Jews of *Yemen and the Babylonian communities. (7) Additional material concerning the Jews in Ereẓ Israel and the role of the *ketubbah* is to be found in a book by M.A. Friedman, *Jewish Marriage in Palestine: A Cairo Genizah Study* in two volumes (1980/81), Vol. 1, *Ketubbah* Tradition in Ereẓ Israel; Vol. 2, Texts.

ALIYAH TO EREẒ ISRAEL. In A. Kupfer's *Konteros Ereẓ Israel* (1968) are included pages from a work written by a sage desirous of immigrating to the Land of Israel, for which purpose he composed a pamphlet to serve as a guide for those contemplating immigration. A. David published new documents from the "late" *Genizah* illuminating life in Ereẓ Israel and its vicinity after the Spanish expulsion.

[Yehoshua Horowitz / Menahem Ben-Sasson (2nd ed.)]

MASORAH. Yeivin has undertaken research into the Babylonian vocalization system. He has examined all the known manuscript sources of Babylonian vocalization and described the linguistic tradition which it reflects. A large proportion of his manuscript sources are from the *Genizah* and contain principally Bible texts, rabbinic texts in Mishnaic Hebrew, and *piyyutim*. Yeivin discovered numerous variations within the Babylonian vocalization system and divided the types of systems which he found in his sources under three headings: (a) Old Babylonian; (b) Middle Babylonian; and (c) Late Babylonian.

The texts using the Old Babylonian system were only partially vocalized, whereas Middle Babylonian vocalization was complete. Late Babylonian is a mixed system consisting essentially of Tiberian vocalization with vestiges of Middle Babylonian pronunciation. With regard to the chronology of the Babylonian system, Yeivin concluded that our earliest sources must date from approximately 800 C.E. Yeivin has also published facsimiles of all *Genizah* Bible fragments with Old Babylonian and Middle Babylonian vocalization and a few with Late Babylonian vocalization. The Spanish scholar Diez Merino has compiled a catalogue of all known Babylonian Bible manuscripts and written a synopsis of the work of former scholars on the Babylonian vocalization system.

Several scholars have collected and studied *Genizah* fragments with Palestinian vocalization. M. Dietrich has edited and analyzed a number of Bible fragments with Palestinian vocalization which he discovered in Cambridge and Oxford *Genizah* collections. E.J. Revell has published two books on Palestinian vocalization. In *Hebrew Texts with Palestinian Vocalization* he analyzes and classifies the pointing of Hebrew texts with this vocalization system. The work is based on non-biblical texts discovered by Dietrich in the Taylor-Schechter New Series and on some 30 other texts, including biblical material, which were found by Revell himself in the Cambridge Genizah Collections. The classification consists of two parts, one of biblical and the other of non-biblical texts, and is based on the number of vowel signs which are used and the manner of their use. According to Revell, in the non-biblical texts there are 11 different types of vocalization, all of which belong to one of two major divisions or dialect groups. In his assessment of the relationship between Palestinian and Ben-Asher Tiberian vocalization, Revell advances the view that the Palestinian system represents a stage of Hebrew which has developed further than that reflected in the Ben-Asher system. This theory is contrary to that of the majority of scholars who maintain that the Palestinian system reflects an earlier stage of Hebrew than the Tiberian. In his more recent book, *Biblical Texts with Palestinian Pointing and their Accents*, Revell lists all known Biblical manuscripts with Palestinian pointing, including several new fragments discovered in the Taylor-Schechter Additional Series, and studies the use of their accent signs. He contradicts P. Kahle, who claimed that Palestinian accent signs did not mark stress. According to Revell, it is quite reasonable to hold that they indicate stress if it is assumed that stress in Palestinian Biblical Hebrew frequently fell on the penultima rather than on the ultima.

B. Chiesa has made a comprehensive study of fragments of biblical texts with Palestinian vocalization. His work includes a summary of previous studies on Palestinian vocalization as well as a catalogue of all the Palestinian Bible fragments which were known to him before the Taylor-Schechter Additional Series became available. He discusses the historical position of the Palestinian system and its cultural milieu and concludes that it was molded by provincial Jewish communities which lacked strong scholarly leadership. Chiesa also collects the variant readings which the Palestinian texts exhibit in comparison with Ben Ḥayyim's Bible as edited by van der Hooght in 1705. These variant readings show that the text of the Palestinian Bible fragments belongs to a textual family which is distinct from that of the Tiberian and Babylonian traditions. It is close to the lost Hebrew tradition whose remains are now to be found in the Greek and related variants.

N. Allony has published facsimiles of 60 *Genizah* fragments of Talmud and *Halakhah* with Palestinian vocalization. None of these fragments is later than the 11th century; they thus invalidate the generally accepted view that vocalized Mishnah texts did not exist before the 14th century (the date of the Kaufmann manuscript).

In his book *Manuscritos hebreos y arameos de la Biblia*, H. Diez Macho discusses the work which has been done on the various vocalization systems and attempts to elucidate many of the problems which these involve. Chapters are devoted to Babylonian, Palestinian, and Tiberian vocalization and also to what he calls "Pseudo Ben-Naphtali" vocalization, i.e., the mixed system of Tiberian and Palestinian vowel signs which Kahle erroneously called Ben-Naphtali. Apart from the standard Tiberian systems, most of our knowledge of these types of vocalization is derived from *Genizah* fragments. The work also includes a catalogue of *Genizah* Bible fragments with "Pseudo Ben-Naphtali" vocalization, which supplements the list published previously by Diez Macho (*Hebrew and Semitic Studies Presented to G.R. Driver*, 1963, pp. 16–52). This new catalogue shows that there are more Bible manuscripts of this type in the *Genizah* than was formerly thought.

GRAMMAR AND LEXICOGRAPHY. Allony has reconstructed Saadiah Gaon's lexicographical work *Ha-Egron* from *Genizah* manuscript fragments and published it in a critical edition. Until the discovery of the *Genizah* this work was known by name only from Abraham Ibn Ezra's introduction to linguistics, *Sefer Moznayim*. The work was designed as a handbook for poets, the entries being arranged both according to their initial letter to assist the writing of acrostics and also according to their final letter in order to help poets find a rhyming word. Allony has also published, in the form of a monograph, *Genizah* fragments of the *Kitāb al-Kāmil* by the Spanish grammarian Jacob ben Eleazar. Previously this work was only known from citations in medieval grammatical treatises and Bible commentaries. The fragments of the original work show that the *Kitāb al-Kāmil* formed the apex of the Spanish school of Hebrew philology. The book was a comprehensive and systematic exposition of grammar, which was more clearly organized than the compendious *Sefer ha-Rikmah* of his illustrious forbear Ibn Janaḥ.

S. Abramson has used *Genizah* sources extensively to reconstruct the *Kitāb al-Tajnīs* (Book of Homonyms) of Judah ibn Bal'am. This is a lexicographical work which lists words with two or more different meanings. *Genizah* fragments have also been used by A. Dotan in his edition of the *Sefer Dikdukei ha-Te'amim* of Aaron ben Asher and by Halkin in his edition of the *Kitāb al-Muhaḍara wa-al-Mudhākara* of Moses Ibn Ezra. The very beginning of the mediaeval linguistic learned works, *Kutub al-Lugha* by Saadya Gaon was reconstructed and edited by A. Dotan.

TARGUM AND VERSIONS. M. Klein has published all the primary sources of the so-called Fragment Targums to the Pentateuch, two of which are *Genizah* manuscripts from the Jewish Theological Seminary of America and the British Museum. The Fragment Targums are not complete verse-by-verse renderings of the Hebrew text but contain only a selection of isolated verses or parts of verses. The two *Genizah* texts are both of Palestinian provenance and are the earliest of the fragment Targum manuscripts (11th–13th century). S. Lund and S.A. Foster have made a study of the Targum traditions as represented in the codex Neofiti 1, which was discovered by Diez Macho in 1956. The codex Neofiti 1 contains the complete text of the Palestinian Targum to the Pentateuch. This text belongs to the same tradition as the *Genizah* fragments of the Palestinian Targum which were published by Kahle in 1930 and also to the same as is represented by the Fragment Targums. The codex also includes a large number of interlinear and marginal notations which constitute two variant Targumic versions of the main text. Lund and Foster correlate these two margin texts with the Palestinian Targum as found in the *Genizah* manuscripts and with the Fragment Targums. They conclude that one of the margin texts is derived from the same tradition as the *Genizah* and Fragment Targums whereas the other belongs to a different tradition, which has certain affinities to the Pseudo-Jonathan Targum to the Pentateuch.

M. Goshen-Gottstein reconstructed parts of the Old Testament in the "Syro-Palestinian" version on the basis of all the known sources. This version was written in Christian Palestinian Aramaic and was used by the Melchite Christian community in Palestine in the first half of the first millennium C.E. The bulk of the source material for this version is provided by palimpsests which have been discovered in the *Genizah*. These contain Hebrew overscripts and Syro-Palestinian underscripts.

MISCELLANEOUS. The *Genizah* has furnished sources for the edition of two important Jewish mystical works. M. Margalioth has reconstructed *Sefer ha-Razim* almost entirely from fragments which were preserved in the *Genizah*. The general contents of this work have long been known, especially from extracts scattered in *Sefer Raziel*. It is only now, however, that we have the text of the original. *Sefer ha-Razim* is an exposition of the names and functions of the angels in the six heavens which precede the supreme heaven, together with an assortment of magic formulae for suppliants of various types. The recently recovered original text shows that the work was heavily indebted to the Greek Gnostic literature of Hellenistic Egypt. It contains many Greek magic terms and even has a prayer to the sun-god Helios. P. Fenton has edited the *Treatise of the Pool* (*al-Maqāla al-Ḥawḍiyya*) by Obadiah Maimonides (1228–1265), the grandson of Moses Maimonides, from *Genizah* fragments and from a manuscript in the Bodleian Library, Oxford. This mystical work is a manual for the spiritual wayfarer along the path to godliness. A man's heart is compared to a cistern or "pool" which is to be filled with pure water. Obadiah's work is permeated by a philosophical mysticism that owes much to the influence of Islamic Sufism. It is therefore an eloquent testimony to the close relationship between Muslim and Jewish mystics in the 13th century. Fenton added more substantial editions of Maimonidean mystical traditions based on sources found in Karaite and Rabbanite *genizot*: *Moreh Derekh ha-Perishut* of David the 2nd Maimuni and several works of earlier generations of this dynasty.

An important contribution to the history of Hebrew printing has been made by H. Dimitrovsky, who has published *Genizah* fragments of incunabula of the Babylonian Talmud from Spain and Portugal. These fragments are valuable because the Expulsion from Spain (1492) and Portugal (1497) and the Christian Inquisition led to the almost complete destruction of Jewish printed books, so that very few examples of early Jewish printing in these countries have come down to us. Moreover the text of the Talmud which these fragments preserve has many particular features which distinguish it from other known texts of the same work. Apparently old texts of the Talmud, which were not preserved elsewhere, reached Spain from Babylonia in early times.

The *Genizah* has preserved the oldest Yiddish work which has so far been attested (14th century). It was first published by Fuks in 1957 and has been critically edited more recently by H.J. Hakkarainen. Hava Turniyanski published a series of letters written in Yiddish.

Scholars of Hebrew paleography have been furnished with abundant source material from the *Genizah*. S.A. Birnbaum and M. Beit-Arié, for instance, have used *Genizah* fragments as representatives of the medieval and, to a lesser extent, post-medieval Oriental and Sephardi scripts. Beit-Arié's work *Hebrew Codicology*, which reports the preliminary conclusions of the Hebrew paleography project of the Israel Academy of Sciences and Humanities, is particularly important. Owing to the mobility of the medieval Jewish population in the Mediterranean area, the form of script used by a manuscript scribe is not by itself a reliable guide to its provenance since the scribe may have had his training in another country. Consequently Beit-Arié has taken into account a wide variety of physical and graphical characteristics of medieval Hebrew manuscripts, which were cumulatively less sensitive to population fluctuations, and established a typology of general codicology. This typology will enable scholars to identify the date and provenance of medieval Hebrew manuscripts with greater accuracy. Edna Engel continues this work and formed types and schools of *Genizah* writers intended to characterize cultural traditions of Oriental communities and to set the basis for future matching projects of fragments from different libraries.

[Geoffrey Khan / Menahem Ben-Sasson (2nd ed.)]

Genizah Material at Cambridge University Library

OLD AND NEW SERIES. At the beginning of the 20th century, a few years after the presentation of the Collection to Cambridge University by Charles Taylor and Solomon Schechter in 1898, a total of some 31,000 fragments had been examined and sorted in a classification series which became known as the Taylor-Schechter Old Series. The fragments were conserved in various ways. Over 2,000 were sealed between glass, almost 7,000 were bound up in volumes, and about 22,000 were individually preserved in paper folders and stored in boxes. The remaining pieces, now known to number approximately 109,000, were left in crates, being considered for the most part of lesser value. It was not until 1955 that their importance was acknowledged and that work began to sort and classify them under the direction of the university librarian, H.R. Creswick. A new classification was adopted for them and they came to be known as the Taylor-Schechter New Series. The sorting of the fragments for the New Series was, however, unsystematic. The bulk of the work was done by visiting scholars who, in the absence of a well-coordinated program, tended to make selections, each according to his own interests, in a rather piecemeal fashion. One reason for this was that, until the appointment of H. Knopf in 1965, no member of the library staff had specific responsibilities for the *Genizah* Collection. The fragments that had been assigned classmarks were stored in boxes like the majority of the Old Series.

Shortly after the initiation of the New Series a program began to microfilm all the classified fragments of the Collection and so enable them to be studied by scholars in academic institutions other than Cambridge. In the late 1960s, on the initiative of the university librarian, Eric Ceadel, a conservationist was appointed to treat the New Series material. The most up-to-date methods were used to ensure that the maximum protection was given to the priceless fragments. They were cleaned, flattened, and repaired. Moreover their storage in boxes was considered unsatisfactory, since they could easily be damaged or misplaced when removed for consultation. Consequently they were placed in a transparent polyester film known as Melinex, sewn onto uniform-sized sheets, and placed in looseleaf binders.

TAYLOR-SCHECHTER GENIZAH RESEARCH UNIT. In 1974 the Taylor-Schechter *Genizah* Research Unit was established under the directorship of S.C. Reif. A ten-year project was initiated, the aims of which were the increase of personnel engaged in work on the Collection, the conservation of the material and its being made available to scholars, the compilation of bibliographical aids for users of the Collection, the initiation of an organized research program in the *Genizah* field, and the publication of material for both the scholarly world and the informed public. Part of the cost of this project was met by Cambridge University Library and the remainder was to be in the form of grants and donations from outside sources. A steering committee was set up for the unit consisting of representatives of the University Library and the Faculty of Oriental Studies, and has ensured the close involvement of the Faculty in the Unit's work.

SORTING. The New Series was terminated after it had come to contain about 42,000 fragments. The material still remaining in 32 crates was sorted in 1974 by a team of scholars in a joint project with the Israel National Academy of Sciences and Humanities. The result of this work was entitled the Taylor-Schechter Additional Series. Since the sorting was coordinated and completed in a short space of time the classification of the fragments in this series was more systematic than that of the New Series. The Additional Series contains about 67,000 fragments and so the total number of pieces in the Collection can now be calculated to be in the region of 140,000, well in excess of Schechter's original estimate of 100,000.

CONSERVATION. A team of full-time conservationists was appointed to deal with the Taylor-Schechter Collection. They continued, with a number of improvements, the modern methods which had been initiated for the treatment of the New Series. After the New Series was completed they treated the newly sorted Additional Series fragments and placed them under Melinex in small manageable binders. Subsequently the Old Series fragments received the same attention. Finally the other *Genizah* fragments which had been acquired by Cambridge University Library before and after Schechter's expedition to Cairo, including the Or. 1080–81 material, were given the same protection as the Taylor-Schechter Collection.

This conservation work was completed in 1981 and now all the material of the Cambridge Genizah Collection is fully accessible to scholars and may be freely consulted without any risk of damage.

RESEARCH AND PUBLICATIONS. From 1974 a systematic-cataloguing program was established in Cambridge. As a result, the first comprehensive catalogues of Cambridge *Genizah* material in a variety of scholarly fields are now making their appearance. The following numbers in the Series have already been published: No. 2. *Hebrew Bible Manuscripts in the Cambridge Genizah Collections*: Volume 1: *Taylor-Schechter Old Series and Other Genizah Collections in Cambridge University Library*, by M.C. Davis, incorporating material compiled by H. Knopf (1978). Volume 2: *Taylor-Schechter New Series and Westminster College Cambridge Collection*, by M.C. Davis (1980).

No. 3. *A Miscellany of Literary Pieces from the Cambridge Genizah Collections*, by Simon Hopkins (1978). *An Introduction to the Cambridge Genizah Collections*, by S.C. Reif. *Hebrew Bible Manuscripts in the Cambridge Genizah Collections*: Volumes 3 and 4: *Taylor-Schechter Additional Series 1–31 and 32–225, with addenda to previous volumes*, by M.C. Davis.

No. 4. *Vocalized Talmudic Manuscripts in the Cambridge Genizah Collections*: Volume 1: *Taylor-Schechter Old Series*, by Shelomo Morag.

No. 5. *Post-Talmudic Rabbinic Manuscripts in the Cambridge Genizah Collections*: Volume 1: *Taylor-Schechter New Series*, by E.J. Wiesenberg.

No. 6. *Published Material from the Cambridge Genizah Collections: A Bibliography* (three volumes).

The *Bibliographies* of publications relating to the Cambridge *Genizah* Collections covers all published material up to 2005. *Genizah* publications are scattered in a wide range of periodicals and books, some of them unavailable in most libraries. Consequently, a scholar who is interested in a fragment is very often unable to trace what has previously been written about it. Each reference to a fragment was checked against the original manuscript and, if necessary, corrected before it was entered into the *Bibliography*.

MICROFILM. The Taylor-Schechter Unit has completed the microfilming of all the fragments in the Cambridge *Genizah* Collections on 320 reels. It has made whole sets of the films available to several institutions around the world including the Hebrew University of Jerusalem, Tel Aviv University, the Jewish Theological Seminary of America, and Yeshiva University in New York. Over the last few years Cambridge University Library has itself acquired microfilms of *Genizah* material held elsewhere. Consequently Cambridge is now a major center for the study of material from all the *Genizah* Collections.

[Stefan C. Reif / Geoffrey Khan / Stuart E. Rosenberg (2nd ed.)]

The Friedberg Genizah Project

The Friedberg Genizah Project was conceived and initiated by Albert D. Friedberg of Toronto, Canada, in 1998 and started to operate in 1999. Mr. Friedberg foresaw the possibilities of harnessing modern technology and international scholarly cooperation in order to advance research into the riches of the Cairo *Genizah* and facilitate the exploitation of these resources within the matrix of both traditional and academic Jewish studies. The *Genizah* contains hundreds of thousands of pages of treatises and documents of all sorts – texts of the Bible and commentaries, biblical and rabbinic dictionaries, halakhic works, poetry and prayer, philosophical and polemic treatises, deeds, documents, official and personal letters, in Hebrew, Aramaic, Judeo-Arabic and Arabic, Judeo-Persian and Yiddish, dating from before the eighth century until the 15th and even later on. The project that resulted from Mr. Friedberg's initiative was made possible by a grant from the Buckingham Foundation of Toronto, Canada.

Specifically, the project's purpose was threefold: (a) to produce a union catalogue of all Cairo *Genizah* fragments, which will eventually be made available online to all interested scholars; (b) to commission transcriptions of as many of those fragments as practicable; and (c) to encourage scholarship on the *Genizah*.

The projected union catalogue will for the first time provide a complete accounting of all *Genizah* fragments from collections all over the world, thus making the rich treasures of the Cairo *Genizah* accessible to all those interested in the history of Jewish texts and contexts from late antiquity to the early modern period. Included in this database will be a flexible search engine that will enable scholars to collate scattered fragments and conduct research on them, as well as a wide variety of searches in all the languages of the *Genizah*. While more than 60% of the *Genizah* has been catalogued in one way or another in the last century, since its discovery and export to libraries all over the world, much remains to be done, and FGP was established in order to bring this task to completion.

Equally important is the effort to produce transcriptions of as many of these fragments as possible. These transcriptions, used in conjunction with the catalogue, will make it possible for those interested in particular subjects to investigate and integrate all relevant texts into their work.

The Project was intended to restore awareness of the importance of the *Genizah* to the general and Jewish scholarly worlds, and, not least important, to attract junior potential scholars to specialize in or utilize this important source for Jewish and general history.

FGP is involved in the continuous efforts of cataloguing at Cambridge University Taylor-Schechter Genizah Research Unit. All already-published catalogues of CUL entries are part of FGP database. FGP has contacted libraries with smaller collections than those at Cambridge or the Jewish Theological Seminary. The John Rylands University Library (JRUL), The University of Manchester, and several other libraries have signaled their willingness to cooperate in the accomplishment of FGP's cataloguing goals. Among these are the British Library, the Bibliothèque Nationale et Universitaire de Strasbourg, the Oestereichische Nationalbibliothek, the National Library of Russia, and the AIU collection in Paris. By its end FGP estimates that the cataloguing of over 170,000 fragments will be completed and the results made available in a union catalogue; it is expected that the remaining 43,000 fragments will be catalogued by the libraries housing these fragments, with the encouragement of the FGP.

In pursuance of its second goal, FGP has set up several units to work on specific areas of *Genizah* transcription, and, when appropriate as in the case of Judeo-Arabic texts, translations. These include units devoted to the entire Talmudic corpus (Mishnah, Tosefta, Babylonian Talmud, Jerusalem Talmud, RIF), *Midrash Halakhah*, *Midrash Aggadah*, Judeo-Arabic halakhic compendia, Judeo-Arabic grammatical and lexical texts, Judeo-Arabic philosophical and polemic texts, liturgical texts, court and economic documents, Geonic responsa. These units are located at Hebrew University, Makhon Ben Zvi, Ben-Gurion University, Tel Aviv University, Bar-Ilan University in Israel, and Princeton University.

FGP also aims at publishing in print the results of its work, catalogues as well as texts. FGP has so far published Professor Menahem Kahana's first volume on *The Genizah Fragments of the Halakhic Midrashim* (Magnes Press, 2005). FGP also participated in the publication of a volume of *Genizah* texts of Maimonides' Commentary on the Mishnah by Dr. Simon Hopkins, a volume of book-lists from the *Genizah* compiled by N. Allony, and further support for other volumes is planned.

The process of transcription has begun to bear substantial fruit and numerous texts have been prepared for eventual distribution, or are in the process of being prepared. Especially significant are important rabbinic fragments and numerous Judeo-Arabic texts that are being transcribed and translated, with the hope of soon being able to make them available to the wider public in a variety of formats. As the Project continues to develop, the scope and significance of this component of its work can be expected to continue to increase, so that a virtual treasure trove of new texts will be available. Coupled with the extensive cataloguing and bibliographical efforts the Project is involved in, we can be assured of opening the *Genizah*'s still unclaimed treasures for academic and religious scholarship.

With all this progress, as well as the opportunity given to many graduate students and others to actually work with *Genizah* texts, a greater interest on the part of students and scholars in researching these texts can already be detected, and thus the third goal of the Project – the further development of the field by encouraging young scholars to enter it – is on the way to fulfillment.

BIBLIOGRAPHY AND CATALOGUING. The Project's Unit of Cataloguing and Bibliography, as its name indicates, has two main roles: one is the preparation of a hand-list as stated in the Project's goals; the second role includes systematic combing of published literature since the discovery of the *Genizah* material, for the purpose of recording the bibliographic references to and cataloguing of fragments from all *Genizah* collections. The focus around which the references are assembled is a unique fragment identifier, while all its varied, old, and erroneous identities in shelf marks, locations, and catalogue numbers are noted as added alternative fields, so as to eliminate as much as possible the confusion that accompanies a researcher's attempt in locating a desired fragment. The bibliographic recording notes the presence of a facsimile or whether a fragment is mentioned, transcribed, translated or fully described, in which case one also includes in the bibliographic records any physical description and cataloguing information that appear in the publication.

1. The Jewish National and University Library has completed the digitizing of JNUL *Genizah* collection and prepared the hand-list for this collection in electronic version.

2. Taylor-Schechter Genizah Research Unit, Cambridge University Cataloguing of T-S Collections: The projects currently receiving full or partial support from FGP are as follows: (a) the preparation of catalogues of the Arabic and Judeo-Arabic items in the New Series and Additional Series of the Cambridge *Genizah* Collections; (b) the compilation of a third volume of bibliography of published items from the Cambridge *Genizah* Collections, covering the years 1980–97.

GINZEI QEDEM. *Ginzei Qedem* is an annual publication devoted to *Genizah* texts and studies. *Ginzei Qedem* is part of the Friedberg Genizah Project, whose aim is to contribute to increased scholarly discussion of *genizot* worldwide, in the hope that the fruits of this discussion will eventually enrich both traditional and academic Jewish studies. The purpose of *Ginzei Qedem* is to provide a specialized venue for scholarly publications in this area. Younger scholars are particularly encouraged to participate alongside their more established colleagues.

In terms of the subject matter to be covered, the rubric "*Genizah* texts and studies" is to be understood in the broadest possible sense to include publications of fragments of literary works and documents from *genizot* in Cairo and elsewhere, as well as studies based on such fragments. Articles may deal with any of the relevant disciplines, including but not limited to biblical studies and exegesis, history, literature (including *piyyut*), Talmud and rabbinics, theology, philosophy, linguistics, science, medicine, and magic.

Contributions may be in Hebrew, English, or other major European languages. Any substantial quotations in a language other than that in which the article is written must be accompanied by a translation.

THE CENTER FOR THE STUDY OF JUDEO-ARABIC CULTURE AND LITERATURE AT THE BEN-ZVI INSTITUTE (JERUSALEM). The Center currently conducts three projects in conjunction with the Friedberg Genizah Project: (1) Judeo-Arabic halakhic literature, (2) Judeo-Arabic biblical exegesis, and (3) Judeo-Arabic philosophical, theological, and polemical works. In addition to these projects, the Friedberg Genizah Project is participating in the institute's ongoing project to catalogue the Judeo-Arabic manuscripts in the Firkovitch Collection.

Judeo-Arabic Halakhic Literature Project. The aim of this project is to reconstruct works relating to halakhic or talmudic topics written in Judeo-Arabic from the geonic period through the 15th century. After reconstruction, these works will be published with an annotated Hebrew translation and introductions. The books concerned include halakhic monographs, works of talmudic methodology and legal theory, talmudic commentaries, commentaries on Maimonides' Mishneh Torah, Books of Commandments, and so on. While work on specific books is currently based on lists of identification made by various scholars, a systematic re-examination and cataloguing of the relevant *Genizah* fragments has also begun.

The following books are at present in varying states of preparation: (1) Hai b. Sherira Gaon, *Kitāb al-Aymān* (Laws of Oaths, known as *Mishpetei Shevuot*); (2) Hai b. Sherira, *Kitab al-Bay' wal-Ashriyah* (Laws of Purchase and Sales, known as *Mekah u-Mimkar*); (3) Samuel b. Hofni Gaon, *Kitāb al-Talāq* (Laws of Divorce); (4) Samuel b. Hofni, *al-Madkhal ila 'Ilm al-Mishnah wal-Talmud* (Introduction to the Study of the Mishnah and Talmud); (5) Samuel b. Hofni, *Kitāb al-Buyū'* (Laws of Sales); (6) Samuel b. Hofni, *Kitāb al-Shurūt* (Laws of Legal Conditions); (7) Samuel b. Hofni, *Kitāb al-Zawjiyah* (Laws of Marriage); (8) Samuel b. Hofni, *Kitāb Ahkām al-Yibbum* (Laws of Levirate Marriage); (9) Samuel b. Hofni, *Kitāb al-'Iddah* (On the period of time a woman must wait between marriages); (10) Samuel b. Hofni, *Kitāb al-Nafaqā* (On Support Payments); (11) Samuel b. Hofni, *Kitāb al-Rahn* (On Pawning); (12) David b. Saadya al-Ger, *Kitāb al-Hawī* (The Comprehensive Work [of *Halakhah*]); (13) Hananel b. Shemuel, Commentary on the Book of Leviticus; (14) Saadiah b. Joseph Gaon, *Sefer Mitzvot* (Book of Commandments).

Judeo-Arabic Biblical Exegesis Project. The goal of this project is similar to that of the *halakhah* project: to reconstruct Judeo-Arabic works of biblical exegesis. In the case of biblical exegesis, however, it has not been possible to begin with a corpus of identified fragments. Further, the number of exegetical fragments is much larger than in the case of the halakhic material. The institute therefore began with a systematic survey of *Genizah* collections, cataloguing the Judeo-Arabic exegetical fragments, surveying the collections of the Bodleian Library and the British Library, the Mosseri collection, and a large part of the Cambridge collections. It is hoped that a detailed description of each fragment's physical, paleographic, codicological details, as well as its content, will eventually enable one to put together fragments of a single manuscript or composition. An attempt at identification of each fragment is already made at this stage. In addition, a start was made to transcribe and translate selected fragments, which from their paleographical, codicological, or orthographic characteristics appear to be relatively early, perhaps pre-Saadianic. As a pilot publication of a reconstructed text Prof. Ben-Shammai is now working on a critical edition of the Judeo-Arabic commentary of Saadiah Gaon on the first part of Exodus (ch. 1–20), based on a large number of fragments in various collections, with annotated Hebrew translation.

Philosophy, Theology, and Polemics. This project is dedicating renewed, concentrated attention to the philosophical, theological, and polemical material in the *Genizah*, mostly in Judeo-Arabic. The intention is to identify, catalogue, and publish works belonging to these branches of thought, in all the *Genizah* collections. Fragments of works that have already been edited are catalogued, and the significant variant readings are noted. These lists will be published independently and used in conjunction with the editions, or will prepare the way for the eventual publication of new, comprehensive critical editions (if the material examined indicates the need for such an undertaking). Fragments that are still unpublished are catalogued, identified, or described in detail in order to facilitate future identification. Several collections have already been catalogued in this way: the Mosseri and AIU collections in Paris, the Kaufman Collection in Budapest, and the collections in Philadelphia and in Oxford, as well as significant parts of the larger collections in the Jewish Theological Seminary (New York) and in Cambridge.

Princeton University Project on Medieval Documents in Judeo-Arabic (Conducted by Prof. Mark Cohen). Under Friedberg funding Princeton will computerize about 4,000 transcriptions of historical documents from the Cairo *Genizah* documents. These documents, mostly unpublished, were originally transcribed by S.D. Goitein and copies of his transcriptions are found in the "S.D. Goitein *Genizah* Research Lab at Princeton" (the original "Lab" is located at the Institute of Microfilmed Hebrew Manuscripts at the Jewish National and University Library in Jerusalem). The Princeton project keyboards Goitein's typed texts, edits them, and provides them with brief catalogue-headers.

Halakhic Midrashim (Project Conducted by Prof. Menahem Kahana, Hebrew University). The first book published by FGP is Professor Kahana's The *Genizah Fragments of the Halakhic Midrashim*, Jerusalem (Magnes Press), 2005.

Judeo-Arabic Documents and Response (Project Conducted by Prof. Mordechai A. Friedman, Tel Aviv University). This group has undertaken the decipherment, translation, and brief annotation of the *Genizah* Judeo-Arabic responsa literature from the geonic period and the classical *Genizah* period (the manuscripts from the latter period will include a few Hebrew responsa) as well as other legal texts: Judeo-Arabic responsa dealing with commercial law, documents and some responsa associated with engagement and betrothal, responsa of Abraham Maimonides and his contemporaries.

Philological Texts, Primarily in Judeo-Arabic (Project Conducted by Prof. A. Maman, Hebrew University). The group working on philology (grammars, dictionaries, and glossaries) which includes among others *Genizah* fragments from Radak's *Sefer Ha-Shorashim* (such as T-S K7/82; T-S AS 141.76B), from Ibn Janah's *Sefer Ha-Shorashim* (Ms. Heb d.33.69; Ms. Heb d.33.70V; TS AR 32.35, TS Ar. 46.36), fragments from Hebrew-Arabic Biblical Glossaries (TS Ar. 5/51; T-S AS 141.44D; T-S AS 141.68B; T-S K7/45), and fragments from Hebrew-Arabic Mishnaic Glossaries (T-S K7/11).

Genizah Cataloguing at JNUL (by Dr. Ezra Chwat, JNUL). This group completed an updated catalogue of the *Genizah* fragments of rabbinic manuscripts in Oxford's Bodleian Library and, for the Oriental Department of the Hungarian Academy of Sciences, a catalogue of the David Kaufman collection in Budapest.

Documents from the Late Middle Ages (by Dr. Avraham David, JNUL). This group completed Cairo *Genizah* documents of the Late Middle Ages (from the second half of the 15th century to the first half of the 17th century).

Aggadic Midrashim (by Prof. Chaim Milikovsky, Bar-Ilan University). A group focusing on *Genizah* texts relating to *Midrash Aggadah*. This group will have two primary goals: (1) the preparation of a database/catalogue of *Genizah* fragments of *Midrash Aggadah*; and (2) the transcription of fragments of *Midrash Aggadah* from all collections of *Genizah* material.

In the beginning of 2006 an interim estimate displays an order of magnitude. The figures, especially in cataloguing, represent records, not necessarily fragments, because of joints and splits. Cataloging (or identifying) records 68,900. About 25 teams (including individual scholars): 42,300 records, in addition to 10 Cambridge computerized catalogues: 24,400 records and 6 additional computerized catalogs: 2,200 records. 6,800 transcriptions; 800 new translations; 23,000 bibliographical items; 4,000 (in process of adding 20,000 jts) digitized images; 167,000 computerized lists of shelf-marks. These are in the process of being loaded into FIST [= FGP Information Storehouse]. FGP has already had an effect on *Genizah*-related activities, certainly in Israel, but also abroad. The number of researchers, and in particular the number of graduate students (both M.A. and Ph.D. students) involved in *Genizah* research today, either cataloguing, transcribing, translating, or in general conducting research on specific topics related to the *Genizah* world is considerably greater than several years ago. Many of these graduate students are now researchers on their own, working in the *Genizah* field. The various teams of researchers in four universities in Israel as well as in the Jerusalem National and University Library, in the Institute for Manuscript Microfilms, and at the Ben-Zvi Institute have created an awareness and induced a flurry of activity very beneficial in itself to the promotion of *Genizah*-related research. Some successful examples are the special session on the FGP at the 14th International Congress of Jewish Studies in Jerusalem (2005), and the publication of the first issue of *Ginzei Kedem*. The same can be said about the awareness and activities in many *Genizah* centers such as Cambridge, Manchester, Princeton, Pennsylvania, and the Jewish Theological Seminary in New York. From this perspective, one of the principal long-term aims of the project is thus being fulfilled.

[Menahem Ben-Sasson (2nd ed.)]

BIBLIOGRAPHY: DOCUMENTS: S.D. Goitein, *A Mediterranean Society*, Vols. I (1967), II (1971), and III (1978); idem, *Letters of Medieval Jewish Traders* (1973); M.A. Michael, *The Archive of Nahray ben Nissim, Businessman and Community Leader in Egypt in the 11th Century* (Hebrew), Ph.D. thesis, Hebrew University, Jerusalem (1967); N.A. Stillman, *East-West Relations in the Islamic Mediterranean in the Early Eleventh Century – A Study in the Geniza Correspondence* *of the House of Ibn ʿAwkal*, Ph.D. thesis, University of Pennsylvania (1970); E. Ashtor, *Histoire des Prix et des Salaires dans L'Orient Médiéval* (1969); H. Rabie, *The Financial System of Egypt A.H. 564–741/ A.D. 1169–1341* (1972); M.R. Cohen, *Jewish Self-Government in Medieval Egypt* (1980); G. Weiss, "Legal Documents written by the Court Clerk Halfon Ben Manasse (dated 1100–1138)" (Ph.D. thesis, University of Pennsylvania, 1970); A.L. Motzkin, "The Arabic Correspondence of Judge Elijah and his Family (Papers from the Cairo Geniza)" (Ph.D. thesis, University of Pennsylvania, 1965); M. Gil, *Documents of the Jewish Pious Foundations from the Cairo Genizah* (1976); M. Friedman, *Jewish Marriage in Palestine* (1980); Y. Stillman, "Female Attire of Medieval Egypt: According to the Trousseau Lists and Cognate Material from the Cairo Geniza" (Ph.D. thesis, University of Pennsylvania, 1972); J. Sadan, *Le Mobilier au Proche Orient Médiéval* (1976); S.D. Goitein, *Palestinian Jewry in Early Islamic and Crusader Times* (Hebrew, 1980); Y. Prawer (ed.), *The History of Eretz-Yisrael under Moslem and Crusader Rule (634–1291)* (Heb., 1981); M. Gil, *The Tustaris: the Family and the Sect* (Heb., 1981); S.D. Goitein, *The Yemenites* (Heb., 1983); N. Golb and O. Pritsak, *Khazarian Hebrew Documents of the Tenth Century* (1983); E. Ashtor, *History of the Jews in Egypt and Syria under the Rule of the Mamluks*, vol. 4 (Heb., 1970); idem, *A Social and Economic History of the Near East in the Middle Ages* (1976); N.A. Stillman, *The Jews of Arab Lands* (1979). POETRY: J. Schirmann, *New Hebrew Poems from the Genizah* (Heb., 1965); A. Mirsky, *The Poems of Yose ben Yose* (Heb., 1977); M. Wallenstein, *Some Unpublished Piyyutim from the Cairo Genizah* (1956); E. Fleischer, *The Pizmonim of the Anonymous* (Heb., 1974); E. Fleischer, *The Poems of Solomon ha-Bavli* (Heb., 1975); D. Jarden, *The Liturgical Poetry of Rabbi Solomon ibn Gabirol* (Heb., 1971); idem, *The Liturgical Poetry of Rabbi Yehuda Halevi* (Heb., 1978); idem, *Divan Samuel ha-Nagid* (Heb., 1966); N. Allony and D. Jarden, *A Collection of the Secular Poems of Solomon ibn Gabirol* (Heb., 1969); H. Brody and J. Schirmann, *Solomon ibn Gabirol, Secular Poems* (Heb., 1974); I. Levin, *The Religious Poems of Abraham ibn Ezra* (Heb., 1975); M.H. Schmelzer, *Isaac ben Abraham ibn Ezra, Poems* (1980); D. Pagis, *The Poems of Levi ibn al-Tabban* (Heb., 1967); Y. David, *The Poems of Joseph Bensuli* (Heb., 1979); A. Mirsky, *The Poems of Isaac Ibn Khalfun* (Heb., 1961); Y. David, *The Poems of Elya Bar Shemaya* (Heb., 1977); D. Jarden, *Ẓefunei Shirah* (Heb., 1967). MASORAH: I. Yeivin, "The Babylonian Vocalization and the Linguistic Tradition it Reflects" (Heb., Ph.D. thesis, Hebrew University, Jerusalem, 1968); idem, *Geniza Bible Fragments with Babylonian Massorah and Vocalization*, 5 vols. (1973); L. Diez Merino, *La biblia babilonica* (1975); M. Dietrich, *Neue Palästinisch Punktierte Bibelfragmente* (1968); E.J. Revell, *Hebrew Texts with Palestinian Vocalization* (1970); idem, *Biblical Texts with Palestinian Pointing and Their Accents* (1977); B. Chiesa, *L'Antico Testamento Ebraico* (1978); N. Allony, *Geniza Fragments of Rabbinic Literature, Mishna, Talmud and Midrash, with Palestinian Vocalization* (1973); H. Diez Macho, *Manuscritos hebreos y arameos de la Biblia* (1971). GRAMMAR: N. Allony, *Ha-Egron: Kitāb ʿUsūl al-Shiʿr al-ʿibrāni by Rav Saadiah Gaon* (Heb., 1969); idem, *Jacob ben Eleazar; Kitāb al-Kāmil* (Heb., 1977); S. Abramson, *R. Judah b. Bal'am's Book of Homonyms* (Heb., 1963); A. Dotan, *The Dikdukei ha-Teʿamim of Aaron ben Moses ben Asher* (Heb., 1967); A.S. Halkin, *Moses ben Jacob ibn Ezra, Kitāb al-Muādara wal-Mudhākara* (Heb., 1975). TARGUM AND VERSIONS: M. Klein, *The Fragment Targums of the Pentateuch According to their Extant Sources* (1968); S. Lund and S.A. Foster, *Variant Versions of Targumic Traditions within Codex Neofiti 1* (1977). **ADD. BIBLIOGRAPHY:** GENERAL: M.A. Friedman, *Cairo Genizah Studies* (1980). This work is the first stage in assembling the research on the *Genizah* in various fields; Talmud, Midrash, poetry, and language. Among the 19 entries are the following: S.D. Goitein: "The Life of our Forefathers as Reflected in the Documents of the Cairo *Genizah*," Y. Sussmann, "Talmud Fragments in the Cairo *Genizah*," Z.M. Rabinowitz, "The Importance of the *Genizah* Fragments for the Study of Talmud and Midrash," E. Fleischer, "The Contribution of the *Genizah* to the Study of Medieval Hebrew Religious Poetry," Y. Schirmann, "Secular Hebrew Poetry in the *Genizah* Manuscripts," M. Gil, "Palestine During the First Period of Muslim Occupation (634–1099) in Light of the Cairo *Genizah* Documents," M. Benayahu, "The Significance of the *Genizah* Documents of the 16th–18th Centuries"; N. Aloni, in: *Sinai*, 79 (1976), 193–210; Sh. Morag, in: *Tarbiz*, 42 (1973), 60–78; *Ginzei Jerusalem – The Teaching of Gaonim and Earlier Rabbinic Sages as compiled from the Ms. stored in the Genizah in Egypt*, 1, new edition by A.J. Wertheimer (1981); A. Scheiber, "*ʿAl Ḥeqer Genizat Kaufmann ve-Ḥashivutah*," in: *Evkonyu* (1977/78), 310–28. BIBLE: S. Abramson, in: KS, 52 (1977), 156–72; G. Weiss, in: *Beth Mikra*, 23 (1978), 341–62. MISHNAH, TALMUD, AND HALAKHAH: J. Agus, in: JQR, 62 (1971/72), 314–6; N. Friedmann, in: *Tarbiz*, 40 (1971), 320–59; N. Aloni, in: *Sinai*, 72 (1973), 11–29; G. Weiss, in: *Gratz College Annual of Jewish Studies*, 2 (1973), 29–42; idem, in: *Meḥkarim be-Toldot Am Israel ve-Ereẓ Yisrael*, 4 (1978), 161–73; R. Mirkin, in: *Sefer Zikkaron to Ḥ. Yalon-Bar Ilan*, 2 (1974), 371–84; E.Ẓ. Melamed, *ibid.*, 385–417; Z.M. Rabinowitz, *ibid.*, 499–511; A.I. Katsh, in: JQR, 61 (1970/71), 1–74; 63 (1972/73), 39–47; 66 (1975/76), 129–42; 69 (1978/79), 16–26, 193–207; 71 (1981), 181–84; idem, in: *Sefer Shazar, Zer li-Gevurot* (1973); S. Abramson, *Koveẓ al Yad*, N.S. 8 (1976); M. Krupp, *Immanuel Freiburger Rundbrief* (1976), 172–76; N. Aloni, in: *Sefer Yaʿakov Gil* (1979), 249–55; S. Morag, in: *Sefer Zikhronot Baneth* (1979), 111–23; M.A. Friedman, in: *Mimizraḥ u-mi-Maʿarav*, 2 (1980), 19–25. MIDRASH: M.B. Lerner, in: KS, 48 (1973), 543–9; A. Scheiber, in: *Acta Orientalia Budapest*, 32 (1978), 231–43; Z.M. Rabinowitz, in: *Mikhtam le-David (Sefer Zikkaron le-ha-Rav D. Ochs)* (1978), 106–19; idem, in: *Bar Ilan*, 16–17 (1979), 100–111. GEONIC PERIOD: Z.M. Rabinowitz, in: *Tarbiz*, 41 (1972), 275–305; M.A. Friedman, in: *Sinai*, 74 (1974), 14–36; *ibid.*, 83 (1978), 250–51; idem, in *Michael*, 5 (1978), 215–42; A. Hurwitz, in: *Hadorom*, 46 (1978), 123–227. MAIMONIDES: A. Hurwitz, in: *Hadorom*, 38 (1974), 4–44; *ibid.*, 40 (1975), 57–122; M.A. Friedman, in: *Tarbiz*, 46 (1977), 145–49. RISHONIM: in: *Hadorom*, 42 (1975), 107–56; A. Hurwitz, in *Hadorom*, 44 (1977), 5–78; *ibid.*, 46 (1978), 4–13; J.H. Lipschitz, in: *Moriah*, 7 (1978), 5–12; *ibid.*, 8 (1978), 2–12. LITURGY: A. Scheiber, in: *Tarbiz*, 42 (1973), 209; N. Wieder, in: *Sinai*, 77 (1975), 116–38; *ibid.*, 82 (1978), 197–221; *ibid.*, 78 (1976), 97–122. POETRY: Z. Malachi, in: *Tarbiz*, 42 (1973), 328–36; idem, *Yahadut Teman* (1976), 321–27; D. Yarden, in: *Sinai*, 79 (1976), 97–101; Z.M. Rabinowitz, *Shai le-Haiman* (1977). HISTORY: S.D. Goitein, in: JQR, 56 (1975/76), 69–88; idem, in: *Sefunot*, 11 (1978), 11–33; B.Z. Kedar, in: *Tarbiz*, 42 (1973), 401–18; D. Baneth, in: *Sugyot be-Toldot Ereẓ Yisrael*, 4 (1976), 103–21; D. Pingree, in: JNES, 36 (1977), 113–45; 38 (1979), 153–76, 231–56; M.A. Michaeli, in: *Michael*, 5 (1978), 168–87; Z. Malachi, *ibid.* 188–91; S. Shaked, in: *Studia Orientalia in memory of Baneth* (1979), 239–44. ALIYAH: S. Abramson, in: *Sinai*, 81 (1977), 181–227. OTHER: M.L. Klein, in: HUCA, 49 (1978), 73–87; 50 (1979), 149–64; A. Scheiber, 277–87; idem, in: AOB, 33 (1979), 113–19; E. Fleischer, in: *Sefunot*, N.S. 47–25 (1979); idem, in: *Kobeẓ al Yad*, 9 (19), (1979), 25–127; idem, in: KS, 55 (1980), 183–90; Z. Falk, in: *Sinai*, 85 (1979), 145–49. MISCELLANEOUS: M. Margalioth, *Sefer ha-Razim* (Heb., 1966); P. Fenton, *The Treatise of the Pool: al-Maqāla al-Ḥawḍiyya* (1981); H. Dimitrovsky, *Seridei Bavli: Fragments from Spanish and Portuguese Incunabula and Sixteenth Century Printings of the Babylonian Talmud and al-Fasi* (Heb., 1979); L. Fuks, *The Oldest Known Literary Documents of Yiddish Literature (c. 1382)* (1957); H.J. Hakkarainen, *Studien zum*

Cambridger Codex (1967); S.A. Birnbaum, *The Hebrew Scripts* (1971); M. Beit-Arié, *Hebrew Codicology* (1976); D. Sklare (with H. Ben-Shammai) (eds.), *Judaeo-Arabic Manuscripts in the Firkovitch Collections: The Works of Yusuf al-Basir*, 1997; D. Sklare (with H. Ben-Shammai) (eds.), Center for the Study of Judaeo-Arabic Culture and Literature: Publications (series): *Judaeo-Arabic Manuscripts in the Firkovitch Collections: The Commentary on Genesis by Yefet ben 'Eli* (Heb., 2000); P.B. Fenton, "Leningrad Treasures," in: *Genizah Fragments*, 10 (1985), 2–3; M. Ben-Sasson, "Firkovich's Second Collection: Remarks on Historical and Halakhic Material," in: *Jewish Studies*, 31 (1991), 47–67 (Heb.); G. Khan, "Documents support Firkovitch theory," in: *Genizah Fragments*, 28 (Oct. 1994), 2; G.D. Cohen, "The Reconstruction of Gaonic History: Introduction to Jacob Mann's Texts and Studies," in the reprint of Mann's *Texts and Studies*, 1, (1972); M. Gil, *The Tustaris: The Family and the Sect* (Heb., 1981); idem, *Palestine during the First Muslim Period* (634–1099), 1–3 (Heb., 1983); M. Ben-Sasson, *The Jews of Sicily 825–1068* (1991); E. Bareket, *The Jews of Egypt 1007–1055* (1995); M. Ben-Sasson, *The Emergence of the Local Jewish Community in the Muslim World – Qayrawan, 800–1057* (Heb., 1996); M. Friedman, *Jewish Marriage in Palestine* (1980–1981); S.D. Goitein, *Jewish Education in Muslim Countries: New Sources from the Geniza* (Heb., 1962); S.C. Reif, *Published Material from the Cambridge Genizah Collections: A Bibliography* (1988), 243; H. Ben-Shammai, "Saadya's Introduction to Isaiah as an Introduction to the Books of the Prophets," in: *Tarbiz*, 60 (1991), 371–404 (Heb.); S.D. Goitein, *Palestinian Jewry in Early Islamic and Crusader Times* (Heb., 1980); Y. Yahalom, "The Leningrad treasures and the Study of the Poetry and Life of Yehuda Halevi," in: *Pe'amim*, 46–47 (1991), 55–74 (Heb.); idem, "Anthology of Ha-Levi poems," in: *Genizah Fragments*, 30 (October 1995); S. Hopkins, "An unpublished autograph fragment of Maimonides's Guide of the Perplexed," in: *Bulletin of the School of Asian and African Studies*, 50 (1987), 465–69; S. Stroumsa, *Dawud ibn Marwan al-Muqammis's Twenty Chapters* (1989); M. Zucker, *Saadia's Commentary on Genesis* (1984); G. Vajda, "Le commentaire kairouanais sur le 'Livre de la Creation'," in: REJ, 105 (1940), 132–40; 107 (1946–47), 99–156; 110 (1949–50), 67–92; 112 (1953), 5–33; 113 (1954), 37–61; 119 (1961), 159–61; 122 (1963), 149–62; A.E. Harkavy, *Zikhron Rav Shemuel ben Hofni* (*Studien und Mittheilungen*, 31) (1880).

GENNAZANO, ELIJAH ḤAYYIM BEN BENJAMIN OF (second half of 15th century), writer and disciple of R. Benjamin of Montalcino. Gennazano wrote (1) *Iggeret Ḥamudot*, on the Kabbalah, dedicated to David b. Benjamin of Montalcino, whom he wished to instruct in Kabbalah (ed. A.W. Greenup, 1912); (2) a poem about women, in which Gennazano arbitrates between Abraham of Sarteano, who published a poem against women, and Avigdor of Fano who composed a poem in their defense (all three ed. by Neubauer in *Israelitische Letterbode*, 10 (1884–85), 97–105); (3) two anti-Christian parodies of the "*Yigdal*" hymn (A. Marx, in JQR, 9 (1918–19), 306–7 and *Freidus Memorial Volume*, 1 (1929), 276ff.); and (4) a polemic against Christianity, a compilation of the arguments he used in a disputation with the monk Francesco da Aquapendente in Orvieto (Ms.).

BIBLIOGRAPHY: HB, 10 (1870), 104; 21 (1881), 21; D. Kaufmann, in: REJ, 34 (1897), 309–11; I. Davidson, *Parody in Jewish Literature* (1907), 32.

[Umberto (Moses David) Cassuto]

GENOA, seaport in N. Italy. There were Jews living in Genoa before 511, since in that year Theodoric the Ostrogoth confirmed through his minister Cassiodorus the Jewish privilege of restoring, but not enlarging, the synagogue, which had been destroyed by Christian fanatics. From 1134 Jews who came to Genoa had to pay toward the illumination of the cathedral – this obviously discouraging their settlement. *Benjamin of Tudela (c. 1165) found only two Jews (brothers) in Genoa, dyers from North Africa. Notarial documents of 1250–74 show a number of Jews established there or in transit. In 1492 refugees from Spain arriving in Genoa in overcrowded ships were allowed to land for three days, but on Jan. 31, 1493, this concession was withdrawn through fear that the Jews had introduced the plague. In following years some well-to-do Jews were allowed to stay in Genoa under the supervision of an "Office of the Jews."

The policy of the Genoese doges and senate toward the Jews subsequently varied, alternately influenced by fear of competition and the need to exploit Jewish experience in overseas trade. The Jews were expelled from the city in 1515, readmitted a year later, and again expelled in 1550. In 1567 the expulsion was extended to the whole territory of the republic. However, between 1570 and 1586, permission to engage in moneylending and to open shops in Genoa was granted four times to the Jews. In 1598 a further decree of expulsion was issued, but many Jews succeeded in evading it. In 1660 the 200 Jews living in Genoa were confined to a ghetto, although two years later many were still living outside it. What is possibly the first polyglot Bible (or part of it) was published here in 1516: the Psalter in the Hebrew original, with the Greek Septuagint, the Latin Vulgate, the Aramaic Targum and its Latin translation, and an Arabic version together with some notes by Bishop Agostino Giustiniani, to whose scholarly initiative this magnificent edition was due. The last decree of expulsion was issued in 1737 but was not rigorously enforced. Finally, in 1752 a more liberal statute was issued, but owing to the uncertain conditions the Jewish population remained small, numbering only 70 in 1763. The number increased during the 19th century, after Genoa's development as Italy's major port, especially after full equality was granted to the Jews in 1848. The community numbered about 1,000 in the middle of the 19th century.

[Attilio Milano]

Holocaust Period

Because of its location and its large and active port, Genoa was an important center for the assistance of Jews in Italy. Until the very last minute, some Jews managed to find boats and escape from the city.

One hundred fifty-three Jews were arrested and deported from the Province of Genoa during the German occupation of Italy. They included many refugees who had fled from Italian-occupied southeastern France at the time of the Italian armistice with the Allies on September 8, 1943, on their way to Switzerland or to the regions of Italy under the Allies.

Many Jewish refugees gathered in Genoa because the city was the headquarters of the Delegazione Assistenza Emigrati Ebrei (DELASEM), which coordinated assistance and rescue programs. The Genovese office of DELASEM was headed initially by Lelio Vittorio Valobra, who later fled to Switzerland and continued to work from there, with Raffaele *Cantoni, to support the organization's activities. Massimo Teglio, a particularly courageous Genovese Jew, remained on the scene and had a central role in helping both Italian and foreign Jews in danger of arrest. Teglio worked closely with Cardinal Pietro Boetto (1871–1946), the archbishop of Genoa, and his secretary, Don Francesco Repetto. Don Repetto recruited local priests and also created a regional rescue network, with help from the archbishop of Turin and priests from other northern Italian cities.

The hunt for Jews began on November 2, 1943, when two German police agents entered the offices of the Jewish community and forced the custodians, Linda and Bino Polacco, to turn over membership lists and summon members to a meeting at the synagogue the following morning. Many members had already left the city, but a majority of those arrested in Genoa were seized at this time. Only a few members who received the summons were able to escape, thanks to a warning received from Teglio. Rabbi Riccardo Pacifici, who until the last moment tried to help refugee Jews, was captured in the Galleria Mazzini, also on November 3. He died at Auschwitz, probably gassed upon arrival on December 11.

[Alberto Cavaglion (2nd ed.)]

Contemporary Period

At the end of World War II, 1,108 Jews were left in Genoa. Subsequently, the Jewish population maintained its size, notwithstanding a constant outnumbering of deaths over births, and in 1965 it numbered 1,036 persons out of a total of 840,000 inhabitants. The port of Genoa was the transit center for various groups of Jewish emigrants who came mainly from Eastern Europe and were heading for Israel. In early 2000s the community numbered a few hundred, operating a synagogue and a Jewish school. The review *La Fiamma* ("The Flame") was published monthly.

[Sergio DellaPergola]

BIBLIOGRAPHY: Milano, Bibliotheca, index, s.v. *Genova*; Roth, Italy, index; idem, in: *Speculum*, 25 (1950), 190–7; idem, *Jews in the Renaissance* (1959), 155; R. Pacifici, *Nuovo Tempio di Genova con illustrazioni e notizie storiche nella comunità nei secoli XVII e XVIII* (1939); Perreau, in: *Vessillo Israelitico*, 29 (1881), 12–14, 37–40, 70–73; D.W. Amram, *Makers of Hebrew Books in Italy* (1909), 266ff.; A. Marx, *Studies in Jewish History and Booklore* (1944), 312; S. Jona, *Persecuzione degli ebrei a Genova* (1965); Musso, G.G., "Documenti su Genova e gli ebrei tra il 'Quattro e il 'Cinquecento," RMI, 36 (1970) 426–435. **ADD. BIBLIOGRAPHY:** G.G. Musso, "Per la storia degli ebrei in Genova nella seconda meta del cinquecento: Le vicende genovesi di R. Josef Hakohen," in: *Carpi* (1967), 101–11; C. Brizzolari, *Gli ebrei nella storia di Genova* (1971); G.N. Zazzu, "Genova e gli ebrei nel basso Medio Evo," RMI, 40 (1974), 248–302; G.N. Zazzu, "Juifs dans le territoire génois au bas moyen-âge," in: WCJS, 6 (1975), 143–51; A. Agosto, "L'Archivio di stato di Genova e le fonti relative alla storia degli Ebrei genovesi dal XV al XVIII secolo," in: *Italia Judaica*, 2 (1986), 91–98; M. Balard, "Les transports maritimes génois vers la Terre Sainte," in: *I comuni italiani* (1986), 141–74; M.L. Favreau-Lilie, "Friedenssicherung und Konfliktbegrenzung; Genua, Pisa und Venedig in Akkon, ca. 1200–1224," in: *I comuni italiani* (1986), 429–47; B.Z. Kedar, "Genoa's Golden Inscription in the Church of the Holy Sepulchre; a Case for the Defence," in: *I comuni italiani* (1986), 317–35; S. Origone, "Genova, Costantinopoli e il Regno di Gerusalemme (prima metà sec. XIII)," in: *I comuni italiani* (1986), 281–316; G. Pistarino, "Genova e il Vicino Oriente nell'epoca del Regno Latino di Gerusalemme," in: *I comuni italiani* (1986), 57–139; R. Urbani, "Nuovi documenti sulla formazione della "Nazione ebrea" nel Genovesato durante il XVII secolo," in: *Italia Judaica*, 2 (1986), 193–209; R. Urbani, "Gli Eccellentissimi Protettori della nazione ebrea a Genova (1658–1797)," in: *Italia Judaica*, 3 (1989), 197–201; R. Urbani, "Considerazioni sull'insediamento ebraico genovese (1600–1750)," in: *Atti della Società Ligure di Storia Patria*, 29:1 (1989), 305–37; O. Limor, "Missionary Merchants; Three Medieval Anti-Jewish Works from Genoa," in: *Journal of Medieval History* 17:1 (1991), 35–51; G.N. Zazzu, *Sepharad addio*, 1492: I profughi ebrei dalla spagna al "ghetto" di Genova, Genova 1991; R. Urbani, "Indizi documentari sulla figura di Joseph Ha Cohen e della sua famiglia nella Genova del XVI secolo," in: *E andammo dove il vento ci spines* (1992), 59–67; R. Urbani, "La riammissione degli ebrei in Genova del 1752; il carteggio tra la Repubblica e la Curia Romana," in: *Wezo't le-Angelo* (1993), 573–91; C. Bricarelli, *Una gioventù offesa: ebrei genovesi ricordano* (1995); G. Jehel, "Jews and Muslims in Medieval Genoa; from the Twelfth to the Fourteenth Century," in: *Mediterranean Historical Review*, 10:1–2 (1995), 120–32; B.Z. Kedar, "A Vaulted East-West Street in Acre's Genoese Quarter?," in: *Atiqot*, 26 (1995), 105–11; G.N. Zazzu, *Una gioventù offesa: ebrei genovesi ricordano* (1995); E. Parma, "Il parato pontificale seicentesco di Genova in San Salvatore di Gerusalemme," in: *Le vie del Mediterraneo* (1996), 35–43; S. Ravera, "Jacopo da Varagine, San Giovanni Battista e le crociate," in: *Le vie del Mediterraneo* (1996), 13–17; R. Urbani, *The Jews in Genoa* (1999). HOLOCAUST PERIOD: C. Brizzolari, *Genova nella seconda guerra mondiale. Una città in guerra (1938–1943)*, 2 vols (1977–78); G.B. Varnier, "Un vescovo per la guerra: L'azione pastorale di Pietro Boetto, arcivescovo di Genova (1938–1946)," in: B. Gariglio (ed.), *Cattolici e Resistenza nell'Italia settentrionale* (1997), 33–57; S. Antonini, *Delasem. Storia della più grande organizzazione ebraica italiana di soccorso* (2000).

GENOCIDE CONVENTION. The Genocide Convention for the prevention of genocide and the punishment of the organizers of genocide arose out of a general reaction to the Nazi crimes against the Jewish people. Though several mass liquidations had already previously occurred in the history of mankind, none of these had reached the proportions and planning of the slaughter of European Jewry by the Third Reich. After World War II, a movement developed demanding that such acts be condemned as an international crime, and their perpetrators be punished. This condemnation was to be upheld by the coordinated activity of all civilized nations. The term "genocide" was coined by the Polish-Jewish lawyer Raphael *Lemkin in his book *Axis Rule in Europe* (1944), 79–95. It was also due to a large extent to his personal efforts over the years that the Convention was later ratified.

The Genocide Convention was directly connected with the trials of the major Nazi war criminals at the International

Military Tribunal at Nuremberg, where the Nazi plan to exterminate Jews wherever possible was publicly revealed in all its brutality. The *United Nations, which in the preamble to its Charter had renewed the affirmation of basic human rights and the recognition of the value of human life, could not ignore what had happened in this sphere. Consequently, at its first session on Dec. 11, 1946, after it had confirmed Resolution No. 95 (I) on the principles of international law which had been introduced by the legislation of the Nuremberg tribunal, the General Assembly adopted Resolution No. 96 (I), condemning genocide as a crime in international law, and determining that all nations have an interest in punishing such cases. After two years of preparation the text of the Convention was unanimously adopted by the General Assembly of the U.N. (Dec. 8, 1948). By January 1969, 67 countries had ratified it, some with important reservations. As of 2000, 132 countries were party to the Genocide Convention.

The Convention outlaws not only mass murder but also several other actions of a less extreme nature, taken against groups of individuals. It does not give a legal definition of the term "genocide." The characteristic trend of all the actions which can be defined as genocide is their inherent intention to destroy, wholly or partially, a national, ethnic, racial, or religious group *per se*. The following actions are classified as genocide: the killing of persons belonging to the group; the causing of grievous bodily or spiritual harm to members of the group; deliberately enforcing on the group living conditions which could lead to its complete or partial extermination; the enforcement of measures designed to prevent birth among the group; the forcible removal of children from one group to another.

Since the Convention aims at the prevention as well as the punishment of genocidal action, it determines that not only those who carry out such actions are liable to punishment, but also those who take certain measures liable to bring about genocide, such as a plot to carry out genocide; direct and public incitement to genocide; an attempt at genocide; participation in such action. This list clearly shows that the activities included within the framework of genocide are related only to the biological and physical existence of the group in question.

One of the main achievements of the Convention is its application to every criminal, regardless of his status, i.e., it applies equally to rulers who bear the legislative responsibility for the act, on public functionaries, and on private individuals. This directive overrrules the argument of an "act of state," which contends that leaders of the state are free of responsibility, performing their action not in their own name but in the name of the state. Although the convention does not deal explicitly with the plea of "superior order," it is clear that this plea is invalid unless it refers to instances in which the intent to murder a group cannot be attributed to the accused. The Convention provided for national implementation (by local courts), for international implementation (by an international penal court, not yet in existence), and for prevention and suppression of genocide by the General Assembly which may be called upon to do so.

The effectiveness of the Convention had in the first 20 years of its existence not been put to the test. Claims of genocide being committed were made, *inter alia*, in regard to blacks in Southern Sudan, to Kurds in Iraq, to Nagas in India, and to communists, Chinese in Indonesia, and the Ibos in the Biafran War in Nigeria, but no attempt was made to "seize" the General Assembly with these claims.

BIBLIOGRAPHY: N. Robinson, *Genocide Convention* (1960); P.N. Drost, *Crime of State*, 2 vols. (1959), incl. bibl.; Perlman, in: *Nebraska Law Review*, 30 (1950); Stanciu, in: *Yad Vashem Studies*, 7 (1968), 185–7; Lemkin, in: *Revue internationale de droit pénal*, 17 (1946); G. Percy, *La Convention pour la prévention et la répression du crime de génocide* (1950); Landsberg, in: *Aussenpolitik* (May 1953), 310–21; Société Internationale de Prophylaxie Criminelle, *La prophylaxie du génocide*, 1 no. 11–13 (1967); 2 no. 14–15 (1968); Fawcett, in: *Patterns of Prejudice* (Nov.–Dec. 1968), 23–25.

[Nehemiah Robinson]

GENTILE, non-Jew. It was only during the later Second Temple period that a sharp distinction and a barrier of separation was erected between the Jew and the gentile. The prohibition of marriage, which in the Bible was limited to the seven Canaanite nations (Deut. 7:1–4), was extended, following the reforms of Ezra, to include all non-Jews; the acceptance of monotheism was made the distinguishing mark of the Jew (Meg. 13a, Esth. R. 6:2); the Jews were regarded as having completely discarded *idolatry which was, however, uniformly characteristic of the non-Jew. In addition to that the low moral, social, and ethical standards of the surrounding gentiles were continuously emphasized, and social contact with them was regarded as being a pernicious social and moral influence. As a result, during this period the world was regarded as divided, insofar as peoples were concerned, into the Jewish people and the "nations of the world," and insofar as individuals were concerned, into "the Jew" and the idolater ("*oved kokhavim u-mazzalot*," usually abbreviated to "*akkum*," literally "a worshiper of stars and planets" but applied to all idolaters). Only considerations of humanity, such as relief of their poor, visiting their sick, affording them last rites (Git. 61a), and discretion ("one greets a gentile on their festivals for the sake of peace" – Tosef. Av. Zar. 1:3) were reasons for breaking the otherwise impenetrable barrier. As a result, the conception of and the attitude toward the non-Jew from the Talmudic period onward are strikingly different from that during the biblical period.

For the biblical period see *Stranger.

In the Talmud

Since talmudic literature spans over half a millennium, covering a wide geographic area, attitudes toward gentiles expressed in it vary considerably. In fact, it reveals a whole spectrum of opinions from the extreme antipathy of the tormented Jew of Hadrian's time – e.g., Simeon b. Yoḥai's statement: The best of gentiles should be killed (TJ, Kid. 4:11, 66c) – to the moderate views expressed in the more friendly atmosphere of early Sassanid Babylon – witness Samuel's making no distinction between Israel and the nations on the Day of Judgment (TJ, RH 1:3, 57a). Thus all such statements must be seen in their specific geographical-historical context. Nevertheless, in general it may be said that the Jew's attitude toward the gentile was largely conditioned by the gentile's attitude toward him (see Esth. R. 2:3), so that a gentile's friendship to a Jew would be warmly and uninhibitedly reciprocated (see BK 38a, and witness the relationships between Meir and Avnimos ha-Gardi, Judah ha-Nasi and Antoninus, Samuel and Sapor, etc.).

Jewish antipathy to the gentile in talmudic times stemmed from a number of causes and functioned on several levels. Thus, gentiles were condemned for their cruelty to Jews (see BK 117a; Av. Zar. 25b, etc.), their morals were considered reprehensible (Yev. 98a; Av. Zar. 22b; Song R. 6:8, etc.), and throughout the period one finds reiterated the (theological) accusation that though they were offered the Torah, they rejected it (Av. Zar. 2b; Tanḥ. B., Deut. 54, etc.). Thus, the Jewish antipathy to the gentile was not due to the fact that he was of non-Jewish stock, i.e., it was not a racial prejudice, but rather motivated by their idolatry, moral laxity, and other such faults (see Av. Zar. 17a–b). Those that were righteous (by Jewish standards), however, were fully entitled to the rewards of the world-to-come (Tosef., Sanh. 13:2; BB 10b), and a further distinction was made by Johanan who declared that gentiles outside Palestine were not really idolaters, but only blind followers of their ancestral customs (Ḥul. 13b).

Terms

In rabbinic literature the distinction between gentile (*goi, akkum*) and Christian (*noẓeri*) has frequently been obscured by textual alterations necessitated by the vigilance of censors. Thus "Egyptian," "Amalekite," "Zadokite" (= Sadducee) and *kuti* (Samaritan) often stand in place of the original *noẓeri*, as well as *goi, akkum*, etc. (see *Paḥad Yiẓḥak*, s.v. *Goi*). Probably when Resh Lakish stated that a gentile (*akkum* etc., in existing texts) who observed the Sabbath is punishable by death (Sanh. 58b), he had in mind Christians (see A. Weiss, in *Bar Ilan*, 1 (1963), 143–8, xxxi–ii). The same may be so in the case of R. Ammi who ruled that one may not teach a gentile Torah (Ḥag. 13a; cf. Sanh. 59a). Numerous anti-Christian polemic passages only make real sense after *noẓeri* has been restored in place of the spurious *kuti* or *ẓedoki*, etc.

In Law

The gentile figures very widely in talmudic law, in various legal categories, such as laws of personal status, marriage and inheritance, proselytization, laws of accession, contract, agency, evidence and damages, purity and impurity, laws concerning the types of property, and offerings he may present to the Temple, to name but a few. The basic assumption is that all non-Jews are subject to certain universal laws, religious, moral, and social (called the seven *Noachide laws): (1) institution of courts of justice; (2) idolatry; (3) blasphemy; (4) incest; (5) homicide; (6) robbery; (7) eating the limb of a living animal, and according to other opinions, castration, mixing of breeds, witchcraft, etc. (Sanh. 56a–b, et al.).

Thus the gentile is a legal personality in Jewish law, and though sometimes discriminated against, is generally treated equitably. Thus, the Talmud relates that once the Roman government sent two officials to learn the Jewish law. After careful study, they said: "We have scrutinized all your laws and found them just (*emet*), except for the following instance. You say that if a Jew's ox gores that of a gentile, the owner is free from damages, while if a gentile's ox gores that of a Jew, he is obliged to pay damages. But if, as you say, 'neighbor' (in Ex. 21:35) excludes the gentile, then he should be free even when his ox gores that of a Jew. And if, on the other hand 'neighbor' includes the gentile, then the Jew should have to pay damages when his ox gores that of a gentile …" (BK 38a).

Where there is legal discrimination against a gentile, it is usually based on objective reasoning, such as the fact that he does not subscribe to the Jewish "social contract" (non-reciprocity). Thus, the Talmud rules that the commandment to restore lost property to its owner (Deut. 22:1–3) does not apply when the gentile is the owner (BK 113b). This is because gentiles do not act reciprocally in such cases. Similarly, a gentile cannot act as witness (BK 15a) because (according to one opinion) he is dishonest and unreliable (cf. Bek. 13b). Here it should be noted that Jews suspected of the same faults were liable to identical discrimination. Other apparently discriminating rulings were intended to discourage intimacy with the non-Jew, or, in other words, primarily to guard the Jews from the dangers of assimilation, such as the interdict against non-Jewish wines and cooked foods, etc. In practice discrimination against gentiles was frowned upon and even forbidden as it might jeopardize friendly relations (*mi-penei darkhei shalom*, Git. 5:8–9; *mi-penei eivah*, Av. Zar. 26a) and bring about a profanation of the Divine Name (*ḥillul ha-Shem*, BK 113b) – so much so, that the Talmud enjoins that gentile poor be supported with charity like Jewish poor (Git. 61a) and does not even tolerate the charging of interest to gentiles (BM 70b).

[Daniel Sperber]

In the Middle Ages

The talmudic laws, referred to above, whose purpose was to minimize contacts between Jews and idolaters ran counter to the social and economic realities of Jewish life in the Middle Ages. Unlike the talmudic period, Jews no longer lived in compact, economically self-sufficient communities. (This historical explanation for lifting many of the talmudic restrictions on Jewish-gentile relationships was already put forth by the tosafists; see Tos. to Av. Zar. 15a, beg. *Eimor.*) Economic – and, as a result, a measure of social – contact with non-Jews was an inevitable necessity. Hence, in daily life, many of the talmudic restrictions in this area simply became dead letters. Taking this fact into cognizance, R. Menahem Meiri could write: "In our times, no one observes these practices, neither gaon, rabbi, sage, pietist, nor pseudo-pietist" (*Bet ha-Beḥirah*, Av. Zar. introd.). Under the circumstances, the halakhists of the period were confronted with the problem of reconciling talmudic law with common practice that patently ignored it. Among the tosafists, this was accomplished by a process of dialectically reinterpreting the talmudic sources. Each specific law was reinterpreted so as to make it conform to the current practice. For example, the talmudic law prohibiting business dealings with gentiles on their festivals was construed as in consonance with doing business with Christians on Sundays (Tos. to Av. Zar. 2a, beg. *Asur*). Rashi (quoted in *Or Zaru'a*, Sanh. 2a) declares that such dealings are forbidden only on Christmas and Easter. A similar attitude is taken by the tosafist R. Elhanan in the matter of renting to a Christian a house owned by a Jew (Tos. to Av. Zar. 21a beg. *Af*; see also Tos. to Av. Zar 13a beg. *Kal va-ḥomer*). Occasionally the discrepancy between law and practice was overcome by drawing a distinction between idolaters referred to in the Talmud and Christians who reside outside the land of Israel (Maharam of Rothenburg, Resp., ed. Berlin, no. 386). While the tosafists declare that "we are certain that the Christians do not worship idols" (Tos. to Av. Zar. 2a beg. *Asur*), an attitude already adumbrated by R. Gershom, they fail to apply the principle categorically. The hesitation of the medieval halakhists to fully accept the implications of an absolute distinction between a Christian and an idolater is apparent in their legal discussions. The prominent tosafist R. Isaac of Dampierre held that since Christians could not be regarded as strict monotheists, according to the *halakhah* they come under the category of Noachides who are not enjoined against trinitarian belief (Tos. to San. 63b beg. *Asur*; Tos. to Bek. 2b beg. *Shema*). Confronted by the exigencies of daily life, the medieval halakhists tended toward leniency in such talmudic prohibitions as the use of gentile bread, butter, and wine. R. Menahem Meiri constitutes the single significant exception to the attitude of the halakhists. Strongly influenced by the rationalistic philosophy of his time, he drew a basic distinction between idolaters and between Christians and Muslims. The latter, he writes, are "peoples disciplined by religion" and, on principle, are to be regarded as Jews insofar as economic and social relations with them are concerned. In these matters, no invidious distinctions are to be made between Jews and Christians (*Bet ha-Beḥirah*, BK 113b; *ibid.*, Av. Zar. 20a). He hesitates however in his practical decisions to waive all the ancient restrictions lest their total abolition lead to a loss of Jewish identity. Maimonides in his role as halakhist offers a position that is at odds both with that of the medieval decisors and with that of R. Menahem Meiri. He flatly states (Yad, Akum 9:4) – deleted by censors in the ordinary editions – that the talmudic limitations on Jewish-pagan relations are applicable in his own time. Moralistic literature of the period, notably, *Sefer Ḥasidim*, displays a marked ambivalence. In a number of instances, it goes far beyond talmudic law in warning against any contact with Christianity and its ritual objects. Thus, while the tosafists broadly qualify and virtually abolish the prohibition against dealing in the ritual objects of an alien faith, *Sefer Ḥasidim* makes the prohibition absolute. Yet, in its moral teachings, the book exhorts to an ethical scrupulosity in dealings with a gentile who observes the seven Noachide commandments. Such a person, it is averred, should be more honored than a Jew who does not engage in the study of Torah. However, such moral promptings were frequently motivated by considerations of expediency. Nevertheless, in a significant passage (no. 58), the book holds up a noble act performed by a Christian as one most worthy of emulation by Jews. A motive frequently invoked in warning against unethical acts committed by Jews toward Christians is that of *ḥillul ha-Shem* (desecration of God's name; no. 1080). Despite a social atmosphere saturated with Christian contempt, repression, and persecution of Jews, R. Moses of Coucy could write: "We have already explained concerning the remnant of Israel that they are not to deceive any one whether Christian or Muslim. Thus, the Holy One, Blessed be He, scatters Israel among the nations so that proselytes shall be gathered unto them; so long as they behave deceitfully toward them (non-Jews), who will cleave to them? Jews should not lie either to a Jew or to a gentile, nor mislead them in any matter" (*Semag Asayim* no. 82).

[Theodore Friedman]

BIBLIOGRAPHY: IN THE TALMUD: G.F. Moore, *Judaism*, 1 (1946), 274–5, 339, 453; 2 (1946), 75; B.M.H. Uzid, in: *Ha-Torah ve-ha-Medinah*, 4 (1952), 9–21; ET, 5 (1953), 286–366; E.E. Urbach, in: IEJ, 9 (1959), 149–65, 229–45; M.D. Herr, in: *Sefer Zikkaron le-Binyamin De Vries* (1968), 149–59; E.E. Urbach, *Ḥazal* (1969), 482–3, 488–9. IN THE MIDDLE AGES: J. Katz, *Exclusiveness and Tolerance* (1961); Y.F. Baer, in: *Zion*, 3 (1937/38), 37–41; E.E. Urbach, *Ba'alei ha-Tosafot* (1955[2]), index, s.v. *Avodah Zarah*; G. Tchernovitz, *Ha-Yaḥas Bein Yisrael la-Goyim le-fi ha-Rambam* (1950).

GENTILI (**Ḥefeẓ**), family in northern Italy, particularly in Gorizia, Trieste, Verona, and Venice. The name Gentili was rendered in Hebrew as Ḥefeẓ, and it is the latter name which appears in the Hebrew writings of the members of this family.

MOSES BEN GERSHOM (1663–1711), rabbinical scholar. Born in Trieste, Moses was active in Venice. He was a pupil of Solomon b. Isaac Nizza, who was active in Venice around 1700, and supported himself by being a private tutor. He dealt with philosophy, mathematics, and the natural sciences. He composed poems, one of which, written when he was 13, can be found in the Venice edition of the Bible (1675–78). His main work was a homiletical-philosophical commentary on the Pentateuch (*Melekhet Maḥashevet*, Venice, 1710, with tables and a portrait of the author; second edition, Koenigsberg, 1819, with super-commentary, *Maḥashevet Ḥoshev*, by Judah Leib Jaffe). Moses also wrote *Ḥanukkat ha-Bayit*, dealing with the construction of the Second Temple (Venice, 1696, with plan). On the occasion of his wedding, the poet Yomtov Valvasson composed a poem (Venice, 1682), and a dirge on his death was published (Ghirondi-Neppi, 241). The beginning of an address by Moses is found in an Oxford manuscript (Neubauer, Cat. 1123).

[Umberto (Moses David) Cassuto]

GERSHOM BEN MOSES (1683–1700), son of Moses b. Gershom. Gershom wrote *Yad Ḥaruzim*, a Hebrew rhyme-lexicon containing an introduction, 12 rules for Hebrew usage in poetry and rhyme scheme, and an appendix devoted to a poetical version of the 613 commandments (*azharot*), according to Maimonides' enumeration. After Gershom's untimely death at the age of 17, the work was published by his father who added an introduction containing his son's biography. A eulogy by Solomon b. Isaac Nizza, Gershom's teacher, appears as an appendix to the work (Venice, 1700; second edition, without the *azharot* and the eulogy, but with additional notes by Simḥah *Calimani, Venice, 1738–45). Moses Gentili quotes some of his son's interpretations in his *Melekhet Maḥashevet*.

[Samuel Abba Horodezky]

BIBLIOGRAPHY: Ghirondi Neppi, 70, 239; Steinschneider, in: *Vessillo Israelitico*, 27 (1879), 204 n.2; Soave, *ibid.*, 28 (1880), 46; Fuenn, Keneset, 219; Cowley, Cat, 212, 469.

GEOGRAPHY.

In the Bible

The geographic horizon in the early biblical period was the *lu'aḥ ha-ammim*, a table of 70 nations listed in Genesis 10. The identification of the names and the location of the countries are the subject of differences of opinion among scholars. It is clear however that included are all of Arabia, Syria, Asia Minor as far as the Caucasus, all the lands of the Tigris and Euphrates, the western part of the highlands of Iran, the regions of the middle and lower Nile including the desert extending to their west, and Greece and its islands (see The Seventy *Nations).

In the Talmud

Scattered throughout the Talmuds, the Targums, and the Midrashim are various geographic references connected with the *halakhah* and with expositions and homilies on the Bible and Midrash. Most of these references are associated with Ereẓ Israel: with laws about "commandments applying to Ereẓ Israel," which are to be observed only in Ereẓ Israel, with praise of the country, and with the identification of biblical place-names.

The *mitzvot* dependent on Ereẓ Israel have full application only within "the territories occupied by those who came back from Babylonia" (Ereẓ Israel); have partial application within the borders of those who came up from Egypt; and refer only marginally to that territory which lies within the wider borders promised to the patriarchs but outside the area of those who came up from Egypt – territory conquered by David on his own responsibility and known in the Talmud as Syria. Within the obligatory territories were exempted enclaves, such as Caesarea in the Sharon, Susita (Hippos) in the Golan, Ashkelon in the Judean coastal lowland, and within the exempted territories obligatory enclaves such as Kefar Ẓemaḥ on the southeastern shore of Lake Kinneret. The boundaries of these areas and also of the enclaves are laid down in the *halakhah* (Shev. 6:1; Tosef., Shev. 6:6–11; Tosef., Oho. 18:14; Sif. Deut. 51; TJ, Shev. 6:1, 36b). In connection with the laws of usucapion, Ereẓ Israel was divided into three districts: Judea, Transjordan, and Galilee (BB 3:2). Concerning the laws for the removal of fruit from the house in the sabbatical year when they had stopped growing in the field, each of the three districts was subdivided into three regions: mountain, valley, and lowland. The phytogeographical features of these were: for mountains the *Cillin* pine, for valleys the palm, and for lowlands the sycamore (*Ficus sycamora*) (Tosef., Shev. 7:11; cf. Shev. 9:2). The area between Judea and Galilee was called "the country of the Cutheans" or contemptuously "the Cuthean Strip" (*Matlit shel Kutim*; Lam. R. 3:7). The question also arose as to whether the law applicable to levitically unclean heathen countries applied also to the country of the Cutheans. The sages decided that the law was applicable in those cities which had been surrounded by a wall since the time of Joshua and in which *Megillat Esther* is read on Adar 15th (Ar. 9:6; Ar. 32a; Meg. 4a; TJ, Meg. 1:1, 70a).

Many identifications of geographic and ethnographic names in the Bible are in the nature of expositions. Onkelos contented himself with a few which he considered to be beyond doubt. Targum Pseudo-Jonathan and the Palestinian Targum frequently identified places solely on the basis of the similarity of names without regard to any geographic considerations. Among the identifications of the table of nations, given in the Midrashim and Targums, none includes all the nations and countries known to the sages. These identifications are frequently inconsistent and contradictory. The equation of Rome with biblical Edom which was apparently intended at first to allow for open criticism of the Roman authorities was later accepted as fact and hence the former and latter halves of the verse: "Behold, of the fat places of the earth shall be thy dwelling, and of the dew of heaven from above" (Gen. 27:39) were interpreted in the Midrash (Gen. R. 67:6) as referring respectively to Italy (Rashi, ad loc., adds "of Greece," i.e., Magna Graecia, southern Italy) and to Bet Guvrin. On the identification of Kenites, Kenizzites, and Kadmonites, who are mentioned in the covenant with Abraham (Gen. 15:19), and who were not conquered by those who came up from Egypt, there are divergent opinions: in a plausible interpretation R. Judah held that they were Arab tribes on the border of the land of the seven nations which the Israelites inherited, whereas R. Eliezer contended that they refer to Asia Minor, Thrace, and Carthage (Gen. R. 44:23, end; BB 56a). The identification of places in Ereẓ Israel, particularly in Galilee, is mostly realistic and is of aid in a scientific study of the historical topography of the country (TJ, Meg. 1:1, 70a, b; TB, Meg 5b).

The sages thought that geographic and hydrologic factors exerted a great influence on man's physical and spiritual being. On Moses' instructions to the spies: "And see the land, what it is; and the people that dwelleth therein, whether they are strong or weak" (Num. 13:18), the *Tanḥuma* (Shelaḥ Lekha, 6) comments: "There is a country that raises strong men, and there is a country that raises weak men." A similar view is expressed in the midrashic statement: "Some springs raise strong, others weak men, some handsome, others ugly men, some modest, others dissolute men." The spring of Shittim (Num. 25:1), which was a place of licentiousness, watered Sodom (Num. R. 20:22).

From the statements of the sages one can reconstruct the geographic concept of the world current in talmudic times. The earth with its seas was seen as a circle ringed around by the ocean (*Okyanos*) with the center of the circle being the **even shetiyyah* ("foundation stone") in the Holy of Holies, which was thought to be in the middle of the earth (*tabbur ha-arez*), not only in a geometrical sense. This was thought to be the beginning of creation. Around the center are concentric circles in order of importance: the Holy of Holies, the Temple, Jerusalem, Ereẓ Israel, and the world (Tanḥ. Kedoshim, 6); this particular idea was devised by a man who had never seen Jerusalem. The idea of the centricity of the Holy Land occurs first in the Apocrypha, influenced by the Greek concept of *omphalos*, which is that the center of Earth is at Delphi. The sages based the idea that the start of creation is with the *even shetiyyah* on biblical passages (Tosef., Yom ha-Kippurim 3:6; Yoma 54b), but not the centricity of Jerusalem, which was not of such great significance to Jews as to Christians who transferred the center to the cross of Jesus, a concept which the Church Fathers based on biblical verses (Ezek. 5:5; 38:12; Ps. 74:12). Thus the center of circular medieval maps is Jerusalem with the cross. The view that Ereẓ Israel is higher than all countries, Jerusalem than the whole of Ereẓ Israel, and the Temple Mount than all Jerusalem (Sif. Deut. 152 and 37; Sanh. 87a) is a literal homiletical interpretation of the verse: "Then shalt thou arise, and get thee up unto the place which the Lord thy God shall choose" (Deut. 17:8). The sages were however not unaware of the fact that the spring of Etam, from which water flowed to the Temple, was higher than the Temple Mount.

An estimate of the size of the "world" ranged between the extremes of 6,000 and 1,440,000 parasangs. But a still more exaggerated view held that the earth was only 1/12,960,000 part of Gehinnom (TJ, Ber. 1:1, 2c; Pes. 94a). On the area of the inhabited world (οἰκουμένη) there were divergent opinions:

(1) a third is inhabited, the remaining two-thirds being sea and desert;

(2) the whole inhabited world is situated under one star;

(3) the inhabited world is located between the Wain and Scorpio, that is, about 80° from north to south (54° north of the equator and 26° south of it);

(4) it extends from east to west, a distance of one hour of the sun's course, that is 15° (Pes. 94a).

Even those sages who were aware that the earth is round did not deal with the problem of the date line. Alexander the Great during his campaigns is said to have risen upward until he saw the earth like a globe partially submerged in an enormous bowl of water, that is, the ocean (TJ, Av. Zar. 3:1, 42c; Num. R. 13:14). The Zohar (Lev., s.v. *ve-im zevaḥ shelamim* (3:1), Soncino ed., 346) states that according to the Book of R. Hamnuna the Elder the earth is a revolving globe, that when it is day on one side, it is night on the other, that there is a place where there is no day and opposite it a place where there is no night. The comprehension of this is said to be the secret of the mystics and not of geographers. How this individual view came to be included in the Zohar is not clear.

The problem of the density of the earth occupied the aggadists. There was a widespread view that the circle of the earth is like a dish that floats on the face of the *deep, namely, the water, and that below the deep are mountains, so that the whole rests on a solid base. Another view holds that the earth rests on pillars which apparently reach down to those mountains. Views on the thickness of the earth range from a thousand cubits (about 500 m. = 547 yds.) to a 50-year journey. There was a generally accepted view that the "water of the deep" is close to the surface of the ground which accounts for the origin of springs and the moistening of the ground: to a handbreadth of rain the deep responds with two handbreadths (Ta'an. 25b). Some thought that these springs originated in the Euphrates. The four rivers that went out of the Garden of Eden were higher than all the rivers in the world, the highest of them being the Euphrates, and hence R. Judah in the name of Rav prohibited all the water in the world to anyone who took a vow not to drink from the Euphrates (Bek. 55a). Hot springs have their origin in the deep, and pass over the entrance to Gehinnom (Shab. 39a). "All the rivers run into the sea, yet the sea is not full … they return (to their source)" (Eccles. 1:7). How do they return? There are three views:

(1) through the channels of the deep;

(2) through vapors that rise from the sea and form clouds, the desalination of the seawater taking place in the deep or in the clouds;

(3) that river water disappears in the ocean because the latter has water which "absorbs water" even if brought up in a barrel on to dry land (a view which is apparently not an exposition of the passage in Ecclesiastes). The phenomenon of how such absorption takes place is not explained (Ta'an. 9b; Gen. R. 13:9; et al.).

The Jordan flows from the Dead Sea to the ocean below the earth (Bek. 55a). The idea that the ocean is higher than the land is apparently based on the homiletic interpretation of biblical verses (Jer. 5:22; Amos 9:6); the sand on the seashore prevents the flooding of the land, which happened twice, once in the generation of Enosh, when the flood reached Calabria, and once in the generation that witnessed the confusion of the tongues when the flood stretched as far as the ends of Barbaria (TJ, Shek. 6:2, 50a; Gen. R. 23:7, end). In the sea there are river-like currents and waves whose height reaches 300 parasangs which is also the distance between one wave and another. Among the big waves there are small ones (BB 73a).

The sages distinguished between floral zones in Ereẓ Israel on the basis of differences in altitude and hence in temperature. But there are other universal reasons for such diversity, *viz.* the distinctive features of water and of soil. Koheleth-Solomon planted in his gardens and parks "trees … of all kinds of fruit" (Eccles. 2:5), which means, according to the *aggadah*, literally all the kinds in the world. That they might flourish he sent demons, over whom he had dominion, to irrigate each tree by bringing water from its country of origin. Another view held that arteries spread out from the center of the earth through the entire world, and Solomon, knowing how to distinguish them, planted on each artery the appropriate trees, even those from Africa and India (Eccles. R. 2:5, no. 1).

From the praise of Ereẓ Israel contained in the *aggadah* it is possible to put together an aggadic geography of the country before its destruction. The love of the Holy Land, the anguish at its impoverishment and at the depletion of its children, and the expectation of its future glory engendered exaggerations that are logically incomprehensible. Ereẓ Israel's situation in the center of the world and its altitude did not change even after the destruction of the Second Temple, nor did the weight of its stones, which was greater than those of the neighboring countries (PdRE 13). The *aggadah* is responsible for the extension of the western boundary up to the Atlantic Ocean, this being, for the aggadist, the interpretation of "the Great Sea" in the verse: "And for the western border, ye shall have the Great Sea for a border" (Num. 34:6). Extravagant conclusions were reached by Targum Pseudo-Jonathan. All the countries on the continent as well as the islands opposite Ereẓ Israel within the limits assigned to the patriarchs (from the Brook of Egypt to Taurus Amanus) up to the "primeval waters" at the furthermost extremity of the world and even the ships sailing the sea are all included in the Promised Land (*ibid.*). It was said that after the destruction of the Second Temple Ereẓ Israel "drew together," i.e., diminished inside. Alexander Yannai had 60 myriad "cities" in the King's Mountain and in each of them were 60 myriad people, except for three in which there were twice as many. To feed this population the country produced enormous crops of excellent quality. By the fourth century, the country had deteriorated to such an extent that it did not produce even a large number of reeds (TJ., Meg. 1:1, 170a; TJ., Ta'an. 4:8, 69a; Git. 57a). In the days of Simeon b. Shetaḥ rain fell at the right time, the grains of wheat were as large as kidneys, the grains of barley like olives, the lentils like golden denarii (Ta'an. 23a). Several species of trees, such as cinnamon, brought from distant lands in the time of Solomon, still grew in the Second Temple period, and Indian pepper continued to grow until the destruction of Bethar (Eccles. R. 2:8). In fulfillment of the biblical passage: "Thou shalt not lack anything in it" (Deut. 8:9), there were exiled with Israel to Babylonia through the channels of the deep 700 species of fish permissible as food and through the air 800 species of locusts permissible as food. The fish and the locusts returned with those who came back from Babylonia (Lam. R., Proem 34).

The fate of the Lost Ten Tribes has stirred the imagination of Jews from the days of the Second Temple to our times. A miraculous existence was invented for them in distant and unknown lands, the legend of the tribes being connected with those of the river *Sambatyon and the Mountains of Darkness. Thus the Ten Tribes were exiled across the Sambatyon, Σαββατείον, the Sabbath river, which rages and hurls stones on six days of the week but rests on the Sabbath, thus proving through nature the holiness of the Sabbath (Sanh. 65b; Gen R. 11:5, 73:6); Josephus describes it as a river in Syria which flows on one day and rests on six days of the week (Jos., Wars, 7:96–99); the origin of the legend being apparently to be found in rhythmically intermittent springs, such as Ein Farah in the Judean desert.

Medieval Jewish Geography

Knowledge of the spherical form of the earth, derived from observing the height of the stars in different latitudes, reached Jewish scholars in Islamic countries through Arab astronomy. The first Jew to consider the earth as a sphere was the Cordovan rabbi, Ḥasan b. Mar Ḥasan ha-Dayyan, in his book on intercalation (end of the tenth cent.). At approximately the same time in Baghdad *Sherira b. Ḥanina Gaon, followed by his son *Hai Gaon, rejected the opinion that the heavens are like a cap over a flat earth. Only fragments remain of the stories of Abraham b. Jacob who traveled in Germany and the Slavic countries in the 950s. The two letters from Joseph b. Aaron, king of the Khazars, to R. *Hisdai ibn Shaprut, which comprise not only historical, but also geographical material, were transmitted by Jewish merchants from Germany (about 950). The books of medieval travelers frequently contained material of geographic interest (see *Travelers).

By the 11th century the spherical form of the earth was accepted among Jewish scholars in Islamic countries, and from there the idea passed to Provence and Italy. Solomon ibn *Gabirol states in *Keter Malkhut*: "The terrestrial globe is divided into two, half is dry land and half water." The first work in Hebrew about the round shape of the earth and its division into climatic regions, together with a list of the countries in each region, was *Sefer Ẓurat ha-Areẓ* ("The Book of the Shape of the Earth" (late 11th or beginning of the 12th century)), by *Abraham b. Ḥiyya. His system, like that of his Muslim teachers, is that of Ptolemy, the Alexandrian (c. 150 C.E.). According to Abraham b. Ḥiyya, the earth, with the seas upon it, is a globe. The western or lower half of the globe is entirely water. The eastern half is mostly dry land (except for seas such as the Mediterranean and the Red Sea), but there is no human settlement except in seven regions. North of latitude 66° there is no settlement because of the cold. In the far south (there are those who say from the equator to the south and those who say from a few degrees south of the equator) there is no populated area because of the heat, which increases as one progresses in a southerly direction. *Ẓurat ha-Areẓ* was published with a Latin translation by D. Schreckenfuchs and notes by Sebastian Muenster (Basle, 1546).

The discoveries at the end of the 15th and the beginning of the 16th century refuted the limitation of the earth's population to seven regions. Information regarding this refutation was conveyed to readers of Hebrew by Abraham b. Mordecai *Farissol in chapter 13 of his book *Iggeret Orḥot Olam* ("Epistle on the Ways of the World," 1525), but geographical ideas derived from legends or books are still to be found in homiletic and ḥasidic works, and they persisted in "scholarly" books until the 19th century. Still in 1550, Mattathias b. Solomon *Delacrut, in his short treatise *Ẓel ha-Olam* ("Shadow of the World"), based on a 13th-century French work, speaks of a quarter of the area of dry land which was not populated and where no human foot trod. As late as the end of the 18th century, Phinehas Elijah *Hurwitz of Vilna in *Sefer ha-Berit* [*ha-Shalem*] ("The [Complete] Book of the Covenant," 1797) maintains that most of the globe is water, either surface or underground, that the waters of the oceans are higher than the land, and that sand prevents their flooding the earth. It served as a basic text to those who wished to learn about nature but were apprehensive of the work of the new *maskilim* who belittled traditional literature. Geographic literature in Hebrew and the part played by Jews in systematic geographic research are slight compared with the Jewish contribution to other branches of science, such as astronomy, mathematics, and medicine.

Geography Textbooks

Abraham Farissol's *Iggeret Orḥot Olam* served as a Hebrew geography textbook until the 19th century. Like other 16th-century Jewish and Christian thinkers, Farissol believed in the existence of the Ten Tribes and the river Sambatyon, and devoted much space to them. Approximately 300 years later, Samson ha-Levi *Bloch, a *maskil* of the Galician school, published *Shevilei Olam* ("The Paths of the World": vol. 1, "Asia," 1822; vol. 2, "Africa," 1827), basing himself on German literature. The treatise is in the rhetorical and witty style of the times. Abraham Menaḥem Mendel *Mohr, still using only German sources, continued the work (1856) after Bloch's death. The information on Jewish communities and Jewish scholars, known to the two authors without having to do any special research, is their original contribution. In the 1780s with the establishment of schools that included secular instruction in the curriculum, special short textbooks began to appear. *Reshit Limmudim* ("The Beginning of Instruction," first ed. 1796; last ed. 1869), by Baruch Linda, the first such textbook in Hebrew, also has chapters on geography. A geography book, *Ha-Kaddur* ("The Globe," Prague, 1831), by Moses S. Neumann, was written partly in Hebrew and partly in German, though in Hebrew characters. Asher Radin's *Ge'ografyah ha-Ketannah* ("The Short Geography," Koenigsberg, 1860), is an abridgment of a German textbook. Two works on the principles of geography: *Meẓukei Ereẓ* ("The Foundation of the Earth," 1878), by Nahum *Sokolow, and *Gelilot ha-Areẓ* ("The Regions of the Earth," 1880), based on German literature, by Hillel Kahana, an experienced pedagogue who is one of the last of the Galician school, appeared about the same time. As was customary among writers who did not know any Western European language other than German, Kahana transcribed French and English names according to the German pronunciation. An innovation was a colored Hebrew map, and sketches and pictures with Hebrew captions. In this way he educated the Hebrew reader to map study and observation.

Writers of textbooks solved problems in Hebrew geographical terminology and paved the way for the teaching of geography in schools in Ereẓ Israel from the end of the 19th century.

[Abraham J. Brawer]

Modern Geography

In modern geography there has been development in the concentration on limited areas and specialization in particular fields of study. One of these limited areas is the city. *Die Stadt Bonn, ihre Lage und raeumliche Entwicklung* (1947), by Alfred *Philippson, a German geographer, is one of the most important works on urban geography. Another significant contribution was made by Norton Sidney *Ginsberg, a U.S. geographer, who at the invitation of the Japanese government studied Tokyo's urban problems and incorporated his findings in "Tokyo Memorandum" (*Reports on Tokyo Metropolitan Planning*, 1962). Another specialized field is economic geography. Julius *Bien, a U.S. cartographer, not only prepared atlases for a number of major cities but carried out a full-scale survey of intercontinental railways for the U.S. War Department. Saul Bernard *Cohen, who specialized in a number of geographic fields, wrote *Store Location Research for the Food Industry* (1961), considered a standard guide. In addition, in the sphere of political geography he wrote *Geography and Politics in a World Divided* (1963).

On physical geography Victor A. *Conrad wrote *Fundamentals of Physical Climatology* (1942) and *Methods in Climatology* (1944); the Israel meteorologist Dov *Ashbel published *A Bio-Climatic Atlas of Israel* (1950) and *Climate of the Great Rift; Arava, Dead Sea, Jordan Valley* (1966). Joseph Ḥefeẓ Gentilli (1912–2000), an Australian geographer, wrote *Australian Climates and Resources* (1947) and *Geography of Climate* (1958). In connection with the study of the geography of soils David *Amiran, an Israeli, edited for UNESCO "Land Use in Semi-Arid Mediterranean Climates" (in *Arid Zones Research*, vol. 26, 1964). Morton Joseph *Rubin, a U.S. meteorologist, did research in oceanography, meteorology, and in glaciology, particularly in connection with his studies on the Antarctic. Another specialized branch of modern geography is biogeography; a monumental work in this field is *Studies in Medical Geography* (7 vols., 1958–67), by Jacques Meyer May (1896–1976), a French-born American scientist. Nautical geography is another division which has drawn the interest of Jewish geographers, among them the Italian Carlo *Errera, who wrote the pamphlet *L'italianità dell' Adriatico* (1914). The modern period has also produced an increasing number of historians of geography. Gustavo Uzielli (1889–1911), an Italian, did extensive research on the explorations of Christopher Columbus, Toscanelli, and Amerigo Vespucci. His best known work is *La vita e i tempi di P. Dal Pozzo Toscanelli* (1894).

A number of geographers have turned their attention to the history of cartography. Roberto *Almagià, one of Italy's most distinguished geographers, edited *Monumenta Italiae Geographica* (1929) and *Monumenta Cartographica Vaticana*

(4 vols., 1944–55). Erwin J. *Raisz, an American, wrote *General Cartography* (1938) and *Principles of Cartography* (1962).

BIBLIOGRAPHY: Neubauer, Géogr; J.Z. Hirschensohn, *Sheva Ḥokhmot* (1912[2]); A.J. Brawer, in: *Yerushalayim*, 10 (1914), 117–32; idem, *Palaestina nach der Agada* (1920); S. Klein, *Zur Geographie Palaestinas in der Zeit der Mischna* (1917); J. Obermeyer, *Die Landschaft Babylonien im Zeitalter des Talmuds…* (1929); J.M. Guttmann, *Ereẓ Yisrael be-Midrash ve-Talmud* (1929); M. Avi-Yonah, *Atlas Karta li-Tekufat Bayit Sheni, ha-Mishnah ve-ha-Talmud* (1966); F. Taeschner, in: ZDMG, 77 (1923), 31–80; Zunz, Schr, 1 (1875), 146–216.

GEONIC LITERATURE. This entry includes the basic books of geonic literature, which were compiled during the geonic period – from the year 600 to 1040, approximately. Geonic literature includes several types of works:

(1) Commentaries on the Bible
(2) Commentaries on the Mishnah and Talmud
(3) Books of *Halakhah*
(4) Jewish Thought and Ethics
(5) Prayers (prayer-books) and Liturgical Poetry
(6) Responsa
(7) Documents and Letters
(8) Language and Grammar

Commentaries on the Bible

COMMENTARIES ON THE PENTATEUCH (TORAH). **Saadiah Gaon.* Torah with Arabic translation (Constantinople, 1546); *Tafsir al-Torah bi-al-Arabiya* (Paris, 1893); *Keter Torah*, known as Taj (Jerusalem, 1894–1901); Commentary on the Torah, Kafaḥ edition (1963); Torah Commentary on Genesis (Zucker edition 1984).

Samuel ben Hophni Gaon. Commentary on the book of Genesis, A. Greenbaum (ed.), 1978. Selections of his commentary on other parts of the Torah have also been published.

COMMENTARIES ON THE PROPHETS AND THE HAGIOGRAPHA. From Saadiah's translation of biblical books, *Tafsir*, there remain those of the Pentateuch, Isaiah, Proverbs, Job, the Five Scrolls, and Psalms, all with commentary. They were published from 1546 to 1970, with new sections of his commentaries on Isaiah, Lamentations, and the Book of Esther appearing more recently.

Saadiah's introduction to his *Pitron Shivim Millim* was printed in N. Allony's *Studies in Medieval Philosophy and Literature I: Saadiah Works* (1986). Various geonic commentaries on the Bible are scattered throughout the geonic responsa and referred to in geonic essays; they were collected in various anthologies.

Commentaries on the Mishnah and Talmud

COMMENTARIES ON THE MISHNAH. (1) The only geonic commentary on the Mishnah extant in its entirety is on the order *Tohorot* (J.N. Epstein edition by E.Z. Melammed, 1982); it is attributed to *Hai Gaon and may be an adaptation of Saadiah's commentary. (2) Geonic commentaries on the Mishnah collected from various sources appear in *Oẓar ha-Geonim* ("The Treasure of the Geonim," 13 vols., 1928–62) by Benjamin M. *Lewin. (3) Saadiah's *Millot ha-Mishnah* ("Words of the Mishnah") appeared in various journals.

COMMENTARIES ON THE TALMUD. (1) Talmud commentaries of the early *geonim* were incorporated into the Talmud. For a long time the geonic commentaries were found among those of the French and Spanish commentators. Some of these were thought irretrievably lost, with fragments being rediscovered only during the past 100 years. They were published in various articles, anthologies, and in Lewin's *Oẓar ha-Geonim*. (2) Talmud commentaries by *Paltoi Gaon, *Sherira Gaon, and *Hai Gaon, mentioned in various sources, have not reached us in their entirety. (3) The Talmudic dictionary of the *gaon* *Samuel ben Ḥophni was published by S. Abramson in *A. Even Shoshan* (1985), 13–65.

INTRODUCTORY BOOKS TO THE TALMUD. These works include material dealing with methodology as well as with history. (1) *Seder Tannaim ve-Amoraim*, compiled c. 884–886, was first published in Leghorn in 1796; an edition by Kalman Kahana appeared in 1935. The author's name is unknown. It contains a summary of the chain of tradition of the oral Law up to the **savoraim*, including regulations for passing halakhic judgments. (2) Saadiah Gaon's Introduction to the Talmud, which has been lost. (3) Samuel ben Hophni's "Introduction to the Talmud" – selected chapters of this work with the Arabic source and Hebrew translation, accompanied by an introduction and notes, were published by S. Abramson (1990). This volume is the second part of the work Samuel b. Hophni called *Mevo li-yedi'at ha-Mishnah ve-ha-Talmud*. Extant from the first part are most of the book's index and several sections from the text (see S. Abramson, in: *Sinai* 88 (1980), 193). (4) *Iggeret Rav* Sherira Gaon was published by B.M. Lewin (1921) in both known versions, the so-called "*nosaḥ Sefarad*" and "*nosaḥ Ẓarefat*," i.e., a "version from Spain" and a "version from France" (in which there is a difference of opinion as to whether the Mishnah was already written down in the time of Rabbi Judah ha-Nasi or merely remembered orally), on the basis of manuscripts and Genizah fragments.

Books of Halakhah

(1) *SHE'ILTOT* (Venice, 1566), by *Aḥa of Shabḥa (680–752), *gaon* of Pumbedita. Robert Brody's *The Textual History of the She'iltot* (1991) is a study aimed at reconstructing as closely as possible the original text of *Sefer ha-She'iltot*. This work prepares the way for a new edition of the *She'iltot* which will contain additional textual vestiges, particularly from the Cairo *Genizah*. (2) The book *Ve-Hizhir*, an imitation of *She'iltot*. (3) Legal decisions by Yehudai *Gaon (head of Sura academy, 757–761), to whom the book *Halakhot Pesukot* is attributed. He is the first *gaon* whose responsa have been preserved. (4) *Halakhot de-Rab Abba*, a student of Yehudai Gaon, excerpts of which were published by J.N. Epstein in *Madda'ei he-Yehadut* (1927). (5) *Halakhot Gedolot. In addition to the 1548 and 1885 editions, a new edition according to a manuscript in the

Ambrosiana Library, Milan, was edited by A. Hildesheimer (grandson of the 1885-edition editor): (a) *Seder Mo'ed* (1972); (b) *Seder Nashim* (first three tractates, 1980), part 3, edited by E. Hildesheimer, introduction, 11–26, and *Hakdamat Halakhot Gedolot*, edited by N.Z. Hildesheimer (1987), 9–52. (See also *Halakhot Gedolot-Halakhot Pesukot*). (6) **Halakhot Pesukot* or *Hilkhot Re'u*, attributed to the disciples of Yehudai Gaon, published in 1886 and in the Sasson Edition (1951). (7) **Halakhot Keẓuvot*, published by M. Margaliot in 1942. (8) Books of *Halakhah* by Saadiah Gaon. Saadiah wrote monographs on various halakhic subjects, but only a small part has reached us in its entirety. A study on Saadiah's *Sefer ha-Edut ve-ha-Shetarot* by M. Ben-Sasson appeared in the *Annual of Jewish Law* (1984–86), 135–278. A new edition of *Sefer ha-Miẓvot*, with commentary by Y.Y.F. Perla, pts. 1–3 appeared 1989. (9) Sherira Gaon who is famous for his *Iggeret* mentioned above. Approximately half of the geonic responsa in our possession were written by Sherira and his son Hai Gaon. Parts of Sherira's commentaries on certain Talmudic tractates have also been preserved. (10) Hai Gaon did not compile any book of *halakhah* on all the Talmudic laws, but devoted a separate composition to each subject, as did Saadiah and Samuel ben Hophni. Five additional chapters of *Sefer ha-Mekkaḥ ve-ha-Mimkar* ("Treatise on Commercial Transactions") were published by S. Abramson in the *Joseph Dov Soloveitchik Festschrift*, vol. 2 (1984), 1312–1379. There is also mention of a Book of Oaths in verse. Chapters of monetary laws of commerce and chapters of oaths in verse have appeared in part in various collections. (11) *Samuel ben Hophni. Of his many works, only a few have reached us. In recent years excerpts have been published of his books from the *Genizah*. He wrote monographs on *halakhah* which are still being published. Mention should be made of the following: Chapters on Blessings (in *Oẓar ha-Geonim*, tractate *Berakhot*, commentaries, pp. 65–77), the Book of Gifts, divorce laws, obligations of religious judges and the Book of Pledge, etc.

Other halakhic essays from the period of the Geonim include (a) *Sefer Metivot*: a book of laws arranged according to the order of tractates of the Talmud. B.M. Levin collected all the citations from the book which were mentioned in earlier books and arranged them in the Talmudic order in this book *Metivot* (1934). (b) *Sefer Ḥefeẓ*: There are many speculations concerning the authorship and place of origin of this book. Many of the early authorities discussing halakhic matters use *Sefer Ḥefeẓ* as their source. Levin is of the opinion that *Metivot* served as an example for *Sefer Ḥefeẓ*. (c) *The Book of Mitzvot of Ḥefetz ben Yatzliaḥ* (B. Halper edition 1915): This book includes all the laws of the Torah, and it is "a treasury of halakhah, philology and philosophy as they were in the time of the author."

HALAKHIC LITERATURE IN EREZ ISRAEL IN THE PERIOD OF THE GEONIM. In recent years, there were discovered in the *Genizah, Hilkhot Tereifot shel Ereẓ Israel* – in the style of *Halakhot Pesukot*. An important find was remnants of *Sefer ha-Ma'asim li-Venei Ereẓ Yisrael*, and parts of this book were published by Levin, Epstein, Mann, and Aptowitzer, between the years 1930–1974. It is assumed that *Sefer ha-Ma'asim* served as a source for the compiler of *Halakhot Gedolot*, and possibly also for *Sefer ha-She'iltot*. There is a theory that *Sefer ha-Ma'asim* is another title for *Sefer ha-She'iltot*. During the Geonic period, important literary activities were undertaken in Ereẓ Israel, such as the translation of works from Aramaic to Hebrew: Rav Yehudai's *Halakhot Pesukot* was translated into Hebrew under the title *Hilkhot Re'u*, taken from the opening words of the book "*Re'u ki Adonai natan lakhem et yom ha-Shabbat....*"

RULES, REGULATIONS AND CUSTOMS. The Geonim set down various legal decisions and customs. At the beginning of the Geonic period, an essay was written by a sage in Erez Israel, under the title: "Controversies between Easterners and those who dwell in Ereẓ Israel" (pub. M. Margaliot, 1938). It includes a list of 55 customs upon which Jews in Babylonia disagreed with Jews in Ereẓ Israel, and this book formed the foundations for all subsequent books of customs. "The Book of Change of Customs" (Müller, 1878) and the "Treasury of Differences of Custom between Babylonian and Palestinian Jewries" (ed. Levin, 1942) are also available.

GEONIC EDICTS (TAKKANOT). Geonim sought to issue decrees based on Talmudic conclusions, and to establish regulations to cover all aspects of Jewish life. In the course of time, it became necessary to supplement Talmudic regulations and to introduce new laws according to the requirements of the period. These laws encompass various areas, and in particular deal with laws of personal status, money matters, oaths, and evidence. The sources for these ordinances are the geonic literature and they are collected in H. Tykocinski's *The Gaonic Ordinances*, translation and notes by H. Ḥavazelet (1959). I. Schipansky's *The Takkanot of Israel*, v. 3, *Geonic Enactments* (1992) contains *takkanot* by sages from Israel and *geonim* of Babylonian yeshivot from the close of the Talmud to the period of the *rishonim* presented in three sections: introduction to geonic *takkanot* by famous *geonim* of Sura and Pumbedita, and other *takkanot* from the same period.

Jewish Thought and Ethics

In this sphere mention must be made of Saadiah Gaon's *Emunot ve-De'ot*, translated from Arabic by Judah Ibn Tibbon (Constantinople, 1562) under the title *Sefer ha-Nivḥar ve-Emunot ve-De'ot* (J. Kappaḥ edition, 1970). Other works are *Rhymes on Moral Instruction attributed to R. Hai Gaon* (ed. H. Gollancz, 1922); Saadiah's "Epistle on Ethics to the Jewish Communities of Spain" (in Saadiah's *Bible Commentary*, Pt. 2, 1960), and *Ethics of the Dayyanim* by Hai Gaon. Other works by Saadiah Gaon: *Esa Meshali*, a rhymed polemic devoted against the teaching of Anan b. David, in: *Devir*, 1 (1923), 180ff; and a polemic against *Ḥiwi al-Balkhi, published by I. Davidson, in the introduction to his edition of this work (1915), 11–37.

Prayers and Liturgical Poetry

Of note are two prayerbooks; the *Siddur* of *Amram Gaon, of which a scientific edition by D. Goldschmidt appeared in 1972, and the *Siddur* of Saadiah Gaon, published 1941.

Geonic Responsa

Scores of collections of geonic responsa exist, comprising thousands of answers sent by the *geonim* to queries received from correspondents throughout the geonic period. A large number of responsa were discovered in the *Genizah* and several excerpts have been published. The first collection of geonic responsa appeared in 1516 in Constantinople. G. Harpnas's *Teshuvot ha-Geonim she-Heishivu Ge'onei Sura u-Pumbedita* ("Responsa of Geonim of Sura and Pumbedita," 1992) has the responsa arranged topically and provides cross references.

Documents and Letters

Many documents and letters of the Geonim have reached us. These were written in answer to specific questions which were addressed to them, or which the Geonim wished to make known among Jewish communities outside Ereẓ Israel – especially as regards specific subjects related to religious fundamentals to taking a stand on current matters. In this connection the *Iggeret* ("Epistle") of *Pirkoi ben Baboi (turn of the ninth century) should be mentioned as it is one of the earliest literary writings from the geonic period and is also the first known instance in the literature advocating the dissemination of the Babylonian Talmud. In this connection, see also the *Iggeret* of Sherira Gaon mentioned above.

Among the many sources of geonic letters are J. Mann, *Texts and Studies I* (1931); L. Ginzberg, *Genizah Studies II* (1929), which contains a collection of all the letters of the Babylonian *geonim*; S. Abramson, *Be-Merkazim u-va-Tefuẓot* (1965).

Throughout the Geonic period, the Geonim occupied themselves with prayerbooks, establishing the versions of prayers, and dealing with the obligation and value of prayer. *Natronai bar Hilai (mid-ninth century) compiled a prayer book, *Me'ah Berakhot* ("Prayer Book of the Hundred Benedictions"), and *Israel ben Samuel bar Hophni (gaon of Sura from about 1017 to 1033) deals with the "obligation to pray." Many liturgical hymns have reached us from the time of the Geonim. Saadiah's *Siddur* contains *bakkashot* (petitions) and *azharot*; "*Otiyyot Rav Saadiah*" contains rhymes on the letters of the alphabet with annotations by Elijah (Baḥur) *Levita at the end of his book *Masoret ha-Masoret* (1538).

Many liturgical hymns of the *geonim* were discovered in the *Genizah* and have appeared in various publications and anthologies.

Language and Grammar

The *geonim* also engaged in the study of Hebrew language and grammar. Saadiah wrote *Ha-Egron* (edition N. Allony, 1969), containing a Hebrew dictionary, with Hebrew grammar rules, and also a summary of the basis of Hebrew poetry. Additional information on geonic Hebrew is in *Ẓaḥut ha-Lashon ha-Ivrit* in: *Allony Studies*, (1986), 20–31.

[Yehoshua Horowitz]

BIBLIOGRAPHY: Ginzberg, *Geonica II. The Halakhic Literature of the Geonim* (1909), 72–200; I.H. Weiss, *Dor Dor ve-Doreshav*, 4 (1911), 1–41, 99–184; I. Halevy, *Dorot ha-Rishonim*, (1923), 147–305; M. Waxman, *History of Jewish Literature*, (1936), 182–86, 253–55, 310–312; H. Graetz. *History of the Jews*, 3 (1939), 86–126, 177–179; on Saadiah, 187–250; on Sherira. 231–33; on Hai, 233–253; V. Aptowitzer, *Meḥkarim be-Sifrut ha-Geonim* (1941); M. Margolis and A. Marx, *History of the Jewish People* (1945), 264–76; H. Tchernowitz (Rav Ẓa'ir), *Toledot ha-Posekim*, 1 (1946), 18–130; S. Assaf, *Tekufat ha-Geonim ve-Sifrutah* (1955); S.W. Baron, *A Social and Religious History of the Jews*, vols. 5–7 (1957/58); see Baron, Index, Geonim and also under individual *geonim*; B. Dinur, *Yisrael ba-Golah*, 1, Bk. 2 (1961), chp. 9, 78–151; chp. 13 (Saadiah), 380–469; *Sefer ha-Mekorot shel ha-Milon ha-Histori le-Lashon ha-Ivrit*, 1 (1963), *Sifrut ha-Geonim*, 76–90; Z. Jawitz, *Toledot Yisrael*, 9 (1963), 82–115; 1–174; M. Elon, *Jewish Law*, 2 (1973), 528–46; 3, 949–64; S. Abramson, *Inyanut be-Sifrut ha-Geonim* (1974); M. Kasher and J. Mandelbaum (eds.) *Sarei ha-Elef* (2 pts.; 1978); A. Kimmelman, "A Guide to commentaries in the Geonic Period," in: *Annual of the Institute for Research in Jewish Law*, 11–12 (1984–86), 463–587; S.Z. Havlin, *Toratan shel Geonim*, 7 vols. (1993). COMMENTARIES ON THE PENTATEUCH (Torah): *Saadiah:* I. Ta-Shema, in: KS, 44 (1969), 442, Y. Ratzaby, in: *Sinai*, 91 (1982), 196–222; idem in *Sinai*, 94 (1984), 4–27; idem in *Sinai*, 95 (1984), 1–26; idem in *Sinai*, 96 (1985), 1–17; idem, in: *Sinai*, 107 (1991), 97–126; A. Kimmelman, in: *Guide*, 475–507. *Samuel b. Hophni:* A. Greenbaum, in the Yechiel Jacob Weinberg Memorial Book (1970), 257–83; idem in: *Areshet*, 5 (1972). 7–33; idem, in: *Ha-Darom*, 3 (1980), 139–41; idem, in: *Introduction to the Commentary on Genesis* (1978), 11–115; idem, in: *Sinai Jubilee Volume*, 100 (1987), 273–90; M. Sokolof, in: *Alei Sefer*, 8 (1980), 137–39; N. Allony, in: *Beth Mikra*, 25 (1980), 85–90; G. Vajda, in: REJ, 139 (1980), 143–47; N. Allony, in: *Immanuel*, 12 (1981), 96–101. COMMENTARIES ON PROPHETS AND HAGIOGRAPHA: *Saadiah:* H. Avenari, in: HUCA, 39 (1968), 145–62; I. Tobi, in: KS, 50 (1975), 654–62; B.Z. Kedar, in *Jerusalem in the Middle Ages* (1979), 107–2; L.E. Gordon, in: *Studies in Jewish Philosophy*, 3 (1982); N. Allony, in: *Studies in Medieval Philology*, I. *Saadia Works* (1986), 9–23; Y. Ratzaby, in: *Sinai*, 89 (1981), 193–216; idem, in: *Sinai*, 90 (1982) 193–231; idem, in: *Sinai*, 93 (1983), 1–116, idem, in: *Sinai*, 105 (1990), 193–211; idem, in *Bar-Ilan*, 20–21 (1983), 349–81; idem, in: *J.B. Soloveitchik Jubilee Volume*, II (1984), 1153–78, *Saadiah*: Hapax Legomena: S. Buber, in: *Oẓar ha-Sifrut*, I (1887), 33–52; B. Klar, in: *Saadiah* COMMENTARIES ON THE MISHNAH: I.N. Epstein, Introduction to commentary on *Seder Tohorot* (1982), 10–146; S. Assaf, *Tekufat ha-Geonim ve-Sifruta* (1955), 137–46; 294–322. *Millot ha-Mishnah – Saadiah:* N. Allony, in: *Leshonenu*, 18 (1953), 176–78, 22 (1958), 147–72; S. Abramson, *Leshonenu*, 19 (1954), 49–50; Y. Ratzaby, *Leshonenu*, 20 (1956), 41–44; 23 (1959) 125–26, *Milon ha-Mishnah – Saadiah:* N. Allony, in: *Studies* (1986), 137–50; A. Kimmelmann, "Guide to Commentaries in the Geonic Period," in: *Annual Jewish Law*, 11–12 (1984–86), 509–87. COMMENTARIES ON THE TALMUD: *Commentary of Saadia to tractate Berakhot*, ed. Wertheimer (1908); I.L. Sachs, in: *Sinai* 13 (1943), 49–54; S.D. Goitein, in: KS, 31 (1956), 368–70; B.M. Lewin, *Marei Makom avur Oẓar ha-Geonim le-Massekhet Bava Batra u-Ḥullin*, in: *Jewish Law Annual*, A. Kimelmann (ed.), 543–56; 565–77. INTRODUCTORY BOOKS TO TALMUD: (1) *Seder Tanaim ve-Amoraim:* S. Assaf, *Tekufat ha-Geonim*, 147–48; Waxmann, 1:315–16; *Sarei ha-Elef*, M. Kasher, J. Mandelbaum (eds.), 1 (1978), 163; 2 (79), 582; S. Abramson, in: *E.Z. Melammed Jubilee*; BOOKS OF HALAKHAH: (1) *Sheiltot*: Aḥa of Shabḥa, *Sarei ha-Elef,* 96–97; 11, 573; A. Kaminka, in: *A. Schwarz Jubilee*; RULES, REGULATIONS, AND CUSTOMS: *Controversies…* M. Margalioth. in: *Mavo* to the book, Assaf, 179; S.H. Kook, *Iyyunim ve-Meḥkarim,* 1 (1959), 286. TAKKANOT: I.H. Weiss, *Dor Dor we-Dorshav,* 4:177–84; Assaf, 62–64; I. Shzipanski, in: *Ha-Darom*, 24 (1967), 135–97; 26 (1968), 203–10; M. Elon, *Jewish Law*, 2 (1973), 531–46; Y. Brody, in: *Annual of Jewish Law,* 11–12 (1984–86), 279–315; A. Shochetman, in: Annual, 655–86. PRAYERS AND LITURGICAL POETRY: (1) *Siddur of Amram Gaon:* D. Goldschmidt, Introduction to his edition of this *siddur,* G. Orman, in: KS, 47 (1972), 376–81; Assaf, 180–184; H.J. Zimmels, in: *Sinai*, 18 (1946), 362–73; *Sarei ha-Elef,* 2 (1979), 394–95. (2) *Prayer Book of Saadiah Gaon:* Introduction to the ed. of Siddur (1941), S. Bernstein, in: *Biẓaron* (1942), 845–57; Review of D. Goldschmidt, B. Klar, in: KS, 18 (1942), 336–48; L. Ginzberg, in: JQR, 33 (1942/3), 315–63; H.J. Zimmels-H. Yalon, in: *Saadia*; LITURGICAL POETRY: *Otiyyot R. Saadiah: Sarei ha-Elef,* 2:420, 659; Baron, Index, 53, 119; 7:63ff, 78, 103, 111f, 132f, 274f. H. Brody, *Yedi'ot ha-Makhon le-Ḥeker ha-Shirah ha-Ivrit,* 3 (1937), 5ff.; idem, in: *Sinai*, 2 (1938), 516ff; Y. Rafael, in: *Sinai*, 12 (1938), 592–676; Habermann, in: *Tarbiz,* 13 (1942), 52–59; M. Zulai, *Ha-Eskolah ha-Paytanit shel R. Saadiah Gaon (Rasag)* (1964); idem, in: *Tarbiz*, 23 (1952), 112–19; I. Tobi, in: *Tarbiz*, 53 (1984), 221–53. RESPONSA: Geonic Period; Assaf, 211–20; Baron, 5:52; 6:29, 115, 339, 385, 8:229; Z. Groner, in: *Sinai*, 79 (1976), 42–229; idem, in: *Alei Sefer*, 8 (1980), 5–22; idem, in: *Alei Sefer,* 13 (1986), contains a list of Hai Gaon's Responsa: M. A Friedmann, in: *Meḥkarim be-Sifrut ha-Talmud* (1983), 71f; J. Lipschitz, in: *Moria*, 7 (1978), 4–5; A. Eisenbach, *Tzefunot*, 1–3 (1989), 4–7; M.A. Friedman, in: *Sinai*, 109 (1992), 125–44. DOCUMENTS AND LETTERS: See Pirkoi B. Baboi, Bibliography; Rav Ẓair, 1:109–12; Baron 5:32; 6:29, 109–116, 339, 381–85. LANGUAGE AND GRAMMAR: *Saadiah's Grammatical Work*: S. Abramson, in: *Tarbiz*, 19 (1948), 104; S.L. Skoss, in: JQR, 23 (1932/33), 329–36; 33 (1942/3), 171–212; 42 (1952), 283–317; idem, in: *Proceedings*, 21 (1952), 75–100; 22 (1953), 65–90; 23 (1954), 59–73; idem, *Saadia Gaon, the Earliest Hebrew Grammarian* (1955); Review in N. Allony, *Studies*, 381–84; N. Allony, *Introduction to ha-Egron* (1969); D. Tene, in: KS, 47 (1972), 545–53; A. Goldenberg, in: *Leshonenu*, 37 (1973), 117–36, 275–90; 38 (1974), 78–90; Y. Eldor, in: *Leshonenu*, 45 (1981), 105–32: N. Allony, *Studies* (1986), 205–31; 233–281; 325–34; Baron, 7:15, 26, 32, 39; S. Abramson, *"Sefer ha-Me'assef le-Rav Hai Gaon,"* in: *Leshonenu*, 41 (1977), 108–16. RESEARCH ON GEONIC LITERATURE: Ḥayyim Loven, in: *The Young Israel Rabbinical Council in Israel Annual*, 2 (1988), 87–123; Y. Blumberg in: *Hebrew Law Annual*, 14–15 (1988/89), 61–87; D. Groner, *Pe'amim*, 38 (1989), 49–57; Y. Horowitz, *Meḥkarei Ḥag*, 1 (1988), 49–56; idem, 3 (1992), 6–14. RESEARCH ON SAADIAH GAON AND HAI GAON: Saadiah Gaon, A. Schlossberg, in: *Shema'tin* (1988), 18–23; idem, in: *Meḥkarei Ḥag*, 4 (1992), 74–82; H. Ben Shammai, *Sefer ha-Yovel li-Shelomo Pines*, 1 (1988), 127–46; Y. Horowitz, in: *Meḥkarei Ḥag*, 2 (1990), 54–62; idem, *Meḥkarei Ḥag*, 4 (1992), 83–87; A. Lasker and D. Lasker, in: *Tarbiz*, 61 (1991), 119–28; Y. Ratzaby, in: *Sinai*, 109 (1992), 97–117; E. Fleischer, in: *Sefer Zikkaron Pagis* (1988), 661–681; Z. Rothstein, in: *Esh Tamid* (1989), 21–30; Y. Gertner, in: *Sinai*, 107 (1991), 202–12.

GEORGE (Cohn), MANFRED (1893–1965), journalist and editor. Born in Berlin, he took a degree in law and became a prominent newspaper editor and writer. George excelled as a political writer and as a film and drama critic. Among his books is *Theodor Herzl, sein Leben und sein Vermaechtnis* (1932). When the Nazis came to power, George went to Prague, worked there for several years, and in 1938 immigrated to the U.S. In New York, he took over *Aufbau* (subtitled "Reconstruction"), founded in 1924, originally the newsletter of the German-Jewish "New World Club." Under his editorship, *Aufbau* became a German-language weekly representing the German-Jewish immigrant community and acquired a circulation of more than 30,000. George was one of the outstanding figures of America's German-Jewish community.

[Frederick R. Lachman]

GEORGE, WALTER LIONEL (1882–1926), French-born English author of half-Jewish parentage. He specialized in labor problems and questions of sex and marriage. George's works include *The City of Light* (1912), *Israel Kalisch* (1913), *A London Mosaic* (1921), and *The Story of Woman* (1925). He also wrote a study of Anatole France (1915).

GEORGIA (Rus. **Gruziya**), republic in W. Transcaucasia. There is a tradition among the Jews of Georgia (the "Gurjim") that they are descended from the Ten Tribes exiled by Shalmaneser, which they support by their claim that there are no *kohanim* (priestly families) among them.

Georgian historical literature had used the term "Georgian Jews" already in the 11th century, but as a firmly established term referring to a specific community it was used only from the early 19th century after Georgia was incorporated in the Russian Empire. The Jews of Georgia call themselves *Ebraeli* and use Georgian language as their spoken and written language of communication, without resorting to the Hebrew alphabet. Georgian Jewish traders developed the jargon *Qivruli* (Jewish), many roots of which originated in Hebrew.

According to the 1897 census 6,407 Jews in the Russian Empire considered Georgian their mother-tongue. According to the 1926 census, the only census where each of the Jewish ethnic and linguistic groups appeared as a separate entity, there were 30,534 Jews in Georgia, among them 20,897 Georgian Jews and 9,637 were Ashkenazim. In the same census 96.6% of the Georgian Jews named Georgian as their mother-tongue, and their literacy rate reached 36.29%. In 1931 the State Planning Committee estimated their number at 31,974. The 1939 census showed 42,300 Jews (Georgian and Ashkenazi), representing 1.2% of the total population. The 1959 census reported that 35,673 Jews considered Georgian their mother-tongue. The 1970 census reported 55,382 Jews. About 70% of them left for Israel in the course of the next decade. There were some Georgian Jews who were registered as Georgians and not as Jews but no reliable estimate of their number was available. The Georgian Jews lived mostly in Tbilisi (Tiflis), capital of Georgia, the other centers being Kutaisi, Kulashi, Tshinvali, Gori, Oni, and Sachkhere.

One historical tradition speaks of the first Jews coming to the country after the conquest of Jerusalem by Nebuchadnezzar 586 B.C.E. It is possible that this reflects the arrival of Jews from Babylonia in Georgia, the southern part of which was

Jewish communities in Georgian S.S.R. after World War II. From M. Neistadt, Yehudei Cruzyah: Ma'avak al ha-Shivah le-Ẓiyyon, *Tel Aviv 1970.*

included in 539 B.C.E. in the ancient Persian state. The Jews presumably spread to the rest of the country from the south.

Archaeological evidence supports the traditions by confirming the existence of Jews in Mtzkheta, the ancient capital of the East Georgian state of Kartli, in the first centuries C.E. Among the first Christian missionaries in the early 4th century, a Jew is mentioned named Eviatar or Abiatar from Urbnisi, as well as his sister Sidonia. Both were sanctified by the Georgian Orthodox Church. Mention is also made of the Jewess Salomea who wrote the life of Nina from Cappadocia who baptized the Georgians.

Georgian sources refer to the arrival of Jews in Western Georgia in the 6th century, evidently from the Byzantine Empire, and the further migration of 3,000 Jews into Eastern Georgia. This information might indicate a mass flight of Jews from the Western regions of Georgia, ruled by the Byzantine Empire – where they were subjected to severe suppression in the 6th century – to the south-eastern regions of Georgia ruled at the time by Persians who tolerated Jews. Sources also speak of Jewish migrations to Georgia from Armenia and Iran. It is likely that the toponym אפריקי mentioned several times in the Babylonean Talmud (e.g., Sanhedrin 94a, Tamid 32a) is to be read as *efirike*, i.e., *Iberika* or *Iberia* which was one of the ancient names of Eastern Georgia, as well as of Georgia as a whole.

After the Arab conquest of considerable territory of Georgia in the second half of the 7th century, it was transformed into a province of the Arab caliphs, although it remained a Christian country. In the late 9th century a Jewish sect emerged in Georgia which denied some laws of *halakhah* including marriage and *kashrut* regulations. The founder of the sect, Abu-ʿImran Musa (Moshe) al-Za'farani, went to Tbilisi (Tiflis) from the Babylonian Empire and was later known as *Abu-ʿImran al-Tiflisi, and the sect as a whole, which existed at least 300 years, was known as the "Tiflis Sect."

In the 9th century, Georgia was bordered to the east and north by the Khazar kingdom (see *Khazars), the elite of which adopted Judaism. There are no authentic data on contacts between the Khazars and the Jews of Georgia, but it is known that in the middle of the 10th century *Ḥisdai Ibn Shaprut wanted to send his famous letter to Joseph, the king of the Khazars, through Georgia which Ibn Shaprut called "Armenia" in accordance with Arabic terminology of the time.

In the early Middle Ages Georgian Jewry was connected mainly with Persian Jewry, and through Iran with Baghdad, the religious center of eastern Jewry.

From the travel diaries of *Pethahiah of Regensburg, written in the second half of the 12th century, it might be concluded that some of the Jews living in "the Ararat country," i.e., in Trans-Caucasus, had emigrated to other countries. He also noted that during his stay in Baghdad he saw the messengers of the kings of "Meshekh Land," and those messengers related that the "Kings of Meshekh and all their Lands became Jews," and also that there were teachers among the inhabitants of Meshekh "educating their children in Torah and in the Jerusalem Talmud." Under the term "Meshekh" one of the Georgian tribes, the Meskhi, might have been meant. However no support has been found for the theory that this tribe as a whole or partially adopted Judaism. Another Georgian tribe, the Hevsures, have up to the present time preserved historical legends connected with Judaism. Chronologically this would accord with the time of Pethahiah's story.

In the 12th century Abraham *Ibn Daud (Rabad I) mentioned Georgia among the countries where the Jews adhered to Rabbinical Judaism and not to Karaism. In the synagogue of the small town of Lailashi in northwestern Georgia, there was preserved up to the 1930s, a Pentateuch manuscript of the 11th or 12th century which was revered not only by the Georgian Jews, but also by the Christian population who attributed to it miraculous properties.

When invaded by the Mongols some of the Jews of eastern and southern Georgia moved to western Georgia, which preserved its independence, and founded new communities there. In the 14th century mention is made of the Jewish community of Gagra on the Black Sea Coast, headed by R. Joseph al-Tiflisi. At the same time the philologist R. Judah ben Jacob either composed or rewrote a Hebrew grammatical work showing traces of influence of the Karaite school of Hebrew grammar.

The impoverished situation of Georgian Jewry after the Mongol invasion contributed to their becoming serfs. Numerous sources refer to their serfdom over a five hundred year period, starting from the end of the 14th century. The process of enslavement accelerated in the 15th–16th centuries when their situation deteriorated as a result of military invasions, first by Timur and then by the armies of Turkey and Persia, and also because of constant inner conflicts. All these events resulted in the disintegrating of the country into three kingdoms and five feudal territories, as from the end of the 15th century. Documents from the early 17th to the mid-19th century attest to the numerous cases of the selling of individual Jews or whole families and groups, or of their changing one owner for another as debt payment or as a gift.

Persistent wars and rebellions devastated entire regions of the country in the late 18th–early 19th century, depriving Jews of their property, and often to escape immediate danger they had to seek the protection of the local feudal lords, but in the final analysis they became enslaved by their protectors. However, one premise of their serfdom was always preserved: the owner was obliged not to force them to convert to Christianity.

The Jewish serfs occupied themselves with agriculture or with the traditional Jewish crafts: fabric weaving and dyeing. Some of them were involved in retail trade and other outside jobs, paying their masters a yearly compensation. As late as 1835, several decades after eastern Georgia had been incorporated in the Russian Empire, many Jews still lived on the estates of their feudal lords, and only a small proportion was engaged in outside jobs in towns. Free Jews who could buy their liberation now also lived in the towns. They were mostly affluent merchants or owners of large stores.

Throughout the period of their serfdom, migration – forced or voluntary – took place. Thus voluntary migrations to the Crimea occurred in the 15th–16th centuries. Jews in the 19th and 20th centuries were still to be found in the Crimea having family names of Georgian origin. In the 17th–18th centuries a forced migration occurred when Georgian Jews were driven out by Persian invaders to Persia together with tens of thousands of non-Jewish Georgians.

The Jewish serfs lived on their masters' estates as small groups, separated from each other. Due to their isolation and the absence of a uniting religious and spiritual center, their Jewish knowledge deteriorated. The German traveler Reineggs who visited Georgia in 1780 wrote about the rural Jews being called "*Canaanites*" by the urban Jewish merchants and weavers because of the former's poor knowledge of the religious laws.

Sometimes Jews converted to Christianity to escape their serfdom. The Georgian Church favored the conversions: documentary evidence exists of cases where the Church paid for the liberation of serfs who wished to convert. There were also cases when the feudal lords, contrary to their obligations, forced their Jewish serfs to convert to Christianity.

According to the Georgian legislation the Jewish serfs of Georgia were divided into three categories: the King's serfs, the Feudal serfs and the Church's serfs. Both groups of Jews, free and enslaved, were not admitted to serve in the army, and instead of military service payed the "army ransom." When in 1801 eastern Georgia was included in the Russian Empire the category of the King's serfs became the "Treasury Serfs" obligated to pay taxes to the Russian treasury. In 1864–1871 serfdom in Georgia was abolished, and the former serfs among Georgian Jews moved to towns where the Jews had been already settled, and became engaged mainly in retail trade.

A comparatively small share of the Jewish population was engaged in various crafts, mainly in shoe and hat making. Before the revolution of 1917 this share did not exceed 3–5% of the Jewish labor force. Women dealt with weaving and dyeing for home and for sale. Some families also possessed land plots, mostly under grape cultivation.

The structure of the Jewish community finally developed following the liberation of Georgian Jews from serfdom and their subsequent urbanization. The liberated serfs coming from the same settlement as a rule moved to the same town where they attempted to establish their own synagogue, settling around it. Usually such a group consisted of a limited number of large families encompassing three or four generations.

Each group elected its *gabbai responsible for all the affairs connected with the synagogue's activity. The *ḥakham* authorized the religious life of the group combining functions of a rabbi, *ḥazzan*, *shoḥet*, *mohel* and teacher of *medreshe* (*ḥeder*). The Georgian Jewish groups from rural settlements lived side by side in a new place of settlement, so the Jewish population concentrated in one part of the town which later turned into the Jewish quarter of the given town.

Open outbursts of antisemitism in Georgia became frequent in the second half of the 19th century. Causes stemmed from the process of urbanization of the Jewish community and the consequent change of occupation by the majority of Jews who now chose trade as their livelihood; from the influence of Russian antisemitism; and from turning the Jew, a weak outsider, into the object of a xenophobia which could not be released against another stranger – the powerful Russian invader.

In the second half of the 19th century, six blood libels occurred in Georgia which at the time constituted the highest concentration of cases not only in the boundaries of the Russian Empire, but in the whole world. The biggest and best known happened in 1878 in the little town of Sachkhere where nine Jews were accused of the ritual killing of a Christian child in anticipation of Passover. The trial of the nine took place in Kutaisi and became known as the "Kutaisi trial" which drew the attention of the civilized world. Although the accused were not found guilty, the local population remained convinced that the Jews used Christian blood for preparing *mazzot*. Other blood libels in Georgia took place in 1852, 1881, 1882, 1883, and 1884. In 1895 the Kutaisi Jews suffered from a severe pogrom. In 1913 a gang headed by the deputy governor of Kutaisi systematically extorted money from the Jews, and those refusing to pay were killed.

One of the most important events in Georgian Jewish life in the 19th century was the establishment of contacts with Russian Ashkenazi Jews who began to settle in Georgia after it was joined to the Russian Empire. For decades the relations between the Georgian Jews and the Ashkenazi communities remained strained: the Georgian Jews considered the majority of the Ashkenazi Jews living in Georgia as godless or insufficiently observant, while the Ashkenazim often looked down on the Georgian Jews. Contacts became closer only at the end of the 19th century, but even then their relations were strained.

At the end of the 1890s R. Abraham ha-Levi Khvoles (1857–1931) – a pupil of the famous Lithuanian Rabbi Isaac Elhanan *Spektor – was elected chief rabbi of the town of Tzkhinvali. His only language for communicating with his congregation was Hebrew, and as time passed the number of Jews of the town using this language increased considerably. In 1906 Khvoles established the first *talmud torah* in Georgia where about 400 pupils studied. He was the first in Georgian Jewish life to introduce education for girls, inviting for this purpose a female Hebrew teacher. To accustom the Jews to crafts and skills he brought in experienced teachers who taught boys shoemaking, leather tanning, soap-boiling, and other skills. He sent some of his best students to the Lithuanian *yeshivot* to continue their education and receive the title of rabbi. In time, such practice became common among the Georgian Jewish communities. Rabbi Khvoles influenced other communities throughout Georgia: for example, in 1902 a school for children was established in Tbilisi where teaching was conducted according to the "Hebrew in Hebrew" system. The teachers for the school came from Vilna.

The Social-Democratic movement which emerged in Georgia at the end of the 19th century had almost no impact on the Jews. One Jewish Social-Democrat, Itzka Rizhinashvili (1885–1906), who became well known, was killed by police in Kutaisi.

From the end of the 19th century Zionist circles sprang up in the Ashkenazi communities, and its members began to propagate Zionist ideas among the Georgian Jews. Rabbi David Baazov, one of the founders of Zionism in the Georgian communities, participated in the Sixth Zionist Congress in 1903. The majority of the Orthodox leaders, the *ḥakhams*, actively struggled against the spreading of Zionist ideas among Georgian Jews. Emissaries of the Ḥabad movement, who arrived in Georgia from 1916, also resisted the penetration of Zionism.

World War I interrupted the process of Georgian *aliyah* to Palestine which had begun in 1863. By 1916, 439 Georgian Jews were living in Palestine, the majority in Jerusalem where they established their own quarter near the Damascus Gate. They had to leave the quarter after the anti-Jewish Arab riots of 1929 had led to its partial destruction.

Most Georgian Jews going to the Holy Land belonged to the poorest strata of the community and engaged in physical labor. In Jerusalem, many were freight-handlers. Only a small number became prominent in trade. These included the Kokiashvili (Kokia) family which owned a network of shops and large land holdings in Jerusalem. The Dabra family (Davarshvili) traded on a large scale, mostly in Jerusalem. The Ḥasidov (Khasidoshvili) and the Khakhamshvili families founded banking businesses.

Despite the fact that the main motivation for *aliyah* was religious, only a small number of *ḥakhams* went to the Holy Land. The well-known *ḥakham* of Akhaltzikhe, Yosef Davidashvili, arrived in the 1890s; Simon ben Moshe Rizhinashvili published in Jerusalem in 1892 a Hebrew-Georgian textbook and conversation book, *Sefer ḥinukh ha-ne'arim* ("The Book for Education of the Youth"), in Hebrew letters; Efraim ben Ya'akov ha-Levi Kokia published in 1877 in Jerusalem the religious and philosophical treatise *Yalkut Ephraim al ha-Torah im Ḥamesh Megillot* ("Comments by Ephraim on the Torah and the Five Scrolls"); he also wrote *Sam Ḥayyim: likkutim u-musarim tovim* ("Elixir of Life: Extracts and Benevolent Morals").

After the October 1917 Revolution, the Georgian population expressed its strong desire for independence, and in May 1918 a democratic republic was established. In the Georgian Executive Assembly, two places were allocated for representatives of the Georgian Jews, and one for the Ashkenazim. In the process of the elections, a small group of young assimilatory Jews, headed by the brothers Yosef and Mikhael Khananishvili were backed by Social Democrats – Mensheviks who formed the coalition government. This group considered the Georgian Jews as Jewish, not from the ethnic point of view, but as Georgians differing from the rest of the population only by their religion. They fought Zionism in concert with some Georgian Jewish religious leaders, supported by members of the Ḥabad movement which had acquired considerable influence in Kutaisi and in several other towns. Kutaisi became the center of the anti-Zionist movement, whose participants abstained from taking part in the All-Jewish Congress in Tbilisi in 1918 where all the Georgian Jewish and Ashkenazi communities of Georgia were represented.

The Association of Zionists of Georgia became the leading group in the congress. The three Jewish representatives elected by the congress to participate in the Executive Assembly were rejected by the Georgian Election Committee which was averse to Zionist representatives and preferred two candidates elected at the Kutaisi congress held at the same time by anti-Zionist groups. The Ashkenazim protested against this action by refusing to elect a new Ashkenazi representative instead of the rejected one.

When the Red Army invaded Georgia in February 1921 the population fled on a mass scale; 1,500–2,000 Jews left Georgia, and about 1,000–1,200 of them arrived in Palestine. The rest settled mainly in Istanbul where a Georgian Jewish community had been in existence from the 1880s. In 1921, there were 1,700 Georgian Jews in Palestine.

At the outset of the Sovietization of Georgia the central Soviet authorities adhered to a policy emphasizing respect of local traditions including religious beliefs. This attitude applied also to Georgian Jewry. The government bodies did not interfere in affairs connected with Jewish religion and synagogues were open as previously. In the early 1920s, Zionist activities also were not impeded. The Zionist school in Tblisi was reopened in 1921 after a short interruption, being now called the Jewish Labor School No. 102, and Hebrew was taught there as the national language of Georgian Jews. In 1924 a Zionist organ appeared in Georgian called *Makabeeli*, but only three issues were published. In 1924–25 the semi-legal ḥalutzic youth organization called "Avoda" managed to function and the youth theater company "Kadima" presented plays on Jewish themes in Georgian.

After an anti-Russian and anti-Soviet rebellion in Georgia was suppressed in 1924, Soviet policy changed for the worse. Legal and semi-legal Zionist activities were cut short. The economic regulations resulted in the bankruptcy of many Jewish traders, large and small. The Zionist group, headed by D. Baazov and N. Eliashvili, appealed to the local authorities to allow Jews to occupy themselves with agriculture, but were turned down. The two leaders then suggested that the authorities should allow those Jews who could not be engaged in Georgian agriculture to leave for Palestine. Two hundred families applied to leave, and in October 1925, 18 of them were allowed to emigrate, under the leadership of N. Eliashvili.

In the mid-1920s industrialization and secularization became the Soviet authorities' main aims for the Jews of Georgia, who were dragged to factories as a working force, or compelled to join craft cooperatives and collective farms.

In 1927–28, OZET (the organization for settling Jewish workers on the land) strengthened its activities, and its Georgian affiliate established branches in many towns. The first Jewish collective farm was formed in 1928 in Tziteli-Gora. By 1933 there were 15 collective farms with a population of 2,314 and land area of 1,540 ha. In 1928 efforts were made to settle some Georgian Jewish communities in *Birobidjan and in certain regions of the Crimea assigned for Jewish agricultural settlement, but these attempts failed. The Jewish collective farms in Georgia contributed to local Jewish welfare, as a means to alleviate their difficult material conditions; moreover they could continue to live according to their religious and communal traditions observing *kashrut*, Sabbath, Jewish festivals, and so on.

From the outset of the 1930s, however, the authorities decided to break the Jewish traditions by eliminating the ethnic homogeneity of the Jewish collective farms; as a result the Jewish community could no longer function. Thus in 1931 in establishing a collective farm in the small town of Mukhrani the Jewish collective farmers were mixed with the Georgians and Armenians, the collective farm being declared "international." Toward 1934 the collective farm in Akhalzikhe, established in 1931 as a Jewish undertaking, lost its ethnic homogeneity.

The policy of integrating the Jewish collective farms was conducted against the background of intermittent blood libels occurring in Sachkhere in 1921, in Tbilisi in 1923, and in Akhalzikhe in 1926. Moreover, the ethnically heterogeneous collective farms became a convenient target for anti-religious campaigns, which had become common in Georgian Jewish life from the end of the 1920s.

From 1938 the Jewish collective farms were united with non-Jewish ones, and the Jewish farmers started to leave them on a large scale. Thus the experiment of turning part of Georgian Jewry into agricultural workers ended, with the sole exception of the first Georgian-Jewish collective farm of Tziteli-Gora which continued to exist up to the beginning of the 1970s.

As its main tool to drive Jews to work in industry and to establish producing cooperatives, the Soviet authorities founded "Evkombed" ("All-Georgian Committee for Assisting the Jewish Poor"). The committee was created in 1928 after a fire in the Jewish quarter of Kutaisi which was burnt to the ground: dozens of people perished and about 6,000 lost their homes.

In 1929 a considerable number of Jews were working in the silk factories in Kutaisi and in Tbilisi. In 1931, 1,430 Jews joined the production cooperatives of shoemakers, hat-makers, leather-tanners, and others, half of them in Tbilisi. The majority of those cooperatives served as cover for the private activities of a large family or several closely connected families; the ethnic homogeneity of the productive cooperatives allowed the members to observe Jewish tradition, and in the first period of their existence Sabbath was the rest day.

The efforts of the authorities to eradicate the religious tradition and to mix nationalities within each co-operative was partially successful. The immediate result was the flight of Jews from mixed co-operatives. On the whole the attempt to industrialize Georgian Jewry failed, and by 1935 only 7,000 Jews were involved in the process.

Religion was considered by the authorities the main ideological impediment to their efforts to influence the Jews, and they accordingly tried all means to secularize the community. From 1927 the authorities established a school network for Georgian Jews with instruction in Georgian. Camps and clubs were created especially for Georgian Jewish youth and in 1933 the "Lavrentii Beria Culture Club" for the working Jews of Georgia was established. All these establishments were conducted in an anti-religious spirit.

For some time the authorities toyed with the idea of creating a Soviet Georgian-Jewish culture, of the same type as the Soviet-Yiddish culture. In 1934 they established a "State History and Ethnography Museum" of the Georgian Jews with the official aim of studying the history and customs of the community and struggling against "survivals of the past in its life." This undertaking attracted a group of young Jewish scholars. About 60 pictures were exhibited in the Museum of Shlomo Koboshvili, an artist of the 1920s, whose pictures depicted Georgian Jewish everyday life and the past of Georgian Jewry. When the museum was closed in the early 1950s, the pictures disappeared. The best-known Georgian author of the 1920s and the 1930s was Herzl *Baazov, novelist and playwright, the subject of whose works was Georgian Jewish life.

In 1937–38 the authorities clamped down on Georgian culture, attacking both Jewish religion and secular Jewish culture. In September 1937 nine *ḥakhams*, of whom two were Ashkenazim, were arrested, in Tzkhinvali (called Staliniri at the time), and killed in prison without trial. In the beginning of 1938 Herzl Baazov perished in prison.

The only Jewish cultural establishment that continued to exist was the History and Ethnography Museum, but in 1948 its director, Aharon Krikheli, was arrested, and soon after, in the early 1950s, the museum was closed.

Thus, the Soviet authorities finally destroyed the non-religious Georgian-Jewish culture which they had assiduously established in the pre-war years. Only from the end of the 1950s did poems and stories by writers belonging to the community and describing its life begin to reappear.

The Soviet rule was far from successful in its efforts to destroy the religious tradition. Even in the 1960s and in the 1970s most Georgian Jews observed religious traditions: visiting synagogues, observing *kashrut*, and conducting their family life according to religious Law. Many of their children studied in illegal *ḥeders*. The authorities were aware of these schools but chose not to notice them.

Although statistical data are lacking, it may be presumed that a considerable proportion of Georgian Jewry became adjusted to the economic situation in Georgia after World War II, viz. the flourishing of private enterprise in trade and small stores under the cover of the state trade and industrial establishments, with the silent acquiescence of the local authorities. The latter used these enterprises to boost the economy of the republic and raise their own affluence.

However whenever they had to organize a show trial of "violators of the Soviet economic laws," demanded by the central authorities, the Jews were always chosen as a scapegoat. Jews predominated among those convicted for economic crimes in Georgia, were punished severely, and sometimes sentenced to death. Community life developed amid continuing blood libels: in 1963 in Tzkhaltubo, in 1964 in Zestafoni, and in 1965 in Kutaisi.

After the *Six-Day War Georgia was the leading region in the Soviet Union for Jewish demonstrations and petitions demanding the right to leave for Israel. The letter of Aug. 6, 1969, by 18 heads of Georgian families to the United Nations containing an appeal to influence the Soviet government to allow them to leave for Israel, was the first document of the *aliyah* movement in the Soviet Union to receive wide publicity in the West. The mass *aliyah* of Georgian Jewry began in 1971; by 1981, about 30,000 of them had immigrated to Israel.

[Michael Zand / The Shorter Jewish Encyclopaedia in Russian]

Participation in Intellectual Life

Georgian Jews took part in the literary, intellectual, and cultural life of Georgia. Among them were Moshe Danieloshvili, a stage producer who translated S. *An-Ski's play *The Dybbuk* into Georgian and produced it at the state theater at Tbilisi; Gyorgi Kokashvili, a poet, playwright, and literary critic, whose play "The Children of the Sea" was performed at the state theater at Tbilisi; Rosa Davidashvili, an ethnologist and author of children's literature of the generation preceding the Revolution; and Shalom Mikhaelashivli, a historian who investigated the history of his native community at Kulashi. Joseph Kotsishvili, wrote an historical novel on the beginning of Jewish settlement in Georgia; he translated Shalom Aleichem into Georgian as well as works by Lion *Feuchtwanger. Other notable Georgian Jews were Herzl Baazov, Nissan *Babalikashvili, Yiẓḥak *Davidashvili, Boris *Gaponov (d. 1972), and Abraham *Mamistabolob.

[Mordkhai Neishtat]

Developments in the Georgian Republic

A CIS republic, Georgia declared its independence in 1991, becoming an arena of military conflict, first between President Zviad Gamsakhurdiia and the opposition, and then, after the former was driven out in January 1992, between the government of Eduard Shevardnadze and separatists in Southern Osetia and Abkhazia. One of Gamsakhurdiia's advisors was Isai Goldshtien, a former refusenik who became an anti Zionist. Most Georgian Jews, however, were reluctant to become involved in the struggles for power.

The Soviet censuses reported 24,800 Jews in 1989; 14,300 of the latter were Georgian Jews who had preserved their ethnic and religious distinctiveness despite speaking the same language as their host nationality. In the mass emigration of Jews that proceeded after the breakup of the Soviet Union, their number dropped to 14,500 in 1993 and under 5,000 in 2000. Approximately 30 Jewish organizations were in operation, including a day school in Tbilisi and supplementary schools in other cities. In February 1993, the first issue of the Jewish newspaper in the Georgian language, *Menora*, was published; the publisher and the editor was Guram Bariashvili.

[Michael Beizer]

BIBLIOGRAPHY: E. Salgaller, in: JSOS, 26 (1964), 195–202; A. Harkavy, *Ha-Yehudim u-Sefat ha-Slavim* (1867), 106–20; J.J. Chorny, *Sefer ha-Massa'ot be-Erez Kavkaz u-va-Medinot asher me-Ever la-Kavkaz* (1884); A.L. Eliav (Ben-Ammi), *Between Hammer and Sickle* (1969), passim; M. Neistadt, *Yehudei Gruzyah* (1970); *Histoire de Géorgie depuis l'antiquité jusqu'au* XIX*e siècle* (attrib. uncertain, trans. M.F. Brosset (Rus. name M.I. Brosse), 7 vols., 1849–58); J. Baye, *Les Juifs des montagnes et les Juifs géorgiens* (1902); A. Katz, *Die Juden im Kaukasus* (1894); D.M. Maggid, in: *Istoriya yevreyskogo naroda*, 12 (1921; = *Istoriya yevreyev v Rossii*, 2 bk. 1) 85–95; M.S. Plisetski, *Religiya i byt gruzinskikh yevreyev* (1931); *Yevreyskaya Biblioteka*, 7 no. 12 (1880), 1–188 (on the Kutaisi blood libel); *Al Yehudei Berit ha-Mo'azot*, published by the Israel Ministry of Education and Culture (1970). THE 1990S: U. Schmelz and S. DellaPergola in AJYB 1995, 478; *Supplement to the Monthly Bulletin of Statistics*, 2 (1995); *Mezhdunarodnaia Evreiskaia Gazeta* (MEG) (1993).

GEORGIA, state in S.E. United States. The Jewish population of Georgia grew tremendously from the 1960s. In 1968, approximately 26,000 Jews resided in the state; by 2001 this figure had risen to 93,500 and showed no sign of abating. With about 92% of the state's Jews concentrated in the metropolitan Atlanta area, the tremendous growth in Georgia's Jewish population is almost solely due to the rise of Atlanta as a national Jewish center. Georgia was first settled at *Savannah by Gen. James Oglethorpe in February 1733. Two shiploads of Jews, about 90 persons, arrived during the same year and were permitted to stay owing to Oglethorpe's personal influence. They were of both Portuguese and German origin, poor and financed by the Jewish community of London. Notable among them were Benjamin Sheftall, Abraham de Lyon, Abraham Minis, and Dr. Nunez who, as the colony's only physician, made himself and his coreligionists more welcome by stemming an epidemic. This pioneer group brought a Torah with them and soon established the colony's first congregation, Mikveh Israel, in 1735. The first settlement failed. By 1741 all but three or four Jewish families had moved north. Most returned during the 1750s, prospered, and reestablished the congregation Mikveh Israel in 1786. Its first president was Philip Minis. His father Abraham Minis probably was the first white male born in Georgia. A Masonic lodge and a welfare society founded by Oglethorpe during the 1750s listed Jews among the charter members.

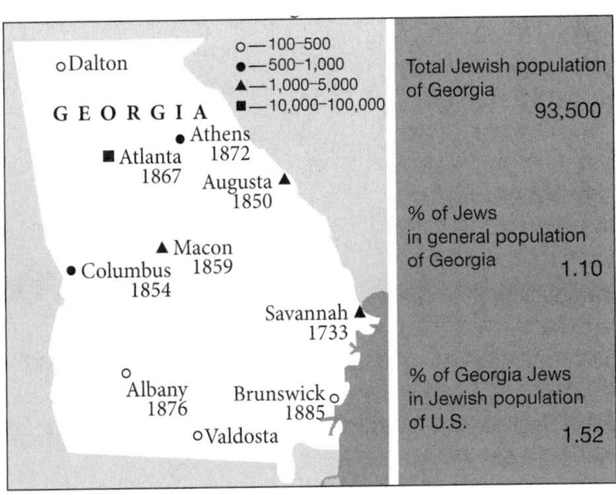

Jewish communities in Georgia and dates of establishment. Population figures for 2001.

There were 400 Jews in the state by 1829; a few families lived in Augusta and isolated areas, while the majority were in Savannah. More rapid growth began during the 1840s with increased immigration from Germany. Jews then settled throughout the state in almost every community, establishing congregations in Augusta in 1850; Columbus, 1854; and Macon, 1859. Although many moved north just before and during the Civil War, they returned in greatly increased numbers immediately after the war. By 1877 there were Jewish communities of 100 or more persons in seven cities, with congregations in *Atlanta; Rome, established in 1871; Athens, 1872; and Albany, 1876. Groups from Eastern Europe began to arrive in the 1880s, settling primarily in Atlanta, Savannah, and Brunswick, which had a congregation by 1885. In 1900 there were 6,400 Jews in Georgia.

Georgian Jews have always enjoyed full civil and religious freedom, including the holding of public office and service in the militia, although the requirement to take a Christian oath restricted them from elective office until 1789. They served as commissioned officers as well as enlisted men in every war, providing all-Jewish companies from Macon and West Point to defend Savannah in 1862. A county is named for David Emmanuel, president of the Georgia Senate in 1797 and governor in 1801, who is believed to have been the first Jewish governor of any U.S. state. Capt. Abraham Simons went to the State Legislature in 1804. Col. Raphael Moses, of Columbus, went to the legislature in 1868 and became chairman of the House Judiciary Committee in 1877. The University of Georgia Law School Building is named for Harold Hirsch (1881–1939), who was a distinguished Atlanta attorney. Several communities have elected Jewish mayors and other city officials. A Jewish woman from Columbus was the first director of the Georgia Department of Public Welfare.

Although relatively free from antisemitism, Georgia Jews have suffered hostility on several occasions. During the Civil War they were temporarily banned from Thomasville, and Jewish-owned stores were broken into in Talbottom. A discriminatory newspaper and the Ku Klux Klan exercised widespread influence in the early 20th century, becoming exceptionally bitter during the Frank case (see Atlanta; Leo *Frank).

Organized Jewish communities exist in the early 21st century in 15 Georgia cities, the major ones in Atlanta, 85,900; Savannah, 3,000; Augusta, 1,300; Columbus, 750; Macon, 1,000; and Athens, 600. Since the 1960s, the state's Jewish community has undergone a significant demographic shift, as the Jewish population in small towns has declined. Small town Jewish merchants once prevalent throughout the state, have retired or sold out due to pressures from national retailing chains. The generations of Jewish merchants have been replaced by a new generation of Jewish professionals, best seen in the tremendous rise of Jewish Atlanta, which has seen the number of its congregations grow from five in 1968 to 38 in 2005. Jewish life is also growing in college towns like Athens, which elected a Jewish mayor, Heidi Davison, in 2002.

There is a home for the aged in Atlanta, serving the entire state, and Jewish community centers exist in Atlanta, Savannah, and Columbus. Two summer camps, one operated by the Southeastern Region of the Union for Reform Judaism and the other by the Atlanta Jewish Community Center, are located at Cleveland. The William Breman Jewish Heritage Museum was opened in Atlanta in 1996 and preserves and displays the history of Jews in the state. There is a Hillel Foundation at Emory University in Atlanta and at the University of Georgia in Athens, and several Anglo-Jewish newspapers published in Atlanta. Jewish Studies programs are also found at the universities with Emory featuring such scholars as David Blumenthal and Deborah Lipstat.

BIBLIOGRAPHY: W.G. Plaut, in: HUCA, 14 (1939), 575–82; M.H. Stern, in: AJHSP, 53 (1963/64), 169–99; L. Huehner, *ibid.*, 10 (1902), 65–95; C.C. Jones, *ibid.*, 1 (1893), 5–12; J.R. Marcus, *Early American Jewry*, 2 (1953), 277–373; J.O. Rothschild, *As But a Day* (1967); B.W. Korn, *American Jewry and the Civil War* (1951), passim.

[Stuart Rockoff (2nd ed.)]

GERAMA AND GARME (Aram. גְּרָמָא, גַּרְמֵי), terms variously used in the Talmud to describe tortious damage caused indirectly by the tortfeasor's person. The following acts are examples cited of *garme* damage: a judge delivering an erroneous decision resulting in damage to another; burning another's bond – thus preventing him from recovering his debt; a banker giving an erroneous valuation of coins – causing them to be acquired at a loss; damaging mortgaged property held by a creditor – thus reducing the value of his security; informing on another's property to bandits – thus causing them to take it away. Opinion is divided in the Talmud over the question of liability for this kind of tort (BK 98b; 100a; 117b); some of the sages maintain that liability does exist, while others exclude it. In other cases – similar to those cited above – the damage is termed *gerama* (BK 48b; 60a; BB 22b), but here liability is excluded. Examples of *gerama* damage are placing a ladder by a pigeon loft, enabling a weasel to climb up and eat the pigeons; setting a fire by means of the wind resulting in a conflagration; allowing an animal to trespass onto another's land, where it falls into a well so that its corpse pollutes the water. Other cases which were later interpreted as *gerama* are bending the stalks of grain in another's field toward an approaching fire so that they catch fire; placing poison in the path of another's animal, causing it to eat this and die; sending a burning object through a minor or an idiot, who is irresponsible and thus causes damage; inciting another's dog to bite a third person; frightening another to the extent that he suffers injury or damage from such fright; leaving a broken vessel on public ground so that the pieces cause injury (BK 24b; 55b–56a). Even the earliest of the post-talmudic commentators found difficulty in explaining the difference between *gerama* damage, for which the Talmud does not impose any liability, and *garme* damage, for which talmudic opinion differs as to whether there is liability or not. According to Rashi (to BB 22b, s.v. *gerama*; see Sh. Ar., ḤM 386:4), there is no difference between the two concepts – and that those sages who exclude liability for *garme* damage also exclude it in cases of *gerama* damage, and vice versa. Some of the tosafists maintain (BB 22b, s.v. *zot omeret*) that, indeed, in strict law there is no distinction and that there is no liability in either case – save that the more common injuries are called *garme* and that those sages who impose liability for *garme* damage do so in the sense of fining the tortfeasor for the sake of public order. However, according to the majority of the tosafists, all indirect damage that is an immediate result of the tortfeasor is termed *garme*, whereas all other acts of indirect damage are called *gerama* – in respect of which the sages are unanimous in excluding liability. There are also further distinctions between *gerama* and *garme* damage, which all present difficulties and which are all less acceptable. It appears that the two categories can be distinguished by using *gerama* to refer to indirect damage that is too remote to have been foreseeable, and *garme* to refer to indirect damage that should have been foreseeable – but which was caused solely by the independent act of a second person who acted negligently following the first person's act, while he could have refrained from doing that which resulted in the damage. In the latter situation, some sages maintain that the first person is exempt from liability, even though he could have foreseen that his act would result in the negligent act of the second person – who is held to be solely responsible. On the other hand, others hold the first person liable, just because he should have foreseen that his own act would result in the negligent act of the second person. According to this distinction, therefore, the loss sustained by someone acting on the advice of an expert is *garme* damage – because he should have realized that other experts should be consulted before he acted on one expert's advice and he was himself negligent in failing to take such second opinions. If, however, the matter is such that only one suitable expert is available and there is no choice but to rely exclusively on his advice, it is not a case of *garme* damage, and it is the unanimous opinion that the expert is liable for the consequences of his negligent advice. The *halakhah* is that a person is liable for *garme* damage, although it is disputed in the codes whether such liability stems from the strict law or is in the nature of a fine for the sake of public order, as mentioned above. The law applicable in the State of Israel is the Civil Wrongs Ordinance, 1947, which makes a person liable for the natural consequences of his conduct – but not if the decisive cause of the damage is the fault of another. An expert is held liable for giving negligent declarations and opinions.

[Shalom Albeck]

Compromise When Payment for Damages Cannot Be Imposed under Tort Law

In recent decisions of rabbinical courts, when damages are of the *gerama* type, i.e., the tortfeasor is only guilty of causing the damage indirectly, and as such damage, there are insufficient grounds for the submission of a legal action. Since no action can be filed for damages classified as *gerama*, no monetary liability can be imposed by the court. Accordingly, the court has on occasion taken the path of compromise in order to effect monetary restitution. This approach has been adopted in other instances as well in which no demand for payment can be imposed under law, such as when there is only liability under Divine law (see *Divine Punishment) or when the damages involve the violation of a negative commandment but do not suffice for the imposition of a monetary liability, such as fraud in the payment of an employee's wages. In such cases, the rabbinical courts, through the use of a compromise settlement, ensure that justice is done when the strict letter of the *halakhah* itself provides no relief. (See, e.g., decisions of the Rabbinic Court for the Kiryat Arba-Hebron District, vol. 1, 205 and index; Rav. Z.N. Goldberg, "In Praise of Compromise," *Mishpetai Ereẓ*, 2002 (Heb.); see *Compromise.)

The Requirement to Terminate the Damage

Even when the damage is only of the *gerama* type and no monetary liability can be imposed under law, it is nonetheless incumbent upon the tortfeasor to terminate the damage in the present and to prevent its recurrence in the future. Thus, the *Rema rules (Sh. Ar., ḤM 386:3) that a ban (see **Ḥerem*) should be imposed on the person causing the damage until he terminates the damage, and R. Jehiel Michael Epstein rules similarly: "Whatever measures the tortfeasor is able to take to save him [i.e., the one who sustained the damage from continued or similar damage] from this point on he is obligated to take, and to rectify that which he perverted; and he should be forced to do so with all means of force until he removes the [source of] damage. And this is the law regarding every *gerama* in the laws of damages" (*Arukh ha-Shulḥan* 386:19).

In the course of adjudicating a suit between spouses regarding the determination of the level of maintenance that a husband was required to pay his wife, the question arose as to whether the fact that she did not rent out the apartment she owned, thereby precluding potential income from rent, should be considered as causing financial damage to her husband (Judgment 325/2/2021, 5 PDR, 279; see *Maintenance). The Rabbinical Court ruled that the wife cannot be obligated to pay for that damage as it belongs to the category of *gerama*. Nevertheless, the *bet din* stated that the husband may delay payment of maintenance until she rents out the apartment, as even in an instance of mere *gerama*, the person causing the damage is responsible for removing the source of the damage (p. 283 of the ruling).

Liability According to Divine Law and the Seizure of Property by the Injured Party

Further on in the above ruling (p. 284), the *bet din* considered the possibility of permitting the husband to withhold maintenance payment according to the rate of the damage she was causing him by not renting out the apartment, in view of the fact that the husband was actually in possession of the maintenance funds. Despite these being damages of the *gerama* type, the exemption from liability for payment of damages is only under human law, while liability does exist under Divine Law (*Divine Punishment). In such cases, the halakhic authorities were divided as to whether to permit seizure of the tortfeasor's property by the injured party as an alternative to the payment of damages. According to some authorities, such seizure is invalid (Resp. Ribash §392), notwithstanding that the court is required to inform the tortfeasor of his liability under Divine Law (*Yam shel Shelomo*, BK 6:6). Contrary to that opinion, Ran and Rashba consider such seizure valid, and the *bet din* cannot confiscate the property seized by the injured party (*Nimmukei Yosef*, BM 28a; *Ḥiddushei R. Akiva Eiger*, Sh. Ar., ḤM 28:1). The rabbinic court ruled that in the case at hand the seizure is effective, due to the existence of an obligation under Divine Law based on *gerama* damages. Consequently, the husband may deduct the amount of those damages from the alimony he owes to his wife.

DISTINCTION BETWEEN GERAMA AND GARME – CONSIDERATIONS OF APPROPRIATE POLICY. The distinction between *gerama* and *garme*, as well as the implications of that distinction for dealing with the subject today, arose in the case of *Mifalei Te'urah* (CF [Jer] 2220/00, *Mifalei Te'urah v. Israel Postal Authority*). The question adjudicated was whether a party could be obligated to pay compensation for the prevention of future profits. In the case at hand, the Postal Authority published a tender for the production of mailboxes. A company that did not win the tender sued the Postal Authority, claiming that it had been prevented from winning the tender owing to flaws in the tender in terms of compliance with the equality requirement under the laws governing tenders. The company sued the Postal Authority for the amount of the anticipated profits that had been denied it by its loss of the tender.

The Jerusalem District Court (Judge Moshe Drori) ruled that under Jewish law compensation is not awarded for this kind of damage, being an instance of *gerama*: "One who negates [i.e., blocks profit from] another's purse, he [the injured party] has no [claim] against him but angry objection" (TJ, BM 5:3). Halakhic authorities explained this exemption as deriving from the classification of the damages as *gerama* (*Piskei ha-Rosh* to BK 2:6; Resp. Maharam §821).

Nevertheless, the court ruled that the Postal Authority should in fact be held liable for payment of damages, relying on the view of Riẓba (Tosafot, BB 22b, s.v. *zot omeret gerama binzikin asur*, and see above) who declared, regarding damages considered *garme*, that "Our Sages of blessed memory levied a fine for any damage that is common and occurs frequently." The reason that they levied these fines was so that people would not go and cause deliberate damage to others and rely on their exemption from liability. (See *Fines.) The court ruled, that since the case involved a public body, as a matter of legal policy it should be declared that the damages in question are "common and occur regularly," thus precluding the possibility of any branch of government ignoring the laws of equality in public tenders and thereby causing damage to a bidder who would otherwise have won the tender (paragraphs 98–99 of the ruling).

The court relied on comments made by Rabbi Aaron *Lichtenstein regarding the distinction between *gerama* and *garme*. In his view, while Maimonides' approach in his treatise on *garme* is to create widely inclusive distinctions between instances that fall under the definition of *gerama*, with no liability for payment of damages, and those that we may consider instances of *garme*, in which there is such liability, the Riẓba's approach is fundamentally different. In the Riẓba's understanding, one should not look for a distinction in principle between the law of *gerama* and that of *garme* other than that in the cases that are considered *garme*, regarding which there is liability for payment of damages, "the Sages felt there was a specific social need to establish liability," because these were instances in which failure to impose liability for damages payment would have negative socio-economic ramifications. According to this approach, the distinction between *gerama* and *garme* is not a "scholarly" distinction originating in the intricacies of talmudic learning, but rather a "practical" distinction from the mundane world, even though it is understood that the decision regarding when to establish liability for payment is based on considerations of values and ethics and not merely on pragmatic convenience (*Shi'urei R. Aharon Lichtenstein – Dina de-garmei* [1999/2000], 198–99).

Using this methodology, the court ruled, as stated, that in a case in which a governmental body treats parties unequally, a legal policy should be established whereby the body is obligated to pay anticipated damages, with the case being treated as one of *garme* and not of *gerama*.

The court further cited Rabbi Lichtenstein, who states that in practice, in the modern era, with its economic, scientific, and technological developments, the social need to regard cases of indirect damage as *garme* and not *gerama* is constantly growing. Lichtenstein suggests that decisors of Jewish law take the step of enacting a *takkanah*, in accordance with the needs of the world of modern commerce, economics, and technology, defining many sorts of damages as *garme*, making the one who inflicts them liable for payment for such damages, in keeping with the Riẓba's outlook, and this would also "bring the Torah greater repute" (*ibid.*, 200).

In addition to the aforementioned, the court suggested other ways in which support can be found for imposing liability under the laws of *gerama* in such cases. One manner of doing so is by invoking the principle that an obligation be imposed upon the public, even when no basis can be found for it in law, in order to uphold the general requirement of "and you shall do that which is right and good" (relying on Resp. Ḥatam Sofer, 2, YD 239). Another way would be, as discussed above, to rely on the fact that there is liability under Divine Law and since causing indirect damage is forbidden, this prohibition may be enforced upon the public as opposed to an individual.

It should be noted that, at the end of his ruling, Judge Drori emphasizes that, according to the Foundations of the Law 5740 – 1980, the court is obliged to apply the *principles* of Jewish law, even if it does not apply all its particular distinctions. In light of this, the court is required to apply Jewish law in a way that brings about desirable results. In the case at hand, this means educating public servants to apply norms of fair governance. Accordingly, we should aspire to subject the public body to a duty of compensation for future damages as well, even when the damage is defined as *gerama*, in cases in which the authority prevented a person from achieving monetary gain as a result of its failure to comply with the principle of equality (paragraphs 101–194 of the ruling).

Evidentiary Damage and the Law of *Garmei*

The modern legal system recognizes the doctrine of "evidentiary damage," i.e., causing harm by damaging evidence that might be beneficial to the opposing party. Under Israeli law, there may be instances in which causing evidentiary damage shifts the burden of proof to the side that caused that damage, and there may even be instances in which one may file direct suit for compensation for evidentiary damages (CA 1171/00, *Cohen v. Kaplan Hospital*, 2 PSM (5762) 298, Judge Neal Hendel). In adjudicating a compensation claim for damages by reason of medical malpractice – viz. the hospital's failure to properly preserve medical records – the Beer Sheva District Court addressed the close similarity between evidentiary damage and the law of *garme*:

"The talmudic tractate *Bava Kamma* discusses the case of one who burns a note belonging to another person. In Rava's view, he is not liable to punishment, 'for he said to him, 'It is only paper that I've burned'' (BK 98a). According to this position, it is only paper that has been burned, and the one who did so has no liability beyond that. Maimonides rules against this position: 'One who burns the notes of another is required to pay the entire debt that was represented by that note, for although the physical note is not money, he caused the loss of that sum of money' (Yad, Hilkhot Ḥovel u-Mazik 7:9). In other words, evidentiary damage is equivalent to actual damage. In the words of R. Joseph b. Haviva, one collects from the person who burned the entire debt attested to by the bond, 'for he caused him to suffer a loss' (see *Nimmukei Yosef* to *Hilkhot ha-Rif*, BK, Ch. 9, 35:1)."

The court goes on to cite R. Aharon Lichtenstein (*Dina de-Garme*, 61–62), who writes that, in practice, the burning of the bond has no effect, positive or negative, regarding the financial obligation to which the certificate itself attests. The only thing that burning it accomplishes is to cause its owner difficulty in proving the existence of that obligation, at the evidentiary level. Thus, one may see a close similarity between the modern doctrine that recognizes evidentiary damage and the principle of *garme*.

[Menachem Elon (2nd ed.)]

BIBLIOGRAPHY: Gulak, Yesodei, 1 (1922), 157; 2 (1922), 24, 182, 206–9; 4 (1922), 162f.; Herzog, Institutions, 2 (1939), 311 (index), s.v.; ET, 6 (1954), 461–97; 7 (1956), 382–96; S. Albeck, *Pesher Dinei ha-Ne-*

zikin ba-Talmud (1965), 43–61; B. Cohen, *Jewish and Roman Law*, 2 (1966), 578–609, addenda 788–92. **ADD. BIBLIOGRAPHY:** M. Elon, *Ha-Mishpat ha-Ivri* (1988), 1:195, 330; *ibid.*, *Jewish Law* (1994), 1:219f, 396; M. Elon and B. Lifshitz, *Mafte'aḥ ha-She'elot ve-ha-Teshuvot shel Ḥakhmei Sefarad u-Ẓefon Afrikah* (legal digest), 2 (1986), 295–96; B. Lifshitz and E. Shochetman, *Mafte'aḥ ha-She'elot ve-ha-Teshuvot shel Ḥakhmei Ashkenaz, Ẓarefat ve-Italyah* (legal digest) (1997), 205; A. Lichtenstein, *Dina de-Garme* (2000); M. Drori, "Causality in Jewish Tort Law: Implementation of Principles in Israeli Public Law," in: *Teḥumin*, 26 (2005).

GERAR (Heb. גְּרָר), a city and region in the Negev in which Abraham and Isaac dwelt (Gen. chs. 20, 26). Gerar was located on the way to Egypt and is mentioned in connection with Kadesh (identified in ancient sources with Petra and now mainly with ʿAyn Qudayrāt) and Shur (the fortifications on the Egyptian frontier). In the north it bordered on the territories of Beersheba and Gaza (Gen. 10:19; 26:1–2; II Chron. 14:12–13). Its area included Rehoboth (which some scholars identify with the later Ruheibah, 12½ mi. (20 km.) south of Elusa, Sitnah, Esek, the valley of Gerar, and the royal city of Gerar. Through Abraham's oath to Abimelech, the land of Gerar was excluded from the territory destined to be conquered by the Israelites (Gen. 21:22–32; cf. Ḥul. 60b) and it was outside the area of Israelite settlement (Josh. 15). According to the patriarchal tradition, the land of Gerar was inhabited by Philistines originating from Casluhim who lived in Gerar as shepherds ruled by a king; a treaty existed between them and the Hebrew Patriarchs (Gen. 10:14; 21:32–34; 26:1, 15ff.). These references to the Philistines, however, are considered an anachronism. Gerar is again mentioned in the time of Asa king of Judah (c. 908–867 B.C.E.) who pursued Zerah the Ethiopian from Mareshah to Gerar and destroyed all the cities in its vicinity (II Chron. 14:8–14). If the Septuagint version of I Chronicles 4:39–41 is correct (reading Gerar instead of Gedor), the land of Gerar was inhabited in the period of the monarchy by remnants of Ham and by Meunim. The name Gerar survived as a geographical term even after the destruction of the city and designated the district occupied by the former land of Gerar. The reference to it in II Chronicles 14:12 may already have this meaning and it certainly has it in II Maccabees 13:24 (cf. I Macc. 11:59). The district was later known by its Greek name Geradike (TJ, Shev. 6:1, 36c; Gen. R. 52:6; 64:3) or Geraritike (Eusebius, Onom. 60:6ff.), which was identified with the biblical Gerar. Eusebius (loc. cit.) locates it 25 Roman miles "from Eleutheropolis (Bet Guvrin) toward the south"; it is similarly represented on the Madaba Map southwest of Beersheba. Various scholars have accordingly proposed to identify it with Tell al-Sharīʿa, 12 mi. (19 km.) northwest of Beersheba or with Tell Yamma further to the west. Y. Aharoni, however, has suggested a site midway between these two mounds – Tell Abu Hurayra (Tell Haror), the largest tell in the area and containing pottery dating from the Middle Bronze Age and later periods.

BIBLIOGRAPHY: Horowitz, Ereẓ Yis, s.v.; I. Ben Zvi, *Sefer ha-Shomeronim* (1935), 116ff.; Grintz, in: *Koveẓ... M. Schorr* (1944), 96ff.; idem, in: *Tarbiz*, 17 (1945/46), 32ff.; 19 (1947/48), 64; Aharoni, in: IEJ, 6 (1956), 26ff.; Aharoni, Land, index.

[Yehoshua M. Grintz]

GERASA (**Jarash**; Heb. גְּרַשׁ; Ar. جَرَش), ancient city in Transjordan, north of the Jabbok River. Its ruins are situated 1,870 feet (570 m.) above sea level near the small Circassian village Jarash between Amman and Irbid in a fertile region with extensive fields, remains of forests, and scenic surroundings. Wadi Jarash (called Chrysorrhoas in antiquity) passed through the ancient city. According to pottery finds, the site was inhabited as early as the Neolithic period in the seventh millennium B.C.E. and settlement continued into the Early Bronze Age (Canaanite period). Although the name Gerasa, of Semitic origin, also testifies to its early occupation, the first mention of the city appears in the Hellenistic period when it was called "Antioch on the River Chrysorrhoas" – a name indicating that the Hellenistic settlement was established under the Seleucid dynasty. It was apparently founded by Antiochus IV, although a Greek legend attributes its establishment to Alexander the Great. The city's jurisdiction extended in the south beyond the Jabbok, in the north beyond Wadi Yābis, in the west as far as Regev (Ragaba, Rājib), and in the east to the desert. During the decline of the Seleucid kingdom, control of Geresa was seized by Zeno and Theodorus, the rulers of Philadelphia (Ammān), from whom it was captured by Alexander Yannai. It remained a Hasmonean possession until the time of Pompey after which a Jewish community continued to live in the city and maintained friendly relations with the other inhabitants. Under Roman rule the importance of the autonomous city of Gerasa increased, especially after the conquest of the Nabatean kingdom by Trajan (105 C.E.) and the establishment of the Province of Arabia. The great highway connecting Boẓrah (*Basrah) with Elath and the Red Sea passed through Gerasa making it one of the centers of the caravan trade. During the disturbances leading to the Jewish War the inhabitants of Gerasa sent the Jewish population away unharmed. Under the emperor Hadrian – who visited the city in 129/30 – and his successors, Gerasa reached the peak of its development and possessed several splendid buildings. In the time of Caracalla in the third century, the title of Roman colony was conferred on Gerasa. In the middle of the century a period of decline set in and continued until the mid-fifth century. Subsequently, however, Gerasa experienced renewed prosperity as a Christian city: its temple of Dionysus was converted into a center of Christian worship and during the years 464 to 611, 11 churches were built, one of them on the ruins of a synagogue. Gerasa's final decline was precipitated by the Muslim conquest (635). In the eighth century the city was destroyed by a series of earthquakes and during the Middle Ages it lay deserted and in ruins until Circassians settled there some time after 1878. The excavation of Gerasa by an Anglo-American expedition began in 1928. It uncovered a triumphal arch, the city wall, a hippodrome, the temple of Zeus, two theaters, the forum (circular marketplace), a columned street 2,624 feet (800 m.) long running through the city, a public fountain (*nymphaeum*), the temple of Artemis with a magnificent entrance connected to the bridge, baths, as well as the ruins of numerous churches containing mosaic pavements, decorated with representations of cities and animal and plant motifs. More than 500 Greek and Latin inscriptions were discovered in the city. The mosaic pavement of a synagogue with a Greco-Jewish inscription recording the names of its donors and representations of animals entering Noah's Ark, a candelabrum, and various sacred objects, was found under the foundations of a church built in 530–33. R. Joshua, "the Garsi," a pupil of R. Akiva (Er. 21b; Lam. R. 3:43, no. 9), may have been named after Gerasa. Since 1982 the Jerash Archaeological Project composed of an international team of investigators has been working at the site, excavating in areas on the western side of the city, particularly the Temples of Artemis and Zeus, the hippodrome, tombs, and other remains.

BIBLIOGRAPHY: Guthe, in: *Das Land Der Bibel*, 3 pt. 1–2 (1919); C.H. Kraeling (ed.), *Gerasa, City of the Decapolis* (1938); G. Lankester Harding, *The Antiquities of Jordan* (1959), 78ff. **ADD. BIBLIOGRAPHY:** I. Browning, *Jerash and the Decapolis* (1982); R.G. Khouri, *Jerash: A Frontier City of the Roman East* (1986); F. Zayadine (ed.), *Jerash Archaeological Project* (1989).

[Michael Avi-Yonah / Shimon Gibson (2nd ed.)]

GERBER, MAYNARD (1947–), cantor. Gerber was born in Chicago where he studied at a *talmud torah* as a child, then at the Hebrew High School of the Chicago Board of Jewish Education, and De Paul University. He attended the cantorial school of the Jewish Theological Seminary in New York and trained as a *mohel* (ritual circumciser) in Jerusalem. From 1971 he was a cantor, serving communities in New Jersey, New York, and Connecticut. Since 1975 (except for a two-year stint as the cantor of Kol Ami congregation in Salt Lake City) he has been the chief cantor of the Jewish Community of Stockholm, Sweden, continuing the tenure of the ḥazzan-composer Leo Rosenbluth. Gerber also appears on radio and television and was one of the first cantors to perform behind the Iron Curtain; in January 1986 he led services in the Great Synagogue in Moscow and in 1988 officiated at prayers in Leningrad. Gerber appeared on Russian television in September 1989 and was also in Tallinn, Estonia conducting services. He has written articles on cantorial and Jewish music and has produced cassettes for use in religious schools. He is a member of the American Cantors Assembly.

[Akiva Zimmerman]

GERCHUNOFF, ALBERTO (1884–1950), Argentine author, essayist, and journalist born in Proskurov, Russia. Gerchunoff arrived in Argentina as a child when his father became a pioneer settler of Moisés Ville, one of the JCA agricultural colonies financed by Baron Maurice de *Hirsch. Young Gerchunoff settled in Buenos Aires, where he became a journalist. In 1908 he joined the staff of *La Nación*, a leading daily, with which he was associated for over 40 years, part of the time as chief editor. Gerchunoff's first, and most famous, book was *Los Gauchos Judíos* (1910; *The Jewish Gauchos of the Pampas*, 1955), a collection of stories describing the life of Jewish colonists in Entre Ríos conceived by him as "a new Zion." This first Spanish account of immigration to the New World remains as the founding work of Jewish Latin American writing, though his intent to show that the return to agriculture was creating a new harmonious Jew who would enjoy full acceptance in Argentina has been strongly criticized by later generations. Gerchunoff also published books of stories such as *Cuentos de ayer* ("Stories of Yesterday," 1919) and *Historias y proezas de amor* ("Stories and Feats of Love," 1926); the autobiographical *Entre Ríos, mi país* ("Entre Ríos, My Country," 1950); and collections of essays such as *El pino y la palmera* ("The Pine and the Palm," 1952) and *La jofaina maravillosa* ("The Wondrous Washbasin," 1923). Gerchunoff was the founder and first president of the Argentine Writers' Association and was an active politician. He was detached from Jewish life for many years. Following the rise of Hitler, however, he became involved in activities against world and local antisemitism and a convinced Zionist. From 1945 onward he canvassed the support of Latin-American statesmen and politicians for the establishment of a Jewish state and was instrumental in securing their aid at the United Nations in 1947–48.

BIBLIOGRAPHY: S. Jaroslasky de Lowy, *Alberto Gerchunoff: Vida y Obra, Bibliografía-Antología* (1957), offprint from *Revista Hispánica Moderna*, 23:3–4 (1957); M. Kantor, *Sobre la obra y el anecdotario de Alberto Gerchunoff* (1960), lists all his published and unpublished work (3,000 articles and essays), offprint from *El hombre importante* (1934); *Davar*, 31–33 (Buenos Aires, 1951), special issue. **ADD. BIBLIOGRAPHY:** E. Aizenberg, *Parricide on the Pampa? A New Study and Translation of Alberto Gerchunoff's* Los gauchos judíos (2000); E. Aizenberg, *Books and Bombs in Buenos Aires. Borges, Gerchunoff and Argentine-Jewish Writing* (2002); M. Kantor, *Sobre la obra y el anecdotario de Alberto Gerchunoff* (1960); N. Lindstrom, *Jewish Issues in Argentine Literature* (1989); D.B. Lockhart, *Jewish Writers of Latin America. A Dictionary* (1997); L. Senkman, *La identidad judía en la literatura argentina* (1983).

[Florinda F. Goldbeg (2nd ed.)]

GEREZ, JOSEF HABIB (1926–), painter, poet. He was the personal secretary of the chief rabbi of Turkey, Rabbi David Asseo, between 1961 and 1985. He published several collections of poems: *Gönülden Damlalar* (1952), *Renklerin Akını* (1954), *Savrulan Zaman* (1955), *Acılı Bitimler* (1960), *Dar Açılar* (1965), *Arayış İçinde* (1967), *Büyük Güzel* (1969), and *Başını Alıp Giden Dünya* (1970), all appearing in Istanbul. He received several awards for his paintings.

GERHARDT, CHARLES FREDERIC (1816–1856), French chemist. Gerhardt, who was born in Strasbourg, was one of the earliest scientists to bring order into the chaos besetting organic chemistry in the first half of the 19th century. He worked in Paris at the beginning of the 1840s as an assistant to Jean Baptiste Dumas (1800–1884) and with Auguste Laurent (1807–1853), and the three of them were mainly responsible for reviving the radical theory of structure. Gerhardt helped Laurent to develop a classification of organic compounds, and it was he who gave the name "phenol" to the acid produced by Laurent from coal tar in 1841. He also produced a detailed exposition of the concept of atoms and molecules. Gerhardt continued to spend much of his time working in Paris after receiving a professorship at the University of Montpellier in 1844, and his appointment was terminated in 1851. He taught chemistry privately in Paris until 1855, when he was appointed professor of chemistry and pharmacy at Strasbourg University. His main works were *Précis de chimie* organique (2 vols., 1844–45) and *Traité de chimie organique* (4 vols., 1853–56). He was also editor of the *Journal chimique*.

[Samuel Aaron Miller]

GERI, JACOB (1901–1974), South African Zionist and Israeli industrialist. Born in Lithuania, he was brought up in South Africa where he studied law. In 1934 he immigrated to Palestine and, after a short spell as a worker in an orange grove, joined the law firm of Dov *Joseph. Shortly after, however, he accepted an invitation to join the African Palestine Investments (API), of which he became chairman in 1956, and devoted himself to other South African commercial enterprises in Israel. His most important achievement in the industrial field was the establishment, by the API, of Savyon, the first garden-city in Israel. In 1950, though belonging to no political party, he was invited by Ben-Gurion to join the cabinet as minister of commerce and industry, the only nonparty member. He resigned in 1953 because of disagreement with Ben-Gurion's policies.

[Louis Isaac Rabinowitz]

GERIZIM, MOUNT (Heb. הַר גְּרִזִּים), mountain in Ereẓ Israel, S. of Shechem. After crossing the Jordan River, the children of Israel were commanded to build a stone altar on Mt. Ebal, to engrave upon it "all the words of this law" (Deut. 27:4–8), and to "set the blessing upon Mt. Gerizim, and the curse upon Mt. Ebal" (*ibid.* 11:29; 27:12–13). According to Joshua 8:30, this was Joshua's first act after the conquest of Ai. Har-Gerizzim (as written in the masoretic text; Har Gerizim, according to *Ben-Asher; usually Hargerizim in the traditional Samaritan text of the Pentateuch) is the present-day Jebel al-Ṭūr (shortened from the Samaritan name Tura Brikha). Mt. Gerizim and Mt. Ebal rise above the city of Shechem (Nablus), in the south and north respectively; Gerizim is approximately 2,600 ft. (881 m.) high and Ebal approximately 2,800 ft. (940 m.). Between them lies the valley of Shechem. Both hills are composed of oolithic limestone, ten springs descending from their slopes to the fertile and well-watered valley. Mt. Ebal has comparatively little vegetation and no water issuing along its southern side, because the slope of the tilted rock is northward; one exception is at the southeast end of Ebal, where a spring makes it possible for the village of Askar to exist. The slopes of Mt. Gerizim, on the other hand, are covered with trees to the very top of the ridge, and the slope of the rock causes the main springs to issue on the side of the valley facing the city of Shechem. The contrast in the amount of water on the two sides of the valley is very marked. A pilgrim's legend from the Middle Ages, which has often been reprinted, relates that Mt. Gerizim, the blessed mountain (Deut. 11:29), is pleasant and fertile, while Mt. Ebal, cursed by divine decree (*ibid.*), is desolate and barren.

The identification of the two mountains is made clear in the Bible (Deut. 11:29–30; cf. Gen. 12:6; Judg. 9:7), and this identification is maintained throughout the sources (Sot. 7:5; Jos., Ant., 4:305; 11:340) down to modern times. As a result of an obscure topographical identification in Deuteronomy 11:30 – "Are they not beyond the Jordan, behind the way of the going down of the sun, in the land of the Canaanites that dwell in the Arabah, over against Gilgal, beside the terebinths of Moreh?" – and apparently in the wake of a dispute with the Samaritans, another tradition, ascribed to R. Eliezer, appears in the Talmud, which identifies the two mountains with two mounds which the children of Israel erected for themselves near Gilgal, and not with the two mountains near Shechem (TJ, Sot. 1:3, 21c; TB, Sot. 33b). This view was later adopted by the fathers of the Christian Church (Eusebius, Onom. 64:1920). On the Madaba Map, both traditions appear: next to Shechem is written Tur Garizin, and next to Jericho Ebal-Gerizin. Apparently, the Bible does not mean to imply that these two mountains are situated in the Arabah near Gilgal, but simply refers to the general direction in order to distinguish between this Arabah and the Arabah associated with the hill-country of the Amorites (Deut. 1:1; 4:49). Perhaps "behind the way of the going down of the sun" indicates the region west of the road which passes through the northern Arabah (from Jericho to Beth-Shean).

Later Mt. Gerizim is mentioned when the Samaritans erected their temple there about the time of Nehemiah (in the time of Alexander the Great, according to Jos., Ant., 11:310–11, but this is apparently a mistake; cf. Neh. 13:28, according to which a man of priestly stock was cast out by Nehemiah for intermarriage with the Samaritans). From then on, the Samaritans considered this temple to be their most holy spot, and their tradition ascribes nearly all of the biblical account of the patriarchs' deeds and the places associated with them (the land of Moriah, Beth-El, etc.) to Mt. Gerizim. There are 13 names for Mt. Gerizim, the "Kibla" of the Samaritans, the place toward which they turn in prayer. The fourth of the five articles in the declaration of their creed proclaims its holiness. *Markah dedicated a whole chapter in his *Memar* to the praise of this mountain (II, 10) in connection with Ex. 15. He enumerates it as one of the choicest things created by God and set apart as divine. The Samaritan text for Deuteronomy 27:4–5 reads: "And it shall be when ye are passed over the Jordan, that ye shall set up these stones, which I command you this day, in Mt. Gerizim" (in place of Mt. Ebal in the masoretic text; cf. Sot. 33b). It is of interest that they even add Mt. Gerizim at the end of the Ten Commandments in both Exodus 20:17 and Deuteronomy 5:21, considering it to be the chosen mountain (*Har ha-Mivḥar*), even from the time of the creation of the world. (The Samaritans read *baḥar*, "has chosen," for the masoretic text *yibḥar*, "will choose," in Deut. 12:14.) The Samaritans gave it the title "mountain of blessing" or "blessed mount" (Tūrbarīk; Samaritan Book of Joshua, ch. 21; Gen. R. 32:10; Song. R. 4:4, no. 5; Tura Brikha; Deut. R. 3:6; Tura Kaddisha) and they claimed that the mountain was not submerged at the time of the Flood (*ibid.*).

Mt. Gerizim became the main point of divergence between the Samaritans and the Jews. (Cf. the end of Kut.: "At what point can the Samaritans be accepted into Judaism? When they reject their belief in Mt. Gerizim.") In the time of Ptolemy I Soter (323–284 B.C.E.), there was an argument over this point between the Samaritans and the Jews of Alexandria (Jos., Ant., 12:1ff.). When Antiochus IV Epiphanes passed decrees against the Jews, he converted the Samaritan temple on Mt. Gerizim into a pagan shrine in honor of Zeus Xenios or Hellenios (II Macc. 5:23; 6:1; Jos., Ant., 12:257ff.). This temple was destroyed in 129 B.C.E. by John Hyrcanus (Jos., Ant., 13:255ff.; cf. Meg. Ta'an. 333). However, it remained a holy site for the Samaritans, and all religious acts were performed "in the name of Mt. Gerizim" (TJ, Yev. 8:1, 9a). Due to the Samaritan belief in the ancient sanctity of the mountain, the Roman procurator Pontius Pilate massacred a large gathering of Samaritans who had assembled to look at vessels which Moses allegedly made for the Tabernacle and which one of the Samaritans claimed he would show them (these vessels had supposedly been concealed on Mt. Gerizim; Jos., Ant., 18:85).

In the war against Rome (66–70), the Samaritans joined the rebellion and assembled on Mt. Gerizim to halt the Romans, in spite of the news they had received that the Jews of Galilee had been defeated. Vespasian sent Cerialis, commander of the fifth legion, against them and he besieged them with 3,000 infantry and 600 cavalry. The Roman troops massacred more than 11,000 of the Samaritans on the 27th of Sivan, 67 C.E. (Jos., Wars, 3:307ff.). After the war of Bar Kokhba (132–135) the emperor Hadrian erected a pagan shrine to Zeus Hypsistos (or to Serapis) on the top of Mt. Gerizim and placed the bronze gates from the Temple in Jerusalem there. From the time of Antoninus Pius onward, this sanctuary appears on the coins of Neapolis, the city which Titus had built on the site of the village of Ma'abarta, near ancient Shechem. In the time of the emperor *Julian, this sanctuary was destroyed and the Samaritans used the bronze gates as the door of the synagogue (*ha-knishah*) called Ḥelkat ha-Sadeh, which their priest Akbon built in the city of Neapolis. Another synagogue was erected by Akbon's predecessor, Baba Rabbah, "near Mt. Gerizim, Beth-El," "below the mountain" (apparently the site of the present-day Rijl al-ʿAmūd), in the time of Theodosius I (379–395 C.E.).

With the predominance of Christianity in the country, the religious status of the Samaritans suffered. Judging from John 4, Gerizim was also a sacred spot for the Christians. After a Samaritan uprising in the time of Zeno (474–491 C.E.), the Samaritans were expelled from the mountain and their synagogue was taken from them by command of the emperor (484 C.E.). The Christians erected a Church of the Virgin Mary there and placed a stone from Calvary in it. Following a Samaritan rebellion in the time of Justinian, the area around the church on Mt. Gerizim was encompassed by a fortified wall. In the time of the caliph al-Manṣūr (754–755), the Christian church was destroyed, and under al-Ma'mūn (813–833) Justinian's wall was razed.

Remains of buildings sacred to the Samaritans still stand on the mountain (Khirbat al-Lūza; al-Ṣakhra ("the rock"); the place of the 12 stones). There are also remains of the Church of the Virgin Mary and Justinian's wall. The remains of the church were excavated by a German expedition during 1927–28 and by the Department of Antiquities of the British Mandatory government in 1946. It is on Mt. Gerizim that the Samaritans still observe all their festivals and all public holy ceremonies, as the sacrifice of the paschal lamb, and prayers on all their feasts and holidays. The entire congregation dwells on its slopes from the tenth of Nisan until the day after the end of the Maẓẓot Festival. Today houses have been built to accommodate them instead of the tents of former years. The offering takes place not on the top of the mountain, the holiest spot where their temple once stood, but at a lower place to the west of it, possibly because the holy spot has been defiled by a Muslim cemetery.

[Yehoshua M. Grintz]

Later Findings

Since 1979 major excavations have been undertaken at the site of Mt. Gerizim under the direction of Yitzhak Magen, in the area of the Samaritan temple and settlement. It is now possible to trace the development of the Samaritan temple, its structure and history, and the cult performed there. Mt. Gerizim served as a religious center which existed parallel to that of the Jerusalem Temple. Various architectural remains, notably carved capitals, date back to the Iron Age. The excavations brought to light substantial portions of the Hellenistic city, with its fortifications, separate quarters, public buildings, and dwellings. On the top of the hill were fortified buildings and a temple esplanade which was approached by a monumental flight of steps. From the Byzantine period are the remains of an enclosure and church from the time of Zeno, and an enclosure from the time of Justinian. About 400 inscriptions, most of a dedicatory character, were brought to light in the recent excavations, written in ancient Hebrew, Aramaic, and Samaritan, with an additional 80 inscriptions in Greek, mostly from the third–fourth centuries B.C.E.

[Shimon Gibson (2nd ed.)]

BIBLIOGRAPHY: N. Adler (ed.), *The Travels of R. Benjamin of Tudela* (1908), 22–23; I. Ben Zvi, *Sefer ha-Shomeronim* (1935); Conder-Kitchener, 2 (1882), 186ff.; J. Montgomery, *The Samaritans* (1907; repr. 1968); Abel, Geog, 1 (1933), 360ff.; A. Reifenberg, in: *Eretz Israel*, 1 (1951), 74ff.; A.M. Schneider, in: ZDPV, 68 (1951), 211ff.; G.E. Wright, *Shechem: The Biography of a Biblical City* (1965). **ADD. BIBLIOGRAPHY:** Y. Magen, "The Church of Theotokos on Mount Gerizim," in: G. Bottini et al. (eds.), *Christian Archaeology in the Holy Land, New Discoveries* (1990), 333–42; idem, "Mount Gerizim – A Temple City: Summary of Eighteen Years of Excavations," in: *Qadmoniot*, 33

(2000), 74–118; E. Stern and Y. Magen, "The First Phase of the Samaritan Temple on Mount Gerizim," in: *Qadmoniot*, 33 (2000), 119–24; Y. Magen et al., "The Hebrew and Aramaic Inscriptions from Mount Gerizim," in: *Qadmoniot*, 33 (2000), 125–32; Y. Magen, "Mount Gerizim During the Roman and Byzantine Periods," in: *Qadmoniot*, 33 (2000), 133–43.

GERMAN LITERATURE.

Biblical and Hebraic Influences

Before the *Aufklaerung* (Age of Enlightenment), Jewish influences in German literature were essentially biblical and Hebraic. The medieval miracle or mystery plays, in Germany as in England and France, dramatized Old Testament themes and treated the Hebrew patriarchs with reverence, but the "passion plays" based on the New Testament made the post-biblical Jew a demonic ally of the Devil. For special historical reasons, this latter portrayal came to have serious popular repercussions. The impact of the Bible itself has been traced to the earliest contact of the Germanic tribes with missionary Christianity. In the fourth century the Gothic bishop Ulfilas (or Wulfila) wrote a Teutonic version of the Bible, from which only a few verses are extant, and, early in the 11th century, Job and the Psalms were translated into Old High German by Notker Labeo of St. Gallen (c. 950–1022), whose Psalter alone is extant. A late 11th-century prose version of the Song of Songs (c. 1065) by Williram familiarized the Germans with its traditional author, King Solomon, whose legendary wisdom, fortified by tales brought back to Europe by the crusaders, soon became a stock literary theme.

BIBLE TRANSLATIONS. The first printed version of the Bible in High German (1466) has been traced to an anonymous 14th-century translator. Based on the Latin (Vulgate) text and printed in Strasbourg, this was the model for 13 subsequent pre-Lutheran editions. The first printed version of the Bible in Low German appeared in 1477. Both German versions, of course, conformed with Roman Catholic doctrine. By contrast, the German reformer Martin *Luther produced a complete translation of the Bible (6 vols., 1534, revised 11 times up to 1545) which was based on the original tongues, notably the Hebrew of the Old Testament. Luther's text injected the thought patterns of the Hebrew Bible into the German language, where the Hebrew simile and metaphor were speedily absorbed. His magnificent version was written in the Saxon dialect, which thus became the principal vehicle of High German language and literature. This was a somewhat curious achievement, since High German was the language of predominantly Catholic south Germany, whereas Low German was spoken in the Protestant north; but the fact that German Catholics found Luther's Bible readily accessible ensured its widespread success. The German Protestant Bible had a greater influence on the language of its readers than any other comparable work except the English Authorized Version. It became the most widely read book in the German tongue, constituted Germany's greatest literary achievement in the 16th century, and was of immeasurable significance in stabilizing the language. Although other German translations were attempted by Luther's contemporaries and successors, it was not until the 20th century that, under Jewish auspices, a comparable version of the Hebrew Bible appeared, published by Martin *Buber and Franz *Rosenzweig.

See also *Bible, Translations.

A post-biblical Hebraic influence on German literature much in evidence during the 16th century was the Kabbalah, the Christian interpretation of which found a pioneer exponent in Johann *Reuchlin. His *De verbo mirifico* (1494) and *De arte cabalistica* (1517), though written in Latin, created a vogue for Hebrew studies in German scholarly circles, and Reuchlin's followers included Wolfgang Fabricius *Capito, Conrad *Pellicanus, Sebastian *Muenster, and Paulus *Fagius. The movement gained its widest support among the Lutherans. Another Protestant, Jacob Boehme (1575–1624), developed a mystical system largely inspired by the Christian Kabbalah.

BIBLICAL DRAMA. Martin Luther and his fellow-reformers fostered the writing of biblical plays in both Latin and German. Sixtus Birck dramatized not only episodes from the Bible – *Zorobabel* (1538), *Ezechias* (1538), and *Joseph* (1539) – but also the apocryphal tales of *Susanna* and *Judith* (both 1532). The Judith story was also dramatized in 1551 by the Nuremberg poet and *Meistersinger*, Hans Sachs. Sachs' biblical plays included among others *Der Wueterich Herodes* (1552) and *Tragedia Koenig Sauls* (1557), and others on themes such as Esther (1530), Job (1547), Adam and Eve (1548), Cain and Abel (1553), and David (1556). A century later, Christian Weise took all the themes of his religious plays from the Old Testament, believing that the figure of Jesus ought not to appear on the stage. His dramas included *Der verfolgte David* (1683), *Nebukadnezar* (1683), *Athalia* (1687), and *Kain und Abel* (1704). Weise was followed by the Swiss poet and playwright Johann Jacob Bodmer, who published a German translation of *Milton's *Paradise Lost* in 1732 and later wrote dramatic poems about Joseph (*Jakob und Joseph*, 1751; *Joseph und Zulika*, 1753), the Flood (*Die Synd-Flut*, 1751), Noah (1752[2]), Adam (1763), Solomon (1764), and Abraham (1778). Bodmer's fellow-Swiss, Solomon Gessner, roused interest in the Cain theme with his sentimental prose epic, *Der Tod Abels* (1758). Its English translation (1761) enjoyed enormous success and is said to have inspired works on the same subject by Coleridge and *Byron. Germany's first major modern poet, Friedrich Gottlieb Klopstock, who was influenced by Milton and Bodmer, is best remembered for his epic *Der Messias* (1749–73). He also wrote the plays *Der Tod Adams* (1757), *Salomo* (1764), and *David* (1772). Another 18th-century Swiss author, Johann Kaspar Lavater, wrote *Abraham und Isaak* (1776). The biblical element in German literature received a valuable stimulus in the late 18th century with the publication by Johann Gottfried *Herder of his two-volume work *Vom Geist der Ebraeischen Poesie* (1782–83). In his *Adrastea* (1802) Herder published a German version of the **Lekhah Dodi* hymn by Solomon *Alkabeẓ. Friedrich *Schiller wrote essays on biblical themes and echoed the Bible in tragedies such as *Die Jungfrau von Orleans* (1802). Johann Wolfgang von *Goethe drew inspiration from the Bible for his great tragedy, *Faust* (1808), whose "Prologue in Heaven" is modeled on the early chapters of Job. Other 19th-century playwrights who wrote on biblical themes were Karl Ferdinand Gutzkow (*Koenig Saul*, 1839), Friedrich Rueckert (*Saul und David*, 1843; *Herodes der Grosse*, 1844), and Austria's leading playwright, Franz Grillparzer (*Esther*, 1877), while a theme from the Apocrypha was dramatized by Otto Ludwig (*Die Makkabaeer*, 1854). Gutzkow's very popular *Uriel Acosta* (1847) entered the Yiddish as well as the German repertoire. Friedrich Hebbel wrote *Judith* (1841), about the heroine of the Apocrypha, but his outstanding "Hebraic" drama was *Herodes und Mariamne* (1850), based on Josephus.

Only a few Jewish writers in 19th-century Germany and Austria dealt with biblical or later historical themes of Jewish interest. Ludwig *Robert wrote the drama *Die Tochter Jephthas* (1820) and Karl *Beck the tragedy *Saul* (1841). Poems on biblical and post-biblical Jewish subjects were written by Heinrich *Heine and Seligmann *Heller, whose works include *Die letzten Hasmonaeer* (1865) and *Ahasver* (1868).

THE BIBLE IN 20TH-CENTURY GERMAN LITERATURE. From 1900 onward there was a considerable increase in German works of biblical inspiration. *Das Buch Joram* (1907) by Rudolf Borchardt, who was of partly Jewish descent, was a pastiche of the Book of Job set in the time of Jesus. *Die juedische Witwe* (1911) by Georg Kaiser, based on the heroic apocryphal tale of Judith and Holofernes, was, unlike so many of these works, a comedy. Jewish writers played an increasingly important role, with Siegfried *Lipiner dramatizing the story of *Adam* (1911), a theme that similarly inspired Arno *Nadel (1917). The same subject was dealt with in some post-World War I poems by the Viennese lyricist Josef Weinheber and in the epic *Erschaffung der Eva* (1941) by the Austrian Franz Karl Ginzkey. The story of Cain prompted a tragedy by another Viennese writer, Anton Wildgans (1920), and that of Noah, Ernst Barlach's drama, *Die Suendflut* (1924). Richard *Beer-Hofmann wrote a mystical drama, *Jaakobs Traum* (1918).

Thomas *Mann's trilogy, *Joseph und Seine Brueder* (1933–42; *Joseph and His Brothers*, 1934–45), was the climax of a vast array of German works based on the story of Joseph, headed by some 26 dramas in the 16th century and by the 17th-century novels of Hans Jakob Christoffel von Grimmelshausen (1667) and Philipp von Zesen (*Assenat*, 1670). Hugo von *Hofmannsthal's only biblical work was *Die Josephlegende* (1914), written for a ballet. The Samson theme was dramatized by Herbert Eulenberg (1910), Frank Wedekind (1914), Hermann Burte (1917), and Karl Roettger (1921). The tragic figure of King Saul attracted Karl *Wolfskehl (1905), Paul *Heyse (1909), and Beer-Hofmann (*Der junge David*, 1933). The romance of David and Bathsheba was dramatized by Lion *Feuchtwanger in *Das Weib des Urias* (1905), and another episode in the life of the Psalmist inspired Arnold *Zweig's *Abigail und Nabal* (1913). Feuchtwanger also wrote a novel on the sacrifice of Jephthah's daughter (1957), a theme previously dramatized by Ernst *Lissauer (1928). The best-known work of Sammy *Gronemann is his comedy *Der Weise und der Narr: Koenig Salomo und der Schuster* (1942).

Other 20th-century writers were drawn to stories from the Prophets and Hagiographa. Jeremiah inspired an anti-war drama by Stefan *Zweig (1917) for which Arno Nadel wrote the music, and Job was the subject of a popular novel by Joseph *Roth (1930). Esther provided the theme of a drama by Felix *Braun (1926), another by Max *Brod (1918), and a Purim play by Sammy Gronemann (*Hamans Flucht*, 1926). Later Jewish historical figures who inspired 20th-century German fiction were Josephus, the hero of a trilogy by Feuchtwanger (1932–42); Rabbi Akiva, in a play by Moritz *Heimann (1922); the hero of Max *Brod's novel, *Rëubeni, Fuerst der Juden* (1925); and the *Jewess of Toledo, who figures in a late novel by Feuchtwanger (*Spanische Ballade*, 1955). The legend of the **golem* formed the theme of a novel by Gustav Meyrink (1915) and Jew Suess was the hero of Feuchtwanger's most famous novel (1925).

Hebrew and Yiddish Influences on the German Language

As with English and French, so in the case of German, certain biblical terms entered the language at a fairly early stage, mainly through the writings of churchmen. Luther's Bible brought a vastly increased number of words and phrases into general usage. Some have become German idioms, including *Kainszeichen* (the mark of Cain, Gen. 4:15); *Suendenbock* (scapegoat, Lev. 16); *Salomonisches Urteil* (the judgment of Solomon, I Kings 3:16ff.); *Gott mit uns* (*Immanuel*, Isa. 7:14); *Menschensohn* (son of man, Ezek. 2:1ff.). Hebrew loanwords also entered German at various periods. These include *Abt* (abbot < Aramaic *abba*), *Ebenholz* (ebony < *even*), *Fratze* (face, mug < *parẓuf*), and *Natro* (soda < *neter*). More than any other European language, not excluding English, German is peculiarly rich in other terms and expressions, mainly slang or colloquialisms, which entered everyday speech through *Yiddish and the *Juden-Deutsch* (West Yiddish) dialect spoken by German Jews. Most of these were, of course, restricted to Jewish circles, including *Schabbes, Jonteff, Mischpoche* or *Muschpoke, Goi, Schickse, Schadchen, meschugge, benschen, daffke*, and *nebbich* (< *nicht bei Euch*). In the 15th and 16th centuries, however, others entered general use, probably by way of thieves' slang; *acheln*, to eat (< *akhal*), *ganfen*, to steal (< *ganav*), *Schaute*, fool (< *shoteh*). The 18th century added words like *Mackes*, blows (< *makkot*), *schmusen*, to chat, *Schmuser*, chatterbox (< *shemu'ot*), and *Stuss*, nonsense (< *shetut*). In the 19th century a host of other such expressions became familiar, notably *Golem, Kaffer*, boor (< *kefar*), *koscher, Rischess*, antisemitism (< *rishut*), *schaechten*, to defraud, overreach (< *shaḥat*), *Schlemihl*, schlemiel (< *Shelumiel*?), and *Zores*, trouble (< *ẓarot*). Despite periodic "purifications" of the German language, a vast number of these Hebraisms and Yiddishisms still occur in German dictionaries and other works of reference. Heine, in his poem "Prinzessin Sabbat" (*Roman-*

zero, 1851), humorously alluding to Schiller's "Ode to Joy," described *tcholent* as "koscheres Ambrosia"; while Adelbert von Chamisso entitled his world-famous story about the man who lost his shadow *Peter Schlemihls wundersame Geschichte* (1814). Conversely, Heine's pathetic "Jewish" refrain in the poem "Gedaechtnisfeier" (in the collection *Romanzero*), "Nicht gedacht soll seiner werden," is taken directly from Luther's translation of Ezek. 21:37.

The Image of the Jew in German Literature

German attitudes toward the Jews, shaped by religious, economic, and social factors, were clearly mirrored in German literature. The earliest recorded Old High German literature, largely written by Christian clerics, depicted Jews as simultaneously God's chosen people and as the "people accursed." On the one hand, Jews were kinsmen of the Christian savior and descendants of revered patriarchs and prophets; on the other, they were supposedly guilty of deicide, had fallen from grace, and had been condemned to eternal scorn and wandering (see also the *Wandering Jew).

THE MEDIEVAL STEREOTYPE. Medieval German drama, from the primitive mystery plays dealing with the life and death of Jesus to the spectacular passion plays staged at Easter, presented a cruel and abhorrent image of the Jew. In these plays Jews were shown to be far more the people of Judas than of Jesus. The most famous of the passion plays – that of Oberammergau, Bavaria – has been performed roughly once every ten years since 1634. It was banned for a time in the 18th century and, strangely enough, during the Hitler era, the Nazis evidently allowing anti-religious policy to outweigh their hatred of the Jews. In 1969 a few textual modifications were made on the recommendation of the Catholic Church in order to remove offensive anti-Jewish passages. Folktales and folksongs also spread the legend that Jews habitually engaged in the crucifixion of Christian boys to provide blood for the Passover ritual. The stories of "Good Werner" (1286) and Simon of Trent (1475) popularized the *blood libel in Germany and provided a counterpart to the English martyrologies of *Hugh of Lincoln and William of Norwich.

Upon the earliest literary image, which had its source in religion, was superimposed another, which had its source in economics: the Jew as usurer. Usury was defined by the Church as the lending of money at interest. Since Christians were forbidden to engage in such moneylending, Jews had a virtual monopoly until the Lombards arrived on the German scene. In the sermons of Berthold von Regensburg (c. 1210–1272), the most popular Franciscan preacher of the mid-13th century, Jew and usurer were synonymous. Easter plays included a comic interlude: the three Marys buying oil to anoint the body of the crucified Jesus from a merchant depicted as a wily, haggling Jew. As an object of ridicule, the Jew also made his entry into the *Fastnachtsspiele* (Shrovetide plays). Hans Folz (c. 1450–c. 1515), a *Meistersinger* of Worms and Nuremberg, was a notable exponent of this genre. In one of his plays rabbinic Judaism is unfavorably contrasted with Christianity and the **Adon Olam* hymn is sung in a German rhymed adaptation. In another farce, a student seduces a Jewess and then mocks her parents and her religion. The Middle High German stereotype of the grasping Jew passed into early New High German literature. In the first published version of the Faust legend – the anonymous *Faustbuch* of 1587 – Faust borrows money from a Jew, who accepts one of his legs as security. Faust saws off the leg, but when he comes to redeem his pledge the Jew cannot return it and has to pay compensation. *Der Jude von Venetien*, a German adaptation by Christoph Bluemel of *Shakespeare's *Merchant of Venice* performed in the 1660s, stressed the greed and hardheartedness of the Jew who insists on his pound of flesh and finally loses his entire investment.

The dominant literary image of the Jew throughout the 16th and 17th centuries was characterized by hostility and ridicule. Though a spirited defense of Hebrew literature was undertaken by Johann Reuchlin and other German humanists in their struggle against the slanders of the apostate Johannes *Pfefferkorn, Martin Luther's embittered diatribe, *Von den Jueden und jren Luegen* (1543), subsequently reinforced the hostile image of the Jew.

18TH-CENTURY ASSESSMENTS. Not until the 18th century was a major breach made in this portrayal. Gotthold Ephraim *Lessing gave the first favorable presentation of Jews in his comedy, *Die Juden* (1749), and later in his internationally famous *Nathan der Weise* (1779). The hero of this philosophical drama, a wise and benevolent Jew, was the mouthpiece for the writer's doctrines of religious tolerance and universal brotherhood. Lessing's model for Nathan was Moses *Mendelssohn, whose mind and character deeply impressed contemporary German intellectuals. "Nathan the Wise" thus became the symbol of the enlightened Jew.

From the late 18th century German Jews and Christians mingled in Berlin salons and influenced each other's religious, philosophical, and literary expression. Jewish salon hostesses inspired German poets and were mirrored in German novels, creating the image of the educated, dignified, and freethinking Jewess. The Romantic movement, which succeeded the Enlightenment, was also ambivalent in its portrayal of Jews. Some Romantic writers, such as Adelbert von Chamisso, Bettina von Arnim, and Karl August Varnhagen von Ense, treated Jewish themes, characters, and legends in a sympathetic manner. On the other hand, some writers – especially those in the Berlin circle of Bettina's husband, Achim von Arnim – regarded Jews with enmity and disdain. Arnim himself perpetuated the idea of the Jew's dual nature as eternal witness and repulsive merchant in his drama, *Halle und Jerusalem* (1811).

THE 19TH-CENTURY PORTRAIT. The intensification of German nationalism during the struggle against Napoleon led writers to depict Jews as outsiders and eternal wanderers. It encouraged virulent antisemitism at a time when Jewish intellectuals were straining toward complete integration in German society, baptism being accepted by many as a corollary of assimilation and as (in Heine's sardonic phrase) "a ticket of admission to German culture." Ludwig *Boerne and Heine both had a profound impact upon the post-Napoleonic generation. As the leaders of *Jungdeutschland* ("Young Germany"), a liberal literary movement, they paved the way for the Revolution of 1848 and both were outspoken champions of Jewish emancipation. Heine's onetime ally, Wolfgang Menzel, derided "Young Germany" as in reality "Young Palestine." While Berthold *Auerbach, in his polemic pamphlet, *Das Judenthum und die neueste Literatur* (1836), defended the Jews against the charge of revolutionary radicalism hurled at them by the apostles of Teutonism, the prominence of Jews among the pioneers of Socialism – men such as Moses *Hess, Karl *Marx, and Ferdinand *Lassalle – reinforced the image of the Jew as a subversive element undermining the established political and social systems. The gifted orator and pamphleteer Gabriel *Riesser denied the existence of a distinct Jewish nationality, but Moses Hess, parting company with the Socialist doctrinaires, strongly affirmed Jewish nationalism in his *Rom und Jerusalem* (1862; *Rome and Jerusalem*, 1918), which called for the reestablishment of a Jewish state in Zion.

During the 19th century Jewish themes increasingly infiltrated German drama and fiction. In her novella *Die Judenbuche* (1842), Annette von Droste-Huelshoff told a grim tale of the avenging of the murder of a Jew, even inserting a cryptic Hebrew phrase into her story. Franz Grillparzer, Friedrich Hebbel, and Otto Ludwig extolled the Jewish past and presented biblical and Jewish historical characters quite different from the old stereotypes. Grillparzer's *Die Juedin von Toledo* (1873), based on the tragic romance of Alfonso VII of Castile and the Jewess of Toledo, was the forerunner of many other treatments of this theme. On the other hand, novelists who dealt with the Jewish present continued to portray the Jew as a villain. Gustav Freytag wrote a best-selling novel, *Soll und Haben* (1854), which reinforced the image of the Jewish usurer, contrasting the noble, loyal, and hardworking Christian apprentice Anton with his rascally Jewish fellow-worker, Veitel Itzig, who comes to a sorry end. In *Der Hungerpastor* (1864), the best-known novel of Wilhelm Raabe, another Jew follows the wicked example of Veitel Itzig; while Felix Dahn's novel, *Ein Kampf um Rom* (1876), extols German racial purity and presents the Jew, Jochem, as cowardly and treacherous.

A somewhat glamorized picture of Jewish life was presented by Leopold *Kompert (*Boehmische Juden*, 1851; *Neue Geschichten aus dem Ghetto*, 1860) and Karl Emil *Franzos (*Die Juden von Barnow*, 1877). The setting of Kompert's tales was Bohemia and that of Franzos', Galicia. Austrian Galicia was also the setting of many novels and stories by the non-Jewish writer, Leopold Ritter von Sacher-Masoch. Sacher-Masoch, whose later erotic works gave rise to the term "masochism," was the son of an Austrian police chief in Letoberg (Lvov), and his early impressions of Jewish life there inspired his *Judengeschichten* (1878), *Polnische Ghetto-geschichten* (1886), and *Juedisches Leben in Wort und Bild* (1890). His obvious sympathy for the East European Jew's tenacious adherence to his religion and culture subjected him to considerable abuse. The works of Kompert, Franzos, and Sacher-Masoch enjoyed quite a vogue as exotic literature, but it was not until Georg *Hermann wrote the novel *Jettchen Gebert* (1906) and its sequel, *Henriette Jacoby* (1909), that cultured German Jewry received adequate treatment in German fiction.

LATER REACTIONS. When Friedrich Nietzsche wrote in 1886 in *Jenseits von Gut und Boese* that he had never yet met a German who was favorably inclined to Jews, he was undoubtedly exaggerating, but he correctly recognized that in Germany the age-old image of the Jew was an unflattering one. Although his close association with Richard *Wagner had brought him into contact with an outspoken antisemite, Nietzsche himself abhorred antisemitism as the revolt of the rabble against culture, and condemned it in the most violent terms. While Nietzsche foresaw a glorious future for Jews on the world scene, another influential German philosopher, Oswald Spengler, held that Judaism had already completed its historic function and was on the verge of disappearing. In *Der Untergang des Abendlandes* (1922) he was at pains to stress the intense mutual hatred between Germans and Jews, and the "inevitable conflict" between a vigorous young culture rooted in the soil and a senile, overripe civilization of landless cosmopolitans. Spengler's vaunted objectivity was soon to supply Nazi ideologists and literary racists with ammunition for their perverted theories.

The late 19th century saw a reaction to German literary antisemitism on the part of a few isolated Jewish writers, notably Max *Nordau and Theodor *Herzl, both of them fathers of the Zionist movement. Nordau's tragedy, *Doktor Kohn* (1898), concluded that assimilation was impossible and that a solution to Jewish misery had to be found elsewhere; while Herzl, in his utopian novel *Altneuland* (1902), projected his answer into an idealized Jewish state. Arthur *Schnitzler, neither a Zionist nor an assimilationist, presented an admirable Jewish physician in his drama *Professor Bernhardi* (1912), which attacked antisemitism. With few exceptions, the major non-Jewish writers sided with the Jews in their battle for self-preservation. Although Artur Dinter anticipated the Nazis with his hate-filled *Die Suende wider das Blut* (1917), modern authors of the stature of Gerhart Hauptmann and Thomas Mann remained aloof from the rising tide of nationalism. In his tragicomedy, *Der rote Hahn* (1901), and in his drama, *Die Finsternisse* (1947), which had to be smuggled out of Nazi Germany, Hauptmann paid tribute to the fruitful liberalism of German Jewry. There were sympathetic Jewish characters in Mann's works, too, especially in *Koenigliche Hoheit* (1909) and *Der Zauberberg* (1924). A certain objectivity characterizes the Jewish portrayals of Ernst Glaeser (*Jahrgang 1902*, 1928) and Gertrud von Le Fort (*Der Papst aus dem Ghetto*, 1930).

PRELUDE TO CATASTROPHE. During the first third of the 20th century, the Jewish influence on German literature reached its climax. The image which Jewish writers incorporated in their works ranged from the self-hatred of Maximilian *Harden, Karl *Kraus, Kurt *Tucholsky, and Otto *Weininger to the strong affirmation of national resurgence by Martin Buber, Richard Beer-Hofmann, Max Brod, and Arnold Zweig. Joseph Roth dramatized the conflict between the authentic and the assimilated Jew; Walter *Mehring identified the Jews with the capitalists responsible for the inflation; and Hans José *Rehfisch and Wilhelm Herzog dramatized European antisemitism in *Die Affaire Dreyfus* (1929). Stefan Zweig saw the Jew as the precursor of the good European and Ernst *Toller fought German racial conceit by espousing cosmopolitanism and utopian Socialism.

Aryan mythmakers from Houston Stewart *Chamberlain to Alfred *Rosenberg propagated the fiction of blood as the determining psychic factor. Nazi writers fed the Germans an image of the Jew as an hereditary criminal, and branded as a fairy tale the possibility that baptism could emancipate the Jew from his criminal tendencies. With the triumph of Nazi ideology in 1933, all favorable images of the Jew were suppressed by literary, stage, and radio censors. Only in exile could Thomas and Heinrich Mann and other writers of non-Jewish origin present a more balanced image of the Jew. Most German émigré writers on Jewish themes were, however, either Jews or of Jewish descent. They included Arthur *Koestler, Lion Feuchtwanger, Karl *Wolfskehl, Arnold Zweig, Hermann *Kesten, Alfred *Doeblin, and Else *Lasker-Schueler. The few courageous voices that were heard from the "Aryan" side included those of the baptized half-Jew Carl *Zuckmayer, who had shown Jewish faults and virtues to be common to all men in such works as his drama *Der Hauptmann von Koepenick* (1930); Wolfgang Langhoff, whose *Die Moorsoldaten* (1935) was the first literary account of Nazi brutality in the concentration camps; and Bertolt Brecht, who developed a similar theme in *Furcht und Elend des Dritten Reiches* (1941). Like their Jewish fellow-writers, however, Zuckmayer, Langhoff, and Brecht were finally compelled to take refuge abroad, and it was not until after World War II that a more dispassionate assessment of the Jewish image in German literature could be attempted.

[Sol Liptzin]

The Jewish Contribution to German Literature

Jews first settled along the Rhine in Roman times and they have thus been an integral element in German culture from its earliest beginnings. In the Middle Ages, the Middle High German which they spoke became interspersed with Hebrew words and, following waves of persecution, was carried eastward to become the Yiddish language (i.e., *Juedisch-Deutsch*). Those Jews who remained in Germany developed a kindred dialect, *Judendeutsch*, and it was in this more distinctly Germanic tongue that Glueckel of *Hameln wrote her famous memoirs at the end of the 17th century. German Jewry can, however, lay claim to one authentic Jewish contributor to medieval German literature – the *Minnesaenger* (minstrel) Suesskind von *Trimberg, who flourished in the first half of the 13th century. The handful of lyrics still extant, notable for their Jewish feeling and inspiration, are of perennial interest to German literary historians. A century later, in 1336, Samson Pine was one of three German writers who collaborated in the translation of a French version of the *Parsifal* romance. The prefatory acknowledgements of his Strasbourg colleagues clearly indicate that Pine was a Jew and that he was responsible for most of the work. In 1519 Johannes *Pauli, a Jew turned Franciscan preacher, published his *Schimpf un Ernst*, an important and influential collection of humorous and didactic anecdotes.

THE AGE OF ENLIGHTENMENT. It was not until 250 years later, during the late 18th century, that Jewish writers first appeared in significant numbers on the German cultural scene, utilizing the German language as their literary medium. The doctrines of tolerance and human equality propounded by the philosophers of the Enlightenment made a profound impression on Jewish intellectuals. The Jewish elite wished to contribute to the stream of German culture, and at first the German elite welcomed them. The finest expression of this rapprochement between the two ethnic groups was the friendship of Moses Mendelssohn, the Jew from Dessau, and Gotthold Lessing, Germany's most influential literary critic, who both stressed the common ethical heritage of Judaism and Christianity. A towering figure of both the German Enlightenment and the Jewish Emancipation, Moses Mendelssohn was also the first modern Jewish writer to master the German idiom in all its subtleties. His philosophical and aesthetic works – notably the *Briefe ueber die Empfindungen* (1755), *Phaedon, oder Ueber die Unsterblichkeit der Seele* (1767), and *Morgenstunden* (1785) – had an enormous impact in Germany itself and abroad. The reputation he came to enjoy in the outside world enhanced his standing within German Jewry, which thereafter involved itself increasingly in German cultural and literary affairs. Mendelssohn also founded German Jewry's first newspaper, *Kohelet Musar* (Berlin, 1750), and in 1778 began publishing an original German translation of the Bible with a Hebrew commentary. German enlightenment found its finest philosophical formulation in the critical reasoning of Immanuel *Kant, and it is no accident that the first enthusiastic adherents of Kantian philosophy were Jews. From Marcus Herz, the friend and physician of Lessing and Mendelssohn, Lazarus *Bendavid, Solomon *Maimon, and David *Friedlaender to the outstanding neo-Kantians of the 20th century – Hermann *Cohen and Ernst *Cassirer – Jews played a leading role in the exposition of Kant's philosophy.

Hartwig *Wessely, who died in 1805, was the last of the Hebrew lyrical poets in Germany, and German steadily replaced Hebrew among the Jewish writers of Central Europe. Moses Ephraim *Kuh attacked antisemitism in witty German epigrams, and the Polish physician Issachar Falkensohn *Behr wrote *Gedichte von einem pohlnischen Juden* (1772), which were reviewed by Goethe. Michael *Sachs, through his translations, introduced the religious poetry of medieval Spanish Jewry to the Jews of Germany.

THE AGE OF ROMANTICISM. During the ensuing Romantic era the German theologian Friedrich *Schleiermacher, who wished to see a revival of religion along with the pursuit of poetry and the fine arts, strenuously opposed all attempts to convert Jews to Christianity, since he doubted the sincerity of the converts. Romanticism delayed the process of Jewish emancipation by developing a nationalist philosophy that led to a new form of antisemitism, based not on religious differences, but rather on differences in national origin. This "Teutonism" condoned hatred of the Jews.

From the 1780s, German Jews and non-Jews had mingled in Berlin salons, where Jewish hostesses of charm, learning, and wit furthered the cultural exchange between statesmen, philosophers, and Romantic artists. The most distinguished salon in Berlin was that of the brilliant Henriette *Herz, wife of the philosopher Marcus Herz and an admirer of Goethe and the Romantics, who fostered the doctrines of the new generation. Other Berlin hostesses were Rahel Varnhagen von Ense (whom Goethe claimed as the first person to understand and recognize him); Moses Mendelssohn's daughter, Dorothea von *Schlegel, who introduced Victor Hugo and Mme. de Staël to the German reader; and Fanny *Lewald, a writer and feminist. Their Viennese counterparts were Fanny, Baroness von *Arnstein; and the von Wertheimsteins, Josephine, her sister Sophie, Baroness Todesco, and her daughter Franziska.

THE AGE OF LIBERALISM. Romanticism promoted the revival of historical studies and taught that history does not merely interpret the past but affords an understanding of the present and guidance to the future. Preeminent among Jewish historians during the first half of the 19th century was Leopold *Zunz, the originator of the *Wissenschaft des Judentums ("Science of Judaism"). Together with Abraham *Geiger, Moses Moser (1796–1838), and Eduard *Gans, he founded in 1819 the *Verein fuer Kultur und Wissenschaft des Judentums. Heine, who joined this organization, gave a detailed record of its achievements in a eulogy of his friend Ludwig Marcus (1798–1843). The impact of Zunz and of the Verein was felt throughout the 19th century. Geiger wrote his three-volume study, *Das Judentum und seine Geschichte* (1864–71), from the standpoint of Reform Judaism, but the concept of Jewish history was broadened when the positive historical (Conservative) school emerged with the *Monatsschrift fuer Geschichte und Wissenschaft des Judentums*, under the editorship of Zacharias *Frankel. The first universal history of the Jewish people in German, *Geschichte der Israeliten* (1820–47) written by Isaac Markus *Jost, paved the way for Heinrich *Graetz, whose *Geschichte der Juden von den aeltesten Zeiten bis auf die Gegenwart* (11 vols., 1853–75) is generally considered one of the outstanding works of historical scholarship in the German language.

Prussian and Austrian reactionaries were the most rabid antisemites, and Jews saw in political liberalism a powerful ally in their battle for emancipation. The aim of German liberalism was to develop the capacities of the individual irrespective of race, sex, class, or economic status; it therefore enabled Jews to develop their talents to the fullest extent. Berthold Auerbach, who was for many years the literary spokesman of German-Jewish liberalism, became the outstanding Jewish master of the sentimental novel and short story. However, although Jews finally succeeded in obtaining full legal rights as citizens of the German states, their inner conflict did not abate. Ferdinand Lassalle, the leading German socialist, summoned his "martyr people" to join the revolutionary working classes in the fight against the common oppressor. Jews in general joined the opposition parties, and some became influential contributors to the liberal and socialist press.

DISILLUSIONMENT. Heinrich Heine, the greatest Jewish poet in the German language, tried to disguise the conflicts arising from his opportunist conversion to Christianity by satirical irony, but at heart he always remained a Jew. Some of his most Jewish poems (e.g., the "Hebraeische Melodien" of his *Romanzero*) were written years after his baptism. Heine and Ludwig Boerne were the originators of the German *feuilleton*, a literary genre of great artistic charm in which Jews – from Moritz Gottlieb *Saphir and Daniel Spitzer (1835–1893) to Herzl, Nordau, Peter *Altenberg, Felix *Salten, and Alfred *Polgar – particularly excelled. Some German revolutionary poets such as Karl *Beck and Moritz *Hartmann were Jewish merely by the accident of birth and both converted. It was only when revolutionary ardor gave way to disappointment verging on despair that these writers turned to authentic Jewish subjects. Karl Emil Franzos discovered *Halbasien* ("Semi-Asia," i.e., Galician Jewry) and described the tension between Eastern and Western Jews.

With few exceptions, 19th-century German dramatists suppressed any Jewish feelings they may have had. Ludwig *Robert, the converted brother of Rahel Varnhagen, was always sensitive to the ambiguities of his position; while Michael *Beer, brother of the composer Giacomo *Meyerbeer, wrote a play, *Der Paria* (1826), which betrays the depressing effect of his Jewish origin. A third playwright, Solomon Hermann von *Mosenthal, in his *Deborah* (1850), dramatized the story of a Jewess living among Christian peasants.

During the first half century of Jewish emancipation, the dichotomy was resolved for many German Jews by assimilation or conversion. Of the direct descendants of Michael *Creizenach, a scholarly advocate of religious reform, his son Theodor (1818–1877), a poet and authority on Goethe, abandoned Judaism, as did Theodor's son Wilhelm (1851–1919), an eminent literary scholar. Friedrich Wolters (1876–1930), who belonged to the circle of Stefan George, was the non-Jewish grandson of the Odessa-born poet and translator Wilhelm Wolfsohn (1820–1865). Heinrich Stieglitz (1801–1849), a melancholic lyricist, was the son of a baptized banker; and Betty

Paoli (Barbara Elisabeth Glueck, 1815–1894) was a Viennese society poet born of a Hungarian nobleman and a Belgian Jewess.

THE STRUGGLE BETWEEN THE TWO SOULS. The novelist Jacob *Wassermann, reviewing his own life in *Mein Weg als Deutscher und Jude* (1921), wrote: "I am a German and a Jew, each as completely as the other; neither can be separated from the other." This held true for most German-Jewish writers of the late 19th and early 20th centuries, although the proportion between the German and the Jewish ingredients of this amalgam varied. Some wished for total assimilation; others were willing to identify themselves within the German-Jewish group but denied all kinship with East-European Jews, whom they considered foreign and inferior. Jewish history was for this class of writer far more remote than the history of the Germans whom they idealized.

Three writers who appear to have been untouched by the problem were the half-Jewish poet Paul Heyse, who was awarded the Nobel Prize for literature in 1910; and two humorists, Julius Stettenheim (1831–1916) and C. Karlweis (Karl Weiss, 1850–1901), an Austrian railroad inspector who wrote popular comedies and short stories. On the other hand, Arthur Schnitzler, the sensitive, delicate analyst of a dying Viennese society, was a vigorous opponent of antisemitism. Stefan Zweig despaired of the survival of European culture, and the European tragedy finally drove him to suicide. He nevertheless felt that Jewry would endure, but he himself was not primarily of it, despite his awareness of Jewish nobility and martyrdom. Some writers were impelled to stress the positive aspects of the Jewish heritage and identity. They include Jacob Loewenberg (1856–1929), whose verse was collected in *Lieder eines Semiten* (1892) and *Aus juedischer Seele* (1901); and the proselyte Nahida Ruth *Lazarus, noted for her expository works conceived in the spirit of Liberal Judaism. Ludwig *Jacobowski, in his novels *Werther der Jude* (1892) and *Loki* (1899), portrayed the struggle between the Jew and his antisemitic surroundings. The pioneer Zionist Samuel *Lublinski emphasized the Jewish thirst for knowledge and truth; another Jewish nationalist, Fritz Mordechai *Kaufmann, became an expert on Yiddish folklore; while Georg Hermann wrote about Berlin's Jewish society with benevolent satire. Two other writers who took a positive Jewish stand were Moritz *Heimann and Alfred *Kerr.

By contrast, several leading literary figures of the era revealed themselves to be either unsympathetic to the fate of their own people or even outspokenly hostile. Carl *Sternheim anticipated the Fascists with his attacks on the Jewish middle classes, but Rudolf Borchardt, who tried to disguise his origin by the adoption of reactionary nationalism, only narrowly escaped deportation to Auschwitz concentration camp. The philosophical father of "Jewish self-hatred" was Otto Weininger; his leading disciple was Arthur *Trebitsch, whose pathological detestation of the Jews and Judaism led him to offer his services as an antisemitic propagandist to the Austrian Nazis. Two other writers influenced by Weininger were Karl *Kraus and Kurt *Tucholsky. Somewhat less violent was the ostentatious Catholic convert Ernst *Lothar. Ernst Lissauer, composer of World War I's notorious "Hymn of Hate" against England, also supported the postwar reactionary nationalists. A double irony attaches to Ferdinand Bronner (1867–1948), a naturalistic dramatist who wrote under the pen name Franz Adamus: he was born in the Polish town of Oświęcim (Auschwitz), and in his comedy, *Schmelz, der Nibelunge* (1905), a son denies his Jewish parentage. His own son, Arnolt Bronnen (1895–1959), swung from support of the extreme left to the far right, and held important radio and television posts under the Nazis. After World War II the erstwhile Nazi became a respectable public figure in Austria and at the end of his life was a drama critic in East Berlin.

THE JEWISH RENAISSANCE. Under the impact of their military disaster in World War I the Germans experienced a temporary spiritual revulsion against war, brutality, lust for power, and materialism. The literary movement of Expressionism thereafter engaged in a fervent struggle for peace, world brotherhood, and the dignity of man. It included a high proportion of Jewish writers, notably Ernst Toller, Alfred Doeblin, Franz *Werfel, Alfred *Mombert, Albert *Ehrenstein, Alfred *Wolfenstein, Jacob von Hoddis (1887–1942), Ludwig *Rubiner, and the Franco-German poet Yvan *Goll.

Together with this rebellious movement in the arts, there arose a second movement aiming at the intellectual, moral, and political rebirth of the Jewish people. Martin Buber and Franz Rosenzweig were the outstanding philosophical leaders of this Jewish renaissance. Richard Beer-Hofmann was the major poet of this German-Jewish revival and gave expression to Jewish suffering and glory in a biblical cycle about King David. His *Schlaflied fuer Miriam* (1897) is regarded as the finest philosophical lullaby in the German language. Karl Wolfskehl, who began his career as a member of the Stefan George circle, also found his way to Jewish poetry. Max Brod, whose Zionism led him to settle in Ereẓ Israel in 1939, considered Judaism a rampart against the black void toward which events were pointing, and felt that his "best service to humanity was to work in all humility for the perfection of my own people." Franz *Kafka and Hermann *Broch broke new ground in German fiction with works on the ultimate goal of human existence. Although their novels never directly touch on Jewish themes, they reflect the Jewish character of their authors. Kafka himself studied Hebrew and even planned to settle in Ereẓ Israel.

Vivid pictures of Jewish life in Germany were painted by the novelists Lion Feuchtwanger (*Jud Suess*, 1925) and Arnold Zweig. Feuchtwanger also wrote a celebrated trilogy based on the story of Josephus. Zweig, long an ardent Zionist, lived in Haifa for many years before settling in East Germany after 1948. In *Der Gezeichnete* (1936), Jacob *Picard portrayed with affection the Orthodox folklore and traditions of Jews long settled in southwest Germany. Else Lasker-Schueler, regarded by many as the greatest German poetess after Annette von Droste-Huelshoff, dreamed of an imagined Oriental world, celebrated the "Land of the Hebrews," and ended her days in Jerusalem. Gertrud *Kolmar, whose poems, some of them in Hebrew, expressed tragic loneliness, remained in Germany and perished in a death camp. A third important woman poet, Nelly *Sachs, who was awarded the Nobel Prize for literature in 1966, expressed both the anxiety and the restlessness of her age and her loyalty to the Jewish people and its destiny.

Jewish writers of the 1930s echoed the torment and despair of their era. On the one hand there was a messianic belief in the future of mankind and, on the other, a nihilistic mistrust of any system of values. The Jews who fled Germany from 1933 and Austria from 1938 included some of the most prominent Jewish writers, although there were many who either chose to remain or could not escape. With the onslaught of the Hitler regime on German-speaking Jewry, the cherished dream of a German-Jewish symbiosis abruptly collapsed and the history of German-Jewish literature was, so far as Europe was concerned, at an end.

LITERARY SCHOLARS. The Jews of Germany and Austria also made an important contribution to literary history and research, many of them writing scholarly works that continue to be regarded as classics. Some outstanding literary historians were the convert Emil Kuh (1828–1876), who "discovered" the dramatist Friedrich Hebbel, editing his works (1866–68) and writing his biography (1877); Julius Leopold *Klein, the Hungarian-born author of a 13-volume *Geschichte des Dramas* (1865–76); Richard Moritz *Meyer, who wrote his *Deutsche Literatur des neunzehnten Jahrhunderts* (1900); Friedrich *Gundolf, an authority on Shakespeare, Goethe, and Kleist; Alfred Kerr, author of *Die Welt im Drama* (1917) and *Die Welt im Licht* (1920); Egon *Friedell, the Austrian playwright, who was also a cultural historian and author of a *Kulturgeschichte der Neuzeit* (3 vols., 1927–31); Hugo *Bieber, who wrote *Der Kampf um die Tradition* (1928) and was an authority on Heine; and Arthur *Eloesser, author of *Die deutsche Literatur vom Barock bis zur Gegenwart* (1930–31).

Other scholars in this field include Julius *Bab, Albert Bielschowsky (1847–1902), Ernst *Heilborn, Rudolf *Kayser, Alfred Klaar (1848–1927), Victor Klemperer (1881–1960), Samuel *Lublinski, Kurt Pinthus (1886–?), Otto Pniower (1859–1932), and Julius Wahle (1861–1940). Two outstanding authorities on Goethe were Michael Bernays (1834–1897), the baptized son of Ḥakham Isaac *Bernays of Hamburg, who was a professor at Munich; and Ludwig *Geiger, a son of the German reformer Abraham Geiger, who was a professor in Berlin and wrote *Die deutsche Literatur und die Juden* (1910). Three other academic scholars were Robert F. Arnold (Robert Frank Levisohn, 1872–1938), who was professor of German literature at Vienna; Jonas *Fraenkel, an expert on Swiss-German literature, who held a chair at Berne; and Fritz *Strich, who was professor successively at Munich and Berne universities. Georg Witkowski (1863–1941), the baptized brother of Maximilian *Harden, wrote *Das deutsche Drama des neunzehnten Jahrhunderts* (1923–25) and ended his career as a professor in Leipzig. Eduard Engel (1851–1938) published a *Geschichte der deutschen Literatur* that reached its 38th edition in 1929; and the Czech anthologist Camill *Hoffmann wrote *Die deutsche Lyrik aus Oesterreich seit Grillparzer* (1912). The literary and dramatic critic Monty Jacobs (1875–1945), who was a coeditor of the *Goldene Klassikerbibliothek*, had an English father and took refuge in London after the Nazis came to power; while Werner Kraft (1896–1991), a German poet, editor, and critic, eventually settled in Israel. An outstanding scholar, Daniel Sanders, published several authoritative German dictionaries, including a *Handwoerterbuch der deutschen Sprache* (3 vols., 1859–65).

From the age of Heine onward, German Jews also distinguished themselves as cultural mediators, especially with the English and French. Heine's contemporary, the royal physician David Ferdinand *Koreff, was also a writer and did much to promote the interchange of ideas between leading authors through his circle in Paris. Later contributions were made by German-Jewish translators from various languages, notably Julius Elias (Ibsen), Alexander Eliasberg (Dostoyevski, Tolstoy), F. Gundolf (Shakespeare), Siegfried *Trebitsch (Shaw), and Stefan Zweig (Verhaeren).

WORKS ON PALESTINE AND ISRAEL. Discounting biblical poems, and plays and novels set in ancient Palestine, most of the literature on the Holy Land written in German was produced by a few German-Jewish authors. One of the very few 19th-century works was *Nach Jerusalem* (1858–60; *The Jews in the East*, 1859), travel sketches by the poet and Viennese communal leader, Ludwig August *Frankl. The *Gesaenge aus der Verbannung* (1829) by Solomon Ludwig *Steinheim anticipated the return to Zion, as did Theodor Herzl's novel, *Altneuland* (1902), three-quarters of a century later. Moshe Ya'akov *Ben-Gavriel (Eugen Hoeflich), who had been an Austrian liaison officer with the Turkish army during World War I, wrote a series of Zionist works based on personal experience, beginning with books such as *Der Weg ins Land* (1918) and *Feuer im Osten* (1920). Rudolf *Lothar included an account of a visit to Palestine in *Zwischen drei Welten* (1926), and other German and Austrian Jews – not always Zionists – brought back glowing reports of Jewish pioneering achievements in Ereẓ Israel. They include Alfred Kerr, who has a chapter entitled "Jeruschalajim" in his *Die Welt im Licht* (1920); Arthur Holitscher, who wrote *Reise durch das juedische Palaestina* (1922); Richard Arnold *Bermann, who collaborated with another non-Zionist, Arthur Rundt, in the publication of *Palaestina* (1923); and Felix Salten (*Neue Menschen auf alter Erde*, 1925). Else Lasker-Schueler's poetic impressions of the land in which she spent her last years, illustrated with her own quaint drawings, were conveyed in *Das Hebraeerland* (1937). Another refugee, the historical biographer Josef *Kastein, wrote many works in Palestine after 1933, including *Jerusalem; Die Geschichte eines Landes* (1937) and *Eine palaestinensische Novelle* (1942).

After World War II, Hans José Rehfisch wrote *Quelle der Verheissung* (1946), a play about German Jews who settled in Ereẓ Israel. Max Brod's novel, *Unambo* (1949), dealt with Israel's War of Independence, while Aryeh Ludwig *Strauss, a refugee poet and literary historian who settled in Palestine and later wrote in Hebrew as well as German, reflected both the Israel scene and his own intimate experience in the lyrical *Heimliche Gegenwart* (1952). M.Y. Ben-Gavriel found a new and valuable outlet for his talents in the many books of anecdotes and travel which became best sellers in post-Hitler Germany, such as *Kumsitz* (1956). His descriptions of life in the State of Israel did much to win sympathy and support for the infant Jewish state in Federal Germany.

[Rudolf Kayser]

The Holocaust and Its Aftermath

The liquidation of German writers of Jewish origin was set in motion almost as soon as the Nazis came to power in 1933. Two early victims were the philosopher Theodor *Lessing (murdered at Marienbad in 1933) and the poet and dramatist Erich *Muehsam (tortured to death at the Oranienburg concentration camp in 1934). The massacre increased after the outbreak of World War II. Ernst Heilborn died at the hands of the Gestapo in Berlin in 1941, Paul *Kornfeld in the Lodz ghetto in 1942, and Gertrud Kolmar somewhere in Eastern Europe in the following year. Writers who perished at *Auschwitz include Georg Hermann (1943), Arno Nadel (1943), and Camill Hoffmann (1944). By a grim irony, Herwarth *Walden, who fled to the U.S.S.R. in 1933, is thought to have been executed during a Soviet purge in 1942. A number of Jewish writers, unable to accept the shattering of their illusions, committed suicide. They include the cultural philosopher and historian Walter *Benjamin (Paris, 1940), Egon Friedell (Vienna, 1938), Ludwig *Fulda (Berlin, 1939), Ernst Toller (New York, 1939), Kurt Tucholsky (Sweden, 1935), Ernst *Weiss (Paris, 1940), Alfred Wolfenstein (Paris, 1945), and Stefan Zweig (Brazil, 1942). In fear of the Nazi invaders, the half-Jewish expressionist poet Walter *Hasenclever took his own life at a detention camp in southern France in 1940.

Many other German and Austrian writers of Jewish birth, more fortunate, found refuge abroad. Among those who settled in England were Felix Braun, Kurt *Hiller, Alfred Kerr, Arthur Koestler, Theodor *Kramer, Robert *Neumann, Hans José Rehfisch, and Carl *Roessler. Karl Wolfskehl died an exile in New Zealand, Nelly Sachs and Peter *Weiss settled in Sweden, while Paul *Adler survived the Holocaust in hiding in Czechoslovakia. Switzerland provided a haven for Efraim *Frisch, Margarete *Susman, Siegfried Trebitsch, and the converted half-Jew, Carl Zuckmayer, who spent the war years in the U.S. By far the largest number fled to the United States or Palestine. Those who immigrated to Ereẓ Israel include Max Brod, Martin Buber, M.Y. Ben-Gavriel, Sammy Gronemann, Josef Kastein, Leo *Perutz, Else Lasker-Schueler, Aryeh Ludwig Strauss, and Arnold Zweig. The U.S. welcomed scores of refugee writers, among them literary figures such as Julius Bab, Richard Beer-Hofmann, Hugo Bieber, Ferdinand *Bruckner, Alfred Doeblin, Lion Feuchtwanger, Manfred *George, Hermann *Kesten, Ernst Lothar, Ludwig *Marcuse, Walter *Mehring, Alfred *Neumann, Alfred *Polgar, Roda Roda (Sandor Rosenfeld, 1872–1945), Felix Salten, Friedrich *Torberg, Berthold *Viertel, Ernst *Waldinger, and Franz Werfel. Refugee writers who returned to Europe after World War II include Braun, Bruckner, Doeblin, Lothar, Marcuse, Rehfisch, Salten, Torberg, and Viertel. Several leftist writers abandoned the West for Iron Curtain countries: from Mexico, Egon Erwin *Kisch, the "rushing reporter," returned to Prague and Anna *Seghers to East Germany; Friedrich *Wolf moved from the U.S.S.R. to East Berlin and was for a time East Germany's envoy in Warsaw; while Arnold Zweig, who left Israel in 1948, also settled in East Berlin. Hans *Habe, who had fought first with the French and later with the U.S. army, finally made his home in Austria. A postwar playwright, Wolfgang Hildesheimer (1916–), was in Ereẓ Israel during the 1930s and World War II, but eventually settled in Munich.

THE LITERATURE OF REMORSE. After the collapse of Nazi Germany, non-Jewish writers of a new, repentant generation experienced a feeling of revulsion against the mass murder of the Jews. They tended to idealize the figure of the Jew, endowing him with biblical grandeur, immense wisdom, and great moral stature. As the prime victim of the European Holocaust, the Jew continued to trouble and preoccupy the conscience of postwar Germany. The poet and novelist Johannes Bobrowski, who had served on the Russian front during World War II, wrote affectionately of the heterogeneous population and folk world of pre-Nazi East Prussia, and spoke of Germany's treatment of the Jews as "a long story of misfortune and guilt, for which my people has been to blame ever since the days of the Teutonic Knights." Similar feelings pervaded the works of postwar novelists such as Heinrich Boell (*Wo warst du, Adam?*, 1951), Albrecht Goes (*Das Brandopfer*, 1954), Guenter Grass (*Die Blechtrommel*, 1959; *Hundejahre*, 1963), Walter Jens (*Der Blinde*, 1951), Wolfgang Koeppen, and Felix Lutzendorf. The anti-Nazi refugee novelist Erich Maria Remarque dealt with the fate of German Jews immediately before and during the Holocaust: *Arc de triomphe* (1946; *Arch of Triumph*, 1946); *Der Funke Leben* (1952; *Spark of Life*, 1952); and *Die Nacht von Lissabon* (1962); and other novels on the theme of anti-Jewish persecution were written by Stefan Andres (*Die Sintflut*, 1949–59), Friedrich Duerrenmatt (*Der Verdacht*, 1953), Hermann Kasack (*Die Stadt hinter dem Strom*, 1947), and Rudolf Lorenzen (*Alles andere als ein Held*, 1959).

The fate of the Jews was also presented on the stage in plays by Stefan Andres (*Sperrzonen*, 1959), Max Frisch (*Andorra*, 1962), Fritz Hochwaelder (*Der Fluechtling*, 1948; *Der oeffentliche Anklaeger*, 1954), Erwin Sylvanus (*Korczak und die Kinder*, 1959), and Martin Walser (*Eiche und Angora*, 1962). The most influential – and controversial – postwar German drama about the Jews in the Nazi era was Rolf *Hochhuth's *Der Stellvertreter* (1963), which condemned Pope Pius XII as an accessory to Hitler's "Final Solution of the Jewish Problem." *Der Stellvertreter* was translated into many languages and was staged in the U.S. as *The Deputy* and in England as *The Representative*. In postwar German literature the Jew thus became a symbol of man's inhumanity to man and an instrument of national self-flagellation. This process was encouraged by the appearance of works in German by Jewish victims of the Hitler era – the moving diary of Anne *Frank; *Das unausloeschliche Siegel* (1946), a novel by the baptized half-Jewess, Elisabeth Langgaesser (1899–1950); *Eine Seele aus Holz* (1962; *A Soul of Wood*, 1964), a grim volume of tales about Hitler's "death doctors" and their victims by Jakov Lind (1927–); the visionary poems of Paul *Celan (1920–1970), a Romanian-born writer and translator, whose works include *Der Sand aus den Urnen* (1948) and *Mohn und Gedaechtnis* (1952); and the poems of Nelly *Sachs. Two half-Jews who saw the problem from both sides of the fence were Carl Zuckmayer, in his plays *Des Teufels General* (1947) and *Das kalte Licht* (1955), and Peter Weiss with *Die Ermittlung*, an oratorio based on the Auschwitz trial held in Frankfurt in 1965 (Eng., *The Investigation*, 1966).

In contemporary Germany, Polish-born Marcel *Reich-Ranicki has established himself as the country's leading literary critic. Other German-language writers of note are Elfriede *Jelinek (Nobel Prize, 2004), Wolfgang *Hildesheimer, and Barbara *Honigmann.

[Sol Liptzin]

BIBLIOGRAPHY: GENERAL: L. Geiger, *Die deutsche Literatur und die Juden* (1910), 1–24. BIBLICAL AND HEBRAIC INFLUENCES: G. Karpeles, *Geschichte der juedischen Literatur*, 2 (1921^{3}), 346–54; E. Tannenbaum, *Philo Zitaten-Lexikon: Worte von Juden, Worte fuer Juden* (1936), 17–61 (includes bibliography); F. Lehner, in: L. Finkelstein (ed.), *The Jews*... 2 (1960^{3}), 1472–86 (includes bibliography). IMAGE OF THE JEW: O.B. Frankl, *Der Jude in den deutschen Dichtungen der 15., 16. und 17. Jahrhunderten* (1905); L. Geiger, *Die deutsche Literatur und die Juden* (1910), 25–45. THE JEWISH CONTRIBUTION: A. Soergel and C. Hohoff, *Dichtung und Dichter der Zeit*, 2 vols. (1961–63), index, s.v. names of authors; G. Karpeles, *Geschichte der juedischen Literatur*, 2 (1921^{3}), 320–43 and index (includes bibliography); G. Krojanker (ed.), *Juden in der deutschen Literatur* (1926); A. Zweig, *Juden auf der deutschen Buehne* (1928); A. Myerson and I. Goldberg, *The German Jew* (1933), 119–42; A. Lewkowitz, *Das Judentum und die geistigen Stroemungen des neunzehnten Jahrhunderts* (1935); E. Tannenbaum, *Philo Zitaten-Lexikon: Worte von Juden, Worte fuer Juden* (1936), 124–44, 149–53 (includes bibliography); F.R. Bienenfeld, *The Germans and the Jews* (1939), 126ff.; R. Kayser, in: D.D. Runes (ed.), *The Hebrew Impact on Western Civilization* (1951), 556–64; C. Roth, *The Jewish Contribution to Civilization* (1956^{3}), 79–80, 93, 94–98, and index (includes bibliography); S. Liptzin, *Germany's Stepchildren* (1944, repr. 1961); A. Zweig, *Bilanz der deutschen Judenheit* (1961), 239–49; S. Kaznelson (ed.), *Juden im deutschen Kulturbereich* (1962^{3}), 1–67; H. Zohn, *Wiener Juden in der deutschen Literatur* (1964); H. Friedmann and O. Mann, *Deutsche Literatur im 20. Jahrhundert*, 2 vols. (1967^{5}), index, s.v. authors' names; H. Zohn, in: *The Jews of Czechoslovakia*, 1 (1968), 468–522 (includes bibliography); W. Jakob, in: *Studies in Bibliography and Booklore*, 6 (1962–63), 75–92 (an extensive bibliography on the subject). THE HOLOCAUST AND ITS AFTERMATH: L. Kahn, in: JBA, 24 (1966), 14–22; I. Elbogen, *A Century of Jewish Life* (1944), 636–74 (includes bibliography); *Exil Literatur 1933–45. Eine Ausstellung aus Bestaenden der deutschen Bibliothek, Frankfurt am Main* (1967^{3}), index, s.v. names of authors. **ADD. BIBLIOGRAPHY:** *Lexikon deutsch-juedischer Autoren*. Archiv Bibliographia Judaica. Redaktionelle Leitung (1992ff.); A.B. Kilcher (ed.), *Metzler Lexikon der deutsch-juedischen Literatur* (2003).

GERMANY, country in north central Europe. The Talmud and the Midrash use "Germania" (or "Germamia") as a designation for northern European countries, and also refer to the military prowess of these peoples and to the threat they posed to the Roman Empire (Meg. 6b; Gen. R. 75:9; etc.). Medieval Jewish sources first refer to Germany as "Allemania" or "Lothir" (Lotharingia); later the biblical term "*Ashkenaz" came into use, and was retained in Hebrew literature and Jewish vernacular until recent times.

Middle Ages

There is no substance to the legends extant in the Middle Ages relating that Jews were present in Germany "before the Crucifixion." Supposedly the first Jews to reach Germany were merchants who went there in the wake of the Roman legions and settled in the Roman-founded Rhine towns. Archaeological evidence suggests that Jews may have lived in Augusta Raurica (Kaiseraugst) and Augusta Treverorum (*Trier). Imperial decrees regarding the duties of Jewish community officials were sent to Colonia Agrippinensis (*Cologne) in 321 and 331 C.E. (Cod. Theod., 16:8, 3–4; Aronius, Regesten, no. 2). There is, however, no evidence of continuous Jewish settlement in Germany from Late Antiquity to the early days of the German Empire. Jews entered Central Europe in this period from the west and the southwest; Jewish merchants from southern Italy and France were welcomed in Germany, and settled in the towns along the great rivers and trade routes. The *Kalonymos family from Lucca established itself in *Mainz in the tenth century. In its early stages German Jewry was closely linked with the Jewish communities of Northern France. A 12th-century Jewish scholar mentions a letter he saw in *Worms, which Rhine Jews had sent to Ereẓ Israel in 960, asking for verification of the rumor that the Messiah had come (REJ, 44 (1902), 238). Ties were also maintained to the academies of Babylonia. Until the end of the 11th century the Jews of Germany engaged in international trade, especially with the East, and were an important element of the urban population. They were concentrated along the west bank of the Rhine, in Lorraine, and in ancient episcopal seats and trade centers, such as Cologne, Mainz, *Speyer, Worms, and Trier, as well as religious and political centers situated more eastward, such as *Regensburg and *Prague. The extant reports of Jewish settlement in Germany are of a haphazard nature, and the dating of such records does not necessarily establish the sequence of settlement. The first mention of Jewish settlement in Mainz dates from c. 900, of Worms from 960, and of Regensburg from 981. Jewish communities in south central Germany (*Bamberg, *Wuerzburg) and *Thuringia (*Erfurt) are mentioned in documents from the 11th century. In *Breslau and *Munich Jews are mentioned at the beginning of the 13th century, in *Vienna in the middle of that century, and in *Berlin (and other places) at its end. At the end of the tenth century (or the beginning of the 11th), *Gershom b. Judah ("Me'or ha-Golah") moved from *Metz to Mainz and that city became noted for Torah learning; the yeshivot of Mainz and Worms became spiritual centers for all the Jews in Central Europe and even attracted students from France, among them the famous *Rashi. For the Jews, the Carolingian Empire, although no longer a political entity, still remained a single social and cultural unit. Their social and legal status was distinct from that of the general population, and, as a small and largely defenseless minority, they required special protection to safeguard their existence. The first reports of persecution of Jews in Germany date from the 11th century (the expulsion of the Jews of Mainz in 1012), and the first written guarantees of rights, granted to them by emperors and bishops, also date from that century. In 1084 the archbishop of Speyer invited them to settle in his enlarged city "in order to enhance a thousandfold the respect accorded to our town" (Aronius, Regesten, 70 no. 168), and granted the Jews far-reaching trading rights and permission to put up a protective wall around their quarters. This evidence of the high value attached to Jews for settlement of a new town and the expansion of its trade precedes by only 12 years the "*gezerot tatnav*" (1096; see below). In 1090 Emperor *Henry IV issued charters of rights to the Jews of Speyer and Worms (*ibid.*, 71–77 nos. 170–1), and succeeding emperors followed his example. All these writs acknowledged the right of the Jews to be judged "by their peers and no others … according to their law" (from a charter of 1090). In another such document, granted to the Jews of Worms in 1157, the emperor reserves for himself the exclusive right of judging the Jews "for they belong to our treasury." The guarantees of rights were given to the community leaders, who were also the spiritual leaders of the community, and were well-to-do men belonging to respected families. Communities that were accorded guarantees already possessed a synagogue (the Worms synagogue was founded in 1034) and public institutions. No reliable figures on the size of these Jewish communities are available; to judge by figures mentioned in the narratives of their martyrdom, there were communities of 2,000 persons (Mainz), but in general they consisted of several hundred, or several dozen. The community regulations enacted by the Jewish communities in Germany, and the commentaries and *piyyutim* written by their scholars (such as Gershom b. Judah and *Simeon b. Isaac) reveal a strong and simple faith, and readiness to die for it (and see *takkanot* of the period).

FIRST CRUSADE. Their faith was put to the supreme test during the first *Crusade, from April to June 1096. The brutal massacres that then took place are remembered in Jewish annuals as the *gezerot tatnav* (i.e., the massacres of 4856 = 1096). The first waves of crusaders turned upon the Jews of the Rhine valley. Although the emperor, the bishops, and Christian neighbors were reluctant to take part in this onslaught and tried to protect the Jews, this defense had small success. Several Hebrew reports written during the first half of the 12th century present a detailed narrative of the indomitable courage and religious devotion of those who chose a martyr's death (**kiddush ha-Shem*). In Mainz, it is related that "in a single day one thousand and one hundred martyrs were slaughtered and died" (A.M. Habermann (ed.), *Gezerot Ashkenaz ve-Ẓarefat* (1945), 32). The martyrdom of Mainz Jewry was preceded by negotiations with the emperor by Kalonymos ben Meshullam; in response, Henry IV published an order in defense of the Jews, but this was of little help. The Jews offered armed resistance and it was only in the final stage that they committed suicide. Similar events took place in many communities on the Rhine and along the crusaders' route; many Jews chose martyrdom; others managed to save their lives by going into hiding (Speyer, Cologne, Worms, *Xanten, Metz). Some accepted temporary conversion, as in Regensburg, where "all were coerced" (*ibid.*, 56). Later the emperor permitted their return to Judaism. The beginning of the Crusades inaugurated far-reaching changes in the social and economic structure of the Christian peoples in Western Europe and in their general outlook, and as a result also mark a turning point in the history of German Jewry. Henceforth physical attacks on Jews were more frequent and widespread, especially in periods of social or religious ferment. The city guilds forced the Jews out of the trades and the regular channels of commerce; this coincided with the stricter appliance of the church ban on usury in the 12th to 13th centuries. The combination of circumstances made *moneylending and pawnbroking the main occupation of Jews in Germany. They also continued in ordinary trade; as late as the 13th century they dealt in wool, attended the Cologne fairs, and traded with Russia and Hungary; during most of the Middle Ages there were even Jewish *craftsmen and Jews had some contact with *agriculture.

However moneylending, conceived by the Church as usury, became the hallmark of Jewish life in Germany. About 100 to 150 years after usury became the main occupation of Jews in England and France, it became central to the livelihood of Jews in Germany also. Jew hatred and the evil image of the Jew as conceived in the popular imagination were nourished by this economic pattern. Owing to the scarcity of money and lack of firm securities the rate of interest was extremely high. In 1244 the Jews of *Austria were given a bill of rights by Duke *Frederick II based on the assumption that interest was the Jews' main source of income; the bill contained detailed regulations on moneylending, and the rate of interest was fixed at 173⅓%. This kind of charter for Jews became typical of those granted in central and eastern Germany (and Poland) in the 13th and 14th centuries. Borrowing money from Jews against pawns became usual among the nobility and the townspeople, and enabled rabble-rousers to accuse the Jews of "sucking Christian blood" and of associating with gentile thieves who pawned their loot with the Jewish moneylenders. The Jews insisted on their right to refuse to return pawns unless reimbursed, a right confirmed as early as 1090. After the end of the 11th century the social status of the Jews steadily deteriorated. The *Reichslandfrieden* ("Imperial peace of the land") issued in 1103 includes the Jews among persons who bear no arms and are therefore to be spared violence and defended. The concepts which had determined the status of the Jews from the beginning of their settlement in Germany were now applied with increasing vigor. The need of the Jews for refuge and protection was now utilized by the urge to oppress and exploit them. A long-drawn-out process of legal and social development was finally summed up in 1236 by Emperor Frederick II, when he declared all the Jews of Germany *Servi camerae nostrae* ("servants of our treasury"; Aronius, Regesten, 216 no. 496). This meant that from the legal point of view the Jews and their property were possessions of the emperor and hence entirely at his mercy. However they never fully experienced the severity of this concept as it was never fully applied to them; in a way, their status as servants of the imperial treasury was even welcomed for it assured them of imperial protection, protection which no other German authority was able or willing to afford them. Long after the concept of the servitude of the Jews had been applied in Germany, *Meir b. Baruch of Rothenburg conceived that "the Jews are not *glebae* [*adscripti* = bound] to any particular place as gentiles are; for they are regarded as impoverished freemen who have not been sold into slavery; the government attitude is according to this" (Responsa, ed. Prague, no. 1001; cf. Tos. to BK 58a). The concepts that Jewish lives were not inviolable and that the Jews were in servitude to the country's rulers led to renewed outbursts of anti-Jewish violence whenever a critical situation arose. The second Crusade (1146) was again accompanied by widespread anti-Jewish agitation and incidents of violent persecution. However the experience of 1096 had taught a lesson both to the Jews and to the authorities: the Jews took refuge in the castles of the nobility, whenever possible having the entire citadel to themselves until the danger passed (see A.M. Habermann, op. cit. 117). The preaching of *Bernard of Clairvaux against doing the Jews physical harm also helped to restrain the masses. Thus a repetition of the earlier terrorization and slaughter did not take place. Between the second Crusade and the beginning of the 13th century the Jews were subjected to numerous attacks and libels but relatively few lost their lives as a result.

SPIRITUAL LIFE. The events of 1096 had shaken German Jewry to the core; its response came in the form of tremendous spiritual and social creativity. Succeeding generations glorified the deeds of the martyrs and created a whole doctrine around the sanctification of God by martyrdom (*kiddush ha-Shem*). The ideas of self-sacrifice, **akedah*, of choosing to meet "the Great Light" rather than apostasy, and of standing up to the attacker, were now formulated and transmitted as permanent principles. A special blessing was inserted into the prayer book to be recited by those who were about to be slain. In the 12th and 13th centuries the *Ḥasidei Ashkenaz ("pious men of Germany") formulated the principles of perfect piety, observance of "Heavenly Law" (*din shamayim*) which is above and beyond the "Law of the Torah," for the latter was given to man taking into account his *yeẓer ha-ra* ("evil inclination"). They taught that one should regard property as being held on trust (from God) only, and that one should abstain from lust without retiring from family and public life. The way of life to which this group adhered was established, in the main, by the members of a single family: *Samuel b. Kalonymos the Ḥasid of Speyer, his son *Judah b. Samuel he-Ḥasid of Regensburg, and their relative *Eleazar b. Judah (ha-Roke'aḥ) of Worms. *Sefer Ḥasidim* and *Sefer ha-Roke'aḥ*, two works written by these men, express the feelings and ideas of the ḥasidim of Germany on the greatness of God, on man's conduct in life, on ghosts and spirits, on sexual temptation and how to withstand it, on the true observance of commandments, and on love of learning as a foremost religious value.

SOCIAL LIFE. During this period further consolidation of the Jewish communal leadership in Germany took place. Jews increasingly restricted themselves to the Jewish quarter in the town, which gave them a greater feeling of security and made possible the development of an intense social life. The *meliores* (leading families) accepted the authority of the most eminent scholars. Torah learning was not interrupted in times of trouble and danger. It even received additional impetus from the need to provide leadership for the Jewish public and guidance to the individual, while the number of outstanding scholars also increased. Even the source of livelihood that was forced upon the Jews – lending money against interest – came to be appreciated as an advantage since it left time to spare for Torah study. Moneylending also determined the artificial structure of Jewish life; the Jews derived their income mainly from non-Jews, and there was hardly any economic exploitation of one Jew by another. As a result, there was a large measure of social cohesion in the German communities. The average community maintained a synagogue, a cemetery (or, if it was too small, obtained burial rights in a neighboring town), a bathhouse, and a place for weddings and other public festivities. A scholar attracted groups of students who lived in his home and were cared for by the scholar's wife (A.M. Habermann, op. cit., 165–6). Meir b. Baruch of Rothenburg attests that his house was spacious and included "a *bet midrash*… a winter house [i.e., the main living quarters]… a courtyard for public use… a cool upper room where I eat in summer and… a room… for each student" (Responsa, ed. Cremona, no. 108). Community institutions developed. The community leaders and scholars – in gatherings on fair-days – issued *takkanot* regulating many spheres of life which were binding upon individual communities or groups of several communities. In the 13th century, *Eliezer b. Joel ha-Levi of Bonn established the principle that a majority decision also obligated the opposing minority, and unanimity was not required (contradicting the 12th-century French scholar Jacob b. Meir *Tam). Communal offices which had come into existence in the 12th and 13th centuries are listed in a document issued by the Cologne community in 1301: *Nos Episcopus, magistratus Judeorum ac universi Judei civitatis Coloniensis* ("We the bishop [i.e., the

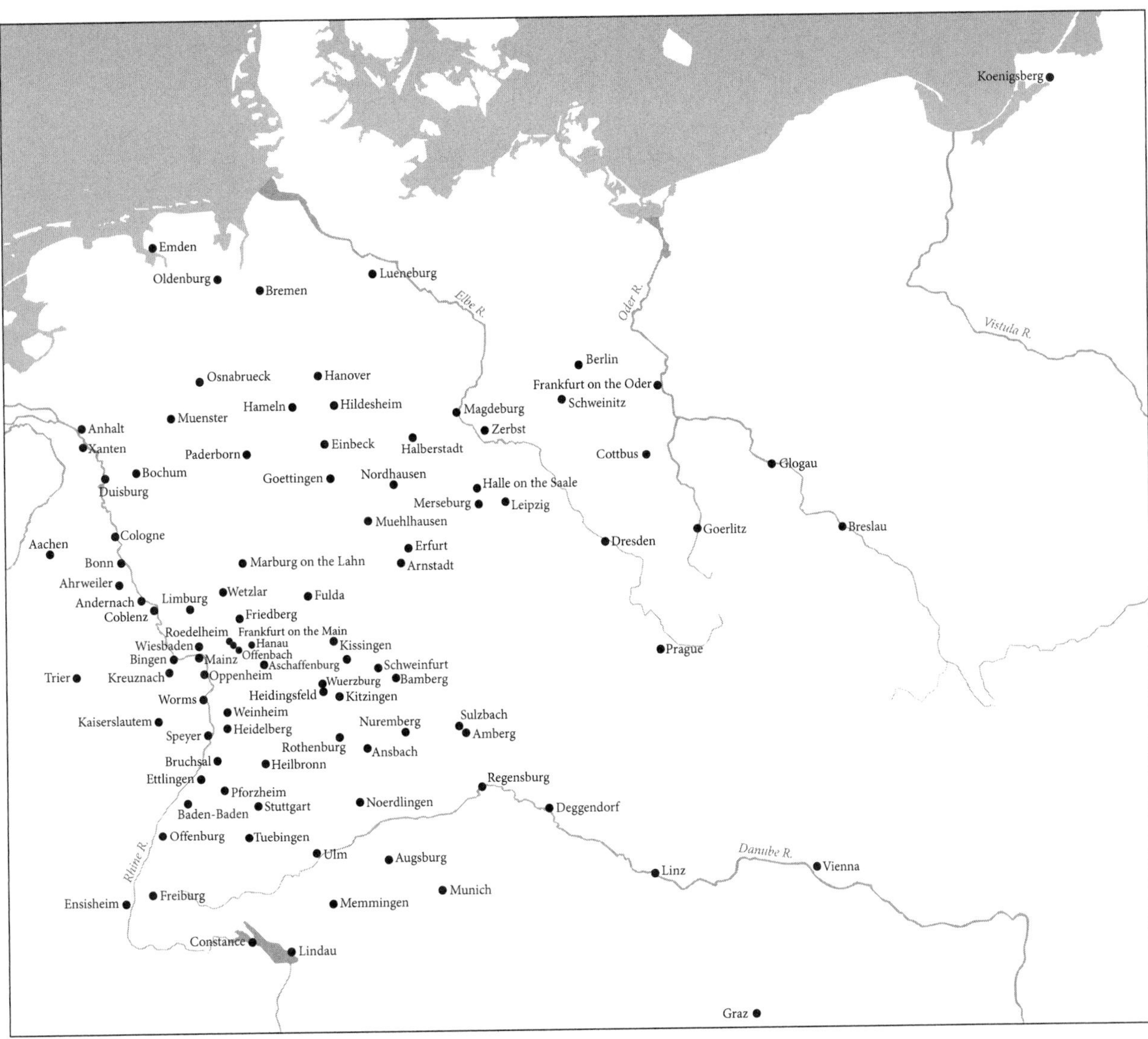

Major medieval Jewish communities in Germany in the 13th century.

leader], and officers of the Jews and the entire Jewish community of Cologne"; see *Judenschreinsbuch*, 92–93). From 1220 onward, the "*Takkanot Shum*," regulations issued by three of the great communities on the Rhine – Speyer, Worms, and Mainz (שו"ם, the initials of the three names) – have been preserved; joint meetings of the leaders of these three communities had a decisive influence on all the Jewish communities in Germany. German Jewry developed an independent leadership with a series of honors and degrees of rank. The intimacy of the small community enabled a person who felt wronged to turn to the public by means of interruption of prayer (see **bittul ha-tamid*) in synagogue until he received redress. Families experienced the usual sorrows and joys, and also had their share of frivolities: "wild young men… who liked gambling" (*Sefer Ḥasidim*, ed. by J. Wistinetzki (1924²), no. 109) and practical jokes at festivities (see also Tos. to Suk. 45a, s.v. *Mi-Yad Tinnokot*). The main purpose of the *takkanot* was to strengthen religious life and especially to provide for increased study of the Torah, the observance of sexual purity laws, of the Sabbath, etc. They also introduced innovations designed to strengthen community life: the obligation on the part of each individual to pay his tax assessment and to refrain from false declarations, and the right of the community officers to transfer funds from one purpose to another, when the common good required it. Considerable emphasis was put on strengthening the authority of the community leadership: members of the community were not permitted to accept appointments by the authorities or to ask the authorities for exemption from community taxes; every dispute between Jews had to be brought before Jewish judges; and Jews were not allowed to apply to non-Jewish courts. Excommunication of an individual required the consent of the community, as did the divorce of a wife. Gambling was outlawed and regulations were issued for the preservation of order in the synagogues and law courts and at public celebrations. Lending money to Jews against the payment of interest, and insulting anyone in public were also prohibited. In the 12th century the Jews still took part in the defense of the towns in which they lived. Eleazar b. Judah tells of "the siege of Worms by a great host on the Sabbath, when we permitted all the Jews to take up arms… for if they had not helped the townspeople they would have been killed… therefore we permitted it" (*Sefer ha-Roke'aḥ* (Cremona, 1557), 23a, *Hilkhot Eruvin*, no. 197). In this period, Jews also moved with the eastward trend of the population, and new Jewish communities were established in the east and southeast. Those who joined in the movement of the urban population eastward encountered the terrors and problems of new colonists: "When you build houses in the forest you find the inhabitants stricken with plague since the place is haunted by spirits… They asked the sage what they should do; he answered: Take the Ten Commandments and a Torah Scroll and stretch out a cord the length of the ground, and bring the Torah Scroll to the cord… and then at the end say: 'Before God, before the Torah, and before Israel its guardians, may no demon nor she-demon come to this place from today and for ever'" (*Sefer Ḥasidim* (ed. Wistinetzki), no. 371).

13TH CENTURY. The 13th century brought new troubles upon the Jews. The Fourth *Lateran Council (1215) decreed that the clergy were to restrict business relations between Christians and Jews, that Jews had to wear signs distinguishing them from the Christians (see *badge), and that they were not to hold any public office. In 1235 the first case of *blood libel occurred in Germany (in *Fulda) and in the second half of the 13th century the libel of *Host desecration began to spread in the country. These accusations were to cost many Jewish lives, to cause Jews much anxiety and anguish, and to bring about further deterioration of their image in the eyes of their Christian neighbors, who now came to regard them as corrupt beings, capable of the most abominable crimes. The acceptance of such views of the Jews by the masses occurred at a time when imperial rule was weakening, and the right to the Jews' "servitude to the treasury" was passed on or transferred in different ways and for differing reasons to various local competencies. Religious fanaticism was rising and caused a social ferment in the cities, where the mob vented their anger on the Jews. In 1241, when the Jews of *Frankfurt on the Main tried to prevent one of their people from converting to Christianity, a *Judenschlacht* (Jews' slaughter) took place, in which the entire community was butchered by the Christian mob. In 1259 a synod of the Mainz archdiocese ordered that Jews within its borders should wear the yellow badge. In 1285 the entire Jewish community of *Munich – some 180 persons – was burned to death, victims of a libel that had been spread against them. The Jews also had a heavy tax burden. A partial list of imperial revenue, dating from 1241, reveals that in 25 Jewish communities the Jews paid 857 marks, amounting to 12% of the entire imperial tax revenue for the year (7,127.5 marks) and 20% of the total raised in the German cities. In addition to the regular taxes the Jews also had to make payments in the form of "presents" and bribes, or money was simply extorted from them. In this period – the second half of the 13th century – German Jewry produced great spiritual leaders. Foremost was Meir b. Baruch of Rothenburg, whose responsa and instructions guided several generations of Jews. He attacked manifestations of injustice or high-handedness in communal affairs, and in his threnodies and other writings gave expression to the sufferings of his people. In the end, his own fate symbolized the distress of the Jews: trying to escape overseas, like other persecuted Jews in Germany, he was arrested, handed over to the emperor, and died in jail in 1293.

PERSECUTIONS OF THE 14TH CENTURY. At the end of the 13th century and the first half of the 14th, anti-Jewish excesses by the mob increased in vehemence and frequency, and the authorities were also increasingly oppressive. In 1342 Louis IV of Bavaria decreed that "every male Jew and every Jewish widow, of 12 years and above, is obliged to pay a yearly tax of one gulden." This poll tax was designed to increase the income that the emperor derived from the Jews, which had declined as the result of their "transfer" to lower authorities, and came in addition to the other taxes exacted from the Jews. In 1356 Emperor *Charles IV transferred his claim over the Jews to the Imperial Electors. Within a period of 50 years the Jews of Germany suffered three devastating blows. In 1298–99, when civil war had broken out in southwest Germany, the Jews were accused of Host desecration, and the Jew-baiter, *Rindfleisch, gathered a mob around him which fell upon the Jews of Franconia, Bavaria, and the surrounding area, destroying no less than 140 communities (including *Rothenburg, Wuerzburg, *Nuremberg, and Bamberg). Many Jews chose a martyr's death and in many places also offered armed resistance. The period 1336–37 was marked by the catastrophe of the *Armleder massacres, in the course of which 110 communities, from Bavaria to Alsace, were destroyed by rioting peasants. Finally, in the massacres during the *Black Death, in 1348–50, 300 Jewish communities were destroyed in all parts of the country, and the Jews either killed, or driven out as "poisoners of wells." The greatest Jewish scholar of the time, *Alexander Suslin ha-Kohen, was among those slain in Erfurt, in 1349. As a result of these three onslaughts, the structure of Jewish life in Germany suffered a severe blow. Nevertheless, only a short while later, Jews were again permitted to take up residence in German cities, where there was no one else to fulfill their function in society of moneylenders. Only a few weeks after the slaughter of the Jews of *Augsburg the bishop permitted some to return to the city; between 1352 and 1355 Jews reappeared in Erfurt, Nuremberg, *Ulm, Speyer, Worms, and Trier. Their residence was now based on contracts which contained severe restrictions and imposed numerous payments on them. There was also increased exploitation of the Jews by the emperor; a moratorium on debts, declared by *Wenceslaus IV in 1385 and again in 1390, dealt a severe blow to the economic situation of the Jews. Jewish vitality, however, was able to assert itself even in the adverse conditions that prevailed after the

Black Death massacres. The scholars assured the continuity of Jewish creativity. In 1365, *Meir b. Baruch ha-Levi established a new school in Vienna, based upon the customs and traditions of the Rhine communities, and his disciples – the "Sages of Austria" – became the spiritual leaders of German Jewry. In east and south Germany, with fewer towns and a relatively backward economy, Jews found it easier to earn their livelihood. This was also the route to *Poland, which gradually turned into a refuge for the Jews. Until the Reformation there was no change in the precarious situation of the Jews of Germany. On the one hand, the disintegration of the Empire prevented large-scale countrywide expulsions: when the Jews were driven out of one locality they were able to bide their time in a neighboring place, and after a short while return to their previous homes; on the other hand, the lack of a central authority put the Jews at the mercy of local rulers. In general, the emperor, the princes, and the leading classes in the towns gave their protection to the Jews; yet a single fanatic anti-Jewish preacher, John of *Capistrano, found it possible to inflame the masses against the Jews and to initiate a new wave of persecutions (1450–59) which culminated in the expulsion of the Jews from Breslau.

15TH CENTURY. The 15th century was generally marked by libels against Jews and their expulsion from certain areas and most major cities: in 1400 the Jews were expelled from Prague; in 1420, 1438, 1462, and 1473 there were successive expulsions from Mainz; in 1420–21 from Austria; in 1424 from Cologne; in 1440 from Augsburg; in 1475 the blood libel was raised in *Trent, resulting in anti-Jewish agitation and riots all over Germany, and the expulsion of the Jews from *Tyrol; in 1492 a Host desecration libel led to the expulsion of the Jews from *Mecklenburg; in 1493 they were driven out of *Magdeburg, and in the period 1450–1500, out of many towns in Bavaria, Franconia, and Swabia; in 1499 from Nuremberg; in 1510 there was another Host desecration libel and expulsion from *Brandenburg; in the same year expulsion from Alsace; and in 1519 from Regensburg. Of the more important cities in Germany, only Frankfurt and Worms still had major Jewish communities after that date. Nevertheless, in the course of the 15th century, amid these tribulations, Jews were also able to branch out into occupations other than moneylending. In the south German communities, there were Jewish wine merchants and petty traders. Jews also began to play a role in the expanding commercial life, acting as intermediaries between the large agricultural producer (such as the monasteries) and the rising city merchant; expelled from the cities and forced to live in the small towns and villages, the Jews bought wool, flax, etc., from the large storehouses and sold these commodities to the wholesale merchant. This was the beginning of a process which culminated in Poland in the 16th and 17th centuries with the Jews entering the service of the nobility as managers of their estates. Jewish life in the small communities of Germany was frequently marked by great material and spiritual hardship. Yet the Jews did all in their power to fulfill the commandments of their faith. Israel *Isserlein's *Pesakim u-Khetavim* (Venice, 1545), para. 52, records a "curious event" in south Germany, when several communities had only a single *etrog* to share among them on the Sukkot festival; they cut the fruit up and sent a piece to each community, and although shriveled by the time it reached its destination, the Jews made the prescribed blessing over their slice of *etrog* on the first day of the festival. Despite their poverty and sufferings, Jews held on to the normal joys of life. Jacob Moses *Moellin permitted "placing tree branches in water on the Sabbath … in order to provide a source of joy for the house" (Jacob b. Moses Moellin, *Maharil* (Cremona, 1558), 38b); when asked about celebrating a wedding in a community where a local ordinance forbade the participation of musicians, the same rabbi advised that the wedding be moved to another community, where music could be made, rather than have the bride and bridegroom forego the pleasure (*ibid.*, 41b). Even at a time when persecutions were actually taking place, the Jews persisted in their way of life and in study of the Torah. Thus Moses *Mintz, while writing a halakhic decision, records that "the time limit given us by the bishop [of Bamberg] for leaving the town has been reached, for he would not allow us a single additional day or even hour" (Resp. Maharam Mintz, para. 48). The rabbis' position became widely acknowledged in this period, and they were regarded as "the leaders." It may be assumed that it was Meir b. Baruch ha-Levi's school that established the custom of *semikhah* (rabbinical ordination) and of awarding the title of *Morenu* ("our teacher") to a graduate rabbi, a custom which Ashkenazi Jews have still retained. At the same time the rabbis often engaged in bitter quarrels over the question of jurisdiction, and the position of the rabbi. These quarrels largely resulted from the difficulties facing the Jewish spiritual leaders, who tried, in a permanent state of insecurity, to rebuild communities that had been destroyed. The rabbinical leaders of this period – Meir b. Baruch ha-Levi and his disciples, Jacob b. Moses Moellin, Israel Isserlein (author of *Terumat ha-Deshen*), Moses Mintz, Israel b. Ḥayyim *Bruna, and others – were dedicated men who did all in their power to establish new yeshivot and spread the study of Torah, but they did not achieve the degree of leadership displayed by their predecessors. An extreme example of a scholar devoted to his yeshivah was that of Jacob b. Moses Moellin "who would live in a house alone with his students, next to the house of his wife the 'rabbanit,' while her sons were with her in her house; nor did he enjoy a mite of his wife's property during her lifetime or eat with her. Only the communal leaders supplied him with sufficient means to support the students of his yeshivah, while he himself earned a livelihood as a marriage broker" (*Maharil*, 76a). His yeshivah was attended not only by poor scholars, but by "those rich and pampered youths who had tables made for them – when they sat down in their seats they could turn the table in any direction they pleased, and kept many books on them" (*Leket Yosher*, ed. by J. Freimann (1903), YD 39). The debate with Christianity did not die down in this period, and Yom Tov Lipmann *Muelhausen raised it to new heights of sharp polemical argument in his *Sefer ha-Niẓẓaḥon* (see *Disputations).

Emperors resorted to the most extreme measures in order to extort money from the Jews. The most extortionate was Sigismund who demanded one-third of their property. In 1407, Rupert of Wittelsbach appointed Israel b. Isaac of Nuremberg to the office of *Hochmeister* (chief rabbi), and sought to give him sole powers of sequestering Jewish property. The communities, however, refused to acknowledge the authority of a Jew appointed by gentiles and eventually the king abandoned his attempt. Sigismund named several "chief rabbis" for the purpose of improving the collection of the oppressive taxes that he imposed upon the Jews, including well-known rabbinical leaders. It is not clear, however, to what extent these appointments were recognized by the communities, and the responsa literature of the period contains no specific references to such appointments. At any rate, a proposal made by Seligmann Oppenheim Bing (see *Bingen) to convene a conference which would create a chief rabbinate was rejected by most of his rabbinical colleagues.

In sum, the last few centuries of the Middle Ages were a period of severe and difficult changes for the Jews of Germany. The center of gravity, both in population and intellectual activity, shifted steadily eastward. From their position as desirable traders the Jews were driven by the religious and social forces which gained ascendancy in the 12th and 13th centuries into the despised occupation of usury. The 50 years from 1298 to 1348 took a tragic toll on both life and property. Despite the trials and tribulations of the Middle Ages the Jews of Germany displayed their own creative powers in halakhic literature and religious poetry, and in the establishment of communal institutions. Although they did not disdain the innocent joys of life, they were exacting in the application of the Law and were imbued with the spirit of ascetic piety. *Kiddush ha-Shem* – martyrdom for the sanctification of God – and their particular pietism (*Ḥasidut Ashkenaz*), in both theory and practice, were authentic contributions of German Jewry to the realm of supreme Jewish values.

[Haim Hillel Ben-Sasson]

From the Reformation To World War I

The age of the Reformation was characterized by upheavals in all spheres of life – political, economic, social, religious, and cultural. It also produced new attitudes to Jews and Judaism often of a conflicting nature. When the Middle Ages came to an end, the Jews had suffered expulsion from most German cities, as well as from many other localities and areas: *Heilbronn 1475, *Tuebingen 1477, Bamberg 1478, *Esslingen 1490, Mecklenburg 1492, Magdeburg 1493, *Reutlingen 1495, Wuerttemberg and Wuerzburg 1498, Nuremberg and Ulm 1499, *Noerdlingen 1507, the state of Brandenburg 1510, Regensburg 1519, Rottenburg 1520, and *Saxony 1537. Jews were prohibited from practicing most occupations. Many now had to earn a livelihood from hawking haberdashery, peddling, moneylending, and pawnbroking in the small towns and villages. Interest rates were subject to severe regulations, and wearing of the humiliating badge was enforced. In various states Jews were prohibited from building new synagogues and from holding discussions on religious questions without Church authorization. However, Emperor *Charles V (at assemblies of the Reichstag in Augsburg 1530, Regensburg 1541, Speyer 1544, and Augsburg 1548) authorized in full the charters granted to the Jews by previous emperors.

At the very time that humanism was coming to the fore, the libels against the Jews, accusing them of using human blood for ritual purposes and of desecrating the Host, were continually resuscitated, and resulted in further killings and expulsions: *Endingen 1470, Regensburg 1476, *Passau 1477, *Trent 1475, Sternberg (Mecklenburg) 1492, Engen (Swabia) 1495, Berlin 1500, Langendenzlingen 1503, Frankfurt 1504, Brandenburg 1520. Some humanists acknowledged the religious and moral values inherent in Judaism and took up its defense, but in folk literature and the mystery plays the Jew was depicted as a usurer and bloodsucker, as the Christ-killer and reviler of the Virgin Mary, an associate of Satan and ally of the Turk. Yet the humanist Johann *Reuchlin led a courageous struggle against the defamation of the Talmud and called for equal rights for the Jews, as "cocitizens of the Roman Empire." Martin *Luther, after failing to win them, showed vehement hatred for the Jews, and in his writings called upon the secular rulers to deprive them of their prayer books and Talmud, to destroy their homes, to put them on forced labor or expel them from the land. There were, however, other reforming movements, especially the Anabaptists, who appreciated the Jewish Bible and Judaism and displayed sympathy and love for the Jews. The Jews were also caught in the struggle between the emperor, on the one hand, and the princes and cities, on the other. The emperors, whose power was on the decline, made efforts to retain their control of the Jews, to protect them against local potentates, and to remain the sole beneficiaries of the taxes paid by the Jews. The opposing forces, bent upon establishing their independence of the emperor, also tried to extend their supremacy over the Jews and tax them. When attacking the Jews the princes and city governments were not only motivated by the traditional hatred, but also by their desire to reduce the emperor's authority and force the Jews to seek protection from them rather than the emperor. As a result, the Jews were often forced to pay taxes to two or even three different authorities. This situation, however, also prevented a general expulsion of the Jews from Germany at a time when this had become the lot of the Jews in most countries of Western Europe. The Jews also became the subject of controversy between the local rulers and the Estates (*Staende*) – the nobility, the ruling clergy, and the privileged townsmen. The latter had the power of levying taxes and tried to extend their power in various ways, including control of the Jews. To some degree the persecutions of Jews in the 15th and 16th centuries, which coincided with a rise in the power of the Estates, were the result of this struggle; thus, the Host desecration libel against Jews in Brandenburg, in 1510, was also an expression of the opposition of the Estates to Elector Joachim I, who had given several Jews permission to settle in the country, despite the Estates' objections. Other internal differences also affected the situation of the Jews, such as the antagonism between the princes and the landed gentry, and the cities. The former would permit Jews who had been expelled from the cities to settle on their lands, thereby gaining additional taxpayers who were also skilled merchants able to compete with the hated townsmen and provide the princes and estate-owners with better and cheaper supplies. The sweeping economic changes that took place in the 16th and 17th centuries also had their effect upon the situation of the Jews. The early manifestations of nascent capitalism caused much suffering among the masses of the people. Failing to grasp the meaning of the social and economic upheaval, they found in the Jew a scapegoat on whom they could blame their troubles, whom they had always been taught to regard as their enemy and exploiter. The demands for equality and justice which emerged from the social unrest in the cities included a call for the expulsion of the Jews "for the devastating harm that their presence brings to the plain people." The patrician class, which had supported the Jews in the cities, made way to the guilds, who adhered to a narrow social and economic outlook and would not tolerate any competition. They were also opposed to foreigners, especially if these were infidels. The numerous instances of expulsion that occurred in this period were to a large degree the outcome of these new developments in the structure of the economy. An outstanding Jewish personality of this period was *Joseph (Joselman) b. Gershon of Rosheim who in the course of his life made tremendous efforts to ease the lot of German Jewry and enable them to withstand the onslaught of the diverse forces arraigned against them.

THE ABSOLUTIST PRINCIPALITIES. Absolutism, followed by enlightened absolutism, and the mercantile system of economy introduced into kingdoms and principalities, brought far-reaching changes in the situation of the Jews. In its enlightened and mercantilist version, the system that now evolved regarded interests of state as supreme and attached the greatest value to money, commerce, and increase of population; it also came to judge the Jews from the point of view of these interests. The taxes paid by the Jews were highly lucrative, for they were among the few paid directly into the coffers of the ruler, and did not depend upon the consent of the Estates. Rulers welcomed wealthy Jews with capital and economic experience who could make important contributions to internal and international trade and to the development of industry. In *Hamburg, Portuguese Jews who had been expelled from their native country founded the Hamburg Bank which promoted commerce with Spain and Portugal and traded in tobacco, wine, textiles, cotton, etc. Saxony invited Jews to the *Leipzig Fair in order to forge new trade links with Switzerland, Holland, Italy, and England. Karl Ludwig, the enlightened elector of the Palatinate – a land which had been devastated by the Thirty Years' War – invited Jews to settle there in order to help restore trade and found industries. In Brandenburg, Frederick William, "the Great Elector," permitted 50 Jewish families who had been driven out of Austria to settle in Berlin and elsewhere, granting them extensive privileges and unrestricted trade throughout the country (1670/71). Jews were allowed to settle in *Frankfurt on the Oder, in order to infuse new life into the fair held in that city; in *Cleves, in order to facilitate transit trade with Holland; in *Pomerania and East Prussia, in order to attract commerce to the eastern portion of the country; and in Berlin itself, in order to make it the commercial center of Brandenburg and northeast Germany. The regime of the absolutist states instituted a system of supervision of the Jews which both regulated every detail of their lives and exploited them (see *Frederick II of Prussia). An unending series of laws and regulations, ordinances, decrees, patents, and privileges, circumscribed the entry and settlement of Jews, the length of their stay, the number of marriages and number of children, matters of inheritance and guardianship, the conduct of business and their moral behavior, their taxes, and even the goods they had to buy, for instance, china – *Judenporzellan* – in Prussia. Violation of these provisions resulted in severe penalties (and see *Austria, *Berlin, *Prussia).

SOCIAL AND SPIRITUAL LIFE. In their internal organization, the Jewish communities, up to the 18th century, continued to base themselves in the main upon the pattern established in the Middle Ages. In many of the communities that had reestablished themselves after an earlier expulsion, leadership became largely a function of wealth. It was not until after the *Chmielnicki massacres of 1648 and the Russian-Polish war (1654–55) that scholars, preachers, and teachers from Poland and Lithuania who took refuge in Germany began to play an important role in Jewish education. At the end of the 17th century the absolutist rulers adopted a policy of interfering in the internal affairs of the communities; as a result, the authority of the autonomous community organs was gradually reduced – a development which corresponded with the abolition of the powers that had previously been vested in the guilds and city councils.

Following upon the Thirty Years' War, proper *conferences of rabbis and community leaders were convened, to which "all the Jewish residents" of the country were invited, in order to decide upon a fair distribution of the tax burden. The powers of these conferences were severely restricted; they could not be held without official permission, and the authorities fought to confine their activities to tax collection. Nevertheless, the conferences in fact became an overall community forum and dealt with all matters that had traditionally been the concern of Jewish autonomous bodies (and see *Landjudenschaft). The authority of the rabbis was reduced in the 18th century by both the secular leaders of the communities and by the authorities, and when *emancipation was introduced, they were divested of their juridical powers. The ferment and crisis caused by the *Shabbateans had a profound effect upon Jewish social and spiritual life in Germany at the end of the 17th century. The two great scholars and spiritual leaders of this period were Jair Ḥayyim *Bacharach and Ẓevi Hirsch *Ashkenazi. The memoirs of *Glueckel of Hameln reflect the life of well-to-do Jews in the 17th to 18th centuries – their business methods, piety, family life, and ties maintained with neighbors. She gives a vivid description of messianic fervor in Germany with the appearance of Shabbetai Ẓevi. *Messianism and *Kabbalah remained at the center of Jewish spiritual life in Germany until the middle of the 18th century as a result of the passions aroused by the fierce controversy between Jonathan *Eybeschuetz and Jacob *Emden. At the same time, affluent Jews in urban communities began to adapt their ways of life to that of the Christian burghers. Around 1700 young women took Italian or French language lessons with Christian teachers, and entertained themselves learning how to draw or play a musical instrument. The deficiencies of the Jewish educational system, which took little if any interest in the education of girls and failed to provide a well-founded and consequential curriculum for boys, were decried by many authors of that time. Towards the close of the early modern era, the social, economic, religious, and cultural profile of German Jewry was highly diversified.

COURT JEWS. A characteristic innovation of the era of absolutism and the mercantile system was the appearance of the *Court Jews. Some of the Court Jews abandoned Jewish tradition and their ties with the Jewish people; others remained faithful and used their wealth and position to help their brethren. In some instances their intervention succeeded in averting anti-Jewish measures; they built synagogues at their expense, published religious books, and founded institutions of learning. Court Jews were instrumental in reestablishing communities that had been destroyed during the Reformation (e.g., in *Dresden, Leipzig, *Kassel, *Brunswick, and *Halle). The precariousness of their position could affect both themselves and the Jewish community; as they were dependent upon the whim of the absolutist ruler, any change in his attitude could mean their downfall, and this was often followed by anti-Jewish measures of a general nature. In fact the Court Jews led a double life, often marked by tragedy – as instanced by such figures as Samuel *Oppenheimer, Samson *Wertheimer, and Joseph Suess *Oppenheimer.

HASKALAH. Toward the end of the 18th century there were significant changes in the situation of German Jewry. Large parts of Poland were incorporated into Prussia and their substantial Jewish population became a reservoir of manpower and spiritual values for German Jewry as a whole. At the same time the growth of the Jewish population in major urban centers – such as Berlin – where the Jewish communities were comparatively new and unencumbered by age-old local tradition and custom furthered the turn toward *assimilation in German society. The background to this development was the Haskalah (enlightenment) movement, which was met in its aspirations by the claims of enlightened gentiles for the "moral and social betterment" of the Jews and the abolishment of all social and legal discrimination (see also C.W. von *Dohm; W. von *Humboldt; *Joseph II; G.E. *Lessing). These developments gave rise to considerable ferment in German Jewry. Moses *Mendelssohn, who wrote and published in Hebrew and German, and whose works made major contributions to pre-Kantian German philosophy as well as to Jewish spiritual life, was widely esteemed as the representative figure of German Jewry in the enlightenment period. Rabbis of the period, such as David Tevele *Schiff of Lissa and Akiva *Eger, took up the struggle against the "enlightened" and the assimilationists, but the bans and excommunications they issued failed to turn the tide.

EFFECTS OF THE FRENCH REVOLUTION. The emancipation granted to the Jews of France by the *French Revolution was soon carried over into Germany by the revolutionary armies. In the states on the left bank of the Rhine, which were incorporated into the French Republic, the Jews became French citizens. When more German states were conquered by *Napoleon, and the Confederation of the Rhine was created, these states, upon French insistence, also declared equal rights for the Jews and granted them freedom to engage in commerce on the same basis as all other citizens (e.g., in Wuerttemberg and the grand duchy of *Berg). Napoleon's "infamous decree" of 1808, which imposed restrictions on Jewish trade and commerce and limited the freedom of movement, was a serious setback to Jewish emancipation in the areas under French domination but was not reinforced in 1818. In Frankfurt and in the Hanseatic cities emancipation was announced in 1811. In 1808 the Jews of *Baden were declared "free citizens of the state for all time" and in 1809 a "Supreme Israelite Council" was formed in that state, which had the task of reforming Jewish education so that the Jews should reach the same cultural and spiritual standards as their environment and eventually achieve full equality. In Prussia, emancipation of the Jews was part of the reforms introduced by H.F.K. von Stein and K.A. *Hardenberg after the defeat suffered by the kingdom in 1806/07. This was followed by the edict of 1812 granting equal rights and privileges to the Jews, and the abolition of the special taxes imposed on them. In Bavaria, the edict of 1813 declared the Jews full citizens of the state but severely restricted their freedom of residence. These regulations, aimed at limiting and, if possible, reducing the number of Jews, were a main factor behind the massive emigration of young Jews from Bavaria to the United States in the following decades.

POST-NAPOLEONIC REACTION. The fall of Napoleon and the victory of the Holy Alliance resulted, almost everywhere, in the restoration of the previous state of affairs and the withdrawal of the equality that the Jews had achieved. Although the Congress of *Vienna had decided that the rights granted to the Jews in the various German states should be retained, the newly restored governments interpreted this decision as not applicable to the rights given to the Jews by the French or by the governments appointed by Napoleon. The "Jewish statutes," enacted by the Prussian provincial governments, repealed the 1812 emancipation edict in fact, although the edict as such was not canceled. Anti-Jewish feelings revived in the post-Napoleonic period, not only because the political and economic emancipation of the Jews was regarded as one of the Napoleonic reforms that had to be removed, but also as part of a spiritual and cultural reaction, an expression of a Christian-Teutonic, romantic and nationalist *Weltanschauung*. The new conservatism sought to replace the ideals of equality of the French Revolution with the harsh tradition of the past, and regarded the patriarchal state and feudal institutions as the natural political way of life for the German people. This view of state and society was accompanied by an emotional religious revival, and the concept of a "Christian-Teutonic" or "German-Christian" state came into being. In the effort to forge a German national identity the Jews, as "strangers within," were often portrayed as the negative counterpart of the Germans. A sharp literary debate was waged over the Jewish problem and the place of the Jews in the German state and society. Opinions on the preconditions, the pace, and the range of further emancipatory steps varied greatly, and the more vehement advocates of a "German-Christian" state rejected such steps altogether unless the Jews would renounce Judaism. The clash between the rationalist and romantic concept of society largely marked the relations between Germans and Jews in the period from 1815 to 1848. Anti-Jewish agitation was especially intense in the years after the Congress of Vienna, and in 1819 the *Hep-Hep riots spread across large parts of Germany and even Denmark.

ASSIMILATION AND REFORM. At the beginning of the 19th century, the social, economic, and legal conditions as well as the religious and cultural horizons of Jewish life were more diverse than ever before in German-Jewish history. The cultural and intellectual reorientation of the Jewish minority was closely linked with its struggle for equal rights and social acceptance. While earlier generations had used solely the Yiddish and Hebrew languages among themselves, and few had possessed even a limited reading ability in German, the use of Yiddish was now gradually abandoned, and Hebrew was by and large reduced to liturgical usage. Elementary schooling was made mandatory for Jewish children – in Baden in 1809, in Prussia in 1824 – and remaining Jewish educational institutions were put under the surveillance of state authorities. The juridical competence of the Rabbinate, already weakened in the era of Absolutism in most German states, was further reduced, as was Jewish communal autonomy in general. While the need for profound changes and an adaptation of Jewish life and Judaism to the circumstances and necessities of the modern era was widely acknowledged, opinions on the nature, the direction, and the extent of such changes differed greatly. Jewish intellectuals like Rachel *Varnhagen, Henriette *Hertz, Eduard *Gans, Friedrich Julius *Stahl, August *Neander, Ludwig *Boerne, and Heinrich *Heine converted to Christianity, but the overall importance of baptism, and the numerical loss it inflicted on German Jewry in this era, have often been overstated. Others sought to preserve what they regarded as the essence of Judaism. They initiated *Reform in Jewish religion, to ease the burden of the precepts which prevented Jews from establishing close relations with the people among whom they lived, and to stress and develop in Judaism spiritual and ethical concepts of faith and life. This was the attitude of the "Society for the Culture and Science of Judaism," among whose founders were Isaac Levin *Auerbach, E. Gans, H. Heine, Isaac Marcus *Jost, Moses *Moser, and Leopold *Zunz. The desire to employ the criteria and methods of modern scholarship in the field of traditional Jewish learning gave rise to the *Wissenschaft des Judentums, which soon made Germany the center of scientific study of Jewish history and culture. The actual reformers – Abraham *Geiger, Samuel *Holdheim, and their associates, sought to reshape the Jewish faith so as to make it compatible with the spirit and culture of the time and facilitate the achievement of equal rights and creation of close relations with Christians. These reformers were violently opposed by the leaders of traditional Judaism of the time, and bitter strife ensued. Other trends emerged which attempted to find a compromise between the two extremes – the "historical-positive" school of Zacharias *Frankel, and "*Neo-Orthodoxy," founded by Samson Raphael *Hirsch and Azriel (Israel) *Hildesheimer. In several places the Neo-Orthodox, who were unwilling to retain organizational ties with their Reform brethren, founded separate communities. In 1876 Prussia adopted the *Austrittsgesetz* ("Law on Withdrawal from the Jewish Community") under which Jews were permitted to dissociate from the existing Jewish community for religious reasons, and yet be recognized as Jews. By this act the compulsory membership of the community, provided for in a law adopted in 1847, was abolished; the "separatist" Orthodox communities (*Austrittsgemeinde*) were legalized and at the same time individual Jews were enabled to leave the organized Jewish community without having to go through formal conversion.

ECONOMIC AND SOCIAL LIFE. From the political and sociological aspect, the history of German Jewry in the first half of the 19th century is marked by their economic and social rise, and by the struggle for emancipation. (See Table: Socio-Economic Structure – Jews.) The political reaction of the "Holy Alliance" period, while succeeding in depriving the Jews of most of their political achievements, had little effect upon their rights in economic and commercial matters. Jews entered all branches of economy in the cities, contributing to the development of industry and capitalism and benefiting from it. At the end of the 18th century most of the German Jews still lived in small towns, their communities rarely exceeding a few dozen families; even in the "large" communities such as Hamburg or Frankfurt they numbered no more than several hundred families (1,000 to 2,000 persons). In the course of the 19th century many Jews left the small towns for the large centers of commerce. Augmented also by the influx of Jews from the east, the communities expanded rapidly, and by the end of the century most of the Jews of Germany lived in the large cities – Breslau, Leipzig, Cologne, in addition to Hamburg and Frankfurt, and particularly in Berlin, which eventually comprised one-third of German Jewry. The standard of living of many Jewish merchants, industrialists, and bankers equaled that of the German middle and upper classes. A large class of Jews in the liberal professions came into being and Jews took an increasingly active part in cultural life, in literature, and science. This development served to step up the Jewish demand for emancipation. Both Reform and Neo-Orthodox felt that the grant of equal rights should not depend upon any demand for diminution of their Jewish identity according to the conceptions of each trend. In this they encountered opposition even on the part of Christian liberals, such as H.E.G. Paulus and H. von *Treitschke, who held that so long as the Jews clung to their religious practice and maintained their specific communal cohesion they were not entitled to participation in the political life of the country. While these liberals did not demand apostasy, they felt that full rights should not be granted to the Jews unless they abandoned their distinctive practices, such as *kashrut*, observance of the Sabbath, and even circumcision. The Jews, on the other hand, encouraged by their economic progress and the rise of their educational level, took strong exception to this view, voicing their opinion that equality was a natural right that could not be withheld from them, whatever the pretext. Convinced that their struggle was intimately connected with the full social and political liberation of the German people and the creation of a free, democratic, and liberal German state, they pleaded their cause before the German public in word and print and took an active part in the German movement for national and political liberation. The chief spokesman of the Jewish struggle for emancipation was Gabriel *Riesser; others were Johann *Jacoby and Ludwig Boerne.

Jewish Socio-Economic Structure, Germany (percent)

	1895	1907
Agriculture	1.4	1.3
Industry and trades	19.3	22.0
Commerce and transportation	56.0	50.6
Hired workers	0.4	0.6
Public services and liberal professions	6.1	6.5
Self-employed with no profession	16.7	19.0

EMANCIPATION. Jews took part in the 1848–49 revolution and there were several Jews among the members of the Frankfurt Parliament (including Gabriel Riesser). The "Basic Laws of the German People" promulgated by this parliament extended equal rights to the Jews by accepting the principle that religious affiliation should in no way influence the full enjoyment of civil and political rights. Ironically, anti-Jewish violence was widespread in many areas during the revolutionary unrest, and often aimed at thwarting further emancipatory steps. The achievements of 1848–49 were curtailed by the reaction that set in during the 1850s, following the collapse of the revolutionary movement; however, the rise of the middle classes, including the Jews, did not come to a halt, and liberal tendencies continued to make headway. Nor did the Jews themselves give up the struggle. In 1869 the North German Confederation abolished the civil and political restrictions that still applied to the members of certain religions; after the 1870 war, the same law was adopted by the south German states and included in the constitution of the newly established German Reich. Many German Jews now felt that the attainment of political and civil equality had also erased their separate Jewish identity, not only in their own estimation but in that of the Germans as well. In the period from 1871 to 1914, German Jews indeed became a part of the German people from the constitutional point of view, and, in a large measure, also from the practical point of view. According to the law, every sphere of German life became open to them, whether economic, cultural, or social, with one exception: they were not permitted to participate in the government of the country. But usually, in spite of the constitutional guarantees, Jews were not appointed to official positions, nor could they become officers in the army. In general, Jews were also barred from appointments as full professors at the universities, although there were large numbers of Jews of lower academic rank. Jews were active in the economy of the country and some became leading bankers, industrialists, and businessmen; there was also a large number of Jews in the liberal professions. Jews were among the founders and leaders of the political parties; the Liberal and Social-Democrat parties usually had a number of Jewish members in the Reichstag. In the sciences and technology, in

Jewish Population in Germany, 1871–2001

Year	Jewish population
1871	512,158
1880	562,612
1890	567,884
1900	586,833
1910	615,021
1925	564,379
1933	503,000[1]
1939	234,000[2]
1941	164,000
1942	51,000
1943	31,910
1944	14,574
1946	156,705[3]
1948	153,000[3]
1949	55,000[3]
1952	23,000
1957	30,000
1964	31,000
1969	30,000
1994	45,000
2001	103,000

1 Jews defined by religion.
2 Jews defined by Nuremberg law.
3 Estimated number includes displaced persons.

literature, the press, the theater and the arts the share of Jews was disproportionately high.

The Jewish population in Germany numbered 512,158 in 1871 (1.25% of the total), 562,612 in 1880 (1.24%), 567,884 in 1890 (1.15%), 586,833 in 1900 (1.04%), and 615,021 in 1910 (0.95%). (See Table: Jewish Population in Germany.) Demographically, German Jewry shared many of the general characteristics of a largely urbanized population element and was among the first communities to feel the effects of the practice of birth control. At the beginning of the 20th century natural increase among German Jewry came to a complete end. It was the steady influx from the east which enabled German Jewry to maintain its numerical strength.

ANTISEMITISM. In the period following the foundation of the German Reich a shadow fell across the tranquility and prosperity enjoyed by German Jewry which darkened increasingly: the manifestation of antisemitism among the German public. Although its virulence varied, it existed throughout this period, and took on the form of political movements. It did not, however, affect the formal legal status of the Jews who therefore regarded antisemitism as mainly a social, cultural, and spiritual problem; its potential political strength and danger were not recognized by either Jews or non-Jews.

INTERNAL LIFE. Despite widespread assimilation, independent Jewish creativity did not come to an end. For a significant part of German Jews, Jewish consciousness retained its strength. The constant influx of Jews from the east ("Ostjuden") was also an important factor in preventing total assimilation. The presence of these newcomers created a certain amount of tension, both among Germans who resented their successful integration into economic life, and among the "old" Jewish families, who disapproved of the Ostjuden manners and of the way they had of making themselves conspicuous in the community. Zionism had an early start among German Jewry. Although small in numbers, the Zionists were well organized and worked effectively for their cause. German Jews were among the leaders of the World Zionist Movement; two of the presidents of the World Zionist Organization – D. *Wolfsohn and O. *Warburg – were German Jews, as was the founder and organizer of agricultural settlement in Ereẓ Israel, A. *Ruppin. After the death of Theodor Herzl, the headquarters of the Zionist Organization was moved to Germany and remained there even during World War I. By their high standard of general education and strict separation from Reform Jews, the German Neo-Orthodox exercised a profound influence upon observant Jews in other parts of the world. They had created a new type of Jew, who could be a qualified professional man, highly educated and versed in the manners of the world, and yet at the same time strictly observant of religious practice. It was men of this type who became the leaders of the world movement of *Agudat Israel after the founding of that organization in 1912. Orthodox chaplains serving in the German forces during World War I did a great deal to spread the principles of Agudat Israel among East European Jews. The confrontation with East European Jewish life also had a profound influence on German Jews serving in the forces; they were attracted by the wholesomeness of the life led by the Jewish masses, and many became convinced Zionists. German Jewish life was well organized. Organizations were established for the consolidation of the communities and for combating antisemitism (see *Centralverein), for social welfare (the *"Hilfsverein"), for research and studies (the rabbinical seminars: the *Breslau Juedisch-theologisches Seminar, established in 1854; the Berlin *Hochschule fuer die Wissenschaft des Judentums, founded in 1872; the *Rabbinerseminar fuer das orthodoxe Judentum in Berlin, also founded in 1872; the Historical Commission established in 1885, etc.). All were active and highly efficient. Throughout the second half of the 19th century and the early years of the 20th, German Jewry occupied a highly respected place among world Jewry, exercising a profound influence on Jewish centers in Eastern and Western Europe, in America, and in Ereẓ Israel.

[Samuel Miklos Stern]

1914–1933

The history of German Jewry in the interwar period is sharply divided into two chapters: the period up to 1933, which was a time of great prosperity; and the period which began in 1933, a year which was to mark the beginning of the tragic end of German Jewry.

Over 100,000 Jews had served in the German army during World War I, and 12,000 Jews fell in battle. At the end of the war, when the monarchy had fallen and a democratic republic was established, it seemed that the Jews had achieved full emancipation. Any restrictions that were still in force were abolished by the Weimar Republic, and Jews could now participate in every sphere of public life. Their share and influence in the political life of the country reached unprecedented proportions. Many of the leaders of the democratic and socialist parties were Jews, as were two of the six "people's commissars" which made up the first post-revolutionary German government (O. *Landsberg and H. *Haase). In Bavaria, Jews played an even more significant role; the head of the revolutionary government was a Jew, Kurt *Eisner, and the majority of the prominent representatives of the two Soviet-type governments set up after Eisner's murder consisted of Jewish intellectuals (Eugen *Leviné, Gustav *Landauer, Ernst *Toller, etc.). The inquiry commission which was to determine the responsibility of the military leadership for Germany's defeat had among its members Oscar *Cohn, a Social Democrat and Zionist. The Weimar Constitution was drafted by a Jew, Hugo *Preuss; another Jew, Walther *Rathenau, first became minister of reconstruction and later foreign minister: his murder by young extremists was motivated largely by antisemitism. Several Jews were appointed to high positions in the civil service, especially in Prussia. The rise of Jews to positions of political power added to their economic and social advance, but also increased hostility among the population. Antisemitic propaganda exploited a series of financial scandals and bankruptcies

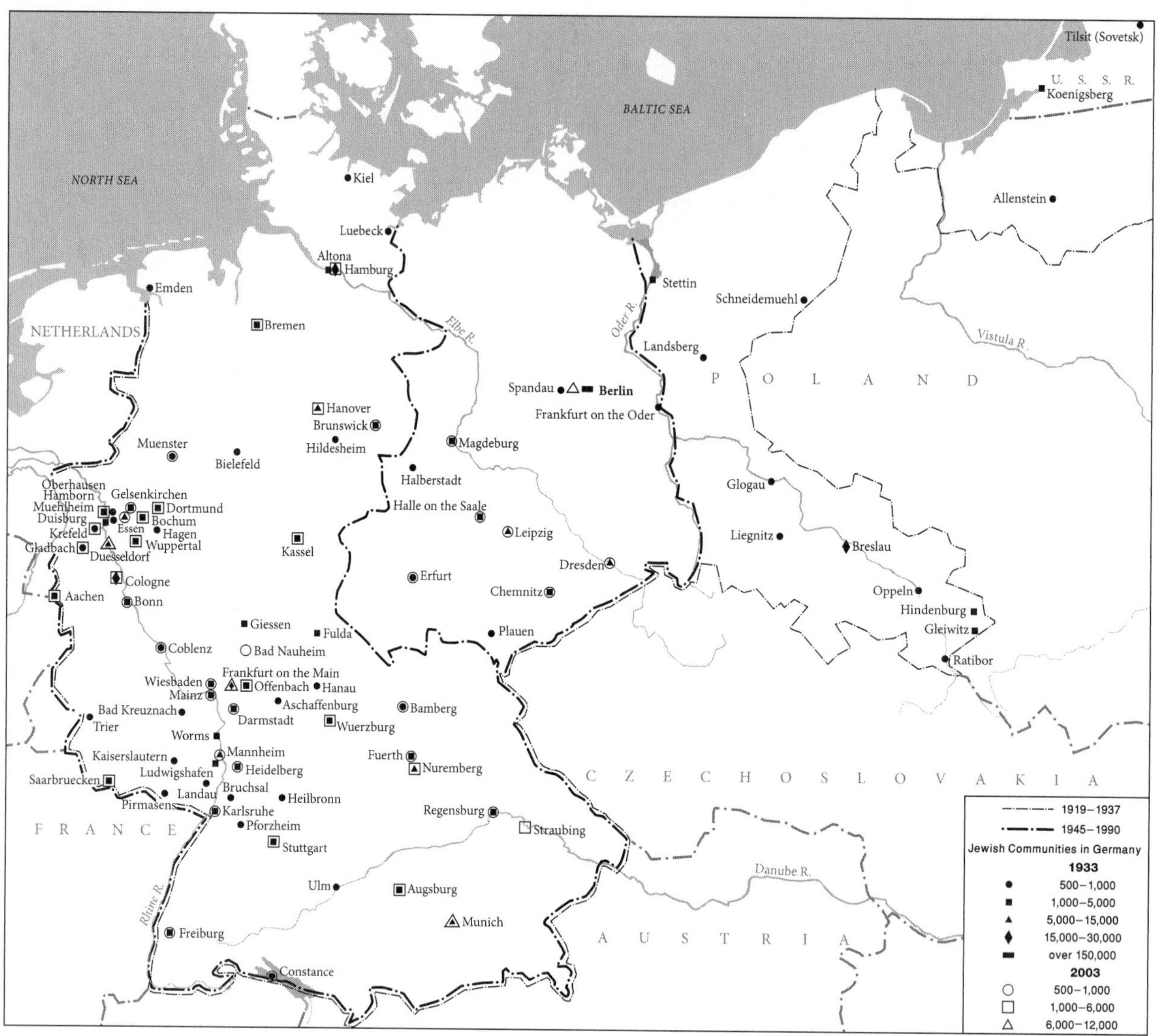

Major Jewish communities in Germany in 1933 and 2003.

in which Jews were involved. The background to these events was the great social and economic crisis which gripped Germany as a result of the terrible inflation after the war. Right-wing circles in Germany, anxious to divert public attention from the real beneficiaries of inflation – the "pure Aryan" industrial and financial barons and their giant enterprises – were more than ready to use the anti-Jewish propaganda for their purposes. The middle class, heavily hit by the economic upheaval, the nobility and the officer class who felt their honor besmirched by the defeat and whose privileges were abolished in the revolution, were all easily swayed by the idea that it was the Jews who were to blame for all of Germany's misfortunes – that "the Jews had stabbed the undefeated German army in the back," and thus forced it to surrender; that Capitalism and "Marxism" (i.e., Bolshevism and Socialism) were the result of the machinations of "World Jewry." In the 1920s, however, the full implications of this antisemitic mood had not yet become apparent, and the situation of the Jews seemed satisfactory. It was not until 1933, when the Nazis came to power and based their program upon the "doctrine of race" – i.e., hatred of Jews – that the role of the "Jewish problem" for the internal historical development of Germany stood fully revealed.

Throughout the Weimar Republic antisemitism did not disappear. Even the assimilationists among the Jews had to acknowledge this fact, and some reacted by over-emphasizing their German nationalism, thereby hoping to set themselves apart from the rest of the Jews. As a result of the large increase of Jewish immigration from Eastern Europe, the old difference between "Eastern" and "Western" Jews became more pronounced and had many practical implications. Jewish organizations did their best to facilitate the absorption of the newcomers and created special institutions for this purpose, such as the Welfare Bureau for Jewish Workers. Among a certain segment of German Jews there was now also deep admiration of an "authentic" East European culture, as can be seen in the enthusiastic reception of Yiddish and Hebrew theater groups, the popularity of Martin Buber's ḥasidic tales, and new cultural creations idealizing East European Jewry, such as Arnold Zweig's *Das Osjüdische Antlitz* ("The Eastern Jewish Countenance") with drawings of Hermann Struck. According to the 1925 census, there were 564,379 Jews in Germany, representing 0.9% of the total population. One-third lived in Berlin, another third in the other large cities, while the remaining third lived in 1,800 different places with organized Jewish communities and another 1,200 places where there were no organized communities. (See Map: Germany.) Most of the Jews made their living in commerce and transportation and in the liberal professions; in the large cities, one-third or even more of the lawyers and doctors were Jews; they also played a prominent role in the press, in literature, in the theater, and in other forms of entertainment. In general, the Jews belonged to the middle class and were well off. Although many had lost their savings in the inflation, they recovered from the effects of this crisis, and when the Nazis came to power, there was again a great deal of capital in the hands of individual Jews and the Jewish communities. The absorption of Jews into all spheres of German life was accompanied by record numbers of mixed marriages, and an increasing number of Jews formally "dissociated" themselves from the community.

COMMUNAL ORGANIZATION. Between the two World Wars, the Jewish communities presented a model of organization. The Weimar Constitution retained official recognition of the Jewish communities as entities recognized by public law and their right to collect dues. In general, a Jewish community had a representative body, elected by the community members, and an executive committee, elected in turn by the representative body and consisting of three to seven members. A point under dispute was the voting rights of Jews of foreign nationality (the Ostjuden), who in some communities amounted to a substantial proportion of the total membership. Although the "foreigners" had equal rights to the religious and social services provided by the community, in some places they had no equal right to vote, or were given that right only after long years of local residence. The fiercest fights for their voting rights were in Saxony, where East European Jews constituted the majority and German Jews insisted on keeping control over the communities by creating separate ballots for the two groups. By the end of the Weimar Republic, however, most communities had given equal voting rights to non-German citizens and women. The longstanding domination of the communities by the Liberals was shattered in a few communities, most notably in Berlin, where in 1926 a coalition of Zionist, Orthodox, and East European Jews received a majority of the votes. In 1930, the Liberals were voted back in. In the various states of which the Reich was made up, there existed "state unions" of Jewish communities. For a long time the need was felt for a national union of Jewish communities, but there were differences of opinion as to the form this should take; some thought that it should be a union of individual communities, others preferred a national union of the state unions, while a third proposal called for a kind of Jewish parliament, elected by direct democratic vote (the last plan was supported by the Zionists). By the time a national union was finally established, shortly before Hitler came to power, the organizational form of the communities, and the tasks they faced, were about to undergo a radical change. Apart from the religious and cultural tasks they performed, the community organizations were most active in social welfare; this was true of the period preceding 1933, and became even more important after that turning point. In 1917 a central welfare bureau for German Jewry was set up, the *Zentralwohlfahrtstelle, whose membership consisted of the communities as well as of many private institutions, trusts, and societies. The bureau cooperated with the main non-Jewish welfare agencies in the country, as well as with the American Jewish *Joint Distribution Committee, and published its own monthly. It supervised hospitals, clinics, counseling centers, bureaus, and a variety of other public institutions, and had some 2,000 welfare agencies affiliated with it. In the large communities expenditure on welfare amounted to as much as 30% of the total budget. Agencies concerned with youth, and with immigrants passing through Germany on their way overseas, also played an important role. In addition to the organizations based on the communities, there were also a large number of other societies, as well as cultural and scientific institutions. Jewish life in general was marked by the struggle between Jewish nationalism and various degrees of assimilation. Zionism succeeded in revolutionizing the life of the communities, and the councils, in addition to "notables," now also contained democratically elected members who represented national-Jewish interests.

The following were the main organizations of German Jewry in the period: Centralverein (CV) deutscher Staatsbuerger juedischen Glaubens ("Central Organization of German Citizens of the Jewish Faith"); Zionistische Vereinigung fuer Deutschland (ZVFD; "Zionist Organization of Germany"); Hilfsverein der deutschen Juden ("Aid Society of German Jews"); the religious organizations – Agudat Israel, Aḥdut, *Vereinigung fuer das liberale Judentum; *B'nai B'rith; *Verband national-deutscher Juden ("Union of Jews of German Nationality"); *Reichsbund juedischer Frontsoldaten ("Reich Association of Jewish War Veterans"); the various rabbinical associations, and associations of teachers and cantors; etc. An important role in the cultural life of German Jewry was played by the academic organizations: *Kartell-Convent (KC) deutscher Studenten juedischen Glaubens ("National Fraternity of German Students of the Jewish Faith"), affiliated to the Centralverein; Bund juedischer Akademiker (BJA, an association of Orthodox academies); Kartell juedischer Verbindungen, the Zionist student organization. A substantial number of Jewish youth in Germany were members of Jewish youth movements. Some of the youth organizations were sponsored by the Centralverein, and others by the Orthodox; a third type were the Zionist youth organizations. The latter encouraged pioneer settlement in Ereẓ Israel, maintained training centers, and supplied a small but steady flow of immigrants. The Centralverein was the largest and most important organization, which published its own newspaper. It advocated a synthesis of Judaism and "Germanism," emphasized defense of Jewish civil rights, and regarded German Jewry as an integral part of the German people. Other periodicals were *Der *Israelit* (published by Agudat Israel); *Juedisch-liberale Zeitung; Der Schild* (published by the veterans' organization); *Der *Jude*, a Zionist monthly, edited by Martin *Buber; and *Der Morgen*, a monthly published by the Centralverein. The official organ of the Zionist movement, **Juedische Rundschau*, a weekly (which in its last years appeared twice a week), eventually became the leading Jewish paper published in Germany.

Despite differences of outlook, there was close cooperation between the various organizations. An outstanding example was the establishment of the *Keren Hayesod in Germany in 1922 which was based on cooperation between Zionists and non-Zionists, and served as a preliminary stage to the enlarged *Jewish Agency (1929). The Zionist Organization included Zionist party organizations (Mizrachi, *Poalei-Zion, *Hapo'el ha-Ẓair-Hitaḥdut, etc.).

CULTURAL AND RELIGIOUS LIFE. The "Jewish Renaissance," a term coined by Martin Buber in 1900, culminated in the Weimar Republic. This brief period witnessed the creation of a modern Jewish adult education system, literary and artistic creations in the German language, the rise of a Jewish youth movement, and the revival of Jewish schools. While only a minority of German Jews was active in the various forms of Jewish cultural creativity, a counter-movement to the still continuing tendency of assimilation could now be observed. In 1920 Franz *Rosenzweig established the Freies Juedisches Lehrhaus ("Free Institute of Jewish Learning") in Frankfurt, which in its heyday attracted over 1,000 adult students who often were assimilated Jews like Rosenzweig himself. Other cultural institutions were the Juedische Volkshochschule ("Jewish College of Adult Education") in most larger cities; the Toynbee Halls, which also served as centers of social work; and the short-lived Juedisches Volksheim ("Jewish Social Center") established in Berlin in 1916. There were Jewish elementary schools in several communities and Jewish teachers' seminaries in Wuerzburg and Cologne. New Jewish elementary and secondary schools, originally maintained by Orthodox Jews only but in later years also supported by the Zionists and even parts of the Liberal Jews, were established, some in cities which for decades had seen no Jewish schools. Both the renewed interest in Jewish culture and increasing antisemitism were behind this increase. All religious and political streams of German Jewry founded their own youth organizations. In a few cities, Jewish museums were established, and the Berlin Jewish Museum was opened in its new home only a few weeks after Hitler came to power. Jewish cultural societies, such as the Soncino Bibliophile Society, were established, Jewish music from all corners of the world enjoyed respectable audiences, and Jewish sports societies were now established even beyond the Zionist spectrum. Most larger communities started their own newspapers, some of them developing into respectable cultural journals.

After World War I, when many Hebrew writers and publishers fled from Russia and took refuge in Germany, the country became a center of Hebrew publishing and Hebrew literature. Some of the greatest Hebrew poets and writers became residents of Germany, and Hebrew and Yiddish publishing houses were established. This was in addition to the many books published in German, on Judaism, Zionism, and Jewish studies. In Berlin and other cities, the Zionist Organization founded schools for the study of modern Hebrew by adults and the youth.

As the economic and political crisis deepened in Germany during the 1920s, a religious revival could be observed in all denominations. Judaism was affected by it as well, as some Jews found refuge in synagogues and study circles. The most prolific Liberal Jewish thinker was Leo *Baeck, who emerged as German Jewry's spiritual leader already in the 1920s. He was careful to keep the balance between radical Reform and Orthodoxy, and thus found a middle ground of moderate Liberal Judaism. It may be symptomatic of the changing times that the new edition of his main prewar work, *Essence of Judaism*, appeared in a revised form in 1922 which gave more weight to mystical and non-rational thought. His younger colleague, Max Wiener, developed the critique of German Jewry's belief in Enlightenment further in his *Judaism in the Time of Emancipation* (1933). Baeck's predecessor as president of the General Rabbinical Association of Germany, the Frankfurt rabbi Anton Nehemias Nobel, reintegrated mystical elements in contemporary Orthodox Jewish thought. Another tendency which became gradually apparent was the rise of women's rights in the synagogue and beyond. While they had fought successfully for their voting rights in most communities, the first synagogue with mixed seating was opened in Berlin in 1929, and in another smaller synagogue service in Berlin a ḥavurah-style egalitarian *minyan* was adopted around the same time. Women were among the students of the Hochschule fuer die Wissenschaft des Judentums, and in 1935 the first woman rabbi, Regine Jonas, was ordained, although she never served a congregation. Due to the financial strains only a few new synagogues were built, most notably the ones in Plauen (1930) and Hamburg (1931) in the Bauhaus style.

[Robert Weltsch]

1933–1939

As a result of the Nazi ascent to power legally through the appointment of Adolf Hitler as chancellor on Jan. 30, 1933, the entire existing structure of Jewish life in Germany collapsed. Personal lives, professional careers, individual freedom, and the very confidence that Germany was their home were thrown into disarray for Jews living in Germany. In response, German Jewry underwent a spiritual awakening and achieved a peak of vitality in Jewish communal life. In the national-socialist racist state, the Jews, branded as an "alien race," were automatically excluded by law from general life. Anti-Jewish measures gradually reduced the Jews to isolation and seclusion; the majority of the Jews were, however, unable unreservedly to sever the ties that had integrated them into German life. The racist decree that "no Jew could be a German" gravely affected the premise for the flourishing life of German Jewry, since the vast majority had considered themselves Germans and were genuinely assimilated in German culture. German was their language, German literature their literature, and German philosophy and values their values.

On April 1, 1933, the first large-scale anti-Jewish demonstration took place, in the form of a boycott of all Jewish-owned shops and offices of Jewish professionals. The yellow *badge was posted on Jewish business concerns and many residences; windows and doors were smeared with antisemitic and indecent cartoons; and SA (storm troop) guards ensured the observance of the boycott. The boycott was abandoned two days later due to sharp reaction from abroad and for fear of potential damage to the economy of the country. Some Germans made it a point of honor to call upon Jewish friends and to patronize Jewish shops. Most were frightened and just stayed away. This demonstration, far from being "a spontaneous eruption of the people's wrath," was organized by the Nazi Party on government orders. In the beginning there were even some signs of resistance among the German public to actions of this sort, until eventually the Nazi Party succeeded in suppressing all opposing political trends and concentrated absolute power in its own hands (see also *SS). This was achieved soon after the Nazi takeover, initiated by a wave of arrests of political opponents, for whose internment concentration *camps were set up. The first victims were political opponents of the regime, or people with whom it had personal accounts to settle, or whom it sought to deprive of their property. On April 7, 1933, the term *Nichtarier* ("non-Aryan") was adopted as legal designation. Jews were expelled from the civil service, including bureaucrats, judges, physicians, and professors. This facilitated the removal, step by step, of the Jews from various professions. The first to suffer were lawyers, judges, public officials, artists, newspapermen, and doctors. (At the beginning, veterans of World War I were not included in the ban, thus dividing the Jewish community.) The Jews were methodically pushed out of their remaining employment.

The adoption of the *Nuremberg Laws on Sept. 15, 1935, marked a new phase. It provided a precise definition of the "Jew" by origin, religion, and family ties; deprived the Jews of their status as citizens of the Reich; and reduced them to "subjects of the state." Intermarriage was prohibited while special provisions were made to deal with already-existing mixed marriages. Sexual intercourse between Jews and non-Jews was branded as *Rassenschande* ("defiling of the race") liable to severe punishment. In order to stigmatize the Jews further and brand them as a licentious people, the employment of "Aryan" maids under the age of 45 in their households was also forbidden. From time to time, addenda were made to the Nuremberg Laws, further reducing the Jews' status, until July 1, 1943, when the 13th such order was promulgated, declaring Germany *judenrein* ("clean of Jews"). Several Nazi leaders declared that with the adoption of the Nuremberg Laws the "regulation of the Jewish problem" was completed, and that the government had no intention of ousting the Jews from the economic positions they still held. Antisemitic slogans and graffiti were removed for the 1936 Olympics, and some Jews felt that they had weathered the worst. The pessimists had emigrated or pursued plans to emigrate and the optimists continued to believe that things would get better; the real Germany they knew would soon be manifest. In the period 1935–37, despite all the destructive measures, a large amount of capital still remained in Jewish hands and some Jews continued to run profit-making enterprises. To an extent, the Jews also benefited from the economic prosperity brought about by rearmament. Confiscation of Jewish capital, or enforced sale of Jewish enterprises (*Arianisierung*) did, however, become more and more frequent, along with arrests and other anti-Jewish measures.

The decisive turning point in Nazi policy against the Jews came in March 1938, when Austria was annexed to the Reich. The anti-Jewish excesses that took place in Austria, especially in *Vienna, were far worse than any that had occurred thus far in Germany, and the general population's part in them was much greater. Little could one see that the German expansion into other countries would make the German policy of cleansing the country of Jews impossible. With each expansion more Jews came under German domination. The Jews in the Sudetenland were to undergo similar persecution when the Nazis annexed it on the basis of the October 1938 Munich Conference. The gravest incident in this stage in the entire area of "Greater Germany" occurred on Nov. 9, 1938 (see **Kristallnacht*). The pretext for this action was the assassination of a member of the German Embassy in Paris by a Jew, Herschel *Grynszpan. A collective fine of one billion marks was also imposed upon the Jews, who, unlike foreign Jews or Aryans, could not collect insurance to repair their property. They were thus victimized by their loss, by their inability to collect insurance, and by the collective fine imposed on the community. These measures put the Jews of Germany in jeopardy and all subsequent measures only further aggravated their situation, culminating in 1941 with the commencement of systematic deportations to extermination camps.

The April 1, 1933, anti-Jewish demonstration filled many with consternation, but only a few Jews were brought to the brink of despair (resulting in some cases in suicide). In the initial stage, both Jews and some non-Jews protested. The Jews sought to remind the Germans of the contributions they had made to Germany's cultural and economic life, of their loyalty to the country, and of the medals they had earned on the field of battle. They soon learned that their efforts were futile. Gradually, the majority of the Jews understood that their fate was bound up with the Jewish people. Their only defenders were the Jews throughout the world who protested against the ill-treatment to which their brethren in Germany were being exposed. Emigration from Germany was their only hope but this too they could not achieve without the aid of international Jewish bodies. Judaism was also their only source of moral comfort. And Jewish institutions within Germany were the one place they were safe from persecution, at least for a while. For some, persecution had an unintended consequence. Instead of internalizing the hatred and loathing they experienced, it aroused in them a sense of pride in being a Jew, which gave them the moral strength to endure.

German Jewry now began to cooperate as a single body because external events erased the differences that had previously divided the assimilationists and those Jews who identified themselves with the Jewish culture and people. The Nazis did not discriminate between pious and secular Jews, between Zionists and assimilated Jews – all were uniformly detested; all were subject to Nazi venom. The anti-Jewish policies were directed against the assimilationist Jews as well, forcing them to recognize that they too were members of the Jewish people. The Nazi doctrine propounded that "blood" determined everything, so even converts and persons of mixed parentage (*mischlinge*) were labeled Jews. Among the latter were persons who for two or three generations had had no spiritual tie with Judaism. Of these "non-Aryan" Christians, or persons not adhering to any religion, only a few found their way back to active Jewish life. Some German churches acquiesced to or enthusiastically supported German racism even when it violated Christian teaching that one who converted to Christianity was a Christian. Only the Confessing Church remained faithful, protesting on behalf of those who had converted. Jews now closed ranks, irrespective of the divergent views they had held in the past. Many who had played important roles in German life, but had been remote from Jewish activities, were now eager and ready to accept Jewish public activity. At first, the existing Jewish organizations united under the Zentralausschuss fuer Hilfe und Aufbau ("Central Committee for Aid and Construction"), providing welfare and emigration services. This was followed by the creation of the *Reichsvertretung der Juden in Deutschland ("Reich Representation of the Jews in Germany") headed by Rabbi Leo *Baeck. (The use of the term "Jews in Germany" was imposed when the Nazis prohibited the term "German Jews.")

From the outset, one of the principal tasks confronting the Reichsvertretung was to organize emigration, which had taken various forms. (See Table: Emigration – Jews from Germany.) There was first of all the spontaneous flight to adjacent countries. In 1933, this was comparatively easy, for the Jews bore German passports which permitted entry to most European countries without visas. Regulations on removal of currency from Germany were not that strict, and a uniform regulation had not as yet been reached. In the course of time, however, the countries of reception placed obstacles in the way of the refugees from Germany, especially by refusing them work permits. Thus, the Swiss government refused such permits to all foreign nationals. In the fall of 1938 it requested that the German government stamp all Jewish passports with the letter *J* so that non-Jewish Germans could be

Emigration of Jews from Germany in the Period April 1933 to May 1939, including Areas Occupied by Germany by May 1939

Country of reception	No. of German immigrants
U.S.A.	63,000
Palestine	55,000
Great Britain	40,000
France	30,000
Argentina	25,000
Brazil	13,000
South Africa	5,500
Italy	5,000
Other European countries	25,000
Other South American countries	20,000
Far Eastern countries	15,000
Other	8,000
Total	304,500

admitted to Switzerland but Jews could be excluded. Only in a few instances were the emigrants able to maintain themselves on the funds they had brought with them. Emigration was also directed to overseas countries, mainly to the United States, but also to South America, Canada, and Australia. The consulates of these countries were thronged, but the existing regulations were not slackened to help the persecuted Jews. Except for Britain in 1938–39, no entry visas were issued outside the scope of existing immigration laws. The third and principal form of emigration was to Palestine. This was more than a simple rescue operation, for it had ideological overtones, reinforced by the feeling of attachment to the "Jewish National Home," while emigration to other countries was dictated by utilitarian reasons only. Most of the Zionists who left Germany made their way to Palestine. A systematic campaign on behalf of *aliyah* was conducted, and as the dangers grew, an immigration certificate to Palestine became a valuable document, coveted also by non-Zionists.

According to estimates of the League of Nations *High Commissioner for Refugees, 329,000 Jews fled from the Nazis in the period 1933–39, of whom 315,000 left Germany itself. In June 1933 there were 503,000 Jews by religion in Germany (including the Saar Region, incorporated in Germany in 1935), while in the first six years of the Nazi regime, the number of Jews was reduced by 289,000, leaving 214,000 Jews in May 1939. According to the census, there were 234,000 Jews (as defined by the Nuremberg Laws) in Germany in 1939, a reduction of 330,000 since 1925.

Efforts were also made to bring about a change in the occupational structure of the Jews, in order to prepare them for emigration. A large part of the Jewish students had been expelled from their German schools and universities and were now taught new trades on farms or in vocational and agricultural schools. Portable skills were essential to success in other countries. Schools to teach Hebrew, English, Spanish, and other languages were also established to prepare Jews for future emigration. *Aliyah* to Palestine, and *hakhsharah*, preparation for *aliyah*, were organized by the Zionist *Palestine Office (*Palaestina-Amt*), which greatly expanded in this period. The Palestine Office acted in an advisory capacity and was in charge of the transfer of capital through the *Ha'avara Company, which, with the approval of the authorities, succeeded in removing Jewish capital from Germany in the form of exports to Palestine, valued at about $16,200,000. Emigrants to the United States were rendered aid primarily by the Hilfsverein der Deutschen Juden and the American Jewish *Joint Distribution Committee. For the Jews in Germany the last few years preceding the war were marked by a desperate race to discover possible emigration outlets. The number of outlets, however, was continually reduced and, when the last exit to safety was finally closed, there was still a sizable Jewish community left in Germany.

In the period 1933–38, the Jews of Germany stepped up in considerable measure their own public and cultural life. They were now called upon to provide not only for their strictly "Jewish" needs, but also to engage in activities of a general nature, especially in education and culture. The Jewish community had to set up its own elementary and high schools for Jewish children, who had been expelled from the public schools. The teaching staff for these new schools consisted of the Jewish teachers who had been dismissed from the German school system. The "Center for Jewish Adult Education," an institution created by Martin Buber under the auspices of the Reichsvertretung, included among its tasks the training of these teachers for their duties in Jewish schools. In general, the educational and cultural activities of the Reichsvertretung may be regarded as the beginning of a Jewish moral resistance movement.

Among the Zionist youth movements, the largest was Ha-Bonim, No'ar Ḥaluẓi, which was founded in 1933 and based on a merger of Kadimah and Berit Olim. Makkabbi Hazair was a General Zionist youth movement, while the Werkleute were absorbed by Ha-Shomer ha-Ẓa'ir. After 1928, religious youth was organized in the Berit Ḥaluẓim Datiyyim. He-Ḥalutz, the largest organization preparing its members for settlement in Ereẓ Israel, established *hakhsharot* – agricultural training centers – with the support of the Reichsvertretung. Non-Zionist youth was organized in the Deutsch-juedische Jugend and Vortrupp societies. The Zionist Organization of Germany, which grew tremendously in strength, gained half of the seats in the community council and the national organizations in 1935.

The Jewish press played a great role in strengthening the spirit of German Jews. The CV *Zeitung* gained a circulation of 40,000 and a similar number subscribed to the *Juedische Rundschau*. (A front-page article of the *Rundschau*, published under the title, *Tragt ihn mit Stolz, den gelben Fleck* ("Wear it proudly, the yellow badge"), electrified the Jews with its call for courage in the face of adversity.) The pro-Zionist *Israelitisches Familienblatt* also jumped to a circulation of 35,000.

In art and literature a similar development took place. Jewish artists and writers who had not succeeded in immediately leaving Germany were forced to restrict their work to the realm of Judaism; in many instances this was a "return to Judaism" in name only, but in others it was accompanied by a profound spiritual change. The *Juedischer Kulturbund was created to organize Jewish cultural life. Jewish newspapers enlarged their scope, Jewish publishing houses increased their activities, and books on Jewish subjects, poetry, history, and essays gained a wide distribution. Like their cultural activities, the publishing activities of Jews were under the official supervision of the Juden-Referat, a separate body established within the framework of Goebbels' Ministry of Propaganda. From time to time certain publications were prohibited and newspaper editions were confiscated. The Zionist organ, *Juedische Rundschau*, was closed down and reopened on numerous occasions. In the course of time, the officials of the Juden-Referat came to show personal interest in the continued functioning of Jewish cultural life. The pogroms of Nov. 9–10, 1938, however, put an end to this situation, and the ensuing months, up to the outbreak of the war, were marked by general alarm among the Jews, cessation of all social activities, mass emigration, and Gestapo persecution of the remaining Jews.

[Robert Weltsch / Michael Berenbaum (2nd ed.)]

World War II

In the course of the war, when German rule was extended over large areas, Jews were sent to, or transferred from, Germany and other European countries. Many German Jews were put to death in Germany itself, along with foreign Jews interned there. In the period 1933–39, the communal and occupational life of German Jewry had undergone a radical change. After expulsion from commercial life and the professions, many Jews switched over to manual labor and agriculture. Although in 1933, 48.12% of German Jews had steady employment, by 1939 this figure had been reduced to 15.6% (Jews "by faith"). Of breadwinners in 1939 who no longer had any regular employment, over 40% were able to live off their capital and property, while others had some income from other sources and insurance. By 1939, thousands of Jews were already imprisoned in concentration camps. The Nazis considered the transfer of German Jews to special reservations in German-occupied territory of Poland or Russia or even the remote island of *Madagascar. But over time and with the capture of more and more Jews in the occupied territories, these plans, even if desired, were simply not feasible. At the beginning of 1942, when the physical destruction of Jews was already in full swing, these plans were finally abandoned. A law passed on July 4, 1939, transformed the Reichsvertretung into the Reichsvereinigung der Juden in Deutschland ("Reich Union of Jews in Germany"), and charged the new organization with promoting Jewish emigration, running the Jewish schools, and social welfare. Leo Baeck remained head of the new organization. The work of the Reichsvereinigung was defined by law, and subject to orders from the minister of the interior. The Nazis regarded it as an instrument which could be maneuvered to rid the country of all its Jews in the shortest possible time. In May 1939, there were still 214,000 Jews left, of whom 90% lived in 200 cities and the rest in 1,800 different places without an organized Jewish community. There were an additional 20,000 persons who had been classified as Jews under the Nuremberg Laws.

The outbreak of the war (Sept. 1, 1939) did not bring about any change in the legal status of the Jews. Until November 1941, i.e., at a time when the mass killing of Jews in Eastern Europe, which had begun as the Germans invaded the Soviet Union in June 1941, some still succeeded in leaving Germany. German Jews were admitted to some neutral countries, others were able to escape across the Atlantic. In fact they reached every corner of the globe, including *Shanghai. Until June 20, 1940, Jews who had some means at their disposal were able to reach Palestine by way of the Italian ports, and until Nov. 11, 1942, they could go to *Lisbon and *Casablanca by way of unoccupied France. On May 1, 1941, there were 169,000 Jews in Germany, and by Oct. 1, 1941, 164,000. In the period that had elapsed since May 1939 their number had therefore been reduced by some 50,000 to 70,000. A substantial number of these had succeeded in leaving Germany, although some of them only moved to countries which soon came under German occupation. About 8,000 Jews were deported by the Nazis, to make room for Germans who were repatriated after the outbreak of war. These Jews were sent in the first shipment to the *Lublin district, and later to unoccupied France. Many Jews were put into the existing concentration camps, or into newly established ones. The mortality rate among the Jews also rose to unprecedented heights.

Some time in 1941, Hitler issued his verbal order for the "Final Solution of the Jewish Question." On Sept. 1, 1941, the Jews were ordered to wear the yellow badge (*Judenstern,* or "Jewish star"). In mid-October 1941, their mass "transfer" ("*Evakuierungen*" or "*Abwanderungen*") to ghettos in Eastern Europe (*Lodz, *Minsk, *Riga, *Kovno) and to concentration and forced labor camps was begun, under Adolf *Eichmann's supervision. By the end of the year, 30,000 Jews had been thus "transferred." In the period from October 1942 to March 1943, Jews from Germany were "transferred" to *Auschwitz and other killing centers, at first by way of concentration camps and, later, directly. Many synagogues were turned into collection points for those about to be deported. It was in this period that the rate of suicide among the Jews took a sudden rise. The property of the "transferred" Jews, or of those who had committed suicide, was taken over by the state, as property of "enemies of the people and the country." So too, the property of Jews who left Germany; no distinctions were made between voluntary departures and forced deportation. Jewish activities were carried on within the framework of the Reichsvereinigung, which in accordance with the law had absorbed all the 1,500 organizations and institutions and the 1,600 religious communal bodies which had existed in Germany in 1939. The last to be absorbed, in January 1943, was the Berlin Community. When emigration ceased, the work of the Reichsvereinigung was restricted to education and social welfare. It supported elementary schools, several high schools and colleges, vocational and agricultural training courses, and language courses, as well as the famous Hochschule fuer die Wissenschaft des Judentums. In July 1942 all Jewish educational institutions were closed down. The Reichsvereinigung also supported Jewish hospitals, children's homes, and homes for the aged. It was forced to assist the Nazis in gathering the Jews who had been earmarked for "transfer." The Reichsvereinigung derived its income from contributions, membership dues, and special taxes imposed on emigrants. In July 1943 the activities of the Reichsvereinigung came to an end. By then, most of its officials, as well as most of those whom it had cared for, had been "transferred" to their deaths, or put into prison. The assets of the Reichsvereinigung (about 170 million marks) were confiscated by the Nazis. A new national body was created, headed by Walter Lustig, at the Jewish hospital in Berlin.

In the "privileged" model concentration camp/ghetto which was known as the *Theresienstadt ghetto, of the 144,000 Jews interned, 42,103 were from Germany. In January 1943, Leo Baeck was interned there. This ghetto allowed the continuation of Jewish life in some measure. But by the end of the war, only 5,639 German survivors were left in the ghetto. Of those 144,000 Jews deported to Theresienstadt, 33,000 died there, while 88,000 were again deported to Auschwitz. Of 15,000 children, only some 100 survived.

By the end of 1942 the number of Jews in Germany had been reduced to 51,000, and by the beginning of April the following year to 32,000. On May 19, 1943, Germany was declared *judenrein*. On Sept. 1, 1944, there were still 14,574 Jews in Germany who were not imprisoned. These were, for the most part (97.8%), the spouses of non-Jews, or "half-Jews," who had been defined as Jews by the Nuremberg Laws. When the tide of battle turned against Germany and concentration and death camps in the East were about to be overrun by Soviet troops, many more Jews were sent to Germany either as slave laborers or on death marches; Germany, which had first tried to be rid of the Jews, was now forced to reabsorb them as they were needed as workers or they were more dangerous to Germany if captured by the Soviets as living witnesses. In January 1945, there were in concentration and forced labor camps in Germany hundreds of thousands of Jews from various European countries. That number grew in the ensuing months until liberation as Jews were forcibly marched back into Germany.

The number of Jews who remained free in Germany – openly or underground – has been estimated at 19,000, and those who returned from the concentration camps after the war (including Theresienstadt) at 8,000. Late (January 1942) and doubtful figures provided by the Nazis state that from the beginning of Nazi rule 360,000 Jews had emigrated from Germany. About 160,000 to 180,000 German Jews are estimated to have been murdered by the Nazis in Germany, or to have died as a result of persecution.

[Jacob S. Levinger / Michael Berenbaum (2nd ed.)]

Early Postwar Period

When the Nazi regime in Germany ended, the general assumption was – in the words of Leo Baeck – that the Holocaust had terminated the thousand-year history of German Jewry and that Jews would not resettle in the country where the massacre of European Jewry had been conceived. This forecast did prove completely accurate. Jews were again living in Germany and they had rebuilt their communal and social organizations; but both numerically and culturally they constituted a faint shadow of the Jewish population of the country at the time of Hitler's rise to power. Although the Jews formed a very diversified group, their relative influence in all spheres of life was negligible. After a period of consolidation the Jews of Germany consisted of three main groups: the remnants of German Jewry who had survived the war in Germany; *Displaced Persons (DPS) who took temporary refuge in Germany after the war, especially in the American Zone; and Jews who returned to Germany or settled there after the war. Those who survived the persecutions and the war in Germany itself had, on the whole, only a tenuous attachment to Judaism. Some had been baptized, and the majority had entered mixed marriages (surviving the Holocaust only with the help of their "Aryan" relatives) and had raised their children as Christians. Among them were also several hundred women who had married Jews, and converted to Judaism. The average age of this group was over 50. The number of Jews in Germany grew in the immediate postwar period, when several thousand German Jews who had survived the concentration camps (especially Theresienstadt) and did not go into DP camps returned to Germany. Soon after, a few thousand were able to immigrate to the United States and several hundred went to other countries. Of those who remained, only a part (estimated by H. Maor between 6,000 and 8,000) joined the reestablished Jewish communities.

The DPS who arrived in Germany after the war were a "community in transit" and did not regard themselves as a part of German Jewry. At the end of 1946, there was a record number of 160,000 Jewish DPS in Germany; the total number of Jewish DPS who spent some time in the country is estimated at over 200,000. Most of them were in the American Zone, where they neither joined the communities nor had much contact with German Jews. The DPS formed their own organization, She'erit ha-Peletah (The Saved Remnant), which had local regional and central committees. In the British Zone (northwest Germany), however, it was the reestablished communities that joined the She'erit ha-Peletah, which had its headquarters at *Bergen-Belsen. In time the refugees, especially those who lived outside the DP camps in the urban DP assembly centers, established contacts with members of the Jewish communities. When the great stream of *aliyah* and emigration of the She'erit ha-Peletah came to an end in the early 1950s, 12,000 former DPS were left in Germany. There were in 1960, according to Maor, about 6,000 former DPS in Germany who had become members of the Jewish communities. They represented a sizable portion of the total membership of some of the communities, e.g., 80% in Munich and 40% in Frankfurt. No precise data are available on the remaining 6,000. Some may have emigrated, others may be listed as returnees, and still others may have severed all links with the organized Jewish community.

The Geographical Distribution of Jews in Germany, 1974

Baden	1,200	Lower Saxony	600
Bavaria	5,200	Cologne	1,200
West Berlin	5,300	North-Rhine	2,700
Bremen	100	Rhineland-Palatinate	600
Hamburg	1,400	Saarland	300
Hesse	1,700	Westphalia	900
Frankfurt	5,000	Wuerttemberg	800

From the end of the war to the beginning of the 1960s, about 6,000 German Jews returned to Germany and some 2,000 Jews from other countries settled there. During the rest of the 1960s, Germany received a few hundred more Jewish immigrants, in addition to several thousand returnees. For the most part, these were people who had not adjusted in the countries to which they had emigrated (including Israel). Others hoped that their presence in Germany would speed up the restitution of their property, or the indemnification payments due to them (see *Restitution and Compensation). Still others were simply attracted to Germany by the prevailing economic prosperity. Some prominent people, mostly artists and men-of-letters, returned to Germany – often to the East – but as a rule they did not join the Jewish communities. In general, the former DPS and the returnees were the more active groups, having much closer ties with Judaism than the group of survivors who never left the country.

REESTABLISHMENT OF JEWISH COMMUNITIES. The reestablishment of Jewish communities began shortly after the war, but in the early stages the means at their disposal were quite limited. Various organizations were operating in Germany to care for the victims of Nazism, and included the Jews in their activities. Among these were the organizations of Nazi victims and the Bavarian Red Cross. In Bavaria, the ministry of the interior established a State Commissariat for the care of people who had been persecuted on the basis of race, religion, or political convictions. (The first commissioner, appointed in the fall of 1945, was a non-Jewish Social Democrat; in 1946 a leading Jew, Philip Auerbach, was appointed to this post.) A bureau of the same kind was also established in Hessen. The American Jewish Joint Distribution Committee helped the communities establish themselves, and gradually they were able to assume the main burden of the religious and social services required by their members. The Berlin Jewish community at this time included the four zones of the city. In June 1947 a coordinating committee of Jewish communities in Germany, covering all the zones of occupation, was formed. When the *aliyah* and emigration of the DPS came to an end, the communities grew in importance. It was at this time that the

German Federal Republic (West) and the German Democratic Republic (East) were established. The interest of the newly founded government of West Germany in strengthening the Jewish communities was shared by the occupation authorities, especially in the American Zone (headed by High Commissioner John J. McCloy). On July 17, 1950, a Zentralrat der Juden in Deutschland ("Central Council of Jews in Germany") was set up with headquarters at Duesseldorf. The formation of the council was encouraged by the authorities, and it became the supreme organ of the Jewish communities in West Germany, achieving that status first in fact and later in law.

While in the immediate postwar years the Jews in Germany had insisted that their stay in the "accursed land" was temporary and that they would soon leave it, by the early 1950s voices began to call for the building of bridges between the Jewish and German peoples. One community leader declared that the Jewish-sponsored idea of dissolving the Jewish communities in Germany should be abandoned, and a rabbi who had returned to Germany even stated that the Jews remaining in the country were charged with reminding the German people of their guilt and their obligation to atone. Such ideas were supported by the government of West Germany and especially by Chancellor Konrad *Adenauer, who felt that in addition to the reparations agreement with Israel, the existence of a Jewish community in Germany and good relations between that community and the German people would be important contributions to the moral and political rehabilitation of Germany in the eyes of the world. To help bring about a reconciliation with the Jewish people, various German organizations and movements, such as the Aktion Suehnezeichen ("Operation Atonement") led by the Protestant theologian Helmut Gollwitzer, the Society for Christian-Jewish Understanding, the Peace With Israel movement headed by Erich Lueth, and others, were formed.

World Jewish organizations, especially the Zionist movement, disapproved of Jewish integration into German life. They regarded it as morally wrong for Jews to be permanently resident in Germany and tried to persuade them to leave the country. When, however, the reparations agreement was signed between the State of Israel, the *Conference on Jewish Material Claims, and the Federal Republic in September 1952, the psychological and political basis for ostracizing the Jews of Germany no longer existed. The Zentralrat became a member of the Claims Conference, and in 1954 the Zionist Executive approved the reestablishment of the Zionist Organization of Germany. (This is not to be confused with the Zionist Organization of the She'erit ha-Peletah, which was disbanded in 1951 as were all other institutions of the She'erit Ha-Peletah.) The Zentralrat also became affiliated with the *World Jewish Congress. Following the reparations agreement and the legislation for indemnification and the restitution of property, the federal government of West Germany and governments of the *Laender* adopted a liberal policy toward the restitution of property to the communities and provided them with regular subsidies for their needs. As a result, the Jewish communities of Germany became among the wealthiest in the world. This process of consolidation was not without its upheavals, struggles, and public scandals, which came before the German courts. Among those sentenced to imprisonment were Aaron Ohrenstein, the rabbi of Munich, and Philip Auerbach, who committed suicide in prison in 1952. There were also court proceedings contesting the legality of several community councils.

Antisemitism continued to exist in the country, perhaps exacerbated by the problem of bringing Nazi criminals to justice and the demand for the exclusion of Nazis from public office and government service. In fact, Neo-Nazi movements sprang up, Jewish cemeteries were desecrated, swastikas were daubed on walls, and antisemitic propaganda was disseminated. On the other hand, there were signs of a genuine change of heart: German youth was educated toward democracy, Jewish literature and literature on Jews appeared on the bookstands, there were exhibitions on Jewish themes, etc. The authorities assisted the communities in the construction of new synagogues and undertook the reconstruction of synagogues of historical value in places where there was no Jewish community (such as the medieval synagogue in Worms).

In October 1967, the number of Jews registered with the Jewish communities in West Germany, including West Berlin, was 26,226 (this includes 1,300 Jews living in Frankfurt who were not members of the community but registered as Jews in the census). According to the figures for Oct. 1, 1966, the largest communities were in West Berlin (5,991 members), Frankfurt (4,168), Munich (3,345), Duesseldorf (1,579), Hamburg (1,500), and Cologne (1,304). (See Map: Germany.) Because of the high average age, the demographic composition of German Jewry was highly abnormal. The death rate greatly exceeded the birth rate, e.g., in 1963–64 there were 482 deaths and only 69 births. In spite of the wide gulf between Jews and Germans, the rate of intermarriage is among the highest in the world. In the period 1951–58, there were 679 marriages in which both partners were Jewish, as against 2,009 mixed marriages; 72.5% of the Jewish men and 23.6% of the Jewish women who married chose non-Jewish partners. (For the period 1901–30 the respective figures were 19.6% for men and 12.2% for women.)

Several aged rabbis returned to Germany, and a few came there from other countries, e.g., the United States, Israel, and Britain, to serve for a limited period. There was a serious scarcity of teachers, religious articles, and community workers. The work of the communities was generally in the hands of a salaried staff. Jewish schools were established in Munich, Frankfurt, Berlin, Duesseldorf, and Hamburg, while elsewhere the community provided religious instruction during after-school hours. There were social welfare departments in the communities and a central welfare office (Zentralwohlfahrtsstelle) in Frankfurt. Many communities maintained homes for the aged and summer camps for children. German-language Jewish weeklies were published in Duesseldorf and Munich, and a Yiddish newspaper in Munich until 1974. The Juedischer Verlag (Jewish Publishing Co.) in Berlin was reestablished, and another publishing house, Ner Tamid, was opened. The Zionist Organization had branches in most of the communities, as did Jewish women's organizations and youth movements. In most places there were local committees of the *Keren Hayesod and the *Jewish National Fund, and in Berlin, Frankfurt, and Munich there were B'nai B'rith Lodges. An outstanding contribution to the postwar rehabilitation of Jews in Germany was made by Karl Marx (1897–1966), who returned to Germany in 1945, joined the Zionist movement, and founded the *Allgemeine Wochenzeitung des Judentums* ("General Jewish Weekly") in Duesseldorf. He regarded as his task the "building of a bridge" between the Jewish people and Israel, on the one hand, and Germany, on the other. He had close connections with the first president of the Federal Republic, Theodor Heuss, with Chancellor Adenauer, and with Social Democratic leaders and tried to serve as a link between them and the leaders of Israel and world Jewry. A number of Jews assumed important public offices. Among them were Paul Hertz, a Social Democratic senator in Berlin; Herbert A. *Weichmann, President of the Bundesrat and mayor of Hamburg; Joseph Neuberger (1902–1977), the minister of justice in North Rhine-Westphalia (who returned to Germany from Israel); and Ludwig Rosenberg, chairman of the Federation of Trade Unions. Several scholars and prominent artists, including the actors Ernst *Deutsch and Fritz *Kortner, also returned to Germany.

Despite their manifold activities, the Jewish communities in Germany rested on weak foundations because of their abnormal demographic structure, the inadequacy of Jewish education, and the abyss that continued to exist between the Jews and German society. The replacement of the expression *Deutsche Juden* ("German Jews") by the term *Juden in Deutschland* ("Jews in Germany") may be taken as an indication of the strangeness that Jews feel in Germany and their anxiety about the future.

[Chaim Yahil]

East Germany (German Democratic Republic)

There was only a tiny remnant of Jews in the German Democratic Republic, among them some prominent writers, such as Arnold *Zweig, Anna Seghers, and Stefan Heym, and Communist politicians returning from exile. A large segment of the Jewish community, including the presidents of the major Jewish communities, fled to the West after the outbreak of the antisemitic Stalinist show trials, culminating in the Prague Slansky Trial of 1952. In the same year the Jewish community of Berlin, which until then was still a unified body in a divided city, split officially. Until his death in 1965, the communities in East Germany were served by Rabbi Martin Riesenburger. Afterwards, the community was mainly served by Hungarian officials. Although there was no ban on religious practice, the Communist regime made an effort to obscure the identity of Jews. They were allowed to publish a periodical, which was mainly of informative character and contained also the obligatory criticism of the State of Israel. Only a few of the public figures who are of Jewish origin retained any connection with organized Judaism. One of these was the author Arnold Zweig who was president of the Academy of Arts.

In the last years of the German Democratic Republic religious and cultural Jewish life were reinforced by the state, mainly motivated by the wish to improve its ties with the United States. This may have been the main motive behind the decision of the Honecker government to renovate the destroyed Oranienburger Street Synagogue in East Berlin. Jews in the GDR could now attain greater visibility. With this new policy, a significant number of individuals, often children or grandchildren of Jewish communists, discovered their Jewish roots, and in East Berlin some of these joined "We for Ourselves," a group of mostly marginally Jewish individuals who stood in an ambivalent relationship to the community; several of its members have since been accepted into the Jewish community. With the Honecker government's new attention to the Jews, a number of important initiatives became possible. East Berlin was able to appoint an American rabbi, Isaak Neuman, who was in office there for a short period from 1987 to 1988. At around the same time, the Weissensee Jewish cemetery, Europe's largest, was rehabilitated, and a descendant of one of the families that belonged to the former Neo-Orthodox community Adass Jisroel, Mario Offenberg, negotiated with the GDR in order to reestablish this community in East Berlin. The restored Neue Synagogue in Berlin's Oranienburger Street was now turned into a cultural center and archive, Centrum Judaicum, financed mostly through small private donations from East German individuals. The community in East Berlin reached the height of activity in 1988 and 1989, the two final years of its full independence: 1988 saw the first large observances of *Kristallnacht*, in a meeting of younger Jews from East and West Germany in East Berlin; an exhibit, *Und lehret sie Gedachtnis*, was shown there in the reconstructed Ephraim Palais, the residence of King Frederick II's Jewish financier; on May 10, 1989, for the first time, *Ha-Tikvah* was sung and a community membership meeting referred to Israel's Independence Day. After the collapse of the Wall, Israel-oriented activities intensified; on November 11, 1989, for the first time, a large Israeli flag was displayed in West Berlin and a GDR-Israel Friendship Society began to be formed. These independent Eastern initiatives came to a halt very soon, however. Very much in step with the rapid unification of East and West Germany, the Western Central Council of Jews and the West Berlin Jewish community took control of their Eastern counterparts, and on January 1, 1991, the East Berlin Jewish community ceased to exist.

The number of members of the Jewish communities in East Germany declined from 2,600 in 1952 to 1,200 in 1967 to 350 (most of them in East Berlin) at the time of the dissolution of the German Democratic Republic in 1989. This count, however, ignores a much higher number of individuals of Jewish ancestry who chose not to register with the communities.

Jewish Life in Unified Germany (Post-1989)

November 9, which once had signified the end of German and European Jewry, received an additional meaning not only in German but also in German-Jewish history in 1989. When the Berlin Wall came down, the doors were opened not only to hundreds of thousands of East Germans from the former GDR and to ethnic Germans from the former Soviet Union but also to more unlikely candidates for immigration. With the upsurge of antisemitic rhetoric and acts, political instability, and economic depression, the Jews of the former Soviet Union began to look for new homes. Despite Israel's negative attitude and despite the fact that officially Germany was a non-immigrant country, it opened its doors to Jewish immigrants and has been trying to integrate them with relatively few bureaucratic impediments. In this respect, there is little disagreement along party lines, and the words of SPD-politician Peter Glotz in the Bundestag debate of October 25, 1990, spoke for the ruling Christian Democrats as well: "The Germans have covered themselves in guilt. I believe that the least we can do now, when Jews express again their wish to return or to come to the land of the Holocaust, is … to solve the problems unbureaucratically and without much fanfare." Initially many Soviet Jewish refugees came to Germany with visitor visas and then applied for political asylum. With the change in the German Basic Law in 1993 this was no longer possible. But even before, Chancellor Helmut Kohl and the governors of the German states had agreed in a meeting on January 9, 1991, that Soviet Jews would be allowed in on humanitarian grounds as quota refugees. After a stay of eight years (according to age) the refugees become eligible for German citizenship. Those who had been admitted by individual German states would be considered as quota refugees retroactively, while allocations were made to the individual states to cover the coming years. There was general agreement that Germany could absorb up to 10,000 Jewish refugees annually. Between 1990 and 1998, 53,559 immigrants from the former Soviet Union joined the Jewish communities: about 1,000 in 1990, an average of 5,000 between 1991 and 1994, and an average of over 8,000 between 1995 and 1998. Between 1998 and 2004 there was almost the same number of Jewish immigrants. The actual number of immigrants from the former Soviet Union is of course much higher (about twice as much), if we consider the (growing) number of non-Jewish family members and the (few) Jews who decided not to join the Jewish communities.

The largest Jewish communities of Germany in 2003 were Berlin (appr. 11,000), Munich (9,000), Duesseldorf and Frankfurt (7,000), and Hanover, Hamburg, and Cologne (5,000). Some of those communities have increased tenfold since unification and have reached the numbers of the 1920s. In a few smaller cities and towns, like Straubing (1,713) or Osnabrueck (1,541) there are now by far more Jews than before 1933. In other places, mainly in East Germany, new Jewish communities have been established which are exclusively or almost exclusively immigrant communities, among them Rostock, Schwerin, and Brandenburg in the East, but also Emmendingen, Lörrach, Delmenhorst, and Hameln in the West. Despite all these accelerated developments, the percentage of Jews in the general German population stands at only about 0.1%, and most Germans still do not know any Jews.

In the attention given to the population explosion of Jews in Germany it has hardly been noted that the "old" Jewish population experienced a steady decline at the same time as the community grew due to immigration. Without the immigrants the Jewish community of Germany would have numbered (in 1999) 22,211 members, which is about 20% less than the 28,081 members of 1990. A second phenomenon is worth noting. The discrepancy between low birth rates and high mortality rates remained constant in the 1990s. Between 1990 and 1998 there was a total of only 1,079 births, as opposed to 4,972 deaths. Thirdly, and connected to this phenomenon, one should take note of the change in age structure. When the first immigrants arrived in the early 1990s, they were mostly younger people, and brought with them a large number of children. By the end of the decade, the older immigrants dominated the scene and the age structure was only slightly younger than in the previous period. In 1998, 20% (18% in 1989) were under 20 years of age, 21% (25%) were between 20 and 40, 30% (24%) between 41 and 60, and 29% (33%) over 60 years old.

Immigration has also changed (for the time being) the occupational structure of German Jewry. In the postwar years the majority of East European Jews took up traditional professions connected to trade and business. Although we do not possess exact statistics it can be assumed that a significant part of the Jewish survivors who came to Germany became small business owners, with some of them expanding them into large enterprises, especially in the areas of textiles and real estate. Many also went into dining and entertainment establishments – restaurants and bars – often in areas with a large American military presence. The occupational structure of the second generation is quite different, with a high proportion of professionals, such as physicians, lawyers, and journalists. There remain a significant number in business, though more in banking and real estate now. The vast majority of German Jews attend not only high schools but also proceed to study at universities in Germany or abroad.

The first Jewish day schools opened in Munich and Frankfurt already in the 1960s, Berlin followed in 1986, Duesseldorf in 1993. Berlin is home to the only Jewish high school in postwar Germany, which consists of a high percentage of non-Jewish pupils. Religious education of two hours a week is compulsory in most German states, and the Jewish community provides those classes in even the smallest communities. It has to be said, however, that it is extremely difficult to recruit qualified teachers with both Jewish knowledge and German-language skills. The Hochschule fuer Juedische Studien in Heidelberg, which was established in 1979 in order to educate new spiritual leaders for Jewish communal life, has graduated in its first 20 years of existence a few teachers, who are now employed in German-Jewish communities, but few rabbis, who mostly continued their studies abroad and did not return to Germany. The first rabbi educated in Heidelberg was employed by the Jewish community of Duesseldorf. Thus, most teachers and basically all rabbis are immigrants to the German-Jewish communities, or at least received their education outside Germany. With the disappearance of the older generation of German-born immigrants who returned to officiate in the German-Jewish communities the language issue becomes more and more significant.

Despite these difficulties and mainly due to the further increase of the Jewish population, the number of rabbis in Germany has grown in recent years. In 2004 there were 34 rabbis listed in the directory of community rabbis, as well as 11 Chabad rabbis, both numbers having doubled as compared to the situation a decade earlier. In a few places, such as Brandenburg, the community rabbi comes from the Lubavitch movement. Chabad developed quite a number of activities in the larger (and now also some smaller) communities, especially child-related. Thus, the only local Jewish summer camps in Germany are run by Chabad, which overcomes the language barrier by recruiting young American women who speak Yiddish to the children. These summer camps have been among their most successful activities in Germany. In recent years, Chabad has also initiated the annual Hanukkah lighting ceremony in German public places.

On the other side of the religious spectrum, the Reform and Conservative movements have made considerable inroads in recent years. Both had developed in 19th-century Germany but virtually disappeared with the destruction of German Jewry in the 1930s. Religious Jewish life in postwar Germany was dominated by East European Jews and therefore led to the establishment of Orthodox synagogues. Only in one Berlin synagogue (Pestalozzistrasse) and in Saarbruecken was the prewar organ tradition revived. However, even there Reform services remained in the tradition of prewar German Liberal Judaism, with separate seating and no active role for women in the service. In the 1980s the first egalitarian services were introduced in Berlin and Frankfurt, followed thereafter in a few other cities. Many of their members originally came from the small American Jewish presence in Germany. Having been established outside the *Einheitsgemeinde* structures, the Berlin and Frankfurt Liberal congregations were granted space within the *Gemeinde* in the later 1990s. Some other Liberal congregations, as in Munich and Cologne, remained outside the *Gemeinde* structure or founded a separate association of communities as in Lower Saxony. In 1995 the small new congregation of Oldenburg in Northern Germany hired the first woman rabbi in Germany, Swiss-born Bea Wyler. In 2005, the Zentralrat reached an agreement with the Union of Progressive Jews and accepted Liberal community associations from northern Germany as members.

Most Jews in Germany are what is often termed "nonpracticing Orthodox." This means they do not attend synagogues on a regular basis but go to Orthodox synagogues during the High Holidays or family celebrations. Developments in recent years show the first signs of a more modern approach to the phenomenon of empty synagogues. Beside the Liberal congregations, which are united in an organization together with their Swiss and Austrian equivalents, there are a few modern Orthodox rabbis trying to replace the more East European-style services in their synagogues. They have initiated youth services, beginners' services, special *Kabbalat Shabbat* events, and regular German sermons. With the few exceptions of the largest communities, there is usually only one synagogue in town. This situation requires a certain amount of compromise in order to serve all community members. Berlin is the only German community which employs an Orthodox and a Liberal rabbi.

Kosher restaurants are integrated in the community centers of Berlin, Frankfurt, and Munich, but most other communities have a kosher kitchen for Sabbath *kiddush* or special events. Several communities maintain old-age homes with a kosher kitchen. *Shoḥets* and *mohels* are extremely rare in Germany, and usually brought from France or Switzerland. In addition to religious activities the larger communities have their own frameworks of secular cultural programs. In Berlin, Frankfurt, and Munich they are organized in adult education institutions which offer language classes, lecture series, and guest lectures with an often very impressive program. In smaller communities these programs have also increased over the years. It is perhaps a peculiar characteristic of the German situation that the audience for these Jewish cultural programs are overwhelmingly non-Jewish. As one consequence some communities, like Munich, established a *Lehrhaus* program which tries to create a more intimate atmosphere for the local Jewish population. Beginning in 2001, a cultural symposium called Tarbut has taken place regularly in the Bavarian Alps on themes of Jewish literature, politics, and arts, with several hundred participants from Germany, Austria, and Switzerland.

There exist a number of other Jewish organizations with regular programs, ranging from student organizations (organized in the German-wide Bundesverband Jüdischer Studenten in Deutschland) to Maccabi sports associations, WIZO, and other women's organizations to senior citizen clubs.

The larger communities run youth centers with a broad range of activities. The lack of leadership is, however, visible in this respect as well. Directors are rare in Germany and are usually recruited from Israel, which means a high rate of turnover, language problems, and often also a gap between a religious leadership and a highly secular clientele. The Zionist Organization, and especially its youth organization, has been among the most active Jewish organizations, organizing seminars and camps, which for many young German Jews become a formative experience in the forging of their Jewish identities.

Jews are a tiny minority in today's Germany, constituting not more than 0.1% of the total population. Their voice, however, can hardly be ignored in the German public. Whenever there are major public debates about the German past, spokespersons of the Jewish community are given prominent space.

It is notable that all leading representatives of postwar German Jewry, from the volatile Bavarian state commissioner, Philipp Auerbach (who committed suicide in 1952 after a spectacular trial against him which failed to prove that he had embezzled restitution money), and the longtime secretary general of the Central Association, Hendrik van Dam, to its most recent presidents, Werner Nachmann, Heinz Galinski, Ignatz *Bubis, and Paul Spiegel, were German-born Jews, while the majority of Germany's Jewish community always remained of East European background. The election of Ignatz Bubis as president of the Central Council of Jews in Germany in 1992 marked a significant change of image for the German-Jewish community. He succeeded the stern Auschwitz survivor Heinz Galinski and his predecessor, Werner Nachmann, who had embezzled millions of marks of reparation money. Bubis, who survived the Holocaust as a child, symbolized a new optimism among German Jews and was one of the best-known figures in the German public. He was even suggested as a candidate for the Federal Presidency in the 1990s. The election of Bubis' successor after his untimely death in 1999 was for the first time a high profile public issue in Germany. Perhaps for the last time a Holocaust survivor, Duesseldorf community president Paul Spiegel, was elected president of the Central Association in January 2000.

In contrast to pre-Nazi Germany there were today only a handful of prominent German Jews in the public sector. For many years not a single professing Jew has been a member of the Bundestag, although there were today a few well-known younger Jews active in political life, such as Michel Friedman for the Christian Democrats and Micha Brumlik for the Greens. Together with the late Ignatz Bubis, a leading member of the Free Democrats, these most visible Jewish politicians all came from Frankfurt.

In the realm of journalism the foremost weekly, *Die Zeit*, had a Jewish publisher in Josef Joffe, and a few other prominent Jewish journalists could be found in the press and television. The most important and influential literary critic in Germany in the last decades of the 20th century was Marcel *Reich-Ranicki. Some observers have noticed an upsurge in German-Jewish literature in recent years. Indeed, there are quite a few young writers of varying quality who increasingly write about Jewish topics and are well known to the German public. At the same time it has to be noted that their audience is almost exclusively non-Jewish.

There exists one German-wide Jewish newspaper, the weekly *Allgemeine Juedische Wochenzeitung*, published by the Zentralrat. Some larger communities, such as Berlin, Frankfurt, and Duesseldorf, issue their own community bulletins. The *Frankfurter Juedische Nachrichten* is only issued a few times a year but remains significant both because of its independence and its high level. By now the Russian immigrants have also established their own press. Jewish student papers such as *Cheschbon* in the 1980s and *Nudnik* in the 1990s had a rather short-lived existence, but student papers continue to exist in varying formats.

The most prominent Jewish representatives of cultural life in Germany are to be found in the realm of music. An impressive list just of conductors can easily be drawn up, ranging from Daniel Barenboim and Vladimir Ashkenazy to James Levine, Lorin Maazel, and Asher Fish. None of them resides permanently in Germany or is affiliated with Jewish life there, but they all have regular appointments and thus put their stamp on German cultural life. Such a list is more than a curiosity: it demonstrates that for a certain sector of society a burgeoning cultural and economic life can overshadow the tragic past. What is true in music is also true in other areas, such as academia, the sciences, and business. Especially where no language barriers exist, increasing mobility makes people move to prosperous and culturally attractive places and stay there, either temporarily or permanently.

Since the 1960s and 1970s German public discourse has been characterized by a culture of memory, which began with modest exhibits and local memorials and reached its peak in the 1990s with the construction of several Jewish museums and the big debate around the Berlin Holocaust Monument. In the 1980s and 1990s the German public began to discuss the less pleasant aspects of the German past with an openness unknown before – ranging from the Historians Debate all the way up to the present debates about the Goldhagen book, the Walser speech, the Wehrmacht exhibit, and the slave labor reparations.

Here again larger German issues were decisive. It was the generation of 1968, and the issues of 1968, which influenced the future outlooks of both progressive and conservative Jewish intellectuals as well. The identification with the student revolt and its causes, just as the later disappointment with an antisemitism often posing as anti-Zionism, shaped the critical Jewish voices emerging first in opposition to the official leadership, but – at least in the Fassbinder scandal – overriding traditional borders. As Jewish intellectuals such as Micha Brumlik, Dan Diner, and Henryk Broder made it clear, their growing disillusionment with the German left caused them to reconsider their Jewish identities. On the other hand, the minority conservative Jewish view (represented for example by TV journalist Richard Loewenthal in the 1960s and 1970s or by the historian Michael Wolffsohn in later decades) was also decisively shaped by its opposition to the student revolt and the values connected to it.

More noticeable than any internal Jewish discourse is the immense German interest in matters Jewish, mainly in the cultural and scholarly spheres. Jewish museums were built in Frankfurt, Berlin, and many smaller places in the 1980s and 1990s and another one in Munich was under construction. Chairs and departments in the field of Jewish Studies spread in the same period. TV films, series, and mini-series on Jewish life are prime time viewing fare. Jewish festivals have become a regular part of local culture in Berlin, Munich, and many other places, Yiddish *klezmer* bands flourish, and Jewish book stores carry on a brisk trade.

[Michael Brenner (2nd ed.)]

Antisemitism

Since the early 1980s, there has been an ever stronger evolution of two countervailing trends in West Germany, and as is now apparent, in East Germany as well. The first one consists of pro-Jewish and sometimes pro-Israeli currents with often strongly idealizing and romanticizing elements; the other, in the wake of growing racism, of more virulent forms of antisemitism. In the past, surveys have shown that the right-wing potential – expressed, for example, in sympathy for the moderate right-wing Republikaner party (roughly equivalent to France's Front National) or by core antisemitic attitudes – has been at about 15%. In recent years, however, the Right has experienced clear gains. This has to do with the traumatic experience of unification for many East Germans, and Germany experiencing the highest growth in foreign population of any state in the European community and far larger absolute numbers of immigrants than Britain or France, former colonial powers. In 1992 alone, willingness to vote for a right-wing party jumped from 12% to 19% in the West, from 8% to 12% in the East; Gerhard Frey's Deutsche Volksunion (DVU), the right of the Republikaner, grew from 22,000 to 24,000 members. In the 2004 state elections of Saxony, the extremist right-wing NPD (Nationaldemokratische Partei Deutschlands) received almost 10% of the vote, and higher percentages among the younger voters. But in the nationwide Bundestag elections of 2005 they fell clearly under 2%.

Blatantly neo-Nazi groups, such as the Deutsche Alternative (AD) of the late Michael Kuhnen, grew from a few dozen members in the 1980s to over 1,000 in the 1990s, with a substantial growth in particular localities in the East. Neo-Nazi, skinhead-type activists increased concurrently from 1,000 to about 6,000 in early 1993, while the total right-wing extremist membership must be estimated at well over 40,000 members. With this growth and the crystallization of right-wing movements into ever more stable parties and other institutions, antisemitism, previously often underground, is now out in the open and acceptable again in some quarters. This goes hand in hand with desecrations of cemeteries, synagogues, monuments, and plaques commemorating the Holocaust (including, for example, the burning of a barracks at Sachsenhausen), with occasional attacks against individual Jews. These sentiments are often located in the lower and lower-middle class, as well as among some noteworthy neo-conservative and right-wing intellectuals. In order to contain the Right within its ranks, the governing CDU has largely downplayed the seriousness of these developments. While they represent a serious threat, as shown in the pogrom-like acts in Moellin, Rostock, or Hoyerswerda, the recent massive resistance against the Right is at least as noteworthy, especially the anniversary of *Kristallnacht* which is turning increasingly into a central day of anti-racist action, with hundreds of thousands in the large cities demonstrating against racism and the asylum policies of the government. Some in the Jewish community, notably Central Council Chair Ignatz Bubis, have been important voices in this regard.

Relations with Israel

Prior to the establishment of diplomatic relations between the State of Israel and the German Federal Republic (West Germany) in March 1965, relations between the two states were confined to the agreement of Sept. 10, 1952, for global recompense of the material damage inflicted on the Jewish people by the National-Socialist regime (see *Restitution and Indemnification). An Israel mission was in charge of the implementation of this agreement as the only official representative of Israel in the Federal Republic. No German counterpart existed in Israel, in view of vehement opposition there to extending relations beyond the commercial limits of the agreement. The Israel mission was, however, authorized to grant entry visas to Israel, where the British consulate, acting for the Federal Republic, granted entry visas to West Germany. The value of Israel's purchases under the agreement amounted to 60–80 million marks annually. As a result of the contact with the large number of suppliers, relations developed and reached far beyond the field of commerce. Consequently, and in view of the Federal Republic's impressive economic and political recovery from 1953 onward, a need was felt for more clearly defined relations, as well as for the presence of an official representative in Israel. In a letter to the Israel mission, written in March 1956, the then foreign secretary, H. von Brentano, officially proposed the establishment of a mission in Israel whose status would be parallel to that of the Israel mission. Although this proposal was accepted by Israel, it was not implemented by Germany, since the German Foreign Office feared the Arab States would react to the establishment of diplomatic relations between Israel and the Federal Republic by recognizing the German Democratic Republic (East Germany) as a second sovereign German state. Such a development would be contrary to the Hallstein Doctrine (adopted in May 1958), whose basic aim was Germany's reunification.

On March 7, 1965 (two years after Ludwig Erhard had become chancellor of the Federal Republic) an offer to establish diplomatic relations with Israel was made; the timing of the offer was due to an official visit to Cairo by Walter Ulbricht, head of the Democratic Republic. Ulbricht's visit was considered by the Federal Republic's government as provocation by President Nasser of the United Arab Republic and an overture to the establishment of diplomatic relations with the Democratic Republic. In consequence of this visit and the publicity campaign initiated by Nasser against the supply of defensive arms to Israel by the Federal Republic (although Egypt received incomparably more weapons from the Soviet Union), diplomatic relations were broken off between Germany and Egypt and most of the Arab States. The Israeli government and the Knesset accepted the West German offer, and on May 12, 1965, diplomatic relations were finally established; exchange of ambassadors followed in July 1965. From July 1965, relations developed satisfactorily between the Federal Republic and Israel. The visit to Israel of the former Chancellor, Konrad Adenauer, in May 1966 was a significant event. It demonstrated his friendship for Israel and for the former prime minister, David *Ben-Gurion. In November 1967 the former chancellor, Professor Erhard, paid a visit to Israel, which also symbolized the gradual normalization of relations. At the inauguration of the new Knesset building in 1966, the Federal Republic was represented by the president of its parliament, Eugen Gerstenmaier. An Israel-German chamber of commerce was established with Walter Hesselbach, a leading figure in the West German economy, and the former minister of finance, Franz Etzel, at its head. Long-term loans for development were granted by the Federal Republic to Israel in 1966 and subsequent years under an agreement of May 12, 1965. Similar loans had been granted for the development of the Negev in the years 1961–65, agreed upon at the historic meeting between Ben-Gurion and Adenauer at the Waldorf Astoria Hotel in New York on March 14, 1960. Visitors from all walks of life subsequently went from the Federal Republic to Israel, and these visits furthered better understanding between the two countries. Even in the five years preceding the establishment of diplomatic relations, about 40,000 young people aged between 18 and 25 years from the Federal Republic had visited Israel. The first German ambassador to Israel, Rolf Pauls, made unceasing efforts for the improvement of relations. Asher Ben-Nathan was Israel's first ambassador to the Federal Republic.

[Felix Eliezer Shinnar]

The policy of the Federal Republic of Germany toward Israel was originally based, to a certain extent, on the assumption that Germany had a unique responsibility in regard to the Jewish State, but this factor has since tended to play a smaller role. Since Germany has no special interests in the Middle East, no political conflicts were created. Germany supported the majority of Israel's requests to strengthen its ties with the European community (e.g., the Common Market). Personal relations between the leaders of both countries have also been strengthened in past years.

The support of Israel by the vast majority of Germans revealed by public opinion polls during the Six-Day War has waned since then, and in New Left circles a radical anti-Israel attitude has evolved. Chancellor Willy *Brandt's official visit to Israel, the first by a German chancellor, in 1973, was an occasion for demonstrations of friendship between the two countries. With his unequivocal anti-Nazi past he stressed the fact that his attitude was not determined by any personal feelings of guilt, but that every German – even of the generation which had not been involved in the Nazi atrocities – must remember the Holocaust for which Germany had been responsible. At the same time, however, Brandt strove for the normalization of relations between the two countries and their citizens.

During the Yom Kippur War, however, Germany not only emphasized her neutrality, but even had a hand in the distinctly pro-Arab resolution adopted by the European Community during the war. To some extent, however, Germany later modified this policy and took up a position midway between the friendly attitude of Holland and the pro-Arab stand of France. In his first official statement to the Bundestag on May 17, 1974, the new chancellor of the Federal Republic, Helmut Schmidt, reaffirmed his predecessor's Middle East policy, indicating his intention of continuing Bonn's balanced approach towards Israel and the Arab countries.

In his address at the United Nations on November 19, 1974, the German representative, Ruediger von Vechmar, expressed, among other things, his government's recognition of the right of the Palestinian people to decide whether they wish an independent authority in the territories to be handed over by Israel. West Germany abstained in the vote on the UN resolution recognizing the right of the Palestinians to fight for their independence by every means. It had earlier abstained on the vote to invite PLO representatives to the General Assembly. It voted against the resolution to grant observer status to the PLO and in common with all other countries condemned the passing of the Jerusalem Law in 1980.

Trade relations between the two countries have continued to develop since the reparations agreement, and in 1972 Germany occupied third place in Israel's foreign trade, after the U.S. and England; 9% of Israel's exports and 12% of her imports were tied up with German trade. Imports from Federal Germany rose from $225.2 million in 1972 to $ 11.8 in 1973, $ 90 million in 1974, and $790.7 million in 1980. Exports from Israel similarly rose from $103.5 million in 1972 to $136.8 million in 1973, but dropped to $135 million in 1974. In 1980 they were $541.9 million.

In 1990, Germany gave Israel DM 63.6 million in development aid in the form of loans and other contributions; while in 1981, imports by Israel amounted to DM 1,724.4 million, by 1991 they had risen to DM 3,036.4 million; Israeli exports to Germany grew from DM 1,077.1 to DM 1,464.4 million. During the Gulf War, the debate between the "pacifists and bellicists" cut across all parties in Germany, and the Israeli public and politicians were angered about the neutral and sometimes anti-Israel stance taken by German politicians and the media, especially in light of the military hardware and poison gas installations given to Iraq by German firms. Partly because of the uproar caused by this, Germany promised Israel $670 million in aid; it supported the war effort with $5.5 billion and sent military goods and gas masks valued at $60 million. These monetary concessions vis-à-vis Israel were complemented by a flurry of visits, including that of Foreign Minister Genscher, to Israel and meetings by Chancellor Kohl and others with major international Jewish organizations.

Apart from the Gulf War and despite all historical obstacles, contacts have been increasing all along. Even before unification, for example, the speakers of both the West and East German parliaments, Rita Süssmuth and Sabine Bergmann-Pohl, in a demonstrative act both for international and domestic consumption, undertook to visit *Yad Vashem in Jerusalem, and the number of mutual political visits in general is steadily growing. Presidents Chaim Herzog and Richard von Weizsaecker made major visits to each other's countries, and there are almost annual visits by the foreign ministers as well as occasional visits by the prime minister of Israel to

Germany and by the German chancellor to Israel. Two Federal presidents, Johannes Rau and Horst Köhler, delivered speeches in the Knesset in German, despite the objections of some Knesset members.

Exchanges also intensified at the cultural and scientific levels. After the death of Herbert von Karajan (whose activities in World War II were regarded with suspicion) in 1989, the Berlin Philharmonic Orchestra could finally visit Israel the following year, and even Gottfried Wagner, great-grandson of Richard Wagner, was invited in 1990 to participate in lectures and discussions. Israeli academics receive study grants to Germany, and the German-Israeli Foundation engenders a wide network of scientific cooperation. Israeli artists, likewise, receive considerable attention in Germany; most noteworthy was the 1990 meeting of Israeli and German authors in Mainz, with Aharon *Meged, Yoram *Kaniuk, Ruth *Almog, and David *Grossman. In 1991 Amos *Oz received the prestigious award of the Frankfurt Book Fair. Tensions between Israel and Germany Jewry have been aggravated by Israeli pressure on the German government not to admit Jews from the former Soviet Union, and by Ignatz Bubis' criticism of Israel's treatment of Palestinians, especially its deportation policy.

Today, in an ironic twist and despite all ambivalences, bitterness, and mutual misunderstandings, the presence of Israel is greater in Germany than in any other European country, and Germany has become the major advocate of Israeli interests and concerns in Europe.

BIBLIOGRAPHY: The major comprehensive work is *German-Jewish History in Modern Times* (1996–98), ed. by Michael A. Meyer, asst. ed. Michael Brenner, which includes bibliographical essays. Earlier bibliographies are *German Jewry* (1958), supplemented by *From Weimar to Hitler: Germany 1918–1933* (1964[2]); *Persecution and Resistance under the Nazis* (1960[2]); and *After Hitler* (1963), all published by the Wiener Library, London. These are brought up to date in the *Yearbooks of the Leo Baeck Institute* (YLBI, 1956ff.). The *Bibliography of Jewish Communities in Europe* (BJCE), compiled by B. Ophir in the Yad Vashem Institute, Jerusalem, is the most complete for an economic, social, and regional history. **ADD. BIBLIOGRAPHY:** Jewish history in specific regions is covered by the series *Bibliographien zur deutsch-juedischen Geschichte*, including volumes on Bavaria (1989), Hamburg (1994), and Silesia (1995–2004). The following periodicals are indispensable: *Aschkenas*; BLBI (since 1992 replaced by *Jüdischer Almanach*); HJ; *Juedische Familien-Forschung*; JJGL; JJLG; JJV; *Menora*; MGADJ; MGWJ; *Zeitschrift fuer Demographie und Statistik der Juden*; ZGJD. GENERAL: J. Reinharz and W. Schatzberg (eds.), *The Jewish Response to German Culture: From the Enlightenment to the Second World War* (1985); H.G. Adler, *Die Juden in Deutschland* (1960); K. Schilling (ed.), *Monumenta Judaica*, 3 vols. (1963); W. Kampmann, *Deutsche und Juden* (1963); I. Elbogen and E. Sterling, *Geschichte der Juden in Deutschland* (1967); H.M. Graupe, *Die Entstehung des modernen Judentums* (1969); M. Kreutzberger (ed.), *Bibliothek und Archiv* (1970). **ADD. BIBLIOGRAPHY:** S.L. Gilman (ed.), *Yale Companion to Jewish Writing and Thought in German Culture* (1997); A. Herzig, *Jüdische Geschichte in Deutschland* (1997). **ADD. BIBLIOGRAPHY:** M. Kaplan (ed.), *Jewish Daily Life in Germany, 1618–1945* (2005). MEDIEVAL: Aronius, Regesten; G. Caro, *Sozial-und Wirtschaftsgeschichte der Juden im Mittelalter*, 2 vols. (1924); Finkelstein, Middle Ages; Germ Jud; G. Kisch, *Jewry-Law in Medieval Germany* (1949); idem, Jews in Medieval Germany (1949); J.R. Marcus, *Jews in the Medieval World* (1960); J. Trachtenberg, *The Devil and the Jews* (1961); C. Roth (ed.), *Dark Ages* (1966), 122–42, 162–74; I.A. Agus, *Heroic Age of Franco-German Jewry* (1969). **ADD. BIBLIOGRAPHY:** E. Zimmer, *Jewish Synods in Germany in the Late Middle Ages* (1978); A. Haverkamp (ed.), *Zur Geschichte der Juden im Deutschland des spaeten Mittelalters und der fruehen Neuzeit* (1981); Th. Metzger, *Juedisches Leben im Mittelalter* (1983); I. Yuval, *Ḥakhamim be-Doram* (1988); M. Toch, *Die Juden im mittelalterlichen Reich* (1998); A. Haverkamp (ed.), *Juden und Christen zur Zeit der Kreuzzuege* (1999); M. Schmandt, *Judei, cives, et incole* (2002). MERCANTILISM AND ABSOLUTISM: J.R. Marcus, *Communal Sick-Care in the German Ghetto* (1947); H. Schnee, *Die Hoffinanz und der moderne Staat*, 6 vols. (1953–67); H. Kellenbenz, *Sephardim an der unteren Elbe* (1958); S. Stern, *Der Preussische Staat und die Juden*, 2 vols. (1962); idem, *Court Jew* (1950). **ADD. BIBLIOGRAPHY:** D. Cohen, *Landjudenschaften als Organe juedischer Selbstverwaltung*, 3 vols. (1996–2001); R. Kiessling and S. Ullmann (eds.), *Landjudentum im deutschen Suedwesten waehrend der Fruehen Neuzeit* (1999); S. Ullmann, *Nachbarschaft und Konkurrenz* (1999); R. Ries and F. Battenberg (eds.), *Hofjuden* (2002). ENLIGHTENMENT AND EMANCIPATION: J. Katz, *Tradition and Crisis* (1961); M.A. Meyer, *Origin of the Modern Jew* (1967). **ADD. BIBLIOGRAPHY:** J. Katz, *Out of the* Ghetto (1973); D. Sorkin, *The Transformation of German Jewry, 1780–1840* (1987); M. Brenner, V. Caron, and U. Kaufmann (eds.), *Jewish Emancipation Reconsidered* (2003); D. Bourel, *Moses Mendelssohn. La naissance du judaisme moderne* (2004). **ADD. BIBLIOGRAPHY:** S. Feiner, *The Jewish Enlightenment* (2004). 19th AND 20th CENTURY: J. Reinharz, *Fatherland or Promised Land; the Dilemma of the German Jew, 1903–1914* (1975); J. Toury, *Die Politschen Orientierungen der Juden in Deutschland* (1966). **ADD. BIBLIOGRAPHY:** J. Toury, *Eintritt der Juden ins deutsche Buergertum* (1972); R. Ruerup, *Emanzipation und Antisemitismus* (1975); J. Toury, *Soziale und politische Geschichte der Juden in Deutschland 1847–1871* (1977); D. Sorkin, *The Transformation of German Jewry, 1780–1840* (1987); Sh. Volkov, *Juden in Deutschland 1780–1918* (1994); J. Ehrenfreund, *Mémoire juive et nationalité allemande* (2000); E. Hamburger and Mosse, Werner (eds.), *Entscheidungsjahr 1932: Zur Judenfrage in der Endphase der Weimarer Republik Juden im oeffentlichen Leben Deutschlands* (1968); U. Tal, *Christians and Jews in Germany* (1975); D.L. Niewyk, *The Jews in Weimar Germany* (1980); S.E. Aschheim, *Brothers and Strangers: The East European Jew in German and German Jewish Consciousness, 1800–1923* (1982); G.L. Mosse, *German Jews Beyond Judaism* (1985); T. Maurer, *Ostjuden in Deutschland 1918–1933* (1986); J. Wertheimer, *Unwelcome Strangers: East European Jews in Imperial Germany* (1987); M. Kaplan, *The Making of the Jewish Middle Class* (1991); H. Lavsky, *Before Catastrophe the Distinctive Path of German Zionism* (1996); M. Brenner, *The Renaissance of Jewish Culture in Weimar Germany* (1996); M. Brenner and D.J. Penslar (eds.), *In Search of Jewish Community* (1998). ANTISEMITISM: P. Massing, *Rehearsal for Destruction* (1949); A. Leschnitzer, *Magic Background of Modern Anti-semitism* (1956); P.G.J. Pulzer, *Rise of Political Anti-semitism in Germany and Austria* (1964); J. Toury, *Mehumah u-Mevukhah be-Mahpekhat 1848* (1968); E. Sterling, *Judenhass* (1969); G.L. Mosse, *Germans and Jews* (1970); I. Schorsch, *Jewish Reactions to German Anti-Semitism* (1972); S. Volkov, *Juedisches Leben und Antisemitismus im 19. und 20. Jahrhundert* (1990); S. Rohrbacher, *Gewalt im Biedermeier* (1993); Ch. Hoffmann, W. Bergmann, and H.W. Smith, *Exclusionary Violence* (2002). HOLOCAUST: R. Hilberg, *Destruction of the European Jews* (1967); G. Reitlinger, *Final Solution* (1968); L. Poliakov and J. Wulf, *Das Dritte Reich und die Juden* (1955); International Military Tribunal, *Trial of the Major War Criminals*, 23 vols. (1949), index; W. Scheffler, *Juden-*

verfolgung im Dritten Reich (1964); idem, *Die Nationalsozialistsche Judenpolitik* (1960). **ADD. BIBLIOGRAPHY:** D. Bankier, *The Germans and the Final Solution: Public Opinion under Nazism* (1992); D. Bankier (ed.), *Probing the Depths of German Antisemitism: German Society and the Persecution of the Jews, 1933–1941* (2000); S. Friedlander, *Nazi Germany and the Jews,* vol. 1 (1997); M. Kaplan, *Between Dignity and Despair* (1998). POSTWAR: L.W. Schwarz, *The Redeemers* (1953); H. Maor, *Ueber den Wiederaufbau der juedischen Gemeinden in Deutschland seit 1945* (1961); N. Muhlen, *The Survivors* (1962); A. Elon, *Journey through a Haunted Land* (1967); K. Gershon, *Postscript* (1969); L. Katcher, *Post Mortem: The Jews of Germany Today* (1968); AJYB (1945–); F.E. Shinnar, *Be-Ol Koraḥ u-Regashot* (1967); *Die Juden in Deutschland 1951/52–1958/59: ein Almanach* (1959); *Vom Schicksal gepraegt…* (1957); H.G. van Dam, *Die Juden in Deutschland seit 1945* (1965); B. Engelmann, *Deutschland ohne Juden* (1970). **ADD. BIBLIOGRAPHY:** H.M. Broder and M.R. Lang (eds.), *Fremd im eigenen Land* (1979); M. Brumlik et. al. (eds.), *Jüdisches Leben in Deutschland seit 1945* (1986); R. Ostow, *Jews in Contemporary East Germany* (1989); A. Nachama and J.H. Schoeps (eds.), *Aufbau nach dem Untergang* (1992); E. Burgauer, *Zwischen Erinnerung und Verdrängung – Juden in Deutschland nach 1945* (1993); A. Königseder and J. Wetzel, *Lebensmut im Wartesaal* (1994); S.L. Gilman, *Jews in Today's German Culture* (1994); Y.M. Bodemann (ed.), *Jews, Germans, Memory* (1996); M. Brenner, *After the Holocaust* (1997); J. Geis, *Übrig sein – Leben "danach"* (1999); Z. Mankowitz, *Life between Memory and Hope* (2002); R. Gay, *Das Undenkbare tun* (2001); H. Lavsky, *New Beginnings: Holocaust Survivors in Bergen-Belsen and the British Zone in Germany* (2002); L. Morris and J. Zipes (eds.), *Unlikely History* (2002); J. Geller, *Jews in Post-Holocaust Germany 1945 – 1953* (2005); W. Bergmann and R. Erb (eds.), *Antisemitismus in der politischen Kultur nach 1945* (1990); F. Stern, *Im Anfang war Auschwitz* (1991). RELATIONS WITH ISRAEL: R. Vogel, *The German Path to Israel* (1969); I. Deutschkron, *Israel und die Deutschen* (1970). **ADD. BIBLIOGRAPHY:** N. Hansen, *Aus dem Schatten der Katastrophe* (2004^2); Y.A. Jelinek, *Deutschland und Israel* (2004).

GERNSHEIM, FRIEDRICH (1839–1916), German composer, conductor, and teacher. Born in Worms, of an old Rhineland family, Gernsheim was a child prodigy, both as performer and composer. He taught and conducted at Cologne and Rotterdam, and from 1890 in Berlin. Finally he became director of a master class in composition at the Prussian Academy of Fine Arts. During his early years as conductor he promoted the works of Brahms. His own compositions, which number over a hundred, include piano and chamber works, four symphonies, cantatas, choral compositions, and songs. Their idiom is generally conservative, although innovations appear in his late period. A renewal of interest in Gernsheim's compositions was noticeable in the 1960s, especially in Germany. His attitude to Judaism seems to have been passive although he gave the subtitle *Mirjam* to his third symphony, op. 54, in which he depicted Miriam's song of triumph at the Red Sea; and he also wrote an *Elohenu* for cello and orchestra or piano (1882). The greater part of his papers and manuscripts were donated in 1966 to the Jewish National and University Library in Jerusalem.

BIBLIOGRAPHY: K. Holl, *Friederich Gernsheim: Leben, Erscheinung und Werk* (1928); Grove, Dict; MGG, s.v. (includes bibliography).

[Bathja Bayer]

GERÖ, ERNÖ (formerly **Singer**; 1898–1980), Hungarian statesman. Gero was born in Budapest and joined the Hungarian Communist Party before the revolution of Béla *Kun (1919). Following the downfall of Kun, he left Hungary for Germany, but returned secretly and served as editor of the Communist underground newspaper. Later he settled in the U.S.S.R. and took part in the Civil War in Spain (1935–36), where, it is assumed, he served as an agent of the NKVD. It is stated that he was responsible for the "guidance" of the Catalan Communists and partly also for the death sentences passed on actual or presumed "deviationists" in the International Brigade, among them Hungarians. He was regarded as more trustworthy even than the Hungarian dictator Mátyas *Rakosi, and it was even rumored that one of his duties was to keep him under surveillance.

Gerö returned to Hungary with the Russian army at the end of 1944. He was appointed minister of transport and placed in charge of the reconstruction of the devastated country and its industry. Among the works attributed to him was the rebuilding of the splendid bridges over the Danube which had been destroyed by the Nazis. He was appointed head of the committee for implementing the Five-Year Plan.

In 1952, Gerö was appointed deputy prime minister and, as a member of the party Politburo and the United Party, was a central figure in the harsh dictatorship. During the period of relaxed rule which followed the historic 20th Congress, at which Khrushchev exposed Stalin and his regime, Gerö was appointed head of the delegation of reconciliation which was sent to meet Marshal Tito in Yugoslavia.

Following the deposition of Rákosi in 1956 Gerö was appointed first secretary of the Communist Party and tried to crush the revolution which broke out on the first day by Stalinist methods. When that failed, he appealed for help to the Soviet army stationed in Hungary. Two days later, he himself was deposed and in 1960 again went to the U.S.S.R., returning to Hungary in 1962, when he was expelled from the Communist Party.

BIBLIOGRAPHY: J. Estebán Vilaro, *El Ocaso de los Dioses Rojas* (1939); H. Thomas, *The Spanish Civil War* (1961), index.

[Baruch Yaron]

GERONA (Catalan, **Girona**; Lat. **Gerunda**; Heb. גירונא), city in Catalonia, northeastern Spain. The Jewish community of Gerona was the second largest in Catalonia, probably dating back to the end of the ninth century. The importance of the community was due to its numerical strength, and no less to its religious and cultural achievements. Houses in the Jewish quarter are mentioned in documents from the mid-tenth century. Jews who owned land in Gerona and its surroundings had to pay a tithe to the Church. In 1160 they were permitted to lease shops built outside the city walls. Remains of the public baths and tombstones have been preserved. In the 13th century the community reached its peak from a demographic point of view, with 1,000 people. Jews began to take part in the administration in the 13th century. Noteworthy were the *baile* (bailiff) Bondia Gracián, *Benveniste de Porta, and Astruc *Ravaya and his son Joseph, both members of the court of Pedro III of Aragon. They served as administrative officers and their signatures in Hebrew appear on numerous documents. Solomon b. Abraham *Adret cooperated with them in the Jewish communal leadership. About 1271 the communities of Gerona and *Besalú, which formed a joint *collecta*, or tax administrative unit, paid a total of 20,000 sólidos, approximately half the sum paid by the community of *Barcelona. In the 13th century the priests of the local cathedral chapter instituted the custom of casting stones on the Jewish quarter from the cathedral tower at Easter, sometimes causing much damage. In 1278 Pedro III threatened to hold the bishop responsible for such actions. At Easter 1331 rioters broke into the Jewish quarter. In 1285 the Jews in Gerona took part in its defense against the French; they suffered when the latter occupied the city, and again when it was recaptured by Pedro III. From the end of the 13th century Jews were forced out of their positions in the local administration, as well as from various economic activities: no further mention is made of Jewish landowners cultivating their own land, and some Jews of Gerona settled in other cities under royal protection. Nevertheless, the Gerona community absorbed Jews expelled from France in 1306.

In 1258 James I of Aragon empowered the Jews in Gerona and nearby Besalú to appoint five persons to punish tax offenders. In 1279 Pedro III granted Benedict Jonah of Gerona and Solomon b. Abraham Adret sole jurisdiction over the community. In 1341 certain notables from Barcelona drafted regulations for the Gerona community concerning the election of trustees, auditors, "criers" (*makhrizim*), and a dual council with 26 members in one section and 16 members in the other. The community was dominated by an oligarchy, which in 1386 was torn by a violent quarrel resulting in the intervention of the authorities. In April 1391 the community of Gerona was given a new constitution, specifying the names of 23 persons entitled to serve on the council, some for life and others for a three-year term. The council was to appoint magistrates (*borerim*), trustees, and a salaried treasurer and tax collector. The latter had to be chosen from among the lesser taxpayers, and relatives of trustees were not eligible for the post. In 1459 John II provided for the election by lot of a treasurer, trustees, two magistrates, and two tax assessors.

During the 1391 persecutions the majority of the Jews of Gerona chose martyrdom. A few were converted to Christianity, mainly merchants and artisans. Some Jews found refuge in the citadel and others managed to escape to *Perpignan. The community had already been reconstituted by 1392. The Jews of Gerona were compelled to send two representatives to the disputation of *Tortosa, which resulted in an intensified tendency to conversion as well as increased attacks on Jews. However, the city authorities and King Ferdinand took action to protect the Jews in Gerona (1413–14). In 1415 the king ordered that the synagogue in Calle San Lorenzo, and the adjoining public bath, should be restored to the Jews. The synagogue was partly destroyed during the civil war in 1462–72.

The decline of the Gerona community continued throughout the 15th century. In 1431 the last treasurer (*gabbai*) of the charitable trust (*hekdesh*) became converted; Alfonso V ordered him to remain in office and to distribute the money at his disposal to both Christian and Jewish poor, but mainly to the Christians as the majority of the Jews had become converted. In 1442 the area of the Jewish quarter was reduced. A reflection of the state of affairs in the community in 1470 is the will of the widow of one Solomon Shalom, expressing the desire that her Jewish son and Christian daughter should live in peace and unity. In 1486 the Jews were prohibited from owning shops with windows and doors facing the main street. When the edict of expulsion of the Jews from Spain was issued in 1492, there was a small community in Gerona. Most of its members went into exile. The remains of the synagogue were sold for ten florins to a canon of the cathedral and the remaining property owned by Jews to the municipal notary and other citizens.

At the height of its prosperity the Gerona community was a center of learning and produced celebrated scholars, many of whom are known by the cognomen "Gerondi," i.e., originating from Gerona: their Italian descendants called themselves *Ghirondi. The primary importance of Gerona in Jewish history is that it became the first center of kabbalistic studies in the Iberian Peninsula. Due to its proximity to Provence, Gerona came under the influence of the Provençal mystics, headed by Isaac the Blind. The center in Gerona came into being at the beginning of the 13th century. The kabbalists of Gerona were instrumental in spreading the Kabbalah among the general public. Ezra ben Solomon, Azriel ben Menaḥem, Meshullam ben Solomon da Piera, Jacob ben Sheshet, and Abraham ha-Ḥazzan were the leading members of the Gerona circle of mystics. Kabbalists of a different school from Gerona were the cousins *Naḥmanides and *Jonah Gerondi. Both of them, but particularly Jonah Gerondi, were involved in the polemics on Maimonides that split the Jews of Provence and Spain in 1232. In the 1230s Gerona was one of the centers of the movement opposing the teachings of *Maimonides. Naḥmanides wrote an account of the disputation of *Barcelona for the bishop of Gerona. Naḥmanides also had connections with their Ḥavurah Kedoshah ("Sacred Association"), which had a decisive influence on the development of Kabbalah. Other noteworthy personalities included Zeraḥiah ha-Levi *Gerondi, who left Gerona while a youth; Jonah Gerondi the Younger (active 1270s); the physician Abraham de Castlar; *Nissim b. Reuben Gerondi (mid-14th century); David Bonjorn, a native of Perpignan (lived in Gerona at the end of the 14th century); Abraham b. Isaac ha-Levi, a distinguished communal leader (14th century); and in the 15th century, Bonastruc Desmaestre and Bonjudah Yeḥasel ha-Kaslari, both of whom took part in the Tortosa disputation.

The Jewish quarter or *call* of Gerona is one of the best preserved in the Iberian Peninsula. Despite the changes that the quarter has undergone since the Middle Ages, it still has part of the original streets, buildings, and remains of its Jewish past. The Jewish quarter and its synagogues make one of the best studies in the entire region. Prior to the 13th century the Jews lived in houses that belonged to the cathedral. These houses were in what is now known as the Plaza de los Apóstoles. In the 13th century the *call* consisted of Força Street, extending from one end of the street up to the building of the Pía Almoina, and from the old city wall, between the street Força and Ballesteríes, reaching the streets Lluis Batle and Oliva I Prat. Made of stones, in several buildings within the medieval *call* one can still see the slots for the *mezuzah*. The earliest synagogue which existed until the beginning of the 13th century was in the Plaza de los Apóstoles, at the corner of the Cathedral and the Bishop's Palace. Another synagogue, which was in Força Street, was closed down in 1415 by the order of Benedict XIII, because it was claimed that it had been previously a church. (This was probably true.) In 1416 King Alfonso V ordered the return of the synagogue to the Jews. Under Juan II the synagogue was in ruins and remained so until the Expulsion. The third synagogue continued to function until 1492. While there is no absolute certainty, it is possible that this synagogue was at No 10 Força Street, which is today included in the Bonastruc Ça Porta or Naḥmanides Center. Most of the tombstones found in the Jewish cemetery are displayed today in this center, where there is also a museum. The entrance to the center is in Sant Llorenç street. The Jewish cemetery was on the hill called, as in Barcelona, Montjuich (The Jews' Mountain).

BIBLIOGRAPHY: Baer, Spain, index; Baer, Urkunden, index; J. Girbal, *Los Judíos de Gerona* (1870); G. Scholem, *Reshit ha-Kabbalah* (1948), 127–61; A. Masiá de Ros, *Gerona en la guerra civil en tiempo de Juan II* (1943); Prats and Millás-Vallicrosa, in: *Sefarad*, 5 (1945), 131ff.; 12 (1952), 297–335; Angeles, *ibid.*, 13 (1953), 287–309; Gallarty, *ibid.*, 19 (1959), 301–20; Prats, *ibid.*, 21 (1961), 48–57; Casanovas, *ibid.*, 23 (1963), 22–25; 25 (1965), 49–58; J. Marqués Casanovas, in: *Anales del Instituto de Estudios Gerundenses* [= AIEG], 22 (1974–5), 1–21; idem, in: AIEG, 25:1 (1979–80), 283–98; idem, in: *Actes, Jornades d'història dels jueus a Catalunya* [= *Actes*] (1990), 225–35; J.M. Madurell Marimón, in: AIEG, 22 (1974–5), 23–49; S. Sobrequés Vidal, *Societat I estructura política de la Girona medieval* (1975), 139–86 (on the Jews of Gerona); J. Ventura Subirats, in: *Cuadernos de Historia Económica de Cataluña*, 14 (1976), 79–131; E. Mirambell Belloç, in: AIEG, 24 (1978), 5–18; idem, in: *Actes* (1990), 237–44; J. Calzada i Oliveras, in: *Annals de l'Institut d'Estudis Gironins*, 25:1 (1979–80), 375–93; R. Alberch i Fugueras and J. Nadal i Farreras, *Bibliografia històrica*, vol. 1 (1982), 169–72; E. Cortés, in: *Revista Catalana de Teología*, 7 (1982), 1–56; 9 (1984), 83–101; 10 (1985), 31–52; J. Marqués Casanovas, *Casals de Girona*, 4 (1984); C. Guilleré, *Diner, poder I societat* (1984), index; J. Riera i Sans, in: *L'Avenç*, 81 (April 1985), 62–64; idem, in: *Actes* (1990), 161–73; R. Alberch i Fugueras and N.G. Aragó, *Els jueus a les terres gironines* (1985); J. Peranau, in: *Arxiu de Textos Catalans Antics*, 4 (1985), 435–44; D. Romano (ed.), *Per a una història de la Girona jueva*, 2 vols. (1988); J. Casanovas, in: *Calls*, 3 (1988–9), 35–44.

[Haim Beinart]

GERONDI (Gerundi), ISAAC BEN JUDAH (13th century), Spanish Hebrew poet. It has been suggested that Gerondi may perhaps be identified with Isaac ha-Nasi of Barcelona (a nephew of Sheshet ha-Nasi) whose poetry is lauded by *Al-Ḥarizi (*Taḥkemoni*, ed. by A. Kaminka (1899), 350–1). Gerondi's surname, Ibn Fasad (בן פשאד), has so far not been satisfactorily explained. The Latin transcription of this name, *Avenpesat*, is that of many Jews of Aragon, Navarre, and Marseilles (Baer, Urkunden, 1 (1929), 1095 s.v. *Avenpesat*). The designation *ha-Nadiv*, found in some of his acrostics, may refer to his father only. About 20 of Gerondi's poems are extant; among these are the individual parts of his *kerovah*, "*Va-Areẓ Etnappal Lifnei Dar Gevohai*" for *Rosh Ha-Shanah. The composition, in which poems by other authors are interpolated, is to be found in the rites of Algiers, Tunis, Constantine, and Tlemcen; and while the text in all four is the same, the incidental poems vary.

BIBLIOGRAPHY: Derenbourg, in: WZJT, 5 (1844), 404, 407, 478; Landshuth, Ammudei, 120–1; Zunz, Lit Poesie, 481–2; Halberstam, in: *Jeschurun*, 7 (1871), 38 (Heb. pt.); Luzzatto, in: *Oẓar Tov*, 3 (1880), 42; Davidson, Oẓar, 4 (1933), 421. **ADD. BIBLIOGRAPHY:** Schirmann-Fleischer, 434 n. 28.

[Jefim (Hayyim) Schirmann]

GERONDI, JACOB BEN SHESHET (mid-13th century), kabbalist in Gerona, Catalonia. His works include *Meshiv Devarim Nekhoḥim* (ed. G. Vajda, 1969), directed against Samuel ibn Tibbon's *Ma'amar Yikkavu ha-Mayim; Sha'ar ha-Shamayim* (published in *Oẓar Neḥmad* (1860), 153–65, and previously in *Likkutim me-Rav Hai Ga'on* (Warsaw, 1798), 15–25) – a treatise also known as *Moshe Kibbel* from its opening words; and *Ha-Emunah ve-ha-Bittaḥon* (first published in *Arzei Levanon* (Venice, 1601)) and in *Kitvei ha-Ramban* (ed. Chavel, 1964). In early manuscripts *Ha-Emunah ve-ha-Bittaḥon* was attributed to *Naḥmanides. Jacob Reifmann suggested that it was written by *Baḥya b. Asher, and other scholars accepted his conjecture. After this had been disproved by A. Tauber, G. Scholem was the first to assign the composition to Jacob b. Sheshet on the basis of comparing *Ha-Emunah ve-ha-Bittaḥon* with *Meshiv Devarim Nekhoḥim*. Recently it has become apparent that in several places in *Meshiv Devarim Nekhoḥim*, Jacob b. Sheshet makes reference to some items, stating "as I have written"; in these cases the subject under discussion is not found in *Meshiv Devarim Nekhoḥim* but in *Ha-Emunah ve-ha-Bittaḥon*. The work has been published in several editions; that by C.B. Chavel retains the errors of previous printings.

Although Jacob b. Sheshet and his works are not widely mentioned in the kabbalistic literature of the late 13th and early 14th century, they had a marked influence on this literature. Large sections of *Ha-Emunah ve-ha-Bittaḥon* were included in the works of Baḥya b. Asher, and Menahem b. Benjamin *Recanati also used the work in several places. *Meshiv Devarim Nekhoḥim*, too, had great influence. Entire homilies were copied by important kabbalists such as Baḥya b. Asher, Recanati, the anonymous author of **Ma'arekhet ha-Elohut*, and Todros *Abulafia. Traces of *Sha'ar ha-Shamayim* have been discovered in the works of Baḥya b. Asher, and *Isaac b. Samuel of Acre copied an important section of it. Jacob b. Sheshet was an outstanding opponent of what he believed to be the heretical tendencies of philosophy, which, he believed, deny: (1) the true essence of the Torah, considering it merely as a sociopolitical theory designed only to regulate the physical needs of the man and society; (2) the creation of the world; (3) divine providence; (4) retribution. Such heresy results in the denial of the value of prayer and of the possibility of man's asking his needs of God.

In *Meshiv Devarim Nekhoḥim* he formulates the kabbalistic meaning of these basic conceptions. A great part of the work is devoted to the question of the creation of the world. Like other kabbalists he is far from holding the traditional conception of creation out of nothing; however, his commentary to Genesis differs from that of his contemporary kabbalists whose works he knew well. Jacob b. Sheshet posits a continuous emanation from the divine realm, i.e., the world of the *Sefirot*, to the physical world. To construct this continuity two main elements, heavenly matter and earthly matter, are found in the world of the *Sefirot*; they evolved until the heavenly and the earthly hylic substances were formed. Thus, according to Jacob b. Sheshet, Genesis is not an expression of a paradigm, i.e., a description of the creation of the physical world which repeats the formation of the world of the *Sefirot*. It is rather a continuous description, beginning with the creation within the world of the *Sefirot* and ending with the physical stage of the primal divine element.

BIBLIOGRAPHY: G. Scholem, *Reshit ha-Kabbalah* (1948), 132; idem, *Ursprung und Anfaenge der Kabbala* (1962), 334–9; G. Vajda, *Recherches sur la philosophie et la Kabbale* (1962), 8–113; idem (ed.), in: J.B.S. Gerondi, *Meshiv Devarim Nekhoḥim* (1969), 11–17, 67–215; E. Gottlieb, *ibid.*, 18–63; idem, *Ha-Kabbalah be-Khitvei R. Baḥya b. Asher* (1970), 10–13, 96–143; idem, in: *Tarbiz*, 37 (1968), 294–317.

[Efraim Gottlieb]

GERONDI, MOSES BEN SOLOMON D'ESCOLA (second half of 13th century), *paytan* of Gerona, Catalonia. Gerondi was related to *Naḥmanides, who in 1267 sent a letter from Jerusalem requesting that his greetings be conveyed to Gerondi – his "son and pupil" – whose poem he had read with great emotion on the Mount of Olives. He may have had in mind the **seliḥah, "Yerushalayim Ir ha-Kodesh,"* printed at the conclusion of Naḥmanides' commentary to the Pentateuch. Gerondi is known to be the author of some other liturgical poems.

BIBLIOGRAPHY: Gross, Gal Jud, 147; Landshuth, Ammudei, 235, 259; Zunz, Gesch, 482; Davidson, Oẓar, 4 (1933), 448.

[Joseph Elijah Heller]

GERONDI, SAMUEL BEN MESHULLAM (c. 1300), scholar of Gerona, Catalonia. Hardly any biographical details are known of him. Gerondi's fame rests primarily on his *Ohel Mo'ed* (1 (Jerusalem, 1886); 2 (Jerusalem, 1904)), a comprehensive code consisting only of such laws as are of practical application. The book is divided into 4 parts: (1) *Ma'arekhet Tamid*, on the reading of the *Shema*, prayer, blessings, *tefillin, mezuzah, ẓiẓit*; appended is a separate section ("gate") devoted to morals and ethics; (2) *Avodat ha-Mishkan*, the laws of ritual slaughter, *terefot*, ritual law, including laws of marriage; (3) *Mishmeret ha-Kodesh*, on the Sabbath and the *eruv; (4) *Yare'aḥ le-Mo'adim*, on the festivals. Each part is subdivided into chapters, sections, and subsections called "gates," "roads," and "paths," respectively. In this work, written after 1320, the author quotes extensively from the early Spanish, Provençal, and German scholars. Like the *Toledot Adam ve-Ḥavvah* of his contemporary, *Jeroham b. Meshullam, Gerondi's work was to a large extent superseded by the *Arba'ah Turim* of *Jacob b. Asher, which fulfilled essentially the same task in a far more comprehensive manner and which was superior both in form and style. Joseph *Caro is almost the sole authority to quote Gerondi. His work, as it has come down, is an abridged version by the author himself of a larger work which is no longer extant.

BIBLIOGRAPHY: Gruenhut, in: JQR, 11 (1898/99), 345–9.

[Israel Moses Ta-Shma]

GERONDI, SOLOMON BEN ISAAC (13th century), Spanish liturgical poet. Gerondi was a student of *Naḥmanides (see *Tashbeẓ*, no. 456). According to L. Zunz he composed five poems which include his variation of a favorite theme among medieval poets, the "Thirteen Attributes of God"; *"Shav min ha-Pesilim,"* a hymn on the patriarch Abraham; and an elegy for the Ninth of *Av (*Shekhurat ve-Lo mi-Yayin*). The latter became very popular among Sephardi and Ashkenazi Jews.

BIBLIOGRAPHY: Zunz, Lit Poesie, 482f.; Zunz, Poesie, 144, 309; Schirmann, Sefarad, 2 (1956), 326–8; Davidson, Oẓar, 4 (1933), 474. **ADD. BIBLIOGRAPHY:** Schirmann-Fleischer, 434 n.28; Feliu, *Poemes Hebraics de Jueus Catalans* (1976), 89–93.

GERONDI, ZERAHIAH BEN ISAAC HA-LEVI (12th century), rabbinical scholar and poet. His father, ISAAC HA-YIẒHARI ben ZERAHIAH HA-LEVI GERONDI, was a Hebrew poet and talmudic scholar in Spain. His poetry was included in the rites of the communities of Avignon, Carpentras, Montpellier, Oran, and Tlemcen. Zerahiah, born in Gerona, Spain, left his native city in his youth, possibly to escape from his many enemies there, and settled in Provence. In Narbonne he studied under *Moses b. Joseph, as well as under *Abraham b. Isaac and Joseph *Ibn Plat. He lived for many years in Lunel, which he was compelled to leave on several occasions because of disputes. In Lunel he was the teacher of Samuel, the son of Judah ibn *Tibbon. Judah characterized Zerahiah as unique in his generation, called him his superior in knowledge, and extolled the stylistic excellence of his letters and poems (I. Abrahams (ed.), *Hebrew Ethical Wills*, 1 (1926), 72). Zerahiah was proficient in Arabic as well as in philosophy and astronomy, having acquired knowledge of the latter in Provence. At the age of 19 he composed a *piyyut* in Aramaic and began to write his chief halakhic work, *Ha-Ma'or* ("The Luminary"), which he completed in the 1180s in Lunel. It is divided into two parts – *Ha-Ma'or ha-Katan* ("The Lesser Luminary" – a play on Lunel, "the moon") on *Berakhot*, many tractates of the order *Mo'ed*, and *Ḥullin*; and *Ha-Ma'or ha-Gadol* ("The Great

Luminary" – a play on his name Zerahiah), on *Nashim* and *Nezikin*. (These have several times been published separately, often together with Isaac Alfasi's commentary, and from 1552 appeared in the Venice edition of the Talmud.) This work, which is deeply critical of *Alfasi, constitutes part of the literature of criticism and is representative of the approach adopted by *Abraham b. David of Posquières in his criticism of Maimonides. *Ta-Shema asserts that *Ha-Ma'or* is not a work of criticism. He demonstrates that the work is really a talmudic commentary. A careful reading of *Ha-Ma'or* reveals that the center of discussion is the talmudic text and not Alfasi's commentary. Over fifty percent of Zerahiah's work does not mention Alfasi altogether. Indeed, Zerahiah discusses halakhic issues ignored by Alfasi because they have no practical application. Many of Zerahiah's disagreements with Alfasi do not concern the practical *halakhah*. Rather, they are about the correct understanding of the talmudic text. Nevertheless, Zerahiah did develop numerous rules for correctly reading and interpreting Alfasi, especially when it is unclear as to how Alfasi decides the law. In many instances Zerahiah preferred the version of the talmudic text as emended by Rashi, and he relied to a considerable extent on the methodology adopted by the northern French commentators, thus combining in his work the principles of the halakhic and exegetical schools of Spain and France which merged in Provence. The *Ma'or* on *Rosh Ha-Shanah* 20b contains a comprehensive exposition on the calendar and the principles of intercalation, Zerahiah having found it necessary to reaffirm the views of the Talmud against those who deviated from it. The language and style of the *Ha-Ma'or* are unique in their exactitude, brevity, and clarity. It is evident from the fine detail – such as the accuracy in citing other sources – that the work was edited carefully and presented as a completed work. Zerahiah was particularly adept at weaving together quotations from various rabbinic sources to make his point. Many generations of halakhists were influenced by the *Ma'or*, which, however, was strongly criticized by several scholars (especially Naḥmanides) who composed works in defense of Alfasi.

One area of particular note that exemplifies Zerahiah's influence on subsequent halakhic decisions is the determination of the halakhic dateline. His discussion of the laws of the New Moon and the necessity for some place in the world other than Jerusalem to experience a full 24 hours of *rosh ḥodesh* (the day of the new moon) led Zerahiah to determine that the halakhic international dateline was 90° east of Jerusalem. He was the first to make such a determination, all the while demonstrating the Talmud's understanding that the earth was round.

Zerahiah also wrote *Sefer ha-Ẓava*, a sequel to his earlier work, in which he endeavored to show that Alfasi had disregarded the accepted principles of talmudic interpretation (see Rabad, *Temim De'im*, 28a–29b, no. 225). In the acrimonious dispute between Abraham b. David and himself, Zerahiah came off second best in a halakhic exchange of letters (D. Crachman, *Divrei ha-Rivot*, 1908). Zerahiah wrote a criticism of Abraham's *Ba'alei ha-Nefesh* (published together with that work, Venice, 1741; Berlin, 1762) and attacked him in *Sela ha-Maḥaloket*, to which Abraham retaliated by severely criticizing *Ha-Ma'or (Katuv Sham*, ed. by I.D. Bergman (1957), introd., 26, 39, 42). Zerahiah was also the author of *Hilkhot Sheḥitah u-Vedikah, Sefer Pitḥei Niddah*, a commentary on the tractate *Kinnim*, and of responsa. *Hilkhot Sheḥitah u-Vedikah* was finally published by Lopiansky and Bordon (1984). The Sephardi *maḥzor* contains 18 of his *piyyutim*, one of which contains a reference to the Crusader rule in Jerusalem.

[Haim Hillel Ben-Sasson / David Derovan (2nd ed.)]

His brother BERECHIAH BEN ISAAC HA-LEVI, also called "Yiẓhari" (12th century), was a Spanish liturgical poet and Talmud scholar. According to Gross, the epithet "Yiẓhari" refers to the name of a Spanish town (perhaps Oliva or Olivares) where his ancestors had lived. He also was born in Gerona (Spain) but lived in Lunel, Provence. In one section of his *Sefer ha-Ma'or*, Zerahiah ha-Levi answers a halakhic question posed by his brother, and he also refers to Berechiah in a poem at the end of his *Hassagot al Sefer Ba'al ha-Nefesh le-ha-Rabad*. Berechiah was the author of a number of *piyyutim*, some extant only in manuscript.

[Joseph Elijah Heller]

BIBLIOGRAPHY: ZERAHIAH: J. Reifmann, *Toledot R. Zeraḥyah ha-Levi* (1853); Marx, in: REJ, 59 (1910), 200–24; S.M. Chones, *Toledot ha-Posekim* (1910), 107–13; Ch. Tchernowitz, *Toledot ha-Posekim*, 1 (1946), 149–63; Urbach, index; Rabad, *Katuv Sham*, ed. I.D. Bergman (1957), introd., 26, 39, 42; I. Twersky, *Rabad of Posquières* (1962), 120ff. and passim; C.B. Chavel, *Ramban, his Life and Teachings* (1960), 20ff. **ADD. BIBLIOGRAPHY:** A. Shoshanah, in: *Sefer Ha-Zikkaron le-Zekher Rabbi Rephael Sorotzkin* (1982), 14–39; A.S. Lopiansky and M.J. Bordon, in: *Sefer Ha-Zikkaron Le-Naran ha-Pahad Yiẓḥak* (1984), 401–32; Y. Ta-Shema, *Rabbi Zeraḥiah ha-Levi Ba'al Ha-Ma'or u-Venei Ḥugo* (1992). BERECHIAH: Zunz, Lit Poesie, 463, 495; Landshuth, Ammudei, 56; Michael, Or, no. 648; Fuenn, Keneset, 202; Gross, Gal Jud, 255–6; Davidson, Oẓar, 4 (1933), 373.

GEROVICH, ELIEZER MORDECAI BEN ISAAC (1844–1913), Russian *ḥazzan* and composer. Gerovich, who was born in the Ukraine, was gifted with a rich tenor voice. At the age of 18 he went to study music at Berdichev where he became assistant *ḥazzan* at the so-called Choral Synagogue (i.e., a synagogue with a choir). After studying cantoral music under Nissan *Blumenthal in Odessa, he attended the St. Petersburg Conservatory. In 1887 he was appointed chief *ḥazzan* at the Choral Synagogue at Rostov-on-Don, a post he held for 25 years. Gerovich became famous for his own compositions of synagogue music, based on traditional Jewish melodies but written in an original style. Most of them were collected in his two-volume *Schire Tefilla* and *Schire Simra* (1897).

BIBLIOGRAPHY: Idelsohn, Music, 310f.; A. Friedmann, *Lebensbilder beruehmter Kantoren*, 3 (1927), 32; E. Zaludkowski, *Kultur-Treger fun der Yidisher Liturgye* (1930), 163–8; H.H. Harris, *Toledot ha-Ḥazzanut be-Yisrael* (1950), 11, 425–7; Sendrey, Music, 368 and 394 (indexes), s.v.; A. Holde, *Jews in Music* (1959), 356 (index), s.v.

[Joshua Leib Ne'eman]

GERSHENZON, MIKHAIL OSIPOVICH (1869–1925), Russian literary historian, philosopher, and essayist. Born in Kishinev, Gershenzon studied in Berlin and Moscow. An anti-Marxist liberal, he nevertheless became the best-known exponent of the thesis that the Bolshevik Revolution would ultimately benefit Russian culture by freeing it from the shackles of tradition. This idea was expressed in his *Perepiska iz dvukh uglov* ("Correspondence From Two Corners," 1921), an exchange of letters with the Symbolist poet Vyacheslav Ivanov. Gershenzon's other works include monographs dealing with several 19th century Russian revolutionaries and men of letters, as well as such major studies as *Mechta I Mysl I.S. Turgeneva*, ("The Dream and Thoughts of Turgenev," 1919), and *Mudrost Pushkina*, ("The Wisdom of Pushkin," 1919). One of the foremost Russian intellectuals of his age, he was the organizer and first chairman of the All-Russian Writers Union. Accused of slavophilism, he replied that he was forever bound to Judaism. Gershenzon was one of the earliest enthusiasts of the revival of Hebrew literature and fought for its recognition as a potentially major contribution to modern writing. He expressed his credo in his foreword to "The Hebrew Anthology" (Russian), and in *The Key to Faith* (Rus.; Eng. translation, 1925). According to Gershenzon, "A free Jew does not cease being a Jew. On the contrary, only a free Jew is fully capable of absorbing Jewish spirit and merging it with his totally liberated humanity." He published an article on *Bialik (1914) and essays on Judaism. He saw in universalism a Jewish spiritual phenomenon and attacked the Zionist movement.

BIBLIOGRAPHY: Y.Z. Berman, *M.O. Gershenzon* (Rus., 1928), includes bibliography.

[Maurice Friedberg / Shmuel Spector (2nd ed.)]

GERSHMAN, JOE (1903–1989), Canadian labor organizer, journalist. Born in the Ukraine, Joshua (Joe) Gershman arrived in Canada in 1921. His father had preceded him by eight years and had settled in Winnipeg. There the young Gershman got his first job as a fur dyer. Radicalized some years before by the Russian Revolution of 1917, Gershman joined the nascent Communist Party of Canada in 1923 and began working as a union organizer among the Jewish workers in Winnipeg's garment industry. After several arrests for his trade union activity, Gershman decided to move to Toronto, where he found work as a textile cutter. But factory work was of no interest to him and within a few weeks he quit to become, in his own description, a "professional revolutionary," which is what he would remain for the next 65 years.

As an organizer for Communist-led unions which were in the forefront of the labor struggles of the period, Gershman was involved in dozens of strikes and demonstrations in the garment districts of Toronto and Montreal. Along with fellow Party members such as Joe *Salsberg and Sam Lipschitz he was elected to the executive of the national bureau of Jewish Communists. In 1935, Gershman found his true craft as a journalist. He became the editor of *Der Kampf* (*The Struggle*), the militant voice of the Jewish labor movement. He was a gifted writer and a tireless polemicist and for the next 40 years he would publish a series of Communist newspapers – all in Yiddish.

Unlike most other Jewish members who deserted the Party after the sordid revelations of Stalin's antisemitism in the early 1950s, Gershman remained and continued to publish a left-wing Yiddish weekly, the *Vochenblatt*, until 1977. Only then, embittered and disappointed, did he leave the Communist Party to protest the relentless anti-Jewish policies of the Soviet government.

[Irving Abella (2nd ed.)]

GERSHOM (Heb. גֵּרְשׁוֹם, גֵּרְשֹׁם), elder son of Moses and Zipporah (Ex. 2:22; 18:3). Gershom was born in Midian. The meaning of the name is unknown, but is explained as "a stranger there," symbolizing Moses' flight from Egypt. According to I Chronicles 23:16 and 26:24, Gershom's son was Shebuel. Since, however, he is described as "the chief officer in charge of the treasuries" in the time of David, Shebuel was very likely a more distant descendant of Gershom. Another descendant was Jonathan who acted as a priest at the idol of Micah (Judg. 18:30; MT has "Moses" deferentially written with a suspended *nun*). The Gershomites had no functions in connection with the Tent of Meeting and no Levitical cities were apportioned to them. They apparently were priests to the tribe of Dan (*ibid.*).

ADD. BIBLIOGRAPHY: J. Wright, in: ABD II, 993–94.

[Nahum M. Sarna]

GERSHOM BEN JUDAH ME'OR HA-GOLAH (c. 960–1028), one of the first great German talmudic scholars and a spiritual molder of German Jewry. Few biographical details are known of Gershom, most of the stories about him being of a legendary nature. He was apparently born in Metz, but his home was in Mainz (Isaac of Vienna, *Or Zaru'a* (1862), 2, 275), where he conducted a yeshivah, and where he wrote in 1013 the *ketubbah* for his second wife Bona, who was a widow. A tombstone in Mainz of which the extant words are "… in memoriam: R. Gershom ben R.…" is thought to be his. Gershom mentions only one of his teachers, Judah b. Meir ha-Kohen Leontin "from whom I received most of my knowledge" (Responsa Meir of Rothenburg (Prague, 1895), 264). His own best-known pupils are Eliezer the Great (*Eliezer b. Issac of Worms), *Jacob b. Jakar, and *Isaac b. Judah, the last two of whom were the teachers of *Rashi. His brother Machir compiled a lexicon known as *Alfa Beta Rabbi Makhir*, now lost. An unconfirmed tradition maintains that Gershom had a son Eliezer, who headed a yeshivah. The *rishonim, however, mention a son who was forcibly converted to Christianity and died before he could repent, yet his father fulfilled the laws of mourning for him (*Or Zaru'a*, *ibid.*, 428). The probable time for this is 1012, when Heinrich II issued an edict of expulsion against the Jews of Mainz. Gershom succeeded in turning Mainz into a major center for Torah study. This status lasted for a number of generations after his demise.

The reverence in which Rabbenu Gershom was held in subsequent generations was already expressed by Rashi: "Rabbenu Gershom, may the memory of the righteous and holy be for a blessing, who enlightened the eyes of the exile, and upon whom we all depend and of whom all Ashkenazi Jewry are the disciples of his disciple" (J. Mueller (ed.), *Teshuvot Ḥakhmei Ẓarefat ve-Lutir* (1881), no. 21). This is apparently also the source of the title "*Me'or ha-Golah*" ("Light of the Exile").

Gershom's name is connected with many *takkanot*, most famous of which is his *ḥerem* ("ban") against bigamy. Well known, too, is the *ḥerem* forbidding the unauthorized reading of private letters. This latter *takkanah* in particular, and several others ascribed to him, may not really be his. Rashi cites only one *takkanah* in his name, the prohibition against reminding forcibly converted Jews, who have repented and returned to the fold, of their transgressions. Jacob *Tam mentions his *takkanah* against emending talmudic texts. The two important *takkanot* enforcing monogamy and prohibiting the divorce of a wife against her will are attributed to him by *Meir of Rothenburg (loc. cit., nos. 866 and 1121), but Eliezer Nathan, who lived in Mainz a century after Gershom, refers to them as communal *takkanot* (*Sefer Raban* (Prague, 1610), 121b). Fifteenth-century scholars attribute to him the ancient *takkanah* known as the *ḥerem ha-yishuv* (Israel of Krems' gloss to Asher b. Jehiel, BB 2:12). It is possible that they were attributed to the great luminary to give these *takkanot* the weight of his great authority. On the other hand, there is no valid reason that *takkanot* ascribed to Gershom should not really be his. The reason for this debate is the fact that no original texts of these *takkanot* have survived. That, coupled with the fact that the scholars of his own generation do not quote Gershom's *takkanot*, raises the question of his authorship. However, later generations recognized the *takkanot* as his, including one individual who wrote to Solomon ben Aderet claiming that his community has an oral tradition regarding the *takkanot*.

Gershom's far-reaching ban on polygamy can be ascribed to the socio-economic situation in Germany of that time. The Jewish community experienced a good deal of economic stability and the rise of a wealthy merchant class. At the same time, the status of women improved. This is evident in the large dowries that were received and in the fact that many women ran their husband's businesses in his absence. An added factor was the increased sensitivity to social injustice. Thus, the time was ripe for a ban on polygamy in the Jewish community.

Rabbenu Gershom's responsa and halakhic decisions are scattered throughout the works of the French and German scholars, and have been collected by S. Eidelberg (1955). Most items deal with civil law. In them he bases himself upon the Bible and Talmud alone, and only seldom refers to the early *geonim*. In one place he writes that he prefers the opinion of his teacher Leontin, who likewise based himself on Scripture and Talmud (Meir of Rothenburg, loc. cit., no. 264), to that of the famous *geonim* Yehudai and Sherira, but the sources of Leontin's teaching are obscure. From his works it appears that Gershom was acquainted with the general German law of his time and was even influenced by it. His legal decisions were regarded as authoritative, particularly by French and German scholars throughout the centuries, and influenced the major direction of the *halakhah* in these countries.

The commentaries attributed to R. Gershom which were published in the Vilna Romm edition of the Talmud to tractates *Bava Batra*, *Ta'anit*, and the whole of *Seder Kedoshim* (except *Zevaḥim*), are now considered not to be his. He probably laid the foundations for them, but the present work is that of his pupils and their pupils. *Nathan b. Jehiel, in the *Arukh*, refers to it sometimes as "the commentary of the sages of Mainz," and sometimes as that of Rabbenu Gershom, but mostly quotes it anonymously (over 550 times). It was superseded by Rashi's commentary and remained almost unknown until the time of Bezalel *Ashkenazi, who was also the first to ascribe them to Rabbenu Gershom.

Gershom transcribed the Mishnah and the *Masorah Gedolah* of the Bible and corrected them. These copies were highly regarded by the *rishonim*, on account of their accuracy. He was the first Franco-German scholar to compose *seliḥot* and other *piyyutim* (collected by A.M. Habermann, 1944). His *seliḥot* were accepted in all German communities; most popular is the *piyyut Zekhor Berit*, included in the *seliḥot* of Rosh Ha-Shanah. They reflect the troubles and tribulations of his generation and are noteworthy for their simplicity and naturalness of expression and the emotion with which they are imbued.

BIBLIOGRAPHY: Epstein, in: *Festschrift... M. Steinschneider* (1896), 115–43; Naphtali b. Shemu'el (J.N. Simḥoni), in: *Ha-Shilo'aḥ*, 28 (1913), 14–22, 119–28, 201–12; Tykocinski, in: *Festschrift... M. Philippson* (1916), 1–5; Finkelstein, Middle Ages, index; idem, in: MGWJ, 74 (1930), 23–31; Baer, *ibid.*, 71 (1927), 392–7; 74 (1930), 31–34; idem, in: *Zion*, 15 (1950), 1–41; A. Aptowitzer, *Mavo le-Sefer Ravyah* (1938), 330–5; Eidelberg, in: *Zion*, 18 (1953), 83–87; Z.W. Falk, *Jewish Matrimonial Law in the Middle Ages* (1966), index s.v. *Gershom*. **ADD. BIBLIOGRAPHY:** S.M. Passamaneck, in: *Journal of Jewish Studies*, 29:1 (1978), 57–74; A. Pichnuk, in: *Shanah be-Shanah* (1972), 220–25; A. Grossman, *Ḥakhmei Ashkenaz ha-Rishonim* (1981), 106–175; idem, in: *Jewish History, Essays in Honor of Chimen Abramsky* (1988), 3–23; S.Z. Havlin, in: *Shenaton ha-Mishpat ha-Ivri*, 2 (1974), 200–57; idem, in: ibid., 11–12 (1984–86), 317–35.

[Shlomo Eidelberg / David Derovan (2nd ed.)]

GERSHOM BEN SOLOMON (13th century), Provençal scholar of Béziers. No biographical details are known about him. He compiled a halakhic work, *Shalman*, giving the halakhic rulings of the Talmud according to the order of the *halakhot* of Isaac Alfasi, and approximating the order of Maimonides in his *Mishneh Torah*. In some sources Gershom's work is erroneously called *Shulḥan* and is not to be confused with the *Sefer Shulḥan* in the Paris National Library (Zotenberg, no. 415; see Benjacob, 583 no. 687, and Lubetzky, bibl.). Gershom's book was completed by his son SAMUEL BEN GERSHOM who also participated in the composition of the earlier portion. Lubetzky corrected the name Meshullam b. Gershom to Samuel b. Gershom in *Bet ha-Beḥirah* (Introduction to *Avot*). The book and its author are referred to in *Mikhtam* by David b. Levi of Narbonne (ed. by A. Sofer (1959), 223), the commentary of Manoah b. Jacob of Narbonne on Maimonides' Yad (Constantinople, 1718, 11b, et al.), *Kol Bo* and *Orḥot Ḥayyim* (see index), *Avudarham* (ed. by C.L. Ehrenreich (1927), 29), and in *Sefer Ba'alei Asufot* (still in manuscript; see Lubetzky). Samuel was the teacher of *Judah b. Jacob, the author of the last-named work.

BIBLIOGRAPHY: Isaac de Lattes, *Sha'arei Ẓiyyon*, ed. by S. Buber (1885), 44; Michael, Or, no. 687; Gross, Gal Jud, 99f.; Meshullam b. Moses of Beziers, *Sefer ha-Hashlamah*, ed. by J. Lubetzky, 1 (1885), introd. xv; Benedikt, in: *Sinai*, 29 (1951), 191–3; idem, in: KS, 27 (1951), 143 and n. 60; Sussman, in: *Koveẓ al Yad*, n.s. 6, pt. 2 (1966), 283, 285.

[Shlomoh Zalman Havlin]

GERSHON, GERSHONITES (Heb. גֵּרְשׁוֹן; in Chron. usually Gershom, גֵּרְשׁוֹם, גֵּרְשֹׁם), the eldest son of Levi, from whom a division of the Levites traced their descent (Gen. 46:11; Ex. 6:16–17; Num. 3:17ff.; Josh. 21:6, 27; I Chron. 5:27; 6:1). The clan descended from Gershon is designated "Gershonites" (Heb. הַגֵּרְשֻׁנִּי; e.g., Num. 3:21). Two sons of Gershon, Libni and Shimei, are also mentioned (Ex. 6:17; Num. 3:18; I Chron. 6:2); in I Chronicles 23:7 and 26:21 Ladan is used in place of Libni. After the exile, very little mention is made of the Gershonites as such. However, the distinguished guild of Asaphites is said to be descended from Gershon (I Chron. 6:24–28 [39–43]), and 128 (Ezra 2:41), or 148 (Neh. 7:44), of the Asaphites are reported to have taken up residence in Jerusalem. They led the music at the laying of the foundation of the Temple (Ezra 3:10) and blew the trumpets at the dedication of the city walls (Neh. 12:35). The traditions that make Gershon the eldest son of Levi presumably originated in a period in which the Gershonite clan was significant. Yet in terms of their position in the levitical hierarchy, the Kohathites seem to rank higher in that they transported the sacred vessels of the tabernacle including the ark (Levine).

The biblical sources describe four stages in the history of the Gershonites. These sources are of mixed historical value.

(1) According to the Book of Numbers, during the desert wanderings, the clans encamped behind the Tabernacle, to the west (Num. 3:23). In the census of the Levites from the age of one month up, the recorded entries of all the Gershonite males came to 7,500 (3:22), and the entries of males from the age of 30 through 50 came to 2,630 (4:39–40). Their duty was to carry the hangings which comprised the Tabernacle proper, the outer coverings and the hangings of the court, with their cords, and the altar and accessories (3:25–26; 4:24–26; cf. 10:17), for which they were assigned two carts and four oxen, as required for their service (7:7). They were under the direction of Ithamar, the youngest son of Aaron the priest. Given the arrangement of the Israelites according to *degel* in these narratives, a feature known from the archives from *Elephantine of the fifth century B.C.E., it is to that period that we must assign the desert traditions concerning the Gershonites. (2) After the settlement in the land, the Gershonites were assigned 13 cities in the tribal territories of the half-clan of Manasseh on the eastern side of the Jordan and of the clans of Issachar, Asher, and Naphtali, on the western side (Josh. 21:6, 27–33; I Chron. 6:47, 56–61). Several scholars date these lists to the eighth century.

(3) According to the Chronicler, at the direction of David the Temple music was conducted partly by Asaph, a Gershonite, and his family (e.g., I Chron. 25:1–2). David also appointed the clan to undertake service in the Temple when he organized the Levites into divisions "according to the sons of Levi" (23:6–11; 26:20ff.).

The last time the Gershonites are mentioned as such is in the list of Levites who took part in the cleansing of the Temple under Hezekiah (II Chron. 29:12–13). Here the Gershonites are moved to third position.

ADD. BIBLIOGRAPHY: W. Propp, in: ABD, 2:994–95; B. Levine, *Numbers 1–20* (1993), 144–51; S. Japhet, *I & II Chronicles* (1993), 920–21.

[Shlomo Balter / S.David Sperling (2nd ed.)]

GERSHON, ISAAC (d. after 1620), scholar and proofreader. His full name was Isaac b. Mordecai Gershon Treves but he is usually referred to simply as Isaac Gershon. Gershon was born in Safed and studied under Moses *Alshekh. He went to Venice not later than 1576, and on his journey there published his *Shelom Esther* (Constantinople, c. 1575–76), an anthology of the commentaries of the French and Spanish scholars to the Book of Esther. For more than 30 years he worked as proofreader of books published in Venice, mainly by the Safed scholars. Among the works he saw through the press were *Beit Elohim* (1576) by Moses di *Trani; *Reshit Ḥokhmah* (1579) by Elijah di Vidas; *Manot ha-Levi* (1585) by Solomon *Alkabeẓ; *Zemirot Yisrael* (1599–1600) by Israel *Najara; the Pentateuch commentary by Moses Alshekh (1601–07); the *Sefer Ḥaredim* (1601) by Eleazar *Azikri; and responsa by Moses Galante (1608). Isaac Gershon was a member of the Venice *bet din* and his signature appears on its resolutions and edicts together with those of the Venice rabbis Ben Zion Sarfaty and Judah Leib *Saraval. He published *Mashbit Milḥamot* (Venice, 1606), containing the rulings of those rabbis who were lenient in connection with the *Rovigo *mikveh*. He wrote commentaries to other books of the Bible; his commentary on Malachi was published in *Likkutei Shoshannim* (*ibid.*, 1602). Together with the other rabbis of Venice, he defended the emissary, Jedidiah b. Moses b. Mordecai Galante, who was accused of embezzling money he had collected for Ereẓ Israel. Some of Isaac's responsa are extant, published in the works of his contemporaries or in manuscript. Toward the end of his life, apparently in the 1620s, he returned to Safed, and died there.

BIBLIOGRAPHY: Montefiore, in: REJ, 10 (1885), 185, 195, 199; Sonne, in: KS, 7 (1930/31), 281f.; 34 (1959), 135f.; idem, *Kobez al Jad*, 5 (15) (1950), 206, 211; Yaari, Sheluḥei, 251, 844; idem, *Meḥkerei Sefer* (1958), 135, 159, 171f., 174, 421; Judah Aryeh of Modena, *Ziknei*

Yehudah, ed. by S. Simonsohn (1956), 37 (introd.); Tamar, in: KS, 33 (1957/58), 377f.

[David Tamar]

GERSHON, KAREN (Kathe Lowenthal; 1923–1993), German-born poet who came to England before World War II without her parents, who died in the camps. Gershon's *Selected Poems* (1966), written under the pseudonym "Karen Gershon," gave powerful expression to the refugee's thoughts and emotions from childhood. She also edited *We Came as Children* (1966), a collective autobiography of young refugees, some of whom, like herself, eventually married English non-Jews; and *Postscript* (1969), an account of Jewish life in West Germany after 1945. She settled in Israel in 1969 but returned to England in 1975 and died in London.

ADD. BIBLIOGRAPHY: ODNB online as "Kathleen Tripp" (her married name).

[William D. Rubinstein (2nd ed.)]

GERSHON, PINCHAS (Pini; 1951–), Israeli basketball coach who led the Maccabi Tel Aviv basketball team to three European championships. Gershon's career as a player ended early, and he then began to coach. In 1993, he guided Galil Elyon to a national championship, the only time in 40 years a team other than Maccabi Tel Aviv had won it. In 1996 he coached Hapoel Jerusalem and took the National Cup. In 1998 he took over Maccabi Tel Aviv, which had had little success in Europe in the preceding years, and led it to the European Final Four. In 2001 Maccabi won the championship, defeating Greek powerhouse Panathinaikos. After taking a break from coaching, and with Tel Aviv slated to host the Final Four, he returned for the 2003/4 season to take Maccabi to a second European championship. In 2004/5 Maccabi took the championship again, becoming the first team since 1991 with back-to-back titles. Gershon was also named Euroleague Coach of the Year, and as a warm-up for the 2005/6 season took the team to the United States, where it split two games against NBA opponents, beating the Toronto Raptors at the buzzer.

Flamboyant and outspoken, Gershon changed the face of European basketball with his offense-minded play and baffling match-up zone. Under his tutelage, Maccabi continued to be the country's leading sports attraction, playing before sellout crowds in Tel Aviv and attracting the cream of local and foreign players.

[Shaked Gilboa (2nd ed.)]

GERSHON BEN SOLOMON OF ARLES (late 13th century), Provençal scholar. There is almost no exact information about his life. The period in which he lived is estimated from the sources he used for his book *Sha'ar ha-Shamayim* (*The Gate of Heaven*, tr. by F.S. Bodenheimer, 1953), the only work by him which is extant, and probably the only one he wrote. It has been estimated that this work was written between 1242 and 1300.

It is now agreed that Gershon lived in Arles in southern France (Provence). The traditional notion that he lived in Catalonia is shown to be incorrect by his own words: "For in the area of Catalonia the sheep and goats are smaller than those in our area" (*Sha'ar ha-Shamayim* (Roedelheim, 1801), 30b, 26–27). Spain is also not his place of residence: "One in our provinces and one in the provinces of Spain" (*ibid.*, 20a, 4). It also appears that Gershon regarded France as outside his homeland (*ibid.*, 16a, 11).

Sha'ar ha-Shamayim is a brief popular summary of the natural sciences, astronomy, and theology of Gershon's day. It is divided into three parts: natural sciences, theology, and astronomy. The first part contains ten treatises, on the following subjects: the four elements (including a discussion of meteorology); inanimate objects; plants; animals; fowls; bees, ants, and spiders; fish; man; parts of the body; sleeping and waking (including a discussion on dreams). The chapters on man include also psychological data, the law of heredity, and even clinical prognoses.

The first part is the longest and most detailed. In the extant editions of the work it takes up five-sixths of the entire book, but in some manuscripts there are obvious additions, which are not found in the printed version.

Gershon lists a great number of Greek, Latin, Arabic, and Jewish authors, and cites from their works. Among the authors cited by him are Homer, Plato, Pythagoras, Aristotle, Galen, Hippocrates, Al-Farabi, Avicenna, and Averroes. It appears that he received this knowledge from Hebrew translations of earlier scientific and philosophic literature rather than from original sources. He states in his introduction that he had "some of the books of the philosophers which had been translated from their languages to his own." He further states, with regard to the second and third parts of the book, that he based it primarily on those writings of *Maimonides and the Arabic scholar Al-Farghani (ninth century), which suited his purposes. It is not known which direct sources were used for the first part of the book.

In addition to citing from written sources, Gershon also set down what he had heard through reports from Jews or Christians. He was not an independent thinker; even where he makes statements in the first person, these are often taken literally from other sources.

Because there were not enough adequate words in Hebrew, and perhaps also in order to make for easier understanding, Gershon expressed many scientific concepts and objects by their foreign names, which he probably found in his sources. These names, usually Latin or Arabic, are an integral part of the text, unlike the foreign usages in other medieval writings, such as the commentaries of *Rashi, whose purpose in using foreign words is merely to clarify the meaning of difficult Hebrew terms.

Sha'ar ha-Shamayim served for hundreds of years as a popular book of sciences for readers of Hebrew. It was widely circulated and is extant in many manuscripts. The extant editions are all imperfect and incomplete in comparison with a few of the manuscripts. The first edition (Venice, 1547) apparently served as a basis for all subsequent editions (Roedelheim,

1801; Zolkiew, 1805; Warsaw, 1876; Jerusalem, 1944), in which corrections were made only on the basis of conjecture.

BIBLIOGRAPHY: L. Kopf, in: *Tarbiz*, 24 (1955), 150–66, 274–89, 410–25; A. Neubauer, in: MGWJ, 21 (1872), 182–4; H. Gross, *ibid.*, 28 (1879), 20ff., Gross, Gal Jud, 82–83, 94; Steinschneider, Uebersetzungen, 9–16; idem, in: REJ, 5 (1882), 278; Renan, Rabbins, 589–91.

[Lothar Kopf]

GERSHOVITZ, SAMUEL (1907–1960), U.S. social worker and Jewish Welfare Board (JWB) executive. Gershovitz was born in New Rochelle, New York, but raised in the Midwest. Gershovitz's association with JWB began in 1939 with his position as field secretary for the Midwest. In 1942 Gershovitz received his first position with national JWB. He became executive director in 1947 and executive vice president in 1952. He traveled widely, organizing USOs, community centers, and similar projects in Europe, Central America, and the Pacific. In Anchorage, Alaska, he set up the first Jewish community council.

GERSHOY, LEO (1897–1975), U.S. historian. Born in Russia, Gershoy was brought to the United States in 1903. He taught at Long Island University (1920–38) and Sarah Lawrence College (1938–46). After serving in World War II, he was professor of history at New York University from 1946. Gershoy's field was French history, specializing in the Ancien Régime and the French Revolution. Among his publications were *The French Revolution and Napoleon* (1933; new annotated biography, 1964); *From Despotism to Revolution, 1763–1789* (1944, 1962[3]); *The Era of the French Revolution, 1789–1799: Ten Years That Shook the* World (1957); and *Progress and Power* (with C. Becker, 1965). In 1975 the American Historical Association established the Leo Gershoy Award, which is presented annually to the author of the most outstanding work published in English on any aspect of 17th- and 18th-century western European history.

[Ruth Beloff (2nd ed.)]

GERSHUNI, GRIGORI ANDREYEVICH (1870–1908), Russian revolutionary; founder and leader of the terrorist arm of the Socialist-Revolutionary (S.-R.) Party. Gershuni was born in Tavrova, an estate in the Kovno province where his father was a tenant. After a short period in *ḥeder* he was educated in a Russian high school in Shavli (Šiauliai), but at the age of 15, before graduating, he was sent by his parents to another town to be a pharmacist's apprentice. He eventually settled in Minsk (1898) where he opened a bacteriological laboratory. There he took part in semi-legal educational activities among working-class people and was gradually drawn into clandestine circles, partly under the influence of Yekaterina Breshkovskaya, the "grandmother of the Russian Revolution." The turning point in his revolutionary career was a fortnight of arrest and interrogation in 1900, when the czarist police officer Zubatov tried to enlist him into the loyalist workers' movement organized by himself as a counterforce to terrorism and revolutionary ideology. The effect on Gershuni was exactly the opposite. He became an ardent supporter of anti-czarist terrorism, and when several revolutionary groups merged into the S.-R. Party, it was Gershuni who organized and headed its terrorist arm, the famous Fighting Organization (Boyevaya Organizatsiya), which, under his personal guidance, assassinated some of the highest and most hated officials and dignitaries, among them the minister Sipiagin and governor Bogdanovich. Yevno *Azeff, who was later unmasked as an *agent provocateur* of the police, became his closest collaborator in leading the Fighting Organization and took it over in 1903, when Gershuni was denounced by another police agent and arrested. A military tribunal sentenced Gershuni to death, but the sentence was later commuted to life imprisonment. He was imprisoned in the old Schluesselburg fortress in 1906, but after having been transported to an eastern Siberian prison, he was smuggled out in a cabbage barrel and in a daring flight, by way of China (where he met Sun Yat-sen) and Japan, he reached the United States. There he addressed socialist mass meetings of Jewish and other workers in many cities and collected funds for the Russian S.-R. Party. Several weeks later he appeared in Finland where he publicly attended the second S.-R. Party congress in 1907. In 1908 Gershuni died in a Zurich hospital after an illness. In his last days he learned about the Azeff affair. His friends arranged for his burial in the Montparnasse cemetery in Paris alongside other famous Russian revolutionaries. His funeral grew into an impressive demonstration of international sympathy for the Russian revolutionary movement.

Gershuni became a legendary figure in his lifetime. Although completely assimilated in Russian language and culture, he was always conscious of being a Jew. In his revolutionary speech before the military tribunal in 1903 he stressed the plight of the Jewish masses in Russia. In his behavior in prison and in his dealings with the czarist authorities he was always proud and courageous, so as not to play into the hands of antisemitic propaganda which tried to present the Jewish revolutionaries as cowardly manipulators behind the scenes. To his friend Chaim *Zhitlowsky he said that after the revolution, when liberty would be achieved in Russia, he would join those who devote themselves completely to Jewish interests. Gershuni's reminiscences *Iz nedavnovo proshlavo* ("From the Recent Past") were published in Paris by the S.-R. central committee (1908).

BIBLIOGRAPHY: A.I. Spiridovich, *Zapiski zhandarma* (1928[2]); V. Chernov (ed.), *Grigory Gershuni: Zayn Leben un Tetikeyt* (1934); M. Rosenbaum, *Erinerungen fun a Sotsyalist-Revolutsyoner*, 2 vols. (1924).

[Binyamin Eliav]

GERSHUNI, MOSHE (1936–), Israeli painter. Gershuni was born in Tel Aviv. His father was a farmer and as a young man Gershuni thought he would be one too. When he was 19 his father was killed in a car accident and young Gershuni had to work in the family orchards. Only when he was 24 did he begin to study art in evening classes at the Avni Institute (1960–64). He studied sculpture and thought of himself as a sculptor. In the 1960s he was one of the young avant-garde artists who exhibited with the support of the Ten Plus group in Tel Aviv and came to the attention of Yona Fisher at the Israel Museum in Jerusalem.

From 1970 to 1978 Gershuni taught at the Bezalel Academy of Art and Design in Jerusalem. As a teacher, in keeping with the spirit of the times, he guided his students toward a Modern-Conceptual art style. Gershuni himself exhibited works in the same style, such as a piece of paper with a piece of margarine on it or torn paper on which he wrote, "The paper looks white but inside it is black." In those years he was a part of a small group of artists, among them Micha *Ullman and Avital Geva, who met with their mentor, Itzhak *Danziger, to talk about art. They worked as a group in peripheral areas and also created political art. As a result of a conceptual-ideological rebellion Gershuni was dismissed from Bezalel at the end of the 1970s. He changed his personal life style as well as his artistic style, which became emotional and expressive. He started to use his fingers as his tools, stained the canvas or the paper with mixed colors, and added scribbling and free handwriting. During these years he began to deal with the subject of homosexuality.

One of the main themes that Gershuni ventured to deal with was the Holocaust. In his complicated way he mixed Yiddish, the swastika, the star of David, and verses from prayer. It was the first time in Israeli art that the swastika was represented, and it courageously reflected Gershuni's desire to get into the very heart of the subject. In the Venice Biennial he used the image of blood, creating a puddle of blood on the floor and writing German words referring to the Holocaust on the walls. In these works he also used cutlery and towels to symbolize the Jewish religious heritage and basic existence, purity and impurity.

With the same daring Gershuni dealt with the wars of the State of Israel. In a series of paintings he scribbled the name Itzhak and wrote repetitive sentences about soldiers and killing together with quotations from Israeli patriotic songs. Gershuni was also one of the first artists to get involved in Judaism, delving deeply into his Jewish identity.

In 2003 Gershuni was awarded the Israel Prize. Gershuni decided to come to the ceremony but for political reasons refused to shake hands with Prime Minister Ariel Sharon and Education Minister Limor Livnat. After much tumult in the media and appeals in the Supreme Court the decision was to deny him the prize.

BIBLIOGRAPHY: Israel Museum, *Moshe Gershuni 1980–1986* (1986); Jerusalem Print Workshop, *Under the Sun* (2003).

[Ronit Steinberg (2nd ed.)]

GERSHWIN, GEORGE (1898–1937), U.S. composer. Born in New York, he wrote his first songs while working as a pianist with a music publishing firm. His first revue, *Half Past Eight* (1918), was followed by the successful *La La Lucille* (1919) and in the same year his song "Swanee," sung by Al *Jolson in the revue *Sinbad*, caused a sensation. He was commissioned by Paul Whiteman to compose a jazz symphony. The resultant work, *Rhapsody in Blue* for piano and orchestra, was first performed in New York in 1924, with the composer at the piano. It made jazz "respectable" for the American concert stage and made Gershwin famous. He composed the *Concerto for Piano in F Major* (1925), *Three Preludes for Piano* (1926), *An American in Paris* (1928), *Second Rhapsody* (1931), and *Cuban Overture* (1932). Gershwin had little formal training, and after the success of the *Rhapsody in Blue*, in which he had received the help of an orchestrator, he studied with Rubin *Goldmark and Joseph *Schillinger.

He continued composing music for films and Broadway shows, his most successful revues being *Lady Be Good* (1924), *Oh Kay* (1926), *Strike Up the Band* (1927), *Girl Crazy* (1930), and *Of Thee I Sing* (1931), a political satire. Most of the lyrics for his revues and songs were written by his brother Ira (1896–1983). His last and greatest work was the folk opera *Porgy and Bess* (1935), based on Du-Bose Heyward's play, *Catfish Row*, about the life of Southern blacks. Gershwin's musical style was rooted in the jazz idiom of his time, and stimulated by the traditions of Southern blacks. Influences of cantorial style may be discerned in certain wide-ranging phrases, notably the clarinet solo which opens *Rhapsody in Blue*.

On February 28, 1973, the U.S. government issued an 8-cent commemorative stamp in honor of George Gershwin as representative of musicians, on the occasion of the 75th anniversary of his birth. It was the first stamp in the American Arts series of commemoratives, and the U.S. Postal Service issued a first day cover featuring him at the piano.

BIBLIOGRAPHY: R. Rushmore, *Life of George Gershwin* (1966); I. Goldberg, *George Gershwin: A Study in American Music* (1931); M. Armitage (ed.), *George Gershwin* (1938); D. Ewen, *A Journey to Greatness, The Life and Music of George Gershwin* (1956); G. Chase (ed.), *American Composer Speaks* (1966), 139–45.

[Josef Tal/Bathja Bayer]

GERSONI, HENRY (Heb., **Gershoni, Ẓevi Hirsch**; 1844–1897), journalist and author. Born in Vilna, he studied in the Vilna Rabbinical Seminary. Moving to St. Petersburg, he married a Christian girl and converted to Christianity. In 1868 he publicly confessed his conversion in *Ha-Maggid*, a leading Hebrew periodical, but announced his repentance and reaffirmed his loyalty to Judaism. After many wanderings, he settled in New York in 1869. In 1874 he became a rabbi in Macon, Georgia. He also served as rabbi in Atlanta and in Chicago, where he published his short-lived weekly *The Jewish Advance* and, later, *The Maccabean*. He returned to New York in 1893 where he lived by his pen until his death.

Devoted to the new Hebrew literature, Gersoni published articles in the leading Hebrew periodicals. He was also a pioneer of the Yiddish press in America, editor of the *Post* in New York (1870), and a contributor to Jewish periodicals in the English language. He translated Turgenev into English and Longfellow's *Excelsior* into Hebrew.

Gersoni wrote on the burning problems of the day: Orthodoxy and Reform, immigration to America and to Palestine, ethical culture, organizational life of Jewry. His subjective and acute observations of the American scene are still of historic importance, e.g., in his *Sketches of Jewish Life and History* (1873).

BIBLIOGRAPHY: J. Kabakoff, *Ḥalutzei ha-Sifrut ha-Ivrit ba-Amerikah* (1966), 79–130.

[Eisig Silberschlag]

GERSON-KIWI, EDITH (**Esther**; 1908–1992), Israeli musicologist. Born in Berlin, she studied with the harpsichordist Wanda *Landowska. Settling in Ereẓ Israel in 1935, she devoted herself to teaching and to ethnomusicological research. Her work was sponsored at different periods by the Hebrew University, by the Ministry of Education and Culture, and by various foundations. It included the collection of musical recordings which, by 1970, comprised 7,000 items. From 1967 she also lectured at Tel Aviv University. Her writings deal with the musical traditions of Jewish communities and the mutual influences to be found in Jewish, Christian, and Muslim music. Her publications include *The Persian Doctrine of Dastga Composition* (1963) and "Vocal Folk Polyphonies of the Western Orient in Jewish Tradition" (in *Yuval*, 1 (1968), 169–93).

BIBLIOGRAPHY: B. Bayer, in: *Bat Kol*, 3 (1961), 33–35.

°**GERSTEIN, KURT** (1905–1945), German anti-Nazi, SS officer and head of the Waffen SS-Institute of Hygiene in Berlin. The son of a bourgeois family, a German nationalist, and a Christian, Gerstein joined the Nazi Party in 1933, while remaining in the Protestant youth movement. He was expelled from the Nazi Party for activities on behalf of the dissident Bekenntniskirche ("Professing Church") and was twice incarcerated in concentration camps (1936 and 1938). Anxious to know more about the Nazis' horrifying activities, he volunteered for the Waffen-SS in March 1941 and became an employee at its Hygiene Service. There are, however, other versions of the reason for his entry into the SS. A professional engineer, Gerstein reached officer's rank and due to his technical abilities was named chief of the disinfection department. He lost a sister-in-law in the so-called euthanasia program. In 1942, as an expert in the use of Zyklon B – a poison gas used in fumigations – Gerstein was sent by the *RSHA to *Belzec and *Treblinka, where his task was to substitute Zyklon B for diesel exhaust fumes as a means of mass murder. At Belzec he witnessed the killing of several thousand Jews from Lvov. Upon his return to Berlin, Gerstein tried to stop the murders, informing Swedish and Swiss legations, the Holy See, and underground Church groups, the German Confessing Church, of his experiences, but despite the accuracy of his reports, he encountered disbelief and indifference. Charged with the task of continuing to supply the murderous gas to the camps, Gerstein succeeded in destroying two consignments. At the end of the war, he submitted to an Anglo-American intelligence team a detailed report in French on Nazi atrocities which was used at the Nuremberg trials. Another, in German, was published after his death in *Vierteljahreshefte fuer Zeitgeschichte* (vol. 1, 1953), entitled "Augenzeugenbericht zu den Massenvergasungen." Arrested by the French as a suspected war criminal, Gerstein was found hanged in his cell on July 25, 1945, victim either of suicide or murder. His testimony remains essential to our understanding of Belzec, where so little first-hand information was available.

BIBLIOGRAPHY: S. Friedlaender, *Kurt Gerstein, the Ambiguity of Good* (1969); idem, in: *Midstream*, 13 no. 5 (1967), 24–29; F. Helmut, *K. Gerstein* (Ger., 1964); R. Hochhuth, *The Representative* (1963), (U.S. title – *The Deputy*). P. Joffroy, *A Spy for God: The Ordeal of Kurt Gerstein* (1971).

[Yehuda Reshef]

GERSTEN, BERTA (1897–1972), Yiddish actress. Born in Cracow, Poland, Gersten started her career in the U.S., in 1908, playing a boy in J. Gordin's *Mirele Efros*. In 1918 she joined Maurice Schwartz's Yiddish Art Theater and remained with Schwartz for 25 years, performing leading roles in New York and on tour, frequently playing opposite Jacob Ben-Ami. She appeared in Yiddish films, among them *Yiskor* (1933), *The Jester* (1937), *Mirele Efros* (1938), *A Letter to Mother* (1938), and *God, Man and Devil* (1950). She also played Benny Goodman's mother, Dora, in the 1955 English-language film *The Benny Goodman Story*. Gersten performed on Broadway in *The World of Sholem Aleichem* (1954), *The Flowering Peach* (1955), *A Majority of One* (1959), and *Sophie* (1963). Her final appearance was in 1971 at the Folksbiene Playhouse in New York, playing opposite her lifelong friend and colleague Ben-Ami in *My Father's Court*.

[Ruth Beloff (2nd ed.)]

GERSTLE, LEWIS (1824–1902), U.S. merchant. Gerstle, born in Ichenhausen, Bavaria, immigrated to America about 1845, settling in Louisville, Ky., and then in California. After prospecting for gold briefly, he joined Louis Sloss and Company of Sacramento, general merchandise dealers. During this time, Gerstle and Sloss married the sisters Hannah and Sarah Greenebaum. Moving to San Francisco in about 1860, Gerstle and Sloss entered the stock brokerage business, bought and sold hides, operated a tannery, and acquired shipping interests. In 1868, after the American purchase of Alaska, they and others organized the highly successful Alaska Commercial Company for trade in the new territory. They received a fur seal concession, established trading posts, and supplied miners during the Klondike gold strike of 1897. Gerstle was a director of Congregation Emanu-El and the Pacific Hebrew Orphan Asylum and Home Society, a member of the Vigilance Committee, and treasurer of the University of California. He promoted manufacturing establishments and directed two banks.

BIBLIOGRAPHY: G. Mack, *Lewis and Hannah Gerstle* (1953); M.A. Meyer, *Western Jewry* (1916); R. Glanz, *Jews in American Alaska (1867–1880)* (1953); L.D. Kitchener, *Flag Over the North* (1954); M. Zarchin, *Glimpses of Jewish Life in San Francisco* (1964).

[Robert E. Levinson]

GERTLER, MARK (1891–1939), English artist. Gertler was born in London, the son of a furrier, but spent part of his early childhood in Poland and America. Gertler was one of the most talented and romantic first generation painters to emerge from the wave of Jewish immigration to England at the turn of the century, and is today one of the most famous of Anglo-Jewish artists. Until he went to school at the age of eight, his only language was Yiddish. Later he began attending evening classes in art and worked for a firm of glass painters. In 1908, on the advice of Sir William *Rothenstein, the Jewish Educational Aid Society sent him to the Slade School of Art. Here he found himself among the brilliant group of Jewish students which included David *Bomberg, Jacob *Kramer, Bernard *Meninsky, and Isaac *Rosenberg. In 1911, before he was 20, he painted one of his finest pictures, *The Artist's Mother*, one of the collection of his works in the Tate Gallery, London. When he left the Slade in 1912, he began to receive important portrait commissions. Handsome, volatile, and a brilliant raconteur, he was taken up by the Bloomsbury Group of intellectuals, and seemed destined for greatness. Gertler's early works were influenced by his life in the Whitechapel ghetto. In addition to the studies of his parents and neighbors, often in fancy dress, these include *Rabbi and Grandchild* (1913) and *Rabbi and Rebbitzen* (1914). Gertler was later influenced by post-impressionism. From 1919 onward he regularly visited the south of France. Gertler was close to many of the famous figures in the Bloomsbury Group, and was briefly the lover of one of its members, the painter Dora Carrington. He was also a friend of many other noted cultural figures of his time, including D.H. Lawrence and Aldous Huxley. His health began to deteriorate and eventually, depressed by his condition, by Hitler's anti-Jewish campaign, and by financial problems resulting from decreasing success, he committed suicide in 1939. Since his death he has become the subject of much interest by biographers and critics.

BIBLIOGRAPHY: Bell, in: M. Gertler, *Selected Letters*, ed. by N. Carrington (1965), introduction; J. Rothenstein, *British Art Since 1900* (1962), 172, plates 85,86. **ADD. BIBLIOGRAPHY:** ODNB online; N. Carrington (ed.), *Mark Gertler: Selected Letters* (1965); S. MacDougall, *Mark Gertler* (2002); J. Woodeson, *Mark Gertler: Biography of a Painter, 1891–1939* (1972).

[Charles Samuel Spencer]

GERTNER, LEVI (1908–1976) and **MEIR** (1905–1976), educationists who profoundly influenced modern Hebrew and Jewish education in Britain. Born in Hungarian Transylvania of ḥasidic parents, they began their education in yeshivot.

From 1929 to 1936 Levi Gertner studied history and philosophy at Berlin University before immigrating to Ereẓ Israel, where he studied at the Hebrew University and taught at the Youth Aliyah village of Geva. He arrived in Britain just before World War II in 1939 and in 1941 began work for the Zionist Federation. In 1950 he became director of the newly established Jewish Agency Education Department and in 1953 was made head of the Zionist Day School movement in Britain. Under his guidance 16 day schools were established.

He organized and participated in 83 full-length and more than 100 weekend seminars of the Hebrew Seminar Movement. These were conducted in a traditional Jewish atmosphere, but attracted both the religious and the non-observant of all ages, including lecturers, teachers and students, family groups and individuals.

Meir Gertner, a philosopical thinker and intellectual, followed a more academic pattern, although he was for a time deputy director of the Education Department of the Jewish National Fund in Jerusalem. After studying at Hamburg and the Hebrew University, he obtained his doctorate at Oxford. He became director of Hebrew studies at Carmel College and succeeded Isidore Wartski as Aḥad Ha-am Lecturer (later Reader) in Modern Hebrew at the School of Oriental and African Studies in London. In 1972 he became J.H. Hertz Fellow at the Oxford Centre for Post-Graduate Hebrew Studies.

He played an active part in Anglo-Jewish communal life as co-chairman of the Jewish Book Council, a founder member of Jewish Book Week, chairman of the Cultural Committee of the World Jewish Congress, and a Council member of the Hillel Foundation.

BIBLIOGRAPHY: *Jewish Chronicle* (July 23, 1976; Aug. 8, 1976).

[Sonia L. Lipman]

GERTSA (Rom. **Herta**), town in N. Bukovina, Chernovtsy district, Ukraine, which passed from Romania to the Soviet Union in 1940. The locality was founded in 1672. Jews of Galician origin, who were craftsmen and merchants, settled in Gertsa in the first quarter of the 18th century.A known local Jewish institution was a *talmud torah* of which a minute-book dating from 1764 has been preserved. The oldest tombstone in the cemetery dates from 1766. The community had four synagogues, of which the oldest was built at the end of the 18th century; a *mikveh* was founded in 1820, and a mixed school was established in the early 20th century. The community numbered 1,200 in 1803, 1,554 (56.4% of the total population) in c. 1859, 1,939 in 1899 (66.1%), 1,876 in 1910, and 1,801 in 1930 (25%). Many of them were ḥasidim, followers of the admor of Buczacz, as well as a local admor. *Maskilim* also lived in the town, among them the bilingual Hebrew-Romanian writer Moise Roman-Ronetti. The bilingual Romanian-French poet Benjamin *Fondane (Fundoianu) was born in Gertsa, describing it in a poem. During the peasants' revolt in 1907 the Jews in Gertsa prevented attacks and pillaging by organizing *self-defense. After the conferment of Romanian nationality in 1919, Jews were elected to the municipal council, and at one time a Jew served as vice mayor. In 1927 the Romanian governing party appointed a communal board from its own adherents, but the Jews boycotted it and two years later ensured its resignation. In 1938 there were seven synagogues, an elementary Israelite-Romanian school, and a Zionist organization. During World War II the Jews in Gertsa (1,600 persons) were deported to *Transnistria. Under the Soviet regime all the Jewish public buildings were secularized and nationalized. In the beginning of the Soviet regime (1940–41) dozens of Jews were deported to Siberia, only some of whom could return to Gertsa in 1960. The majority of Jews immigrated to Israel in the 1970s. Only a few Jews remain in Gertsa in the beginning of the 21st century.

BIBLIOGRAPHY: E. Schwarzfeld, *Impopularea, reimpopularea şi intemeires tîrgurilor şi tîrguşoarelor în Moldova* (1914), 63, 79; V. Tufescu, *Tîrguşoarele din Moldava şi importanţa lor economiaš* (1942), 115, 118, 140. **ADD. BIBLIOGRAPHY:** S. David (ed.), *Generatii de iudaism si sionism: Dorohoi, Mihaileni, Darabani, Herta*, 5 vols. (1992–2000).

[Lucian-Zeev Herscovici (2nd ed.)]

GERTZ, ELMER (1906–2000), U.S. lawyer. Gertz, who was born in Chicago and received his law degree from the University of Chicago, practiced law in his native city from 1930. He became known for his vigorous opposition to capital punishment, his defense of freedom of expression, and his fight for civil rights and liberties. In 1958, taking over the case begun in 1924 by legendary litigator Clarence Darrow, he obtained parole for Nathan Leopold, who had been convicted of murder and served 34 years in prison. In 1962 he secured commutation of the death sentence of William Crump for murder, on the grounds that Crump had been rehabilitated in prison while surviving nine stays of execution. Gertz helped to save the life of William Witherspoon, another convicted murderer, when the U.S. Supreme Court (1968) upheld his contention that prospective jurors should not have been challenged for their conscientious scruples against imposing the death penalty. He was also instrumental in the setting aside of the death penalty imposed on Jack *Ruby (1966). Gertz's court pleas brought about the removal of the ban, on account of obscenity, on the sale of Frank Harris' *My Life and Loves*, Henry Miller's *Tropic of Cancer* (1964), and the works of the Marquis de Sade. He also secured the abolition by the U.S. Supreme Court of the Chicago motion picture censorship ordinance (1968). In the 1940s, as special counsel for the National Association for the Advancement of Colored People, Gertz was successful in a test case to make housing restrictions in Illinois illegal. He helped secure passage of the Illinois Fair Employment Practices Law and defended its validity before the Illinois Supreme Court in the late 1950s.

Active in many Jewish communal affairs, Gertz was president of the Greater Chicago Council of the American Jewish Congress (1959–63). He served as an officer of the Society of Midland Authors and the Illinois Freedom to Read Committee. From 1970 until his death, he taught civil rights courses at the John Marshall Law School.

While serving as chairman of the Illinois Bill of Rights Committee of the Illinois Constitutional Convention (1969–70), Gertz helped draft what has been called the strongest bill of rights of any state constitution in the country. Gertz also chaired the civil rights committees of the Illinois State Bar Association and the Chicago Bar Association (1978–80) and was president of the First Amendment Lawyers Association (1978–79). In 1983, he won a 14-year legal battle against the John Birch Society by suing its magazine publisher, Robert W. Welch, for libel in regard to an article written about him. This landmark case increased the instances in which a plaintiff could be deemed a private citizen and thus entitled to more protection against the press.

Among his many honors, Gertz was a national trustee of the City of Hope, for which he received the Golden Key Award in 1966. He received the State of Israel Prime Minister's Medal in 1972 (which he considered his greatest accomplishment), and Educator of the Year in 1975. In 2000, he was honored posthumously with the Illinois State Bar Association Medal of Merit. The association's highest honor for a practicing attorney, it is awarded only in extraordinary circumstances for exemplary accomplishments.

Books written by Gertz include *Frank Harris: A Study in Black and White* (1931, with A.I. Tobin), *The People vs. The Chicago Tribune* (1942), *A Handful of Clients* (1965), *Moment of Madness: The People vs. Jack Ruby* (1968), *Quest for a Constitution* (1984), *To Life:* The Story of a Chicago Lawyer (1990), *Errors, Lies, and Libel* (with P. Kane, 1991), and *Gertz v. Robert Welch, Inc.: The Story of a Landmark Libel Case* (1992).

BIBLIOGRAPHY: M. Myerson and E.C. Banfield, *Politics, Planning, and Public Interest* (1955). **ADD. BIBLIOGRAPHY:** E. Gertz and F. Lewis (eds), *Henry Miller: Years of Trial & Triumph, 1962–1964: The Correspondence of Henry Miller & Elmer Gertz* (1978).

[Morton Mayer Berman / Ruth Beloff (2nd ed.)]

GERUSIA (Gr. γερουσία), council of elders, common throughout the Hellenistic world (e.g., Sparta, Cyrene). Since the "elders" or "city elders" (*Ziknei ha-Ir*) are mentioned repeatedly in the Bible (cf. Deut. 19:12, 21:2ff.; Josh. 20:4; Judg. 8:14; I Sam. 9:3; I Kings 21:8,11; Ruth 4:2ff.), Josephus concludes that the earliest Jewish *Gerusia* dates back to biblical times, functioning as a high court together with the high priest and prophets (Ant. 4:218). During the Hellenistic period the *Gerusia* appears not merely as a legislative and judicial body, but as representative of the Jewish population of Judea. Thus in the famous edict of Antiochus III the Great, following his conquest of Palestine, the Seleucid monarch describes the splendid reception given him by the Jews – in the person of the *Gerusia* (and not, as might have been expected, the high priest). As a result, the members of the *Gerusia* were exempted from a number of taxes, together with officials of the Temple (Ant. 12:138ff.). Similarly, Antiochus IV Epiphanes, in an epistle to the Jews, addresses his remarks to the *Gerusia* and not the high priest (II Macc. 11:27). That the Jews of this period considered the *Gerusia* their official representative body is further apparent from the correspondence of "those in Jerusalem and Judea, the *Gerusia*, and Judah" to their brethren in Egypt during the early years of the Hasmonean rebellion (II Macc. 1:10). When Jonathan became leader of the Jewish nation, the office of high priest was apparently formally recognized as representative of the people, and thus in a correspondence with the Spartans "Jonathan the high priest and the *Gerusia*" are listed together (I Macc. 12: 6; Jos., Ant. 13, 166).

It would be a mistake, however, to identify the *Gerusia*, which appears to be a permanent representative body of elders dating back to the Persian period (cf. Judith 4:8, 11: 14, 15:8), with the "Great Assembly" (*keneset ha-gedolah*), a body representing the total Jewish population of Palestine, and convened only when important constitutional decisions were taken. The "elders" are thus mentioned as a part of the Great Assembly that appointed Simeon high priest and leader of the Jewish nation (I Macc. 14:28). It is feasible, however, that the *Gerusia* eventually evolved into what became known as the "Sanhedrin" of Jerusalem, although the precise date of the introduction of this term is unknown (cf. H. Mantel, *Studies in the History of the Sanhedrin* (1961), 49–50, 61–62, for a summation of the numerous views on this problem). According to Philo (Flaccus, 10:74) there also existed a Jewish *Gerusia* in Alexandria, which during the rule of Augustus replaced the previous form of local Jewish leadership, the ethnarchate.

BIBLIOGRAPHY: S.B. Hoenig, *Great Sanhedrin* (1953); Y.M. Grintz, *Sefer Yehudit* (1957), 105.

[Isaiah Gafni]

GERY, a small group of ethnic Russians who adhere to Judaism. As a separate religious group the Gery emerged in the early 19th century from the sect of the Subbotniki (Sabbatarians) and in the late 19th–early 20th centuries adopted Orthodox Judaism. The Gery strive to observe all the commandments of the Jewish religion and to merge totally with Jews of Jewish ethnic origin, including by marriage. Many Gery sent their children to **yeshivot*. They lived scattered through many districts of Russia (Astrakhan, Saratov, Tambov, Voronezh) on the Don, in the Kuban, in the northern Caucasus and Transcaucasus, and in Siberia where they were sent as exiles. They were persecuted by the czarist government and the Russian Orthodox Church which considered "Judaizing" sects especially dangerous. Cases are known of Jews serving the Gery as rabbis, ritual slaughterers, and teachers. Important roles in their religious education were played by an anonymous Jewish distiller from Tambov district who lived among the Gery from 1805 and in the 1880s by a Lithuanian Jew, David Teitelbaum. Many Gery families settled in the land of Israel in the 19th century, particulary in Galilee (Yesud ha-Ma'alah, Bet-Gan, etc.) and within two to three generations were completely assimilated into the surrounding Jewish populations. After the Russian proclamation of the freedom of religion in 1905, the Gery, now known as "sabbatarians of the Jewish faith," gained the right to legal recognition of their communities and the right to build synagogues (e.g., at Stantsiya Zima in the Irkutsk district, Tiflis). Although the number of Gery has significantly declined, they still continue to exist (in the Voronezh district, on the Don, in the northern Caucasus, and elsewhere).

In Israel the Gery are recognized as Jews both from the point of view of *Halakhah* and by the laws of the state. Many Gery in the Soviet Union are actively fighting for emigration to Israel and a number of Gery families left for Israel between 1971 and 1980. Twenty families from the village of Il'inka, Talov county, Voronezh district, who moved to Israel in 1973–76 evidently have a Gery background.

[*Shorter Jewish Encylopaedia in Russian*]

GESANG, NATHAN-NACHMAN (1886–1944), one of the leaders and president of the Zionist Organization and of the Keren Hayesod of Argentina. Born in Cracow, Gesang went to Berlin to study and became active in the Zionist movement. When he moved to Britain (in 1909) he became secretary of the British Zionist Organization. In 1910 he settled in Argentina and after a short while became the first hired secretary of the local "Zionist Party." He was one of the leaders of Argentine Jewry and served as president of the Zionist Federation (General Zionists) in 1922–23, 1930–31, and 1941–1944. Gesang was active in the propagation of Zionism from the very beginning of its work, with his speeches and organizational work in Buenos Aires as well as in the province communities, in cities, and in agricultural settlements. He represented the Argentine Zionist Federation at some Zionist Congresses. In 1937 he supported a kind of cooperation with Jabotinsky and the Revisionists who had seceded from the World Zionist Organization and were organized in Ha-Ẓohar. In the 1930s Gesang promoted the establishment of a representation of the Jewish Agency in Argentina. He participated in the promotion of Hebrew language and culture and published articles in Hebrew, Yiddish, and Spanish on Zionist affairs and Jewish studies. Among his published books are *Der Hoveve Tzionism un der Politisher Tzionizm* ("Ḥovevei Zion Movement and Political Zionism," Yid. and Sp., 1937) and a new edition of the *Kuzari* by Judah Halevi, with a detailed introduction (1943).

BIBLIOGRAPHY: S. Schenkolewski-Kroll, *Ha-Tenu'ah ha-Ẓionit ve-ha-Miflagot ha-Ẓiyyoniyyot be-Argentina – 1935–1948* (1996).

[Getzel Kressel / Efraim Zadoff (2nd ed.)]

GESELLSCHAFT DER FREUNDE (Ger. "Society of Friends"), German mutual aid society. The society was founded in 1792 by Berlin bachelors, among them Isaac *Euchel, Aaron Wolfssohn, and Joseph Mendelssohn. It officially aimed at mutual aid in cases of illness, poverty, business problems, and death. However, during the first decades of its existence the Gesellschaft also served as the main organization of the late Berlin *Haskalah and was successfully involved in the ongoing fight against the ritual of early burial.

During the first decades of the 19th century, the character of the Gesellschaft der Freunde changed. Instead of being an organization of just one social group, it became the cultural center of all of Berlin Jewry. The association bought a big house in the city center, near the synagogue in Heidereuterstrasse, where other organizations, schools, and private parties used the dining rooms, ballrooms, and large garden for their dinners, examinations, or wedding celebrations as well. The spectrum ranged from the Reform community to the neo-Orthodox Adass Jisroel, from the social Geselliger Verein der Handwerker to the religious Talmud-Verein. The personal connection with the leadership of the Berlin Jewish community was especially close during this period.

After 1880, the Gesellschaft der Freunde withdrew from public attention. It had to sell its house and became an organization where leading Jewish bankers, entrepreneurs, merchants, and managers met. The *Mendelssohns, *Liebermanns, *Ullsteins, *Mosses, *Rathenaus, and *Bleichroeders all were members. During the 1920s, dozens of non-Jewish economic leaders joined the association, most of whom resigned, however, after 1933. In 1935, the Gesellschaft der Freunde was closed down by National Socialist officials; most of its members succeeded in emigrating to the U.K., the U.S., Switzerland, and other countries.

BIBLIOGRAPHY: H. Baschwitz, *Rueckblick auf die hundertjaehrige Geschichte der Gesellschaft der Freunde zu Berlin und Nachtrag zur Chronik bis zum Schluss des Jahres 1891* (1892); L. Lesser, *Chronik der Gesellschaft der Freunde in Berlin zur Feier ihres Fünfzigjaehrigen Jubilaeums. Nebst einem Nachtrag 1842–1872 von Martin Steinthal* (1842/1872); S. Panwitz, *Die Gesellschaft der Freunde (1792–1935) in Berlin.*

[Sebastian Pannwitz (2nd ed.)]

GESELLSCHAFT DER JUNGEN HEBRAEER (Ger. "Society of Young Hebrews"), society founded in Prague at the beginning of the 19th century by two young enlightened Jews, Judah and Ignaz *Jeiteles. Unlike the Gesellschaft der Freunde in Berlin, on which it was modeled, the society's aim was not only to provide mutual aid for its members, but also to propagate the ideas of the Haskalah among the working youth and uneducated members of Jewish society in Prague. Thus their *Yidish Daytshe Monatshrift*, of which six numbers appeared in 1802, was published neither in Hebrew nor in German but in *Vayber-Daytsh* ("Women's German," i.e., the Yiddish language of *Ẓe'enah u-Re'enah* printed in the Hebrew alphabet). Both the society and its periodical were forerunners of the particular Bohemian brand of Haskalah that was influenced by rising Czech nationalism, Jewish consciousness, and loyalty to the house of Hapsburg.

BIBLIOGRAPHY: R. Kestenberg-Gladstein, in: *Molad*, 23 (1965), 221 33; idem, *Neuere Geschichte der Juden in den boehmischen Laendern*, 1 (1969), 191–253.

[Meir Lamed]

GESELLSCHAFT ZUR FOERDERUNG DER WISSENSCHAFT DES JUDENTUMS (Ger. "Society for the Advancement of Jewish Scholarship"), Jewish scholarly society in Berlin, Germany, 1902–1938. The primary objective of the Gesellschaft was to raise the level of Jewish academic scholarship, thereby earning the respect of disenfranchised Jewish intellectuals and Christian Protestant scholars alike. As Jewish theology was not a recognized academic discipline at German universities, the founders attempted to create a financially viable forum for Jewish scholars to conduct research and to publish their works. The immediate incentive for the establishment of the Gesellschaft was the unequaled success enjoyed by Harnack's *Das Wesen des Christentums* and the perceived inability of the Jewish scholarly community to counter his unfavorable portrayal of post-biblical Judaism.

While Hermann *Cohen was the driving force behind foundation of the Gesellschaft, the initiative came from Rabbi Leopold Lucas of Glogau. The society's first chairman was historian Martin Philippson. Membership was open to both individuals and organizations, with a membership exceeding 1,700 in the early 1920s.

In pursuit of the advancement of Jewish scholarship, the Gesellschaft held annual meetings featuring scholarly lectures and published and subsidized scholarly volumes. It adopted the prestigious **Monatsschrift fuer die Geschichte und Wissenschaft des Judentums*, as its official organ, rescuing the publication from financial ruin by broadening its appeal to the general public. Equally important and innovative was the monetary support of individual Jewish scholars and the financing of research trips to various countries.

The most lofty endeavor of the Gesellschaft, which was never completed, was the "Grundriss der Gesamtwissenschaft des Judentums," projected to be a systematic and comprehensive collection of Jewish scholarship to encompass 36 volumes. The first volume to be published was Leo Baeck's classic *Das Wesen des Judentums* (1905). Among the other important publications were M. Guedemann, *Juedische Apologetik* (1906); M. Philippson, *Neueste Geschichte des juedischen Volkes* (1907–11); G. Caro, *Die Sozial-und Wirtschaftsgeschichte der Juden* (1908–20); K. Kohler, *Grundriss einer systematischen Theologie des Judentums* (1910); S. Krauss, *Talmudische Archäologie*, 3 vols. (1910, 1911, 1912); I. Elbogen, *Der juedische Gottesdienst* (1913); E. Mahler, *Handbuch der jüdischen Chronologie* (1916); H. Cohen, *Die Religion der Vernunft aus den Quellen des Judentums* (1919); A. Lewkowitz, *Das Judentum und die geistigen Stömungen des 19. Jahrhunderts* (1935); the incomplete *Corpus Tannaiticum and Germania Judaica*; and two volumes of a trilogy on Maimonides(1908, 1914).

The establishment of the society marked an important step towards the professionalization of *Wissenschaft des Judentums, and can be regarded as a limited success; for more than a generation it provided impetus and organization for all branches of Jewish scholarship, earning respect in both Jewish and non-Jewish academic circles. The society was forced to cease its activities following the *Kristallnacht riots.

BIBLIOGRAPHY: L. Lucas, in: MGWJ, 71 (1927), 321–31; I. Elbogen, MGWJ, 72 (1928), 1–5; Z.W. Falk, "Juedisches Lernen und die Wissenschaft des Judentums," in: K.E. Groetzinger (ed.), *Judentum im deutschen Sprachbereich* (1991), 347–56; F.D. Lucas and M. Heitmann, in: *Stadt des Glaubens: Geschichte und Kultur der Juden in Glogau*

(1991); C. Wiese, in: *Wissenschaft des Judentums und protestantische Theologie im wilhelminischen Deutschland: Ein Schrei ins Leere?* (1999); D. Adelmann, "Die Religion der Vernunft im Grundriss der Gesamtwissenschaft des Judentums," in: H. Holzhey, G. Motzkin and H. Wiedebach (eds), *Religion of Reason out of the sources of Judaism: Tradition and the Concept of Origin in Hermann Cohen's Later Work* (2000), 3–35; H. Soussan, " Gesellschaft zur Förderung der Wissenschaft des Judentums,1902–1915," in: LBIYB, 46 (2001).

[Henry Soussan (2nd ed.)]

°**GESENIUS, HEINRICH FRIEDRICH WILHELM** (1786–1842), German Orientalist, lexicographer, and Bible scholar. Born at Nordhausen, he taught in several German towns (Helmstedt, Goettingen, Heiligenstadt), and was appointed professor of theology at the University of Halle in 1811. He wrote a number of studies on Semitic languages including *Versuch ueber die maltesische Sprache…*, Leipzig (1810); *De Pentateuchi Samaritani origine, indole et auctoriate…*, Halle (1815); *De Samaritanorum theologia ex fontibus ineditis commentatio*, Halle (1822); *Palaeographische Studien ueber phoenizische und punische Schrift* (1835); *Scripturae linguaeque phoeniciae monumenta quotquot supersunt edita et inedita* (1837). Gesenius' main field of interest was the scientific investigation of biblical Hebrew based on comparison with other Semitic languages and his studies remained basic for subsequent research. His work was the first in a field of research that freed the study of Hebrew from theological considerations. His most important contributions to the knowledge of Hebrew language and grammar are (1) *Hebraeisch-deutsches Handwoerterbuch…*, in two volumes (Leipzig, 1810–12); an improved edition *"Hebraeisches und chaldaeisches Handwoerterbuch ueber das Alte Testament"* (Leipzig, 1815; after the tenth edition *aramaeisches* was substituted for *chaldaeisches*). The book has appeared in German in 16 editions. The 16th edition (1915) was reprinted several times. The standard, though greatly outdated BDB (*A Hebrew and English Lexicon of the Old Testament*, ed. F. Brown, S.R. Driver, and Ch. A. Briggs, 1907²; corrected impression 1963) is based on Gesenius' work. (2) *Thesaurus philologicus criticus linguae Hebraeae et Chaldaeae veteris testamenti* (started to appear in 1829 but was completed only posthumously by his pupil E. Roediger, in 1858). In this dictionary, Gesenius drew on talmudic sources and quotes Jewish Bible commentators such as *Rashi, Abraham *Ibn Ezra, and David *Kimḥi. (3) *Hebraeische Grammatik* (Halle, 1813), a Hebrew grammar which appeared in German in 29 editions (editor G. Bergstraesser, 1929²⁹; 29th edition not completed) and was also translated into English (*Gesenius' Hebrew Grammar*, ed. A.E. Cowley, 1910²). (4) *Hebraeisches Lesebuch* ("A Hebrew Reader," Halle, 1814); (5) *Geschichte der hebraeischen Sprache und Schrift* ("A History of the Hebrew language and script," Leipzig, 1815). (6) *Ausfuehrliches grammatisch-kritisches Lehrgebaeude der hebraeischen Sprache mit Vergleichung der verwandten Dialekte* (Leipzig, 1817). In it, he explained his scientific linguistic system based on comparative Semitic philology. Gesenius wrote one exegetical work, a commentary (together with a translation) on Isaiah, in three volumes (Leipzig 1820–21, 1829²). Gesenius was a close friend of W. de *Wette, who greatly influenced his work on the authorship of biblical books and Israelite religion. His rationalism aroused the ire of orthodox supernaturalists. Some negative assessments of Judaism in his work were hardly unique to Gesenius' in his own time.

BIBLIOGRAPHY: E.F. Miller, *The Influence of Gesenius on Hebrew Lexicography* (1927); R. Haym, *Gesenius, eine Erinnerung fuer seine Freunde* (1842). **ADD. BIBLIOGRAPHY:** J. Rogerson, in: DBI, 1:445.

[Irene Garbell]

GESHEM, GASHMU, an "Arab," one of the chief opponents of *Nehemiah, who, together with *Sanballat and Tobiah, opposed the rebuilding of the walls of Jerusalem (c. 450 B.C.E.). When Geshem and his allies heard of Nehemiah's intention to rebuild the wall of Jerusalem, they mocked and scorned him (Neh. 2:10–20). Later, when the wall was completed and all but the gateways fully repaired, they sought by various means to dispose of Nehemiah personally or to compromise his position within the country. These efforts also failed, and Nehemiah's opponents were forced to admit that the task was divinely supported (Neh. 6).

Geshem's designation as an "Arab" is supported by the name's widespread attestation in North Arabia. From the context of Nehemiah 6 it is clear that Geshem was an influential figure. He may be identical with a "king" of the same name mentioned in an Aramaic votive inscription on a silver bowl found in the temple of the Arab goddess Han-'Illat at Tell al-Maskhuta, in the neighborhood of Ismailia in Egypt (now in the Brooklyn Museum), which, on paleographical and archeological grounds, was dated as belonging to the fifth century B.C.E. This inscription reads in translation: "What Qaynu son of Geshem, King of Kedar, brought (as offering) to (the goddess) Han'Illat." On this basis, it has been suggested that Geshem King of Kedar is identical with Nehemiah's enemy. The name appears also in Safaitic inscriptions, and on a Nabatean inscription as "Gashmu, which like Nehemiah 6:6 preserves the old Semitic case ending.

BIBLIOGRAPHY: A. Alt, in: PJB, 27 (1931), 73ff.; J. Rabinowitz, in: JNES, 15 (1956), 2, 5–9, and pls. 6, 7; W.F. Albright, in: *Geschichte und Altes Testament* (A. Alt anniversary volume, 1953), 4, 6; F.W. Winnett, *A Study of the Lihyanite and Thamudic Inscriptions* (1937), 14, 16, 50–51; H. Grimme, in: OLZ, 44 (1941), 343; W.C. Graham, in: AJSLL, 42 (1926), 276ff.; W. Rudolph, *Esra und Nehemia* (1949), 112ff.; EM, s.v. GESHEM; G. Ryekmans, *Les noms propres sud-semitiques*, 1 (1934), 64, 259, 290. **ADD. BIBLIOGRAPHY:** B. Porten, in: TAD, 4 (1999), 23–33; idem, in: COS, 2, 175–76.

[Yuval Kamrat / S. David Sperling (2nd ed.)]

GESHER (Heb. גֶּשֶׁר), kibbutz in the Jordan Valley, Israel, near the confluence of the Jordan and Yarmuk Rivers, affiliated with Ha-Kibbutz ha-Me'uḥad. Its land, belonging to the Palestine Jewish Colonization Association, was previously settled by another group which later established itself permanently at *Ashdot Ya'akov. Gesher was taken over in 1939 by Youth Aliyah graduates from Germany joined by Israeli-born youth and settlers from various countries. In the War of Independence (1948) Gesher held out against a heavy bombardment when the Arabs attempted to cross the Jordan in order to reach Haifa. After the Six-Day War, it became a target of frequent artillery attacks from the other side of the Jordan. Gesher developed intensive farming and operated a gypsum plant. Subsequently, it initiated a joint venture with the Israeli Electric Corporation – a visitor's center with an audio-visual representation of Israel's early generation of electricity from the Yarmuk and Naharayim Rivers. In 2002 its population was 494. The name of the kibbutz, "Bridge," refers to a Roman bridge nearby and to modern railway and road bridges spanning the Jordan and Jarmuk.

WEBSITE: www.gesher.org.il.

[Efraim Orni]

GESHER BENOT YA'AKOV (Heb. גֶּשֶׁר בְּנוֹת יַעֲקֹב; "Bridge of the Daughters of Jacob"), a bridge on the Jordan situated at the southern end of the Huleh Valley where the riverbed enters the valley about 6 mi. (9 km.) E. of Rosh Pinnah, near kibbutz Gadot. In excavations conducted near the bridge by M. Stekelis (1935–36), remains of the Early Stone Age were uncovered including remains of elephants. Built of basalt arches, the original bridge was erected at the end of the 13th century on the site of a natural ford of the Jordan (cf. Isa. 8:23) which served as one of the most important links between Ereẓ Israel and Damascus via Galilee and the Golan. A branch of the ancient route, the Roman *Via Maris*, passed through the ford. The name of the bridge is derived from an Arab tradition according to which the patriarch Jacob crossed the Jordan here and his daughters were buried nearby. The crusaders called the ford Vadum Jacob. Because of its strategic importance, it was the scene of several famous battles. In 1157 Baldwin III, crusader king of Jerusalem, was defeated there by the Muslim ruler of Damascus, Nur al-Din. A fortress ("chastellet"), remains of which still stand, erected by Baldwin IV in 1178 and assigned to the Knights Templar, was captured by Saladin within a year of its construction. In 1799 soldiers of Napoleon were stationed at the bridge to prevent reinforcements from Damascus from reaching Acre which his army was besieging. A battle between British and Turkish forces took place at the bridge in 1918. It was one of the bridges blown up by members of the *Haganah* on the night of June 17, 1946. In May 1948 the Syrians entered Israel near the bridge and captured *Mishmar ha-Yarden, but later withdrew under the cease-fire agreements. After the Six-Day War (June 1967) the bridge served traffic to the Golan Heights.

BIBLIOGRAPHY: Stekelis, in: BRCI, 9 (1960), 61–88.

[Yehoshoua Ben-Arieh]

GESHER HA-ZIV (Heb. גֶּשֶׁר הַזִּיו), kibbutz in the northern Coastal Plain (Acre Valley) of Israel, N. of *Nahariyyah, affiliated with Iḥud ha-Kibbutzim. It was founded in 1949 by members of the former kibbutz Bet ha-Aravah evacuated during the War of Independence (1948). The founding members, some from Central Europe and some Israeli-born, were later joined by pioneers from North America, South Africa, and other countries. The kibbutz engaged in highly intensive farming (avocado and banana plantations, citrus groves, field crops, and poultry) and had guest rooms and a gas station. The regional school of the area's settlements was located in the kibbutz. In 1968 its population was 328, rising to 491 in 2002. Gesher ha-Ziv, meaning "Bridge of Splendor," commemorates a unit of 14 Haganah men who fell in the area on June 17, 1946, when they blew up a bridge over the Keziv River, during the struggle against the British; the name also refers to the nearby ancient city *Achzib.

[Efraim Orni]

GESHURI, MEIR SHIMON (1897–1977), writer on music. Born in Myslowitz, Silesia, Geshuri went to Ereẓ Israel in 1920. He was active in the founding of the Ha-Po'el ha-Mizraḥi, but his main interest was research into Jewish music, particularly ḥasidic song. He was one of the founders of the Israel Institute for Sacred Music (1958). Geshuri was the author of numerous articles and published his main researches in *Ha-Niggun ve-ha-Rikkud ba-Ḥasidut* (3 vols., 1956–59). A bibliography of his writings was edited by B.M. Cohen in 1966.

°GESSIUS FLORUS, the last procurator of Judea before the Jewish War; governed from 64–66 C.E. He was appointed on the recommendation of Nero's consort Poppaea Sabina (Tacitus, Historiae, 5:10). Florus showed himself to be an oppressive and rapacious ruler. On the occasion of a visit to Jerusalem of the Roman governor of Syria, *Cestius Gallus Gaius, the Jews complained bitterly to him of the procurator's conduct. On his departure the situation deteriorated. With the renewal of the quarrel at Caesarea between the Jews and the Syrians over the local synagogue, Florus promised the Jews his support but later adopted an anti-Jewish attitude (TJ, Bik. 2:3, 65d). The arrest of Jewish leaders who had come to Sebaste to enlist his aid, and his plundering of 17 talents from the Temple treasury, aroused the anger of the people against him, and the Jews sarcastically collected money in the streets of Jerusalem for the "indigent procurator." Florus demanded that those responsible should be handed over to him for punishment and finally ordered his soldiers to sack Jerusalem, paying no attention to the intercession of *Berenice, the sister of *Agrippa II. For a while the leading citizens were able to calm the people, but when Florus led his troops on the city the Jews rose in arms and succeeded in halting the Roman advance. Fearing a second attempt, the Jews now broke down the porticoes connecting the Temple Mount with the fortress of Antonia, whereupon Florus returned to Caesarea. Agrippa tried to calm the people, but they refused to submit any more to the orders of the procurator. Both Florus and the Jews gave the governor of Syria their own version of what had taken place. The latter sent an emissary to Jerusalem to learn the truth of the matter and subsequently informed Nero that the blame for the outbreak of war rested on Florus. There is no doubt that Florus's conduct was one of the chief causes of the ensuing war which resulted in the destruction of the Second Temple.

BIBLIOGRAPHY: Jos., Ant., 20:252–68; Jos., Wars, 2:277ff., 558; Schuerer, Gesch, 1 (1901[4]), 585,601ff.; Pauly-Wissowa, 13 (1910), 1325–28, no. 5.

[Lea Roth]

GESTAPO (abb. **Geheime Staats Polizei**; "Secret State Police"), the secret police of Nazi Germany, their main tool of oppression and destruction, which persecuted Germans, opponents of the regime, as well as Jews at the outset of the Nazi regime and later played a central role in carrying out the "*Final Solution"; originally the Prussian domestic intelligence, which became a quasi-Federal Bureau of Investigation, though initially with much less power. The right-wing revolution in Prussia in late 1932 brought about a sweeping purge of "left-wing and Jewish elements" in its political police and paved the way for the changes of the Nazi era. After Hitler's ascent to power, he appointed Hermann Goering as the new Prussian minister of the interior and Goering completed the purge and gave the secret police executive powers, transforming it from a shadowing and information agency into a wide executive arm to persecute enemies of the Nazi regime. The head office of the secret state police – the Geheimes Staatspolizeiamt, or Gestapa – was given powers to shadow, arrest, interrogate, and intern; however, it had to struggle against the Nazi Party organizations, the SA (Storm Troops) and *SS, which also "fought" the regime's opponents, but without the supervision of traditional state bodies.

Simultaneously, with relatively few changes in the Prussian political police, the *Reichsfuehrer* of the SS, Heinrich *Himmler, achieved control over the Bavarian political police and established direct ties between the SS, the political police, and concentration camps. Thus Himmler snatched the secret police administration out of the hands of the state conservatives and in collaboration with the Bavarian minister of justice, Hans *Frank, and with Hitler's direct support, created an independent organization for shadowing, interrogation, arrest, imprisonment, and execution along the lines of the Nazi ideology (see SS and *SD, and *Hitler). The Bavarian political police under Reinhard *Heydrich's direction was able to evade the laws that still applied in Germany in order to influence individuals, disband political parties, and liquidate trade unions. It led campaigns through the newspapers and radio against political opponents, interrogated individual "enemies," and sent them to the central concentration camp *Dachau. The officials of the political police all remained civil servants but were simultaneously drafted into the SS and subordinated to Himmler, both through the civil service and Nazi Party. Many of the officials had never been members of the Nazi Party, as was the case of Heinrich *Mueller, an old Weimar secret police man who became Heydrich's assistant and eventually headed the Gestapo.

From the outset Heydrich's prisoners included many Jews, most of whom were intellectuals or active in left-wing parties. During 1933 the political police began shadowing and investigating Jewish organizations and Jewish community life and thus set up its own network for imprisonment and uniform repression of all the Jews of Bavaria, in the wake of the policy of isolating Jews that was part of the first stage and was followed by exerting pressure, openly and insidiously, on the Jews to emigrate.

Unification of the Political Police

From August 1933, Himmler managed to rise from his starting point in Bavaria to take over the political police of the various *Laender*, including Prussia. From the head office of the Prussian Gestapo in Berlin, which also became the headquarters of the SS, Himmler and Heydrich directed all the political police services in Germany. The Gestapo then became the authority that investigated, along with the SD, every aspect of life in Germany, and especially watched over the regime's "enemies of alien race." The Jews headed the list. Until the end of 1939, the Gestapo's Jewish Department was directed by Karl Haselbacher, a lawyer who was among those who drafted the first anti-Jewish laws. Until the outbreak of World War II, most of the murders in the camps were carried out on Gestapo orders under various cover-ups, such as "killed while attempting escape," but eventually these pretenses were dispensed with, especially where Jews were concerned.

From 1938

As an institution in charge of shadowing, interrogating, arresting, and imprisoning "enemies of the Reich," the Gestapo became a massive authority employing thousands of government officials and SS men who together persecuted the regime's "enemies" or other opponents. Various groups in the population were turned over and left to the Gestapo's sole discretion; they were subjected to "neutralization" in camps without prior trial or forced to emigrate or face physical liquidation. From 1938 onward, the Gestapo began increasingly to deal with Jews who had previously been subject to other Nazi authorities. It had a hand in the **Kristallnacht* and enforced Jewish emigration. In competitive cooperation with the SD, the Gestapo set up the Zentralstelle fuer juedische Auswanderung in annexed Austria, directed by Adolf *Eichmann and headed by Mueller. Other centers for forced emigration were set up in 1939 in the Protectorate of Bohemia-Moravia and in Germany proper to accelerate the emigration of Jews by eviction and persecution, impoverishment, and degradation. When the Gestapo and part of the SD were joined under the *RSHA of the SS in November 1939, Office IV (Gestapo) of the new main office acquired sole authority over all Jews who were not yet imprisoned in camps.

During World War II the Gestapo, along with the SD and Security Police, constituted part of the *Einsatzgruppen* (mobile killing units) in Poland and other occupied countries. These units dealt with the murder and internment of numerous Jews and especially with the expulsion of the inhabitants of the small towns in Poland to mass concentration centers. Afterward Gestapo officials were appointed supervisors over the mass concentration of Jews. In Berlin headquarters the Gestapo in the first year of the war laid plans for various temporary "solutions for the Jewish problem," such as the establishment of a "reservation" in Poland or the mass transfer of Jews to Madagascar. At the end of 1940, when the Jews in Eastern Europe were interned in ghettos, the Gestapo, along with the German occupational civil administration, was charged with guarding and supervising the ghettos, imposing forced labor, and causing starvation and disease in an effort to decimate the ghetto inhabitants. In the Western occupied countries the Gestapo saw to registering the Jews and isolating them from the rest of the population for purposes of their eventual removal from economic life and confiscation of property. Under Eichmann, Section IVB4 of the Gestapo was "*federfuehrend*" (leading) in the "Final Solution."

The *Einsatzgruppen*

After the invasion of Russia in 1941, the *Einsatzgruppen*, headed by Gestapo men and directly responsible to Heydrich and Mueller, renewed the massacres on an enormous scale. The *Einsatzgruppen* carried out executions of Jews in the Baltic states and in Belorussia and wiped out part of the Ukrainian Jews. Later in 1941, the decision was made to kill all the Jews of Europe in gas chambers and the Gestapo was to supervise the dispatch of the Jews to the camps specially adapted or constructed for the program of mass murder (see *Holocaust, General Survey). The Gestapo section headed by Eichmann was in charge of the dispatch of Jews to the camps, and it also directly supervised at least one camp, *Theresienstadt, in Czechoslovakia. The section also supplied some of the gas used in the chambers, negotiated with countries under German domination to accelerate the murder, and dealt with Jewish leaders, especially in Hungary (see *Kasztner) in an effort to smooth the process of the impending destruction of various Jewish communities (see *Judenrat). The local Gestapo offices in Germany supervised the dispatch of Jews to death trains and the confiscation of their property. The Gestapo was largely responsible for the actual implementation of the dispatch orders and could choose its victims. It especially held the fate of people of mixed parentage (*Mischlinge*) in its hands. It excelled in its unabated and premeditated cruelty, in its ability to delude its intended victims as to the fate that awaited them, and in the use of barbaric threats and torture to lead the victims to their death, all as part of the "Final Solution."

At the same time the Gestapo acted as the principal executive arm of the Nazi regime in all the campaigns of terror, liquidation, looting, starvation, confiscation of property, and theft of cultural treasures (see Desecration and Destruction of *Synagogues; *Poland) throughout Europe. The Gestapo also repressed the anti-Nazi partisan movement and stamped out resistance in the Western European countries. Thus the term Gestapo became an accepted synonym for horror. After the war, very few of the important members of the Gestapo were caught and brought to trial. The courts in the Federal German Republic from 1969 discussed the question of several principal contingents of the Gestapo.

BIBLIOGRAPHY: G. Reitlinger, SS, *Alibi of a Nation* (1956); H. Hoehne, *The Order of the Death's Head: The Story of Hitler's* SS (1969); K.D. Bracher, W. Saver, and W. Schulz, *Die Nationalsozialistische Machtergreifung* (1968); S. Aronson, *Reinhard Heydrich und die Fruehgeschichte von Gestapo und* SD (1970); H. Krausnick et al., *Anatomy of the* SS *State* (1968); F. Zipfel, *Gestapo und* SD *in Berlin* (1961); R. Hilberg, *Destruction of the European Jews* (1961, 1985[2], 2003[3]). **ADD. BIBLIOGRAPHY:** R. Gellately, *Gestapo and German Society: Enforcing Racial Policy* (1991); E. Johnson, *Nazis Terror: The Gestapo and Ordinary Germans* (1999); G. Broder, *Hitler's Enforcers: The Gestapo and* SS *Security Service in the Nazi Revolution* (1996); S. Aronson, *The Beginnings of the Gestapo System: The Bavarian Model* (1970).

[Shlomo Aronson]

GESTETNER, DAVID (1854–1939), British industrialist. Born in Csorna, Hungary, he was the inventor of the cyclostyle duplicating process and was credited with being the founder of modern stencil duplicating. At 17, chafing at the monotony of clerking on the Vienna Stock Exchange, he went to New York, where, after experimenting with papers for duplicating, he moved on to London to sell his invention and set up business. The firm he founded now has worldwide branches and factories, employing thousands of people. Entering communal life, he was a founder of the Green Lanes Synagogue, London (1897). SIGMUND (1897–1956), David's son, was chairman and managing director of the Gestetner business when he was 23, and made a name as a progressive industrialist. Influenced by Chaim Weizmann, he was a devoted Zionist, and as chairman of the *Keren Hayesod in England at the time of the Nazi regime in Germany, he helped Jewish craftsmen to escape, and through the *Central British Fund for German Jewry and the Children's Movement, he helped to resettle refugees. He served in the army in World War I, and in World War II his factory did war work and he organized the Balfour Club for the Jewish Forces in London. He was treasurer of the Jewish National Fund in Britain in 1949 and became its president in 1950. He was treasurer of the Joint Palestine Appeal and honorary treasurer of the Weizmann Institute Foundation. He was also a successful farmer, and loaned his farm to the Zionist movement for training agricultural pioneers bound for Ereẓ Israel.

BIBLIOGRAPHY: *The Times*, London (March 16, 1939; April 21, 1956). **ADD. BIBLIOGRAPHY:** ODNB online; DBB, 2, 519–25.

[John M. Shaftesley]

GESUNDHEIT, JACOB BEN ISAAC (1815–1878), Polish rabbi and author. Gesundheit was born in Praga, a suburb of Warsaw. He studied there under Leib Zinz of Plotsk. On the death of Dov Berush b. Isaac Meisels, rabbi of Warsaw, Gesundheit was chosen to succeed him (1870). Possessed of considerable means, he had not previously held a rabbinic post despite the fact that he was a great talmudist, headed a yeshivah, and had already written a number of books. Gesundheit fought strongly against *Ḥasidism, which was on the increase in Warsaw. The Ḥasidim fought back and together with the assimilationists under Ludwig Nathanson compelled him to resign from the rabbinate after four years. He died four years later. All his published books are entitled *Tiferet Ya'akov*. He wrote novellae on the Shulḥan Arukh (1842–1926), and on tractates *Gittin* (1858) and *Ḥullin* (2 pts., 1867–1910). His responsa and other talmudic novellae have remained in manuscript.

BIBLIOGRAPHY: Fuenn, Keneset, 542f.; "Toledot Rabbenu Ya'akov Gesundheit," in: *Reshimat ha-Sefarim mi-Sifriyyat Gesundheit* (1939), 5–8.

[Itzhak Alfassi]

GETZ, STAN (1927–1991), U.S. tenor saxophonist. Getz was one of those rare figures in jazz who manages to achieve huge commercial successes without compromising considerable artistic abilities. Like his first major influence, Lester Young, he had a light yet huge sound and a natural sense of swing. He was one of jazz's great ballad players and a superb melodist. Of the latter skill he once said, "The saxophone is actually a translation of the human voice, in my conception. All you can do is play melody. No matter how complicated it gets, it's still a melody." Born in Philadelphia but raised in the Bronx, Getz manifested his musical skills early, playing bass in junior high school and bassoon in high school, where he was selected for the all-city orchestra. He recalled, "I was a withdrawn, hypersensitive kid. I would practice the saxophone in the bathroom, and the tenements were so close together that someone from across the alleyways would yell, 'Shut that kid up,' and my mother would say, 'Play louder Stanley, play louder.'" He turned down a possible scholarship to Juilliard at age 15 to go on the road with the Jack Teagarden band. Shortly after, he moved to Los Angeles, where he quickly found work in the Stan Kenton Orchestra, but he quit when Kenton made disparaging remarks about Lester Young. He would not stay unemployed for long, working with Benny *Goodman and Tommy Dorsey before he landed the job that first brought him stardom, as one of the "Four Brothers" sax section in the Woody Herman band known as the Second Herd. He quickly became one of the stars of this be-bop influenced band, with his solo on "Early Autumn" earning him major accolades. Regrettably, he also acquired a heroin habit that would plague him throughout the 1950s, leading him to a brief retirement and exile in Denmark in 1958–61. Getz came roaring back the following year with a series of Brazilian-influenced recordings that would bring his greatest commercial success, including a session with Joao and Astrud Gilberto that included "The Girl From Ipanema," one of the biggest-selling jazz singles of all time. He continued playing and recording steadily until his death from liver cancer at age 64. Elected to the Down Beat Hall of Fame in 1986 by the magazine's readers, Getz was also held in high esteem by his peers; John Coltrane, the most influential tenor player of the post-World War II era, said of him, "We would all like to play like Stan Getz, if we could."

BIBLIOGRAPHY: B. Case and S. Britt, "Stan Getz," in: *The Illustrated Encyclopedia of Jazz* (1978); D.L. Maggin, *Stan Getz: A Life in Jazz* (1996); B. Priestly (ed.), *The Sax and Brass Book* (1998); "Stan Getz," Down Beat Magazine archives at www.downbeat.com.; "Stan Getz," MusicWeb Encyclopaedia of Popular Music, at www.musicweb.uk.net.

[George Robinson (2nd ed.)]

GE'ULEI TEIMAN (Heb. גְּאוּלֵי תֵּימָן; "The Redeemed from Yemen"), moshav and housing quarter in the Ḥefer Plain, Israel, founded in 1947 by settlers from Yemen as an extension of the neighboring village of *Elyashiv. The farming community was affiliated with Ha-Po'el ha-Mizrachi Moshavim Association (from 1967). Its population was 181 in 1968 and 311 in 2002.

[Efraim Orni]

GE'ULIM (Heb. גְּאוּלִים; "Redeemed Ones"), moshav in central Israel, S.E. of *Netanyah, affiliated with Tenu'at ha-Moshavim, founded in 1938 by settlers from Yemen. Its population in 1968 was 480, expanding to 545 in the mid-1990s, and 670 in 2002. Ge'ulim engaged in intensive farming, including citrus groves, fruit plantations, poultry, and flowers.

[Efraim Orni / Shaked Gilboa (2nd ed.)]

GE'ULLAH (Heb. גְּאֻלָּה; "Redemption"), title of several prayers. That section in the morning and evening prayer which is recited between the *Shema and the *Amidah is known as *Ge'ullah*. This ancient prayer is mentioned in the Mishnah (Ber. 1:4; 2:2; Tam. 5:1) and referred to as *Ge'ullah* in the Talmud (Pes. 117b). The original text was probably much shorter; according to Zunz it contained only 45 Hebrew words. The present wording varies considerably in different rites. The prayer starts with the words "*emet ve-emunah*" ("true and trustworthy") in the evening prayer and with "*emet ve-yaẓiv*" ("true and firm") in the morning prayer (Ber. 12a). It opens with a profession of faith, enumerates the miracles of the redemption of Israel from Egypt, and closes with a plea to the Redeemer of Israel to deliver them again. In some Sephardi rituals, however, there is a longer variant ending. The Talmud (Ber. 4b, 9b) insists that there be no interruption between *Ge'ullah* and the *Amidah* and so even the response "Amen" is omitted after the *Ge'ullah* benediction in the morning prayer. In the evening prayer *Hashkivenu is inserted between them, the interruption being permitted because the recitation of the evening prayer was not considered obligatory in the Talmud.

The name *Ge'ullah* applies also to the *piyyutim* which are inserted before the closing formula of this prayer on special Sabbaths and on the three pilgrimage festivals.

The Mishnah uses the term *Ge'ullah* for the benediction recited at the end of *Hallel* during the Passover *seder* (Pes. 10:6).

The term *Ge'ullah* is also used to designate the seventh benediction of the *Amidah* which ends with the words "the Redeemer of Israel."

BIBLIOGRAPHY: ET, 5 (1953), 43–46; Elbogen, Gottesdienst, 22ff., 101, 211f., 514; Eisenstein, Dinim, 67f.; Idelsohn, Liturgy, 41, 92, 99.

GEVA (Heb. גֶּבַע; "Hill"), kibbutz in the Valley of Jezreel, Israel, affiliated with Iḥud ha-Kevuẓot ve-ha-Kibbutzim, and founded in 1921 by Third Aliyah pioneers from Russia who were later joined by new settlers from different countries. In 1968 the kibbutz had 510 inhabitants, engaged in highly intensive mixed farming. In 2002 the population was 542. Baccara Automation Control, a factory manufacturing solenoid valves, was founded in 1964. Shkediya Geva Industries produced almond products and a therapeutic horse stable was located in the kibbutz. Geva is also the home of the Gevaton Singers, founded in 1948 and among the country's most popular performers of Israeli pioneer music.

[Efraim Orni / Shaked Gilboa (2nd ed.)]

GEVARAM (Heb. גְּבַרְעָם; "the People Overcomes"), kibbutz in the southern coastal plain of Israel, S. of Ashkelon, affiliated with Ha-Kibbutz ha-Me'uḥad, founded in 1942. The settlers, mainly pioneers from Slovakia, Austria, Holland, and Germany, previously maintained a transitory camp at *Kefar Sava as hired agricultural workers. They initially suffered from lack of water, but by deep drilling a rich groundwater table was discovered sufficient for local needs and to supply other settlements. The siege of the Egyptian army during the War of Independence was lifted in Operation Ten Plagues (October 1948). Gevaram's economy was based on intensive and largely irrigated farming, dairy cattle, and a metal factory. Its population was 240 in 1968 and 311 in 2002.

[Efraim Orni]

GEVAT (Heb. גְּבַת), kibbutz in northern Israel, in the *Jezreel Valley, at the foot of the *Nazareth Hills, affiliated with Ha-Kibbutz ha-Me'uḥad. It was founded in 1926 by pioneers from Pinsk, Poland. The kibbutz participated in the draining of the Jezreel Valley swamps. With the split in Ha-Kibbutz ha-Me'uḥad in 1951–52, some of its members established a separate kibbutz, Yifat, further east. In 1968 Gevat had 625 inhabitants and its economy was based on field crops and dairy cattle. The kibbutz also produced plastic and rubber products. In 2002 its population was 658. Gevat is a historical name, mentioned by Eusebius (Onom. 70:9ff.) in its Aramaic form Gabata.

[Efraim Orni]

GÉVAUDAN, region in France, corresponding to the present department of Lozère. Jews were first recorded in Gévaudan in 1229, in the town of Mende, and they were also found in Marvejols and Meyrueis. The supposition that the names of localities like Salmon, Gimel, etc. indicate an earlier presence of Jews can be dismissed as fantasy. However, it is probable that the place name Montjézieu derives from an earlier name *mons judaeus*. Gulielmus Durandus, bishop of Mende (1285–96), enforced in his diocese the canonical laws prohibiting Christians from entering the service of Jews and forbidding Jews to appear in public during Easter or to work on Sundays and Christian holidays; they were also compelled to wear the *badge. When they were expelled in 1306, Gévaudan's Jews had an estimated capital of 15,000 livres. A few Jews were living in Marvejols in 1322.

BIBLIOGRAPHY: N. Pinzuti, in: *Archives Juives*, 2, no. 3 (1965/66, 2ff.)

[Bernhard Blumenkranz]

GEVIM (Heb. גְּבִים), kibbutz in the coastal plain of Israel, 8 mi. (13 km.) E. of Gaza, affiliated with Iḥud ha-Kevuẓot ve-ha-Kibbutzim, founded in August 1947. Gevim was one of the first links in the settlement chain extending to the south and Negev that had to defend itself against the Egyptian forces in the Israeli *War of Independence (a few months after its establishment). The founding members were Israeli-born and *Youth Aliyah graduates from Central Europe. Farming included field crops, avocado plantations, poultry, and dairy cattle. However, its economic mainstay became factories producing plastics and flutes. Its population was 372 in 2002. Gevim means "Water Holes," an allusion to the first Negev water pipeline, which passes through the kibbutz.

[Efraim Orni]

GEVIRTZ, STANLEY (1929–1988), U.S. Bible scholar. Gevirtz received his B.A. at Brooklyn College and earned his Ph.D. at the University of Chicago in 1959. He remained at Chicago at its Oriental Institute until 1972. He then left Chicago for the Los Angeles campus of Hebrew Union College, where he taught until his death from cancer. As a young man Gevirtz had studied drama and world literature. As a result he earned a reputation as an outstanding classroom teacher and captivating public lecturer, whose public delivery bordered on the poetic. His monograph, *Patterns in the Early Poetry of Israel* (1963), illustrates Gevirtz's literary sensibility and his far-ranging knowledge of ancient Semitic poetic style and syntax. Especially incisive are Gevirtz's studies of ancient biblical poetry.

BIBLIOGRAPHY: *MAARAV*, 7–8 (1991–92); list of Gevirtz's publications, *MAARAV*, 8, 377–79.

[S. David Sperling (2nd ed.)]

GEVULOT (Heb. גְּבוּלוֹת), kibbutz in southern Israel, 20 mi. (32 km.) W. of Beersheba, affiliated with Kibbutz Arẓi ha-Shomer ha-Ẓa'ir, founded in 1943 as the first of the three "observation outposts" established to explore settlement conditions in the Negev (the other two were *Bet Eshel and *Revivim). The sandy loess soil of the region proved cultivable despite the severe lack of water. In 1946, on the basis of Gevulot's successful experiments, 11 additional settlements were erected in the south and the Negev. In the *War of Independence (1948) the isolated kibbutz held out against the long Egyptian siege until Operation Ten Plagues (October 1948). With water made available through the Yarkon-Negev pipeline in the 1950s, the kibbutz developed intensive farm branches such as field crops, dairy cattle, poultry, and flowers. Its factory made polymers products. The kibbutz also made a living from tourism, including a guesthouse and its Watch Tower tourist site. In 2002 its population was 251. Gevulot's name, "Borders," was chosen as the kibbutz was, at the time of its founding, the Jewish settlement nearest to the Egyptian border.

[Efraim Orni]

GEZER (Heb. גֶּזֶר).

(1) Major city in ancient times located in the northern Shephelah at Tell Jazar (also called Tell Abu-Shūsha). Gezer was first settled in the Chalcolithic period (fourth millennium B.C.E.); in the Early Bronze Age I it was occupied by a non-Semitic people who followed the custom of burning their dead. Semitic settlers established there in the Early Bronze Age II–IV (3rd millennium B.C.E.) enclosed the city with a wall. The Canaanite occupation reached its peak of prosperity in the Middle Bronze and Late Bronze I Ages (20th–14th centuries B.C.E.), when a stone wall 10 ft. (3 m.) wide with square towers was built around the city. This period at Gezer also yielded objects testifying to links with Egypt as well as a potsherd in ancient Canaanite script. The city is first mentioned in Egyptian documents in the list of cities captured by Thutmose III (c. 1469 B.C.E.). The importance of Gezer in the 14th century is evident from the Tell *el-Amarna letters. Milkilu, king of Gezer, and his successor Yapahu controlled an extensive area which also included Aijalon and Zorah; their chief rival was the king of Jerusalem. The capture of Gezer is mentioned in the "Israel stele" of Pharaoh Merneptah (c. 1220 B.C.E.) together with Ashkelon and Yeno'am. During the Israelite conquest, Horam, king of Gezer, was defeated in battle by the Israelites (Josh. 10:33). His city was assigned to the Levites in the territory of Ephraim but its population remained predominantly Canaanite (Josh. 16:3; 21:21). Pharaoh Siamun (?) conquered Gezer and ceded it to Israel "for a portion unto his daughter, Solomon's wife." Commanding the approaches to Jerusalem, the city became one of the major strongholds of Solomon who built a gate there identical in plan with gates he erected at Hazor and Megiddo (I Kings 9:15–17). Part of the Solomonic city gate, built of dressed stones, and an adjacent casemate wall have been discovered there. A stepped tunnel 216 ft. (66 m.) long cut to provide access to the water table may date to this period. Also found there is a small contemporary stone tablet of seven lines ("the *Gezer Calendar"). Gezer was conquered by Shishak according to that Pharaoh's inscriptions (c. 924 B.C.E.) and archaeological finds indicate that the city declined at that time. Tiglath-Pileser III's capture of the city (probably in 733 B.C.E.) is depicted on a relief found at Calah. In the Assyrian period Gezer's population was augmented by foreign settlers; contracts of two of these, written in cuneiform from the years 651 and 649 B.C.E., have survived. The city recovered in the Persian period and under the Hellenistic kings it again became an important royal fortress. During the Hasmonean wars Gezer was a major Greek base and remained in Greek hands until its capture in 142 B.C.E. by Simeon, who expelled the aliens. He refortified the city and made it the military center of his state, under the command of his son John Hyrcanus, second only to Jerusalem (I Macc. 4:15; 9:52; 13:43; 16:19). A Hasmonean palace discovered there was apparently built by Greek prisoners of war; a curse was found scratched on one of its stones: "May fire descend from heaven and devour the house of Simeon." Gezer's importance declined after the Hasmonean period and the center of the district was transferred to Emmaus. Eusebius mentions it as a village four miles north (this should read "south") of Emmaus (Onom. 66:19ff.). It does not appear in other ancient sources but a Roman bathhouse and several Christian lamps found there testify to its continued occupation. On the Madaba Map, the legend "Gedor also Gidirtha" apparently refers to Gezer. It was known as Montgisart in the crusader period; there King Baldwin IV defeated the forces of Saladin in 1177 but by 1191 it was in the hands of the Muslims and served as their headquarters in the war against Richard the Lionhearted.

After crusader times the site was completely forgotten. It was re-identified by C. Clermont-Ganneau in 1873 and investigated in excavations conducted at Tell Jazar by R.A.S. Macalister from 1902 to 1912, and A. Rowe in 1934–35.

[Michael Avi-Yonah]

Later Excavations at Gezer

A ten-year project of archaeological excavations was initiated and carried out between 1964 and 1974 under different directors, G.E. Wright, W.G. Dever, and J.D. Seger. An additional season of work at the site was made by Dever in 1984. One of the goals of the expedition was to re-investigate the gates and walls previously uncovered by Macalister as well as to obtain a good stratigraphical sequence. Twenty-six strata were uncovered dating from approximately 3500 B.C.E. to 100 C.E. Five final reports have been published on the results of the excavations as well as numerous articles.

The earliest remains from Gezer, including architectural remains and caves, date from the Chalcolithic and Early Bronze Age and represent the remains of small villages. During the Early Bronze II the city expanded but was still not surrounded by a city wall. Following a period of abandonment, Gezer was resettled at the beginning of the Middle Bronze Age, growing into a large urban site during the Middle Bronze Age II (c. 1750 B.C.E.) with the construction of structures on terraced slopes. During the latter part of the Middle Bronze II (c. 1650 B.C.E.) the site was fortified with an encircling wall and rectangular towers, one of which was built of cyclopean stones. A three-entryway monumental gate with a mud-brick superstructure and a glacis of tamped chalk and debris were also excavated. The "high place" with ten massive standing stones (*masseboth*) excavated by Macalister also dates from the Middle Bronze Age. The Middle Bronze Age city was destroyed in a violent fire and this has been attributed to Pharoah Thutmosis III who mentioned Gezer in the Karnak Inscription. A cache of gold jewelry and much pottery was found within the destroyed houses. Following another period of abandonment, Gezer's fortunes revived during the Late Bronze IIA (c. 1400 B.C.E.). A large building – perhaps a palace or Egyptian-style residency – was uncovered. Ten of the Amarna tablets written by kings of Gezer date from this time. One of the excavators (Dever) has suggested that the site was fortified at that time, but this has been contested by others who have suggested an Iron Age date instead. A tomb with 68 individuals was uncovered, containing numerous luxury items and imports. Late Bronze Age Gezer declined, and it was probably conquered in 1207 B.C.E. during the campaign of Pharoah Merneptah. From about 1200 the first typical Philistine pottery appears at Gezer. One building from this period was destroyed in a violent fire (c. 1150 B.C.E.).

The Iron Age stratum from the tenth century B.C.E. includes the fortifications previously excavated by Macalister. In the present excavation they were redated to Solomonic times, following a suggestion by Yadin that these fortifications resembled gates and walls found at Hazor and Megiddo. The fortifications of the site were rebuilt in the eighth century B.C.E. and dwellings from this period were also unearthed. The destruction of this stratum probably took place in c. 733 B.C.E. at the time of the campaign of Tiglath Pileser III, and it may very well have been depicted on a relief in the Assyrian king's palace at Nimrud, which depicts a town by the name of *gaz(ru)*. The city of the late eighth to sixth centuries B.C.E. was more modest than the previous city, and it too was destroyed with the Babylonian invasion of Judah in 598–586 B.C.E. Remains of settlements from the Persian, Hellenistic, and Roman periods were also found. Gezer was the residence of Simon Maccabaeus for a time, as well as the headquarters of John Hyrcanus. A number of boundary stones have been found in the fields around the site, one referring to the "the boundary of Gezer" and another to the landlord of an agricultural estate by the name of "Alkios."

[Shimon Gibson (2nd ed.)]

(2) Gezer is a kibbutz in central Israel, E. of *Ramleh, and is affiliated with Iḥud ha-Kevuẓot ve-Kibbutzim. Its land was originally acquired by the Ancient Order of Maccabaeans in England because of its proximity to *Modi'in. The settlement was founded in 1945 by settlers from Central Europe together with Israel-born youth. In the Israel *War of Independence (1948), Gezer, located in the thin chain of settlements connecting Jerusalem with the Coastal Plain, was involved in a hard battle with the Arab Legion and served as a vantage point in Operation Dani (July 1948), which resulted in the inclusion of the towns of Ramleh and Lydda in the State of Israel. Gezer ran various farms branches and had a factory for adhesives. It also operated a special educational park, Ginat Shorashim, dedicated to peace and the environment and rooted in Jewish sources and Jewish soil. A pumping station of the Yarkon-Negev water pipeline is located nearby. In the mid-1990s, the population was approximately 280, increasing to 340 by 2002.

[Efraim Orni / Shaked Gilboa (2nd ed.)]

BIBLIOGRAPHY: Clermont-Ganneau, Arch, 2 (1899), 224ff.; R.A.S. Macalister, *Excavation of Gezer*, 3 vols. (1912); Abel, in: RB, 35 (1926), 513ff.; Rowe, in: PEFQS, 67 (1935), 19ff.; EM, 2 (1965), 465–71; A. Malamat (ed.), in: *Bi-Ymei Bayit Rishon* (1961), 35ff.; Yadin, *ibid.*, 66ff.; idem, in: IEJ, 8 (1958), 80ff.; W.G. Dever, in: *Jerusalem Through the Ages* (1968), 26–32; idem, in: *Qadmoniot*, 3 (1970), 57–62; idem, in: *The Biblical Archaeologist*, 30 (1967), 47–62; H. Lance, in: *ibid.*, 34–47; J. Ross, in: *ibid.*, 62–71. **ADD. BIBLIOGRAPHY:** W.G. Dever, et al., *Gezer I: Preliminary Report of the 1964–66 Seasons* (1970); idem, *Gezer II: Preliminary Report of the 1967–70 Seasons in Fields I and II* (1974); W.G. Dever, "Solomonic and Assyrian 'Palaces' at Gezer," in: IEJ, 35 (1985), 217–30; S. Gitin, *Gezer III: A Ceramic Typology of the Late Iron Age II, Persian and Hellenistic Periods at Tell Gezer* (1990); W.G. Dever et al., *Gezer IV: The 1969–71 Seasons in Field VI, the "Acropolis"* (1986); J.D. Seger, *Gezer V: The Field I Caves (*1988); W.G. Dever, "Further Evidence on the Date of the Outer Wall at Gezer," in: BASOR, 289 (1993), 33–54. **WEBSITE:** www.gezer.org.il.

GEZER CALENDAR, a Hebrew inscription of seven lines, engraved on a limestone tablet written in ancient Hebrew script; discovered in Gezer by R.A.S. *Macalister in 1908. The Gezer Calendar is dated by its script to the tenth century B.C.E. and cites an annual cycle of agricultural activities that seem to begin with the month of Tishri. The word *yrḥ* ("month") or *yrḥw* ("two months") precedes the name of each month. According to an accepted view, the inscription first lists two months of fruit picking, particularly olives (Tishri–Ḥeshvan). Then follow two months of grain sowing (Kislev–Tevet), two months concerned with the late sowing (Shevat–Adar), one month of flax harvest (by uprooting with a mattock; Nisan), one month of barley harvest (Iyyar), a month of wheat harvest (Sivan), two months of vine pruning or of vintage (Tammuz–Av), and, at the end, the month of *qayiẓ*, i.e., the picking or drying of figs (Elul). In the left lower edge of the inscription "*Aby* […]" is written vertically. It is possible that the name indicates the owner of the inscription or its author. The nature and purpose of the calendar are not clear, and many different explanations have been proposed. According to some scholars, the calendar was written as a schoolboy exercise in writing. This view derives from the fact that the script is rather crude. Another view holds that the Gezer Calendar was designated for the collection of taxes from farmers. It is also possible that the content of the inscription is a popular folk song, listing the months of the year according to the agricultural seasons. The original is in the Istanbul archeological museum.

BIBLIOGRAPHY: R.A.S. Macalister, *Excavation of Gezer*, 2 (1912), 24–28; Albright, in: BASOR, 92 (1943), 16–26; L. Finkelstein, *ibid.*, 94 (1944), 28–29; Wright, in: BA, 18 (1955), 50–56; Segal, in: JSS, 7 (1962), 212–21; Talmon, in: JAOS, 83 (1963), 177–87; Wirgin, in: *Eretz Israel*, 6 (1960), 9–12 (Eng. section); Rathjen, in: PWQ, 93 (1961), 70–72; Honeyman, in: JRAS (1953), 53–58; Pritchard, Texts, 320; Pritchard, Pictures, 272; EM, 2 (1965), 471–4 (incl. bibl.). **ADD. BIBLIOGRAPHY:** S. Ahituv, *Handbook of Ancient Hebrew Inscriptions* (1992), 149–52.

[Bustanay Oded]

GEZERTA, term used by the *geonim* for the oath of imprecation that they instituted in place of the oath by God's name or by a divine attribute (*kinnuy*). Geonic responsa describe the *gezerta* as a series of imprecations intended to intimidate the deponent (see *Teshuvot ha-Geonim* [Assaf], 1927, #106). The term is first mentioned in a responsum by *Natronai, *gaon* of Sura (853–58), who ascribes it to an earlier *gaon*, *Ẓadok Mar bar Ishi of Sura (816–18; *Teshuvot ha-Geonim Ḥemdah Genuzah* #22). *Gezerta* was employed as a substitute for biblical or mishnaic oaths only, not for post-mishnaic oaths such as the "consuetudinary oath" (*shevu'at hesset*). Its institution was the culmination of a gradual process, which began with the use of an imprecation even when there was no obligation to impose a biblical or mishnaic oath (see *ḥerem setam*). The transition from an oath by God's name to an oath of imprecation led to an extension of the use of oaths to matters in which a biblical or mishnaic oath could not be administered. The change enabled the *geonim* to resume the previous practice of administering an oath (of imprecation) to a widow demanding her *ketubbah* payment in cases that did not warrant a mishnaic oath (Git. 3:4); or an oath with respect to landed property, which is not possible in mishnaic law (Shevu. 6:5; and see TB Ket. 87a, and the geonic responsum in *Sha'arei Ẓedek* 73a #9). The *gezerta* was used, in particular, in the case of destitute debtors, who were required to take an oath that they had no means to repay their debt (Rav Hai Gaon, in *Teshuvot ha-Geonim* [Harkavy], #182; see also his *Mishpetei Shevu'ot*, p. 102).

The *gezerta* was not instituted through a special geonic enactment (*takkanah*) but was based mainly on the geonic practice of evading oaths by God's name or *kinnuy* and replacing it by an oath of biblical imprecation – a process which may date back to the talmudic period. This explains the prevalence in geonic sources of phraseology such as "it is our custom," "they were accustomed to…," in relation to the *gezerta*; terminology attesting to enactment is used only in relation to the ceremony accompanying the imposition of *gezerta*: "They enacted that rams' horns should be brought and blown in the presence of the deponent, and he is threatened as well with excommunication and other decrees" (*Ḥemdah Genuzah, ibid.*).

The *geonim* suspended the administration of biblical and mishnaic oaths because of the increased taking of false oaths and disrespect for oaths, as well as the talmudic principle that punishment for a false oath applies to the entire world (TB, Shevu. 39b) – an explanation offered by many *geonim*. As Rav Natronai writes: "But now, because of the deceivers… the courts refrained from imposing oaths [sworn] on a Torah scroll,… and the courts saw that people were swearing false oaths and bringing calamity upon the world, they refrained from imposing the biblical oath and abolished it entirely" (see *Ḥemdah Genuzah* #22, and further responsa in, e.g., *Teshuvot ha-Geonim* [Assaf], 1927, p. 97, etc.). Rav Saadiah Gaon writes in his commentary to the Torah (*Ḥayyei Sarah*, ed. Zucker, p. 412): "…In our nation they did not discontinue swearing this oath, that is, by the Lord God of heaven and earth, until there were many who swore falsely, and earlier authorities abolished the oath by God's name, because they knew that punishment might be visited upon the entire world. They then began to administer the oath of imprecation, punishment for which is imposed only upon the person who swears, [and we follow] their tradition to this day." Similarly, Rav Hai Gaon (*Mishpetei Shevu'ot*, p. 11) writes: "Our rabbis are now accustomed not to administer the oath by God's name, for the entire world may suffer and the punishment for [violation] is severe…." The imprecation was a useful substitute for the oath, because of the use of a curse and an imprecation was taken more seriously, in addition to the power of excommunication and the accompanying ceremony to deter people from lying: "Wherever a person is required to swear a biblical oath, he is now made to hold a Torah scroll… and inflated water skins are brought, as well as a bier on which the dead are borne… and lighted candles… and wood ashes… and sacks are placed in the center… and a ram's horn is blown together with the imprecation" (responsum by Rav Sherira and Rav Hai, *Teshuvot ha-Geonim* [Assaf], 1927, #3; see also responsum by Rav Paltoi, Gaon of Pumbedita, in *Teshuvot ha-Geonim* [Lyck], #10). Perhaps, moreover, it was in view of the prevalent use by the Muslims of oaths in God's name – they in fact refer in their writings to the Jewish oath – that the *geonim* were motivated to avoid a formula similar to that used in the Muslim oath.

The renunciation of oaths and their replacement by imprecation did not affect the actual obligation to take an oath, which was still considered as having biblical force, as declared by Rav Sherira Gaon in a responsum (*Sha'arei Ẓedek*, p. 71a, #3). The basic elements of the administration of oaths were not abandoned, and the imprecation "inherited" the various practices involved, such as holding an object (generally a Torah scroll) while swearing. These practices were still the hallmark of biblical (and mishnaic) oaths as against later rabbinic oaths (such as the "consuetudinary oath"), in which the Torah scroll was held not by the deponent but by the person administering the oath (the scroll might also be placed on a chair; see, e.g., *Teshuvot ha-Geonim* [Harkavy], #550). The *gezerta* also retained certain other elements of the oath, such as naming the suspicious party, answering "amen," etc.

The identification of the oath with the imprecation known as *gezerta* may be attributed to Saadiah Gaon. He cites a series of passages from the Bible to stress that the *gezerta* was not innovated by the *geonim* but could already be found in biblical tradition. This was indeed Saadiah's tendency in other contexts as well – to demonstrate that everything was rooted in the Bible, in order to reject Karaite criticism of the Rabbanite approach (see, e.g., *Sha'arei Ẓedek* 41b, #38). Saadiah makes systematic use of *gezerta* in connection with oaths of biblical force (such as the oath imposed on a defendant who admits part of a claim, or the oath required to rebut the evidence of a single witness), and mishnaic oaths (such as the oath of a widow or of partners). The identification of the oath with imprecation around the time of Saadiah enabled the *geonim* to innovate the institution of *ḥerem setam*, which was imposed when there was no obligation to administer an oath.

The provisions of the *gezerta* as instituted by the *geonim* were accepted in their time by communities outside Babylonia (Iraq) as well. In the transitional period between the *geonim* and the later rabbis, the *gezerta* still continued in use, though without its ceremonial accoutrements, in the Jewish centers of North Africa (R. Hananel), Spain (R. Joseph b. Abitur, R. Isaac Alfasi), and even Italy (R. Kalonymus and Meshullam b. Kalonymus), France, and Germany (R. Gershom Me'or ha-Golah, R. Judah ha-Kohen (author of *Sefer ha-Dinim*), Rashi, R. Eliezer b. Nathan of Mainz, R. Isaac the Elder), as implied by the works of the major authorities of those countries. However, as time passed, a marked change is observed in rabbinical literature. The *gezerta* with its special practices became increasingly rare, until it was virtually abandoned and the use of real oaths (by God's name or *kinnuy*) was resumed, even in regard to the post-mishnaic oath (*shevu'at hesset*). The change is first evident in Spain and Provence, as follows from the writings of Naḥmanides, R. Shelomo b. Adret, R. Yom Tov b. Abraham Ishbili, R. Isaac bar Abba Mari (author of *Sefer ha-'Ittur*), R. Abraham b. David of Posquières, and others, continuing later, around the end of the 13th century, in Germany and France. In Germany and France, however, when oaths by God's name or *kinnuy* were discontinued, the rule requiring an object to be held and the "amen" response during the administration of the oath were also almost completely abolished. When the use of oaths was resumed, there was still no requirement to hold an object while taking the oath. The early rabbis of Spain, where the oath by God's name (or *kinnuy*) had been resumed, found it necessary to permit the defendant to request that a *ḥerem setam* be imposed upon the plaintiff, lest the latter unnecessarily demand that an oath be administered to the former. In contemporary Franco-Germany, however, where the use of God's name in oaths had not yet been resumed, there was no need for such protection of the defendant. Only later do we find a return to oaths by God's name in France and Germany and, consequently, the possible imposition of *ḥerem setam* upon the plaintiff.

BIBLIOGRAPHY: G. Libson, "*Gezerta* and *Herem Setam* in the Gaonic and Early Medieval Periods" (Heb.; dissertation, Hebrew University, Jerusalem 1979); idem, "The Use of a Sacred Object in the Administration of a Judicial Oath," in: *Jewish Law Association Studies*, 1 (1985), 53–60; B. Lifshitz, "Evolution of the Court-Oath with Imprecation," in: *Shenaton ha-Mishpat ha-Ivri*, 11–12 (1984–86), 393–406 (Heb.); H. Tykocinski, *The Geonic Ordinances* (Heb.; 1959).

[Gideon Libson (2nd ed.)]

°GHAZĀLĪ, ABU ḤAMID MUḤAMMAD IBN MUḤAMMAD AL-TŪSĪ AL- (1058–1111), Persian Muslim theologian, jurist, mystic, and religious reformer, who wrote mainly in Arabic.

Al-Ghazālī's best-known work is his *Iḥyā' 'Ulūm al-Dīn* ("Revival of the Religious Sciences," 1096–7), in which he successfully reconciled orthodox Islam and *Sufism.

In his early career, al-Ghazālī wrote his famous *Tahāfut al-Falāsifa* ("Incoherence of the Philosophers," 1095) in which he directly confronted the claims of the philosophic systems of al-*Fārābī and *Avicenna. The book is divided into 20 topics, the most important of which is the discussion of the creation of the world. At the end of his work, he offers the legal opinion that the philosophers are guilty of heresy and are liable to the death penalty on three counts: they believe in the eternity of the world, they disbelieve in the omniscience of God, and they do not accept the dogma of bodily resurrection.

Al-Ghazālī had summed up the philosophic system of al-Fārābī and Avicenna in his *Maqāṣid al-Falāsifa* ("Intentions of the Philosophers," 1094), which was supposed to serve as an introductory volume to his "Incoherence," but was used as a handy, independent compendium of philosophy.

In his *Al-Munqidh min al-Ḍalāl* ("Deliverance from Error," 1108) he discussed his initial skepticism concerning the possibility of knowledge, and then his search for enlightenment in *Kalām (scholastic theology), philosophy, the doctrine that there exists an authoritative Imām, or religious guide, to absolute knowledge (Isma'ilism), and finally Sufism, in which he found the solution to his quest for certainty through prophecy.

The four large volumes of al-Ghazālī's *Revival of the Religious Sciences* constitute one of the major works of Sunni Islam. While the first part deals with knowledge and the requirements of faith imposed on the individual (such as ritual purity, prayer, charity, fasting, pilgrimage, recitation of the *Koran) and part two concentrates mainly on duties relating to social interrelations (such as practices relating to eating, marriage, earning a living, friendship), parts three and four are dedicated to the inner life of the soul and deepen the perspective of the first two parts. As a result of al-Ghazālī's endeavor, some of the warmth and emotional religious feeling inherent in Islamic mysticism was infused into the legalistic approach of Sunni Islam.

Al-Ghazālī found the strictness of exacting logical tools especially effective for the renovation and revival of the religious sciences. In addition to a systematic description of logic in his introduction to his writing on legal theory entitled *al-Mustaṣfā min 'Ilm al-Uṣūl* ("The Essentials of Islamic Legal Theory," 1109), he dedicated three other works to Aristotelian logic: *Mi'yar al-'Ilm* ("The Standard Measure of Knowledge," 1095), *Miḥakk al-Naẓar fī al-Manṭiq* ("The Touchstone of Proof in Logic," 1095) and *al-Qisṭās al-Mustaqīm* ("The Just Balance," 1095–96). The first two were written shortly after the *Tahāfut* in the same momentum of thought, and the third was composed after his retirement.

Along with his magnum opus, *Iḥyā 'Ulūm al-Dīn*, al-Ghazali's sincere commitment to Sufism yielded a number of distinctive works on Sufism and ethics, such as *Mīzān al-'Amal* ("The Balance of Action," 1095), *Kitāb al-Arba'īn fī Uṣūl al-Dīn* ("The Forty Chapters on the Principles of Religion"), which is an abbreviation of the *Revival*, *Mishkāt al-Anwār* ("The Niche of the Lights," 1106–7), on the guidance of the inner light to divine intellectualism, and others. In these writings, al-Ghazālī presents his unique perception of man's ultimate goal: an intellectual or spiritual nearness to God instead of the imaginary and metaphorical sensuous pleasures depicted in the Koran and in the Traditions. Al-Ghazālī's conversion to Sufism is not only a move from practical orthodoxy to the internal worship of God, but also a move from a formal conservative form of faith, expressed through practicing the Islamic law, to a learned mode of faith, expressed through an intellectual-mystical progression. In the same token, his revival of the religious sciences on the basis of Sufism, is a move from naïve belief to a learned belief based on semi-philosophical grounding.

Influence on Jewish Philosophy

Al-Ghazālī's influence on Jewish thought falls into two periods: (1) through the 13th century, when he influenced Jewish thinkers who thought and wrote in Arabic, and (2) from the 13th century onward, when a number of his works were translated into Hebrew, some more than once, commented on, and read by the Jewish thinkers of Provence and Spain, who did not know Arabic.

In the first period al-Ghazālī influenced *Judah Halevi, who followed al-Ghazālī's *Incoherence* in attacking the Aristotelian philosophy then current in Spain. One of Judah Halevi's main arguments refers to the difference of opinion among philosophers, except in matters of mathematics and logic, to which al-Ghazālī had already referred. However, in a more general and profound sense, al-Ghazālī made apparent the great danger of philosophy for revealed religion, and it is in this sense that Judah Halevi, and later on Ḥasdai *Crescas, were true disciples of their great Islamic predecessor. Judah Halevi also quotes textually from an early work of al-Ghazālī that sums up the dogmatic bases of the belief of a religious person. This early work of al-Ghazālī was later incorporated into his *Revival* (D. Baneth, *Knesset*, 7 [1942], p. 317 [Hebrew]). Unlike Halevi, who was mostly influenced by the anti-philosophical tone of al-Ghazālī, Ibn Da'ud who wrote his *Emunah Ramah* ("The Exalted Faith") in 1160 was mainly influenced by al-Ghazālī's reliable account of philosophy in his concise reworking of the Aristotelian-Avicennian definitions in his *Intentions*.

Although it cannot be demonstrated conclusively, most probably *Maimonides had read al-Ghazālī's *Incoherence* and was influenced by it in formulating the contrasting conceptions of a God of religion, who exercises free will, and a God of philosophy, who is restricted by the immutability of the order of nature (Maimonides, *Guide of the Perplexed*, ed. by S. Pines [1963], cxxvii). The parallel between al-Ghazālī, who attempted to reconcile Islam and Sufism in his *Revival*, and *Maimonides, who attempted to reconcile the law of Judaism with philosophy in his *Guide*, is instructive, and Maimonides' idea of an all-inclusive legal work including non-legal aspects may have been influenced by al-Ghazālī's *Revival* as well. S. Harvey has pointed to particular similarities between al-Ghazālī's "*Book of Knowledge*," the first book of the *Revival of the Religious Sciences* and Maimonides' *Book of Knowledge*, the first book of the *Mishneh Torah*. This scholar and others have shown that Maimonides was also influenced by al-Ghazālī's supreme way to approach God, such as his concepts of divine love, spiritual pleasures, and the world to come.

The number of works of al-Ghazālī translated into Hebrew during the 13th century indicates his popularity during the preceding period, in which they had become well known and were considered worth translating. His *Intentions of the Philosophers* was translated into Hebrew three times. The first Hebrew translation of al-Ghazālī's *Maqāṣid* was made by Isaac *Albalag (1292). Yet, this translation, known as *Sefer Tikkun ha-De'ot* (or *De'ot ha-Filosofim*) includes only two parts of the original; namely, logic and metaphysics. The third part of this Hebrew version was completed in 1307 by Isaac Pulgar. Albalag, who advocated the philosophy of Averroes, chose al-Ghazālī's compendium of the Avicennian-oriented Aristotelianism out of pedagogical considerations and used it as a point of departure for his own views, which he expressed in excursuses appended to his translation.

The second translation is that of Judah ben Solomon Nathan, who translated the work twice, under the title *Kawwanot ha-Filosofim* sometime between 1330 and 1340; and the third one is an anonymous translation composed at the first half of the 14th century, to which *Moses of Narbonne composed a full commentary (c. 1349). In his commentary on the *Maqāṣid*, Narboni insists that al-Ghazālī wrote a small work entitled *Maqāṣid al-Maqāṣid* (*Kawwanot ha-Kawwanot*), where he confronts the metaphysical issues he challenged in the *Maqāṣid*. In some Hebrew manuscripts, the *Tahāfut* is followed by a small treatise, in which al-Ghāzalī answers the objections which he himself had raised. Narboni's commentary was the object of further comments and commentaries, from the 14th century to the beginning of the 16th century, such as the 14th-century encyclopedia *Ahavah ba-Ta'nugim* by *Moses ben Judah Nogah (1353–56). Even a poetical, rhymed, and abridged version based on selected passages from Judah ben Solomon Nathan's translation was composed in the second half of the 14th century (1367) by *Abraham ben Meshulam Avigdor, under the title *Segullat Melakhim*. Al-Ghazālī's *Intentions of the Philosophers* became a very popular and frequently quoted text in the 15th and 16th centuries and over 50 manuscripts of the Hebrew translations from these centuries are extant. Partial commentaries were written by Moses Rieti (1388–1460), Isaac ben Shem-Ṭob (metaphysics), and (probably) by Elijah Habillo (metaphysics and physics), and there is evidence that the *Maqāṣid* was studied at the schools of Judah Messer Leon and Abraham Bibago and even among the learned Jews of Bohemia and Poland. In addition, there are about 11 anonymous commentaries on the *Maqāṣid* in various European libraries. David ben Judah Messer Leon in his *Ein ha-Kore'* says that Maimonides drew his Peripatetic theories from the *Maqāṣid* (Steinschneider, *Hebr. Bibl.* ii. 86). Moses Almosnino cites a commentary by Elijah Mizraḥi which is no longer extant. The last commentary on the *Maqāṣid al-Falasi-*

fah was by the Karaite Abraham Bali (1510). In his criticism of Aristotelian philosophy, Ḥasdai Crescas preferred to use al-Ghazālī's *Intentions* rather then his *Incoherence* in order to refute the Averroistic-Aristotelian argumentation. Following Ibn Da'ud's historical exemplar, he treated the *Intentions* as a dependable sourcebook for philosophical definitions and suppositions.

Al-Ghazālī's *Tahāfut al-Falāsifah* was translated by Zerahyah ha-Levi in 1411 under the title *Happalat ha-Filosofim*. Isaac ben Nathan of Cordova translated in the 14th century a small treatise by Al-Ghazālī under the title *Ma'amar bi-Teshuvot She'elot Nish'al Mehem*, in which he answers philosophical questions (published by H. Malter, Frankfurt-on-the-Main, 1897). Jacob ben Makhir (d. 1308) translated, under the title *Moznei ha-Iyyunim*, a work in which al-Ghazālī refuted the philosophical arguments contradicting simple religious faith. Simon Duran (d. 1444) cites a passage from *Moznei ha-Iyyunim* in his *Keshet u-Magen*. Al-Ghazālī's *Mishkāt al-Anwār fī Riyāḍ al-Azhar* was translated by Isaac ben Joseph Alfasi under the title *Maskit ha-Orot be-Pardes ha-Nizzanim*. Moses ibn Ḥabib quotes the *Mishkat* in his commentary on *Beḥinat Olam*, where he makes the sun a metaphor to the Law. Johanan Alemanno compares the hierarchy of lights in al-Ghazālī's paradigm to the symbolic system of the Kabbalah in his *Ḥeshek Shelomoh*.

Al-Ghazālī's ethical teachings were studied by Jewish thinkers of the Middle Ages. *Mīzān al-'Amal* (*Moznei Ẓedek*) was translated by Abraham ibn Ḥasdai ben Samuel ha-Levi of Barcelona, who replaced the Koranic quotations with parallel Biblical and Talmudic verses. The *Mīzān* served as a source for Abraham Ibn Da'ud's parable of the pilgrim in his *Emunah Ramah*, used originally by Al-Ghazālī to illustrate the importance of different scientific disciplines.

Altogether, at least six works ascribed to al-Ghazālī were translated into Hebrew during the Middle Ages. Transliterations into Hebrew letters of al-Ghazālī's *Intentions*, *Incoherence*, and *Deliverance* are extant, which is another indication of al-Ghazālī's popularity among the Jewish intellectuals who knew Arabic.

It is interesting to note that on the flyleaf of a manuscript containing some of his works in Arabic letters, the contents are described in Hebrew letters as being by "Abū Ḥāmid al-Ghazālī, the memory of the righteous be blessed," the usual designation for a pious Jew. This illustrates how congenial his general outlook was felt to be by Jewish medieval thinkers and is a striking example of Jewish-Islamic medieval symbiosis. Al-Ghazālī greatly influenced distinguished Jewish thinkers who wrote in Arabic and Hebrew. His case presents an example of Jewish assimilation of Islamic thought during the Middle Ages.

BIBLIOGRAPHY: PRIMARY SOURCES: *Iḥyā' 'Ulūm al-Dīn* (*The Revival of the Religious Sciences*) (1937–38), 5 vols; partial translations can be found in E.E. Calverley, *Worship in Islam: al-Ghazali's Book of the Ihya' on the Worship* (1957); N.A. Faris, *The Book of Knowledge, Being a Translation with Notes of the Kitab al-ilm of al-Ghazzali's Ihya' 'Ulum al-Din* (1962); idem, *The Foundation of the Articles of Faith: Being a Translation with Notes of the Kitab Qaw'id al-'Aqa'id of al-Ghazzali's Ihya' 'Ulum al-Din* (1963); L. Zolondek, *Book XX of al-Ghazali's Ihya' 'Ulum al-Din* (1963); T.J. Winter, *The Remembrance of Death and the Afterlife: Book XL of the Revival of Religious Sciences* (1989); K. Nakamura, *Invocations and Supplications: Book IX of the Revival of the Religious Sciences* (1990); M. Bousquet, *Ihya' 'ouloum ed-din ou vivification de la foi, analyse et index* (1951); I.A. Qubukçu and H. Atay (eds.), *Al-Iqtisad fi'l-'tiqad* (*The Middle Path in Theology*) (1962); partial trans. A.R. Abu Zayd, *Al-Ghazali on Divine Predicates and Their Properties* (1970); M.A. Palacios, *El justo medio en la creencia* (1929); S. Dunya (ed.), *Maqasid al falasifa* (*The Intentions of the Philosophers*) (1961); S. Dunya (ed.), *Mizan al-'amal* (*The Balance of Action*) (1964); H. Hachem (tr.), *Ghazali: Critere de l'action* (1945); S. Dunya (ed.), *Mi'yar al-'ilm* (*The Standard Measure of Knowledge*) (1961); M. al-Nu'mani (ed.), *Mihakk al-nazar fi'l-mantiq* (*The Touchstone of Proof in Logic*) (1966); V. Chelhot (ed.), *Al-Qistas al-mustaqim* (*The Just Balance*) (1959); V. Chelhot (tr.), "Al-Qistas al-Mustaqim et la connaissance rationnelle chez Ghazali," in: *Bulletin d'Etudes Orientales*, 15 (1955–57), 7–98; D.P. Brewster (tr.), *Al-Ghazali: The Just Balance* (1978); A.L. Tibawi (ed. and tr.), *Al-Risala al-Qudsiyya* (*The Jerusalem Epistle*) "Al-Ghazali's Tract on Dogmatic Theology," in: *The Islamic Quarterly*, 9:3–4 (1965), 62–122; A. Afifi (ed.), *Mishkat al-anwar* (*The Niche of the Lights*) (1964); W.H.T Gairdner (tr.), *Al-Ghazzali's Mishkat al-Anwar* (1924; repr. 1952); R. Deladriere, *Le Tabernacle des lumierès* (1981); A.E. Elschazli, *Die Nische der Lichter* (1987); J. Saliba and K. Ayyad (eds.), *Al-Munqidh min al-ḍalāl* (*The Deliverer from Error*) (1934); W.M. Watt (tr.), *The Faith and Practice of al-Ghazali* (1982); R.J. McCarthy (trans.), *Freedom and Fulfillment: An Annotated Translation of al-Ghazali's al-Munqidh min al-Dalal and Other Relevant Works of al-Ghazali* (1980); M. Bouyges (ed.), *Tahāfut al falāsifa* (*The Incoherence of the Philosophers*) (1927); S.A. Kamali (trans.), *Al-Ghazali's Tahafut al-Falasifah* (1963); second English translation by M.E. Marmura, *The Incoherence of the Philosophers: Tahafut al-falasifah: A Parallel English-Arabic Text* (1997). SECONDARY SOURCES: B. Abrahamov, *Divine Love in Islamic Mysticism, the Teachings of al-Ghazali and al-Dabbagh* (2003); M.E. Marmura, "Al-Ghazālī," in: P. Adamson and R.C. Taylor (eds.), *The Cambridge Companion to Arabic Philosophy* (2005), 137–54. INFLUENCE ON JEWISH THOUGHT: M. Steinschneider, *Uebersetzungen* (1893, [1956]), 296–348. CIRCULATION OF THE "INTENTIONS OF THE PHILOSOPHERS": "Issac Albalag," in: *Sefer Tiqqun ha-De'ot*, ed. Georges Vajda (1973); S. Harvey, "Why Did Fourteenth-Century Jews Turn to Al-Ghazali's Account of Natural Science?" in: JQR, 91:3–4 (January–April 2001), 359–76. INFLUENCE OF THE "INCOHERENCE": B.S. Kogan, "Al-Ghazali and Halevi on Philosophy and the Philosophers," in: *Medieval Philosophy and the Classical Tradition* (2002), 64–80; H. Malter, Die Abhandlungen des Abu Hamid al-Gazzali Antworten auf Fragen, die an ihn gerichtet wurden (1894); J. Wolfsohn, *Der Einfluss Gazālī's auf Chisdai Crescas* (1905). ETHICAL WRITINGS: Abraham ibn Ḥasdai ben Samuel ha-Levi, *Moznei Ẓedek*, ed. J. Goldenthal (1839). POSSIBLE INFLUENCE ON MAIMONIDES: A. Eran, "Al-Ghazali and Maimonides on the World to Come and Spiritual Pleasures," in: *Jewish Studies Quarterly*, 8 (2001), 137–66; H.A. Davidson, *Proofs for Eternity, Creation and the Existence of God in Medieval Islamic and Jewish Philosophy* (1987), 196–203; S. Harvey, "Alghazali and Maimonides and their Books of Knowledge," in: J.M. Harris (ed.), *Be'erot Yitzhak – Studies in Memory of Isadore Twersky* (2005), 99–117; S. Pines, "The Philosophic Sources of the Guide of Perplexed," in his translation of *Maimonides' Guide of Perplexed*, 1 (1963), cxxvi–cxxxi.

[Amira Eran (2nd ed.)]

GHELERTER, LUDWIG LITMAN ("Leon"; 1873–1945), physician; one of the pioneers of the general and Jewish socialist movements in Romania. Born in Jassy, Ghelerter studied medicine in his native town, where he joined the socialist movement. His doctoral thesis was on a problem of social medicine: Alcool si alcoolism ("Alcohol and Alcoholism," 1899). In 1895 he was among the founders in Jassy of *Lumina, ("The Light"), the first Jewish socialist society in Romania, with a journal of the same name, and signed the memorandum of the society to the London Congress of the Second International (1896). He was also active in the struggle for civil rights of Jews deprived of Romanian citizenship, thus coming into conflict with the official leadership of the party. A notable speaker, organizer, and writer, Ghelerter continued to uphold his views during the disintegration of the movement and assisted in the reorganization of the Jewish socialist society in Jassy in 1915 and in publication of a weekly, *Der Veker*. After World War I he moved to Bucharest and founded a new party, Partidul Socialist Unitar ("The United Socialist Party"). Although Ghelerter held similar views to those of the Bund, he did not join that movement. He established the Socialist Workers' Party of Romania (1929) which was affiliated to the Fourth International but rejoined the Social Democratic Party of Romania on the eve of World War II. Ghelerter founded and headed the Jewish hospital of Bucharest (1926) and helped promote popular Jewish cooperative credit banks. He accepted non-Jewish patients also in his hospital, named Iubirea de oameni ("Love of People"). While not a Zionist, he was sympathetic toward pioneering enterprises in Palestine, especially cooperatives and kibbutzim. Romanian immigrants named a New York branch of the Workmen's Circle after him.

BIBLIOGRAPHY: J. Kisiman, Shtudien tsu der Geshikte fun Rumenishe Yidn in 19-tn un Onheb 20-tn Yorhundert (1994); LNYL, 2 (1958), 310. **ADD. BIBLIOGRAPHY:** G. Bratescu, in: *Contributia evreilor din Romania la cultura si civilizatie* (1996), 166–7.

[Isac Bercovici and Moshe Mishkinsky / Lucian-Zeev Herscovici (2nd ed.)]

GHENT (Flemish **Gent**; Fr. **Gand**), city in N.W. Belgium. That there was a Jewish settlement in Ghent in the eighth century, as indicated in some early Christian chronicles, is difficult to believe. The Jews were expelled from the city as from the rest of Flanders in 1125, but they were apparently permitted to return in the 13th century. The Jews were again expelled during the *Black Death, 1348–49. Jews began to settle again only in the 18th century. In 1724, the municipal council decided on a special formula of oath for the Jews. However, by 1756, only one Jewish resident, a jeweler, was still in Ghent. When the area passed to France, at the end of the 18th century, the Jewish population increased. It numbered 20 families (107 persons) in 1817, and maintained a synagogue. The majority were peddlers, some of whom were lottery-ticket dealers. Apparently the Jewish street (*Jodenstraatje*) received its name at this time. In 1847, the municipal council granted a plot of land to the community for establishing a Jewish cemetery. In May 1940, before the Nazi occupation, the Jewish population numbered 300. In 1941 the Nazis prohibited the Jews of Belgium to live outside Brussels, Antwerp, Liège, and Charleroi, so that any Jews who remained in Ghent did so illegally. After the liberation in September 1944, there were 150 Jews in Ghent. There were an estimated 80 Jews living in Ghent in 1969.

BIBLIOGRAPHY: E. Ouverteaux, *Notes et documents sur les Juifs de Belgique sous l'ancien régime* (1885), 21, 27; E. Ginsburger, *Les Juifs de Belgique au XVIIIe siècle* (1932), 86–97; S. Ullmann, *Histoire des Juifs en Belgique jusqu'au 19e siècle* (1934), 37–49, 50, 58; E. Sperling-Levin, in: *Regards* (Dec. 1970), 20–27.

GHERON, YAKKIR MORDECAI BEN ELIAKIM (d. 1817), Turkish rabbi (the Italian branch of the family write the name Ghiron, and the Turkish, Gheron). Gheron succeeded his father as rabbi and *dayyan* of Adrianople and district in 1800. He devoted himself particularly to the building of synagogues and supervised the studies in a *talmud torah* which he had established during his period of office in Adrianople. A certain scholar who had converted to Islam was found burnt to death, and the pasha of the town accused the Jews of having been responsible. Gheron was imprisoned and sentenced to death. The pasha's secretary, to whom the rabbi had previously shown kindness, succeeded in having the death sentence repealed, and in its stead a fine was imposed on the Jewish community. In 1812 he went to Jerusalem and was appointed a member of the *bet din* of Jacob Moses *Ayash. His name appears as a signatory to a *takkanah of 1814 with reference to milk milked by gentiles. His responsa appear in the *Dera Dakhya* (Salonika, 1819) of Mordecai b. Menahem *Bekemoharar. He wrote an approbation for the *Nimmukei Yosef* (Leghorn, 1795) of Josef ibn Habib.

BIBLIOGRAPHY: S. Marcus, in: *Sinai*, 41 (1957), 49–52.

[Simon Marcus]

GHETTO, urban section serving as compulsory residential quarter for Jews. Generally surrounded by a wall shutting it off from the rest of the city, except for one or more gates, the ghetto remained bolted at night. The origin of this term has been the subject of much speculation. It was probably first used to describe a quarter of Venice situated near a foundry (*getto*, or *ghetto*) and which in 1516 was enclosed by walls and gates and declared to be the only part of the city to be open to Jewish settlement. Subsequently the term was extended to all Jewish quarters of the same type. Other theories are that the word derives from the Hebrew *get* indicating divorce or separation; from the Greek γέιτων (neighbor); from the German *geheckter* [*Ort*], or fenced place; or from the Italian *borghetto* (a small section of the town). All can be excluded, except for *get* which was sometimes used in Rome to mean a separate section of the city. In any case the institution antedates the word, which is commonly used in several ways. It has come to indicate not only the legally established, coercive ghetto, but also the voluntary gathering of Jews in a secluded quarter, a process known in the Diaspora time before compulsion was exercised. By analogy the word is currently used to describe similar homogeneous quarters of non-Jewish groups, such as immigrant quarters, Black quarters in American cities, native quarters in South African cities, etc.

For historical survey see *Jewish Quarter.

In Muslim Countries

In Muslim countries the Jewish quarter (Arab. *ḥāra*) in its beginnings never had the character of a ghetto. It was always built on a voluntary basis, and it remained so in later times in the vast Ottoman Empire. Istanbul (Constantinople) was the classic example of a capital in which the Jewish quarters were scattered all over the city. In Shīʿite countries (Persia, Yemen) and in orthodox North Africa (Malikite rite) all non-Muslims were forced to live in separate quarters – for religious reasons (ritual uncleanness). Embassies from Christian countries had to look for their (even temporary) dwellings among the Jews. Christian travelers and pilgrims to the Holy Land always remark that in case there was no Christian hospice in a town, they had to look for hospitality among the Jews. After the regulations compelling the Jews to dwell in separate quarters had been repealed (in the 19th and 20th centuries), and they could freely move out, the majority voluntarily remained in their old quarters. Only after the establishment of the new independent states in North Africa did most of the Jews abandon their old dwellings.

See *Jewish Quarter, in Muslim Countries.

Holocaust Period

THE CRYSTALLIZATION OF GERMAN POLICY. While ghettos were traditionally permanent places of Jewish residence, in Poland, under the Nazis, the ghettos were viewed as a transitional measure. "I shall determine at which time and with what means the ghetto, and thereby the city of Lodz, will be cleansed of Jews," boasted Hans Biebow, the Nazi official who ran the Lodz ghetto. "In the end … we must burn out this bubonic plague."

A secret memo issued on September 21, 1939, by Reinhard *Heydrich, the chief of the Security Police, to the chiefs of all task forces operating in the conquered Polish territory, established the basic outlines of German policy in the territories.

Heydrich distinguishes between the ultimate goal (*Endziel*), which would require some time to implement, and the intermediate goals, which must be carried out in the short term. He said: Some goals cannot yet be implemented for technical reasons and some for economic reasons. Room was left for innovation.

He wrote: "The instructions and directives below must serve also for the purpose of urging chiefs of the *Einsatzgruppen* to give practical consideration to the problems involved."

His language was specific: the *Endziel,* the final goal, must be distinguished from the language that is later to be used, the *endlossen*, or final solution, a polite euphemism for the murder of Jewish men, women, and children. The ultimate goal was unarticulated.

The first intermediate goal was concentration. Jews were to be moved from the countryside into the larger cities. Certain areas were to become *Judenrein*, free of Jews, and smaller communities were to be merged into the larger ones.

Heydrich ordered local leaders to establish a Council of Jewish Elders, 24 men to be appointed from the local leaders and rabbis that are to be made *fully responsible*, "in the literal sense of the word," to implement future decrees. A census must be taken and leaders are to be personally responsible for the evacuation of Jews from the countryside. It was unnecessary to indicate what personal responsibility implied; clearly, the lives of individual *Judenrat members were at risk.

Due priority was given to the needs of the army and to minimize economic dislocation, not of the Jews, but of industries essential to German economic interest. Businesses and farms were to be turned over to the locals, preferably Germans, and, if essential and no Germans were available, even to Poles.

The *Einsatzgruppen* were to issue reports, a census of people, an inventory of resources, industries, and personnel.

It is within this framework that the Jewish Councils were established and that the work of securing the occupied territory began. A second decree dated two months later and signed by Hans *Frank, the head of the General Government, further specified the role of the Jewish Council, which was to have a chairman and a deputy.

"The Jewish Council is obliged to receive through its chairman and his deputy the order of the German official agencies. Its responsibility will be to see that the orders are carried out completely and accurately." Jews were ordered to obey the orders of the Jewish Councils.

In retrospect, but only in retrospect, it can be seen that the ghetto was a holding pen, intended to concentrate Jews and hold them captive until such time as an infrastructure was created that could solve the Jewish problem.

The ghetto originally had two goals. The Germans created a situation in which hard labor, malnutrition, overcrowding, and substandard sanitary conditions contributed to the death of a large number of Jews. One in ten died in Warsaw in 1941, before the deportations, before shots were fired. This policy was at odds with the other use of the ghetto as a source of cheap labor that could be of benefit to the Reich and also to individual commanders. In the end, and often only in the end, even the availability of cheap labor gave way to the "Final Solution."

The lifespan of some ghettos was extended because they provided a large reservoir of cheap labor; but while this consideration might forestall the murder process, it did not prevent it. Thus the commander of Galicia, for example, sent out an order in the fall of 1942 to decrease the number of ghettos from 1,000 to 55, and in July 1943 Himmler decided to transfer the surviving inhabitants of ghettos throughout *Ostland* to concentration camps. The last ghetto on Polish soil (*Lodz), which had been in existence since April 1940, was liquidated in August 1944.

Special ghettos were established for Jews deported from Romania to Transnistria and resettled in cities or towns and in neighborhoods or on streets that had been occupied by Jews who had been murdered shortly before by the German army. One exception was the ghetto at *Theresienstadt, which was established at the end of 1941 to house Jews from Bohemia and Moravia and later Jews from Germany and other Western countries were deported there as well. The Germans intended Theresienstadt to be a showcase to the world of their mass treatment of the Jews and thus to mask the crime of the "Final Solution." Still Theresienstadt was actually a ghetto – a holding pen for captive Jews – a concentration camp where conditions of imprisonment prevailed, and a transit camp: of the 144,000 Jews sent to Theresienstadt, 88,000 were shipped from there to Auschwitz, while 33,000 died in the ghetto. Of the 15,000 children sent to Theresienstadt, fewer than 100 survived.

There were several crucial differences between ghettoization in Poland and ghettoization in former Soviet territories. In Poland, ghettoization began shortly after the onset of war, before mass killings and before the murderous intentions of the Germans were clear to all. In former Soviet territories, ghettoization occurred only after the *Einsatzgruppen* murders; Jews were certain that German rule would be murderous even if the nature of German intensions was unclear. Some ghettos were situated near forests which could facilitate escape and a chance, however remote, of survival.

THE JEWISH REACTION TO THE ESTABLISHMENT OF THE GHETTOS. In Poland, the Jews, who were unaware of the Nazis' intentions, resigned themselves to the establishment of ghettos and hoped that living together in mutual cooperation under self-rule would make it easier for them to overcome the period of repression until their country would be liberated from the Nazi yoke. They gave a name to their strategy of survivor, *iberleben*, to live beyond, beyond German rule until liberation. If within the ghetto, they presumed they would somehow be safer, as they would no longer interact with non-Jews in quite the same way and be freed of daily humiliations and dangers. Based on past experience and also on rational calculations or economic self-interest, it seemed to them that by imprisoning Jews in ghettos, the Nazis had arrived at the final manifestation of their anti-Jewish policy. If the Jews would carry out their orders and prove that they were beneficial to the Nazis by their work, they would be allowed to organize their community life as they wished. In addition, the Jews had practically no opportunity to offer armed opposition that would prevent the Germans from carrying out their plans. The constant changes in the composition of the population (effected by transfers and roundups) and in living quarters made it more difficult to express opposition; the hermetic imprisonment from the outside world prevented the acquisition of arms; and conditions in the ghetto (malnutrition, concern for one's family, etc.) weakened the strength of the opposition. On the other hand, the Germans had the manpower and technical equipment to repress any uprising with ease, and the non-Jewish population collaborated with them, or at best remained apathetic. Any uprising in the ghettos, even if it could be pulled off, was thus doomed to military failure. Any attempt at resistance was risky as the German practice of collective responsibility and disproportionate punishment left the remaining ghetto population at risk. Thus uprisings, when they occurred, were usually last stands undertaken when all hope for collective survival was lost and when the only question was what could be done in the face of impending death.

TYPOLOGY OF THE GHETTOS. In most cases, the ghetto was located in one of the poor neighborhoods of a city that had previously housed a crowded Jewish population. Moving large numbers of widely dispersed people into ghettos was a chaotic and unnerving process. In Lodz, where an area already housing 62,000 Jews was designated as the ghetto, an additional 100,000 Jews were crowded into the quarter from other sections of the city. Bus lines had to be rerouted. To avoid the disruption of the city's main transportation lines, two streets were walled off so trolleys could pass through. Polish passengers rode through the center of the Lodz ghetto on streets that Jews could only cross by way of crowded wooden bridges overhead.

In Warsaw, the decree establishing the ghetto was announced on October 12, 1940 – Yom Kippur, the Jewish Day of Atonement. Moving schedules were posted on billboards. Whole neighborhoods were evacuated. While Jews were forced out of Polish residential neighborhoods, Poles were also evicted from the area that would become the ghetto. During the last two weeks of October 1940, according to German figures, 113,000 Poles (Christians) and 140,000 Jews had to be relocated, bringing with them whatever belongings they could pile on a wagon. All abandoned property was confiscated. In every Polish city, the ghettos were overcrowded. Jews were transferred from the other neighborhoods in the city, and in many cases from nearby villages, to housing there, while the non-Jewish inhabitants of the neighborhood were forced to move to another area. These transfers caused great overcrowding from the outset. In Lodz, for example, the average was six people to a room; in Vilna there were even eight to a room during one period. Whenever the overcrowding lessened because of the deporting of Jews to extermination camps, the area of the ghetto was reduced significantly.

At first there were two types of ghettos: open ones, which were marked only by signs as areas of Jewish habitation; and closed ones, which were surrounded by fences, or in some cases even by walls (as in *Warsaw). This difference, however, lost all significance during the period of deportations before an open ghetto was destroyed, or what the Germans called liquidated. In advance all access roads were blocked by the German police, whereas in closed ghettos shifts of German police or their aides constantly guarded the fences and walls. A more significant distinction was the fact that the Germans regarded the closed ghettos as large concentration camps, and therefore most of them were liquidated later than the open ghettos. In contrast to these ghettos, which were all in Polish and Russian territory, the ghettos in Transnistria were not predestined for liquidation. Neither was the ghetto in Theresienstadt. Transnistria even succeeded in maintaining contact with the outside world and received assistance from committees in Romania. Theresienstadt was, in fact, cut off from the world (except for the transports that came in and went out), but the standard of living was higher there than in Eastern European ghettos.

JEWISH ADMINISTRATION. For every ghetto, the German authorities appointed a Judenrat, which was usually composed of Jewish leaders acceptable to the community. The Judenrat was not a democratic body, and its power was centered in one person, not always the chairman, who was responsible for its cooperation in matters relating to the ghetto. The leader of the Judenrat was subordinate to the German authorities, who delegated to him much authority with regard to the Jews but treated him disrespectfully and often cruelly. Many Jews appointed to the Judenrat believed that they were placed in their position in order to serve the Jewish people in its time of great need. They faced two masters. To the Germans they represented Jewish needs and to the Jews they represented German authority. The Germans were uninterested in meeting Jewish needs and German authority was eventually lethal for the Jews.

Ghetto life was one of squalor, hunger, disease, and despair. Rooms and apartments were overcrowded, with 10 or 15 people typically living in space previously occupied by four. Daily calorie allotments seldom exceeded 1,100. Without smugglers who brought in food, starvation would have been rampant. The smugglers' motto: "Eat and drink for tomorrow we die," was only too apt.

There were serious public health problems. Epidemic diseases were a threat, typhus the most dreaded. Dead bodies were often left on the street until the burial society came. Beggars were everywhere. Perhaps most unbearable was the uncertainty of life. Ghetto residents never knew what tomorrow would bring.

In the ghetto, life went on. Families adjusted to new realities, living in constant fear of humiliation, labor conscription, and deportation. Survival was a daily challenge, a struggle for the bare necessities of food, warmth, sanitation, shelter, and clothing. Clandestine schools educated the young. Religious services were held even when they were outlawed. Cultural life continued with theater and music, poetry and art offering a temporary respite from squalor.

From the beginning, the Jewish leadership was faced with the impossible task of organizing ghetto life under emergency conditions and under the ceaseless pressure of threats of cruel punishment. Jewish institutions, to the extent that they existed, continued to function, either openly, such as the institutions that fulfilled religious needs, or in secret, such as the various political parties. The major function of the leadership, however, was the provision of sustenance and health and welfare services (including hospitals) and sanitation, and this had to be accomplished without adequate means. Raul *Hilberg likened their task to a small isolated municipal government living in hostile territory. The authority of leaders always derived from the Germans. To provide these services, they taxed those who still had some resources and worked those who had none. They practiced the time-honored traditions of their people honed by centuries of exile and persecution. Decrees were evaded or circumvented. They tried to outwit the enemy and alleviate the awful conditions of the ghetto, at least temporarily. Some behaved admirably; others became infatuated with their power and imposed it on the powerless, captive population.

Despite what was often their best effort, in the course of time these institutions collapsed in most ghettos. It was even more difficult to establish those services which had not existed within the Jewish community before the Holocaust, such as police, prisons, and courts. The authority vested in these institutions was broad within the narrow autonomous framework that existed in the ghettos, and in many instances they were, of course, not properly utilized under conditions of the life-and-death struggle imposed on the inhabitants of the ghetto.

LIQUIDATION OF THE GHETTOS. The lifespan of the Polish ghettos was brief; formed in 1940, most were destroyed beginning in 1942 shortly after the *Wannsee Conference. The destruction of the ghettos was conducted as part of the policy of the "Final Solution," for which purpose the Germans prepared special death camps, what they called extermination camps. When it was decided to liquidate a ghetto, they would call on the Jews to present themselves voluntarily to be transferred to labor camps (sometimes with false promises of improved living conditions), but if deception proved unsuccessful, they would round up the residents and bring them by force to assembly areas, from where they would be transported, usually by train, to their destination. Ghetto leaders faced the ultimate decision. For a time they could save some but only at the sacrifice of others. *Rumkowski in Lodz saved the able-bodied and shipped the children to Chelmno, reasoning that the best chance of survival was if the ghetto was transformed into a work camp, productive for the Wehrmacht. "Survival by work" was his motto. In Warsaw, *Czerniakow tried to save the children; when he could not, he killed himself rather than participate in their deportation. Jewish police were employed to send Jews to the trains. In some ghettos – but not many – the leadership chose suicide rather than cooperation. The great majority of the ghetto inhabitants were killed immediately upon their arrival in the camps; a minority, the young and the able-bodied, women without children, were employed in forced labor and were killed after a short time by one of the regular means of extermination. Only a very small number remained alive, sometimes after having been shunted from camp to camp.

See also *Holocaust. For more information on specific ghettos see *Kovno, *Lodz, *Lublin, *Theresienstadt, and *Warsaw.

[Michael Berenbaum (2nd ed.)]

BIBLIOGRAPHY: G. Reitlinger, *Final Solution* (1968²), index; R. Hilberg, *Destruction of the European Jews* (2003³), index; P. Friedman, in: JSOS, 16 (1954), 61–88 (incl. bibl.). **ADD. BIBLIOGRAPHY:** E. Sterling, *Life in the Ghettos during the Holocaust* (2005); I. Gutman, *The Jews of Warsaw 1939–1943* (1982); A. Tory, *Surviving the Holocaust: The Kovno Ghetto Diary* (1990); L. Dobroszycki, *The Chronicles of the Lodz Ghetto 1941–44* (1984); I Trunk, *Judenrat* (1972).

GHETTO FIGHTERS' HOUSE (Heb. בֵּית לוֹחֲמֵי הַגֵּטָאוֹת, *Beit Loḥamei ha-Getta'ot*), a ghetto uprising and Holocaust remembrance authority, established in kibbutz *Loḥamei ha-Getta'ot, on April 19, 1950, by a group of former ghetto fighters and partisans. The house serves as a memorial and research and documentation center on the Holocaust period, and on Jewish resistance under Nazi rule in Europe. It contains an important historical archive on the Holocaust, and particularly on organized resistance; papers left by the poet Itzhak *Katzenelson, after whom it is named; documents from the *He-Ḥalutz archives in the Warsaw and Bialystok ghettos; a collection of the publications of the Jewish underground in occupied Poland; on the Jewish underground in Holland and France; a register of names of Jewish partisans who fought in Italy and Yugoslavia; and photographs, films, and pictures. It also contains the papers of Yitzhak *Zuckerman and Miriam Nocitch, a collection of 60 diaries in different languages, and several thousand testimonies of Holocaust survivors. The museum maintains a permanent display as well as special exhibits dealing with different aspects of the Holocaust and Jewish resistance; models of the Warsaw ghetto and the *Treblinka death camp are on show. In 2005 the Museum's permanent exhibition underwent a significant upgrading that will take several years to complete. On the national Holocaust Remembrance Day in Israel (27th of Nisan), a mass memorial assembly is held at the amphitheater outside the museum. The Ghetto Fighters' House has published a series of books and periodicals, *Dappim le-Ḥeker ha-Sho'ah ve-ha-Mered* (1951–52, 1969); and *Yedi'ot Beit Loḥamei ha-Getta'ot al shem Yiẓḥak Katzenelson* (1951–60).

The Museum also has a highly acclaimed children's exhibition, Yad la-Yeled, designed to tell the story of the Holocaust to younger children. Designed by Ram Karmi, the exhibit is semicircular, descending into the depths of the earth. It unfolds section by section, not allowing the visitor to take in the entire exhibition at once, and tells the story of the Holocaust through the testimonies of those who were children during the Holocaust and through documents and imaginative reconstructions that suggest the magnitude of what happened in a manner that children can understand. At the center of the exhibition is a Janusz *Korczak room, based on the work of the famed Polish-Jewish educator and physician who ran an orphanage in the ghetto. This world of imagination and the empowerment of children here contrast boldly with the contents of the rest of the Museum. Educational activities in arts and crafts, drama, and music enable children to process what they have experienced. Among the other activities of the Museum, aside from those related to the Holocaust, are the international book-sharing project and work in democracy and pluralism that attracts neighboring Arab and Jewish communities in Galilee.

GHEZ, Tunisian family, whose most eminent members were DAVID (second half of 18th century), author of a number of works of which only one, *Ner David*, part 1 (Leghorn, 1868), has been published; the others include a commentary to the tractates *Shabbat, Pesaḥim*, and *Sukkah*, as well as novellae to various other tractates. MOSES (end of 18th century) wrote commentaries to the tractate *Shevu'ot* and Elijah *Mizrachi's supercommentary on Rashi to the Pentateuch under the titles *Yeshu'at Ya'akov* and *Yedei Moshe*. He also wrote *Yismaḥ Moshe* (Leghorn, 1863), a commentary to the Passover *Haggadah*, notes on the Pentateuch, and three poems. JOSEPH (b. 1800), son of David, was a kabbalist. He left numerous works in manuscript, including a commentary to Maimonides' *Mishneh Torah*, sermons, glosses on the Talmud, on the Zohar, etc. In *Pi ha-Medabber* (Leghorn, 1854), his kabbalistic commentary to the Passover *Haggadah*, he cites explanations by his cousin Ḥayyim Ghez.

Another member of the family was MATHILDA GHEZ (1918–1990), a communal leader in Tunisia. In 1957 she moved to Israel and was elected to the Knesset (in 1965 representing Rafi, and in 1969, the Israel Labor Party).

BIBLIOGRAPHY: D. Cazès, *Notes Bibliographiques sur la Littérature Juive-Tunisienne* (1893), 194–205 (= *Mizraḥ u-Ma'arav*, 2 (1928), 353–6).

°**GHILLANY, FRIEDRICH WILHELM** (1807–1876), German theologian. A municipal librarian in Nuremberg, Ghillany wrote on various historical subjects but he was chiefly concerned with religious questions, and adopted the teachings of G.F. Daumer (1800–1875), a deist in search of "true religion." Following the Damascus blood libel, Ghillany wrote *Die Menschenopfer der alten Hebraeer* (Nuremberg, 1842), in which he accused the Jews of "cannibalism" and "molochism" in both ancient and modern times and of the ritual murder of Jesus. He gave further expression to his antisemitism in *Die Judenfrage; eine Beigabe zu Bruno Bauer's Abhandlung ueber diesen Gegenstand* (*ibid.*, 1843), and *Das Judenthum und die Kritik* (*ibid.*, 1844). Both Daumer and Ghillany were praised by Nazi propagandists.

BIBLIOGRAPHY: L. Poliakov, *Histoire de l'antisémitisme*, 3 (1968), 425–6; R.W. Stock, *Die Judenfrage durch fuenf Jahrhunderte* (1939), 391–427; V. Eichstaedt, *Bibliographie zur Geschichte der Judenfrage 1750–1848* (1938), index; M. Loewengard, *Jehowa, nicht Moloch, war der Gott der alten Hebraeer…* (1843).

GHIRON, family of scholars whose name derives from Gerona in N. Spain. Among its most important members are:

JOHANAN GHIRON (1646–1716), born in Casale Monferrato, Italy. Johanan was rabbi of Florence for 34 years, and was given the title *Alluf Torah* ("Master of the Torah") in appreciation of his great erudition. Though by upbringing and inclination he sided with the Shabbatean movement, he willingly signed the excommunication on Nehemiah *Ḥayon. After his death, all the *takkanot* he had instituted were repealed. Johanan was the author of (1) *Mishtaḥ ha-Ramim*, an apology for his attitude in connection with the dispute over Ḥayon, with an appendix consisting of his letters (still in manuscript); (2) prayers, on the occasion of the earthquakes in Lugo in 1688 and in Ancona in 1690. The prayer on Ancona was also recited in Florence on the occasion of the earthquake in Leghorn in 1742. It was published in the *Shever ba-Meẓarim* of Raphael Meldola (Leghorn, 1742); (3) responsa mentioned in the *Paḥad Yiẓḥak* of Isaac *Lampronti, in the *Shemesh Ẓedakah* of Samson Morpurgo, and elsewhere (Montefiore collection); (4) glosses on the *Arba'ah Turim* and halakhic novellae (unpublished).

JUDAH ḤAYYIM GHIRON, his son, was born in Casale Monferrato and was rabbi of Florence from 1719 to 1738. His *Mekor Dimah*, on his father's activities in connection with Nehemiah Ḥayon and on his *takkanot*, together with a selection of letters on Nehemiah Ḥayon and an appendix to his father's *Mishtaḥ ha-Ramim*, are still in manuscript. JUDAH ḤAYYIM LEONTI GHIRON (1739–1761) was rabbi of Casale. His halakhic correspondence with contemporary scholars is preserved in the Asiatic Museum in Leningrad. SAMUEL ḤAYYIM GHIRON (1829–1895) was born in Ivrea. In 1854 he qualified as a teacher of literature and in 1877 was appointed rabbi of Turin. He published a prayer book according to the Italian rite, with an Italian translation (Leghorn, 1879). In the National Library, Jerusalem, there is an elegy on the death of Hillel Cantoni in Italian and Hebrew, the latter by Samuel Ghiron (Turin, 1857). In 1880, with the assistance of B. Peyron, he published a catalog of the Hebrew manuscripts in Turin. He also wrote essays, sermons, and poems. ISAIAH GHIRON (1837–1888), director of the Braidense Library in Milan, wrote books in Italian on Hebrew numismatics and inscriptions. In 1874 he was editor of *Rivista di Lettere, Scienze ed Arti*.

BIBLIOGRAPHY: Ghirondi-Neppi, 161; Levi, in: RI, 8 (1911), 169–85; Mortara, Indice, 27; Nacht, in: *Zion Me'assef*, 6 (1934), 121; Sonne, in: *Zion*, 4 (1938/39), 86–88; Wilensky, in: KS, 24 (1946/47), 195 no. 68.

[Simon Marcus]

GHIRONDI, MORDECAI SAMUEL BEN BENZION ARYEH (1799–1852), Italian scholar and biographer. Ghirondi was a descendant of a rabbinic family. His grandmother Mazal-Tov Benvenida Ghirondi (c. 1760), wife of Mordecai, rabbi of Cittadella, was famous for her Jewish learning and educated many disciples to a relatively high grade of knowledge. Ghirondi was born in Padua. He taught theology at the rabbinical college of Padua, where he had studied, beginning in 1824. He was assistant rabbi of Padua 1829–31, and from 1831 to his death was chief rabbi.

Apart from a juvenile moral treatise, *Tokho Raẓuf Ahavah* (1818), Ghirondi's minor works include some scattered essays and a number of unpublished works, mainly in the Montefiore collection and in the Jewish Theological Seminary of America. His major work is *Toledot Gedolei Yisrael* (1853), a biographical dictionary of Jewish scholars and rabbis composed as an extension of *Zekher Ẓaddikim li-Verakhah*, a similar biographic work by Hananel Graziadio *Neppi. The *Toledot* was published by Ghirondi's son Ephraim Raphael (1834–57) at Trieste. Although naive and badly proportioned, the work retains its importance for information, based in some entries on personal acquaintance or oral tradition, on Italian rabbis of the 18th and early 19th centuries; these are the vast majority of the entries. Ghirondi also annotated *Azulai's *Shem ha-Gedolim* (publ. in E. Gartenhaus, *Eshel ha-Gedolim*, 1958).

Ghirondi was a notable book collector; many of his manuscripts are in the Montefiore Library in Jews' College, London, and his printed books and some manuscripts are in the Jewish Theological Seminary in New York.

BIBLIOGRAPHY: Ghirondi-Neppi, 56, 374–6.

[Cecil Roth]

GHIRSHMAN, ROMAN (1895–1979), French archaeologist, specialist in Iranian studies. Ghirshman was born and educated in Paris. He had his first experience in excavation at Tello in Iraq in 1930. In 1931 he was sent to Iran as leader of an expedition and this was the beginning of a long series of successful excavations of important early settlements in Iran and Afghanistan. These included Tepe Giyan, Tepe Sialk, and Tchoga Zanbil in Elam. Ghirshman, who held a professorship at the University of Aix-en-Provence, was head of the French archaeological mission to Afghanistan from 1941 to 1943, and director of the Suse mission in Iran from 1946 to 1967. His numerous publications on Iranian art, history, and culture include *Fouilles de Tépé Giyan 1931 et 1932* (with G. Contenau, 1935), *Foullies de Sialk* (2 vols., 1938–39), *Iran: From the Earliest Times to the Islamic Conquest* (1954), and *Iran:* From the Origins to Alexander the Great (1964).

[Penuel P. Kahane]

GIBBETHON (Heb. גִּבְּתוֹן).

(1) Town in the territory of Dan, mentioned with Eltekeh and Baalath (Josh. 19:44). It is also listed as a levitical city of the Kohathite family (*ibid.* 21:23) and was thus apparently a Davidic administrative center (its name is absent in the parallel text of levitical cities in I Chron. 6). Gibbethon appears twice in the Book of Kings as a Philistine city that was besieged by Nadab and "all Israel" and again by Elah; both sieges, however, were interrupted by revolutions in the besieging armies and were unsuccessful (I Kings 15:27; 16:15). It may also be included in the list of cities captured by Thutmose III in c. 1469 B.C.E. (no. 103). Gibbethon is generally identified with Tel al-Malāt (now called Tell Gibbethon), southwest of Gezer, a prominent mound containing pottery from the Chalcolithic to the Arabic periods.

[Michael Avi-Yonah]

(2) Moshav Gibbethon (Givton) in central Israel, near *Reḥovot, affiliated with Tenu'at ha-Moshavim, was founded in 1933 by settlers from Eastern Europe as one of the villages of the "Thousand Families Settlement Scheme." Citriculture constitutes a prominent farm branch. Modern Gibbethon does not seem to lie on the ancient site. In the mid-1990s, the population was approximately 215, while in the end of 2002 it grew to number 290 residents.

[Efraim Orni]

BIBLIOGRAPHY: Von Rad, in: PJB, 29 (1933), 30ff., 35; EM, 1 (1963), 354.

GIBBOR, JUDAH BEN ELIJAH (b.c. 1460), Karaite author and poet living in Constantinople. His writings include a poetical commentary on the Pentateuch *Minḥat Yehudah* (published in the Karaite ritual, Venice, 1529). In this poem, often commented upon by Karaite scholars, Gibbor refers with deep respect to Maimonides; it deals with the three pillars of Karaism – Scripture, analogy, and (Karaite) tradition. He also wrote three works which are no longer extant: *Hilkhot Sheḥitah*, on the laws of ritual slaughter, *Sefer Mo'adim*, regulations for the festivals, and *Mo'ed Katan*, on the secondary festivals, which also contained the essential teachings of the Kabbalah. Gibbor's eldest son, ELIJAH SHUBSHI (1483–1501), who died at the age of 18, wrote a commentary on *Shesh Kenafayim*, an astronomical work by Immanuel b. Jacob *Bonfils of Tarascon.

BIBLIOGRAPHY: Danon, in: JQR, 15 (1924/25), 313–5; 17 (1926/27), 179–81; Mann, Texts, 2 (1935), 296, n. 7, 732, n. 176, 1177, 1421.

[Isaak Dov Ber Markon]

GIBBS, TERRY (**Julius Gubenko**; 1924–), U.S. vibraphonist, drummer. The Brooklyn-born Gibbs grew up in a musical family. His brother Sol taught him to play drums and vibes and the two boys worked for their father, Abe, whose band, the Radio Novelty Orchestra, was a fixture on the Depression-era bar mitzvah-wedding circuit. It was a training ground that gave him a healthy respect for Jewish music and for the business side of the music industry. But it was while he was on a two-week furlough from the U.S. Army during WWII that Gibbs had a life-changing encounter, slipping into a jazz club to hear Charlie Parker play the new jazz music called "be-bop." One night turned into two weeks as the young GI spent every night of his furlough at Minton's Playhouse absorbing the new sounds. His first stop upon his discharge from the army was 52nd Street again, where he took up the vibes in earnest in a bebop quintet that featured tenor saxophonist Allen Eager and drummer Max Roach. Gibbs's major career break followed shortly after when he was hired by Woody Herman as part of the clarinetist's legendary Second Herd, a bop-oriented band that featured a powerhouse sax section whose members included Eager, Al Cohn, and Stan *Getz. After Herman dissolved that group, Gibbs went to work for a succession of excellent leaders, most prominently Benny *Goodman. Eventually he relocated to the West Coast, where he started his own group and divided his time between jazz jobs and studio and television work. Gibbs remained active into his seventies.

BIBLIOGRAPHY: "Terry Gibbs: Jazz Profiles from NPR," at: www.npr.org; B. Priestly, "Terry Gibbs," in: *Jazz: The Rough Guide* (1995); J. Ephland., "Terry Gibbs," *Down Beat Magazine* archives at: www.downbeat.com.

[George Robinson (2nd ed.)]

GIBEAH, GEBA (Heb. גִּבְעָה, גֶּבַע; "hill"), a central city in the territory of Benjamin and the royal capital at the time of Saul. It was situated on the main road from Judah to Mount Ephraim (Judg. 19:11–13), near the Jerusalem–Shechem road. The territory of the tribe of Benjamin is characterized by a hilly terrain. The biblical sources relating to this territory contain a large number of place names based on the root *g-b-ʿ*, the stem for the Hebrew word meaning "hill." These include the name Gibeon, Geba (I Sam. 14:5), and Gibeah (Judg. 19.12; I Sam. 14:2), the latter thought to be identified at Tell el-Ful. There are also longer versions of these names such as Geba of Benjamin (I Sam. 13:16), Gibeah of Benjamin (I Sam. 13:2), and Gibeath Haelohim (I Sam 10:5).

According to the story in Judges 19–21 the city was destroyed during the civil war that ensued as a result of the atrocities committed by the people of Gibeah against the concubine from Judah. Later Gibeah became one of the Philistines strongholds in the highlands (I Sam 10:5). According to I Samuel 10:26; 11:4 Saul came from Gibeah; however, the genealogical lists in I Chronicles 8:29; 9:35 suggest that Saul's ancestral home was at Gibeon. After the battle of Michmash (I Sam. 13–14) Gibeah became Saul's capital and was renamed after him as "Gibeah of Saul" (I Sam. 15:34).

After the schism Gibeah became an important strategic city on the northern border of Judah. It is also mentioned in Isaiah 10:29 in Sennacherib's march through the region north of Jerusalem.

The modern site of Tell el-Ful is situated 3.5 miles (5.5 km.) north of the Damascus Gate in Jerusalem. It is located on the crest of the watershed, with deep valleys extending to the east and west. The hill rises with steep terraces on the east, south and north, but on the west the slope is more gradual. The ancient road from Judah to Mount Ephraim extended along the base of the tell. This was the main north-south route of central Palestine and the tell, 2,755 ft. (840 m.) above sea level, commanded it. The top was relatively flat, about 500 ft. (150 m.) north to south by 300 ft. (90 m.) east to west.

Edward Robinson (1841, 14–15) first identified Gibeah at the village of Jabaʿ, but later changed his mind and identified it with Tell el-Ful. Although the identification of Gibeah with Tell el-Ful is generally accepted, it is still a matter of debate among some scholars. Hence, more recently J.M. Miller (1975) and P.M. Arnold (1990) have challenged this identification and proposed that Gibeah should be identified with Geba (modern Jabaʿ). But this proposal has been rejected due to the fact that Gibeah belonged to a group of sites whose precise location was already lost in ancient times. The name Gibeah was transferred as Geba to the place now known as Jabaʿ. Moreover, there is no archaeological evidence to support Miller or Arnold's claims, and in recent surveys Jabaʿ produced ceramics of the Iron Age II as well from the Persian period, but none from the Iron Age I. Tell el-Ful, however, produced ample evidence from the Iron Age I. Tell el-Ful is also an extremely commanding and important site; the view from the summit covers a wide area. The strong fortress (or tower) at the summit is situated on the main trade route leading from Jerusalem to the north, and from the coast in the west to Moab and Ammon in the east. No other proposed site in the vicinity has such obvious advantages.

Tell el-Ful was excavated by W.F. Albright (in 1922–23, and in 1933) and by P.W. Lapp (1964). Five phases of occupation were uncovered, from the Iron Age I period to the Roman Period. These include a new fortress from the fourth century B.C.E. which survived until the second century B.C.E. (Josephus, Wars, 5:51 mentions Gibeah as a settlement situated 30 ris (3.5 miles) north of Jerusalem; Titus camped there on his way to Jerusalem, and eventually his troops destroyed it.) The site continued to exist until the time of *Bar Kokhba (132–35 B.C.E.). The earliest occupation, however, appears to have been in the Middle Bronze II (c. 2000–1550 B.C.E.) as is indicated by pottery and a mace-head. No building remains dating from earlier than the Iron Age have been discovered on the summit of the hill, though MB buildings were excavated in 1995–96 on the lower east slope. The stratum with archaeological remains most relevant to our topic is from the Iron Age I and was divided into three "periods":

1. Period I: miscellaneous constructions that antedated the foundation of the fortress and which were destroyed by fire
2. Period II: Fortress I, destroyed by a massive fire
3. Period II: Fortress II, a second fortress which was a reconstruction of the first one, and eventually abandoned.

Paul Lapp's main objection to Albright's result was the suggestion that during Period II at Tell el-Ful an entire fortress existed at the site. In addition, Albright suggested that towers were built at each one of the four corners of the fortress which, when reconstructed, measured 203 × 187 ft. (62 × 57 m.). However, in actual fact the contour of the mound precludes such an extension of the fort eastwards; and since the tower which Albright discovered stood at a height of 10 ft. (3 m.) and was well preserved; it is not clear why traces of the fort have not been discovered elsewhere at the site.

The evidence so far indicates that there was only one solitary massive tower, not a fortress, during Tell el-Ful Period II (i.e., the period of Saul). It is possible, however, that at the time of Saul *only* the tower was necessary and that additional walls were added later.

The main reason for the uncertainty in dating the early archaeological periods at Tell el-Ful stems from the attempts to correlate the archaeological finds with the biblical story in Judges 19–21. Albright (1924, 45) dated the foundation of Tell el-Ful to 1230 B.C.E. and the fortress to 1200 B.C.E. Albright was convinced that the archaeological results supported the story as it appears in Judges and dated the destruction of Gibeah in this story to 1100 B.C.E. Albright based this on the assumption that the Benjaminites' war must have occurred long before Saul's accession to kingship; by which time the atrocities at Gibeah would have been forgotten. The second period Albright (1933, 8) assigned to the time of Saul on the evidence of potsherds attributed to the last phase of Iron I and before the transition to Iron II period in the 10th century.

However, the archaeological data from Tell el-Ful does not provide enough substantial evidence from which an accurate chronology may be deduced. Therefore, consideration should be made of A. Mazar's (1981, 1–36) dating considerations at the site of Giloh. The settlement at Giloh (south of the Rephaim Valley, and a twin site of Tell el-Ful) was founded about the time Lachish was destroyed in the reign of Rameses III, c. 1184–1153, i.e., in the first half of the 12th century B.C.E. It is not possible to determine whether this was a few years before or after the destruction. Some of the vessels which appear at Giloh have parallels at Lachish, but other types especially the "collared rim" jars and some of the cooking pots do not appear at Lachish. Taking this dating into consideration one may assume that Period I at Tell el-Ful (like Giloh) was constructed some time around 1153 B.C.E. at the latest, even though there is no clear indication as to how long the Period I settlement survived or how many years elapsed between Period I and Period II at Tell el-Ful.

Lapp's excavation results allowed Period I to run for 50 years from 1200 to 1150, though a slight modification must also be made. Thus 50 years should be allowed for Period I, from 1153 B.C.E., placing Period II (i.e., Saul's period) roughly about 1100 B.C.E. It is generally accepted that Saul reigned for a period of about 20 years. It has been argued (Shalom Brooks, 1997) that there was a gap of at least 17 years between Saul's death and David's accession to the throne. Hence, taking away about 40 years from 1100 B.C.E. brings us closer to the date of c. 1060–1050 B.C.E., the time which marks the end of the rule of the house of Saul, contrary to the generally accepted dates for Saul, i.e., 1025–1005 B.C.E.

In concluding this discussion it is possible to propose that the end of Period I at Tell el-Ful (most probably a Philistine post, defeated by Saul as described in I Samuel 13–14), ended by fire some time before or around 1100 B.C.E. It is possible also that Saul built the large tower (Period II, fortress I) and that it ended with a violent destruction after Saul's death. The second fortress (Period II fortress II) was built almost immediately after the first one was destroyed as a rebuilding of the first fortress. This fortress, according to the archaeological finds, survived for a short period of about 10 years. Because the fortress was built immediately after the first one had been destroyed, with the building following almost exactly the same plan, it might be suggested that the builder was possibly closely connected with Saul. That person may have been Abner, Saul's uncle, or Ishbaal, Saul's son. Is it possible that they tried to rebuild Saul's tower in order to resettle Saul's town?

Abner was murdered a few years later (II Sam 3:27), which would explain why fortress II was abandoned.

The archaeological evidence shows that Gibeah stood in ruins until the eight century B.C.E. No attempts were made to rebuild or inhabit the site. Perhaps it was during this period that the story in Judges was written to explain why Gibeah had been destroyed.

BIBLIOGRAPHY: W.F. Albright, *Excavation and Results at Tell el-Ful (Gibeah of Saul)*, Annual of the American School of Oriental Research, 4 (1924); idem, "A New Campaign of Excavation at Gibeah of Saul," in: *Bulletin of the American School of Oriental Research*, 52 (1933), 6–12; P.M. Arnold, *Gibeah, In Search of a Biblical City (Journal for the Study of the Old Testament* Supplement 79, 1990); N.L. Lapp, *The Tale of a Tell* (1975); idem, *The Third Campaign at Tell el-Ful: Excavations of 1964*, Annual of the American School of Oriental Research, 45 (1981); A.Mazar, "Giloh: An Early Israelite Site Near Jerusalem," in: IEJ, 31:1–36; J.M. Miller, "Geba/Gibeah of Benjamin," in: VT, 25 (1975), 145–66; E. Robinson, *Biblical Researchers in Palestine, Mount Sinai and Arabia Petraea. A Journal of Travels in the Year 1838* (1852); S. Shalom Brooks, "Was There A Concubine at Gibeah?"in: *Bulletin of the Anglo-Israel Archaeological Society*, 15 (1996–97) 31–40; idem, *Saul and the Monarchy: A New Look* (2005).

[Simcha Shalom Brooks (2nd ed.)]

GIBEON (Heb. גבעון), the largest and best-known city in the territory of the tribe of Benjamin, resembling a royal city (Josh. 10.2).

Biblical Gibeon has been identified with modern el-Jib, 6 miles (9 kms.) north of Jerusalem. The first proper scientific identification of the place with modern el-Jib was made in 1838 by Edward Robinson. During the archaeological excavations of 1956, 1957, and 1959, directed by J.B. Pritchard (1962, 24–52), this identification was confirmed by the discovery of 56 jar handles inscribed with the name Gdn (or Gdd).

Gibeon was first mentioned in Joshua 9 in an incident which tells how the Hivite inhabitants of Gibeon deceived Joshua into making a peace covenant with them. When the deception was discovered, the Gibeonites were sentenced to become "hewers of wood and drawers of water" (Josh. 9:21, 23). Later when the Amorite king Adoni-Zedek attacked Gibeon for siding with the Israelites, Joshua was obliged to protect them and chased the Amorites down the pass of Beth-Horon supported by "hailstones and the sun standing still upon Gibeon" (Josh. 10:1–14; Isa. 28:21). However, the reference to this story in Joshua 9 presents a problem since there is no archaeological evidence for a settlement at Gibeon during the Late Bronze Age, the period in which the conquest stories in Joshua are placed.

In Joshua 18:25 and 21:17 Gibeon is described as a levitical city. The section in II Samuel 2:12–17 describes the scene of the contest at the "pool of Gibeon" between the two opponents groups; that of Abner (Saul's supporters) and that of Joab (David's supporters). In that contest 12 men of each group were "thrusted through" by the swords of their opponents. In II Sam. 20:8 Joab slew Amasa at Gibeon; in II Sam. 21:1–10 seven of Saul's sons were executed, i.e. two of Ritzpah, Saul's concubine, and five of Michal from her marriage to Paltiel (and not Adriel as mentioned in II Samuel 21:8; Adriel is the Aramaic version of the Hebrew Paltiel (see Z. Ben-Barak 1991, 87)). According to the narrative, the execution had to be carried out to end the three-year famine during David's reign, caused by Saul's violation of the covenant with the Gibeonites, not recorded anywhere else in the Bible.

It is stated (I Kings 3:4–5) that the people were sacrificing at the high place at Gibeon; Solomon offered one thousand burnt offerings on the altar; and Solomon's famous inaugural dream is placed at the high place at Gibeon. According to I Chronicles 16:39; 21:29 the "tabernacle" was there, too.

Examining the textual material Shalom Brooks (2005) has argued that Gibeon played an important role in Israelite cultic life before Solomon, i.e. since the time of Saul. Firstly, it is not plausible that Gibeon was insignificant during the time extending from Samuel and Saul to David; its cultic popularity does not make sense unless the sanctuary had a long history behind it. Secondly, the description of the worship held at Gibeon makes sense and is convincing particularly since Gibeon is described as a levitical city (Josh 21.17). This view can be supported by Blenkinsopp (1974) who proposed that the sanctuary that David visited (II Sam. 21:1) was at Gibeon; and that the first altar that Saul built to Yahweh (I Sam 14:33) was in the Gibeonite region and must be a great stone which is at Gibeon (II Sam. 20:8). This story has cultic significance (Josh. 24:26; I Sam. 6:14–16) and may be identified with the altar on which Solomon offered sacrifices (I Kings 3:4).

In Jeremiah 28:1 Gibeon is mentioned as the home of the false prophet Hananiah; and the "great pool" of Gibeon is mentioned again as the site of a bloody combat when Johanan unsuccessfully attacked Ishmael, Gedaliah's assassin. A reference from the post-exilic period is found in Nehemiah 3:7. It indicates that the men from Gibeon assisted in the rebuilding of the city wall of Jerusalem. The earliest extra-biblical reference to Gibeon is found at Karnak, in a list of cities either captured or visited during the campaign Sheshonk (biblical Shishak, I Kings 14:25) made in Canaan, c. 924 B.C.E.

The archaeological data from el-Jib indicates that there was no Late Bronze Age (c. 1550–1200 B.C.E.) settlement at Gibeon, i.e. prior to the settlement in the Iron Age I Period (Pritchard II, 1976, 449–50). However, the site was occupied in the EB I (c. 3300–3050 B.C.E.), and MB II (c. 2300–2000 B.C.E.), and these periods are only represented by pottery and other artifacts discovered in tombs on the west side of the mound. It should be noted that late Bronze Age pottery was also found, though these were found in eight of the tombs only. During the 1960s an additional 18 burial caves were uncovered. These had been hewn out of the limestone western slopes of the hill and were in use during the MB I and LB I periods.

The Iron Age I Period (c. 1200–1000 B.C.) at the site consisted of a massive city wall, 10.5–11 ft. (3.2–3.4 m.) in width, which was built around the hill. Two water systems were discovered; they were constructed in the Iron Age to provide the inhabitants of the city with water in the time of siege. The first system was a rock-hewn shaft, 37 ft. (11.3 m.) in diameter and 35.5 ft. (10.8 m.) deep. A spiral staircase (79 steps) was cut along the north and east sides of the pool. At the bottom, the stairs continued into a tunnel to provide access to the water chamber which lies 44.5 ft. (13.6 m.) below the floor of the pool. Thus the inhabitants had access to water lying 80 ft. (24.4 m.) below the level of the city. It has been estimated that 3,000 tons of limestone were quarried and removed to create the "pool of Gibeon" mentioned in II Sam. 2:13. The second system was the stepped tunnel which led from inside the city to the spring of the village. This system was constructed later in the Iron Age II, possibly due to the flow of the water into the chamber which was deemed inadequate.

The wealth of Gibeon may be demonstrated by the winery discovered there; the flat lands around the site were suitable for agricultural production and the slopes beyond were suitable for vineyards. The Karstic character of the soil meant there were many springs, of which the largest was at Gibeon. This flourishing economy is evidenced by the large number of pots found, as well as by the frequent occurrences of wine cellars. About 40 such cellars have been discovered. These were cistern-like constructions, each 6 ft. (2 m.) deep and dug out of the rock. The jars inside each cellar held about 45 liters of wine. In the same area wine presses were also found; they were carved from the rock with channels for conducting the grape juice into fermentation tanks. It is estimated that the cellars provided storage space for jars containing 25,000 gallons of wine. There were smaller jars which had been used to export the wine produced at Gibeon. Stoppers and a funnel for filling the jars were also found.

The studies by Demsky (1971) and Yeivin (1971) have demonstrated that there is a link between the names inscribed on the jar handles and Saul's genealogy lists in I Chronicles (8:29–40; 9:35–44). The studies of these genealogies provide some evidence relating to the Benjaminites' settlement in their territory. Demsky attests that these lists present at one and the same time the history of the branch of the Ner family, as well as the clans and villages that depended on Gibeon both culturally and administratively. This list is also an illustration of the relationship of the clans to each other and to Gibeon, one which would not have changed from the time of the initial Benjaminites settlement until the Exile. Yeivin suggests that after the Benjaminites' penetration there must have been a considerable integration with the local inhabitants, mainly through marriage, the results of which are reflected in the genealogical lists in Chronicles. These lists are not concerned with the Gibeonites at Gibeon, but with the Benjaminite group which came to settle at Gibeon in the course of time. Their eponymous ancestor is called "the father of Gibeon" in I Chronicles 8:29–40 and its duplicate in 9:35–44). In the first list his personal name is not given, whereas in the second list he is named as Yehiel.

The most interesting aspect of these lists is the naming of the wife of "the father of Gibeon" as Maacah. This name does not appear as an Israelite name, but is the name of an Aramean principality in the Golan. When it appears as a personal name it always represents a non-Israelite or someone of non-Israelite descent. This reference to the non-Israelite Maacah may express itself in intermarriage with the local women. Such intermarriages probably resulted in acquisition of rights of heritage and property. The "father of Gibeon" could indicate the head of a large family, quite wealthy and influential. Saul's ancestors are recorded as Kish, Ner … and Benjamin, that is, in ascending order from the smaller to the larger unit. Also in I Samuel 9:1 Kish, Saul's father, is described as *gibbor ḥayil*, which is also taken to mean a man of wealth.

BIBLIOGRAPHY: Z. Ben-Barak, "The Legal Background to the Restoration of Michal to David", in: D.J.A. Clines and T.C. Eskenazi (eds.), *Telling Queen Michal's Story* (JSOTS sup. 119), 74–90; J. Blenkinsopp, *Gibeon and Israel* (1972); idem, "Did Saul Make Gibeon his Capital," in: *Vetus Tesamentum* 24 (1974), 1–7; A. Demsky, "The Genealogy of Gibeon (1 Chronicles 9.35–44): Biblical and Epigraphic Considerations," in: *Bulletin of the American School of Oriental Research* 202 (1971), 16–23; J.B. Pritchard, *Gibeon Where the Sun Stood Still* (1962); idem, "Gibeon," in: M. Avi-Yona and E. Stern (eds.), EAEHL (OUP, 1976), 446–50; S. Shalom Brooks, *Saul and the Monarchy: A New Look* (2005); S. Yeivin, "The Benjaminite Settlement in the Western Part of Their Territory," in: IEJ 21 (1954), 141–54;

[Simcha Shalom Brooks (2nd ed.)]

GIBEONITES AND NETHINIM (Heb. גִּבְעֹנִים, נְתִינִים). The Gibeonites, residents of four important cities in the vicinity of Jerusalem, feared that they might share the fate of Jericho and Ai, which were destroyed by the Israelites, and tricked *Joshua into a treaty that would spare them (Josh. 9). Had Joshua known that these people were actually Canaanites whom he was pledged to dispossess, he would not have concluded a treaty with them, but the Gibeonites had disguised themselves as coming from a distant land, and had made overtures of devotion to the God of Israel. As they were returning to their nearby cities, the ruse was discovered, but by that time the Israelites were bound by the treaty, and could not drive them out or destroy their cities, which were strategically located to control access to Jerusalem and the roads through the Judean mountains. As a result of this treaty, five Canaanite rulers immediately formed a coalition under the king of Jerusalem and attacked Gibeon. Under the terms of the treaty, the Gibeonites called upon Joshua to come to their aid, and he routed the Canaanite coalition (Josh. 10; cf. 11:19). Thus deceived by the Gibeonites, the Israelites adopted an alternative measure, that of forced labor: "On that day Joshua gave them over to be hewers of wood and drawers of water for the assembly and for the altar of the Lord until this day, at the place which He will choose" (Josh. 9:27). The Gibeonites appear again in connection with a famine during the reign of *David (II Sam. 21). David learned that the famine was a punishment for an offense committed by *Saul, who had put a number of Gibeonites to death out of zeal for Israel and Judah, but in violation of Israel's ancient oath. In expiation, David was obliged to hang seven of Saul's descendants on a hill at Gibeath-Shaul, where Saul had resided, and where at least some of his descendants undoubtedly still lived.

The designation Nethinim is derived from the Hebrew verb *natan* ("to give over"), which can mean devoting someone to cultic service. The verb is used in this sense with respect to Joshua's action toward the Gibeonites in Joshua 9:27, where cultic servitude is involved ("for the altar of the Lord"). The Book of Ezra (8:20) states that David and his commanders "devoted" (Heb. *natan*) the Nethinim "to the service of the *levites" which may reflect the ancient practice of committing captives and conquered peoples to temple slavery, which was a widespread phenomenon in the ancient Near East. The Bible itself offers other indications of its operation in ancient Israel. Many modern scholars consider that such was the status of the Nethinim, and cite certain data in support of this view. The Nethinim are listed together with "the sons of the servants of Solomon" in the census of Israelites returning from Babylonia in about 538 B.C.E. (Ezra 2 = Nehemiah 7), and the latter are generally considered to have been royal slaves. Furthermore, a large number of foreign names in the list of Nethinim suggests that they were captives of war.

There are, however, counterindications. It is possible that "servants of Solomon" were not slaves but royal merchants (see: Servants of *Solomon). The verb *natan*, discussed above, need not necessarily imply servitude, but was used to designate other types of cultic devotion as well. It was applied to the levites, who were hardly temple slaves, and was used to characterize a relationship to the cultic establishment which was primarily administrative and religious; one not based on the economic institution of temple property, under which temple slaves are to be classified.

A later tradition identifies the Gibeonites of Joshua's time with the Nethinim mentioned in the post-Exilic literature. This tradition probably arose in Palestine during the late Hellenistic or early Roman period, at a time when the Jews had become familiar with temple slavery among the pagans, especially in the form of sacred prostitution. It was probably known to the historian Josephus of the first Christian century who translates the term Nethinim in Ezra, chapter 2, by the Greek term *hierodoulos* (from δούλοι ʿιεροί, "sacred slaves"). On the other hand, it probably arose after the completion of the Septuagint translation to the Bible which never renders Nethinim as *hierodoulos*, but either translates the term literally into Greek as *dedomenoi* (so in I Chron. 9:2), or uses Greek transcriptions of the original Hebrew term. Modern scholarship, though recognizing that identification of the Gibeonites with the Nethinim represents a later tradition, nevertheless tends to accept the identification of the Nethinim as "uncircumcised" temple personnel, such as those referred to by Ezekiel (44:7). Conclusive clarification of the exact social status and precise cultic functions of the Nethinim must await further evidence, but the possibility that they represented a guild of free cultic practitioners should not be disregarded.

I Chronicles 9:1–2 states that in the days of David the Nethinim were among the first settlers in the land, but they are never actually mentioned in the pre-Exilic books of Samuel and Kings, nor in any other biblical book presumed to be pre-Exilic. Some scholars claim that this term occurs in Numbers 3:9 and 8:19, which speaks of the dedication of the levites; however, this is unlikely, and it is better to take the repeated *netunim netunim* ("devoted, yea, devoted") as mere passive participles. Although Ezra 8:20 associates the Nethinim with the levites, they are left as two separate groups elsewhere in the Bible (cf. Ezra 2; 7:7; Neh. 10:29; 11:3; I Chron. 9:2). However, there is evidence to support the tradition of I Chronicles 9 concerning the pre-Exilic existence of the Nethinim. A hoard of Hebrew ostraca dating from the last days of the kingdom of Judah has been uncovered at the site of ancient *Arad in the Negev, where an Israelite sanctuary was in use throughout most of the pre-Exilic period. An official named "the Kerosite" appears in one of the ostraca. The personal name Keros otherwise occurs only once, and that in the list of Nethinim in Ezra 2:44 (= Neh. 7:47): "the sons of Keros." Therefore it is probable that the Kerosite at Arad was a member of a group of Nethinim, who would logically be located at a sanctuary. If true, this would be the first contemporary attestation of the existence of Nethinim in the pre-Exilic period. Evidence of a comparative nature also suggests that the Nethinim were a very ancient group. The administrative archives at Ugarit have yielded a list of *ytnm*, the Ugaritic form of Hebrew *nethinim* (C.H. Gordon, *Ugaritic Text-Book*, 301:1, 1). They are also mentioned in a poetic ritual text (*ibid.*, 52:3) and it is reasonable to consider them some sort of cultic personnel, as in Palestine. One of the families or groups of *ytnm* at Ugarit had the same name as a group of Nethinim listed in Ezra (cf. Ugaritic *bn ḥgby, ibid.*, 301:2, 5 with *benei Hagab, Hagabah* in Ezra 2:45–46). It is therefore possible that the Nethinim were an international group of persons skilled in certain cultic arts, who had attached themselves to the Israelites at an early period. The manner in which they are listed suggests that they were organized according to family groups, as was customary.

Akkadian sources also throw light on the semantic and institutional background of the Nethinim. Neo-Babylonian documents refer to members of a religious order dedicated to the service of different Babylonian deities, called *širku*, "devotees, oblates" (from Akk. *šarāku*, "to give, present"). This word is the semantic equivalent of the Hebrew Nethinim, and the members of both orders were temple servitors (Speiser). The Bible provides several more references to the Nethinim which are instructive. About the middle of the fifth century B.C.E. Ezra recruited Nethinim along with other personnel preparatory to his return to Judah (Ezra 7:7, 24; 8:1–20). Nehemiah 3 describes the resettlement of Jerusalem, whose recruited population of skilled persons included Nethinim. In about 438 B.C.E. the leaders of the people convoked a great assembly in Jerusalem to ratify a new covenant (Neh. 10:1–40), and the Nethinim were among the principal signatories (10:29; cf.

11:3). Only *bona fide* Israelites would have been admitted to the covenant, especially at a time when there was great concern in rooting out foreign strains from the community.

[Baruch A. Levine]

Post-Biblical Period

Nothing more is heard of the Nethinim until they appear in the legislation of the Mishnah which classes them with proselytes, freedmen, *mamzerim*, waifs, and foundlings with whom alone they are permitted to intermarry (Kid. 4:1). The Mishnah (Hor. 3:8), however, classifies the Nethinim as being one level lower than *mamzerim* but preceding proselytes and freedmen. They were regarded as the descendants of the Gibeonites (Yev. 78b–79a) and the prohibition in their marrying Jews of pure pedigree as having been established by King David (*ibid.* 78b) and reconfirmed by Ezra (Num. R. 8:4). It is impossible to explain this loss of status since the days of Nehemiah. It is possible that, in employing the classification Nethinim, the talmudic sages did not have the actual biblical group in mind at all, but merely reapplied an ancient term to contemporary groups of declassed persons who were the subject of their own legislation, thus stigmatizing them with traditional associations. An attempt by the rabbis to abolish the inferior status of the Nethinim was rejected by Judah ha-Nasi on the grounds that when the Temple was rebuilt it would be deprived of hewers of wood and drawers of water, and the matter was relegated to "the time to come" (Yev. 79b). Maimonides, too, regards the Nethinim as the descendants of the Gibeonites (Yad, Issurei Bi'ah 12:23–24).

Gibeonites in the *Aggadah*

Although the Gibeonites deserved no better fate than all the rest of the Canaanite nations, in that the covenant made with them was obtained through subterfuge, Joshua nevertheless kept his promise to them, in order to show the world the sanctity of an oath to Israel (Git. 46a). He hesitated to defend them when they were attacked, but God reminded him, "If you estrange those who are distant you will ultimately estrange also those who are near" (Num. R. 8:4). In the course of time it became obvious that the Gibeonites were not worthy of being received into the Jewish fold and Joshua, therefore, left their fate to be decided by the one who was to build the Temple (TJ, Sanh. 6:9, 23c–d).

During David's reign Israel suffered from a drought which was ascertained to be God's punishment for the murder of seven Gibeonites by the descendants of Saul. When David sought to make restitution through ransom, the Gibeonites firmly refused, insisting upon lives from the household of Saul. This cold-bloodedness clearly demonstrated to David the absence in the Gibeonite character of Israel's three basic attributes – mercy, humility, and benevolence – and he consequently excluded them from the assembly of Israel (TJ, Kid. 4:1, 65c). Ezra renewed the edict, which is to be in force even in the Messianic era (*ibid.*).

BIBLIOGRAPHY: B.A. Levine, in: JBL, 82 (1963), 207–12 (incl. bibl.); idem, in: IEJ, 19 (1969), 49–51; M. Haran, in: VT, 11 (1961), 159–69; E.A. Speiser, in: IEJ, 13 (1963), 69–73; Ginzberg, Legends, index.

GIBRALTAR, British crown colony, south of *Spain. Jews lived in Gibraltar in the 14th century, and in 1356 the community issued an appeal for assistance in the ransoming of Jews captured by pirates. In 1473, a number of Marranos fleeing from Andalusia applied for permission to settle in Gibraltar. The Treaty of Utrecht (1713), which ceded the fortress to England, excluded the Jews from Gibraltar in perpetuity. However, by an agreement in 1729 between England and the sultan of Morocco, his Jewish subjects were empowered to come there temporarily for the purpose of trade, and the establishment of a permanent community was not long delayed. The majority of the Jewish settlers were from adjacent parts of North Africa. By 1749, when the legal right of Jewish settlement was recognized, the community numbered about 600, being about one-third of the total number of civilian residents, and there were two synagogues. During the siege of 1779–83, many took refuge in London, reinforcing the Sephardi community there. Subsequently, the community in Gibraltar resumed its development. During the period of the Napoleonic wars, Aaron Nuñez *Cardozo was one of the foremost citizens of Gibraltar; his house on the Almeida subsequently became the city hall. In the middle of the 19th century, when the Rock was at the height of its importance as a British naval and military base, the Jewish community numbered about 2,000 and most of the retail trade was in their hands, but thereafter the number declined. During World War II, almost all the civilian population, including the Jews, was evacuated to British territories, and not all returned. In 1968, the community numbered 670 (out of a total population of 25,000); it still maintained four synagogues and many communal organizations. Sir Joshua A. *Hassan was the first mayor and chief minister of Gibraltar from 1964 to 1969. In 2004, about 600 Jews lived in Gibraltar, with the same four synagogues and a communal rabbi. Almost all Jewish children attended the community's primary schools and girls went to the Jewish secondary school. The community published a weekly newsletter.

BIBLIOGRAPHY: A.B.M. Serfaty, *Jews of Gibraltar under British Rule* (1958[2]); H.W. Howes, *The Gibraltarian*: Origin and Development of the Population of Gibraltar from 1704 (1950); Beinart, in: *Sefunot*, 5 (1961), 87–88; Cano de Gardoqui and Bethencourt, in: *Hispania*, 103 (1966), 325–81; Hirschberg, in: *Essays Presented … I. Brodie* (1968), 153–81; JYB (1968), 140. **ADD. BIBLIOGRAPHY:** M. Benady, "The Settlement of Jews in Gibraltar, 1704–1783," in: JHSET, 26 (1974–78), 87–110.

[Cecil Roth]

GIDAL, TIM (Ignaz Nachum Gidalewitsch; 1909–1996), photographer. Gidal was born into an Orthodox family of Russian immigrants in Munich. From 1929 he was among the pioneers of modern photojournalism and became one of its leading historians. Based in Jerusalem between 1936 and 1947, and again from 1970, he has achieved an international reputation.

Gidal started taking photographs during his studies (1928–1935) at the universities of Munich, Berlin, and Basle. His photographs were published in the foremost illustrated weeklies in Germany. In 1936 Gidal immigrated to Palestine where he continued his work. In 1938 he moved to London, where he worked for *Picture Post*, the magazine in which the new medium reached its zenith. Between 1942 and 1944 he served as Chief Staff Reporter for *Parade*, the Eighth Army magazine. In 1947 he found a new base in New York where he stayed until 1970, the time of his return to Jerusalem. During this period Gidal and his first wife Sonia traveled the world and produced a series of 23 photographic books, entitled *My Village*. He also served as consultant for *Life* magazine and taught at the New School for Social Research in New York. From 1971, he taught at the Hebrew University of Jerusalem and produced scholarly works and compilation albums including his seminal *Modern Photojournalism: Origin and Evolution 1910–1933* (1972); *Ewiges Jerusalem/Eternal Jerusalem* 1840–1914 (1980) (one of the most beautiful published collections of photographs on Jerusalem); and in 1988, a major work of illustrated history, *The Jews in Germany from Roman Times until the Weimar Republic* (in German). During this period, he also published and exhibited his work in Israel, Europe and the U.S., and in 1983 was awarded the prestigious Dr. Erich Salomon Prize in Germany. His photo-history of Palestine/Israel appeared in the *Encyclopaedia Judaica Year Books* 1973, 1974, and 1975 and were subsequently published in *The Land of Israel: 100 Years Plus 30 (1978).*

Critics have said about Gidal's photography that "it has about it a visual innocence going straight for the subject photographed," but describing his photographs as innocent does not mean that they are necessarily simplistic or naive. Speaking of his own pictures, Gidal insists that he is not an artist. "An artist adds to nature. His personality is an ingredient of his painting. With my camera, I can only use what is already there. Art is expression of the inner self. Photography is a depiction of the outer world."

Gidal sees his photographs "as a variation on the everlasting theme of the tragicomedy of daily life, facts of the human condition. I do not wait until the selected moment satisfies a constructivist formal urge. I am directed more by participating and by intuition." His photography communicates an accomplished sense for simplicity and straightforwardness, representing a balance between his keen sense of form and construction and his respect for the subject itself.

His brother, George Gidal (1908–1931), was also a pioneer photojournalist in Germany whose promising career was cut short by his death in a car accident.

BIBLIOGRAPHY: N. Trow, *Tim Gidal in the Forties* (1981); idem, *Tim Gidal: A Visual Ethic* (1982).

[Yeshayahu Nir]

GIDDAL (end of third century C.E.), Babylonian *amora*. He was one of the best-known younger pupils of *Rav. Most of Giddal's sayings in the Talmud are in the name of this teacher, often via Ḥiyya b. Joseph, but a few in the name of Ḥiyya b. Joseph himself. Once Giddal defended himself by swearing on the Holy Scripture and Prophets that his saying was that of Rav (Er. 17a). After Rav's death he studied in the academy of *Huna in Sura, and there came into contact with *Zeira (Ber. 49a). He appears to have had heated debates with Huna ("Giddal became impotent through the discourses of Huna": Yev. 64b). However, he was also ruled by the decisions of Judah b. Ezekiel of Pumbedita (Av. Zar. 11b). Later in life he went to Palestine (Kid. 59a). He interpreted Song of Songs 5:13 in an allegorical way, to teach that one should not study lightheartedly. "Any scholar who sits before his teacher and his lips do not drip bitterness shall be burnt" (Shab. 30b). He interpreted Psalms 39:7 to the effect that anyone who quotes a saying should imagine himself as standing in the presence of the one who originally said it (TJ, Shab. 1:2, 3a et al.). A man who writes a Torah Scroll was regarded by Giddal as if he had received it at Mount Sinai (Men. 30a). His keen sense of justice is revealed in the story about a field which he intended to buy but was anticipated by another buyer. When Isaac Nappaḥa (the Palestinian) ruled that the owner of the field should sell it to Giddal, he declined even to accept it as a gift (Kid. 59a). This explains his sharp critique of people who dealt unjustly (although he gives it in the name of Rav): "If an inhabitant of Naresh has kissed you, then count your teeth. If a man of Nehar Pekod accompanies you, it is because of the fine garments he sees on you. If a Pumbeditan accompanies you, then change your quarters" (Ḥul. 127a). Giddal was accustomed to sit at the gates of the ritual bath and to instruct the women about the rules of immersion. When asked whether he was not afraid lest his passion get the better of him, he replied that to him the women looked like so many white geese (Ber. 20a).

BIBLIOGRAPHY: Bacher, Pal Amor; Hyman, Toledot, s.v.

GIDEON (Heb. גִּדְעוֹן, derived from גדע; "to cast down"), also called Jerubaal (Heb. יְרֻבַּעַל; "let Baal contend," or "let Baal replace," Judg. 6:32), son of Joash, the Abiezrite from *Ophrah, in the area of the tribe of Manasseh. Gideon is regarded as one of the *Judges although his biography (Judg. 6:11–8:32) does not contain the usual formula that "he judged Israel." He was appointed to leadership in an angelic revelation reinforced by signs and wonders of folkloristic nature, which were intended to confirm his divinely ordained mission and to emphasize his charismatic personality (6:34).

Gideon was destined to deliver Israel from the Midianites and their allies, Amalek and "the children of the east" (6:3; cf. *Midian, *Amalek, *Kedemites (*Benei Kedem*)), described as camel-mounted bedouin who came marauding from the fringes of the desert into the cultivated areas west of the Jordan. In the course of their invasions they menaced those Israelite tribes, especially Manasseh, whose settlements bordered on the Valley of Jezreel. These areas made good targets for plunder, and provided convenient passage to the interior and to the coast. Gideon's brothers appear to have been among those killed in such an attack (8:18–19). At first, only

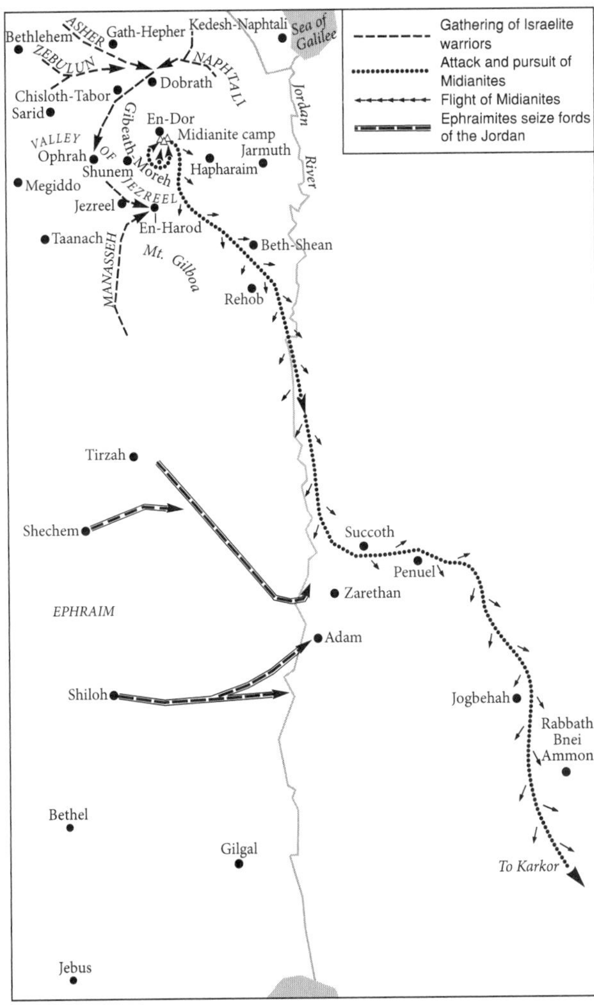

The war of Gideon against the Midianites. After Y. Aharoni and M. Avi-Yonah, Macmillan Bible Atlas, *Carta, Jerusalem, 1968.*

the Abiezrites responded to his call, but he was later joined by the tribes of Asher, Zebulun, and Naphtali (6:34–35; cf. 7:23). From more than 30,000 followers, a carefully selected force of 300 men was assembled at his camp at *En-Harod (7:2–7). Upon gathering intelligence as to the state of the enemy's morale, Gideon struck with a surprise night attack that wrought havoc in the Midianite camp. The Midianites and their allies withdrew eastward to the Jordan, and Gideon summoned support from Naphtali, Asher, Manasseh, and Ephraim to block the escape routes, thereby ambushing the retreating enemy. In the pursuit, two Midianite princes, Oreb and Zeeb, were captured and beheaded (7:25; cf. Ps. 83:12–13). At this point, the Ephraimites complained about their exclusion from the original operations, but Gideon diplomatically settled the affair (Judg. 8:1–3). Gideon then resumed the pursuit of the enemy beyond the Jordan, requesting material support, meanwhile, from the non-Israelite cities of Succoth and Penuel. The rulers of these cities refused, fearing Midianite reprisals should Gideon fail. After decisively defeating the enemy, who retreated deeper into the desert, Gideon returned to Succoth and Penuel to settle accounts there (8:4–21). The military victory over the Midianites was remembered and cited for many generations (Isa. 9:3; 10:26; Ps. 83:10; cf. I Sam. 12:11).

There can be no doubt about the outstanding position Gideon occupied prior to the founding of the monarchy. Not only are his exploits recorded with unwonted detail, but also, and most exceptionally, the narrative is concerned with his post-military activities. Clearly, he enjoyed some special leadership status, though its precise nature is unclear. It is in Gideon's time that we encounter a desire for change from tribal, charismatic rule to a more comprehensive, hereditary type when the "men of Israel" offer to make Gideon the founder of a dynasty (Judg. 8:22). However, it should be noted that the verb employed is "rule" (*mshl*) rather than "reign" (*mlkh*), the word usually employed for kingship. Apparently, the incident represents an intermediary stage in the movement toward the establishment of a permanent monarchy.

Despite his refusal of the offer, Gideon continued to play a leading role. He had a large harem and fathered 70 sons (8:30). Through his concubine in Shechem (8:31) he was related to some of the leading families in that town (9:1–4), and a son born of the union, *Abimelech, was later crowned king of that city-state (9:6). Gideon also exercised authority in the sphere of the cult. At the outset of his career he had built an altar to the Lord at Ophrah and had dared to destroy a local Baal altar, an act which earned him the name *Jerubaal (6:24–32; cf. I Sam. 12:11; II Sam. 11:21). Subsequent to his military victories he fashioned an *ephod from the spoils of war (Judg. 8:24–27), which, while it did not meet with the approval of the editor of Judges, illustrates the deeply religious character of Gideon.

[Nahum M. Sarna]

In the Aggadah

Gideon, Jephthah, and Samson were the three least worthy of the Judges (RH 25a and b). Because on the eve of one Passover Gideon said of the Lord, "Where are all the miracles which God did for our fathers on this night" (Judg. 6:13), he was chosen to save Israel (Yal. Judg. 62) and that victory was also gained on Passover (cf. Yannai, *"Az Rov Nissim,"* Passover *Haggadah*). Another reason was his filial piety (Mid. Hag., Gen. 48:16). When Gideon sacrificed his father's bullock after the angel appeared to him, he would have transgressed no less than seven commandments, were it not that he was obeying an explicit divine command (TJ, Meg. 1:14, 72c). The cake of barley bread seen by the Midianite soldier in his dream (Judg. 7:13) indicated that the children of Israel would be vouchsafed victory as a reward for bringing the offering of an omer of barley (Lev. R. 28:6). On the breastplate of the high priest the tribe of Joseph was represented by Ephraim alone. To remove this slight upon his own tribe Manasseh, he had a new ephod made after his victory, bearing the name of Manasseh. Although he consecrated it to God, after his death it became an object of adoration (Yalkut, Judg. 64). He is identified with Jerubaal of I Samuel 12:11 and from the juxtaposition of this name in that verse with that of Samuel, the rabbis deduce that even the most worthless of individuals, once he is appointed as leader of the community, is to be accounted as the greatest (RH 25a and b).

In the Arts

Literary works on this theme have tended to stress Gideon's heroism and patriotic motivation. Probably the first treatment occurs in the early 17th-century Old Testament dramatic cycle known as the *Stonyhurst Pageants*, in which an English writer devoted some 300 lines to the Hebrew judge. Several works in verse and prose dealt with the subject from the 18th century onward, including *Gideon; or the Patriot* (London, 1749), a fragmentary epic poem by the English dramatist Aaron Hill, a rival of Alexander Pope. In the 20th century, Grete Moeller wrote the verse play *Gideon* (Ger., 1927), two other dramas being August Schmidlin's *Gedeon, biblisches Heldendrama… aus der Zeit der Richter* (1932) and *Gideon* (1953), a "tragedy in 22 scrolls" by the Yiddish writer David *Ignatoff. An unusual modern interpretation of the story was the U.S. writer Paddy *Chayefsky's play *Gideon* (1962), which dramatizes man's alternate dependence on and rebellion against God.

In art the typology of Gideon is particularly subtle. The miracle of the fleece was interpreted as a symbol of the Jews, first chosen and favored (or wet), and then rejected (or dry). The fleece also became the emblem of the Burgundian Order of the Golden Fleece, one of the supreme honors of knighthood. Gideon is usually represented as a knight in armor, helmeted, and with a broken pitcher in his hand, as in the 17th-century statue in Antwerp Cathedral. Narrative cycles are rare (though Chartres offers a 13th-century sequence of four episodes) with most representations concentrating on the appearance of the angel, the miracle of the fleece and the dew, the selection of the 300 warriors, or the victory over the Midianites. The angel's appearance and Gideon's incredulity, seen as a prefiguration of the Annunciation, are depicted at Chartres and in the tapestry of La Chaise-Dieu (1510). The miracle of the fleece occurs frequently at Chartres; in the Amiens and Avignon cathedrals (15th century); in the *Petites Heures d'Anne de Bretagne* (15th century); in a 16th-century fresco in Chilandari, Mount Athos; and in a fresco by Salvator Rosa (1615–1673) in the Quirinal. The selection of the warriors is illustrated in the French *Psalter of Saint Louis* and the English *Queen Mary's Psalter* (both dating from the 13th century) and by Federico Zuccaro (1540/43–1609) in a drawing at the Louvre. The victory is again portrayed at Chartres.

An early musical interpretation of the Gideon theme occurs in *Daz Gedeones wollenvlius* ("Gideon's Woollen Fleece"), an allegorical song by the *minnesaenger* Rumelant (c. 1270), which typically combines the search for biblical prototypes of the knightly ideal with the mystical concept of divine love. The martial atmosphere also prevails in at least some of the later compositions on this subject, beginning with "Gideon – Der Heyland Israels," the fifth of J. Kuhnau's *Biblische Sonaten* for keyboard instrument (1700). Johann Mattheson's oratorio *Der siegende Gideon*, written for the Hamburg celebration of Prince Eugene of Savoy's victory at Belgrade (1717), was begun, completed, and performed in the record time of 11 days. One of J. Chr. Smith's oratorios for which the music was taken wholly or largely from Handel was his *Gideon* (1769). Other compositions inspired by the subject include oratorios by Friedrich Schneider (1829) and Charles Edward Horsley (1959) and a choral work for eight male voices, *Les soldats de Gédéon* (1868), by Camille Saint-Saëns.

BIBLIOGRAPHY: Bright, Hist, index; S. Tolkowski, in: JPOS, 5 (1925), 69–74; Malamat, in: PEQ, 85 (1953), 61–65; Yeivin, in: *Zion Me'assef*, 4 (1930), 1ff.; idem, in: *Ma'arakhot*, 26–27 (1945), 67ff.; idem, in: BIES, 14 (1949), 85ff.; Kutscher, *ibid.*, 2 (1934), 40–42; Kaufmann Y., Toledot, 2 (1942), 118; M. Buber, *Koenigtum Gottes* (19362), 3–12, 27–30; Ginzberg, Legends, 4 (1913), 39f.; 6 (1928), 199f. **IN ART:** G. Reese, *Music in the Middle Ages* (1940), 235–6; L. Réau, *Iconographie de l'art chrétien*, 2 pt. 1 (1956), 230–4. **ADD. BIBLIOGRAPHY:** R. Boling, in: ABD, 2:1013–15.

GIDEON, MIRIAM (1906–1996), U.S. composer of choral and orchestral works. Gideon was born in Greeley, Colorado, to Abram Gideon, a professor of philosophy and ordained rabbi, and Henrietta Shoninger Gideon, a teacher. Gideon's choice of a career in music was influenced by her uncle Henry Gideon, an organist and choir director at Temple Israel in Boston, with whom she spent summers. She studied piano and composition while attending Boston University, graduating in 1926 with a degree in French and mathematics. Gideon continued her musical studies in New York City, ultimately earning an M.A. from Columbia in 1946. She taught at several institutions in New York City, including City College, the Jewish Theological Seminary (1955–91), and the Manhattan School of Music (1967–91). In 1970, she received a Doctorate of Sacred Music in Composition, from the Jewish Theological Seminary. She married Frederick Ewen, an English professor, in 1949.

Gideon wrote over 50 compositions covering the gamut from orchestral to vocal chamber works. Her early choral settings include *Slow, Slow Fresh Fount* (1941) and *Sweet Western Wind* (1943). She turned to contrapuntal vocal chamber work with *The Hound of Heaven* (1945). In 1948, she was awarded the Bloch Prize for choral work for *How Goodly Are Thy Tents – Psalm 84* (1947), a work in a modal idiom with Jewish melodic contours. Early orchestral works were *Lyric Piece for String Orchestra* (1944) and a full orchestral work, *Symphonia Brevis* (1953). Works with Jewish themes included *May the Word of My Mouth* (premiere, 1938), *Adon Olom* (1954), *Three Biblical Masks* (1958), and the cantata *The Habitable Earth* (1965), based on the Book of Proverbs. Her more important vocal chamber works include *The Condemned Playground* (1963), *Questions on Nature* (1964), *Rhymes from the Hill* (1968), and *Nocturnes* (1976).

Gideon was the first woman ever commissioned to set Jewish liturgy. She completed *Sacred Service for Sabbath Morning* (1971), based on Reform liturgy, for The Temple, Cleveland, Ohio. *Shirat Miriam L'Shabbat,* for Conservative liturgy, was completed in 1974 for Park Avenue Synagogue and published in 1976. Later Jewish text settings include *Eishet Chayil (A Woman of Valor)* (1982). Her sacred compositions reflect the influences of her exposure to synagogue music, yet remain introspective and personal. Awards include an ASCAP, for symphonic music (1958); National Federation of Music Clubs (1969); and a National Endowment for the Arts Award (1974). In 1975, she became the second woman ever admitted to the American Academy and Institute of Arts and Letters.

[Judith S. Pinnolis (2nd ed.)]

GIDEON, SAMSON (originally **Gideon Abudiente**; 1699–1762), English financier. His father Reuel Gideon Abudiente (c. 1655–1722), a West India merchant in London, was descended from the Hamburg scholar of the same name. Gideon early made a considerable fortune by speculation. In the mid-18th century, he was the principal agent for raising English government loans. His advice helped to preserve the financial stability of the country during the Jacobite rebellion in 1745. During the Seven Years' War (1755–63), he advised the English government in financial matters, and in 1758 was thanked by the king for his services in raising a loan for Hanover. Gideon left more than £500,000. In his younger days he supported the synagogue, and in 1720 contributed a sonnet in English to the Spanish translation of the Psalms by D. Lopez *Laguna. Subsequently, however, he bought a country estate, married out of the faith, had his children baptized, and, on the pretext of disapproving of the Jewish Naturalization Bill (1753), resigned his synagogue membership. He continued nevertheless to contribute to the synagogue secretly and left it a large legacy on the condition that he would be buried in its cemetery. By 1750 Gideon had obtained a coat of arms for himself and was a substantial landowner. In 1757 his daughter married Viscount Gage. In 1759 he obtained the title of baronet for his son, also SAMSON GIDEON (1745–1824), who became Lord Eardley in 1789. The son had no contacts with Judaism. In 1770 he was elected to Parliament, the first member of Parliament to have known Jewish ancestry. He was also the first person of known Jewish ancestry to be granted a peerage in Britain. Among his descendants was Hugh Culling Eardley Childers (1827–1896), who was chancellor of the Exchequer in 1882–85.

BIBLIOGRAPHY: Sutherland, in: JHSET, 17 (1953), 79–90; A.M. Hyamson, *Sephardim of England* (1951), 128–33; C. Roth, *Anglo-Jewish Letters* (1938), 130–2, 176. **ADD. BIBLIOGRAPHY:** ODNB online; Katz, England, 248–49, 267–71; T. Endelman, *Jews of Georgian England*, 28–31, 139–40, 255–56; M. Jolles, *Directory of Distinguished British Jews*, 75.

[Cecil Roth / William D. Rubinstein (2nd ed.)]

GIEHSE, THERESE (1898–1975), German actress. Giehse was born as Therese Gift to the textile merchant Salomon Gift and his wife, Gertrude, in Munich. Between 1918 and 1920 she took acting lessons and made her debut at the Buehnenverein in Munich (1920). She adopted the name Giehse, and after engagements at various provincial theaters worked under Paul Barnay (1884–1960) in Breslau (now Wroclaw, Poland). Otto Falckenberg (1873–1947), then director of the Muenchner Kammerspiele, invited her to join his ensemble in 1925 where she stayed until 1933 and also got to know the *Mann family. Giehse, Erika Mann, and Klaus Mann founded the Literarische Cabaret – "Die Pfeffermuehle" in 1933 in response to the Nazi rise to power. She immigrated via Austria to Switzerland in March 1933 because of the increasing political pressure and refounded Die Pfeffermuehle. During her exile in Zurich (1933–37) she also toured in various European and American cities and through her marriage to British actor John Hampson-Simpson became a British citizen (1936). From 1937 on she worked at the Zuericher Schauspielhaus and starred in the world premieres of Bertold Brecht's plays *Mutter Courage und ihre Kinder* (1941), *Der gute Mann von Sezuan* (1943), and *Herr Puntila und sein Knecht Matti* (1948). She performed at various theaters in Munich, Berlin, and Zurich from 1949 to 1952 and had successes with major roles in plays by Friedrich Duerrenmatt like *Der Besuch der alten Dame* (1956) and *Die Physiker* (1962). In 1954 she returned to Munich and had various roles in film, radio, and theater productions. She was awarded the Bundesfilmpreis/Filmband in Silber (1955).

BIBLIOGRAPHY: W. Drews, *Die Schauspielerin Therese Giehse* (1965); M. Sperr, *Therese Giehse – "Ich hab nichts zum Sagen"* (1973); M. Piekenbrock, *Therese Giehse 1898–1998* (Deutsches Theatermuseum Muenchen, 2000); I. Hildebrandt, "Pfeffer ueber Zuerich – Therese Giehse, Erika Mann und die Pfeffermuehle," in: I. Hildebrandt (ed.), *Frauen die Geschichte schreiben* (2002), 235–62; M. Karl, "Therese Giehse – Die Mutter Courage," in: M. Karl (ed.), *Bayerische Amazonen* (2004), 151–67.

[Bjoern Siegel (2nd ed.)]

GIESSEN, city in Hesse, Germany. A persecution of the Jews took place there in 1350. Jews are again mentioned in 1375. In the 17th century the few dozen Jews of Giessen were compelled to listen to missionary sermons by Christian preachers. In 1662 they were expelled from the town. Jews were permitted to return and to settle in Giessen in 1708. Some Hebrew printing took place in Giessen during the 17th and 18th centuries, most of it by non-Jewish printers. The community numbered 200 in 1828, 458 in 1871, and 1,035 (3.3% of the total population) in 1925. In 1933, under the Nazi regime, Richard Laqueur, rector of the university, was dismissed from his office because he was Jewish, as were F.M. *Heichelheim, K. *Koffka, Erich *Stern, and Margarete *Bieber. The synagogues erected in 1867 and 1899 were destroyed during *Kristallnacht in November 1938. By the end of the year 730 of the out of the 1,265 Jews living in Giessen and its environs in 1933 had left. The last Jews were deported in September 1942. There were 27 Jews living in Giessen in 1967 and around 200 at the beginning of the 21st century.

BIBLIOGRAPHY: Germ Jud, 2 (1968), 278–9; PK; A. Freimann, *A Gazetteer of Hebrew Printing* (1946).

[Akiva Posner]

GIFT, the transfer of legal rights without any consideration or payment. It is essentially no more than a sale without payment and all the principles of the law of sale apply (see *Sale).

The *Da'at* of the Parties

The decision (*gemirat ha-da'at*) of the parties to conclude a gift transaction – the intention of one to give and the other to receive – is established by means of an act of *kinyan*, i.e., by the performance of one of the recognized acts whereby property is acquired (see *Acquisition, Modes of). Upon performance of the *kinyan*, ownership of the property passes from the donor to the donee and neither may any longer withdraw from the transaction. The test as to whether or not the *gemirat ha-da'at* exists is an objective one, namely: if the parties performed an act customarily performed by people in order to conclude such a transaction and if in the particular circumstances of the case there existed no reason why most people would not conclude the transaction, the gift will be effective (Kid. 49b). A gift may be conferred on a person without his knowledge, because it is assumed that he agrees to get a benefit, the rule being that "a benefit may be conferred on a person in his absence, but an obligation may only be imposed on him in his presence" (Git. 11b). Similarly, the *gemirat ha-da'at* of the parties does not require a *consensus ad idem* between the parties. If it is manifest that the donor made up his mind to effect the gift, whereas the donee has not made up his mind to receive it, the latter may retract but the former may not, since the *gemirat ha-da'at* of a party to a transaction precludes him from retracting from it. Consequently, when a person confers a gift on another through a third party, the donee may refuse to accept it until it has reached his hands, even if he has heard of the intended gift – but the donor may not withdraw, since the person acquiring the gift on behalf of the donee performed a *kinyan* whereby the donor's decision to conclude the transaction was made (Yad, Zekhiyyah 4:2). If the donee should discover a defect in the gift, and it is of such nature that people would generally not want such a gift, the donee may retract even after the gift has come to his hands (*Kesef Mishneh*, Zekhiyyah 4:1, concl.).

When it is manifest to all that there was an absence of *gemirat ha-da'at* on the part of both parties, the transaction will be void. A person cannot transfer to another, by way of a gift, something which is not yet in existence, or which is not his own; nor can a gift be conferred on someone who is not yet born; nor can a gift be conferred of something which one owns but which is not at the present time in his possession, such as where the owner has been robbed (see *Theft and Robbery). According to some scholars, however, even these kinds of gifts may validly be conferred in certain circumstances (see *Sale). Similarly, if a person promises a valuable gift to another verbally, but without a *kinyan*, so that the latter does not rely on the promise, there would not even be any moral sanction against him if he should withdraw (BM 49a).

If it is clear, notwithstanding an act of *kinyan*, that the donor did not really intend to effect the gift (for example, he was compelled to make the gift under duress), it will be void. Even if there was no duress, but prior to the gift the donor had declared before witnesses that he was not making it of his own free will, the transaction will also be void, even if the witnesses were not themselves aware of any duress exercised against him, because by his declaration he manifests an intention of not making the gift (Yad, Zekhiyyah 5:4; see **Ones*). Moreover, as a gift must be made openly and publicly, an undisclosed gift is invalid, since "the donor is not presumed to have made up his mind to a gift, but is scheming for the loss of other people's property" (*ibid.* 5:1). Similarly, if a person makes a written disposition of all his property to one of his sons, the latter does not acquire it all since the assumption is that the father intended to do no more than appoint this son administrator so that his brothers should accept his authority. This is also the case if he made a disposition in favor of his wife. However, where he disposes of only part of his assets to his wife or son, or where he expressly states that an absolute gift is intended, the gift will be effective (*ibid.* 6:2–4). A gift by a woman before her marriage by way of a written disposition in favor of a person other than her prospective husband becomes ineffective if the latter should die or be divorced from her, since the disposition of her assets to another was made in order to keep these from her husband in the event of his inheriting her (*ibid.* 6:12). On the other hand, one who gives money for *kiddushin* (*marriage) which is known to be invalid, e.g., to one's own sister, intends to do so for the sake of gift (Kid. 46b). According to another opinion he gives the money as bailment.

A deaf-mute, an idiot, and a minor lack the legal capacity to make a gift, since they have no *da'at*, but the scholars prescribed that minors or deaf-mutes, depending on the degree of their understanding of the nature of the transaction, may effectively make certain gifts, by virtue of the rule of "for the sake of his sustenance" (Yad, Mekhirah 29; see *Sale). According to many opinions, they may also receive gifts, even in terms of biblical law (Tos. to Kid. 19a). The sages also prescribed that someone may acquire and receive a gift on behalf of a minor, even if the latter is no more than one day old (Rashbam to BB 156b).

Conditions of the Gift

The donor may make the gift conditional upon certain terms, failing which the gift will be void (see *Conditions). As in the case of a sale, the stipulating party must impose his conditions in such a manner as to make it clear and known to all that he intends in all seriousness that the gift be considered void if the conditions should not be fulfilled and that he is not merely making a statement at large (Yad, Zekhiyyah 3:6–7). When it is apparent from the circumstances that he intends to make his gift subject to the happening of certain events, the condition will be operative even if not expressly stated and, at times, even if not stated at all (Tos. to Kid. 49b). Thus a gift would be void if made by a person who transfers all his assets to another on hearing of his son's death, but subsequently finds out that his son is still alive – since the circumstances show that he would not have given away all his assets if he had known that his son was really alive (BB 164b). Similarly, a gift made to the family of one's bride is returnable, if the marriage should fail to take place and the gift was not of a perishable kind (*ibid.*). So too, where it is customary for wedding gifts to be sent to a friend in order that the latter shall give his own similar gifts to the donor upon his own marriage; the latter may claim such from the former if they are not given, gifts of this kind being regarded as similar to loans (Yad, Zekhiyyah 7).

The donor may stipulate that the gift is to be returned, in which event the gift is valid but the recipient is obliged to return it after the expiry of the stipulated period. During this stipulated period, however, this gift is the property of the recipient, like all his other property; but after the stipulated period, the recipient must return the property to its former owner, and failure to do so will amount to the nonfulfillment of a condition, voiding the transaction of a gift *ab initio* (Sh. Ar., ḤM 241:6). Similarly, the donor may stipulate that he is making a gift, first for the benefit of one person and then for another (see *Wills). Where the true intention of the donor is in doubt, his ultimate purpose may be deduced with the aid of the rule that "he who gives a gift gives in a liberal spirit." Thus if one says, "give to so-and-so a house capable of holding 100 barrels," and it is found to hold 120 barrels, the donee will have acquired the whole house (BB 71a). Generally, no responsibility is imposed in connection with the gift, and if it should be foreclosed, the donee will have no recourse against the donor, unless expressly provided for between the parties (Yad, Shekherim 13:1).

In the State of Israel the rules of gift are ordered in terms of the Gift Law, 1968, consisting of six material paragraphs. On the question of the degree of its reliance on Jewish law, see Elon in bibliography.

[Shalom Albeck]

In the State of Israel

INTERSPOUSAL GIFT. Issues involving the Gift Law frequently arise in the rabbinical courts in the context of division of property between a husband and wife in the course of divorce (see *Divorce; *Joint Property).

In File 2319/42, 13 PDR 144, the wife claimed that she was entitled to 50 percent of the rights in the apartment, based on the fact that the apartment was registered in the Land Registry Office in the name of both spouses. The husband claimed that the apartment was purchased with his money and that it was mistakenly registered in the wife's name as well, since he did not know at the time that she was mentally ill, and upon becoming aware of her mental illness he had immediately filed for divorce. The District Rabbinical Court in Tel Aviv ruled that, even if the apartment was purchased exclusively with the husband's money, he could not have done so without the loan that he received from the Housing Ministry, and this loan is only granted if the apartment is registered in the name of both spouses. Consequently, registration of the apartment in both of their names must be regarded as an unconditional gift made by the husband to his wife. The rabbinical court accordingly held that half the apartment did indeed belong to the wife.

An additional question in this field arose before the Supreme Court in the case of *Boehm* (HCJ 609/92 *Boehm v. The Rabbinical Court of Appeals*, 47(3) PD 288). A petition was filed to reverse the decision of the Rabbinical Court of Appeals, ruling that the apartment of a couple divorced as a result of the wife's infidelity would belong solely to the husband, because the half-interest in the apartment given by the husband to his wife was given on the condition that she not betray her husband. Even though this condition had not been expressly written or stipulated orally, the rabbinical court inferred that there had been an implied condition to that effect, based on the parties' presumed intention. (In addition, the Court ruled that the husband's offer to give the wife 30% of the value of the apartment as a compromise was not binding upon him once the wife refused the offer.) The appellant's argument was that the decision violated civil law principles in effect in the State of Israel, regarding equal rights of women as expressed in the Woman's Equal Rights Law, 5711 – 1952, and provisions of the Gift Law, 5728 – 1968, with respect to the possibility of revoking a gift. It also contradicted the provisions of the Basic Law: Human Dignity and Freedom.

The Supreme Court (*per* Justice Menachem Elon) ruled that, "as a factual finding had been made that the apartment was purchased with the husband's money, and that legally, the act constituted an interspousal gift, the Court's task was solely to ascertain what the parties presumably intended to accomplish by that act." As such, the issue did not concern the woman's equal rights or basic rights (p. 294 of the decision, *ibid.*). In addition, the Court ruled that, since the rabbinical court has jurisdiction to decide the matter, it must rule according to Jewish law. On the basis of these findings, the Court denied the petition, holding that the rabbinical court ruled according to Jewish religious law and that, accordingly, this gift must be viewed as a conditional gift. "He did not make the gift with the intention that she should leave him (i.e., the gift was given on the condition that if she leaves him he would not confer her any rights)" (*ibid.*).

Justice Elon noted further that, even under the provisions of the Gift Law, a gift may be given conditionally, and one can infer that such a condition exists on the basis of the presumed intention of parties, as evidenced by the circumstances. Indeed, in a number of cases the Supreme Court ruled regarding interspousal gifts, that circumstances occasionally indicate that the gift was given conditionally, and once the judicial forum has construed the gift contract as being conditional, the condition becomes an integral part of the contract. By the same token it is clear that the rabbinical court was entitled to interpret the contract as including a condition, pursuant to Jewish law.

The Supreme Court further stated in its decision that the rabbinical court had ruled that a gift between spouses is given on the condition that they will not divorce, even in the reverse situation – i.e., where the wife gave half-ownership in the apartment to her husband. In that case too the husband must return his half-ownership of the apartment to the wife (see also under *Condition).

A GIFT FROM A LIVING PERSON AND A WILL. The Supreme Court also considered the laws pertaining to gifts under Jewish law in the case of *Abergil* (CA 2555/98 *Abergil v. The Estate of Ben Yair*, 53(5) PD 673, *per* Justice Yitzchak Englard). In that case, a man gave his house as a gift to the appellant, by means of a written deed of gift signed by witnesses and certified by a notary. His intention was for the gift to be effective according to both the laws of the State and Jewish law. The giver wrote in the gift deed that he was giving his apartment as a gift to the appellant "from this time while I am alive until one hour before my death." The Supreme Court discussed the use of this formulation in halakhic literature. Its purpose is to effect conveyance of the gift in such a manner that title in the gift would be given at the time of the conveyance of the deed of gift, while its proceeds – the right to use the gift – would not be conveyed until after the death of the giver (*ibid.*, p. 681).

The Supreme Court notes that the "Jewish legal tradition … does not allow a person to bequeath property to "one who is not competent to inherit from him" and similarly does not allow for "disinheriting of an heir" (Sh. Ar, ḤM 281, A). Hence, the only permissible way under Jewish law to allocate an estate in deviation from the rules of inheritance is through a living gift – that is, by using language of a gift and not of inheritance. Consequently, the Court ruled that in essence this was a will pursuant to the Israeli law: "From a substantive perspective, and pursuant to the Succession Law, a gift that becomes effective upon death of the donor is a will … the essence of the transaction must be viewed as a true will within the meaning of the civil Succession Law. Therefore, since the will did not conform with a number of requirements prescribed by the Succession Law, 5725 – 1965, such as the requirement that the will not benefit any one person involved in drafting it (section 35 of the Law), it is void." The Court also stated that according to these holdings, "a Jewish person wishing to dispose of his estate in accordance with *halakhah* must ensure that he complies with the provisions of the civil law regarding wills and that there are formulations that satisfy the requirements of both legal systems" (*ibid.*, p. 686; see also under *Wills; *Succession).

See also, HP 138/98, *Medina v. Medina* (Haifa Dist. Ct., Judge Yaakobi-Shvili), regarding a fictitious gift; Civil File 443/94, *Mizrachi v. Mizrachi* (Jlm. Dist. Ct., Judge E. Rubinstein), regarding a gift that is subject to an implicit condition.

[Menachem Elon (2nd ed.)]

BIBLIOGRAPHY: M. Bloch, *Das mosaisch-talmudische Erbrecht* (1890), 40ff.; idem, *Der Vertrag nach mosaisch-talmudischen Rechte* (1893), 87–90; Gulak, Yesodei, 1 (1922), 39, 76 n. 3, 118, 129ff.; 2 (1922), 159–63; Gulak, Oẓar, xxii, 38, 182–91, 346f.; Herzog, Instit, index; ET, 1 (1951³), 165f., 216f., 219, 291; 3 (1941), 203; 5 (1953), 400–3; 6 (1954), 89–92, 550f., 606f., 613f., 619, 625–31; 7 (1956), 30, 43f., 57, 170–3; 8 (1957), 435f.; 9 (1959), 161f.; 10 (1961), 64–66; 12 (1967), 140–6; B. Cohen, in: *Wolfson Jubilee Volume*, 1 (1965), 227f.; M. Elon, in: ILR, 4 (1969), 96–98. **ADD. BIBLIOGRAPHY:** M. Elon, *Ha-Mishpat ha-Ivri* (1988), 1:101f., 133, 327, 346, 476, 481, 536, 572; 3:1404, 1412, 1450; idem, *Jewish Law* (1994), 1:113f., 149f., 416f.; 2:580, 586, 652, 705; 3:1673, 1681f, 1724; idem, *Jewish Law (Cases and Materials)* (1999), 398–404; M. Elon and B. Lifshitz, *Mafte'aḥ ha-She'elot ve-ha-Teshuvot shel Ḥakhmei Sefarad u-Ẓefon Afrikah* (legal digest), 2 (1986), 255–65; B. Lifshitz and E. Shochetman, *Mafte'aḥ ha-She'elot ve-ha-Teshuvot shel Ḥakhmei Ashkenaz, Ẓarefat, ve-Italyah* (legal digest) (1997), 185–87.

GIFTER, MORDECAI (1916–1991), U.S. rabbi and talmudic scholar. Gifter was born in Richmond, Virginia, but he moved to Baltimore with his family, when his father realized that his son could not be adequately taught in a city with such limited Torah resources. He studied at Yeshiva College and at the Rabbi Isaac Elchanan Theological Seminary (RIETS) in New York under Rabbi Moshe Halevi Soloveitchik. On the advice of his uncle, Reb Yehuda Leib Zer, one of the directors of the RIETS, a newly ordained Rabbi Gifter went to study in the Telz yeshivah of Lithuania in the winter of 1932. He became very close to the *rosh yeshivah*, Reb Avrohom Yitzchok Bloch. With the expansion of the Ner Yisroel yeshivah in Baltimore by Rabbi Jacob Isaac Ruderman, Rabbi Gifter was invited to teach there. In 1943, Rabbi Gifter became rabbi in Waterbury, Connecticut, and one year later, his uncles, R. Eliyahu Meir Bloch and R. Chaim Mordechai Katz, founded the Telz yeshivah in Cleveland. They asked him to join them.

Gifter moved to Israel in 1976, founding the Telz yeshivah in Kiryat Telz-Stone near Jerusalem with the support of Irving Stone, Cleveland philanthropist. However, three years later, the *rosh yeshivah* of Telz in Cleveland, Rabbi Boruch Sorotzkin, died, and Gifter returned to Cleveland to succeed him. He remained at Telz until his death. The growth of Telz mirrored the growth and self confidence of ultra-Orthodoxy. A gifted speaker in Yiddish and English, Gifter was known for his humility. Introduced as a *gaon* in a local synagogue, he spent the first part of his discourse refuting the compliment and speaking of the denigration of learning and the inflation of compliments over the generations.

Among the works he wrote were *Hirhurei Teshuvah* (1977), *Torah Perspectives* (1986), and *Sefer Pirkei Moed* (1992).

[Michael Berenbaum (2nd ed.)]

GIKATILLA (Chiquitilla; Heb. גיקטיליא**), ISAAC IBN** (fl. second half of 10th century), Spanish Hebrew poet and grammarian. A student of *Menahem b. Jacob ibn Saruq, he took part in the controversy on grammar between him and *Dunash b. Labrat. Moses *Ibn Ezra in his *Kitab al-Muhadara wal-Mudhakara* (published by A. Halkin (1975), 31a) states that Isaac ibn Gikatilla and his contemporary the poet R. Isaac Mar Saul surpassed their immediate predecessors – Dunash b. Labrat, Menahem ibn Saruk, and other contemporary poets in nobility and eloquence, and that "both came from Lucena and had similar skills, but Ibn Gikatilla was superior because of his greater knowledge of Arabic culture." Moses ibn *Tibbon in his commentary (still in manuscript) to the *azharot* of

Solomon ibn *Gabirol mentions that Isaac ibn Gikatilla had also written some *azharot*. Only in 1950, however, were four manuscripts containing the majority of these *azharot* published by M. Zulay. The influence of *Saadiah Gaon is strongly marked in these poems. This type of *azharah* is the first of its kind to be written in Spain, and at the end of each the name "Isaac" appears. Besides this work, Moses ibn Ezra ascribed another verse to Gikatilla. This ascription has been authenticated by a number of scholars.

Isaac ibn Gikatilla, together with Judah ibn Daud (Ḥayyuj?) and Isaac ibn Kapron, who were also students of Menahem ibn Saruk, actively defended their teacher against the attacks of Dunash b. Labrat. In their reply (ed. together with Yehudi ben Sheshet's reply by S.G. Stern and by S. Benavente, see bibl.), they praise the grammatical works of Menahem, enumerate some of Dunash's errors, and try to invalidate his system of comparison between Hebrew and other Semitic languages, Arabic and Aramaic. In their criticism of the new metrical system introduced by Dunash adapting the Arabic basic elements, they accuse Dunash of having corrupted the Hebrew language by adapting it to the Arabic meter. *Yehudi b. Sheshet, the pupil of Dunash, replied and from his words "Behold, the greatest among you, ben Gikatilla" (Stern, pt. 2, p. 17) it can be deduced that Gikatilla was presumably the most outstanding scholar among his colleagues. Yehudi b. Sheshet's enumeration of the errors of Gikatilla makes it possible to estimate the extent of the latter's contribution to the jointly written reply of Menahem's disciples. Gikatilla was a teacher of the grammarian Jonah *Ibn Janaḥ whom he encouraged in the study of the Arabic language. Ibn Janaḥ, in many of his own works, cites Gikatilla without, however, mentioning the source. Other grammarians of the Middle Ages, such as Judah *Ibn Bal'am, also quote him.

BIBLIOGRAPHY: S. Pinsker (ed.), *Likkutei Kadmoniyyot* (1860), in: Supplements 159, 161, 165; S.G. Stern (ed.), *Sefer Teshuvot Talmidei Menaḥem ve-Talmidei Dunash*… (1870), lxxv (introd.); Jonah ibn Janaḥ, *Sefer ha-Shorashim*, ed. by W. Bacher (1896), x (introd.); D. Yellin, *Toledot Hitpatteḥut ha-Dikduk ha-Ivri* (1945), 94–106; Zulay, in: *Tarbiz*, 20 (1949/50), 161–76; Schirmann, Sefarad, 2 (1956), 702, s.v. *Azharot*. **ADD. BIBLIOGRAPHY:** E. Ashtor, *The Jews of Moslem Spain*, I (1973), 259, 393–4; S. Benavente and A. Sáenz-Badillos (eds),. *Tĕšubot de los Discípulos de Mĕnaḥem contra Dunaš ben Labraṭ* (1986); A. Sáenz-Badillos, in: *Sefarad*, 46 (1986), 421–31.

[Nissan Netzer]

GIKATILLA (Chiquatilla), JOSEPH BEN ABRAHAM (1248–c. 1325), Spanish kabbalist whose works exerted a profound and permanent influence on kabbalism. Gikatilla, who was born in Medinaceli, Castile, lived for many years in Segovia. Between 1272 and 1274 he studied under Abraham *Abulafia, who praises him as his most successful pupil. Gikatilla, who was at first greatly influenced by Abulafia's ecstatic, prophetic system of kabbalism, soon showed a greater affinity for philosophy.

His first extant work, *Ginnat Egoz* (1615), written in 1274, is an introduction to the mystic symbolism of the alphabet, vowel points, and the Divine Names. The title derives from the initial letters of the kabbalistic elements *gematria* ("numerology"), *notarikon* ("acrostics"), *temurah* ("permutation"). In common with his mentor, Gikatilla also links this mystic lore with the system practiced by *Maimonides. This work makes no suggestion of the theosophical doctrine of *Sefirot* or "spheres" (see *Kabbalah), later adopted by Gikatilla. The *Sefirot* here are identified with the philosophical term "intelligences." On the other hand, the author shows himself familiar with the revelatory mysticism of *Jacob b. Jacob ha-Kohen, although the latter is not mentioned by name. Several of Gikatilla's other writings also deal with the theory of letter combinations and alphabetical mysticism. However, in the 1280s, Gikatilla evidently made contact with *Moses b. Shem Tov de Leon, and thereafter the two exerted a mutual influence on each other's kabbalistic development.

Before writing *Ginnat Egoz*, Gikatilla had written a commentary on the Song of Songs (but not the one in the Paris manuscript 790 which bears indications that Gikatilla wrote it in 1300 in Segovia). The later work endorses the doctrine of *Shemitot*, a theory of cosmic development based on the sabbatical year, as expounded in the Sefer ha-*Temunah. Gikatilla also compiled *Kelalei ha-Mitzvot*, explaining *mitzvot* by a literal interpretation of *halakhah* (Ms. Paris 713); a number of *piyyutim* (Habermann, in *Mizraḥ u-Ma'arav*, 5 (1932), 351; Gruenwald, in *Tarbiz*, 36 (1966/67), 73–89), some devoted to kabbalistic themes; and *Sefer ha-Meshalim*, a book of proverbs to which he added his own commentary, whose ethical precepts were close to kabbalistic principles. (The proverbs alone published by I. Davidson, in *Sefer ha-Yovel shel "Hadoar"* (1927), 116–22; the book with commentary, in Ms. Oxford 1267). While Gikatilla wrote numerous works on Kabbalah, many others have been attributed to him erroneously. A. Altmann, for instance, has shown that Gikatilla was not the author of the lengthy *Sefer Ta'amei ha-Mitzvot*. Written by an unknown kabbalist about 1300 (Cambridge Ms.) and also attributed to Isaac ibn Farḥi, it had a wide circulation. A number of treatises await clarification as to authorship.

Gikatilla's most influential kabbalistic work, written before 1293, is his *Sha'arei Orah* (1559), a detailed explanation of kabbalistic symbolism and the designations of the ten *Sefirot*. He adopted a system intermediate between that of the Geronese school of kabbalists and the *Zohar. This is one of the first writings to disclose knowledge of portions of the Zohar, although it departs from its approach in several fundamental respects.

Sefer Sha'arei Ẓedek (1559) provides another explanation of the theory of *Sefirot*, reversing their normal succession. Other published works by Gikatilla are *Sha'ar ha-Nikkud* (1601), a mystical treatise on vocalization; *Perush Haggadah shel Pesaḥ*, a kabbalistic commentary on the Passover *Haggadah* (1602); a number of essays on various subjects (publ. in *Sefer Ereẓ ba-Levanon*, ed. by Isaac Perlov, Vilna, 1899); kabbalistic works remaining in manuscript are: mystical treatises on certain *mitzvot*; a commentary on the Vision of the

Chariot of Ezekiel (numerous manuscripts); and considerable portions of a biblical commentary continuing the system followed in *Ginnat Egoz* (manuscript in JTS, New York, Deinard 451). A work on disciplines ("*pe'ulot*") in practical Kabbalah was extant in the 17th century (Joseph Delmedigo, *Sefer Novellot Ḥokhmah* (1631), 195a). A collection of kabbalistic responsa on points of *halakhah* from the second half of the 14th century has been erroneously ascribed to Gikatilla. Joseph *Caro made use of them in his *Beit Yosef.* Problems of Kabbalah put to Joshua b. Meir ha-Levi by Gikatilla are in manuscript, Oxford, 1565. Also extant are a number of prayers, such as *Tefillat ha-Yiḥud, Me'ah Pesukim* ("100 Verses," on the *Sefirot*), and *Pesukim al-Shem ben Arba'im u-Shetayim Otiyyot* ("Verses on the 42-Lettered Divine Name"). Commentaries were written on *Sha'arei Orah* by an anonymous 15th-century kabbalist (publ. by G. Scholem, in his *Kitvei Yad be-Kabbalah* (1930), 80–83) and by Mattathias *Delacrut (mainly included with the work). A summary was translated into Latin by the apostate Paul Riccius (1516).

Gikatilla made an original attempt to provide a detailed yet lucid and systematic exposition of kabbalism. He was also the originator of the doctrine equating the infinite, **Ein Sof,* with the first of the ten *Sefirot*. The conception was rejected by the majority of kabbalists from the 16th century onward, but his works continued to be highly esteemed and were published in many editions.

[Gershom Scholem]

Since 1970 a series of books by Gikatilla has been printed from manuscripts. The outstanding among them is the *Commentary on the Merkavah* (eds. D. Abrams and A. Farber Ginnat, Cherub Press, Los Angeles, 2005). The possible contribution of Gikatilla to the book of the Zohar has been discussed by Y. Liebes, *Studies in the Zohar* (SUNY Press, Albany, 1993), 98–105.

[Moshe Idel (2nd ed.)]

BIBLIOGRAPHY: S. Sachs, *Ha-Yonah* (1850), 80–81; G. Scholem, *Kitvei Yad ba-Kabbalah* (1930), 218–25; idem, in: *Sefer ha-Yovel le-Ya'akov Freimann* (1937), 163–70 (Heb. section); Altmann, in: KS, 40 (1965), 256–76, 405–12; idem, in: *Sefer ha-Yovel le-Israel Brodie* (1967), 57–65; Weiler, in: HUCA, 37 (1966), 13–44 (Heb. section); Steinschneider, Cat Bod, 1461–70; A. Jellinek, *Beitraege zur Geschichte der Kabbala*, 2 (1852), 57–64; Scholem, Mysticism, 194–5, 405–6; Werblowsky, in: *Zeitschrift fuer Religion und Geistgeschichte*, 8 (1956), 164–9.

GIKATILLA (Chiquatilla/Chiquitilla), MOSES BEN SAMUEL HA-KOHEN (11th century), Spanish Jewish liturgical poet, Hebrew translator, and grammarian. Born in Córdoba of good family, he lived principally in Saragossa and, it seems, traveled extensively. One of a group of youths favored and supported by *Samuel ha-Nagid, Gikatilla wrote poems of praise dedicated to his benefactor and to the latter's son Joseph. Most of his works in the fields of grammar, Bible exegesis, and other subjects have been lost except for quotations in the works of others, and are now known only through laudatory or critical references to them. Abraham *Ibn Ezra refers to him as the "greatest of the grammarians." From the quotations ascribed to him, it can be deduced that he wrote commentaries in Arabic to most of the books of the Bible. He mentions, always with a note of criticism, *Saadiah Gaon, Hayyuj, Samuel ha-Nagid, Ibn Janaḥ, Yeshu'ah, the Oriental *paytanim*, Midrashim, Christian translations of Psalms, and others. He made extensive use of the Targum. His Arabic commentary on Psalms still remains in manuscript; the only incomplete copy has the commentaries on Psalms 12, 42, 44, 69, 74, 78, 104, 109, 119, 141, and 144 (in fragmentary versions); the commentaries on Psalms 43, 70–73, 79–103, 110–118, and 145–150 are lost. The text of this copy is the work of Ibn Gikatilla, as is shown by his own quotations in his treatise on masculine and feminine Hebrew gender. Ibn Gikatilla says explicitly that he had written earlier commentaries on Job, Isaiah, and possibly on Jeremiah and Amos. The passages in this unique copy demonstrate that Ibn Gikatilla's commentary has four levels, paying attention to semantics, morphology, syntax, and exegesis. Although the two first levels continue the line of the Andalusian Hebrew grammarians from the 10th century, especially of the *Kitab al-Nutaf* by Hayyuj, they combine the oldest rabbinical tradition with the intellectual trends of his time. The original exegetic method developed by Ibn Gikatilla was very critical, of high intellectual quality, and had a profound influence on other Andalusian authors. According to Ibn Gikatilla, the Psalms are prayers and songs. He usually adopted the literal meaning (*haqiqa*) of the text and used the figurative meaning (*majaz*) for unusual texts like Psalm 26:7: "Gates, raise yours heads." Ibn Gikatilla usually rejects miracles; he is probably the most rationalistic of all medieval commentators. Ibn Bilam accused him of "agnosticism." Other extant fragments of his exegetical writings suggest also that he was a bold and original commentator. He was among the few who explained the aspirations of the prophets as applying to their own times and not to those of the Messiah. He was the first exegete to attribute the chapters from Isaiah 40 onward to a prophet other than Isaiah. On Isaiah 41, the following is reported in his name: "These first consolations, from the middle of the book onward, refer to the Second Temple" (i.e., not to the messianic age). Concerning Psalm 106:47 he said, "This psalmist was in Babylon." Similar comments on other chapters are also cited in his name. He wrote a *Sefer Dikduk* ("Book of Grammar"): *The Book on the Masculine and Feminine* (*Kitab al-Tadkir wal-Ta'nit*). This monographic lexicographical work, probably inspired in the Muslim book by Anbary from Basra, became quite famous, and it is quoted in other Andalusian works as "small but tasty." Gikatilla also translated from Arabic into Hebrew the work of Ḥayyuj on weak and geminate Hebrew verbs for non-Arabic-speaking Jews from North Spain, and possibly also some works of Samuel ha-Nagid. As a translator, he innovated and fixed the Hebrew terminology for Hayyuj's theories, which is still used today. He added hundreds of glosses to the original Arabic version, sometimes reducing and sometimes extending the text, and also included some explicit criticism on Hayyuj. In that way Gikatilla offered an updated version of the original Arabic work.

The scanning excerpts of Gikatilla's commentaries were collected by S. Poznański. Of his Hebrew hymns and poems, only ten have been published. Moses *Ibn Ezra said of him: "He was among the greatest of the exalted rhetoricians and poets in both languages, but he had a soft spot that damaged his privileged position" (*Kitab al-Muhadara wal-Mudhakara*, ed. A. Halkin (1975), 36a). His poems, which are rhymed and stylistically characteristic of his time, include religious compositions, friendship and love poems, and drinking songs; they were published by Brody (1937). His commentary on Psalms has been preserved in the manuscript Firk I-3583 (Finkel edited and translated three of them into Hebrew). His Hebrew translation of Hayyuj's grammatical works was edited by Nutt. The fragments belonging to his *Treatise on Hebrew Gender* were translated into Hebrew and published by Allony. Bacher edited an Arabic Targum commentary on Job that may also be his work.

BIBLIOGRAPHY: N. Allony, in: *Sinai*, 24 (1949), 34–67, 138–47; Brody, in: YMḤSI, 3 (1937), 64–90; S. Poznański, *Moses b. Samuel ha-Kohen Chiquitilla nebst den Fragmenten seiner Schriften* (1895). **ADD. BIBLIOGRAPHY:** Eldar, in: *Ben Ever le-Arav* (1998), 95–111; Finkel, in: *Horeb*, 3 (1936–7), 153–62; M. Haran, in: *Hebrew Bible–Old Testament: The History of its Interpretation*, 1–2: *The Middle Ages* (2000), 261–81; M. Delgado, in: MEAH, 51 (2002), 119–57; idem, in: MEAH, 52 (2003), 201–41; Nutt, *Two Treatises on Verbs Containing Feeble and Double Letters by R. Yehuda Hayug of Fez, Translated into Hebrew from the original Arabic by R. Moses Gikatilia of Cordova* (1870); Schirmann, Sefarad (1956), 294–7; S. Poznański, in: ZFAVG (1912), 38–60; U. Simon, *Four Approaches to the Book of Psalms: From Saadiah Gaon to Abraham Ibn Ezra* (1991); A. Watad, *Mishnato ha-Leshonit shel R. Hayyuj: mi Be'ad le-Munaḥab bi-Mekoram ha-Aravi u-be-Tirgumam ha-Ivrit* (1984); del Valle, in: *Judaísmo hispano*, 1 (2002), 81–88.

[Abraham Meir Habermann / José Martínez (2nd ed.)]

GIKOW, RUTH (1915–1982), U.S. artist, known primarily as a figurative painter of murals and easel paintings. Gikow was also involved in socially conscious organizations, worked on WPA-sponsored murals, and held several gallery exhibitions before her death.

Gikow was born in Russian Ukraine to Boris and Lena Gikow. Her family fled after a pogrom and spent the first years of Ruth's life wandering in Eastern Europe, at one point living in a gypsy camp outside Bucharest. They immigrated to New York City in 1920, when Ruth was five years old. After graduating from Washington Irving High School with honors in art, Gikow won admission to Cooper Union, where she studied with regionalist painter John Steuart Curry. A scholarship enabled her to study with social realist painter Raphael Soyer, whose progressive sympathies were more to Gikow's political tastes. Another lasting influence was Cooper Union's director Austin Purvis, who took students into the urban streets, encouraging them to represent daily life in their art. Gikow began to paint scenes of common people on the street, in stores, and in parks, exhibiting a dedication to figurative art and humanity that would characterize her art throughout her life. During the 1930s Gikow became involved with activist artists' organizations like the Artists' Union and the American Artists' Congress. In the late 1930s she taught at the American Artists School, successor to the radical left-wing John Reed Club Art School.

In 1940, while working with the Mural Division of the New York City WPA Art Project, Gikow executed a mural for the children's wing of Bronx Hospital. Entitled *Children's Indoor and Outdoor Activities*, the mural depicted a world with children and animals living together in harmony. In 1943, the artist was featured in live demonstrations of mural painting at the World's Fair, in which Gikow stood on a 12-foot scaffolding while visitors watched her paint and listened to her explain the process. She also painted commercial murals for retail stores, including Macy's. By 1946, when the artist held her first one-person show of oil paintings, she had participated in group shows at the A.C.A. Gallery and elsewhere, designed textiles, and produced illustrations for such books as *Crime and Punishment* and *History of the Jews in America* (a children's text). Gikow was a strong colorist, often mixing her oil paints with turpentine to achieve a more fluid effect.

In 1946 she married painter Jack Levine and had one daughter. Her paintings were purchased by major art museums including the Metropolitan, the Whitney, the Museum of Modern Art, and the National Institute of Arts and Letters in New York, the Smithsonian Institute in Washington, the Philadelphia Museum of Art, and the Tel Aviv Museum, as well as collections at Brandeis University, New York University, and elsewhere. By the time of her death, Gikow had received several honors, including a National Institute of Arts and Letters grant in 1959, two Childe Hassam awards, and a Smith College citation as one of America's ten outstanding women artists.

[Lauren B. Strauss (2nd ed.)]

GILADI, ALEX, Israeli member of the International Olympic Committee and vice president for global operations at NBC. Giladi began his career as a sportswriter in 1964. He worked until 1972 at *Yedioth Ahronoth*, and then moved to Israeli TV, becoming head of the sports department in 1975. In 1981 he became vice president for global operations at NBC, responsible for all of the network's foreign sports coverage. In 1985 he became a member of the TV and Radio Committee of the international Olympic Committee. In 1993 he was named president of KESHET, one of the commercial TV networks that run Israel's Channel 2. In 1994 he became Israel's first and only delegate to the International Olympic Committee. In that capacity he had the honor of handing out medals to Israeli athletes in the Olympic Games. He was also the first Israeli to carry the Olympic torch, in Athens in 2004.

WEBSITE: olympic.achla.co.il.

[Shaked Gilboa (2nd ed.)]

GILADI (Butelbroit), ISRAEL (1886–1918), pioneer in Ereẓ Israel and leader of *Ha-Shomer. Born in Calarasi, Bessarabia, Giladi was a member of Po'alei Zion and an advocate of

Jewish self-defense. In 1905 he went to Ereẓ Israel and joined the Jewish laborers in the settlements. In 1907 he was one of the founding members of the Bar Giora secret defense society and a year later joined the collective labor group in *Sejera. When Ha-Shomer was founded in 1909, Giladi was elected to its committee and put in charge of the defense of settlements in Galilee, Samaria, and Judea. He became acting head of the organization in 1913 when Israel *Shochat, its leader, left for Constantinople. During World War I he proposed the establishment of an agricultural settlement to serve as a base for Ha-Shomer and, in the summer of 1917, he and a group of friends established Kefar Bag (named after the Bar Giora society) south of Metullah. He died in an influenza epidemic. Giladi was the author of *Divrei Yemei ha-Aguddah* ("History of the Association"), a source for the history of Ha-Shomer (published in *Koveẓ ha-Shomer*, 1937). After his death, the village he had helped found, Kefar Giladi, was named after him.

BIBLIOGRAPHY: Dinur, Haganah, index; J. Yaari-Poleskin, *Ḥolemim ve-Loḥamim* (1946), 363–9; S. Sheva, *Shevet ha-No'azim* (1969).

[Yehuda Slutsky]

GILĀN, province of Iran situated in the southern part of the Caspian Sea and to the north of Alborz Mountains at the delta of the river Sefid-Rud. Gilān's population density, within its present borders, is 14,000 people per square mile and at the beginning of the 20th century had a population of about half a million, a majority of whom were the original Gilān people who spoke the Gilaḳi dialect and minorities who were Armenians, Gypsies, Jews, and a few thousand immigrants from Russia.

The beginning of the Jewish settlement in Gilān is not known, but the first reference to Jews living in Chākhān, a place north of the city of Lāhijān, appears in Mir Zahir al-Din's writings (1441/2). The second source is the Chronicle of *Bābāi ben Lutf (Ms JTS 401, fol. 20b) referring to the city of Rasht (17th century). The third source belongs to the Armenian Bishop Arakel (17th century), who mentions the city of Fuman. The fourth source is the record of Ya'kov Dilmanian regarding the transfer of the Jews from Gilān and Deylamān to Mashhad (see *Mahshad). Jaubert (p. 435) and Rabino (pp. 70–71) mention that about 50 Jewish families lived in Rasht in miserable conditions (during 1806–09).

In the plague of 1830 about one third of the then 60,000 inhabitants of Rasht perished. According to Curzon (vol.2, p. 385) the city of Rasht looked like a ghost town. The plague certainly affected the local Jews, too. Levy (p. 1005) claims that many Jews in Rasht perished in the massacre which, according to him, occurred around 1750. There is a place in Rasht called Yehudi-Tappeh (Jewish Height) but no one remembers exactly when it was populated by Jews.

Another important city in Gilān is Siyāhkal whose Jewish population holds a tradition saying that they were the descendants of King David. Unlike the Jews of Rasht, the Jews of Siyāhkal speak Gilaki among themselves, which may indicate their antiquity in Gilān. According to Rabino (pp. 33, 80) there were between 15 and 20 Jewish families in Siyāhkal working as petty merchants at the beginning of the 20th century. There was a pogrom in Siāhkal in which many Jews were killed, some converted to Islam, and others left the city to live in Rasht. It is possible that this pogrom occurred around the year 1880 (Netzer, Siyāhkal).

Threre are also general references to the existence of Jews in several settlements in Gilān such as Eframjān, Khomām, Yahud-Kelayeh, Lāhijān, Fumanāt, Rudbār, and others about which we know very little (Netzer, Siyāhkal).

Up to 1948, Rasht and the sea port Pahlavi were relatively the most populated cities as far as Jews, Armenians, and Muslims were concerned. Most of the Jews were immigrants from *Kashan, *Isfahan, and Siyāhkal, almost all of whom worked in textile business. At that time, Rasht had about 30 Jewish families, one synagogue, and one elementary school called Koresh. The Jewish population of Pahlavi numbered less than half of that of Rasht. After the Islamic Revolution in Iran there remained only one Jewish family in Rasht. There are no reports on the existence of Jewish communities in the early 21st century in other cities and towns of the province of Gilān.

BIBLIOGRAPHY: G.N. Curzon, *Persian and the Persian Question*, 1–2 (1892), index; A.P. Jaubert, *Voyage en Arménie et Perse fait dans les années 1805 et 1806* (1821); H. Levy, *History of the Jews of Iran*, 3, *Teheran* (1960); A. Netzer, "*Yehudim be-Gilān*," in: *Yeẓirah ve-Toladot* (1994), 215–32; idem, "Jews of Siyāhkal," in: *Shofar* (a monthly Jewish-Persian magazine), 274 (December 2003), 22ff.; 275 (January 2004), 22ff.; L. Rabino, *Les provinces caspiennes de la Perse* (1917).

[Amnon Netzer (2nd ed.)]

GILBERT, BRAD (1961–), U.S. tennis player, winner of 20 singles titles and successful pro coach. Born in Oakland, California, the youngest of three children in a family of tennis prodigies, Gilbert attended Pepperdine University, where he was the 1982 NCAA singles runner-up. Though saddled with a weak backhand, an average net game, and little natural ability, Gilbert's court smarts, preparation, tenacity, and an ability to engage in mental warfare on the court helped him win 20 singles titles and three doubles titles during his 14-year career. Gilbert never made it past the quarterfinals (1987 U.S. Open, 1990 Wimbledon) of any of the four major tournaments, but he was consistently ranked among the top 40 players, peaking at No. 4 in January 1990. Gilbert compiled a lifetime 519–288 career record, including 10–5 in Davis Cup play. He won a bronze medal in men's singles at the 1988 Olympics, and won gold at the 1989 Maccabiah, defeating Amos Mansdorf.

Gilbert began coaching at the end of his playing career, guiding Andre Agassi and later Andy Roddick to No. 1 world rankings. Gilbert's knowledge of the tactical side of tennis – how to recognize and attack an opponent's weaknesses – resulted in his being regarded as one of the top five coaches in the game. Gilbert, inducted into the Intercollegiate Tennis Association Men's Hall of Fame in 2001, is the author of *Winning*

Ugly (1993), and *I've Got Your Back – Coaching Top Performers from Center Court to the Corner Office* (2004).

[Elli Wohlgelernter (2nd ed.)]

GILBERT, FELIX (1905–1991), U.S. historian. Born in Baden, Germany, Gilbert immigrated to the U.S. in 1936. During World War II he served as research analyst in the Office of Strategic Services and the U.S. Department of State (1943–46). In 1946 he joined the faculty of Bryn Mawr College, rising to the position of professor of history in 1948. From 1962 he was professor at the School of Historical Studies at the Institute for Advanced Study in Princeton.

Gilbert's principal scholarly interests were the Italian Renaissance and diplomatic history of the 18th and 20th centuries. Among his major works were *Hitler Directs His War* (1951), *To the Farewell Address: Ideas of Early American Foreign Policy* (1961), *Niccolò Machiavelli e la vita culturale del suo tempo* (1964), *Machiavelli and Guicciardini: Politics and History in Sixteenth-century Florence* (1965), *The End of the European Era: 1890 to the Present* (1970), *The Pope, His Banker, and Venice* (1980), and *A European Past: Memoirs, 1905–1945* (1988). With G.A. Craig he edited *The Diplomats, 1919–1939* (2 vols, 1953–63), and he was the general editor of the *Norton History of Modern Europe* (1971).

ADD. BIBLIOGRAPHY: H. Lehmann, *Felix Gilbert as Scholar and Teacher* (1992).

[Oscar Isaiah Janowsky / Ruth Beloff (2nd ed.)]

GILBERT, INA (1932–), Canadian painter and president of the Society of Canadian Artists. Born into a family of painters in Toronto, Gilbert graduated in political science and economics. Later she took up interior design, began painting at night, and studied techniques of etching. Her works display a bold sense of color and a quality of whimsy. They are executed in acrylic paint on canvas or on sheets of plexiglass where she creates an appearance of depth by using two or three superimposed sheets.

GILBERT, SIR MARTIN (1936–), British historian. Born in London, the son of a jeweler, Gilbert was educated at Highgate School and Magdalen College, Oxford. His earliest work concerned British foreign policy in the 1930s, which in 1962 brought him into contact with Randolph Churchill. Between 1962 and 1968 he worked as research assistant to Randolph Churchill on the official biography of Sir Winston Churchill. From 1968 Gilbert was the sole author of what became the most voluminous biography ever written, totaling over nine million words and running to six volumes plus an as yet unfinished set of companion volumes containing documents. Appointed a fellow of Merton College, Oxford, in 1962, Gilbert remained on an extended sabbatical while engaged in the biography; during this time he also produced a series of major studies on the creation of the State of Israel, the Holocaust, and World War II. A tireless worker on behalf of Soviet Jewry, he was at one time writing over a dozen letters a day to "refuseniks" and became personally known to many Russian Jews during his frequent visits to the U.S.S.R. He has written on the situation of Soviet Jewry and authored a biography of Anatoly Shcharansky. In 1987 he was a non-governmental representative on the U.N. Commission on Human Rights (43rd session) in Geneva. He is a highly popular author, although some historians have criticized his preference for pure narrative history. He has defended his choice to abstain from judgments and has said that "by what you select you make plain your views." Volume 6 of the Churchill biography, *Finest Hour, 1939–41*, won the 1983 Wolfson Award. In 1988 he was awarded the Ka-Zetnik Prize for Literature by Yad Vashem and the Holocaust Memorial Foundation. Since 1978 Gilbert has been a governor of the Hebrew University of Jerusalem. He has homes in London and Jerusalem.

In addition to the Churchill biography, completed in 1988, Gilbert's publications include *The Appeasers* (with Richard Gott; 1963); *The European Powers 1900–45* (1965); *The Roots of Appeasement* (1966); *Exile and Return: A Study of the Emergence of Jewish Statehood* (1978); *Churchill: A Photographic Portrait* (1974); *Churchill's Political Philosophy* (1981); *Auschwitz and the Allies* (1981); *The Jews of Hope: The Plight of Soviet Jewry Today (1984); Jerusalem, Rebirth of a City* (1985); *Shcharansky: Hero of Our Time* (1986); *The Holocaust: The Jewish Tragedy* (1986); *Second World War* (1989); three edited collections of documents; and 12 historical atlases including *Atlas of Jewish History* and *Atlas of the Holocaust.* More recently, he completed a three-volume history of the 20th century and *The Righteous* (2003). Gilbert received a knighthood in 1995.

[David Cesarani]

GILBERT, MELISSA ELLEN (1964–), U.S. actress. Born in Los Angeles, Calif., Gilbert was adopted the day after her birth by comedian Paul Gilbert and his actress wife Barbara (née Crane). Melissa Gilbert's grandfather, Harry Crane, was creator and writer of *The Honeymooners*. She first appeared in a commercial for baby clothes at the age of two, but her parents decided to keep her out of show business until she turned seven. She then started filming more than 30 commercials, including sports for McDonald's and Crest. At nine, in the summer of 1973, she was cast in the role of Laura Ingalls for the NBC TV series *Little House on the Prairie*, which ran until 1983. In 1979, she starred as Helen Keller opposite Patty Duke as Annie Sullivan in *The Miracle Worker*, which won an Emmy Award, and in 1980 Gilbert played Anne Frank in the NBC adaptation of *The Diary of Anne Frank*. She became involved with Rob Lowe in 1981 and moved to Manhattan after *Little House*. In 1985, Gilbert became the youngest person to ever receive a star on the Hollywood Walk of Fame, and in 1987 she earned an Outer Critic's Circle Award for best debuting actress in the off-Broadway show *A Shayna Maidel*. Gilbert and Lowe ended their relationship in 1987, and soon after in 1988 she married actor Bo Brinkman. The two had a son, Dakota Paul, but the couple divorced in 1992. Gilbert returned to Hollywood, where she continued to act, mostly in television.

She married actor Bruce Boxleitner in 1995 and the two had a son together, Michael Garrett. In November 2000, Gilbert was elected to the Screen Actors Guild board and then became its third female president. On November 2, 2001, she was elected a vice president of the AFL-CIO, and in 2002 was re-elected as SAG president. Gilbert also has two stepsons, Sam Boxleitner and Lee Davis Boxleitner, and her siblings include actress-director Sara Gilbert and actor Jonathan Gilbert.

BIBLIOGRAPHY: "Gilbert, Melissa," in: *Almanac of Famous People* (2003[8]). "Gilbert, Melissa," in: *Contemporary Theatre, Film and Television*. Vol. 38 (2002).

[Adam Wills (2nd ed.)]

GILBERT, MILTON (1909–1979), U.S. economist. Gilbert, who was born in Philadelphia, joined the U.S. Department of Commerce in 1938 as editor of the department's *Survey of Current Business*, later becoming director of national and statistical accounts. He also worked at the Organization for European Economic Cooperation (OEEC), and from 1960 to 1975 served as economic adviser to the Bank of International Settlements in Basle. His major interests were social accounting, business fluctuations, foreign exchange, and international finance. He strongly advocated that an increase in the official price of gold was essential to bringing about the repair of the international monetary system.

Gilbert's publications include *International Comparison of National Products and the Purchasing Power of Currencies* (1954), *Problems of the International Monetary System* (1966), *The Gold-Dollar System* (1968), *Export Prices and Export Cartels* (1971), and *Quest for World Monetary Order* (1980).

[Joachim O. Ronall / Ruth Beloff (2nd ed.)]

GILBERT, SHLOMO (1885–1942), Yiddish writer. Born in Radzymin to a ḥasidic family, he spent his adult years in Warsaw before perishing in Treblinka. His realistic tales and short dramas, which reflected his own kabbalistic-mystical tendency, appeared from 1907 in the Yiddish journals *Haynt* and *Literarishe Bleter*. In addition to the collection *Noveln* ("Short Stories," 1922), he published *"Meshiekhs Trit"* ("The Steps of Messiah," 1924), a dramatic poem in three acts in the Hebrew journal *Ha-Tekufah*, and the comedy, *Der Keler* ("The Cellar," 1927). A definitive edition of his works appeared in 1954, with an introduction and evaluation by the critic S. *Niger.

BIBLIOGRAPHY: LNYL, 2 (1958), 209ff.; M. Ravitch, *Mayn Leksikon*, 1 (1945), 52–54.

[Melech Ravitch / Edward Portnoy (2nd ed.)]

GILBERT, WALTER (1932–), U.S. molecular biologist and Nobel laureate. Gilbert was born in Boston and graduated from Harvard University (B.A. 1953, M.A. 1954) and received his doctorate from Cambridge University in mathematics in 1957. Appointed assistant professor of physics at Harvard from 1959 to 1964, he was an associate professor in biophysics from 1964 to 1969 and professor of molecular biology from 1969 to 1972; during that period he was an American Cancer Society professor. He left Harvard in 1981 to become CEO of Biogen, N.V. Returning to Harvard (1985–2002), he was the Carl M. Loeb University Professor. As emeritus, he was a managing partner of Bioventures Investors in 2005, a venture capital fund investing in biotechnology. He has founded many biotechnology companies. Among them are Biogen, Myriad Genetics, Memory Pharmaceuticals, and Paratek Pharmaceuticals.

He is a member of the National Academy of Science, the American Academy of Arts and Sciences, the American Physics Society, and the American Society of Biological Chemistry. He is an overseer of the Museum of Fine Arts, Boston and on the collections committee of the Fogg Museum of Art, Harvard.

Gilbert's research has been in the fields of biophysics, genetic control mechanism, and protein DNA interaction. He worked extensively in the field of the early evolution of genes. He is the recipient of many awards, culminating in the Nobel Prize in chemistry in 1980, along with Frederick Sanger and Paul *Berg.

Gilbert is married to Celia Gilbert, poet and painter, who is the daughter of I.F. *Stone.

GILBOA (Heb. גִּלְבֹּעַ), mountain ridge branching off to the N.E. from the Samarian Hills and lying on a S.E.–N.W. axis. The ridge is an upfaulted block that drops precipitously to the Beth-Shean Valley in the east and the Harod Valley in the northeast and more gradually to the southern Jezreel Valley in the west. Along the fault lines at the mountain's foot in the east and the northeast are some of the most plentiful natural springs in Israel. The entire length of the ridge is 10½ mi. (about 17 km.). The summit is 479 m. high, lying 1¼ mi. (about 2 km.) south of Kafr Faqūʿa. It is from this village that the Arabic name for the mountain, Jebel Faqūʿa, was derived.

Mt. Gilboa was the scene of the battle in which Saul and his sons were killed (I Sam. 31:1–6). David cursed the mountain in his lament over Saul and his sons (II Sam. 1:21): "Ye mountains of Gilboa, let there be no dew nor rain upon you, neither fields of choice fruits." The ancient name is preserved in the present-day Arab village of Jalbūn, situated southeast of Kafr Faqūʿa. Jalbūn is mentioned by Eusebius as Gelbous (Onom., 72:10). In September 1921 kibbutz *En-Harod was established at the foot of the mountain, next to the En-Harod spring (the kibbutz was transferred in 1929 to the northern side of the Harod Valley; on the side of the mountain itself is moshav Gidonah – established in 1949 – which initially bore the name Gilboa). In the time of the British Mandate, especially between 1936 and 1939, Gilboa served as a base for Arab raids on the Jewish settlements in the Harod and Beth-Shean Valleys. Similarly, the Arab Legion and irregulars fortified positions on Mt. Gilboa during the *War of Independence in the spring of 1948, with the aim of cutting off the Harod and Beth-Shean Valley settlements from the west. This danger was overcome with the occupation of the villages of Zarʿīn (see *Yizreʾel) and Mazār by a *Palmaḥ detachment. The 1949 armistice border, following the military front, gave Israel a foothold on the northern and eastern rims of the mountain and left to Jordan most of its inhabited parts in the west and south. After the *Six-Day War, this border marked the northeastern corner of the occupied region of Samaria.

Apart from the new villages founded in the 1950s and 1960s at the foot of Mt. Gilboa in the west, north, and east, five settlements came into being on the mountain proper – Nurit, established in 1950 as a moshav and later transformed into a *Gadna training camp and nature study center; Ma'aleh Gilboa, founded in 1962 as a Naḥal outpost, which became a civilian kibbutz affiliated with *Ha-Kibbutz ha-Dati in 1967; Kibbutz Meirav, also affiliated with Ha-Kibbutz ha-Dati; Malkisuah, a drug rehabilitation village founded in 1990; and Gan Ner, a community founded in 1985. The Jewish National Fund planted a forest on Mt. Gilboa with over 3,000,000 trees – one of the country's largest – and built many access roads and paths opening the mountain for tourism. A large area has been declared a nature reserve where plant species exclusive to Mt. Gilboa are afforded protection.

BIBLIOGRAPHY: Weitz, in: *Bikat Beit-She'an* (1962), 124–8; Levinsohn, *ibid.*, 96–101; EM, 2 (1965), 486.

[Abraham J. Brawer / Shaked Gilboa (2nd ed.)]

GILBOA, AMIR (1917–1984), Israeli poet. Born in Radzywilow, Volhynia, Gilboa went to Palestine in 1937, working initially as a laborer. He began to publish poetry while serving in the Jewish Brigade during World War II. The accent on linguistic sensitivity in the 1940s prompted Gilboa to abandon flowery rhetoric, but he nevertheless preserved the multilevel allusions inherent in this style. His poetry with its developed lyrical sense and complex structure speaks with compassion, and his blending of personal and national motifs is reminiscent of Bialik. Gilboa sensitively and at times enigmatically describes the feelings of the individual within the crowd in a surrealistic dream atmosphere. These feelings range from the fear and expectation of the apocalypse to an expression of wild and childlike joy. A similar atmosphere distinguishes his poems about biblical characters, but the aura of nightmare is present as the landscapes and figures of his childhood and youth are darkened by the Holocaust and the death of his relatives. Gilboa's use of various levels of language without the perspective of distance or irony draws him into a confrontation with the primordial element in Hebrew poetry, particularly the Psalms. His confidence in his own personal vision enables him to create poems wherein ancient words and experiences are suffused with wonder and freshness. The same compassion that typifies his attitude toward human beings is also seen in Gilboa's relationship with trees and plants, their tactile values and biological vitality replacing human attributes. He received the Israel Prize in 1982 for Hebrew poetry.

Gilboa's four volumes of poetry are *Le'ut* ("Fatigue," 1942); *Sheva Rashuyyot* (1949); *Shirim ba-Boker ba-Boker* (1953); *Keḥulim va-Adumim* (1963); and "*Raẓiti Likhtov Siftei Yesheinim*" (1968). His *Collected Works* appeared in 1987. Selected poems in English translation appeared under the title *The Light of Lost Suns* (1979). Warren Bargad wrote a study in English entitled *To Write the Lips of Sleepers: The Poetry of Amir Gilboa* (1994). For English translations of his works, see Goell, Bibliography, 24.

BIBLIOGRAPHY: D. Tsalka (ed.), *Amir Gilboa: Mivḥar Shirim u-Devarim al Yeẓirato* (1962); Sachs, in: S. Burnshaw et al. (eds.), *The Modern Hebrew Poem Itself* (1965), 136–47. **ADD. BIBLIOGRAPHY:** H. Be'er, "*Shirat Ish Yehudi*," in: *Moznayim*, 29 (1969), 236–40; A. Balaban, *Amir Gilboa, Mivḥar Ma'amrei Bikkoret al Yeẓirato* (1972); L. Hakak, *Darkhei Irgun be-Ḥarizah ḥofshit ba-Shirah ha-Ivrit ha-Modernistit: Iyyunim be-Shirim shel Ben Yitzhak, Gilboa. Zach ve-Zamir* (1974); H. Barzel, "*Temurot be-Shirat A. Gilboa*," in: *Moznayim*, 40 (1975), 379–94; S. Sandbank, in: *Davar* (Oct. 14, 1977); L. Barak, *Ha-Tashtit ba-Shir ha-Ḥadash lefi Shirei Amir Gilboa, T. Ruebner ve-Y. Amichai* (1978); A. Lipsker, "*Mivneh u-Mashma'ut be-Shirat A. Gilboa*," in: *Biẓaron*, 24–25 (1985), 17–32; H. Barzel, *Amir Gilboa, Monografyah* (1985); A. Balaban, "*A. Gilboa*," in: *Ha-Do'ar*, 63, 38 (1985), 637–39; Y. Haefrati, "*Al Shenei Shirim shel A. Gilboa*," in: *Alon la-Moreh le-Sifrut*, 12 (1991), 33–50; E. Zoritte, *Ha-Ḥayyim, ha-Aẓilut: Perakim Biografiyim ve-Iyyunim ba-Markivim ha-Kabbaliyim-Ḥasidiyyim shel Shirat Amir Gilboa* (1988); M. Fruchtman, "How Do I know that You Mean what You Mean when You State: You Mean what I Mean. Two Linguistic Models of Modern Hebrew Poetry," in: *Language and Style*, 24:1 (1991), 91–102; H. Shaham, *Hedim shel Niggun* (1997); Y. Abrabanel, *Lada'at Me'ayin u-Le'an: Iyyun ba-Kovez ha-Kol Ḥolekh Le-Amir Gilboa* (2001); D. Laor, "Prodigal Sons: Desertion and Reconciliation in Contemporary Israeli Writing," in: *Midstream*, 50:4 (2004), 33–37.

[Dan Tsalka]

GILBOA, JACOB (1920–), Israeli composer. Born in Czechoslovakia, he studied architecture in Vienna and continued his studies at the Haifa Technological Institute after immigrating to Israel in 1938. Later he studied composition with Josef *Tal and Paul *Ben-Haim and graduated from the Jerusalem Music Academy and Teachers Seminary in 1947. In 1963 he took classes with Stockhausen and Pousseur at the Cologne new music courses. His early style was post-Romantic with Mediterranean elements and later he combined avant-garde style with Oriental elements. His style is unique and difficult to define. Among his many awards were the Israel Composers and Authors Association Prize on four occasions and the Prime Minister's Award in 1983. He has also represented Israel at the ISCM festival four times (1969, 1973, 1978, 1989). His works include *Seven Little Insects* for piano (1955); *Chagall Windows* (1965); *Crystals* (1967); *From the Dead Sea Scrolls* (1972); *Cedars* (1972); *Reflections on 3 Chords of Alban Berg* for piano (1979), *3 Lyric Pieces in Mediterranean Style* for orchestra (1984), *Steps of Spring* for children's/women's chorus (1986); and works with tape such as *3 Vocalises for Peter Breughel*, (1979) and *The Grey Colours of Käthe Kollwitz* (1990). Gilboa also wrote lyrics for many Israeli folk songs.

ADD. BIBLIOGRAPHY: Grove Music Online; O. Tourny, *Jacob Gilboa: Compositeur israelien contemporain* (1988).

[Uri (Erich) Toeplitz and Yohanan Boehm / Gila Flam and Israela Stein (2nd ed.)]

GILEAD (Heb. גִּלְעָד), the central region east of the Jordan, approximately between the river Yarmuk in the north and the northern end of the Dead Sea in the south. The name Gilead is explained in the Bible as deriving from Gal-ed, in Aramaic Yegar-Sahadutha (Gen. 31:47), and there are some scholars who relate its meaning to the Arabic *Jalʿad*, meaning "harsh," "rude," because of the mountainous and rocky nature of the region.

According to the Bible, Israelite Transjordan was divided in three main regions: the plain, Gilead, and the Bashan (Deut. 3:10; Josh. 20:8; II Kings 10:33). The plain is the flat height north of the Arnon which was the scene of constant battle between Israel and Moab. The Bashan is the northern part of Transjordan north of the Yarmuk, for which Israel competed with the Arameans. Gilead is the clearly Israelite section of Transjordan and, therefore, in its broad meaning, encompassed central Transjordan, on both sides of the Jabbok, from the Sea of Galilee to the Dead Sea (Gen. 37:25; Josh. 22:9, 15; II Sam. 2:9; II Kings 10:33; Ezek. 47:18; Amos 1:3; etc.). Different parts of the Bible mention the two halves of Gilead, north and south of the Jabbok (Deut. 3:12; Josh. 12:2, 5; 13:31).

The allotted settlements of tribes on the other side of the Jordan are described according to this geographic division: "From Aroer, which is by the valley of Arnon, and half the hill-country of Gilead, and the cities thereof, gave I unto the Reubenites and to the Gadites; and the rest of Gilead, and all Bashan, the kingdom of Og … gave I unto the half-tribe of Manasseh" (Deut. 3:12 13).

On the other hand, there are some places in the Bible from which it appears that the name Gilead designates a smaller area. Numbers 32:1 separates the land of Jazer from the territory Gilead. In Deuteronomy 3:15–16 the name Gilead includes only the northern part, between the Jabbok and the Yarmuk (though "from the Gilead to the valley of Arnon" is not separated – it is a part of the territory of the tribes of Reuben and Gad). On the other hand, "the land of Gilead" which is enumerated among the 12 regions of Solomon (I Kings 4:19) is in southern Transjordan, including the plain. In place of "the land of Gilead," however, the Septuagint reads "the land of Gad."

In light of these different descriptions several scholars have concluded that the name Gilead originally comprised a more limited area and broadened only with the continuation of Israelite settlement.

According to R. Smend, the name Gilead originally referred to ʿAjlūn, the region between the Jabbok and the Yarmuk. He bases this opinion on the names of the cities Jabesh-Gilead and Ramoth-Gilead, both of which belong to this region, and also on the genealogical lists of Manasseh which mention Gilead, the son of Machir (Num. 26:29; Josh. 17:1; see *Manasseh). R. de Vaux, on the other hand (and also M. Noth), prefers a more southerly location, between al-Ṣalt and the Jabbok, because of the present-day Jebel Jalʿad, Khirbat Jalʿad, and Khirbat Jalʿud, which preserved the name, as well as various biblical statements (especially Num. 32).

Gilead was described in the Bible as pasturage land (Num. 32:1; Jer. 50:19; Micah 7:14). It was known for its spices, among other things (Jer. 8:22; 46:11). There are iron deposits in the vicinity of the Jabbok that were exploited in early times. Archaeological research has shown that the first great settlement of Gilead flourished around the 24th–21st centuries B.C.E. During the 20th century B.C.E. there was a definite decline in the settlement of Gilead and the southern parts of Transjordan, and it seems that these areas were occupied mainly by a nomadic population. This decline was not present in the Bashan and in northern Gilead, up to the area of Bet Arbel (Irbid), around 20 mi. (30 km.) south of the Yarmuk. Heavy population of the whole Gilead and the southern regions of Transjordan was resumed around the beginning of the 13th century, with the establishment of the kingdoms of Amman, Moab, and Edom. According to biblical tradition most of the areas of Gilead were then occupied by two Amorite kings, Og king of Bashan and Sihon king of Heshbon, from whom these areas were conquered by the settling Israelite tribes (Num. 21:32; Deut. 1:4; 3:10–13; Josh. 1:12–15; 9:10; 12:1–6; Judg. 11; etc.). The southern part of Gilead was settled by the tribes of Reuben and Gad, and north of the Jabbok – the half-tribe Manasseh. The latter comprised several family units, such as Machir and the villages of Jair (I Kings 4:13), and the Gadites, too, spread southward up to the Sea of Galilee (Josh. 13:27). According to biblical tradition, the name Israel was given to Jacob at Peniel which is on the Jabbok in central Gilead (Gen. 32:29–31).

The Bible records the war, during the time of the judges, between the Gileadites and Amman, under the leadership of Jephthah the Gileadite (Judg. 11), which resulted in bloody conflict between the Gileadites and the Ephraimites (*ibid.* 12:1–6). This period saw the weakening of the bonds between the tribes of the Gilead and western Ereẓ Israel, as can also be seen from their nonparticipation in the war of Deborah (*ibid.* 5:17) and from the building of the altar by the tribes from the other side of the Jordan "over against the land of Canaan in the borders of Jordan" (Josh. 22:11).

Nevertheless, the Ammonites' attempt to conquer Jabesh-Gilead and its being saved by Saul were the direct motivations for the establishment of the Israelite monarchy (I Sam. 11). The mountainous nature of the Gilead and its broad pasture-lands helped preserve desert customs and early Israelite traditions to which prophetic vision became attached. It is not, therefore, a coincidence that this was the place of origin of Elijah the Gileadite whose spirit greatly affected the development of prophecy.

The Gileadites remained loyal to the ruling house of Israel that protected them from their neighbors in the east and plunderers from the desert. In time of trouble the Israelite kings sought refuge in Mahanaim and Penuel on the Jabbok (II Sam. 2:8; I Kings 12:25). The Gilead is mentioned as one of three places over which Abner son of Ner appointed Ish-Baal (Ish-Bosheth) son of Saul as king (II Sam. 2:8–9). In the time of Solomon Transjordan was divided into three areas (I Kings 4:13–14, 19): (1) the vicinity of Ramoth-Gilead, the village of

Jair in the Gilead and the region of Argob in the Bashan, i.e., northern Gilead and the Bashan; (2) the vicinity of Mahanaim, i.e., central Gilead on both sides of the Jabbok; (3) "the land of Gad" according to the Septuagint (masoretic text, "the (southern) land of Gilead"), i.e., southern Gilead and the plain up to the Arnon River.

With the division of the kingdom Gilead remained in the area of northern Israel. However, the Bashan and the northern part of Gilead were quickly conquered by the Arameans (I Kings 22; II Kings 9:14; II Chron. 18), and Ramoth-Gilead thereafter became an area of perpetual conflict between them and Israel. The Arameans also took the opportunity to broaden their boundaries in Gilead (Amos 1:13). In around 814 B.C.E. Hazael of Aram Damascus conquered the whole land of Gilead from Israel (II Kings 10:32–33). At the beginning of the eighth century Damascus was weakened under Assyrian pressure (*ibid.* 13:5), and the Gilead was restored to the area of Israel (*ibid.* 13:25; 14:25, 28). In 733 the Gilead was conquered by Tiglath-Pileser III, king of Assyria, and many of its inhabitants were exiled to Assyria (*ibid.* 15:29; I Chron. 5:26). The Assyrian satrapy Gal'aza (= Gilead) was established in the place, except for the regions of southern Gilead which were occupied by the Ammonites (Jer. 49:1).

Gilead in the Persian period was included in the fifth satrapy called Abirnahara ("beyond the river," i.e., Transeuphrates) whose capital was at Damascus. During the rule of the Ptolemies the name Galaaditis (Gilead) designated a small district in Transjordan and in the Seleucid period it was the name of one of the four large eparchies into which Coele-Syria was organized (I Macc. 5:17–45).

BIBLIOGRAPHY: R. de Vaux, in: RB, 47 (1938), 398ff.; idem, in: *Vivre et Penser*, 1 (1941), 16ff.; N. Glueck, in: AASOR, 18–19 (1939), passim; 25–28 (1951), passim; M. Noth, in: PJB, 37 (1941), 50ff.; idem, in: ZDPV, 75 (1959), 14ff.; Abel, Geog, 1–11, passim; Aharoni, Land, passim.

[Yohanan Aharoni]

GILEAD, ZERUBAVEL (1912–1988), Hebrew poet, writer, and editor. Born in Bendery, Bessarabia, his family immigrated to Palestine in 1922 and settled in the newly founded kibbutz *En-Harod, where he grew up. He was active in the Ha-No'ar ha-Oved and He-Ḥalutz youth movements, served as an emissary of the latter in Poland, and was information officer of the *Palmaḥ and a member of its general staff during Israel's War of Independence. His poems, stories, and articles appeared in numerous journals and newspapers from 1929. His works include *Ne'urim* (poems, 1936), *Marot Gilbo'a* (sketches, 1943), *Aggadot Yaldut* (poems, 1947), *Siḥah al ha-Ḥof* (stories, 1954), *Nahar Yarok* (poems, 1956), *Siḥah she-Lo Tammah* (essays, 1965), *Yam shel Ma'alah* (poems, 1967), *Ha-Kikhli* (poems, 1978), *Or ha-Har* (poems, 1986), and *Be-Ẓel ha-Te'enah* (poems, 1988). From 1956, he was one of the editors of *Mi-Bifenim*, a periodical of Ha-Kibbutz ha-Me'uḥad, and was an editor of the Kibbutz ha-Me'uḥad publishing house. An English translation of his selected poems appeared in 1983. For further English translations, see Goell, Bibliography, index.

BIBLIOGRAPHY: G. Yardeni, *Siḥot im Soferim* (1961), 133–42; D. Sadan, *Avenei Boḥan* (1951), 140–5; Sadan, in: *Bein Din le-Ḥeshbon* (1963), 115–23; Y. Keshet, *Maskiyyot* (1953), 273–81. **ADD. BIBLIOGRAPHY:** U. Shavit, "*El mul Shorshei ha-Naḥal*," in: *Moznayim*, 44 (1977), 309–12; Y. Zemora, "*Einav Aẓuvot gam ke-she-Meẓalẓel Kolo*," in: *Moznayim*, 47:6 (1979), 419–21; M. Ben Shaul, in: *Maariv* (Aug. 22, 1980); U. Shavit, in: *Davar* (Aug. 22, 1980); A. Brakai, in: *Al ha-Mishmar* (Nov. 11, 1980).

[Getzel Kressel]

GILELS, EMIL GRIGORYEVICH (1916–1985), Russian pianist. Born in Odessa, he became a teacher at the Moscow Conservatory in 1939 and in that same year won the first prize at the international piano competition in Brussels. He was awarded the Stalin Prize in 1946 and the Lenin Prize in 1962. Gilels became popular on concert platforms all over the world. The virtuosity of his early days was enhanced by a depth of interpretation and range of expression that made him one of the foremost pianists of the time.

BIBLIOGRAPHY: V. Delson, *Emil Gilels* (Rus., 1959); S.M. Khentova, *Emil Gilels* (Rus., 1967^2).

[Michael Goldstein]

GILGAL (Heb. גִּלְגָּל), name indicating an ancient sacred site on which a circle of large stones was erected. *Gilgalim* ("circles") were constructed in Canaan from very early times; the Bible mentions several places called Gilgal which were named after *gilgalim* in their vicinity.

(1) The best-known Gilgal is the place "on the east border of Jericho" where the Israelites encamped after crossing the Jordan. There Joshua set up the 12 stones which the Israelites had taken from the Jordan (Josh. 4:19–20). At Gilgal *Pesaḥ* (Passover) was celebrated and those born in the desert were circumcised. "This day have I rolled away (*galloti* from root *galol*) the reproach of Egypt from off you" is the biblical explanation given for the place-name (5:7–10). The camp at Gilgal served as a base during Joshua's wars (9:6; 10:6–9; 14:6). After the conquest of Canaan, the site continued to be sacred; in times of national crisis sacrifices were offered there; Samuel judged Israel there; and Saul was crowned king at Gilgal (I Sam. 10:8; 7:16; 11:14–15). Later its cult aroused the wrath of the prophets (Hos. 4:15; Amos 4:4; 5:5). In the period of the Second Temple it was called Beth-Gilgal and was inhabited by levites who were sons of the Temple singers (Neh. 12:29). The 12 stones in Gilgal are mentioned in the Talmud (Sot. 35b). Eusebius locates it east of Jericho (Onom. 64:24ff.). The Madaba Map shows a church, in which the stones have been embodied, east of the tell of Jericho. Khirbat al-Mafjar or Khirbet al-Athala have been suggested for its identification.

(2) Another Gilgal is perhaps referred to in the verse: "in the Arabah, over against Gilgal, beside the terebinths of Moreh" (Deut. 11:30); its location is not clear.

(3) The Gilgal from which "they went down to Beth-El" which is associated with the activities of Elisha (II Kings 2:1–2;

4:38–44) is identified by some scholars with Jaljūliya, north of Ramallah; others suggest that it is identical with Gilgal (1).

(4) The Gilgal mentioned in the description of the frontier of Judah near "the ascent of Adummim" (Josh. 15:7; but called Geliloth in Josh. 18:17) is unidentified.

(5) The Gilgal whose king Joshua defeated (Josh. 12:23; LXX – "Galilee") is also unidentified.

BIBLIOGRAPHY: Maisler (Mazar), in: BJPES, 11 (1945), 35–41; S. Klein, *Ereẓ ha-Galil* (1946), 13; E. Sellin, *Gilgal* (1917); Albright, in: BASOR, 11 (1923), 7ff.; M. Noth, *Das Buch Josua* (1953²), 32–33; Abel, Geog, 2 (1938), 336–8; Kelso, in: BASOR, 121 (1951), 6ff.; Kelso and Baramki, in: AASOR, 29–30 (1955).

[Michael Avi-Yonah]

GILGUL (Heb. גִּלְגּוּל; "transmigration of souls," "reincarnation," or "metempsychosis"). There is no definite proof of the existence of the doctrine of *gilgul* in Judaism during the Second Temple period. In the Talmud there is no reference to it (although, by means of allegoric interpretations, later authorities found allusions to and hints of transmigration in the statements of talmudic rabbis). A few scholars interpret the statements of Josephus in *Antiquities* 18:1, 3, and in *Jewish Wars* 2:8, 14 on the holy bodies which the righteous merit, according to the belief of the Pharisees, as indicating the doctrine of metempsychosis and not the resurrection of the dead, as most scholars believe. In the post-talmudic period *Anan b. David, the founder of Karaism, upheld this doctrine, and in some of his statements there is an echo and a continuation of the ancient sectarian traditions. The doctrine of transmigration was prevalent from the second century onward among some Gnostic sects and especially among Manicheans and was maintained in several circles in the Christian Church (perhaps even by Origen). It is not impossible that this doctrine became current in some Jewish circles, who could have received it from Indian philosophies through Manicheism, or from Platonic and neoplatonic as well as from Orphic teachings.

Anan's arguments on behalf of *gilgul*, which were not accepted by the Karaites, were refuted by *Kirkisani (tenth century) in a special chapter in his *Sefer ha-Orot*; one of his major points was the death of innocent infants. Some Jews, following the Islamic sect of the Muʿtazila and attracted by its philosophic principles, accepted the doctrine of transmigration. The major medieval Jewish philosophers rejected this doctrine (*Saadiah Gaon, *The Book of Beliefs and Opinions*, treatise 6, ch. 7; Abraham ibn Daud, *Emunah Ramah*, treatise 1, ch. 7; Joseph *Albo, *Ikkarim*, treatise 4, ch. 29). *Abraham b. Ḥiyya quotes the doctrine from neoplatonic sources but rejects it (*Meditations of the Sad Soul*, 46–47; *Megillat ha-Megalleh*, 50–51). *Judah Halevi and *Maimonides do not mention *gilgul*, and *Abraham b. Moses b. Maimon, who does refer to it, rejects it completely.

In Early Kabbalah

In contrast with the conspicuous opposition of Jewish philosophy, metempsychosis is taken for granted in the Kabbalah from its first literary expression in the *Sefer ha-*Bahir* (published in late 12th century). The absence of any special apology for this doctrine, which is expounded by the *Bahir* in several parables, proves that the idea grew or developed in the circles of the early kabbalists without any affinity to the philosophic discussion of transmigration. Biblical verses (e.g., "One generation passeth away, and another generation cometh" (Eccles. 1:4), taken as meaning that the generation that passes away is the generation that comes) and talmudic *aggadot* and parables were explained in terms of transmigration. It is not clear whether there was any connection between the appearance of the metempsychosic doctrine in kabbalistic circles in southern France and its appearance among the contemporary Cathars (see *Albigenses), who also lived there. Indeed the latter, like most believers in transmigration, taught that the soul also passes into the bodies of animals, whereas in the *Bahir* it is mentioned only in relation to the bodies of men.

After the *Bahir* the doctrine of *gilgul* developed in several directions and became one of the major doctrines of the Kabbalah, although the kabbalists differed widely in regard to details. In the 13th century, transmigration was viewed as an esoteric doctrine and was only alluded to, but in the 14th century many detailed and explicit writings on it appeared. In philosophic literature the term *ha'atakah* ("transference") was generally used for *gilgul*; in kabbalistic literature the term *gilgul* appears only from the *Sefer ha-*Temunah* onward; both are translations of the Arabic term *tanāsukh*. The early kabbalists, such as the disciples of *Isaac the Blind and the kabbalists of Gerona, spoke of "the secret of *ibbur*" ("impregnation"). It was only in the late 13th or 14th centuries that *gilgul* and *ibbur* began to be differentiated. The terms *hitḥallefut* ("exchange") and *din benei ḥalof* (from Prov. 31:8) also occur. From the period of the *Zohar on, the term *gilgul* became prevalent in Hebrew literature and began to appear in philosophic works as well.

Biblical verses and commandments were interpreted in terms of *gilgul*. The early sects to whom Anan was indebted saw the laws of ritual slaughter (*sheḥitah*) as biblical proof of transmigration in accordance with their belief in transmigration among animals. For the Kabbalists the point of departure and the proof for *gilgul* was the commandment of levirate marriage (see *Ḥaliẓah*): the brother of the childless deceased replaces the deceased husband so that he may merit children in his second *gilgul*. Later, other *mitzvot* were interpreted on the basis of transmigration. The belief in metempsychosis also served as a rational excuse for the apparent absence of justice in the world and as an answer to the problem of the suffering of righteous and the prospering of the wicked: the righteous man, for example, is punished for his sins in a previous *gilgul*. The entire Book of Job and the resolution of the mystery of his suffering, especially as stated in the words of Elihu, were interpreted in terms of transmigration (e.g., in the commentary on Job by *Naḥmanides, and in all subsequent kabbalistic literature). Most of the early kabbalists (up to and including the author of the Zohar) did not regard transmigration as a universal law governing all creatures (as is the case in the Indian belief) and not even as governing all human beings, but saw it rather as connected essentially with offenses against procreation and sexual transgressions. Transmigration is seen as a very harsh punishment for the soul which must undergo it. At the same time, however, it is an expression of the mercy of the Creator, "from whom no one is cast off forever"; even for those who should be punished with "extinction of the soul" (*keritut*), *gilgul* provides an opportunity for restitution. While some emphasized more strongly the aspect of justice in transmigration, and some that of mercy, its singular purpose was always the purification of the soul and the opportunity, in a new trial, to improve its deeds. The death of infants is one of the ways by which former transgressions are punished.

In the *Bahir* it is stated that transmigration may continue for 1,000 generations, but the common opinion in the Spanish Kabbalah is that in order to atone for its sins, the soul transmigrates three more times after entering its original body (according to Job 33:29, "Behold, God does all these things, twice, three times, with a man"). However, the righteous transmigrate endlessly for the benefit of the universe, not for their own benefit. As on all points of this doctrine, opposing views also exist in kabbalistic literature: the righteous transmigrate as many as three times, the wicked, as many as 1,000! Burial is a condition for a new *gilgul* of the soul, hence the reason for burial on the day of death. Sometimes a male soul enters a female body, resulting in sterility. Transmigration into the bodies of women and of gentiles was held possible by several kabbalists, in opposition to the view of most of the Safed kabbalists. The *Sefer Peli'ah* viewed proselytes as Jewish souls which had passed into the bodies of gentiles, and returned to their former state.

GILGUL AND PUNISHMENT. The relationship between transmigration and hell is also a matter of dispute. Baḥya b. *Asher proposed that transmigration occurred only after the acceptance of punishment in hell, but the opposite view is found in the *Ra'aya Meheimna*, in the Zohar, and among most of the kabbalists. Because the concepts of metempsychosis and punishment in hell are mutually exclusive, there could be no compromise between them. Joseph of Hamadan, Persia, who lived in Spain in the 14th century, interpreted the entire matter of hell as transmigration among animals. The transmigrations of souls began after the slaying of Abel (some claim in the generation of the Flood), and will cease only with the resurrection of the dead. At that time the bodies of all those who underwent transmigrations will be revived and sparks (*niẓoẓot*) from the original soul will spread within them. But the other answers to this question were proposed by many kabbalists, especially in the 13th century. The expansion of the notion of transmigration from a punishment limited to specific sins into a general principle contributed to the rise of the belief in transmigration into animals and even into plants and inorganic matter. This opinion, however, opposed by many kabbalists, did not become common until after 1400. Transmigration into the bodies of animals is first mentioned in the *Sefer ha-Temunah*, which originated in a circle probably associated with the kabbalists of Gerona. In the Zohar itself this idea is not found, but some sayings in *Tikkunei Zohar* attempt to explain this concept exegetically, indicating that this doctrine was already known to the author of that work. *Ta'amei ha-Mitzvot* (c. 1290–1300), an anonymous work on the reasons for the commandments, records many details (partly quoted by Menahem *Recanati) on the transmigration of human souls into the bodies of animals, the great majority of which were punishments for acts of sexual intercourse forbidden by the Torah.

In the Later and the Safed Kabbalah

A more general elaboration of the entire concept appears in the works of Joseph b. Shalom *Ashkenazi and his colleagues (early 14th century). They maintain that transmigration occurs in all forms of existence, from the *Sefirot* ("emanations") and the angels to inorganic matter, and is called *din benei ḥalof* or *sod ha-shelaḥ*. According to this, everything in the world is constantly changing form, descending to the lowest form and ascending again to the highest. The precise concept of the transmigration of the soul in its particular form into an existence other than its original one is thus obscured, and is replaced by the law of the change of form. Perhaps this version of the doctrine of *gilgul* should be seen as an answer to philosophical criticism based on the Aristotelian definition of the soul as the "form" of the body which consequently cannot become the form of another body. The mystery of true *gilgul* in this new version was sometimes introduced instead of the traditional kabbalistic teaching as found in *Masoret ha-Berit* (1916) by David b. Abraham *ha-Lavan (c. 1300). The kabbalists of Safed accepted the doctrine of transmigration into all forms of nature and, through them, this teaching became a widespread popular belief.

In Safed, especially in the Lurianic Kabbalah, the idea of *niẓoẓot ha-neshamot* ("sparks of the souls") was highly developed. Each "main" soul is built in the spiritual structure of "mystical limbs" (parallel to the limbs of the body), from which many sparks spread, each of which can serve as a soul or as life in a human body. The *gilgulim* of all the sparks together are aimed at the restitution of the hidden spiritual structure of the "root" of the principal soul; it is possible for one man to possess several different sparks belonging to one "root." All the roots of the souls were in fact contained in Adam's soul, but they fell and were scattered with the first sin; the souls must be reassembled in the course of their *gilgulim* which they and their sparks undergo and through which they are afforded the opportunity to restitute their true and original structure. The later Kabbalah developed much further the idea of the affinity of those souls which belong to a common root. In the kabbalistic commentaries on the Bible many events were explained by such hidden history of the transmigration of various souls which return in a later *gilgul* to situations similar to those of an earlier state, in order to repair damage which they had previously caused. The early Kabbalah provides the basis of this idea: there Moses and Jethro, for example, are considered the reincarnations of Abel and Cain; David, Bathsheba, and Uriah, of Adam, Eve, and the serpent; and Job, of Terah, the father of Abraham. The anonymous *Gallei Razayya* (written 1552; published partly Mohilev, 1812), and *Sefer ha-Gilgulim* (Frankfurt, 1684) and *Sha'ar ha-Gilgulim* (1875, 1912) by Ḥayyim *Vital present lengthy explanations of the histories of biblical characters in the light of their former *gilgulim*. *Luria and Vital expanded the framework to include talmudic figures. The transmigrations of many figures are explained in *Gilgulei Neshamot* by Menahem Azariah da *Fano (edition with commentary, 1907). Many kabbalists dealt in detail with the function that was fulfilled by the several *gilgulim* of Adam's soul; they also explained his name as an abbreviation of Adam, David, Messiah (first mentioned by Moses b. Shem-Tov de *Leon).

Ibbur

In addition to the doctrine of *gilgul*, that of *ibbur* ("impregnation") developed from the second half of the 13th century. *Ibbur*, as distinct from *gilgul*, means the entry of another soul into a man, not during pregnancy nor at birth but during his life. In general, such an additional soul dwells in a man only for a limited period of time, for the purpose of performing certain acts or commandments. In the Zohar it is stated that the souls of Nadab and Abihu were temporarily added to that of Phinehas in his zeal over the act of Zimri, and that Judah's soul was present in Boaz when he begat Obed. This doctrine was a respected one in the teachings of the kabbalists of Safed, especially in the Lurianic school: a righteous man who fulfilled almost all of the 613 *mitzvot* but did not have the opportunity to fulfill one special *mitzvah* is temporarily reincarnated in one who has the opportunity to fulfill it. Thus the souls of the righteous men are reincarnated for the benefit of the universe and their generation. The *ibbur* of a wicked man into the soul of another man is called a *Dibbuk in later popular usage. The prevalence of the belief in *gilgul* in the 16th and 17th centuries also caused new disputes between its supporters and detractors. A detailed debate on the doctrine of transmigration took place in about 1460 between two scholars in Candia (Ms. Vatican 254). Abraham ha-Levi ibn Migash disputed against the doctrine of *gilgul* in all its manifestations (*Sefer Kevod Elohim*, 2, 10–14, Constantine, 1585) and Leone *Modena wrote his treatise *Ben David* against transmigration (published in the collection *Ta'am Zekenim*, 1885, pp. 61–64). In defense of transmigration, Manasseh Ben *Israel wrote *Sefer Nishmat Ḥayyim* (Amsterdam, 1652). Works of later kabbalists on the subjects are *Midrash Talpiyyot, Anaf Gilgul* (Smyrna, 1736) by Elijah ha-Kohen ha-Itamari, and *Golel Or* (Smyrna, 1737) by Meir *Bikayam.

BIBLIOGRAPHY: S. Rubin, *Gilgulei Neshamot* (1899); S. Pushinski, in: *Yavneh*, 1 (1939), 137–53; G. Scholem, in: *Tarbiz*, 16 (1945), 135–50; S.A. Horodezki, *Torat ha-Kabbalah shel ha-Ari ve-Ḥayyim Vital* (1947), 245–52; S. Poznański, in: *Semitic Studies in Memory of A. Kohut* (1897), 435–56; N.E. David, *Karma and Reincarnation in Israelitism* (1908); G. Scholem, *Von der mystischen Gestalt der Gottheit* (1962), 193–247, 297–306; E. Gottlieb, in: *Sefunot*, 11 (1969), 43–66.

[Gershom Scholem]

GILLIGAN, CAROL FRIEDMAN (1936–), U.S. social psychologist. Daughter of William E. Friedman and Mabel (Caminez) Friedman, Carol Gilligan spent her early years in New York City. Her mother was a teacher and therapist and her father an attorney. Gilligan, who describes her Jewish identity as rooted in Reconstructionist Judaism, celebrated her bat mitzvah at the Society for the Advancement of Judaism in New York. She received her B.A. in literature in 1958 from Swarthmore College, M.A. in 1960 from Radcliffe College in clinical psychology, and doctorate in 1964 from Harvard University in social psychology. After a departure from academia to a world of dance, motherhood, and political activism, Gilligan returned to teaching, at the University of Chicago in 1965–66 and then at Harvard in 1968. Gilligan became a full professor at Harvard in 1986 and in 1997 was named Harvard's first professor of gender studies, occupying the Patricia Abjerg Graham Chair. In 1999, Gilligan returned to her childhood home of New York City and became a visiting professor at New York University, where she was named university professor in 2002.

Carol Gilligan's work fundamentally altered the world of psychological theory and research by demonstrating that gender was a central component in human behavior and development. Beginning with her groundbreaking book, *In a Different Voice: Psychological Theory and Women's Development* (1982) and culminating in *The Birth of Pleasure* (2003), Gilligan proposed that women's moral and personal development did not conform to patterns of maturation that had been observed for men. She suggested that mainstream psychological theories about human growth reflected a male bias that ignored female identity and experience. During the 1980s, Gilligan founded the Harvard Project on Women's Psychology and Girls' Development and conducted two longitudinal studies tracing the relational worlds of girls between ages six and seventeen. This research profoundly influenced understanding of the tensions and dilemmas girls face in American society. Together with her graduate students, Gilligan edited or coauthored five books that stemmed from these and related studies in coeducational and urban public schools, *Mapping the Moral Domain: A Contribution of Women's Thinking to Psychological Theory* (1988); *Making Connections: The Relational World of Adolescent Girls at Emma Willard School* (1990); *Women, Girls and Psychotherapy: Reframing Resistance* (1991); *Meeting at the Crossroads* (1992) (*New York Times* Notable Book of the Year); and *Between Voice and Silence: Women and Girls, Race and Relationship* (1995). In the late 1990s, Gilligan turned her attention to the development of boys, with special focus on the early childhood years and parental relationships.

Gilligan received numerous awards, including a Grawemeyer Award for her contributions to education (1992), a Heinz Award for her contributions to understanding the human condition (1998), and a senior research award from the Spencer Foundation (1989–93). In 1996 she was named one of the 25 most influential Americans by *Time* magazine.

BIBLIOGRAPHY: A. Medea, "Gilligan, Carol," in: P.E. Hyman and D.D. Moore (eds.), *Jewish Women in America*, vol. 1 (1997), 512–4.

[Miriam B. Raider-Roth (2nd ed.)]

GILLMAN, NEIL (1933–), U.S. scholar in Jewish thought and philosophy. Born in Quebec City, Quebec, Canada, Gillman earned his B.A. from McGill University (1954), and received both a master's degree in Hebrew literature and rabbinic ordination from the Jewish Theological Seminary of America (JTSA; 1960). He also received a Ph.D. in philosophy from Columbia University (1975) and later held the Aaron Rabinowitz and Simon H. Rifkind Chair in Jewish Philosophy at JTSA, where he served in various faculty and administrative roles.

From the 1970s, Gillman primarily taught Conservative Jews how to hold the dynamic tensions among belief, behavior, and community. Students at the Jewish Theological Seminary are taught by Gillman that they must create a personal philosophy that serves them both as an individual and as a member of the Jewish community, and that their philosophy will likely evolve over time. Gillman's extensive experience teaching adults in synagogues throughout America has broadened the impact of his work by bringing the scholarship of Jewish thought from the principal academic institution of the Conservative movement in Judaism to people of all ages and backgrounds.

From his scholarly works on death and dying, such as "Coping with Chaos: Jewish Theology and Ritual Resources in Death, Bereavement, and Mourning" (2005) to widely read articles in popular Jewish periodicals, including "I Believe" (*Sh'ma*, 1993), Gillman has demonstrated the ability to articulate the challenges facing modern Jews. His ability to help others clarify their personal philosophy and to see how their relationship to God is magical comes not only by sharing his knowledge of those who came before him and how they were able to change their own thinking, but also through sharing his own personal, evolving story.

Gillman's books on Jewish thought include *Sacred Fragments: Recovering Theology for the Modern Jew* (1990), which won the National Jewish Book Award in Jewish Thought; *The Death of Death: Resurrection and Immortality in Jewish Thought* (1997); *The Way Into Encountering God in Judaism* (2000); and *Traces of God: Seeing God in Torah, History and Everyday Life* (2005).

Committed to creating materials that are accessible to a variety of audiences, Gillman's publications also include scholarly monographs such as "Mordechai Kaplan and the Ideology of Conservative Judaism" (*Proceedings of the Rabbinical Assembly*, 1984) and "Covenant and Chosenness in Postmodern Jewish Thought" (*Covenant and Chosenness in Mormonism and Judaism*, 2001), as well as other writings targeted at a broader audience, such as "Why Can't I Pray and What Can I Do About It" (*Moment*, 1990) and "On Teaching Jewish Theology" (*The Melton Journal*, 1994). In 1991, Gillman began writing a column, *Sabbath Week*, in New York newspaper *The Jewish Week*.

[Donna Fishman (2nd ed.)]

GILLMAN, SID (1911–2003), innovative U.S. football coach, recognized as a leading authority on passing theories and tactics, influential in changing the downfield passing game and in the use of film footage as a preparatory tool for coaching; the only coach elected to both Pro (1983) and College (1989) Football Halls of Fame.

Born and raised in a traditional kosher home in Minneapolis, Minn., to Sara (Dickerson), who was born in New York, and David, born in Austria. Gillman played college football from 1931 to 1933 at Ohio State University, where he was a Grantland Rice AP All-American honorable mention, 1932–33. He also played in the inaugural College Football All-Star Game in 1934. While working as a movie theater usher at his father's theater, he would remove the football segments from newsreels and take them home to study. Gillman was the first coach to analyze game footage, something practiced by all coaches today.

Gillman played one year in the National Football League for the Cleveland Rams, then began coaching, first as an assistant coach at Denton University (1935–37, 1941), Ohio State (1938–40), and the University of Miami of Ohio (1942–43), before being named head coach at Miami of Ohio (1944–47). He led Miami to a 31–6–1 record, including a 13–12 victory in the 1947 Sun Bowl. After a year as assistant coach at Army in 1948, Gillman was named head coach at the University of Cincinnati (1949–54), which he led to three Mid-American Conference titles, two bowl games, and a 50–13–1 record, resulting in a remarkable .814 winning percentage (81–19–2) in his college coaching career.

In 1955, after failing to receive the Ohio State head-coaching job – which Gillman always suspected was because he was Jewish – he moved to the pros as head coach with the Los Angeles Rams, where he compiled a 28–31–1 record in 1955–59 and led the team to the NFL championship game in 1955. When the American Football League debuted in 1960, Gillman was named head coach of the Los Angeles Chargers, which moved to San Diego in 1961. He led the team to five Western Division titles, one league championship – in 1963, beating the Boston Patriots 51–10 – and an 82–47–6 record in the first six years of the league's existence. He also coached the Houston Oilers in 1973–74, winning Coach of the Year honors in 1974. Gillman, who finished with a 123–104–7 professional record, is credited with putting names on the backs of jerseys, and with first suggesting the idea of a "Super Bowl" game between champions of the NFL and AFL.

[Elli Wohlgelernter (2nd ed.)]

GILMAN, ALFRED G. (1941–), U.S. pharmacologist and Nobel laureate in medicine. Gilman was born in New Haven, Connecticut, and received his B.Sc. in biochemistry from Yale in 1962 and M.D. and Ph.D. from Case Western Reserve University, Cleveland, in 1969. He was a research associate at the National Institutes of Health, in 1969–71, and worked at the University of Virginia, Charlottesville, in 1971–81, where he became professor of pharmacology. From 1981 he was professor and chairman of the department of pharmacology at the University of Texas Southwestern Medical Center in Dallas, Texas. Gilman's life-long research interests concern the ways in which cells respond to external stimuli transmitted from the surrounding plasma membrane. Sutherland's discovery of the cyclic AMP system introduced the concept of transduction in the plasma membrane and the generation of a second messenger initiating cellular responses. The discovery of the G protein family (shorthand for guanine nucleotide-binding regulatory proteins) by Gilman and his colleagues greatly expanded knowledge of the plasma membrane events which signal appropriate responses to an enormous range of external stimuli including hormones and bacterial toxins. In 1994 he and Martin Rodbell were awarded the Nobel Prize for medicine for this work. His subsequent work largely concerned the distribution and properties of the different members of the G protein family, and the cyclic AMP system. Gilman took over the editorship of the world's best-known textbook of pharmacology (*The Pharmacological Basis of Therapeutics*) from his distinguished pharmacologist father. His honors include membership in the U.S. National Academy of Sciences and the Gairdner and Lasker Awards.

[Michael Denman (2nd ed.)]

GILYONOT (Heb. גִּלְיוֹנוֹת), an independent literary monthly published in Tel Aviv from 1934 to 1954, founded and edited by Yiẓhak *Lamdan. Lamdan's strong Zionist and socialist ideas were expressed both in his literary and editorial policy. He viewed modern Hebrew literature as a "continuation of the Hebrew literature" of the past. In addition to recognized Hebrew writers, Lamdan encouraged younger writers to publish in *Gilyonot* and several contemporary writers of stature published their first works in its pages (S. *Yizhar, for example). He also invited the participation of Hebrew writers living in Europe and the U.S. He manifested great interest in U.S. Jewry, devoting an issue of *Gilyonot* to that community (vol. 31, no. 8–10). Of interest also is the 18th anniversary issue (vol. 26, no. 5–6), which dealt with the history of Hebrew periodical literature. The final issue of *Gilyonot* appeared after Lamdan's death and was dedicated to his memory.

[Getzel Kressel]

GIMBEL, U.S. merchant family. ADAM GIMBEL (1817–96), who emigrated from Bavaria, settled in New Orleans in 1835. Six brothers and two sisters followed him to the United States. Adam was a peddler along the Mississippi River before opening a dry goods store in Vincennes, Indiana, in 1842. By the time he sold his firm 40 years later, he owned four stores in Vincennes. He was a member of the city council from 1842 to 1866. The two eldest of Adam's seven sons, JACOB (1851–1922) and ISAAC GIMBEL (1857–1931), established a department store in Danville, Illinois, in the 1880s. When they found the undertaking unprofitable, they moved to Milwaukee, Wisconsin, where they founded Gimbel Brothers. In 1894 they opened a second department store in Philadelphia, which was run by their brothers CHARLES (1861–1932) and ELLIS GIMBEL (1865–1950). The Gimbels' first New York venture came in 1910 with the establishment of a department store at Herald Square, which grew rapidly when two older firms were merged with it. In 1923 Gimbel Brothers bought Saks and Co. and shortly thereafter built a Saks subsidiary on Fifth Avenue. The Gimbel chain was further extended in 1926, when it took over Kaufman and Baer of Pittsburgh.

In the next decades, Saks branches were opened in Chicago, Detroit, Beverly Hills, and San Francisco. BERNARD F. GIMBEL (1885–1966), Isaac's son, became president of Gimbel Brothers in 1927. He was a distinguished civic figure who played a large part in the organization and direction of New York City's World Fairs in 1939 and 1964–65. He was a generous contributor to a number of scholarly institutions and was active in the work of the National Conference of Jews and Christians. Bernard's son, BRUCE A. GIMBEL (1913–1980), succeeded his father as president of Gimbel Brothers, Inc. in 1953. Sales during the fiscal year ending January 31, 1961, in a total of 53 urban and suburban stores in the chain, reached a record $61.6 million. Ten additional stores were opened over the next three years. However, in 1973 the company was absorbed by Brown and Williamson Tobacco Corp. and later by BAT Industries PLC. The last Gimbel's store closed its doors in 1987.

Maintaining the family's dedication to philanthropy, the Bernard F. and Alva B. Gimbel Foundation, established in 1943, supports services, programs and advocacy efforts in New York City that deal with education, workforce and economic development, civil legal services, criminal justice, reproductive rights, and the environment.

[Hanns G. Reissner Ruth Beloff (2nd ed.)]

GIMMEL (Heb. ג; גִּמֶל), third letter of the Hebrew alphabet; its numerical value is therefore 3. The basic shape of this letter consists of two strokes forming an angle: thus in the Proto-Sinaitic ∟, Proto-Canaanite ⌃. and Proto-Arabian ˥ scripts. In the tenth-century B.C.E. Phoenician script two types occur: ˥ and ⌃. The first type was adopted by the ancient Hebrew and Greek scripts (cf. the gamma Γ), while the second one prevailed in the later Phoenician and Aramaic scripts. From the Aramaic ∧ developed the Jewish λ, Syriac ⦣, and Arabic ⦣. The modern Hebrew cursive *gimmel* evolved as follows: ג → λ → ɕ. See *Alphabet, Hebrew.

[Joseph Naveh]

GINGOLD, HERMIONE (1897–1987), British actress. Born in London, the daughter of a stockbroker from Austria, Hermione Gingold had a varied career on the London and New York stage, lasting over 60 years, from 1908 until 1973, usually appearing in comedies and reviews. A second career in Hollywood saw her star in such films as *Gigi* (1958), and a further career in American television found her typecast as a delightful eccentric. Twice married, her first husband was the British Jewish literary agent and publisher MICHAEL JOSEPH (1897–1958), whom she married in 1918 and divorced in 1926.

His firm, Michael Joseph Ltd., published the works of such famous writers as Michael Arlen, Daphne DuMaurier, and Dick Francis. Gingold wrote a posthumously published autobiography, *How to Grow Old Gracefully* (1988). There is a biography of her husband, *Michael Joseph: Master of Words* (1986), which never mentions the fact that he was Jewish.

[William D. Rubinstein (2nd ed.)]

GINGOLD, PINCHAS M. (1893–1953), U.S. Labor Zionist and Yiddish educator. Gingold was born near Grodno, Lithuania, and immigrated to the United States at the age of 16. A founder of the Jewish Legion at the start of World War I, Gingold enlisted and saw action with the British Army in Palestine. Upon his return to New York (1920), he joined the Labor Zionist movement and was active in the American and the World Jewish Congress. During the 1920s and 1930s Gingold was the director of the Yiddish Teachers Seminary. In 1932 he edited the *Yidishe Dertsiung*, an educational journal sponsored by the Jewish National Workers' Alliance (Farband). After 1930 he headed the national committee of the Jewish Folk Schools. The committee published the *Pinchas Gingold Book* (1955), a commemorative Yiddish volume containing Gingold's essays on Jewish education and culture and his reminiscences of the Jewish Legion.

GINIEWSKI, PAUL (1926–), French editor and author. Born in Vienna, Giniewski went to France in 1940 and from 1943 to 1945 was a member of the French Resistance. He served as chairman of the press committee of the Zionist Federation of France and in 1951 became editor in chief of the French Jewish periodical, *La Terre Retrouvée*. His books include *Quand Israël combat* (1957), *Israël devant l'Afrique et l'Asie* (1958), *Le Bouclier de David* (1960), *Bantustans: A Trek Towards the Future* (1961), and *Une autre Afrique du Sud* (1962).

GINNEGAR (Heb. גִּנֵּיגַר), kibbutz on the northern rim of the Jezreel Valley, Israel, S.W. of Nazareth, affiliated to Iḥud ha-Kevuẓot ve-ha-Kibbutzim. It was founded in 1922 by pioneers of the Third Aliyah. Its settlers had previously set up kibbutz Deganyah Gimmel in the Jordan Valley. Ginnegar was one of the earliest Jezreel Valley settlements, and in the initial years of struggle, the settlers were employed in the planting of the Balfour Forest, at the time the largest *Jewish National Fund forest in the country, located on the slopes above the kibbutz. The kibbutz economy was based on highly intensive farming and it owned a factory manufacturing plastic products. In 2002 its population was 448. Ginnegar is a historical name mentioned, in forms like Neginegar (נְגִינֵגַר) in the Talmud (TJ, Er. 1:9, 19c; Kil. 4:4, 29b; et al.), and is preserved in the Arabic name of the site Jinjār.

WEBSITE: www.ginegar.co.il.

[Efraim Orni]

GINNOSAR (גִּנּוֹסַר), kibbutz on the shore of Lake Kinneret, Israel, founded by Israel-born youth and Youth Aliyah graduates of *Ben Shemen. The kibbutz was set up at the time of the Arab riots early in 1937, serving initially as a guard outpost on *Palestine Jewish Colonization Association (PICA) lands. In spite of PICA's opposition, the settlement became permanent. Before 1948, in the pre-State period, Ginnosar served as a training and organizational center of the *Palmaḥ. It developed subtropical intensive farming (bananas, avocado, mango, and litchi), field crops, dairy cattle, and fishery. In addition, the kibbutz operated a banana plant nursery and also opened a large guesthouse and restaurant. Yigal Allon House, a memorial museum, is located inside the kibbutz. It features the so-called "Jesus boat," constructed in around 40 B.C.E. and salvaged from Lake Tiberias in 1986. In 2002 the population of Ginnosar was 483.

BIBLIOGRAPHY: www.ginosar.net/history.html.

[Efraim Orni / Shaked Gilboa (2nd ed.)]

GINNOSAR, PLAIN OF (Heb. בִּקְעַת גִּנּוֹסַר), narrow plain on the N.W. shore of Lake *Kinneret. The plain extends c. 3½ mi. (5½ km.) along the coast and its width in the center from the sea to the edge of the alluvial soil and the foot of the hills is c. 1¼ mi. (2 km.). In antiquity the name Ginnosar apparently also applied to the rim of the hills since Josephus states that it is 2½ mi. (3.7 km.) wide (Wars, 3:516ff.). Its area covers over 1,600 acres (6,450 dunams). The plain of Ginnosar was created by alluvial soil deposited by three brooks which pass through the plain: Naḥal Ammud and Naḥal Zalmon, perennial brooks, and Naḥal Arbel, a brook flowing intermittently. The extreme fertile basaltic red soil washed down from the hills to which the sea added moisture and dew produced the famous fruits praised by Josephus (*ibid.*) and the Talmud. The fruits are described as being large, easily digested, and causing the skin to become smooth. Several interesting anecdotes are told about rabbis who partook of them, including a story about *Simeon b. Lakish whose mind began to wander (Ber. 44a). The plain of Ginnosar was included in the territory of Naphtali and the Talmud attributes the blessings of Jacob and Moses to Naphtali to this plain: "It is the plain of Ginnosar which hastens its fruits like a hind [which runs swiftly]" (Gen. R. 99:12); "Naphtali, satisfied with favor, and full with the blessing of the Lord: that is the plain of Ginnosar" (Sif. Deut. 355). The name appears in ancient sources in various forms of which the most correct appears to be the Greek form Gennesar as in I Maccabees 11:67 and in talmudic sources, but the form Ginnosar is most frequently used and has become generally accepted. The lands of the plain of Ginnosar are now cultivated by the settlements of *Migdal and *Ginnosar.

[Abraham J. Brawer]

GINOSSAR (née **Hacohen**), **ROSA** (1890–1979), Zionist women leader. Daughter of the writer Mordecai ben Hillel *Hacohen, Rosa Ginossar was born in Gomel, Belorussia and immigrated with her family to Ereẓ Israel in 1907 with the Second Aliyah. She studied law there and succeeded in having the ban against the admission of women to the Palestine bar removed, becoming the first practicing woman lawyer in Ereẓ

Israel. She married Shlomo, the son of Aḥad *Ha-Am (Asher Hirsch Ginsberg), Israel's first ambassador to Italy (1949–51), who hebraized his name to Ginossar. Rosa Ginossar joined *WIZO at its inception in 1920, becoming its first secretary, and was actively associated with the organization throughout its history. After serving as treasurer for many years, she was elected chairman of the World Executive in 1951 and president in 1963. On her retirement from active work in 1970, she was appointed honorary president.

GINOTT, HAIM G. (1922–1973), U.S. psychologist. Ginott was born in Tel Aviv but immigrated to the United States, where he received his doctorate from Columbia University in 1952. He specialized in group psychotherapy, especially with children, practicing as chief clinical psychologist at the Child Guidance Clinic at Jacksonville, Florida, from 1952 to 1960 and lecturing at Jacksonville University from 1955 to 1958. In 1960 he was appointed an adjunct associate professor and supervisor of child psychotherapy at New York University. In 1966 he was appointed associate clinical professor in the postdoctoral program at Adelphi University in Garden City, Long Island, N.Y. He served as UNESCO expert in guidance and counseling to the government of Israel from 1965 to 1966.

Ginott was best known for his practical and commonsense approach to child psychotherapy. In his *Group Psychotherapy with Children* (1961), he stressed the importance of the details of play therapy, such as the selection of children, how to equip a playroom, etc. Nor did he overlook the parent, including the screening of the parents of prospective clients and ways of conducting parent guidance groups. He addressed himself to those colleagues who "knew about Oedipus and Electra, but were puzzled when confronted with children's incestuous approaches; they knew about transference and resistance, but had difficulty in transferring a resisting child from the waiting room to the playroom."

From 1967 Ginott devoted himself to writing authoritative books for the nonspecialist, and his *Between Parent and Child* (1967) made him the public's favorite expert on child psychology. His later books dealt with the teenager (*Between Parent and Adolescent*, 1969) and the school-age child (*Teacher and Child*, 1972).

BIBLIOGRAPHY: G.D. Goldman and G. Stricker (eds.), *Practical Problems of a Private Psychotherapy Practice* (1972).

[Helmut E. Adler (2nd ed.)]

GINSBERG, ALLEN (1926–1997), U.S. poet and leader of the mid-20th century "Beat Movement," an aesthetic and political movement marked by its rebellion against the claustrophobic culture and repressive politics of Cold War 1950s America. He was born Irwin Allen Ginsberg in Newark, New Jersey. His mother, Naomi, was a Russian Jewish immigrant and communist whose lifelong battle with mental illness became the focus of his highly regarded poem "Kaddish." His father, Louis, was a Jewish-American socialist, high school teacher, and published poet (see below). Ginsberg attended Columbia University, where he studied with Lionel *Trilling, and during which time he met and established lasting friendships with such future Beat writers as Jack Kerouac, author of *On the Road*, and William Burroughs, author of *Naked Lunch*. During this time Ginsberg also had a life-altering vision. While reading William Blake's poem "Ah! Sunflower," he heard Blake speak to him and experienced a profound mystic awareness of the divinity of all creation. His prophetic vision convinced him that he was meant to become an ecstatic poet, writing "open breath poetry" in the mystical, hermetic tradition of Blake and Walt Whitman. While writing his early poems, he worked as a dishwasher, spot-welder, night porter, actor, and market research worker.

Ginsberg finally entered the popular imagination with "Howl," which, from his first public reading of the poem in San Francisco in 1955, quickly came to be considered the central spiritual, prophetic poem of his alienated generation. "Howl," with its famous opening line "I saw the best minds of my generation destroyed by madness, starving hysterical naked," was both a powerful Lament at the grief and suffering of his fellow artists and visionaries – "angelheaded hipsters" – and a Jeremiad against the dehumanization of the industrialized, tranquilized, repressive culture of Eisenhower and McCarthy's 1950s. "Howl" turned Ginsberg into a well-known public poet and personality, especially after its publication as part of his first book of verse, *Howl and Other Poems* (1955). *Howl* involved its publisher in a highly publicized obscenity trial, which only added to Ginsberg's rising fame. He came to specialize in readings of his own works in coffee shops and on college campuses, as well as later playing music with famous rock and folk artists including Bob *Dylan.

Ginsberg's later works include *Empty Mirror* (1960); *Kaddish and Other Poems 1958–60* (1960); *Reality Sandwiches 1953–60* (1963); *The Fall of America: Poems of These States, 1965–1971* (1973); *White Shroud: Poems 1980–1985* (1986); and *Cosmopolitan Greetings: Poems 1986–1992* (1995). Stylistically, much of his work is notable for its jazz rhythms and surrealist imagery, and for his candid, vivid descriptions of madness, homosexuality, drug-induced hallucinations, and physical anguish, all illuminated by an exalted Blakean vision of man's perfectibility in innocence. Some of the poems also reveal the author's bizarre, even apocalyptic, sense of humor.

Ginsberg often referred to himself as a "Buddhist Jew," and while he never rejected his Jewish heritage, he did often criticize both American Jews and the State of Israel. In fact, he saw this critique as central to his Jewishness. Ginsberg writes about his Jewish family members, the Holocaust, Israel, and Jewish themes such as memory, loss, and reconciliation in his poems "Visiting Father and Friends," "Jaweh and Allah Battle," "To Aunt Rose," and "Kaddish," his marvelous transformation of the Jewish prayer of mourning and memory into a painfully honest elegy for his dead mother. In his later poem "Yiddishe Kopf," Ginsberg explores the complex nature of his Jewish identity and its roots in Jewish food, history, intellectualism, alienation, and radical political activism. Additionally, his poetic style was greatly influenced by Jewish forms, namely cantorial chanting and Hebraic poetry, with their long lines and anaphoric opening repetitions, as well as being influenced by the prosody of Blake, Whitman, and William Carlos Williams and by American jazz. While many of his works deal with Jewish themes, many more explore his fascination with Eastern religious practices and religious syncretism. His later works *Wichita Vortex Sutra* (1966) and *Planet News* (1968) reflect Buddhism's mystical notion of man's oneness with a benevolent universe. Ginsberg also helped establish the Naropa Institute, a Buddhist university in Boulder, Colorado.

In addition to producing important poetic and prose works to the end of his life, Ginsberg also was active in the love-ins, anti-Vietnam War protests, drug experimentation, and gay rights movements of the 1960s and 1970s, becoming increasingly involved in progressive political movements in his later years. He traveled widely, visiting Martin Buber in Jerusalem in 1961 and traveling to every part of the globe. Ginsberg was elected a fellow of the American Academy of Arts and Sciences in 1992 and awarded the Chevalier l'ordre des Arts et de Lettres in France. By the time of his death, his poetry had been translated into dozens of languages, and his balding head, black beard, bespectacled face, and patriarchal demeanor had became familiar to millions all over the world. His father, LOUIS GINSBERG (1896–1976), was born in New Jersey and published two books of poetry, *The Attic of the Past and Other Lyrics* (1920) and *The Everlasting Minute and other Lyrics* (1937), which at their best give literary freshness and color to everyday things.

BIBLIOGRAPHY: *Midstream*, 7:4 (1961); J. Kramer, *Allen Ginsberg in America* (1969); B. Miles, *Ginsberg: A Biography* (1989); A. Ginsberg, *Journals Mid-Fifties 1954–1958*, ed. G. Ball (1995).

[David Ignatow / Rohan Saxena and Craig Svonkin (2nd ed.)]

GINSBERG, EDWARD (1917–1997), U.S. attorney and business executive. Born in New York City, Ginsberg moved with his family to Cleveland, Ohio. He received his B.A. from the University of Michigan (1938) and his Juris Doctor from Harvard University (1941). After graduation, he returned to Cleveland, where he practiced law for more than 50 years. He was a partner in the Cleveland law firm of Gottfried, Ginsberg, Gruen & Merritt. He was also a director of Rusco Industries, and a board member of Orlite, an Israeli company.

Active in Jewish communal life, Ginsberg devoted himself to Israeli and Jewish activities in the U.S. and around the world. After World War II, he played an important role in raising funds for the establishment and support of the Jewish state. He was a general chairman and then president of the National United Jewish Appeal, president of the *American Jewish Joint Distribution Committee, and a leader in the Cleveland Jewish Community Federation, and the *United Jewish Appeal. He served as vice president of the Jewish Telegraphic Agency and was the founder of the *Cleveland Jewish News*. He served as a life trustee of the Jewish Community Federation of Cleveland and was president of the Fairmount Temple. He sponsored many educational programs at the Hebrew University of Jerusalem, which made him an honorary founder. Hebrew Union College and Hebrew University in Jerusalem awarded him honorary degrees, and he was awarded the Eisenman Award for humanitarianism by the Jewish Community Federation.

He was also involved in many business activities, including directorships of El Al Israel Airlines and the First Israel Bank and Trust Company. A lifelong sports enthusiast, Ginsberg was a partner in the New York Yankees and a director of the Chicago Bulls.

The Edward Ginsberg Center for Community Service and Learning, named in his memory at the University of Michigan, is dedicated to engaging students and faculty members in a process that combines community service and academic learning to promote civic participation, build community capacity, and enhance education.

[Ruth Beloff (2nd ed.)]

GINSBERG, HAROLD LOUIS (1903–1990) U.S. Bible scholar and Semitist. Born in Montreal (Canada), Ginsberg, at the urging of his parents, spent two years in medical school. With their premature deaths, he decided to move to mandatory Palestine in the early 1920s, where he taught Hebrew and English. In Palestine Ginsberg became interested in Semitic languages. Because the Hebrew University had not yet opened, Ginsberg, aided financially by his uncles, was able to study at Jews College and the University of London. He returned to Palestine, where he completed the writing of his London doctoral thesis on the Hebrew verb. By this time the Hebrew University had opened and Ginsberg was able to study talmudic philology with J.N. *Epstein. In addition he was able to work with W.F. *Albright of the American School of Oriental Research in Jerusalem. In 1936 Ginsberg was invited to the Jewish Theological Seminary of America, where, from 1941, he was professor of Bible at the Jewish Theological Seminary of America, New York. While the bulk of his publications in the biblical field are philological – word studies, text restorations, and exegesis – he also elucidated problems of biblical history and religion. Ginsberg made significant contributions to Aramaic linguistics and was a pioneer in the interpretation of Ugaritic texts and their application to the Bible. His Semitistic and exegetical skills are combined luminously throughout his work.

Ginsberg was an editor of the new Bible translation of the American Jewish Publication Society (editor in chief of the translation of the Prophets from 1962). He edited the Bible division of the *Encyclopaedia Judaica*.

Ginsberg was a fellow of the American Academy for Jewish Research (vice president, 1969–70) and was the honorary president of the American Society of Biblical Literature (1969). He was a member of the Israel Academy for the Hebrew Language.

His works include *Kitvei Ugarit* (1938); *The Legend of King Keret* (1946); *Studies in Daniel* (1948); *Studies in Koheleth* (1950); a new Hebrew commentary on Ecclesiastes (1961);

and translations from Aramaic and Ugaritic in J.B. Pritchard (ed.), *Ancient Near Eastern Texts Relating to the Old Testament* (1950; 1955²; 1969³). He also edited *The Five Megilloth and the Book of Jonah* (JPS, 1969).

In Ginsberg's days at the Jewish Theological Seminary there was no Ph.D. program but Ginsberg's classes influenced several generations of rabbis to become biblicists and academicians.

ADD. BIBLIOGRAPHY: B. Levine, in: PAAJR, 5 (1991), 57.

[Moshe Greenberg / S. David Sperling (2nd ed.)]

GINSBERG, MITCHELL I. (1915–1996), U.S. social worker and educator. Ginsberg, a native of Boston, received his B.S. (1937) and his M.A. in education and psychology (1938) from Tufts University and his M.S. in social work from Columbia University (1941). He served in the U.S. Army from 1942 to 1946 as supervisor of a psychiatric social work unit. He was a social worker in Manchester, New Hampshire, and in Boston, then moved to the personnel and training bureau of the National Jewish Welfare Board in New York. He joined the faculty of the Columbia University School of Social Work, and in 1953 he became full professor, serving as associate dean (1960–66). He was a consultant in various training programs of the U.S. Peace Corps project and to the City of New York. In 1966 Ginsberg was appointed commissioner of the New York City Department of Social Services under Mayor John Lindsay. During his two-year tenure, he initiated several reforms, including the elimination of expensive investigations of welfare applicants and late-night inspections of recipients' homes. In 1968 he held the position of administrator of the city's Human Resources Commission, serving also as consultant on the community action program of the U.S. Office of Economic Opportunity.

Ginsberg returned to Columbia in 1971 as dean of the School of Social Work and special assistant to the president for community affairs. During the next 10 years, he helped launch Columbia Community Services, a cooperative project that provides health and social services to the homeless. When he retired in 1986, Ginsberg was designated professor and dean emeritus, continuing to teach and serving as co-director of Columbia's Center for the Study of Human Rights and chairman of the citywide Emergency Alliance for Homeless Families and Children.

In recognition of his lifelong work on behalf of the underprivileged, Columbia established in 1991 the Mitchell I. Ginsberg Professorship in Contemporary Urban Problems, which provides research on preventive policies and practical solutions to homelessness and other urban problems. The Ida R. and Mitchell Ginsberg Social Policy Endowed Fund was established at Columbia to support further studies in social policy by students at the School of Social Work.

[Joseph Neipris / Ruth Beloff (2nd ed.)]

GINSBERG, MORRIS (1889–1970), English sociologist. Born in Lithuania, Ginsburg immigrated to England, entering University College, London, in 1910. At that time he knew little or no English. Nevertheless, he was appointed lecturer in philosophy at University College, where he remained from 1914 to 1923. From 1929 to 1954, he was professor of sociology at the London School of Economics. Ginsberg's position in sociology was derived from the evolutionary theory of his teachers Hobhouse and Westermarck. His works deal with the systematic evaluation of sociology, the study of social structures, institutions and groups, and the comparative study of custom and religion in a variety of cultures. Ginsberg was actively interested in Jewish problems. His book *The Jewish People Today,* a survey of the structure and the institutions of contemporary Jewish life, appeared in 1956. He was associated with the World Jewish Congress and was an editor of *The Jewish Journal of Sociology.* His works include *The Material Culture and Social Institutions of the Simpler Peoples* (with L.T. Hobhouse and G.C. Wheeler, 1915), *The Psychology of Society* (1921), *L.T. Hobhouse: His Life and Work* (with J.A. Hobson, 1931), *Studies in Sociology* (1932), *Sociology* (1934), *Moral Progress* (1944), *Reason and Unreason in Society* (1947), *The Idea of Progress: A Reevaluation* (1953), *Essays in Sociology and Social Philosophy* (3 vols., 1956–61), *Reason and Experience in Ethics* (1956), *Law and Opinion in England in the 20th Century* (1959), *Evolution and Progress* (1961), and *Nationalism: A Reappraisal* (1961). In 1974, R. Fletcher edited *The Science of Society and the Unity of Mankind: A Memorial Volume for Morris Ginsberg.*

ADD. BIBLIOGRAPHY: ODNB online.

[Werner J. Cahnman]

GINSBURG, CHRISTIAN DAVID (1831–1914), Bible scholar. Born in Warsaw, he converted to Christianity in 1846 and soon afterward moved to England. Through two successive marriages to women of wealth he was able to pursue scholarship without ever holding an academic post. In England Ginsburg devoted himself to research on the masoretic text of the Bible; *The Massorah* (his magnum opus), published between 1880–1905 in four volumes, is the fruit of his labor. In the first two volumes, the original text of the masorah (in Hebrew) is arranged alphabetically with many additional notes drawn from manuscripts. The third volume contains supplements, and some masoretic tractates; the fourth renders into English all Hebrew entries of the first volume up to the letter "*yod,*" with explanatory notes. In his work, Ginsburg amassed rich and rare material; some of it, however, is not accurate. He also published two standard editions of the Hebrew Bible (1894, 1911) based on the same research. In *Introduction to the Massoretico-Critical Edition of the Hebrew Bible* (1897, repr. 1966) and in *A Series of 15 Facsimiles of MSS of the Hebrew Bible* (1897; second edition: *A Series of 18 Facsimiles…,* 1898), he explains his system. In 1904, on the occasion of its centennial, the British Bible Society entrusted Ginsburg with the publication of a new critical Hebrew Bible text; it was completed only in 1926. Before his death, however, he edited and published the Pentateuch (1908), Isaiah (1909), the Prophets

(1911), and Psalms (1913). In his research he based himself on 75 manuscripts and 25 earlier Bible editions.

Ginsburg also wrote commentaries on the Song of Songs (1857), Ecclesiastes (1861), Leviticus (1882); and published *The Karaites, their History and Literature* (1862); *The Essenes* (1864); *The Kabbalah, Its Doctrines, Development and Literature* (1863, 1920^2); *Massoret ha-Massoret*, by Elijah *Levita, with an English translation and critical explanatory notes (1867); Jacob b. Chajim ibn Adonijah's Introduction to the *Mikra'ot Gedolot* Bible edition (Hebrew and English) with explanatory notes (1867, repr. 1968); *The Moabite Stone* (1870). He also published the New Testament in Hebrew, translated by the convert J.E. Salkinson (1885). Ginsburg spent the last years of his life in Middlesex. His collection of Bible manuscripts is in the possession of the British Bible Society.

BIBLIOGRAPHY: C.D. Ginsburg, *Introduction to the Massoretico-Critical Edition of the Hebrew Bible* (1966), introduction by H.M. Orlinsky; C.D. Ginsburg, *Commentary to Jacob ben Chajim ibn Adonijah's Rabbinic Bible and E. Levita's Massoret ha-Massoret* (1968), introduction by N. Snaith. **ADD. BIBLIOGRAPHY:** J. Hayes, in: DBI, 1, 448–49.

GINSBURG, DAVID (1920–1988), Israel organic chemist. Born in New York, Ginsburg immigrated to Israel in 1948. He worked at Weizmann Institute of Science in Reḥovot until 1954, when he became professor of chemistry at Haifa Technion where he was acting president 1961–62. He wrote *Opium Alkaloids* (1962), and edited *Non-Benzenoid Aromatic Compounds* (1960). His research covered polynuclear aromatic compounds, heterocyclic nitrogen compounds, reactions with tertiary butyl hypochlorite, morphine, colchicine, and conformational analysis. Ginsburg was awarded the Israel Prize for exact sciences in 1972.

GINSBURG, EVGENIA SEMIONOVA (1906–1978), Russian writer; mother of the writer Vasili Axenov. She was born in Kazan and spent the years 1937–48 in prisons were she wrote the poem "And again like grown white Jews" (I vnov kak sedye evreii) on 31 of October 1937. The refrain of the poem says: /Next year in Jerusalem/. In the Samizdat she published her memoirs from the prisons and camps *Krutoi Marshrut* (*Into the Whirwind*). It was published in all European languages abroad in the 1970s. In 1966 the journal *Yunost* published her documentary novel about the students in the 1920s. Various items of her writings were published in the Soviet press under the pseudonym Ye. Axsenova.

GINSBURG, JEKUTHIEL (1889–1957), mathematician and Hebrew writer, brother of Simon and Pesaḥ *Ginzburg. Born in Russia, he emigrated to the United States in 1912, studied at Columbia University and, later, taught mathematics at Teachers College of Columbia University. In 1930 he was appointed professor and head of the department of mathematics at Yeshiva College. In 1932 he founded the quarterly *Scripta Mathematica*, edited the *Scripta Mathematica Library*, and coauthored (with D.E. Smith) the *History of Mathematics in America before 1900* (1936). His Hebrew feuilletons appeared in *Hadoar* under the pseudonym of J.L. Gog. His articles on the role of Jews in mathematics were collected in his *Ketavim Nivḥarim* ("Selected Writings," 1960), which includes his biography and data on his literary and scientific works.

BIBLIOGRAPHY: Kressel, Leksikon, 1 (1965), 472f.

[Eisig Silberschlag]

GINSBURG, NORTON SIDNEY (1921–), U.S. geographer. Ginsburg was born in Chicago. In World War II he served in the U.S. Navy and participated in actions with the Sixth Marine Division in north China. After the war he remained in the Far East as chief of the Research and Intelligence Center at Shanghai. In 1947 he taught geography at the University of Chicago (full professor, 1960). His major interests lay in urban geography, political geography, and economic development, with particular stress on East and Southeast Asia. In 1961 he was appointed director of the Association for Asian Studies. Apart from many papers, he published (with C.F. Roberts) *Malaya* (1958), was the co-author and editor of *Pattern of Asia* (1958), and edited *Essays on Geography and Economic Development* (1960). In 1961 he compiled the *Atlas of Economic Development*. The Japanese government invited him in 1962 to study Tokyo's urban problems, on which he reported in the *Tokyo Memorandum: Reports on Tokyo Metropolitan Planning* (1962). In 1980 he co-authored with Chi-Keung Leung *China: Urbanization and National Development*. He also coauthored *Geographic Perspectives on the Wealth of Nations* (with J. Osborn and G. Blank, 1986). In 1990 he published *The Urban Transition: Reflections on the American and Asian Experiences*. He edited A. Harmann's *Historical Atlas of China* (1968, new edition) and *China: The '80s Era* (1984). Ginsburg has also co-edited with Elizabeth Borgese 12 volumes of the *Ocean Yearbook* series (1979–96), a publication devoted to ocean-related issues.

[Ruth Beloff (2nd ed.)]

GINSBURG, RUTH JOAN BADER (1933–), U.S. lawyer and Supreme Court justice. Born in Brooklyn, the daughter of Nathan Bader and Celia Amster Bader, Ginsburg graduated from Cornell University in 1954. Following her graduation she married classmate Martin Ginsburg, who was already a law student at Harvard. In 1956, Ruth Bader Ginsburg also entered Harvard Law School, one of nine women in her class. During the next two years, she coped with an infant daughter and her husband's diagnosis and recovery from a severe form of cancer while excelling academically in an environment which was less than welcoming to female students. Following her husband's graduation and employment in New York City, Ginsburg completed her studies at Columbia Law School. She was elected to the law reviews of both institutions, and was recommended as a law clerk by Albert Sachs, dean of Harvard Law School, to Supreme Court Justice Felix *Frankfurter in 1960. Frankfurter refused to employ Ginsberg because she was a woman, a pattern repeated by New York City law firms. She was ultimately hired as a law clerk by a district court judge in New York.

In 1963, following her participation in a comparative law project in Sweden sponsored by Columbia University, she became the second woman to join the law faculty of Rutgers University. At Rutgers, Ginsburg became increasingly committed to addressing social conditions that denied women choices and opportunities open to men. Appointed as the director of the Women's Rights Project of the American Civil Liberties Union in 1972, Ginsburg looked for sex discrimination cases that raised issues amenable to change through legislation. She often employed the strategy of using male plaintiffs to show that laws that discriminated between men and women – even when supposedly designed to benefit women – were based on negative and unfair stereotypes that perpetuated the prevailing notion that women were generally dependent on men. Seeking to persuade a majority of the Supreme Court that sex-based legal distinctions demanded heightened judicial scrutiny, Ginsburg won five out of the six major women's rights cases she argued. The Supreme Court's ruling in *Craig vs. Boren* in particular – a 1976 case for which Ginsburg filed the brief – made it far more difficult to enact laws based on sexual stereotypes.

In 1980, eight years after being appointed the first tenured woman law professor at Columbia University, Ginsburg was elected to the United States Court of Appeals for the District of Columbia Circuit. There she earned respect for clear thinking, careful reasoning, and assiduous preparation of her cases. In June 1993, when President Clinton proposed her to replace Justice Byron R. White, she became the first Supreme Court justice to be nominated by a Democratic president in 26 years; she was confirmed by the Senate in August 1993. On the Court, Ginsburg was a strong supporter of women's rights and civil liberties in general.

Her husband, MARTIN D. GINSBURG, an expert in tax law, was the lawyer to Ross Perot, billionaire oil magnate and 1992 presidential candidate, for many years. He was an economic adviser to Perot during his campaign. Ginsberg taught at Georgetown University Law School, to which Perot donated $1 million in his honor in 1986.

BIBLIOGRAPHY: E. Ayer, *Ruth Bader Ginsburg: Fire and Steel on the Supreme Court* (1994); A. Leigh Campbell, *Raising the Bar: Ruth Bader Ginsburg and the ACLU Women's Rights Project* (2004); M. Halberstam, "Ginsburg, Ruth Bader," in: P.E. Hyman and D.D. Moore (eds.), *Jewish Women in America*, vol. 1 (1997), 515–20.

[Judith R. Baskin (2nd ed.)]

GINSBURG, SAUL (1866–1940), author and historian of Russian Jewry. Born in Minsk, he received a traditional Jewish as well as secular education. He graduated in 1891 from the law faculty of Peterburg University. He was active in the Ḥovevei Zion movement. Ginsburg became a contributor to *Voskhod* in 1892, and in 1896 published a historical study in that journal, "*Zabytaya epokha*" ("A Forgotten Era"), concerning the first Russian-Jewish periodical *Razsvet*. The following year he began contributing a regular review of the Hebrew press (under the pseudonym of "Ha-Kore") to *Voskhod*, as well as a literary column, and in 1899 was appointed to the editorial board. Together with P. *Marek he published *Yevreyskiye narodnye pesny* ("Jewish Folk Songs," 1901), which became a landmark in the study of Jewish folklore. In 1903 Ginsburg established *Der Fraynd*, the first Yiddish daily in Russia, which played an important role in the development of Yiddish journalism and was noted for its high literary standards. In 1908 Ginsburg left *Der Fraynd* to devote himself completely to the study of the cultural history of the Jews in Russia. He took part in the historical periodical *Perezhitoye* (4 vols., 1908–13). In 1913 he published *Yevrei i otechestvennaya voyna 1812 goda* ("Jews and the War of 1812"), a study of the history of Russian Jews during the Napoleonic Wars, and was a cofounder of the Jewish Literary and Scientific Society (which was closed down by the authorities in 1910). He graduated in 1891 from the law faculty of Peterburg University.When the Bolshevist Revolution broke out, Ginsburg was one of a small group who strove to carry on independent Jewish scientific work under the Soviet regime. From 1922 to 1928 he edited *Yevreyskaya mysl* ("Jewish Thought") and *Yevreyski vestnik* ("Jewish Herald"). In this period several of his studies on the history of Russian Jews also appeared in *Zukunft*, the New York Yiddish monthly. In 1930 Ginsburg left the Soviet Union and was able to take his voluminous archive with him. He first settled in Paris, but moved to New York in 1933. Here the Yiddish daily *Forward* regularly published his popular historical essays. A collection of his studies, *Historishe Verk*, appeared in three volumes in 1937-38 with a bibliography by I. Rivkind. Two posthumous volumes were *Amolike Peterburg* ("Petersburg as It Was," 1944), and *Meshumodim in Tsarishn Rusland* ("Jewish Apostates in Czarist Russia," 1946). Some of his articles and studies are devoted to personal memoirs.

BIBLIOGRAPHY: Rejzen, Leksikon, 1 (1926) 567–72; LNYL, 2 (1958), 227–9.

[Yehuda Slutsky]

GINSBURGER, ERNEST (1876–1943), French rabbi and Jewish historian; born in Héricourt (Haute-Saône), France. During World War I he volunteered as rabbi of the French 18th Army Corps and was awarded the Médaille Militaire. He was subsequently chief rabbi of Geneva, Belgium, and Bayonne. Arrested in March 1942, he was interned at Compiègne and deported to a death camp in February 1943. Ginsburger left valuable essays on Jewish history, including *Les Juifs de Belgique au XVIIIe siècle* (1932), "*Les Juifs de Frauenberg*" (in REJ, 47 (1903), 87–122), and *Le Comité de Surveillance de Jean-Jacques Rousseau – Saint-Esprit-les-Bayonne* (1934), based on the minutes of the only committee in revolutionary France with a majority of Jewish members.

GINZBERG, ELI (1911–2002), U.S. economist and social planner. Ginzberg was born in New York City, the son of rabbinic scholar Louis *Ginzberg. He studied economics at Columbia University and in 1935 was appointed to the Columbia School of Business, where he was A. Barton Hepburn Professor of Economics until 1979. In addition to his teaching duties, Ginzberg was an adviser to several U.S. presidents, from Franklin D. Roosevelt through Jimmy *Carter. He was named director of the Eisenhower Center for the Conservation of Human Resources, when it was established in 1950. Under his guidance the Center was responsible for pioneering research efforts in employment and health policy. He also served with the United States War Department (1942–44 and 1946–48), the Surgeon General's Office, the White House Conference on Children and Youth (1959–63), and the National Manpower Council, of which he became chairman in 1962. His activities as a consultant, which were widely sought, embraced the United States Departments of State, Defense, Labor, and Health, Education and Welfare, the Hoover Commission, and the National Advisory Mental Health Council.

From 1953 to 1959 he was a governor of the Hebrew University of Jerusalem.

In 1978, on the verge of retirement from Columbia, Ginzberg accepted an appointment to direct the Revson Fellows Program on the Future of the City of New York at Columbia. For the next 20 years he oversaw the selection of 240 Revson Fellows and guided them into positions of leadership.

A specialist in labor economics, Ginzberg was particularly interested in problems of manpower utilization and economic growth, especially as they affected underdeveloped countries and minority groups. He was a leading expert on the economic aspects of African-American inequality in the United States, and he frequently traveled abroad in an advisory capacity to the governments of developing nations, especially Israel.

Among his more than 100 publications are *The House of Adam Smith* (1934), *Grass on the Slag Heaps: The Story of the Welsh Miners* (1942), *Agenda for American Jews* (1950), *The Potential* (1956), *Manpower Utilization in Israel* (1962), *The Great Society: Lessons for the Future* (1974), *Beyond Human Scale: The Large Corporation at Risk* (1985), *My Brother's Keeper: Reflections on Jews, Social Science & Public Policy* (1989), *The Medical Triangle: Physicians, Politicians, and the Public* (1992), and *Tomorrow's Hospital: A Look to the Twenty-First Century* (1998). He edited a wide series of studies for the Columbia Conservation of Human Resources Department, including *The Uneducated* (1953), *Life Styles of Educated Women* (1966), and *Manpower Strategy for the Metropolis* (1968). His biography of his father, *Keeper of the Law*, was published in 1966.

BIBLIOGRAPHY: *Current Biography Yearbook, 1966* (1967), 126–9. **ADD. BIBLIOGRAPHY:** I. Horowitz (ed.), *Eli Ginzberg: The Economist as a Public Intellectual* (2002).

[Mark Perlman / Ruth Beloff (2nd ed.)]

GINZBERG, LOUIS (1873–1953), one of the outstanding Talmud scholars of the first half of the 20th century; leader and the major halakhic authority of the Conservative movement in North America. Born in Kovno, Lithuania, Ginzberg received a typical East European Jewish education: private tutors, four years of study at the Telz and Slobodka yeshivot, and academic studies at three German universities. After studying with *Noeldeke at Strassburg, he received his doctorate from the University of Heidelberg in 1898 for his study of the midrashim quoted by the Church Fathers.

Ginzberg was a direct descendant (sixth generation) of Abraham, brother of *Elijah, the Gaon of Vilna. He was acutely aware of his ancestry and refers to the Gaon frequently as "*dodi zekeni*" (my great uncle), "the pride of our family," my famous ancestor, and the like. Ginzberg's father and mother were extremely pious Jews and even though he became more liberal when he left home at age 15, he remained an observant Jew for the rest of his life. Nonetheless, he was plagued until his death by a certain ambivalence about following the path of *Wissenschaft des Judentums*.

Ginzberg was a brilliant polymath, "a walking encyclopedia." He knew most of the Bible by heart at age seven and had mastered much of rabbinic literature by age 14. His *magnum opus, The Legends of the Jews*, contains 36,000 references which Ginzberg kept in his head. In addition to rabbinics, Ginzberg was an expert in philosophy, Kabbalah, and mathematics and he knew at least 12 languages.

In 1899, Ginzberg immigrated to the United States at the invitation of Rabbi Isaac Mayer *Wise to accept a position as preceptor in Biblical Exegesis at *Hebrew Union College in Cincinnati, but the invitation was withdrawn by the time he arrived. Wise changed his mind because he heard that Ginzberg was an adherent of higher criticism of the Bible and, paradoxically, because he was afraid that Ginzberg was too observant. He was hired by *The Jewish Encyclopedia* from 1900 to 1902, writing 400 articles, many of which have remained classics until today. In 1902, Solomon *Schechter invited Ginzberg to become professor of Talmud at the newly re-organized *Jewish Theological Seminary (JTS). There Ginzberg made his academic and spiritual home for the next 51 years until the day he died.

As professor of Talmud at JTS, Ginzberg had tremendous influence on the development of Jewish studies at JTS and throughout the world. He brought young scholars such as H.L. *Ginsberg, Saul *Lieberman, Shalom *Spiegel, and A.J. *Heschel to JTS. He was one of the founders of the American Academy for Jewish Research in 1919 and served as its president until 1947. He raised substantial sums of money for classics such as *Kasovsky's concordance of the Mishnah and Tosefta, B.M. *Lewin's *Oẓar ha-Ge'onim*, and *Schreiber's *Meiri*. He helped found the Institute for Jewish Studies at the Hebrew University and taught there in 1928–29. Finally, he played a major role in training and ordaining 650 rabbis over the course of two generations.

Ginzberg devoted most of his academic scholarship to three fields: *Aggadah*, the Jerusalem Talmud, and Geonica. In the realm of *Aggadah*, *The Legends of the Jews* (7 vols., 1909–38) remains unsurpassed. It also appeared in Hebrew translation (6 vols., 1966–75) and in a one-volume abridgement called *Legends of the Bible* (1956). It retells the story of the Bible from Adam to Chronicles, weaving together thousands of *aggadot* culled from early and late Midrashim, Philo, Josephus, the Apocrypha, and the Church Fathers. In other words, Ginzberg systematically collected and rearranged the *aggadah,* as Maimonides had the *halakhah* in his *Mishneh Torah.* In addition to his *Legends*, his dissertation was devoted to *Die Haggada bei den Kirchenvatern* (1899–1900) and in 1928 he published over 40 **Genizah* fragments of Midrash in *Ginzei Schechter,* volume 1.

In the realm of the Jerusalem Talmud, his *Seridei Yerushalmi* (1909) remains the only published volume of *Genizah* fragments of this basic rabbinic work. His *Perushim ve-Ḥidushim ba-Yerushalmi* on *Berakhot*, Chapters 1–5 (1941–61) remains one of the only scientific commentaries to the *Yerushalmi.* He also wrote commentaries on several other tractates; his commentary on *Pesaḥim* was scheduled for publication in 2005–6, over 50 years after his death.

In the realm of Geonica, the first volume of *Geonica* (1909) remains one of the few English language introductions to the field. The second volume of *Geonica*, as well as *Ginzei Schechter,* volume 2, contain over 100 *Genizah* fragments of geonic responsa and commentaries and early Karaite works.

Ginzberg also wrote a book of biographies (*Students, Scholars and Saints*, 1928), an early study of the Zadokite Fragment from the *Genizah* which later turned out to be one of the Dead Sea Scrolls (*Eine Unbekannte Judische Sekte*, 1922; *An Unknown Jewish Sect*, 1976), and two volumes of collected articles (*On Jewish Law and Lore*, 1955; *Al Halakhah ve-Aggadah*, 1960).

Ginzberg was a leading proponent of the "Positive-Historical School," which later became the Conservative movement. In an essay from 1901 about Rabbi Zacharias *Frankel (1801–1875), the founder of this school of thought in Germany, Ginzberg describes Frankel's historical Judaism, which was really Ginzberg's own: "We may now understand the apparent contradiction between the theory and practice of the positive-historic school. One may, for instance, conceive of the origin and idea of Sabbath rest as the professor of Protestant theology at a German university would conceive it, and yet minutely observe the smallest detail of the Sabbath observances known to strict Orthodoxy. For an adherent of this school, the sanctity of the Sabbath reposes not upon the fact that it was proclaimed on Sinai, but on the fact that the Sabbath idea found for thousands of years its expression in Jewish souls." In other words, the authority of Jewish law does not derive from a one-time event of revelation at Mt. Sinai but from the fact that *Kelal Yisrael*, the collective Jewish people, observed Jewish law for thousands of years.

Ginzberg believed that it was not possible to understand Jewish history and culture without a thorough knowledge of Jewish law ("The Significance of the Halachah for Jewish History," 1929). Furthermore, we now know from a recently published volume (*The Responsa of Professor Louis Ginzberg*, 1996) that Ginzberg was a prolific *posek* (decisor) for the Conservative movement between 1913 and 1953. He wrote over 100 responsa, first as chair of the Committee on the Interpretation of Jewish Law of the *United Synagogue (1917–27), and then as a private *posek.* From his responsa, one can learn about his approach to Jewish law. On the one hand, he was quite strict with regard to liturgical and synagogue-related issues: "I am not one of those who likes 'new things,' and I have a special aversion to changes in the customs of the synagogue" (*ibid.*, p. 99).

On the other hand, he usually judged a case on its own merits and frequently arrived at a lenient decision. Ginzberg occasionally prohibited something not because it was technically forbidden by Jewish law, but in order to preserve the "spirit of the law" or to prevent "*mar'it ayin*" (the appearance of impropriety) or "*ḥillul ha-shem*" (the desecration of God's name). He opposed introducing the organ into the synagogue because it would cut off American Jewry from *Kelal Yisrael.*

In Ginzberg's opinion, Jewish law is determined by the Talmud and the **rishonim* (early authorities ca. 1000–1500 C.E.) and not by Midrashim, later customs, or the **aḥaronim* (1500ff.).

Ginzberg was a lifelong Zionist. His second article, published in Dutch in 1899, was a "Plea for Zionism." He was a ZOA delegate to the Zionist Congress in Basel in 1905. In 1918, he said that the United Synagogue of America "should take an active part in the work for the restoration of Palestine." He believed that the State of Israel must respect the Sabbath and *kashrut* and leave matters of marriage and divorce to the rabbinate. But he was opposed to religious coercion of the State against Jews who do not recognize the authority of *halakhah.* He was opposed to mixing religion with politics because it would lead to the weakening of religion and the corruption of politics. According to Historical Judaism, Jewish nationalism without religion is like a tree without fruit, and Jewish religion without nationalism is like a tree without roots.

BIBLIOGRAPHY: D. Druck, *R. Levi Ginzberg* (Heb., 1934); A. Marx et al. (eds.), *Louis Ginzberg Jubilee Volume*, 2 vols. (1945), incl. bibl. by B. Cohen; E. Ginzberg, *Keeper of the Law: Louis Ginzberg* (1966, 1996[2]); D. Golinkin, *The Responsa of Professor Louis Ginzberg* (1996), incl. intro. and extensive bibl.

[David Golinkin (2nd ed.)]

GINZBURG, ISER (1872–1947), Hebrew and Yiddish journalist, short story writer, and editor. Ginzburg was born in Develtov (Russia), and as a youth became influenced by the ideals of the *Haskalah. He settled in the U.S. in 1893, and graduated from Cornell University Medical School in 1900. Influenced by radical politics, he contributed articles to American-Yiddish publications, including the *Fraye Arbeter Shtime* and *Tsukunft*, and was on the staff of the *Forverts*. Ginzburg also remained active as a Hebrew-language journalist, contributing to publications such as *Hatoren* and *Hadoar.* He wrote on contemporary problems and reviewed books dealing with Jewish religion, literature, and history. His major works are *Der Tal-*

mud, Zayn Antshteyung un Antviklung ("The Talmud, Its Origins and Development," 1910); *Di Antshteyung fun Kristntum* ("The Origin of Christianity," 1917); *Yidishe Denker un Poeten in Mitlelter* ("Jewish Thinkers and Poets in the Middle Ages," 2 vols., 1918–9); *Maimonides* (1935).

BIBLIOGRAPHY: LNYL, 2 (1958), 223f. **ADD. BIBLIOGRAPHY:** H. Rogoff, *Der Gayst fun Forverts* (1954), 107–14.

[Elias Schulman / Marc Miller (2nd ed.)]

GINZBURG, NATALIA (1917–1991), Italian novelist and playwright. Natalia Ginzburg, who was born in Palermo, was the daughter of the biologist, Giuseppe Levi, and a non-Jewish mother. She studied in Turin, where her associates were the Jewish anti-fascist intellectuals who were active in the Italian resistance. Her first husband, Leone Ginzburg, a victim of the Nazis, died in a Roman prison in 1944. Her first story, *La strada che va in città* (1942; *Road to the City*, 1949), appeared under the pen name "Alessandra Tornimparte." Later works are *È stato così* (1947), the novel *Tutti i nostri ieri* (1952; Eng. ed. *Dead Yesterdays*, 1956; U.S. ed. *A Light for Fools*, 1957), the short story volume *Valentino* (1957), *Le voci della sera* (1961; *Voices in the Evening*, 1963), and *Le piccole virtù* (1962). Natalia Ginzburg's characters, who are lonely, persecuted, and engaged in a hopeless quest for sympathy and understanding, include many Jews. Her deep pessimism was overcome, for once, in her outstanding work, *Lessico famigliare* (1963; *Family Sayings*, 1967). This is a psychological novel based on the author's recollections of her own family and the events of her youth. The characters range from the bourgeois, assimilated Jews of the late 19th century, personified by her father, to the anti-fascist circles of Turin and her first friends. But the book's main achievement lies in the distinctive language of the narrative. Natalia Ginzburg uses her family's private phraseology, including many expressions from Spanish- and German-Jewish dialects, in such a way that it plays a leading role in recreating the flavor of an age. Natalia Ginzburg's three plays are *Ti ho sposato per allegria, La segretaria*, and *L'inserzione*. The last was produced as *The Advertisement* by the National Theater in London.

BIBLIOGRAPHY: O. Lombardi, *La giovane narrativa* (1963); G. Romano, in: *Scritti in memoria di L. Carpi* (1967), 202–4; S. Pacifici, *A Guide to Contemporary Italian Literature* (1962), index. **ADD. BIBLIOGRAPHY:** E. Clementelli, *Invito alla lettura di Natalia Ginzburg* (1996); A.O. Bullock, *Natalia Ginzburg: Human Relationships in a Changing World* (1991); I. Giovanna, *Natalia Ginzburg: la casa, la città, la storia* ((1996); M.L. Quarsiti, *Natalia Ginzburg: bibliografia 1934–1992* (1996); M. Pflug, *Natalia Ginzburg: arditamente timida* (1997); idem, *Natalia Ginzburg:una biografia* (1997); G. Borri, *Natalia Ginzburg* (1999); A. Jeannet, G. Sanguinetti Katz (eds.), *Natalia Ginzburg, a Voice of the Twentieth Century* (2000); C. Borrelli, *Notizie di Natalia Ginzburg* (2002); C. Nocentini, "Racial Laws and Internment in Natalia Ginzburg's 'Lessico famigliare,'" in: *The Most Ancient of Minorities* (2002), 147–55; T.L. Picarazzi, *Maternal Desire: Natalia Ginzburg's Mothers, Daughters and Sisters* (2002); N. Ginzburg, *It's Hard to Talk about Yourself* (2003).

[Giorgio Romano]

GINZBURG, SIMON (1890–1944), poet and critic. Ginzburg was born in the village of Lipniki, Volhynia, where he received a traditional education. He published his first poem in *Ha-Shilo'aḥ* in 1910. In 1912 he settled in the U.S., studied at Columbia University, and obtained a doctorate from Dropsie College in 1923. He immigrated to Palestine in 1933, but returned to America shortly before World War II as the emissary of the Hebrew Writers' Association. He was one of the editors of *Ha-Toren* (1913–15) and *Lu'aḥ Aḥi'ever* in 1918, and a contributor to numerous Hebrew publications. Both in content and language, Ginzburg was greatly influenced by Bialik to whom he dedicated his book of poems *Shirim u-Fo'emot* ("Songs and Poems," 1931). Essentially a romantic poet, the American rural landscape attracted him, but he was repelled by the noise of New York. In *Ahavat Hoshe'a* ("Love of Hosea," 1935), he reveals dramatic ability; the twilight of the Northern Kingdom and the regeneration of the Jews on the eve of disaster are used to suggest a significant lesson for contemporary Jewry. In addition to a biography in English of Moses Ḥayyim Luzzatto (1931), Ginzburg published three of his plays, with critical notes, including *Ma'aseh Shimshon* from a manuscript in the New York Public Library, his poetry, *Sefer ha-Shirim* ("Book of Poems," 1944–45), and an edition of his letters, under the title *R. Moshe Ḥayyim Luzzatto u-Venei Doro* ("R. Moshe Ḥayyim Luzzatto and His Contemporaries," 1936). These works, and his critical essays on the poet, are a major contribution to Luzzatto scholarship. His other critical essays were collected in *Be-Massekhet ha-Sifrut* ("In the Web of Literature," 1945). He translated Coleridge's *The Rime of the Ancient Mariner* into Hebrew, as well as D.H. Lawrence's *Sons and Lovers*, and poems by Tennyson, Hood, Byron, and Poe.

His younger brother PESAH (1894–1947), also born in the village of Lipniki, studied in Odessa, and lived for a time in the United States (1913–18), England, Canada, and the Scandinavian countries before settling in Palestine in 1922. He published several newspapers, which were, however, short-lived; edited various magazines; and was a night editor of *Haaretz* for about 20 years. Pesaḥ's poems, short stories, and articles appeared in the Hebrew press, a number of them also as separate booklets, including *Regina Ashkenazi* (1919) and *Sippur Ereẓ Yisraeli* (1945). He translated extensively, mainly Scandinavian and English literary works.

BIBLIOGRAPHY: A. Epstein, *Soferim Ivriyyim ba-Amerikah*, 1 (1952), 92–103; Waxman, Literature, 4 (1960^2), 1067–69.

[Eisig Silberschlag]

GINZBURG, VITALY LAZAREVICH (1916–), Russian physicist and Nobel laureate. Ginzburg was born in Moscow and obtained his Ph.D. in physics (1940) from Moscow State University. In 1941 he joined the Lebedev Physical Institute of the U.S.S.R. Academy of Sciences (FIAN), where he remained, including the period in World War II when the Institute was evacuated to Kazan. He research was greatly influenced by the Russian physicists I.E. Tamm and L.D. *Landau (Nobel Prize in physics in 1962). Ginzburg won the Nobel Prize in physics in 2003 for his contributions to understanding superconductivity, which allows electric currents to pass through some metals and other materials (superconductors) at very low temperatures. Type 1 superconductors displace magnetic flow to allow the passage of electric currents. Type 2 superconductors allow the passage of electric currents despite the persistence of magnetic fields. The distinction is important to the practical applications of superconductivity such as magnetic resonance imaging (MRI) in medicine. His main theoretical contribution was to recognize the role of wave function in superconducting materials. Ginzburg also made important contributions to the design of Soviet thermonuclear weapons, especially by suggesting ^{6}lithium as the source for generating tritium^3 hydrogen in the reaction. He had a broad interest in the development and applications of theoretical physics and astrophysics. He succeeded in becoming a corresponding member (1953) and a full member (1966) of the U.S.S.R. Academy of Sciences despite the antisemitism of the Stalinist era. He was editor of Russia's principal physics journal (*Physics-Uspekhi*) from 1998. His democratic and pro-Israel views are set out in his autobiography.

[Michael Denman (2nd ed.)]

°**GIORGIO (Zorzi), FRANCESCO (Franciscus Georgius Venetus**; 1460–1540), kabbalist of the Franciscan Order of Minor Friars. Giorgio was the author of *De Harmonia Mundi* (1525) and *In Scripturam Sacram et Philosophos Tria Millia Problemata* (1536), which was placed on the *donec corrigatur* ("till it is corrected") list of prohibited books. After the censorships of G. Contarini, *Sixtus of Siena, R. Bellarmino, etc., the most famous is that of Marin Mersenne, *Quaestiones…in Genesim, cum…textus explicatione. In volumine Atheir…expugnatur, et F. Georgii…cabalistica dogmata…repelluntur* (1623). Giorgio was a cousin of Marino Sanuto, who mentions him in his *Diarii*, a friend of Gershom *Soncino, and the sponsor of several converts; his Hebrew library awakened the interest of H.C. Agrippa and Egidio da Viterbo. He was one of the active intermediaries in the controversial divorce case of Henry VIII of England. His pupil Archangelus of Burgunuovo, the defender of Giovanni *Pico della Mirandola, plagiarized his works. A disciple of G. *Postel, Guy *Le Fèvre de la Boderie, translated the *De Harmonia* into French in 1578 and dedicated it to a member of the heterodox Family of Love. A manuscript of his detailed commentaries on the kabbalistic theses of Pico della Mirandola is in the National Library in Jerusalem (Yahuda Collection).

BIBLIOGRAPHY: C. Vasoli, *Testi scelti* (1955); *Biographie Universelle*, s.v. *Georges*; A. Mercati and A.P.M.J. Pelzer, *Dizionario Ecclesiatico*, 3 (1958), s.v. *Zorzi*; D.W. Amram, *The Makers of Hebrew Books in Italy* (1909); L. Thorndike, *A History of Magic and Experimental Science*, 6 (1941); R. Wittkower, *Architectural Principles in the Age of Humanism* (19622); F. Secret, *Le Zôhar chez les Kabbalistes chrétiens* (1958); idem, *Les kabbalistes chrétiens de la Renaissance* (1964); idem, in: *Bibliothèque d'Humanisme et Renaissance*, 30 (1968).

[Francois Secret]

GIOVANNI MARIA (c. 1470–c. 1530), Italian lute player, born in Germany. His original Jewish name is unknown and when, after settling in Florence, he was baptized, he took his new name in honor of Cardinal Giovanni de' Medici. He was still often referred to, however, as "Giovanni Maria, the Jew." In 1492 he was condemned to death for murder, but fled to Rome, where he entered the service of the Cardinal de' Medici. When the cardinal became Pope Leo X, Giovanni Maria was given the revenues of the township of Verrocchio, with the title of count. He subsequently entered the service of Pope Clement VII, the doge of Venice, and the dukes of Mantua and Urbino. A few of Giovanni Maria's own compositions were published and he is referred to with admiration in various literary works of the period. His son Camillo was also a musician in the papal service.

BIBLIOGRAPHY: Pirro, in: *Mélanges … H. Hauvette* (1934); C. Roth, *The Jews in the Renaissance* (1959), 281–3; U. Cassuto, *Gli Ebrei a Firenze nell' età del Rinascimento* (1918), 192f.

[Cecil Roth]

GIRGASHITES (Heb. גִּרְגָּשִׁי), one of the nations inhabiting the land of Canaan (Gen. 15:21; Deut. 7:1; Josh. 3:10; Neh. 9:8). The name also appears as that of the fifth ethnic group descended from Canaan (Gen. 10:16; I Chron. 1:14). Although the Girgashites are not referred to in the narrative of the wars of conquests, and their locality is not stated, they are named by Joshua among the peoples the Israelites dispossessed (24:11).

They have been uncertainly identified with the Qaraqisha, allies of the Hittites in their wars with Ramses II. If that identification is correct the Girgashites would have been part of the southward migrations from Anatolia of peoples displaced by the fall of the Hittite empire ca. 1200 B.C.E. A personal name *grgš* appears in Ugaritic, but its connection with this people is unknown. The sibilant termination of the biblical name suggests a Hurrian origin.

BIBLIOGRAPHY: B. Maisler (Mazar), in: ZAW, 50 (1932), 86–87; E.A. Speiser (ed.), *Genesis* (Eng., 1964), 69. **ADD. BIBLIOGRAPHY:** S. Ahituv, *Joshua* (1995), 93.

GIROUD, FRANÇOISE (France Gourdji; 1916–2003), French journalist and writer. Born in Geneva, Switzerland, Giroud, an ardent polemicist, was a major figure in the political press in France. In 1953, she co-founded with Jean-Jacques Servan-Schreiber one of France's first news magazines, *L'Express*, which began as a weekly supplement of *Les Echos*, a daily newspaper specializing in economics, but soon became a mainstay of France's political landscape. Giroud's journalistic motto was "understanding quickly how things work, and helping people to understand quickly." *L'Express* was aimed at revolutionizing the French press by "telling people the truth," in Servan-Schreiber's words; important writers took part in the project, including left-wing thinkers like Camus and Sartre and center-right writers like Malraux and Mauriac. From the beginning, *L'Express* voiced strong and clear opinions against colonial wars, which were often met with censorship from the

State. Giroud, a journalist and political columnist for most of her life, also held government positions as secretary of state for the condition of women (1974) and secretary of state for culture (1976–79). An outspoken, but moderate feminist, she played a vital role in the creation of a feminist press in France, and directed the monthly women's magazine *Elle*. From 1983 on, she was an editorialist and columnist on the center-left weekly *Le Nouvel Observateur*. Her published books include *Lou, histoire d'une femme libre* (2004), *Les taches du léopard* (2005), and *Une Femme honorable* (1982).

BIBLIOGRAPHY: F. Giroud, *Profession journaliste, conversations avec Martine de Rebaudy (2001).*

[Dror Franck Sullaper (2nd ed.)]

GISCALA (Gush Halav; Heb. גּוּשׁ חָלָב), ancient Jewish city in Upper Galilee, today the Christian-Arab village of al-Jish, 5 mi. (c. 8 km.) N.W. of Safed. According to the Mishnah, "the acropolis of Gush Ḥalav" was surrounded by a wall built in the time of Joshua (Ar. 9:6). Canaanite and Israelite remains from the Early Bronze and Iron Ages have been uncovered there but the city is first mentioned (as Giscala) in connection with the history of the Jewish War (66–70/73). It was the birthplace of the Zealot leader *John (Johanan) b. Levi of Giscala, a dealer in oil, who fortified the city at his own expense and escaped to Jerusalem with his followers when the Romans surrounded it; Giscala thereupon surrendered – the last city in Galilee to fall to the Romans (Jos., Wars, 2:275, 590; 4:92–120, 208; Life, 70, 75, 189). After the destruction of the Second Temple, during the days of the *amoraim* and *tannaim*, Jews also lived there. The city was situated in the center of an olive-growing district and derived its main livelihood from oil; the inhabitants also engaged in the production of silk (Tosef., Shev. 7:15; Eccl. R. 2:8, no. 2). A Jewish community continued into the Middle Ages, at least until the 13th century. The village was severely damaged by an earthquake in 1873.

On the summit of the hill on which Giscala stands is a Maronite church with the remains of an ancient synagogue beneath it and, at its foot, near a spring, are the ruins of a second synagogue, excavated by H. Kohl and C. Watzinger in 1916, in which an Aramaic inscription was found on a column mentioning a certain Yose son of Tanhum. The latter synagogue was excavated in 1977–78 by E. Meyers, J.F. Strange, and C. Meyers, and dated to between 250–551 C.E. A hoard of Roman coins was also found in the village. Numerous rock tombs are scattered through the village and its vicinity; according to an unsubstantiated local tradition, these include the graves of *Shemaiah and *Avtalyon. A monumental tomb built of masonry and with a large sarcophagus was excavated in 1973 by G. Edelstein and F. Vitto.

[Michael Avi-Yonah / Shimon Gibson (2nd ed.)]

Modern Period

In October 1948 when it was taken by the Israeli army, the Muslims left and the Christian inhabitants of the neighboring Kafr Bir'im came to settle in the village soon afterwards. Since then, the village population has been made up almost exclusively of members of the Maronite sect, forming Israel's major Maronite community. In 1968, it had 1,650 inhabitants. Its economy was based on olives, figs, deciduous fruits, vineyards, tobacco fields, and beef cattle. The historical name Gush Ḥalav ("Milk Clod") assumedly points to the production of milk and cheese for which the village has been famous at least since the early Middle Ages; some scholars, however, assume that the name refers to the light color of the local limestone, in contrast with the dark-reddish basalt rock of the neighboring village Ra's al-Aḥmar ("Red Mountain Top"), today moshav Kerem Ben Zimrah.

BIBLIOGRAPHY: Y. Aharoni, *Hitnaḥalut Shivtei Yisrael ba-Galil ha-Elyon* (1957), 14; S. Klein (ed.), *Sefer ha-Yishuv*, 2 vols. (1939–44), s.v.; H. Kohl and C. Watzinger, *Antike Synagogen in Galilaea* (1916), 107ff.; Hamburger, in: IEJ, 4 (1954), 201ff. **ADD. BIBLIOGRAPHY:** S.J. Saller, *Second Revised Catalogue of the Ancient Synagogues of the Holy Land* (1972), 49; E. Meyers, "Ancient Gush Halav (Giscala), Palestinian Synagogues and the Eastern Diaspora," in: J. Gutman (ed.), *Ancient Synagogues. The State of Research* (1981), 61–77; Z. Ilan, *Ancient Synagogues in Israel* (1991), 25–27; Y. Tsafrir, L. Di Segni, and J. Green, *Tabula Imperii Romani. Iudaea – Palaestina. Maps and Gazetteer* (1994), 136; B. Bagatti, *Ancient Christian Villages of Galilee* (2001), 190–95.

GISER, MOSES DAVID (Moyshe; 1893–1952), Yiddish writer and editor. Born in Radom (Poland), Giser was deported during World War I for labor in Germany. In 1919, he published his first poem in *Der Yidisher Arbeter* (Vienna). Returning to Warsaw in 1921, he joined the Yiddish expressionistic group *Khaliastre. He emigrated to Argentina in 1924, where he taught in Yiddish schools, continued publishing his works (many under his pseudonym David Bender), operated a printing press, and edited the Yiddish publications *Zid-Amerike*, *Pasific*, and *Dos Yidishe Vort*. While his early lyrics focused on Polish Jews in cities and villages, his later lyrics dealt with Latin American scenes and people. A posthumous edition of his selected works appeared as *Dos Gezang fun a Lebn* ("The Song of a Life," 1953).

BIBLIOGRAPHY: LNYL, 2 (1958), 241–3; M. Ravitch, *Mayn Leksikon*, 1 (1945), 55ff; **ADD. BIBLIOGRAPHY:** Talush, *Yidishe Shrayber* (1953).

[Melech Ravitch / Marc Miller (2nd ed.)]

GISSIN, AVSHALOM (1896–1921), pioneer in the military defense of the *yishuv*. Born in Petaḥ Tikvah, Gissin studied at the officers' school of the Turkish Army in Istanbul and Damascus. At the end of World War I he returned to Palestine and founded *Maccabi and the scout movement in Petaḥ Tikvah, where he schooled local youth in the use of arms. When Arab riots broke out in 1921, Gissin left his work as a surveyor in the south and returned to his home to organize the defense of the settlement. He was killed with three others in battle while defending Petaḥ Tikvah against armed Bedouins. Maccabi Avshalom, the Petaḥ Tikvah soccer team, is named after him. His grandfather, EPHRAIM GISSIN (1835–1898), born in

Mohilev, Belorussia, was an early member of Ḥovevei Zion and went to Ereẓ Israel in 1895, joining his three sons and daughter who had settled in Petaḥ Tikvah.

BIBLIOGRAPHY: Tidhar, 2 (1947), 741–2, 770.

GISZKALAY (Gush Halav), JÁNOS (pseudonym of **Dávid Widder**; 1888–1951), Hungarian poet and journalist, and leader of the Hungarian and Transylvanian Zionist movements. Born in Nyitra, Giszkalay worked in Budapest, where he contributed to the Jewish press and, from 1918, edited the Zionist newspaper, *Zsidó Szemle*. During the "White Terror" which followed the defeat of Béla *Kun in 1918, he wrote justifying a Jewish girl's protest in a school essay against the Hungarian persecution of the Jews. Giszkalay maintained that antisemites had no moral right to demand patriotism of the oppressed Hungarian Jews. This led to an order for his arrest and he fled to Romania, where he joined the staff of *Uj Kelet*, the Hungarian-language Jewish daily in Kolozsvár (Cluj), Transylvania. Giszkalay's verse betrays the influence of E. Ady, the leading modern Hungarian poet, who was himself greatly influenced by the Bible. Outstanding for their enthusiasm and richness of language, Giszkalay's poems deeply impressed Zionist youth. His best-known poems were *Kezét fel az égre, ki férfi ki bátor*! ("Whoever is a man, whoever is courageous, let him raise his hand!"); *A messiás heroldja* ("The Herald of the Messiah"); and *Péntek a háboruban* ("A Wartime Friday Night"). Anthologies of his poems include *Új próféciák* ("New Prophecies," 1923). He also wrote a children's story, *Vitéz Benája három utja* ("Three Journeys of Knight Benayahu," 1928). Giszkalay's Zionist activities encouraged many Hungarian Jews to settle in Ereẓ Israel. In 1941 he immigrated to Palestine, where he worked as a shepherd on kibbutz Ma'agan. Later he moved to Haifa, where he translated his own works into Hebrew.

BIBLIOGRAPHY: H. Danzig, in: *Davar* (April 13, 1951); *Magyar Zsidó Lexikon* (1929); *Száz év zsidó magyar költői* (1943), 241, 243.

[Baruch Yaron]

GITAI, AMOS (1950–), Israeli film director. Gitai made over 46 movies and regularly showed his films at prestigious international festivals, where they often won awards. He triumphed at the Cannes Film Festival in 2005 when Hanna Laslo, the leading actress in his film *Free Zone*, won the Best Actress Award, the first time an Israeli actress has been so honored. Born in Haifa, Gitai studied architecture and earned a doctorate at the University of California, Berkeley. In the 1970s, while studying in the U.S., he began making documentaries, then moved to Paris for more than ten years. He continued to direct documentaries and also began making features. His films usually focus on Jewish history or crises in Israel and express his strong left-wing perspective. His 1989 film, *Berlin Jerusalem*, a look at friends in Germany in the 1920s who move to Palestine, won the critics' prize at the Venice International Film Festival. In 1993, he returned to Israel. While he is celebrated abroad, his films generally receive a less enthusiastic reaction in Israel. His 1999 film, *Kadosh*, is about ultra-Orthodox sisters; in 2000, he drew on his own experiences in the Yom Kippur War in the film, *Kippur*; and his 2002 film, *Kedma*, examines the fate of a group of immigrants to Palestine just before the establishment of the state. His other films include *Yom Yom* (1998), *Eden* (2001), and *Promised Land* (2004).

[Hannah Brown (2nd ed.)]

GITIN, SEYMOUR (**Sy**; 1936–), U.S. archaeologist. Gitin was born in Buffalo, New York. He earned a B.A. in ancient history at the University of Buffalo and studied ancient Near Eastern languages and literature in the rabbinic program at the Hebrew Union College–Jewish Institute of Religion in Cincinnati, Ohio. There he earned a B.A. (1959) and an M.A. in Hebrew letters as well as receiving ordination (1962). During this period, he spent a year in Jerusalem at the Hebrew University, studying ancient Hebrew texts and archaeology, and in 1961 he participated in the archaeological survey of the Western Negev directed by Nelson *Glueck.

In the late 1960s, he continued his archaeological studies with Nelson Glueck and with William G. Dever at the Hebrew Union College, first in Cincinnati and then in Jerusalem. From 1970 through 1975, he studied Near Eastern languages at the Hebrew University with Jonas Greenfield and epigraphy and paleography with Joseph Naveh, and completed an intensive tutorial archaeological research program with faculty members of the Hebrew University and his dissertation supervisor William G. Dever. In 1970, he joined the Tell Gezer excavation staff, where he was a senior field archaeologist from 1971 to 1975. In 1971, he also served as senior field archaeologist for the Jebel Qa'aqir excavations. In 1976, he became director of the Gezer Publications Program and during 1977–78 was assistant professor of the archaeology of the Land of Israel at the Jerusalem campus of the Hebrew Union College. In 1979, he was awarded a Ph.D. from the Hebrew Union College–Jewish Institute of Religion in Cincinnati. His dissertation, *A Ceramic Typology of the Late Iron Age, Persian, and Hellenistic Periods at Tell Gezer*, appeared as an Annual of the Nelson Glueck School of Biblical Archaeology. In 1980, he was appointed as the fifth long-term director and professor of archaeology at the W.F. Albright Institute of Archaeological Research, where in 1994 he became the Dorot director and professor of archaeology.

As Albright director, Gitin has been the creative force behind the establishment of the institute as an international center for the study of cultural and economic interconnections in antiquity in the Eastern Mediterranean basin. He also developed a doctoral and post-doctoral fellowship program in ancient Near Eastern studies at the Albright, which is one of the most extensive research programs of its kind in the world. Despite the complex political climate of the region, this program has successfully promoted academic ties and collaboration between students and scholars of different cultural and religious backgrounds. Today, the Albright is the only such institute in the Middle East where foreign, Israeli, and Palestinian scholars continue to interact and exchange information on a friendly and congenial basis.

Gitin's own research has resulted in major contributions to the field of archaeology, as seen in his groundbreaking work in late Philistine studies of the Iron Age II, which has dramatically altered the traditional perception of the history of the Philistines. His research is based on the results of the Tel Miqne-Ekron excavations, jointly sponsored by the Albright Institute and the Hebrew University, and directed by Gitin for 14 seasons during the years 1981–96 with his colleague Trude *Dothan. Contrary to conventional wisdom, Gitin has demonstrated that around 1000 B.C.E., the Philistines had not assimilated into one of the major culture groups, the Canaanites, Phoenicians, or Israelites. Rather they continued to exist for another 400 years, at the end of which the Philistines of *Ekron achieved the zenith of their economic development under the influence of the Neo-Assyrian empire. In his more than 60 publications on the development of Philistine material culture, best summarized in his 1997 article "The Neo-Assyrian Empire and its Western Periphery: The Levant, with a Focus on Philistine Ekron," Gitin has shown that it was a process of acculturation which ultimately contributed to the disappearance of the Philistines from the pages of history. This is supported by his publications, "A Royal Dedicatory Inscription from Ekron" (1998, with T. Dothan and J. Naveh), analyzing one of the most important archaeological finds of the 20th century, and "Israelite and Philistine Cult and the Archaeological Record: The 'Smoking Gun' Phenomenon" (2003). These and his other publications on the unique assemblage of incense altars from Ekron have helped to establish a new perception of Philistine cultic practices and their *sitz im leben* in the ancient Near East.

Gitin also created and directs the international research project "The Neo-Assyrian Empire in the 7th Century BC: A Study of the Interactions between Center and Periphery." The project, under the aegis of the Council of American Overseas Research Centers, located at the Smithsonian Institution in Washington, D.C., is designed to investigate the growth and development of the first "world market" in history and involves 50 scholars working in Bahrain, Cyprus, Egypt, Greece, Iran, Iraq, Israel, Jordan, Spain, Syria, Tunisia, and Turkey.

In recognition of his archaeological experience, Gitin was appointed editor of the three-volume work in progress, *The Ancient Pottery of Israel and Its Neighbors from the Neolithic through the Hellenistic Period*, which is destined to become the archaeologist's "ceramic bible." The project is sponsored by the Israel Exploration Society, the Albright Institute, the Israel Antiquities Authority, and the American Schools of Oriental Research.

Gitin is the recipient of the University of Buffalo's Distinguished Alumni award (1998), a doctorate of human letters, *honoris causa*, from the Hebrew Union College (2003), and the Israel Museum's Percia Schimmel Award for Distinguished Contributions to the Archaeology of Eretz Israel and the Lands of the Bible (2004).

BIBLIOGRAPHY: B. Boone, "In Search of a Lost World (Archaeologist Seymour Gitin, '56, Makes a Historic Discovery about the Long-Elusive City of Ekron, Ancient Capital of the Philistines)," in: *UB Today*, State University of New York at Buffalo (1997), 34–35; J.A. Blakely, "The Albright Institute 1980–2000, Establishing a Vision (S. Gitin's Directorship)," in: J.D. Seger, *An ASOR Mosaic, A Centennial History of the American Schools of Oriental Research* (2000), 175–217; S.W. Crawford, "Introduction and Appreciation," in: S.W. Crawford et al., *Festschrift in Honor of Seymour Gitin* (2006).

[Shimon Gibson (2nd ed.)]

GITLIN, JACOB (1880–1953), South African communal leader. For half a century Gitlin was the moving spirit in Zionist activities in *Cape Town, where he arrived from Vilna, Lithuania, in 1902. His furniture business became the unofficial headquarters of the Zionist movement there. As chairman of the Western Province (Cape) Zionist Council, he helped to make the organization one of the most influential Zionist centers in South Africa. Active in many spheres, he helped to found the Cape Board of Jewish Education.

BIBLIOGRAPHY: M. Gitlin, *The Vision Amazing* (1950), index.

[Louis Hotz]

GITLOW, BENJAMIN (1891–1965), U.S. Socialist and one-time Communist. Gitlow was born in New Jersey. He early became active in the Socialist Party and in the Retail Clerks Union of New York. Nominated in 1917 by the Socialist Party for the New York assembly, Gitlow was elected but became convinced that more revolutionary action was necessary and helped form the American Communist Labor Party. Elected to its Labor Committee at its 1919 founding convention, Gitlow was arrested that same year for publishing revolutionary material and served a three-year term. Gitlow then became a member of the Communist International executive committee and presidium, and also held a high position in the American Communist Party. While serving as general secretary in 1929, he and some associates were expelled by Moscow for not following the international communist line. In 1933, along with Lazar Becker, a colleague, he formed the Workers Communist League, later the Socialist Party. Disillusioned with Marxism, he became involved in investigations to expose the Communist movement and eventually wrote a bitter attack on the movement in his autobiography, *I Confess: The Truth About American Communism* (1940).

[Albert A. Blum]

GITTAIM (Heb. גִּתַּיִם), biblical city in the northern Shephelah. Its name is derived from Gath, and some of the biblical verses mentioning Gath may, in fact, refer to Gittaim (e.g., I Sam. 7:14; I Kings 2:39; II Kings 12:18; I Chron. 7:21; 8:13; II Chron. 26:6). Since, according to the Bible, the Beerothites of the tribe of Benjamin fled to Gittaim (II Sam. 4:3), the city must have been situated in the vicinity of this tribe. It is mentioned together with Hadid, Neballat, Lydda, and Ono in Nehemiah 11:33. Some scholars identify Gi-im-tu, the city captured by

Sargon II in 712 B.C.E., with Gittaim, and not Gath. Eusebius locates it between Antipatris and Jabneh (Onom. 72:2–3); it appears as Gitta on the Madaba Map. Recent studies have shown that it was probably located at Tel Ra's Abu Ḥumayd near Ramleh, a large site of some 100 dunams containing surface pottery dating from the Early Iron Age to the Arab period.

BIBLIOGRAPHY: Mazar, in: IEJ, 4 (1954), 227–35.

[Michael Avi-Yonah]

GITTELSOHN, ROLAND BERTRAM (1910–1995), U.S. rabbi. Gittelsohn, who was born in Cleveland, Ohio, was ordained at the Hebrew Union College in 1936. After serving as rabbi from 1936 to 1953 at the Central Synagogue of Nassau County in Long Island, he was appointed rabbi of Temple Israel, Boston, Mass. in 1953 and served there for the remainder of his career. Gittelsohn served as a U.S. Navy chaplain from 1943 to 1946 where he was the first Jewish chaplain in U.S. history assigned to the Marine Corps. He received three ribbons for his role in the Iwo Jima campaign and preached the address of dedication of the Jewish section of the Iwo Jima cemetery. He was a prominent communal leader serving on President Harry S. Truman's Committee on Civil Rights in 1947 and on the Governor's Commission in Massachusetts, including the Governor's Commission on Abolition of the Death Penalty (1957–58), the Governor's Committee on Migratory Labor (1960–62) and the Governor's Committee to Survey Operations of Massachusetts Prisoners (1961–62). Long active in Reform movement affairs, in 1968 he was elected president of the Central Conference of American Rabbis. He was also president of the Association of Reform Zionists of America and was a member of the Zionist General Council of the World Zionist Organization. During the late 1960s and early 1970s, he repeatedly called on the American Jewish community to adopt a more activist position on social and political issues, particularly in opposition to the war in Vietnam. Gittelsohn wrote *Modern Jewish Problems* (1935), *Little Lower than the Angels* (1955), *Man's Best Hope* (1961), *My Beloved Is Mine* (1969) on the Jewish view of marriage; and *Fire in My Bones* (1969).

[Abram Vossen Goodman]

GITTIN (Heb. גִּטִּין; "divorces"), sixth tractate of the order *Nashim* in the Mishnah, Tosefta, and Babylonian and Jerusalem Talmuds. *Gittin* is placed before *Kiddushin* because of the custom of arranging the tractates in the order of their length, *Gittin* containing nine chapters and *Kiddushin* only four. From a statement of Rashi (Git. 71b, s.v. *ta'ama*) and others, it seems that there was a different order of chapters, the present seventh chapter, according to Rashi, preceding the sixth. But from the *geonim, tosafot* (to Git. 62b, s.v. *ha-omer*), and Naḥmanides (in his novellae at the end of chapter 6) it appears that the present order is correct. The entire tractate deals with bills of divorce, with few digressions on other topics. The first chapter deals with the bringing of a bill of divorce *(get)* from outside Ereẓ Israel, the bearer of which has to testify that "it was written and signed in my presence." The question of the borders of Ereẓ Israel is dealt with in this connection. The first Mishnah of the second chapter, in fact, is a continuation of the first chapter and deals with the same topic. A similar phenomenon also occurs at the beginning of the seventh chapter; its first two *mishnayot* are a direct continuation of the theme of *agency in the writing and delivery of a *get* dealt with in the sixth chapter. The second chapter discusses the materials used for writing a *get* and the persons who may write and deliver it. The third chapter contains a group of *halakhot* based upon the principle that a previous condition may be presumed to exist: e.g., "If a man brings a *get* and has left the husband aged or sick, he may deliver it on the presumption that he is still alive" (3:3); the possibility of his death and the consequent invalidity of the *get*, necessitating a levirate marriage if he is childless, is ignored.

The fourth and fifth chapters cite a series of *halakhot* enacted for "general welfare" or in the interests of peace; e.g., "Scrolls of the Law, **tefillin*, and **mezuzot* should not be bought from gentiles at more than their value, for the general good" (4:6), i.e., so that gentiles should not be encouraged to steal such religious requisites from Jews; similarly, "one does not prevent the gentile poor from gathering gleanings, the forgotten sheaf, and the corner of the fields in the interest of peace" (5:8). The sixth chapter discusses agency and clarifies the difference between an agent for the delivery of a *get*, in which case the woman is not divorced until the *get* reaches her, and an agent for the reception of the *get*, where the agent represents the wife with the result that she is divorced as soon as the agent receives the *get*. The seventh chapter deals with the laws of conditional divorces. The eighth chapter, which derives from the Mishnah of R. Meir ("the whole of this chapter is R. Meir" – TJ, 8:5, 49c), contains a list of invalid divorces; should the woman remarry on the strength of them, she would need to receive a divorce from both husbands (a formula repeated in *mishnayot* 5–9). The ninth chapter contains parts of formulae of bills of divorce (9:3), from which it may be inferred that in early days there was no fixed formula (cf. also Tosef., Git. 9:6; Kid. 5b) and that divorces were written in Aramaic or Hebrew. The tractate concludes with a dispute between Bet Shammai and Bet Hillel about the grounds on which a man is permitted to divorce his wife. "Bet Shammai says, 'a man may not divorce his wife unless he has found unchastity in her,' while Bet Hillel says, 'even if she spoilt his food.'" According to Akiva, he may even divorce his wife if he finds another more attractive. This additional opinion is not a third one but an explanation of the words of Bet Hillel (see also Halevy, Dorot, 1, pt. 3 (1923), 569), and the radical wording is apparently intended to reject the views of Christians, who forbade divorce entirely (Mark 10:2–12, et al.).

The Tosefta, which in the printed edition contains seven chapters (the Mss. have nine like the Mishnah), supplements the Mishnah and gives the continuation of the development of the *halakhah*. Thus Mishnah 7:8 teaches: "(If the husband said) 'This is your *get* if I do not return within 12 months,' and he died within 12 months, it is not valid" – for the *get* only becomes effective at the end of 12 months and a divorce cannot be effected after death. To this the Tosefta (7:11) adds: "but our rabbis permitted her to marry." The Babylonian and Jerusalem Talmuds remark: "who are meant by 'our rabbis'? *Judah Nesiah …," Judah (II) the son of Gamaliel and the grandson of Judah ha-Nasi redactor of the Mishnah (76b; TJ, 7:3, 48d). This is one of three instances in which Judah Nesiah is called "our rabbi," although in general "our rabbis" refers to the generation of quasi-*tannaim* following Judah ha-Nasi (see Epstein, Tannaim, 231). Tosefta 5:4–5 affords information about cooperation between Jews and gentiles in the field of social welfare. In a city containing Jews and gentiles the communal leaders collect from both in the interest of peace. The gentile poor are supported together with the Jewish poor, in the interest of peace. Eulogies are delivered over them; when in mourning they are comforted; and their burial is undertaken in the interest of peace.

From the tractate it is possible to prove that there existed a kind of official recognition by the government of Jewish civil jurisdiction and that government sanctions were invoked to execute the decisions of the Jewish courts. Thus the Mishnah (9:8) teaches: "A bill of divorce given under compulsion is valid if ordered by a Jewish court, but if by a gentile court it is invalid; but if the gentiles beat him and say, 'Do what the Jews bid thee,' it is valid." Thus even a bill of divorce arranged by gentiles can also be valid, i.e., if the Jewish court requests the gentile court forcefully to compel the husband to give a divorce. So too in the Jerusalem Talmud (9:10, 50d) "and if gentiles compel on the initiative of (the *bet din* of) Jews, it is valid." The Jerusalem and Babylonian Talmuds explain and clarify the subjects raised in the Mishnah; e.g., Mishnah 4:2 cites a **takkanah* of Rabban Gamaliel the Elder that for the general good the husband is forbidden to annul a bill of divorce that has been handed over to a messenger but has not yet reached the wife. According to Simeon b. Gamaliel in a *baraita* (33a), should the husband disobey the *takkanah* and annul the divorce, the annulment is of no effect, and the divorce is valid. On this, the Talmud asks: "And is it possible that where a divorce has been annulled according to Torah law, we should, to uphold the authority of the court, allow a married woman to remarry?" To this the Babylonian Talmud replies: "Yes. When a man betroths he does so on the conditions laid down by the rabbis, and in this case the rabbis annul his betrothal." The Jerusalem Talmud (4:2), however, holds that the rabbis do have the power to annul Torah law, even without the premise that all who betroth do so on the conditions laid down by the rabbis.

Aggadic sayings are sometimes interwoven with the *halakhah*. Mishnah 5:6 quotes various *takkanot* in connection with the law of buying land from the sicaricon (i.e., those usurping the owner's land by decree of the Roman government), the purpose of these *takkanot* being to normalize economic conditions and the purchase of property. In connection with this, the Talmud (55bff.) cites a collection of interesting *aggadot* relating to events connected with the destruction of the Temple and its causes (67bff.). The beginning of the seventh chapter enumerates a long list of popular remedies, and the passage includes the story of *Asmodeus (Ashmedai) and his demons.

Mishnah 5:8 lays down, "in the interest of peace," the order in which men are called to the public reading of the Pentateuch: "A priest reads first, after him a levite, and after him an Israelite." The Babylonian Talmud (60a) completes the order in which Israelites are called to the reading of the law. From this list the degree of importance of the functionaries in Jewish society can be inferred: "First scholars appointed *parnasim* over the community, then scholars fit to be appointed *parnasim* over the community, then the sons of scholars whose fathers have been appointed *parnasim* over the community, after them heads of synagogues and the general public." The Babylonian Talmud (67a) quotes a *baraita* specifying the distinctive merits of scholars: "Meir was wise and a scribe; Judah was wise when he desired to be; Tarfon was like a heap of nuts; Ishmael was like a well-stocked shop; Akiva was like a storehouse with compartments; Johanan b. Nuri was like a basket of fancy goods; Eleazar b. Azariah was like a basket of spices; the Mishnah of Eliezer b. Jacob is scant but clear. Yose always had his reasons; Simeon used to grind much and produce little … and what he discarded was only the bran" (cf. ARN[1] 18, 68). The following dicta and apothegms are worthy of note: **dina de-malkhuta dina*, "the law of the government is binding" (a halakhic rule of great importance in the Diaspora; 10b); "a man should not terrorize the members of his household" (6b); "The words of the Torah abide only with one who sacrifices himself for their sake" (57b); "If a man divorces his first wife, even the altar sheds tears" (90b). In the Soncino translation of the Talmud tractate *Gittin* was translated by M. Simon (1936). For the commentators, editors, and translations of the tractate, see *Talmud.

BIBLIOGRAPHY: Ḥ. Albeck (ed.), *Shishah Sidrei Mishnah*, 3 (*Seder Nashim*, 1954), 265–72.

[Yitzhak Dov Gilat]

°GIUSTINIANI, AGOSTINO (Pantaleone; 1470?–1536), Italian Orientalist and Hebraist. Born in Genoa, Giustiniani, a friend of Erasmus, *Pico della Mirandola, and Sir Thomas More, taught in Bologna, and in 1513 wrote a kabbalistic work inspired by J. *Reuchlin's *De verbo mirifico* and *De arte cabalistica*. He then made a bold, but unsuccessful, attempt to publish the first modern polyglot Bible, of which only the first part, *Psalterium octaplum* (Genoa, 1516), appeared. This contained the Hebrew text of Psalms, the Targum, an Arabic translation, two Greek and two Latin translations, and a commentary based largely on rabbinic sources. On Psalm 19:5 there is a curious marginal allusion to Christopher *Columbus (Giustiniani's Genoese compatriot) and his voyages of discovery, which is the first such allusion in Hebrew literature. Although this Psalter, dedicated to Pope Leo X, was well received, it did not enjoy great commercial success, and the project then came to an end.

In 1514 Giustiniani was made bishop of Nebbio in Corsica, but political considerations led to his acceptance of the chair of Hebrew in Paris. From 1517 until 1522 he taught at the new College of the Three Languages, founded by Francis I, and published various works, including an edition of R. David *Kimḥi's Hebrew grammar (*Liber Viarum Linguae Sanctae*, Paris, 1520?), and *Rabi Mossei Dux seu Director dubitantium aut perplexorum* (Paris, 1520), a Latin version of the *Guide of the Perplexed* of *Maimonides. The latter, which Giustiniani produced with the aid of Jacob *Mantino, was marred by its reliance on faulty texts. Many of his kabbalistic writings appeared in the *De arcanis catholicae veritatis* (Ortona, 1518) of P. Columna *Galatinus. Giustiniani bequeathed his library of rare books and manuscripts to Genoa. Little is known about the last years of his life. In 1536, on a trip to Corsica, he was lost at sea.

BIBLIOGRAPHY: Steinschneider, Cat Bod, 5 no. 1564–66; C. Roth, *The Jews in the Renaissance* (1959), 124f., 155; F. Secret, *Le Zôhar chez les Kabbalistes Chrétiens de la Renaissance* (1964²), 30ff.; idem, *Les Kabbalistes Chrétiens de la Renaissance* (1964), 99–102.

[Godfrey Edmond Silverman]

°GIUSTINIANI, MARCO ANTONIO (fl. 16th century), printer of Hebrew books in Venice, Venetian patrician. His master printer Cornelius *Adelkind printed a fine edition of the Babylonian Talmud (1546–51). Soon, this very active press faced a formidable competitor in the house of *Bragadini which issued Maimonides' *Mishneh Torah*, with the notes of Meir Katzenellenbogen. Giustiniani then printed the full text of that code without R. Meir's notes. The mutual recriminations that the rivals engaged in at the Papal Court ultimately resulted in the confiscation and burning of all Hebrew books (1553).

BIBLIOGRAPHY: D W. Amram, *Makers of Hebrew Books in Italy* (1909), index.

GIVAT ADA (Heb. גִּבְעַת עָדָה), moshavah in central Israel on the slopes of the Manasseh Hills. Founded in 1903 by the Jewish Colonization Association (ICA) on land purchased by Baron Edmond de Rothschild, after whose wife Ada (Adelaïde) it was named, it provided homesteads for the children of farmers from *Zikhron Ya'akov. The village's progress was very slow and it suffered from attacks during the Arab riots of 1920 and 1936–39. After World War II additional families received land at Givat Ada, and after 1948, when the village received the status of a municipal council, new immigrants were absorbed, from Yemen, Hungary, Turkey, Romania, and other countries. In 1962–64 new immigrants from North Africa arrived. In 1968 Givat Ada had 1,330 inhabitants, in the mid-1990s approximately 1,510, and at the end of 2002, 2,540, on an area of 4.2 sq. mi. (11 sq. km.). The population's growth rate was a very high 4% per year, with its economy based on vineyards, fruit orchards, field and garden crops, and cattle. In 2003 the municipality of Givat Ada was united with the municipality of *Binyaminah.

[Efraim Orni / Shaked Gilboa (2nd ed.)]

GIVATAYIM (Heb. גִּבְעָתַיִם; "Two Hills"), township in central Israel, between Tel Aviv and Ramat Gan, founded in 1922 as a workers' suburb named Shekhunat Borochov (after Ber (Dov) *Borochov). In 1942 this quarter was united with four others in the vicinity to form the municipal unit of Givatayim. In 1959 Givatayim received municipal status. The town's population increased from 7,000 in 1947 to 42,100 in 1968 and 47,400 in 2002. Compared with other urban communities, Givatayim's population was characterized in 1969 by an exceptionally high percentage of Israeli-born and veteran Israelis (over 70%), while among those born abroad, 79.6% originated from Europe and America. At the beginning of the 21st century, Givatayim had the highest senior citizen population in Israel (21.8%). Standards of living and education were above average. The municipality pays particular attention to the environment. Buildings in Givatayim tend to be low, and 10% of the city's area consists of green zones, including 26 public parks and squares. In 2003 Givatayim was chosen as the best cared for city in Israel.

The city is situated within the Tel Aviv conurbation and its built-up area links up with that of the neighboring municipalities. Its area includes 1.2 sq. mi. (3.211 sq. km.).

WEBSITE: www.givatayim.muni.il.

[Efraim Orni / Shaked Gilboa (2nd ed.)]

GIVAT BRENNER (Heb. גִּבְעַת בְּרֶנֶר), kibbutz in central Israel, south of *Reḥovot, affiliated with Ha-Kibbutz ha-Me'uḥad. It was founded in 1928 by pioneers from Lithuania and Italy who were later joined by immigrants from Germany and several other countries. The members initially derived a livelihood mainly as hired laborers on farms and in industries nearby, but they quickly developed their own intensive farming branches (plant nurseries, field crops, and orchards) and industrial enterprises (including plants for metal sprinkler parts, textiles, fruit and vegetable preserves, ceramics, furniture, baby food), and became the largest collective settlement in the country. Following the split in *Ha-Kibbutz ha-Me'uḥad in 1951–52, a number of its members joined a new kibbutz, *Neẓer Sereni. In 1968, Givat Brenner had 1,520 inhabitants, declining to approximately 1,340 in the mid-1990s, and 1,180 in 2002. Its Bet Yesha rest home and resort was the first of its kind in a labor settlement. The kibbutz has a cultural center named after Enzo *Sereni, who was one of its members. The settlement is named after Joseph Ḥ. *Brenner.

WEBSITE: www.gbrener.org.il.

[Efraim Orni /Shaked Gilboa (2nd ed.)]

GIVAT HA-SHELOSHAH (Heb. גִּבְעַת הַשְּׁלוֹשָׁה), kibbutz in central Israel, east of Petaḥ Tikvah, affiliated with Ha-Kibbutz ha-Me'uḥad, first founded in 1925 on a site west of Petaḥ Tikvah by pioneers from Eastern Europe. The kibbutz initially subsisted mainly on its members' wages as hired laborers in local farms and industry. Gradually it developed its own farm branches and industrial enterprises. With the urbanization of the vicinity, the kibbutz was allocated a new site in rural surroundings of Rosh ha-Ayin further east. The transfer also made possible the establishment of two separate kibbutzim for the two sectors created as a result of the 1951–52 split in Ha-Kibbutz ha-Me'uḥad (the kibbutz that joined Iḥud ha-Kevuẓot ve-ha-Kibbutzim assumed the name Einat). In 1968, Givat ha-Sheloshah had 510 inhabitants, dropping to 439 in 2002. Its farming was highly intensive, with citrus and other orchards, irrigated crops, and dairy cattle. The kibbutz had a shoe factory and a plant for building materials. The name, "Hill of the Three," commemorates three Jewish laborers from the Petaḥ Tikvah area who were executed by the Turks during World War I.

[Efraim Orni]

GIVAT ḤAYYIM (Heb. גִּבְעַת חַיִּים), two kibbutzim in central Israel 4 mi. (6 km.) south of Ḥaderah. The founding settlers from Austria and Czechoslovakia were among the first pioneers on the Ḥefer Plain lands. They worked on drainage of the local swamps and planted eucalyptus groves. In 1932, the group established a kibbutz and was joined by immigrants from other countries. They developed intensive farming and set up a cask factory and a food preserves plant. Givat Ḥayyim was affiliated with Ha-Kibbutz ha-Me'uḥad, and after a split in that movement in 1951–52, was partitioned into two neighboring kibbutzim – Givat Ḥayyim and Givat Ḥayyim Bet. In 1968, Givat Ḥayyim (Ha-Kibbutz ha-Me'uḥad) numbered 705 persons and Givat Ḥayyim Bet (Iḥud ha-Kevuẓot ve-ha-Kibbutzim) had 690 inhabitants. In 2002, their populations were 960 and 801, respectively. Each had a one-third interest in the Pri-Gat juice company. The name commemorates Chaim *Arlosoroff.

WEBSITE: www.gat.co.il.

[Efraim Orni]

GIVAT ḤEN (Heb. גִּבְעַת ח"ן), moshav in central Israel near *Ra'ananah, affiliated with Tenu'at ha-Moshavim, founded in November 1933 in the framework of the "Thousand Families Settlement Scheme" by settlers from Eastern Europe who had become agricultural workers in Ra'ananah. They began by developing auxiliary farms which later became full-fledged farmsteads mainly based on citriculture, vegetable gardens, and dairy cattle. Later, some of the farmers went into organic farming. In 2002 the moshav's population was 331. The moshav's name is composed of the initials of Ḥayyim Naḥman *Bialik's first names.

[Efraim Orni /Shaked Gilboa (2nd ed.)]

GIVAT SHEMUEL (Heb. גִּבְעַת שְׁמוּאֵל), town in central Israel, located east of *Bene-Berak on land purchased from the Arab village of Ibn-Ibrāk. Givat Shemuel was founded in 1944 by a group of Romanian Jews, with a committee running the settlement as an association. In 1948, with the expansion of the settlement and the creation of the new neighborhood of Kiryat Yisrael, the association became a municipal council. Over the years additional neighborhoods were built and by the end of 2002 the population of Givat Shemuel had grown to 15,200 in a mixed religious and secular population, on a land area of 1.4 sq. mi. (3.5 sq. km.). The town is named after Samuel *Pineles, a Romanian Zionist leader.

WEBSITE: www.gshmuel.gov.il.

[Shaked Gilboa (2nd ed.)]

GIVAT ZE'EV (Heb. גִּבְעַת זְאֵב), urban settlement east of Jerusalem. In 1977 a group of settlers including native-born Israelis and immigrants from the U.S.S.R. occupied a deserted Jordanian army camp near ancient Giv'on nearby. After a few failed efforts to found a settlement, the Israeli government took over in 1981 and in 1983 the first new settlers began to arrive. By 2002 the population had reached 10,600, on a land area of 0.04 sq. mi. (1 sq. km.), and enjoyed municipal status. The majority of the population consists of young families and was expanding rapidly with another 2,000 apartments under construction in 2004. Givat Ze'ev is named for Ze'ev (Vladimir) *Jabotinsky, the leader of the *Betar movement.

WEBSITE: www.givat-zeev.muni.il.

[Shaked Gilboa (2nd ed.)]

GIVENS, PHILIP (1922–1995), Canadian politician and Jewish community leader. Givens was born in Toronto to Polish immigrants Hyman and Mary Gevertz. After completing Jewish parochial school, he graduated from the University of Toronto in 1945 with a degree in political science and economics and Osgoode Hall Law School in 1949. A member for the Liberal Party from youth, Givens gave up legal practice for politics. A long-time member of the Toronto city council, in 1961 Givens was elected as controller of the City of Toronto. A forceful, progressive, and energetic promoter of the city, after only one term as controller he was elected mayor of Toronto in 1963 – the second Jewish mayor of Toronto. His term as mayor was marked by the rapid expansion of Toronto's cultural and transportation infrastructure. Especially controversial was his championing the purchase of an abstract sculpture, *The Archer*, by Henry Moore, for the plaza of the new City Hall. Opponents branded Given's support for public art as ugly and a waste of money but Givens had his way. While the sculpture has since become a source of community pride, the controversy rebounded against Givens and he was defeated in his 1966 re-election bid. Givens turned his attention to the federal politics and was elected to Parliament in the 1968 Pierre Trudeau landslide. Givens resigned in 1971 before completing his term, after a dispute with Prime Minister Pierre Trudeau over issues that affected the Jewish community and out of disappointment at not being made a member of Cabinet. Givens ran for the Liberal Party in the 1971 Ontario provincial sphere and remained in the Ontario legislature until he retired from electoral politics in 1977. He subsequently held a number of judicial appointments.

Givens was a committed member of the Toronto Jewish community. A Yiddishist and Zionist, he was founding president of the Upper Canada Lodge of B'nai B'rith and president of the Toronto Zionist Council and member of the national executive of the Zionist Organization of Canada. He chaired the United Israel Appeal in Toronto and was active in the Canadian Jewish Congress, the Canadian Council of Christians and Jews, and a number of other community organizations. Givens is fondly remembered for his flamboyant style and devotion to the preservation of Yiddish language and culture.

[Frank Bialystok (2nd ed.)]

GIVET (Vichniac), JACQUES (1917–), Swiss poet. Born in Moscow, Givet became prominent in Swiss intellectual circles. His verse collections, at first influenced by surrealism, include *Nous n'irons plus au bois* (1938), *Les cicatrices de la peur* (1954), and *L'eau et la mémoire* (1963). Givet also published a remarkable polemical tract on neo-antisemitism, *La gauche contre Israël* (1968).

GLADIATOR, professional fighter in Roman public games. Little information is available about the gladiatorial contests held in the Middle East under Roman imperial rule. The performances were arranged by the authorities of cities with a predominantly Hellenistic culture; in Judea, for instance, they were sponsored by *Herod in *Caesarea. The Jewish sources make mention of Jews in this connection, and it was common knowledge that gladiators were bought for "large sums" (TJ, Git. 4:9, 46a–b). Rabbinical opinion was in general opposed to providing a ransom for a man who had sold himself as a gladiator, although an opinion is expressed that he should be ransomed since his life was in danger (Git. 46b–47a). "It is the accepted custom that a gladiator does not make a will," since he might be killed at any moment (Gen. R. 49:1, ed. by Theodor and Albeck, 1200). Some Jewish gladiators deliberately infringed the dietary laws to annoy their coreligionists and lived in Roman style (Git., loc. cit.). Others, however, were obliged to sell themselves out of financial stress "in order to exist" (TJ, loc. cit.). The expression "meal for gladiators" denoted an early repast consisting of an enriched diet (Pes. 12b; Shab. 10a). It is related of the *amora* Resh Lakish (see *Simeon b. Lakish) that he sold himself as a gladiator but that by combining courage with guile he managed to outwit the promoters of the contest and kill them all (Git. 47a). The rabbinical attitude toward the gladiatorial contests is clear from their association in the Midrash with brothels, gaming, and sorcery (Tanh. B., Gen. 24).

BIBLIOGRAPHY: Schuerer, Gesch, 2 (1907[4]), 60f.; Krauss, Tal Arch, 3 (1912), 114f.; S. Lieberman, *Greek in Jewish Palestine* (1942), 148f.

[Haim Hillel Ben-Sasson]

GLAGAU, OTTO (1834–1892), antisemitic German writer. Glagau was born in Koenigsberg, Prussia. As a journalist and political writer he had already made quite a reputation when he began, in the *Gartenlaube* of 1873, a series of articles on fraudulent stock-jobbing which were so full of invective that the editor discontinued them. Glagau had lost heavily in unfortunate speculations, and was very bitter against the stock exchange. In this spirit he wrote *Der Boersen- und Gruendungsschwindel in Berlin* and *Der Boersen- und Gruendungsschwindel in Deutschland* (Leipzig, 1877), in which he made some exposures of dishonest business methods, but in general caricatured rather than described the German business world. He naturally became involved in numerous libel suits. In these books he attacked the Jews vehemently as the perpetrators of all questionable financial transactions. It may be said that these books inaugurated the antisemitic movement.

GLANTZ, JACOBO (Yaakov Glanz; 1902–1982), Yiddish Mexican poet. He was born in Novovitebsk, Ukraine, into a family of religious farmers. He studied both in a traditional Jewish school and in Russian secular schools, and taught Yiddish language and literature at ORT schools in Odessa. Glantz wrote poetry in Russian and was part of literary bohemian groups of the Russian Revolution. In 1925 he immigrated to Mexico, where he worked in many occupations. In 1927 he started to publish in the first Yiddish newspaper in Mexico, *Meksikaner Yiddish Lebn,* and in 1927 he authored with Itzhak Berliner and Moshe Glikovsky the first book of poems in Yiddish to appear in Mexico: *Dray Vegn*. In 1936–46 Glantz was the literary editor of the newspaper *Der Veg*. In 1939 he suffered a lynch attempt by a fascist local group. Most of his poetry was in Yiddish, but he also wrote in Spanish and on Latin American subjects (such as his long poem *Cristóbal Colón*). He published essays on the Yiddish poet H. Leivick and on Novo-Vitebsk (1950).

BIBLIOGRAPHY: I. Berliner, J. Glantz and M. Glikovsky, *Dray Vegn. Lider un poemes* (1927); J. Glantz, *Vaticinios* (1963); *Voz sin pasaporte: Voice without Passport* (bilingual edition, 1965); *Balade fun Mein Ersten Cholem / Balada de mi primer sueño* (bilingual edition, 1979); M. Glantz, *Las genealogías* (1981; *The Family Tree*, 1991).

[Florinda F. Goldberg (2nd ed.)]

GLANTZ, MARGO (1930–), Mexican author and critic. The daughter of Yiddish poet Jacobo *Glantz, she grew up in an atmosphere of both Jewish European and Mexican Christian and popular culture. Her books reflect this complex double identity as well as the strife of an independent woman in a man-ruled culture. Glantz's best-known book, *Las genealogías* (1981; *The Family Tree*, 1991), retells her family's and her own memories. Since *Las mil y una calorías* ("One Thousand and One Calories," 1978), her narrations defy the traditions of the genre by means of fragmentation and irony. Among them: *Síndrome de naufragios* ("Shipwreck Syndrome," 1984); *Zona de derrumbe* ("Zone of Collapse," 2001); *El rastro* (2002; *The Wake*, 2005); *Historia de una mujer que caminó por la vida con zapatos de diseñador* ("History of a Woman who Walked through Life with Designer Shoes," 2005). Her essay "De la amorosa inclinación a enredarse en cabellos" ("On the Loving Tendency to Entangle Oneself in Hair," 1984) satirizes Jewish Orthodoxy related to woman's hair and submission. Glantz contributes to the Mexican press and media. She published critical essays on Mexican literature, which she also taught at Mexican, American, and European universities. She received several awards for her literary and critical works.

BIBLIOGRAPHY: R. DiAntonio and N. Glickman, *Tradition and Innovation: Reflections on Latin American Jewish Writing* (1993); M. García Pinto, *Women Writers of Latin America: Intimate Histories* (1991); D. Meyer, *Reinterpreting the Spanish American Essay: Women Writers of the 19th and 20th Centuries* (1995).

[Florinda F. Goldberg (2nd ed.)]

GLANVILLE, BRIAN LESTER (1931–), English novelist and journalist. Glanville's first novel was *The Reluctant Dictator* (1952). He emerged as the leading young Anglo-Jewish novelist of the decade with *The Bankrupts* (1958) which exposed the sham culture of Anglo-Jewry's nouveaux riches, but proved controversial. Glanville was attacked in various quarters for his unsympathetic attitude toward and relative ignorance of Judaism. *A Bad Streak* (1961) and *Diamond* (1962) also incorporate critical portrayals of Jewish types. Three later novels on general themes were *The Director's Wife* (1963), *A Roman Marriage* (1966), and *The Olympia* (1969). Glanville became a sports writer for the *Sunday Times* in 1960, remaining in that position for 30 years. He published books on soccer, including *A History of the World Cup* (2002).

GLANZ, LEIB (1898–1964), cantor and composer. He was born in Kiev, where his father was cantor at the synagogue of the Talna Ḥasidim. He led congregational prayers at the age of eight. After holding cantorial posts at Kishinev and in Romania, he immigrated to the United States in 1926 to become cantor of the Ohev Shalom Synagogue in Brooklyn, N.Y. Glanz had a lyric tenor voice which had great appeal both in its technical range and warmth of expression. He rebelled against the "sobbing" style favored in his time by many cantors and disapproved of the excessive use of the minor scale. The music he arranged for the synagogue had grace as well as devotional fervor. While holding his post at Brooklyn, he toured extensively and then accepted a post as cantor of Heikhal Sinai Synagogue and the Sha'arei Tefillah Synagogue in Los Angeles. In 1954 he settled in Israel and was chief cantor of the Tiferet Ẓevi Synagogue in Tel Aviv until his death. Glanz regarded the pentatonic scale as the ancient basis of Jewish music. He did research on liturgical melodies, and arranged choral music in the ḥasidic style. He aimed at creating a new tradition of *ḥazzanut*, and for this purpose founded the Tel Aviv Institute of Religious Jewish Music, to which the Cantorial Academy he headed became affiliated. He left more than 100 compositions in manuscript form and many recordings of his own performances.

BIBLIOGRAPHY: E. Steinmann (ed.), *Zoharim* (1965); E. Zaludkowski, *Kulturtreger fun der Yidisher Liturgie* (1930), 263; Sendrey, Music, index.

[Joshua Leib Ne'eman]

GLANZ-LEYELES, AARON (1889–1966), U.S. Yiddish poet and essayist. Born in Vloclawek, Poland, he was educated in his father's *talmud torah* in Lodz, studied literature at the University of London (1905–08) and, after immigrating to New York in 1909, at Columbia University (1910–13). He taught at Yiddish schools, lectured on Yiddish literature, edited Yiddish journals, and for more than half-a-century wrote articles on literary, social, and political events for the New York daily *Der Tog*. His prose appeared primarily under the name, A. Glanz, and his verse under the pseudonym A. Leyeles. In 1919, together with Jacob *Glatstein and N.B. *Minkoff, he founded the *In-Zikh ("Introspectivist") movement of Yiddish poetry and the literary organ *In Zikh* for the propagation of the Inzikhist credo. While his first book of poetry, *Labirint* ("Labyrinth," 1918), rejected impressionistic effects and intricate traditional forms, his second book, *Yungharbst* ("Young Autumn," 1922), followed the Inzikhist doctrines. It was followed by *Rondos un Andere Lider* ("Rondos and Other Poems," 1928) and *Tsu Dir – tsu Mir* ("To You – to Me," 1933). *Fabius Lind* (1937), an autobiography in verse, told the story of his spiritual odyssey and was prefaced by a restatement of his literary beliefs. *A Yid Oyfn Yam* ("A Jew at Sea," 1947) consisted of lyrics composed under the impact of the European Jewish catastrophe. It was followed by the volume of poems *Baym Fus Fun Barg* ("At the Foot of the Mountain," 1957), in which he again emphasized his opposition both to abstract poetry stripped of emotional content and to poetry as the expression of untamed feeling devoid of intellectual content. He held that poetry must always be concrete, the direct or indirect expression of a real experience, in which thought and feeling were intertwined. In the lyrics of *Amerike un Ikh* ("America and I," 1963), he voiced his faith in the historical ideals of the U.S. Of his experiments in poetic drama, only *Shlomo Molkho* (1926), which dealt with the conflict between the two messianic figures David *Reuveni and Solomon *Molcho, aroused significant interest. While Reuveni sought to redeem the Jewish people by force of arms and to restore them to a normal existence on their ancestral soil, Molcho, influenced by kabbalistic lore, wished the Jews to remain in the Diaspora and to become the self-sacrificing redeemers of all mankind. Through this 16th-century Marrano martyr, Glanz-Leyeles voiced the Territorialist philosophy with which he had been long associated. In a second drama, *Asher Lemlen* (1928), he dealt with the conflict between Jewish messianic longing and the reality of political and social life. A Hebrew translation of the two plays was made by Shimshon Melzer and a Hebrew rendering of selected poems by B. Ḥrushovski (Harshav; 1960), with a literary analysis by Dov Sadan; Harshav also translated his verse into English (*American-Yiddish Poetry*, 1986). Glanz-Leyeles translated works from English, Russian, and Polish into Yiddish, most notably the works of Edgar Allen Poe. In the volume *Velt un Vort* ("World and Word," 1958), Glanz-Leyeles collected the best of his important essays on poets, novelists, and memoirists. In his criticism, he maintained that a critic should call attention to the way in which a work enriched literature rather than to its failings. In his 75th year, he visited Israel for the first time and was stimulated to a new burst of lyric creativity.

BIBLIOGRAPHY: Rejzen, Leksikon, 2 (1927), 255–8; LNYL, 5 (1963), 330–8: N.B. Minkoff, *Literarishe Vegn* (1955), 219–49; J. Glatstein, *In Tokh Genumen*, 1 (1947), 97–105, 295–302; 2 (1956), 291–6; S. Lestchinsky, *Literarishe Eseyen* (1955), 116–26; S. Bickel, *Shrayber fun Mayn Dor* (1958), 84–98; Waxman, Literature, 5 (1960), 93–5; *Jewish Book Annual*, 25 (1968), 116–22. **ADD. BIBLIOGRAPHY:** D. Sadan, in: *Shirim ve-Ḥezyunot me-Et Aharon Gelants-Liles* (1960), 9–35.

[Sol Liptzin / Anita Norich (2nd ed.)]

GLAPHYRA (first century B.C.E.), daughter of Archelaus, king of Cappadocia. Glaphyra's first husband was *Alexander, son of Herod the Great. After Alexander's execution (7 B.C.E.) Herod returned her to her father. However, her two sons by the marriage, Tigranes and Alexander, remained with the king. Glaphyra then married Juba, king of Libya. This marriage seems to have ended abruptly, and the princess returned home again. There she met Archelaus, son of Herod, who immediately divorced his wife Mariamne and married her. This marriage constituted a transgression of Jewish law, since Glaphyra had already borne children to the brother of Archelaus. Glaphyra died shortly after her arrival in Judea.

BIBLIOGRAPHY: Jos., Ant., 16:11, 193, 206, 303, 328–32; 17:12, 341, 349–53; Jos., Wars, 1:476–8, 552f.; 2:114–6; Schuerer, Hist, 152, 154, 176; A.H.M. Jones, *Herods of Judaea* (1938), index; Klausner, Bayit Sheni, 4 (1950²), 154ff., 179.

[Isaiah Gafni]

GLASER, DONALD ARTHUR (1926–), U.S. physicist and Nobel laureate. Glaser was born in Cleveland, Ohio, and received his B.Sc. in physics from the Case Institute of Technology (1946) and his Ph.D. in physics and mathematics from the California Institute of Technology (1949). He joined the physics department of the University of Michigan (1949), becoming professor (1957) before moving to the University of California at Berkeley as professor of physics (1959) and of physics and neurobiology from 1989. Glaser's early research interests, for which he was awarded the Nobel Prize (1960), concerned the properties of high-energy particles. He designed the bubble chamber for tracking these particles as a method superior to the cloud chambers previously in use. Subsequently he worked on computational models of the human visual system supported by physical and psychological observations of visual perception.

[Michael Denman (2nd ed.)]

GLASER, EDUARD (1855–1908), scholar, archaeologist, and explorer. Born in Deutsch-Rust (Czech Republic), Glaser was, along with another Jewish scholar, Joseph *Halévy, the leading 19th century scholarly researcher in south Arabia and the pioneer of Sabaean studies and pre-Islamic history. His thorough knowledge of the Arabic language, of Oriental customs, and especially of Islam was the secret of his research success. His journeys through *Yemen represent the most important scholarly research ever carried out in this part of the world after Halévy. Despite great financial problems and dangers, he undertook four expeditions to Yemen between 1882 and 1895, disguised as a Muslim. He reached remote historical places in Yemen never visited before by Western scholars, such as Mārib, the capital of the ancient Kingdom of Sheba. The southern Arabian inscriptions he collected are of fundamental importance for all research on ancient Yemen. The analysis of his still unpublished scholarly works is far from finished. The collection of almost 660 objects from southern Arabia that he brought back from his fourth journey into Yemen in 1895 formed the nucleus of the "Oriental" or Near Eastern section in the Kunsthistorischen Museum in Vienna; he also brought hundreds of Yemeni-Arabic manuscripts to the National Library in Vienna. He was a great lover of the Jewish people and the Zionist movement. He corresponded with *Herzl and proposed to him the establishment of the Jewish state in Yemen. In Sana he became close to the local Jewish scholar, R. Yiḥye *Kafaḥ and strengthened his enlightened attitude toward the Jewish religion. In a series of articles published in the REJ, written as a part of his spirited debate with Halévy, Glaser expressed his uncompromising view that the pre-Islamic Himyari kingdom was indeed a Jewish kingdom, based on his interpretation of some on the inscriptions he found in Yemen.

BIBLIOGRAPHY: E. Glaser, "Meine Reise durch Arhab und Haschid," in: *Petermanns Mitteilungen* 30 (1884), 170–83, 204–13 (Eng. tr. with intro., notes, and indices by D.M. Varisco, "My Journey through Arhab and Haashid" (1993)); C.J. Robin, "Le judaïsme de Himyar," in: *Arabia*, 1 (2003), 98–99; idem, "Von Hodeida nach Sanaa vom 24 April bis 1 May 1885," in: *Petermanns Mitteilungen*, 32 (1886), 1–10, 33–48; idem, *Ethnographica Jeminica: Auszuege aus den Tagebuechern Eduard Glasers*, ed. Walter Dostal (1993); S.D. Goitein, in: *Shevut Teman* (1945), 149–59; Y. Nini, in: *Ha-Ẓiyyonut*, 5 (1975), 299–310; Y. Tsurieli, in: *Le-Ammim*, 65 (1996), 57–76.

[Yosef Tobi (2nd ed.)]

GLASER, JOSEPH (1925–1994), U.S. Reform rabbi. Glaser was born in Boston, Massachusetts. His education was interrupted by World War II, where he served in combat infantry and earned a Purple Heart. He returned to the United States and received his B.A. from UCLA (1948) and his law degree from the University of San Francisco before entering Hebrew Union College-Jewish Institute of Religion, where he was ordained in 1956. His first assignment was a pulpit in Ventura, California, and he served as registrar and instructor at the Los Angeles campus of the Hebrew Union College, which opened in the mid-1950s to accommodate the rapid expansion of the California Jewish community. Glaser left his congregation in 1959 to become the Northern California/Pacific Region director of the *Union of American Hebrew Congregations, the congregational arm of the Reform movement. He moved to New York in 1971 to serve as executive vice president of the *Central Conference of American Rabbis. He remained in that position until his retirement. Within a few years Rabbi Alfred *Gottschalk was to head the Hebrew Union College and Alexander *Schindler the UAHC, thus giving the Reform movement stable and experienced leadership during most of the last quarter of the 20th century.

Glaser directed the activities of the CCAR, an organization of 1,700 rabbis, mainly in North America. He played an important role in the 1990 decision of the Reform Rabbinate to open membership to rabbis without regard to their sexual orientation, balancing that with a reaffirmation of the ideal of a monogamous, procreative marriage.

A social activist, he was an advocate for Native Americans and Tibetan refugees, as well as for Israel. He served as chairman of Religion in American Life, the first Jew to preside over the non-sectarian organization designed to fortify the American people's faith in God. He also served on the executive committee of the Synagogue Council of America and the Union of American Hebrew Congregations. He was on the board of American Jewish World Service and other organizations.

[Michael Berenbaum (2nd ed.)]

GLASER, JULIUS ANTON (**Joshua**; 1831–1886), Austrian jurist. Born in Poestelberg, Bohemia, he converted to Christianity in his youth. He obtained doctorates in law from the universities of Zurich and Vienna. In 1856 he was appointed assistant professor of criminal law at Vienna University and four years later became full professor. From 1871 to 1879 he was minister of justice and later attorney general. Glaser's principal contribution to Austrian jurisprudence was the introduction of a new penal code in 1873. The code was largely concerned with protecting the rights of the accused and remained in force in Austria until 1938. Among his numerous legal publications are *Das englischschottische Strafverfahren* (1850); *Anklage, Wahrspruch und Rechtsmittel im englischen Schwurgerichtsverfahren* (1866). In addition, he coedited the *Allgemeine Oesterreichische Gerichtszeitung*.

ADD. BIBLIOGRAPHY: M.G. Losano, *Der Briefwechsel Jherings mit Unger und Glaser* (*Abhandlungen zur rechtswissenschaftlichen Grundlagenforschung*, vol. 78) (1996); ADB, vol. 49, 372–80.

[Guido (Gad) Tedeschi]

GLASGOW, city in S.W. Scotland. The first Jew to settle in the city was Isaac Cohen in 1812; however there was no sizable community or synagogue until 1833, when services were held in the house of the *shoḥet*, Moses Lisenheim. By 1831, 47 Jews lived in the city, most of them originating from Eastern Europe, though six had already been born in Glasgow. Four years later the community acquired its first burial ground, which was used until 1851. There was a split in the congregation in 1842 when a hall attached to Anderson College was leased for religious services; a minority of community members objected, arguing that since human bodies were dissected at the college, it was an unfit place for a synagogue. Subsequent bitterness between the two groups led to court proceedings over the right to use the cemetery; the majority won the case. However, at the election of Nathan Marcus *Adler as chief rabbi of Great Britain in 1844, both parties exercised a vote. By 1850 there were 200 Jews in the city and eight years later they consecrated a new synagogue, known as the Glasgow Hebrew Congregation. In 1879 a synagogue was built for the community at Garnethill, with E.P. Phillips as minister; it was soon followed by two others in the South Side. (In 1979 the Garnethill Synagogue celebrated its centenary.) As elsewhere in Britain, an influx of immigrants followed the Russian persecutions of 1881; in 1897 there were 4,000 Jews in the city and in 1902, 6,500. Many of the newcomers, who settled in the Gorbals district, were tailors or furriers.

The community was always active in Zionism, supporting Ḥovevei *Ẓion in the 19th century and Zionist associations in modern times. Mainly because of the stimulus of the *Habonim movement, a large number of young Glasgow Jews settled on kibbutzim in Israel. A charity board originally known as the Glasgow Hebrew Philanthropic Society (1858) and later called the Glasgow Jewish Board of Guardians also helped in the organization of the Jewish Old Age Home for Scotland, situated in the south of the city. The Glasgow *talmud torah* and Board of Jewish Religious Education organized classes for children (as do the individual synagogues), directed the Hebrew College (for post-bar mitzvah Jewish education), and assisted in running the yeshivah. In 1970 there was a Jewish day school at the primary level and Hebrew was taught in two municipal secondary schools; Glasgow University taught both biblical and modern Hebrew.

The Jewish Echo (weekly, established in 1928) was Scotland's only Jewish newspaper until 1965, when *The Jewish Times* (later renamed *Israel Today*) was established. The community had many organizations of Jewish interest, e.g., Bnei Akiva, ORT, and the Jewish Lad's Brigade (which claimed the world's only Jewish bagpipe band). Ten Orthodox and one Reform synagogue served the community. Religious leaders of note included Samuel I. *Hillman, Kopul Rosen, I.K. Cosgrove (1903–1973), and Wolf Gottlieb (b. 1910). Among the community's outstanding members were Sir Maurice *Bloch, Sir Isaac *Wolfson, Sir Ian M. *Heilbron, Sir Myer Galpern (b. 1903, lord provost and lord lieutenant of Scotland (1958–60) and Labor M.P. (1959)), Samuel Krantz (b. 1901) and L.H. *Daiches. Notable in the university as well as in the community were Noah Morris (professor of medicine), Michael Samuel (professor of English language), and David Daiches Raphael (professor of political and social theory).

In 1969 the Jewish population numbered about 13,400 (out of a total of 1,045,000). In the mid-1990s the Jewish population dropped to approximately 6,700. In 2001 the British census recorded a Jewish population of 4,224. Dr. Kenneth E. Collins has written a number of important studies of Glasgow Jewry, including *Second City Jewry* (1990). At the beginning of the 21st century, six synagogues functioned in Glasgow, which also had a range of Jewish institutions, mainly in the city's southern suburbs. (See also Oscar *Slater.)

BIBLIOGRAPHY: A. Levy, *Origins of Glasgow Jewry, 1812–1895* (1949); idem, *Origins of Scottish Jewry* (1959), 27–29; idem, in: JHSET, 19 (1960), 146–56; C. Roth, *Rise of Provincial Jewry* (1950), index; J. Gould and S. Esh (eds.), *Jewish Life in Modern Britain* (1964), index; C. Bermant, *Troubled Eden* (1969), index; idem, in: *Explorations*, 1 (1967), 99–106. **ADD. BIBLIOGRAPHY:** K.E. Collins, *Be Well! Jewish Health and Welfare in Glasgow, 1860–1914* (2001); idem., *Glasgow Jewry: A Guide to the History and Community of the Jews* (1993).

GLASHOW, SHELDON LEE (1932–), U.S. physicist. Glashow was born in New York. He graduated from Cornell University in 1954, received his M.A. from Harvard in 1955 and his doctorate in 1959. After serving as assistant professor at Stanford University in 1961, he received a similar appointment at Berkeley (1961–66), where he was then named associate professor (1966–67); in 1967 he was appointed professor at Harvard. He is a member of the National Academy of Science, the American Academy of Arts and Sciences, the American Physics Society, and Sigma Xi. Glashow's research has been in the fields of theory of elementary particles and the interactions between them: a unified conception of strong and weak electrodynamic interaction and the identification of basic constituents of matter. He is the recipient of many awards, culminating in the Nobel Prize in physics in 1979 for his "contributions to the theory of the weak and electromagnetic interactions between elementary particles including, inter alia, the predictions of weak currents."

GLASMAN, BARUCH (1893–1945), Yiddish novelist, short story writer, and essayist. Glasman was born in Kapitkevich, Belorussia, and raised in nearby Mozyr. When he was 13 his family moved to Kiev, where he attended a Russian secondary school. In 1911, he emigrated to the U.S. and received a B.A. from Ohio State University in 1918, after which he served in the U.S. Army (1918–19). He began his literary career in English, publishing short stories in the Anglo-Jewish journal *Menorah*. He soon turned to writing in Yiddish and published his works in *Tsukunft, Der Yidisher Kemfer, Der Tog, Morgn-Zhurnal*, and *Forverts*. In 1924, he moved to Poland, where he toured, lecturing to audiences on the subject of Yiddish literature in America. In 1930, he returned to New York, where he remained until his death in 1945. Glasman is best known for his novels, including *A Trep* ("A Step," 1917), *Af an Inzl* ("On an Island," 1927), and *In Goldenem Zump* ("In the Golden Swamp," 1940). His selected works appeared in eight volumes (1927–37).

BIBLIOGRAPHY: LYNL, 2 (1958), 249–52; A. Beckerman, *Baruch Glasman* (1944); B. Rivkin, *Undzere Prozaiker* (1951), 274–84; S.D. Singer, *Dikhter un Prozaiker* (1959), 145–52; A. Tabachnik, *Dikhter un Dikhtung* (1965), 441–51. **ADD. BIBLIOGRAPHY:** Y. Kisin, *Lid un Esay* (1953), 249–54; R.R. Wisse, *A Little Love in Big Manhattan* (1988), 166.

[Melech Ravitch / Marc Miller (2nd ed.)]

GLASNER, MOSES SAMUEL (1856–1924), rabbi and early leader of the *Mizrachi movement in Hungary and Transylvania. Glasner, a great-grandson of R. Moshe *Sofer, was born in Pressburg. From 1878 until 1923, when he settled in Ereẓ Israel, he was the rabbi of Klausenburg. He was one of the two Orthodox rabbis in Hungary (the other being Moses Aryeh Roth) who joined the Zionist movement and Mizrachi, and at the founding convention of Mizrachi (Pressburg, 1904) he spoke out against the Orthodox Hungarian rabbis for their attacks upon Zionism and the Mizrachi. He propagated the Zionist idea in speeches and writings among Orthodox circles. He also published several halakhic works (*Or Bahir*, 1908; *Halakhah le-Moshe*, 1912; *Dor Revi'i*, 1921) and a work on the *aggadah, Shevivei Esh* (1903). In Jerusalem, he took part in the educational and cultural activities of Mizrachi and was especially close to Rabbi A.I. *Kook.

BIBLIOGRAPHY: L. Jung (ed.), *Men of the Spirit* (1964), 459–66; EẒD, 1 (1958), 523–7.

[Getzel Kressel]

GLASS.

Earliest Times

The earliest manufacture of glass does not antedate the late third millennium B.C.E., when the first glass beads were made in Mesopotamia and Egypt. The invention of glass vessel-making dates to the mid-second millennium B.C.E., when the first core-formed glass vessels appear almost simultaneously in Egypt and Mesopotamia. Egypt's glass industry was particularly flourishing in the el-Amarna period (the first half of the 14th century B.C.E.). Some Mesopotamian glass vessels have been found in northern Syria, though none in Palestine, but several Palestinian sites have yielded Egyptian glass vessels of the 14th–13th centuries B.C.E. A rich collection of such vessels was found in the small Canaanite Fosse Temple at Lachish; others were found at Beth Shean and Tell Dayr ʿAllā (the ancient Sukkoth). Egyptian glass vessels were also found in tombs at Tell al-ʿAjūl, Beth Shemesh, and Ẓahrat al-Ḥumrāya south of Jaffa. Gezer and Megiddo yielded similar glass vessels. There is no positive evidence that there was any manufacture of glass vessels in Canaan in the Late Bronze Age. A complete decline in glassmaking set in toward the end of the second millennium B.C.E. and it is only in the second half of the eighth and the seventh centuries B.C.E. that glass vessels appear again. None of the molded and cut luxury glass bowls and other colored vessels of that period has come to light in Palestine, but a core-formed vessel of the seventh century was found in a tomb at Achzib. Glass-inlay pieces of the late ninth and eighth centuries were found together with the ivories in the palace of the kings of Israel at Samaria, but whether they were made of Syrian or imported glass is not known. An active production center of core-formed glass vessels, probably on the island of Rhodes, began making small amphoriskoi, aryballoses (short-necked flasks), alabastra, and juglets late in the seventh century B.C.E., and specimens have been found in an early sixth-century tomb at Gibeah, north of Jerusalem, and in Ammonite tombs in Jordan. Other vessels of this type have been found in Israel at Athlit, Achzib, Hazor, Beth Shean, and En Gedi. Molded and cut luxury glass vessels continued to be made in the Achaemenid period (sixth to fourth centuries) and the remains of an alabastrum of this type were found in a tomb at Athlit. Core-formed glass vessels of the Hellenistic period have occasionally been found in Palestine. The fragments of molded bowls found in second- and first-century B.C.E. levels at Ashdod, Jerusalem, Samaria, and other sites, may be products of local glass factories, possibly situated somewhere along the coast. There is, however, no indication whatsoever that Jews had any connection with glassmaking during the Hellenistic period, either in Palestine or in the Diaspora.

Glass in Hellenistic and Roman Periods

Glass is mentioned only once in the Bible, in Job 28:17, where it is equated with gold. This reflects the early situation when glass was of great value. The obscure statement in Deuteronomy 32:18–19 about Zebulun's hidden treasures in the sand was explained by Targum Jonathan as referring to glass, but this seems anachronistic. The Septuagint followed a very different line when it chose to render this passage as close as possible to Genesis 49:13. This probably indicates that when the Greek version of the Bible was prepared, this area had not had the obvious connection with glass that it had later on. A very early tradition seems to be preserved in the Palestinian Talmud (TJ, Pes. 1:6, 27b) and in the Babylonian Talmud (Shab. 14b, 15a), according to which Yose b. Joezer and Yose b. Johanan, who lived in the first half of the second century B.C.E., declared that glass vessels are liable to become impure. The U.S. talmudist Louis Ginzberg suggested that this declaration had an economic basis – it was meant to protect local pottery and metal ware from competition with foreign glass imports. Glass was, however, rare and valuable all through the Hellenistic period, and could not have presented competition to any local products. An explanation must therefore be sought in the cultural-religious sphere. The edict is contemporary with the first large-scale production of glass drinking bowls, and the two Jewish authorities may have objected to them because they identified them with Hellenistic influence, manners, and customs.

A revolutionary event was the invention of glassblowing toward the end of the first century B.C.E., which made it possible to produce glass vessels cheaply and in great variety. The invention seems to have taken place during the reign of Augustus (31 B.C.E.–14 C.E.) somewhere along the Phoenician coast, perhaps at Sidon, an area where a glass production center was apparently already in existence. The fame of Sidonian glass must have been considerable, since glassmakers working in Rome in the first century C.E. boasted of their Sidonian origin when they stamped the handles of their canthari in Greek or Latin, as, for example, Artas Sidon.

Several Jewish tombs of the first and second centuries C.E. have yielded glass vessels. Glass vessels are relatively rare in ossuary tombs around Jerusalem, which are no later than 70 C.E. A tomb excavated at Ramat Raḥel in 1931 (Tomb I) contained a small bottle with a spheric body and a short cylindrical neck. Several tombs in a cemetery on the Mount of Olives yielded simple, small glass bottles with pearshaped bodies and elongated necks. All these glass vessels are typical of the first-century vessels common throughout the Roman Empire. A Jewish tomb of the middle of the first century at Carthage yielded a shallow glass bowl of a shape very common in the early imperial period. So-called "candlestick" bottles which have small convex bodies and long tubular necks were found in a few ossuary tombs in and around Jerusalem which can be dated to the second century. To the relatively limited testimony from Jewish tombs were added in 1960–61 the finds from the Judean desert caves in which fugitives of the Bar Kokhba revolt took refuge. The finds included typical glass vessels of the early part of the second century C.E. It appears, then, that the only Jewish glass vessels of this period were the normal ware of the day. It stands to reason that some of the vessels, perhaps even many of them, were made by Jews but this is no more than a logical assumption. The Mishnah includes passages which refer specifically to glassmaking. *Kelim* 8:9 mentions עוֹשֵׂי זְכוּכִית – those who make glass (the "metal") – and זַגָּגִין – those who make glass vessels and their furnaces. Makers of glass vessels are also mentioned in *Kelim* 24:8. The Mishnah would not have included regulations about these trades if they had not been part and parcel of the daily life in Palestine, at any rate in the second century C.E. and possibly earlier. This, then, proves the existence of Jewish glassmakers in this period.

GOLD GLASS. The first group of glass vessels which is distinctly Jewish by reason of its decoration is the famous gold glass with Jewish symbols. The term is used to describe decorations of thin gold foil encased between two layers of glass medallion; and must not be confused with gilding, where the gold is left uncovered. The commonest type of gold glasses are those which were used, in the third and the fourth centuries C.E., as a decorated base of very shallow plates, bowls, or beakers. The thinly hammered gold foil was pasted on a round piece of clear or dark blue glass, within the boundaries of a low raised glass base. The outlines and the designs of the desired pictures, patterns, and inscriptions were prepared by removing the superfluous gold from the background, and leaving the designs in gold. Enamel paints were used at times to enrich the decoration. In the final stage the decorated base was reheated and joined to the outer surface of a large, hot, clear glass "bubble" which was later given the shape of the required bowl. A similar method was used to decorate the body of a vessel by smaller medallions of gold foil on blue glass. This technique was not exclusively Jewish. In the third and fourth centuries C.E. this particular craft flourished on an unprecedented scale. The center of the industry was Rome, and most of the pieces were found in pagan, Christian, or Jewish catacombs in and around the city. The vessels were broken deliberately, often skillfully chiseled around the edges, and stuck into the plaster near or on the graves of the deceased. The reasons for this custom have not yet been convincingly explained. Of the 500 bases and decorative medallions that have survived, only about a dozen bear definitely Jewish symbols. The earliest was found in 1882 in the catacomb of the saints Peter and Marcellinus (now in the Vatican Museum) and another around 1894 in the catacomb of Saint Ermete. A gold glass now in Berlin is said to have been found in the Jewish catacomb of Vigna Randanini in Rome and another which is now in the Cologne City Museum is said to have come from the Villa Torlonia catacomb. Other Jewish gold glass pieces are now in the Vatican and in the British, the Ashmolean, the Metropolitan, the Wuerzburg University, and the Israel museums. Most of the Jewish gold glass bases have their decorations presented in two registers. These include representations of the Ark of the Covenant flanked by a pair of lions or doves, temple vessels like *menorot*, amphorae, and *shofarot*, and objects relating to Sukkot, the Feast of the Temple, such as *lulavim, etrogim*, and motifs found in other Jewish objects and catacombs of the period. Of a different type is the Vatican fragment found in 1882. This bears a miniature painting of a tetrastyle temple inside a peristyle court surrounded by palm trees. The temple is approached by four steps and on the tympanum of the gable is a *menorah*. In front of the temple are a *lulav*, an *etrog*, two amphorae, and other objects. The temple is flanked by two free-standing columns. Most scholars seem to agree that this is a representation of Solomon's Temple, and it can be assumed that it was copied from an early illuminated Bible manuscript. This fragment bears a Greek inscription. Other Jewish gold glasses have inscriptions in Latin, similar to those found on the non-Jewish glasses such as *ANIMA DULCIS* ("sweet soul"). Only one Jewish small gold glass medallion is known. This shows a *shofar* between two *etrogim*. It is now in the Vatican Library. These Jewish gold glasses are generally thought to have been drinking vessels, perhaps for ritual purposes. The fragment with Solomon's Temple may tentatively be attributed to the third or early fourth century C.E.; the rest are more likely to be of the fourth century. Their decoration has numerous parallels in Jewish art. It is possible to assume that they were made by Jews.

In addition to the gold glasses and cut bowls from Rome there are further specimens worth noting: Moshe *Schwabe and Adolf *Reifenberg uncovered and published in 1935 a Jewish gilded glass sepulchral inscription in Greek ending with *Shalom* in Hebrew, with a *menorah* below the inscription and a *shofar* on its right. They also published a stamped glass medallion from Rome bearing a *menorah* and the name of the glassmaker: *EX OF [FICINA] LAVRENTI.*

The Eastern Mediterranean: Third Century to Arab Conquest

The excavations at the Jewish cemeteries at Beth She'arim have yielded some finds of glass. Several vessels and many fragments were found in catacombs 12–20 and date to the third and first half of the fourth century C.E. These are, with very few exceptions, fragments of various common types of receptacles of the period, mainly bottles, and do not have any characteristics which could identify them as Jewish. An exceptional decorated glass plate was discovered in catacomb 15. With a diameter of 52 cms. (c. 20 ins.), it is unusually large, and engraved on its exterior are 13 arches under which are vessels, tools, doors, and hanging lamps and several unidentified objects. Although this may represent a temple facade, nothing in the designs on the plate is specifically Jewish. The remains of a glass factory were found at Beth She'arim during the excavations in 1940 and were attributed to the first half of the fourth century C.E. and to the Byzantine period. A large slab of glass – 3.40 × 1.94 × 0.45 m. (11 × 6½ × 1½ ft.) – apparently the bottom of a glassmaker's tank, was also discovered in a cistern. This too possibly dates to the Byzantine period. It is therefore reasonable to assume that some of the vessels found in the cemeteries around the site were local products. Several glass vessels, also of contemporary Palestinian types, were found in a Jewish tomb of the late fourth to fifth centuries at Gezer (Tomb 201). Glass lamps having three handles for suspension and cups of the type used for bronze polycandela were in use in Palestinian synagogues of the Byzantine period. Lamps suspended from seven-branched candlesticks are depicted on the mosaic pavement of the synagogue of Naaran (sixth century C.E.). Several other synagogue mosaic pavements have representations of seven-branched candlesticks with glass lamps. A complete glass lamp and many fragments of lamps of various types were found in the Beth-Shean synagogue. They belong to its last phase in the first half of the seventh century and are now in the collection of the Israel Department of Antiquities. Similar fragments of lamps from the late sixth or early seventh centuries were also found in the synagogue of Maon near Nir Am, southeast of Gaza. Exactly the same types of lamp were used in contemporary churches in Palestine and Syria, so the glass finds in such Jewish contexts as the catacombs of Beth She'arim, Gezer (Tomb 201), or the ruins of synagogues do not differ from the normal glassware of their times. Between the late fourth and early seventh centuries there are a few groups of ornamental glass objects such as pendants and bracelets, bearing symbols which identify them as specifically Jewish. In a tomb excavated at Tarshīḥā in western Galilee a small circular pendant of greenish glass with a loop for suspension was found stamped with a *menorah*. The tomb was in use in the fourth and fifth centuries. The pendant is now in the Rockefeller Museum, Jerusalem (31.286B). The British Museum has a pendant made of light brownish glass, said to be from Tyre, with a *menorah*, a *shofar* on the left, and a *lulav* and *etrog* on the right. There are similar pendants in the Israel Museum and in the Reifenberg collection. Of unknown provenance is a small greenish glass medallion in the Jewish Museum, New York, representing a *menorah* in a wreath. It was originally applied to a vessel and dates to the fourth century C.E. An identical piece from Egypt is in the Israel Museum. A fragment of a blue glass bracelet with the *menorah* stamped on it several times was found in the western part of the Jezreel Valley. It is now in a private collection. A complete bracelet of blue glass with 14 impressions of a *menorah* and *shofar* on its right side was acquired in New York in 1965. It is said to be of east Mediterranean provenance. Both the fragment and the complete example are probably of the fourth or fifth century. Another bracelet of very dark green glass with similar impressions but of unknown provenance is in the Museum Haaretz, Tel Aviv.

HEXAGONAL BOTTLES FROM PALESTINE. By far the most interesting Jewish glass from Palestine are the mold-blown hexagonal and octagonal small jugs or jars. These were blown into hexagonal or octagonal metal molds which were open top and bottom. The designs which were hammered into the molds appeared on the lower part of the jug, as an impression and not as a relief. Some hexagonal jugs have a long neck and a handle while others have a short neck and outsplayed rim. Nearly all these vessels were made of a bubbly brown glass, but there are a few known examples made of greenish glass. Of many such mostly Christian jugs, only about 30 survived bearing Jewish symbols, such as *menorot*, often with a *shofar* on the left, and a *lulav* and *etrog* on the right, sometimes with an incense shovel on the right. The other sides are decorated with trees, arches, and other objects or patterns. Similar jugs and jars bearing Christian symbols have identical features, indicating that they were made in the same workshops. They are believed to have been used as containers for oil taken from the lamps of the Church of the Holy Sepulcher to be blessed at Golgotha, and there can be no doubt that they were made in Jerusalem. These are attributed to the late sixth or early seventh century, and by analogy the Jewish vessels can be attributed to the same period. It can be assumed that Jewish pilgrims used the vessels for carrying away oil from lamps at their center of veneration – probably the Western Wall. During the excavations at Ephesus in Asia Minor a bottle was found on which are painted in black a *menorah*, a *shofar*, a *lulav*, and an *etrog*. Though this seems to be the only known Jewish glass vessel from the eastern Mediterranean area, apart from Palestine and Syria, the existence of Jewish glassmakers in the region in the sixth century C.E. can be deduced from two popular Byzantine fables of that time, one from Emesa (Homs), the other from Constantinople, in both of which the central figure is a Jewish glassmaker.

In the East from Medieval to Modern Times

The fact that Jews were active in glassmaking in medieval times is borne out by references in sources of the period. Arab historians have preserved the interesting information that the Khalif ʿAbd al-Malik (685–705) employed a group of Jews to make the glass lamps and vessels for the Mosque in Jerusalem but that Omar ibn Abd al-Aziz deprived them of this office. Very important data have been preserved in the *Cairo *Genizah*. A document signed in the spring of 1011 deals with a dispute over the payment for a consignment of 50 "bales of glass" sent by three Jews from Tyre to Cairo. This ties up with a statement made by *Benjamin of Tudela, who visited Palestine in 1170, that at Tyre were "Jews, makers of good glass which is called Tyrian glass and is famous in all countries." Benjamin of Tudela also mentions that at Antioch "are about ten Jews and they are glassmakers." In an article on the Cairo *Genizah* published in 1961, S.D. Goitein mentions four contracts of partnership in glass workshops, one of which refers to a Jewish glassmaker who arrived in Cairo "from the west." He appears to have traveled overland from Tunis. Goitein believes that Jews were connected with the issue of the well-known Islamic glass weights. However, no actual survivals of Jewish glass manufactured in this period are known.

It has been suggested that Jews were connected with the age-old glass works at Hebron. The first to mention these works seems to have been the Augustine monk, Jacob of Verona, who visited Hebron in 1335; but he made no reference to any Jews there, although production was already on a large scale.

[Dan P. Barag]

L.A. Mayer assumed that a group of clumsily inscribed Syro-Egyptian glass mosque lamps were executed by "Jewish craftsmen, who were literate, but in a different script." During the Ottoman period, in the 17th century, there was in Damascus a Jewish center for the manufacturing of similar glass lamps. One such lamp in the Jewish Museum in London bears a Hebrew inscription and dates from 1694. Of Middle Eastern 18th-century origin are bottles of opaque glass, which have Hebrew dedicatory inscriptions cut in them. One which belonged to the Charles Feinberg Collection is now in the Israel Museum. Another specimen in the Victoria and Albert Museum in London has a metal top and decorative chains. These were probably used as oil or wine containers.

In the West From Medieval to Modern Times

The art of glassmaking was reintroduced into Europe during the period of the Crusades. Numbers of Eastern glassmakers settled in northern Italy, Spain, and southern France. Jewish craftsmen may have been among them; though it cannot be proven.

EASTERN EUROPE. There were, however, Jewish glassmakers in Central and Eastern Europe after the 15th century. There are also records of Jewish glaziers and glassmakers in Bohemia and Moravia from the 15th century onward, and the craft was frequently practiced by Bohemian Jews in the latter half of the 16th century.

From glass vessels and from contracts between Jewish glassmakers and the aristocracy it is clear, for instance, that the Jews took an active part in the flowering of glassmaking in Hungary in the 17th and 18th centuries.

Ḥevra Kaddisha Beakers. In the 17th and 18th centuries Hungarian and Bohemian Jews apparently participated in the general practice of manufacturing decorated jugs or beakers for special occasions. Among them were prominent beakers used by members of a guild or a fraternity at their annual banquets and given each year by the men chosen head of the guild. Interesting are some painted and cut-glass beakers which were executed for the Jewish Burial Society, the *ḥevra kaddisha*, in some German and Bohemian communities. Several such beakers survived, mostly in the Jewish Museum in Prague. Their most common decoration is the burial procession. One such beaker dated 1692 is now in the New York Jewish Museum.

In modern times too Jews were prominent in the marketing and industrial production of Czechoslovakian glass, centered in Bohemia. In the period between the world wars there were many Jewish firms which produced sheet glass, plate glass, and mirrors, as well as glass pastes for artificial jewelry. When Hitler occupied Czechoslovakia some of the leading Jewish producers of artificial gems and costume jewelry moved their firms to the United States.

ENGLAND. In the late 18th and 19th centuries Lazarus Jacobs (d. 1796) of Bristol and his son Isaac (d. 1833) were important glass manufacturers and merchants, the latter holding a royal appointment as glass manufacturers to George III. They were especially celebrated for their opaque white, and the elegant royal blue glassware for which Bristol was famous. Another eminent Jewish glassmaker was Meyer Oppenheim, who came from Pressburg in Hungary. He invented a ruby flint glass which he produced in Birmingham from 1756 to 1775. A number of Jews were associated with the glass industry in Birmingham, where the lead glass used for artificial gems was known as "Jew's glass" in the middle of the 19th century.

THE UNITED STATES. The earliest known American glass cutter was a Jew named Lazarus Isaacs who arrived from England in 1773. He was employed by Stiegel at his factory at Manheim, Pennsylvania, where the first fine glassware in America was produced. Jews do not reappear in American glassmaking until the late 19th century, when Lazarus Straus and Sons of New York was a leading producer of high quality cut glass in the United States and Europe (see *Straus family).

ISRAEL. On their return to Ereẓ Israel, the Jews revived the glass industry on the Phoenician coast, where it existed in ancient times. In the late 19th century, the Baron de *Rothschild set up a glass factory at Tantura near the site of the Phoenician harbor of Dor to provide bottles for the nascent wine industry, and in 1934 Phoenicia, the Israel Glass Works, was founded in the Haifa Bay Area. Under the patronage of Baroness Bathsheva de Rothschild, a new style of art glass was evolved in the early 1960s, based on forms of the talmudic period.

From the end of the 19th century a school of primitive glass paintings developed in Safed, Jerusalem, and other centers. One of its later offsprings is the painter Shalom of Safed. Their subjects were *holy places, *Mizraḥ* panels, amulets, and biblical topics.

BIBLIOGRAPHY: Mayer, Art, index, s.v. *glass, glass blowing, glass bottle, glass cutters, glass makers, gold glasses*; Goodenough, 1 (1953), 168–77; 2 (1953), 108–119, 218; Krauss, Tal Arch, 2 (1911), 285–8; A.B. Engle, in: *Miscelanea de Estúdios Arabes y Hebráicos* (1969), 15–16; E.H. Bryrne, in: JAOS, 38 (1918), 176–87; C.J. Lamm, *Mittelalterliche Glaeser und Steinschnitt-Arbeiten aus dem Nahen Osten*, 1 (1930), 522–44 (a general bibliography); J.C. Pick, in: *The Jews of Czechoslovakia*, 1 (1968), 379–400; Roth, Art, 242–3, 355.

GLASS, MONTAGUE MARSDEN (1877–1934), U.S. humorist. Glass, who was born in Manchester, England, was taken to the U.S. at the age of 13. He studied and practiced law in New York, but in 1909 abandoned his profession to become a full-time writer. The Jewish clients whom Glass met in his law office inspired a series of short stories which he began publishing in various magazines in 1908. The first collection, *Potash and Perlmutter*, appeared in 1910 and this was followed a year later by *Abe and Mawruss*. Though treated humorously, the two clothing manufacturers, Abe Potash and Morris Perlmutter, were sympathetically presented and their entertaining foibles and typically Jewish family virtues endeared them to Jewish readers. Both story collections became the basis of stage successes. The first *Potash and Perlmutter* play, produced in 1913, had long runs in New York and London. Glass also wrote *Elkan Lubliner – American* (1912), *Worrying Won't Win* (1918), and *You Can't Learn Them Nothing* (1930).

BIBLIOGRAPHY: Waxman, Literature, 4 (1960^2), 974–5; S. Liptzin, *Jew in American Literature* (1966), 116–7.

[Jo Ranson]

GLASS, PHILIP (1937–), U.S. composer and performer. Born in Baltimore, Glass began to study violin at six and flute at eight. At 12, he started composing while working at his father's record shops after school. At 15, he entered the University of Chicago (where he received a B.A. in liberal arts, 1956). Later he studied composition at Juilliard with Bergsma and Persichetti (receiving a M.A. in composition, 1961). Awarded a Fulbright scholarship, he went to Paris to study for two years with Nadia Boulanger. There he made the acquaintance of Indian musician Ravi Shankar, whose music Glass adapted for the film score of *Chappaqua*. After leaving Paris, he traveled in North Africa and the Indian subcontinent. Non-European music became one of the sources of his own style, named repetitive music (or minimalism), which was founded by him in the 1960s together with Riley, *Reich, and La Monte Young. Minimalistic music is based on a short melodic formula and its numerous varied repetitions over time. In Glass's view, such music required a special type of reception: "When it becomes apparent that nothing 'happens' in the usual sense, but that, instead, the gradual accretion of musical material can and does serve as the basis of the listener's attention, then he can perhaps discover another mode of listening.... It is hoped that one would then be able to perceive the music as 'presence,' freed from dramatic structure, a pure medium of sound" (P. Glass, 1974).

In the late 1960s and early 1970s Glass wrote a great number of chamber pieces and established his own Philip Glass Ensemble that had the exclusive right to perform his instrumental music. Performances at this time were held in New York lofts (Glass's in Greenwich Village, sculptor Donald Judd's in SoHo), private art galleries (those of Leo Castelli and Paula Cooper), and museums (the Guggenheim and the Whitney). Occasionally, Glass had to work as a plumber or taxi driver in order to survive when not touring with his ensemble throughout the U.S., Canada, and Europe. However, the seminal work of this period, *Music in Twelve Parts,* was premiered in the traditional atmosphere of New York's Town Hall, hired by the composer himself. This opus includes 12 sections and lasts over four hours. Being the culmination of Glass's minimalism, it shows the transition to greater vertical complexity, up to traditional functional harmony in the conclusion of the piece.

From the late 1970s the composer produced numerous scores for music theater, film, and dance. A great public success was *Einstein on the Beach,* the opera that was named a "theater of visions" because of its lack of narration. Instead of plot, there are series of dramatized icons (like Einstein's violin, or the trains symbolizing the theory of relativity). The following operas return little by little to narrative music theater (*Satyagraha,* 1980, on Gandhi, and *Akhnaten,* 1984, on the Egyptian pharaoh who introduced monotheism). Afterwards, in the second opera trilogy based on the films of Cocteau, Glass used his individual multimedia forms (for example, the film is accompanied by a new soundtrack composed by Glass).

Glass also scored numerous films over the last two decades, from the wordless, visionary cinema of Godfrey Reggio, Paul Schrader's experimental *Mishima,* and Errol Morris's intense documentary *The Thin Blue Line* to Hollywood war films (*Hamburger Hill*) and horror films (*Candyman* and its sequel). His score for *Kundun* received an Oscar nomination, while *The Truman Show* won him a Golden Globe. Glass collaborated with pop singers Paul *Simon, David Byrne, Suzanne Vega, and Laurie Anderson in the song-cycle *Songs from Liquid Days.* Other collaborations were with Allen Ginsberg in *Hydrogen Jukebox,* with Ravi Shankar in *Passages,* and with Doris Lessing on two science-fiction operas, *The Making of the Representative for Planet 8* and *The Marriages between Zones Three, Four and Five.* His work influenced rock and film music as well as classical music. As an example of reciprocal influence, it is worth mentioning that Glass wrote symphonic versions of the art-rock albums *Low* and *Heroes* by David Bowie and Brian Eno, who, in turn, were influenced by Glass at the end of the 1970s. Glass became one of the best known and commercially successful composers of his generation.

BIBLIOGRAPHY: NG²; MGG²; E. Strickland, *Minimalism: Origins* (1993); R. Kostelanetz (ed.), *Writings on Glass: Essays, Interviews, Criticism* (1996, incl. writings by Glass); K.R. Schwarz, *Minimalists* (1996); K. Potter: *Four Musical Minimalists: La Monte Young, Terry Riley, Steve Reich, Philip Glass* (2000).

[Yulia Kreinin (2nd ed.)]

GLATSTEIN (Gladstone), JACOB (1896–1971), Yiddish poet, novelist, and critic. Born in Lublin, Poland, Glatstein was encouraged by his father to read widely in contemporary Yiddish literature. Like many Yiddish writers of his generation, he visited I.L.*Peretz in Warsaw. As a result of violent outbreaks of antisemitism in Lublin, Glatstein convinced his parents to let him immigrate to the U.S. (1914). His debut as a Yiddish writer was the short story "Di Geferlekhe Froy" ("The Terrible Woman") in the journal *Fraye Arbeter Shtime.* In the 1920s and 1930s, he published more than 100 short stories in the style of Guy de Maupassant and Abraham *Reisen under the pseudonym Y. Yungman in the Yiddish daily *Morgn Zhurnal.* In 1920, together with Aaron *Glanz-Leyeles and N.B. *Minkoff, Glatstein inaugurated the *Inzikhist* ("introspectivist") movement in U.S. Yiddish poetry. Taking their name from the journal *In Zikh,* which was to appear irregularly (1920–39), and from the group anthology, *In Zikh, A Zamlung Introspektive Lider* ("Introspection, a Collection of Introspective Poems," 1920), the *Inzikhistn* announced their mission of revitalizing and modernizing Yiddish poetry. The key words in the introspectivists' manifesto (1921) were *kaleidoscopic, contradictory,* and *chaotic.* They rebelled against the aestheticism of *Di Yunge,* which they considered ivory tower art-for-art's-sake, removed from truth and life. The introspectivists rejected decorum and formal elegance in favor of free verse whose rhythms were to be correlates of unique, individual experience. Like their Anglo-American contemporaries, whose work they knew well, the introspectivists emphasized the concrete image and favored suggestion and association. They distrusted metrical regularity and fixed patterns and sought to capture the rhythms of the human voice and modern urban life. From his earliest poems onward Glatstein was the poet in love with his medium, the Yiddish language. No poet in Yiddish has been so richly inventive in coining new words and word combinations. No poet in Yiddish has had a better ear for folk idiom and, indeed, for the sound structure of Yiddish generally. Many of Glatstein's poems seem to grow out of the latent powers hidden in the shape, sound, and history of individual words. The introspectivists early declared that a Yiddish poem was Jewish by virtue of its medium; no subject was barred. They often wrote on themes far removed from Jewish life.

Glatstein's reputation rests primarily on his poetry. Critics divide his work into two periods: the first includes his four books of poetry: *Yankev Glatshteyn* (1921), *Fraye Ferzn* ("Free Verse," 1926), *Kredos* ("Credos," 1929), *Yidishtaytshn* ("Yiddish-Meanings," 1937); and the second, his books of poetry and criticism from 1943 to 1978 (the last two posthumous), including *Gedenklider* ("Remembrance Poems," 1943), *Shtralendike Yidn* ("Radiant Jews," 1946), *Dem Tatns Shotn* ("My Father's Shadow," 1953), *Fun Mayn Gantser Mi* ("The Fruits of My Labor," 1965), *Di Freyd fun Yidishn Vort* ("The Joy of the Yiddish Word," 1961), and *A Yid fun Lublin* ("A Jew from Lublin," 1966). In poems such as "Zing Ladino" ("Sing Ladino"), "Mir, di Vortproletarier" ("We, the Word Proletariat"), and "Tsum Kopmayster" ("To the Headmaster") from the collection *Yidishtaytsn,* Glatstein crafted some of the most experimental, "wild" modernist poems ever written in Yiddish. These poems are both part of the main trends of European and American modernism, and deeply rooted in the phonetics, semantics, and cultural specificity of Yiddish. He was, however, also a distinguished writer of both imaginative and critical prose. There are no novelistic travel narratives in Yiddish literature comparable to *Ven Yash iz Geforn* ("When Yash Set Out," 1938; Eng. *Homeward Bound*, 1969) and *Ven Yash iz Gekumen* ("When Yash Arrived," 1940; Eng., *Homecoming at Twilight*, 1962). These loosely autobiographical works, part of a projected trilogy inspired by his nine-week journey to Lublin to visit his dying mother in summer 1934, inaugurated the second phase of his artistic career; they are notable for their poetic style and their brooding sense of impending catastrophe. Because he remained independent of political allegiances, he was able to give a compelling portrait of Polish Jewry on the eve of the Holocaust in these novels. *Emil un Karl* (1940), a novel of a Jewish and a Christian boy in Hitler-occupied Austria, is particularly suited to the young reader. The war years and the Holocaust transformed Glatstein into one of the great elegists of Eastern European Jewish life. It became his major poetic purpose to meditate on, mourn, and celebrate a shattered way of life. Already in "A Gute Nakht, Velt" ("Good Night, World," 1938), he bitterly rejects European culture and defiantly and joyously declares his return to the narrow confines of traditional Jewish life. No American Yiddish poem has aroused as much comment as this anti-universalist poem of execration and affirmation.

As columnist for the New York daily *Tog-Morgn Zhurnal* and as regular contributor of the column *In Tokh Genumen* to the weekly *Yidisher Kemfer* (1945–57) and other periodicals, Glatstein commented on virtually every significant event in Jewish literary and cultural life and on world literature generally. As critic of Yiddish literature he exerted great influence and helped to raise the level of critical awareness both among writers and readers. His essays and reviews appeared in a series of volumes entitled *In Tokh Genumen* ("The Heart of the Matter," 1947; 1956; 1960), continued in *Mit Mayne Fartogbikher* ("With My Dawn Journals," 1963) and *Oyf Greyte Temes* ("On Ready Themes," 1967).

Glatstein's poetry revolutionized Yiddish modernism and added a cosmopolitan, intellectual voice to the chorus of Yiddish avant-garde poetry. His greatest contribution to Yiddish poetry were his Holocaust poems, the Bratslaver poems, and his homage to the Yiddish language. He once quipped: "What does it mean to be a poet of an abandoned culture? It means that I have to be aware of Auden but Auden need never have heard of me" (I. Howe, *A Margin of Hope* (1982), 264). Although Glatstein lived in New York for more than half a century and published more than 20 books, he remained virtually unknown outside Yiddish literary circles. In a tribute to the poet, Cynthia Ozick recognized his crucial role in the rise of Jewish American literature (1972): "…if Jacob Glatstein had not lived and written his splendid poetry, and if there were no other Yiddish writers present to write as only they can about our lives and our natures there would be no hope for a Jewish literature of any kind in America."

BIBLIOGRAPHY: D. Sadan, in: J. Glatstein, *Mi-Kol Amali: Shirim u-Fo'emot* (1964), 28–32 (bibl.); LNYL, 2 (1958), 256–61 (bibl.); I. Howe and E. Greenberg, *A Treasury of Yiddish Poetry* (1969), 245–56, 326–37. **ADD. BIBLIOGRAPHY:** J. Glatstein, in: *Yiddish*, 1 (1973), 30–9; J. Hadda, in: *Prooftexts*, 1 (1981), 192–200; I. Howe, in: *Commentary*, 53 (Jan.1972), 75–7; C. Ozick, in: *Jewish Heritage* (Spring 1972), 58–60; Y. Rappoport, *Oysgerisene Bleter* (1957), 97–137; B. Harshav (ed.), *American Yiddish Poetry* (1986), 773–805; R. Fein (ed.), *Selected Poems of Yankev Glatshteyn* (1987); B. Zumoff (ed.), *I Keep Recalling: The Holocaust Poems of Jacob Glatstein* (1993); J. Schwarz, in: *Yiddish After the Holocaust* (2004), 74–91; J. Schwarz, in: *Imagining Lives: Autobiographical Fiction of Yiddish Writers* (2005), 98–126.

[Leonard Prager / Jan Schwarz (2nd ed.)]

GLATZER, NAHUM NORBERT (1903–1990), scholar, teacher, and editor. Glatzer was born in Lemberg (Lvov), and pursued his higher education in Germany and at the Breuer Yeshivah in Frankfurt on the Main (1920–22). He became a disciple and associate of Franz *Rosenzweig, whose life and work so influenced him that he decided to devote himself to scholarship rather than pursue a career in the rabbinate. In 1932 he succeeded another mentor, Martin *Buber, in the University of Frankfurt's chair of Jewish philosophy and ethics. In fact, Glatzer had been Buber's only doctoral student during his years at the university (1924–33). In 1933 Glatzer left Germany for Israel, where he taught at Bet Sefer Reali in Haifa. From 1938 he was in the United States, teaching at several colleges before joining the faculty of Brandeis University in 1950. He served as editorial adviser to *Schocken Books, where he was chief editor (1945–51), and was a director of the Leo Baeck Institute from 1956. Before retiring from Brandeis in 1973, Glatzer served as the Michael Tuch Professor of Jewish History and Samuel Lane Chair in Jewish History and Social Ethics, as well as chair of the NEJS Department from 1957 to 1969. He was also the first faculty member to receive Brandeis's honorary degree.

In his doctoral dissertation, *Untersuchungen zur Geschichtslehre der Tannaiten* (1933), Glatzer maintained that the rabbis of the first and second centuries C.E. retained their faith in the God of history in the face of apocalyptic tendencies and the consequent denigration of this world. Glatzer's *Geschichte der Talmudischen Zeit* (1937) elaborates and continues his earlier work. He wrote a number of studies on particular problems of talmudic history.

Glatzer wrote, translated, and edited more than 50 books, with a range of expertise that extended from the Bible to existentialism. He also wrote extensively on the history of 19th-century Jewry, especially on the history of the Wissenschaft des Judentums. His book *Franz Rosenzweig: His Life and Thought* (1953, 1961^2) is considered the definitive volume on Rosenzweig. Glatzer edited more than a dozen anthologies, which are used widely in teaching Jewish history and ideas.

Among his many works are *Hillel the Elder* (1956, 1962), *Anfaenge des Judentums* (1966), *The Rest Is Commentary* (1961, 1969^2), *Faith and Knowledge* (1963, 1969^2), *Dynamics of Emancipation* (1965, 1969^2), *The Dimensions of Job* (1969), *Language of Faith* (1974), *The Loves of Franz Kafka* (1986), and *The Quest for the Cities of Gold*, vol.16 (1987). He edited *A Jewish Reader* (1961, 1966²), *Hammer on the Rock* (1962), *Parables and Paradoxes* by Franz Kafka (1961), and *The Essential Philo* (1970).

In 1992 the Nahum Glatzer Archives were donated to Brandeis; they include his correspondence with colleagues worldwide, manuscripts of his books, and his lecture notes.

BIBLIOGRAPHY: A. Altmann, in: *Judaism*, 12 (1963), 195–202, contains a list of Glatzer's writings. **ADD. BIBLIOGRAPHY:** M. Fishbane and J. Glatzer Wechsler (eds.), *The Memoirs of Nahum N. Glatzer* (1998).

[Abram Leon Sachar / Ruth Beloff (2nd ed.)]

GLAUBER, ROY J. (1925–), U.S. physicist and Nobel laureate. Glauber was born in New York and gained his B.S. (1946), M.A. (1947), and Ph.D. in physics (1949) from Harvard University. He worked on the Manhattan Project at Los Alamos (1944–46), at the Institute for Advanced Studies at Princeton University (1949–51), and the California Institute of Technology, Pasadena (1951–52) before returning to the Harvard physics department (1952). He was professor of physics (1962–76) and the Mallinckrodt Professor of Physics from 1976. His research concerned the behavior of light particles and the adaptation of quantum theory to describe the detection process irrespective of the nature of the light source. The resulting quantum theory of optical coherence helped to inspire the burgeoning field of quantum optics. It has important practical applications as a method of achieving extraordinarily precise physical measurements in fields such as chronology and the application of laser techniques for medical purposes. He was awarded the Nobel Prize in Physics (2005) with John L. Hall and Theodor W. Hänsch. His further research concerned the behavior of matter at extreme density, conditions prevailing at the Universe's inception. Glauber is also renowned for his undergraduate and postgraduate teaching. His many honors include the Michelson Medal of the Franklin Institute (1985), the Max Born Award of the American Optical Society (1985), and election to the American Academy of Arts and Sciences, the American Physical Society, and the U.S. National Academy of Sciences.

[Michael Denman (2nd ed.)]

GLAZER, NATHAN (1923–), U.S. sociologist. Born in New York, Glazer attended the City College of New York, the University of Pennsylvania, and Columbia University, where he received his Ph.D. in sociology. He was a member of the editorial staff of *Commentary* (1945–53) and worked in publishing at Doubleday and Random House. He was an urban sociologist with the Housing and Home Finance Administration in Washington, D.C., and a lecturer and instructor at the universities of Chicago and California and at Bennington and Smith Colleges. From 1963 to 1968 he was professor of sociology at the University of California at Berkeley.

Glazer then went to Harvard in 1968 as professor of sociology and education. In 1969 he became a fellow of the American Academy. In 1983 he taught in India as Distinguished Fulbright Lecturer. He also served on the United States Board of Foreign Scholarships (1984–89), which supervises the Fulbright Program, with special responsibility for South Asia. In 1993 he became professor emeritus of sociology and education at Harvard and subsequently became engaged in a research project on Indian federalism and democracy and studied Indian government policy affecting minority groups.

Glazer, who has written extensively on issues of ethnicity and race in American society, is co-editor of *The Public Interest* magazine and a contributing editor at *The New Republic*.

Glazer published numerous papers and articles on housing problems and on problems of American ethnic groups, including papers on the specific problems of American Jews; the latter appeared chiefly in *Commentary*. He wrote and also contributed the article "Social Characteristics of American Jews" to *Jews: Their History, Culture and Religion 1694–1735* (vol. 2 (1960³), ed. by L. Finkelstein).

He co-authored *The Lonely Crowd* (with David Riesman and Reuel Denney, 1950); *Faces in the Crowd* (with Riesman, 1952), and *The Social Basis of American Communism* (with Daniel Patrick Moynihan, 1961). He also wrote *American Judaism* (1957); *Beyond the Melting Pot* (1963), an analysis of the persistence of ethnic groups – African-Americans, Puerto Ricans, Jews, Italians, and Irish – in the New York metropolitan area; *Remembering the Answers* (1970); *Affirmative Discrimination: Ethnic Inequality & Public Policy* (1975); and *We Are All Multiculturalists Now* (1998). He co-edited *Conflicting Images: India and the United States* with his wife, Sulochana Raghavan Glazer (1990).

BIBLIOGRAPHY: *Contemporary Authors*, 5–6 (1963), 179–80. **ADD. BIBLIOGRAPHY:** M. Miller and S. Gilmore (eds.), *Revolution at Berkeley: The Crisis in American Education* (1965); P. Steinfels, *The Neo-Conservatives* (1979).

[Werner J. Cahnman / Ruth Beloff (2nd ed.)]

GLAZER, SIMON (1878–1938), U.S. Orthodox rabbi and author. Glazer, who was born in Ezwillig, Lithuania, was ordained in 1896 by Rabbi Alexander Mose Lapidus and Rabbi Isaac Rabinowitz. He fled from service in the Russian army; unable to receive permission to stay in Koenigsberg, he left for Palestine, where he was unable to earn a living and therefore immigrated to the U.S. in 1897 where he served as a cantor in Buffalo while mastering English and subsequently served as rabbi in several cities in the Midwest before becoming chief rabbi of the United Synagogues of Montreal and Quebec (1907–18). He worked to improve Jewish education, helped establish a Federation of Jewish charities and helped found the YMHA. He believed in using whatever means possible to interest Jewish children in Jewish education. He also approved of Sunday school education believing that it was better than the lack of all Jewish education. He moved to New York in 1923 and was rabbi of Beth Hamidrash Hagadol (1923–27) in Harlem; Temple Beth-El, Brooklyn (1927–30); and the Maimonides Synagogue (1930–38). A profilic writer and journalist, Glazer was a founder (1907) and the first editor of the Yiddish daily, the *Canadian Jewish Eagle* (*Kanader Adler*) and was active in rabbinic and Zionist organizations. His published works include: *Jews of Iowa* (1904); *Guide of Judaism* (1917); *The Palestine Resolution* (1922); *History of Israel* (6 vols., 1930), a reworking of Graetz's *History of the Jews*; and *Visions of Isaiah* (1937), a collection of sermons. He also wrote on *Techina Book: Containing Prayers and Religious Duties for the Daughters of Israel* (1930).

His son, B. BENEDICT GLAZER (1902–1952), was a prominent Reform rabbi in the U.S. He was rabbi of Temple Beth El in Detroit, Michigan, from 1942 until his death.

ADD. BIBLIOGRAPHY: M.D. Sherman, *Orthodox Judaism in America: A Bibliographical Dictionary and Sourcebook* (1996).

GLICENSTEIN, ENRICO (Henoch; 1870–1942), sculptor, painter, and print maker. The son of a tombstone carver, Glicenstein was born in Turek, Poland, and began studying for the rabbinate. After working as a sign painter and woodcarver in Lodz he went to study art in Munich, where he won the Prix de Rome in 1894 and 1897. He went to live in Italy in 1897 with his wife, Helen, daughter of the painter Samuel Hirshenberg, but had to leave the country in 1928 because of his refusal to join the Fascist Party and settled in New York. He died in an automobile accident. Glicenstein, who had been elected an honorary member of the Société des Beaux-Arts in 1906 on Rodin's recommendation, had one-man shows in nearly all the art centers of the world including the 15th Venice Biennale (1928). Glicenstein was predominantly a carver. The majority of his works were done in wood, mostly oak or walnut. Spurning mechanical aids, he preferred the arduous, time-consuming method of cutting directly into his material. He created stern monolithic pieces, in solid, sturdy forms, devoid of any unnecessary detail. Like the expressionists, he felt free to exaggerate, to abbreviate, to elongate, and to distort, although he showed that a sculpture can be expressive while maintaining a firm equilibrium between form and content. Form is maintained, too, in Glicenstein's drawings, etchings, and his few paintings. As a draftsman, he was never indecisive. Likewise, the mastery of a knowledgeable hand is seen in the prints, cut with a needle into copper by vigorous strokes that aim straight to the core of a face, action, or scene. Among his dry points, more than 60 plates for the *Book of Samuel* must be singled out for mention. Among the outstanding men of his time who sat for Glicenstein's portrait busts were Ludwig *Mond, Hermann *Cohen, Gabriele D'Annunzio, Sir Israel *Gollancz, Ignace Paderewski, and Franklin D. Roosevelt. His works were acquired by many museums and a Glicenstein Museum containing his library was established in Safed, Israel. His son, EMANUEL ROMANO (1897–1985), was a painter. Born in Rome, he changed his name and in 1928 immigrated to New York with his family. Romano was best known for his portraits but also did murals for many buildings. He was an outstanding colorist.

BIBLIOGRAPHY: J. Cassou, *Glicenstein* (Eng., 1958), album with introd. by J. Cassou; F. Orestano, *Enrico Glicenstein e la sua arte* (1926).

[Alfred Werner]

GLICK, DAVID (1908–2000), U.S. biochemist. Born in Homestead, Pennsylvania, he received a B.S. in chemistry 1929 and a Ph.D. in biochemistry in 1932, both from the University of Pittsburgh. He held many positions in his career, spanning academics, industry, and hospital laboratories. Among Glick's hospital positions were Hernsheim Research Fellow at Mount Sinai Hospital, N.Y., chief chemist at Mount Zion Hospital, San Francisco, and at Beth Israel Hospital, Newark, N.J. Throughout his career, Glick was a visiting researcher at the Carlsberg Laboratory in Copenhagen, Denmark. He worked with Linderstrom-Lang, who was a pioneer in the development of microchemistry. He also conducted research as a visiting research scientist at the Stazione Zoologica, Naples, Italy, and at the Karolinska Institute, Stockholm, Sweden. Glick became professor of physiological chemistry at the University of Minnesota in 1950. In 1961 he became professor of pathology and head of the division of histochemistry at Stanford University Medical School, California. He served as acting head of the Department of Pathology from 1964 to 1965, and became emeritus professor in 1973. Thereafter Glick remained an active scientist in the Cancer Biology Research Laboratory in the Department of Radiology. Glick was internationally recognized for his work in quantitative histochemistry and cytochemistry. He was a founder of the Histochemical Society and had an important impact on its early development, serving as president from 1951 to 1957 and again from 1968 to 1970. Glick was also president of the International Committee for Histochemistry and Cytochemistry (ICHC) from 1972 to 1976. He served on the editorial boards of several histochemistry and cytochemistry journals and was the editor for *Methods of Biochemical Analysis* from 1954 to 1986. In 1971, he was listed as one of the 50 most cited authors in a survey of world science literature reported by *Current Contents–Life Sciences*. He wrote more than 275 publications. Glick received many other honors, including the Van Slyke Medal and Award, the Ames Award from the American Association of Clinical Chemistry, and a Career Award from the U.S. Public Health Service. Additional recognition of his stature as a scientist were his elections as an honorary member of both the Royal Danish Academy of Sciences and Letters and the Finnish Histochemical Society. The David Glick Lectureship was established in 1982 by the International Federation of Societies for Histochemistry and Cytochemistry (IFHSC). Glick not only had a keen mind and a creative and entrepreneurial spirit but exhibited an unusual openness toward students and colleagues. These traits, together with his analytical acumen and eloquence, made him a much sought-after lecturer and board member.

BIBLIOGRAPHY: *Stanford Report* (2004).

[Bracha Rager (2nd ed.)]

GLICK, HIRSH (1922–1944), Yiddish poet and editor. Glick was born in Vilna and, as a teenager, became active in Ha-Shomer ha-Ẓa'ir. In 1935 he began composing original verse in Hebrew. He joined the circle of the Yung Vilne group of Yiddish writers and, in 1939, edited and published four issues of the literary journal *Yungvald.* Glick spent the war years in the Vilna ghetto and forced labor camps nearby, where he continued to compose Yiddish poems, including the work for which he is best known, "Zog nit Keynmol" ("Never Say"), which became the official hymn of the Vilna partisan fighters. The poem was subsequently translated into many languages, including Hebrew (by the poet A. Shlonsky), Dutch, English, Polish, Romanian, and Spanish. In October 1943, Glick was transferred to the concentration camp at Goldfield (Estonia), from which he escaped the following year; he died in combat against the Nazis in the forest nearby.

BIBLIOGRAPHY: LNYL, 2 (1958), 271–3; N. and M. Ausubel (eds.), *A Treasury of Jewish Poetry* (1957), 270, 445; N. Mayzl, *Hirsch Glick un Zayn Lid "Zog Nisht Keyn Mol"* (1949); M. Dvorjetski, *Hirshke Glick* (1966). **ADD. BIBLIOGRAPHY:** Sh. Katsherginski, *Ikh Bin Geven a Partizan* (1947), 104–9; Sh. Lastik, *Mitn Ponem Tsum Morgn* (1952), 157–58; B. Mark, *Umgekumene Yidishe Shraybers fun di Getos un Lagern* (1954), 215–16.

[Elias Schulman / Marc Miller (2nd ed.)]

GLICK, IRVING SRUL (1934–2002), Canadian composer. Born in Toronto, Glick was raised with music. He learned about cantillation from his father, a Russian-born cantor; the Western classical repertoire from his brother, a professional clarinetist; and Jewish folk music from the Habonim Zionists.

When Glick graduated from the University of Toronto with a bachelors and masters of music in theory and composition, he firmly believed in the international, non-denominational nature of music. After studying with composers Louis Saguer, Darius *Milhaud, and Max Deutsch, he began changing this view. Contemplating his existence as a composer and his personal Jewish identity, he concluded that his Jewish roots were deeper than his desire to compose universal music.

This reassessment allowed Glick to incorporate ancestral musical motifs into his compositions. At times, as in his only ballet *Heritage Dance Symphony,* he attempted to synthesize dance music and jazz rhythms with Hebraic lyricism. Alternately, he layered textural and chordal density with Jewish folk tonality. Through experimentation, Glick developed a complex personal idiom combining Jewish and classical traditions into openly lyrical, emotional music. For example, Glick's song cycle, *I Never Saw Another Butterfly,* addressed the Holocaust by using the poetry of the Theresienstadt concentration camp children. Harmonic dissonance contrasts the children's tragic deaths with the thirst for life in their writing. Conversely, Glick's 1998 composition *Old Toronto Klezmer Suite,* honoring his mother's memory and the remembered splendor of his childhood community, represents his fusion style and playful idealism.

In 1969, Glick became choir director at Toronto's Beth Tikvah, work he considered a labor of love, beauty, and inspiration. In 1978, he became the synagogue's composer-in-residence. While working as a Canadian Broadcasting Corporation producer, he also taught composition at York University and the Royal Conservatory of Music in Toronto. By the time of his death in 2002, Glick had written several hundred pieces of music.

[Deborah Hopper (2nd ed.)]

GLICKMAN, DANIEL ROBERT (Dan; 1944–), U.S. secretary of agriculture (1995–2001) and congressman (D-KS, 1976–1994). Glickman, a native of Wichita, Kansas, received his B.A. from the University of Michigan and his law degree from George Washington University. He began his public service as member and president of the Wichita School Board. He was a partner in the law firm of Sargent, Klenda and Glickman and served as a trial attorney for the U.S. Securities and Exchange Commission.

During his 18 years in Congress, Glickman served on the House Agriculture Committee, House Judiciary Committee, and the House Permanent Select Committee on Intelligence. For six years he chaired a key Agriculture Subcommittee which oversaw nearly 75% of the Agriculture Department's farm program budget. On the House Judiciary Committee, he staked out his leadership on aviation policy and authored landmark legislation creating product liability protection for small airplane manufacturers. He also was a member of the Intellectual Property Subcommittee. As chairman of the House Permanent Select Committee on Intelligence, he led the effort to demystify and make more publicly accessible the activities of the U.S. intelligence community, and he presided over the committee's investigation of the Aldrich Ames case, the FBI agent convicted of spying for the Soviet Union.

He is the author of several major legislative proposals, including the law authorizing the United States Institute of Peace and several measures promoting alternative energy uses. Glickman also wrote the legislation that increases criminal penalties for the destruction of religious property.

His tenure as secretary of agriculture under Clinton was noted for the modernization of food safety regulations, an expansion of international trade agreements to open foreign markets to U.S. products, policies aimed at preserving forest lands and conservation, and an improved commitment to civil rights. Glickman was an advocate for farmers and ranchers in the face of the turbulent farm economy.

In 2004 Dan Glickman succeeded Jack Valenti, becoming only the fourth person to head the Motion Picture Association of America, the trade association founded in 1922 to advocate on behalf of the major motion picture studios. Immediately prior to his joining MPAA, Glickman was director of the Institute of Politics at Harvard University's Kennedy School of Government.

Glickman served on the board of directors of the Chicago Mercantile Exchange; Hain – Celestial Corporation; Ready

Pac Produce Corporation; Communities in Schools; America's Second Harvest; Food Research and Action Center; the RFK Memorial Foundation; and Mazon, A Jewish Response to Hunger. He also is on the International Advisory Board of the Coca-Cola Company and co-chairs the U.S. Consensus Council (with former Governor Marc Racicot) and the Pew Initiative on Food and Biotechnology (with former Congressman Vin Weber).

[Melissa Patack (2nd ed.)]

GLICKMAN, MARTIN IRVING ("**Marty**"; 1917–2001), U.S. sprinter, radio broadcaster, founding father of basketball on radio, and a track star who was pulled from the 1936 Berlin Olympics because he was Jewish; member of the basketball Hall of Fame.

Glickman was born in the East Bronx, New York, to Harry, a cotton-goods salesman, and Molly, who knew each other in Jassy, Romania, and met again and married in New York. When Glickman was five the family moved to Brooklyn, where Glickman became a football star for James Madison High School on their New York City championship team in 1935, while also winning the city, state, and national sprint champion.

The next year, as a freshman at Syracuse University, Glickman won a spot on the 1936 United States Olympic 4x100-meter relay team. But in one of the ugliest chapters in U.S. Olympic history, Glickman and Sam Stoller, the other Jewish athlete on the track team, were suddenly told in Berlin on August 8, the morning of the qualifying trials, that two other runners, Jesse Owens and Ralph Metcalfe, were replacing them. While it was never proved, it was Glickman's contention and many others' belief that their being denied a chance to compete was a case of blatant antisemitism: Avery Brundage, chairman of the U.S. Olympic Committee, was an enthusiastic supporter of Hitler's regime, and he and assistant U.S. Olympic track coach Dean Cromwell were members of America First, an isolationist political movement that attracted American Nazi sympathizers.

"Joseph Goebbels, head of the Ministry of Propaganda, had contacted Avery Brundage," Glickman said years later on ESPN. "[Goebbels] didn't want to have Jews run for the United States or on that track before 120,000 people, [to] keep them from embarrassing Adolf Hitler."

His Olympic snub remained a central part of his life, sparking this reaction upon his return to Olympic Stadium in Berlin in 1985:

"As I walked into the stadium, I began to get so angry. I began to get so mad. It shocked the hell out of me that this thing of 49 years ago could still evoke this anger. I mean I was fucking mad. I was cussing – I was with people, colleagues of mine, and I was cussing. I was really amazed at myself, at this feeling of anger. Not about the German Nazis, that was a given. But anger at Avery Brundage and Dean Cromwell for not allowing an 18-year-old kid to compete in the Olympic Games just because he was Jewish."

He returned to Syracuse as a sophomore, where his long and distinguished broadcasting career began in 1937: After Glickman scored two touchdowns to help upset Cornell, a local haberdasher hired him to do a sports broadcast on radio for $50 to capitalize on his sudden fame. After graduating in 1939, and a stint in the Marines, Glickman broadcast college basketball games, and was the first radio announcer for the New York Knicks, beginning on November 7, 1946.

Glickman was a pioneer in the technical precision of describing basketball and establishing the precise geometry of the court, using a language and terminology – the key, the lane, the top of the circle, the mid-court stripe, between the circles – that survives to this day. With his unmistakable greeting – "Hello, fans! I'm Marty Glickman" – and his famous calls – "Swish!," "It's high enough, it's deep enough, it's good!," and "It's good ... like Nedicks!" – Glickman was the radio voice of the Knicks for 11 years, the football Giants for 19 years, and the New York Jets for 11. He broadcast horse races at Yonkers Raceway for 12 years, did pre- and post-game shows for the Brooklyn Dodgers and New York Yankees for 22 years, college basketball for 21 years, Paramount newsreels for 15 years, as well as doing track meets, wrestling matches, high school football, roller derbies, rodeos, four marbles tournaments, and even described the circus to an audience of blind children.

Novelist Jack Kerouac, in *On The Road*, wrote: "Man, have you dug that mad Marty Glickman announcing basketball games – up-to-midcourt-bounce-fake-set-shot, swish, two points. Absolutely the greatest announcer I ever heard."

Glickman was awarded the Basketball Hall of Fame's Curt Gowdy Award in 1991, elected to the National Sportscasters and Sportswriters Hall of Fame in 1992, and the American Sportscasters Hall of Fame in 1993. In 1996 he published *The Fastest Kid on the Block: The Marty Glickman Story*.

[Elli Wohlgelernter (2nd ed.)]

GLID, NANDOR (1924–1997), Yugoslav sculptor. Glid was born in the town of Subotica. During the Nazi occupation he was in a forced labor camp and later fought with the Yugoslav partisans. After the war he studied at the Academy of Fine Arts in Belgrade. He began as a portrait sculptor but later worked on monuments to commemorate concentration camp victims. He was commissioned to carry out his projects for monuments in the former Nazi camps of Mauthausen and Dachau. The monument in Subotica to a group of anti-Nazis (mainly Jews) who were hanged there is also his work. He has exhibited monotype graphics on war and camp subjects.

BIBLIOGRAPHY: A. Rieth, *To the Victims of Tyranny – Den Opfern der Gewalt* (1968), 45–47, pls. 53, 75.

[Zdenko Lowenthal]

GLIÈRE, REINHOLD MORITZEVICH (1874–1956), Soviet Russian composer and conductor. He was born in Kiev where his father, following a family tradition, was a maker of musical instruments. Glière began composing at 14, entered the Kiev Music School in 1891 and the Moscow Conservatory in 1894. He taught for some time in St. Petersburg, spent two years (1905–07) in Berlin, and became director of the Kiev Conservatory in 1914. In 1920 he went to the Moscow Conservatory as professor and held this post until his death. Glière was a prolific composer. He studied the folk music of various national groups and used folklore elements in his compositions. His symphonic works reflect Russian traditional harmony. Prokofieff, Miaskovsky, and Mossolov were among his pupils. A tireless conductor, Glière appeared in remote regions of the country. From 1938 to 1948 he was chairman of the Union of Soviet Composers. His major works are: three symphonies (1900, 1907, and 1911), several operas, among them *Shah-Senem* (1923–34) on an Azerbaijan subject, and *Rachel* (1943) after Maupassant's novel. His ballets include: *Cleopatra* (1925), *Red Poppy* (1927), *The Bronze Horseman* (1949), and *Taras Bulba* (1952). His concerto for harp and orchestra (1938) and especially the concerto for voice and orchestra (1942) won great popularity. He composed chamber music, songs, and piano works. Glière received many awards, including the Order of Lenin and the Stalin Prize.

BIBLIOGRAPHY: I.F. Belza, *R.M. Glière* (Russ., 1962); N.E. Petrova, *Reyngold Moritsevich Gliere* (1962); S.V. Katanova, *Balety R.M. Gliera* (1960); R.M. Glière, *Statyi, vospominaniya, materialy* (1965); MGG, s.v.; Rieman-Gurlitt, s.v.; Grove, Dict, s.v.

[Michael Goldstein]

GLIKIN, MOSHE (1874–1973), Zionist and *yishuv* leader. Born in Moscow, in 1892 Glikin went to Ereẓ Israel, where he worked as a laborer at Ein Zeitim. He returned to Russia in 1894 and later studied in Leipzig, where he was secretary of a student Zionist association. He attended the Fifth and Sixth *Zionist Congresses and voted against the *Uganda Scheme. He directed the office of the Zionist *Democratic Fraction in Berlin in 1902 and later worked at the offices of various Zionist periodicals in Russia. In 1908 Glikin returned to Ereẓ Israel, where he worked first in the Atid edible oil factory in Haifa and then at the Bezalel School of Arts and Crafts in Jerusalem. From 1910 he was director of *Migdal Farm. During World War I, he was exiled by the Ottoman authorities to Nazareth. In 1920 he was a delegate to the first Asefat ha-Nivḥarim ("the Elected Assembly" of the *yishuv*) and was a founder of the Hadar ha-Karmel, the new Jewish quarter of Haifa, where he then lived.

BIBLIOGRAPHY: I. Klausner, *Oppoziẓyah le-Herzl* (1960), index; Tidhar, 1 (1947), 479–80.

[Israel Klausner]

GLINYANY (Pol. Gliniany; Yid. Gline), small town in Lvov district, Ukraine. An organized Jewish community existed from 1474. The first settlers were leaseholders. The Jews of Glinyany suffered during the Tatar raids and Cossack massacres in 1624, 1638, and 1657, and particularly in 1648–49 (see *Chmielnicki). The first synagogue, built of wood, was erected there in 1704. Glinyany was a stronghold of the Shabbateans and later of the Frankists (see Jacob *Frank); in 1758 King Augustus III assigned Glinyany to the latter as one of their places of residence before baptism. In the 18th century Glinyany became a center of Ḥasidism when R. Jehiel Michael Moskovich (great grandson of Jeciel Michael of Zloczow) established his court there. A Jewish-German school in Glinyany, established under Joseph II after Austrian annexation of Galicia, remained open until 1806. A public school in the name of Baron Hirsch existed there from 1816 to 1914, and among the teachers was the historian Meir Balaban. The center of Zionist activity was a club, "National Home," founded in 1906, and a Hebrew school was opened in 1909. Between the world wars the economic situation deteriorated due to Ukrainian and Polish competition and antisemitism. The community numbered 688 in 1765, 1,708 in 1880 (out of a total population of 3,695), 2,177 in 1900 (out of 4,906), 1,679 in 1921 (out of 4,355), 1,906 in 1931, and 2,300 in 1939.

Holocaust Period

Under Soviet rule (1939–41), the communal bodies were disbanded and all political activity outlawed. In 1940 the former political leaders and important businessmen were arrested. In spring 1941 young Jews were drafted into the Soviet army and placed in special work units. The city fell to the Germans on July 1, 1941. On July 27 a pogrom broke out, led by the Ukrainian populace in which the Jews were murdered and robbed, and their sacred literature was burned. A provisional Jewish committee was set up in an attempt to prevent further persecution. The community had to pay a fine of 1,000,000 zlotys, but could not raise such a sum. Emissaries were sent to the German authorities in Peremyshlyany in an effort to lower the sum and delay payment, but met with partial success. The Jews of Glinyany were sent to a labor camp in Kurwice. The *Judenrat, headed by Aaron Hochberg, considerably assisted the community until the period between Nov. 20, 1942, and Dec. 1, 1942, when the remaining Jews were interned in Peremyshlyany ghetto. They perished there when it was liquidated in the summer of 1943. A few groups of Jews tried to hide in bunkers in the woods but were hunted down, mostly by the Ukrainians, and killed. A group of 40 resisted and fought when discovered. The city of Glinyany was taken by Soviet forces in August 1944, at which time only 20 Jewish survivors were found there. These left Glinyany in 1946.

[Aharon Weiss]

BIBLIOGRAPHY: M. Balaban, in: YE, 6 (c. 1910), 586; *Bleter far Geshikhte*, 4 pt. 3 (1953), 163; H. Halpern (ed.), *Megiles Gline* (1950); *Khurbn Gline* (1964); A. Korech (ed.), *Kehillat Glina 1473–1943, Toledoteha ve-Ḥurbanah* (1950).

GLIWICE (Ger. **Gleiwitz**), city in Silesia, Poland. It passed to Prussia in 1742, reverting to Poland in 1945. A "Jewish Street" is mentioned there in the Middle Ages. In 1587 the city council opposed further Jewish settlement and those already resident probably left soon afterward. In 1715 a Jew acquired the liquor privileges in Gliwice and built a home there; he converted to Christianity, and in 1753 opposed the acceptance of additional Jewish residents. However, the community grew from 62 in 1795, to 178 in 1812 (6.9% of the total population), and numbered 2,009 (16.5%) in 1867, 1,962 (3.17%) in 1905, and 2,200 (2%) in 1921, the industrialized city having grown much more rapidly than the Jewish community. The first synagogue, in use from 1812, was replaced in 1861. In 1932 the community maintained a *mikveh*, library, school (100 pupils), home for the aged (founded 1926), seven charitable and nine social organizations.

Holocaust and Contemporary Periods

There were 1,845 Jews living in Gliwice in 1932. When the Nazis came to power in 1933 the community was subjected to the same antisemitic persecution as in the rest of Germany, causing around 400 to leave. On Nov. 10, 1938 (**Kristallnacht*), the Nazis burned down the large synagogue, and arrested all male Jews between the ages of 18 and 60. After two days of torture in prison, they were deported to *Buchenwald concentration camp where some died. The rest were sent home after three or six months' imprisonment. All the women were forced to do hard, humiliating work in the city. Jews were also compelled to leave their homes and settle in densely crowded living quarters with a minimum of one family per room. Deportation to the East commenced in May 1942, leaving just 40 intermarried Jews in the city. After the war a small number of Jews from Poland settled there. There were 200 Jews living in the town in 1950. The new community had its own producers' cooperative (1962). A number emigrated after the Six-Day War.

[Stefan Krakowski]

BIBLIOGRAPHY: B. Nietsche, *Geschichte der Stadt Gleiwitz* (1886), 599–606; FJW (1932–33), 104; M. Grinwald, in: *Zion*, 9 (1944), 143–5; S. Wenzel, *Juedische Buerger und kommunale Selbstverwaltung in preussischen Staedten, 1808–1845* (1967), 265; AJYB (1962). **ADD. BIBLIOGRAPHY:** P. Maser et al., *Juden in Oberschlesien*, 1 (1992), 96–106.

GLOBES, Israeli financial daily, established in 1983. Its founding editor was Uri Gotleib and its owners from 1984 were Haim Bar-On and Eliezer Fishman. The newspaper expanded over the years from supplying mostly financial data about the Israeli Stock Market to covering the gamut of Israeli finance, industry, and economics and key economic developments abroad. During Matti Golan's editorship in 1988–92, its circulation climbed to 22,500.

The newspaper's growth coincided with Israel's economic crisis in the 1980s caused by rampant inflation and subsequently the economic growth that accompanied the Likud's free market economics. *Globes*' growth spurred other Israeli dailies to add economic supplements, but this, in turn, limited *Globes*' potential readership growth from beyond the country's economic and industrial sector to the wider Israeli public. The newspaper succeeded in withstanding competition from a short-lived financial rival, the *Telegraph* (1993–96), edited by Golan after he left *Globes*. In 1996 Haggai Golan was appointed *Globes*' editor. It is a subscriber-only newspaper, published in the early evening after the closure of the Tel Aviv Stock Market. 3.4% of Israelis read the newspaper in 2005, according to a TGI Teleseker survey. Other estimates put their circulation at 35,000. The newspaper has Internet editions in Hebrew and English; according to *Globes* the Hebrew edition has 200,000 registered users.

[Yoel Cohen (2nd ed.)]

°GLOBOCNIK, ODILO (1904–1945), Nazi executioner of Polish Jewry. Born in Trieste, Italy, Globocnik joined the Nazi Party in Austria in 1922 and the then illegal Austrian SS in 1934. He was nominated *Gauleiter* of Vienna in reward for his part in the preparation of Austria's annexation in 1938, but was later dismissed for embezzlement. Recognizing the usefulness of his ideological fanaticism and ambition, his longtime friend Heinrich Himmler brought him back from disgrace and appointed him SS and police leader for the Lublin District on November 1, 1939. In the fall of 1941 – just months before the Wannsee Conference – Himmler authorized Globocnik to organize what became known as *Aktion Reinhard*. He organized Jewish slave labor camps as industrial enterprises of the SS, and in April 1942 he was put in charge of "Action Reinhard" (see *Holocaust, General Survey) to annihilate Polish Jewry and confiscate their property. He organized the death camps of *Belzec, *Sobibor, *Majdanek, and *Treblinka. At the end of 1942, he directed the brutal resettlement of Poles from the Zamość region. In September 1943, he and other SS party officials who worked on *Aktion Reinhard* were transferred to Trieste. Globocnik committed suicide shortly after his arrest by British troops in Austria in May 1945. His role in the "Final Solution" was central and provides key information on the decision-making process for the murder of the Jews. The decision to annihilate the Jews in the Generalgouvernment (GG) was made as early as the first half of October 1941. On October 17, 1941, during a conference in Lublin in the presence of Hans Frank, SS and police leader for the Lublin District, Odilo Globocnik said that *Reichsführer-SS* Heinrich Himmler and Hitler ordered the "evacuation of Jews beyond the Bug river," a statement that meant the physical elimination of Jews from the GG. Globocnik also planned to resettle all the Poles from the Lublin District and even spoke about the resettlement of Poles from the entire GG. Ethnic Germans were to take their place.

BIBLIOGRAPHY: R. Hoess, *Commandant of Auschwitz* (1960); J. Tenenbaum, *Race and Reich* (1956), index; R.M.W. Kempner, *Ha-Mikẓo'a Hashmadah* (1963), index; J. Wulf, *Das Dritte Reich und seine Vollstrecker* (1961); Hilberg, *Destruction of the European Jews* (1961), index; Reitlinger, *Final Solution* (1953), index.

[Yehuda Reshef]

GLOBUS, YORAM (1941–), Israeli movie producer who founded and ran the international production company, the Cannon Group, with his cousin, Menachem *Golan. From the late 1970s to the late 1980s, they produced hundreds of low-brow movies of all kinds, specializing in action films such as *The Delta Force* (1986) with Chuck Norris and *Death Wish II* (1982) starring Charles Bronson. Golan and Globus' willingness to wheel and deal earned them the nickname "the Go-Go boys." Globus balanced box-office hits with the occasional art-house drama and produced such films as Jean-Luc Godard's *King Lear* (1987) and Robert Altman's *Fool for Love* (1985). Born in Tiberias, Globus began making movies with Golan in the 1960s in Israel. Among his Israeli credits are the popular *Eskimo Limon* (1978) comedy and its sequels, as well as such classics as the 1974 musical *Kazablan* and *Operation Thunderbolt* (1977), the story of the IDF's hostage rescue at Entebbe, which was nominated for an Academy Award. After the Cannon Group was sold in the late 1980s, Golan and Globus went their separate ways, although they occasionally worked together later. Globus went on to run Globus-United, which includes the largest movie theater chain in Israel, production facilities, and a distribution company.

[Hannah Brown (2nd ed.)]

GLOCK, CHARLES Y. (1919–), sociologist and author. Born in New York City, Charles Glock earned his bachelor's degree from New York University (1940), his master's degree from Boston University (1941), and his doctorate from Columbia University (1952). He served in the U.S. Army Air Forces in World War II and was awarded the Bronze Star and the Legion of Merit.

Glock served as the executive director of the Bureau of Applied Research at Columbia beginning in 1947, becoming managing director in 1949 and director in 1952. He taught at Columbia as professor of sociology from 1956 to 1958, then at the University of California, Berkeley, from 1958 to 1978. He also served as director of Berkeley's Survey Research Center from 1958 to 1967 and as director of an extensive research program on religion and society from 1962 through 1979. Glock was named professor emeritus at Berkeley in 1978.

Glock is perhaps best known for his 1966 work, with co-author Rodney Stark, *Christian Beliefs and Anti-Semitism*, in which Glock and Stark suggest an inherent relationship between Christian beliefs and religious and secular antisemitism. They contend that, because of the traditional Christian claim of universal truth, a strong belief in Christianity leads to the belief that Christianity is the only true religion, which in turn leads to unfavorable images of those who practice other religions, especially Jews, who are considered to have rejected Jesus. The authors also claim that differences in degrees of antisemitism among Christian denominations correspond to differences in Christian beliefs among the denominations. Critics suggested that Glock and Stark did not sufficiently address nonreligious causes of antisemitism, and that therefore the relationship between Christian beliefs and antisemitism was not necessarily inherent.

In 1968 Glock and Stark published *American Piety: The Nature of Religious Commitment*, which was considered a significant contribution to the study of American religion. *The New Religious Consciousness*, edited by Glock and Robert Bellah in 1976, which examined religious groups associated with the counterculture movement of the 1960s, was also well received. Glock's other works include *Prejudice, U.S.A.* (with Ellen Siegelman, 1969), *Adolescent Prejudice* (with Robert Wuthnow, Jane Piliavin, and Metta Spencer, 1975), and *Anti-Semitism in America* (with Harold E. Quinley, 1979). Glock received the Roots of Freedom Award from the Anti-Defamation League of B'nai B'rith in 1977.

[Dorothy Bauhoff (2nd ed.)]

GLOGAU (Pol. **Głogó**), town in Silesia, W. Poland. Jews are first mentioned there in 1280. In 1299 the duke of Gross-Glogau granted them a charter of privileges. The community possessed a cemetery, a synagogue, inhabited a "Jews' lane," and engaged in moneylending, and the cloth and fur trade. The Jews of Glogau escaped persecution during the *Black Death, 1348–49, but in 1401 two Jews were burned to death for an alleged *Host desecration, and the synagogue and other buildings were destroyed in a riot by the populace in 1442. The community subsequently recovered and prospered until 1488, when Duke Hans, after first taxing them heavily, expelled them. Nevertheless, a few Jews continued to live outside the city bounds. After the expulsion of Silesian Jewry in 1582 the family of Israel Benedict was allowed to live in Glogau and received a letter of privilege in 1598. Protected by this, other members of his family and numerous fictitious relatives flocked to the city from Poland and Prague. A Jewish quarter was organized and a synagogue built in 1636. Despite the sufferings caused by the Thirty Years' War, the plague, a general conflagration in 1678, and local opposition, the community grew from 81 families in 1673 to 1,564 persons in 1725. After it returned to Prussia in 1745. *Frederick II confirmed the limited rights of the community. One of the most prosperous communities in Central Europe, Glogau Jewry overshadowed that of *Breslau. From the beginning of the 18th century, the community possessed its own seal. The Jewish population gradually outgrew the confines of the Jewish quarter and totaled 2,000 in 1791 (one-fifth of Silesian Jewry). In the 19th century, the community decreased from 1,516 in 1812 (12% of the total population) to 1,010 in 1880 (5.4%), and 716 in 1900. Solomon and Eduard *Munk, Michael *Sachs, and David and Paulus *Cassel were born in Glogau. Solomon *Maimon was buried in the old cemetery. The community remained approximately the same size (around 600) until 1933. Many left during the Nazi persecutions and their numbers had declined to 120 by 1939. Most were deported to the East from March 1942. The community was not reestablished after World War II.

BIBLIOGRAPHY: R. Berndt, *Geschichte der Juden in Gross-Glogau* (1873); M. Brann, *Geschichte der Juden in Schlesien* (6 vols. (1896–1917), passim; Brilling, in: *Juedische Zeitung fuer Ostdeutschland*, 8 (Nov. 6, 1931); FJW, 97; Germ Jud, 2 (1968), 279–80; Blaschke, in: *Ost und West*, 16 (1916), 185–92.

GLOGAU, JEHIEL MICHAEL BEN ASHER LEMMEL HA-LEVI (c. 1740–1818), rabbi in Burgenland (Austria).

Glogau took his name from his birthplace, where his father served as *dayyan*, before becoming rabbi in Eisenstadt. Around 1780 Glogau served as preacher of the *ḥevra kaddisha* of Vienna. On the death of his father in 1789 he succeeded him at Eisenstadt. He was in halakhic correspondence with Moses *Sofer, who held him in high esteem (*Ḥatam Sofer* OḤ, nos. 40, 80). His son MOSES (d. 1837), who served as rabbi of Liben near Prague and then in Deutschkreutz (Burgenland), published the commentaries on *aggadah* of his father and grandfather together with his own work entitled *Ḥut ha-Meshullash bi-She'arim* (Vienna, 1821). The work contains sermons on the weekly readings of the Torah, each consisting of three parts: the sermons of his grandfather, entitled *Sha'ar Asher*; of his father, entitled *Sha'ar ha-Mayim*; and his own, *Sha'ar ha-Katan*.

BIBLIOGRAPHY: M. Markbrieter, *Beitraege zur Geschichte der juedischen Gemeinde Eisenstadt* (1908), 53f.; J.J. (L.) Greenwald (Grunwald), *Ha-Yehudim be-Hungaryah* (1913), 73f.; P.Z. Schwartz, *Shem ha-Gedolim me-Ereẓ Hagar*, 1 (1913), 45a no. 127, 3 (1915), 17a no. 6; B. Wachstein, *Die Inschriften des alten Judenfriedhofes in Wien*, 2 (1917), 194 n. 1, 564 n. 17; idem, *Die Inschriften des alten Judenfriedhofs in Eisenstadt* (1922), 152 no. 426, 188 no. 594; idem, *Urkunden und Akten zur Geschichte der Juden in Eisenstadt* (1926), 469–71, 714; Patai, in: *Arim ve-Immahot be-Yisrael*, 1 (1946), 54.

[Yehoshua Horowitz]

GLOTZ, GUSTAVE (1862–1935), French historian. He was born at Haguenau and taught at the lycée in Nancy (1886–92), and Paris (1892–1907). In 1907 he became professor of Greek history at the Sorbonne. In 1920 he became a member of the Académie des Inscriptions et Belles Lettres, and in 1928 president of the *Institut de France*. Well known as a French patriot and as a fine scholar and a popular teacher, he was honored at his Sorbonne jubilee in 1932, when the *Mélanges Gustave Glotz* (2 vols., including bibliography) was presented to him. His work is notable for its special study of ancient Greek social and economic life. He directed the publication of the *Histoire générale*, in which the first three volumes of the *Histoire grecque* (1925–36) are his work in collaboration with Robert Cohen. He contributed to the *Dictionnaire des antiquités grecques et romaines*. His other works include *Etudes sociales et juridiques sur l'antiquité grecque* (1906), *Le travail dans la Grèce ancienne* (1920; Eng. 1926), *La civilisation égéenne* (1923, Eng. 1925), and *La cité grecque* (1928; Eng. 1929). He was an editor of the *Revue des Etudes Grecques*.

[Irwin L. Merker]

GLOUCESTER, county town in N. England. Its Jewish community is first mentioned in the financial records of 1158–59. It was again mentioned in connection with an alleged ritual murder in 1168. The Jewry was situated in the present East Gate Street, the synagogue being on the north side. Josce of Gloucester, a prominent financier under Henry II, apparently financed an illegal raid on Ireland. Under John, the community suffered greatly from royal exaction. Gloucester possessed an *archa. It was one of the dower-towns of Queen Dowager Eleanor from which the Jews were expelled in 1275. The members of the community, first transferred to *Bristol, were afterward scattered. A small community was reestablished at the close of the 18th century but decayed in the middle of the 19th century. The last survivor died in 1886.

BIBLIOGRAPHY: J. Jacobs, *Jews of Angevin England* (1893), 45–47, 376; Rigg-Jenkinson, Exchequer, passim; H.G. Richardson, *English Jewry under Angevin Kings* (1960), passim; C. Roth, *Rise of Provincial Jewry* (1950), 67–70; Roth, England, index.

[Cecil Roth]

GLUBOKOYE (Pol. **Głębokie**), Molodechno district, Belarus, in Poland until 1793 and from 1921 to 1939. Jews are mentioned there in the middle of the 16th century. Within the framework of the Council of Lithuania (see *Councils of the Lands) Glubokoye came under the jurisdiction of the *Smorgon community. Samuel *Mohilever was rabbi there from 1848 to 1856. Jews traded in lumber, farm products, and bristles, exporting them to Poland and Russia. They also owned flour mills and hide-processing factories. Most identified themselves with the Chabad Ḥasidism. The community numbered 755 in 1766, 3,917 in 1897 (70% of the total population), and 2,844 in 1921 (63%). After WWI Jewish trade was only partially revived. In 1927 a Hebrew Tarbut school was opened.

Holocaust Period

In September 1939 Glubokoye was annexed to the Soviet Belorussian Republic. All Jewish public life ceased and Jewish institutions were closed. The town was occupied by the Germans on July 2, 1941. In the first days several Jews accused of being Communists were put to death. When many of the prisoners in the Soviet jail of nearby Berezwiecz were found dead the blame was placed on the Jews and a pogrom was prevented only after intercession by R. Josef Ha-Levi Katz. In early November 1941 a ghetto was set up in the town and the Jews there were grouped into two categories: those fit for work, and the sick and the aged. Jews from the nearby towns of Sharkovshchisna, Postawy, and Plissa were also brought to the ghetto and its population reached 6,000. On March 25, 1942, 105 Jews were arrested and shot. Following this *Aktion*, the youth tried to organize and make contact with the partisans. On June 19, 1942, about 2,500 Jews classified "unfit for work" were murdered in the Borek forest. In 1943 Soviet partisans attacked targets in the vicinity of Glubokoye. The Germans, fearing that contact might be established between the ghetto and the partisans, began to deport the Jews and liquidate the ghetto. On August 20, 1943, members of the *Judenrat* were ordered to organize the Jews for deportation. Upon entering the ghetto, the Germans met with armed resistance by Jewish groups. Some Jews tried to break through the siege, but few succeeded. In order to break the resistance and to prevent a mass escape, the Germans set the ghetto on fire and left 5,000 dead. Jews from Glubokoye who managed to escape joined partisan units, including the Kaganovich unit.

About 100 survived the Holocaust. The community was not reconstituted after World War II.

BIBLIOGRAPHY: *Lite*, 1 (1951), 1551–53; *Yahadut Lita*, 1 (1959), index; Yad Vashem Archives.

[Aharon Weiss]

GLUCK, ALMA (born **Reba Fiersohn**; 1884–1938), U.S. soprano. Born in Bucharest, Romania, she was taken to New York as a child. When she left school, she worked as a secretary, and it was not until her marriage to Bernard Gluck, in 1906, that she began taking singing lessons. In 1909 she obtained an engagement at the Metropolitan Opera, New York, where she remained for four years. Subsequently, after studying in Berlin with Marcella Sembrich, she concentrated on concert work. Her great success was enhanced by her recordings. In 1914, having divorced her first husband, she married the violinist Efrem Zimbalist. Her home in New York became the meeting place of distinguished musicians and she was a principal figure in the founding of the American Guild of Musical Artists. Her daughter by her first marriage became the novelist Marcia *Davenport.

BIBLIOGRAPHY: M. Davenport, *Too Strong for Fantasy* (1967), index; G. Saleski, *Famous Musicians of Jewish Origin* (1949), 587–9; Baker, Biog Dict.

GLUCK, HANNAH (1895–1978), British painter. Hannah Gluck, widely known as "Gluck," was born in London and belonged to the well-known *Gluckstein family. She attended St. Pauls Girls' School but, refusing to go to the university, she enrolled in the St. John's Wood Art School, London, which she left after one year and was thereafter self-taught. In 1916, while on a holiday in Cornwall, she met a group of distinguished artists, including Munnings and Harold and Lora Knight, and this made her more determined to become a genuine artist. She eventually studied music, but after a promising beginning returned to painting. In 1926, the Fine Art Society of London held an exhibition of her work entitled "Stage and Country," which included landscapes as well as theater scenes and portraits. Its success led to other successful exhibitions in 1932 and 1937. Nothing was heard of Gluck for some 35 years, during which time she was living in the country, painting very slowly, and, having no financial means, not bothering to exhibit. In 1973, however, the Fine Art Society persuaded her to hold another show, which included the portrait of her grandfather done in 1915, a series of works from 1917 to 1937, as well as paintings covering the period from World War II. It proved a thrilling exhibition and Gluck was hailed as a minor master.

During the subsequent five years, until her death, Gluck was reestablished both as a painter in her own right and as part of the reassessment of English art in the 1920s and 1930s.

ADD. BIBLIOGRAPHY: ODNB online; D. Souhami, Gluck, 1895–1978: *Her Biography* (1988).

[Charles Samuel Spencer]

GLUCK, LOUISE (1943–), U.S. poet. Gluck was born in New York City to a father who never acted on his dream of being a writer and a mother who fought to attend Wellesley College before women's education was accepted. Honed by inner wounds from the death of an older sister, and by her battle with anorexia, years of psychoanalysis, and study with Stanley Kunitz, Gluck's poetic voice is lyrical yet reticent, cloaking the confessional in the classical. Her poetry explores the intimate drama of family tragedies resonating through the generations and the relationship between human beings and their creator. Although her poetry shows the strong influence of psychoanalysis and classical mythology, she also draws on Jewish tradition for mythic images and stories. Her works include an award-winning collection of essays on the theory and practice of poetry, *Proofs & Theories* (1994), as well as her many books of poetry, most notably, *The House on Marshland* (1975), *Descending Figure* (1980), *Ararat* (1990), and *The Seven Ages* (2001). In *The Triumph of Achilles* (1985), she creates her own midrashic interpretation of a story from the Midrash Rabbah and measures her immigrant grandfather's life against that of Joseph in Egypt. *The Wild Iris* (1992), an entire book in the voice of one of the Hebrew prophets translated to a modern sensibility, won the Pulitzer Prize. She writes with passion restrained by intelligence in a voice of controlled elegance, and luminous mystery. Although her use of myth and story to illuminate the individual heart and the archetypal family, as well as her recurrent attempts to understand God, have led some to call her work cryptic or harsh, she has received multiple awards for her poetry, and her critical recognition as one of America's finest poets resulted in her term as U.S. poet laureate in 2003.

BIBLIOGRAPHY: F. Diehl (ed.), *On Louise Gluck: Change What You See* (2005).

[Linda Rodriguez (2nd ed.)]

GLUCKMAN, HENRY (1893–1987), South African physician and politician who was the only Jew to hold a cabinet post in the Union of South Africa. He represented a Johannesburg division in Parliament from 1938 until 1958, when he retired from politics to devote himself to industrial interests. Largely as a result of his work as chairman of the government's National Health Services Commission (1942–44), whose report influenced future health policy, the prime minister, General J.C. Smuts, in 1945 appointed him minister of health and housing. He held this position until 1948 when Smuts' government left office. Gluckman was chairman of the Central Health Services and Hospitals Coordinating Council (1943–45) and of the National Nutrition Council (1945–48). He was a regional vice president of the World Parliamentary Association. He served in the South African Medical Corps in both world wars and was president of the National War Memorial Health Foundation, and vice president of the Jewish Ex-Service League.

Gluckman was an executive member of the Jewish Board of Deputies and vice president of the Zionist Federation. Particularly interested in the Hebrew University, he was on its board of governors and was chairman and lifetime president of the South African Friends of the Hebrew University.

[Louis Hotz]

GLUCKMAN (Herman), MAX (1911–1975), social anthropologist. Born and educated in Johannesburg, South Africa, and Rhodes scholar to Oxford, 1934, he was assistant anthropologist to the Rhodes Livingston Institute in North Rhodesia (now Zambia) from 1939 to 1941 and its director from 1941 to 1947. In 1947 he was appointed lecturer in social anthropology at Oxford and in 1949 professor of social anthropology at the University of Manchester. He did field research in Zululand from 1936 to 1938; in Barotseland from 1939 to 1941; Tonga in North Rhodesia in 1944; and Lamba in 1946. Gluckman became an expert on African societies, the political systems of tribal society, and more generally political anthropology. His *Custom and Conflict in Africa* (1955) paid special attention to cultural change and the significance of conflict, which he regarded as a basic element in society. He was chairman of the Association of Social Anthropologists of the British Commonwealth from 1962 to 1966. He wrote *Administrative Organization of the Barotse Native Authorities* (1943), *Rituals of Rebellion in South-East Africa* (1954), *Custom and Conflict in Africa* (1955), *Order and Rebellion in Tribal Africa* (1963), *Politics, Law, and Ritual in Tribal Society* (1965), and *The Ideas in Barotse Jurisprudence* (1965). Gluckman died in Jerusalem, where he was a visiting scholar at the Hebrew University.

ADD. BIBLIOGRAPHY: ODNB online.

[Ephraim Fischoff]

GLUCKSMAN, HARRY L. (1889–1938), U.S. communal worker. Glucksman was born in New York. A founder of the Jewish center movement in the U.S. and Canada, he joined the *National Jewish Welfare Board in 1917 when it was organized as a war service agency and was executive director for 19 years until his death. Previously, Glucksman had served in executive capacities with the Jewish Big Brothers (in N.Y.), the 92nd Street YMHA (also in N.Y.), and the New Orleans YMHA. An able administrator and organizer, Glucksman was widely consulted on various aspects of Jewish community life. He was a supporter of Zionism and was prominent in the American Jewish Committee, the New York YMHA, and the Jewish Board of Guardians.

GLUCKSTEIN, English family of caterers. In 1872 ISIDORE GLUCKSTEIN (1851–1920) opened a small tobacconist's shop in London with his brother-in-law Barnett *Salmon. This concern developed into Salmon and Gluckstein, the largest firm of retail tobacconists in England, which was then purchased by the Imperial Tobacco Company in 1904. In 1887 Isidore Gluckstein was also one of the founders of the catering firm, J. Lyons and Company, together with his brother MONTAGUE GLUCKSTEIN (1854–1922), Alfred Salmon, son of Barnett Salmon, and Sir Joseph *Lyons. Montague Gluckstein conceived the idea of this popular catering establishment and played a leading part in its development, based on the principle of offering good food at moderate prices. He succeeded to the chairmanship of the company on the death of Lyons in 1917. ISIDORE MONTAGUE GLUCKSTEIN (1890–1975) was chairman of the company 1956–60, and president 1961–68.

Other members of the family were SIR SAMUEL GLUCKSTEIN (1880–1958), who was active in the London Country Council and occupied many posts in executive committees and was mayor of Westminster 1920–21; and SIR LOUIS HALLE GLUCKSTEIN (1897–1979), Conservative member of parliament from 1931–45, chairman of the Greater London Council in 1968, and president of the Liberal Jewish Synagogue from 1944.

ADD. BIBLIOGRAPHY: "Montague Gluckstein," in: DBB, II, 578–81; S. Aris, *The Jews in Business* (1970), index.

GLUECK, ABRAHAM ISAAC (1826–1909), Hungarian rabbi. Glueck was born in Vertes and served as rabbi of Tolcsva for almost 50 years, until his death. His published works are *Be'er Yiẓḥak* on tractate *Ḥullin* (1896), and on *Gittin* in two parts (1909–10), and responsa *Yad Yiẓḥak*, in three parts (1902–08). R. Joseph ha-Kohen Schwartz published a complete volume entitled *Ẓafenat Pa'ne'aḥ* (1909), consisting of notes to the third part. Glueck also published the *Parashat Mordekhai* (1889) of Mordecai Benet, together with his own glosses. Many of his works were apparently lost in the Holocaust.

BIBLIOGRAPHY: B.Z. Eisenstadt, *Dorot ha-Aḥaronim* (1913), 99f.; P.Z. Schwartz, *Shem ha-Gedolim me-Ereẓ Hagar*, 1 (1913), 8a-b, no. 71; *Magyar Zsidó Lexikon* (1929), s.v.

[Naphtali Ben-Menahem]

GLUECK, NELSON (1900–1971), U.S. archaeologist and president of *Hebrew Union College. Glueck, who was born in Cincinnati, Ohio, received his rabbinic ordination from the Hebrew Union College there in 1923. Continuing his studies in Germany, Glueck received his Ph.D. at Jena in 1927. In 1928–29 he studied at the American School of Oriental Research in Jerusalem. Glueck began teaching Bible at Hebrew Union College in 1929, and while still a member of the faculty resumed his connection with the American School of Oriental Research. He was director of the Jerusalem School during 1932–33, 1936–40, and 1942–47, and field director of the Baghdad School in 1942–47. During World War II Glueck worked with the U.S. Office of Strategic Services, then was director of the Union of American Hebrew Congregations, to which he had been appointed in 1941.

A conspicuous figure among American archaeologists, Glueck undertook systematic excavations throughout Transjordan. In 1937 he uncovered the Nabatean Temple at Jebel el-Tannur, and in 1938 he began excavating the Iron Age site of Tell-el-Kheleifeh (Ezion-Geber), near Akaba. From 1952 onward he surveyed ancient sites in the Negev.

In 1947 Glueck was elected president of Hebrew Union College. The college, isolated geographically from the main centers of American Jewish life, also tended to be overshadowed by the burgeoning activities of its patron, the Union of American Hebrew Congregations. Avoiding philosophical controversy, Glueck successfully fought to maintain the independence of the college, and at the same time transformed its structure. In 1949 he succeeded Stephen Wise as president of the Jewish Institute of Religion in New York, and the amalgamation of the two schools followed. Branches of the combined institution were opened in Los Angeles and Jerusalem largely due to Glueck's enthusiasm. The buildings in Cincinnati were greatly enlarged and the granting of fellowships for postgraduate studies, particularly to Christian students of Judaica, was increased considerably.

In addition to contributions to learned journals, Glueck has published *Das Wort Ḥesed im alttestamentlichen Sprachgebrauche* (1927); *Explorations in Eastern Palestine* (4 vols., 1934–51); *The Other Side of the Jordan* (1940); *The River Jordan* (1946); *Rivers in the Desert* (1959); and *Deities and Dolphins: The Story of the Nabateans* (1966). On his 70th birthday, the festschrift *Near Eastern Archeology in the Twentieth Century* was published in his honor.

BIBLIOGRAPHY: D. Lazar, *Rashim be-Yisrael*, 1 (1953), 322–6; *Current Biography*, 30 (July 1969), 28–30; *Time* (Dec. 13, 1963).

GLUECK, SHELDON (1896–1980), U.S. criminologist. Born in Warsaw, Glueck was taken to the United States in 1903. In 1925 he became an instructor in criminology at Harvard and was professor of law from 1931. A member of the advisory committee on Rules of Criminal Procedure of the U.S. Supreme Court, he was also an adviser at the Nuremberg war crimes trials after World War II.

Glueck's work in criminology was largely accomplished with the help of his wife, ELEANOR GLUECK-TOUROFF (1898–1972), who held research posts in criminology at Harvard from 1928 to 1953. For over 30 years they carried out unique follow-up investigations of delinquent and criminal behavior to determine the effectiveness of various forms of correctional treatment. The research resulted in several important publications including *One Thousand Juvenile Delinquents* (1934). Later research into the early identification of delinquency and recidivism led to the development of prognostic tables to predict post-offense behavior of criminal offenders. The Glueck system of prediction enabled them to determine which children in the first grade would probably become persistent delinquents unless there was timely and effective intervention. The predictions were based on certain factors in the social background of the children such as parental discipline, relationship with parents, and the cohesiveness of the family. Validation studies of these prediction tables generally confirmed their accuracy, and were approved by a number of eminent criminologists and social scientists.

Among their many publications were *Unraveling Juvenile Delinquency* (1950), in which the Glueck Social Prediction Table is described, and *Predicting Delinquency and Crime* (1959), which incorporates various tables of prediction for different types of criminal and delinquent behavior. They also wrote *Ventures in Criminology* (1964). Among Sheldon Glueck's other writings were: *Mental Disorder and the Criminal Law* (1925); and *The Nuremberg Trial and Aggressive War* (1946).

[Zvi Hermon]

GLUECKEL OF HAMELN (1646/47–1724), merchant, wife, mother, and Yiddish memoirist. David Kauffman, who edited her Yiddish text, was the first to call her "Glueckel von Hameln"; she signed herself as "Glikl bas Judah Leib." Glikl was born in Hamburg to the merchant Judah Leib and the businesswoman Beila Melrich. Judah Leib, one of the original Ashkenazim to settle in Hamburg, never had the status of that city's great Sephardi financiers; he became a prosperous trader and a notable of the German-Jewish community based in the adjacent town of Altona. At 14, Glikl married Ḥayyim ben Joseph, a native of Hameln. After briefly boarding with their families, Glikl and Ḥayyim established their own household in the Ashkenazi section of Hamburg. The couple had 14 children; 12 lived long enough to marry and all but one had children of their own. Using as his public names either Hamel or Goldschmidt, Ḥayyim traded successfully in gold, silver, pearls, and money, attended the German fairs, and arranged sales from Moscow to London. Glikl helped with the account books, local pledges, and contracts. In 1689, Ḥayyim died from a fall, leaving Glikl with eight children still at home. After marrying off some children nearby and others in distant cities, such as Berlin and Metz, she continued Ḥayyim's business with much success.

In 1699, Glikl married Hirsch Levy, a wealthy widower, provisioner to the armies of Louis XIV, and a leader of the Metz Jewish community. Less than two years later, Levy went bankrupt and the couple had to live in straitened circumstances. After Hirsch's death in 1712, Glikl moved in with her daughter Esther and her banker son-in-law Moses Schwabe and watched her grandchildren grow up until her own death in 1724.

Glikl began to record her reflections and incidents from her life in the "melancholy" period following Ḥayyim's death and gave her writings final form several years after the death of her second husband. This carefully crafted text, interspersed with relevant folk tales, is the first surviving extensive written document by a Jewish woman. However, Glikl was drawing from an established practice of self-description, by women as well as men, in ethical wills and personal narratives. She also drew upon her wide reading in Yiddish printed books, such as women's prayers, moral teachings, extracts from the Bible, and story collections, and from sermons heard from the women's section of the synagogue. Through her book, she could tell her children about their past and also reflect on the ups and downs in her life, her sins and strengths, and the meaning of suffering. Her autobiography, a woman's presentation of family life, the relations between generations, religious sensibility, business activities and values, and the messianic hopes of the 17th century, is an invaluable source for Yiddish language and literature and for early modern Jewish history.

It is important to point out that all of the translations of Glikl's memoirs, in German, French, Hebrew, and English omit as much as two-thirds of the actual text, based on various editorial principles shaped by the translator's approach to the material at hand. This has meant that the genre and the significance of Glikl's writings for her time and audience are still far from adequately understood. Although some of the core issues of the problem have been discussed by C. Turniansky, much room remains for further research, analysis, and full translation.

BIBLIOGRAPHY: D. Kaufmann (ed.), *Zikhronot Marat Glikl Hamil mi-Shnat t"z [!] ad ta"t* (1896); *Die Memoiren der Glueckel von Hameln*, tr. B. Pappenheim (1994); *The Life of Glückel of Hameln, 1646–1724, Written by Herself*, tr. and ed. B.Z. Abrahams (1963). N.B. Minkoff, *Glikl Hamil* (Yid., 1952); D. Bilik, "The Memoirs of Glikl of Hameln: The Archeology of the Text," in: *Yiddish*, 8 (1992), 5–22; C. Turniansky, "Vegn di Literatur-Mekoyrim in Glikl Hamels Zikhroynes," in: I. Bartal, et al. (eds.), *Keminhag Ashkenaz ve-Polin: Sefer Yovel le-Khone Shmeruk, Studies in Honour of Chone Shmeruk* (Yid., 1993), 153–77; idem, "Tsu voser literarishn zshaner gehert Glikls shafung," in: *Proceedings of the Eleventh World Congress of Jewish Studies*, vol. 3 (1994), 283–90; N.Z. Davis, *Women on the Margins: Three Seventeenth-Century Lives* (1995), 5–62; G. Jancke, "Die Sichronot der juedischen Kauffrau Glueckel von Hameln zwischen Autobiographie, Geschichtsschreibung und religiösem Lehrtext," in: M. Heuser (ed.), *Autobiographien von Frauen* (1996), 93–133; M. Richarz (ed.), *Die Hamburger Kauffrau Glikl. Juedische Existenz in der Fruehen Neuzeit* (2001).

[Natalie Zemon Davis (2nd ed.)]

°GLUECKS, RICHARD (1889–1945), SS-*Brigadefuehrer* (major general), charged with participation in the mass murder of Jews in the "Final Solution" (see *Holocaust, General Survey). A native of Dusseldorf, he served as an artillery officer during World War I, and then became a merchant. After Hitler came to power, Gluecks became a member of the Nazi Party and the SS. In 1936 he was appointed chief of staff under Theodor Eike, inspector of concentration camps, and succeeded him in 1940. In 1941, when the Inspection Authority was absorbed into the "Economic and Administrative Main Office" (WVHA) of the SS, Gluecks became head of Amtsgruppe D, which supervised the concentration camps (see Concentration *Camps). Gluecks was responsible for the establishment of Auschwitz and the construction of gas chambers. Under his jurisdiction, exploitation of prisoner's labor was introduced in the camps. He died in Flensburg, seemingly by suicide.

BIBLIOGRAPHY: R. Hoess, *Commandant of Auschwitz* (1961), index; R. Hilberg, *Destruction of the European Jews* (1961), 605, 706, and index; IMT, *Trial of the Major War Criminals*, 24 (1949) index.

[Yehuda Reshef]

GLUECKSOHN (Glickson), MOSHE (1878–1939), Hebrew journalist and Zionist leader. Born in Cholynka, near Grodno, Gluecksohn began his Zionist activity in Western Europe among Jewish students. He was a delegate to the Sixth Zionist Congress (1903) and later congresses, joining the opposition to the Uganda Scheme. From 1908 to 1914 he was the secretary of the Ḥovevei Zion committee in Odessa. In 1910 Gluecksohn began to publish articles in Hebrew in *Haolam* and later also in *Ha-Shiloaḥ*. After the February Revolution, 1917, he edited the Moscow Hebrew daily *Ha-Am*. After the Bolshevik Revolution he left for Palestine (autumn 1919). From 1923 to 1938 he edited the daily *Haaretz*, and during his period of editorship the paper became an important Zionist organ, supporting the policy of Chaim Weizmann and the Zionist leadership and strongly opposing Revisionism. Gluecksohn was the ideological leader of Ha-No'ar ha-Ẓiyyoni and of progressive Zionism. He wrote monographs on Aḥad Ha-Am (1927) and Maimonides (1935). Active in public life as a leader of the General Zionist Party in Palestine, he was also a member of the Zionist General Council, Va'ad ha-Lashon ha-Ivrit (Hebrew Language Committee), and the Board of Governors of the Hebrew University. Kibbutz *Kefar Glickson is named after him. His *Ishim ba-Madda u-va-Sifrut* ("Personalities in Science and Literature") appeared after his death (1940–41; 2nd ed. 1963, with a preface by his wife). Two volumes of his collected works appeared posthumously: *Ishim ba-Ẓiyyonut* ("Zionist Personalities," 1940), and *Im Ḥillufei Mishmarot* ("Changing the Guard," 1965).

BIBLIOGRAPHY: Bergman, in: *Haaretz* (July 2, 1943); G. Kressel, *Toledot ha-Ittonut ha-Ivrit be-Ereẓ Yisrael* (1964), index; A. Carlebach, *Sefer ha-Demuyot* (1959), 306–11; Rabbi Binyamin (pseud.), *Keneset Ḥakhamim* (1960), 358–80.

[Baruch Shohetman]

GLUECKSTADT, town in Schleswig-Holstein, N.W. Germany; until 1864 under Danish rule. It was founded in 1616 by Christian IV of Denmark who in 1619 granted special privileges to induce a group of Hamburg Jews to settle there. By 1650, 130 Sephardi Jews had taken residence in the town. They opened a sugar refinery, a soap factory, and saltworks, and were active in foreign trade. The leader of the newly settled Sephardi community, Albertus *Denis, received permission to operate a mint. The Jews, known as members of the "Portuguese nation," had two representatives on the city council, and possessed a synagogue, school, cemetery, and printing press. The first rabbi was Abraham de Fonseca, who later moved to Hamburg. Due to the rising prosperity of *Altona, the city declined economically in the early 18th century and many Jews left; their privileges lapsed in 1732. Although the synagogue was completely rebuilt in 1767 only 20 families remained by then. The last rabbi died in 1813, and the synagogue was dismantled in 1895.

BIBLIOGRAPHY: Cassuto, in: JJLG, 21 (1930), 287–317; idem, in: *Jahrbuch fuer die juedischen Gemeinden Schleswig-Holsteins*, 2 (1930–31), 110–8; H. Kellenbenz, *Sephardim an der unteren Elbe* (1958), index; M. Grunwald, *Portugiesengraeber auf deutscher Erde* (1902), index; Baron, Social2, 14 (1969), 278ff.

GLUECKSTADT, ISAAC HARTVIG (1839–1910), Danish financier. Glueckstadt, who was born in Fredericia, Denmark, started his business career as a private banker in Christiania (Oslo) in 1865; five years later he was made manager of the

Norwegian Credit Bank. In 1872 he was recalled to Copenhagen as director of the new Landmandsbanken, which developed into the largest bank in Scandinavia under his farsighted management. From the outset, Glueckstadt recognized the importance of international connections and did not confine himself to banking alone. Many important Danish commercial enterprises, among them the Copenhagen Free Port and the East Asiatic Company, owed a great deal to his initiative and support. For many years he was chairman of the board of delegates of the Jewish Community

BIBLIOGRAPHY: *Dansk Biografisk Leksikon*, 8 (1936), 179–82; J. Schovelin, *Landmansbanken 1871–1921* (Copenhagen, 1921).

[Julius Margolinsky]

GLUSK (Glosk), ABRAHAM ABBA (second half of 18th century), Haskalah pioneer. According to one opinion, he was born in Glussk (Lublin province), and to another, in the town bearing the same name in the province of Minsk. He is also identified with the "Glusker Maggid" whose works were burned for heresy in the courtyard of the Vilna synagogue. Glusk, who acquired a wide knowledge of philosophy and secular learning, left his native land in search of free ideas. After a long period spent wandering from city to city, he reached Berlin where he met Moses *Mendelssohn. However he was persecuted by local Orthodox circles and the head of the Berlin community asked the authorities to expel him from the city on the pretext that he had no right of residence. Mendelssohn, however, who considered Glusk a profound thinker, enabled him to remain. Glusk later traveled in Germany, Holland, France, and England before returning home. His subsequent fate is unknown. The German poet A. von Chamisso wrote a poem dedicated to Glusk (1832).

BIBLIOGRAPHY: Stanislavsky, in: *Voskhod*, 12 (1887), 122–8; *Ha-Karmel* (1871), 234–5; A. Kohut, *Mendelssohn und seine Familie* (1886), 51–53.

GLUSKA, ZEKHARYAH (1895–1960), leader of the Yemenite community in Ereẓ Israel. Born in Nadir, Yemen, Gluska moved to Ereẓ Israel with his parents who settled in the Neveh Ẓedek quarter in Jaffa in 1909. In 1911 he joined the Ha-Po'el ha-Ẓa'ir Party and became one of the first members of the Histadrut. In 1921 he helped form the Ẓe'irei ha-Mizraḥ movement, which was founded to integrate Yemenite youth in Ereẓ Israel, and he acted as its representative in the first Asefat ha-Nivḥarim. Gluska was a founder of Hitaḥdut ha-Teimanim ("Union of Yemenites") in Ereẓ Israel and its chairman from 1925. He became its representative in the central *yishuv* bodies and at Zionist Congresses. In 1949 he was elected on behalf of the Yemenite list to the First Knesset.

BIBLIOGRAPHY: Tidhar, 3 (1958), 1515–16.

[Benjamin Jaffe]

GLUSKIN, ZE'EV (1859–1949), Zionist. Born in Slutsk, Belorussia, Gluskin joined the Ḥovevei Zion in Warsaw in the 1880s, became a member of *Benei Moshe, and was among the founders of the Menuḥah ve-Naḥalah society, which established the settlement of Reḥovot. He was also one of the founders of the Aḥi'asaf publishing house, which introduced innovations in the publishing and distribution of Hebrew books. He participated in the establishment of the Carmel society (1896), which marketed and exported the wine produced in the settlements, and was its first director. In 1901 Gluskin took part in a Ḥovevei Zion deputation to Baron Edmond de Rothschild to persuade him to continue his settlement activities in Ereẓ Israel. In 1904 he was among the founders of the Geulah Company, which was established for the private purchase of land in Ereẓ Israel.

Gluskin went to Ereẓ Israel late in 1905 and took over the directorship of Agudat ha-Koremim ("Vintners Association") and of its wine cellars in Rishon le-Zion and Zikhron Ya'akov. When World War I broke out, he went to Alexandria and helped organize aid both for the refugees from Ereẓ Israel and for Jews who had remained there. He supported the volunteer movement for the establishment of a Jewish regiment in the British Army from among the Ereẓ Israel refugees. He was director of the Geulah Company from 1925–46. He published his memoirs (1946), which contain valuable material on the history of the Jews and of Zionism in Russia and Ereẓ Israel.

BIBLIOGRAPHY: D. Idelovitch, *Rishon le-Ẓiyyon* (1941), index; M.Smilansky, *Mishpaḥat ha-Adamah*, 3 (1954), 194–206; Y. Pogrebinsky, *Sefer "Ge'ullah"* (1956), 131ff., 233–5.

[Yehuda Slutsky]

GLUSSK (Yid. **Hlusk**), town in Polesie district, Belarus. Jews settled in Glussk in the third quarter of the 17th century. Jehiel b. Solomon *Heilprin was rabbi there and compiled the regulations of its *ḥevra kaddisha*. In 1717 the Jews paid a 600 zloty poll tax. In 1819 they numbered 1,405, in 1847 – 3,148, in 1897 – 3,801 (71% of the total population), and in 1926 – 2,581 (58.3%). Glussk had no industry. Some of the Jews produced a special kind of tea (called Glussk tea) but most were gardeners, carpenters, horse merchants, and small traders. In the mid-1920s 40 families earned their livelihoods from farming, the others were artisans, and some still engaged in trade. A Yiddish school and Jewish council were in operation. In 1939 the Jews numbered 1,935 (38% of the total population). The Germans occupied Glussk on July 3, 1941. In December 1941 and January 1942 the Jews were murdered near Khvastovichi. Some who escaped to the forest fought in partisan units.

BIBLIOGRAPHY: *Słownik geograficzny Królestwa Polskiego* 3 (1882), 78–79; *Yevrei v SSSR* (1929[4]), 51; *Sefer ha-Partizanim*, 1 (1958), 648–9; Y. Slutzky (ed.), *Sefer Bobruisk*, 2 (1967), 764–8.

[Shmuel Spector (2nd ed.)]

GNAT, tiny insect. Included among the plagues of Egypt is *arov*, identified by one *tanna* as "a swarm of gnats" and "hornets" and by others as "a mixture of animals" (Ex. R. 11:3). In the Septuagint *arov* is rendered by the Greek word for "flies." In Egypt there are many species of gnats or mosquitoes, in particular *Culex* and the *Anopheles*, a conveyor of malaria.

Their eggs are laid in bodies of water and the gnat develops by stages – larval, pupal, imaginal. Despite the inconvenience caused by the gnat, the rabbis stated that it, too, is important in the complex of ecological relations between creatures (Shab. 77b). They also declared that even "if all mortals were to gather together to create one gnat," they would fail to do so (Sif. Deut. 32).

BIBLIOGRAPHY: Tristram, Nat Hist, 327; J. Feliks, *Animal World of the Bible* (1962), 125.

[Jehuda Feliks]

GNESIN, MIKHAIL FABIANOVICH (1883–1957), Russian composer, musicologist, and teacher. Born in Rostov-on-Don, he studied with Lyadov and Rimsky-Korsakov at the St. Petersburg Conservatory. From 1910 to 1923 he taught at Rostov, Yekaterinodar, and Petrograd, and undertook study trips to Greece, Italy, France, Germany, and Palestine (in 1914 and 1921) and worked in Meyerhold's St. Petersburg studio. He also made a survey of music education in the Jewish schools on behalf of the *Odessa Committee. During 1921 he stayed in Palestine, and then went to Germany where he was one of the founders of the Jibneh music publishing house and reorganized the activities of the *Society of Jewish Folk Music of which he had been one of the founders in 1908.

From 1923 to 1935 he was professor of composition at the Moscow Conservatory, where he also served as head of the pedagogical faculty and of the "studios for the development of the national music of the Soviet peoples." From 1935 to 1945 he taught composition at the Leningrad Conservatory, and from 1945 to 1951 headed the composition department at the music school, which bore his name and that of his sister who was also a musician. Gnesin's pedagogical activity included the creation of the basic plan for teaching music composition, which is still followed in the Soviet Union. In addition to his memoirs, he published a number of books on composition, aesthetics, Jewish music, and a study of Rimsky-Korsakov. Among his students were Khachaturian and Khrennikov. As a composer, he pioneered the new Russian symphonic style, and the use of material from the various peoples of the U.S.S.R. Of the 68 items in the list of his works, about a quarter bear "Jewish" titles. The sources for these were, as he himself declared, threefold: tunes of his maternal grandfather, the Vilna *badḥan* and singer Shayke Fayfer (Isaiah Fleytsinger); the synagogue tradition which he received from his first teacher, Eliezer *Gerovich; and the melodies he had collected in Palestine. The publication of his Jewish compositions ended in 1929 (see list, up to this date, in Sendrey, Music). Of his later works, the most noteworthy are *Song of the Old Homeland*, for orchestra, op. 30; *Wolochs* for string quartet and clarinet, op. 56, in two versions (1938, 1951); *Pastoral Elegy* for piano trio, op. 57 (1940); the opera *Abraham's Youth*, to his own libretto, op. 36 (1921–23); and the suite *A Jewish Orchestra at the Mayor's Ball*, from his music to Gogol's *Revizor* ("The Government Inspector"). His opera *Bar Kokhba*, to a libretto by Samuel Halkin, remained unfinished.

BIBLIOGRAPHY: NG[2]; Baker's Biographical Dict; Riemann-Gurlitt Dic; L. Saminsky: 'O tvorcheskom puti M. Gnesina' [The work of the composer], in: *Muzyka* (1913), no. 3 pp. 5–8; A.N. Drozdov, *Michail Fabianowitsch Gnessin* (Rus. and Ger., 1927); I. Ryzhkin: 'O tvorcheskom puti Mikhaila Gnesina', in: *Sovetskaya muzyka* (1933), no. 6 pp. 32–49; M. Bronsaft [Gorali], *Ha-Askolah ha-Musikalit ha-Yehudit* (1940), 52–59.

[Haim Bar-Dayan]

GNESSIN, MENAHEM (1882–1952), Israeli actor and pioneer of the Hebrew theater. Menahem Gnessin, a brother of Uri Nissan *Gnessin, went to Palestine from theUkraine in 1903 and for some years was a laborer and teacher in the villages. In 1907 he founded the Amateur Dramatic Arts Company for the presentation of plays in Hebrew. He staged Chirikov's *The Jews*, Gutzkow's *Uriel Acosta*, and other plays in Jaffa, Jerusalem, and the Judean settlements. Returning to Moscow in 1912, Gnessin and N. *Zemach established a Hebrew group which formed the nucleus of *Habimah. By 1923 Gnessin was in Berlin, organizing the Te'atron Ereẓ Yisraeli, which performed a one-act play, *Belshazzar* by H. Roche, with great success. In 1924 he took the group to Palestine and worked as an actor, teacher, and director. When Habimah reached Palestine in 1928, he joined the company. Gnessin wrote articles on the theater and published his memoirs *Darki im ha-Te'atron ha-Ivri, 1905–26* ("My Career in the Hebrew Theater," 1946).

BIBLIOGRAPHY: M. Kohansky, *The Hebrew Theatre in Its First Fifty Years* (1969), index.

[Gershon K. Gershony]

GNESSIN, URI NISSAN (1881–1913), Hebrew author who was the first to introduce the psychologically oriented prose style into Hebrew literature. Born in Starodub, Ukraine, Gnessin spent his childhood and youth in Pochep, a small town in the province of Orel. His father was head of a yeshivah and Gnessin studied in a *ḥeder*, later at his father's yeshivah where J.H. *Brenner was also a student. Besides his religious studies, Gnessin was interested in secular subjects, studying classical and modern languages and literatures. As a boy, he wrote poems and at 15 began publishing, together with Brenner, a literary monthly and a literary weekly for a small circle of friends and readers. These served as a forum for many of his early works. Nahum *Sokolow invited the young poet, then 18, to join the editorial staff of *Ha-Ẓefirah in Warsaw; this marks the beginning of a productive period in his literary career. Gnessin published poems, literary criticism, stories, and translations in *Ha-Ẓefirah*. A small collection of short stories and sketches, *Ẓilelei ha-Ḥayyim* ("The Shadows of Life"), appeared in 1904.

At this time Gnessin began wandering from city to city, unable or unwilling to strike permanent roots. After a year's stay in Warsaw he moved to Yekaterinoslav, then to Vilna, where he worked for a time for the periodical *Ha-Zeman*, and then went to Kiev. Gnessin tried to study abroad but was not accepted by various schools since he did not have a formal education. Financial distress, hunger, and an inner restlessness beset Gnessin during his stay in Kiev, yet it was the time of his greatest prolificacy. However, plans to found a Hebrew literary organ and a publishing house did not materialize. In 1907 Gnessin left Kiev and at Brenner's invitation went to London (via Warsaw and Berlin, where he stayed for a short time) to co-edit *Ha-Me'orer with Brenner. The periodical failed and there were violent disagreements between him and Brenner. London proved to be a severe disillusionment in other ways – the spiritual life of London Jewry was disappointing and his later fatal heart disease, probably contracted in Kiev, began to affect him. In the autumn he immigrated to Ereẓ Israel but was unable to adjust. The country was a bitter experience for the young writer; his painful impressions found expression only in his letters however. He ascribes his disappointment at times to himself, at times to his environment which he saw as "Jews who trade in their Judaism." In the summer of 1908 Gnessin returned to Russia. He died in Warsaw four years later.

Gnessin's work, one of the major landmarks in Hebrew prose, is characterized by modern literary techniques and devices which he introduced into Hebrew literature. The interior monologue through which the reader receives an unmediated impression of the hero's continuous flow of ideas, sensations, feelings, and memories as they come into his consciousness was one of the main literary vehicles used by Gnessin to convey the psychological anxieties of his characters. He was among the first Hebrew writers to probe the problems of alienation and uprootedness, particularly as they affected the Jew in the modern age. Among his works four stories of his middle period are most outstanding and their impact on Hebrew prose is felt to this day: *"Haẓiddah"* ("Aside," 1905); *"Beinatayim"* ("Meanwhile," 1906); *"Be-Terem"* ("Before," 1909); and *"Eẓel"* ("By," 1913). His early work, *Ẓilelei ha-Ḥayyim*, fails to reveal an individualistic literary character, while later stories, like *"Ba-Gannim"* ("In the Gardens," 1909) and *"Ketatah"* ("A Quarrel," 1912), mark the transition to a new psychological style. Brenner, G. *Shofman, and Gnessin were among the first to cast the problems of the Jew of the age in a literary context. Gnessin poignantly describes the dilemma of the Jew whose world outlook is rooted in the values and spirit of the Jewish East European town, but who, at the same time, adopted the characteristics of a "citizen of the world" sharing the achievements and the deterioration of 20th-century culture. Gnessin's treatment of the theme is close to that of *Berdyczewski.

The four stories are autobiographical and Gnessin, under the guise of different names, is the protagonist. The plots, variations of the same theme, are about a man who leaves home, travels to distant lands, and becomes a "citizen of the world" only to find himself uprooted. A cosmopolitan, he is now completely alienated and lonely. After traveling far and wide, he returns home only to be faced by the awful realization that he has become an alien in his own homeland. At times he may only go as far as the next town, a center somewhat larger than his own hamlet, but the experience uproots and alienates him. The past becomes irretrievable, the gap unbridgeable, and he is cast in a strange, complex, and confusing world. The theme, apparently peculiar to contemporaneous Jewish intellectuals who had rejected religious tradition, merges in Gnessin with the more universal theme of perplexity, cultural strangeness, loss of God, and loss of roots. Out of his anguish, the lost son, wishing to comfort himself, cries: "Father, there is a God in heaven, isn't there, and He is so good!" (*"Be-Terem"*). The very names of the stories imply the protagonist's detachment from time and place.

Scandinavian literature and the stories of Chekhov, his favorite author, had a marked influence on Gnessin. His sense of time as a factor in the life of man and of society resembles that of Marcel Proust. Through the associative technique, Gnessin focused the past and future in the present, rendering the present less real than the past. He broke with the realistic trend then current in the Hebrew short story and became a "modern" author in the spirit of developments in world literature after World War I.

Gnessin's style involves a flow of lyrical patterns which approaches poetic rhythm. His lyricism, however, is neither ambiguous nor vague and his description of details, objects, characters, and scenery is vivid and precise. One of Gnessin's stylistic devices is to reflect the inner world of his characters in all that surrounds them. This demands a descriptive realism and an avoidance of rhetoric. His language, despite certain Russianisms, captured the rhythms of the spoken tongue. His critical essays, which he signed U. Esthersohn, show a close affinity to the 19th-century school of symbolism. Among the works he translated are prose poems by Baudelaire and works by Chekhov, Heinrich Heine, S. Obstfelder, M. Spektor, and J. Wassermann. An edition of his collected works (*Kitvei*) appeared in 1982. The story "Sideways" appeared in A. Lelchuk and G. Shaked (eds.), *Eight Great Hebrew Novels* (1983); "Uproar" is included in G. Abramson (ed.), *The Oxford Book of Hebrew Short Stories* (1996). For further translations into English, see Goell, Bibliography, 2102.

BIBLIOGRAPHY: J.Ḥ. Brenner (ed.), *Haẓiddah* (memorial volume, 1917); B. Katz (Benshalom), *Uri Nissan Gnessin* (1935); S.Y. Penueli, *Brenner u-Gnessin ba-Sippur ha-Ivri shel Reshit ha-Me'ah ha-Esrim* (1965); Y. Zmora, *Ha-Mesapper Kav le-Kav* (1951); Z. Fishman, in: *Ha-Toren*, 10 (1923), 89–95; S. Nashkes, in: *Kitvei U.N. Gnessin*, 3 (1946), 221–35; Kressel, Leksikon (1965), 494–6. **ADD. BIBLIOGRAPHY:** G. Shaked, *Lelo Moẓa: Al Brenner, Berdyczewski, Shoffman, Gnessin* (1973); L. Rattok (ed.), *U.N. Gnessin: Mivḥar Ma'amrei Bikkoret al Yeẓirato* (1977); H. Bar-Yosef, *Ha-Lashon ha-Figurativit bi-Yeẓirato ha-Sippurit shel U.N. Gnessin* (1984); I. Even Zohar, "Gnessin's Dialogue and Its Russian Models," in: *Slavica Hierosolymitana*, 7 (1985), 17–36; D. Miron and D. Laor (eds.), *U.N. Gnessin: Meḥkarim u-Te'udot* (1986); Y. Bakon, *Brenner u-Gnessin ke-Sofrim du Leshoniyim* (1986); A. Balaban, "Gnessin Revisited," in: *Prooftexts*, 9:2 (1989), 177–84; D. Steinhart, "Is Anybody There? The Subjectivism of U.N. Gnessin Reconsidered," in: *Prooftexts*, 11:2 (1991), 131–51; H. Herzig, *Ha-Sippur ha-Ivri bi-Reshit ha-Me'ah ha-Esrim* (1992); D. Steinhart, "Shabtai and Gnessin: A Comparative Reading," in: *Prooftexts*, 14:3 (1994), 233–47; D. Miron, *Ha-Ḥayyim be-Appo shel Neẓaḥ: Yeẓirato shel U.N. Gnessin* (1997); A. Zemaḥ: *Be-Emẓa: Keri'ah bi-Shenei Sippurim shel U.N. Gnessin* (2000); A. Holtzman, *Temunah le-neged Ei-*

nai (2002); A. Petrov Ronell, "Reading Gnessin's 'Sideways' in Its Russian Context," in: *Journal of Modern Jewish Studies*, 3:2 (2004), 167–82; D. Aberbach, "Gnessin's Anguish," in *Jewish Quarterly*, 196 (2004–2005), 63–64.

[Lea Goldberg]

GNIEZNO (Ger. **Gnesen**), city in Poland; first capital of Poland and center of the Catholic Church in that country until the beginning of the 14th century. Jews are mentioned there in 1267. Various charters of privilege granted to individual Jews or the community giving them rights of residence, and permission to organize defense and engage in commerce (1497, 1499, 1519, 1567, 1571, 1637, 1661) were destroyed in fires that periodically devastated the town. From the 13th to the middle of the 17th centuries, Gniezno Jewry remained one of the smaller communities in the kingdom, numbering 100 people in 30 houses at the end of the period. A representative from Gniezno participated in the provincial (*galil*) council of the communities of Great Poland in 1519. Several such councils were convened at Gniezno (in 1580, 1632, 1635, 1640, 1642). Local and visiting merchants and their agents dealt in wool and rags and collected tolls at the biannual fairs, and even attempted to carry on business outside the Jewish quarter (1643). The synagogue, built in 1582, was modeled after the one in Poznan. Eliezer *Ashkenazi was among the rabbis of Gniezno. The events surrounding the Swedish War (1655–59), as well as attacks led by the Jesuits and by the troops of Stephan *Czarniecki, ended with the destruction of the community. In 1661 it reorganized outside the city walls. A new synagogue was built in 1680. In the first half of the 18th century the community suffered during the Northern War, and there was an outbreak of fire as well as cases of *blood libel (1722, 1738). There were 60 Jews living in Gniezno in 1744. The community increased from the second half of the 18th century, particularly after Gniezno came under Prussian rule with the second partition of Poland in 1793, growing from 251 in the beginning of the period to 1,783 in the middle of the 19th century. It had cultural and welfare institutions, craftsmen's associations, a school, and a synagogue. The talmudic scholar Moses Samuel *Zuckermandel officiated as rabbi in Gniezno from 1864 to 1869. Subsequently many Jews emigrated to the German states and from the second half of the 19th century to America, especially after Gniezno was incorporated within independent Poland in 1919. The community numbered 750 in 1913 and approximately 150 in the 1930s.

[Dov Avron]

Holocaust Period

Before World War II nearly 150 Jews lived in Gniezno. During the Nazi occupation, the town belonged to Warthegau. During the first four months of the occupation, the town was emptied of all its Jewish inhabitants. A certain number escaped before and after the Germans entered, but the majority were deported on orders given on Nov. 12, 1939, by Wilhelm Koppe, the Higher SS and Police Leader of Warthegau. The orders called for the deportation of the entire Jewish population of Gniezno by the end of February 1940 to the territory of the Generalgouvernement. On Dec. 13, 1939, 65 Jews from Gniezno, probably the last of the community, arrived in Piotrkow Trybunalski in the Radom district. After the removal of the Jews from Gniezno, the Germans blew up the synagogue and razed the old Jewish cemetery, using it as the site of a warehouse. No Jews resettled in the town after World War II.

[Danuta Dombrowska]

BIBLIOGRAPHY: Halpern, Pinkas, index; idem, *Yehudim ve-Yahadut be-Mizrah Eiropah* (1968), index: B.D. Weinryb, *Te'udot le-Toledot ha-Kehillot ha-Yehudiyyot be-Polin* (1950), index (= PAAJR, 19 (1950), Hebrew and English text); D. Avron, *Pinkas ha-Kesherim shel Kehillat Pozna* (1967), index; A.B. Posner, *Le-Korot Kehillat Gnesen* (1958); A. Heppner and J. Herzberg, *Aus der Vergangenheit und Gegenwart der Juden und der juedischen Gemeinden in den Posener Laendern* (1909), 405–13; D. Dąbrowska, in: BŻIH, 13–14 (1955), passim (on Holocaust). **ADD. BIBLIOGRAPHY:** E.B. Posner, *Le-Korot Kehillat Gnesin* (1958).

GNOSTICISM, designates the beliefs held by a number of nonorthodox Christian sects flourishing in the first to second centuries C.E., which developed mystical systems of philosophy based on the *gnosis* (Gr. "knowledge") of God. These systems were syncretic, i.e., mixtures of pagan magic and beliefs from the Babylonian and Greek world as well as from the Jewish. Judaism made an important contribution to the conceptions and the developments of gnosticism. One way in which Jewish motifs were infused into gnosticism was through the Bible, which was holy to Christianity and likewise through other Jewish literature – in Hebrew, Aramaic, and Greek – which was used by the Christians. The chapters on the Creation in Genesis were also of special influence. Special importance was also attributed to the account of the first man and his sin, which is interpreted by gnosticism as the downfall of the divine principle into the material world. From their negative attitude toward the world of natural existence and moral law which is meant to regulate man's behavior in this world, the gnostics came to a view of the God of Israel, the creator of the universe, as the god of evil, or an inferior god, and they strongly rejected his Law and its commandments. They interpreted the stories in the Bible in a way opposite to their meaning and intention: thus, for example, the original serpent is often seen by them as the bearer of the true "knowledge," of which God intends to deprive man; and Cain becomes a positive figure persecuted by God, etc.

Jewish influence on gnosticism is also evident in the use of names, concepts, and descriptions taken from the Hebrew or Aramaic, e.g., God, the creator of the universe, is called in some gnostic systems *Yaldabaot* (*Yalda Bahut*, according to some "the Child of Chaos"); other mythological or symbolic figures in gnosticism are *Barbelo* (*Be-arba Eloha*, "in four gods," i.e., the father, the son, the female principle in the divine, and the first man), *Edem* (Eden), *Akhamot* (*ḥokhmot*, "wisdom," according to Prov. 9:1); the name of the gnostic Naassene sect is derived from *naḥash* ("serpent"); the mysterious words "*Ẓav la-ẓav ẓav la-ẓav kav la-kav kav la-kav ze'eir sham* ze'eir sham" (Isa. 28:10, 13) serve as the mystical designation of the three gnostic *Sefirot*.

In addition to these contributions unwittingly and unintentionally made by Judaism to gnosticism, there existed in Judaism itself, at the end of the Second Temple period, emotional and intellectual attitudes which were close to the spiritual world of gnosticism. It is possible that these had a more direct influence on the emergence of gnosticism or, at least, that they served as seeds for a few of its ideas. There are indications of this in the literature of the Dead Sea Sect. Common to both gnosticism and the Dead Sea Scrolls is the view of esoteric "knowledge" as a redemptive factor, which enables a group of select people to bridge the abyss separating the human from the divine, and to rise "from a spirit perverse to an understanding of you and to stand in one company before you with the everlasting host and the spirits of knowledge, to be renewed with all things that are and with those versed in song together" (Thanksgiving Psalms, 1QH 11:13–14), and to be those "who heard the glorious voice and saw the holy angels, men whose ears are opened and hear deep things" (War Scroll, 1QM 10:11).

The literature of the sect also reflects a dualistic outlook on the world conceiving a schism between the principle of good (the light) and the principle of evil (the darkness) each with its own hosts of angels and spirits. This view, however, in contrast to its expression in gnosticism, does not step beyond the framework of Jewish belief in divine unity. Even the feeling of disgust and revulsion with man and the impurity of his material basis ("the mystery of the flesh is iniquity"; Manual of Discipline, 1QS 11:9) does not culminate in the notion of distinction between matter per se and the divine spiritual world; "For the world, albeit now and until the time of the final judgment it go sullying itself in the ways of wickedness owing to the domination of perversity" (*ibid.*, 4:19), but God "created man to rule the world" (*ibid.*, 3:17–18). Thus, despite a certain spiritual kinship between the writings of the sect and the world of gnosticism, the former are not records of a "gnostic Judaism," but rather reflect certain general attitudes of mind shared at that time by others including Jews, which could be the point of departure for truly gnostic speculations.

There is no explicit mention in talmudic literature of gnosticism and its history. It is possible, however, that the appellation **Minim* refers in some instances to gnostics.

For the influence of gnosticism on the history of Jewish mysticism, see *Kabbalah.

BIBLIOGRAPHY: H. Graetz, *Gnostizismus und Judentum* (1846); C.W. King, *The Gnostics and Their Remains* (1872[2]); G. Scholem, *Jewish Gnosticism, Merkabah Mysticism, and Talmudic Tradition* (1960); Scholem, Mysticism, index; R.M. Grant, *Gnosticism and Early Christianity* (1959); K. Schubert, in: *Kairos*, 3 (1961), 2–15 (Ger.); M. Friedlaender, *Der vorchristliche juedische Gnostizismus* (1898).

[David Flusser]

GOA, city and district on the W. coast of India, about 250 miles (400 km.) S. of Bombay, a Portuguese province from 1510 until 1961. The first Jew to be mentioned in Goa was Gaspar da *Gama who was kidnapped by Vasco da Gama in 1498 and baptized. From the early decades of the 16th century many New Christians from Portugal came to Goa. The influx soon aroused the opposition of the Portuguese and ecclesiastical authorities, who complained bitterly about the New Christians' influence in economic affairs, their monopolistic practices, and their secret adherence to Judaism. As a result of these complaints the Portuguese Inquisition was established in Goa in 1560, and lasted, apart from a temporary suspension from 1774 to 1778, for almost 250 years. Even before the Inquisition was formally established, a physician named Jeronimo Diaz had been burned in 1543 for maintaining heretical opinions. Many prominent New Christians became victims of the Inquisition in Goa. The great scientist Garcia de *Orta was not affected during his lifetime, but 12 years after his death, in 1580, his remains were exhumed, burned, and the ashes thrown into the ocean. In the latter part of the 16th century Coje *Abrahão served as interpreter to the Portuguese viceroys, despite ecclesiastical objections. Eighteenth-century travelers refer to the existence of a synagogue and organized Jewish communal life, but this is doubtful.

BIBLIOGRAPHY: Roth, Mag Bibl, 105–6; Roth, Marranos, 394; E.N. Adler, *Auto De Fé and Jew* (1908), 139–51; J.M.T. de Carvalho, *Garcia d'Orta* (Sp., 1915); A. Baião (ed.), *A inquisiçào de Goa*, 2 vols. (1945); Fischel, in: JQR, 47 (1956/57), 37–45.

[Walter Joseph Fischel]

GOAT. The classification of the domesticated goat bred in Israel is disputed among scholars, some maintaining that it originates from the wild goat *Capra hircus*, hence the name of the domesticated goat as *Capra hircus mambrica*, others, that it originates from the wild *Capra prisca*, the name of the domesticated goat therefore being *Capra prisca mambrica*. The wild goat is apparently the *akko* mentioned as one of the permitted wild animals (Deut. 14:5). The goat of Ereẓ Israel has recurved horns, those of the he-goat being branched. Its bones have been found in excavations at *Megiddo and a drawing of it in excavations at *Gezer (dating from about 3,000 years ago). The goat has black hair (cf. Song 4:1), but a few have black hair with white or brown spots (cf. Gen. 30:32). This black hair may have symbolized sin, and for this reason it was chosen as a sin offering and for the scapegoat (see *Azazel; Lev. 16:8 ff.). The expression *sa'ir* (lit. "hairy") for a he-goat (*ibid.*, 4:24) and *se'irah* for a she-goat (4:28) is connected with their long hair. The curtains of the Tabernacle were made of goat's hair, as were the black tents of the Bedouin – "the tents of Kedar" (Song 1:5). The she-goat is called *ez*, but *izzim* is also a general expression for the species, the kid being referred to as *gedi izzim* (Gen. 38:17) or *seh izzim* (Deut. 14:4); he-goats are called *attudim* (Num. 7:17) or *teyashim* (Gen. 30:35). The he-goat usually leads the flock and hence apparently the reference to it as "stately in going" (Prov. 30:29, 31). Another name for the he-goat is *ẓafir* (Dan. 8:5).

The importance of the goat lay in its flesh, that of the kid being particularly delicious (Gen. 27:9; 38:20; Judg. 13:15). Ancient peoples apparently boiled a kid in milk on idolatrous fertility festivals, the prohibition of seething "a kid in its mother's milk" (Ex. 23:19; 34:26; Deut. 14:21) being connected with this. From its threefold repetition, the sages deduced a general prohibition against eating meat with milk, as well as its concomitant laws (Kid. 57b). Goat's milk was widely used (cf. Prov. 27:27), being also regarded as a remedy for chest trouble. A *baraita*, however, tells of a pious man who reared a goat in his home for this purpose, but because he transgressed the prohibition of the sages against the breeding of goats, his colleagues rebuked him, calling the goat an "armed robber" (BK 80a), the goat being regarded as a robber since it jumps over fences and damages plants. A Greek inscription prohibiting the breeding of goats has been uncovered at Heracleas. According to the Mishnah (BK 7:7) "small cattle (goats and sheep) are not to be bred in Ereẓ Israel, but may be bred in Syria or in the deserts of Ereẓ Israel." After the destruction of the country's agriculture, especially following the Muslim conquest, goats were imported to Ereẓ Israel, and they increased in number. Some maintain that they were responsible for the erosion of the land by ruining the terraces, destroying the natural vegetation, and creating fissures on the slopes. The eroded soil was deposited in the valleys, blocking the flow of rivers to the sea and forming marshes such as those of the Valley of Jezreel, which were drained by Jews only in the present century. Even now goats, still kept in large numbers by the Bedouin, cause damage to Israel's natural woods by chewing the young shoots, thereby preventing them from growing to full height.

In the 1940s, the Jewish settlers introduced into the country the white European goat, distinguished for its yield of milk. In the Diaspora, particularly in Eastern Europe, the Jews in the towns and villages raised goats so as to have an independent supply of milk. In popular Jewish folklore the goat is a well-known motif which finds expression in jokes ("the rabbi and the goat"), in folk songs ("the child and the goat," see *Ḥad Gadya), as also in poems and paintings (e.g. those of *Chagall).

BIBLIOGRAPHY: Dalman, Arbeit, 4 (1935), 171; 6 (1939), 186ff.; F.S. Bodenheimer, *Animal and Man in Bible Lands* (1960), 224, index, s.v. *Capra*; Feliks, in: *Teva va-Areẓ*, 7 (1964/65), 330–7. **ADD BIBLIOGRAPHY:** Feliks, *Ha-Ẓome'aḥ*, 260.

[Jehuda Feliks]

°GOBINEAU, JOSEPH ARTHUR, COMTE DE (1816–1882), French diplomat and essayist. Of his abundant literary efforts, only his *Essai sur l'inégalité des races humaines* (1853–55) is now remembered. In this essay Gobineau simplified to the extreme current opinions on the "racial factor" in history and the hierarchy of races, white, yellow, and black. According to him, only the white or "Aryan" race, the creator of civilization, possessed the supreme human virtues, such as honor, love of freedom, etc., qualities which could be perpetuated only if the race remained pure. Though he held the Jews in no particular aversion, Gobineau believed that the Latin and Semitic peoples had degenerated in the course of history through various racial intermixtures. Only the Germans had preserved their "Aryan purity," but the evolution of the modern world condemned them too to crossbreeding and degeneracy. Western civilization must be resigned to its fate. The success of the *Essai* was posthumous and, predictably, assured by Gobineau's German admirers. Chief of these was Richard *Wagner, who shared his cultural pessimism, and the literary society of Bayreuth, followed by a group of authors and anthropologists who founded the Gobineau-Vereinigung in 1894. Gobineau's influence on recent history, and especially on antisemitic ideology, was due less to his dilettante philosophy of history than to the construction given it by German and other fanatics.

BIBLIOGRAPHY: L.I. Snyder, *The Idea of Racialism...* (1962); J. Buenzod, *La formation de la pensée de Gobineau et l'Essai sur l'inégalité des races humaines* (1967). **ADD. BIBLIOGRAPHY:** M.D. Biddiss, *Father of Racist Ideology: The Social and Political Thought of Count Gobineau* (1970); J. Bossel, *Gobineau, 1816–1882, un Don Quichotte tragique* (1981).

[Leon Poliakov]

GOD.

IN THE BIBLE

The Bible is not a single book, but a collection of volumes composed by different authors living in various countries over a period of more than a millennium. In these circumstances, divergencies of emphasis (cf. Kings with Chronicles), outlook (cf. Jonah with Nahum), and even of fact (cf. Gen. 26:34 with 36:2–3) are to be expected. These factors have also affected the biblical presentation of the concept of God. There are passages in which Israel's monotheism is portrayed in unalloyed purity and incomparable beauty (I Kings 19:12; Isa. 40:18), and there are other verses in which folkloristic echoes and mythological reflexes, though transmuted and refined, appear to obscure the true character of the Hebrew concept of the divine (Gen. 2 and 3). Notwithstanding these discrepancies the Bible is essentially a unity; its theology is sui generis and must be studied as a whole to be seen in true perspective. This total view of biblical doctrine does not seek to blur differences and to harmonize the disparate; rather it resolves the heterogeneous elements into a unitary canonical ideology – the doctrine of the final editors of the Bible. It blends the thoughts, beliefs, and intuitions of many generations into a single spiritual structure – the faith of Israel – at the heart of which lies the biblical idea of God. It is this complete and ultimate scriptural conception of the Deity that will be described and analyzed in this section.

The One, Incomparable God

God is the hero of the Bible. Everything that is narrated, enjoined, or foretold in biblical literature is related to Him. Yet nowhere does the Bible offer any proof of the Deity's existence, or command belief in Him. The reason may be twofold: Hebrew thought is intuitive rather than speculative and systematic, and, furthermore, there were no atheists in antiquity. When the psalmist observed: "The fool hath said in his heart 'There is no God'" (Ps. 14:1), he was referring not to disbelief in God's existence, but to the denial of His moral governance. That a divine being or beings existed was universally accepted. There were those, it is true, who did not know YHWH (Ex. 5:2), but all acknowledged the reality of the Godhead. Completely new, however, was Israel's idea of God. Hence this idea is expounded in numerous, though not necessarily related, biblical passages, and, facet by facet, a cosmic, awe-inspiring spiritual portrait of infinite magnitude is built up. Paganism is challenged in all its aspects. God is One; there is no other (Deut. 6:4; Isa. 45:21; 46:9). Polytheism is rejected unequivocally and absolutely (Ex. 20:3–5). There is no pantheon; even the *dualism of Ormuzd and Ahriman (of the Zoroastrian religion) is excluded (Isa. 45:21); apotheosis is condemned (Ezek. 28:2ff.). Syncretism, as distinct from identification (Gen. 14:18–22), which plays a historical as well as a theological role in paganism, is necessarily ruled out (Num. 25:2–3; Judg. 18). Verses like Exodus 15:11 – "Who is like Thee, O Lord, among the gods?" – do not lend support to polytheism, but expose the unreality and futility of the pagan deities. The thought is: Beside the true God, how can these idol-imposters claim divinity? The term "sons of gods" in Psalms 29:1 and 89:7 refers to angels, the servants, and worshipers of the Lord; there is no thought of polytheism (see E.G. Briggs, *The Book of Psalms* (ICC), 1 (1906), 252ff.; 2 (1907), 253ff.). The one God is also unique in all His attributes. The prophet asks: "To whom then will ye liken God? Or what likeness will ye compare unto Him?" (Isa. 40:18). Though the question is rhetorical, the Bible in a given sense provides a series of answers, scattered over the entire range of its teaching, which elaborate in depth the incomparability of God. He has no likeness; no image can be made of Him (Ex. 20:4; Deut. 4:35). He is not even to be conceived as spirit; the spirit of God referred to in the Bible alludes to His energy (Isa. 40:13; Zech. 4:6). In Isaiah 31:3, "spirits" parallels "a god" (*'el*, a created force), not the God, who is called in the verse YHWH. Idolatry, though it lingered on for centuries, was doomed to extinction by this new conception of the Godhead. It is true that the Torah itself ordained that images like the cherubim should be set up in the Holy of Holies. They did not, however, represent the Deity but His throne (cf. Ps. 68:5[4]); its occupant no human eye could see. Yet the invisible God is not a philosophical abstraction; He manifests His presence. His theophanies are accompanied by thunder, earthquake, and lightning (Ex. 19:18; 20:15[18]; Hab. 3:4ff.). These fearful natural phenomena tell of His strength; He is the omnipotent God (Job 42:2). None can resist Him (41:2); hence He is the supreme warrior (Ps. 24:8). God's greatness, however, lies not primarily in His power. He is omniscient; wisdom is His alone (Job 28:23ff.). He knows no darkness; light ever dwells with Him (Dan. 2:22); and it is He, and He only, who envisions and reveals the future (Isa. 43:9). He is the source of human understanding (Ps. 36:10[9]), and it is He who endows man with his skills (Ex. 28:3; I Kings 3:12). The classical Prometheus and the Canaanite Kôthar-and-Ḥasis are but figments of man's imagination. The pagan pride of wisdom is sternly rebuked; it is deceptive (Ezek. 28:3ff.); but God's wisdom is infinite and unsearchable (Isa. 40:28). He is also the omnipresent God (Ps. 139:7–12), but not as *numen*, *mana*, or *orenda*. Pantheism is likewise negated. He transcends the world of nature, for it is He who brought the world into being, established its laws, and gave it its order (Jer. 33:25). He is outside of time as well as space; He is eternal. Everything must perish; He alone preceded the universe and will outlive it (Isa. 40:6–8; 44:6; Ps. 90:2). The ever-present God is also immutable; in a world of flux He alone does not change (Isa. 41:4; Mal. 3:6). He is the rock of all existence (II Sam. 22:32).

The Divine Creator

God's power and wisdom find their ultimate expression in the work of creation. The miracles serve to highlight the divine omnipotence; but the supreme miracle is the universe itself (Ps. 8:2, 4 [1, 3]). There is no theogony, but there is a cosmogony, designed and executed by the divine fiat (Gen. 1). The opening verses of the Bible do not conclusively point to *creatio ex nihilo*. The primordial condition of chaos (*tohu* and *bohu*) mentioned in Genesis 1:2 could conceivably represent the *materia prima* out of which the world was fashioned; but Job 26:7 appears to express poetically the belief in a world created out of the void (see Y. Kaufmann, Religion, 68), and both prophets and psalmists seem to substantiate this doctrine (Isa. 42:5; 45:7–9; Jer. 10:12; Ps. 33:6–9; 102:26; 212:2). *Maimonides, it is true, did not consider that the Bible provided incontrovertible proof of *creatio ex nihilo* (*Guide*, 2:25). The real criterion, however, is the overall climate of biblical thought, which would regard the existence of uncreated matter as a grave diminution of the divinity of the Godhead. God is the sole creator (Isa. 44:24). The celestial beings ("sons of God") referred to in Job 38:7, and the angels who, according to rabbinic *aggadah* and some modern exegetes, are addressed in Genesis 1:26 (cf. 3:22) were themselves created forms and not co-architects or co-builders of the cosmos. Angels are portrayed in the Bible as constituting the heavenly court, and as taking part in celestial consultations (I Kings 22:19ff.; Job 1:6ff.; 2:1ff.). These heavenly creatures act as God's messengers (the Hebrew *mal'akh* and the Greek ἄγγελος, from which the word "angel" is derived, both mean "messengers") or agents. They perform various tasks (cf. Satan, "the Accuser"), but except in the later books of the Bible they are not individualized and bear no names (see *Angels and Angelology). Nor are they God's only messengers; natural phenomena, like the wind (Ps. 104:4), or man himself, may act in that capacity (Num. 20:16). Some scholars think that since the Bible concentrated all divine powers in the one God, the old pagan deities, which represented various forces of nature, were demoted in Israel's religion to the position of angels. The term *shedim* (Deut. 32:17; Ps. 106:37), on the other hand, applied to the gods of the nations, does not, according to Y. Kaufmann, denote demons, but rather "no-gods," devoid of both divine and demonic powers. The fantastic proliferation of the angel population found in pseudepigraphical literature is still unknown in the Bible. It is fundamental, however, to biblical as well as post-biblical Jewish angelology that these celestial beings are God's creatures and servants. They fulfill the divine will and do not oppose it. The pagan notion of demonic forces that wage war against the deities is wholly alien and repugnant to biblical theology. Even Satan is no more than the heavenly prosecutor, serving the divine purpose. The cosmos is thus the work of God above, and all nature declares His glory (Ps. 19:2, 13ff.). All things belong to Him and He is the Lord of all (I Chron. 29:11–12). This creation theorem has a corollary of vast scientific and social significance: the universe, in all its measureless diversity, remains a homogeneous whole. Nature's processes are the same throughout the world, and underlying them is "One Power, which is of no beginning and no end; which has existed before all things were formed, and will remain in its integrity when all is gone – the Source and Origin of all, in Itself beyond any conception or image that man can form and set up before his eye or mind" (Haffkine). There is no cosmic strife between antagonistic forces, between darkness and light, between good and evil; and, by the same token, mankind constitutes a single brotherhood. The ideal is not that of the ant heap. Differentiation is an essential element of the Creator's design; hence the Tower of Babel is necessarily doomed to destruction. Although uniformity is rejected, the family unity of mankind, despite racial, cultural, and pigmentary differences, is clearly stressed in its origin (Adam is the human father of all men) and in its ultimate destiny at the end of days (Isa. 2:2–4). The course of creation is depicted in the opening chapter of the Bible as a graduated unfolding of the universe, and more particularly of the earth, from the lowest levels of life to man, the peak of the creative process. God, according to this account, completed the work in six days (that "days" here means an undefined period may be inferred from Gen. 1:14, where time divisions are mentioned for the first time; cf. also N.H. Tur-Sinai, in EM, 3 (1958), 593). The biblical accounting of the days, however, is not intended to provide the reader with a science or history textbook but to describe the ways of God. Running like a golden thread through all the variegated contents of the Bible is the one unchanging theme – God and His moral law. Of far greater significance than the duration of creation is the fact that it was crowned by the Sabbath (Gen. 2:1–3), bringing rest and refreshment to the toiling world. The concept of the creative pause, sanctified by the divine example, is one of the greatest spiritual and social contributions to civilization made by the religion of Israel. The attempts to represent the Assyro-Babylonian *šabattu* or *šapattu* as the forerunner of the Hebrew Sabbath are without foundation. The former was a designation for the ill-omened 15th day of the month, and the notions associated with it are as polarically different from those of the Sabbath, with its elevating thoughts of holiness and physical and spiritual renewal, as a day of mourning is from a joyous festival.

God in History

The Sabbath did not mark the retirement of the Deity from the world that He had called into being. God continued to care for His creatures (Ps. 104), and man – all men – remained the focal point of His loving interest (Ps. 8:5[4]ff.). The divine providence encompasses both nations (Deut. 32:8) and individuals (e.g., the Patriarchs). Cosmogony is followed by history, and God becomes the great architect of the world of events, even as He was of the physical universe. He directs the historical movements (*ibid.*), and the peoples are in His hands as clay in the hands of the potter (Jer. 18:6). He is the King of the nations (Jer. 10:7; Ps. 22:29). There is a vital difference, however, between the two spheres of divine activity. Creation encountered no antagonism. The very monsters that in pagan mythology were the mortal enemies of the gods became in the Bible creatures formed in accordance with the divine will (Gen. 1:21). Nevertheless, the stuff of history is woven of endless strands of rebellion against the Creator. Man is not an automaton; he is endowed with free will. The first human beings already disobeyed their maker; they acquired knowledge at the price of sin, which reflects the discord between the will of God and the action of man. The perfect harmony between the Creator and His human creation that finds expression in the idyll of the Garden of Eden was disrupted, and never restored. The revolt continued with Cain, the generation of the Flood, and the Tower of Babel. There is a rhythm of rebellion and retribution, of oppression and redemption, of repentance and grace, and of merit and reward (Jer. 18:7–10). Israel was the first people to write history as teleology and discovered that it had a moral base. The Bible declares that God judges the world in righteousness (Ps. 96:13); that military power does not presuppose victory (Ps. 33:16); that the Lord saves the humble (Ps. 76:10) and dwells with them (Isa. 57:15). The moral factor determines the time as well as the course of events. The Israelites will return to Canaan only when the iniquity of the Amorite is complete (Gen. 15:16); for 40 years the children of Israel wandered in the wilderness for accepting the defeatist report of the ten spies (Num. 14:34); Jehu is rewarded with a dynasty of five generations for his punitive action against the house of Ahab; and to Daniel is revealed the timetable of redemption and restoration (Dan. 9:24). It is this moral element in the direction of history that makes God both Judge and Savior. God's punishment of the wicked and salvation of the righteous are laws of the divine governance of the world, comparable to the laws of nature: "As smoke is driven away, so drive them away; as wax melts before fire, let the wicked perish before God…" (Ps. 68:2–3; cf. M.D. Cassuto, in *Tarbiz*, 12 (1941), 1–27). Nature and history are related (Jer. 33:20–21, 25–26); the one God rules them both. The ultimate divine design of history, marked by universal peace, human brotherhood, and knowledge of God, will be accomplished in "the end of days" (Isa. 2:2–4; 11:6ff.), even as the cosmos was completed in conformity with the divine plan. Man's rebellions complicate the course of history, but cannot change the design. God's purpose shall be accomplished; there will be a new heaven and a new earth (Isa. 66:22), for ultimately man will have a new heart (Ezek. 36:26–27).

God and Israel

Within the macrocosm of world history there is the microcosm of Israel's history. It is natural that in the context of national literature the people of Israel should receive special and elaborate attention, although the gentile world, particularly in prophetic teaching, is never lost sight of. The Bible designates Israel *'am segullah*, "a treasured people," which stands in a particular relationship to the one God. He recognized Israel as His own people and they acknowledge Him as their only God (Deut. 26:17–18). He redeems His people from Egyptian bondage, brings them to the promised land, and comes to their aid in periods of crisis. Israel's election is not, however, to be interpreted as a form of favoritism. For one thing, the Exodus from Egypt is paralleled by similar events in the histories of other peoples, including Israel's enemies (Amos 9:7). In truth, Israel's election implies greater responsibility, with corresponding penalties as well as rewards: "You only have I singled out of all the families of the earth; therefore I will visit upon you all your iniquities" (Amos 3:2; see *Chosen People). The choice of the children of Israel as God's people was not due to their power or merit; it was rather a divine act of love, the fulfillment of a promise given to the Patriarchs (Deut. 7:7–8; 9:4–7). The Lord did, however, foresee that the spiritual and moral way of life pioneered by Abraham would be transmitted to his descendants as a heritage. Subsequently this concept found material expression in the covenant solemnly established between God and His people at Sinai (Ex. 24:7ff.). This covenant demanded wholehearted and constant devotion to the will of God (Deut. 18:13); it was an everlasting bond (Deut. 4:9). Thus to be a chosen people it was incumbent upon Israel to become a choosing people (as Zangwill phrased it). The rhythm of rebellion and repentance, retribution and redemption, is particularly evident in the story of Israel. Yet the fulfillment of the divine purpose is not in doubt. God's chosen people will not perish (Jer. 31:26–27). It will be restored to faithfulness, and in its redemption will bring salvation to the whole earth by leading all men to God (Jer. 3:17–18). Until that far-off day, however, Israel will remain God's witness (Isa. 44:8).

The Divine Lawgiver

The covenant that binds the children of Israel to their God is, in the ultimate analysis, the Torah in all its amplitude. God, not Moses, is the lawgiver; "Behold, I Moses say unto you" (cf. Gal. 5:2) is an inconceivable statement. It would not only be inconsistent with Moses' humility (Num. 12:3), but would completely contradict the God-given character of the Torah. However, notwithstanding its divine origin, the law is obligatory on Israel only. Even idolatry, the constant butt of prophetic irony, is not regarded as a gentile sin (Deut. 4:19). Yet the Bible assumes the existence of a universal moral code that all peoples must observe. The talmudic sages, with their genius for legal detail and codification, speak of the seven Noachian laws (Sanh. 56a). Although the Bible does not specify the ethical principles incumbent upon all mankind, it is clear from various passages that murder, robbery, cruelty, and adultery are major crimes recognized as such by all human beings (Gen. 6:12, 13; 9:5; 20:3; 39:9; Amos 1:3ff.). It would thus appear that the Bible postulates an autonomous, basic human sense of wrongdoing, unless it is supposed that a divine revelation of law was vouchsafed to the early saints, such as assumed by the apocryphal and rabbinic literatures (and perhaps by Isa. 24:5). The Torah – which properly means "instruction," not "law" – does not, in the strict sense of the term, contain a properly formulated code; nevertheless, detailed regulations appertaining to religious ritual, as well as to civil and criminal jurisprudence, form an essential part of pentateuchal teaching. The halakhic approach is reinforced by a number of the prophets. For instance, Isaiah (58:13), Jeremiah (34:8ff.), Ezekiel (40ff.), and Malachi (1:8; 2:10) lent their authority to the maintenance of various religious observances. Ezra and Nehemiah rebuilt the restored Jewish community on Torah foundations. Yet paradoxically the Bible also evinces a decidedly "anti-halakhic" trend. In Isaiah the Lord cries: "What to Me is the multitude of your sacrifices… I have had enough of burnt offerings of rams and the fat of fed beasts… who requires of you this trampling of My courts?… Your new moons and your appointed feasts My soul hates… When you spread forth your hands, I will hide My eyes from you; even though you make many prayers, I will not listen" (1:11–15). Jeremiah not only belittles the value of the sacrifices (7:22); he derides the people's faith in the Temple itself: "The temple of the Lord, the temple of the Lord, the temple of the Lord are these" (7:4). Even the Book of Psalms, though essentially devotional in character, makes an anti-ritual protest: "I do not reprove you for your sacrifices… I will accept no bull from your house… For every beast of the forest is Mine, the cattle on a thousand hills… If I were hungry, I would not tell you; for the world and all that is in it is Mine. Do I eat the flesh of bulls, or drink the blood of goats?" (50:8–13). These and similar passages represent a negative attitude towards established cultic practices. No less inconsonant with Torah law seems the positive prophetic summary of human duty formulated by Micah (6:8): "He has told you, O man, what is good; and what does the Lord require of you but to do justice, and to love lovingkindness, and to walk humbly with your God?" A similar note is sounded by Hosea (2:21–22 [19–20]): "I will espouse you with righteousness and with justice, with steadfast love, and with mercy. I will espouse you with faithfulness; and you shall be mindful of the Lord"; by Amos (5:14): "Seek good, and not evil, that you may live"; and by Isaiah (1:17): "Learn to do good; seek justice, correct oppression; defend the fatherless, plead for the widow." The emphasis here is on moral and spiritual conduct; the ceremonial and ritualistic aspects of religion are conspicuously left unmentioned. The paradox, however, is only one of appearance and phrasing. Inherently there is no contradiction. The ostensibly antinomian statements do not oppose the offering of sacrifices, prayer, or the observance of the Sabbath and festivals. It is not ritual but hypocrisy that they condemn. Isaiah (1:13) expresses the thought in a single phrase: "I cannot endure iniquity and solemn assembly." Organized religion must necessarily have cultic forms; but without inwardness and unqualified sincerity they are an affront to the Deity and fail of their purpose. The underlying motive of the precepts is to purify and elevate man (Ps. 119:29, 40, 68). The Torah (Wisdom) is a tree of life and its ways are ways of peace (Prov. 3:17, 18). Sin does not injure God (Job 7:20), but is a disaster to man (Deut. 28:15 ff.). It is heartfelt devotion that saves the *mitzvah* from becoming a meaningless convention and an act of hypocrisy (Isa. 29:13). The specific commandments are in a sense pointers and aids to that larger identification with God's will that is conterminous with life as a whole: "In all your ways acknowledge Him" (Prov. 3:6). Just as the divine wonders and portents lead to a deeper understanding of the daily miracles of providence, so the precepts are guides to the whole duty of man. Biblical religion is thus seen to be an indivisible synthesis of moral and spiritual principles, on the one hand, and practical observances on the other.

The Biblical Theodicy

The moral basis of providence, reinforced by the ethic of the Torah, also raises another kind of problem. Can the biblical theodicy always be justified? The issue is raised already in the Bible itself. Abraham challenges the divine justice: "Shall not the Judge of all the earth do right?" (Gen. 18:25). Moses echoes the cry in another context: "O Lord, why hast Thou done evil to this people?" (Ex. 5:22). The prophets are no less perplexed: "Why does the way of the wicked prosper? Why do all who are treacherous thrive?" (Jer. 12:1). The psalmist speaks for the individual and the nation in many generations, when he cries: "My God, my God, why hast Thou forsaken me?" (22:2[1]), and the Book of Job is, in its magnificent entirety, one great heroic struggle to solve the problem of unwarranted human suffering. The biblical answer appears to point to the limitations of man's experience and understanding. History is long, but individual life is short. Hence the human view is fragmentary; events justify themselves in the end, but the person concerned does not always live to see the denouement. In the words of the psalmist: "Though the wicked sprout like grass and all evildoers flourish, they are doomed to destruction forever" (92:8–10; cf. 37:35–39). The brevity of man's years is further complicated by his lack of insight. God's purpose is beyond his comprehension: "For as the heavens are higher than the earth, so are My ways higher than your ways and My thoughts than your thoughts" (Isa. 55:9). In the final analysis, biblical theodicy calls for faith: "But the righteous shall live by his faith" (Hab. 2:4); "they who wait for the Lord shall renew their strength" (Isa. 40:31). It is not an irrational faith: – *Certum est quia impossibile est* (Tertullian, *De Carne Christi*, 5), but is necessitated by innate human intellectual limitations. In another direction the problem is even more formidable. God, the Bible states categorically, hardened Pharaoh's heart; nevertheless the Egyptian ruler was punished for this. Indeed his obduracy was induced in order to provide the occasion for his punishment (Ex. 7:3). Here the fundamental norms of justice by any standards are flagrantly violated. The explanation in this sphere of biblical theodicy is not theological but semantic. Scripture ascribes to God phenomena and events with which He is only indirectly concerned. However, since God is the author of all natural law and the designer of history, everything that occurs is, in a deep sense, His doing. Even in human affairs the king or the government is said to "do" everything that is performed under its aegis. Thus God declares in Amos 4:7: "And I caused it to rain upon one city, and I caused it not to rain upon another city," although the next clause uses passive and impersonal verbal forms to describe the same occurrences. The processes of nature need not be mentioned, since the laws of the universe are dictates of God. Similarly Exodus states indiscriminately that "Pharaoh hardened his heart" (8:28), that "the heart of Pharaoh was hardened" (9:7), and that "the Lord hardened the heart of Pharaoh" (9:12). In the end it is all one; what God permits He does. This interpretation does not, however, fit another area of divine conduct. Uzzah, the Bible states, was struck dead for an innocent act that was motivated by concern for the safety of "the ark of God" (II Sam. 6:6–7). Wherein lay the iniquity? Here the reason appears to be of a different character. Even innocent actions may in certain circumstances be disastrous. Uzzah's attempt to save the ark from falling was well meant, but it was conducive to irreverence. Man needs God's help; God does not require the help of man (Sot. 35a; for a similar thought cf. Ps. 50:12; another explanation is given by Kimḥi, II Sam. 6:6). In one thoughtless moment Uzzah could have reduced the sacred ark in the eyes of the people to the impotent level of the idols, which the prophets depicted with such scathing mockery. The same principle operated in the tragedy of Nadab and Abihu, and Moses explained the underlying principle in the words: "I will show Myself holy among those who are near Me" (Lev. 10: 1–3).

The Limitation of the Infinite God

Is the Godhead subject to restriction? The irresistible conclusion to be drawn from biblical teaching is that such a limitation exists. Man's freedom to resist or obey the will of God is a restriction of the Deity's power that is totally unknown in the physical universe. It must be added, however, that this restriction is an act of divine self-limitation. In His love for man God has, so to speak, set aside an area of freedom in which man can elect to do right or wrong (Deut. 5:26; 30:17). In rabbinic language: "Everything is in the power of Heaven except the reverence of Heaven" (Ber. 33b). Man is thereby saved from being an automaton. It adds a new dimension to the relationship between God and man. Man may defect, but when, on the other hand, he chooses the path of loyalty, he does so from choice, from true love. Needless to say, without such freedom there could be neither sin nor punishment, neither merit nor reward. The divine humility, which permits human dissent, is also the grace to which the dissenter succumbs in the end. Man is a faithful rebel, who is reconciled with his Maker in the crowning period of history. God's self-limitation is thus seen as an extension of His creative power. Other biblical concepts that might be construed as restrictions of God's infinitude are, on closer scrutiny, seen not to be real limitations. The association of the Lord with holy places like the Tent of Meeting, the Temple, Zion, or Sinai does not imply that He is not omnipresent. In prophetic vision Isaiah saw the divine train fill the Temple, and at the same time he heard the seraphim declare: "the whole earth is full of His glory" (6: 1–3). God's geographical association, or His theophany at a given place, signifies consecration of the site, which thus becomes a source of inspiration to man; but no part of the universe exists at any time outside God's presence. Sometimes God is depicted as asking man for information (Gen. 3:9; 4:9). On other occasions He is stated to repent His actions and to be grieved (Gen. 6:6). These are mere anthropomorphisms. The Lord knows all (Jer. 11:20; 16:17; Ps. 7:10), and unlike human beings He does not repent (Num. 23:19). Genesis 6:6 is not a contradiction of this thesis; its "human" terminology does not imply a diminution of God's omniscience, but emphasizes the moral freedom granted to man. In addition to spiritual option, the Creator, as has been stated, gave man knowledge. This finds expression, inter alia, in magical powers, which, in as much as they are "supernatural," constitute a challenge to God's will. In Moses' protracted struggle with Pharaoh, the Egyptians actually pit their magical powers against the Almighty's miracles. In the end they acknowledge their relative weakness and admit that they cannot rival "the finger of God" (Ex. 8:15). This is to be expected, for the divine wisdom is unbounded (Job 11:7), whereas human understanding is finite. Nevertheless the use of all forms of sorcery, even by non-Israelites, is strongly denounced (Isa. 44:25); to the Israelite, witchcraft is totally forbidden (Deut. 18:10–11). The differentiation between magic and miracles had deep roots in Hebrew monotheism. To the pagan mind magical powers were independent forces to which even the gods had to have recourse. The miracle, on the other hand, is regarded in the Bible as a manifestation of God's power and purpose. It is an attestation of the prophet's mission (Isa. 7:11); whereas divination and sorcery are either forms of deception (Isa. 44:25) or, where magic is effective, as in the episode of the witch of Endor (I Sam. 28:7ff.), it represents an abuse of man's God-given knowledge. There is no independent realm of witchcraft, however; all power, natural and supernatural, emanates from the one God. To the Israelite all that happens is wrought by God.

The Divine Personality

Though inconceivable, God is portrayed throughout the Bible as a person. In contradistinction to the idols, who are dead, He is called the living God (II Kings 19:4, 16). He is neither inanimate nor a philosophical abstraction; He is the living source of all life. Anthropomorphisms abound in the Bible, but it is not by these that the divine personality, so to speak, is depicted. Anthropomorphic figures were intended to help early man to grasp ideas that in philosophical terms transcended the human intellect. God's essential personality is primarily reflected in His attributes, which motivate His acts. He is King, Judge, Father, Shepherd, Mentor, Healer, and Redeemer – to mention only a few of His aspects in His relationship to man. Different biblical teachers conceived God's character from different historical angles. Amos was conscious of God's justice. Hosea underscored the Lord's love, and made forgiveness and compassion the coefficient, as it were, of divinity: "I will not execute My fierce anger… for I am God and not man" (11:9). Ezekiel stresses that God does not desire the destruction of the wicked but that through repentance they may live (18:23). The heart of the matter is clearly stated in the Torah: "The Lord passed before him (Moses), and proclaimed, 'The Lord, the Lord, a God merciful and gracious, slow to anger, and abounding in steadfast love and faithfulness, keeping steadfast love for thousands, forgiving iniquity and transgression and sin, but who will by no means clear the guilty…" (Ex. 34:6–7). Maimonides was philosophically justified in insisting that God has no attributes and that the epithets applied to Him in the Bible really represent human emotions evoked by His actions (*Guide*, 2:54). The Bible, however, which is little interested in the speculative approach to the Deity, but teaches practical wisdom and religion as life, without the help of catechism or formulated dogmas, prefers to endow God with personality to which it gives the warmth and beauty of positive characterization. In sum, the divine nature is composed of both justice and love. The Bible recognizes that without justice love itself becomes a form of injustice; but in itself justice is not enough. It can only serve as a foundation; the superstructure – the bridge between God and man – is grace.

Between Man and God

Grace is the divine end of the bridge; the human side is existential devotion. Otherwise, what M. Buber felicitously called the "I-Thou" relationship cannot come into being. Hence, underlying all the commandments is the supreme precept: "And you shall love the Lord your God with all your heart, and with all your soul, and with all your might" (Deut. 6:5). This love is unqualified: "You shall be whole-hearted with the Lord your God" (Deut. 18:13). It calls for complete surrender; but this is not conceived as a narrow, if intense, religious attitude. It is broad-based enough to allow for deep-rooted spiritual communion. Man pours out his heart in prayer to God; it is to Him that he uplifts his soul in thanksgiving and praise; and it is also to Him that he addresses his most searching questions and most incisive criticism of life and providence. Sincere criticism of God is never rebuked. God reproaches Job's friends, who were on His side; but Job is rewarded despite his searing indictment of God's actions. The God-man relationship flowers in an evolutionary process of education: Man is gradually weaned from his own inhumanity, from atrocities, like human sacrifice (Gen. 22:2–14), from bestial conduct, and from wronging his fellowman. The goal again is love: "You shall love your neighbor as yourself" (Lev. 19:18). It is a corollary of the love of God: "I am the Lord." Reward and retribution play a role in the divine educational procedures; but their functions are limited – they are not ultimates. The eternal fires of hell are never used as a deterrent, though punishment of the wicked after death is obscurely mentioned (Isa. 66:24; Dan. 12:2), nor is paradise used as an inducement. The Torah-covenant is an unquenchable spiritual light (Prov. 6:23); but the "I-Thou" relationship does not end with the written word. God communes with man directly. The prophet hears the heavenly voice and echoes it; the psalmist knows, with unfaltering conviction, that his prayer has been answered and that salvation has been wrought before he actually experiences it. At one with God, man finds ultimate happiness: "In Thy presence is fullness of joy, in Thy right hand bliss for evermore" (Ps. 16:11).

The Hebrew term for the love that binds man to God (as well as to his fellowman) is *ʾahavah*; but sometimes the Bible uses another word, *yirʾah* (literally: "fear"), which seems to turn the "I-Thou" nexus into an "It" relationship. The psalmist declares: "The fear of the Lord is the beginning of wisdom" (111:10), and Ecclesiastes comes to the conclusion: "The end of the matter; all has been heard. Fear God, and keep His commandments, for this is the whole duty of man" (12:13). The picture is thus completely changed. The heavenly Father suddenly becomes a divine tyrant, before whom man cowers in terror, as does the unenlightened pagan before the demonic force that he seeks to appease. This might be consonant with the notion of "the jealous God" (Ex. 34:14), but it would appear to be irreconcilable with the concept of the God of *ḥesed* ("lovingkindness," "grace"). Here, too, this is not a theological but a semantic problem. *Yirʾah* does not signify "fear"; it is best rendered by "reverence." "Love" and "reverence" are not antithetic but complementary terms. They are two aspects of a single idea. *ʾAhavah* expresses God's nearness; *yirʾah* the measureless distance between the Deity and man (see *Love, Love and Fear of God). God spoke to Moses "mouth to mouth" (Num. 12:8), yet in his human frailty the Hebrew leader could not "see" his divine interlocutor (Ex. 33:20). The inner identity of "love" and "reverence" is reflected in the Torah's religious summary: "And now, Israel, what does the Lord your God require of you but to revere the Lord your God, to walk in all His ways and to love Him, and to serve the Lord your God with all your heart and with all your soul" (Deut. 10:12). Talmudic Judaism (Shab. 120a) drew a distinction between *ḥasidut* (steadfast love of God) and *yirʾat shamayim* ("reverence of Heaven"), but this represents a later development. In the Bible this bifurcation does not exist; "reverence of God" is by and large the biblical equivalent of "religion."

Likewise there is no spiritual contradiction between the "gracious" and the "jealous" God. "Jealousy" is an anthropomorphic term used to define God's absolute character, which excludes all other concepts of the Godhead. It does not detract from the divine love and compassion; it serves only to protect them. The sum of all the divine attributes finds expression in the epithet "holy." It is the highest praise that prophet and psalmist can give to the Lord (Isa. 6:3; Ps. 22:4[3]), and since man is created in the image of God (Gen. 1:26), the attribute of holiness becomes the basis of the concept of "the imitation of God": "You shall be holy; for I the Lord your God am holy" (Lev. 19:2). The Bible makes it clear, however, that, in seeking to model himself on the divine example, it is primarily God's moral attributes that man must copy. Even as God befriends the sojourner and acts as the father of the fatherless and as the judge of the widow, so must man, on his human scale, endeavor to do (Deut. 10:18–19; cf. Sot. 14a). Indeed all that uplifts man, including the Sabbath and abstention from impurity, is comprised in the concept of the imitation of God. At the highest level Israel's ethic and theology are indissolubly linked.

To sum up: The biblical conception of God was revolutionary both in its theological and its moral implications. The pagan world may occasionally have glimpsed, in primitive form, some of the higher truths inherent in Israel's ethical monotheism. Egypt for a brief span attained to monolatry (Akhenaton's heresy); Babylon had a glimmering of a unified cosmic process; Marduk, Shamash, and Aton punished evildoers; and some Greek philosophers commended the imitation of the godhead. Yet no cult in antiquity even remotely approached the elevated conceptions associated with the one God of the Bible. This spiritual revolution not only eventually brought paganism to an end, but its inner dynamic gave birth, in time, to two daughter religions, Christianity and Islam, which, despite their essential differences from Judaism, are deeply rooted in biblical thought.

[Israel Abrahams]

IN HELLENISTIC LITERATURE

Certain Jewish concepts of God were apparently known to the circle of Aristotle. His pupil Theophrastus (fourth century B.C.E.) said of the Jews that they were "the philosophers among the Syrians," because of their concept of the unity of God. The skeptic *Hecataeus of Abdera, the first of the Greek thinkers to attempt to define the substance of the Jewish concept of God, states that the Jews do not give form or image to God, because they regard the cosmos – which includes everything – as God. Their idea of the unity of God, according to Hecataeus, includes all existing things. Megasthenes, a Greek writer of the early third century, also notes that the important philosophers, outside of Greece, were the wise men of Israel. He arrived at this conclusion because of the fact that the unity of God was an accepted idea in Israel. Thus the Greek thinkers regarded the Jewish notion of divine unity as a view founded upon philosophic meditation in the spirit of the ideas common in their own circles, and in the spirit of the Ionian monists.

However, the primary quality of God according to Jewish teachings – ethical personalism – was not considered by the Greek writers. This idea of God's ethical will, which is beyond the universe and beyond nature and has absolute dominion over nature and over man, was far from the Greek mode of thought. Strangely no signs of influence of the Greek concept of God's unity are found in the early Jewish compositions in

Greek. In the Septuagint, for instance, there is a recognizable tendency to avoid anthropomorphism (e.g., "And they saw the God of Israel" (Ex. 24:10) is translated as: "And they saw the place where the God of Israel stood"). This tendency, however, has deep roots in the Jewish concepts of God during the period of the Second Temple, which found expression in the abstention from uttering the Tetragrammaton or in applying to God terms taken from everyday usage. This should not be regarded as intentional avoidance of anthropomorphism, as there are no signs of such avoidance in the Bible. It rather expresses a reverence for the majesty of God, which compelled the choosing of special expressions relating to divine matters. In any event the Septuagint contains no trace of the terms or linguistic usages current in Greek philosophic literature. All those terms to which the philosophers gave a special abstract connotation, such as Nous ("Mind"), Cosmos ("Universe"), Psyche ("Divine Soul"), occur in the Septuagint not in their abstract philosophical sense but in their normal concrete daily usage. Even in the apocryphal Wisdom of Solomon – a book undoubtedly influenced by Greek philosophy – the concepts of God are no different from those found in the Bible. Although the author of the Wisdom of Solomon praises the value of Wisdom in his book and regards it as a sort of partner in the creation of the world, this idea does not in the slightest detract from the concept of the unity of God for God is the Creator of the world, and Wisdom is not regarded as an independent or separate entity from God. The moral value of Wisdom in the life of man is particularly stressed as a force which refines the spirit of man and elevates him to a higher intellectual moral level. In so doing the author reduces the importance of Wisdom as a cosmic force. Man, according to the Wisdom of Solomon, seeks a personal closeness with God; God reveals Himself by signs and wonders in the history of the Jewish nation and by utilizing reward and punishment. All this accords with what is found in the Bible. Yet in contrast to the later Jewish view, the author of the Wisdom of Solomon regards God as a creator from existent material (not *ex nihilo*) as in the doctrine of matter and form found in Plato. The philosopher *Aristobulus of Paneas (first half of second century B.C.E.) already clearly expressed his opposition to anthropomorphism, and explains such expressions as "the hand of God," or "the voice of God" allegorically (see *Allegory) as the power of God, the expression of God's power of dominion in the world, etc. In the teaching of Aristobulus there is already a clear attempt to make the Jewish view of God correspond to the teaching of the Greek philosophers, even though it is difficult to determine to which school of philosophy Aristobulus himself belonged. The author of the Letter of *Aristeas too was influenced by Greek philosophy. God rules over all creatures and all are dependent upon Him, while He himself is not dependent upon any creature. The author of the Letter of Aristeas lays down that all men are aware of the unity of God as the Creator of everything, the director of everything, and the ruler over everything, but different peoples designate Him by different names (Letter of Aristeas 16). The name of the chief god current among the Greeks, Zeus, indicates his character as the source of life in nature and it too therefore is nothing else but a term for the one God.

Philo

The influence of Greek philosophy is especially strong on *Philo. Philo, under the influence of Plato, frequently uses for God the terms τό ὄν, τό ὄν ὄντως which in the teaching of Plato signify "existence" or "true existence" (see Timaeus, 27D–29D). Philo points to a basis for these in the expression "I am that I am" (cf. Som. 1:230–31, Ex. 3:14). There is no hint of such terminology in the Septuagint (the sentence used by the Septuagint for "I am that I am" has no connection with the above-mentioned terms used by Plato and Philo). Philo also uses such terms as "the one," "unity," etc., for the purpose of stressing God's transcendence over perfection, over all concepts of the good and the beautiful, and for His being above human comprehension. Such a degree of philosophic abstraction in the conception of God rules out any possibility of personal relations between man and God, examples of which are found in the Bible and the later literature. However as a Jew Philo was unable to content himself with mere abstraction, and he frequently raises the question of the relations of man to God, particularly on the methods by which man can come to apprehend God. Apprehension of God is possible, according to Philo, from two aspects: that of His existence, and that of His subsistence. A conception of God's existence can be achieved without great difficulty, since His works testify to this: the universe, man, and all other creatures.

However many aberrations occur in such a conception, since many people do not distinguish the ruler of the world from the powers subject to him; these people are compared to one who ignores the chariot driver and thinks that the horses are directing the movement toward the goal with their own powers; in such a manner the distorted concepts of God current in the circles of idolaters are created. Philo battled with exceptional vehemence against the views of those who regard the various heavenly powers or other hidden forces as independent active causes. It is his opinion that sound human intelligence has the power to avoid such aberrations in the understanding of God and this was achieved, according to Philo, by the greatest of the Greek philosophers whose names he mentions with much respect. However, this recognition of God's existence founded upon contemplation of the material world is very far from perfect, since it judges the uncreated from the created, whereas it is impossible to judge the reality of God by the creatures He created. A more perfect apprehension of God's reality is attained by those who "apprehended him through Himself, the light through the light." This was achieved only by the few intimates of God who are in no need of external analogies as aids to the apprehension of God. This type of person is called by Philo, "Israel," i.e., according to his etymology, "seers of God" (Praem. 43 ff.). This level of understanding of the Divine existence was attained by Moses. The conceptual level of apprehension of the Divine existence is the highest that a mortal can attain. For as a result of the frailty of human nature man does not possess the power to apprehend anything of the nature of the Divine. Even the sharpest vision is not capable of seeing Him who was not created, since man possesses no instrument which could prepare him to apprehend His image, and the most man can attain is the apprehension that the nature of God is not within the bounds of human apprehension. Nevertheless the attempt at such apprehension is not in vain. For even though the results of such effort will always be negligible, the effort itself elevates man and lifts him to a high degree of spiritual purity. Examples of such endeavor by man to apprehend the Divine nature are described in Philo's writings. After human intellect investigates everything to be found on earth, it turns to the contemplation of heavenly causes and partakes of their harmonious motion. From there it rises to the sphere of the intelligibles and at the time it contemplates the ideas of sensible things and absorbs their spiritual splendor, "a sober intoxication" (νηφάλια μέθη) assails it and elevates it to the level of prophecy. With a spirit full of supramundane yearnings it is elevated to the highest level of the intelligible world and already beholds itself approaching the King Himself in His glory. Now, however, when the craving for vision is greatest, dazzling beams of abounding light pour themselves over it and the brilliance of their glitter dims the eye of reason (Op. 69–72; Praem. 36f.). The impossibility of direct contact between God's nature and the sensible world created the concept of duality in Philo's understanding of the world, a concept much influenced by Plato. According to this view it does not become the majesty and elevation of God to be in direct contact with matter, and the forces within God or the activities overflowing from him fulfill the function of the intermediaries. The great gap between the sublime God and the perceptible world is bridged in Philo's teaching by the idea of level and intermediaries which serve as a connection between the absolute being of God and the changing level of the perceptible world. Angel, Idea, Logos – are the terms utilized by Philo to formulate the principles of the theory of levels whose influence upon subsequent religious thought was enormous.

[Joshua Gutmann]

IN TALMUDIC LITERATURE

Abstract philosophical concepts, such as are found in Philo, are foreign to the thought system of the rabbis of the Talmud and Midrash. However, a marked tendency is discernible among them to present an exalted picture of God, as well as to avoid expressions that could throw the slightest shadow on the conception of His absolute Oneness. In the *Targums, the early Aramaic translations of Scripture, the name God is frequently rendered "*memra* ('word') of God." It is certain that no connection whatsoever is intended between this word and the "logos," or with the idea of an intermediary between God and the world. Were this the intention, the word "*memra*" would have been used in the Targum to such verses as: "The Lord sent a word unto Jacob" (Isa. 9:7); "so shall My word be that goeth forth out of My mouth" (*ibid.* 55:11); "He sent His word and healed them" (Ps. 107:20). It is precisely in these verses that the Targum employs the word *pitgam* ("word") or *nevu'ah* ("prophecy"). Even in the verse "By the word of the Lord were the heavens made" (Ps. 33:6) "word" is rendered by the Targums as *milta* ("word") of God. Nor is there any mention of the expression "*memra*" in the Targums of the account of creation. It is therefore certain that this word, which occurs only in the Targums, but not in the Talmud and the Midrash, was used only to guard against any idea which (in the minds of the common people for whom the Targum was intended) might militate against the exalted conception of the Divinity or tend to diminish the pure concept of God. For the same reason one finds many euphemisms employed as substitutes for the names of God, such as *Ha-Gevurah* ("Might"), *Raḥmana* ("the Merciful"), *Ha-Kadosh Barukh Hu* ("The Holy One, blessed be He"), or such terms as *Shamayim* ("Heaven"), *Ha-Makom* ("Omnipresent"), *Ribbono shel Olam* ("Lord of the Universe"), *Mi-she-Amar ve-Hayah ha-Olam* ("He who spoke, and the Universe came into being"), *Avinu she-ba-Shamayim* ("Our Father in heaven"), *Mi she-Shikken Shemo ba-Bayit ha-Zeh* ("He who caused His name to dwell in this house"). A special significance was given by the rabbis to the tetragrammaton, and to *Elohim*, the tetragrammaton denoting the attribute of mercy, and *Elohim*, that of judgment (Gen. R. 33:3). That this was a time-honored distinction is evident from its occurrence in Philo where, however, in conformity with the tradition of the Septuagint to translate the tetragrammaton by the Greek word κύριος which corresponds more closely to the concepts of rule and judgment, the name is regarded as the symbol of the attribute of judgment, and the name *Elohim* (translated in the Septuagint by θεός) as a symbol of the attribute of mercy. The idea of the unity of God, which was widely discussed in non-Jewish circles at the time, receives strong emphasis in the *aggadah*. The concept of the unity of God is based upon the premise that the cosmos, with all its activities, is inconceivable without the existence of a single power which determines and directs it in accordance with a preordained plan and in conformity with a definite purpose. In order to give concrete expression to this idea, the rabbis of the *aggadah* utilized various parables, whose prototypes are found in Philo. They were particularly fond of the parable of "the ship and the captain," or of "the building and its owner," or of "the building and its director" (Sif. Deut. 341; Gen. R. 12:12; Mid. Ps. 23 to 24:1ff.; Gen. R. 39:1). Just as it is impossible for the ship, for example, to reach its destination without a captain, so administration of the cosmos and of individuals is impossible without a directing and supervising force. Other parables frequently found in the *aggadah* were intended to bring about reverence for the might of God, whose awesomeness is rendered even greater for the very reason that it defies man's powers of comprehension. If the brilliance of the sun blinds the human eye, how much more so the light of God (Ḥul. 59b). Man is unable to observe more than a particle of His grandeur and sublimity. The rabbis of the *aggadah* also use the soul as an example in teaching this doctrine. If a man's own soul, the source of his life, is beyond his intellectual comprehension, how much less can he comprehend the Creator of the universe and the source of its life (Mid. Ps. to 103:1; Lev. R. 4:3).

The recognition of the oneness of God is regarded by the scholars of the Talmud as a cardinal principle of religion, concerning which mankind as a whole was commanded, the seven precepts binding upon Noachians including idolatry (see *Noachide Laws).

If there is any difference between the biblical concept of God and that of the Talmud it lies in the fact that the God of the Talmud is more "homey," so to speak, than the God of the Bible. He is nearer to the masses, to the brokenhearted, to the ordinary person in need of His help. Only in this sense, does He at times appear to be an even greater epitomization of ethical virtues than the God of Scripture.

One finds no echo in the *aggadah* of the arguments for and against idolatry, such as occur in the Greek literature of that period. The *aggadah*'s attacks on idolatry are much more extreme than those of the biblical period, the dominant note being one of contempt and disdain for those who presume to desecrate in a degrading and crude manner that which is most holy in human life – the service of God. In the course of their violent attacks on idolatry, the rabbis did not shrink from denouncing with equal vehemence the cult of emperor-worship, a type of idolatry for which Nimrod, Sisera, Sennacherib, Hiram, and Nebuchadnezzar served as the prototypes.

In apocalyptic circles, among those who expounded *Merkabah mysticism and those who entered *paradise, there is no discernible variation from the aggadic concept of God, the restrictions that the scholars of the Talmud placed upon the study of the esoteric doctrine of the *Ma'aseh Merkavah* and upon those of whom it was said that they "entered paradise" having a great deal to do with this. Despite this there were many in these circles "who looked and became demented," or "who cut down the saplings" (i.e., led astray the youth). The Talmud applied to them the term **minim* ("sectarians"), a term which also included Christians, Gnostics, and other sectarians, whom the rabbis regarded either as complete disbelievers (Sif. Deut. 32, 39) or as rejecting the oneness of God. Regardless of whether these sectarians were Jews or whether they wished to identify themselves with them, the rabbis made every effort to exclude them from the fold, at times taking drastic measures to do so. The reaction of the rabbis to the varying concepts of God that were widespread in their time was thus characterized by exceptional vigilance. Even more significant, however, was the complete absence, in their doctrine of the Deity, of any materialistic elements. Though, according to the rabbis, angels play an important role in the lives of human beings, this does not in the least affect the closeness of God to every person in his daily life: "When trouble comes upon a man, he does not burst upon his patron suddenly, but goes and stands at his door… and he calls his servant who announces: 'so and so is at the door'.… Not so, however with regard to the Holy One, blessed be He. If trouble comes upon a man, he should cry out neither to Michael nor to Gabriel, but let him cry out to me, and I shall answer him immediately" (TJ, Ber. 9:1, 13a).

The nearness of God is the predominating idea of the Talmud and Midrash. God mourns because of the evil decrees He has pronounced upon Israel; He goes into exile with His children; He studies Torah and gives His view on halakhic topics, and is overjoyed if the scholars triumph over him in *halakhah*. Every generation of Israel has been witness to the nearness of God. God revealed Himself at the Red Sea as a warrior; at Sinai as a sage filled with mercy; after the incident of the golden calf, as a congregational reader draped in a *tallit* ("prayer shawl"), instructing the people how to pray and repent. These metaphors are not intended anthropomorphically, but are rather devices for driving home the idea of God's nearness to his people, by the use of striking and daring images. The sages see no difference between God's closeness to Israel in the past and in the present. The idea of the selection of Israel and the greatness of its destiny stands, both in the past and in the present, at the very center of the relationship between God and His people, and complete confidence therefore exists that God will answer His people whenever they seek Him. The concept of God's nearness to man is also enshrined in the ethical teaching of the time, the rabbis enjoining man to imitate the attributes of God: "Just as He is merciful and compassionate, be thou too merciful and compassionate" (Mekh., be-Shallaḥ 14:2; Sifra 19:1).

[Yehoshua M. Grintz]

IN MEDIEVAL JEWISH PHILOSOPHY

Medieval Jewish philosophy concentrated very heavily on problems concerning the existence and nature of God, His knowability, and His relationship to man and the world. Neither the Bible nor rabbinic literature contain systematic philosophic treatments of these topics, and it was only under the stimulus of Greek and Arabic philosophy that Jews engaged in such inquiries. In natural philosophy, metaphysics, and theology Jewish thought was influenced by *Kalām thinkers and by Arabic versions of neoplatonism and Aristotelianism. Fundamental to Jewish philosophic speculation about God was the conviction that human reason is reliable (within its proper limits), and that biblical theology is rational. Most medieval Jewish philosophers considered intellectual inquiry essential to a religious life, and were convinced that there could be no real opposition between reason and faith. Thus, *Saadiah Gaon held that, "The Bible is not the sole basis of our religion, for in addition to it we have two other bases. One of these is anterior to it; namely, the fountain of reason…" (*Book of Beliefs and Opinions*, 3:10). *Baḥya ibn Paquda believed that it is a religious duty to investigate by rational methods such questions as God's unity, because, of the three avenues which God has given us to know Him and His law, "the first is a sound intellect" (*Ḥovot ha-Levavot*, introduction; cf. 1:3). Even *Judah Halevi, who distrusted philosophy, said, "Heaven forbid that there should be anything in the Bible to contradict that which is manifest or proved" (*Kuzari*, 1:67). This attitude toward the relationship between reason and faith dominated medieval Jewish philosophy. It reached its highest, most elaborate, and most familiar expression in the thought of *Maimonides, and was reaffirmed by later philosophers, such as *Levi b. Gershom and Joseph *Albo.

The Existence of God

The first task of philosophical theology is to prove the existence of God, though medieval philosophers did not always begin their treatises with this topic. Of the familiar philosophic arguments for the existence of God, the ontological argument, i.e., that God's existence follows necessarily from a definition of what He is, seems to have been unknown to medieval Jewish thought. Emphasis was placed on the cosmological argument, according to which the existence of God was derived from some aspect of the world, such as the existence of motion or causality. Some attention was also given to the teleological argument, according to which the existence of God was derived from order existing in the world.

TELEOLOGICAL ARGUMENT. The simplest form of the teleological argument, the argument from design, was used by Saadiah and Baḥya. Both derided those who claim that the world arose by chance without an intelligent and purposive creator. They pointed out the high improbability (in their view, incredibility) that the extremely complex and delicately balanced order of the universe could have come about accidentally, since even ordinary artifacts are known to require an artisan. A more sophisticated version of this argument was offered by Levi b. Gershom. From the teleological nature of all existing things, i.e., the fact (as he supposed) that each thing is moved toward the realization of its own proper end, he concluded that all things together move toward their common ultimate end. This is the final cause of the world, namely God.

COSMOLOGICAL ARGUMENT. In Saadiah's versions of the cosmological argument, following the Kalām closely, he deduced the existence of God from the creation of the world. He first demonstrated that the world must have been created in time out of nothing, and he then showed that such a world could only have been created by an omnipotent God whose essence is an absolute unity. Baḥya followed a similar method. His basic argument was that since the world is composite, it must have been put together at some point in time; it could not have made itself, because nothing can make itself; therefore, it must have been created, and the creator of the world we call God. The earliest Jewish philosopher to turn away from the Kalām in favor of a stricter Aristotelianism was Abraham *Ibn Daud, and the most prominent by far was Maimonides (see *Aristotle and Aristotelianism). In contrast to the followers of the Kalām, Maimonides rejected the view that proofs for the existence of God are contingent on proofs of the creation of the world. He showed that in principle one cannot prove either that the world is eternal or that it was created, but went on to argue that even if we grant the eternity of the world, we can still demonstrate the existence of God. The arguments he used, two of which had already been set forth in Abraham Ibn Daud's *Emunah Ramah*, are essentially cosmological. The most familiar of Maimonides' arguments is the argument from motion. Since things in the world are in motion and no finite thing can move itself, every motion must be caused by another; but since this leads to an infinite regress, which is unintelligible, there must be an unmoved mover at the beginning of the series. This unmoved mover is God. Another of Maimonides' arguments begins from the fact that the existence of all things in our experience is contingent, i.e., their existence begins and ends in time, so that each thing can be conceived as not existing. Contingent existence is unintelligible, unless there is at least one necessary existence, one being whose existence is eternal and independent of all cause, standing behind it. Maimonides laid great stress on the conception of God as necessary existence. This argument was the only one that Ḥasdai *Crescas found acceptable, though he was a severe critic of the Aristotelianism of his predecessors. In addition to other arguments, Saadiah and Judah Halevi offered a non-philosophical argument. Since the revelation at Sinai took place in the presence of 600,000 adults, there is public evidence that places the fact of God's existence beyond all reasonable doubt.

The Nature of God

For Judaism, the proof of God's existence is incomplete unless it also establishes His absolute unity. Though Jewish philosophers conceived this unity in different ways, none deviated from the fixed belief in God's unity. In reflecting on this question, practically all Jewish philosophers of the Middle Ages came to the conclusion that the unity of God necessarily implies that He must be incorporeal. This conclusion then required them to set forth figurative or metaphorical interpretations of the many biblical passages that ascribe bodily characteristics to God, because no proper philosophical understanding of God can accept a literal reading of these anthropomorphisms. As Abraham Ibn Daud pointed out, Jewish thinkers were particularly sensitive to this problem because many non-Jews held the slanderous opinion that the Jews believe in a corporeal God. Thus, it is understandable that medieval Jewish philosophers devoted much attention to arguments for God's incorporeality and the detailed exegesis of anthropomorphic passages in Scripture. Some scholars even suggest that the primary purpose of Saadiah's philosophical work was to refute all claims that God is corporeal. Maimonides began his *Guide of the Perplexed* with an elaborate and comprehensive effort to refute all literal interpretations of passages in the Bible that speak of God as having corporeal features.

Divine Attributes

Having rejected the literal meaning of biblical statements about God, the medieval philosophers had to determine what may be considered a legitimate description of God. Can attributes of God, such as goodness, mercy, wisdom, and justice be predicated of Him positively? The bulk of medieval opinion held that one cannot properly say anything positive about God, for two reasons. First, ascribing multiple attributes to Him compromises His unity. Second, human language reflects the limitations of the human perspective, so that describing God by way of human predicates reduces Him to the finiteness of man. Therefore, a majority of the medieval philosophers held that nothing positive can be said about God. However, since there is no choice but to talk about God in some way, despite the limitations of human language, they had to find some interpretation of the divine attributes which would not be a positive one. The most widely accepted solution was to understand all the essential attributes, such as living, wise, powerful, which describe the divine nature, as negative, so that every seemingly positive assertion about God only says what He is not. For example, the statement, "God is wise," can only mean that He is not ignorant. In this way one may speak of God's nature in the language of men without compromising His unity and without reducing Him to human form. Because God transcends all knowledge and all experience, one can only affirm that He exists and even this must be interpreted as negating that He lacks existence and describes what He is solely in terms of negative attributes. This view was held with minor variations by Saadiah, Baḥya, *Joseph ibn Ẓaddik, Judah Halevi, Ibn Daud, and Maimonides. Besides these descriptions of God's nature which were interpreted as negative attributes, there are others, such as merciful and just, which appear to describe what God does rather than what He is. These could also not be interpreted positively since such positive predication of these descriptions, too, could compromise God's unity. These descriptions were therefore interpreted as attributes of action, i.e., as describing God's effects without, however, attempting to account for a property in God which causes these effects. This non-positive predication of the attributes of action again safeguards divine unity. Maimonides gave the most subtle and comprehensive treatment to the problem of attributes. While holding rigorously to the negative interpretation of essential attributes, he also followed some of his predecessors in affirming the doctrine of attributes of action. Thus, a great calamity may be interpreted in human eyes as an expression of God's anger, and a seemingly miraculous rescue of men from danger will be understood as an instance of God's love and compassion. Two major figures of the late medieval period rejected the doctrine of negative attributes. Both Levi b. Gershom and Ḥasdai Crescas argued in favor of the view that if God is to be intelligible, His attributes must be understood as positive predications. They did not think that positive predication compromises the divine unity and perfection. Moreover, Levi b. Gershom believed that positive predicates could be applied to God literally because their primary meaning is derived from their application to God, while their human meaning is secondary. The position of Joseph Albo, the last of the medieval Jewish philosophers, is ambiguous. Although he affirmed the doctrine of negative attributes, he also tried to argue that the divine attributes have a descriptive-positive meaning.

Relation of God to Man and the World

In denying God's corporeality and in developing the doctrine of negative attributes, the philosophers went far toward protecting the unity of God. However in proclaiming this absolute metaphysical unity they also generated serious problems. If God is conceived as the metaphysical One, eternal, absolute, unique, and incomparable, how should His relationship to man and the world be understood? In every relation there is multiplicity, and in relations with the corporeal world there is also inescapable temporality. With respect to *creation the problem was often solved (or at least avoided) by invoking various forms of neoplatonic theories of emanation.

DIVINE PROVIDENCE. The issue was particularly acute with respect to the question of divine providence and God's relationship to man. To remain consistent with the Bible and rabbinic teaching, the philosophers had to affirm the doctrine of *reward and punishment and, thus, support the view that God knows and is concerned about individual human life and action. Yet, such a God seems to be a temporal, changing being, not the absolute, eternal One. In a most radical statement Maimonides asserted that, "the relation between us and Him, may He be exalted, is considered as non-existent" (*Guide of the Perplexed*, 1:56). Maimonides tempered this view, however, and developed a theory according to which God shows providence to the human species. God is removed from any direct involvement with individual animals or with inanimate objects: "For I do not by any means believe that this particular leaf has fallen because of a providence watching over it; nor that this spider has devoured this fly because God has now decreed and willed something concerning individuals" (*ibid.*, 3:17). Moreover, according to Maimonides, the providential care of man is totally dependent on the level of the individual's intellectual development. As the human intellect develops in its highest form, it is brought into progressively closer contact with the divine nature which overflows toward it; for the individual human intellect is only a particularization of the divine overflow. "Now if this is so, it follows necessarily… that when any human individual has obtained… a greater proportion of this overflow than others, providence will of necessity watch more carefully over him than over others… Accordingly, divine providence does not watch in an equal manner over all the individuals of the human species, but providence is graded as their human perfection is graded… As for the ignorant and disobedient, their state is despicable proportionately to their lack of this overflow, and they have been relegated to the rank of the individuals of all the other species of animals" (*ibid.*, 3:18). Maimonides solved the problem by making providence an extension of the divine nature in the perfected human intellect, and thus succeeded in preserving God's unity and eternity. Similar views were held by Levi b. Gershom and Abraham *Ibn Ezra. While the medieval Jewish philosophers succeeded in meeting the challenge of their intellectual environment, many Jews felt that in the process they had sacrificed the spiritual satisfactions of simple piety. As the French philosopher Pascal (17th century) once observed, the God of the philosophers is no substitute for the God of Abraham, Isaac, and Jacob. Many great Jewish teachers opposed such philosophical conceptions of God, because they felt that they robbed the Jew of his intimate relationship with a God who is loving and compassionate, as well as stern, judging, and commanding. In the centuries since the Middle Ages, Judaism has made room for both the God of the philosophers and the God who lives in the emotions and aspirations of simple, non-philosophical men.

[Marvin Fox]

IN KABBALAH

The kabbalistic view of God is in principle a derivation from the desire to abolish the contradiction between the two concepts: God's unity and God's existence. The emphasis of God's unity leads the philosopher to reject anything that could undermine that absolute unity – any attribute, determination, or quality that can be interpreted as an addition to His unity and as evidence for plurality. On the other hand, the emphasis on God's life which is characteristic of religious faith endangers His unity, since life is variegated by its very nature: it is a process and not a state. In the opinion of many kabbalists the divinity should be conceived of in the following two fundamental aspects:

(1) God in Himself who is hidden in the depths of His being;

(2) the revealed God who creates and preserves his creation.

For kabbalists these two aspects are not contradictory but complement one another. Regarding God Himself the first aspect suffices, and in the opinion of some (Moses *Cordovero, and the Chabad Ḥasidism), one could doubt whether from this point of view anything at all exists apart from God. It is precisely the second view, however, that is required by religious faith: namely, a revealed God who can be recognized by His action and revelation.

In terms of God Himself, He has neither a name nor an attribute and nothing can be said of Him except that He is. This absolute divinity is usually called in Kabbalah **Ein-Sof* ("the Infinite"). *Ein-Sof* lacks any attributes, even more than, if one may say so, does the God of Maimonides. From the sayings of some early kabbalists, it is apparent that they are careful not even to ascribe personality to God. Since He is beyond everything – beyond even imagination, thought, or will – nothing can be said of Him that is within the grasp of our thought. He "conceals Himself in the recesses of mystery"; He is "the supreme cause" or "the great existent" (in *Berit Menuḥah*, Amsterdam, 1648), appellations which contain a negation of the personal nature of God. There were also kabbalists, however, who wished to give a personality to *Ein-Sof*, though in their opinion too this personality was indefinable: according to them the *Ein-Sof* is *ba'al ha-raẓon*, "the possessor of will" (Menaḥem Azariah da *Fano), hence it is possible to say of Him, as do faithful pious Jews, "Blessed be He"; "May He be blessed and exalted," etc. Both these conceptions are met with in the pages of the *Zohar. In favor of the personal character of *Ein-Sof* weighed the argument that even without the existence of emanations, the *Sefirot*, and the worlds, His perfection would not lack anything, hence one should not think that God acquired personality through the emanation of the "attributes" or the *Sefirot*, which determine for us the personal character of God. It should be said that, in the opinion of all kabbalists the *Ein-Sof* is divinity itself, but some kabbalists doubt whether it is also "God." For the life of the *Ein-Sof* is concealed within itself and is not revealed, while the religious man seeks the revelation of this concealed life. This revelation comes through the emanation of the *Sefirot*, which are the domain of the life of the revealed God. This emanation is not a necessity, according to the nature of the *Ein-Sof*; it is a voluntary activity of the emanator.

The special difficulty in connection with this view is that according to kabbalistic doctrine the ten *Sefirot* or worlds of heavenly *Parẓufim* ("configurations," in the Lurianic Kabbalah) are not created regions distinct from the *Ein-Sof*, like other creations, but are included within the divine unity (see *Emanation). The *Sefirot* are also attributes (and some kabbalists explicitly identify them with the "attributes of action" of the philosophers) but in actual fact they are more than attributes: they are the various stages at which God reveals Himself at the time of creation; they are His powers and His names. Each quality is one facet of his revelation. Hence every name applied to the divine is merely one of these qualities: *Eheyeh, Yah, El, Elohim, Ẓeva'ot, Adonai* – each points to a special aspect in the revealed God, and only the totality of all these qualities exhausts the active life of God. It is this totality, its order, and its laws, in which the theology of the Kabbalah is fundamentally interested. Here the personality of God is manifested even if it is not developed: God revealed himself not only at Mt. Sinai; He revealed Himself in everything since the beginning of the creation, and will continue to reveal Himself until the end of time; His act in creation is His main revelation. From this position stems a certain dualism in the realm of the revelation of the divine: on the one hand there is *Ein-Sof* which is transcendental and its traces are not discernable in the creatures; yet on the other hand the traces of the living God, who is embodied in the world of the *Sefirot*, are found in everything and discernable in everything – at least to the mystic who knows how to interpret the symbolic language of outer reality. God is in His creation, just as He is outside of it. And if the *Sefirot*, active in the creation, are the "souls" and the inwardness of everything, then the *Ein-Sof* is the "soul of the souls." By the mere fact of being a creature, no creature is divine, though nevertheless something of the divine is revealed in it. The world of *Sefirot* then is the region of divine revelation per se, for the flow of divine life rises and descends in the stages of the *Sefirot*. The divine revelation emanates also upon the region of creation, through the "clothing" of the *Sefirot* in the mundane world.

In critical literature on Kabbalah opinions vary on the question to what extent the formulations of this fundamental standpoint are pantheistic. At various times a pantheistic view of God had been attributed in particular to the Zohar, to Moses Cordovero, and to Abraham *Herrera. Important in the theology of the Kabbalah is the new view of the divine presence, which is no longer a synonym for God Himself, but a name for the last *Sefirah* which is the passive and receptive element in God, although it is simultaneously active and emanating upon the creatures. The unity of God in the *Sefirot* is dynamic and not static and all explanations by kabbalists of the *Shema* ("Hear O Israel") testify to this: this is the unity of the stream of life flowing from the *Ein-Sof*, or, according to some opinions, from the will which is the first *Sefirah* (See *Kabbalah).

[Gershom Scholem]

IN MODERN JEWISH PHILOSOPHY

Moses Mendelssohn

Moses *Mendelssohn, the first modern Jewish philosopher, believed that, "Judaism knows nothing of a revealed religion in the sense in which Christians define this term." The truths of religion, particularly those that have to do with the existence and nature of God, are principles of reason and, as such, are available to all men. Through rational reflection we know that God exists, that He is a necessary and perfect being, creator of the world, omnipotent, omniscient, and absolutely good. These truths, which constitute the essential grounds of salvation, are the elements of a natural religion shared by all men. What is peculiarly Jewish is not religion at all, but only divine legislation, God's revealed law, which binds and obligates the Jewish people alone and is the necessary condition of their salvation. True religion, on the other hand, is universal. God has made known to all men, through reason, the essential and eternal truths about His nature and the world He created.

Solomon Formstecher

Solomon *Formstecher was especially indebted to the idealist philosopher *Schelling for the metaphysical foundations of his theology. He conceived God as the "world-soul," which is the ultimate ground of the unity of all reality. While nature is the open manifestation of God in the world of our experience, it is only as spirit that God can truly be conceived. His essence is beyond all human knowledge, and to restrict God to the necessarily anthropomorphic conceptions of man borders on paganism. Formstecher believed that the world-soul is not in the world, but is prior to and independent of it. God is an absolutely free spirit, whose freedom is most clearly evident in His activity as creator of the world. Because of His absolute freedom, God is understood as the ultimate ethical being and as the ideal that man should strive to imitate and realize in his own ethical life.

Samuel Hirsch

Samuel *Hirsch taught a doctrine similar to that of Formstecher, although he was more dependent on the philosophy of *Hegel. He emphasized the centrality of the ethical even more than Formstecher did. Man discovers his freedom in his own self-consciousness. He knows himself, not as part of nature, but as an "I" who stands in freedom over against the world. God is conceived, on this human model, as a being who is absolutely free and supreme in power over all that exists. Through the miracles that He performs, God exhibits to man His absolute power and freedom. For Hirsch, Judaism is, above all, the religion of the spirit. Its highest purpose is the actualization of human freedom in the ethical life, because only in free and moral acts does man truly serve God.

Solomon Ludwig Steinheim

Unlike most of his contemporaries, Solomon Ludwig *Steinheim thought that philosophy and religion are radically opposed. He held that the true knowledge of God can be acquired only through revelation, and that scriptural revelation contradicts the canons of human reason. If God is conceived in purely rational terms, then His freedom must necessarily be denied, because rationality entails causal necessity. The God of reason is subject to causal rules, since, even as first cause, He is limited to that which reason finds possible. Such a God is not absolutely free. Neither is He a true creator, for according to the principle that nothing comes from nothing, He could not have created the world freely and *ex nihilo*. Steinheim rejected reason in favor of revelation, denied the principle of causality, and represented God as the true and free creator who stands above the limitations of rational necessity. Only through such a theology does man become free. Freedom is possible for man only if he subordinates his reason to the God of revelation, whose creative freedom provides the sole ground of genuinely human existence.

Nachman Krochmal

Nachman *Krochmal, although living in Eastern Europe, was more fully Hegelian than his Western Jewish contemporaries. They modified the prevailing philosophy to accommodate the personal God of traditional Judaism, but Krochmal developed a doctrine which borders on pantheism. He conceived God as Absolute Spirit, containing in itself all reality. Absolute Spirit has none of the characteristics of a personal God. Even as cause, He is impersonal: He causes the world only in the sense that He is its totality. The world is derived from God through emanation, which Krochmal understood as a form of divine self-limitation. In this Krochmal was affected by kabbalistic doctrines, which he combined with Hegelianism.

Hermann Cohen

Three figures of major importance appeared in the late 19th and early 20th centuries, Hermann *Cohen, Franz *Rosenzweig, and Martin *Buber. In his early years Cohen thought of God as a philosophical construct that served as the guarantor of morality and moral progress. The existence of God, according to this conception, cannot be proved. He is beyond all positive descriptions, and is thought of only as an "idea" in the technical Kantian sense. Though His nature is absolutely unknown to us, God as idea is the one absolutely necessary ground of morality. His reality is affirmed because the alternative of denying morality cannot be accepted. In his later years Cohen adopted more traditional language as he became more deeply concerned for Judaism. He then spoke of God as the Creator, the God of love, and the source of all being, who is absolutely one and unique.

Franz Rosenzweig

In Rosenzweig's view, God is not known through philosophic inquiry or rational demonstration. He is met in direct existential encounter, which is true revelation. In the anguished consciousness of his own creaturely contingency, man encounters God, who is the creator of the world, and above all he encounters dependence. This meeting reveals God as an all-powerful and loving father. His love for man results in commandments that bind every individual for whom the divine-human encounter is a reality.

Martin Buber

Like Rosenzweig, Buber stressed, above all, the personal quality of God. He is the Eternal Thou, whom one meets as the supreme partner in dialogue. This is not the depersonalized God of the philosopher-theologian, whose nature is expressed in a set of formal propositions. Man knows Him only as the Ever-Present, who meets him in true encounter. No effort to give a consistent definition of God succeeds. "Of course God is the 'wholly Other'; but He is also the wholly Same, the wholly Present. Of course He is the *Mysterium Tremendum* that appears and overthrows; but He is also the mystery of the self-evident, nearer to me than my I" (*I and Thou* (1937), 79).

Mordecai Kaplan

In the United States Mordecai *Kaplan developed a naturalistic view of God in conscious opposition to the traditional, supernatural views. Convinced that modern science makes it impossible to believe in a transcendent, personal God, Kaplan nevertheless saw value in retaining the idea and the name "God." He conceived God simply as that power in nature which makes possible the fulfillment of man's legitimate aspirations. Despite his commitment to scientific naturalism, Kaplan believed that the world is so constituted that valid human ideals are supported and helped toward realization by the cosmic process. It is this force making for human salvation that Kaplan called God.

[Marvin Fox]

ATTRIBUTES OF GOD

The discussion in Jewish philosophy of the attributes or predicates (Heb. *te'arim*; Arab. *ṣifāt*) of God is based on the problem of how God, whose essence is presumed to be unknowable, can be spoken of in meaningful terms.

Philo

Philo was the first to introduce the doctrine of the unknowability of God, which he derived from the Bible (see C. Siegfried, *Philo* (1875), 203–4; H.A. Wolfson, *Philo*, 2 (1947), 86–90, 119–26). He interprets Moses' prayer, "Reveal Thyself to me" (according to the Septuagint version of Ex. 33:18) as a plea for a knowledge of God's essence, and God's answer as pointing out that only His existence, and not His essence, can be known (Wolfson, op. cit., 86–87). From God's unlikeness to any other being follows His simplicity, i.e., essential unity, indivisibility, and His being "without quality," i.e., without "accidents" such as inhere in corporeal objects, and without "form," such as inheres in matter. God belongs to no class. He is without genus or species, and consequently no concept can be formed of Him (*ibid.*, 97–110). The scriptural passages describing God in anthropomorphic and anthropopathic terms must, therefore, be understood as serving a merely pedagogical purpose. Since God's essence is unknowable, all the predicates of God in Scripture describe Him only by what is known of Him through the proofs of His existence, and they refer only to the causal relation of God to the world. Philosophical discussion of the problem of God's attributes gained new impetus under the influence of Muslim philosophy, especially the Kalām.

Kalām

The most elaborate Jewish Kalām discussion of attributes is found in Saadiah's *Emunot ve-De'ot* (*Book of Beliefs and Opinions*, tr. by S. Rosenblatt, 1948). Saadiah finds in Scripture the following attributes assigned to God: He is one, living, omnipotent, omniscient, and unlike any other being. His unity and incomparability follow logically from the notion of "Creator" (1:1), as do the notions of existence, omnipotence, omniscience. The latter three attributes do not imply diversity in God. Just as the attribute of "Creator" does not add anything to the essence of God, but merely expresses His causal relation to the world, so do these three attributes, which explain the term Creator, add nothing to His essence, but merely denote the existence of a world created by Him (1:4). It would seem to follow that these three attributes are active, not essential attributes, but this is not Saadiah's ultimate meaning. Since these attributes, when applied to God (unlike the case when they are applied to man) are not distinct from God's essence, Saadiah upholds positive essential attributes (existence, omniscience, omnipotence), but reduces their meaning to that of God's causality as Creator. He does, however, distinguish between these essential attributes and attributes of action. Attributes such as merciful, gracious, jealous, and avenging are attributes of action in the sense that they express a certain affection for the creatures produced by the causality of God (1:12).

Neoplatonism

Jewish neoplatonic writings are marked by a new emphasis on the unity of God. At the same time the notion of the will of God was injected into the discussion. The extant writings of Isaac *Israeli, the earliest Jewish neoplatonist, contain few references to the attributes (see A. Altmann and S.M. Stern, *Isaac Israeli* (1958), 151–8). Solomon ibn *Gabirol's views are more explicit. In his *Mekor Ḥayyim* and his poem *Keter Malkhut*, Ibn Gabirol emphasizes God's unity (*Mekor Ḥayyim*,

3:4; 5:30). Negative terms are used particularly with reference to the "mystery" (*sod*) of the divine unity, concerning which we do not know "what it is," but which may be described as unaffected by plurality or change, or by attribute (*to'ar*) and designation (*kinnui*). His negative interpretation of the divine attributes is, however, complicated by Ibn Gabirol's doctrine that matter and form, the two principles which constitute all created beings, derive from the essence and the will of God respectively. Matter (which is originally "spiritual" matter) proceeds from the very essence of God, and form is impressed upon, and diffused in matter by virtue of God's will. Ibn Gabirol's will tends to assume the character of an intermediate between God and the world and, in certain respects, shares in the divine absoluteness (*ibid.*, 5:37–9; 4:20). Baḥya ibn Paquda's elaborate treatment of the attributes in the "*Sha'ar ha-Yiḥud*" ("Chapter on Unity") of his *Ḥovot ha-Levavot* starts from the thesis that from the existence and order of the universe, the existence of one single creator can be inferred. Like Aristotle (*Metaphysics*, 5, 5, 1015b, 16–7), Baḥya distinguishes between the "accidental" and "absolute" senses of the term "one" and concludes that the truly One is God alone, who is incomparable and unique (1:8–9). Having established God's unity in the neoplatonic sense, Baḥya proceeds to discuss the meaning of the attributes, which may again be classified under two heads: essential attributes and attributes of action. The essential attributes are existence, unity, and eternity. They do not imply a plurality in God's essence, but must be interpreted negatively, i.e., God is not nonexistent; there is no plurality in Him; He is not a created thing. The attributes of action which describe God's actions either in anthropomorphic terms or in terms of corporeal motions and acts are used by Scripture in order to establish a belief in God in the souls of men (1:10), i.e., for pedagogical reasons.

Aristotelianism

In Jewish Aristotelianism the discussion of the divine attributes reached a new level, reflecting the influence of Avicenna and, subsequently, of *Averroes. The notion of God as the "necessary being" which was introduced by Avicenna, contested by al-*Ghazālī, and modified by Averroes, replaced, in some measure, the neoplatonic concept of the One. Moreover, the problem of the meaning of terms like "one" and "being" came to the fore, for even though these terms were predicated of God in a peculiar sense, they seemed also to bear a generic sense in which they were predicated of other beings as well. Al-*Fārābī held the notion that common terms of this kind are predicated of God "firstly" or "in a prior manner," and of other beings "secondly" or "in a posterior manner," i.e., that the perfections implied by the particular predicate derive from God as their cause or exemplar. According to Avicenna, the term "one" is predicated of God and other beings "in an ambiguous sense" (see H.A. Wolfson, in *Homenaje a Millás-Vallicrosa*, 2 (1956), 545–71), which implies the doctrine of the "analogy" of being (A.M. Goichon (tr.), *Ibn Sina, Livre des Directives et Remarques* (1951), 366–9, n. 2), a view which was not adopted by the first Jewish Aristotelians (Abraham ibn Daud and Maimonides), who substituted for it the notion of the purely homonymous character of these terms, that is that terms applied to God and other beings share only the name but not the meaning. Only under the influence of Averroes did the doctrine of the "analogy" of being eventually command the assent of Jewish Aristotelians (notably Levi b. Gershom, see below). Abraham Ibn Daud, in his *Emunah Ramah* (ed. by S. Weil (1852), 48–57), follows Avicenna in establishing the existence of God as "the necessary being" in the sense that God's essence necessarily implies His existence, while in the case of all other beings their existence is only "possible" and extrinsic to their essence. True unity is therefore established in the case of God alone by virtue of His intrinsic necessary existence. Ibn Daud enumerated seven positive attributes: unity, truth, existence, omniscience, will, omnipotence, and being. These neither imply definitions of God nor constitute a plurality in Him. They have to be interpreted as either negations or as asserting God's causality. Unlike Avicenna, he asserts the homonymity of the term "being" in the case of God as compared with its application to all other beings. God's being is true and necessary because it alone has an underived and independent existence. The other eight attributes are explained by Ibn Daud as negative.

MAIMONIDES. The most incisive treatment of the attributes is found in Maimonides' *Guide of the Perplexed* (1:50–60). Maimonides argues that every attribute predicated of God is an attribute of action or, if the attribute is intended for the apprehension of His essence and not of His action, it signifies the negation or privation of the attribute in question (1:58). There cannot be affirmative essential attributes, i.e., affirmative predications relating to the essence of God which is unknowable (1:60). The anthropomorphic and anthropopathic descriptions of God in Scripture have to be understood as attributes of action, or as assertions of God's absolute perfection (1:53). Novel elements in Maimonides' discussion of attributes are his fivefold classification; his rejection of relational attributes; and his interpretation of negative attributes. Maimonides lists and discusses five kinds of attributes:

(1) A thing may have its definition and through it its essence is predicated of it. In the case of God, who cannot be defined, this kind of attribute is impossible.

(2) A part of a definition may be predicated. This, again, is inapplicable to God; for if He had a part of an essence, His essence would be composite.

(3) A quality subsisting in an essence may be predicated. None of the genera of quality is applicable to God.

(4) A relation to something other than itself (to time, place, or another individual) may be predicated of a thing. This is inadmissible in the case of God who is not related to time or place and not even to any of the substances created by Him.

(5) The action performed by a certain agent may be predicated of him. This kind of attribute makes no affirmation of

his essence or quality and is therefore admissible in the case of God (1:52).

The "13 attributes of mercy" revealed by God to Moses (Ex. 34:6–7) are attributes of action. They do not denote affections (e.g., compassion) on the part of God, but merely express the actions proceeding from Him in terms drawn from analogous human experience. Maimonides makes the point that not only the many attributes of God used in Scripture, but also the four intellectually conceived attributes of existence, omnipotence, omniscience, and will are attributes of action and not essential attributes (1:53). Because of God's absolute uniqueness and unlikeness to anything else, God's essence is unknowable (1:55). The only correct way of speaking of God's essence is that of negation. Maimonides lists eight terms (existence and life, incorporeality, firstness, omnipotence, omniscience, will, and unity), all of which are interpreted as negative in meaning and as expressing the dissimilarity between God and all other beings, e.g., "God exists" means "God is not absent"; "He is powerful" means "He is not weak." The negation means that the term in question (e.g., "weak") is inapplicable to God. It also means that the affirmative term (e.g., "powerful") is equally inapplicable, and that it can only be used in an equivocal sense. Maimonides' doctrine of attributes reflects, fundamentally, Avicenna's position as represented by al-Ghazālī in his *Tahāfut al-Falāsifa'* (i.e., denial of essential attributes based on the concept of God's "necessary existence," which, in turn, is based on the Avicennian ontological distinction between essence and existence in the cases of all beings except God), but goes beyond Avicenna in rejecting relational attributes.

Post-Maimonidean Philosophy

In post-Maimonidean Jewish philosophy the influence of Averroes became increasingly pronounced. Averroes' attack on Avicenna's ontological distinction between essence and existence (*Tahāfut al-Tahāfut*, ed. by S. van den Bergh (1954), 179–81, and passim) achieved particular prominence and led to the adoption of the theory that the divine attributes did not imply homonymous terms, but rather that essence and existence are identical in all beings, including God.

LEVI BEN GERSHOM (Gersonides). The full implications of Averroes' critique of Avicenna appear in the doctrine of Levi b. Gershom (*Milḥamot Adonai*, 3:3). The attributes are not to be interpreted as equivocal in meaning. They are to be understood *secundum prius et posterius* (both by a priori and a posteriori reasoning). They do not thereby imply a kind of relation and similarity between God and other beings, nor do they involve plurality: "For not every proposition in which something is affirmed of something implies plurality of that thing" (see H.A. Wolfson, in JQR, 7 (1916/17), 1–44, 175–225). Gersonides quotes scriptural passages affirming God's oneness (Deut. 6:4) and existence (Ex. 3:14), and he concludes from them the attributes of intellect, life, goodness, omnipotence, and will must likewise be predicated of God in a positive sense.

ḤASDAI CRESCAS. The last significant development of the doctrine of divine attributes in medieval Jewish philosophy is found in Ḥasdai Crescas (*Or Adonai*, 1:3, 1–6). He distinguishes between the essence of God, which is unknowable, and essential predicates which are knowable. The latter are neither identical with God's essence nor merely accidental to it, but inseparable from it in the sense that the one cannot be thought of without the other. This distinction is not in conflict with the notion of God's absolute simplicity. Nor is God's unlikeness to any other being thereby denied. The attributes of omnipotence and omniscience may be predicated of God *secundum prius et posterius*. There are, however, some attributes which are, in the final analysis, negative in meaning, namely existence, unity, and eternity. These too apply to God and all other beings *secundum prius et posterius* and are thus not equivocal. Crescas thus firmly rejects denial of affirmative attributes, and suggests that such denial may be interpreted as really referring only to God's essence, where it is legitimate, but not to His essential attributes (1:3,3 end).

Modern Philosophy

In modern Jewish philosophy the divine attributes are no longer discussed with the stringency imposed by the medieval tradition as inherited from Philo and the neoplatonists and modified by the Aristotelians. Nevertheless, the concepts evolved by the medieval thinkers are not entirely lost. Both Moses Mendelssohn and Hermann Cohen reflect in different ways, according to their respective positions, essential elements of the earlier discussion. Mendelssohn deals with the attributes particularly in his small treatise *Die Sache Gottes oder die gerettete Vorsehung* (1784). He asserts in the name of "the true religion of reason" the conjunction in God of his "greatness" and His "goodness." The greatness of God contains two parts: His power or omnipotence and His wisdom or omniscience. Mendelssohn's discussion of the divine attributes (he does not use this term) is directed towards the problem of theodicy. The essential point is that the infinite wisdom of God is allied to His infinite goodness, which constitutes God's "justice." In its highest degree justice is "holiness" in which equity and mercy are included. The concept of the goodness of God implies that God's punishment of the sinner is meant for the sake of the sinner's improvement. Hermann Cohen presents his concept of the attributes of God in much closer dependence on the medieval Islamic and Jewish philosophers, particularly on Maimonides. The concept of the unity of God in Judaism, according to Cohen, must not be confounded with that of mere "oneness," which is merely negative in meaning. Cohen adopts the term "uniqueness" (*Einzigheit*), which denotes God as the only Being in the true sense of the word, and signifies also His incomparability (Isa. 40:25), eternity, and causality (*Religion der Vernunft* (1929), 51–54, 70), as well as the concept of God as creator (*ibid.*, 73–77). He interprets Maimonides' theory of negative attributes as the absolute negation of negativity and the affirmation of positivity. Thus, propositions such as "God is not weak" are given in the logical form "God is not non-active" (*Juedische Schriften*, 3 (1924), 252, 257; *Religion der Vernunft*, 72–73). Moreover, he links this interpretation with his own concept of *Ursprung* (*principium*; Gr. *arché*) as the thinking which alone can produce what may be considered as being, and which does not depend on the data of sense experience. Cohen interprets Maimonides' attributes of action as expressing the "correlation" between God and men (see A. Altmann, *In Zwei Welten* (1962), 377–99). They denote exemplars for man's action rather than qualities in God (*Religion der Vernunft*, 109ff., 252, 313). The attributes of action can be reduced to two: love and justice which, in Cohen's ethical monotheism, become "concepts of virtue for man" (*ibid.*, 475, 480).

[Alexander Altmann]

JUSTICE AND MERCY OF GOD

Central among the biblical affirmations about God are those that emphasize His justice (*mishpat*) and righteousness (*ẓedakah*) on the one hand, and His mercy (*raḥamim*) and lovingkindness (*ḥesed*) on the other. God's justice and mercy are both affirmed in God's proclamation to Moses at Sinai before the giving of the Decalogue: "The Lord, the Lord, a God compassionate and gracious, slow to anger, abounding in kindness and faithfulness, extending kindness to the thousandth generation, forgiving iniquity, transgression, and sin; yet He does not remit all punishment, but visits the iniquity of the fathers upon children and children's children, upon the third and fourth generations" (Ex. 34:6–7). Justice and mercy are the bases of the covenant between God and the Israelites. God's mercy is revealed in the fact that he redeemed the people of Israel from slavery in Egypt to make them His people and contract a covenant with them: "When Israel was a child, I loved him, out of Egypt I called my son" (Hos. 11:1). His justice is revealed in the fact that He punishes the Israelites if they sin and do not uphold their side of the covenant: "You only have I known of all the families of the earth; therefore I will punish you all your iniquities"(Amos 3:2). Both the justice and mercy of God are evident in the biblical portrayal of God's relationship with Israel; "I will betroth you to me in righteousness and in justice, in steadfast love and in mercy" (Hos. 2:19). In exercising justice and punishing the people of Israel when they sin God reveals His power and lordship not only to Israel but to the world as a whole. God's justice is often tempered by His mercy: "My heart recoils within me, My compassion grows warm and tender. I will not execute My fierce anger, I will not again destroy Ephraim; for I am God and not man…" (Hos. 11:8–9). By exercising His mercy God hopes to encourage the people of Israel to uphold their side of the covenant and fulfill His demands as expressed in the Torah. The relationship between justice and mercy in God's attitude toward the people of Israel is intricate and varied, and while some biblical verses emphasize His justice and others, His mercy, it is impossible to say that one or the other is predominant.

In Post-biblical Judaism

This same intermingling of justice and mercy is to be discerned in the works of Philo and other post-biblical writings (see G.F. Moore, *Judaism in the First Centuries of the Christian Era*, 1 (1927), 386–400). In rabbinic Judaism a vivid expression of this intermingling is found in a parable in *Genesis Rabbah* (12:15) comparing God to a king who in order to prevent a fragile goblet from shattering must mix hot and cold water when filling it. Thus the world exists because of the admixture of the attributes of mercy and justice (*middat ha-raḥamim* and *middat ha-din*). Behind this parable lies a complex development of biblical ideas in which the two divine appellations, the Tetragrammaton (YHWH) and *Elohim*, were understood to refer to the two main manifestations of God's providence: the first, to express the attribute of mercy; the second, that of justice (see A. Marmorstein, *The Old Rabbinic Doctrine of God*, pt. 1 (1927), 43–53, 181–208). The presence of both names in Genesis 2:4 signifies that mercy and justice were both necessary in order to make creation possible. *Genesis Rabbah* 39:6 expresses a similar notion: "If thou desirest the world to endure, there can be no absolute justice, while if thou desirest absolute justice the world cannot endure.…" Insofar as God's justice and mercy are necessary for creation it is not only the community of Israel that is the major object of these divine activities but the world as a whole. Nonetheless, it must be recognized that rabbinic Judaism was more concerned with the divine activities of mercy and justice as they were directed toward the community of Israel. The fate of the Jewish people in the Roman period was a tragic impetus to this discussion. Faced, too, with the problem of the suffering of the righteous and the prosperity of the wicked, the rabbis examined the concept of divine justice and advanced a number of new interpretations of it in an effort to justify the apparent imbalance of suffering and prosperity in the world. It was suggested that ultimate reward and punishment would take place in the *afterlife, that suffering was a process of purification (*yissurin shel ahavah*), and that the individual often suffered for the sins of his ancestors or of the community at large.

While various trends in medieval Jewish philosophy and mysticism interpreted the divine attributes of justice and mercy differently, they all affirmed that these were qualities of God. In the face of the Holocaust in the 20th century, some thinkers, for example, R. Rubenstein, have seriously questioned the concept of divine justice and mercy, while others, for example, Emil Fackenheim, maintain that it is a major obligation of Jewish religious thought to rediscover the meaning of the concept in the face of the contemporary situation.

[Lou H. Silberman]

CONCEPTIONS OF GOD

Monotheism

The normative Jewish conception of God is theism, or more exactly, *monotheism. It conceives of God as the creator and sustainer of the universe, whose will and purposes are supreme. He is the only being whose existence is necessary, uncaused, and eternal, and all other beings are dependent on Him. God as conceived by Judaism transcends the world, yet He is also present in the world, and "the whole earth is full of His glory" (Isa. 6:3). He is a personal God, whom man can love with the highest and most complete love, while confronting Him as father, king, and master. He loves man and commands him, and His commandments are the criterion of the good. He is absolutely one, admitting no plurality in His nature, and absolutely unique, so that no other existing thing can in any way be compared to Him. This is essentially the picture of the biblical God as it was developed and understood in classical Jewish thought.

This conception of God contrasts sharply with the mythological gods, who have parents and children, eat and drink, have desires and passions. Judaism categorically rejected the mythological gods. However, a variety of more sophisticated conceptions of God confronted Judaism, presenting challenges and evoking responses.

Atheism

It might be supposed that the greatest threat to monotheism would be atheism, but throughout most of Jewish history this was not the case. In the Bible there is no awareness of genuine atheism. The biblical authors attacked idolatry and other mistaken conceptions of God. Frequently, they attacked those who deny that God is concerned with man and the world, but seemed unaware of men who did not believe in a superior power.

Atheism was known in the Middle Ages, and was countered by the various proofs for the existence of God that were common to all medieval philosophical theology. Yet, since the dominant medieval culture was overwhelmingly religious, atheism constituted only a minor threat. In modern times atheism became a significant and widely held doctrine, based on and reinforced by naturalistic scientific ideas and scientifically oriented philosophy. The classical proofs for God's existence have been largely discredited and no longer provide a satisfactory ground for theism. Modern theists usually offer arguments for the existence of God, but do not claim that they have proofs. These arguments, though not decisive, provide a justification for the theistic option, since it is claimed that these are matters about which no demonstrative certainty is possible. In the 20th century theistic belief usually rests on a combination of admittedly incomplete intellectual evidence and personal faith and commitment.

Polytheism and Dualism

Polytheism, the belief that there are many gods, was never a serious threat to normative Judaism, because it is a form of idolatry which could not be readily confused with biblical doctrine. Wherever polytheism appeared among Jews, recognized authorities rejected it vigorously.

Dualism was the only version of polytheism which made serious inroads into the cultural world of the Jews. Dualism teaches that there are two cosmic powers, each of which has dominion over one portion of the universe. The Zoroastrian version has a god of light and a god of darkness, while the Gnostics taught that there is a hidden god who is beyond all knowledge and the evident god who created and formed the world. Dualism is soundly rejected in a classical biblical passage which says, "I am the Lord, and there is none else, beside me there is no God… I form the light and create the darkness; I make peace and create evil; I am the Lord that doeth all these things" (Isa. 45:5, 7). This forceful denial of dualism is repeated in a slightly modified form in the daily liturgy. The Talmud challenges the heresy of dualism explicitly with strong prohibitions against any deviations from standard liturgy that might have dualistic implications. Rabbinic rulings proscribe any form of prayer that suggests that there are *shetei reshuyot*, two independent powers controlling the world (Ber. 33b).

The medieval philosophers also argued against dualism. Saadiah Gaon dealt with the problem explicitly, offering three arguments against the dualistic position. He first showed that if the doctrine of one God is abandoned, there is no reason to restrict the cosmic powers to two. Arguments can then be made for almost any number one chooses. A second objection is that dualism makes unintelligible the fact that there is an ordered world, since, presumably, each power could frustrate the designs of the other. Finally, he argued that we cannot conceive of such powers as gods at all, since each would limit the other (*Beliefs and Opinions*, 2:2). Other medieval philosophers attacked dualism indirectly through their arguments for the necessary unity of God.

Though there are similarities between Kabbalah and *Gnosticism, the kabbalists did not succumb to the temptations of dualism. "On the contrary," says Gershom Scholem, "all the energy of 'orthodox' Kabbalistic speculation is bent to the task of escaping from dualistic consequences; otherwise they would not have been able to maintain themselves within the Jewish community" (Scholem, Mysticism, 13).

Trinity

The Trinitarian conception of God is associated especially with *Christianity. Though Christian theologians normally intepret the Trinity as a doctrine of one God in three persons, Jewish thinkers rejected it categorically as a denial of the divine unity. Since only heretical Jewish sects could even entertain the possibility of a Trinitarian God, most Jewish anti-Trinitarian polemics were directed specifically against Christianity. Occasionally, kabbalistic doctrines seem to have a Trinitarian cast, as is the case in the thought of Abraham *Abulafia (*ibid.*, 123ff.). However, these Trinitarian formulations are always interpreted in such ways that they clearly do not refer to a triune God. Some Shabbateans (see *Shabbetai Ẓevi) developed a trinity consisting of the unknown God, the God of Israel, and the *Shekhinah* ("Divine Presence"; *ibid.*, 287ff.). Their heresy was vigorously attacked by official Jewish spokesmen.

Pantheism

A far more complex problem is posed by Jewish attitudes toward pantheism. This doctrine teaches that God is the whole of reality and that all reality is God. Because it does not involve any polytheistic notions and seems, therefore, compatible with standard Jewish doctrines about God's unity, pantheism found occasional followers among even highly respected Jewish thinkers. It also evoked great opposition, because it denies some of the fundamentals of Jewish monotheism. The pantheistic God is not a separate being who transcends the world, nor is he even a being who is immanent in the world. He is identical with the totality of the world. He is not a personal God; he neither commands men nor seeks their obedience. Consequently, there are almost no instances of pure pantheism within the normative Jewish tradition, though pantheistic tendencies have appeared at various times. They derive from an overemphasis on the immanence of God or an excessive stress on the nothingness of the world. They must be considered in any account of Jewish conceptions of God. Hermann Cohen expressed the extreme view of many thinkers when he stated categorically "Pantheism is not religion" (see *Ethik des reinen Willens* (1921[2], 456–66). Nevertheless, one can find various traces of pantheistic thought, if not actual pantheism, in many deeply pious Jewish thinkers. Some scholars attempted to put a pantheistic interpretation on the rabbinic use of *Makom* ("Place") as a name for God because "He is the place of the world, but the world is not His place" (Gen. R. 68). (The original significance of *Makom* as a divine name has no pantheistic connotations.) Philo also spoke of God as "Place" and for this reason is considered by some interpreters to have a pantheistic doctrine. H.A. Wolfson however, argues that for Philo the doctrine that God is the place of the world means that "God is everywhere in the corporeal world, thereby exercising His individual providence, but He is no part of the corporeal world and is unlike anything in it" (see his *Philo* (1947), 245ff.). The elements of pantheism which appeared periodically in the history of Jewish thought were almost always tempered by the use of theistic language and adjustments to theistic claims. Solomon ibn Gabirol conceived of reality as a graded continuum, moving from the Godhead through a series of levels of being down to the corporeal world (*Mekor Ḥayyim*, passim). His system seems pantheistic, because it treats all reality as one continuous emanation of the divine substance. Nevertheless, in his general religious orientation he returns to standard conceptions of a personal God who is the creator of the world. The thought of Abraham Ibn Ezra exhibits a similar ambiguity. He used purely pantheistic language when he said that "God is the One. He is the creator of all, and He is all… God is all and all comes from Him" (Commentary to Genesis, 1:26; to Exodus, 23:21). Yet, there are countless places in his writings where he also uses strictly conventional theistic terminology. Wherever there is strong neoplatonic influence on Jewish thought a suggestion of pantheism is usually present. Pantheism also appears in mystical doctrines that stress the immanence of God. In the Kabbalah there is an ongoing struggle between pantheistic and theistic tendencies. The former often provide the doctrinal base of a kabbalistic system, while the latter determine the language in which the system is expressed. Scholem states, "In the history of Kabbalism, theistic and pantheistic trends have frequently contended for mastery. This fact is sometimes obscured because the representatives of pantheism have generally endeavored to speak the language of theism; cases of writers who openly put forward pantheistic view are rare… The author of the Zohar inclines toward pantheism… On the whole, his language is that of the theist, and some penetration is needed to lift its hidden and lambent pantheistic core to the light" (Mysticism, 222). The same tendency can be observed in Ḥasidism. In a key passage R. *Shneur Zalman of Lyady asserted that "there is truly nothing besides Him" (*Tanya, Sha'ar ha-Yiḥud ve-ha-Emunah*, ch. 3); yet, he can hardly be called a pure pantheist when we consider the many conventional theistic formulations in his writings. Only in the case of Nachman Krochmal does there seem to be an instance of genuine Jewish pantheism. Krochmal ascribed true existence only to God, who is Absolute Spirit. In his thought only the Absolute Spirit truly exists, and he denies any other mode of existence. Krochmal was far less inclined than earlier Jewish thinkers to adopt language appropriate to a doctrine of a personal, theistic God.

Deism

Deism was still another conception of God that confronted Jewish theology. Deistic doctrine contains two main elements. First is the view that God, having created the world, withdrew himself from it completely. This eliminates all claims of divine providence, miracles, and any form of intervention by God in history. Second, deism holds that all the essential truths about God are knowable by unaided natural reason without any dependence on revelation. The vast bulk of Jewish tradition rejected both deistic claims. It is hardly possible to accept the biblical God and still affirm the deistic view that he is not related to the world. Numerous rabbinic texts are attacks on the Greek philosophers who taught such a doctrine. Similar attacks continued throughout the history of Jewish philosophy. Of the medieval philosophers, only Levi ben Gershom seems to have had deistic tendencies.

Among modern Jewish thinkers, Moses Mendelssohn is sometimes classified as a deist because he held that there is a universal natural religion, whose doctrines are known by reason alone. It does not seem correct, however, to identify Mendelssohn's God with the deistic God, because he ascribes to God qualities of personality and involvement with the world that are hardly in accord with standard deism (see Guttmann, Philosophies, 291ff.). However, Mendelssohn is open to varying interpretations, and Leo *Baeck was not alone when he propounded the view that for Mendelssohn "Judaism had become merely a combination of law and deistic natural religion." Over the centuries of its history Judaism has been exposed to a variety of conceptions of God, but none has ever been strong enough to overcome the basic Jewish commitment to monotheism. Other doctrines have influenced Jewish thought and have left their traces, yet, the monotheistic faith has consistently emerged as the normative expression of Jewish religion.

[Marvin Fox]

BIBLIOGRAPHY: IN THE BIBLE: Kaufmann Y., Toledot (incl. bibl.); Kaufmann Y., Religion; M. Buber, *I and Thou* (1937); EM, 1 (1950), 297–321; U. Cassuto, *The Documentary Hypothesis* (1961); A.J. Heschel, *The Prophets* (1962); R. Gordis, *The Book of God and Man* (1965). IN HELLENISTIC LITERATURE: J. Klausner, *Filosofim ve-Hogei De'ot*, 1 (1934); H.A. Wolfson, *Philo*, 2 vols. (1947). IN TALMUDIC LITERATURE: Ginzberg, Legends, index; M. Lazarus, *Ethics of Judaism*, 2 vols. (1900–01); G.F. Moore, *Judaism*, 2 vols. (1927), index; C.G. Montefiore and H. Loewe, *A Rabbinic Anthology* (1938), index; A. Marmorstein, *The Old Rabbinic Doctrine of God* (1927, repr. 1968); A. Cohen, *Everyman's Talmud* (1932), 1–71 and index; M. Guttmann, *Das Judentum und seine Umwelt* (1927); H. Cohen, *Religion der Vernunft aus den Quellen des Judentums* (1929²); P. Kuhn, *Gottes Selbsterniedrigung in der Theologie der Rabbinen* (1968). IN MEDIEVAL JEWISH PHILOSOPHY: Guttmann, Philosophies, index; Husik, Philosophy, index; D. Kaufmann, *Attributenlehre* (1875). IN THE KABBALAH: Scholem, Mysticism, index; idem, *Reshit ha-Kabbalah* (1948); I. Tishby, *Mishnat ha-Zohar*, 1 (1949), 95–282; M. Ibn Gabai, *Derekh Emunah* (1890, repr. 1967); M. Cordovero, *Elimah Rabbati* (1881, repr. 1961), Ma'ayan 1. IN MODERN JEWISH PHILOSOPHY: J.B. Agus, *Modern Philosophies of Judaism* (1941); Guttmann, Philosophies, index; S.H. Bergman, *Faith and Reason: An Introduction to Modern Jewish Thought* (1961). ATTRIBUTES OF GOD: D. Kaufmann, *Attributenlehre* (1875); idem, *Gesammelte Schriften*, 2 (1910), 1–98; H.A. Wolfson, in: *Essays and Studies in Memory of Linda R. Miller* (1938), 201–34; idem, in: *Louis Ginzberg Jubilee Volume* (1945), 411–46; idem, in: *Harvard Studies in Classical Philology*, 56–67 (1947), 233–49; idem, in: HTR, 45 (1952), 115–30; 49 (1956), 1–18; idem, in: *Mordecai M. Kaplan Jubilee Volume* (1953), 515–30; idem, in: JAOS, 79 (1959), 73–80; idem, in: *Studies and Essays in Honor of Abraham A. Neuman* (1962), 547–68; A. Altmann, in: BJRL, 35 (1953), 294–315; idem, in: *Tarbiz*, 27 (1958), 301–9; Guttmann, Philosophies, passim; S. Rawidowicz, in: *Saadya Studies* (1943), 139–65; A. Schmiedl, *Studien ueber juedische, insondere juedische-arabische Religionsphilosophie* (1869), 1–66; G. Vajda, *Isaac Albalag, Averroiste Juif, Traducteur et Annotateur d'Al-Ghazali* (1960), 34–129, and passim; idem, in: *Jewish Medieval and Renaissance Studies* (1966), 49–74. **ADD. BIBLIOGRAPHY:** G. Scholem, *Origins of Kabbalah*; M. Idel, *Kabbalah: New Perspectives*, 112–55; S.O. Heller-Willensky and M. Idel (eds.), *Studies in Jewish Thought* (Heb.; 1989), 7–230.

GOD, NAMES OF. Various Hebrew terms are used for God in the Bible. Some of these are employed in both the generic and specific sense; others are used only as the personal name of the God of Israel. Most of these terms were employed also by the Canaanites, to designate their gods. This is not surprising, since the early Israelites arose in Canaan and spoke "the language of Canaan" (Isa. 19:18). It must be noted, however, that in the Bible these various terms, when used by the Israelites to designate their own deity, refer to one and the same god, the God of Israel. When Joshua told the tribes of Israel, assembled at Shechem, that their ancestors had "served other gods" (Josh. 24:2), he was referring to the ancestors of Abraham, as is clear from the context. The God who identified Himself to Moses as YHWH said He was "the God of Abraham, the God of Isaac, and the God of Jacob" (Ex. 3:6). Therefore, the terms "the Fear of Isaac" (perhaps rather, "the Kinsman of Isaac," Gen. 31:42, 53) and "the Mighty One of Jacob" (Gen. 49:24; Isa. 49:26), are synonymous with YHWH.

ʾEl

The oldest Semitic term for God is *ʾel* (corresponding to Akkadian *ilu*(*m*), Canaanite *ʾel* or *ʾil*, and Arabic *ʾel* as an element in personal names). The etymology of the word is obscure. It is commonly thought that the term derived from a root *ʾyl* or *ʾwl*, meaning "to be powerful" (cf. *yesh le-el yadi*, "It is in the power of my hand," Gen. 31:29; cf. Deut. 28:32; Micah 2:1). But the converse may be true; since power is an essential element in the concept of deity, the term for deity may have been used in the transferred sense of "power."

In Akkadian, *ilu*(*m*), and plural *ilū* and *ilānu*, is used in reference to any individual god as well as to divine beings in general; but it is not employed as the personal name of any god. In Ugaritic Canaanite, however, *il* occurs much more frequently as the personal name of the highest god *el* than as the common noun "god" (pl., *ilm*; fem., *ilt*). In the Ugaritic myths El is the head of the Canaanite pantheon, the ancestor of the other gods and goddesses, and the creator of the earth and its creatures; but he generally fades into the background and plays a minor role in the preserved myths.

In the Bible *ʾel* is seldom used as the personal name of God, e.g., *ʾEl-ʾElohei-Yisrael*, "El, the God of [the Patriarch] Israel" (Gen. 33:20; cf. Ps. 146:5). Almost always, *ʾel* is an appellative, with about the same semantic range as *ʾelohim* (see below). The word can thus be preceded by the article: *ha-ʾel*, "the [true] God" (e.g., Ps. 18:31, 33, 48; 57:3). Like *ʾelohim*, *ʾel* can be employed in reference to an "alien god" (Deut. 32:12; Mal. 2:11) or a "strange god" (Ps. 44:21; 81:10). It can also have the plural form *ʾelim*, "heavenly beings" (Ex. 15:11). In contrast to the extremely common word *ʾelohim*, *ʾel* occurs relatively seldom, except in archaic or archaizing poetry, as in Job and Psalms. But *ʾel* and, rarely, *ʾelohim* are used when the term is modified by one or more adjectives, e.g., "a jealous god" (e.g., Ex. 20:5; 34:14), "a god compassionate and gracious" (e.g., Ex. 34:6; Ps. 86:15). Moreover, *ʾel*, not *ʾelohim*, is used when the divine is contrasted with the human (Num. 23:19; Isa. 31:3; Ezek. 28:9; Hos. 11:9; Job 25:4). As an element in theophoric names, *ʾel*, not *ʾelohim*, is used often as the first element, e.g., Elijah, Elisha, and Elihu, and even more often as the last element, e.g., Israel, Ishmael, and Samuel. Of special interest are the divine names of which El is the first element: *ʾEl ʿElyon*, *ʾEl ʿOlam*, *ʾEl Shaddai*, *ʾEl Roʾi*, and *ʾEl Berit*.

ʾEl ʿElyon

The Hebrew word *ʿelyon* is an adjective meaning "higher, upper," e.g., the "upper" pool (Isa. 7:3), the "upper" gate (II Kings 15:35), and "highest," e.g., the "highest" of all the kings of the earth (Ps. 89:28). When used in reference to God, the word can rightly be translated as "Most High." Since in reference to God *ʿelyon* is never preceded by the article *ha*- ("the"), it must have been regarded as a proper noun, a name of God. Thus, it can be used as a divine name meaning "the Most High" (e.g.,

Deut. 32:8; Isa. 14:14; Ps. 9:3) or in parallelism with YHWH (e.g., Ps. 18:14; 21:8; 83:19), El (Num. 24:16; Ps. 107:11), and Shaddai (Ps. 91:1).

Among the Canaanites, *ʾEl* and *ʿElyon* were originally distinct deities. El is attested over 500 times in texts from Ugarit (Ras Shamra) in Northwest Syria from the later second millennium. In a list of gods in an Aramaic treaty of the eighth century B.C.E. from Sefire in Syria we have *ʾl wʿlyn*, which has been interpreted by some scholars as "El and Elyon," that is, two distinct gods, and by others as "El, who is Elyon," which would approximate Genesis 14:18–20. *Eusebius, bishop of Caesarea in the fourth century, cites the first-century author Philo of Byblos, who himself cites the "Phoenician Theology" of one Sanchuniathon, to the effect that Elioun was the name of a deified mortal, who became the ancestor of Zeus Demarous. According to Genesis 14:18–20, Melchizedek, king of Salem, was "a priest of God Most High [*ʾEl ʿElyon*]," and he blessed Abraham by "God Most High, Creator of heaven and earth." Abraham accepted the title "Most High" as merely descriptive of his own God; he swore by "YHWH, God Most High, Creator of heaven and earth." Greek inscriptions refer to *Zeus Hypsistos*, a reflection of Semitic terminology. Whereas for the pagans the term referred to the god who was supreme over the other gods, in Israel it referred to the transcendent nature of the one true God.

ʾEl ʿOlam

According to Genesis 21:33, "Abraham planted a tamarisk at Beer-Sheba, and invoked there the name of YHWH, the everlasting God." The Hebrew for "the Everlasting God" is *ʾel ʿolam*, literally, "the God of an indefinitely long time." Perhaps it was the title of El as worshiped at the local shrine of Beer-Sheba (cf. El Bethel, "the El of Bethel," in Gen. 35:7). Then Abraham would have accepted this Canaanite term as descriptive of his true God. In any case, the epithet is logical in the context, which concerns a pact meant for all times. The term by which Abraham invoked YHWH at Beer-Sheba is apparently echoed in Isaiah 40:28, where YHWH is called "the Everlasting God [*ʾelohei ʿolam*], the Creator of the ends of the earth" (cf. Jer. 10:10, *melekh ʿolam*, "the everlasting King"; Isa. 26:4, *ẓur ʿolamim*, "an everlasting Mountain"). In Deuteronomy 33:27, where "the ancient God" (*ʾelohei qedem*) parallels "the everlasting arms" (*zeroʿot ʿolam*), the text is uncertain. Only in the late passage of Daniel 12:7 (probably translated from Aramaic) is the article used with *ʿolam*: "The man clothed in linen… swore by Him that liveth for ever (*be-ḥei ha-ʿolam*)."

ʾEl Shaddai

According to the literary source of the Pentateuch that the critics call the "Priestly Document," YHWH "appeared to Abraham, Isaac, and Jacob as El Shaddai" (Ex. 6:3). The traditional English rendering of the obscure Hebrew term *ʾEl Shaddai* as "God Almighty" goes back to ancient times. The Septuagint renders Shaddai as *Pantokrator*, "All-powerful"; this is followed by the Vulgate's *Omnipotens*, "Omnipotent." Apparently, this rendering is based on an ancient rabbinic interpretation, *sha*, "who," and *dai*, "enough," i.e., "He who is self-sufficient" (e.g., Ḥag. 12a); thus, the Jewish translators Aquila and Symmachus in the early centuries C.E. translated *shaddai* by Greek *hikanos*, "sufficient, able." But this definition can hardly be taken as the true etymology of the term. No fully satisfactory explanation of it has yet been accepted by all scholars. The term is often explained as a cognate of the Akkadian word *šadū*, "mountain," either in the sense that *ʾEl Shaddai* would mean "God the Mountain" (cf. *ẓur*, "Mountain," an epithet of God, e.g., Deut. 32:4, 30, 37); the abode of "ʾEl of Heaven," or *ʾEl Shaddai* could mean "ʾEl-of-the-Mountain," i.e., of the cosmic mountain, the abode of "ʾEl. of Heaven." The ending *-ai* of *shaddai* would be adjectival, as in Ugaritic *ʾrṣy* (to be vocalized *ʾarṣai*), "She of the Earth," the name of one of the three daughters of the Ugaritic *ʾEl*. No Ugaritic equivalent of *ʾEl Shaddai* has yet been found. Deities known as *šdyn* are mentioned in the ninth-eighth century *Balaam text unearthed at Deir Alla (probably biblical Sukkoth) in Jordan. In the Bible the full name, *ʾEl Shaddai*, is used only in connection with Abraham (Gen. 17:1), Isaac (Gen. 28:3), and Jacob (Gen. 35:11; 43:14; 48:3). The word Shaddai alone occurs as God's name in the ancient oracles of Balaam (Num. 24:4, 16), in poetic passages (Isa. 13:6; Ezek. 1:24; Joel 1:15; Ps. 68:15; 91:1; and 31 times in Job), and even in archaizing prose (Ruth 1:20–21). Moreover, Shaddai is an element in Israelite names with parallels in ancient sources, such as Ammishaddai ("My Kinsman is Shaddai"; Num. 1:12) and Zurishaddai ("My Mountain is Shaddai"; Num. 1:6).

ʾEl Roʾi

The divine name *ʾEl Roʾi* occurs in Genesis 16:13. After Hagar was driven away by Sarai (Sarah) and fled into the western Negev, at a certain spring or well she had a vision of God, "and she called YHWH who spoke to her, 'You are *ʾEl Roʾi*.'" The meaning of the word "Roʾi" in this context is obscure. By itself it can be either a noun, "appearance" (I Sam. 16:12), "spectacle" (Nah. 3:6), or a participle with a suffix of the first person singular, "seeing me," i.e., who sees me (Job 7:8). Therefore, *ʾEl Roʾi* could mean either "the God of Vision" (who showed Himself to me) or "the God who sees me." The explanation of the divine name that is given in the second half of the same verse (Gen. 16:13b) is equally obscure. As the Hebrew text now stands, it is usually rendered as "She meant, 'Have I not gone on seeing after He saw me [*aḥarei roʾi*]?'" (JPS, 1962), or, "She meant, 'Did I not go on seeing here [*halom*] after He had seen me?'" (E.A. Speiser, *Genesis* (1964, 117). In the following verse (16:14) it is stated: "Therefore the well was called *Beʾer-Laḥai-Roʾi*." This name is explained in a footnote as "Apparently, 'The Well of the Living One Who sees me'" (JPS). However, on the basis of the name of the well, E.A. Speiser (op. cit., p. 119) would emend the unvocalized Hebrew text of Genesis 16:13, *hgm hlm rʾyty ʾḥry rʾy*, to read *hgm ʾlhm rʾyty wʾḥy*, "Did I really see God, yet remain alive?" The name of the well he would then take to mean, "Well of living sight." Since the well was in the region occupied by the Ishmaelites (and Hagar was the mother of Ishmael), the divine name, *ʾEl Roʾi*, may have been proper to the Ishmaelites rather than to the Israelites.

ʾEl Berit

The divine name *ʾEl Berit* ("God of the Covenant") occurs only in Judges 9:46, where mention is made of "the house [i.e., temple] of *ʾEl Berit*" at Shechem. This is certainly the same sanctuary that is called "the house [i.e., temple] of *Baʿal Berit*" in 9:4. From the treasury of the temple of Baal-Berith the citizens of Shechem gave 70 silver shekels to Abimelech, the son of Jerubbaal (another name of Gideon) to aid him in his fight for the sole kingship of Shechem against the other sons of Jerubbaal (*ibid.*). A few years later, the rebellious citizens of Shechem were burned to death by Abimelech in the temple of El-Berith where they had taken refuge (9:46–49).

The Deuteronomist editor of the Book of Judges regarded Baal-Berith as a pagan god. But the case is not quite that simple. First of all, in early Israel the word *baʿal*, meaning "owner, master, lord," was often regarded more or less as a synonym of *ʾadon*, "lord" (see below under "*ʾAdonai*"), and so it could be used legitimately as a title of YHWH. Among the sons of King Saul, who was certainly not a worshiper of a pagan god, were those who bore the names of Merib-Baal, "the Lord contends" (?), and Eshbaal (originally, *ʾish-baʿal*), "man of the Lord," I Chron. 8:33, 34; 9:39, 40; and even one of King David's sons was called Beeliada (originally *baʿal-yadaʿ*), "the Lord knows" (I Chron. 14:7), who is called Eliada (*ʾel-yadaʿ*), "God knows," in II Samuel 5:16. Only after the time of Solomon was the word "Baal" recognized in Israel as the specific title of the Canaanite storm-god Hadad, and thereafter avoided by true Israelites as a title for YHWH. (Scribal tradition later changed the *baʿal* in older Israelite names to *boshet* ("shame") in the Books of Samuel and Kings; see *Euphemism and Dysphemism.) It is likewise uncertain what the *berit* ("covenant") refers to in the words Baal-Berith or El-Berith. Shechem was regarded as a sacred site by Abraham and Jacob, each of whom erected an altar there (Gen. 12:6–7; 33:19–20). In addition, Jacob's acquisition of land at Shechem (Gen. 33:19; cf. 48:22) and the connubium between the sons of Jacob and the sons of Hamor (as the Shechemites were then called) imply certain covenant agreements. Moreover, the strange name, "sons of Hamor" (*benei ḥamor*, "sons of the ass"), who is said to be the "father of Shechem" (Gen. 34:6), seems to have something to do with covenant making. From the *El-Amarna Letters (c. 1400 B.C.E.) it is known that there was a strong Hurrian element in Shechem. The Septuagint is therefore probably correct in reading *hḥry* ("the Horite," i.e., the Hurrian) instead of *hḥwy* ("the Hivite") of the Masoretic Text in describing the ethnic origin of "Shechem" (Gen. 34:2); moreover, the uncircumcised Shechemites (Gen. 34:14, 24) were most likely not Semitic Canaanites (see E.A. Speiser, op. cit., 267). It is also known that the slaughtering of an ass played a role among the Hurrians in the making of a covenant. Thus, Baal-Berith or El-Berith may have been regarded by the Shechemites as the divine protector of covenants.

Did the early Israelites perhaps regard El-Berith as the God of the covenant made between YHWH and Israel? It is a noteworthy fact that Joshua made a covenant with all Israel precisely at Shechem, the city sacred to El-Berith, "the God of the Covenant" (Josh. 8:30–35; 24:1–28). Therefore, even though the late Deuteronomist editor of the Book of Judges considered Baal-Berith one of the pagan Canaanite *Baʿalim*, this term may well have been regarded in early Israel as one of the titles of YHWH. A god *ilbrt*, found in a second millennium hymn, has been interpreted variously as El-berith and as Ilabrat, an old Semitic deity.

ʾELOAH, ʾElohim

The word *ʾeloah* "God" and its plural, *ʾelohim*, is apparently a lengthened form of *ʾEl* (cf. Aramaic *ʾelah*, Arabic *ʾilāh*). The singular *ʾeloah* is of relatively rare occurrence in the Bible outside of Job, where it is found about 40 times. It is very seldom used in reference to a foreign god and then only in a late period (Dan. 1137ff.; II Chron. 32:15). In all other cases it refers to the God of Israel (e.g., Deut. 32:15; Ps. 50:22; 139:19; Prov. 30:5; Job 3:4, 23). The plural form *ʾelohim* is used not only of pagan "gods" (e.g., Ex. 12:12; 18:11; 20:3), but also of an individual pagan "god" (Judg. 11:24; II Kings 1:2ff.) and even of a "goddess" (I Kings 11:5). In reference to Israel's "god" it is used extremely often – more than 2,000 times – and often with the article, *ha-ʾelohim*, "the [true] god." Occasionally, the plural form *ʾelohim*, even when used of the god of Israel, is construed with a plural verb or adjective (e.g., Gen. 20:13; 35:7; Ex. 32:4, 8; II Sam. 7:23; Ps. 58:12), especially in the expression *ʾelohim ḥayyim*, "the living God." In the vast majority of cases, however, the plural form is treated as if it were a noun in the singular. The odd fact that Hebrew uses a plural noun to designate the god of Israel has been explained in various ways. Some scholars take it as a plural that expresses an abstract idea (e.g., *zekunim*, "old age"; *neʿurim*, "time of youth"), so that *ʾElohim* would really mean "the Divinity." More likely, however, it came from general Canaanite usage. In the el-Amarna Letters Pharaoh is often addressed as "my gods [*īlānīʾya*] the sun-god." In the ancient Near East of the second half of the second millennium B.C.E. there was a certain trend toward quasi-monotheism, and any god could be given the attributes of any other god, so that an individual god could be addressed as *ʾelohai*, "my gods," "my pantheon," or *ʾadonai*, "my lords." The early Israelites felt no inconsistency in referring to their god in these terms. The word *ʾelohim* is employed also to describe someone or something as godlike, preternatural, or extraordinarily great, e.g., the ghost of Samuel (I Sam. 28:13; cf. Isa. 8:19 "spirits"), the house of David (Zech. 12:8), and Rachel's contest with her sister (Gen. 30:8).

Adonai

The Hebrew word *ʾadon* is correctly rendered in English as "lord." In the Bible it is often used in reference to any human being who had authority, such as the ruler of a country (Gen. 42:30), the master of a slave (Gen. 24:96), and the husband of a wife (Gen. 18:12). In formal polite style a man, not necessarily a superior, was addressed as "my lord" (*ʾadoni*; e.g., Gen. 23:6, 15; 24:18); and several men could be addressed as "my lords" (*ʾadonai*; e.g., Gen. 19:2). Since God is "Lord [*ʾadon*] of all the earth" (Josh. 3:11), He is addressed and spoken of as "my Lord" – in Hebrew, *ʾAdonai* (literally, "my Lords," in the plural in keeping with the plural form, *ʾElohim*, and always with the "pausal" form of a long *ā* at the end). Originally, "*ʾadonai*," especially in the combined form "*ʾadonai* YHWH" (e.g., Gen. 15:2, 8; Deut. 3:24; 9:26), was no doubt understood as "my Lord." But later, "*ʾAdonai*" was taken to be a name of God, the "Lord."

YHWH

The personal name of the God of Israel is written in the Hebrew Bible with the four consonants YHWH and is referred to as the "Tetragrammaton." At least until the destruction of the First Temple in 586 B.C.E. this name was regularly pronounced with its proper vowels, as is clear from the *Lachish Letters, written shortly before that date. But at least by the third century B.C.E. the pronunciation of the name YHWH was avoided, and Adonai, "the Lord," was substituted for it, as evidenced by the use of the Greek word *Kyrios*, "Lord," for YHWH in the Septuagint, the translation of the Hebrew Scriptures that was begun by Greek-speaking Jews in that century. Where the combined form ʾAdonai YHWH occurs in the Bible, this was read as ʾAdonai ʾElohim, "Lord God." In the early Middle Ages, when the consonantal text of the Bible was supplied with vowel points to facilitate its correct traditional reading, the vowel points for ʾAdonai with one variation – a *sheva* with the initial *yod* of YHWH instead of the *ḥataf-pataḥ* under the *aleph* of *ʾAdonai* – were used for YHWH, thus producing the form YeHoWaH. When Christian scholars of Europe first began to study Hebrew, they did not understand what this really meant, and they introduced the hybrid name "Jehovah." In order to avoid pronouncing even the sacred name ʾAdonai for YHWH, the custom was later introduced of saying simply in Hebrew *ha-Shem* (or Aramaic *Shemāʾ*, "the Name") even in such an expression as "Blessed be he that cometh in the name of YHWH" (Ps. 118:26). The avoidance of pronouncing the name YHWH is generally ascribed to a sense of reverence. More precisely, it was caused by a misunderstanding of the Third Commandment (Ex. 20:7; Deut. 5:11) as meaning "Thou shalt not take the name of YHWH thy God in vain," whereas it really means either "You shall not swear falsely by the name of YHWH your God" (JPS) or more likely, "Do not speak the name of YHWH your god, to that which is false," i.e., do not identify YHWH with any other god.

The true pronunciation of the name YHWH was never lost. Several early Greek writers of the Christian Church testify that the name was pronounced "Yahweh." This is confirmed, at least for the vowel of the first syllable of the name, by the shorter form Yah, which is sometimes used in poetry (e.g., Ex. 15:2) and the *-yahu* or *-yah* that serves as the final syllable in very many Hebrew names. In the opinion of many scholars, YHWH is a verbal form of the root *hwh*, which is an older variant of the root *hyh* "to be." The vowel of the first syllable shows that the verb is used in the form of a future-present causative *hiphʿil*, and must therefore mean "He causes to be, He brings into existence." The explanation of the name as given in Exodus 3:14, *Eheyeh-Asher-Eheyeh*, "I-Am-Who-I-Am," offers a folk etymology, common in biblical explanation of names, rather than a strictly scientific one. Like many other Hebrew names in the Bible, the name Yahweh is no doubt a shortened form of what was originally a longer name. It has been suggested that the original, full form of the name was something like *Yahweh-Asher-Yihweh*, "He brings into existence whatever exists"; or *Yahweh Ẓevaʾot* (I Sam. 1:3, 11), which really means "He brings the hosts [of heaven – or of Israel?] into existence." "The Lord of Hosts," the traditional translation of the latter name, is doubtful.

According to the documentary hypothesis, the literary sources in the Pentateuch known as the Elohist and the Priestly Document never use the name Yahweh for God until it is revealed to Moses (Ex. 3:13; 6:2–3); but the Yahwist source uses it from Genesis 2:4 on and puts the name in Eve's declaration, "I along with Yahweh have made a man," thus implying that it was known to the first human generation (Gen. 4:1; cf. 4:26). The apparent purpose of Exodus 6:2–3 is to glorify Moses at the expense of the patriarchal traditions.

Divine Epithets

Besides the above-mentioned divine names, the god of Israel is also given several epithets or appellatives that are descriptive of His nature. Yahweh shares several of these epithets with other ancient divinities. Only a few of these can be mentioned here.

Israel's god is "Creator of heaven and earth" (Gen. 14:19, 22). He is also called "the Creator of Israel (Isa. 43:15 – unless this is to be emended to "the Mighty One of Israel; cf. Isa. 1:24); for His creative activity was regarded, not only as His initial bringing of the world into existence, but also as His continuous governing of the world (Isa. 29:16; 45:9; 64:7; Jer. 27:5; 31:35–36). Like some of his Canaanite and Phoenician contemporaries He is called "the Holy One" (Isa. 40:25; Hab. 3:3); Yahweh is specifically, "the Holy One of Israel" (e.g., Isa. 1:4; 5:19, 24). In common with numerous Mesopotamian gods, Yahweh is called "Shepherd." He cares for his flock as loving care for "the Shepherd of Israel" (Ps. 80:2; cf. 28:9; Hos. 4:16). Another common title that YHWH shares with Mesopotamian gods is "the Mountain" (e.g., Deut. 32:4, 18, 31, 37; I Sam. 2:2; II Sam. 22:32 (= Ps. 18:32); Isa. 44:8), thus emphasizing Yahweh's enduring power and the place where one finds refuge. The God of Israel is very often spoken of or addressed as "King" or "King of Israel," thus describing His sovereign rule over His Chosen People, to give them peace, happiness, and salvation (e.g., Isa. 41:2; 44:6; 52:7). The so-called "Enthronement Psalms of YHWH" (Ps. 47; 93; 96–99) emphasize the Lord's kingship over Israel. Prophetic oracles are proclaimed as pronouncements made by His Royal Majesty (Jer. 46:18; 48:15;

51:57). Although before the time of Saul, Israel generally rejected the idea of human kingship as an encroachment on the Lord's sole rule over Israel (I Sam. 8:7; 12:12), at a later period the Chronicler did not hesitate to speak of the Davidic kings as the Lord's representatives seated on the royal "throne of YHWH" (e.g., I Chron. 17:14; 28:5; 29:23). Not only the nation, but also individual Israelites addressed the Lord as "King" (Ps. 5:3; 44:5; 84:4). It is disputed whether the term "King" was used of YHWH before the monarchical period in Israel. This title for YHWH is rare in the Pentateuch (Ex. 15:18; Num. 23:21; Deut. 33:5). Gideon, in refusing to "rule over" Israel, does not speak of YHWH as the king of Israel but says, "It is YHWH who is to rule over you" (Judg. 8:22–23). The term "King" is not mentioned in this passage. The phrase "Ancient of days," which is employed as an epithet of God in modern times, is biblical in origin (Dan. 7:9, 13, 22). A careful reading of these passages shows that "Ancient of Days" was yet an epithet of Yahweh. For the use of the names of God as a basis for the documentary hypothesis see *Bible, cols. 906–7.

Apocrypha

In the Apocrypha, as in the Hebrew Bible, the most common names are "God" (Gr. *Theos*; in Ben Sira usually *ʾElohim* but sometimes *ʾEl*), "Lord" (Gr. *Kyrios*, which no doubt generally stands for *ʾAdonai*; but Ben Sira commonly has *YHWH*, represented by three *yods* in the medieval mss.), "the Most High" (Gr. *ho Hypsistos*, probably for Heb. *ʿElyon*, but perhaps at times for *Ha-Gavoha* as in the Talmud), "the Lord Almighty" (Gr. *Kyrios Pantokrator* for Heb. *YHWH Ẓevaʾot*) or simply "the Almighty" (Gr. *ho Pantokratōr* for Heb. *Ẓevaʾot* alone), "the Eternal One" (Gr. *ho Aionios* (I Bar. 4:20, 22, 24, etc.) for Heb. *ʾEl ʿOlam*), etc.

Among the terms used for God that are more or less peculiar to the Apocrypha are "the God of Truth" (I Esd. 4:40); "the Living God of Majesty" (Add. Esth. 16:16; cf. Talmudic Heb. *Ha-Gevurah*); "King of Gods and Ruler of every power" (Add. Esth. 14:12); "Sovereign Lord" (Lat. *Dominator Dominus*; IV Ezra 6:11); "Creator of all" (Heb. *Yoẓer ha-Kol*; Ecclus. 24:8; 51:12); and such terms as "the Praiseworthy God" (*El ha-Tishbaḥot*), "Guardian of Israel" (*Shomer Yisrael*), "Shield of Abraham" (*Magen Avraham*), "Rock of Isaac" (*Ẓur Yiẓḥaq*), and "King over the king of kings" (*Melekh Malkhei ha-Melakhim*), which are found in that passage of Ben Sira, inserted after 51:12 in the Greek, that has been preserved only in Hebrew.

An interesting passage occurs in IV Ezra 7:62 (132)–70 (140), where, based on Exodus 34:6–7, the author of this book lists seven names of the Most High: "I know that the Most High is called 'the Compassionate One,' because He has compassion on those who have not yet come into the world; and 'the Merciful One,' because He has mercy on those who repent and live by His law; and 'the Patient One,' because He is patient toward those who have sinned, since they are His creatures; and 'the Bountiful One,' because He would rather give than take away; and 'the One Rich in Forgiveness,' because again and again He forgives sinners, past, present, and to come, since without His continued forgiveness there would be no hope of life for the world and its inhabitants; and 'the Generous One,' because without His generosity in releasing sinners from their sins not one ten-thousandth part of mankind could have life; and 'the Judge,' because if He did not grant pardon to those who have been created by His word by blotting out their countless offenses there would probably be only a very few left of the entire human race."

The earliest occurrences (except for Dan. 4:23: "It is Heaven that rules") of the substitution of the word "Heaven" (God's abode) for "God" (Himself) are found in the Apocrypha: "In the sight of Heaven" (I Macc. 3:18), "Let us cry to Heaven" (I Macc. 4:10), "They were singing hymns and glorifying Heaven" (I Macc. 4:24), "All the people… adored and praised Heaven" (I Macc. 4:55), "With the help of Heaven" (I Macc. 12:15), and "From Heaven I received these [sons]" (II Macc. 7:11). In the Christian Gospels this usage is especially common in the Judeo-Christian Gospel of Matthew, where, e.g., "the kingdom of Heaven" corresponds to "the kingdom of God" in the parallel passages of Mark and Luke (Matt. 3:2 = Mark 1:15; Matt. 5:3 = Luke 6:20; et al.), but also in Luke 15:18, 21: "I have sinned against Heaven." This usage still persists in such modern English expressions as "Heaven help us!"

[Louis F. Hartman / S. David Sperling (2nd ed.)]

In the Talmud

The subject of the names of God in the Talmud must be considered under two heads, the prohibition of using the biblical divine names, and the additional names evolved by the rabbis.

The Prohibition of Use of the Names of God

The prohibition applies both to the pronunciation of the name of God and its committal to writing, apart from its use in sacred writings. The prohibition against the pronunciation of the name of God applies only to the Tetragrammaton, which could be pronounced by the high priest only once a year on the Day of Atonement in the Holy of Holies (cf. Mishnah Yoma 6:2), and in the Temple by the priests when they recited the Priestly Blessing (Sot. 7:6; see also Ch. Albeck (ed.), *Seder Nashim* (1954), 387). As the Talmud expresses it: "Not as I am written am I pronounced. I am written *yod he vav he*, and I am pronounced *alef dalet" (nun yod*, i.e., *ʾAdonai*; Kid. 71a). The prohibition of committing the names of God to secular writing belongs to a different category. Basing themselves on Deuteronomy 12:4, the *Sifrei* (ad loc.) and the Talmud (Shev. 35a) lay it down that it is forbidden to erase the name of God from a written document, and since any paper upon which that name appears might be discarded and thus "erased," it is forbidden to write the name explicitly. The Talmud gives an interesting historical note with regard to one aspect of this. Among the decrees of the Syrians during the persecutions of *Antiochus Epiphanes was one forbidding the mention of the name of God. When the *Hasmoneans gained the victory they not only naturally repealed the decree, but demonstratively ordained that the divine name be entered even in monetary bonds, the opening formula being "In such and such a year of Johanan, high priest to the Most High God." The rabbis, however, forbade this practice since "tomorrow a man will pay his debt and the bond (with the name of God) will be discarded on a dunghill"; the day of the prohibition was actually made an annual festival (RH 18b).

It is, however, specifically stated that this prohibition refers only to seven biblical names of God. They are *ʾEl, ʾElohim* (also with suffixes), "I am that I am" (Ex. 3:14), *ʾAdonai*, the Tetragrammaton, *Shaddai*, and *Ẓevaʾot* (R. Yose disagrees with this last, Shev. 35a–b). The passage states explicitly that all other names and descriptions of God by attributes may be written freely. Despite this, it became the accepted custom among Orthodox Jews to use variations of most of those names in speech, particularly *ʾElokim* for *ʾElohim*, and *Ha-Shem* ("the Name"; and, for reasons of assonance, *ʾAdoshem*) for Adonai. The adoption of *Ha-Shem* is probably due to a misunderstanding of a passage in the liturgy of the Day of Atonement, the *Avodah*. It includes the formula of the confession of the high priest on that day. Since on that occasion he uttered the Ineffable Name, the text has "Oh, *Ha-Shem*, I have sinned," etc. The meaning is probably "O [here he mentioned the Ineffable Name] I have sinned," and from this developed the custom of using *Ha-Shem* for *ʾAdonai*, which is in itself a substitute for the Tetragrammaton (see also Allon, Meḥkarim, 1 (1957), 194ff.; S. Lieberman, *Tosefta ki-Feshutah (Moʿed)*, 4 (1962), 755).

*Shabbetai b. Meir ha-Kohen (first half 17th century) states emphatically that the prohibition of erasure of the divine name applies only to the names in Hebrew but not the vernacular (*Siftei Kohen* to Sh. Ar., YD 179:8; cf. *Pitḥei Teshuvah* to YD 276:9), and this is repeated as late as the 19th century by R. Akiva Eger (novellae, ad loc.). Jehiel Michael Epstein, however, in his *Arukh ha-Shulḥan* (ḤM 27:3) inveighs vehemently against the practice of writing the Divine Name even in vernacular in correspondence, calling it an "exceedingly grave offense." As a result the custom has become widespread among extremely particular Jews not to write the word God or any other name of God, even in the vernacular, in full.

Rabbinical Names of God

The rabbis evolved a number of additional names of God. All of them, without exception, are references to His attributes, but curiously enough they are not included in the list of the permitted names enumerated in the passage in *Shevuʿot*: "the Great, the Mighty, the Revered, the Majestic," etc. (35a–b). The most common is *Ha-Kadosh barukh Hu* ("the Holy One, blessed be He"; in Aramaic, *Kudsha berikh Hu*). It is an abbreviation of "the Supreme King of kings, the Holy One blessed be He." The full formula is found in the Mishnah (e.g., Sanh. 4:5; Avot 3:1), but more often the abbreviation is found (e.g., Ned. 3:11; Sot. 5:5; Avot 3:2; 5:4; and Uk. 3:12); it is by far the most common appellation of God in the Midrash. Another name is *Ribbono shel Olam* ("Sovereign of the Universe"), normally used as an introduction to a supplication, as in the prayer of *Onias ha-Meʿaggel for rain (Taʿan. 3:8). One of the most interesting names is *Ha-Makom* (lit. "the place," i.e., the Omnipresent; Av. Zar. 40b; Nid. 49b; Ber. 16b), and it is explained in the Midrash: "R. Huna in the name of R. Ammi said, 'Why do we use a circumlocution for the name of the Holy One, blessed be He, and call him *Makom?* Because He is the place of His world, but this world is not His [only] place'"(Gen. R. 68:49). The name *Ha-Raḥaman* ("the All-Merciful") is commonly used in the liturgy, particularly in the *Grace after Meals. In the Talmud, the Aramaic form, *Raḥmana*, is also found (Git. 17a; Ket. 45a), as it is in several prayers from the geonic period. So also *Shamayim* ("heaven") as in *Yirat Shamayim* ("Fear of God"; Ber. 16b), however *Avinu she-ba-Shamayim* ("Our Father in Heaven"; Yoma 8:9) is also used. According to the Talmud (Shab. 10b) *Shalom* ("Peace") is also one of the names of God, as is the word *Ani* ("I") in Mishnah *Sukkah* 4:5, and in Hillel's statement (Suk. 53a) "If *Ani* is here, all is here," it is given the same connotation.

Reference is made to a "Name of 12 letters" and a "Name of 42 letters" (Ked. 71a). Of the former, it is stated that "it used to be entrusted to everyone, but when unruly men increased, it was confided only to the pious of the priesthood and they used to pronounce it indistinctly ("swallowed it") while their priestly brethren were chanting the benediction." R. Tarfon, who was a kohen, states that he once heard the high priest thus muttering it. Similarly the 42-lettered Name is entrusted only to those of exceptionally high moral character. Rashi (ad loc.) states that these names have been lost. According to the kabbalists the prayer *Anna be-Khoʾaḥ*, found in the prayer book, and consisting of 42 words, is connected with this latter name. Finally it should be mentioned that to the rabbis it is definite that the Tetragrammaton denotes God in His attribute of mercy and *ʾElohim* (which in fact means a "judge" (cf. Ex. 22:8, 27)) denotes Him in His attribute of justice.

[Louis Isaac Rabinowitz]

In Kabbalah

The names of God play different roles in the kabbalistic literature. According to a magical tradition adopted by *Naḥmanides, there is a reading of the Torah as a continuum of divine names. Though he asserted that this reading is lost, other kabbalists, especially the ecstatic ones, adopted this theory in order to interpret the biblical verses as combinations of divine names. Following some discussions found in *Ḥasidei Ashkenaz, in this kabbalistic school, the divine names, the Tetragrammaton, and the name of 72 letters, serve as a vital part of the mystical technique. According to the theosophical-theurgical kabbalists, the various divine names point to each of the divine powers, or *sefirot*, and they serve both as symbols for those powers and instruments to unify them. In a few cases, kabbalists assume that in the Bible there is no name that points to the highest divine realm. In practical Kabbalah, recipes based on divine names, imagined to achieve a variety of magical acts, abound.

[Moshe Idel (2nd ed.)]

In Medieval Jewish Philosophy

The multiple names of God in the Bible posed a special problem for medieval Jewish philosophers. Concerned to defend and explicate God's absolute unity, they found it necessary to treat the divine names in a way that eliminates any suggestion of plurality in God's being. They either reduced the multiple names to a single common meaning or showed that, among the numerous names, one alone was the proper and exclusive name of God. *Saadiah Gaon held that the two most widely used scriptural names, YHWH and *'Elohim*, have a single meaning. This is in marked contrast to the above-mentioned teaching that one name stands for God's attribute of mercy and the other for His attribute of justice.

*Judah Halevi, Abraham *Ibn Daud, *Maimonides, and Joseph *Albo all emphasized the Tetragrammaton as the only proper name of God. Judah Halevi held that all the other names "are predicates and attributive descriptions, derived from the way His creatures are affected by His decrees and measures" (*Kuzari*, 2:2; 4:1–3).

Maimonides declared that, except for YHWH, "All the names of God that are to be found in any of the books derive from actions" (*Guide of the Perplexed*, 1:61–64), but only the Tetragrammaton "gives a clear and unequivocal indication of His essence," a view which is shared by Albo (*Sefer ha-Ikkarim*, 2:28). For Halevi the meaning of YHWH is hidden, and for Ibn Daud it refers to God as master of the universe. The philosophers identified God as creator, first cause, first mover, first being, or necessary existence, but none of these technical philosophic terms can be considered names of God.

In Modern Jewish Philosophy

From Moses *Mendelssohn through Martin *Buber, modern Jewish philosophy exhibits two main tendencies with respect to the names of God. One line, moving from Mendelssohn through such thinkers as Solomon *Formstecher, Samuel *Hirsh, Nachman *Krochmal, and Hermann *Cohen, treats the names of God as primarily metaphysical. In his German translation of the Bible, Mendelssohn renders YHWH as "the Eternal"; Formstecher speaks of God as the "World-Soul"; and Krochmal conceives Him as "Absolute Spirit." In his extensive discussion of the traditional divine names, Cohen interprets all of them as pointing to God's unity and His uniqueness. YHWH refers to God as absolute Being; *Ehyeh-asher-ehyeh* (Ex. 3:14) relates to His eternal and unchanging nature; and **Shekhinah*, translated by Cohen as "Absolute Rest," refers to the unchanging divine nature.

In contrast, Franz *Rosenzweig and Martin Buber view the names as primarily religious and personalistic. In their translation of the Bible, they render YHWH by the personal pronouns YOU or HE. *Ehyeh* names the God who is always present to man and constantly participates in human concerns. Thus, Buber interprets Exodus 3:14 as saying, "I again and again stand by those whom I befriend; and I would have you know indeed that I befriend you." They consider the philosophic interpretation of the names as seriously inadequate in its failure to grasp the personal-religious reality which is fundamental to Judaism. Turning in a radically different direction, Mordecai *Kaplan developed a purely naturalistic conception of God. He refers to Him as "The Power that makes for salvation" and interprets this as "The Power that makes for the fulfillment of all valid ideals."

[Marvin Fox]

BIBLIOGRAPHY: IN THE BIBLE: A.E. Murtonen, *Philological and Literary Treatise on Old Testament Divine Names* (1952); M. Pope, *El in Ugaritic Texts* (1955); Albright, in: JBL, 54 (1935), 173–93; 67 (1948), 377–81; Freedman, *ibid.*, 79 (1960), 151–6; Abba, *ibid.*, 80 (1961), 320–8; Bailey, *ibid.*, 87 (1968), 434–8; Cohon, in: HUCA, 23 (1950–51), 579–604; Mowinckel, *ibid.*, 32 (1961), 121–33; Cross, in: HTR, 55 (1962), 225–9; Maclaurin, in: VT, 12 (1962), 439–63; Rendtorff, in: ZAW, 78 (1966), 277–92; Hyatt, in: JBL, 86 (1967), 369–77; A. Alt, *Der Gott der Väter* (1929); Finkelstein, in: *Conservative Judaism*, 23 (1969), 25–36. IN THE TALMUD: S. Esh, *Ha-Kadosh Barukh Hu: Der Heilige Er sei gepriesen* (1957); A. Marmorstein, *The Old Rabbinic Doctrine of God: The Names and Attributes of God* (1968²), 17–145. **ADD. BIBLIOGRAPHY:** IN THE BIBLE: K. Tallqvist, *Akkadische Götterepitheta* (1974); E. Urbach, *The Sages …* (1987); L. Jacobs, in: *Encyclopedia of Religion* (2004²), 3547–552; J. Neusner, *ibid.*, 7583–90; B. Becking, in: DDD, 44–55; *ibid.*, 292–93; W. Herrmann, *ibid.*, 274–80; W. Rőllig, *ibid.*, 28––81; D. Pardee, *ibid.*, 285–88; A. de Pury, *ibid.*, 288–92; E. Elnes and P. Miller, *ibid.*, 293–99; E.A. Knauf, *ibid.*, 749–53; K. van der Toorn, *ibid.*, 910–19; S. David Sperling, in: IDBSUP, 608–9; idem, *Encyclopedia of Religion* (2004²), 3537–43. IN KABBALAH: M. Idel, "Allegory and Divine Names in Ecstatic Kabbalah," in: J. Whitman (ed.), *Interpretation and Allegory, Antiquity to the Modern World* (2000), 317–47.

GODAL, ERIC (1898–1969), German cartoonist. Born in Berlin, Godal began drawing topical illustrations and cartoons for Acht Uhr Abendblatt when in his twenties. He drew some of the first cartoons of Hitler and his stormtroopers, and when the Nazis seized power in 1933 escaped from Berlin when the men sent to arrest him surrounded the wrong house. Godal went to Prague, where he worked for the anti-Nazi daily *Prager Mittag* and for the satirical weekly *Der Simplicus* which had been founded as an answer to the famous weekly *Simplicissimus* of Munich, which had by then accepted the Nazi line. Godal reached the U.S. before World War II and contributed to various papers there. He returned to Germany in 1954 and worked for the *Hamburger Abendblatt* and the woman's magazine *Constanze*. Together with Rolf Italiaander he published the book *Teenagers* in 1958, combining essays and illustrations which attempted to explain the feelings of the first generation born after World War II. Godal visited Israel in 1968 to write a series of illustrated articles. His memoirs, *Kein Talent zum Tellerwaescher*, were published in 1969.

GODDARD, PAULETTE (Pauline Marion Levy; 1911–1990), U.S. film actress. Born in Long Island, New York, Goddard was the only child of a Mormon mother and a Jewish father. She began her public career as a child model at a local department store and debuted in the Ziegfeld Follies at age 13. She went to Hollywood in 1931, where she had bit parts in several films. In 1932 she appeared as one of the 20 original chorus girls, known as the "Goldwyn Girls," in the Eddie Cantor film *The Kid from Spain*, along with such young starlets as Lucille Ball, Betty Grable, and Jane Wyman. That year, Charlie Chaplin chose her to star opposite him as the waif in *Modern Times* (1936). They were subsequently secretly married, but by 1940 the couple split up and they were divorced in 1942. In 1939 her performance in the films *The Women* and *The Cat and the Canary* landed her a 10-year contract with Paramount, and she rose to become one of the studio's top film stars during the 1940s. She starred once again with Chaplin in his first talking film, *The Great Dictator* (1940). In 1944 she married actor-director Burgess Meredith (they divorced in 1950). They produced and starred in *Diary of a Chambermaid* (1946). Among Goddard's other films were *The Ghost Breakers* (1940); *Northwest Mounted Police* (1940); *Second Chorus* (1940); *Pot o' Gold* (1941); *Hold Back the Dawn* (1941); *Nothing but the Truth* (1941); *The Lady Has Plans* (1942); *Reap the Wild Wind* (1942); *The Forest Rangers* (1942); *So Proudly We Hail* (1943), for which she was nominated for a Best Supporting Actress Oscar; *The Crystal Ball* (1943); *Standing Room Only* (1944); *I Love a Soldier* (1944); *Kitty* (1945); *Suddenly It's Spring* (1947); *Unconquered* (1947); *An Ideal Husband* (1947); *On Our Merry Way* (1948); *Hazard* (1948); *Bride of Vengeance* (1949); *Anna Lucasta* (1949); *Charge of the Lancers* (1954); and *The Unholy Four* (1954).

Goddard left the film industry in the mid-1950s and moved to Europe, where, in 1958, she married novelist Erich Maria Remarque. She made her last film appearance in 1964 in *Time of Indifference* and in 1972 performed in the TV movie *The Snoop Sisters*. Upon her death, she bequeathed a large amount of money to the Hebrew University and to New York University.

BIBLIOGRAPHY: J. Morella, *Paulette: The Adventurous Life of Paulette Goddard* (1985); C. Chaplin, *My Autobiography*, (1993); J. Gilbert, *Opposite Attraction: The Lives of Erich Maria Remarque and Paulette Goddard* (1995).

[Ruth Beloff (2nd ed.)]

GODEFROI, MICHAEL HENRI (1813–1882), Dutch lawyer and statesman, who was the first Jew to hold a cabinet post in Holland and the first Jewish member of the Second Chamber of Parliament. Born into an emancipated Jewish family in Amsterdam, Godefroi became a judge of the Provincial Court of North Holland in 1846 and in 1849 entered the Second Chamber of the Dutch Parliament where he remained until 1881. He became minister of justice from 1860 to 1862 after having rejected earlier offers to become a minister, and drafted a new legal code on the Council of State. Through his sister he was connected to the *Asser family. Godefroi was active in Jewish affairs as a member of the Hoofdcommissie tot de Zaken der Israëlieten from 1844 to 1860, serving as its chairman from 1854. In 1857 he induced the Dutch government to defer its trade agreement with Switzerland until that country granted equal rights to her Jews. Likewise, in 1876 he successfully opposed the ratification of the Dutch-Romanian commercial agreement because of Romania's persecution of Jews.

[Henriette Boas / Bart Wallet (2nd ed.)]

GODIK, GIORA (1918–1977), Israeli impressario. Born in Warsaw, Godik reached Palestine during World War II, and later established himself as manager of soloists from abroad. He presented *West Side Story* performed by an American company, and then started production of musicals in Hebrew. *My Fair Lady* was a financial success in 1964, and was surpassed two years later by *Fiddler on the Roof*. Godik then promoted musicals written in Israel with less financial success; in 1967 he presented *Casablan*. In 1972 he moved to West Germany.

GODINER, SAMUEL NISSAN (**Shmuel Nisn**; 1893–1942), Soviet Yiddish poet. Born in Telchan, Belorussia, Godiner moved to Warsaw as a teenager, became active in the Russian Social Revolutionary movement, was recruited into the Russian army in 1912, and was wounded in battle two years later. In 1918, he was taken prisoner by the Austrian army but escaped and rejoined the Russian army. From 1921 to 1923 he attended a Soviet literary institute in Moscow. His first short stories, published after 1921, dealt with the Russian civil war and employed the impressionistic symbolic style of the Kiev novelists Dovid *Bergelson and *Der Nister. His later short stories followed the requirements of socialist realism. Godiner's most popular novel was *Der Mentsh mit der Biks* ("The Man with the Rifle," 2 vols., 1928). He translated Russian novels into Yiddish and wrote a drama *Dzhim Kuperkop* ("Jim Coopercop," 1930). Godiner traveled to Birobidzhan several times and helped found Jewish schools and libraries there. In June, 1941, when the Germans invaded Russia, he left Moscow to fight with the partisans and died in battle. His short novel, *Zaveler Trakt* ("Blocked Highway," 1938), was reprinted posthumously in New York in 1950.

BIBLIOGRAPHY: LNYL, 2 (1958), 3f.; Y. Levin, in: S.N. Godiner, *Zaveler Trakt* (1950), 5–8. **ADD. BIBLIOGRAPHY:** Y. Bronshteyn, *Atake* (1931), 194–218; A. Abtshuk, *Etyudn un Materyaln* (1932), 27–29, 50–51, 61.

[Sol Liptzin / Marc Miller (2nd ed.)]

GODÍNEZ, FELIPE (c. 1585–c. 1639), Spanish playwright. Born in Moguer, Godínez became famous as a preacher in Seville. Jewish sympathies remained strong in his "New Christian" family: one of his grandparents was penanced by the Inquisition and an uncle fled to North Africa, where he reverted to Judaism. Old Testament themes inspired a number of Godínez' plays – *El divino Isaac, Las lágrimas de David, Amán y Mardoqueo o la reina Esther, Los trabajos de Job*, and *Judit y Holofernes*. Of these, *Los trabajos de Job* is memorable for its pathetic evocation of the trials of its hero. Godínez also wrote works on the lives of Christian saints, as well as some comedies of intrigue typical of the period, notably *Aun de noche alumbra* *el sol*. The biblical works are considered his best. Godínez was arrested by the Inquisition and in November 1624 appeared at an auto-de-fé – one of the very few dramatists of the Spanish Golden Age to appear at an auto-de-fé in person. His property was confiscated, and he was deprived of his ecclesiastical offices and imprisoned for two years. After his release he moved to Madrid, where he was accepted in literary circles, although writers like Lope de Vega (1562–1635) satirized him because of his Jewish origin. Godínez nevertheless agreed to deliver Lope de Vega's funeral oration.

BIBLIOGRAPHY: M. Méndez Bejarano, *Histoire de la Juiverie de Séville* (1922), 195–213; A. Valbuena Prat, *Historia de la literatura española*, 2 (1946), 148–9, 151; E. Diez Echarri and J.M. Roca Franquesa, *Historia de la literatura española e hispanoamericana* (1960), 513–4; C. Menéndez Onrubia, in: *Segismundo*, 25–26 (1977), 89–130; M.S. Carrasco Urgoiti, in: *Nueva Revista de Filología Hispánica*, 30 (1981), 546–73; P. Bolaños Donoso, *La obra dramática de Felipe Godínez; trayectoria de un dramaturgo marginado* (1983); G. Vega García-Luengos, *Problemas de un dramaturgo del Siglo del Oro. Estudios sobre Felipe Godínez, con dos comedias inéditas: La Reina Ester, Ludovico el Piadoso* (1986).

[Kenneth R. Scholberg]

GODOWSKY, LEOPOLD (1870–1983), pianist. Born in Soshly near Vilna, he was a child prodigy and early embarked on a widely acclaimed international concert career. His enquiries into the fundamentals of pianistic technique led him to the composition of etudes and pieces for both the elementary and virtuoso level, with special attention to left-hand technique. He also edited some of the standard etude works.

His son, also called LEOPOLD GODOWSKY (1900–1983), was a U.S. violinist and co-inventor, with Leopold *Mannes, of the Kodachrome color process. Though photography was only Godowsky's hobby, he was best known for his pioneering work in the development of color film. He was born in Chicago, but spent much of his youth in Berlin and in Vienna, where his father held prominent positions for several years. Godowsky met Leopold Mannes in a school in Connecticut when they were both 16 years old. While still at school, they began experimenting to find a successful method of producing color film. They built a camera with three lenses and three filters, one for each primary color, and superimposed them on a single plate. Eventually, they produced a double-layered plate on which part of the spectrum could be photographed. Working at the Eastman Kodak laboratories in Rochester, N.Y., they succeeded by 1935 in developing three-color motion-picture film, and soon after followed with the process for stills. In 1938 they initiated research for Kodacolor, Ektacolor, and Ektachrome film and in 1939 they left Rochester. Godowsky built his own laboratory on his estate in Connecticut for further experiments. In addition, Godowsky was the first violinist of the San Francisco Symphony Orchestra and played in the Los Angeles Philharmonic.

°**GOEBBELS, PAUL JOSEF** (1897–1945), Nazi leader and propaganda minister. Exempted from military service during World War I because of his clubfoot, Goebbels received a Ph.D. in literature and history in 1920. After some political searching, he made several unsuccessful attempts to write for liberal papers, most of which happened to be owned by Jews. He joined the Nazi Party in 1922. He never forgot his failure with liberal newspapers. After some soul-searching, Goebbels resolutely backed Hitler in the party's factional intrigues. In 1926 he was appointed *Gauleiter* ("district head") of Berlin, where he succeeded in building a strong party organization out of insignificant beginnings. The Nazi success at the polls in the early 1930s was due to a considerable extent to the propagandist genius of Goebbels, who had become chief of the party's propaganda department at the beginning of 1929. Appointed minister for people's information and propaganda after the Nazi accession to power, he became virtual dictator of Germany's communications media and artistic life. Goebbels' Manichean philosophy of a charismatic hero-leader opposed by powers of darkness (the latter personified by the Jew) was reflected in his propaganda. He was one of the instigators of the anti-Jewish boycott of April 1, 1933, and of **Kristallnacht* (1938), organizing the latter in Berlin and participating in the Nazi conference dealing with the aftermath of the pogrom, in which heavy sanctions were imposed on the Jews. Continually demanding new oppressive measures against the Jews, he was among the initiators of the *Final Solution (see *Holocaust, General Survey), doing his best to incite the killers by various propaganda methods. As *Gauleiter* of Berlin he strove to make it *judenrein*, i.e., "cleanse" it of its Jewish population. Goebbels stayed with Hitler to the end, killing himself and his family after Hitler's suicide.

BIBLIOGRAPHY: L.P. Lochner, *Goebbels' Diaries 1942–1943* (1948); H. Heiber, *Josef Goebbels* (Ger., 1962); R. Manvell and H. Fraenkel, *Doctor Goebbels* (1960); E.K. Bramstead, *Goebbels and National Socialist Propaganda 1925–1945* (1965).

[Yehuda Reshef]

°**GOERING, HERMANN WILHELM** (1893–1946), Nazi leader. A fighter pilot during World War I, Goering was awarded the highest military decoration ("Pour le Mérite"). In 1922 he joined the Nazi Party, becoming the first leader of its storm troops (SA). He was at Hitler's side during the Munich putsch of Nov. 9, 1923, and suffered a thigh wound, which caused his life-long drug addiction. He stood by Hitler through all the party's vicissitudes, boasting of being his leader's most faithful paladin. He participated in the intrigues that brought the Nazis to power and was appointed Hitler's minister of air transport and Prussian prime minister. In the latter capacity he formed the *Gestapo. Goering created the Nazi Air Force (Luftwaffe) and planned its strategies; he was as much responsible for its initial successes as for its later failures. In 1936 he was appointed "Plenipotentiary for the Four-Year Plan" to prepare Germany economically for war. Goering decided to use the property of German Jewry for financing Germany's rearmament, and he utilized his office to organize its expropriation. In the spring of 1938 he promulgated a set of orders obliging German Jewry, which by then included the Jews of Austria, to declare and register their property. The *Kristallnacht in 1938 gave him the opportunity to realize his plans and set his "aryanization" into action to expropriate Jewish businesses and property. On Nov. 12, 1938, Goering convened a conference of Nazi officials and experts, including Josef *Goebbels and Reinhard *Heydrich. The conference decided to impose a fine of a billion marks on Germany's Jews to expiate the murder of vom Rath. Furthermore, all Jewish property was to be taken over by the Reich and the owners indemnified with government low-interest bonds at a price lower than the real value. Goering's expropriation methods later served as a pattern for looting Jewish property in the countries occupied during World War II. Continuing the policy set by the November Conference, on Jan. 24, 1939, Goering appointed Heydrich head of the newly formed central organization for Jewish emigration, the "Zentralstelle fuer juedische Auswanderung." At the start of World War II, Goering was appointed Hitler's successor. He organized the plunder of the occupied countries, especially the Soviet Union. He collaborated with Alfred *Rosenberg in confiscating Jewish collections of art and used the loot to enlarge his own private collection. On July 31, 1941, Goering charged Heydrich with the implementation of Hitler's decision on the "Final Solution" (see *Holocaust, General Survey). He sent a representative to attend the *Wannsee Conference. He was involved in every phase of the destruction of European Jews and knew their fate. He was a fanatical antisemite (see his remarks at the Nov. 12, 1938 conference), but according to some authorities he saved individual Jews, at least before the start of the destruction process. With the decline of Germany's fortunes, Goering's influence waned. The failures of his Luftwaffe and his indolence and corruption made Hitler lose faith in him. Before committing suicide, Hitler stripped him of all his offices and had him arrested. Goering was condemned to death by the Nuremberg International Military Tribunal as a major war criminal, specific reference being made to his decisive role in the extermination of the Jews. He poisoned himself before the execution could take place.

BIBLIOGRAPHY: *The Trial of the Major War Criminals* (1947), index; *Nazi Conspiracy and Aggression* (1949; includes indictment of Goering); W. Frischauer, *Rise and Fall of Hermann Goering* (1951); R. Manuell and H. Fraenkel, *Hermann Goering* (1962); E. Davidson, *Trial of the Germans* (1966), ch. 3; C. Bewley, *Hermann Goering and the Third Reich* (1962), 337–54; G.M. Gilbert, *Nuremberg Diary* (1947), 185–216.

[Yehuda Reshef]

GOERITZ, MATHIAS (1915.–1990), Mexican artist and architect. Born in Danzig, Germany, the grandson of a painter, Goeritz studied in Berlin. Art historian in the National Gallery of Art in Berlin, he was forced to leave Germany in 1941 by the Nazis. He lived two years in Spain and in 1949 went to the University of Guadalajara, Mexico, where he helped construct a museum and later executed the plan for two 195 feet (60 meters) high towers on the north highway to Mexico City. He was interested in religious motives and liturgical art. He also took part in the design of the Magen David Synagogue of Mexico City.

GOERLITZ, town in Silesia, Germany. The earliest extant sources attest to the presence of a Jewish community at the beginning of the 14th century but it was probably even older. It is known that there was a *Judengasse* on which both Jews and non-Jews were living in 1307. The cemetery dates from 1325, and the community owned a bathhouse and a synagogue as well. In this period the only occupation pursued by Jews which is attested in the sources was that of moneylending. The persecutions in the wake of the *Black Death brought the community to an end in 1349, but it was reestablished in 1364. After their expulsion in 1389, Jews were permitted to stay in Goerlitz only to participate in trade fairs.

Shortly before 1849 a new community was founded. A cemetery was acquired in 1850; the first synagogue was consecrated in 1870 and the second in 1911; the latter was destroyed in 1938. In 1880 there were 643 Jews in Goerlitz. In 1932, even before the Nazi regime, ritual slaughter was prohibited in Goerlitz. Separate areas for Jewish merchants were set up in the marketplace on Aug. 30, 1935. The number of Jews decreased rapidly, from 600 in 1931 to 376 in 1933 and 134 in 1939. The remnants of the community were wiped out during World War II.

BIBLIOGRAPHY: FJW, 98–99; Germ Jud, 1 (1963), 504; 2 (1968), 282–3; Neubauer, Cat, no. 194.

[Bernhard Brilling]

°GOETHE, JOHANN WOLFGANG VON (1749–1832), German writer. As a boy, Goethe acquired a thorough knowledge of *Luther's translation of the Bible, which left its mark on his conversation, letters, and literary work. Among his youthful projects were a "biblical, prose-epic poem" *Joseph* and several dramatic pieces on biblical subjects (*Isabel, Ruth, Selima, Der Thronfolger Pharaos*), none of which has been passed on to us; only fragments of the tragedy *Belsazar*, written in alexandrine verse, have survived. Goethe also mentions, among "youthful sins" which he condemned to the fire, a work inspired by the history of Samson. His notebooks show him wrestling with the Hebrew alphabet and with the Judeo-German dialect (*Judendeutsch*) which he heard on visits to the *Judengasse* of his native Frankfurt. He records how, on one such occasion, when part of the ghetto burned down, he helped to quench the flames while other youngsters jeered at the hapless Jews. Goethe even planned a novel in which seven brothers and sisters were to correspond in seven languages, including *Judendeutsch*; a surviving *Judenpredigt* written in that dialect has been dated on 1768. In 1771 he reviewed Isachar Falkensohn *Behr's *Gedichte eines polnischen Juden*. He thought very highly of the poetic quality of the Hebrew bible; his own translation of the Song of Songs (1775) proves his knowledge of the original text.

Goethe's *Faust* has almost 200 passages containing biblical parallels, beginning with the "Prologue in Heaven," for which the first chapters of Job served as a model, and ending with the final scene of Faust's death, which was inspired by the biblical and talmudic accounts of the death of Moses. In the explanatory prose parts of his late collection of poems *West-östlicher Divan* he integrated an extensive study on *Israel in der Wüste*, which deals with the role of Moses and the Israelite people.

After he moved to Weimar in 1775, Goethe's social life brought him into contact with many Jewish and converted Jewish intellectuals and artists, including Heinrich *Heine, who did not impress him, and Felix Mendelssohn-Bartholdy, whom he loved. Goethe allowed the artist Moritz *Oppenheim to paint his portrait and to illustrate his poetic idyll *Hermann und Dorothea* (1798). He opposed legislation aimed at liberalizing the position of Jews in German society. In general, however, contemporary Judaism did not play a major role in his work. Goethe's many Jewish biographers include Albert Bielschowsky, Ludwig Geiger, Richard Moritz Meyer, Eduard Engel, Georg Simmel, Emil *Ludwig, Friedrich *Gundolf, Georg *Brandes, Richard Friedenthal and Hans Mayer.

BIBLIOGRAPHY: L. Deutschlaender, *Goethe und das Alte Testament* (1923), incl. bibl.; H. Teweles, *Goethe und die Juden* (1925); G. Janzer, *Goethe und die Bibel* (1929), incl. bibl.; M. Waldman, *Goethe and the Jews* (1934); R. Eberhard, *Goethe und das Alte Testament* (1935), incl. bibl.; A. Spire, in: E.J. Finbert (ed.), *Aspects du génie d'Israël* (1950), 183–99. **ADD. BIBLIOGRAPHY:** W. Barner, "150 Jahre nach seinem Tod: Goethe und die Juden," in: BBI, 63 (1982), 75–82; A. Muschg, "Mehr Licht für ein Aergernis. Goethe und die Juden," in: FAZ, Nr. 223 (Sept. 26, 1987); N. Oellers, "Goethe und Schiller in ihrem Verhaeltnis zum Judentum," in: H.O. Horch und H. Denkler (eds), *Conditio Judaica. Judentum, Antisemitismus und deutschrsprachige Literatur vom 18. Jh. bis zum Ersten Weltkrieg.* Part 1 (1988), 108–30; W. Barner, *Von Rahel Varnhagen bis Friedrich Gundolf. Juden als deutsche Goethe-Verehrer* (1992); F.R. Lachman, "Was das Judentum dazu sagt: Goethe u. das Judentum," in: *Aufbau*, America's only German-Jewish publication, 58:7 (1992), 17, 20; G. Hartung, "Goethe und die Juden," in: *Weimarer Beiträge*, 40 (1994), 398–416; K. Feilchenfeldt, "Goethe im Kreis seiner Berliner Verehrergemeinde 1793–1832," in: C. Perels (ed.), *"Ein Dichter hatte uns alle geweckt": Goethe und die literarische Romantik* (1999), 201–14. J. Stenzel and O. Hoeher, "Die Verschrobenheit eines veralteten Unsinns. Goethes, Judenpredigt," in: JBDFDH (2000), 1–26; A. Weber (ed.), *"Außerdem waren sie ja auch Menschen." Goethes Begegnung mit Juden und dem Judentum* (2000).

[Sol Liptzin / Anne Bohnenkamp-Renken (2nd ed.)]

GOETSCHEL, JULES (1908–1981), Swiss lawyer, educated in Basle and Paris, politician and communal leader. Under the impact of National Socialism Goetschel turned to the Social Democratic party and was elected member of the cantonal parliament of Basle-city (1949–68) and its president for 1967–68. In his inauguration speech he spoke of the long route of Basle Jews towards gaining social acceptance. He was active in the affairs of the Basle Jewish community, especially for the Jewish home for the aged, La Charmille.

BIBLIOGRAPHY: H. Wichers, "Juedinnen und Juden in der Politik," in: H. Haumann (ed.), *Achthundert Jahre Juden in Basel* (2005), 223f.

[Uri Kaufmann (2nd ed.)]

GOETTINGEN, city in Germany. Jews are first mentioned there in the 13th century. The community, composed of a dozen families, had a synagogue and paid 4½% of the city's taxes. It was destroyed in 1350 during the *Black Death persecutions, but in 1370 a charter giving protection to the Jews of the city was re-endorsed. In 1591 the Jews were expelled from Goettingen. Several resettled in the city at the end of the 17th century, and in 1718 Jews were given permission to acquire real property. In the university quarter their numbers were limited to three families. Some Hebrew printing took place in Goettingen. Abraham Jagel's *Lekaḥ Tov* was published there in 1742, and Hebrew type was also used in A.G. Wachner's *Antiquitates Hebraeorum* (1742–43). The community numbered 43 in 1833, 265 in 1871, 661 (1.75% of the total population) in 1910, 410 in 1933, and 173 in 1939. In 1859 there was appointed at Goettingen University the first Jew to become a professor in a German university, the mathematician Moritz Abraham *Stern. The university was noted for its biblical scholars, most of whom were champions of the documentary hypothesis, from J.G. *Eichhorn and G.H.A. *Ewald to Paul de *Lagarde and Julius *Wellhausen. When James *Franck, the Nobel prizewinner, resigned his chair in 1933, a number of professors demanded that he be tried for sabotage; six other Jewish professors were put on compulsory leave, among them the mathematicians Otto *Neugebauer and Richard *Courant, as well as Nikolaus *Pevsner, and Eugen *Caspary. The synagogue was burned down on Kristallnacht. In March and June 1942, 150 Jews were deported; including those who had sought refuge in other localities, 267 local Jews were murdered by the Nazis during the Holocaust. There were 26 Jews living in Goettingen in 1965, bolsterd in the 1990s by immigrants from the former Soviet Union.

BIBLIOGRAPHY: Germ Jud, 2 (1968), 296–8; Yad Vashem Archives; PKG.

GOFFMAN, ERVING MANUAL (1922–1982), Canadian sociologist and ethnographer. The son of Ukrainian Jewish immigrants, Goffman was born in Mannville, Alberta, and raised in Dauphin, Manitoba, near Winnipeg. He was educated at the University of Manitoba, the University of Toronto (B.A., 1945) and the University of Chicago (M.A., 1949; Ph.D., 1953). He held academic appointments at the University of Chicago (1952–54), the National Institute of Mental Health, Bethesda, Maryland (1954–57), the University of California, Berkeley (1958–68; full professor, 1962); and the University of Pennsylvania, where he was the Benjamin Franklin Professor of Anthropology and Sociology from 1968 until his death from cancer in 1982.

Goffman practiced a form of sociology that he developed largely in opposition to the prevailing "value-free" quantitative methods in favor in the 1940s and 1950s. Using qualitative methods of subtle, sophisticated critical observation, he focused on personal interactions in public places and developed a system of classification and categorization of everyday behaviors, which he referred to as the "interaction order." He understood these behaviors in terms of a strategic "presentation of self," of "impression management" and interpersonal "dramaturgy." Though Goffman's work was immensely influential among sociologists, the quality of his writing as well as the ironies implicit in his portraits of people performing or representing their own identities made his work influential with a wider, more literary, audience outside academic sociology.

Goffman's first major book, and probably still his best known, was *The Presentation of Self in Everyday Life* (1959), in which he set forth his basic insights and established the metaphorical language he was to use in all of his published work. *Asylums* (1961) was based on an ethnographic study he had conducted at St. Elizabeth's, a federal mental hospital in Washington, D.C., in 1955–57, under the sponsorship of the National Institute of Mental Health. Here he developed his ideas about the deforming effects on those caught in "total institutions" – not only the inmates but the managers as well. It is safe to say that these two books are among the most influential sociological publications of the post-World War II era. His other major publications, *Stigma* (1963), *Behavior in Public Places* (1963), *Strategic Interaction* (1969), *Relations in Public: Micro-Studies of the Public Order* (1971), *Frame Analysis: Essays on the Organization of Experience* (1974), *Gender Advertisements* (1979), and *Forms of Talk* (1981), extend and elaborate his observations and theory.

Goffman's interest in acting and game behaviors extended beyond his published work. He is said to have been an avid poker and blackjack player, and while at Berkeley in the 1960s he actually trained as a blackjack dealer and worked at a Las Vegas casino.

[Drew Silver (2nd ed.)]

GOFNAH (**Gufnah**, or **Bet Gufnin**; Heb. גָּפְנָה), town in N. Judea that is first mentioned in the Second Temple period. The Talmud refers to it as Bet Gufnin, a name derived from the Hebrew root *gefen* ("vine"). Gofnah replaced Timnah as the center of a toparchy in the time of Herod and continued to occupy this position in later times (Jos., Wars, 1:45; 3:55; Pliny, *Historia Naturalis*, 5:15, 30). In the middle of the first century B.C.E., the inhabitants of Gofnah were sold into slavery by the Roman general Cassius for failure to pay taxes, but they were freed shortly afterward by Antonius. The city was part of the area under the command of Hananiah b. Johanan in 66 C.E. during the Jewish War. Vespasian occupied it in 68 C.E., established a garrison there, and concentrated the priests and other important persons who had surrendered to him in the city (Jos., Wars, 6:115). Gofnah is also mentioned in the Talmud as a city of priests (Ber. 44a; TJ, Ta'an. 4:8, 69a). In the Middle Ages it continued to exist as Gafeniyyah. It is marked as a road station on the Peutinger Map; Eusebius places it 15 miles (24 km.) north of Jerusalem on the road to Neapolis (Onom. 168:16). Remains found there include a Jewish tomb with inscribed ossuaries, one of which mentions a Judah, son of Eleazar (in Aramaic); a Greek inscription, Salome daughter of Iakeimos, in a burial cave; a Roman villa; and a Byzantine church.

On the site of historical Gofnah there is now the Arab village of Jifnā, which in 1967 had 655 inhabitants, of which 538 were Christians and the rest Muslims (for the number of inhabitants in the 19th century, see Bagatti's figures). There were 961 residents in 1997. One of the folk legends about Jifna refers to the hill opposite the village called Jebel ed-Dik ("Mount of the Rooster"). Apparently a Jew from Jifna was in Jerusalem during the final days of Jesus. When he perceived that Jesus had risen from the dead, he immediately converted and when arriving back home told his wife what had happened. She replied that she could not believe it, unless the rooster she had just killed and half-plucked would come back to life. Suddenly the rooster revived and flew away to the mountain. Its Greek Orthodox church of St. George stands on medieval and Byzantine foundations. Another church may exist close to the village. Tombs, buildings, installations, and other remains are also visible in the vicinity.

ADD. BIBLIOGRAPHY: Y. Tsafrir, L. Di Segni, and J. Green, *Tabula Imperii Romani. Iudaea – Palaestina. Maps and Gazetteer* (1994), 137; B. Bagatti, *Ancient Christian Villages of Samaria* (2002), 135–40.

[Michael Avi-Yonah and Efraim Orni / Shimon Gibson (2nd ed.)]

GOG AND MAGOG (Heb. גּוֹג וּמָגוֹג). Gog and Magog are first mentioned together in Ezekiel 38–39 in the vision of the end of days, where the prophet describes the war of the Lord against "Gog, of the land of Magog, the chief prince of Meshech and Tubal." After the ingathering of Israel Gog will come up against Israel with many peoples from the furthest north to plunder it and carry away spoil. The Lord Himself will go to war against Gog and punish him "with pestilence, and with blood, and with overflowing rain," and His name will be magnified and sanctified in the eyes of many nations. Gog will die in the land of Israel and his place of burial will be called "the valley of *hamon Gog*" and for seven years the inhabitants of Israel will use the weapons of the enemy for fuel.

Since, in the list of the sons of Noah (Gen. 10:2), Magog is mentioned as the brother of Gomer and Madai, the most reasonable identification put forward is with Giges, also known as Gogo, king of Lydia, and Magog, with his country. That, however, does not affect in any way the symbolic nature of the name and the special character of Ezekiel's vision. Gog and his people are not historical enemies of Israel, like Babylonia and Assyria. They will attack simply out of a lust for violence and with the intention of destroying a peaceful kingdom. Indeed, other prophets prophesied about a people that would come up from the north to besiege Israel in the end of days, but Ezekiel, who prophesied after the destruction of the Temple, fixed the date of the last war after the ingathering of the exiles and the rebuilding of Jerusalem.

In the Septuagint the name Gog appears in two other places where it is not mentioned in the Hebrew text. In Numbers 24:7, Gog appears instead of Agag, and in Amos 7:1, the reading is "Gog," instead of *gizei* ("the mowings"). These variants indicate the antiquity of the connection between the war of Gog and the advent of the Messiah. Descriptions of the decisive, final war occupy an important place in the Apocrypha (En. 56:5; IV Ezra 13:5), but the names Gog and Magog appear only in the vision of the Hebrew Sibylline Oracles (3:319 and 512), and even there only as the name of a country between the rivers of Ethiopia, a country saturated with blood, for which a bitter fate is in store. In the *aggadah*, the names Gog and Magog were reserved for the enemy of Israel in the end of days, but the details are very different from those in Ezekiel. In Ezekiel, Gog is the king of Magog; in the *aggadah*, Gog and Magog are two parallel names for the same nation. Moses had already seen Gog and all his multitude coming up against Israel and falling in the valley of Jericho (Mekh. Be-Shalaḥ, 2), and Eldad and Medad prophesied concerning them (Sanh. 17a). The war of Gog and Magog is in essence a war against the Lord, and the whole of Psalm 2 is interpreted as referring to it (Av. Zar. 3b; Tanh. Noah 18; Pd-RK 79); God Himself will do battle with this enemy. The last of "the ten occasions of the Shekhinah's descent to the world" will be in the days of Gog and Magog (ARN[1], 34, 102). R. Akiva was of the opinion that the judgment of Gog would endure for 12 months (Eduy. 2:10). This judgment will bring great calamities upon Israel that will cause all previous calamities to fade into insignificance (Tosef., Ber. 1:13). Eliezer b. Hyrcanus connects it with the pangs of the Messiah and the great day of judgment (Mekh., Be-Shalaḥ 4: Shab. 118a). The war of Gog and Magog will be the final war, after which there will be no servitude, and it will presage the advent of the Messiah (Sif. Num. 76, Deut. 43; Sanh. 97b). In the Palestinian Targums the Messiah plays an active role in this war. Gog and Magog and their armies will go up to Jerusalem and fall into the hands of the Messianic king, but the ingathering of the exiles – contrary to what is said in Ezekiel – will come only after the victory (Targ. Yer., Num. 11:26; *ibid.*, Song 8:4). A kind of compromise is found in the Targum, namely, that the house of Israel will conquer Gog and his company through the assistance of Messiah the son of Ephraim (Targ. Yer., Ex. 40:11; cf. also Targ. Song 4:5). In the New Testament vision of John (Rev. 20), the war of Gog and Magog takes place at the end of a millennium after the first resurrection, and in *Sefer Eliyahu* ("Book of Elijah"; J. Kaufmann (Even Shemuel), ed.), *Midreshei Ge'ullah* (1954[2]), 46) Gog and Magog come after the days of the Messiah but before the final day of judgment.

From the biblical sources and the tradition of the rabbis, the stories about Gog and Magog passed to the Church Fathers. At the time of the Gothic migrations it was customary to identify the Goths with Gog and Magog. An ancient Christian tradition also identified Gog and Magog with the barbarian peoples whom Alexander the Great locked away behind iron gates next to the Caspian Sea but who are destined to break forth in the end of days. During the Islamic conquests, Christians identified the Muslim armies with Gog and Magog.

BIBLIOGRAPHY: Kaufmann Y., Toledot, 3 (1954), 578–83; Ginzberg, Legends, index; P. Volz, *Die Eschatologie der juedischen Gemeinde im neutestamentlichen Zeitalter* (1934), 150ff.; J. Klausner, *The Messianic Idea in Israel* (1955); M. Waxman, *Galut u-Ge'ulah* (1952), 218–33. **ADD. BIBLIOGRAPHY:** J. Lust, in: DDD, 373–75.

GOIIM (Heb. גּוֹיִם), name appearing in the Bible as "king of Goiim." Genesis 14:1, 9 mentions "Tidal king of Goiim," as one of the kings participating in a war during the time of Abraham. It has been suggested that Tidal is Tudḫaliya, the name of five Hittite kings (Heb. תִּדְעָל; Ugaritic transliteration Tidʿl, Tṯʿl). Given the unhistorical character of Genesis 14, which lumps together names from different periods, it is probably futile to attempt to identify the biblical character with a specific Hittite Tudhaliya. Another possibility is that Tidal of Genesis 14 is borrowed from a Mesopotamian source opposed to Sennacherib king of Assyria (705–681), in which he was called Tudhula, "evil offspring" in Sumerian. This would be in keeping with the other midrashic names in the chapter already observed by medieval Jewish scholars, Bera, "in evil," and Birsha, "in wickedness." The word *goyim* is also used to indicate "nations" in general. There is an opinion that the connection between the two usages of the word *goyim* resembles that of *ummān-Manda* ("the horde, the armies of '*Manda*'"), an ancient term applied to various groups including the barbarian nation that helped the Babylonians destroy Harran in 610 B.C.E. Thus, there is reason to believe that the name Goiim in Hebrew corresponds to *ummān*, and simply means "nations," and is incomplete for "the nations of…," the actual name of Tidal's realm having been omitted in translation or lost in transmission. The usage in Joshua 12:23 is probably a corruption of Goiim to Gilgal (according to LXX), that is, the king Gilgal of Galilee instead of the king of Goiim of Gilgal (cf. Isa. 8:23).

BIBLIOGRAPHY: M. Cassuto, in: EM, 2 (1954), 457–8; D. Wiseman, *Chronicles of Chaldaean Kings* (1956), 81, n. to 1. 38; Jean Bottero, in: *Archives Royales de Mari*, 7 (1957), 224–5; E.A. Speiser, *Genesis* (Eng., 1964), 107–8; N.M. Sarna, *Understanding Genesis* (1966), 113. **ADD. BIBLIOGRAPHY:** H. Tadmor, in: EM, 8:435–36; N. Sarna, *JPS Torah Genesis* (1989), 103–4; M. Astour, in: ABD, 6:551–52.

GOITEIN, BARUCH BENEDICT (c. 1770–1842), Hungarian rabbi and author. Goitein was born in the town of Kojetin, Moravia and studied in the yeshivah of Moses *Mintz in Budapest. He was appointed rabbi in Hőgyesz, in Hungary. Goitein's fame rests upon his *Kesef Nivḥar*, 3 parts, Prague, 1827–28; repr. of 2nd ed., 1966, an examination of, and commentary on, 160 talmudic themes. Although a product of the Hungarian method of study, the close approximation of his method with that customary in the Lithuanian yeshivot made his work very popular in talmudic circles. He resigned from his rabbinical office in 1841 and was succeeded the following year by his son ẒEVI HIRSCH (Hermann; 1805–1860) author of *Yedei Moshe* (1905) on the 613 commandments.

BIBLIOGRAPHY: P.Z. Schwartz, *Shem ha-Gedolim me-Ereẓ Hagar*, 1 (1914), 216 no. 20.

[*Encyclopaedia Hebraica*]

GOITEIN, SHLOMO DOV (**Fritz**; 1900–1985), Orientalist. Descended from a Hungarian family of rabbis, Goitein was born in Burgkunstadt, a small village in southern Germany. He acquired an extensive Jewish education before his student years at the University of Frankfurt (1918–23). There he studied Arabic and Islam with the scholar Josef *Horovitz, while continuing his talmudic training. Upon completing his doctoral dissertation, he fulfilled his long-time Zionist ambition to live in Palestine. He immigrated there in 1923, and, like so many other European university-trained immigrants, taught for four years at the Reali School in Haifa. In 1928, three years after the founding of the Hebrew University, he joined the faculty of the Institute of Oriental Studies there. He was appointed professor in 1947 and continued to teach at the Hebrew University until 1957, when he became professor of Arabic at the University of Pennsylvania, Philadelphia, until his retirement in 1971. In the same year he became a long-term member of the School of Historical Studies at the Institute for Advanced Study in Princeton, where he lived the remainder of his life.

From 1938–48 Goitein served the British Mandatory government in Palestine as senior education inspector. He maintained his early devotion to education in later years. In addition to his works in Arab and Judeo-Arabic studies, Goitein published works on biblical research, including *Iyyunim ba-Mikra* (1958), and works on pedagogy, such as *Hora'at ha-Tanakh* (1942) on the teaching of Bible in elementary and secondary schools and *Hora'at ha-Ivrit* (1958). In his twenties, he composed a play based on the story of a famous Jewish woman in the court of one of the counts of medieval France, *Pulcellina* (1927). He also wrote and published Hebrew poems.

Goitein was a prolific scholar, whose output and influence should rightly be compared with that of his contemporary, Gershom *Scholem – with whom he made the journey from Germany to Palestine on the same boat in 1923. His bibliography (published by the Ben-Zvi Institute, second, expanded edition, 2000) contains 737 items.

Roughly speaking, three more or less distinct periods of Goitein's scholarly career can be discerned, though there was considerable overlap of subjects. During the first period, Goitein published a series of investigations of the religious institutions of Islam, such as prayer (*Das Gebet im Qoran* (1923), a summary of his German dissertation), and the Ramadan month of fasting, among others. The crowning achievement of his studies of early Islam was the publication of the fifth volume of al-Balādhurī's (9th century) historical work *Ansāb al-ashrāf* (1936).

During the second period of his research, Goitein dealt primarily with the cultural legacy of the Jews of Yemen, a by-product of his intensive contact with and ethnographic work among Yemenite Jews in Palestine. Among the results of this work were *Jemenica*, a collection of proverbs from central Yemen (1934; *From the Land of Sheba*, 1947) and the publication of the account by Ḥayyim Ḥabshush, who accompanied Joseph *Halevy, on his explorations in Yemen (Ar. text, 1941; Heb. tr., 1939). His studies of contemporary Yemenite Jewry, whom he considered the "most Jewish and most Arab of all Jews," had a profound influence on his research on medieval Arab Jewry as well.

In his third period, Goitein was mainly engaged in publishing documentary texts from the Cairo *Genizah, from which he derived conclusions about the history of the Jews in Mediterranean countries and about the general history of these texts. Many of his views about relations between Jews and Arabs had already begun to form earlier, in articles published in the 1930s and 1940s and in his popular book *Jews and Arabs – Their Contacts through the Ages* (1955; 1974; reprinted with new preface by Mark R. Cohen, 2005). But from the 1950s on, he concentrated all his energies on researching the "historical documents" of the Genizah, a term he coined to differentiate the letters, legal documents, marriage contracts, bills of divorce, and lists from the literary material. In his work he continued and deepened the research begun earlier by such scholars as Jacob *Mann. Goitein went far beyond his predecessors, however, because he was a trained Arabist. He opened the door to the study of the mass of Judeo-Arabic documents from everyday life, something done only sporadically by those who came before him.

Goitein "discovered" the Genizah on a trip to the Hungarian Academy of Sciences in Budapest in 1948, among the manuscripts that had previously belonged to the private collection of David *Kaufmann (1852–1899). A few years later in Cambridge and in Oxford he came upon legal documents from the Genizah relating to the then largely undocumented subject of the medieval India trade. He decided to research this topic and continued to work on it after his move to the United States in 1957. But, as he later wrote, he soon realized that to understand the world of the India merchants, he had first to survey the whole Mediterranean. This occupied him for the rest of his life, resulting in hundreds of articles and his magnum opus, *A Mediterranean Society* (5 volumes, 1967–88; Index volume 1993).

A Mediterranean Society is a masterpiece, comparable in European history to the work of Fernand Braudel on the Mediterranean during the early modern period (Goitein wrote that he did not read Braudel until he completed his own work). The first volume describes "economic foundations." Here the Jewish merchants and craftsmen of Egypt and other Mediterranean lands come forth, representing not just their ethnic and religious group, but also their economic class. Their activities are fully representative of the economic life of the majority Muslim population. Thanks to Goitein, the value of the Genizah as a source for Islamic history was therefore demonstrated. In the second volume, "The Community," we see especially inner Jewish life and also how a minority group viewed Muslim government. Even if diachronic factors prevailed in Jewish communal life, as Goitein maintained, a reflection of the environment is visible in many of the pages of this book, too. The "Family" takes centerstage in the third volume. Even this fundamental cell of Jewish life shows the imprint of the Islamic milieu, as Goitein himself saw. In "Daily

Life" (vol. 4), Goitein surveyed material culture as reflected in the Genizah. His discussions of the city, domestic architecture, clothing, food, as well as other aspects of quotidian existence – similar to the "structures of everyday life" portrayed in the first volume of Braudel's *Civilisation matérielle, économie et capitalisme: XVe–XVIII siècle* (1967) make this volume, like the one on economic foundations, as much a contribution to general as to Jewish history. In the final volume, "The Individual," Goitein writes a fascinating study of the *mentalité* of the Mediterranean Arabic-speaking Jew.

The period covered by *A Mediterranean Society,* roughly 1000 to 1250, was a particularly lenient period of Jewish history under Islam. Goitein wrote the entire work while living in the United States and conceded (in the introduction to vol. 2) that his experience living in open, capitalist America had had an impact on his reconstruction of life in the Genizah world. He was sometimes criticized for this and for being anachronistic (H.H. Ben-Sasson in *Zion,* 40 (1975)). His lasting achievement, however, is to have surveyed every aspect of life during this period, the most thoroughly documented period of medieval Jewish history, and to have laid the groundwork for students and other followers to expand upon the foundations he laid. Directly or by inspiration, Goitein trained most of the major senior scholars of the historical Genizah working in the field in the late 20th and early 21st centuries.

No sooner did Goitein deliver the manuscript of the final volume of *A Mediterranean Society* to the publisher in December 1984 than he returned to the project with which he had begun his Genizah career, to the extensive notes and the more than 400 texts he had identified over the years related to the India trade. He died two months later, leaving the "India Book" to be completed by others. (Part One, containing roughly half of the opus, was edited by Mordechai Akiva Friedman for publication by the Ben-Zvi Institute.)

In 1980 Goitein was the recipient of the Harvey Prize of the Haifa Technion (jointly with Michael Rabin and Efraim Racker). Other awards included the Haskins Medal of the Medieval Academy of America, the Levi Della Vida Prize of the Gustave E. von Grunebaum Center for Near Eastern Studies (University of California), and, just two years before his death in 1985, a MacArthur Laureate Fellowship.

ADD. BIBLIOGRAPHY: H.H. Ben-Sasson, in: *Zion 40 (1975);* M.R. Cohen, in: *American Philosophical Society Yearbook* (1987); idem, in: *Middle Eastern Lectures No. 4* (Moshe Dayan Center, Tel Aviv University) (2001); S.D. Goitein, in: *Religion in a Religious Age* (1974); M.A. Friedman, in: *Yedi'on ha-Igud ha-Olami le-Mada'ei ha-Yahadut,* 26 (1986); idem, in: *Sefunot,* n.s. 20 (1991); J.L. Kraemer, in: *Zemanim,* 34–35 (1990); G. Libson, in: *The Jewish Past Revisited: Reflections on Modern Jewish Historians* (1998); S. Morag, in: *Pe'amim,* 22 (1985); S. Shaked, in: ibid.; A.L. Udovitch, Foreward to Goitein, *A Mediterranean Society,* vol. 5 (1988).

[Mark R. Cohen (2nd ed.)]

GOLAN (Heb. גּוֹלָן), a town of the half-tribe *Manasseh in *Bashan that was set aside as a city of refuge (Deut. 4:43; Josh. 20:8) and a levitical city of the family of Gershon (Josh. 21:27; I Chron. 6:56). It is mentioned as Giluni in the *El-Amarna Letters. Although situated in Bashan, the city seems to have given its name to the entire district of Golan (or Gaulan) to the west of it. According to Eusebius it was a large village in Batanaea in the fourth century B.C.E. (Onom. 64:68). Schumacher has identified it with Sakhm al-Jawlān, a village 5 miles (8 km.) east of the Nahr al-ʿAllān (ʿAllān River), the eastern boundary of Gaulanitis. This identification conforms with the assumption that the city was located outside the district named for it, which ended at Nahr al-ʿAllān. D. Urman has cast doubt on the Sakhm al-Jawlān identification owing to the fact that Bronze and Iron Age remains have not yet been found there. Other scholars have proposed a more northerly location for Golan, in the region of *Maacah. W.F. Albright, however, was of the opinion that the biblical city must have been situated within the region of the present-day Golan. Josephus was the first to use the name Golan not only as the name of a town but also of a region. There are several references to Golan in the Talmud; these, however, seem to refer to the district and not to the city (TJ, Meg. 3:1, 73d).

For geography, archaeology, and settlement of the region see *Ramat ha-Golan.

BIBLIOGRAPHY: R. Dussaud, *Topographie historique de la Syrie…* (1927), 335, 343f.; Albright, in: *L. Ginsberg Jubilee Volume* (1945), 57 (Eng. section); EM, s.v. **ADD. BIBLIOGRAPHY:** D. Urman, *The Golan: A Profile of a Region During the Roman and Byzantine Periods* (1985).

[Michael Avi-Yonah / Shimon Gibson (2nd ed.)]

GOLAN, MENAHEM (1929–), Israeli producer-director. Born to Polish immigrants Noah Globus and Deborah (née Godman) in Tiberias, Israel, Golan served as an air force pilot and at 19 changed his surname in honor of the Golan Heights. Following his military service, he went to London to study at the Old Vic Theatre School. Golan spent many years directing Israeli theater productions. In the early 1960s, he went to the United States to study film in New York. While serving as an assistant on the Roger Corman film *The Young Racers* (1963) he became a protégé of the low-budget director. Golan returned to Israel again to collaborate with his cousin, Yoram Globus, and the two wrote and directed the film *El Dorado* (1963). The cousins went on to form Noah Films to produce features for the Israeli market. In 1964, their production of Ephraim Kishon's *Sallah Shabati,* starring Chaim *Topol, received Oscar and Golden Globe nominations for best foreign film. In 1978, Golan immigrated to the United States, and a year later the cousins bought controlling interest in the failing production company, Cannon Group, Inc. Golan and Globus produced a few high-quality independent films, like *Barfly* and *The Hanoi Hilton* in 1987, but the majority of its success was built on such action pictures as *Breakin'* (1984), *Missing in Action* (1984), *Cobra* (1986), *The Delta Force* (1986), and *Superman IV: The Quest for Peace* (1987). In the 1980s Golan and Globus were called "The Go-Go Boys" and were famous for selling movies at the Cannes Film market solely on the basis of a poster. Cannon was eventually sold to Pathe Communications in 1989. While the cousins stayed on, a falling-out led Golan to start the 21st Century Film Corporation, which released *Captain America* (1991). In 1999, Golan established New Cannon, Inc.

[Adam Wills (2nd ed.)]

GOLB, NORMAN (1928–), scholar of Jewish history. Born in Chicago, Golb received his early education there; in 1954 he earned his doctorate in Judaic and Semitic studies from Johns Hopkins University. He was the recipient of several fellowships, including the Warbury Fellowship for Research in Judaic and Semitic Studies at the Hebrew University of Jerusalem (1955–57), and he was a visiting faculty member at the University of Wisconsin (1957–58), Harvard University (1966), and Tel Aviv University (1969–70). Golb was a faculty member of the Hebrew Union College in Cincinnati from 1958 to 1963; in 1963 he joined the faculty of the University of Chicago, where he became, in 1988, the Ludwig Rosenberger Professor of Jewish History and Civilization. He was also chairman of the university's Aronberg Judaica Lectureship Committee.

Golb's many fellowships and research awards have included Guggenheim Fellowships (1964, 1966) and grants from the National Endowment for the Humanities, the American Philosophical Society, and the Littauer Foundation. His studies have appeared in numerous academic journals over the years and involve significant interpretations of archaeological discoveries. He identified *Obadiah the Proselyte as the author of the oldest Hebrew musical manuscript, uncovered the earliest extant legal record of the Jews of Sicily, identified a Hebrew document concerning the First Crusade, and discovered manuscripts pertaining to the Jews of medieval Normandy.

Golb's 1976 work in Hebrew, *Toledot ha-Yehudim be-Ir Rouen bi-Ymei ha-Benayim* ("History and Culture of the Jews of Medieval Rouen"), was followed by studies of archaeological discoveries made in 1976 and 1982 in the Street of the Jews in Rouen. In 1985 he published *Les Juifs de Rouen au Moyen Age: Portrait d'une culture oubliée*, for which he received the Grand Medal of the City of Rouen. In 1987 he was granted an honorary doctorate by the University of Rouen and was awarded the Medal of the Region of Haute Normandie.

Golb took an active role in the campaign to make available the Dead Sea Scrolls for academic study, and he was one of the organizers of an international conference on the scrolls for the New York Academy of Sciences and the Oriental Institute. His later works include *Who Wrote the Dead Sea Scrolls? The Search for the Secret of Qumran* (1995) and *The Jews of Medieval Normandy: A Social and Intellectual History* (1998). Among other honors, he is a fellow of the American Academy for Jewish Research.

[Dorothy Bauhoff (2nd ed.)]

GOLCUV JENIKOV (Czech. **Golčův Jeníkov**; Ger. **Goltsch-Jenikau**), town in E. Bohemia, Czech Republic. Jews appear to have settled in Golcuv Jenikov at the end of the 16th century. Documents indicate that there was a synagogue in 1659 which was rebuilt in 1806 and 1870; it continued in existence after World War II. Because of plague the Jews settled temporarily outside the town in 1681. In 1724 there were 28 families in Golcuv Jenikov; there were 613 Jews there in 1847 (27.8% of the total population), and 79 (3.9%) in 1931. The community had a Jewish German-language school from 1797 to 1907. R. Aaron *Kornfeld, whose yeshivah was the last in Bohemia, lived in Golcuv Jenikov. Those members of the community, who had not succeeded in leaving by 1942, were deported to Nazi extermination camps. The synagogue accessories were transferred to the Central Jewish Museum in Prague. After the Holocaust, some Jews returned to Golcuv Jenikov, where the Jewish quarter (rebuilt after a fire in 1808) and cemetery (the oldest monument dates from 1726) still existed in 1970. The synagogue was put at the disposal of the Prague State Jewish Museum in 1969. In nearby Habry (Habern), a Jewish community was founded in the 14th century. Its synagogue dates from 1650. Habry had 21 Jewish families in 1724; 120 families in 1848; 143 persons in 1893; and 79 in 1930. In 1898 it was incorporated in the Golcuv Jenikov community. Other than the few who emigrated in World War II, the Jews of Golcuv Jenikov were deported to the death camps of Poland via Theresienstadt in 1942.

BIBLIOGRAPHY: Maximovič, in: H. Gold (ed.), *Die Juden und Judengemeinden Boehmens in Vergangenheit und Gegenwart* (1934), 152–7; O. Kosta, in: *Židovská ročenka* (1970/71), 71–79.

[Jan Herman]

GOLD, BENJAMIN (1898–1983), U.S. labor leader. Gold, who was born in Bessarabia, Russia, was taken to the United States in 1910. In the following year, he started to work in the fur industry. Gold joined both the Socialist Party and the Fur Workers Union, where he became identified with the union's left wing. During the 1920s a struggle took place between the union's left wing led by Gold (who had joined the Communist Party by 1925) and the more conservative wing. Gold, who became the general manager of the union's New York joint board in 1925, led a bitter strike in 1926 that lasted 17 weeks. The strike ended with the union winning only one of its major demands, a 40-hour work week. The American Federation of Labor then investigated the joint board and charged it with being Communist-controlled and corrupt. As a result of these charges, the union's executive council expelled Gold and his fellow officers. Gold and other left-wing needle trade unionists then formed the Needle Trades Industrial Union and the Fur Workers Industrial Union.

During the Depression, Gold attended the Lenin School of Moscow. In 1935 the Fur Workers Industrial Union was disbanded and its members joined the new CIO International Fur Workers Union (which later became known as the International Fur and Leather Workers Union). In 1937 Gold became the union's president, while continuing to play an important role in the Communist Party. Regarded by many as the most incorruptible figure in the needle trade, Gold was held in high esteem by the manufacturers because he brought reliable production as well as high wages and good benefits to the industry.

In 1948 the union was forced to leave the CIO as a result of that organization's investigation into Communist influence in a number of its member unions. Shortly afterward, Gold, in order to be eligible to sign the Taft-Hartley Act's loyalty pledge which, in turn, would provide his union with the legal protection afforded by the act, resigned from the Communist Party. Gold continued as union president until he resigned in 1954. After resigning, he worked as a fur cutter until his retirement.

Gold wrote *Avreml Broide* (1944), *Mentshn, dertseylungen fun Ben Gold* (1948), and *Memoirs* (1985).

[Albert A. Blum]

GOLD, HENRY RAPHAEL (1893–1965), U.S. rabbi and psychiatrist. Born in Grajewo, Poland, Gold was ordained rabbi by the Jewish Theological Seminary in 1916. He held rabbinical positions in Memphis (1916–18), Boston (1918–24), New Orleans (1924–28), and Dallas (1928–43). While in Dallas, he took up the study of medicine, receiving an M.D. from Baylor University in 1934 and later teaching medical psychiatry there. He also served as a commissioner of the Dallas Housing Authority. On giving up his rabbinate in Dallas, he moved to New York and entered private practice as a psychiatrist and psychologist. Gold was an active Zionist. At various times he served as president of Hapoel Hamizrachi and the National Council for Torah Education and as vice president of the Union of Orthodox Jewish Congregations and of the Zionist Organization of America.

BIBLIOGRAPHY: *New York Times* (Jan. 7, 1965).

[Sefton D. Temkin]

GOLD, HERBERT (1924–), U.S. novelist. Gold, who was born in Cleveland, recollected that "we were just about the only Jewish family in Lakewood at the time." He served in the U.S. Army during World War II. After the war he studied in Columbia and in Paris, finally settling in San Francisco, and eventually was appointed professor at the University of California at Berkeley. Gold's books deal with the search for love between men and women, parents and children. He has claimed that his writing is a need "to make the world magic" and his style – witty yet compassionate – reflects this. His most successful characters are young people who affect cynicism without being cynical, and who hide their real sensitivity behind a conventional mask. Gold's humor stems from the relentless truthfulness of his description of male and female relationships. His novels include *The Birth of a Hero* (1951), *The Prospect Before Us* (1954), *The Man Who Was Not with It* (1956), and *The Optimist* (1959). *Therefore Be Bold* (1960) is a humorous Jewish work set in the Middle West; *Love and Like* (1960) a collection of short stories; and *Salt* (1963) a satirical novel dealing with life in the impersonal metropolis. Gold also published essays on the contemporary American scene titled *The Age of Happy Problems* (1962). His "family" works are spun around the substance of his life: *Fathers* (1966), in which the novelist drew upon his own family experiences to tell of the Jewish immigrants who sought fulfillment in the United States; *My Last Two Thousand Years* (1972), and *Family* (1981). These memoirs are also mediations about the informing power (or lack of such) of place, tradition, class, and gender – this last especially in *Family*.

BIBLIOGRAPHY: B. Kretzer, *Idealitat und Realitat der Frauenfiguren im modernen amerikanischen Roman: Saul Bellow, Herbert Gold, John Hawkes*. **ADD. BIBLIOGRAPHY:** J. Troiano, "Herbert Gold's Golden State," at: www.sanfranciscoreader.com.

[Sylvia Rothchild / Lewis Fried (2nd ed.)]

GOLD, HUGO (1895–1974), publisher and historian. Gold was born in Vienna. He studied philosophy at the University of Vienna and soon after was drafted into the army. With the beginning of World War I, Gold served as a commander on the Eastern Front. He was captured by the Russian Army and sent to Siberia, from where he returned in 1918. In 1924 he became the head of the publishing house Juedischer Buch- und Kunstverlag, formerly owned by his uncle Max *Hickl. From 1924 to 1939 he was the publisher and editor of the journal *Juedische Volksstimme*, and from 1931 to 1936 of the historical journal *Zeitschrift fuer die Geschichte der Juden in der Tschechoslowakei*. In 1940 Gold settled in Palestine. After World War II he established in Tel Aviv the Olamenu publishing house, which concentrated on books in the German language relating to Central European Jewry. From 1964 he published and edited the *Zeitschrift fuer die Geschichte der Juden* (Tel Aviv). Gold's main contributions as a historian are works on the history of the Jews in Czechoslovakia, Austria, and Bukovina, including *Die Juden und Judengemeinde Bratislava in Vergangenheit und Gegenwart* (1932); *Geschichte der Juden in Wien* (1966); *Max Brod, Ein Gedenkbuch 1884–1968* (1969); and *Gedenkbuch der untergegangenen Judengemeinden des Burgenlandes* (1970). The works he wrote and edited are a major source of information about the destroyed Jewish communities in Central Europe.

ADD. BIBLIOGRAPHY: E. Gottgetreu, in: *Illustrierte Neue Welt*, 8/9 (1975), 46; E. Pistiner, in: *Illustrierte Neue Welt*, 3 (1988), 15–16.

GOLD, MICHAEL (Irwin Granich; 1893–1967), U.S. Communist author and journalist. Born in New York to poor immigrant parents from Romania, Gold left school at the age of 13 and worked at various odd jobs to help support his family. He later attended City College night school and began to write his first sketches and poems, which from the start were politically radical in tone. After a brief and unhappy tenure as a special student at Harvard and an extended stay in Mexico in 1916–17, he returned to New York where he worked as a copy editor on the Socialist *Call* and contributed articles and poetry to *Masses*. He joined the Communist Party soon after its formation and became editor first of the *Liberator* (1920–22) and later of *New Masses* (1928–32), both of which were devoted to "proletarian" literature and culture. Gold also worked closely in these years with the left-wing New Playwrights' Theater and himself wrote several plays and a collection of short stories, *120 Million* (1929). In 1930 he published his autobiographical novel of the Lower East Side, *Jews Without Money*, whose stark imagistic prose has made it one of the best-known accounts of Jewish immigrant life in New York. Throughout the 1930s and 1940s Gold wrote a regular column for the Communist *Daily Worker* but produced little of literary value. During the last years of his life he lived in San Francisco, where he contributed to the radical West Coast publication, *The People's World*. His books include *The Hollow Men* (1941) and *Change the World!* (1937), a collection of his newspaper columns.

BIBLIOGRAPHY: M. Gold, *Mike Gold Reader*, ed. by S. Sillen (1954); Folsom, in: D. Madden (ed.), *Proletarian Writers of the Thirties* (1968), 221–51; C. Angoff, *Tone of the Twenties* (1966), 182–8; D. Aaron, *Writers on the Left* (1961), 84–90, 453.

GOLD, PHILIP (1936–), Canadian medical researcher. Gold was born in Montreal and studied at McGill University from which he holds both an M.D. degree and a Ph.D. From 1973 he was professor of medicine, and subsequently Douglas G. Cameron Professor of Medicine, at McGill, where he was also a professor in the Department of Physiology and the Department of Oncology. Among the other major academic and research appointments that he held were director of the McGill Cancer Center, director of the McGill University Clinic and physician-in-chief of the Montreal General Hospital, chairman of McGill's Department of Medicine, and executive director of the Clinical Research Center of the McGill University Health Center.

Gold is widely known for his development of an important diagnostic (CEA) test for cancer; his work won him international renown and brought him numerous awards. He is a Companion of the Order of Canada and a Fellow of the Royal Society of Canada. In his professional work Gold has written numerous scientific papers and is co-editor of *Clinical Immunology*. He served as president of the Canadian Society of Immunology from 1975–77.

GOLD, WOLF (**Ze'ev**; 1889–1956), rabbi, leader of religious Zionism. Born in Sczcyczyin, Poland, and descended from a long line of rabbis, Gold was ordained at the age of 17 by Rabbi Eliezer Rabinowitz after having studied at the Yeshiva in Mir and succeeded his father-in-law as rabbi in Juteka. In 1907 he emigrated to the U.S., where he served in several congregations: South Chicago, Scranton, Pennsylvania, Williamsburg, New York, San Francisco (where he strenuously fought Reform), and Brooklyn, New York. A man of handsome presence with a beautiful speaking voice, he was a powerful orator and capable organizer. Everywhere he engaged in educational and communal activities, founding a Hebrew school (Williamsburg Talmud Torah), a yeshivah ("Torah Vada'at"), a hospital ("Beth Mosheh," Brooklyn) which he established when the Jewish hospital abandoned its *kashrut* superivision, a Hebrew teachers training college (San Francisco), and an orphanage (also in Brooklyn). Gold was from the beginning in the forefront of Zionist workers in the U.S. – in the Order of the Sons of Zion, and the Zionist funds; he was a delegate to all Zionist Congresses and a member of the Zionist General Council from 1923. From 1913 he was active in the *Mizrachi movement, which, together with his lifelong friend M. *Bar-Ilan (Berlin), he organized in the U.S.; he served as president of the American Mizrachi 1932–35. His contract specified that he could work three months a year on Zionist activities, which involved extensive travel. From 1945 he represented the Mizrachi on the executive of the Jewish Agency and was a member of the Jewish delegation at the United Nations in 1946. Already in 1924 Gold went to Ereẓ Israel to assist in the religious propaganda work of the chief rabbinate and the Mizrachi in the new settlements. His experience led him to the idea of an agricultural yeshivah which was founded eventually (1938) in *Kefar ha-Ro'eh. He settled in Ereẓ Israel in 1935. With the establishment of the State of Israel he became a member of the Provisional Council of State and for some time headed the Jewish Agency's Department for the Development of Jerusalem and in 1951 the Department for Torah Education and Culture. In that capacity Gold did much for the establishment of schools and other educational institutions in various parts of the Diaspora – in North Africa in particular. He worked on the plans for a training institute for rabbis, teachers, youth leaders, etc. for the Diaspora, which after his death came into being as the Z. Gold Institute for Jewish Studies and Teachers' Seminary. A volume of his sermons, articles etc. was published in 1949 (*Nivei Zahav*), and a memorial volume of sermons in 1963 (*Ẓiyyon min ha-Torah*, ed. Z. Tabori).

BIBLIOGRAPHY: EẒD, 1 (1958), 464–9, incl. bibl.; *Netivot*, no. 6 (1956), 7–16; S. Daniel, in: *Gevilim*, 1 (1957), 84–102; J.B. Soloveitchik, in: *Ẓiyyon min ha-Torah* (1963), 31–43; *Shanah be-Shanah 5731* (1970), 192–201; Z. Gold, *Lessons in Talmud* (1956), introd. What Would Ezra Say? An Open Letter to the Rabbinical Assembly (1935); *Shuva Yisrael* (1936). **ADD. BIBLIOGRAPHY:** M.D. Sherman, *Orthodox Judaism in America: A Bibliographical Dictionary and Sourcebook* (1996).

GOLDBERG, ABRAHAM (1881–1933), Yiddish and Hebrew journalist. Born in Brest-Litovsk into a *maskilic* family, the eldest brother of the Yiddish poet Menahem *Boraisha, his education combined both traditional and secular elements. His journalistic career, which complemented his early Zionist activity, began in the Hebrew press at the turn of the century, although he later wrote primarily in Yiddish. He was one of the chief contributors to the Yiddish daily **Haynt* from its foundation in 1908, and when the paper was reorganized after World War I he became its editor-in-chief. During this period Yiẓḥak *Gruenbaum returned to Poland from Russia, and Goldberg became his right-hand man in the communal and Zionist struggle in Poland. Under Goldberg's editorship, *Haynt* became the main advocate for Jewish rights and protagonist of Polish Zionism, exercising great influence on the Jewish masses. Goldberg consistently maintained that it was the duty of the press not only to provide information, but also to serve as an instrument for the amelioration of the condition of the Jewish people. He convinced Russian émigrés to protest the Mendel *Beilis trial in Kiev. Goldberg played a leading role in the Zionist Organization of Poland and was a delegate to a number of Zionist congresses. Although he wrote mainly in Yiddish, he supported the weekly *Ba-Derekh*, published by *Haynt*, the last Hebrew newspaper in Poland.

BIBLIOGRAPHY: I. Gruenbaum, *Penei ha-Dor* (1957), 270–2; Y. Zineman, *In Gerangl* (1952), 114–9; LNYL 2 (1958), 43–4; G. Kressel, Leksikon, 1, 410. **ADD. BIBLIOGRAPHY:** Rejzen, Leksikon, 1 (1928), 477–9.

[Getzel Kressel / Jerold C. Frakes (2nd ed.)]

GOLDBERG, ALEXANDER (1906–1985), Israel chemical engineer. Goldberg, who was born in Vilna, went to England in 1914. He graduated in mining engineering and chemical engineering at the Royal School of Mines, London. He was a pioneer in the development of techniques of crop preservation, and subsequently worked with the raw-material group of the Hawker-Siddeley organization. During World War II he was responsible for producing metallic magnesium from seawater, and later for the production of the aluminum used in Britain's postwar prefabricated houses. In 1948 he went to Israel and headed Chemicals and Phosphates Ltd. thereby becoming a key figure in Israel's developing chemical industry. In 1965 he became president of the Haifa Technion.

[Samuel Aaron Miller]

GOLDBERG, ARTHUR JOSEPH (1908–1990), U.S. labor lawyer, secretary of labor, Supreme Court justice, and ambassador to the United Nations. Goldberg, who was born in Chicago, was the youngest of 11 children. After graduating from Northwestern University Law School (1929) at the head of his class, Goldberg began practicing law in Chicago. He soon developed a national reputation in labor law, a field then rapidly expanding in the wake of the intensive labor strife and legislation of the depression years and Roosevelt's New Deal. During World War II, he was appointed head of the labor division of the U.S. Office of Strategic Services (OSS), for which he helped to establish intricate clandestine operations with anti-Fascist trade union leaders behind Nazi lines. In 1948 Goldberg was appointed general counsel of the Congress of Industrial Organizations (CIO). In this capacity he played a crucial role in the prolonged negotiations between the CIO and its warring rival the AFL (American Federation of Labor) and was instrumental in drafting the merger agreement between them in 1955, after which he returned to private practice. His book *AFL-CIO: Labor United* was published the following year.

An early supporter of the presidential aspirations of John F. Kennedy, Goldberg was appointed to the cabinet as secretary of labor upon Kennedy's inauguration in 1961. Unlike his immediate predecessor, Goldberg took an activist view of the office. He vigorously strove to raise the national minimum wage and to increase federal unemployment benefits, while at the same time seeking to arbitrate a wide range of labor-management conflicts in order to implement Kennedy's anti-inflationary program by discouraging excessive wage hikes. His activities in this area alienated many of his old labor colleagues, causing the magazine *New Republic* to summarize his two years as labor secretary by remarking, "His contribution to the Kennedy administration has been notable for his forthright disregard of old ties with organized labor in shaping a new doctrine of the national interest in labor-management disputes."

In 1962 Goldberg was chosen by President Kennedy to replace the retiring Felix Frankfurter as a justice on the United States Supreme Court. During his term on the Court, Goldberg consistently voted with its liberal majority and wrote several key decisions protecting the rights of naturalized American citizens. The most significant decision written by him, however, was in the famous Escobedo Case of 1964, in which the Court ruled by a 5–4 majority that every accused prisoner had the constitutional right to be advised by a lawyer during police interrogation, thereby working a revolution in American criminal law.

In 1965 Goldberg resigned from the Court to become United States permanent representative to the United Nations. The high point of his UN career came during the Arab-Israel war of 1967, when throughout the six days of fighting he repeatedly and successfully argued the American position calling for a cease-fire without previous Israel withdrawal. He thereby earned the enmity of the Arab nations, who accused him of influencing American foreign policy on behalf of Jewish interests. Goldberg was also said to have had a major hand in the drafting of the November 1967 Security Council resolution which served as a basis for the Jarring Mission to the Middle East. In 1968 he resigned from his position, reportedly dissatisfied with President Johnson's "hawkish" policies in Vietnam and his own inability to moderate them. Leaving Washington, he settled in New York City, where he opened a law practice while taking an active behind-the-scenes role in local and statewide Democratic Party politics. In 1970 he ran unsuccessfully for the office of governor of New York State. Goldberg, who was active in Zionist and Jewish affairs, was president of the American Jewish Committee (1968–69) and chairman of the Jewish Theological Seminary's board of overseers (1963–69). In July 1978 Goldberg was awarded the Presidential Medal of Freedom by President Carter for his efforts in the "Middle East and for human rights."

BIBLIOGRAPHY: J.P. Frank, *The Warren Court* (1964), 165–85; D.P. Moynihan (ed.), *The Defenses of Freedom: The Public Papers of Arthur J. Goldberg* (1966).

[Arnold Beichman]

GOLDBERG, BAER (Dov) BEN ALEXANDER (known by his acronym **Bag**; 1800–1884), Polish scholar. Goldberg was born in Chlodna, near Lomza, Poland, and was orphaned at an early age. He studied Torah in dire poverty, but earned a reputation as a prodigy. Having tried his hand at business and teaching, in 1830 Goldberg became a private tutor for the family of the wealthy and learned Gershon Litinski in one of the villages of Suwalki district. When after some time the entire Litinski family converted to Christianity, he was slandered as having influenced them.

In 1843 he went to Berlin, where he was favorably received by the *maskilim*. However, lacking a formal education, he could not find employment there, and in 1847 went to England, where he managed with great difficulty to earn a living copying and publishing Hebrew manuscripts from the Oxford libraries. In 1853 he settled in Paris, earning his living there by copying and publishing Hebrew and Arabic manuscripts from the National Library. Altogether, Goldberg published 17 books and pamphlets and hundreds of articles in Hebrew periodicals, writing mainly under the name "Divrei Bag" ("Words of Bag") and "Gam Elleh Divrei Bag" ("These also are the words of Bag"). His writings exemplified all the virtues and weaknesses of one who is self-taught: diligence and an abundance of detail but written in ornate language and lacking organization.

Goldberg's main contribution to scholarship was the editing of such medieval works as *Ḥefes Matmonim* (1845), a collection of medieval texts; Isaac Israeli's *Yesod Olam* (1848); Ibn Janaḥ's *Sefer ha-Rikmah* in Judah ibn Tibbon's translation (1857); *Iggeret Sherira Ga'on* (1873); *Risalat R. Judah b. Koraish* (1867); and Abraham b. Moses b. Maimon's *Birkat Avraham* (1860, repr. 1960).

BIBLIOGRAPHY: I.I. Goldbloom, in: *Oẓar ha-Sifrut*, 4 (1892), 542–51; B. Wachstein, *Hebraeische Publizistik in Wien* (1930), 71 (incl. bibl.); Kressel, Leksikon, 1 (1965), 412–3.

GOLDBERG, BEN ZION (**Benjamin Waife**; 1895–1972), Yiddish journalist. Born in Golshany (Lithuania), a descendant of prominent rabbinical families, Goldberg studied at the Lida and Volozhin *yeshivot* before immigrating to the U.S. in 1907. In 1917 he married the youngest daughter of *Sholem Aleichem. He studied psychology at Columbia University and wrote articles on that subject and on foreign policy for the daily *Der Tog*, of which he became managing editor (1924–40). He helped to organize the U.S. branch of YIVO. As a daily columnist for more than 40 years, he was influential and controversial, particularly with his pro-Soviet orientation – which ended with the purges that exterminated Soviet Jewish leaders. His books in English include *Sacred Fire: The Story of Sex in Religion* (1930), and *The Jewish Problem in the Soviet Union* (1961).

BIBLIOGRAPHY: LYNL, 3 (1960), 45–8. **ADD. BIBLIOGRAPHY:** I. Oren (ed.), *Kratkaia evreĭskaia entsiklopediia*, 2 (1982), 157.

[S.L./ Jerold C. Frakes (2nd ed.)]

GOLDBERG, BERTRAND (1913–1997), U.S. architect. Born in Chicago, Goldberg studied at Harvard, at the Bauhaus in Berlin, and at the Armour Institute of Technology (now Illinois Institute of Technology) in Chicago. He specialized in industrial design and city planning. The acting principal of Bertrand Goldberg Associates in Chicago from 1937, Goldberg established a branch office of the company in Boston in 1964.

He believed that the modern rectilinear style of architecture had been superseded by the new structural shapes made possible through the recent development in reinforced concrete. To that end, he created circular designs in concrete shell structures, which he believed would serve activity better and help create community. He also maintained that circular buildings provide more efficient wind resistance, more direct mechanical distribution, and more usable footage. Over the years, he developed a theory of kinetic space based on non-parallel walls that set a space in motion. Goldberg introduced several shapes to skyscraper architecture, many of which can be recognized by their rounded lobes and oval windows.

Among his chief works in Chicago are the Astor Tower (1962); Marina City (1963), featuring round, 60-story residential towers; the Raymond Hilliard Homes (1966); the Prentice-Stone Pavilion (1975); St. Joseph's Hospital (1975); SUNY Hospital and SUNY Basic Science and Clinical Science Towers (1976); and River City (1986).

Goldberg was elected to the College of Fellows of the American Institute of Architects in 1966 and was awarded the Officier de l'Ordre des Arts et des Lettres from the French government in 1985.

In 2002, Goldberg's family donated his entire architectural archive to the Art Institute of Chicago. It includes his architectural plans, drawings, photos, and models, as well as lectures, articles, and construction photos.

BIBLIOGRAPHY: J. and K. Cook, *Conversations with Architects* (1973).

[Ruth Beloff (2nd ed.)]

GOLDBERG, BORIS (1865–1922), economist and Zionist. Born in Shaki (Sakiai), Lithuania, Goldberg studied at Hanover, where he graduated in 1891 as a chemical engineer. In 1898 he moved to Vilna. He joined the Ḥibbat Zion movement at an early age, and when the Zionist Organization was founded, joined it at once. Goldberg was an ardent supporter of practical settlement work in Ereẓ Israel. He contributed articles to all existing Jewish periodicals in Russia, was a member of the editorial board of *Razsvet* and *Ha-Olam*, and published studies on the demographic and social composition of Russian Jewry. Goldberg was a member of the Central Office of the Zionist Organization in Vilna, and, together with his brother I.L. *Goldberg, he headed the illegal Zionist activities in the Vilna region, for which he was imprisoned on several occasions. In 1906 he took part in the work of the League for Equal Rights for Russian Jews, and in 1917 he was a member of the National Council of Russian Jews. He left Russia in 1919 as a representative of Russian Jews to the Comité des Délégations Juives, which represented the Jewish people at the Versailles Peace Conference. He helped to transfer the capital of Russian Jews to Palestine and was one of the founders of the Ha-Boneh Company and the Silikat building materials factory in Tel Aviv. He was wounded during the Arab riots of 1921 and died a year later in Tel Aviv.

BIBLIOGRAPHY: N. Sokolow, *History of Zionism*, 2 (1919), index; I. Klausner, *Mi-Kattoviz ad Basel*, 2 vols. (1965), index; Tidhar, 1 (1947), 293, 483–4.

[Yehuda Slutsky]

GOLDBERG, EMANUEL (1881–1970), photographic scientist. Goldberg was born in Moscow and graduated from Moscow University before moving to Leipzig, where he obtained his doctorate in photochemistry (1906). After appointments at the University of Leipzig and the Military Academy of Berlin, he moved to Dresden (1917), where he became managing director of the Zeiss Ikon optical company and professor at the Technical University. He was kidnapped by the Nazis but his employers recognized his inventive genius and arranged his release into exile in Paris (1933), where he worked in their subsidiary company. He immigrated to Palestine (1937), where he established a laboratory for precision instruments which became the basis of the optical industry in Israel. Goldberg was a pioneer in many photographic and related fields, notably high-resolution microfilms, microdot technology, hand-held movie cameras, sound movies, television, and electronic systems for document storing and retrieval. He worked on military applications of his inventions for the Allied governments in World War II and for the Haganah and the Israeli government. Goldberg's original contributions were recognized by the award of the Peligot Medal by the French Photographic Society (1931) but were subsequently obscured by the Nazis and Communists for political reasons and by later inventors anxious to establish their own priority. He was awarded the Israel Prize for exact sciences (1968).

[Michael Denman (2nd ed.)]

GOLDBERG, HARVEY E. (1939–), U.S. anthropologist. Born in New York City, Goldberg received his bachelor's degree from Columbia University in 1961 and his doctorate from Harvard in 1967. He taught at the University of Iowa from 1966 as an assistant professor, then from 1969 to 1972 as associate professor. He was a research fellow at Columbia University in 1968 and 1969, and a visiting scholar at Cambridge and at the University of Texas. From 1972 he was a member of the faculty of the Hebrew University of Jerusalem, where he was named the Sarah Allen Shaine Professor of Sociology and Anthropology. Goldberg was also a fellow of the American Anthropological Association and a member of the New York Academy of Sciences and the Middle East Studies Association of North America.

A leading anthropologist of Jewish culture, Goldberg wrote numerous works that center on Jewish life in the Middle East, both in Israel and elsewhere. His books include *Cave Dwellers and Citrus Growers: A Jewish Community in Libya and Israel* (1972), *Greentown's Youth: Disadvantaged Youth in a Development Town in Israel* (1984), *Jewish Life in Muslim Libya* (1990), *Sephardi and Middle Eastern Jewries* (as editor, 1996), *Life of Judaism* (as editor, 2001), and *Jewish Passages: Cycles of Jewish Life* (2003).

Jewish Passages has been well received by a wide audience. In this work, Goldberg examines both individual practice and collective identity as he considers the ways in which Jews from many traditions celebrate the cycles of life. The work includes an exploration of Sephardi and Ashkenazi traditions; it examines ritual, custom, and a range of events, from circumcision to identity-seeking tourism.

Goldberg wrote numerous articles for academic journals, including the *Jewish Journal of Sociology, Hagar: International Social Science Review*, and *Jerusalem Studies in Jewish Folklore*. He also contributed to various texts and reference works, including the *Oxford Handbook of Jewish Studies* (2002), *Global Religions* (2003), and *Key Texts in American Jewish Culture* (2003). Goldberg's subsequent research focused on the Jews of Libya and Ethiopia, seeking to integrate historical and sociological perspectives in understanding cultural diversity within Israeli society.

[Dorothy Bauhoff (2nd ed.)]

GOLDBERG, ISAAC (1887–1938), U.S. author. Born in Boston, Goldberg wrote *Sir William S. Gilbert* (1913); *The Story of Gilbert and Sullivan* (1928); *George Gershwin* (1931); *Major Noah: American-Jewish Pioneer* (1936); and *Queen of Hearts* (1936), a biography of Lola Montez. He did pioneering work in his surveys, *Studies in Spanish-American Literature* (1920) and *Brazilian Literature* (1922). Goldberg also translated into English some of the major Yiddish authors, such as David Pinski, Scholem Asch, and Yehoash. From 1923 to 1932 he was literary editor of *The American Freeman*.

BIBLIOGRAPHY: Ewen, in: *American Hebrew* (Nov. 5, 1937). **ADD. BIBLIOGRAPHY:** A. Crandall, *Isaac Goldberg, An Appreciation* (1934).

[Sol Liptzin]

GOLDBERG, ISAAC LEIB (1860–1935), Zionist leader and philanthropist in Russia and Ereẓ Israel; brother of Boris *Goldberg. After studying at the Kovno yeshivah, he settled in Vilna, where he joined his uncle's business. One of the first members of the *Ḥibbat Zion movement (1882), he founded the Ohavei Zion society in Vilna. At the Ḥovevei Zion meeting in Druzgenik in 1887, he sought to effect a compromise between the views of the Orthodox and the *maskilim*. He represented the Ḥovevei Zion committee in Vilna and was a member of *Benei Moshe. His home in Vilna became the center of Zionist and Jewish national activities. His wife, Rachel, was among the founders of Yehudiyyah Hebrew Girls School.

Goldberg was a delegate to the First Zionist Congress, representing the Ḥovevei Zion of Vilna; in 1900 he was appointed representative of the *Zionist Organization in the Vilna district. He took part in the establishment of the Geulah Company, whose aim it was to acquire land in Ereẓ Israel for private ownership, and of the Carmel Company for the marketing of wine produced in the Jewish settlements in Ereẓ

Israel. In 1908 he established a farm at Hartuv and purchased the first plot of land on Mount Scopus in Jerusalem for the future *Hebrew University. In 1906 he became a member of the Zionist Central Committee in Russia, and its office was located in his home. He lent his support to the Zionist periodicals in Vilna *Ha-Olam* and *Dos Yidishe Folk*. During World War I the Russian authorities forced him to live in Moscow, where he continued his Zionist activities. In 1919 he settled in Palestine, engaged in growing oranges, and made important contributions to improving the packing and marketing of citrus products. He was one of the founders of the *Haaretz* daily newspaper, which he supported financially. Goldberg was also a supporter of the Hebrew Language Committee. He left half his estate for the establishment of a fund for the Promotion of Hebrew Literature and Hebrew Culture in Ereẓ Israel, which was eventually handed over to the *Jewish National Fund, which devoted the income to Hebrew cultural projects.

BIBLIOGRAPHY: N. Sokolow, *History of Zionism*, 2 (1919), index; S. Eisenstadt, *I.L. Goldberg…* (Heb., 1945); I. Klausner, *Mi-Kattoviẓ ad Basel*, 2 vols. (1956), index; Tidhar, 1 (1947), 293, 483–4.

[Yehuda Slutsky]

GOLDBERG, J.B. (1884–1946), Soviet army commander. In 1919, Lenin personally entrusted him with the command of the reserves and with the task of setting up a corps of reserves for the whole of the Red Army fighting on the Eastern front. Within two years Goldberg created a force of half a million men. In 1922 he was appointed deputy head of the air force.

GOLDBERG, JEANNETTE MIRIAM (1868–1935), U.S. Jewish educator. Goldberg, a charismatic organizer, was the first field secretary of the National Council of Jewish Women (NCJW) and the longtime executive secretary of the Jewish Chautauqua Society (JCS). For three decades, she guided the Chautauqua Society, which popularizes Judaic learning among English-speaking Jews and non-Jews.

A native Texan whose parents had emigrated from Russia to Louisiana in 1860 and then to Texas after the Civil War and whose father, Louis, was among the founders in 1873 of Jefferson's Hebrew Sinai Congregation, Goldberg enrolled in Vassar College's preparatory division in 1883. She received an A.B. from New York's Rutgers Female Institute, where she was class valedictorian. Goldberg taught literature at women's finishing schools in Birmingham, Ala. and Dallas, Waco, and Sherman, Tex. She worked as a Sabbath School superintendent in Houston and Jefferson.

In 1896, she attended the Council of Jewish Women's first triennial in New York. Appointed vice president for Texas, she helped organize her state's first Council chapters in Tyler, Dallas, Waco, Beaumont, and Fort Worth. In 1902, she was elected a national director of the council and carved out a role as field secretary. In that capacity, she traveled cross-country organizing chapters and motivating co-religionists who had grown indifferent toward Judaism. "We have had enough lullaby and slumber in religious life," she exhorted. "[W]e now need wakefulness and spirit, to revivify the dry bones of American Judaism."

In 1905, the Jewish Chautauqua Society, headquartered in Philadelphia, hired Goldberg as its field secretary, a position similar to her volunteer role with the NCJW. When the Chautauqua's home secretary retired in 1910, the two positions merged, with Goldberg shouldering both roles. Under Goldberg's leadership, the JCS launched study circles, assemblies, and a national correspondence school to train Sabbath School teachers. In her travels throughout the U.S., Goldberg helped organize congregations and recruit rabbis to lead them. The JCS opened religious schools in the Dakotas and in the south New Jersey farm colonies started with Baron de *Hirsch funds. The Chautauqua Society also initiated a university lecture circuit – still in operation in the 21st century – featuring rabbis speaking to non-Jewish audiences about Judaism.

Rabbi Julian *Feibelman, who became acquainted with Goldberg when he was a Mississippi boy enrolled in Chautauqua correspondence classes, maintained that she "kept her hand on the pulse of virtually every congregation" in the nation. She was "instrumental in helping many rabbis [including himself] to advancement in pulpits." He lauded Goldberg as "one of the two Jewish women in America capable of addressing an audience on Jewish subjects – the other was Sadie *American" (the first executive secretary of the NCJW). When Goldberg died on February 28, 1935, she was eulogized in the *Philadelphia Exponent* as "a modern Miriam" and a "high priestess" of Judaism. Unmarried, she outlived her siblings and had no survivors.

BIBLIOGRAPHY: J.B. Feibelman, *The Making of a Rabbi* (1980), 56, 266–68; M.E. Berkowitz, *The Beloved Rabbi: An Account of the Life and Works of Henry Berkowitz. D.D.* (1932), 144–47, 171, 180; H.A. Weiner, "The Jewish Junior League: The Rise and Demise of the Fort Worth Council of Jewish Women" (M.A. thesis, University of Texas at Arlington, 2004); "Report of Miss Goldberg on Organizing," in: *Proceedings of the Council of Jewish Women, Fourth Triennial Convention, Chicago, Illinois, December 5 to 12, 1905*, 149; P. Kronsberg Pearlstein. "Understanding through Education: One Hundred Years of the Jewish Chautauqua Society, 1893–1993" (Dissertation, George Washington University, 1993).

[Hollace Ava Weiner (2nd ed.)]

GOLDBERG, LEA (1911–1970), Hebrew poet and critic. Born in Koenigsberg, Eastern Prussia, she spent the early years of her childhood in Russia but after the Revolution her family returned to their home in Kovno, Lithuania. While still a schoolgirl, Lea Goldberg began to write Hebrew verse and her first poem was published in *Hed Lita* in 1926. She attended the universities of Kovno, Berlin, and Bonn. Arriving in Tel Aviv in 1935, she joined the circle of modernist authors, whose mentor was Avraham *Shlonsky, and began publishing her poetry in *Turim*, the literary forum of the group. Shlonsky helped her compile her first volume of poetry *Tabbe'ot Ashan* ("Smoke Rings," 1935). After a career as a schoolteacher, she joined the editorial staffs of *Davar and later *Mishmar* in the capacity of theater critic and eventually became editor of

Al ha-Mishmar's literary supplement. She also served on the staff of *Davar li-Yladim*, a popular children's magazine, was the children's book editor of Sifriyyat Po'alim, and the literary adviser to *Habimah, Israel's national theater. In 1952 she was invited to organize the Department of Comparative Literature at the Hebrew University of Jerusalem, holding the chair until her death. As Goldberg was a prolific and versatile writer, her literary talent found expression in many genres. Primarily a poet, she was also a literary critic, wrote a number of children's works, was a copious translator, and the author of a novel and a play.

Poetry

All of Goldberg's poetry is written in the modern mode set by the school of younger poets that developed in Ereẓ Israel during the Mandate period. Influenced by the Russian Acmeist poets (a literary trend which rejected symbolism, aiming at concrete imagery and a clear unadorned style), she used traditional verse forms, expressing her modernism through a conversational style which eschewed the ornate rhetoric of many of her predecessors and the bombastic expressionism of her contemporaries. Her language though symbolic is simple and familiar, in which ordinary words, images, rhythms, and rhymes have an astonishing freshness. The later verse is stripped of all "literary" pretensions; the poet thus strove to evolve a style of direct and unencumbered statement of the poetic experience. Goldberg's tendency toward aesthetic intellectualism is modified by a lyrical delicacy. She refused to write ideological verse and unlike her contemporaries she rarely touched upon Jewish themes. Only in the aftermath of the Holocaust did she express her feelings in a Jewish framework (*Mi-Beiti ha-Yashan*, "From My Old Home," 1944). Universal in her approach, she wrote on childhood, nature, love (especially unfulfilled love), the quest for aesthetic expression, aging, and death. In her later years her central themes were resignation to the tragedy of existence and finding solace in the poetry unexpectedly discovered in ordinary phenomena. Among her outstanding poems are "Mi-Shirei ha-Naḥal" ("The Songs of the Stream," in *Al ha-Periḥah*, 1948) in which she employed natural symbols such as river, stone, tree, moon, and blade of grass to serve as a vehicle for the poetic presentation of aesthetic problems of the creative artists; "Be-Harei Yerushalayim" ("In the Hills of Jerusalem," in *Barak ba-Boker*, 1956), one of her best landscape poems, set in Jerusalem, the city in which she resided for many years; and "Ahavatah shel Teresa di Mon" ("The Love of Therese du Meun," in *Barak ba-Boker*), a series of sonnets purportedly written in the 17th century by an aging aristocrat on her unconfessed love for her children's young tutor.

Criticism

An avid reader, Goldberg was at home in the literature of all the major European languages. She was most familiar with Russian literature and wrote *Aḥdut ha-Adam ve-ha-Yekum bi-Yẓirat Tolstoy* ("The Unity of World and Man in Tolstoy's Works," 1959), as well as a collection of essays on Pushkin, Lermontov, Gogol, Turgenev, Herzen, and Chekhov entitled *Ha-Sifrut ha-Rusit ba-Me'ah ha-Tesha-Esreh* (1968). The latter was to have been part of a general history of the literature of the period, but she abandoned the project. Goldberg was also well versed in Italian literature and wrote an introduction to Dante's *Divine Comedy (Mavo la-Komedyah ha-Elohit*, mimeograph, 1958) and a preface to her translation of selected poems by Petrarch (1957). In *Ḥamishah Perakim bi-Ysodot ha-Shirah* ("Five Chapters in the Elements of Poetry," 1957), a more systematic attempt at studying the problems of poetry, she discusses poetic theory, meter, rhyme, and symbol. Each chapter begins with a close reading of a Hebrew poem which is used to illustrate the specific hypothesis she has posited. In contrast to her generalizations about poetry, which reflect accepted literary criteria, the interpretations of specific works show an original and creative poetic mind. The same can be said about her study *Ommanut ha-Sippur* ("The Art of the Short Story," 1963).

Children's Literature

Goldberg was one of Israel's most successful children's writers. She was able to enter the world of children, communicate with them, and establish a bond of friendship with all children not only through the written word but by live contact. She wrote about 20 works for children. A whole generation of Israelis grew up on her stories and poems (see *Children's Literature).

Prose Works

Mikhtavim mi-Nesi'ah Medummah ("Letters from an Imaginary Journey," 1937) and *Ve-Hu ha-Or* ("He Is the Light," 1946), the two major prose works of Goldberg, are mainly autobiographical. The latter is set in Lithuania and describes the struggle of a young and sensitive girl student for identity, despite insecurities rooted in a background of mental illness in her immediate family. The earlier work, *Mikhtavim mi-Nesi'ah Medummah,* hardly a novel because of its weak structure, refers to a later period in the author's life and gives an insight into her basically aristocratic view of the arts. The struggle between leftist politics and art is the theme of her single play *Ba'alat ha-Armon* ("Lady of the Manor," 1956) which is set in postwar Europe. The play (in English translation) was staged in New York but was not a critical success. Goldberg's diaries were published in 2005.

Translations

Among the many European classics that Goldberg translated into Hebrew are: Tolstoy's *War and Peace* (1958), Chekhov's *Stories* (1945), Gorki's *Childhood* (1943), several plays and poems by Shakespeare (1957), selected poems by Petrarch (1957), Ibsen's *Peer Gynt* (1958), and *Aucassin et Nicolette* (1966). Together with Shlonsky she edited an anthology of Russian poetry (1942). Goldberg started to paint in her later years and she illustrated several of her own books (*Aucassin et Nicolette*, for example).

Goldberg's poems have been translated into various languages. Poems in English translation are included in T. Carmi (ed.), *The Penguin Book of Hebrew Verse* (1981) as well as in *The Modern Hebrew Poem Itself* (2003). *Mikhtavim mi-Nesi'ah Medummah* was translated into German (*Briefe von einer imaginaeren Reise*, 2003). For further English translations of her works, see Goell, Bibliography, index.

BIBLIOGRAPHY: E. Spicehandler, in: *Israel* (Spring 1961), 61–80; G. Yardeni, *Siḥot im Soferim* (1961), 119–32; G. Shaked, in: *Moznayim*, 3 (1956) no. 3, 86–190; idem, in: *Orot*, 38 (Jan. 1960), 45–49; D. Sadan, in: *Yerushalayim, Shenaton le-Divrei Sifrut ve-Ommanut* (1970), 17–22; R. Alter, in: *Commentary*, 49, 5 (1970), 83–86. **ADD. BIBLIOGRAPHY:** R. Sherwin, "Two New Translations: The Poems of L Goldberg and D. Ravikovich as Good English Poems," in: *Modern Hebrew Literature* 3/1–2 (1977), 38–42; O. Baumgarten-Kuris, *Emẓa'im Sifrutiyim be-Shiratah shel L. Goldberg* (1979); T. Ruebner, *L. Goldberg, Monografyah* (1980); A.B. Jaffe, *Pegishot'im L. Goldberg* (1984); L. Hovav, *Yesodot be-Shirat ha-Yeladim bire'i Yeẓiratah shel L. Goldberg* (1986); H. Shoham, "Fichte und Landschaft: Ein romantisches und ein zionistisches Modell. Vergleichende Betrachtung eines Gedichtes von Heinrich Heine und Lea Goldberg," in: *Conditio Judaica* 1 (1988), 329–38; Y. Nave, *Biblical Motifs Representing the "Lyrical Self" in the Works of Scholem Aleichem, N. Alterman, Lea Goldberg, Ariela Deem, Shulamit Har-Even* (1987); A.B. Jaffe, *Lea Goldberg: Tavei Demut li-Yeẓiratah* (1994); A. Lieblich, *El Lea* (1995); S. Neumann, *Mokedim ba-Lashon ha-Figurativit shel Shirat L. Goldberg* (1996); N.R.S. Gold, "Rereading *It Is the Light,* L. Goldberg's Only Novel," in: *Prooftexts* 17/3 (1997), 245–59; M.E. Varela Moreno, "Hypotexts of Lea Goldberg's Sonnets," in: *Jewish Studies at the Turn of the Twentieth Century* 2 (1999), 236–43; R. Kartun-Blum and A. Weisman (eds.), *Pegishot im Meshoreret: Masot u-Meḥkarim al Yeẓiratah shel L. Goldberg* (2000); H. Barzel, *Shirat Ereẓ Yisrael: Shlonsky, Alterman, Goldberg* (2001); O. Yaglin, *Ulai Mabat Aher: Klasiyut Modernit u-Modernizm be-Shirat L. Goldberg* (2002).

[Ezra Spicehandler]

GOLDBERG, MARSHALL (**"Biggie," "The Elkins Express," "Mad Marshall,"** the **"Hebrew Hillbilly"**; 1917–), U.S. football player, starring in college at the University of Pittsburgh and in the NFL with the Chicago Cardinals, and member of College Football Hall of Fame. Goldberg was born and raised in Elkins, West Virginia, a town of five Jewish families in a community of 7,500 people. Goldberg's father, Saul, had immigrated from Uman, Romania, and ran a ladies' clothing store before becoming owner of the town's movie theater. Goldberg was a high school legend, captaining his school's football, basketball, and track teams in 1935, and was selected All-State in each sport. He led Pitt to a Rose Bowl title in 1936 after leading the nation in rushing with 886 yards, and to the National Championship the following year. Goldberg was named Grantland Rice All-America honorable mention in 1936, and a consensus All-America halfback in 1937 and fullback in 1938, finishing third in the Heisman Trophy voting in 1937 and second in 1938. Goldberg ended his career at Pitt holding all the school's rushing records, including total rushing yards with 1,957. Goldberg then played with NFL Chicago Cardinals for eight years, and was considered the greatest defensive back of his time. He led the team to the NFL championship in 1947, and made all-pro at two positions – as a halfback in 1941 and as a defensive back in 1946, 1947, and 1948. Goldberg led the league in 1941 with seven interceptions, and in kickoff returns that year with a 24.2-yard average, and the following year with a 26.2-yard average. He was inducted into the College Football Hall of Fame in 1958.

[Elli Wohlgelernter (2nd ed.)]

GOLDBERG, OSCAR (1885–1952), scholar and author, born in Berlin. Goldberg first studied medicine, but on the basis of personal parapsychological experiments he turned to esoteric mysticism. After Hitler's rise to power he immigrated to France and subsequently to the United States. He later returned to France and died in Nice. His first work, *Die fuenf Buecher Mosis, ein Zahlengebaeude* (1908) is an attempt to prove (in accordance with kabbalistic opinion) that the entire Torah is based on the letters of the Tetragrammaton. His basic theories are expressed in the works: *Die Wirklichkeit der Hebraeer* (vol. 1, 1925; no more were published); *Maimonides* (1935); and articles on Greek mythology in the monthly *Mass und Wert* (1937). Goldberg assumed that there were "metaphysical" peoples whose biological center was their "god" as opposed to peoples or groups who had lost their metaphysical power and were merely biological groups. *Die Wirklichkeit der Hebraeer* ("The Reality of the Hebrews") shows the Hebrews to be the outstanding example of a metaphysical people, which activates the vital link between it and its "center," i.e., its god, via the magical power of ritual and makes its god dwell within the world. The metaphysical reality of the genuine Hebrews consisted in the activation of the laws and statutes of the Torah (which must be understood in its most literal and exact interpretation). Later Judaism, beginning with "the religion of the prophets," was based on the deterioration of the magical powers of the Hebrews and the loss of the basic tools for the activation of their magical reality: the Tabernacle and the Ark of the Covenant. Every metaphysical people has a national god, and among these gods, which had perfect reality, the God of Israel is but the strongest. As the real magical power of metaphysics was weakened, there begins the process of the transformation of the ritual which possessed formal and material precision into an abstract universal "religion." The histories of religions constitute decline and not progress. The decline of true Hebraism, which worked miracles not according to circumstance but by order and fixed ritual, began during the reigns of David and Solomon. It reached its nadir in the "religiosity" of the Psalms. The transition from worship in the Temple to that in the synagogue typifies the decline of the metaphysical power to nothingness.

Goldberg accepted only the Pentateuch as a divine document in all its details and signs, and interpreted it magically, not "theologically." The Revelation of God is not an act of free grace to His creatures, but springs from the need of God Himself to find a dwelling place (*mishkan*) on earth. Goldberg views the system of Maimonides as the final expression of complete alienation from the true mission of the Hebraic existence, and as an intended blurring and abolition of the realistic principle which is the power to work miracles in favor of moralistic and abstract prattle. According to this system, Goldberg interpreted all details of other mythologies. He advocated the organization of the remnants of magical power which remained here and there, in order to find a way for the renewal of divine revelation. He stated his magical views in a clearly rationalistic way and linked them with modern biological philosophy. The kabbalistic origins of his thought are conspicuous and Goldberg himself recognized this despite his attempts to define specific differences between the spheres of the Torah and that of Kabbalah. Goldberg was hostile to Zionism, which he viewed as a secular renewal of a Jewish people without a metaphysical basis according to his definition.

For many years Goldberg led a small group which propagated his views in writing and orally. His most important disciple in philosophy was Erich Unger (d. 1951 in London). For some time his works and thoughts had considerable influence on circles of both Jewish and gentile intellectuals, scholars and writers such as the paleontologist E. Dacque, and the writer Thomas Mann. The latter depicted Goldberg in his novel *Doctor Faustus* (1947) as the character Dr. Chaim Breisacher.

BIBLIOGRAPHY: J. Schechter, *Mi-Madda le-Emunah* (1953), 213–29; E. Unger, *Politik und Metaphysik* (1922); idem, *Das Problem der mythischen Realitaet* (1926); idem, *Wirklichkeit, Mythos, Erkenntnis* (1930); A. Caspary, *Die Maschinenutopie* (1927).

[Gershom Scholem]

GOLDBERG, RUBE (1883–1970), U.S. cartoonist. Reuben Lucius Goldberg, satirist of American folkways and creator of improbable and outlandish devices and inventions, was born in San Francisco, Calif. His father insisted he go to college to become an engineer. After graduating from the University of California at Berkeley, Goldberg went to work for the San Francisco Water and Sewers Department. After six months, Goldberg joined the sports department of a San Francisco newspaper and kept submitting drawings and cartoons to its editor, until he was finally published. He moved to New York, drawing daily cartoons for *The Evening Mail.* At first he was a sports cartoonist and sportswriter, but one day, with a little space left over from his cartoon, he filled it with "Foolish Question No. 1," which showed a man who had fallen from the Flatiron Building being asked if he was hurt. "No, I jump off this building every day to limber up for business," he replied. The Foolish Question caught on, and Goldberg wound up doing thousands of them. Many of his ideas came from readers, fascinated with the nearly probable. As comic strips grew in popularity, Goldberg conceived the character Boob McNutt, a simple-looking fellow who was in love with a beautiful girl named Pearl. Their blunder-filled courtship went on from 1916 to 1933. Goldberg also created the strip *Lala Palooza*, about a woman of ample girth. His most enduring creation was Professor Lucifer Gorgonzola Butts, the inventor of marvelously complicated contraptions designed to accomplish fairly simple ends. An exhibition of these nonexistent and zany gadgets opened at the National Museum of History and Technology of the Smithsonian Institution in Washington in 1970. The Goldbergs of yesterday were catalogued under the show title "Do It the Hard Way: Rube Goldberg and Modern Times." There were cartoons, comic strips, and oddly ingenious doodads that might have been invented by Goldberg himself. The cartoonist's ludicrous inventions became so widely known that Webster's Third International Dictionary listed the adjective "rube goldberg" and defined it as "accomplishing by extremely complex roundabout means what actually or seemingly could be done simply."

In the middle 1930s, comic strips declined in popularity and at the age of 55 Goldberg embarked on a career as an editorial cartoonist for *The New York Sun* and later the *New York Journal-American*, for which he drew 5,000 cartoons. One of his cartoons, "Peace Today," warning of the perils of atomic weapons, which appeared in *The Sun*, won a Pulitzer Prize in 1948.

[Stewart Kampel (2nd ed.)]

GOLDBERG, SZYMON (1909–1993), violinist and conductor of Polish birth. He studied with Mihailowicz in Warsaw, and with Flesch in Berlin. After his debut in Warsaw (1921), he appeared with the Berlin PO (1924) and was leader of the Dresden Philharmonic (1925–1929). From 1929 to 1934 he formed a string trio with Hindemith and *Feuermann and was appointed concertmaster of the Berlin Philharmonic. He then toured as soloist and as sonata partner with Lili *Kraus. While on a tour of Asia, Goldberg was interned in Java by the Japanese (1942–1945). After the war he resumed his career and played in Australia, South Africa, the Americas, and Israel. He became an American citizen (1953) and taught at the Aspen Music School (1951–1965) where he formed the Festival Quartet, which achieved wide recognition in concerts and on records. Goldberg played trios with Casals and R. *Serkin during the Prades Festival (1954) and became permanent conductor and musical director of the Netherlands Chamber Orchestra (1955), which he led with notable distinction for 22 years. From 1969 he lived in London, conducted the Manchester Camerata (1977–1982), taught at Yale University, the Juilliard School, the Curtis Institute of Music, and the Manhattan School of Music. From 1990 until his death he conducted the New Japan Philharmonic in Tokyo. He was an officer of the Order of Oranje Nassau. A masterly violinist Goldberg's tone was warm and pure, his interpretations stressed refinement, intimacy and a noble intensity. His recordings include a distinguished set of the Brandenburg Concertos and, with Radu Lupu, 16 Mozart sonatas. He was also a sensitive performer of Bartók, Berg, and Hindemith.

BIBLIOGRAPHY: Grove Music Online; MGG²; Baker's Biographical Dictionary (1997); B. Gavoty. *Szymon Goldberg* (Geneva, 1961),

[Naama Ramot (2nd ed.)]

GOLDBERGER, IZIDOR (1876–1944), Hungarian rabbi and scholar. Goldberger, who was born in Bátorkeszi, Hungary, held appointments in Sátoraljaujhely (1903–1914) and Tata

(1912–1944). He wrote on the history of Hungarian Jewry, especially on that of the Jews in Zemplén County (1910), and in the city of Tata (1914). He also wrote on the emancipation of Hungarian Jewry. Goldberger translated into Hungarian excerpts from the Mishnah (1905) and from the Midrash (1907).

BIBLIOGRAPHY: *Dr. Goldberger Izidor tatai rabbi irodalmi működése, 1904–1914* (1915); *Magyar Zsidó Lexikon* (1929), 318; Wininger, Biog, 2 (1927), 441; 7 (1936), 14.

[Jeno Zsoldos]

GOLDBERGER, JOSEPH (1874–1929), U.S. physician and public health specialist. Goldberger, who was born in Giralt, Hungary, immigrated to the U.S. at an early age. From 1899 until his death he served in the U.S. Public Health Service in Washington, D.C. Goldberger's greatest contribution was his discovery of the etiology and therapy of pellagra and his introduction of nicotinic acid as a means of preventing the disease. He also made significant contributions in the study of infectious diseases and public health, particularly in the field of welfare of the poor.

BIBLIOGRAPHY: S.R. Kagan, *Jewish Medicine* (1952), 549; *Biographisches Lexikon der hervorragenden Aerzte*, 1 (1932), s.v.

[Suessmann Muntner]

GOLDBLOOM, Montreal family noted for their involvement in medicine, research, teaching, and publishing, as well as political activity, social activism, and community work.

Renowned for his pioneering work in children's health, ALTON GOLDBLOOM (1890–1968) was a founder of the Canadian Pediatric Society. During his career, he was a professor (emeritus) of pediatrics at McGill University and physician-in-chief at the Montreal Children's Hospital. His many publications include his autobiography, *Small Patients* (1959), and *The Care of the Child* (1928).

The elder son, VICTOR CHARLES (1923–), graduated from McGill University and worked as a pediatrician. In 1966, he was elected to the National Assembly of Quebec, and after re-election in 1970, he became the first Jewish member of a provincial cabinet in Quebec. Remaining in the National Assembly until 1979, he served as minister of the environment as well as minister of municipal affairs. He later worked as the executive director of the Canadian Council of Christians and Jews and several other ecumenical and intercultural organizations. From 1991 to 1999, he served as official languages commissioner of Canada. Among his many distinctions, he was named a Companion of the Order of Canada and an Officer of the Order of Quebec. His wife, SHEILA BARSHAY, a McGill graduate and professor of social work, was actively involved in several public organizations and was named Member of the Order of Canada in 1998.

His brother, RICHARD GOLDBLOOM (1924–) graduated from McGill University, taught pediatric medicine at Dalhousie University in Halifax, Nova Scotia, and was appointed chancellor of the University in 2001. He published over 200 articles and books, including a textbook, *Pediatric Clinical Skills*. In recognition of his dedication to both general and Jewish community organizations, as well as his university and medical career, he was named an Officer of the Order of Canada in 1987. His wife, RUTH MIRIAM SCHWARTZ, a graduate of McGill, among other public and benevolent appointments served to coordinate the renovations to Pier 21 in Halifax. She was named an Officer of the Order of Canada in 2000.

BIBLIOGRAPHY: R.C. Goldbloom, "Family Ties," in: *Canadian Medical Association Journal*, 158 (1998), 1167–70; E. Gottesman, *Who's Who in Canadian Jewry* (1965); E. Lipsitz, *Who's Who in Canadian Jewry: Canadian Jewry at Year 2000 and Beyond* (2000).

[Steven Lapidus (2nd ed.)]

GOLDBLOOM, JACOB KOPPEL (1872–1961), Zionist leader. Born in Kletsk, then Poland, Goldbloom went to London in 1892, joined the Ḥovevei Zion and, after meeting Herzl, began to found Zionist societies in Whitechapel. He introduced the "*Ivrit be-Ivrit*" method of Hebrew teaching and taught many thousands of youngsters who enrolled in his "Redman's Road Talmud Torah" over the decades. From 1901 onward Goldbloom attended almost every Zionist Congress and was a member of the Zionist General Council. In 1935 he became chairman of the European executive of the Confederation of General Zionists. He served Herzl, Wolffsohn, Otto Warburg, Weizmann, Sokolow, and Nahum Goldmann with loyalty and devotion. Goldbloom was one of the architects of the British Zionist Federation and of its Synagogue Council. He wrote a utopian work in Hebrew entitled *Ḥag ha-Bikkurim be-Ereẓ Yisrael bi-Shenat 2016* ("Festival of the First Harvest in Ereẓ Israel in the Year 2016," 1920). In 1963 his remains were buried in Jerusalem.

[Josef Fraenkel]

GOLDBLUM, ISRAEL ISSER (**Isidore**; 1864–1925), Polish Hebrew writer and bibliographer. Goldblum was born in Vilna and studied in an East European yeshivot. He devoted himself to the study and publication of Hebrew manuscripts in Berlin, Paris, London, Oxford, and Rome. The result of his research he published under the pseudonym Yafag mainly in the periodical *Ha-Maggid*. He corresponded with the leading Jewish scholars of his time and published a collection of these letters (*Kevuẓat Mikhtavim*, 1895). He also published *Mi-Ginzei Yisrael be-Paris* (1894) on the Paris Hebrew manuscripts and *Ma'amar Bikkoret Sefarim* (1891). Some of his writings and letters exist in manuscript form at the Jewish Theological Seminary of America.

BIBLIOGRAPHY: Kressel, Leksikon, 1 (1965), 409–10.

GOLDBLUM, JEFF (1952–), U.S. film actor. Goldblum started on the New York stage, but soon went to Hollywood. Goldblum played small roles in such films as *California Split*, *Nashville*, *Next Stop Greenwich Village*, and *Annie Hall*, before landing his first leading role in a remake of the classic sci-fi adventure *Invasion of the Body Snatchers* (1978). Goldblum was soon recognized for the off-beat authenticity he gave his characters in such films as *The Big Chill* (1983), *The Right Stuff* (1983), *Into the Night* (1985), *Silverado* (1985), *The Fly* (1986), *Beyond Therapy* (1987), *Vibes* (1988), *The Tall Guy* (1989), *Earth Girls Are Easy* (1989), *Mister Frost* (1990), *The Player* (1992), *Deep Cover* (1992), and *Fathers and Sons* (1992). He appeared in *Jurassic Park* (1993) and *Independence Day* (1996), two of the most financially successful movies ever made. Later films include *Igby Goes Down* (2002) and *The Life Aquatic with Steve Zissou* (2004).

[Jonathan Licht]

GOLDBLUM, NATAN (1920–2001), Israeli virologist. Born in Poland, Goldblum immigrated to Palestine in 1938 as a student at the Hebrew University, where later he became professor of virology. His early work on malaria and West Nile fever was accompanied by his own efforts to eradicate these diseases in the Hulleh Valley in Galilee, Israel. With the establishment of the Israeli Defense Forces in 1948, he joined the medical corps and took part in the medical treatment of Yemenite immigrants. His activity was largely responsible for preventing the dangerous spread of malaria, among other diseases. He served in the beginning of the 1950s as head of the Department of Epidemiology of Hemed, the Military Research Institue, and subsequently became director of the Virus Laboratories of the Ministry of Health. He studied the preparation of polio vaccine with Jonas *Salk and Albert *Sabin in the United States and upon his return to Israel applied this knowledge to produce the vaccine with which some 60,000 Israeli children were inoculated. He joined the Hebrew University in 1960, where he was appointed professor of virology and head of the Department of Virology. He was vice president of the university in 1974–77. For over 30 years he continued research on polio. Among his other research subjects were Israeli snake venom, molecular identification of viruses transmitted by insects, and hoof-and-mouth disease. Goldblum joined the WHO consulting team on the eradication of viral diseases and traveled to African and other countries to help solve public health problems. In 1988 he was awarded the Israel Prize for life sciences, on the 40th anniversary of the founding of the State of Israel.

[Fern Lee Seckbach]

GOLDEMBERG, ISAAC (1945–), Peruvian poet, novelist, and lecturer. The son of a Catholic Peruvian mother and a Jewish immigrant, he was alternately raised in both cultures. He studied in Spain and the U.S., lived for two years in Israel, and settled in New York in 1964. Goldemberg taught at various universities and was a professor at the Hostos Community College and the Graduate School of CUNY, where he founded and directed the Latin American Writers Institute. His novels and poems reflect, in a personal and unconventional way, the conflicts of an always unfinished identity made up of contradictory cultures, of exiles, and the desire to belong. He published the following: novels – *La vida a plazos de don Jacobo Lerner* (1978; *The Fragmented Life of Don Jacobo Lerner*, 1976), selected by the National Yiddish Book Center among the greatest Jewish literary works; *Tiempo al tiempo* (1984; *Play by Play*, 1984); *El nombre del padre* ("The Name of the Father," 2001); Poetry – *Tiempo de silencio* ("Time of Silence," 1970); *Hombre de paso/Just Passing Through* (bilingual, 1981); *Cuerpo del amor* ("Body of Love," 2000); *La vida son los ríos* ("Lives are the Rivers," fiction & poetry, 2005); *Peruvian Blues* (2001); *Memorias* ("Memories," 2005); plays – *Hotel Amérikka* (2000); *Golpe de gracia* ("Coup of Death," 2003). In 2003 appeared *Señas y contraseñas: Antología personal. Poesía, narrativa, teatro* ("Signs and Passwords: Personal Anthology. Poetry, Fiction, and Theater"). In 1998 he edited *El Gran Libro de América Judía* ("The Great Book of Jewish America," a huge anthology of Latin American Jewish writing).

BIBLIOGRAPHY: L. Baer Barr, *Isaac Unbound. Patriarchal Traditions in the Latin American Jewish Novel* (1995); E. González Viaña, *Identidad cultural y memoria colectiva en la obra de Isaac Goldemberg* (2001); J. Paredes Carbonell, *Isaac Goldemberg ante la crítica: Una visión múltiple* (2004); D. Sheinin and L. Baer Barr, *The Jewish Diaspora in Latin America: New Studies on History and Literature* (1996); I. Stavans, *The Hispanic Condition. Reflections on Culture & Identity in America* (1995); S. Sosnowski, *Isaac Goldemberg: The Esthetics of Fragmentation* (2003); M.A. Zapata, *Luces de la memoria: Conversaciones con Isaac Goldemberg* (2003).

[Florinda F. Goldberg (2nd ed.)]

GOLDEN, HARRY LEWIS (Herschel Goldhurst; 1902–1981), U.S. author, editor, and publisher. One of five children of immigrants from Austria-Hungary, Golden was born on New York's Lower East Side. His father was an editor of the *Jewish Daily Forward*. Golden studied English literature, but left the university without completing his degree. During the "Roaring Twenties" he was sentenced to five years imprisonment for running a Wall Street gambling den. On his release he moved south, changing his name to Golden and becoming a successful journalist. Golden is best known for his one-man newspaper, *The Carolina Israelite*, which he published from 1942 to 1969. He was much admired by American liberals for his witty and courageous stand in favor of black integration, attacking race hatred as absurd rather than criminal. His best-selling books *Only in America* (1958), *For 2¢ Plain* (1959), and *Enjoy* (1960) were drawn from some of his editorials. Much of their charm lies in his folkloristic description of Jewish immigrant life. His other works include *Mr. Kennedy and the Negroes* (1964); *So What Else Is New* (1964); and an autobiography, *The Right Time* (1969). In 1965 he published *A Little Girl Is Dead* about the Leo *Frank case.

BIBLIOGRAPHY: M. Levin (ed.), *Five Boyhoods* (1962), 37–78; T. Solotaroff, in: *Commentary*, 31 (1961), 1–13; *Current Biography Yearbook 1959* (1960), 150–2.

[Milton Henry Hindus]

GOLDEN, JOHN (1874–1955), U.S. songwriter and theatrical producer. Born in New York City, Golden was educated at New York University. He began songwriting in collaboration with

Irving Berlin, Oscar Hammerstein, and Douglas Fairbanks. The songs that brought him the most fame and money were "Poor Butterfly" and "Goodbye Girls, I'm Through." In 1914 he and Winchell Smith went into partnership as play producers, made a hit with *Turn to the Right* (1916) and again with *Lightnin'*, which ran for 1291 performances on Broadway. He was a charter member of ASCAP (American Society of Composers, Authors, and Publishers) and its director in 1914–15, as well as the organization's first treasurer.

Golden subsequently produced more than a hundred plays. Some of his Broadway productions included *Susan and God, Turn to the Right, Three Wise Fools, The First Year, Seventh Heaven, Counselor-at-Law, When Ladies Meet, As Husbands Go, Let Us Be Gay, Claudia, Skylark, The Male Animal,* and *They Knew What They Wanted.* As a composer, he wrote the scores for the Broadway shows *The Candy Shop*; *Over the River*; *Hip, Hip, Hooray*; *The Big Show*; *Cheer Up*; and *Everything.*

In 1943 he conducted a play competition in the U.S. Army and presented the five winners as "The Army Play by Play." He was also the founder of the Stage Door Canteen and the Stage Relief Fund. The U.S. Army gave him the highest civilian decoration for distinguished service. His will established a fund for the advancement of playwriting, The John Golden Fund Inc. The intimate, 80-seat John Golden Theater on Broadway was named in his honor.

[Ruth Beloff (2nd ed.)]

GOLDENBERG, BAERISH (1825–1898), Hebrew scholar, teacher, and poet. Born in Vishnevets (Volhynia), he studied in Tarnopol in the school established by Joseph *Perl, and in 1850 opened his own school there. The rest of his life was devoted to teaching, mainly in Tarnopol, but also for some time in other towns in Galicia and Romania. He published many linguistic studies in the Hebrew journals of his time, articles and books (in German) on ancient Jewish history, and Hebrew poetry. His two major Hebrew books are *Ohel Yosef* (a biography of Joseph Perl and a history of his Tarnopol school, 1860) and *Or Ḥadash* (biblical commentaries and linguistic studies, 10 vols., 1889–97). He also edited the journal *Nogah ha-Yare'aḥ* (1872–80).

BIBLIOGRAPHY: G. Bader, *Medinah va-Ḥakhameha* (1934), 59–60; N.M. Gelber, *Toledot ha-Tenu'ah ha-Ẓiyyonit be-Galiẓyah* (1958), 261; *Sefer Tarnopol* (1955), 94–95.

[Getzel Kressel]

GOLDENBERG, CHARLES ROBERT (**"Buckets"**; 1911–1986), U.S. football player; helped lead the Green Bay Packers to three NFL championships. Born in Odessa, Ukraine, Goldenberg grew up in Milwaukee, where he was a star as a tackle and tailback at North Division High School, and then an outstanding back at the University of Wisconsin from 1930 to 1933. He received a Knute Rockne All-America honorable mention and Knute Rockne All-Western in 1930, and AP All-Western Conference second team in 1932. After graduating in 1933, Goldenberg played fullback, blocking back, guard, linebacker, and defensive back from 1933 to 1945 with the Green Bay Packers, which won the championship in 1936, 1939, and 1944 and the Western Conference title in 1938. Goldenberg was named All-Pro guard in 1939, 1940, and 1942, and was named to the NFL's All-1930s Team. Goldenberg holds the oldest record in Packers history with five touchdowns as a rookie, set in 1933, and his 13 seasons is tied for fifth-longest tenure in team history.

[Elli Wohlgelernter (2nd ed.)]

GOLDENBERG, SAMUEL LEIB (1807–1846), Hebrew journalist. Born in Bolechow (Bolekhov) into a wealthy family, he was one of the pioneers of the Haskalah in Galicia. In 1833 Goldenberg launched the periodical *Kerem Ḥemed which was almost entirely devoted to scholarly articles (in the form of letters) and marked a development in Hebrew periodical literature. The leading modern Jewish scholars of the first half of the 19th century contributed to it.

BIBLIOGRAPHY: Klausner, Sifrut, 2 (1952), 37–38.

[Getzel Kressel]

GOLDENBERG-GETROITMAN, LAZAR (1846–1916), Russian revolutionary and one of the first Jewish socialists in Russia. Goldenberg was born in the Kherson district. He joined the revolutionary movement as a young man, when he was studying at the Technological Institute in Peterburg. He was arrested for incitement of the farmers not to pay taxes. He escaped to Switzerland where he became secretary of the Slavic department of the International League of Socialist Revolutionaries. After he was expelled from Switzerland he went to London in 1876 and established the Agudat ha-Soẓialistim ha-Ivrim (the Jewish Socialist Organization) with Aaron *Lieberman, which was probably the first of its kind in the world. On a visit to Romania in 1881, Goldenberg was seized and handed over to the Russian authorities but managed to escape a second time. He tried to live in Paris but was expelled for his revolutionary activities. He lived for ten years in New York, where he organized the Russian revolutionary activities abroad and for many years afterward managed a publishing house in London which produced books on socialist subjects in Russian, among them Khaim Zhitlovskis' "Jews to Jews." From 1891 to 1900 Goldenberg published an English monthly *Free Russia*. His memoirs appeared posthumously (1924) in Russian in the Moscow periodical *Katorga i ssylka* (nos. 3, 4, 5, 6).

GOLDENBURG, SAMUEL (**Sholem Goldstein**; 1886–1945), Yiddish actor. Son of a lumber merchant in Russia, Goldenburg joined a Yiddish company and at 20 toured with Sigmund Feinman in Europe. In 1917 he acted with Thomashefsky in New York, but later joined Maurice Schwartz's Jewish Art Theater, playing the lead in L. Feuchtwanger's *Jew Suess* and I.I. Singer's *Di Brider Ashkenazi* (*The Brothers Ashkenazi*, 1936). With Celia *Adler he did a 32-week season at the Amphion Theater, Brooklyn, in a repertory of 20 plays, among which were *The Dybbuk* and *Camille* (1925–26).

GOLDEN CALF (Heb. עֵגֶל מַסֵּכָה, Ex. 32:4; עֶגְלֵי זָהָב I Kings 12:28), the golden image made by Aaron at the behest of the Israelites and venerated near Mount Sinai (Ex. 32). Exodus 32 relates that the Israelites, anxious about Moses' prolonged absence, demanded that *Aaron provide a god to lead them. Complying, Aaron collected the golden ornaments of the people and fashioned the gold into the shape of a calf or a small bull. The image was immediately hailed by the people as a representation of the God who had brought Israel out of Egypt. Aaron then built an altar, and on the following day sacrifices were offered and the people feasted and danced and played. Thereupon the Lord told Moses of the apostasy of the "stiff-necked people," whom He proposed to destroy. Moses, however, interceded on behalf of the Israelites and persuaded the Lord to renounce His intended punishment. Carrying the Tablets of the Covenant down from Mt. Sinai, Moses saw the people dancing around the golden calf. In great anger Moses smashed the Tablets, melted down the image of the calf, pulverized the precious metal, and scattered the powdered gold over the available source of water, thus making the people drink it (verse 20); and there is doubtless a causal nexus between this and the plague that is reported in verse 35 (see Ordeal of *Jealousy).

Exodus 32 relates that Moses then upbraided Aaron for having "brought great guilt" upon the people. The parallel account in Deut. 9:20 relates that but for Moses' supplication on behalf of Aaron the Lord would have destroyed Aaron. Stern punishment was, however, meted out to the calf-worshipers, 3,000 of whom were slain by the *Levites who had responded to Moses' call for volunteers. Henceforth the Levites were consecrated to the service of the Lord. Despite Moses' prayer for divine forgiveness, the Lord threatened that on the day of His visitation punishment would overtake the people. Soon afterward a plague broke out among the Israelites (see above). In addition the Lord announced that He would no longer abide amid this "stiff-necked people." The Israelites mourned the departure of the Divine presence and stripped themselves of their ornaments (Ex. 33:1–6).

Critical View

The extant text of Exodus 32 is according to certain Bible critics an expansion of a basic narrative into several strata by secondary additions; for another interpretation see Cassuto (Exodus, ad loc.). The critical view does not see the chapter as a literary unity on the basis of inconsistencies. Others, however, believe that Aaronic authorship (and divine sanction) of the practice of calf symbolism was claimed from the very beginning by Jeroboam I and the priesthoods of Bethel and Dan, and that the version in Exodus 32, in boldly "representing Aaron, the ancestor of Israel's priestly caste, as a man of somewhat feeble character" (H.L. Ginsberg, in JBL, 80 (1961), 345) is motivated by a desire to discredit the practice which he instituted.

Calf and Bull Symbolism

The narrative of the golden calf cannot be understood without relating it to the erection of two golden calves in the temples of *Beth-El and *Dan by *Jeroboam I of Israel (I Kings 12:26ff.). Not only are the general features of the story similar in both accounts, but the explanatory formula in Exodus 32:4b, 8b – "These are your gods, O Israel, who brought you up out of the land of Egypt" – is virtually identical to the one in I Kings 12:28b. Scholars are divided on the question of the chronological relationship of the two accounts. The traditional view is that the Jeroboam incident is dependent on the Exodus story (see Cassuto, loc. cit.). Other scholars, however, hold the view that Exodus 32 presupposes I Kings 12.

The bull had an important role in the art and religious texts of the ancient Near East. The storm-god *Hadad is frequently represented standing on a bull. Taking these facts into account it is generally assumed (after H. Th. Obbrick) that Jeroboam's calves corresponded to the *cherubim of Solomon's Temple, i.e., they were regarded as seats or pedestals upon which the Lord was thought to stand invisible to human eyes. M. Haran remarks that if Jeroboam's calves were considered pedestals, then they were not meant to be an exact replica of cherubim connected with the *Ark of the Covenant because the Ark and its cherubim were kept in the publicly inaccessible Holy of Holies while the calves were placed in the courts of the Temple, where the people could see and kiss them (cf. Hos. 13:2). It is also possible that the calves were, from the beginning, meant to represent the Lord like the images in the sanctuaries of Micah and Dan (Judg. 17:4; 18:14, 15–31; cf. M. Haran, in B. Zvieli (ed.), *Siḥot ba-Mikra*, 1 (1968), 214; idem, in: *Biblica*, 50 (1969), 264).

In any case Jeroboam's initiative must have had some basis in an old tradition, otherwise he could not have succeeded in his enterprise. Jeroboam's bulls, contrary to the Ark symbolism, were meant to be accessible to worshipers in the temples (cf. I Kings 12:27); and thus they developed from symbols of the Lord to fetishes in their own right (cf. e.g., II Kings 17:16; Hos. 8:5–6; 10:5; 13:2).

In the Aggadah

The rabbinic attitude toward the episode of the golden calf is guided by the need to explain how the Children of Israel could demand an idol so soon after hearing the Ten Commandments and giving liberally to the erection of the Sanctuary and how Aaron could agree to the construction of the calf and still not forfeit his future role as high priest. The initiative in demanding the idol is attributed by some rabbis to the mixed multitude who joined the Israelites at the time of the Exodus (Ex. 12:38). Forty thousand of them, accompanied by two Egyptian magicians, *Jannes and Mambres, came to Aaron and claimed that it already was the sixth hour of the 40th day since Moses had left, the hour which he previously had designated for his return. They claimed that since he had not yet appeared he would never come. Satan added to the state of helplessness of the people by showing them a vision of Moses' bier which convinced them that he had died. Only then did they demand that Aaron produce a god for them (Shab. 89a; Tanh. B., Ex. 112–3). The error of the people consisted in including in their calculation the day of the ascent, whereas Moses had excluded it (Rashi, Shab. 89a). God was also blamed since He enslaved them in Egypt where they were exposed to the most idolatrous of ancient civilizations (Ex. R. 43:7) and for giving them an abundance of gold and silver when they left Egypt (Ber. 32a). *Hur, who is regarded as the son of Miriam and Caleb, attempted to dissuade the people from the sin and was put to death by them. Aaron feared that he would share the same fate (Lev. R. 10:3; Tanh. B., Ex. 112–3) and in accordance with his passion for the pursuit of peace (Avot 1:12; see *Aaron in the aggadah), felt it better to acquiesce than to permit the people to commit the unpardonable sin of slaying two leaders on the same day (Sanh. 7a). Hoping to gain time, he ordered them to bring the golden ornaments of their wives, relying on their known piety to refuse. The men thereupon donated their own jewelry (PdRE 45). Aaron then threw the gold into the fire, still hoping that Moses would return. Instantly, however, a calf appeared, alive and skipping, the result of a splinter which was thrown into the fire by the wicked Micah. This splinter, containing the words עלה שור (*aleh shor*, "Come up, Ox"; Joseph being compared to an ox; cf. Deut. 33:17), had previously been thrown into the Nile by Moses when he desired that Joseph's coffin rise to the surface so that he could transport his remains to Ereẓ Israel (Tanḥ. *Ki Tissa*, 19). According to another version, the Egyptian magicians made the calf move as if it were alive (Song R. 1:9, no. 3). Aaron then postponed the celebration to the next day again to gain time. Since God knew that Aaron was motivated by good intentions the high priesthood was not withheld from him (Lev. R. 10:3; Ex. R. 37:2). Nevertheless, he still was severely punished in that the subsequent death of two of his sons was attributed to his role in this incident (Lev. R. 10:5).

The tribe of Levi (Yoma 66b) and its 12 heads (PdRE 45) did not join the worship of the calf. The remaining Israelites were severely punished. Whoever sacrificed and burned incense died by the sword; whoever embraced and kissed the calf died by the plague; and whoever rejoiced in his heart died of dropsy (Yoma 66b). "There is not a misfortune that Israel has suffered which is not partly a retribution for the sin of the calf" (Sanh. 102a).

[Aaron Rothkoff]

In Christianity

During the Roman period and long after, the golden calf episode was a source of embarrassment to the Jews in their relations with the increasingly aggressive Church, which fully exploited the story in its polemics with the Synagogue. Even Josephus, who was concerned only with pagan antisemitism, was evidently afraid that the biblical account might be employed by Alexandrian antisemites to lend credence to their allegation that the Jews worshiped an ass's head in the Temple (cf. Apion 2:80, 114, 120; Tacitus, Histories 5:4). Josephus accordingly omits the entire golden calf episode from his account of the Israelite migrations in the desert. Instead, he graphically depicts the deep anxiety of the Israelites concerning Moses and their joy when at last he came down from Mount Sinai (Ant. 3:95–99). Not only did Moses not break the tablets, but he actually displayed them to the rejoicing people (3:101–2). Josephus also omits any reference to Aaron, and the same is true of Philo who does not, however, completely suppress the golden calf narrative (Mos. 2:161–74, 271).

As early as the immediate post-crucifixion era, Stephen, the first Christian martyr, sharply denounced the Jews (but not Aaron who was held in veneration by the Church) for having made the golden calf, which became the fountainhead of Jewish crimes throughout their history, culminating in the crucifixion of Jesus (Acts 7:41–52). For the Church the golden calf episode served as proof that the divine covenant with Israel had never been consummated, so that the Jewish claim to a special relationship with the Almighty was unacceptable (see Smolar in bibl., p. 91). By worshiping the golden calf, the Jews had revealed their foolish, stubborn, unrepentant, and immoral character (*ibid.*, 100). Augustine also associated the calf cult with the worship of the devil, and the Jews who had drunk the water into which the powder of the golden calf had been cast with the body of the devil (*ibid.*, 100–1). The medieval identification of the Jew with the devil was no doubt influenced by this extreme patristic interpretation (*ibid.*, 101, n. 12).

While the rabbinic reaction to such violent attacks by the Church was bound to be militant, as has been seen, some of the criticism was frankly accepted, and the seriousness of the offense was by no means played down: Israel was compared to "a shameless bride who plays the harlot within her bridal canopy" (Shab. 88b).

[Moses Aberbach]

See also *Aaron in the *aggadah*; *Hur in the *aggadah*. For Golden Calf in the arts see *Moses in the Arts.

BIBLIOGRAPHY: IN THE BIBLE: O. Eissfeldt, in: ZAW, 17 (1940–41), 199ff.; Albright, Stone, 228ff.; U. Cassuto, *A Commentary on the Book of Exodus* (1965[4]), 284–97; T.J. Meek, *Hebrew Origins* (1960), 135ff.; M. Aberbach, in: JBL, 86 (1967), 129–40; L. Smolar and M. Aberbach, in: HUCA, 39 (1968), 91–116; S.E. Loewenstamm, in: *Biblica*, 48 (1967), 481–90. IN THE AGGADAH: Ginzberg, Legends, 3 (1954[4]), 119–34; 6 (1959[4]), 50–56. In CHRISTIANITY: Smolar and M. Aberbach, loc. cit. **ADD. BIBLIOGRAPHY:** S. Loewenstamm, *Comparative Studies in Biblical and Ancient Oriental Literatures* (1980), 242–45; S. Gevirtz, in: *Biblica*, 65 (1984), 377–81; J. Spencer, in: ABD, 2:1065–69 (with bibliography); S.D. Sperling, *Original Torah* (1998), 91–112.

GOLDENE KEYT, DI ("The Golden Chain"), Israel Yiddish quarterly. It was founded under Histadrut (Labor Federation) auspices in 1949 and until 1955 edited by Avrom *Sutskever and Abraham *Levinson. In that year Sutskever became sole editor, with Eliezer Pines serving as assistant editor until his death in 1984. Other editorial staff included Aleksander

*Shpiglblat, Mendl *Man, and Meylekh Karpinovitsh. In the rich first issue Joseph *Sprinzak and other prominent figures called for an end to the antagonism between Hebrew and Yiddish. The journal published works by Yiddish masters and by young writers in Israel and the Diaspora, Yiddish translations of Hebrew literature, research into literary and linguistic problems, and surveys of Jewish cultural events. Long before its last issue (no. 141) appeared in 1995, *Di Goldene Keyt* was recognized as the preeminent literary organ of Yiddish writers. It continues to be an invaluable source of Yiddish belles lettres and scholarship.

[Sol Liptzin / Leonard Prager (2nd ed.)]

GOLDENSON, SAMUEL HARRY (1878–1962), U.S. Reform rabbi. Goldenson was born in Kalvarija, Poland, and was taken to the United States in 1890. He was ordained at the Hebrew Union College in 1904, then led congregations in Lexington, Kentucky (1904–06), and Albany, New York (1906–18). In 1918 Goldenson moved to Temple Rodef Shalom, Pittsburgh, where he established his reputation nationally. In 1934 he was appointed senior rabbi of Temple Emanu-El, New York, also serving as president of the Central Conference of American Rabbis (1933–35). Becoming rabbi emeritus in 1947, he devoted the last years of his career to preaching in small communities under the auspices of the Union of American Hebrew Congregations. Goldenson adhered to the older standpoint in American Reform Judaism, emphasizing the universal message of the prophets and showing little sympathy for Jewish nationalism and the revived interest in ceremonial matters. He was a lifelong advocate of social justice and was active in campaigns for civic betterment.

BIBLIOGRAPHY: *New York Times* (Sept. 1, 1962).

[Abram Vossen Goodman]

GOLDENTHAL, JACOB (1815–1868), Austrian Orientalist. Goldenthal was born in Brody and became principal of the Jewish school in Kishinev, Russia, in 1843; in 1846 he settled in Vienna and taught Oriental languages, rabbinics, and literature at the University of Vienna from 1848 until his death. Beside his regular teachings he offered a theological program for rabbinical candidates.

Goldenthal published several articles on medieval Jewish literature in *Kokhevei Yiẓḥak* (5, 1846; 24, 1858). He edited the following medieval texts: Abraham ibn Ḥasdai's Hebrew translation of al-Ghazālī's Arabic *Mīzān al-ʿAmal, Sefer Moznei Ẓedek* (1939); Averroes' commentary on Aristotle's *Rhetoric*, translated into Hebrew as *Be'ur Ibn Rushd le-Sefer ha-Halaẓah le-Aristo* (1842); *Mesharet Moshe* (1845), an exposition of Maimonides' teaching on the concept of providence; Nissim b. Jacob's *Mafte'aḥ shel Manulei ha-Talmud* (1847), dealing with Talmud methodology; Moses Rieti's poem *Mikdash Me'at* (1851), on ancient philosophy and the history of Jewish literature; and Moses Narboni's commentary on Maimonides' *Guide, Be'ur le-Sefer Moreh Nevukhim* (1852). Goldenthal tried to revive Jost and Creizenach's periodical *Zion*, but only one issue, *Neue Zion* (1845), appeared. His correspondence with S.D. *Luzzatto was published in *Kokhevei Yiẓḥak*. He also published the first Hebrew textbook for the study of Arabic, *Sefer Maspik li-Ydi'at Dikduk Lashon Arvi* (1857), and a textbook for the study of Turkish (1865); he compiled a catalog of forty Hebrew manuscripts at the National Library of Vienna (1851). Some of his works were published in the *Denkschriften* of the Vienna Academy of Sciences.

BIBLIOGRAPHY: J. Fuenn, in: *Knesset Yisrael*, 1 (1866), 541–2; Gelber, in: *Arim ve-Immahot be-Yisrael*, 66 (1955), 204–5. **ADD. BIBLIOGRAPHY:** A. Bruell, in: ADB, 9 (1879), 332; S. Mannheimer, in: JE 6 (1904), 23.

[Samuel Miklos Stern / Gregor Pelger (2nd ed.)]

GOLDENWEISER, ALEXANDER ALEXANDROVICH (1880–1936), U.S. anthropologist. Born in Kiev, Russia, the son of Alexander Solomonovich *Goldenweiser, Goldenweiser studied anthropology under Franz *Boas, and later taught anthropology and other social sciences at various institutions including Columbia University, the New School for Social Research, and the University of Oregon in Portland. He followed Boas in his attacks on certain intellectual positions then prevalent, such as unilinear evolutionism, geographical and biological determinism, and extreme diffusionism. Described by a contemporary as "the most philosophical of American anthropologists," Goldenweiser did little field work except for several brief trips to the Grand River Iroquois Reservation in Ontario. His main contributions were to anthropological and social theory, as in his article "The Principle of Limited Possibilities in the Development of Culture" in the *Journal of American Folklore,* 26 (1913), in which he sought to explain convergences among traits of different cultures as the result of a natural limitation on the number of possible forms. In addition, he contributed to the elucidation of such basic concepts as culture, culture patterns, and especially, totemism, the subject of his best-known monograph in which he rejected Durkheim's theory of the totemic origin of religion. He concerned himself too with various themes in the history of thought and helped organize the *Encyclopedia of Social Science*, for which he wrote a number of articles.

BIBLIOGRAPHY: DAB, 22 (1958), 244–5; IESS, 6 (1968), 196–7.

[Ephraim Fischoff]

GOLDENWEISER, EMANUEL ALEXANDROVICH (1883–1953), U.S. economist. Goldenweiser was born in Kiev, immigrated to the United States in 1902, studied at Columbia and Cornell Universities, and, in 1907, joined the U.S. government service as an economist and statistician. He first served with the Immigration Commission and then with the Census Bureau and the Department of Agriculture. In 1919 he began working for the Federal Reserve Board, and from 1927 until his retirement was its director of research. He developed the Board's statistical services, frequently represented the Federal Reserve System nationally, and served on the government's principal technical committees on economics and finance. He was, moreover, one of the main U.S. designers of the International Monetary Fund and the World Bank. His many publications include: *Immigrants in Cities* (1909), *Farm Tenancy in the United States* (1924), *The Federal Reserve System in Operation* (1925), and *Monetary Management* (1949).

[Joachim O. Ronall]

GOLDFADEN, ABRAHAM (**Avrom Goldfodem**; 1840–1908), Yiddish poet, dramatist, and composer, founder of the modern Yiddish theater (see *Theater, Yiddish). Born into a watchmaker's family in Staro Konstantinov, Ukraine, he received not only a thorough Hebrew education but also acquired a knowledge of Russian, German, and secular subjects. To avoid the draft, Goldfaden was sent to a government school at 15 and there came under the influence of Abraham Baer *Gottlober, *maskil* and author of Hebrew and Yiddish satires, including the scathing anti-ḥasidic comedy *Der Dektukh, Oder Tsvey Khupes in Eyn Nakht* ("The Bridal Veil, or Two Weddings in One Night"), which exerted a strong influence on Goldfaden's early comedies. Upon graduation in 1857, Goldfaden entered the rabbinical seminary at Zhitomir, which trained rabbis, teachers, and Jewish officials for government service. Under the guidance there of *maskilic* leaders such as E.Z. Zweifel, H.S. Slonimsky, and Gottlober, he composed Hebrew lyrics, the first of which were published in *Ha-Meliẓ* (1862). A year later his first Yiddish poems appeared in *Kol Mevaser*. In 1865 he published a Hebrew collection, *Ẓiẓim u-Feraḥim* ("Buds and Flowers"), and upon his graduation, his first Yiddish collection, *Dos Yudele* ("The Little Jew," 1866), offering rich material for **badḥanim* and folksingers. It was followed by a supplementary volume, *Di Yidene* ("The Jewish Woman," 1869), which included his first efforts at writing drama: a short two-character sketch, and the full-length comedy *Di Mume Sosye* ("Aunt Sosya"), closely modeled on Shloyme Ettinger's comedy *Serkele*. Goldfaden knew the latter play intimately, having played the title (female) role in the seminary's all-male production, which was the toast of Zhitomir.

In 1875 he joined his former classmate Isaac Joel *Linetzki in founding and editing in Lemberg a short-lived humorous magazine, *Der Alter Yisrolik*. Goldfaden then moved to Romania, where, in Jassy, he came in contact with the *Broder Singers, who were singing and acting out Yiddish songs, including his own, in wine cellars and restaurant gardens. He then conceived the idea that the dramatic effect of the songs and impersonations could be heightened if combined with prose dialogues and woven into an interesting plot. The first performances, at Shimen Mark's Pomul Verde cafe in October 1876, starring the veteran performer Israel Grodner and his young co-star, Sokher Goldstein, launched the professional Yiddish theater. Encouraged by the enthusiastic reception accorded his performances in Jassy, Goldfaden engaged wandering minstrels and cantors' assistants as additional actors, toured other Romanian cities, including Bucharest, and then went to Odessa. By 1880 his troupe was giving performances throughout Russia, and his phenomenal success was encouraging theatrical ventures by other enterprising actors and librettists. Of Goldfaden's early plays, the most successful were the musical comedies *Shmendrik* (1877), a satire whose titular anti-hero became a synonym for a foolish person; *Di Kishefmakherin* ("The Sorceress," 1879), which includes many of Goldfaden's most popular songs; and *Der Fanatik oder di Tsvey Kuni Leml* ("The Fanatic, or the Two Kuni Lemls," 1880), the apotheosis of the *maskilic* farces Goldfaden had been writing for the previous few years. All three of these plays retained uninterrupted stage popularity for decades in both their original forms and in a variety of adaptations. Though not a trained musician, Goldfaden had been writing songs for most of his life, and the music in his plays is a combination of original composition and artful selection of pre-existing music. He drew upon varied sources – synagogue chants and Jewish folksong, the non-Jewish folk and popular music of Eastern Europe, and Italian and French operatic arias. Many of his songs became enormously popular among Yiddish speakers. Among other types of songs, Goldfaden composed popular lullabies ("Rozhinkes mit Mandlen" / "Raisins and Almonds"), occasional songs (like "Tsu Dayn Geburtstog," the Yiddish "Happy Birthday"), allegories of God's relationship with the Jewish people ("A Pastekhl" / "A Shepherd"), and songs that poignantly captured a sense of aspiration for self-fulfillment on both individual and national levels ("Faryomert, Farklogt" / "Lamented, Mourned"; "Shabes, Yontev, un Rosh Khoydesh" / "Sabbath, Festival, and New Moon").

The Russian pogroms of the early 1880s prompted Goldfaden, like many other Jewish writers, to reassess Jewish life and politics, and a more serious tone becomes evident in his work beginning at this point. The romantic operetta *Shulamis* (1880) tells an epic story set in late antiquity and following the fortunes of a shepherdess and the soldier who falls in love with, abandons, and ultimately returns to her. In *Doktor Almosado* (1882), Goldfaden reacted to the pogroms of 1881, and even though he transposed the scene of the dramatic action to 14th-century Palermo, his audience sensed its timeliness and its veiled references to their sad plight. In *Bar Kokhba* (1883), a historical opera depicting the last desperate revolt of the Jews against their Roman oppressors, Goldfaden – an adherent of the Ḥovevei Zion movement – tried to stir his people with visions of ancient national grandeur and heroism.

The Yiddish theater expanded and flourished in Eastern Europe until 1883, when the Russian government, fearing this new mass medium, banned performances in Yiddish. This action compelled many authors, actors, and producers to migrate to other lands, though some remained in Russia and found various ways to sidestep the ban. Those who left helped establish Yiddish theaters in Warsaw, Paris, London, and New York, among other places. In 1887 Goldfaden was invited by some of his actors who had moved to New York to join them, but when he arrived he encountered severe competition from producers who had preceded him and from playwrights like Joseph Lateiner and Moyshe Hurwitz, who were even more prolific than he. During this American sojourn, he composed his successful biblical dramas *Akeydes Yitskhok* ("The Binding of Isaac," 1887) and *Kenig Akhashveyresh* ("King Ahasuerus," 1887), but professional disappointments drove him back to Europe. He led a troupe at the Princess Club Theatre in London for several months during 1889, but soon moved to Paris and then on to Lemberg (Lvov), where he remained for most of the 1890s.

As he grew older, Goldfaden's commitment to Zionism became increasingly prominent in his life and work. In 1900, he served as Paris delegate to the World Zionist Congress in London. Many of his plays and poems reflect his political views. The epic play *Meshiekhs Tsaytn!?* ("The Messianic Era?!," 1891), for example, takes the characters on spiritual and physical journeys resulting from pogroms and ultimately concludes that the Land of Israel is the only suitable home for the Jews. His last play, *Ben Ami* (1907), reaches a similar conclusion. To a large extent an adaption of George Eliot's novel *Daniel Deronda, Ben Ami* transposes the action to pogrom-ridden Odessa, and the philo-Semitic English aristocrat becomes a Russian baron. The play ends with the pogrom victims and their noble savior experiencing regeneration as pioneers of Jewish national redemption on the soil of Zion.

In spite of the enormous popularity and influence of his plays, Goldfaden and his wife, Paulina, perpetually struggled to stay out of poverty. His final years brought continued wandering and declining health, ultimately bringing him to his deathbed as *Ben Ami* was running in New York theaters during the closing weeks of 1907; he died there on January 9, 1908. The following day, 100,000 mourners were said to have greeted his funeral procession to Washington Cemetery. His death ended one era and inaugurated another – that of the reinterpretation of his works by other artists. Avant-garde productions of his work were mounted by notable companies like the Moscow State Yiddish Theater, which offered a groundbreaking, Sovietized reinvention of *Di Kishefmakherin* in 1922; the Yiddish Art Theater in New York, which produced three ambitious revivals of Goldfaden plays in the mid-1920s; and Warsaw's Yung Teater, with *Trupe Tanentsap* ("The Tanentsap Troupe," 1933), a play-within-a-play revolving around a fictional production of *Di Tsvey Kuni-Leml* during the early years of the professional Yiddish theatre. Other prominent playwrights who would take up the challenge of adapting Goldfaden's plays included Shmuel *Halkin (*Shulamis* and *Bar Kokhba*) and Itsik *Manger (*Hotsmakh-shpil* / "Hotsmakh Play," 1947), an original work based on characters from *Di Kishefmakherin*).

[Sol Liptzin / Joel Berkowitz (2nd ed.)]

Music

Goldfaden himself furnished the tunes to his plays, although he was unable to write music and played no instrument. He drew upon the most varied sources – synagogue chants and Jewish folksong, the non-Jewish folk and popular music of Eastern Europe, and Italian and French operatic arias. Many of the songs from his plays have remained popular: some were folksongs initially (such as the cradle song *Rozhinkes mit Mandlen* which he adapted and put into *Shulamis*, from where it achieved its fame), and others became folksongs. Goldfaden described his musical activity with engaging frankness in his short autobiography; A.Z. *Idelsohn's analysis of the melodies in *Shulamis* and *Bar Kokhba*, and his conclusions, are a fair appraisal both of Goldfaden's musical shortcomings and his merits. For the performance of *Di Kishefmakherim* ("The Witch") by the Jewish Chamber Theater of Petrograd in 1922, the music was rearranged by Josef *Achron. In 1947, "The Witch" was staged in Tel Aviv in Hebrew by the *Ohel Theater, on the 70th anniversary of its first performance. The text was adapted by Abraham Levinson as a play within a play – bringing Goldfaden himself and his contemporary audience on the stage – and the music was arranged by Marc *Lavry.

[Bathja Bayer]

BIBLIOGRAPHY: J. Shatzky (ed.), *Goldfaden-Bukh* (1926); Idelsohn, Music, 229, 447–53; Z. Zylbercweig, *Leksikon fun Yidishn Teater* 1 (1931), 275–367; N. Meisel, *Avrom Goldfaden* (1938); J. Shatzky (ed.), *Hundert Yor Goldfaden* (1940); N.B. Minkoff, *Literarishe Vegn* (1955), 29–40; LNYL, 2 (1958), 77–87; Sendrey, Music, indexes; S. Liptzin, *Flowering of Yiddish Literature* (1963), 33–51. **ADD. BIBLIOGRAPHY:** B. Gorin, *Di Geshikhte fun Yidishn Teater* (1923); N. Oyslender and U. Finkel, *A. Goldfadn: Materyaln far a Biografye* (1926); J. Shatzky (ed.), *Arkhiv far der Geshikhte fun Yidishn Teater un Drame* (1930), 255–301; Y. Dobrushin, *Di Dramaturgye fun di Klasiker* (1949), 6–52; A. Quint, "The Botched Kiss: Abraham Goldfaden and the Literary Origins of the Yiddish Theatre" (diss. 2002); P. Bertolone, *L'esilio del teatro: Goldfadn e il moderno teatro yiddish* (1994); J. Berkowitz (ed.), *Yiddish Theatre: New Approaches* (2003), 77–104, 139–55.

GOLDFARB, ISRAEL (1879–1967), Polish-born American rabbi, cantor, and influential composer. Born in Sieniewa, Galicia, Poland, Goldfarb came to New York at the age of 14 and within a decade graduated from Columbia University. He was ordained by the Jewish Theological Seminary in New York (1902). Receiving musical training at the Institute for Musical Arts, the forerunner of the famed Juilliard School, Goldfarb then began his service, his dual calling as rabbi and cantor of the Kane Street synagogue, which was founded in 1856 and is the oldest continuously operating synagogue in Brooklyn. Goldfarb served the congregation for more than half a century (1904–56) and was rabbi emeritus until his death. He died knowing that his grandson Henry Michelman was to be named his successor. When he came to the congregation it had just completed a merger and was moving to new quarters in a converted church on Kane Street. His music united divergent parts of the congregation and eased the many transitions. The congregation became known as mother congregation of Brooklyn and led to the formation of other Brooklyn synagogues such as Union Temple, East Midwood Jewish Center, and Flatbush Jewish Center. Goldfarb became known as the father of congregational singing.

He tested his compositions in his synagogue and at his Sabbath table where many of his compositions were first sung. From there they spread throughout the Jewish world. He formed a youth choir of boys and girls, which was rare in those days and served a social as well as a spiritual function. Many of his compositions, especially his high holiday melodies, have been so widely chanted that they have come to be regarded as traditional.

Goldfarb was also among the founders of the Cantor's Institute at the Jewish Theological Seminary, where he taught for decades. He is best known for his compilation of Jewish music for schoolchildren, *The Jewish Songster*, and for composing the melodies to "*Shalom Aleichem*" (1918) and to "*Magen Avot*," which are sung in nearly every Ashkenazi synagogue in North America. His work continues to be performed in concerts and recorded by musicians, including Celtic guitarist Tony McManus and Jewish violinist Itzhak Perlman. Goldfarb's work can be heard in many homes and synagogues by people who acknowledge the mastery of his composition without knowing the master who composed it. At his funeral, his son-in-law Rabbi Irving Lehman said that Goldfarb's most beautiful melody was the song of his life.

BIBLIOGRAPHY: H. Michaelman, "The Journey of a Hebrew Melody: Rabbi Israel Goldfarb's Shalom Aleichem," in: *Rayonot: A Journal of Ideas*; I. Lehman, "Rabbi Israel Goldfarb, z"l," in: *Proceedings of the Rabbinical Assembly* (1967).

[Henry Michaelman (2nd ed.)]

GOLDFEDER, FISHEL (1912–1981), U.S. Conservative rabbi. Goldfeder was born in Pittsburgh, educated at Orthodox yeshivot in Brooklyn and Lithuania, and ordained at the Jewish Theological Seminary in 1944, the same year he earned a B.A. from New York University. After acting as substitute rabbi at Kadimah Synagogue in Springfield, Mass., while the permanent rabbi was serving as a chaplain during World War II, Goldfeder became assistant rabbi at the "conservadox" Congregation Adath Israel in Cincinnati in 1945. In 1949, Goldfeder – whose philosophy was "the life of a rabbi's is the life of his people" – became senior rabbi, remaining in that post until his retirement 31 years later. In the 1950s, the congregation became embroiled in a very public dispute over whether the synagogue – which followed many Orthodox practices, but was affiliated with United Synagogue and was gradually adopting Conservative innovations – should move from separate seating to mixed seating; the case even reached the secular courts, and monopolized an entire issue (Fall, 1956) of *Conservative Judaism*. Goldfeder articulated his opinion that one of the *raisons d'etre* of the Conservative movement was precisely to provide houses of worship for Jews who wanted less strict interpretations of *halakhah*. His view ultimately prevailed: the disgruntled Orthodox minority departed and Goldfeder steered Adath Israel firmly into the Conservative mainstream. By the time Goldfeder was elected rabbi emeritus in 1980, the congregation had grown to 1,000 members, making it one of the largest in Cincinnati – a city whose Jewish community Goldfeder had served in many realms. He was instrumental in founding Yavneh Day School, Chofetz Chaim Day School, Jewish Culture and Art Series, and the first city-wide Jewish Youth Council. He served as president of the Board of Rabbis and of the Zionist Federation; chairman of the Soviet Jewish Committee and of the Southern Ohio Region of Israel Bonds; and co-chairman of the Jewish Welfare Fund. On a national level, he served on the Executive Committee of the Jewish Community Relations Council; the National Advisory Council of the United Jewish Appeal; the Israel Bonds National Rabbinic Cabinet; and the Executive Committee of the Rabbinical Assembly, as well as the RA's Committee on Jewish Law and Standards. Goldfeder passed away in Jerusalem less than a year after his retirement.

BIBLIOGRAPHY: P.S. Nadell, *Conservative Judaism in America: A Biographical Dictionary and Sourcebook* (1988).

[Bezalel Gordon (2nd ed.)]

GOLDFLAM, ARNOŠT (1946–), Czech playwright, writer, director, screenwriter, and actor. Born to Holocaust survivors in Brno (Moravia), Goldflam studied theater directing at the Janáček Academy of Music Arts. He worked in various theaters until 1992, when he began freelancing. He was involved in many performances at home and abroad. Goldflam is the author of more than 25 plays, such as *Horror* (1981); *Biletářka* ("The Ticket Girl," 1983); *Útržky z nedokončeného románu* ("Scraps of an Unfinished Novel," 1985); *Agatománie* ("Agathomania," 1987); *Písek* ("The Sand," 1987); and *Smlouva* ("The Contract," 1999). Goldflam's plays oscillate between the tragic and the comic, the realistic and the dreamlike, between a dramatic construction and real life, often combined with the absurd.

He is influenced by his Jewish heritage. One of his plays, *Sladký Theresienstadt* ("Sweet Theresienstadt," 1996), is based on a diary from the Terezín concentration camp. In his work, Goldflam is also drawn to Jewish authors. His dramatic adaptations comprise works by Franz *Kafka, Franz *Werfel, Joseph *Roth, and Karel *Poláček. He was active as a theater and film actor, wrote stories and fairytales, and taught at the Faculty of Drama in Brno.

BIBLIOGRAPHY: J. Lehár a kol., *Česká literatura od počátků k dnešku* (1998); A. Mikulášek et al., *Literatura s hvězdou Davidovou*, vol. 1 (1998).

[Milos Pojar (2nd ed.)]

GOLDHAMMER-SAHAWI, LEO (later **Aryeh**; 1884–1949), leader of the Zionist Organization in Austria, author, and journalist. Born in Mihaileni, Romania, Goldhammer moved to Vienna in 1902 and became an adherent of Herzl. He devoted himself primarily to statistical-economic studies of the Jews, particularly those of Austria. He established and edited the early Zionist periodicals in Vienna, *Die Stimme* and *Die Hoffnung*. In 1907 he moved back to Romania, returning to Vienna after World War I. Goldhammer was president of the Zionist Organization of Austria for many years. He took part, with B. *Borochov, in founding the World Union of *Po'alei Zion. He continued his Zionist activities until after the Nazi invasion of Austria (1938), finally settling in Haifa in 1939 and taking an active part in municipal affairs and the Aliyah Ḥadashah

Party. Among his books are *Kleiner Fuehrer durch die Palaestina-Literatur* (1919), *Die Juden Wiens* (1927); a monograph on the Jews of Vienna in volume 1 of *Arim ve-Immahot be-Yisrael* (1946); and *Leopold Plaschkes – Zwei Generationen österreichischen Judentums* (1943).

BIBLIOGRAPHY: MB (Aug. 5, 1949).

[Getzel Kressel]

GOLDHAR, PINCHAS (1901–1947), Australian writer of Yiddish fiction. Born in Lodz, Goldhar migrated to Melbourne, Australia, in 1928. His early death (of heart disease) was said to have been aggravated by hard physical work in his father's dye factory. Goldhar wrote many short stories, chiefly in Yiddish, which are regarded as among the best ever written by a Jewish writer in Australia. They focus on the loneliness (as was the case at the time, before the arrival of large numbers of Yiddish-speaking Holocaust survivors) of East European Jews in remote Australia, and the relative lack of culture in that country. Goldhar also edited Yiddish supplements in Australian Jewish newspapers and a collection of short stories, *Dertseylungen fun Oystrale,* in 1939. In recent years there has been a considerable revival of interest in his work.

BIBLIOGRAPHY: P. Maclean, "The Convergence of Cultural Worlds – Pinchas Goldhar: A Yiddish Writer in Australia," in: W.D. Rubinstein (ed.), *Jews in the Sixth Continent* (1986); idem., "The Australian-Yiddish Writer, Pinchas Goldhar (1901–47)," in: *Southerly,* 55, 29–34; W.D. Rubinstein, Australia II, 326–27.

[William D. Rubinstein (2nd ed.)]

GOLDIN, DANIEL SAUL (1940–), U.S. space administrator. New York-born and Bronx-bred, Goldin earned a bachelor of science degree in mechanical engineering from the City College of New York in 1962. Inspired in his freshman physics class by a professor's blackboard reminder ("Sputnik is watching you") as the Russians orbited the world's first artificial satellite, Goldin directed his attention to space. After graduation, he applied to the National Aeronautics and Space Administration, newly created amid the East-West space race. He joined NASA's Lewis Research Center in Cleveland, Ohio, because, he said, "they were working on electric propulsion for going to Mars." His work led to a major discovery. The ion engine he was working on for space propulsion could be converted to a radio transmitter powerful enough to beam television signals from a satellite to Earth, speeding them across thousands of miles of space. His advancement of that idea eventually won a United States patent and helped give birth to direct-broadcast satellites, which increasingly circle the Earth.

In 1967 Goldin was hired by the conglomerate TRW, a maker of military and civilian spacecraft. He moved to its California divisions and stayed there for 25 years, rising through the ranks to become vice president and general manager. He led projects that conceptualized and produced advanced communication spacecraft, space technologies, and scientific instruments. Between 1976 and 1983 he managed several top-secret programs involving such projects as spy satellites. During that period, TRW was the prime contractor on photographic spy satellites, then the nation's most powerful. The company also developed a satellite known as Magnum, which, instead of using a camera, unfurls a giant antenna in space to monitor missile tests, radio, telephone, radar, and other military and diplomatic communications. Under his stewardship, TRW also built early warning and communications satellites as well as scientific probes like NASA's Gamma Ray Observatory.

Goldin was selected by President George H.W. Bush in 1992 to become the ninth head of NASA. His appointment was seen as a way to shake up an agency that the administration found unresponsive to its direction. Goldin arrived when NASA had been in a tailspin since the 1986 *Challenger* disaster, which killed seven astronauts, including a high school teacher. Its wobbly state became apparent two months after his nomination when balky hardware aboard the space shuttle *Endeavor* forced three astronauts to reach out with nothing but their gloved hands to snare a wayward satellite in space. After that Goldin ordered a study to see if added rehearsals and training were needed for the agency's greatest impending challenge, repair of the $1.6 billion Hubble Space Telescope. Eventually, shuttle astronauts conducted a record three preparatory space walks. In December 1993, with Bill Clinton as president, the repair went with surprising ease, giving the agency a major boost in confidence. Goldin's tenure at NASA lasted through nine months of the administration of President George W. Bush, to November 2001; he was its longest-serving administrator.

Over the nine years of his administration, with lower budgets, Goldin initiated a "faster, better, cheaper" approach that included aggressive management reforms. The human space flight funding was reduced from 48 percent of the agency's budget to 38 percent and funds for science and aerospace technology were increased from 31 to 43 percent. The civil service workforce was reduced by about a third, while the headquarters civil service and contractor workforce was reduced by more than half, all without forced layoffs. In space exploration, he initiated the Origins Program, to understand how the universe has evolved, to learn how life began, and to see if life exists elsewhere. He was a vigorous proponent for increased exploration of Mars and established a series of robotic missions to visit the planet every two years over a decade. The missions, designed to determine if life and water may have existed on Mars, featured planetary rovers, penetrators, and sample returns. Goldin also played a pivotal rote in redesigning the International Space Station. Starting with the Space Shuttle program, Goldin established a goal to transfer day-to-day space operations to the private sector. He was also instrumental in promoting cooperative endeavors with the Russian Space Agency to the point where Russia became a full partner in the International Space Station program.

After leaving NASA in 2001, Goldin engaged in robotics research at the Neurosciences Institute in La Jolla, Calif. In November 2003, Goldin was selected by Boston University, the fourth largest private university in the United States, to succeed its longtime president and chancellor, John Silber. However, shortly before his inauguration, the university trustees withdrew its contract offer, which called for a salary of $600,000 for five years and had other provisions. Goldin threatened to sue. The university settled with Goldin for a reported payment of $1.8 million.

[Stewart Kampel (2nd ed.)]

GOLDIN, EZRA (1868–1915), Hebrew and Yiddish author. Born in Luna, Grodno district, Goldin lived in Warsaw from 1886 to 1893 and then moved to Lodz. His first publication was a collection of poems, *Shirei No'ar* ("Poems of Youth," 1887). Subsequently he turned to writing fiction, and his stories appeared in Hebrew and Yiddish literary journals, including *Ha-Ẓefirah* and *Ha-Meliẓ*. Several of his stories were published as separate books. In 1896 he published *Ha-Zeman*, a literary anthology to which many leading Hebrew writers of the day contributed. At the beginning of the century he abandoned his literary activity, took up commerce, and became a prosperous merchant. During World War I he fled from the approaching German army and spent his last days in Riga. Goldin's short stories idealized the traditional Jewish way of life, particularly its devotion to Torah. In his view the secularized Judaism of the new nationalism had yet to prove its legitimacy as a replacement for the old faith.

BIBLIOGRAPHY: B.Z. Eisenstadt, *Dor, Rabbanav ve-Soferav*, 1 (1895), 12f.; H.I. Yanovsky, *Le-Dorotai*, 2 (1938), 180f.; Waxman, Literature, 4 (1960²), 151–4.

[Getzel Kressel]

GOLDIN, HYMAN ELIAS (1881–1971), U.S. rabbi, educationist, and author. Goldin was born in Lithuania and studied at the Yeshivah of Vilna where he was ordained as a rabbi in 1900. He immigrated to the United States in the following year. In a chance visit to a study group in a synagogue, the destitute scholar so impressed those present with his erudition that they immediately established a fund to aid him in his studies. He graduated from the New York University Law School in 1909.

Goldin served successively as principal of the Machzike Talmud Torah, the Hebrew Academy of Boro Park, both in Brooklyn, N.Y., and the Glens Falls Hebrew Academy. Passionately devoted to education, he established summer camps for children and later a camp for adults at Blue Sky.

From 1932 to 1947 Goldin served as chaplain of the Great Meadow Prison in Comstock, N.Y., and his experience there served as the basis for his unique volume *The Dictionary of American Underworld Lingo*. His main literary activity, however, was devoted to spreading Jewish knowledge and combating antisemitism. His *The Case of the Nazarene Re-Opened* (1948), which he regarded as his *magnum opus*, was the fruit of research in the New Testament, on which he became an acknowledged expert.

Among his other publications were *Universal History of Israel* (4 vols., 1935), *Hebrew Criminal Law* (1952), and a translation of Ganzfried's *Kiẓẓur Shulḥan Arukh*. He also wrote introductory books for Hebrew. Goldin published no fewer than 80 books for children based on rabbinic and medieval Jewish literature.

[Irwin Mirkin]

GOLDIN, JUDAH (1914–1998), U.S. scholar and teacher. Goldin was born in New York City. He received his B.S.S. from the City College of New York and his B.H.L. from the Seminary College of Jewish Studies at the Jewish Theological Seminary of America (1934). He received his M.A. in English literature from Columbia University and an M.H.L. and D.H.L. from the Jewish Theological Seminary. Ordained by the JTS in 1939, he was also dean and professor of *aggadah*.

He then taught religion, Jewish literature, and history at several institutions. He held faculty positions at Duke University and the University of Iowa before moving on in 1958 to a 15-year stint at Yale University, teaching classical Judaica. Then, for an even longer period, he was professor of post-biblical Hebrew literature at the University of Pennsylvania. Upon his retirement in 1985, he became professor emeritus there.

Goldin was a fellow of the American Academy for Jewish Research and chairman of the Yale Judaica Research Committee. He was also a Guggenheim Fellow and a Fulbright Research Scholar and served as a consultant on Judaica to the *Encyclopedia Britannica*.

Goldin's particular scholarly concern was rabbinic Judaism, and he was a skillful and graceful translator. For many years he served as editor of the Yale Judaica Series and he edited *The Jewish Expression* (1970) and *Shirta: The Song at the Sea Midrash* (1971), among other books. In 1988 the Jewish Publication Society inaugurated its Scholars of Distinction series with Goldin's book of collected essays, *Judah Goldin: Studies in Midrash and Related Literature*. In 1996 he received the National Foundation for Jewish Culture's Jewish Cultural Achievement Award for Textual Scholarship.

Among Goldin's works are *The Fathers According to Rabbi Nathan* (1955), an annotated translation; *The Living Talmud* (1957), a compendium of medieval commentaries on *Pirkei Avot;* and "The Period of the Talmud" (in L. Finkelstein (ed.), *The Jews...*, 1 (1960³), 115–215).

[Jack Reimer / Ruth Beloff (2nd ed.)]

GOLDIN, NAN (1953–), U.S. photographer. Shortly after she was born in Washington, D.C., Goldin and her family moved to a suburb of Boston, where Goldin spent several primarily unhappy years before moving away from her family. In 1965 her older sister, Barbara Holly Goldin, committed suicide. It had a profound effect on her life and she sought comfort in her friends. Deciding that conventional family life and traditional schooling did not suit her, Goldin moved in with a series of foster families and began studies at an alternative school called Satya Community School. There, in Lincoln, Mass., she met two people, David Armstrong and Suzanne Fletcher, who were to become influential throughout her early career. To capture memories of the past, she began to photograph friends documenting their lives and her own. With Armstrong and Fletcher, she used photography to reinvent herself and those around her, particularly by photographing her companions dressing up for one another in gender-bending attire. This early experimentation on the line separating the genders shaped her lifelong fascination with the underground subculture.

In the early 1970s she photographed drag queens and became friends with many transvestites. She depicted her subjects in a nonjudgmental way; she saw drag as a way to reinvent oneself. During this period, she enrolled at the Boston School of Fine Arts and her photographic style changed from black and white, primarily from available light, to color, which became an integral part of her style. She illuminated her subjects with careful use of flash, achieving bright deep hues. She moved to the Bowery in New York City in 1978 and her career and personal life underwent a significant change. Her images of the time reflected her lifestyle: excessive drug and alcohol use and abusive relationships. Goldin documented everything in this demi-monde: drunken parties, beatings, sex. In 1979 Goldin put together a slide show of her photographs, added music and showed them at punk rock clubs for her friends and photographic subjects to see. The show, later called "The Ballad of Sexual Dependency," was made up of color photographs lit with flash and ran for 45 minutes. To some, the 800-image "ballad," a sweeping, diaristic and critical account of life within the photographer's milieu, reflected the same dissatisfaction with contemporary life evident in Robert *Frank's *The Americans* of the 1950s. Over the years, the format remained the same, but the show grew in size and artistic ambition as Goldin continued to photograph her surroundings. In 1985 the show was included in the Whitney Biennial, a major exhibition of avant-garde work.

By 1988 Goldin's drug and alcohol abuse took a toll on her life and work, and she entered a detoxification clinic. There she created many images of herself, including "My Bedroom at the Lodge," "Self-Portrait in Front of Clinic" and "Self-Portrait With Milagro." She even showed herself battered by her boyfriend, her face bruised and swollen, her eyes filled with blood ("Nan After Being Battered"). During this time many of her close friends were dying of AIDS. One of her closest friends, Cookie Mueller, a writer and dancer whom she had known since 1976, when she started her career, was stricken. Goldin's series, "The Cookie Portfolio," consists of 15 portraits, from those taken at parties in their youth to her funeral in 1989. A critic said Goldin's work did not glamorize her sensationalist subjects but tried to humanize them. In 1996 the Whitney Museum of American Art held a retrospective of her work called "I'll Be Your Mirror." It was composed of photographs from every period of her career, which included a series with her own parents, landscapes, couples, friends' children, formal and informal. She produced several books, including one based on her "ballad" with 130 photographs, and *The Devil's Playground* in 2003.

[Stewart Kampel (2nd ed.)]

GOLDING, LOUIS (1895–1958), English novelist. Born in Manchester and educated at Oxford, Golding joined an ambulance unit during World War I and served in Macedonia and France. *Sorrow of War* (1919), a book of poems, was followed by his first novel, *Forward from Babylon* (1920). During the 1920s Golding traveled widely and the many books reflecting his experiences include *Sicilian Noon* (1925); *Those Ancient Lands: Being a Journey to Palestine* (1928); *In the Steps of Moses the Lawgiver* (1937); *In the Steps of Moses the Conqueror* (1938); and a late work, *Good-bye to Ithaca* (1955). Golding made his reputation, however, with *Magnolia Street* (1931), the first of a cycle of novels about Anglo-Jewish life. *Magnolia Street*, which was an international best-seller and was adapted for the stage, was based on his memories of Manchester, which in his books became "Doomington." The novel portrayed the tensions and sympathies governing the relations between Jewish and non-Jewish inhabitants of one particular street between 1910 and 1930. Golding projected himself into the book through his alter ego, the emancipated painter Max Emmanuel, whose brother (like the novelist's) died while on active service in France in World War I. The second of the Doomington novels, *Five Silver Daughters* (1934), was set against the background of the Bolshevik Revolution and post-war Germany. Golding's ideal of racial harmony was personified by the eponymous hero of *Mr. Emmanuel* (1939), which was later made into a film of the same name (1945), while *The Glory of Elsie Silver* (1945) reflected his response to Nazism and his sympathy for Zionism. These he had already revealed in two studies: *The Jewish Problem* (1938) and *Hitler Through the Ages* (1939).

Not all Golding's novels were concerned with Jewish themes: *The Camberwell Beauty* (1935) dealt with black magic and the Mafia in Sicily; and *The Loving Brothers* (1952) told the story of two pairs of brothers, one of each pair being brilliant and the other criminal. Golding also wrote radio plays and books on sport. His other works include the novel *Day of Atonement* (1925); *James Joyce* (1933), a study; and *To the Quayside* (1954). He also wrote an autobiography, *The World I Knew* (1958).

BIBLIOGRAPHY: J.B. Simons, *Louis Golding, A Memoir* (1958). **ADD. BIBLIOGRAPHY:** ODNB online.

[Renee Winegarten]

GOLDMAN, family of U.S. investment bankers descended from Bavarian-born MARCUS GOLDMAN (1821–1904) and JOSEPH *SACHS, both of whom arrived in the United States in 1848. Goldman was a peddler in Pennsylvania and a clothing merchant in Philadelphia before he began his financial career in New York in 1869. Later he was joined by his son, HENRY GOLDMAN (1857–1937), and by Joseph Sachs's sons, SAMUEL SACHS, who married Marcus Goldman's daughter LOUISE, and HARRY SACHS. They formed the banking firm of Goldman, Sachs & Co., which cooperated with the London bankers Kleinwort and Japhet in channeling European capital into U.S. investments.

Friendship between Henry Goldman and the *Lehman Brothers partner, Philip Lehman, engendered joint underwritings for companies engaged in the manufacture and distribution of consumer goods. Henry Goldman, staunchly pro-German in World War I, retired in 1918. Under the guidance of Joseph *Duveen, he assembled an impressive art collection. Only two members of the Sachs family remained in the business as limited partners: Walter Edward Sachs (1884–1980) and Howard Joseph Sachs (1891–1969).

BIBLIOGRAPHY: S. Birmingham, *Our Crowd* (1967), index; J. Wechsberg, *The Merchant Bankers* (1966), 285, 303–6; S.N. Behrman, *Duveen* (Eng., 1951), 286–90.

[Hanns G. Reissner]

GOLDMAN, AHARON HALEVI (1854–1932), rabbi of the Jewish agricultural colony Moisesville, Argentina. Goldman was born in Podolia, Russia. When he was 18 years old he was ordained and worked as a *shoḥet*. Goldman accepted the role of spiritual leader of the first organized group of 120 families that planned to establish themselves in Argentina as farmers. The group arrived in Buenos Aires on board the *Wesser* on August 14, 1889. Goldman immigrated with his wife and five children. The group established an agricultural colony in Palacios, province of Santa Fe; in 1890 they moved to a new home, close to the railway, which Aharon Goldman called Kiryat Moshe or Moises-Ville, referring to Moshe Rabbeinu, who liberated the Israelites from slavery in Egypt, as a symbol of the liberation of the settlers from the oppressive situation that they had suffered in Russia.

In his role as rabbi in Moisesville Goldman tried to maintain observance, especially *kashrut* and the Sabbath. He succeeded in obtaining the recognition by the authorities of the Sabbath as the weekly day of rest and Sunday as a weekday. Goldman was also *gabbai ẓedakah* in charge of the collection of money for the local needy and for the yeshivot in Ereẓ Israel and the Diaspora. He studied 18 hours a day. A large part of his responsa was dedicated to the various problems facing the Jews in a new social and geographical environment. He solved halakhic problems with respect to the different seasons in the southern part of the globe, as well as the different fauna not mentioned in the Torah with respect to the dietary laws. His responsa were published posthumously by his grandson Dr. David Goldman, in *Divrei Aharon* (Jerusalem, 1981). Goldman maintained a wide correspondence with prominent rabbis of his generation: Isaac Elhanan *Spektor, Samuel *Salant, *Ḥafeẓ Ḥayyim, Abraham Isaac ha-Kohen *Kook, and Samuel *Mohilever. His rabbinical authority was recognized throughout Argentina and was accepted also by Shaul Setthon Dabbah, rabbi of the Aleppan community of Buenos Aires.

One of his sons, MORDECHAI GOLDMAN, was *shoḥet* in Moisesville and died in 1981 in Jerusalem.

[Efraim Zadoff (2nd ed.)]

GOLDMAN, BERNARD (1841–1901), Polish patriot and militant supporter of assimilation. Goldman was born in Warsaw, where his father was a Hebrew *maskil* and owned a printing press; his grandfather Jacob was a rabbi in Amsterdam. Goldman played an active role in the Polish revolutionary movements against czarist rule. After the demonstration held in Warsaw in 1861, he was exiled to Siberia, but escaped and returned to Warsaw to take part in the uprising of 1863. After its suppression he went abroad, traveled through Germany, and reached Paris, where he contributed to the cause of the Polish émigrés. He went to Vienna in 1867 and completed his law studies. In 1870 he settled in Lemberg where he initiated an extensive program for promoting education among the Jewish masses in Galicia. He organized cultural activities, including courses and libraries for spreading Polish culture and combating the pro-Austrian centralist movement. In opposition to the aspirations of the Shomer Yisrael society of German orientation, he founded the rival Doreshei Shalom and published a newspaper *Zgoda*. This resulted in the establishment of the *Agudat Aḥim, which later became the most prominent center of assimilationist activity in Poland.

In 1876 Goldman took his seat in the national Sejm (parliament) of Galicia as the delegate for Lemberg and in 1883 was elected to the Lemberg municipal council. Goldman was also active within the framework of the community administration, founding an organization of artisans, Yad Ḥaruẓim. In particular he promoted the development of a school network, which was named after him. This network provided a Polish-oriented education combined with the teaching of religious observance.

BIBLIOGRAPHY: EG, 4 (1956), 314–5; N.M. Gelber, *Die Juden und der polnische Aufstand 1863* (1923), 221; M. Balaban, *Dzieje Żydów w Galicji* (1914); M. Bertold, *Żydzi w powstaniu 1863* (1913), 21–22, 30–31; Estreicher, *Almanach i leksykon żydostwa polskiego*, 1 (1937), 67–69; J.K. Urbach, *Udział żydów w walce o niepodległość Polski* (1938), 102–3; 150–1; *Polski słownik biograficzny*, 8 (1959–60), 210–1.

[Moshe Landau]

GOLDMAN, EDWIN FRANKO (1878–1950), U.S. bandmaster, brother of Mayer Clarence *Goldman. Goldman was born in Louisville, Kentucky, and studied music at the National Conservatory, New York, where Anton Dvořak taught him composition. He began his career as solo cornetist in the Metropolitan Opera orchestra, and in 1911 formed his own band, which from 1918 gave outdoor concerts on university campuses and in New York public parks. The band toured the U.S. and in 1945 performed for the U.S. armed forces in the Philippines and Japan. It had a high standard of performance and an unusually extensive repertoire, and hence exerted a great influence on bands throughout the U.S. Goldman was a founder and first president of the American Bandmasters' Association. He was assisted by his son and associate conductor RICHARD FRANKO GOLDMAN (1910–1980).

GOLDMAN, ELIEZER (1918–2002), Israeli philosopher. Born in Brooklyn, New York, Goldman pursued his undergraduate education at Yeshiva University and was a student of Rabbi M. *Soloveitchik and his son Rabbi J.B. *Soloveitchik, with whom he studied both Talmud and philosophy. His wide-ranging interests included *halakhah*, philosophy, Jewish thought, mathematics, physics, literature, economics, and music. His grounding in Talmud would serve him, in later life, for his interest in philosophy of *halakhah*. In the late 1930s Goldman immigrated to what was then Palestine and became a member of kibbutz Sedeh Eliyahu in the Bet Shean Valley. In his own words, his *aliyah* resulted less from Zionism in the political sense than from his search to fulfill Jewish religious socialism and establish a socialist Jewish society based on traditional Jewish sources. Only later in life was he able to complete his graduate studies at Bar-Ilan University, where he taught for many years and became professor of philosophy. Many of his writings are only now being prepared for posthumous publication in three volumes: the first volume deals with his research into classical Jewish thought; the second on Rav Kook; and the third on social, economic, and cultural thought. Goldman was, however, no ivory tower academic. Many of his writings relate to the social, economic, and cultural life of the religious kibbutz.

Goldman's thought is characterized by a continual dialogue with his teacher J.B. Soloveitchik, and with his friend Yeshayahu *Leibowitz; he agreed with them regarding the centrality of the *halakhah* to understanding the Jewish world of life (*lebenswelt*). Together with Soloveitchik and Leibowitz, Goldman contributed to a dramatic shift in contemporary Jewish thought, away from theological-metaphysical theory to halakhic practice. Unlike the other two, however, who employed general philosophy to analyze the *halakhah*, and who wrote about the *halakhah* from a philosophical point of view, Goldman sought to overcome the problem of imposing a foreign perspective onto the Jewish tradition itself, preferring what may be called a phenomenological methodology, based on precise examination of the sources themselves. His philosophic work was an attempt to describe carefully and critically the Jewish tradition as it reveals itself, and not as it can be imagined from an external theoretical perspective. Goldman was thus the founder of a new field, philosophy of the *halakhah*, in which philosophy is used to analyze the *halakhah* itself. Goldman's collected essays, *Expositions and Inquiries: Jewish Thought in Past and Present* (1996), was edited by Avi Sagi and Daniel Statman.

Goldman was both an academic scholar and a constructive thinker, who (together with Soloveitchik and Leibowitz) had a seminal impact on Orthodox thought's response to modernity. His research interests focused especially on Saadiah Gaon and Maimonides, but he went beyond neutral research in also seeking existential relevance in their thought. For example, in his view, Maimonides' philosophic positions did not outlive their time, but his method is still largely useful in working out the relationship between philosophy and science, and the sources of religion. In contrast with Soloveitchik and Leibowitz, for whom there is always a fundamental tension between Jewish sources and the external world, Goldman's thought is shaped by the Maimonidean harmony of the Torah and philosophy, and rejects the distinction between "internal" and "external"; each person, including the religious person, reflects his or her socio-cultural environment in his or her understanding of tradition.

Goldman also distanced himself from Soloveitchik's view, especially in his later writings, concerning the feeling of alienation of the individual from nature and society, a feeling of alienation Goldman did not share. In contrast with both Soloveitchik and Leibowitz, Goldman's thought emphasized the multi-cultural and multi-contextual situation of human life. A person does not establish a religious world or halakhic commitment autonomously, independently of the other contexts in which he or she lives.

A consistent theme in Goldman's thought over the years was the problem of the relationship between the Torah and the conditions of life. For Goldman, this is not an ideological question, but an existential one: what do we expect of the *halakhah*, and how can we interpret it so that it accords real conditions? How does the *halakhah* actually function, and how can it harmonize its norms with external realities? Goldman's approach thus sharply contrasts with that of Leibowitz, for whom the *halakhah* is a closed system, which functions autonomously and independently of external conditions, focusing exclusively on the service of God. Leibowitz's approach leads to a split personality in the believer: he or she can either be a believer serving God, or a person committed to political, social, and moral values and conceptions. In the framework of Leibowitz's thought, the believer can never unite these two separate worlds. Goldman, by contrast, proposed a more complex model based on his analysis of the *halakhah* itself. In 1958 he proposed a new category, "meta-halakhic norms." These norms are not behavioral, but are principles for interpreting and implementing the *halakhah* itself. The existence of these meta-halakhic norms also undermines the prevalent tendency to describe the *halakhah* in closed, formal categories of jurisprudence, without any reference to external considerations. Such tendencies, Goldman argued, are contradicted by great halakhic decisors over the ages, who responded to real, practical needs, referring to such concepts as "what most of the community cannot sustain" in making their decisions. Goldman maintained that the contemporary tendency in *ḥaredi* (ultra-Orthodox) ideology, which reduces a halakhic decision to formal, theoretical truth, results in an abject failure to relate to the needs of the time. Another sociological factor in the problem of the *halakhah* in our day is the status attached to the yeshivot, which emphasize theoretical study of the *halakhah*, at the expense of involvement in public life and practical halakhic study. The *halakhah* thus becomes a theoretical construct rather than a real phenomenon.

The problem, then, is that the *halakhah*, like any other system of thought, cannot incorporate within itself all the principles required for it to operate, and can only function when we apply meta-halakhic principles. In a series of articles on "Ethics, Religion and Halakhah," Goldman attempted, accordingly, to derive these meta-halakhic principles guiding great halakhic decisiors from the halakhic literature itself, in particular from the vast responsa literature. In his view, these meta-halakhic principles mediate between the *halakhah* and human existence.

This approach also led Goldman to criticize Leibowitz's reductionism regarding the religious "paradox" underlying the *halakhah* and the dichotomy Leibowitz posited between the *halakhah* and existence. On the one hand, the *halakhah* represents utter heteronomy – the acceptance of the divine will as expressed in the written and oral Torah. On the other hand, since the *halakhah* no longer relies on prophetic instruction, the moment one attempts to realize and implement the Torah in concrete life situations, one is forced to employ autonomous human reason. The *halakhah*, which is thus founded on heteronomous authority, operates by means of autonomous human reason. It does not originate in human culture, but is directed towards human culture, which it endows with religious significance, and can only be implemented within a cultural context. In this way, the Torah is a product not only of divine revelation, but also, and not less, of its being transmitted to real people in a concrete social-cultural situation, which in many respects precedes the Torah and guides its interpretation. The Torah thus does not exist independently of the community which lives according to its teachings, but also lives according to values reflecting its concrete human situation. The sources of meta-halakhic principles are, therefore, not necessarily the divine will, i.e., the halakhic system itself, but human value judgments based on social and cultural reality, a reality the *halakhah* both reflects and is intended to order.

In these ways Goldman advocated what he called "Judaism without illusions," in which religious propositions reflect the believer's own insights and not transcendent being. This, in turn, forms a basis for a pluralistic religious outlook.

BIBLIOGRAPHY: A. Sagi, "Religious Language in the Modern World: An Interview with Eliezer Goldman," in: M. Roth (ed.), *Religious Zionism in a Renewed Perspective* (Heb., 1998); idem, *A Challenge: Returning to Tradition*, ch. 4 (2003).

[Avi Sagi (2nd ed.)]

GOLDMAN, EMMA (1869–1940), U.S. anarchist writer and lecturer, leading advocate of anarchism in the United States. Goldman, born in Kovno, Lithuania, grew up there and in Koenigsberg and St. Petersburg, immigrating to the United States in 1885. Her independent spirit emerged early, and disputes with teachers and her father cut short her formal education. For the most part she was self-educated, particularly in anarchist thought. Her long and close association with Alexander *Berkman was the most significant influence on her thought and deed. Unlike many anarchists, she moved beyond the small radical immigrant community, and her lectures and her journal *Mother Earth* (1906–18) aimed to illuminate the injustice and immorality of American society.

Goldman became an open advocate of birth control in the years before World War I, which led to considerable notoriety. However, it was her vigorous opposition to conscription during the war that finally led the United States government to imprison her and ban *Mother Earth* from the mails. Goldman had long been considered dangerous, and the combination of a technical weakness in her citizenship status and legislation that broadened the grounds for action against undesirable aliens led to her deportation to the Soviet Union in 1919. By 1921 she fled that country, repelled by the suppression of the individual, which seemed as complete under Bolshevism as under capitalism.

While she continued to write and lecture, her active political career was ended except for vigorous efforts on behalf of the Catalonian anarchists in the Spanish Civil War. Her life was one of commitment to anarchism in theory, and to personal independence and radical political action in practice.

Goldman continuously focused on the basic contention that the state was a coercive force that destroyed the differences among individuals and eliminated genuine freedom in defense of the conformity required by society. She stressed the freedom of the individual, responsive to self-developed standards of love and justice. Her demand for individual freedom never wavered, and she detested capitalism because of its inherent inequalities, which doomed the majority of persons to a toilsome and regimented life focused on material matters. She favored communism as the ultimate form of economic emancipation to break the link between work and income that enslaved men in Western capitalist states. To Goldman, anarchism conformed to man's basic nature, and it would prove to be a workable and orderly system.

Goldman's writings include *Anarchism and Other Essays* (1910), *The Social Significance of the Modern Drama* (1914), *The Psychology of Political Violence* (1917), *My Disillusionment in Russia* (1923), *My Further Disillusionment in Russia* (1924), *Living My Life* (2 vols., 1931), and *The Traffic in Women and Other Essays on Feminism* (1971).

BIBLIOGRAPHY: R. Drinnon, *Rebel in Paradise* (1961). **ADD. BIBLIOGRAPHY:** *Nowhere at Home: Letters from Exile of Emma Goldman and Alexander Berkman* (1975); *Red Emma Speaks: An Emma Goldman Reader* (1984); A. Wexler, *Emma Goldman in America* (1989); M. Duberman, *Mother Earth: An Epic Drama of Emma Goldman's Life* (1991); A. Wexler, *Emma Goldman in Exile* (1992); J. Chalberg, *Emma Goldman: American Individualist* (1997).

[Irwin Yellowitz]

GOLDMAN, ERIC FREDERICK (1915–1989), U.S. historian. Goldman was born in Washington, D.C. He was professor of history at Princeton where he taught from 1940. Goldman served as president of the Society of American Historians from 1962 to 1969. He was a member of the academic council of the American Friends of the Hebrew University. Goldman's field of specialization was American history of the 20th century. His best-known books are: *Rendezvous With Destiny: A History of Modern American Reform* (1952) and *Crucial Decade, America 1945–1955* (1956), revised as *Crucial Decade – and After, America 1945–1960* (1961). In 1964 President

Johnson named Goldman special consultant to the president. After his resignation (1966) Goldman published *The Tragedy of Lyndon Johnson* (1968).

[Oscar Isaiah Janowsky]

GOLDMAN, HETTY (1881–1972), U.S. archaeologist. Born in New York, Goldman studied at Bryn Mawr College (1903) and at Radcliffe (1910), where she received her M.A. and later (1916) her Ph.D. Her excavation of the necropolis of Halae, in the ancient Greek district of Boeotia, was followed by excavations at the Ionian city of Colophon in Asia Minor and at Eutresis, a Bronze Age settlement in Boeotia. These were interrupted by the Greco-Turkish war in 1922. The peak of her career was her excavation at the south Anatolian city of Tarsus, birthplace of the apostle Paul, which had been a flourishing site in the Bronze and Iron Ages as well as during Hellenistic and Roman times. Hetty Goldman's main interest was the relationship between the Oriental cultures of the Eastern Mediterranean and the culture of the Greek world. She was one of the first members of the Institute for Advanced Study, Princeton, New Jersey. Her published works include *Excavations at Eutresis in Boeotia* (1931) and *The Acropolis of Halae* (in *Hesperia*, 9 (1940), 381–514). She edited *Excavations at Gözlü Kule, Tarsus*, 3 vols. (1950–63).

BIBLIOGRAPHY: S.S. Weinberg (ed.), *The Aegean and the Near East* (1956), studies presented to Hetty Goldman (includes bibliography). **ADD. BIBLIOGRAPHY:** M.J. Mellink, "Goldman, Hetty," in: B. Sicherman and C.H. Green (eds.), *Notable American Women* (1980), 280–82.

[Penuel P. Kahane / Shimon Gibson (2nd ed.)]

GOLDMAN, ISRAEL (1904–1979), U.S. Conservative rabbi. Born in Poland, Goldman immigrated to the United States with his parents and earned his B.A. at the City College of New York (1924) and was ordained by the Jewish Theological Seminary in 1926 where he later earned his D.H.L. (1937). While still at the Seminary, he served Temple Emmanu-El in Providence, Rhode Island, for the High Holidays and then was brought back as its full-time rabbi. He introduced many of the innovations common to the Conservative Movement of his generation, late Friday evening services and the bat mitzvah, but his primary interest was in Jewish education, at all levels. He organized a Sunday school, a PTA, and an innovative adult education program that enrolled 350 students in 1941 alone. His local success with adult Jewish education brought him national attention and he proposed and directed the National Academy for Adult Jewish Studies, created under the auspices of the Seminary. It published books and created adult institutes called Kallot. Goldman was president of the *Rabbinical Assembly from 1946 to 1948 where he tried to create a regional structure for the rabbinic organization and also for its international expansion. He also pushed the Rabbinical Assembly into social action by forming the Social Justice Commission. "Going national" was not without its tensions with his Providence congregation. Goldman resolved them by leaving in 1948 and moving to Baltimore, where he took Chizuk Amuno congregation and moved it to the nearby suburb of Pikesville. With suburbanization came a threefold growth in membership. Goldman was a leader in the civil rights movement and served as vice chairman of the Maryland Commission on Interracial Relations. He received significant support for his civil rights efforts from his congregation. In 1963 he was arrested in a protest against segregation, a mark of honor in his career.

He was the author of two books *The Life and Times of Rabbi David ibn Abi Zimra* (1970), a book about Jewish life in the post-Spanish expulsion Ottoman Empire, and *Lifelong Learning among Jews: Adult Education in Judaism from Biblical Times to the 20th Century* (1975).

BIBLIOGRAPHY: P.S. Nadell, *Conservative Judaism in America: A Biographical Dictonary and Sourcebook* (1988).

[Michael Berenbaum (2nd ed.)]

GOLDMAN, MARTIN JACOB (Mordechai; 1917–1991), rabbi, Jewish educator. In his youth Goldman was known as the Yerushalmi Ilui (prodigy in Talmud) in the Hebron Yeshivah. At the age of 18 he was tested by the greatest rabbis in Jerusalem – Ezekiel Sarna, R. Isaac Herzog, R. Issur Zalman Meltzer, R. Eliyahu Rom, R. Katz, and R. Moshe Mordecai Epstein – who gave him the ordination of "*Yore Yore, Yadin Yadin*."

When he followed his family to New York and realized that he would need a broader education, he taught Talmud to some of the faculty at the Jewish Theological Seminary in return for rooms at the dorm so he could study for his bachelor's degree at New York University. He earned his M.A. and Ph.D. (1963) at Harvard, working under Harry *Wolfson.

After teaching at the Hebrew Teachers' College in Boston for 20 years, he became the Maxwell Abell Professor of Talmud in Chicago and the Dean of the College of Jewish Studies there, which soon became Spertus College.

Realizing that there were no departments of Jewish studies in the Chicago academic scene, he instituted a consortium of seven Chicago area universities and colleges with Spertus College serving as their department of Jewish studies. Joint degrees were awarded to students who could study Jewish subjects on the same level as their other subjects.

The most popular of his courses at Spertus was "The Talmud in Contemporary Society." Some of the subjects covered in this course were psychology, marriage, civil law, business, sex, medicine, and government, and it was frequented by lawyers, judges, and physicians in the Chicago community.

He wrote on many burning contemporary medical issues, such as his work "Abortion in Jewish Law" and articles on transplants and the time of death. He was called upon frequently to represent the authentic Jewish voice in Interfaith Conferences and was routinely consulted by other rabbis on talmudic questions.

[Celia Goldman (2nd ed.)]

GOLDMAN, MAYER CLARENCE (1874–1939), U.S. lawyer, born in New Orleans. Goldman became convinced that achievement of the American ideal of equality before the law required the state to provide qualified legal counsel for poor defendants. He vigorously advocated establishment of the office of public defender by state and local governments. He gave speeches and wrote for legal periodicals in support of this cause. He wrote a book, *The Public Defender* (1917), and was coauthor of a movie script on the subject. Goldman chaired the public defender committees of the American Lawyers Guild, the American Institute of Criminal Law and Criminology, and the New York State Bar Association. He initiated the public defender movement in New York and drafted public defender bills introduced in the state legislature from 1915 to 1931.

[Barton G. Lee]

GOLDMAN, MOISES (1902–1997), physician and Jewish community leader in Argentina. Goldman was born in Palacios, province of Santa Fe. His grandfather was Rabbi Aharon *Goldman of Moisesville. He graduated as a pharmacist and then as a surgeon from the University of Cordoba, Argentina. Goldman headed many central Jewish community organizations in Argentina and Latin America: *DAIA – Delegación de Asociaciones Israelitas Argentinas (the central representative organization of Argentinean Jewry) for two consecutive terms – under the military government (1943–46) and during the first presidency of Juan D. Perón; *AMIA – Asociación Mutual Israelita Argentina (Ashkenazi Community of Buenos Aires); the Va'ad ha-Kehiloth (federative central organization of all the communities) from its foundation in 1952; Maccabi Sports Organization; Latin American Jewish Congress; Instituto de Intercambio Cultural Argentino-Israelí. He also was honorary vice president of the World Jewish Congress. Goldman participated in many national and international conferences in his profession as well as in public affairs promoting the eradication of discrimination and antisemitism and the strengthening of democracy.

[Efraim Zadoff (2nd ed.)]

GOLDMAN, MOSES HA-KOHEN (1863–1918), U.S. Hebrew teacher and journalist. A native of Pinsk, he studied at the Volozhin yeshivah and then under R. Isaac Hirsch *Weiss, in Vienna. Later he journeyed to London and, in 1890, settled in the United States where he became a teacher, a printer, and, finally, a journalist. He founded the short-lived Hebrew journal *Ha-Moreh* in 1894 and then edited (1901–02), first together with Nahum Meir *Schaikewitz, then by himself *Ha-Le'om*, which began as a Hebrew-Yiddish monthly and then appeared only in Hebrew. In 1909 he edited the first American Hebrew daily *Ha-Yom* which ceased publication after 90 days but reappeared briefly in 1913. The *Proverbs of the Sages* which he first published in *Ha-Le'om* with translations in English was republished in a separate book in New York (1916).

BIBLIOGRAPHY: B.Z. Eisenstadt, *Ḥakhmei Yisrael ba-Amerika* (1903), 26f.; J.D. Eisenstein, *Oẓar Zikhronotai*, 1 (1929), 138; Kressel, Leksikon, 1 (1965), 421.

[Eisig Silberschlag]

GOLDMAN, PAUL L. (1904–1973), U.S. Labor Zionist leader. Goldman was born in Poland and even in his youth was involved in Zionist-Socialist work, influenced by the ideology of Dov Ber *Borochov. In 1920, he immigrated to America, where he worked in a shop and, at the same time, attended high school at night, later studying law and graduating from St. John's Law School in 1928. He became identified with Aḥdut ha-Avodah and Po'alei Zion, and for 40 years played a leading role in Zionist and associated agencies. For many years he was general secretary of Aḥdut ha-Avodah-Poalei Zion and served as editor or associate editor of the party organ, *Unzer Tsayt*. Goldman helped bring the movement into the United Labor Zionist Organization of America and later into the Labor Zionist Alliance. He was a member of the presidium of the World Zionist Organization and of the commission to reorganize that body. One of the founders and leaders of the Jewish Labor Committee, he was actively identified with the Workmen's Circle (Arbeiter Ring) and was one of the founders of the American Zionist Federation in 1970. Goldman was highly regarded for his qualities of leadership and his lifelong devotion to Zionist causes and the furtherance of Jewish culture.

[Milton Ridvas Konvitz (2nd ed.)]

GOLDMAN, SOLOMON (1893–1953), U.S. Conservative rabbi. Goldman, who was born in Volhynia, Russia, was taken to the U.S. in 1902. He studied at the Rabbi Isaac Elchanan Yeshivah and at the Jewish Theological Seminary where he was ordained (1918) and later received his DHL (1936). After serving in Brooklyn, he moved to the Cleveland Bnai Jeshurun Congregation, which he could not convince to become a synagogue center so he moved to the Cleveland Jewish Center, which had been refashioned as a synagogue center with excellent sports facilities and auditorium. He was a wonderful orator and an innovative organizer who worked to establish a large school and a serious adult education program. He moved the synagogue from its Orthodox origins toward the Conservative tradition, meeting with serious opposition and a legal suit in which the change was upheld by the court. But after seven years, he left to go to Chicago where he became rabbi of the Anshe Emet Synagogue of Chicago (1929) and held that position until his death. He became widely known as an orator, communal leader, and scholar who popularized the cause of Zionism. Among the positions of leadership he held were the presidency of the Histadrut Ivrit (1936–38), presidency of the Zionist Organization of America (1938–40), and cochairmanship of the United Jewish Appeal. He was a founder of National Hillel and served on the board of the Jewish Theological Seminary. Goldman edited a series of texts in modern Hebrew literature and wrote *Romance of a People*, a pageant performed at the Chicago World's Fair in 1933. Among his books are *A Rabbi Takes Stock* (1931), *The Jew and the Universe* (1936), *Crisis and Decision* (1938), and *Undefeated* (1940), all dealing with the Jewish people in modern times. In his last years he began the publication of a study of the Bible and its influence on world literature, of which three volumes were completed: *The Book of Books* (1948), *In the Beginning* (1949), and *From Slavery to Freedom* (1958).

BIBLIOGRAPHY: L.P. Gartner, *History of Jews of Cleveland* (1978); S. Vincent and J. Rubinstein, *Merging Traditions: Jewish Life in Cleveland* (1978); J.L. Weinstein, *Solomon Goldman: A Rabbi's Rabbi* (1973); P.M. Nadell, *Conservative Judaism in America: A Biographical Dictionary and Sourcebook* (1988).

[Jack Reimer / Michael Berenbaum (2nd ed.)]

GOLDMAN, WILLIAM (1931–), U.S. novelist-screenwriter. Born to businessman Maurice Clarence and Marion Goldman (née Weil) in Chicago, Illinois, Goldman grew up in suburban Highland Park, spending his time at the Alcyon Theater watching films. He studied writing at Oberlin College. After receiving his bachelor's degree in 1952, he did a two-year stint in the U.S. Army. Following his discharge as a corporal in 1954, he did graduate work in English at Columbia University, graduating in 1956. During the summer he wrote the novel *The Temple of Gold* in 10 days. Accepted by Alfred A. Knopf, it was published in 1957. He went on to write *Your Turn to Curtsy, My Turn to Bow* (1958), and *Soldier in the Rain* (1960). Goldman followed those first novels with *No Way to Treat a Lady* (1964) and *Boys and Girls Together* (1964). Goldman was hired to adapt the novel *The Moving Target*, which became the Paul Newman film *Harper* (1966), but continued to focus on novels. In 1961, Goldman began the screenplay for *Butch Cassidy and the Sundance Kid*; released in 1969, the film earned Goldman an Oscar for best original screenplay. His next two works were adaptations, *The Stepford Wives* (1975) and *All the President's Men* (1976), which earned him another Oscar. He continued to write novels during this time, including *Marathon Man* (1975) and *Magic* (1976), both of which were adapted for film. His screenplays for *The Princess Bride* (based on his 1973 novel) and his adaptation of Stephen King's *Misery* (1990), both for director Rob Reiner, received critical acclaim. Goldman also had success with his screenplay for the Clint Eastwood film *Absolute Power* (1997). More recent produced work includes *The General's Daughter* (1999), *Hearts in Atlantis* (2001), and *Dreamcatcher* (2003). Goldman also established himself as an authority on the ways of Hollywood with his books *Adventures in the Screen Trade* (1983) and *What Lie Did I Tell?* (2000).

[Adam Wills (2nd ed.)]

GOLDMAN, YA'AKOV BEN ASHER (1856–1931), Hebrew journalist. Goldman was born in Jerusalem where he studied at the Eẓ Ḥayyim yeshivah. Influenced by the Haskalah at an early age, he contributed articles to the Hebrew press, including *Yehudah vi-Yrushalayim, Ha-Ẓefirah, Ha-Asif, Ha-Maggid, Ha-Meliẓ*, and *Ḥavaẓẓelet*. In 1890 he moved to Jaffa, where he was among the leading figures in the Ashkenazi Jewish community and one of the founders of the Neveh Ẓedek quarter. For a time he served as chief Palestine correspondent for *Ha-Ẓefirah* and acting editor of *Ḥavaẓẓelet*. His articles include detailed historical accounts of modern Jewish settlement in Ereẓ Israel. At the turn of the century, Goldman became extremely religious. He abandoned his secular writing and devoted himself to biblical research. Late in life, he published two books on various topics (talmudic, religious, etc.).

BIBLIOGRAPHY: Kressel, Leksikon, 1 (1965), 419.

[Getzel Kressel]

GOLDMANN, LUCIEN (1913–1970), literary and philosophical writer. Born in Bucharest, Romania, Goldmann settled in Paris, where he became director of studies at the Ecole Pratique des Hautes Etudes in 1958. His major work, *Le Dieu caché* (1955), deals with the tragic vision of life underlying the writings of *Pascal and Racine. He also wrote *Sciences humaines et philosophie* (1952), *Jean Racine dramaturge* (1956), *Recherches dialectiques* (1959), and *Pour une sociologie du roman* (1964).

GOLDMANN, NAHUM (1895–1982), statesman and Zionist leader, born in Visznevo, Lithuania. When Goldmann was five years old his family moved to Germany – first to Koenigsberg and from there to Frankfurt. His father, Solomon Ẓevi Goldmann, was a writer and Hebrew teacher, and young Goldmann grew up in an atmosphere suffused with the spirit of Judaism. At the age of 15 he published an anonymous article attacking Solomon *Reinach, the vice president of *Alliance Israélite Universelle, that contributed to Reinach's resignation from his post. In 1913 Goldmann spent several months in Ereẓ Israel and reported his impressions in *Eretz Israel, Reisebriefe aus Palaestina*, published in 1914. During World War I he joined the staff of the Jewish section of the German Foreign Ministry. At that time Goldmann supported a pro-German orientation of the Zionist movement and sought means of gaining the Kaiser's support for the Zionist cause. After the war, Goldmann joined with Jacob *Klatzkin in publishing *Freie Zionistische Blaetter*, a Zionist periodical (1921–22). At this time the two men also conceived the idea of publishing a German-language Jewish encyclopedia, and in 1925 they founded a publishing house, "Eshkol," for this purpose. Three years later the first volume of the *Encyclopaedia Judaica* appeared. Hitler's rise to power prevented the completion of the venture, and when publication of the encyclopedia had to be interrupted, a total of ten volumes in German and two in Hebrew had been issued. (In the 1960s, Goldmann took the initiative in inaugurating the English-language *Encyclopaedia Judaica*.)

In the early 1920s Goldmann joined Ha-Po'el ha-Ẓa'ir, but later left the party and became a member of the Zionist "radical" faction and in 1926 was elected its representative on the Zionist Actions Committee. He was critical of Weizmann's plan to coopt non-Zionists to the *Jewish Agency. He also denounced the Zionist leadership for its lack of interest in the political and cultural problems of Jewish masses in the

Diaspora. As Ereẓ Israel would not be capable of absorbing the entire Jewish people; it should serve as an inspiration to the Jewish people and be a symbol and the principal instrument of its renascence.

Goldmann was the chairman of the Political Committee at the 17th Zionist Congress (1931) and played a decisive role in forging a majority to oppose the reelection of Weizmann as president of the Zionist Organization. Two years later, however, when the Radical faction was disbanded, Goldmann began to lean toward Weizmann and eventually to cooperate with him. In the same year, Goldmann was forced to leave Germany, and in 1935 he was deprived of German citizenship and became a citizen of Honduras. At the end of 1933, upon the death of Leo *Motzkin, he was elected chairman of the Comité des Délégations Juives, and in 1935 he became the representative of the Jewish Agency at the League of Nations. Together with Stephen *Wise, he organized the *World Jewish Congress and at the first conference of the Congress, in 1936, was appointed chairman of its executive board. Shortly after the outbreak of World War II, he moved to New York where he established the Zionist Emergency Council for political work and represented for years the Executive of the Jewish Agency, later becoming the chairman of the American Section upon its establishment.

During the Mandatory period Goldmann supported the idea of establishing a Jewish State. In 1931, during the debate on the "final goal" of Zionism and in 1935, as the head of the *General Zionist faction, he declared that the principal task of the Zionist Movement was to create among the Jewish people the momentum for the establishment of a Jewish State in Ereẓ Israel. In 1937, he was among the most ardent supporters of the Partition Plan, preferring sovereignty to territory. This attitude also prompted him to support *Ben-Gurion at the *Biltmore Conference. Henceforth, until May 1948, he took an active and sometimes decisive part in the diplomatic and public relations activities designed to bring about the immediate establishment of a Jewish state. When the State of Israel came into being, Goldmann was elected one of the two chairmen of the Executive of the Zionist Organization (Berl Locker was the other), and in 1956 he was elected president of the organization. Upon the death of Stephen Wise, he was also elected president of the World Jewish Congress. He held that position until 1977, when he relinquished it and was named founder-president.

Goldmann was largely responsible for initiating negotiations with the Federal Republic of Germany on the payment of *reparations to Israel and indemnification for Nazi victims. It was primarily Goldmann who arranged for the secret preliminary contact with German statesmen, mainly with Chancellor Konrad *Adenauer, before the official negotiations took place. It was also mostly at his initiative that the Claims Conference, which became the most comprehensive and representative world Jewish body, was established. He was elected president of the Conference and led its delegation in the negotiations with Germany. Goldmann subsequently conducted similar negotiations with Austria. As a result of the work done by the Claims Conference, a Memorial Foundation for Jewish Culture was established in 1965, with Goldmann as its president. He initiated the creation of the Conference of Jewish Organizations (COJO) and became its president, founded the World Council of Jewish Education, took an active part in organizing the Conference of Presidents of Major American Jewish Organizations for Israel, was the chairman of the first international conference for Soviet Jewry (Paris, 1960), etc.

In the field of Zionist affairs, Goldmann participated in the formulation of the Jerusalem Program (1951; see *Basle Program) and conducted the negotiations with the Israel government that preceded the enactment of the law on the status of the World Zionist Organization and the signing of a covenant between the State of Israel and the Zionist Organization. He supported the concept of the centrality of the State of Israel in the life of the Jewish people, but opposed any attitude that negated the Diaspora (while at the same time refusing to accept the view held by many American Zionists that the American Diaspora was no longer to be regarded as an exile). Goldmann regarded the continued existence of the Jewish people in the Diaspora as threatened not by antisemitism, but by assimilation as a result of full emancipation and by the unparalleled prosperity of the Jews in most countries since World War II. He believed that the struggle of the Jewish people should now be directed to uphold the right of the Jews to be different from other peoples and preserve their uniqueness. This task, primarily an educational one, should be the main concern of the Jewish people and its leaders.

In 1962 Goldmann left the United States and became a citizen of Israel. He did not, however, take an active part in the internal political life of the country. He subsequently spent part of his time in Israel and part in Europe. In 1968 Goldmann took on Swiss citizenship but continued to be active throughout the Jewish world.

Goldmann frequently voiced criticism of Israel's leadership, which he accused of narrow-mindedness, overestimating the power of the state and its military forces, lacking the proper attitude toward the Jewish people in the Diaspora, and of pursuing an inflexible policy. He advocated a more elastic and moderate policy toward the Arab states and also recommended that Israel moderate her criticism of Soviet policy vis-à-vis the Middle East and Jews living in the U.S.S.R. Declarations made by Goldmann in this vein periodically caused friction between him and leading Israel personalities; furthermore, the various offices held by Goldmann also raised the question of whether his criticism represented the view of the Zionist Organization, the World Jewish Congress, some other Jewish body, or only his personal opinion. Relations between Goldmann and Israel leaders took a further turn for the worse after the *Six-Day War, when the impression was created that Goldmann's identification with the State of Israel was rather less than that of many other Jewish leaders. It was against this background that several Zionist parties began to oppose his continuance in office as president of the organization, and at the 27th Zionist Congress (1968), Goldmann did not put forward his candidacy for the presidency. The *Autobiography of Nahum Goldmann* appeared in 1969. In 1970, a controversy was aroused by Goldmann's approach to the Israel prime minister in connection with a possible meeting between himself and *Nasser. When the Israel government expressed its disapproval, the matter was dropped.

Selections of Goldmann's articles and speeches have been published in two volumes: *Dor shel Ḥurban u-Ge'ullah* (1968) and *Be-Darkhei Ammi* (1968).

[Chaim Yahil]

Goldmann relinquished the presidency of the World Jewish Congress in November 1977, but despite his age continued to be a controversial figure, and in 1978 was severely criticized because of his support of Egypt's attitude in the peace negotiations. A number of such actions indicated his growing dissociation from Zionism and the State of Israel. In 1978 *Foreign Relations of the U.S. 1950*, Vol. 5, *The Near East, South Asia and Africa* was published, consisting of nearly 2,000 previously top-secret documents of the U.S. State Department. The publication revealed that in 1950 Goldmann – then president of the WJC – told the State Department that he would use his influence to prevent American Jews from exerting pressure on the U.S. government with regard to its policy toward Israel.

BIBLIOGRAPHY: J. Draenger, *Nachum Goldmann*, 2 vols. (Ger., 1959, Fr., 1956); A. Carlebach, *Sefer ha-Demuyyot* (1959), 172–5; R. Vogel (ed.), *The German Path to Israel* (1969).

GOLDMANN, SIDNEY (1903–1983), U.S. jurist and Jewish civic leader. When he died, an editorial in the local (Trenton) newspaper said that Goldmann was a respected historian, a community leader of tremendous stature, and a brilliant judge. Born in Trenton, New Jersey, of immigrant parents, Goldmann graduated from Harvard College with a brilliant record as a mathematician. After graduating from Harvard Law School in 1927, he practiced law in Trenton, where he was appointed city attorney and acting city manager. From 1942 to 1944 he was executive secretary to Governor Charles Edison. He resigned this position to become New Jersey State Librarian, and after three years he became head of the New Jersey State Archives and History Bureau. In 1947, when work began on a new constitution for the State of New Jersey, he became librarian and archivist for the State Constitutional Convention and chairman of the Governor's Commission for Preparatory Research for the Constitutional Convention, and at the same time he became a member of the New Jersey Commission of Revision of Statutes. At the end of the convention, he edited its proceedings in five volumes. His contributions to the new constitution of the State of New Jersey were inestimable.

In 1949 Goldmann started a new career. He was appointed Standing Master of the New Jersey Supreme Court, and two years later he was named a judge of the state's Superior Court, and in 1951 he was assigned to its Appellate Division. From 1954 to 1971 he served as presiding judge of the court, and for two years he was also the court's administrative judge. He retired in 1971, at age 68. He then became a member of the Supreme Court Committee on opinions and chairman of the State Election Law Enforcement Commission. He served frequently as special hearing commissioner in important public-interest cases. He edited 116 volumes of court cases and 43 volumes of New Jersey Equity Reports. When he retired from the bench in 1971, he estimated that he had written over 2,000 judicial opinions.

Goldmann was known as a progressive judge. While giving due weight to judicial precedents, he was not timid about striking out along a new path, and at least one of his opinions was cited with approval several times by the United States Supreme Court.

Goldmann was active in Trenton's public affairs as a trustee of the Public Library, head of the city's Council of Social Agencies, president of the Trenton Council of Human Relations, cofounder of the Trenton Symphony Orchestra, coauthor of a history of the city – indeed, he was identified with almost every aspect of the civic life of his community.

At the same time he was Trenton's leading Jewish citizen. He served as president of the Jewish Community Center, the Jewish Federation, Jewish Family Service, and the home for the aged. He was active in the American Jewish Committee and was a life member of its Board of Governors.

A measure of the esteem in which he was held may be seen in the fact that when he retired from the bench, three former governors spoke at the dinner in his honor.

[Milton Ridvas Konvitz (2nd ed.)]

GOLDMARK, Viennese and U.S. family. JOSEPH GOLDMARK (1819–1881), Austrian revolutionary leader and U.S. physician and chemist, was born in the province of Warsaw. He studied at Vienna University (1838), entered medical school in 1840, and took a research post in chemistry in 1845. When revolution broke out in Vienna in 1848 Goldmark was a hospital intern. He enlisted in the Academic Legion, became president of the Students Union, and was elected to the Reichstag. Accused of complicity in the murder of Minister of War Latour (for which he was later sentenced to death in absentia), Goldmark fled the country, and in 1850 left France for New York. In 1868 he was acquitted after voluntarily returning to Austria to stand trial on the murder charge. Goldmark first practiced as a physician in New York but achieved greater prominence through the practical application of his knowledge of chemistry. In 1857 he took out a patent for manufacturing mercury compound, and in 1859 he established a highly successful factory for making percussion caps and cartridges. Of his ten children, one married Louis D. *Brandeis and another Felix *Adler. A third daughter, PAULINE GOLDMARK (1874–1962), was a well-known social worker and served as secretary of the national and New York consumer leagues. A son, HENRY GOLDMARK (1857–1941), was a civil engineer engaged in railroad construction, and was the designer of the locks for the Panama Canal. The composer KARL *GOLDMARK was a half brother of Joseph Goldmark. RUBIN GOLDMARK (1872–1936),

U.S. musician, nephew of Karl Goldmark, was born in New York. Moving to Colorado for reasons of health, he directed the Conservatory of Music at Colorado College from 1895 to 1901. From 1902 he lived in New York, teaching piano and harmony and giving numerous lecture recitals throughout the United States and Canada. In 1911 he became director of the department of theory of the New York College of Music, and in 1924 head of the department of composition of the Juilliard Graduate School. While Goldmark was known in his day as a composer (in 1910 his piano quartet won the Paderewski Chamber Music Prize), his influence as a teacher was more considerable. His pupils included Aaron *Copland, George *Gershwin, and Efrem *Zimbalist, and he was highly respected for his intellectual honesty, artistic integrity, and broad general culture. In 1956 City College, New York, named its music building in his honor.

BIBLIOGRAPHY: J. Goldmark, *Pilgrims of '48* (1930); *New York Times* (March 7, 1936); DAB, 22 (1958), 249–50; Grove, Dict, 3 (1954[5]), 699–701; MGG, 5 (1956), 481–5; O. Thompson (ed.), *Cyclopedia of Music and Musicians* (1956[7]), 682–3; Baker, Biog Dict (1958[5]), 583–4.

GOLDMARK, KARL (1830–1915), composer. Goldmark, the son of a cantor in the small town of Keszthely, was sent to study in Vienna. He was financed by his half-brother Joseph, who, however, was involved in the revolutionary activities of 1848 and had to leave the country. Karl himself was led out to be shot as a rebel, but was saved by the intervention of a friend. He settled in Vienna as a teacher, conductor, and composer, and displayed his great talent for orchestration in the overture *Sakuntala* (1865) and his *Laendliche Hochzeit* (1876) symphony. His opera *Die Koenigin von Saba* (1875) with a libretto by S.H. *Mosenthal, on which he worked for ten years, was an immediate success in Vienna and many other cities. Goldmark wrote other operas that had limited success, violin concertos, chamber music, choral music and songs. For a short time he was the teacher of Sibelius, and did much to encourage the performance of Wagner in Austria. His autobiography, *Erinnerungen aus meinem Leben* (1922), was translated into English in 1927 as *Notes from the Life of a Viennese Composer*.

BIBLIOGRAPHY: O. Keller, *Karl Goldmark* (Ger., 1901); MGG; Riemann-Gurlitt; Grove, Dict; Baker, Biog Dict.

[Marc Rozelaar]

GOLDMARK, PETER CARL (1906–1977), U.S. television engineer. Born in Hungary, Goldmark went to the U.S. in 1933 and joined CBS as chief TV engineer in 1936, becoming president of its laboratories division in 1954. He developed systems of color television, one of which was adopted for a time in New York in 1951.

GOLDSCHEID, RUDOLF (1870–1932), Austrian sociologist and pacifist. Born in Vienna, where he lived throughout his life, Goldscheid was representative of a strongly ethically oriented group whose interest was in the problems of sociology and social philosophy. A cofounder of the German Sociological Society ("Deutsche Gesellschaft fuer Soziologie," 1909), he sided with the approach of the "Kathedersozialisten" (academic social reformers) against Max Weber's emphasis on a strictly objective, "value-free" orientation in the social sciences. As editor of the *Friedenswarte*, he was one of the most influential European pacifists. He was also editor of the *Annalen fuer Natur-und Kulturphilosophie*. His publications include *Zur Ethik des Gesamtwillens* (1902), *Verelendungs-oder Meliorationstheorie* (1906), *Monismus und Politik* (1912), *Hoeherentwicklung und Menschenoekonomie* (1911), *Frauenfrage und Menschenoekonomie* (1913), and *Staatssozialismus und Staatskapitalismus* (1917).

ADD. BIBLIOGRAPHY: NDB, vol. 6 (1964), 607; G. Witrisal, *Der Soziallamarckismus von Rudolf Goldscheid – Ein milieutheoretischer Denker zwischen humanitärem Engagement und Sozialdarwinismus* (2004).

[Werner J. Cahnman]

GOLDSCHMIDT, ERNST DANIEL (1895–1972), librarian and scholar of Jewish liturgy. Goldschmidt was born in Koenigshuette (now Chorzow, Poland), where his father was rabbi. He served from 1926 to 1935 as librarian in the Prussian State Library, Berlin. Immigrating to Palestine in 1936, he joined the staff of the Jewish National and University Library (1936–62). Goldschmidt prepared critical editions of various liturgical texts. His various Passover *Haggadot* (with German translation, introduction, and notes, 1936, 1937; Hebrew, 1947, 1960[2]) became very popular; the *Haggadah* by N.N. Glatzer (Eng., 1953, 1969[2]) is based on Goldschmidt's work. In 1959 his edition of Maimonides' prayer text appeared; it was followed by *Siddur Tefillat Yisrael* (two rites) in 1964; *Seliḥot* according to both the Lithuanian and Polish rites in 1965; *Kinot* (liturgy for the Ninth of Av, Polish rite) in 1968; S.D. Luzzatto's introduction to his edition of the *Maḥzor Roma* was reissued by Goldschmidt (1966) with notes and an essay on the Roman rite. His edition of the High Holiday *maḥzor* (1970), which is a compendium of all the Ashkenazi rites, is of particular importance.

[Alexander Carlebach]

GOLDSCHMIDT, GUIDO (1850–1915), Austrian organic chemist. Goldschmidt was born in Trieste. From 1874 to 1891 he worked at the University of Vienna, becoming professor there in 1890. In 1891 he became professor of chemistry at the German University of Prague. In 1907 he was elected rector of the university, but declined to accept the position, partly because he thought that it might precipitate antisemitic manifestations. He returned to the University of Vienna in 1911. He was one of the earliest organic chemists to elucidate the structure of an alkaloid, in his case papaverine; later he worked on other alkaloids, on polynuclear hydrocarbons (fluoranthene and others), on aldehyde condensations, etc.

BIBLIOGRAPHY: *Berichte der Deutschen Chemischen Gesellschaft*, 49 (1916), 893–932; *Chemiker-Zeitung*, 39 (1915), 649; *Proceedings of the American Academy of Arts and Science*, 77 (1950).

[Samuel Aaron Miller]

GOLDSCHMIDT, HANS (1861–1923), German industrial chemist. He was born in Berlin, and was awarded his doctorate at Heidelberg in 1886. He became a partner with his brother in the firm of tin smelters and metallurgists founded by his father in Essen. In 1894 he invented the "Thermit" process, still used for welding heavy sections of iron and steel. Although industrial chemists were not really welcome in German learned societies, he became chairman of the Bunsengesellschaft fuer Angewandte Physikalische Chemie and of the Liebig Stipendien Verein.

[Samuel Aaron Miller]

GOLDSCHMIDT, HEINRICH JACOB (1857–1937), chemist. Born in Prague, Goldschmidt became professor at Heidelberg in 1896 and was appointed professor of chemistry at Oslo University in 1900. In 1929 he was back in Goettingen, but returned to Oslo when the Nazis came to power. He was the first Jew to receive the Norwegian Order of St. Olaf. His research centered on organic and physical chemistry, his best-known work being the constitution of aromatic compounds and the kinetics of reactions in organic chemistry.

GOLDSCHMIDT (née **Benas**), **HENRIETTE** (1825–1920), German suffragette and educator; wife of Rabbi Abraham Meir Goldschmidt of Leipzig. She was one of the founders of the German Women's League (Allgemeiner Deutscher Frauenverein) in 1865, organized petitions on behalf of women's rights to higher education and entry in professions (1867), and was a signatory to a petition to the Reichstag for protecting children born out of wedlock. In 1871 she founded the Society for Family Education and for People's Welfare (Verein fuer Familienerziehung und Volkswohl) in Leipzig, and was instrumental in the establishment of a municipal educational institution which eventually comprised kindergartens, a seminary for kindergarten teachers, and a vocational school for girls with teachers' training courses. In 1911 she founded the first institution of higher education for girls in Germany. Henriette Goldschmidt wrote *Die Frauenfrage, eine Kulturfrage* (1870), as well as on education, publicizing the ideas of Froebel. Her works include *Was ich von Froebel lernte und lehrte* (1909).

BIBLIOGRAPHY: H. Lange and G. Baeumer (eds.), *Handbuch der Frauenbewegung* (1901), index; J. Siebe and J. Pruefer, *Henriette Goldschmidt…* (Ger., 1922); M. Mueller, *Frauen im Dienste Froebels* (1928). **ADD. BIBLIOGRAPHY:** A. Kemp, "Henriette Goldschmidt – Vom Frauenrecht zur Kindererziehung," in: *Judaica Lipsiensia* (1993), 33–53; I.M. Fassmann, *Juedinnen in der deutschen Frauenbewegungen 1865–1919* (*Haskala – wissenschaftliche Abhandlungen*, vol. 6) (1996).

[Otto Immanuel Spear]

GOLDSCHMIDT, HERMANN (1802–1866), French astronomer and artist. Born in Frankfurt, Goldschmidt studied painting in Munich and in 1836 settled in Paris where he became eminent as a vivid painter of historical events and portraits. In spite of his great artistic activity, astronomy became his hobby and love. An enthusiastic observer of the sky, Goldschmidt worked with simple devices and modest optical instruments. In the nine years between 1852 and 1861 he discovered 14 asteroids (or minor planets as these were then called). He also observed variable stars, double stars, comets, nebulae, and in 1860, in Spain, a total solar eclipse; his report was accompanied by three impressive oil paintings. In 1857 he received the Cross of the Legion of Honor and in 1861 the Royal Astronomical Society in London awarded him its Gold Medal.

[Arthur Beer]

GOLDSCHMIDT, HUGO (1859–1920), musicologist. Born in Breslau, Goldschmidt was co-director of the Scharwenka-Klindworth Conservatory in Berlin and subsequently professor at this conservatory until he retired because of ill health. Goldschmidt was an authority on the art of singing and on early operatic history. His writings include *Die italienische Gesangsmethode des 17. Jahrhunderts* (1890), *Handbuch der deutschen Gesangspaedagogik* (1896), *Die Musikaesthetik des 18. Jahrhunderts und ihre Beziehungen zu seinem Kunstschaffen* (1915), and *Studien zur Geschichte der italienischen Oper im 17. Jahrhundert* (2 vols., 1901–04), which has remained a basic reference work.

GOLDSCHMIDT, JAKOB (1882–1955), banker, born in Eldagsen, Hanover. His parents Marcus and Lina Bachrach Goldschmidt could not afford to send him to university, and he became an apprentice at the Hanover banking house of H. Oppenheimer. Thanks to his exceptional talents, he was able to work his way up and make a fortune in the banking business. In 1910 he formed his own brokerage firm, Schwartz, Goldschmidt & Company, and became one of Germany's leading bankers. In 1918 he became managing director of the Nationalbank fuer Deutschland which later merged with the Deutsche Nationalbank and the Darmstaedter Bank to form the Darmstaedter und Nationalbank (Danatbank). Owing to his position at the bank, which played an important role as a financier of industry, he sat on the boards of a wide range of companies that included shipping, steel, power, mining, insurance, and aviation. Although regarded as an upstart and speculator by his more traditional banking colleagues, he nevertheless exercised great influence in Weimar economic affairs. He was also a major art collector, and also was devoted to Jewish causes, rescuing the *Encyclopedia Judaica* from financial collapse in 1926. In July 1931 the Danatbank fell prey to the fraudulent actions of the Lahusen brothers, who ran one of its main customers, the North German Wool Company. The Danat was forced to close its doors after the other great banks abandoned it, while the Reichsbank would not grant it support either. Having become a major target of Nazi attacks, Goldschmidt left Germany in 1933 and settled in the United States in 1936, where he had a successful if more modest career in business. He once again became an art collector, and supported many philanthropies and cultural institutions, including the New York Metropolitan Museum and the Museum of Modern Art.

[Joachim O. Ronall / Gerald Feldman (2nd ed.)]

GOLDSCHMIDT, JOHANNA SCHWABE (1806–1884), author and social activist. Goldschmidt was born in Hamburg. Her father, Marcus Herz Schwabe, was one of the founders of the Hamburg Reform Temple in 1817 and Johanna attended its first confirmation class. Johanna married Moritz Goldschmidt in 1827. The couple had eight children and their care effectively kept Johanna from any outside activity for 20 years. In 1847 she launched a career as a writer and social activist with her first book, *Rebekka and Amalia*, written as a series of letters between a young Jew, Rebekka, and a Christian aristocrat named Amalia. The general topic of the work was the problem of Jewish conversion and assimilation, but in one of its chapters, Goldschmidt focused on a plan for an organization in which rich women would help poorer women to improve themselves by means of lectures and instruction. Within one year of the publication of *Rebekka and Amalia*, Johanna Goldschmidt, together with her friend Amalie Westendarp, founded the Women's Association to Combat and Reduce Religious Prejudice, an organization that promoted the early, non-sectarian education of children. Goldschmidt's second book, *Mothers' Worries and Mothers' Joys* (1849), led to more social activism and the founding of a seminary to train teachers in the new methods pioneered by educator Friedrich Froebel. In this project she worked closely with liberal Christian women. Goldschmidt remained active in both the Women's Association and the seminary and also continued writing sporadically. Her play, "A Look at the Family," opened in Hamburg in 1864.

BIBLIOGRAPHY: I. Fassmann, *Juedinnen in der deutschen Frauenbewegung* (1996); M. Keyserling, *Die juedischen Frauen in der Geschichte, Literatur und Kunst* (1879; repr. 1991); E. Taitz, S. Henry, and C.Tallan, *The JPS Guide to Jewish Women: 600 B.C.E.–1900 C.E.* (2003).

[Emily Taitz (2nd ed.)]

GOLDSCHMIDT, LAZARUS (1871–1950), scholar, bibliophile, and translator of the Talmud into German. Goldschmidt, who was born in Plongian, Lithuania, studied first at the Slobodka yeshivah at Kaunas (Kovno) and later at the universities of Berlin and Strasbourg. His early studies were devoted to Ethiopian language and its literature. He published the Ethiopic version of the Book of Enoch (I Enoch) with Hebrew translation (1892) and *Biblioteca Ethiopica* (1895). Goldschmidt published an edition of the *Sefer Yeẓirah* (1894), a Hebrew translation of the Koran (1916), and prepared a new edition of Jacob Levy's *Woerterbuch zum Talmud und Midrasch* (1924). On the rise of Hitler to power in 1933 Goldschmidt left Germany for England and lived in London. His bibliographical works include *Hebrew Incunables* (1948), and the *Earliest Editions of the Hebrew Bible* (1950). Some of his works were published under the pseudonym Arselaj bar Bargelaj.

Goldschmidt's major contribution was his translation of the entire Babylonian Talmud into German. It appeared in two editions, a nine-volume work containing the original text and variant readings (1897–1935) and a 12-volume edition without the original text (1929–36). This translation, which was severely criticized by David Zvi *Hoffman (ZHB 1, 1896), was nevertheless considered to be an important and standard work in talmudic studies. Goldschmidt also prepared a subject concordance to the Babylonian Talmud which was published posthumously (1959). He also published a facsmile edition of the Hamburg manuscript of the order *Nezikin* of the Babylonian Talmud (1913). A controversial figure who engaged in sharp personal polemics against leading scholars of his time (Immanuel Loew, David Hoffman, and others), he published a number of pamphlets attacking his adversaries. In his youth, he published as a practical joke an Aramaic text entitled *Baraita de-Ma'aseh Bereshit* (1894), which he claimed to be an old *midrash*. Later he admitted that this was a parody. Goldschmidt was a collector of rare books. Because of his forced emigration to London in 1933 the Royal Library in Copenhagen bought his collection, which is known as the Goldschmidt Collection..

BIBLIOGRAPHY: E. Neufeld, in: *Synagogue Review*, 16 (Dec. 16, 1941), no. 4.

GOLDSCHMIDT, MEIR ARON, (1819–1887), Danish novelist, political writer, and journalist. Born in Vordingborg, Zealand, Goldschmidt was sent to Copenhagen for a year as a child and was impressed by the Jewish life of the capital. Although he matriculated in 1836, religious prejudice prevented him from studying medicine. He accordingly turned to journalism and in 1837 founded a liberal provincial weekly, *Nestved Ugeblad* (later renamed *Sjællandsposten*), whose policy brought him a heavy fine and a year's censorship. He later moved to Copenhagen and in 1840 founded *Corsaren*, a successful satirical weekly with a radical outlook. The paper attacked Denmark's conservative establishment, especially the absolute monarchy and the powerful civil service. Goldschmidt began his literary career with the novel *En Jøde* (1845; *The Jews of Denmark*, 1852). This told the story of a Danish Jew whose break with traditional Orthodoxy provokes his father's curse. His romance with a Christian girl ends unhappily and the hero ultimately becomes a moneylender. *En Jøde* contains some picturesque descriptions of Jewish customs and festivals, as does the story *Aron of Esther* in the collection *Fortællinger* ("Tales," 1846). During the years 1847–59 Goldschmidt published the periodical *Nord og Syd*, which largely consisted of his own articles on literature, theater, art, and politics. After the failure of the magazine *Hjemme og Ude*, which appeared briefly in 1861, he moved to England, but returned to Denmark in 1863, resolved to abandon his political involvements. The central figure of his long novel *Hjemløs* (1853–57), which he himself adapted into English as *Homeless, or a Poet's Inner Life* (1861), is a Danish gentile, but Goldschmidt introduces a cultured English Jew who teaches the hero that happiness and misery are balanced in each person's life and that men's sins must be atoned for on earth. The novelist called this ethical system "Nemesis," and it dominates his later works. These include two novels, *Arvingen* (Eng., *The Heir,* both 1865), and *Ravnen* ("The Raven," 1867); three Jewish short stories, "*Maser*" (1858), "*Avrohmche Nattergal*" (1871; English version in *Denmark's Best Stories*, 1928), and "*Levi og Ibald*" (1883); and *Livserindringer og Resultater* ("Memoirs and Results," 2 vols., 1877). He was an outstanding storyteller and the worldly yet pious and decent hero of his stories, Simon Levy, is one of the outstanding figures of Danish fiction.

BIBLIOGRAPHY: G. Brandes, *Samlete Skrifter,* 2 (1900), 447–68; H. Kyrre, *M.A. Goldschmidt* (Danish, 1919); *Dansk Biografisk Leksikon*, 8 (1936).

[Frederik Julius Billeskov-Jansen]

GOLDSCHMIDT, NEIL EDWARD (1941–), U.S. politician. Goldschmidt was born in Eugene, Oregon, and graduated from the University of Oregon in 1963 and from the University of California at Berkeley Law School in 1967. Entering political life at an early age, in his twenties he became a city commissioner of Portland, Oregon (1971–73). In 1973, at age 32, he became mayor of Portland, the youngest mayor of a major U.S. city, serving until 1979. He was referred to by Richard Corner, mayor of Peoria, Illinois, then president of the United States Conference of Mayors, as "one of the best of a new breed." In July 1979 he was appointed secretary of transportation by President Carter and served until the end of the Carter administration. Goldschmidt returned to Oregon in 1981, where he served as international vice president of Nike until 1985. In 1986–87 he was president of the running shoe company's Canadian subsidiary, Nike Canada.

Goldschmidt served as governor of Oregon from 1987 to 1991. He helped create in 1991 the Oregon Children's Foundation, and SMART (Start Making a Reader Today), which places 10,000 volunteers in Oregon schools to read to children. He also established the law and consulting firm Neil Goldschmidt, Inc. in Portland, specializing in international business. Goldschmidt was an active member of the local Reform congregation.

In 2004 he resigned from his positions with the Oregon Board of Higher Education, the Oregon Electric Utility Company, and the state bar. His resignation was prompted by an imminent newspaper article that was to reveal his sexual misconduct while he was mayor of Portland. On May 6, 2004, Goldschmidt announced – and apologized – publicly that in 1975 he had engaged in a nine-month sexual relationship with a 14-year-old girl. In his statement he said, "For almost thirty years, I have lived with enormous guilt and shame about this relationship.... I have sat in my place of worship each year at Yom Kippur ... searching for personal peace."

Goldschmidt wrote *The Oregon Book of Juvenile Issues* (with G. Johnson, 1989).

[Ruth Beloff (2nd ed.)]

GOLDSCHMIDT, RICHARD BENEDICT (1878–1958), German geneticist. Goldschmidt, who was born in Frankfurt, became a lecturer at Munich University in 1904. In 1913 he was selected to head a genetics department at the newly organized Kaiser Wilhelm Institute for Experimental Biology in Berlin. Before assuming his duties he went to Japan to obtain material for his studies on sex determination in the gypsy moth. World War I broke out while he was on his way home; as a result he spent three of the war years as a visiting professor at Yale University and the fourth interned as an enemy alien. Returning to Berlin after the war, he worked at the Kaiser Wilhelm Institute from 1919 to 1936, except for two years as a visiting professor at the University of Tokyo (1924–26). In 1936, as a result of the Nazi persecution, he emigrated to the United States. He was professor of zoology at the University of California in Berkeley until his retirement in 1948. In the course of his studies on the gypsy moth Goldschmidt discovered that sex is determined by a balance between genetic factors for maleness and femaleness present in all individuals. He found that the strength of these factors differed in different geographic races, and he was able to produce predictable degrees of intersexuality by appropriate interracial hybridizations. These findings led him to conclude that the genes are responsible for determining the rate of physiological processes. He rejected the concept of linearly linked unitary genes; instead he regarded the chromosome as a single giant molecule. Mutations, in his view, were caused by breakages and rearrangements of the chromosomal material ("position effects"). Goldschmidt's views on evolution were also unorthodox; he maintained that new types evolved not through the selection and accumulation of small genetic differences but rather by major, single-step mutations ("hopeful monsters") that produced drastic changes in development. Although he stood almost alone as a dissenter, he was widely respected as a brilliant critic and eloquent polemicist. Goldschmidt's scientific works include *Mechanismus und Physiologie der Geschlechtsbestimmung* (1920; *The Mechanism and Physiology of Sex Determination*, 1923); *Physiologische Theorie der Vererbung* (1927; *Physiological Genetics*, 1938); *The Material Basis of Evolution* (1940); *Theoretical Genetics* (1955); and a number of textbooks, among them *Ascaris* (Ger., 1922; *Ascaris, The Biologist's Story of Life*, 1937). He also wrote *Portraits from Memory: Recollections of a Zoologist* (1956) and the autobiographical *In and Out of the Ivory Tower* (1960).

BIBLIOGRAPHY: E. Caspari, in: *Genetics* (Jan. 1960), 1–5; A.V. Howard (ed.), *Chamber's Dictionary of Scientists* (1958), 191–2.

[Mordecai L. Gabriel]

GOLDSCHMIDT, RICHARD HELLMUTH (1883–1968), German psychologist. Born in Posen, Goldschmidt became professor of psychology at Muenster in 1919. Just before World War II he managed to leave for England, where he was a fellow of Oxford University's Institute of Psychology from 1939 to 1945. He returned to the university at Muenster in 1949, remaining for the rest of his career. His early research dealt with the psychology of visual perception with regard to color schemes. He published *Postulat der Farbwandelspiele* (1928), and later wrote *Ahnung und Einsicht* (1967). Other areas of Goldschmidt's scientific interest were the psychology of religion and aesthetics.

GOLDSCHMIDT, VICTOR (1853–1933), German crystallographer and inventor. Goldschmidt, who was born in Mainz, was appointed teacher at Heidelberg University in 1888, and professor in 1893. Among his publications were *Index der Krystallformen der Mineralien* (3 vols., 1887–91), a catalog of the forms on the crystals of minerals, and *Krystallographische Winkeltabellen* (1897), a collection of tables of angles in crystal formation. His chief work, however, was his *Atlas der Krystallformen* (1913–23), a compilation of all published figures of crystals of minerals, in nine volumes. His researches into number series appearing in crystal symbols resulted in his formulation of a theory of number and harmony involving a consideration of musical and color harmonies. Goldschmidt was the inventor of the bicircular goniometer, used in measuring angles. He was baptized.

BIBLIOGRAPHY: L. Milch, in: *Festschrift Victor Goldschmidt* (1928), includes bibliography; C. Palache, in: *American Mineralogist*, 19 (1934), 106–11 (includes bibliography); L.J. Spencer, in: *Mineralogical Magazine*, 24 (1936), 287–9; *Neue Deutsche Biographie*, 6 (1964).

GOLDSCHMIDT, VICTOR MORITZ (1888–1947), Norwegian mineralogist, crystallographer, and geochemist. Goldschmidt was born in Zurich, son of Heinrich Jacob Goldschmidt (1857–1937) who became professor of chemistry at Oslo University in 1901. In 1914 Victor Goldschmidt was appointed professor of crystallography, mineralogy, and petrography at Oslo University. In 1929 he was appointed director of the mineralogical-petrographical institute at Goettingen, but in 1935 left Nazi Germany to return to Oslo. He was chairman of the Norwegian Friends of the Hebrew University in 1937. After the invasion of Norway in 1940, Goldschmidt was hunted by the Nazis and was arrested on several occasions. The underground succeeded in smuggling him to Sweden in December 1942 and from there he was flown to England, where he devoted himself to work connected with atomic energy. He returned to Oslo in 1946. Goldschmidt was one of the great mineralogists and crystallographers of his generation and is recognized as the founder of the new science of geochemistry. Already in his doctoral thesis in 1911 on the "Phenomena of Metamorphosis" he established a basis for classifying the metamorphic minerals according to general physico-chemical laws, proposed the concept of "stability limits" of minerals, and developed the idea of mineral facies that became the central idea in mineralogy-petrography. Later he developed the notion of type relationships of rocks and laid the foundations of genetic classification of magnetic rocks. Besides these main fields of work, he also explained the distribution of chemical elements in the earth's crust and defined the laws of distribution that result from the natural factors in elements themselves. Goldschmidt was also interested in problems of practical research including the formation of mineral pigments, the production of aluminum from silicates, the use of biotite as a fertilizer, and the use of olivine as a raw material for the production of materials resistant to chemical and heat reactions. Goldschmidt's main works were *Die Kontaktmetamorphose im Kristianiagebiet* (1911); *Geologisch-petrographische Studien…* (5 vols. 1912–21); *Geochemische Verteilungsgesetze der Elemente* (9 parts, 1923–38).

BIBLIOGRAPHY: D. Oftedal, in: Geological Society of America, *Proceedings 1947* (1948), 149–54, includes bibliography; C.E. Tilley, in: Royal Society of London, *Obituary Notices…*, 17 (1948), 51–66; Norwegian Academy of Science, *Årbok 1947* (1948), 85–102.

[Yakov K. Bentor]

GOLDSMID, English family, descended from AARON GOLDSMID (d. 1782), who settled in London in the second quarter of the 18th century and was active in the affairs of the Great Synagogue. BENJAMIN GOLDSMID (1755–1808) and ABRAHAM GOLDSMID (1756–1810), sons of Aaron, became prominent financiers in the City of London during the French revolutionary wars, when their competition with the old-established non-Jewish bankers resulted in the issue of treasury loans on terms much more favorable to the government, and thereby initiated a new era in public finance. The brothers were active in the affairs of the Jewish community and in general philanthropy. They served in all the offices of the Great Synagogue and were associated with the establishment of both the Jews' Hospital and the Royal Naval Asylum. Their close familiarity with the sons of George III did much to break down social prejudice against Jews in England and to pave the way for emancipation. They were considered by Lord Nelson among his closest friends. Both of the brothers committed suicide. Their activity marked the displacement of the Sephardi element in London from their former hegemony. ALBERT GOLDSMID (1793–1861), Benjamin's son, entered the army in 1811. He fought in the Peninsular War at Waterloo, and reached the rank of major general. SIR ISAAC LYON GOLDSMID (1778–1859), son of Aaron Goldsmid's second son Asher, made a large fortune, partly by financing railway construction. He was made a baronet in 1841, being the first professing Jew to receive an English hereditary title. He was prominent in the struggle for Jewish emancipation in England and was one of the founders of the nonsectarian University College, London. He took a leading part in the establishment of the Reform synagogue. In 1846 he was named Baron de Palmeira by the king of Portugal. SIR FRANCIS HENRY GOLDSMID (1808–1878), the eldest son of Isaac Lyon, was the first Jewish barrister in England and for many years a member of Parliament, as was his brother FREDERICK DAVID GOLDSMID (1812–1866). SIR JULIAN GOLDSMID (1838–1896), the son of Frederick David, succeeded to the title and was for many years a member of Parliament and at one time deputy speaker. Like his father, he was also active in communal affairs as chairman of the Reform synagogue, of the *Anglo-Jewish Association, and others. On his death, the baronetcy was transferred to his cousin, Sir

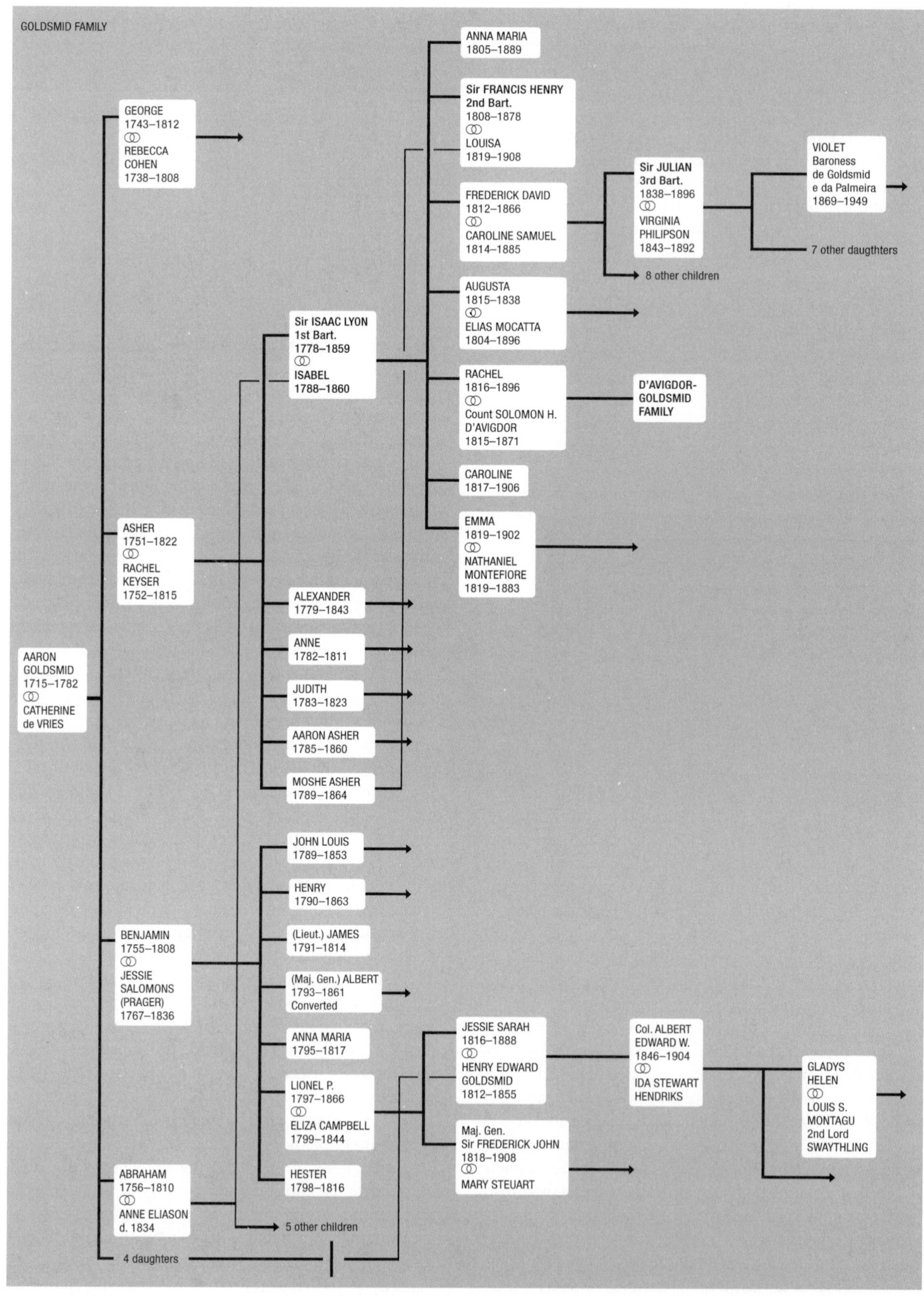
GOLDSMID FAMILY
AARON GOLDSMID 1715–1782 ⚭ CATHERINE de VRIES
GEORGE 1743–1812 ⚭ REBECCA COHEN 1738–1808
ASHER 1751–1822 ⚭ RACHEL KEYSER 1752–1815
BENJAMIN 1755–1808 ⚭ JESSIE SALOMONS (PRAGER) 1767–1836
ABRAHAM 1756–1810 ⚭ ANNE ELIASON d. 1834
4 daughters
Sir ISAAC LYON 1st Bart. 1778–1859 ⚭ ISABEL 1788–1860
ALEXANDER 1779–1843
ANNE 1782–1811
JUDITH 1783–1823
AARON ASHER 1785–1860
MOSHE ASHER 1789–1864
JOHN LOUIS 1789–1853
HENRY 1790–1863
(Lieut.) JAMES 1791–1814
(Maj. Gen.) ALBERT 1793–1861 Converted
ANNA MARIA 1795–1817
LIONEL P. 1797–1866 ⚭ ELIZA CAMPBELL 1799–1844
HESTER 1798–1816
5 other children
ANNA MARIA 1805–1889
Sir FRANCIS HENRY 2nd Bart. 1808–1878 ⚭ LOUISA 1819–1908
FREDERICK DAVID 1812–1866 ⚭ CAROLINE SAMUEL 1814–1885
AUGUSTA 1815–1838 ⚭ ELIAS MOCATTA 1804–1896
RACHEL 1816–1896 ⚭ Count SOLOMON H. D'AVIGDOR 1815–1871
CAROLINE 1817–1906
EMMA 1819–1902 ⚭ NATHANIEL MONTEFIORE 1819–1883
Sir JULIAN 3rd Bart. 1838–1896 ⚭ VIRGINIA PHILIPSON 1843–1892
8 other children
D'AVIGDOR-GOLDSMID FAMILY
VIOLET Baroness de Goldsmid e da Palmeira 1869–1949
7 other daugthters
JESSIE SARAH 1816–1888 ⚭ HENRY EDWARD GOLDSMID 1812–1855
Maj. Gen. Sir FREDERICK JOHN 1818–1908 ⚭ MARY STEUART
Col. ALBERT EDWARD W. 1846–1904 ⚭ IDA STEWART HENDRIKS
GLADYS HELEN ⚭ LOUIS S. MONTAGU 2nd Lord SWAYTHLING

Osmond *D'Avigdor. ANNA MARIA GOLDSMID (1805–1889), daughter of Isaac Lyon, made a name as philanthropist and poet. SIR FREDERICK JOHN GOLDSMID (1818–1908), who belonged to the baptized branch of the family, was a distinguished Orientalist, a major general in the army, constructed the first telegraph lines in Persia, and established the administrative system in the Congo (see also *D'Avigdor family).

BIBLIOGRAPHY: A.J. Prijs, *Pedigree of the Family Goldsmit-Cassel of Amsterdam, 1650–1750* (1937); Hyamson, in: JHSET, 17 (1951–52), 1–10; Emden, *ibid.*, 14 (1935–39), 225–46; D. Marks and A. Loewy, *Memoir of Sir Francis Henry Goldsmid* (1882); Cope, in: *Economica*, 9 (1942), 180–206. **ADD. BIBLIOGRAPHY:** ODNB online for Abraham Goldsmid, Benjamin Goldsmid, Sir Isaac Lyon Goldsmid, Sir Francis Henry Goldsmid, Anna Maria Goldsmid, Sir Frederick John Goldsmid; Bermant, *The Cousinhood*, 17–24, index; Jolles, *Directory of Distinguished British Jews* (2002), index; Katz, *Jews in Britain*, index.

[Cecil Roth]

GOLDSMID, ALBERT EDWARD WILLIAMSON (1846–1904), English soldier. Born at Poona, India, Goldsmid entered the British Army in 1866, reached the rank of colonel in 1894, and served with distinction in the Boer War. Born of a long-assimilated family connected with the illustrious *Goldsmid family by marriage (though he was not descended from it), he became attracted to Judaism in maturity and was henceforth active in the life of Anglo-Jewry. In 1892 he went temporarily to the Argentine to supervise the *Jewish Colonization Association (ICA) colonies established there by Baron de *Hirsch. He was one of the founders of the *Maccabeans and of the Jewish Lads Brigade (see *Scouting) in London. A prominent member of the English Ḥovevei Zion (see *Ḥibbat Zion) movement, as early as 1891 he advocated the revival of Hebrew as a spoken language, welcomed Herzl's proposals with enthusiasm, became an ardent Zionist, and was a member of the *El-Arish Commission in 1903. Herzl was deeply impressed by him and thought of him as occupying a high office in the Jewish State when it was established. Goldsmid is said to have been the model for George *Eliot's character Daniel Deronda.

BIBLIOGRAPHY: Fraenkel, in: *Herzl Yearbook*, 1 (1958), 145–53; N. Sokolow, *History of Zionism* (1919); index; T. Herzl, *Diaries*, ed. by M. Lowenthal (1956), index. **ADD. BIBLIOGRAPHY:** Bermant, *The Cousinhood*, 242–43.

[Cecil Roth]

GOLDSMID-STERN-SALOMONS, SIR DAVID LIONEL (1851–1925), British innovator in electronics and automobiles. He was born in London, the son of Philip Salomons (1796–1867) and the nephew of Sir David *Salomons; his mother was the daughter of Jacob *Montefiore. He was educated at Cambridge and, in 1873, succeeded his uncles as second baronet. Salomons was a barrister and a local government official, serving as mayor of Tunbridge Wells in 1895, but was wealthy enough to pursue full time his passion for mechanical and scientific research. This he did at his large private laboratory at his estate at Broomhill, Kent. Salomons took out numerous patents in the electrical field and was the author of *Electric Light Installations*, a textbook which went through many editions. He also served as vice president of the Institute of Electrical Engineers. He is best remembered, however, for his role as a pioneer of automobiles in England. In October 1895 he imported the second gasoline-driven car to appear in Britain, and he was responsible for removing many of the legal restrictions on the use of the motor car in England. He was also one of the founders of the Royal Automobile Club, the oldest British motoring body. He gained his triple surname in 1899 when he inherited a legacy from the relatives of his wife, a daughter of Hermann, Baron de *Stern, and added "Goldsmid-Stern" to his name.

BIBLIOGRAPHY: ODNB online.

[William D. Rubinstein (2nd ed.)]

GOLDSMITH, HORACE WARD (1894–1980), U.S. businessman and philanthropist. Goldsmith was born in Chicago, but moved to New York as a youth and in 1927 he bought a seat on the New York Stock Exchange and founded the brokerage firm of H.W. Goldsmith and Company. He held the Stock Exchange seat for half a century until his retirement in 1977 to Phoenix, Arizona, where he died.

Goldsmith was a generous benefactor of many Jewish institutions in the United States and Israel. Appointed a member of the international board of governors of the Technion, the Israel Institute of Technology, Haifa, he established the Goldsmith Institute of Industrial Microbiology there. Other benefactions in Israel included the Jerusalem Great Synagogue, the Hebrew University of Jerusalem, and the Grace Goldsmith Physical Education Center at Boys' Town Jerusalem. His benefactions in the United States included the Goldsmith Hall at the Jewish Theological Seminary, the Horace Goldsmith Mathematics Building at Brandeis University, and contributions to the Scholarship Foundation of NYU. He is said to have contributed at least $250,000 annually for the last 40 years of his life and in his will made provisions for further generous bequests.

GOLDSMITH, LEWIS (c. 1763–1846), English political journalist. Goldsmith, who was born in London of Portuguese Jewish descent, was never associated with Judaism and was probably baptized as a young man. His *The Crimes of Cabinets* (1805) censured the attempts to suppress the French Revolution. Later he took refuge in Paris where he established *The Argus*, an anti-English journal. The journal was suspended when he refused to attack the English royal family. Returning to England in 1809, he was tried for high treason but was acquitted. He then started the violently patriotic *Anti-Gallican* (subsequently *The British Monitor*), advocating the assassination of Napoleon. On the restoration of Louis XVIII, he returned to Paris where he became interpreter to the Tribunal of Commerce. Goldsmith published his *Statistics of France* in 1832. His daughter Georgiana (1807–1901) became the second wife of Baron Lyndhurst, Lord Chancellor of England, and a noted political hostess.

BIBLIOGRAPHY: *Nouvelle Biographie Générale*, s.v.; Rubens, in: JHSET, 19 (1955–59), 39–43. **ADD. BIBLIOGRAPHY:** ODNB online.

[Cecil Roth]

GOLDSMITH, RAYMOND WILLIAM (1904–1988), U.S. economist. Born in Brussels, Belgium, Goldsmith received a Ph.D. from the University of Berlin (1927) and then studied at the London School of Economics and Political Science. He lived in the U.S. from 1930 and during the years 1934–48 he served with the U.S. Securities and Exchange Commission, the War Production Board, and the National Bureau of Economic Research. He was U.S. adviser on the 1946 German currency reform and on the 1947–48 Austrian treaty negotiations. Goldsmith became professor of economics, first at New York University (1958–59) and later at Yale (from 1960). Money and banking were his major interests. In an effort to find the means by which to measure wealth, he devised such methods as balance sheets, which tracked the flow of capital among various segments of the economy.

His works include *The Changing Structure of American Banking* (1933), *A Study of Saving in the United States* (3 vols., 1955–56), *Financial Intermediaries in the American Economy* (1958), *The National Wealth of the United States in the Postwar Period* (1962), *Financial Structure and Development* (1969), *The National Balance Sheet of the United States, 1953–1980* (1982), *The Financial Development of India, Japan, and the United States* (1983), and *Comparative National Balance Sheets: A Study of Twenty Countries, 1688–1979* (1985).

[Joachim O. Ronall / Ruth Beloff (2nd ed.)]

GOLDSMITH, SAMUEL ABRAHAM (1893–1987), U.S. social worker. Goldsmith was born in New York. Following service as a field worker for the YMHA and the Jewish Welfare Board in New York City, Goldsmith served for ten years as executive director of the Bureau of Jewish Social Research. In this capacity he conducted detailed surveys of Jewish social services in many American cities. Their findings and recommendations profoundly affected the direction of American Jewish social and communal work. In 1930 Goldsmith was appointed executive director of the Jewish Federation and Jewish Welfare Fund of Chicago, a position he held until his retirement. Shortly after accepting that position, he helped organize the Community Fund of Chicago, a forerunner of the United Way. He served as president of the National Conference on Jewish Social Welfare (1928–29). During the 1930s he was a charter member of the Joint Emergency Relief Fund and chairman of the Health Division of the Council of Social Agencies. In 1936 he helped establish and served as executive director of the Jewish Welfare Fund of Chicago, which raised funds for European Jews during the Holocaust. The JWF merged with other organizations, becoming in 1950 the Jewish Federation of Metropolitan Chicago. Goldsmith served as its executive vice president. An active leader and speaker within the American Jewish community, Goldsmith encouraged American Jewry to support the needs of Jews abroad and the development of a modern State of Israel.

[Kenneth D. Roseman / Ruth Beloff (2nd ed.)]

GOLDSMITHS AND SILVERSMITHS. The two closely related professions of refining, casting, beating, and filigreeing silver and gold have occupied Jewish craftsmen uninterruptedly from biblical times to the present. The highly skilled nature of the work, the relatively constant value of the two precious metals and the universal demand for artifacts made of them, their ready transportability, and not least, their use throughout the ages in Jewish ritual and ceremonial objects, all help account for the fact that Jewish goldsmiths and silversmiths can be found in almost every period of Jewish history wherever Jewish communities existed. However, because their creations were so often melted down or plundered for their metallic worth, no identifiable work of any Jewish craftsman has survived from before late medieval times, except for the artifacts and cult objects that have been excavated.

Antiquity

Apart from archaeological finds – ear and finger rings, anklets, pendants, beads, eating and drinking utensils, and figures of gods and goddesses such as those uncovered at Beth-Shean, Tell al-ʿAjjūl, and Tell al-Faraḥ – there is ample literary evidence from the Bible that both silver and gold were worked by Israelite craftsmen from the earliest times; indeed, according to the biblical narrative, the first two Jewish goldsmiths and silversmiths were the builders of the Tabernacle, *Bezalel and Oholiab. The many biblical injunctions against making silver and gold idols point in themselves to the widespread manufacture of such objects from the time of the Israelite conquest on, as borne out also by stories like that of Micah and his idol of silver (Judg. 17) or Jeroboam's golden calves (I Kings 12). Numerous passages in the Bible refer to silver and gold artifacts of all kinds and to the many silver and gold utensils in the Temple. Though neither of these metals was ever mined in Palestine, both were available throughout the ancient Near East; the Bible speaks of *Ophir and *Tarshish as sources, and this has been partly corroborated by a recently found eighth-century B.C.E. ostracon on which appear the words "gold from Ophir." Israelite craftsmen most probably learned to work both gold and silver directly from the Canaanites among whom they settled. In the time of Ezra and Nehemiah, to judge by two verses in the Book of Nehemiah (3:8, 31–32), they were organized into guilds. Such societies undoubtedly persisted later in the Second Temple period, and it is known that in the years preceding the destruction of the Temple goldsmiths occupied their own quarters in Jerusalem. The Mishnah (Mid. 3:8) and Josephus (Ant., 15:395) write of a golden vine with grape clusters "a marvel of size and artistry" adorning the Herodian Temple. Several references to Jewish goldsmiths and silversmiths occur in the Mishnah and Talmud. Rabbi

Eliezer, a *tanna* living in the first half of the second century, ruled that Jewish craftsmen could not make ornaments for idols but could supply gentile customers with "necklaces, earrings, and finger rings" – a clear indication that such artisans competed for the non-Jewish trade as well. The Talmud (Sot. 49b; Shab. 59a) twice refers to a specific piece of gold jewelry, the "city of Jerusalem" (*yerushalayim shel zahav*) or "city of gold," apparently a pendant, engraved with an illustration of a wall encircling a city, that was customarily given to young brides. The first record of Jewish gold- and silversmiths active outside Palestine comes from the description in Suk. 51b of the great synagogue of Alexandria. It is stated that various groups of artisans, among them silversmiths and goldsmiths, sat each in their own pews, "so that when a poor man [i.e., artisan] entered there, he recognized the members of his own craft and turned to them to find means for the maintenance of himself and his family." This presumably refers to organized guilds. That Alexandria continued to harbor many Jewish gold- and silversmiths as late as the eve of the Muslim conquest, by which time the Jewish population of the city had greatly dwindled, is known from the writings of the sixth-century monk and geographer Cosmas Indicopleustes, who also mentions an even greater concentration of such Jewish craftsmen in Medina, where, he writes, 300 Jewish gold- and silversmiths lived in one quarter of the city. Presumably this records the beginnings of a tradition of Jewish gold and silver work in the southern Arabian peninsula.

Middle Ages and Modern Times

Like the practice of *crafts in general by Jews in the Middle Ages, the intricate craft of the goldsmith and silversmith continued to be a widespread Jewish occupation south of the Pyrenees and in the Mediterranean lands, while there was little activity among Jews in this profession north of this demarcation line. The specific combination of skills and financial acumen needed for the goldsmith's trade is evidenced in the information that has been preserved about the plying of this craft by Jews in Muslim countries. The records of the *Genizah* of Cairo show that goldsmithing was a common, lucrative, and highly specialized profession of Jews in Egypt and the surrounding area as far as Aden in the 11th and 12th centuries. In Iraq, Persia, Yemen, and the Maghreb many of the goldsmiths were Jews. That this was a widespread Jewish occupation in Muslim countries may be explained by the contempt in which artisans were held by the Arabs. In pre-Islamic Arabia there was a tribe of Jewish goldsmiths, the Zuaynuga, who were defeated and forced to accept Islam by Muhammad. The preponderance of Jews in goldsmithing and silversmithing, particularly in the manufacture of jewelry, continued well into the modern period. In Baghdad, in 1844, 250 of 1,607 Jewish families employed in industry and trade were goldsmiths by profession. In Yemen in particular, the Jewish artisans attained a high standard of skill and artistry. Jews there even believed that the few Muslim goldsmiths were descendants of Jews who had been forcibly converted. The mass immigration to Israel after 1948 of the Jews of Yemen and other Arab countries helped to develop a local jewelry industry.

Jewish goldsmiths are among the first Jews mentioned in Muslim Spain, and are repeatedly referred to there in the following centuries. In Christian Spain Jewish goldsmiths were to be found in practically every sizable town; they were employed by the royal households and occupied their own row of shops in large cities like Tudela and Pamplona. The Augustinian eremites of Barcelona in 1399 commissioned a Jewish artisan to make them a silver reliquary. Jews manufactured Christian religious artifacts in violation of Jewish law and the antipope Benedict XIII in 1415 had to forbid Spanish Jews to produce such objects as goblets and crucifixes. Jewish silversmithing was expressly permitted in the 15th century: in Aragon in 1401 and in Castile in 1419. A magnificent pair of silver **rimmonim*, decorated with semiprecious stones and executed by a Spanish Jewish artist in Camarata (Sicily) in the 15th century, still survives in the Cathedral treasury in Palma de Mallorca. Delicate filigree work surrounds the horseshoe arched repoussé areas and the Hebrew inscriptions. The expulsion from Spain in 1492 left many *Marranos in the Iberian peninsula and Balearic islands who now engaged freely in silversmithing and goldsmithing. Numbers of the exiles from Spain and Portugal entered these crafts in the Ottoman Empire. This was recognizable particularly in Walachia where Jews sometimes even headed the silversmith guilds. In Ereẓ Israel, in particular in Safed, goldsmithing was considered one of the profitable crafts for Jews in the 16th century. In Italy the refugees from Spain met local well-established Jews in the craft. An apostate of Ferrara, Ercole dei Fideli (before baptism, Solomon de Sessa), was celebrated in this renaissance environment for the ornamental daggers and other works he produced (1465–1519). The gold- and silversmith Abraham b. Moses Ẓoref ("goldsmith") is mentioned in Venice in the early 18th century. Jewish goldsmiths are found in Rome in 1726. In Bohemia-Moravia gold- and silversmithing developed as a flourishing craft among Jews from the 16th century. Emperor Rudolf II appointed Isaac Goldscheider ("gold refiner") elder of Bohemian Jewry in 1560. He was followed in the craft by his son Jacob. The profession became widespread there, as attested by the frequent appearance of the name Ẓoref on Prague tombstones until 1740. In the 18th century Jewish goldsmithing was combined with the Jewish trade in precious stones and metals centered in Amsterdam and Hamburg. The craft continued to develop. There were eight goldsmiths among the Jews who returned to Prague in 1749. Several families practiced the craft for successive generations. The program of "enlightenment" and "productivization" of the Jews, animating the legislation of Emperor *Joseph II, encouraged practice of the craft among Jews; a separate Jewish guild came into existence in 1805 and continued until the abolition of the guilds in 1859. There were 29 Jewish apprentices recorded in Prague in 1804 and in 1830 there were 55 goldsmiths. In Germany, Jews did not begin to enter the craft until the middle of the 19th century when, however, the general developments in Jewish society were tending to deflect them from occupation in crafts. Silesia was an exception, for Jewish goldsmiths and silversmiths were working there in the second half of the 18th century. In Poland-Lithuania Jews entered this craft as they entered others, as a result of the weakness of the guilds and the activities of Jews in the private towns of the nobility. In 1664 Hirsch Jelenowicz was officially called "goldsmith to His Majesty" in Poland. With the mass emigration of Jews from Eastern Europe to Western Europe and the Americas, Jewish goldsmiths – now combining the profession with watchmaking – joined the few Sephardi goldsmiths who had arrived there earlier. The most noted of early Jewish goldsmiths in the United States was Myer *Myers. Between 1725 and 1837, 50 Jewish goldsmiths are recorded in England. Thus in modern times Jewish goldsmiths in Northern and Central Europe severed the old connection with moneylending and pawnbroking and the trade became allied with formal banking, on the one hand, and with the making of delicate instruments and the watch trade, on the other. Jewish *art, in particular, the ornamentation of Torah scrolls, *mezuzot*, and similar cult objects, was influenced by the Christian artisans who did the work for Jews, especially in Northern, Central, and Eastern Europe in the early Middle Ages. Family names like Goldschmidt, Goldsmith, Goldsmid, Ẓoref or Soref, and Orefice (Italian) generally indicate that at some stage in its history the family derived its livelihood from goldsmithing.

[Henry Wasserman]

Many Jewish goldsmiths and silversmiths became celebrated during the 19th century: best known was Israel Roukhomovsky, who worked in a small townlet near Odessa (Russia) at the turn of the century. In 1896 he was asked by a friend to make a golden tiara decorated with scenes from the *Iliad*, scenes in the daily life of the Scythians, and inscriptions referring to the gift of a tiara to King Saitaphornes by the people of Olbia. In 1898 this work was sold to the Louvre as an archaeological find by a Viennese merchant. When in 1903 Roukhomovsky was invited to Paris, and there produced a similar work with his primitive tools, he managed to convince a team of archaeologists headed by Clermont-Ganneau that he was the craftsman who made the alleged Saitaphornes tiara.

In Palestine the *Bezalel School of Arts and Crafts, established by Boris *Schatz in 1906, created a style of its own by adapting the traditional artistry of the Yemenites to western forms and tastes. This "Bezalel style" continued to be produced in Israel, especially in the manufacture of ritual objects as well as jewelry. Among modern goldsmiths and silversmiths in Israel and the U.S.A. were many important artists; most renowned in the production of ritual objects, both in Jerusalem and New York, were Wolpert and Gumbel.

[Bezalel Narkiss]

Contemporary Developments

The narrowing of the gap between the well-designed manufactured product and the handmade craft or art continued into the 1980s. In those fields where artistic expression is of particular importance, there are signs that a new type of patron is emerging who will consider commissioning a delicate piece of jewelry, silver for a special occasion, or a contemporary piece of Judaica for the synagogue, and studios with an emphasis on individual design and originality are being set up in many parts of the world.

In August 1977 the first international conference dedicated to Jewish art, under the auspices of the Oxford Centre for Postgraduate Hebrew Studies, in conjunction with the Tarbuth Foundation of America, organized by Isaiah Shachar, who died tragically a month later, entitled "The Visual Dimension – Aspects of Jewish Art," took place in Oxford. There emerged from this conference a tremendous worldwide interest in Jewish art, a desire to record the past, and an interest in encouraging a high standard of contemporary Judaica.

Museums and academic institutions devoted to Jewish art in general and ritual objects in particular have proliferated in many parts of the world, such as the Jewish Museum, New York, which encourages a contemporary approach to Judaica through its own workshops. A new dimension is already apparent in the work of some contemporary gold- and silversmiths.

In May 1978 an Anglo-Jewish Silver Exhibition was organized by the Victoria & Albert Museum of London, under the auspices of the Jewish Historical Society of England. The exhibition aimed at exhibiting the various types of Jewish ritual plates produced, principally by English silversmiths for synagogue and domestic worship, following the resettlement of the Jews in England in 1656. Also included were the fine cups and salvers dating from the reign of William III to that of George III presented as tributes to various Lord Mayors of London by members of the Spanish and Portuguese community. An unusual Victorian table centerpiece by J.S. Hunt, which was presented to Sir Moses Montefiore in 1841, created considerable interest.

There was also an important modern section, and among the silversmiths were represented two famous non-Jews: Prof. Gerald Benney (1930–), professor of silversmithing and jewelry at the Royal College of Art since 1974, and Leslie Durbin (1913–). Benney, who has developed his own technique of texturing and enameling, holds Royal Warrants of Appointment to the Royal Family, is a member of the Government Craft Advisory Committee, and was elected to the Faculty of Royal Designers for Industry. Benney has created some beautiful examples of Jewish ritual art.

In 1978 the department of goldsmithing, silversmithing, and jewelry of the Bezalel Academy of Arts and Design, Jerusalem, exhibited the works of 29 students and the head of their department, Professor Arie *Ofir. It consisted of 100 items of jewelry and 20 items of gold- and silversmithing, some in Judaica. The works showed originality, not only in the use of traditional materials, but with combinations of leather, rope, wood, and acrylics. The exhibition was first shown at the unique Pforzheim Museum of Jewelry in Germany in March 1978 and subsequently at the Deutsches Goldschmiedehaus in Hanau. It then moved to the Diamond Museum in Antwerp, the Electrum Gallery in London, the Arnolfini Gallery in Bristol and, finally, to several centers in the United States.

[Amia Raphael]

BIBLIOGRAPHY: L.A. Mayer, *Bibliography of Jewish Art* (1967), index, s.v. *Goldsmith* and *Ceremonial Art*; A. Wolf in: MGJW, 9 (1902), 12–74; 15 (1905), 1–58; 24 (1907), 103–17; M. Gruenwald, *ibid.*, 74 (1925), 419f.; Y. Bronner, in: *Zeitschrift fuer die Geschichte der Juden in der Tschechoslowakei*, 1 (1931), 243–7; H. Flesch, in: *Die juedischen Denkmaeler in der Tschechoslowakei* (1933), 32–33; Baer, Urkunden, index; Baer, Spain, index; Y.W. Rosenbaum, *Myer Myers, Goldsmith* (1954); A.G. Grimwalde, in: JHSET, 18 (1953–55), 113–26; C. Roth, *The Jews in the Renaissance* (1959), 195–8; S. Simonsohn, *Toledot ha-Yehudim be-Dukkasut Mantova*, 2 vols. (1962–64), index, s.v. *Ẓorefim*; M. Wischnitzer, *A History of Jewish Crafts and Guilds* (1965); A. Ben-Yakob, *Yehudei Bavel mi-Sof Tekufat ha-Ge'onim ad Yamenu* (1965), index, s.v. *Ẓorefim*; O. Muneles (ed.), *Prague Ghetto in the Renaissance Period* (1965), 108–25; Ashtor, Korot, 1 (1966), 180; J. Hrasky, in: *Judaica Bohemiae*, 2 (1966), 19–40, 97–106; H. Bentov, in: *Sefunot*, 10 (1966), 413–83; J.M. Landau, *Ha-Yehudim be-Miẓrayim ba-Me'ah ha-Tesha-Esreh* (1967); S.D. Goitein, *A Mediterranean Society* (1967), index; W. Pillich, in: *Zeitschrift fuer die Geschichte der Juden*, 4 (1967), 79–82; B. Brilling, *ibid.*, 5 (1968), 21–26; 6 (1969), 137–46; idem, *Geschichte der juedischen Goldschmiedwerke in Schlesien* (1969); I. Roukhomovsky, *Zikhroynes fun mayn Leybn un fun mayn Shtetl* (1930); A. Kanoff, *Jewish Ceremonial Art* (1970).

GOLDSTEIN, ABRAHAM SAMUEL (1925–), U.S. lawyer and educator. Goldstein, who was born in New York City, received his LL.B. from Yale University in 1949 and was admitted to the Washington, D.C., bar. After two years as a law clerk to U.S. Circuit Court Judge David *Bazelon (1949–51), he practiced privately with a Washington law firm from 1951 to 1956. In the latter year, he was appointed a member of the Yale Law School faculty. Goldstein, an expert in U.S. criminal law and procedure, became a professor in 1961. He served as dean of Yale Law School from 1970 to 1975. From 1975 he served as Sterling Professor at Yale, teaching criminal law and criminal procedure. He served as a consultant to the President's Commission on Law Enforcement (1966–67), was a member of the Connecticut State Board of Parole (1967–69), and a member of the Governor's Planning Commission on Criminal Administration (1967–71).

Active in Jewish affairs, Goldstein was a member of the board of directors of the New Haven Jewish Community Council. In 1978 he was appointed provost of Yale University, the second highest post in the university. He was the first Jew to attain this position, which is that of chief educational and administrative officer after the president. He was a visiting professor at the Hebrew University of Jerusalem in 1975 and at Tel Aviv University in 1986. He was senior vice president of the American Jewish Congress (1978–84) and served on its governing council from 1976 to 1994. He was also a member of the Executive Committee of the National Jewish Community Relations Advisory Council (1985–89). From 1990 he served on the board of directors of Hillel at Yale.

Goldstein wrote *The Insanity Defense* (1967), *Crime, Law, and Society: Readings* (with J. Goldstein, 1971), *Criminal Procedure: Cases and Materials on the Administration of Criminal Law* (with L. Orland, 1974), and *The Passive Judiciary: Prosecutorial Discretion and the Guilty Plea* (1981).

[Ruth Beloff (2nd ed.)]

GOLDSTEIN, ALEXANDER (1884–1949), Russian Zionist leader. Born in Minsk, Goldstein studied law at the University of St. Petersburg and took an active part in Zionist student circles. In 1903 he published his first article (in Russian) and eventually became one of the outstanding writers on Zionist affairs, contributing to the Zionist monthly, *Yevreyskaya Zhizn*, and primarily to *Razsvet*, when this weekly was founded in 1907. He also traveled throughout Russia in order to promote the Zionist idea. He was one of the originators of the Helsingfors Program which sought to incorporate Diaspora activities into the Zionist program. At the Seventh Convention of Russian Zionists, held in Petrograd in 1917, Goldstein submitted a proposal to hold a national "referendum," which would demand equal rights for the Jews in the Diaspora as well as a national home for the Jews in Ereẓ Israel. In 1919 he left Russia, and, when Keren Hayesod was established, he entered its service and traveled extensively on its behalf. In 1933 he settled in Palestine, where he continued his work for Keren Hayesod.

BIBLIOGRAPHY: Tidhar, 2 (1947), 793; *He-Avar*, 14 (1967), 3–87.

[Getzel Kressel]

GOLDSTEIN, ANGELO (1889–1947), politician and Zionist leader in Czechoslovakia. The son of a rabbi in Bohemia, he graduated in law. He was wounded during his service in the Austro-Hungarian army in World War I and after the war he practiced as an advocate in Prague. An active Zionist from his student days, he was among the founders of the Jewish party. At the death of Ludwig *Singer (1931) he took his place in parliament, and was reelected in 1935. An outstanding orator, he fought all attempts at discrimination against Jews. Goldstein was bitterly opposed by assimilationists and extreme Orthodox Jews. He acted as counsel in libel actions brought against the Jewish party (e.g., as counsel of Emil *Margulies in the Hirschler-Weber case in 1928). Goldstein was one of the main propagandists of Zionism in the Czech language. He served on the Zionist General Council (1931–35) on behalf of the Progressive General Zionist faction. In 1939 he left for Palestine where he practiced as a lawyer.

BIBLIOGRAPHY: *The Jews of Czechoslovakia* (1969), index.

[Yehuda Gera]

GOLDSTEIN, ELYSE (1955–), rabbi, educator, feminist activist. Born in Scranton, Pennsylvania, to Terry and Abe Goldstein, Elyse Goldstein earned a B.A. from Brandeis University in 1978 and an M.A. from Hebrew Union College in 1981. She was ordained at Hebrew Union College-Jewish Institute of Religion in 1983 and from 1991 served as the founding director of Kolel: The Adult Centre for Liberal Jewish Learning in Toronto, Ontario.

Goldstein's first rabbinic position was as assistant rabbi at Holy Blossom Temple in Toronto between 1983 and 1986. One of the first female rabbis in Canada, she was also an outspoken feminist committed to Reform Judaism. From 1986 to 1991, she served as rabbi of Temple Beth David of Canton, Massachusetts, before returning to Toronto to become the primary architect of the Kolel, first Reform institute for advanced adult learning. Through her pioneering educational work at Kolel, Rabbi Goldstein made a unique contribution to Liberal Judaism in North America by enabling Jews of diverse backgrounds and affiliations to study Judaism as adults in a yeshiva-like environment that is not Orthodox. Goldstein is the author of *Re-Visions: Seeing Torah through a Feminist Lens* (1998), and edited *The Women's Torah Commentary* (2000) and *The Women's Haftorah Commentary* (2003). She also published a study guide on women and Judaism, *Seek Her Out: A Textual Approach to the Study of Women and Judaism* (2004). She is one of seven women featured in the groundbreaking 1989 National Film Board of Canada documentary *Half the Kingdom*.

Elyse Goldstein received many honor and awards, including the 2005 Covenant Award and the 2004 UJA Rabbinic Achievement Award. In 2001 she was named ORT Woman of the Year.

BIBLIOGRAPHY: N. Joseph, "Jewish Women in Canada: An Evolving Role," in: R. Klein (ed.), *From Immigration to Integration, the Canadian Jewish Experience: A Millennium Edition* (2001), 182–95; F. Zuckerman (ed.), *Half the Kingdom: Seven Jewish Feminists*, (1992).

[Norma Baumel Joseph (2nd ed.)]

GOLDSTEIN, EUGEN (1850–1931), German physicist. Goldstein was born at Gleiwitz in Upper Silesia and became a student of the German scientist Herman von Helmholtz (1821–1894). Most of Goldstein's research was devoted to radiant emissions, first at the University of Berlin and later at the Potsdam Observatory. He is best remembered for his studies of high-vacuum cathode ray tubes, leading to his discovery of "Kanalstrahlen," known in English as "canal rays." He found that these rays travel in the opposite direction from normal cathode rays. This was highly significant for the understanding of radiation in general, as it was shown later that such rays consist of positively charged particles and this in turn led Rutherford to prove that these particles, called protons, must exist alongside uncharged neutrons to make up the nucleus of every atom.

BIBLIOGRAPHY: I. Asimov, *Biographical Encyclopedia of Science and Technology* (1964), 403–4; Huntress, in: *Proceedings of the American Academy of Arts and Sciences*, 78 (1950), 29–30.

[J. Edwin Holmstrom]

GOLDSTEIN, FANNY (1888–1961), U.S. librarian. Born in Kamenets-Podolsk, Russia, Fanny Goldstein was taken to the United States at an early age. She entered the Boston public library system in 1913 and served as librarian of the West End branch from 1922 until her retirement in 1957, developing there a notable Judaica collection later housed in the main library. In 1954 she was appointed curator of Judaica, the first woman in America to receive this title.

Throughout her career she was active in promoting interest in Jewish books and writers among Jews and non-Jews alike. In 1925 she introduced the celebration of Jewish Book Week in Boston; it was subsequently made a national event. In 1940 she became the first chairman of the National Committee for Jewish Book Week and in 1941 was made honorary president of its successor organization, the Jewish Book Council of America. She was well known for her listings of Judaica published by the Boston Public Library, and those which appeared in the *American Jewish Year Book* (43 (1941–42), 499–517) and the *Jewish Book Annual* (5 (1946–47), 84–100; also vols. 11–16, 1952–59). In 1958 she presented her own large collection of Judaica to the Boston Public Library, where it is now maintained as the Fanny Goldstein Collection.

BIBLIOGRAPHY: C. Angoff, in: JBA, 20 (1962/63), 70–72.

[Harry J. Alderman]

GOLDSTEIN, HERBERT S. (1890–1970), U.S. rabbi. Goldstein was born and educated in New York City, receiving his B.A. (1911) and M.A. (1912) degrees from Columbia University. He graduated from the *Jewish Theological Seminary in 1914, when such ordination did not necessarily mark one as a Conservative rabbi and was also ordained by Rabbi Shalom Jaffe, vice president of the *Union of Orthodox Rabbis. While still a seminary student, he assisted Rabbi Moses Z. Margolies at the prestigious Kehilath Jeshurun Congregation in New York on the Upper East Side where he succeeded Mordecai *Kaplan. Like Kaplan, he believed that an English-speaking, secularly educated rabbinate was essential to the survival of Judaism and that the synagogue must remain the center of Jewish life. Unlike Kaplan, who moved to the left, Goldstein remained firmly within the Orthodox camp. After graduation, he pioneered a new synagogue in Harlem, which was then populated by first-generation Jewish immigrants. To attract their American-born children, Goldstein organized a youth *minyan* and gradually evolved the congregation into a new form: an institutional synagogue which comprised social, educational, and sports activities in addition to religious services. After Harlem became a totally black neighborhood in the 1930s, he transferred his activities to the West Side (1937), where he had previously established a branch known as the West Side Institutional Synagogue. It was a combination of a synagogue, *talmud torah*, and YMHA. Although a Seminary graduate, Goldstein also served as professor of homiletics at the Rabbi Isaac Elchanan Theological Seminary of *Yeshiva University, and was president of the *Synagogue Council of America, *Rabbinical Council of America, and the *Union of Orthodox Jewish Congregations. He was also active in the *Agudat Israel movement, and continually visited Eretz Israel to aid the activities of the Harry Fischel Institute for Research in Jewish Law and the Rabbi Herzog World Academy of Jewish Studies. Both these projects were supported by the philanthropic foundation established by his father-in-law, Harry *Fischel. He also wrote several books, including a commentary to the 613 commandments, and edited his father-in-law's autobiography. Despite the fact that he was a graduate of the Jewish Theological Seminary, Goldstein was a strictly Orthodox rabbi, belonging to the right wing of the English-speaking Orthodox rabbinate, and in this respect was unique.

ADD. BIBLIOGRAPHY: J. Gurrock, *When Harlem Was Jewish* (1979); M.D. Sherman, *Orthodox Judaism in America: A Biographical Dictionary and Sourcebook* (1996), 79–81.

GOLDSTEIN, ISRAEL (1896–1986), U.S. Conservative rabbi and Zionist. He was born in Philadelphia, received his Jewish education at Yeshiva Mishkan Israel and Gratz College, studying for a time at a ḥeder in Riga. He was a graduate of the University of Pennsylvania (1914) and ordained by the Jewish Theological Seminary in 1918. He received his D.H.L. from the Seminary as well (1927). In that year he was appointed rabbi of the prominent Congregation B'nai Jeshurun in New York, where he served until 1961. Begun in 1825, B'nai Jeshurun was one of the oldest congregations in New York and badly in need of revitalization. Goldstein instituted late Friday evening services, expanded its school and educational outreach, and began the community center directed by Louis Levitsky. During his four decades of leadership, he established B'nai Jeshurun as a respected and progressive congregation. An ardent Zionist, Goldstein was president of the Jewish National Fund of America (1933–43), and vice president (1934–43) and president (1943–45) of the Zionist Organization of America, and enjoyed the reputation of an outstanding orator and administrator.

A member and officer of several Jewish, interfaith, and public organizations and commissions, he was a founder of the National Conference of Christians and Jews (1928) and of Brandeis College (1946). Elected first president of the World Confederation of General Zionists (1946), he served as chairman of both the United Jewish and Palestine Appeals (1947–48), treasurer of the Jewish Agency (1948–49) while on Sabbatical from his congregation, and first president of Amidar, the Israel national housing company (1948–49). During Goldstein's tenure as president of the American Jewish Congress (1951–58) that organization vigorously opposed McCarthyism and the restrictive McCarran-Walter Immigration Act, supported equal rights for American blacks, and attempted to counter Arab anti-Israel propaganda. In 1961 Goldstein moved to Jerusalem and became world chairman of the Keren Hayesod-United Israel Appeal, serving in that capacity until 1971, when he also retired from the co-presidency of the World Confederation of General Zionists, of which he was appointed honorary president. His books include a history of his congregation *Century of Judaism in New York* (1930); sermons and essays, *Towards a Solution* (1940) and *American Jewry Comes of Age* (1955); and *Transition Years, New York–Jerusalem, 1960–1962* (1962); *Israel at Home and Abroad* (1973); *Jewish Justice and Conciliation: History of the Jewish Conciliation Board of America. 1930–1968* (1981); and a two-volume autobiography, *My World as a Jew* (2 vols., 1984); and *Jewish Perspectives: Selected Addresses, Sermons, Broadcasts and Articles, 1915–1984*, edited by Gabriel A. Sivan (1985). He was also honorary president of the American Jewish Congress, the JNF of America, and the Israel Interfaith Committee. His wife BERTHA (1895–1996) was national president of the *Pioneer Women Organization (1947 to 1951) and was active in many women's organizations.

With his wife Israel Goldstein instituted the Bert and Israel Goldstein Jerusalem Prize for Good Citizenship. Both Goldsteins were *yekirei Yerushalayim* (Distinguished Citizens of Jerusalem).

BIBLIOGRAPHY: H. Schneiderman (ed.), *Two Generations in Perspective: Notable Events and Trends, 1896–1956* (1957).

GOLDSTEIN, JENNIE (1896–1960), U.S. actress. Born in New York, Jennie Goldstein appeared in *Khanele di Nayterin* at the age of six. At 15 she performed with David *Kessler in *Dos Yidishe Harts* and played the leading role in Jacob Gordin's *Di Yesoyme*. At 16 she married the actor-playwright Max Gabel, who wrote plays for the two of them. After their divorce in 1930, she toured in vaudeville. She appeared on the English-language stage in George Abbott's *The Number* (1951) and in Tennessee Williams' *Camino Real* (1953).

GOLDSTEIN, JOSEF (1837–1899), *ḥazzan* and composer. Goldstein was born and brought up in Hungary. His father, known as "Shmelke Ḥazzan," was *ḥazzan* of the town of Neutra, and Josef sang in his choir at the age of six. His father died when Josef was 10, and when he was 13, though still at school, he was made *ḥazzan* of the community. During the next five years, he conducted services in many Hungarian towns and at the Polish synagogue in Vienna, studied music in Prague, Florence, and Padua, and sang in concerts in Budapest and elsewhere. At the age of 18 he was appointed chief *ḥazzan* of the Leopoldstadt Synagogue in Vienna, and served there for over 40 years. He introduced the Polish-Jewish style of singing, which he also used for the songs in his book *Schire Jeschurun* (3 vols., 1862). The work contains melodies for all the services of the synagogue and settings of psalms for choir with organ accompaniment.

BIBLIOGRAPHY: Idelsohn, Melodien, 6 (1932), 196–209, nos. 15–30; Friedmann, Lebensbilder, 2 (1921), 102–8; E. Zaludkowski, *Kultur-Treger fun der Yidisher Liturgie* (1930), 120–4; Sendrey, Music, index.

[Joshua Leib Ne'eman]

GOLDSTEIN, JOSEPH LEONARD (1940–), U.S. medical geneticist and Nobel laureate. Goldstein was born in Sumter, South Carolina, and graduated with a B.S. in chemistry from Washington and Lee University in Lexington, Virginia (1962), and an M.D. from the University of Texas Southwestern Medical School at Dallas (1966). After medical training at Massachusetts General Hospital, Boston (1966–68), where he met his long-term collaborator Michael *Brown, he began his research career at the National Institutes of Health, Bethesda (1968–70). He worked in the laboratory of Marshall Nirenberg and with Donald Fredrickson, clinical director of the National Heart Institute (1968–70) whose patients with lipid disorders stimulated his interest in cholesterol metabolism. His genetic studies with Arno Motulsky at the University of Washington, Seattle (1970–72) clarified the link between inherited abnormalities of lipid metabolism, especially high blood cholesterol levels, and susceptibility to heart disease. He also learned techniques for culturing readily accessible cells called fibroblasts which he subsequently used to study normal and abnormal lipid metabolism. In 1972 he joined the faculty of the Southwestern Medical School, Dallas, initially as head of the division of medical genetics, progressing to professor (1974) and Paul J. Thomas Professor of Medicine and Genetics, chairman of the department of medical genetics from 1977, and regent professor of the University of Texas (1985). He continued his collaboration with Michael Brown throughout this period in Dallas, and they shared the Nobel Prize for physiology or medicine (1985) for the research which identified the receptors on cell surfaces which normally regulate blood levels of low-density lipoproteins. They further showed that low density lipoproteins within cells control the enzyme coenzyme A reductase which governs cholesterol synthesis, especially by the liver. They characterized the genetic defects in these receptors which lead to high blood levels of low-density lipoproteins and cholesterol. This results in excessive lipid deposition in blood vessel walls predisposing to disease, especially in coronary arteries. These observations led to a greater understanding of the regulatory role of receptors in general. They also underlie the modern clinical practice of reducing abnormally high cholesterol levels by dietary means or drugs. His subsequent collaborative work with Michael Brown identified other metabolic defects resulting in high blood lipoprotein levels dependent upon high blood insulin levels and insulin resistance. His many honors include election to the U.S. National Academy of Sciences (1980), the Gairdner Award (1981), presidency of the American Society for Clinical Investigation (1985–86), and the Lasker Award in Basic Medical Science (1985).

[Michael Denman (2nd ed.)]

GOLDSTEIN, JUDAH JAMISON (1886–1967), U.S. judge and civic leader. Goldstein, who was born in Ontario, Canada, went with his family to New York's Lower East Side when a child. He began practicing law in 1907 and in 1911 became secretary to Alfred E. Smith, then majority leader of the New York State Assembly. In the wake of the Seabury probe of municipal corruption, Goldstein assisted in the investigation of New York City's magistrate courts and was then appointed to this court by Mayor Walker. In 1936 he received an interim appointment to the General Sessions Court and in 1939, despite the opposition of Tammany Hall, won a full term on that court. Defeated as the Republican-Liberal-Fusion candidate for mayor in 1945, he was reelected to the court in 1953. On the bench, Goldstein was a socially conscious and innovative justice who advocated more understanding and lenient treatment for youthful offenders. Prominent in Jewish community, welfare, and philanthropic activities, Goldstein was an active Zionist, a trustee of the Federation of Jewish Philanthropies, a member of the board of the Joint Distribution Committee, and a founder with Lillian *Wald of the East Side Neighborhood Association. He was president (for 32 years) of the well-known Grand Street Boys, the philanthropic organization composed of members who rose from slum childhoods to positions of power and prominence in New York City life. Goldstein wrote *The Family in Court* (1934), dealing with the requirements of the Family Court.

[Richard Skolnik]

GOLDSTEIN, JULIUS (1873–1929), German philosopher. Born in Hamburg, he taught at the Technische Hochschule in Darmstadt from 1901. He edited the literary journal *Der Morgen*, which dealt with Jewish topics, from 1925 until his death. Philosophically he was close to William James, whose *A Pluralistic Universe* he translated (1914). He wrote a great deal on contemporary civilization and culture. Goldstein's major works are *Untersuchungen zum Kulturproblem der Gegenwart* (1899); *Die empiristische Geschichtsauffassung David Humes…* (1902); *Wandlungen in der Philosophie der Gegenwart…* (1911) on James, Bergson and Eucken; *Die Technik* (1912); *Rasse und Politik* (1921), dealing with the Jewish question; *Aus dem Vermaechtnis des neunzehnten Jahrhunderts…* (1922); and *Deutsche Volks-Idee und deutsch-voelkische Idee* (1927).

BIBLIOGRAPHY: *Der Morgen*, 5 (1929), no. 4.

[Richard H. Popkin]

GOLDSTEIN, KURT (1878–1965), neurologist and psychiatrist; coformulator of a test which measures the impairment of function in the case of brain injury in regard to abstract and concrete thinking, known as the Goldstein-Sheerer test. Goldstein, who was born in Katowice, Poland, was educated and worked in Germany. During World War I, he headed a special hospital for treating brain injuries. After the war, he was appointed professor at Frankfurt University and in 1931 at Berlin University. With the coming of the Nazis, he was dismissed from his post, imprisoned, and then released. He then emigrated to the U.S. He headed a research laboratory at the Montefiore Hospital, New York from 1936 to 1940. Then he taught for five years at Tufts Medical College in Boston, and from 1946 was professor of psychology at the City College of New York. Through his medical work on patients with brain damage, Goldstein formed a holistic approach and questioned the idea that the brain was an assembly of mechanisms that performed particular functions. He conceived the brain as a single unit in whose every function, the whole personality is reflected. His many investigations covered problems of localization in the brain, the methods of adaption of an organism to injuries, and the behavior of patients with brain damage.

His findings were collected in his books: *Psychologische Analysen hirnpathologischer Faelle*, written in collaboration with A. Gelb (1920), and *Der Aufbau des Organismus* (1934, *The Organism*, written in collaboration with A. Gelb, 1963²), which have become classic works in neurology. From his own wide and varied experience with speech disorders, resulting from central defects and lesions, he published *Ueber Aphasie* (1927), *The Organism* (1939), *Human Nature in the Light of Psychopathology* (1940), *After-effects of Brain Injuries in War* (1942), and *Language Disturbances* (1948).

[Lipman Halpern]

GOLDSTEIN, MORITZ (**Egon Distel**, **Michael Osten**, **Inquit**; 1880–1977), German journalist and writer. Following his studies in German literature in Berlin, Goldstein, born into an assimilated family, intended to become a writer. Following the advice of Gustav Karpeles, he wrote in 1898–1900 the play *Alexander in Jerusalem* (published 1921) and from then on continued writing plays, stories, and novels, of which only a few were published (e.g., *Die zerbrochene Erde*, 1927; *Katastrophe*, 1927). Whereas Goldstein remained without any success as an author, he was widely known for spurring the debate about the role of Jews in German culture with the publication of his essay "Deutsch-juedischer Parnass" (1912) in *Der Kunstwart* (hence known as the "*Kunstwart* debate"). As early as 1906 Goldstein published the essay "Geistige Organisation des Judentums," where he followed the cultural-Zionist demand for a new Hebrew culture. In his *Kunstwart* essay, however, he moved away from a clear Zionist position. He still emphasized the need for the Jews to rebuild their own culture set against the politics of assimilation. Nevertheless, he doubted the possibility of a renaissance of Hebrew language and literature and instead proposed a new Jewish national literature in the German language. This compromise was controversial: Assimilated Jews (e.g., Ernst *Lissauer) and Zionists (e.g., Ludwig Strauss) both criticized Goldstein, demanding a radical either/or answer – either to become German or Jewish. Goldstein, surprised by the strong reaction to his essay, defended his position in *Begriff und Programm einer juedischen Nationalliteratur* (1913). After the World War I Goldstein continued working as a journalist, mainly for the *Vossische Zeitung*. In 1933 he fled to Italy, where he worked on a political-philosophical analysis of power (only the second part was published under the title *Fuehrers Must Fall: A Study of the Phenomenon of Power from Caesar to Hitler*, 1942) and on a historical analysis of the Jews, *Die Sache der Juden* (unpublished). In 1938 Goldstein fled to America. Until his death in 1977, he lived in New York, never feeling at home, as he described it in the autobiographical novel *Die Goetter von Manhattan* (written 1954, unpublished).

BIBLIOGRAPHY: A. Kilcher, in: *Weimarer Beiträge*, 45 (1999); S. Aschheim, in: S. Gilman (ed.), *Yale Companion to Jewish Writing and Thought in German Culture* (1997); J.H. Schoeps (ed.), *Deutsch-juedischer Parnass. Rekonstruktion einer Debatte* (2002).

[Andreas Kilcher (2nd ed.)]

GOLDSTEIN, RAYMOND (1953–), Israeli composer, arranger, and conductor. Born in Capetown, where he completed his musical studies. Goldstein was on the faculty of the Rubin Academy of Music from 1978, specializing, among other subjects, in opera. He also holds the post of arranger/composer (associate conductor) in the Jerusalem Great Synagogue Choir, where he has over 550 works to his credit.

In 1991 he was appointed senior teacher at the Tel Aviv Cantorial Institute.

As musical director/accompanist, he frequently appears on stage, radio, and television in Israel and has made concert tours in Australia, the U.S., and Western Europe. He has made professional recordings with international cantors and singers, and as accompanist and/or arranger, his name appears on more than a 150 CDs, cassette tapes, and videos. His compositions include a chamber opera, two cantatas, a concert *Kabbalat Shabbat Service*, orchestrations, works for chamber ensemble, and numerous arrangements (more than 1,500 in all), sacred and secular.

[Amnon Shiloah (2nd ed.)]

GOLDSTEIN, REBECCA (1950–). U.S. philosopher and novelist, Goldstein was born in White Plains, New York. Her father was the cantor at the Hebrew Institute of White Plains. After going to public school, Goldstein wanted to go to a yeshivah, and thought of "plunging … into religiosity." She went to the Esther Schoenfeld High School on the Lower East Side of New York City, and recollected that it cured her of her "religious phase." She graduated from Barnard College in 1972 and received her doctorate in philosophy from Princeton (1997). Her dissertation, supervised by Thomas Nagel, is titled *Reduction, Realism and the Mind.* Her fictional works usually have as their protagonists gifted and spirited women who are often forced to explore their commitments (for example to Judaism, to the possibilities of love, to family) against the claims of philosophical schools (for instance, to Spinoza, to Plato). Her novels are graceful and lucid explanations of what these relations mean to her protagonists, and how such characters envision themselves within such traditions. *The Mind-Body Problem* appeared in 1983, followed by *The Late-Summer Passion of a Woman of Mind* (1989); *The Dark Sister* (1991); a volume of stories titled *Strange Attractors* (1993); *Mazel* (1995), which received the National Jewish Book Award, as well as the Edgar Lewis Wallant Award; and *Properties of Light* (2000). Her *Incompleteness: The Proof and Paradox of Kurt Godel* was published in 2005. She is a MacArthur Foundation Fellow and a fellow of the American Academy of Arts and Sciences.

[Lewis Fried (2nd ed.)]

GOLDSTEIN, RICHARD FRANK (1904–1966), British organic chemist and chemical engineer, born in London. Goldstein worked for Imperial Chemical Industries (1927–46), first in dyestuffs division and then on development studies in petrochemicals. His *Petroleum Chemicals Industry* (1949) became a standard. He joined the British Oxygen Company (1946) and became its managing director (1965).

GOLDSTEIN, RUBY (Reuven, "The Jewel of the Ghetto"; 1907–1984), U.S. boxing referee, one-time fighter, member of the International Boxing Hall of Fame and World Boxing Hall of Fame. Born and raised by his widowed mother – his father had died when he was 10 days old – on the Lower East Side of New York City, the 5′ 4½″ Goldstein began boxing as an amateur at the Educational Alliance Building, fighting his first professional fight on December 30, 1924, and winning his first 23 fights, 13 by knockout. A hard puncher with a glass jaw, the welterweight fought his last fight on August 10, 1937, and retired with a 56–6–0 record, including 39 KOS. Goldstein began refereeing while in the Army in World War II and went on to a 21-year career that included officiating 39 world championship fights in all divisions – more than any other referee in history. They included the 1946 Zony Zale vs. Rocky Graziano classic; the first Joe Louis-Jersey Joe Walcott bout in 1947; Louis' last fight, against Rocky Marciano, in 1951; the Sugar Ray Robinson-Joey Maxim light heavyweight fight in 1952, when Goldstein collapsed in the 104-degree heat after the 10th round and could not finish the fight; and the first Floyd Patterson-Ingemar Johansson world heavyweight fight in 1957. Goldstein is perhaps famous for being third man in the ring in the controversial championship fight between Benny "Kid" Paret and Emile Griffith on March 26, 1962. In that nationally televised encounter, Griffith pinned Paret in a corner in the 12th round and delivered a six-second barrage of 18 unanswered punches. When Goldstein finally intervened, Paret slumped to the canvas, unconscious, and died 10 days later. It was the first ring death seen by millions on American national television. While Goldstein was blamed for not stopping the fight, interviews years later with Paret's widow and son show that the family did not blame Goldstein for the death, but rather Paret's manager. Goldstein wrote an autobiography, *Third Man in the Ring* (1959).

[Elli Wohlgelernter (2nd ed.)]

GOLDSTEIN, SALWIAN (1855–1926), Russian historian. Goldstein was born in Warsaw to an assimilated family. In 1888 he began lecturing on Polish and Lithuanian antiquities at the Imperial Archaeological Institute at St. Petersburg. In 1908 he was among the founders of the Jewish Historical-Ethnographical Society and was in charge of its archives. Goldstein's main activity was the collection of documents and other material on the history of Russian Jewry. He organized the archives of S. *Bershadsky and cooperated in the preparation and editing of the collections of documents *Regesty i nadpisi* (3 vols., 1899–1913) and *Russko-yevreyskiy arkhiv* (vol. 3, 1903). He published studies in *Yevreyskaya starina* and similar publications and was a contributor to the *Yevreyskaya Entsiklopediya*, the Russian-Jewish encyclopedia. Goldstein belonged to the small group of scholars who endeavored to maintain some sort of independent Jewish scholarship under Soviet rule.

BIBLIOGRAPHY: YE, 6 (1910), 660–1; *Yevreyskaya starina*, 12 (1928), 404–5.

[Yehuda Slutsky]

GOLDSTEIN, SIDNEY (1903–1989), mathematician and aerodynamicist. Goldstein, who was born in Hull, England, was lecturer in mathematics at Manchester University, and then a fellow of St. John's College, Cambridge (1931–45). Goldstein became a fellow of the Royal Society in 1937. He was chairman of the Aeronautical Research Council (1946–49), and professor of applied mathematics at Manchester University 1945–50. Goldstein went to Israel in 1950, as vice president of the Technion in Haifa and dean of the department of aeronautical engineering. In 1955 he became professor of applied mathematics at Harvard University in the U.S. Goldstein wrote numerous papers on applied mathematics (most dealing with aeronautics), and he was editor and coauthor of *Modern Developments in Fluid Dynamics* (1938) and *Lectures in Fluid Mechanics* (1960).

[Samuel Aaron Miller]

GOLDSTEIN, SIDNEY EMANUEL (1879–1955), U.S. Reform rabbi. Goldstein, who was born in Marshall, Texas, was ordained at the Hebrew Union College in 1905. From 1905 to 1907 he held the position of assistant superintendent at New York's Mount Sinai Hospital. When the Free Synagogue was founded by Stephen S. Wise in 1907, Goldstein became associate rabbi and established and directed its Social Service department. The services instituted by Goldstein included a child-placement service and a program for assisting former mental patients to readjust to life outside the institution. Goldstein was a vigorous supporter of the labor, woman's suffrage, and civil rights movements, regarding the rabbi as a pioneer in social and community reform and the synagogue as the instrument for implementing them. A founder of the Jewish Institute of Religion, Goldstein was professor of social service at the Institute from 1922. Long interested in the field of marriage counseling, Goldstein served as chairman of both the New York State Conference on Marriage and the Family from 1936 to 1947 and the Jewish Institute on Marriage and the Family from 1937. His numerous public activities included: chairman of the Central Conference of American Rabbis' Commission on Social Justice (1934–36); chairman of the executive committee of the War Resisters League of America (1930–40); chairman of the Joint Committee on Unemployment (1930–34); and executive committee member of the State of New York Committee on Discrimination in Employment (1941–44). His book, *The Synagogue and Social Welfare* (1955), studied the meaning of the synagogue and its relation to American life.

GOLDSTONE, RICHARD JOSEPH (1938–), South African judge and international war crimes prosecutor. Born in Boksburg, South Africa, Goldstone was appointed judge of the Transvaal Supreme Court in 1980 and judge of the Appellate Division of the Supreme Court in 1989. In July, he was appointed to the newly established Constitutional Court of South Africa, a position he held until 2003. From 1991 to 1994, he served as chairperson of the Commission of Inquiry regarding Public Violence and Intimidation, which came to be known as the Goldstone Commission. This led to his appointment as chief prosecutor of the United Nations International Criminal Tribunals for the former Yugoslavia and Rwanda (1994–96). He was chairman of the committee that drafted a Declaration of Human Duties and Responsibilities for the director general of UNESCO (the Valencia Declaration) in 1998 and afterwards was chairman of the International Independent Inquiry on Kosovo (1999–2001). In April 2004, he was appointed by the secretary-general of the United Nations to the Independent International Committee to investigate the Iraq Oil for Food program. In December that year, he was appointed as co-chairman of the council for the International Bar Association's Human Rights Institute. Goldstone was further involved in many areas of public life, in both the Jewish and general community. He was a governor of the Hebrew University of Jerusalem and from 1997 to 2004 served as president of World ORT, an international Jewish education and training charity. His autobiography, *For Humanity: Reflections of a War Crimes Investigator*, appeared in 2000.

[David Saks (2nd ed.)]

GOLDSTUECKER, EDUARD (1913–2000), Czech literary historian and critic, author, and diplomat. Goldstuecker was born in Podbiel, Slovakia. In his youth he was active in the Ha-Shomer ha-Ẓa'ir movement in Slovakia but later became a Communist. Following the Nazi occupation of Czechoslovakia in 1938, Goldstuecker fled to England, where he studied at Oxford. In 1945 he returned to Prague, joined his country's diplomatic service, and, after a tour of duty in London, was appointed Czechoslovakia's first minister to Israel (1949–51). Goldstuecker later figured in the *Slánský trial and in 1952 was sentenced to life imprisonment for "anti-state" activities. Released after four years, he was appointed professor of the history of German literature at Charles University in Prague in 1963 (vice rector 1968–69). An outspoken critic of the Party's interference in cultural affairs, Goldstuecker published a collection of studies on Franz *Kafka, *Na téma Franz Kafka* (On Franz Kafka, 1964). He organized two international conferences on Kafka and on Prague's German literature in Liblice in 1963 and 1965. As a result of his efforts Kafka, who until then was taboo in the Communist world, was "rehabilitated" in Czechoslovakia and some other states of the Communist bloc. After the liberalization of the Czechoslovak regime in January 1968, Goldstuecker was elected president of the Czechoslovak Writers' Union and a member of the Czech National Council. After the Soviet invasion of Czechoslovakia in August 1968, Goldstuecker was a major target of criticism by the anti-liberal elements. He left the country and accepted a visiting professorship at the University of Sussex (1969–78) and the University of Brighton (1978–90), England. In 1970 Goldstuecker was one of several Czechoslovak public figures accused of being agents of "Zionism and Imperialism" and tried in absentia. Goldstuecker for his part maintained that his Jewish origin was a major reason for his persecution by "Stalinist ruling circles" in Czechoslovakia. He returned to Prague in 1991.

Goldstuecker published dozens of studies and articles on Prague's German literature and its major figures, such as Franz Kafka, Franz *Werfel, R.M. Rilke, and E.E. *Kisch, including *Rainer Maria Rilke and Franz Werfel* (1960) with prefaces and epilogues to translations from German literature (Thomas *Mann, Karl *Kraus, etc.). He also edited works by J.W. Goethe. During his second exile, (1969–91) he published *The Czech National Revival, the Germans and the Jews* (1973) and *Prozesse: Erfahrungen eines Mitteleuropäers* (Trials: Experiences of an Inhabitant of Central Europe, 1989). In Czechoslovakia, he published studies on Czech antisemitism, relations between Czechs, Germans and Jews, and on the Prague Spring of 1968. Goldstuecker took stock of his life in a volume of memoirs, *Vzpomínky (1913–1945)*, published in 2003. The second part remained unpublished.

ADD. BIBLIOGRAPHY: A. Mikulášek et al., *Literatura s hvězdou Davidovou*, vol. 1 (1998).

[Avigdor Dagan / Milos Pojar (2nd ed.)]

GOLDWASSER, ISRAEL EDWIN (1878–1974), U.S. educator, financier, and philanthropist. Goldwasser was born in New York City, and began public school teaching in 1897. He eventually became a principal and the youngest district superintendent of schools in New York City (1914–17), publishing several educational works, including *Method and Methods in Teaching English* (1912) and *Yiddish English Lessons* (with Joseph Jablonower, 1914). In 1920 Goldwasser entered business as a factor, becoming president of an investment firm during the 1930s, and retired in 1954 after nearly 15 years with the Commercial Factors Corporation. Subsequently he served as an economic consultant and took a special interest in economic projects in Israel. Goldwasser was a leading figure in many Jewish communal organizations, such as the Federation of Jewish Philanthropies, of which he was the first executive director (1917–20). His son, EDWIN L. GOLDWASSER (1919–), was co-director of the National Accelerator Laboratory in Weston, Illinois, the world's largest atom smasher. Professor emeritus of physics at the University of Illinois at Urbana-Champaign, he also served as vice chancellor for academic affairs. He is a fellow of the American Association for the Advancement of Science; the American Physical Society; and the J.S. Guggenheim Foundation. He wrote *Optics, Waves, Atoms, and Nuclei: An Introduction* (1965).

GOLDWATER, family of early settlers in Arizona and the American West. Originally named "Goldwasser," the first of the family to reach America were the brothers MICHAEL and JOSEPH, who were born in Konin, Poland, in the 1820s. They immigrated first to Germany, then to England, where they worked as cap makers, and in 1852, along with Michael's young wife, to the United States. Attracted by the gold rush, they went West, selling whiskey and hardware to the miners and then settling in Los Angeles, where they operated a combined general store and saloon. In 1862 Michael Goldwater led a mule train to the gold-rush settlement of La Paz, Arizona, along the Colorado River. He remained in the area and later founded the town of Ehrenburg, which he named after a friend who had been killed by Indians. Subsequently he was joined by his brother Joseph and the two opened a large store in Phoenix and another in Prescott. Michael retired in 1883 and died in 1903, leaving the business, Goldwater Inc., to his sons MORRIS and BARON. Baron married an Episcopalian. Their son, BARRY M. GOLDWATER (1909–1998), served as U.S. senator from Arizona from 1952 to 1964 and again from 1968, and was the unsuccessful presidential candidate of the Republican Party in 1964. In 1968 he won back his seat in the Senate. After serving three more terms as one of the Senate's most respected members, he retired in 1987. Goldwater wrote *The Coming Breakpoint* (1976) and his autobiography, *With No Apologies* (1979).

BIBLIOGRAPHY: O. Jensen, in: *American Heritage* (June 1964).

GOLDWATER, JOHN L. (1916–1999), U.S. comic-book artist. An orphan from East Harlem, N.Y., Goldwater hitchhiked west in the Depression and invented prototypical teenage America in the comics. His creations – Archie Andrews, Jughead, Betty, and Veronica – were always 16 years old, going on 17. Millions worldwide came to chuckle over Archie's misadventures at school with his spinster teacher and fussy principal; his intractable romantic triangle with the sweet Betty and spoiled, rich Veronica; a hamburger obsession of the nerdy Jughead, and rivalry with the handsome, conceited Reggie. "He's basically a square," Goldwater said of Archie, "but in my opinion the squares are the backbone of America. If we didn't have squares we wouldn't have strong families." The comic strip ran in 750 newspapers and comic book sales sometimes reached 50 million a year.

In the 1940s and 1950s, Goldwater catapulted to the pinnacle of the comics world, with a publishing empire, Archie Comics Publications, one of the industry's big three, and radio and television shows and a movie.

Goldwater dreamed up Archie, a hapless teenage Everyman, in 1941, placing him in the mythical and idyllic town of Riverdale. He found a young artist, Bob Mantana, who provided what became indelible faces. He went to a magazine publisher and offered to buy his outdated issues at a penny each. Then he shipped them abroad to an avid market. The business prospered and Goldwater soon joined forces with a pulp magazine publisher, Louis Silberkleit, to found a magazine publishing business in 1941, just as the war was restricting paper supplies. Their Archie venture began as a four-page insert in another comic but proved an immediate hit and Archie and friends got their own comic.

In 1954, with national critics decrying brutality, vulgarity, and sex in comics, Goldwater helped found the Comics Magazine Association of America, whose Comics Code Authority persuaded magazines to voluntarily weed out offensive material as well as ads for guns, knives, and war weapons. Goldwater served as president for 25 years.

In 1973 Goldwater licensed Archie for evangelical Christian messages. Although Jewish, Goldwater said the sentiments were in line with his wholesome family message.

[Stewart Kampel (2nd ed.)]

GOLDWATER, SIGMUND SCHULZ (1873–1942), U.S. consultant in hospital administration and design. Goldwater was born in New York City. Joining Mount Sinai Hospital in New York, he rose to the position of director, a post he held from 1917 to 1929. At the same time, Goldwater became a registered architect, and gained an international reputation as an expert consultant in hospital design and administration. In 1914 New York Mayor John Mitchell appointed him health commissioner, later citing his accomplishments in reorganizing the department. Goldwater served as commissioner of hospitals under Mayor La Guardia for six years starting in 1934, and worked to rejuvenate the city's aging facilities. An advocate of extending private health insurance to lower income groups, Goldwater became president of the Associated Hospital Service in 1940.

[Richard Skolnik]

GOLDWYN (Goldfish), SAMUEL (1882–1974), U.S. motion-picture producer. Born in Warsaw, Poland, he immigrated to the U.S. at the age of 13. He worked in a glove factory, and at the age of 30 owned a successful glove company. In 1913 Goldwyn entered the motion-picture industry as an associate of his brother-in-law, Jesse L. Lasky, and Cecil B. DeMille. Their first production, *The Squaw Man* (1914), perhaps the first feature-length film made in Hollywood, was an instant success. Two years later Goldwyn joined Edgar and Archibald Selwyn to form the Goldwyn Pictures Corporation (using the first syllable of Goldfish and the last of Selwyn), adopting the name as his own. In 1922 Goldwyn was fired from the company, which later merged with Metro Pictures and Louis B. Mayer Productions to become Metro-Goldwyn-Mayer. Goldwyn became an independent producer, acquiring a reputation that none of his competitors could match. He endowed his films with talent and imagination, leaving his own distinctive mark on them. He introduced and produced many popular actors and hired distinguished writers, including Maurice Maeterlinck, Robert Sherwood, and Lillian *Hellman. His stars included Ronald Colman, Vilma Banky, Eddie *Cantor, Gary Cooper, David Niven, and Danny *Kaye.

Goldwyn became a legend in the film industry, and many malapropisms were attributed to him, such as "Include me out" and "a verbal contract isn't worth the paper it's written on." Between 1917 and 1959, Goldwyn produced more than 100 films. Some of his productions include *Arrowsmith* (1931), *The Kid from Spain* (1932), *Wuthering Heights* (1939), *The Little Foxes* (1941), *The Pride of the Yankees* (1942), *The Best Years of Our Lives* (1946), *The Secret Life of Walter Mitty* (1947), *Enchantment* (1948), *Hans Christian Anderson* (1952), *Guys and Dolls* (1955), and *Porgy and Bess* (1955).

Goldwyn was nominated for seven Academy Awards. In 1946 he won the Oscar for *The Best Years of Our Lives* and received the Irving G. Thalberg Memorial Award. In 1957 he was honored with the Academy's Jean Hersholt Humanitarian Award and in 1973 he won the Golden Globe's Cecil B. DeMille Award for outstanding contribution to the entertainment field. Goldwyn wrote *Behind the Screen* (1923). He assigned his film profits to the Samuel Goldwyn Foundation for assisting scholars and philanthropic causes.

ADD. BIBLIOGRAPHY: A. Marx, *Goldwyn: A Biography of the Man Behind the Myth* (1976); M. Freedland, *The Goldwyn Touch* (1986); S. Berg, *Goldwyn: A Biography* (1989); C. Easton, *The Search for Sam Goldwyn: A Biography* (1989).

[Jo Ranson / Ruth Beloff (2nd ed.)]

GOLDZIHER, IGNAZ (**Isaac Judah**; 1850–1921), Hungarian scholar, one of the founders of modern Islamic scholarship. Goldziher, born in Szekesfehervar (Stuhlweissenburg), studied Arabic manuscripts at Leyden and Vienna, and traveled in Egypt, Palestine, and Syria before becoming a lecturer at the University of Budapest in 1872. As his university teaching was unpaid until he became a professor in 1904, he earned his living as secretary of the Budapest Neolog Jewish community for 30 years. In 1900 he succeeded D. *Kaufmann as professor of religious philosophy at the Budapest Rabbinical Seminary. Goldziher was elected a member of the Hungarian Academy of Sciences long before his appointment to a professorship in the university. He was respected by Muslim scholars and received queries from them; he was invited to lecture at Fuad University in Cairo but did not accept the position. When the Jewish National Home was established in Palestine after World War I, it was hoped that Goldziher would use his influence in the Muslim world to help bring about a rapprochement between Jews and Arabs, but he was far from being a Zionist, and refused to act on this matter. Goldziher was the first to describe critically and comprehensibly the history of Islamic oral tradition (*ḥadith) and the various Islamic sects; he published many studies, still valuable, on pre-Islamic and Islamic culture, the religious and legal history of the Arabs, and their ancient and modern poetry. He was one of the initiators of the *Enzyklopaedie des Islām* (4 vols., 1913–36), and was among its contributors. Goldziher's principal works in this field are *Beitraege zur Literaturgeschichte der Schiʿa und der sunnitischen Polemik* (1874), *Die Zâhiriten…* (1884), *Muhammedanische Studien* (2 vols., 1889–90), Eng. tr. *Muslim Studies*, ed. by S.M. Stern (1967), *Abhandlungen zur arabischen Philologie* (2 vols., 1896–99), *Vorlesungen ueber den Islam* (1910, 1925²), and *Die Richtungen der islamischen Koranauslegung* (1920). Goldziher also made valuable contributions to Jewish scholarship. At the age of 12 he published *Si'aḥ Yiẓḥak*, an essay on the Jewish prayers. His doctoral dissertation was devoted to the 13th-century Arab-Jewish philologist and Bible commentator *Tanḥum Yerushalmi. He wrote for Hungarian and German Jewish periodicals and in various Festschriften on problems of Jewish scholarship, in particular about the relations between Islam and Judaism, and on Muslim criticism of the Pentateuch, the Talmud, and the "people of the book" in general. Goldziher's Islamic and Jewish studies complemented each other; he was able to draw many parallels between the two religions, pointing out their differences as well.

Among his major publications in Jewish studies are *Der Mythos bei den Hebraeern…* (1876; *Mythology among the Hebrews…*, 1877), "Mélanges judéo-arabes" (in REJ, vols. 43–60, 1901–10), and "Islamische und juedische Philosophie des Mittelalters" and "Religion des Islams," in *Die Kultur der Gegenwart* (vol. 1 pt. 3, 1906). With W. Wundt and H. Oldenberg he edited *Allgemeine Geschichte der Philosophie* (1909). Goldziher reviewed critically various editions of the Arabic originals of important medieval philosophical and halakhic texts and he himself edited pseudo-Baḥya's *Kitâb Maʿânî al-Nafs* (1907). He also wrote on modern Hebrew poetry (in JQR, 14 [1902], 719–36). His general views on Judaism were presented in *A zsidóság lényege és fejlödése* ("Essence and Evolution of Judaism," 2 vols., 1923–24), and in a lecture delivered in Stockholm ("Tradition und Dogma" in AZDJ, 78 (1914), 6–8, 22–23, 33–35; Eng. tr. in *Reform Advocate*, 47 (1914), 39–42). Goldziher served on the editorial board of the *Jewish Encyclopedia* (1901–06), to which he contributed many articles. An *Ignace Goldziher Memorial Volume* was published in two parts (1948–58) by S. Loewinger, J. Somogyi, and A. Scheiber. A collection of his writings was edited in three volumes by J. Somogyi as *Gesammelte Schriften* (1967–69), and a bibliography of his works was published by B. Heller, *Bibliographie des oeuvres…* (1927) and of his Hebrew writings was compiled by S.D. Goitein (in KS, 23 (1946/47), 251–7). His memoirs, covering the years 1890–1919, were edited by A. Scheiber and published as *Tagebuch* in 1978. After his death, Goldziher's valuable library and his extensive scholarly correspondence were acquired by the National and University Library in Jerusalem.

BIBLIOGRAPHY: H. Loewe, *Ignaz Goldziher* (Ger., 1929); A.S. Yahuda, in: JC Literary Supplement (April 25, 1924); idem, in: *Der Jude*, 8 (1924), 575–92; L. Massignon, in: B. Heller, *Bibliographie des oeuvres de Ignace Goldziher* (1927), introduction; M. Plessner, in: I. Goldziher, *Harẓa'ot 'al ha-Islam* (1951), 289–309; J. Nemeth, in: *Acta Orientalia Academiae Hungariae*, 1 (1950–51), 7–24; S. Loewinger, in: S. Federbusch (ed.), *Ḥokhmat Yisrael be-Ma'arav Eiropah* (1958), 166–81. **ADD. BIBLIOGRAPHY:** L.I. Conrad, "Ignaz Goldziher …," in: M. Kramer (ed.), *The Jewish Discovery of Islam* (1999), 137–80).

[Martin Meir Plessner]

GOLEM (Heb. גֹּלֶם), a creature, particularly a human being, made in an artificial way by virtue of a magic act, through the use of holy names. The idea that it is possible to create living beings in this manner is widespread in the magic of many peoples. Especially well known are the idols and images to which the ancients claimed to have given the power of speech.

Among the Greeks and the Arabs these activities are sometimes connected with astrological speculations related to the possibility of "drawing the spirituality of the stars" to lower beings (see *Astrology). The development of the idea of the *golem* in Judaism, however, is remote from astrology: it is connected, rather, with the magical exegesis of the *Sefer *Yeẓirah* ("Book of Creation") and with the ideas of the creative power of speech and of the letters.

The word "*golem*" appears only once in the Bible (Ps. 139:16), and from it originated the talmudic usage of the term – something unformed and imperfect. In philosophic usage it is matter without form. Adam is called "*golem*," meaning body without soul, in a talmudic legend concerning the first 12 hours of his existence (Sanh. 38b). However, even in this state, he was accorded a vision of all the generations to come (Gen. R. 24:2), as if there were in the *golem* a hidden power to grasp or see, bound up with the element of earth from which he was taken. The motif of the *golem* as it appears in medieval legends originates in the talmudic legend (Sanh. 65b): "Rava created a man and sent him to R. Zera. The latter spoke to him but he did not answer. He asked, 'Are you one of the companions? Return to your dust.'" It is similarly told that two *amoraim* busied themselves on the eve of every Sabbath with the *Sefer Yeẓirah* (or in another version *Hilkhot Yeẓirah*) and made a calf for themselves and ate it. These legends are brought as evidence that "If the righteous wished, they could create a world." They are connected, apparently, with the belief in the creative power of the letters of the Name of God and the letters of the Torah in general (Ber. 55a; Mid. Ps. 3). There is disagreement as to whether the *Sefer Yeẓirah* or *Hilkhot Yeẓirah*, mentioned in the Talmud, is the same book called by these two titles which we now possess. Most of this book is of a speculative nature, but its affinity to the magical ideas concerning creation by means of letters is obvious. What is said in the main part of the book about God's act during creation is attributed at the end of the book to *Abraham the Patriarch. The various transformations and combinations of the letters constitute a mysterious knowledge of the inwardness of creation. During the Middle Ages, *Sefer Yeẓirah* was interpreted in some circles in France and Germany as a guide to magical usage. Later legends in this direction were first found at the end of the commentary on the *Sefer Yeẓirah* by *Judah b. Barzillai (beginning of the 12th century). There the legends of the Talmud were interpreted in a new way: at the conclusion of profound study of the mysteries of *Sefer Yeẓirah* on the construction of the cosmos, the sages (as did Abraham the Patriarch) acquired the power to create living beings, but the purpose of such creation was purely symbolic and contemplative, and when the sages wanted to eat the calf which was created by the power of their "contemplation" of the book, they forgot all they had learned. From these late legends there developed among the Ḥasidei Ashkenaz in the 12th and 13th centuries the idea of the creation of the *golem* as a mystical ritual, which was used, apparently, to symbolize the level of their achievement at the conclusion of their studies. In this circle, the term "*golem*" has, for the first time, the fixed meaning indicating such a creature.

In none of the early sources is there any mention of any practical benefit to be derived from a *golem* of this sort. In the opinion of the mystics, the creation of the *golem* had not a real, but only a symbolic, meaning; that is to say, it was an ecstatic experience which followed a festive rite. Those who took part in the "act of creation" took earth from virgin soil and made a *golem* out of it (or, according to another source, they buried that *golem* in the soil), and walked around the *golem* "as in a dance," combining the alphabetical letters and the secret Name of God in accordance with detailed sets of instructions (several of which have been preserved). As a result of this act of combination, the *golem* arose and lived, and when they walked in the opposite direction and said the same combination of letters in reverse order, the vitality of the *golem* was nullified and he sank or fell. According to other legends, the word *emet* (אמת; "truth"; "the seal of the Holy One," Shab. 55a; Sanh. 64b) was written on his forehead, and when the letter *alef* was erased there remained the word *met* ("dead"). There are legends concerning the creation of such a *golem* by the prophet *Jeremiah and his so-called "son" *Ben Sira, and also by the disciples of R. *Ishmael, the central figure of the *Heikhalot* literature. The technical instructions about the manner of uttering the combinations, and everything involved in the rite, proves that the creation of the *golem* is connected here with ecstatic spiritual experiences (end of commentary on *Sefer Yeẓirah* by *Eleazar of Worms; the chapter *Sha'ashu'ei ha-Melekh* in N. Bachrach's *Emek ha-Melekh* (Amsterdam, 1648); and in the commentary on *Sefer Yeẓirah* (Zolkiew, 1744–45) attributed to *Saadiah b. Joseph Gaon). In the legends about the *golem* of Ben Sira there is also a parallel to the legends on images used in idol worship which are given life by means of a name; the *golem* expresses a warning about it (idol worship) and demands his own death. It is said in several sources that the *golem* has no intellectual soul, and therefore he lacks the power of speech, but opposite opinions are also found which attribute this power to him. The opinions of the kabbalists concerning the nature of the creation of the *golem* vary. Moses *Cordovero thought that man has the power to give "vitality" alone to the *golem* but not life (*nefesh*), spirit (*ru'aḥ*), or soul proper (*neshamah*).

In the popular legend which adorned the figures of the leaders of the Ashkenazi ḥasidic movement with a crown of wonders, the *golem* became an actual creature who served his creators and fulfilled tasks laid upon him. Legends such as these began to make their appearance among German Jews in the 15th century and spread widely, so that by the 17th century they were "told by all" (according to Joseph Solomon *Delmedigo). In the development of the later legend of the *golem* there are three outstanding points:

(1) The legend is connected with earlier tales of the resurrection of the dead by putting the name of God in their mouths or on their arm, and by removing the parchment containing the name in reverse and thus causing their death.

Such legends were widespread in Italy from the tenth century (in *Megillat *Aḥima'az*).

(2) It is related to ideas current in non-Jewish circles concerning the creation of an alchemical man (the "homunculus" of Paracelsus).

(3) The *golem*, who is the servant of his creator, develops dangerous natural powers; he grows from day to day, and in order to keep him from overpowering the members of the household he must be restored to his dust by removing or erasing the *alef* from his forehead.

Here, the idea of the *golem* is joined by the new motive of the unrestrained power of the elements which can bring about destruction and havoc. Legends of this sort appeared first in connection with Elijah, rabbi of Chelm (d. 1583). Ẓevi Hirsch *Ashkenazi and his son Jacob Emden, who were among his descendants, discussed in their responsa whether or not it is permitted to include a *golem* of this sort in a *minyan* (they prohibited it). Elijah Gaon of Vilna told his disciple Ḥayyim b. Isaac of *Volozhin that as a boy he too had undertaken to make a *golem*, but he saw a vision which caused him to desist from his preparations.

The latest and best-known form of the popular legend is connected with *Judah Loew b. Bezalel of Prague. This legend has no historical basis in the life of Loew or in the era close to his lifetime. It was transferred from R. Elijah of Chelm to R. Loew only at a very late date, apparently during the second half of the 18th century. As a local legend of Prague, it is connected with the Altneuschul synagogue and with an explanation of special practices in the prayers of the congregation of Prague. According to these legends, R. Loew created the *golem* so that he would serve him, but was forced to restore him to his dust when the *golem* began to run amok and endanger people's lives.

[Gershom Scholem]

Descriptions of creations of artificial anthropoids quite reminiscent of the medieval Jewish *golem* are found in Arabic magic predating Ḥasidei Ashkenaz and were available to some Jewish authors. In the Ḥasidei Ashkenaz and in the Jewish French esoterica, there are a variety of recipes for and views of the *golem*, which point to earlier traditions. In Kabbalah the *golem* legend has been interpreted in different ways, either as an entity created by astro-magic, or as a figure to be visualized in different colors, or even a symbol of the divine sphere. In Italian Renaissance, an interest in the subject of the *golem* is evident both in Jewish and Christian sources.

[Moshe Idel (2nd ed.)]

In the Arts

The legends concerning the *golem*, especially in their later forms, served as a favorite literary subject, at first in German literature – of both Jews and non-Jews – in the 19th century, and afterward in modern Hebrew and Yiddish literature. To the domain of belles lettres also belongs the book *Nifla'ot Maharal im ha-Golem* ("The Miraculous Deeds of Rabbi Loew with the Golem," 1909), which was published by Judah Rosenberg as an early manuscript but actually was not written until after the *blood libels of the 1890s. The connection between the *golem* and the struggle against ritual murder accusations is entirely a modern literary invention. In this literature questions are discussed which had no place in the popular legends (e.g., the *golem*'s love for a woman), or symbolic interpretations of the meaning of the *golem* were raised (the unredeemed, unformed man; the Jewish people; the working class aspiring for its liberation).

Interest in the *golem* legend among writers, artists, and musicians became evident in the early 20th century. The *golem* was almost invariably the benevolent robot of the later Prague tradition and captured the imagination of writers active in Austria, Czechoslovakia, and Germany. Two early works on the subject were the Austrian playwright Rudolf *Lothar's volume of stories entitled *Der Golem, Phantasien und Historien* (1900, 1904[2]) and the German novelist Arthur *Holitscher's three-act drama *Der Golem* (1908). The Prague German-language poet Hugo *Salus published verse on "Der hohe Rabbi Loew" and by World War I the theme had gained widespread popularity. The outstanding work about the *golem* was the novel entitled *Der Golem* (1915; Eng., 1928) by the Bavarian writer Gustav Meyrink (1868–1932), who spent many years in Prague. Meyrink's book, notable for its detailed description and nightmare atmosphere, was a terrifying allegory about man's reduction to an automaton by the pressures of modern society. Other works on the subject include Johannes Hess' *Der Rabbiner von Prag (Reb Loeb)*... (1914), a four-act "kabbalistic drama"; Chayim Bloch's *Der Prager Golem: von seiner "Geburt" bis zu seinem "Tod"* (1917; *The Golem. Legends of the Ghetto of Prague*, 1925); and *Ha-Golem* (1909), a story by the Hebrew writer David *Frischmann which later appeared in his collection *Ba-Midbar* (1923). The Yiddish dramatist H. *Leivick's *Der Golem* (1921; Eng., 1928) was first staged in Moscow in Hebrew by the Habimah Theater. Artistic and musical interpretations of the theme were dependent on the major literary works. Hugo Steiner-Prag produced lithographs to accompany Meyrink's novel (*Der Golem*; *Prager Phantasien*, 1915), the book itself inspiring a classic German silent film directed by Paul Wegener and Henrik Galeen (1920), and a later French remake by Julien Duvivier (1936). The screenplay for a post-World War II Czech film about the *golem* was written by Arnost *Lustig. Music for Leivick's drama was written by Moses *Milner; and Eugen d'Albert's opera *Der Golem*, with libretto by F. Lion, had its première at Frankfurt in 1926, but has not survived in the operatic repertory. A more lasting work was Joseph *Achron's *Golem Suite* for orchestra (1932), composed under the influence of the Habimah production. The last piece of this suite was written as the first movement's exact musical image in reverse to symbolize the disintegration of the homunculus. *Der Golem*, a ballet by Francis Burt with choreography by Erika Hanka, was produced in Vienna in 1962.

BIBLIOGRAPHY: Ch. Bloch, *The Golem* (1925); H.L. Held, *Das Gespenst des Golems* (1927); B. Rosenfeld, *Die Golemsage und ihre Verwertung in der deutschen Literatur* (1934); G. Scholem, *On* *the Kabbalah and its Symbolism* (1965), 158–204; F. Thieberger, *The Great Rabbi Loew of Prague: His Life and Work and the Legend of the Golem* (1954). **ADD. BIBLIOGRAPHY:** E. Bilsky (ed.), *Golem! Danger, Deliverance and Art*, foreword by Isaac Bashevis Singer, with essays by M. Idel and E. Ledig (1988); M. Idel, "Golems and God: Mimesis and Confrontation," in: O. Krueger, R. Sarioender, A. Deschner (eds.), *Mythen der kreativitaet* (2003), 224–68; idem, *Golem; Jewish Magical and Mystical Traditions on the Artificial Anthropoid* (1990); H.J. Kieval, "Pursuing the Golem of Prague; Jewish Culture and the Invention of a Tradition," in: *Modern Judaism*, 17:1 (1997), 1–23; P. Schaefer, "The Magic of the Golem; the Early Development of the Golem Legend," in: *Journal of Jewish Studies*, 46 (1995), 249–61; B.L. Sherwin, *The Golem Legend: Origins and Implications* (1985); idem, *Golems Among Us: How a Jewish Legend Can Help Us Navigate the Biotech Century* (2004).

GOLIATH (Heb. גָּלְיָת), Philistine warrior from the city of Gath (I Sam. 17:23) who advanced from the ranks of the Philistines when they faced the Israelites in battle in the Valley of Elah (I Sam. 17). Because of Goliath's great size, he is described as a *rafah* (Raphah; II Sam. 21:19–20; I Chron. 20:8), the *Rephaim being among the ancient people of Canaan who were regarded as giants (Deut. 2:11). The story combines the elements of fairy tales in which an underdog wins a surprise victory against a daunting foe, with the theological message that victory or defeat depends not on might or power but on divine will (Rofé). Goliath was equipped with heavy armor and weapons – a bronze helmet, a coat of mail, bronze greaves, a bronze javelin slung between his shoulders, and a heavy spear with a head of iron. This fighting equipment does not correspond with what was typically carried by warriors from the countries of the Aegean Sea, the region from which the *Philistines came. It is rather an eclectic description meant to emphasize Goliath's stature as a warrior (Galling). Goliath's defiant call for the battle to be decided by the outcome of a duel with a warrior from the enemy's camp (I Sam. 17:8–10) is quite rare. The most famous parallel to the battle of the champions in I Samuel 17 is found in the third book of the Iliad, in which Paris fights Menelaus. The appearance of Goliath, and his boastful words struck terror into the poorly armed Israelite warriors. In contrast to his armed and experienced opponent, David is armed only with courage, faith, and agility. But young *David manages to kill Goliath with a slingstone aimed at the Philistine's forehead (*ibid.* 17:50). David's victory caused the rout of the Philistine army (17:51–53). Goliath's head was brought to Jerusalem (17:54), an obvious anachronism given that Jerusalem was still a non-Israelite city. Goliath's sword was hung up and kept in the temple at Nob (21:10; 22:10). *Ahimelech the priest later returned the sword to David when he arrived at Nob in his flight from King Saul (21:10). In II Samuel 21:19 it is stated that Elhanan the Beth-Lehemite, one of David's captains, slew Goliath. This contradiction was noticed by the author of Chronicles, who attempted to resolve it by representing Elhanan as having killed "Lahmi, the brother of Goliath the Gittite" (I Chron. 20:5). Some scholars hold that Elhanan was David's original name, which was later changed to David. It is more likely, though, that in the course of time Elhanan's exploit was transferred to the more famous David. There are significant differences between the Hebrew version and the Septuagint. In addition, whereas the Goliath narrative depicts David as unskilled in battle (I Sam. 17:39) and unknown to the king (I Sam. 17:55–58), the previous chapter had already placed him in Saul's court (I Sam. 16:21–3) as the king's armor bearer. A weak attempt at harmonization was made in I Samuel 17:15. Although the tale of David and Goliath is one of the best-known Bible stories, various linguistic, stylistic, and theological elements point to a post-exilic date for this tradition about David (Rofé).

[Bustanay Oded / S. David Sperling (2nd ed.)]

In the Aggadah

Goliath was related to his vanquisher David, being descended from Orpah, Ruth's sister-in-law (Sot. 42b). Orpah was a woman of low character and morals, but as a reward for the 40 steps which she took in following Naomi before leaving for Moab, Goliath was permitted to flaunt his strength for 40 days before his downfall (Ruth R. 2:20). Goliath appeared "morning and evening," when the *Shema* was to be recited, to make Israel omit this affirmation of faith (Sot. 42b). The name Goliath is interpreted allegorically as a reflection of effrontery (*gillui panim*) in profaning the name of God. He is described as "*ish ha-beinayim*" ("champion") because he was built like a *binyan* ("building"; *ibid.*). "When David looked at Goliath and saw that he was a mighty man armed with all kinds of weapons, he said, 'Who can prevail against such as he?' But when David saw him reviling and blaspheming, he said: 'Now I shall prevail against him, for there is no fear of God in him'" (Mid. Ps., 36:2). David cast upon him the evil eye and he was struck with leprosy which rooted him to the ground (Lev. R. 21:2). When he fell, an angel pressed his face into the ground, choking the mouth which had blasphemed God (*ibid.* 10:7).

In Islam

In connection with the war of *Saul, who is known as Ṭālūt in the Koran, Muhammad relates that a number of the people of Israel doubted whether they could overcome Jālūt (Goliath) and his army. Allah however granted them courage and strength, and Da'ūd (see *David) killed Goliath (Sura 2:250–2). The details of the duel between David and Goliath are retold in the post-Koranic literature as they are stated in the Bible. Muslim legend relates that Jālūt was one of the kings of Canaan; this is linked to the legend that he came from the Amalekites-Berbers. Goliath is briefly mentioned in the *Qaṣīda*, which is attributed to al-Samaw'al ibn 'Adiyā: "and on the misfortune of 'Ifrīs when he rebelled against God and on Goliath when his fate caught up with him." According to J.W. (H.Z.) Hirschberg, the name 'Ifrīs is similar in form to Idrīs-Iblīs (Satan), which is a strange change of the Philistine name. However, it is possible that this is an allusion to the *aggadah* tracing Goliath's descent from Orpah (see above). According to Horowitz (see bibliography), the name Jālūt was influenced by the word *galut*, which Muhammad often heard in Medina. There is a spring in the valley of Jezreel (Israel) which is known to the Arabs as ʿAyn Jālūt (today En-Harod; cf. Judg. 7:1).

For Goliath in the Arts see *David, In the Arts.

[Haïm Z'ew Hirschberg]

BIBLIOGRAPHY: Y. Yadin, *The Art of Warfare in Biblical Lands*, 2 (1963), 265ff.; idem, in: *Eretz Israel*, 4 (1956), 68ff.; Sukenik (Yadin), in: JPOS, 21 (1948), 114–6; de Vaux, in: *Biblica*, 40 (1959), 495–508 (Fr.); de Boer, in: OTS, 1 (1942), 78–104. IN THE AGGADAH: Ginzberg, Legends, index. IN ISLAM: J.W. Hirschberg, *Der Dīwān des As-Samauʾal ibn ʿAduja...* (1931), 2, 61; EIS^3, 2 (1965), 406 s.v. *Djālūt*, incl. bibl.; J. Horovitz, *Koranische Untersuchungen* (1926), 106. **ADD. BIBLIOGRAPHY:** K. Galling, in: VTSup, 15 (1966), 150–69; A. Rofé, in: J. Neusner et al. (eds.), *Judaic Perspectives on Ancient Israel* (1987), 117–51; C. Ehrlich, in: ABD, 2:1073–74; S. Bar-Efrat, 1 *Samuel* (1996), 219–36.

GOLINKIN, DAVID (1955–), Conservative rabbi, leader, and *posek* (halakhic authority), was born and raised in Arlington, Virginia. After moving to Israel in 1972, he earned a B.A. in Jewish History and two teaching certificates from Hebrew University in Jerusalem. He then received an M.A., rabbinical ordination, and a Ph.D. in Talmud from the *Jewish Theological Seminary (JTS) in New York where he taught Talmud from 1980–82.

Upon returning to Israel in 1982, he taught Talmud and Jewish Law at Neve Schechter, the Jerusalem branch of JTS, until 1990. In 1987, he began to teach Jewish Law at the Seminary of Judaic Studies (later renamed the *Schechter Institute of Jewish Studies) which was founded in 1984 in order to train Israeli Conservative/Masorti rabbis. After serving as assistant dean and then dean of the Schechter Institute beginning in 1990, he was chosen as president in 2000.

Golinkin played a large part in the growth of the Schechter Institute during those years, as it grew rapidly from a small rabbinical school into four *amutot* (non-profits): the Schechter Institute of Jewish Studies, an accredited Israeli graduate school; the Schechter Rabbinical Seminary for Israelis and for visiting Conservative rabbinical students from JTS, the *University of Judaism, and the *Seminario Rabinico Latinoamericano; the TALI Education Fund which provides enriched Jewish education to 25,000 Israeli children in 140 TALI schools and pre-schools; and Midreshet Yerushalayim which teaches Jewish studies to Russian immigrants in Israel and to Jews in Ukraine and Hungary. Golinkin stated that his dream is to provide every Israeli and Eastern European Jew with a Jewish education.

Golinkin has published widely in various fields of Jewish studies. He is the author or editor of 31 books and almost 200 articles including *Rediscovering the Art of Jewish Prayer* (1997); *Ginzei Rosh Hashanah: Manuscripts of Bavli Rosh Hashanah from the Cairo Genizah* (2000); *Megillat Hashoah*, a liturgy for Yom Hashoah (2003); *Insight Israel: The View from Schechter* (2003); and works by Theodore *Friedman, Gershon *Levi, and Hayyim *Kieval.

Golinkin, however, is known primarily as one of the leading *posekim* in the worldwide Conservative/Masorti movement. He served on the *Vaʿad Halakhah* (Law Committee) of the Rabbinical Assembly of Israel from its inception in 1985 and has served as its chair for most of those years. Golinkin authored many of the responsa published by the *Vaʿad* and edited volumes 4–6.

Golinkin also authored a column entitled "Responsa" which appeared in *Moment* magazine from 1990–96. Those responsa were collected in *Responsa in a Moment* (2000).

Golinkin felt that it was very important to publish or republish Conservative responsa. To that end, he published *An Index of Conservative Responsa and Practical Halakhic Studies 1917–1990* (1992); *The Responsa of Professor Louis Ginzberg* (1996); *Proceedings of the Committee on Jewish Law and Standards of the Conservative Movement 1927–1970* (1997); and *Responsa and Halakhic Studies* by Rabbi Isaac Klein (2005). He also founded the Institute of Applied Halakhah at the Schechter Institute in 1996 in order to publish a library of halakhic works in various languages for the worldwide Conservative/Masorti movement.

Golinkin viewed the status of women in Jewish law as one of the main halakhic challenges of our time. He therefore devoted many responsa to this topic and helped found the Center for Women in Jewish Law at the Schechter Institute in 1999. In that capacity, Golinkin authored *The Status of Women in Jewish Law: Responsa* (2001) and edited *The Jewish Law Watch* (2000–03), *To Learn and To Teach* (2004ff.), and *Zaʿakat Dalot: Halakhic Solutions for the Agunot of our Time* (2006), all of which were published by the Center.

Golinkin's responsa and halakhic studies are known for their thoroughness, examining all sides of every issue using a wide range of talmudic, medieval, and modern sources. In *Halakhah for Our Time: A Conservative Approach to Jewish Law* (1991), Golinkin maintains that there are six characteristics of Conservative responsa, including preference for a *kula* (leniency) over a *humra* (stringency), the use of a historic-scientific approach, and an emphasis on the ethical component in Jewish law. Golinkin is firmly committed to the halakhic tradition but allows for change and flexibility in Jewish law, provided that such change is well-grounded in talmudic and halakhic sources.

BIBLIOGRAPHY: J. Adler, *The Jerusalem Post* (November 10, 2000), B12; S. Berkovic, *The Jerusalem Post* (May 3, 2002), B12; R. Brody, JQR XCII/1–2 (July–October 2001), 182–184; D. Ellenson, *Between Tradition and Culture* (1994), 101–114; Sh. Freedman, *In the Service of God* (1995), 61–73; M.Z. Fuchs, *Madaʿei ha-Yahadut* 40 (5760), 211–215; M.S. Geller, *Conservative Judaism*, 55:4 (Summer 2003), 92–93; G. Lichtman, *In Jerusalem* (October 6, 2000), 4; Sh. L. Sappir, *JTS Magazine*, 10:2 (Winter 2001), 16–17; Y. Sheleg, *Haaretz* (July 7, 2000), B7; Z. Zohar, *Tarbiz*, 68:2 (5759), 303–308; idem, *Nashim*, 7 (2004), 240–246.

[Monique Susskind Goldberg (2nd ed.)]

GOLINKIN, MORDECAI (1875–1963), conductor and pioneer of opera in Israel. Golinkin was born in Izluchistaya in the Ukrainian province of Kherson and as a boy sang in the choir of Phinehas *Minkowsky. In 1918 he became conductor at the Maryinsky Opera Theater in Petrograd. He conceived the idea of establishing an Opera in Palestine and gave a concert with the singer Chaliapin to raise funds for the project on which he published a pamphlet in 1920. In 1923 Golinkin immigrated to Palestine and in July of that year staged a performance in Hebrew of *La Traviata*, with local and guest singers, in Tel Aviv. His company, the Palestine Opera, gave intermittent opera performances until 1948, when he became conductor of the Israel Opera, a post he held until 1953. Golinkin's writings include *The Temple of Art* (1927, Hebrew and English), a volume of memoirs *Me-Heikhalei Yefet le-Oholei Shem* ("From the Palaces of Japheth to the Tents of Shem," 1947), and *Ha-Historyah ba-Opera* ("History in the Opera," 1961).

[Yemima Gottlieb]

GOLINKIN, MORDECHAI YA'AKOV (1884–1974), Orthodox rabbi, religious Zionist, *av bet din*. Born in the Kherson district of Ukraine and orphaned at a young age, Golinkin studied in the Lithuanian yeshivot of Lomza, Tiktin, and Lida, where he was called "the Khersoner Ilui" (prodigy). He was ordained in 1904 by Rabbi Mordechai (Slonimer) Oshminer and Rabbi Binyamin Ze'ev Zakheim of Yekaterinoslav.

In 1913 he published a book of sermons (*Derashot Harim*, Jerusalem, 2001^2). He then became the *av bet vin* and *de facto* chief rabbi of Zhitomir, capital of the Volyn (Volhynia) district of Ukraine where he developed a youth organization called Tiferet Bakhurim for 1,200 young men. Golinkin developed a good relationship with the governor of Volyn. As a result, Golinkin persuaded him to exempt from the Russian draft the yeshivah students of Novaredok who had fled to Zhitomir and he also prevented a blood libel in Zhitomir at the time of the *Beilis blood libel in Kiev in the fall of 1913.

After the February Revolution of 1917, Golinkin and Rabbi Solomon *Aronson of Kiev (later of Tel Aviv) and Rabbi Judah Leib *Zirelson of Kishinev formed Aḥdut, which proclaimed the religious and cultural rights of the Jews of Russia. After the October Revolution of 1917 and the subsequent pogroms of *Petlyura, Golinkin and his family fled to Vilna, where he worked at a number of Jewish institutions. Golinkin served as rabbi of Dokshitz near Vilna, where he founded a Yavneh religious Zionist day school and traveled to other cities to found Yavneh schools. From 1936 to 1939 he served as chief rabbi and *av bet din* of the Free State of Danzig, where he supervised the *kashrut* on the many ships embarking from Danzig and Gdynia. Since the Nazis forbade kosher slaughter, he arranged *sheḥitah* in the Polish town of Ossawa. After most of the Jews of Danzig fled before the Holocaust, Golinkin escaped to the United States in 1939, where he served as rabbi of Worcester, Massachusetts, until his death.

In October 1943, Golinkin participated in the historic March on Washington demanding action to save the Jews of Europe.

Golinkin also served as *av bet din* of the Orthodox Rabbinical Court of Justice of the Associated Synagogues of Massachusetts for over two decades, presiding over cases of national prominence. In 1969–1970, the Boston *bet din* spent 10 months studying the subject of civil disobedience and conscientious objection in light of the Vietnam War. In January 1970, it issued a 54-page responsum to the seven major questions. The Boston *bet din* showed that a rabbinic court could function as an activist court, which could go way beyond the domain of family matters.

Golinkin's son Rabbi Noah *Golinkin, a Conservative rabbi, was an activist during the Holocaust and a prominent Hebrew educator in North America.

BIBLIOGRAPHY: R. Medoff, *The Jewish Chronicle* (of Worcester), 77:20 (Sept. 25, 2003), 1, 21; A.Z. Rand (ed.), *Toledot Anshei Shem* (1950), 8; R. Gelmis, *Look Magazine* (April 1, 1969), 69; H. Levine and L. Harmon, *The Death of an American Jewish Community* (1992), 184–193; *Newsweek* (April 17, 1972), 54–55; I.M. Schaeffer, *The National Jewish Monthly*, 89:3 (November 1974), 28–38.

[David Golinkin (2nd ed.)]

GOLINKIN, NOAH (1914–2003), U.S. rabbi. After studying at various yeshivot and earning a law degree in Vilna, Noah Golinkin emigrated from his native Poland to the United States in 1938. He earned a master's degree in American history at Clark University before enrolling as a rabbinical student at the Jewish Theological Seminary in New York City.

In late 1942, Golinkin and fellow JTS students Jerome Lipnick and Moshe "Buddy" Sachs, Golinkin established the "European Committee of the Student Body of the Jewish Theological Seminary," to publicize the plight of Europe's Jews. Their first public program was a Jewish-Christian inter-seminary conference on European Jewry, in February 1943. Several hundred students and faculty, including representatives of eleven Christian seminaries, attended the sessions, which alternated between JTS and the nearby Union Theological Seminary. Speakers included prominent Jewish and Christian leaders and relief experts.

In a series of letters and articles in the spring of 1943, Golinkin and his colleagues took American Jewry to task for not actively pressing the Roosevelt administration to rescue Jews from Hitler. Their words of rebuke made a strong impression on the Synagogue Council of America, the national umbrella group for Orthodox, Conservative, and Reform synagogues. Shortly after meeting with Golinkin, Lipnick, and Sachs, the Synagogue Council established an emergency committee to raise Jewish and Christian awareness of the Nazi genocide and urge Allied intervention.

Closely following suggestions made by the students, the Synagogue Council undertook a nationwide campaign to coincide with the traditional seven weeks of semi-mourning between Passover and Shavuot. Numerous synagogues adopted the proposals to recite special prayers for European Jewry, limit "occasions of amusement," observe partial fast days and moments of silence, write letters to political officials and

Christian religious leaders, hold memorial rallies, and wear black armbands.

The rallies, held around the country on May 2, 1943, in many instances were jointly sponsored by Reform, Conservative, and Orthodox rabbis. The Federal Council of Churches organized memorial assemblies at churches in a number of cities on the same day, although Christian participation overall was modest. The gatherings received significant media coverage and increased public awareness of the Nazi slaughter of European Jewry.

After the war, Golinkin held pulpits in Virginia, Maryland, and elsewhere, and was the founding director of the Board of Jewish Education of Greater Washington, D.C. Fearing that the Hebrew language would become as little known to American Jews as Latin is to most Catholics, Golinkin created the Hebrew Literacy Campaign in 1963. In twelve weeks, every adult in the synagogue could read the prayer book, and the synagogue won the Solomon Schechter Award. He later expanded his efforts and convinced the National Federation of Jewish Men's Clubs to adopt the program. Golinkin's textbook *Shalom Aleichem* (1978) has sold over 100,000 copies, and the 1981 sequel, *Ein Keloheinu*, which teaches the Shabbat morning service, has been translated into Russian and Hungarian. His 1987 book, *While Standing on One Foot*, used in conjunction with a program he called the Hebrew Reading Marathon, teaches adults how to read Hebrew in one day. This book has been used by over 700 synagogues in 45 states, Canada, and Australia. It is estimated that more than 150,000 Jewish adults have learned how to read Hebrew in the two Golinkin programs since the 1960s.

Golinkin was also the originator, in 1989, of the custom, observed by a number of synagogues and Jewish organizations, to plant yellow tulips on Holocaust Remembrance Day as a reminder of the yellow star that Jews were forced by the Nazis to wear on their clothing.

BIBLIOGRAPHY: N. Golinkin et al, "The Holocaust Period," in: *The Reconstructionist*, 9:2 (March 5, 1943), 19–21; R. Medoff, in: *Holocaust and Genocide Studies*, 11:2 (Fall 1997); N. Golinkin, "The Hebrew Programs" in: *Proceedings of the Rabbinical Assembly*, 39 (1977), 62–67; 41 (1979), 193–196; 49 (1987), 226–230; *The Washington Post* (March 8, 2003), B7; D. Golinkin, *Insight Israel: The View from Schechter* (2003), 157–67.

°GOLITSYN, COUNT NIKOLAI NIKOLAYEVICH (1836–1893), Russian author and government official. While holding governmental positions in the *Pale of Settlement, and as editor of the semiofficial newspaper *Varshavskiy Dnevnik*, Golitsyn undertook an inquiry into the Jewish problem in Russia. He wrote studies and articles on the subject with an anti-Jewish approach during the 1870s, achieving the rep-utation among upper government circles of being an expert on the Jewish problem, and in 1883 was appointed by the ministry of the interior a member of the "High Commission for the Revision of the Current Laws Concerning the Jews" (the Von Pahlen Commission). In this connection, Golitsyn prepared a series of studies and memoranda, the most important of which was *Istoriya russkogo zakonodatelstva o yevreyakh 1649–1825 gg.* ("History of Russian Legis-lation Concerning the Jews 1649–1825"). The book, of 1,116 pages, provides an abundance of documents drawn from archives and is therefore of value. It was published in 1886 in 300 copies. Despite his anti-Jewish outlook, Golitsyn agreed with the conclusions of the Commission which recommended the gradual abolition of the restrictions against the Jews (1888).

BIBLIOGRAPHY: YE, 6 (c. 1910), 623; Dubnow, Hist Russ, 1 (1916), 392ff.; 2 (1918), 74ff.; I. Levitats, *Jewish Community in Russia, 1772–1844* (1943), 91, 102–4.

[Yehuda Slutsky]

GOLL, CLAIRE (1891–1977), German writer, journalist, and translator. Goll was born Clarisse Liliane Aischmann in Nuremberg into a strict family. In 1911, after the suicide of her brother and because of the mental disorder of her mother, she left her family and married the publisher Heinrich Studer. Her first publications, *Mitwelt* (1918), an anthology of poems, and her narratives *Die Frauen erwachen* (1918), were influenced by her family tragedies and focused on the suffering and mortified human being. Her texts are also committed to pacifism and can be classed as expressionistic. In the late 1910s Goll studied philosophy at the University of Geneva, broke up with her husband, and had a love affair with Rainer Maria Rilke. The correspondence between Rilke and Goll was published under the title *Ich sehne mich sehr nach deinen blauen Briefen* (2000). This exchange of letters contains seven poems in French from Rilke that were published as *Verges* in the journal *Nouvelle Revue Française* and the forgotten manuscript *Gefuehle* from Claire Goll.

In 1921 Goll married Yvan *Goll. With him she participated in the Dadaist meetings in Zurich and later invited Surrealists to their apartment in Paris. In 1927 Goll published *Eine Deutsche in Paris* (1927), which deals with the life and failure of a woman in Paris in the late 1920s. Her novel *Arsenik* (1932) also emphasizes the life of a woman around this period of time caught between love, failure, jealousy, and murder. Her own life with Yvan Goll was marked by a volatile relationship which both worked through in their *Poèmes d'amours* (1925), *Poèmes de la jalousie* (1926), and *Poèmes de la vie et de la mort* (1926). Most of Goll's texts had been written originally in French and translated by Goll herself. In 1939 Goll immigrated to the United States, returning in 1947 to Paris, where Yvan Goll died. After his death Goll became a disputatious editor of her husband's works and published her autobiography, *Ich verzeihe keinem: Eine literarische Chronique scandaleuse unserer Zeit* (1976). In 1953 she confronted Paul *Celan with the accusation of plagiarism, claiming that Celan had copied from Yvan Goll's *Traumkraut*. Her own novels *Der gestohlene Himmel* (1962) and *Traumtänzerin* (1971) went unnoticed. They link up with her early writings narrating her childhood and youth.

BIBLIOGRAPHY: C. Pleiner, *Du uebtest mit mir das feuer-*

feste Lied: Eros und Intertextualität bei Claire und Iwan Goll (1999); V. Mahlow, *Die Liebe, die uns immer zur Hemmung wurde: weibliche Identitätsproblematik zwischen Expressionismus und Neuer Sachlichkeit am Beispiel der Prosa Claire Golls* (1996); E. Robertson (ed.), *Yvan Goll-Claire Goll: Texts and Contexts* (1997).

[Ann-Kristin Koch (2nd ed.)]

GOLL, YVAN (Isaac Lang; 1891–1950), Franco-German poet and author. Born in Saint-Dié des Vosges, Goll studied law at the universities of Strasbourg and Paris. Even though French was his native language he at first wrote in German. Under the nom de plume Iwan Lazang he made his debut with *Lothringische Volkslieder* (1912). Two years later his collection of poems *Der Panamakanal* (1914) was published and owed some of its material to the expressionist circles he belonged to. With the beginning of World War I Goll as a committed pacifist moved to Switzerland, where he continued his studies in Lausanne and he kept company with Romain Rolland, Stefan *Zweig, Hermann Hesse, Franz *Werfel, and René Schickele. His sympathies transcended political boundaries, and he followed his *Requiem pour les morts de l'Europe* (1916) with a German version, *Requiem fuer die Gefallenen von Europa* (1917). *Der Torso* (1918) is a collection of poems that display Goll's pacifist beliefs and are written in an expressionist style. Not only could he share his pacifist ideas with like-minded intellectuals but he also met Dadaists like Hans Arp and Tristan *Tzara, who influenced his writings and later led to the publication of two essays portraying Arp: "Der Homer unserer Zeit" (1927) and "Aus dem Leben eines Genies" (1932). After World War I Goll published articles and poems in left-wing journals on political themes, such as the revolution in *Die letzten Tage von Berlin* (1919) and social inequity in the poems of *Die Unterwelt* (1919). In 1919 Goll settled in Paris, where he married the writer Claire Aischmann (see preceding entry). He soon turned away from expressionism, criticizing its political ineffectiveness and its tendency to sentimentality in his essay "Der Expressionismus stirbt" (1921). Goll became interested in surrealism and in 1924 established the magazine *Surréalisme*. He also published poems in *Der Eiffelturm* (1924) which took on the main characteristics of this literary movement, such as montage and the imitation of visual signs and the rapidity of film.

During the time in Paris Goll became a friend of James Joyce and Stefan *Zweig and published the first German translation of Joyce's novel *Ulysses*. Until 1925 he continued to write in German, his books including *Das Herz des Feindes* (1920), and the drama *Der Stall des Augias* (1924). Together with his wife, Goll published three anthologies of French verse: *Poèmes d'amour* (1925), *Poèmes de jalousie* (1926), and *Poèmes de la vie et de la mort* (1926). In the 1930s Goll was friendly with the Austrian lyricist Paula Ludwig, resulting in the *Chansons malaises* (1934). Goll started writing his novels in the late 1920s and focused on social problems. *Le Microbe de l'Or* (1927), for example, can be read as a coming to terms with his family. In *Die Eurokokke* (1928) and *Der Mitropäer* (1928) Goll sketches the decay of European culture and modernity per se. Especially *Sodome et Berlin* (1929) is a sharply etched caricature of civil society in Berlin.

Jewish themes constantly recur in the rich and complex work of this cosmopolitan poet. Prominent among them are loneliness, eternal wandering between two worlds and three languages, the haunting presence of poverty, war, and death, and the search for salvation in occult and kabbalistic speculation. The figures of Job and of the *Wandering Jew merge with the homeless poet himself in a major verse collection *La Chanson de Jean sans Terre* (3 vols., 1936–39), where the only certainty in a foundering universe is total annihilation. In 1939 Goll and his wife fled to the U.S. While they were living in New York he published the literary magazine, *Hémisphères*, and a volume of English poems, *Fruit from Saturn* (1946), as a literary response to the dropping of the atomic bomb on Hiroshima. In 1947 Goll and his wife returned to Paris, where he struggled with leukemia. On his sickbed Goll reverted to writing in German. Two volumes of poetry appeared after his death: *Traumkraut* (1951), a collection of poems dealing with his experience of illness and death, and *Neila* (1954). Two other posthumous works were *Abendgesang* (1954) and a play, *Melusine* (1956). Other late works of Yvan Goll are *Le Char Triomphal de l'Antimoine* (1949), *Les Géorgiques parisiennes* (1951), and *Les Cercles magiques* (1951). His scattered publications were collected by his widow in *Dichtungen: Lyrik, Prosa, Drama* (1960) and also in a collection of poems in *Yvan Goll: 100 Gedichte* (2003).

ADD. BIBLIOGRAPHY: Y. Goll, in: *Europe 899* (2004); C. Pleiner, *"Du uebtest mit mir das feuerfeste Lied": Eros und Intertextualitaet bei Claire und Iwan Goll* (1999); H. Schmidt, *Art mondial: Formen der Internationalität bei Yvan Goll* (1999); M. Mueller-Lentrodt, *Poetik fuer eine brennende Welt: Zonen der Poetik Yvan Golls im Kontext der europaeischen Avantgarde* (1997); M. Knauf, *Yvan Goll: ein Intellektueller zwischen zwei Laendern und zwei Avantgarden* (1996); J. Phillips, *Yvan Goll and Bilingual Poetry* (1984).

[Claude (Andre) Vigee / Ann-Kristin Koch (2nd ed.)]

GOLLANCZ, SIR HERMANN (1852–1930), rabbi and teacher. Gollancz was born in Bremen and was the brother of Sir Israel *Gollancz. He officiated at the Bayswater Synagogue (1892–1923) and taught Hebrew at University College, London (1902–24). In 1897, when he received the rabbinic diploma on the Continent from three Galician rabbis, he became the center of a controversy over whether the rabbinic title should be a recognized qualification for the Anglo-Jewish clergy with the ultimate result that the title was so recognized. Gollancz published a number of critical editions and translations from Hebrew, Aramaic, and Syriac, including a Hebrew and English edition of *Sefer Mafte'aḥ Shelomo* (1914) and also of Joseph Kimḥi's *Shekel ha-Kodesh* (1919). Hermann was the first English rabbi to receive a knighthood (1923).

BIBLIOGRAPHY: Loewe, in: DNB (1922–1930), 350–1; H. Gollancz, *Personalia* (includes bibliography); P.H. Emden, *Jews of Britain* (1943), 123–5.

[Cecil Roth]

GOLLANCZ, SIR ISRAEL (1864–1930), English literary scholar. Gollancz, son of the Rev. Samuel Marcus Gollancz, minister of the Hambro Synagogue in London and a brother of Rabbi Sir Hermann *Gollancz, was lecturer in English at University College, London (1892–95), and then at Cambridge. In 1903 he was appointed professor of English at King's College, London. An outstanding Shakespearean scholar, Gollancz also made important contributions to the study of early English literature and philology. His works include an edition and translation of the 14th-century alliterative poem, *Pearl* (1891), an edition of Marlowe's *Dr. Faustus* (1897), *The Sources of Hamlet* (1926), and *The Caedmon MS of Anglo-Saxon Biblical Poetry…* (1927). He was also general editor of the Temple Classics and of the highly successful Temple Shakespeare. Gollancz did not confine his activities to the area of English literature. In 1902 he helped to found the British Academy, of which he remained secretary until his death. In this capacity he was instrumental in establishing the British School of Archaeology in Jerusalem in 1920. He was knighted in 1919. He took an interest in Jewish affairs, especially in the training of rabbis. He also served on the council of Jews' College, London, for some years.

ADD. BIBLIOGRAPHY: ODNB online.

[Harold Harel Fisch]

GOLLANCZ, SIR VICTOR (1893–1967), English publisher and author. The grandson of a *ḥazzan* and nephew of Rabbi Sir Hermann *Gollancz and Sir Israel *Gollancz, Victor Gollancz early rejected his family's religious Orthodoxy and all middle-class conservatism. Appalled by poverty and suffering, he sought to combat these ills through socialism and, later, pacifism. While an undergraduate at Oxford, he took a brief interest in Liberal Judaism, but was increasingly drawn to Christianity, although he never formally converted. After a period as a classics teacher, Gollancz entered publishing, and in 1928 founded his own publishing house. In 1936, together with John Strachey and Harold *Laski, he established the Left Book Club, whose aim was to expose Nazism and to "halt Hitler with war." Their success in providing informative books at low cost was a remarkable feat of political publishing. The club, which became a nationwide social and political movement, had some 60,000 members at its peak, but did not survive the Nazi-Soviet pact of 1939, which for Gollancz was an intolerable betrayal.

During World War II Gollancz was one of the founders and leading members of the National Committee for Rescue from Nazi Terror, an organization which tried to save some of Hitler's victims, and was one of the first people in Britain to understand and internalize the horrors of the Holocaust. Later he sponsored other humanitarian causes, such as the "Save Europe Now" campaign to alleviate starvation in Germany in the post-World War II period, the Association for World Peace (later known as "War on Want"), and the British campaign against capital punishment. Although from 1945 onward he fought the Palestine policy of British foreign secretary Ernest Bevin and endeavored to secure the admission of Jewish refugees to Palestine, Gollancz behaved characteristically when he headed an organization for relief work for the Arabs during Israel's War of Independence and later for Arab refugees in the Gaza Strip. He advocated reconciliation between Jews and Germans and between Jews and Arabs. At the same time he was on the board of governors of the Hebrew University in Jerusalem from 1952 to 1964.

A bon vivant with mystical longings, a successful businessman who opposed capitalism, an idealist tortured by a guilt complex, Gollancz wrote on many subjects. His books include *The Brown Book of the Hitler Terror* (1933); a translation (1943) of *Why I Am A Jew* by Edmond *Fleg; two autobiographical works addressed to his grandson, *My Dear Timothy* (1952) and *More for Timothy* (1953); *The Case of Adolf Eichmann* (1961), which expressed his total opposition to the trial of the Nazi criminal; and several religious anthologies and essays on music. He was knighted in 1965. Some of his views were considered bizarre by many Jews.

ADD. BIBLIOGRAPHY: ODNB online; DBB, II, 591–95; R.D. Edwards, *Victor Gollancz: A Biography* (1987); S. Hodges, *Gollancz: The Story of a Publishing House* (1978); P. Duff, *Left, Left, Left* (1971); W.D. Rubinstein, *Great Britain*, 266–67, index.

[Renee Winegarten]

GOLLER, IZAK (1891–1939), English author and rabbi. Born in Lithuania, Goller was taken to England as a child. He served congregations in Manchester, London, and finally the Hope Place Synagogue in Liverpool, where his advanced social views and outspoken addresses led to his dismissal in 1926. With characteristic defiance, Goller subsequently reestablished himself in the Young Israel (Zionist) Synagogue in Liverpool. His verse collection, *The Passionate Jew and Cobbles of the God-Road* (1923), violently denounced the atrocities committed against the Jews of Eastern Europe after World War I. It was followed by *A Jew Speaks!* (1926), a book of poetry and prose which, like many of Goller's subsequent publications, was illustrated with the author's original "cartoons." Goller's novel, *The Five Books of Mr. Moses* (1929), was dramatized as *Cohen and Son* (1937), a Jewish mystery play in "three acts, ten scenes, and a melody," and first performed in London in 1932. Other plays on Jewish themes were *Judah and Tamar, Modin Women*, and *A Purim Night's Dream* (all in 1931), and *The Scroll of Lot's Wife* (1937). A statement of his faith as a Jew was contained in *First Chapter – A Summary of the History of My People from Abraham of Ur to Herzl of Budapest* (1936).

BIBLIOGRAPHY: Temkin, in: JC (June 30, 1939); G.E. Silverman, in: *Liverpool Jewish Gazette* (June 24, 1960); idem, in: *Niv ha-Midrashiyyah* (Spring 1970), 74–81, English section.

[Godfrey Edmond Silverman]

GOLLUF, ELEAZAR (d. 1389), courtier and agent of the royal family of Aragon; member of a prominent Saragossa family. In 1376 he was permitted to carry arms and exempted from wearing the Jewish *badge. From 1383 he served as agent of the infante John, son of Pedro IV of Aragon, and of his wife Violante. After John ascended the throne in 1387 Golluf served as "chief agent of the queen" – in fact her chief treasurer – a position that had not been held by a Jew in Aragon for a century. His ledgers are not preserved, and may have been intentionally destroyed even before the end of the Middle Ages. A devoted Jew, Golluf's activities in Jewish affairs extended beyond his own community. After Golluf's death, his son ISAAC converted to Christianity, first obtaining the king's promise that he should nevertheless inherit his father's property. His name as a Christian was Juan Sánchez de Calatayud. He was the grandfather of Gabriel *Sánchez, a leading official during the reign of Ferdinand and Isabella and a supporter of Christopher Columbus.

BIBLIOGRAPHY: Baer, Spain, index, s.v. *Alazar Golluf*; Baer, Urkunden, 1 (1929), 610–6; M. Serrano y Sanz, *Orígenes de la dominación española en America*, 1 (1918), 138, 502f.; Lóz de Meneses, in: *Sefarad*, 14 (1954), 110.

GOLOBOFF, GERARDO MARIO (1939–), writer and literary critic. Born in Carlos Casares, one of the agricultural colonies established by the Jewish Colonization Association in Argentina, Goloboff was formally trained as a lawyer but dedicated his life to literature. He wrote books on renowned Argentine authors such as Roberto Arlt, Jorge Luis Borges, and Julio Cortázar. He taught literature for almost 20 years in France. He later resided in Argentina.

Goloboff's first book was *Entre la diáspora y octubre* (1966), a collection of poetry. It was followed by the novel *Caballos por el fondo de los ojos* (1976), published the same year that the military coup d'état occurred. He is best known for his trilogy of novels that takes place in the fictional town of Algarrobos: *El criador de palomas* (1988), *La luna que cae* (1989), and *El soñador de Smith* (1990). Together the novels recreate, to a certain extent, the author's own experience growing up in the countryside. Goloboff manages to insert Jewish specificity into a long tradition of literary myth-making begun in the 19th century that arises from the Pampa, mainly in the form of gauchesque literature. The novels have been widely praised for the author's lyrical style of story-telling that combine biblical imagery with the allegorical representation of Argentine socio-historical reality, while at the same time weaving a mystery for the main character, El Pibe, to unravel in an attempt to uncover his past. Although his most recent novel, *Comuna Verdad* (1995), also takes place in Algarrobos it is not part of the aforementioned trilogy. This fifth novel is based more strictly on historical circumstances and events, namely the formation of an agricultural commune by an anarchist group of primarily immigrant origins. Nevertheless, all four of these last titles are gathered together in English translation under the title *The Algarrobos Quartet* (2002).

[Darrell B. Lockhart (2nd ed.)]

GOLODNY, MIKHAIL (Mikhail Semyonovich Epshtein; 1903–1949), Russian poet. Golodny was first inspired by the heroism of the civil war and wrote verse distinguished for its simplicity and song-like quality. His World War II collections include *Pesni i ballady Otechestvennoy voyny* ("Songs and Ballads of… War," 1942) and *Stikhi ob Ukraine* ("Poems about the Ukraine," 1942). Golodny's *Stikhi, ballady, pesni* ("Poems, Ballads, Songs") appeared in 1952.

GOLOMB, ABRAHAM (1888–1982), Yiddish writer and educator. Born in Lithuania, Golomb studied at yeshivot and at the University of Kiev. In 1921–31 he directed the Yiddish Teachers' Seminary in Vilna. He settled as a teacher in Palestine (1932), before moving to Winnipeg, Manitoba, Canada, (1938) to become the principal of the Peretz School, to Mexico City (1944) to head Yiddish schools there, and finally to Los Angeles (1964–82). In his hundreds of articles and many books he expounded his ideology of "Integral Jewishness," which includes the language, festivals, religious observances, family relationships, and ideals of the Jews, which collective experience he deemed essential for the continued existence of the Jewish people. Like Simon *Dubnow and *Aḥad Ha-Am, Golomb stressed the need for retaining Jewish distinctiveness in the Diaspora, holding that this will remain a continuing fact of Jewish historic life, no matter how much the Jewish center in Israel grows. Golomb called for maximum efforts to retain both Yiddish and Hebrew as national languages of the Jewish people. Diaspora communities which were giving up Yiddish were becoming fossilized and fragmented into the scattered dying remnants of a people. He advocated the canonization of the finest works of Yiddish literature, as had been done with earlier holy works in Hebrew. Golomb enriched the Yiddish vocabulary of science and psychology and supplemented his theoretical discourses with practical classroom texts. His selected works *Geklibene Shriftn* ("Selected Works") appeared in six volumes (1945–48).

BIBLIOGRAPHY: Rejzen, Leksikon, 1 (1926), 464–6; S. Kahan, *Literarische un Zhurnalistische Fartseykhnungen* (1961), 259–62. **ADD. BIBLIOGRAPHY:** T. Soxberger, in: G. Estraikh and M. Krutikov (eds.), *Yiddish and the Left* (2001), 195–207.

[Sol Liptzin / Gennady Estraikh (2nd ed.)]

GOLOMB, ELIYAHU (1893–1945), leader of Jewish defense in Palestine and main architect of the *Haganah. Born in Volkovysk, Belorussia, Golomb went to Ereẓ Israel in 1909 and was a pupil in the Herzlia High School's first graduating class of 1913. He organized his fellow graduates into the Histadrut Meẓumẓemet (approximately "The Inner Circle") for agricultural training, service in Jewish settlements, and the realization of Zionist ideals, and himself went to train at *Deganyah. At the outbreak of World War I he opposed the enlistment of young Jews as officers in the Turkish Army and insisted on the formation of an independent Jewish defense force. In 1918 Golomb was a founder and leading member of the movement to encourage volunteers for the *Jewish Legion, in which he served as a corporal. He hoped that the Legion would form the basis for a permanent official Jewish militia. While serving in the army, he became friendly with Berl *Katznelson and joined the *Aḥdut ha-Avodah Party upon its foundation in 1919. After his demobilization he became a member of the committee to organize the Haganah and was active in dispatching aid to the defenders of *Tel Ḥai (1920).

In contrast to the *Ha-Shomer policy, Golomb realized that Jewish defense was a matter for the Jewish population at large, and not the concern of an elite of fighters. He successfully propagated this idea among the leaders of the *yishuv*. From 1921 Golomb was a member of the Haganah Committee of the *Histadrut and, in 1922, was sent abroad to purchase arms; he was arrested by the Vienna police in July of that year. He purchased arms and organized pioneering youth in Europe until 1924. In 1931 he was one of the three representatives of the Histadrut in the Mifkadah ha-Arẓit, the parity National Command of the Haganah.

Golomb regarded the Haganah as the arm of the nation and of the Zionist Movement and thus brought it under the auspices of the national institutions, although these were unable to express their opinions on defense matters openly. In consequence, he was violently opposed to the dissident armed organizations, *Irgun Ẓeva'i Le'ummi and *Loḥamei Ḥerut Israel (Leḥi), but tried to avoid futile hatred and attempted to find ways of reuniting them with the main body. In 1939 and 1940 he and Berl Katznelson tried to reach an agreement with Vladimir *Jabotinsky and the Revisionists over the reunification of the Zionist movement and the formation of a single defense command.

During the Arab riots of 1936–39 Golomb was one of the initiators of the "field units" (*pelugot sadeh*) that went out to confront Arab terrorists in combat. He thus supported active defense and the punishment of terrorists; but, for both moral and tactical reasons, he opposed indiscriminate reprisals against the Arab population. Golomb supported all forms of cooperation with the British authorities that permitted secret stockpiling of weapons and military training, but never forgot the fundamental conflict existing between the alien regime and the clandestine Haganah. He always opposed giving information to the British concerning the strength and equipment of the Haganah. Golomb was among those who supported the enlistment of volunteers into the British Army during World War II and proposed the parachuting of Jews into occupied Europe. He was one of the founders and builders of the *Palmaḥ and prepared the Haganah for the future struggle of the Jewish people in Palestine. He inspired and educated many commanders of the Haganah and future officers of the Israel Defense Forces.

Golomb was active in Ereẓ Israel public life. He was a leader of Aḥdut ha-Avodah (later of *Mapai), and of the Histadrut, a member of the Va'ad Le'ummi as well as a delegate to Zionist congresses. His articles appeared in the Hebrew labor press, and a number of them were collected into two volumes, *Ḥevyon Oz* (1950–54), which also included memoirs and reminiscences by his friends. His home in Tel Aviv was turned into a Haganah museum.

BIBLIOGRAPHY: Dinur, Haganah, index; Z. Shazar, *Or Ishim* (1964^2), 182–8; S. Avigur, *Im Dor ha-Haganah* (1962^3), 143–73; M. Sharett, *Orot she-Kavu* (1969), 13–25; Y. Allon, *The Making of the Israeli Army* (1970).

[Yehudah Erez and Haim Hillel Ben-Sasson]

GOLOMBEK, HARRY (1911–1995), British writer on chess and grandmaster. Born in London to recent immigrants from Poland, Golombek became British chess champion five times and served as a senior official at many World Championship matches. He was best known, however, as a chess writer and journalist, the author of more than 30 books on chess, and the chess correspondent of the London *Times* newspaper from 1945 until 1989. In these decades he was almost certainly the best-known chess writer in Britain, although he made less of an impact in the United States. He was known for his excellent writing style and conscientious annotations and commentary.

BIBLIOGRAPHY: ODNB online.

[William D. Rubinstein (2nd ed.)]

GOLOVANEVSK, town in Odessa district, Ukraine. Jews settled there in the middle of the 18th century and numbered 456 in 1790. Their number rose to 1,974 in 1847, and 4,320 (53% of the total population) in 1897. In 1910 a Jewish school for boys opened. During the civil war of 1918–19 the community formed a strong *self-defense organization which deterred the peasants of the surrounding region from pogroms, and 2,000 refugees from neighboring localities found refuge in Golovanevsk. At the end of 1919, however, armed bands of peasants led by the hetman Sokolowski broke into the town, overcame the self-defense units, and carried out pogroms in which over 200 Jews lost their lives. There were 3,474 Jews (86% of the population) living in Golovanevsk in 1926. Many Jewish families were occupied in farming. A Yiddish school operated there. By 1939 the number of Jews had dropped to 1,393. Golovanevsk was occupied on August 1, 1941, by the Germans, who soon executed 100 Jews. In September the Germans with help of the Ukrainian police murdered 776 Jews, raping young girls and hurling infants alive into the burial pits. On January 3, 1942, they murdered 36 children from a nearby children's home and in February 1942 they killed another 168 Jews, including 49 children.

BIBLIOGRAPHY: I. Klinov, *In der Tekufah fun Revolutsye* (1923), 157–210; A.D. Rosental, *Megillat ha-Tevaḥ*, 2 (1931), 3–16.

[Yehuda Slutsky / Shmuel Spector (2nd ed.)]

GOLSCHMANN, VLADIMIR (1893–1972), conductor. Born in Paris to Russian parents, Golschmann founded the Concerts Golschmann in 1919, which gave many important first performances. In 1920, he conducted performances for Diaghilev's Ballet Russe, as he was later to do for Pavlova. He made guest appearances with leading French orchestras in New York (1924) and Glasgow (from 1928). From 1931, he was principal conductor of the St. Louis Symphony Orchestra, a post he held for more than 25 years until his resignation in 1958. From 1964 until his retirement in 1970, he was conductor of the Denver Symphony Orchestra. Golschmann was awarded the Ordre des Arts et des Lettres and became an Officier de la Legion d'Honneur.

[Max Loppert (2nd ed.)]

GOLUB, LEON (1922–2004), U.S. painter and printmaker. Chicago-born Golub received a B.A. in art history from the University of Chicago (1942) and a BFA (1949) and MFA (1950) from the Art Institute of Chicago. Although he did not experience combat, his experience in the army during World War II as a cartographer of reconnaissance maps influenced his art during the postwar years, which frequently focused on the abuse of power and victimization. Based on newspaper photographs of Holocaust victims, the expressionistic lithograph *Charnel House* (1946) shows a mass of anguished figures twisting helplessly in ambiguous space. Similarly, *Damaged Man* (1955, private collection) from the Burnt Man series (1954–55; 1960–61) references the Holocaust; the painting presents a single flayed human figure isolated at the center of the canvas. Finding the United States inhospitable to his figurative, socially conscious work, Golub and his artist-wife Nancy *Spero moved to Paris in 1959, where they remained until 1964 when they took up permanent residence in New York City.

War and man's inhumanity to man remained a constant theme for his entire career. His style and subject work together; since 1951, Golub frequently scraped down and reworked his heavily applied paint, often brutalizing the surface of his large canvases as deeply as the oppressed figures he painted. Golub based his figures on classical art, such as the Hellenistic Altar of Pergamon, and from around 1956–57 he added contemporary news photographs to his source material. He often employed several photographs for single figures, amalgamating data to create the most effective composite of gestures, postures, and expressions to convey a theme. In 1970 Golub ceased placing his canvases on stretchers, instead nailing the unstretched canvas on a wall of his studio. At this time he also began cutting out portions of the canvas to draw attention to aspects of the composition.

He typically produced cycles of paintings on a theme, including the Combat (1962–65), Vietnam (1972–73), and Interrogation (1980–81) series, all of which explored the condition of victims and tyrants through the successive wars and struggles of his era. From 1976 to 1979, Golub made several hundred portraits of powerful figures such as Henry Kissinger and Fidel Castro, often in several versions.

BIBLIOGRAPHY: D. Kuspit, *Leon Golub: Existential/Activist Painter* (1985); G. Marzorati, *A Painter of Darkness: Leon Golub and Our Times* (1990); S. Horodner, *Leon Golub: While the Crime is Blazing, Paintings and Drawings, 1994–1999* (1999); J. Bird, *Leon Golub: Echoes of the Real* (2000).

[Samantha Baskind (2nd ed.)]

°GOLUCHOWSKI, AGENOR SEN., COUNT (1812–1875), Austrian politician, minister of the interior, and three times governor of Galicia. A conservative and a fervent Polish patriot, he was an opponent of Jewish emancipation. Claiming to "discover" conflicts among the Jews, he aspired to lead the "enlightened" Jews against the Orthodox. However, in parliament, he was leader of those conservatives who, while masking their antisemitism, fought against any changes in the condition of the Jews. When the Lvov municipality had twice rejected the right of the Jews to quit the ghetto (1846, 1855), the problem came before Goluchowski as minister of interior; he gave the casting vote against the Jews. In 1857 he forbade Jews to employ Christian servants. While he introduced a project granting Jews the right to acquire real property in 1865, when his project was passed to a commission he made no attempt to defend it and it never became law.

ADD. BIBLIOGRAPHY: T. Andlauer, *Die juedische Bevoelkerung im Modernisierungsprozess Galiziens 1867–1918* (2001); Y. Ben-Avner, "The Civil State of Jews in the Austrian Empire in the First Decade of the Reign of Emperor Francis Joseph I (1849–1859)" (Diss., Ramat Gan 1978); M. Fagard, "La question juive en Autrich-Hongrie (1867–1918)" (Diss., Paris 1996); Ph. Friedman, *Die galizischen Juden im Kampfe um ihre Gleichberechtigung, 1848–1868* (1929), index.

GOMBERG, MOSES (1866–1947), U.S. organic chemist, born in Yelizavetgrad (now Kirovograd), Russia. In 1884 his father was accused of anti-czarist activities and fled with his family to Chicago, U.S.A. In spite of financial hardship, Moses graduated at the University of Michigan. In 1896–97 he went to Germany to work with Baeyer at Munich and Victor Meyer at Heidelberg. He subsequently returned to the University of Michigan where he became professor of chemistry. During World War I, he undertook the (to him abhorrent) task of working out commercial production of mustard gas, and as a major in the ordinance department advised on the manufacture of smokeless powder and high explosives. Of his various activities in organic chemistry – including the diazo reaction that bears his name – he is best known for his work on free radicals and his demonstration that carbon can exhibit a valency of three instead of the normal four. He was president of the American Chemical Society in 1931.

BIBLIOGRAPHY: Schoepele and Bachmann, in: *Journal of the American Chemical Society*, 69 (1948), 2921–25; E. Farber (ed.), *Great Chemists* (1962), 1211–17.

[Samuel Aaron Miller]

GOMBINER, ABRAHAM ABELE BEN ḤAYYIM HA-LEVI (c. 1637–1683), Polish rabbi. After the death of his parents during the Chmielnicki massacres of 1648, Abraham left his birthplace, Gombin. In 1655 he went to Lithuania, and there studied with his relative, Jacob Isaac Gombiner. Later he went to Kalisz, where he was appointed head of the yeshivah and *dayyan* of the *bet din*. Abraham is best known for his *Magen Avraham* (Dyhernfurth, 1692), a commentary on the Shulḥan Arukh *Oraḥ Ḥayyim*, highly esteemed throughout Poland and Germany by scholars who followed it in their halakhic decisions, at times against the opinions of other codifiers. In his work Abraham reveals his acumen, depth of insight, and comprehensive knowledge of the entire halakhic literature. Abraham's main purpose was to reach a compromise between the decisions of Joseph *Caro and the glosses of Moses *Isserles, but he upholds the latter where no compromise can be arrived at. He regarded all Jewish customs as sacred and endeavored to justify them even where they were at variance with the views of the codifiers. He also thought highly of the Zohar and of the kabbalists Isaac Luria and R. Isaiah Horowitz, occasionally accepting their decision against that of the codifiers. *Magen Avraham* is written in a terse style, which scholars were at times hard put to understand until the appearance of R. Samuel ha-Levi *Kolin's extensive commentary, *Maḥaẓit ha-Shekel.*

Abraham is also the author of *Zayit Ra'anan* (Dessau, 1704), a commentary on the *Yalkut Shimoni*, published together with some of his homilies on Genesis, *Shemen Sason. Zayit Ra'anan* was also published in abridged form in the margins of the *Yalkut*, in the 1876 edition and in all subsequent editions. His short commentary on the Tosefta of *Nezikin* was published by his grandson under the title *Magen Avraham* at the end of the *Leḥem ha-Panim* (Amsterdam, 1732) of his son-in-law, Moses Jekuthiel Kaufmann. A commentary to Job, Proverbs, and Ecclesiastes was attributed in error to him, having in fact been taken from the *Beit Avraham* of Abraham b. Samuel *Gedaliah.

BIBLIOGRAPHY: Landshuth, Ammudei, 2; Fuenn, Keneset, 17, s.v. *Avraham b. Ḥayyim ha-Levi Gombiner*; M. Freudenthal, *Aus der Heimat Mendelssohns* (1900), 20f.; S. Knoebil, *Toledot Gedolei Hora'ah* (1927), 99–103; Ḥ. Tchernowitz, *Toledot ha-Posekim*, 3 (1947), 164–72; J.L. Maimon, in: Y. Raphael (ed.), *Rabbi Yosef Caro* (Heb., 1969), 62f.; M. Strashun, *Mivḥar Ketavim* (1969), 323–3.

[Shmuel Ashkenazi]

GOMBRICH, SIR ERNST HANS (1909–2001), British historian of art. Probably the best-known historian of art in modern Britain, Gombrich was born into a cultured Jewish household in Vienna – Freud and Mahler were family friends – where he studied and worked as a museum curator. He was also a member of the famous Vienna Circle of philosophers. Gombrich immigrated to Britain in 1936. He spent virtually all of his professional life at the Warburg Institute in London, serving as its director from 1959 to 1976, and was professor of the history of art at London University. His best-known works include *The Story of Art* (1950), which has been translated into 20 languages; *Art and Illusion* (1960); and *Meditations on a Hobby Horse* (1963). A collection of his writings, *The Essential Gombrich,* edited by Richard Woodfield, appeared in 1996. Gombrich was knighted in 1972 and appointed to the Order of Merit (O.M.) in 1988.

BIBLIOGRAPHY: J.B. Trapp, *E.H. Gombrich: A Bibliography* (2000).

[William D. Rubinstein (2nd ed.)]

GOMEL (**Homel**; in Jewish sources, *Homiyyah*), district capital in Belarus. The beginning of Jewish settlement is apparently connected with the annexation of the town to Lithuania in 1537. The community of Belitsa (which became a suburb of Gomel in 1854) is mentioned in 1639 as one of the Lithuanian communities. During the *Chmielnicki massacres in 1648 many refugees from the Ukraine fled to Gomel, but the Cossack armies reached the city and massacred about 2,000 Jews there. Many saved their lives by converting to Christianity, but returned to Judaism when the Poles returned in 1665 and the Jewish community was renewed. By 1765 there were 658 Jews living in the city. *Ḥabad Ḥasidism won many converts there, and in the mid-19th century one of its leaders, Isaac b. Mordecai *Epstein, served as rabbi.

The city was given the status of district capital in 1852, its geographical situation and position as a railroad junction making it an important commercial center. The annual fair attracted many Jewish merchants. The community increased from 2,373 in 1847, with an additional 1,552 in Belitsa, to 20,385 in 1897 (56.4% of the total population). It had 30 synagogues, including the great synagogue built by Count Rumyantsev in the middle of the 19th century; only two remained by 1941. While a few wealthy Jews in Gomel traded in forest products or were government contractors, many thousands of poor families lived in the "Rov," the valley described by J.Ḥ. *Brenner in his *Me-Emek Akhor* (1900). Toward the end of the 19th century a Jewish revolutionary movement, centered on the Bund, developed in Gomel. Zionism also gained many adherents there and several Hebrew schools were established. Zionists from Gomel settled in Ereẓ Israel and participated in the building of Ḥaderah; many were pioneers of the Second and Third Aliyah. In the summer of 1903 there was a pogrom in Gomel in which eight Jews were killed, many wounded, and much Jewish property looted. A *self-defense group was organized under the command of Yeḥezkel Henkin in which the Jewish political parties participated. Subsequently, 36 of its members were prosecuted by the authorities, in company with the perpetrators of the pogroms, and charged with committing pogroms against the Russian population. During World War I, thousands of refugees from the war zone took refuge in Gomel and several yeshivot moved there from Poland and Lithuania. In the 1917–1926 period many Zionist groups were active. They ran two Hebrew kindergartens and a Hebrew high school.

After the consolidation of the Soviet regime, Jewish religious and nationalist elements struggled against the Communist campaign to win over the masses. Nevertheless, the *ḥadarim* were closed down, beautiful synagogues were converted to secular purposes, and Jewish communal life came to an end. The rabbi of Gomel, R. Borishanski, was arrested for opposing the Communist suppression of the Jewish religion. The community decreased from 47,505 in 1910 (55%) to 37,745 in 1926 (43.7%). Most of the city's artisans were Jews. Among the Jewish working population in 1926, 3,482 were factory hands, 4,057 white-collar workers, 3,235 artisans, and 5,046 worked the land. In 1930 there were eight Jewish kolkhozes near the city, where 1,889 Jews (400 families) farmed 21,000 acres of land. In the 1920s 6 Yiddish schools, and two kindergartens were in operation. There was also a Yiddish teachers college, but it was moved to Smolensk in 1929. In 1939 the Jewish population in Gomel was 40,880 (29% of the total). In the beginning of the German-Soviet war, many Jews succeeded in escaping into the Soviet interior. The Germans entered the city on August 19, 1941. The Jews were concentrated to four ghettos, under conditions of overcrowding, starvation, and disease. Three labor camps housing 1,500 Jews were set up in the city. In October 1941, 2,365 Jews were murdered. By December 1941, 4,000 had been killed. Women and children were gassed in vans. In the following months the Germans proceeded to murder the remaining Jews.

The Jewish population of the entire district numbered 45,000 in 1959; the number of Jews in Gomel was estimated at about 20,000 in 1970, of which only a few thousand remained in the early 21st century after the mass emigration of the 1990s. There is no synagogue in the city. (In 1963 a *minyan* was interrupted by the police, who dispersed those at prayer and took away two Torah scrolls and all religious articles.) There is a separate Jewish cemetery. A monument was erected in the vicinity of the city to the memory of local Jews massacred by the Nazis.

BIBLIOGRAPHY: Nathan Hannover, *Yeven Meẓulah*; L.H. Kahanovich, in: *Arim ve-Immahot be-Yisrael*, 2 (1948), 187–269; idem, *Mi-Homel ad Tel Aviv* (1952); S. Levin, in: *Royte Bleter* (1929); I. Halpern, *Sefer ha-Gevurah*, 3 (1950), 46–62; B.G. Bogoraz-Tan (ed.), *Yevreyskoye mestechko v Revolyutsii* (1926), 157–219; M. Zinowitz, *Ha-Ẓofeh* (March 3, 1944; April 4, 1944).

[Yehuda Slutsky / Shmuel Spector (2nd ed.)]

GOMEL, BLESSING OF (Heb. בִּרְכַּת הַגּוֹמֵל, i.e., "He who bestows"), a thanksgiving benediction recited by those who have been saved from acute danger to life. Those who have crossed the sea or a wilderness, have recovered from illness, or been released from prison are especially obligated to pronounce this blessing (Ber. 54b). The Talmud (*ibid.*) derives the duty to recite the *Gomel* from the verses: "Let them give thanks unto the Lord for His mercy, And for His wonderful works to the children of men!" (Ps. 107:8, 15, 21,31); and "Let them exalt Him also in the assembly of the people, And praise Him in the seat of the elders" (Ps. 107:32). The blessing should preferably be said in the presence of ten men (an "assembly of the people"), two of whom should be rabbis (recited at the "seat of the elders"; Sh. Ar., OḤ 219:3), and should be pronounced within three days after the person has been delivered from danger. It has become customary to recite this blessing after being called to the Reading of the Law in the synagogue on Mondays, Thursdays, or Sabbaths. In many communities it is recited by women after childbirth in front of the Ark after the service. The wording suggested by the Talmud is: "Blessed is He who bestows lovingkindness" (Ber. 54b). The accepted text for the benediction is "Blessed art Thou… Who doest good unto the undeserving, and Who hast dealt kindly with me" (Yad, Berakhot 10:8). The congregation responds "He who hath shown thee kindness, may He deal kindly with thee for ever" (Hertz, Prayer, 487). A *Gomel* benediction can be recited by an entire community. In Israel, this benediction is also recited by military reservists after a stretch of active service.

BIBLIOGRAPHY: Idelsohn, Liturgy, 114f.

GOMELSKY, ALEXANDER YAKOVLEVICH (1928–2005), Russian basketball coach. Born in Kronstadt, Gomelsky graduated from the trainers' college attached to the Lesgaft Institute for Physical Education in Leningrad (1945–48) and from the Military Institute of Physical Culture (1949–52). His first coaching job was with Leningrad's Spartak (1949–52). In 1953–66 he was head coach of SKA Riga, where he won U.S.S.R. championships five times and the European Cup in 1957, 1958, and 1959. In 1966–88 Gomelaky was head coach of the CSKA armed forces basketball team, another U.S.S.R. powerhouse. Gomelsky also coached the Soviet national team in the 1962–88 period, with a break in 1970–76, winning an Olympic gold medal in 1988 as well as eight European and two world championships (1967, 1982). Outspoken as a Jew, he was kept from going to Munich for the 1972 Olympic Games by the KGB, which feared he would defect to Israel, and thus denied his rightful place as coach in the historic and controversial victory of the U.S.S.R. over the U.S. for the gold.

In 1991–92 Gomelsky was president of the Russian Basketball Federation and in 1997 became president of the CSKA basketball club. He created a sports dynasty of sorts. His brother EVGENY (1938–) coached the Russian women's basketball team that won the 1992 Olympic championship and then became coach of Israel's national women's team. Three of Gomelsky's sons are also active in sports. Gomelsky was a popular sports commentator on TV and the author of a series of books on basketball. In 1995 he was inducted into the Basketball Hall of Fame.

[Naftali Prat (2nd ed.)]

GOMER (Heb. גֹּמֶר), the firstborn son of *Japheth; the father of Ashkenaz, Riphath, and Togarmah (Gen. 10:2–3; I Chron. 1:5–6); and the name of a nation (Ezek. 38:6). Gomer is nowadays identified with the *Gi-mir-ra-a* of the Assyrian sources who are the Κιμμέριοι of the Greek sources. This migratory people, who made their first historical appearance in Eastern Asia at the end of the eighth century B.C.E., shook Asia Minor with campaigns of conquest in the seventh century.

On Gomer, daughter of Diblaim, see *Hosea.

BIBLIOGRAPHY: M.J. Mellink, in: IDB, 2 (1962), 440 (incl. bibl.). **ADD. BIBLIOGRAPHY:** D. Baker, in: ABD, 2, 1074; A. Birley and S. Hornblower, in: OCD (3rd ed.), 331.

GOMEZ, family of prominent early U.S. merchants. LEWIS MOSES (c. 1660–1740), who was the founder of this New York family, was probably born a Marrano in Madrid, and lived in France and England before settling in New York about 1703. Three years later he was made a freeman of New York City, where he prospered in the import and export trade. Together with his sons he purchased considerable real estate in the city and in Ulster and Orange counties. Of Gomez' six sons, one died at sea in 1722; the other five, all merchants, figured prominently in community affairs. MORDECAI (1688–1750) was made a freeman in 1715 and was appointed interpreter to the Admiralty Court. DANIEL (1695–1780) became a freeman in New York in 1727; he died in Philadelphia. DAVID (1697?–1769) carried on a considerable fur trade with the Indians and became a naturalized British subject in 1740. ISAAC (1705–1770) bought a distillery in the Montgomerie Ward in the city in 1763, together with BENJAMIN (1711–1772), who lived in Charleston for a time. In 1729 Gomez and his sons, except Benjamin, purchased land which included the site of what was to be the Shearith Israel cemetery off Chatham Square. They posted a bond that the land would be a "burying place" for the use of the "Jewish nation." The family was among the original founders of Congregation Shearith Israel. The elder Gomez was one of the trustees who purchased land for the Mill Street Synagogue and was president of the congregation in 1730, when the synagogue was dedicated. Benjamin Gomez served as *parnas* four times, and during the period between 1730 and the Revolution, seven members of the Gomez family served as president.

BIBLIOGRAPHY: H. Simonhoff, *Jewish Notables in America*… (1956), 112–6; D. de Sola Pool, *Portraits Etched in Stone* (1952), index; L. Hershkowitz (comp.), *Wills of Early New York Jews* (1967), index; Rosenbloom, Biogr Dict, s.v. *Gomez, Benjamin*[1], *Gomez, David*[1], *Gomez, Isaac*[1], *Gomez, Lewis (Louis) Moses*, incl. bibl. on all of them.

[Leo Hershkowitz]

GÓMEZ DE SOSSA, ISAAC (late 17th century), *Marrano literary figure. Gómez de Sossa lived and worked in Amsterdam and, according to Miguel de *Barrios, was a Latin poet and an imitator of Virgil. He composed poems in praise of the works of other writers, and was responsible for a Spanish translation of Saul Levi *Morteira's Hebrew work on the divine origin of the Law. He was a member of the Academia de los Sitibundos, a literary society founded in 1676 by Manuel de Belmonte, and was one of the judges of its poetry contests. His younger brother, Benito Gómez de Sossa, was a minor writer in Amsterdam. Their father, Abraham Gómez de Sossa, had once served as physician-in-ordinary to the infante Fernando, the son of Philip III of Spain and governor of the Netherlands in 1632. Abraham Gómez de Sossa died in Amsterdam in 1667, and Isaac composed a Latin epitaph for his tombstone.

BIBLIOGRAPHY: M. de Barrios, *Relación de los Poetas y Escritores Españoles de la Nación Judaica Amstelodama* (n. d.); Kayserling, Bibl, 74, 104; idem, *Sephardim* (Ger., 1859), 292.

[Kenneth R. Scholberg]

GOMPERS, SAMUEL (1850–1924), U.S. trade unionist. Gompers was born in London and after a few years of primary school was apprenticed in the cigar-making trade. When Gompers' family immigrated to America in 1863, settling on the Lower East Side of New York City, he joined a local of the Cigar Makers' National Union. From this point Gompers' life centered on trade union activities. He became a leader of the cigar makers' union in the 1870s, playing a major role in its reorganization (1879) through increased dues, sickness and death benefits, and substantial control of locals by the national officers. Gompers helped to establish the American Federation of Labor in 1886, and became its president. He also edited the official journal of the Federation from 1894 until his death. Most of Gompers' public activities were related to his position in the American Federation of Labor. From 1900 he served as a vice president of the National Civic Federation, which sought to promote stable labor relations through collective bargaining and personal contact between labor leaders, industrialists, and bankers. Gompers received considerable criticism from labor sources because of these associations. He also played a prominent role in winning strong support from American trade unions for President Woodrow Wilson's war policies in 1917 and 1918; and he did much to protect organized labor's interests during World War I.

Gompers was a formative influence upon the American labor movement, as well as a spokesman for it. Although he would have preferred the former role, the decentralized American labor movement did not permit any one individual to exercise much influence over the constituent trade unions. Gompers often had to rely upon his reputation and influence in order to be effective, and he often had to accept the role of spokesman even when his own views differed. Thus, for instance, despite his personal belief in organizing black workers, Gompers acquiesced in the refusal of the AFL to attempt to enforce an anti-discrimination policy upon its affiliates. However, in most matters, his views became almost synonymous with those of the leading unions in the Federation.

Gompers argued that the improvement of workers' wages, hours, and employment conditions could only be accomplished through the formation of strong trade unions to exert direct economic pressure on the employer. The resulting collective bargaining agreements protected the basic interests of the worker. Such labor organizations must be independent of control by politicians, intellectuals, or any non-labor source. This viewpoint in effect acknowledged that organized labor lacked the political power to achieve its objectives through legislation, and that the climate of opinion in the United States was usually hostile to trade unions so that apparent victories might be reversed quickly. Moreover, Gompers believed that men view economic and social questions in terms of their material interests, which meant that the worker could not expect continuing support from the middle class, since their objectives would inevitably conflict. Workers must therefore avoid dependence on legislation or political action.

Gompers maintained a vitriolic hostility to socialism almost throughout his presidency of the AFL. The socialists called for industrial unionism and political action, as opposed to Gompers' belief in craft unionism dedicated to the immediate interests of a relatively homogenous membership. The socialists viewed the labor organization as only the first step in the workers' struggle for social justice. Ultimately, Gompers accepted capitalism, providing it could guarantee an adequate standard of living for the worker, and he had little patience with claims that the entire economic system had to be reordered to accomplish this.

Despite his immigrant background, Gompers demanded the restriction of immigration in order to protect the competitive position of workers in America. Although he called for the unionization of all workers, he basically accepted the decision of the AFL to concentrate on the skilled and retain the craft basis for organizing, which maintained the position of the existing trade unions. Clearly, Gompers was an effective leader for organized workers, but for the greatest part of the labor force his program had little validity since these workers were unorganized and likely to remain so. Gompers' career was thus marked by the paradox that he was an able trade unionist but a largely ineffective labor leader.

Gompers wrote *American Labor and the War* (1919), *Labor and the Common Welfare* (1919), *Labor and the Employer* (1920), and *Party of the Third Part: The Story of the Kansas Industrial Relations Court* (with H. Allen, 1921). His autobiography, *Seventy Years of Life and Labor* (2 vols.), was published posthumously in 1925.

BIBLIOGRAPHY: B. Mandel, *Samuel Gompers* (1963); F.C. Thorne, *Samuel Gompers* (1957); R.H. Harvey, *Samuel Gompers* (1935); L. Reed, *Labor Philosophy of Samuel Gompers* (1930); DAB, 7 (1931), 369–73. **ADD. BIBLIOGRAPHY:** H. Livesay, *Samuel Gompers & Organized Labor in America* (1978); W. Dick, *Labor and Socialism in America: The Gompers Era* (1972); W. Chasan, *Samuel Gompers: Leader of American Labor* (1971).

[Irwin Yellowitz]

GOMPERTZ, English family, closely associated with the Hambro Congregation in London and known in the synagogue as Emmerich, after the family's place of origin. JOSEPH GOMPERTZ (1731–1810) was an early member of the *Board of Deputies of British Jews. The sons of his brother SOLOMON BARENT GOMPERTZ (1729–1807) attained distinction in different spheres. BENJAMIN GOMPERTZ (1779–1865) was a mathematician of genius, Fellow of the Royal Society, and writer on astronomy. When he was refused the post of actuary to the Guardian Insurance Office because of his faith, his brother-in-law N.M. *Rothschild established the Alliance Insurance Company (1824) in which he filled that position until 1848. He developed a mathematical law of human mortality which is still used in actuarial calculations. He proposed a plan for the amalgamation and reorganization of the Jewish charities in London. His brother EPHRAIM GOMPERTZ (1776–1876) wrote *Theoretic Discourse on the Nature and Property of Money* (London, 1820), a pioneering work in the field of economics. ISAAC GOMPERTZ (1774–1856) was among the earliest Anglo-Jewish poets and was compared in his day to Dryden and Pope. His works include *Time or Light and Shade* (London, 1815), *The Modern Antique or, the Muse in the Costume of Queen Anne* (London, 1813), and *Devon, a Poem* (Teignmouth, 1825). He spent his last years in Devonshire and is buried in the Jewish cemetery of Exeter. LEWIS GOMPERTZ (1784–1861), the youngest of the Gompertz brothers, was an inventor who devoted himself to the cause of the humane treatment of animals. His *Moral Enquiries on the Situation of Men and Brutes* (London, 1824) led to the foundation of the Society (later Royal Society) for the Prevention of Cruelty to Animals, which he served devotedly as secretary. However, when it was reorganized on Christian sectarian lines in 1832, he resigned and then founded the Animals' Friend Society, with its influential periodical, *The Animals' Friend*, which he managed successfully until 1846, when his health failed and the society was disbanded. Gompertz was responsible for a number of patented inventions, many designed to lessen the sufferings of animals. His expanding chuck is still widely used in industry. In more recent times, the Gompertz family, no longer attached to Judaism, produced many army officers and the violinist RICHARD GOMPERTZ (1859–1911).

BIBLIOGRAPHY: D. Kaufmann and M. Freudenthal, *Familie Gompertz* (1907), 318–25; Roth, in: JHSET, 14 (1935–39), 8, 10, 14; P. Emden, *Jews of Britain* (1943), 167–74; Roth, Mag Bibl, index; *The Times* (July 12, 1965). **ADD. BIBLIOGRAPHY:** ODNB online for Benjamin Gompertz, Lewis Gompertz; T. Endelman, *The Jews of Georgian England* (1989), 261–64, index.

[Cecil Roth]

GOMPERZ, name of a family widely dispersed throughout Central Europe. In records of the 14th century the old-German form of the name "Gundbert" began appearing as a surname for persons with the name Ephraim or Mordecai. Occurring in variant spellings as Gumpert, Gumpertz, Gomperts, Gumpel, etc., it became associated with a specific family prominent in the late 15th century, in the duchy of Juelich-Cleves, when SOLOMON BEN MORDECAI GUMPEL received the right of residence in Emmerich. His immediate descendants settled in nearby Cleves, Wesel, and Nijmegen; branches of the family were eventually found in England, Amsterdam, Berlin, Frankfurt on the Main, Prague, and the United States (Samuel *Gompers). David *Kaufmann, who married into the Budapest branch, traced, in cooperation with Max Freudenthal, the genealogy of the family (see bibliography).

Solomon's grandson ELIJAH (d. 1689) founded the family banking business in Wesel (Cleves) which soon became one of the largest in Prussia. His son REUBEN ELIAS assisted in the rapid expansion of business. After moving to Berlin he became the first Jew to serve as a government official in Brandenburg; he subsequently became the chief inspector of taxes payable by the Jews in the duchies of Mark and Cleves (about 1700). He also acted as supplier to the army and to the court, and through these transactions came into contact with all the important Jewish court suppliers of his time, including Samuel *Oppenheimer, Leffmann *Behrends, and Behrend *Lehmann. Falsely accused of the attempted murder of Samson *Wertheimer, he was arrested by order of Frederick I and released a year later after payment of 20,000 talers.

Two members of the third generation of Court Jews in this family, MOSES LEVI and ELIJAH, established a bank-

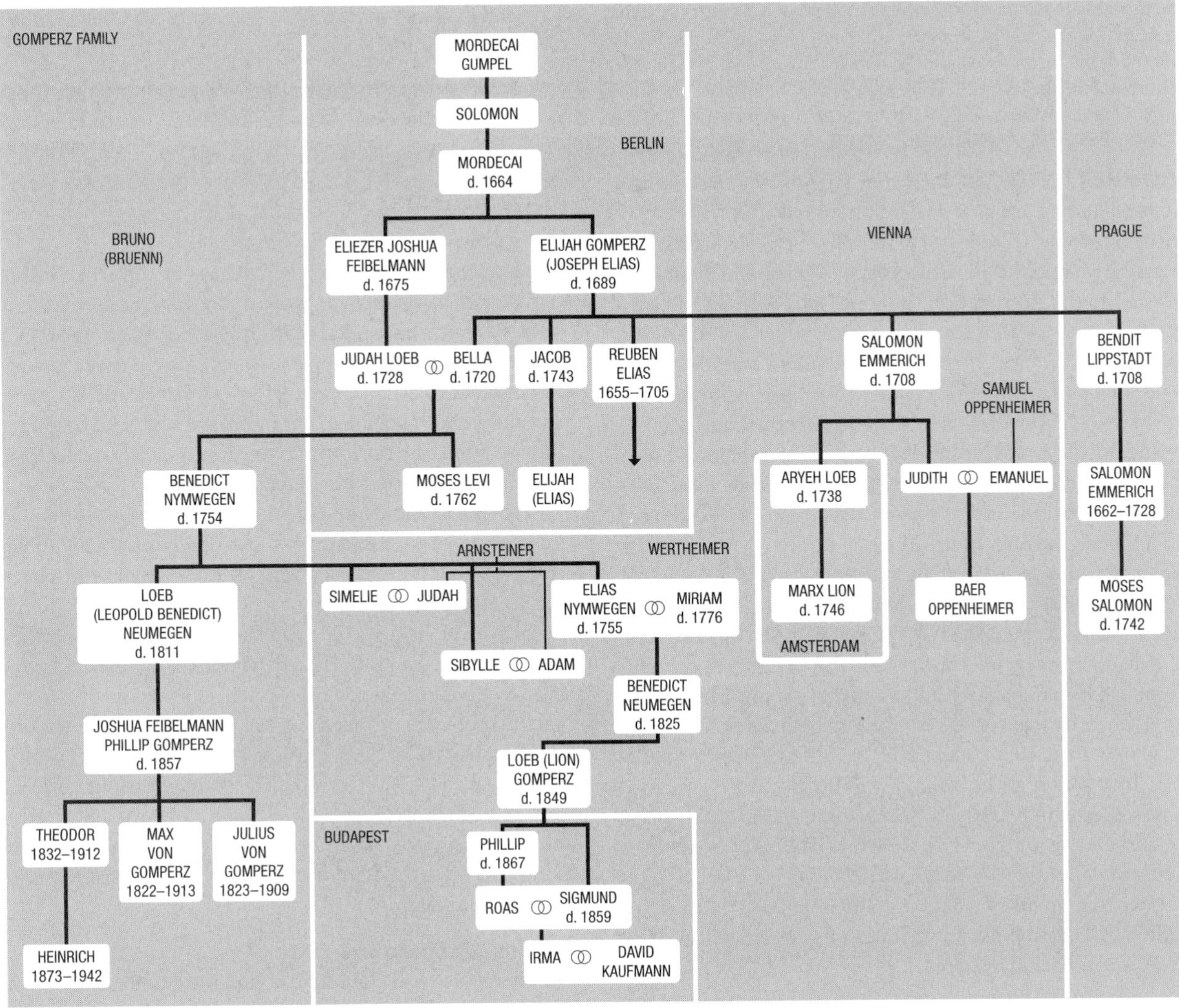

ing and business house in Berlin at the beginning of the 18th century. In Prussia, members of the Gomperz family served as court purveyors to six rulers in the course of five generations. To Frederick I (1688–1713), the luxury-loving first king of Prussia, they supplied jewels, and to the soldier-king, Frederick William I (1713–1740), "tall fellows" for his guard. At the time of Frederick the Great (1740–1786), they changed their activities to minting. In conjunction with the Court Jew Daniel *Itzig they rented the minting monopoly. In Berlin, AARON ELIAS GOMPERZ, physician, writer, and teacher of Moses Mendelssohn, became celebrated. Members of the Gomperz family also served as *Landesrabbiner* (Cleves and Silesia) and *Oberrabbiner* (Ansbach). Many created influential positions for themselves, aided by their family relations with other Court Jews.

In Bohemia-Moravia a noteworthy member of the family was SALOMON (SALMAN) EMMERICH (1662–1728), who studied medicine at Leiden and practiced in Metz and Soest before establishing himself in Prague. He was the first Prague Jew to be freed by imperial order from wearing the obligatory neck-frill. His son MOSES SALOMON GOMPERZ (d. 1742) was permitted to practice medicine by Prague University after passing an examination, and was the first Jew to graduate from a German university, in Frankfurt on the Oder, in 1721.

The Bruenn (Brno) branch of the Gomperz family was founded by LOEB BEN BENDIT (LEOPOLD BENDIT or BENEDICT) NEUMEGEN, from Nijmegen, Holland. His son PHILLIP GOMPERZ founded a successful bank. Three of his sons became celebrated: Theodor *Gomperz (1832–1912), classical philologist and historian of Greek philosophy; MAX VON GOMPERZ (1822–1913), industrialist, financier, and politician; JULIUS VON GOMPERZ (1823–1909), president of the Jewish community from 1869, who initiated the Moravian communities organization and was active on behalf of the Jewish communities in Parliament. A hereditary title was conferred on him in 1879. Theodor's son HEINRICH GOMPERZ (1873–1942) was also a classical philologist.

BIBLIOGRAPHY: D. Kaufmann and M. Freudenthal, *Familie Gompertz* (1907); S. Stern, *The Court Jew* (1950), index; idem, *Der* *preussische Staat und die Juden* (1962), index s.v. *Gumperts*; H. Schnee, *Die Hoffinanz und der moderne Staat*, 3 (1955), index; G. Kisch, in: MGWJ, 78 (1934), 350–63; idem, in: HJ, 8 (1946), 169f., 175, 180; A. Shochat, *Im Ḥillufei Tekufot* (1960), index.

[Michael J. Graetz and Henry Wasserman]

GOMPERZ, THEODOR (1832–1912), Austrian classical philologist and historian of ancient philosophy. He was born in Bruenn, Moravia. From 1873 to 1901 Gomperz was professor of classical philology at the University of Vienna, and in 1882 was elected to the Academy of Sciences. His *Griechische Denker*, 3 vols. (1896–1909), is a monumental work which sets Greek philosophy, from its beginnings until after Aristotle, within the context of a history of science and of the general development of ancient civilization. This work has been translated into many languages and is considered one of the basic works in its field. The author's empiricist-positivist bias is evident throughout. Gomperz, also active in public affairs and politics, served as a Liberal member of the Austrian upper house. In Jewish affairs, he took an extreme assimilationist stand and was violently opposed to Herzl and Zionism. His biography, letters, and notes were published by his son Heinrich as *Briefe und Aufzeichnungen* (1936). HEINRICH (1873–1942) was also a philosopher. He was baptized and was a professor in Vienna until 1934 when he was compelled to retire because of his refusal to join Dolfuss' Fatherland Front. In 1938 he emigrated to the U.S. In addition to the biography of his father, he published a new edition of his father's *Griechische Denker* (1922–31). He published a comprehensive study of Greek philosophy, *Die Lebensauffassung der griechischen Philosophen und das Ideal der inneren Freiheit* (1904), and *Philosophical Studies* (1953, edited by D.S. Robinson), which is a psychoanalytical study of Parmenides and Socrates.

BIBLIOGRAPHY: THEODOR GOMPERZ: *Neue Deutsche Biographie*, 6 (1964); *Oesterreichisches Biographisches Lexikon*. HEINRICH GOMPERZ: Topitsch, in: *Wiener Zeitschrift fuer Philosophie, Psychologie und Paedagogik*, 5 (1954–55), 1–6; W. Ziegenfuss (ed.), *Philosophen-Lexikon*, 1 (1949). **ADD. BIBLIOGRAPHY:** R.A. Kann, *Theodor Gomperz – Ein Gelehrtenleben in der Franz-Josefs-Zeit* (1974); A. Weinberg, *Theodor Gomperz and John Stuart Mill* (1963).

[Otto Immanuel Spear]

GÖNDÖR, FERENC (1928–), Holocaust survivor and memoirist. Göndör waited 30 years before committing the story of his early life to paper in *A 6171; Ett judiskt levnadsöde* ("A 6171: The Story of a Jew," 1984). In it he describes his idyllic childhood in a small town in Hungary and his internment as a 16-year-old in Auschwitz. The book was later made into a film. In 1986 he was awarded the coveted Torgny Segerstedt prize and in 1993 the Liberal Immigrant Association's culture prize. In 1994 he received a special grant from the Linköping municipality for his work in publicizing the horrors of the Holocaust and making an entire generation of schoolchildren aware of the dangers of the Nazi evil and its implications for the present. Like many other survivors in Sweden, Göndör spends much time visiting schools and talking about the Holocaust. For many years he also worked as a sound engineer for Swedish Radio.

BIBLIOGRAPHY: Megilla-Förlaget: *Svensk-judisk litteratur 1775–1994* (1995).

[Ilya Meyer (2nd ed.)]

GOOD AND EVIL.

In the Bible

A major corollary of the Jewish belief in the One God is that, seen in its totality, life is good. Viewing the cosmos as it emerged from chaos, God said, "It is good" (Gen. 1:10). In a monotheistic world view, a persistent problem is to account for the existence of evil in its many forms – natural catastrophes, pain and anguish in human life, moral evil, and sin. These facts must be fitted somehow within the design of the Creator as it is realized in the course of human history.

The problem of the existence of evil in the world was not given great prominence in the earlier books of the Bible, which are mainly concerned with positing general ethical-religious norms. In the later books, however, when the status of the individual vis-à-vis God gains in importance, it becomes necessary to account for the existence of evil in a world governed by a benevolent and omnipotent God. Jeremiah asks the perennial question concerning the prosperity of the wicked and the adversity of the righteous. This problem appears also in the Books of Isaiah, Job, and the Psalms. Various answers were given, which were later elaborated by the talmudists and the philosophers, but it should be noted that the idea of a heavenly reward is never mentioned in the biblical writings as a possible solution.

In Talmudic Literature

For the rabbis of the talmudic period the existence of evil in a world created by a merciful and loving God posed a number of theological problems, which they attempted to solve in a variety of ways. Although these solutions do not add up to a coherent theodicy, some of the more representative discussions indicate the general lines of rabbinic thought on the matter. First there is the issue of the existence of evil itself. The rabbis insisted that as good derives from God so, ultimately, does evil. This insistence was intended to discount any implications of duality, the idea of a separate deity from whom evil springs being complete anathema to the rabbis, who even say, "Man should bless God for the evil which occurs in the same way that he blesses Him for the good" (Ber. 33b). The same antidualistic motif is contained in the verse, "I am the Lord, there is none else; I form the light, and create darkness; I make peace, and create evil" (Isa. 45:6–7). (In the liturgy this is changed to "makes peace and creates all that exists," implying that evil itself is perhaps not a positive phenomenon at all, but mainly the absence of good.) Another vexing problem is why there is no just distribution of good and evil to the righteous and wicked respectively. This problem is dealt with in a number of different ways. On the one hand one finds the view that the issue is beyond the grasp of man's intellect, in support of which the verse, "I will be gracious to whom I will be gracious, and will show mercy on whom I will show mercy" (Ex. 33:19) is quoted (cf. Ber. 7a). On the other hand, a series of more partial solutions is proffered: the righteous man who suffers in this world is not wholly righteous, and the wicked man who prospers is not wholly wicked; or alternately the former is perhaps not a descendant of righteous ancestors, while the latter prospers because of the merit of his fathers (Ber. 7a); or evil is blamed on Satan and various malicious demons who are at the root of the trouble caused to the righteous (Ber. 6a; Gen. R. 84:3).

Perhaps the most widespread explanation of suffering in this world is that what the righteous undergo is punishment for every small sin they may have committed so that they will enjoy their full reward in paradise, while the wicked are rewarded in this world for any small amount of good they have to their credit so that in the world to come they will reap the full measure of the punishment they deserve (Ber. 4a; Eruv. 19a; Ta'an. 11a; Kid. 39b; Avot 2:16; Gen. R. 33:1; Yal., Eccles. 978). The sufferings of the righteous are also seen as a form of trial, "afflictions of love," enabling them to develop virtues such as patience and faith (Ber. 5a; BM 85a; Gen. R. 9:8; *Tanna de-Vei Eliyahu Zuta* 11). Support for this view is found in biblical verses such as "Happy is the man whom Thou disciplineth, O Lord, And teacheth out of Thy Law" (Ps. 94:12) and "It is good for me that I have been afflicted, in order that I might learn Thy statutes" (*ibid.* 119:71).

Another aspect concerning the evil caused by man himself is dealt with by viewing evil as the product of, if not identical with, the evil inclination (Ḥag. 16a). The evil inclination is a necessary factor in the continued existence of the world, for without it no man would build a house, marry, raise a family, or engage in trade (Gen. R. 9:9). Nevertheless, it is within man's grasp to control his evil inclination, against whose power the Torah was seen as an antidote (Kid. 30b). This control enables man to serve God with both his good and evil urges (Ber. 9:5); the one enabling him to continue in his this-worldly pursuits and the other helping him to grow in holiness. Despite an acute awareness of the extent of evil and suffering, both in the natural world and in the world of interhuman relations, and notwithstanding the limitations of the explanations they were able to offer by way of theodicy, the rabbis continually reaffirm the ultimate goodness of God and of His creation. This affirmation is even contained in the burial service, in a series of refrains emphasizing the perfection of God's world (Hertz, Prayer, 1074). The rabbis advise man to accustom himself to say, "All that the Merciful One does is for the good" (Ber. 60b); and they assure him that the measure of God's reward exceeds that of His punishment (Yoma 76a). One *tanna* – *Nahum of Gimzo (Ish Gamzu) – was even renowned for his response to every occurrence: "This too is for the best" (Ta'an. 21a).

In Medieval Jewish Philosophy

The answers given by *Philo to the problem of evil correspond, in certain respects, to those of the rabbis. If some righteous men suffer, he states, it is because they are not really perfect in their righteousness. Furthermore, the good which befalls the wicked is not a real good. Also, the suffering of the righteous may come from God as a trial or test, or because of the sins of their ancestors.

The need to account for the existence of evil in the world became even more acute with the manifestation of dualistic movements. Saadiah Gaon strongly rejects these dualist doctrines and affirms God's unity. Steeped as he was in the *Kalām tradition, he states that God conducts the world with infinite justice and wisdom. God, according to Saadiah, would not have created evil because evil does not have a separate existence *sui generis* but is nothing more than the absence of good. The sufferings of the righteous are either a requital for the few sins which they have committed, or they serve as an instrument of chastisement or trial, for which reward will be given in the afterlife. Saadiah thus upholds the doctrine of "afflictions of love."

The answer of Joseph al-*Basir, the 11th-century Karaite, is that the infliction of pain may, under certain circumstances, be a good instead of an evil, for it may ultimately result in a greater advantage. Thus, disease and suffering are either punishment for offenses committed, or are imposed with a view to later reward. Similarly, *Abraham b. Ḥiyya expresses the view that the righteous suffer in this world in order to try them and to increase their ultimate reward (*Meditation of the Sad Soul* (1969), 117ff.). Joseph ibn *Ẓaddik sees the evil which happens to the righteous as often being a natural occurrence without reference to reward and punishment. Sometimes, too, this evil is inflicted upon the good man for his sins, but ultimate reward and punishment are in the future life. Abraham *Ibn Ezra sees the whole world as good. From God, he states, comes only good. Evil is due to the defect of the object receiving higher influence. To argue that because of a small part of evil the whole world, which is good, should not have been created, is foolish. Abraham *Ibn Daud argues that it is impossible either according to reason or according to the Bible and tradition that evil or defect should come from God. If both good and evil come from God, He would have to be a composite. Besides, the majority of evils are negations, and cannot have been produced by any agent.

*Maimonides also views evil as a nonexistence, namely the absence of good, which could not have been produced by God. He distinguishes between three different kinds of evil. The first category is that of natural evils which befall man, such as landslides, earthquakes, and floods, or his having been born with certain deformities. The cause of this type of evil is the fact that man has a body which is subject to corruption and destruction. This is in accordance with natural law and is necessary for the continuance and permanence of the species. The second kind of evil is within the social realm, such as wars. This type of evil, Maimonides says, occurs infrequently and, of course, being wholly within the control of man, could not have been caused by God. Though difficult, its remedy is within the hands of man. The third class of evil, the largest and most frequent class, is the evil which the individual brings upon himself through his vices and excessive desires. Again the remedy is within man's power. Maimonides rejects the notion of "afflictions of love," holding instead that even the minutest pain is a punishment for some previous transgression. He explains that the tests mentioned in the Bible, such as God's request to Abraham to offer up his son, have a didactic purpose, to teach the truth of God's commandments and how far one must go in obeying them.

Joseph *Albo holds that perfect saints may have to endure agonies in order to atone for their people or for the entire world.

[Jacob Bernard Agus]

In Modern Jewish Philosophy

For Hermann *Cohen suffering stirs man's conscience and prods him to ethical action. Israel's election by God is tied up with the idea of Israel as the "suffering servant," i.e., the eternal prod of mankind's conscience. Evil in a metaphysical sense did not interest Cohen. He castigated metaphysical speculation about evil as an attempt to cover the existence of evil in society and as perverting the intent of suffering which should be to arouse sympathy in men.

The problem of evil played an important role in the philosophy of Martin *Buber. For Buber the source of evil was the failure to enter into relation, and conversely evil can be redeemed by the reestablishment of relations. "Good and evil, then, cannot be a pair of opposites like right and left or above and beneath, 'good' is the movement in the direction of home, 'evil' is the aimless whirl of human potentialities without which nothing can be achieved and by which, if they take no direction but remain trapped in themselves, everything goes awry" (*Between Man and Man* (1966[4]), 103). Man is not evil by nature, but his misuse of his nature generates evil. Some men can carry evil so far as to give it a kind of independent quality. However, evil is never an independent entity but such men crystallize it into a perverse resistance to the individual's self-fulfillment in relation. After World War II Buber did question the possibility of addressing God as "kind and merciful" in the light of what had happened to the Jews in Europe, but he nevertheless maintained the possibility of man redeeming evil. He denied the gnostic dualistic approach and maintained that man had it in his power to sanctify the world.

Abraham J. *Heschel, referring to a midrash about Abraham seeing a castle in flames (Gen. R. 39:1), asks: "The world is in flames, consumed by evil. Is it possible that there is no one who cares?" (*God in Search of Man* (1961[3]), 367). After considering the horrors of Auschwitz he questions: "What have we done to make such crimes possible? What are we doing to make such crimes impossible?" (*ibid.*, 369). According to him nothing in the world is wholly good or wholly evil, everything is a mixture. Man's nature, his ego, and the relative rewards of evil in this world help evil to prevail. Fortunately, God is concerned about man's separating the good from the evil. God commands man and gives him the *mitzvot*, which are the tools by which man can overcome evil. "Evil is not man's ultimate problem. Man's ultimate problem is his relation to God.... The biblical answer to evil is not the good but the holy. It is an attempt to raise man to a higher level of existence, where man is not alone when confronted with evil" (*ibid.*, 376).

For Mordecai *Kaplan God is identical with certain principles in the universe whose analogues in human society lead to salvation, i.e., the achievement of the good for all mankind. The existence of evil in the world is due to the failure of man to act in accord with God, i.e., those principles. "When the conscience operates simultaneously through creativity, responsibility, honesty, and loyalty or love, it is the source of Divine Revelation.... The function of conscience is not to philosophize or theologize concerning the problem of evil in the world. Conscience is the pain of the human spirit. The function of spiritual pain is not to have us speculate about it but to eliminate the cause ... it is rather to impel us to make a religion of combating the man-made evils that mar human life ..." (M.M. Kaplan, in *The Reconstructionist*, May 1963).

[Michael J. Graetz]

BIBLIOGRAPHY: IN TALMUDIC LITERATURE: K. Kohler, *Jewish Theology* (1918); A. Marmorstein, *The Doctrine of Merits in Old Rabbinical Literature* (1920); A. Buechler, *Studies in Sin and Atonement* (1928); E.E. Urbach, *Ḥazal, Pirkei Emunot ve-De'ot* (1969). IN ANCIENT AND MEDIEVAL JEWISH PHILOSOPHY: Guttmann, Philosophies, index, s.v. *evil*; Husik, Philosophy, index, s.v. *Evil, Problem of*; H.A. Wolfson, *Philo*... (1947), index, s.v. *Evil*. IN MODERN JEWISH PHILOSOPHY: J.B. Agus, *Modern Philosophies of Judaism* (1941), 94–6, 108ff.; M.S. Friedman, *Martin Buber* (1960[2]), 11–15, 101–58; F.A. Rothschild, *Between God and Man* (1959), 191–7.

GOODBLAT, MORRIS (1901–1978), Conservative rabbi and educator. Born in Mlawa, Poland, he came to the United States in 1912. He was educated at the Rabbi Jacob Joseph School and the Mizrachi Teachers Institute. He received his B.A. from City College of New York (1924) and was ordained at the Jewish Theological Seminary of America (1927). He earned his DHL there in 1944.

For more than four decades, he served as a rabbi at Congregation Beth Am Israel in Philadelphia, where he focused on Jewish education. His congregation produced many young men who entered the rabbinate and many more who were educated Conservative Jews. He was president of the Jewish National Fund and the Board of Rabbis of Greater Philadelphia and regional president of the Rabbinical Assembly for the Greater Philadelphia area.

In 1960 he established the Academy of Judaism to tutor perspective students for conversion; thus, establishing a regional program for what had until then been the individual responsibility of the local rabbi. He served as dean and director of the academy. The model of a regional program has been adopted in many communities throughout the U.S. as it is an excellent use of resources and an important way of imposing and enforcing standards.

Goodblat co-chaired the United Synagogue Commission on Jewish Education, which tried to standardize congregational curricula and published and developed material for the afternoon hebrew school, which was instrumental in Jewish education. He headed its publication committee and helped hire Abraham Millgram as the Commission's educational director.

He was chairman of the Rabbinical Assembly's special Committee on Ritual Surveys, which compiled a detailed picture of the way in which Conservative Judaism was being practiced in the synagogue and in the major ceremonies from Bar and Bat-Mitzvah and Confirmation to funeral practices. He also chaired the membership committee of the Rabbinical Assembly that opened membership to non-seminary graduates, which facilitated the transformation of some Orthodox congregations and their rabbis to the then rapidly growing Conservative movement. He also served on the prestigious Committee on Jewish Law and Standards for the Rabbinical Assembly.

As a scholar, he wrote *Jewish Life in Turkey in the XVI Century as Reflected in the Legal Writings of Samuel De Medina* in 1952, about the immediate post-expulsion period in which Jews fleeing from Spain found a haven in Turkey.

BIBLIOGRAPHY: P.S. Nadell, *Conservative Judaism in America: A Biographical Dictionary and Sourebook* (1988).

[Michael Berenbaum (2nd ed.)]

°GOODENOUGH, ERWIN RAMSDELL (1893–1965), U.S. scholar who specialized in the study of Judaism in the Hellenistic period. Goodenough was born in Brooklyn, New York, and was raised in a family with Methodist fundamentalist beliefs. Following studies at the Garrett Biblical Institute, he studied at Harvard for three years under the influential historian of religion, George F. Moore, receiving his Ph.D. in Oxford in 1923, and then began teaching history at Yale University. Throughout his life Goodenough was active in many scholarly organizations, and edited the *Journal of Biblical Literature* from 1934 to 1942. While preparing his doctoral thesis, published as *The Theology of Justin Martyr* (1923), Goodenough came to the conclusion that many Hellenistic elements of early Christianity were derived not from the pagan world directly but from the already hellenized Judaism through which Christianity was first disseminated. Most of his later work was devoted to the study of this hellenized Judaism, especially *The Jurisprudence of the Jewish Courts in Egypt* (1929), *By Light, Light: The Mystic Gospel of Hellenistic Judaism* (1935), *The Politics of Philo Judaeus* (1938), *An Introduction to Philo Judaeus* (1940), and *Jewish Symbols in the Greco-Roman Period* (13 vols., 1953–68). Goodenough's reconstruction of Hellenistic Judaism from literary sources was often speculative. His account of the teachings of Philo, in particular, must be corrected in the light of H.A. *Wolfson's analysis of Philo's philosophy and demonstration of its many similarities to rabbinic teaching. But *Jewish Symbols in the Greco-Roman Period*, by its collection of Greco-Roman archaeological remains and its confrontation of these with pagan parallels, revealed an entire world of Judaism that previously had been known only in fragments and generally neglected. Consequently, this work began a new epoch in the study of ancient Judaism – this in spite of the fact that Goodenough's interpretation of the material has been questioned (Avi-Yonah, Smith, and others). One of Goodenough's supporters, J. *Neusner, wrote (in 1988) that "Goodenough asks when a symbol is symbolic. He wants to know how visual symbols speak beyond words and despite words. We find ourselves surrounded by messages that reach us without words, that speak to and even for us beyond verbal explanation. Goodenough studied ancient Jewish symbols because he wanted to explain how that happens and what we learn about the human imagination from the power of symbols. It is difficult to point to a more engaging and critical problem in the study of humanity than the one Goodenough took for himself. That is why, twenty years after the conclusion of his research, a new generation will find fresh and important the research and reflection of this extraordinary man."

ADD. BIBLIOGRAPHY: M. Avi-Yonah, "Goodenough's Evaluation of the Dura Paintings: A Critique," in: J. Guttman (ed.), *The Dura-Europas Synagogue* (1973); M. Smith, "Goodenough's Jewish Symbols in Retrospect," in: J. Guttman (ed.), *The Synagogue: Studies in Origins, Archaeology and Architecture* (1975); J. Neusner, "Editor's Foreward," in E.R. Goodenough, *Jewish Symbols in the Greco-Roman Period* (1988). For a complete bibliography of Goodenough's writings, see J. Neusner (ed.), *Religions in Antiquity. Essays in Memory of Erwin Ramsdell Goodenough* (1968).

[Morton Smith / Shimon Gibson (2nd ed.)]

GOODHART, ARTHUR LEHMAN (1891–1978), U.S. jurist. Born in New York, Goodhart studied in America and Britain and was an officer in the United States Army during World War I. In 1919 he became a lecturer in law at Cambridge University and was editor of the *Cambridge Law Journal* from 1921 to 1925. In 1931 Goodhart was appointed professor of jurisprudence at Oxford University. In this position he exercised considerable influence both as a lecturer and writer, and his lucid exposition of legal problems, particularly in the field of contracts and torts, earned him a reputation as an outstanding jurist. He also served on several government legal committees, including the Royal Commission on the Police, the Monopolies Commission, and the Law Revision Committee.

In 1951 Goodhart was appointed master of University College, Oxford, the first Jew and the first American citizen to become master of an Oxford college. He was also the recipient of many other honors. He was made a king's counsel in 1943 and awarded a knighthood (honorary by virtue of his American citizenship). He was chairman of the International Law Association. His writings include *Essays in Jurisprudence and the Common Law* (1931); *Precedent in English and Continental Law* (1934); *The Government of Great Britain* (1946); and *Five Jewish Lawyers of the Common Law* (1950). He was also editor of the *Law Quarterly Review*, one of the most authoritative legal magazines in the world.

Goodhart took an interest in Jewish affairs and was a strong supporter of Israel. After the *Six-Day War he wrote several articles justifying the Israeli position in international law. His son PHILIP J. GOODHART (1925–) was a Conservative Member of Parliament and a member of the British delegation to the Council of Europe and the United Nations.

BIBLIOGRAPHY: *Current Biography Yearbook 1964* (1964), 159–61.

[Israel Finestein]

GOODMAN, ALLEGRA (1967–) U.S. novelist and short story writer. Goodman, the daughter of academics, was born in Brooklyn, raised in Hawaii, and educated at Harvard and Stanford. She has written works that are at ease with Jews who are urban as well as urbane. Her focus is invariably on the nature of community and its ability to transmit a Judaism that can maintain the allegiance – both ritualistically as well as personally – of her characters. She has pointed out that George Eliot's *Middlemarch*, with its treatment of a "whole community" containing individuals that are "so alive, so real," was an inspiration. Goodman's works often do just that. *Total Immersion* (1989), a widely praised collection of stories, was followed by *Family Markowitz* (1996), a series of related stories about a family's adjustment to the ruptures as well as blandishments of modern life. Her *Kaaterskill Falls* (1998) deals with the political and religious conflicts of an Orthodox Jewish community whose characters must not only accept a new leadership but also adjust their ambitions to a regulated life. *Paradise Park* (2001), with its pathos and humor, offers readers the God-seeking but all-too-human Sharon Spiegelman, seeking revelation in her travels, beginning in Hawaii. In 2006 she published *Intuition*, set in a Cambridge, Mass., research institution.

BIBLIOGRAPHY: D. Welch, "Author Interviews: Allegra Goodman," at: Powells.com.

[Lewis Fried (2nd ed.)]

GOODMAN, ANDREW (1907–1993), U.S. merchant. Bergdorf Goodman was already one of New York City's most elegant fashion emporiums when Andrew Goodman inherited it. But it was he who transformed it from a store that catered to the carriage trade to one that expanded its appeal to "people who have more taste than money and are on the way up." Goodman's father, Edwin, founded the store early in the 20th century. He came to New York City in 1899 and went into business with a tailor named Herman Bergdorf. After buying out Bergdorf in 1906 – but keeping his name as part of the business – the elder Goodman moved the shop from lower Fifth Avenue further uptown, branching out as a furrier and dressmaker. In 1926, Andrew Goodman, who had spent an uneventful year and a half at the University of Michigan, was summoned home by his father and sent to Paris to apprentice at the house of couturier Jean Patou. Goodman came back to the U.S. a year later and joined the family business, which was beginning to undergo an important transition. Instead of limiting itself to custom-made clothing, Bergdorf Goodman began offering clothing off the rack. The concept was a hit and by 1928 annual volume was $5 million. Ready to expand, Bergdorf's moved into a new marble and sandstone building on Fifth Avenue and 57th Street. Inside, the store looked like the genteel home of a moneyed family. Its fashions were from top U.S. and European designers, its clients were the wealthy and well known, and its saleswomen often exuded a snobbishness that could be terrifying. After service in the U.S. Navy during World War II, Goodman returned to the store, becoming president in 1951. When his father died, in 1953, Goodman inherited the store and the title of chairman. He also began reaching out to women who might have been put off by Bergdorf's intimidating image. In 1955, Goodman opened the Miss Bergdorf Shop, which featured more moderately priced merchandise. It quickly became highly popular. He also added antiques, a beauty salon, and an art gallery presided over by his wife, Nena. Bergdorf's kept expanding, eventually doubling in size to 120,000 square feet. By 1969, it was the nation's only large high-quality specialty store that was independently owned, but in 1972, Goodman sold the business to Broadway Hale Stores. He retained the real estate as well as the 16-room penthouse above the store, where his family lived, and he remained as president until 1975. Active in philanthropic and civic affairs, Goodman was a chairman of the Fifth Avenue Association and the Better Business Bureau of New York. He was vice president of the American Jewish Committee and served on the boards of various other Jewish organizations.

BIBLIOGRAPHY: *New York Times* (April 5, 1993); *W* magazine (Nov. 2003).

[Mort Sheinman (2nd ed.)]

GOODMAN, ARNOLD ABRAHAM, LORD (1913–1995), British lawyer and legal advisor. Goodman was born in London to middle-class, middle-of-the-road Orthodox parents and had a brilliant career at Cambridge and in his law studies. He was created a Life Peer in 1965. Lord Goodman was personal legal advisor to many leaders of Britain's three political parties – in itself a unique position. He first came to public prominence in 1967 when the Labour government called on him to arbitrate and settle a serious strike of television workers. He was successful, and from that point forward, both the Labour and subsequent Conservative administrations used his services as unofficial envoy in a number of industrial disputes as well as in Britain's constitutional dispute with Rhodesia. He was so successful in gaining the confidence of the workers in the newspaper industry that the powerful Newspaper Proprietors' Association made him its chairman. He held many other public and semipublic offices, the most important of which was chairman of the semiofficial Arts Council (1965–72), which encourages all the arts, including literature, and disburses official funds to theaters, etc. He was also a member of a number of royal commissions and committees of enquiry, and prochancellor of Warwick University. Until 1986, he was Master, University College, Oxford. He also spoke on behalf of Jewish charities and without being a formal Zionist showed active sympathy toward Israel. In 1973, he was appointed chairman of the Housing Corporation and the National Building

Agency, both government bodies. His autobiography, *Tell Them I'm on My Way*, appeared in 1993.

Goodman was one of the most famous *eminences grises* in postwar Britain. Like all men credited with backstairs influence, his powers were often exaggerated. Nevertheless, Goodman met, on a weekly, confidential basis, with Harold Wilson during his 1964–70 term as prime minister, sharing many secrets with him. Wilson greatly valued Goodman's advice, and used him as a sounding board for proposed actions. From 1993, Goodman's life was overshadowed by a lawsuit brought against him by the Portman family, London landowners, who claimed that he had siphoned off funds from their family trust. After Goodman's death, his law firm paid the Portmans £500,000 without any admission of guilt.

BIBLIOGRAPHY: *Not for the Record* (selected speeches and writings by Lord Goodman:, 1972). **ADD. BIBLIOGRAPHY:** ODNB online; B. Brivati, *Lord Goodman* (1999); D. Selbourne, *Not an Englishman: Conversations With Lord Goodman* (1993).

[Michael Wallach / William D. Rubinstein (2nd ed.)]

GOODMAN, BENNY (Benjamin David; 1909–1986), U.S. clarinetist and band leader. He learned to play the clarinet as a child in Chicago in a music instruction program fostered by a local synagogue. When he turned professional, he played in various well-known bands until he organized his own orchestra in 1933. Goodman became one of the founders of the "swing" style prevalent in the 1930s, and was called the "King of Swing." His was the first jazz ensemble in which both white and black musicians played together. At the same time he developed a technical mastery that led to his appearances with symphony orchestras and chamber ensembles. Bartok dedicated his clarinet trio "Contrasts" to him in 1938, and Hindemith (1947) and *Copland (1948) each wrote a clarinet concerto for him. He wrote an autobiography, *The Kingdom of Swing* (1961), and authorized *Benny Goodman's Own Clarinet Method* (1941), edited by Charles Hathaway.

BIBLIOGRAPHY: D.R. Connor, BG – *Off the Record* (1958); P. Maffei, *Benny Goodman* (1961); E. Condon and R. Gehman (eds.), *Eddie Condon's Treasury of Jazz* (1956), 258–74; N. Shapiro and N. Hentoff (eds.), *Jazz Makers* (1957), 175–86.

[Claude Abravanel]

GOODMAN, MARTIN DAVID (1953–), British professor of Jewish Studies. Educated at Oxford, Goodman is a major, much-respected historian of ancient Jewry and the ancient world in the Roman era. He is the author of many works, including *The Ruling Class of Judea* (1987), *Mission and Conversion: Prosteltyzing in the Religious History of the Roman World* (1994), and the editor of *Jews in a Graeco-Roman World* (1998), which often aims to place the history of Roman-era Judea in a wider context. He is also the editor of the comprehensive *Oxford Handbook of Jewish Studies* (2002). Goodman is professor of Jewish Studies at Oxford University, a fellow of Wolfson College, Oxford. He was president of the British Association for Jewish Studies.

[William D. Rubinstein (2nd ed.)]

GOODMAN, NELSON (1906–1998), U.S. philosopher. Born in Somerville, Massachusetts, Goodman received his B.S. magna cum laude (1928) and his Ph.D. (1941) from Harvard University. From 1929 to 1941 he ran the Walker-Goodman Art Gallery in Boston, and remained an avid collector of ancient and modern art. He served in the U.S. Army from 1942 to 1945.

He taught at Tufts College (1945–46), the University of Pennsylvania (1946–64), and Brandeis University (1964–67). In 1968 he was named professor of philosophy at Harvard. His philosophical studies ranged over many areas, including logic, epistemology, and aesthetics.

Two of Goodman's important early works are *The Structure of Appearance* (1951) and *Fact, Fiction and Forecast* (1955). In the late 1950s he turned his attention to the theory of simplicity, which was the main theme of his many contributions to philosophical journals. In attempting to eliminate superfluous entities in any complete description of the world, Goodman's work shows the influence of Bertrand Russell and W. Van Orman Quine.

In 1967, as a research associate at Harvard's Graduate School of Education, Goodman founded Project Zero. The program's purpose was to understand and enhance learning, thinking, and creativity in the arts, as well as humanistic and scientific disciplines, at both the individual and institutional level. He served as the project's director until 1971, engaging in basic research into education and the arts, while also producing a number of programs in film, dance, music, theater, and poetry. For example, Goodman created *Hockey Seen* in collaboration with choreographer Martha Gray, composer John Adams, and artist Katharine Sturgis – Goodman's wife. It was performed at Harvard in 1972 and was filmed there in 1984.

Articles about Goodman and his work frequently appeared in the European press, such as *Le Monde, Frankfurter Allgemeine,* and other leading international newspapers. Among his many awards and honors, Goodman received the Guggenheim Award in 1946 and 1947. Other books by Goodman include *Problems and Projects* (1972), *Ways of Worldmaking* (1978), *Of Mind and Other Matters* (1984), *Reconceptions in Philosophy and Other Arts and Sciences* (with C. Elgin, 1988), and *The Languages of Art* (1997).

BIBLIOGRAPHY: A. Hausman and F. Wilson, *Carnap and Goodman, Two Formalists* (1967). **ADD. BIBLIOGRAPHY:** C. Elgin, *The Philosophy of Nelson Goodman* (1997).

[Avrum Stroll / Ruth Beloff (2nd ed.)]

GOODMAN, PAUL (1875–1949), British Zionist and public figure. Born in Dorpat, Estonia, Goodman went to England in 1891. He was for many years secretary of the Spanish and Portuguese Congregation. Goodman became an active Zionist after hearing Theodor *Herzl address his first meeting in London (1896), and from that time until his death he served the Zionist Organization. He occupied various important positions in the Zionist Movement of London and was honorary secretary of the Political Committee, appointed by Chaim

*Weizmann and Naḥum *Sokolow, before the *Balfour Declaration was issued. Together with Arthur D. Lewis he edited the volume *Zionism: Problems and Views* (1916), was editor of the *Zionist Review* (1920–26 and 1934–38), and was a contributor to various Jewish encyclopedias and Zionist periodicals. Among his works are *The Synagogue and the Church* (1908), *History of the Jews* (1911), *Moses Montefiore* (1925), *Zionism in England* (1930), and *The Jewish National Home* (1943). He also edited *Chaim Weizmann: A Tribute on His Seventieth Birthday* (1945). A memorial tribute to him, entitled *The Rebirth of Israel* (1952), was published by the Zionist Federation of Great Britain.

BIBLIOGRAPHY: *Paul Goodman on his Seventieth Birthday* (1945); *Current Biography Yearbook 1968* (1969), 153–7. **ADD. BIBLIOGRAPHY:** S.A. Cohen, *English Zionists and British Jews: The Communal Politics of Anglo-Jewry, 1895–1920* (1982), index.

[Josef Fraenkel]

GOODMAN, PAUL (1911–1972), U.S. author, psychotherapist, and educator. The youngest of three children deserted by their father, Goodman was born and educated in New York City. At City College he was most influenced by the philosopher Morris Raphael *Cohen and by his reading of the Russian revolutionary author Kropotkin. A versatile writer, Goodman published verse collections such as *Stop-Light* (1942), *The Lordly Hudson* (1963), and *Hawkweed* (1967); novels including *The Empire City* (1959); plays (notably *Faustina*, 1949); short stories (*The Facts of Life*, 1946); and criticism. An account of life in New York over the previous three decades, *The Empire City*, was notable for its mingled comedy and sadness. From his earliest years Goodman's intelligence and experimental attitude toward literature gave him a place in the radical avant-garde, but it was only with the publication of *Growing Up Absurd* in 1960 that he became known to the wider public. The book is an indictment of the American "rat race" and a defense of those young people who do not choose to enter it. In the years that followed, Goodman came to be described as "the father-figure of the New Left" and as "a communitarian anarchist pacifist of protean intellect and prolific pen." Some other works of Goodman are *Communitas* (1947), written in collaboration with his brother, the architect Percival *Goodman, which became a standard work on cities; *The Community of Scholars* (1962), a critique of the U.S. academic scene; *Utopian Essays and Practical Proposals* (1962); *The Society I Live in Is Mine* (1963); *Compulsory Mis-Education* (1964); and *Like a Conquered Province: The Moral Ambiguity of America* (1967); he also contributed to F. Perls, *Gestalt Therapy* (1951). Goodman taught at several universities and at the Institute for Gestalt Therapy (New York City and Cleveland). From 1964 to 1966 he was a full professor at the University of Wisconsin and then at San Francisco State College's experimental college. In the Massey Lectures, delivered over the Canadian broadcasting network, he described what he called an "empty society," which had "a tendency to expand meaninglessly for its own sake, and … to exclude human beings as useless." In 1967 Goodman published a journal, *Five Years: Thoughts in a Useless Time.*

BIBLIOGRAPHY: *Current Biography Yearbook 1968* (1969), 153–7; R. Kostelanetz, in: *New York Times Magazine* (April 5, 1966), 70–71; S.J. Kunitz, *Twentieth Century Authors, First Supplement* (1955); G. Steiner, in: *Commentary*, 36 (1963), 158–63.

[Milton Henry Hindus]

GOODMAN, PERCIVAL (1904–1989), U.S. architect. Goodman was born in New York; he studied there, and after receiving the Society of Beaux-Arts Architects Paris Prize, he enrolled in the Ecole des Beaux Arts in Paris, in France. He was a versatile architect, an expert on city planning, and a professor of architecture at Columbia University, a position he held from 1946 to 1971. Goodman designed furniture for mass production, wrote a book (*Communitas*, 1947), and illustrated the *Golden Ass* of Apuleius (1932). In 1977 he published his work *The Double E*, on the relationship of ecology to city planning. He had no previous religious background when he embarked on his fruitful career as a builder of synagogues. He said that the Nazi atrocities together with his readings of Martin Buber gave him the need for concrete expression of kinship, describing himself as "an agnostic who was converted by Hitler."

Goodman's synagogues are brightly lit and tend to be small and intimate, as Goodman felt this encouraged a feeling of unity in the congregation and a sense of participation in the service. He humanized his design with the use of warm materials such as wood. He regarded the artist as an indispensable collaborator, and gave him an important place in his projects. In this respect he acted as a pioneer and helped to bring into being a flourishing modern synagogal art in the United States.

Between 1936 and 1979 Goodman designed over 50 synagogues and religious buildings. These included the Fifth Avenue Synagogue in New York, Shaarey Zedek in Detroit, the B'nai Israel Synagogue in Millburn, New Jersey, and Temple Beth-El in Springfield, Massachusetts. In addition, he designed many houses, schools, and public buildings, including Public School 92 on West 134th Street in Manhattan (1935) and the Queensborough Community College administration building (1977).

An urban theorist who believed that rational planning could produce better cities, he criticized the planning efforts of his home city New York as timid and short-sighted. Named a fellow by the American Institute of Architects, he nonetheless argued that the institute was irrelevant since it failed to take up moral or political positions.

Goodman's brother was the writer Paul *Goodman.

BIBLIOGRAPHY: R. Wischnitzer, *Synagogue Architecture in the United States* (1955), 141ff.; A. Kampf, *Contemporary Synagogue Art* (1966), 37ff.

[Rohan Saxena (2nd ed.)]

GOODMAN, TOBIAS (d. 1824), English scholar. Goodman, who was born in Bohemia, went to England at the close of the 18th century. In 1806 he was a schoolmaster in *Liverpool, where he is said to have preached the earliest synagogue sermons delivered in English. He was subsequently associated with the Westminster Synagogue in London, where he delivered various addresses, the earliest both delivered and published in English, on the death of the Princess Charlotte (1817) and of King George III (1820). Goodman published Jedaiah Penini's *Beḥinat Olam* with an English translation (1806). He was an active religious controversialist.

BIBLIOGRAPHY: A. Barnett, *Western Synagogue through Two Centuries (1761–1961)* (1961), 48–51; Benas, in: *Transactions of the Historic Society of Lancashire and Cheshire*, 51 (1901), offprint, p. 17. **ADD. BIBLIOGRAPHY:** Katz, England, 275.

[Cecil Roth]

GOODRICH, FRANCES (1890–1984) and **HACKETT, ALBERT** (1900–1995), U.S. writers. Born in Belleville, New Jersey, Goodrich attended Passaic High School. She graduated from Vassar College in 1912, and then spent a year at the New York School of Social Work. She first appeared on stage in Massachusetts in 1913, and her first Broadway show was *Come Out of the Kitchen* (1916). Hackett was born to professional actors Maurice Hackett and Florence (née Spreen) in New York. He first took to the stage at the age of six. The couple met while performing together in Denver, Colorado, in 1927. Goodrich and Hackett began writing plays together; their first hit, *Up Pops the Devil*, was adapted into a film in 1931. The couple married in 1931; the marriage was the third for Goodrich, the first for Hackett. After a string of less than successful screenplays for MGM, Goodrich and Hackett enjoyed their first box-office success adapting Dashiell Hammett's *The Thin Man* (1934), which earned them their first of four career Oscar nominations. Goodrich and Hackett followed up with two more *Thin Man* films – *After the Thin Man* (1936) and *Another Thin Man* (1939). In 1941, the couple returned to Broadway with the long-running *Mr. and Mrs. North*. After the play's run, the couple returned to Hollywood to work for Paramount adapting *Lady in the Dark* (1944). Goodrich and Hackett were known for sophisticated comedy, but also worked on Frank Capra's classic *It's a Wonderful Life* (1946). After *The Pirate* (1948), *Easter Parade* (1948), *Father of the Bride* (1950) and *Seven Brides for Seven Brothers* (1954), the couple once again took an uncharacteristic turn to drama with a stage production of *The Diary of Anne Frank* (1956), which won the Pulitzer Prize for drama and two Tony Awards, and which was adapted to film in 1959. Goodrich and Hackett's final collaboration was *Five Finger Exercise* (1962).

[Adam Wills (2nd ed.)]

GOOR (Grasovski), YEHUDAH (1862–1950), educator and lexicographer. Born in Pohost, Belorussia, he studied at the yeshivah of Volozhin and in 1887 immigrated to Ereẓ Israel. At first he worked as an agricultural laborer and watchman in Rishon le-Zion and, after a year, as a clerk in Jaffa. He later became secretary of the *Benei Moshe society, participated in editing its publication *Ha-Mikhtavim me-Ereẓ Yisrael*, and then a teacher. With D. Idelovitch he founded the first Histadrut ha-Morim ha-Ivrim (Hebrew Teachers' Association) in Ereẓ Israel. Goor was one of the pioneers of the *Ivrit be-Ivrit* method whereby Hebrew is taught without using any other language. He wrote several manuals on the study of Hebrew, Jewish history, natural sciences, the geography of Ereẓ Israel, and translated into Hebrew several of Hans Christian Andersen's tales, Daniel Defoe's *Robinson Crusoe*, and stories by Mark Twain, Dickens, and Jules Verne. In 1893, together with Eliezer Ben-Yehuda and D. Idelovitch, he edited a newspaper for children, *Olam Katan* ("Small World"). From 1906 to 1929, he worked for the Anglo-Palestine Company, at first in Beirut (until 1911), and then in Jaffa-Tel Aviv. His activities with this institution included the purchase of lands for the *yishuv* in Tel Aviv and Haifa. While in Beirut, he helped to open a Hebrew kindergarten. During World War I, he and his family were exiled to Damascus, where he engaged in many beneficial activities for refugees in Palestine.

Goor is best known for his work in Hebrew lexicography. Already in 1903, he prepared (together with Y. Klausner) a "pocket dictionary" and later several other small dictionaries (Hebrew–Hebrew, Hebrew–English, etc.). In 1920, he and *D. Yellin published an illustrated Hebrew dictionary, and from 1937 he was occupied with his major work, the *Millon ha-Safah ha-Ivrit* ("Dictionary of the Hebrew Language," published in an enlarged edition in 1947). In 1939, he prepared a *Leksikon le-Millim Zarot* ("Lexicon of Foreign Words"). Goor's was the first Hebrew dictionary in which Hebrew words were traced to the period in which they originated.

BIBLIOGRAPHY: *Yehudah Grasovski Ish ha-Gevurot* (1942); Pograbinsky, in: KS, 28 (1952/53), 110–20 (bibliography).

[Irene Garbell]

GOOSE. The *barburim avusim* (AV, JPS "fatted fowl") included among the daily provision for Solomon's table (I Kings 5:3) have been identified with the goose, the word *barbur* being explained as derived from *bar* ("pure," "white"), and *avus* ("fattened"). Some, however, identify *barburim* ("swans" in modern Heb.) with hens (BM 86b) or with a variety of fowl that came from Barbaria, that is North Africa (Eccl. R. 2:7). The breeding of geese in Ereẓ Israel is extremely old, a picture of them being fattened having been preserved on a ninth-century B.C.E. ivory tablet found in excavations at Megiddo. In ancient Egypt geese were extensively bred and fattened. The Mishnah mentions goose breeding (Shab. 24:3; Ḥul. 12:1), and a distinction was made between the wild and the domesticated goose (TJ, BK 5: 10, 5a: TB, BK 55a). According to folklore, "if a man sees a goose in a dream, he may hope for wisdom" (Ber. 57a).

BIBLIOGRAPHY: F.S. Bodenheimer, *Animal and Man in Bible Lands* (1960), index, s.v. *Anser*; J. Feliks, *Kilei Zeta'im ve-Harkavah* (1967), 133–4.

[Jehuda Feliks]

GOPHNA, RAM (1928–), Israeli archaeologist, who made a major contribution to the study of the proto-history of Israel, with a special interest in spatial archaeology and environmental history. Gophna was born in Tel Aviv and was educated at the Ḥadash High School during 1943–46. In 1946, before the War of Independence, he joined the *Palmaḥ. As one of the first students of the Department of Archaeology of the Hebrew University in Jerusalem, Gophna's teachers were B. *Mazar, N. *Avigad, M. *Avi-Yonah, and M. *Stekelis. He completed his B.A. in 1954 and his M.A. in 1956. Following his studies Gophna worked for the Israel Department of Antiquities from 1958 to 1974 as a district archaeologist for the southern region, the Negev, and the southern coastal plain. In 1968 Gophna was one of the team leaders during the survey of the hills of Ephraim and Manasseh in the West Bank. Gophna eventually joined the staff of the Department of Archaeology of Tel Aviv University in 1971 in parallel with his work as district archaeologist. In 1974 he completed his Ph.D. dissertation, supervised by Yohanan *Aharoni, entitled "The Settlements of the Coastal Plain of Eretz-Israel During the Early Bronze Age." Gophna conducted a great number of archaeological surveys and excavations in Israel, with his most important and pioneering work carried out at En Besor between 1970 and 1983, which laid the foundations for a new discipline of research, namely the study of the interrelationship between Egypt's Dynasties "0" and I and Canaan in the Early Bronze Age I. As a professor of archaeology (since 1981) at Tel Aviv University, where he taught for nearly 20 years, Gophna was an influential mentor for a large number of undergraduate and graduate students. Gophna has more than 100 research articles to his credit, with his first article appearing in 1963. Key articles include "The Rural Aspect of the Settlement Patterns of the Coastal Plain in the Middle Bronze Age II" (*Tel Aviv*, 8 (1981), with P. Beck); "The Settlement Landscape of Palestine During the Early Bronze II–III and Middle Bronze Age II" (IEJ, 34 (1984)); "Man's Impact on the Natural Vegetation of the Central Coastal Plain of Israel During the Chalcolithic and the Bronze Age" (*Tel Aviv*, 13–14 (1987), with N. Liphschitz and S. Lev-Yadun). He was also the editor of two important monographs on his excavations at En Besor and Tel Dalit. In 2002 a collection of studies (see Bibliography, below), many by his students, was presented to Gophna on the occasion of his retirement from Tel Aviv University.

BIBLIOGRAPHY: E.C.M. van den Brink and E. Yannai (eds.), *In Quest of Ancient Settlement and Landscapes; Archaeological Studies in Honour of Ram Gophna* (2002).

[Shimon Gibson (2nd ed.)]

GORA KALWARIA (Yid. **Ger**; Heb. **Gur**), town 19 mi. (30 km.) S.E. of Warsaw, Poland. The town, known popularly as Nowy Jeruzalem, obtained a charter in 1670 which included a clause prohibiting the settlement of Jews there. Jews were first permitted to settle in the town after it passed to Prussian rule in 1795. Subsequently Gora Kalwaria became celebrated as the seat of the ḥasidic Gur dynasty, founded by Isaac Meir Alter and headed by his successors (see below). The community numbered 2,919 in 1897 (55.1% of the total population) and 2,691 in 1921 (48.9%).

Holocaust Period

On the eve of World War II there were approximately 3,500 Jews living in Gora Kalwaria. When the German Army entered on Sept. 8, 1939, a reign of terror began for the Jewish population. During April and May 1940 several hundred Jews from Lodz and nearby Pabianice and Aleksandrow were deported to Gora Kalwaria. In January 1941 all the Jewish inhabitants of the small localities around Gora Kalwaria, numbering approximately 300, were also concentrated there. On Feb. 25–26, 1941, all the Jews in the town were transferred to the Warsaw ghetto where they shared the fate of Warsaw Jewry, hundreds dying of disease and starvation and the rest deported to the death camps in August 1942. The Jewish community was not reconstituted after the war.

[Stefan Krakowski]

Gur Dynasty

The Gur (Yid. *Ger*) ḥasidic dynasty, one of the most celebrated of the dynasties, existed in Poland from 1859 to 1939; subsequently the center moved to Ereẓ Israel, under the Gur rabbi residing in Jerusalem.

Gur Ḥasidism is based primarily on the trend in Ḥasidism developed by *Jacob Isaac of Przysucha (Peshiskha) and *Menahem Mendel of Kotsk (Kock) but has taken an individual direction. It also derives ideologically from the philosophy of *Judah Loew b. Bezalel of Prague (the Maharal).

The founder of the dynasty was ISAAC MEIR ROTHENBERG ALTER (1789–1866), whose father R. Israel was a disciple of *Levi Isaac of Berdichev and rabbi of Gur. Isaac Meir grew up under the tutelage of Israel Hofstein, the *maggid* of *Kozienice, who influenced Isaac considerably. At an early age he distinguished himself in Torah study, showing originality and intellectual acumen. He subsequently studied under Aryeh Leib Zinz, rabbi of Polotsk, and won a reputation as a brilliant young scholar.

After the death of the *maggid* of Kozienice, and a short period with the latter's son and successor Moses, Isaac Meir left him to become a disciple of *Simḥah Bunem of Przysucha, and after his death, of Menahem Mendel of Kotsk. He continued to give unreserved support to Menahem Mendel throughout the stormy controversy which divided Kotsk Ḥasidism and during the period when Menahem Mendel was in isolation, enabling Kotsk Ḥasidism to survive its acute internal crisis. After Mendel's death in 1859 Isaac Meir was acknowledged as their rabbi by the majority of the Kotsk Ḥasidim. His work entitled *Ḥiddushei ha-Rim* (Warsaw, 1875), novellae on Talmud tractates and the Shulḥan Arukh, became basic texts for study in the yeshivot and are still acknowledged as classic works on the *pilpul* (dialectical) method of exposition. Isaac Meir is frequently referred to by the name of his work as "Ḥiddushei ha-Rim." Isaac Meir displayed a ready awareness of public needs and was well acquainted with Jewish problems in Poland. He fought uncompromisingly to preserve the traditional Jewish way of life and headed opposition to the regulations imposing changes in dress issued by the government and upheld in Jewish circles by the *maskilim*, refusing to make concessions even when imprisoned by the authorities. During the Polish uprising of 1830 he was suspected of sympathizing with the Polish loyalists. He changed his name from Rothenberg to Alter. In his private life he experienced considerable suffering, losing his 13 children during his lifetime.

Although Isaac Meir derived the principal part of his teaching from the Przysucha-Kotsk school of Ḥasidism, in practice it revealed radical divergences. Instead of withdrawing from contact with the masses he tried to win them over, and interested himself in day-to-day problems. He made himself available to all who sought him out, receiving them kindly. However, like the Kotsk school he placed Torah study at the center of spiritual life. As one of the most eminent scholars in Poland of his day he developed among his followers enthusiasm for Torah learning. He also followed the Kotsk method in emphasizing profundity of thought in the search after truth and the inner promptings of the heart, and in continuous striving after self-perfection.

The period of his leadership, which lasted only seven years, had a formative influence on the development of Ḥasidism in Poland. Gur Ḥasidism became a powerful element in Orthodox Polish Jewry, and retained a leading position until the Holocaust.

JUDAH ARYEH LEIB ALTER (1847–1905) son of Abraham Mordecai (the eldest son of Isaac Meir), was orphaned as a child and brought up and educated largely by his grandfather. In 1870, after the death of *Ḥanokh of Aleksandrow, the successor of Isaac Meir as Gur rabbi, Judah Aryeh Leib became the head (*admor*) of Gur. In this position he wielded a wide influence and established the leadership of Gur Ḥasidism in Congress Poland. A distinguished scholar, modest in behavior, Judah Aryeh Leib won the confidence of rabbis and communal leaders throughout Jewry. Like his grandfather he also played a role in public affairs, concerning himself with contemporary Polish Jewish problems. Through his influence Ḥasidism in Poland dissociated itself from Zionism. Judah Aryeh Leib devoted much energy promoting Torah study and attracted many of the youth. His writings are collected under the title *Sefat Emet* (2 vols., 1905–08), after which he is also known. The five sections on the Pentateuch include addresses on Sabbaths and festivals, distinguished by the profundity of their ideas and clarity of exposition, and reflect the marked influence of Judah Loew b. Bezalel (the Maharal) of Prague. The sections on the Talmud, on tractates *Mo'ed* and *Kiddushin*, evidence his wide Jewish scholarship and ability to penetrate to the intended meaning and provide a lucid exposition of the problem, in contrast to the dialectical *pilpul* method followed by his grandfather.

Judah Leib was succeeded by his eldest son, ABRAHAM MORDECAI ALTER (1866–1948), the last of the dynasty in Poland. Under his leadership Gur Ḥasidism reached the height of its influence. He restored the recitation of morning prayer to the regular time and enjoined a break during the Sabbath service for public study. A lover of order and precision, he gave Gur Ḥasidim an organized framework.

In the period preceding the Holocaust Abraham Mordecai was the most prominent figure in European Orthodox Jewry and one of the founders of *Agudat Israel. Particularly sympathetic toward young people and concerned with their needs, he was instrumental in establishing schools and youth organizations. As well as being a scholar, he was an ardent bibliophile. He visited Ereẓ Israel many times and acquired property there. On the outbreak of World War II he escaped from Gur to Warsaw, and finally to Ereẓ Israel in 1940. During and after the Holocaust he was active in rescue work and in the material and spiritual rehabilitation of refugees. He died on Shavuot at the height of the siege of Jerusalem in 1948 and was buried in the precincts of Yeshivah Sefat Emet which he had founded.

Abraham Mordecai's son, ISRAEL ALTER (1892–1977), succeeded him as Gur rabbi. A noted scholar of great personal charm, he had an influence far beyond the immediate circle of his followers. As head of the various Gur institutions and yeshivot he did much to enhance the reputation and influence of Gur Ḥasidism. Thousands of visitors traveled to his court in Jerusalem each year to see him and receive his blessing.

Two sons of Abraham Mordecai, SIMḤAH BUNEM (1898–1992) and PINḤAS MENAHEM (1926–1996), took over after the death of Israel Alter, and were in turn succeeded by YA'AKOV ARYEH (1936–), eldest son of Simḥah Bunem. In the early 21st century, in addition to Israel, Gur ḥasidim were concentrated in the Boro Park section of Brooklyn, New York.

[Abram Juda Goldrat]

BIBLIOGRAPHY: *Bleter far Geshikhte*, 1 pt. 3–4 (1948), 146–8; *Megiles Poyln*, 5 pt. 1 (1961; Heb. and Yid.), 303, 305; T. Brustin-Bernstein, in: *Bleter far Geshikhte*, 4 no. 2 (1951), 103–19, passim; S. Weiss, in: *Sinai*, 8 (1941), 174–89; L. Grossman, *Shem u-She'erit* (1943), 20–21: O.Z. Rand (ed.), *Toledot Anshei Shem*, 1 (1950), 2–3; A.I. Bromberg, *Mi-Gedolei ha-Ḥasidut*, 2 (1951); 22 (1966); I. Alfasi, *Gur* (1954); A.I. Alter, *Me'ir Einei ha-Golah* (1954); M. Schwartzman, *Ha-Ma'or ha-Gadol* (1966); I. Frenkel, *Men of Distinction*, 1 (1967), 127–34; 2 (1967), 95–102; M.A. Lipschitz, "Hassidic School of Gur" (diss., Univ. of Wisconsin, 1964).

GORCEY, LEO (1917–1969), U.S. actor. Bowery Boy Leo Gorcey was born in New York to an Irish mother, Josephine Condon, and a Russian-born Jewish father, BERNARD (1886–1955), an actor who played Papa Cohen in *Abie's Irish Rose* on Broadway. Gorcey dropped out of school to apprentice in his uncle's plumbing shop. However, in 1935 his father encouraged Leo and his brother DAVID (1921–1984) to try out for the Broadway drama *Dead End*; both were cast as New York street toughs. Gorcey was later tapped for the role of "Spit" in the 1937 feature film adaptation that starred Humphrey Bogart and Joel McCrea. The Dead End Kids would appear in a slate of dramas, including *Angels with Dirty Faces* starring James Cagney, which spoke to such issues as social injustice. In

1940 the name of the gang was changed to the East Side Kids, and Monogram Studios decided to play the kids for laughs, upping the slapstick in several low-budget hour-long films in which Gorcey played "Muggs McGinnis" and his brother played "Peewee." The group was renamed a second time as the Bowery Boys in 1946, with Gorcey playing roughneck leader "Terence 'Slip' Mahoney," his brother "Chuck," and his father "Louie," the sweet shop owner. Gorcey, his brother, and father often shot four to five Bowery movies a year until 1956, when Bernard died after a car accident in Los Angeles in 1955. Gorcey, upset by the death of his father, retired from films and moved to a ranch near Red Bluff, Calif. He married five times between 1939 and 1968, and had three children. Gorcey died in Oakland, Calif., two years after writing his autobiography, *An Original Dead End Kid Presents: Dead End Yells, Wedding Bells, Cockle Shells, and Dizzy Spells.*

[Adam Wills (2nd ed.)]

GORDIMER, NADINE (1923–), South African novelist, Nobel Prize laureate. Gordimer occupied a preeminent position in South African letters, was internationally acclaimed, and was the first South African writer to receive a Nobel Prize (1991). She was born in Springs, near Johannesburg, and published her first volume of short stories, *Face to Face*, in 1949. During her long writing career she published over 200 short stories, among the finest in South African writing, and 14 novels. *The Lying Days* (1953), her first novel, established her as a realist, a genre in which she is best known. Her unerring eye for detail is apparent in all her work, but her realism also charts an inner landscape and constitutes a mirror of the intensity of feeling, suffering, and conflict during the troubled situation under apartheid. Together with her fiction, her numerous essays and studies on culture and politics contribute a general social critique, and all her writing reflects her own commitment to the liberation movement and to social transformation. She has been hailed as a courageous and authoritative voice of conscience during the years of silence and repression, her work sometimes being banned in her own country. *A Guest of Honour* (1970) won the James Tait Black Memorial Prize in 1973. *The Conservationist* (1974) won the Booker Prize for Fiction. Her numerous other awards include the Modern Language Association Award, the Commonwealth Prize for distinguished service to literature, and the Royal Society of Literature Medal. She insisted that she did not regard herself as a feminist but as a "white African." Many readers and critics are either unaware of her Jewish background or disregard it. She herself asserts that she had no sense of identity with the Jewish community, and that being Jewish has not influenced her thinking or writing in any way. The central character of *A Sport of Nature* (1987) is a Jewish girl who marries two black revolutionaries, but generally there are few Jewish characters in her work and those are presented in stereotypical fashion. Her vigorous anti-racial stance is not always clearly evident in the presentation of Jewish storekeepers on the mines in her early work.

In a story of 1991, "My Father Leaves Home," a Jew (seemingly largely based on the history of her own father, a Lithuanian immigrant) is stigmatized on racial grounds and becomes himself a racist. Perhaps this illustrates her awareness of one facet of the fractured identity of some South African Jews. She continued to chronicle South African life after apartheid. She has been the subject of deep admiration and scrutiny from leading critics and has been translated into several languages, including Hebrew. The intense focus of her vision of the complex and troubled situation of a country beset by seemingly insoluble racial and political problems and gradually undergoing transformation is universally valued. Some detractors see her apparent detachment and coldness as a fault. None, however, deny her immaculate craftsmanship or underestimate her incomparable contribution to South African letters.

BIBLIOGRAPHY: N.T. Bazin and M.D. Seymour (eds.), *Conversations with Nadine Gordimer* (1990); S. Clingman, *The Novels of Nadine Gordimer: History from the Inside* (1986); J. Cooke, *The Novels of Nadine Gordimer: Private Lives, Public Landscapes* (1985); D. Driver et al., *Nadine Gordimer: A Bibliography* (1993), A.V. Ettin, *Betrayals of the Body Politic: The Literary Commitments of Nadine Gordimer* (1993); N. Gordimer, "A South African Childhood: Allusions in a Landscape," *New Yorker* (16 October 1954); S. Gray, *Indaba: Interviews with South African Writers* (2005); R.F. Haugh, *Nadine Gordimer* (1974); D. Head, *Nadine Gordimer* (1994); R.J. Nell, *Nadine Gordimer, Novelist and Short Story Writer: A Bibliography of her Works and Selected Literary Criticism* (1964); J. Newman, *Nadine Gordimer* (1988); A.W. Oliphant (ed.), *A Writing Life: Celebrating Nadine Gordimer* (1998); R. Pettersson, *Nadine Gordimer's One Story of a State Apart* (1995); R. Smith (ed.), *Critical Essays on Nadine Gordimer*, (1990); P. Stein and R. Jacobson, *Sophiatown Speaks* (1986); B. Temple-Thurston, *Nadine Gordimer Revisited* (1999); M. Wade, *Nadine Gordimer* (1978); K.M. Wagner, *Rereading Nadine Gordimer: Text and Subtext in the Novels* (1994).

[Marcia Leveson (2nd ed.)]

GORDIN, ABBA (1887–1964), Yiddish and Hebrew writer. Born in Michalishek (Belorussia), Gordin received a traditional Jewish education and was self-taught in general subjects. He wrote in Hebrew, Russian, and English as well as in Yiddish. He remained true to his anarchist convictions even in Communist Russia. Resident in Moscow and Leningrad, in 1926 he escaped to New York, where he edited *Yidishe Shriftn* (1941–46). The last seven years of his life he lived in Israel and edited the Hebrew-Yiddish *Problemot*. In his early writings, he sought a synthesis of biblical Judaism and classical anarchism. He wrote *Sotsiale Ibergloyberay un Kritik* ("Social Superstitions and Criticism," 1941), *Eseyen* ("Essays," 1951). *In Gerangl far Frayhayt: Rusland* ("In Struggle for Freedom: Russia," 1956); and *S. Yanovsky (1864–1939)*, a memorial volume for the anarchist leader (1957). His memoirs of the post-1917 years, *Zikhroynes un Kheshboynes 1917–1924* ("Reminiscences and Reckonings 1917–1924," 1955–57) and *Draysik Yor in Lite un Poyln: Oytobiografye* ("Thirty Years in Lithuania and Poland: Autobiography," 1958) are of particular interest to students of the Bolshevik Revolution.

BIBLIOGRAPHY: LYNL, 2 (1958), 139–40.

[Melech Ravitch / Leonard Prager (2nd ed.)]

GORDIN, JACOB (1853–1909), Yiddish playwright and journalist. Born in Mirgorod, Ukraine, Gordin was writing for the Russian press at 17. Though tutored in secular subjects at home, he was essentially self-educated. He tried his hand at business but failed and became in turn a farm laborer, a stevedore, and an actor in a Russian itinerant troupe, all the while writing for the Russian press and deeply involved in utopian political movements. He finally settled in Yelizavetgrad (Kirovograd) as a teacher in the local "russified" Jewish school. Gordin's first political ideal was nurtured in a circle devoted to Ukrainian independence. Later, influenced by Tolstoy and by the dissident Stundists (a non-Orthodox Christian Evangelical sect in Russia), as well as by Russian populist and Jewish enlightenment currents, he founded his own sect, the *Dukhovno-Bibliĭskoe Bratstvo* ("The Spiritual Biblical Brotherhood"), in 1880. He and his followers rejected post-biblical Judaism, claimed the Bible as the source for their rationalist ethics, repudiated commerce, and saw in agriculture the sole healthy and virtuous occupation. Gordin's obsession with occupational reform led him to write an article which grossly offended the Jewish community. Soon after the April 1881 pogroms, he published in the Russian press an open letter "To My Jewish Brethren" in which he argued that Jewish usury, love of money, and middleman occupations were to blame for Russian antisemitism. The "Brotherhood" was ineffectual: its efforts to build a communal colony failed. In 1891, the czarist police decided to disband the group, and Gordin, forewarned, fled to the U.S. Shortly after arriving in New York, which was to become his permanent home, Gordin applied to the Baron de Hirsch *Fund for aid in establishing a communal farm and was refused. Family obligations, a pregnant wife, and eight (eventually 14) children to support, made Gordin turn to journalism; he soon began writing for the New York daily *Di Arbeter Tsaytung*. When that work proved insufficient to support his growing family, he turned to playwriting. Prior to his arrival in America, at the age of 38, Gordin had never written in Yiddish nor ever written a play.

His first drama, *Sibirya* ("Siberia," 1891), though an apprentice piece, reveals many of those qualities for which Gordin was to earn the title "Reformer of the Yiddish Stage." The Yiddish theater, as Gordin found it, was one of vulgar burlesque and of absurd and garish "historical operettas." In *Sibirya*, as in all of Gordin's plays, the characters speak colloquial Yiddish rather than the affected Germanized Yiddish favored by the bombastic style of the day. Gordin disciplined the ad-libbing comic actors and banned, or at least modified, the rhymed-couplet, song-and-dance routine. He built suspense into his plays and made spectacle secondary to dramatic action. *Sibirya*, however, also heralds Gordin's characteristic tendentiousness, stereotyping, moralizing, and excessive pathos. Yet the gentile judge in *Sibirya* is presented as a human being rather than as a caricature, something of an innovation, and indicative of the way in which Gordin's earnest view of the theater as school and temple yielded aesthetic fruit. But his melodramatic plays never ceased to be vehicles for his social gospel; he valued his art mainly for what it might teach. Gordin's first great popular success, *Der Yidisher Kenig Lir* ("The Yiddish King Lear," 1892), made his reputation. It also added further luster to the acting career of Jacob P. *Adler in the title role, and it was Adler's star power and popularity with the audience that helped them accept a play that dispensed with or modified many of the norms of Yiddish drama up to that point. Henceforth, Gordin was to write many plays for virtuosi. He created the lead roles in *Der Vilder Mentsh* ("The Wild Man," 1893) and *Elisha ben Abuye* (1906) for Adler; those in *Mirele Efros* (1898), *Di Shkhite* ("The Slaughter,"1899), and *Khasye di Yesoyme* ("Khasye the Orphan Girl," 1903) for Keni Liptzin; and those in *Safo* ("Sappho," 1899) and *Kraytser Sonate* ("Kreutzer Sonata," 1902) for Bertha *Kalish. Great actors respected Gordin, and he in turn wrote great roles for them. His use of borrowed plots was to become typical, and despite his open avowal of his sources, he was plagued with accusations of plagiarism. He adopted plots from Hugo, Hauptmann, Schiller, Gogol, Gorki, Sudermann, Grillparzer, Ibsen, Lessing, Gutzkow, Ostrovski, and others. From *Shakespeare he took the skeletal plot of *King Lear* for his *Yidisher Kenig Lir* – the title itself acknowledging the debt. The latter is essentially a Jewish play, a didactic melodrama which probes the problem of conflict between generations. The impulse behind its female analogue, *Mirele Efros*, one of the most popular dramas in the Yiddish repertoire, came from Gordin's own Lear play rather than from Shakespeare. The world of *Mirele Efros* is a Jewish world, yet the play was performed successfully in nine languages. Gordin was frequently attacked for introducing alien matter into the Yiddish theater; some critics denied he was a Jewish writer at all. Among his other popular plays may be mentioned *Got, Mensh un Tayvl* ("God, Man, and Devil," 1900), *Di Shvue* ("The Oath," 1900), and *On a Heym* ("Homeless," 1907). Only about a quarter of his plays have been printed, some in pirated editions, while many survive only in manuscript or have been lost. Gordin also wrote a score of one-act plays, largely to encourage amateur performers, as well as serious essays on the theater. He also wrote widely for the press. His stories and sketches are invariably characterized by socialist moralizing.

In his stormy 18 years in America, Gordin wrote more than 100 plays for the Yiddish stage, most of which have been forgotten. Yet he must be reckoned the most important formative influence, after *Goldfaden, in the history of the modern Yiddish theater. Gordin came to love Yiddish but denied it the status of "national tongue." He viewed with pessimism the future of the American Yiddish theater whose temporary decline he lived to witness. His dying words were "finita la commedia." A quarter of a million Jews attended his funeral in New York City. His works have not been well edited. The four basic collections are *Yankev Gordins Ertseylungen* ("J. G.'s Stories," 1908); *Ale Shriftn* ("Works," 4 vols., 1910); *Yankev Gordins Dramen* ("J.G.'s Dramas," 2 vols., 1911); *Yankev Gordins Eynakters* ("J.G.'s One Act Plays," 1917).

BIBLIOGRAPHY: M. Winchevsky, *A Tog mit Yankev Gordin* (1909); A. Cahan, *Bleter fun Mayn Lebn*, 3 (1926), 186–94; 4 (1928), 344–77; B. Gorin, *Di Geshikhte fun Yidishn Teater*, 2 (1923), 107–26; Z. Zylbercweig (ed.), *Leksikon fun Yidishn Teater* 1 (1931), 391–461; idem, *Di Velt fun Yankev Gordin* (1964); S. Niger, *Dertseylers un Romanistn* (1946), 193–203; K. Marmor, *Yankev Gordin* (1953), incl. bibl.; LNYL, 2 (1958), 142–53; L. Prager, in: *American Quarterly*, 18 (1966), 506–16. **ADD. BIBLIOGRAPHY:** N. Sandrow, *Vagabond Stars: A World History of Yiddish Theater* (1977); L. Rosenfeld, *Bright Star of Exile: Jacob Adler and the Yiddish Theatre* (1977); S. Cassedy, *To the Other Shore: The Russian Jewish Intellectuals Who Came to America* (1997); J. Adler, *A Life on the Stage* (1999); J. Berkowitz, *Shakespeare on the American Yiddish Stage* (2002), 31–72; N. Warnke, "Reforming the New York Yiddish Theater...1887–1910" (diss. 2001).

[Leonard Prager / Joel Berkowitz (2nd ed.)]

GORDIN, JACOB (1896–1947), religious philosopher. Gordin was born in Dvinsk, Latvia, and received his general and Jewish education in St. Petersburg. During the Russian Revolution and civil war, he wandered from one village to the next and took the opportunity to increase the depth of his knowledge of Jewish mysticism by becoming acquainted with Ukranian Jewish kabbalists.

In 1923 he settled in Germany where he became part of the Akademie der Wissenschaft des Judenstums. It was in Berlin that he published his major work on general philosophy, *Untersuchungen zur Theorie des unendlichen Urteils.* During the same period he published several important entries on Jewish Philosophy for the *Encyclopedia Judaica* of Berlin, including those on Crescas, J. Kaspi, Kant, Hermann Cohen, and God in Jewish Religious Philosophy, which was republished later in the *Encyclopaedia Hebraica.*

Gordin immigrated to France in 1933 after the advent of the Nazis and became librarian of the Alliance Israélite Universelle. His significant articles on Spinoza, Maimonides, and others were then published in French in the *Cahiers Juifs* of Alexandria. After the Nazi occupation of France, the Eclaireurs Israélites (Jewish Scouting Movement) of France opened educational training centers for its leaders and children's homes in the Vichy "free zone." They called upon Gordin to organize the Jewish training of their educators and he thereby reaffirmed the Jewish consciousness of a significant number of members of the Jewish Resistance. It is from this time that he began to influence Leon *Poliakov.

He returned to Paris after the Liberation of France and for three years – until his death at age 50 – played an increasingly important role in Jewish education at the highest level of the young intellectuals who were searching for their roots after the terrible years of the war. Gordin gave up writing in order to dedicate himself entirely to oral instruction, as master to disciple following an ancient Jewish tradition. Among his best-known disciples were Robert Gamzon (Castor), Léon Ashkenazi (Manitou), and Renée Neher-Bernheim. He introduced them to a knowledge of Jewish mysticism in its most exalted philosophical aspects. After he became seriously ill, his students came to his home to study, fascinated by the extent of his knowledge and the depth of his thinking. Long after his death his disciples have continued to disseminate the teachings of their master in France and in Israel.

[Leon Poliakov / Renee Neher-Bernheim]

GORDIS, ROBERT (1908–1992), U.S. Bible scholar, author, and rabbi. Gordis was born in New York City. He wrote his Ph.D. dissertation on Masoretic *qere* and *ketib* at Dropsie College, where his primary teacher was the renowned textual critic Max *Margolis. With prospects of academic employment curtailed by the Great Depression, Gordis decided to become a Conservative rabbi and was ordained at the Jewish Theological Seminary in 1932. He served as rabbi of Temple Beth El of Rockaway Park, N.Y., from 1931 until his retirement in 1968, and while there established the first Conservative day school in the United States. Gordis did not abandon academic life. Invited in 1937 as an annual lecturer to the Seminary, Gordis served as professor of Bible beginning in 1940. Gordis also taught at Columbia University (1948–57), the (Protestant) Union Theological Seminary (1960), and Temple University. He served as editor of the periodical *Judaism*, president of the Rabbinical Assembly and of the Synagogue Council of America, and consultant to the Center for the Study of Democratic Institutions.

Gordis' biblical scholarship has been in three major areas: Wisdom literature with special emphasis on the Books of Ecclesiastes and Job, to both of which he composed book-length commentaries; the forms of rhetoric and biblical poetry; and aspects of the masorah and the preservation of the biblical text. Gordis employed his considerable knowledge of rabbinic literature as a tool in biblical lexicography. Within the Conservative movement he was a spokesman for the centrist position, advocating change within the framework of the law. He also wrote on the relationship of Judaism to contemporary problems, on the pertinent insights of the Jewish tradition to the issues facing Western civilization, and on the status of Judaism in the modern age. Among his books are *Koheleth: the Man and His World* (1951), *Judaism for the Modern Age* (1955), *Faith for Moderns* (1960) *Root and the Branch* (1962), *Book of God and Man: A Study of Job* (1965), and *Judaism in a Christian World* (1966).

ADD. BIBLIOGRAPHY: S.D. Sperling, in: DBI, 1;456.

[Jack Reimer / S. David Sperling (2nd ed.)]

GORDON, ABRAHAM (1874–1941?), socialist, active in Vilna. From a poor family, Gordon became an engraver, from which profession he derived his Russian pseudonym "Rezchik." He took an active part in the Jewish workers' circles in Vilna and was influenced by populism. In the early 1890s Gordon led the opposition against the shift in aims of the workers' circles – from spreading general education and explaining socialist ideology in the Russian language to conducting propaganda in Yiddish on economic problems and the organization of strikes. Gordon fought the influence of the Social-

Democrat intelligentsia (who later founded the *Bund) on the workers' movement. Even without supporters, he continued to advocate his ideas for many years, and published a number of pamphlets. He was last reported in Vilna in 1940. The circumstances of his death are unknown.

BIBLIOGRAPHY: E. Mendelssohn, in: *International Review of Social History*, 10 (1965), 271–3; LNYL, 2 (1958), 116–7; N.A. Buchbinder, *Di Geshikhte fun der Arbeter-Bavegung in Rusland* (1931), 69–70.

[Moshe Mishkinsky]

GORDON, AHARON DAVID (1856–1922), Hebrew writer and spiritual mentor of that wing of the Zionist labor movement which emphasized self-realization through settlement on the land (the *ḥalutzim*); born in Troyanov, Russia. Gordon's grandfather was a noted scholar, and his father worked as a clerk for his famous relative, Baron Joseph *Guenzburg. Gordon studied Talmud, Bible, and Hebrew grammar with private tutors, as well as Russian and secular subjects on his own. As he was the only survivor of five children, his parents were anxious to have him exempted from military service, but he insisted on presenting himself for examination. When he was found medically unfit, he married and was given a responsible post in the financial management of Baron Guenzburg's estate, which he held, with interruptions, for 23 years. He was respected by the workers and junior officials, whose interests he tried to protect, often at the expense of his own. During this period he was active in educational and cultural work, especially among the youth. At first he was antagonistic to the modern Hebrew literature of his time, especially because of the hostility of many writers to Jewish religious tradition. In 1903, the village in which Gordon worked was sold to a new owner, and he had to find other employment. In this crisis, he decided, despite the opposition of his parents and his wife's family, to settle in Ereẓ Israel, and in 1904 he set out alone, bringing his wife and daughter over only five years later.

In Ereẓ Israel

Although he was now 48 and had never done physical work, he insisted on tilling the soil with his own hands. He worked as a manual laborer in the vineyards and orange groves of *Petaḥ Tikvah and *Rishon le-Zion and, after 1912, in various villages in Galilee, suffering all the tribulations of the pioneers: malaria, unemployment, hunger, and insecurity. From 1909 he wrote numerous articles, most of them published in **Ha-Po'el ha-Ẓa'ir*, embodying his original outlook on labor, Zionism, and the Jewish destiny, which became widely known as "the religion of labor," though he did not use the term. He spent his last years in *Deganyah, where he died in 1922.

Although Gordon was a delegate to the Eleventh Zionist Congress in 1913 and the Ha-Po'el ha-Ẓa'ir conference in Prague in 1920, he was never interested in political affairs as such. He believed that salvation for the Jewish people could come about only through the efforts of the individual to change himself. Thus, he was not enthusiastic about the *Balfour Declaration and the World War I *Jewish Legion. He opposed *Po'alei Zion and *Aḥdut ha-Avodah because of their ties with international socialism, believing that the Jewish workers in Ereẓ Israel must find their own way to a just, productive society through a life of labor. Although he held no official position, Gordon exercised a profound influence on the Jewish labor movement the world over through his writings and, even more, through his personal example. The *Gordonia youth movement, founded in 1925, was named after him and based largely on his ideas.

Gordon's Philosophy

Gordon's world view is rooted in the conviction that the cosmos has unity, that nature and man are one, and that all men are organic parts of the cosmos. Man is molded by the cosmos in two different ways: through his knowledge of the world and through his intuitive perception of the world, which can never be consciously known, yet can be lived. What we know is merely a fragment of what we are. A man becomes an individual by the way in which he opens himself to the immediacy of the experience of life. The human soul is related to a hidden part of the cosmos. It is in this "hidden" life that each man's individuality is rooted.

Gordon was conscious of the fact that his theory sets up a dichotomy between rational "knowledge" and "life." He compared their dualism with the relationship between the flame and the oil in a burning lamp. Consciousness and knowledge are the flame; life itself is the oil which nourishes it. The intellect achieves clarity by concentrating its light on a single sector of reality. However, the intellect pays a price for this clarity: it cuts off the living relationship between the sector which it investigates and the totality of the cosmos. The more a man penetrates nature with his knowledge, the less he can live it with his whole being. Yet the ultimate source of our deepest certainties is not the knowledge we may accumulate, but life itself. Living intuition speaks where our intellect fails us. The intellect is an important weapon in the struggle for survival. At the same time, however, it tends to isolate and alienate man from the cosmos as a whole.

In this tension Gordon discovers the source of religion. Through religion man begins to feel once again that he is an organic part of creation. God cannot be approached through the intellect, but man can reach God in an immediate living relationship. With the psalmist, Gordon says, "My soul thirsteth for God, the living God." A mystery to the intellect, God cannot be known, but He can be experienced and lived.

Gordon's friends found it difficult to accept his religious notions. For them religion had become ossified, irrelevant, a thing of the past. He attempts to meet their objections by making a distinction between form and content in religion. He concedes that as far as form is concerned, religion has lost much of its vitality. The content of religion originates in the religious individual; it is the expression of his sense of cosmic unity and purpose. But men tend to sanctify religious forms at the expense of religious content. Gordon claims that, though present-day religious thinking may be dead, God Himself can never die. He is a hidden mystery, yet we encounter Him in all we experience. Religion will not die so long as men live and think and feel. Its time has not passed – its time has not yet even come. True religion is of the future.

Man cut himself off from this source of rejuvenation when he left the soil and moved to the city. Nature is no longer the source of his inner renewal; he has reduced nature to a quantity of corn, or grain, or wood, which he buys or sells. Man's relationship with other men, things, and nature have become purely utilitarian. Authentic religion cannot live in such an atmosphere. If man is to rediscover religion, the proper balance between the two powers of the human soul – intellect and intuition – must be restored. The task of the intellect is to be the servant – the *shammash* – of intuition, not to overpower it. The proper balance between master and servant can be restored only by man's return to a direct relationship with nature.

"Our road leads to nature through the medium of physical labor." The return to nature through labor will enable man to rediscover religion and to regain a sense of cosmic unity and holiness. Gordon's religion has been defined as a "religion of labor." Gordon was strongly influenced by Tolstoy, who preached a similar return to nature; but unlike Tolstoy, Gordon attempted to practice what he preached.

Gordon opposed socialism in its Marxist form. He regarded Marxism as merely another creation of the intellect, a product of a technological and capitalistic civilization. The aim of Marxism is the reorganization of the social order, not the renewal of the human spirit. It seeks to change man by changing the regime, instead of seeking to change the regime by changing man. All attempts to transform human life through the introduction of a new social order are doomed to failure if they do not begin with what must come first: the living human being. A genuine inner renewal of society can be achieved not by an accidentally related mass, but only by an organically united community – the people. Nature has created the people as the connecting link between the cosmos and the individual. Mankind represents the unity not of states but of peoples. A people is a natural community embodying a living cosmic relationship.

For this reason cosmopolitanism must be replaced by what Gordon calls cosmo-nationalism. Cosmopolitanism is based on the assumption that the individual can be a citizen of mankind directly, without being a member of a specific historic people. This assumption is an illusion. Such an individual and such a mankind are mere abstractions. There are only men who are Russians, Germans, Frenchmen.

Gordon uses the phrase *am-adam* ("people-humanity," "people-incarnating humanity") to express his thinking on the role of the people in the fulfillment of man's destiny. Man was created in the image of God, and Gordon adds that the people has to be created in the image of God too. This "people-incarnating humanity" is the new ideal which Israel, returning to its land, is to exemplify in the eyes of all mankind. Gordon's cosmo-nationalism has genuine universalistic implications. No people must ever be permitted to place itself above morality. A people incarnates humanity only to the extent to which it obeys the moral law.

Here Gordon saw the challenge which the Jew faced in Ereẓ Israel. The recreation of such a nation – its realization – was to be the contribution of the reborn Jewish people to mankind. The creation of a nation which, at the same time, would be an integral part of humanity, is an extension of the original act of creation:

"We were the first to proclaim that man is created in the image of God. We must go farther and say: the nation must be created in the image of God. Not because we are better than others, but because we have borne upon our shoulders and suffered all which calls for this. It is by paying the price of torments the like of which the world has never known that we have won the right to be the first in this work of creation."

He saw the crucial test in the attitude of the Jews toward the Arabs:

"Our attitude toward them must be one of humanity, of moral courage which remains on the highest plane, even if the behavior of the other side is not all that is desired. Indeed their hostility is all the more a reason for our humanity."

Gordon's writings, entitled *Ketavim* (1951–54), appeared in three volumes, including a bibliography. There is also a selection of his writings in English entitled *Selected Essays* (1937).

BIBLIOGRAPHY: S.H. Bergman, *Faith and Reason* (1961), 98–120; idem, *A.D. Gordon, l'homme et le philosophe* (1962); Ẓemaḥ Duran, in: A.D. Gordon, *Ha-Ummah ve-ha-Avodah* (1952), 11–52; M.M. Buber, *Israel and Palestine: The History of an Idea* (1952), last chapter; E. Schweid, *Ha-Yaḥid: Olamo shel A.D. Gordon* (1969); H.H. Rose, *The Life and Thought of A.D. Gordon* (1964); A. Hertzberg, *The Zionist Idea* (1960), 368–86; Rose in: *Judaism*, 10 (1961), 40–48.

[Samuel Hugo Bergman]

GORDON, ALBERT I. (1903–1968), U.S. rabbi and sociologist. Gordon, who was born in Cleveland, Ohio, earned his B.A. from New York University (1927), was ordained by the Jewish Theological Seminary (1929), and received a Ph.D. from the University of Minnesota (1949). He served as a rabbi in Temple Israel in Washington Heights, New York, and then in Congregation Kneset Israel-Beth Shalom in Kansas City before he moved to Adath Jeshurun Synagogue, Minneapolis, Minnesota (1930–46), a congregation in transition between generations. He modernized the services and attracted new members, increasing the congregation more than fourfold to 400 families. He was also active in the community, serving the War Labor Board and conducting a weekly radio broadcast. He left the congregation to serve as executive director of the United Synagogue of America (1946–50), where he expanded lay involvement and helped found the first Camp Ramah in Wisconsin under the initiative of the Chicago Council of United Synagogue. He left after considerable success and significant expansion but also in great frustration and returned to the pulpit as rabbi of Temple Emanuel, Newton, Massachusetts (1950–68). Under his leadership, which coincided with the suburbanization of American Jews, the school there expanded more than threefold to 1,000 students who studied four days a week. The synagogue expanded its building and classroom facilities. He was a member of the faculty of neighboring Andover Newton Theological School and taught sociology at Boston University, and held many positions in the Jewish community. He wrote four sociological studies, which constitute a substantial contribution to the study of American Jewry: *Jews in Transition* (1949); *Jews in Suburbia* (1959); *Intermarriage: Interfaith, Interethnic and Interracial* (1964); and *The Nature of Conversion* (1967). He also wrote a series of booklets on marriage.

BIBLIOGRAPHY: M. Sklare, *Conservative Judaism* (1955, rev. 1972), 219–22; P.S. Nadell, *Conservative Judaism in America: A Bibliographical Dictionary* (1988), 117–18.

[Jack Reimer / Michael Berenbaum (2nd ed.)]

GORDON, CYRUS HERZL (1908–2001), U.S. Semitic scholar. Gordon was born into a Zionist family in Philadelphia, hence the middle name Herzl. He worked as a field-archaeologist in Jerusalem and Baghdad from 1931 to 1935, after which he taught Semitics at Johns Hopkins University (1935–38), Bible at Smith College (1938–41), at Princeton (1939–42) Assyriology and Egyptology at Dropsie College (1946–56). From 1956 to 1973 Gordon was at Brandeis, where he taught Mediterranean Studies, an area that reflected his conception that the Aeagean had to be included in the study of the ancient Near East. His final academic appointment was at New York University where he taught biblical and Semitic studies from 1973 to 1990.

His *Ugaritic Grammar* (1940) and *Ugaritic Handbook* (1947) which revised the grammar and provided transliterated texts and glossaries were pioneer works in the field, as were his *Ugaritic Literature* (1949) and later his *Ugaritic Manual* (1955; revised as *Ugaritic Textbook*, 1965). Other significant contributions to Semitics were his work on the Akkadian of Nuzi, the Aramaic magic bowls, and the language of *Ebla in Syria first recovered in the 1970s.

Gordon's other major contribution was in "Helleno-Semitics," the comparison of Eastern and Western civilizations, mainly through the study of early Greece and the ancient Near East. His works on this subject include *Before the Bible* (1962; revised as *The Common Background of Greek and Hebrew Civilizations*, 1965), in which Gordon examined ancient Greek mythology in comparison to the biblical stories. In *Homer and the Bible* (1967) he tried to show the common background of all the East Mediterranean cultures.

These interests led him to regard the undeciphered Minoan tablets of Crete (Linear A) as possibly written in a language of Semitic origin. He suggested a translation of the Phaestos Disk of Crete and of Eteocretan inscriptions on the basis of Semitic linguistics. In 1966 he published these studies in *Ugarit and Minoan Crete and Evidence for the Minoan Language*. Other works on Semitics and archaeology include *Nouns in the Nuzi Tablets* (1936); *Numerals in the Nuzi Tablets* (1938); *The Living Past* (1941), a summary of his studies on important excavations in the Middle East; and *Lands of the Cross and Crescent* (1948). He also wrote *The Relationship between Modern and Biblical Hebrew* (1951); *Smith College Tablets* (1952), in which he published 110 cuneiform texts from the college collection; *Introduction to the Old Testament Times* (1953, revised as *The World of the Old Testament*, 1958); *Hammurabi's Code* (1957); *Adventures in the Nearest East* (1957), a popular description of important discoveries in the Middle East from the Dead Sea Scrolls to Ugaritic; *New Horizons in Old Testament Literature* (1960); *Ancient Near East* (1965); *Mediterranean Literature* (1967); and *Forgotten Scripts* (1968).

In 1968 Gordon declared that new knowledge about Phoenician word usage had made it likely that a previously rejected Phoenician tablet (found in 1872) was genuine and that the Phoenicians had gone to America from Ezion-Geber in the 19th year of Hiram, king of Tyre. Given the vastly broad nature of his interests it was inevitable that some of Gordon's work was considered overly speculative but could never be ignored.

ADD. BIBLIOGRAPHY: W. Kaiser, Jr., in: DBI, 1:456–57; C. Gordon, in: M. Lubetski et al. (eds.), *Boundaries of the Ancient Near Eastern World* (1998), 533–54 (Gordon's publications classified); G. Rendsburg, in: JQR, 112 (2001), 137–43.

GORDON, DAVID (1831–1886), Hebrew journalist and editor; one of the early supporters of Ḥibbat Zion. Born in Podmerecz near Vilna, he studied in a yeshivah and later turned to Haskalah and took up secular studies. In 1849 he settled in Sergei (Serbei), earning a meager livelihood as a teacher. In the mid-1850s he moved to England, where he remained until 1858, teaching Hebrew and German. In 1858 Gordon moved to Lyck when Eliezer Lipmann Silbermann invited him to become assistant editor of the first Hebrew weekly, *Ha-Maggid*. In 1880 he officially became the editor of *Ha-Maggid*, a position he had long occupied unofficially. From 1879 to 1881 he published a weekly literary and scientific supplement to *Ha-Maggid*, called *Maggid Mishneh*. He also edited a German paper, *Lycker Anzeiger*, and wrote for the *Times* and *Jewish Chronicle*. His articles in *Ha-Maggid* calling for Jewish national revival in Palestine were the first of their kind in Hebrew. When the Ḥibbat Zion movement was established in the early 1880s, he became one of its leading members and under his editorship *Ha-Maggid* became the Hebrew voice of the movement. Gordon also published several books and contributed to various Hebrew and Yiddish journals.

BIBLIOGRAPHY: Waxman, Literature, 3 (1960), 335–7; G. Kressel (ed.), *Mivḥar Kitvei Gordon* (1942), with introd. and bibl.

[Getzel Kressel]

GORDON, ELIEZER (1840–1910), rabbinical scholar. Gordon was born in the district of Minsk, and while still a young man was invited by R. Israel *Salanter to succeed him in Kovno as teacher of the younger pupils. Appointed in 1874 as rabbi of Kelme and head of its yeshivah, which now attracted many students, he became renowned as one of Lithuania's greatest and most pious rabbinical scholars. In 1884 he was appointed rabbi of Telz (*Telsiai) and head of its yeshivah, which, after the closing of the yeshivah of Volozhin, in 1858, became the spiritual center of Lithuanian Jewry. Gordon was one of the first to adopt what was known in Lithuanian yeshivah circles as "the method of logical comprehension," his lectures being distinguished for their penetrating analysis and their original and logical interpretations. He was also one of the first heads of a Lithuanian yeshivah to introduce the study of *musar* (ethics) into the curriculum, and he appointed adherents of the *Musar movement as *mashgiḥim* (student "supervisors"). Gordon took a special interest in the financial upkeep of the institution and was personally attentive to the needs of each of his students. So deep an attachment existed between them that even those of his students who later became estranged from his outlook and way of life continued to hold him in great personal esteem. As rabbi of Telz Gordon displayed great dedication and resoluteness. At times he would forgo his salary; he interceded with the authorities to protect the rights of Russian Jewry; and he played an active part in internal Jewish matters. At every assembly of Russian rabbis Gordon was one of the principal speakers. In Vilna, in 1904, seeking to establish an organization that would embrace all of Orthodox Jewry, he helped found the Keneset Israel organization, regarded by some as the forerunner of *Agudat Israel. In 1910 the Telz yeshivah was destroyed by fire, and Gordon died in the same year, while on a visit to London, where he had gone to raise funds for its rebuilding, and was buried there. His only published work is *Teshuvot Rabbi Eli'ezer* (2 vols., 1912, 1940).

BIBLIOGRAPHY: S. Assaf, in: *Ha-Ẓofeh* (Feb. 24, 1950); idem, in: *He-Avar*, 2 (1954), 34–45; D. Katz, *Tenu'at ha-Musar*, 2 (1950), 426–36; Z.A. Rabiner, *Ha-Ga'on Rabbi Eli'ezer Gordon* (1969).

[Zvi Kaplan]

GORDON, GEORGE, LORD (1757–1793), English proselyte. A younger son of the third duke of Gordon, he entered Parliament in 1774 but attracted little notice until 1779 when he became president of the United Protestant League which opposed measures in relief of Catholic disabilities (1779). After the violent London "No-Popery" Riots (1780), Gordon was tried for high treason but was acquitted. He again appeared as Protestant champion in 1784 in the quarrel between the Dutch and Joseph II. He subsequently developed an interest in Judaism. Although rebuffed by the London rabbinical authorities, he was circumcised in 1787, either in Holland or in Birmingham (where he lived for a time), assuming the name of Israel b. Abraham. He became scrupulous in religious observance, growing a long beard and rebuking those who were not as devout as himself. He was tried for libels on the British government and Marie Antoinette of France and sentenced in 1788 to imprisonment in Newgate, London. Here he surrounded himself with foreign Jews, ate only specially prepared food, refused to see any Jew who was not bearded, and held regular services with a *minyan* in his apartment. He died in prison, but was buried not in the Jewish cemetery but in his family's burial plot. Paradoxically, Gordon was one of the best-known British Jews of his time.

BIBLIOGRAPHY: P. de Castro, *Gordon Riots* (1926); Solomons, in: JHSET, 7 (1915), 222–71; P. Colson, *Strange History of Lord George Gordon* (1937); C. Roth, *Essays and Portraits in Anglo-Jewish History* (1962), 183–210; Roth, Mag Bibl, index. **ADD. BIBLIOGRAPHY:** ODNB online; Katz, England, 304–10, index.

[Cecil Roth]

GORDON, HAROLD (1907–1979), U.S. rabbi and administrator. Gordon, who was born in Minneapolis, Minn., was ordained in Palestine. During World War II, he was chaplain in the North Atlantic Division of the Air Transport Command, flying over 250,000 miles to military bases in North America and Europe. Gordon was elected general secretary and chaplaincy coordinator of the New York Board of Rabbis, the metropolitan organization of Orthodox, Conservative, and Reform rabbis, in 1946 and executive vice-president in 1956. As such, he directed a network of chaplains in hospitals, prisons, and other institutions, and coordinated the work of one of the largest rabbinic bodies in the world. He initiated the establishment of the International Synagogue at Kennedy Airport, the Brit Milah School, and the Brit Milah Board of New York.

[Jack Reimer]

GORDON, JACOB (1877–1934), Canadian rabbi. Gordon was born in Dunilovitch (Dunilowicze), Vilna (Vilnius) district, Belarus. He apparently attended Volozhin yeshivah toward the end of 1895 or early in 1896 for several months, then relocated to Minsk and later to Kovno (Kaunas) in order to pursue his religious studies. During the 1880s or 1890s, Gordon's parents moved to Smorgon and in the summer of 1904 Gordon immigrated to America together with his wife and first daughter, serving initially as a fund-raiser for an East European yeshivah. In February 1905, Gordon arrived in Toronto, where he stayed until his death.

A few months later, Gordon was appointed as rabbi of the Lithuanian-oriented congregation Goel Tzedec, and served also at congregation Chevra Tehillim (Beth Hamidrash Hagadol as of 1905). Over the following years, Gordon served additional congregations such as Knesseth Israel, Anshei Lida, and Yavneh Zion. Gordon gained a central position in the local Orthodox community due to his ongoing communal involvement and activities in Jewish education, the Free Burial Society, the Associated Hebrew Charities, the *Mizrachi* movement, and *Va'ad Harabanim*. In addition, Gordon developed various connections with non-Orthodox local organizations such as the Ladies' Garment Workers' Union of Toronto, as well nationwide Canadian Jewish organizations such as the Central Division of the Canadian Jewish Congress.

Gordon was a supervisor in the kosher meat industry, and was part of several disputes, some of which involved legal action. Gordon also supervised other food products, such as vegetable oil and salad oil manufactured by various companies.

In addition to articles in the Jewish press and several entries he contributed to the *Hebrew Encyclopedia* and the *Oẓar Yisrael Encyclopedia*, Gordon published a book of sermons in Hebrew, entitled *Minḥat Ya'akov* (Safed, 1914). He persumably wrote another book, *Dovev Siftei Yeshenim*, and an essay on vegetarianism entitled *Nezirut min ha-Basar* that remained unpublished.

BIBLIOGRAPHY: E. Gottesman, *Who's Who in Canadian Jewry 1964* (1964), 114; A.D. Hart, *The Jew in Canada* (1926), 130.

[Kimmy Kaplan (2nd ed.)]

GORDON, JACOB (1902–1943), philosopher. Gordon was born in Vilna. After graduating from the Jewish gymnasium founded by the Society for the Promotion of Culture among Jews, he studied philosophy, history, and psychology at the University of Hamburg (1920–24). His doctoral thesis, a comparative study of Kant's and Hermann *Cohen's philosophies, was published in 1926 with the aid of the Hermann Cohen Fund of the Akademie fuer die Wissenschaft des Judentums and Albert Einstein. Gordon returned to Vilna, where he worked in the *Yivo Institute of Jewish Research and on scholarly journals in Yiddish. In World War II, during the Nazi occupation, he was employed by the Vilna Judenrat, during which time he continued his philosophical studies. In January 1943 he addressed a letter in Yiddish to the Writers' and Artists' Committee of the Vilna Ghetto in which he outlined his plan to write a study on the "*a priori* foundations of history" and on "Kant and Schopenhauer," but pointed out that nobody "could concentrate on *a priori* idealist matters while living under empirical, realistic conditions where getting money to buy a piece of bread assumes the weight and somberness of a fateful event." In September, a month before the liquidation of the ghetto, Gordon was deported to the Vaivara camp in Estonia, where he died as a result of malnutrition.

Apart from his doctoral thesis, all of Gordon's works were written in Yiddish. He edited the academic journals *Etyuden* and *Kultur un Problemen* and published a Yiddish translation of Kant's *Prolegomena*. During the ghetto years he wrote an essay on the "Specificity of History." Most of his collected writings were published in Israel in Hebrew in 1961 under the title *Yaḥid ve-Ḥevrah ba-Historyah* ("Individual and Society in History"), with an introduction by S.H. Bergman.

GORDON, JEKUTHIEL BEN LEIB (18th century), kabbalist. Gordon went from Vilna to study medicine at the University of Padua. He became acquainted with Moses Ḥayyim *Luzzatto in Padua. At that time, Luzzatto was organizing his group for study and messianic activity. Gordon, who became his foremost disciple, was one of the first seven who signed the "regulations" of Luzzatto's circle around 1728. In 1729 Gordon wrote a letter in which he related in detail the activities of Luzzatto, especially the revelation of the *maggid*, the divine revelatory agent which disclosed to Luzzatto the *Zohar Tinyana* ("second Zohar"). Gordon described Luzzatto's many mystical powers and told of how various *ẓaddikim* were revealed to him. This letter fell into the hands of Moses *Ḥagiz, who saw that the activities recounted in the letter were close to Shabbatean practices, and asked the rabbis of Venice to intervene and stop them. Gordon supported Luzzatto in the ensuing controversy. He probably discontinued his medical studies to devote his energy to the activities of the group. A poem written by Luzzatto seems to indicate, with other sources, that Gordon was believed by Luzzatto and his circle to be a reincarnation (*gilgul) of the soul of the hero Samson, who would be revealed in messianic times as Serayah from the tribe of Dan, and would be one of the leaders of the Israelite army in the apocalyptic wars. Gordon returned to Eastern Europe after Luzzatto had to cease his activities in Padua, but he probably continued to preach Luzzatto's teachings.

BIBLIOGRAPHY: S. Ginzburg, *Ramḥal u-Venei Doro* (1937), 18–20 and passim; I. Tishby, *Netivei Emunah u-Minut* (1964), 169–72, 192–6; Y. David, in: *Tarbiz*, 31 (1961/62), 102–4; J. Dan, *ibid.*, 412–3.

[Joseph Dan]

GORDON, JUDAH LEIB (**Leon**; 1831–1892), Hebrew poet, writer, critic, and allegorist. One of the outstanding poets of the 19th century, Gordon was also a witty, incisive journalist who courageously militated against the ills in Jewish society. He advocated social and religious reform and fiercely denounced the rigidness of its leaders, especially the rabbis. His wrath was vented most directly in his poetry and in satirical feuilletons. Probably the severest critic of his time and a fiery exponent of the *Haskalah, Gordon is rightly considered one of its key spokesmen. He embodied an age which ended with him, but at the same time he paved the way for such poets as Ḥayyim Naḥman *Bialik, Saul *Tchernichowsky, and others whom he had influenced. Bialik, his great admirer and successor as the "poet laureate" of Hebrew literature, called him "the mighty hammer of the Hebrew language."

Childhood and Education

Gordon was born in Vilna. His father was "a cultured and erudite man" who engaged as Judah Leib's first teacher Rabbi Lipa, the pupil of a disciple of the Gaon of Vilna. The boy was taught according to the Gaon's method which involved first the study of the Bible and Hebrew grammar, and then the study of Talmud (an unusual procedure in traditional Jewish education at that time). At 14, he already had the reputation of a prodigy. He was permitted to study without the guidance of a teacher and soon became thoroughly versed in rabbinic literature. His brother-in-law, the Yiddish poet Mikhel *Gordon, exercised a considerable influence on Judah Leib, who, at 17, began studying European culture and languages (Russian, German, Polish, French, and English). At 22, he graduated from the government teachers seminary in Vilna and in 1853 began his teaching career in various Jewish government schools in the Kovno province (Lithuania): in Ponevezh (1853–60); in

Shavli (1860–65) where he taught French and other secular subjects in the higher grades of the government secondary school; and in Telz (1865–72).

First Steps in Literature (Ponevezh and Shavli Periods)

Mikhel Gordon introduced Judah Leib to the Vilna circle of Hebrew *maskilim* whose leading members were Abraham Dov *Lebensohn, the outstanding Hebrew poet of the generation, and his son, the poet Micah Joseph *Lebensohn (Michal), Gordon's contemporary and friend. Both of them influenced his early literary efforts. At the behest of A.D. Lebensohn, Gordon transcribed Micah Joseph Lebensohn's manuscript poems, making minor editorial emendations, and when the latter died in 1852 at the age of 24, Gordon composed a eulogy to his memory, "*Hoi Aḥ*" ("O, Brother").

Gordon's first poems, *Shirei Higgayon* and *Shirei Alilah* (1851), were written under the influence of A.D. Lebensohn and his son. His first major work, *Ahavat David u-Mikhal* ("The Love of David and Michal," 1857), an epic, he dedicated to the "high priest," Lebensohn, who proofread and corrected it. Lebensohn also wrote a *haskamah* (a laudatory introduction) in verse to Gordon's book *Mishlei Yehudah* ("Judah's Parables," Vilna, 1859) which contains mostly translations and adaptations of works by Aesop, Phaedrus, La Fontaine, Lessing, and Krylov, as well as a few fables whose themes, while derived from the Bible, the *aggadah*, and the Midrash, are original in their rendering. The work became very popular and its reputation extended beyond the Hebrew reading public of Russia. Some of the fables were included in Karaite children's collections (in the Crimea and the Caucasus), and a chrestomathy compiled by M. *Steinschneider (Berlin, 1861) for D. Sassoon's Jewish school in Bombay includes many of Gordon's fables.

At this time, Gordon, besides composing poetry, already wrote polemic essays. In an article in the Hebrew periodical *Ha-Maggid* (signed "Dan Gabriel"), he advocated the translation of general literary works of universal human interest into Hebrew and denounced the opponents of such projects, accusing them of wishing "to drive out our Hebrew language from the lands of the living…." Gordon also reproached the German Jewish scholars, who published their Jewish studies in German, for their indifference to the Hebrew language. Thus already in the 1850s Gordon used the Hebrew language as a cudgel with which to rap Jewish society, especially the *maskilim* who failed to see in the revival of Hebrew a renaissance of the people itself.

Besides *Ha-Maggid*, Gordon published in *Ha-Karmel*, in L. Philippson's *Allgemeine Zeitung des Judenthums*, and in Russian-Jewish periodicals (e.g., *Raszvet, Den*). His articles in the non-Hebrew press were mostly on Hebrew literature. During the blood libel case in Shavli in which two Jews were accused of the murder of a little peasant girl (1861), he strongly denounced prejudice in the Jewish and in the general press, writing especially for *Golos*, a liberal Russian paper which came out for the rights of Jews, and on whose staff Gordon was employed.

Later Haskalah Activity

In 1865 Gordon became the principal of the Hebrew public school of Telz and later established a girls' school in that city. He gave up teaching in 1872 and moved to St. Petersburg where he was secretary of the Jewish community and director of the *Society for the Promotion of Culture among the Jews. He held these offices simultaneously from 1872 to 1879 when he was incarcerated for purported anti-czarist activities. While imprisoned, and in banishment in Pudozh in the province of Olonets, he wrote *Ẓidkiyyahu be-Veit ha-Pekuddot* ("King Zedekiah in Prison," 1879), a historical biblical poem which reflects his prison experiences. Exonerated in 1880, he returned to St. Petersburg but was not reappointed to his former position. The passiveness with which the Jewish community leaders of St. Petersburg reacted to his imprisonment, with their failure to reinstate him after his release, was a blow to Gordon. Lacking any other income, he accepted A. *Zederbaum's invitation to become editor of the Hebrew daily *Ha-Meliẓ*.

Gordon was a prolific and versatile writer and editor. Besides editing, he wrote editorials and various columns ("*Halikhot Olam*" and "*Be-Mishkenot Ya'akov be-Ḥuẓ la-Areẓ*") anonymously, and published stories, feuilletons, and book reviews under diverse pseudonyms. He turned the Hebrew feuilleton into an effective vehicle of expression. His poetry imitates the form of the biblical verse, but his prose style (stories and feuilletons) is a synthesis of biblical, talmudic, midrashic, and later Hebrew literature. Characterized by typical Hebrew scholarly humor, the style contains many puns and Gordon's literary and conceptual associations range over the whole body of Hebrew literature.

Gordon was also the science editor and literary critic of the Russian Jewish monthly *Voskhod* (1881–82), writing under the pseudonym "*Mevakker*" (Hebrew for "critic"). In "The History of Jewish Settlement in St. Petersburg," and "Attempts at Reforming the Jewish Religion," two articles published in *Voskhod*, he denounced basic reforms in the Jewish religion and the negative attitude to the Talmud taken by some. At the same time, however, he advocated moderate changes. Following a disagreement with his publisher, Gordon resigned from *Ha-Meliẓ* in May 1883 and began editing a collection of his poems which was published by the Jubilee Committee (4 vols., 1884), established in 1881 to honor the 25th anniversary of his writing career. He also worked on the staff of the 82-volume Russian encyclopedic dictionary, published by F. Brockhaus and I. *Efron, to which he contributed articles on Jewish history and Hebrew literature. Gordon's poetry of this period, which he published in the annual *Ha-Asif*, was mostly satirical and included some biting verse against Zederbaum, the publisher of *Ha-Meliẓ*. This, however, did not stop the latter from recalling Gordon to the editorship of his paper. Gordon returned in December 1885 and, having meanwhile been completely cleared by the Russian secret police, his name now appeared on the masthead. He continued as editor for two years (December 1885–88), during which time *Ha-Meliẓ* became a daily.

Literary Periods in Gordon's Work

Gordon's work falls into three periods: (1) the romantic period; (2) the realistic period; (3) the period of national awakening.

THE ROMANTIC PERIOD. Influenced by the Haskalah and its exponents, he wrote long epics on biblical themes during this period, e.g., *Ahavat David u-Mikhal* (Vilna, 1857), "*David u-Varzillai*" (written between 1851 and 1856), and "*Asenat Bat Potifera*" (publ. in 1868). They are imbued with the Haskalah spirit and are of allegorical tenor, yet echo yearnings for a distant and enchanting biblical past.

THE REALISTIC PERIOD. In his poetry as well as in his polemical articles, Gordon was the foremost combatant against the ills of Jewish society and the intransigent religious conservatism of its leaders who, in his view, disregarded the reality of the modern age. He fearlessly chided the people and their leaders. In one of his letters he called himself "the national prosecutor." He became an advocate of the common people, the poor, and the oppressed. Among those whose cause he championed was the Jewish woman whom he saw deprived of rights and subordinate to the male. The heroine of the poem "*Kozo shel Yod*" ("The Point on Top of the *Yod*," completed in 1876) is the beautiful Bat-Shu'a (Gen. 38:12) who, after much suffering and hardships, succeeds in obtaining a divorce from her husband Hillel, a ne'er-do-well who had gone abroad to seek his fortune and had deserted her and their two children. An educated young man, a government employee, wants to marry Bat-Shu'a, but "Rav Vafsi ha-Kuzari" (the name being an anagram of the letters of the then well-known Rabbi Joseph Zechariah [Stern]) invalidates the divorce bill because the husband's name "Hillel" had not been signed in *plene*, lacking the letter *yod*. Bat-Shu'a therefore remains an *agunah and poor. The poem is an outcry against the lot of the Jewish woman who, because of the "point of a *yod*," is denied happiness. In fighting for the rights of Jewish women, Gordon was influenced by the powerful Russian women's liberation movement of the 1860–70s. "*Kozo shel Yod*" became a catchword quoted by the fighters for women's rights: "Hebrew woman, who knows your life? / In darkness you came and in darkness shall go; / Your sorrow, your joy, your misfortune, your desires / In you are born, in you they die."

THE PERIOD OF NATIONAL AWAKENING. Gordon, like the *maskilim* of his generation, at first believed that isolation was at the root of all the troubles that plagued the Jews. "Be a Jew in your home and a man in the street," a line from his poem *Hakizah Ammi* ("My People Awake"), became the motto for a whole generation of *maskilim*. The source of the evil was the rabbis whom he considered intransigent and rigid adherents to the *halakhah* and to old customs and tradition. The only solution for Russian Jewry was to leave its narrow, confined existence and to adapt itself to the wider environment. He urged Jews to stop speaking Yiddish, which he regarded as a jargon, and to adopt Russian. He advocated universal general education, reform of religious customs, and prompted Jews to engage in more productive occupations, such as crafts, industry, and agriculture. Caught up in the liberal spirit that swept Russia at the time, Gordon firmly believed in Russian liberalism, especially after serfdom was abolished in 1861 and the Jews were granted some rights. He thought that adaptation to the non-Jewish environment would lead to a relationship of friendship and brotherhood between Jews and the people among whom they lived.

Gordon was to become disillusioned in Russian liberalism and in his whole conception of the viability of Jewish life in the Diaspora. This led him to reexamine his ideas and values in the light of everyday reality. With the growth of the antisemitic movement in Russia and in light of the ineptness of Russian liberalism, Gordon despaired of the Russian Jewish community ever integrating within the Russian environment and cultural milieu. He was also disappointed in the Jewish *maskilim*, particularly the young, who were carried away by the assimilationist trend, rejecting indiscriminately and forsaking Jewish values and the Hebrew language which Gordon loved and championed without reservation. In his poem "*Le-Mi Ani Amel*" ("For Whom Do I Labor?") he cries out in despair: "My enlightened brothers have learned science. / They mock the old mother who holds the distaff / Forsake it [Hebrew] and let us each follow the language of his country." He concludes on an ominous note of dejection: "Oh, who can tell the future, who can tell me? / Perhaps I am the last of Zion's poets / And you, the last readers." Thus he protested against the assimilationist trend as well as against his adversaries who accused him of preaching russification.

The 1881 pogroms in southern Russia (instigated with the knowledge and perhaps the support of the government) completely crushed Gordon's spirit. He began to look upon emigration to Western countries as the only salvation for Russian Jewry. Gordon did not believe that the Erez Israel of his time, under the yoke of a degenerate and cruel Turkish rule which closed the country to Jewish immigration, could absorb all the Jews who would want to settle there. He therefore advocated immigration to Western countries, particularly to the United States. In his powerful poem "*Aḥoti Ruḥamah*" ("Ruhamah, My Sister"), written in 1882 after the Russian pogroms, he pleaded for "the honor of Jacob's daughter whom the son of Hamor had violated." The use of biblical names – Dinah, daughter of Jacob, and Shechem, son of Hamor – enabled the poet to evade Russian censorship and to publish his poem of wrath against the Russian rioters in *Migdanot*, a literary supplement to *Ha-Meliz*. Gordon thunders in his wrath: "Abel's blood marks Cain's forehead! / And your blood too all shall behold / A mark of Cain, disgrace and eternal shame / On the forehead of the murderous villains."

He ends his poem: "Come, let's go, my sister Ruḥamah!" In "*Bi-Ne'areinu u-vi-Zekeneinu Nelekh*" ("We Shall Go, Young and Old"), a poem also written in the aftermath of the Russian atrocities, he calls out to the Jewish people: "Fear not, Jacob, be not dejected, / Thousands slaughtered will not deter! / Our God's voice calls from the storm / 'Let's go, young and old.'"

Gordon's changed attitude is manifest in his articles and feuilletons written when he returned as editor of *Ha-Meliẓ* which had become the organ of the *Ḥibbat Zion movement. He was sharply attacked by *Ha-Ẓefirah and *Ha-Yom, rival Hebrew newspapers. They accused him of disavowing the views he had preached all his life and of submitting, for material reasons, to the dictates of the owner of *Ha-Meliẓ*. Gordon, however, never actually joined the Ḥibbat Zion movement and did not explicitly endorse emigration to "Turkish" Ereẓ Israel as a solution for Russian Jewry. Settlement in Ereẓ Israel, without the renaissance of the nation, in his view, would be ineffectual, and such a revival depended on religious and cultural modifications: "Our redemption can come about only after our spiritual deliverance" (*Ha-Meliẓ*, 18 (1882), 209–16).

His writings, in which he fervently urged the revival of Hebrew and which express his great love for the Jews as a people, undoubtedly influenced the movement for national revival and later the Zionist movement. In his introduction to *Al Parashat Derakhim* ("At the Crossroads," 1895), Aḥad *Ha-Am, father of spiritual Zionism, notes his indebtedness to Gordon. Gordon's call, "O House of Jacob, come ye, and let us walk" (Isa. 2:5), in his article in *Ha-Karmel* (1866), in which he advocated enlightenment and rapprochement to Europe, eventually became the motto of the first *Bilu pioneers who turned their back on Europe and its enlightenment and immigrated to Ereẓ Israel (1882) to rebuild its wilderness. Gordon, while not committing himself formally, actively upheld the Zionist cause. Thus his criticism (in Hebrew and Russian) of L. *Pinsker's *Autoemancipation* (1882) was favorable, as was his view on Britain's occupation of Egypt in 1882. Realizing that the occupation would increase Palestine's importance "as a corridor to Egypt and a center for Asian trade and that the British rule would attract many of our brethren throughout the Diaspora to Palestine to till the soil, build railways, and introduce new life in trade, property, and arts and crafts," he proposed the founding of "the society for those going to Palestine" in his article in *Ha-Meliẓ* (1882).

Gordon's place in Jewish literature as the poet of the Haskalah is undisputed. The aesthetic value of his writings, however, was questioned soon after his death and is still being contended. The dispute grew out of a literary atmosphere which had reexamined the values of the past. The last decade of the 19th century had witnessed cultural changes in society in general, and the Jewish community in particular, that affected literature and modified aesthetic taste. It was debated whether Gordon was a poet or merely a versifier. Strong views were voiced by both his admirers and his detractors but the former always prevailed.

There was no conflict between Gordon, the poet and visionary, and the Gordon who attempted to forge a new style, had mastered several languages, both classical and modern, and was a gifted translator. Among his translations are Byron's *Hebrew Melodies (Zemirot Yisrael*, 1884), the Pentateuch (from Hebrew into Russian, 1875), and classical fables which he translated from Russian into Hebrew (*Mishlei Mofet*). Gordon also wrote in Russian and German on Judaism and Hebrew literature. His light, humoristic poems in Yiddish, a language he had always disparaged, were published in *Kol Mevasser*, a Yiddish weekly supplement (1862–72) to *Ha-Meliẓ*. At the request of friends, the poems were collected in a book and published under the title *Siḥat Ḥullin* ("Small Talk," 1887, 1889[2]). At home in all of Jewish literature, Gordon was able to draw on its sources with remarkable versatility and ease. He invested obsolete expressions and idioms with fresh meaning and created new syntactical units. Bialik called him one of the greatest wizards in Hebrew of all times – a title his prodigious mastery and control of the language have deservedly earned.

Kitvei J.L. Gordon (2 vols., 1953–60), his collected works (prose and poetry), includes an autobiography and diary. His letters were published by I.J. Weissberg (*Iggerot Y.L. Gordon*, 2 vols., 1894). S. Werses edited the correspondence *Yedidato shel ha-Meshorer: Iggerot Miryam Markel-Mendelson el Y.L. Gordon* (2004).

BIBLIOGRAPHY: A.B. Rhine, *Leon Gordon: An Appreciation* (1910), incl. bibl.; Waxman, Literature, 3 (1960[2]), 234–55; *Kitvei J.L. Gordon*, 1 (1953), introd. by J. Fichmann; *Meḥkarim bi-Leshon Bialik vi-Yhudah Leib Gordon* (1953); Klausner, Sifrut, 4 pt. 2 (1942); *Leksikon fun der Yidisher Literatur un Prese* (1914); J.S. Raisin, *Haskalah Movement in Russia* (1913), index; *Sefer Zikkaron le-Soferei Yisrael ha-Ḥayyim Ittanu ka-Yom* (1889), 19–20; *Ha-Asif*, 6 (1893), 1855–56; Spiegel, *Hebrew Reborn* (1930), index; G. Karpeles, in: AZDJ, no. 43 (1892); YE, vol. 6, pp. 690–5. **ADD. BIBLIOGRAPHY:** M. Duvshani, *Yalag u-Mendele* (1961); S. Kottek, "*Y.L. Gordon al ha-Rofe'im*," in: *Korot*, 7/5–6 (1978), 515–20; J. Strauss, *Yehuda Leib Gordon: poète hébru* (1980); T. Cohen, "*Ereẓ lo Noda'at*," in: *Zehut*, 2 (1982), 145–53; M. Stanislwaski, *For Whom Do I Toil? Jehuda Lieb Gordon and the Crisis of Russian Jewry* (1988); S. Nash, "The Discussion over YaLaG' s Legacy," in: *Jewish Book Annual*, 49 (1991), 152–57; Y. Itzhaki, "Zionist Roots in Haskala Literature. The Case of Y.L. Gordon," in: *Jewish Affairs* 47/4 (1992), 21–27; Z.J. Goodman, "Traced in Ink: Women's Lives in '*Qotzo shel Yud*' by YaLaG and '*Mishpacha*' by D. Baron," in: *Gender and Judaism* (1995), 191–207; U. Shavit, "*Shirei Y.L. Gordon ki-Nekudat Mifneh ba-Hitpatḥut ha-Ide'it shel ha-Shirah ha-Ivrit*," in: *Akhshav*, 61 (1995), 101–09; Z. Shamir, *Iyyunim bi-Yeẓirat Y.L. Gordon* (1998); U. Shavit, "*Intertextualiyut ke-Even Boḥan le-Ma'avar mi-Tekufah li-Tekufah: YaLaG ke-Historyon Ḥadash*," in: *Sadan*, 3 (1998), 11–25; Z. Karniel, "*Bein YaLaG le-Sokolov*," in: *Sadan*, 3 (1998), 323–30; S. Werses, "*Deyukano shel Y.L. Gordon ba-Aspaklariya shel Igrotav*," in: *Sadan*, 3 (1998), 187–210; Y. Friedlander, "*Ha-Pulmus ha-Satiri bein YaLaG le-Rabanei Lita*," in: *Bein Halakhah le-Haskalah* (2004), 181–93.

[Aharon Zeev Ben-Yishai]

GORDON, MAX (Mechel Salpeter; 1892–1978), U.S. theatrical manager and producer. In his early years Gordon was linked with Sam Harris in productions of *Welcome Stranger*, *The Jazz Singer*, and *Rain*. From 1930 he produced upward of 30 plays, among them *Design for Living* (1933), *Dodsworth* (1934), *Pride and Prejudice* (1935), *The Women* (1936), *Othello* (1937), *My Sister Eileen* (1940), *Junior Miss* (1941), and *Born Yesterday* (1946). His final Broadway presentation was *The*

Solid Gold Cadillac (1953). Gordon also produced the films *A Trip to Paris* (1938), *Abe Lincoln in Illinois* (1940), and *My Sister Eileen* (1942). His autobiography, *Max Gordon Presents*, was published in 1963 (with Lewis Funke).

BIBLIOGRAPHY: M. Harriman, *Take Them Up Tenderly: A Collection of Profiles* (1944).

[Ruth Beloff (2nd ed.)]

GORDON, MICHAEL (1909–1993), U.S. director. Born in Baltimore, Gordon began directing feature films in 1942 and was highly successful critically and commercially with films such as *The Web* (1947); *Another Part of the Forest* (1948); *An Act of Murder* (1948); *Woman in Hiding* (1950); and his adaptation of Rostand's *Cyrano de Bergerac* (1950). Gordon was blacklisted because of the House Un-American Activities Committee hearings. Away from Hollywood for a decade, he returned with an unrecognizable but successful style, directing slick, glossy films, such as *I Can Get It for You Wholesale* (1951); *The Secret of Convict Lake* (1951); *Pillow Talk* (1959); *Portrait in Black* (1960); *Boy's Night Out* (1962); *For Love or Money* (1963); *Move Over, Darling* (1963); *A Very Special Favor* (1965); *Texas across the River* (1966); *The Impossible Years* (1968); and *How Do I Love Thee?* (1970). He was also one of the directors of the television series *Decoy* (1957) and *Anna and the King* (1972).

[Jonathan Licht / Ruth Beloff (2nd ed.)]

GORDON, MIKHL (1823–1890), Hebrew and Yiddish poet and essayist. Born in Vilna, he early came under the influence of the *Haskalah* circle of A.D. *Lebensohn. He began his literary career in 1847 with a Hebrew elegy on the death of Mordecai Aaron *Guenzburg, a member of this circle, and continued with Hebrew articles in various periodicals and the publication of two books in Hebrew. He rose to fame with his Yiddish songs which circulated in manuscript in the 1850s and 1860s and for which he also composed melodies. He published some of these Yiddish songs in *Di Bord... un andere... Yidishe Lider* ("The Beard ... and other ... Yiddish Songs," 1868), issued anonymously so as not to endanger his reputation as a Hebrew poet. His song "*Shtey oyf Mayn Folk*" ("Arise My People") was composed in 1869 and has generally been regarded as the classical poetic expression in Yiddish of the spirit of Jewish enlightenment in Russia. That year he also published a history of Russia in Yiddish. His late, pessimistic mood, intensified by his poverty and loneliness, is reflected in his final poems, published in 1889. His wife was the sister of the Hebrew and Yiddish poet J.L. *Gordon.

BIBLIOGRAPHY: Rejzen, Leksikon, 1 (1926), 510–8; LNYL, 2 (1958), 129–34; I. Manger, *Noente Geshtalten* (1938), 150–63; Y. Charlash, in: *S. Niger Bukh* (1958), 56–71; S. Liptzin, *Flowering of Yiddish Literature* (1963), 63–6. **ADD. BIBLIOGRAPHY:** L. Wiener, *The History of Yiddish Literature in the Nineteenth Century* (1899), 82–85 (also 1972 with intro. by E. Schulman).

[Sol Liptzin]

GORDON (Goldberg), MILTON M. (1918–), U.S. sociologist. Born in Gardiner, Maine, Gordon taught at the University of Pennsylvania, Drew University, and Haverford and Wellesley Colleges before being appointed professor of sociology at the University of Massachusetts in 1959. In 1986 he became professor emeritus of sociology.

A specialist in the fields of social stratification and inter-group relations, he became widely known through his books *Social Class in American Sociology* (1958) and *Assimilation in American Life* (1964). The latter, which analyzes the role of race, religion, and national origin in American social organization, is remarkable for its differentiation between cultural and structural pluralism and the formulation of the concept of the "ethclass," referring to social ranking within an ethnic group.

Gordon dealt with subjects of Jewish interest in several of his many papers and essays. They include "The Nature of Assimilation and the Theory of the Melting Pot," in *Current Perspectives in Social Psychology* by E.P. Hollander and R.G. Hunt (1967[2]) and "Marginality and the Jewish Intellectual," in *The Ghetto and Beyond: Essays on Jewish Life in America* (ed. Peter I. Rose, 1969). He was general editor of the *Ethnic Group in American Life* series. Other books by Gordon include *Human Nature, Class, and Ethnicity* (1978) and *The Scope of Sociology* (1993). He also edited *America as a Multicultural Society* (with R. Lambert, 1981).

[Werner J. Cahnmen / Ruth Beloff (2nd ed.)]

GORDON, NATHAN (1882–1938), rabbi, lawyer, community activist. Gordon was born in New Orleans. He was educated in the public schools there but his secondary and post-secondary education was in Cincinnati. In 1906 he earned both a B.A. from the University of Cincinnati and his rabbinical ordination from the Hebrew Union College. Several months after graduation he became the spiritual leader of Montreal's Reform Temple Emanu-El. He strongly supported the Reform ideal of social activism and became an active voice against corruption in Montreal's governance and the attendant neglect to social services. He also participated in the creation of the Mount Sinai Sanatorium in Ste. Agathe in 1913, and helped in its subsequent maintenance. Unlike most of his American colleagues, and his predecessors in Montreal, Gordon was both a Reform Jew *and* a Zionist, and spoke for Zionist groups in Jewish communities in Ontario and Quebec.

In 1916, Gordon earned a law degree from Laval University in Montreal (now the Université de Montréal) and left the pulpit. He first practiced with the well-known Jewish lawyer Peter Bercovitch; in 1919, however, he became the prosecuting attorney of the city of Montreal, a position he held until 1921 when he returned to private practice. Gordon remained concerned about the social welfare of Montrealers and was a member of the Non-Catholic Juvenile Court Committee. He also stayed active in Temple Emanu-El, and served as its president for a number of years. In the 1930s he took part in the reorganization of the Canadian Jewish Congress and served as president of its Eastern Division.

Gordon had an interest in academic Jewish studies. He earned an M.A. in 1909 at McGill, writing on capital punishment in biblical and rabbinic texts. In 1913 he earned a Ph.D., with his thesis titled "Prolgomena to the Social Customs of Mishna." In 1909 he was appointed lecturer in the Department of Oriental Languages and Literature at McGill.

BIBLIOGRAPHY: A. Hart (ed.), *The Jew in Canada* (1926): 125; G. Tulchinsky, *Taking Root* (1992); L. Tapper, *Biographical Dictionary of Canadian Jews* (1992), 6, 28, 93, 111.

[Richard Menkis (2nd ed.)]

GORDON, SAMUEL (1871–1927), English novelist. Gordon began his literary career while secretary of the London Great Synagogue. His *Sons of the Covenant: A Tale of London Jewry* (1900) saw the best solution to the "ghetto" problem in a combination of religious Orthodoxy and social and educational advancement. Gordon also wrote stories of Jewish life in Russia: *The New Galatea* (1901), and *The Lost Kingdom; or, the Passing of the Khazars* (1926), a historical romance.

GORDON, SAMUEL LEIB (1865–1933), Hebrew writer and Bible scholar. Born in Lithuania, he immigrated to Palestine in 1898 and taught at the Jaffa Boys School. When the school was taken over by the *Alliance Israélite Universelle, he left for Warsaw (1901) where he established a Hebrew school for boys. In 1924, he returned to Palestine and devoted the latter years of his life to the composition of an extensive commentary on the Bible. Gordon contributed poems, articles, and translations to the Hebrew periodicals of the late 19th century, and also wrote extensively for children. His books include *Kinnor Yeshurun* (3 vols., 1891–93); *Torat ha-Sifrut* (2 vols., 1900), which was reprinted many times; and a revised edition of his poems, *Shirim u-Fo'emot* (with foreword by S. Halkin), which was published in 1955. He translated three books by I. *Zangwill, La Fontaine's *Fables*, and Shakespeare's *King Lear*. Gordon's textbooks played a vital role in Hebrew education in the Diaspora at the turn of the century; *Ha-Lashon* (3 vols., 1910–19) was one of his most popular works. He also edited several journals for the young: *Olam Katan* (1901–05), *Ha-Ne'urim* (1904–05), as well as *Ha-Pedagog* (1903–04), a journal of education to which the best writers of his generation contributed.

[Getzel Kressel]

From 1907 he worked on a vocalized Bible commentary which was to provide a "new scientific pedagogical interpretation for advanced students and teachers, edited in the accepted traditional spirit." Known as *Shalag* after the initials of his name, it was largely based on German Bible criticism. Gordon explained words and subject matter simply and fully enough for school pupils and teachers without elaborating on the religious significance of the Bible. His introduction to the prophetic and hagiographic books deal with the literary aspect as well as with personalities and events. Gordon's commentary is still used extensively in the secondary schools in Israel, with the exception of those which are religiously oriented.

[Jacob S. Levinger]

BIBLIOGRAPHY: Ḥ.N. Bialik, *Devarim she-be-Al-Peh* (1935), 242–3; M. Gluecksohn, *Ishim ba-Madda u-va-Sifrut* (1941), 309–12; J. Fichmann, *Be-Terem Aviv* (1959); idem, *Ruḥot Menaggenot* (1953), 383–6; *Kitvei A. Levinson*, 1 (1957), 161–5; M.Y. Fried, *Yamim ve-Shanim*, 2 (1939), 147–50; H.A. Kaplan, *Pezurai* (1937), 198–201.

GORDON, SHMUEL (1909–1998). Soviet Yiddish prose writer. Gordon was born in Lithuania to a family related to the Hebrew poet Judah Leib *Gordon, but grew up in Jewish orphanages in the Ukraine. In 1928 he was a student of the Yiddish department at the Second Moscow State University. A tyro poet, he showed some of his works to Aaron *Kushnirov, who advised him to send the poems to the Warsaw *Literarishe Bleter*, where they appeared on December 28, 1928, and provoked a scandal in the Soviet press, signaling the complete isolation of the Stalinist Yiddish literary world. Following Gordon's letters of repentance, he was allowed to graduate two years later from the Moscow Teachers Training Institute. For a couple of years he worked as a teacher before becoming a Yiddish journalist and writer. His first story was published in 1930 (under the pseudonym Sh. Dongar) by the Kharkov journal *Di Royte Velt*. During World War II, Gordon served in the army and worked for the Jewish *Anti-Fascist Committee. In 1944 he was accepted as a member of the Writers' Union. Some of his stories written during the war were included in his 1946 book *Milkhome-tsayt* ("War Time"). He was imprisoned in 1949 and was sent to the Gulag as a Jewish nationalist. After Stalin's death he returned to literary activities, became a leading contributor to *Sovetish Heymland* and the author of a score of volumes. His prose represented an attempt to register the last sparks of traditional Jewish life in the Soviet Union. In 1988 he began to write his last novel, *Yizker* ("Commemorating the Dead"), which is matchless for a background understanding of the persecution of Soviet Yiddish literati in the 1940s and 1950s. Initially serialized in *Sovetish Heymland*, it was published in Israel in 2003 thanks to the endeavors of Gershon Winer's Foundation for the Advancement of Yiddish Studies.

BIBLIOGRAPHY: T. Gen, in: *Sovetish Heymland*, no. 11 (1969), 20–29; G. Estraikh and M. Krutikov, *The Shtetl* (2000), 152–68.

[Gennady Estraikh (2nd ed.)]

GORDON, SID (1917–1975), U.S. baseball player. Gordon was born in the Brownsville section of Brooklyn to Rose (Meyerson) and Morris, who emigrated from Russia and became a plumber and a coal dealer in the United States. After moving to Flatbush, Gordon attended Samuel Tilden High School, where he was a star baseball player. Gordon played his first game for the New York Giants on September 11, 1941, and ten days later on September 21, just hours before Rosh Hashanah, he was one of four Jewish players to appear in the Giants' lineup, an unprecedented occasion: Gordon and Morrie Arnovich played in the outfield; Harry Feldman, who had just debuted himself on September 10, pitched a shutout for his first major league win; and Harry "the Horse" Danning was behind the plate. Gordon joined the Giants full-time in 1943, and after two years in the Coast Guard, he rejoined them, playing mostly outfield and third base throughout his career, with occasional stints at first and second. Gordon became a very popular player with the many Jewish fans in New York, even being honored in 1949 by the citizens of Brooklyn at Ebbets Field, though he played for the hated rival Giants. His best year was 1948, when he hit.299 with 30 homers and 107 RBI. Gordon was named to the All-Star team that year and again in 1949, when he homered twice in one inning. In 1950 Gordon hit four grand slams, which was then the record. He was traded after the 1949 season to the Boston Braves, and then to the Pittsburgh Pirates in 1954. In 1955 he was back with the Giants, where he ended his baseball career. Gordon hit.283 with 202 HRs and 805 RBIs in his 13-year career, including 731 walks against only 356 strikeouts. He finished in the top ten in home runs, on-base percentage, slugging percentage, and walks from 1948 to 1952. He died of a heart attack while playing softball in Central Park in New York.

[Elli Wohlgelernter (2nd ed.)]

GORDON, WILLY (1918–2003), sculptor. Gordon was born in Latvia, but at the age of five was taken to Sweden where his father was cantor at the Malmo synagogue. An infant prodigy, he began his art studies in Malmo at the age of 10 and exhibited when he was 12 years old. At the age of 14 he decided to concentrate on sculpture and studied with William Zadig, a distinguished Swedish Jewish sculptor and teacher. Awarded a travel scholarship, Gordon returned to his birthplace in Latvia, where he spent six months studying the Orthodox Jewish way of life. A further scholarship enabled him to study at the Swedish Royal Academy of Art for seven years. In 1943 the purchase by the late Prince Eugene of his "Head of a Jewish Child" brought Gordon into public prominence. The extermination of members of his family in Eastern Europe during World War II led him to concentrate on Jewish subjects, the first being his bronze statue "Flight with Torah," copies of which are in the Karlstadt Museum and the Histadrut Building in Israel. In 1947, Gordon moved to Paris and studied under the famous Russian-Jewish sculptor Ossip *Zadkine. At the end of that year he was commissioned to create the Jewish Martyrs' monument for the Malmo Jewish community. A number of other important public commissions followed, including one from the Swedish Labor Party. In 1950, Gordon paid his first visit to Israel and held exhibitions of his work in Jerusalem, Tel Aviv, and Haifa. He completed a series of portrait busts of leading Israel personalities, including the then Speaker of the Knesset Joseph *Sprinzak which was presented to the Knesset by the Swedish Friends of Israel. Returning to Stockholm, Gordon consolidated his position as one of the country's leading monumental sculptors. He regularly holds exhibitions in Sweden, Europe, Israel, and the United States and is represented in leading museums in Sweden and Israel.

[Charles Samuel Spencer]

GORDONIA, pioneering Zionist youth movement that was founded at the end of 1923 in Galicia from small cells and grew into a world movement. The first groups of Gordonia were created under the influence of *Hitaḥadut, on the one hand, and by members who had left *Ha-Shomer ha-Ẓa'ir, on the other. The official name of the movement was chosen at the first world conference in Danzig (November 1928) as Histadrut ha-No'ar ha-Amamit ha-Ḥalutzit Gordonia (the People's Pioneering Association of Youth – Gordonia). The principles of the movement, which were set down at the same conference, were the "building up of the homeland, education of members in humanistic values, the creation of a working nation, the renaissance of Hebrew culture, and self-labor (*avodah aẓmit*)."

From its beginnings, the movement developed around two ideological bases. It aimed at reaching the lower classes of Jewish society (artisans, farmers and villagers, poor people, which constituted a large percentage of Galician Jewry), in contrast to Ha-Shomer ha-Ẓa'ir, which was composed principally of students; and it wished to mold these youth in the spirit of A.D. *Gordon's personality and teachings. Although Gordon, as a historical figure, was recognized by all the pioneering youth movements, Gordonia regarded his philosophy as its principal ideological source and adopted his world view. In contrast to the dogmatic attachment of Marxist movements to Marx, the relationship of Gordonia to Gordon was characterized by its lack of dogmatism, as reflected in Gordon's personality itself. Gordon's ideological image was not distinguished from his personality, and the combination of both was viewed as expressing free humanistic creativity (influenced by both the world at large and the Jewish world) that perpetuates independent, original thought which is always related to all facets of life. This philosophy was particularly attractive to those who had been disappointed by Marxism and did not believe that it was relevant to a youth movement wishing to build its future in Ereẓ Israel on the basis of labor. The Danzig Conference established 13 standards for the behavior of the individual in his personal life and in the movement, and in his relationship to the Jewish people, Ereẓ Israel, labor, socialism, etc. Although it had taken much from other youth movements, especially German ones, Gordonia meticulously maintained its unique character as a Jewish, Zionist, and Ereẓ Israel-oriented movement.

From Galicia Gordonia spread to the rest of Poland, Romania, and the United States and, by World War II, had close to 40,000 members. At all its conferences, it stressed its identification with the Ereẓ Israel labor movement and its fundamental principle – personal fulfillment through *aliyah* and settlement within the framework of collective living and labor. The first Gordonia groups began to settle in Ereẓ Israel shortly after the riots of 1929, first in Ḥaderah and later in other places.

These groups laid the foundation for kevuẓot of Gordonia in the rebuilt *Ḥuldah, which became the movement's center in Ereẓ Israel and contains the central archive of Gordonia, and in Kefar ha-Ḥoresh, Massadah, Ma'aleh ha-Ḥamishah, Nir Am, Ḥanitah, and elsewhere. These groups, which first merged into Iggud Gordonia, joined Ḥever ha-Kevuẓot in 1933 and also provided new members for established kevuẓot (such as Deganyah Alef and Bet, Geva, Ginnegar).

Later followed the merger of Gordonia with Maccabi ha-Ẓa'ir, which developed as a Jewish scouting movement in Germany and Czechoslovakia and whose members began to settle in Ereẓ Israel in 1932–33. Maccabi ha-Ẓa'ir set up its first settlements (Kefar ha-Maccabi, Ma'yan Ẓevi) in the framework of Ḥever ha-Kevuẓot in 1941, integrated with Gordonia, and thereafter the two movements served as a single framework for pioneering Jewish youth from Eastern and Western Europe. In 1937 a Gordonia movement came into being among Jewish youth in Palestine, and in 1945 it united with part of Maḥanot ha-Olim and founded Ha-Tenu'ah ha-Me'uḥedet (full name, Ha-Tenu'ah ha-Kelalit shel ha-No'ar ha-Lomed). After the Holocaust, attempts were also made abroad to unite pioneering youth movements with aims similar to those of Gordonia, and finally, when the *Iḥud ha-Kevuẓot ve-ha-Kibbutzim was created (in 1951), and after a series of mergers with Gordonia, *Iḥud Habonim was founded.

Gordonia played a heroic role in Nazi-occupied Poland during World War II. In Warsaw, under the leadership of Israel Zeltzer and Eliezer Geller, a secret center of the movement was established on 23 Nalewki Street, which organized a considerable network of underground educational activities among its members of all age groups. The center, mainly through Geller's visits in the ghettos of Czestochowa, Opoczno, Bendin, Sosnowiec, Opatow, and other towns, contributed greatly to the resistance movement and also to the preparations for active revolts, particularly in Warsaw in 1943. Gordonia's Polish-language underground paper in Warsaw, *Słowo Mlodych,* was published in Hebrew translation in 1966 by the archives of Gordonia-Maccabi ha-Za'ir. From its foundation, the movement published newspapers and literature in a number of languages. Pinḥas *Lavon (Lubianiker) was the head of the movement from its foundation throughout its existence. He served as Israel's minister of defense from 1953 to 1955.

BIBLIOGRAPHY: P. Lubianiker, *Yesodot* (1941); idem, in: *Derekh ha-No'ar* (1930), 47–73; idem, in: G. Chanoch (ed.), *Darkhei ha-No'ar* (1937), 17–26; Mandel, in: J. Cohen and D. Sadan (eds.), *Pirkei Galiẓyah* (1957), 270–81; A. Avnon (ed.), *Ittonut Gordonia be-Maḥteret Getto Varshah* (1966); I. and G. Kressel, *Mafte'aḥ le-ha-Po'el ha-Ẓa'ir (5668–5717)* (1968), s.v.; *Gordonia Report* (1938). **ADD. BIBLIOGRAPHY:** Y. Margalit, *Gordonia be-Polin* (1980).

[Meir Mandel]

GORELIK, SHEMARYA (1877–1943), Yiddish, German, and Hebrew journalist and essayist. Born in Lokhvitsa, Ukraine, he came to Vilna in 1890 and engaged in literary activities in the Russian press. For several years he sympathized with the *Bund, but in 1905 he joined the Zionist movement, and in 1906 he started publishing articles and essays in the Yiddish Zionist weekly *Dos Yudishe Folk*. In 1908 he joined S. *Niger and A. Veiter in founding and editing *Literarishe Monatshriften*, a Vilna literary monthly which attracted writers of diverse ideologies, and in the following years contributed numerous feuilletons and essays about modern literature to various Yiddish publications in Poland and the U.S. During World War I, Gorelik lived in Switzerland, participated in pacifist publications, and was sentenced to prison for six months. He later described his experiences during these years in *Fünf Jahre im Lande Neutralien* (1919). After the war, he lived in Germany, except for one year spent in New York, and contributed to German Jewish periodicals, until forced to leave in 1933. He then settled in Palestine and wrote for the Hebrew press. His literary sketches first appeared in book form in 1912. His Yiddish essays which offered interesting insights into the work of most prominent European writers were collected in four further volumes. A posthumous selection, with an introduction by his brother, M. Horelik, appeared in Los Angeles in 1947. A Hebrew translation of Gorelik's essays by A. *Shlonsky, was published in Tel Aviv (*Massot*, 1937).

BIBLIOGRAPHY: Rejzen, Leksikon, 1 (1926), 539–42; LNYL, 2 (1958), 163–5; J. Glatstein, *In Tokh Genumen* (1956), 98–102; S. Liptzin, in: *Maturing of Yiddish Literature* (1970), 75–7.

GOREN, CHARLES HENRY (1901–1991), U.S. bridge expert. Goren, who was born in Philadelphia into a Russian immigrant family, earned an LL.B. in 1922 and a master's degree in 1923 at McGill University in Montreal. He was admitted to the Pennsylvania bar in 1923 and practiced law in Philadelphia. He had taken up bridge during his student days and eventually achieved master status, abandoning the law in order to play and write about bridge. Goren won the National Bridge Championship of America 34 times. His many books and newspaper columns earned him widespread recognition. Goren's bridge methods are known for their simplicity and teachability. He cleverly synthesized the "honor trick" strategy of Culbertson with the "point-count" invented by Milton Work.

Known as "Mr. Bridge," Goren was a popular teacher and author who traveled extensively as a professional, a lecturer, and a TV personality. He was a regular contributor to *McCalls* and *Sports Illustrated*, had a syndicated newspaper column, led bridge cruises, and appeared on his own TV show, *Bridge with Charles Goren* (1959–64). Before his retirement from active competition in 1966, he had captured virtually every major bridge trophy in U.S. tournament play. As his health and eyesight began to fail, he settled into a quiet life in Southern California. Goren established a charitable trust during his lifetime. After his death, it became the Charles Goren Foundation.

His books include *Winning Bridge Made Easy* (1936), *Point Count Bidding in Contract Bridge* (1949), *New Contract Bridge in a Nutshell* (1959), *An Evening of Bridge with Charles H. Goren* (1959), *Goren's Hoyle Encyclopaedia of Games* (1961),

The Sports Illustrated Book of Bridge (1961), *Bridge Is My Game: Lessons of a Lifetime* (with J. Olsen, 1965), *Goren on Play and Defense* (1974), *100 Challenging Bridge Hands for You to Enjoy* (1976), *Goren Settles the Bridge Arguments* (1985), and *Goren's New Bridge Complete* (1986).

[Gerald Abrahams / Ruth Beloff (2nd ed.)]

GOREN (Gruenblatt), NATAN (1887–1956), Hebrew author, journalist, and critic. Born in Vidzy, in the Kovno district of Lithuania, he moved to Vilna in 1903. He became active in Jewish revolutionary circles and was imprisoned several times during 1906–08. In 1910 he moved to Odessa, joining the prominent group of Hebrew and Yiddish writers who lived there. Subsequently he lived in Moscow, where he worked for the Stybel publishing house and for the journal *Ha-Am*. In 1921 he returned to Lithuania, taking up a leading position in Jewish education and in Hebrew and Yiddish letters. In 1935 he settled in Tel Aviv, where he taught in secondary schools, was active in the Writers' Association, and continued his literary work.

His articles, stories, and poems appeared, beginning in 1911, in numerous Hebrew and Yiddish journals in Europe, Palestine, and the United States. He published his first novel, *Feyvush*, in 1901, several other novels, and two collections of essays on modern Hebrew writers, *Mevakkerim be-Sifrutenu* ("Critics in Our Literature," 1944), and *Demuyyot be-Sifrutenu* ("Figures in Our Literature," 1953).

BIBLIOGRAPHY: Z. Harkavi (ed.), *Sefer Natan Goren* (1958).

[Getzel Kressel]

GOREN, SHLOMO (1917–1994), Israel rabbi. Born in Zambrow, Poland, he was taken in 1925 to Palestine where his father was one of the founders of Kefar Ḥasidim. At the age of 12, Goren entered the Hebron Yeshivah in Jerusalem where he soon became famous as a prodigy. He published his first work, titled *Nezer ha-Kodesh* (1935) on Maimonides' *Mishneh Torah*, at the age of 17. In 1939, Goren published *Sha'arei Tohorah* on the laws of *mikveh*. He joined the Haganah in 1936, and fought in the Jerusalem area during the War of Independence. During this war, he was appointed by the two chief rabbis, Herzog and Ouziel, as chief chaplain of the newly formed army. He subsequently distinguished himself for his bravery, qualified as a paratrooper, and rose to the rank of brigadier-general. He accompanied the troops during both the Sinai Campaign and the Six-Day War, and was the first to conduct a prayer service at the liberated Western Wall in 1967. Goren was responsible for the organization of the military chaplaincy and worked out the regulations for total religious observance in the army. Rabbi Goren succeeded in establishing a unified prayer service, combining Ashkenazic and Sephardic ritual, in the IDF, which is used to this day. He published a *Siddur* with the unified service in 1971, followed by a Passover *Haggadah* in 1974. He was responsible for numerous original responsa concerning specific problems of observance due to conditions of active warfare and technological progress. He also developed the principles for permitting the assumed widows (*agunot*) of missing soldiers to remarry. Particularly noteworthy were his decisions permitting the remarriage of the widows of those men who perished on the destroyer *Eilat* and the submarine *Dakar* in 1967-68.

In 1961 Goren received the Israel Prize for the first volume (on the order *Berakhot*) of his comprehensive commentary on the Jerusalem Talmud, entitled *Yerushalmi ha-Meforash* (1961). A collection of his halakhic and philosophical essays, mainly concerning the Festivals and Holy Days, was published in 1964 under the title of *Torat ha-Mo'adim*. In 1968, he was elected Ashkenazi chief rabbi of Tel Aviv-Jaffa, taking up his duties only in 1971, and on October 16, 1972, was elected Ashkenazi chief rabbi of Israel. Shortly after his election he was involved in a violent controversy stemming from the unconventional manner in which he solved the problem of a brother and sister who had been declared *mamzerim* by the rabbinical courts, including the Bet Din of Appeals. An ad hoc *bet din*, which Goren had assembled, assented to a responsum he had published (in a limited edition) that they were free from the taint of *mamzerut*. He subsequently arranged their immediate marriages. The secrecy surrounding the military-like operation and his refusal to reveal the names of the *dayyanim* aroused violent opposition from the heads of the yeshivot and prominent rabbis, including the Lubavitch Rabbi. He published a detailed volume consisting of 200 pages (*Pesak Din B'Inyan ha-Aḥ ve-ha-Aḥot*, Jerusalem, 1973), to justify his ruling. In April 1980 a law was passed by the Knesset issuing new regulations with regard to the future of the Chief Rabbinate. It included a provision that the period of service of both incumbents be extended to 1983, after which, however, they would be precluded from offering themselves for reelection.

During the summer of 1981 Rabbi Goren became involved in a public controversy over his ruling that Area G in the archeological excavations in the City of David near the Western Wall had been the site of an ancient Jewish cemetery and that no excavations should be undertaken there. The Israeli academic world rejected that claim and leading scholars stated that no Jewish cemetery had been there in the past. A special session of the Knesset was called during the summer recess, but no action was taken. Work was suspended in the area for a few weeks by order of the Minister of Education and Culture Zevulun Hammer, and the Supreme Court was asked to rule on the situation. On September 15, 1981, the Supreme Court made known its decision that the rabbinate has no legal right to determine state policy. The season's excavation work ended soon thereafter. Excavation of the area continued until 1985 and no actual cemetery was discovered.

Another controversial issue that occupied Rabbi Goren throughout the second half of his life was the question of Jewish access to the Temple Mount. As IDF chief rabbi, Goren was one of the first soldiers to reach the Western Wall during the Six-Day War in 1967. At that time, he also ascended the Temple Mount and is reported suggesting to Central Command Head General, Uzi Narkiss, that the IDF blow up the Dome of the Rock, thereby establishing Israeli/Jewish sovereignty on the Temple Mount (*Haaretz*, December 31, 1997). In the months following the Six-Day War, Goren called for the destruction of the mosques on the Temple Mount and the building of the third Temple. This was in direct opposition to the majority of the rabbis on the Chief Rabbinate Council and the chief rabbis, Unterman and Nissim, themselves, who were of the halakhic opinion that the Temple Mount was to be placed off-limits to Jews. Just after the Six-Day War, Goren held seminars for IDF reservists on the Mount, as well as full religious services on Tisha B'Av. Over time, Goren modified his views and privately encouraged scholars and others to ascend to the Temple Mount, but refrained from issuing a public decree permitting Jews to ascend. During his tenure as chief rabbi, he did approach then prime minister, Menaḥem Begin, to ease the government's stance restricting the access of Jews to the Temple Mount. Goren's extensive research into the Temple Mount and the exact placement of the Temple, *Har ha-Bayit*, was finally published in 1992, almost 20 years after he finished his research because of the controversial nature of the subject and his opinions.

Rabbi Goren published numerous other works during his lifetime: *Torat ha-Shabbat ve-ha-Moed* (1982); *Sefer ha-Yerushalmi ve-ha-Gra* (1991) on the relationship between the Gaon of Vilna and the Jerusalem Talmud; *Sefer Moadei Yisrael* (1993); and posthumously, *Meshiv Milḥamah* (1996), responsa dealing with war; *Torat ha-Mikra* (1996), essays on the weekly Torah reading; *Torat ha-Philosophia* (1998), essays on Jewish philosophy; *Mishnat ha-Medinah* (1999), the halakhic perspectives on the major political issues facing the State of Israel; and *Torat ha-Refuah* (2001), on Jewish medical ethics.

BIBLIOGRAPHY: Ehrlich, in: *Panim el Panim* (Oct. 4, 1967); D. Lazar, *Rashim be-Yisrael*, 2 (1955), 86–91. **ADD. BIBLIOGRAPHY:** Y. Alfasi (ed.), *Ha-Maalot Le-Shlomo* (1996); Y. Cohen in: *Jewish Political Studies Review*, 11:1–2 (1999).

[Mordechai Piron]

°**GORGIAS**, Seleucid general in the war against the forces of *Judah Maccabee. Together with two other generals, *Ptolemy Macron and *Nicanor, Gorgias was sent against the Jews in 165 B.C.E. with a force of 40,000 foot soldiers and 7,000 cavalry. Gorgias set out from his camp near Emmaus with 6,000 soldiers, hoping to surprise Judah by night. Judah, however, succeeded in evading the Greek army and destroyed its main camp at Emmaus, after which Gorgias retreated in disorder. When, two years later, Judah and his brother *Simeon set out to Gilead and Galilee in order to protect the hard-pressed Jewish settlements there, they left the armies of Judea under the inexperienced command of *Joseph and Azariah, sons of Zechariah. Hoping to acquire a reputation for valor, the two commanders attacked the armies of Gorgias, who was at that time in command at Jamnia, but suffered a disastrous defeat.

BIBLIOGRAPHY: Jos., Ant., 12:298, 305–12, 351; I Macc. 3:38; 4:1ff.; 5:55; II Macc. 10:14; 12:32–37; Schuerer, Hist, 31, 35; Klausner, Bayit Sheni, 1 (1951^2), 57; 3 (1950^2), 21, 23.

[Isaiah Gafni]

GORIN, BERNARD (pseudonym of **Isaac Goido**; 1868–1925), Yiddish playwright, translator, editor, and drama critic. Born in Lida (Lithuania), Gorin published his first story, "*Zikhroynes fun Kheyder*" ("Memoirs From the Ḥeder," 1889), in Mordecai Spektor's *Hoyzfraynd*, followed by "*Shakhne un Shrage*" ("Shakhne and Shrage," 1890), in I.L. Peretz's *Yidishe Bibliotek*. He edited a Yiddish series entitled *Kleyne Ertseylungen*, which included works by I.L. Peretz and David Pinsky (1893) and translated Dickens's *David Copperfield* (1894), leaving that same year for New York, where he became active in the literary and theatrical world, contributing to both the Yiddish and English language press. In 1908 he began reviewing plays for the *Morgn-Zhurnal*. In addition to writing original plays, Gorin adapted numerous foreign language works for the Yiddish stage. He is best known as a historian of the Yiddish theater, his most important work being *Di Geshikhte fun Yidishn Teater* ("History of the Yiddish Theater," 2 vols., 1918) which lists 2,000 plays produced on the Yiddish stage. In 1927 Gorin's stories were collected and published in three volumes.

BIBLIOGRAPHY: Rejzen, Leksikon, 1 (1928), 531–7; Schulman, *Geshikhte fun der Yidisher Literatur in Amerike* (1943), 110–6; LNYL, s.v. **ADD. BIBLIOGRAPHY:** Sh. Niger, *Dertseylers un Romanistn* (1946), 154–56.

[Elias Schulman / Marc Miller (2nd ed.)]

GORIZIA, city in Friuli, N.E. Italy. Gorizia was part of the Austrian empire until 1918 though for centuries its culture had been Italian. Jews were first mentioned in the county in the years 1299–1363. Only in 1548, however, did Jews sign the first charter with the local authorities. In 1624 the first Jew from Gorizia, Joel Pincherle, obtained from Emperor Ferdinand II the title of Hoffaktor. In 1696 Emperor Leopold I legislated the erection of the ghetto, activated in 1698. The community followed the Ashkenazi rite. Until the 18th century the Jews of Gorizia were mostly moneylenders. The most important banking families were that of Pincherle, Gentili, and Morpurgo. In the 18th century Jews engaged in the manufacture of silk and wax (the latter by a certain Aron and the Morpurgo brothers), which dominated the city's economy. In 1756 the synagogue in the Via Ascoli was consecrated. After they had been expelled from the smaller Venetian towns in 1777, more Jews moved to Gorizia. The 1781 *Toleranzpatent* of Joseph II allowed the Jews to be even more integrated in civic life. In 1788 the town's Jewish population numbered 270.

The intellectual life of Gorizia Jews at the end of the 18th century and at the beginning of the 19th was dominated by the figures of two rabbis, Isacco Samuele Reggio and his son Abram Vita Reggio.

During the 19th century the community slowly developed. In 1846 there were 266 Jews living in Gorizia. In 1900 there were already 865 living there.

[Attilio Milano / Samuele Rocca (2nd ed.)]

Holocaust Period

In 1938, there were 183 Jews in Gorizia, mostly engaged in business, commerce, and services. Of these, 109 were Italians and 76 were foreigners, primarily from Central and Eastern Europe. Since the beginning of the century, the population of Gorizian Jews had decreased, that of foreign Jews had significantly increased, and assimilation had grown. A strong demographic decline occurred soon after the appearance of the racial laws of 1938, caused especially by the exodus of the foreign Jews and by conversions or withdrawal from the community. After the German occupation in September 1943, Jews most aware of the danger moved elsewhere or went into hiding, while the old, the sick, and those without adequate means remained at home and were arrested and deported. The first arrests and imprisonments occurred in September 1943. There followed the roundup of November 23, in which 22 people were arrested, imprisoned at Coroneo in Trieste, and deported to Auschwitz on December 7. In the following months, other Gorizian Jews who had gone into hiding there or in other Italian towns and cities, such as Ferrara, Florence, Genova, and San Cesario sul Panaro, were caught. In all, 47 Jews from Gorizia were deported, of whom only two, Iris Steinmann and Giacomo Jacoboni, returned. Because of the drastic decrease in the number of Jews in Gorizia after the war, the historic local Jewish nucleus of the Isonzo area was incorporated into the Jewish community of Trieste in 1969.

[Adonella Cedarmas (2nd ed.)]

BIBLIOGRAPHY: G. Bolaffio, in: RMI, 23 (1957), 537–46; 24 (1958), 30–40, 62–74, 132–41. **ADD. BIBLIOGRAPHY:** S.G. Cusin, and P.C.I. Zorattini, *Friuli Venezia Giulia, Itinerari ebraici, I luoghi, la storia, l'arte* (1998), 48–57; C.L. Budin, *Vita e cultura ebraica nella Gorizia del Settecento*, (1995); A. Cedarmas, *La Comunità israelitica di Gorizia (1900–1945)*, Udine: Istituto Friulano per la Storia del Movimento di Liberazione (1999).

GORKI (until 1932 and again from 1992 **Nizhni Novgorod**), city on the Volga River, Belorussia. It served as an entrepôt for the merchants of Russia and Russian Central Asia from the early 19th century. From 1835 Jewish merchants were permitted to attend its celebrated fairs where they were allowed to purchase goods and, with the exception of imported articles, sell them wholesale. A permanent Jewish community was founded by soldiers discharged from the army of Nicholas I (see *Cantonists), and in 1873 received permission to maintain a house of worship. On June 7, 1884, pogroms resulting in murder and looting broke out in Kanavino, a suburb of the city. The Jewish community of Gorki numbered 2,377 in 1897 (2.5% of the total population). It increased during World War I when refugees from the war zone arrived there, and in 1926 numbered 9,328 (5.2% of the total). In 1939 there were 14,319 Jews in Gorki (2.2%). According to the census of 1959 the Jewish population of Gorki district was 17,827; the majority apparently lived in the capital. In 1970 the Jewish population was estimated at about 30,000. Most left for Israel and the West during the mass emigration of the 1990s. There was a Jewish cemetery, but no synagogue.

[Yehuda Slutsky]

°**GORKI, MAXIM** (pseudonym of **Aleksey Maksimovich Peshkov**; 1868–1936), Russian author. Gorki was the outstanding pre-Revolutionary Russian writer who sided with Lenin and the Bolsheviks, but he also distinguished himself as a vigorous champion of the oppressed Jewish people in Russia. Raised in a primitive environment, where the Jews were seen through a strange accumulation of folklore, fantasy, and superstition, Gorki was intellectually at odds with such notions, although emotionally and artistically he sometimes could not help expressing them. His early revolutionary position – which despite periods of dissent and opposition to the Bolsheviks and even voluntary exile, eventually made him a supporter of the Soviet regime – was closely linked with his deep revulsion against Jew-baiting and pogroms, and his warm friendship for many Jewish writers and intellectuals. His story *Pogrom* (1918), inspired by the *Kishinev outrages of 1903, was no isolated example of Gorki's preoccupation with the Jewish fate in Russia; and in *Detstvo* (1914; *My Childhood*, 1915), the first part of his autobiography, Gorki movingly recalled a Jewish boy encountered in his youth. In 1916 Gorki coedited *Shchit*, an anthology of statements in defense of the Jews drawn from Russian literature, in which he made it clear that he saw in the question of Jewish rights the whole issue of injustice under the Czarist system.

Gorki also showed sympathy for the Hebrew renascence and for Zionist aspirations in Ereẓ Israel. Most of Gorki's impassioned denunciations of antisemitism were omitted from the 30-volume Soviet edition of his works (1949–55). Most of these omissions have been cataloged (B. Suvarin, in *Dissent*, winter 1965; B.D. Wolfe, *The Bridge and the Abyss* (1967), 162–3n.). Works not published in this edition include an article on the Hebrew poet *Bialik; another on the Kishinev pogrom; and an appeal to save the *Habimah theater, then still in the U.S.S.R.

His wife, EKATERINA PESHKOVA (née VOLZHINA, 1876–1965), was, after the October Revolution, for many years a kind of guardian angel of the political prisoners in the U.S.S.R. in her capacity as chairman of the "Political Red Cross." She was warmly remembered by many Jews, particularly Zionists, whom she helped in various ways during their imprisonment, sometimes obtaining for them the permission to emigrate to Palestine.

BIBLIOGRAPHY: A.S. Kaun, *Maxim Gorky and His Russia* (1932); I. Weil, *Gorky: His Literary Development and Influence on Soviet Intellectual Life* (1966), contains bibl. of works in translation; I. Maor, in *Niv Hakevutzah*, vol. 5 (Oct. 1956), 643–654; B. Shochetman, in *Heavar*, 3 (1955). **ADD. BIBLIOGRAPHY:** D.L. Levin, *Stormy Petrel:*

The Life and Work of Maxim Gorky (1986); T. Yedlin, *Maxim Gorky: A Political Biography* (1999).

[Irwin Weil]

GORLICE, town in S.E. Poland. In the early period of Polish rule Gorlice belonged to the district of Nowy Sacz where all the towns had been granted the privilege of excluding Jews (*de non tolerandis Judaeis*), excepting Nowy Sacz itself, where a Jewish community existed. A few Jewish families were living in Gorlice in 1765 and 1784. Jews settled there in the 19th century, living in an area near the marketplace. By 1880 the Jewish population formed half of the total of 5,000, and by 1900 their number had grown to 3,297 (51.2%). They dealt mainly in wine and corn. The town suffered severely during World War I. In 1921 there were 2,300 Jews (41%) living in Gorlice.

Holocaust Period

At the outbreak of World War II the Jewish population numbered between 4,500 and 5,000. Most of them fled to the Soviet-occupied part of Poland before the Germans entered on Sept. 6, 1939. The Germans immediately took hostages among Jews and Poles and detained them for a long time in prison. On the eve of Rosh Ha-Shanah, the Germans ordered that all Jews between 18 and 35 years old should appear daily at the magistrate's office for work. On the eve of the Day of Atonement, the Germans destroyed the interior of the main synagogue and later converted it into a stable. Religious Jews were singled out for particular persecution: Jews caught praying in small *minyanim* were killed; the *shoḥet*, who continued to slaughter poultry in secret, was shot with his family.

During the German occupation, a *Judenrat* consisting of seven members was set up in Gorlice. Its first president, Henryk Arnold, a man of integrity, was harassed by the Gestapo and finally killed in the *Judenrat* office for disobedience to German orders. The Jewish police in Gorlice were honest and helpful in protecting the population. A Jewish labor office was established to supply the Germans regularly with manpower. After the outbreak of the German-Soviet war (1941) a ghetto was established. An influx of refugees from larger towns, such as Cracow, caused an acute housing shortage. Disease spread, but there was no Jewish doctor available until a physician arrived from Cracow some time later. The *Judenrat* established a primitive hospital. A Jewish elementary school functioned, possibly also in the ghetto, where Hebrew was taught clandestinely.

In the spring of 1942 about 70 members of Zionist organizations were executed in Gorlice and the neighboring town of Biecz. In June 1942 a large fine was levied on the community, and houses were searched in order to confiscate valuables. In the summer increased numbers of young men were sent to distant labor camps in *Plaszow, Pustchow, and Frysztak. In early August, Jews from nearby Bobowa and Biecz were brought to Gorlice. On Aug. 12, 1942, another heavy fine, of 250,000 zlotys, was imposed for immediate payment. On the night of Aug. 13–14, 1942, the ghetto was surrounded by German and Ukrainian units. In the morning the Gestapo selected about 700 old and infirm people and others. They were taken to Garbic, where a mass grave was prepared. They were ordered to undress and were shot at the edge of the grave together with children. The majority of the remaining Jews were sent to the death camp at Belzec. Many Jews managed to escape during the *Aktion* to fields, woods, or villages in the vicinity: encountering no help, most of them returned and were executed on the spot or included in the transport.

After this, about 700 able-bodied Jews remained in Gorlice. In the period to mid-September two further "selections" were made and most of the remaining Jews were sent to Belzec; after Sept. 14, 1942, there remained only the factory workers who lived in the factory buildings, and on Jan. 6, 1943, they were sent to the labor camps of Muszyna and Rzeszow.

After the war approximately 30 Jewish families returned to Gorlice. They found that their property had been looted, and that tombstones from the cemetery had been taken to construct pavements. An attempt was made at rehabilitation, and goods sent by the Landsmannschaft in the United States were distributed by a committee. However, antisemitism among the local population caused them to leave shortly afterward.

[Danuta Dombrowska]

BIBLIOGRAPHY: An-Ski, *Der Yidishe Khurbn Fun Poyln, Galitsye un Bukovine* (1922); *Sefer Gorliẓeh* (1962).

GORLIN, ALEXANDER (1955–), U.S. architect. Gorlin is a graduate of the Yale School of Architecture and Cooper Union School of Architecture. The firm Alex Gorlin, Architects was founded in 1987. Gorlin taught at the Yale School of Architecture as a critic from 1980 to 1990. His early work was influenced by Classicism but he gradually became influenced by Modernism. Gorlin is now known for his Urban Modernism. With unusual versatility, he has designed projects in New York, Santa Fe, New Mexico, Denver, Colorado, and Palm Beach, Florida. He was awarded the Rome Prize Fellowship in 1983–84, the Cooper Union Distinguished Alumni Award in 1998, and the Chicago Athenaeum Architecture Award for the Yale University Boathouse. He served as a member of the board of directors of CityArts, New York City, and held a summer internship at Cooper Union in New York in 1994. In January 2002, *Architectural Digest* named Gorlin one of the Top 100 designers and architects in the U.S. The Ruskin Place townhouse in Seaside, Florida, won the 1996 New York State AIA Award for Excellence in Design. Chosen for his knowledge of Jewish tradition and expertise in synagogue design, Gorlin planned the one million dollar remodeling of the United Synagogue of Hoboken, New Jersey, and also the North Shore Synagogue in Long Island, New York. Gorlin was the architect for the North Shore Hebrew Academy, King's Point, New York, and a synagogue for the Young Israel of Plainview, New York. Always imaginative, he once designed a tree house, and created plans for a city apartment for architect Daniel *Libeskind in the Tribeca district of Manhattan. In Denver, Colorado, Gorlin designed a 10,000 square foot house built as a cross between an Irish barn and an Indian stone dwelling. Gorlin said his inspiration came in part from Dante's "Inferno." By contrast, on tiny Allison Island off the shore of South Beach, Miami, Florida, Gorlin built for the AQUA planned community a midrise building which is an example of the new "Tropical Urbanism" that is part of the "New Urbanism." One of the features of this trend spreads the highrise building out horizontally. Gorlin's building is 11 stories high with ample space around it, wide areas of window glass, and spacious balconies. According to Vincent Scully, noted architectural historian, "Gorlin's work is simple openhearted appreciation and wonder, an excitement that enlivens everything."

BIBLIOGRAPHY: P. Goldberger, *Alexander Gorlin: Buildings and Projects* (1997).

[Betty R. Rubenstein (2nd ed.)]

GORNI (pl. **Grana**), term used for the Jewish immigrants from Leghorn (Livorno), who began to settle in North Africa, especially in Tunisia, from the 17th century on. Livorno was called Leghorn(a) in Jewish sources (e.g., David Reuveni), as well as by English sailors, and Jews and Arabs in the Maghreb. The first syllable *Le* was used as an article, making al-Ghorn(a); from this came the appellative (al-)Gorni. The Grana were essentially merchants; their commercial activity was strictly connected with the Jews of Livorno. They were 400 or 500 in 1821, their number rose to 2,500 or 3,000 in 1893 and to about 5,000 in 1938. Until the 1940s the Gorni constituted separate congregations in Tunis and in other towns of Tunisia, with their own administration, *bet din*, and communal institutions. At all times, the Grana considered themselves as belonging to the European culture (besides Arabic, they spoke Spanish, Italian, and French) and felt separate from the "Tuansa," i.e., the old Jewish residents of Tunisia.

BIBLIOGRAPHY: A. Milano, in: *Miscellanea di studi in memoria di Dario Disegni* (1969), 139–51; R. Attal, in REJ, 141:1–2 (1982), 223–35; Y. Abrahami, *Pinkas ha-Kehillah ha-Yehudit ha-Portugesit be-Tunis: 1710–1944* (1997); L. Lévy, *La Communauté juive de Livourne. Le dernier des Livournais* (1996); idem, *La Nation Juive Portugaise. Livorno, Amsterdam, Tunis 1591–1951* (2003).

[Haïm Z'ew Hirschberg / Alessandro Guetta (2nd ed.)]

GORNICK, VIVIAN (1935–), U.S. author. A product of New York City's vibrant, multi-ethnic, and often socialist urban environment, Gornick attended City College and received her master's degree from New York University. A veteran journalist, she has written for the *Village Voice*, the *Atlantic Monthly*, the *Washington Post*, *The Nation*, *Ms* magazine, the *New York Times Book Review* and *Sunday Magazine*, *The Three Penny Review*, and *The New Yorker*. She also taught at the University of Colorado and Pennsylvania State University.

Gornick rose to prominence in the early 1970s as one of the most articulate of the feminist writers. Her essay "Woman as Outsider" in *Women in Sexist Society: Studies in Power and Powerlessness* (1971), which she edited, paints an unflattering portrait of women's role "in the fierce unjoyousness of Hebraism." Later books explored a variety of subjects, including *In Search of Ali Mahmoud: An American Woman in Egypt* (1973); *The Romance of American Communism* (1977); *Essays in Feminism* (1978); *Women in Science: Recovering the Life Within* (1983); and the novel/memoir *Fierce Attachments* (1987). Gornick also wrote *Women in Science: 100 Journeys Into the Territory* (1990); *Approaching Eye Level* (1996); *The End of the Novel of Love* (1997); and *The Situation and the Story: The Art of Personal Narrative* (1999).

In 1989, she became a tenured professor at the University of Arizona. She was also a literary critic and writer of memoirs. In her research, she explored the interrelationship of feminism, psychoanalysis, and literature.

In the early 2000s, in conjunction with a group of New York artists and activists, Gornick helped found *THEA*, the House of Elder Artists. THEA was planned as a not-for-profit senior residence in Manhattan for men and women in the arts who continue to engage in a working relationship with New York City, thereby enriching its cultural life. The 100-unit apartment building was designed to enable residents to give public readings, performances, and master classes based on the wealth of knowledge and the expertise they had accumulated over a lifetime.

[Sylvia Barack Fishman / Ruth Beloff (2nd ed.)]

GORODENKA (Pol. **Horodenka**), city in Stanislav district, Ukraine. Jews first settled there under Polish rule during the middle of the 17th century, but an organized community was only formed in the beginning of the 18th century. In 1743 the Polish landowner granted them by a privilege the right to live in the town and to engage in commerce (excluding trade in Christian religious appurtenances) and crafts. The community received land for building a synagogue and for a cemetery. Jews of Gorodenka were dealers in grain, timber, and salt, wine makers, distillers of brandy, beer brewers, tavern keepers, and leasers and managers of estates. According to the census of 1765, 863 Jews lived in Gorodenka and 133 in 14 villages in the vicinity, affiliated to the Gorodenka community. In the middle of the 18th century there was a group of Shabbateans and Frankists in the town. During the 1760s most of the Jews in Gorodenka joined the ḥasidic movement, among them *Naḥman of Horodenko, one of the closest disciples of *Israel b. Eliezer Ba'al Shem Tov.

The city passed to Austria in 1772. In 1794, 30 Jews in Gorodenka (12 families) joined to found an agricultural settlement. Despite their economic difficulties, the rate of taxation levied upon the Jewish population was five times higher than that for the Christian population. According to data of 1890, 4,340 of the 11,162 inhabitants of the town and 7 of the 18 members of the municipal council were Jews. By the end of the 19th century a local *Benei Zion society had been founded, which by 1897 consisted of about 150 members. A Jewish boys' school financed by Baron *Hirsch functioned from 1898 until 1914. The first Hebrew school was opened in 1907. At the beginning of the 20th century, the community had a great synagogue and a number of *battei midrash* and ḥasidic prayer houses. In World War I the Jews in Gorodenka suffered severely under the Russian occupation. In 1916 Jewish houses were set on fire and nine local Jews were hanged on a charge of espionage.

Gorodenka was within Poland between the two world wars. The Jewish population was 3,048 (out of 9,907) in 1921 and 3,256 in 1931. World War I left in its wake 200 widows and 220 orphans, and postwar competition with the Poles and Ukrainians was a cause of economic hardship for the Gorodenka Jews. Subsequently, many emigrated to the United States, Canada, and South America, and hundreds of others to Ereẓ Israel.

[Arthur Cygielman]

Holocaust Period

Within a few days of the outbreak of war between Germany and the U.S.S.R., Gorodenka was occupied by Hungarian troops. The local Ukrainian populace immediately attacked the Jewish inhabitants, murdering and robbing them. Subsequently, Jews from Carpatho-Ruthenia (which had been annexed by Hungary) arrived in Gorodenka, having been driven from their homes. A local Jewish committee was set up to deal with the situation. Aid was extended to the local Jews and refugees. When the city came under German administration in September 1941 conditions deteriorated. Anti-Jewish measures were enacted, including restriction on free movement on the streets, compulsory wearing of the yellow *badge, and the institution of slave labor. In November the Jews were concentrated in a ghetto. On Dec. 4, 1941, they were assembled, allegedly to receive immunization against typhus, but were guarded by the Germans and their Ukrainian collaborators in the great synagogue. The following day they underwent a "*Selektion*," and those classed as "nonproductive" – 2,500 Jews – were taken to mass graves dug between the villages of Michalcze and Simakowce, and murdered. On April 13, 1942, a second *Aktion* was carried out in which 1,500 were sent to the death camp of Belzec and murdered there. In May and June hundreds of Jews were taken from Gorodenka to Kolomyya, where they shared the fate of the Jews there. Some of the inmates fled to Tlusta, where they found temporary refuge. The liquidation of the ghetto started in July and was completed on Sept. 6, 1942. The last Jews were sent to the Janowska labor camp in Lvov. During the Aktionen, some Jews escaped; some joined partisan groups, and 40 succeeded to flee to Romania. On March 24, 1944, Soviet forces returned to Gorodenka, but by then only a few Jews were left. They subsequently left for Poland in transit to Palestine.

[Aharon Weiss / Shmuel Spector (2nd ed.)]

BIBLIOGRAPHY: M. Bałaban, *Spis Żydów i Karaitów ziemi Halickiej i powiatów Trembowelskiego i Kołomyjskiego w roku 1765* (1909), 18; M. Freudental, *Leipziger Messegaeste* (1928), 141; W. Tokarz, *Galicya w początkach ery józefińskiej…* (1909), 356–7; B. Wasiutyński, *Ludność żydowska w Polsce w wiekach xix i xx* (1930), 100, 122; *Sefer Horodenka* (Heb. and Yid., with Eng. introduction, 1963).

GORODOK (Pol. **Gródek Jagielloński**, Yid. **Greiding**), city in Lvov district, Ukraine, within Poland until 1772 and between the two world wars. The earliest information on the presence of Jews there dates from 1444. Jews were responsible for collection of customs and taxes in Gorodok for short periods. In 1550 King Sigismund II Augustus granted the town the privilege to exclude Jews (*de non tolerandis Judaeis*), but probably those already there remained. In 1662, after Gorodok had been devastated during the Crimean Tartars' invasions, the local governor (*starosta*) encouraged Jews to settle in the town and rehabilitate it; because of the objections of the townsmen, he assigned them a special quarter, "the Gnin." King John III Sobieski confirmed their right of residence in 1684. According to the census of 1765, there were 788 Jews living in the "Jewish town of Gnin" and 251 in neighboring villages. As a result of the difficult economic situation, the debts of the community increased, amounting to 3,212 zlotys in 1784. Gorodok had a beautiful synagogue and a famous collection of books as well a *bet midrash* and yeshivah. Belz ḥasidim dominated, opposing Haskalah and Zionism.

The community numbered 2,952 in 1880 (29% of the total population), and 3,610 in 1900, with an additional 3,478 living in villages in the district. In World War I the Jews of Gorodok and its surroundings suffered severely during the fighting between the Russian and Austrian armies in 1915, and subsequently in 1918–19 during the struggle between the Poles and Ukrainians. There were 2,545 Jews living in the city itself (24% of the population) and 1,414 in the villages in 1921, and 3,281 in 1931. Between the two world wars most of them were occupied in crafts, hawking, and trade in agricultural products.

[Arthur Cygielman]

Holocaust Period

With the German invasion of Poland on Sept. 1, 1939, many Jewish refugees from western Poland arrived in the city, and by 1941 the Jewish population numbered over 5,000. From October 1939 until the outbreak of the German-Soviet war in June 1941 the city was occupied by the Soviets. On June 29, 1941 the Germans captured Gorodok, and neighboring farmers, mainly Ukrainians, attacked the Jews there, and looted their property. Conscription into forced labor camps in Jaktorow and Winniki continued through the autumn of 1941 and 1942. On May 7, 1942, several hundred Jews were deported to Janowska camp in Lvov. On August 13, half the Jews were deported to the extermination camp in Belzec. On December 26, 1942, 1,300 Jews were murdered outside the town and on January 27, 1943, the ghetto was finally liquidated, in an *Aktion* that lasted three days. A labor camp was established in March 1943, but it was liquidated in May 1943. The last Jews of Gorodok were shot and buried in mass graves near Artyszczow.

[Aharon Weiss / Shmuel Spector (2nd ed.)]

BIBLIOGRAPHY: B. Wasiutyński, *Ludnoüeć żydowska w Polsce…* (1930), 107, 115, 147, 151, 196, 212; I. Schiper, *Studya nad stosunkami gospodarczymi żydów w Polsce podczas sredniowiecza* (1911), 154, 239, 243.

GORODOK, town in Vitebsk district, Belarus, The Jewish community was founded during the 18th century. In 1772, when Belorussia was annexed by Russia after the first partition of Poland, the town had 400 Jews, the majority of the population. In 1897 there were 3,413 Jews in Gorodok (68% of the total population), and in 1926, 2,660 (48.3%), most of whom were *Chabad ḥasidim. Jews were petty traders and artisans. In the Soviet period a Yiddish school was in operation. In 1939 the Jews numbered 1,584 (21.7% of the total population). Gorodok was occupied by the Germans on July 9, 1941. The Jews were herded into open fields outside the town, joined by others from the vicinity In August 1941, 2,000 were murdered; the rest on October 14.

BIBLIOGRAPHY: Surkin, in: B. Karu (Krupnik) (ed.), Sefer Vitebsk (Heb., 1957), 233–4.

[Yehuda Slutsky / Shmuel Spector (2nd ed.)]

GORODOK (Pol. **Grodek Wilenski**), town in *Molodechno district, Belarus. Jews started to settle there in the beginning of the 19th century. In 1897, they numbered 1,230, constituting 75% of the population. They owned most of the stores and many had auxiliary farms. Between the two world wars the town belonged to Poland. In 1921 the Jews numbered 990. Most of the children attended the Tarbut Hebrew school. Gorodok was occupied in June 1941. The approximately 1,500 Jews were imprisoned in a ghetto on March 13, 1942. Two hundred were sent to the Krasne labor camp and 400 followed on July 11, when the remaining 900 were murdered. The Krasne camp was liquidated in March 1943. Fugitives from the ghetto played an active role in the local partisan movement.

BIBLIOGRAPHY: *Sefer ha-Partizanim ha-Yehudim*, 1 (1958), 479.

[Yehuda Slutsky / Shmuel Spector (2nd ed.)]

GOROKHOVSKAYA, MARIA (1921–), Soviet gymnast, winner of seven medals at the 1952 Olympics. Born in Yevpatoria, Ukraine, Gorokhovskaya volunteered for military service in World War II, serving in hospitals in Leningrad (now St. Petersburg) during the Nazi siege of the city. She was decorated with the Order of the Great Patriotic War, as well as other honorable citations.

Gorokhovskaya won her first U.S.S.R. gymnastic title on the balance beam in 1948. Four years later the Soviet Union made its debut at the 1952 Olympics in Helsinki, and Gorokhovskaya's gold medals were the first ever won by the Soviet Union. Altogether Gorokhovskaya – at the advanced age of 30 – won gold medals in the individual and team all-around events, and silver medals in the vault, parallel bars, balance beam, floor exercise, and team hand apparatus. Her seven medals are the most ever won by one woman at one Olympic Games.

At the 1954 World Championships, Gorokhovskaya finished third in the floor exercise, fourth in the vault, and seventh in the all-around, and helped the Soviet Union capture the gold medal in the team event. It was her final international competition.

Gorokhovskaya was the world's top-ranked female gymnast in 1952 and 1953, No. 3 in 1954, and No. 2 in 1955. The Soviet Union awarded her its highest sports honor, the Order of Red Banner, and the Honorary Master of Sport.

Gorokhovskaya immigrated to Israel in 1990, and only then was it revealed that she was Jewish – she had kept her identity a lifelong secret in the Soviet Union so as not to hurt her gymnastic career.

[Elli Wohlgelernter (2nd ed.)]

GORSHMAN, SHIRA (**Shirke**, née **Grigorevna**; 1906–2001), Soviet Yiddish prose writer. Born in Lithuania, Gorshman immigrated to Palestine in 1924. In 1929, she went to the Soviet Union with a group of disillusioned members of the *Gedud ha-Avodah* ("Labor Brigade"). Led by Mendl Elkind, they established the commune of Vojo Nova ("New Way" in Esperanto) in the Crimea. Gorshman soon met and married the artist Mendl (Mikhail) Gorshman (1902–1972), whose Moscow circle of friends included Yiddish writers such as Leib *Kvitko, who encouraged Gorshman to become a Yiddish writer. Her stories began to appear in Soviet Yiddish periodicals. Her first collection of works, *Der Koyekh fun Lebn* ("The Power of Life"), appeared in 1948, when the Kremlin supported Israel, which enabled the volume to include stories set in both the Crimea and Palestine. Her second book, *33 Noveln* ("33 Stories," 1961), was published in Warsaw. In the 1960s–1990s, *Sovetish Heymland* regularly published her works and translations from Russian into Yiddish. Her 1974 collection of stories, *Lebn un Likht* ("Life and Light"), represents her output of the 1940s–1960s. In 1990, she again immigrated to Israel, where she published edited versions of her works, most notably her autobiographic novel *Khanes Shof un Rinder* ("Hannah's Sheep and Cattle," 1993), and wrote documentary stories about her life in Palestinian and Crimean communes. Volumes of her stories in Russian translation appeared in 1963, 1979, and 1983.

BIBLIOGRAPHY: F. Forman et al. (eds.), *Found Treasures: Stories by Yiddish Women Writers* (1994); S. Bark (ed.), *Beautiful as the Moon, Radiant as the Stars: Jewish Women in Yiddish Stories* (2003).

[Gennady Estraikh (2nd ed.)]

GÓRSKA (**Endelman**), **HALINA** (1898–1942), Polish novelist and social worker. Active in the League for the Defense of the Rights of Man, Halina Górska fought antisemitism and helped to found the Socialist periodical *Sygnały*. Her four major novels were *Nad czarną wodą* ("Over the Black Water," 1931), *Chłopcy z ulic miasta* ("Boys from the Streets," 1934), *Druga brama* ("The Other Gate," 1935), and, the two-part *Barak płonie* ("The Burning Hut," 1937–39). She was arrested and shot by the Gestapo.

GORZOW WIELKOPOLSKI (Ger. **Landsberg an der Warthe**), town in Poland, before 1945 in Brandenburg. A

Jewish quarter and synagogue are first mentioned in 1557, though the community probably originated in the 14th century. It ceased to exist in 1573 when Jews were expelled from the whole of Brandenburg. Toward the middle of the 17th century, Jews attended the Landsberg fairs and soon after renewed their permanent settlement in the city. In 1662 Solomon Kajjem Kaddish was rabbi of the city and in 1672 his authority was extended to include all Brandenburg. He was succeeded by Benjamin Wolff Liebmann. In 1690, 21 Jewish families lived in the city; their number had increased to 417 persons by 1717. In that year, however, all Jews without right of domicile were banished and only 96 remained. They were active in the wool trade and the leather industry. A synagogue was built in 1755 and was used until 1854. The community grew from 304 in 1817 to 730 in 1871 but declined to 435 in 1933. Six charitable organizations, a school, and a cemetery were maintained in 1932 as well as an old-age home which had been opened in 1928. The community diminished during the Nazi era to 180 in 1936 and 95 in 1939; eight of the community were deported to Czechoslovakia on Aug. 27, 1942.

BIBLIOGRAPHY: B. Elsass, in: MGJV, 16 (1905), 95–103; MGADJ, 1 (1909), 9–29; FJW, 66; O. Lassaly, in: MGWJ, 80 (1936), 406–24; E. Keyser (ed.), *Deutsches Staedtebuch* (1939), 776; PK Germanyah; S. Stern, *Der Preussische Staat und die Juden*, 1 (1962), Akten, index; 2 (1962), Akten, nos. 45, 146, 170, 171, 172, 252, 269, 294. Part of the communal archives (1717–1912) are in the CAHJP, Jerusalem.

ABBREVIATIONS

GENERAL ABBREVIATIONS

This list contains abbreviations used in the Encyclopaedia (apart from the standard ones, such as geographical abbreviations, points of compass, etc.). For names of organizations, institutions, etc., in abbreviation, see Index. For bibliographical abbreviations of books and authors in Rabbinical literature, see following lists.

*	Cross reference; i.e., an article is to be found under the word(s) immediately following the asterisk (*).
°	Before the title of an entry, indicates a non-Jew (post-biblical times).
‡	Indicates reconstructed forms.
>	The word following this sign is derived from the preceding one.
<	The word preceding this sign is derived from the following one.
ad loc.	*ad locum*, "at the place"; used in quotations of commentaries.
A.H.	*Anno Hegirae*, "in the year of Hegira," i.e., according to the Muslim calendar.
Akk.	Addadian.
A.M.	*anno mundi*, "in the year (from the creation) of the world."
anon.	anonymous.
Ar.	Arabic.
Aram.	Aramaic.
Ass.	Assyrian.
b.	born; *ben, bar.*
Bab.	Babylonian.
B.C.E.	Before Common Era (= B.C.).
bibl.	bibliography.
Bul.	Bulgarian.
c., ca.	Circa.
C.E.	Common Era (= A.D.).
cf.	*confer*, "compare."
ch., chs.	chapter, chapters.
comp.	compiler, compiled by.
Cz.	Czech.
D	according to the documentary theory, the Deuteronomy document.
d.	died.
Dan.	Danish.
diss., dissert,	dissertation, thesis.
Du.	Dutch.
E.	according to the documentary theory, the Elohist document (i.e., using Elohim as the name of God) of the first five (or six) books of the Bible.
ed.	editor, edited, edition.
eds.	editors.
e.g.	*exempli gratia*, "for example."
Eng.	English.
et al.	*et alibi*, "and elsewhere"; or *et alii*, "and others"; "others."
f., ff.	and following page(s).
fig.	figure.
fl.	flourished.
fol., fols	folio(s).
Fr.	French.
Ger.	German.
Gr.	Greek.
Heb.	Hebrew.
Hg., Hung	Hungarian.
ibid	*Ibidem*, "in the same place."
incl. bibl.	includes bibliography.
introd.	introduction.
It.	Italian.
J	according to the documentary theory, the Jahwist document (i.e., using YHWH as the name of God) of the first five (or six) books of the Bible.
Lat.	Latin.
lit.	literally.
Lith.	Lithuanian.
loc. cit.	*loco citato*, "in the [already] cited place."
Ms., Mss.	Manuscript(s).
n.	note.
n.d.	no date (of publication).
no., nos	number(s).
Nov.	Novellae (Heb. *Ḥiddushim*).
n.p.	place of publication unknown.
op. cit.	*opere citato*, "in the previously mentioned work."
P.	according to the documentary theory, the Priestly document of the first five (or six) books of the Bible.
p., pp.	page(s).
Pers.	Persian.
pl., pls.	plate(s).
Pol.	Polish.
Port.	Potuguese.
pt., pts.	part(s).
publ.	published.
R.	Rabbi or Rav (before names); in Midrash (after an abbreviation) – *Rabbah.*
r.	recto, the first side of a manuscript page.
Resp.	Responsa (Latin "answers," Hebrew *She'elot u-Teshuvot* or *Teshuvot)*, collections of rabbinic decisions.
rev.	revised.

Rom.	Romanian.
Rus(s).	Russian.
Slov.	Slovak.
Sp.	Spanish.
s.v.	*sub verbo, sub voce*, "under the (key) word."
Sum	Sumerian.
summ.	Summary.
suppl.	supplement.
Swed.	Swedish.
tr., trans(l).	translator, translated, translation.
Turk.	Turkish.
Ukr.	Ukrainian.
v., vv.	*verso*. The second side of a manuscript page; also verse(s).
Yid.	Yiddish.

ABBREVIATIONS USED IN RABBINICAL LITERATURE

Adderet Eliyahu, Karaite treatise by Elijah b. Moses *Bashyazi.

Admat Kodesh, Resp. by Nissim Ḥayyim Moses b. Joseph |Mizraḥi.

Aguddah, Sefer ha-, Nov. by *Alexander Suslin ha-Kohen.

Ahavat Ḥesed, compilation by *Israel Meir ha-Kohen.

Aliyyot de-Rabbenu Yonah, Nov. by *Jonah b. Avraham Gerondi.

Arukh ha-Shulḥan, codification by Jehiel Michel *Epstein.

Asayin (= positive precepts), subdivision of: (1) *Maimonides, *Sefer ha-Mitzvot;* (2) *Moses b. Jacob of Coucy, *Semag.*

Asefat Dinim, subdivision of *Sedei Ḥemed* by Ḥayyim Hezekiah *Medini, an encyclopaedia of precepts and responsa.

Asheri = *Asher b. Jehiel.

Aeret Ḥakhamim, by Baruch *Frankel-Teomim; pt, 1: Resp. to Sh. Ar.; pt2: Nov. to Talmud.

Ateret Zahav, subdivision of the *Levush*, a codification by Mordecai b. Abraham (Levush) *Jaffe; *Ateret Zahav* parallels Tur. YD.

Ateret Ẓevi, Comm. To Sh. Ar. by Ẓevi Hirsch b. Azriel.

Avir Ya'akov, Resp. by Jacob Avigdor.

Avkat Rokhel, Resp. by Joseph b. Ephraim *Caro.

Avnei Millu'im, Comm. to Sh. Ar., EH, by *Aryeh Loeb b. Joseph ha-Kohen.

Avnei Nezer, Resp. on Sh. Ar. by Abraham b. Ze'ev Nahum Bornstein of *Sochaczew.

Avodat Massa, Compilation of Tax Law by Yoasha Abraham Judah.

Azei ha-Levanon, Resp. by Judah Leib *Zirelson.

Ba'al ha-Tanya – *Shneur Zalman of Lyady.

Ba'ei Ḥayyei, Resp. by Ḥayyim b. Israel *Benveniste.

Ba'er Heitev, Comm. To Sh. Ar. The parts on OḤ and EH are by Judah b. Simeon *Ashkenazi, the parts on YD AND ḤM by *Zechariah Mendel b. Aryeh Leib. Printed in most editions of Sh. Ar.

Baḥ = Joel *Sirkes.

Baḥ, usual abbreviation for *Bayit Ḥadash*, a commentary on Tur by Joel *Sirkes; printed in most editions of Tur.

Bayit Ḥadash, see *Baḥ*.

Berab = Jacob Berab, also called Ri Berav.

Bedek ha-Bayit, by Joseph b. Ephraim *Caro, additions to his *Beit Yosef* (a comm. to Tur). Printed sometimes inside *Beit Yosef*, in smaller type. Appears in most editions of Tur.

Be'er ha-Golah, Commentary to Sh. Ar. By Moses b. Naphtali Hirsch *Rivkes; printed in most editions of Sh. Ar.

Be'er Mayim, Resp. by Raphael b. Abraham Manasseh Jacob.

Be'er Mayim Ḥayyim, Resp. by Samuel b. Ḥayyim *Vital.

Be'er Yiẓḥak, Resp. by Isaac Elhanan *Spector.

Beit ha-Beḥirah, Comm. to Talmud by Menahem b. Solomon *Meiri.

Beit Me'ir, Nov. on Sh. Ar. by Meir b. Judah Leib Posner.

Beit Shelomo, Resp. by Solomon b. Aaron Ḥason (the younger).

Beit Shemu'el, Comm. to Sh. Ar., EH, by *Samuel b. Uri Shraga Phoebus.

Beit Ya'akov, by Jacob b. Jacob Moses *Lorberbaum; pt.1: Nov. to Ket.; pt.2: Comm. to EH.

Beit Yisrael, collective name for the commentaries *Derishah, Perishah*, and *Be'urim* by Joshua b. Alexander ha-Kohen *Falk. See under the names of the commentaries.

Beit Yiẓḥak, Resp. by Isaac *Schmelkes.

Beit Yosef: (1) Comm. on Tur by Joseph b. Ephraim *Caro; printed in most editions of Tur; (2) Resp. by the same.

Ben Yehudah, Resp. by Abraham b. Judah Litsch (ליטש) Rosenbaum.

Bertinoro, Standard commentary to Mishnah by Obadiah *Bertinoro. Printed in most editions of the Mishnah.

[Be'urei] Ha-Gra, Comm. to Bible, Talmud, and Sh. Ar. By *Elijah b. Solomon Zalmon (Gaon of Vilna); printed in major editions of the mentioned works.

Be'urim, Glosses to Isserles *Darkhei Moshe* (a comm. on Tur) by Joshua b. Alexander ha-Kohen *Falk; printed in many editions of Tur.

Binyamin Ze'ev, Resp. by *Benjamin Ze'ev b. Mattathias of Arta.

Birkei Yosef, Nov. by Ḥayyim Joseph David *Azulai.

Ha-Buẓ ve-ha-Argaman, subdivision of the *Levush* (a codification by Mordecai b. Abraham (Levush) *Jaffe); *Ha-Buẓ ve-ha-Argaman* parallels Tur, EH.

Comm. = Commentary

Da'at Kohen, Resp. by Abraham Isaac ha-Kohen. *Kook.

Darkhei Moshe, Comm. on Tur Moses b. Israel *Isserles; printed in most editions of Tur.

Darkhei No'am, Resp. by *Mordecai b. Judah ha-Levi.

Darkhei Teshuvah, Nov. by Ẓevi *Shapiro; printed in the major editions of Sh. Ar.

De'ah ve-Haskel, Resp. by Obadiah Hadaya (see *Yaskil Avdi).*

Derashot Ran, Sermons by *Nissim b. Reuben Gerondi.
Derekh Ḥayyim, Comm. to *Avot* by *Judah Loew (Lob., Liwa) b. Bezalel (Maharal) of Prague.
Derishah, by Joshua b. Alexander ha-Kohen *Falk; additions to his *Perishah* (comm. on Tur); printed in many editions of Tur.
Derushei ha-Ẓelah, Sermons, by Ezekiel b. Judah Halevi *Landau.
Devar Avraham, Resp. by Abraham *Shapira.
Devar Shemu'el, Resp. by Samuel *Aboab.
Devar Yehoshu'a, Resp. by Joshua Menahem b. Isaac Aryeh Ehrenberg.
Dikdukei Soferim, variae lections of the talmudic text by Raphael Nathan*Rabbinowicz.
Divrei Emet, Resp. by Isaac Bekhor David.
Divrei Ge'onim, Digest of responsa by Ḥayyim Aryeh b. Jeḥiel Ẓevi *Kahana.
Divrei Ḥamudot, Comm. on *Piskei ha-Rosh* by Yom Tov Lipmann b. Nathan ha-Levi *Heller; printed in major editions of the Talmud.
Divrei Ḥayyim several works by Ḥayyim *Halberstamm; if quoted alone refers to his Responsa.
Divrei Malkhi'el, Resp. by Malchiel Tenebaum.
Divrei Rivot, Resp. by Isaac b. Samuel *Adarbi.
Divrei Shemu'el, Resp. by Samuel Raphael Arditi.

Edut be-Ya'akov, Resp. by Jacob b. Abraham *Boton.
Edut bi-Yhosef, Resp. by Joseph b. Isaac *Almosnino.
Ein Ya'akov, Digest of talmudic *aggadot* by Jacob (Ibn) *Habib.
Ein Yiẓḥak, Resp. by Isaac Elhanan *Spector.
Ephraim of Lentshitz = Solomon *Luntschitz.
Erekh Leḥem, Nov. and glosses to Sh. Ar. by Jacob b. Abraham *Castro.
Eshkol, Sefer ha-, Digest of *halakhot* by *Abraham b. Isaac of Narbonne.
Et Sofer, Treatise on Law Court documents by Abraham b. Mordecai *Ankawa, in the 2nd vol. of his Resp. *Kerem Ḥamar.*
Etan ha-Ezraḥi, Resp. by Abraham b. Israel Jehiel (Shrenzl) *Rapaport.
Even ha-Ezel, Nov. to Maimonides' *Yad Ḥazakah* by Isser Zalman *Meltzer.
Even ha-Ezer, also called *Raban* of *Ẓafenat Pa'ne'aḥ*, rabbinical work with varied contents by *Eliezer b. Nathan of Mainz; not identical with the subdivision of Tur, Shulḥan Arukh, etc.
Ezrat Yehudah, Resp. by *Isaar Judah b. Nechemiah of Brisk.

Gan Eden, Karaite treatise by *Aaron b. Elijah of Nicomedia.
Gersonides = *Levi b. Gershom, also called Leo Hebraecus, or Ralbag.
Ginnat Veradim, Resp. by *Abraham b. Mordecai ha-Levi.

Haggahot, another name for *Rema.*
Haggahot Asheri, glosses to *Piskei ha-Rosh* by *Israel of Krems; printed in most Talmud editions.
Haggahot Maimuniyyot, Comm,. to Maimonides' Yad Ḥazakah by *Meir ha-Kohen; printed in most eds. of Yad.
Haggahot Mordekhai, glosses to *Mordekhai* by Samuel *Schlettstadt; printed in most editions of the Talmud after *Mordekhai.*
Haggahot ha-Rashash on Tosafot, annotations of Samuel *Strashun on the Tosafot (printed in major editions of the Talmud).
Ha-Gra = *Elijah b. Solomon Zalman (Gaon of Vilna).
Ha-Gra, Commentaries on Bible, Talmud, and Sh. Ar. respectively, by *Elijah b. Solomon Zalman (Gaon of Vilna); printed in major editions of the mentioned works.
Hai Gaon, Comm. = his comm. on Mishnah.
Ḥakham Ẓevi, Resp. by Ẓevi Hirsch b. Jacob *Ashkenazi.
Halakhot = Rif, *Halakhot.* Compilation and abstract of the Talmud by Isaac b. Jacob ha-Kohen *Alfasi; printed in most editions of the Talmud.
Halakhot Gedolot, compilation of *halakhot* from the Geonic period, arranged acc. to the Talmud. Here cited acc. to ed. Warsaw (1874). Author probably *Simeon Kayyara of Basra.
Halakhot Pesukot le-Rav Yehudai Ga'on compilation of *halakhot.*
Halakhot Pesukot min ha-Ge'onim, compilation of *halakhot* from the geonic period by different authors.
Ḥananel, Comm. to Talmud by *Hananel b. Ḥushi'el; printed in some editions of the Talmud.
Harei Besamim, Resp. by Aryeh Leib b. Isaac *Horowitz.
Ḥassidim, Sefer, Ethical maxims by *Judah b. Samuel he-Ḥasid.
Hassagot Rabad on Rif, Glosses on Rif, *Halakhot*, by *Abraham b. David of Posquières.
Hassagot Rabad [on Yad], Glosses on Maimonides, *Yad Ḥazakah*, by *Abraham b. David of Posquières.
Hassagot Ramban, Glosses by Naḥmanides on Maimonides' *Sefer ha-Mitzvot;* usually printed together with *Sefer ha-Mitzvot.*
Ḥatam Sofer = Moses *Sofer.
Ḥavvot Ya'ir, Resp. and varia by Jair Ḥayyim *Bacharach
Ḥayyim Or Zaru'a = *Ḥayyim (Eliezer) b. Isaac.
Ḥazon Ish = Abraham Isaiah *Karelitz.
Ḥazon Ish, Nov. by Abraham Isaiah *Karelitz
Ḥedvat Ya'akov, Resp. by Aryeh Judah Jacob b. David Dov Meisels (article under his father's name).
Heikhal Yiẓḥak, Resp. by Isaac ha-Levi *Herzog.
Ḥelkat Meḥokek, Comm. to Sh. Ar., by Moses b. Isaac Judah *Lima.
Ḥelkat Ya'akov, Resp. by Mordecai Jacob Breisch.
Ḥemdah Genuzah, , Resp. from the geonic period by different authors.
Ḥemdat Shelomo, Resp. by Solomon Zalman *Lipschitz.
Ḥida = Ḥayyim Joseph David *Azulai.
Ḥiddushei Halakhot ve-Aggadot, Nov. by Samuel Eliezer b. Judah ha-Levi *Edels.
Ḥikekei Lev, Resp. by Ḥayyim *Palaggi.
Ḥikrei Lev, Nov. to Sh. Ar. by Joseph Raphael b. Ḥayyim Joseph Ḥazzan (see article *Ḥazzan Family).
Hil. = Hilkhot … (e.g. *Hilkhot Shabbat).*
Ḥinnukh, Sefer ha-, List and explanation of precepts attributed (probably erroneously) to Aaron ha-Levi of Barcelona (see article **Ha-Ḥinnukh*).
Ḥok Ya'akov, Comm. to Hil. Pesaḥ in Sh. Ar., OḤ, by Jacob b. Joseph *Reicher.
Ḥokhmat Sehlomo (1), Glosses to Talmud, *Rashi* and Tosafot by Solomon b. Jehiel "Maharshal") *Luria; printed in many editions of the Talmud.
Ḥokhmat Sehlomo (2), Glosses and Nov. to Sh. Ar. by Solomon b. Judah Aaron *Kluger printed in many editions of Sh. Ar.
Ḥur, subdivision of the *Levush*, a codification by Mordecai b. Abraham (Levush) *Jaffe; *Hur* (or *Levush ha-Hur)* parallels Tur, OḤ, 242–697.
Ḥut ha-Meshullash, fourth part of the *Tashbeẓ* (Resp.), by Simeon b. Zemaḥ *Duran.

Ibn Ezra, Comm. to the Bible by Abraham *Ibn Ezra; printed in the major editions of the Bible *("Mikra'ot Gedolot").*
Imrei Yosher, Resp. by Meir b. Aaron Judah *Arik.
Ir Shushan, Subdivision of the *Levush,* a codification by Mordecai b. Abraham (Levush) *Jaffe; *Ir Shushan* parallels Tur, ḤM.
Israel of Bruna = Israel b. Ḥayyim *Bruna.
Ittur. Treatise on precepts by *Isaac b. Abba Mari of Marseilles.

Jacob Be Rab = *Be Rab.
Jacob b. Jacob Moses of Lissa = Jacob b. Jacob Moses *Lorberbaum.
Judah B. Simeon = Judah b. Simeon *Ashkenazi.
Judah Minz = Judah b. Eliezer ha-Levi *Minz.

Kappei Aharon, Resp. by Aaron Azriel.
Kehillat Ya'akov, Talmudic methodology, definitions etc. by Israel Jacob b. Yom Tov *Algazi.
Kelei Ḥemdah, Nov. and *pilpulim* by Meir Dan *Plotzki of Ostrova, arranged acc. to the Torah.
Keli Yakar, Annotations to the Torah by Solomon *Luntschitz.
Keneh Ḥokhmah, Sermons by Judah Loeb *Pochwitzer.
Keneset ha-Gedolah, Digest of *halakhot* by Ḥayyim b. Israel *Benveniste; subdivided into annotations to *Beit Yosef* and annotations to Tur.
Keneset Yisrael, Resp. by Ezekiel b. Abraham Katzenellenbogen (see article *Katzenellenbogen Family).
Kerem Ḥamar, Resp. and varia by Abraham b. Mordecai *Ankawa.
Kerem Shelmo. Resp. by Solomon b. Joseph *Amarillo.
Keritut, [Sefer], Methodology of the Talmud by *Samson b. Isaac of Chinon.
Kesef ha-Kedoshim, Comm. to Sh. Ar., ḤM, by Abraham *Wahrmann; printed in major editions of Sh. Ar.
Kesef Mishneh, Comm. to Maimonides, *Yad Ḥazakah,* by Joseph b. Ephraim *Caro; printed in most editions of *Yad Ḥazakah.*
Keẓot ha-Ḥoshen, Comm. to Sh. Ar., ḤM, by *Aryeh Loeb b. Joseph ha-Kohen; printed in major editions of Sh. Ar.
Kol Bo [*Sefer*], Anonymous collection of ritual rules; also called *Sefer ha-Likkutim.*
Kol Mevasser, Resp. by Meshullam *Rath.
Korban Aharon, Comm. to *Sifra* by Aaron b. Abraham *Ibn Ḥayyim; pt. 1 is called: *Middot Aharon.*
Korban Edah, Comm. to Jer. Talmud by David *Fraenkel; with additions: *Shiyyurei Korban;* printed in most editions of Jer. Talmud.
Kunteres ha-Kelalim, subdivision of *Sedei Ḥemed,* an encyclopaedia of precepts and responsa by Ḥayyim Hezekiah *Medini.
Kunteres ha-Semikhah, a treatise by *Levi b. Ḥabib; printed at the end of his responsa.
Kunteres Tikkun Olam, part of *Mispat Shalom* (Nov. by Shalom Mordecai b. Moses *Schwadron).

Lavin (negative precepts), subdivision of: (1) *Maimonides, *Sefer ha-Mitzvot;* (2) *Moses b. Jacob of Coucy, *Semag.*
Leḥem Mishneh, Comm. to Maimonides, *Yad Ḥazakah,* by Abraham [Ḥiyya] b. Moses *Boton; printed in most editions of *Yad Ḥazakah.*
Leḥem Rav, Resp. by Abraham [Ḥiyya] b. Moses *Boton.
Leket Yosher, Resp and varia by Israel b. Pethahiah *Isserlein, collected by *Joseph (Joselein) b. Moses.
Leo Hebraeus = *Levi b. Gershom, also called Ralbag or Gersonides.
Levush = Mordecai b. Abraham *Jaffe.
Levush [Malkhut], Codification by Mordecai b. Abraham (Levush) *Jaffe, with subdivisions: [*Levush ha-] Tekhelet* (parallels Tur OḤ 1–241); [*Levush ha-] Ḥur* (parallels Tur OḤ 242–697); [*Levush] Ateret Zahav* (parallels Tur YD); [*Levush ha-Buẓ ve-ha-Argaman* (parallels Tur EH); [*Levush] Ir Shushan* (parallels Tur ḤM); under the name *Levush* the author wrote also other works.
Li-Leshonot ha-Rambam, fifth part (nos. 1374–1700) of Resp. by *David b. Solomon ibn Abi Zimra (Radbaz).
Likkutim, Sefer ha-, another name for *[Sefer] Kol Bo.*

Ma'adanei Yom Tov, Comm. on *Piskei ha-Rosh* by Yom Tov Lipmann b. Nathan ha-Levi *Heller; printed in many editions of the Talmud.
Mabit = Moses b. Joseph *Trani.
Magen Avot, Comm. to *Avot* by Simeon b. Ẓemaḥ *Duran.
Magen Avraham, Comm. to Sh. Ar., OḤ, by Abraham Abele b. Ḥayyim ha-Levi *Gombiner; printed in many editions of Sh. Ar., OḤ.
Maggid Mishneh, Comm. to Maimonides, *Yad Ḥazakah,* by *Vidal Yom Tov of Tolosa; printed in most editions of the *Yad Ḥazakah.*
Maḥaneh Efrayim, Resp. and Nov., arranged acc. to Maimonides' *Yad Ḥazakah* , by Ephraim b. Aaron *Navon.
Maharai = Israel b. Pethahiah *Isserlein.
Maharal of Prague = *Judah Loew (Lob, Liwa), b. Bezalel.
Maharalbaḥ = *Levi b. Ḥabib.
Maharam Alashkar = Moses b. Isaac *Alashkar.
Maharam Alshekh = Moses b. Ḥayyim *Alashekh.
Maharam Mintz = Moses *Mintz.
Maharam of Lublin = *Meir b. Gedaliah of Lublin.
Maharam of Padua = Meir *Katzenellenbogen.
Maharam of Rothenburg = *Meir b. Baruch of Rothenburg.
Maharam Shik = Moses b. Joseph Schick.
Maharash Engel = Samuel b. Ze'ev Wolf Engel.
Maharashdam = Samuel b. Moses *Medina.
Maharḥash = Ḥayyim (ben) Shabbetai.
Mahari Basan = Jehiel b. Ḥayyim Basan.
Mahari b. Lev = Joseph ibn Lev.
Mahari'az = Jekuthiel Asher Zalman Ensil Zusmir.
Maharibal = *Joseph ibn Lev.
Mahariḥ = Jacob (Israel) *Ḥagiz.
Maharik = Joseph b. Solomon *Colon.
Maharikash = Jacob b. Abraham *Castro.
Maharil = Jacob b. Moses *Moellin.
Maharimat = Joseph b. Moses di Trani (not identical with the Maharit).
Maharit = Joseph b. Moses *Trani.
Maharitaẓ = Yom Tov b. Akiva Ẓahalon. (See article *Ẓahalon Family).
Maharsha = Samuel Eliezer b. Judah ha-Levi *Edels.
Maharshag = Simeon b. Judah Gruenfeld.
Maharshak = Samson b. Isaac of Chinon.
Maharshakh = *Solomon b. Abraham.
Maharshal = Solomon b. Jeḥiel *Luria.
Mahasham = Shalom Mordecai b. Moses *Sschwadron.
Maharyu = Jacob b. Judah *Weil.
Maḥazeh Avraham, Resp. by Abraham Nebagen v. Meir ha-Levi Steinberg.
Maḥazik Berakhah, Nov. by Ḥayyim Joseph David *Azulai.

*Maimonides = Moses b. Maimon, or Rambam.
*Malbim = Meir Loeb b. Jehiel Michael.
Malbim = Malbim's comm. to the Bible; printed in the major editions.
Malbushei Yom Tov, Nov. on *Levush,* OḤ, by Yom Tov Lipmann b. Nathan ha-Levi *Heller.
Mappah, another name for *Rema.*
Mareh ha-Panim, Comm. to Jer. Talmud by Moses b. Simeon *Margolies; printed in most editions of Jer. Talmud.
Margaliyyot ha-Yam, Nov. by Reuben *Margoliot.
Masat Binyamin, Resp. by Benjamin Aaron b. Abraham *Slonik
Mashbir, Ha- = *Joseph Samuel b. Isaac Rodi.
Massa Ḥayyim, Tax *halakhot* by Ḥayyim *Palaggi, with the subdivisions *Missim ve-Arnomiyyot* and *Torat ha-Minhagot.*
Massa Melekh, Compilation of Tax Law by Joseph b. Isaac *Ibn Ezra with concluding part *Ne'ilat She'arim.*
Matteh Asher, Resp. by Asher b. Emanuel Shalem.
Matteh Shimon, Digest of Resp. and Nov. to Tur and *Beit Yosef,* ḤM, by Mordecai Simeon b. Solomon.
Matteh Yosef, Resp. by Joseph b. Moses ha-Levi Nazir (see article under his father's name).
Mayim Amukkim, Resp. by Elijah b. Abraham *Mizraḥi.
Mayim Ḥayyim, Resp. by Ḥayyim b. Dov Beresh Rapaport.
Mayim Rabbim, , Resp. by Raphael *Meldola.
Me-Emek ha-Bakha, , Resp. by Simeon b. Jekuthiel Ephrati.
Me'irat Einayim, usual abbreviation: *Sma* (from: *Sefer Me'irat Einayim*); comm. to Sh. Ar. By Joshua b. Alexander ha-Kohen *Falk; printed in most editions of the Sh. Ar.
Melammed le-Ho'il, Resp. by David Ẓevi *Hoffmann.
Meisharim, [*Sefer*], Rabbinical treatise by *Jeroham b. Meshullam.
Meshiv Davar, Resp. by Naphtali Ẓevi Judah *Berlin.
Mi-Gei ha-Haregah, Resp. by Simeon b. Jekuthiel Ephrati.
Mi-Ma'amakim, Resp. by Ephraim Oshry.
Middot Aharon, first part of *Korban Aharon,* a comm. to *Sifra* by Aaron b. Abraham *Ibn Ḥayyim.
Migdal Oz, Comm. to Maimonides, *Yad Ḥazakah,* by *Ibn Gaon Shem Tov b. Abraham; printed in most editions of the *Yad Ḥazakah.*
Mikhtam le-David, Resp. by David Samuel b. Jacob *Pardo.
Mikkaḥ ve-ha-Mimkar, Sefer ha-, Rabbinical treatise by *Hai Gaon.
Milḥamot ha-Shem, Glosses to Rif, *Halakhot,* by *Naḥmanides.
Minḥat Ḥinnukh, Comm. to *Sefer ha-Ḥinnukh,* by Joseph b. Moses *Babad.
Minḥat Yiẓḥak, Resp. by Isaac Jacob b. Joseph Judah Weiss.
Misgeret ha-Shulḥan, Comm. to Sh. Ar., ḤM, by Benjamin Ze'ev Wolf b. Shabbetai; printed in most editions of Sh. Ar.
Mishkenot ha-Ro'im, Halakhot in alphabetical order by Uzziel Alshekh.
Mishnah Berurah, Comm. to Sh. Ar., OḤ, by *Israel Meir ha-Kohen.
Mishneh le-Melekh, Comm. to Maimonides, *Yad Ḥazakah,* by Judah *Rosanes; printed in most editions of *Yad Ḥazakah.*
Mishpat ha-Kohanim, Nov. to Sh. Ar., ḤM, by Jacob Moses *Lorberbaum, part of his *Netivot ha-Mishpat;* printed in major editions of Sh. Ar.
Mishpat Kohen, Resp. by Abraham Isaac ha-Kohen *Kook.
Mishpat Shalom, Nov. by Shalom Mordecai b. Moses *Schwadron; contains: *Kunteres Tikkun Olam.*
Mishpat u-Ẓedakah be-Ya'akov, Resp. by Jacob b. Reuben *Ibn Ẓur.
Mishpat ha-Urim, Comm. to Sh. Ar., ḤM by Jacob b. Jacob Moses *Lorberbaum, part of his *Netivot ha-Mishpat;* printed in major editons of Sh. Ar.
Mishpat Ẓedek, Resp. by *Melammed Meir b. Shem Tov.
Mishpatim Yesharim, Resp. by Raphael b. Mordecai *Berdugo.
Mishpetei Shemu'el, Resp. by Samuel b. Moses *Kalai (Kal'i).
Mishpetei ha-Tanna'im, Kunteres, Nov on *Levush,* OḤ by Yom Tov Lipmann b. Nathan ha-Levi *Heller.
Mishpetei Uzzi'el (Uziel), Resp. by Ben-Zion Meir Hai *Ouziel.
Missim ve-Arnoniyyot, Tax *halakhot* by Ḥayyim *Palaggi, a subdivision of his work *Massa Ḥayyim* on the same subject.
Mitzvot, Sefer ha-, Elucidation of precepts by *Maimonides; subdivided into *Lavin* (negative precepts) and *Asayin* (positive precepts).
Mitzvot Gadol, Sefer, Elucidation of precepts by *Moses b. Jacob of Coucy, subdivided into *Lavin* (negative precepts) and *Asayin* (positive precepts); the usual abbreviation is *Semag.*
Mitzvot Katan, Sefer, Elucidation of precepts by *Isaac b. Joseph of Corbeil; the usual, abbreviation is *Semak.*
Mo'adim u-Zemannim, Rabbinical treatises by Moses Sternbuch.
Modigliano, Joseph Samuel = *Joseph Samuel b. Isaac, Rodi (Ha-Mashbir).
Mordekhai (Mordecai), halakhic compilation by *Mordecai b. Hillel; printed in most editions of the Talmud after the texts.
Moses b. Maimon = *Maimonides, also called Rambam.
Moses b. Naḥman = Naḥmanides, also called Ramban.
Muram = Isaiah Menahem b. Isaac (from: Morenu R. Mendel).

Naḥal Yiẓḥak, Comm. on Sh. Ar., ḤM, by Isaac Elhanan *Spector.
Naḥalah li-Yhoshu'a, Resp. by Joshua Ẓunẓin.
Naḥalat Shivah, collection of legal forms by *Samuel b. David Moses ha-Levi.
*Naḥmanides = Moses b. Naḥman, also called Ramban.
Naẓiv = Naphtali Ẓevi Judah *Berlin.
Ne'eman Shemu'el, Resp. by Samuel Isaac *Modigilano.
Ne'ilat She'arim, concluding part of *Massa Melekh* (a work on Tax Law) by Joseph b. Isaac *Ibn Ezra, containing an exposition of customary law and subdivided into *Minhagei Issur* and *Minhagei Mamon.*
Ner Ma'aravi, Resp. by Jacob b. Malka.
Netivot ha-Mishpat, by Jacob b. Jacob Moses *Lorberbaum; subdivided into *Mishpat ha-Kohanim,* Nov. to Sh. Ar., ḤM, and *Mishpat ha-Urim,* a comm. on the same; printed in major editions of Sh. Ar.
Netivot Olam, Saying of the Sages by *Judah Loew (Lob, Liwa) b. Bezalel.
Nimmukei Menaḥem of Merseburg, Tax *halakhot* by the same, printed at the end of Resp. Maharyu.
Nimmukei Yosef, Comm. to Rif. *Halakhot,* by Joseph *Ḥabib (Ḥabiba); printed in many editions of the Talmud.
Noda bi-Yhudah, Resp. by Ezekiel b. Judah ha-Levi *Landau; there is a first collection *(Mahadura Kamma)* and a second collection *(Mahadura Tinyana).*
Nov. = Novellae, Ḥiddushim.

Ohel Moshe (1), Notes to Talmud, *Midrash Rabbah,* Yad, *Sifrei* and to several Resp., by Eleazar *Horowitz.

Ohel Moshe (2), Resp. by Moses Jonah Zweig.
Oholei Tam. Resp. by *Tam ibn Yaḥya Jacob b. David; printed in the rabbinical collection *Tummat Yesharim.*
Oholei Ya'akov, Resp. by Jacob de *Castro.
Or ha-Me'ir Resp by Judah Meir b. Jacob Samson Shapiro.
Or Same'aḥ, Comm. to Maimonides, *Yad Ḥazakah,* by *Meir Simḥah ha-Kohen of Dvinsk; printed in many editions of the *Yad Ḥazakah.*
Or Zaru'a [the father] = *Isaac b. Moses of Vienna.
Or Zaru'a [the son] = *Ḥayyim (Eliezer) b. Isaac.
Or Zaru'a, Nov. by *Isaac b. Moses of Vienna.
Orah, Sefer ha-, Compilation of ritual precepts by *Rashi.
Oraḥ la-Ẓaddik, Resp. by Abraham Ḥayyim Rodrigues.
Oẓar ha-Posekim, Digest of Responsa.

Paḥad Yiẓḥak, Rabbinical encyclopaedia by Isaac *Lampronti.
Panim Me'irot, Resp. by Meir b. Isaac *Eisenstadt.
Parashat Mordekhai, Resp. by Mordecai b. Abraham Naphtali *Banet.
Pe'at ha-Sadeh la-Dinim and Pe'at ha-Sadeh la-Kelalim, subdivisions of the *Sedei Ḥemed,* an encyclopaedia of precepts and responsa, by Ḥayyim Hezekaih *Medini.
Penei Moshe (1), Resp. by Moses *Benveniste.
Penei Moshe (2), Comm. to Jer. Talmud by Moses b. Simeon *Margolies; printed in most editions of the Jer. Talmud.
Penei Moshe (3), Comm. on the aggadic passages of 18 treatises of the Bab. and Jer. Talmud, by Moses b. Isaiah Katz.
Penei Yehoshu'a, Nov. by Jacob Joshua b. Ẓevi Hirsch *Falk.
Peri Ḥadash, Comm. on Sh. Ar. By Hezekiah da *Silva.
Perishah, Comm. on Tur by Joshua b. Alexander ha-Kohen *Falk; printed in major edition of Tur; forms together with *Derishah* and *Be'urim* (by the same author) the *Beit Yisrael.*
Pesakim u-Khetavim, 2nd part of the *Terumat ha-Deshen* by Israel b. Pethahiah *Isserlein' also called *Piskei Maharai.*
Pilpula Ḥarifta, Comm. to *Piskei ha-Rosh, Seder Nezikin,* by Yom Tov Lipmann b. Nathan ha-Levi *Heller; printed in major editions of the Talmud.
Piskei Maharai, see *Terumat ha-Deshen,* 2nd part; also called *Pesakim u-Khetavim.*
Piskei ha-Rosh, a compilation of *halakhot,* arranged on the Talmud, by *Asher b. Jehiel (Rosh); printed in major Talmud editions.
Pitḥei Teshuvah, Comm. to Sh. Ar. by Abraham Hirsch b. Jacob *Eisenstadt; printed in major editions of the Sh. Ar.

Rabad = *Abraham b. David of Posquières (Rabad III.).
Raban = *Eliezer b. Nathan of Mainz.
Raban, also called *Ẓafenat Pa'ne'aḥ* or *Even ha-Ezer,* see under the last name.
Rabi Abad = *Abraham b. Isaac of Narbonne.
Radad = David Dov. b. Aryeh Judah Jacob *Meisels.
Radam = Dov Berush b. Isaac Meisels.
Radbaz = *David b Solomon ibn Abi Ziumra.
Radbaz, Comm. to Maimonides, *Yad Ḥazakah,* by *David b. Solomon ibn Abi Zimra.
Ralbag = *Levi b. Gershom, also called Gersonides, or Leo Hebraeus.
Ralbag, Bible comm. by *Levi b. Gershon.
Rama [da Fano] = Menaḥem Azariah *Fano.
Ramah = Meir b. Todros [ha-Levi] *Abulafia.
Ramam = *Menaham of Merseburg.
Rambam = *Maimonides; real name: Moses b. Maimon.
Ramban = *Naḥmanides; real name Moses b. Naḥman.
Ramban, Comm. to Torah by *Naḥmanides; printed in major editions. ("Mikra'ot Gedolot").
Ran = *Nissim b. Reuben Gerondi.
Ran of Rif, Comm. on Rif, *Halakhot,* by Nissim b. Reuben Gerondi.
Ranaḥ = *Elijah b. Ḥayyim.
Rash = *Samson b. Abraham of Sens.
Rash, Comm. to Mishnah, by *Samson b. Abraham of Sens; printed in major Talmud editions.
Rashash = Samuel *Strashun.
Rashba = Solomon b. Abraham *Adret.
Rashba, Resp., see also; *Sefer Teshuvot ha-Rashba ha-Meyuḥasot le-ha-Ramban,* by Solomon b. Abraham *Adret.
Rashbad = Samuel b. David.
Rashbam = *Samuel b. Meir.
Rashbam = Comm. on Bible and Talmud by *Samuel b. Meir; printed in major editions of Bible and most editions of Talmud.
Rashbash = Solomon b. Simeon *Duran.
*Rashi = Solomon b. Isaac of Troyes.
Rashi, Comm. on Bible and Talmud by *Rashi; printed in almost all Bible and Talmud editions.
Raviah = Eliezer b. Joel ha-Levi.
Redak = David *Kimḥi.
Redak, Comm. to Bible by David *Kimḥi.
Redakh = *David b. Ḥayyim ha-Kohen of Corfu.
Re'em = Elijah b. Abraham *Mizraḥi.
Rema = Moses b. Israel *Isserles.
Rema, Glosses to Sh. Ar. by Moses b. Israel *Isserles; printed in almost all editions of the Sh. Ar. inside the text in Rashi type; also called *Mappah* or *Haggahot.*
Remek = Moses Kimḥi.
Remakh = Moses ha-Kohen mi-Lunel.
Reshakh = *Solomon b. Abraham; also called Maharshakh.
Resp. = Responsa, *She'elot u-Teshuvot.*
Ri Berav = *Berab.
Ri Escapa = Joseph b. Saul *Escapa.
Ri Migash = Joseph b. Meir ha-Levi *Ibn Migash.
Riba = Isaac b. Asher ha-Levi; Riba II (Riba ha-Baḥur) = his grandson with the same name.
Ribam = Isaac b. Mordecai (or: Isaac b. Meir).
Ribash = *Isaac b. Sheshet Perfet (or: Barfat).
Rid= *Isaiah b. Mali di Trani the Elder.
Ridbaz = Jacob David b. Ze'ev *Willowski.
Rif = Isaac b. Jacob ha-Kohen *Alfasi.
Rif, *Halakhot,* Compilation and abstract of the Talmud by Isaac b. Jacob ha-Kohen *Alfasi.
Ritba = Yom Tov b. Abraham *Ishbili.
Riẓbam = Isaac b. Mordecai.
Rosh = *Asher b. Jehiel, also called Asheri.
Rosh Mashbir, Resp. by *Joseph Samuel b. Isaac, Rodi.

Sedei Ḥemed, Encyclopaedia of precepts and responsa by Ḥayyim Ḥezekiah *Medini; subdivisions: *Asefat Dinim, Kunteres ha-Kelalim, Pe'at ha-Sadeh la-Dinim, Pe'at ha-Sadeh la-Kelalim.*
Semag, Usual abbreviation of *Sefer Mitzvot Gadol,* elucidation of precepts by *Moses b. Jacob of Coucy; subdivided into *Lavin* (negative precepts) *Asayin* (positive precepts).
Semak, Usual abbreviation of *Sefer Mitzvot Katan,* elucidation of precepts by *Isaac b. Joseph of Corbeil.

Sh. Ar. = *Shulḥan Arukh*, code by Joseph b. Ephraim *Caro.
Sha'ar Mishpat, Comm. to Sh. Ar., ḤM. By Israel Isser b. Ze'ev Wolf.
Sha'arei Shevu'ot, Treatise on the law of oaths by *David b. Saadiah; usually printed together with Rif, *Halakhot;* also called: *She'arim of R. Alfasi.*
Sha'arei Teshuvah, Collection of resp. from Geonic period, by different authors.
Sha'arei Uzzi'el, Rabbinical treatise by Ben-Zion Meir Ha *Ouziel.
Sha'arei Ẓedek, Collection of resp. from Geonic period, by different authors.
Shadal [or Shedal] = Samuel David *Luzzatto.
Shai la-Moreh, Resp. by Shabbetai Jonah.
Shakh, Usual abbreviation of *Siftei Kohen*, a comm. to Sh. Ar., YD and ḤM by *Shabbetai b. Meir ha-Kohen; printed in most editions of Sh. Ar.
Sha'ot-de-Rabbanan, Resp. by *Solomon b. Judah ha-Kohen.
She'arim of R. Alfasi see *Sha'arei Shevu'ot.*
Shedal, see Shadal.
She'elot u-Teshuvot ha-Ge'onim, Collection of resp. by different authors.
She'erit Yisrael, Resp. by Israel Ze'ev Mintzberg.
She'erit Yosef, Resp. by *Joseph b. Mordecai Gershon ha-Kohen.
She'ilat Yaveẓ, Resp. by Jacob *Emden (Yaveẓ).
She'iltot, Compilation arranged acc. to the Torah by *Aḥa (Aḥai) of Shabḥa.
Shem Aryeh, Resp. by Aryeh Leib *Lipschutz.
Shemesh Ẓedakah, Resp. by Samson *Morpurgo.
Shenei ha-Me'orot ha-Gedolim, Resp. by Elijah *Covo.
Shetarot, Sefer ha-, Collection of legal forms by *Judah b. Barzillai al-Bargeloni.
Shevut Ya'akov, Resp. by Jacob b. Joseph Reicher.
Shibbolei ha-Leket Compilation on ritual by Zedekiah b. Avraham *Anav.
Shiltei Gibborim, Comm. to Rif, *Halakhot*, by *Joshua Boaz b. Simeon; printed in major editions of the Talmud.
Shittah Mekubbeẓet, Compilation of talmudical commentaries by Bezalel *Ashkenazi.
Shivat Ẓiyyon, Resp. by Samuel b. Ezekiel *Landau.
Shiyyurei Korban, by David *Fraenkel; additions to his comm. to Jer. Talmud *Korban Edah;* both printed in most editions of Jer. Talmud.
Sho'el u-Meshiv, Resp. by Joseph Saul ha-Levi *Nathanson.
Sh[ulḥan] Ar[ukh] [of Ba'al ha-Tanyal], Code by *Shneur Zalman of Lyady; not identical with the code by Joseph Caro.
Siftei Kohen, Comm. to Sh. Ar., YD and ḤM by *Shabbetai b. Meir ha-Kohen; printed in most editions of Sh. Ar.; usual abbreviation: *Shakh.*
Simḥat Yom Tov, Resp. by Tom Tov b. Jacob *Algazi.
Simlah Ḥadashah, Treatise on *Sheḥitah* by Alexander Sender b. Ephraim Zalman *Schor; see also *Tevu'ot Shor.*
Simeon b. Ẓemaḥ = Simeon b. Ẓemaḥ *Duran.
Sma, Comm. to Sh. Ar. by Joshua b. Alexander ha-Kohen *Falk; the full title is: *Sefer Me'irat Einayim;* printed in most editions of Sh. Ar.
Solomon b. Isaac ha-Levi = Solomon b. Isaac *Levy.
Solomon b. Isaac of Troyes = *Rashi.

Tal Orot, Rabbinical work with various contents, by Joseph ibn Gioia.
Tam, Rabbenu = *Tam Jacob b. Meir.
Tashbaẓ = Samson b. Zadok.
Tashbeẓ = Simeon b. Zemaḥ *Duran, sometimes also abbreviation for Samson b. Zadok, usually known as Tashbaẓ.
Tashbeẓ [*Sefer ha-*], Resp. by Simeon b. Ẓemaḥ *Duran; the fourth part of this work is called: *Ḥut ha-Meshullash.*
Taz, Usual abbreviation of *Turei Zahav*, comm., to Sh. Ar. by *David b. Samnuel ha-Levi; printed in most editions of Sh. Ar.
(Ha)-Tekhelet, subdivision of the *Levush* (a codification by Mordecai b. Abraham (Levush) *Jaffe); *Ha-Tekhelet* parallels Tur, OḤ 1-241.
Terumat ha-Deshen, by Israel b. Pethahiah *Isserlein; subdivided into a part containing responsa, and a second part called *Pesakim u-Khetavim* or *Piskei Maharai.*
Terumot, Sefer ha-, Compilation of *halakhot* by Samuel b. Isaac *Sardi.
Teshuvot Ba'alei ha-Tosafot, Collection of responsa by the Tosafists.
Teshjvot Ge'onei Mizraḥ u-Ma'aav, Collection of responsa.
Teshuvot ha-Geonim, Collection of responsa from Geonic period.
Teshuvot Ḥakhmei Provinẓyah, Collection of responsa by different Provencal authors.
Teshuvot Ḥakhmei Ẓarefat ve-Loter, Collection of responsa by different French authors.
Teshuvot Maimuniyyot, Resp. pertaining to Maimonides' *Yad Ḥazakah;* printed in major editions of this work after the text; authorship uncertain.
Tevu'ot Shor, by Alexander Sender b. Ephraim Zalman *Schor, a comm. to his *Simlah Ḥadashah*, a work on *Sheḥitah.*
Tiferet Ẓevi, Resp. by Ẓevi Hirsch of the "AHW" Communities (Altona, Hamburg, Wandsbeck).
Tiktin, Judah b. Simeon = Judah b. Simeon *Ashkenazi.
Toledot Adam ve-Ḥavvah, Codification by *Jeroham b. Meshullam.
Torat Emet, Resp. by Aaron b. Joseph *Sasson.
Torat Ḥayyim, , Resp. by Ḥayyim (ben) Shabbetai.
Torat ha-Minhagot, subdivision of the *Massa Ḥayyim* (a work on tax law) by Ḥayyim *Palaggi, containing an exposition of customary law.
Tosafot Rid, Explanations to the Talmud and decisions by *Isaiah b. Mali di Trani the Elder.
Tosefot Yom Tov, comm. to Mishnah by Yom Tov Lipmann b. Nathan ha-Levi *Heller; printed in most editions of the Mishnah.
Tummim, subdivision of the comm. to Sh. Ar., ḤM, *Urim ve-Tummim* by Jonathan *Eybeschuetz; printed in the major editions of Sh. Ar.
Tur, usual abbreviation for the *Arba'ah Turim* of *Jacob b. Asher.
Turei Zahav, Comm. to Sh. Ar. by *David b. Samuel ha-Levi; printed in most editions of Sh. Ar.; usual abbreviation: *Taz.*

Urim, subdivision of the following.
Urim ve-Tummim, Comm. to Sh. Ar., ḤM, by Jonathan *Eybeschuetz; printed in the major editions of Sh. Ar.; subdivided in places into *Urim* and *Tummim.*

Vikku'aḥ Mayim Ḥayyim, Polemics against Isserles and Caro by Ḥayyim b. Bezalel.

Yad Malakhi, Methodological treatise by *Malachi b. Jacob ha-Kohen.

Yad Ramah, Nov. by Meir b. Todros [ha-Levi] *Abulafia.
Yakhin u-Vo'az, Resp. by Ẓemaḥ b. Solomon *Duran.
Yam ha-Gadol, Resp. by Jacob Moses *Toledano.
Yam shel Shelomo, Compilation arranged acc. to Talmud by Solomon b. Jehiel (Maharshal) *Luria.
Yashar, Sefer ha-, by *Tam, Jacob b. Meir (Rabbenu Tam); 1st pt.: Resp.; 2nd pt.: Nov.
Yaskil Avdi, Resp. by Obadiah Hadaya (printed together with his Resp. *De'ah ve-Haskel).*
Yaveẓ = Jacob *Emden.
Yehudah Ya'aleh, Resp. by Judah b. Israel *Aszod.
Yekar Tiferet, Comm. to Maimonides' *Yad Ḥazakah,*by David b. Solomon ibn Zimra, printed in most editions of *Yad Ḥazakah.*
Yere'im [ha-Shalem], [Sefer], Treatise on precepts by *Eliezer b. Samuel of Metz.
Yeshu'ot Ya'akov, Resp. by Jacob Meshullam b. Mordecai Ze'ev *Ornstein.
Yiẓhak Rei'aḥ, Resp. by Isaac b. Samuel Abendanan (see article *Abendanam Family).
Ẓafenat Pa'ne'aḥ (1), also called *Raban* or *Even ha-Ezer,* see under the last name.
Ẓafenat Pa'ne'aḥ (2), Resp. by Joseph *Rozin.
Zayit Ra'anan, Resp. by Moses Judah Leib b. Benjamin Auerbach.
Ẓeidah la-Derekh, Codification by *Menahem b. Aaron ibn Zerah.
Ẓedakah u-Mishpat, Resp. by Ẓedakah b. Saadiah Huẓin.
Zekan Aharon, Resp. by Elijah b. Benjamin ha-Levi.
Zekher Ẓaddik, Sermons by Eliezer *Katzenellenbogen.
Ẓemaḥ Ẓedek (1) Resp. by Menaham Mendel Shneersohn (see under *Shneersohn Family).
Zera Avraham, Resp. by Abraham b. David *Yiẓḥaki.
Zera Emet Resp. by *Ishmael b. Abaham Isaac ha-Kohen.
Ẓevi la-Ẓaddik, Resp. by Ẓevi Elimelech b. David Shapira.
Zikhron Yehudah, Resp. by *Judah b. Asher
Zikhron Yosef, Resp. by Joseph b. Menahem *Steinhardt.
Zikhronot, Sefer ha-, Sermons on several precepts by Samuel *Aboab.
Zikkaron la-Rishonim . . ., by Albert (Abraham Elijah) *Harkavy; contains in vol. 1 pt. 4 (1887) a collection of Geonic responsa.
Ẓiẓ Eliezer, Resp. by Eliezer Judah b. Jacob Gedaliah Waldenberg.

BIBLIOGRAPHICAL ABBREVIATIONS

Bibliographies in English and other languages have been extensively updated, with English translations cited where available. In order to help the reader, the language of books or articles is given where not obvious from titles of books or names of periodicals. Titles of books and periodicals in languages with alphabets other than Latin, are given in transliteration, even where there is a title page in English. Titles of articles in periodicals are not given. Names of Hebrew and Yiddish periodicals well known in English-speaking countries or in Israel under their masthead in Latin characters are given in this form, even when contrary to transliteration rules. Names of authors writing in languages with non-Latin alphabets are given in their Latin alphabet form wherever known; otherwise the names are transliterated. Initials are generally not given for authors of articles in periodicals, except to avoid confusion. Non-abbreviated book titles and names of periodicals are printed in *italics.* Abbreviations are given in the list below.

AASOR	*Annual of the American School of Oriental Research* (1919ff.).
AB	*Analecta Biblica* (1952ff.).
Abel, Géog	F.-M. Abel, *Géographie de la Palestine,* 2 vols. (1933-38).
ABR	*Australian Biblical Review* (1951ff.).
Abr.	Philo, *De Abrahamo.*
Abrahams, Companion	I. Abrahams, *Companion to the Authorised Daily Prayer Book* (rev. ed. 1922).
Abramson, Merkazim	S. Abramson, *Ba-Merkazim u-va-Tefuẓot bi-Tekufat ha-Ge'onim* (1965).
Acts	Acts of the Apostles (New Testament).
ACUM	*Who is who in ACUM [Aguddat Kompozitorim u-Meḥabbrim].*
ADAJ	*Annual of the Department of Antiquities, Jordan* (1951ff.).
Adam	Adam and Eve (Pseudepigrapha).
ADB	*Allgemeine Deutsche Biographie,* 56 vols. (1875–1912).
Add. Esth.	The Addition to Esther (Apocrypha).
Adler, Prat Mus	I. Adler, *La pratique musicale savante dans quelques communautés juives en Europe au XVIIe et XVIIIe siècles,* 2 vols. (1966).
Adler-Davis	H.M. Adler and A. Davis (ed. and tr.), *Service of the Synagogue, a New Edition of the Festival Prayers with an English Translation in Prose and Verse,* 6 vols. (1905–06).
Aet.	Philo, *De Aeternitate Mundi.*
AFO	*Archiv fuer Orientforschung* (first two volumes under the name *Archiv fuer Keilschriftforschung)* (1923ff.).
Ag. Ber	*Aggadat Bereshit* (ed. Buber, 1902).
Agr.	Philo, *De Agricultura.*
Ag. Sam.	*Aggadat Samuel.*
Ag. Song	*Aggadat Shir ha-Shirim* (Schechter ed., 1896).
Aharoni, Ereẓ	Y. Aharoni, *Ereẓ Yisrael bi-Tekufat ha-Mikra: Geografyah Historit* (1962).
Aharoni, Land	Y. Aharoni, *Land of the Bible* (1966).

Ahikar — Ahikar (Pseudepigrapha).
AI — *Archives Israélites de France* (1840–1936).
AJA — *American Jewish Archives* (1948ff.).
AJHSP — *American Jewish Historical Society – Publications* (after vol. 50 = AJHSQ).
AJHSQ — *American Jewish Historical (*Society) *Quarterly* (before vol. 50 =AJHSP).
AJSLL — *American Journal of Semitic Languages and Literature* (1884–95 under the title *Hebraica,* since 1942 JNES).
AJYB — *American Jewish Year Book* (1899ff.).
AKM — Abhandlungen fuer die Kunde des Morgenlandes (series).
Albright, Arch — W.F. Albright, *Archaeology of Palestine* (rev. ed. 1960).
Albright, Arch Bib — W.F. Albright, *Archaeology of Palestine and the Bible* (1935^3).
Albright, Arch Rel — W.F. Albright, *Archaeology and the Religion of Israel* (1953^3).
Albright, Stone — W.F. Albright, *From the Stone Age to Christianity* (1957^2).
Alon, Meḥkarim — G. Alon, *Meḥkarim be-Toledot Yisrael bi-Ymei Bayit Sheni u-vi-Tekufat ha-Mishnah ve-ha Talmud,* 2 vols. (1957–58).
Alon, Toledot — G. Alon, *Toledot ha-Yehudim be-Ereẓ Yisrael bi-Tekufat ha-Mishnah ve-ha-Talmud,* I (1958^3), (1961^2).
ALOR — Alter Orient (series).
Alt, Kl Schr — A. Alt, *Kleine Schriften zur Geschichte des Volkes Israel,* 3 vols. (1953–59).
Alt, Landnahme — A. Alt, *Landnahme der Israeliten in Palaestina* (1925); also in Alt, Kl Schr, 1 (1953), 89–125.
Ant. — Josephus, *Jewish Antiquities* (Loeb Classics ed.).
AO — *Acta Orientalia* (1922ff.).
AOR — *Analecta Orientalia* (1931ff.).
AOS — American Oriental Series.
Apion — Josephus, *Against Apion* (Loeb Classics ed.).
Aq. — Aquila's Greek translation of the Bible.
Ar. — *Arakhin* (talmudic tractate).
Artist. — Letter of Aristeas (Pseudepigrapha).
ARN[1] — *Avot de-Rabbi Nathan,* version (1) ed. Schechter, 1887.
ARN[2] — *Avot de-Rabbi Nathan,* version (2) ed. Schechter, 1945^2.
Aronius, Regesten — I. Aronius, *Regesten zur Geschichte der Juden im fraenkischen und deutschen Reiche bis zum Jahre 1273* (1902).
ARW — *Archiv fuer Religionswissenschaft* (1898–1941/42).
AS — *Assyrological Studies* (1931ff.).
Ashtor, Korot — E. Ashtor (Strauss), *Korot ha-Yehudim bi-Sefarad ha-Muslemit,* 1(1966^2), 2(1966).
Ashtor, Toledot — E. Ashtor (Strauss), *Toledot ha-Yehudim be-Miẓrayim ve-Suryah Taḥat Shilton ha-Mamlukim,* 3 vols. (1944–70).
Assaf, Ge'onim — S. Assaf, *Tekufat ha-Ge'onim ve-Sifrutah* (1955).
Assaf, Mekorot — S. Assaf, *Mekorot le-Toledot ha-Ḥinnukh be-Yisrael,* 4 vols. (1925–43).
Ass. Mos. — Assumption of Moses (Pseudepigrapha).
ATA — Alttestamentliche Abhandlungen (series).
ATANT — Abhandlungen zur Theologie des Alten und Neuen Testaments (series).
AUJW — *Allgemeine unabhaengige juedische Wochenzeitung* (till 1966 = AWJD).
AV — Authorized Version of the Bible.
Avad. — *Avadim* (post-talmudic tractate).
Avi-Yonah, Geog — M. Avi-Yonah, *Geografyah Historit shel Ereẓ Yisrael* (1962^3).
Avi-Yonah, Land — M. Avi-Yonah, *The Holy Land from the Persian to the Arab conquest (536 B.C. to A.D. 640)* (1960).
Avot — *Avot* (talmudic tractate).
Av. Zar. — *Avodah Zarah* (talmudic tractate).
AWJD — *Allgemeine Wochenzeitung der Juden in Deutschland* (since 1967 = AUJW).
AZDJ — *Allgemeine Zeitung des Judentums.*
Azulai — Ḥ.Y.D. Azulai, *Shem ha-Gedolim,* ed. by I.E. Benjacob, 2 pts. (1852) (and other editions).

BA — *Biblical Archaeologist* (1938ff.).
Bacher, Bab Amor — W. Bacher, *Agada der babylonischen Amoraeer* (1913^2).
Bacher, Pal Amor — W. Bacher, *Agada der palaestinensischen Amoraeer* (Heb. ed. *Aggadat Amora'ei Ereẓ Yisrael),* 2 vols. (1892–99).
Bacher, Tann — W. Bacher, *Agada der Tannaiten* (Heb. ed. *Aggadot ha-Tanna'im,* vol. 1, pt. 1 and 2 (1903); vol. 2 (1890).
Bacher, Trad — W. Bacher, *Tradition und Tradenten in den Schulen Palaestinas und Babyloniens* (1914).
Baer, Spain — Yitzhak (Fritz) Baer, *History of the Jews in Christian Spain,* 2 vols. (1961–66).
Baer, Studien — Yitzhak (Fritz) Baer, *Studien zur Geschichte der Juden im Koenigreich Aragonien waehrend des 13. und 14. Jahrhunderts* (1913).
Baer, Toledot — Yitzhak (Fritz) Baer, *Toledot ha-Yehudim bi-Sefarad ha-Noẓerit mi-Teḥillatan shel ha-Kehillot ad ha-Gerush,* 2 vols. (1959^2).
Baer, Urkunden — Yitzhak (Fritz) Baer, *Die Juden im christlichen Spanien,* 2 vols. (1929–36).
Baer S., Seder — S.I. Baer, *Seder Avodat Yisrael* (1868 and reprints).
BAIU — *Bulletin de l'Alliance Israélite Universelle* (1861–1913).
Baker, Biog Dict — *Baker's Biographical Dictionary of Musicians,* revised by N. Slonimsky (1958^5; with Supplement 1965).
I Bar. — I Baruch (Apocrypha).
II Bar. — II Baruch (Pseudepigrapha).
III Bar. — III Baruch (Pseudepigrapha).
BAR — *Biblical Archaeology Review.*
Baron, Community — S.W. Baron, *The Jewish Community, its History and Structure to the American Revolution,* 3 vols. (1942).

Baron, Social	S.W. Baron, *Social and Religious History of the Jews,* 3 vols. (1937); enlarged, 1-2(1952^{2}), 3-14 (1957–69).
Barthélemy-Milik	D. Barthélemy and J.T. Milik, *Dead Sea Scrolls: Discoveries in the Judean Desert,* vol. 1 *Qumram Cave* I (1955).
BASOR	*Bulletin of the American School of Oriental Research.*
Bauer-Leander	H. Bauer and P. Leander, *Grammatik des Biblisch-Aramaeischen* (1927; repr. 1962).
BB	(1) *Bava Batra* (talmudic tractate). (2) *Biblische Beitraege* (1943ff.).
BBB	Bonner biblische Beitraege (series).
BBLA	*Beitraege zur biblischen Landes- und Altertumskunde* (until 1949–ZDPV).
BBSAJ	*Bulletin,* British School of Archaeology, Jerusalem (1922–25; after 1927 included in PEFQS).
BDASI	*Alon* (since 1948) or *Hadashot Arkheʾologiyyot* (since 1961), bulletin of the Department of Antiquities of the State of Israel.
Begrich, Chronologie	J. Begrich, *Chronologie der Koenige von Israel und Juda* (1929).
Bek.	*Bekhorot* (talmudic tractate).
Bel	Bel and the Dragon (Apocrypha).
Benjacob, Oẓar	I.E. Benjacob, *Oẓar ha-Sefarim* (1880; repr. 1956).
Ben Sira	see Ecclus.
Ben-Yehuda, Millon	E. Ben-Yedhuda, *Millon ha-Lashon ha-Ivrit,* 16 vols (1908–59; repr. in 8 vols., 1959).
Benzinger, Archaeologie	I. Benzinger, *Hebraeische Archaeologie* (1927^{3}).
Ben Zvi, Eretz Israel	I. Ben-Zvi, *Eretz Israel under Ottoman Rule* (1960; offprint from L. Finkelstein (ed.), *The Jews, their History, Culture and Religion* (vol. 1).
Ben Zvi, Ereẓ Israel	I. Ben-Zvi, *Ereẓ Israel bi-Ymei ha-Shilton ha-Ottomani (1955).*
Ber.	*Berakhot* (talmudic tractate).
Beẓah	*Beẓah* (talmudic tractate).
BIES	Bulletin of the Israel Exploration Society, see below BJPES.
Bik.	*Bikkurim* (talmudic tractate).
BJCE	Bibliography of Jewish Communities in Europe, catalog at General Archives for the History of the Jewish People, Jerusalem.
BJPES	Bulletin of the Jewish Palestine Exploration Society – English name of the Hebrew periodical known as: 1. *Yediʿot ha-Ḥevrah ha-Ivrit la-Ḥakirat Ereẓ Yisrael va-Attikoteha* (1933–1954); 2. *Yediʿot ha-Ḥevrah la-Ḥakirat Ereẓ Yisrael va-Attikoteha* (1954–1962); 3. *Yediʿot ba-Ḥakirat Ereẓ Yisrael va-Attikoteha* (1962ff.).
BJRL	*Bulletin of the John Rylands Library* (1914ff.).
BK	*Bava Kamma* (talmudic tractate).
BLBI	*Bulletin of the Leo Baeck Institute* (1957ff.).
BM	(1) *Bava Meẓia* (talmudic tractate). (2) *Beit Mikra* (1955/56ff.). (3) British Museum.
BO	*Bibbia e Oriente* (1959ff.).
Bondy-Dworský	G. Bondy and F. Dworský, *Regesten zur Geschichte der Juden in Boehmen, Maehren und Schlesien von 906 bis 1620,* 2 vols. (1906).
BOR	*Bibliotheca Orientalis* (1943ff.).
Borée, Ortsnamen	W. Borée *Die alten Ortsnamen Palaestinas* (1930).
Bousset, Religion	W. Bousset, *Die Religion des Judentums im neutestamentlichen Zeitalter* (1906^{2}).
Bousset-Gressmann	W. Bousset, *Die Religion des Judentums im spaethellenistischen Zeitalter* (1966^{3}).
BR	*Biblical Review* (1916–25).
BRCI	*Bulletin of the Research Council of Israel* (1951/52–1954/55; then divided).
BRE	*Biblical Research* (1956ff.).
BRF	*Bulletin of the Rabinowitz Fund for the Exploration of Ancient Synagogues* (1949ff.).
Briggs, Psalms	Ch. A. and E.G. Briggs, *Critical and Exegetical Commentary on the Book of Psalms,* 2 vols. (ICC, 1906–07).
Bright, Hist	J. Bright, *A History of Israel* (1959).
Brockelmann, Arab Lit	K. Brockelmann, *Geschichte der arabischen Literatur,* 2 vols. 1898–1902), supplement, 3 vols. (1937–42).
Bruell, Jahrbuecher	*Jahrbuecher fuer juedische Geschichte und Litteratur,* ed. by N. Bruell, Frankfurt (1874–90).
Brugmans-Frank	H. Brugmans and A. Frank (eds.), *Geschiedenis der Joden in Nederland* (1940).
BTS	*Bible et Terre Sainte* (1958ff.).
Bull, Index	S. Bull, *Index to Biographies of Contemporary Composers* (1964).
BW	*Biblical World* (1882–1920).
BWANT	*Beitraege zur Wissenschaft vom Alten und Neuen Testament* (1926ff.).
BZ	*Biblische Zeitschrift* (1903ff.).
BZAW	*Beihefte zur Zeitschrift fuer die alttestamentliche Wissenschaft,* supplement to ZAW (1896ff.).
BŻIH	*Biuletyn Zydowskiego Instytutu Historycznego* (1950ff.).
CAB	*Cahiers d'archéologie biblique* (1953ff.).
CAD	*The [Chicago] Assyrian Dictionary* (1956ff.).
CAH	*Cambridge Ancient History,* 12 vols. (1923–39)
CAH^{2}	*Cambridge Ancient History,* second edition, 14 vols. (1962–2005).
Calwer, Lexikon	*Calwer, Bibellexikon.*
Cant.	Canticles, usually given as Song (= Song of Songs).

Cantera-Millás, Inscripciones — F. Cantera and J.M. Millás, *Las Inscripciones Hebraicas de España* (1956).
CBQ — *Catholic Biblical Quarterly* (1939ff.).
CCARY — Central Conference of American Rabbis, *Yearbook* (1890/91ff.).
CD — *Damascus Document* from the Cairo *Genizah* (published by S. Schechter, *Fragments of a Zadokite Work*, 1910).
Charles, Apocrypha — R.H. Charles, *Apocrypha and Pseudepigrapha . . .*, 2 vols. (1913; repr. 1963–66).
Cher. — Philo, *De Cherubim*.
I (or II) Chron. — Chronicles, book I and II (Bible).
CIG — *Corpus Inscriptionum Graecarum*.
CIJ — *Corpus Inscriptionum Judaicarum*, 2 vols. (1936–52).
CIL — *Corpus Inscriptionum Latinarum*.
CIS — *Corpus Inscriptionum Semiticarum* (1881ff.).
C.J. — Codex Justinianus.
Clermont-Ganneau, Arch — Ch. Clermont-Ganneau, *Archaeological Researches in Palestine*, 2 vols. (1896–99).
CNFI — *Christian News from Israel* (1949ff.).
Cod. Just. — Codex Justinianus.
Cod. Theod. — Codex Theodosinanus.
Col. — Epistle to the Colosssians (New Testament).
Conder, Survey — Palestine Exploration Fund, *Survey of Eastern Palestine*, vol. 1, pt. I (1889) = C.R. Conder, *Memoirs of the . . . Survey*.
Conder-Kitchener — Palestine Exploration Fund, *Survey of Western Palestine*, vol. 1, pts. 1-3 (1881–83) = C.R. Conder and H.H. Kitchener, *Memoirs*.
Conf. — Philo, *De Confusione Linguarum*.
Conforte, Kore — D. Conforte, *Kore ha-Dorot* (1842^2).
Cong. — Philo, *De Congressu Quaerendae Eruditionis Gratia*.
Cont. — Philo, *De Vita Contemplativa*.
I (or II) Cor. — Epistles to the Corinthians (New Testament).
Cowley, Aramic — A. Cowley, *Aramaic Papyri of the Fifth Century B.C.* (1923).
Colwey, Cat — A.E. Cowley, *A Concise Catalogue of the Hebrew Printed Books in the Bodleian Library* (1929).
CRB — *Cahiers de la Revue Biblique* (1964ff.).
Crowfoot-Kenyon — J.W. Crowfoot, K.M. Kenyon and E.L. Sukenik, *Buildings of Samaria* (1942).
C.T. — Codex Theodosianus.

DAB — *Dictionary of American Biography* (1928–58).
Daiches, Jews — S. Daiches, *Jews in Babylonia* (1910).
Dalman, Arbeit — G. Dalman, *Arbeit und Sitte in Palaestina*, 7 vols.in 8 (1928–42 repr. 1964).
Dan — Daniel (Bible).
Davidson, Oẓar — I. Davidson, *Oẓar ha-Shirah ve-ha-Piyyut*, 4 vols. (1924–33); Supplement in: HUCA, 12–13 (1937/38), 715–823.
DB — J. Hastings, *Dictionary of the Bible*, 4 vols. (1963^2).
DBI — F.G. Vigoureaux et al. (eds.), *Dictionnaire de la Bible*, 5 vols. in 10 (1912); Supplement, 8 vols. (1928–66)
Decal. — Philo, *De Decalogo*.
Dem. — *Demai* (talmudic tractate).
DER — *Derekh Ereẓ Rabbah* (post-talmudic tractate).
Derenbourg, Hist — J. Derenbourg *Essai sur l'histoire et la géographie de la Palestine* (1867).
Det. — Philo, *Quod deterius potiori insidiari solet*.
Deus — Philo, *Quod Deus immutabilis sit*.
Deut. — Deuteronomy (Bible).
Deut. R. — *Deuteronomy Rabbah*.
DEZ — *Derekh Ereẓ Zuta* (post-talmudic tractate).
DHGE — *Dictionnaire d'histoire et de géographie ecclésiastiques*, ed. by A. Baudrillart et al., 17 vols (1912–68).
Dik. Sof — *Dikdukei Soferim*, variae lections of the talmudic text by Raphael Nathan Rabbinovitz (16 vols., 1867–97).
Dinur, Golah — B. Dinur (Dinaburg), *Yisrael ba-Golah*, 2 vols. in 7 (1959–68) = vols. 5 and 6 of his *Toledot Yisrael*, second series.
Dinur, Haganah — B. Dinur (ed.), *Sefer Toledot ha-Haganah* (1954ff.).
Diringer, Iscr — D. Diringer, *Iscrizioni antico-ebraiche palestinesi* (1934).
Discoveries — *Discoveries in the Judean Desert* (1955ff.).
DNB — *Dictionary of National Biography*, 66 vols. (1921–222) with Supplements.
Dubnow, Divrei — S. Dubnow, *Divrei Yemei Am Olam*, 11 vols (1923–38 and further editions).
Dubnow, Ḥasidut — S. Dubnow, *Toledot ha-Ḥasidut* (1960^2).
Dubnow, Hist — S. Dubnow, *History of the Jews* (1967).
Dubnow, Hist Russ — S. Dubnow, *History of the Jews in Russia and Poland*, 3 vols. (1916 20).
Dubnow, Outline — S. Dubnow, *An Outline of Jewish History*, 3 vols. (1925–29).
Dubnow, Weltgesch — S. Dubnow, *Weltgeschichte des juedischen Volkes* 10 vols. (1925–29).
Dukes, Poesie — L. Dukes, *Zur Kenntnis der neuhebraeischen religioesen Poesie* (1842).
Dunlop, Khazars — D. H. Dunlop, *History of the Jewish Khazars* (1954).

EA — El Amarna Letters (edited by J.A. Knudtzon), *Die El-Amarna Tafel*, 2 vols. (1907 14).
EB — *Encyclopaedia Britannica*.
EBI — *Estudios biblicos* (1941ff.).
EBIB — T.K. Cheyne and J.S. Black, *Encyclopaedia Biblica*, 4 vols. (1899–1903).
Ebr. — Philo, *De Ebrietate*.
Eccles. — Ecclesiastes (Bible).
Eccles. R. — *Ecclesiastes Rabbah*.
Ecclus. — Ecclesiasticus or Wisdom of Ben Sira (or Sirach; Apocrypha).
Eduy. — *Eduyyot* (mishanic tractate).

EG	*Enziklopedyah shel Galuyyot* (1953ff.).
EH	*Even ha-Ezer.*
EHA	*Enziklopedyah la-Ḥafirot Arkheologiyyot be-Ereẓ Yisrael,* 2 vols. (1970).
EI	*Enzyklopaedie des Islams,* 4 vols. (1905–14). Supplement vol. (1938).
EIS	*Encyclopaedia of Islam,* 4 vols. (1913–36; repr. 1954–68).
EIS^{2}	*Encyclopaedia of Islam, second edition (1960–2000).*
Eisenstein, Dinim	J.D. Eisenstein, *Oẓar Dinim u-Minhagim* (1917; several reprints).
Eisenstein, Yisrael	J.D. Eisenstein, *Oẓar Yisrael* (10 vols, 1907–13; repr. with several additions 1951).
EIV	*Enziklopedyah Ivrit* (1949ff.).
EJ	*Encyclopaedia Judaica* (German, A-L only), 10 vols. (1928–34).
EJC	*Enciclopedia Judaica Castellana,* 10 vols. (1948–51).
Elbogen, Century	I Elbogen, *A Century of Jewish Life* (1960^{2}).
Elbogen, Gottesdienst	I Elbogen, *Der juedische Gottesdienst ...* (1931^{3}, repr. 1962).
Elon, Mafte'aḥ	M. Elon (ed.), *Mafte'aḥ ha-She'elot ve-ha-Teshuvot ha-Rosh* (1965).
EM	*Enziklopedyah Mikra'it* (1950ff.).
I (or II) En.	I and II Enoch (Pseudepigrapha).
EncRel	*Encyclopedia of Religion*, 15 vols. (1987, 2005^{2}).
Eph.	Epistle to the Ephesians (New Testament).
Ephros, Cant	G. Ephros, *Cantorial Anthology,* 5 vols. (1929–57).
Ep. Jer.	Epistle of Jeremy (Apocrypha).
Epstein, Amora'im	J N. Epstein, *Mevo'ot le-Sifrut ha-Amora'im* (1962).
Epstein, Marriage	L M. Epstein, *Marriage Laws in the Bible and the Talmud* (1942).
Epstein, Mishnah	J. N. Epstein, *Mavo le-Nusaḥ ha-Mishnah,* 2 vols. (1964^{2}).
Epstein, Tanna'im	J. N. Epstein, *Mavo le-Sifruth ha-Tanna'im.* (1947).
ER	*Ecumenical Review.*
Er.	*Eruvin* (talmudic tractate).
ERE	*Encyclopaedia of Religion and Ethics,* 13 vols. (1908–26); reprinted.
ErIsr	*Eretz-Israel,* Israel Exploration Society.
I Esd.	I Esdras (Apocrypha) (= III Ezra).
II Esd.	II Esdras (Apocrypha) (= IV Ezra).
ESE	*Ephemeris fuer semitische Epigraphik,* ed. by M. Lidzbarski.
ESN	*Encyclopaedia Sefaradica Neerlandica,* 2 pts. (1949).
ESS	*Encyclopaedia of the Social Sciences,* 15 vols. (1930–35); reprinted in 8 vols. (1948–49).
Esth.	Esther (Bible).
Est. R.	*Esther Rabbah.*
ET	*Enziklopedyah Talmudit* (1947ff.).
Eusebius, Onom.	E. Klostermann (ed.), *Das Onomastikon* (1904), Greek with Hieronymus' Latin translation.
Ex.	Exodus (Bible).
Ex. R.	*Exodus Rabbah.*
Exs	Philo, *De Exsecrationibus.*
EẒD	*Enziklopeday shel ha-Ẓiyyonut ha-Datit* (1951ff.).
Ezek.	Ezekiel (Bible).
Ezra	Ezra (Bible).
III Ezra	III Ezra (Pseudepigrapha).
IV Ezra	IV Ezra (Pseudepigrapha).
Feliks, Ha-Ẓome'aḥ	*J. Feliks, Ha-Ẓome'aḥ ve-ha-Ḥai ba-Mishnah* (1983).
Finkelstein, Middle Ages	L. Finkelstein, *Jewish Self-Government in the Middle Ages* (1924).
Fischel, Islam	W.J. Fischel, *Jews in the Economic and Political Life of Mediaeval Islam* (1937; reprint with introduction "The Court Jew in the Islamic World," 1969).
FJW	*Fuehrer durch die juedische Gemeindeverwaltung und Wohlfahrtspflege in Deutschland* (1927/28).
Frankel, Mevo	Z. Frankel, *Mevo ha-Yerushalmi* (1870; reprint 1967).
Frankel, Mishnah	Z. Frankel, *Darkhei ha-Mishnah* (1959^{2}; reprint 1959^{2}).
Frazer, Folk-Lore	J.G. Frazer, *Folk-Lore in the Old Testament,* 3 vols. (1918–19).
Frey, Corpus	J.-B. Frey, *Corpus Inscriptionum Iudaicarum,* 2 vols. (1936–52).
Friedmann, Lebensbilder	A. Friedmann, *Lebensbilder beruehmter Kantoren,* 3 vols. (1918–27).
FRLT	*Forschungen zur Religion und Literatur des Alten und Neuen Testaments* (series) (1950ff.).
Frumkin-Rivlin	A.L. Frumkin and E. Rivlin, *Toledot Ḥakhmei Yerushalayim,* 3 vols. (1928–30), Supplement vol. (1930).
Fuenn, Keneset	S.J. Fuenn, *Keneset Yisrael,* 4 vols. (1887–90).
Fuerst, Bibliotheca	J. Fuerst, *Bibliotheca Judaica,* 2 vols. (1863; repr. 1960).
Fuerst, Karaeertum	J. Fuerst, *Geschichte des Karaeertums,* 3 vols. (1862–69).
Fug.	Philo, *De Fuga et Inventione.*
Gal.	Epistle to the Galatians (New Testament).
Galling, Reallexikon	K. Galling, *Biblisches Reallexikon* (1937).
Gardiner, Onomastica	A.H. Gardiner, *Ancient Egyptian Onomastica,* 3 vols. (1947).
Geiger, Mikra	A. Geiger, *Ha-Mikra ve-Targumav*, tr. by J.L. Baruch (1949).
Geiger, Urschrift	A. Geiger, *Urschrift und Uebersetzungen der Bibel* 1928^{2}).
Gen.	Genesis (Bible).
Gen. R.	*Genesis Rabbah.*
Ger.	*Gerim* (post-talmudic tractate).
Germ Jud	M. Brann, I. Elbogen, A. Freimann, and H. Tykocinski (eds.), *Germania Judaica,* vol. 1 (1917; repr. 1934 and 1963); vol. 2, in 2 pts. (1917–68), ed. by Z. Avneri.

GHAT	*Goettinger Handkommentar zum Alten Testament* (1917–22).
Ghirondi-Neppi	M.S. Ghirondi and G.H. Neppi, *Toledot Gedolei Yisrael u-Ge'onei Italyah ... u-Ve'urim al Sefer Zekher Ẓaddikim li-Verakhah . . .*(1853), index in ZHB, 17 (1914), 171–83.
Gig.	Philo, *De Gigantibus.*
Ginzberg, Legends	L. Ginzberg, *Legends of the Jews,* 7 vols. (1909–38; and many reprints).
Git.	*Gittin* (talmudic tractate).
Glueck, Explorations	N. Glueck, *Explorations in Eastern Palestine,* 2 vols. (1951).
Goell, Bibliography	Y. Goell, *Bibliography of Modern Hebrew Literature in English Translation* (1968).
Goodenough, Symbols	E.R. Goodenough, *Jewish Symbols in the Greco-Roman Period,* 13 vols. (1953–68).
Gordon, Textbook	C.H. Gordon, *Ugaritic Textbook* (1965; repr. 1967).
Graetz, Gesch	H. Graetz, *Geschichte der Juden* (last edition 1874–1908).
Graetz, Hist	H. Graetz, *History of the Jews*, 6 vols. (1891–1902).
Graetz, Psalmen	H. Graetz, *Kritischer Commentar zu den Psalmen*, 2 vols. in 1 (1882–83).
Graetz, Rabbinowitz	H. Graetz, *Divrei Yemei Yisrael*, tr. by S.P. Rabbinowitz. (1928 1929²).
Gray, Names	G.B. Gray, *Studies in Hebrew Proper Names* (1896).
Gressmann, Bilder	H. Gressmann, *Altorientalische Bilder zum Alten Testament* (1927²).
Gressmann, Texte	H. Gressmann, *Altorientalische Texte zum Alten Testament* (1926²).
Gross, Gal Jud	H. Gross, *Gallia Judaica* (1897; repr. with add. 1969).
Grove, Dict	*Grove's Dictionary of Music and Musicians,* ed. by E. Blum 9 vols. (1954⁵) and suppl. (1961⁵).
Guedemann, Gesch Erz	M. Guedemann, *Geschichte des Erziehungswesens und der Cultur der abendlaendischen Juden,* 3 vols. (1880–88).
Guedemann, Quellenschr	M. Guedemann, *Quellenschriften zur Geschichte des Unterrichts und der Erziehung bei den deutschen Juden* (1873, 1891).
Guide	Maimonides, *Guide of the Perplexed.*
Gulak, Oẓar	A. Gulak, *Oẓar ha-Shetarot ha-Nehugim be-Yisrael* (1926).
Gulak, Yesodei	A. Gulak, *Yesodei ha-Mishpat ha-Ivri, Seder Dinei Mamonot be-Yisrael, al pi Mekorot ha-Talmud ve-ha-Posekim*, 4 vols. (1922; repr. 1967).
Guttmann, Mafte'aḥ	M. Guttmann, *Mafte'aḥ ha-Talmud*, 3 vols. (1906–30).
Guttmann, Philosophies	J. Guttmann, *Philosophies of Judaism* (1964).
Hab.	*Habakkuk* (Bible).
Ḥag.	*Ḥagigah* (talmudic tractate).
Haggai	*Haggai* (Bible).
Ḥal.	*Ḥallah* (talmudic tractate).
Halevy, Dorot	I. Halevy, *Dorot ha-Rishonim,* 6 vols. (1897–1939).
Halpern, Pinkas	I. Halpern (Halperin), *Pinkas Va'ad Arba Araẓot* (1945).
Hananel-Eškenazi	A. Hananel and Eškenazi (eds.), *Fontes Hebraici ad res oeconomicas socialesque terrarum balcanicarum saeculo XVI pertinentes*, 2 vols, (1958–60; in Bulgarian).
HB	*Hebraeische Bibliographie* (1858–82).
Heb.	Epistle to the Hebrews (New Testament).
Heilprin, Dorot	J. Heilprin (Heilperin), *Seder ha-Dorot,* 3 vols. (1882; repr. 1956).
Her.	Philo, *Quis Rerum Divinarum Heres.*
Hertz, Prayer	J.H. Hertz (ed.), *Authorised Daily Prayer Book* (rev. ed. 1948; repr. 1963).
Herzog, Instit	I. Herzog, *The Main Institutions of Jewish Law,* 2 vols. (1936–39; repr. 1967).
Herzog-Hauck	J.J. Herzog and A. Hauch (eds.), *Real-encyklopaedie fuer protestantische Theologie* (1896–1913³).
HḤY	*Ha-Ẓofeh le-Ḥokhmat Yisrael* (first four volumes under the title *Ha-Ẓofeh me-Ereẓ Hagar)* (1910/11–13).
Hirschberg, Afrikah	H.Z. Hirschberg, *Toledot ha-Yehudim be-Afrikah ha-Zofonit*, 2 vols. (1965).
HJ	*Historia Judaica* (1938–61).
HL	*Das Heilige Land* (1857ff.)
ḤM	*Ḥoshen Mishpat.*
Hommel, Ueberliefer.	F. Hommel, *Die altisraelitische Ueberlieferung in inschriftlicher Beleuchtung* (1897).
Hor.	*Horayot* (talmudic tractate).
Horodezky, Ḥasidut	S.A. Horodezky, *Ha-Ḥasidut ve-ha-Ḥasidim,* 4 vols. (1923).
Horowitz, Ereẓ Yis	I.W. Horowitz, *Ereẓ Yisrael u-Shekhenoteha* (1923).
Hos.	Hosea (Bible).
HTR	*Harvard Theological Review* (1908ff.).
HUCA	*Hebrew Union College Annual* (1904; 1924ff.)
Ḥul.	*Ḥullin* (talmudic tractate).
Husik, Philosophy	I. Husik, *History of Medieval Jewish Philosophy* (1932²).
Hyman, Toledot	A. Hyman, *Toledot Tanna'im ve-Amora'im* (1910; repr. 1964).
Ibn Daud, Tradition	Abraham Ibn Daud, *Sefer ha-Qabbalah – The Book of Tradition,* ed. and tr. By G.D. Cohen (1967).
ICC	International Critical Commentary on the Holy Scriptures of the Old and New Testaments (series, 1908ff.).
IDB	*Interpreter's Dictionary of the Bible,* 4 vols. (1962).
Idelsohn, Litugy	A. Z. Idelsohn, *Jewish Liturgy and its Development* (1932; paperback repr. 1967)
Idelsohn, Melodien	A. Z. Idelsohn, *Hebraeisch-orientalischer Melodienschatz,* 10 vols. (1914 32).
Idelsohn, Music	A. Z. Idelsohn, *Jewish Music in its Historical Development* (1929; paperback repr. 1967).

IEJ — *Israel Exploration Journal* (1950ff.).
IESS — *International Encyclopedia of the Social Sciences* (various eds.).
IG — *Inscriptiones Graecae,* ed. by the Prussian Academy.
IGYB — *Israel Government Year Book* (1949/50ff.).
ILR — *Israel Law Review* (1966ff.).
IMIT — *Izraelita Magyar Irodalmi Társulat Évkönyv* (1895 1948).
IMT — International Military Tribunal.
INB — *Israel Numismatic Bulletin* (1962–63).
INJ — *Israel Numismatic Journal* (1963ff.).
Ios — Philo, *De Iosepho.*
Isa. — Isaiah (Bible).
ITHL — Institute for the Translation of Hebrew Literature.
IZBG — *Internationale Zeitschriftenschau fuer Bibelwissenschaft und Grenzgebiete* (1951ff.).

JA — *Journal asiatique* (1822ff.).
James — Epistle of James (New Testament).
JAOS — *Journal of the American Oriental Society* (c. 1850ff.)
Jastrow, Dict — M. Jastrow, *Dictionary of the Targumim, the Talmud Babli and Yerushalmi, and the Midrashic literature,* 2 vols. (1886 1902 and reprints).
JBA — *Jewish Book Annual* (19242ff.).
JBL — *Journal of Biblical Literature* (1881ff.).
JBR — *Journal of Bible and Religion* (1933ff.).
JC — *Jewish Chronicle* (1841ff.).
JCS — *Journal of Cuneiform Studies* (1947ff.).
JE — *Jewish Encyclopedia,* 12 vols. (1901–05 several reprints).
Jer. — Jeremiah (Bible).
Jeremias, Alte Test — A. Jeremias, *Das Alte Testament im Lichte des alten Orients* 1930[4]).
JGGJČ — *Jahrbuch der Gesellschaft fuer Geschichte der Juden in der Čechoslovakischen Republik* (1929–38).
JHSEM — Jewish Historical Society of England, *Miscellanies* (1925ff.).
JHSET — Jewish Historical Society of England, *Transactions* (1893ff.).
JJGL — *Jahrbuch fuer juedische Geschichte und Literatur* (Berlin) (1898–1938).
JJLG — *Jahrbuch der juedische-literarischen Gesellschaft* (Frankfurt) (1903–32).
JJS — *Journal of Jewish Studies* (1948ff.).
JJSO — *Jewish Journal of Sociology* (1959ff.).
JJV — *Jahrbuch fuer juedische Volkskunde* (1898–1924).
JL — *Juedisches Lexikon,* 5 vols. (1927–30).
JMES — *Journal of the Middle East Society* (1947ff.).
JNES — *Journal of Near Eastern Studies* (continuation of AJSLL) (1942ff.).
J.N.U.L. — Jewish National and University Library.
Job — Job (Bible).
Joel — Joel (Bible).
John — Gospel according to John (New Testament).
I, II and III John — Epistles of John (New Testament).
Jos., Ant — Josephus, *Jewish Antiquities* (Loeb Classics ed.).
Jos. Apion — Josephus, *Against Apion* (Loeb Classics ed.).
Jos., index — *Josephus Works,* Loeb Classics ed., index of names.
Jos., Life — Josephus, *Life* (ed. Loeb Classics).
Jos, Wars — Josephus, *The Jewish Wars* (Loeb Classics ed.).
Josh. — Joshua (Bible).
JPESB — Jewish Palestine Exploration Society Bulletin, see BJPES.
JPESJ — Jewish Palestine Exploration Society Journal – Eng. Title of the Hebrew periodical *Kovez ha-Ḥevrah ha-Ivrit la-Ḥakirat Erez Yisrael va-Attikoteha.*
JPOS — *Journal of the Palestine Oriental Society* (1920–48).
JPS — Jewish Publication Society of America, *The Torah* (1962, 1967[2]); *The Holy Scriptures* (1917).
JQR — *Jewish Quarterly Review* (1889ff.).
JR — *Journal of Religion* (1921ff.).
JRAS — *Journal of the Royal Asiatic Society* (1838ff.).
JHR — *Journal of Religious History* (1960/61ff.).
JSOS — *Jewish Social Studies* (1939ff.).
JSS — *Journal of Semitic Studies* (1956ff.).
JTS — *Journal of Theological Studies* (1900ff.).
JTSA — Jewish Theological Seminary of America (also abbreviated as JTS).
Jub. — Jubilees (Pseudepigrapha).
Judg. — Judges (Bible).
Judith — Book of Judith (Apocrypha).
Juster, Juifs — J. Juster, *Les Juifs dans l'Empire Romain,* 2 vols. (1914).
JYB — *Jewish Year Book* (1896ff.).
JZWL — *Juedische Zeitschift fuer Wissenschaft und Leben* (1862–75).

Kal. — *Kallah* (post-talmudic tractate).
Kal. R. — *Kallah Rabbati* (post-talmudic tractate).
Katz, England — *The Jews in the History of England, 1485-1850 (1994).*
Kaufmann, Schriften — D. Kaufmann, *Gesammelte Schriften,* 3 vols. (1908 15).
Kaufmann Y., Religion — Y. Kaufmann, *The Religion of Israel* (1960), abridged tr. of his *Toledot.*
Kaufmann Y., Toledot — Y. Kaufmann, *Toledot ha-Emunah ha-Yisre'elit,* 4 vols. (1937 57).
KAWJ — *Korrespondenzblatt des Vereins zur Gruendung und Erhaltung der Akademie fuer die Wissenschaft des Judentums* (1920 30).
Kayserling, Bibl — M. Kayserling, *Biblioteca Española-Portugueza-Judaica* (1880; repr. 1961).
Kelim — *Kelim* (mishnaic tractate).
Ker. — *Keritot* (talmudic tractate).
Ket. — *Ketubbot* (talmudic tractate).

Kid.	*Kiddushim* (talmudic tractate).
Kil.	*Kilayim* (talmudic tractate).
Kin.	*Kinnim* (mishnaic tractate).
Kisch, Germany	G. Kisch, *Jews in Medieval Germany* (1949).
Kittel, Gesch	R. Kittel, *Geschichte des Volkes Israel,* 3 vols. (1922–28).
Klausner, Bayit Sheni	J. Klausner, *Historyah shel ha-Bayit ha-Sheni,* 5 vols. (1950/512).
Klausner, Sifrut	J. Klausner, *Historyah shel haSifrut ha-Ivrit ha-Ḥadashah,* 6 vols. (1952–582).
Klein, corpus	S. Klein (ed.), *Juedisch-palaestinisches Corpus Inscriptionum* (1920).
Koehler-Baumgartner	L. Koehler and W. Baumgartner, *Lexicon in Veteris Testamenti libros* (1953).
Kohut, Arukh	H.J.A. Kohut (ed.), *Sefer he-Arukh ha-Shalem,* by Nathan b. Jehiel of Rome, 8 vols. (1876–92; Supplement by S. Krauss et al., 1936; repr. 1955).
Krauss, Tal Arch	S. Krauss, *Talmudische Archaeologie,* 3 vols. (1910–12; repr. 1966).
Kressel, Leksikon	G. Kressel, *Leksikon ha-Sifrut ha-Ivrit ba-Dorot ha-Aḥaronim,* 2 vols. (1965–67).
KS	*Kirjath Sepher* (1923/4ff.).
Kut.	*Kuttim* (post-talmudic tractate).
LA	Studium Biblicum Franciscanum, *Liber Annuus* (1951ff.).
L.A.	Philo, *Legum allegoriae.*
Lachower, Sifrut	F. Lachower, *Toledot ha-Sifrut ha-Ivrit ha-Ḥadashah,* 4 vols. (1947–48; several reprints).
Lam.	Lamentations (Bible).
Lam. R.	*Lamentations Rabbah.*
Landshuth, Ammudei	L. Landshuth, *Ammudei ha-Avodah* (1857–62; repr. with index, 1965).
Legat.	Philo, *De Legatione ad Caium.*
Lehmann, Nova Bibl	R.P. Lehmann, *Nova Bibliotheca Anglo-Judaica* (1961).
Lev.	Leviticus (Bible).
Lev. R.	*Leviticus Rabbah.*
Levy, Antologia	I. Levy, *Antologia de liturgia judeo-española* (1965ff.).
Levy J., Chald Targ	J. Levy, *Chaldaeisches Woerterbuch ueber die Targumim,* 2 vols. (1967–68; repr. 1959).
Levy J., Nuehebr Tal	J. Levy, *Neuhebraeisches und chaldaeisches Woerterbuch ueber die Talmudim . . .,* 4 vols. (1875–89; repr. 1963).
Lewin, Oẓar	Lewin, *Oẓar ha-Ge'onim,* 12 vols. (1928–43).
Lewysohn, Zool	L. Lewysohn, *Zoologie des Talmuds* (1858).
Lidzbarski, Handbuch	M. Lidzbarski, *Handbuch der nordsemitischen Epigraphik,* 2 vols (1898).
Life	Josephus, *Life* (Loeb Classis ed.).
LNYL	*Leksikon fun der Nayer Yidisher Literatur* (1956ff.).
Loew, Flora	I. Loew, *Die Flora der Juden,* 4 vols. (1924 34; repr. 1967).
LSI	*Laws of the State of Israel* (1948ff.).
Luckenbill, Records	D.D. Luckenbill, *Ancient Records of Assyria and Babylonia,* 2 vols. (1926).
Luke	Gospel according to Luke (New Testament)
LXX	Septuagint (Greek translation of the Bible).
Ma'as.	*Ma'aserot* (talmudic tractate).
Ma'as. Sh.	*Ma'ase Sheni* (talmudic tractate).
I, II, III, and IVMacc.	Maccabees, I, II, III (Apocrypha), IV (Pseudepigrapha).
Maimonides, Guide	Maimonides, *Guide of the Perplexed.*
Maim., Yad	Maimonides, *Mishneh Torah (Yad Ḥazakah).*
Maisler, Untersuchungen	B. Maisler (Mazar), *Untersuchungen zur alten Geschichte und Ethnographie Syriens und Palaestinas,* 1 (1930).
Mak.	*Makkot* (talmudic tractate).
Makhsh.	*Makhshrin* (mishnaic tractate).
Mal.	Malachi (Bible).
Mann, Egypt	J. Mann, *Jews in Egypt in Palestine under the Fatimid Caliphs,* 2 vols. (1920–22).
Mann, Texts	J. Mann, *Texts and Studies,* 2 vols (1931–35).
Mansi	G.D. Mansi, *Sacrorum Conciliorum nova et amplissima collectio,* 53 vols. in 60 (1901–27; repr. 1960).
Margalioth, Gedolei	M. Margalioth, *Enẓiklopedyah le-Toledot Gedolei Yisrael,* 4 vols. (1946–50).
Margalioth, Ḥakhmei	M. Margalioth, *Enẓiklopedyah le-Ḥakhmei ha-Talmud ve-ha-Ge'onim,* 2 vols. (1945).
Margalioth, Cat	G. Margalioth, *Catalogue of the Hebrew and Samaritan Manuscripts in the British Museum,* 4 vols. (1899–1935).
Mark	Gospel according to Mark (New Testament).
Mart. Isa.	Martyrdom of Isaiah (Pseudepigrapha).
Mas.	Masorah.
Matt.	Gospel according to Matthew (New Testament).
Mayer, Art	L.A. Mayer, *Bibliography of Jewish Art* (1967).
MB	*Wochenzeitung* (formerly *Mitteilungsblatt*) *des Irgun Olej Merkas Europa* (1933ff.).
MEAH	*Miscelánea de estudios drabes y hebraicos* (1952ff.).
Meg.	Megillah (talmudic tractate).
Meg. Ta'an.	*Megillat Ta'anit* (in HUCA, 8 9 (1931–32), 318–51).
Me'il	*Me'ilah* (mishnaic tractate).
MEJ	*Middle East Journal* (1947ff.).
Mehk.	*Mekhilta de-R. Ishmael.*
Mekh. SbY	*Mekhilta de-R. Simeon bar Yoḥai.*
Men.	*Menaḥot* (talmudic tractate).
MER	*Middle East Record* (1960ff.).
Meyer, Gesch	E. Meyer, *Geschichte des Alterums,* 5 vols. in 9 (1925–58).
Meyer, Ursp	E. Meyer, *Urspring und Anfaenge des Christentums* (1921).
Mez.	*Mezuzah* (post-talmudic tractate).
MGADJ	*Mitteilungen des Gesamtarchivs der deutschen Juden* (1909–12).
MGG	*Die Musik in Geschichte und Gegenwart,* 14 vols. (1949–68).

MGG[2]	*Die Musik in Geschichte und Gegenwart, 2nd edition (1994)*
MGH	*Monumenta Germaniae Historica* (1826ff.).
MGJV	*Mitteilungen der Gesellschaft fuer juedische Volkskunde* (1898–1929); title varies, see also JJV.
MGWJ	*Monatsschrift fuer Geschichte und Wissenschaft des Judentums* (1851–1939).
MHJ	*Monumenta Hungariae Judaica,* 11 vols. (1903–67).
Michael, Or	H.Ḥ. Michael, *Or ha-Ḥayyim: Ḥakhmei Yisrael ve-Sifreihem,* ed. by S.Z. Ḥ. Halberstam and N. Ben-Menahem (1965^2).
Mid.	*Middot* (mishnaic tractate).
Mid. Ag.	*Midrash Aggadah.*
Mid. Hag.	*Midrash ha-Gadol.*
Mid. Job.	*Midrash Job.*
Mid. Jonah	*Midrash Jonah.*
Mid. Lek. Tov	*Midrash Lekaḥ Tov.*
Mid. Prov.	*Midrash Proverbs.*
Mid. Ps.	*Midrash Tehillim* (Eng tr. *The Midrash on Psalms* (JPS, 1959).
Mid. Sam.	*Midrash Samuel.*
Mid. Song	*Midrash Shir ha-Shirim.*
Mid. Tan.	*Midrash Tanna'im* on Deuteronomy.
Miége, Maroc	J.L. Miège, *Le Maroc et l'Europe,* 3 vols. (1961 62).
Mig.	Philo, *De Migratione Abrahami.*
Mik.	*Mikva'ot* (mishnaic tractate).
Milano, Bibliotheca	A. Milano, *Bibliotheca Historica Italo-Judaica* (1954); supplement for 1954–63 (1964); supplement for 1964–66 in RMI, 32 (1966).
Milano, Italia	A. Milano, *Storia degli Ebrei in Italia* (1963).
MIO	*Mitteilungen des Instituts fuer Orientforschung* 1953ff.).
Mish.	Mishnah.
MJ	*Le Monde Juif* (1946ff.).
MJC	see Neubauer, Chronicles.
MK	*Mo'ed Katan* (talmudic tractate).
MNDPV	*Mitteilungen und Nachrichten des deutschen Palaestinavereins* (1895–1912).
Mortara, Indice	M. Mortara, *Indice Alfabetico dei Rabbini e Scrittori Israeliti ... in Italia ...* (1886).
Mos	Philo, *De Vita Mosis.*
Moscati, Epig	S, Moscati, *Epigrafia ebraica antica* 1935–1950 (1951).
MT	Masoretic Text of the Bible.
Mueller, Musiker	[E.H. Mueller], *Deutisches Musiker-Lexikon* (1929)
Munk, Mélanges	S. Munk, *Mélanges de philosophie juive et arabe* (1859; repr. 1955).
Mut.	Philo, *De Mutatione Nominum.*
MWJ	*Magazin fuer die Wissenshaft des Judentums* (18745 93).
Nah.	Nahum (Bible).
Naz.	*Nazir* (talmudic tractate).
NDB	*Neue Deutsche Biographie* (1953ff.).
Ned.	*Nedarim* (talmudic tractate).
Neg.	*Nega'im* (mishnaic tractate).
Neh.	Nehemiah (Bible).
NG[2]	*New Grove Dictionary of Music and Musicians* (2001).
Nuebauer, Cat	A. Neubauer, *Catalogue of the Hebrew Manuscripts in the Bodleian Library ...,* 2 vols. (1886–1906).
Neubauer, Chronicles	A. Neubauer, *Mediaeval Jewish Chronicles,* 2 vols. (Heb., 1887–95; repr. 1965), Eng. title of *Seder ha-Ḥakhamim ve-Korot ha-Yamim.*
Neubauer, Géogr	A. Neubauer, *La géographie du Talmud* (1868).
Neuman, Spain	A.A. Neuman, *The Jews in Spain, their Social, Political, and Cultural Life During the Middle Ages,* 2 vols. (1942).
Neusner, Babylonia	J. Neusner, *History of the Jews in Babylonia,* 5 vols. 1965–70), 2nd revised printing 1969ff.).
Nid.	*Niddah* (talmudic tractate).
Noah	Fragment of Book of Noah (Pseudepigrapha).
Noth, Hist Isr	M. Noth, *History of Israel* (1958).
Noth, Personennamen	M. Noth, *Die israelitischen Personennamen. ...* (1928).
Noth, Ueberlief	M. Noth, *Ueberlieferungsgeschichte des Pentateuchs* (1949).
Noth, Welt	M. Noth, *Die Welt des Alten Testaments* (1957^3).
Nowack, Lehrbuch	W. Nowack, *Lehrbuch der hebraeischen Archaeologie,* 2 vols (1894).
NT	New Testament.
Num.	Numbers (Bible).
Num R.	*Numbers Rabbah.*
Obad.	Obadiah (Bible).
ODNB online	*Oxford Dictionary of National Biography.*
OḤ	*Oraḥ Ḥayyim.*
Oho.	*Oholot* (mishnaic tractate).
Olmstead	H.T. Olmstead, *History of Palestine and Syria* (1931; repr. 1965).
OLZ	*Orientalistische Literaturzeitung* (1898ff.)
Onom.	Eusebius, *Onomasticon.*
Op.	Philo, *De Opificio Mundi.*
OPD	*Osef Piskei Din shel ha-Rabbanut ha-Rashit le-Ereẓ Yisrael, Bet ha-Din ha-Gadol le-Irurim* (1950).
Or.	*Orlah* (talmudic tractate).
Or. Sibyll.	Sibylline Oracles (Pseudepigrapha).
OS	*L'Orient Syrien* (1956ff.)
OTS	*Oudtestamentische Studien* (1942ff.).
PAAJR	*Proceedings of the American Academy for Jewish Research* (1930ff.)
Pap 4QS[e]	A papyrus exemplar of IQS.
Par.	*Parah* (mishnaic tractate).
Pauly-Wissowa	A.F. Pauly, *Realencyklopaedie der klassichen Alertumswissenschaft,* ed. by G. Wissowa et al. (1864ff.)

PD — *Piskei Din shel Bet ha-Mishpat ha-Elyon le-Yisrael* (1948ff.)
PDR — *Piskei Din shel Battei ha-Din ha-Rabbaniyyim be-Yisrael.*
PdRE — *Pirkei de-R. Eliezer* (Eng. tr. 1916. (1965^2).
PdRK — *Pesikta de-Rav Kahana.*
Pe'ah — *Pe'ah* (talmudic tractate).
Peake, Commentary — A.J. Peake (ed.), *Commentary on the Bible* (1919; rev. 1962).
Pedersen, Israel — J. Pedersen, *Israel, Its Life and Culture,* 4 vols. in 2 (1926–40).
PEFQS — *Palestine Exploration Fund Quarterly Statement* (1869–1937; since 1938–PEQ).
PEQ — *Palestine Exploration Quarterly* (until 1937 PEFQS; after 1927 includes BBSAJ).
Perles, Beitaege — J. Perles, *Beitraege zur rabbinischen Sprach- und Alterthumskunde* (1893).
Pes. — *Pesaḥim* (talmudic tractate).
Pesh. — Peshitta (Syriac translation of the Bible).
Pesher Hab. — Commentary to Habakkuk from Qumran; see 1Qp Hab.
I and II Pet. — Epistles of Peter (New Testament).
Pfeiffer, Introd — R.H. Pfeiffer, *Introduction to the Old Testament* (1948).
PG — J.P. Migne (ed.), *Patrologia Graeca,* 161 vols. (1866–86).
Phil. — Epistle to the Philippians (New Testament).
Philem. — Epistle to the Philemon (New Testament).
PIASH — *Proceedings of the Israel Academy of Sciences and Humanities* (1963/7ff.).
PJB — *Palaestinajahrbuch des deutschen evangelischen Institutes fuer Altertumswissenschaft,* Jerusalem (1905–1933).
PK — *Pinkas ha-Kehillot,* encyclopedia of Jewish communities, published in over 30 volumes by Yad Vashem from 1970 and arranged by countries, regions and localities. For 3-vol. English edition see Spector, *Jewish Life.*
PL — J.P. Migne (ed.), *Patrologia Latina* 221 vols. (1844–64).
Plant — Philo, *De Plantatione.*
PO — R. Graffin and F. Nau (eds.), *Patrologia Orientalis* (1903ff.)
Pool, Prayer — D. de Sola Pool, *Traditional Prayer Book for Sabbath and Festivals* (1960).
Post — Philo, *De Posteritate Caini.*
PR — *Pesikta Rabbati.*
Praem. — Philo, *De Praemiis et Poenis.*
Prawer, Ẓalbanim — J. Prawer, *Toledot Mamlekhet ha-Ẓalbanim be-Ereẓ Yisrael,* 2 vols. (1963).
Press, Ereẓ — I. Press, *Ereẓ-Yisrael, Enẓiklopedyah Topografit-Historit,* 4 vols. (1951–55).
Pritchard, Pictures — J.B. Pritchard (ed.), *Ancient Near East in Pictures* (1954, 1970).
Pritchard, Texts — J.B. Pritchard (ed.), *Ancient Near East Texts* ... (1970^3).
Pr. Man. — Prayer of Manasses (Apocrypha).
Prob. — Philo, *Quod Omnis Probus Liber Sit.*
Prov. — Proverbs (Bible).
PS — *Palestinsky Sbornik* (Russ. (1881 1916, 1954ff).
Ps. — Psalms (Bible).
PSBA — *Proceedings of the Society of Biblical Archaeology* (1878–1918).
Ps. of Sol — Psalms of Solomon (Pseudepigrapha).

IQ Apoc — The *Genesis Apocryphon* from Qumran, cave one, ed. by N. Avigad and Y. Yadin (1956).
6QD — *Damascus Document* or *Sefer Berit Dammesk* from Qumran, cave six, ed. by M. Baillet, in RB, 63 (1956), 513–23 (see also CD).
QDAP — *Quarterly of the Department of Antiquities in Palestine* (1932ff.).
4QDeut. 32 — Manuscript of Deuteronomy 32 from Qumran, cave four (ed. by P.W. Skehan, in BASOR, 136 (1954), 12–15).
4QEx[a] — Exodus manuscript in Jewish script from Qumran, cave four.
4QEx[α] — Exodus manuscript in Paleo-Hebrew script from Qumran, cave four (partially ed. by P.W. Skehan, in JBL, 74 (1955), 182–7).
4QFlor — *Florilegium,* a miscellany from Qumran, cave four (ed. by J.M. Allegro, in JBL, 75 (1956), 176–77 and 77 (1958), 350–54).).
QGJD — *Quellen zur Geschichte der Juden in Deutschland* 1888–98).
IQH — *Thanksgiving Psalms* of *Hodayot* from Qumran, cave one (ed. by E.L. Sukenik and N. Avigad, *Oẓar ha-Megillot ha-Genuzot* (1954).
IQIs[a] — Scroll of Isaiah from Qumran, cave one (ed. by N. Burrows et al., *Dead Sea Scrolls ...,* 1 (1950).
IQIs[b] — Scroll of Isaiah from Qumran, cave one (ed. E.L. Sukenik and N. Avigad, *Oẓar ha-Megillot ha-Genuzot* (1954).
IQM — The *War Scroll* or *Serekh ha-Milḥamah* (ed. by E.L. Sukenik and N. Avigad, *Oẓar ha-Megillot ha-Genuzot* (1954).
4QpNah — Commentary on Nahum from Qumran, cave four (partially ed. by J.M. Allegro, in JBL, 75 (1956), 89–95).
IQphyl — Phylacteries *(tefillin)* from Qumran, cave one (ed. by Y. Yadin, in *Eretz Israel,* 9 (1969), 60–85).
4Q Prayer of Nabonidus — A document from Qumran, cave four, belonging to a lost Daniel literature (ed. by J.T. Milik, in RB, 63 (1956), 407–15).
IQS — *Manual of Discipline* or *Serekh ha-Yaḥad* from Qumran, cave one (ed. by M. Burrows et al., *Dead Sea Scrolls ...,* 2, pt. 2 (1951).

IQS[a] — The *Rule of the Congregation or Serekh ha-Edah* from Qumran, cave one (ed. by Burrows et al., *Dead Sea Scrolls* ..., 1 (1950), under the abbreviation IQ28a).
IQS[b] — *Blessings* or *Divrei Berakhot* from Qumran, cave one (ed. by Burrows et al., *Dead Sea Scrolls* ..., 1 (1950), under the abbreviation IQ28b).
4QSam[a] — Manuscript of I and II Samuel from Qumran, cave four (partially ed. by F.M. Cross, in BASOR, 132 (1953), 15–26).
4QSam[b] — Manuscript of I and II Samuel from Qumran, cave four (partially ed. by F.M. Cross, in JBL, 74 (1955), 147–72).
4QTestimonia — Sheet of Testimony from Qumran, cave four (ed. by J.M. Allegro, in JBL, 75 (1956), 174–87).).
4QT.Levi — *Testament of Levi* from Qumran, cave four (partially ed. by J.T. Milik, in RB, 62 (1955), 398–406).

Rabinovitz, Dik Sof — See Dik Sof.
RB — *Revue biblique* (1892ff.)
RBI — *Recherches bibliques* (1954ff.)
RCB — *Revista de cultura biblica* (São Paulo) (1957ff.)
Régné, Cat — J. Régné, *Catalogue des actes . . . des rois d'Aragon, concernant les Juifs* (1213–1327), in: REJ, vols. 60 70, 73, 75–78 (1910–24).
Reinach, Textes — T. Reinach, *Textes d'auteurs Grecs et Romains relatifs au Judaïsme* (1895; repr. 1963).
REJ — *Revue des études juives* (1880ff.).
Rejzen, Leksikon — Z. Rejzen, *Leksikon fun der Yidisher Literature*, 4 vols. (1927–29).
Renan, Ecrivains — A. Neubauer and E. Renan, *Les écrivains juifs français* ... (1893).
Renan, Rabbins — A. Neubauer and E. Renan, *Les rabbins français* (1877).
RES — *Revue des étude sémitiques et Babyloniaca* (1934–45).
Rev. — Revelation (New Testament).
RGG[3] — *Die Religion in Geschichte und Gegenwart*, 7 vols. (1957–65[3]).
RH — *Rosh Ha-Shanah* (talmudic tractate).
RHJE — *Revue de l'histoire juive en Egypte* (1947ff.).
RHMH — *Revue d'histoire de la médecine hébraïque* (1948ff.).
RHPR — *Revue d'histoire et de philosophie religieuses* (1921ff.).
RHR — *Revue d'histoire des religions* (1880ff.).
RI — *Rivista Israelitica* (1904–12).
Riemann-Einstein — *Hugo Riemanns Musiklexikon*, ed. by A. Einstein (1929[11]).
Riemann-Gurlitt — *Hugo Riemanns Musiklexikon*, ed. by W. Gurlitt (1959–67[12]), Personenteil.
Rigg-Jenkinson, Exchequer — J.M. Rigg, H. Jenkinson and H.G. Richardson (eds.), *Calendar of the Pleas Rolls of the Exchequer of the Jews*, 4 vols. (1905–1970); cf. in each instance also J.M. Rigg (ed.), *Select Pleas* ... (1902).
RMI — *Rassegna Mensile di Israel* (1925ff.).
Rom. — Epistle to the Romans (New Testament).
Rosanes, Togarmah — S.A. Rosanes, *Divrei Yemei Yisrael be-Togarmah*, 6 vols. (1907–45), and in 3 vols. (1930–38[2]).
Rosenbloom, Biogr Dict — J.R. Rosenbloom, *Biographical Dictionary of Early American Jews* (1960).
Roth, Art — C. Roth, *Jewish Art* (1961).
Roth, Dark Ages — C. Roth (ed.), *World History of the Jewish People*, second series, vol. 2, *Dark Ages* (1966).
Roth, England — C. Roth, *History of the Jews in England* (1964[3]).
Roth, Italy — C. Roth, *History of the Jews in Italy* (1946).
Roth, Mag Bibl — C. Roth, *Magna Bibliotheca Anglo-Judaica* (1937).
Roth, Marranos — C. Roth, *History of the Marranos* (2nd rev. ed 1959; reprint 1966).
Rowley, Old Test — H.H. Rowley, *Old Testament and Modern Study* (1951; repr. 1961).
RS — *Revue sémitiques d'épigraphie et d'histoire ancienne* (1893/94ff.).
RSO — *Rivista degli studi orientali* (1907ff.).
RSV — Revised Standard Version of the Bible.
Rubinstein, Australia I — *H.L. Rubinstein, The Jews in Australia, A Thematic History, Vol. I (1991).*
Rubinstein, Australia II — *W.D. Rubinstein, The Jews in Australia, A Thematic History, Vol. II (1991).*
Ruth — Ruth (Bible).
Ruth R. — *Ruth Rabbah.*
RV — Revised Version of the Bible.

Sac. — Philo, *De Sacrificiis Abelis et Caini.*
Salfeld, Martyrol — S. Salfeld, *Martyrologium des Nuernberger Memorbuches* (1898).
I and II Sam. — Samuel, book I and II (Bible).
Sanh. — *Sanhedrin* (talmudic tractate).
SBA — Society of Biblical Archaeology.
SBB — *Studies in Bibliography and Booklore* (1953ff.).
SBE — *Semana Biblica Española.*
SBT — *Studies in Biblical Theology* (1951ff.).
SBU — *Svenkst Bibliskt Uppslogsvesk*, 2 vols. (1962–63[2]).
Schirmann, Italyah — J.Ḥ. Schirmann, *Ha-Shirah ha-Ivrit be-Italyah* (1934).
Schirmann, Sefarad — J.Ḥ. Schirmann, *Ha-Shirah ha-Ivrit bi-Sefarad u-vi-Provence*, 2 vols. (1954–56).
Scholem, Mysticism — G. Scholem, *Major Trends in Jewish Mysticism* (rev. ed. 1946; paperback ed. with additional bibliography 1961).
Scholem, Shabbetai Ẓevi — G. Scholem, *Shabbetai Ẓevi ve-ha-Tenu'ah ha-Shabbeta'it bi-Ymei Ḥayyav*, 2 vols. (1967).
Schrader, Keilinschr — E. Schrader, *Keilinschriften und das Alte Testament* (1903[3]).
Schuerer, Gesch — E. Schuerer, *Geschichte des juedischen Volkes im Zeitalter Jesu Christi*, 3 vols. and index-vol. (1901–11[4]).

Schuerer, Hist	E. Schuerer, *History of the Jewish People in the Time of Jesus,* ed. by N.N. Glatzer, abridged paperback edition (1961).
Set. T.	*Sefer Torah* (post-talmudic tractate).
Sem.	*Semaḥot* (post-talmudic tractate).
Sendrey, Music	A. Sendrey, *Bibliography of Jewish Music* (1951).
SER	*Seder Eliyahu Rabbah.*
SEZ	*Seder Eliyahu Zuta.*
Shab	*Shabbat* (talmudic tractate).
Sh. Ar.	J. Caro Shulḥan Arukh. OḤ – *Oraḥ Ḥayyim* YD – *Yoreh De'ah* EH – *Even ha-Ezer* ḤM – *Ḥoshen Mishpat.*
Shek.	*Shekalim* (talmudic tractate).
Shev.	*Shevi'it* (talmudic tractate).
Shevu.	*Shevu'ot* (talmudic tractate).
Shunami, Bibl	S. Shunami, *Bibliography of Jewish Bibliographies* (1965^{2}).
Sif.	*Sifrei Deuteronomy.*
Sif. Num.	*Sifrei Numbers.*
Sifra	*Sifra* on Leviticus.
Sif. Zut.	*Sifrei Zuta.*
SIHM	Sources inédites de l'histoire du Maroc (series).
Silverman, Prayer	M. Silverman (ed.), *Sabbath and Festival Prayer Book* (1946).
Singer, Prayer	S. Singer *Authorised Daily Prayer Book* (1943^{17}).
Sob.	Philo, *De Sobrietate.*
Sof.	*Soferim* (post-talmudic tractate).
Som.	Philo, *De Somniis.*
Song	Song of Songs (Bible).
Song. Ch.	Song of the Three Children (Apocrypha).
Song R.	*Song of Songs Rabbah.*
SOR	*Seder Olam Rabbah.*
Sot.	*Sotah* (talmudic tractate).
SOZ	*Seder Olam Zuta.*
Spec.	Philo, *De Specialibus Legibus.*
Spector, Jewish Life	*S. Spector (ed.), Encyclopedia of Jewish Life Before and After the Holocaust (2001).*
Steinschneider, Arab lit	M. Steinschneider, *Die arabische Literatur der Juden* (1902).
Steinschneider, Cat Bod	M. Steinschneider, *Catalogus Librorum Hebraeorum in Bibliotheca Bodleiana,* 3 vols. (1852–60; reprints 1931 and 1964).
Steinschneider, Hanbuch	M. Steinschneider, *Bibliographisches Handbuch ueber die . . . Literatur fuer hebraeische Sprachkunde* (1859; repr. with additions 1937).
Steinschneider, Uebersetzungen	M. Steinschneider, *Die hebraeischen Uebersetzungen des Mittelalters* (1893).
Stern, Americans	M.H. Stern, *Americans of Jewish Descent* (1960).
van Straalen, Cat	S. van Straalen, *Catalogue of Hebrew Books in the British Museum Acquired During the Years 1868–1892* (1894).
Suárez Fernández, Docmentos	L. Suárez Fernández, *Documentos acerca de la expulsion de los Judios de España* (1964).
Suk.	*Sukkah* (talmudic tractate).
Sus.	Susanna (Apocrypha).
SY	*Sefer Yeẓirah.*
Sym.	Symmachus' Greek translation of the Bible.
SZNG	*Studien zur neueren Geschichte.*
Ta'an.	*Ta'anit* (talmudic tractate).
Tam.	*Tamid* (mishnaic tractate).
Tanḥ.	*Tanḥuma.*
Tanḥ. B.	*Tanḥuma.* Buber ed (1885).
Targ. Jon	Targum Jonathan (Aramaic version of the Prophets).
Targ. Onk.	Targum Onkelos (Aramaic version of the Pentateuch).
Targ. Yer.	Targum Yerushalmi.
TB	Babylonian Talmud or Talmud Bavli.
Tcherikover, Corpus	V. Tcherikover, A. Fuks, and M. Stern, *Corpus Papyrorum Judaicorum,* 3 vols. (1957–60).
Tef.	*Tefillin* (post-talmudic tractate).
Tem.	*Temurah* (mishnaic tractate).
Ter.	*Terumah* (talmudic tractate).
Test. Patr.	Testament of the Twelve Patriarchs (Pseudepigrapha). Ash. – Asher Ben. – Benjamin Dan – Dan Gad – Gad Iss. – Issachar Joseph – Joseph Judah – Judah Levi – Levi Naph. – Naphtali Reu. – Reuben Sim. – Simeon Zeb. – Zebulun.
I and II	Epistle to the Thessalonians (New Testament).
Thieme-Becker	U. Thieme and F. Becker (eds.), *Allgemeines Lexikon der bildenden Kuenstler von der Antike bis zur Gegenwart,* 37 vols. (1907–50).
Tidhar	D. Tidhar (ed.), *Enẓiklopedyah la-Ḥalutẓei ha-Yishuv u-Vonav* (1947ff.).
I and II Timothy	Epistles to Timothy (New Testament).
Tit.	Epistle to Titus (New Testament).
TJ	Jerusalem Talmud or Talmud Yerushalmi.
Tob.	Tobit (Apocrypha).
Toh.	*Tohorot* (mishnaic tractate).
Torczyner, Bundeslade	H. Torczyner, *Die Bundeslade und die Anfaenge der Religion Israels* (1930^{3}).
Tos.	*Tosafot.*
Tosef.	Tosefta.
Tristram, Nat Hist	H.B. Tristram, *Natural History of the Bible* (1877^{5}).
Tristram, Survey	Palestine Exploration Fund, *Survey of Western Palestine,* vol. 4 (1884) = *Fauna and Flora* by H.B. Tristram.
TS	*Terra Santa* (1943ff.).

TSBA	*Transactions of the Society of Biblical Archaeology* (1872–93).
TY	*Tevul Yom* (mishnaic tractate).
UBSB	United Bible Society, *Bulletin.*
UJE	*Universal Jewish Encyclopedia*, 10 vols. (1939–43).
Uk.	*Ukẓin* (mishnaic tractate).
Urbach, Tosafot	E.E. Urbach, *Ba'alei ha-Tosafot* (1957[2]).
de Vaux, Anc Isr	R. de Vaux, *Ancient Israel: its Life and Institutions* (1961; paperback 1965).
de Vaux, Instit	R. de Vaux, *Institutions de l'Ancien Testament,* 2 vols. (1958 60).
Virt.	Philo, *De Virtutibus.*
Vogelstein, Chronology	M. Volgelstein, *Biblical Chronology (1944).*
Vogelstein-Rieger	H. Vogelstein and P. Rieger, *Geschichte der Juden in Rom,* 2 vols. (1895–96).
VT	*Vetus Testamentum* (1951ff.).
VTS	*Vetus Testamentum* Supplements (1953ff.).
Vulg.	Vulgate (Latin translation of the Bible).
Wars	Josephus, *The Jewish Wars.*
Watzinger, Denkmaeler	K. Watzinger, *Denkmaeler Palaestinas,* 2 vols. (1933–35).
Waxman, Literature	M. Waxman, *History of Jewish Literature,* 5 vols. (1960[2]).
Weiss, Dor	I.H. Weiss, *Dor, Dor ve-Doreshav,* 5 vols. (1904[4]).
Wellhausen, Proleg	J. Wellhausen, *Prolegomena zur Geschichte Israels* (1927[6]).
WI	*Die Welt des Islams* (1913ff.).
Winniger, Biog	S. Wininger, *Grosse juedische National-Biographie* ..., 7 vols. (1925–36).
Wisd.	Wisdom of Solomon (Apocrypha)
WLB	*Wiener Library Bulletin* (1958ff.).
Wolf, Bibliotheca	J.C. Wolf, *Bibliotheca Hebraea*, 4 vols. (1715–33).
Wright, Bible	G.E. Wright, *Westminster Historical Atlas to the Bible* (1945).
Wright, Atlas	G.E. Wright, *The Bible and the Ancient Near East* (1961).
WWWJ	*Who's Who in the World Jewry* (New York, 1955, 1965[2]).
WZJT	*Wissenschaftliche Zeitschrift fuer juedische Theologie* (1835–37).
WZKM	*Wiener Zeitschrift fuer die Kunde des Morgenlandes* (1887ff.).
Yaari, Sheluḥei	A. Yaari, *Sheluḥei Ereẓ Yisrael* (1951).
Yad	Maimonides, *Mishneh Torah (Yad Ḥazakah).*
Yad	*Yadayim* (mishnaic tractate).
Yal.	*Yalkut Shimoni.*
Yal. Mak.	*Yalkut Makhiri.*
Yal. Reub.	*Yalkut Reubeni.*
YD	*Yoreh De'ah.*
YE	*Yevreyskaya Entsiklopediya,* 14 vols. (c. 1910).
Yev.	*Yevamot* (talmudic tractate).
YIVOA	*YIVO Annual of Jewish Social Studies* (1946ff.).
YLBI	*Year Book of the Leo Baeck Institute* (1956ff.).
YMḤEY	See BJPES.
YMḤSI	*Yedi'ot ha-Makhon le-Ḥeker ha-Shirah ha-Ivrit* (1935/36ff.).
YMMY	*Yedi'ot ha-Makhon le-Madda'ei ha-Yahadut* (1924/25ff.).
Yoma	*Yoma* (talmudic tractate).
ZA	*Zeitschrift fuer Assyriologie* (1886/87ff.).
Zav.	*Zavim* (mishnaic tractate).
ZAW	*Zeitschrift fuer die alttestamentliche Wissenschaft und die Kunde des nachbiblishchen Judentums* (1881ff.).
ZAWB	*Beihefte* (supplements) to ZAW.
ZDMG	*Zeitschrift der Deutschen Morgenlaendischen Gesellschaft* (1846ff.).
ZDPV	*Zeitschrift des Deutschen Palaestina-Vereins* (1878–1949; from 1949 = BBLA).
Zech.	Zechariah (Bible).
Zedner, Cat	J. Zedner, *Catalogue of Hebrew Books in the Library of the British Museum* (1867; repr. 1964).
Zeitlin, Bibliotheca	W. Zeitlin, *Bibliotheca Hebraica Post-Mendelssohniana* (1891–95).
Zeph.	Zephaniah (Bible).
Zev.	*Zevaḥim* (talmudic tractate).
ZGGJT	*Zeitschrift der Gesellschaft fuer die Geschichte der Juden in der Tschechoslowakei* (1930–38).
ZGJD	*Zeitschrift fuer die Geschichte der Juden in Deutschland* (1887–92).
ZHB	*Zeitschrift fuer hebraeische Bibliographie* (1896–1920).
Zinberg, Sifrut	I. Zinberg, *Toledot Sifrut Yisrael,* 6 vols. (1955–60).
Ẓiẓ.	*Ẓiẓit* (post-talmudic tractate).
ZNW	*Zeitschrift fuer die neutestamentliche Wissenschaft* (1901ff.).
ZS	*Zeitschrift fuer Semitistik und verwandte Gebiete* (1922ff.).
Zunz, Gesch	L. Zunz, *Zur Geschichte und Literatur* (1845).
Zunz, Gesch	L. Zunz, *Literaturgeschichte der synagogalen Poesie* (1865; Supplement, 1867; repr. 1966).
Zunz, Poesie	L. Zunz, *Synogogale Posie des Mittelalters,* ed. by Freimann (1920[2]; repr. 1967).
Zunz, Ritus	L. Zunz, *Ritus des synagogalen Gottesdienstes* (1859; repr. 1967).
Zunz, Schr	L. Zunz, *Gesammelte Schriften,* 3 vols. (1875–76).
Zunz, Vortraege	L. Zunz, *Gottesdienstliche vortraege der Juden* ... 1892[2]; repr. 1966).
Zunz-Albeck, Derashot	L. Zunz, *Ha-Derashot be-Yisrael*, Heb. Tr. of Zunz Vortraege by H. Albeck (1954[2]).

TRANSLITERATION RULES

HEBREW AND SEMITIC LANGUAGES:

	General	*Scientific*
א	not transliterated[1]	ʾ
בּ	b	b
ב	v	v, b̲
גּ	g	g
ג		ḡ
דּ	d	d
ד		ḏ
ה	h	h
ו	v – when not a vowel	w
ז	z	z
ח	ḥ	ḥ
ט	t	ṭ, t
י	y – when vowel and at end of words – i	y
כּ	k	k
כ, ך	kh	kh, k̲
ל	l	l̲
מ, ם	m	m
נ, ן	n	n
ס	s	s
ע	not transliterated[1]	ʿ
פּ	p	p
פ, ף	f	p, f, ph
צ, ץ	ẓ	ṣ, ẓ
ק	k	q, k
ר	r	r
שׁ	sh[2]	š
שׂ	s	ś, s
תּ	t	t
ת		ṯ
ג׳	dzh, J	ğ
ז׳	zh, J	ž
צ׳	ch	č
◌ָ		å, o, ȯ (short) â, ā (long)
◌ַ	a	a
◌ֲ		a, ^{a}
◌ֵ		e, ẹ, ē
◌ֶ	e	æ, ä, ę
◌ֱ		œ, ĕ, ^{e}
◌ְ	only *sheva na* is transliterated	ə, ĕ, e; only *sheva na* transliterated
◌ִ ◌ִי	i	i
◌ֹ וֹ	o	o, o, o
◌ֻ וּ	u	u, ŭ û, ū
◌ֵי	ei; biblical e	
‡		reconstructed forms of words

1. The letters א and ע are not transliterated.
An apostrophe (') between vowels indicates that they do not form a diphthong and are to be pronounced separately.
2. *Dagesh ḥazak* (forte) is indicated by doubling of the letter, except for the letter שׁ.
3. Names. Biblical names and biblical place names are rendered according to the Bible translation of the Jewish Publication Society of America. Post-biblical Hebrew names are transliterated; contemporary names are transliterated or rendered as used by the person. Place names are transliterated or rendered by the accepted spelling. Names and some words with an accepted English form are usually not transliterated.

YIDDISH

א	not transliterated
אַ	a
אָ	o
ב	b
בֿ	v
ג	g
ד	d
ה	h
ו, וּ	u
וו	v
וי	oy
ז	z
זש	zh
ח	kh
ט	t
טש	tsh, ch
י	(consonant) y (vowel) i
יִ	i
יי	ey
ײַ	ay
כּ	k
כ, ך	kh
ל	l
מ, ם	m
נ, ן	n
ס	s
ע	e
פּ	p
פֿ, ף	f
צ, ץ	ts
ק	k
ר	r
שׁ	sh
שׂ	s
תּ	t
ת	s

1. Yiddish transliteration rendered according to U. Weinreich's Modern *English-Yiddish Yiddish-English* Dictionary.
2. Hebrew words in Yiddish are usually transliterated according to standard Yiddish pronunciation, e.g., חזנות = *khazones.*

LADINO

Ladino and Judeo-Spanish words written in Hebrew characters are transliterated phonetically, following the General Rules of Hebrew transliteration (see above) whenever the accepted spelling in Latin characters could not be ascertained.

ARABIC

ء ا	a[1]	ض	ḍ
ب	b	ط	ṭ
ت	t	ظ	ẓ
ث	th	ع	c
ج	j	غ	gh
ح	ḥ	ف	f
خ	kh	ق	q
د	d	ك	k
ذ	dh	ل	l
ر	r	م	m
ز	z	ن	n
س	s	ه	h
ش	sh	و	w
ص	ṣ	ي	y
ـَ	a	ـَا ى	ā
ـِ	i	ـِي	ī
ـُ	u	ـُو	ū
ـَو	aw	ـِيّ	iyy[2]
ـَي	ay	ـُوّ	uww[2]

1. not indicated when initial
2. see note (f)

a) The EJ follows the *Columbia Lippincott Gazetteer* and the *Times Atlas* in transliteration of Arabic place names. Sites that appear in neither are transliterated according to the table above, and subject to the following notes.

b) The EJ follows the *Columbia Encyclopedia* in transliteration of Arabic names. Personal names that do not therein appear are transliterated according to the table above and subject to the following notes (e.g., Ali rather than ʿAlī, Suleiman rather than Sulayman).

c) The EJ follows the *Webster's Third International Dictionary, Unabridged* in transliteration of Arabic terms that have been integrated into the English language.

d) The term "Abu" will thus appear, usually in disregard of inflection.

e) Nunnation (end vowels, *tanwīn*) are dropped in transliteration.

f) Gemination (*tashdīd*) is indicated by the doubling of the geminated letter, unless an end letter, in which case the gemination is dropped.

g) The definitive article *al-* will always be thus transliterated, unless subject to one of the modifying notes (e.g., El-Arish rather than al-ʿArīsh; modification according to note (a)).

h) The Arabic transliteration disregards the Sun Letters (the antero-palatals (*al-Ḥurūf al-Shamsiyya*).

i) The *tā-marbūṭa* (o) is omitted in transliteration, unless in construct-stage (e.g., *Khirba* but *Khirbat Mishmish*).

These modifying notes may lead to various inconsistencies in the Arabic transliteration, but this policy has deliberately been adopted to gain smoother reading of Arabic terms and names.

GREEK

Ancient Greek	*Modern Greek*	*Greek Letters*
a	a	*Α; α; ᾳ*
b	v	*Β; β*
g	gh; g	*Γ; γ*
d	dh	*Δ; δ*
e	e	*Ε; ε*
z	z	*Ζ; ζ*
e; e	i	*Η; η; ῃ*
th	th	*Θ; θ*
i	i	*Ι; ι*
k	k; ky	*Κ; κ*
l	l	*Λ; λ*
m	m	*Μ; μ*
n	n	*Ν; ν*
x	x	*Ξ; ξ*
o	o	*Ο; ο*
p	p	*Π; π*
r; rh	r	*Ρ; ρ; ῥ*
s	s	*Σ; σ; ς*
t	t	*Τ; τ*
u; y	i	*Υ; υ*
ph	f	*Φ; φ*
ch	kh	*Χ; χ*
ps	ps	*Ψ; ψ*
o; ō	o	*Ω; ω; ῳ*
ai	e	*αι*
ei	i	*ει*
oi	i	*οι*
ui	i	*υι*
ou	ou	*ου*
eu	ev	*ευ*
eu; ēu	iv	*ηυ*
–	j	*τζ*
nt	d; nd	*ντ*
mp	b; mb	*μπ*
ngk	g	*γκ*
ng	ng	*νγ*
h	–	ʽ
–	–	ʼ
w	–	*Ϝ*

RUSSIAN

А	A
Б	B
В	V
Г	G
Д	D
Е	E, Ye[1]
Ё	Yo, O[2]
Ж	Zh
З	Z
И	I
Й	Y[3]
К	K
Л	L
М	M
Н	N
О	O
П	P
Р	R
С	S
Т	T
У	U
Ф	F
Х	Kh
Ц	Ts
Ч	Ch
Ш	Sh
Щ	Shch
Ъ	omitted; see note [1]
Ы	Y
Ь	omitted; see note [1]
Э	E
Ю	Yu
Я	Ya

1. Ye at the beginning of a word; after all vowels except ***Ы***; and after **Ъ** and ***Ь***.
2. O after ***Ч***, ***Ш*** and ***Щ***.
3. Omitted after ***Ы***, and in names of people after ***И***.

A. Many first names have an accepted English or quasi-English form which has been preferred to transliteration.
B. Place names have been given according to the *Columbia Lippincott Gazeteer*.
C. Pre-revolutionary spelling has been ignored.
D. Other languages using the Cyrillic alphabet (e.g., Bulgarian, Ukrainian), inasmuch as they appear, have been phonetically transliterated in conformity with the principles of this table.

GLOSSARY

Asterisked terms have separate entries in the Encyclopaedia.

Actions Committee, early name of the Zionist General Council, the supreme institution of the World Zionist Organization in the interim between Congresses. The Zionist Executive's name was then the "Small Actions Committee."

***Adar**, twelfth month of the Jewish religious year, sixth of the civil, approximating to February–March.

***Aggadah**, name given to those sections of Talmud and Midrash containing homiletic expositions of the Bible, stories, legends, folklore, anecdotes, or maxims. In contradistinction to **halakhah.*

***Agunah**, woman unable to remarry according to Jewish law, because of desertion by her husband or inability to accept presumption of death.

***Aharonim**, later rabbinic authorities. In contradistinction to **rishonim* ("early ones").

Ahavah, liturgical poem inserted in the second benediction of the morning prayer *(*Ahavah Rabbah)* of the festivals and/or special Sabbaths.

Aktion (Ger.), operation involving the mass assembly, deportation, and murder of Jews by the Nazis during the *Holocaust.

***Aliyah**, (1) being called to Reading of the Law in synagogue; (2) immigration to Ereẓ Israel; (3) one of the waves of immigration to Ereẓ Israel from the early 1880s.

***Amidah**, main prayer recited at all services; also known as *Shemoneh Esreh* and *Tefillah.*

***Amora** (pl. **amoraim**), title given to the Jewish scholars in Ereẓ Israel and Babylonia in the third to sixth centuries who were responsible for the **Gemara.*

Aravah, the *willow; one of the *Four Species used on *Sukkot ("festival of Tabernacles") together with the **etrog, hadas,* and **lulav.*

***Arvit**, evening prayer.

Asarah be-Tevet, fast on the 10th of Tevet commemorating the commencement of the siege of Jerusalem by Nebuchadnezzar.

Asefat ha-Nivḥarim, representative assembly elected by Jews in Palestine during the period of the British Mandate (1920–48).

***Ashkenaz**, name applied generally in medieval rabbinical literature to Germany.

***Ashkenazi** (pl. **Ashkenazim**), German or West-, Central-, or East-European Jew(s), as contrasted with *Sephardi(m).

***Av**, fifth month of the Jewish religious year, eleventh of the civil, approximating to July–August.

***Av bet din**, vice president of the supreme court (*bet din ha-gadol*) in Jerusalem during the Second Temple period; later, title given to communal rabbis as heads of the religious courts (see **bet din*).

***Badḥan**, jester, particularly at traditional Jewish weddings in Eastern Europe.

***Bakkashah** (Heb. "supplication"), type of petitionary prayer, mainly recited in the Sephardi rite on Rosh Ha-Shanah and the Day of Atonement.

Bar, "son of . . . "; frequently appearing in personal names.

***Baraita** (pl. **beraitot**), statement of **tanna* not found in *Mishnah.

***Bar mitzvah**, ceremony marking the initiation of a boy at the age of 13 into the Jewish religious community.

Ben, "son of . . . ", frequently appearing in personal names.

Berakhah (pl. **berakhot**), *benediction, blessing; formula of praise and thanksgiving.

***Bet din** (pl. **battei din**), rabbinic court of law.

***Bet ha-midrash**, school for higher rabbinic learning; often attached to or serving as a synagogue.

***Bilu**, first modern movement for pioneering and agricultural settlement in Ereẓ Israel, founded in 1882 at Kharkov, Russia.

***Bund**, Jewish socialist party founded in Vilna in 1897, supporting Jewish national rights; Yiddishist, and anti-Zionist.

Cohen (pl. **Cohanim**), see Kohen.

***Conservative Judaism**, trend in Judaism developed in the United States in the 20th century which, while opposing extreme changes in traditional observances, permits certain modifications of *halakhah* in response to the changing needs of the Jewish people.

***Consistory** (Fr. *consistoire*), governing body of a Jewish communal district in France and certain other countries.

***Converso(s)**, term applied in Spain and Portugal to converted Jew(s), and sometimes more loosely to their descendants.

***Crypto-Jew**, term applied to a person who although observing outwardly Christianity (or some other religion) was at heart a Jew and maintained Jewish observances as far as possible (see Converso; Marrano; Neofiti; New Christian; Jadīd al-Islām).

***Dayyan**, member of rabbinic court.

Decisor, equivalent to the Hebrew *posek* (pl. **posekim*), the rabbi who gives the decision (*halakhah*) in Jewish law or practice.

***Devekut**, "devotion"; attachment or adhesion to God; communion with God.

***Diaspora**, Jews living in the "dispersion" outside Ereẓ Israel; area of Jewish settlement outside Ereẓ Israel.

Din, a law (both secular and religious), legal decision, or lawsuit.

Divan, diwan, collection of poems, especially in Hebrew, Arabic, or Persian.

Dunam, unit of land area (1,000 sq. m., c. ¼ acre), used in Israel.

Einsatzgruppen, mobile units of Nazi S.S. and S.D.; in U.S.S.R. and Serbia, mobile killing units.

***Ein-Sof**, "without end"; "the infinite"; hidden, impersonal aspect of God; also used as a Divine Name.

***Elul**, sixth month of the Jewish religious calendar, 12th of the civil, precedes the High Holiday season in the fall.

Endloesung, see *Final Solution.

***Ereẓ Israel**, Land of Israel; Palestine.

***Eruv**, technical term for rabbinical provision permitting the alleviation of certain restrictions.

***Etrog**, citron; one of the *Four Species used on *Sukkot together with the **lulav, hadas,* and *aravah.*

Even ha-Ezer, see Shulḥan Arukh.

***Exilarch**, lay head of Jewish community in Babylonia (see also *resh galuta*), and elsewhere.

***Final Solution** (Ger. *Endloesung*), in Nazi terminology, the Nazi-planned mass murder and total annihilation of the Jews.

***Gabbai**, official of a Jewish congregation; originally a charity collector.

***Galut**, "exile"; the condition of the Jewish people in dispersion.

*__Gaon__ (pl. **geonim**), head of academy in post-talmudic period, especially in Babylonia.

Gaonate, office of *gaon.

*__Gemara__, traditions, discussions, and rulings of the **amoraim*, commenting on and supplementing the *Mishnah, and forming part of the Babylonian and Palestinian Talmuds (see Talmud).

*__Gematria__, interpretation of Hebrew word according to the numerical value of its letters.

General Government, territory in Poland administered by a German civilian governor-general with headquarters in Cracow after the German occupation in World War II.

*__Genizah__, depository for sacred books. The best known was discovered in the synagogue of Fostat (old Cairo).

Get, bill of *divorce.

*__Ge'ullah__, hymn inserted after the **Shema* into the benediction of the morning prayer of the festivals and special Sabbaths.

*__Gilgul__, metempsychosis; transmigration of souls.

*__Golem__, automaton, especially in human form, created by magical means and endowed with life.

*__Ḥabad__, initials of *ḥokhmah, binah, da'at*: "wisdom, understanding, knowledge"; ḥasidic movement founded in Belorussia by *Shneur Zalman of Lyady.

Hadas, *myrtle; one of the *Four Species used on Sukkot together with the **etrog*, **lulav*, and *aravah*.

*__Haftarah__ (pl. **haftarot**), designation of the portion from the prophetical books of the Bible recited after the synagogue reading from the Pentateuch on Sabbaths and holidays.

*__Haganah__, clandestine Jewish organization for armed self-defense in Ereẓ Israel under the British Mandate, which eventually evolved into a people's militia and became the basis for the Israel army.

*__Haggadah__, ritual recited in the home on *Passover eve at seder table.

Haham, title of chief rabbi of the Spanish and Portuguese congregations in London, England.

*__Hakham__, title of rabbi of *Sephardi congregation.

*__Hakham bashi__, title in the 15th century and modern times of the chief rabbi in the Ottoman Empire, residing in Constantinople (Istanbul), also applied to principal rabbis in provincial towns.

Hakhsharah ("preparation"), organized training in the Diaspora of pioneers for agricultural settlement in Ereẓ Israel.

*__Halakhah__ (pl. **halakhot**), an accepted decision in rabbinic law. Also refers to those parts of the *Talmud concerned with legal matters. In contradistinction to **aggadah*.

Ḥaliẓah, biblically prescribed ceremony (Deut. 25:9–10) performed when a man refuses to marry his brother's childless widow, enabling her to remarry.

*__Hallel__, term referring to Psalms 113-18 in liturgical use.

*__Ḥalukkah__, system of financing the maintenance of Jewish communities in the holy cities of Ereẓ Israel by collections made abroad, mainly in the pre-Zionist era (see *kolel*).

Ḥalutz (pl. **ḥalutzim**), pioneer, especially in agriculture, in Ereẓ Israel.

Ḥalutziyyut, pioneering.

*__Ḥanukkah__, eight-day celebration commemorating the victory of *Judah Maccabee over the Syrian king *Antiochus Epiphanes and the subsequent rededication of the Temple.

Ḥasid, adherent of *Ḥasidism.

*__Ḥasidei Ashkenaz__, medieval pietist movement among the Jews of Germany.

*__Ḥasidism__, (1) religious revivalist movement of popular mysticism among Jews of Germany in the Middle Ages; (2) religious movement founded by *Israel ben Eliezer Ba'al Shem Tov in the first half of the 18th century.

*__Haskalah__, "enlightenment"; movement for spreading modern European culture among Jews c. 1750–1880. See *maskil*.

*__Havdalah__, ceremony marking the end of Sabbath or festival.

*__Ḥazzan__, precentor who intones the liturgy and leads the prayers in synagogue; in earlier times a synagogue official.

*__Ḥeder__ (lit. "room"), school for teaching children Jewish religious observance.

Heikhalot, "palaces"; tradition in Jewish mysticism centering on mystical journeys through the heavenly spheres and palaces to the Divine Chariot (see Merkabah).

*__Ḥerem__, excommunication, imposed by rabbinical authorities for purposes of religious and/or communal discipline; originally, in biblical times, that which is separated from common use either because it was an abomination or because it was consecrated to God.

Ḥeshvan, see Marḥeshvan.

*__Ḥevra kaddisha__, title applied to charitable confraternity (**ḥevrah*), now generally limited to associations for burial of the dead.

*__Ḥibbat Zion__, see Ḥovevei Zion.

*__Histadrut__ (abbr. For Heb. **Ha-Histadrut ha-Kelalit shel ha-Ovedim ha-Ivriyyim be-Ereẓ Israel**). Ereẓ Israel Jewish Labor Federation, founded in 1920; subsequently renamed Histadrut ha-Ovedim be-Ereẓ Israel.

*__Holocaust__, the organized mass persecution and annihilation of European Jewry by the Nazis (1933–1945).

*__Hoshana Rabba__, the seventh day of *Sukkot on which special observances are held.

Ḥoshen Mishpat, see Shulḥan Arukh.

Ḥovevei Zion, federation of *Ḥibbat Zion, early (pre-*Herzl) Zionist movement in Russia.

Illui, outstanding scholar or genius, especially a young prodigy in talmudic learning.

*__Iyyar__, second month of the Jewish religious year, eighth of the civil, approximating to April-May.

I.Ẓ.L. (initials of Heb. *__Irgun Ẓeva'i Le'ummi__; "National Military Organization"), underground Jewish organization in Ereẓ Israel founded in 1931, which engaged from 1937 in retaliatory acts against Arab attacks and later against the British mandatory authorities.

*__Jadīd al-Islām__ (Ar.), a person practicing the Jewish religion in secret although outwardly observing Islām.

*__Jewish Legion__, Jewish units in British army during World War I.

*__Jihād__ (Ar.), in Muslim religious law, holy war waged against infidels.

*__Judenrat__ (Ger. "Jewish council"), council set up in Jewish communities and ghettos under the Nazis to execute their instructions.

*__Judenrein__ (Ger. "clean of Jews"), in Nazi terminology the condition of a locality from which all Jews had been eliminated.

*__Kabbalah__, the Jewish mystical tradition:
Kabbala iyyunit, speculative Kabbalah;
Kabbala ma'asit, practical Kabbalah;
Kabbala nevu'it, prophetic Kabbalah.

Kabbalist, student of Kabbalah.

*__Kaddish__, liturgical doxology.

Kahal, Jewish congregation; among Ashkenazim, *kehillah*.

*__Kalām__ (Ar.), science of Muslim theology; adherents of the Kalām are called *mutakallimūn*.

*__Karaite__, member of a Jewish sect originating in the eighth century which rejected rabbinic (*Rabbanite) Judaism and claimed to accept only Scripture as authoritative.

*__Kasher__, ritually permissible food.

Kashrut, Jewish *dietary laws.

*__Kavvanah__, "intention"; term denoting the spiritual concentration accompanying prayer and the performance of ritual or of a commandment.

*__Kedushah__, main addition to the third blessing in the reader's repetition of the *Amidah* in which the public responds to the precentor's introduction.

Kefar, village; first part of name of many settlements in Israel.

Kehillah, congregation; see *kahal*.

Kelippah (pl. **kelippot**), "husk(s)"; mystical term denoting force(s) of evil.

*__Keneset Yisrael__, comprehensive communal organization of the Jews in Palestine during the British Mandate.

Keri, variants in the masoretic (*masorah) text of the Bible between the spelling (*ketiv*) and its pronunciation (*keri*).

*__Kerovah__ (collective plural (corrupted) from **kerovez̩**), poem(s) incorporated into the **Amidah*.

Ketiv, see *keri*.

*__Ketubbah__, marriage contract, stipulating husband's obligations to wife.

Kevuz̩ah, small commune of pioneers constituting an agricultural settlement in Erez̩ Israel (evolved later into *kibbutz).

*__Kibbutz__ (pl. **kibbutzim**), larger-size commune constituting a settlement in Erez̩ Israel based mainly on agriculture but engaging also in industry.

*__Kiddush__, prayer of sanctification, recited over wine or bread on eve of Sabbaths and festivals.

*__Kiddush ha-Shem__, term connoting martyrdom or act of strict integrity in support of Judaic principles.

*__Kinah__ (pl. **kinot**), lamentation dirge(s) for the Ninth of Av and other fast days.

*__Kislev__, ninth month of the Jewish religious year, third of the civil, approximating to November-December.

Klaus, name given in Central and Eastern Europe to an institution, usually with synagogue attached, where *Talmud was studied perpetually by adults; applied by Ḥasidim to their synagogue ("*kloyz*").

*__Knesset__, parliament of the State of Israel.

K(c)ohen (pl. **K(c)ohanim**), Jew(s) of priestly (Aaronide) descent.

*__Kolel__, (1) community in Erez̩ Israel of persons from a particular country or locality, often supported by their fellow countrymen in the Diaspora; (2) institution for higher Torah study.

Kosher, see *kasher*.

*__Kristallnacht__ (Ger. "crystal night," meaning "night of broken glass"), organized destruction of synagogues, Jewish houses, and shops, accompanied by mass arrests of Jews, which took place in Germany and Austria under the Nazis on the night of Nov. 9–10, 1938.

*__Lag ba-Omer__, 33rd (Heb. **lag**) day of the **Omer* period falling on the 18th of *Iyyar; a semi-holiday.

Leḥi (abbr. For Heb. ***Loḥamei Ḥerut Israel**, "Fighters for the Freedom of Israel"), radically anti-British armed underground organization in Palestine, founded in 1940 by dissidents from *I.Z.L.

Levir, husband's brother.

*__Levirate marriage__ (Heb. *yibbum*), marriage of childless widow (*yevamah*) by brother (*yavam*) of the deceased husband (in accordance with Deut. 25:5); release from such an obligation is effected through *ḥaliz̩ah*.

LHY, see Leḥi.

*__Lulav__, palm branch; one of the *Four Species used on *Sukkot together with the **etrog*, *hadas*, and *aravah*.

*__Ma'aravot__, hymns inserted into the evening prayer of the three festivals, Passover, Shavuot, and Sukkot.

Ma'ariv, evening prayer; also called **arvit*.

*__Ma'barah__, transition camp; temporary settlement for newcomers in Israel during the period of mass immigration following 1948.

*__Maftir__, reader of the concluding portion of the Pentateuchal section on Sabbaths and holidays in synagogue; reader of the portion of the prophetical books of the Bible (**haftarah*).

*__Maggid__, popular preacher.

*__Maḥzor__ (pl. **maḥzorim**), festival prayer book.

*__Mamzer__, bastard; according to Jewish law, the offspring of an incestuous relationship.

*__Mandate, Palestine__, responsibility for the administration of Palestine conferred on Britain by the League of Nations in 1922; mandatory government: the British administration of Palestine.

*__Maqāma__ (Ar. pl. **maqamāt**), poetic form (rhymed prose) which, in its classical arrangement, has rigid rules of form and content.

*__Marḥeshvan__, popularly called Ḥeshvan; eighth month of the Jewish religious year, second of the civil, approximating to October–November.

*__Marrano(s)__, descendant(s) of Jew(s) in Spain and Portugal whose ancestors had been converted to Christianity under pressure but who secretly observed Jewish rituals.

Maskil (pl. **maskilim**), adherent of *Haskalah ("Enlightenment") movement.

*__Masorah__, body of traditions regarding the correct spelling, writing, and reading of the Hebrew Bible.

Masorete, scholar of the masoretic tradition.

Masoretic, in accordance with the masorah.

Meliz̩ah, in Middle Ages, elegant style; modern usage, florid style using biblical or talmudic phraseology.

Mellah, *Jewish quarter in North African towns.

*__Menorah__, candelabrum; seven-branched oil lamp used in the Tabernacle and Temple; also eight-branched candelabrum used on *Ḥanukkah.

Me'orah, hymn inserted into the first benediction of the morning prayer (*Yoz̩er ha-Me'orot*).

*__Merkabah__, *merkavah*, "chariot"; mystical discipline associated with Ezekiel's vision of the Divine Throne-Chariot (Ezek. 1).

Meshullaḥ, emissary sent to conduct propaganda or raise funds for rabbinical academies or charitable institutions.

*__Mezuzah__ (pl. **mezuzot**), parchment scroll with selected Torah verses placed in container and affixed to gates and doorposts of houses occupied by Jews.

*__Midrash__, method of interpreting Scripture to elucidate legal points (*Midrash Halakhah*) or to bring out lessons by stories or homiletics (*Midrash Aggadah*). Also the name for a collection of such rabbinic interpretations.

*__Mikveh__, ritual bath.

*__Minhag__ (pl. **minhagim**), ritual custom(s); synagogal rite(s); especially of a specific sector of Jewry.

*__Minḥah__, afternoon prayer; originally meal offering in Temple.

*__Minyan__, group of ten male adult Jews, the minimum required for communal prayer.
*__Mishnah__, earliest codification of Jewish Oral Law.
Mishnah (pl. **mishnayot**), subdivision of tractates of the Mishnah.
Mitnagged (pl. *__Mitnaggedim__), originally, opponents of *Ḥasidism in Eastern Europe.
*__Mitzvah__, biblical or rabbinic injunction; applied also to good or charitable deeds.
Mohel, official performing circumcisions.
*__Moshav__, smallholders' cooperative agricultural settlement in Israel, see moshav ovedim.
Moshavah, earliest type of Jewish village in modern Ereẓ Israel in which farming is conducted on individual farms mostly on privately owned land.
Moshav ovedim ("workers' moshav"), agricultural village in Israel whose inhabitants possess individual homes and holdings but cooperate in the purchase of equipment, sale of produce, mutual aid, etc.
*__Moshav shittufi__ ("collective moshav"), agricultural village in Israel whose members possess individual homesteads but where the agriculture and economy are conducted as a collective unit.
Mostegab (Ar.), poem with biblical verse at beginning of each stanza.
*__Muqaddam__ (Ar., pl. **muqaddamūn**), "leader," "head of the community."
*__Musaf__, additional service on Sabbath and festivals; originally the additional sacrifice offered in the Temple.
Musar, traditional ethical literature.
*__Musar movement__, ethical movement developing in the latter part of the 19th century among Orthodox Jewish groups in Lithuania; founded by R. Israel *Lipkin (Salanter).
*__Nagid__ (pl. **negidim**), title applied in Muslim (and some Christian) countries in the Middle Ages to a leader recognized by the state as head of the Jewish community.
Nakdan (pl. **nakdanim**), "punctuator"; scholar of the 9th to 14th centuries who provided biblical manuscripts with masoretic apparatus, vowels, and accents.
*__Nasi__ (pl. **nesi'im**), talmudic term for president of the Sanhedrin, who was also the spiritual head and later, political representative of the Jewish people; from second century a descendant of Hillel recognized by the Roman authorities as patriarch of the Jews. Now applied to the president of the State of Israel.
*__Negev__, the southern, mostly arid, area of Israel.
*__Ne'ilah__, concluding service on the *Day of Atonement.
Neofiti, term applied in southern Italy to converts to Christianity from Judaism and their descendants who were suspected of maintaining secret allegiance to Judaism.
*__Neology; Neolog; Neologism__, trend of *Reform Judaism in Hungary forming separate congregations after 1868.
*__Nevelah__ (lit. "carcass"), meat forbidden by the *dietary laws on account of the absence of, or defect in, the act of **sheḥitah* (ritual slaughter).
*__New Christians__, term applied especially in Spain and Portugal to converts from Judaism (and from Islam) and their descendants; "Half New Christian" designated a person one of whose parents was of full Jewish blood.
*__Niddah__ ("menstruous woman"), woman during the period of menstruation.
*__Nisan__, first month of the Jewish religious year, seventh of the civil, approximating to March-April.
Niẓoẓot, "sparks"; mystical term for sparks of the holy light imprisoned in all matter.
Nosaḥ (**nusaḥ**) "version"; (1) textual variant; (2) term applied to distinguish the various prayer rites, e.g., *nosaḥ Ashkenaz*; (3) the accepted tradition of synagogue melody.
*__Notarikon__, method of abbreviating Hebrew works or phrases by acronym.
Novella(e) (Heb. **ḥiddush (im)*), commentary on talmudic and later rabbinic subjects that derives new facts or principles from the implications of the text.
*__Nuremberg Laws__, Nazi laws excluding Jews from German citizenship, and imposing other restrictions.
Ofan, hymns inserted into a passage of the morning prayer.
*__Omer__, first sheaf cut during the barley harvest, offered in the Temple on the second day of Passover.
Omer, Counting of (Heb. *Sefirat ha-Omer*), 49 days counted from the day on which the *omer* was first offered in the Temple (according to the rabbis the 16th of Nisan, i.e., the second day of Passover) until the festival of Shavuot; now a period of semi-mourning.
Oraḥ Ḥayyim, see Shulḥan Arukh.
*__Orthodoxy__ (Orthodox Judaism), modern term for the strictly traditional sector of Jewry.
*__Pale of Settlement__, 25 provinces of czarist Russia where Jews were permitted permanent residence.
*__Palmaḥ__ (abbr. for Heb. *peluggot maḥaẓ*; "shock companies"), striking arm of the *Haganah.
*__Pardes__, medieval biblical exegesis giving the literal, allegorical, homiletical, and esoteric interpretations.
*__Parnas__, chief synagogue functionary, originally vested with both religious and administrative functions; subsequently an elected lay leader.
Partition plan(s), proposals for dividing Ereẓ Israel into autonomous areas.
Paytan, composer of **piyyut* (liturgical poetry).
*__Peel Commission__, British Royal Commission appointed by the British government in 1936 to inquire into the Palestine problem and make recommendations for its solution.
Pesaḥ, *Passover.
*__Pilpul__, in talmudic and rabbinic literature, a sharp dialectic used particularly by talmudists in Poland from the 16th century.
*__Pinkas__, community register or minute-book.
*__Piyyut__, (pl. **piyyutim**), Hebrew liturgical poetry.
*__Pizmon__, poem with refrain.
Posek (pl. *__posekim__), decisor; codifier or rabbinic scholar who pronounces decisions in disputes and on questions of Jewish law.
*__Prosbul__, legal method of overcoming the cancelation of debts with the advent of the *sabbatical year.
*__Purim__, festival held on Adar 14 or 15 in commemoration of the delivery of the Jews of Persia in the time of *Esther.
Rabban, honorific title higher than that of rabbi, applied to heads of the *Sanhedrin in mishnaic times.
*__Rabbanite__, adherent of rabbinic Judaism. In contradistinction to *Karaite.
Reb, rebbe, Yiddish form for rabbi, applied generally to a teacher or ḥasidic rabbi.
*__Reconstructionism__, trend in Jewish thought originating in the United States.
*__Reform Judaism__, trend in Judaism advocating modification of *Orthodoxy in conformity with the exigencies of contemporary life and thought.

Resh galuta, lay head of Babylonian Jewry (see exilarch).

Responsum (pl. ***responsa**), written opinion (*teshuvah*) given to question (*she'elah*) on aspects of Jewish law by qualified authorities; pl. collection of such queries and opinions in book form (*she'elot u-teshuvot*).

***Rishonim**, older rabbinical authorities. Distinguished from later authorities (**aharonim*).

***Rishon le-Zion**, title given to Sephardi chief rabbi of Ereẓ Israel.

***Rosh Ha-Shanah**, two-day holiday (one day in biblical and early mishnaic times) at the beginning of the month of *Tishri (September–October), traditionally the New Year.

Rosh Hodesh, *New Moon, marking the beginning of the Hebrew month.

Rosh Yeshivah, see *Yeshivah.

***R.S.H.A.** (initials of Ger. *Reichssicherheitshauptamt*: "Reich Security Main Office"), the central security department of the German Reich, formed in 1939, and combining the security police (Gestapo and Kripo) and the S.D.

***Sanhedrin**, the assembly of ordained scholars which functioned both as a supreme court and as a legislature before 70 C.E. In modern times the name was given to the body of representative Jews convoked by Napoleon in 1807.

***Savora** (pl. **savoraim**), name given to the Babylonian scholars of the period between the **amoraim* and the **geonim*, approximately 500–700 C.E.

S.D. (initials of Ger. *Sicherheitsdienst*: "security service"), security service of the *S.S. formed in 1932 as the sole intelligence organization of the Nazi party.

Seder, ceremony observed in the Jewish home on the first night of Passover (outside Ereẓ Israel first two nights), when the *Haggadah is recited.

***Sefer Torah**, manuscript scroll of the Pentateuch for public reading in synagogue.

***Sefirot, the ten**, the ten "Numbers"; mystical term denoting the ten spheres or emanations through which the Divine manifests itself; elements of the world; dimensions, primordial numbers.

Selektion (Ger.), (1) in ghettos and other Jewish settlements, the drawing up by Nazis of lists of deportees; (2) separation of incoming victims to concentration camps into two categories – those destined for immediate killing and those to be sent for forced labor.

Seliḥah (pl. ***seliḥot**), penitential prayer.

***Semikhah**, ordination conferring the title "rabbi" and permission to give decisions in matters of ritual and law.

Sephardi (pl. ***Sephardim**), Jew(s) of Spain and Portugal and their descendants, wherever resident, as contrasted with *Ashkenazi(m).

Shabbatean, adherent of the pseudo-messiah *Shabbetai Ẓevi (17th century).

Shaddai, name of God found frequently in the Bible and commonly translated "Almighty."

***Shaḥarit**, morning service.

Shali'aḥ (pl. **sheliḥim**), in Jewish law, messenger, agent; in modern times, an emissary from Ereẓ Israel to Jewish communities or organizations abroad for the purpose of fund-raising, organizing pioneer immigrants, education, etc.

Shalmonit, poetic meter introduced by the liturgical poet *Solomon ha-Bavli.

***Shammash**, synagogue beadle.

***Shavuot**, Pentecost; Festival of Weeks; second of the three annual pilgrim festivals, commemorating the receiving of the Torah at Mt. Sinai.

***Sheḥitah**, ritual slaughtering of animals.

***Shekhinah**, Divine Presence.

Shelishit, poem with three-line stanzas.

***Sheluḥei Ereẓ Israel** (or **shadarim**), emissaries from Ereẓ Israel.

***Shema** ([Yisrael]; "hear… [O Israel]," Deut. 6:4), Judaism's confession of faith, proclaiming the absolute unity of God.

Shemini Aẓeret, final festal day (in the Diaspora, final two days) at the conclusion of *Sukkot.

Shemittah, *Sabbatical year.

Sheniyyah, poem with two-line stanzas.

***Shephelah**, southern part of the coastal plain of Ereẓ Israel.

***Shevat**, eleventh month of the Jewish religious year, fifth of the civil, approximating to January–February.

***Shi'ur Komah**, Hebrew mystical work (c. eighth century) containing a physical description of God's dimensions; term denoting enormous spacial measurement used in speculations concerning the body of the **Shekhinah*.

Shivah, the "seven days" of *mourning following burial of a relative.

***Shofar**, horn of the ram (or any other ritually clean animal excepting the cow) sounded for the memorial blowing on *Rosh Ha-Shanah, and other occasions.

Shoḥet, person qualified to perform **sheḥitah*.

Shomer, *Ha-Shomer, organization of Jewish workers in Ereẓ Israel founded in 1909 to defend Jewish settlements.

***Shtadlan**, Jewish representative or negotiator with access to dignitaries of state, active at royal courts, etc.

***Shtetl**, Jewish small-town community in Eastern Europe.

***Shulḥan Arukh**, Joseph *Caro's code of Jewish law in four parts:
Oraḥ Ḥayyim, laws relating to prayers, Sabbath, festivals, and fasts;
Yoreh De'ah, dietary laws, etc;
Even ha-Ezer, laws dealing with women, marriage, etc;
Ḥoshen Mishpat, civil, criminal law, court procedure, etc.

Siddur, among Ashkenazim, the volume containing the daily prayers (in distinction to the **maḥzor* containing those for the festivals).

***Simḥat Torah**, holiday marking the completion in the synagogue of the annual cycle of reading the Pentateuch; in Ereẓ Israel observed on Shemini Aẓeret (outside Ereẓ Israel on the following day).

***Sinai Campaign**, brief campaign in October–November 1956 when Israel army reacted to Egyptian terrorist attacks and blockade by occupying the Sinai peninsula.

Sitra aḥra, "the other side" (of God); left side; the demoniac and satanic powers.

***Sivan**, third month of the Jewish religious year, ninth of the civil, approximating to May–June.

***Six-Day War**, rapid war in June 1967 when Israel reacted to Arab threats and blockade by defeating the Egyptian, Jordanian, and Syrian armies.

***S.S.** (initials of Ger. *Schutzstaffel*: "protection detachment"), Nazi formation established in 1925 which later became the "elite" organization of the Nazi Party and carried out central tasks in the "Final Solution."

***Status quo ante** community, community in Hungary retaining the status it had held before the convention of the General Jewish Congress there in 1868 and the resultant split in Hungarian Jewry.

***Sukkah**, booth or tabernacle erected for *Sukkot when, for seven days, religious Jews "dwell" or at least eat in the *sukkah* (Lev. 23:42).

***Sukkot**, festival of Tabernacles; last of the three pilgrim festivals, beginning on the 15th of Tishri.

Sūra (Ar.), chapter of the Koran.

Ta'anit Esther (Fast of *Esther), fast on the 13th of Adar, the day preceding Purim.

Takkanah (pl. ***takkanot**), regulation supplementing the law of the Torah; regulations governing the internal life of communities and congregations.

***Tallit (gadol)**, four-cornered prayer shawl with fringes (*ẓiẓit*) at each corner.

***Tallit katan**, garment with fringes (*ẓiẓit*) appended, worn by observant male Jews under their outer garments.

***Talmud**, "teaching"; compendium of discussion on the Mishnah by generations of scholars and jurists in many academies over a period of several centuries. The Jerusalem (or Palestinian) Talmud mainly contains the discussions of the Palestinian sages. The Babylonian Talmud incorporates the parallel discussion in the Babylonian academies.

Talmud torah, term generally applied to Jewish religious (and ultimately to talmudic) study; also to traditional Jewish religious public schools.

***Tammuz**, fourth month of the Jewish religious year, tenth of the civil, approximating to June-July.

Tanna (pl. ***tannaim**), rabbinic teacher of mishnaic period.

***Targum**, Aramaic translation of the Bible.

***Tefillin**, phylacteries, small leather cases containing passages from Scripture and affixed on the forehead and arm by male Jews during the recital of morning prayers.

Tell (Ar. "mound," "hillock"), ancient mound in the Middle East composed of remains of successive settlements.

***Terefah**, food that is not **kasher*, owing to a defect on the animal.

***Territorialism**, 20th century movement supporting the creation of an autonomous territory for Jewish mass-settlement outside Ereẓ Israel.

***Tevet**, tenth month of the Jewish religious year, fourth of the civil, approximating to December–January.

Tikkun ("restitution," "reintegration"), (1) order of service for certain occasions, mostly recited at night; (2) mystical term denoting restoration of the right order and true unity after the spiritual "catastrophe" which occurred in the cosmos.

Tishah be-Av, Ninth of *Av, fast day commemorating the destruction of the First and Second Temples.

***Tishri**, seventh month of the Jewish religious year, first of the civil, approximating to September–October.

Tokheḥah, reproof sections of the Pentateuch (Lev. 26 and Deut. 28); poem of reproof.

***Torah**, Pentateuch or the Pentateuchal scroll for reading in synagogue; entire body of traditional Jewish teaching and literature.

Tosafist, talmudic glossator, mainly French (12–14th centuries), bringing additions to the commentary by *Rashi.

***Tosafot**, glosses supplied by tosafist.

***Tosefta**, a collection of teachings and traditions of the *tannaim*, closely related to the Mishnah.

Tradent, person who hands down a talmudic statement on the name of his teacher or other earlier authority.

***Tu bi-Shevat**, the 15th day of Shevat, the New Year for Trees; date marking a dividing line for fruit tithing; in modern Israel celebrated as arbor day.

***Uganda Scheme**, plan suggested by the British government in 1903 to establish an autonomous Jewish settlement area in East Africa.

***Va'ad Le'ummi**, national council of the Jewish community in Ereẓ Israel during the period of the British *Mandate.

***Wannsee Conference**, Nazi conference held on Jan. 20, 1942, at which the planned annihilation of European Jewry was endorsed.

Waqf (Ar.), (1) a Muslim charitable pious foundation; (2) state lands and other property passed to the Muslim community for public welfare.

***War of Independence**, war of 1947–49 when the Jews of Israel fought off Arab invading armies and ensured the establishment of the new State.

***White Paper(s)**, report(s) issued by British government, frequently statements of policy, as issued in connection with Palestine during the *Mandate period.

***Wissenschaft des Judentums** (Ger. "Science of Judaism"), movement in Europe beginning in the 19th century for scientific study of Jewish history, religion, and literature.

***Yad Vashem**, Israel official authority for commemorating the *Holocaust in the Nazi era and Jewish resistance and heroism at that time.

Yeshivah (pl. ***yeshivot**), Jewish traditional academy devoted primarily to study of rabbinic literature; *rosh yeshivah*, head of the yeshivah.

YHWH, the letters of the holy name of God, the Tetragrammaton.

Yibbum, see levirate marriage.

Yiḥud, "union"; mystical term for intention which causes the union of God with the **Shekhinah*.

Yishuv, settlement; more specifically, the Jewish community of Ereẓ Israel in the pre-State period. The pre-Zionist community is generally designated the "old yishuv" and the community evolving from 1880, the "new yishuv."

Yom Kippur, Yom ha-Kippurim, *Day of Atonement, solemn fast day observed on the 10th of Tishri.

Yoreh De'ah, see Shulḥan Arukh.

Yoẓer, hymns inserted in the first benediction (*Yoẓer Or*) of the morning **Shema*.

***Ẓaddik**, person outstanding for his faith and piety; especially a ḥasidic rabbi or leader.

Ẓimẓum, "contraction"; mystical term denoting the process whereby God withdraws or contracts within Himself so leaving a primordial vacuum in which creation can take place; primordial exile or self-limitation of God.

***Zionist Commission (1918)**, commission appointed in 1918 by the British government to advise the British military authorities in Palestine on the implementation of the *Balfour Declaration.

Ẓyyonei Zion, the organized opposition to Herzl in connection with the *Uganda Scheme.

***Ẓiẓit**, fringes attached to the **tallit* and **tallit katan*.

***Zohar**, mystical commentary on the Pentateuch; main textbook of *Kabbalah.

Zulat, hymn inserted after the **Shema* in the morning service.